The Complete Guide
to Videocassette Movies

The Complete Guide to Video

cassette
Movies

Conceived and edited by Steven H. Scheuer

MANAGING EDITORS: Mark Harris · Gregory Martino
ASSOCIATE EDITORS: M. Faust · Eric Monder · Dennis Myers
CONTRIBUTING EDITOR: Robert J. Pardi

An Owl Book
HENRY HOLT AND COMPANY
NEW YORK

Copyright © 1987 by Steven H. Scheuer
All rights reserved, including the right to reproduce this
book or portions thereof in any form.
Published by Henry Holt and Company, Inc.,
521 Fifth Avenue, New York, New York 10175.
Published in Canada by Fitzhenry & Whiteside Limited,
195 Allstate Parkway, Markham, Ontario L3R 4T8.

Library of Congress Cataloging-in-Publication Data
The complete guide to videocassette movies.
"An Owl book."
1. Video recordings—Catalogs. 2. Moving-pictures—
Catalogs. 3. Video recordings—Reviews. 4. Moving-
pictures—Reviews. I. Scheuer, Steven H.
PN1992.95.C66 1987   016.79143'75   87-7571
ISBN 0-8050-0110-7

Printed in the United States of America
10 9 8 7 6 5 4 3 2 1

ISBN 0-8050-0110-7

For Nikki—for everything, during so many wondrous years.

Acknowledgments

In addition to our staff's reviews, this volume is greatly enhanced by the work of many talented free-lance contributors. We would like to thank the Boston Phoenix for providing us with their extensive collection of capsule reviews. In particular, our gratitude goes to Phoenix reviewers Owen Gleiberman, Charles Taylor, and Steve Vineberg for their always insightful criticism. As well, we are grateful to be able to include many of the fine reviews of former Phoenix critics David Chute, David Denby, Janet Maslin, Stephen Schiff, and Michael Sragow. We also thank the Metro Cinema in New York and the Everyman Cinema in London for their film notes. We could not have begun to cover the often obscure field of horror films without the expertise of Maitland McDonagh's reviews; Karen and Bill Palmer were similarly essential to our martial arts coverage. We also thank Mary Lugo, Suzanne Fedak, Daniel Schweiger, Jeremy Pomeroy, Jennifer Jordan, Elizabeth Wrenn, Rachel Bow, Clif Garboden, John Ferguson, Herbert Reynolds, Tim Clinton, Christine Spisak, Robert Norden, Martin Kihne, Amy Asch, Steve Brindberg, Susan Glasser, Maria Oghanian, Sarah Connor, Chris Minichino, Edmond Grant, and Matthew Boyle, all of whom gave generously of their time and talent. Thanks to Jeffrey Gustavson for his inestimable copyediting and scrupulous proofreading, and to Nongluk Phoonkeao and Johanna Thompson for their flawless typing.

The publishers express their appreciation to the following companies for use of videocassettes and promotional material: Twentieth Century Fox; ABC Motion Pictures; Allied Artists Picture Corporation; American Cinema; American International Pictures; Arts and Entertainment Network; BLT Productions; Bravo; Buena Vista; Channel 13; Cinema Five; Cinematheque Collection; Cinemax; Columbia Pictures; DDL Pictures; Discovery Film; The Disney Channel; Embassy Home Entertainment; EMI; The Film Society of Lincoln Center; HBO; Landau Company; Levitt-Pickman Film Corporation; Lorimar; MCA; Media Home Entertainment; MGM/UA; National General Pictures Release; National Screen Service Corporation; New World Pictures; NTA; Orion; Paramount; PBS; Polygram; Republic; RKO; The Movie Channel; Group 1 and The Rank Organization; Saturn; Tri-Star; United Artists; United Film Distribution Company; Universal Studios; Vestron Video; Walt Disney; Warner Brothers and Ladd Company; World Entertainment Corporation; WTBS.

About the Editor

Steven H. Scheuer is the author of numerous critically acclaimed books about motion pictures and television, including *Movies on TV*; *The Movie Book*, a pictorial history of world cinema; and *The Television Annual*. Mr. Scheuer is also the editor and publisher of "TV Key," the most widely syndicated TV newspaper column in the country, appearing daily in over two hundred papers. He has contributed to many magazines including *TV Guide*, and lectures throughout the world on motion pictures, television, and home video.

Mr. Scheuer is the president and editorial director of a new international business called VBS, Video Buyers Service, the first comprehensive informational and transactional service covering virtually all programming available in videocassette form in America and abroad. He is the executive producer and moderator of the long-running, award-winning weekly TV series called *All About TV*, the only television program in the United States dealing candidly with television itself. For three years Mr. Scheuer was the television critic of the CBS Radio Network.

Mr. Scheuer is a native New Yorker and a graduate of Yale University. He has done graduate work at the London School of Economics and Political Science, and has taught college and university courses about film, TV, and popular culture. He is a member of the Communications Media Committee of the American Civil Liberties Union, the Society of Fellows of the Aspen Institute for Humanistic Studies, the Royal Television Society, and the International Institute of Communications and is a vice president of International Film Seminars.

Mr. Scheuer participates in many sports and is a nationally ranked squash tennis player.

Preface

This reference work is the definitive consumer guide to films on video—a single, inexpensive volume that encompasses the widest range and largest number of available titles published to date, and that contains only movies that are on video. We have tried to save your time and your money with a comprehensive, honest book that evaluates films that run the gamut from the brilliant to the bad, and, in some cases, the ugly. This book is for all those owners of videocassette recorders understandably puzzled by the staggering array of choices before them, as well as for fans wondering if their favorite movie is indeed on tape, and if so, where to buy it. We are confident that it will help discriminating home viewers to make intelligent choices, or jaded movie buffs who think—usually incorrectly—that they've seen it all, or jaundiced cinematic thrill-seekers always in search of the new. Everything—well, almost everything as of the winter of 1987—is reviewed here in an easy-to-use format containing over five thousand critiques newly written by a team of movie experts and cinema scholars. We have included virtually every theatrical or made-for-television film available on videocassette in the United States or scheduled for release by the fall of 1987, with the conspicuous exception of pornographic entries.

From the beginning of our work on this mammoth project, we have set ourselves a special goal. Alfred H. Barr, the founding director of the Museum of Modern Art in New York City, who was also a connoisseur, art historian, pioneer and teacher, once defined his task as "the conscientious, continuous, resolute distinction of quality from mediocrity." That definition is our precise task as well!

An illustrious critic in a different field whose writings we much admire—the late Winthrop Sergeant, the music critic of *The New Yorker* magazine for over two decades—made an illuminating comment on the role of the critic in the arts. "The critic's function," he once wrote, "is not to lay down incontrovertible laws or pronounce absolute truths. It is to reflect his personal taste, for what it is worth, and try to stimulate his readers into accepting or rejecting it according to their own lights. Music, in particular, is an art that invites intuitive and passionate reactions rather than cold-blooded appraisals."

We think that this is also demonstrably true of a much newer art—motion pictures, arguably the most pervasive and influential art of our time throughout the world. Sergeant's concerns and point of view toward his music criticism are tenets we endorse unreservedly. They most assuredly are also discerning guidelines for film criticism.

All attempts by market researchers or commentators on American popular culture to predict, in the mid-1980s, the dramatic and still unchecked growth and importance of the homevideo phenomenon have fallen far short of the flabbergasting truth. Nearly sixty percent of American TV households own a videocassette recorder, and they will spend over five billion dollars in 1987 on the rental and purchase of prerecorded videotapes. What television was to America in the 1950s, the videocassette recorder is to the late 1980s throughout the world—a form of entertainment and education that will not only increasingly revolutionize many aspects of our culture, but will also create, to our considerable benefit, a whole new generation of artists and audiences.

Certainly the most pervasive and popular form of entertainment now available on video is the feature film, a movie produced for and originally exhibited in movie theaters. Even the smallest mom-and-pop rental outlets now sometimes stock a modest selection of the best-known movie classics, in addition to the obligatory multiple copies of the current box office smash hits. A few of the large video supermarkets house virtually everything under the cinematic sun: obscure horror movies, classics of the silent screen, meretricious examples of low-budget eroticism, treasures from Hollywood's golden era (whatever period you consider that to be), the highs and lows of the international cinema repertoire, and avoid-at-all-cost gory trash.

Whatever your penchant, predilection, or fancy, *The Complete Guide to Videocassette Movies* should help you fulfill it. And whether your store stocks five hundred movie titles or considerably more than that, we'll try to steer you toward the winners and away from the losers.

Each review in this volume contains all the information you will need to make what we hope will be the perfect informed decision for either purchase or rental. Films are listed alphabetically by title, and all alternate titles have been carefully cross-referenced. Let's say that you're trying to remember the name of an old Cary Grant film, *Amazing Adventure*. Whether you look for it under its original U.S. release title, *Riches and Romance*, or its alternate titles, *The Amazing Quest of Ernest Bliss* or *Romance and Riches*, our book will refer you to the proper entry.

Below the title, each listing contains the year of the film's original release, its country of origin, and, for films released since 1969, its MPAA rating. Films made for network or cable television are designated by *TV* following the date. In addition, the cast, director, and running time are noted.

Each film has also received a star rating. Ratings range from one-half to four stars, chosen to reflect the overall quality of the film.

THE RATING SYSTEM

☆☆☆☆ The best! Great cinematic entertainment, ranging from an acknowledged classic like *Citizen Kane* to rip-roaring fun like *Back to the Future*.

☆☆☆½ Excellent. *Monkey Business*, *Lawrence of Arabia*, *A Hard Day's Night*—this side of paradise.

☆☆☆ Good. *Mister Roberts*, *Legal Eagles*, *Racing with the Moon*—a thoroughly satisfying movie.

☆☆½ Above average. With movies like *California Suite*, *Magnum Force*, and *High Society*, you may not be thrilled, but you won't be wasting your time either.

☆☆ Fair. Competent filmmaking that falls short of the mark (*Gung Ho*), or bad films with redeeming features (*Blame it on Rio*).

☆½ Barely escapes being awful. A tired formula retread like *National Lampoon's Class Reunion* or *The Stuff*, or an overblown epic like *Midway*.

☆ Just plain bad. Everything from major bores like *The Greek Tycoon* to minor-league piffle like *Caged Women* and *Doctor Butcher, M.D.*

½☆ The worst. *Santa Claus Conquers the Martians*, *Ilsa, Harem Keeper of the Oil Sheiks*—movies like these constitute assault in seventeen states.

By drawing on the resources of experts in their fields, we have assembled by far the most complete, the widest-ranging, and the most current collection of critical evaluations of movies available on videocassettes. Our attention to usually overlooked genre films—martial arts, B westerns, horror and science fiction—is, we modestly believe, unsurpassed. We also provide information of specific importance to video consumers. If a film has been edited since its theatrical release, we note the time discrepancy. If two versions of a film are available, we often comment on the differences between them and make a recommendation. *Crimes of Passion*, for example, can be seen in both the R-rated version shown in theaters and a more explicit, more coherent unrated version, available only on video.

Since the 1950s, when wide-screen movies became popular, difficulties have arisen in trying to fit the long rectangular image onto the almost square television screen. When a film originally shot in Cinemascope or Panavision is transferred to videotape, more than fifty percent of the image is usually lost. When a transfer has proven exceptionally damaging to the quality of a film, as it did with *Lawrence of Arabia*, we provide a warning. Conversely, in the rare instances when the entire image is preserved, as it is in *Manhattan*, we applaud the conscientiousness of the distributor.

The question of what constitutes the *definitive* version of a film also has special importance to homevideo viewers. There are many instances in which a film will be substantially trimmed after its initial release—George Cukor's *A Star Is Born*, which lost twenty-seven minutes, is but one example. Other films, however, will include up to an hour of footage not seen in theaters—many of Universal's adventure or disaster films of the 1970s, like *Earthquake* and *Midway*, had entire subplots and characters added for their network telecasts, only parts of which were included in the homevideo versions. Occasionally, a director will decide to add footage that he wanted in the original release of a film, as when Steven Spielberg refashioned a "special edition" of his hit *Close Encounters of the Third Kind* for theatrical rerelease. Some studios have had directors simultaneously shoot two versions of a film, one "hot" for overseas release in countries where rating codes are more lax, and one toned down for domestic or television viewing. Finally, hundreds of very old films or more recent B pictures have entered the public domain—meaning that any enterprising video company can release them, with no regard to their print quality or completeness.

With well over two hundred video companies releasing feature films, it's often hard to tell which ones are the best. Generally, but not always, the names you recognize are the names you can trust. All of the studio-affiliated video companies have track records of good prints and complete versions, and Vestron, Embassy, and Thorn/EMI (later HBO/Cannon) are just a few of the independent companies that are generally reliable. As for judging a video by its packaging, slick artwork and big boxes are no guarantee of quality, but the reverse is often true—if a box looks cheaply thrown together, chances are that the film will be, too!

Film buffs and the more discerning among you will, we trust, appreciate the wealth of lore, trivia, and inside information included in hundreds of the reviews. In what film did Betty Grable sub for the ailing Alice Faye and break through to stardom? What film co-starred Kurt Russell and Goldie Hawn fifteen years before *Swing Shift*? In what movie did Jimmy Durante first perform his signature song "Inka Dinka Doo"? You can find the answers to these cosmic questions in our reviews of *Down Argentine Way*, *The One and Only Genuine Original Family Band*, and *Joe Palooka*.

Our reviews were written to entertain you, but they're also designed to do more—the lively, witty, and pointed opinions offered herein will give you a clear idea of what to expect, let you know how we reacted, and *most importantly*, give you the opportunity to make your own selections with the requisite information and reviews readily available. Our reviews don't just give you dry rehashes of the plot, nor do they simply lavish praise or condemnation on the flicks in question. If we think a film is excellent, we'll tell you that, but we've also tried to tell you *why*. Just as it's true that not all films are for everyone, it's important to remember that not all four-star films will please every viewer. Similarly, we often find unexpected chuckles in one-star movies; nothing livens up a party better than a really great bad movie. Well, *almost* nothing!

Finally, a note about two things you *won't* find in this book. The first is prices. Videos can cost anywhere from $8 (as is the case with many titles in the public domain) to $300 (one example would be a multi-cassette version of a TV miniseries). Many films that are released at a list price of $80 or $90 will have their prices slashed six months later when their companies rerelease them. In addition, every Christmas season brings with it special and often substantial discounts on hundreds of the most popular feature films. Alert consumers should keep a watchful eye on the constant fluctuations in pricing and the great video bargains that result.

The other information you won't find in this volume is whether a film has undergone colorization. As we go to press, dozens of Hollywood's black-and-white classics have already been subjected to this pernicious practice, with Ted Turner and the Hal Roach Studios merely the most prominent among the many perpetrators. With hundreds of other films slated for colorizing, several lawsuits against the colorization companies are pending, and virtually every creative guild in Hollywood has denounced the process as artistic defacement. As the questions of copyrights and legalities become more entangled, colorized films will continue nonetheless to appear with increasing frequency in the homevideo marketplace. We urge you to avoid, if possible, these computer-painted (and, we think, tainted) prints: a colorized film is always a violation of the original work, no matter how much some younger viewers prefer to see movies in color.

Colorization is not the only unpleasant development in the homevideo marketplace in 1987. One of the principal reasons millions of Americans have bought videocassette recorders in the past decade was precisely to avoid those maddening and often idiotic commercials which inundate nearly all parts of free television in America. Now, alas, commercials are being added to some video movies, even huge box-office hits. Paramount Pictures had a triumphant theatrical success in 1986 with *Top Gun*; when the film was released on video in March of 1987, Diet Pepsi shared part of the costs of the marketing campaign, and in exchange for their benefactions was given a one-minute commercial placed just before the start of *Top Gun* in the videocassette. Maybe if enough purchasers of the *Top Gun* video write rude letters to their local Pepsi distributor, this new merchandising racket will come to a timely demise.

Another unique feature of this guide is the free phone number 1-800-VIDEOS-1 to call to purchase any movie listed in this book, or any *other* videocassette you want. Many of the good films reviewed in this first edition may not be available in your local video store. So just pick up the phone for easy access to these often elusive treasures.

—Steven H. Scheuer
Mark Harris
Gregory Martino

A Note to the Reader

Each film reviewed in this book has been assigned a subject category and corresponding symbol. The list of symbols is provided below.

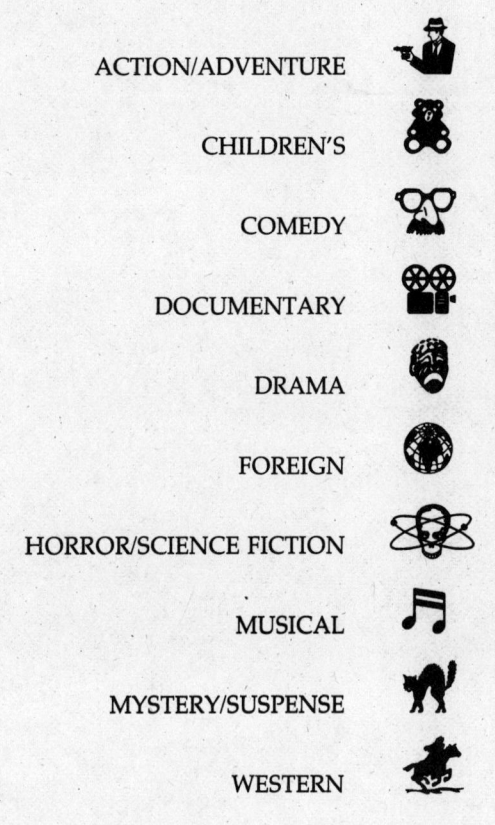

ACTION/ADVENTURE

CHILDREN'S

COMEDY

DOCUMENTARY

DRAMA

FOREIGN

HORROR/SCIENCE FICTION

MUSICAL

MYSTERY/SUSPENSE

WESTERN

Films are indexed by subject category starting on page 643.

The Complete Guide to Videocassette Movies

A

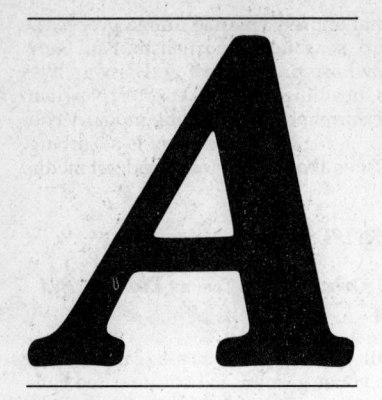

AARON LOVES ANGELA ★★½
1975, USA, R
Kevin Hooks, Irene Cara, Moses Gunn, Robert Hooks, Ernestine Jackson, Jose Feliciano, Walt Frazier. Directed by Gordon Parks, Jr. 99 min.

An updating of the Romeo and Juliet plot, filmed and set in New York City with a pre-*Fame* Irene Cara in the Juliet role. Unfortunately, director Parks didn't seem to believe that a movie for black audiences could succeed without large doses of violence, so there is also a major subplot involving some of the seedier aspects of street life. The result is an uneven mixture of comedy, romance, action, and exploitation that succeeds just enough to make you disappointed when it doesn't.

ABBOTT AND COSTELLO IN HOLLYWOOD ★★½
1945, USA
Bud Abbott, Lou Costello, Francis Rafferty, Robert Stanton, Mike Mazurki, "Rags" Ragland. Directed by S. Sylvan Simon. 83 min.

Abbott and Costello show themselves to be the true progenitors of Lenny and Squiggy (we already knew they were the grandpappies of lowbrow queens Laverne and Shirley) as they forsake their careers as a barber and shoeshine boy to become talent agents in Hollywood. They're promoting a singer played by Bob Stanton; we hear him trill a few numbers like "On the Midway" and "As I Remember You." MGM, producing its last A & C vehicle, provided a bigger budget and some fun cameos, and Bud and Lou show their gratitude by pouring on the energy and creating a slightly more adult-oriented comedy.

ABBOTT AND COSTELLO MEET CAPTAIN KIDD ★★½
1952, USA
Bud Abbott, Lou Costello, Charles Laughton, Hillary Brooke, Bill Shirley, Leif Erickson, Fran Warren. Directed by Charles Lamont. 70 min.

Charles Laughton and Lou Costello really work up a sweat trying to out-ham each other, and the result is more laughter than the usual Abbott and Costello film supplies. The boys are stranded on Tortuga and get their hands on a treasure map. Captain Kidd (Laughton) is in hot pursuit, along with a luscious female pirate played by A & C regular Hillary Brooke. Director Lamont had a sloppy style that was perfect for these movies, but here he's a bit hampered by six musical numbers.

ABBOTT AND COSTELLO MEET DR. JEKYLL AND MR. HYDE ★★★
1953, USA
Bud Abbott, Lou Costello, Boris Karloff, Craig Stevens, Reginald Denny, Helen Westcott, John Dierkes. Directed by Charles Lamont. 76 min.

This one's right up there with *Meet Frankenstein* and *Meet the Invisible Man* as the drooling-boob duo's best! They're a couple of bumbling bobbies out to capture the terror of London town. Karloff, as the doctor and company, seems to have taken lessons from Charles Laughton (*Meet Captain Kidd*) in how to play opposite Lou—he's like Raymond Massey in *Arsenic and Old Lace*. There are two outstanding sequences—one in a wax museum and another when Costello gets a dose of the doctor's juice.

ABBOTT AND COSTELLO MEET FRANKENSTEIN ★★★
1948, USA
Bud Abbott, Lou Costello, Lon Chaney, Jr., Bela Lugosi, Glenn Strange. Directed by Charles T. Barton. 82 min.

The first of innumerable A & C-meet-somebody-or-other movies is easily the best, an enjoyable romp with most of the then-defunct Universal stable of horror icons (except the Mummy, who got an "A & C Meet" all to himself). Dracula wants to replace the Frankenstein monster's brain with Lou's; Larry Talbot, when not transformed by the full moon into a wolf ("Yeah, you and about a million other guys," comments Costello), tries to warn the duo away. Vincent Price does a cameo as the Invisible Man at film's end.

THE ABDUCTION ★½
1975, USA, R
Gregory Rozakis, Judith-Marie Bergan, David Pendleton, Dorothy Malone, Leif Erickson. Directed by Joseph Zito. 100 min.

A disagreeable melodrama that plays fast and loose with our attitudes toward the Patty Hearst kidnapping. In its defense, however, the film is supposedly based on the book *Black Abductors*, which was written before the SLA grabbed Patty and turned her into Tania the bank robber. Yet everything about the film is geared to remind us of the real-life kidnapping of the rich girl by political terrorists. It's one of those films designed to cash in on a briefly topical news story but that holds little interest once the headlines have faded.

THE ABDUCTORS ★
1972, USA
Cheri Caffaro, Jennifer Brooks. Directed by Don Schain. 88 min.

Just what the world clamored for—a sequel to *Ginger*. Just as inept as before, but with more nudity and brutality—the bad guys this time around are a group of white slavers who kidnap (sorry, *abduct*) innocent young girls to become "mistresses" to rich men. Of course, they have to provide them with some experience first. *Note*: The recommendation ostensibly from *Variety* that adorns the sleeve of this cassette does not appear anywhere in the *Variety* review of this sleaze.

ABDULLA'S HAREM

See *Abdulla the Great*

ABDULLA THE GREAT ★½
1954, Great Britain/Egypt
Gregory Ratoff, Kay Kendall, Sidney Chaplin, Alex D'Arcy. Directed by Gregory Ratoff. 89 min.

Russian-born actor and director Gregory Ratoff produced this tale featuring himself as an Egyptian monarch (don't *all* Egyptian monarchs have Russian accents?) who falls in love with an English model. Of course, she despises him for his despotic ways, giving her heart instead to a young officer plotting to overthrow him. King Farouk sued to prevent this from being shown. (a.k.a: *Abdulla's Harem*)

ABE LINCOLN IN ILLINOIS ★★★
1940, USA
Raymond Massey, Ruth Gordon, Gene Lockhart, Mary Howard, Dorothy Tree, Howard da Silva, Minor Watson, Alan Baxter. Directed by John Cromwell. 110 min.

Robert E. Sherwood wrote some of Hollywood's more literate screenplays, including *Idiot's Delight*, *The Best Years of Our Lives*, and this adaptation (with Grover Jones) of his 1938 play. It tones down the camp of D.W. Griffith's *Abraham Lincoln* and the melodrama of John Ford's *Young Mr. Lincoln* in favor of historicity and a more attuned conception of Lincoln's politics. Raymond Massey lacks Henry Ford's sensitivity but makes up for it in sheer physical verisimilitude (interestingly, Massey played abolitionist John Brown that same year in *Santa Fe Trail*), and he gets rugged, solid support from everyone except Ruth Gordon, who overdoes it as Mary Todd. Accomplished camera work by James Wong Howe makes the film more than a vehicle for the screenplay.

ABILENE TOWN ☆☆
1946, USA
Randolph Scott, Ann Dvorak. Directed by Edwin L. Marin. 89 min.

Randolph Scott plays a tough but good-hearted marshall facing a violent dispute between the cattlemen and the homesteaders in his Kansas town. Ann Dvorak shines as a dance-hall entertainer in this rollicking, action-packed B Western.

THE ABOMINABLE DR. PHIBES ☆½
1971, Great Britain
Vincent Price, Joseph Cotton, Terry-Thomas, Virginia North. Directed by Robert Fuest. 90 min.

A glossy exercise in camp horror from the director of *The Devil's Rain* and *The Last Days of Man on Earth*. In 1930s London, doctors who failed to save the life of Victoria Phibes are killed in bizarre ways by her deranged (and presumed dead) husband, Anton. Not one of Vincent Price's greater moments in schlock horror.

ABOUT LAST NIGHT... ☆☆☆
1986, USA, R
Rob Lowe, Demi Moore, James Belushi, Elizabeth Perkins, George DiCenzo, Michael Alldredge. Directed by Edward Zwick, 116 min.

This adaptation of David Mamet's corrosively cynical play *Sexual Perversity in Chicago* actually jettisons about 95 percent of his dialogue, but the result is something of a cornball triumph—a messy, searching look at contemporary men and women as they struggle to live down the legacy of a singles-bar society. Lowe and Moore play the young couple whose one-night stand leads them into a love affair; Belushi and Perkins are their respective friends who do their best to jostle them out of it. A decade after *Annie Hall*, much of the terrain seems overly familiar, and the movie itself is jarringly impure, slick one minute, raw the next, crammed with nasty one-liners and earnest reconciliations that don't quite mesh. Yet much of this smart, flawed, slightly gushy romance is unexpectedly moving. Belushi has never registered on screen with this kind of blustery force, Perkins makes a very bright debut, and Moore is a revelation—in several scenes, she pushed the film toward something like a moment of truth.

ABRAHAM LINCOLN ☆☆☆
1930, USA
Walter Huston, Una Merkel, Kay Hammond. Directed by D. W. Griffith. 97 min.

This dramatization of Lincoln's life relies heavily on Huston's fine acting and Stephen Vincent Benét's screenplay. Although this was Griffith's first sound film, he seems uninterested in the challenges of the new medium. The movie lacks the dynamic visual style that characterized the great director's earlier, silent works.

ABSENCE OF MALICE ☆☆☆
1981, USA, R
Paul Newman, Sally Field, Bob Balaban, Melinda Dillon, Luther Adler, Barry Primus. Directed by Sydney Pollack. 116 min.

Pollack's scorching but not entirely credible drama probes the shoddy practices of cheap, sensational journalism. Paul Newman is a Miami businessman whose professional and private lives are victimized by an ambitious, headline-hunting reporter. Newman contributes one of his better performances in this contemporary cousin to Billy Wilder's classic *Ace in the Hole*. The story is absorbing, and it raised some important issues about print and broadcast media.

THE ABSENT-MINDED PROFESSOR ☆☆☆
1961, USA, G
Fred MacMurray, Nancy Olson, Keenan Wynn, Tommy Kirk. Directed by Robert Stevenson. 90 min.

Walt Disney's delightful comedy is about a likeable science instructor who invents a gooey gasoline substitute called Flubber, which has powerful antigravity properties. The Professor (Fred MacMurray) first uses the substance for a practical need—on the shoes of a hopeless basketball team. Later, Flubber causes hilarious chaos when the Professor uses it in his car and flies over Washington, D.C., throwing the bewildered Air Force into panic.

ABSOLUTE BEGINNERS ☆☆☆
1986, Great Britain, PG-13
Eddie O'Connell, Patsy Kensit, David Bowie, James Fox, Steven Berkoff, Sade, Ray Davies, Anita Morris. Directed by Julien Temple. 107 min.

This roaringly energetic, visually striking British musical is set in the London of 1958, envisioned by director Julien Temple as the year when teenagers began to discover themselves as a group, and their music, clothes, and ever-changing style ruled the streets. The whole first hour—with the camera gliding sinuously through the glitter of the gorgeous sets and a fine rock score pulsing on the soundtrack—has more sustained energy than almost any screen musical in years. Temple, in an astonishing directorial debut, couples the split-second imagemaking of rock videos with the scope and grace of an old-fashioned spectacular. Unfortunatley, the leads are terrible bland—as faceless and generically wholesome as their American counterparts, Frankie and Annette—and the very simple story collapses into a tangle of race riots and cynicism that its feathery premise can't support. See it, though, for the spine-tingling style and the delightful cameos by Sade, Bowie, and, best, the Kinks's Ray Davies singing "Quiet Life." Based on a novel by Colin MacInnes.

ACCIDENT ☆☆½
1967, Great Britain
Dirk Bogarde, Stanley Baker, Jacqueline Sassard, Delphine Seyrig, Alexander Knox, Michael York, Vivien Merchant. Directed by Joseph Losey. 105 min.

A stylish but pretentious Joseph Losey–Harold Pinter collaboration filled with pregnant pauses that, if eliminated, would have reduced this film's running time to half an hour. As played by a superb cast completely in tune with Pinter's ultra-cryptic writing, this somewhat intriguing film ambles along dispensing mysterious hints about the characters' motivations. The complicated script concerns an Oxford don having an affair with a student *femme fatale*, who seems to have snared several other men in her spare time. Expert performances help fill in the hidden meanings the director and screenwriter thrive on.

THE ACCIDENT ☆☆
1983, Canada
Michael Hogan, Frank Perry, Fiona Reed, Terence Kelly. Directed by Donald Brittain. 104 min.

A disaster movie with a difference. When a stadium collapses during a hockey game, many of the attendees are trapped and many die before rescue teams can reach them. Uninterested in the usual special-effects syndrome, this melodrama eschews the all-star cameo approach to the spectacle of disaster and concentrates on human interest in the intimate stories unfolding in this emotion-charged life-and-death situation. Though fairly engrossing, the movie has the look and sensibility of a telefilm.

ACQUA E SAPONE ☆½
1985, Italy, PG
Carlo Verdone, Natasha Hovey, Florinda Bolkan, Fabrizio Bracconeri. Directed by Carlo Verdone. 105 min.

This innocuous, annoyingly mawkish Italian comedy concerns a bashful, tubby teacher who, stricken with love for a beautiful American teenage model, poses as a priest to become her tutor. The constant mugging of writer-director-star Carlo Verdone is so hammy it's almost unnerving—the vanity of his characterization is appalling and rather funny. The rest of the film (the few minutes when Verdone is offscreen) is less emphatic but just as dull.

ACROSS 110TH STREET ☆☆
1972, USA, R
Anthony Quinn, Yaphet Kotto, Paul Benjamin, Antonio Fargas, Anthony Franciosa. Directed by Barry Shear. 102 min.

Shrill, violent film about a war between a Harlem gang and the mob. Quinn and Kotto are two cops caught in the middle as they investigate. Only about half a step up from bad blaxploitation mostly because of higher production values and a good performance from Kotto.

ACROSS THE GREAT DIVIDE ☆☆
1976, USA, PG
Heather Rattray, Mark Hall, Robert Logan, George Flower. Directed by Stewart Raffill. 102 min.

After their grandfather dies and they are robbed, two orphans must traipse across the Oregon wilderness. That's only the beginning of the tykes' misfortunes in this Pacific International family feature. They also encounter wild animals, a roving gang, and a trickster gambler. Won't somebody give these innocent kids a break? At least the scenery is nice.

THE ACT ☆½
1983, USA, R
Robert Ginty, Sarah Langenfeld, Nick Surovy, Eddie Albert, Pat Hingle, Jill St. John. Directed by Sig Shore. 94 min.

The producer of *Superfly* shows that he didn't learn much about the technical aspects of filmmaking in the ten years between that feature and this incomprehensible crime drama. It all has something to do with a union leader/mobster who pays the President of the United States a $2-million "campaign contribution" in return for granting a pardon to his ex-partner. Afraid of losing face, the mobster then sets out to steal his money back. Astoundingly enough, this features songs by John Sebastian, one of the least cynical singers ever to strum a guitar, that are totally out of place here.

ACT OF PASSION ☆☆☆☆
1984, USA (TV)
Marlo Thomas, Kris Kristofferson, Jon DeVries, George Dzundza. Directed by Simon Langton. 104 min.

A superb TV film that bears favorable comparison with the German film that inspired it (*The Lost Honor of Katharina Blum*). A hardworking divorcée with little social life meets a dangerously handsome stranger at a party and, for once in her life, decides to throw caution to the wind. However, after spending the night with him, she discovers he's a suspected terrorist and subsequently pays for her night of passion. Placed under police scrutiny, she becomes suspect, is treated like a criminal, suffers business reverses, and is persecuted by the press. Strangely, even as the film documents her harrowing experiences and serves as a reminder of the failures of the legal system to protect witnesses, the film still carries the undercurrent of the woman's romantic involvement. Provocative and enjoyable on several levels; TV movies don't come any better. (a.k.a: *The Lost Honor of Kathryn Beck*)

ADAM ☆☆☆
1983, USA (TV)
Daniel J. Travanti, Jobeth Williams, Martha Scott, Richard Masur, Paul Regina, Mason Adams. Directed by Michael Tuchner. 104 min.

A grim TV docudrama about missing children that is far more powerful than most of its kind is passionately performed by Travanti and Williams. They play Jon and Reve Walsh, a young couple who successfully spearheaded the lobby for the Missing Children's Bill in Congress after their own young son was kidnapped and murdered. Alan Leicht's teleplay starts shortly before the tragedy that galvanized the Walshes into action, and the agonizing impact of their son's loss is impressively conveyed, despite inevitable near-lapses into ordinary melodrama. Several Emmy nominations went to the original telecast, which ended with snapshots of fifty missing kids, several of whom were located as a result.

ADAM HAD FOUR SONS ☆☆½
1941, USA
Ingrid Bergman, Warner Baxter, Susan Hayward, Fay Wray, Richard Denning, Johnny Downs. Directed by Gregory Ratoff. 81 min.

An entertaining, slightly unwieldy domestic drama spanning several years in the life of a French family. When a man's ailing wife expires, he relies heavily on the family governess to put his house and children in order. Years later, after financial reverses, the father rebuilds his fortune and discovers that he needs the governess more than ever. The household is ripped apart when one of his daughters-in-law takes a fancy to her brother-in-law. Based on Charles Bonner's *Legacy*, the film is an overstuffed drama that affords the pleasure of a good book, with solid storytelling and compelling characterizations.

ADAM'S RIB ☆☆☆☆
1949, USA
Spencer Tracy, Katharine Hepburn, Judy Holliday, Tom Ewell, Jean Hagen, David Wayne. Directed by George Cukor. 101 min.

One of Cukor's greatest comedies and probably the finest of the many films that paired Hepburn and Tracy, *Adam's Rib* concerns a couple of married lawyers who bring the courtroom home when she defends and he prosecutes a wife accused of trying to murder her philandering husband. The legal theatrics and marital battles in Ruth Gordon and Garson Kanin's bright screenplay provide some sharp-edged commentary on sexual double standards, and, as always, Hepburn and Tracy show an intelligent, romantic chemistry amid even the most far-flung plot contrivances. Cukor's understated direction wisely allows the crisp dialogue and performances to take center stage. Ewell, Holliday, and Hagen all made their film debuts here, giving their two great stars worthy support.

ADDITION ☆½
1985, France, R
Richard Berry, Richard Bohringer, Victoria Abril, Fadrid Chopel, Daniel Sarky. Directed by Denis Amar. 93 min.

Unwieldly morality play that's just one more trip on that old "Midnight Express" to sadomasochism and other examples of poor prison conditions. A skirt-chasing romantic is jailed on a minor charge but gets embroiled in a prison break in which a guard is crippled and seeks revenge. The convoluted plot is almost impossible to follow and the writers' and directors' intentions are just as hard to decipher. A creepy descent into the inhuman prison universe that writers like Jean Genet have explored with formal elegance and meaning. This one is an obtuse, philosophical muddle.

THE ADMIRAL WAS A LADY ☆☆½
1950, USA
Edmond O'Brien, Wanda Hendrix, Rudy Vallee, Johnny Sands, Garry Owen. Directed by Albert S. Rogell. 85 min.

Passably enjoyable comedy about four ex-soldiers who devote time to avoiding work and pursuing Miss Hendrix, an ex-WAVE. Vallee turns in his usual eccentric performance, this time as a jukebox magnate who threatens to cancel their schemes and put them to work if they don't help him.

THE ADULTRESS ½☆
1973, USA
Tyne Daly, Eric Braeden, Greg Morton, Lynn Roth. Directed by Norbert Meisel. 85 min.

A ghastly bomb with a pre-"Cagney and Lacey" Tyne Daly as a sex-starved wife whose impotent hubby hires a gigolo as a stand-in—so to speak. Feeble, implausible junk.

ADVENTURE FOR IMPERIAL TREASURE ☆½
Hong Kong
Wang Dao, Lung Fei, Cheng Hwei-Lou, Yieh Hai-Fang. Directed by Hsieh Yu-Chen.

Historical kung fu adventure with a band of villains out to steal the treasures of the Ming Dynasty. Our hero (Dao) becomes involved after the baddies kill his father. Good production values, better-than-average story and action.

THE ADVENTURE OF SHERLOCK HOLMES' SMARTER BROTHER ☆☆☆
1975, USA, PG
Gene Wilder, Marty Feldman, Madeline Kahn, Dom DeLuise, Leo McKern, John Le Mesurier, Thorley Walters. Directed by Gene Wilder. 91 min.

Having learned the parody genre from collaborating with Mel Brooks on *Blazing Saddles* and *Young Frankenstein*, first-time director Wilder took with him most of the Brooks regulars to produce this amiable, funny spoof on Sherlock Holmes movies. (Perhaps not coincidentally, the quality of Brooks's own films went downhill after Wilder left.) Aside from writing and directing, Wilder also stars as the blindly jealous but considerably duller younger sibling of the famous sleuth (*not* Mycroft, the brother of whom Arthur Conan Doyle wrote, but Sigerson, whom Doyle somehow overlooked). Leo McKern is splendid as Professor Moriarty, here shown to be a mathematical genius who can't remember what you do with the decimal point in long division.

THE ADVENTURES OF BUCKAROO BANZAI ACROSS THE EIGHTH DIMENSION ☆☆☆
1984, USA, PG
Peter Weller, Ellin Barkin, John Lithgow, Jeff Goldblum. Directed by W. D. Richter. 103 min.

"What's going on here?" a character demands when confronted by a scene of considerable mayhem. "Lectroids from Planet 10 by way of the Eighth Dimension," comes the terse reply. Apocalyptic black comedy in which all aliens are named John, the President of the United States is offered the short form for the declaration of war, and the fate of the world rests on the capable shoulders of Buckaroo Banzai—brain surgeon, scientist, and world-famous rock musician. A cult hit from which science-fiction fanatics will derive a great deal of pleasure, the movie is also a good example of the deadpan, post-hip movies that go for the tone of a Pynchon novel. (a.k.a.: *Buckaroo Banzai*)

THE ADVENTURES OF CAPTAIN FABIAN ☆½
1951, USA
Errol Flynn, Micheline Presle, Vincent Price, Agnes Moorehead, Victor Francen. Directed by William Marshall. 97 min.

Almost all of the easy, daring charm that made Flynn a matinee idol of the thirties and early forties had vanished by the time he wrote and starred in this inept vehicle about a sea captain who comes to the rescue of a New Orleans servant girl accused of murder. The dialogue is unbearable even for a cut-rate adventure, and the melodramatic ending is downright ludicrous. After this film, Flynn began drifting into gradual retirement—small wonder.

ADVENTURES OF DON JUAN ☆☆½
1948, USA
Errol Flynn, Viveca Lindfors, Robert Douglas, Alan Hale, Romney Brent, Ann Rutherford, Una O'Connor, Raymond Burr. Directed by Vincent Sherman. 110 min.

This glossy Technicolor epic puts Flynn through his standard heroic paces, though with tongues held firmly in cheek by all concerned. After dallying with a few already-spoken-for ladies in England, Don Juan is shipped back to Spain for reassignment by Queen Margaret as an instructor in a fencing academy, where he runs afoul of a plot against the royal family. Flynn hauls out his sword anytime the action threatens to die down, and Viveca Lindfors, an actress who has never gotten her due, is very good as the queen, the one thespian in the cast who plays a straight part.

THE ADVENTURES OF FRONTIER FREMONT ☆½
1976, USA
Dan Haggerty, Denver Pyle. Directed by Richard Friedenberg. 106 min.

A sort of follow-up to *The Life and Times of Grizzly Adams*, which was a TV movie and also a series. It concerns a disgruntled tinsmith who heads for the forests to live off the land away from all those dirty city slickers. A pitiful, moth-eaten excuse for a family film, the movie seems intended for the children of survivalists. Lots of gentle humor plus the excitement of watching Frontier Fremont (or is it really Grizzly Adams in disguise?) befriend forest animals, wash in mountain streams, and flash his smile as he communes with nature.

THE ADVENTURES OF HUCKLEBERRY FINN (1939)

See *Huckleberry Finn* (1939)

THE ADVENTURES OF HUCKLEBERRY FINN ☆½
1981, USA (TV)
Kurt Ida, Dan Monahan, Brock Peters, Forrest Tucker, Larry Storch, Lurene Tuttle, Jack Kruschen, Michele Marsh, Mike Mazurki, Cliff Osmond. Directed by Jack B. Hively. 100 min.

This "Classics Illustrated"–style presentation of Twain's classic was made two years before its premiere. Either NBC did not want it confused with the 1975 made-for-TV *Huckleberry Finn* (with Ron Howard) or the 1974 musical feature *Huckleberry Finn* (with Jeff East), or they were just too embarrassed to air it at all. "F-Troop" fans will enjoy seeing Forrest Tucker and Larry Storch reteamed, playing the Duke and Dauphin. Otherwise, a children's pop-up book version could beat this one in suspense and surprises.

THE ADVENTURES OF MARK TWAIN ☆☆
1985, USA, G
Animated: James Whitmore, Chris Ritchie, Gary Krug, Michele Mariana. Directed by Will Vinton. 90 min.

The Claymation animation process is certainly an intriguing one. Some day an enchanting children's film will be made utilizing it, but this oddity is not it. Somehow the story line is one of more interest to adults, which rather limits the film's appeal (unless, of course, there are advanced Twain scholars running around our grammar schools). The plot concerns the adventures of several characters from Twain books (Tom Sawyer, Huck Finn, Becky Thatcher) who go on a balloon trip with their creator, Mark Twain, who is in search of his late wife. Along the way, Twain lifts everyone's spirits by spinning some of his favorite short stories, which will not exactly make the kiddies sit up and take notice. A nice try, but at whom exactly is this aimed?

THE ADVENTURES OF NELLIE BLY ☆½
1981, USA (TV)
Linda Purl, Gene Barry, John Randolph, Cliff Osmond, J. D. Cannon. Directed by Henning Schellerup. 100 min.

A standard, sanitized TV bio-pic about the celebrated female journalist who was "liberated" long before the word became fashionable. As played by perky Linda Purl, Nellie is a perpetually smiling crusader who single-handedly cleans up the scummy city streets without getting any grime on her skirt. Girl Scouts in need of a role model are probably the best audience for this account of Bly's do-gooding activities; others will doze between her journalistic junkets.

THE ADVENTURES OF ROBIN HOOD ☆☆☆☆
1938, USA
Errol Flynn, Olivia de Havilland, Basil Rathbone, Claude Rains, Patric Knowles, Eugene Pallette, Alan Hale. Directed by Michael Curtiz. 105 min.

Everything about this swashbuckler—the lush production, the rich, vibrant use of Technicolor, the rousing Erich Korngold score—adds up to superior, sustained entertainment, a film that remains, after fifty years, a pleasure for young and old alike. Flynn plays Robin Hood with such panache that you're not likely to care that he turned the character into little more than a Sherwood Forest variant of Captain Blood. De Havilland makes an unduly frosty Maid Marian, but she's just a sidelight. The dueling scene between Flynn and the wonderfully evil Rathbone is the high point. Both men did their own sword work, and the film was edited to make them look astonishingly fast and dexterous.

THE ADVENTURES OF SHERLOCK HOLMES ☆☆½
1939, USA
Basil Rathbone, Nigel Bruce, Ida Lupino, George Zucco, Terry Kilburn, Alan Marshal, Henry Stephenson, E. E. Clive. Directed by Alfred Werker. 85 min.

After the unexpected success of *The Hound of the Baskervilles*, featuring the original teaming of Rathbone and Bruce as Holmes and Watson, this was rushed into completion and released in the same year; it and *Hound* are the only two of the Holmes series not to have been updated to the 1940s. The goings-on seem much more acceptable in the proper Victorian milieu. Here Holmes battles a scheme by the infamous Professor Moriarty (Zucco) to steal the crown jewels.

THE ADVENTURES OF TARTU ☆☆☆
1943, Great Britain
Robert Donat, Valerie Hobson, Glynis Johns, Martin Miller, Walter Rilla. Directed by Harold S. Bucquet. 103 min.

After *Goodbye Mr. Chips*, Robert Donat passed up a series of major screen roles before he starred in this relatively minor adventure-comedy. He plays a chemist who joins Czech freedom fighters in order to blow up a Nazi gas laboratory. Though director Bucquet successfully mixes comedy, suspense, and melodrama, it's Donat's delightful screen presence that pulls it all together. Not another *Thirty-Nine Steps*, but good enough. (a.k.a.: *Tartu*)

THE ADVENTURES OF THE AMERICAN RABBIT ☆☆½
1986, USA, G
Animated: Bob Arbogast, Pat Freley, Ken Mars, Bob Holt, Anne Underwood, Linda Stewart. Directed by Fred Wolf and Noutaka Nishizawa. 85 min.

Pleasant animated fare about a Super Rabbit and the hare-raising adventures he endures in order to become a superhero. This cute-as-a-cottontail plot-line involves the bunny's attempts to curtail the activities of some nefarious jackals. Sweet-tempered, the film is not very distiguished as animation, but the drawings are serviceable and the story hops along energetically. Good songs by Howard Kaylan and Mark Volman (ex-Turtles Flo and Eddie) help.

THE ADVENTURES OF THE WILDERNESS FAMILY ☆½
1975, USA, PG
Robert F. Logan, Susan Damante Shaw, Hollye Holmes, Ham Larsen. Directed by Stewart Raffill. 94 min.

In the mid-seventies, there was Ivory soap, Breyer's ice cream, and Pacific International's Wilderness Family. The getting-back-to-nature plot that has provided a framework for many a Hollywood comedy becomes straight-faced treacle in this family entertainment. The animals are cute and the Utah scenery eye-pleasing, but one episode of "Wild Kingdom" is preferable to this drawn-out "Waltons"-type movie.

THE ADVENTURES OF TOM SAWYER ☆☆½
1938, USA
Tommy Kelly, Jackie Moran, May Robson, Walter Brennan, Ann Gillis, Victor Jory. Directed by Norman Taurog. 93 min.

Like Aunt Polly's fence, this version of Mark Twain's classic novel gets a good whitewashing. Producer David O. Selznick coats the production with an early, vivid use of three-step Technicolor but lacquers over Twain's earthy satire and paints the adult characters with grotesquely broad brush-strokes. Many of the classic episodes are retained, including Tom and Becky Thatcher's flight in the cave from Injun Joe. Still, children would do better to read the book, or have it read to them. Taurog's film is less stilted than his *Huckleberry Finn*, and he makes the most of the Technicolor palette, but the Twain color has definitely been thinned out.

ADVISE AND CONSENT ☆☆☆
1962, USA
Henry Fonda, Walter Pidgeon, Charles Laughton, Don Murray, Burgess Meredith, Franchot Tone, Lew Ayres, George Grizzard, Gene Tierney. Directed by Otto Preminger. 139 min.

This long, complex film will entertain those with an insatiable appetite for behind-the-scenes political maneuvering. Henry Fonda plays a newly appointed secretary of state who undergoes an arduous confirmation hearing. Perhaps viewers will not be leaping out of their seats with excitement, but this is an intelligent film made by a great director and the cast are all seasoned professionals. In an interesting sidelight, Otto Preminger had a role for a black senator (though no black person was serving in the Senate at that time) and he offered the part to Reverend Martin Luther King. Although Preminger felt that the part offered the chance to create a positive role model, King turned down the offer, fearing white hostility and a possible backlash against the cause of civil rights.

THE AFFAIR ☆☆
1973, USA (TV)
Natalie Wood, Robert Wagner, Bruce Davison, Pat Harrington. Directed by Gilbert Cates. 74 min.

A beautiful lyricist, crippled by polio, finds her great love with a handsome lawyer in a sentimental TV movie that's too often awash in its own tears, but enjoyable on a very simplistic level. It's of interest as Wood and Wagner's only costarring venture after *All the Fine Young Cannibals*, and they play well together, though not well enough to keep this corny old vehicle from stalling out.

THE AFFAIRS OF ANNABEL ☆☆
1938, USA
Lucille Ball, Jack Oakie, Ruth Donnelly, Bradley Page, Fritz Feld, Thurston Hall, Elizabeth Risdon. Directed by Ben Stoloff. 73 min.

An overcooked farce that strains for laughs but draws only a few chuckles from Ball's comic timing and Oakie's buffoonery. He's an inventive but callous publicist who puts actress Lucy into wacky situations parallel to those of her films; e.g., if she's in a prison film, Oakie gets her arrested and put in jail. Everyone works very hard to overcome these strained contrivances, but they succeed only at the film's hilarious finale, in which a manic Fritz Feld is duped into staging a police rescue when he's told that it's his big chance to direct a "realistic" film.

THE AFRICAN QUEEN ☆☆☆☆
1951, USA
Katharine Hepburn, Humphrey Bogart, Robert Morley, Peter Bull, Theodore Bikel. Directed by John Huston. 105 min.

One of the classics of the American popular cinema, from a script by film critic James Agee. The story of a crabby steamboat captain and a spinstery missionary who unite forces to destroy a German gunboat controlling the Congo River. Somewhere along the line, the two fall in love, and Hepburn and Bogart wind up creating one of the screen's most marvelously mismatched pairs. Both stars emote a lot, and their chemistry overcomes a too-pat plot and an unconvincing ending. A lively, lovable movie that proves Hollywood was still capable of turning them out in 1951. Shot on magnificent location in Africa, *Queen* remains a sentimental favorite, and it won Bogart his only Best Actor Oscar.

AFRICA SCREAMS ☆☆
1949, USA
Bud Abbott, Lou Costello, Hillary Brooke, Max Baer, Buddy Baer, Clyde Beatty, Frank Buck, Shemp Howard, Joe Besser. Directed by Charles Barton. 79 min.

Sensitive souls would probably be offended by this crude view of Africa—hungry cannibals after meaty little Lou—but why would a sensitive soul be watching an Abbott and Costello feature? Lou seems to recall this old map of a lost diamond mine, and a gang of bad guys takes him into the jungle to find it. Clyde Beatty, the lion tamer, and Frank Buck play themselves with little effect; sometimes-Stooges Shemp Howard and Joe Besser are much better—they show real comic ability.

AFTER HOURS ☆☆☆☆
1985, USA, R
Griffin Dunne, Rosanna Arquette, Verna Bloom, Teri Garr, John Heard, Thomas Chong, Cheech Marin, Catherine O'Hara, Linda Fiorentino. Directed by Martin Scorsese. 97 min.

A lacerating, bleak, surreal, and very funny comedy about a night full of nightmares on the mean streets of SoHo and Chelsea. Director Scorsese doesn't abandon the shades of paranoia, isolation, and desperation that marked his earlier work; he simply transposes them to a farcical framework and lets all hell break loose. His hero-victim is Paul Hackett (Dunne, who also produced), an amiable fellow whose chance date with a mercurial young woman (Arquette) leads to encounters with thieves, dominatrixes, punks, time-warped barmaids, and vigilante mobs. As written by Joseph Minion and perfectly orchestrated by the director, it's never predictable. Nothing else of the clever, snaky plot should be revealed. It's an uneven film, veering between out-and-out laughs, mordant wit, and melodrama; but even its lows are high. The superb supporting performance, especially the verbal pirouetting of Arquette, Garr, O'Hara, and Fiorentino, are well matched by Dunne's fine work in the central role. A special nod goes to cinematographer Michael Ballhaus, who has made *After Hours* one of the most beautiful-looking American comedies in years. It's also one of the best.

AFTER THE FALL OF NEW YORK ½☆
1985, Italy/France, R
Michael Sopkiw, Valentine Monnier, Anna Kanakis, Roman Geer, George Eastman, Edmund Purdom. Directed by Martin Dolman. 95 min.

A big bomb about the Big Bomb and its aftermath in the Big Apple, which has been shriveled from radiation. The sound quality is particularly poor, which, in light of the dismal performances, is a blessing.

AFTER THE FOX ☆☆½
1966, USA/Great Britain/Italy
Peter Sellers, Akim Tamiroff, Victor Mature, Britt Ekland. Directed by Vittorio De Sica. 103 min.

Sellers, the Marlon Brando of comedy, sleepwalks his way through another mid-sixties comedy, this time as an Italian crook known as the Fox. In attempting to smuggle in a load of stolen gold, he pretends to be a famous film director so that the people of a small Italian fishing town will aid him. Sellers is sporadically funny, but the most consistent laughs come from, of all places, Victor Mature as a has-been movie star enlisted to play the lead in a movie being shot with no film in the cameras. Neil Simon wrote the screenplay.

AFTER THE REHEARSAL ☆☆☆½
1984, Sweden, R
Erland Josephson, Ingrid Thulin, Lena Olin. Directed by Ingmar Bergman. 72 min.

Originally made for Swedish television, Bergman's latest contains all of the major themes of his recent films—the meaning of love, work, and their relationship to each other. One evening, after a rehearsal of Strindberg's *A Dream Play*, an eminent director (Josephson) is confronted by two of his actresses—one at the end of her career, the other just beginning—each forcing him to face questions in his own life. The impeccable work of Bergman's fine cast gives this brief, intimate look at a life in the theater surprising emotional muscle. It may seem talky and confusing to those unfamiliar with the Strindberg play, which is given an important thematic role here. Subtitled.

AFTER THE THIN MAN ☆☆☆½
1936, USA
William Powell, Myrna Loy, James Stewart, Elissa Landi, Joseph Calleia, Jessie Ralph, Alan Marshall, Teddy Hart, Sam Levene, Dorothy McNulty. Directed by W. S. Van Dyke. 110 min.

William Powell and Myrna Loy were one of the screen's most charming and sophisticated couples, and no vehicles served their breezy, insouciant style better than the *Thin Man* films, in which they played Dashiell Hammett's amateur detectives Nick and Nora Charles. This was the second and perhaps the best of the six. The script, by Frances Goodrich and Albert Hackett, has the pair investigating the disappearance of one of Nora's relatives and stumbling into a murder scheme along the way. The mystery is thin, but the comedy is rich and still hilarious, especially in the opening scenes and the frequent byplay with their dogs Asta and a new arrival, Mrs. Asta. A delight.

AGAINST A CROOKED SKY ☆
1975, USA, G
Stewart Peterson, Richard Boone, Geoffrey Land, Jewel Blanch. Directed by Earl Bellamy. 89 min.

Offensive, almost racist tale of a young boy who sets out to find his sister after she has been abducted by Indians. Joined by grizzled old trapper Richard Boone, the boy learns such valuable lessons as how to say "Dag nab it" when the going gets tough. It's hard to believe that this cornball melodrama was made in 1975—one would have thought that these sensibilities had gone the way of road-show productions of *Uncle Tom's Cabin*.

AGAINST ALL ODDS ☆
1969, Spain, R
Richard Greene, Christopher Lee, Shirley Eaton. Directed by Jess Franco. 89 min.

Against All Odds is the last of Christopher Lee's Fu Manchu series that is watchable. This one lacks the strong adversarial characterization that Nigel Greene brought to the Nayland Smith role. Richard Greene is at least restrained in his inherited role. Unfortunately, the well-done period flavor of the earlier films is missing; the tone is curiously like the Vincent Price *Dr. Goldfoot* series. Lee, however, makes it all tolerable.

AGAINST ALL ODDS ☆☆½
1984, USA, R
Jeff Bridges, Rachel Ward, James Woods, Alex Karras, Jane Greer, Richard Widmark, Dorian Harewood, Swoosie Kurtz, Saul Rubinek, Pat Corley, August Darnell (Kid Creole). Directed by Taylor Hackford. 125 min.

Hackford's remake/update of Jacques Tourneur's 1947 *film noir* classic *Out of the Past* has a seedy ex–football pro (Bridges) and a Los Angeles hood (Woods) vying for the love of a mysterious, beautiful, and treacherous heiress (Ward). It's not nearly up to the original, and Ward's character is conceived with a halfheartedness that nearly destroys the film, but it still functions as an effective, clever, and sexy entertainment, with strong performances from everyone in the large, varied cast. Film buffs in search of a genuine *noir* atmosphere or sensibility will, however, be sorely disappointed. Jane Greer, who played Ward's role in Tourneur's film appears here to fine effect as the character's mother; the lovely title lament was composed and sung by Phil Collins.

AGATHA ☆☆☆½
1979, Great Britain, PG
Vanessa Redgrave, Dustin Hoffman, Timothy Dalton, Helen Morse, Celia Gregory. Directed by Michael Apted. 98 min.

Redgrave's luminous performance makes this charming speculation about the eleven-day disappearance of mystery writer Agatha Christie in 1926 well worth a look. Arthur Hopcraft and Kathleen Tynan's script portrays Christie as an ungainly wallflower trapped in a terrible first marriage; when she flees to a health spa, pursued by a tenacious American reporter determined to uncover her secret, reality ends, and a very engaging literary fantasy begins. The miscast Hoffman is blustery and one-dimensional, but it's Redgrave's show, and, as always, she creates a vivid and memorable character. Excellent, low-key direction by Michael Apted (*Coal Miner's Daughter*) and lush cinematography by Vittorio Storaro.

AGENCY ☆
1981, Canada, R
Robert Mitchum, Lee Majors, Valerie Perrine, Saul Rubinek. Directed by George Kaczender. 93 min.

The notion that advertising agencies could be using subliminal messages in order to make us buy certain products is a potentially intriguing idea for an article in *Psychology Today* magazine, or maybe for a TV skit. As a basis for a movie, though, there's nothing particularly visual or dramatic about it. The viewer is also asked to believe Lee Majors as a frustrated writer turned marketing whiz and (we save the best for last) Valerie Perrine as a doctor. Silly, full of cliché, and pointless. Mitchum, who could have been the film's saving grace, hardly spends enough time on screen to justify his star billing.

AGENT ON ICE ½☆
1986, USA, R
Tom Ormeny, Clifford David, Louis Pastore, Matt Craven, Debra Mooney, Donna Forbes, Jennifer Leak. Directed by Clark Worswick. 97 min.

It seems that everyone is out to kill a down-and-out former CIA agent, John Pope (played by Tom Ormeny, a rank unknown among an entire cast of unknowns), including his corrupt ex-CIA bosses and a Mafia big shot who's supposed to be dead. (Since when did a powerful Mafia boss become inept at executing a simple hit himself?) Even if you're in the mood to forgive the plot flaws and the boring-beyond-all-reason story, no one could forgive casting Ormeny, who resembles nothing so much as the Pillsbury Dough Boy, in a lead role. Worthless.

AGNES OF GOD ☆☆☆
1985, USA, PG-13
Jane Fonda, Anne Bancroft, Meg Tilly, Anne Pitoniak, Winston Rekert. Directed by Norman Jewison. 99 min.

Jewison's direction and some fine acting makes this stage-adopted melodrama about Catholic mysticism and disbelief more effective and less hokey than it might have been. The setting is a Calgary convent, and, as in the director's previous *A Soldier's Story*, the drama's moral issues are couched within the device of a murder investigation. Doing battle for the soul of a troubled young nun (Tilly) who may or may not have murdered her baby are court psychiatrist and lapsed Catholic Martha Livingston (Fonda) and smart, practical Mother Miriam Ruth (Bancroft). While their conversation too often sounds like issues-and-answers regurgitations of doctrine and dispute, John Pielmeir's script is leaner and more perceptive than it was onstage, and its central conflict remains compelling. Fonda plays a huffy, taut career women in a dull reduplication of her work in a half-dozen other films but Bancroft is tough, impassioned, and admirably unsentimental. To see her experience coupled with Tilly's beautifully controlled, vibrant work is invigorating. Sven Nykvist did the handsome, austere cinematography.

AGUIRRE, THE WRATH OF GOD ☆☆☆☆
1972, West Germany
Klaus Kinski, Ruy Guerra, Helena Rojo, Cecilia Rivera, Peter Heiling, Del Negro. Directed by Werner Herzog. 90 min.

Hallucinatory is the best word to describe the strange voyage of a power-mad conquistador rafting down the Amazon. Klaus Kinski inhabits the role of Aguirre with a snarling, narcissistic intensity: he seems to believe that only he could play the Spanish soldier who would crown the emperor of El Dorado. Director Werner Herzog shot the film on location in South America, inflicting primitive conditions on his cast and crew like another Aguirre, wringing desperation, dysentery, and dislocation out of every frame. Startlingly beautiful, with incredible scenery, this should really be seen on a big screen. Arguably the best film from the flowering of the New German Cinema.

AIR FORCE ☆☆☆
1943, USA
John Garfield, John Ridgely, Gig Young, Charles Drake, Harry Carey, Arthur Kennedy, George Tobias, Edward S. Brophy. Directed by Howard Hawks. 124 min.

A Howard Hawks film with lots of exciting aerial footage and the usual fast-paced action. The adventure revolves around an airplane heading for the Pacific on December 6, 1941, and the action heats up as expected. For some tastes, the buddy-buddy heroics and hard-to-digest jingoism will be detrimental, but the slick Hollywood craftsmanship and the well-rounded characters of the bomber crew engage our sympathies nonetheless. A salty, muscular World War II adventure.

AIRPLANE! ☆☆☆½
1980, USA, PG
Robert Hays, Julie Hagerty, Kareem Abdul-Jabbar, Lloyd Bridges, Peter Graves, Leslie Nielsen, Robert Stack, Ethel Merman, Jimmie Walker, Barbara Billingsley, Maureen McGovern. Directed by Jim Abrahams, David Zucker, Jerry Zucker. 88 min.

A delightfully silly, flippant, and energetic send-up of the disaster genre, Airplane! probably has more jokes per foot of film than any other recent American comedy. That inevitably means that there are also more *bad* jokes, but most of them whiz by before you have a chance to wince. Writer-directors Abrahams, Zucker, and Zucker have created a seamless *Mad* magazine–style parody that punctures the pretension of every trouble-in-the-skies film from *The High and the Mighty* to *Airport '79*. Most impressively, they've cast it with a gallery of TV's greatest stone faces, and Bridges, Nielsen, Stack, and Graves lampoon their own images with the acid expertise of born comedians. Hays and Hagerty are, in their own way, just as good playing the stoically dim-witted pilot and stewardess who must overcome shell shock, sexual passion, and an unusual drinking problem to guide the jet to safety. No matter what your tastes, you're almost guaranteed, at least once, to laugh out loud. Followed by *Airplane II: The Sequel*.

AIRPLANE II: THE SEQUEL ☆☆½
1982, USA, PG
Robert Hays, Julie Hagerty, Sonny Bono, Lloyd Bridges, Raymond Burr, Chuck Connors, John Dehner, Rip Torn, Chad Everett, Peter Graves, Kent McCord, William Shatner. Directed by Ken Finkleman. 85 min.

Better than you'd expect. The trio of savvy young comics who made *Airplane!* flew off to friendlier skies, but they left the crew in the hands of a capable copilot—writer/director Finkleman, who has the hip, anything-goes tone of the first movie down cold. The plane's a lunar shuttle this time out, but the movie's still a spritz of high silliness—ninety minutes of cynical *Saturday Night Live*–generation humor delivered with the head-on effrontery of a TV commercial. Hays and Hagerty reprise their roles from the first film, and William Shatner shows up for a delightful Captain Kirk parody.

AIRPORT ☆☆½
1970, USA, G
Burt Lancaster, Dean Martin, Jean Seberg, Jacqueline Bisset, George Kennedy, Helen Hayes, Van Heflin, Maureen Stapleton, Lloyd Nolan, Barbara Hale. Directed by George Seaton. 137 min.

A lumpy, slow, but amiable disaster movie about a bomb on board a jet and the secret lives of the jeopardized all-star cast, *Airport* was a hugely popular and, surprisingly, critical success when it opened. Since then, the already dated film has been rendered virtually irrelevant by the sequels, rip-offs, and parodies it spawned. It functions best as a sort of "Love Boat" with intrigue instead of romance, and if Arthur Hailey's insipid, simplistic plot bores you, the cast remains entertaining. Best among them are Helen Hayes, who won an Academy Award as a generically feisty old lady, and Maureen Stapleton, who invests a stock role with startling emotional intensity. The sequels were *Airport 1975*, *Airport '77*, and *Airport '79—The Concorde*.

AIRPORT 1975 ☆
1974, USA, PG
Charlton Heston, Karen Black, George Kennedy, Gloria Swanson, Helen Reddy, Efrem Zimbalist Jr., Susan Clark, Sid Caesar, Linda Blair, Dana Andrews, Nancy Olson, Roy Thinnes, Myrna Loy, Larry Storch, Norman Fell, Jerry Stiller, Beverly Garland, Erik Estrada. Directed by Jack Smight. 107 min.

A stupefyingly bad movie in which the cast is the only interesting thing about this mess: Nancy Olson, for instance, who played the mother of the Girl on Her Way to a Vital Operation, was in *Sunset Boulevard* with Gloria Swanson, who's also on hand here. Of the numerous plots, the most ridiculous has Karen Black as a stewardess trying to work the contols of a 747 after its pilots have been incapacitated, providing a study in hysteria that Freud would have drooled over; she's rescued by granite-jawed lover Chuck Heston in one of the most ludicrous *deus ex machina* resolutions ever put on film. Other drolleries include Helen Reddy as a singing nun, pudgily pubescent Linda Blair as the aforementioned Girl on Her Way, Myrna Loy and Norman Fell as jolly drunks, and Erik Estrada as navigator Julio. At its best/worst, even funnier than *Airplane!*, which, however was *trying* to be funny.

AIRPORT '79—THE CONCORDE ☆
1979, USA, PG
Alain Delon, Susan Blakely, Robert Wagner, Sylvia Kristel, George Kennedy, Eddie Albert, Bibi Andersson, Charo, John Davidson, Andrea Marcovicci, Martha Raye, Cicely Tyson, Jimmie Walker, David Warner, Mercedes McCambridge, Avery Schreiber, Sybil Danning, Nicolas Coster. Directed by David Lowell Rich. 123 min.

This is not quite as bad as *Airport 1975* (faint praise if ever there was any), but the casting is, again, truly amazing. Casting Bergman star Bibi Andersson alongside the likes of Charo, Sylvia Kristel, and Sybil Danning may be ridiculous, but it takes a really demented mind to choose Miss Andersson from among that quartet to play a hooker. In keeping with the times, 747s have been dispensed with for the supersonic Concorde, the real star of this mess. It contends with an electronic missile, an attack by a French fighter jet, and other tribulations caused by billionaire Robert Wagner, who is trying to kill his girlfriend on board. There have to be easier ways to break up!

AIRPORT '77 ☆☆
1977, USA, PG
Jack Lemmon, James Stewart, Lee Grant, Brenda Vaccaro, Joseph Cotten, George Kennedy, Olivia de Havilland, Darren McGavin, Christopher Lee, Robert Foxworth, Robert Hooks, Monte Markham, Kathleen Quinlan, Gil Gerard, Arlene Golonka, Tom Sullivan, M. Emmet Walsh, Michael Pataki, George Furth. Directed by Jerry Jameson. 114 min.

Especially compared to what came before and after it (*Airport 1975* and *Airport '79—The Concorde*), this entry in the *Airport* series is one of the best of the lot, second only to the original. What helps is that, in choosing the two dozen or so recognizable faces to populate the aisles this time, the producers got actors who were able to bring some conviction to this kind of hokey suspense-melodrama. Jack Lemmon in particular has it down to a T. He has top billing as the pilot of a private 747 loaded with art treasures and wealthy friends that is hijacked over the Bermuda Triangle and crashes into the Atlantic Ocean; it's his job to get the passengers out before pressure breaks open the cabin. Of the rest of the cast, standouts include M. Emmet Walsh as a veterinarian and Christopher Lee playing nicely against type as a henpecked husband.

THE ALAMO ☆½
1960, USA
John Wayne, Richard Widmark, Laurence Harvey, Frankie Avalon, Patrick Wayne, Linda Cristal, Chill Wills, Denver Pyle, Richard Boone. Directed by John Wayne. 192 min.

John Wayne produced, directed, cowrote the original story for, and starred in, this story about the men who defended the fort that Texans will never forget, the Alamo. As a producer, he had the sense to hire a solid bunch of Hollywood craftsmen to mount this expensive attempt at American mythologizing; unfortunately, as its director, he doesn't seem to know exactly where he wants to go, constantly pursuing irrelevant tangents through most of the film's three-hour-plus running time. The final battle sequence is fine, but it takes far too long to get there. Not as bad as *The Green Berets*, Wayne's other pet project, but not as much lamebrained fun, either.

ALAMO BAY ☆½
1985, USA, R
Amy Madigan, Ed Harris, Ho Nguyen, Donald Moffat. Directed by Louis Malle. 105 min.

Malle's film about Vietnamese refugees horning in on the ancestral fishing grounds of Texan bigots could have been a latter-day Capra film had Malle felt any bond with either of the communities he portrays. But the director has as little rapport with his innocent Vietnamese as with his racist rednecks. Screenwriter

Alice Arlen draws the battle lines between Shang (Harris), a Vietnam vet who's about to lose his boat because he can't keep up with his payments, and Dinh (Nguyen), who's hustling to buy a boat of his own. Glory (Madigan), the daughter of a fish wholesaler who employs the immigrants, has to choose between them; both, however, serve less as characters than as ethical options. Madigan is a credible heroine, but she sticks out in Malle's heap of hayseeds.

ALBINO ☆
1976, West Germany/South Africa
James Faulkner, Christopher Lee, Trevor Howard, Horst Frank, Sybil Danning. Directed by Juergen Goslar. 96 min.

Not a horror movie, as the lurid packaging of the videocassette implies, but a dull revenge-chase melodrama set in an unnamed African country. The white settlers are beset by terrorists who use magic to gain the loyalty of the local native. When the fiancée of an ex-policeman is raped and murdered by the leader of the terrorists, an albino Negro (it's amazing what the makeup people can do with a little Pillsbury) sets off across the desert in pursuit. Both fans of Sybil Danning will wish to note that she gets bumped off, rather unpleasantly, after about ten minutes. Fans of Christopher Lee and Trevor Howard will wish to note that the two have very little to do here except sit around and chat about the plot.

THE ALCHEMIST ½☆
1985, USA, R
Robert Ginty, Lucinda Dooling, John Sanderford, Viola Kate Stimpson, Robert Glaudini. Directed by James Amante. 84 min.

A woman and a male hitchhiker are sucked into a weird world of alchemy and ancient curses when she begins hallucinating about a previous life as the wife of a nineteenth-century farmer, seduced away from him by a backwoods sorcerer. This low-budget thriller tries for bigger special effects than it can afford and stars genre veterans Robert Ginty (*The Exterminator*) and Robert Glaudini (*Parasite*). The end result is claustrophobic and not terribly interesting.

ALEXANDER NEVSKY ☆☆☆☆
1938, USSR
Nikolai Cherkassov, Nikolai Okhlopkov, Andrei Abrikosov, Dmitri Orlov. Directed by Sergei Eisenstein. 112 min.

Something of a Russian national epic, this historical saga is one of the most important and influential films of the early sound era. The plot concerns the 1242 defeat of the invading Teutons by Prince Nevksy. In this 1938 film, Eisenstein coordinated screen parallels to the advancing German armies of the day. After the subsequent Russian–German nonaggression pact the film was withdrawn from release until 1941, when the pact was broken. The film has often been compared to a film opera in both the scope of its presentation and its classic score by Sergi Prokofiev. This was also the film in which Eisenstein, the greatest of Russian filmmakers, moved away from his usual depiction of the masses to center on one character. The final battle scene on an icy lake is the highlight.

ALEXANDER THE GREAT ☆☆½
1956, USA
Richard Burton, Fredric March, Claire Bloom, Danielle Darrieux, Peter Cushing, Barry Jones, Helmut Dantine. Directed by Robert Rossen. 143 min.

Although produced, written, and directed by Robert Rossen, this bio-spectacle is less personal than either *All the King's Men* or *Lilith*. The story of Alexander, the fourth century B.C. world conqueror, should have been a great motion picture, and with Burton as the charismatic warrior, March as his father, and Claire Bloom as his true love, the characters should also have come to life. Yet Rossen seemed determined to tell the man's entire story and has difficulty negotiating between the spectacular battles and personal drama. Aside from the Technicolor-Cinemascope battle footage (which is severely diminished on video), this historical epic offers nothing that you couldn't get in *The Adventures of Marco Polo*, *King Richard and the Crusaders*, and so on.

ALFIE ☆☆☆
1966, Great Britain
Michael Caine, Shelley Winters, Millicent Martin, Vivien Merchant. Directed by Lewis Gilbert. 114 min.

Michael Caine became a star with his witty portrayal of a cockney womanizer who gets a harsh comeuppance in this hard-edged comedy of modern manners. Like most films determined to be contemporary, this one has become somewhat dated, but Caine's enthusiasm and quippy asides to the audience still work, and the cast of women who support him is excellent. Oscar nominations went to the film, Caine, Vivien Merchant, and Burt Bacharach's title song. The version on video includes an introduction by Joan Collins. Followed by a sequel, *Oh Alfie* (also known as *Alfie Darling*).

ALFIE DARLING

See *Oh, Alfie*

ALGIERS ☆☆½
1938, USA
Charles Boyer, Hedy Lamarr, Sigrid Gurie, Joseph Calleia, Alan Hale, Gene Lockhart, Johnny Downs. Directed by John Cromwell. 98 min.

Pépé le Moko, holed up in the Casbah, is invulnerable from police capture yet feels as though he's been buried alive. Charles Boyer won the Oscar for his portrayal of Pépé, and Hedy Lamarr, in her Hollywood debut, shines as the fatal attraction who lures Pépé out of hiding. The film, a recreation of Julien Duvivier's French film *Pépé le Moko*, succeeds today mostly on its hallucinatory atmosphere, a tribute to the cinematography of James Wong Howe.

ALICE ADAMS ☆☆☆½
1935, USA
Katharine Hepburn, Fred MacMurray, Fred Stone, Evelyn Venable, Frank Albertson. Directed by George Stevens. 99 min.

George Stevens's masterful screen translation of a Booth Tarkington novel has avoided some of Tarkington's stickiness and even manages to keep a rein on young Hepburn's mannerisms. (Even if you admire Hepburn tremendously, you may want to turn away from a few of her thirties films, where her fluttering eyelids and tremulous hands make you want to sedate her.) Here she is perfection, since all of those affectations are part of the character of Alice, a social climber who puts on airs that she doesn't have the money or position to justify. With deft strokes, the film presents a cruelly accurate portrait of the aspiration of the middle class. Some critics carp about a happy ending that is implausible given the tribulations Alice has undergone, but such is Hepburn's appeal that the audience must see Alice resign her wallflower status and capture her Galahad.

ALICE DOESN'T LIVE HERE ANYMORE ☆☆☆☆
1975, USA, PG
Ellen Burstyn, Kris Kristofferson, Diane Ladd, Jodie Foster, Alfred Lutter, Vic Tayback, Harvey Keitel. Directed by Martin Scorsese. 113 min.

Scorsese's searing vision of a woman in search of herself goes from city streets to suburban bleakness to create a unique, bittersweet portrait of a newly widowed wife who decides to hit the road with her smart-aleck son and resume the singing career she abandoned for marriage. It's a moving and often funny tale, bolstered by seriocomic vignettes of a woman in pursuit of the American dream. Ellen Burstyn won an Academy Award for her vibrant, multifaceted portrayal of Alice, and country singer Kristofferson gives his most honest performance as her earthy lover. This important movie was the basis for the mediocre television sitcom "Alice."

ALICE GOODBODY ☆½
1976, USA, R
Sharon Kelly, Daniel Kaufman, Keith McConnell. Directed by Tom Scheuer. 83 min.

This typical, dumb, soft-core sex comedy had a naive young girl working as a hamburger waitress and waiting for her Big Break to come along. Eventually, she gets an offer to appear in "the seventh most expensive movie ever made." Guess on what basis she gets the part. This type of thing really needs a drive-in around it for the proper ambience.

ALICE IN WONDERLAND ☆☆☆
1950, France/USA
Stephen Murray, Pamela Brown, Carol Marsh, Felix Aylmer, Ernest Milton, David Reed, Raymond Bussières. Directed by Dallas Bower. 83 min.

Lou Bunin's version of the Alice story is a meticulously crafted labor of love that was out of circulation for many years, and one has to be thankful that it was not lost entirely. That said, there are problems with the film that make viewing it primarily of interest to cinema buffs and animation enthusiasts. Bunin used a combination of live action and puppet animation that is almost unique in film history and bears resemblance only to the works of Ray Harryhausen and some of the Russian and Eastern European animators. In addition, Bunin constructed his own figures, and their striking, blocky appearances make them strange and utterly individual artworks. As a film, the movie suffers from poor story direction and mediocre music. Though it is faithful to the texts, it lacks the magic of Carroll. Because the video was made from a rare, surviving print, there is an understandable plethora of scratches and color fading (an outmoded, unstable color process, Ansco, was used). The film was released at the same time as Disney's version and the ensuing legal wrangles hurt this film in its initial release.

ALICE IN WONDERLAND ☆☆☆
1951, USA
Animated: Kathryn Beaumont, Ed Wynn, Sterling Holloway, Richard Haydn, Jerry Colonna, J. Pat O'Malley, Verna Fulton, Bill Thompson. Directed by Clyde Geronomi, Hamilton Luske, Wilfred Jackson. 75 min.

Walt Disney drew on the classic Lewis Carroll books and Sir John Tenniel's famous illustrations for an animated feature film that he had been dreaming about for over two decades. The result is a movie that does not rank with the best of Disney but remains a visual and aural treat. Children, especially, may tire as the film skips thoughtlessly from one episode to the next; but along the way there are several masterful sequences. Perhaps the best scene is the Mad Hatter's tea party, where the anarchy of what is seen is ironically played against the tightly constructed vaudeville patter of Ed Wynn and Jerry Colonna—it's downright dizzying! Other gems include the Walrus and the Carpenter, the Cheshire Cat, and the original-with-Disney talking flowers. The supporting cast is tremendous, and they can really put over the movie's memorable score, including favorites like "I'm Late," "A Very Merry Un-birthday," and "A E I O U." The character of Alice, played by young Beaumont, is the weakest link of the film, failing to provide an emotional focus. All in all, though, well worth seeing.

ALICE'S RESTAURANT ☆☆½
1969, USA
Arlo Guthrie, James Broderick, Pat Quinn, Michael McClanathan, Tina Chen. Directed by Arthur Penn. 111 min.

Arthur Penn followed up *Bonnie and Clyde* with this loose, surprisingly lackluster tale of life among the hippies. Built around Arlo Guthrie's song about the draft, littering, and counterculture mores, the movie manages some deft, funny moments, but its meandering style and breezy liberal attitudes have dated considerably.

ALICE, SWEET ALICE ☆☆☆
1977, USA, R
Brooke Shields, Tom Signorelli, Louis Horton, Paula Sheppard, Lillian Roth. Directed by Alfred Sole. 96 min.

This visually intriguing and thematically complex horror film has so much going on that it's no wonder the director can't resolve all the loose ends. But what a pleasure to see a horror film that has more on its mind than bumping off teenagers. Dealing with the transference of guilt and intense sibling rivalry that affects two generations of sisters, the film probes human emotion with amazing intensity. In its exploration of the influence of the Catholic Church on its members' personal lives, saddling them with guilt, the film is uncomfortably on target. When her lovable sister is found burned to death on her Communion Day, a jealous sibling is suspected; the shadow of this crime follows her throughout childhood. Cruel and incisive, the film would have been a classic if the false leads had been juggled more persuasively (a.k.a.: *Communion* and *Holy Terror*)

ALIEN ☆☆½
1979, USA, R
Sigourney Weaver, Tom Skerritt, John Hurt, Yaphet Kotto, Veronica Cartwright, Harry Dean Stanton, Ian Holm. Directed by Ridley Scott. 105 min.

Ridley Scott's moody outer-space horror film has an intergalactic garbage truck accidentally picking up an omnivorous, metamorphic monster as cargo. *Alien* benefits from a fine cast, Scott's high style, and up-to-the-minute special effects by a team that included Carlo (*E.T.*) Rambaldi and H. R. Giger. Scott's view of the cosmos as a series of grubby dumping grounds for the refuse of civilization is unusual enough to be refreshing, and Sigourney Weaver, in her film debut, makes a formidable heroine. There are well-calculated shrieks and explosions of gore throughout, but as the alien picks off the *Nostromo*'s crew members one by one, the story underlying this superabundance of technique emerges as a hackneyed old mad-slasher plot. Among its greater and more annoying pretensions is an intentionally muffled dialogue soundtrack.

ALIEN CONTAMINATION ☆
1980, Italy
Ian McCulloch, Louise Monroe, Martin Mase. Directed by Luigi Cozzi. 90 min.

It is well-known to connoisseurs of bad horror movies that, since the heyday of the Mexicans in the late fifties and the Japanese in the sixties, the best and most consistent producers of laughably unfrightening monster movies with cheapo beasties, unfathomable plots, and asynchronous dubbing have been the Italians. Such fans will not be disappointed by this silliness about eggs from Mars that squirt goop all over people, causing them to disintregate. Only for the extremely jaded.

THE ALIEN FACTOR ☆
1976, USA
Don Leifert, Tom Griffith, Richard Dyszel, Mary Mertens. Directed by Donald M. Dohler. 80 min.

This ultra-low-budget monster movie was sold directly to television and later released on videocassette, apparently without ever having played in a theater. None of this will surprise you, should you happen to watch it. A small town finds itself beset by a series of alien beasties, who are then set upon by a self-appointed monster hunter. The special effects range from not bad to just okay. The acting, however, lends new meaning to the phrase "on-location shooting."

ALIEN PREY
1983, USA, R ☆
Barry Stokes, Sally Faulkner, Glory Annan, Sandy Chaney. Directed by Norman J. Warren. 85 min.

Into a lesbian ménage on an isolated country estate wanders a humanoid alien, who is quickly drawn into the hothouse world the two women have created for themselves. He stirs up deadly sexual jealousy between them before showing his true, horrifying nature: he is a cannibal from space, scouting Earth as a possible food source for his planet, and he likes what he finds very, very much.... Cross *The Fox* with director Warren's *Horror Planet* (a.k.a.: *Inseminoid*) and this is more or less what you get: how amusing you find it depends. Lots of blood, lots of sex, lots of stranger-in-a-strange-land clichés.

ALIENS
1986, USA, R ☆☆☆
Sigourney Weaver, Michael Biehn, Carrie Henn, Lance Henriksen. Directed by James Cameron. 137 min.

This sequel to Ridley Scott's harrowing 1979 film suffers from few of the traditional afflictions of sequels; in fact, it's better than the original—the story is logical, the pacing is brisk, and the action never lets up. It is fifty-seven years after the destruction of the spaceship *Nostromo* when Officer Ripley (Weaver), the sole survivor, is salvaged, and emerges from her hibernation to find that no one will believe her story—in fact, the deserted planet has been colonized in the interim with no trouble from the purported aliens. But she and we know better, and when contact with the colony is lost, marines-of-the-future travel to the planet to take a look. What they find are ... great special effects by Stan Winston and ferocious nonstop adventure courtesy of director-writer James Cameron (*The Terminator*).

ALIENS FROM SPACESHIP EARTH
1977, USA, PG ☆½
Donovan, Lynda Day George. Directed by Don Como. 107 min.

Have you ever longed for a film that asks some of the same burning questions as *Plan 9 from Outer Space*, with slightly better production values? Have you ever wondered whatever became of Donovan, the sixties hippie folksinger? Has it ever occurred to you that many of the great men in human history may have been extraterrestrials sent here to influence the course of human development? Well, no one else has thought about it either, which could be why the yo-yos who made this junk felt that they didn't have to work too hard at answering any of these questions. This pseudodocumentary with dramatic enactments from history is in the Sun Classics mold, and about as classic.

ALISON'S BIRTHDAY
1983, USA ☆½
Joanne Samuel, Lou Brown. Directed by David Hannay. 99 min.

Alison is not at all amused, at her nineteenth birthday party, to find out that her family is a coven for devil worshipers. Not that we can blame her, but c'mon, she should try to put petty differences aside on occasions like birthdays and Easter and Arbor Day.

ALL ABOUT EVE
1950, USA ☆☆☆½
Bette Davis, Anne Baxter, George Sanders, Gary Merrill, Marilyn Monroe, Hugh Marlowe, Celeste Holm. Directed by Joseph L. Mankiewicz. 138 min.

This humorous study of New York theater life has a still-fascinating plot and enough sharp performances to overcome its few minor flaws. Although Joseph L. Mankiewicz won Oscars for both his screenplay and his direction, the screenplay, despite some sharp lines, is shakily structured, and the direction is surprisingly ordinary. Essentially, the cast is the thing. Baxter plays Eve, a manipulative young woman who plots to dethrone Margo Channing (Davis), the toast of Broadway. Before Margo knows what's happening, Eve is understudying her current role, replacing her in the next project and cuddling up to her director-boyfriend (Davis's then-husband, Gary Merrill). Bette Davis gives a bravura, scenery-chewing performance as the dynamic but aging star and Anne Baxter's wolf-in-sheep's-clothing is a perfect foil. The other women shine, particularly Marilyn Monroe as a starlet, and George Sanders tops them all as an acid-spewing critic. It is unfortunate, however, that the two male leads (Merrill and Marlowe) are practically interchangeable. The juiciest of the film's many juicy moments occurs when Sanders reveals to both Baxter and the audience her fraudulent past.

ALLAN QUATERMAIN AND THE LOST CITY OF GOLD
1987, USA, PG ☆
Richard Chamberlain, Sharon Stone, James Earl Jones, Richard Donner. Directed by Gary Nelson. 99 min.

For those six or seven Americans who were breathlessly awaiting the sequel to the Richard Chamberlain–Cannon Films remake of *King Solomon's Mines*, this cheap, cheesy swashbuckling adventure is it. Back from the first film are Chamberlain and Sharon Stone (not surprising, since much of this was shot at the same time), contending with new villains, not-quite-hairsbreadth escapes, and a fresh array of bargain-basement action sequences and tepid special effects.

ALLEGHENY UPRISING
1939, USA ☆☆
John Wayne, Claire Trevor, George Sanders, Brian Donlevy, Wilfrid Lawson, Moroni Olsen, Chill Wills. Directed by William A. Seiter. 98 min.

Pre-Revolutionary War action, with Big John the leader of a group of Pennsylvanians determined to put a stop to the selling of firearms and fire water to the Indians by British-supported profiteers. Wayne and Trevor are rematched after *Stagecoach* earlier that year, but director Seiter is no John Ford. The set and costume designers have, at least, concocted a reasonably valid period piece.

ALLEGRO NON TROPPO
1976, Italy, PG ☆☆☆½
Animated. Directed by Bruno Bozzetto. 75 min.

A consistently witty send-up of Disney's *Fantasia* that's more than mere parody of the juicier moments from that classical-music cartoon. In its own right, this animated laugh-in satirizes symphonic orchestra pretension much more adeptly than Fellini did in *Orchestra Rehearsal*; and yet it still has comic energy enough left for some brilliant animation. Somehow, the brilliance of the artwork and the wicked wit of the conception do not serve to diminish the impact of *Fantasia*; perhaps Disney's film is better enjoyed with a little of its hot air let out.

ALLEY CAT
1984, USA, R ☆☆
Karin Mani, Robert Torti, Britt Helfer, Michael Wayne, Jon Greene. Directed by Edward Victor (Eduardo Palmos, Victor Ordonex, Al Valletta). 82 min.

If you're a fan of sleazy revenge films about tormented but beautiful women, this is for you. A young L.A. women refuses to give in to a gang that won't stop bothering her when she jogs at night, and she ultimately takes them to court. Of course, given the type of movie this is, the judge is a wimp who lets the thugs go and then throws Our Heroine in jail for contempt of court. After a brief foray into the Women-in-Prison genre, she gets out and takes matters into her own hands. It's all made a little more palatable by the casting of Karin Mani, who is not only robustly sexy but actually seems to be doing her own fighting.

ALL GOD'S CHILDREN ★★★
1980, USA (TV)
Richard Widmark, Ned Beatty, Ruby Dee, Ossie Davis, Mariclare Costello, Ken Swofford, Trish Van Devere. Directed by Jerry Thorpe. 100 min.

A provocative, carefully wrought TV problem pic about the still-controversial forced school-busing issue. Sometimes these torn-from-today's-headlines TV dramas are obviously shallow attempts to cash in on topicality, but this film sensitively illuminates the heated conflict. An entire neighborhood finds itself divided over the fate of its children. In fact, the film painstakingly points out that friends and families find themselves on opposite sides of the philosophical fence. Thoughtful direction and passionate performances from actors who care about the film's message add to the quality.

ALLIGATOR ★★★
1980, USA, R
Robert Forster, Robin Riker, Jack Carter, Henry Silva, Dean Jagger, Perry Lang, Sidney Lassick, Mike Mazurki, Sue Lyon, Angel Tompkins. Directed by Lewis Teague. 94 min.

Screenwriter John Sayles wrote a lot of this kind of thing to provide funds for his own films. Here he took the old canard about what happens to those cute little baby alligators that parents flush down the toilet before they get too big to care for (they grow to full size in the sewers, as any eight-year-old can tell you) and gave it a suitable tongue-in-cheek treatment. The result, while never a comedy (there are enough gory scenes to merit keeping the weak of stomach away from this), is full of jokes and lots of fun for fans of the genre. Director Lewis Teague gets in on the game as well, making the best of a low budget to keep you glued to your seat as thirty-five-foot-long Ramone (the gator) feeds on the bodies of dogs used in hormone growth experiments, attacks a sewer worker named Ed Norton, and finally bursts out to terrorize the town. You'll want to keep your fingers on the freeze-frame button so you can read the graffiti on the sewer walls.

ALL MINE TO GIVE ★★
1956, USA
Glynis Johns, Cameron Mitchell, Rex Thompson, Patty McCormack, Ernest Truex, Hope Emerson, Alan Hale, Sylvia Field. Directed by Allen Reisner. 103 min.

A heavy-handed but ultimately effective tearjerker about a horde of moppets who must go into different foster homes after their mother dies. The performances are good, if tending toward the maudlin, and the resolution is, of course, upbeat. With the advent of the TV movie, this sort of lump-in-the-throat material was permanently consigned to the small screen; in fact, a somewhat similar plot was handled with much more grace in the 1983 telefilm *Who Will Love My Children?*

ALL NIGHT LONG ★★½
1981, USA, R
Gene Hackman, Barbra Streisand, Diane Ladd, Dennis Quaid, Annie Girardot, Kevin Dobson. Directed by Jean-Claude Tramont. 100 min.

This low-key comedy-drama about a businessman going through a mid-life crisis contains one outrageous and obtrusive element—the casting of Barbra Streisand as the man's Kewpie-doll mistress. Streisand stepped in at the last minute, took second billing, and donned a blonde wig for the occasion. Though she tries for a sort of Marilyn Monroe innocence, she comes off uncertain and affected. Her best moment comes when she sits down to the piano and sings off key. Hackman is excellent, and the rest of the cast work well together. However, the film wobbles from comedy (a slapstick fight in the supermarket) to drama (Kevin Dobson as Streisand's violent husband) without proper grounding. An admirable failure. The video contains twelve minutes not seen in theatrical release.

ALL OF ME ★★★½
1984, USA, PG
Steve Martin, Lily Tomlin, Victoria Tennant, Richard Libertini. Directed by Carl Reiner. 93 min.

Arguably the best so far of the Reiner-Martin collaborations, *All of Me* tells the story of a rich, dying dowager (Tomlin) whose nasty grouch of a soul decides to inhabit one side of the body of her unwitting lawyer (Martin). What could have been a succession of dumb sex jokes becomes instead a snappy, exuberant farce that gives Steve Martin a chance to demonstrate his astounding physical dexterity as both actor and comedian. His consistently inventive split-personality performance creates a characterization richly funny enough to have earned him several critics' circle awards for best actor. He and Tomlin (who isn't on screen nearly long enough) turn *All of Me* into a comedy that fully lives up to a very bright premise.

ALL OVER TOWN ★★½
1937, USA
Ole Olsen, Chic Johnson, Mary Howard, Franklin Pangborn, James Finlayson, Harry Stockwell, Stanley Fields. Directed by James Horne. 62 min.

Bizarre B comedy with everything from a performing seal to a hallucinating hobo to a guy who can't keep his pants up. When Olsen and Johnson made *Hellzapoppin*, a comedy (based on the Broadway revue) full of cinematic tricks, they inadvertently set themselves up as the darlings of film students, who discover postmodernist self-consciousness in the pair's jokes on the cinematic process. At heart, though, the boys are strictly buffoons; this earlier film, too, has them involved in show business, but they're just bouncing gags off a plot about a girl, a theater, and a couple of murders. Olsen and Johnson are a very strange vaudeville duo. They look a little like starved-mad Abbott and Costellos, and they never get involved in the story—they're always giggling at the other characters' troubles, and they often seem flat-out psychotic. The ventriloquism number, with Chic playing a very creepy dummy, must be seen to be believed. A good, obscure discovery for the distributor, Kartes Video.

ALL QUIET ON THE WESTERN FRONT ★★★★
1930, USA
Louis Wolheim, Lew Ayres, John Wray, Raymond Griffith, George "Slim" Summerville. Directed by Lewis Milestone. 105 min.

A group of young German men grow from students to battle veterans to trench corpses in this beautiful, horrifying indictment of war. Based on Erich Maria Remarque's pacifist classic, the film succeeds in combining the intensely felt personal tragedies of the individual young men with an understanding of a country's war machine. There is a stunning, extended scene between Lew Ayres and former silent film comedian Raymond Griffith, who find themselves sharing a fox hole. The entire war becomes encapsulated in this sequence of two enemies thrown together, and surprise is replaced by suspicion and fear. Ayres's guilt (you'll see why) leads to a heartbreaking, failed reconciliation. This film was one of Carl Laemmle, Jr.'s bids to make Universal a top studio, and the assembled cast and crew carried the Academy Award for best picture. Within a couple of years, however, Universal was best known for cranking out horror movies.

ALL QUIET ON THE WESTERN FRONT ★★★½
1979, USA (TV)
Richard Thomas, Patricia Neal, Ian Holm, Donald Pleasence, Ernest Borgnine. Directed by Delbert Mann. 155 min.

It isn't often that a TV remake can hold its own with a recognized movie classic, but this expertly crafted and memorably acted drama bears comparison with the illustrious 1930 Hollywood original. Although it lacks the power of its distinguished predecessor, this creditable production touches our emotions and shakes us out of our complacency as it unfolds the tale of an idealistic German student turned soldier who comes of age on a World War battlefield. The pain and anger of Remarque's antiwar novel is captured with force and incisiveness, making this another enduring pacifist drama.

ALL SCREWED UP ☆☆½
1974, Italy
Luigi Diberti, Lina Polito, Nino Bignamini, Sara Rapisarda. Directed by Lina Wertmüller. 105 mi.

Not nearly as screwed up as Wertmüller's later films, which overflow with half-baked philosophical twaddle, this film's humane values are part of the fabric of the film: we really care about the two bumpkin farmers who flee the sticks and discover that they are unprepared to handle big-city living. The film was made after the splendidly funny *Seduction of Mimi* but before the overwrought but acclaimed *Seven Beauties*, in which Wertmüller's political bent and penchant for grossness established her personal directorial trademark.

ALL THAT JAZZ ☆☆½
1979, USA, R
Roy Scheider, Jessica Lange, Ann Reinking, Leland Palmer, Cliff Gorman, Ben Vereen. Directed by Bob Fosse. 123 min.

Roy Scheider gives one of his best performances in Fosse's lavish, indulgent autobiographical musical drama about a brilliant, pill-popping filmmaker in the fast lane. Fosse may have chosen an ugly subject—himself—but he directed some scenes in a glitzy, colorful style. Most of the dance sequences, which Fosse choreographed, are highly imaginative. The final number is painfully drawn out and unpleasant. Oscars went to the costume design and musical score.

ALL THAT MONEY CAN BUY

See *The Devil and Daniel Webster*

ALL THE KING'S MEN ☆☆☆☆
1949, USA
Broderick Crawford, John Ireland, Joanne Dru, Mercedes McCambridge, John Derek, Shepperd Strudwick, Ralph Dumke, Anne Seymour. Directed by Robert Rossen. 109 min.

Writer-director Robert Rossen adapted the Robert Penn Warren Pulitzer-prize novel for this still-compelling political drama, the study of Willie Stark (Broderick Crawford), a backwoods man-of-the-people who runs for the governorship of a Southern state and becomes a monomaniacal dictator once in office. Rossen's film looks like few others to come out of Hollywood in the 1940s—the locations seem unusually real, and the powerful, dense montages that accompany Willie's rise to power show Rossen as a filmmaker in firm control of the medium. The film is dark, impassioned, and almost as insightful in today's world as it was forty years ago. Winner of Academy Awards for Best Picture, Best Actor (Crawford), and Best Supporting Actress (Mercedes McCambridge, in a superb screen debut as one of Stark's most devious advisers).

ALL THE MARBLES ☆☆☆
1981, USA
Peter Falk, Vicki Frederick, Laurene Landon, Burt Young, Tracy Reed, Ursaline Bryant-King. Directed by Robert Aldrich. 113 min.

Director Aldrich's last film was packaged as a sexy comedy about women wrestlers, but it really studies the vicious manipulations of their low-life manager. The camera predictably devotes a great deal of attention to the female body, but Frederick and Landon can act as well as wrestle. Falk, as their wheeling-dealing manager, captures Aldrich's gritty, hard-nosed flair, and the film is genuinely entertaining and quickly paced.

ALL THE PRESIDENT'S MEN ☆☆☆☆
1976, USA, PG
Robert Redford, Dustin Hoffman, Jason Robards, Jack Warden, Martin Balsam, Hal Holbrook, Jane Alexander. Directed by Alan J. Pakula. 138 min.

A courageous attempt to present how *Washington Post* reporters Carl Bernstein (Dustin Hoffman) and Bob Woodward (Robert Redford) uncovered the 1972 Watergate scandal that forced Richard Nixon to resign. William Goldman's Oscar-winning screenplay, based on Woodward and Bernstein's book, details everything from the actual break-in at National Democratic headquarters to Woodward's clandestine meetings with White House source "Deep Throat," to the editorial meeting that nearly killed the story, to the final break on the eve of Nixon's oath of office. Alan J. Pakula admirably creates a suspenseful detective thriller out of the predetermined story line, and, while the performances (especially Best Supporting Actor Jason Robards as *Post* editor Ben Bradlee) are competent and credible, it is the brillant re-creation of the 1972 *Post* newsroom that is most enthralling about the film. A well-deserved Oscar went to art director George Jenkins and set decorator George Gaines.

ALL THE RIGHT MOVES ☆☆½
1983, USA, R
Tom Cruise, Lea Thompson, Craig T. Nelson, Charles Cioffi, Gary Graham. Directed by Michael Chapman. 91 min.

An inspirational melodrama that succeeds on its own hollow terms. Cruise plays Stefan Djordjevic, a high school football player who's gunning for a college scholarship so he can get the hell out of Steeltown, Pennsylvania. Nelson is the coach who also wants out, and he collides with Stef when the young player takes to defending one of his teammates. Both are fine, as is Thompson as the loyal girlfriend/cheerleader. Directing for the first time, ace cinematographer Michael Chapman disguises his lack of experience as a filmmaker with shrewd camera placement. His shooting of the Big Game is a small classic, and the whole film looks and plays like a male *Flashdance*—but he can't shake the essential hokiness of the material.

ALL THE WAY, BOYS ☆½
1973, Italy, PG
Terence Hill, Bud Spencer, Cyril Cusak, Michele Antoine. Directed by Giuseppe Colizzi. 105 min.

Lamebrained reteaming of those *They Call Me Trinity* boys, but comic lightning doesn't strike twice here. This time, their escapades involve risking life and limb flying over the Andes on the lookout for treasure. The rousing adventure elements work better than the slack comedy scenes.

ALL THIS AND HEAVEN TOO ☆☆☆
1940, USA
Bette Davis, Charles Boyer, Jeffrey Lynn, Barbara O'Neil, Virginia Weidler, Henry Daniell, George Coulouris, Montagu Love, June Lockhart, Ann Todd, Fritz Leiber, Helen Westley. Directed by Anatole Litvak. 140 min.

The book that knocked *Gone with the Wind* off the top of the best-seller list is turned into an absorbing, well-mounted Hollywood historical drama. Charles Boyer and Bette Davis turn in remarkably restrained performances as the Duc de Praslin and the governess of his household, who in 1847 were accused of murdering the Duc's wife in order to continue an affair they were rumored to be having. Although the actual murderer's identity was never satisfactorily ascertained, the film takes the position that the Duc and the governess were innocent, both of the killing and of any illicit affair, so the two stars have to carry a burden of conveying passion as an abstract quality. Barbara O'Neil steals the show, though, as the Duchesse. Litvak directs with his usual style and moderation, a rarity in a project of such epic proportions.

ALMOST ANGELS ☆☆½
1962, USA
Peter Weck, Hans Holt, Fritz Eckhardt, Bruni Lobel, Vincent Winter. Directed by Steve Previn. 93 min.

Another Disney heart-tugger about a deep friendship that develops between two youngsters in the Vienna Boys Choir. If sentimentality annoys you, then close your eyes and just listen to the music. This is a sweet but not inordinately sticky kids' film with a prankish sense of humor to alleviate all that Viennese schlag.

AN ALMOST PERFECT AFFAIR ☆☆½
1979, USA, PG
Keith Carradine, Monica Vitti, Raf Vallone, Christian De Sica. Directed by Michael Ritchie. 93 min.

Michael Ritchie is a director who has consistently and amusingly taken lighthearted yet cynical looks at various institutions: beauty pageants in *Smile*, baseball in *The Bad News Bears*, and football and faddish self-help therapy in *Semi-Tough*. In *An Almost Perfect Affair*, Ritchie turns his camera 180 degrees to observe the film industry in a romantic farce set during the Cannes Film Festival. It's about a filmmaker (Carradine) who falls in love with a producer's wife (Vitti) while exhibiting his first feature at the festival. The stars are attractive and the setting is beautiful and intriguing, but the Walter Bernstein–Don Peterson script is not up to the witty heights of previous Ritchie vehicles. Ultimately, the film is best in its more contemplative moments.

ALMOST YOU ☆½
1985, USA, R
Griffin Dunne, Brooke Adams, Karen Young, Marty Watt, Christine Estabrook, Josh Mostel, Laura Dean, Miguel Pinero, Spalding Gray. Directed by Adam Brooks. 96 min.

This trite romantic comedy-drama concerns yuppie love in the Big Apple. Griffin Dunne and Brooke Adams are attractive performers who manage to wring some nice moments out of this all-too-predictable tale of romantic complications, but neither can overcome the self-analysis, self-obsession, and just plain selfishness of their upwardly mobile, brattish characters. Adams is as underutilized here as she was in the similarly ridiculous *Key Exchange*. A waste of time and talent.

ALOHA, BOBBY AND ROSE ☆½
1975, USA, PG
Paul Le Mat, Dianne Hull, Tim McIntire, Leigh French, Robert Carradine. Directed by Floyd Mutrux. 89 min.

Two young lovers flee the Sunset Strip for Mexico when a foolish joke tragically misfires. The film also misfires, failing both to engage our sympathies toward the protagonist and to provoke our anger towards the antagonist. Paul Le Mat and screen newcomer Dianne Hull mechanically portray the hard-luck couple, and writer-director Mutrux's substitutions of chic *mise-en-scène* for grainly realism doesn't help matters.

ALONE IN THE DARK ½☆
1982, USA, R
Jack Palance, Martin Landau, Donald Pleasence, Dwight Schultz. Directed by Jack Sholder. 92 min.

Three escaped psychopaths seek revenge on their psychiatrist. If that doesn't sound enticing, check out the cast: Jack Palance, Martin Landau, and Donald Pleasence.

ALONG CAME JONES ☆☆☆
1945, USA
Gary Cooper, Loretta Young, William Demarest, Dan Duryea, Frank Sully, Russell Simpson. Directed by Stuart Heisler. 90 min.

Lively performances by Cooper, Demarest, and Duryea add some sparkle to what might otherwise have been a flat frontier tale of guns, cows, and mistaken identity. Cooper, who made his debut as a producer with this movie, turned *Along Came Jones* into a wry, good-natured spoof of Westerns and his own screen image.

ALONG THE NAVAJO TRAIL ☆☆
1945, USA
Roy Rogers, George "Gabby" Hayes, Dale Evans, Estelita Rodriguez. Directed by Frank McDonald. 60 min.

Roy Rogers poses as a singing cowboy in an effort to unravel a murder and break an outlaw syndicate out on the prairie. Good tunes, riding, and shooting by the ever personable Rogers—combined with comely love interests Evans and Rodriguez—make this an enjoyable, good-natured Western.

ALPHABET CITY ☆½
1984, USA, R
Vincent Spano, Kate Vernon, Michael Winslow, Zohra Lampert. Directed by Amos Poe. 98 min.

Lots of flash and glitter, but little sense characterize this tale of a Manhattan drug pusher whose empire crumbles around him during the course of one night. Director Poe desperately tries to stylize New York's infamous Avenues A, B, and C by lighting the ghetto in designer neon blues and pinks. While *Alphabet City* does look good, it suffers from the lack of a credible plot and from an overdose of bizarre street characters. Good young actor Vincent Spano of *Baby It's You* is wasted by the hackneyed script. Only Michael Winslow *(Police Academy)* provides interest as a human sound-effects machine. For a much classier rendition of the same type of story, check out the British film *The Long Good Friday*.

THE ALPHA INCIDENT ☆½
1977, USA, PG
Ralph Meeker, Stafford Morgan, John Goff, Carole Irene Newell. Directed by Bill Rebane. 84 min.

A deadly growth from Mars is brought back to Earth without due consideration for the consequences. Of course the stuff gives off dangerous radiation. Although the filmmakers have seen their share of outer-space paranoia flicks, they haven't been inspired to try anything remotely new or exciting with the genre.

ALSINO AND THE CONDOR ☆☆☆
1982, Nicaragua/Mexico/Cuba/Costa Rica
Dean Stockwell, Alan Esquivel, Carmen Bunster, Alejandro Parodi. Directed by Miguel Littin. 89 min.

In the first fiction feature ever made in Nicaragua, a twelve-year-old peasant takes a nighmarish tour of his war-torn countryside. He dreams of flying over the turmoil like a bird, but from his godlike perch he can see the full horror of the devastation visited on his people. This allegory becomes engrossing as the boy falls out of a tree and becomes hunchbacked; only by joining the guerrilla fighters is he able to find the freedom of his dreams again. Somewhat primitive in ideology and execution, the film is nonetheless remarkably moving.

ALTERED STATES ☆☆½
1980, USA, R
William Hurt, Blair Brown, Charles Haid, Bob Balaban, Thaao Penghlis. Directed by Ken Russell. 102 min.

This cinematic head trip sets the soul-searching spirit of the sixties in the academic world of the eighties. William Hurt is a psychophysiologist who uses himself as a guinea pig in complex experiments dealing with isolation tanks and psychosomatic de-evolution. The script is hardly intelligible and the muddled dialogue tends to alienate, but Hurt plays his role with such conviction that he commands interest and renders even the most skeptical viewers curious. The real power of this film, though, rests on director Russell's wildly inventive cinematic talent: psychedelic visual effects and hallucination sequences may nearly work you into an altered state of your own. As Hurt returns to a prehuman bestial form, the film becomes a virtual horror movie, though one tempered by sensuality and scientific intrigue.

ALVAREZ KELLY ☆☆½
1966, USA
William Holden, Richard Widmark, Janice Rule, Patrick O'Neal, Roger C. Carmel, Arthur Franz, Harry Carey, Jr. Directed by Edward Dmytryk. 110 min.

Good location photography and an exciting cattle stampede don't balance out the slowness of this Civil War adventure. Holden, as the half-Mexican, half-Irishman of the title, sells his herd of cattle to the Yankees. Confederate colonel Widmark kidnaps him and forces him to help him steal the herd to help feed the South, suffering under a food blockade.

ALWAYS ☆☆☆
1986, USA, R
Henry Jaglom, Patrice Townsend, Amnon Meskin, Bud Townsend, Bob Rafelson, Joanna Frank, Alan Rachins, Michael Emil. Directed by Henry Jaglom. 105 min.

Henry Jaglom (*Sitting Ducks, Can She Bake a Cherry Pie?*) records his own divorce, putting all the principals on film but changing the names to protect himself against charges of *cinéma vérité*. When Judy stops by David's house to sign the papers that will finalize their divorce, she suffers an allergic reaction and is forced to spend the entire weekend, thus giving the pair and assorted friends and relatives the chance to talk things out *ad infinitum*. Jaglom and ex-wife Patrice Townsend play David and Judy, Patrice's father plays Judy's father, Henry's brother Michael Emil plays David's brother, and so on. It's a sort of West Coast, low-budget *Annie Hall*, except instead of looking at the past through flashbacks we listen to everyone discuss it. This isn't as bad as it sounds, because the Jaglom clan includes some fascinating, bizarre conversationalists; much of the dialogue is improvised, presumably consisting of actual reminiscences. Be forewarned, however, that Jaglom is very much an acquired taste.

AMADEUS ☆☆☆☆
1984, USA, PG
F. Murray Abraham, Thomas Hulce, Elizabeth Berridge, Simon Callow, Jeffrey Jones, Christine Ebersole. Directed by Milos Forman. 158 min.

Winner of Oscars for Best Picture, Director, Actor (Abraham over Hulce, who was also nominated), Cinematography (Miroslav Ondricek), Score, Costumes, and whatever else they give out Oscars for, this adapation of Peter Shaffer's popular stage play all but abandons the play's theme of the conflict between genius and mediocrity about halfway through in order to become a sumptuous re-creation of the latter works of Mozart, all produced with a high degree of historical verisimilitude. The best performance is from Jeffrey Jones as a slightly daffy Emperor Joseph II.

AMARCORD ☆☆☆☆
1974, Italy/France, R
Puppela Maggio, Magali Noel, Armando Brancia, Bruno Zanin. Directed by Federico Fellini. 123 min.

Fellini's nostalgic, semiautobiographical portrait of the small Italian town where he grew up is touching and remarkably free of the artifice and stylization of many of his other films. It's a gentle, generous coming-of-age comedy with a serious undertone: to the people of those provinces, Mussolini's fascist rule is an abstract but growing threat. *Amarcord*'s tone is one of good-natured vulgarity—although the adults here are fairly grotesque, they're also quirky and likable. The sumptuous production design is by longtime Fellini collaborator Danilo Donati.

THE AMATEUR ☆☆½
1982, Canada, R
John Savage, Christopher Plummer, Marthe Keller, Arthur Hill, Ed Lauter. Directed by Charles Jarrott. 111 min.

Computer whiz Savage blackmails the U.S. government into letting him sneak into East Berlin in order to kill an international terrorist who murdered his girlfriend during a hostage situation. Implausible but fast-moving in the finale, it's reasonably entertaining. Plummer overacts outrageously as a Shakespeare-quoting terrorist honcho.

THE AMAZING ADVENTURE ☆½
1936, Great Britain
Cary Grant, Mary Brian, Peter Gawthorne, Henry Kendall, Leon M. Lion. Directed by Alfred Zeisler. 61 min.

Creaky Cary Grant vehicle that casts him as a rich cad who finds out who his true friends are only when he's forced into the pretense of making an honest living. Grant is fine, although little is asked of him, but the rest of the cast is grating, and the story had whiskers on it fifty years ago. The version on video is twenty minutes shorter than the original British release. The film has been released at various lengths under the titles *Amazing Quest, The Amazing Quest of Ernest Bliss, Riches and Romance,* and *Romance and Riches*.

THE AMAZING DOBERMANS ☆☆
1976, USA, G
Fred Astaire, James Franciscus, Barbara Eden, Jack Carter, Billy Barty. Directed by Byron Chudrow. 96 min.

Just how amazing are they? Can they overcome a cast that includes both Jack Carter and Billy Barty? Well, they're pretty amazing, and the cast isn't as annoying as it could be. A kiddie movie with funny villains, animals helping the police, and a hero who doesn't end up with the girl, this is hard to get excited about, but nominally entertaining. A sequel to *The Doberman Gang* and *The Darling Dobermans*, and better than both.

THE AMAZING HOWARD HUGHES ☆☆
1977, USA (TV)
Tommy Lee Jones, Ed Flanders, James Hampton, Tovah Feldshuh, Lee Purcell, Sorrell Booke, Howard Hesseman, Morgan Brittany, Ed Harris. Directed by William A. Graham. 215 min.

The only thing worse than Hollywood biographies of legendary figures are made-for-television biographies of legendary figures. In this one, Tommy Lee Jones plays Howard Hughes, the enigmatic entrepreneur who became involved with as many business ventures as Hollywood starlets. Based on Bob Thomas and Noah Dietrich's *Howard: The Amazing Mr. Hughes*, the film covers Hughes's life from his late teens to his death in 1976 and is potentially fascinating. But with Tovah Feldshuh as Katherine Hepburn and Sorrell Booke as Fiorello LaGuardia, it becomes *Citizen Kane* meets *Gable and Lombard*. Stick with *Melvin and Howard*; there's less Hughes but more entertainment.

AMAZING QUEST

See *The Amazing Adventure*

THE AMAZING QUEST OF ERNEST BLISS

See *The Amazing Adventure*

THE AMBUSH MURDERS ★★½
1982, USA (TV)
Dorian Harewood, James Brolin, Alfre Woodard, Robert Denison, Louis Giambalvo. Directed by Steven Hilliard Stern. 100 min.

A fairly compelling factual drama based on a book by distinguished newspaper (*Washington Post*) editor Ben Bradlee. A liberal white attorney jeopardizes his career by taking the case of a Black Panther-type accused of slaying two policemen. As the black activist with a chip on his shoulder, dynamic Dorian Harewood uses his electric screen presence to transform a cliché into a multidimensional character. Without him, this would be just another typical TV film, if a bit talkier than most.

AMERICAN ANTHEM ★½
1986, USA, PG-13
Mitch Gaylord, Janet Jones, Michael Pataki, Tiny Wells, Patrice Donnelly, John Aprea. Directed by Albert Magnoli. 100 min.

Albert Magnoli, the director of *Purple Rain*, combines music, good looks, and muscles in this pretty but dimwitted vehicle for Mitch Gaylord, the Olympic gymnast. Playing a gymnast here (he took months of acting lessons), Gaylord isn't awful, but he's more likely to reap gold medals than gold statuettes. The film itself is a golden turkey, a leaden rehash of *Purple Rain*'s dreary father-and-son-in-conflict plot with only some spectacular gymnastics work to redeem it.

AN AMERICAN CHRISTMAS CAROL ★½
1979, USA (TV)
Henry Winkler, David Wayne, Chris Wiggins, R. H. Thomson, Susan Hogan. Directed by Eric Till. 98 min.

As the title subtly indicates, this is an updated version of Charles Dickens's *A Christmas Carol*, for all those who have been sitting around saying, "Boy, that Chuck Dickens sure could spin a great yarn, but I just can't identify with all of that merry-old-England stuff." Winkler, with the assistance of mega-makeup, plays crotchety old Mr. Slade, who remembers his youth in Depression-era New England. Recommended only if none of the other versions, including the Mr. Magoo one, are left in stock.

AMERICAN COMMANDOS ★
1986, USA/Philippines, R
John Philip Law. Directed by Robbie Suarez. 85 min.

Released in the wake of Arnold Schwarzenegger's hit *Commando*, *American Commandos* is pure exploitation that fails to deliver on any level. (Even the poster—which grafted the head of slender John Philip Law onto a grotesquely muscled, *Rambo*-ish torso, was a lie.) The plot involves drug dealing, the supporting cast is composed of unknowns and the unfortunate Law, whose mild success in the 1960s has not carried over. Rape, murder, and mayhem, badly shot and badly edited, are the "bankable" elements here; viewers in search of well-crafted action should look elsewhere.

AMERICAN DREAM ★★★
1981, USA (TV)
Karen Carlson, Michael Hershewe, Stephen Macht, Hans Conried, John McIntire, Scott Brady. Directed by Mel Damski. 74 min.

This superlative drama was a pilot for a series that did a fast and undeserved fade-out. Perhaps it was too difficult to sustain the premise of an upper-middle-class family that abandons the white-bread suburbs for the challenge of living in an integrated inner-city neighborhood, but this original TV drama can't be faulted in its execution. The story unfolds with subtlety and conviction, and, mercifully, preachiness does not get the upper hand.

AMERICAN DREAMER ★★
1984, USA, PG
Jobeth Williams, Tom Conti, Giancarlo Giannini, Coral Browne, Huckleberry Fox, James Staley. Directed by Rick Rosenthal. 104 min.

Pallid, featureless comedy-adventure about a dreamy young housewife (Williams) who wins a trip to Paris in a writing contest, and, after a concussion, wakes up believing that she's the intrepid heroine of the trashy novels she loves. Spy shenanigans ensue, as well as a romantic liaison with the charmingly nonplussed Conti. Williams, a lovely, light performer, milks the script for all the style it has, but the writing team of Jim Kouf and David Greenwalt (perpetrators of *Class* and *Gotcha*) seems intent on turning out formulaic drivel without one sparkle of originality. No one in *American Dreamer* lives as anything but a cliché, but the attractive leads almost pull it off.

AMERICAN EMPIRE ★★½
1942, USA
Richard Dix, Leo Carillo, Preston Foster, Frances Gifford. Directed by William McGann. 82 min.

In this post–Civil War Western drama with exciting range-riding sequences, the leads gallop to glory by establishing an empire of grade-A beef. Punching cows and wrangling steers, Dix and Foster ensure that life on the lone prairie will never be dull. Not exceptional, but a reassuringly straightforward presentation of Western lore.

AMERICAN FLYERS ★★
1985, USA, PG-13
Kevin Costner, David Grant, Janice Rule, Rae Dawn Chong, Alexandra Paul. Directed by John Badham. 114 min.

A disappointing try for another uplifting sports film in the vein of *Breaking Away*. Two brothers, one of whom is terminally ill, compete in a grueling do-or-die bicycling event. A lot of attractive performers are wasted in this "you-can-do-anything-you-set-your-mind-to" hooey. When the film turns into a maudlin soap opera (since we know one of the brothers isn't going to make it), the slight plot drowns in the tears Badham jerks from us.

THE AMERICAN FRIEND ★★★★
1977, Germany/France
Bruno Ganz, Dennis Hopper, Gérard Blain, Lisa Kreuzer, Nicolas Ray, Samuel Fuller. Directed by Wim Wenders. 123 min.

Wenders's philosophical thriller has what so many works from the New German cinema have lacked: suspense, character, and the avid storytelling one associates with American films. Spacey, dangerous-seeming Dennis Hopper is a mobster, and quiet, saddened Bruno Ganz is the ailing art restorer he tricks into committing a pair of anonymous gangland murders. The movie is drowned in the cruel amorality of Patricia Highsmith's source novel, *Ripley's Game*. Wenders is an expert at bringing out his characters' eerie psychological states, and his murder scenes are as taut and disturbing as anything in the American films to which *The American Friend* pays homage. Look for legendary directors Nicholas Ray as Prokasch and Samuel Fuller as The American.

AMERICAN GIGOLO ★½
1980, USA, R
Richard Gere, Lauren Hutton, Hector Elizondo, Nina Van Pallandt, K Callan, Bill Duke. Directed by Paul Schrader. 117 min.

Paul Schrader's film is as elegantly dressed as its opaque protagonist, a paid consort (impassively played by Richard Gere) whom Schrader imagines to be a Dostoevskian hero. Accused of murdering one of his clients, Gere faces a dilemma: he may not be guilty of the crime, but being a gigolo and all, he sure is Guilty. Schrader finds this existential conundrum earthshaking; most viewers, we suspect, will find it pretty dull, especially since Gere's Nietzschean supertramp is made out to be a superior being on the basis of his good taste in apparel and his knowledge of antiques. There is an excellent synth/disco score by Giorgio Moroder.

AMERICAN GRAFFITI ☆☆☆½
1973, USA, PG
Ron Howard, Richard Dreyfuss, Cindy Williams, Paul Le Mat, Charles Martin Smith, Candy Clark, Mackenzie Phillips, Harrison Ford, Wolfman Jack, Suzanne Somers. Directed by George Lucas. 109 min.

For this bittersweet nostalgia, George Lucas ransacks his memories of high school graduation night in California circa 1962 to come up with a thin but superlatively evocative portrait of an era. Featuring greasers, cuddly carhops on roller skates, and that time-honored American ritual, cruising. Almost every one of the actors in the talented young cast went on to something bigger, if not necessarily better; watching it now, you may find yourself reminiscing as much about '73 as about '62.

AN AMERICAN IN PARIS ☆☆☆½
1951, USA
Gene Kelly, Oscar Levant, Leslie Caron, Nina Foch, Georges Guétary. Directed by Vincente Minnelli. 113 min.

Vincente Minnelli's Oscar-winning musical represents the apotheosis of the director's ingenuity; camera tricks, larger-than-life characters, and flamboyant stylizations beef up a thin plot in which Gene Kelly, as an ex-GI artiste, has to choose between patroness Nina Foch and the gamine he really loves—Leslie Caron in her beguiling debut. The celebrated *American in Paris* ballet, a seventeen-minute extravaganza influenced by the painting style of Dufy, Utrillo, Rousseau, Renoir, Toulouse-Lautrec, and Van Gogh, is still impressive, but it overburdens this slight, engaging musical. The film's best moments aren't the cultural ballet, but Kelly's romantic *pas de deux* with Caron by the River Seine. Whether Broadway and ballet merge successfully in Kelly's choreography for the big number is open to question, but Kelly's assured charm as a performer overrides any quibbles about his ambition.

AMERICAN JUSTICE ☆
1986, USA, R
Jack Lucarelli, Jameson Parker, Gerald McRaney, Wilford Brimley, Jeannie Wilson. Directed by Gary Grillo. 95 min.

TV's Simon and Simon bid for big-screen stardom and lose. Parker and McRaney are both better actors than their series reveals, but trapped in this hokey action drama about a vicious killer knocking off illegal aliens in a dusty border town, they come off as vacuous. McRaney fares slightly better as the nemesis than does Parker as the hero, but you'd have to be a diehard fan to sit through this nonsense.

AMERICAN NINJA ☆½
1985, USA, R
Michael Dudikoff, Steve James, Judie Aronson, Guich Koock, John Fujioka. Directed by Sam Firstenberg. 95 min.

Krunch! Pow! Kick! Those few words could serve as a screenplay for much of the running time of this film, which would more aptly be titled *Uncle Sam in the Philippines*. A mean, lean fighting machine for the USA takes on an army of nasty ninjas as he battles corruption and outwits his enemies. A simpleminded combination of ninjitsu, karate, tae kwon do, and every other leggy defense system making the world safe for future martial-arts films.

THE AMERICANO ☆☆½
1955, USA
Glenn Ford, Cesar Romero, Frank Lovejoy, Abbe Lane, Ursula Thiess. Directed by William Castle. 85 min.

A Brazilian locale spruces up this exotic Western. No, Carmen Miranda's not in it, but Glenn Ford is, and he's adept at playing tight-lipped Western loners squinting into the blazing sun and riding the range against desperadoes. As he rides deeper into their double dealings, Glenn discovers that these South American hombres are just as deadly as their North American counterparts and even more underhanded. Fast-paced and refreshingly off the beaten track.

THE AMERICAN SOLDIER ☆☆
1970, West Germany
Karl Scheydt, Elge Sorbas, Jan George. Directed by Rainer Werner Fassbinder. 80 min.

This early, rather awkward Fassbinder film brims with adoring movie references and in-jokes and boasts a brooding *noir* atmosphere. Beyond that, there's very little going on. Tough guy Karl Scheydt plays Ricky, a German-born American who returns to Munich after a stint in Vietnam and is hired by a trio of cops to commit a series of murders. There are some funny scenes between Ricky and his mother and brother, but for the most part this is third-rate Fassbinder.

AN AMERICAN TAIL ☆☆½
1986, USA, G
Animated: Phillip Glasser, Amy Green, Cathianne Blore, Dom DeLuise, Nehemiah Persoff, Christopher Plummer, John Finnegan. Directed by Don Bluth. 80 min.

This animated musical comedy about the experience of European immigrants in America at the end of the nineteenth century, with cats as the oppressors and mice as the heroes, is elaborate and heavy-handed. The focus is on the Mousekewitz family, who make the journey from Russia to America after their house is destroyed in a pogrom. During a storm at sea, little Fievel is tossed overboard, and the movie follows his struggles to find his family. The animation is a try at classic Disney, but as with most contemporary traditional animation, it is visually mediocre. And if the story has a jagged edge of danger and cynicism, it's finally too flimsy—and sentimental—to support its social and political pretensions. Produced by Steven Spielberg's company.

AN AMERICAN WEREWOLF IN LONDON ☆☆☆½
1981, USA, R
David Naughton, Griffin Dunne, Jenny Agutter, John Woodvine, Brian Glover. Directed by John Landis. 97 min.

A hard one to categorize, but devilishly entertaining, this film mixes horror and romance with a distinctly American sense of humor. After two teenage backpackers from New York are attacked on the English moors, one of them (Naughton) becomes a werewolf and unknowingly terrorizes modern-day London. Jenny Agutter is particularly appealing as the young British woman who falls for Naughton in his confusion. The inspired, gruesome makeup effects, however, ultimately steal the show. Much credit goes to John Landis's colorful, creative direction and to a great pop soundtrack (including several well-used versions of "Blue Moon") that complements the film's upbeat, wry flavor. All in all, it's a refreshing deviation from the beaten path of most horror films.

AMERICATHON ☆½
1979, USA, PG
Peter Reigert, Harvey Korman, Fred Willard, Zane Busby, Nancy Morgan, John Ritter, Richard Schall, Elvis Costello, Chief Dan George, Meat Loaf, Jay Leno. Directed by Neal Israel. 85 min.

The premise of this tired, scattershot farce isn't a bad one: in 1998, the U.S. government has run aground under the leadership of a young, dopey president and must hold a telethon to save itself from being bought out by a manufacturer of jogging suits. Unfortunately, it goes nowhere as a satire of politics, television, contemporary mores, or anything else. Director Neal Israel (*Bachelor Party*) crams the film with so many stupid gags that you won't even notice the few good ones, and the diverse comic talents of the cast go largely to waste. One of the major jokes identifies Fred Silverman, program chieftain of ABC and NBC in the 1970s and early 1980s as the president (1980–88) who first brought America to financial ruin, which should clue you in as to how quickly the whole thing has become stale.

AMIN—THE RISE AND FALL ☆☆½
1981, Kenya, R
Joseph Olita, Geoffrey Keen, Denis Hills, Leonard Trolley, Andre Maranne, Diane Mercier. Directed by Sharad Patel. 101 min.

Count on the predictable brutality inherent in a topic such as this—it's there, but there's no denying the serious intent behind this docudrama of Idi Amin's seven-year reign of terror in Uganda: the director's relatives were among the 75,000 Asians expelled from that nation as a slap at British authority. Re-creating his own role is Denis Hills, the journalist sentenced to death for his reference to Amin as a "village tyrant." Actor Olita bears a fearful likeness to the dictator who proved to be so murderous (as the film reports, he slaughtered half a million of his countrymen). Its concentration on factual horrors robs this film of any dramatic shape, but Amin's life, after all, is hardly a subject for high art. A more serious shortcoming is the lack of historical context or information about events leading up to Amin or following in his wake.

THE AMITYVILLE HORROR ☆½
1979, USA, R
James Brolin, Margot Kidder, Rod Steiger, Don Stroud, Murray Hamilton, John Larch, Helen Shaver. Directed by Stuart Rosenberg. 117 min.

Nothing much happens—horrible or otherwise—in this allegedly true story of a Long Island dream house possessed by demons. Although director Rosenberg (*Voyage of the Damned*) does manage to keep us knotted with tension at the mere prospect of being frightened, the film is flat, dull, and literal-minded. Kidder is as wired and sexy as ever, although here she often seems to be looking around nervously for something to do. Brolin, as her husband, driven bats by the resident malign forces, appears much more comfortable—like many other TV veterans, he seems perfectly content to do nothing. As for Steiger, he does way too much. Based on Jay Anson's bestseller it was followed by a "prequel": *Amityville II: The Possession*.

AMITYVILLE: THE DEMON ☆
1983, USA, R
Tony Roberts, Candy Clark, Tess Harper, Robert Joy. Directed by Richard Fleischer. 98 min.

Dull, formulaic second sequel to the 1979 hit was released theatrically as *Amityville 3D* to no particular good effect. A journalist and a photographer aim to prove that the haunted house in Amityville is no such thing. They soon regret their skepticism as paranormal manifestations lay waste to their lives.

AMITYVILLE 3D

See *Amityville: The Demon*

AMITYVILLE II: THE POSSESSION ½☆
1982, USA, R
Burt Young, Rutanya Alda, James Olson, Jack Magner, Diane Franklin, Ted Ross, Andrew Prine, Moses Gunn. Directed by Damiano Damiani. 104 min.

The "prequel" to *The Amityville Horror* (1979) is a clumsy and often ludicrous devil-possession movie that nevertheless cuts deeper than one might expect. Here the poltergeist serves to heighten the tensions and neuroses of the Montellis, a quarrelsome family whose eldest son (Magner) is being tempted by the devil to turn on his loved ones. The film is truly vile, because it disarms you with silliness and then taps into a domestic agony that you just can't laugh off. Watching it is like finding a razor blade in your Halloween candy.

AMOK

See *Schizo*

AMONG THE CINDERS ☆½
1984, New Zealand/West Germany, R
Paul O'Shea, Derek Hardwick, Amanda Jones, Rebecca Gibney, Yvonne Lawley. Directed by Rolf Haedrich. 99 min.

This story of a sixteen-year-old boy growing up in New Zealand is taken from Maurice Shadbolt's coming-of-age novel. There are the normal sexual crises to be faced, and some mortal ones—as when a boyhood friend, a Maori, dies in an accident for which the hero believes himself responsible. Shortly, however, most everything is resolved on a long hike with his grandfather. Disappointing.

AMOS ☆☆☆
1985, USA (TV)
Kirk Douglas, Elizabeth Montgomery, Dorothy McGuire, Pat Morita, Ray Walston, Jerry Hausner, Don Keefer. Directed by Michael Tuchner. 100 min.

A compelling TV-movie with an excellent performance by Kirk Douglas as an aged retiree who's put in a rest home and soon comes in conflict with the conniving nurse (Montgomery) who manages the place. When he begins to suspect that her methods of efficiency include killing patients as their treatment becomes too costly, he begins a race against time to expose her. Gripping and efficient, with Emmy-nominated performances by Douglas, McGuire, and Morita.

THE AMSTERDAM CONNECTION ☆
1979, Hong Kong
Jason Pai Piu, Milan, Yang Sze, Kid Sherrif. Directed by Lo Ke and Fang Mui San. 90 min.

For dull kung fu and gangster action in Amsterdam, watch Big Louie and his henchman Ah-Bun try to boost their gambling den business by putting their main competitor out of the market by acting as informers to the police on his illegal drug-smuggling ring. The pits.

THE AMSTERDAM KILL ☆☆
1977, Hong Kong, R
Robert Mitchum, Bradford Dillman, Richard Egan, Leslie Nielsen, Keye Luke. Directed by Robert Clouse. 93 min.

Robert Mitchum comes out of police retirement to do battle with the international drug trade, which provides an excuse for a lot of chases around Europe. He seems to have remained awake throughout, though it *is* hard to tell at times.

AMY ☆☆½
1981, USA, PG
Jenny Agutter, Barry Newman, Kathleen Nolan, Nanette Fabray. Directed by Vincent McEveety. 100 min.

There are moments when this Walt Disney feature about deaf children becomes a very moving children's version of *The Miracle Worker*—though without the battle of the wills that made the Helen Keller story such an intense experience. Agutter (*Walkabout*) has the Annie Sullivan role. She plays a young woman who arrives at a ramshackle Appalachian school in 1913 to teach the deaf students to speak, despite the opposition of the school's stiff-necked administrators. There's a tiresome subplot about Amy's abandoned husband, but the story is still very appealing, and the issues the film raises about the relative merits of sign language and speech are pressing ones. Made for TV, but released theatrically instead.

ANATOMY OF A MURDER ☆☆☆☆
1959, USA
James Stewart, Ben Gazzara, Lee Remick, George C. Scott, Eve Arden, Arthur O'Connell, Joseph Welch, Murray Hamilton. Directed by Otto Preminger. 160 min.

A riveting Otto Preminger film which shows off his fondness for ambiguity and his directorial finesse. Despite being confined to the courtroom for long stretches, this film is fluidly directed and its energy never flags. James Stewart won the New York Film Critics Circle award for his subtle rendering of a wily defense attorney not always sure of his client's veracity. The case involves an army officer accused of murdering the man who allegedly raped his wife. Controversial at the time because of its sexual terminology, the story is no longer shocking but has lost none of its dramatic punch. Uniformly fine performances, with the film's judge played by Joseph Welch, who in real life opposed McCarthy in the Army-McCarthy Senate hearings.

THE ANDERSON TAPES ☆☆☆
1971, USA, PG
Sean Connery, Dyan Cannon, Martin Balsam, Alan King, Ralph Meeker, Christopher Walken, Margaret Hamilton, Scott Jacoby, Conrad Bain. Directed by Sidney Lumet. 98 min.

Sidney Lumet directs two kinds of films: tough, realistic dramas (*Serpico, Prince of the City*) and slicker entertainments (*Murder on the Orient Express, The Wiz, Deathtrap*). *The Anderson Tapes* is a blend of the two, a crafty and funny heist yarn about an ex-con (Sean Connery on a James Bond sabbatical) who elaborately plans to rob a Manhattan apartment building. The colorful cast, especially Martin Balsam as an aging homosexual, somehow makes the wobbly tone work. Easily outclasses the similar *Thomas Crown Affair* and *The Hot Rock*.

AND GOD CREATED WOMAN ☆☆
1957, France
Brigitte Bardot, Jean-Louis Trintignant, Curt Jurgens. Directed by Roger Vadim. 90 min.

In its time a daringly frank, erotic film about a young waif who becomes caught among three men, this is a slow-moving melodrama that depends entirely on the ravishing appeal of Brigitte Bardot. Roger Vadim exploited his young wife's sensational looks for their joint debut in movies. While Bardot went on to become a huge star, Vadim continued making opulent sexy films, eventually exploiting *another* young wife—Jane Fonda.

...AND HOPE TO DIE ☆½
1972, USA/France, PG
Robert Ryan, Jean-Louis Trintignant, Lea Massari, Jean Gaben, Aldo Ray. Directed by René Clément. 95 min.

Adapting David Goodis's strange, taut crime novel *Black Friday*, director Clément might have made an equally compelling caper film about a disoriented fugitive (Trintignant) who becomes embroiled in a heist conspiracy led by a mysterious old man (Ryan). We say "might have" because the version released in the United States (and now on video) is forty-five minutes shorter than the French release. What remains is jumpy, confused, and piecemeal—and at times simply unwatchable. This kind of cutting is not uncommon with foreign films, but video is the ideal place to restore missing footage, and it's a pity it didn't happen here. Those interested in Clément's idiosyncratic career would be advised to haunt repertory houses in search of the full-length version. (a.k.a.: *La Course du Lièvre à Travers les Champs*)

AND JUSTICE FOR ALL ☆☆½
1979, USA, R
Al Pacino, Christine Lahti, John Forsythe, Jack Warden, Lee Strasberg, Craig T. Nelson, Jeffrey Tambor. Directed by Norman Jewison. 119 min.

Al Pacino shines as an idealistic lawyer battling the injustices of our legal system. Unfortunately, what Pacino's character lacks is what the whole film lacks—control. The characters' emotional outbursts occur indiscriminately: whether hotheaded Pacino is jailed for contempt of court or is made to defend the villainous judge played by John Forsythe, the viewer is repeatedly thrown out of the dramatic situations and into comedy scenes. The film is gripping at times but it ultimately lacks believability and consistency.

AND NOTHING BUT THE TRUTH ☆☆☆
1982, Great Britain
Glenda Jackson, John Finch, Kenneth Colley, James Donnelly. Directed by Karl Francis. 90 min.

Writer/director Karl Francis drew upon his years of making current-affairs documentaries for British television in this behind-the-scenes drama set at a television network. The two central characters (Jackson and Finch) are reporters, each working on stories they consider important and necessary. The film's point, however, is that the reporter has no control over what is actually seen on a network newscast in its final form—stories are reworked or cut due to lack of time, pressure from sponsors or politicians, or simply bad decisions by their superiors. This is not a particularly dramatic film, but it is a thought-provoking one about an important quesion: how much credence can we place in what is, for many of us, our major source of information about the outside world?

AND NOW FOR SOMETHING COMPLETELY DIFFERENT ☆☆☆½
1972, Great Britain, PG
Graham Chapman, John Cleese, Eric Idle, Terry Jones, Michael Palin, Terry Gilliam. Directed by Ian McNaughton. 89 min.

If you don't already like the British satirical troupe Monty Python, this film, their first, probably won't convert you. If you're a fan though, this treasure of some of their funniest sketches is worth seeking out. *And Now* may be the sharpest of all the Python revue films, with often hilarious interplay between members of the tight ensemble and fair-to-great material written by the performers. The "dead parrot" skit may be the funniest; if you don't see how anything involving a dead parrot could be amusing, you aren't the type to get much of a charge out of the wrestlers in drag or the cannibal babies either. Alternately sophisticated and sophomoric, and very, very British. Terry Gilliam directed the striking animation sequences.

AND NOW MY LOVE ☆☆☆
1975, France
Marthe Keller, Charles Denner, André Dussolier, Carla Gravina. Directed by Claude Lelouch. 121 min.

In one of director Lelouch's more delectable confections, he seems to be straining to create musical films with little bits of drama, whimsy, humor, and music all tossed in. But he's never managed to find the audience he had for his mega-hit *A Man and a Woman*, another sentimental, music-drenched drama. A terrific makeout movie, this one deals with love breaking down class restrictions as an aristocratic dame and a sexy loafer find each other more and more irresistible. In these cynical times, the ultraromantic Lelouch is refreshing; and though he sometimes swings wildly for effects, he hits the sublime as often as the ridiculous.

AND NOW THE SCREAMING STARTS ☆☆½
1973, Great Britain, R
Peter Cushing, Herbert Lom, Ian Ogilvy, Stephanie Beacham, Patrick Magee. Directed by Roy Ward Baker. 87 min.

In this lesser but still entertaining Amicus horror production, the new young bride of Lord Fengriffen falls under the spell of the family curse (his, not hers, which presumably makes it a curse-in-law). There are lots of corpses and other things to go bump in the night. Roy Ward Baker directs in his usual craftsmanlike way.

ANDREW'S RAIDERS

See *The Great Locomotive Chase*

ANDROID
1984, USA, PG ☆☆½
Klaus Kinski, Don Opper, Brie Howard, Norbert Weisser, Crofton Hardester, Kendra Kerchner. Directed by Aaron Lipstadt. 81 min.

In a dark, lonely space station off the beaten flight tracks, Dr. Daniel (Kinski) is struggling to create the perfect female android; meanwhile, one of the doctor's earlier creations, Max 404 (Opper), plays video games, listens to sixties soul music, and longs for the company of a woman. Not much of a story, but the wit and intelligence of director Aaron Lipstadt help take this sci-fi comedy beyond its low-budget restrictions.

THE ANDROMEDA STRAIN
1971, USA, G ☆☆½
Arthur Hill, David Wayne, James Olson, Paula Kelly. Directed by Robert Wise. 130 min.

Michael Crichton's authentic-seeming best-seller about a group of scientists attempting to contain a deadly alien virus becomes an opulently mounted, overlong film by Robert Wise. But the final suspense sequence—a race against the clock, the virus, and a nuclear detonation system—is a doozy. The cast is solid and modest.

AND THEN THERE WERE NONE
1945, USA ☆☆☆
Walter Huston, Barry Fitzgerald, Louis Hayward, June Duprez, Roland Young, Richard Haydn, C. Aubrey Smith, Judith Anderson, Mischa Auer. Directed by René Clair. 97 min.

One of the better Agatha Christie mysteries on film. Dudley Nichols adapted Christie's *Ten Little Niggers* (known in America as *Ten Little Indians*) and René Clair directed the story of ten houseguests on a mysterious island who are murdered successively. Although Louis Hayward and June Duprez are dreary romantic leads, the rest of the cast gives the almost mechanical structure of the narrative style and color. Standouts include Barry Fitzgerald, Walter Huston, and Judith Anderson. Plodding at times, but the film is brilliant compared to the 1966 and 1974 remakes.

AND THE SHIP SAILS ON
1984, Italy ☆☆☆☆
Freddie Jones, Barbara Jefford, Victor Poletti, Peter Cellier, Norma West, Janet Suzman, Sarah Jane Varley, Fiorenzo Serra, Pina Bausch. Directed by Federico Fellini. 128 min.

A grand film from one of cinema's grand masters. On the eve of World War I, an ocean liner carrying royalty and the royalty of the opera world sets out on a voyage to scatter the ashes of the world's greatest singer. The film begins as a silent, black-and-white movie; color and sound bleed onto the screen, gently serving as a reminder that this is Fellini, directly addressing his audience. Soon a narrator appears (Freddie Jones, in a stellar performance), and he comments on the action and offers an entrée into a world that is wildly expressive, theatrical, and utterly artificial. Fellini's genius lies in blending the passion of spectacle with the detachment of observation: in this film, he turns his attention to the dying *Belle Époque* and the gathering thunderclouds of nationalistic strife and individual dispossession. The reveling singers find themselves on a ship of discontented workers, and though the proletariat can't *really* upset them, the ship is forced to take on a load of Serbian refugees and everyone aboard becomes caught in the jaws of history. But none of this really accounts for the magic of the film, studded as it is with music, singing, marvelous comic turns, rich action, and visually breathtaking direction.

ANDY WARHOL'S BAD
1977, USA, R ☆☆☆½
Carroll Baker, Perry King, Susan Tyrrell, Brigid Polk, Geraldine and Maria Smith. Directed by Jed Johnson. 105 min.

"A movie with something to offend absolutely everybody," wrote one indignant critic upon *Bad*'s release. Typical of the exuberantly deranged spirit of the film, its producers used that line as an advertising come-on. It's pretty close to the truth—if the soiled diapers, bigoted characters, and lewd dialogue don't send you packing, the baby dropped out of the window (impact shot included) probably will. If you can stomach it, you'll be treated to one of the smartest, nastiest urban satires of the 1970s, a film that succeeds with just about every disgusting risk it takes. Carroll Baker gives a near-perfect performance as Hazel Aiken, a no-nonsense businesswoman who runs an electrolysis salon by day and an assassination agency by night. "We need the income," she sighs, with the resignation of a modern-day Mildred Pierce. The grimy look and deadpan acting are wholly appropriate to *Bad*'s dry look at a New York whose residents seem to be members of a mutual insanity pact. The satirists know their business here—they mean to appall you and then make you question that reaction. If you're very open-minded, they succeed.

ANDY WARHOL'S DRACULA
1975, Italy/France, X ☆½
Joe Dallesandro, Udo Kier, Arno Juerging, Vittorio De Sica, Roman Polanski, Maxime McKendry. Directed by Paul Morrissey. 106 min.

It seems there's a bloodsucker born every minute in movieland, but Paul Morrissey's version must be the most enervated. Perhaps that's appropriate to the subject, but it makes for a soporific horror film. Udo Kier is the ineffectual Count who requires not just blood but virgin blood, and Joe Dallesandro is the stud hired hand whose priapic adventures make Dracula's needs even harder to satisfy. As a whole, the film is less gory than the director's previous *Frankenstein* and somewhat more successful in sustaining its low-camp tone. Directors De Sica and Polanski make brief, pleasing appearances.

ANDY WARHOL'S FRANKENSTEIN
1974, Italy/W. Germany/France, X ☆½
Joe Dallesandro, Monique Van Vooren, Udo Kier, Srdjan Zelenovic, Dalila Di Lazzaro, Arno Juerging. Directed by Paul Morrissey. 95 min.

Morrissey's perverse, soft-core version of the great horror story seems intent on exploiting its one original device: the meretricious exhibition of entrails, human and otherwise, in living Day-Glo color. Joe Dallesandro does his beefcake-zombie number, and Udo Kier scowls. On the dull side. Despite the title, Warhol had little to do with the film. Originally shown in 3-D.

ANGEL
1984, USA, R ☆☆☆
Donna Wilkes, Cliff Gorman, Susan Tyrrell, Dick Shawn, Rory Calhoun. Directed by Robert Vincent O'Neil. 92 min.

This sleaze classic is not nearly as sleazy as it sounds. The title character, a fourteen-year-old Hollywood hooker who attends an honors high school during the day, becomes the target of one of those innumerable slashers with some kind of a mother fixation. (The only clue to his motivation is a scene in which he sucks a raw egg out of its shell; as the camera focuses in on a faded photograph of an unidentified female in the background, he smashes the egg into his face.) Along the way, Angel is assisted by a Tough But Caring Cop, a Grandfatherly Cowboy, a Foul-Mouthed Lesbian, and her adopted "Mother"—Dick Shawn as a transvestite who does Eddie Cantor when dodging the slasher. The totally ridiculous fun climaxes with a cowboy shoot-out on Hollywood Boulevard. This is the kind of film made by young smartasses who stop the camera momentarily when the mad killer ducks into a porno theater so that you can see that the visible letters of the marquis overhead spell out "D-I-E S-L-E-A-Z-E." The sequel was *Avenging Angel*.

ANGELA ☆☆
1977, Canada
Sophia Loren, John Huston, Steve Railsback, John Vernon. Directed by Boris Sagal. 91 min.

Despite the impressive star roster, this overcooked incestuous-love tale fails to have much impact. The superb actors do, however, bring great conviction to a dreary romance between a mother and her son who've been separated for twenty-three years. Naturally, they don't know they're related, but this uninspired film would hardly be more interesting even if they did. In one of the melodramatic plot strands, a revenge-seeking hubby wants to gun Angela down for turning him in to the cops. All the action footage can't obscure the blandness of the drama.

ANGEL AND THE BADMAN ☆☆½
1947, USA
John Wayne, Gail Russell, Harry Carey, Bruce Cabot. Directed by James Edward Grant. 107 min.

John Wayne starred in and produced this sensitive, exciting, and well-acted tale of a gunman who finds romance and redemption when a Quaker family takes him in after he collapses, wounded, on their doorstep.

ANGEL FROM H.E.A.T. ☆½
1982, USA, R
Marilyn Chambers, Stephen Johnson, Mary Woronov, Dan Jesse. Directed by Myril Schreibman. 93 min.

This inane, soft-core spy parody has nothing more going for it than the appearance of Mary Woronov, ex-Warhol star and B-movie queen of the past decade. Unfortunately, she doesn't have much to do here, being only a member of an antiterrorist group (headed by Marilyn Chambers) out to stop yet another mad scientist. Chambers is able to do exactly one thing well on film, but, this having only an R rating, there's none of that.

ANGELO MY LOVE ☆☆☆½
1983, USA, R
Angelo Evans, Michael Evans, Ruthie Evans, Tony Evans. Directed by Robert Duvall. 115 min.

Director-actor Duvall's outrageously funny portrait of a super-sharp, pint-sized Gypsy dynamo named Angelo and the wildly exotic milieu that he inhabits is told in a high-pitched, frenetic style. *Angelo* follows a fabulous cast of actual gypsies (who virtually play themselves) through their secret meetings and rituals. A rare, non-Hollywood ethnic study that is simultaneously funny, fascinating, and energizing, the film was made by Duvall after he developed a friendship with Angelo Evans in his Manhattan neighborhood.

ANGEL ON MY SHOULDER ☆☆½
1946, USA
Paul Muni, Claude Rains, Anne Baxter, Erskine Sanford, Hardie Albright. Directed by Archie Mayo. 101 min.

This post–World War II fantasy about a gangster who is killed but is then given a second chance at life by Satan secures the talents of the author (Harry Segall) and star (Claude Rains) of the similar *Here Comes Mr. Jordan*, but it fails to pack the same punch. Muni is relatively restrained (for Muni) as the gangster who is reincarnated as an evil judge to carry out the devil's plans, and Rains is better cast as Satan than he was as the angelic Mr. Jordan. Still, the plot and character development are predictable, and Baxter was never well-suited for ingenue roles. This familiar, mild hokum was remade for television in 1980.

ANGEL ON MY SHOULDER ☆☆
1980, USA (TV)
Peter Strauss, Richard Kiley, Barbara Hershey, Janis Paige, Seymour Cassel, Scott Colomby. Directed by John Berry. 100 min.

Another one of those *Here Comes Mr. Jordan* fantasies, this one originally made with Paul Muni in 1946. In this update, Strauss plays a recently bumped-off gangster who's sent back to earth by Lucifer to make more mischief but finds that this time around he may prefer being a good guy. Aside from Strauss's expert performance, this comedy is run-of-the-mill.

ANGELS DIE HARD ☆½
1970, USA, R
Tom Baker, William Smith, R. G. Armstrong, Alan De Witt, Gary Littlejohn. Directed by Richard Compton. 87 min.

Better than most of the many imitative biker movies that followed in the success of *Easy Rider*, this movie is still watchable only if you have a predilection for the genre. Former Andy Warhol star Tom Baker is the head of a motorcycle gang, one of whom is murdered in a small California town. The townspeople want them out, but the Angels want to know who killed their buddy. Just like every other biker movie, this features real-life Hell's Angel Gary Littlejohn as one of the gang.

ANGELS HARD AS THEY COME ☆½
1971, USA, R
Gary Busey, Scott Glenn, Charles Dierkop, Gilda Texter, Janet Wood. Directed by Joe Viola. 90 min.

Vroom! Vroom! go the motorcycles. Pant! Pant! go the motorcyclists. These vehicular hot mamas seem more eager to go for a ride with Scott Glenn (in his first film) than you'll be. It's a tedious adventure flick with the proverbial hard-riding leather loners and leatherettes peeling rubber and engaging in other mobile macho activities.

ANGELS OVER BROADWAY ☆☆½
1940, USA
Douglas Fairbanks Jr., Rita Hayworth, Thomas Mitchell, John Qualen, George Watts, Ralph Theodore. Directed by Ben Hecht; co-directed by Lee Garmes. 78 min.

The great screenwriter Ben Hecht made his directorial debut with this odd, gritty tale of New York nightlife in and around Times Square. Four down-and-out types meet up in an all-night cafe and decide to go for one last shot at the big time (something different for each of them). The punchy, Runyonesque dialogue is fun to hear, but the hokey melodramatics bog the story down and Hecht, who rarely directed after this, doesn't have a sure hand.

ANGELS WITH DIRTY FACES ☆☆☆½
1938, USA
James Cagney, Pat O'Brien, Humphrey Bogart, Ann Sheridan, George Bancroft, Huntz Hall, Leo Gorcey. Directed by Michael Curtiz. 97 min.

Nowadays, when people say that they don't make them like they used to, *Angels with Dirty Faces* is the kind of old-fashioned, rip-snorting, melodramatic movie they mean. This may be the only film the Dead End Kids ever made that can be watched without wincing by a sober grown-up. Thanks is due not to the kids, but to James Cagney, as the gangster they misguidedly worship, and to Pat O'Brien, as the priest who sets them straight. The climactic scene, in which Cagney is dragged off to the electric chair, lives on in a thousand traumatized hearts.

ANGRY HARVEST ☆☆☆☆
1985, Germany
Armin Mueller-Stahl, Elisabeth Trissenaar, Kathe Jaenicke. Directed by Agnieszka Holland. 107 min.

A stunningly acted and deeply moving character study that uses a Holocaust backdrop in depicting man's continuing struggle to dominate the opposite sex. The chauvinistic oppressor here is Leon, a simple and lonely Polish farmer who sees the chance to keep the woman of his dreams when a beautiful Jew wanders onto his land after escaping from a concentration camp transport. When he takes Rosa in, however, Leon discovers that the battle of the sexes won't be so easily won. While Holland gets in a number of angry jabs at the abhorrent practice of hiding refugees for profit during World War II, her greatest skill is at developing her poignant characters and their twisted relationship. This superb mood piece was deservedly nominated for the Best Foreign Film Oscar.

THE ANGRY RED PLANET ☆☆
1959, USA
Gerald Mohr, Nora Hayden, Les Tremayne, Jack Kruschen, Paul Hahn. Directed by Ib Melchior. 83 min.

Not to be confused with the camp classic *Red Planet Mars*, this is a straightforward, dated sci-fi flick about the incredible sights awaiting some space travelers headed toward Mars. Despite decent special effects, the film suffers from the usual 1950s low-budget cheesiness; you'll want to escort the spacemen to Stanley Kubrick or George Lucas to get them better outfits and ships. A quaint artifact of sci-fi Space Paranoia.

ANGST
See *Fear*

ANIMAL CRACKERS ☆☆☆☆
1930, USA
Groucho, Harpo, Chico and Zeppo Marx, Margaret Dumont, Lillian Roth, Louis Soren. Directed by Victor Heerman. 98 min.

The Brothers' second film was, like *Cocoanuts* before it, based on a hit Broadway play, so it suffers a tiny bit from staginess and unimaginative direction. But the dialogue (by Morrie Ryskind, adapting his and George S. Kaufman's play) is enough to carry the movie, and it would have taken a much stronger director than Heerman to do anything with the camera except turn it on and set the Marxes in front of it. The mildly intrusive plot has art thieves planning to steal a famous oil painting from Mrs. Rittenhouse (Margaret Dumont, in peak form), who is having a weekend party to celebrate the unveiling. More importantly, this is the one in which Groucho sings "Hooray for Captain Spaulding" and "Hello, I Must Be Going," dictates a letter to his lawyer, Mr. Hungadunga, and offers a discourse on how what the country needs is an eight-cent nickel; Chico explains that his orchestra cannot arrive on time because Groucho couldn't afford their rehearsal rates (or even worse, their rates for *not* rehearsing); and Harpo loses an entire silver service from his sleeves while shaking a detective's hand. This may not be their best, but it's pretty close.

ANIMAL FARM ☆☆☆
1954, Great Britain, PG
Animated. Voices of Maurice Denham, Gordon Heath. Directed by Joy Batchelor and John Halas. 75 min.

Perhaps the only way to adapt George Orwell's bleakly funny political allegory about a populist revolution in a barnyard was in cartoon form, and this animated feature scores points for its inventive, splashy artwork and its refusal to lighten the book's mood. But, inevitably, much of the subtlety and spare style of Orwell's writing was lost, and at times the film becomes something the book never was, a mere procession of talking beasts. It's nonetheless a largely clever attempt to bring a difficult novel to the screen.

ANIMALS ARE BEAUTIFUL PEOPLE ☆☆
1974, South Africa, G
Directed by Jamie Uys. 92 min.

This feature documentary about African wildlife is from the maker of *The Gods Must Be Crazy*, who has been writing, producing, directing, photographing, and editing his own films for thirty years. The Disney-like series of bits about various adorable birds, boars, fish—with the occasional villainous hyena thrown in for drama—is great for family audiences, but it's nothing you'd want to watch without a ten-year-old in the room.

ANNABEL TAKES A TOUR ☆☆½
1939, USA
Lucille Ball, Jack Oakie, Ruth Donnelly, Bradley Page, Ralph Forbes. Directed by Lew Landers. 66 min.

This agreeable sequel to *The Affairs of Annabel* is the frenetic tale of a tempestuous film star who, hungry for notoriety, embarks on a personal appearance tour. She eagerly gets her name in the papers by ensnaring a titled nobleman who's got his own line of novels to plug. In this bubbly B comedy, Oakie and Ball made a good team, but Lucy lacked the comic finesse she would later exhibit on television.

ANNA CHRISTIE ☆☆½
1930, USA
Greta Garbo, Charles Bickford, George F. Marion, Marie Dressler. Directed by Clarence Brown. 74 min.

Based on an early, tedious play by Eugene O'Neill, this early talkie tells the tale of Anna (Garbo), a jaded ex-prostitute, and her troubled father, a sailor played by George Marion. The camerawork and the screenplay are equally stilted; Garbo alone makes this film noteworthy. *Anna Christie* was Garbo's first talkie. With her Swedish accent and raspy, sensual voice, Garbo succeeds with style. At the age of twenty-four, Garbo conveyed that sense of *angst* and allure that became her trademark.

ANNA KARENINA ☆☆☆
1935, USA
Greta Garbo, Fredric March, Freddie Bartholomew, Basil Rathbone, Maureen O'Sullivan. Directed by Clarence Brown. 95 min.

Anna Karenina is one of cinema's great melodrama warhorses, yet none of the four features made from Leo Tolstoy's novel is especially moving. Perhaps the heroine's tragic end is an outdated coda to her otherwise contemporary attitudes and its inevitability fits too snugly into the Production Code thinking of the time. In any case, this particular Greta Garbo version (she did the silent, happy-ending *Love* in 1927) is meticulously well-made and cast. Garbo, as photographed by William Daniels, is the epitome of the bored bourgeois wife and mother who leaves her uncaring husband (Rathbone) for a sensitive Russian count (March). David O. Selznick's production bogs down slightly in the ballroom scenes, but remains admirably faithful to Tolstoy's story. The problem is that director Brown lacks the grace and finesse of Max Ophuls, who made a much more moving and humorous film out of similar material in *The Earrings of Madame de . . . .*

ANNE OF THE THOUSAND DAYS ☆☆½
1969, Great Britain
Richard Burton, Geneviève Bujold, Irene Papas, Anthony Quayle, John Colicos, Michael Hordern, Katherine Blake, William Squire. Directed by Charles Jarrott. 145 min.

Somewhere between *The Lion in Winter* and *Mary, Queen of Scots* came this slice of monarchic life depicting the ill-starred love affair of Henry VIII (Burton) and Anne Boleyn (Bujold). Director Charles Jarrott went on to mount the ignominious remake of *Lost Horizon* and *The Other Side of Midnight*, and he doesn't seem quite at home with this sort of dialogue-heavy, costume-draped historical pageantry. *Anne* doesn't have the emotional or intellectual acuity to make it another *Man for All Seasons*, but fine work from the two stars makes the long film, based on a 1948 play by Maxwell Anderson, less draggy than it might otherwise seem.

ANNIE ☆☆½
1982, USA, PG
Aileen Quinn, Carol Burnett, Tim Curry, Albert Finney, Bernadette Peters, Ann Reinking, Geoffrey Holder, Edward Herrmann, Toni Ann Gisondi. Directed by John Huston. 128 min.

Thanks to a shrewd combination of elements (and a fifty-million-dollar budget), the smash Broadway musical of the seventies has been turned into a lavish wish-fulfillment fantasy—the ultimate Shirley Temple movie! And because it celebrates the unbridled enthusiasm of American movies, the film triumphs over its weaker links: a lackluster script, serviceable but uninspired direction by Huston, and the aggressively adorable Quinn as Little Orphan Annie. Adults will enjoy the outstanding caricature-performances of Burnett as the boozy head of the orphanage and Curry and Peters as ne'er-do-well villains.

ANNIE HALL ☆☆☆☆
1977, USA, PG
Woody Allen, Diane Keaton, Tony Roberts, Paul Simon, Carol Kane, Colleen Dewhurst, Christopher Walken. Directed by Woody Allen. 95 min.

Woody Allen's touching, bittersweet comedy tells a tale of life and love in New York City. Allen plays Alvy Singer, a neurotic, Jewish comedian. Diane Keaton is Annie Hall, Alvy's unlikely love interest. Allen employs a wide array of cinematic devices in chronicling the rise and demise of their romance. The film uses flashbacks, a split screen, animation, and other techniques to explore the minds of his protagonists and the reasons that their relationship finally fails. At one point, the dialogue is accompanied by hilarious subtitles that clue us in to what the characters are *really* feeling. The result of all this movie magic is one of the warmest, funniest, and most consistent works Allen has ever given us. The Academy chose wisely that year and awarded *Annie Hall* Oscars for Best Picture, Best Direction, Best Original Screenplay (Allen and Marshall Brickman), and Best Actress (Diane Keaton).

ANNIE OAKLEY ☆☆☆
1935, USA
Barbara Stanwyck, Preston Foster, Melvyn Douglas, Pert Kelton, Andy Clyde. Directed by George Stevens. 88 min.

Barbara Stanwyck is a perfect Annie Oakley, the star sharpshooter of Buffalo Bill's Wild West Show who romances two different men in the troupe. The script and direction don't quite live up to the idea, but the film recreates Cody's nineteenth century American institution with authenticity, splendor, and more comedy than the moviemakers probably intended.

THE ANNIHILATORS ☆
1985, USA, R
Gerrit Graham, Lawrence Hilton Jacobs, Paul Koslo, Christopher Stone, Andy Wood, Sid Conrad, Dennis Redfield, Jim Antonio. Directed by Charles E. Sellier, Jr. 87 min.

The title characters in this plodding tale of vigilante justice are four Vietnam veterans who decide to make the streets of Atlanta safe for decent folk after a gang of thugs murders their crippled buddy. Uplifting music clogs the soundtrack as we view dewy montages of the Annihilators busting heads, kicking butts, and being kind to children and old ladies. Very standard, somewhat violent exploitation, with a ridiculous prologue that makes Vietnam combat look like a rumble in a city park.

ANN VICKERS ☆☆½
1933, USA
Irene Dunne, Walter Huston, Bruce Cabot, Edna May Oliver. Directed by John Cromwell. 72 min.

This juicy adaptation of a Sinclair Lewis novel is strictly in the tradition of the 1930s woman's film, in which a long-suffering female chokes back her tears alone while sacrificing her personal happiness to that of most of the members of the cast. Irene Dunne is properly noble as the warden of a prison, and soap-opera fanciers will forgive the film's dated quality and get out their Kleenexes for a good cry.

À NOS AMOURS ☆☆☆
1984, France, R
Sandrine Bonnaire, Maurice Pialat, Évelyne Ker, Cyr Boitard. Directed by Maurice Pialat. 99 min.

A fifteen-year-old girl goes through a series of loveless sexual encounters in order to escape her hateful family, in an almost sickeningly harsh drama by Maurice Pialat. Few recent films dared to depict family life as a waking nightmare, an endless succession of face slappings and castigations. This one goes all the way: the scenes last forever, and much of the most lacerating dialogue and action was reportedly improvised as the cameras rolled. It all has a stomach-churning power, but universal contempt can take a movie only so far; Pialat seems to find all of his characters (including the father, whom he plays) either despicable or pathetic. There are extraordinary moments and raw, emotional performances all the way. Subtitled.

ANOTHER COUNTRY ☆☆½
1984, Great Britain, R
Rupert Everett, Colin Firth, Anna Massey. Directed by Marek Kanievska. 90 min.

Based on the life of British spy Guy Burgess, *Another Country* (an adaptation of a long-running English play) is a very British story of homosexuality and Marxism nurtured in an exclusive boys' school. Rupert Everett, repeating his stage role of the flamboyant gay figure, plays with skill but misjudges how far to go for the camera: He is neither spontaneous nor subtle. Furthermore, he and the other students look at least ten years too old. Anna Massey is sharp as Everett's overprotective mother.

ANOTHER TIME, ANOTHER PLACE ☆☆☆
1983, Great Britain, R
Phyllis Logan, Giovanni Mauriello, Denise Coffey, Tom Watson, Gian Luca Favilla, Gregor Fisher, Paul Young. Directed by Michael Radford. 102 min.

This muted but gripping love story benefits from its understated approach to overheated passions. In an insular community in Northern Scotland during 1944, a married woman trapped in a loveless marriage finds emotional and sexual release with a charming Italian POW in a brief, illicit affair. Phyllis Logan's incandescent performance lifts *Another Time* above the ordinary, although the film also has a keen sense of time and place in relating to this particular wartime environment. For those reasons, this low-key romance elicits a considerable emotional response.

À NOUS LA LIBERTE ☆☆☆☆
1931, France
Raymond Cordy, Henri Marchand, Rolla France, Paul Olivier, Jacques Shelly. Directed by René Clair. 87 min.

René Clair's musical satire, loosely based on the career of French record magnate Charles Pathé, traces the careers of two ex-cons (Cordy and Marchand), one of whom becomes an industrialist. The futuristic style of the sets and the outsized machinery, the spirited, operettalike music, and some delightful business with factory equipment run amok all contribute to an exhilarating experience. The film was an inspiration for Chaplin's *Modern Times*; René Clair forced his own producers to drop a lawsuit against Chaplin when the film was released. Clair felt that he certainly owed as much to Chaplin's Tramp as *Modern Times* may have owed to *À Nous*. (a.k.a.: *Freedom for Us*)

ANTARCTICA ★★★
1984, Japan, PG
Ken Takakura, Tsunehhiko Watase, Eji Okada. Directed by Koreyoshi Kuraha. 112 min.

Ranking with *E.T.* as Japan's all-time biggest box-office hit, this is an enthralling wilderness tale of man's relationship with his proverbial best friend. It derives its power from being based on a true story that has, over the years, taken on the semblance of a legend in Japan. A scientific exploration team in the frozen wasteland encounters tremendous hardships, but their spirits are buoyed by their faithful sled dogs. Unfortunately, they have to abandon their companions temporarily, with every intention of returning; fate intervenes and the dogs are left to fend for themselves. The dogs who survive become sort of folk heroes to the Japanese people. Beautifully photographed and quite moving, if a bit too long.

ANTS ★★
1977, USA (TV)
Suzanne Somers, Robert Foxworth, Myrna Loy, Lynda Day George, Bernie Casey, Moosie Drier, Steve Franken, Brian Dennehy, Stacy Keach, Sr. Directed by Robert Scheerer. 88 min.

After dining on a dandy lunch of high-octane pesticide, hordes of ants descend upon a resort manor for a dinner of TV stars. The fact that Suzanne Somers is top-billed should warn you that she does *not* get eaten early on; hence, she's likely to be on-screen for most of the hour and a half. (a.k.a.: *Panic at Lakewood Manor* and *It Happened at Lakewood Manor*)

ANYTHING FOR LOVE

See *11 Harrowhouse*

ANTHONY ADVERSE ★★½
1936, USA
Fredric March, Olivia de Havilland, Donald Woods, Anita Louise, Edmund Gwenn, Claude Rains, Gale Sondergaard, Louis Hayward, Akim Tamiroff, Fritz Leiber. Directed by Mervyn LeRoy. 136 min.

This is what audiences hungry for big-screen spectacle gobbled up in 1936: a long, improbable, and deliriously silly historical drama set in late-eighteenth-century France, Northern Italy, Scotland, Switzerland, Havana, and even darkest Africa. Warner Brothers rounded up all the sets and extras it could find to film Hervey Allen's 1200-page novel about a foundling, abandoned by a Spanish nobleman, who grows to maturity and goes through all manner of misadventures before finding the road to wealth and happiness. Fredric March is a sturdy and appealing Anthony, and Olivia de Havilland is fine, though a somewhat odd casting choice for an Italian peasant's opera-singing daughter. The story plays like a fiercely compressed TV miniseries, and some of the plot turns are ludicrous, but the sweep and grandeur are still entertaining. Academy Awards went to Gale Sondergaard (it was the first Best Supporting Actress statuette), the rousing and everpresent score by Erich Wolfgang Korngold, the cinematography, and the editing.

ANY WHICH WAY YOU CAN ★★
1980, USA, PG
Clint Eastwood, Ruth Gordon, Sondra Locke, Geoffrey Lewis, Harry Guardino. Directed by Buddy Van Horn. 116 min.

The further adventures of Philo Beddoe (Eastwood), Clyde the orangutan, and their pals has, in several aspects (notably the writing and direction, by Stanford Sherman and Buddy Van Horn, respectively) more style than its predecessor, *Every Which Way But Loose*. The characters, not the cars, are still the show, and the film keeps bouncing along, amiably and sometimes hilariously. True, the silly shenanigans of the Black Widow motorcycle gang are wearying; this is one film that needs no comic relief. But Gordon, Locke, and Lewis offer first-class support, and Clyde is the first simian superstar of the Reagan era; Bonzo, look to your laurels!

APACHE ★★½
1954, USA
Burt Lancaster, Jean Peters, John McIntire. Directed by Robert Aldrich. 91 min.

One Indian's historic crusade against the U.S. Army is sensitively portrayed here by the combined efforts of Lancaster in the leading role and Aldrich in the director's chair. Characterized by all the stuff of an action-filled Western, this one is uniquely sympathetic to the Indian plight. Rugged outdoor locations, vividly photographed, enhance the film's heroics. Jean Peters, as an Indian woman, lends it humanity. Lancaster and Aldrich went on to do *Vera Cruz* together in the same year.

THE APARTMENT ★★★★
1960, USA
Jack Lemmon, Shirley MacLaine, Fred MacMurray, Ray Walston, Edie Adams, Jack Kruschen, David White. Directed by Billy Wilder. 125 min.

Billy Wilder combines the sexual cynicism of *Double Indemnity* with the unabashed romanticism of *Love in the Afternoon* and somehow pulls it off; he took away Oscars for Best Picture, Best Director, and Best Screenplay. Junior executive Lemmon hopes to rise to the top of his profession (we never find out exactly what he does, but he works in a building full of rows of desks with other people doing the same thing) by loaning out his bachelor apartment to the higher-level executives. He makes the mistake, however, of falling in love with MacLaine, who has just been dumped by the boss. MacMurray makes a terrifically sleazy philanderer, and MacLaine was never better than she is here.

APE ★
1976, Korea, PG
Rod Arrants, Joanne De Verona, Alex Nichol. Directed by Paul Leder. 87 min.

They call it Chutzpah: Dino De Laurentiis, who should have been hiding in shame when his version of *King Kong* came out in 1976, was spending part of his time in court suing the distributors of this giant ape rip-off for trying to cash in on the publicity campaign of his own giant ape rip-off. Poetic justice aside, this is real junk, with some bozo in a gorilla suit stomping on toy boats and buildings while the film's leading lady struggles in a flimsy giant ape hand and pleads "Be gentle, big fella!" Originally released in 3-D.

THE APE ★½
1940, USA
Boris Karloff, Maris Wrixon, Gertrude Hoffman, Henry Hall. Directed by William Nigh. 63 min.

A mediocre Karloff vehicle, this is recommended only if you have a yen for low-budget shockers. As yet another mad doctor, he is at work on a serum to cure paralysis, which he hopes to use to cure the wheelchair-bound Miss Wrixon. Because he needs spinal fluid for the serum, he disguises himself as an ape and murders townspeople whom he has judged unfit to live. Given that Karloff was over six feet tall, rather large for a gorilla, we can safely assume that a double was used to play the ape.

THE APE MAN ★½
1943, USA
Bela Lugosi, Wallace Ford, Louise Currie, Henry Hall. Directed by William Beaudine. 64 min.

Almost so bad that it's amusing, but not quite, this is yet another in the long series of $1.39 movies that Lugosi made after *Dracula*. Here he's a scientist who discovers that by injecting himself with the spinal fluid of apes he can turn himself into a half-human/half-gorilla creature. (Discovering this is one thing; why anyone would actually *do* so is beyond us!) There's a ridiculous running gag featuring an unknown character who is always popping up telling the rest of the cast what do do; at the film's end, he reveals himself to be—well, we won't say; you might as well have *something* to look forward to.

APOCALYPSE NOW ☆☆☆☆
1979, USA, R
Martin Sheen, Marlon Brando, Robert Duvall, Frederic Forrest, Sam Bottoms, Dennis Hopper, Harrison Ford, G. D. Spradlin. Directed by Francis Ford Coppola. 153 min.

A flawed masterpiece. Coppola's years-in-the-making reworking of Joseph Conrad's *Heart of Darkness* becomes the epic hallucination of the Vietnam War—Vietnam as the ultimate trip. The effect is so vivid and unnerving that it almost doesn't matter if the acting is variable and the script (especially Michael Herr's "hard-boiled" narration) uneven. Coppola released several different versions of this—the 35mm and 70mm copies were different lengths—and developed an elaborate sound presentation. It *should* be seen in a theater and will lose immeasurably on a television screen. A small-screen viewing, however, could be useful for a serious dissection, and Marlon Brando's very strange performance might be easier to take a bit at a time. The highlight: a flabbergasting helicopter-attack sequence, in which Coppola forges nightmare beauty out of sheer destruction.

APOLOGY ☆☆
1986, USA (TV)
Lesley Ann Warren, Peter Weller, John Glover, Jimmie Ray Weeks, George Loros, Garrett M. Brown, Harvey Fierstein. Directed by Robert Bierman. 98 min.

An inventive premise goes nowhere in this slick but empty made-for-cable thriller set among New York's would-be avant-garde artistic community. Lesley Ann Warren plays a SoHo performance artist creating a "piece" out of the confessions she hears on her apology hot line—the idea is based on a real number anyone can call to expiate his sins anonymously. When a string of unsolved murders and a handsome detective enter the picture, scripter Mark Medoff's bland prattle about victims, responsibility and the electronic age takes over, and the film becomes a dull, conventional melodrama whose aspirations to greater things go unfulfilled.

THE APPLE ☆
1980, USA, PG
Catherine Mary Stewart, Allan Love, George Gilmour, Joss Ackland. Directed by Menahem Golan. 90 min.

Incredibly bad. A futuristic Faustian rock musical about a group called "The Bim" that has the world's record-buying public enslaved to a wicked (and relentlessly droning) beat. But then along comes a sweet-voiced duo (sort of like the Carpenters crossed with Donnie and Marie Osmond) who threaten to swing popular taste back to melodic songs. Before you can do the "Bim" dance, a devilish promoter tries to get the singing saps to sign their souls away for fame and fortune. A hellish experience!

THE APPLE DUMPLING GANG ☆☆½
1975, USA, G
Bill Bixby, Susan Clark, Don Knotts, Tim Conway, Slim Pickens, Harry Morgan, Clay O'Brien, Brad Savage, Stacy Manning. Directed by Norman Tokar. 100 min.

Bill Bixby is the handsome gambler who wins three kids in a poker game in this light, pleasant Disney Western. Don Knotts and Tim Conway steal the show with their bumbling antics (and they came back for the idiotic sequel, *The Apple Dumpling Gang Rides Again*). Although the movie isn't sidesplitting, children will enjoy watching the three likable moppets tangle with bad guys, find a huge gold nugget, and win the gambler's heart.

THE APPLE DUMPLING GANG RIDES AGAIN ☆
1979, USA, G
Tim Conway, Don Knotts, Tim Matheson, Kenneth Mars, Jack Elam, Harry Morgan, Ruth Buzzi, Richard X. Slattery, Cliff Osmond. Directed by Vincent McEveety. 89 min.

A homogenized family-exploitation picture from the Walt Disney studios, in which Don Knotts and Tim Conway mug desperately while playing two idiots bumbling their way across the Old West. The movie makes a fetish out of predictability. The viewer is glassy-eyed before the Polaroid-snapshot color, the Western sets that seem molded out of Styrofoam, and the sagging, hopeless faces of the second-rate TV actors (Kenneth Mars, as a self-worshipping, dandified lawman, is a blessed exception). There's a degree of polish in the execution—the picture isn't slapdash—but it's the polish of machine-tooled bric-a-brac, of plastic lawn animals.

APPOINTMENT IN HONDURAS ☆☆½
1953, USA
Glenn Ford, Ann Sheridan, Zachary Scott, Rodolfo Acosta, Jack Elam. Directed by Jacques Tourneur. 79 min.

When given compelling material, as he was with *Cat People* and *Out of the Past*, Jacques Tourneur was capable of turning out brooding, dark, emotionally charged work without calling undue attention to his own directorial flourishes. But when handed pulp like the chase-through-the-jungle plot of *Appointment in Honduras* and a star as resolutely unromantic as Glenn Ford, there was little he could do but run the tired story through its paces. There are intermittent demonstrations of his flair for the macabre, and the story moves quickly enough that you won't be completely bored, but you may not be very interested, either.

THE APPRENTICESHIP OF DUDDY KRAVITZ ☆☆☆½
1974, Canada, PG
Richard Dreyfuss, Micheline Lanctot, Jack Warden, Randy Quaid, Joseph Wiseman, Denholm Elliott, Joe Silver. Directed by Ted Kotcheff. 121 min.

Richard Dreyfuss's first starring role was the flip side of the sunny smartass character he made so popular later in the seventies; here he's a Jewish youth in the anti-Semitic Montreal of the 1940s, an unprincipled, albeit charming, climber who is determined to make it to the top one way or another. It's mostly very funny, especially when Duddy enlists a drunken, blacklisted British director in a scheme to make Bar Mitzvah films, resulting in something called "Happy Bar Mitzvah, Bernie!"—consisting of shots of the blessed event intercut with Nazi rallies and Zulu rituals. The screenplay was by Mordecai Richler from his story "What Makes Duddy Run?"

THE APRIL FOOLS ☆☆
1969, USA
Jack Lemmon, Catherine Deneuve, Myrna Loy, Charles Boyer, Peter Lawford, Sally Kellerman, Harvey Korman. Directed by Stuart Rosenberg. 95 min.

Can an unhappily married man (played by Lemmon with more *angst* than a light comedy can support) chuck a lifetime of responsibility and run away to a happy ending with a walking perfume ad (played by Deneuve with more glacial reserve than a light comedy can support)? Boyer and Loy are charming as a fairy godcouple who bestow their blessings on this improbable union. Maybe Lemmon should have watched their old romantic films, or some of his own. The direction is hopelessly overemphatic, and Deneuve acts as if she were about to confer knighthood on the other cast members.

APRIL FOOL'S DAY ☆
1986, USA, R
Deborah Foreman, Deborah Goodrich, Griffin O'Neal, Clayton Rohner, Amy Steel, Ken Olandt, Leah King Pinsent. Directed by Fred Walton. 90 min.

A group of college students spending the weekend in an isolated island mansion disappears, one by one. Is the culprit a crazed maniac on the loose, the hostess' evil identical twin, or producer Frank Mancuso, Jr., whose previous contribution to the art of film was the *Friday the 13th* series? We won't give away the final twist to his inept horror-comedy, but if you look at the title and think really hard, you can probably guess what it is.

ARABESQUE ☆☆☆
1966, USA
Gregory Peck, Sophia Loren, Alan Badel, George Coulouris, Kieron Moore. Directed by Stanley Donen. 105 min.

In this delicious spy comedy-thriller with oodles of picturesque settings and smashing photographic trickery, the plot twists and turns so much that you'll be dizzy trying to fit the pieces of intrigue together. Peck plays a language expert who stumbles into a hornet's nest of spies eager to have him misuse his knowledge. Those who claim that Loren is the world's most beautiful woman can certainly point to this film to support their argument.

THE ARCHER: FUGITIVE FROM THE EMPIRE ☆½
1981, USA (TV)
Lane Caudell, Belinda Bauer, Victor Campos, Kabir Bedi, George Innes, Priscilla Pointer, George Kennedy. Directed by Nicholas Corea. 97 min.

Sword-and-sorcery comic books were the inspiration for this failed television-series pilot. Lane Caudell plays a young warrior in a medieval fantasy world who must find a legendary sorcerer to avenge his father's murder. The inane script plays up the worst aspects of such comic books—their slow pace, pompous portent, and lack of imaginative characterization—and the amateurish performances don't help.

ARCH OF TRIUMPH ☆☆½
1948, USA
Ingrid Bergman, Charles Boyer, Charles Laughton, Louis Calhern. Directed by Lewis Milestone. 120 min.

Enterprise, that short-lived, left-wing production company of the late 1940s, gave us a handful of commercial disasters before it quietly folded. Some are better films than was once thought (e.g., *Caught*); others, including this adaptation of Erich Maria Remarque's World War II novel, are mediocre. The production credits are highly impressive and the plot about a French refugee who falls for a suicidal streetwalker while hunting down the Nazi doctor who persecuted him is good, gritty stuff. The execution, however, is woefully synthetic and slow-moving. Russell Metty gives the studio sets a real workout with his dazzling camera movements, but the drama still rings hollow.

ARE YOU IN THE HOUSE ALONE? ☆½
1978, USA (TV)
Kathleen Beller, Blythe Danner, Tony Bill, Robin Mattson, Dennis Quaid. Directed by Walter Grauman. 96 min.

A high school coed is stalked by some demented soul, who is intent on pushing her off the deep end. This clanky TV movie thriller was not worthy of the neat suspense novel on which it was based. If you inflict this on your friends, *you* may end up in the house alone.

L'ARGENT ☆☆☆☆
1984, France
Christian Patey, Sylvie Van Den Elsen, Michel Briguet. Directed by Robert Bresson. 83 min.

In his fourteenth film in fifty years, Robert Bresson once again charts the progress of a soul from deprivation through sin and judgment to resignation and grace. Adapted from a story by Tolstoy, *L'Argent* is about a deliveryman (Christian Patey) arrested for innocently passing a counterfeit bill. After being released from prison, he descends into a life of crime and despair, until he is ready to commit murder for a few francs. Bresson treats this lurid-sounding tale with the formal symmetry of a stained-glass window; the result is an austere but powerful fable of spiritual redemption.

ARIZONA DAYS ☆½
1937, USA
Tex Ritter, Ethelind Terry, Syd Saylor, Snub Pollard. Directed by Jack English. 56 min.

A cowboy comes up with a dangerous scheme to save a show in this low-budget Western. Ritter provides a credible performance with a few good tunes, including "High, Wide, and Handsome."

ARIZONA RAIDERS ☆☆½
1965, USA
Audie Murphy, Michael Dante, Ben Cooper, Buster Crabbe, Gloria Talbott. Directed by William Witney. 90 min.

Considering that the Western had gone through the psychologizing of Anthony Mann (*The Naked Spur*, *The Man from Laramie*), the demythologizing of Sam Peckinpah (*Ride the High Country*), and the stripping tragic starkness of Budd Boetticher (*Ride Lonesome*, *Comanche Station*) this old-fashioned adventure yarn holds up pretty well. Murphy plays a young Confederate prisoner who is offered freedom if he'll help hunt down his old commanding officer, Quantrell. With a good script, workmanlike direction, and credible performances by Crabbe and Cooper, it has as a bonus perhaps the best Indian torture since the old burial-in-a-fire-ant-mound—namely, the famous Yaqui cactus torture.

THE ARIZONA RANGER ☆½
1948, USA
Tim Holt, Jack Holt, Nan Leslie, Richard Martin. Directed by John Rawlins. 57 min.

Jack Holt—Tim Holt's on-screen and real-life father—comes into conflict with his son, who refuses a partnership on the family ranch and joins the Arizona Rangers. This B Western has enough good action to keep everything moving.

ARMED AND DANGEROUS ☆☆½
1986, USA, PG-13
John Candy, Eugene Levy, Robert Loggia, Kenneth McMillan, Meg Ryan. Directed by Mark L. Lester. 88 min.

John Candy and Eugene Levy have built up such a reservoir of goodwill that audiences will forgive them anything, even their inability to pick good scripts. (Why haven't any of the brilliant talents from SCTV appeared in a film that even approaches the wittiness of their television sketches?) Here, Levy is at half-mast as a befuddled attorney seeking job security as a night watchman, but Candy is quite amusing as a roly-poly cop bounced unfairly off the force. Seeking vindication, the two expose corruption in the security guard business. The biggest laugh comes when Candy leaves an adult bookstore in drag, putting Divine and Milton Berle to shame. Harmless fun, but not worthy of the stars.

ARMORED CAR ROBBERY ☆☆
1950, USA
Charles McGraw, Adele Jergens, William Talman, Douglas Fowley, Steve Brodie. Directed by Richard Fleischer. 67 min.

This solid, no-frills crime drama is about a hard-nosed cop trying to crack a ring of thieves planning a heist at Chicago's

Wrigley Field. Veteran director Fleischer was generally better at this sort of slightly *noir* police procedural than at the epics and period pieces that marked his later career, and genre fans will find this an effective if unexceptional entry. The requisite bad girl with a conscience is played by Adele Jergens.

ARNOLD ☆½
1973, USA, PG
Stella Stevens, Roddy McDowall, Shani Wallis, Jamie Farr. Directed by George Fenady. 95 min.

An English lord's last request is to be wed after death to his airline stewardess girlfriend (Stevens). A predictable onslaught of murders follow, as greedy relatives try in vain to change the terms of his will. An unsavory mix of the macabre and the merry, the tight-budgeted film relies heavily upon bird droppings for the latter. Familiar faces from yesterday (Elsa Lanchester, Farley Granger, Victor Buono and John McGiver) all look as if they'd rather have stayed between jobs.

AROUND THE WORLD IN 80 DAYS ☆☆☆½
1956, USA, G
David Niven, Cantinflas, Robert Newton, Shirley MacLaine; cameos by Charles Boyer, John Carradine, Charles Coburn, Ronald Colman, Noel Coward, Andy Devine, Marlene Dietrich, John Gielgud, Hermione Gingold, Trevor Howard, Buster Keaton, Victor McLaglen, Robert Morley, Jack Oakie, George Raft, Frank Sinatra, Red Skelton, others. Directed by Michael Anderson. 175 min.

Under the supervision of Michael Todd, who invented his 70-mm Todd-AO process for the occasion, Jules Verne's comic adventure became the first of the all-star giant-screen spectaculars. It is less giant and less spectacular, but almost as entertaining, on video. The film was directed by veteran hack Anderson (who went on to oversee such latter-day folderol as *Logan's Run*), but Todd remained in charge, festooning his *chef d'oeuvre* with lavish props and costumes, travelogue-style location photography, and cutesy cameos by forty stars. David Niven is charming as Phineas Fogg, the Victorian gentleman who bets his whist club that he can make the trip in the allotted time; Cantinflas plays his worthy servant, Passepartout. With a screenplay by S. J. Perelman, James Poe, and John Farrow, the film won five Academy Awards, including Best Picture.

AROUND THE WORLD UNDER THE SEA ☆½
1966, USA
Lloyd Bridges, Shirley Eaton, David McCallum, Keenan Wynn. Directed by Andrew Marton. 117 min.

This adventure film is really wet. The direction is soggy; the cast of TV pros is drippy; and the screenplay seems watered down from dozens of other action sci-fi films. Into the briny depths, a team of scientists sound out the ocean floor for signs of earthquake tremors. Good for small fry who want to be oceanographers when they grow up.

THE AROUSERS ☆
1973, USA
Tab Hunter. Directed by Curtis Hanson. 85 min.

A pretty hot number considering its star, former wholesome heartthrob Tab Hunter, who is cast in the lead role as a sex-crazed sickie. Tab plays a sexually frustrated physical-education teacher who starts to get his exercise and his kicks cutting up young women. Whether you'll be aroused by such scenes as Tab inducing a prostitute to dress up as his dead mother is a matter of personal taste or tastelessness, but he's actually quite persuasive, given the sleazy sexploitative nature of this lowbrow enterprise.

THE ARRANGEMENT ☆☆☆
1969, USA, R
Kirk Douglas, Deborah Kerr, Faye Dunaway, Richard Boone, Hume Cronyn. Directed by Elia Kazan. 127 min.

Elia Kazan (*Gentleman's Agreement, A Streetcar Named Desire, East of Eden*) directed *The Arrangement* from his own screenplay based on his best-selling 1967 novel of the same name. The results are frustrating and, at times, uncomfortable to watch, but nonetheless there are rewards. Kirk Douglas (as a thinly disguised Kazan) plays an ad executive who chucks the comforts of his home, job, and wife (Deborah Kerr) for a relationship with a free-spirited woman (Faye Dunaway). It is hard to accept plastic Dunaway as a sort of sexy flower child, but Douglas and Kerr excel as the rich, thwarted married couple. Kazan's uses of flashback and cross-cutting are alternately explosive and confusing. The film feels almost twice as long as its actual running time, but Kazan's insightful, bitter, and slashingly funny self-exploration is an experience well worth viewers' time and trouble.

ARSENIC AND OLD LACE ☆☆☆½
1944, USA
Cary Grant, Josephine Hull, Jean Adair, Raymond Massey, Jack Carson, Peter Lorre, Priscilla Lane. Directed by Frank Capra. 116 min.

This no-holds-barred farce stars Cary Grant as a mild-mannered drama critic thrown into a comic frenzy by the astonishing news that his sweet and kindly aunts Abby and Martha have the longstanding, but rather disturbing, habit of murdering people. Capra, who usually directs warmer and sweeter comedies, fuses the strange and macabre with the funny and sentimental in this high-energy, high-quality comedy.

ARTHUR ☆☆☆½
1981, USA, PG
Dudley Moore, Liza Minnelli, John Gielgud, Geraldine Fitzgerald, Jill Eikenberry, Stephen Elliott, Barney Martin, Anne DeSalvo. Directed by Steve Gordon. 97 min.

This enchanting, beautifully performed romantic comedy is reminiscent of Hollywood's classic screwball farces. Arthur (Dudley Moore) is a permanently inebriated, irresponsible, and irrepressible millionaire due to inherit a $750 million fortune from his father if he marries a bland socialite, but doomed to lose it all when, instead, he falls in love with a dirt-poor shoplifter from Queens (Liza Minnelli). Will the triumph be one of true love, true greed, or both? Writer-director Steve Gordon gives *Arthur* almost everything a comedy could want: wit, sarcasm, countless laughs, and a heart of gold. Seldom has drunkenness been as entertaining as in Moore's riotous performance, but John Gielgud steals the film with a sublime turn as Arthur's hilariously haughty butler-nanny Hobson. (Meeting Arthur's true love, he bows and says, "One must usually frequent a bowling alley to meet a woman of your stature.") Gielgud and the title song (performed by Christopher Cross) won Academy Awards.

ASHANTI—LAND OF NO MERCY ☆½
1979, USA, R
Michael Caine, Peter Ustinov, Beverly Johnson, Kabir Bedi, Omar Sharif, Rex Harrison, William Holden. Directed by Richard Fleischer. 117 min.

This slow, bloated adventure, shot on location in Kenya, concerns an Arab slave trader (the woefully miscast Peter Ustinov) who kidnaps the wife of a U.N. doctor (Michael Caine). Hampered by the loss of its original star, Telly Savalas, and the original director, Richard Sarafian, during production, *Ashanti* looks like what it is, a halfhearted, sloppily made action film whose story was rewritten during shooting. An often offensive bore, despite its fine cast.

ASHES AND DIAMONDS
1958, Poland   ☆☆☆☆
Zbigniew Cybulski, Ewa Krzyzanowska, Waclaw Zastrzezynski, Adam Pawlikowski. Directed by Andrzej Wajda. 104 min.

A chilling and sorrowful account of the last day of the Second World War, the first day of peace, and the final, ironic murder that has to be committed in 1944 Poland. *Ashes and Diamonds* is the best of Wajda's early films. Though some knowledge of the country's wartime politics is helpful, the film can be appreciated by anyone for Wajda's attention to atmosphere and for the gently nuanced performances of his cast. *Ashes* is just as powerful as the director's later and better-known work and is more controlled.

THE ASPHALT JUNGLE
1950, USA   ☆☆☆☆
Sterling Hayden, Sam Jaffe, Louis Calhern, Jean Hagen, Marilyn Monroe, James Whitmore, Marc Lawrence. Directed by John Huston. 112 min.

The Asphalt Jungle is not only a *film-noir* classic, it is the last *film noir* directed by John Huston. As such, it cuts deeper into *noir*'s emotional core of hopelessness and desperation while Huston refines his visual thinking toward a sparer and more realistic look. The story, from the W. R. Burnett (*Little Caesar*) novel, is the venerable chestnut about a sophisticated heist that goes wrong. Sterling Hayden plays a small-time hood who is brought in on his first big score, and the film is his story of a criminal's rock-bottom disillusionment—he learns that big-time crime means big-time corruption, venality, and double crosses. Marilyn Monroe has a small part. Brilliant score by Miklos Rozsa.

THE ASSAM GARDEN
1985, Great Britain   ☆☆½
Deborah Kerr, Madhur Jaffrey, Alec McCowen, Zia Mohyeddin, Anton Lesser, Iain Cuthbertson. Directed by Mary McMurray. 92 min.

After a fifteen-year absence from films, Deborah Kerr returned to give a typically graceful, perceptive performance in this somewhat tepid, very low-key drama. Elisabeth Bond's screenplay is a character study of a privileged woman, newly widowed, whose obsessive tending of her late husband's elaborate garden forces her to take on an Indian woman (Jaffrey). The exploration of Britain's relationship to India is interesting though not especially fresh; the exploration of gardening is very tedious. It's worth seeing only for Kerr and Madhur Jaffrey, who work well with and against each other.

ASSASSINATION
1987, USA, PG-13   ☆
Charles Bronson, Jill Ireland, Stephen Elliott, Jan Gan Boyd, Randy Brooks, Michael Ansara. Directed by Peter Hunt. 88 min.

This lumbering, logy action film stars Charles Bronson as a security expert assigned to protect Jill Ireland (Mrs. Bronson), the First Lady who seems to be the target of an assassination conspiracy from within. Bronson is way past his prime as an action hero, and he and Ireland aren't even the Lunt and Fontanne of the exploitation set (that, of course, would have to be Sylvester Stallone and Brigitte Nielsen). Has its moments, but the gunplay, chases, and narrow escapes are awfully wheezy, even for this genre.

ASSAULT
1971, Great Britain   ☆☆
Suzy Kendall, Frank Finlay, Freddie Jones, James Laurenson, Lesley-Anne Down, David Essex. Directed by Sidney Hayers. 90 min.

This awfully dull British crime story is redeemed only partially by an exciting ending. Someone has been attacking schoolgirls in a wooded area near the school, and a local detective and the art teacher, who was almost attacked herself, team up to track down the assailant. (a.k.a.: *In the Devil's Garden* and *Tower of Terror*)

ASSAULT ON AGATHON
1976, Great Britain/Greece   ☆☆
Nico Minardos, Nina Van Pallandt, John Woodvine, Marianne Faithfull, Kostos Baladimos. Directed by Laslo Benedek. 96 min.

Photogenic Aegean locations almost make up for the convoluted plot of this action film about an Interpol agent who discovers that a World War II mercenary thought to have died is masterminding a series of bank robberies in Greece. The pyrotechnic finale may please viewers who've made it through the labyrinthine and often dull buildup (which apparently underwent heavy editing). Look for singer Marianne Faithfull, excellent in a small role.

ASSAULT ON PRECINCT 13
1976, USA, R   ☆☆☆½
Darwin Johnson, Austin Stoker, Nancy Loomis, Kim Richards. Directed by John Carpenter. 90 min.

Director John Carpenter's reworking of Howard Hawks's *Rio Bravo* has a group of policemen and convicts trapped inside of an abandoned precinct station by dozens of gang members. Carpenter slowly builds up the action and has it violently explode in a series of exciting gun battles. A lot of notable characterizations are on hand from the cast of unknowns. Carpenter exhibits the dark style that made his next movie, *Halloween*, into a gigantic hit. *Assault* shows this director at the top of his form.

AS SUMMERS DIE
1986, USA (TV)   ☆☆
Jamie Lee Curtis, Bette Davis, Scott Glenn, Penny Fuller, Beah Richards. Directed by Jean-Claude Tramont. 88 min.

Back in the 1950s, audiences had a predilection for steamy melodramas set in the deep and dirty South. How strange to see a retrograde slice of the same Southern Gothicana served up anew in a made-for-cable movie. Closer to *Desire in the Dust* than to *The Long Hot Summer*, this competently made but wholly unoriginal scandal drama deals with a collection of venal rich folk trying to bilk a little old black lady out of her legitimate claim to part of their land. She's a noble type who respects the earth and prattles on about tradition, but she faces an uphill battle against the slimy aristocrats who have dollar signs stamped on their souls. Scott Glenn plays the maverick attorney with a yen for spiting the gentry and for romancing Jamie Lee Curtis, the one family member who believes in justice. Passable, and Bette Davis shines in her brief, carefully framed role as an addled grand dame who holds the key to the entire courtroom fracas that breaks out over the property.

ASTÉRIX LE GAULOIS
1978, France   ☆☆
Animated. 67 min.

A reasonably amusing animated feature about France's most popular comic-strip heroes—the pint-sized ancient Gaul, Astérix, and his hulking, chowhound sidekick Obelix. Written and designed by Goscinny and Uderzo, who draw the strip.

THE ASTRO-ZOMBIES
1967, USA   ½☆
Wendell Corey, John Carradine, Tom Pace, Tura Satana. Directed by Ted V. Mikels. 83 min.

This incredibly inept horror garbage is on a level with *Plan Nine from Outer Space*. Director/producer/coscreenwriter Mikels has made lots of these (*The Corpse Grinders, Blood Orgy of the She-Devils*), never once learning from his mistakes. Mad doctor Carradine babbles on and on about the zombies he has created, while foreign agents scurry about and FBI agent Wendell Corey coordinates the efforts of the Free World. This was cowritten and produced by Wayne Rogers, Trapper John on television's "M*A*S*H"!

ASYLUM ★★★
1972, Britain, PG
Peter Cushing, Britt Ekland, Herbert Lom, Patrick Magee, Barry Morse, Charlotte Rampling, Barbara Parkins, Robert Powell. Directed by Roy Ward Baker. 88 min.

Another Amicus horror anthology and the third to be released in the United States in less than a year, *Asylum* has once again the setting of a lunatic asylum, where the new director is given the task of interviewing four of the inmates in order to determine which one is his predecessor. Of course, each of the four has quite a story to tell. . . . The screenplay is by Robert Bloch, with all the same crew behind the cameras as *Tales from the Crypt* and *The House that Dripped Blood*.

ASYLUM OF SATAN ½★
1972, USA, R
Charles Kissinger, Nick Jolly, Sherry Stein, Carla Borelli. Directed by William Girdler. 82 min.

This cheap, sleazy, and hopelessly amateurish gorefest was made on a visibly tiny budget. The tedious plot has an acolyte of Satan in charge of a mental hospital, and running afoul of the Evil One when he offers up a less-than-genuine virgin as a sacrifice. Some hideously dismembered bodies are on display, but it's too poorly made to be at all frightening.

AS YOU LIKE IT ★★½
1936, Great Britain
Laurence Olivier, Elisabeth Bergner, Henry Ainley, Felix Aylmer, Aubrey Mather, Sophie Stewart. Directed by Paul Czinner. 96 min.

Laurence Olivier had his first on-screen fling with Shakespeare in this British version of the comedy about court and country, love and cross-dressing. He's fine, but this overproduced, truncated handling of the Bard's work (based on an earlier adaptation by J. M. Barrie) isn't one for the actor's time capsule. Visually pleasing but static, the film was produced and directed by Czinner, who miscast his wife, Elisabeth Bergner, in the leading role of Rosalind. As a result, the film is more a curiosity than anything approaching a definitive version.

L'ATALANTE ★★★★
1934, France
Jean Dasté, Dita Parlo, Michel Simon, Giles Margarites. Directed by Jean Vigo. 89 min.

Completed shortly before Vigo's early death at age twenty-nine, *L'Atalante*, along with *Zero for Conduct*, established him as one of cinema's great masters. Told with Vigo's poetic purity, the gentle story of a simple riverboat master whose new bride begins to yearn for life in the city becomes a transcendent paean to love and longing. The film is constructed as a mosaic of many brief, telling moments, and characters' behaviors are not carefully executed, consistent portraits; they are jumbled, human responses to situations and quicksilver emotions. The continually shifting perspectives create a distance that often works against the film's emotive content. Michel Simon delivers an earthy, quirky performance as the eccentric, sentimental sailor.

AT CLOSE RANGE ★★½
1986, USA, R
Sean Penn, Christopher Walken, Mary Stuart Masterson, Christopher Penn, Eileen Ryan, Millie Perkins, Tracey Walter, Candy Clark, Crispin Glover. Directed by James Foley. 115 min.

James Foley's second film (his first was *Reckless*) is based on the horrifying true story of a shiftless young man whose father lured him into a criminal gang and then targeted him for murder when he thought the boy might turn witness. On screen, it's squalid and violent, which was probably necessary, but it's also dull and unrevealing, which certainly wasn't. Working in a rural setting, Foley drenches each scene with visual beauty—languid, gorgeous, and wholly inappropriate. As a result, the climactic moments become production numbers and play as comically overwrought set pieces. Christopher Walken, looking hollow-eyed and vicious, is truly scary as the father, and a beefed-up, very blond Sean Penn is excellent as the son. The rest of the cast mumbles in yokel accents that are unintelligible at least half the time. It's finally powerful in a very crude way, but Foley fights against the content throughout. The screenplay was written by Nicholas Kazan, son of the great film and theater director Elia Kazan. (The theme song "Live to Tell" features Mrs. Penn—a.k.a. Madonna.)

AT GUNPOINT ★★½
1955, USA
Fred MacMurray, Dorothy Malone, Walter Brennan, Tommy Rettig, Skip Homeier, Whit Bissell, John Qualen. Directed by Alfred Werker. 80 min.

Watch this one for the crowd of familiar actors working well together. The *High Noon* plot line isn't much, and Werker's direction is clunky and pedestrian, but MacMurray is just fine as a meek store owner who shoots a marauding bank robber and finds himself alone when the gang comes looking for vengeance. Other cast standouts are Malone, Brennan, and Bissell, and Homeier as the killer. Originally in CinemaScope.

ATLANTIC CITY ★★★★
1981, France/Canada, R
Burt Lancaster, Susan Sarandon, Kate Reid, Michel Piccoli, Hollis McLaren, Robert Joy, Al Waxman, Robert Goulet, Wallace Shawn. Directed by Louis Malle. 105 min.

Louis Malle's highly acclaimed melodrama set in contemporary Atlantic City—a visually evocative mélange of crumbling Victoriana and slapped-up casinos—stars Burt Lancaster as a stylish old numbers runner and Susan Sarandon as a dreamy croupier. As an aging punk who has almost come to believe in the heroic veneer he has constructed for himself, Lancaster has the best role of his career. His scenes with Kate Reid, as a bedridden woman who supports him and abuses him, are chilling. Sarandon is first rate, too. Lancaster, Malle, and screenwriter John Guare were all given awards by the National Society of Film Critics. Curiously, the film was shot in 1977 but was not released until 1981.

ATOLL K

See *Utopia*

THE ATOMIC CAFE ★★★★
1982, USA
Directed by Kevin Rafferty, Jayne Loader, Pierce Rafferty. 88 min.

A long overdue antidote to greasy fifties nostalgia, this film serves up the dark side of Cold War America in all its paranoia and conformism. Artfully culled from newsreel footage and government archives, the film is a mind-boggling compilation of government misinformation aimed at selling nuclear war to the American public like a new brand of laundry detergent. *Cafe* is especially remarkable in its exquisite use of scathing humor to underscore the horrifying unreality and impracticality of America's civil-defense posture.

ATOR

See *Ator, the Fighting Eagle*

ATOR, THE FIGHTING EAGLE ★
1983, USA, PG
Miles O'Keeffe, Sabrina Siani, Edmund Purdom. Directed by David Hill. 98 min.

Just about the worst of the sword-and-sorcery genre that had a brief spell of popularity after *Conan the Barbarian*. In this one, our superhuman prehistoric hero battles all sorts of obstacles on a quest to rescue his bride-to-be from the Spider King. The script, production, and direction are all bad enough, but, worst of all, the star is Miles O'Keeffe, previously Tarzan in the Bo Derek version of *Tarzan the Ape Man*. There at least he wasn't given any lines to speak.

AT SWORD'S POINT ☆☆
1952, USA
Cornel Wilde, Maureen O'Hara, Robert Douglas, Gladys Cooper, Dan O'Herlihy, Alan Hale Jr., Blanche Yurka. Directed by Lewis Allen. 81 min.

The sons (and one daughter) of the original Four Musketeers take to the battlefields of France to halt a revolutionary plot against their aging queen, in this appendix to the classic adventure story. The lush period sets and swordplay are fun, but of all of the actors in Hollywood who've ever played a musketeer—Don Ameche, the Ritz Brothers, even Michael York—Cornel Wilde may be the least compelling personality. Swashbuckler fans may enjoy it, but they'd do better to see almost any version of the original story, especially Richard Lester's 1973-74 two-parter.

ATTACK FORCE Z ☆☆½
1981, Australia/Taiwan
John Phillip Law, Sam Neill, Mel Gibson, John Waters. Directed by Tim Burstall. 84 min.

This fast-paced, brutal action flick drags out World War II once again as a backdrop for more rat-a-tat, rapid-fire adventure. It's strange that they should still make these Son of John Wayne films as if the propaganda machines of the Second World War were still going great guns. If you can forget we're now allies with Japan, you may get your fill of macho mayhem in this compact tale of a rescue mission organized to bring back survivors of a plane crash on a Japanese-occupied island.

THE ATTACK OF THE CRAB MONSTERS ☆☆
1957, USA
Richard Garland, Pamela Duncan, Russell Johnson, Mel Welles, Jonathan Haze, Ed Nelson. Directed by Roger Corman. 64 min.

No, it's not the ultimate in sexually transmitted diseases (the world had to wait for the collected works of David Cronenberg for that) but one of Roger Corman's legendary fifties drive-in specials. Giant crabs eat the heads of scientists, assimilating their brains so that they can use their voices to lure new victims. Need we even say that the little crustaceans got to be so big as the result of that favorite fifties hazard, nuclear radiation? Featuring Mel Welles and Jonathan Haze of *Little Shop of Horrors*, Russell Johnson of "Gilligan's Island," and Ed Nelson as the crab.

ATTACK OF THE 50 FOOT WOMAN ☆
1958, USA
Allison Hayes, William Hudson, Yvette Vickers, Roy Gordon, George Douglas, Ken Terrell. Directed by Nathan Hertz. (a.k.a. Nathan Juran). 65 min.

She's taken an overdose of gamma rays, and her footloose hubby might get trodden underfoot. This tacky science-fiction hoot-fest isn't as much fun as it should be; the special effects, in particular, are both transparent (literally) and distinctly lacking in pizazz.

ATTACK OF THE KILLER TOMATOES ☆
1979, USA, PG
David Miller, Sharon Taylor, George Wilson, the San Diego Chicken. Directed by John De Bello. 87 min.

Splat! Bountiful beefsteaks terrorize the populace in this witless satire of giant-monster flicks. It's intentional camp, which by definition is seldom very funny.

AT THE CIRCUS ☆☆☆
1939, USA
Harpo, Groucho, and Chico Marx, Margaret Dumont, Florence Rice, Kenny Baker, Eve Arden. Directed by Edward Buzzell. 87 min.

Ironically, while the indefatigable Marx Brothers are the plot's key to saving a circus from financial trouble, they turn in one of their less impressive film performances. Even at their low point, however, the trio cannot fail to evoke laughter with their lawless brand of musical slapstick. As usual, Margaret Dumont is an apt foil for their antics. Groucho gets the showstopper with his song "Lydia, the Tattooed Lady." Middling Marx is still better than top marks from lesser mortals. (a.k.a.: *The Marx Brothers at the Circus*)

AT THE EARTH'S CORE ☆☆☆
1976, Great Britain, PG
Doug McClure, Peter Cushing, Caroline Munro, Cy Grant. Directed by Kevin Connor. 89 min.

An enjoyable re-creation of the Saturday-afternoon adventure that avoids the self-consciousness or overt parody that marks most such efforts of the past decade. Peter Cushing is a doddering Victorian scientist who invents an earth-boring machine. During a test run, he and assistant McClure accidentally drill their way down to a prehistoric civilization beneath the earth's surface, where they are taken captive by bird-men and undergo various thrills, chills, and spills. This is the second in a series that also included *The Land That Time Forgot* and *The People That Time Forgot*, all from stories by Edgar Rice Burroughs.

THE ATTIC ☆½
1979, USA
Ray Milland, Carrie Snodgress, Ruth Cox, Francis Bay, Rosemary Murphy. Directed by George Edwards. 97 min.

Here's a sort of unappetizing horror-movie version of *The Barretts of Wimpole Street* with an old maid who's stored her sexuality along with a few other antiques up in the attic. A happy ending with Robert Browning is not in store, however. As titles go, this one doesn't hold a candle to the wonderful (and perhaps apocryphal) *Debasement in the Attic*.

ATTICA ☆☆☆½
1980, USA (TV)
Henry Darrow, Charles Durning, Joel Fabiani, Morgan Freeman, George Grizzard, David Harris, Roger E. Mosley, Arlen Dean Snyder, Glynn Turman, Anthony Zerbe. Directed by Marvin J. Chomsky. 100 min.

This harrowing made-for-TV docudrama was adapted from Tom Wicker's book about the 1971 uprising and subsequent slaughter at New York's Attica State Prison. The film benefits from superb performances, sensitive, well-attuned direction (Chomsky won an Emmy), and the diligent attention to fact and detail in James Henerson's teleplay. Years later, this film and the events it depicts still have the power to shock and outrage—this is the "issue" TV-movie at its finest.

AT WAR WITH THE ARMY ☆☆½
1950, USA
Dean Martin, Jerry Lewis, Polly Bergen. Directed by Hal Walker. 93 min.

In 1946, an ex-prizefighter/singer and a twenty-year-old Borscht Belt entertainer decided to throw in together, and the legendary team of Martin and Lewis was born. By the end of the forties they were one of the most popular acts in America, and a movie contract with Paramount naturally followed. In this, their first starring vehicle, their roles were already solidified—Dino was the romantic smoothie and Jerry was the anxious boob. Problems with a woman cause the high-ranked Martin to depend on comically inept Lewis in a military farce. Throughout the series, the boys continually reenacted their potent chemistry and, as in the Hope–Crosby vehicles, locale changes supplied the variety.

AUDREY ROSE
1977, USA, PG ☆
Marsha Mason, Anthony Hopkins, John Beck. Directed by Robert Wise. 113 min.

Marsha Mason, hiccuping her lines between maternal sobs, and stalwart John Beck star as an incredibly thick-skulled couple whose eleven-year-old daughter, Ivy (Susan Swift), turns out to be the result of a botched reincarnation: previously killed in a car crash, she was born again before her soul had a chance to "free itself." Director Robert Wise and screenwriter Frank De Felitta are determined to make a horror movie out of this not particularly scary notion, so they subject poor Ivy to a series of repetitious nightmares during which we watch her stumble around the house like a clown at the rodeo. The film is soporifically paced and its ludicrous defense of reincarnation turns a fairly plausible notion into just another horror-movie bugaboo, like google-eyed monsters.

AUNTIE MAME
1958, USA ☆☆☆
Rosalind Russell, Forrest Tucker, Coral Browne, Fred Clark, Roger Smith, Peggy Cass, Pippa Scott. Directed by Morton DaCosta. 143 min.

The adventures of Mame Dennis, perennial bohemian who believes that "life is a banquet and most poor suckers are starving to death." She weathers the Great Depression, buries her rich husband, surrounds herself with the oddest assortment of characters she can find, and teaches her young nephew how to enjoy life. The role almost seems written for Russell, who made a long-overdue comeback here; although the supporting cast (especially Peggy Cass) is strong, Rosalind is still the entire show. Don't confuse this with 1974's *Mame*, the musical remake with Lucille Ball.

AUTHOR! AUTHOR!
1982, USA, PG ☆
Al Pacino, Dyan Cannon, Tuesday Weld, Alan King, Bob Dishy, Bob Elliot, Ray Goulding, Eric Gurry. Directed by Arthur Hiller. 100 min.

There isn't a believable moment in this niggardly light comedy about an aspiring Broadway playwright (Al Pacino) and his five cutesy kids. Neither sharp enough to be funny nor involving enough to be dramatic, the movie is basically the self congratulatory fantasy of screenwriter Israel Horovitz, who has conceived Pacino's character as a sort of souped-up Horovitz. A waste of a good cast; however, Bob and Ray get off a good moment, and Bob Dishy hits all of his comic marks.

THE AUTOBIOGRAPHY OF MISS JANE PITTMAN
1974, USA (TV) ☆☆☆
Cicely Tyson, Thalmus Rasulala, Richard Dysart, Michael Murphy. Directed by John Korty. 110 min.

Cicely Tyson ages from 19 to 110 in this fictional story of a woman who began life as a slave and survived to see the civil-rights movement of the 1960s. Dramatically and visually, it's unmistakably a TV movie, but Tyson's performance is a big-screen-sized splendor, always convincing, never deliberately ingratiating. She won one of nine Emmys that went to *Pittman*, as did Rick Baker and Stan Winston for their aging makeup work on her, the most convincing that had ever been seen. It's a good chance to see an undervalued actress at her best.

AUTOPSY
1973, Spain ☆
Juan Luis Galiardo, Emiliano Redondo, Jack Taylor, Maria Jose Cantudo. Directed by Juan Logar. 91 min.

An autopsy is shown being performed from beginning to end, interspersed with interviews with people on the street about their thoughts on death, comments on Vietnam, classical music, and quotes from Shakespeare and Goethe. If you want to give this the benefit of the doubt, you could assume that it is a seriously intended, if failed, meditation on human mortality that employs the most forceful possible way to put across its point. On the other hand, maybe the producers just got hold of some footage of a real autopsy and clumsily padded it out. If you want to see real dead bodies being cut up, well, maybe you should go to medical school.

AUTOPSY
1974, Italy, R ☆½
Mimsy Farmer, Barry Primus, Ray Lovelock. Directed by Armando Crispini. 89 min.

Reputedly, this originally contained scenes of a real autopsy being performed. Those scenes aren't there now, and what's left is a dull murder mystery about a young girl whose friends seem to be killing themselves at an alarming rate. The only redeeming factor is the music by Ennio Morricone, the Italian Bernard Herrmann.

AUTUMN LEAVES
1956, USA ☆☆☆
Joan Crawford, Cliff Robertson, Vera Miles, Lorne Greene, Ruth Donnelly, Shepperd Strudwick. Directed by Robert Aldrich. 107 min.

A good performance by Joan Crawford lends luster to this melodramatic, but effective, soap opera about a middle-aged spinster who finds love in the arms of a younger man (Robertson) only to discover that he is a married psychotic nearing a breakdown. It's a dark version of Douglas Sirk's *All That Heaven Allows* that has "1950s Women's Picture" stamped all over it, but it's well mounted and energetically told. Credit goes to Robert Aldrich, one of the few directors who knew how to rein in Crawford's tendency toward histrionic hysteria (he later directed her in *Whatever Happened to Baby Jane?*). Nat King Cole sings Johnny Mercer's now-standard title song.

AUTUMN SONATA
1978, Sweden, PG ☆☆☆☆
Ingrid Bergman, Liv Ullmann. Directed by Ingmar Bergman. 97 min.

Ingrid Bergman gives a wrenching performance as a concert pianist who returns home to visit her oldest daughter (Ullmann), a grown woman who still aches with the memory of her mother's neglect of her as a child. Overwhelmed by feelings of guilt and resentment, the women approach an emotional climax in which each tries to understand the power and significance of the past. One of Ingmar Bergman's most moving films, *Autumn Sonata* features remarkable, intelligent performances by two great actresses. It was dubbed by Bergman and Ullmann.

AVALANCHE
1978, USA ☆½
Rock Hudson, Mia Farrow, Robert Forster, Jeanette Nolan, Barry Primus, Steve Franken. Directed by Corey Allen. 91 min.

The disaster movie died a long-overdue death with this Roger Corman New World release. All the usual soap-opera plot permutations, this time taking place at a ski lodge, are interrupted by—you guessed it—snow sliding all over the place. The avalanche sequences themselves, which are easily the best part of the movie, were directed and edited by Lewis Teague (*Alligator, Jewel of the Nile*).

AVENGING ANGEL ☆½
1985, USA, R
Betsy Russell, Susan Tyrrell. Directed by Robert Vincent O'Neil. 92 min.

This rush-released sequel to *Angel* is an enormous disappointment in light of the cheap thrills of its predecessor; and unforgivably so, given that both films had the same writer-director. Angel, now in her first year of law school (and doing legal research most third-year students would have trouble with), sets out to avenge the murder of the cop who first got her off the streets. The first problem is that Angel is here played by Betsy Russell, an actress of no discernible talent. The second is that the script is played almost entirely for laughs, with a few scenes of unmitigated violence to balance out. The few good scenes toward the end, when Angel and company try to return a gangster's son without Dad catching on that Junior is dead, don't compensate for a first hour full of embarrassingly stupid slapstick.

AVENGING BOXER ☆☆
Hong Kong
Peter Chen, Casanova Wong.

Another sequel to *Angel*, in which the hero this time learns the fine art of pugilism in order to clean up the Hollywood strip? Not really; this is a kung fu revenge tale, in which our hero sets his sights on the baddie who killed his father and stole the Gold Plate, their symbol of trust and leadership. An exciting finale in a booby-trapped warehouse makes this better than average. (a.k.a.: *Fearless Young Boxer*)

AVENGING FORCE ☆½
1986, USA, R
Michael Dudikoff, Steve James, James Booth, John P. Ryan, Bill Wallace. Directed by Sam Firstenberg. 103 min.

A Cannon ninja film by any other name is still exactly what you'd expect. The director and stars of *American Ninja* reteamed for this very similar action outing about a pair of macho heroes taking on a group of deranged right-wing cultists who are trained in the art of fighting fists and flying feet. It's nice to see an exploitation film with a "liberal" slant, although when it comes to issues such as the right to a lawyer, fair trial or *any* trial, ripply-muscled Dudikoff and James are more in line with the Rambo philosophy.

THE AVIATOR ☆½
1985, USA, R
Christopher Reeve, Rosanna Arquette, Tyne Daly, Scott Wilson, Sam Wanamaker, Jack Warden. Directed by George Miller. 98 min.

A mundane star vehicle for Reeve that tries desperately to be a head-in-the-clouds romance but ends up with its prosaic feet planted firmly in the ground. Set during the earliest days of air travel, this adventure pic chronicles the ordeal of the burned-out airborne mailman who's forced to fly one of the first commercial travelers (who's traveling by air for no discernible reason). Naturally, the plane crashes, and adversity forces the two scrapping souls together, so that, when rescued, they are better people. Reeve tries hard to act like Clark Gable. Arquette, among the most overrated actresses of modern times, pushes her chipmunky appeal to its tiny limit.

THE AWAKENING ☆☆½
1980, USA, R
Charlton Heston, Stephanie Zimbalist, Susannah York, Patrick Drury, Jill Townsend. Directed by Mike Newell. 102 min.

Mummy movies may be silly, but this one updates the genre effectively, offering suggestive thrills and some chillingly kinky embellishments. It's based on Bram Stoker's obscure novel *The Jewel of Seven Stars*. Despite an affected English accent that rivals Marlon Brando's in *Mutiny on the Bounty*, Heston is credible and usually restrained as a trespassing Egyptologist whose daughter (Zimbalist) is assaulted by the spirit of vengeful Queen Kara, dead these last 2000 years. Mike Newell, who went on to direct *Dance with a Stranger*, puts some nice, fresh wrappings on this long-dead genre.

THE AWAKENING OF CANDRA ☆
1983, USA (TV)
Blanche Baker, Cliff De Young, Richard Jaeckel, Jeffrey Tambor, Paul Regina. Directed by Paul Wendkos. 100 min.

Candra may be awake, but you're going to have trouble staying that way viewing this soporific TV pic. Out in the great outdoors, a dewy-eyed bride is captured on her honeymoon by a psychotic, but, judging from her idealized relationship with her bland hubby, it was probably the most exciting thing that could have happened to her. Moral: If you go on a honeymoon, don't spend it in the woods.

THE AWFUL TRUTH ☆☆☆☆
1937, USA
Irene Dunne, Cary Grant, Ralph Bellamy, Cecil Cunningham, Mary Forbes, Joyce Compton. Directed by Leo McCarey. 92 min.

This splendid romantic farce has the kind of polished comic teamwork of which the modern cinema seems virtually incapable. Dunne and Grant shine as a bickering couple who can't live with each other and then discover that living apart is worse. Of course, this gives Cary a chance to court Irene all over again, only he has to get past her new fiancé first. It's a delectable comedy about making it to the altar the second time around. (And you get Asta, the famous *Thin Man* dog, too; he's almost as funny as Grant and Dunne.)

AZTEC MUMMY DOUBLE FEATURE ☆
1959, Mexico
Ramon Gay, Rosita Arenas, Crox Alvarado, Luis Aceves Cantaneda. Directed by Rafael Portillo. 130 min.

Here are two indistinguishable sequels to the original *The Aztec Mummy*, all with the same director and cast. In *The Robot vs. the Aztec Mummy*, Dr. Krupp (a.k.a. the Bat), breaks into an ancient tomb with one of the silliest-looking robots since *Robot Monster* helping him to steal the treasure that comes with every ancient tomb. The fight between the mummy and the robot is a lot more exciting if you hit the fast-forward control—neither of these guys is a speed demon. In *The Curse of the Aztec Mummy*, more desecration of his tomb brings the mummy out cruisin' for a bruisin', which he gets from superhero Angel. The mummy, Popoca, has long hair and looks like what's left of a leg cast after someone has been wearing it for about a year. He made a comeback in 1964's *The Wrestling Women vs. the Aztec Mummy*, this time as a good guy. No, we're not making any of this up.

B

BABES IN ARMS ☆☆☆
1939, USA
Mickey Rooney, Judy Garland, Margaret Hamilton. Directed by Busby Berkeley. 93 min.

🎵 "Hey kids, let's put on a show!"—this was the original one. *Babes in Arms* is based on the Rodgers and Hart Broadway hit, but MGM's version omits the play's best songs, including "My Funny Valentine" and "The Lady Is a Tramp." The plot is even more wispy than on stage—just efforts to put on the big show. Luckily, the movie does retain "Where or When" and adds two good songs, "I Cried for You" and "Good Morning." It's also worth seeing for Mickey Rooney and Judy Garland. Rooney won an Oscar nomination for his role, Garland is irresistible, and together they make a great team.

BABES IN TOYLAND ☆☆☆½
1934, USA
Stan Laurel, Oliver Hardy, Charlotte Henry, Henry Brandon, Felix Knight, Jean Darling. Directed by Gus Meins and Charles Rogers. 73 min.

🧸 Six-foot-tall wooden soldiers march against the apelike Bogeymen in this timeless children's fairy-tale film. Laurel and Hardy are particularly endearing as toymakers who try to help two young lovers. Enchanting songs, a mystical Toyland set, and plenty of thrills still bring out the kid in every viewer. (a.k.a.: *March of the Wooden Soldiers; Wooden Soldiers; Laurel and Hardy in Toyland*)

THE BABY ☆☆½
1973, USA, R
Anjanette Comer, Ruth Roman, Marianna Hill. Directed by Ted Post. 86 min.

☠ *The Baby* has an intriguing plot for a low-budget exploitation film, and Anjanette Comer offers a genuinely subtle performance as a social worker involved with the case of an adult man who is treated like a child by his warped family. Once started, viewing to the very end is recommended.

BABY DOLL ☆☆☆☆
1956, USA
Karl Malden, Carroll Baker, Eli Wallach, Mildred Dunnock, Lonny Chapman, Eades Hogue, Noah Williamson. Directed by Elia Kazan. 114 min.

🎭 This infamous film about a white-trash cotton-gin owner (Karl Malden) living in a run-down Mississippi mansion with his child-wife (Carroll Baker) is definitely steamy—but even more than that, it's sly, subtle, and mockingly funny. Malden's poor slob of a farmer got to marry his young sweetheart on the condition that she'd stay a virgin till her twentieth birthday. When a new cotton gin ruins his business, he burns the place down, and the plantation's Sicilian manager (Eli Wallach) seeks revenge—partly by seducing Baby Doll. Adapted from a pair of Tennessee Williams one-acters, this mixture of gothic melodrama and nursery/bedroom comedy is one of Hollywood's rare authentic inroads into rural terrain. Malden does blubbery wonders with his lowly character, Wallach is sharp and flashy, and Carroll Baker, in her one great role, is astonishing: her strength and comic timing help turn this down-home Lolita into a dirt-poor cousin of Ibsen's Nora.

BABY LOVE ☆
1969, Great Britain
Linda Hayden, Keith Barron, Ann Lynn, Derek Lamden, Diana Dors. Directed by Alastair Reid. 92 min.

🐈 This ultra-sleazy soft-core titillation seems tame today. A Lolita-type baby-sitter infiltrates a household to exact revenge on a man she thinks might have been the father who abandoned her. If you get your kicks watching middle-aged men suck in their guts to simulate lust, and if the thought of a teenage temptress reducing everyone around her to mush sounds like hot stuff, you may want to give this a gander. It's a tired businessman's special, about as exciting as using a vibrating bed in a run-down motel.

BABY... SECRET OF THE LOST LEGEND ☆☆
1985, USA, PG
William Katt, Sean Young, Patrick McGoohan, Julian Fellowes, Kyalo Mativo, Hugh Quarshie. Directed by B. W. L. Norton. 95 min.

🕵 This fantasy-adventure about a young American couple who stumble upon a baby brontosaurus in the African jungles and then risk their lives to protect it from evil scientists follows the age-old Disney formula of first sundering and then reconstituting a cozy family group. It's surefire kid stuff, but in pursuit of the young teen market, director B. W. L. Norton has inserted a series of sub-Spielberg/Lucas chases and some "adult" romantic byplay, and the film lurches to a stop every few minutes to pander to a different segment of the audience.

THE BABYSITTER ☆☆½
1980, USA (TV)
William Shatner, Patty Duke Astin, Quinn Cummings, Stephanie Zimbalist, John Houseman, David Wallace, Kenneth Tigar. Directed by Peter Medak. 104 min.

☠ A well-chosen cast enlivens this made-for-TV gothic about a family whose lives are imperiled when they hire a sweet-faced but demonic baby-sitter (Stephanie Zimbalist) to care for their daughter. John Houseman, who often seems best when his material is least challenging, scores as the grandfatherly neighbor, and, as Dad and Mom, William Shatner and Patty Duke Astin are both unusually restrained. Effectively creepy at times, but completely unsurprising.

BABY THE RAIN MUST FALL ☆☆☆
1965, USA
Lee Remick, Steve McQueen, Don Murray, Paul Fix, Ruth White. Directed by Robert Mulligan. 100 min.

🎭 This trim, unpretentious drama, an excursion into writer Horton Foote's land of lost opportunities made long before *1918* and *Tender Mercies*, has gritty integrity and deft characterizations that show Foote at his best. It deals with a jailbird's return to his hometown, and his troubled period of adjustment as he tries to quell his wanderlust and re-cement his family ties. Unfortunately overlooked at the time of its release, this is a beautifully crafted film whose rustic virtues have improved with age.

THE BACHELOR AND THE BOBBYSOXER ☆☆☆
1947, USA
Cary Grant, Myrna Loy, Shirley Temple, Ray Collins, Rudy Vallee, Harry Davenport. Directed by Irving Reis. 95 min.

🤓 Sidney Sheldon's screenplay, absurd as it might seem, did win an Oscar, but it is by far the weakest element in this lightweight Cary Grant comedy. Teenaged Shirley Temple (in her only decent adult performance) plays a high school student who develops a crush on painter and ladies' man Grant. Myrna Loy (incomprehensibly cast as Temple's older sister) plays the judge who looks askance at the situation. It's the cast that makes the thin plot work. Grant has a particularly good time teasing his matinee-idol image, and he and Loy share some great knowing glances (though their *Mr. Blandings Builds His Dream House*, also made that year, is better). Frothy amusement but rarely hilarious. (a.k.a.: *Bachelor Knight*)

BACHELOR BAIT ☆½
1934, USA
Stuart Erwin, Rochelle Hudson, Pert Kelton, Skeets Gallagher, Berton Churchill. Directed by George Stevens. 80 min.

This is a routine, very dull comedy about the head of a small matchmaking agency whose business is encroached upon by a Boss Tweed–like politician who wants a piece of the action. The plot wears and George Stevens's direction (it was only his second feature) shows none of the confidence that he later demonstrated in everything from *Swing Time* to *Giant*.

BACHELOR KNIGHT

See *The Bachelor and the Bobbysoxer*

BACHELOR MOTHER ☆☆☆½
1939, USA
Ginger Rogers, David Niven, Charles Coburn, Frank Albertson, E. E. Clive, Elbert Caplen Jr., Ernest Truex. Directed by Garson Kanin. 81 min.

This tale of a merry series of misunderstandings involving a shop girl and an abandoned baby is one of Garson Kanin's most vivacious comedies. Rogers is enormously appealing and her combination of innocent eyes with a knowing voice is delicious. Niven may be a little undernourished as her love interest, but *Bachelor Mother* is not really a romantic story; instead, it is refreshing, unsentimental, and very funny. Subtlety is lacking, but high spirits carry the day.

BACHELOR PARTY ☆½
1984, USA, R
Tom Hanks, Tawny Kitaen, George Grizzard, Adrian Zmed, Bibi Besch. Directed by Neal Israel. 106 min.

Tom Hanks may be the only young actor who could bring off a scene in which he's asked to whir an eggbeater at his girlfriend as though it were a hand-powered vibrator. This comedy about a groom-to-be on his last night out pokes fun at shacking up and marriage, orgies and bridal showers, all the while following a young couple (Hanks and Tawny Kitaen) trying to slog through the erotic confusion. Hanks proves a charismatic hero (he's like a less oily Bill Murray), but the attempt at satire quickly gives way to moronic sight gags, exhausting genitalia jokes, and "Flintstones"-era sexism.

BACK FROM ETERNITY ☆☆
1956, USA
Robert Ryan, Anita Ekberg, Rod Steiger, Phyllis Kirk, Gene Barry, Keith Andes, Beulah Bondi, Fred Clark, Jesse White. Directed by John Farrow. 97 min.

This is a remake of John Farrow's *Five Came Back*. Jonathan Latimer's screenplay (based on the original by Nathanael West, Dalton Trumbo, and Jerry Cady) tells what happens when only five of eight passengers can return from a South American jungle after their plane crashes. The philosophical and psychological possibilities of the tale are left generally unexplored in favor of a lot of scenery chewing by the cast. Competent melodrama, but a theme better handled elsewhere.

BACK ROADS ☆☆
1981, USA, R
Sally Field, Tommy Lee Jones, David Keith, Miriam Colon, Michael V. Gazzo, Dan Shor, M. Emmet Walsh, Nell Carter. Directed by Martin Ritt. 94 min.

After the success of *Norma Rae*, Martin Ritt and Sally Field made the mistake of reteaming for this dreary, weary social comedy about a hooker and a drifter who meet up and cruise through Mobile, Alabama, getting into all sorts of uninteresting trouble. Alternately snide and sentimental, the film treats its characters with a bizarre combination of mistiness and contempt. Tommy Lee Jones has some good moments as the bum-in-the-making, but Field is completely charmless, as is always the case when she tries too hard.

BACK STREET ☆☆½
1932, USA
Irene Dunne, John Boles, June Clyde, George Meeker, ZaSu Pitts, Doris Lloyd. Directed by John M. Stahl. 93 min.

Audiences seem to love watching strong-willed career women chuck it all to become the "back-street" mistresses of married men. This is the first of three versions of Fannie Hurst's best-selling novel, which also influenced countless variations (*Letter from an Unknown Woman*, *About Mrs. Leslie*). Melodrama specialist John M. Stahl (*Imitation of Life*, *Magnificent Obsession*) actually creates some lively sequences, and Karl Freund's camera movements are remarkably fluid for Hollywood in 1932, but neither they nor charming Irene Dunne as the masochistic heroine can make this tearjerker anything more than a creaky, old-fashioned sudser. Remade in 1941 and 1961.

BACK STREET ☆☆
1961, USA
Susan Hayward, John Gavin, Vera Miles, Charles Drake, Virginia Grey, Reginald Gardner, Tammy Marihugh. Directed by David Miller. 107 min.

The third and weakest version of Fannie Hurst's thirties weepie concerns the grand passion of an extramarital affair ruined by the man's alcoholic wife (Vera Miles). In the role of the lover, previously played by Irene Dunne and Margaret Sullavan, Susan Hayward is fine; she seems built to suffer and grieve. But notwithstanding her work and Ross Hunter's cloyingly lush production, this is tedious nonsense that was dated twenty-five years ago; it's neither improved with age nor ripened into camp since then.

BACK TO BATAAN ☆☆
1945, USA
John Wayne, Anthony Quinn, Beulah Bondi, Fely Franquelli, Richard Loo. Directed by Edward Dmytryk. 95 min.

This typical John Wayne war movie finds the Duke as a colonel organizing a Filipino invasion of Japanese-held Bataan. Since no one pairs off with Big John (the closest he comes to a romance is his relationship with Beulah Bondi, who plays an American schoolteacher), Anthony Quinn and Fely Franquelli portray the obligatory love interests. Bland, competent Edward Dmytryk direction of a grim, jingoistic screenplay by Ben Barzman and Richard Landau. Not a sequel to MGM's *Bataan*.

BACK TO SCHOOL ☆☆☆
1986, USA, PG-13
Rodney Dangerfield, Keith Gordon, Sally Kellerman, Robert Downey, Jr., Burt Young, Sam Kinison, Adrienne Barbeau. Directed by Alan Metter. 90 min.

Rodney Dangerfield trades in his bitingly foulmouthed characterization from *Easy Money* for the friendly and mostly harmless guise of Thornton Melon, a sarcastic self-made millionaire who leaves his business and his sadistic second wife to take courses at his son's college. Upon arrival, Thornton wastes no time ingratiating himself with the shapelier students and bringing down the wrath of the stuffier professors when he hits the parties instead of the books. There are some great comic bits and knowing jabs at higher education, but this particular cinematic institution delivers more affable entertainment than real laughs. A likable picture that gets a B and a pat on the head for good behavior.

BACK TO THE FUTURE ☆☆☆☆
1985, USA, PG
Michael J. Fox, Christopher Lloyd, Lea Thompson, Crispin Glover. Directed by Robert Zemeckis. 115 min.

Director Robert Zemeckis's hip tale of time travel is a witty blend of comedy, manic characterizations, and special effects that pumps new life into the familiar time-travel genre. Everyteenager Marty McFly (Michael J. Fox) is transported back to 1955 and meets his nerdy father and lascivious mother as young adults. It's up to Marty to attract these two opposites to one another, or he will cease to exist before he can get "back to the future." Even though the movie telegraphs its plot twists, Zemeckis vigorously works around his self-imposed barriers to create one of the wackiest, most original science-fiction films in recent years—a picture that mixes nuclear-powered DeLoreans, Libyan terrorists, sock hops, and malt shops. Its obvious that everyone loves the material they're working with— especially Christopher Lloyd as the maddest scientist since Dr. Frankenstein. *Back to the Future* is an irresistibly enthusiastic film made in the Spielberg tradition, and produced by the master himself.

BAD

See *Andy Warhol's Bad*

BAD BOYS ☆☆☆
1983, USA, R
Sean Penn, Esai Morales, Reni Santoni, Eric Gurry, Ally Sheedy. Directed by Rick Rosenthal. 120 min.

This story of juvenile delinquents in prison is the most powerful teen-rebel movie in years. Sean Penn is a violent J.D. who's sent to prison after accidentally killing a young Hispanic boy: Esai Morales is the dead boy's teenage brother who comes looking for revenge. Penn is a revelation as the mostly silent hero. There are echoes of James Cagney and Robert de Niro, but the snarling nihilism of this performance is Penn's alone.

BAD COMPANY ☆☆☆½
1972, USA, PG
Jeff Bridges, Barry Brown, Jim Davis, David Huddleston, John Savage, Jerry Houser. Directed by Robert Benton. 93 min.

Robert Benton's directorial debut is a period piece in two senses—it evokes both the outlaw spirit of the West during the Civil War, when it takes place, and the cynical disillusionment of so many American films of the early 1970s, when it was made. Certainly, it's among the most thoughtful and intelligent of the so-called anti-Westerns, films which turned genre conventions and clichés about honor, duty, and heroism inside out. The "good guys" in *Bad Company* are a timid young Methodist (Barry Brown) who flees to Virginia City to avoid the draft, and the amoral AWOL soldier (Jeff Bridges) with whom he forms a very uneasy alliance. Before he knows it, they run afoul of both sides of the law and head for the unexpectedly bleak frontier. Funny, sad, and consistently surprising, with excellent performances from all and cinematography by Gordon Willis that is in itself a complex portrait of the old West.

BADGE 373 ☆
1973, USA, R.
Robert Duvall, Eddie Egan, Verna Bloom, Henry Darrow, Felipe Luciano, Tina Cristiani. Directed by Howard W. Koch. 116 min.

This violent, narrow-minded police drama is reportedly based on the real-life exploits of Eddie Egan, the cop whose career also inspired *The French Connection*. Robert Duvall plays the Egan role, Egan himself appears as a sergeant, and the screenplay is by noted New York journalist Pete Hamill. Downbeat, shoddily crafted, less interesting than any of the people involved, and consistently, unapologetically racist, the film was picketed by Hispanic activists at the time of its release.

BAD GUYS ½☆
1985, USA, PG
Adam Baldwin, Mike Jolly, Michelle Nicastro, Ruth Buzzi, James Booth, Sergeant Slaughter. Directed by Joel Silberg. 86 min.

A cheap-looking, moronic comedy for undiscriminating wrestlemaniacs. Adam Baldwin (with a bad blond dye job) and Mike Jolly play L.A. cops who get busted from the force. After brief careers as construction workers and male strippers, they decide to become tag wrestlers, acquire screechy Ruth Buzzi as their trainer, and go up against the Kremlin Krushers, a Russian team. Unremittingly stupid, and guaranteed to bore even—and perhaps especially—those who take the showy sport seriously. The script is co-credited to "Joe Gillis," which happens to be the name of the writer-turned-gigolo in *Sunset Boulevard;* whoever chose the pseudonym (if it is one) had more wit than he showed in *Bad Guys.*

BADLANDS ☆☆☆☆
1973, USA, PG
Martin Sheen, Sissy Spacek, Warren Oates. Directed by Terence Malick. 94 min.

Using the actual 1950s killing spree of Charles Starkweather and Caril Fugate, Malick has fashioned a film of cool, stark beauty. Both stars are marvelous: Sheen manages to be boyishly open while retaining a mysterious, murderous undertone, and Spacek provides a deadly, dispassionate voice-over narration that undercuts her naive, wholesome screen persona. An astonishing directorial debut for Malick, who also wrote and produced this low-budget stunner.

BAD MANNERS ☆
1984, USA, R
Martin Mull, Karen Black, Edy Williams. Directed by Bobby Houston. 85 min.

An oppressive, imitation-underground comedy, this film takes the derisive black humor of directors like John Waters and the pre-1970s Roger Corman and packages it like laundry detergent. A crew of delinquent teenage orphans lives in a Catholic orphanage run by glittery-eyed sadists. When one of the kids is adopted by a wealthy suburban couple (played with no-stops nastiness by Martin Mull and Karen Black), four of his friends break out and try to rescue him. Director Bobby Houston has stuffed this anarchic scenario full of cult-movie trappings (gross-outs, a trash cameo by Russ Meyer superstar Edy Williams, the usual hip parody of suburbia), but his meat-grinder amorality is so shamelessly calculated that the result is about as subversive as a sitcom.

BAD MAN'S RIVER ☆☆
1972, Spain, PG
Lee Van Cleef, Gina Lollobrigida, James Mason, Diana Lorys. Directed by Gene Martin. 89 min.

In this Western action along the Tex-Mex border, a gang of bank robbers is offered a job by a Mexican revolutionary who wants them to blow up the arsenal of the Mexican army. A double-cross arrives in the person of the gang leader's ex-wife. There is neither enough comedy nor enough adventure to make this very interesting; did James Mason lose a bet with the producer that forced him to appear here?

BADMAN'S TERRITORY ★★½
1946, USA
Randolph Scott, Ann Richards, George "Gabby" Hayes, Ray Collins, James Warren, Chief Thundercloud, Lawrence Tierney, Tom Tyler, Isabel Jewell, Morgan Conway. Directed by Tim Whelan. 97 min.

A hard-riding sheriff goes into outlaw territory looking for his brother. He meets the Daltons, the James Gang, and Belle Starr, but it turns out they're all amiable folks just looking to get along. Could it be that the real villain is the crafty U.S. marshal? Ann Richards hits all the right notes as a lady editor, and Randolph Scott was one of the best cowboys ever—stoic and mannerly, with just a hint of menace. Although it's hard to pick out Gabby Hayes's best performance, this is prime Gabby.

BAD MEDICINE ★★
1985, USA, PG
Steve Guttenberg, Julie Hagerty, Alan Arkin, Julie Kavner, Bill Macy, Curtis Armstrong, Robert Romanus. Directed by Harvey Miller. 96 min.

This starts out promisingly enough as a *Police Academy*–style spoof set in a Central American medical school for students who can't get into any other med school. There are the usual assorted zany characters, including "pharmaceutical specialist" Dennis Gladstone (*Revenge of the Nerds*). Before long, however, the movie becomes over-serious, as the students decide to raid the school's medical supplies in order to set up their own clinic to care for the impoverished residents of a nearby pueblo. Alan Arkin suffers from a wildly inconsistent part: At times, he's supposed to be a greedy, power-mad businessman, whose only motive in operating the school is to make a name for himself; at others, though, he is presented as a sympathetic character whose frustrations stem from loneliness since the death of his wife.

THE BAD NEWS BEARS ★★★½
1976, USA, PG
Walter Matthau, Tatum O'Neal, Jackie Earle Haley, Vic Morrow, Joyce Van Patten, Alfred Lutter. Directed by Michael Ritchie. 102 min.

Director Michael Ritchie brings his wonderfully offbeat, ironic sense of humor to this box-office hit about a losing Little League team that makes a miraculous turnaround when female pitcher Tatum O'Neal joins their ranks and inspires home-run hitter Jackie Earle Haley to play too. Walter Matthau is perfectly cast as the grumbling, beer-guzzling coach who learns a little bit about life from his motley crew of hilarious, pint-sized misfits. It's a delightful chunk of foul-mouthed but family-style Americana.

THE BAD NEWS BEARS GO TO JAPAN ★½
1978, USA, PG
Tony Curtis, Jackie Earle Haley, Tomisaburo Wakayama, Lonny Chapman. Directed by John Berry. 91 min.

Why didn't they go farther away—like to the moon? The original entry in this series had some freshness and verve, but hardly enough originality to sustain two sequels. This time, the by-now-familiar Little League team is being promoted by Tony Curtis, a money-grubbing small-timer who sets out to exploit the little batters before grudgingly realizing that he's a good guy at heart. Simpleminded comedy that belongs in the dugout.

THE BAD NEWS BEARS IN BREAKING TRAINING ★½
1977, USA, PG
William Devane, Clifton James, Jackie Earle Haley, Jimmy Baio, Chris Barnes, Erin Blunt, Alfred Lutter, Dolph Sweet. Directed by Michael Pressman. 99 min.

For the wit in Michael Ritchie's original *The Bad News Bears*, this sequel (sans Ritchie, screenwriter Bill Lancaster, and stars Walter Matthau and Tatum O'Neal) substitutes sentimentality—gobs of it. The story of a California Little League team's trip to a championship game in the Houston Astrodome, it embraces all the smarm and kitsch Ritchie's film mocked. Even the kids, many of them the same charmers as in the original, seem lifeless. Badly directed, they perform like trained fleas. A rousing Big Game sequence is too little, too late.

BAD RONALD ★★½
1974, USA (TV)
Scott Jacoby, Pippa Scott, John Larch, Dabney Coleman, Kim Hunter, John Fiedler. Directed by Buzz Kulik. 78 min.

In this taut, surprisingly creepy thriller, a teenaged killer (Scott Jacoby) resides in a secret room in his late family's house. The new tenants don't know about their uninvited boarder, and veteran TV director Buzz Kulik wrings the plot for all of its grotesquerie and suspense. Network restrictions hamper the tale, but a fair number of shivers are generated within its constraints and Jacoby is very effective as the increasingly deranged boy.

THE BAD SEED ★★★
1956, USA
Patty McCormack, Nancy Kelly, Henry Jones, William Hopper, Eileen Heckart, Evelyn Varden. Directed by Mervyn LeRoy. 129 min.

Precious little Rhoda Penmark is a pigtailed Miss Perfect with a bad habit of getting away with murder. Based on William March's bestseller and play, Mervyn LeRoy's film follows the fascinating story of Rhoda's corpse-strewn life-style and eventual come-uppance by treating it as all-stops-out melodrama; it works beautifully despite the staginess of LeRoy's direction. Like Veda in *Mildred Pierce*, Rhoda is all-American evil incarnate—the perfect child as sociopath—and McCormack won well-deserved stardom for her chilling portrayal. Good for horror fans, and a feast for camp followers in search of overwrought performances and juicy dialogue. And if Rhoda ever saw the awful TV remake of this, she'd have known what to do with the perpetrators.

BAFFLED ★½
1972, Great Britain (TV)
Leonard Nimoy, Susan Hampshire, Vera Miles, Rachel Roberts. Directed by Phillip Leacock. 74 min.

Although not a *guarantee* of mediocrity, the fact that *Baffled* was an unsuccessful television series pilot does anticipate a certain formulaic approach to the plot and characterization! Leonard Nimoy and the lovely Susan Hampshire are game participants in an ESP story laced with horror elements. English locations and a talented guest cast, including Vera Miles and Rachel Roberts, give this a little class. But the villain is a nonentity, reducing some suspenseful play elements to mere unpleasantries.

LE BAL ★★★
1982, France/Italy/Algeria
Etienne Guichard, Regia Bouquet, Francesco de Rosa, Liliane Delval, Arnault Le Carpentier. Directed by Ettore Scola. 112 min.

Set entirely inside a Parisian dance hall, this all-dancing, no-talking extravaganza attempts to weave together snippets of the past four decades of French history in dance and romance. Scola's trying to create a fatalistic Gallic romanticism, but the film's political pronouncements are a bit shallow. Instead, we watch this project for its grandiose sweep and the pleasure we derive from watching the stylish actors strutting their stuff in this choreographic time capsule. A unique film in a period when there are far too few musicals for adult tastes.

LA BALANCE ★★½
1983, France, R
Nathalie Baye, Philippe Léotard, Richard Berry, Christophe Malavoy, Jean-Paul Connart. Directed by Bob Swaim. 102 min.

This gritty, effective police thriller concerns a hooker and a small-time thief who form an unlikely alliance with the cops to find a killer. American expatriate director Bob Swaim provides plenty of local color and keeps the film moving at a very brisk clip, although it finally degenerates into a splashy but conventional shoot-out. Nice performances from Nathalie Baye and Philippe Léotard as the romantic odd couple make it worth a look. (Note: the title is French *argot* for "informer.")

BALLAD IN BLUE ☆½
1965, Great Britain
Ray Charles, Tom Bell, Mary Peach, Dawn Addams, Piers Bishop. Directed by Paul Henreid. 88 min.

Ray Charles's only feature-film acting role is in this painfully mawkish "inspirational" drama in which he plays himself, rather stiffly. Ray's job here is to help an adorable little blind boy who's being overprotected by his worried mother. Whatever chance the film might have had to make a positive statement about living with blindness is vitiated by the ridiculously upbeat ending.

BALLAD OF A SOLDIER ☆☆☆½
1959, USSR
Shanna Prokhorenko, Vladimir Ivashov, Antonina Maximova, Nikolai Kruchkov. Directed by Grigori Chukrai. 89 min.

One of the seminal Soviet films of the 1950s, this is the romantic tale of a young soldier who receives a week's leave during World War II and falls (chastely) in love with a young girl. Very moving, though the scope and emotions are somewhat simpler and less impressively conveyed than in Mikhail Kalotozov's similar film *The Cranes Are Flying*. Shanna Trokhorenko and Vladimir Ivashov are both outstanding.

THE BALLAD OF CABLE HOGUE ☆☆☆½
1970, USA
Jason Robards, Stella Stevens, David Warner, Strother Martin, Slim Pickens, L. Q. Jones, R. G. Armstrong. Directed by Sam Peckinpah. 120 min.

Sam Peckinpah's beautiful, introspective, and surprisingly gentle capitalist fable is the only film he totally controlled, and it died at the box office. Jason Robards is Hogue, a prospector robbed and left to perish in the desert, who discovers a water hole and builds a profitable business around it—only to be done in by the encroachments of the machine age. (Like Peckinpah's previous effort, *The Wild Bunch*, *Hogue* is set in the last days of the frontier, circa 1900.) Stella Stevens has rarely had a funnier (or sexier) role than as Cable's ex-hooker mistress.

THE BALLAD OF GREGORIO CORTEZ ☆☆½
1982, USA
Edward James Olmos, Brian James, William Sanderson, Bruce McGill. Directed by Robert M. Young. 99 min.

This righteous tale of racial prejudice and miscarried justice is set in the waning days of the legendary American frontier. An anti-Western whose historically based narrative serves as the framework for a series of set pieces aimed at debunking the romanticized cinematic image of the Old West. Extremely serious, sometimes to its detriment, but full of striking images. Although *The Ballad of Gregorio Cortez* was made for PBS's "American Playhouse" series, it was first given a theatrical release.

BALL OF FIRE ☆☆☆½
1941, USA
Gary Cooper, Barbara Stanwyck, Dana Andrews, Oscar Homolka, S. Z. "Cuddles" Sakall, Dan Duryea. Directed by Howard Hawks. 111 min.

Howard Hawks directed this screwball variation on *Snow White and the Seven Dwarfs* from a script by Billy Wilder and Charles Brackett. Barbara Stanwyck is the Snow White, a flashy nightclub singer who is fleeing the police in order to prevent herself from testifying against her gangster boyfriend (Dana Andrews). She decides to hide out in a house inhabited by seven stuffy professors who are in the process of rewriting the encyclopedia and need someone like her to complete their section on slang. Before long, Babs is leading the men (including a shy and bumbling Gary Cooper) in conga lines and wild parties. (Hawks must have liked the premise since he used it again six years later in the musical *A Song Is Born*.) Although the stars work hard, the six other professors (played by character actors like S. Z. "Cuddles" Sakall and Oscar Homolka) are cute (maybe too cute), and the pace is fast, the film ultimately lacks the necessary lines and situations to make it consistently funny. Cooper's delirious slapstick fight scene toward the end nearly pulls it all together.

THE BALTIMORE BULLET ☆☆½
1980, USA, PG
James Coburn, Omar Sharif, Bruce Boxleitner, Ronee Blakely, Jack O'Halloran, Calvin Lockhart. Directed by Robert Ellis Miller. 103 min.

This hybrid of *The Hustler* and *The Flim-Flam Man* has its amusing moments, and you might even enjoy it if you have any affinity for the charms of James Coburn and Bruce Boxleitner. They play a team of pool sharks who travel around small towns getting into games with local hustlers, on the morally questionable justification that it's okay to cheat someone who is trying to cheat you. The object is to raise the $20,000 Coburn needs to get into a game with his old nemesis Omar Sharif, the acknowledged pro in the hustling field. From the screenwriter of *Angel*.

THE BAMBOO SAUCER ☆½
1968, USA
Dan Duryea, Lois Nettleton, John Ericson. Directed by Frank Telford. 100 min.

When a flying saucer is reported by agents hidden in a Red Chinese peasant village, a team of Americans is sent to investigate. Along the way they meet a similarly minded Soviet team, and both band together in the name of science. Dan Duryea's last film is a sophomoric attempt to link the Cold War with extraterrestrials, succeeding neither as a plea for unilateral cooperation nor as a genre thriller. Scripted by Rip Von Runkel, this flat, uninteresting yarn will put even the most wide-awake insomniac to sleep. Lois Nettleton's impersonation of a Russian scientist is as awful as you might expect.

THE BANANA MONSTER

See *Schlock*

BANANAS ☆☆☆☆
1971, USA, PG
Woody Allen, Louise Lasser, Carlos Montalban, Howard Cosell. Directed by Woody Allen. 82 min.

Mild-mannered products tester Fielding Melesh (Woody Allen), dying to impress his activist girlfriend (Louise Lasser), visits a banana republic and winds up leading a revolution. This sprawling, hilarious early film from one of America's greatest directors features scores of one-liners and sight gags, most of which are on the mark. Howard Cosell narrates the fall of a dictator, and Sylvester Stallone appears briefly as a thug.

THE BANDITS ☆½
1967, Mexico
Robert Conrad, Jan-Michael Vincent, Roy Kenson, Pedro Armindariz, Jr., Manuel Lopez Ochoa. Directed by Robert Conrad and Alfredo Zacharias. 88 min.

Three American bandits are saved from the executioner by a Mexican outlaw. They escape to the south of the Rio Grande, where they resume their gunslinging ways. Forgive us if we sound unexcited. Made in Mexico in 1967 but unreleased in the United States until much, much later.

BANDITS, PROSTITUTES, AND SILVER ☆☆
Hong Kong
Don Wong Dao, Angela Mao, Lo Lieh, Wang Hsieh, Mao Ren, Wen Chiang Chung. Directed by Kao Pao Shu.

Here, at last, is a movie that really lives up to its title! Don Wong Dao plays a humble carriage driver who's trying to earn enough money to buy his girlfriend from a brothel. Watch this one for its choreographed martial arts and above-average costumes and sets.

BAND OF THE HAND ☆☆
1986, USA, R
Stephen Lang, Michael Carmine, Lauren Holly, John Cameron Mitchell, Daniele Quinn, Larry Fishburne, James Remar. Directed by Paul Michael Glaser. 109 min.

Michael Mann produced this extremely slick, violent, and boring action thriller, and he might as well have called it *Miami Vice Versa*. The good guys in this version of the city are really ex-bad guys, a group of teenagers suddenly paroled from juvenile hall, taken into the Everglades jungles and trained in survivalism, vigilantism, and hand-to-hand combat, and then let loose on the Miami streets to act as an anticrime squad. (Where are trigger-happy Crockett and Tubbs when you need them most?) For a better indication of Mann's talents, check out the underappreciated *Manhunter*; *Band of the Hand* has all of the deficiencies of his overly decorative, underplotted style, and none of the excitement he can generate under better circumstances.

BANDOLERO! ☆☆
1968, USA
James Stewart, Dean Martin, Raquel Welch, George Kennedy, Andrew Prine, Will Geer, Denver Pyle, Harry Carey. Directed by Andrew V. McLaglen. 107 min.

The opening third of this Western, in which James Stewart ingeniously rescues brother Dean Martin from the hangman, almost makes up for the rest of the film; the long sequence is engrossing and exciting, qualities lacking in what comes afterward. It's all downhill as soon as Raquel Welch shows up, complete with a horrendous Mexican accent. Martin is fair—this being no better and no worse than the average picture he made—but Stewart is wasted. Fans of the death of Hollywood and loyalists of the new Hollywood of Coppola, Spielberg, etc., should get some perverse pleasure out of this bloated, aging miasma of clichés.

THE BAND WAGON ☆☆☆☆
1953, USA
Fred Astaire, Cyd Charisse, Nanette Fabray, Oscar Levant, Jack Buchanan, James Mitchell. Directed by Vincente Minnelli. 112 min.

Among the greatest of the MGM musicals, *The Band Wagon* brought together some of the biggest names in the business. Arthur Freed, the man behind all of the studio's most important musicals in the 1940s and 1950s, produced. Betty Comden and Adolph Green, whose earlier collaborations included *On the Town* and *Singin' in the Rain*, penned the screenplay. Vincente Minnelli (*Meet Me in St. Louis*, *An American in Paris*) directed. Fred Astaire plays Tony Hunter, an aging dancer who winds up starring opposite an acclaimed ballerina (Cyd Charisse) in an outrageously pretentious Faustian musical under the direction of a megalomaniacal, pseudo-intellectual director (Jack Buchanan). Tony finally seizes the helm of the musical-within-the-musical, adding such song-and-dance numbers as "Dancing in the Dark," "I Guess I'll Have to Change My Plans," and the *film noir* parody "Girl Hunt Ballet." Although *The Band Wagon* incorporates many of the traditional elements of the Hollywood musical—with its classic romance and the anthemic "That's Entertainment"—it reaches beyond the genre's conventions, addressing such uncharacteristically dark issues as loneliness, isolation, and anarchy beneath its veneer of Hollywood happiness.

BANG THE DRUM SLOWLY ☆☆☆½
1973, USA, PG
Michael Moriarty, Robert DeNiro, Vincent Gardenia, Phil Foster, Anne Wedgeworth, Tom Ligon, Selma Diamond. Directed by John Hancock. 98 min.

Powerhouse performances by Robert DeNiro and Michael Moriarty draw every emotive possibility from the sad story of a big-league catcher's fatal disease. DeNiro is immersed in the role of the slow-thinking, tobacco-chewing Pearson, and Moriarty gives just the right toughness to his thoughtful, golden-boy pitcher. There is a great sense of each actor continually changing character nuances to act as a foil for the other. What is less obvious, but no less affecting, is the incipient humor of the film, delicately nudged along by Vincent Gardenia, Selma Diamond, and the rest of the expert cast. The film is based on Mark Harris's excellent baseball novel of 1956, and Harris worked on the screenplay.

THE BANK DICK ☆☆☆☆
1940, USA
W. C. Fields, Cora Witherspoon, Una Merkel, Evelyn Del Rio, Jessie Ralph, Franklin Pangborn, Shemp Howard, Grady Sutton, Richard Purcell, Russell Hicks, Jack Norton. Directed by Eddie Cline. 74 min.

One of the classic W. C. Fields comedies, this is the hilariously funny story of Egbert Souse—grumpy family man, patron of the Black Pussycat Café, professional moviegoer, replacement film director, contest winner, and slogan suggester—who accidentally captures a bank robber and becomes "the bank dick." The plot, from a screenplay by Mahatma Kane Jeeves (Fields), is nothing more than a string of absurd situations that Egbert escapes with adroitness, bluff, or a modicum of violence. The movie works not only because of Eddie Cline's expert direction, but also because of Fields's brilliantly off-kilter dialogue and his utter defiance in the face of his ugly little family and crackpot town. A marvelous satire on the ambitions of American life, where success can come even to a blowhard chiseler, brought to life wonderfully by a perfect supporting cast.

BARABBAS ☆☆
1962, Italy
Anthony Quinn, Silvana Mangano, Arthur Kennedy, Vittorio Gassman, Jack Palance, Ernest Borgnine, Katy Jurado, Harry Andrews. Directed by Richard Fleischer. 144 min.

Nobel Prize-winner Pär Lagerkvist's austere, thoughtful novel is splashed thinly across a very broad canvas by Dino De Laurentiis. The gladiator and colosseum routine, which was de rigueur for spectacle movies after *Spartacus*, has aged rather badly, and on video, without wide-screen effects, it has no effect at all. Anthony Quinn plays with a dull, brooding intensity and fails to convey the crisis of conscience of his character—in the novel, Barabbas, whose life was spared in place of Christ's, underwent a series of trials and hardships that eventually led him to his own small-scale redemption, but Quinn just seems like a sullen lout spoiling for a fight. The religious genuflections are heaped on, but they are entirely insincere, and the film's length, which is supposed to signify seriousness, is merely numbing. This was the kind of movie that made television so popular.

BARBARELLA ☆☆½
1967, France/Italy
Jane Fonda, John Phillip Law, Anita Pallenberg, Milo O'Shea, David Hemmings, Marcel Marceau, Ugo Tognazzi, Claude Dauphin. Directed by Roger Vadim. 98 min.

Jane Fonda, in what seems centuries away from *Tout Va Bien* and light-years from her *Workout* tape, plays a scantily clad astronaut of the fortieth century sent on a mission to rescue a demented scientist. Roger Vadim (the director and Jane's then-husband) clearly has talent, as he demonstrates in set pieces involving carnivorous dolls, a deadly estuary, and an apocalyptic explosion. Unfortunately, his stylish sense of humor cannot sustain the many dull stretches in Terry Southern's adaptation of Jean-Claude Forest's book. The members of the cast, especially John Phillip Law as a blind angel and Anita Pallenberg as a one-eyed lesbian queen, seem to be enjoying themselves, but *Barbarella* never recovers from the opening sequence in which Jane strips off her space suit to a wacky title tune.

BARBAROSA ☆☆☆
1982, USA, PG
Willie Nelson, Gary Busey, Isela Vega, Gilbert Roland, Danny De La Paz. Directed by Fred Schepisi. 90 min.

Australian director Fred Schepisi (*The Chant of Jimmie Blacksmith*) directed this offbeat, cautious American Western about a heroic loner and a young farmhand on the lam in the Old West. Country-and-Western iconoclast Willie Nelson brings depth and warmth to the character of Barbarosa, and Gary Busey is excellent as his overawed sidekick. A sedate movie about what it takes to be a legend. Its lessons tend to be drawn in broad, melodramatic strokes that occasionally work against the modest performances of the two stars.

BARBARY COAST ☆☆½
1935, USA
Edward G. Robinson, Miriam Hopkins, Joel McCrea, Walter Brennan, Frank Craven, Brian Donlevy, Donald Meek. Directed by Howard Hawks. 91 min.

Howard Hawks made some great films (*His Girl Friday*, *The Big Sleep*). He also made some duds, such as this period yarn. It's not a poorly made film; the evocation of California's gold-rush days is, in fact, often brilliant. But the Ben Hecht–Charles MacArthur screenplay covers overly familiar territory (see *San Francisco* and *Nob Hill*) as Edward G. Robinson plays a nightclub owner determined to make a star out of the girl he loves (Miriam Hopkins). The Robinson-Hopkins chemistry leaves something to be desired—Robinson reportedly had to stand on crates during the love scenes—but at least the supporting cast is up to snuff. A good example of a well-made bore.

THE BAREFOOT CONTESSA ☆☆½
1954, USA
Humphrey Bogart, Ava Gardner, Edmond O'Brien, Marius Goring, Rossano Brazzi, Valentina Cortesa. Directed by Joseph L. Mankiewicz. 128 min.

Joseph L. Mankiewicz wanted to do to Hollywood in *The Barefoot Contessa* what he had done so successfully to theater in *All About Eve*. He didn't. Despite some sharp dialogue in the first half and two excellent performances by the male leads (Humphrey Bogart, Edmond O'Brien), this is a sadly disjointed and overlong saga of a Spanish dancer's rise to Hollywood stardom. Ava Gardner, no dancer, is at least ten years too old to play the quasi-tragic Rita Hayworth–type starlet. Also, the flashback technique is confusing and unnecessary, and the second half becomes a deadly serious diatribe against the evils of the Hollywood Dream Factory. Bogie's burnt-out director, O'Brien's unscrupulous agent (a role for which he won an Oscar), and assorted pungent insights point up by contrast the shallowness of the rest of the film.

THE BAREFOOT EXECUTIVE ☆☆
1971, USA, G
Kurt Russell, Joe Flynn, Wally Cox, Harry Morgan, Hayden Rorke, Raffles, John Ritter. Directed by Robert Butler. 96 min.

In this low-grade Disney comedy, a young network page (Kurt Russell) discovers that his girlfriend's pet chimpanzee is a better program director than the company president. The complications that ensue are more tiresome than funny. The adults are portrayed as bumbling buffoons, and Russell is wholesome and dull. Disney Studios churned out these halfheartedly wacky comedies by the dozen in the late 1960s and early 1970s; this wasn't their worst, but even their best weren't that good.

BAREFOOT IN THE PARK ☆☆☆
1967, USA
Robert Redford, Jane Fonda, Mildred Natwick, Charles Boyer, Herb Edelman. Directed by Gene Saks. 105 min.

Neil Simon's early Broadway hit about young marrieds adjusting to life in a Greenwich Village walk-up is given a shapeless but still pleasing adaptation by director Gene Saks. The sweetly played urban romance is more human and less machine-gun-rapid than in many of Simon's more recent works, and young stars Jane Fonda, as the bon vivant wife, and Robert Redford, as the prim, preppy husband, make a sparkling and unself-conscious team.

THE BARON AND THE KID ☆½
1984, USA (TV)
Johnny Cash, Greg Webb, Darren McGavin, June Carter Cash, Tracy Pollan, Richard Roundtree, Claude Akins. Directed by Gary Nelson. 100 min.

This is a schmaltzy, overlong drama about a father-son rift and reconciliation down South. Dad (Johnny Cash) is the Baron, a legendary pool player who may or may not have won his fame by fraud. The Kid (Greg Webb) is the son he never knew, all grown up now and ready to take on the old man. Cash, though no actor, has a cold, rock-jawed presence that gives the film a flicker of life. Other than that, this one is a misfire from the homespun homilies to the trumped-up climax.

BARON BLOOD ☆½
1972, Italy
Joseph Cotten, Elke Sommer, Rada Rassimov, Massimo Girotti, Alan Collins, Antonio Cantafora, Humi Raho. Directed by Mario Bava. 90 min.

A descendant of the infamous Baron Otto Von Kleist returns to his mansion in Austria and succeeds in raising his dead ancestor with an ancient incantation; getting him back in the grave, however, proves somewhat more difficult. Mario Bava's horror exercise isn't one of his best; despite a plot with a few clever twists, there's too much talk, erratic camerawork, a dearth of genuine scares, and distractingly poor postdubbing. Joseph Cotten, however, turns in an amusingly camp performance, and the end may surprise you.

BARRY LYNDON ☆☆☆½
1975, Great Britain, PG
Ryan O'Neal, Marisa Berenson, Patrick Magee, Hardy Kruger, Michael Hordern. Directed by Stanley Kubrick. 185 min.

With his tenth feature film, Kubrick splendidly and faithfully re-creates Thackeray's eighteenth-century tale about an ambitious, provincial Irish boy who becomes worldly and finally jaded after marrying into wealth. O'Neal's cool portrayal of Lyndon is right on the mark, as is Leonard Rosenman's evocative musical score. But most memorable of all is John Alcott's Oscar-winning cinematography, which artistically captures the lushness of Ireland's landscapes. Unfortunately, some of this visual magic is lost on the small screen.

BARRY MCKENZIE HOLDS HIS OWN ☆
1976, USA
Barry Crocker, Barry Humphries, Donald Pleasence. Directed by Bruce Beresford. 93 min.

Barry Crocker is, allegedly, Australia's answer to Monty Python. In this episode, he travels around Europe, gets involved in a case of mistaken identity, drinks Foster's beer, and winds up in Transylvania with the wicked Eric, Count Plasma (Donald Pleasence). Unfortunately, your local store probably won't have enough Foster's to get you drunk enough to enjoy this. Must be a major embarrassment for director Bruce Beresford (*Breaker Morant*, *Tender Mercies*).

BASIC TRAINING ☆
1986, USA, R
Ann Dusenberry, Rhonda Shear, Angela Ames, Will Nye, Walter Gotell. Directed by Andrew Sugarman. 91 min.

This lame service comedy is just what you'd expect from a Playboy Enterprises production: an embarrassing stab at a plot about a curvy Secretary of Defense (Ann Dusenberry) who backs her male underlings into every corner of the Pentagon. Thoroughly inane and proud of it, this should appeal to voyeurs who enjoy generous portions of female nudity soft-pedaled to them in the guise of a film.

THE BASILEUS QUARTET ☆☆½
1982, France/Italy, R
Pierre Malet, Hector Alterio, Omero Antonutti, Michel Vitold. Directed by Fabio Carpi. 118 min.

This small-scale drama is about three aging musicians and the young violinist who profoundly disrupts their lives when he replaces a recently deceased companion in their string quartet. A European travelogue filled with weary observations about life, love, art, youth, old age, and death. It's "Masterpiece Theatre"–style entertainment for the art-film fan, but Pierre Malet's vibrant performance goes a long way toward redeeming it.

BASKET CASE ☆☆½
1982, USA
Kevin Van Hentenryck, Terri Susan Smith, Beverly Bonner, Lloyd Pace. Directed by Frank Henenlotter. 91 min.

Here is an exceptional example of the power of kinky imagery to overcome technical deficiencies. Sweet-faced Duane from upstate New York moves into a sleazy Times Square hotel with a large wicker basket in tow. Inside: his dwarfed, mutated, and insanely vengeful Siamese-twin brother, from whom he was separated as a child. Low-budget, violent, and perverse—it's related in subject matter to Brian De Palma's *Sisters*, but it's even more willing to satisfy the morbid curiosity of its viewers.

BATAAN ☆☆☆
1943, USA
Robert Taylor, George Murphy, Thomas Mitchell, Lloyd Nolan, Robert Walker, Lee Bowman, Desi Arnaz, Barry Nelson. Directed by Tay Garnett. 114 min.

Robert Walker makes a strong screen debut in this tough wartime drama from underrated director Tay Garnett (*The Postman Always Rings Twice*). The action centers on a cutoff platoon attempting to defend the Bataan peninsula from a much larger Japanese force. The movie generates a fair amount of tension from the fighting sequences and squeezes out a lot of atmosphere from the malarial jungle setting. Good performances all around and a terrific last-stand death scene for Robert Taylor.

BATMAN ☆☆
1966, USA
Adam West, Burt Ward, Cesar Romero, Frank Gorshin, Burgess Meredith, Lee Meriwether, Alan Napier, Neil Hamilton. Directed by Leslie Martinson. 105 min.

Fans of the classic TV series will be disappointed by this feature version starring the Caped Crusaders. Many of the regulars are here—Batman, Robin, the Joker, the Penguin, the Riddler, Catwoman (played here by Lee Meriwether and not Julie Newmar)—but the campy flavor of the series is missing and the extended length is self-defeating. This is one case where a TV series is far more inventive than its theatrical film counterpart.

BATTERED ☆☆½
1978, USA (TV)
Karen Grassle, Mike Farrell, LeVar Burton, Chip Fields, Joan Blondell, Howard Duff, Diana Scarwid. Directed by Peter Werner. 100 min.

Wife-beating gets the telefilm treatment in this absorbing, tough-minded drama, which interweaves the stories of three unhappy couples. Although the script, coauthored by star Karen Grassle, occasionally descends into didacticism, instructing when it should engage, the grim narrative will hold your attention. Best in the cast are Joan Blondell in one of her last roles and Mike Farrell in a surprisingly effective switch from his nice-guy image.

BATTLE BENEATH THE EARTH ☆☆½
1967, Great Britain
Kerwin Matthews, Viviane Ventura, Robert Ayres, Peter Arne, Bessie Love. Directed by Montgomery Tully. 91 min.

This especially silly sci-fi adventure is a relic of that brief period at the end of the 1960s when Cold War neuroses shifted from the Russians to the more distant and inscrutable Chinese. Their dastardly plot here is to dig a network of tunnels under the United States, wipe us out from below, and then take over to establish a new Chinese homeland! Fortunately, Commander Jonathan Shaw is on hand to preserve the future of democracy. Unlikely to be taken seriously by anyone, which aids in enjoying this on a pulp level.

BATTLE BEYOND THE STARS ☆☆☆
1980, USA, PG
Richard Thomas, George Peppard, Sybil Danning, Robert Vaughn. Directed by Jimmy T. Murakami. 104 min.

John Sayles (*The Brother from Another Planet*) cowrote this clever combination of *Star Wars* and *The Seven Samurai*. A Luke Skywalker–ish hero must recruit intergalactic mercenaries to rescue his defenseless planet from the hordes of an evil space conqueror. Tongue in cheek, with lots of enjoyable comic moments and eccentric characters to go along with the space dogfight sequences. George Peppard's portrayal of a "space cowboy" is priceless.

BATTLE CREEK BRAWL

See *The Big Brawl*

BATTLE CRY ☆☆½
1955, USA
Van Heflin, Aldo Ray, Tab Hunter, Raymond Massey, Dorothy Malone, Mona Freeman, Nancy Olson, James Whitmore, Anne Francis, Fess Parker. Directed by Raoul Walsh. 147 min.

Warner Brothers' big-budget version of Leon Uris's novel is a war film with more action in the bedroom than on the battlefield. Aldo Ray's lumberjack hooks up with Nancy Olson's war widow; Tab Hunter's young recruit negotiates between Dorothy Malone's older woman and Mona Freeman's girl back home; and John Lupton's intellectual gets serious about Anne Francis's socialite. Oh, yes, between the love scenes, the men are World War II Marines led by Van Heflin's gruff major. Though the film is technically uneven and makes poor use of Cinemascope, director Raoul Walsh does manage some gritty scenes.

BATTLE FOR THE PLANET OF THE APES ☆☆
1973, USA, G
Roddy McDowall, Claude Akins, Natalie Trundy, Severn Darden, Paul Williams, John Huston. Directed by J. Lee Thompson. 88 min.

The fifth and final installment of the *Planet of the Apes* series is a disappointing, sloppy closer, with the mutated humans returning for violent conflict with the apes, who are still enslaving the healthy ones. Paul Dehn, who wrote parts two, three, and four, only planned the story for this one, and the absence of his skilled hand is felt. The series as a whole is one of the few multipart film stories in which the sequels flesh out the original rather than rehash it. The five films are best viewed in the order in which they were made, but can also be rearranged in terms of when they take place. Start with *Escape* (part three), then watch *Conquest* (part four), and *Battle*, then go back to the original, and conclude with *Beneath* (part two); that film leads directly into *Escape* again.

BATTLE HELL ☆☆☆
1956, Great Britain
Richard Todd, Akim Tamiroff, William Hartnell, Donald Huston, Keye Luke, Robert Urquhart. Directed by Michael Anderson. 113 min.

This tense, exciting war film is based on a real incident that took place just after the end of World War II: A British ship, on a legal mission in Red China delivering supplies to the British embassy, is fired upon by the Chinese. Attempts to bring medical aid to the wounded are thwarted, and the Chinese refuse to let the ship leave unless its captain takes the blame for the incident (so that it can be turned into propaganda for the Chinese). Akim Tamiroff is outstanding as the Chinese leader, but the film's main virtues are in its production (on-board scenes were shot on the *Amethyst*, the actual ship involved in the incident) and its stirring, tense direction. (a.k.a.: *Yangtse Incident*)

BATTLE OF AUSTERLITZ ☆½
1960, France/Italy
Claudia Cardinale, Martine Carol, Leslie Caron, Vittorio De Sica, Jean Marais, Jack Palance. Directed by Abel Gance. 123 min.

It may be unfair to judge this film at its present length because it's been drastically recut. Considering Abel Gance's reputation based on films like his silent masterpiece *Napoleon*, this unspectacular spectacle is a disappointment—one of those all-star international productions where the backing has been raised in dribs and drabs and the cutting of corners shows in the final product. The title refers to the Little Emperor's triumph at Austerlitz. The cast and crew do not have similar luck in re-creating that historic assault in this sagging epic.

BATTLE OF EL ALAMEIN ☆☆
1968, Italy/France
Frederick Stafford, Ettore Manni, Robert Hossein, Michael Rennie, George Hilton. Directed by Calvin Jackson Padgett (Giorgio Ferroni). 105 min.

This action-packed war film reflects the other guy's viewpoint but is not a pacifist tract like *All Quiet on the Western Front*. Here the British are the baddies, with Italy and Germany banding together to rout the limeys out of North Africa. If you were to view this film after seeing *Mrs. Miniver* or *The Sands of Iwo Jima*, you might go into propaganda shock, for this is not the American-history-book approach to studying World War II that we're used to. Aside from this twist, it's a standard against-all-odds adventure with excellent battle scenes and the benefit of a novel perspective.

THE BATTLE OF NERETVA ☆☆
1971, USA/Yugoslavia/Italy/Germany
Yul Brynner, Serge Bondarchuk, Curt Jurgens, Hardy Kruger, Orson Welles, Franco Nero. Directed by Veljko Bulajik. 102 min.

Good things don't necessarily come in small packages. You will be hard-pressed to figure out how this choppy film was once an Academy Award nominee for Best Foreign Film. Its original length was three hours, and most of its atmosphere and characterizations have been sacrificed to fit a condensed running time. As it stands, it is a difficult-to-follow "war is hell" spectacle about those indefatigable Nazis adding Yugoslavia to their trophy shelf of conquered countries. The emphasis is on the awe-inspiring battle scenes, because depth and logic have ended up a casualty on the cutting-room floor.

BATTLE OF THE BULGE ☆☆½
1965, USA
Henry Fonda, Robert Shaw, Robert Ryan, Dana Andrews, George Montgomery, Ty Hardin, Charles Bronson, Pier Angeli, James MacArthur, Telly Savalas. Directed by Ken Annakin. 167 min.

There's no reason why you can't get in some aerobics while watching this almost-three-hour-long re-creation of one of the pivotal final battles of World War II. Push it to the limit while German tank commander Robert Shaw barks out orders! Jog in place and share the agony of thousands of Cinerama foot soldiers marching to their doom! Feel your lungs explode in time with the bombs on screen!

BATTLE OF THE COMMANDOS ☆½
1969, Italy
Jack Palance, Diana Lorys, Curt Jurgens, Tomas Hunter. Directed by Umberto Lenzi. 94 min.

Although in the tradition of *The Dirty Dozen* and *The Guns of Navarone*, this film is really only a poor imitation. Jack "Bare-Those-Teeth" Palance hams it up as a commander of a do-or-die mission to sabotage a German cannon that could be a key factor in the D-day landing. The usual gung-ho heroics, with a cast from all over the world and a script that wanders all over the place.

BATTLE OF THE SEXES ☆☆☆
1960, Great Britain
Peter Sellers, Constance Cummings, Robert Morley. Directed by Charles Crichton. 88 min.

Peter Sellers gives one of his less adventurous performances as an elderly Edinburgh accountant who contemplates murdering a meddlesome efficiency expert (Constance Cummings). Amusing but, given the premise, surprisingly tame.

BATTLESHIP POTEMKIN ☆☆☆☆
1925, USSR
Alexander Antonov, Vladimir Barsky, Grigori Alexandrov, Mikhail Goronorov. Directed by Sergei Eisenstein. 65 min.

Sergei Eisenstein's creative retelling of several episodes during the 1905 Russian Revolution is one of the greatest and most eloquent of all Russian films and a peak in the 1920s' Russian formalist school of filmmaking headed by Eisenstein, Pudovkin, and Dovzhenko. The incomparable Odessa Steps sequence alone makes this film, which was produced to celebrate the twentieth anniversary of the Revolution, a landmark event. Eisenstein uses both his unconventional brand of crosscutting and many elegantly composed shots to underscore his theme of group over individual. Other highlights include the sailors' mutiny over the rotted meat aboard the *Potemkin* and the mass mourning for the slaughtered peasants. An artistically poetic and politically vital film.

BATTLE SHOCK ☆☆
1956, USA
Ralph Meeker, Janice Rule, Paul Henreid, Rosenda Monteros, Fanny Schiller. Directed by Paul Henreid. 88 min.

This fairly intriguing mystery is batted around by some wooden performers and balled up with bad dialogue. Ralph Meeker plays an off-kilter artist suspected of murdering his model, a cantina waitress. Some really strange character touches by Meeker, and one good supporting performance by Rosenda Monteros as a venal maid. The Acapulco locations and fifties look are nicely realized in Republic's lurid Trucolor—a fine print was used for the video. (a.k.a.: *A Woman's Devotion*)

BATTLESTAR: GALACTICA ☆☆
1979, USA
Lorne Greene, Jane Seymour, Richard Hatch, Dirk Benedict, Ray Milland, Lew Ayres, Patrick MacNee. Directed by Richard Colla. 125 min.

This is the three-hour pilot episode of the TV series, re-edited and released as a movie. But they can't fool us!

BATTLING HOOFER

See *Something to Sing About*

THE BAY BOY ☆☆☆
1984, Canada/France, R
Kiefer Sutherland, Liv Ullmann, Peter Donat, Mathieu Carriere, Alan Scarfe. Directed by Daniel Petrie. 107 min.

Daniel Petrie wrote and directed this autobiographical saga about a seventeen-year-old maturing in a Cape Breton town in 1937. The protagonist is a religious kid who's torn between the priesthood and his libido, and his path to manhood is dogged by a gay priest and a murder committed by the father of his beloved girl-next-door. The film is by far the most personal work Petrie (*Beat the Drum Slowly*, *A Raisin in the Sun*) has ever done. The film has its pleasures, and they come with soupcons of grace, understanding, and style. Liv Ullmann, as usual, is splendid.

BAY OF BLOOD ☆☆½
1972, Italy, R
Claudine Auger. Directed by Mario Bava.

This is an early body-count film featuring an effect stolen by both *Friday the 13th* and *Friday the 13th, Part 2*: squirming lovers impaled together on a phallic spear. Directed by Mario Bava, whose stylish efforts include the extraordinary *Blood and Black Lace* and *Black Sunday*, *Bay of Blood* involves various relatives, land developers, and sundry other parties who slaughter one another over a valuable piece of waterfront property. Pretty solid entertainment for stalk-and-slash fans. (a.k.a.: *Twitch of the Death Nerve* and *Last House on the Left Part II*)

BAYOU

See *Poor White Trash*

BEACH BLANKET BINGO ☆☆½
1965, USA
Annette Funicello, Frankie Avalon, Deborah Walley, Harvey Lembeck, Linda Evans, Don Rickles, Paul Lynde, Buster Keaton. Directed by William Asher. 100 min.

Here's more grooviness on the high seas, or at least the beaches of Malibu, with a plot irresistible to nostalgia or camp fans: Dee Dee (Annette Funicello) must fight to keep Frankie (Frankie Avalon) when his head is suddenly turned by the appearance of a curvaceous, broad-shouldered cutie named Sugar Kane (you guessed it, Linda Evans) on their sandy shores. Not hooked yet? Throw in Eric Von Zipper and the Rat Pack, Don Rickles, Paul Lynde, and a Buster Keaton cameo, and you have grade-A teen kitsch from a bygone era. Followed by *How to Stuff a Wild Bikini*; preceded by *Beach Party* and *Muscle Beach Party*, among others.

THE BEACH BOYS—AN AMERICAN BAND ☆☆☆
1985, USA
The Beach Boys. Directed by Malcolm Leo. 105 min.

This is an authorized documentary following the legendary band's career, from the early 1960s to the present. Members of the band openly discussed the problems that have plagued their twenty-five-year career (leader Brian Wilson's emotional instability, the death by drowning of Dennis Wilson just after shooting began) and contributed a great deal of film footage from their personal collections. Some of the found footage includes a music-video–style film for an unreleased song from their *Smile* album and a home movie of a birthday party for Brian with Paul McCartney. Premiered on video and went into a limited theatrical run.

THE BEACHCOMBER ☆☆☆
1938, Great Britain
Charles Laughton, Elsa Lanchester, Tyrone Guthrie, Robert Newton, Dolly Mollinger. Directed by Erich Pommer. 90 min.

Critical consensus may never consider the Laughtons the Alfred Lunt–Lynn Fontannes of the silver screen, but in *The Beachcomber*, the famed acting team gives it a good go. The story, based on W. Somerset Maugham's "Vessel of Wrath," is a sort of British *African Queen*. In it, drunken good-for-nothing Chuck is marooned on an atoll in the East Indies with priggish schoolteacher Elsa; opposites attract. Producer Erich Pommer directed for the first and only time in his career, keeping the story moving and giving free rein to Laughton's antics. Not *The African Queen*, but far superior to the 1955 Beachcomber starring Robert Newton, who has a supporting role in this version. (a.k.a.: *Vessel of Wrath*)

THE BEACH GIRLS ½☆
1982, USA, R
Debra Blee, Val Kline, Jeana Thomasina. Directed by Pat Townsend. 91 min.

A prim teenage girl and her two whoring friends borrow the uncle's beach house during summer vacation. A wretched sexual exploitation comedy with no sex, no laughs, and poor production values.

BEACH HOUSE ☆
1982, USA, PG
Ileana Seidel, John Cosola, Kathy McNeil, Richard Duggan. Directed by John Gallagher. 75 min.

This is an amazing soft-core teen-porn movie. What's amazing about it is that there is no sex or nudity in it, just the mindless dancing and jokes that usually accompany this kind of drive-in fodder. The plot, all seventy-five minutes of it, has to do with a bunch of Brooklyn kids and a bunch of Philadelphia kids who meet at an Ocean City beach house, where they dance and . . . well, they just dance a lot. No jokes to speak of, and no drama; reportedly, the producers thought of splicing in some footage of a monster rising out of the ocean to add a little zest, but they never got around to it—otherwise, we would have had a remake of *The Horror of Party Beach* on our hands.

BEACH PARTY ☆☆½
1963, USA
Robert Cummings, Frankie Avalon, Annette Funicello, Harvey Lembeck, Dorothy Malone, Jody McCrea, Morey Amsterdam, Eva Six. Directed by William Asher. 104 min.

This is the original. Everything is here: Frankie and Annette, out to make each other jealous. Eric Von Zipper and his Rats and Mice. Surfing. Tunes at the Sugar Bowl. There's even a plot, with Robert Cummings as an anthropologist studying the mating habits of the American teenager. Wigged out!

BEAR ISLAND ☆☆
1980, Great Britain/Canada, PG
Donald Sutherland, Vanessa Redgrave, Richard Widmark, Christopher Lee, Barbara Parkins, Lloyd Bridges, Lawrence Dane. Directed by Don Sharp. 118 min.

This dozy thriller is based on Alastair MacLean's equally narcotic novel, about a polar expedition team that comes up against a cadre of Nazis in an attempt to retrieve a fortune in gold from a sunken U-boat. More suspense is generated in seeing which cast member will fare the worst with his/her accent (Vanessa Redgrave's crypto-Swedish takes bottom honors) than in awaiting the final unraveling of the interminable plot. Technically efficient, but very, very slow.

THE BEARS AND I ☆☆
1974, USA, G
Patrick Wayne, Chief Dan George, Andrew Duggan, Michael Ansara. Directed by Bernard McEveety. 89 min.

In this more-than-competent Disney family flick, Vietnam vet Patrick Wayne takes to the great outdoors to find himself and winds up becoming mother to three orphaned bear cubs. For a subplot there's also an Indian tribe that refuses to be relocated by the government, which wants to turn their land into a national park. Loses half a star for the John Denver theme song, "Sweet Surrender."

THE BEAST IN THE CELLAR ☆
1971, Great Britain
Beryl Reid, Flora Robson, John Hamill, Tessa Wyatt. Directed by James Kelly. 87 min.

This soporific British film tries for atmosphere but fails to provide any substance. Two spinster sisters hide their brother, a maniac, in the basement to save him from the lawful penalties of his crime. The big mystery here is how the producers lured Beryl Reid and Flora Robson, two distinguished British stage actresses, into this talky bit of nothing. *Note:* The version on videocassette is fourteen minutes shorter than the theatrical release.

THE BEASTMASTER ☆☆
1982, USA, PG
Marc Singer, Tanya Roberts, John Amos, Rip Torn, Rod Loomis. Directed by Don Coscarelli. 120 min.

This beefcake-barbarian movie is basically a scene-for-scene retread of *Conan the Barbarian*, but it's livelier and more amusing than *Conan*, because the director, Don Coscarelli (*Phantasm*), has a sense of humor. He seems to understand that the spectacle of a blond *Playgirl*-centerfold-type running around in a loincloth and swinging a broadsword is at least vaguely amusing. Marc Singer plays the hero, a tawny-skinned Adonis who commands a trio of animals, and onetime Charlie's Angel Tanya Roberts is his ladylove.

THE BEAST MUST DIE ☆☆
1974, Great Britain, PG
Calvin Lockhart, Peter Cushing, Charles Gray, Anton Diffring, Marlene Clark, Ciaran Madden. Directed by Paul Annett. 93 min.

A wealthy man, convinced that one of his friends is a werewolf, has his house wired for pictures and sound ("I am *not* a voyeur," he snaps when his assistant suggests that he tune into one of the bedrooms) and invites all of his friends out for the weekend. Much mayhem ensues, and there is a "werewolf break" to allow the audience to place last-minute bets on the identity of the lycanthrope. Moderately suspenseful.

THE BEAST OF THE YELLOW NIGHT ☆½
1972, USA/Philippines, R
John Ashley, Mary Wilcox. Directed by Eddie Romero. 87 min.

In this typically awful Eddie Romero Filipino horror, coproducer John Ashley stars as a degenerate who sells his soul to the devil and becomes some kind of "weremonster" who kills others and absorbs their evil. The executive producer was Roger Corman, who had just launched his New World Pictures; presumably, this is one of those movies he would point to as having paid the bills for the more prestigious foreign films that New World also released. Which means that you should rent this only if you feel extremely philanthropic toward the world of the foreign film.

THE BEAST WITHIN ☆½
1982, USA, R
Ronny Cox, Bibi Besch, Paul Clemens, Don Gordon, R. G. Armstrong, Kitty Moffat, L. Q. Jones. Directed by Philippe Mora. 98 min.

Raped on her wedding night by a deformed maniac in a Southern swamp, a woman gives birth to a fine son who never gives her a moment's trouble until he reaches the age of seventeen. Then all hell breaks loose as he is transformed into a slimy, flesh-eating monster, out to decimate the town whose ugly little secret is the cause of all his troubles. Special effects by Tom (*Cat People*) Burman enliven a silly story that's not as gross as the advertising would have one believe, but is still pretty disgusting. Screenplay by Tom Holland, author of *Psycho II* and *Fright Night*.

BEATLEMANIA—THE MOVIE ½☆
1981, USA, PG
Mitch Weissman, Ralph Castelli, David Leon, Tom Teeley. Directed by Joseph Manduke. 86 min.

This film of the concert/slide show performed by Beatles look-and-sing-alikes has to qualify as one of the most pointless musical undertakings in screen history. Only occasionally do these stooges sound anything like the Fab Four, and if you think Mitch Weissman looks like Paul McCartney, well, you should *see* Paul McCartney—in *A Hard Day's Night* or *Help!* "Not the Beatles, but an incredible simulation!" screamed the ads. It's incredible, all right.

BEAT STREET ☆☆½
1984, USA, PG
Jon Chardiet, Guy Davis, Robert Taylor, Rae Dawn Chong. Directed by Stan Lathan. 104 min.

This big-budget dramatic musical tries, with some success, to capture the electricity, pulse, and action of break dancing, graffiti art, and rap music. Produced by Harry Belafonte, *Beat Street* follows the dreams and despairs of a group of ghetto kids trying for a career in these new performing arts, and features great performances by such well-known hip-hop stars as the N.Y.C. Breakers, the Rock Steady Crew, and the Magnificent Force. It's got a good, dirty urban texture. Between the production numbers you'll have to endure a preachy, melodramatic story that drags the film down considerably.

BEAT THE DEVIL ☆☆☆
1954, USA
Humphrey Bogart, Jennifer Jones, Gina Lollobrigida, Robert Morley, Peter Lorre, Edward Underdown. Directed by John Huston. 89 min.

John Huston pulled out all the stops in making this satiric comedy, and what he gained in inspired performances and quiet laughs he lost in cohesion, sense, and story. The film makes fun of the international thriller genre, and the cast is suitably offbeat in accents and behavior. The plot is something about a loose-knit gang that can't seem to get out of Italy en route to swindling a uranium lode in Africa. Bogart is nicely stiff as a reluctant conman, and Jennifer Jones steals her share of scenes as a pathological liar; however, viewers may best remember Peter Lorre as a quack doctor of philosophy. Truman Capote cowrote the script with Huston—they allegedly made it up as they shot on location. This is one of those movies that ultimately makes you mad: its's so good, you can't help being wildly frustrated with its many flaws.

LE BEAU MARIAGE ☆☆☆
1982, France
Beatrice Romand, Arielle Dombasle, André Dussolier, Feodor Atkine, Patrick Lambert. Directed by Eric Rohmer. 97 min.

From the simplest of premises comes an often exquisite comedy of contemporary manners, directed by the genre's master. The film's protagonist is Sabine (Beatrice Romand), a bright but capricious and utterly self-obsessed young woman who decides suddenly and irrevocably that she wants to marry. Her object—or rather target—is a Parisian lawyer (André Dussolier) who proves unexpectedly skillful at resisting her questionable charms. As are all of Rohmer's films, this one is slow and full of talk, but at its best, the characters come alive in a way that few other filmmakers can manage. (*Note: Le Beau Mariage* is the second film in Rohmer's series of *Comedies and Proverbs* begun with *The Aviator's Wife*.)

BEAU-PÈRE ☆☆½
1981, France
Patrick Dewaere, Nathalie Baye, Ariel Besse, Maurice Ronet, Nicole Garcia, Maurice Risch. Directed by Bertrand Blier. 125 min.

Director Bertrand Blier (*Get Out Your Handkerchiefs*) makes light of a taboo subject in this amusing, warm comedy about the love affair of a twenty-nine-year-old cocktail-lounge pianist (Patrick Dewaere) and his fourteen-year-old stepdaughter (Ariel Besse). Dewaere is droll and touching in one of the last performances he gave before his death, but Blier is so enraptured with the idea of treating a shocking subject in a whimsical manner that the story never seems believable. It's still entertaining and, at times, surprisingly thoughtful.

BECAUSE OF THE CATS ☆
1973, Belgium/Netherlands
Bryan Marshall, Alexandre Stewart, Alex Van Rooyen, Leo Beyers. Directed by Fons Rademakers. 88 min.

Fons Rademakers, who previously hit the heights with the critically acclaimed *Mira*, hits rock bottom in this always-reaching but never-touching account of an Amsterdam youth gang called the Crows. Made up entirely of rich kids whose parents don't understand (whose do?), the Crows try to garner our sympathy simply because they don't steal—instead, they wreck opulent homes, rape middle-aged women, and consort with a bunch of sadistic girls called the She-Cats. It is within this framework that a ritualistic murder occurs, if for no other reason than to provoke a series of grand confessions. It is all rather emotionally facile, continually substituting the horrible for what should have been harrowing.

BECKET ☆☆☆½
1964, Great Britain
Richard Burton, Peter O'Toole, John Gielgud, Martita Hunt, Pamela Brown, Donald Wolfit, Paola Stoppa, Sian Phillips. Directed by Peter Glenville. 149 min.

This is a rare treat: an intellectual costume epic. Jean Anouilh's sparring match of a play between Thomas Becket and Henry II is turned into a stage-bound but still lively film. Richard Burton and Peter O'Toole are at their best playing the archbishop and king, respectively. Others in the cast are reduced to stereotypes, but Burton and O'Toole flesh out their roles with relish. They even outclass the Paul Scofield–Robert Shaw interchanges in *A Man for All Seasons*. Edward Anhalt's Oscar-winning screenplay admirably keeps the anachronisms to a minimum and delicately treats the homosexual subtext. A film both edifying and entertaining.

BECKY SHARP ☆☆½
1935, USA
Miriam Hopkins, Cedric Hardwicke, Frances Dee, Billie Burke, Nigel Bruce, Alison Skipworth. Directed by Rouben Mamoulian. 83 min.

Rouben Mamoulian's celebrated use of color (*Blood and Sand*, *Summer Holiday*) was first seen in this adaptation of Thackeray's *Vanity Fair*. The problem is that the color design is more exciting than the action it's used to paint. Miriam Hopkins is perfect as the woman who schemes her way through Regency society, but the Francis Edward Faragoh screenplay is neither trashy enough for camp nor literate enough for solid, incisive drama; it scores somewhere in a dullish middle ground. The recently restored Technicolor print of this film is *not* yet available on videotape.

BEDAZZLED ☆☆☆½
1967, Great Britain
Peter Cook, Dudley Moore, Raquel Welch, Eleanor Bron, Alba, Barry Humphries. Directed by Stanley Donen. 107 min.

Peter Cook and Dudley Moore are very funny as a Satan hell-bent on raining on everyone's parade and a Faust who can't seem to get his soul sold in this 1960s-flavored comedy. Raquel Welch plays Lust. The film is based on a story by Peter Cook; Moore composed the music. This was the team's elevation to film leads, following on the heels of their revue, *Beyond the Fringe*.

THE BEDFORD INCIDENT ☆☆☆
1965, USA
Richard Widmark, Sidney Poitier, James MacArthur, Martin Balsam, Wally Cox, Eric Portman, Donald Sutherland. Directed by James B. Harris. 102 min.

Richard Widmark coproduced and starred in this film, in which he gives one of the best performances of his career as a U.S. submarine captain who discovers a Russian sub in the North Atlantic and decides to pursue it, a decision that causes much tension among his subordinate officers and crew. His character is similar to—though done with less satire than—Sterling Hayden's mad Colonel Ripper in 1964's *Dr. Strangelove*: both have the capacity to start World War III all by themselves. As a reporter covering a general-interest story on the ship who sets out to learn what makes its commander tick, Sidney Poitier is also good, but he relies a bit too much on standard wise-guy journalist jargon. An absorbing Cold-War drama that is marred somewhat by an unsatisfactory ending. Watch for Donald Sutherland in a small part as a hospital worker.

BEDKNOBS AND BROOMSTICKS ☆☆☆
1971, USA, G
Angela Lansbury, David Tomlinson, Roddy McDowall, Sam Jaffe, John Ericson. Directed by Robert Stevenson. 117 min.

This Disney comedy-fantasy is much better than most of the syrup that poured out of the studio in the early 1970s, thanks to a winning turn by Angela Lansbury and a nicely developed sense of period from veteran director Robert Stevenson. The story, set in World War II London, has good-witch-in-training Eglantine Price (Lansbury) squiring a brood of moppets around Merrie Olde England as it comes magically to life. Very sweet-natured, perhaps too much so for older kids, but the mix of animation and live action will enthrall young ones.

BEDLAM ☆☆☆
1946, USA
Boris Karloff, Anna Lee, Billy House, Glenn Vernon, Jason Robards, Sr., Joan Newton. Directed by Mark Robson. 78 min.

This creepy, lurid treat from the RKO horror vaults is the last of producer Val Lewton's superbly crafted B horror films for that studio. Along the lines of his *Cat People*, *I Walked with a Zombie*, and *The Body Snatcher*, *Bedlam* depends more on atmosphere and suggestion than outright shock, and it's ghoulishly effective. Karloff plays the sinister head of an asylum in eighteenth-century London, and Anna Lee is the young actress ripped from the aristocracy and caged among the loonies. Some of the inmates, most notably the Queen of the Artichokes, are hysterically ridiculous, but Karloff's performance is sublime.

BEDROOM EYES ☆☆
1986, USA, R
Kenneth Gilman, Dayle Haddon, Barbara Law, Christine Cattell. Directed by William Fruet. 90 min.

This cheesy little thriller, with voyeurism as its theme, occasionally threatens to become interesting. The eyes of the title belong to Harry, a jittery young stockbroker whose nightly jogging ritual comes to include extended peeps into the boudoir of a sexually adventurous temptress. Is that criminal violence he sees one night, or just kinky sex? Will his voluptuous psychiatrist cure him of his obsession or give him another? Do you care? The screenplay by Michael Alan Eddy makes the least of every possibility, but it's really no less clever, though much less slick, than the somewhat similar *Body Double*.

THE BEDROOM WINDOW ☆☆☆
1987, USA, R
Steve Guttenberg, Elizabeth McGovern, Isabelle Huppert, Wallace Shawn, Paul Shenar, Carl Lumbly, Brad Greenquist. Directed by Curtis Hanson. 111 min.

Entertaining in a clinical, anonymous way, this smartly plotted thriller set in Baltimore concerns a yuppie (Steve Guttenberg) who faces the dread prospect of seeing his affair with the boss' wife (Isabelle Huppert) dragged out in public after she witnesses an attempted homicide from his bedroom window. When another young woman turns up dead a few blocks away, Guttenberg goes to the police in Huppert's place and soon finds himself a suspect in a string of murders. The fun of the movie is that, as in Hitchcock, the crime-story plot becomes a heightened version of the hero's romantic dilemmas. It's pleasing to see a contemporary thriller that's reasonably well assembled and has some of the cleverness of vintage studio-system thrillers. Unfortunately, this one is utterly without their dark, subterranean atmosphere—it's thin. Guttenberg projects an eager-to-please passivity and turns in his most creditable performance since *Diner*, but there's still something too smooth and callow about him. Huppert gives the film the requisite slinkiness; and Elizabeth McGovern, as the righteous assault victim, has an appealing, no-frills sexiness.

BEDTIME FOR BONZO ☆☆½
1951, USA
Ronald Reagan, Diana Lynn, Walter Slezak, Lucille Berkely, Herbert Heyes. Directed by Frederick de Cordova. 83 min.

Watching the fortieth president of the United States hanging outside a window ledge, trying to catch his pet chimp, will strike you as either hilarious or frightening—regardless of your politics. Speaking of politics, Ronald Reagan plays a liberal scientist trying to prove that children are affected predominantly by environment. He uses a mischievous chimpanzee as his guinea pig. Minor farce with a few laughs becomes a postmodern classic of sorts, thanks to Reagan's presence. Director de Cordova is the longtime director of the "Tonight" show.

BEER ☆½
1985, USA, R
Loretta Swit, Rip Torn, Kenneth Mars, David Alan Grier, William Russ, Saul Stein, Dick Shawn. Directed by Patrick Kelly. 82 min.

This halfhearted and finally offensive satire picks a very easy target—the advertising industry—and misses. Loretta Swit (who replaced Sandra Bernhard during shooting) plays an ambitious exec who revamps a failing beer company's ad campaign and makes stars out of three would-be tough guys with the slogan "Whip out your Norbecker." The many commercial parodies are too close to the real thing to be effective satire, and when the writers run out of ideas, they resort to a stream of racist and antigay putdowns that are as good a explanation as any of why *Beer* was shelved after a minimal theatrical release.

THE BEES ☆½
1978, USA, PG
John Saxon, Angel Tompkins, John Carradine, Claudio Brook. Directed by Alfredo Zacharias. 83 min.

This low-budget rip-off of *The Swarm* is distinguishable from other "killer bee" movies only by the occasional nagging feeling you get that they may have *intended* parts of this to be funny. Even John Carradine, as a German bee expert, almost seems to be overacting on purpose this time. But then again, maybe not.

BEFORE I HANG ☆☆½
1940, USA
Boris Karloff, Evelyn Keyes, Bruce Bennett, Edward van Sloan, Ben Taggart, Pedro de Cordoba. Directed by Nick Grind. 62 min.

This is a mad scientist flick with a couple of twists. Karloff plays a scientist condemned to death for a mercy killing. While in prison he gets permission to continue his experiments on counteracting the effects of aging. Using blood from a merciless killer to prepare a serum, he injects himself with it and absorbs the homicidal properties of the stuff, setting himself off on a killing spree. Absorbing, but by no means Karloff's best.

THE BEGUILED ☆☆☆
1970, USA
Clint Eastwood, Geraldine Page, Elizabeth Hartman, Jo Ann Harris, Darleen Carr, Mae Mercer. Directed by Don Siegel. 105 min.

Director Don Siegel and Clint Eastwood both work against their usual inclinations by suppressing action and emphasizing mood. A dreamy, creepy gothic film about a wounded Confederate soldier who finds refuge at an all-girl seminary. The movie is dominated by Geraldine Page and Elizabeth Hartman playing two neurotic spinsters who realize that they hold the life of an attractive young man in the sweaty palms of their grasping hands. A strange, expressionistic film told with rare flair, but marred by a lack of dramatic buildup. This was Eastwood's first box-office failure.

BEHIND THE RISING SUN ☆☆☆
1943, USA
Margo, Tom Neal, J. Carrol Naish, Robert Ryan, Gloria Holden, Don Douglas, George Givot. Directed by Edward Dmytryk. 89 min.

One of the most curious products of the World War II period, it purports to give an inside look at the growth of fascist militarism that turned Japan into an aggressive enemy. The focus is on the emotional and political rift that divides a right-wing Japanese publisher (J. Carrol Naish) from his liberal-minded, Americanophile son (Tom Neal) during the Japanese excursions into China in the 1930s.

BEHOLD A PALE HORSE ☆☆☆
1964, USA
Gregory Peck, Anthony Quinn, Omar Sharif, Mildred Dunnock, Paolo Stoppa, Raymond Pellegrin. Directed by Fred Zinnemann. 121 min.

Fred Zinnemann's films (*High Noon*, *A Man for All Seasons*) are occasionally more interesting as think pieces than as entertainments. In this slow but provocative tract, Zinnemann explores the effects of war on individuals and the problem of divided loyalties. Gregory Peck, in a change-of-pace role, plays a soldier who seeks out a ruthless police chief (Anthony Quinn) twenty years after the Spanish Civil War has ended. The story, based on Emeric Pressburger's *Killing a Mouse on Sunday*, resembles *Les Misérables*, but this is a politically aware film that eschews Hugo's romanticism. The film's politics are so explicitly liberal, in fact, that Spain's Franco government banned this and all other Columbia films. Offbeat and worth sitting through.

THE BEING ½☆
1980, USA, R
Martin Landau, Rexx Coltrane, Dorothy Malone, José Ferrer, Ruth Buzzi. Directed by Jackie Kong. 79 min.

Pottsville, Idaho, is plagued by a series of strange occurrences that seem to date from right around the time a nuclear dump site was installed on the outskirts of town. A ridiculous, convoluted plot, a boggle-eyed monster (a rip-off from *Forbidden World*, itself cloned from *Alien*), and many stars who have seen better days contribute to the sleazy atmosphere. "What is it?" demanded the ads. "Man? Animal? Extraterrestrial? Fiend? It's disgusting! To survive, it consumes human beings!" What more needs to be said?

BEING DIFFERENT ☆☆☆
1985, USA
Directed by Harry Rasky. 102 min.

This gives a fascinating and ultimately sympathetic look at people who are disabled enough to be labeled "freaks" by an uncomprehending world. Although the movie seems to be sold as a voyeuristic morbid-interest piece, the dignity and articulateness of these people cut through the rather shallow narration (by Christopher Plummer), the silly padding, and the slightly sensationalistic packaging. Our favorite person: the sideshow fat man who declares, "I think that the jolly fat man is a myth. . . . Heart disease, liver problems . . . what the hell do we have to be jolly about?"

BEING THERE ☆☆☆☆
1979, USA, PG
Peter Sellers, Shirley MacLaine, Melvyn Douglas, Jack Warden, Richard Dysart, Richard Basehart, David Clennon. Directed by Hal Ashby. 130 min.

Peter Sellers is wonderful in this, his last major film before his untimely death. He plays a character who watches endless amounts of television and who is literally without character, an imbecile who has spent all of his fifty-odd years inside the house of a benefactor. Kicked out into the real world by lawyers after the old man's death, he accidentally falls in with a series of increasingly powerful people who see in his silence and reticence a tacit wisdom; he becomes all things to all people simply by innocently echoing them. Based on Jerzy Kosinski's novel, the film is very funny and frequently poignant, and has something important to say about the often deadening effect of television on our citizenry and body politic. Beautiful soft-focus photography by Caleb Deschanel (*The Natural*). Melvyn Douglas won the Best Supporting Actor Oscar; Sellers was nominated for Best Actor.

BELA LUGOSI MEETS A BROOKLYN GORILLA

See *The Boys from Brooklyn*

THE BELARUS FILE ☆☆☆
1985, USA (TV)
Telly Savalas, Suzanne Pleshette, Max Von Sydow, George Savalas. Directed by Robert Markowitz. 104 min.

Savalas returned to the role of Kojak in good form in this taut murder mystery with a Nazi manhunt subplot. Kojak keeps running into walls of official indifference while investigating the deaths of Russian immigrants who have lived in America since the end of World War II and have all shared a terrible secret. Thwarted by the State department, Kojak stops at nothing to solve this mystery, whose surprising resolution caps a fast-paced detective film.

BELIZAIRE THE CAJUN ☆☆☆
1986, USA, PG-13
Armand Assante, Gail Youngs, Michael Schoeffling, Stephen McHattie, Will Patton, Robert Duvall. Directed by Glen Pitre. 95 min.

This film is an ambitious and not uninteresting attempt to depict a much-maligned minority, Louisiana's Cajun population. Armand Assante plays the title character, a faith healer and medicine man living in Louisiana in the years before the Civil War. Filled with evocative music, detail, and characterization, the film is a little too unstructured to hold one's attention, but writer-director Glen Pitre's evocation of an almost unknown world is admirable.

BELL, BOOK AND CANDLE ☆☆½
1958, US
Kim Novak, James Stewart, Elsa Lanchester, Jack Lemmon, Ernie Kovacs, Hermione Gingold, Janice Rule. Directed by Richard Quine. 103 min.

Another bright and funny play is brought to the screen with only middling results. Daniel Taradash adapted John Van Druten's play about a witch in contemporary Manhattan who casts a love spell on her neighbor but loses her magical powers in the process. It's no better or worse than three or four "Bewitched" episodes strung together—except for the presence of a highly skilled cast. Kim Novak was once critically burned at the stake for her "mishandling" of this and other comedy roles. Actually, she balances the more frenetic style of the supporting cast very nicely. Perhaps a stronger director than Richard Quine would have brought out more in the material, but at least he had the good sportsmanship to belittle himself in the tongue-in-check graphics of the credits sequence; you'll see what we mean.

THE BELLBOY ☆☆☆
1960, U.S.
Jerry Lewis, Alex Gerry, Bob Clayton, Bill Richmond, Milton Berle, Walter Winchell, Joe Levitch, Maxie Rosenbloom, Joe E. Ross, Sammy Shore. Directed by Jerry Lewis. 72 min.

Fans of Jerry Lewis the director will, of course, see this as a watershed film. Not only is this his first directorial effort, he has also abandoned a story line, cut out all lines of dialogue for himself (except one parting shot), and made his sheer goofiness the star of the film. Jerry plays a bellboy who messes up his various work assignments—a motif he was to mine again and again, in movies ranging from *The Errand Boy* and *Who's Minding the Store?* to *Hardly Working*. Unfortunately, Lewis's work does seem to need a narrative; the funniest gags in *Who's Minding the Store?*, for example, spring from the character's deepest fears as he finds himself in love—without his anxiety about marriage, his recurrent beatings at the hands of shrewish, middle-aged dames wouldn't be half so telling, scary, or hilarious. This isn't a sidesplitting film, nor a Lewis classic along the lines of *The Nutty Professor* or *Hollywood or Bust*, but it is beautifully directed. Lewis's elegant use of Miami's Fontainebleau Hotel is arresting and some of the gags are diverting. The director's father, Joe Levitch, appears with the Novelties.

LA BELLE ET LA BÊTE ☆☆☆☆
1946, France
Jean Marais, Josette Day, Mila Parley, Marcel Andre, Michel Auclair. Directed by Jean Cocteau. 90 min.

French cinema and the cinema of Jean Cocteau (*Blood of a Poet*, *Orpheus*) both reached peaks with this timeless beauty. Not only has Cocteau retold Charles Perrault's classic fairy tale in a light, engaging way, he has also incorporated many surreal touches that give both depth and unexpected humor to the simple fable; when the poor farm girl, Beauty, enters the beast's castle—where she becomes a live-in guest to keep a promise made by her father—she is greeted by disembodied arms holding candelabras, busts with roving eyes and smiling faces, and a princely but furry beast who burns at first sight of her (and is eventually transformed by her love). Part comedy, horror, and Freud-laced melodrama, and all fantasy, *La Belle et la Bête* is one of the most successful combinations of art direction (Christian Bérard), camerawork (Henri Alekan), lighting (Raymonde Meresse), and costume (Marcel Escoffier) to create a fairy-tale effect (Georges Auric's score, however, is too romantic). It is also to Cocteau's credit that he does not use soft-focus or other traditional oneiric devices and that his sense of humor is of a modernist stripe. Avoid shorter, execrably dubbed versions; Goldwyn Classics has recently released a restored print.

THE BELLES OF ST. TRINIAN'S ☆☆☆½
1954, Great Britain
Alistair Sim, Joyce Grenfell, George Cole, Hermione Baddeley, Beryl Reid, Joan Sims. Directed by Frank Launder. 91 min.

The first of several very popular movies, featuring the less-than-well-behaved young ladies of the boarding school of St. Trinian's, this film is based on a popular British comic strip by Ronald Searle. Alistair Sim stars in two roles, as the matron of the school and as her no-good brother, a bookie who wants to turn a profit on the nearly bankrupt institution. Really not much of a plot, but lots of wonderful, bratty gags. The sequels, which went straight downhill after Sim left, were *Blue Murderer at St. Trinian's*, *The Pure Hell of St. Trinian's*, and *The Great St. Trinian's Train Robbery*.

BELLISSIMA ☆☆☆
1951, Italy
Anna Magnani, Walter Chiari, Tina Apicella, Gastone Renzelli. Directed by Luchino Visconti. 109 min.

The wonderful Anna Magnani stars in this comedy-drama as the star-struck wife of a worker in Rome. She hears about an open casting call for a child's role in a major movie and rushes her small daughter into the spotlight. The child is not quite as anxious about the movie as she is and they both end up learning a lesson about the film business. *Bellissima* is a bit too long and shifts focus too often, but Magnani is brilliant: she can be instantly heartbreaking or hilarious; a truly gifted actress.

THE BELL JAR ☆
1979, USA, R
Marilyn Hassett, Julie Harris, Anne Jackson, Barbara Barrie, Robert Klein, Donna Mitchell, Mary Louise Weller, Jameson Parker, Thaao Penghlis. Directed by Larry Peerce. 112 min.

A virginal intellectual is driven mad by philistines, lechers, and lesbians in a film that could be called *The Perils of Sylvia Plath*. This adaptation of the poet's autobiographical novel, an account of her brush with madness and suicide while a student at Smith in the early 1950s, is a true story without a single believable scene. The movie fairly crawls with heartless anti-intellectuals and sex fiends, and every time sex rears its ugly head, Hassett goes nuts. We know she's going nuts because she keeps opening her mouth wide and yelling, "Aargh! Aargh! Aargh!" This Esther injects snatches of Plath's famous *Ariel* poems into her daily conversation, even spouting a choice line or two on the way to shock therapy.

BELLS ARE RINGING ☆☆☆☆
1960, USA
Judy Holliday, Dean Martin, Fred Clark, Eddie Foy, Jr., Jean Stapleton. Directed by Vincente Minnelli. 126 min.

Vincente Minnelli's pleasant version of the sparkling Judy Holliday stage vehicle proved to be Holliday's final film. Her portrayal of an answering-service operator who falls for the voice of Dean Martin (as a writer of show tunes) is a gas, and so is Betty Comden and Adolph Green's slightly sappy script. Minnelli's graceful use of Cinemascope is lost on small screens; however, aficionados probably won't get a chance to see this in the theaters. Besides, as long as the camera is on the spirited Holliday, she's all you need to see.

BELLS OF CORONADO ☆½
1950, USA
Roy Rogers, Dale Evans, Pat Brady, Trigger, the Riders of the Purple Sage. Directed by William Witney. 67 min.

This serviceable horse opera about uranium-robbing on the prairie features some wholesome tunes from Roy and Dale, including "Save a Smile for a Rainy Day." William Witney, Rogers's most frequent director, smoothly handles the B-level action.

THE BELLS OF ROSARITA ☆½
1945, USA
Roy Rogers, George "Gabby" Hayes, Dale Evans, Wild Bill Elliott, the Sons of the Pioneers, Trigger. Directed by Frank McDonald. 68 min.

All of Republic's star B players show up in this silly Western songfest. Roy Rogers plays—not badly—Roy Rogers saving a young innocent from a mean swindler's nefarious plotting. Low energy and typically saintly characterizations—even Gabby Hayes is less chipper than usual.

THE BELLS OF ST. MARY'S ☆☆☆
1945, USA
Bing Crosby, Ingrid Bergman, Henry Travers, William Gargan, Ruth Donnelly. Directed by Leo McCarey. 126 min.

Once again, Leo McCarey turns Der Bingle's collar around to play the lovable but self-righteous Father O'Malley. With Barry Fitzgerald's Father Fitzgibbon gone, O'Malley's sparring matches are now opposite Ingrid Bergman's Sister Benedict. Apparently, the two have different approaches to raising funds for their Catholic school. Cutesy touches such as Bergman (in habit) trying to teach a student to box, tend to overwhelm this sequel to the equally sappy but somehow superior *Going My Way*, but the hint of romance and the star byplay keep things afloat.

BELOW THE BELT ☆☆☆
1980, USA, R
Regina Baff, Mildred Burke, John C. Becher, Annie McGreevey, Shirley Stoler, Dolph Sweet, Ric Mancini. Directed by Robert Fowler. 89 min.

Shot for the most part in 1974, this took six years to get the limited release that it did, and even then it was a film ahead of its time, sort of. Although you'll probably find this pseudo-documentary about women wrestlers in the Hulk Hogan–Rowdy Roddy Piper section of your video store, this is actually a comparatively realistic treatment of the world of wrestling. Regina Baff is very good as a New York City waitress who looks for fame and fortune on the wrestling circuit, but the real interest is in the sleazy, low-budget ambience with which director Robert Fowler has photographed this fringe area of society. An upbeat musical score keeps the whole project from getting too depressing; all in all, it's a welcome relief from the comic antics of the World Wrestling Federation people.

THE BELSTONE FOX ☆☆½
1973, USA, G
Eric Porter, Rachel Roberts, Jeremy Kemp, Bill Travers, Dennis Waterman. Directed by James Hill. 103 min.

Fans of *Born Free* might wish to check out this feature from the same producer, writer, and director, dealing again with an animal raised away from its natural environment. This time it's a fox, raised by a professional huntsman along with his hounds. Comes the time, of course, when they must be pitted against each other. Nature lovers may be distressed that the film does not condemn the ancient British pastime of the fox hunt; while it doesn't support it either, the amount of time devoted to it in the context of this film seems rather excessive. (a.k.a.: *Free Spirit*)

BEN ☆
1972, USA, PG
Lee Harcourt Montgomery, Joseph Campanella, Arthur O'Connell, Rosemary Murphy, Meredith Baxter, Kaz Garas. Directed by Phil Karlson. 95 min.

You've seen the story a hundred times before: boy meets rat, boy gets rat, boy loses rat . . . all right, maybe not a *hundred* times, and certainly never done with the hilarious ineptitude that characterizes this sequel to *Willard*. Willard (the boy) is gone, but Ben (the rat) is back, leading an army of four thousand rodent pals in a terrorist rampage through Los Angeles, and befriending a little boy (Lee Harcourt Montgomery) with a bad heart. The mawkish scenes with Montgomery are so bad that they really are funny; by the time he sits down to compose a ballad for his new best friend, you'll laugh out loud. (The tune, sung by Michael Jackson, is, as far as we know, the only love song about a rat to be nominated for a Best Song Oscar.)

BEND OF THE RIVER ★★★½
1952, USA
James Stewart, Arthur Kennedy, Julia Adams, Rock Hudson, Jay C. Flippen, Stepin Fetchit, Lori Nelson, Henry Morgan. Directed by Anthony Mann. 91 min.

Jimmy Stewart's tremulous authority makes him the perfect actor for this tale of an outlaw attempting to reform himself only to have his past catch up with him and overwhelm his hope for redemption. His performance is shocking in its intensity and harrowing to the viewer: When he confronts an unregenerate ex-cohort, Stewart's hysterical diatribe shows him in an unheroically strident light, and when he is beaten, humiliated, and abandoned on a mountaintop, it is genuinely difficult to keep one's eyes on the screen. This story of a man guiding a wagon train through the Oregon territory contains the usual episodic incidents—Indian attacks, battles with his "friends," hazardous river crossings—but it also has the power and coherency of a developing, personal story. Anthony Mann fruitfully collaborates with writer Borden Chase (*Winchester '73*, *The Far Country*), and he adds his own lush visual style and trademark fluid camera.

BENEATH THE PLANET OF THE APES ★★½
1970, USA, G
James Franciscus, Kim Hunter, Maurice Evans, Linda Harrison, Charlton Heston, Natalie Trundy. Directed by Ted Post. 95 min.

Number two in the *Planet of the Apes* cycle is, perhaps inevitably, a letdown, but moderately exciting nevertheless. Picking up where the original left off, this much grimmer story has the apes battling the grotesque mutant humans who live under the postnuclear earth and worship the Bomb, while astronaut James Franciscus arrives to hunt down the missing Taylor (Charlton Heston). All of the original cast members reprise their roles here except for Roddy McDowall, who was replaced by David Watson but who returned to the series in part three. The screenplay by Paul Dehn (who also wrote the next two films) culminates in apocalypse, but don't be fooled—the mere destruction of a planet couldn't stop the producers from churning out three more sequels to this money machine. Great makeup, once again, by John Chambers and Dan Striepeke. Followed by *Escape from the Planet of the Apes*.

BENEATH THE 12-MILE REEF ★★
1953, USA
Robert Wagner, Terry Moore, Gilbert Roland, J. Carrol Naish, Peter Graves. Directed by Robert Webb. 102 min.

This average skin-diving tale was a 1950s attempt to compete with early TV by offering lush travelogue scenery and eye-filling location camerawork. Off Key West, two sponge-diving dynasties compete for profits while their offspring fall madly in love with each other. It's a briny version of *Romeo and Juliet*, starring that white-bread duo, Terry Moore and Robert Wagner, who manage to tan throughout the film with more skill than they act. A picture-pretty romance where the scenery is the real star.

BEN HUR ★★½
1959, USA
Charlton Heston, Stephen Boyd, Hugh Griffith. Directed by William Wyler. 217 min.

William Wyler capped the decade of spectaculars with 1959's *Ben Hur*, winning an Oscar for his work and seeing the film set box-office records. Yet time hasn't accorded the film much favor. It lacks the camp appeal of *The Ten Commandments* and the visual panache of *El Cid*. Rather, *Ben Hur* is the most tastefully vulgar monstrosity ever produced. Charlton Heston won an Oscar for his role as the Jewish nobleman living in the time of Christ who endures physical and mental ordeals and struggles against social tyranny. It must have been the breadth of Heston's three-hour performance that turned the Oscar tide over Jack Lemmon in *Some Like It Hot*. Stephen Boyd is believably decadent. Hugh Griffith is likewise lively in this reverent, cold setting. The much-vaunted chariot race is skillfully edited, and all praise to the stuntmen, but *Ben Hur* is a very impoverished human drama.

BENJI ★★
1974, USA, G
Higgins (Benji), Cynthia Smith, Allen Fiuzak, Peter Breck, Frances Bavier. Directed by Joe Camp. 89 min.

Yes, the dog outacts the humans, and there *is* a sticky-sweet theme song, and the plotting isn't going to exercise anybody's intellect, but children will adore both the film and the resourceful canine who stars in it, and adults will groan less often than they might expect. The animal antics are expertly engineered by Camp and trainer Frank Inn, and if the story is a little thin, it could be worse—at least he's a dog and not a Smurf.

BERLIN ALEXANDERPLATZ ★★★★
1983, West Germany
Gunter Lamprecht, Hanna Schygulla, Barbara Sukowa, Gottfried John. Directed by Rainer Werner Fassbinder. 921 min.

It's fitting that the final work of Fassbinder's incredibly prolific, if brief, career should be this fifteen and one-half-hour epic. A massive, remarkable near-masterpiece, originally made for German television but shown theatrically in this country, *Berlin Alexanderplatz* is an adaptation of a well-known German novel of the post–World War I era. It opens with the release of Gunter Lamprecht from prison and follows this corrupt Candide through incidents of rape, murder, alcoholism, and a host of lesser transgressions against the bourgeois world. It concludes with a hallucinatory 116-minute segment rife with images both trite and dense. Less overtly stylized than much of Fassbinder's late work (*Lola*, *Veronika Voss*), this is an engrossing, audacious achievement, though parts of it are supremely self-conscious exercises in melodramatic excess.

BERLIN EXPRESS ★★★★
1948, USA
Merle Oberon, Robert Ryan, Charles Korvin, Paul Lukas, Robert Coote, Reinhold Schunzel, Roman Toporow, Peter von Zerneck, Otto Waldis. Directed by Jacques Tourneur. 86 min.

Director Jacques Tourneur's eyes and ears register the details of the Third Reich's ruination with an appalling objectivity, giving a superb documentary flavor to this engrossing story about a representative (Paul Lukas) of the democratic forces in Germany who is kidnapped by a surviving Nazi faction (led by Charles Korvin). The international cooperation that led to the Allied victory is inoffensively symbolized by the group of acquaintances—an American (Robert Ryan), a Frenchwoman (Merle Oberon), an Englishman (Robert Coote), and a Russian (Roman Toporow)—who undertake to rescue Lukas. Apart from its cinematographic excellence, it also works well as an out-and-out spy thriller, and admirably holds its own against later entries in the genre. There's nothing else quite like it.

BEST DEFENSE ★
1984, USA, R
Dudley Moore, Eddie Murphy, Kate Capshaw, Michael Scalera, George Dzundza. Directed by Willard Huyck. 94 min.

Dudley Moore plays a lowly arms engineer who stumbles upon a plan for the "DYP gyro" and tries to palm it off as his own; Eddie Murphy is the young American lieutenant who's been chosen to test the weapon—and who accidentally drives his tank into the middle of a war between Iraq and Kuwait. Screenwriter

Gloria Katz and director Willard Huyck have plunged into nuclear-age "absurdity" without touching on any feelings of dread or peril. Their satire isn't merely witless; it's out of control—and as wearyingly overblown—as the Reagan defense budget.

BEST FOOT FORWARD   ★★★
1943, USA
Lucille Ball, William Gaxton, Virginia Wiedler, Tommy Dix, Nancy Walker. Directed by Edward Buzzell. 95 min.

This is a rollicking film version of the stage success about a movie star whose visit to a military school drives the student body wild when she accepts a cadet's invitation to be his prom date. A minor musical, but the infectious high spirits of the cast and the zippy choreography make this a delightful diversion—with Lucille Ball having a ball and Nancy Walker stealing the show.

BEST FRIENDS   ★★★
1982, USA, PG
Burt Reynolds, Goldie Hawn, Jessica Tandy, Barnard Hughes, Audra Lindley, Keenan Wynn, Ron Silver, Richard Libertini. Directed by Norman Jewison. 116 min.

Burt Reynolds and Goldie Hawn team up in this comedy about a pair of successful screenwriters who tie the knot after years of living together, and find their relationship falling apart during a cross-country pilgrimage to meet their respective in-laws. The movie stays stubbornly on the surface (and Reynolds's coy mugging is tiresome), yet the pain and desperation at its center lend the sight gags an unusual edge. This is a serious sitcom about the strangeness of new families, and about the horror of discovering you're suddenly a link in the long line of couples who marry and procreate and march grimly toward death. As the parents, Jessica Tandy, Barnard Hughes, Audra Lindley, and Keenan Wynn are wonderful. Written by Barry Levinson (*Diner*) and Valerie Curtin.

THE BEST LEGS IN THE EIGHTH GRADE   ★★
1984, USA (MTV)
Tim Matheson, Annette O'Toole, Kathryn Harrold, Jim Belushi. Directed by Tom Patchett. 48 min.

Originally an "HBO Comedy Playhouse" special, this superficial comedy plays like a one-act romance tailor-made for a dinner-theater production in the boondocks. A formerly nerdish yuppie redesigns himself at a health club and pursues the girl who had the best legs in the eighth grade while his long-suffering girlfriend pumps iron in the background and chokes back her tears. Almost all of the cast is attractive and the level of wit is sophomoric but passable. Unfortunately, one of the cast members, Kathryn Harrold, seems to be permanently locked in a smug self-embrace.

THE BEST LITTLE GIRL IN THE WORLD   ★★
1981, USA (TV)
Eva Marie Saint, Charles Durning, Melanie Mayron, Jennifer Jason Leigh, Jason Miller, Viveca Lindfors. Directed by Sam O'Steen. 100 min.

In this "disease-of-the-week" TV movie, a pretty girl with everything that upper-middle-class money can buy develops anorexia nervosa, a disease that causes its victims to slowly starve themselves to death. The film zeros in on the horror of the situation, rather than offering insight into the problems of ultralow self-esteem inextricably linked with this illness. The adult actors are persuasive, but the titular anorectic gives an undernourished performance; Jennifer Jason Leigh pouts her way through every crisis.

THE BEST LITTLE WHOREHOUSE IN TEXAS   ★½
1982, USA, R
Burt Reynolds, Dolly Parton, Dom De Luise, Charles Durning, Jim Nabors, Robert Mandan, Lois Nettleton, Theresa Merritt, Noah Beery. Directed by Colin Higgins. 114 min.

For all its busts and buttocks, Colin Higgins's god-awful version of the hit Broadway musical about a Texas bordello squirms at the merest suggestion of naughtiness or eroticism—it's a puritanical outcry against puritanism. Like the show, the movie centers on the attempt of a consumer watchdog (Dom De Luise) to shut down the infamous Chicken Ranch whorehouse, run by the virtuous Miss Mona (Dolly Parton). The score is mostly galumphing, imitation-hoedown music, and though Burt Reynolds, as Miss Mona's longtime lover, tries hard to act sweet and sensitive, you can feel him straining not to turn the movie into a Dolly Parton joke. Almost worth seeing, though, for Charles Durning's song-and-dance number "Sidestep."

THE BEST OF POPEYE   ★★★
1983, USA
Animated compilation. Various directors. 56 min.

This is a compilation of several of the Max Fleischer animations from the 1930s, based on Elzie Segar's "Thimble Theater" comic strip. Included are several of the best short Popeyes—"Goonland," "Have You Seen a Dream Walking," and "Lost and Foundry"—and two longer films in Technicolor, *Popeye the Sailor Meets Sinbad the Sailor* and *Popeye Meets Aladdin and His Wonderful Lamp*, which showcase an innovative form of 3-D animation that was rarely employed again. Children will love it, and animation enthusiasts will appreciate the quirky pictorial style.

THE BEST OF TIMES   ★★
1986, USA, PG-13
Robin Williams, Kurt Russell, Pamela Reed, Holly Palance, Donald Moffat, M. Emmet Walsh, R. G. Armstrong, Dub Taylor, Carl Ballantine, Kathleen Freeman. Directed by Roger Spottiswoode. 103 min.

There's a good movie to be made about the obsession of the adult American male with football and adolescence, but this isn't it. Kurt Russell and Robin Williams play, respectively, the quarterback who almost won Taft High School's annual game against their archrivals, and the nerd who fumbled the pass and lost the game. After spending fifteen years obsessed with his failure, Williams decides he can regain his (and the town's) self-respect by replaying the game. None of this is explained in any kind of satisfactory way—why, for instance, should the rest of the town care about this game in particular, and not the countless other games the two teams played? Williams plays his character as a prissy stereotype; Russell is better, but he has less of a part. There are some remarkably erotic scenes between the two men and their wives that would have served as a wonderful subtext if only this were a better movie. But British director Roger Spottiswoode seems to be ill at ease with so American a subject, and the final replay of the Big Moment is shamelessly milked.

THE BEST YEARS OF OUR LIVES   ★★★★
1946, USA
Dana Andrews, Fredric March, Myrna Loy, Teresa Wright, Virginia Mayo, Cathy O'Donnell, Harold Russell, Hoagy Carmichael, Ray Collins. Directed by William Wyler. 182 min.

Samuel Goldwyn's grandiose meditation on the post–World War II mood is a high-class tearjerker that still delivers a wallop. Robert E. Sherwood's screenplay, based on MacKinlay Kantor's *Glory for Me*, minutely describes the trials and tribulations faced by three returning servicemen: Fredric March's sergeant is being retired from his bank; Dana Andrews's officer is cuckolded by his wife; and Harold Russell's handicapped GI faces prejudice at home. The pace is deliberate and the length a little excessive, yet the film works thanks to superb performances, heartrending Hugo Friedhofer music, crisp, smooth Gregg Toland photography, and several outstanding lump-in-the-throat sequences: the three men returning home in the plane, Russell removing his prosthesis for his sweetheart, and Andrews reliving a moment from the war. The film represents Hollywood's social-conscience filmmaking at its finest. *Best Years* won an Oscar for Best Picture and others for Sherwood, William Wyler, Friedhofer, March, and Russell.

LA BÊTE HUMAINE ★★★½
1938, France
Jean Gabin, Simone Simon, Fernand Ledoux, Blanchette Brunoy, Jean Renoir. Directed by Jean Renoir. 105 min.

Renoir adapted Emile Zola's classic novel for this dark, brooding study of a locomotive engineer with an obsessive urge to kill. This well-wrought drama from the greatest of all French directors remains faithful to the spirit of Zola's work in its penetrating look at the psychological and hereditary origins of its main protagonist's passions. The opening montage, shot on location, of Jean Gabin driving a train from Le Havre to Paris, is among the most elegant in the Renoir catalog. (a.k.a.: *The Human Beast, Judas Was a Woman*)

BETRAYAL ★★★
1983, Great Britain, R
Jeremy Irons, Patricia Hodge, Ben Kingsley. Directed by David Jones. 95 min.

Harold Pinter's small, severe play takes an archetypal tale of love, marriage, and adultery and turns it on its head, telling the familiar story backward. The result is a theatrical exercise in which the various interlocked betrayals function as structure, not as drama, and in which the inner churnings of the characters seem beside the point. Ben Kingsley, with his incessant staring, gives a curious performance as the wormy, cuckolded husband.

THE BETSY ★★½
1978, USA, R
Laurence Olivier, Robert Duvall, Katherine Ross, Tommy Lee Jones, Jane Alexander, Lesley-Anne Down, Joseph Wiseman, Kathleen Beller, Edward Herrmann. Directed by Daniel Petrie. 125 min.

Harold Robbins's cheesy novel about lust and betrayal in a family of auto magnates becomes a fairly entertaining pre-"Dynasty" soap opera, thanks to a cast that knows it's better than the material but still relishes every sleazy plot machination. Best of all is Lord Larry as the patriarch, giving what may be his only out-and-out camp performance (wait until you hear his Southern accent). Not a moment of art will be found here, but it's ideal trash for those who like a low-rent plot with a classy veneer.

BETTER LATE THAN NEVER ★★
1982, USA
David Niven, Maggie Smith, Art Carney, Catherine Hicks, Kimberley Partridge. Directed by Bryan Forbes. 95 min.

Does the title refer to the laughs registered? Fans of polished comedy teamwork will want to catch the three leads marking time here in a flimsy plot about two aging rapscallions trying to worm their way into the heart of a miniature Miss Moneybags, a ten-year-old poor little rich girl. Those delightful sophisticates David Niven and Maggie Smith, who traded quips so beautifully in *Murder by Death*, have precious little to work with here, allowing Art Carney to win the scene-stealing competition. If you're in the mood for a comedy, better this than nothing.

BETTER OFF DEAD ★★½
1985, USA, PG
John Cusack, Amanda Wyss, Diane Franklin, Curtis Armstrong. Directed by Savage Steve Holland. 100 min.

For a while, director Savage Steve Holland (yes, that's his name) really has something going for him—a crazily surrealistic style that twists the sodden reality of teen comedies inside out. Every one of the grim young hero's nightmares comes true: his math teacher wants to go out with his girlfriend, and his doodles come alive from the notebook paper to chastise him. But when Savage Steve opts for a familiar, unsurprising romance at the picture's midpoint, he blows what could potentially have become a lowbrow classic. Still, the first half is so outrageously hilarious that it may make the rest of the movie worth watching.

BETTY BLUE ★★★
1986, France
Jean-Hugues Anglade, Beatrice Dalle, Gerard Darmon, Consuelo de Havilland. Directed by Jean-Jacques Beineix. 117 min.

Jean-Jacques Beineix, the director who debuted brilliantly with *Diva* only to follow it with the disastrous *Moon in the Gutter*, returns to form with his third film, a very sexy, obsessively stylish melodrama about a passion so strong that it overwhelms reality and reason. Betty (Beatrice Dalle) is an erotic tornado who whirls into the beachhouse and life of an unpublished writer (Jean-Hugues Anglade). Between bouts of torrid sex, she manages to throw his furniture out the window, his job into jeopardy, and his emotional life into utter chaos. Beineix uses a new actress, the impossibly sultry Beatrice Dalle, as a wild exaggeration of the tempestous, flighty coquette that's a staple of so many French films. Her entire character is whim, fury, and eroticism, and her extreme nature is exploited for both comic and tragic effect. The jumpy narrative will frustrate many, and some of the dialogue is unbearably purple—Betty's lover calls her "a flower with a psychic antenna and a tinsel heart"—but Beineix's alternately dreamy and nightmarish vision of contemporary France is unlike any other, and well worth seeing.

BETWEEN FRIENDS ★★★
1983, USA (TV)
Elizabeth Taylor, Carol Burnett. Directed by Lou Antonio. 100 min.

Not one member of the supporting cast of this film will be recognizable to even an ardent film buff, but the two leading players are more than enough. *Between Friends* is a contrived but involving story of two divorcées, one timid and one adventurous, who develop a strong friendship. In the hands of two lesser stars, this would be ordinary stuff, but if you hold any feelings for these ladies, *Between Friends* is a winner. Elizabeth Taylor gives one of her best performances, and Carol Burnett proves once again her great range as an actress. These women have such enormous appeal that the film is hard to resist.

BETWEEN GOD, THE DEVIL AND A WINCHESTER ★½
1970, Italy/Spain
Richard Harrison, Gilbert Roland, Dominique Boschero, Enio Girolami, Roberto Camardiel. Directed by Dario Silvestri. 98 min.

This is a spaghetti Western without enough garlic. Or, for that matter, basil, oregano, bay leaf, onion, or tomato paste. A stranger rides into town fleeing from the bandits who robbed the treasure of the mission of the Virgin of Guadalupe. Before he dies, he passes the map to a young boy, who is assisted by the padre in recovering the treasure.

BETWEEN THE LINES ★★★½
1977, USA, R
John Heard, Jill Eikenberry, Lindsay Crouse, Jeff Goldblum, Gwen Welles, Michael J. Pollard, Marilu Henner. Directed by Joan Micklin Silver. 101 min.

A precursor of Lawrence Kasdan's *The Big Chill* and John Sayles's *Return of the Secaucus Seven*, *Between the Lines* follows a group of slightly shell-shocked veterans of 1960s radicalism who are now publishing a weekly antiestablishment newspaper. The then-unknown cast offers some splendid ensemble acting, and Joan Micklin Silver's sensitive direction, coming on the heels of her work on *Hester Street*, keeps the loose-limbed narrative on track to create a meditative comedy for grown-ups.

BEVERLY HILLS COP ★★★
1984, USA, R
Eddie Murphy, Lisa Eilbacher, Steven Berkoff, Judge Reinhold, Ronny Cox, John Ashton, Bronson Pinchot. Directed by Martin Brest. 105 min.

If you haven't seen this box-office monster already, you may expect something a lot funnier than what Martin Brest and screenwriter Daniel Petrie, Jr., actually deliver. It's not a straightforward comedy, but rather a mildly funny action film that shot into the stratosphere on the strength of its star's very engaging presence. Eddie Murphy plays a sort of inversion of his *48 HRS.* character. This time he's a cop, not a crook, who finds himself out of place while tracking his friend's killer in the land of the "Lifestyles of the Rich and Famous." The plot tends to skid to a halt whenever Murphy goes into one of his routines; most of them are dazzling displays of comic cockiness, although the antigay jokes are both stale and crass. Very good support from Judge Reinhold and Steven Berkoff and a scene-stealing cameo by Bronson Pinchot will also hold your attention, as will the well-integrated pop score. See it by all means, but from the film that topped *Tootsie* as the highest-grossing comedy in history, we expected more. Incidentally, Murphy's part was originally to go to Sylvester Stallone. Followed by a sequel in 1987.

BEWARE! THE BLOB ☆½
1971, USA, PG
Robert Walker, Gwynne Gilford, Godfrey Cambridge, Richard Stahl, Carol Lynley, Shelley Berman, Burgess Meredith, Larry Hagman. Directed by Larry Hagman. 88 min.

In between appearances on *I Dream of Jeannie* and *Dallas*, Larry Hagman directed this low-budget sequel to the horror classic *The Blob*. It's just as campy as the original, but in a self-conscious and heavy-handed way. The plot is a virtual retread of the 1958 film of a man and a woman trying to warn the police of the deadly gelatin menace. The attack scenes are still fun, but Hagman obviously forgot that it was young Steve McQueen and the funky title song that made the original film a hit. (a.k.a.: *Son of Blob*)

BEYOND A REASONABLE DOUBT ☆☆☆½
1956, USA
Dana Andrews, Joan Fontaine, Sidney Blackmer, Philip Bournouf, Shepperd Strudwick. Directed by Fritz Lang. 80 min.

Lang, the creator of *Metropolis* and *M*, directed this gripping, thought-provoking suspense thriller. It is the story of a writer, Tom Garrett (Dana Andrews), who helps plant circumstantial evidence to frame himself for a murder, thus exposing the shakiness of "truth" and the inadequacy of the legal system. The plotters keep film records of their actions, planning to reveal Garrett's innocence only after he has been sentenced to death. But things go terrifyingly awry. Douglas Morrow's screenplay, with its stunning plot twists, establishes the film as importantly different from Fritz Lang and Alfred Hitchcock's other explorations of the theme of an innocent man who is captured and destroyed by an overpowering, impersonal system. The film within the film, and the questions it raises about cinema and truth, constitute a crucial subtext to this taut, exciting Lang classic.

BEYOND ATLANTIS ½☆
1973, USA/Philippines
Patrick Wayne, John Ashley, George Nader, Lenore Stevens. Directed by Eddie Romero. 89 min.

This film is not to be confused with *Atlantis the Lost Continent* or Patrick Duffy's swim to fame in *The Man from Atlantis*. Unlike the fabled submerged continent, it would be better off left unexplored, or perhaps viewed only by schools of fish on the ocean floor. Has a good film ever been spawned in the Philippines? The film does offer deep philosophical speculation about why some cities decline and fall and provides an answer to the question, what has George Nader been doing since his heyday at Universal Studios? Beyond redemption!

BEYOND EVIL ☆☆½
1980, USA, R
John Saxon, Lynda Day George, Michael Dante, Janice Lynde, David Opatoshu. Directed by Herb Freed. 94 min.

Certain horror films play like TV movies in the predictable way in which they wind toward their conclusions, but we know they aren't telefilms because of the high violence quotient. So don't be confused by this generic thriller, even though small-screen queen Lynda Day George heads the cast. In this familiar but not uninteresting tale, a foolish couple makes the mistake of invading the home turf of a restless spirit who doesn't want to share her haunting space with the living. If you can suppress the urge to scream at these people, then the flick may be good for a few goose bumps. Fair "Fright Night" fodder.

BEYOND OBSESSION ☆
1982, Italy
Tom Berenger, Marcello Mastroianni, Eleonora Giorgi. Directed by Liliana Cavani. 116 min.

In this embarrassing "international" production, an American construction worker (Tom Berenger) in Marrakesh becomes ensnared in a mysterious woman's web of deceit. Berenger, speaking English, and Eleonora Giorgi, speaking Italian, act as if they can barely understand themselves, let alone each other, and Marcello Mastroianni looks, quite appropriately, sheepish that he's in this film at all. Unexciting, unsuspenseful, unerotic, and, from director Liliana Cavani (*The Night Porter*), unsurprising.

BEYOND REASONABLE DOUBT ☆☆½
1980, New Zealand, PG
David Hemmings, John Hargreaves, Martyn Sanderson, Diana Rowan. Directed by John Laing. 127 min.

An engrossing pseudodocumentary, the film is based on a true case in which a New Zealand couple was murdered. In order to obtain a conviction, the investigating officer planted incriminating evidence to frame an innocent man, who was found guilty of the crime after an unprecedented two trials, but who was later released. This was made for an audience that was intimately familiar with all of the principal characters, having read about them in the daily newspapers for years, so it has a lessened effect on international audiences; even given that hurdle, though, it holds one's interest, provided one has a reasonable attention span.

BEYOND THE DOOR ☆
1975, USA/Italy, R
Juliet Mills, Richard Johnson, Elizabeth Turner, David Colin, Jr., Gabriele Lavia. Directed by Oliver Hellman. 100 min.

This is a confused and confusing tale of demonic possession, satanism, and unnatural childbirth from Italy by way of *The Exorcist*. A couple with two children—a little boy who drinks pea soup out of the can and a foulmouthed little girl—are surprised when the wife finds herself pregnant again despite taking the Pill. Her pregnancy is a nonstop nightmare and her baby, when born, has no mouth. *Beyond the Door II*, a far superior picture directed by Mario Bava, is a sequel in name only.

BEYOND THE DOOR II ☆☆
1977, USA, R
Daria Nicolodi, John Steiner, David Colin, Jr., Ivan Rassimov. Directed by Mario Bava. 92 min.

A woman, her small son, and her second husband move to the house she inhabited with her first husband, an apparent suicide whose body was never found. She begins to suffer what may be hallucinations or psychic warnings, her child may or may not be possessed, and things come quickly to a bloody pass. Evocative horror from the director of *Blood and Black Lace, Twitch of the Death Nerve*, and others; only vaguely a sequel to Oliver Hellman's 1975 film *Beyond the Door*, although it was so marketed. (a.k.a.: *Shock*)

BEYOND THE LIMIT ☆☆☆
1983, Great Britain, R
Richard Gere, Bob Hoskins, Michael Caine, Elpidia Carrillo, Joaquim De Almeida. Directed by John MacKenzie. 103 min.

In this extraordinarily faithful version of Graham Greene's grim, downbeat novel *The Honorary Consul*, Richard Gere, underacting for once, plays a self-absorbed doctor who is drawn into a kidnapping plot masterminded by a crew of clumsy Paraguayan revolutionaries. The movie is low-key and novelistic, with crisp, understated dialogue and marvelous performances from Bob Hoskins, as the police chief who trails Gere like a dapper Latin-American Columbo, and Michael Caine as the drunken, bleary-eyed Charley Fortnum—one of the most memorable roles in Caine's career.

BEYOND THE POSEIDON ADVENTURE ☆½
1979, USA, PG
Michael Caine, Sally Field, Telly Savalas, Peter Boyle, Jack Warden, Shirley Jones, Shirley Knight, Karl Malden, Slim Pickens, Veronica Hamel. Directed by Irwin Allen. 116 min.

Producer-director Irwin Allen should have let the sleeping ship lie instead of trying to dredge it up for this almost unrelated sequel about a salvage team checking out the sunken *Poseidon* and running into undersea trouble themselves. Since this sequel was made for a different studio, there are no references to the original and a completely new cast has been assembled, but the spectacular effects and genuine suspense of the original are wholly absent here.

BEYOND THE VALLEY OF THE DOLLS ☆
1970, USA, X
Dolly Read, Cynthia Meyers, Marcia McBroom, John LaZar, Edy Williams, Michael Blodgett. Directed by Russ Meyer. 109 min.

A title of sublime irrelevance is attached to a film that verges on the unbelievable. The Carrie Nations—a lively all-girl rock band—travel to Los Angeles, where they meet enigmatic rock mogul Z-Man Barzel and plunge headlong into his wild world of drugs, parties, and kinky sex. Garish nonsense directed by soft-core pornographer, Russ Meyer, and written by Chicago *Sun-Times* movie critic Roger Ebert. The film's final scenes are tasteless and incompetent to an almost perversely funny degree.

BEYOND THE WALLS ☆☆½
1984, Israel, R
Arnon Zadok, Muhamad Bakri, Assi Dayan, Rami Danon, Boaz Sharaabi, Adib Jahashan. Directed by Uri Barbash. 104 min.

This schematic melodrama concerns life behind bars in an Israeli maximum-security prison, where Arab and Jewish factions cast aside their differences in an effort to expose the cruelty and corruption of their oppressors. More effective as a prison genre piece than as a particularly significant statement on race relations, the film eventually bogs down in a morass of clichés and hackneyed situations.

BEYOND TOMORROW ☆☆
1940, USA
Harry Carey, C. Aubrey Smith, Charles Winninger, Maria Ouspenskaya, Rod LaRoque, Richard Carlson, Jean Parker. Directed by A. Edward Sutherland. 84 min.

This highly unbelievable tale of spirits and romance is burdened with a cumbersome screenplay, awkward direction, and lackluster acting. The story becomes mildly touching when Jean Parker and Richard Carlson fall in love on Christmas Eve, but the film has little else to recommend it.

THE BIBLE ☆☆☆
1966, Italy/USA
George C. Scott, Peter O'Toole, Richard Harris, Franco Nero, Ava Gardner, Stephen Boyd, Michael Parks, Ulla Bergryd. Directed by John Huston. 174 min.

John Huston's sprawling, highly uneven, but sometimes inspired epic covers the first twenty-two chapters of Genesis. The best episodes include the Noah's Ark sequence, with Huston himself as Noah (all by itself, this is one of the most enjoyable animal—or kids'—movies ever made), and the long sequence with George C. Scott as Abraham, in which Isaac's near-sacrifice achieves a tragic grandeur. The limpid cinematography is by Giuseppe Rotunno. A Dino De Laurentiis superproduction, this then-extravagant, eighteen-million-dollar epic was planned as the first installment of the complete cinematic Bible. Plans subsequently collapsed. Shot in a 70 mm wide-screen process.

THE BICYCLE THIEF ☆☆☆☆
1949, Italy
Lamberto Maggiorani, Lianella Carell, Enzo Staiola, Elena Altieri. Directed by Vittorio De Sica. 90 min.

This is one of the masterpieces from Vittorio De Sica's great Neorealist period. Working with his favorite scenarist, Cesare Zavattini, and a cast of nonactors, he created a timeless story out of the travails of a common worker whose bicycle—on which he depends for his livelihood—is stolen. With its humble inner-city settings and stripped-down plot, the film has extraordinary visual eloquence and stunning emotional resonance.

BIG BAD MAMA ☆☆
1974, USA
Angie Dickinson, William Shatner, Tom Skerritt, Susan Sennett. Directed by Steve Carver. 85 min.

Roger Corman produced this slick, sporadically entertaining rip-off of *Bonnie and Clyde* about a pistol-packing mom and her two daughters who become Depression-era outlaw leaders. As with many films in which Corman had a hand, energetic, sharp direction and inventive cinematography help to compensate for a "while-you-wait" script; *Big Bad Mama* is enjoyable even when its plot sags, which is almost always. William Shatner and Angie Dickinson are painfully uncharismatic screen presences.

THE BIG BRAWL ☆☆☆
1980, USA
Jackie Chan, José Ferrer, Kristine De Bell, Mako, Lenny Montana, Ron Max, H. B. Haggerty. Directed by Robert Clouse. 95 min.

This amusing American-made martial-arts movie comes from the writer-director and producer of *Enter the Dragon*. The slightly built Chan is the biggest kung fu star since Bruce Lee, but of a different, more accessible acting style. In this story, set in 1930s Chicago, Chan comes to the aid of his restaurateur uncle, who is being shaken down by local gang lord José Ferrer. Done with humor and even charm: kung fu for people who don't usually like kung fu. (a.k.a.: *Battle Creek Brawl*)

THE BIG BUS ☆☆½
1976, USA, PG
Joseph Bologna, Stockard Channing, John Beck, Rene Auberjonois, Ned Beatty, Bob Dishy, José Ferrer, Ruth Gordon, Larry Hagman, Sally Kellerman, Richard Mulligan, Lynn Redgrave, Stuart Margolin, Howard Hesseman, Vic Tayback. Directed by James Frawley. 89 min.

This poke at disaster movies also takes swipes at priests, doctors, soda, cemeteries, and the Donner party. *Bus* is a pre-*Airplane* jokefest that never quite holds to its off-center center. A nuclear-powered superbus travels cross-country with an offbeat load of passengers and two cursed drivers. Rene Auberjonois (of TV's "Benson") is very funny as a priest with a grudge against God. The movie is acerbically funny in parts, but the huge cast is given, for the most part, pretty tame material.

THE BIG CAT ☆☆½
1949, USA
Lon McCallister, Peggy Ann Garner, Preston Foster, Forrest Tucker, Irving Bacon. Directed by Phil Karlson. 75 min.

This exciting outdoors feature, set in Depression-era Utah, brings city-raised Lon McCallister, desperate for a job, back to the town of his mother's kin. There he finds an ongoing feud between his uncle and another old mountaineer (Forrest Tucker and Preston Foster, who have a terrific fight scene). The denouement has McCallister tracking down the cougar that has killed a few of the locals. Director Phil Karlson shows a sure hand for action and scenery, but it wasn't until the 1950s that he hit his stride with such urban crime classics as The Phoenix City Story and 99 River Street.

THE BIG CHILL ☆☆☆☆
1983, USA, R
Glenn Close, William Hurt, Kevin Kline, Tom Berenger, Mary Kay Place, Jeff Goldblum, JoBeth Williams, Meg Tilly, Don Galloway. Directed by Lawrence Kasdan. 103 min.

Big warmth emanates from this intelligent, insightful sketch about a mid-life reunion between seven old college friends who are brought together by a suicide. Magnificent ensemble acting brings wit, nostalgia, and intimacy to life as the male and female characters rediscover their need for each other. A sensational 1960s soundtrack lends itself to the creation of an atmospheric film that you can easily sit through more than once. Winner of a Best Picture Oscar nomination.

THE BIG COMBO ☆☆☆½
1955, USA
Cornel Wilde, Richard Conte, Brian Donlevy, Jean Wallace, Robert Middleton, Lee Van Cleef, Earl Holliman, Helen Walker. Directed by Joseph Lewis. 89 min.

A man pinions himself to a woman's body, alternately kissing her and mumbling crude remarks. He's a mobster, she's a society girl out for kicks. A pair of hired killers make eyes at each other while they slowly, systematically torture a detective. In a misty, dark airplane hanger, violent death explodes in a web of shadowy betrayal. This is the world of *film noir*, and *Combo* is the real, raw thing. Cornel Wilde is taut and cool as the dick out to separate the whipped crime boss from his imperious girl friend; catching him breaking the law is only secondary to stealing his dame. John Alton (*I, The Jury, Slightly Scarlet*) evokes the lost look of *noir*, photographing with some hard-edged, high-key lighting. Joseph Lewis knows the turf.

THE BIG DOLL HOUSE ☆
1971, USA, R
Judy Brown, Pam Grier, Roberta Collins, Brooke Mills, Sid Haig, Pat Woodell, Christiane Schmidtamer. Directed by Jack Hill. 93 min.

The first exploitation film about women in a jungle prison is a must-see for fans of this violent, often campy genre; however, this lacks a real punch. There are the usual scenes of women being brutalized by sadistic guards and rebelling against their voyeuristic commandant, but it's all two-dimensional sleaze—never threatening and always pandering. Pam Grier and Sid Haig, at least, know how to turn in very overripe—that is to say, rotten—performances; they'll draw the only appreciative chuckles.

THE BIG FIX ☆☆☆½
1978, USA, PG
Richard Dreyfuss, Susan Anspach, Bonnie Bedelia, John Lithgow, Nicolas Coster, F. Murray Abraham, Fritz Weaver. Directed by Jeremy Paul Kagan. 108 min.

Richard Dreyfuss had his best role yet in this updated private-eye thriller. Based on a character created by Roger L. Simon (who also wrote the screenplay), Dreyfuss's Moses Wine is an ex-sixties Berkeley radical, law school dropout, and divorced father who now pursues the standard Sam Spade/Philip Marlowe trade in Los Angeles. He is hired by an old girlfriend to find out who is trying to ruin an honest politician by passing around leaflets of endorsement purportedly written by a terrorist-in-hiding. The film has telling points to make about how the "love generation" became the "me generation," especially in the person of the ex-terrorist (an early role by *Amadeus*'s F. Murray Abraham). There is also one very touching scene in which Wine, looking for clues, examines archival footage of student riots at Berkeley. A big surprise from director Jeremy Paul Kagan, whose previous film (*Heroes*) gave no hint of this much talent.

BIG FOOT ☆½
1971, USA, R
John Carradine, Joi Lansing, John Mitchum, Chris Mitchum, Joy Wilkerson. Directed by Robert Slatzer. 94 min.

This is a Sasquatch spectacular. Sasquatch, of course, is just another name for Bigfoot, well known to fans of the *National Enquirer*, the pages of which abound with terrifying stories of his exploits. Here the furry, ill-tempered creature is making life a living hell for those intrepid campers who haven't read the *Enquirer* and thus don't know enough to stay out of the woods. Of the many shaggy horror films featuring this fiend of the forest, this is the best; but that's not saying much.

THE BIG HEAT ☆☆☆½
1953, USA
Glenn Ford, Gloria Grahame, Lee Marvin, Jocelyn Brando. Directed by Fritz Lang. 90 min.

Ford plays a good cop whose battle against a crime syndicate sends him on an obsessive quest for revenge in this gripping *film noir* melodrama. Among the best of Fritz Lang's American films, *The Big Heat* conveys a mood of shadowy malevolence, punctuated with sharp, realistic drama. A pot of coffee hurled into Gloria Grahame's face provides a shocking central image for a dark, violent tale. As in many of the German-born director's films, Lang's theme is that of a well-meaning man embroiled in and corrupted by a massive, overpowering impersonal system. Mobs and machines rob Lang's protagonists of their humanity.

BIG JAKE ☆☆½
1971, USA, PG
John Wayne, Richard Boone, Maureen O'Hara, Patrick Wayne, Chris Mitchum, Bobby Vinton, Bruce Cabot, Harry Carey, Jr., John Agar, John Ethan Wayne. Directed by George Sherman. 109 min.

Like all John Wayne movies made after about 1965, this is half action, half comedy, but it doesn't work as well as the usual. When his grandson (played by Wayne's own son, one of four celebrity offspring in the cast) is kidnapped, big John, or Jake, or whomever, rides off in pursuit. Most of the film consists of watching the male cast interact in particularly macho ways—snarling, fighting, boozing. More violent than the usual Wayne opus, especially in the opening and closing bloodbaths.

BIG MO ☆☆
1973, USA, G
Bernie Casey, Bo Svenson, Janet MacLachlan, Stephanie Edwards. Directed by Daniel Mann. 113 min.

This mawkish sudser dramatizes the relationship between former Cincinnati Royals basketball star Maurice Stokes, who suffered paralyzing injuries at the height of his career, and teammate Jack Twyman, who spent ten years trying to raise money to rehabilitate his friend. The listless script never explores the complexities and growth of either man, substituting manipulative music for character motivation. Ex–pro-footballer Bernie Casey has little to work with as the fallen hero, and Bo Svenson's self-sacrificing Twyman has all the dimension of a plywood angel. A poor man's *Brian's Song*. (a.k.a.: *Maurie*)

THE BIG RASCAL ☆½
Hong Kong, 1980
Chi Kuan-Chun, Wang Chen, Chi Kang, Peng Kang, King Kung. Directed by Chi Kuan-Chun. 92 min.

Writer-director-star Chi Kuan-Chun seeks revenge after his brother is killed by a gang boss. The usual plotless plot, saved here by superlative martial-arts action.

BIG RED ☆☆½
1962, USA
Walter Pidgeon, Gilles Payant, Emile Genest, Janett Bertrand, Doris Lussier. Directed by Norman Tokar. 89 min.

There are more tears than treacle in this Disney movie about a boy who wins the love of a champion Irish setter. Walter Pidgeon remains adorable throughout as the crusty trainer who hires the boy, then fires him, then tries to put an injured Big Red to sleep, and finally adopts the youngster. Viewers will cheer as the stalwart setter and his mate Mollie fight off a dangerous mountain lion. The location shooting in Quebec is up to the Disney standards and the film, with its French-Canadian actors and songs in French, has a nice Continental flavor to it.

THE BIG RED ONE ☆☆☆
1980, USA, R
Lee Marvin, Mark Hamill, Robert Carradine, Bobby DiCicco. Directed by Samuel Fuller. 113 min.

Lee Marvin plays a sergeant who leads his young squadron of soldiers into battle during World War II, including D day and the liberation of the concentration camps. A gritty and powerful war film that substitutes violent battlefield realism for John Wayne–type heroics, it marked director Samuel Fuller's return to the Hollywood fold, and his driving style is apparent in all of the spectacular fight sequences. Marvin gives a stalwart performance as the tough-as-nails warrior and is helped along by the sparkling young cast.

THE BIG SCORE ☆½
1983, USA, R
Fred Williamson, John Saxon, Richard Roundtree, Michael Dante, Bruce Glover, Nancy Wilson. Directed by Fred Williamson. 85 min.

In a city where the bad guys are named Jumbo and Huge, Fred Williamson is the biggest private eye in town. He can't help developing a bad attitude: He's tired of seeing drug dealers walk and cops laughed at. Dated before it was made, with no more action than an average TV cop show, *Score* was produced from a rejected *Dirty Harry* script. Nancy Wilson delivers a torch song, but even Fred walks out on it.

THE BIG SHOW ☆☆
1937, USA
Gene Autry, Smiley Burnette, Kay Huges, the Sons of the Pioneers. Directed by Mark Wright. 70 min.

This music-filled extravaganza has Gene Autry playing a comic double role. *The Big Show* has little to do with the West; however, it does give a glimpse behind the scenes of the making of a Western movie. Autry plays the double of a Western star who, through a series of mix-ups, is chased by gangsters and gets engaged to two women.

THE BIG SLEEP ☆☆☆☆
1946, USA
Humphrey Bogart, Lauren Bacall, Martha Vickers, John Ridgely, Dorothy Malone, Elisha Cook, Jr., Charles Waldron. Directed by Howard Hawks. 114 min.

Humphrey Bogart stars as Philip Marlowe, the tough but vulnerable private eye, in Howard Hawks's classic adaptation of Raymond Chandler's hard-boiled page-turner. Marlowe moves through a tawdry universe of violence and corruption in his effort to unravel all sorts of complicated goings-on involving a nymphomaniac named Carmen (Martha Vickers) and her beautiful, dissipated sister, Vivien (Lauren Bacall). Bacall provided the on- and off-screen romantic interest for Bogart. William Faulkner helped—reportedly with great difficulty—to write the film's notoriously convoluted screenplay. Midway though production, the filmmakers realized that they had no idea who had committed one of the murders. Chandler didn't know either, and it doesn't matter one bit.

THE BIG SLEEP ☆☆
1978, Great Britain, R
Robert Mitchum, Sarah Miles, Candy Clark, Richard Boone, James Stewart, Joan Collins, Edward Fox, Oliver Reed, John Mills. Directed by Michael Winner. 99 min.

Setting Raymond Chandler's overheated novel in the dessicated atmosphere of contemporary London is a fatal error all by itself; you keep longing for the juicy decadence of Los Angeles. But Michael Winner's unpleasant—and totally unnecessary—remake doesn't stop there. It actually tries to make sense of the notoriously incomprehensible plot. An enervated bastardization; thank God we've still got Howard Hawks's 1946 version. This has Robert Mitchum as Philip Marlowe, Sarah Miles in the Lauren Bacall role, and Candy Clark in a career-wrecking performance as the younger sister. A sequel to the far better *Farewell, My Lovely*.

THE BIG TREES ☆☆
1952, USA
Kirk Douglas, Eve Miller, Patrice Wymore, Edgar Buchanan, John Archer. Directed by Felix Feist. 89 min.

Kirk Douglas chews the bark, offering another of his antihero portraits to this lackluster remake of *Valley of the Giants*. He plays a lumberjack who gets mixed up with Quakers while striking it rich in Northern California redwood territory. Technicolor and two attractive leading ladies make the film pretty, but the story line is unexceptional and the melodrama is as cardboard as some of the backdrops.

BIG TROUBLE ☆☆☆
1986, USA, R
Alan Arkin, Peter Falk, Beverly D'Angelo, Charles Durning, Paul Dooley, Richard Libertini, Robert Stack, Valerie Curtin. Directed by John Cassavetes. 93 min.

This screwball comedy (or rather a comedy about screwballs) finds director John Cassavetes in an uncharacteristically silly, loose-jointed mood (he replaced writer Andrew Bergman during shooting; the screenplay is pseudonymously credited to "Warren Bogle"). An insurance salesman (Alan Arkin) wants to ensure that his sons, musically gifted triplets, get to go to Yale, but where's a middle-class papa going to earn that kind of money? One way is to fall in with the kind of bad company that will introduce him to the wonderful world of grand larceny, in an upward spiral of wacky schemes. Arkin is quickly seduced into a life of crime in an outrageous parody of *Double Indemnity* that doesn't work out as expected. Like that other bizarrely funny but uneven comedy *Finders Keepers*, *Big Trouble* is about the American dream of getting rich quickly and illegally. The superb teamwork of Arkin, Peter Falk, and Beverly D'Angelo gives shape to this relaxed diversion, which garners enough laughs to make it worth seeing.

BIG TROUBLE IN LITTLE CHINA ☆½
1986, USA, PG-13
Kurt Russell, Kim Cattrall, Dennis Dun, James Hong, Victor Wong, Kate Burton. Directed by John Carpenter. 100 min.

Desperately trying to fashion a hip parody of martial-arts pictures, with a little of *Indiana Jones* and *Buckaroo Banzai* thrown in, John Carpenter ends up with a noisy mishmash. Kurt Russell is a trucker who helps rescue his best buddy's fiancée from an evil two-thousand-year-old spirit who lives beneath Chinatown. Along the way, there are rival gangs, monsters, a trio of mystical "furies," and endless rounds of ninja combat. The script was rewritten by *Banzai*'s W. D. Richter, and it's hard to think of a director less suited to his arch, woobly humor than Carpenter, who's slavishly attached to the workings of plot. The joke of the movie is supposed to be Russell's confused reaction to the goings-on, but it backfires—you'll wind up every bit as baffled as he is.

BIG WEDNESDAY ☆☆
1978, USA, PG
Jan-Michael Vincent, William Katt, Gary Busey, Patti D'Arbanville, Lee Purcell, Robert Englund, Reb Brown. Directed by John Milius. 126 min.

There are a few appealing elements in this overlong film: the excellently photographed surfing sequences at the film's end (Bruce Surtees is the cinematographer), and some of the vignettes in the lives of the three California surfers whose growth we follow. On the whole, though, this is incredibly pretentious stuff; if you must use surfing as a metaphor for coming of age, leave it in a two-minute spot on "Wide World of Sports." With a pre–*Buddy Holly Story* Gary Busey (who is also lighter by seventy or so pounds) and, as "Fly," Robert Englund, whom you might not recognize as Freddy Krueger of *Nightmare on Elm Street* and its sequels.

BIKINI BEACH ☆☆
1964, USA
Annette Funicello, Frankie Avalon, Keenan Wynn, Martha Hyer, John Ashley, Harvey Lembeck, Jody McCrea. Directed by William Asher. 100 min.

Frankie and Annette kick up a sandstorm in this beach romp with lots of time out for innocuous love songs and close-ups of wriggling bikinied derrieres (absolutely essential for any beach movie). Remaining pure and chaste while frugging and twisting their hearts out, suntanned Muscle Beach dropouts and curvaceous sand bunnies interact in what can only be regarded as a dating ritual 1960s style, before the hippies made all this innuendo passé.

BILITIS ☆½
1977, France, R
Patti D'Arbanville, Mona Kristensen, Bernard Giraudeau. Directed by David Hamilton. 95 min.

This is a picture-perfect depiction of Sapphic love on the Mediterranean shot by famed photographer David Hamilton, who does a great job with stills of naked young women, but just can't make them move with any fluidity in his first directorial effort. Everything's shot in such muted soft-focus photography that the images at times seem to disappear.

BILL ☆☆☆
1981, USA (TV)
Mickey Rooney, Dennis Quaid, Largo Woodruff. Directed by Anthony Page. 104 min.

A middle-aged, retarded innocent attempts to carve out an independent life-style after his release from an institution. Mickey Rooney won an Emmy for his portrayal of Bill, as did the script. Both the screenplay and the performances are far above those of the average TV movie. Followed by a lesser sequel, *Bill: On His Own*.

BILL AND COO ☆☆☆
1947, USA
Narrated by Ken Murray. Directed by Dean Riesner. 61 min.

Veteran vaudeville star Ken Murray was an amateur cameraman in his spare time, which was when he made this Oscar-winning short feature that critic James Agee called, not unkindly, "the God-damnedest thing ever seen." *Bill and Coo* is populated entirely by birds, wearing hats and other garments, waddling around miniature sets enacting a plot about life in "Chirpendale." For family viewing and not too bad for adults, depending on your tolerance level for cuteness.

BILL COSBY—"HIMSELF" ☆☆½
1983, USA, PG
Bill Cosby. Directed by Bill Cosby. 105 min.

This concert film, edited from four of Bill Cosby's 1981 performances at Toronto's Hamilton Performing Arts Center, presents a funny if somewhat lackluster series of monologues on the comedian's most familiar themes: growing up, marriage, kids, middle age. Cosby is clearly on comfortable ground here, but as a solo performer he's not as witty or engaging as he is in a sitcom context, and he seems to offer his best material grudgingly.

BILLION DOLLAR HOBO ☆
1978, USA, G
Tim Conway, Will Geer, Eric Weston, Sydney Lassick, John Myhers. Directed by Stuart E. McGowan. 96 min.

This billionth retread of the old rich-man-must-learn-to-live-like-a-poor-man-in-order-to-become-a-richer-man plot is strictly for undemanding kids. Tim Conway plays the hapless hero, and his monotonous, dreadfully slow performance will wear out its welcome and then numb you into a woozy dream state. Variations on this theme have been worked with greater success in everything from *Sullivan's Travels* to *Brewster's Millions*; this one, with a grade-Z crime caper and cute dog thrown in, is a loser.

BILLY BUDD ☆☆☆½
1962, USA/Great Britain
Peter Ustinov, Terence Stamp, Robert Ryan, Melvyn Douglas, Paul Rogers, David McCallum. Directed by Peter Ustinov. 112 min.

This is a haunting, expressionistic version of Herman Melville's novella about a young man who is too good for this world. Terence Stamp inhabits the titular role of the beautiful innocent with gravity and grace. Robert Ryan, playing the blighted Claggart, foils the young man with a performance that is positively satanic. The story, simplicity itself, details the extreme punishment meted out for Billy's assault on his brutal superior officer. Those who are not fans of Melville may find the story sluggish and obscure, but Peter Ustinov's tight direction never lets things get sloppy. Robert Krasher did the black-and-white photography, and its studied, angular look contributed to the movie's art-house feel. Another Cinemascope film that would have benefited from being presented full-frame on video. (See Woody Allen's *Manhattan* for an example of the right way to put wide screen onto the small screen).

BILLY JACK ☆☆
1971, USA, PG
Tom Laughlin, Delores Taylor, Clark Howat, Bert Freed, Julie Webb. Directed by Tom Laughlin, using pseudonym T. C. Frank. 114 min.

With its muddleheaded mixture of issues-of-the-hour (Vietnam, drugs, Indian rights), exploitative violence, preachy pacifism, and antiestablishment clamor, *Billy Jack* emerged as the surprise hit of the early 1970s. Despite its amateurish performances and uneven production, the film struck a nerve among the nation's young. With that nerve no longer quite so raw, contemporary audiences may see this film and rightfully wonder what made it such a hit in 1971—about all *Billy Jack* brings off now is a low-grade action with protracted polemical blather. The thin story involves rape and retribution at an Indian reservation, and Tom Laughlin (who also wrote and directed) proves self-conscious and silly in all three departments. Technically a sequel to *The Born Losers* (1967), *Billy Jack* was followed by the unsuccessful *Trial of Billy Jack* (1974) and the barely released *Billy Jack Goes to Washington*.

BILLY LIAR ☆☆☆½
1963, Great Britain
Julie Christie, Tom Courtenay, Wilfred Pickles, Mona Washbourne, Ethel Griffies. Directed by John Schlesinger. 98 min.

A breakthrough film for both director John Schlesinger and Julie Christie (whom Schlesinger would make into a full-fledged star two years later, in *Darling*), this amiable seriocomedy stars Courtenay as a working-class English Walter Mitty constantly fantasizing about escapes from the life he leads as an undertaker's assistant. From the moment she walks onscreen, Christie is the embodiment of the "new" English woman of the 1960s. Based on a classic "angry young man" novel by Keith Waterhouse (who collaborated with Willis Hall on the screenplay; they also teamed with Schlesinger on *A Kind of Loving*). In Cinemascope.

BILLY THE KID RETURNS ☆½
1938, USA
Roy Rogers, Smiley Burnette, Lynn Roberts. Directed by Joe Kane. 53 min.

In Roy Rogers's second starring role, he plays an ordinary cowpoke who is mistaken for the famous outlaw Billy the Kid. Some well-staged gun battles are mixed with several songs, including "Born to the Saddle." Smiley Burnette plays Roy's sidekick and supplies a little harmony.

BILLY THE KID VS. DRACULA ☆
1966, USA
John Carradine, Chuck Courtney, Melinda Plowman, Roy Barcroft, Harry Carey, Jr. Directed by William Beaudine. 95 min.

B Western meets B horror film, and the two genres wander around confused, occasionally bumping into each other. This was the prolific William Beaudine's one hundred seventy fourth feature, and his technique hadn't changed much since his first in 1915. John Carradine plays the slightly over-the-hill Count who plans to foil the Kid's plans to marry his niece Betty. Will Dracula catch them necking? Will Billy have a silver bullet handy? Stay tuned if you're ten or under.

THE BINGO LONG TRAVELING ALL-STARS AND MOTOR KINGS ☆☆☆
1976, USA, PG
Billy Dee Williams, James Earl Jones, Richard Pryor, Rico Dawson, Stan Shaw. Directed by John Badham. 111 min.

A sly comedy with a social conscience, *Bingo* looks at the pre–Jackie Robinson era, when black players were relegated to the Negro League baseball teams. The movie contends that the black athletes were victimized as much by their own people—in the form of corrupt teams owners—and their negative self-image as they were by an oppressive white society. Consequently, the movie is able to spend its time in a well-drawn, complex black universe. Billy Dee Williams heads the cast as a dissatisfied pitcher who forms his own barnstorming team. Of course, Richard Pryor steals his share of scenes as a player learning Spanish so that he can pass into the majors as a Cuban. Director John Badham (*Saturday Night Fever*, *War Games*) makes a good feature-film debut, giving the movie a feel for its shabby, small-town locations.

BIOHAZARD ☆½
1983, USA, R
Aldo Ray, Angelique Pettyjohn, William Fair, Frank McDonald, Christopher Ray. Directed by Fred Olen Ray. 84 min.

Here's yet another horror flick that never would have seen the light of day were it not for the miracle of videocassette. The army, the world of science, the fourth estate, and a psychic all combine their efforts to battle a beastie that they've somehow brought here from another dimension. The monster is another cheap rip-off of the one in *Alien*. The film ends with ten minutes of outtakes, some of which are less inept than the stuff that they *did* use. Aldo Ray fans might as well get *Bog* while they're at it and make an evening of it.

THE BIONIC WOMAN ☆
1975, USA (TV)
Lee Majors, Lindsay Wagner, Richard Anderson. Directed by Richard Moder. 96 min.

This series pilot is right up there with earth shoes, disco dancing, and Watergate among the important reasons we should all be embarrassed that the 1970s ever happened. We admit it: we preferred Lindsay Wagner running in slow motion as Jaime Sommers to robot Lee Majors as robot Steve Austin, but really! Wagner's winsomeness doesn't overcome the nonsensical plot. This is what you bought a VCR to escape.

THE BIRDMAN OF ALCATRAZ ☆☆☆½
1962, USA
Burt Lancaster, Karl Malden, Thelma Ritter, Neville Brand, Telly Savalas, Edmond O'Brien, Whit Bissell. Directed by John Frankenheimer. 147 min.

Lancaster is excellent as Robert Stroud, a convict imprisoned for murder at Alcatraz for fifty-three years, forty-three of them in solitary confinement; at the time of the film's making, he was still imprisoned. The justice of the sentence is not in question: Stroud killed two men, one of them a prison guard, and never shows any sign of remorse. Rather, the film examines how a human being can withstand an enforced incarceration of such length. Frankenheimer manages to maintain visual interest even though he's limited by the story to minimal, drab backgrounds.

BIRD OF PARADISE ☆☆
1932, USA
Joel McCrae, Dolores del Rio, John Halliday, Skeets Gallagher. Directed by King Vidor. 80 min.

The original King Vidor version of the classic adventure-romance is now on video complete with its Busby Berkeley production number. Too bad the story of an American traveler (Joel McCrae) who falls for a South Seas island girl (Dolores del Rio) is slow, uninvolving, and bland (it could use some Technicolor). Dolores del Rio's beauty remains intact. An equally dull but more lavish remake was done in 1951.

THE BIRDS ☆☆☆½
1963, USA
Tippi Hedren, Rod Taylor, Jessica Tandy, Suzanne Pleshette, Veronica Cartwright, Ethel Griffies. Directed by Alfred Hitchcock. 120 min.

Alfred Hitchcock's dark meditation on nature and chaos contains some of the most horrifying and technically brilliant sequences ever filmed. As birds begin to mass against and attack the citizens of a small, seaside town, Hitchcock gives us a glimpse of a universe gone awry. Hitchcock employed hundreds of real, trained birds, as well as many mechanical and animated ones, to achieve the film's terrifying, convincing power. *The Birds* received an Oscar nomination for its phenomenal special effects and should have won the award. The climactic two-minute sequence in the attic took a week to shoot. Tippi Hedren, in her screen debut, spent that time tied down, fending off multitudes of live birds. Filming ultimately had to be interrupted for a week when the dedicated young actress suffered a physical and emotional breakdown from the strain.

BIRDS OF PREY ☆☆
1973, USA (TV)
David Janssen, Ralph Meeker, Elayne Heilveil, Harry Klekas. Directed by William Graham. 81 min.

Action and suspense highlight this television drama. Traffic-helicopter pilot David Janssen witnesses a bank robbery and becomes involved in ensuing dangers. Some cutthroat suspense and fancy helicopter stunts will hold your attention.

THE BIRD WITH THE CRYSTAL PLUMAGE ☆☆½
1969, Italy/West Germany
Tony Musante, Suzy Kendall, Eva Rienzi, Mario Adorf. Directed by Dario Argento. 98 min.

A psychopathic sex killer stalks Rome, and an American writer finds himself witness to one of the maniac's non-fatal attacks. Asked by the police to remain in the country, the writer begins his own investigation, which endangers his girlfriend's life and plunges him into a morass of madness and murder. This is a stylized first feature from Italian director Dario Argento, whose later films became increasingly baroque and bizarrely violent manifestations of a disturbingly warped worldview. Unsettling and entertaining. (a.k.a.: *The Phantom of Terror*)

BIRDY ☆☆☆☆
1984, USA, R
Nicolas Cage, Matthew Modine, John Harkins, Sandy Baron. Directed by Alan Parker. 120 min.

Alan Parker's haunting film is a simple but powerful tale of male bonding. Set during the Vietnam war, *Birdy* follows the desperate attempts of the physically and psychologically scarred Al (Nicolas Cage) to resurrect his friend Birdy (Matthew Modine), who is suffering from catatonia at a mental hospital. While the veteran goes about his seemingly impossible task, *Birdy* flashes back to their upbringings on the streets of Philadelphia, where Al's main preoccupation is girls, and Birdy is obsessed with turning himself into one of his feathered companions. *Birdy* is one of the most moving and humorous pictures in recent years, portraying the friendship that is the only thing that these young men have left after their spirits have been shattered in Vietnam. Cage and Modine give honest and greatly affecting performances. Under Parker's sensitive direction, they help to make *Birdy* an altogether superior film.

BIRGITT HAAS MUST BE KILLED ☆☆☆
1981, France
Philippe Noiret, Jean Rochefort, Lisa Kreuzer, Bernard Le Coq, Michel Beaune. Directed by Laurent Heynemann. 105 min.

This espionage drama resembles the more widely seen *La Balance* in that both films view the evils of political corruption from the vantage point of personal and sexual relationships that are abused and manipulated by the power holders. A promiscuous German terrorist is set up to be assassinated in a roundabout plot concocted by French agency head Philippe Noiret: he will plant an unsuspecting stooge in proximity to the terrorist and wait for them to inevitably tumble into bed, at which point the woman will be killed by a hired murderer—leaving the stooge to take the blame. Rather involved, but the cast brings a nice world-weary air to this typically French outlook on international politics.

THE BIRTH OF A NATION ☆☆☆☆
1915, USA
Lillian Gish, Mae Marsh, Henry Walthall, Miriam Cooper, Josephine Crowell, Spottiswood Aiken, J. A. Beringer, John French. Directed by D. W. Griffith. 180 min.

D. W. Griffith's epic chronicle of the Civil War and its aftermath remains one of the most audacious and evocative historical spectacles in screen history. Some of today's audiences may have trouble with the film's length, Victorian sentimentality, formal performance, and—last, but far from least—the bizarrely racist attitudes that impel audiences to root for the Ku Klux Klan. Still, anyone even vaguely aware of filmmaking technique will be able to appreciate Griffith's remarkable editing—including some breathtaking battle scenes that remain unparalleled to this day. Formally great if ideologically offensive, *Nation* is still a film that demands to be seen. *Note*: Most video versions are transferred at a higher speed, which cuts down the running time; viewers who are wary of this dense epic may want to try the interesting ninety-three-minute video released by Kartes Video Classics—it's edited highlights, but it is a cut approved by Griffith (for a rerelease in the 1930s), and is clear, crisp, nicely tinted, and orchestrally scored.

THE BISHOP'S WIFE ☆☆☆
1947, USA
Cary Grant, Loretta Young, David Niven, Monty Woolley, James Gleason, Gladys Cooper, Elsa Lanchester, Regis Toomey. Directed by Henry Koster. 106 min.

This is one of those entertaining comedy-fantasies that always pops up around the holiday season. Cary Grant plays a dapper angel sent to earth to restore some humanity to David Niven, an Episcopalian bishop who has become so caught up in his plans to build a new cathedral that he's beginning to lose touch with his parishioners and his wife. A prime cast of supporting players lends color to what might finally be too sentimental a story for some.

THE BITCH ☆½
1979, Great Britain, R
Joan Collins, Michael Coby, Kenneth Haigh, Ian Hendry, Carolyn Seymour, Mark Burns. Directed by Gerry O'Hara. 90 min.

Joan Collins takes her talent slumming again in this tale of a rich bitch down at the high heels. Obsessed with climbing into bed with her social inferiors and climbing out of debt by cultivating her betters, the Bitch goes hot-and-heavy over a two-bit gambler while trying to rebuild her disco dynasty. This sequel to *The Stud* is like an extended commercial for the disco way of life; it's soft-core pornography of interest primarily to Collins's fans.

BITE THE BULLET ☆☆☆½
1975, USA, PG
Gene Hackman, James Coburn, Candice Bergen, Ben Johnson, Jan-Michael Vincent, Ian Bannen, Robert Donner. Directed by Richard Brooks. 131 min.

This exciting offbeat Western, blessed with Richard Brooks's directorial craftsmanship, is expertly scripted. The rugged adventure details the rivalry of several competitors engaged in a six-hundred-mile horse race at the turn of the century. There's no letup in the action as the burly horsemen attempt to nose ahead of each other and capture the prize. Superlative on-location photography enhances the tale. Staunch and sturdy action picture.

BITTERSWEET LOVE ☆½
1976, USA, PG
Lana Turner, Robert Lansing, Celeste Holm, Robert Alda, Scott Hylands, Meredith Baxter Birney. Directed by David Miller. 92 min.

This brackish soap opera, which the cynical may have fun with, cries out for the sort of Blackglama glamour Ross Hunter would have brought to it. Instead, this cloth-coat bore deals with love affairs and incest in a cheesily photographed production. A couple about to wed discovers they may be brother and sister because of the youthful indiscretions of their parents. Everyone in this threadbare work looks as if he or she needs a face lift, even the ingenue.

BIZARRE, BIZARRE ☆☆☆½
1939, France
Louis Jouvet, Françoise Rosay, Michel Simon, Jean-Pierre Aumont. Directed by Marcel Carné. 84 min.

This still-funny farce from Carné and scriptwriter Jacques Prévert was made at the height of their creative powers. Michel Simon plays a mystery writer and head of a middle-class French family thrown into turmoil by the arrival of a distant cousin. Like the best farces, it builds slowly but steadily until the complications begin to unravel in all directions at once.

THE BLACK ARROW ☆☆☆
1948, USA
Louis Hayward, Janet Blair, George MacReady, Edgar Buchanan. Directed by Gordon Douglas. 76 min.

Louis Hayward was less handsome than Tyrone Power and had less swagger than Errol Flynn, but he really knew how to convey the devil-may-care spirit of the swashbuckler in films like *Man in the Iron Mask*, *Son of Monte Cristo*, and this undeservedly obscure adventure film. Taking a breather from courting his lady fair, this lovesick knight in shining armor must throw his jousting pole in George MacReady's villainous direction in order to ensure that knighthood will remain in flower. This *Arrow* scores a bull's-eye as a fast-paced tournament of thrills, and if you're a knight aficionado, you'll want to catch Hayward's dashing presence in an action film that exhibits real panache.

BLACKBEARD'S GHOST ☆☆
1968, USA
Peter Ustinov, Dean Jones, Suzanne Pleshette, Elsa Lanchester, Joby Baker. Directed by Robert Stevenson. 107 min.

This Disney comedy features a meddlesome ghost who helps some elderly ladies save their inn from being converted into a casino. The cute but predictable shenanigans are like an extended version of "Bewitched" or "The Ghost and Mrs. Muir" helped somewhat by the ladies in the cast. Otherwise, Dean Jones is as bland as Peter Ustinov is hammy. Best for the younger set.

BLACK BEAUTY ☆☆☆
1946, USA
Mona Freeman, Richard Denning, Evelyn Ankers, Terry Kilburn, Arthur Space. Directed by Max Nosseck. 74 min.

This is one of those semiclassic children's perennials like *Heidi* that still make decent entertainment for kids. Although nothing in this film is exceptional, the story is strong enough to delight any youngsters who are crazy about horses. With few exceptions (like *The Black Stallion* or *National Velvet*), these films aren't as memorable as the books they're based on. This film falls into that category, along with *My Friend Flicka*. Still, the subject matter is pretty surefire, and you can overlook the fact that the actors seem too polished for the rural roles they're assuming. Just sit back with the entire family and enjoy this nicely balanced yarn about the girl who tamed an untamable stallion.

BLACK BEAUTY ☆☆½
1971, Great Britain, PG
Mark Lester, Walter Slezak, Pete Lee Lawrence, Ursula Glas. Directed by James Hill. 106 min.

Black Beauty comes galloping back for the umpteenth time (counting films, TV specials, and cartoons) in a classily produced but rather mechanical retelling of this favorite animal lovers' classic. The process whereby a youngster's love domesticates a hellion horse possessed more charm in its 1946 version, but kids who love horse stories will probably enjoy this retelling, too.

BLACK BELT JONES ☆½
1974, USA, R
Jim Kelly, Gloria Hendry, Scatman Crothers, Alan Weeks, Eric Laneuville. Directed by Robert Clouse. 85 min.

It could have been a great meeting of the two best B genres of the early 1970s—martial arts and black exploitation. Unfortunately, it's just a substandard entry in both departments, with Kelly as the eponymous hero taking on the evildoers who want to padlock Scatman Crothers's kung fu practice gym. Flying feet! Furious fists! Crashing bore!—and disappointingly so, given the fact that Robert Clouse (*Enter the Dragon*) directed.

THE BLACK BIRD ☆½
1975, USA, PG
George Segal, Stephane Audran, Lionel Stander, Elisha Cook, Jr., Lee Patrick, Signe Hasso, Richard B. Schull. Directed by David Giler. 98 min.

There's something wrong when a parody is less funny and witty than what it is supposed to be sending up. There's more than that wrong with this movie, a spoof of *The Maltese Falcon*, featuring George Segal as Sam Spade, Jr. You'll have to be a *Falcon* fan to begin with to get half of the in-jokes; but if you are, you'll probably be offended at the shoddy treatment given the (uncredited) Dashiell Hammett. There will be a few laughs for those who don't remember the original.

THE BLACK CAT ☆☆
1934, USA
Bela Lugosi, Boris Karloff, David Manners, Jacqueline Wells. Directed by Edgar G. Ulmer. 65 min.

This deluxe Universal horror stars both Boris Karloff and Bela Lugosi. Edgar G. Ulmer directed the bizarre plot about a nefarious Art Deco architect who casts a spell on a young man's fiancée and the vengeful doctor who is out to stop him. The use of classical music only heightens the camp hilarity but it's not enough to put this on a par with *Frankenstein*, *Dracula*, and the rest. No relation to Edgar Allan Poe's novel. (a.k.a.: *House of Doom*)

THE BLACK CAULDRON ☆☆½
1985, USA, PG
Animated: Grant Bardsley, Freddie Jones, John Hurt, John Byner. Directed by Ted Berman and Richard Rich. 80 min.

The Disney studio labored for ten years and spent twenty-five million dollars to make a visually spectacular return to the kind of classic animation seen in *Sleeping Beauty* and *Pinocchio*. What these talented technicians *haven't* come up with is a credible story to back up their gorgeously detailed images. They have opted instead for typical fantasy plot line about a boy who must stop an evil king from gaining possession of a magical cauldron that will give life to an army of skeletal soldiers. Unfortunately, this is the kind of movie where the bad guys are far more interesting than the good ones. One can always watch the masterful animation when nothing else makes sense.

BLACK CHRISTMAS ☆☆½
1974, Canada, R
Olivia Hussey, Keir Dullea, Margot Kidder, John Saxon, Douglas McGrath, Marian Waldman, Art Hindle. Directed by Bob Clark. 93 min.

Bob Clark (*Porky's*) directed this equally tasteless but perversely engrossing horror quickie that's a good deal fresher than its premise—sorority sisters being stalked by a mad killer—might suggest. Good performances, especially Margot Kidder's bawdy turn, help, and the slasher film clichés are handled with more care than usual. (a.k.a.: *Stranger in the House*, *Silent Night Evil Night*)

BLACKENSTEIN ½☆
1973, USA, R
John Hart, Ivory Stone, Liz Renay. Directed by William Levey. 87 min.

Wounded in Vietnam, Eddie allows brilliant, Nobel Prize-winning Dr. Stein to go out on a limb with an experimental operation, but Dr. Stein's brilliant assistant Malcolm has the hots for Eddie's girlfriend, a brilliant medical woman herself, so he replaces

Eddie's DNA injection and *voilà*—Blackenstein! This films one-two punch of soporific story line and repellent gore (the monster eats the internal organs of his female victims) may leave you feeling woozy. With its canned music, its "Ask Mr. Wizard" lab sets, and its performances of the maybe-if-we-don't-even-try-to-act-no-one-will-remember-we-were-in-this-bomb variety, *Blackenstein* has been assembled from the picked-over bones of other grade-Z horror pics and it deserves to rest undisturbed in the bad-movie graveyard.

BLACK FURY ☆☆½
1935, USA
Paul Muni, Karen Morley, Barton MacLane, John Qualen, J. Carroll Naish, Mae Marsh, Ward Bond, Akim Tamiroff. Directed by Michael Curtiz. 93 min.

Paul Muni is memorable, as always, as a Polish mine worker in Pennsylvania who is forced by the corruption around him to become involved in union politics. Somewhat dated but still effective.

THE BLACK GODFATHER ☆½
1974, USA, R
Rod Perry, Damu King, Jimmy Witherspoon, Don Chastain, Diane Sommerfield. Directed by John Evans. 96 min.

Would that writer-producer-director John Evans had hired Ossie Davis to stuff his cheeks with cotton balls and sit around mumbling throughout this movie. But no, we just get the standard black exploitation. The only difference between the good guys and the bad guys here, aside from the fact that the former are black and the latter aren't, is that the "good" guys don't push dope, and want to push out the "bad" Mafia guys who are polluting the ghetto with drugs. Otherwise, all concerned parties do approximately equal amounts of head bashing.

THE BLACK HAND ☆☆
1976, USA
Lionel Stander, Mike Placido. 90 min.

In turn-of-the-century New York City, an Italian immigrant is theatened by a gang of Irishmen before testifying in a controversial court case. Although unrelated to a 1980 Spanish spy film bearing this title, it is quite similar in theme and setting to a 1950 MGM film of the same title starring Gene Kelly. Standard, slow-moving melodrama.

THE BLACK HOLE ☆☆½
1979, USA, PG
Joseph Bottoms, Maximilian Schell, Yvette Mimieux, Anthony Perkins. Directed by Gary Nelson. 97 min.

Disney's answer to *Star Wars* has a group of scientists finding a gigantic spaceship on the fringes of a menacing black hole. Inside the craft is a mad scientist (Maximilian Schell) who eyes his visitors as guinea pigs for bizarre experiments. A sprawling big-budget effort with great special effects, but one that's hampered by its juvenile approach and cutesy R2D2-like robots. Still, *The Black Hole* provides a lot of silly fun. Notable matte work by Peter Ellinshaw.

BLACK JACK ☆
1951, USA/France
George Sanders, Patricia Roc, Herbert Marshall, Agnes Moorehead, Marcel Dalio. Directed by Julien Duvivier. 105 min.

This cheaply made melodrama wastes a good cast, most of whom probably just wanted to vacation in Spain, where this was filmed. George Sanders is his usual cyncial self as a smuggler out to make one last big score so he can retire.

BLACK LIKE ME ☆☆½
1964, USA
James Whitmore, Roscoe Lee Browne, Sorrell Booke, Will Geer, Dan Priest. Directed by Carl Lerner. 107 min.

A potentially powerful drama is seriously marred by James Whitmore's portrayal of a white man who, in order to experience prejudice firsthand, takes a drug that changes his pigmentation to black. Whitmore's performance is not bad, but he *looks* unconvincing as a black man. It is hard to believe that the film's other characters could be fooled by his sloppy blackface makeup job, thus undermining important scenes. This low-budget film, based on a true story that ended tragically (the man died from the drug), also gets cluttered in its latter stages, but the admirable intent generally shines through.

BLACK MAGIC ☆☆
1949, USA
Orson Welles, Akim Tamiroff, Raymond Burr, Nancy Guild. Directed by Gregory Ratoff. 105 min.

Orson Welles began his long descent into movie hamdom here playing the Italian magician Cagliostro, who plots to rise to power in the eighteenth century. He assisted in the direction, without credit; whatever he may have contributed is not apparent in this standard melodrama.

BLACKMAIL ☆☆☆½
1929, Great Britain
Anny Ondra, Sara Allgood, John Longden, Charles Paton, Cyril Richard, Donald Calthrop. Directed by Alfred Hitchcock. 86 min.

Recognized as a landmark when it was released over five decades ago, this early Alfred Hitchcock was the first talkie for the director and for his native England. Hitchcock began shooting the film as a silent movie and switched to sound midway through production. An innovative, beautifully filmed tale of treachery, deception, murder, and sexual politics, it established Hitchcock's position among the world's foremost directors. The famous sequence where the guilt-ridden Alice (Anny Ondra) begins hallucinating about knives represents a stunning exploitation of the possibilities of sound in cinema.

THE BLACK MARBLE ☆☆½
1980, USA, PG
Robert Foxworth, Harry Dean Stanton, Paula Prentiss, Barbara Babcock, Raleigh Bond. Directed by Harold Becker. 113 min.

Author Joseph Wambaugh (*The Onion Field*) attempts to go beyond the practical issues of police stress he's dealt with before to consider their ultimate implications. Wambaugh's hero, a susceptible, romantic Russian-American cop in L.A. (Robert Foxworth), has witnessed atrocities that have convinced him "there's no heaven and no hell; nothing but a big sewer." Wambaugh, rather than jettisoning pulp best-seller conventions to grope for something genuine, merely turns the clichés on their heads, or else treats them satirically; the result is pretty much a mess. The mix of genres is audacious, but few of the strokes actually come off; you can always tell exactly what effect a given scene isn't having on you.

BLACK MOON RISING ☆☆
1986, USA, R
Tommy Lee Jones, Robert Vaughn, Richard Jaeckel, Bubba Smith, Dan Shor, William Sanderson, Keenan Wynn, Nick Cassavetes. Directed by Harley Cokliss. 100 min.

The prototype of a futuristic car is stolen in a sweep by a sophisticated gang of car thieves. The inventors want it back in time to strike a deal with a foreign auto manufacturer, and they team up with a professional thief who has his own stake in the matter: hidden in the car is a tape wanted by the U.S. government, and he stands to inherit some serious trouble if it isn't delivered on time.

Lots of high-tech caper moves here, along with some hot sex, psychopathic bad guys, and very cool cars, but it doesn't amount to very much in the end, despite the participation (on the screenplay) of John Carpenter (*Halloween*).

BLACK NARCISSUS ★★★
1947, Great Britain
Deborah Kerr, Sabu, David Farrar, Flora Robson, Esmond Knight, Jean Simmons. Directed by Michael Powell and Emeric Pressburger. 100 min.

This is a heated, visually splendid story of English nuns who face a harsh climate and earthly temptation on a mission to the Himalayas. Kerr gives a powerful performance as the Sister Superior who tries to hold her wilderness convent together.

BLACK ORPHEUS ★★★★
1959, France/Portugal
Marpessa Dawn, Bruno Mello, Lea Garcia, Adhemar Da Silva. Directed by Marcel Camus. 98 min.

The ultimate samba film is a glorious modern retelling of the Orpheus-Eurydice myth set during Rio's Carnival. A fabulous explosion of color, music, celebration, and tragedy, this film stars Brazilian soccer star Bruno Mello and American dancer Marpessa Dawn as the entranced lovers whose passion is stalked by Death in a Carnival disguise. The film understands the starkness of the tragic myth and it attempts to frame myth within a complicated, unmythic real world. Ultimately, the colorful explosions of the Carnival seem to represent the devastation wreaked on the world by love and sadness.

THE BLACK PIRATE ★★★
1926, USA
Douglas Fairbanks, Billie Dove, Tempe Pigott, Fred Becker, Donald Crisp. Directed by Albert Parker. 88 min.

Douglas Fairbanks, Sr., is in top form in this silent classic. The plot isn't much to speak of—the standard buckling of swashes for an hour and a half—but then Fairbanks is the entire show, performing all sorts of acrobatic stunts, including the famous sliding-down-the-mainsail-with-sword bit. Originally released in experimental Technicolor.

THE BLACK ROOM ★★★
1935, USA
Boris Karloff, Marian Marsh, Robert Allen, John Buckler. Directed by Roy William Neill. 67 min.

In this above-average Gothic thriller, Karloff plays twin brothers—one good, one evil (of course). The bad one inherits the family baronetcy; when the good one returns home and the townspeople clamor for him to take over, the evil one plots to take his place. Atmospheric and well photographed.

BLACK SABBATH ★★★½
1964, Italy
Boris Karloff, Mark Damon, Suzy Anderson, Jacqueline Pierrieux. Directed by Mario Bava. 99 min.

One of master horror stylist Mario Bava's most fully realized works. (Perhaps working on three compact tales reined in his often excessive visual overkill.) The result is a shuddery evening for fans of the macabre. The first tale is about a woman who steals a ring from a corpse, the second concerns mysterious death threats by phone, and the third deals with a family of vampires that feeds only on its close relatives. Guaranteed nightmares; some scenes, such as that of the first story's vengeful dead woman rising to reclaim her possession, linger in the memory.

THE BLACK SIX ★★½
1974, USA, R
Gene Washington, Carl Eller, Lem Barney, "Mean" Joe Greene, Willie Lanier, Rosalind Miles. Directed by Matt Cimber. 90 min.

This attempt to do for a half-dozen football stars what promoters these days are doing with wrestling stars—turn them into movie idols—has enough going for it in the script that you wish some of its other elements were more successful. Our heroes are a band of Vietnam veterans who have forsaken city life for choppers and the road. When the brother of one of them is killed in a Southern town, and the police refuse to go after the killer, the six are compelled to put aside their nonviolent ways. Surprisingly, this is all written, in a relatively subdued, nonracist manner—violence is convincingly shown as a last resort, used only in self-defense. Unfortunately, the whole thing is slow and drawn out—this *is* supposed to be an action movie. Gets an extra half star for the character names, which include Frenchy La Boise, Jr., Brother Williams, Moose King, and Thor.

THE BLACK STALLION ★★★½
1979, USA, G
Teri Garr, Kelly Reno, Mickey Rooney, Clarence Muse, Hoyt Axton. Directed by Carroll Ballard. 118 min.

In his first fiction feature, Carroll Ballard brings Walter Farley's classic 1941 children's novel to life in a way that may enrapture grown-ups even more than their kids. The first half of the movie, in which the stallion and his young friend (Kelly Reno) are marooned on a gorgeous, rocky island, is a ravishing visual show. When the story returns to America, some of the wonder is lost, though Mickey Rooney is delightful as the avuncular horse trainer.

THE BLACK STALLION RETURNS ★½
1983, USA, PG
Kelly Reno, Vincent Spano, Allen Goorwitz, Jodi Thelen, Teri Garr. Directed by Robert Dalva. 103 min.

In the sequel to 1979's *The Black Stallion*, young Alec Ramsay (Kelly Reno) stows away on a Pan Am clipper and crosses the Sahara on a camel, trying to retrieve his kidnapped horse from its original Berber owners. We're supposed to feel Alec has mastered his exotic surroundings (as he did in the far superior first film), but the story and dialogue are so silly that you wish the kid would return home to his mother.

BLACK SUNDAY ★★★
1961, Italy
Barbara Steel, John Richardson, Ivo Garrani, Andrea Checchi. Directed by Mario Bava. 83 min.

A terrific atmospheric horror film, it is photographed in eerie black and white without gore but with many moments that are still shocking to jaded 1980s audiences. Set in the nineteenth century, the story concerns a witch, accidentally resurrected by two doctors, who sets about gaining vengeance on the descendants of those who sent her to the stake. Exceptional first feature from ex-cinematographer Bava.

BLACK SUNDAY ★★★
1977, USA, R
Bruce Dern, Marthe Keller, Robert Shaw, Fritz Weaver, Steven Keats, Bekim Fehmiu, Michael V. Gazzo, William Daniels. Directed by John Frankenheimer. 143 min.

The John Frankenheimer–Robert Evans movie about Black September terrorists who harness the Goodyear blimp to bombard the Super Bowl is among the best of a very tired breed: the disaster thriller. Taut and suspenseful, abounding with clever scenes and skillfully orchestrated action, it remains gripping throughout, due largely to the momentarily rejuvenated Frankenheimer's inspired directorial strategies: he gets us rooting for both teams at once and lets us have our disaster and its interception, too.

But Bruce Dern's imaginative, quirky performance as the blimp's ex-POW pilot, half backslapping glad-hander and half twisted loser, is good enough to make us wish for similarly rich characterizations from the film's other two principals: Marthe Keller as a glamorous terrorist and Robert Shaw as the Israeli general on her trail. Unfortunately, they remain one-dimensional. Screenplay by Ernest Lehman, based on a novel by Thomas Harris.

BLACK WIDOW ☆☆☆
1987, USA, R
Debra Winger, Theresa Russell, Sami Frey, Dennis Hopper, Nicol Williamson, Terry O'Quinn, James Hong, Diane Ladd, Lois Smith, Mary Woronov, D.W. Moffett, David Mamet. Directed by Bob Rafelson. 110 min.

Black Widow is a tantalizing suspense thriller with a welcome sense of humor; in fact, at times one could almost call it a black comedy. A Justice Department investigator (Debra Winger) tries to nail an elusive murderess fond of wedding, bedding, and dispatching men who are as wealthy as they are unsuspecting. The cat-and-mouse game is beautifully played by Winger and Theresa Russell, but one wishes that the exceptional supporting cast had more to do.

THE BLACK WINDMILL ☆☆
1974, Great Britain, PG
Michael Caine, Donald Pleasence, Delphine Seyrig, Clive Revill, John Vernon, Joss Ackland, Janet Suzman. Directed by Don Siegel. 106 min.

A slothful spy-versus-spy-versus-spy drama, it starts strongly but ends in a morass of clichés. Michael Caine plays an operative whose son is kidnapped by one of his own men, who turns the suspicion on Caine himself. The complex plot is well established but fails to build to an exciting or even coherent conclusion.

BLACULA ☆½
1972, USA, R
William Marshall, Vonetta McGee, Denise Nicholas, Thalmus Rasulala. Directed by William Crain. 92 min.

Black exploitation meets low-budget horror. Count Dracula puts the bite on a cultured African prince and turns him into an enemy of the people. Blacula wakes up in L.A. after being imported with the rest of his furniture, and he hits the bars to find some fresh blood. Not that scary, and cheaply made. Followed by *Scream, Blacula, Scream*.

BLADE ☆☆
1973, USA, PG
John Marley, Jon Cypher, William Prince, John Schuck, Kathryn Walker. Directed by Ernest Pintoff. 90 min.

A woman-hating killer stalks his quarry while a grizzled New York veteran cop sets his cap for the devious murderer. The traditional psychopathic slasher genre gets a workout here, back in the days when all madmen dedicated themselves to the memory of Jack the Ripper and weren't out terrorizing tumescent teens at summer camps. Urban local color is captured with gritty élan, and this atmosphere serves to remind us of how our teeming cities seem to breed psychotics, as well as providing enough holes for them to hide in.

THE BLADE MASTER ☆½
1984, USA, PG
Miles O'Keeffe, Lisa Foster, Charles Borromel, Chen Wong. Directed by David Hills. 92 min.

This is a plodding kids' movie with lots of important messages and correct behavior on the part of the hero, and some hacking sword work done to various anatomical parts of the bad guys. Miles O'Keeffe (*Tarzan, the Ape Man*) has a washboard stomach and an ironing board screen presence; however, he does manage to act the animal skins off Charles Borromel and the eternally stunned Lisa Foster. Strictly background noise for a rainy day; if the kids are really misbehaving, make them sit through the original *Ator, the Fighting Eagle*, too.

BLADE RUNNER ☆☆☆½
1982, USA, R
Harrison Ford, Rutger Hauer, Sean Young, Joe Turkel, Daryl Hannah, Joanna Cassidy. Directed by Ridley Scott. 114 min.

This film is a truly great neo-*noir* science-fiction vision of the future, through the cinematic past, darkly. Obsessed, murderous androids are loose in decaying Los Angeles, and only retired cop Rick Deckard can stop them. *Blade Runner* is complex, allusive, and amazing to look at, and it's hampered only slightly by Deckard's deliberately hokey voice-over narration. The production design, by Lawrence G. Paull, creates a vast and magnificently seedy underworld tableau.

BLAME IT ON RIO ☆☆
1984, USA, R
Michael Caine, Joseph Bologna, Michelle Johnson, Valerie Harper, Demi Moore. Directed by Stanley Donen. 110 min.

This soft-core sex romp about a recently separated middle-ager (Michael Caine) who has a torrid affair with his best friend's teenage daughter may be vile at its core, but it's also crudely enjoyable. Caine and Joseph Bologna play coffee execs who've taken their daughters on a vacation in Rio de Janeiro. Michelle Johnson plays a dreamy Valley Girl nymph who wastes no time making her "Uncle Matthew" erotic offers he can't refuse. There's enough skin on display for a *Playboy* spread, but the movie's real subject is a friendship on a collision course, and Stanley Donan's spit-and-polish craftsmanship keeps the gags hopping.

BLAME IT ON THE NIGHT ☆½
1984, USA, PG
Nick Mancuso, Byron Thames, Richard Bakalyan, Leslie Ackerman, Billy Preston, Merry Clayton. Directed by Gene Taft. 84 min.

This is a corny story about a rock star who discovers that the mother of his thirteen-year-old son has died. In a fit of loneliness or altruism or something, he decides to take the boy, who has lived in a military boarding school since the age of five and whom he has never met, on the road with him. Nick Mancuso is badly miscast as a rock star, although the songs written for him by Ted Neely and Tom Scott hardly qualify as rock, anyway. The premise can't help but evoke a few tears for those predisposed to like this type of soap opera, but the rest is a drag.

THE BLAZING NINJA ☆½
1985, Hong Kong
Philip Cheung, Sony Tanaka, Ronny Lee, Tim Chen, Sandy Peng. Directed by Godfrey Ho. 86 min.

There's nothing like a Japanese occupation to get up the dander of Chinese patriots, and there's plenty of hard-hitting fighting in this Godfrey Ho kung fu film. Virulently anti-Japanese, with no sense of the war period, the movie has nothing to do with ninjas—the title intends only to capitalize on the ninja craze. Poor production values and a chopped-off print.

BLAZING SADDLES ☆☆☆☆
1974, USA, R
Cleavon Little, Gene Wilder, Madeline Kahn, Harvey Korman, Slim Pickens, Mel Brooks, David Huddleston, Dom DeLuise. Directed by Mel Brooks. 93 min.

An outrageously irreverent comedy that dismantles all the myths of the Old West with great, nasty flair, *Blazing Saddles* was the first and remains one of the best of Mel Brooks's genre spoofs. The sketchy story concerns a black sheriff assigned to the unfriendly, un-black Western town of Rock Ridge, but it's no more than an excuse for a machine-gun succession of gags that upend every cowboy convention. The cast is wonderfully hammy, with top honors going to Madeline Kahn as Lili Von Shtupp, a barroom chanteuse whose world-weary solo would put Marlene Dietrich to shame. Andrew Bergman (*Fletch*) and Richard Pryor were among those who contributed to the uneven screenplay, whose humor treads a delicate line between spoofing racism and falling prey to it.

BLESS THE BEASTS AND CHILDREN ★★★½
1972, USA, PG
Bill Mumy, Barry Robins, Miles Chapin, Darel Claser, Bob Kramer. Directed by Stanley Kramer. 101 min.

A message picture that never preaches is definitely a plus, but when real characterizations are added and an interesting story glides the movie along, an exceptional film is created. *Bless* is the funny, genuinely touching story of a gang of misfits who band together to fight a government-sponsored buffalo hunt. Directed by Stanley Kramer with a good feel for his actors and a fine sense of satire. Based on the fine juvenile novel by Glendon Swarthout.

BLIND DATE ★★½
1984, USA, R
Joseph Bottoms, Kirstie Alley, Keir Dullea, James Daughton. Directed by Nico Mastorakis. 99 min.

An advertising executive (Joseph Bottoms) is accidentally blinded while pursuing a long-lost love. After a doctor implants a computer inside his skull that allows him to see, the executive uses his newfound abilities to catch a psychopathic killer who is trailing her. Skillfully directed by Nico Mastorakis, *Blind Date* has a lot of innovative visual touches, but doesn't start to really get going until its midpoint, when the picture replaces superfluous slashings with nail-biting suspense. Kirstie Alley shines as Bottoms's concerned girlfriend, while the rest of the beautiful females in the cast gleefully shed their clothing before getting killed.

BLIND FIST OF BRUCE ★★
Hong Kong
Ho Tsun Tao, Yuen Shui Tu, Tiger Yeung, Lam Kin Min, Simon Yuen, Chaing Tao. Directed by Kam Bo.

Despite the title, Ho Tsun Tao is not in his usual role of a Bruce Lee imitator, and he proves to be an interesting actor in his own right. Here he plays a bank owner who learns kung fu from a blind teacher in order to save the town from a gang of thugs.

BLIND MAN'S BLUFF

See *Cauldron of Blood*

BLIND RAGE ★
1978, Philippines, R
D'Urville Martin, Leo Fong, Fred Williamson, Tony Adair. Directed by Efren C. Pinon. 80 min.

Blind rage is what you'll feel after watching this. Five blind men (representing several different nationalities, character types, etc.) decide that the best way to prove their ability to fit into society is to behave like a growing number of the populace, i.e., to become criminals. Once again, the Philippines proves filmmaking is not its forte by delivering an inept, slapdash action film that does nothing toward appreciating the plight of the blind.

BLISS ★★★
1985, Australia, R
Barry Otto, Lynette Curran, Helen Jones, Miles Buchanan, Gia Carides, Tim Robertson. Directed by Ray Lawrence. 111 min.

In this audacious, unsettling black comedy from Australia, Harry Joy (Barry Otto), an advertising executive who suffers a heart attack, has a vision of damnation, and comes back to life convinced he's living in Hell—and he's determined to prove it. The evidence, at first, is overwhelming, but Harry finds salvation in the form of a holistic hooker named Honey Barbara (Helen Jones). This is the first feature directed by Ray Lawrence, and there's a charge to his surrealistic imagery and a visionary undertone not unlike that of Buñuel. But whereas Buñuel's films teem with blasphemous fury, *Bliss* is imbued with the righteous zeal of the true believer. Winner of the Australian Academy Award for Best Picture.

THE BLOB ★★★
1958, USA
Steve McQueen, Aneta Corsaut, Earl Rowe, Olin Howlin. Directed by Irvin S. Yeaworth, Jr. 85 min.

A small ball of slime comes from outer space and begins to engulf the inhabitants of a little town. Only our stalwart teen heroes Steve and Judy can stop this red menace, but how? The central premise of this cheap scare film is Jell-O on the rampage, and it makes for good gooey horror, with Steve McQueen appropriately stolid in his first big role. Probably because it deliriously embraces every cliché of its genre, *The Blob* has ascended to minor classic status. Whether or not that's justified, it remains good, hokey fun.

BLOCK-HEADS ★★★½
1938, USA
Stan Laurel, Oliver Hardy, Patricia Ellis, Minna Gombell, Billy Gilbert, Jimmy Finlayson. Directed by John G. Blystone. 58 min.

In this first-rate Laurel and Hardy feature, World War I has been over for twenty years, but someone forgot to tell Stan; he's still guarding the trenches. Ollie takes him home, where the two of them get into some strange encounters with an automatic garage door, a dump truck, and a long flight of stairs.

BLONDE VENUS ★★½
1932, USA
Marlene Dietrich, Cary Grant, Herbert Marshall, Dickie Moore, Sidney Toler. Directed by Josef Von Sternberg. 89 min.

This film is a real oddity—a typically opulent Dietrich-Von Sternberg vehicle cross-pollinated with a 1930s mother-love weepie. Neither genre gets the upper hand and the movie gets lost in the shuffle, but Josef Von Sternberg's direction and the cast are not devoid of interest. Marlene Dietrich needs dough to pay for hubby Herbert Marshall's operation and (horror of horrors!) she has to sacrifice herself to Cary Grant to get it. Only the silliest movie would then have her suffer at the hands of her husband, who can't forgive and forget when he finds out. Still, if you can overlook the constraints of this plot, Dietrich is something to behold in her "Hot Voodoo" number, which she performs while peeling herself out of an ape suit! This makes up for the fact that she's just not comfortable playing a suffering mother figure cast aside by society.

BLOOD AND BLACK LACE ★★½
1965, Italy/France/West Germany, R
Cameron Mitchell, Eva Bartok, Thomas Reiner, Arianna Gonni. Directed by Mario Bava. 88 min.

The lurid preoccupations of this slick psycho-thriller were some years ahead of movie trends. The models of Countess Christina's house of high fashion design are, one by one, the victims of gruesome murder. Who could the black-gloved killer be, and what is his twisted motivation? From the director of *Black Sunday*, *Twitch of the Death Nerve*, *Beyond the Door II*, *Lisa and the Devil*, and others.

BLOOD AND SAND
1922, USA ★★★
Rudolph Valentino, Lila Lee, Nita Naldi, George Field, Walter Long, Rose Rosanova, Leo White. Directed by Fred Niblo. 80 min.

Rudolph Valentino whips up a hot Spanish wind as a poor boy who becomes a famous matador. Nowadays his flagrant sexuality and constant preening may seem ridiculous; however, in his own time Valentino touched off a national debate about whether American men could really be sexy. Judge for yourself. The bullfighting sequences are exciting, the story is very simple, and the scenes of Rudolph being pursued by an amorous widow (Nita Naldi) are ripe. Neither this version nor the 1941 Tyrone Power vehicle really do justice to the Vincente Blasco Ibañez novel, but they are both fun to watch.

BLOOD AND SAND
1941, USA ★★½
Tyrone Power, Linda Darnell, Rita Hayworth, Nazimova, Anthony Quinn, J. Carroll Naish, John Carradine, Laird Cregar, George Reeves. Directed by Rouben Mamoulian. 123 min.

This remake of the old Rudolph Valentino bullfight melodrama is pretty hoary stuff, but it's worth seeing for the spectacular color photography. Although the film is in Technicolor, it is much more realistic and less lurid than other films in that process tended to be at the time. That aside, the story is mildly interesting, but Tyrone Power is not optimally cast as a Spaniard and the film as a whole is a bit too long, with several unnecessary songs thrown in to pad the length.

BLOOD BEACH
1980, USA, R ★
David Huffman, Mariana Hill, John Saxon. Directed by Jeffrey Bloom. 90 min.

This film is predicated on one of the dumbest ideas for a horror film ever—killer sand. Production values are nonexistent on this one, unless one counts suntan lotion.

THE BLOOD BEAST TERROR
1967, Great Britain ★
Peter Cushing, Robert Flemyng, Wanda Vantham, Venessa Howard, David Griffin. Directed by Veron Sewel. 88 min.

Peter Cushing took over the starring role in this dreary period horror film after the death of Basil Rathbone; he plays, in his reliable way, a mad country scientist who has turned his daughter into a gigantic moth (!) with vampire tendencies. As he busily goes about creating a mate for his little princess, a heroic young entomologist wanders by and begins to realize what's happening. Will goodness triumph, or will everyone have huge holes in his clothes for the rest of his natural life? (a.k.a.: *The Vampire Beast Craves Blood*)

BLOODBROTHERS
1978, USA, R ★
Paul Sorvino, Tony Lo Bianco, Richard Gere, Lelia Goldoni, Yvonne Wilder, Kenneth McMillan, Marilu Henner. Directed by Robert Mulligan. 116 min.

The stifling closeness of his working-class Italian-American family threatens to turn teenage hothead Stony DeCoco (Richard Gere) into a blowhard small-timer like his father and uncle. Italian soap operas are probably more interesting than WASP ones because they're genuinely operatic, but this one is full of cheap melodrama and preposterously hammy performances, and Bill Conti's noisily upbeat score is perhaps the worst one written in the 1970s. Robert Mulligan doesn't hit a single convincing note. From the movie-influenced novel by Richard Price (*Ladies' Man*). (a.k.a.: *A Father's Love*)

BLOODED TREASURY FIGHT
Hong Kong ★★½
David Chaing, Tan Tao-Liang, Chen Hui-Min, Wang Chun, Hsia Kuang-Li, Tsia Hung. Directed by Pao Husueh.

To obtain his freedom, a criminal (David Chaing) signs on for a dangerous government mission to find a fortune in hidden pearls. Unfortunately for them, an evil general (Chen Hui-Min) is also after the treasure. Above-average martial arts, and a nicely twisted plot.

BLOOD FEAST
1961, USA ½★
Thomas Wood, Mal Arnold, Connie Mason, Scott H. Hall. Directed by Herschell Gordon Lewis. 58 min.

In this crude, gross, and silly film, the status-conscious Mrs. Fremont engages exotic Egyptian caterer Fuad Ramses to create a special twenty-first birthday party for her daughter Suzette. Ramses prepares a blood feast using parts of girls he has murdered and mutilated for the purpose. Perfect entertainment of its—admittedly unambitious—kind. Director Herschell Gordon Lewis pioneered the splatter movie form, and has also been responsible for such disgusting pictures as *2000 Maniacs*, *Color Me Blood Red*, *The Wizard of Gore*, and *The Gruesome Twosome*.

BLOOD FEUD
1983, USA (TV) ★★★½
Robert Blake, Cotter Smith, Danny Aiello, Edward Albert, Brian Dennehy, Ernest Borgnine, Forrest Tucker, José Ferrer. Directed by Mike Newell. 200 min.

This is a powerful enactment of the years of battle between Teamsters big shot Jimmy Hoffa and U.S. Attorney General Robert Kennedy. Within the framework of the power plays of the labor movement and the political maneuvering, the film also creates a vivid portrait of the personalities of the two men locking horns over the law. Robert Blake is extraordinary as the pint-sized dictator; like his work in *In Cold Blood*, this shows him at the height of his acting powers.

BLOOD FIEND

See *Theatre of Death*

BLOOD IN THE STREETS
1974, France/Italy, R ★★
Oliver Reed, Fabio Testi, Agostina Belli. Directed by Sergio Sollima. 111 min.

Kidnappers hold the wife of an Italian prison official (Oliver Reed) as ransom for an inmate in his charge (Fabio Testi). But when he learns that the terrorists plan to murder the prisoner once he's released, the warden forms an alliance with the prisoner to vanquish their common enemies. Precious little of the comely Agostina Belli, but heaps of blood and chases until the finale, which is mired in philosophizing about the ethics of political assassinations, an Italian preoccupation for the past two decades.

BLOOD LEGACY
1973, USA ★★
John Carradine, Faith Domergue, Jeff Morrow, Merry Anders, Buck Kartalian. Directed by Carl Monson. 77 min.

Just when you think they've used up every possible plot under the sun, some young genius thinks up something new to thrill and chill us with. Get this: the children of an old millionaire must spend a night in his spooky mansion in order to claim the inheritance. Wow! Not only are they terrified of the creepy place, but someone is out to kill them! If it were any worse, the film might be worth watching for laughs, but it's mildly competent—and therefore incredibly dull. The only virture is a good cast that includes

John Carradine, Faith Domergue and Jeff Morrow, two venerable icons of many a 1950s sci-fi epic, and the immortal Buck Kartalian, star of *Please Don't Eat My Mother*. *Legacy of Blood* was the original release title of this film, but it was also the title of an awful Andy Milligan gore film with almost exactly the same plot. (a.k.a.: *Legacy of Blood*)

BLOODLINE ☆☆
1979, USA, R
Audrey Hepburn, Ben Gazzara, James Mason, Claudia Mori, Irene Papas, Michelle Phillips, Maurice Ronet, Romy Schneider, Omar Sharif, Beatrice Straight, Gert Frobe, Marcel Bozzuffi. Directed by Terence Young. 116 min.

This dull, all-star fluff is based on a novel by trashmaster Sidney Sheldon about a glamorous pharmaceutical heiress, a string of prostitute murders, a stock takeover, and the sexual ups and downs of a family with closets full of skeletons and *haute couture*. Although *Bloodline* had the potential to be an entertaining sleaze wallow, director Terence Young makes the fatal mistake of trying to make some narrative sense out of it. The result is two hours of utter boredom, redeemed only in part by the efforts of a cast that takes it all quite seriously. Audrey Hepburn, in one of her rare latter-day screen appearances, is only adequate, and a bit old for the ingenueish leading role, but her fans will be pleased. Her costumes are by Givenchy; this is the kind of film in which that credit is among the most important.

BLOOD MANIA ½☆
1970, USA, R
Peter Carpenter, Maria De Aragon, Vikki Peters, Alex Rocco. Directed by Robert O'Neil. 88 min.

An evil blond vixen arranges to have her father killed in order to get his inheritance so she can pay off her boyfriend's blackmailer. Unfortunately, it turns out that her sister inherits everything. The final sequence has some violent and gory killings, if that's what you're into, but you'll have to sit through the other seventy minutes of this soporific sleaze first.

BLOOD OF A POET ☆☆☆☆
1930, France
Lee Miller, Pauline Carton, Odette Talazac. Diected by Jean Cocteau. 58 min.

Surreal, mannered, theatrical fun from Jean Cocteau (his first film), this is a series of four dreamy, death-obsessed episodes that take place in the split second before a crumbling chimney hits the ground. Many of Cocteau's familiar images and icons are here, such as the linking of sexual desire and the "danger of death." The result is occasionally artificial, but is more often sublime. Not as dramatically satisfying as Cocteau's narratives (*La Belle et la Bête, Orpheus*), but in some ways even more haunting. (a.k.a.: *Le Sang d'un Poète*)

BLOOD OF DRACULA'S CASTLE ☆
1967, USA
Alex D'Arcy, Paula Raymond, John Carradine, Ray Young, Vicki Volante. Directed by Al Adamson and Jean Hewitt. 84 min.

About the only reason you could ever have for watching an Al Adamson movie is if you're a serious student of the great cinematographers of our time, since both Vilmos Zsigmond and Laszlo Kovacs got their start filming Adamson's abysmal low-budget cheapies. This one was shot by Kovacs, but it's not even interesting for that. The production is too cheap, and the final film is so grainy that it looks as if it were shot on secondhand stock. The typically feeble plot has Dracula and his bride (here called Count and Countess Townsend) chaining up young women and draining their blood with a hypodermic needle so they can drink it as cocktails. The exact function of codirector Jean Hewitt is not clear; his presence certainly didn't raise Adamson's standards. (a.k.a.: *Dracula's Castle*)

BLOOD OF THE DRAGON ½☆
Hong Kong
Jimmy Wang Yu, Chiao Chiao, Nu Lang, Yang Yang. Directed by Kao Pao Shu.

This is yet another kung fu movie about an attempt to get through enemy lines with the rebels' plans. This one's marginally enlivened by lots of swordplay. (a.k.a.: *Desperate Chase*)

BLOOD OF THE DRAGON PERIL ½☆
Hong Kong
Jerry Chan, Philip Cheung, Marty Chui, Robby Ban, Edie Wang, Judy Suh, Edwin Lau. Directed by Rocky Man. 86 min.

A masked fighter, "Doll Bright," is helping the villagers against the Japanese. Too bad he couldn't help this movie. Poor choreography, an overabundant use of trampolines and wires, terrible camerawork, an unbelievable story line, and horrible acting.

BLOOD OF THE UNDEAD

See *Schizo*.

THE BLOOD ON SATAN'S CLAW ☆☆½
1970, Great Britain, R
Linda Hayden, Patrick Wymark, Barry Andrews. Directed by Piers Haggard. 93 min.

A plowman uncovers a "deformed anatomy" in his field in seventeenth-century rural England, unleashing the very devil among his friends and neighbors. The young people, led by the bewitching Angel Blake, take to heathen forms of worship, and a local judge with a city education must try to put a stop to the deviltry. Creepy period piece full of lurking evil and understated beauty. (a.k.a.: *Satan's Skin*)

BLOOD ON THE MOON ☆☆☆
1948, USA
Robert Mitchum, Barbara Bel Geddes, Robert Preston, Walter Brennan, Phyllis Thaxter, Tom Tully. Directed by Robert Wise. 86 min.

One of the postwar "new" Westerns, this is not always successful but is still worth checking out. Cowboy Robert Mitchum rides into the middle of a range war between ranchers and settlers, and hires himself out to an old acquaintance who is plotting to use the skirmishes to his own advantage. The main theme, as in so many postwar, pre-McCarthy Hollywood films, is conscience, but director Robert Wise doesn't let it predominate to the point where it gets in the way of the action.

BLOOD ON THE SUN ☆☆☆
1945, USA
James Cagney, Sylvia Sidney, Wallace Ford, Rosemary De Camp, Robert Armstrong, John Emery. Directed by Frank Lloyd. 98 min.

Believe it or not, James Cagney was once considered a Communist sympathizer; therefore, as if to remove any doubt about his actual politics, he made a series of ultrapatriotic pictures like this one about a journalist in 1930s Tokyo who uncovers Japan's plan for world conquest. Interestingly, Lester Cole, who wrote the screenplay, was later blacklisted as a Communist sympathizer; he was one of the Hollywood Ten. Politics aside, the film is a swift, appropriately coarse-textured examination of embryonic totalitarianism. Overly melodramatic at times, but rarely unexciting.

BLOOD ON THE SUN ☆☆
Hong Kong
Chang Ching Ching, Tieng Peng, Yang Hsiao Ping, Yu Yuan. Directed by James Kong.

China, 1936: the Phoenix Martial Arts Club is smuggling saltpeter, used in the manufacture of gunpowder, to munitions plants during the Japanese occupation. Potentially intriguing adventure is cluttered with foul language and exceedingly violent action. Good for those with cast-iron stomachs, less so for the kiddies. Not to be confused with the James Cagney film bearing this title.

BLOOD ORGY OF THE SHE-DEVILS ☆
1973, USA
Lila Zaborin. Directed by Ted V. Mikels. 73 min.

A witch commands a "wolf pack of voluptuous virgins" and consigns those who displease her to "a terrifying, screaming plunge to the depths of hell" by means of the black arts. Cheap, stupid, and badly made; from the director of *The Corpse Grinders* and *Astro Zombies*.

BLOOD SIMPLE ☆☆
1984, USA, R
John Getz, Frances McDormand, Dan Hedaya, M. Emmet Walsh, Samm-Art Williams. Directed by Joel Coen. 97 min.

A tepid, rather ordinary tale of lust and murder in Texas whose twists depend on the stupidity of its characters, *Blood Simple* was made independently by two N.Y.U. film grad brothers, and garnered unwarranted critical attention. Director Joel Coen has drenched the movie in stylistic flourishes and homages to virtually every *noir* filmmaker in history, and what results is a slick, "knowing" enterprise without one original moment. The violence is undeniably well handled, so exaggerated that it becomes funny. As for the rest, it's disturbingly eager to subvert its hackneyed scenes with show-offy camerawork. It's not enough for Coen and his writer-brother Ethan to prove that they can pull off an old-fashioned betrayal-and-reversal piece; they also keep telling you that they're too cool not to smirk at it. This is a rip-off, in style and substance, that asks you to applaud its awarenesss of its own secondhand nature. Whatever charms that holds, creativity isn't one of them.

BLOOD SISTERS

See *Sisters*

THE BLOOD-SPATTERED BRIDE ☆½
1969, Spain
Simon Andrew, Maribel Martin, Alexandra Bastedo. Directed by Vincent Aranda. 82 min.

This is one of the subgenre of lesbian-vampire films that flourished in the early 1970s, most of them deriving in some part from the novel *Carmilla* by Sheridan Le Fanu. A newlywed couple are trapped in an ancient castle where their hostess is the reincarnation of a long-dead murderess. Some strange, jolting sexual imagery, but, on the whole, a weak attempt. (a.k.a.: *Bloody Fiancée*)

THE BLOODSUCKERS ☆☆½
1970, Great Britain, PG
Patrick MacNee, Patrick Mower, Peter Cushing, Imogen Hassall. Directed by Robert Hartford-Davies. 90 min.

A young woman in Greece loses her fiancé to the undead. He is a college professor who gets lured into a coven of vampires by their ability to satisfy his odd sexual fetishes. A peculiar, seldom-seen film, not wholly successful—but different. Not to be confused with *Return from the Past/Dr. Terror's Gallery of Horrors*, which uses the same title as another alternate. (a.k.a.: *Incense for the Damned* and *Doctors Wear Scarlet*)

BLOODSUCKING FREAKS ½☆
1978, USA, R (originally X)
Niles McMaster. Directed by Joel M. Reed. 89 min.

In this repellent, clumsy attempt at gross-out humor, an S & M theater in New York's SoHo district uses real victims, even though the audience thinks it's all fake. Fingers are chopped off, nipples are electrified, and there's a notorious scene in which a sicko drills into a woman's head and sucks out the insides with a straw. Need we say more? (a.k.a.: *The Incredible Torture Show!*)

BLOODTHIRSTY BUTCHERS ☆
1970, USA, R
John Miranda, Annabella Wood, Berwick Kaler. Directed by Andy Milligan. 80 min.

Andy Milligan and his 16 mm camera leave Staten Island for once and go to England, where he turns out another cheap gore film that is indistinguishable from his homegrown ones. This is another version of "The Demon Barber of Fleet Street," the story that was also the basis for the Broadway musical *Sweeney Todd*, which is much better company than Milligan deserves to be in. In his version, the emphasis is on the blood and guts spilled by the barber and baker who decide to fill a meat shortage by producing human meat pies. No songs, no thrills, no fun.

BLOOD TIDE ☆
1982, Great Britain/Greece, R
James Earl Jones, José Ferrer, Lila Kedrova, Deborah Shelton, Martin Kove, Mary Louise Weller. Directed by Richard Jefferies. 82 min.

Some young Americans in Greece become involved in a cult ritual that calls forth a rubbery sea monster. Whatever potential gloom lay in this idea is quickly dispelled by the radiant clarity of the Greek coast, the languor of the people enjoying it, and the hamming of James Earl Jones as a treasure-seeking onetime Shakespearean. José Ferrer and Lila Kedrova are the other misplaced guest stars.

BLOOD WEDDING ☆☆☆
1981, Spain
Antonia Gades, Cristina Hoyos, Juan Antonio Jiminez, Pilar Cardenas, Carmen Villena. Directed by Carlos Saura. 70 min.

Carlos Saura's spare, intense adaptation of the Garcia Lorca play isn't as visually rich or as masterfully handled as his *Carmen*, but he fills the screen with enough superb choreography to satisfy most dance enthusiasts. The film is framed as a dance rehearsal, and the self-consciousness of Saura's techniques make *Blood Wedding* more suitable for viewers already familiar with the narrative than for newcomers to the work.

BLOODY FIANCÉE

See *The Blood-Spattered Bride*

THE BLOODY FIGHT ½☆
Hong Kong
Alan Tang, Tan Chin, Fu In-In. Directed by Ng Tien Tsu.

The pre–Bruce Lee fighting and choreography of this film may put you to sleep. If that fails, there's a plot about the Japanese beating up the locals that's sure to succeed.

THE BLOODY FIST ☆½
1969, Hong Kong
Chen Hsing, Chen Kuan-Tai, Lui Ta Chuan, San Lau, Fong Yeh. Directed by Yuen Wo Ping.

A plague hits a Japanese town and fugitives help by capturing a panacea called "Dragon Herb" and by destroying the town leader. Low-grade kung fu activity has a fair plot but lame action footage.

BLOODY MAMA ☆☆½
1970, USA, R
Shelley Winters, Pat Hingle, Robert De Niro, Don Stroud. Directed by Roger Corman. 92 min.

The title is no exaggeration: the bloody exploits of Ma Barker and her legendary clan of criminal sons constitute a violent depiction of crime during the Depression years. Some will call it a trashy imitation of *Bonnie and Clyde*, but the staging is dynamic, and Shelley Winters, Don Stroud, and young Robert De Niro deliver strong performances as the brutal public enemies. Because of its visual and thematic potency, the film epitomized Roger Corman's works as an auteur.

BLOOMFIELD

See *The Hero*

BLOW OUT ☆☆☆☆
1981, USA, R
John Travolta, Nancy Allen, Dennis Franz, John Lithgow. Directed by Brian De Palma. 108 min.

Brian De Palma's suspense drama about a film sound editor who inadvertently tapes a politician's murder owes less to Alfred Hitchcock than does most of his other work, and is his best film so far. It's a heady mélange of *Blow-Up*, *The Conversation*, and Chappaquiddick, full of cinematic flourish and clever, dynamic editing—and, for once, the self-conscious technical dazzle serves a purpose, since film technology is the actual subject of *Blow Out*. Travolta is fine as the audio wizard whose penchant for eavesdropping has gotten him into trouble once before, and the versatile John Lithgow has a grand time wth the role of a baby-voiced psychotic killer. You may quarrel with *Blow Out*'s ending, but its deliberate contrivance is right in line with the rest of the film.

BLOW-UP ☆☆☆☆
1966, Great Britain/Italy, R
David Hemmings, Vanessa Redgrave, Peter Bowles, Sarah Miles, John Castle, Verushka, Harry Hutchinson, the Yardbirds. Directed by Michelangelo Antonioni. 111 min.

On the surface, this is a uniquely elegant vision of swinging 1960s London and maybe the most fun that any art movie can give. David Hemmings stars as a mod fashion photographer who may have accidentally photographed an anonymous murder in his pursuit of the beautiful and elusive Vanessa Redgrave. When the film is developed and the image enlarged, he becomes obsessed with penetrating its mystery. Underneath it all is Antonioni's search for meaning in a senseless, chaotic world. A very free adaptation of a Julio Cortázar short story, the film retains the source's gloomy, provisional point of view but adds the ironically bright, kinetic, and overadorned surface. The object of the game is to get below the frosting without becoming blinded by one's own desire to see certain things. Nice camerawork by Carlo di Palma, music by Herbie Hancock, and a smashing performance by the Yardbirds.

THE BLUE AND THE GRAY ☆☆½
1982, USA (TV)
John Hammond, Stacy Keach, Colleen Dewhurst, Lloyd Bridges, Diane Baker, Kathleen Beller, Penny Peyser, Gregory Peck, Sterling Hayden, Robert Vaughn, Paul Winfield, David Doyle, Warren Oates, Geraldine Page. Directed by Andrew V. McLaglen. 245 min.

Originally telecast as an eight-hour miniseries, this adaptation of Bruce Catton's brilliant Civil War history is just what you'd expect: one part plodding historical pageantry, one part fictionalized subplots, and more than a dash of self-importance. The story is told through the eyes of a young illustrator (John Hammond) who becomes a journalist and is thus privy to almost every major event of the war—he even gets some free career advice from President Lincoln (Gregory Peck). *Note:* The version on video has been shortened by more than two hours from the original telecast length.

THE BLUE ANGEL ☆☆☆☆
1930, USA
Marlene Dietrich, Emil Jannings, Kurt Gerron, Rosa Valenti. Directed by Josef Von Sternberg. 90 min.

Josef Von Sternberg was at his best when manipulating intricate images rather than maneuvering through story-line complexities, extracting telling looks and gestures rather than eliciting talky performances, and it's no wonder that *The Blue Angel* is one of his stellar achievements. He had just plucked a withdrawn Maria Magdalene (Marlene Dietrich) out of the ranks of Berlin actresses, and every bit of her transformation to the demimonde goddess Marlene is evident on the screen. Although the film stands as a monument to the creation of a sensual treasure, the story concerns the degradation of a man through sensuous attraction. Emil Jannings is fine as the desktop autocrat who becomes destroyed through his attraction to cabaret star Lola (Dietrich). A perfect movie for the video recorder—you should stop and examine each of Von Sternberg's crowded frames. Von Sternberg himself felt that his movies should be played backward to eliminate the distractions of narrative. Beware cut or cheap versions.

BLUEBEARD ☆☆☆
1944, USA
John Carradine, Jean Parker, Nils Asther. Directed by Edgar Ulmer. 73 min.

Lady-strangler John Carradine terrorizes the streets but then does himself in by falling for a bright and beautiful shop owner who realizes that something is amiss. The effectiveness of this suspense-thriller is testimony to Edgar Ulmer's frequently overlooked ability as a director.

BLUEBEARD ☆
1972, France/Italy/West Germany, R
Richard Burton, Raquel Welch, Joey Heatherton, Virna Lisi, Sybil Danning. Directed by Edward Dmytryk. 124 min.

Richard Burton portrays an impotent baron who methodically does away with seven beautiful wives. If only he had done away with the script. No need to mince words: the film is bad, a totally unsuccessful blend of high camp and cheap exploitation. Joey Heatherton is particularly awful—a man in a trenchcoat's answer to Sandra Dee. Look, if you must, for a young Sybil Danning as a prostitute.

BLUE CITY ☆
1986, USA, R
Judd Nelson, Ally Sheedy, Scott Wilson, David Caruso, Paul Winfield, Anita Morris. Directed by Michelle Manning. 83 min.

Welding together a *film noir* story line skimmed from Ross MacDonald's 1947 novel and the teen-sheen appeal of stars Judd Nelson and Ally Sheedy, the makers of this abysmal thriller have come up with an ungodly new subgenre: Brat Pack *noir*. Nelson is a rich troublemaker who returns to his Florida hometown to attempt a reconciliation with his father (who's the mayor), only to discover that Dad's been killed. Without wasting time investigating, he decides the guilty party is the local gambling kingpin (the quivering Scott Wilson), who's taken up with his stepmother, and proceeds to wage a one-man war. The film serves up the vigilantism that's a rote part of any Eastwood potboiler as the latest form of teen hipsterism. To a terminal smartypants like Nelson, cool redeems all sins.

BLUE COLLAR ☆☆½
1978, USA, R
Richard Pryor, Harvey Keitel, Yaphet Kotto, Ed Begley, Jr. Directed by Paul Schrader. 114 min.

Paul Schrader's first directorial effort, scripted with his brother Leonard, is a realistic, hard-driving portrait of three Detroit auto workers caught in a frustrating whirlpool of bitterness, mounting debts, and rampant union corruption. Although the film begins strongly, with a rarely seen Hollywood look at the proletariat, it quickly slips into a rather tired caper film. A nice Carter-era film of the deteriorating manufacturing class.

BLUE FIN ☆½
1978, Australia
Hardy Kruger, Greg Rowe, Elspeth Ballantyne, Liddy Clark. Directed by Carl Schultz. 90 min.

Here's a film with a slight edge. Sailing over the bounding main, a father and his estranged son go fishing and try to patch up their differences. Uninspired, but it's refreshing to see a family movie in which domestic problems aren't easily solvable in the Disney tradition. Stunning photography is an asset, too.

BLUE FIRE LADY ☆☆
1978, Australia
Cathryn Harrison, Mark Holden, Pete Cummins, Marion Edward, John Wood. Directed by Ross Dimsey. 95 min.

Much of the appeal of this Down Under version of a *National Velvet*–type story will be lost on American youngsters: male lead Mark Holden, an Australian pop star of the time, is unknown here, and the numerous references to local personalities and events only confuse matters. The basic story is straightforward: a girl sets out to rescue a horse, Blue Fire Lady, from its cruel trainer, even though everyone else thinks that it's an untamable beast. You've seen it before, but maybe the kids haven't, and they shouldn't object.

BLUE HAWAII ☆☆
1961, USA
Elvis Presley, Joan Blackman, Jenny Maxwell, Angela Lansbury, Roland Winters. Directed by Norman Taurog. 101 min.

Art imitates life . . . up to a point. Returning GI Elvis Presley plays a returning GI in this Paramount travelogue of the fiftieth state. He also plays a tour guide to the islands who gets mixed up with two women. Fifteen songs, including "Ku-U-I-Po" and "Rock-a-Hula Baby," interrupt the thrilling action. Angela Lansbury plays Elvis's mother (now *that's* inspired casting). Norman Taurog directed Elvis for the second of seven times.

THE BLUE KNIGHT ☆☆
1975, USA (TV)
George Kennedy, Alex Rocco, Glynn Turman, Verna Bloom, Joseph Wambaugh, Howard Hesseman. Directed by J. Lee Thompson. 72 min.

In this pilot for the 1975–76 television series, George Kennedy plays big, tough L.A. cop Bumper Morgan; he resists being retired by the force while hunting down the killer of his buddy. It's the plot of *Beverly Hills Cop*, but with Kennedy in the lead it plays like *Winterset* or worse. Kennedy, incidentally, replaced William Holden, who starred in the 1973 *Blue Knight* telefeature. Based on the book by Joseph Wambaugh (who has a walk-on in the film).

THE BLUE LAGOON ☆
1980, USA, R
Brooke Shields, Christopher Atkins, Leo McKern, William Daniels. Directed by Randal Kleiser. 104 min.

This second film by Randal Kleiser (whose first was *Grease*) speculates on how two ignorant children, shipwrecked on a tropical island, might grow into teenagers, discovering sex the way Mother Nature intended. Brooke Shields and Christopher Atkins ineptly play the kids, and quite apart from the absurdity of using a nude stand-in for the actress (when nudity is meant to seem clean and natural), Kleiser's effort to update an essentially Victorian view of sexual liberation is a spectacle of confusion. At times, the combination of turn-of-the-century mores, 1980s characters who resemble castaways from "Happy Days," and the kitschiest 1930s-style romantic imagery boggles the mind. And rarely has the dialogue of a studio movie provided more accidental whimsy. Based on a 1903 novel by Henry DeVere Stackpoole, first filmed in 1949.

BLUE LAMP ☆☆½
1950, Great Britain
Jack Warner, Jimmy Hanley, Dirk Bogarde, Patric Doonan, Bernard Lee, Tessie O'Shea. Directed by Basil Dearden. 82 min.

This is a solid British pseudodocumentary about the crime wave that arose in that country after World War II and the efforts of the constabulary to deal with it. Even though it's pretty much a support piece for the local bobby, Dirk Bogarde steals the movie as the main bad guy. Music-hall legend Tessie O'Shea has a cameo role as herself in a saloon scene.

THE BLUE MAX ☆☆☆
1966, USA, PG
George Peppard, James Mason, Ursula Andress, Jeremy Kemp, Carl Schell. Directed by John Guillermin. 156 min.

Despite impressive aerial pyrotechnics, this surprisingly tangy aviation drama doesn't allow the stuntwork to dwarf the drama. Of all the films featuring daredevil heroes testing their mettle in the wild blue yonder, this film maintains the most satisfying balance of stratospheric vistas and down-to-earth storytelling. If you're in the mood for a head-in-the-clouds romance and adventure, catch this first. It's a World War I drama about dogfighting and other "Curses, Red Baron!" pursuits, as told from the viewpoint of the German flying corps. Lots of fun.

BLUE MONEY ☆☆½
1984, Great Britain (TV)
Tim Curry, Debby Bishop, Billy Connolly, Dermot Crowly, Frances Tomelty. Directed by Colin Bucksey. 82 min.

This ramshackle caper comedy, about a London cabbie who suddenly finds himself in possession of an underworld kingpin's briefcase full of money, is less watchable for its silly plot than for the showcase it gives to Tim Curry. He's delightful and unexpectedly versatile in the role of the small-time driver whose big-time showbiz dreams don't quite mesh with the realities of child support and limited income. Curry's extraordinary musical mimicry of everyone from Mick Jagger to Ray Charles is reason enough to see this oddball, often charming fable, and there's nice support from Debby Bishop as his girlfriend.

THE BLUES BROTHERS ☆☆½
1980, USA, R
John Belushi, Dan Aykroyd, Carrie Fisher, James Brown, Henry Gibson, Aretha Franklin, Kathleen Freeman, Cab Calloway. Directed by John Landis. 133 min.

This is Keystone Kops taken to the nth degree. One can just feel the thirty-three-million-dollar budget going into each massive car crash (and each massive star salary). In suits, ties, and dark glasses, John Belushi and Dan Aykroyd are the modern-day Robin Hoods who stop at nothing to aid an orphanage. The saving graces are a series of numbers from such performers as Aretha Franklin (in the showstopper "Think"), James Brown, and Cab Calloway. As for the rest, no amount of money could disguise the mediocrity of the material. Directed (sloppily) by John Landis; written by Landis and Aykroyd.

BLUE SKIES AGAIN ☆½
1983, USA, PG
Harry Hamlin, Robyn Barton, Mimi Rogers, Kenneth McMillan, Dana Elcar. Directed by Richard Michaels. 110 mins.

In this dull, dim-witted sports film, a young woman is determined to make it in baseball's major leagues. "Absolutely not! It's out of the question! But wait . . . that girl can hit!" Every move is predictable, third-rate, and uninspiring. Most Valuable Player goes to the wasted Kenneth McMillan as the team's manager. Worst Error goes to Warner Bros. for producing and distributing this mess.

BLUE STEEL ☆
1934, USA
John Wayne, Eleanor Hunt, George "Gabby" Hayes, Yakima Canutt, George Nash. Directed by Robert N. Bradbury. 54 min.

In this very standard Monogram Western starring John Wayne, an undercover U.S. marshal tries to foil a mischievous plot to displace settlers from gold-rich land. Genre fans should appreciate the work of stalwarts as Yakima Canutt and Gabby Hayes, but, really, there's nothing much here.

BLUE SUNSHINE ☆☆☆
1976, USA, R
Zalman King, Deborah Winters, Mark Goddard, Robert Walden, Charles Siebert. Directed by Jeff Lieberman. 97 min.

Eerie moments abound in this capably directed shocker about delayed reactions to an experimental drug ingested ten years earlier. First, people start losing their hair; then they start losing their minds, doing bizarre things like murdering their friends and stuffing them into fireplaces. The film's a curious hybrid of detective thriller and horror flick as a man accused of the murders tries to track down the chemical motivations behind these gruesome slayings. Like the same director's *Squirm*, the film is enticingly original, delivering imaginative thrills on a low budget.

BLUE THUNDER ☆☆½
1983, USA, R
Roy Scheider, Malcolm McDowell, Candy Clark, Daniel Stern, Warren Oates. Directed by John Badham. 108 min.

You'll pay more attention to the 'copters than the characters in this high-tech thriller about an L.A. police pilot (Roy Scheider) who's handed a new assignment—the testing of the government's ultimate surveillance/attack weapon, code-named "Blue Thunder." The flight footage is dynamic, and there's a terrifically crusty performance (his last) by Warren Oates. But *Blue Thunder*'s relentless action finally undercuts the cogent message about questionable SWAT tactics that it means to impart.

BLUE VELVET ☆☆☆
1986, USA, R
Kyle MacLachlan, Laura Dern, Isabella Rossellini, Dennis Hopper, Dean Stockwell, Hope Lange, Jack Lance, Brad Dourif, Priscilla Pointer. Directed by David Lynch. 119 min.

After adapting the material of other writers in *The Elephant Man* and *Dune*, David Lynch got his first chance since *Eraserhead* to vent his own vision with *Blue Velvet*. The result, an obsessive look at sexual rot in small-time America, is neither a masterpiece nor a disgrace—with its baroque flourishes and uneasy voyeurism, it may be the most expensive and elaborate cult movie ever made. *Dune*'s Kyle MacLachlan plays the hero, a clean-cut Midwesterner who stumbles upon a severed human ear in a field and decides to investigate. The idyllic tranquillity of his small town is shattered as his search takes him into realms of sadomasochism, sexual obsession, and murder. Lynch, who won an Oscar nomination, handles the bizarre twists with panache and gets an astonishing performance out of Dennis Hopper, playing a villain of almost unearthly evil. But he may be a director who can deal *only* with the *outré*; his intentionally overlit day scenes grow tiresome, and the dialogue he gives his fresh-scrubbed ingenues means to be arch but is merely banal.

BLUME IN LOVE ☆☆☆☆
1973, USA, R
George Segal, Susan Anspach, Kris Kristofferson, Marsha Mason, Shelley Winters, Donald F. Muhich, Paul Mazursky. Directed by Paul Mazursky. 115 min.

Paul Mazursky takes a gentle, acerbic look at shattering marital traditions amid 1960s Southern California chic. George Segal plays an adulterer whose wife, gloriously played by Susan Anspach, leaves him. For him, his extracurricular fling was a trifle, but for her it meant the end. Trouble is, Segal is madly, madly in love with her, and she no longer seems to have the slightest interest in him. Mazursky's best film, *Blume in Love* aches: Its characters suffer from tragic passions reduced to absurdity by the heedless shiftings of culture. Segal has never been better, and *Blume* is the perfect embodiment of his standard character: the crass, shameless Lothario who knows he's an S.O.B. and suffers for it. A film that seems to grow with the passage of time.

BOARDING HOUSE ½☆
1982, USA, R
Hawk Adley, Alexandra Day. Directed by John Wintergate. 85 min.

It's amateur night at the slaughterhouse, as nubile boarders in a house once inhabited by psychic researchers are done to death in a variety of disgusting—though ineptly realized—ways. Parapsychological nonsense and gross slasher clichés combine to no good effect in this incompetent exercise in bottom-of-the-barrel exploitation.

BOARDING SCHOOL ☆☆
1978, West Germany, R
Nastassja Kinski, Gerry Sundquist, Carolin Ohrner, Marion Kracht, Veronique Delbourg, Sean Chapman. Directed by Andre Farwagi. 100 min.

Don't be fooled by the soft-core come-ons used to advertise this early Nastassja Kinski film rereleased to cash in on her fame. She plays an American girl, a new arrival at a European boarding school, who becomes smitten with a British youth at a neighboring boys' school. Each is the leader of a group that spends much time *discussing* sex, though the film contains only a little nudity, all tastefully done. No cheap thrills here. (a.k.a.: *Passion Flower Hotel*)

THE BOAT ☆☆☆½
1982, West Germany, PG
Jurgen Prochnow, Herbert Gronemeyer, Klaus Wennemann, Hubertus Bengsch, Martin Semmelrogge. Directed by Wolfgang Petersen. 145 min.

New German cinema director Wolfgang Petersen captures the drama and intensity of life aboard a German U-boat stationed in the Atlantic during World War II. Produced on an epic scale, *The Boat* was one of the most celebrated new German films to emerge in recent years. The dubbing is well done, but you would be better off watching the subtitled version, *Das Boot*.

THE BOAT IS FULL ☆☆☆☆
1981, Switzerland
Martin Walz, Curt Bois, Gerd David, Simone Laurent, Renate Steiger, Klaus Steiger. Directed by Markus Imhoof. 101 min.

This heartrending political film hammers home its horror tale in a simple, unemphatic manner. Instead of the usual catalog of blustery Nazi henchmen or smug polemics about the failure of civilized nations to head off the Holocaust, this film tries to define the situation without explaining it away or pointing fingers of guilt in a way to make audiences sleep easier. It deals with the deep-rooted prejudices of the neutral Swiss toward Jewish refugees seeking sanctuary in their country; the film's accomplishment is to make us comprehend what that horrendous epoch was like for both the homeless Jews and the gentiles who didn't want their well-ordered existence upset. Thought-provoking and quietly powerful without the all-star grandstanding of *Ship of Fools* or *Voyage of the Damned*. Academy Award nomination for Best Foreign Film.

THE BOATNIKS ☆☆
1970, USA, G
Robert Morse, Stefanie Powers, Phil Silvers, Don Ameche. Directed by Norman Tokar. 104 min.

The Boatniks is a slightly-better-than-normal Disney live-action film. Robert Morse is at least more professional than Dean Jones, the usual star of these opuses, and Stefanie Powers has such a genuinely attractive personality that the pair is really quite charming. Their charm has to go a long way in face of some fiercely overplayed shtick by Phil Silvers and Don Ameche. Nevertheless, the kids will like it and a reasonably tolerant adult will survive it.

BOB AND CAROL AND TED AND ALICE ☆☆☆
1969, USA, R
Natalie Wood, Robert Culp, Elliott Gould, Dyan Cannon. Directed by Paul Mazursky. 104 min.

Paul Mazursky's films (*Blume in Love*, *An Unmarried Woman*, *Willie and Phil*) generally deal with sexual mores, but none has been as famous as his first, *Bob and Carol and Ted and Alice*. Two California couples decide that they could get in touch with each other better if they merely swapped partners. Neither the sexual content nor the satiric jousts are anything to get excited over. The material is dated and harmless by today's standards, but it is also well handled, providing some amusing moments. Natalie Wood pushes too hard as a comedienne, but everyone else is exactly right at playing basically old-fashioned married people trying to adjust to the sexual revolution. The highlight is a scene between Dyan Cannon and her psychiatrist. A former ground breaker that now works as a lightweight sex comedy.

BOBBY DEERFIELD ☆½
1977, USA, PG
Al Pacino, Marthe Keller, Anny Duperey, Walter McGinn, Romolo Valli, Stephan Meldegg. Directed by Sydney Pollack. 124 min.

Sydney Pollack's romance about a "cold, calculating" Grand Prix champion and a terminally ill beauty who teaches him the joy of living was supposed to be the "new woman's film," a dignified message movie without treacle. But, as it turns out, *Bobby Deerfield* is a pretentious, clumsily written series of errors. Pollack and screenwriter Alvin Sargent have drained the performances of life and color and left them floating listlessly on an ocean of suds—Dave Grusin's schmaltzy bossa nova music, Henry Decae's postcard-pretty Swiss views, and lots of symbolically soaring balloons. Al Pacino gives a leading performance so woefully inept it would destroy a less popular actor's career, and Marthe Keller is unable to transcend the problems inherent in her character, whose truculent, manic behavior makes a ridiculous role model for the glum racer she's supposed to be inspiring.

BOBBY JO AND THE OUTLAW ☆
1976, USA, R
Marjoe Gortner, Lynda Carter, Jesse Vint, Gerrit Graham. Directed by Mark L. Lester. 88 min.

This stupid, unpleasant rural crime spree has nothing to recommend it except a nude skinny-dipping scene featuring the pre–"Wonder Woman" Lynda Carter.

BOB LE FLAMBEUR ☆☆☆½
1955, France
Roger Duchesne, Isabelle Corey, Daniel Cauchy, Howard Vernon, Guy Decomble. Directed by Jean-Pierre Melville. 95 min.

Jean-Pierre Melville's elegant homage to American gangster films preceded Godard's *Breathless*—in which he made a cameo appearance—by three years, and influenced an entire generation of French New Wave filmmakers. Roger Duchesne plays Bob, an aging and relentlessly cool ex-gangster with a chance at pulling the biggest heist of his life. Melville traces Bob's movements through the shadowy, picturesque underworld of Paris. Auguste Le Breton and Melville penned the terse, piquant dialogue.

BOBO ☆☆
1977, Hong Kong
Yang Sze, Jason Pai Piao, Wong Ha, Chin Yet Sun, San Kwei, Lau Yet Fan, Chaing Tao, Milan. Directed by Yang Sze.

Yang Sze, abandoning his usual villain's role, makes an excellent comedian playing the lovable dimwit, Bobo. He is imprisoned by corrupt village officials, but his insatiable appetite causes his jailers to beg and, finally, pay him to leave. He and his partner Ma (Jason Pai Piao) recover some stolen money and donate it to the local hospital. (a.k.a.: *Bolo the Brute*)

THE BOBO ☆☆☆
1967, USA, R
Peter Sellers, Britt Ekland, Rossano Brazzi, Adolfo Celi, Hattie Jacques. Directed by Robert Parrish. 103 min.

Not high on the best Sellers list, this does nevertheless have sufficient sight gags and another Peter Sellers ethnic impersonation to keep fans happy. He plays a singing bullfighter, not particularly skilled at either profession but (like Inspector Clouseau) supremely sure of himself. He comes to Madrid to brashly demand a week's singing engagement at the best local club. Both amused and impressed by Sellers's tenacity, the club owner agrees, but only if Sellers can seduce Britt Ekland, the city's most beautiful and icy maiden, within three days. Sellers's ability to carry on despite any and evey rejection and reasonable appeal to his good sense is both hilarious and, in a later scene, quite touching.

BODY AND SOUL ☆☆☆☆
1947, USA
John Garfield, Lilli Palmer, Hazel Brooks, Anne Revere, William Conrad. Directed by Robert Rossen. 104 min.

John Garfield's most popular and archetypical performance as the slum boy who becomes boxing champion is only one of the allures of this exceedingly good film. Robert Rossen directed the entire enterprise with vivid economy and almost palpable mood. James Wong Howe deserves kudos for his cinematography, but for most viewers it will be Garfield at his most intense and sympathetic that will enthrall.

BODY AND SOUL ☆½
1981, USA, R
Leon Isaac Kennedy, Jayne Kennedy, Michael Gazzo, Perry Lang, Peter Lawford, Muhammad Ali. Directed by George Bowers. 109 min.

Leon the Lover is a great amateur boxer who has no desire to go pro; he has too much promise as a brilliant med student. But his little sister needs an operation and he has to raise the money . . . the only way he knows how . . . with his two fists! Leon Isaac Kennedy wrote the screenplay and viewers constantly hear all the other characters tell Leon that he's a great lover, man, brother, fighter. Jayne Kennedy looks good, but all she has to do is adore. Muhammad Ali has a small role as a trainer.

BODY DOUBLE ☆☆½
1984, USA, R
Craig Wasson, Melanie Griffith, Gregg Henry, Deborah Shelton, Dennis Franz. Directed by Brian De Palma. 100 min.

This lurid hybrid of *Vertigo* by way of *Rear Window* is set in the world of pornographic filmmaking and is informed by enough references to Alfred Hitchcock to keep a generation of film students in thesis topics for years to come. Brian De Palma weaves a flashy, gory web of carefully plotted deceit that is ultimately too flimsy to support the weight of allusion heaped upon it and proves again that it's one thing to tease your audience and very much another—less appealing—thing to actively cheat on it. Some striking images, but shallow and unexpectedly restrained.

BODY HEAT ☆☆☆
1981, USA, R
William Hurt, Kathleen Turner, Richard Crenna, Ted Danson, J. A. Preston, Mickey Rourke. Directed by Lawrence Kasdan. 113 min.

Lawrence Kasdan's paean to *film noir* tends to recycle the genre's clichés, but also presents much that is fresh and original. A couple involved in a steamy affair plot to knock off the woman's husband, with unexpected results. Billy Wilder did more with this premise in *Double Indemnity*, but the dialogue still crackles and the story sears. *Body Heat* marked a promising debut for Kasdan (*The Big Chill*), for Kathleen Turner, and for Mickey Rourke.

BODY ROCK ☆☆½
1984, USA, PG-13
Lorenzo Lamas, Vicki Frederick, Cameron Dye, Ray Sharkey, Michelle Nicastro. Directed by Marcelo Epstein. 93 min.

A schlock classic! Lorenzo Lamas (of "Falcon Crest") joins a distinguished list of nonmusical stars—including Joan Crawford in *Dancing Lady*, Jimmy Stewart in *Born to Dance*, and Lana Turner in *Dancing Co-ed*—who threw caution to the winds and headlined a major Hollywood musical. Lorenzo was smart enough to get hold of a script that makes light of the fact that he can't dance, sing, emote, or rap. Lamas fans will be in ecstasy, of course, watching him break-dance in the latest cutoff T-shirts and baggy jumpsuits. The story, which is secondary to the incredible musical moments, casts Lorenzo as a tough street kid who learns how to break-dance in order to break into show business. You haven't seen explosive acting until you've seen Lorenzo, dressed in a black leather cape, get kissed by a lecherous male record producer in a gay bar. Warning: non-Lamas buffs will enjoy Robby Muller's psychedelic color photography, but after they hear Lorenzo "rap" they may want to "scratch" their videocassette. Not to be confused with *Beat Street* or the *Breakin'* movies.

THE BODY SNATCHER ☆☆☆½
1945, USA
Boris Karloff, Henry Daniell, Bela Lugosi, Edith Atwater. Directed by Robert Wise. 79 min.

This is an excellent scary movie without any monsters, the specialty of RKO producer Val Lewton (*I Walked with a Zombie*, the original *Cat People*). Based on a story by Robert Louis Stevenson, this is about the infamous Scottish grave robbers Burke and Hare, rolled together into one in the person of Boris Karloff. He begins by raiding graves at night in order to supply fresh cadavers for a medical school (an illegal practice); once he discovers how lucrative it is, however, he decides that he might as well save himself the trouble of having to dig them up. This is a classy production, with an especially frightening dream sequence. Bela Lugosi, who received second billing, has only a very small part. Other versions of the same story include *The Flesh and the Fiends* and the more recent *The Doctor and the Devils*.

BOG ☆
1984, USA, PG
Gloria DeHaven, Aldo Ray, Marshall Thompson, Leo Gordon, Jeff Schwaab. Directed by Don Keeslar. 90 min.

Hey, just because you made your own movie and it turned out to be so awful that no one, not even Troma or New Line, would release it theatrically, that doesn't mean you have to eat the loss. Sell it to the video! The producers of this cheapo monster flick no doubt needed the money to pay salaries owed to a cast of luminaries that includes Gloria DeHaven, Marshall Thompson (star of *Fiend without a Face*) and Aldo Ray, who must have the same agent as John Carradine and José Ferrer. Somewhere in darkest Wisconsin, a fisherman using some novel techniques arouses a prehistoric monster resting on the bottom of a lake. Apparently influenced by *The Creature from the Black Lagoon* and *Dracula*, and usurping the more lurid elements of *Humanoids from the Deep*, the filmmakers have this monster suck the blood of various passersby and then go in search of human women to, er, reproduce with. All offscreen, mind you, which is a good place to keep the entire film.

BOGIE: THE LAST HERO ☆
1980, USA (TV)
Kevin O'Connor, Anne Wedgeworth, Kathryn Harrold, Patricia Barry, Alfred Ryder. Directed by Vincent Sherman. 100 min.

Originally titled *Bogie*, this insipid bio-pic is a bore under any name. As usual, the star's career and unique screen presence are given short shrift in order to trot out tawdry details of his private life. The film's best sequences revolve around the hard-drinking star's troubled marriage to fiery actress Mayo Methot (superbly played by Anne Wedgeworth), but its most unfortunate moments are those involving the legendary Humphrey Bogart–Lauren Bacall coupling. Kevin O'Connor adequately fills the Bogart bill, but Kathryn Harrold makes a wretched Bacall, sullen instead of sultry.

BOHEMIAN GIRL ☆☆☆
1936, USA
Stan Laurel, Oliver Hardy. Directed by James V. Horne and Charles R. Rogers. 74 min.

Comedy and opera go together well here, but of course the real team is Laurel and Hardy. Traveling with gypsies in the Alps, featherbrained Stan and short-tempered Ollie demonstrate their timeless brand of buffoonery, consistently getting themselves into trouble but somehow managing to help an abandoned girl. The magic is in the duo's formula, not in the plot.

THE BOILING POINT ☆☆
1932, USA
Hoot Gibson. Directed by George Melford. 62 min.

In an entertaining and relatively unusual Western, Hoot Gibson plays a chronic troublemaker who must avoid fighting for thirty days if he is to inherit his uncle's ranch. Gibson works to foil a bank robbery and win over the heroine—who cannot understand his apparent cowardice.

BOLERO ☆☆☆
1981, France, R
James Caan, Geraldine Chaplin, Robert Hossein, Nicole Garcia, Evelyn Bouix. Directed by Claude Lelouch. 173 min.

Do not confuse this with the identically titled filmic centerfold display designed for Bo Derek. This *Bolero* is one of dreamy romanticist Claude Lelouch's more ambitious concoctions. It attempts to intertwine the stories of characters from France, Russia, and America over a fifty-year period and the mulilingual mishmash isn't totally successful. The actors each play more than one role without differentiating their characters sufficiently; but the film is beautifully shaped and wonderfully scored. The bold strokes of this sweeping drama hold our interest, as does the multistoried structure.

BOLERO ½☆
1984, USA, X
Bo Derek, Andrea Occhipinti, George Kennedy, Ana Obregon, Olivia D'Abo, Greg Benson. Directed by John Derek. 106 min.

Bo Derek and her director-husband, John, persist in selling Bo as the Ultimate Woman, though with her towering bronze physique she comes on more like a Barbie doll as sculpted by Rodin—

she's got precious little in the way of movable parts. This mock-1920s fable about a young woman who journeys to Spain to lose her virginity isn't as uproariously inept as the 1982 Bo bonanza, *Tarzan*, but it's still shameless enough to earn a place on the all-time honor roll of tacky T & A. The Dereks have pioneered a new subgenre in pornography: call it limp-core. Don't be fooled by the self-imposed X; although the nudity here is interminable, it's no more explicit than that of many films rated R.

BOLO THE BRUTE

See *Bobo*

THE BONE CRUSHING KID ☆☆☆
Hong Kong
Pan Yin Tze, Chin Lung, James Tien. Directed by Hsieh Shing.

This entertaining, humorous Monkey-style kung fu film is heavily indebted to Jackie Chan's *Snakes in the Eagle's Shadow*. Crisp choreography, nicely executed forms, and convincing acrobatics make this tale of a dull-witted student and his crippled master fresh and exciting. Enthusiasts consider this *the* definitive Chin Lung film.

BONNIE AND CLYDE ☆☆☆½
1967, USA, R
Warren Beatty, Faye Dunaway, Estelle Parsons, Michael J. Pollard, Gene Hackman, Gene Wilder. Directed by Arthur Penn. 111 min.

This politically ambiguous film tends to heroize and mythologize the infamous 1930s bank robbers by equating them with 1960s radicals and by casting Warren Beatty and Faye Dunaway in the leads. If one gets over this problem, the film is an exciting adventure, from Bonnie and Clyde's first meeting to their bullet-showered car-ride finale. Beatty and Dunaway are pretty faces more than great actors, but the supporting cast has some memorable moments. The film has been considered a classic by many and should be seen, but a critical eye is necessary.

BONNIE'S KIDS ☆½
1982, USA, R
Tiffany Bolling, Steve Sandor, Robin Mattson, Scott Brady. Directed by Arthur Marks. 105 min.

In a competent and minimally offensive exploitation quickie, Tiffany Bolling and Robin Mattson are two sisters who kill their father in retaliation for his sexual abuse of them, then go to stay with their more conventionally criminal uncle, whom they plan to rob.

BON VOYAGE CHARLIE BROWN (AND DON'T COME BACK!) ☆☆☆
1980, USA, G
Animated: Daniel Anderson, Casey Carlson, Patricia Patts, Arrin Skelley. Directed by Bill Melendez. 76 min.

Few of the "Peanuts" cartoon features are as clever as Charles Schultz's comic strip, but this is a fairly pleasant outing in which Charlie Brown and his pals go to France as exchange students and get into all sorts of trouble. Great for children.

THE BOOGEYMAN ☆☆
1980, USA, R
Suzanna Love, Ron James, John Carradine. Directed by Ulli Lommel. 86 min.

A sister and brother, traumatized by his murder of their mother's brutal lover, return to their childhood home to exorcize their nightmares. But the man's malevolent spirit lives on in a large mirror, and when it is broken each piece carries his evil influence. Weird but unsuccessful attempt to break away from genre clichés, directed by Fassbinder-trained Ulli Lommel, star of *Effi Briest* and director of *The Tenderness of Wolves*. Followed by *The Boogeyman II*.

THE BOOGEYMAN II ☆
1982, USA, R
Suzanna Love. Directed by Ulli Lommel. 90 min.

The survivor of *The Bogeyman* goes to Hollywood, where her sleazy friends suggest that the story of her experiences would make a great exploitation film. More murders ensue. Boring film extensively padded with flashback footage from the first picture.

BOOM IN THE MOON ☆½
1945, Mexico
Buster Keaton, Angel Grassa, Virginia Serret, Fernando Sotto, Luis Barreiro. Directed by Jaime Salvador. 83 min.

If you believe the cover of this video, this is "an excellent example of this master comedian at his best"; however, if you watch the film, you'll discover a sordid exploitation of a comic genius in a stupid Mexican B comedy. In the mid-forties, while Buster Keaton was employed as a gag writer at the studio that destroyed his career, he accepted most acting offers that came his way. Producer Alexander Salkind managed to lure him south for this mistake. He plays a dazed, lost soldier mistaken for a dangerous criminal—a modern Bluebeard. Although much of the film is virtually silent, there is little wit. A sad, rare curiosity piece for Keaton admirers.

BOOTS AND SADDLES ☆☆
1937, USA, PG
Gene Autry, Smiley Burnette, Judith Allen. Directed by Joseph Kane. 60 min.

Gene Autry and Smiley Burnette have a nice rapport, and Smiley's comic efforts are used here to good effect. The plot is nothing to speak of but there is a nice romance between Autry and Judith Allen. The movie also contains a classic staging of Autry, on his horse with the setting sun behind him, singing "Give Me My Boots and Saddle."

THE BORDER ☆☆☆
1982, USA, R
Jack Nicholson, Harvey Keitel, Valerie Perrine, Warren Oates, Elipidia Carrillo. Directed by Tony Richardson. 107 min.

Jack Nicholson is fine in a more sedate role than usual. He plays a police officer who accepts a position as a Texas border guard. Although his sympathies begin to grow for the wretchedly poor Mexicans he is supposed to keep out of the country, he faces pressures from his materialistic wife and corrupt fellow officers to augment his income by ripping off the wetbacks. Excellent Tex-Mex musical score by Ry Cooder.

BORDERLINE ☆☆
1980, USA, PG
Charles Bronson, Bruno Kirby, Bert Remsen, Michael Lerner, Ed Harris. Directed by Jerrold Freedman. 105 min.

This is a borderline Charles Bronson flick, not as memorably gruesome as the thrill-packed *Death Wish*, but not as slipshod as many of his other films. Bronson stoically portrays a border patrol officer who's hot on the trail of a killer; he glides back and forth in pursuit without being influenced by American corruption on one side or Mexican desperation on the other. Pausing only to ripple a muscle or play a bad guy, Chuck conquers all. Bronson had a long reign as the king of movie machismo, but films like this demonstrate why he doesn't have the staying power of Clint Eastwood. Old vigilantes never die; they just fade into convictionless formula films.

BORDER ROMANCE
1930, USA ☆
Armida and Don Terry, Wesley Barry. Directed by Richard Thorpe. 58 min.

Soldiers, cattle rustling, and murder provide the backdrop for an American man's courtship of a pretty, young Mexican girl. A few amusing sequences help out this otherwise thin and awkward film, an early sound Western.

BORN AGAIN
1978, USA ½☆
Dean Jones, Anne Francis, Jay Robinson, Dana Andrews, Raymond St. Jacques, George Brent. Directed by Irving Rapper. 110 min.

This is a meretricious true-life account of how Chuck Colson, Nixon's special counsel, found God and a best-seller after his involvement in the scandalous Watergate affair. It's sad to see Hollywood veterans like Anne Francis, George Brent, and Dana Andrews reduced to this religious advertisement disguised as a film, but Dean Jones, a Disney Studios refugee, fits into this schlocky sermonizing perfectly. Boasting some of the worst set design and lighting in film history, the film looks more dead than born again. It's hard to believe director Irving Rapper once put Bette Davis through her paces in *Deception*.

BORN AMERICAN
1986, USA/Finland, R ½☆
Mike Norris, Steve Durham, David Coburn, Thalmus Rasulala, Albert Salmi. Directed by Renny Harlin. 95 min.

A group of brash college boys vacations sans invitation in the Soviet Union and then can't get out. This derivative claptrap doesn't even succeed as a mindless patriotism binge, because the script doesn't make a jot of sense. The country-crashing bozos elude the entire Red army, wreak havoc in a typical small town in the Ukraine, are falsely accused of raping a proletarian girl, survive KGB tortures that would have made Sylvester Stallone wince, and eventually escape—no thanks to a villainous CIA operative. Made in English by a Finnish director, producer, and writers; what does this say about the Finnish perception of American tastes?

BORN FREE
1966, Great Britain ☆☆☆½
Virginia McKenna, Bill Travers, Geoffrey Keen, Peter Lukoye, Omar Chambati. Directed by James Hill. 95 min.

This is an extraordinarily touching, well-made family film about Kenya animal researcher Joy Adamson and Elsa, the lioness cub she domesticated and then prepared for her return to the wild. Sustaining both a credible documentary tone and a dramatic drive that will keep adults interested and children enthralled down to the heartwrenching ending, *Born Free* is that rare film that really is suitable for the whole family and not just its younger members.

BORN INNOCENT
1974, USA (TV) ☆½
Linda Blair, Joanna Miles, Kim Hunter, Richard Jaeckel, Allyn Ann McLerie. Directed by Donald Wrye. 100 min.

Poor Linda Blair: as if to chastise her for her devilish doings in *The Exorcist*, NBC put her through the paces in this tedious, predictable prison movie. Linda plays a fourteen-year-old who pits herself against tough wardens and equally tough inmates in a women's detention home. Though made for television and less explicit than her later theatrical films like *Chained Heat*, there *is* a famous scene in which our heroine is raped with a broom handle. The sequence was cut after its initial showing, but it is restored here for home video viewing.

BORN INVINCIBLE
1984, Hong Kong ☆☆½
Carter Huang, Luo Lieh, Ling Fei. Directed by Joseph Kuo. 90 min.

This entertaining, well-made kung fu epic is about the original son of the Tai Chi family and his nearly superhuman powers. An original *Gunfighter*-type story line, attractive production values, and several excellent action sequences put this way above the average. Filmed in Hohwa Scope (please do not write in inquiring about Hohwa Scope).

THE BORN LOSERS
1967, USA, PG ☆☆
Tom Laughlin, Elizabeth James, Jeremy Slate, Robert Tessier, Jane Russell. Directed by Tom Laughlin, using the pseudonym T.C. Frank. 112 min.

Tom Laughlin made his first appearance as Billy Jack, a sort of neofascist pacifist who's violently antibloodshed (unless it's for a good cause), in this motorbike sleazefest from American International Pictures. He's a strong if dull presence, and *Losers* manages to pack a punch despite its fly-by-night production quality and dreary dialogue. Very much of a piece with other AIP films, *The Born Losers* became a hit only in its 1974 rerelease following the huge success of *Billy Jack*. The second film was slightly more polished; this one, on its own rather low level, is more fun.

BORN YESTERDAY
1950, USA ☆☆☆☆
Judy Holliday, William Holden, Broderick Crawford, Howard St. John, Frank Otto. Directed by George Cukor. 103 min.

Judy Holliday was the most sparkling comedienne of her day, and in George Cukor's crackling adaptation of Garson Kanin's play, she re-creates her Broadway role as a born-yesterday blond bombshell who is reeducated by a cynical newsman (William Holden). Not enough can be said about Holliday's Academy Award–winning performance, and the famous card-playing scene remains a classic. The story centers on the developing political awareness of the young woman as she comes to see the corruption of her power-hungry boyfriend, but the charm of the film lies in its deft comedic tone and slow-dawning romance.

BORROWED TROUBLE
1948, USA ☆☆
William Boyd, Andy Clyde, Rand Brooks, Elaine Riley, John Kellogg, Helen Chapman. Directed by George Archainbaud. 61 min.

Hopalong Cassidy fans will appreciate this change of pace as the easygoing cowpoke takes on a comedy script. Hopalong has to rescue a schoolmarm who's managed to get on the bad side of a few fellas who don't have a good side (seems she objected to them placing a saloon smack dab next to the schoolhouse). Above average.

THE BOSS'S SON
1978, USA ☆☆☆
Asher Brauner, Rudy Solari, Rita Moreno, James Darren, Richie Havens, Piper Laurie, Elena Verdugo. Directed by Bobby Roth. 97 min.

A popular late-night TV item, it's quite watchable. This is one of those well-intentioned shoestring productions where the limits of the modest execution are in sympathy with the film's ambitions rather than resulting in the filmmakers' overreaching themselves. Every point remains on target here. If you've ever suffered through a miserable summer job given you by a relative, or been coerced into following in your parents' footsteps, you'll appreciate the plight of the boss's son who has trepidations about hitching his star to his dad's carpet firm. A vivid exploration of whether this boy is cut from the same wall-to-wall shag as his old man; a very similar theme was used as a subplot in Bobby Roth's later *Heartbreakers*.

THE BOSTONIANS
1984, Great Britain, PG ★★★
Vanessa Redgrave, Christopher Reeve, Madeleine Potter, Jessica Tandy, Nancy Marchand, Maura Moynihan. Directed by James Ivory. 120 min.

Henry James's atypically gritty novel about feminism in 1870s Boston becomes a dry and cautious, but still compelling film. The tormented heroine (Vanessa Redgrave) is a fanatic reformer who vies with her chivalrous Southern cousin (Christopher Reeve) for the affections of a beautiful young feminist orator (Madeleine Potter). James Ivory and screenwriter Ruth Prawer Jhabvala don't dramatize enough of James's tantalizing ambiguities, and only Redgrave escapes their overly refined treatment; she stunningly conveys the self-lacerating horror of a fractured, alienated personality.

THE BOSTON STRANGLER
1968, USA ★★★
Henry Fonda, Tony Curtis, George Kennedy, Mike Kellin, Hurd Hatfield, Sally Kellerman, Murray Hamilton. Directed by Richard Fleischer. 118 min.

Echoing the documentary-style *noir* films of the late 1940s, like *The House on 92nd Street* and *13 Rue Madeleine*, this slick 1960s update (complete with multiple screen imagery) is surprisingly effective. Henry Fonda (with a mustache) is sturdy as the police chief out to nab the infamous "Boston strangler" and Tony Curtis is excellent as the killer himself. Thankfully, the brutal sex killings are less explicit than more contemporary depictions, but they disturb nonetheless. What could have been another slasher movie becomes a taut and incisive study.

LA BOUM
1981, France ★★
Claude Brasseur, Brigitte Fusey, Sophie Marceau, Denise Grey, Bernard Giraudieu. Directed by Claude Pinoteau. 100 min.

This French domestic drama, which broke box-office records there, is a sensitive but unexceptional study of a teenage girl trying to shut out the angry sound made by her bickering parents. The adolescent psychology is handled well enough, but we've seen these generational failure-to-communicate dramas before. What seems perceptive in a foreign language with subtitles may really be the equivalent of just another TV movie with Valerie Bertinelli.

BOUND FOR GLORY
1976, USA ★★★½
David Carradine, Ronny Cox, Melinda Dillon, Gail Strickland, Randy Quaid. Directed by Hal Ashby. 147 min.

No Depression-era period piece since *The Grapes of Wrath* tasted so much of dirt and grit and sat so heavy on the heart. In this startling and brilliantly lensed (by Haskell Wexler) adaptation of Woody Guthrie's autobiography, Guthrie (David Carradine) hops onto the battered freight train too common at the time. Driven to the western edge of the continent by the Dust Bowl, he finds human nobility among the migrant workers in California's central valleys. Eventually Guthrie's congruence with the times is expanded by the emergence of his talents; his balking turns to talking when he begins careers in radio, political activism, and conscientious songwriting. A long film, it is bound together by taut direction, an omnipresent and strong-lunged Carradine (who does his own singing) and a deliciously delineated performance by Melinda Dillon as Guthrie's sporadic mate.

THE BOUNTY
1984, Great Britain, PG ★★½
Anthony Hopkins, Mel Gibson, Laurence Olivier, Edward Fox, Daniel Day Lewis. Directed by Roger Donaldson. 130 min.

This ambitious rethinking of history's most notorious mutiny reshapes the story to make the indominatable Captain Bligh (Anthony Hopkins) and the humanistic Fletcher Christian (Mel Gibson) figures of pure reason and pure impulse, respectively. The opening sections are crisp and intelligent, as Hopkins's vigorous Bligh, during his court-martial, recalls the ship's voyage. But when Gibson's dewy-eyed, ingenuous Christian takes center stage in Tahiti, the movie loses its bearings; it doesn't succeed in casting the spell that turned the men into mutineers, and it dramatizes their rebellion with vague, expressionistic flourishes. Roger Donaldson directs in a closed-in style that, though punchy, denies the audience any sense of wonder.

BOXCAR BERTHA
1972, USA, R ★★★
Barbara Hershey, David Carradine, Bernie Casey. Directed by Martin Scorsese. 97 min.

Barbara Hershey plays an innocent who robs trains with a band of drifters during the Depression. It isn't long until the railroad bosses come after them with a vengeance. Director Martin Scorsese's first notable film, made under the aegis of producer Roger Corman, shows the beginning of the slick, violent style that Scorsese later employed in *Taxi Driver*. A fast-moving, low-budget film that never takes itself too seriously, complemented by some great action scenes. The best of the AIP *Bonnie and Clyde* rip-offs.

A BOY AND HIS DOG
1975, USA, R ★★★
Don Johnson, Susanne Benton, Jason Robards, L. Q. Jones. Directed by L. Q. Jones. 87 min.

This wild, kinky tale of survival in the year 2024 traces the exploits of Vic and his talking canine companion Blood in a dried-mud, postatomic wilderness where a man's life consists of hunting for food, arms, and an occasional female. When the young hero ventures to a materialistic underground society that wants the teenager for his sperm, the movie wittily starts to treat life after the bomb as being some kind of capitalistic nightmare. The film, based on Harlan Ellison's novella, is a cult favorite among science-fiction enthusiasts. Don't miss its great violent punch line.

BOY, DID I GET A WRONG NUMBER!
1966, USA ★★★★
Bob Hope, Elke Sommer, Phyllis Diller, Marjorie Lord, Cesare Danova. Directed by George Marshall. 99 min.

Boy, Did I Get a Wrong Number! was the beginning of the Bob Hope–Phyllis Diller trilogy that continued with *Eight on the Lamb* and *The Private Navy of Sergeant O'Farrell*. Some of the stylistic and ideological concerns of Hope were already emerging in *Wrong Number* and would flower in the later films: the playful use of Diller as a dark contrast to charming and elegant actresses like Elke Sommer and Jill St. John and an elaboration of the Hitchcockian theme of the wrongly accused man. Bob Hope plays a real-estate agent who dials a number and gets mixed up with Sommer, an actress who refuses to do bubble baths. Marjorie Lord, sensitively playing Hope's wife, jumps to the wrong conclusions. Hope's Tom Meade is apparently a simple character, but the actor invests the role with a depth and fragility reminiscent of Charlie Chaplin. George Marshall's direction masterfully combines Frank Tashlin's comic-book style and Fellini's eccentricity.

THE BOY IN BLUE
1986, Canada, R ★
Nicolas Cage, Cynthia Dale, Christopher Plummer, David Naughton, Sean Sullivan, Melody Anderson. Directed by Charles Jarrott. 97 min.

This tepid, "inspirational" sports drama attempts to do for scull-racing what *Chariots of Fire* did for footracing, but never gets both of its oars in the water. A woefully miscast Nicolas Cage is Ned Hanlan, a muscular, somewhat brutish Canadian rower circa 1900 who comes south to Philadelphia to show up the snobs and college boys in the first of many regattas. In voice and appearance, Cage is one of our most contemporary actors, and he crashes through this period role like a bull in a china shop. Since there isn't an exciting or honestly felt moment in the film, however, the weakness of his performance doesn't much matter.

THE BOY IN THE PLASTIC BUBBLE ☆☆
1976, USA (TV)
John Travolta, Glynnis O'Connor, Diana Hyland, Ralph Bellamy, Robert Reed. Directed by Randal Kleiser. 103 min.

A young John Travolta, then a heartthrob on "Welcome Back Kotter," made a strong impression in this weepy, simplistically effective drama about a teenager, born without immunities, who's lived in an isolated environment all his life. Finally, he "escapes" in a TV-style resolution that denies reality while pretending to face it. Travolta and Diane Hyland are appealing; the film is considerably less so. Randal Kleiser, who directed, went on to work with Travolta on *Grease*.

A BOY NAMED CHARLIE BROWN ☆☆
1969, USA, G
Animated: Peter Robbins, Pamelyn Ferdin, Glenn Gilger, Andy Pforsich. Directed by Bill Melendez. 85 min.

They're lovable and funny in four cartoon panels every day, but somehow, when the Peanuts gang is brought to animated life on screen, their humor turns unexpectedly melancholy, and the characters begin to look like tiny existential philosophers with large heads and sad souls. This feature has Charlie Brown off to New York to compete in a national spelling bee. Will he be the hero or the goat? The answer will remind you that sometimes, when Shultz means to be touching, he's merely bleak.

THE BOYS FROM BRAZIL ☆☆
1978, USA, R
Gregory Peck, Laurence Olivier, James Mason, Lilli Palmer, Uta Hagen, Steve Guttenberg, Denholm Elliott, Rosemary Harris, John Dehner, John Rubinstein, Anne Meara, Bruno Ganz, Michael Gough. Directed by Franklin J. Schaffner. 123 min.

This handsomely filmed but cloddishly brutal thriller, from Ira Levin's prefab best-seller, supposes that Auschwitz butcher Dr. Josef Mengele (Gregory Peck) is still puttering around somewhere in the South American jungle, plotting to loose wicked clones upon an unsuspecting world. Franklin J. Schaffner tries for a lurid, horror-movie quality, but he's defeated by the pasted-together plot, the logy pace, and Peck's dull, competent, ultimately ludicrous attempt to play a fiend inflamed by a monstrous vision. Only in the reactions of Laurence Olivier, as the aging Nazi-hunter who's pursuing Mengele, is there a genuine sensation of evil. Olivier, as a mean-spirited, obstinate old man lent stature only by his lifelong obsession, is fascinating and exciting.

THE BOYS FROM BROOKLYN ½☆
1952, USA
Bela Lugosi, Duke Mitchell, Sammy Petrillo, Charlita, Muriel Landers. Directed by William Beaudine. 74 min.

This horror-comedy may be the worst film of Bela Lugosi's career (and remember, that career included *Plan 9 from Outer Space*). Here he plays Dr. Zabor, a mad scientist seeking to reverse the human evolutionary process. When he stumbles on Duke Mitchell and Sammy Petrillo, whose brief claim to fame consisted of startlingly good impersonations of Dean Martin and Jerry Lewis, he has the perfect guinea pigs for his diabolical experiments (as if Jerry Lewis imitators weren't already the lowest beings on the evolutionary ladder). Almost painfully stupid, the film sent Lugosi spiraling downward into obscurity, and effectively ended the careers of his costars when Jerry Lewis actually sued Petrillo for personality infringement. Pee Wee Herman clones, beware. (a.k.a.: *Bela Lugosi Meets a Brooklyn Gorilla*)

THE BOYS IN COMPANY C ☆☆
1978, USA/Hong Kong, R
Stan Shaw, Andrew Stevens, James Canning, Michael Lembeck, Scott Hylands, James Whitmore, Jr., Santos Morales, Lee Ermey. Directed by Sidney J. Furie. 125 min.

This confused movie follows five young Marines from induction through combat in Vietnam. The boot-camp scenes are graphic, profane, and splendidly acted. But then the boys traipse into the jungle, and instead of watching the film unfold, you watch it unravel. Santos Morales and Lee Ermey, who play drill sergeants, save the first third of the film, but the rest of it piles on so many clichés from World War II pictures and so many pious misconceptions about Vietnam that you suspect it was made with the advice and consent of the U.S. Marine Corps public relations office.

THE BOYS IN THE BAND ☆☆
1970, USA, R
Kenneth Nelson, Cliff Gorman, Fredrick Combs, Leonard Frey, Laurence Luckinbill, Peter White, Reuben Greene. Directed by William Friedkin. 117 min.

Mart Crowley adapted his Off-Broadway hit and the original cast was retained for the making of this once ground-breaking, now dated film about the emotional fireworks at a homosexual birthday party. The film may embarrass viewers with its endless superficial psychology and its "honest" depictions of gay character types. However, the sincere performances by Cliff Gorman, Leonard Frey, Frederick Combs, and especially Kenneth Nelson eventually bring this one-set, mechanically plotted film to life.

THE BOYS NEXT DOOR ☆☆☆
1985, USA, R
Maxwell Caulfield, Charlie Sheen, Patti D'Arbanville, Christopher McDonald, Hank Garrett. Directed by Penelope Spheeris. 95 min.

From *Rebel without a Cause* to *Over The Edge*, youth-in-revolt films have examined the problems of their alienated protagonists with a certain degree of Hollywood decorum. Not here. Director Penelope Spheeris takes the gloves off and beats the audience to a pulp with her disturbing, intensely violent tale of two All American teens on a rampage. Maxwell Caulfield and Charlie Sheen are both excellent as the middle-class youths who have been abused by their parents and classmates, and decide to take out their frustrations on humanity at large when they paint Los Angeles red with the blood of everyone they encounter. The movie is told from a point of view that takes chauvinism to psychotic extremes, where women are only good for sex and gays are deserving of death. Hearing the twisted philosophy of these "boys" is chilling; watching them carry it out is terrifying. This is the kind of no-holds-barred dive into anarchy that the studios wouldn't dare to make, and the director of *Suburbia* handles her low budget superbly. Well worth seeing, if you can stomach it.

THE BOY WHO COULD FLY ☆☆☆½
1986, USA, PG
Lucy Deakins, Jay Underwood, Bonnie Bedelia, Fred Savage, Colleen Dewhurst, Fred Gwynne, Mindy Cohn. Directed by Nick Castle. 114 min.

This melancholy fable exercises restraint and remains rooted in a recognizable reality throughout, even in its wildest flights of fancy. Remaining true to its modest virtues, the film never resorts to cuteness or overproduced blandness like so many of today's quasi-Spielberg adventures. After his parents' death in a plane crash, a grief-stricken boy retreats into autism but exhibits evidence of an ability to fly, an occurrence that no one can readily believe. A year later, when a new family moves next door, the troubled teen begins to build a relationship with a girl his own age; as he starts to come out of his shell, the young couple must fight well-meaning bureaucrats who want to institutionalize him and explain the magic away. This special film about believing in miracles is sensitively written and unafraid to cope with the pain and discouragement of its characters. Slow in spots and not structured as tightly as it could be, this is a lovely film that the entire family can watch together—that is, if people can still appreciate subtlety and intimacy in fantasy films.

THE BOY WITH GREEN HAIR ☆☆☆
1948, USA
Pat O'Brien, Robert Ryan, Barbara Hale, Dean Stockwell, Richard Lyon. Directed by Joseph Losey. 82 min.

Unexpected adventures occur after a schoolboy wakes up one morning to find his hair has turned green. What begins as a clever children's movie becomes, in the hands of producer Dore Schary and directory Joseph Losey, a provocative statement about pacifism, as the boy learns to combat the prejudice against him. Even in his first feature and within the confines of Hollywood genre, Losey exhibits sociopolitical concerns and a personal filmmaking style, most evidently in a bizarre dream sequence with war orphans. He also gets excellent work from Pat O'Brien as the grandfather and Dean Stockwell as the boy; and the production values, particularly George Barnes's Technicolor cinematography, are outstanding.

BRADY'S ESCAPE ☆☆
1984, USA/Hungary
John Savage, Kelly Reno, Ildiko Bansagi, Ferenc Bacs, Laszlo Mensaros. Directed by Pal Gabor. 96 min.

This elemental action-adventure teams *The Deer Hunter*'s John Savage with *The Black Stallion*'s Kelly Reno. Obviously, no better scripts were forthcoming. Savage plays a World War II U.S. Air Force pilot befriended by a band of cowboys while trying to flee Nazi-occupied Hungary. It's good versus evil with the usual quota of macho heroics and war film clichés, but director Pal Gabor (*Angi Vera*) does manage to inject a modicum of suspense.

THE BRAIN ☆☆☆
1965, West Germany/Great Britain
Peter Van Eyck, Anne Heywood, Cecil Parker, Bernard Lee. Directed by Freddie Francis. 85 min.

This rather brainy sci-fi chiller delves into the gray areas of gray matter, thus touching on such philosophical issues as the responsibility of modern science in human experimentation, and whether the evil that men do can indeed live on after them. In this convincing retread of the popular 1953 thriller *Donovan's Brain*, a driven man of science is dominated by the brain of an avaricious, power-mad wheeler-dealer that the doctor has kept alive artificially in his laboratory. A frightening portrait of experimentation degenerating into madness and a potent demonstration that evil is the greatest monster that mankind can unleash in the world. Next to this dead man's cruel spirit, Dracula and Frankenstein seem like amateurs at death and destruction.

THE BRAIN ☆☆
1969, France/USA
Jean-Paul Belmondo, David Niven, Bourvil, Eli Wallach, Fernand Valois. Directed by Gérard Oury. 100 min.

Not to be confused with any of the numerous horror films sporting similar titles, this is an affable heist film played for suspense and laughs. Debonair David Niven plays the brains behind a foolproof plan to stick up a train. He's ably flanked by some international actors known for their scapegrace charm, but he is not so well served by the clunky emoting of heavy-breathing Eli Wallach, not known for scoring high grades on comedy aptitude tests. Passable, and unlikely to overtax anyone's brains.

THE BRAIN FROM PLANET AROUS ☆☆
1958, USA
John Agar, Joyce Meadows, Robert Fuller, Henry Travis. Directed by Nathan Juran. 70 min.

Fans of trashy horror movies should get a low-grade kick out of this. The title is somewhat misleading because there are actually *two* brains from planet Arous, an evil one (Gor) and a good one (Vol). (One can just imagine Glinda the Good Witch asking, "Are you a *good* brain, or a *bad* brain?") Gor takes over the body of John Agar, who probably wasn't doing anything better with it at the time, and sets about conquering our puny planet. Vol arrives, takes over Agar's dog, and instructs his girlfriend how to kill the bad brain. From the director of *Attack of the Fifty-Foot Woman*.

THE BRAINIAC ☆☆
1961, Mexico
Abel Salazar, Ariadne Wekter, Mauricio Garces, German Robles, Rosa Maria Gallardo. Directed by Chano Urveta. 77 min.

This is one of the best Mexican horror movies ever made; but, given the competition, that is faint praise. An evil baron who was burned at the stake during the Inquisition for practicing black magic returns to gain vengeance on the descendants of his accusers. Ordinarily normal in appearance, when he strikes he turns into a monster with a long, snaky tongue; the effect, depending on your mood, can be very silly or quite scary. Abel Salazar, who was connected with just about every horror movie made in Mexico during this boom era, also served as producer here.

BRAINSTORM ☆☆☆½
1983, USA, PG
Christopher Walken, Louise Fletcher, Natalie Wood, Cliff Robertson. Directed by Douglas Trumbull. 106 min.

A headphonelike machine that can record any human sensation, experience, dream, or nightmare and then transmit it to the wearer is the subject of this wildly visual thriller dominated by special effects. Super performances from Christopher Walken and Louise Fletcher as the scientists who don't want their invention turned into a weapon, and fine work from Natalie Wood in her last, never-completed film appearance, will keep your attention. Some of the story's inconsistencies may have arisen from the production halt and rewrites that followed Wood's death; they're not easy to overlook.

THE BRAIN THAT WOULDN'T DIE ☆☆☆
1959, USA
Jason Evers, Virginia Keith, Adele Lamont, Leslie Daniel. Directed by Joseph Green. 81 min.

This is a classic of inept, low-budget horror. The difference between this and a so-bad-it's-funny flick like, say, *Bride of the Monster* is that, in its sleazy, gross way, this is actually scary. (It's hard to believe that such an incredibly *lurid* film was made in 1959, although it *is* understandable that it wasn't generally released until over three years later.) Brilliant surgeon Jason Evers, who has been assembling, from leftover bits and pieces he gets during his operations, a monster he keeps locked in a closet at home, goes wacko when his fiancée is decapitated in an auto accident. He takes her head home and keeps it alive while he looks for a replacement body. The head isn't too happy about this, and starts communicating with the monster in the closet, to the chagrin of the doctor's crippled assistant. Featuring a great girl-fight between two strippers, and a nihilistic ending that you won't want to see alone at three in the morning.

BRAIN WASH ☆☆☆
1983, USA
Yvette Mimieux, Christopher Allport, Cindy Pickett, John Considine, Fran Ryan, Scott Marlowe. Directed by Bobby Roth. 103 min.

This compelling but little-known film made the rounds on cable and has appeared under several titles, but it does not deserve obscurity. Big business has always enjoyed placing its employees in a position of submit-or-die (dismissal being tantamount to death). Here some execs and their willing wives demonstrate how difficult it is to snap the employment umbilical cord as they allow themselves to be subjected to a series of cruel and demeaning workshops, clearly modeled on once-popular techniques. The training is supposed to make them better people, but seems rather to instill a more insidious brand of conformity. An incisive exposé of mind-control techniques that crush individuality even as they preach self-awareness.

BRAINWAVES ☆☆½
1982, PG
Keir Dullea, Suzanna Love, Tony Curtis, Vera Miles, Percy Rodrigues, Paul Willson. Directed by Ulli Lommel. 80 min.

A woman who's just been killed in an accident is returned to life through an unusual and dangerous new treatment. In this interesting chiller, the woman is given a new lease on life after receiving the brain waves of a murdered girl. Unfortunately, she also may have inherited the girl's memory. When the killer discovers this, he sets out to murder the unexpected "witness." Not the brainiest of sci-fi, but the suspense builds consistently and satisfyingly.

BRANNIGAN ☆☆
1975, Great Britain, PG
John Wayne, Richard Attenborough, Judy Geeson, John Vernon, Mel Ferrer. Directed by Douglas Hickox. 111 min.

In a late-career change of pace, John Wayne plays a Chicago cop who goes to London in pursuit of a fugitive mobster (John Vernon), and his rock-solid, no-frills presence enlivens an otherwise subroutine adventure. Wayne might have been a little too old (sixty-eight) to play the brawling, blustery Brannigan, but the film is tailor-made to his tough persona, so much so that there's little suspense as to whether—or even how—the good guys will triumph. Nice use of London locations, but pedestrian direction by Douglas Hickox.

THE BRASS TARGET ☆☆
1978, USA, PG
John Cassavetes, Sophia Loren, George Kennedy, Max von Sydow, Bruce Davison. Directed by John Hough. 111 min.

This all-star action flick fizzles, despite its interesting—but underdeveloped—premise. The film speculates that General Patton was assassinated by his underlings in order to facilitate a major gold theft. The liberties taken with history would be more forgivable if the script managed enough flashes of cleverness. As it is, it's a mildly enjoyable what-if movie, but surely all those big names should have added up to something a little more on target.

THE BRAVE LION ☆
Hong Kong
Wei Tzi Yung, Wong Fei, Cheng Fu Hsiung, Tsai Hung. Directed by Ng Fei Chien.

During the occupation of China in the 1940s, the Japanese take over a lumberyard for the timber needed by the army. This film was probably made in the late 1960s and is typical of that period: poor or nonexistent sets, costumes, acting, and martial arts.

THE BRAVE ONE ☆☆☆
1956, USA
Michel Ray, Rodolfo Hoyos, Elsa Cardenas, Carlos Navarro. Directed by Irving Rapper. 100 min.

This is a sentimental-sounding story that has enough true charm and human emotion to make it palatable to most audiences. A young boy saves the life of a calf during a storm and raises the grateful animal as a pet. When it has matured into a fighting bull, however, it is taken away from him and sent into the bullring. Filmed in Mexico on authentic locations with champion matador Fermin Rivera playing himself, the story is based on a true incident. The film won an Academy Award for Best Original Screenplay that went unclaimed until 1973 because "Robert Rich," the screen-writer listed in the credits, was actually Dalton Trumbo, one of the blacklisted Hollywood Ten.

THE BRAVEST FIST ☆☆
1980, Hong Kong
Chen Wei-Min, Hsu Hsiao Feng, Chaing Tao, Fang Yeh, Yuh Lung, Johnny Chang. Directed by Luk Pang.

An escaped convict sets up operations that our hero (Chen Wei-Min) is forced to stop in this middle-gear martial arts movie. The kung fu is not as sophisticated as in other Chen Wei-Min flicks, but Johnny Chang does make a cameo appearance as the heavy.

BRAZIL ☆☆☆☆
1985, Great Britain, R
Jonathan Pryce, Kim Griest, Michael Palin, Robert De Niro. Directed by Terry Gilliam. 131 min.

In former Monty Python member Terry Gilliam's highly eccentric and visually audacious fantasy, a hapless government official wanders across a nightmarish totalitarian society to find his elusive "dream" woman. This is a paranoid epic that takes Orwellian themes to bizarre extremes. The basic story is continually overwhelmed by a series of hilarious vignettes and horrific images concerning the incompetence and brutality that afflict this future world, and all of it's done wih great imagination. Rarely has such original brilliance been milked from such a familiar idea. A searingly immediate film with enough symbolism and startling techniques to make it worthy of repeated viewing.

BREAKER, BREAKER ½☆
1977, USA, PG
Chuck Norris, George Murdock, Terry O'Connor, Don Gentry. Directed by Don Hulette. 86 min.

Chuck Norris raises a ruckus against some small-town baddies in Texas as he searches for his missing brother, who's being held unfairly by a sadistic judge. It's not Chuck's finest action hour, and CB fans will also want to run this idiotic action flick off the road.

BREAKER MORANT ☆☆☆½
1979, Australia, PG
Edward Woodward, Jack Thompson, John Waters, Bryan Brown, Charles Tingwell, Vincent Ball, Lewis Fitz-Gerald. Directed by Bruce Beresford. 107 min.

This absorbing courtroom drama deals with three soldiers accused of killing prisoners of war during the Boer War. Bruce Beresford's film is an engrossing account of the dangerous moral territory of guerrilla warfare: the three accused men never denied killing prisoners, but they insisted that they were acting on orders. The men felt that their trial and punishment was intended as a conciliatory gesture aimed toward bringing the Boers to the bargaining table. The film, based on the book *Scapegoats of Empire* by one of the defendants, is emotional, bitter, and self-consciously heroic. Edward Woodward gives a star-making performance as Breaker Morant, the roguish British soldier and poet who is the leader and spokesman of the three accused.

BREAKFAST AT TIFFANY'S ☆☆☆
1961, USA
Audrey Hepburn, George Peppard, Mickey Rooney, Patricial Neal, Martin Balsam, Buddy Ebsen, Villalonga. Directed by Blake Edwards. 115 min.

Blake Edwards (*Victor/Victoria*, *Mickey and Maude*) has glossed and lacquered Truman Capote's charming novella about a serious young writer who seeks to tame a Manhattan playgirl. The bowdlerized screen expansion isn't all that bad. There are cute supporting performances by Patricia Neal, Buddy Ebsen, and Martin Balsam and, until the contrived climax, a lovely one by Audrey Hepburn, perfectly cast as Holly Golightly; a haunting theme song in Henry Mancini's "Moon River"; and some genuine surprises in George Axelrod's uneven screenplay. A good-looking but less-than-entrancing lark.

THE BREAKFAST CLUB ☆☆☆
1985, USA, R
Emilio Estevez, Molly Ringwald, Ally Sheedy, Anthony Michael Hall, Judd Nelson, Paul Gleason. Directed by John Hughes. 97 min.

Five high school kids, including a jock, a punk, a nerd, a prom queen, and a psycho, are sentenced to spend Saturday detention together in this very funny, unusually perceptive look at the traumas of teenhood. Nicknamed *The Little Chill* by some, this seminal Brat Pack opus verges on giving young emotions an undeservedly tragic weight, and the filming, almost entirely in one room, is somewhat stagy and overreliant on confessional monologues. But writer-director John Hughes has a remarkable ear for the sound of adolescence, and his talented young cast does generally sterling work.

BREAKFAST IN HOLLYWOOD ☆☆
1946, USA
Tom Breneman, Bonita Granville, Beulah Bondi, Eddie Ryan, Billie Burke, ZaSu Pitts, Hedda Hopper, Spike Jones and his City Slickers, the Nat King Cole Trio. Directed by Harold Schuster. 90 min.

Strictly a nostalgia package, this feature is based on a hit radio talk show featuring folksy host Tom Breneman. Unless you're a particular fan of Breneman, though, this is pretty thin: too much of a plot purporting to show a typical day in his life (getting ready for his show, talking to old ladies, straightening out a young romance) and not enough of the guest stars. But Spike Jones and his band are amusing, as always, and there's a look at Nat "King" Cole from before he became a popular crooner, when he was the pianist-leader of a jazz trio.

BREAKHEART PASS ☆☆½
1976, USA, PG
Charles Bronson, Ben Johnson, Jill Ireland, Richard Crenna, Charles Durning, Ed Lauter, David Huddleston, Archie Moore. Directed by Tom Gries. 94 min.

Charles Bronson's fans will like this slow but enjoyable change-of-pace film, set in the old West, in which he plays an undercover government agent doing battle with gunrunners on a treacherous railroad trip. Alastair MacLean adapted the surefooted script from his own novel, and veteran stunt stager Yakima Canutt sets up some well-orchestrated action sequences, including a thriller with Bronson and Archie Moore atop the train. Standard, pleasant action fare.

BREAKIN' ☆☆
1984, USA, PG
Lucinda Dickey, Adolfo "Shabba-Doo" Quinones, Michael "Boogaloo Shrimp" Chambers. Directed by Joel Silberg. 90 min.

This quickie cash-in on the then-popular break-dancing sensation brought the craze to Main Street, USA. The simple plot—concerning a chorus girl who teams up with some breakers to further their careers—is superseded by the energy and humor of the dancing acrobatics, especially by Shabba-Doo and Boogaloo Shrimp. A not-quite-streetwise successor to the silly, happy kind of musicals MGM used to churn out.

BREAKING AWAY ☆☆☆½
1979, USA, PG
Dennis Christopher, Dennis Quaid, Daniel Stern, Jackie Earle Haley, Barbara Barrie, Paul Dooley. Directed by Peter Yates. 100 min.

This very appealing film set in Bloomington, Indiana, follows four recent high school graduates as they try to decide what to make of their immediate futures. Central conflicts are with their families and with the supercilious students at the local college, with a bicycle race as the final proving ground. Dennis Christopher is especially amusing as a youth who decides that—as all the best cyclists are Italian—he must become Italian to win the race. The scenes with his parents trying to deal with a son who has suddenly developed wild hand gestures and an affection for the opera are priceless. Screenwriter Steve Tesich won an Oscar, and later wrote the similar *American Flyer*.

BREAKING GLASS ☆☆½
1980, Great Britain, PG
Hazel O'Connor, Phil Daniels, Jon Finch, Jonathan Pryce, Mark Wingett. Directed by Brian Gibson. 94 min.

A rising young singer goes from the small clubs to superstardom but discovers that success doesn't bring happiness. Does this plot sound familiar? This is the New Wave version, with lots of seedy London locations and feverish musical performances by punk singer Hazel O'Connor. She, along with Phil Daniels and especially Jonathan Pryce, move this somewhat above the oh-so-familiar plot.

BREAKING THE ICE ☆½
1938, USA
Bobby Breen, Charlie Ruggles, Dolores Costello, Robert Barrat, Billy Gilbert, Margaret Hamilton, Jonathan Hale. Directed by Edward F. Cline. 80 min.

Bobby Breen, the male answer to Shirley Temple, tugs at your heartstrings as a boy who runs away from his stern Mennonite uncle and finds a job singing at an ice show in Philadelphia, where the main attraction is Irene Dare, billed as the world's youngest ice skater. The song score, which was nominated for an Oscar, includes "Happy as a Lark," "Put Your Heart in a Song," and that instant standard, "Telling My Troubles to a Mule."

BREAKIN' II: ELECTRIC BOOGALOO ☆☆½
1984, USA, PG
Lucinda Dickey, Adolfo "Shabba-Doo" Quinones, Michael "Boogaloo Shrimp" Chambers, Susie Bono. Directed by Sam Firstenberg. 94 min.

This sequel to *Breakin'*, rushed out only a few months after the original, is more of the same, with even less plot and characterization but with more and better break dancing. (For the curious, the story is remake #637 of Mickey Rooney and Judy Garland in "We need money—what'll we do—hey, let's put on a show of our own!") The depiction of lower-class urban life is unreal and cartoonish. Bland and inoffensive, great for children, and pretty much all the break dancing you'll ever need or want to see for the rest of your life.

BREAK OF HEARTS ☆½
1935, USA
Charles Boyer, Katherine Hepburn, John Beal, Jean Hersholt. Directed by Phillip Moeller. 78 min.

Girl meets internationally acclaimed orchestra conductor. Girl falls in love with IAOC. Girl and IAOC cavort happily around Europe. Girl and IAOC break up, but find each other at end. Would have been justifiably forgotten were the girl not played by Katharine Hepburn, at a time in her career before she had evinced her full talent.

BREAKOUT ☆☆
1975, USA, PG
Charles Bronson, Jill Ireland, Robert Duvall, John Huston, Randy Quaid, Sheree North, Alejandro Rey. Directed by Tom Gries. 96 min.

This action drama about a prison break caused a brief sensation when a real escape modeled on the film nearly succeeded. That exploit had to be more exciting than this very routine Charles Bronson vehicle, which has the great stone-face snoozing through his role. He's an ace pilot who engineers the liberation of his friend (Robert Duvall, whose talents are wasted) from a Mexican jail. John Huston provides some color as a corrupt patriarch, but not enough to keep the interest of anyone who isn't a Bronson buff.

BREAK-OUT FROM OPPRESSION ½☆
Hong Kong
Lir Chia-Hui, Li Lim Lim, Chin Pai.

In this lifeless story, a young man, pressed into the army, escapes and hires on to protect a town. Mediocre actioner is marred by poor production values.

BREAKTHROUGH ☆☆
1978, West Germany, PG
Richard Burton, Rod Steiger, Robert Mitchum, Curt Jurgens, Helmut Griem. Directed by Andrew V. McLaglen. 110 min.

This so-so sequel to *Cross of Iron*, focuses on German sergeant Steiner (Richard Burton) and his involvement in a plot to assassinate Adolf Hitler that comes to involve both American and German officers. The acting and characterization are above average for this sort of big-stars-in-uniform production, but Andrew McLaglen's direction doesn't have the grit or viscerality that Sam Peckinpah brought to part one. A passable entertainment for genre fans. (a.k.a.: *Sergeant Steiner*)

BREATHLESS ☆☆☆☆
1959, France
Jean-Paul Belmondo, Jean Seberg, Daniel Boulanger, Liliane David. Directed by Jean-Luc Godard. 89 min.

One of the seminal films of the French New Wave, Jean-Luc Godard's brilliant first feature combines the erratic, exhilarating visuals and melancholy eroticism that have become the director's trademark. The narrative chronicles a few murky days in the lives of a cool Parisian thug (Jean-Paul Belmondo) and his pretty, pensive American girlfriend (Jean Seberg). Belmondo launched his film career with his unforgettable performance. Godard's film evokes the rough energy and stylized romanticism of American gangster movies and *film noir*. Belmondo's bearing and gestures pay tribute to the archetypical gangster, Humphrey Bogart.

BREATHLESS ☆☆
1983, USA, R
Richard Gere, Valerie Kaprisky, Art Metrano. Directed by Jim McBride. 105 min.

Richard Gere breaks through his usually sullen screen façade with a kinetic portrayal of a gyrating rock-and-roll stud on the lam in this otherwise pointless remake/update/Americanization of Jean-Luc Godard's 1959 New Wave classic. Neon-lit L.A. backdrops, adrenalin-pumping music, and the smoldering combination of Gere and French newcomer Valerie Kaprisky make this *Breathless* sporadically enjoyable. The screenplay, however, is a mess, and the film won't ever come close to tarnishing your memories of Belmondo, Seberg, or the extraordinary visual inventiveness of Godard.

A BREED APART ☆☆
1984, USA
Rutger Hauer, Powers Boothe, Kathleen Turner, Donald Pleasence, John Dennis Johnston. Directed by Philippe Mora. 101 min.

A weirdly obscure item considering its high-powered cast, this one seems born for the shelves of video stores. A lunatic millionaire (Donald Pleasence) indulges in the expensive habit of collecting rare bird eggs. Powers Boothe is a bold mountain climber in need of capital to finance his next ascent. Rutger Hauer is a conservationist who's rich enough to own an island and obsessive enough to wound or kill humans who mess with his endangered species. Everyone has a hobby to pursue or an ax to grind except for Kathleen Turner, who simply wants to domesticate Hauer. Uninterestingly directed, the film moves toward its climax without surprises; it's not a bad movie, but viewers will be bothered by the underuse of the cast's talents. As for Turner, now ensconced as a glamorous star, she's so cruelly lit and photographed that she looks here as if she's the one who's been killing the animals and eating them.

BREWSTER McCLOUD ☆☆☆
1970, USA, R
Bud Cort, Sally Kellerman, Shelley Duvall, Michael Murphy, William Windom, Rene Auberjonois, Stacy Keach, John Schuck, Margaret Hamilton, Jennifer Salt, William Baldwin. Directed by Robert Altman. 105 min.

Robert Altman's *M*A*S*H* follow-up is this peculiar social comedy about a young man who is teaching himself to fly while living beneath the Houston Astrodome. When the recluse looks like the prime suspect in several murder cases, a hotshot detective is soon on his trail. Bud Cort (the strange young man in *Harold and Maude*) is perfect as Brewster, and the rest of the cast, including many Altman regulars, is excellent. Doran William Cannon's (*Skidoo*) screenplay is engagingly offbeat. The only drawback is that Altman's camera strays too often from the main action. Not the director's funniest or most profound work, but an intriguing effort nonetheless.

BREWSTER'S MILLIONS ☆☆½
1945, USA
Dennis O'Keefe, Helen Walker, Eddie "Rochester" Anderson, June Havoc, Gail Patrick, Mischa Auer, Thurston Hall. Directed by Allan Dwan. 79 min.

One of the most oft-told tales is the one about the young man who must spend a million dollars in two months in order to inherit eight times that amount. This is at least the fourth film version of the 1907 play, and it shows in Allan Dwan's lack of original contributions to the formula. The breezy, small-scale production gets mileage—or, footage, anyway—out of the familiar plot, but it never overcomes a certain mustiness.

BREWSTER'S MILLIONS ☆☆
1985, USA, PG
Richard Pryor, John Candy, Lonette McKee. Directed by Walter Hill. 98 min.

The umpteenth remake of this particular story has Richard Pryor as a down-and-outer who must spend $30 million in one month in order to inherit the grand sum of $300 million. The film is unevenly made, and not nearly as funny as it should be given the talent involved. Action director Walter Hill (*48 HRS.*) is totally out of place here, and he isn't helped by the mediocre script. A lame performance by Pryor, but Lonette McKee stands out as his love interest.

BRIAN'S SONG ☆☆☆
1970, USA (TV), G
James Caan, Billy Dee Williams, Jack Warden, Shelly Fabares. Directed by Buzz Kulik. 73 min.

This drama about Chicago Bears running back Brian Piccolo and his battle with cancer, based on a book by his friend and teammate Gale Sayers, is perhaps the most lastingly popular of all TV movies. Blame it if you want for creating the disease-of-the-week genre that spawned dozens of mediocre films, but note as well that this one earns its tears rather than jerking them. William Blinn's teleplay rarely slips into the maudlin, and James Caan is extraordinarily controlled and touching in the central role.

THE BRIDE ☆½
1985, Great Britain, PG-13
Sting, Jennifer Beals, Clancy Brown, David Rappaport, Geraldine Page. Directed by Franc Roddam. 118 min.

This is a serious, humane, and very, very dull film. Franc Roddam has taken off from Mary Shelley's novel by way of *Pygmalion* to come up with a musty gothic morality play, a kinked-up "Masterpiece Theatre"–style episode that wags a scolding finger at its bad-boy protagonist and then comes down squarely on the side of love, friendship, and kindness. If *The Bride* generates any suspense, it's not over the outcome of the story but over the all-important question of whether Sting (as Baron Frankenstein) and Jennifer Beals (as his perfect-lady creation)—a match made in hype heaven—will end up in the sack. The creaky script gives Sting no chance to parade the demonic, bent-choirboy perversity he was cast for; Beals is beautiful, but her line readings are pure tin.

THE BRIDE OF FRANKENSTEIN ☆☆☆½
1935, USA
Boris Karloff, Colin Clive, Elsa Lanchester, Valerie Hobson, Ernest Thesiger. Directed by James Whale. 85 min.

The first and only worthwhile sequel to *Frankenstein* surpasses the original in the eerie elegance of its set design and the craftiness of its scares, tossing in some subtle black comedy as well. The evil Dr. Praetorius (Ernest Thesiger) bullies Frankenstein into constructing a mate for his monster, and when the Bride meets her man, sparks fly—literally. The best moments in this outstanding achievement in horror artistry come from Elsa Lanchester, of the mesmerizing electric hairdo and roof-rattling scream (she also plays Mary Shelley in the film's often-trimmed prologue). Her first encounter with Karloff may be one of the funniest, strangest romantic scenes you'll ever see onscreen.

BRIDE OF THE MONSTER ☆½
1956, USA
Bela Lugosi, Tor Johnson, Tony McCoy, Loretta King, Nancy B. Dunne, George Becwar, Don Nagel. Directed by Edward D. Wood, Jr. 69 min.

This disappointingly accomplished film by the director of *Plan 9 from Outer Space* is just inept enough to be awful and not inept enough to be funny. Bela Lugosi plays a mad scientist who tinkers with enlarging people. At least there's a superbly ludicrous climax, in which the emaciated Lugosi and a woefully limp fake octopus wrestle for world supremacy in a ditch. Followed by *Night of the Ghouls*.

THE BRIDGE OF SAN LUIS REY ☆☆
1944, USA
Lynn Bar, Louis Calhern, Nazimova, Akim Tamiroff, Blanche Yurka, Francis Lederer. Directed by Rowland V. Lee. 85 min.

This is an ambitious but flawed treatment of Thornton Wilder's famous novel, which might have seemed like surefire screen material. In some ways, it could be viewed as the ultimate disaster movie, long before the days of *The Poseidon Adventure* or *The Towering Inferno*. Predictably, Wilder's philosophizing about the meaning of fate is given short shrift, so all we're left with is the tale of five people traveling across a bridge when it collapses.

THE BRIDGE ON THE RIVER KWAI ☆☆☆☆
1957, USA
Alec Guinness, Sessue Hayakawa, William Holden, Jack Hawkins, James Donald, Geoffrey Horne, Andre Morell. Directed by David Lean. 161 min.

David Lean's memorable World War II epic is about a crew of British POWs in Burma who are ordered by their captors to build a sprawling, strategically important bridge. Mostly, it's about the efforts of their leader (Alec Guinness) to maintain their pride as soldiers, even if it means building a better bridge than the Japanese could build themselves. The movie is pictorially stunning, and its antimilitary sentiments are anything but routine. It includes outstanding performances by Guinness as the honor-obsessed Captain Nicholson, Sessue Hayakawa as the Japanese martinet, and William Holden as the American commando who returns to destroy the bridge. The screen credit says Pierre Boulle adapted his own novel; but the screenplay was actually written largely by the then-blacklisted writer Michael Wilson, who received—belatedly and properly—a posthumous Oscar.

A BRIDGE TOO FAR ☆☆½
1977, Great Britain, PG
Dirk Bogarde, James Caan, Michael Caine, Sean Connery, Edward Fox, Elliott Gould, Gene Hackman, Anthony Hopkins, Hardy Kruger, Laurence Olivier, Ryan O'Neal, Robert Redford, Maximilian Schell, Liv Ullmann. Directed by Richard Attenborough. 175 min.

This war movie, epic in scale and length, is on an unlikely subject—the disastrous Allied defeat at Arnhem in 1944, when U.S., British, and Polish troops tried to push through to a German industrial center and went "a bridge too far." It's very slow and simple, but genuinely spectacular in scope, and producer Joseph E. Levine's all-star cast makes it quite entertaining; World War II never had so many square jaws or pretty faces. The performances range from excellent (Gene Hackman, Anthony Hopkins, Laurence Olivier) to miscast (Liv Ullmann) to simply awful (Ryan O'Neal), and some of the biggest names appear so briefly that it might be unwise to blink. Overall, the film settles for sweep and grandeur at the cost of a compelling narrative; but, as war movies go, *Bridge* is worth seeing if only because it may be the biggest.

BRIEF ENCOUNTER ☆☆½
1975, USA (TV), PG
Richard Burton, Sophia Loren, Jack Hedley, Rosemary Leach, Ann Firbank. Directed by Alan Bridges. 76 min.

Richard Burton and Sophia Loren make an attractive romantic couple, but both look distracted and bored in this pallid, pointless TV remake of David Lean's 1946 classic about two married strangers who meet and fall in love on a train. Alan Bridges's direction is polite and occasionally sensitive, but his complete restraint mutes the slight story to the point of nonexistence. *Note*: The version on videocassette is the seventy-six-minute original telecast cut, not the one hundred and three-minute European release cut that often turns up on television.

BRIGADOON ☆☆½
1954, USA
Gene Kelly, Cyd Charisse, Van Johnson, Barry Jones, Jimmy Thompson. Directed by Vincente Minnelli. 108 min.

Though it's nicer to have this heavy-going MGM film preservation of Lerner and Loewe's 1947 Broadway show than none at all, it still disappoints. Gene Kelly plays an American businessman who falls in love with a Scottish girl in a town that wakes up only every one hundred years. What had been essentially a singing show became a dancing movie in the hands of producer Arthur Freed and director Vincente Minelli. So, while the dances to "Heather on the Hill" and "Almost Like Being in Love" take off and soar in their full Anscocolor and Cinemascope splendor, the singing of them leaves a lot to be desired, and the syrupy romantic plot draws the film to a halt between numbers. Some incidental pleasures come from Van Johnson as Kelly's cynical best friend, and from Minnelli's staging of a climactic chase and a scene in a New York bar. Otherwise, one gets cross-eyed staring at goats in front of cardboard backdrops.

BRIGHTON BEACH MEMOIRS ☆☆
1986, USA, PG-13
Jonathan Silverman, Blythe Danner, Bob Dishy, Judith Ivey, Stacey Glick, Brian Drillinger, Lisa Waltz, Fyvush Finkel. Directed by Gene Saks. 117 min.

Neil Simon's autobiographical story (adapted from his play) about a teenage Jewish boy's family in 1937 Brooklyn suggests Clifford Odets's *Awake and Sing!* as rewritten by Hallmark. During a single week, Eugene (Jonathan Silverman) watches his father (Bob Dishy) suffer a minor heart attack, his brother (Brian Drillinger) get fired, and his mother (Blythe Danner) and aunt (Judith Ivey) have a terrible fight. Simon softens his usual socko formula here: the one-liners aren't as funny as usual, and the sentimentality starts oozing well before the end. Danner gives her role some depth, but the character is such a nag you can't work up much sympathy for her, and the gifted comic Dishy is stuck in a humorless role. Only Judith Ivey's Blanche has any real juice; she gives the role a girlish tentativeness that's both charming and touching. Silverman's shtick-in-your-throat performance is also convincing—it's easy to believe that this pain in the ass could grow up to be Neil Simon.

BRIGHTY OF THE GRAND CANYON ☆☆½
1967, USA
Joseph Cotten, Pat Conway, Karl Swensen, Dick Foran. Directed by Norman Foster. 89 min.

This is an easygoing adventure about a benevolent burro who bestows his deep knowledge of survival and large capacity for affection on a grizzled prospector. The scenic wonders of the Grand Canyon are more breathtaking than any drama derived from this sentimental yarn, but kids may cotton to the idea of a donkey befriending an old codger and teaching him a trick or two as they both wend their way into the southwestern sunset.

BRIMSTONE AND TREACLE ☆☆
1982, Great Britain, R
Sting, Denholm Elliott, Joan Plowright, Suzanna Hamilton. Directed by Richard Loncraine. 85 min.

In this frequently interesting but finally oppressive mixture of grotesque cynicism and syrupy sentimentality, Sting, in his first major movie role, plays a mysterious young man who insinuates himself into a middle-class British family for the sadistic pleasure of wielding power over their lives. Charming the parents, and then, at select opportunities, sexually molesting their twenty-four-year-old daughter, a frothing, twisted vegetable, he's a self-styled English Antichrist whose evil turns out to be a catalyst for renewal. The movie wants to be satanically hip (and Sting's cool, studied performance fits the bill), but its tone is repellent. Fine supporting work from Denholm Elliott and Joan Plowright.

BRING ON THE NIGHT ☆☆☆
1985, USA, PG-13
Sting and the Blue Turtles Band (Omar Hakim, Darryl Jones, Kenny Kirkland, Branford Marsalis, Dolette McDonald, Janice Pendarvis). Directed by Michael Apted. 97 min.

Michael Apted, one of the few contemporary directors to work in both the documentary and narrative fields with equal success, brings a storyteller's instinct to this engrossing look at pop superstar Sting's attempt to form a more jazz-based, improvisational band after his split with the Police. There's plenty of music to please fans, including concert performances of music from both the Police repertoire and Sting's *Dream of the Blue Turtles* solo album; in addition, there are funny and revealing glimpses behind the scenes at the band's rehearsal in a French chateau, and a great deal (perhaps too much) of Sting himself, often pompous and arrogant, but also articulate and engaging.

THE BRINK'S JOB ☆☆½
1978, USA, PG
Peter Falk, Peter Boyle, Allen Goorwitz (Garfield), Warren Oates, Gena Rowlands, Paul Sorvino, Sheldon Leonard, Kevin O'Connor. Directed by William Friedkin. 104 min.

The Brink's Job is a crime movie that in the end is just too realistic for its own good. The story—a true one, about a group of small-time crooks who just about stumbled into the biggest cash robbery ($2.7 million) in history—has become a bit of American folklore in the thirty-five years since it took place. Director William Friedkin pulls a switch from his prior high-action films (*French Connection, Sorcerer*) by keeping the violence and gunplay to a minimum. He makes his characters (reduced in number from the eleven who actually participated to seven for filmic economy) not quite lovable, but certainly understandable and human. And although he chopped out over twenty minutes of downbeat material fom the final print, the film as a whole still tends to waver between low comedy, crime drama, and crime-doesn't-pay existentialism. Worth seeing—Friedkin is such a craftsman that anything he makes is worth seeing—but don't get your hopes up.

BRITANNIA HOSPITAL ☆☆½
1982, Great Britain, R
Graham Crowden, Malcolm McDowell, Joan Plowright, Mark Hamill, Leonard Rossiter. Directed by Lindsay Anderson. 116 min.

This follow-up to *If . . .* and *O Lucky Man!* came as a disappointment to many of Lindsay Anderson's admirers. It's a rather obvious allegory about Great Britain, set on the day of the five-hundredth anniversary of the Britannia Hospital. The Queen Mother is due to visit, but the hospital administration is beset with innumerable problems, including labor strikes, a scandal-hunting reporter, international terrorists, and the peculiarly Frankensteinian projects of the hospital's chief of surgery. There are no likable characters, but satirists from Swift to Evelyn Waugh have proved that they aren't necessary. Anderson was widely condemned for his maliciousness here, but satire requires a blunt edge. This is not a genteel British comedy: it is gleefully nasty, graphically gory (even more so than *Monty Python's Meaning of Life*), and willfully offensive. It is also quite often very funny. Watch for Alan Bates in a cameo as a dead body.

BROADWAY DANNY ROSE ☆☆☆½
1984, USA, PG
Woody Allen, Mia Farrow, Nick Apollo Forte, Milton Berle, Sandy Baron, Howard Storm, Corbett Monica, Jackie Gayle, Morty Gunty, Will Jordan. Directed by Woody Allen. 86 min.

Endearing and innovative, this is another of the "small" films that Woody Allen has been turning out fairly rapidly since he got psychoanalytical comedy out of his system in the late 1970s. Here he plays a small-time New York talent agent who gets caught up with the mistress of one of his clients as she is trying to escape from the gunmen of a mafioso who she jilted. Mia Farrow is unrecognizable as the vulgar, brassy woman, and Nick Apollo Forte is the real thing, a nightclub singer of Italian songs who'd never heard of Allen when he was cast in this film. The Catskills comics appear in a frame story as themselves, reminiscing about the story we're seeing.

BROADWAY MELODY OF 1936 ☆☆☆
1935, USA
Jack Benny, Eleanor Powell, Robert Taylor, Una Merkel, Buddy Ebsen. Directed by Roy Del Ruth. 110 min.

This genial, splashily produced MGM musical features glorious Arthur Freed–Nacio Herb Brown tunes like "Broadway Rhythm." The serviceable plot involves a scheming columnist who tries to get the goods on a producer and uses a luscious dancer (Eleanor Powell) to make his dirty work a little easier. It would have been a journeyman musical without Powell, who was definitely filmdom's best female tap dancer. Her work here is exhilarating as she executes whirlwind steps seemingly faster than the speed of light. The original ads billed this musical as, "So new, it's a year ahead of time!"

BROADWAY MELODY OF 1938 ☆☆½
1937, USA
Eleanor Powell, George Murphy, Sophie Tucker, Judy Garland, Robert Taylor, Buddy Ebsen, Sid Silvers, Billy Gilbert, Raymond Walburn. Directed by Roy Del Ruth. 110 min.

♪ In this standard but entertaining MGM musical spectacular, the thin plot is a barely serviceable excuse for the generous musical numbers. The highlight here is a very young Judy Garland clutching Clark Gable's picture and singing the adaptation of "You Made Me Love You" entitled "Dear Mr. Gable," but we also like Eleanor Powell's lively "Broadway Rhythm" number, mama Sophie Tucker's "Some of These Days," and any scene with loose, lanky Buddy Ebsen. As for lead Robert Taylor, don't ask.

BROKEN BLOSSOMS ☆☆☆☆
1919, USA
Lillian Gish, Donald Crisp, Richard Barthelmess, Edward Piel, Arthur Howard. Directed by D. W. Griffith. 68 min.

Based on a Thomas Burke story, *Broken Blossoms* is extremely sensitive in its racial attitudes. Richard Barthelmess's young Chinese nobleman is the most developed and sympathetic character in the movie. D. W. Griffith's evocation of Burke's London slums, realized by cameraman Billy Bitzer, is starkly beautiful. Both Lillian Gish and Barthelmess are wonderful—intensely controlled and poignant without becoming grim. The film's desperate air is still shocking, and its conclusion is as brutal as anything made today. The film was originally tinted.

BROKEN HEARTS AND NOSES

See *Crimewave*

BRONCO BILLY ☆☆☆
1980, USA, PG
Clint Eastwood, Sondra Locke, Geoffrey Lewis, Scatman Crothers, Bill McKinney. Directed by Clint Eastwood. 119 min.

Clint Eastwood may be the only working actor to have established three separate successful screen personae: the supercool cop of the *Dirty Harry* films, the iconic cowboy of Sergio Leone's spaghetti Westerns, and Clint the Cuddly in the films he's directed himself. This outing is so far the best of that third group, with Eastwood affectionately lampooning his own Western image as a part-time shoe salesman who also runs a ramshackle Wild West road show. The story is low-key but pleasing and emotionally resonant. Most impressively, Eastwood's direction (this is his seventh feature) is consistently efficient and crisp. Still, *Bronco Billy*'s resolutely gentle nature may please you more if you don't like the star's other work than if you do.

BRONSON LEE, CHAMPION ☆
1978, USA, PG
Tadashi Yamashita, Yoko Horikoshi, Dale Ferguson. Directed by Yukio Noda. 80 min.

A dull, talky martial arts film, this offers, as its contribution to the genre, karate instead of kung fu. A Japanese-American fighter with no sense of humor travels to the fatherland to compete in a big international tournament featuring contestants wielding an exotic assortment of weapons.

BRONZE VENUS ☆☆
1938, USA
Lena Horne, Duke Davis, Ralph Cooper, Basin Street Boys, Rubber Neck Holmes, Cats and the Fiddle, Harlemania Orchestra. Directed by William Nolte. 80 min.

♪ Lena Horne fans will gobble up almost anything the lady has done, including this, her first film, a scrappy, low-budget musical. At age twenty, Horne looks like she's still carrying some baby fat, and her singing voice lacks the powerhouse range she would later acquire. Still, it's curious to see her starring in a film made well before her Hollywood successes. She plays the star attraction of a traveling variety show ("Sepia Scandals") who breaks with her manager-boyfriend when he sells her to a Broadway producer. The real star of the film is Duke Davis, playing the boyfriend; unfortunately, Davis is about exciting as George Brent. Specialty acts abound, ranging in quality from tasteless (a jungle dance number) to excellent (a trio vocally imitating musical instruments). Technically inept, the production looks as if it weren't rehearsed enough; in fact, it was made in two weeks. Is it also possible that the filmmakers were insulting their back audience by keeping the written intertitles on the screen for such unconscionably long periods of time? Originally titled *The Duke Is Tops*, but changed in 1940 to emphasize Horne's presence.

THE BROOD ☆☆☆½
1979, Canada, R
Oliver Reed, Art Hindle, Samantha Eggar, Robert Silverman. Directed by David Cronenberg. 92 min.

This film of warped horror comes from Canada's reigning genre filmaker, who also directed *They Came from Within*, *Rabid*, *Scanners*, *Videodrome*, and *The Dead Zone*. Exponents of Dr. Hal Raglan's psychoplasmic school of therapy are encouraged to give their psychic malaises physical manifestations in the form of lesions and sores. One creates freestanding embodiments of her murderous rage, with bloody results. Witty and repellent in equal parts.

THE BROTHER FROM ANOTHER PLANET ☆☆☆½
1984, USA, PG
Joe Morton, Darryl Edwards, Steve James, Maggie Renzi, John Sayles. Directed by John Sayles. 110 min.

John Sayles's wise, generous comedy-drama about a black extraterrestrial who escapes the slavery of his world only to land in Harlem is rich in characterization and detail, and manages to say much about racial isolation without being didactic. The inner-city dwellers welcome the mute Brother (played with great delicacy by Joe Morton) as just another oddball in their already strange lives. By its end, the film becomes a touching plea for a better world, and stands as one of the only films of the last ten years to explore black issues even tangentially. Unsurprisingly, Sayles made it outside the Hollywood mainstream; it is the best of his independent features yet.

BROTHER SUN, SISTER MOON ☆½
1973, Italy/Great Britain, PG
Graham Faulkner, Judi Bowker, Michael Feast, Alec Guinness. Directed by Franco Zeffirelli. 121 min.

Probably perturbed that Andrew Lloyd Webber and Tim Rice had already come up with a hip Jesus set to a modern song score, the producers of this postbiblical epic came up instead with a hippie St. Francis of Assisi. Meteoric young star Graham Faulkner burned out after playing Francis, a sensitive young man who rejects the materialistic life-style of his merchant father in order to lead a communal life with his followers. The whiny songs provided by Bob Dylan manqué Donovan are full of such couplets as, "Through the meadows there go I/As the flowers please my eye." As in any Zeffirelli film, the locations and camerawork are often breathtakingly beautiful; it's so annoying that he always has to have these silly actors running around in front of them, blocking your view. Co-written by Lina Wertmuller.

BRUBAKER ☆☆☆
1980, USA, R
Robert Redford, Yaphet Kotto, Jane Alexander, Murray Hamilton, David Keith, Morgan Freeman, Richard Ward, M. Emmet Walsh. Directed by Stuart Rosenberg. 127 min.

A heroic liberal prison warden (Robert Redford) discovers corruption, mistreatment, and the murder of inmates within the walls of his Southern penitentiary, and comes under fire when he tries to institute reforms. Director Stuart Rosenberg (*Cool Hand Luke*) uses a Martin Ritt–ish tone of populist sincerity rather than moral outrage, a calculated choice that keeps the film free of preachiness but makes it slightly less rabble-rousing than was called for, particularly since the story is true. Generally fine nonetheless, with Redford, as always, giving an earnest and carefully understated performance that's generous to the fine supporting cast, among them Jane Alexander as a political prison official, Yaphet Kotto and Richard Ward as prisoners, and the inimitable character actor M. Emmet Walsh as a venal local merchant.

BRUCE AND SHAOLIN KUNG FU PART I ☆
Hong Kong
Bruce Le (Huang Kin-Lung), Chen Hsing, Chang Li, Chaing Tao, James Nam. Directed by James Nam.

Bruce Le's teacher has been killed by the Japanese, and Bruce must travel to Korea for revenge. Martial arts direction by Tang Te-Hsiang, from a script by kung fu director Joseph Velasco.

BRUCE AND THE DRAGON FIST ☆½
1979, Hong Kong
Bruce Le, Nelson Lee, Chaing Tao. Directed by Zackey Chan. 88 min.

This is thoroughly undistinguished kung fu with Bruce Lee–imitator Bruce Le out to rescue the wife of an instructor at a kung fu school who has been kidnapped by a rival school. Martial arts direction by Mu Lo Chiba.

BRUCE, KUNG FU GIRLS ☆½
1984, Hong Kong
Sun Kuan, Lih Feng, Sun Kuan Yue, Betty Pei. Director not credited. 90 min.

Five two-fisted Gidgets grow bored with running their health club and decide to help the police chase an invisible burglar. Marginally entertaining, perky fun and games, with a little fighting and no Bruce in sight. The film is padded with lots of awful, dubbed songs and some nice landscape scenery.

BRUCE LE'S GREATEST REVENGE ☆½
1978, Hong Kong
Bruce Le, Yang Sze, Ku Feng, Michelle. Directed by Tu Lu-Po. 94 min.

This is a retelling of Bruce Lee's *The Chinese Connection*. Chen (Bruce Le) comes home to find that his martial arts teacher has been killed by the Japanese. No reason to prefer it to the original. (a.k.a.: *Dragon's Greatest Revenge*)

BRUCE LI IN NEW GUINEA ☆
1977, Hong Kong
Bruce Li (Ho Tsung-Tao), Chen Hsing, Dana, Yang Sze. Directed by C.Y. Yang. 98 min.

Chang Wan-Li (Bruce Li) must confront the king of the Snake Cult (Chen Hsing) to rescue his girlfriend and obtain the legendary Snake Pearl. Diverting location shooting in New Guinea in an otherwise run-of-the-mill kung fu story.

BRUCE VS. BILL ☆
Hong Kong
Bruce Le, Bill Lonie, Angela Yu (Ching), Alexandre. Directed by Lam Kwok Cheung. 90 min.

The key to a safe that contains a fortune is missing, and two kung fu experts (Bruce Le, Bill Lonie) battle for its possession. The arrogant Le nicely balances out the low-key, charming Lonie. Script by Chan Rai Yin.

THE BRUTE MAN ☆☆
1946, USA
Rondo Hatton, Jane Adams, Tom Neal, Jan Wiley. Directed by Jean Yarbrough. 48 min.

This film is the final chapter in the sad story of Rondo Hatton, an actor who enjoyed a career as a supporting player in films of the 1930s before he was stricken with acromegaly, a glandular disease that horribly distorted his features and hospitalized him for years. Rather than quit the movies, he decided to capitalize on his ugliness by taking roles where he could play characters as monstrous as he now looked. This was his last (and only starring) role, as a scientist who is disfigured and maddened by acid in a chemistry lab, leading him to go on a spree of vengeance against his former schoolmates. Hatton died of the disease soon after this was completed; depending on which version of the story you choose to believe, Universal Studios gave this over to poverty-row PRC to release either because they no longer wished to put out B movies or because they were actually ashamed of its exploitativeness.

BUCK AND THE PREACHER ☆☆☆
1972, USA, PG
Sidney Poitier, Harry Belafonte, Ruby Dee, Cameron Mitchell. Directed by Sidney Poitier. 102 min.

Sidney Poitier's directorial debut is a loose, likable post–Civil War Western, with a strong measure of 1970s black consciousness thrown in. Although the territory is familiar, the faces who inhabit it aren't. Poitier plays Buck, a no-nonsense trail guide who rules the plains, protecting former slaves who seek to homestead the West. Working both as entertainment and social awareness, the film suffers a bit from a plot filled with more holes than some of the bullet-ridden villains. Harry Belafonte successfully shakes off his matinee-idol background, stealing the show as a hard-drinking, fast-talking preacher who reluctantly joins forces with Buck.

BUCKAROO BANZAI

See *The Adventures of Buckaroo Banzai Across the Eighth Dimension*

BUCK PRIVATES ☆☆☆
1941, USA
Bud Abbott, Lou Costello, the Andrews Sisters, Lee Bowman, Alan Curtis, Jane Frazee, Nat Pendleton. Directed by Arthur Lubin. 82 min.

One of the first service-camp comedies was also the first commercially successful feature for Abbott and Costello. There's the usual batch of songs (the Andrews Sisters sing "Boogie Woogie Bugle Boy") and love triangle filler, but the highlights, of course, are the tireless, beautifully timed vaudeville sketches performed by Bud and Lou in their prime. Livelier and funnier than many of their later pairings.

BUCK ROGERS IN THE 25TH CENTURY ☆½
1979, USA, PG
Gil Gerard, Erin Gray, Pamela Hensley, Tim O'Connor, Henry Silva, Joseph Wiseman, Felix Silla, Mel Blanc (voice). Directed by Daniel Haller. 89 min.

This pilot for the short-lived television series was released theatrically, but it's strictly small-screen in scope and therefore not as completely disappointing on video. Gil Gerard is appropriately stolid as Buck, but there are better science-fiction films, better nostalgia items, better comic-strip adaptations, and better things to do than watch this.

BUDDY BUDDY ☆½
1981, USA, R
Walter Matthau, Jack Lemmon, Paula Prentiss, Klaus Kinski. Directed by Billy Wilder. 96 min.

This Billy Wilder film is a rude, leaden farce that sadly marks a total collapse of taste and craftsmanship. Walter Matthau plays an aging hit man who holes up in a hotel room to fulfill his last contract, and Jack Lemmon is his suicidal next-door neighbor. The film is a series of thudding gags, most of them centering on bathroom humor and failed suicide attempts, and Matthau and Lemmon both hit new lows; howling and yowling, they're the Odd Couple turned into a dog-and-cat fight.

THE BUDDY SYSTEM ☆☆
1984, USA, PG
Richard Dreyfuss, Susan Sarandon, Nancy Allen, Jean Stapleton, Wil Wheaton, Edward Winter. Directed by Glenn Jordan. 110 min.

A sappy romantic comedy with a twist; the two leads, an inventor (Richard Dreyfuss) and a single mother (Susan Sarandon), make goo-goo eyes at each other, but after sleeping together they agree the experience was a disaster, have a few giggles at each other's expense, and shake hands as friends. Cementing their relationship is Sarandon's precociously wise kid (Wil Wheaton), who's been given the usual adorably foulmouthed dialogue. Dreyfuss and Sarandon both give natural, easygoing performances (in fact, this is Dreyfuss's best work in years), but the script is just a series of predictable situations.

BUEK
See *Happy New Year*

BUFFALO BILL AND THE INDIANS, ☆½
OR SITTING BULL'S HISTORY LESSON
1976, USA, PG
Paul Newman, Burt Lancaster, Joel Grey, Harvey Keitel, Geraldine Chaplin, Will Sampson, Kevin McCarthy, E. L. Doctorow, Shelley Duvall. Directed by Robert Altman. 120 min.

Very loosely based on Arthur Kopit's play *Indians*, this was Robert Altman's statement on American history in the year of the Bicentennial. As you might expect, the screenplay by Altman and Alan Rudolph concerns a variety of topics—show business, politics, Richard Nixon, the demise of America—in fact, almost everything *except* William F. Cody. Long and diverse; pretty much for Altman's devoted followers.

BUG ☆☆
1975, USA, PG
Bradford Dillman, Joanna Miles, Jamie Smith Jackson, Patty McCormack. Directed by Jeannot Szwarc. 101 min.

Thomas Page's "The Haphaestus Plague" becomes a slow-moving, occasionally effective thriller about a biology professor who breeds incendiary, foot-long insects. The final sequences have a nightmarish intensity, but the rest is just routine. Produced by schlock-horror movie master William Castle.

THE BUGS BUNNY/ROAD RUNNER MOVIE ☆☆☆
1979, USA, G
Animated: Mel Blanc. Directed by Chuck Jones. 92 min.

A collection of some of the best Looney Tunes ever turned out by the Warner Bros. animation department, this has a *real* all-star cast: Bugs, Road Runner, Wile E. Coyote, Daffy Duck, Elmer Fudd, and, for foreign flavor, Pepe le Pew. If that roster doesn't grab you, the delightfully self-parodic pictorials of Chuck Jones, Friz Freleng, and other masters should. The collection is presented with a newly drawn framing story that demonstrates only that Bugs's glory days have passed, and ninety minutes of any cartoon becomes a little nerve-racking, but for aficionados, it's a delight. Followed by *The Looney Looney Looney Bugs Bunny Movie*.

BUGS BUNNY'S 3RD MOVIE: ☆☆☆
1,001 RABBIT TALES
1982, USA, G
Animated: Mel Blanc, others. Directed by Fritz Freleng and Robert McKimson. 74 min.

Probably the best of the compilations of Warner Bros.' classic Looney Tunes, this has a gallery of stars, including Bugs, Tweety, Sylvester, Daffy Duck, and Elmer Fudd, and with outstanding work from Yosemite Sam. The film should hold any right-thinking child's attention, and adults will have the unexpected pleasure of discovering the wry sophistication that went into these little gems. Best of the bunch are two all-time classics, one in which Bugs is adopted by a family of gorillas, and the other featuring a frog in white tie and tails who sings "I'm Just Wild About Harry."

BUGSY MALONE ☆☆☆
1976, Great Britain
Scott Baio, Jodie Foster, Florrie Dugger, John Cassisi, Martin Lev. Directed by Alan Parker. 93 min.

One of the more intriguing musicals of the 1970s, *Bugsy Malone* is a send-up of Warner Bros.' backstagers-and-gangsters melodramas. The audacious twist is that the entire cast is made up of children in adult roles and dubbed by adults in the musical numbers. The results range from irritatingly strained to fascinatingly clever, but writer-director Alan Parker, in his first feature, should be commended for tenaciously sticking to his concepts. The film is certainly both ambitious and experimental enough to entertain adults as well as children.

BULLDOG DRUMMOND COMES BACK ☆☆½
1937, USA
John Barrymore, John Howard, Louise Campbell, J. Caroll Naish, Reginald Denny. Directed by Louis King. 64 min.

In action-movie circles, the ever-popular character Bulldog Drummond kept coming back as late as the 1960s with such films as *Deadlier than the Male* and *Some Girls Do*; he began his career in 1929 with *Bulldog Drummond*, starring Ronald Colman, still the best of the Drummond interpreters. Long before Indiana Jones, Drummond, an ex–British Army officer, fought his way into moviegoers' hearts against a background of international intrigue, and thwarted the menace presented by an impressive array of movie villains. Unlike the original A productions with Colman, this fast-paced programmer is a B movie with the attractive but less-than-dynamic John Howard playing the title. One of those likable, forgettable productions without an ounce of dramatic fat on the bones of its screenplay and no wasted motion in its brief running time.

BULLDOG DRUMMOND'S BRIDE ☆☆½
1939, USA
John Howard, Heather Angel, H. B. Warner, Reginald Denny, Eduardo Cianelli. Directed by James Hogan. 55 min.

The ace detective (best personified by Ronald Colman in two early talkies) is up to his neck in mayhem in this smoothly filmed adventure tale. Here John Howard lends his congenial presence to the role of the ex–Army officer perpetually hearing the call of adventure. Any romancing of damsels in distress is shelved as he acquires a better half in this energetic entry in the series. Fast-paced, no-frills B-movie entertainment with a grade-A supporting cast, including the ultrasinister Eduardo Cianelli.

THE BULLFIGHTER AND THE LADY ☆☆☆
1951, USA
Gilbert Roland, Robert Stack, Joy Page, Katy Jurado, John Hubbard, Virginia Grey. Directed by Budd Boetticher. 87 min.

This unusual, visually expressive work about the psychology of bullfighting is an incisive examination of the factors that draw certain personalities into the bullring. While vacationing in Mexico, a sports buff branches out into bullfighting by studying under the auspices of the world's finest matador. The amateur's overeager desire to triumph instantaneously results in disaster in this pungent drama that conveys the power of the sport with startling immediacy. Academy Award nominee for best motion picture story.

THE BULLFIGHTERS
1945, USA ★★★
Stan Laurel, Oliver Hardy, Margo Woode, Richard Lane, Carol Andrews, Diosa Costello. Directed by Mal St. Clair. 61 min.

This may leave Laurel and Hardy fans shouting *Olé!* In their later screen ventures, the laughs were often few and far between, but this film is a return to form without being as hilarious as their early efforts. As mistaken-identity comedies go, this is amusing nonsense in which the legendary duo manages to take the proverbial bull by the horns. Laurel is a dead ringer for a celebrated matador and almost ends up a *dead* dead ringer as circumstances push him into the arena. Amusement is a sure thing for L & H fans as they stick a comic sword into the thick masculine mystique of bullfighting.

BULLIES
1986, USA, R ★½
Jonathan Crombie, Janet Laine Green, Dehl Berti, Stephen B. Hunter. Directed by Paul Lynch. 96 min.

In this supercharged slop, a Canadian family leaves the nightmares of urban life only to find a hell on earth in a remote resort town presided over by resident bullies. A romance ensues between newcomer boy and local girl that turns the film into a "Romeo and Juliet Meet Deliverance."

BULLITT
1968, USA ★★★
Steve McQueen, Robert Vaughn, Jacqueline Bisset, Don Gordon, Robert Duvall, Norman Fell, Simon Oakland. Directed by Peter Yates. 112 min.

Steve McQueen stars in this dynamic police procedural as the tough, hip detective assigned to protect a hoodlum testifying against the Mafia. As McQueen bites off every line, underplaying for maximum effect, he has a look on his face as if a weasel were gnawing on his leg. It is one of the most popular action films, with a satisfyingly gloomy air. The movie's climax is an unforgettable behind-the-wheel chase scene through the San Francisco hills.

BULLWHIP
1958, USA ★★★
Guy Madison, Rhonda Fleming, James Griffith, Don Beddow, Peter Addams, Dan Sheridan. Directed by Harmon Jones. 81 min.

A man about to be hanged is given an interesting proposition: if he agrees to marry a mysterious woman, he will be set free. After the nuptials, the woman disappears, and he sets off to discover her secret. Whip-cracking Rhonda Fleming, as the half-Indian woman out to become the fur-trading queen of the West, will undoubtedly remind viewers of Joan Crawford in *Johnny Guitar*. However, she is fierce and lovely in her own right. A splashy, colorful Western with a sense of humor.

BUNCO
1985, USA (TV) ★½
Robert Urich, Tom Selleck, Donna Mills, Michael Sacks, Will Geer, Arte Johnson, James Hampton, Bobby Van. Directed by Alexander Singer. 90 min.

Made for TV consumption, this movie trades on the names of the cast of TV stars in the crime/suspense format. On an investigation, police detectives Robert Urich and Tom Selleck are joined by plainclotheswoman Donna Mills, who soon becomes the center of attention when she is threatened by the demented Michael Sacks. As for entertainment—it's bunk.

BUNDLE OF JOY
1956, USA ★★
Debbie Reynolds, Eddie Fisher, Adolphe Menjou, Tommy Noonan, Nita Talbot. Directed by Norman Taurog. 98 min.

Once upon a time, before Carrie Fisher and *Star Wars*, even before Elizabeth Taylor, there was little Eddie and Debbie, and they made one film together during their blissful *Better Homes and Gardens*–style union. It's a Technicolor remake of Ginger Rogers's *Bachelor Mother*, with Debbie now as the saleslady who finds a baby on her doorstep. If you can stomach Eddie Fisher walking around a department store singing songs like "What's So Good about Morning" and "Worry about Tomorrow Tomorrow," this will suffice as family entertainment.

BURDEN OF DREAMS
1982, West Germany ★★★½
Directed by Les Blank. 94 min.

Perhaps fearing that it would be the only record of his dream project, German filmmaker Werner Herzog invited Les Blank to shoot a documentary on the filming of *Fitzcarraldo*. Herzog's epic had one of the most tortured production histories of any recent film. Beyond its value as an introduction to that work, *Burden of Dreams* is a fascinating probe of an artist driven to extremes to achieve his vision—including a sequence of hundreds of Peruvian Indians pulling a 320-ton steamship over a small mountain in a remote Amazonian jungle without special effects or models.

BURIAL GROUND
1979, Italy ½★
Karin Well, Gian Luigi, Simone Mattioli, Antonietta Antinori, Roberto Caporali, Peter Bark. Directed by Andrea Bianchi. 85 min.

Amateurish horror trash, this one is about a large family whose stay in a country mansion is rudely interrupted by local zombies. Said zombies are none too scary—they move like turtles and their masks keep slipping. The unattractive Italian actors are dubbed, awfully, in ridiculously overcultured American voices; when they speak while having sex, they sound like the "Father Knows Best" kids committing incest.

BURN!
1968, Italy/France ★★★½
Marlon Brando, Norman Hill, Evaristo Marquez. Directed by Gillo Pontecorvo. 112 min.

Gillo Pontecorvo (*The Battle of Algiers*) directed this electrifying saga of a nineteenth-century Caribbean isle's struggle for independence against white colonialists. The film is marred by a muddled script, but his use of fast, energizing devices and nonactors in key roles provides momentum, as does Brando's extravagant performance as a treacherous Britisher. This is among the most exciting political thrillers ever made. (a.k.a.: *Queimada!*)

THE BURNING
1981, USA, R ★
Brian Backer, Shelley Bruce, Brian Matthews, Leah Ayres, Larry Joshua. Directed by Tony Maylam. 90 min.

There is terror in upstate New York, where a fellow known as the Cropsy Maniac is taking revenge on the innocent campers at Camp Blackfoot. It seems our mad hero was badly incinerated while a gardener at summer camp; now if he so much as sees a teenager, he experiences hot flashes of blood lust. While *Friday the 13th* crowds will enjoy the way the plot heats up, horror fans who prefer subtlety and shadow to gore and obviousness will be burned up by the rampant predictability.

THE BURNING BED
1984, USA (TV) ★★½
Farrah Fawcett, Paul LeMat, Richard Masur, Grace Zabriskie, Jame Callahan. Directed by Robert Greenwald. 96 min.

Farrah Fawcett won acclaim for her strong, deglamorized portrayal of Francine Hughes, a housewife who endures fifteen years of battering and finally ends it by setting her sleeping husband's bed afire, in this powerful but predictable TV movie. Robert Greenwald directs the scenes of abuse in compelling close-up, and Fawcett gives a low-key, wary performance that never degenerates into hysteria; it's not her fault that Paul LeMat steals the show as the helplessly monstrous husband.

THE BURNING QUESTION

See *Reefer Madness*

BURNT OFFERINGS
1976, USA, PG ☆☆
Oliver Reed, Karen Black, Bette Davis, Eileen Heckart, Burgess Meredith. Directed by Dan Curtis. 116 min.

Dan Curtis was responsible for TV's scary "Dark Shadows," but he doesn't fare too well with *Burnt Offerings*. A couple, their son, and the husband's aunt rent a summer house from some weird people. Sure enough, once they move in, they, too, are affected—doors are slamming and murder is on their minds. It's all very predictable and a total waste of Bette Davis. With special billing ("and Bette Davis as Aunt Elizabeth"), she starts out the film looking okay but before long is madly bugging her eyes out.

BURY ME AN ANGEL
1971, USA, R ☆☆
Dixie Peabody, Terry Mace, Clyde Ventura, Dan Haggerty, Gary Littlejohn. Directed by Barbara Peeters. 86 min.

This revenge film has the unusual quality of being told from a woman's point of view. Even more unusual, this was written and directed by a woman, Barbara Peeters, a New World staffer who went on to direct *Humanoids from the Deep*. The film itself is pretty standard, if done with the customary New World panache. The poster for the film, which would have done director Russ Meyer proud, features its gun-toting star, the statuesque Dixie Peabody, described as "a howling hellcat humping a hot steel hog on a roaring rampage of revenge"—after which the movie itself is totally anticlimactic.

THE BUS IS COMING
1971, USA, PG ☆☆
Mike Simms, Stephanie Faulkner, Burl Bullock, Eddie Kendricks. Directed by Wendell James Franklin. 109 min.

In this obscure racial-tension melodrama, filmed in the riot-torn neighborhood of Watts, a leader of a black group is killed by a racist policeman. Militant members of the group try to enlist the dead man's brother, a newly returned Vietnam vet, in a plan to make a martyr of him. The police chief, meanwhile, is torn between defending his men and sympathy for the black community. Non-sensationalistic, reasonably well made, but tied to current events of the time that leave it lacking in context to modern audiences.

BUS STOP
1956, USA ☆☆☆☆
Marilyn Monroe, Don Murray, Arthur O'Connell, Betty Field, Eileen Heckart, Hope Lange, Hans Conried, Casey Adams, Robert Bray. Directed by Joshua Logan. 96 min.

The lady gives what may be her finest performance in William Inge's acclaimed comedy-drama. An exuberant young cow-poke (Don Murray), en route to a rodeo in the big city, decides he's going to find himself an angel. Instead he finds Cherie (Marilyn Monroe), a chanteuse who sings at the Blue Dragon, the quintessential smoke-filled dive. What starts out as a fierce, funny battle of the sexes ultimately turns to love while the two are snowbound overnight at a roadside restaurant. Murray's depiction of the rambunctious cowboy is perhaps the greatest performance of his career. But Monroe, of course, steals the show. Her sympathetic portrayal of an essentially sweet girl who's "been around" represented a critical breakthrough for the mythical sex goddess.

BUSTER AND BILLIE
1974, USA, R ☆☆½
Jan-Michael Vincent, Joan Goodfellow, Pamela Sue Martin, Clifton James, Robert Englund. Directed by Daniel Petrie. 100 min.

Bucolic beauty and brutal violence mix uneasily in this romance between Buster (Jan-Michael Vincent), a handsome, popular boy at the local high school, and Billie (Joan Goodfellow), a slightly dim-witted, abused farmgirl who regularly submits to rape by the horny local boys. When Buster jilts his steady and starts dating Billie, who's been mislabeled the town tramp, the repercussions are bloody and, in context, unbelievable. Still, the well-focused performances and Petrie's decent period evocation of Georgia in the 1940s may hold your attention.

BUSTIN' LOOSE
1981, USA, R ☆☆½
Richard Pryor, Cicely Tyson, Robert Christian, George Coe, Bill Quinn, Roy Jenson, Fred Carney. Directed by Oz Scott. 94 min.

A slight, sloppy, sentimental comedy, this film succeeds by providing enough opportunities for its star, Richard Pryor, to get into his act. Playing a parolee who's been recruited to drive a busload of maladjusted kids across the country, Pryor uses every predicament—be it an encounter with a Doberman pinscher or one with the KKK—to create a sort of instant theater: with one electrified glance, or a twitch of his nose, he musters up more conviction, wit, and drama than either Roger L. Simon's screenplay or Oz Scott's direction can provide. As a prim, dedicated social worker, Cicely Tyson gives Pryor class—and he gives her comedy. By the final chase scene, the two of them are tossing sight gags back and forth with the élan of a seasoned comedy team.

BUTCH AND SUNDANCE: THE EARLY DAYS
1979, USA, PG ☆☆☆
William Katt, Tom Berenger, Jeff Corey, John Schuck, Michael C. Gwynne, Peter Weller, Brian Dennehy, Christopher Lloyd, Jill Eikenberry, Arthur Hill, Vincent Schiavelli. Directed by Richard Lester. 110 min.

A "prequel" to *Butch Cassidy and the Sundance Kid* (well, they couldn't exactly make a sequel with the same two characters, could they?) follows the teams' exploits as fledgling outlaws. In the Robert Redford and Paul Newman roles, William Katt and Tom Berenger do better than might have been expected, and a large supporting cast of familiar faces helps, but Richard Lester's direction is below his best work—competent but uninspired. Enjoyable enough, though it doesn't compare to the original.

BUTCH CASSIDY AND THE SUNDANCE KID
1969, USA, PG ☆☆☆☆
Paul Newman, Robert Redford, Katherine Ross, Strother Martin, Henry Jones, Jeff Corey, George Furth, Cloris Leachman, Ted Cassidy, Kenneth Mars, Sam Elliott. Directed by George Roy Hill. 112 min.

Butch Cassidy and the Sundance Kid is simply one of the most enjoyable films to come out of Hollywood in the last few decades. Paul Newman and Robert Redford created an archetype for male relationships in American movies—an archetype whose perfect obverse was Dustin Hoffman and Jon Voight in *Midnight Cowboy*, released at the same time in late 1969. The dialogue by William Goldman is superb, as is the photography of the American West. The film has adventure, romance, comedy, and even a bit of mythologizing, but all without most of the self-conscious parody that ultimately mars the Steven Spielberg and George Lucas blockbusters of more recent years. For pure entertainment, Butch and Sundance can't be beat. If you worked really hard at it, you could maybe find some captious things to say about this film. For instance, the scene where we're set up to think that Katherine Ross is about to be raped has a vague misogyny to it. And it's probably not such a good idea to make being an outlaw look like so much fun. But if you have that great a need to find fault with things, go pick on the national debt and leave *Butch* alone.

BUTTERFLIES ARE FREE ☆☆½
1972, USA, PG
Goldie Hawn, Edward Albert, Eileen Heckart, Michael Glasser. Directed by Milton Katselas. 109 min.

Eileen Heckart won a Best Supporting Actress Oscar playing the overbearing mother of a blind young man (Edward Albert), and she is excellent in the monstrous role. Otherwise, this adaptation by Leonard Gershe of his Broadway play is coy and obvious. Gershe manages some cute Neil Simonesque one-liners in the early part of the film, but his writing soon becomes strained and serious. Goldie Hawn was able to get away with her kooky blonde routine in those days, and she does provide some refreshment as the man's neighbor. However, even her character grows tiresome to watch. A failed attempt at the bittersweet.

BUTTERFLY ☆
1982, USA, R
Pia Zadora, Stacy Keach, Orson Welles, Lois Nettleton, Edward Albert, James Franciscus, Stuart Whitman, June Lockart, Ed McMahon. Directed by Matt Amber. 108 min.

This inept adaptation of the almost equally inept novel by James M. Cain is too turgid to qualify for camp immortality, but it does feature one of the all-time preposterous performances: that of Pia Zadora. In her first starring role, this freakish-seeming creature, who has the face of a four-year-old and the squirmy body of a nubile teen, plays the long-lost daughter of a dim-witted miner (Stacy Keach), whom she promptly seduces; what she's really after, of course, is the mother lode. The movie has a notorious bathtub scene, which proves notable less for its explicitness than for the sublimely demented look on Keach's face as he succumbs to Zadora's squeaky-clean charms. And no movie whose supporting cast includes Orson Welles *and* Ed McMahon should be ignored completely.

THE BUTTERFLY AFFAIR ☆☆
1970, France/Italy, PG
Henri Charrière, Georges Arminel, Leroy Haynes, Claudia Cardinale. Directed by Jean Herman. 100 min.

Henri Charrière, whose book *Papillon* became a hit film, somehow acquired the clout to star in his own screenplay here, but his onscreen charisma level is nowhere near that of Steve McQueen. This *Butterfly* remains artistically in the larval stage, as it unfolds a tale of a big diamond heist and the double-dealing complications arising among the caper's coconspirators. Strenuously directed, but all the plot twists can't disguise the familiarity of this material, nor redeem it from the commonplace. (a.k.a.: *Popsy Pop*)

BYE BYE BIRDIE ☆☆☆
1963, USA
Ann-Margret, Dick Van Dyke, Janet Leigh, Maureen Stapleton, Paul Lynde, Bobby Rydell, Ed Sullivan, Jesse Pearson. Directed by George Sidney. 112 min.

This musical about teen idol-worship is still as energetic as ever. Ann-Margret stars as a lovestruck high-school girl who drops her steady beau, Hugo (Bobby Rydell), when the country's reigning rock star, Conrad Birdie, comes to town for his last appearance before going into the Army. It's a merry and occasionally sharp spoof of Elvis-mania, shot in the cartoon-bright style of a 1960s sitcom. Best-known song: "Put on a Happy Face."

BYE BYE BRAZIL ☆☆☆
1980, Brazil/France
Betty Faria, Jose Wilker, Fabio Junior, Zaria Zambelli. Directed by Carlos Diegues. 100 min.

This sexy, sarcastic comedy is about a low-rent traveling carnival wending its way across 9,000 miles of Brazilian countryside. Director Carlos Diegues finds the cultural chaos of his homeland at once hilarious and enraging, and the squalid Brazilian landscape itself becomes a string of black jokes. One of the most popular foreign films of the past decade.

BY DESIGN ☆☆
1981, Canada, R
Patty Duke Astin, Sara Botsford, Saul Rubinek. Directed by Claude Jutra. 90 min.

Claude Jutra's gentle comedy tells of the complications that ensue when one half of a lesbian couple, still very much in love with her partner, decides that she wants to have a baby. Rejecting artificial insemination, she and her lover go in search of good genes. It's nicely acted and rarely goes for cheap laughs, but one wishes Jutra hadn't burdened an interesting and sympathetic portrayal with a low-comedy pretext.

C

CABARET
1972, USA, PG ☆☆☆☆
Liza Minnelli, Joel Grey, Michael York, Helmut Griem, Marisa Berenson, Fritz Wepper. Directed by Bob Fosse. 124 min.

Bob Fosse's dynamite, provocative film version of the Broadway stage musical artfully sets the story of a divinely decadent American girl against the solemn political backdrop of Hitler's rise in old Berlin. Liza Minnelli's energetic, captivating portrayal of Sally Bowles, which won her an Academy Award, remains her trademark role. Joel Grey earned a Best Supporting Actor Oscar for his penetrating performance as the sinister emcee of the Kit Kat Klub, and Michael York adroitly plays an American bisexual who gets involved with both Minnelli and German playboy Helmut Griem. With great acting, social commentary, and evocative atmosphere, *Cabaret* is a drama with music, not music tied together by a plot. Fosse's ingenious staging of musical numbers is another benefit. Winner of eight Academy Awards.

THE CABINET OF DR. CALIGARI
1919, Germany ☆☆☆☆
Conrad Veidt, Werner Krauss, Lil Dagover. Directed by Robert Wiene. 69 min.

As the high-water mark of German Expressionist filmmaking, this is quite probably one of the most influential films ever made; just for openers, its progeny includes almost every *film noir* and horror film to follow. Werner Krauss as the original Mad Doctor (or is he?) and Conrad Veidt as Cesare the Somnambulist act in the best Expressionist manner, which is to say very stylized in a way that would be ludicrous were it not for the equally fantastic and surrealistic sets and photography. Of course, the film appears very dated, but its fragmented, distorted visuals still suggest the power that it exerted at its original release: it no longer frightens, but the fetid images remain compelling.

CABIN IN THE SKY
1943, USA ☆☆☆½
Ethel Waters, Lena Horne, Eddie "Rochester" Anderson, Rex Ingram, Louis Armstrong, Kenneth Spencer, John "Bubbles" Sublett, Butterfly McQueen, Duke Ellington and His Orchestra. Directed by Vincente Minnelli. 100 min.

An all-black Hollywood musical, this movie is less condescending than others of its ilk (*Hallelujah, The Green Pastures, Stormy Weather*). Joseph Shank's adaptation of Lynn Root's 1940 Broadway fantasy play retained the clever framing battle between Good (Kenneth Spencer) and Evil (Rex Ingram), as well as the central story, in which Lena Horne is unleashed as a satanic temptress who lures hapless Eddie "Rochester" Anderson away from homey Ethel Waters. That plot becomes the cue for a series of catchy, artfully staged songs, the highlights of which are: Waters's and Anderson's brookside duet to the title number; John "Bubbles" Sublett's "Shine" specialty; Duke Ellington's "Things Ain't What They Used to Be"; and Waters's definitive, scalding hot "Honey in the Honeycomb." Horne, in one of her few full-scale roles, had her best number (something in a bubble bath) cut by the censors. Vincente Minnelli's stylish, intimate mise-en-scène (this was his first feature) was exactly right for this MGM project, and it provided audiences with relief from Busby Berkeley's kaleidoscopic spectacles. Ironically, an uncredited Berkeley staged one of the numbers for this film.

CABOBLANCO
1980, USA, R ☆
Charles Bronson, Jason Robards, Jr., Dominique Sanda, Fernando Rey, Denny Miller, Simon MacCorkindale. Directed by J. Lee Thompson. 87 min.

Any resemblance to the title of the classic film *Casablanca* is obviously intended, but comparisons are odious and so is the film. *Caboblanco* features a lot of senseless but fairly exciting action sequences revolving around the beefy presence of stolid Charles Bronson, a man of few words and many retaliations. Sometimes, as he glares interminably in a close-up, you may get the feeling that silent movies have returned. *Casablanca* fans may note the many superficial resemblances and want to have this film buried in North Africa.

CACTUS
1986, Australia ☆☆
Isabelle Huppert, Robert Menzies, Norman Kaye, Monica Maughan, Banduk Marika, Sheila Florance, Peter Aanensen. Directed by Paul Cox. 95 min.

In this glum, arid romantic drama from Down Under, Isabelle Huppert plays a Frenchwoman who's partially blinded in a car accident and must face the possibility of total loss of sight. Gradually, she becomes involved with a young blind man (Robert Menzies) who's every bit as prickly as the cacti he loves to study. Slow, dry as dust, and often unnecessarily elliptical, *Cactus* is helped by Huppert's intriguing presence and some visually pleasing directorial flourishes, but the story is flimsy and predictable.

CACTUS FLOWER
1969, USA ☆☆½
Walter Matthau, Ingrid Bergman, Goldie Hawn, Jack Weston, Rick Lenz. Directed by Gene Saks. 103 min.

This is an amusing but predictable farce about a dentist (Walter Matthau) who tricks his girlfriend (Best Supporting Actress Goldie Hawn) into thinking he is married to his secretary (Ingrid Bergman). The screenplay by I. A. L. Diamond is slick and intermittently sophisticated, but it lacks the great cynical wit and clever plot twists he provided in his screenplays for director Billy Wilder (*Love in the Afternoon, Some Like It Hot, The Apartment*). Diamond was constricted, no doubt, by having to remain faithful to the play by Abe Burrows, which was in turn based on a French original by Pierre Barillet and Jean Pierre Gredy. The results are like average Neil Simon, but the three stars play it charmingly.

CADDIE
1976, Australia, PG ☆☆½
Helen Morse, Takis Emmanual, Jack Thompson. Directed by Donald Crombie. 107 min.

This early Australian-feminist film is about a woman (Helen Morse) who walks out on her faithful husband and is faced with the task of supporting herself and her two children. With no job skills or financial resources to speak of, she takes a job as a barmaid in a Sydney pub. Through the first half, director Donald Crombie's style is hard, humorous, and pointed. But somewhere during the middle of the film, all the intelligence seeps out of it. The photography goes fuzzy, and when Caddie meets a handsome Greek in the silk business, we might as well be watching a soap opera. The movie manages to stumble into all the pitfalls of straight autobiography: it lacks the consistent point of view and scrupulous design of a well-told story, and demonstrates an uncanny ability to mimic the soaps. Comic highlight: a depiction of a now-defunct Aussie tradition, the six o'clock swill.

CADDYSHACK ☆☆½
1980, USA, R
Chevy Chase, Bill Murray, Rodney Dangerfield, Ted Knight, Michael O'Keefe, Albert Salmi, Brian Doyle-Murray. Directed by Harold Ramis. 90 min.

One of the few post–Animal House, youth-anarchy comedies that's actually funny, though not nearly so much as a perusal of the cast might lead you to hope. At a snobby WASP country club, the uppity golfers (led by a rampaging Ted Knight) have it out with the forces of weirdness, which include Bill Murray as a grungy gardner and Rodney Dangerfield as an irresistibly crazed millionaire. The story (about a teen caddy who wants to win a scholarship) is pretty lame stuff, but when the comics take over, the movie hits some wild highs. Written by National Lampoon/Second City/Saturday Night Live alumni Doug Kenney, Harold Ramis, and Brian Doyle-Murray.

CAESAR AND CLEOPATRA ☆☆☆
1946, Great Britain
Vivien Leigh, Claude Rains, Stewart Granger, Flora Robson, Francis L. Sullivan, Cecil Parker. Directed by Gabriel Pascal. 135 min.

George Bernard Shaw's witty play gets an overly reverent treatment here, resulting in a stodgy, self-consciously "important" film that loses some of the play's wit and style. Claude Rains is a fine Caesar, and Vivien Leigh makes a satisfactory Cleopatra, but Shaw's light-spirited writing deserved a less-ponderous handling. (A later television version with Rex Harrison and Geneviève Bujold was far better.)

CAFÉ EXPRESS ☆☆½
1981, Italy
Nino Manfredi, Adolfo Celi, Vittorio Mezzogiorno, Luigi Basagaluppi, Silvio Spaccesi, Gigi Reder. Directed by Nanni Loy. 90 min.

Nino Manfredi stars in a spiritual (if not actual) sequel to Bread and Chocolate. Once again, he portrays a meek, softhearted, occasionally scheming soul trying to eke out a living by waiting on people. This time, he's an unauthorized coffee vendor aboard the second-class section of the Naples-to-Salerno express train. The movie, which takes place almost entirely aboard the moving train, is basically a series of anecdotes involving Manfredi's encounters with assorted passengers and with the police, who are hot on his tail. Director Nanni Loy cowrote the screenplay with Elvio Porto. The version on videocassette is fifteen minutes shorter than the original release print.

CAFÉ FLESH ☆☆☆
1982, USA, X
Pia Snow, Kevin Jay, Marie Sharp, Darcy Nycols. Directed by Rinse Dream. 80 min.

This is a unique low-budget shocker masquerading as pornography. The creative team had to promise to deliver hard-core penetration scenes in order to finance the kind of film they wanted to make. Although the X-rated insertions aren't titillating, they constitute part of the underground appeal of this cult film about a post–nuclear war wasteland. In a seedy cabaret, an impotent MC announces the live onstage sex acts performed by lucky "performers," who still have what it takes to entertain an audience consisting of nuclear holocaust survivors who can no longer have sex. The acting's not first-rate, but still above-average for porn, and the memorable pulsating rock score plus some clever directorial touches all help to flesh out this visually arresting movie. Not for the fainthearted, or for those planning an experimental excursion into "dirty movies."

LA CAGE AUX FOLLES ☆☆☆☆
1978, France, R
Michel Serrault, Ugo Tognazzi, Michel Galabru, Remy Laurent. Directed by Edouard Molinaro. 91 min.

This often hysterical and occasionally poignant farce is based on a French stage play about a young man who brings his respectable fiancée home to meet the folks—his middle-aged gay father and Dad's prima donna transvestite lover, Zaza. The kid asks both to play it straight for a night, and complications ensue. Although the film's portrayal of homosexuality ranges from mild condescension to pure camp, Ugo Tognazzi and Michel Serrault prove to be one of the cinema's great comic-romantic duos, and the warmth and compassion of their work (especially Serrault's) give the laughs a backbone of drama and humanity. Only three or four other foreign films have even approached La Cage's popularity in the United States, and one reason may be that its plot and humor translate so easily across different film cultures. All in all, it's far funnier and wiser than the lame sequels and glitzy Broadway musicalization it inspired, and well worth a look.

LA CAGE AUX FOLLES II ☆☆½
1980, France/Italy, R
Ugo Tognazzi, Michel Serrault, Gianni Frisoni, Marcel Bozzuffi, Michel Galabru, Paola Borboni, Benny Luke. Directed by Edouard Molinaro. 101 min.

This sequel to Edouard Molinaro's popular farce uses a heavy-handed spy-chase plot as an excuse for some more skits featuring Serrault and Tognazzi. When Albin, the cuddly transvestite, inadvertently acquires a top-secret microfilm capsule, our heroes are pursued by both the French government and a host of enemy agents. By the end of the movie almost everyone is scampering around in drag, and the novelty of the idea wears thin. The two stars are still highly effective, even though Francis Veber's screenplay lacks the symmetrical precision of his first.

LA CAGE AUX FOLLES III: THE WEDDING ☆
1985, France/Italy, PG-13
Michel Serrault, Ugo Tognazzi, Michel Galabru, Benny Luke, Stephane Audran. Directed by Georges Lautner. 87 min.

In what will, we fervently hope, be the last sequel to the popular farce, the homophobic underpinnings that made the poignant original such a hit become ever more apparent. Clubowner Renato stands to inherit a fortune if he can marry and produce an heir within eighteen months, but screaming queen Albin will have nothing to do with so "respectable" a life-style. Writer Francis Veber and director Edouard Molinaro, who gave the two previous entries some humanity along with the condescension, are absent here, and director Lautner and his six coscenarists are more than happy to trundle out the thinly veiled, cheap jokes.

CAGED HEAT ☆☆½
1974, USA, R
Barbara Steele, Erica Gavin, Juanita Brown, Roberta Collins, Rainbeaux Smith. Directed by Jonathan Demme. 84 min.

Any movie featuring Barbara Steele as a repressed, wheelchair-bound prison matron deserves the serious attention of film buffs. But this early effort of Jonathan Demme (Melvin and Howard, Stop Making Sense) has other unexpected pleasures to offer. It mocks the conventions of Women's Prison pics without ribbing them into parody. All the requisite violence is here, but it's stylized; all the voluptuous Big House Babes are present, but the nude scenes don't degrade women. As they unite against Nazi-like prison experiments and lousy chow, these resourceful convicts escape from both jail and the constrictions of a usually sexist genre. An extremely strange John Cale score adds to Demme's unconventional sound montage. (a.k.a.: Renegade Girls)

CAGED WOMEN ½☆
1984, Italy/France, R
Laura Gemser, Gabriele Tinti, Jack Stany. Directed by Vincent Dawn. 97 min.

This exceedingly violent exploitation picture wastes Laura Gemser (*Emanuelle the Queen, Emanuelle in America*) as a journalist who poses as a prostitute in order to expose the corruption inside a women's prison. Our heroine is beaten, poisoned, raped, attacked by rats and, in the film's most disgusting sequence, thrown into a pile of human excrement. Of course there are the obligatory vicious wardens and lesbian inmates, but they play second fiddle to the film's other atrocities.

CAHILL, U.S. MARSHALL ☆½
1973, USA, PG
John Wayne, Gary Grimes, George Kennedy, Neville Brand, Clay O'Brien. Directed by Andrew V. McLaglen. 102 min.

This film is a dismal account of a lawman (Wayne) who's so caught up in the business of catching bad guys that he neglects his two young sons. The youngsters, seeking attention, assist in a bank robbery while Dad's away, leaving it up to the Duke to . . . well, you can figure out the rest. Disjointedly directed by McLaglen, this soggy horse opera lacks the staying power of the then sixty-two-year-old Wayne. Pilgrims be warned.

THE CAINE MUTINY ☆☆☆☆
1954, USA
Humphrey Bogart, Jose Ferrer, Van Johnson, Fred MacMurray, Tom Tully, E. G. Marshall, Lee Marvin, Claude Akins, Jerry Paris, Whit Bissell. Directed by Edward Dmytryk. 123 min.

Herman Wouk's best-seller about a World War II naval mutiny and its courtroom aftermath is given a solid Preminger-like treatment in Edward Dmytryk's best film after *Crossfire* (1947). But the movie belongs to its stars, particularly Humphrey Bogart in his last great performance, a splendidly moving portrayal of the paranoid Captain Queeg. Fine acting from Van Johnson, Fred MacMurray, and especially Jose Ferrer as the defense lawyer.

CAL ☆☆☆½
1984, Ireland, R
John Lynch, Helen Mirren, Donal McCann, John Kavanagh, Ray McAnally, Stevan Rimkus. Directed by Pat O'Connor. 102 min.

A sullen, nineteen-year-old Ulster Catholic, guilt-torn over his involvement in the murder of a Northern Ireland policeman, is drawn into an affair with the Protestant cop's Catholic widow, but she remains unaware of the boy's IRA past. Director Pat O'Connor provides convincing details of the violence and grinding daily prejudice in Northern Ireland, and he's greatly aided by the superb, understated performances of John Lynch and Helen Mirren. Adapting his novel, Bernard MacLaverty has conveyed the horror of Ireland's "troubles" in a hushed, grieving tone that is no less effective for being somewhat schematic, and Mark Knopfler, of the rock band Dire Straits, has provided an exceptionally beautiful score. Well worth seeing.

CALIFORNIA DREAMING ☆☆
1979, USA, R
Glynnis O'Connor, Seymour Cassel, Dennis Christopher, Dorothy Tristan. Directed by John Hancock. 92 min.

Although this latter-day American International film contains all of the standard beach party props—surfing, volleyball, a publicity stunt, some innocent sex—the movie is unrelentingly downbeat in its portrayal of the dead-end lives of these beachless bums. The promised land has been moved to Hawaii, and the California kids are trapped at the edge of the continent where the sky is overcast and even the sand looks dirty. Dennis Christopher is strong as the serious kid from Chicago who gets taken in by the healthy beach gloss, and Glynnis O'Connor does a lot with her role as the sexy kid who sees the underlying moral rot.

CALIFORNIA GOLD RUSH ☆☆½
1981, USA (TV)
Robert Hays, Henry Jones, John Dehner, Gene Evans, Ken Curtis. Directed by Jack Hively. 100 min.

This fairly engrossing Wild West saga has a nodding acquaintance with Bret Harte's tales "The Luck of Roaring Camp" and "The Outcasts of Poker Flats." Action is the operative word here as money-grubbing gold prospectors converge on a town while newshound Robert Hays tries to put all the lively goings-on down on paper. This honest attempt to capture the colloquial twang and flavor of the Old West is partially successful, and the actors adept at playing regional types make the concept palatable.

CALIFORNIA SUITE ☆☆½
1978, USA, PG
Alan Alda, Michael Caine, Bill Cosby, Jane Fonda, Walter Matthau, Elaine May, Richard Pryor, Maggie Smith. Directed by Herbert Ross. 103 min.

Neil Simon's slick but uneven series of sketches set in a Los Angeles luxury hotel is in the vein of his own *Plaza Suite*, and about as funny. Bickering is the theme here, as Jane Fonda and Alan Alda trade barbs and snarls over their daughter, Bill Cosby and Richard Pryor go head-to-head (with extremely disappointing results) as buddies on a weekend trip with their wives, and Michael Caine and Maggie Smith chew over the remains of their sad marriage. The fourth sketch, with Walter Matthau and Elaine May, is an achingly tired bedroom farce. Much of the writing is just above "Love Boat" level, but Simon does pull off one lovely seriocomic vignette, about an actress in town for her nerve-racking shot at an Academy Award. (In real life Smith won an Oscar as Best Supporting Actress for her delicately etched portrayal—in the film she loses.)

CALIGULA ½☆
1980, USA, self-imposed X
Malcolm McDowell, Helen Mirren, John Gielgud, Peter O'Toole. Directed by Tinto Brass. 156 min.

Historically semi-accurate tale of the mad Roman emperor's reign of terror provides an excuse for *Penthouse* editor and movie producer Bob Guccione to insert hard-core sex and moments of nauseating violence. Between these shocking sequences, *Caligula* is a dull, talky movie about imperial intrigue. Malcolm McDowell behaves like an enfant terrible, and the rest of the excellent cast (including Peter O'Toole) is similarly wasted. The repugnance of the movie caused screenwriter Gore Vidal to have his name removed from the credits. Made for the then whopping cost of $15 million.

CALLIE AND SON ☆☆
1981, USA (TV)
Lindsay Wagner, Jameson Parker, Dabney Coleman, Joy Garrett, Michelle Pfeiffer, John Harkins, James Sloyan, Andrew Prine. Directed by Waris Hussein. 97 min.

In this soapy, mildly entertaining TV melodrama, Lindsay Wagner tries—and fails—to fill Joan Crawford's shoulder pads as a young mother who works her way up the social ladder and will stop at nothing to ensure the fortunes of her teenaged son (Jameson Parker). Wagner is too young for her role, and Parker too old for his; the juicy story by Texas-trash chronicler Tommy Thompson (*Blood and Money*) becomes bogged down in TV-movie clichés. The heavily edited video version eliminates over forty-five minutes of the overlong original and concentrates on the second, better half.

CALL OF THE CANYON ☆☆
1942, USA
Gene Autry, Smiley Burnette, Ruth Terry, the Sons of the Pioneers. Directed by Joseph Santley. 71 min.

This above-average Gene Autry Western combines a tale of a treacherous cattle buyer with a young woman's attempt to start a singing-cowboy radio show. Though the film contains little action, the plot integrates the musical numbers, which include support from the Sons of the Pioneers.

THE CALL OF THE WILD ☆½
1972, West Germany/Spain/Italy/France/Great Britain
Charlton Heston, Raimund Harmsdorf, Michele Mercier, George Eastman. Directed by Ken Annakin. 100 min.

This is a mediocre version of the often-filmed Jack London novel about two prospectors in the Klondike gold rush days, saved from many a scrape by their faithful guide dog Buck. Although technically well-made, with some beautiful location shooting (in Finland), this is mostly a drag; the 1935 Clark Gable version, while not as faithful to the book, is much better.

THE CALL OF THE WILD ☆☆☆
1976, USA (TV)
John Beck, Bernard Fresson, Michael Pataki, Billy Green Bush, Donald Moffat. Directed by Jerry Jameson. 100 min.

Boasting a well-honed script by James Dickey (*Deliverance*), this compelling TV treatment of the Jack London classic is faithful to the book with a no-holds-barred depiction of man's struggle for survival in the wilderness. A gritty examination of the effects of gold fever, this film chronicles the difficulties of panning for gold in the Klondike while battling the forces of nature. Not as much fun as the gussied-up 1935 Hollywood version, but it has more impact.

CALL OUT THE MARINES ☆☆
1942, USA
Victor McLaglen, Edmund Lowe, Franklin Pangborn. Directed by Frank Ryan and William Hamilton. 66 min.

Victor McLaglen, John Ford's favorite brawling Irishman, and suave Edmund Lowe team up for this good-natured but thoroughly mediocre service comedy. The two rejoin the marines, chase after girls, and engage in far too many tiresome antics. The movie aims for a wisecracking style, but the writing isn't good enough to make it work. A few cute tunes make this period piece occasionally amusing.

CALL TO GLORY ☆½
1984, USA (TV)
Craig T. Nelson, Cindy Pickett. Directed by Thomas Carter. 98 min.

This film was the slow-moving pilot for the 1984–85 series. Set in the turbulent times of 1962, the story centers on a dedicated U.S. Air Force colonel (Craig T. Nelson) and his family. You get a flavor of life in the early 1960s, but political issues are merely skimmed over while family melodrama rules.

CAMELOT ☆½
1967, USA, PG
Richard Harris, Vanessa Redgrave, Franco Nero. Directed by Joshua Logan. 178 min.

Joshua Logan's botched version of *Camelot* is not likely to dissuade anyone from listening to the Broadway cast album. Alan Jay Lerner and Frederick Loewe wrote a lovely score for this retelling of the story. Richard Harris is so heavily made up as to suggest *La Cage aux Folles*; the extraordinary number of grating close-ups of Harris while he shouts the songs must be rated as perhaps the low point of the 1960s musicals. Vanessa Redgrave is of course much better as Guinevere, but Logan's vulgarity infuses her also; the actress is skittish much of the time and only in some of her wordless reaction shots does she suggest her skill. Further, one keeps longing for Marni Nixon's return after hearing Redgrave's undubbed voice. *Camelot*, with its withered, gnarled settings and Las Vegas–on–the–Thames style of costumes, is an extraordinarily ugly film.

CAMILA ☆☆☆
1984, Argentina/Spain
Susu Pecoraro, Imanol Arias, Hector Alterio, Elena Tasisto, Carlos Muñoz, Hector Pellegrini, Juan Leyrado, Cecilio Madanes, Mona Maris. Directed by Maria Luisa Bemberg. 105 min.

This film is a lavishly mounted period drama with surprising political and erotic punch, based on a real-life incident in which a well-bred young woman and a priest caused a national scandal in 1847 by falling in love. First-time director Maria Luisa Bemberg, filming during the loosening of cultural restrictions after the downfall of Argentina's military government, creates some incisive parallels between Camila and Gutierrez's suffering under a church-state patriarchy and her country's current political situation. Many of these parallels may be lost on an American audience, but the narrative remains an enticing blend of romanticism and anger, with stars Susu Pecoraro, Imanol Arias, and Hector Alterio doing exceptionally distinguished work. Ignore the syrupy, mitigating coda and enjoy the rest of the film.

CAMILLE 2000 ☆☆
1969, USA
Daniele Gaubert, Nino Castelnuovo, Eleanora Rossi Drago. Directed by Radley Metzger. 116 min.

Like Russ Meyer, Radley Metzger figured that there was money to be made in the 1960s by bringing sex and nudity out of stag films and into "real" movies. But where Meyer took his inspiration straight from those stag films and all other things American, Metzger looked to the Europeans; his films are generally lavish, glossy, melodramatic, and pretentious, the idea being that "it's OK if they're naked because it's Art." This is probably the best of his output, a retelling of the Dumas tearjerker in a futuristic setting. Although the film is an American production in English, it was made in Rome with a top-notch Italian crew, so it does *look* good. But that's just background, and what's going on in the foreground is tame by today's standards. Using the pseudonym Henry Paris, Metzger went on to make some of the first hard-core films to gain wider public respectability (*Opening of Misty Beethoven, The Private Afternoons of Pamela Mann*).

THE CANDIDATE ☆☆☆
1972, USA, PG
Robert Redford, Melvyn Douglas, Peter Boyle, Don Porter, Allen Garfield, Karen Carlson. Directed by Michael Ritchie. 110 min.

The casting of Robert Redford as the epitome of political sincerity, always ready to give autographs, shake hands, knit his brow with concern, or just flash his white teeth, is *The Candidate*'s coup—his presence gives this inconsistent and finally insubstantial study of show-biz politics a real edge. Jeremy Larner's Oscar-winning script has him playing a young California Democrat, recruited to run for the Senate, whose ideals diminish as his standing in the polls moves from underdog to front-runner. The film deserves credit for having a defined perspective; it's unabashedly liberal, anti-"system" and anti–Nixon era politics. But Michael Ritchie's direction is wobbly in tone, stumbling between mordant comedy, serious indictment, and flashy farce. Some of the film's targets may seem rather tame as well, since the intervening years have seen a glut of political satire. But fine performances, especially from Redford and Melvyn Douglas as an ex-governor who'd sell his grandmother down the river, give *The Candidate* an entertaining charge.

CANDLESHOE ☆☆½
1977, USA, G
David Niven, Helen Hayes, Jodie Foster, Leo McKern, Vivian Pickles. Directed by Norman Tokar. 101 min.

The folks at Walt Disney Studios didn't seem especially bothered by the fact that Jodie Foster's most recent film prior to this had been *Taxi Driver*, in which she played a pre-deb hooker; this is somewhat more standard fare, with Foster as a tomboy being passed off by a British con man as the long-lost granddaughter of a rich old dowager (Helen Hayes). Prime interest, assuming you're not just looking for something unobjectionable to plop the kids down in front of, comes from David Niven, playing four roles in a nice Peter Sellers/Alec Guinness–ish turn.

CANDY STRIPE NURSES ☆½
1974, USA, R
Candice Rialson, Robin Mattson, Maria Rojo, Kimberly Hyde, Dick Miller. Directed by Allan Holleb. 80 min.

This is a lukewarm sex comedy from Roger Corman's stable. Some pretty volunteer nurses handle their patients with shocking familiarity. It's doubtful that even a tired businessman will experience a rise in temperature due to the ministrations of these cuties, but a cast of R-rated veterans tries hard to resuscitate all the expected innuendos.

CAN I DO IT . . . TIL I NEED GLASSES? ☆½
1980, USA, R
Roger Behr, Debra Klose, Moose Carlson, Walter Olkewicz, Robin Williams, Roger and Roger. Directed by I. Robert Levy. 73 min.

Apart from the different titles, this "sequel" to *If You Don't Stop It, You'll Go Blind* may as well be the same movie. Like its predecessor, this film consists of a small cast of moderately talented comedians acting out a series of very old dirty jokes. It's not actually that bad, but it is pretty pointless—watchable in a pinch, as long as you've got a reasonable tolerance for forced bawdiness. This flick was the subject of a lawsuit by Robin Williams, who filmed one segment for it; on the strength of his name, the picture was rereleased in 1979.

CANNERY ROW ☆½
1982, USA, PG
Nick Nolte, Debra Winger, Audra Lindley, Frank McRae, M. Emmet Walsh. Directed by David S. Ward. 120 min.

This treacly adaptation of John Steinbeck's *Cannery Row* and *Sweet Thursday* deals in part with the romance of a marine biologist and a would-be hooker in the old cannery town of Monterey, California. A canned screenplay stuffed with clichés and a ludicrously overelaborate production design consign this allegedly whimsical love story to the junk pile. The corniest elements of Steinbeck's stories about love among the low-lifes are sweetened up with cheap sentiment and stickiness that the attractive brio of the two leads cannot dispel. Strictly from Torpor-ville.

CANNONBALL ☆☆☆
1976, USA, PG
David Carradine, Bill McKinney, Veronica Hamel, Gerrit Graham, Robert Carradine. Directed by Paul Bartel. 93 min.

Black comedy and relentless action characterize a cross-country auto race, as contestants who'll do anything to win vie for the $100,000 grand prize. Director Paul Bartel invests *Cannonball* with the same over-the-top energy he put into *Death Race 2000*, which also starred David Carradine. Here, fancy sci-fi gadgetry is replaced by seemingly infinite and surprisingly entertaining variations on the car-crash theme, and a good, mean-spirited story pulls it along. Cameos by Joe Dante, Martin Scorsese, Roger Corman, and Sylvester Stallone; virtually remade in 1981 as *The Cannonball Run*, without all the fun.

THE CANNONBALL RUN ☆½
1981, USA, PG
Burt Reynolds, Dom DeLuise, Farrah Fawcett, Roger Moore, Dean Martin, Sammy Davis, Jr., Jack Elam, Adrienne Barbeau, Terry Bradshaw, Bert Convy, Jamie Farr, Peter Fonda, George Furth, Bianca Jagger, Molly Picon, Mel Tillis. Directed by Hal Needham. 95 min.

To judge by what's on screen, Burt Reynolds, Hal Needham, and their pals had such a good time making this moronic comedy that the movie itself was only an afterthought. Buried deep in the film is a great idea for a chase comedy: the Cannonball Sea-to-Shining-Sea Memorial Trophy dash is an actual (and highly illegal) cross-country racing competition held every two years. But the movie, which is devoid of interesting incidents, leaves us with nothing more than a handful of character actors sending up their screen images, which are caricatures to start with. There is one good thing to be said for it: at least it's better than the sequel.

CANNONBALL RUN 2 ½☆
1984, USA, PG
Burt Reynolds, Dom DeLuise, Shirley MacLaine, Marilu Henner, Sammy Davis, Jr., Dean Martin, Frank Sinatra, Susan Anton, Catherine Bach. Directed by Hal Needham. 108 min.

Could any film be worse than *Cannonball Run*? Yes. The first car-crashing bore crossbred the *Smokey and the Bandit* formula of rural humor and car chases with the *Around the World in 80 Days* formula of now-you-see-'em-now-you-don't movie star cameos—over twenty of them. This low comedy of the highway drives along that same familiar road as another cross-country race is waged in a film littered with stalled jokes, wrecked cars, and big-name actors whose performances here can only be listed as fatalities. It's like "Hee Haw" played on a bad stretch of road.

CAN SHE BAKE A CHERRY PIE? ☆☆½
1983, USA
Michael Emil, Karen Black, Michael Margotta, Martin Harvey Friedberg. Directed by Henry Jaglom. 90 min.

Lily Tomlin once remarked that it would be nice if someone could take all those aimless people wandering around big cities talking to themselves and pair them off so that they looked like they were having conversations. This seems to be what director/writer Henry Jaglom has done here, with Karen Black and Michael Emil incessantly at each other about relationships past and present. Surprisingly, Black is much more restrained here than she is in more tightly scripted films. Emil, however, is a hit-and-miss case; a non-cute hybrid of Woody Allen and Wallace Shawn, he spends most of the movie sprawled out in bikini underwear (someone get this man a robe, please!) rattling on and on and on and . . . Good music, anyway.

CANTONEN IRON KUNG FU ☆☆
Hong Kong
Liang Jia-Ren, Wang Chung. Directed by Li Chao.

This film is a tremendously paced, dynamic cliché-fest carried entirely by the powerful Liang Jia-Ren. His Iron Bridge kung fu style is more than a match for the bad guy's Eagle kung fu.

CAN'T STOP THE MUSIC ☆
1980, USA, PG
The Village People, Steve Guttenberg, Bruce Jenner, Tammy Grimes, Valerie Perrine, June Havoc, Paul Sand. Directed by Nancy Walker. 118 min.

The unstoppable Allan Carr put together this lavish musical that purports to tell how the disco group the Village People came to be. That singing group is used in this unspeakably tacky film the way blacks playing family retainers were used in films of the thirties and forties. Although the filmmakers have the best intentions in being fair rather than "broadminded," the Village People was always a gay group for heterosexuals. Today, the group is a faded memory. If only the film were too, but this homophobic mess is on tape for you to watch to your endless amazement. This is recommended only for those with a curiosity for the awesomely awful, and for those members of a secret underground movement awaiting the return of disco music to the pop mainstream. We suspect this bomb was not made in cooperation with the Young Men's Christian Association.

CAN YOU HEAR THE LAUGHTER?: THE STORY OF FREDDIE PRINZE ★★
1979, USA (TV)
Ira Angustain, Kevin Hooks, Julie Carmen. Directed by Burt Brinckerhoff. 106 min.

Hollywood's instinct for cannibalization remains unerring; after comedian Freddie Prinze shot to stardom in the mid-seventies on the NBC sitcom "Chico and the Man," then fell victim to cocaine and, perhaps accidentally, killed himself, his rise and fall became the fodder for just one more TV movie. Ira Angustain does a fair Prinze impersonation and a good job at conveying the frustrations that drove the young star to ruin, but the film is slick and shallow, offering no insights or surprises.

CAPRICORN ONE ★★
1978, USA, PG
Elliott Gould, James Brolin, Brenda Vaccaro, Sam Waterston, O. J. Simpson, Hal Holbrook, David Huddleston, Karen Black, Telly Savalas. Directed by Peter Hyams. 127 min.

The premise of this film is terrific—the first Mars landing has been faked to save face and funding of the U.S. space program. But apart from Elliott Gould as a rumpled, chain-smoking investigative reporter, Telly Savalas as a crabby biplane pilot, and one good aerial chase sequence, it's practically a complete text on how *not* to make a big-budget thriller. The casting of the astronauts—the men we're supposed to care about—is a disaster (James Brolin as a tormented idealistic hothead?). Gould's task as a detective is made far too easy to generate real tension, and the one trace of a satisfying theme (is lofty illusion better for the country than sordid, demoralizing truth?) is just milked for a while and then dropped. Peter Hyams went on to direct *Outland* and *2010*.

CAPTAIN AMERICA ★½
1979, USA (TV)
Reb Brown, Heather Menzies, Len Birman, Steve Forrest, Robin Mattson. Directed by Rod Holcomb. 98 min.

A lackluster attempt to bring the popular comic book hero Captain America to the small screen, this pilot for a proposed series didn't catch fire. Reb Brown plays the ex-marine crimefighter who must use all of his powers to combat a maniac threatening to destroy Phoenix with a neutron bomb. This is unimaginative, unexciting, and fatally lacking in the most important quality for a live-action comic-strip fantasy: a sense of humor. A made-for-TV sequel followed (see below).

CAPTAIN AMERICA II: DEATH TOO SOON ★½
1979, USA (TV)
Reb Brown, Len Birman, Connie Sellecca, Katherine Justice, Christopher Lee. Directed by Ivan Nagy. 88 min.

The second of two attempts to make a small-screen superhero out of Reb Brown is marginally better than the first, thanks primarily to the presence of Christopher Lee as an archvillain threatening to spread a plague with a drug that accelerates the aging process. Lee does his best to enliven the tepid tale, but he's no match for the sluggish story and lethal lack of imagination.

CAPTAIN APACHE ★★
1971, Spain/USA
Lee Van Cleef, Carroll Baker, Stuart Whitman, Percy Herbert, Hugh McDermott. Directed by Alexander Singer. 94 min.

It's hard to tell just exactly how the filmmakers want you to take this Spaghetti Western: is it intended to be a parody of the genre, or is it just badly overloaded with clichés? The opening titles and song, as sung by star Lee Van Cleef, seem to point toward self-conscious parody, but they could have been tacked on afterward; and director Alexander Singer, who apprenticed with Stanley Kubrick, has usually been deadly serious in his other features. You'll probably enjoy this film most if you adopt a cynical attitude toward the proceedings. Van Cleef plays an Indian officer with the Union Army tracking down the killer of a U.S. agent. His drugged-out dream sequence is a choice bit of leftover 1960s pseudo-psychedelia.

CAPTAIN BLOOD ★★★½
1935, USA
Erroll Flynn, Olivia de Havilland, Lionel Atwill, Basil Rathbone, Guy Kibbee, Donald Meek, J. Carroll Naish. Directed by Michael Curtiz. 119 min.

Errol Flynn burst into the minds and hearts of the masses—and especially the ladies—with his portrayal of a doctor forced into piracy in this adaptation of Rafael Sabatini's swashbuckler. The exhilaration of it all hasn't faded largely because of the crisp, well-paced direction by Michael Curtiz. Lionel Atwill and Basil Rathbone are, as always, nicely snide bad guys, and a wonderful Erich Korngold score helps things along.

CAPTAIN CAUTION ★★
1940, USA
Victor Mature, Louise Platt, Leo Carillo, Bruce Cabot, Miles Mander, Alan Ladd. Directed by Ricard Wallace, 84 min.

This film chronicles the trials and tribulations of an American sailing ship during the period around the War of 1812. On its way back home with a hold of valuable cargo, the ship is seized by the British and put to use as a prison vessel. Along the way the captain is killed and his daughter (Louise Platt), aided by romantic interest Victor Mature, takes his place. For the Mature devotees who wouldn't rest comfortably until this was released on videocassette.

CAPTAIN KIDD ★★½
1945, USA
Charles Laughton, Randolph Scott, Barbara Britton, Reginald Owen, John Carradine, Gilbert Roland, John Qualen, Sheldon Leonard, Miles Mander. Directed by Roland V. Lee. 89 min.

This is a stylish, if occasionally dull, pirate adventure. Enlisted by the Crown to guard treasure-laden ships, Captain Kidd decides to double-cross king and country. Worth seeing for the overacting of a shipful of choice character actors, led by that prize ham Charles Laughton, and for the direction of Roland V. Lee (*Son of Frankenstein*).

CAPTAIN KRONOS: VAMPIRE HUNTER ★★★
1974, Great Britain, R
Horst Janson, John Carson, Shane Briant, Caroline Munro, Ian Hendry. Directed by Brian Clemens. 91 min.

This Hammer Studio horror, produced at about the time the studio was going under, is an admirable attempt to inject new life into an old genre. In fact, this is so unlike the typical vampire film that one hesitates to call it one. For instance, these vampires kill the young to obtain their youth, cutting off their lips instead of biting their necks. And the hero, Captain Kronos, a veteran of the War of 1812, instead of being a scientific Van Helsing type, is more a cross between Erroll Flynn and the Lone Ranger; he dispatches the monster not with a stake but in a swordfight. The ideas are more admirable than interesting. A nice try, anyway. Writer/director Brian Clemens got his start writing scripts for "The Avengers," which will give you a fair idea of the ambience you can expect here. (a.k.a.: *Kronos*)

CAPTAIN NEWMAN M.D. ★★★
1963, USA
Gregory Peck, Tony Curtis, Angie Dickinson, Larry Storch, Bethel Leslie, Robert Duvall, Bobby Darin. Directed by David Miller. 126 min.

A rather entertaining service melodrama with comic interludes, this film deals with an idealistic psychiatrist battling the little military minds who don't understand the problem of mental illness where their fighting men are concerned. Set on an American air base during World War II, the film is saved by its good-hearted expansiveness, even if it's scarcely an improvement over those psychological dramas of the 1930s in terms of depth. (It also suffers from that distinctive plastic Universal Studios sheen that always makes its films seem a few steps away from being TV movies.) Expertly acted, and Bobby Darin's surprisingly good turn netted him an Oscar nomination.

CAPTAIN SCARLETT ☆
1953, USA
Richard Greene, Leonora Amar, Nedrick Young, Manolo Fabregas. Directed by Thomas Carr. 75 min.

This film chronicles the adventures of another Robin Hood manqué, this one operating in France after the fall of Napoleon. (The film was shot in Mexico, but what the heck, all of those foreign countries look alike anyway, right?) The only reason we can think of that the marketing people decided to release this on videocassette, aside from appealing to the Richard Greene Appreciation Society, is that the rights were cheap and they thought that someone might think it was an Errol Flynn movie. It isn't.

CAPTAINS COURAGEOUS ☆☆☆
1937, USA
Freddie Bartholomew, Spencer Tracy, Lionel Barrymore, Melvyn Douglas, Mickey Rooney, John Carradine. Directed by Victor Fleming. 115 min.

This film dramatizes Rudyard Kipling's story of a spoiled rich kid (Freddie Bartholomew) who grows up and gets tough on board a fishing schooner. The tone of Kipling's novel, a moralistic adventure story for boys, is retained in this handsome, wholesome movie (directed by *Gone with the Wind*'s Victor Fleming). Spencer Tracy won an Oscar for his portrayal of a kindly Portuguese fisherman.

THE CAPTAIN'S PARADISE ☆☆☆
1953, Great Britain
Alec Guinness, Celia Johnson, Yvonne de Carlo, Charles Goldner, Miles Malleson. Directed by Anthony Kimmons. 89 min.

This charming farce (and the inspiration for many a TV sitcom) finds Alec Guinness playing a sea captain who travels between two wives stationed in different ports, each satisfying needs that the other cannot. The twist is that the wives change personalities and the captain is sunk. Alec Coppel's Oscar-nominated original story uses the bigamy theme for laughs and gets away with it, but the story is better than the film, which is played too smugly by Guinness for comfortable laughs. At least four films that have borrowed this plot are *Coffee, Tea or Me*, *A Touch of Class*, *Having It All*, and *My Other Husband*.

THE CAR ☆
1977, USA, PG
James Brolin, Kathleen Lloyd, John Marley, R. G. Armstrong, John Rubinstein. Directed by Elliot Silverstein. 98 min.

As automotive monster movies go, this cheapie about a driverless four-door with a vengeful streak can't measure up to *Christine*—why, the villainous auto here doesn't even have a first name! It does, however, have a nifty smoked-glass windshield, the better to look anonymous while pursuing its victims. With James Brolin playing the deputy sheriff who tries to stop this madness, you'll be rooting solidly for vehicular manslaughter.

CARAVAGGIO ☆
1986, Great Britain
Nigel Terry, Sean Bean, Garry Cooper, Spencer Leigh, Tilda Swinton, Michael Gough. Directed by Derek Jarman. 93 min.

Derek Jarman's flaccid pop biography, which has something to do with the life of the famous Renaissance painter, is like a Ken Russell movie without a sense of humor. Jarman includes ersatz-Fellini masques, gay beefcake models, and anachronistic images of typewriters and telephones—and he wants you to take it all seriously. The film is structured as a series of flashbacks from the agonized artist's deathbed, over which we hear semicoherent, erotic-philosophical narration. As a screenwriter Jarman is hopeless, and as a director he's perverse: the idea of staging scenes from the life of a celebrated painter as a collection of tableaux is one of those obvious art-and-life concepts that a filmmaker with any sense of forward movement would have instantly discarded. The result is pretty much what you'd expect—a silly, pretentious movie that's hell to sit through.

CARBON COPY ☆½
1981, USA, PG
George Segal, Susan Saint James, Jack Warden, Denzel Washington, Paul Winfield. Directed by Michael Schultz. 92 min.

This film is a rock-bottom comedy about a white businessman who meets the black teenage son he never knew he fathered. Issues of racial prejudice and tolerance are explored with the subtlety of flashcards, and the results manage to be at once treacly and offensive. Denzel Washington (of TV's "St. Elsewhere") does surprisingly well with the uncertain role of the son, but George Segal is shrill, unfunny, and overbearing in an increasingly familiar way.

THE CARDINAL ☆☆½
1963, USA
Thomas Tryon, Romy Schneider, Carol Lynley, Maggie McNamara, John Huston, Cecil Kellaway, John Saxon, Robert Morse, Dorothy Gish, Burgess Meredith, Ossie Davis, Jill Haworth, Chill Wills. Directed by Otto Preminger. 175 min.

Overlength may not be a cardinal sin in Catholicism, but it is in filmmaking, and this mammoth melodrama about the rise of a young Irish-Catholic from Back Bay priest to cardinal has some atoning to do. Otto Preminger uses the international locations and star-filled cast to keep the story moving as quickly as is feasible, but three hours is simply too much to devote to a melodrama which, for all its pretense at grappling with Big Questions, is pretty shallow. Thomas Tryon's dull performance in the leading role makes the film rough going, but stick around for John Huston's Oscar-nominated turn as an older cardinal.

THE CARE BEARS MOVIE ☆☆½
1985, USA, G
Animated: Mickey Rooney, Georgia Engel. Directed by Arna Selznick. 75 min.

Practically everything goes right with this colorful cartoon treat for tykes except for the emotionally uplifting grizzlies themselves. The animation is way above current Saturday morning standards, the colors are unbelievably pretty (as if you'd stepped into a kaleidoscope), and the story line about the buttinsky bears teaching two cynical kids how to trust holds interest. But the cuddly bears have no individual personalities as they gambol across the screen stamped with different markings on their chests (like convict ID numbers). Perhaps they should have just been marked "Sold," but in all fairness, this is agreeable tuneful fare for the Mister Rogers set. We just hope that every stuffed animal on the shelves of better card shops everywhere doesn't have a secret desire to end up in its own movie.

CARE BEARS MOVIE TWO: ☆☆
A NEW GENERATION
1986, USA, PG
Animated: Hadley Kay, Chris Wiggins, Cree Summer Francks, Alyson Court. Directed by Dale Schott. 77 min.

The cutesy, cuddly Care Bears are back, but this film is geared a bit too noticeably toward all those merchandising tie-ins.

(Perhaps the film should be evaluated by how many Care Bears toys it sold.) The film traces the beginnings of the Care Bear clan and the ways in which they brought plushy goodness to the world; here they try to stop Dark Heart from poisoning the minds of little summer campers by espousing a bad sport philosophy in place of the Care Bears homilies. While grown-up cynics may be rooting for the forces of evil, small fry will probably enjoy the pastel bears, the bright cartoon drawings, and the bouncy tunes.

CAREFREE ☆☆☆
1938, USA
Ginger Rogers, Fred Astaire, Ralph Bellamy, Luella Gear, Jack Carson, Clarence Kolb. Directed by Mark Sandrich. 83 min.

There is more plot than usual in this Fred Astaire–Ginger Rogers teaming, but the then-new use of psychoanalysis as a story machination wears thin. Rogers is amusing in some of her screwball scenes, but the magic is mostly lacking during the infrequent, impersonal dances.

CAREFUL, HE MIGHT HEAR YOU ☆☆☆
1983, Australia, PG
Wendy Hughes, Nicholas Gledhill, Robyn Nevin, John Hargreaves. Directed by Carl Schultz. 113 min.

This melodrama about an adorable six-year-old caught in a brutal custody fight floors the emotional accelerator until you're either hissing or cheering every scene. The winner of eight Australian Oscars, *Careful* was one of the biggest hits to come out of that country's revitalized film industry. It presents an endearingly clear-cut story of Good and Evil, with the former represented by the orphaned boy's poor but loving relations and the latter by one rich, powerful, mean aunt. As the tyrannical Vanessa, Wendy Hughes is grandly malicious and funny, creating one of the most convincing child-haters since the Wicked Witch of the West. You may quarrel with the extremity of the movie's depictions, but you'll probably be swept up all the same.

CARMEN ☆☆☆☆
1983, Spain, R
Antonio Gades, Laura del Sol, Paco de Lucia, Christina Hoyos. Directed by Carlos Saura. 102 min.

Of the flood of screen *Carmen*s in the early eighties, Carlos Saura's multilayered, structurally complex flamenco retelling is the most fiery, pleasurable, and satisfying. As in his other films, Saura creates a seductive seesaw between dream and reality, desire and fulfillment, and past and present, set within the story of a director/choreographer whose search for the perfect Carmen ends with a maddeningly elusive, untried dancer—named Carmen. As the rigors of rehearsal become ever more intense, actress and director both find the story of seduction and treachery beginning to take over their lives. Georges Bizet's great music is the starting point for the entrancing, erotic choreography, which weds dance, drama, and film more successfully than almost any movie of its time, including Saura's own earlier work.

CARMEN ☆☆½
1984, France/Italy
Julia Migenes-Johnson, Placido Domingo, Ruggero Raimondi, Faith Esham, Jean-Philippe Lafont, Gerard Garino. Directed by Francesco Rosi. 152 min.

Shot on location in Andalusia, Francesco Rosi's version of the Georges Bizet opera features an array of breathtaking settings—but it's odd to see singers and choruses lined up against the natural backdrops to face the audience in the most banal blocking since *A Night at the Opera*. Bizet's rhythmic energy and cheek are antithetical to the French Salon–painting imagery that Rosi evokes and to his jarring editing rhythms. As Carmen, Julia Migenes-Johnson is a forceful and intelligent actress who's been prodded in the direction of coarseness and vulgarity. As Don José, Placido Domingo sings up a storm and flares his nostrils when he gets upset.

CARMEN JONES ☆☆☆
1954, USA
Dorothy Dandridge, Harry Belafonte, Olga James, Joe Adams, Pearl Bailey, Diahann Carroll, Brock Peters. Directed by Otto Preminger. 105 min.

Otto Preminger's lumbering latter-day style was already forming as he mounted this Cinemascope version of Oscar Hammerstein II's all-black Broadway production. That's unfortunate, because the material would have made an excellent forties musical starring someone like Lena Horne. Here it's still good but never great. Dorothy Dandridge plays the tragic factory worker suspected of infidelity by her GI boyfriend (Harry Belafonte). The best thing about the film is the preservation of the score, which Hammerstein adapted from Georges Bizet's *Carmen*, but some viewers may feel uncomfortable with the way the racially derogatory lyrics are at odds with Harry Kleiner's dialogue. Dandridge is dubbed by Marilyn Horne, Belafonte (inexplicably) by Laverne Hutchinson, and Diahann Carroll by Bernice Peterson. Choreography by Herbert Ross and Herschel Burke Gilbert.

CARNAL KNOWLEDGE ☆☆☆½
1971, USA
Jack Nicholson, Art Garfunkel, Candice Bergen, Ann-Margret, Rita Moreno, Cynthia O'Neal, Carol Kane. Directed by Mike Nichols. 96 min.

The comic horror of male-female relationships is the subject of Mike Nichols's early 1970s classic about the sexual despair of two college roommates over three morally, politically, and carnally tumultuous decades. The screenplay, by the masterful comic-strip artist Jules Feiffer, hits some of its points very heavily; however, the film remains one of the few treatments of the toll sexism takes on men.

CARNIVAL STORY ☆½
1954, USA
Anne Baxter, Steve Cochran, Lyle Bettger, George Nader, Jay C. Flippen. Directed by Kurt Neumann. 94 min.

This melodrama was filmed in Munich, Germany, against a carnival background. The high-diving star has an affair with the show's agent, then drops him when she realizes what a heel he is, but can't shake him off. Decent performances help, but the sought-after thrills of watching numerous high-dives from a 100-foot-high platform won't do much for a modern audience.

CARNY ☆☆☆
1980, USA, R
Gary Busey, Jodie Foster, Robbie Robertson, Meg Foster, Kenneth McMillan, Elisha Cook, Jr. Directed by Robert Kaylor. 105 min.

This offbeat story of two carnival pros (Gary Busey and Robbie Robertson) involved with teenage runaway Jodie Foster slides from one formula to another: domestic thriller, buddy picture, even a sort of circusy *Camille*, with Busey coughing his way through Greta Garbo's part. But director Robert Kaylor has style and flash, and you get caught up in the film's rotting moral ambience. Foster gives an amazingly sexy performance.

CAROUSEL ☆☆½
1956, USA
Gordon MacRae, Shirley Jones, Cameron Mitchell, Gene Lockhart, Barbara Ruick, Robert Rounseville. Directed by Henry King. 128 min.

Yet another Rodgers and Hammerstein show becomes a slow-moving, "theatrical" film. Screenwriters Phoebe and Henry Ephron have meticulously retained the story of a New England carnival barker who is killed in a robbery but returns from heaven to guide his troubled family. They failed, however, to capture the frail whimsy of Ferenc Molnár's *Liliom*, filmed by Fritz Lang in 1934, or the offbeat charm of Rodgers and Hammerstein's 1945 Broadway show, directed by Rouben Mamoulian. Twentieth Century–Fox reteamed *Oklahoma*'s Gordon MacRae and Shirley Jones, but without that film's rich supporting cast and earful of standards to sing, they look wooden and pallid. The best number is still "June Is Busting out All Over." The wide-screen (Cinemascope 55) splendor will be lost to home-video viewers.

THE CARPETBAGGERS ☆½
1964, USA
George Peppard, Alan Ladd, Bob Cummings, Martha Hyer, Elizabeth Ashley, Lew Ayres, Martin Balsam, Leif Erickson, Carroll Baker, Arthur Franz, Tom Tully. Directed by Edward Dmytryk. 150 min.

Cut this up into a few pieces, add your own commercials, and whammo, you've got four episodes of a new nighttime soap! George Peppard plays the ruthless businessman; Alan Ladd (in his last film role) is his best friend; Elizabeth Ashley is his long-suffering wife; Carroll Baker is the sexpot actress—you get the idea. Fashion freaks take note of the gowns by Edith Head. From the novel by Harold Robbins, author of *The Lonely Lady*, and almost as much of a camp classic.

CARRIE ☆☆☆☆
1976, USA, R
Sissy Spacek, Piper Laurie, Amy Irving, John Travolta, Nancy Allen, Betty Buckley. Directed by Brian De Palma. 97 min.

Brian De Palma's usually overbearing abundance of style is, for once, beautifully controlled in this brilliant depiction of taunting, cruel high-school terror, an adaptation and substantial alteration of Stephen King's first novel. Sissy Spacek stars as a timid, tortured teenager who—through telekinesis—gives her gum-snapping tormentors a bloody comeuppance. The acting, including Spacek's and Piper Laurie's Oscar-nominated mother-and-daughter turn, is extraordinary for a horror film, and none in the genre has since challenged it as perhaps the most maliciously scary adolescent revenge-fantasy ever put on screen.

CARRINGTON, V.C. ☆☆☆
1954, Great Britain
David Niven, Margaret Leighton, Victor Maddern, Maurice Denham. Directed by Anthony Asquith. 106 min.

A British war hero (David Niven), faced with a court-martial for embezzling his company's funds, must oppose the conservative military hierarchy to clear himself of all charges. Anthony Asquith, among the best of all British filmmakers, infuses just the right amount of intrigue into the plot to tighten the tension in this involving trial drama. (a.k.a.: *Court Martial*)

CARRY ON BEHIND ☆☆
1975, Great Britain
Kenneth Williams, Elke Sommer, Joan Sims, Bernard Bresslaw, Kenneth Connor, Liz Fraser, Peter Butterworth, Jack Douglas. Directed by Gerald Thomas. 90 min.

Fewer of the usual *Carry On* gang are on hand in this, one of the last in the long-running series, although a new scriptwriter does help inject a bit more life and fresher gags into this one. The setting this time is a British vacation camp (there already was a *Carry on Camping*, which otherwise would have been the appropriate title here), with plenty of double entendres and time-tested sexual farce (though nothing explicit, mind you). Elke Sommer is actually competently amusing as a Russian archaeologist at a dig next to the camp.

CARRY ON, CLEO ☆☆½
1964, Great Britain
Sidney James, Kenneth Williams, Kenneth Connor, Charles Hawtrey, Joan Sims, Jim Dale, Amanda Barrie, Jon Pertwee. Directed by Gerald Thomas. 92 min.

No doubt inspired by the big-budget disaster *Cleopatra* of the previous year, this is more of the usual shenanigans from the *Carry On* company. Those familiar with the film being parodied, or Shakespeare's play, or even the historical situation, will pick up on a few in-jokes. Otherwise, its only claim on our attention is that music-hall vulgarity that so captivated Roland Barthes.

CARRY ON, JACK ☆☆½
1964, Great Britain
Bernard Cribbins, Kenneth Williams, Juliet Mills, Charles Hawtrey, Jim Dale, Peter Gilmore. Directed by Gerald Thomas. 91 min.

The title says it all: another *Carry On* entry. Most of the usual participants (Joan Sims, Kenneth Connor, Sidney James, Bob Monkhouse) are absent, but this is still a better-than-average entry in the series, with the usual nonstop slapstick and gags much fresher than in later films. (a.k.a.: *Carry on, Venus*)

CARRY ON NURSE ☆☆☆
1959, Great Britain
Kenneth Connor, Kenneth Williams, Charles Hawtrey, Terence Longdon, Bill Owen, Wilfrid Hyde-White, Hattie Jacques, Joan Hickson, Shirley Eaton, Joan Sims. Directed by Gerald Thomas. 90 min.

The second in the *Carry On* series (and the earliest one available on videocassette), this is one of the better ones. There is virtually no plot at all, just an endless series of vaudeville-style gags and situations set in a hospital. As usual, puns, slapstick, and jokes arising out of confusion and subterfuge abound, and if you're in the mood for a good, unencumbered dose of low (but not vulgar or offensive) humor, this is for you.

CARRY ON, VENUS

See *Carry on, Jack*

THE CARS THAT ATE PARIS

See *The Cars That Eat People*

THE CARS THAT EAT PEOPLE ☆☆½
1974, Australia, PG
Terry Camilleri, John Meillon, Melissa Jaffa, Kevin Miles, Max Gillies, Peter Armstrong. Directed by Peter Weir. 91 min.

Peter Weir's first work was this bizarre, uneven comedy-horror film about the residents of a small Australian town that earns its livelihood by causing car wrecks and then scavenging the drivers for valuables and the vehicles for salable spare parts. The ironic, surreal tone will remind you less of Weir's later films than of Bill Forsyth's work, but it's a fairly auspicious debut on a comparatively low budget. Only toward the end, when wit gives way to standard scare machinations, does the film turn commonplace. (a.k.a.: *The Cars That Ate Paris*)

CAR WASH ☆☆½
1976, USA, PG
Franklin Ajaye, Sully Boyar, George Carlin, Ivan Dixon, Antonio Fargas, Richard Pryor, Garrett Morris, The Pointer Sisters, Melanie Mayron, Irwin Corey. Directed by Michael Schultz. 97 min.

This film is a funky, money-making comedy about a day in the life of a low-down car wash. *Car Wash* borrows heavily from *M*A*S*H* and *American Graffiti*, and in comparison it's not nearly as good as either. But, for the undemanding, it is a pleasant movie, with good turns from Garrett Morris and Richard Pryor. Antonio Fargas gives his role as a drag queen a lot of energy.

CASABLANCA ☆☆☆☆
1942, USA
Humphrey Bogart, Ingrid Bergman, Paul Henreid, Claude Rains, Conrad Veidt, Sydney Greenstreet, Peter Lorre, Dooley Wilson. Directed by Michael Curtiz. 102 min.

You must remember this timeless favorite. Humphrey Bogart stars as Rick, the strong but ever-so-vulnerable proprietor of Rick's Café, a haven for wartime refugees. The luminous and enigmatic Ingrid Bergman is the woman he loved and lost in Paris. The script, by Julius J. Epstein, Philip G. Epstein, and Howard Koch, was written and revised as the shooting progressed, and no one knew how the story would end until the film was nearly completed. But Michael Curtiz's balanced direction and the passionate, subtle performances of an entirely outstanding cast miraculously resulted in one of the most unforgettable Hollywood melodramas. The film won Oscars for Best Picture, Best Direction, and Best Screenplay.

THE CASE OF JONATHAN DREW

See *The Lodger*

A CASE OF LIBEL ☆☆☆
1983, USA (TV)
Ed Asner, Daniel J. Travanti. Directed by Eric Till. 90 min.

A hard-hitting courtroom drama based on a play that was in turn based on Louis Nizer's best-selling memoirs. This impassioned play of ideas deals with a slimy newspaper columnist more interested in a juicy story than the truth and a dedicated liberal attorney who gets his day in court against him. Daniel J. Travanti, cast against type as the muckraker who brands a respected war correspondent with a Communist label, and Asner, as the concerned advocate, bring the issues involved to vivid life.

CASEY'S SHADOW ☆☆☆
1978, USA, PG
Walter Matthau, Alexis Smith, Robert Webber, Murray Hamilton. Directed by Martin Ritt. 117 min.

Walter Matthau plays a struggling Cajun horse trainer preparing a prize quarter horse for the million-dollar All American Futurity race in this family film directed by Martin Ritt. This relaxed homey entertainment has the appeal of snuggling up in a favorite bathrobe to breeze through a good book. The film delivers the pleasures of a good story, well told. It's undemanding but reassuring; Ritt (*Hud*, *The Long Hot Summer*) is an old hand at delineating the Southern temperament, and the cast of pros keeps the film from flagging in the homestretch.

CASINO ROYALE ☆☆½
1967, Great Britain
David Niven, Peter Sellers, Ursula Andress, Orson Welles, George Raft, Joanna Pettet, Woody Allen, William Holden, Charles Boyer, John Huston, Jacqueline Bisset, Jean-Paul Belmondo, Deborah Kerr, Peter O'Toole. Directed by John Huston, Ken Hughes, Val Guest, Robert Parrish, and Joe McGrath. 131 min.

Any comedy with a cast this good and a source—the James Bond novels and films—so ripe for parody ought to be a lot funnier than *Casino Royale*. The gargantuan production has many moments of levity—how could it not?—but its potential is fulfilled only in the scenes pitting Bond (David Niven) against his crazed nephew. As young Jim, who wants to control the world and all of its beautiful women by killing all males over fifty-four inches tall, Woody Allen walks away with the film; many of the other big names have only cameo roles. It's as uneven as any film with five directors must be, but worth seeing as a curiosity, the kind of extravagant all-star spoof that has, perhaps for the better, gone out of style.

THE CASSANDRA CROSSING ☆½
1977, USA, R
Sophia Loren, Burt Lancaster, Richard Harris, Ava Gardner. Directed by George Pan Cosmatos. 125 min.

Any movie that has a cameraman who can do something with Ava Gardner circa 1976 and even allows her some funny lines is not a complete washout, but *The Cassandra Crossing* could use a lot more of her sexy insouciance. Instead, a carefully lit Sophia Loren looks scared while Burt Lancaster and Ingrid Thulin look pained and Richard Harris looks at the camera. The plot can be understood only if diagrams are used. If one turns up the sound only for Gardner, the time passes pleasantly.

CAST A GIANT SHADOW ☆☆☆
1966, USA
Kirk Douglas, Senta Berger, Angie Dickinson, Frank Sinatra, Yul Brynner, John Wayne, Luther Adler, (Chaim) Topol. Directed by Melville Shavelson. 144 min.

This is the Hollywoodized saga of Colonel David "Mickey" Marcus, the American military lawyer and ex-cop who participated in the founding of the state of Israel in the late 1940s. Frank Sinatra, Yul Brynner, and John Wayne (whose son coproduced) contribute little more than cameo parts. It is worth seeing; director Melville Shavelson has a certain visual flair, particularly in the battle scenes.

THE CASTAWAY COWBOY ☆☆☆
1974, USA, G
James Garner, Vera Miles, Robert Culp, Eric Shea, Gregory Sierra. Directed by Vincent McEveety. 91 min.

Here is an enjoyable Disney family film, the kind they made when they weren't trying too hard. Dislocated Texas cowboy James Garner, stuck in Hawaii, agrees to help a woman convert her failing farm into the first Hawaiian cattle ranch. The plot is predictable, but there are nice touches along the way, as when Garner devises a novel way to transport the cattle off the island. Gregory Sierra, in the best tradition of Hollywood ethnic verisimilitude, has a small role here as a native Hawaiian.

CASTLE OF EVIL ☆½
1966, USA
Scott Brady, Virginia Mayo, Lisa Gaye, Hugh Marlowe. Directed by Francis D. Lyon. 80 min.

The producers of this low-budget item must have been nostalgic for all of those Poverty Row mad-doctor films of the 1940s, because that's what this most resembles. After this mad doctor dies, those who were present when he was scarred by acid are summoned to his island and told that they will be allowed to split up his fortune—as soon as they weed out the one responsible for his disfigurement. Passable chills if your standards are low.

THE CASTLE OF FU MANCHU ☆
1968, West Germany/Spain/Italy/England
Christopher Lee, Richard Greene, Maria Perschy, Gunther Stoll. Directed by Jess Franco. 92 min.

This film is the last in the Fu Manchu series—fortunately, because it's pretty bad. In fact, it wasn't even released until five years after it was made, and then only as a second feature for a kung-fu movie. Fu, with the help of his loving daughter, develops a formula that instantly turns water into ice, and he threatens the powers of the world with naval destruction via iceberg if they don't accede to his demands. Director Jess Franco has made dozens of Spanish horror movies, almost all of them atrocious.

THE CATAMOUNT KILLING ☆☆½
1974, West Germany
Horst Bucholz, Ann Wedgeworth, Chip Taylor, Louise Clark, Patricia Joyce, Polly Holliday. Directed by Krzysztof Zanussi. 93 min.

Krzysztof Zanussi, one of the most highly regarded of Polish directors, shot this psychological crime drama in Vermont with a mostly American cast. A bank manager and an innkeeper in a small town rob the local bank, murder a girl, and try to have the whole thing blamed on the bank's manager. The bulk of the film is concerned with the pair's reactions after the crime has been committed, and should appeal to art-house patrons who didn't catch it upon its initial release.

THE CAT AND THE CANARY ☆☆½
1927, USA
Laura La Plante, Creighton Hale, Forrest Stanely, Tully Marshall, Gertrude Astor. Directed by Paul Leni. 75 min.

German director Paul Leni's first American feature was this adaptation of a very popular stage melodrama, a whodunit with all of the suspects gathered in a house full of panels, passageways, and skeletons in the closet. Its spooky, stylized photography is unexpectedly beautiful, but what's left of the plot (there are intertitles but no dialogue) is for the birds. Remade as a Bob Hope comedy in 1939, and again in 1977.

THE CAT AND THE CANARY ☆
1978, Great Britain
Honor Blackman, Carol Lynley, Michael Callan, Edward Fox, Peter McEnery, Wendy Hiller, Olivia Hussey, Beatrix Lehmann, Wilfrid Hyde-White. Directed by Radley Metzger. 98 min.

Beware of movies that play on airplanes *before* they show up in theaters. This one, shelved for four years after its completion, is a remake of the old chestnut about eccentrics gathered in a spooky British manor for a will-reading. Several things quickly start going bump in the night, but you'll sleep through it all, thanks to former soft-core-porn director Radley Metzger's unimaginative eye and slack pacing. Children might enjoy the broadly played melodramatics, but film buffs should hunt down the 1927 original or wait for the 1939 Bob Hope remake to turn up.

CAT AND MOUSE ☆½
1975, France
Serge Reggiani, Michèle Morgan, Philippe Léotard, Valérie Lagrange, Philippe Labro, Jacques François. Directed by Claude Lelouch. 108 min.

What may have been conceived as urbane and knowing ends up smelling like Gallic charm gone rancid. Inspector Lechat (Serge Reggiani) has fallen in love with a widow (Michèle Morgan) who is also his prime suspect in the case of her husband's murder. Lechat pockets holdup money, tortures suspects, and yet is consistently presented as a mature, tolerant, and essentially honest man. What's more, writer/director Claude Lelouch doesn't respect mystery conventions—he just piles on his usual lyrical-romantic mannerisms.

CAT BALLOU ☆☆½
1965, USA
Jane Fonda, Lee Marvin, Michael Callan, Dwayne Hickman, Nat "King" Cole, Stubby Kaye, John Marley, Jay C. Flippen, Reginald Denny, Bruce Cabot, Burt Mustin. Directed by Elliot Silverstein. 97 min.

Not the earthshaking lampoon it was hailed as at its release, Elliot Silverstein's frontier comedy nevertheless has a good deal of flair, even if today its cutesy screenplay seems better suited to a sitcom. Jane Fonda plays the lady outlaw, and Lee Marvin won an Oscar for his dual role as a soused, has-been gunslinger and the villain he's been hired to track down. A fine supporting cast of character actors keeps the pace lively.

CATCH ME A SPY ☆☆
1971, Great Britain/France
Kirk Douglas, Marlene Jobert, Trevor Howard, Tom Courtenay, Bernard Blier, Patrick Mower. Directed by Dick Clement. 94 min.

This film is a no-big-deal spy saga performed with tongues at least partly in cheek. Genial smuggler Kirk Douglas, mistaken for a spy, gets caught up in an espionage plot that Tom Courtenay, as the real spy, is too inept to deal with. French actress Marlene Jobert is an appealing leading lady, but this sinks or swims on your tolerance for a mediocre Kirk Douglas vehicle. (a.k.a.: *To Catch a Spy*)

CATCH-22 ☆☆☆½
1970, USA, R
Alan Arkin, Martin Balsam, Richard Benjamin, Jack Gilford, Art Garfunkel, Bob Newhart, Anthony Perkins, Paula Prentiss, Jon Voight, Orson Welles, Martin Sheen, Bob Balaban, Buck Henry, Norman Fell, Charles Grodin, Austin Pendleton, Peter Bonerz, Richard Libertini, Liam Dunn. Directed by Mike Nichols. 121 min.

Like most such attempts at filming great novels, this movie ultimately fails because it tries to cram too much of Joseph Heller's dense, sprawling masterpiece onto too small a canvas. Were it an hour longer, it might have gone over the top; the style of the book is admirably adapted for film, but director Mike Nichols and screenwriter Buck Henry finally sacrifice exposition for incident. For those unfamiliar with the book, or willing and able to consider the film separately, this spiraling collage of insanities set on a World War II U.S. base in the Mediterranean is a potpourri of comic performances held together by Alan Arkin as Yossarian, Heller's Everyman. Entertaining on a surface level, which makes possible the several viewings it will take before the design starts to become clear.

THE CAT FROM OUTER SPACE ☆☆½
1978, USA, G
Ken Berry, Sandy Duncan, McLean Stevenson, Roddy McDowall, Harry Morgan. Directed by Norman Tokar. 104 min.

Those expecting *E.T.* with furballs will be disappointed by this lightweight fantasy. Youngsters in the mood for a Disney comedy about an extraterrestrial feline in need of spaceship repairs to return to his home planet will be amused. As for adults, if they can muster tolerance for the mugging of the supporting players and overlook the blandness of the leads (excepting the talented title performer), they will find that this tall cat tale is passable family entertainment.

CATHERINE THE GREAT ☆☆½
1934, USA
Elisabeth Bergner, Douglas Fairbanks, Jr. Directed by Paul Czinner. 91 min.

The director's wife, Elisabeth Bergner, who plays the ruthless Russian Czarina, saves this otherwise ponderous, humorless historical drama. Douglas Fairbanks, Jr., also performs well as the twisted and pathetic Grand Duke Peter. Josef Von Sternberg's *The Scarlet Empress*, although similarly stilted, provides a far more fascinating and better-crafted enactment of Catherine's rise to power.

CATHOLICS ☆☆☆
1973, USA (TV)
Trevor Howard, Martin Sheen, Raf Vallone, Cyril Cusack, Andrew Keir, Michael Gambon. Directed by Jack Gold. 78 min.

The early scenes of this made-for-TV movie, based on a novel by Brian Moore, have an uncomfortably distant air bordering on condescension; a Latin Mass is viewed in a manner that is splendid but indicates something antiquated. Fortunately, that bit of scenery out of the way, this turns into a thoughtful drama about Catholic monks in an Irish monastery struggling to maintain their ways and faith in the wake of growing permissiveness within the Church.

CATHY'S CURSE ☆½
1977, Canada, R
Alan Scarfe, Randi Allen, Beverly Murry. Directed by Eddy Matalon. 90 min.

"She has the power to terrorize," claimed the posters, but that's not quite the case. She (Cathy) has the power to embody the worst of the post-*Exorcist* horror-movie clichés and bore viewers in a serious way. This Canadian possession picture features a little girl taken over by the spirit of an aunt burned to death in a car crash; people die, supernatural manifestations abound (within certain budgetary constraints), and few viewers are likely to be thrilled.

CAT ON A HOT TIN ROOF ☆☆☆½
1958, USA
Elizabeth Taylor, Paul Newman, Burl Ives, Judith Anderson, Jack Carson. Directed by Richard Brooks. 108 min.

Tennessee Williams's favorite of all his plays, this fiery saga of a tortured Southern family had its themes of impotence and homosexuality washed clean for the screen. You're asked to believe that one man's "hero worship" for another can cause his marriage to fail, but Williams's intent emerges despite the studio's then-ridiculous attempts to veil it. His lively, ferocious dialogue is put across by the unforgettable performances of Elizabeth Taylor as Maggie the Cat, Paul Newman as her troubled husband Brick, and Burl Ives as the overwhelming Big Daddy. It's one of the most dynamic screen adaptations of Williams's work and considerably better than the 1984 cable production (which, ironically, worked from an improved version of the text).

CAT ON A HOT TIN ROOF ☆☆½
1984, USA (TV)
Jessica Lange, Tommy Lee Jones, Rip Torn, Kim Stanley, Penny Fuller. Directed by Jack Hofsiss. 144 min.

In 1973, Tennessee Williams rewrote the ending of *Cat on a Hot Tin Roof* to bring what had been a subtext of homosexuality into clearer light. The tougher, smart version of the play that resulted is the one used for this otherwise disappointing cable adaptation. Its main attraction is Jessica Lange, who gives a wildly stylized but very fiery performance as Maggie: her drawl and even her movements take some getting used to, but she's worth accommodating. Not so with the rest of the actors, a jumble of mumbles (Tommy Lee Jones), miscasting (Rip Torn), and fidgetiness (Kim Stanley). The show was videotaped and kept confined to one set, but the actors give theater-sized performances, playing to the back row all the way. After two-and-a-half hours, you're likely to become as itchy as Maggie herself.

CAT PEOPLE ☆☆☆
1942, USA
Simone Simon, Kent Smith, Jane Randolf, Tom Conway. Directed by Jacques Tourneur. 73 min.

A stylish triumph of evocative material over low-budget adversity, this film concerns a young woman who believes herself to be descended from a race of women who become killer cats when their passions are aroused. Simone Simon is particularly effective as Irena, a sweet little pussycat of a wife whose metaphorical claws are all too real. Her American husband and his coworker/confidant are no-nonsense types whose imaginations don't extend to problems like Irene's. Her psychiatrist—George Sanders's insinuating brother Tom Conway—is an amoral lecher, and her apartment is so close to the zoo that she can hear the panthers scream at night; it's no wonder that she can't get ahold of herself and act like a normal person. (The film demonstrates internationalist Hollywood's effect on world culture: the creepy classic, directed with Gallic moodiness by Jacques Tourneur, was remade forty years later with exotic Nastassja Kinski; and the film formed the emotional core of Manuel Puig's Argentinian novel *Kiss of the Spider Woman*, which was in turn made into a film by a Brazilian director starring American William Hurt.)

CAT PEOPLE ☆☆
1982, USA, R
Nastassja Kinski, Malcolm McDowell, John Heard, Annette O'Toole. Directed by Paul Schrader. 118 min.

This film is an overblown remake of the forties B movie, updated with lashings of perverse sex and graphic violence. A young Eastern European woman raised in orphanages is brought to New Orleans by the sinister older brother who has devoted his life to locating her. She finds herself in the middle of a dark dream of death and night and blood, cast as an incestuous cat woman who must devour her lovers if they are not also flesh of her flesh. Dreamy, erotic, and utterly illogical, with a soundtrack by David Bowie and Giorgio Moroder.

CAT'S EYE ☆☆½
1985, USA, PG-13
Drew Barrymore, James Woods, Alan King, Kenneth McMillan, Robert Hays, Candy Clark, James Naughton, Mary D'Arcy. Directed by Lewis Teague. 94 min.

In the third segment of this Stephen King anthology, Drew Barrymore is reunited with E.T.—only this time, the critter is a snuffling little troll with an irresistible urge to stuff its fingers up her nostrils. You may root for him to have his way with her as the pouty, pajama-clad actress coos for her champion, an American tabby who pads through the entire film, to come to the rescue. The cat is supposed to connect King's three tales—the first a sadistic satire about a quit-smoking therapist who comes on like a Nazi Godfather, the second a thriller about a gambler who forces his wife's lover to circumnavigate a skyscraper ledge; but the connection is a forced, dumb contrivance. The individual segments aren't bad, but they're more funny than frightening. Adapted in part from King's collection *Night Shift*. (a.k.a.: *Stephen King's Cat's Eye*)

CATTLE ANNIE AND LITTLE BRITCHES ☆☆☆
1980, USA, PG
Diane Lane, Amanda Plummer, Burt Lancaster, Scott Glenn, Rod Steiger, John Savage, Perry Lang. Directed by Lamont Johnson. 98 min.

Amanda Plummer makes a sensational screen debut in this comic-elegiac Western about a young woman who looks for the untamed frontier and discovers that the West isn't as wild as it used to be. All she can find is a pair of old men who used to be members of the Dalton gang, but she latches onto them anyway for one last adventure. As one of the aging outlaws, Burt Lancaster is forceful, wry, and funny, and the supporting cast is so full of pleasing, idiosyncratic actors that you may not realize, or care, just how thin the story that surrounds them really is.

CATTLE QUEEN OF MONTANA ☆½
1954, USA
Barbara Stanwyck, Ronald Reagan, Gene Evans, Lance Fuller, Jack Elam. Directed by Allan Dwan. 89 min.

This second-rate Western is one of the last of more than 400 films directed over a fifty-year period by Allan Dwan, who must have been getting tired by this point: the movie is all talk and clichés, with precious little action. Renegade Indians and a rival rancher conspire to keep Barbara Stanwyck from establishing her Montana ranch; undercover agent Ronald Reagan tries to weed out the bad redskins. This is the movie on the 1950s marquee in *Back to the Future*.

CAUGHT ☆☆☆
1949, USA
Barbara Bel Geddes, James Mason, Robert Ryan. Directed by Max Ophuls. 88 min.

An all-star cast stretches this taut romantic triangle to the breaking point. Barbara Bel Geddes, one of the best and most underutilized actresses of her time, is a young innocent who convinces herself that she is in love with a millionaire. Robert Ryan gives a vicious severity to the role of the millionaire, whose neuroses are inflamed by his dependent, nervous wife. James Mason portrays the cool, romantic doctor who offers the rebellious wife a direction. Ophuls's handling of the material is both visually stunning and emotionally drenched.

CAULDRON OF BLOOD ☆½
1967, USA/Spain, PG
Boris Karloff, Viveca Lindfors, Jean-Pierre Aumont, Jacqui Speed. Directed by Santos Alcocer (Edward Mann). 95 min.

One of four movies that Karloff made simultaneously in Mexico the year before he died, this wasn't released until 1971. Fans can derive some small comfort from the fact that he never saw it. He plays a blind sculptor who doesn't know that the forms for his works are the skeletons of people his wife has murdered. Viveca Lindfors, a good actress who seldom got good roles in movies, has a few hammy moments as his wife. (a.k.a.: *Blind Man's Bluff* and *Children of Blood*)

CAVEGIRL ½☆
1985, USA, R
Daniel Roebuck, Cindy Ann Thompson, Bill Adams, Larry Gabriel, Jeff Chayette, Valerie Greybe. Directed by David Oliver. 87 min.

This inane, low-budgeted comedy concerns a high-school anthropology nerd transported back to the prehistoric era, where he hooks up with a comely cavewoman and learns the ways of love and self-respect in the process. There is no difference between this film and any contemporary sex comedy except for the exceptionally poor production values, the utter unattractiveness of the leads, and the utter lack of even one good laugh. Or chuckle. Or smile.

CAVEMAN ☆☆
1981, USA, PG
Ringo Starr, Barbara Bach, John Matuszak, Dennis Quaid, Shelley Long, Avery Schreiber. Directed by Carl Gottlieb. 94 min.

Ringo Starr is featured as the first *homo erectus* in this freewheeling comedy about the halcyon days of prehistoric man. On an acting level, the best performance comes from a wonderfully animated dinosaur that happens to graze on some prehistoric cannabis and gets stoned in a most unterrifying way. The whole film is pretty much like Ringo: goofy and dumb, and while you may get bored with it, you can't really dislike it.

C.C. AND COMPANY ☆☆☆
1970, USA, R
Joe Namath, Ann-Margret, William Smith, Jennifer Billingsley, Don Chastain. Directed by Seymour Robbie. 94 min.

Years from now, this film will be unearthed and appreciated as a great neo-Hollywood, mythic artifact. Conceived in a plush suite at the Vegas Flamingo, the product of a sacred union between a pro-football god and a showgirl goddess, *C.C. and Company* was anointed by the producers, who proclaimed from on high: it shall have "loving, brawling and bustin' it up!" Ann-Margret and Namath shoot sparks as a pair of lovers who meet at a gang rape. Surprisingly, Namath is fine as a lone-wolf biker who hangs out with a cool gang, The Heads, but dumps them for an upscale fashion writer. Flashily directed—you'll love it as disco dancing becomes intercut with flash frames of the couple making love, while Wayne Cochran belts out Otis Redding songs.

CEASE FIRE ☆☆
1985, USA, R
Don Johnson, Lisa Blount, Robert F. Lyons, Richard Chavres. Directed by David Nutter. 95 min.

A muddled, overwrought post-Vietnam adjustment film noteworthy only because Don Johnson made it before his "Miami Vice" fame. Adapted from the play *Vietnam Trilogy*, this film deals with a veteran who suffers from battle flashbacks and soon begins terrifying his family with violent outbursts. However, once a skeleton in his 'Nam closet comes out in therapy, everything is hunky-dory. He's cured just in time to provide a happy ending to a film that seems to be suffering from delayed stress, too.

CELEBRITY ☆☆☆
1984, USA (TV)
Michael Beck, Joseph Bottoms, Ben Masters, James Whitmore, Hal Holbrook, Karen Austin, Tess Harper, Dinah Manoff, Debbie Allen, Ned Beatty, Jennifer Warren, Claude Akins. Directed by Paul Wendkos. 313 min.

American miniseries seem to be at their best when they cast aside pretension, history, and educational value in favor of juicy, scandal-packed plot lines and showy, overheated performances. *Celebrity* is trashy TV melodrama at its near-best, the visual equivalent of a good beach read (which is exactly what Tommy Thompson's source novel was). The story spans twenty-five years in the lives of three high school friends who gain fame and fortune respectively as a movie star, a journalist, and a faith healer. But a dark secret links them together—a sordid murder in their past. You'll be enthralled as the drama moves toward its lurid climax; the version on video omits nothing from the original telecast but the commercials.

CENTERFOLD GIRLS ☆
1974, USA
Andrew Prine, Tiffany Bolling, Aldo Ray, Ray Danton, Francine York. Directed by John Peyser. 93 min.

A fulsome, mad-killer marathon about a bevy of scantily clad cuties being bumped off rather peremptorily by another woman-hating nut case. Very sleazy, with some venerable movie pros trying to disguise the obviousness of it all. The TV movie *The Calendar Girl Murders* covers the same titillating territory with a bit more panache.

CERTAIN FURY ☆☆½
1985, USA, R
Tatum O'Neal, Irene Cara, Nicholas Campbell, Peter Fonda, Moses Gunn, George Murdock. Directed by Stephen Gullenhaal. 88 min.

A middle-class black girl and an illiterate streetwise white girl find themselves on the run together after two lesbian psychopaths shoot up the courtroom where they're all being arraigned; their feature-length wallow in the neon slime makes for very energetic exploitation entertainment. As Tatum and Irene race through sewers, back alleys, and shooting galleries, meeting killers, pimps, junkies, rapists, and the occasional mere eccentric, an uneasy alliance begins to form. We could do without an incongruous happy ending, but Stephen Gullenhaal sustains a relentless standard of action until then; we wish all films this sleazy were also this much fun.

A CERTAIN SACRIFICE ½☆
1979, USA, R
Jeremy Pattnosh, Madonna, Charles Kurtz. Directed by Stephen Jon Lewicki. 60 min.

Cine Cine Productions released this execrable old film in order to cash in on the fact that Madonna does, indeed, appear as a topless, skinny twenty-year-old. Aside from that, it's strictly a student film that must have been made in a remedial class, complete with an oh-so-tough antihero, a rape and revenge, the usual boy-meets-girl, and evil adults. Everything is *very* decadent and *very* serious (and, consequently, absolutely absurd)—the climax of the film is a cannibalistic sacrifice conducted during a punk performance.

All in all, it's New York's East Village as envisioned by a Boy Scout with a dirty mind.

CÉSAR ☆☆☆
1933, France
Raimu, Pierre Fresnay, Orane Demazis, Charpin, Milly Mathis, André Fouché. Directed by Marcel Pagnol. 170 min.

This film is the last chapter in Marcel Pagnol's touching trilogy about the tempestuous love affair of Fanny (Orane Demazis) and Marius (Pierre Fresnay), and the only one of the films to have been directed by Pagnol himself. Much more sentimental and self-consciously "touching" than either *Marius* or *Fanny*, *César* will nonetheless please those who enjoyed the others. Pagnol, however, is not a director of the caliber of *Fanny*'s Marc Allegret.

CHAINED HEAT ☆½
1983, USA/West Germany, R
Linda Blair, Sybil Danning, John Vernon, Stella Stevens, Henry Silva. Directed by Paul Nicholas. 97 min.

There are only three possible reactions to this film: (1) moral outrage at the sexual stereotyping and use of violence as an aphrodisiac; (2) leering satisfaction at the sexual stereotyping and the use of violence as an aphrodisiac; or (3) helpless laughter. Did you know that our penal system is nothing but a front for prostitution rings transporting inmates to Playboy mansions? Can you believe Linda Blair as a virginal interior-decorating student up for manslaughter, even though she looks more hardened than those "we-won't-take-no-for-an-answer" lesbians accosting her in the showers? Were you aware that the entire female prison populace suffers from an incurable Jayne Mansfield disease, placing a tremendous burden on taxpayers, who must pay for letting out the chests of their uniforms? Never have so many clichés served time together.

CHAIN REACTION ☆☆½
1980, Australia
Steve Bisley, Anna-Maria Winchester, Ross Thompson, Ralph Cotterill. Directed by Ian Barry. 87 min.

Another graduate of the *China Syndrome/Silkwood* school, this cautionary fable focuses on the fate of a nuclear scientist exposed to deadly radiation. Aided by a concerned couple, he tries to wake up the world to the dangers of atomic power. A decent thriller that scores its point but is unduly fond of melodramatics.

THE CHAIRMAN ☆☆½
1969, USA
Gregory Peck, Anne Heywood, Arthur Hill, Alan Dobie, Conrad Yama, Bert Kwouk, Keye Luke. Directed by J. Lee Thompson. 104 min.

A Nobel Prize–winning American scientist is sent to Red China to learn the facts about a scientific breakthrough that can grow food in previously unarable regions. He is equipped with a transmitting device in his skull that will relay all information he receives back to Washington; what he doesn't know is that the device is also a bomb that can be exploded should he be caught. This Cold War remnant (in which, ironically, the Russians are on our side and the Chinese take the part of the Godless Commies) is mostly talk, though it generates reasonable suspense toward the end.

THE CHALLENGE ☆☆☆
1982, USA, R
Scott Glenn, Toshiro Mifune, Donna Kei Benz, Atsuo Nakamura, Calvin Young, Clyde Kusatsu. Directed by John Frankenheimer. 106 min.

John Frankenheimer's solid direction and John Sayles's intelligent screenplay make this samurai adventure film much more entertaining than you might expect. Scott Glenn, who looks here like a younger, more talented Charles Bronson, plays a drifter who becomes embroiled in a long-standing battle between two Japanese brothers for possession of a treasured sword. At times, the director's brooding, reflective style and Sayles's verbal bric-a-brac and movie allusions work against each other, but everything comes together in the dazzling, violent action sequences, and Toshiro Mifune's mere presence gives the story dramatic weight.

CHALLENGE THE DRAGON ½☆
Hong Kong
Tarng Long, Shane Guam, Horng Ing, Ou Yang Jong. Directed by Li Chan Yang.

The villains try to take over King Shao's land. Oh, just give them the damned real estate.

CHALLENGE TO BE FREE ☆
1975, USA, G
Mike Mazurki, Jimmy Kane, Fritz Ford, Tay Garnett. Directed by Tay Garnett, Ford Beebe. 88 min.

This poorly made nature film was the last movie directed by Hollywood veteran Tay Garnett; it was originally made in 1972 and would seem to have been heavily reedited. What's left consists half of trapper Mike Mazurki wandering around communing with the animals and half of him being chased after accidentally killing a state trooper. The whole thing is tied together with narration by actor John McIntire.

CHAMBER OF FEAR ½☆
1968, USA/Mexico
Boris Karloff, Isela Vega, Juan Ibañez, Jack Hill, Carlos East. Directed by Jack Hill and Juan Ibañez. 88 min.

A scientist (Karloff) discovers a living rock; his degenerate assistants torment young women and feed their blood to the stony organism. That's about all there is here in the way of plot. In one of his last film roles, Karloff is largely absent from this dull, barely coherent mélange of monster movie clichés and Mexican madness, written and codirected by Roger Corman protégé Jack Hill (*Track of the Vampire, Spider Baby*). With a dwarf, girls in black bras, and not much more. (a.k.a.: *The Fear Chamber*)

THE CHAMP ☆☆☆
1931, USA
Wallace Beery, Jackie Cooper, Irene Rich, Roscoe Ates, Edward Brophy, Hale Hamilton, Jesse Scott, Marcia Mae Jones. Directed by King Vidor. 85 min.

Get out your handkerchiefs! There are at least three major crying stops in this compellingly sentimental yarn about a washed-up fighter and his ever-faithful son. Ten-year-old Jackie Cooper tugs at the heartstrings just by showing up in his raggedy clothes and big grin; when his father pretends that he doesn't like him so as to get the boy to live with his rich mother—watch out for the waterworks. Wallace Beery won an Academy Award (tying with Fredric March) for his portrayal of the boozing, brawling father who wins the kid a racehorse, only to lose it at the gambling tables. It's a tremendous, nonstop scenery-eater of a performance, but within the movie's wildly pathetic story, it's never less than believable and always affecting. The main plot follows the Champ's ill-advised return to the ring and the son's attempt to remain a part of his life. King Vidor wisely directs this all very simply, letting the action carry the greatest load, and viewers will delight in this world of Tijuana bars, dingy jails, racetracks, and back rooms. Accept no remakes.

THE CHAMP ☆
1979, USA, PG
Jon Voight, Faye Dunaway, Ricky Schroder, Jack Warden, Arthur Hill, Strother Martin, Joan Blondell, Elisha Cook, Jr. Directed by Franco Zeffirelli. 121 min.

Franco Zeffirelli dredges up his inarguable skills as a director of live opera by blowing up this remake of the 1931 Wallace

Beery tearjerker to operatic proportions, replete with misty landscapes and enormous sniffling faces. Better someone had blown up the whole project before it hit the screen. Jon Voight is the punch-drunk boxer who gives his all in the ring for his scrappy young son, played with precocious expertise and unbearable cuteness by eight-year-old Ricky Schroder. Voight, trying with his whole body to act like an oaf, seems graceless for the first time in his career. And Faye Dunaway, as the boy's estranged mother, a neurotic fashion designer, is plain embarrassing.

CHAMPAGNE FOR CAESAR ☆☆☆☆
1950, USA
Ronald Colman, Vincent Price, Celeste Holm, Art Linkletter, Barbara Britton. Directed by Richard Whorf. 99 min.

This sidesplitting farce fully lives up to its great premise about a genius who plans to bankrupt a cash-giveaway game-show sponsor. Colman is a delight to watch as the dapper egghead who slickly and methodically takes Vincent Price's soap company empire for all it's worth, and the rest of the cast is reminiscent of the sort of ensembles Preston Sturges used to put together in his films (e.g., Art Linkletter steps in for Rudy Vallee). Additionally, the satire on big business and television game shows is consistently funny and relevant today. Only the tacky, low-budget production values can be faulted in this much-underrated film.

CHAMPION ☆☆☆☆
1949, USA
Kirk Douglas, Marilyn Maxwell, Arthur Kennedy, Paul Stewart, Ruth Roman. Directed by Mark Robson. 99 min.

This bleak boxing drama made a star of Kirk Douglas, and rightly so. He plays a young man from an impoverished background who punches his way to the top, losing his soul in the bargain. The film's strongest scene occurs with his crippled brother, who is upset over the changes the boxer is undergoing. Producer Stanley Kramer manages to take the low budget and make it work in his favor, producing a realistic portrait of inner-city life. A superior forerunner to such fifties boxing exposés as *Requiem for a Heavyweight* and *The Harder They Fall*.

CHAMPION OF DEATH ½☆
1975, Hong Kong
Sonny Chiba

When legendary karate exponent Masutatsu Oyama made a rare appearance in Madison Square Garden in 1975, he astonished the American audience with his speed and grace. For his life story, unfortunately, they used the heavy-limbed sledgehammer Sonny Chiba to play the master. What a woeful piece of casting, and what a horrible film.

CHAMPIONS ☆☆½
1983, Great Britain
John Hurt, Edward Woodward, Ben Johnson. Directed by John Irvin. 115 min.

In this earnest inspirational flick about a determined jockey riding the recovery trail while grappling with cancer, the hero must overcome all hurdles and eventually win the big race that everyone says a sick man could never win. John Hurt is superb as the jockey racing against time, and the workmanlike script jerks a few tears, but if there's a type of film that has drained dry the cup of inventiveness, it's the "athlete with a halo" category. If you liked *Brian's Song* or *The Terry Fox Story* or dozens of other films about sports figures beating the odds, you'll appreciate this true-life embodiment of heroism. The non-horsey set of cynics should skip this and wait for the first movie about a fatally ill marble shooter.

CHANEL SOLITAIRE ☆☆
1981, France/Great Britain, R
Marie-France Pisier, Timothy Dalton, Rutger Hauer, Karen Black, Brigitte Fossey, Leila Frechet, Katherine Alcover. Directed by George Kaczender. 124 min.

To spare theatrical audiences some unrelieved boredom, twelve minutes were trimmed from the final cut of this movie. Guess what—they're back for the video version. Little enough is learned about the artistic life of one of the world's most famous fashion designers; as recompense, more than enough is learned about her love life. (Although, given Coco Chanel's reputation for evasive, contradictory, and "creative" information about her past, it might be going too far to say we learn anything.) Another bloated international coproduction.

THE CHANGELING ☆☆½
1979, Canada, R
George C. Scott, Trish Van Devere, Melvin Douglas, John Colicos, Jean Marsh, Barry Morse. Directed by Peter Medak. 107 min.

In this stylish horror-thriller George C. Scott plays a composer whose wife and daughter have been killed in a car accident. When he moves into a spooky old Seattle house, a ghostly child seeks him out and makes demands upon him. Casting a man as imposing as Scott as the victim of a haunted mansion is daring indeed, but it works for a while—certainly until the end of the brilliant séance set piece during which the ghost's intentions become clear. Alas, those intentions ruin the film. The ghost sends Scott off on a vengeful hunt for politician Melvyn Douglas, whereupon the film quickly becomes distasteful, for Douglas himself is an innocent victim of past skullduggery; watching him hounded to death by our heroic composer is not an amusing spectacle.

CHANGE OF HABIT ☆☆
1969, USA, G
Elvis Presley, Mary Tyler Moore, Barbara McNair, Jane Elliott, Edward Asner, Regis Toomey. Directed by William Graham. 93 min.

This was Elvis Presley's last film as an actor, indicating that after thirty-one movies in fourteen years, even he was getting tired of his movies. Actually, this may be even better than, say, *Fun in Acapulco*, if you can accept him in a mostly serious role as a concerned urban doctor working in a slum clinic. The title refers to the pressing decision faced by Mary Tyler Moore, who plays a nun assigned to help out Dr. El: should she renounce her vows or return to the church and give up the doc? (Of course, you know in *advance* what really happens—she runs away to Minneapolis with costar Ed Asner.) Fans need not worry—Elvis still finds time to sing two songs.

A CHANGE OF SEASONS ☆½
1980, USA, R
Shirley MacLaine, Anthony Hopkins, Bo Derek, Michael Brandon, Mary Beth Hurt, Ed Winter. Directed by Richard Lang. 102 min.

This film sings another chorus of the middle-aged blues, already sung into the ground in *10*, *Serial*, *Loving Couples*, et al. Even by those low standards, this New Morality sex farce is the pits. Shirley MacLaine and Anthony Hopkins are a fortyish academic couple dallying with a couple of students (it's a lousy deal, though, since he gets Bo Derek and she has to settle for a woodsy Michael Brandon). Only Mary Beth Hurt, as the level headed daughter, is a skillful enough farceur to transcend the mirthlessly banal dialogue, much of which was written by *Love Story*'s Erich Segal.

CHAPTER TWO ☆☆½
1979, USA, PG
James Caan, Marsha Mason, Valerie Harper, Joseph Bologna, Alan Fudge. Directed by Robert Moore. 124 min.

Neil Simon may write the funniest, most one-upping comic exchanges in the business, but his inability to resist them is almost crippling—too often, snappy one-liners replace real feeling and communication. That's the case with this otherwise sensitive comedy-drama about a writer (James Caan) who finds romance with an actress (Marsha Mason) after his wife dies. Simon's semiautobiographical story, adapted from his hit play, has moving moments and several well-realized scenes, but its litany of wisecracks and cute situations causes it to evaporate almost instantly. It's perfectly acceptable light entertainment and no more, with a standard but very pleasant performance from Mason (then married to Simon) and a weak, frustrated one from the miscast Caan.

CHARADE ★★★½
1963, USA
Cary Grant, Audrey Hepburn, Walter Matthau, James Coburn, George Kennedy, Ned Glass. Directed by Stanley Donen. 113 min.

Stanley Donen's ersatz Hitchcock thriller is a bit too suave for its own good, but the humorously grisly homicides, the slick performances, and a soupçon of very real suspense make for a pleasantly stylish film. The memorable score by Henry Mancini doesn't hurt, either. Bet you don't guess the surprise ending.

THE CHARGE OF THE LIGHT BRIGADE ★★½
1936, USA
Errol Flynn, Olivia de Havilland, Patric Knowles, Donald Crisp, Nigel Bruce, Henry Stephenson, David Niven, Spring Byington. Directed by Michael Curtiz. 115 min.

Gunga Geste? The Lives of a Bengal Feather? This Warner Brothers production of Tennyson's poem is a fairly good film, but is highly derivative and a lousy history lesson. Michel Jacoby and Rowland Leigh's screenplay exchanges the poet's bitter attack on British military incompetence for an imperialistic viewpoint and tacks on a hollow, phony love story to the charge itself. Errol Flynn plays a major in the Crimean War who leads his lancers from India to Balaklava to fight the Russians. A rousing, brilliantly edited battle sequence (directed by B. Reeves Eason) is the highlight of the film. Remade (poorly) in 1968 by Tony Richardson.

CHARIOTS OF FIRE ★★★★
1981, Great Britain, PG
Ben Cross, Ian Charleson, Nigel Havers, Nicholas Farrell, Alice Krige, Cheryl Campbell, Ian Holm, John Gielgud, Lindsay Anderson, Patrick Magee, Nigel Davenport, Dennis Christopher, Brad Davis. Directed by Hugh Hudson. 123 min.

This beautifully made, inspirational film follows the passionate careers of British track stars Eric Liddell and Harold Abrahams from their days of early training to their bids for glory on the Olympic track in 1924. Their personal stories—Liddell as a struggling Scottish preacher and Abrahams as one of the first Jews at Cambridge—unfold with a depth, deliberateness, and elegance that made this rousing film an international success and the Oscar-winner for Best Picture. Hudson makes a remarkable feature debut, directing Charleson and Cross to powerful performances in the leads. Forgivable for its indulgent use of slow motion, *Chariots* takes grand advantage of Vangelis's dramatic score; the theme song is enough to make anyone want to go for a jog.

CHARLEY VARRICK ★★★½
1973, USA, PG
Walter Matthau, Joe Don Baker, Felicia Farr, Andy Robinson. Directed by Don Siegel. 111 min.

This is a fast, funny, and absorbing thriller about a former air-circus pilot turned bank robber. The larcenous activities begin as small, "paying-the-rent" jobs, but trouble enters when a modest, family-style stickup becomes a $750,000 heist of Mafia money. Walter Matthau shines in the uncustomarily dramatic role of a man caught between a rock (the Mob) and a hard place (the police). Don Siegel's direction is right on target, dynamically fusing a sense of thematic entrapment with exhilarating, fast-paced action. The final sequence is a stunner.

CHARLIE CHAN AND THE CURSE OF THE DRAGON QUEEN ★
1981, USA, PG
Peter Ustinov, Lee Grant, Angie Dickinson, Richard Hatch, Brian Keith, Roddy McDowall, Michele Pfeiffer. Directed by Clive Donner. 97 min.

A tired-looking Peter Ustinov plays Charlie Chan in this feeble, stupid, and most dishonorable comedy. The Chan movies were very mild amusements to begin with; this one is mild but with no amusement. Critic say: he who parody Charlie Chan movie hasn't a clue.

CHARLOTTE'S WEB ★★★
1973, USA, G
Animated: Debbie Reynolds, Paul Lynde, Henry Gibson, Agnes Moorehead, Pamelyn Ferdin, Danny Bonaduce, Dave Madden. Directed by Charles A. Nichols and Iwao Takamoto. 94 min.

E. B. White's children's classic about the friendship between Wilbur the pig and Charlotte the spider is very hard to resist—it's sweet and touching without ever being mawkish or cloying, and it can charm and move children without boring adults. Even though this animated adaptation is little more than serviceable, it's worth seeing simply for the literary charms it transfers to the screen. *Charlotte's Web* could do without the gooey Richard and Robert Sherman song score, and the artwork, by Hanna-Barbera, doesn't approach the level of a Disney film. But Henry Gibson and Debbie Reynolds are in perfect voice as the hero and heroine, and the wrenching conclusion is a real tearjerker.

CHARLY ★★★
1968, USA, PG
Cliff Robertson, Claire Bloom, Dick Van Patten, Lilia Skala, Ralph Nelson. Directed by Ralph Nelson. 103 min.

Cliff Robertson won an Oscar for his portrayal of a retarded-man-turned-genius in this mechanical adaptation of the Daniel Keyes novella *Flowers for Algernon*. Kids may respond to Robertson's Sweet Jesus innocence, but on the whole this is pretty insufferable stuff—particularly the gushy romantic subplot featuring Claire Bloom.

THE CHASE ★★½
1966, USA
Marlon Brando, Robert Redford, Jane Fonda, Angie Dickinson, Robert Duvall, E. G. Marshall, Janice Rule, James Fox, Miriam Hopkins, Martha Hyer. Directed by Arthur Penn. 135 min.

Marlon Brando stars in Arthur Penn's overblown but powerful Deep South melodrama. On a hot summer night, Brando's beleaguered small-town sheriff tries to contain the forces unleashed when a local criminal (Robert Redford) returns to town after making a prison break. Penn's striking direction (especially in the final shootout in an automobile graveyard) sets off the work of a stunning cast, notably Jane Fonda (as Redford's old girlfriend) and E. G. Marshall (as the town's most powerful landowner). The film strains to be a fable of mass violence and Southern brutality but, scene for scene, Penn's effects are impressive. Lillian Hellman wrote the screenplay (which she later disowned), adapting a play by Horton Foote.

CHASE STEP BY STEP ½★
Hong Kong
Chee Fung, Wang Kuan-Hsing. Directed by Yu Min Sheung.

In this ineptly made martial-arts flick, thieves chase a couple carrying a cargo of gold. The rotten action sequences alone qualify this as one of the worst of the genre.

CHATTANOOGA CHOO CHOO ☆½
1984, USA, PG
Barbara Eden, George Kennedy, Joe Namath, Melissa Sue Anderson, Bridget Hanley, Parley Baer. Directed by Bruce Bilson. 102 min.

A dumb movie that aims to be a down-home version of *Silver Streak* but seldom rises above TV-sitcom level. Small-town mogul George Kennedy wants to build a football stadium for his team. He can get $1 million from his father-in-law's will if he restores the old man's favorite train and gets it from New York to Chattanooga in twenty-four hours. Along for the ride are his wife, mistress, daughter, daughter's jilted fiancé and her new one, and sundry other characters. Everything in the film is in some pastel shade of purple, blue, or lavender, but it's the kind of film where it doesn't really make any difference. Were it not for the inclusion of a few mild expletives, this could easily have been a made-for-TV movie, in which case it would at least have an excuse.

THE CHEAP DETECTIVE ☆☆
1978, USA, PG
Peter Falk, Ann-Margret, Eileen Brennan, Sid Caesar, Stockard Channing, James Coco, Dom DeLuise, Louise Fletcher, John Houseman, Madeline Kahn, Fernando Lamas, Marsha Mason, Phil Silvers, Abe Vigoda, Nicol Williamson, Vic Tayback, Scatman Crothers, Paul Williams. Directed by Robert Moore. 92 min.

This film is a good example of variety-show tedium, despite a slick surface. Writer Neil Simon intended this wan comedy to send up every *film noir*, police procedural, and spy/counterspy drama of the 1940s; in spite of an astonishing cast and a look that's anything but cheap, the film falls almost completely flat. The plot is a series of shakily connected sketches that let many of the ripest comic talents go to waste, although John Houseman (in the Sydney Greenstreet role) and Stockard Channing are seen to good advantage.

CHEAPER TO KEEP HER ☆½
1980, USA, R
Mac Davis, Tovah Feldshuh, Priscilla Lopez, Jack Gilford, Art Metrano, Ian McShane, Rose Marie. Directed by Ken Annakin. 92 min.

Just what the moviegoing world was clamoring for—Mac Davis as a romantic lead. In his only starring vehicle thus far, the pudgy country-and-western crooner plays a rakish young devil dallying with a sizzling secretary (Priscilla Lopez) and a cold-as-ice attorney (Tovah Feldshuh). The film's attitude toward women is adequately summed up in its title, and is mightily reinforced in the familiar sexual tomfoolery that keeps the film trotting along its well-worn path. Cheaper, need we say, to miss it.

CHECK AND DOUBLE CHECK ☆½
1930, USA
Freeman F. Gosden, Charles V. Correll, Sue Carol, Charles Morton, Irene Rich, Duke Ellington and His Orchestra. Directed by Melville Brown. 71 min.

Enlightened audiences will have trouble sitting through the only screen teaming of radio's Amos and Andy. Freeman F. Gosden and Charles V. Correll, two white men in blackface, were once the most popular comics in the business but, aside from historical interest, they warrant little attention today. The plot has Amos and Andy trying to get Duke Ellington (the only reason to see the film) to play at a society birthday party. The humor (such as it is) never transcends the racial stereotypes.

CHEECH AND CHONG'S NEXT MOVIE ☆☆☆
1980, USA, R
Richard "Cheech" Marin, Thomas Chong, Evelyn Guerrero, Edie McClurg, Pee-Wee Herman (Paul Reubens). Directed by Thomas Chong. 99 min.

This film is even scruffier, grosser, and patchier than the dope-struck duo's first movie, *Up in Smoke*, and funnier too. The film, written by the pair and directed by Chong, is simply a single wild day, and an even wilder night, in the lives of our favorite welfare recipients, cruising L.A. in search of good grass, good sex, and the ultimate power chord. There's a great deal of concealed artistry under *Next Movie*'s disordered surface—especially in the pacing and construction of individual routines—but the film is bound to be too frenzied, too crude, and above all too noisy for some. And that's as it should be. Cheech and Chong have made the first masterpiece in the comedy of cacophony. Scoff if you will, but these two may be the Marx Brothers of our time.

CHEECH AND CHONG'S NICE DREAMS ☆☆☆
1981, USA, R
Richard "Cheech" Marin, Thomas Chong, Stacey Keach, Evelyn Guerrero, Pee-Wee Herman (Paul Reubens), Timothy Leary. Directed by Thomas Chong. 110 min.

Had they chopped out the twenty or so minutes devoted to the unnecessary plot in this, their third film, Cheech and Chong would have had a much better movie along the lines of their almost plotless and totally hilarious second film. Even as is, though, there are a lot of unexpected, senseless, and very funny bits in here, half from the stars and the rest from the astounding assortment of loonies they've surrounded themselves with—like Stacey Keach, the ultra-right-wing narc from *Up in Smoke*, now gone to the opposite extreme; the inimitable Pee-Wee Herman, who is to C&C what Franklin Pangborn would have been to the Marx Brothers had he played the Margaret Dumont role; and the guy who does an incredible Jimi Hendrix impression—without a guitar.

CHEECH AND CHONG'S STILL SMOKIN'

See *Still Smokin'*

CHEECH AND CHONG'S THE CORSICAN BROTHERS ☆☆
1984, USA, R
Richard "Cheech" Marin, Thomas Chong, Roy Dotrice, Shelby Fiddis, Rikki Marin, Edie McClurg, Robbi Chong, Rae Dawn Chong. Directed by Thomas Chong. 90 min.

The funniest and most typical part of this, the first Cheech and Chong movie with no drug jokes, is the brief prologue and epilogue, in which the boys travel around Paris in a van, stop in the most effete neighborhoods, and blast out a raucous version of "Nadine" until the annoyed and unwilling audiences pay them to stop. The main part of the movie is a parody of the old Dumas yarn about the two brothers, separated at birth, who are reunited during the French Revolution. They get a surprising amount of laughs out of one running gag—the spiritual bond between them is so deep that any blow inflicted on one is felt by the other—thanks to Chong's insufferable deadpan bravery and Cheech's amphetamine cowardice. Overall, though, the duo's poorest outing, too tied to plot (presumably in an effort to gain a wider audience) to really let them loose. (a.k.a.: *The Corsican Brothers*)

CHEERLEADERS WILD WEEKEND ☆½
1979, USA, R
Jason William, Kristine De Bell, Anthony Lewis, Ann Wharton, Janet Blythe. Directed by Jeff Werner. 88 min.

This is the sort of drivel that gets to the nudity before the opening credits are finished; that continually uses a low-angle camera setup to get panty shots; that starts as a vulgar comedy, then takes an ugly turn (a busload of cheerleaders is kidnapped by disgruntled ex-football players); that ends on a note of wild improbability (the cheerleaders help one of the guys escape the police). What can be said? Miss it!

CHEERS FOR MISS BISHOP ★★½
1941, USA
Martha Scott, William Gargan, Edmund Gwenn, Sterling Holloway, Sidney Blackmer, Marsha Hunt, Rosemary DeCamp. Directed by Tay Garnett. 94 min.

In this distaff *Goodbye Mr. Chips*, Martha Scott plays a Midwestern teacher who spends over fifty years in the public school system. The adaptation of Bess Streeter Aldooch's novel is predictably episodic, covering the spinster teacher's problems with her students and the details of two failed love affairs. Scott is a competent actress and ages well in the part, but she is not a magnetic personality. The film really needed a Katharine Hepburn or a Bette Davis to make it work.

CHESTY ANDERSON U.S. NAVY ½★
1975, USA, R
Shari Eubank, Dorri Thomson, Rosanne Katon, Timothy Carey, Fred Willard, Frank Campanella, Scatman Crothers. Directed by Ed Forsyth. 83 min.

This is a film for truly desperate brassiere fetishists only. Busty WAVES search for a missing friend. Highly billed Fred Willard and Scatman Crothers make extremely small, shamefaced appearances.

CHEYENNE AUTUMN ★★★★
1964, USA
Richard Widmark, Carroll Baker, Karl Malden, Sal Mineo, Dolores Del Rio, Ricardo Montalban, Gilbert Roland, Arthur Kennedy, James Stewart, Edward G. Robinson, Patrick Wayne, John Carradine, Victor Jory. Directed by John Ford. 156 min.

John Ford's epic elegy to the passing of a great Native American nation partially redresses Hollywood's long history of portraying Indians as simple savages. Nowadays, the casting of Sal Mineo and Ricardo Montalban as Cheyenne leaders seems strange, but both are credible, if not exactly inspired. And Ford's adaptation of Mari Sandoz's book is a beautifully realized telling of the story of the "Trail of Tears," the forced march of the Cheyenne from their Wyoming homelands to a desolate reservation in Oklahoma. The camerawork is pure and perfect; however, the wide-screen compositions are not translatable for the video version. More problematic is the film's sprawling structure: viewers who lose the threads of one of the various stories may lose interest in the whole movie. For fans of Ford, this is a masterwork. The casual viewer will derive more pleasure from the large-scale performances of the cast members (especially Jimmy Stewart's ripe, comic portrait of Wyatt Earp).

CHEYENNE RIDES AGAIN ★½
1938, USA
Tom Tyler, Lucille Browne, Jimmy Fox, Creighton Chaney, Roger Williams, Ed Cassidy. Directed by Bob Hill. 60 min.

Tom Tyler was no John Wayne or Bob Livingstone, but this is an okay B Western. An undercover detective infiltrates a gang and raises heck. Jimmy Fox is a better-than-average comic support, and he even warbles a tune.

CHEYENNE TAKES OVER ★½
1948, USA
Lash LaRue, Al "Fuzzy" St. John, Nancy Gates, George Cheesebro, Lee Morgan, John Merton, Steve Clark. Directed by Ray Taylor. 58 min.

If a sagebrush star has earned the sobriquet "Lash," one can reasonably expect a whip to be used to discipline a few assorted malefactors. Alas, this is not the case here—Mr. LaRue uses his gun, though he does *carry* a whip.

THE CHICKEN CHRONICLES ½★
1977, USA, PG
Steven Guttenberg, Phil Silvers, Ed Lauter, Lisa Reeves. Directed by Francis Simon. 92 min.

Even if you actually want to see one more movie about a horny adolescent boy pursuing a beautiful airhead, make it *The Last American Virgin, Secret Admirer, Porky's*—anything but *The Chicken Chronicles*. Not only does it fail to distinguish itself even within its own mutated subgenre, but it inflates itself with pompous pontifications about the 1960s, wastes the great Phil Silvers in a pathetic lecher role, and gives that unbearable mugger Steve Guttenberg his first lead. "He appears in virtually every scene, a dream assignment for a young actor," trumpeted the press release. For anyone else, it's a nightmare.

CHIEFS ★★★½
1983, USA (TV)
Charlton Heston, Keith Carradine, Brad Davis, Wayne Rogers, Billy Dee Williams, Paul Sorvino, Stephen Collins. Directed by Jerry London. 200 min.

This fascinating miniseries is set in the Deep South, where murders and cover-ups seem to go hand in hand. Covering a time period from the twenties through the sixties, the film deals with the detective work of three different police chiefs trying to solve a perplexing series of homosexual murders. Working on several different levels, *Chiefs* offers a shrewd appraisal of the seamy side of politics and how it can impede due process of law. This is first and foremost a slam-bang crime drama that will have viewers on the edge of their seats as they try to figure out whodunit and how long he can get away with it.

CHILD BRIDE OF SHORT CREEK ★★½
1981, USA (TV)
Conrad Bain, Diane Lane, Christopher Atkins, Helen Hunt, Dee Wallace, Kiel Martin. Directed by Robert Michael Lewis. 104 min.

This film is sometimes cogent drama that delves into cult psychology. Set in the 1950s, the sharply scripted and mildly sensationalized exposé examines the phenomenon of polygamy by concentrating on one father-son contretemps over the issue. Dad wants to add a teenage girl to his harem, but Junior, who's seen something of the world during the Korean War, returns to his community and states his opposition.

THE CHILDREN ★
1980, USA, R
Martin Shaker, Gil Rogers, Gale Garnett, Jesse Abrams, Tracy Griswold, Joy Glacum, Suzanne Barnes, Rita Montone. Directed by Max Kalmanowicz. 90 min.

A school bus passes through a radioactive cloud that turns its small passengers into black-nailed zombies whose embrace imparts sizzling death. The young menaces can be stopped only if their hands are lopped off, an enterprise too horrifying for most of the town's adult population to contemplate—though they realize that the alternative is also fairly unappealing. Derivative and mean-spirited, with little in the special-effects department to offer by way of compensation.

CHILDREN OF A LESSER GOD ★★½
1986, USA, R
William Hurt, Marlee Matlin, Piper Laurie, Philip Bosco, Alison Gompf, John F. Cleary. Directed by Randa Haines. 119 min.

William Hurt's versatile, inventive performance as a teacher of the deaf is a triumph and, in another way, so is that of hearing-impaired actress Marlee Matlin as the willful, unspeaking worker with whom he falls in love. Unfortunately, the charismatic performers are stuck in a script with the rhythm and pace of an average TV movie, in which every scene goes on too long, makes exactly one point, and then gives way to the next predictable interchange. The real problems of the deaf are presented with a cheerful sitcom patina that suggests too many easy answers, and the love story between Hurt and Matlin grows wearisome—it's really one long monologue, since he speaks, signs, and translates her lines. To Hurt's great credit, his presence is never overinsistent, but the film is slick and predictable.

THE CHILDREN OF AN LAC ☆☆☆½
1980, USA (TV)
Ina Balin, Shirley Jones, Alan Fudge, Beulah Quo, Ben Piazza, Len Paul. Directed by John Llewellyn Moxey. 100 min.

This film is the absorbing real-life saga of three women who organize and carry out the evacuation of hundreds of Vietnamese orphans from Saigon. The time is 1975, right before the city fell to the Communists, and the women fight fiercely to have these children flown to freedom. In an interesting twist, actress Ina Balin, who was involved in the airlift, plays herself. This dramatic and heartrending race against the clock to save the children is rendered here without reliance on trumped-up melodramatics, and the effect is quite moving.

CHILDREN OF BLOOD

See *Cauldron of Blood*

CHILDREN OF THE CORN ☆☆
1984, USA, R
Peter Horton, Linda Hamilton, R. G. Armstrong, Courtney Gains, Robby Kiger. Directed by Fritz Kiersch. 93 min.

Although some of Stephen King's novels have been turned into good feature-length movies, his short stories tend to look awfully bloated onscreen. For this outing, the producers took a little tale about a band of zombie-eyed rural kids who happen upon human sacrifices in the form of two stranded motorists and expanded it into a big, boring mess. A couple of the child actors give appealingly creepy performances, but leads Peter Horton and Linda Hamilton barely register, and even the screams are tedious. Don't blame King—the script is by George Goldsmith.

CHILDREN OF THE DAMNED ☆☆
1964, Great Britain
Ian Hendry, Alan Badel, Barbara Ferris, Alfred Burke, Sheila Allen. Directed by Anton Leader. 90 min.

This follow-up to the haunting horror film *Village of the Damned* is not a continuation of that film's story, but rather a much less interesting variation on the same theme. Here, six telepathic tots are collected from around the world and brought to London for study. The timorous adults soon decide that the prodigious kids are better off dead than empowered, and the conflict that follows, though not entirely predictable, is tiresome and preachy. John Briley, who later won an Academy Award for *Gandhi*, wrote the screenplay.

CHILDREN OF DIVORCE ☆☆½
1980, USA (TV)
Barbara Feldon, Lance Kerwin, Olivia Cole, Kim Fields, Carmine Caridi, Stella Stevens, Fritz Weaver, Billy Dee Williams, Zohra Lampert, Greg Mullavey. Directed by Joanna Lee. 101 min.

The title pretty much tells the story—this is a sensitively handled TV "issue" movie that studies the effects of the marital breakups of three different families on the kids fought over, ignored, or left behind. Unfortunately, the anthological style doesn't allow writer-director Joanna Lee to go into enough depth in any of her several plot lines, although fine acting makes each drama compelling in its own way.

THE CHILDREN OF SANCHEZ ☆☆½
1978, USA/Mexico, R
Anthony Quinn, Dolores Del Rio, Katy Jurado, Lupita Ferrer. Directed by Hall Bartlett. 126 min.

The magnificent book by sociologist Oscar Lewis comes to the screen with a diluted impact, thanks to pedestrian direction and a journeyman screenplay. Despite the dream casting of Anthony Quinn and Dolores Del Rio, the film never attains the power this tale of familial devotion had on the printed page. Quinn, everyone's favorite ethnic type, is excellent if a bit obvious as the Job-like peasant whose greatest satisfaction in life would come from somehow unifying the many children he has fathered into an unorthodox but loving family unit. A disappointment, but there is a good Chuck Mangione score.

THE CHILDREN OF THEATER STREET ☆☆☆½
1978, USA/USSR
Directed by Robert Dornhelm and Earle Mack. 100 min.

Superlative Academy Award–winning documentary that manages the considerable feat of communicating the joy of dancing to its audience. The effect is not that of viewing a stodgy documentary but rather of dropping in at a dance recital. We participate in the spectator sport of dance-watching as we witness the backbreaking work and ultimate triumphs of three students dedicated to the art of ballet at the world-famous Kirov school in Leningrad. Narrated by Grace Kelly.

CHILDREN SHOULDN'T PLAY WITH DEAD THINGS ☆½
1972, USA
Alan Ormsby, Anya Ormsby, Valerie Mauches, Jane Daly. Directed by Benjamin Clark. 85 min.

A troupe of actors, led by their tyrannical director, play at invoking the dead on a deserted island. To their surprise and dismay, their game is all too successful, and they are besieged by the cannibal dead. An uneasy mixture of humor and horror makes the first half tough going, but once the dead rise from their graves, it's pure post–*Night of the Living Dead* zombie fun. From the director of *Deathdream* and *Black Christmas*, and the screenwriter of *Deathdream* and *Deranged*.

CHILLY SCENES OF WINTER ☆☆☆☆
1979, USA, PG
John Heard, Mary Beth Hurt, Peter Riegert, Kenneth McMillan, Nora Heflin, Gloria Grahame, Griffin Dunne, Mark Metcalfe, Ann Beattie. Directed by Joan Micklin Silver. 93 min.

Despite the Bergmanesque title, this is the best film about lost love since *Annie Hall*, and it's quite often just as funny. Charles, a member of the generation that just missed Woodstock, works as a minor civil servant and spends his time mooning over Laura, a married woman with whom he had an affair a year before. Director Joan Micklin Silver (*Hester Street*), who wrote the screenplay based on a novel by Ann Beattie (here seen in a bit part as a waitress), has a marvelous eye for detail in the lives of these characters, and gets equally wonderful performances from the principals, especially John Heard and Mary Beth Hurt as Charles and Laura, Peter Riegert (*Local Hero*) as Charles's equally ungrounded best friend, and Gloria Grahame as Charles's senile mother. This film was originally released (under the title *Head over Heels*) with a more upbeat ending, insisted on by the studio; it was rereleased with the proper title and ending after a few years' struggle by the director. Funny, charming, moving, and true: this one is well worth hunting down.

CHIMES AT MIDNIGHT ☆☆☆½
1966, Spain/Switzerland
Orson Welles, John Gielgud, Jeanne Moreau, Norman Rodway, Keith Baxter, Margaret Rutherford. Directed by Orson Welles. 113 min.

Pieced together from five of Shakespeare's plays, Orson Welles's little-seen "lament for Merrie England" is, despite its shoestring budget, one of his richest, most stirring films. Welles, whose portrayal of Falstaff is well nigh definitive, creates an authentically gritty Elizabethan atmosphere, moving from the coarse lightheartedness of the taverns to a comic but rather grim battle sequence (breathtakingly directed) and finally into a dark, infected world of death and decay. The wretchedly post-synced soundtrack makes the going difficult at times, but the film's rewards are well worth the trouble. (a.k.a.: *Falstaff*)

CHINA SEAS ☆☆☆
1935, USA
Clark Gable, Jean Harlow, Wallace Beery, Rosalind Russell, Lewis Stone, C. Aubrey Smith, Robert Benchley. Directed by Tay Garnett. 90 min.

Although by 1935 Clark Gable was getting prestige assignments like the role of Fletcher Christian in *Mutiny on the Bounty*, he was still being worked overtime in well-cast trash like this more up-to-date nautical adventure. (Irving Thalberg was quoted at the start of production as saying, "The hell with art this time. I'm going to produce a picture that will make money.") Gable plays the captain of a luxury liner who has troubles with both his women and some modern-day pirates. Rosalind Russell can be faulted for her veddy English milady, but Gable and Jean Harlow sizzle like they did in *Red Dust*; while they look better suited for screwball comedy, they put over the melodramatics with zest. Best scene has Wallace Beery torturing Gable with a foot press.

THE CHINA SYNDROME ☆☆☆
1979, USA, PG
Jane Fonda, Jack Lemmon, Michael Douglas, Scott Brady, James Hampton, Peter Donat, Wilford Brimley. Directed by James Bridges. 123 min.

A reporter (Fonda) and a cameraman (Douglas) stumble upon the cover-up of a near-meltdown at a nuclear plant in James Bridges's riveting, thought-provoking film. Although the drama is sometimes heavy-handed and the film sometimes becomes too preachy, the message is real and the performances make the story credible. Bridges's film, which preceded Three Mile Island by a matter of weeks, has proven all too prescient.

CHINATOWN ☆☆☆☆
1974, USA, R
Jack Nicholson, Faye Dunaway, John Huston, John Hillerman, Perry Lopez, Burt Young. Directed by Roman Polanski. 131 min.

Roman Polanski's sweatily erotic, perversely cruel *film noir* stars Jack Nicholson as a slick, small-time private eye who is led into a kinky maze of murder, corruption, and incest by his beautiful and mysterious client (Faye Dunaway). Polanski set this bleak, brilliant film in 1930s Los Angeles, the hard-boiled milieu of Raymond Chandler. Nicholson, like Chandler's detective Philip Marlowe, is a loner—sharp, tough, and honest—operating in a universe that is corrupt, deceitful, and malevolent. But Polanski doesn't merely rehash the genre's conventions; rather, he manipulates them, using the Chandleresque setting to reflect his dark, original vision of a world where even the last spark of hope and integrity is ultimately extinguished.

THE CHINESE CONNECTION ☆☆☆½
1973, Hong Kong, R
Bruce Lee, Nora Miao, Lo Wei, Robert Baker. Directed by Lo Wei. 107 min.

Bruce Lee (along with Bob Marley) is the only Third World hero to achieve mass success in the West by practicing an indigenous art without sacrificing his own cultural values. He communicated, instead, a very individual blend of mysticism, action, and a call for independence. *The Chinese Connection* is Lee's most overt ideological statement—he plays an oppressed Chinese fighter rebelling in Japanese-controlled Shanghai. His rhetoric is located in his hands, his feet, and his nunchaku—when he sees a sign that says "No dogs or Chinese," he kicks it in half. More importantly, Lee's intensity and brilliance as a martial artist mark him as a quintessential loner/hero. He's the most deeply affected student mourning his murdered teacher, and he's the only one who *can* get to the villains—all the villains. Blazing fighting; this is probably Lee's greatest film and definitely one of the greatest martial arts movies of all time.

CHINO ☆☆½
1973, Italy/USA
Charles Bronson, Jill Ireland, Vincent Van Patten, Marcel Bozzuffi, Fausto Tozzi. Directed by John Sturges. 98 min.

This rawhide Western is not one of Charles Bronson's better-known assignments, but it's more enticing than a lot of his urban brass-knuckles adventures. The barrel-chested brawler is cast as a heroic half-breed getting a lot of flak from the prejudiced locals, who are understandably peeved that they are no longer the head honchos of the horse-ranching set. Bronson's a bit more sympathetic than usual as the beleaguered rancher; we're drawn into his quest for peace on the prairie.

CHISUM ☆☆☆
1970, USA, G
John Wayne, Forrest Tucker, Geoffrey Duel, Patric Knowles, Pamela McMyler, Ben Johnson, Glenn Corbett, Christopher George, Richard Jaeckel. Directed by Andrew V. McLaglen. 111 min.

This autumnal John Wayne Western tells the story of an aging ranch owner who almost sits by and watches as a villain takes over a town. It's a good-looking, heartfelt cowboy film built on the classic theme of one man's stand against the corruption of the range. Good performances all around, including Forrest Tucker as a surprisingly menacing bad guy. There is also a nice romantic subplot involving Chisum's niece, Billy the Kid, and Pat Garrett.

CHITTY CHITTY BANG BANG ☆½
1968, Great Britain, G
Dick Van Dyke, Sally Ann Howes, Lionel Jeffries, Robert Helpmann, Gert Frobe, Benny Hill. Directed by Ken Hughes. 145 min.

James Bond's writer (Ian Fleming) and producer (Albert R. Broccoli) came up with one of the more nauseating children's musicals of the 1960s. Dick Van Dyke plays the bumbling inventor of a magic car that, among other things, swims and flies. Although the Roald Dahl–Ken Hughes screenplay is based on a collection of stories by Fleming, it owes more to films like *The Sound of Music* and *Mary Poppins*; however, it fails to provide any charms of its own. The film is overcute and overlong, and contains no memorable songs (the title tune is catchy, but in an irritating sort of way). It is directed by Ken Hughes, who would later direct another "musical masterpiece," Mae West's *Sextette*. Children will be justifiably grumpy after two-and-a-half hours of this treacle.

CHOICE OF ARMS ☆☆½
1983, France
Yves Montand, Gérard Depardieu, Catherine Deneuve. Directed by Alain Corneau. 114 min.

In Alain Corneau's complex and ultimately unsatisfactory thriller, Yves Montand plays a retired criminal whose past comes back to haunt him when a maniacal prison escapee (Gérard Depardieu) hides out at his mansion. Corneau seems determined to throw his characters into situations that smack more of old movies than of clever plotting; although all three principals become tools of his conceits and Deneuve is simply wasted, it's nonetheless a film of interesting twists and flourishes.

CHOICES
☆½
1984, USA
Paul Carafotes, Victor French, Lelia Goldoni, Val Avery. Directed by Silvio Narizzano. 90 min.

Substance is sorely missed in this sentimental drama. An extension of *Reckless* and *All the Right Moves*, *Choices* is about a teenage football star and violinist, John Carluccio, who is forced to alter his life because of the school board's decision to bar him from contact sports because of a hearing impairment. Watching Carluccio behave like a delinquent through most of the film is neither uplifting nor entertaining. Even on the most fundamental level, the film fails to adequately address its main theme of personal choices.

THE CHOIRBOYS
☆½
1977, USA, R
Charles Durning, Louis Gossett, Jr., Perry King, Tim McIntyre, Stephen Macht, Randy Quaid, Burt Young, Blair Brown, Charles Haid, Jim Davis, Barbara Rhoades. Directed by Robert Aldrich. 119 min.

This film is a repulsive, mean-spirited comedy about a group of cops who are anything but L.A.'s finest. These foul-mouthed, drunken, brawling pathetics were real characters in Joseph Wambaugh's sharp novel; in this episodic, wildly overlong film adaptation, they're just as reprehensible but totally uninteresting as well. Wambaugh's wit is missing, and what's left plays like an installment of *Police Academy* with cruelty substituting for stupidity.

CHOKE CANYON
☆½
1986, USA, PG
Stephen Collins, Janet Julian, Lance Henriksen, Bo Svenson, Victoria Racimo, Nicholas Pryor. Directed by Chuck Bail. 94 min.

In this low-budget action-adventure set near a Utah canyon, an idealistic scientist (stolid Stephen Collins) who wants to harness energy from the approaching Halley's Comet must do battle with the illegal toxic-waste dumpers who are soiling his outdoor lab site with radioactive gunk. Outlandish, at times moronic, and played too broadly to be taken seriously, *Choke Canyon*'s mildly exciting stuntwork is its only redeeming feature.

C.H.O.M.P.S.
☆½
1979, USA, G
Valerie Bertinelli, Wesley Eure, Conrad Bain, Chuck McCann, Red Buttons, Hermione Baddeley, Jim Backus, Robert Q. Lewis, Regis Toomey. Directed by Don Chaffey. 89 min.

C.H.O.M.P.S. is an acronym for Canine Home Protection System, a mechanical dog that the malignant owner of an electronics firm sets out to steal. A mechanical dog is also an apt description for this film, a dopey comedy written by Joseph Barbera, of Hanna-Barbera infamy. Chuck McCann and Red Buttons embarrass themselves as two bumbling burglars, parts that look like they were written with Tim Conway and Don Knotts in mind.

CHOOSE ME
☆☆☆½
1984, USA, R
Geneviève Bujold, Keith Carradine, Lesley Anne Warren, Rae Dawn Chong, Patrick Bauchau, John Larroquette. Directed by Alan Rudolph. 106 min.

Jumping off from the Teddy Pendergrass title tune, Alan Rudolph's romantic psychodrama is like a long, sultry jazz riff that's at its best when it works around the edges of dissonance. Keith Carradine is a former asylum inmate who gets involved with a bar owner (Lesley Anne Warren) and her new psychologist housemate (Geneviève Bujold), a prim, virginal type who gives advice to the sexlorn on a hot radio talk show. Rudolph's desperate characters seem to have walked in from the soaps, but his actors imbue their mannered roles with shades of unexpected urgency and wit.

CHOPPING MALL
½☆
1986, USA, R
Kelli Maroney, Tony O'Dell, John Terlesky, Russell Todd, Paul Bartel, Mary Woronov, Dick Miller, Barbara Crampton. Directed by Jim Wynorski. 76 min.

An anorectic little horror film about teenagers trapped in a shopping mall with three murderous robots on their trail, this inept entry in the exploitation market has barely enough meat on its bones to qualify as a feature; almost anything else on the horror shelf would offer you a better time. Sole positive note: Paul Bartel and Mary Woronov appear very briefly, reprising their *Eating Raoul* characters Paul and Mary Bland. Also known as *R.O.B.O.T.* and *Killbots*.

A CHORUS LINE—THE MOVIE
☆☆½
1985, USA, PG
Michael Douglas, Janet Jones, Audrey Landers, Vicki Frederick, Nicole Fosse, Terrence Mann. Directed by Richard Attenborough. 110 min.

Director Richard Attenborough is a masterly overseer of such world-class epics as *Young Winston* and *Gandhi*, but put him in a theater filled with young dancers and he falls all over himself. Much of the blame for this disappointing, boring translation of the fabulous Broadway show can be put on the usually talented Englishman, who focuses his camera everywhere but on the feet during the dance sequences and revives backstage clichés left behind with *42nd Street*. Thankfully, the energetic songs and footwork of the spirited cast more or less pull the show together. The young talents (particularly Janet Jones and Audrey Landers) act miles ahead of "name" star Michael Douglas. How Hollywood could have labored so long to bring this story to the screen, and have ended up with such muddled results, is a difficult question to answer.

THE CHOSEN

See *Holocaust 2000*

THE CHOSEN
☆☆☆
1981, USA, PG
Maximilian Schell, Rod Steiger, Robby Benson, Barry Miller. Directed by Jeremy Paul Kagan. 108 min.

Chaim Potok's novel about the clash of values between secular and Hasidic Jews during World War II has been given a respectful treatment—though at times the movie's pivotal conflict seems to have less to do with Judaism than with actual technique. Playing the progressive father and son who want to feel connected to both their roots and to the twentieth century, Maximilian Schell and Barry Miller give fine performances; unfortunately, as the Hasidim who've immersed themselves in their traditional discipline, Rod Steiger and Robby Benson turn on the histrionics.

CHRISTIANE F.
☆☆☆
1981, West Germany
Natja Brunckhorst, Thomas Haustein, David Bowie. Directed by Ulrich Edel. 120 min.

This film is a gritty, harrowing, relentlessly downbeat look at Germany's decadent new youth culture. The heroine, Christiane (Natja Brunckhorst), is a pretty, sad-faced fifteen-year-old who falls in with the zonked-out kids she meets at a local rock club and then slides into heroin addiction and prostitution. Director Ulrich Edel refuses to moralize: the movie follows Christiane straight into the gutter, but the point is that she hasn't fallen in with the "wrong crowd"—in Germany, it's the only crowd. The story is too long by half an hour, and the scenes in which Christiane and her addict boyfriend go cold turkey are not for the squeamish. But the film has a kind of rancid integrity at its core. David Bowie appears in several concert scenes—the only vaguely uplifting moments in the entire movie. The video version has apparently been slightly trimmed to fit on a two-hour cassette.

CHRISTINE ☆☆
1983, USA, R
John Stockwell, Keith Gordon, Alexandra Paul, Robert Prosky. Directed by John Carpenter. 110 min.

This slick adolescent horror-fantasy, based on the novel by Stephen King, was directed by genre expert John Carpenter, who is also responsible for *Halloween, The Fog, Escape from New York,* and *Starman,* among others. The plot centers around a candy-colored vermillion Plymouth Fury that takes over the life of an ultra-nerd. As he refurbishes the car, he becomes handsome and cool, but he also becomes as nasty as the car, which brings woe to all her owners. Dullish, subpar King.

A CHRISTMAS CAROL ☆☆½
1938, USA
Reginald Owen, Gene Lockhart, Kathleen Lockhart, Terry Kilburn, Leo G. Carroll, Lynne Carver. Directed by Edwin L. Marin. 69 min.

Just as Lionel Barrymore was about to play Scrooge (the meatiest role of his career), he became ill and MGM replaced him with Reginald Owen in this version of Dickens's Christmas classic. Too bad, because Owen gives an acceptable but predictable reading and the rest of the film is stodgy and sentimental in the 1930s "prestige film" manner. For a darker, more complex *Carol,* see below. Children, however, will be satisfied with this rendering. Footnote: the Lockharts were married to each other in real life.

A CHRISTMAS CAROL ☆☆☆½
1951, Great Britain
Alastair Sim, Kathleen Harrison, Jack Warner, Michael Hordern, Mervyn Johns, Hermione Baddeley, Patrick Macnee, Glyn Dearman, Ernest Thesiger. Directed by Brian Desmond Hurst. 86 min.

Until George C. Scott delivered his wonderful characterization of Scrooge in a TV movie, this was easily the finest film version of Dickens's Yuletide classic, with Alastair Sim as a sly, rascally, oddly spunky Scrooge—a vast improvement over Reginald Owen's maudlin portrayal in the 1938 version. Overall, it's a bleaker, darker tale than you may remember, the last ten minutes notwithstanding. Patrick Macnee appears as the young Marley.

CHRISTMAS EVIL ½☆
1983, USA
Brandon Maggart, Jeffrey De Munn. Directed by Lewis Jackson. 90 min.

Oh, you'd better watch out, I'm telling you why, Santa has a big ax this year, and if you're in his Book of Bad Boys and Girls under "negative body hygiene" or "impure thoughts," this Christmas is going to be a downer. This indescribably stupid horror opus doesn't even have the violence it promises—just a script that must have been written on the back of a cocktail napkin and the nerve to try to make an antihero of sorts out of its crazed St. Nick. After all, he says, kids like discipline, ho, ho, ho. (a.k.a.: *You Better Watch Out*)

CHRISTMAS IN JULY ☆☆½
1940, USA
Dick Powell, Ellen Drew, Raymond Walburn, Alexander Carr, William Demarest, Ernest Truex, Franklin Pangborn. Directed by Preston Sturges. 66 min.

This early Preston Sturges comedy, while not up to the brilliance of some of his other work, is full of interesting touches and remarkable for the current of bitterness and misery that runs through its comedy. Dick Powell plays an impoverished office boy who constantly dreams of making it big and is then tricked into believing that he's won a $25,000 slogan contest. By the time he finds out the truth, he's already run up a hefty bill in becoming his neighborhood's benefactor. Sturges's tone is often uncertain and the ending rings false, but Powell brings a startling, angry forcefulness to his role.

CHRISTMAS LILIES OF THE FIELD ☆☆☆
1979, USA (TV)
Billy Dee Williams, Maria Schell, Fay Hauser, Judith Piquet, Lisa Mann. Directed by Ralph Nelson. 100 min.

In the celebrated Oscar-winning classic *Lilies of the Field,* wayfaring wanderer Homer Smith was charmed by some nuns into helping them build a chapel in the desert. In this generally agreeable seasonal treat, Homer returns fifteen years later (played by Billy Dee Williams instead of Sidney Poitier), this time to construct an orphanage. A lovely, often spirited study of interracial brotherhood at work.

A CHRISTMAS STORY ☆☆½
1983, USA, PG
Melinda Dillon, Darren McGavin, Peter Billingsley, Ian Petrella, Scott Schwartz, R. D. Robb. Directed by Bob Clark. 98 min.

This film is a bizarre mixture of forties nostalgia and eighties cynicism whipped into a slapstick froth by director Bob Clark (*Porky's*). Based on Jean Shepherd's popular 1966 novel *In God We Trust, All Others Pay Cash,* it's a domestic black comedy about a cheerfully devious nine-year-old (played by pudgy Peter Billingsley, a crack scene stealer) who desperately wants a Red Ryder BB gun for Christmas. Clark crams the story with the sort of loud, brazen, exaggerated satire one remembers from *Mad* magazine's Dave Berg. It doesn't work exactly, but there are some moments of impish wit, as well as a streak of toasty Yuletide sentimentality that seems borrowed from some other, far more innocent film.

A CHRISTMAS TO REMEMBER ☆☆☆
1978, USA (TV)
Jason Robards, Jr., Eva Marie Saint, Joanne Woodward, George Perry, Bryan Englund. Directed by George Englund. 100 min.

This meaty drama delves into the gradual development of family ties between an obstreperous grandfather and his confused grandson, an urbanite who doesn't fit into the old man's scheme of things. This is a holiday film to remember. It doesn't ply you with saccharine Christmas pudding sentiments, and it dares to acknowledge that holidays can also be painful times for many people.

THE CHRISTMAS TREE ☆½
1969, France/Italy, G
William Holden, Virna Lisi, André Bourvil, Brook Fuller, Madeline Damien. Directed by Terence Young. 110 min.

Boo hoo. American millionaire William Holden, separated from his wife, has never gotten to know his ten-year-old son. On a trip to Corsica, the boy is exposed to a fatal dose of radioactivity, and Dad sets out to make his last few months happy by spoiling the kid rotten. Dad, by the way, didn't suffer any ill effects from the radiation because he was underwater at the time, so remember, if the Bomb ever falls in your neighborhood, just jump in the pool and you'll be safe.

A CHRISTMAS WITHOUT SNOW ☆☆½
1980, USA (TV)
Michael Learned, John Houseman, Ramon Bieri, James Cromwell, Valerie Curtin. Directed by John Korty. 100 min.

This holiday story of an urban divorcée (Michael Learned) who moves to a small Nebraska town and finds unexpected challenge in the church choir is steered away from overt sentiment by John Korty's sensitive direction, and by good performances from Learned and John Houseman as the crusty, imperious choirmaster (a characterization that "Paper Chase" devotees will find completely familiar). Predictable but effective material.

CHRISTOPHER STRONG ★★½
1933, USA
Katharine Hepburn, Colin Clive, Billie Burke, Helen Chandler, Jack LaRue. Directed by Dorothy Arzner. 77 min.

In her first starring role, Katharine Hepburn portrays Lady Cynthia Carrington, a daredevil pilot forced to choose between her career and the married man she loves, Sir Christopher Strong (Colin Clive). This early film by Dorothy Arzner, Hollywood's most important female director of the thirties, has aged poorly, but Hepburn's headstrong performance remains vibrant, and the image of her in a silver lamé body stocking is striking indeed.

CHRIST STOPPED AT EBOLI ★★★★
1979, Italy/France
Gian Maria Volonte, Paolo Bonacelli, Alain Cuny, Lea Massari, Irene Papas, François Simon, Luigi Infantino. Directed by Francesco Rosi. 120 min.

In the mid-thirties, writer-physician-painter Carlo Levi was exiled from his home in Turin to a remote corner of Southern Italy. His experiences in a land that was cut off from the rest of the world, where Christianity itself supposedly penetrated no further than the town of Eboli, resulted in a memoir that became a classic of Italian literature. Rosi's version, originally produced for Italian television, was more than twice as long as the film available on video, and naturally the shorter movie lacks the texture and impact of the original. Nonetheless, it remains a moving document about one man, a victim of politics and history, confronting a world in which his problems are incomprehensible and his only solace is simple communication on a very elementary level. Gian Maria Volonte is very good as Levi, showing his character's initial diffidence and alienation gradually giving way to empathy and involvement. The movie is beautifully photographed and has the lyrical realism that is the hallmark of Italian cinema. (a.k.a.: *Eboli*)

CHU CHU AND THE PHILLY FLASH ★★
1981, USA, PG
Alan Arkin, Carol Burnett, Jack Warden, Danny Glover, Ruth Buzzi. Directed by David Lowell Rich. 100 min.

The gifted Alan Arkin and Carol Burnett can't save a fourth-rate script (by Mrs. Arkin) that casts them as two street eccentrics in San Francisco. Arkin is an ex–baseball player and Burnett a former dancer who both think they've found a lucky thing in a briefcase filled with secret government papers. These two actors, equally at home with comedy or drama, have some sensitive moments when going over their failed lives, but most of the comedy simply falls flat.

C.H.U.D. ★★
1984, USA, PG
John Heard, Daniel Stern, Christopher Curry. Directed by Douglas Cheek. 88 min.

This is an entertaining exploitation film about what *really* lives under the sidewalks of New York City, and what might happen if they decided they were tired of staying down there. Paranoid, clever, and not too serious; a romp through genre clichés in the best of spirits.

A CHUMP AT OXFORD ★★½
1940, USA
Stan Laurel, Oliver Hardy, Forrester Harvey, Wilfred Lucas, Forbes Murray, Peter Cushing, James Finlayson. Directed by Alfred Goulding. 63 min.

This short Laurel-and-Hardy feature almost seems like two two-reelers pasted together, with the second half much better than the first. In the earlier section, the duo are servants in the home of a rich man (James Finlayson) and the predictable slapstick confusion ensues. The movie picks up, though, when the two land in stuffy old England; the comedy is more verbal than physical, and of a reasonably high order. Peter Cushing makes his film debut as one of the Oxford students.

CIAO! MANHATTAN ★★
1973, USA, R
Edie Sedgwick, Wesley Hayes, Isabel Jewell, Geoff Briggs, Paul America, Baby Jane Holzer, Roger Vadim, Jean Margouleff. Directed by John Palmer and David Weisman. 90 min.

"They will never make a film that encompasses more of the 1960s," said one of the stars of *Ciao! Manhattan* on its 1983 rerelease. That may well be true. As a movie, it's horrible (and horrifying); as a cultural artifact, it's completely compelling. Shot between 1967 and 1971, when its star overdosed on heroin, the film is a barely fictional look at the high life of Edie Sedgwick, the socialite-model-starlet who came out of Andy Warhol's "Factory" to shimmer briefly as a celebrity-for-celebrity's-sake sensation. As you watch her turn from a wide-eyed ingenue to a dope-addicted alcoholic, you see virtually everything short of her sadly predictable death. How much of it is acting? Not enough for the film to be anything other than exploitative, and that's just what makes much of it genuinely frightening: it's truer than even the filmmakers must have intended. Unless you have an abiding interest in the Warhol era, a lot of patience, and a very strong stomach, stay away.

THE CICADA

See *The Cricket*

LA CICALA

See *The Cricket*

EL CID ★★★½
1961, USA/Spain
Charlton Heston, Sophia Loren, Raf Vallone, Geneviève Page, Hurd Hatfield. Directed by Anthony Mann. 184 min.

The problem with most romantic epics is that the central love story is dwarfed by the gargantuan set design and special effects, but not in this superb film. Most biblical and historical epics shove their loving couples behind the nearest pillar as the panorama of historic events whizzes by like the chariots in *Ben-Hur*. In *El Cid*, Charlton Heston and Sophia Loren strike passionate sparks, and their affair is part of the main attraction of this three-ring spectacle handsomely filmed in Spain. Heston is a Spanish lord who loves the sensual Loren but can't overcome her bitterness toward him for his responsibility in her father's death. As the lovers rail at each other, the Spanish-Moorish wars clang away in the background. An extravaganza with striking battle sequences, an impassioned love story, and a startlingly memorable finale.

THE CINCINNATI KID ★★★
1965, USA
Steve McQueen, Ann-Margret, Edward G. Robinson, Karl Malden, Joan Blondell, Tuesday Weld, Rip Torn, Jack Weston. Directed by Norman Jewison. 113 min.

Often referred to as the poor man's *The Hustler*, this film deserves a lot better than that flip dismissal. It's a juicy gambling melodrama with a lot of dynamic high-stakes suspense (and a sidecar of romance unconvincingly tossed in). Building to a climactic winner-takes-all poker game, the film is flashy, colorful, and engrossing. Whenever slow spots diminish the effectiveness of this game of chance, the movie is revitalized by those veteran scene stealers Joan Blondell and Edward G. Robinson. Steve McQueen's at his tight-lipped best, but Ann-Margret, licking her lips as she spills out of her red dress at a cockfight, is, shall we say, excessive.

CINDERFELLA ★★★
1960, USA
Jerry Lewis, Ed Wynn, Judith Anderson, Anna Maria Alberghetti, Henry Silva, Robert Hutton, Count Basie and His Orchestra. Directed by Frank Tashlin. 88 min.

As children's entertainment, Jerry Lewis's slightly twisted, splashy fairy tale holds up remarkably well. The Fella is an orphan bedeviled by deliciously wicked stepmother Judith Anderson; he beats out insipid stepbrother Robert Hutton for pretty, singing Anna Maria Alberghetti. Kids will always appreciate Jerry's inspired mugging, and he performs a jazzy dance solo to the music of Count Basie's Orchestra. Mavens of the Frank Tashlin/Jerry Lewis collaboration, which produced classics like *Hollywood or Bust* and *Rock-a-Bye Baby*, will be disappointed by the lack of sharp satire, and viewers with any prejudice against Jerry's narcissism may well faint. The film looks gorgeous, thanks partly to the art direction of Hal Pereira and Henry Bumstead and to Edith Head's updated costuming, and also to Tashlin's elegant moving camera.

CIRCLE OF DECEIT ★★★½
1981, France/Germany
Bruno Ganz, Hanna Schygulla, Jean Carmet, Jerzy Skolimowski. Directed by Volker Schlondorff. 108 min.

This icily effective political drama mixes a documentary-like approach in recounting the death-soaked atmosphere of war-torn Lebanon with a detached account of the travails of a journalist who can't relinquish his intense feelings for a widow in Beirut. With complexity and escalating power, the film delves into the reporter's psyche; it gives us a frightening glimpse of the price he pays for his personal and professional detachment. Somehow, his uncharacteristically passionate affair with the widow is linked with the life-and-death struggles of the civil war in Lebanon. Disturbing, timely film.

CIRCLE OF IRON ★★½
1979, USA, R
David Carradine, Jeff Cooper, Roddy McDowall, Eli Wallach, Christopher Lee. Directed by Richard Moore. 102 min.

Fans of David Carradine in the television series "Kung Fu" will be happy to see that he has been promoted here to the role of teacher of the Eastern arts. Actually, he plays four roles, each a character encountered by young, knowledge-seeking Cord (Jeff Cooper) as he travels across a desert in search of wisdom. It's better than it sounds (several steps above the usual kung-fu nonsense), but if you're really into the martial arts it's going to strike you as somewhat silly. Bruce Lee, who wrote the original story along with actor James Coburn, was originally set to play the Carradine roles.

CIRCLE OF TWO ★★
1980, Canada, PG
Richard Burton, Tatum O'Neal, Kate Reid, Robin Gammell, Patricia Collins. Directed by Jules Dassin. 90 min.

Bad-movie fans the world over were salivating in anticipation of this collaboration between Tatum and Burton (especially after Dick's triumph with that other Junior Miss thespette, Linda Blair, in *Exorcist II: The Heretic*) in a story that sounds like a cross between *Manhattan* and *Endless Love*. Unfortunately, HUAC expatriate director Jules Dassin ruined all of their fun by turning this into a sincere attempt at an unconventional soap opera. It's still not good, mind you, just not bad enough to be fun. A sixteen-year-old schoolgirl meets a retired artist at a porno movie; they fall in love, and she convinces him to resume his work, but her parents object to his age. Watch for Ryan O'Neal (undoubtedly chaperoning his daughter on the set) and Lee Majors in the audience at the porno house.

THE CIRCUS ★★★★
1928, USA
Charlie Chaplin, Merna Kennedy, Allan Garcia, Harry Crocker, Henry Bergman, Betty Morrissey. Directed by Charles Chaplin. 72 min.

Certainly Chaplin's most underrated silent-comedy feature and long regarded as his most purely funny film, *Circus* has become, with time, even more emotionally satisfying while remaining just as hilarious. Charlie's Tramp evokes a man who can be funny only when he is trying to be most serious, providing a poignant link with the later masterpiece *Limelight*. In that movie, the clown Calvero tries desperately but can no longer amuse. Here, the Tramp wanders into a traveling circus, becomes the unwitting star, and falls in love with the beautiful bareback rider. Chaplin's tightrope-walking scene is one of the funniest sequences in cinema history, and the movie contains several other brilliant pieces set variously in a hall of mirrors, a lion's cage, and the center ring. To make this film, Chaplin constructed an entire circus and kept it standing for a full year, and *The Circus* authentically captures the hurdy-gurdy atmosphere of the big top. Highly publicized problems in Chaplin's personal life—his young second wife divorced him, and her complaints against Chaplin led to a ban on his films—overshadowed the movie's release and may have cast an unfair pall over this great work. Playhouse Video has released a very good-looking version of this movie that includes Chaplin's own music (recorded in 1970; he even sings the title song) and the First National Short *Sunnyside*.

CIRCUS WORLD ★
1964, USA
John Wayne, Rita Hayworth, Claudia Cardinale, John Smith, Lloyd Nolan, Richard Conte. Directed by Henry Hathaway. 138 min.

A fine cast is wasted in this true turkey from the generally gifted Henry Hathaway. John Wayne plays a circus owner who attempts to keep his daughter from finding out about her mother's scarlet past. Vulgar production values (despite Super Technirama), atrocious acting (especially Claudia Cardinale's), and an idiotic script (by Ben Hecht, Julian Halevy, and James Edward Grant) make this unquestionably the worst in the not terribly distinguished cycle of fifties and sixties circus melodramas, which included *The Greatest Show on Earth, Carnival Story, Trapeze, The Big Circus,* and *The Big Show*.

THE CISCO KID RETURNS

See *Guns of Fury*

THE CITADEL ★★★
1938, Great Britain
Robert Donat, Rosalind Russell, Ralph Richardson, Emlyn Williams, Rex Harrison, Penelope Dudley-Ward. Directed by King Vidor. 113 min.

Before "Masterpiece Theatre" did it, A. J. Cronin's *The Citadel* was nicely made by MGM's British studios. Robert Donat sensitively plays the poor but ambitious young doctor who is lured from his mining town to a more lucrative practice treating hypochondriacs. Rosalind Russell (with a British accent) is poorly cast as the heroine, but Ralph Richardson is perfect as a colleague. Spencer Tracy starred in the quasi-remake, *Take This Woman*. Ponderous in spots and patly resolved, but the carpentry is solid.

CITIZEN KANE ★★★★
1941, USA
Orson Welles, Joseph Cotten, Dorothy Comingore, Everett Sloane. Directed by Orson Welles. 119 min.

The extraordinary genius of the twenty-five-year-old Orson Welles makes *Citizen Kane* one of the most exciting, cinematically revolutionary films of all time. A landmark of stylistic virtuosity, the film details the life of newspaper magnate Charles Foster Kane through dynamic editing, imaginative camera angles, deep-focus photography, and an ever-shifting narrative perspective. Welles's *roman-à-clef* treatment of the life of newspaper tycoon William Randolph Hearst created a scandal at the time of *Citizen Kane*'s release, and the film's indictment of the individual's power over media and government remains fresh and relevant today. One of the great achievements in the history of cinema.

THE CITY
1977, USA (TV)　　★★
Robert Forster, Don Johnson, Ward Costello, Jimmy Dean, Mark Hamill, Susan Sullivan, William Conrad. Directed by Harvey Hart. 78 min.

L.A. Vice? It could have happened if this series pilot starring baby-faced Don Johnson as a street cop in the City of Angels had taken off. It didn't, and it's easy to see why; the plot is pure tedium. Johnson and co-cop Robert Forster are assigned to hunt down and capture a psychotic killer who has targeted a country-and-western singer (Jimmy Dean) for assassination. Routine action, with Forster sleepwalking through his role and Johnson (whose many TV movies have started to surface on video since "Miami Vice"'s success) failing to show a bit of charisma.

CITY HEAT
1984, USA, PG　　★
Clint Eastwood, Burt Reynolds, Jane Alexander, Madeline Kahn, Rip Torn, Irene Cara, Richard Roundtree, Tony LoBianco. Directed by Richard Benjamin. 97 min.

This film is a botch. Director Richard Benjamin couldn't decide whether to make a knockabout comedy, an ersatz-Bogart gangster flick, or a contemporary shoot-'em-up, and the result is ninety minutes of dull, ludicrous confusion. The film is set up as a *Sting*-style Prohibition Era adventure, with Reynolds as a private detective stalking rival gangs of hoodlums and Eastwood as a police lieutenant working on the same case, two steps behind. Box-office arithmetic aside, pairing up Reynolds and Eastwood was an unlikely bet to begin with, and the two stars end up not acting together at all. Instead, each performs a *pas de deux* with his own screen clichés.

CITY IN FEAR
1980, USA (TV)　　★★★
David Janssen, Robert Vaughn, William Daniels, Susan Sullivan, Perry King, Pepe Serna, Mickey Rourke. Directed by Alan Smithee (pseudonym for Jud Taylor). 135 min.

Any resemblance between this gritty telefilm and New York's notorious "Son of Sam" murder case is purely opportunistic, but *City in Fear* isn't merely a psycho-killer drama—it's also a sharp, incisive look at the way newspapers can manipulate criminals and victims to get a juicier story. In his last role, David Janssen played a worn-out reporter pressed into duty by a ruthless publisher (Robert Vaughn) eager to boost circulation. Well-acted and often surprisingly pointed.

CITY LIGHTS
1931, USA　　★★★★
Charlie Chaplin, Virginia Cherill, Harry Myers, Florence Lee, Allan Garcia, Hank Mann, Henry Bergman, Albert Austin. Directed by Charles Chaplin. 87 min.

Charlie Chaplin's warmest film has to be the sentimental favorite of his legion of admirers. The appeal of its story about a tramp who falls in love with a blind girl remains undiminished and sparkling clear. What may be less obvious is the beautiful organization of its parallel stories. The poignancy of the blind girl who doesn't know that her hero is a bum finds an echo in the low-comedy story of the millionaire who finds a fast friend in the Tramp when intoxicated, but wakes up the next morning and doesn't recognize him at all. As the little Tramp struggles throughout the film to raise money to help the girl (ironically squandering tons of the stuff with the alcoholic millionaire), the film creates opportunities for several great Chaplin set pieces. The rescue of the millionaire from his suicide attempt is priceless. The boxing match, with the Tramp matched against a huge, hostile opponent, is an oft-excerpted classic. Last, but far from least, the closing sequence is an unsurpassed heart-tugger. This film, though scored by Chaplin himself, is virtually a silent movie, and although made at a time when the film industry had switched over to dialogue-heavy projects, it became an audacious, unexpected success.

CITY OF THE WALKING DEAD
1980, Spain/Italy, R　　½★
Hugo Stiglitz, Laura Trotter, Fancisco Rabal, Maria Rosaria Omaggio, Mel Ferrer. Directed by Umberto Lenzi. 92 min.

In this execrable Spanish/Italian rip-off of *Night of the Living Dead*, a remote nuclear accident turns people into bloodthirsty zombies who take over a whole city; meanwhile, the military, under the auspices of a distraught Mel Ferrer, attempts to contain the outbreak. There is lots of hacking, cutting, and clawing—and watch for an unintentionally hilarious scene in which the ghouls run wild on a "Solid Gold"-type television show. This film was made in 1980 but not released here for four years. (a.k.a.: *Nightmare City*)

CITY ON FIRE
1979, Canada, R　　★½
Barry Newman, Susan Clark, Shelley Winters, Leslie Nielsen, James Franciscus, Ava Gardner, Henry Fonda, Movor Moore. Directed by Alvin Rakoff. 101 min.

This is a disaster movie made by rote (but then, aren't they all?); within two minutes of meeting each character, you know whether he or she is going to die or survive, and even at about what point into the movie. The disaster at hand is a sort of horizontal version of *The Towering Inferno*—a fire in a new refinery spreads throughout an entire city because the mayor has been cutting costs. Some of the special effects are pretty good, and there's always the soap-opera appeal of these things. Unfortunately, also like *Towering Inferno*, the film has an unpleasant tendency to linger over scenes of people before, during, and after burning to death, which makes it difficult to enjoy this for the cornball entertainment it is.

THE CITY'S EDGE
1983, Australia　　★½
Hugo Weaving, Katrina Foster, Mark Lee, Tommy Lewis, Ralph Cotterill, Frederic Abbott, Martin Harris. Directed by Ken Quinnell. 86 min.

MGM/UA Home Video's deceptive packaging makes this out to be a suspense thriller; would that there were any suspense or thrills to be had. Instead, this gloomy drama is a character study of someone without much character. A young would-be writer from the outback arrives in Sydney and takes a room in a seedy boardinghouse, trying to soak up enough interesting experiences to have something to write about. He insinuates himself into the lives of a young junkie (*Gallipoli*'s Mark Lee, in a touching performance), his overly protective sister, and a black superintendent with a chip on his shoulder. Things end tragically, but not unpredictably.

CLAIR DE FEMME
1979, France/Italy/Germany　　★★½
Romy Schneider, Yves Montand, Romolo Valli, Lilia Kedrova. Directed by Constantine Costa-Gavras. 105 min.

Costa-Gavras is perhaps the best director of serious political thrillers we have; unfortunately, as a maker of romantic melodramas he's out of his depth. Yves Montand and Romy Schneider play a couple drawn together by death (his wife's, her daughter's). Like Truffaut's *The Green Room*, which also concerns two characters obsessed by their dead, this is a gloomy, obsessive film that you need to be in the right mood to sit through. May you live long, prosper, and very seldom be in that mood.

THE CLAIRVOYANT

See *The Evil Mind*

THE CLAN OF THE CAVE BEAR
1986, USA, R　　★½
Daryl Hannah, Pamela Reed, James Remar, Thomas G. Waites, John Doolittle; Salome Jens (narration). Directed by Michael Chapman. 98 min.

Looking for someone to make a film of Jean M. Auel's massive anthro-trash novel about a sexy Cro-Magnon-ette who teaches her Neanderthal pals modern ways, the producers of this laugher inexplicably chose John Sayles, whose films are cultural anthropologies of a somewhat different sort. Sayles's dialogue here is on the order of "Grrrmggrmphmph?" "Gibi! Gibi!" and the accompanying subtitles are only a couple of steps more literate. One of the cheesiest earthquake scenes in recent history provides a bit of merriment; an unnecessarily brutal rape scene does not. Most strangely, the action, though shot by skilled cinematographer Jan De Bont and directed by skilled cinematographer Michael Chapman, looks as phony as it sounds.

CLASH BY NIGHT ★★★½
1952, USA
Barbara Stanwyck, Paul Douglas, Robert Ryan, Marilyn Monroe, J. Carroll Naish. Directed by Fritz Lang. 105 min.

This is a Fritz Lang film from a very strong period, when the German director had fully mastered the mechanics of Hollywood moviemaking. The source, an early working-class melodrama by Clifford Odets, is an odd one for Lang, but the result is one of his warmest films. As the "woman with a past" who makes a last bid for security with rough-hewn fisherman Paul Douglas, Barbara Stanwyck adds new depths to the sort of tough-cookie role she had played often before. Worth seeing.

CLASH OF THE TITANS ★★
1981, Great Britain, PG
Laurence Olivier, Claire Bloom, Maggie Smith, Ursula Andress, Harry Hamlin, Judi Bowker, Burgess Meredith, Flora Robson, Freda Jackson, Tim Pigott-Smith. Directed by Desmond Davis. 120 min.

This kiddie-show version of the myth of Perseus and Andromeda is one of those bad movies whose strange artificiality casts a spell of its own. The film garbles Greek mythology, the blank-faced actors (notably "L. A. Law" 's Harry Hamlin and Judi Bowker as Perseus and Andromeda) spout blank dialogue with all the exaggerated verve of guest stars on "Captain Kangaroo," and the sets look like the scenery for a toy train kit. Even the animated monsters—created by fifties special-effects wizard Ray Harryhausen—are jerky and rubbery and have ridiculously hyperactive tails. Yet the very clumsiness of the effects has a charming quaintness. Watching this amusingly anachronistic spectacle, you never forget you're at the movies. With Laurence Olivier camping it up as Zeus.

CLASS ★★
1983, USA, R
Rob Lowe, Andrew McCarthy, Jacqueline Bisset, Cliff Robertson. Directed by Lewis John Carlino. 98 min.

Shy, awkward Jonathan and rich, blue-blooded Skip are prep-school roommates and best friends—until Jonathan has an affair with an older woman who turns out to be Skip's alcoholic nymphomaniac mom. Is this, you may ask, the premise of a movie that, apparently without irony, calls itself *Class*? It's one quality that's decidedly lacking in this coming-of-age ode to vicarious Oedipalism, and there isn't much humor or skill to make up for it. Preening, pouty Rob Lowe is harder to take than Andrew McCarthy, who manages to inject a couple of sly moments into this humdrum comedy-drama. But Jacqueline Bisset, more or less reprising her *Rich and Famous* role as a dissatisfied woman craving teenage sex in public places, is an embarrassment.

CLASS OF '44 ★★
1973, USA, PG
Gary Grimes, Jerry Houser, Oliver Conant, William Atherton, Sam Bottoms, Deborah Winters. Directed by Paul Bogart. 95 min.

In anticipation of the teenage sex comedies of the eighties, this lukewarm sequel to *Summer of '42* contains such high jinks as a student being expelled from college for bringing a prostitute to his fraternity. The bittersweet nostalgia and wry observation of teenage growing pains that was so lovingly evoked in the earlier film looks flat and artificial here. Paul Bogart (an *All in the Family* director) does a competent but thoroughly artless job, and much of the (now older) cast has lost a lot of its youthful appeal. Yet another misbegotten follow-up to a good movie.

THE CLASS OF MISS MacMICHAEL ★★
1978, Great Britain/USA, PG
Glenda Jackson, Oliver Reed, Michael Murphy, Rosalind Cash, Phil Daniels. Directed by Silvio Narizzano. 100 min.

An outstanding cast can't do anything of note with a rehash of the old story about the dedicated teacher in the underprivileged school. Not nearly as good as *Blackboard Jungle* or *To Sir, With Love*, though it's not as bad as the repulsive *Class of 1984*; it's just not much of anything. Phil Daniels, who plays one of the students, went on to fame as Jimmy in *Quadrophenia*.

CLASS OF 1984 ★½
1982, USA/Canada, R
Perry King, Timothy Van Patten, Keith Knight, Roddy McDowall, Lisa Langlois, Michael J. Fox. Directed by Mark Lester. 93 min.

This violent story of juvenile delinquency is meant to be a sort of modern, punk version of *Blackboard Jungle*. Instead, it's a rather dull exploitation/revenge pic. Perry King plays a high-school teacher who's menaced by a psychopathic, piano-pounding student. What would you do if four of your students raped your pregnant wife? Yes, it's one of those. Music by the L.A. band Fear.

CLASS OF '63 ★★½
1973, USA (TV)
James Brolin, Joan Hackett, Cliff Gorman, Ed Lauter. Directed by John Korty. 90 min.

Joan Hackett is excellent as a wife who considers rekindling a college romance during a campus reunion. This film is more incisive and exploratory than most made-for-TV movies of the period, though it leans toward a love triangle melodrama with the usual sort of conclusion. Cliff Gorman lends fine support as the husband.

CLASS REUNION

See *National Lampoon's Class Reunion*

THE CLASS REUNION MASSACRE ★
1977, USA, R
T. G. Finkbinder, Jeanetta Arnette, Mel Lenzi. Directed by Constantine S. Gochis. 84 min.

There is undoubtedly a large market, consisting of people who were traumatized for life by high school, for a movie about a tenth class reunion in which a maniac locks his ex-classmates into the venerable old school and begins to slaughter them one by one. And this is just the kind of junk that market deserves. If *Carrie* wasn't cathartic enough for you, get counseling, or at least write Ann Landers.

CLAUDINE ★★★
1974, USA, PG
Diahann Carroll, James Earl Jones, Lawrence Hilton-Jacobs, Tamu, Yvette Curtis, Adam Wade. Directed by John Barry. 94 min.

In the mid-1970s, when it sometimes seemed that the only blacks in American movies were whores, superstuds, junkies, or clowns, this touching romance about a divorced mother in Harlem who falls for a local garbageman took everyone by surprise. Though some of its plot pretexts (the daughter who becomes pregnant by young Abdulla X, the son who gets a vasectomy for "revolutionary" reasons) are a bit much, the film is still a charmer, thanks to James Earl Jones and Diahann Carroll. He is wonderfully low-key and funny, and she has a comic and dramatic intensity that may surprise you. *Claudine* skirts as many issues as it faces, but tries harder and succeeds more often than many similar films.

THE CLAY PIGEON ☆☆½
1949, USA
Bill Williams, Barbara Hale, Richard Loo. Directed by Richard O. Fleischer. 97 min.

An ex–P.O.W. on the lam attempts to discover whether he really was responsible for the torture/murder of his buddy. The husband-and-wife team of Bill Williams and Barbara Hale, parents of actor William Katt, generate interest, but Richard Fleischer's static, stagy direction is smothering. The film is saved by an intriguing script by Carl Foreman, who would go on to write *High Noon* before being blacklisted in the early fifties. Richard Loo growls and struts his way through the role of the Japanese heavy. The use of Chinatown locations is visually interesting, but the climax in Glendale fizzles.

CLEAN SLATE

See *Coup de Torchon*

CLEOPATRA ☆½
1963, USA
Elizabeth Taylor, Richard Burton, Rex Harrison, Pamela Brown, George Cole, Hume Cronyn, Martin Landau, Roddy McDowall. Directed by Joseph L. Mankiewicz. 243 min.

The biggest film and biggest mistake of Joseph L. Mankiewicz's distinguished career was this whale-sized retelling of the Cleopatra legend. What started six years earlier with Joan Collins, Stephen Boyd, and Peter Finch (under the direction of Rouben Mamoulian) swelled into a monster starring Elizabeth Taylor, Richard Burton, and Rex Harrison. Nothing on screen is nearly as interesting as the "behind-the-scenes" story of the film and, on video, the Todd-AO original loses most of its big-budget splendor. What's left is a lot of Queen Liz shrieking at sleepy Dick's Mark Antony. Despite severe cutting by Twentieth Century–Fox, most of the blame lies with Mankiewicz. It is difficult to say which is worse: his bungled use of the wide screen or his laughable screenplay (cowritten with Ronald MacDougall and Sidney Buchman). It sure ain't Shakespeare, or Shaw!

CLEOPATRA JONES ☆☆½
1973, USA, PG
Tamara Dobson, Shelley Winters, Bernie Casey, Brenda Sykes, Esther Rolle, Bill McKinney. Directed by Jack Starrett. 88 min.

Statuesque Tamara Dobson plays the flamboyant, karate-chopping, pistol-toting, astonishing-to-behold government agent in this fast-moving, charmingly campy entry in the black female exploitation sub-subgenre. On the international drug trade beat, she must contend with pushers, dealers, junkies, thugs, and, best of all, Shelley Winters as a fright-wigged lesbian-dominatrix crime boss. Very funny, often unintentionally, with sex and gore kept to a minimum in favor of cartoony action. Followed by a sequel, *Cleopatra Jones and the Casino of Gold*.

THE CLINIC ☆☆
1985, Australia
Chris Haywood, Simon Burke, Gerda Nicholson, Rona McLeod. Directed by David Stevens. 93 min.

A venereal-disease clinic is the setting for this low-budget comedy about the exploits of a gay doctor and his straight assistant. The format is sketchy, and most of the sketches don't work; what's worse is the rather graphic descriptions of some pretty unseemly symptoms. Still, the cast does try for an ensemble feel.

CLOAK AND DAGGER ☆☆☆
1984, USA, PG
Henry Thomas, Dabney Coleman, Michael Murphy, Christina Nigra, John McIntire, Jeanette Nolan. Directed by Richard Franklin. 101 min.

In this engaging, at times disturbing, fantasy, a kid who loves role-playing games like Dungeons and Dragons gets tangled up in a real-life espionage caper. On the way to pick up some Twinkies, Davey (Henry Thomas), an earnest eleven-year-old tyke, stumbles upon a nasty spy murder. The dying man passes him a cartridge secretly encoded with plans for an invisible bomber, and Davey tries to persuade the grown-up world that he's no longer playing a game—while dodging the silenced bullets of thugs. Watching Davey outsmart the slower adults is fun, but director Richard Franklin doesn't flinch from showing that mixing fantasy and daily life is a serious, potentially deranging business.

THE CLOCK ☆☆
1945, USA
Judy Garland, Robert Walker, James Gleason, Keenan Wynn, Marshall Thompson, Ruth Brady. Directed by Vincente Minnelli. 90 min.

A soldier (Walker) on leave in Manhattan meets, falls in love with, and marries a girl (Garland), all within the forty-eight hours of his furlough. Director Minnelli, at the time Garland's husband, has added a lot of Capra-esque flavor to this, and the location shooting on the streets of New York will appeal to many, but the story itself is unbelievable and not made persuasive by the principals. The perennial boyish insecurity of Walker and the still-present girlishness of Garland do not play well together, and as they are on screen constantly, the film is weighed down.

THE CLOCKMAKER ☆☆☆☆
1973, France
Philippe Noiret, Jean Rochefort, Jacques Denis. Directed by Bertrand Tavernier. 105 min.

This film is as intricately designed and well-crafted as the mechanism of an antique clock. Bertrand Tavernier, who was also responsible for stunning films like *Coup de Torchon* and *Let Joy Reign Supreme*, demonstrates his exceptional directorial control in this, his first feature film. Based on a Georges Simenon novel, the film examines the attempts of a clockmaker to put his life back together after it's dismantled by the shocking arrest of his son. Analytic and restrained, this meticulous character study stirs both our thoughts and feelings as the old man painstakingly endeavors to understand his son's involvement in a political murder, despite the boy's having shown no prior evidence of political activism. Exemplary filmmaking.

CLOCKWISE ☆☆½
1986, Great Britain, PG
John Cleese, Alison Steadman, Stephen Moore, Sharon Maiden, Penelope Wilton, Joan Hickson. Directed by Christopher Morahan. 105 min.

John Cleese plays an obsessively punctual headmaster who misses his train on the way to a speaking engagement and becomes involved in a series of mishaps. The fun of watching Cleese is waiting for the tremors of outrage to shake his outwardly normal frame. But director Christopher Morahan takes almost an hour to get him to the boiling point, and there isn't much for Cleese to do along the way. The movie stays on the same meandering farce level when it should be getting crazier, and it's not much fun watching the subversively funny Cleese get smoothed down. The often witty screenplay is by playwright Michael Frayn.

A CLOCKWORK ORANGE ☆☆☆½
1971, Great Britain, R
Malcolm McDowell, Patrick Magee, Adrienne Corri, David Prowse, Aubrey Morris, James Marcus. Directed by Stanley Kubrick. 137 min.

Stanley Kubrick's most controversial film, a hypnotic future-shock parable of England in the not-too-distant future, has grown less outrageous and more prophetic with the years. The episodic narrative follows Alex, a reckless gang member played by Malcolm McDowell. McDowell makes Alex a buoyant, winning character, lending Kubrick's usual pyrotechnics an emotional focus, but he becomes so charismatic at times that "liking" him becomes a moral dilemma. Alex's gleeful rendition of "Singin' in the Rain," as he rapes an author's wife and assaults the author, is still the most unsettling sequence in the film. (The author's character, as played by Patrick Magee, is supposedly based on Anthony Burgess.) Alex is sent to prison for his crimes, and rehabilitation changes him into a passive milquetoast. As a commentary on modern society and human behavior, Kubrick's film makes some acute observations, but his point of view is fuzzy and he rarely captures the eccentricity of Burgess's novel (which includes its own futuristic language, only minimally incorporated into the movie). But it's still a major film achievement, well worth seeing. With a memorable score by Walter Carlos of "Switched-on Bach" fame.

THE CLONES OF BRUCE LEE ☆
1980, Hong Kong, R
Dragon Lee, Bruce Le, Bruce Lai, Bruce Thai, John Benn, Yang Tze. Directed by Joseph Kong. 87 min.

Three men are cloned from the brain cells of Bruce Lee. It's unnatural! It's terrifying! It's three guys with the same haircut! They're battling men of bronze! (But don't worry, the Bruces force them to eat some poison grass!) Meanwhile, their enemy, an evil kingpin, relaxes with three naked girls—he cruelly makes one of them dance and he laughs!

THE CLONUS HORROR ☆½
1979, USA, R
Tim Donnelly, Dick Sargent, Peter Graves, Paulette Breen, David Hooks. Directed by Robert S. Fiveson. 90 min.

There are many insidious clones in Southern California, one of which is this movie. Set in the sunny suburbs where a dark technobureaucratic storm threatens to drown all America in a sea of clones, it proves that *1984* plus *Fahrenheit 451* equals *THX1138*. A feisty rebel attempts to expose the plot but eventually decides there's no place like clone. People have trouble distinguishing substitute clones from real people, which might offend some Californians. Technically and directorially competent, but we've seen it all before. (a.k.a.: *Parts: The Clonus Horror*)

CLOSE ENCOUNTERS OF THE THIRD KIND ☆☆☆☆
1977, USA, PG
Richard Dreyfuss, Melinda Dillon, François Truffaut, Teri Garr. Directed by Steven Spielberg. 138 min. (Original 135 min, reissue 132 min.)

One of the best science-fiction films to emerge from the special-effects morass of the late seventies, *Close Encounters of the Third Kind* is a canny and enchanting mixture of technical sophistication and childlike wonder. As awe-inspiring as the visuals get here, they never overtake the solid, suspenseful, and, above all, human story of a telephone repairman who receives a subliminal message after seeing some UFOs. This urging compels him to tear asunder his normal life in an effort to reach a particular spot where earthlings will have their first contact with extraterrestrials. Spielberg loads his story with imaginative pop images of consumerism and household humor; this is one picture dealing with the fantastic that takes place in the "real" world. He's also set up the likable star Richard Dreyfuss as the everyman who must sacrifice all to achieve his dreams, and the actor's emotional and lightly comic performance makes it all believable. The sequence in which he actually gets to go inside the alien mother-ship was added for the reissue. Spielberg used the same idea of friendly spacemen for his most popular film, *E.T.*

CLOSELY WATCHED TRAINS ☆☆☆☆
1966, Czechoslovakia
Vaclav Neckar, Jitka Bendova, Vladimir Valenta. Directed by Jiri Menzel. 89 min.

This film is a tender, ironic masterpiece about the world of a provincial railway station in occupied Czechoslovakia during World War II. Its constant inhabitant, a shy seventeen-year-old trainee, longs to prove his manhood. Unfortunately, his first chance for sexual fulfillment carries a heavy political price tag, and he finds himself facing death just as life has begun. Bohumil Hrabal, the writer and screenwriter for the film, creates a funny, all-too-human world wherein the young man's life swings precipitously between comedy and tragedy. *Closely Watched Trains* was one of the watersheds of the Czech New Wave, and its cautionary lessons of the necessity and danger of direct political action are especially poignant in light of the subsequent and continuing repression of Czech culture.

CLOUD DANCER ☆½
1980, USA, PG
David Carradine, Jennifer O'Neill, Joseph Bottoms, Albert Salmi, Salome Jens, Nina Van Pallandt. Directed by Barry Brown. 108 min.

The title *Cloud Dancer* refers to stunt flying, the occupation and obsession of the protagonist, as played in his usual unsympathetic style by David Carradine. The director-producer-writer, a flyer himself, wants you to like this character—we see him being nice to his mentally retarded brother and helping a fellow flier kick a drug habit—but the single-mindedness of his life is not really very interesting. The flying scenes are well handled, but not well enough to carry this wispy cloud.

THE CLOWN ☆☆☆
1952, USA
Red Skelton, Tim Considine, Jane Greer, Loring Smith, Philip Ober, Lou Lubin, Fay Roope, Steve Forrest. Directed by Robert Z. Leonard. 91 min.

This is the second, very loose version of the Wallace Beery film *The Champ*, and it is distinguished by the casting of Red Skelton in a heavyweight dramatic role. Skelton is surprisingly effective as a washed-up, alcoholic comic attempting to make a comeback and hold on to his son. It's unabashed corn, but Skelton is seen to good advantage as both comedian (his famous sketch from *Bathing Beauty* is presented in a flashback) and dramatic actor, and he is well supported by Tim Considine and Jane Greer. Charles Bronson has a bit part.

THE CLOWNS ☆☆☆½
1971, Italy/France
Mayo Morin, Lima Alberti, Alvaro Vitali, Gasparmo. Directed by Federico Fellini. 91 min.

Federico Fellini's fourteenth film is an affectionate coda to the alternately hilarious and tragic world under the big top. Austere in its composition, the movie is actually a semidocumentary focusing not only on clownish antics but on the film crew's response to it all. Fellini fans will obviously see allusions to other works, notably *8½* and *Nights of Cabiria*, but if you question thematic elements too hard here you might find yourself in a similar position to that of a journalist in the film who asks about the meaning underneath a bucket of water. Originally commissioned by Italian television, the theatrical release runs thirty minutes longer than its small-screen counterpart.

CLUB PARADISE ☆½
1986, USA, PG-13
Robin Williams, Peter O'Toole, Rick Moranis, Eugene Levy, Jimmy Cliff, Twiggy, Adolph Caesar, Andrea Martin, Brian Doyle-Murray. Directed by Harold Ramis. 107 min.

Despite its all-star cast and exotic locale, this is a low-grade rehash of the slob humor used to much better effect in *Stripes* and *Animal House*. Harold Ramis has taken the very familiar low road. Among the actors struggling with the infantile script are a surprisingly restrained Robin Williams as a Chicago fireman who opens up an island resort, Adolph Caesar as a hysterically ranting police chief, and Peter O'Toole as the last remnant of the British Empire who won't let the sun set on his island. Amiable in fits and starts, but an appalling waste of several comic talents.

CLUNY BROWN ☆☆☆½
1946, USA
Jennifer Jones, Charles Boyer, Helen Walker, Peter Lawford, Reginald Gardner, Reginald Owen, C. Aubrey Smith. Directed by Ernst Lubitsch. 100 min.

Ernst Lubitsch, one of Hollywood's great comedy masters (*To Be or Not to Be, Ninotchka*), creates a devilishly clever comedy of manners based on Margery Sharp's novel. He draws a deft comedy performance from super-suave Charles Boyer as a displaced person in pre–World War II England, and draws something of a miraculous comedy turn from Jennifer Jones, best known for her dewy-eyed dramatics. With grace and affability, Jones portrays a plumber's niece who forgets that in genteel circles one just doesn't mention the fact that indoor plumbing and bathrooms actually exist. Never able to assume the hypocrisy of polite society, Cluny nonetheless captures the heart of fellow nonconformist Boyer in this airy, sophisticated trifle.

COACH ☆
1978, USA, PG
Cathy Lee Crosby, Michael Biehn, Keenan Wynn. Directed by Bud Townsend. 100 min.

This film is a lame excuse to watch Cathy Lee in a pair of gym shorts. An ex–Olympic runner, Crosby, is accidentally hired to coach a boys' bottom-of-the-barrel basketball team. Will Cathy Lee transform the losers into winners? Will the boys come to accept Cathy Lee as a coach first and a sex object second? High schoolers who look more like college seniors, basketball sequences executed with the finesse of an elephant ballet, and an unintelligible cameo by ex-pro Sidney Wicks are among *Coach*'s many lowlights.

COAL MINER'S DAUGHTER ☆☆☆½
1980, USA, PG
Sissy Spacek, Tommy Lee Jones, Beverly D'Angelo, Levon Helm, Phyllis Boyens. Directed by Michael Apted. 125 min.

The rags-to-riches career of country-music queen Loretta Lynn is the subject of this sensitive but never over-sentimental screen biography. With precision and grace, British director Michael Apted illuminates indigenously American locales ranging from dirt-poor dwellings in the hills of Appalachia to the Grand Ole Opry in Nashville. Sissy Spacek won an Academy Award for her portrayal of Lynn, creating a lovely characterization in quick strokes and convincingly singing many of Lynn's songs in a voice that's half-impersonation, half-tribute, and very engaging. Tommy Lee Jones is almost as good playing her troubled husband, and Beverly D'Angelo is marvelous as Lynn's country-and-western mentor Patsy Cline. The story is standard show-biz-biography material, but it's handled with class in all departments.

COAST TO COAST ☆
1980, USA, PG
Robert Blake, Dyan Cannon, Quinn Redeker, Michael Lerner. Directed by Joseph Sargent. 98 min.

Dyan Cannon is very funny as a hysteric whose husband is trying to have her committed; unfortunately, that promising plot line disintegrates after about fifteen minutes. What replaces it is a painfully humorless cross-country road trip during which she hooks up with a trucker and becomes involved in numerous dull misadventures. The premise is as old as the hills, and Robert Blake gives the kind of domineering, loudmouthed performance that only a mother could love.

COBRA ☆
1981
Bruce Lei, Peter Chen Lau, Wong Ko Leong. Directed by Joseph Velasco. 90 min.

This is the dull story of a student seeking revenge for the murder of his teacher and classmates. Why is this such a common theme in kung-fu movies? Bruce Lei is Bruce Le, actually Hwang King Lung, under any name a better fighter than actor.

COBRA ½☆
1986, USA, R
Sylvester Stallone, Brigitte Nielsen, Reni Santoni, Andrew Robinson, Val Avery, Brian Thompson. Directed by George P. Cosmatos. 90 min.

It's hard to decide what's most sickening about this macho fantasy: Stallone's titanic ego or the gut-wrenching violence and fascist ideals. Mr. Beefcake gets the chance to revel in slime here as a hard-boiled and soft-brained cop who shoots first and doesn't ask questions. Stallone gets a better body count than his psycho ax-killer enemies, but it's the viewer who will fall victim to the incomprehensible editing and the nonsensical ending. Despite the movie's occasional attempts at black humor, this is irredeemable garbage.

THE COCA-COLA KID ☆☆☆
1985, Australia, R
Eric Roberts, Greta Scacchi, Bill Kerr, Tim Finn, Chris Haywood, Max Gilles, Rebecca Smart, Colleen Clifford. Directed by Dusan Makavejev. 94 min.

This is a film that, at least superficially, bears a striking resemblance to Bill Forsyth's *Local Hero*: a hotshot American business whiz goes to a country where relaxed people speak English with funny accents and tries to pave the way for the wonders of capitalism, but he soon finds himself succumbing to this strange way of life. However, Yugoslavian director Dusan Makavejev (*Montenegro, WR: Mysteries of the Organism*) has a distinctly different outlook, though this is much more low-key and conventional than his previous work. The main characters are always doing things that surprise you—just when you think you've got a handle on them, they turn around and do something quite perplexing. Why? Well, sex has a great deal to do with it. As the titular whiz, Eric Roberts is more restrained than in past roles, but still peculiar in ways that are alternately engaging and repellent. Greta Scacchi, however, is amazingly and heartbreakingly sexy. Good song score by Tim Finn and the Australian band Split Enz.

COCAINE COWBOYS ☆
1979, USA, R
Jack Palance, Andy Warhol, Tom Sullivan, Suzanna Love, Ester Oldham-Farfan, the Cowboy Island Band. Directed by Ulli Lommel. 86 min.

Former Rainer Werner Fassbinder compatriot Ulli Lommel made this low-budget turkey before going on to such "class" productions as *The Boogeyman*. An aspiring rock band, needing money to fund their musical endeavors, starts smuggling drugs, much to the annoyance of the mob. Jack Palance snarls and Andy Warhol, at whose house this was filmed, looks as though he's more concerned about the lawn than anything else. Lacking even camp value.

COCAINE FIENDS ☆
1937, USA, PG
Lois January, Noel Madison. Directed by W. A. Connor. 74 min.

In this campy period piece from the thirties, your friends in the government warn you about the evils of the snow you sniff, which include such invariable results as prostitution and heroin addiction. Not as funny as *Reefer Madness*, though pretty much in the same vein.

COCAINE: ONE MAN'S SEDUCTION ☆☆☆
1983, USA (TV), PG
Dennis Weaver, Karen Grassle, Pamela Bellwood, David Ackroyd. Directed by Paul Wendkos. 97 min.

This timely, well-meaning TV movie unfortunately falls prey to an overdose of overdramatization as the story reaches its conclusion. The details of Dennis Weaver's downfall are devastatingly portrayed as the salesman tries to revive his shattered spirits and wavering ambitions by increasingly relying on hits of nose candy. What he realizes too late is that his habit has developed into a full-blown addiction that will destroy his business and damage his relations with his family. Cast against type, Weaver is so persuasive and moving that the film becomes even more terrifying and takes on the dimensions of a horror film. The way he conveys the changes in the man's personality are so disturbing that this becomes a searing cautionary tale.

COCAINE WARS ☆
1986, USA, R
John Schneider, Kathryn Witt, Federico Luppi, Royal Dano. Directed by Hector Olivera. 85 min.

Unremittingly sleazy but mercifully brief, this cheap action thriller about drug trafficking south of the border was produced by drive-in king Roger Corman, and stars ex-Duke of Hazzard John Schneider as the Mexican-busting hero. There's the requisite graphic violence and soft-core sex; we have nothing against exploitation films except when they're as resolutely dull as this one.

THE COCKEYED CAVALIERS ☆☆☆
1934, USA
Bert Wheeler, Robert Woolsey, Thelma Todd, Dorothy Lee, Noah Beery, Franklin Pangborn, Snub Pollard. Directed by Mark Sandrich. 72 min.

One of almost twenty films that ex–stage comedians Bert Wheeler and Robert Woolsey made in the decade in which they worked together, this is about average for them. They play a pair of vagabonds in sixteenth-century England who are taken into the court of the Duke of Weskit when they are mistaken for the king's physicians. It has about as much plot as a Marx Brothers movie, which is to say just enough to let the star duo go through their routine of upsetting everything around them. Some of the gags meant for thirties audiences (a parody of a famous scene in Greta Garbo's *Queen Christina*, for example, and a great deal of then-current slang used as a comic contrast to the medieval setting) may be lost on postwar audiences, but overall this is an entertaining package.

THE COCKFIGHTER ☆☆½
1974, USA
Warren Oates, Richard B. Shull, Troy Donahue, Harry Dean Stanton. Directed by Monte Hellman. 83 min.

This is probably the only movie you'll ever see that deals with a man raising fighting cocks in Georgia. It captures the underground existence of cockfight fanciers and breeders with a great deal of vitality and with no apologies tendered for this bloodletting sport. An above-average entry with a then-archetypal low-budget movie cast all doing topflight work. The plot is refreshingly off the beaten path; the direction is hard-edged.

COCKLESHELL HEROES ☆☆½
1955, Great Britain
Jose Ferrer, Trevor Howard, Victor Maddern, Anthony Newley, David Lodge, Peter Arne, Christopher Lee. Directed by Jose Ferrer. 97 min.

The British, it sometimes seems, made exactly two types of films in the fifties: black comedies about murder, infidelity, and drinking, usually starring Alec Guinness, and flag-raisers about how stiff they kept their upper lips during World War II. This, unfortunately, is one of the latter. The operation at hand involves training eight Royal Marines to canoe into German waters and mine Nazi boats. It's all well and good, but you've seen it before and after. The script was written by Bryan Forbes, who went on in the sixties to write and direct black comedies about murder, infidelity, and drinking, usually without Alec Guinness. Christopher Lee has a small part as a submarine commander.

THE COCOANUTS ☆☆☆
1929, USA
The Marx Brothers (Groucho, Harpo, Chico, and Zeppo), Mary Eaton, Oscar Shaw, Margaret Dumont, Cyril Ring. Directed by Joseph Santley, Robert Florey. 90 min.

The Marx Brothers's first movie is a very straightforward and often funny adaptation of their stage success of the same name, and a must for proponents of mise-en-scène over montage; as one later critic noted, the directors here seem merely to have set the camera down and turned it on. And that's good enough. The story concerns the Florida land-development boom, with Groucho as a shady hotel manager trying to get in on the action. The best-remembered scene is Groucho and Chico's "Why a Duck?" routine. Morrie Ryskind adapted the screenplay from the stage show by George S. Kaufman, and Irving Berlin wrote some forgettable songs for the film.

COCOON ☆☆☆
1985, USA, PG-13
Don Ameche, Wilford Brimley, Hume Cronyn, Brian Dennehy, Jack Gilford, Steve Guttenberg, Maureen Stapleton, Jessica Tandy, Gwen Verdon, Tahnee Welch, Tyrone Power, Jr. Directed by Ron Howard. 118 min.

A group of Florida retirees discovers that the Fountain of Youth is a swimming pool just a trot away from their rest home, in a large-scale fantasy spectacle that, at its best, is a humanely funny sci-fi parable about getting old. Director Ron Howard shows a very sure hand when dealing with the venerable performers who become the film's heart and soul—although he invites comparisons to Steven Spielberg too often, his film has a more decidedly bittersweet edge, and he isn't afraid to let real and complex emotions intermingle with the dazzlement. Only in the last third does he push *Cocoon* into a predictable and disappointing pigeonhole, a crowd-pleaser that undermines his earlier precision. All of the performers, especially Brian Dennehy as a polite extraterrestrial and Jack Gilford as the one old man who wants nothing to do with eternal life, are top caliber and provide more than enough reason to see the film. If you liked *Splash* or the "Kick the Can" episode of *Twilight Zone—The Movie*, *Cocoon* will afford you a familiar but pleasant experience.

CODE NAME: DIAMOND HEAD ☆☆
1977, USA (TV)
Roy Thinnes, France Nuyen, Zulu, Ward Costello, Don Knight, Ian McShane. Directed by Jeannot Szwarc. 78 min.

This film is a pilot for a TV series that never got off the ground. Roy Thinnes plays the hero, an American agent in Hawaii assigned to prevent a toxic-gas formula from falling into the wrong hands; Ian McShane has some good moments as his crafty, disguise-donning adversary. Competent but uninspired action, and certainly no better than the average contemporary police series.

CODE NAME: TRIXIE

See *The Crazies*

CODE NAME: WILDGEESE ☆
1985, USA, R
Ernest Borgnine, Lewis Collins, Lee Van Cleef, Klaus Kinski, Manfred Lehmann, Mimsy Farmer. Directed by Anthony M. Dawson (Antonio Margheriti). 101 min.

This is cheap exploitation about a gang of brutal mercenaries on the warpath in the jungle. The cast of semi-big names might seem to be a draw at first, but try to remember the last time you saw any of them give a good performance. Like everything else about this shoddy, violent production, the title smacks of rip-off: this bears no real relation to either *The Wild Geese* or its sequel. Good explosive effects by Margheriti.

CODE OF SILENCE ★★½
1985, USA, R
Chuck Norris, Henry Silva, Bert Remsen, Mike Genovese, Nathan Davis, Joseph Guzaldo, Ralph Foody. Directed by Andy Davis. 102 min.

Now that age is making his bones brittle, Chuck Norris (of the flailing fists and flying legs) has changed his persona into that of a more traditional adventure hero. *Code of Silence* is a moderately well-crafted detective movie—a by-the-numbers imitation, in fact, of Clint Eastwood's cop films. Norris plays a Chicago policeman facing both a burgeoning gang war and a conspiratorial cover-up in his own department. The film is no *Dirty Harry*, but it is a satisfactory entertainment—even if Norris, as always, skulks through the action like molasses dripping off a spoon.

COLD FEET ★½
1984, USA, PG
Griffin Dunne, Marissa Chibas, Blanche Baker, Mark Cronogue. Directed by Bruce van Dusen. 96 min.

Two unhappy professionals (Dunne and Chibas) try to make sense out of their vacuous lives by droning on to one another about sex, love, family, etc. Despite all of the gabbing that's going on, nothing of real importance is ever said in this smarmy social comedy. Two very good young actors are wasted on the inane dialogue.

THE COLDITZ STORY ★★★
1954, Great Britain
John Mills, Eric Portman, Christopher Rhodes, Lionel Jeffries, Bryan Forbes, Ian Carmichael, Anton Diffring, Theodore Bikel. Directed by Guy Hamilton. 97 min.

During World War II, Colditz Castle was used by the Germans as a prison camp for enemy officers who had tried to escape from other camps. Located in the heart of Saxony, it was considered perfectly escape-proof. Of course, this feature can only be considered a challenge, and the various enemy officers held there make attempt after attempt until they finally get out. The excellent British cast helps provide an occasional touch of unforced levity, and Guy Hamilton, directing one of his first films, turns in a smart effort, lacking the slickness that he developed when he worked on the later James Bond films.

THE COLD ROOM ★★½
1984, Great Britain (TV)
George Segal, Amanda Pays, Anthony Higgins, Warren Clarke, Renee Soutendijk, Clifford Rose. Directed by James Dearden. 95 min.

It's things-that-go-bump-in-the-night time as a hotel room in West Berlin holds the key to a mystery. George Segal, who's trying to mend a relationship with his estranged daughter, is plunged into intrigue and mystery after his daughter discovers a man hiding behind furniture in her hotel room. Nicely chilling, with a nifty premise that will keep viewers on pins and needles until the end.

THE COLLECTOR ★★★
1965, USA
Terence Stamp, Samantha Eggar, Mona Washbourne, Maurice Dallimore. Directed by William Wyler. 117 min.

This psychological drama about romantic and sexual obsession is somewhat overdirected by William Wyler, a fault of much of his later work, but it still stands up as a compelling character study. Terence Stamp, a sexually repressed young bank clerk whose hobby is collecting butterflies, kidnaps a beautiful young woman and locks her up in the basement of a secluded farmhouse. He tells her that he will supply her with all her needs and with luxuries besides, and will then release her in two months; he will not touch her, but he wants her to fall in love with him. The intensity of the main theme is diminished by the need to develop suspense—will the girl escape?—so it's not as satisfying as one might hope. Based on the novel by John Fowles; excellent technical credits include the photography by Bruce Surtees and music by Maurice Jarre.

COLLEGE ★★★½
1927, USA
Buster Keaton, Anne Cornwall, Flora Bramley, Buddy Mason, Harold Goodwin, Grant Withers, Snitz Edwards. Directed by James W. Horne. 63 min.

Buster Keaton enrolls in the college comedy curriculum covered by Harold Lloyd in *The Freshman*, and though this isn't quite a classic, Keaton does deliver some A+ laughs. He plays a scholar who disdains athletics until he needs to impress a muscle-hungry coed. Look for the ingenious rib-tickling spoofs of baseball, high jumping, hurdling, and sprinting. Keaton was a talented athlete who always did his own stunt work, and he was reportedly very distressed when he could not pull off a pole vault here—the result of years of hard knocks and, perhaps, hard drinking.

COLONEL EFFINGHAM'S RAID ★★★
1945, USA
Charles Coburn, Joan Bennett, William Eythe, Allyn Joslyn, Donald Meek, Thurston Hall, Cora Witherspoon, Roy Roberts. Directed by Irving Pichel. 70 min.

This is a pleasant, misleadingly titled comedy that shows that you *can* fight City Hall. Retired Southern colonel Charles Coburn returns to his hometown and doesn't like what he sees going on in local government. Accepting an assignment to write a column on military matters for the local newspaper, he uses it as a launching pad to attack corruption. Coburn capably commands the entire show, with Joan Bennett around for eye candy.

COLORADO SERENADE ½★
1946, USA
Eddie Dean, David Sharpe. Directed by Robert E. Tansey. 68 min.

Eddie Dean sings "Home on the Range" and "Riding down to Rawhide." The story's even more hackneyed than you would expect.

COLOR ME BLOOD RED ★
1965, USA
Don Joseph, Candi Conder, Evelyn Warner, Patricia Lee, Scott H. Hall. Directed by Herschell Gordon Lewis. 70 min.

Even those who enjoyed Herschell Gordon Lewis's two earlier gore groundbreakers, *Blood Feast* and *Two Thousand Maniacs*, won't find anything worthwhile in this. At least in those films he was trying to scare audiences, but in *Color Me Blood Red* it's obvious that even Lewis isn't taking himself seriously any more—it's loaded with annoyingly arch "jokes," stupid pseudo-hipster dialogue, and rabid nonacting. The plot, about an artist who finds that the shade of red he has been searching for can only be obtained by using blood, is a variant on the mad-artist horror subgenre; there are very few gory scenes, and they're all depicted on the videocassette jacket. Lewis didn't even have enough material to sustain a feature that runs a mere hour and ten minutes: at least fifteen minutes in the middle are sheer padding. Neither frightening nor campy, just dull and bad.

COLOR ME DEAD ☆½
1969, Australia
Tom Tryon, Carolyn Jones, Rick Jason, Patricia Connolly, Tony Ward. Directed by Eddie Davis. 97 min.

Color this ordinary. A dying man spends his last moments trying to bring his poisoners to justice. A dead-on-its-feet remake of the semiclassic *D.O.A.* (1949). Tom Tryon's a better writer than an actor; Carolyn Jones, as usual, redeems whatever trash she's cast in.

THE COLOR OF MONEY ☆☆☆½
1986, USA, R
Paul Newman, Tom Cruise, Mary Elizabeth Mastrantonio, Helen Shaver, John Turturro, Bill Cobbs. Directed by Martin Scorsese. 119 min.

This is a gritty, highly entertaining sequel to the 1961 back-alley classic *The Hustler*. Richard Price's sharp screenplay recaptures the character of Fast Eddie Felson after twenty-five years of enforced exile from the game of pool. Now a successful liquor salesman, he prowls bars and back rooms in search of an up-and-comer who might revitalize his own interest in the game. He finds one in the flaky hotshot Vince Lauria, and their partnership turns the film into an unpredictable duel of hustlers, with style, flash, and unexpected irony. Reprising the role of Eddie, Paul Newman gives a superbly sly, relaxed performance that allows Tom Cruise's ambitious young pool wizard a chance to share, but never steal, the spotlight. Martin Scorsese directs with typical subtlety and unusual attention to the women in his cast, led by Mary Elizabeth Mastrantonio's razor-edged portrayal of Vince's shrewd girlfriend. Michael Ballhaus's stunning cinematography helps make this a pleasure to watch, especially after revisiting *The Hustler*.

THE COLOR PURPLE ☆☆
1985, USA, PG
Danny Glover, Whoopi Goldberg, Margaret Avery, Oprah Winfrey, Rae Dawn Chong, Adolph Caesar, Desreta Jackson. Directed by Steven Spielberg. 152 min.

Steven Spielberg's "Kick the Can" episode in *Twilight Zone—The Movie* was only an embryonic form of the kind of false, sugary humanism he presents here. Alice Walker's Pulitzer Prize–winning novel about forty years (1909–1949) in the life of a Southern black woman becomes sloppy and sentimental under Spielberg's care. Hollywood's "boy genius" may be a wizard with action scenes and special effects, but when it comes to dramatic situations, he comes up dry. The bittersweet saga of the much-abused heroine becomes unintentionally funny, thanks to pointless slapstick comedy in the midst of tragic situations, artsy, obtrusive camera movements, and weak, unclear story development. The cast, with the exception of Desreta Jackson as the young Celie, is unconvincing; but who can blame them, under the circumstances? Nominated for eleven Academy Awards.

COMA ☆½
1978, USA, R
Geneviève Bujold, Michael Douglas, Richard Widmark, Elizabeth Ashley. Directed by Michael Crichton. 108 min.

Michael Crichton's careless direction of his actors prevents *Coma* from being worthwhile artistically, but the film plays successfully on an almost universal fear of hospitals with its icy mise-en-scène. Elizabeth Ashley is briefly disturbing as an inhuman nurse, but Geneviève Bujold is more like Nancy Drew than a figure of supposed medical brilliance. Star-watchers might enjoy seeing Tom Selleck in a brief role.

THE COMANCHEROS ☆☆½
1961, USA
John Wayne, Stuart Whitman, Lee Marvin, Ina Balin, Nehemiah Persoff, Michael Ansara, Patrick Wayne, Bruce Cabot, Joan O'Brien, Jack Elam, Edgar Buchanan, Henry Daniell, Roger Mobley, Bob Steele. Directed by Michael Curtiz. 107 min.

Texas Ranger John Wayne and gambler Stuart Whitman set out to stop the dirty varmints who are supplying firearms and firewater to the Comanches and getting them all riled up. In the best Hollywood tradition, the Indians are portrayed by the likes of Nehemiah Persoff, though it's hard to get too upset about such clichés in a Western that refuses to take anything seriously. Lee Marvin walks off with the movie in a few brief scenes as a half-scalped gunrunner.

COME AND GET IT ☆☆½
1936, USA
Edward Arnold, Joel McCrea, Frances Farmer, Walter Brennan, Andrea Leeds, Frank Shields. Directed by William Wyler and Howard Hawks. 105 min.

Those who know Frances Farmer only from her two screen biographies shouldn't miss her in this sprawling adaptation of Edna Ferber's novel about life in the lumbermills—she plays a dance hall woman in the film's first half and her daughter in the second. Her work here is compelling, biting, and unusually direct, much better than the cornball story or stolid players around her deserve. The film itself is dated and poorly paced, notwithstanding its inflated reputation—see it for Farmer and for Walter Brennan's reliable character work, which won him the first of three Oscars.

THE COMEBACK ☆½
1978, Great Britain
Jack Jones, Pamela Stephenson, David Doyle, Bill Owen, Sheila Keith. Directed by Pete Walker. 100 min.

This cheesy, no-chills slash-bash features pop singer Jack Jones in an unwelcome dramatic change of pace. If you're saying "I didn't know he could act," you're right: he can't. Who is responsible for framing the fading pop star (played by Jones) for a series of murders? Is the singer freaking out again or is someone trying to keep him off the charts permanently? Who cares? Featuring one of those rapidly paced denouements that leaves you hopelessly confused as it tries to tie up the loose ends of a sloppy script.

COME BACK CHARLESTON BLUE ☆☆
1972, USA, PG
Raymond St. Jacques, Godfrey Cambridge, Peter De Anda, Jonelle Allen, Maxwell Glanville. Directed by Mark Warren. 100 min.

This sequel to the popular *Cotton Comes to Harlem* puts detectives Grave Digger Jones and Coffin Ed Johnson back on the uptown beat, trying to stop a war between drug dealers that's about to explode onto the streets. Their unconventional crime-busting methods aren't as clever or funny here as they were in the original, and director Warren's filming of the violent action is strictly by the book. Screenplay by Ernest Kinoy, using the name Bontsche Schweig, and Peggy Elliott.

THE COMEBACK KID ☆☆
1980, USA (TV)
John Ritter, Susan Dey, Doug McKeon, James Gregory, Jeremy Licht, Dick O'Neil, Patrick Swayze. Directed by Peter Levin. 100 min.

The saccharine silliness of this film pushes beyond the limits of John Ritter's charm. He's the title character of this telefilm about a baseball player who starts coaching a team of underprivileged kids after he's bounced from the minor leagues. When he's called back, his already shaky conscience is torn between the moppets, the minors, and the ministrations of the sexy playground supervisor (Susan Dey). Dey and Ritter are likable, but this vehicle is very rusty.

COME BACK TO THE FIVE AND DIME, JIMMY DEAN, JIMMY DEAN ☆☆½
1982, USA, R
Cher, Sandy Dennis, Karen Black, Kathy Bates, Marta Heflin, Sudie Bond. Directed by Robert Altman. 109 min.

Robert Altman brings the diffuse elements of his stage production into sharper focus for the film version. Set in a dusty Texas dime store, the story concerns the myriad revelations made by an aging group of James Dean fans at an anniversary reunion. Cher, in the film's best-defined part, does not do much acting in the conventional sense, but she is extraordinarily winning in her depiction of the chesty, good-natured waitress whose own secret is both deeper and less complicated than those of her friends. Karen Black's acting is the most bound to the play's theatrical origins, although in all fairness her character is playacting from her first entrance. Sandy Dennis, however, is a disaster, twitching and pausing over every line until she becomes unbearable. Robert Altman does achieve a nice balance among the supporting cast, and Sudie Bond in particular elevates her stock performance to the level of artistry by blending into the group effort as well. *Come Back to the Five and Dime* is about people who have either gone nowhere or else made the wrong turn; it is to Altman's credit that the film does not stagnate.

COME BACK TO ME

See *Doll Face*

COMES A HORSEMAN ☆☆☆
1978, USA, R
Jane Fonda, James Caan, Richard Farnsworth, Jason Robards. Directed by Alan J. Pakula. 119 min.

Richard Farnsworth's moving, Oscar-nominated performance as an old cowpoke is the only distinguished element of this Western set in the 1940s. Fonda and Caan try to outwit land baron Jason Robards and retain Fonda's farm; they should have concentrated on enacting a believable relationship. Caan is distracted throughout, and Fonda is dreadful—straining for effects and never in period.

COMFORT AND JOY ☆☆☆☆
1984, Scotland/Great Britain, PG
Bill Paterson, Eleanor David, C. P. (Clare) Grogan, Alex Norton, Rikki Fulton, Patrick Malahide, Roberto Bernardi. Directed by Bill Forsyth. 106 min.

After having attained a devoted following with his first three films (*That Sinking Feeling*, *Gregory's Girl*, and *Local Hero*), comedies from a territory also inhabited by Frank Capra and François Truffaut but still utterly unique, Scottish director Bill Forsyth disappointed a lot of his fans with this disarmingly low-key tale about a Glasgow DJ trying to find meaning in his life—or at least get through the Christmas holidays—after his girlfriend suddenly and inexplicably walks out on him. But give this film another chance; it doesn't at first seem as beguiling as *Local Hero*, but it is actually a fuller exploration of Forsyth's pet theme, that the usually unnoticed, peripheral details of daily life are really what life is all about. In other hands than his, that notion would probably be treated cynically, but Forsyth handles it with subtlety and affirmation. Alan Bird, the DJ, is dealing with a problem that everyone faces and no one, including Forsyth, knows how to handle. So he just survives it, albeit through a comic involvement in a contrived situation that is the film's only drawback. It hardly matters, though, in a film whose only real message is that time heals all wounds. What makes this so wonderful is that Forsyth persuades you that such a mundane, shopworn truism can provide you what the title promises, in details that you may not notice until the tenth or so time you've watched it.

THE COMIC ☆☆½
1969, USA
Dick Van Dyke, Michele Lee, Mickey Rooney, Cornel Wilde, Steve Allen, Gavin MacLeod, Carl Reiner. Directed by Carl Reiner. 95 min.

After Dick Van Dyke's long-running TV series came to an end, he and Carl Reiner reteamed for this uneven but interesting look at the silent comedy era, as narrated by clown Billy Bright (Van Dyke) years later at his own funeral. Much of it is awfully sentimental, reviving every tears-of-a-clown cliché since *Pagliacci*, and the script unconvincingly turns Bright into an amalgam of about half a dozen real-life comedians. But Van Dyke and Michele Lee both have a good feel for slapstick, and Reiner's fondness for his subject is evident throughout.

COMIC MAGAZINE ☆☆½
1986, Japan
Yuya Uchida, Yumi Asou, Hiromi Go, Beat Takeshi, Yoshio Harada. Directed by Yojiro Takita. 120 min.

This edgy, energetic Japanese comedy concerns the journalist as terrorist in modern society. Kinameri (writer and star Yuya Uchida) is a wildly ambitious, rude, dogged TV reporter, the kind who specializes in thrusting microphones in the faces of unsuspecting victims and asking hilariously incriminating questions. The savagery of the script's attack on yellow journalism wears a little thin, but flashy technique and some very funny moments merit a look.

COMING ATTRACTIONS

See *Loose Shoes*

COMING HOME ☆☆½
1978, USA, R
Jon Voight, Jane Fonda, Bruce Dern, Penelope Milford, Robert Ginty, Robert Carradine. Directed by Hal Ashby. 127 min.

The first half of Hal Ashby's anti-Vietnam War movie is an enjoyable romance, but as a political parable the movie is hopeless—a sanctimonious "greening-of-America" film that stacks the deck so clumsily that its social message is reduced to a silly equating of liberalism with lovemaking dexterity. Jane Fonda plays the prim wife of gung-ho Marine captain Bruce Dern; after Dern embarks for Vietnam, she falls into an affair with an antiwar paraplegic (Jon Voight). Voight brings a dazzling mixture of ravaged integrity and boyish sexuality to his role but, as a character, he is to paraplegics (and Vietnam vets) what Sidney Poitier once was to blacks. The use of period music is particularly grating, but Voight and Fonda both won Academy Awards for their almost redemptive performances.

COMMANDO ☆☆
1985, USA, R
Arnold Schwarzenegger, Rae Dawn Chong, Vernon Wells, Dan Hedaya. Directed by Mark L. Lester. 90 min.

While watching Arnold Schwarzenegger bash in the brains of an opponent, costar Rae Dawn Chong adequately sums up this movie with her comment: "I'm tired of your macho bullshit!" Schwarzenegger enters the cinematic parade of he-men with big guns as an ex-commando who fights an evil South American despot to free his kidnapped daughter. This gives The Incredible Bulk an excuse to perform heroics that would make even Rambo blink with amazement, and morticians smile with glee. While the film does provide some warped fun, its bread-and-butter scenes of violence are all mediocre in execution and astoundingly unbelievable. *Commando* ultimately tries to come across as a self-parody, but it's a markedly unfunny rip-off.

THE COMMIES ARE COMING, THE COMMIES ARE COMING ☆☆☆
1956, USA
Jack Kelly, Jack Webb, Jean Cooper, Peter Brown, Patricia Woodell, Andrew Duggan, Robert Conrad. Directed by George Waggner. 60 min.

The scene: a normal college campus. Suddenly, Jack Webb appears and cautions the viewer that although this may *look* like a normal college campus, it's actually a secret spy-training school located deep in the heart of the Soviet Union. C'mon, Jack . . . it's a studio backlot located deep in the heart of L.A. This cautionary tale, originally called *Red Nightmare*, is one man's guilt-induced dream occasioned by his ducking an important civic meeting for an evening's snooze; next thing he knows, the Ruskies are lining them up in the streets. Best moment: after forcing his bratty kids—pint-size Stalinists—to go to church, they discover that the homey little chapel has been turned into a museum for cheapjack, unionist goods. We bet he won't be missing any more PTA meetings.

THE COMMITTEE ☆☆☆
1969, USA
Don Sturdy, Howard Hesseman, Carl Gottlieb, Christopher Ross, Jessica Myerson, Peter Bonerz, Melvin Stewart, Garry Goodrow, Barbara Bosson. Directed by Del Jack. 90 min.

Like the Chicago and Toronto Second City troupes that have flourished in the last decade, San Francisco's Committee was an improvisational comedy group that served as a breeding ground for up-and-coming comedians. This is simply a filmed record of one of their live performances—no props, no staging, just various groupings of the eight performers on stage. The film is a bit misleading because it includes little political material, which was the group's specialty, perhaps because the film was not released until eighteen months after it was made. (Topicality counted a lot, and there had been a presidential election in the interim.) Most of the sketches, though, are still quite funny. Favorites include a group of potential draftees trying to persuade an army psychiatrist that they're insane; a blind date who really is blind, giving her evening's escort a chance to freely check her out; and a confrontation between a nasty old man and an equally vile motorcycle punk. (a.k.a.: *A Session with The Committee*)

COMMUNION

See *Alice, Sweet Alice*.

THE COMPANY OF WOLVES ☆☆
1984, Great Britain, R
Angela Lansbury, David Warner, Stephen Rea, Tusse Silberg, Sarah Patterson, Graham Crowden, Terence Stamp. Directed by Neil Jordan. 95 min.

It's one thing to read "Little Red Riding Hood" as a parable about adolescent sexuality, and another to rewrite it that way for the screen. Jung and Company recommended that we mine psychological truth from fairy stories—not surgically implant it there. Angela Carter's screenplay takes us into the bedroom of a young English girl who tosses and sweats on her mattress and dreams furiously about handsome men who turn into slavering wolves. Alas, she never wakes up, and thus there's no real life for her dreams to illuminate. The film keeps sinking deeper into fables and fables-within-fables; it's all metaphor and no substance. English director Neil Jordan narrates like a literary critic—eyes always on the subtext. But the film's drowsy, painterly look, with bows to Brueghel and the Pre-Raphaelites, is memorable.

LES COMPERES ☆☆☆½
1984, France
Gérard Depardieu, Pierre Richard, Anny Duperey. Directed by Francis Veber. 92 min.

This very funny, charming, and entertaining comedy comes from the writer and director of *La Cage aux Folles*. After a woman's son disappears and the police prove to be of no help, she goes to two old lovers, tells each that the boy is his son, and sends them out after him. One of the two (Gérard Depardieu) is a hotheaded, ready-fisted crime reporter; the other (Pierre Richard) is a suicidal, timid poet. As farce it succeeds admirably, but there's more: Depardieu and Richard play off their characters' differences and inevitable friendship in an understated, believable manner. *Les Comperes* can be faulted slightly for a few of Francis Veber's usual bugaboos—all of his women, for instance, are bitches or whores—but overall it's Veber's best, most sustained effort, far superior to his earlier film with Depardieu and Richard, *Le Chevre*.

THE COMPETITION ☆½
1980, USA, PG
Richard Dreyfuss, Amy Irving, Lee Remick, Sam Wanamaker, Priscilla Pointer. Directed by Joel Oliansky. 129 min.

Like *The Turning Point*, this film seeks to reassure us that those who move in the rarefied circles of ballet or (in this case) classical music are exposed to the same banalities as the rest of us. Against a backdrop redolent of culture (the musical interludes, in particular, are staged with obvious care and respect), two entrants in a prestigious piano competition (Richard Dreyfuss and Amy Irving) become entangled in an affair worthy of the soaps. Irving's quivery mannerisms ossify her into visual platitudes, and Dreyfuss gives a sniveling, spineless performance. Though these two don't have a clue about their characters, there's something lurid in their acting that holds our interest. Irving's music teacher is played by Lee Remick, who has a field day cursing a blue streak. (Priscilla Pointer, for those of you interested in trivia, is Irving's mother.)

THE COMPLEAT BEATLES ☆☆☆
1982, USA
Paul McCartney, John Lennon, Ringo Starr, George Harrison, George Martin, Gerry Marsden. Narrated by Malcolm McDowell. Directed by Patrick Montgomery. 120 min.

This documentary is a sprightly, satisfying overview of the Fab Four's career. It begins with a history of the band's lesser-known, mid-fifties days and moves on to Beatlemania, *Sergeant Pepper*, the Maharishi, Yoko Ono—the works. Also featured is a fascinating interview with George Martin, the spry, aristocratic producer who oversaw all the group's recordings. The unspoken message is that the Beatles are now ancient history—a disquieting realization indeed. Incidentally, *The Compleat Beatles* was the first movie to be made for home video; two years later, it was released in theaters.

COMPROMISING POSITIONS ☆☆☆
1985, USA, R
Susan Sarandon, Raul Julia, Edward Herrmann, Judith Ivey, Mary Beth Hurt, Ann DeSalvo, Joe Mantegna, Josh Mostel, Deborah Rush. Directed by Frank Perry. 98 min.

Susan Isaacs's witty adaptation of her novel begins as a delicious suburban comedy of bad manners—Long Island's top periodontist is murdered, presumably by one of the dozens of rich housewives whom he bedded and then photographed in S&M gear. It's up to the most intrepid of the women, an ex-journalist (Susan Sarandon), to retake her pen and pad and solve the thing. But the film fluctuates uneasily between its rather half-baked mystery and the more biting humor that fills it out, and Frank Perry's direction is unsure and uninventive. The slight story loses steam as it goes along, and the ending is a letdown, but the large cast of New York–based actors performs beautifully. Sarandon has her best role in years as the would-be sleuth, and her comic timing is explosively funny (although her scenes with Edward Herrmann, who badly plays her insufferable husband, almost kill the movie). Stage actress Judith Ivey is very sharp as her acid-tongued friend, and Josh Mostel, Ann DeSalvo, and Deborah Rush make up a bizarrely comic family you may not forget.

THE COMPUTER WORE TENNIS SHOES ☆☆
1969, USA, G
Kurt Russell, Cesar Romero, Joe Flynn, William Schallert. Directed by Robert Butler. 90 min.

Grown-ups are entitled to see mindless action films of no artistic value; in the late 1960s the Disney studios decided to extend the privilege to children as well. The result was a series of Kurt Russell comedies, of which this is probably the most fun. Here he plays a college kid who accidentally has a computer's memory bank zapped into his brain, and thereby becomes extremely intelligent. Naturally, he appears on a game show, gets involved in a series of car chases, and foils the nefarious plans of evildoer Cesar Romero. And so would we, if we had the chance and were under ten years old.

CONAN THE BARBARIAN ☆
1982, USA, R
Arnold Schwarzenegger, James Earl Jones, Sandahl Bergman, Max von Sydow, Mako. Directed by John Milius. 115 min.

John Milius has envisioned his lavish adaptation of the Conan comics as a larger-than-life spectacle—a gladiator movie laced with the philosophy of G. Gordon Liddy. But with its logy, impassive performance by Arnold Schwarzenegger, *Conan* doesn't feel "mythic"; it's just long, solemn, and dull, with more religious symbolism than the entire Vatican art collection. The sequel, *Conan the Destroyer*, is far less pretentious and surprisingly enjoyable.

CONAN THE DESTROYER ☆☆½
1984, USA, PG
Arnold Schwarzenegger, Grace Jones, Wilt Chamberlain, Mako, Tracey Walter, Olivia D'Abo, Sarah Douglas. Directed by Richard Fleischer. 103 min.

Arnold Schwarzenegger decapitates or disembowels a dozen or so foes and a couple of monsters in order to protect a virgin princess and forestall the end of the world. Sound like fun? It is—much more so, in fact, than the overblown John Milius original. This time, our hero teams up with Wilt Chamberlain and disco androgyne Grace Jones, and Jones almost steals the movie; looking perfectly at ease with a ponytail hanging from her rump, she's such a lithe, snarling figure that you wish Conan would get it on with her instead of pining away for his lost Aryan goddess. Very undemanding entertainment.

THE CON ARTISTS ☆½
1977, Italy, PG
Anthony Quinn, Adriano Celentano, Corinne Clery. Directed by Sergio Corbucci. 86 min.

This film is an attempt to re-create, à la *The Sting*, the lighthearted roar of the twenties and the freewheeling life of lovable con men. Unfortunately, there isn't the talent here to support the endeavor, and the high jinks become screechy and irritating. Sergio Corbucci is a capable director, but there is no story. Anthony Quinn is lost in another bad role. Dubbed.

THE CONCERT FOR BANGLA DESH ☆☆½
1972, USA, G
George Harrison, Bob Dylan, Eric Clapton, Ringo Starr, Billy Preston, Leon Russell, Klaus Voorman, Badfinger. Directed by Saul Swimmer. 99 min.

Before there was Live Aid, Band Aid, Farm Aid, or any of those other kool aids, George Harrison put together this all-star benefit to raise money for victims of famine in Bangla Desh. Harrison was such a thoroughly nice guy about it that no one had the heart to ask him not to pronounce it *Bongla* Desh, which he does constantly. Unfortunately, thanks to various legal and other foul-ups, almost none of the money raised ever seems to have gotten to the intended recipients. Performances range from OK to outstanding (Bob Dylan and Leon Russell).

THE CONCORDE

See *Airport '79—The Concorde*

CONCRETE JUNGLE ☆☆
1982, USA, R
Jill St. John, Barbara Luna, Tracy Bregman, Nina Talbot, June Barrett. Directed by Tom De Simone. 101 min.

Framed for cocaine smuggling, sweetly naive Elizabeth is thrown into the Big House for a year and soon realizes that her sisters behind bars are pretty tough customers—rapists, killers, drug dealers—and that's just while they're *inside* prison. This not-bad exploitation flick places itself squarely in the women's prison genre with obligatory shower scenes and lesbian encounters, but it's got a better story and sharper acting than most. (Barbara Luna is particularly good as Cat, the queen bee of the creeps.) Although *Concrete Jungle* isn't complete sleaze, it certainly isn't any kind of art. One longs for Sybil Danning and Linda Blair to trash things up, but they weren't jailed until the sequel, *Chained Heat*.

THE CONDEMNED OF ALTONA ☆☆
1962, Italy/France
Maximilian Schell, Fredric March, Sophia Loren, Robert Wagner. Directed by Vittorio De Sica. 114 min.

A convoluted theatrical piece by Jean-Paul Sartre is given the all-star college try here, but De Sica's direction fails to overcome built-in deficiencies in the play's structure. A terminally ill businessman cannot resolve the difficulties stemming from the skeleton he has stashed away in the family closet—a crazed son fond of dressing up in Nazi drag. The philosophical implications of the theme are obscured by the sluggish treatment, but the languor is offset by some impressive hamming by Maximilian Schell and Fredric March. Sophia Loren and Robert Wagner get lost in the big-theme-and-important-message shuffle. Screenplay by Abby Mann.

CONDORMAN ☆½
1981, USA/Great Britain, G
Michael Crawford, Oliver Reed, James Hampton, Barbara Carrera, Dana Elcar. Directed by Charles Jarrott. 90 min.

This wan, witless parody of the James Bond pictures may well represent a new low for Walt Disney Studios. The movie regurgitates Bondian situations with blunt literal-mindedness and then adds "goofy" high jinks: spies dressed as Arab oil sheikhs, a car that turns into a speedboat, the hero (Michael Crawford) taking to the air on homemade wings. The result isn't merely dumb; it's less funny than the movies it's supposedly satirizing.

CONDUCT UNBECOMING ☆☆½
1975, Great Britain, PG
Michael York, Richard Attenborough, Trevor Howard, Stacy Keach, Christopher Plummer, Susannah York, James Faulkner. Directed by Michael Anderson. 107 min.

A solid, slightly stiff courtroom drama, adapted from a play about a British officer posted in Victorian India who is accused of assaulting a superior officer's widow. The dramatic focus is not on the defendant, but rather on his heroic counsel (Michael York), who sways the judge's opinion as he gradually begins to uncover the real identity of the culprit and the nature of the offense. The climactic revelation is abominably muddled, but until that point director Michael Anderson creates a nicely atmospheric study of manners and mores in the colonialist class structure, filled with strong, unshowy performances.

CONFESSIONS OF A POLICE CAPTAIN ☆☆½
1971, Italy
Martin Balsam, Franco Nero, Marilu Tolo, Claudio Gora, Luciano Lorcas. Directed by Damiano Damiani. 101 min.

This film comes from the school of early seventies Italian political awareness that also produced *The Conformist* and *Investigation of a Citizen above Suspicion*. Damiano Damiani's film follows a veteran policeman's efforts to bring to justice certain influential criminals (the word "Mafia" is never used) who have remained free because of personal power and connections in high places. Both Martin Balsam, as the commissioner, and Franco Nero as a young DA who seems to be engaged in corrupt practices, turn in fine performances.

CONFIDENTIALLY YOURS ☆☆½
1983, France
Fanny Ardant, Jean-Louis Trintignant, Philippe Laudenbach, Caroline Sihol. Directed by François Truffaut. 111 min.

This François Truffaut film might be described as paint-by-numbers Hitchcock. It's got a guilty-seeming protagonist (Jean-Louis Trintignant) accused of double homicide, a breezy heroine (Fanny Ardant) who helps him solve the crime, voyeuristic black-and-white photography (by Nester Almendros), a bevy of comic/sinister sideline characters, and a story that skips through locations faster than a Riviera bus tour. What the movie doesn't have is wit, energy, or suspense.

THE CONFORMIST ☆☆☆☆
1970, France/Italy/West Germany, R
Jean-Louis Trintignant, Stefania Sandrelli, Dominique Sanda, Pierre Clementi, Gastone Moschin, Enzo Taroscio. Directed by Bernardo Bertolucci. 115 min.

Bernardo Bertolucci's version of Alberto Moravia's celebrated novel tells the story of Clerici (Jean-Louis Trintignant), a young, passionless Fascist official in thirties Italy who's assigned to murder his former professor and winds up falling for his intended victim's wife (Dominique Sanda). Bertolucci turns the novel into a baroque melodramatic thriller full of dazzling compositions, ravishing lighting and color, and elliptical plot twists. The effect is to trap the cold-blooded monster in a swirling, impassioned milieu. Trintignant—stiff, suspicious, almost obscenely narcissistic—gives the finest performance of his career. The stunning, thoughtful cinematography is by Vittorio Storaro.

THE CONGRESSMAN

See *El Diputado*

A CONNECTICUT YANKEE IN KING ARTHUR'S COURT ☆☆
1949, USA
Bing Crosby, Rhonda Fleming, William Bendix, Cedric Hardwicke, Henry Wilcoxon. Directed by Tay Garnett. 107 min.

This disappointing musical-fantasy, based on the novel by Mark Twain, moves too slowly to be effective. Bing Crosby plays a modern-day blacksmith who finds himself in the land of King Arthur after being knocked unconscious. Nice Technicolor and good songs, but Bing isn't Will Rogers (who did it in 1931) and King Arthur's Court isn't Oz. Add a drippy Rhonda Fleming (as Lady Alesande) and the film sinks under its own weight. Songs include "Once and for Always" and "If You Stub Your Toe on the Moon." Remade by Disney as *Unidentified Flying Oddball*.

THE CONQUEROR ½☆
1956, USA
John Wayne, Susan Hayward, Agnes Moorehead, Pedro Armendariz, John Hoyt, William Conrad. Directed by Dick Powell. 111 min.

Hot-blooded Genghis Khan risks his empire for the seductive charms of titian-tressed Tatar princess Bortai, in Howard Hughes's grandest folly, one of the worst and most unintentionally funny films ever perpetrated. Picture John Wayne looking like a road show Charlie Chan as the fierce warrior, plus Susan Hayward as a very Irish-looking barbarian babe. Add to this the mock biblical dialogue that beggars description (how did the Mongols take time off from pillaging to develop so flowery a language?) and cap it off with a cast of thousands, most of whom look like they'd be more comfortable in *Flower Drum Song* than impersonating rugged barbarians. A camp classic, but also famous for being filmed near a nuclear test site; dozens of the film's cast and crew eventually died of cancer.

CONQUEST ☆
1983, Italy/Spain/Mexico, R
George Rivero, Andrea Occhipinti, Conrado San Martin, Violeta Ceta, Sabrina Sellers. Directed by Lucio Fulci. 92 min.

Perhaps you can imagine a film written by three kids in the seventh grade: Eddie, the nerd, insists on lots of villains that look just like Chewbacca; Bobby, the one with the acne who loves Spielberg, wants a plot about a magic sword, a long journey, and a cynical sidekick; and Joey, the kid with the *Playboy* magazines hidden in his locker, insists that all of the women be topless. Lucio Fulci (*Zombie Flesh Eaters*, *City of the Living Dead*) makes sure that there are a few zombies thrown in for good measure. In spite of its puerility, this movie might have been fun if the cinematography weren't so achingly, artily obscure.

CONQUEST OF THE PLANET OF THE APES ☆☆½
1972, USA, G
Roddy McDowall, Don Murray, Natalie Trundy, Ricardo Montalban, Severn Darden. Directed by J. Lee Thompson. 87 min.

The enslaved apes revolt against their human captors in part four of the series, marked by unusually complex references to the preceding films and a prolonged bloody finale. This time Roddy McDowall plays the ape Caesar, the son of the character he originated, and Natalie Trundy (wife of series producer Arthur Jacobs) also returns, playing her *third* character. Oddly enough, this installment, set in 1990, is now the most dated of the five, due in part to its design as a comment on the tense race relations of the early 1970s. The G rating here seems particularly inappropriate, since this sequel is far more violent and frightening than the already borderline original. That will matter little to fans of the series who have already come this far. Followed by *Battle for the Planet of the Apes*.

CONRACK ☆☆½
1974, USA, PG
Jon Voight, Paul Winfield, Madge Sinclair, Tina Andrews, Antonio Fargas, Ruth Attaway, James O'Reare, Hume Cronyn. Directed by Martin Ritt. 106 min.

Pleasing but simplistic Southern-liberal humanism from director Martin Ritt mines the same vein of togetherness and populism as many of his other films, most notably *Norma Rae*. The story, based on Pat Conroy's autobiographical *The Water Is Wide*, has teacher Jon Voight as the great white hope of students at a horrifyingly neglected black grade school in a South Carolina backwater. The resulting transition is too large a lump of sugar to swallow without gagging a little—within weeks, the kids who used to barely know their own names are spouting Shakespeare, and the hero's blond locks begin to take on a halo-like glow. But the film's heart and mind are in the right place, and Voight does everything you could reasonably ask with the title role. Nice, uplifting stuff, but don't look too closely.

CONTEMPT ☆☆☆☆
1963, France/Italy
Brigitte Bardot, Jack Palance, Michel Piccoli, Fritz Lang. Directed by Jean-Luc Godard. 103 min.

Jean-Luc Godard's most accessible film can be viewed as a satire on moviemaking, a caustic but sad description of marital love, and an honest attempt to use Brigitte Bardot as an actress. Fritz Lang is delightful in the small role of a grandiose director working on a glossy production of *The Odyssey*. Jack Palance, in the most stereotyped role, gives a humanized, vivid portrayal. Godard's style is not for everyone, but this is one of his strongest, most emotionally charged creations. (a.k.a.: *Le Mepris*)

CONTINENTAL DIVIDE
★★½
1981, USA, PG
John Belushi, Blair Brown, Allen Goorwitz, Val Avery. Directed by Michael Apted. 103 min.

This light entertainment falls far short of its goal of emulating the romantic comedies of the thirties and forties. John Belushi is cast against type as a tough, wisecracking journalist assigned to do a story on a beautiful ornithologist (Blair Brown). Stuck in a cabin in the middle of nowhere, these two toss insults at each other, play with sex-role reversals, and—of course—fall in love. The script, by Lawrence Kasdan (*Body Heat*), is clever but in predictable ways, and Belushi doesn't show much of a gift for light comedy.

THE CONVERSATION
★★★★
1974, USA, PG
Gene Hackman, Allen Garfield, John Cazale, Frederic Forrest, Teri Garr, Cindy Williams, Harrison Ford, Robert Duvall. Directed by Francis Ford Coppola. 113 min.

This Watergate-era masterpiece concerns a veteran surveillance expert (Gene Hackman) whose tape recording of a hauntingly ambivalent conversation causes him to become emotionally concerned, for the first time in his career, with a client's motives. Taking a pause between *Godfathers*, Francis Ford Coppola picked up a script he had begun in 1966 and made his most personal, mature, and technically brilliant essay. Hackman's acting is astonishingly precise as he portrays the ingrained, implosive alienation and loneliness of a professional listener, and Bill Butler's camerawork and a dense, multilayered soundtrack make *The Conversation* a film that not only rewards repeated viewings, but demands them. As suspense, drama, and social commentary, it's a fully realized tour de force, and one of the finest films of the last two decades. Credit soundman Walter Murch with piecing the film together from a number of alternative storylines during postproduction; Coppola has called him the film's coauthor. Winner of the Cannes Film Festival's Palme d'Or.

CONVERSATION PIECE
★★★
1975, France/Italy
Burt Lancaster, Silvana Mangano, Helmut Berger, Claudia Marsani, Stefano Patrizi, Dominique Sanda, Claudia Cardinale. Directed by Luchino Visconti. 120 min.

This film is an immaculately designed and well-executed miniature from a director previously obsessed with the plummeting of grandiose dynasties (*The Damned*, *Ludwig*, *The Leopard*). Sparsely set in two apartments in Rome, it carefully and slowly draws the portrait of an erstwhile American academic (Burt Lancaster) who grapples with an intrusive woman who has moved her lover and family into the spare rooms of his home. On this claustrophobic but tasteful canvas, the characters sometimes seem merely sketched, while their dialogue is slopped on. But Luchino Visconti, who directed from a wheelchair after suffering a stroke, has applied a sure hand to this rich and colorful picture, giving the whole frame a surprisingly effective hue.

CONVOY
★★
1978, USA, PG
Kris Kristofferson, Ali MacGraw, Ernest Borgnine, Burt Young, Madge Sinclair, Frankin Ajaye, Seymour Cassel, Cassie Yates. Directed by Sam Peckinpah. 110 min.

This action film was designed to capitalize on the late-seventies CB craze. The stunts are immaculately staged, and everything is photographed in the airy gold-and-sky-blue style of director Sam Peckinpah's earlier films. Yet *Convoy* seems embarrassed by its own beauties; it plays like a bloated, less-spontaneous *Smokey and the Bandit*. All of Peckinpah's virtuosity has gone into running cars off the road—here he becomes a cooperative hack director, and his favorite themes have become embellishments. Kris Kristofferson, as the renegade trucker Rubber Duck, is allowed to walk through his role; we never understand him, much less what the convoy he's leading is supposed to stand for. B. W. L. Norton's screenplay is based on the fluke hit song "Convoy" by C. W. McCall.

COOGAN'S BLUFF
★★★
1968, USA
Clint Eastwood, Lee J. Cobb, Susan Clark, Tisha Sterling, Don Stroud, Betty Field, Tom Tully, Melodie Johnson. Directed by Don Siegel. 94 min.

This above-average police procedural comes from the hit (and kick) team of Don Siegel and Clint Eastwood. In a few years they would go on to create the Dirty Harry character, and much of Harry's ruthless forcefulness is present in the character of Coogan, an Arizona lawman let loose in the Big Apple to extradite a killer. The hippies-and-dope milieu may seem a trifle dated, or they may strike you as a good period feel. At any rate, the action and Eastwood never let up and never disappoint.

COOLEY HIGH
★★★
1975, USA, PG
Glynn Turman, Lawrence Hilton-Jacobs, Garrett Morris, Cynthia Davis, Corin Rogers. Directed by Michael Schultz. 107 min.

This episodic comedy-drama about ghetto teenagers growing up in 1964 Chicago was billed as a black *American Graffiti*, and comes pretty close to that film's style and tone. Offbeat performances by a young, promising cast, good locations, and a soundtrack percolating with every sixties Motown group from the Marvelettes to the Four Tops combine to make *Cooley High* a winning, heartwarming experience; you may want to turn it off before the unbearably maudlin, schematic ending ruins it all. Watch for one great scene involving the kind of catastrophic Friday-night party that everyone who attended high school has lived through at least once. Note: the film was the basis for the TV series "What's Happening."

COOL HAND LUKE
★★★½
1967, USA, PG
Paul Newman, George Kennedy, J. D. Cannon, Strother Martin, Lou Antonio, Jo Van Fleet, Luke Askew. Directed by Stuart Rosenberg. 129 min.

A tremendous performance from Paul Newman as a screwed-down prisoner keeps building the pressure in this explosive chain-gang film. The movie is an endgame play—Luke Jackson is the kind of loser who never gives up trying to win. His refusal to submit to the authority of the guards, his continuing escape attempts, and his stoic resistance to punishment gradually begin to give him the mythic status that is usually conferred by absolute success. George Kennedy won an Academy Award for Best Supporting Actor. Look for the faces of Dennis Hopper, Harry Dean Stanton, Ralph Waite, Anthony Zerbe, and Joe Don Baker.

COPACABANA
★★½
1947, USA
Carmen Miranda, Groucho Marx, Steve Cochran, Gloria Jean, Andy Russell, Ralph Sanford, Earl Wilson. Directed by Alfred E. Green. 92 min.

This is one of those musical curiosities that simply must be seen to be believed. Groucho Marx and Carmen Miranda team up in Hollywood's most creative pairing since Mae West and W. C. Fields. Groucho plays a sleazy agent who gets Miranda (his only client) into the Copacabana on the condition that she appear as both a Latin-American bombshell and a French singer. Scenes of Miranda in a veil and blond wig, and of Groucho jitterbugging with her in the finale, make this a bad-musical-lover's delight. Apparently, the writers thought so too, or they wouldn't have turned the love interest between Steve Cochran and Gloria Jean into a satire.

COPACABANA ★★½
1985, USA (TV)
Barry Manilow, Annette O'Toole, Estelle Getty, Joseph Bologna, Andra Akers. Directed by Waris Hussein. 100 min.

🎵 It's so invigorating to see an old-fashioned 1940s-style musical again that even those who are not fans of Barry Manilow will be tapping their toes, especially since the production design captures the studio-bound charm of the old Twentieth Century–Fox musicals. Unfortunately, Annette O'Toole (who sings and dances superbly but without much dynamism) is no Alice Faye, and Manilow isn't even a Don Ameche. Despite the less-than-breathtaking performances by the leads, you'll be glad to find out how Lola the Copa showgirl lost her faithful piano-playing swain to a bullet from a psychotic gangster. The bonus is a wickedly funny supporting performance by Andra Akers as a lascivious divorcée able to indulge her penchant for handsome gigolos.

THE COP KILLER

See *Corrupt*

CORNBREAD, EARL AND ME ★★½
1975, USA, PG
Moses Gunn, Rosalind Cash, Bernie Casey, Madge Sinclair, Keith (Jamaal) Wilkes, Tierre Turner, Larry Fishburne III. Directed by Joe Manduke. 94 min.

What starts as a warm, affecting study of ghetto life becomes an obvious and predictable melodrama, despite sensitive acting and welcome attention to atmosphere and detail. Cornbread is a high-school basketball star idolized by the two young friends of the title. He's on the verge of moving up and out when fate intervenes in the form of two cops who claim they saw a gun in his hand. It's a story familiar to anyone who lives in a big city, and well worth telling, but when the courtroom scenes begin, the writing nosedives. Excellent performances from the entire cast except for NBA pro Wilkes, who's engaging but amateurish as Cornbread.

CORNERED ★½
1945, USA
Dick Powell, Micheline Cheirel, Walter Slezak, Morris Carnovsky. Directed by Edward Dmytryk. 103 min.

This film is yet another tremendously overrated Edward Dmytryk *noir* melodrama. Dick Powell plays a French-Canadian pilot in Buenos Aires who seeks out the man who killed his wife. John Wexley's convoluted plot resembles Margharita Laski's *Little Boy Lost*, but lacks the warmth of that novel (and the George Seaton film). This kind of thing was the *Dirty Harry* of its day: dark, grim, cold, and not particularly well made.

THE CORN IS GREEN ★★★½
1979, USA (TV)
Katharine Hepburn, Ian Saynor, Bill Fraser, Patricia Hayes, Anna Massey, Artro Morris. Directed by George Cukor. 100 min.

George Cukor is a better director than Irving Rapper, and Katharine Hepburn is a more appropriate choice than Bette Davis to play Lilly Moffat; yet, this made-for-TV remake of the 1945 film is no real improvement on the original, although touching nonetheless. The central problem is that the play by Emlyn Williams, about a spinster schoolteacher who attempts to educate a promising pupil in a Welsh mining town at the turn of the century, is too pat to stir up much interest. The Ivan Davis adaptation is too politically docile to illustrate the problems of education on anything other than a personal plane. This was, however, Cukor and Hepburn's tenth union in thirty-seven years, and they demonstrate that a TV movie can be just as elegantly made and acted as any feature film.

THE CORPSE GRINDERS ★
1971, USA
Sean Kenny, Monika Kelly, Sanford Mitchell, J. Byron Foster. Directed by Ted V. Mikels. 72 min.

The director of *The Astro-Zombies* and *Blood Orgy of the She-Devils* scores again with this endearing horror-comedy about a cat-food company that uses human meat in its product. When cats eat it, they turn into killer kitties and massacre their masters, who in turn go into the cat-food grinder. Isn't capitalism wonderful? Ted V. Mikels not only produced and directed, but also edited and did the music—all badly, of course. The grinder of the title is a cardboard box with holes in one side through which someone pushes hamburger meat. Written by Arch Hall, producer/director of the classic *Eegah!*

THE CORPSE VANISHES ★★
1942, USA
Bela Lugosi, Luana Walters, Tristram Coffin, Elizabeth Russell, Minerva Urecal, Angelo Rossitto. Directed by Wallace Fox. 64 min.

Love, Lugosi style. Happily ensconced in a marriage of many decades, Bela keeps his bride young and beautiful by kidnapping young virgins on the eve of their marriage and sucking them dry of hormones. Unfortunately, a dopey plot about a peppy young reporter investigating the unusual practice keeps getting in the way, but there are still scenes of Lugosi sleeping in a coffin, and an appearance by the inimitable Angelo Rossitto as his dwarf henchman. Campy fun.

CORRUPT ★★
1983, Italy/USA, R
Harvey Keitel, John Lydon, Sylvia Sidney, Nicole Garcia. Directed by Roberto Faenza. 99 min.

This weird thriller concerns the exchange of guilt between a corrupt police detective and a pale, peculiar young man who may be a psychotic murderer preying on members of the narcotics squad. The intriguing idea is undercut by weak production values, but buoyed by intense performances by Harvey Keitel and John Lydon (formerly of the Sex Pistols) in the leads.

THE CORRUPT ONES ★½
1966, West Germany/France/Italy
Robert Stack, Elke Sommer, Nancy Kwan, Christian Marquand, Werner Peters. Directed by James Hill. 92 min.

This dull, overly familiar crime melodrama was produced to cash in on the European success of reruns of Robert Stack's television series "The Untouchables." That fact is more interesting than anything in this film, which is about two rival gangs out to raid an ancient Chinese burial tomb. From the director of *Born Free*, who unfortunately has no cute lions to work with here.

THE CORSICAN BROTHERS ★★½
1941, USA
Douglas Fairbanks, Jr., Ruth Warrick, Akim Tamiroff, J. Carroll Naish, H. B. Emery, Henry Wilcoxon, Veda Ann Borg, Gloria Holden. Directed by Gregory Ratoff. 111 min.

Douglas Fairbanks, Jr., was never quite as winning as his father, but he came so close in looks and mannerisms alone that he gives an excellent impression of what Doug Sr. might have been like as a major sound-film star. In this loose adaptation of the Alexandre Dumas story, he plays twins who, after years of separation, join forces to avenge the murder of their parents. Fairbanks's zest and the "doubling" feature are the only elements that set this apart from the usual costume picture derring-do. Harry Stradling's photography is excellent, but color would have helped. OK for committed fans.

THE CORSICAN BROTHERS (1984)

See *Cheech and Chong's the Corsican Brothers*

CORVETTE SUMMER ☆½
1978, USA, PG
Mark Hamill, Kim Milford, Annie Potts, Eugene Roche, Richard McKenzie. Directed by Matthew Robbins. 105 min.

Mark Hamill's first film after *Star Wars* was this undistinguished car-chase comedy, in which he plays an eighteen-year-old whose high-school shop class's prize Corvette is stolen. His pursuit of the car links him up with a gabby, good-hearted hooker (Annie Potts, the only cast member here who makes a stab at acting). First-time director Matthew Robbins seems to like his characters and story; if only they weren't so tedious and familiar, we might too.

COSI COME SEI

See *Stay As You Are*

THE COSMIC MONSTER ☆
1958, Great Britain
Forrest Tucker, Martin Benson, Gaby André, Wyndham Goldie, Hugh Latimer. Directed by Gilbert Gunn. 75 min.

Yet another mad scientist mucks around with Things Best Left Alone and blows a big hole in the ionosphere. This, of course, lets in cosmic rays that cause insects to grow to gigantic proportions. It also lets in a visitor from another dimension who pulls our fat out of the fire. This film was based on a BBC serial, which just goes to show that everything the British watch on the telly is not "Upstairs Downstairs." (a.k.a.: *The Strange World of Planet X*)

THE COTTON CLUB ☆☆☆½
1984, USA, R
Richard Gere, Gregory Hines, Diane Lane, James Remar, Bob Hoskins, Nicolas Cage, Fred Gwynne, Lonette McKee, Julian Beck. Directed by Francis Ford Coppola. 128 min.

Francis Ford Coppola's extravagant collage of the singers, dancers, and gangsters that inhabited Harlem's Cotton Club in the 1930s is pure visual dazzlement wedded to the unlikeliest of entertainments—a *Godfather* with splashy production numbers. The multiple plot lines wedged into two hours allow Coppola to embrace an astonishing variety of genres—musical, fantasy, cops-and-robbers, and show-biz romance, among others. Somehow, despite the rampant inaccuracies and occasional sloppiness, just about all of it comes together. He even draws passable performances out of Richard Gere and Diane Lane, although their romance scenes can't help but look like a mating of mannequins. Excess drips from each frame of this $45 million film, but a couple of virtuoso sequences show that Coppola at last found the right movie to embody his increasing interest in visual grandeur and technical wizardry. Whatever else, you won't be bored—*The Cotton Club*'s energy borders on the ecstatic.

COTTON COMES TO HARLEM ☆☆½
1970, USA, R
Raymond St. Jacques, Godfrey Cambridge, Calvin Lockhart, Vinnette Carroll, Redd Foxx, Cleavon Little, Judy Pace. Directed by Ossie Davis. 97 min.

This action-comedy about detectives Grave Digger Jones and Coffin Ed Johnson was one of the first black-oriented films to achieve box-office success with white as well as black audiences, thus paving the way for scores of black exploitation films in the early seventies. This isn't as bad as most of what followed, although its humor, relying primarily on unexpected racial reversals and the novelty of its black cops, has dated badly. Good acting by Godfrey Cambridge and Raymond St. Jacques, who play a sort of mean-mouthed, updated version of Abbott and Costello, partially compensates for the low-comedy premise, which has them searching for a cache of loot buried in a bale of cotton somewhere above 125th Street.

COUNTDOWN ☆☆½
1968, USA
James Caan, Joanna Moore, Robert Duvall, Barbara Baxley, Steve Ihnat. Directed by Robert Altman. 101 min.

Robert Altman's third film, and his first Hollywood feature, is a science-fiction potboiler about the first manned moon landing. Robert Duvall is an obsessive military astronaut who loses the moon assignment to civilian James Caan. The film—based on Hank Searles's novel *The Pilgrim Project*—is notable for its elaborate aerospace hardware, which accurately anticipated the real Apollo gear of the following year. Altman initiated the project himself, but was fired before it was edited; his overlapping dialogue was eliminated, and a new, upbeat ending was shot to replace the somber one. "(Jack) Warner cut the picture for kids," Altman has said, "which was the reverse of what I was going for . . . it became a lot of flag-waving."

COUNT DRACULA ☆
1970, Italy/West Germany/Spain
Christopher Lee, Klaus Kinski, Herbert Lom, Soledad Miranda, Maria Rohm, Fred Williams, Jack Taylor. Directed by Jess Franco. 100 min.

Purportedly a faithful adaptation of Bram Stoker's novel by a wildly prolific purveyor of Spanish exploitation films, *Count Dracula*—needless to say—is just another of the dozens of second-rate vampire films that trade on the genre's most famous name. Unattractive photography and poor dubbing don't help matters, but the intense Klaus Kinski is exceptional as Renfield, the lunatic whose bloodlust derives from his empathetic relationship with the vampire count.

THE COUNT OF MONTE CRISTO ☆☆☆½
1934, USA
Robert Donat, Elissa Landi, Louis Calhern, Sidney Blackmer, Raymond Walbern. Directed by Rowland V. Lee. 119 min.

There have been five cinematic versions of Alexandre Dumas's great escape classic; this is the third and best. Englishman Robert Donat is convincing as the prisoner who masterminds his own deliverance and wreaks vengeance on the three men who framed him. A large, fine cast supports Donat, making the film far more than a one-man show.

THE COUNT OF MONTE CRISTO ☆☆☆
1976, Great Britain
Richard Chamberlain, Tony Curtis, Trevor Howard, Louis Jordan, Donald Pleasence, Kate Nelligan, Anthony Dawson. Directed by David Greene. 103 min.

Yet another version of the Alexandre Dumas tale about the innocent sailor sent to prison on trumped-up charges who escapes after fifteen years and sets about to gain revenge on those responsible. Unlike Richard Lester's *The Three Musketeers*, this is played perfectly straight in a handsome production emphasizing the heroics and moral tragedy: it's corn, but at least it's *sincere* corn. Richard Chamberlain is much better here than he was in the similarly made *Hamlet*. Originally shown in this country on television.

COUNTRY ☆☆☆
1984, USA, PG
Jessica Lange, Sam Shepard, Wilford Brimley, Sandra Seacat. Directed by Richard Pearce. 109 min.

This somber drama about a farm family threatened with displacement, despite schematic events and characters, never degenerates into tear-jerking excess, largely because of the uniformly high level of the performances, including Jessica Lange's Oscar-nominated effort. This is a successful problem picture, better than but eclipsed by two other films with the same theme released the same year: the sentimental *Places in the Heart* and the lushly romanticized *The River*. *Country* took a more overtly political stance about the plight of the farmer and may have suffered at the box office for it.

COUNTRY GENTLEMAN ☆☆
1936, USA
Ole Olsen, Chic Johnson, Joyce Compton, Lila Lee, Pierre Watkin, Donald Kirke. Directed by Ralph Staub. 66 min.

This seldom-seen feature is a bit more subdued than the usual Olsen and Johnson vehicle—the former functions almost entirely as a romantic lead/straight man here, which throws the team's chemistry off. They play con men selling worthless stock who find themselves in jail on a phony kidnapping charge. As usual, the plot is secondary to the duo's antics, though in the first half the story does seem as though it's about to sink them. Look for *All over Town* instead.

THE COUNTRY GIRL ☆☆☆
1954, USA
Bing Crosby, Grace Kelly, William Holden, Anthony Ross, Gene Reynolds. Directed by George Seaton. 104 min.

Grace Kelly won the Oscar, but it's Bing Crosby who delivers the goods. Clifford Odets's play about a washed-up actor making a comeback, his seemingly cold wife, and a concerned director who tries to figure out their relationship makes an interesting, if theatrically calculated, film. Despite the pat ending, Odets is highly skillful at manipulating to be part of the process. George Seaton, not known for his visual flair, won an Oscar for faithfully transcribing the play to the screen, and he is greatly assisted by his cast in making it work. Kelly tries hard in the key role of the wife, but her New England diction and looks belie her tattered outfits. Bill Holden also does well, but he too is overshadowed by Crosby's vivid, heartrending portrayal of the alcoholic actor. It's his best work and should not be missed.

THE COUNTRY GIRL ☆☆☆
1981, USA (TV)
Faye Dunaway, Dick Van Dyke, Ken Howard. Directed by Bernie Dodd. 137 min.

An effective, adeptly acted TV version of the famous Clifford Odets play that won Grace Kelly an Oscar in 1954. Faye Dunaway skillfully portrays the ultimate backstage wife who patches up her husband's tattered ego and prepares him for his comeback. Ken Howard makes a good foil for Dunaway as the director who believes she's responsible for her husband's alcoholic downfall, and Dick Van Dyke almost erases memories of Bing Crosby in the difficult role of the destructive, self-pitying Frank Elgin.

COUNT YORGA, VAMPIRE ☆☆☆
1970, USA, PG
Robert Quarry, Roger Perry, Michael Murphy, Donna Anders, Judith Lang. Directed by Robert Kelljan. 91 min.

American-International's low-budget attempt to create a new vampire character surprised everyone by being offbeat, a little hip, and a little scary—all in all, not bad. Basically, it's *Dracula* all over again—a civilized, distinguished Count arrives in a big city under mysterious circumstances and engages in disdainful ripostes with his human adversary, a doctor who is on to him. In this version, however, the city is Los Angeles, and director Kelljan manages to use its sleazy ambience without going for laughs or campiness. The sequel, *The Return of Count Yorga*, was just as good.

COUP DE FOUDRE

See *Entre Nous*

COUP DE GRACE ☆☆
1976, West Germany/France
Margarethe Von Trotta, Matthias Habich, Rudiger Kirschstein, Matthieu Carrière. Directed by Volker Schlöndorff. 95 min.

Volker Schlöndorff has adapted a fine, neglected novel by Marguerite Yourcenar (*Memoirs of Hadrian*), a study of the pressurized relationships among a group of young Germans fighting with the White Russians in the last-ditch holding action against the Bolsheviks. The performers, particularly Schlöndorff's fortyish wife, Margarethe Von Trotta, are uniformly "mature" for their roles, so the book's essentially adolescent sexual psychology now makes very little sense. And the movie has been shot (in handsome black-and-white) as a respectful, almost academic homage to the early films of Jean-Pierre Melville, especially in *La Silence de la Mer*. Like Schlöndorff's more recent *Swann in Love*, adapted from Marcel Proust's *Remembrance of Things Past*, the result is a film that can't stand on its own for people who don't know the book, and fails to illuminate the story for those who do.

COUP DE TORCHON ☆☆☆½
1981, France, R
Philippe Noiret, Isabelle Huppert, Guy Marchand, Stephane Audran, Irene Skobline, Eddy Mitchell. Directed by Bertrand Tavernier. 128 min.

This cruel and funny morality tale is based on Jim Thompson's *Pop.1280* and is another estimable work from French director Bertrand Tavernier (*The Clockmaker*, *Let Joy Reign Supreme*). While Philippe Noiret's performance doesn't convey the full-throttle madness of the protagonist of the novel, it masterfully sets the tone of detachment for this cool, polished work about a worm-who-turns policeman in French Equatorial Africa. This "little" man is crushed by his superiors, his wife, and his own inadequacies, but he acquires a social conscience that compels him to rid the world of evil—starting with all those who've stepped on him. The director plays on our delight in watching this poor slob get the best of his oppressors, but Tavernier also creates a masterful study in irony, since the man ends up more callous than his enemies and just as impotent as ever. Unfortunately, the tape is marred by poor transfer of nighttime scenes, which are difficult to see on VHS. (a.k.a.: *Clean Slate*)

THE COURAGE OF BLACK BEAUTY ☆☆½
1957, USA
Johnny Crawford, Diane Brewster, J. Pat O'Malley, John Bryant. Directed by Harold Schuster. 77 min.

This time Black Beauty's owner is a boy, and somehow the story worked better with a female owner in 1946. Everyone tries hard, but it's obvious that the celebrated stallion is now flaring its nostrils at a much lower budget. Although the original film still leads the pack as the most winning member of the Black Beauty stable, this modest programmer has its own homey virtues. It won't leave a lasting impression, but it's a film the whole family will enjoy, on the level of Saturday morning live-action TV series of the fifties like "My Friend Flicka" and "Fury."

LA COURSE DU LIEVRE À TRAVERS LES CHAMPS

See *... And Hope to Die*

THE COURT JESTER ☆☆☆☆
1956, USA
Danny Kaye, Glynis Johns, Basil Rathbone, Angela Lansbury, Cecil Parker, Mildred Natwick, Robert Middleton, John Carradine, Edward Ashley. Directed by Norman Panama and Melvin Frank. 101 min.

It's hard to know where to begin with a comedy this good. First there's Danny Kaye, who regrettably hasn't achieved the status of classic comedian that he so richly deserves. In this, his best film, he is everywhere, bouncing his quips off a great supporting cast, dominating every scene with his manic intensity. He gets a good run for his money from Angela Lansbury, for one; she plays her role of a lecherous princess like a confident, plump cat stalking a nervous, skinny mouse. Basil Rathbone, John Carradine, and Mildred Natwick, too, are comic adepts. Perhaps best of all, this film accomplishes the ultimate rarity: its farcical plot, with ever-escalating improbabilities, works by a wacky and precise logic. A lowly pot boy in an outlaw band becomes involved in a plot to rethrone an infant monarch named the Purple Pimpernel. He falls under a spell that makes him instantly change from an inept coward into a courageous, romantic hero. Everything is confidently handled by writer/directors Norman Panama and Melvin Frank. All in all, a surpassing spoof of the classic Douglas Fairbanks/Errol Flynn swashbucklers and a treasure trove of insights into Hollywood's ability to create beautifully blended confections from wide-ranging resources.

COURT MARTIAL

See *Carrington, V.C.*

COUSIN, COUSINE ☆☆☆
1975, France, R
Victor Lanoux, Marie-Christine Barrault, Guy Marchand, Marie-France Pisier. Directed by Jean-Charles Tacchella. 95 min.

A couple having an adulterous affair become cousins by marriage in Jean-Charles Tacchella's frothy and sometimes poignant comedy about upper-middle-class lives and loves. *Cousin, Cousine* is on surer footing when it aims for a light and charming look at infidelity; the slice-of-life family scenes are brought off with an unevenness of tone that disrupts the film. Nonetheless, Victor Lanoux and Marie-Christine Barrault (an Academy Award nominee) make an attractively down-to-earth pair of lovers, and Guy Marchand and Marie-France Pisier are extremely funny cuckolds (her attempted-suicide scene is, against all odds, the film's comic high point). *Cousin, Cousine* was a huge and unexpected hit in the United States, becoming the highest-grossing foreign film (except for Z) released here until that time.

COWARD OF THE COUNTY ☆☆½
1981, USA (TV)
Kenny Rogers, Frederic Lehne, Largo Woodruff, Mariclare Costello, Ana Alicia. Directed by Dick Lowry. 100 min.

Good news for Kenny Rogers fans, although non-fans will be blanded-out by his role as a preacher with a troubled relation. The plot, based on one of his hit tunes, concerns Rogers's nephew, a conscientious objector who is labeled a coward when he refuses to join up during World War II. The small-town atmosphere is well captured, adding nostalgic appeal to a pacifist story line about following the dictates of one's conscience.

THE COWBOY AND THE SENORITA ☆
1944, USA
Roy Rogers, Mary Lee, Dale Evans, Fuzzy Knight, the Sons of the Pioneers. Directed by Joseph Kane. 77 min.

Roy had greater moments in cinema history than this dim-witted yarn about buried treasure. As always, there's an angelic young woman and an unscrupulous older man. Fortunately, the guitar-slinging cowboy rights all wrongs before the end credits roll. A yawn.

THE COWBOYS ☆☆
1972, USA, PG
John Wayne, Roscoe Lee Browne, Bruce Dern, Colleen Dewhurst, Sarah Cunningham, Slim Pickens, Allyn Ann McLerie. Directed by Mark Rydell. 128 min.

A group of boys ranging in age from nine to fifteen learn to be men on a cattle drive, in a garbled Western lent more authority than it deserves by the granite presence of John Wayne. Just craggy enough to look like a monument without yet seeming like an old man, Wayne almost makes you believe the nonsensical poop he spouts about morality, manhood, and murder, all of which become the same thing in the inappropriately bloody climax. Director Mark Rydell doesn't make anything interesting out of the film's only fresh idea, which is using kids as cowboys; for the most part, he emphasizes the hoariest plot lines, right down to the black chuck-wagon cook who just glows with the folk wisdom of the ages.

THE CRACKER FACTORY ☆☆½
1979, USA (TV)
Natalie Wood, Perry King, Peter Haskell, Vivian Blaine, Juliet Mills, Marian Mercer. Directed by Burt Brinkerhoff. 100 min.

This film is an uneven but compassionate study of a neurotic woman following a downward path of destruction because of alcoholism and instability. Natalie Wood is quite moving as the suburban woman forced to come to terms with her mental problems in the "Cracker Factory," her nickname for the place she is sent to be cured. Cataloguing the details of someone's breakdown is not an easy task, and too often this film falls back on dramatic shorthand and clichés. Luckily, the finely tuned acting of the ensemble gives added refinement to the script.

CRACKERS ☆½
1984, USA, PG
Donald Sutherland, Jack Warden, Sean Penn, Wallace Shawn, Larry Riley, Trinidad Silva, Christine Baranski, Irwin Corey. Directed by Louis Malle. 92 min.

Something went wrong with this, and it's anyone's guess just what that might have been. The film has a fine, eccentric cast, a very good director, and a promising scriptwriter with one solid previous credit (Jeffrey Fiskin, *Cutter's Way*) who based the scenario on a very funny Italian comedy, *Big Deal on Madonna Street*. But none of it works, at least not in any way that seems to have been intended. As a mismatched gang of down-and-outs who decide to rob the local pawnshop, the cast displays no ability for ensemble work and is able to pull off only a few isolated solo moments apiece. Best of the lot is Christine Baranski as a feckless meter maid; all the others, even the usually reliable Donald Sutherland, seem to be floundering.

CRACKING UP ☆☆½
1983, USA, PG
Jerry Lewis, Herb Edelman, Bill Richmond, Milton Berle, Sammy Davis, Jr. Directed by Jerry Lewis. 90 min.

Jerry Lewis's overwhelming screen persona, his refusal to give up the gag, and his outrageous disregard for story line have gradually eroded his audience. Jerry has become more and more indulgent of his comic routines, and viewers will probably find this series of gags to be an unmatched set of overlarge rhinestones strung together in a gaudy necklace. Essentially, however, the film works; this is the story of a guy whose life is breaking into a million jagged pieces and, told from his point of view, it makes sense that nothing will hold to the center. Jerry's initial confrontation with his psychiatrist's plastic and Naugahyde office is a beautiful literalization of an insecure man's trip through life.

CRAIG'S WIFE ☆☆☆
1936, USA
Rosalind Russell, John Boles, Billie Burke, Jane Darwell, Dorothy Wilson, Alma Kruger, Thomas Mitchell. Directed by Dorothy Arzner. 75 min.

In 1950, Joan Crawford delighted a generation of camp followers with her performance as a domineering, compulsively neat, and materialistic housewife in *Harriet Craig*. That film was a remake of this one, and the original, with Rosalind Russell in Crawford's role, is a better but less entertaining movie. Dorothy Arzner, one of the very few women to work steadily as a director in early Hollywood, invests the driven central character with a degree of sympathetic interest not found in other, similar films.

THE CRANES ARE FLYING ☆☆☆☆
1957, USSR
Tatiana Samoilova, Alexei Batalov, Vasili Merkuriev. Directed by Mikhail Kalatozov. 94 min.

This realistic romantic drama about a woman who desperately awaits the return of her lover from the World War II battlefront transcends its genre to become a very moving study of the tragic effects of war on both soldiers and civilians. Mikhail Kalatozov directs spectacular tableaux of action and intimate emotional moments with equal skill and restraint, making *Cranes* all the more powerful for its steadfast refusal to wallow in sentimental excess. Tatiana Samoilova's gentle, masterful performance is the centerpiece of a top-notch production. The film's lyrical tone and penetrating insight into character marked the thaw of the rigid code of "Socialist Realism" and signaled the rebirth of Russian cinema.

THE CRASH OF FLIGHT 401

See *The Ghost of Flight 401*

CRATER LAKE MONSTER ☆
1977, USA, PG
Richard Cardella, Glenn Roberts, Mark Siegel, Bob Hyman. Directed by William R. Stromberg. 85 min.

A few minutes of decent stop-motion animation by David Allen, who created the monsters in *Flesh Gordon* and lots of commercials, isn't reason enough to sit through the rest of this cheap, terribly acted feature. The monster is a dinosaur that hatches from an egg at the bottom of Crater Lake after soaking up radiation from a meteor. In the heart-pounding finale, the critter does battle with—a snowplow!

THE CRAWLING EYE ☆☆½
1958, Great Britain
Forrest Tucker, Laurence Payne, Janet Munro, Jennifer Jayne, Derek Sydney. Directed by Quentin Lawrence. 85 min.

The producers and star of *The Cosmic Monster* bounce back with another feature derived from a BBC television show; this one is better than most, though, thanks mostly to a screenplay by Hammer Films' Jimmy Sangster. The titular terror doesn't so much crawl as float, encased in a cloud, from which it occasionally reaches forth with a creepy tentacle to decapitate some helpless earthling. Forrest Tucker, in his salad days before going on to fame and glory as Sgt. O'Rourke in "F-Troop," plays the stalwart American who saves the day.

THE CRAWLING HAND ☆½
1963, USA
Peter Breck, Kent Taylor, Rod Lauren, Sirry Steffen, Alan Hale, Jr., Allison Hayes. Directed by Herbert L. Strock. 89 min.

No, this isn't the movie containing the sequence, directed by Luis Buñuel, in which the disembodied hand crawls out of the fire and strangles Peter Lorre. (That was *The Beast with Five Fingers*.) This is a cheap B feature about a living hand—all that remains of an astronaut who died in an explosion—that strangles a few people and then takes over a medical student, obviously realizing that two hands (not to mention a head) are better than one. B horror fans will be heartened by the presence of Allison Hayes (*Attack of the 50 Foot Woman*) and director Herbert Strock (*I Was a Teenage Frankenstein*).

CRAWLSPACE ☆
1986, USA/Italy, R
Klaus Kinski, Talia Balsam, Barbara Whinnery, Carol Francis, Tane, Sally Brown. Directed by David Schmoeller. 78 min.

This grubby, unpleasant horror film concerns a murderous landlord (Klaus Kinski) molesting and mangling his tenants. Kinski's blank, sullen performance suggests that he's toiled in one too many low-budget horror films, and the rest of the no-name cast is completely forgettable. Gore fans will be disappointed in the timidity of the bloodletting, and those who crave serious scares should look elsewhere.

CRAZE ☆
1973, Great Britain, R
Jack Palance, Diana Dors, Julie Ege, Edith Evans, Hugh Griffith, Trevor Howard, Michael Jayston. Directed by Freddie Francis. 96 min.

An antiques dealer makes blood sacrifices to a wooden idol, convinced that he has discovered the path to wealth and prosperity in the modern world. Skilled director of photography Freddie Francis (*The Innocents*, *Dune*) applies his leaden directorial hand (*Dracula Has Risen from the Grave*, *Torture Garden*) to this British thriller starring the always-wonderful Jack Palance, who emotes with gravelly fervor.

THE CRAZIES ☆☆
1973, USA
Lane Carroll, W. G. McMillan, Harold Wayne Jones, Lloyd Hollar. Directed by George Romero. 103 min.

Although this film has its partisans, the amateurishness of the acting undercuts the tension much more than did the ragged acting in *Night of the Living Dead*. George Romero himself is an uneven talent who's only twice committed a consistently terrifying vision to celluloid, in *Night of the Living Dead* and *Martin*. Biological warfare breaks out unexpectedly in Pennsylvania when the locals are exposed to a germ plague and go crazy when the army arrives to make sure that the pestilence doesn't leave the town. There are some scary moments as the infected citizenry runs amok, but much of it plays like a rehash of his *Living Dead* films, with bio-crazies replacing zombies. Although the basic premise no longer seems that farfetched, the film is so overwrought that none of it seems remotely believable. (a.k.a.: *Code Name: Trixie*)

THE CRAZY FAMILY ☆☆☆½
1985, Japan
Katsuya Kobayashi, Mitsuko Baisho, Yoshiki Arizono, Yuki Kudo, Hitoshi Ueki. Directed by Sogo Ishii. 106 min.

Whether this film offers, even in parodic hyperbole, any valid assessments on the state of family relationships in modern Japan is unknown to us; what we can tell you, though, is that this is one grotesque and funny film. A middle-class Japanese family moves into their first house. The overprotective father, who is convinced that the rest of his family is mentally ill, works himself into a frenzy trying to "shelter" them and ends up as the most wacked-out of the bunch: he tries to induce them all to commit suicide one night when he can no longer stand it, initiating a nightlong spree in which each family member tries to kill all the others with power tools, cooking implements, and other items. Director Sogo Ishii comes to film from the world of rock videos, and this whole project has a speeded-up, garish, occasionally abrasive feel that fits the material perfectly—were it treated more realistically, it would be horrifying; as it is, it is detached and very weird.

CRAZY MAMA ☆☆
1975, USA, PG
Cloris Leachman, Ann Sothern, Linda Purl, Donny Most. Directed by Jonathan Demme. 82 min.

This early Jonathan Demme film (he also directed *Melvin and Howard* and *Stop Making Sense*) strikes a familiar chord as a watered-down *Bonnie and Clyde*. Three generations of women shoot their way across America in a sadistic unveiling of empty lives. Although not without some merit, the film is basically as empty as the lives it focuses on. A major problem stems from the corn-pone Southern dialogue, particularly when mouthed by the not-so-belle Sothern.

CREATION OF THE HUMANOIDS ☆
1962, USA
Don Megowan, Erica Elliott, Dudley Manlove. Directed by Wesley E. Barry. 75 min.

Andy Warhol once called this his favorite movie, presumably because it looks like a lot of his own early movies: it's filmed very statically on minimal sets. Set in the post–World War II world, it has survivors of the holocaust being served by intelligent but subservient androids who begin to rebel after a rogue scientist begins to inject them with human blood. Jack Pierce, who created the fabulously elaborate makeup jobs in all of the Universal horror films of the thirties and forties (including the Frankenstein monster and the Wolfman), came out of a fifteen-year retirement to work on this. He obviously forgot a lot in the meantime. One of the worst.

CREATOR ☆☆½
1985, USA, R
Peter O'Toole, Vincent Spano, Mariel Hemingway, Virginia Madsen, John Dehner, David Ogden Stiers. Directed by Ivan Passer. 107 min.

A terrific cast and a slew of lively and original ideas add up to depressingly little in Ivan Passer's comedy-turned-melodrama about an eccentric scientific genius and his young assistant, both of whom try to bring loved ones back from the dead. The film has much to say about the helpless lunacy of romantic attachment, and Passer and writer Jeremy Leven superbly render the alternately mellow and hypertense atmosphere of a Cal Tech–ish university. But all this and the splendid if familiar work of Peter O'Toole, Vincent Spano, and Virginia Madsen can't save a film that asks you not to respond but to "LAUGH," "CRY," or "THINK" at the flick of a switch. Many people resented the sudden mood changes in the much better *Terms of Endearment*; those at least had structural justification and emotional resonance. In *Creator* the laughs may be real but the tears are crocodile, and the ludicrous ending denies all of the intelligent thought and offhand excellence that has gone before.

CREATURE ☆½
1985, USA, R
Klaus Kinski, Stan Ivar, Wendy Schaal, Marie Laurin, Lyman Ward. Directed by William Malone. 100 min.

Stranded on an apparently barren planet, a group of space travelers find the wreck of the ship that housed an earlier German expedition. Hiding inside is an awful, slimy monster that immediately embarks on the slaughter of all the interlopers. The survivors of the first attack are greeted with further onslaughts at every turn and must also cope with their own failing equipment and internal differences, as well as the rather sinister presence of a sardonic German who has no satisfactory explanation for surviving the fate that befell his fellow crew members. *Creature* is deeply indebted to *Alien* for its basic plot structure, which it overlays with considerable gore and gratuitous sex. The result is not unamusing, but it is desperately predictable and unlikely to entertain any but the serious fans of this sort of picture. Some fairly gross special effects are a plus. (a.k.a.: *Titan Find*)

THE CREATURE FROM THE BLACK LAGOON ☆☆☆
1954, USA
Richard Carlson, Julia Adams, Richard Denning, Antonio Moreno, Whit Bissell, Nestor Paiva, Bernie Gozier, Henry Escalante. Directed by Jack Arnold. 79 min.

This fifties chiller is both prime and primal stuff. It's prime because its story of anthropological expedition that travels to the Amazon is a masterfully executed drama of hunters becoming the hunted, and because it's such a quintessential piece. From the dedicated scientist, to the pretty girl in a white bathing suit, to the prehistoric creature who seems smarter than the whole human crew—everything is snapped perfectly into place. It is primal because of the marvelous secondary story of a woman who, isolated in a jungle with a gang of men, becomes the object of uncontrollable desires. The lagoon itself is rendered as a beautifully spooky, silent place, and the monster, by Bud West and Jack Keven, became an instant fixture in American pop culture.

CREATURE FROM BLACK LAKE ☆
1976, USA
Dub Taylor, Jack Elam, Dennis Fimple, John David Carson. Directed by Joy Houck, Jr. 97 min.

In this low-budget, low-mentality thriller, two young city slickers venture foolishly into an eerie-looking swamp and run smack dab into Big Foot, that popular favorite of fans of the *National Enquirer*. Have you ever seen Big Foot or spotted a UFO? Then this movie is for you. Those viewers with a less-personal interest in the subject matter may end up feeling that the monster just needs a few sessions at a good electrolysist and that the filmmakers need a few years at the nearest film school.

THE CREATURE FROM THE HAUNTED SEA ☆☆
1960, USA
Antony Carbone, Betsy Jones-Moreland, Edward Wain, Edmundo Rivera Álvarez, Robert Beam. Directed by Roger Corman. 60 min.

This is one of those films that you should give thanks to the great god VCR for having resurrected from the dead. If you've seen either Roger Corman's *Little Shop of Horrors* or *A Bucket of Blood* (and if you've seen them, and liked them), then you must get this, because it sort of forms a trilogy with the other two, and it's been all but impossible to see for years. The story goes that Corman was in Puerto Rico making two quickie movies with the same cast and production crew. When he was done he figured, well, why not stay another week, seeing as all the necessary people are here, and make another one? So he called Charles Griffith, author of *Little Shop* and *Bucket*, and asked if he could write another comedy-horror film that afternoon. This is the result. A gangster agrees to use his boat to transport a group of political refugees off a revolution-torn island. When he discovers that they've taken the national treasury with them, he decides to kill them off, blame the deaths on the local sea monster, and keep the loot himself. Of course, there turns out to be a *real* sea monster (not that the thirty-nine-cent costume will fool you for a minute) who claims his revenge; the final shot in the film is the beastie picking his teeth after finishing off the crew. Robert Beam, who plays one of the crew members, was promoted to actor from boom man when Corman, who was supposed to play the role himself, decided that it was too tough.

THE CREATURE WASN'T NICE

See *Spaceship*

CREEPERS ☆☆
1985, Italy/USA, R
Jennifer Connolly, Daria Nicolodi, Donald Pleasence, Eleanora Giorgi. Directed by Dario Argento. 83 min.

This visceral, offbeat horror film was directed by genre demigod Dario Argento, whose prior efforts have won cult audiences and a degree of acclaim. Set in and around a European boarding school, where an unseen maniac is dismantling the student body, the film is only a journeyman effort until the action moves into the countryside, where an overnight trip for our heroine becomes a descent into hell. Buffs will enjoy the monkeys, maggots, and midgets in a climax that's better than the buildup.

THE CREEPING FLESH
1972, Great Britain ☆
Peter Cushing, Christopher Lee. Directed by Freddie Francis. 89 min.

One wonders whether Christopher Lee and Peter Cushing could tell one of these Hammer films apart from the other. Certainly, only the die-hard fans bothered to seek out this one. Actually, its tale is a bit confused—something about the transference of evil—but the visuals are rather good, courtesy of Freddie Francis's direction. The late Hammer sense of complete boredom and vague disgust is absent from this one, courtesy perhaps of Cushing and Lee, who perform their adversarial roles with the sense of two old friends having a lark.

THE CREEPING TERROR
1964, USA ☆
Vic Savage, Shannon O'Neill, William Thourlby, Robin James. Directed by Argyle Nelson, Jr. 81 min.

Grab this if you're in the mood for a good laugh. Two priapic monsters, obviously made out of used vacuum cleaner hoses, carpet remnants, and whatever else was laying around the producer's house, emerge from a spaceship and attack Lake Tahoe. No doubt foreshadowing the popular trend of late seventies slasher movies, they attack teenagers at a drive-in movie and a wild party. This looks like it was never finished; there's hardly any dialogue, just a narrator to tell us what's going on. The star is actually the director under a different name, and the screenwriter went on to write *The Incredibly Strange Creatures Who Stopped Living and Became Crazy Mixed-up Zombies*.

CREEPSHOW
1982, USA, R ☆☆½
Viveca Lindfors, Carrie Nye, Stephen King, E. G. Marshall, Hal Holbrook, Fritz Weaver. Directed by George A. Romero. 120 min.

Just-desserts stories in a lurid comic-book framework: a murdered man returns from the grave to punish his grasping relatives; a dim-witted farmer is consumed by weeds from space; a henpecked professor feeds his shrewish wife to a monster in a crate; a cuckolded husband murders his wife and her lover; a fastidious sadist is killed by swarming cockroaches; a small boy uses a mail-order voodoo doll to deal with his overbearing stepfather. Tame but flashy tribute to E. C. comics, with an original screenplay by Stephen King.

THE CRICKET
1982, Italy ☆☆☆
Anthony Franciosa, Virna Lisi, Clio Goldsmith, Renato Salvatori, Barbara de Rossi, Mario Marangana. Directed by Alberto Lattuada. 130 min.

What begins as a knockout comedy about two women on the road becomes a scathing melodrama ending in violence and death. A young, free-spirited woman attaches herself to an aging singer-cum-prostitute and learns a little about friendship and life. When the older woman marries a café owner, all three settle down into a life of work and bourgeois security. Of course, sexual jealousy, that bane of the middle class, rears its pretty head in the form of the woman's teenage daughter, who comes to the café and sets her sights on her stepfather. Director Alberto Lattuada served his apprenticeship with the neorealists, and his stylistic consistency and gritty feel for the slightly tattered characters and their tired truck-stop prevent the film from falling prey to either an inconsistent tone or meandering sloppiness. His shading toward the vagabond life and the excess of the ending reveal, too, an interesting sympathy for the underdog and a mistrust of economic success. Virna Lisi and Clio Goldsmith are outstanding, and the young Goldsmith, in her first role, shows a sultry, sullen charm that bodes well for her future. Anthony Franciosa is a notch above his usual television woodenness. Embassy Home Entertainment is to be commended for showcasing this underrecognized Italian director; perhaps they can be forgiven for packaging this as a sex drama and supplying incorrect information as to running time and date. Subtitled. (a.k.a.: *La Cicala* and *The Cicada*)

CRIES AND WHISPERS
1972, Sweden, R ☆☆☆☆
Harriet Andersson, Kari Sylwan, Ingrid Thulin, Liv Ullmann. Directed by Ingmar Bergman. 94 min.

A mature masterpiece from a great director, this film eschews the straightforward movement of narrative and works by means of a continually shifting series of images clustered around a central theme. Ingmar Bergman's belief that the soul can be imagined as a damp red membrane becomes incarnated in this film, awash with a blood-red decor, fade-outs to complete red separating the scenes, bleeding from self-inflicted wounds, and the central figure's slow death from cancer of the uterus. The story revolves around a trip home by two married sisters to the deathbed of their unmarried sibling. Familiar Bergman themes of individual isolation and the guilt over failed communication are here amplified by the isolated closure of the country manor, the unsparing revelation of the relations of sisters, and the grim end game of a deathwatch. Each image becomes amplified, diminished, and changed by every other image; the devastating fantasy of the servant woman (Kari Sylwan) cradling the dying, bereft Agnes (Harriet Andersson) cuts through the earlier scenes of alienation between the sisters, giving the film a wrenching, emotional climax. A beautiful, pensive work of art located somewhere between the expressionist scream of Edvard Munch and the repressed psychological explosions of August Strindberg.

CRIME AND PASSION
1976, USA/West Germany, R ½☆
Omar Sharif, Karen Black, Joseph Bottoms, Bernhard Wicki, Heinz Ehrenfreund. Directed by Ivan Passer. 92 min.

Jesse Lasky, Jr., and Pat Silver adapted this James Hadley Chase novel about the lusts of a financial consultant (Omar Sharif); there was also an Alan Trustman–David M. Wolf version hammered into shape by director Ivan Passer and William Richert. Somehow these scripts were glued together. And that's only the beginning of the inanity. Even if it's the last movie in the world, read a book—how about something by Dostoevsky!

CRIME SCHOOL
1938, USA ☆☆
Humphrey Bogart, the Dead End Kids (Billy Halop, Bobby Jordan, Gabe Dell, Huntz Hall, Leo Gorcey, Bernard Punsley), Gale Page, Milburn Stone. Directed by Lewis Seiler. 90 min.

This film is an unofficial continuation of the *Dead End Kids–Angels with Dirty Faces* genre of the thirties, here with the entire bunch of Dead End Kids in a state reformatory. The school is just as tough as the kids, and procedure calls for dealing with rebelliousness with lashings until new warden Humphrey Bogart decides to adopt more constructive measures. In return, the kids come around to his side and save him from a political plot to discredit him. From the time when the Dead End Kids still *were* kids.

CRIMES OF PASSION
(two versions)
1984, USA ☆☆☆
Kathleen Turner, Anthony Perkins, John Laughlin, Annie Potts. Directed by Ken Russell. 101 min. (R-rated theatrical version); 105 min. (unrated version).

Kathleen Turner is astonishing as a repressed fashion designer who dons a platinum-blond wig each night to become China Blue, the best, busiest hooker in town. It's a completely unexpected, adventurous performance from a major actress, and the best reason to see *Crimes of Passion*, a lurid but fascinating drama about sexual hang-ups and deviants. In addition to China, there's a knife-wielding street reverend gone bonkers and a dissatisfied suburban jock and his frigid wife. The plot is a mess, but the dialogue is hilariously

raunchy. Unlike Paul Schrader's *Hardcore*, this film makes no bones about its lewd appreciation of the scum it features.
NOTE: *Crimes of Passion* is about sex, and the acts it depicts, including the sodomization of a cop with his own nightstick, are actually integral to the plot. If this sort of thing offends you, stay away from the film altogether. If it doesn't, see the unrated version, which is the version favored by the director and the one that makes more sense.

CRIMES OF THE HEART ☆☆
1986, USA, PG-13
Diane Keaton, Jessica Lange, Sissy Spacek, Sam Shepard, Tess Harper, David Carpenter, Hurd Hatfield, Beeson Carroll. Directed by Bruce Berseford. 105 min.

This flaccid all-star adaptation of Beth Henley's comic play works so hard at being a relaxed ensemble piece that you can practically see the sweat. Henley's work is a wobbly, occasionally amusing Southern Gothic farce, a sort of chicken-fried *Three Sisters* that can't begin to support the tidal wave of acting talent that it so conspicuously displays. Of the three stars, Sissy Spacek fares the best with her amiably gaminelike recreation of Babe, the sister who says she shot her no-good husband "because I didn't like his stinking looks." Jessica Lange, however, seems distracted and remote, and Diane Keaton never gets beyond her ill-conceived Southern accent. While none of the actresses can be accused of scenery-chewing or scene-hogging, there's a sort of reverse vanity to their calculated underplaying that's more detrimental than hamminess; they're so busy passing the ball to each other that none really gets a chance to shine. Not without its moments, but slow and painfully heavy-handed.

CRIMEWAVE ☆☆½
1985, USA, PG
Louise Lasser, Paul Smith, Brion James, Edward R. Pressman, Sheree J. Wilson, Bruce Campbell. Directed by Sam Raimi. 83 min.

A meek young man meets the girl of his dreams, only to find their already less-than-perfect date turned into a nightmare by two psychopathic exterminators, who, as their Yellow Pages ad ominously asserts, kill *all sizes*. *Crimewave* is the second film by Sam Raimi, whose *The Evil Dead* was widely praised by genre fans who responded to its combination of gross-out theatrics and sophisticated in-jokes; his cowriters for this film are Joel and Ethan Coen (*Blood Simple*). Though sometimes clever, *Crimewave*'s viciousness is undercut by a tendency to be silly, and the constant mockery of *film noir* conventions is just a little smug. Among its major assets are some glorious neon-colored lighting and outrageously amplified sound effects. Filmed under the title *The XYZ Murders*. (a.k.a.: *Broken Hearts and Noses*)

THE CRIMINAL CODE ☆☆☆
1931, USA
Walter Huston, Phillips Holmes, Constance Cummings, Boris Karloff, Mary Doran. Directed by Howard Hawks. 96 min.

Presumably, the rerelease of *Scarface* led to interest in and the subsequent release to video of this long-unseen early Howard Hawks feature. Adapted from a popular Broadway melodrama of the time, the film version is still a bit too stage-bound, but Hawks does a good job of keeping things moving, especially in comparison with the typical filmed plays of the time. Prison warden Walter Huston's daughter falls in love with an unjustly convicted young man sent to prison by Huston when he was a district attorney. The boy is under pressure both from prison officials and his fellow inmates because he knows who committed a murder in the big house. Boris Karloff is good in a pre-*Frankenstein* part. The ending was "happified" for the movies, but it doesn't really change the content.

CRIMINAL COURT ☆☆☆
1946, USA
Tom Conway, Martha O'Driscoll, June Clayworth, Robert Armstrong. Directed by Robert Wise. 63 min.

This snappy courtroom melodrama has enough twists to fill up a feature twice its length. Brash lawyer Tom Conway is running for the office of district attorney, boosted by public recognition for his flashy courtroom tactics. When he accidentally kills a racketeer who wants to keep him out of office, his fiancée is blamed for the murder and he has to persuade a jury that he is the guilty party!

THE CRIMSON PIRATE ☆☆☆
1952, USA
Burt Lancaster, Nick Cravat, Eva Bartok, Torin Thatcher, Christopher Lee. Directed by Robert Siodmak. 104 min.

This film is a rarity that delivers the thrill of a rough-and-tumble action picture along with the buoyant energy that derives from satirizing the action genre. Lancaster's wall-to-wall smile has never flashed as brilliantly as it does here in this athletic yarn about a fearless buccaneer who, on occasion, is not above fighting for principles instead of booty. The sinewy star puts his early off-screen career as a circus acrobat to good use as he swaggers with braggadocio, swordfights with bravado, and manages at all times to communicate the good time he's experiencing in the flashy title role. A delight for the entire family.

CRISIS AT CENTRAL HIGH ☆☆☆½
1981, USA (TV)
Joanne Woodward, Charles Durning, Henderson Forsythe, Calvin Levles. Directed by Lamont Johnson. 124 min.

The uproar surrounding the 1957 integration of Central High in Little Rock, Arkansas, is the subject of this well-made, poignant TV docudrama, which focuses on the wrenching emotions felt by one teacher and two students. Veteran director Lamont Johnson provides convincing period detail and atmosphere. As the embattled instructor, Joanne Woodward is, as always, quietly excellent. The "crisis" is resolved with too much tidiness and optimism, but that's almost endemic to this TV genre.

CRITICAL CONDITION ☆½
1987, USA, R
Richard Pryor, Rachel Ticotin, Ruben Blades, Joe Dallesandro, Sylvia Miles, Bob Dishy, Joe Mantegna, Bob Saget, Randall (Tex) Cobb, Garrett Morris. Directed by Michael Apted. 90 min.

This weak, sloppy comic vehicle for Richard Pryor casts him as a mental patient masquerading as a doctor in a city hospital that's stuck in an overnight blackout. No comic actor could overcome the feeble, shopworn script, but Pryor is particularly poor here—it's almost impossible to associate his halfhearted clowning and pained expression with the fiery brilliance of his concert films. Some funny moments from the supporting players, but a saddening misuse of Pryor's talent.

CRITICAL LIST

See *Terminal Choice*

CRITTERS ☆☆
1986, USA, PG-13
Dee Wallace Stone, M. Emmet Walsh, Billy Green Bush, Scott Grimes, Nadine Van Der Velde, Don Opper. Directed by Stephen Herek. 86 min.

This film is a quickie *Gremlins* rip-off about a bunch of small, furry, cannibalistic aliens who terrorize a farm family. Director Herek mixes up Spielbergian family fare, irreverent humor, and some fairly gruesome horror to scattershot effect. With their pointy teeth forever going for toes and fingers, and their steel, porcupinelike quills lodging in necks and open wounds, the nasty little furballs provide a few nifty moments. Most of the time, though, the humor and horror just cancel each other out.

CROCODILE
1979, Thailand/Korea, R ☆
Nat Puvanai, Tany Tim. Directed by Sompote Sands. 95 min.

Exploitation producer Herman Cohen bought this *Jaws* rip-off for U.S. distribution in the wake of the success of *Alligator*. Although the monster is a giant crocodile (increased in size by that favorite fifties growth formula, a nuclear explosion), the plot is literally straight out of *Jaws*, with the beastie eating the locals until a trio including a grizzled old sea captain go after it. No redeemable qualities.

"CROCODILE" DUNDEE
1986, Australia, PG-13 ☆☆
Paul Hogan, Linda Koslowski, John Meillon, Mark Blum, Michael Lombard, David Gulpilil. Directed by Peter Faiman. 94 min.

"Visit beautiful Australia!" seems to be the message of this witless picaresque adventure, a record-breaker Down Under (where it outgrossed *E.T.*) and a surprise blockbuster here. Professional Australian Paul Hogan (a TV pitchman and tourism-board personality) stars as adventurer Mick "Crocodile" Dundee, whose encounter with a New York reporter (Linda Koslowski) leads to his spending a week in a ridiculously contrived Manhattan. Hogan, like Maurice Chevalier, is a self-appointed national representative who ingratiates himself by playing an unctuous cartoon version of his countrymen. As the supposedly savvy female who discovers that she needs a real man to take care of her, Koslowski is continually made the butt of the joke, but Hogan (whose naïveté about the city is meant to be charming) is man enough to handle whatever perils are thrown at him. The film is predictable and dull, with Russell Boyd's airy outback cinematography as a saving grace. Note: the quotation marks in the title were added by the American distributor to improve the film's box-office chances. Studios work in mysterious ways . . .

THE CROSS AND THE SWITCHBLADE
1970, USA ☆½
Pat Boone, Erik Estrada, Jackie Giroux. Directed by Don Murray. 106 min.

Rural preacher Pat Boone is transplanted to a big-city ghetto area, where he converts members of street gangs to The True Way. Although the plot is based on a true story, there's no way that squeaky-clean Boone can convince you he'd ever last five minutes in this neighborhood. The film strives for inspiration at the expense of realism. The degree to which this will make you feel good is the degree to which you're willing to be blind to the problems of poverty. Featuring a pre-"CHiPs" Erik Estrada as one of the gang leaders.

CROSS COUNTRY
1983, Canada, R ☆½
Richard Beymer, Nina Axelrod, Michael Ironside, Brent Carver, Michael Kane. Directed by Paul Lynch. 95 min.

At the same time that a young woman is brutally murdered (in graphic detail, of course), her neurotic boyfriend comes down with a case of wanderlust and is tracked down by an overzealous cop who wants to convict him. While driving around aimlessly, our hero picks up two hitchhikers who are inordinately fond of sexual fun-and-games, leading the audience to two conclusions: (1) don't pick up hitchhikers unless you're in the mood to stop at a lot of motels, and (2) don't watch sleazy slasher movies unless you want to be irritated and bored.

CROSS CREEK
1983, USA, PG ☆☆½
Mary Steenburgen, Rip Torn, Peter Coyote, Alfre Woodard, Dana Hill, Malcolm McDowell. Directed by Martin Ritt. 120 min.

This film is a sentimentalized biography of Marjorie Kinnan Rawlings, the writer who abandoned her native North to record the lives of white trash in the swamps of Florida and who eventually wrote *The Yearling*. As the hillbilly patriarch Marsh Turner, Rip Torn whoops up a storm of compassion, mixing gentility and barbarism as offhandedly as he pours moonshine into his coffee. You almost wish the story were focused on him instead of on Mary Steenburgen's halting, demure Rawlings. Alfre Woodard won an Oscar nomination as the housekeeper. Screenplay by Dalene Young.

CROSSED SWORDS
1978, USA ☆☆½
Mark Lester, Charlton Heston, Oliver Reed, Raquel Welch, George C. Scott, Rex Harrison. Directed by Richard Fleischer. 113 min.

This *Sword*'s edge is a bit blunted, but fans of swashbucklers, especially streamlined modern ones like Richard Lester's *The Three Musketeers*, will be entertained by the lavish production trappings, the exceptional supporting cast, and the ample swordsmanship. The film could have used a consistently tongue-in-cheek tone to help audiences maintain interest in this familiar tale, and this retread of Twain's *Prince and the Pauper* also suffers from Mark Lester having outgrown his boyish charm in the major role. Still, it's produced on a grand scale, and if the 1937 version isn't on TV, this costume drama will suffice.

CROSSFIRE
1947, USA ☆☆☆
Robert Young, Robert Ryan, Robert Mitchum, Gloria Grahame, Paul Kelly, Sam Levene, Steve Brodie. Directed by Edward Dmytryk. 86 min.

Crossfire was overlooked in 1947 because the big social conscience picture condemning anti-Semitism that year was *Gentleman's Agreement*. Today *Crossfire*'s reputation stands higher, but only by default. It's not that good, but it is less pat and slack than the Elia Kazan film. The mystery plot details how three soldiers are suspected of killing a Jew. Interestingly, the Richard Brooks novel on which John Paxton's screenplay is based involved the killing of a homosexual. The film has a *noir*ish look that complements the grim subject matter, and Robert Ryan is properly chilling as a psychopathic soldier. Unfortunately, Robert Mitchum as another soldier seems thrown in for star value, and Robert Young, as a detective, gives a climactic speech about racial tolerance that is patronizing and laughable.

CROSS OF IRON
1977, USA/Great Britain/West Germany, R ☆☆☆
James Mason, James Coburn, Maximilian Schell, David Warner. Directed by Sam Peckinpah. 133 min.

In this bleak, rat-eyed look at the stagnating battle on the Russian front, James Coburn plays a weary, canny sergeant supplying the valor for his dug-in German unit. The film uses Sam Peckinpah's patented graceful violence for the battle scenes and continues the director's exploration into the group dynamics of loyalty and heroics. The German soldiers are reminiscent of the tired Western professionals in *The Wild Bunch*, and David Warner is especially cynical as a dyspeptic scarecrow aide-de-camp. Beautifully photographed in muted tones by John Coquillon.

CROSSOVER DREAMS
1985, USA ☆☆☆
Ruben Blades, Shawn Elliot, Tom Signorelli, Elizabeth Pena. Directed by Leon Ichaso. 86 min.

A simple moralistic tale is rescued from banality by real-life salsa star Ruben Blades: he's witty, bitingly intelligent, wry—a true artist. Cowriter and star, Blades plays a sharp Spanish Harlem inmate who gets a chance for fame in the white musical world; he grabs for it, turning his back on his old neighborhood, his girl (Elizabeth Pena), and his family. When the record ends up in cutout bins, he's forced to swallow some pride and return to the world he rejected. By turns callous and admirable, Blades provides an intriguingly sexy core. The rest of the cast is solid (especially the comic Pena), and the whole film is well-orchestrated. With songs by Blades.

CROSSROADS
☆½
1986, USA, R
Ralph Macchio, Jami Gertz, Joe Seneca, Robert Judd, Joe Morton. Directed by Walter Hill. 100 min.

This uneven, dishwatery drama concerns a neophyte white-bread musician (Ralph Macchio) with delusions of becoming a real bluesman. After helping a cutely crotchety old black musician escape from a nursing home, the wimpy teen guitarist receives instruction in enough living and loving to qualify him as a soul musician. Despite the heapings of hard-driving blues music on the soundtrack, the film is convictionless and mopey throughout. The out-of-left-field climax, in which Macchio must play the blues to save his old pal's soul, turns the film into "The Karate Kid Meets Faust." Real blues aficionados will, of course, be outraged at the spectacle of cheering black fans rooting for white rip-off artists and will undoubtedly miss authentic blues music (though the Ry Cooder score is passable). Joe Seneca alone, of all the cast, is first-rate.

CROWDED PARADISE
☆☆½
1956, USA
Hume Cronyn, Nancy Kelly, Frank Silvera, Enid Rudd. Directed by Fred Pressburger. 94 min.

This seldom-seen feature is an interesting antiracism piece, photographed in superb semidocumentary style by legendary Russian cameraman Boris Kaufman, who had won an Academy Award for his similar work on *On the Waterfront*. Set on New York City's Upper East Side, in a Puerto Rican slum, the over-melodramatic story follows a newly immigrated young man who wants to get work in New York so he can marry his sweetheart. Complications arise in the person of the building superintendent, who takes out his personal frustrations on his tenants. Not a great success, but worth a look.

CRUCIBLE OF HORROR
☆☆½
1971, Great Britain, PG
Michael Gough, Yvonne Mitchell, Sharon Gurney, Simon Gough. Directed by Viktors Ritelis. 91 min.

This surprisingly chilling British murder movie is not as lurid as its title would imply. Michael Gough plays the sadistic head of a family. One day, after a particularly grueling breakfast, his family decides they can no longer tolerate him. They set about to kill him; but then, we all know that such crimes never go unpunished, right? Reminiscent of *Diabolique* in its tone, this sags a bit toward the end, but is worth checking out if you're in the mood for a good old-fashioned shocker. (Just be careful you don't get *Crucible of Terror*, below, instead.) (a.k.a.: *Velvet House*)

CRUCIBLE OF TERROR
☆
1971, Britain, R
Mike Raven, Mary Maude, James Bolam, Ronald Lacey, Betty Alberge. Directed by Ted Hooker. 90 min.

A mad sculptor gets the brilliant idea of covering dead bodies in bronze and then passing them off as statues. Of course, he has to get the dead bodies from somewhere . . . Prior to the advent of the slasher film, this had to be the single most popular plot device in horror movies, from 1933's *Mystery in the Wax Museum*, to *House of Wax*, to *Color Me Blood Red*, to *Bucket of Blood*, etc., etc., any one of which has far more to offer than this. (Did we mention *Nightmare in Wax*? Or . . .)

THE CRUEL SEA
☆☆☆
1953, Great Britain
Jack Hawkins, Donald Sinden, John Stratton, Denholm Elliott, Stanley Baker, John Warner, Bruce Seton, Virginia McKenna, Alec McCowan, Moira Lister. Directed by Charles Frend. 120 min.

"The heroes are the men. The heroines are the ships. The villain is the cruel sea." So says the narrator. Ealing Studios, traditionally a maker of light farces, did an about-face with this World War II drama based on a novel by Nicholas Monsarrat. A British ship sets out with a crew that includes only one experienced officer—the captain—and a load of raw recruits from civilian life who rushed to join up and serve their country when the war began. They are forced to deal with a storm, enemy activity, and a final disaster at sea. The film is overlong, but on the whole this is a better-than-average naval adventure for World War II buffs.

CRUISE INTO TERROR
☆
1978, USA (TV)
Dirk Benedict, Frank Converse, John Forsythe, Lynda Day George, Ray Milland, Christopher George. Directed by Bruce Kessler. 100 min.

There are episodes of "The Love Boat" that offer more seagoing thrills than this un-terrifying thriller. The preposterous script features an ancient sarcophagus on board, along with some nefarious passengers out to wreak havoc. Playing the would-be victims, who seem to have drifted in from an Irwin Allen disaster picture, are a cast of TV veterans who seem more afraid of the dialogue they have to deliver than of any supernatural terrors concocted by the scriptwriter.

CRUISING
☆
1980, USA, R
Al Pacino, Paul Sorvino, Karen Allen, Don Scardino, Joe Spinell, Sonny Grosso. Directed by William Friedkin. 106 min.

William Friedkin didn't invent homosexuality or sadomasochism or leather bars, but he certainly invented the grotesque versions of them that appear in this film, a murder mystery set among Manhattan's S&M crowd. His fiendish creations might seem droll if they didn't float by us in the gloomiest colors imaginable, and if they weren't accompanied by music (created by Jack Nitzsche) that sounds like the creakings of the medieval rack. In *Cruising*, monsters have overrun New York, and if you hang around long enough, you begin to turn into one. It's *Invasion of the Body Snatchers* in drag. The body being snatched here belongs to Al Pacino, who portrays a heterosexual rookie cop sent undercover into the gay netherworld to ferret out a killer. When Pacino seems to be turning both gay and violent at the same time, is Friedkin suggesting that the homosexual milieu breeds murders? Probably, although the film has been so shoddily slapped together that it's hard to tell what (if anything) was intended.

A CRY FOR LOVE
☆☆☆½
1980, USA (TV)
Susan Blakely, Powers Boothe, Charles Siebert, Herb Edelman, Edie Adams, Fern Fitzgerald, Lainie Kazan, Gene Barry. Directed by Paul Wendkos. 100 min.

This searing drama about two lost souls clinging to each other as their lives fall apart is based on Jill Schary Robinson's autobiographical *Bed/Time/Story*. The film is a devastating account of a pill-popping divorcée and an alcoholic who try desperately to overcome the weaknesses in their characters that led to their addictions, but keep backsliding into self-destructive behavior. It's not just another judgmental look at the outwardly successful and inwardly damaged well-to-do; it's an honest and painfully frank examination of human failure. Susan Blakely gives her best performance ever, and Powers Boothe is extraordinary.

CRY OF THE INNOCENT
☆☆
1980, USA (TV)
Rod Taylor, Joanna Pettet, Nigel Davenport, Cyril Cusack, Walter Gottell, Jim Norton. Directed by Michael O'Herlihy. 105 min.

Frederick Forsyth wrote the original story for this better-than-average TV movie. Ex–Green Beret Rod Taylor, now an insurance executive (now *there's* a frightening idea!), sets out after those responsible when he discovers that the plane crash that killed his family was no accident. Vigilante fans of the *Commando* school will note that, being a made-for-television movie, this is pretty tame, though the Irish scenery helps.

CRYPT OF THE LIVING DEAD ☆½
1972, USA
Andrew Prince, Mark Damon, Patty Sheppard. Directed by Ray Danton. 93 min.

An archaeologist working on a small Greek island uncovers the grave of a vampire queen, and his son must help return her to it before she decimates the entire community. Dull and predictable. Ray Danton also directed the far more interesting *The Deathmaster*. (a.k.a.: *Hannah—Queen of the Vampires*)

CUBA ☆☆½
1979, USA, R
Sean Connery, Brooke Adams, Jack Weston, Hector Elizondo, Martin Balsam, Chris Sarandon. Directed by Richard Lester. 122 min.

Though less Eurocentric than one might expect from someone like Richard Lester, this political melodrama is also a lot less exciting. Sean Connery plays a British businessman who travels to Cuba, only to get caught up in the fall of the Batista regime. He falls for a former love, an Eva Peron–type played by Brooke Adams. The cast is a likable ensemble (playing unlikable characters), the re-creation of late fifties Cuba is impressively authentic, and the politics are ambiguous without being offensively partisan. It's too bad, then, that the drama spurts and sputters all over the place without ever being compelling or suspenseful.

CUBA CROSSING

See *Kill Castro*

CUJO ☆☆
1983, USA, R
Dee Wallace, Daniel Hugh-Kelly, Danny Pintauro, Christopher Stone. Directed by Lewis Teague. 94 min.

A woman and her small son find themselves trapped in a crippled car by a rabid St. Bernard in this claustrophobic adaptation of a novel by Stephen King. The film is essentially a tale of domestic discontent whose *monstrum ex machina* does little more than further stir up some very muddy waters. Although nicely produced, it is more than a little dull. From the director of the delightful *Alligator* and the so-so *Cat's Eye*.

THE CULPEPPER CATTLE CO. ☆☆½
1972, USA, PG
Gary Grimes, Billy "Green" Bush, Luke Askew, Bo Hopkins, Geoffrey Lewis, Wayne Sutherlin, Charlie Martin Smith, Hal Needham, Royal Dano, Gregory Sierra. Directed by Dick Richards. 92 min.

When the Western made a brief comeback in the late sixties, it was in two forms: the revisionist, grubbier efforts best exemplified by Sergio Leone and Sam Peckinpah, and the Western-as-metaphor, usually for "growth," either of an individual or of the United States as a whole. This film takes a bit of both approaches, and thus never really finds an audience of its own. A teenager (Gary Grimes, who played a similar coming-of-age part in *Summer of '42*) joins a cattle drive as a cook's helper and discovers some bitter truths about life. Many of the images, though unpleasant, are remarkable, and some of it is violent in a realistic and unembellished way. The film appeals mostly to serious fans of the Western. The stunt coordinator was Hal Needham, who went on to become an action director himself in the late seventies.

CURSE OF THE BLACK WIDOW ☆½
1977, USA (TV)
Tony Franciosa, Donna Mills, Patty Duke Astin, June Lockhart, June Allyson, Max Gail, Jeff Corey, Vic Morrow, Sid Caesar, Roz Kelly. Directed by Dan Curtis. 100 min.

This kind of all-star whodunit was done with more aplomb on the old series "Burke's Law." The stellar cast must deal with the deadliness of the script as well as imminent death from a killer fond of bundling up victims in a spider web. Given the staleness of the acting (by the likes of June Allyson and Roz Kelly in particular), perhaps the killer should have wrapped the cast in Saran Wrap. Certainly this moldy script should have been kept under wraps and not filmed.

THE CURSE OF THE CAT PEOPLE ☆☆½
1944, USA
Kent Smith, Simone Simon, Jane Randolph, Julia Dean, Ann Carter. Directed by Robert Wise, Gunther von Fritsch. 70 min.

After coediting *Citizen Kane*, Robert Wise (*West Side Story*, *The Sound of Music*) got his break as a director by finishing this film started by Gunther von Fritsch. The results were genuinely unexpected. Unlike producer Val Lewton's original *Cat People*, the film was not horror but rather a meditation on childhood fantasy and wish fulfillment. The tenuous connection to the Jacques Tourneur film was in casting "cat person" Simone Simon as the apparition of her previous character who comforts the young daughter of her mortal ex-lover (Kent Smith). The intention to do something different is apparent, and the film does have a likeable, offbeat charm. Finally, though, Wise and company are hampered by poor acting and some compromised ideas. It remains a minor curiosity piece.

THE CURSE OF THE CRYING WOMAN ☆
1961, Mexico
Rosita Arenas, Abel Salazar, Rita Macedo, Carlos Lopez Moctezuma. Directed by Rafael Baledon. 74 min.

This is one of the duller Mexican horror films, all of which look like the worst low-budget Poverty Row productions of the forties. (You expect to see Bela Lugosi or George Zucco pop up at any moment.) A young woman and her husband visit her ancestral home where, unbeknownst to them, a centuries-old witch plots to take over her body. There is so much atmosphere, you could cut it with a knife—and you'll probably be tempted to. Regarded as a camp classic.

CURSE OF THE DEMON ☆☆☆½
1957, Great Britain
Dana Andrews, Peggy Cummins, Niall MacGinniss, Maurice Denham, Athene Seyler. Directed by Jacques Tourneur. 80 min.

This beautifully crafted, extremely effective horror film is one of the best in director Jacques Tourneur's canon of moody thrillers (he also directed the original *Cat People* and *I Walked with A Zombie*). Dana Andrews plays a psychologist who travels to England to investigate reports of a "black magic" phenomenon; the monsters and brutality are left offscreen and the story is all the more chilling for its restraint. A genre gem from a director all too frequently overlooked.

THE CURSE OF FRANKENSTEIN ☆☆☆
1957, Great Britain
Peter Cushing, Christopher Lee, Hazel Court, Robert Urquhart. Directed by Terence Fisher. 83 min.

Baron Victor Frankenstein pursues his unholy studies in his isolated ancestral mansion. He creates a creature that is less successful than he had hoped, but he is undaunted to the tune of five sequels, beginning with *The Revenge of Frankenstein*. This is English Hammer Films's first foray into lush gothic horror, quickly followed by *Horror of Dracula*; also the first pairing of stars Peter Cushing and Christopher Lee. It is colorful, exciting, and stylish. Lee hasn't too much to do as the monster, and his makeup, especially created *not* to resemble the Boris Karloff monster, is unmemorable, but Cushing is great fun as the single-minded Dr. Frankenstein.

THE CURSE OF KING TUT'S TOMB ☆½
1980, USA (TV)
Eva Marie Saint, Robin Ellis, Raymond Burr, Harry Andrews, Wendy Hiller, Angharad Rees, Tom Baker. Directed by Philip Leacock. 100 min.

If there's any truth to the notorious curse, perhaps it's been visited on this unintentionally hilarious TV movie about digging up trouble at the celebrated crypt. Creepy things crawl through the tomb as chief baddie Raymond Burr plots dirty deeds with hammy abandon. If the pharaohs had been locked up with this film through the centuries, they'd have really known what it is to be cursed.

CURSE OF THE LIVING CORPSE ☆☆
1964, USA
Helen Warren, Roy Scheider, Margo Hartman, Hugh Franklin, Candace Hilligoss. Directed by Del Tenney. 84 min.

From director Del Tenney, who helmed the unforgettable *The Horror of Party Beach*, this is a standard shocker with a somewhat firmer grasp of film technique than his other drive-in classic. What differentiates the film from other scare flicks of its day is the high violence quotient; some of the murder sequences are rather gruesome. Roy Scheider made his film debut in this "get the heirs" mystery about a dead man who seems to have abandoned his final resting place in order to eliminate as many relatives as he can. Sometimes scary; often grotesque; never distinguished.

CURSE OF THE MUMMY

See *Aztec Mummy Double Feature*

CURSE OF THE PINK PANTHER ☆☆
1983, Great Britain, PG
Ted Wass, David Niven, Robert Wagner, Herbert Lom, Joanna Lumley, Capucine, Robert Loggia, Harvey Korman, Burt Kwouk, Roger Moore, Graham Stark. Directed by Blake Edwards. 109 min.

In 1968, when Peter Sellers decided he'd had enough of Inspector Clouseau, the character was farmed out to Alan Arkin and director Bud Yorkin for *Inspector Clouseau*. Not having learned from the enormous failure of that attempt, Blake Edwards here tries to keep the series going by bringing in a replacement, an American equivalent to Clouseau. While Ted Wass does have a flair for physical comedy, he just isn't able to stand up to Sellers. And because, in the later Pink Panther films, it was Sellers who kept the proceedings lively against increasingly dull plots, this is an almost total washout. This was filmed at the same time as the frame scenes used in the previous year's compilation, *Trail of the Pink Panther*, which does lend a mercenary air to the entire project. Hopefully, Edwards will henceforth let the series rest in peace. The voice of the ailing David Niven was dubbed by impressionist Rich Little.

THE CURSE OF THE WEREWOLF ☆☆☆
1961, Great Britain
Oliver Reed, Clifford Evans, Yvonne Romain, Anthony Dawson, Michael Ripper. Directed by Terence Fisher. 91 min.

You may have seen this listed in one of those "Films That the Stars Would Like to Forget" features: Oliver Reed's first starring role was playing Leon the Werewolf in this Hammer production. (We think Reed would much rather forget *Two of a Kind*.) Don't let that fool you, though; this is one of the best films on the werewolf theme, with many surprising touches and the typical Hammer opulence. Instead of the usual gypsy curse stuff, Leon's lycanthropy springs from his father, a beggar thrown into a dungeon in eighteenth-century Spain and left to rot for years; he rapes a servant girl thrown into his cell for a cruel joke, and Leon is the resultant child. The exposition is quite long and intricate, but it provides suitable atmosphere for this exemplary shocker.

CURTAINS ☆½
1983, Canada, R
John Vernon, Samantha Eggar, Sandra Warren, Linda Thorson, Anne Ditchburn. Directed by Jonathan Stryker (Richard Ciupka). 89 min.

Another Veg-o-matic flick. So many plot strands are left dangling in this muddled slasher movie that it seems to have been reedited by the film's mad killer. The idea of a movie director inviting six actresses to his creepy mansion to test for a film role "worth killing for" is gimmicky but promising, and the actresses are all good enough to merit curtain calls. But the concept goes the way of all flesh as the lovely ladies are disposed of in gruesome detail, according to the tedious, prescribed pattern of *Friday the 13th* and its kin.

CUTTER AND BONE

See *Cutter's Way*

CUTTER'S WAY ☆☆☆☆
1981, USA, R
Jeff Bridges, John Heard, Lisa Eichhorn, Ann Dusenberry, Stephen Elliott. Directed by Ivan Passer. 105 min.

Beautiful performances and a thoughtful, literate screenplay highlight this quietly suspenseful story of two California losers who try to beat the system by blackmailing a wealthy murderer. Czech émigré director Ivan Passer has a real feeling for locations that, whether sleazy or upper-crust, are indigenously American, and he allows his bleak but compassionate tale to unfold with leisure. John Heard and Lisa Eichhorn, as a crippled veteran and his alcoholic wife, give performances of astounding integrity, never pushing too hard to make their characters likable, and Jeff Bridges is just as good as the lazy bum who doesn't want to get involved. The film has much to say about the bitterness of post-Vietnam America, and does so with compelling grace and impact. Released as *Cutter and Bone*, it bombed, but the retitled, unchanged film quickly and deservingly resurfaced as an art-house hit.

CYCLOPS ☆½
1957, USA
James Craig, Gloria Talbot, Lon Chaney, Jr., Tom Drake, Dean Parkins. Directed by Bert I. Gordon. 75 min.

This is a typical, cheap fifties sci-fi/horror, a genre synonymous with the name of Bert I. Gordon, who wrote, produced, and directed this. Gloria Talbot hires Lon Chaney, Jr., to fly her into the Mexican jungles to look for her lost brother. Thanks to radiation, which in fifties sci-fi was blamed for everything except lower SAT scores, brother has grown into a fifty-foot monster, losing his hair, one eye (hence the title), and half his face in the process. In fact, he looks just like the monster in *War of the Colossal Beast*, another Gordon opus with the same actor. Amusing only to the arrantly supercilious.

CYRANO DE BERGERAC ☆☆½
1950, USA
José Ferrer, Mala Powers, William Prince, Morris Carnovsky, Lloyd Corrigan. Directed by Michael Gordon. 112 min.

José Ferrer won a well-deserved Oscar for transcending this juiceless adaptation of Edmond Rostand's play. The tragic romantic triangle between seventeenth-century poet and swordsman Cyrano, his cousin Roxane, and the soldier she loves is filmed as cheaply and unimaginatively as possible. Fortunately, Ferrer's abrasive and hammy mannerisms are perfectly suited to the material and undercut the absurdly masochistic and sentimental aspects of his character. He's all the more to be applauded for doing exciting work without having a single decent actor to play scenes against. Conventionally directed by Michael Gordon (*Pillow Talk*, *Portrait in Black*) and produced by Stanley Kramer on the eve of his own mediocre directorial career.

D

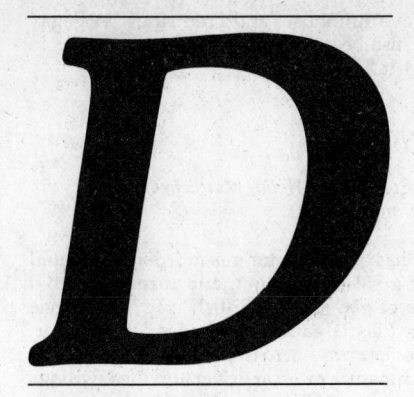

DADDY LONG LEGS ☆☆½
1955, USA
Fred Astaire, Leslie Caron, Terry Moore, Thelma Ritter, Fred Clark, Charlotte Austin, Larry Keating. Directed by Jean Negulesco. 126 min.

The frail fairy-tale plot about a wealthy playboy anonymously sponsoring the American education of a French waif is bloated out of proportion in this lengthy, sluggish Cinemascope musical. Leslie Caron was still getting away with her gamine-like charm at this time, and Fred Astaire isn't too offensive as her fatherly benefactor-turned-lover. But they don't belong together—on the dance floor or off—and Roland Petit's lumbering choreography only emphasizes the disparity of their respective styles. Johnny Mercier's score, including the hit "Something's Got to Give," supplies the tonic.

DAFFY DUCK'S MOVIE: FANTASTIC ISLAND ☆½
1983, USA
Animated: Mel Blanc. Directed by Friz Freleng. 78 min.

Like that other quarrelsome quacker, Donald, Daffy Duck has always functioned best as a foil to calmer, more subdued top bananas. Unfortunately, Daffy is less successful as a central focus. As lovable as he is, his charm begins to pale here. Perhaps that's because this is the blandest bunch of Warner Bros. cartoons assembled and they fail to show off the anarchic duck to his best advantage. Not much animated fun here, and who thought up that lame-duck linking device dealing with the TV series "Fantasy Island"? You may end up wishing this film had flown south for the winter.

THE DAIN CURSE ☆☆
1978, USA (TV)
James Coburn, Hector Elizondo, Jason Miller, Jean Simmons, Beatrice Straight. Directed by E. W. Swackhamer. 118 min.

The videotape version has been cut down from a six-hour television movie, and the resulting confusions make the convoluted plot hard to follow. James Coburn, in his return to television, stars in this measured adaptation of the Dashiell Hammett novel. Although it drags, it is palatable. (The long TV version didn't win any critical hosannas either.)

DAISY MILLER ☆☆½
1974, USA, G
Cybill Shepherd, Barry Brown, Cloris Leachman, Mildred Natwick, Eileen Brennan. Directed by Peter Bogdanovich. 91 min.

Bogdanovich's rendering of the Henry James novella, slightly reimagined as a showcase for the talents of his onetime protégée Cybill Shepherd, is nowhere near the debacle that many called it, but it's not exactly a success, either. The sumptuous production design, strong supporting performances, and generally faithful script (by Frederic Raphael) all serve to highlight Shepherd's star turn, and the results are iffy. In light of her more recent successes, one has to assume that Shepherd's nasal, sing-songy delivery is the result of interpretation rather than incompetence; although she overdoes it, it's much closer to the character of Daisy than it at first appears. The real letdown is Bogdanovich's direction, which evinces more of a feeling for his leading lady than for the time, place, or story he's trying to depict.

DAKOTA ☆☆
1945, USA
John Wayne, Vera Ralston, Walter Brennan. Directed by Joseph Kane. 81 min.

John Wayne becomes embroiled in a battle over Dakota land. Wayne is suave, the story interesting.

DAKOTA INCIDENT ☆☆½
1956, USA
Linda Darnell, Dale Robertson, Ward Bond, Regis Toomey, Skip Homeier, Irving Bacon. Directed by Lewis R. Foster. 88 min.

This dependable Western about a disparate group of travelers pinned down by a band of renegade Indians *is* reminiscent of *Stagecoach*; however, the cast, especially the sultry Linda Darnell as a woman of easy virtue, is engaging. Also helping the cause is Lewis Foster's steady direction, and location shooting rendered in Republic's strangely beautiful Trucolor process.

THE DAM BUSTERS ☆☆☆
1954, Great Britain
Michael Redgrave, Ursula Jeans, Stanley Van Beers, Hugh Manning, Basil Sidney, Laurence Naismith, Richard Todd. Directed by Michael Anderson. 119 min.

This semidocumentary recounting of a major British military triumph during World War II will be a little vague for American audiences, who will not be as familiar with the operation as the British audiences for whom this was intended. Still, it is an exciting and involving film. The problem at hand is to destroy the dams on the Ruhr River in Germany, which feeds several significant factories. At least three-quarters of the film is devoted to the intricate scientific and engineering planning for the mission, and it's quite absorbing stuff.

DAMES ☆☆☆
1934, USA
Joan Blondell, Dick Powell, Ruby Keeler, ZaSu Pitts, Guy Kibbee. Directed by Ray Enright. 90 min.

The plot is the same old let's-put-on-a-show stuff you've seen a million times, but the choreography is by Busby Berkeley, and it ranges from the outrageous (a little number called "When You Were a Smile on Your Mother's Lips and a Twinkle in Your Daddy's Eye") to the sublime ("I Only Have Eyes for You"). The stars are the usual gang of chuckleheads—Dick Powell, Ruby Keeler, ZaSu Pitts—but, let's face it, you're here for the dancing or you're not here at all.

DAMIEN—OMEN II ☆☆
1978, USA, R
William Holden, Lee Grant, Jonathan Scott-Taylor, Robert Foxworth, Lucas Donat, Nicholas Pryor, Lew Ayres, Sylvia Sidney. Directed by Don Taylor. 109 min.

Following the death of his "parents," young Damien Thorne passes into the care of his industrialist uncle—the better for him to achieve eventual world domination through economic tyranny—and continues, with his ever-increasing cult of worshipers, to destroy those who oppose him. The limitations of the material are painfully evident in this sequel to *The Omen*, but it is still superior to the last entry in the series, *Omen III—The Final Conflict*. Jonathan Scott-Taylor here replaces Harvey Stephens as Damien.

DAMIEN: THE LEPER PRIEST ☆½
1980, USA (TV)
Ken Howard, William Daniels, Mike Farrell, Wilfrid Hyde-White, David Ogden Stiers, Irene Tsu. Directed by Steve Gethers. 100 min.

Ken Howard, a late replacement for the deceased David Janssen, makes a decent Father Damien, but the film never gets beyond its dewy-eyed pieties and unconvincing controversies. This television movie fails to generate a realistic portrayal of this tough, crusty, coarse savior.

DAMNATION ALLEY ☆☆½
1977, USA, PG
George Peppard, Dominique Sanda, Paul Winfield, Jan-Michael Vincent. Directed by Jack Smight. 91 min.

World War III one more time. After the Earth gets nuked, a team of scientists and adventurers set out across the desolate landscape in search of paradise—which turns out to be a still-verdant New Jersey. On the road to salvation, the rugged heroes encounter such bizarre menaces as mutants and killer cockroaches. Twentieth Century-Fox spent a lot of money on this picture, but *Alley* still isn't able to shake off a comfortable but cheap backlot feeling. This is unimaginative but sporadically enjoyable postnuclear fun in the tradition of *The Day the World Ended*. Based on the novel by Roger Zelazny.

THE DAMNED ☆☆☆
1969, Italy/West Germany, X
Helmut Berger, Ingrid Thulin, Dirk Bogarde, Helmut Griem, Charlotte Rampling. Directed by Luchino Visconti. 155 min.

In loving detail, Luchino Visconti painstakingly unveils his operatic vision of the prelude to Nazi domination of Germany, mirrored by the downfall of a rich industrialist family. All the famous set pieces, such as the Night of the Long Knives, are staged impeccably. In some ways, Visconti's conception of a decadent post–World War I Germany sliding down into Nazism is excessive and overstated, and the grotesque horrors are piled one on top of the other. However, the decadence does exert an inescapable pull on the audience as Helmut Berger graduates from mimicking Dietrich in drag to proving his manhood by vindictively destroying his mother and her lover, before aligning himself with Hitlerian evils.

DAMN YANKEES ☆☆☆
1958, USA
Tab Hunter, Gwen Verdon, Ray Walston, Russ Brown, Jean Stapleton, Shannon Bolin. Directed by George Abbott and Stanley Donen. 110 min.

George Abbott and Stanley Donen's film of the Broadway musical about a baseball fan (Tab Hunter) who sells his soul to the devil in exchange for stellar playing ability. Hamster-eyed Hunter is a very odd choice for the leading role, but Gwen Verdon could hardly be better as Satan's sexiest minion. With Ray Walston as the Devil and crisp choreography by young Bob Fosse.

DAMSEL IN DISTRESS ☆☆½
1937, USA
Fred Astaire, George Burns, Gracie Allen, Joan Fontaine, Reginald Gardiner, Constance Collier, Ray Noble. Directed by George Stevens. 101 min.

Who would believe that a film starring Fred Astaire, with the comedy of Burns and Allen and a score by the Gershwins could be so dull? The problem is not the loss of Ginger Rogers (she was busy doing *Stage Door* and *Vivacious Lady* that year), nor the find of Joan Fontaine (who can't dance to save her life). It's George Stevens's direction, which pauses over the already musty, lethargic screenplay by P. G. Wodehouse, Ernest Pagaon, and S. K. Lauren (from the play by Wodehouse and Ian Hay). The plot has Fred as an American dancer in London who comes to the aid of a modern-day princess. Stuffy, but not without charming set pieces: Fred, George, and Gracie dance in a funhouse, and Fred sings "A Foggy Day" in haunting mist and also beats the hell out of some drums in "Nice Work If You Can Get It."

DANCE WITH A STRANGER ☆☆☆☆
1985, Great Britain, R
Miranda Richardson, Rupert Everett, Ian Holm, Matthew Carroll. Directed by Mike Newell. 102 min.

Director Mike Newell has taken a notorious murder that would make for the stuff of great pulp fiction, and turned it into a superb and stylish example of *film noir* the British way. The movie is based on the life of Ruth Ellis, a gaudy, hard-edged, and determined woman who tramps her way across postwar England, attracting the attention of an immature race-car driver and the fawnings of a sexually repressed businessman. Because of her involvement in this odd love triangle, Ruth is beaten, nearly raped, and finally moved to kill one of her admirers, an act which results in her being the last woman to be hanged in Britain. Miranda Richardson makes a remarkable film debut as the abused murderess, giving a complex and understanding performance that lets Ruth remain more sympathetic than sluttish. Her sexually impulsive ways are depicted in a neat and nasty way by Newell, who's more concerned with his blighted characters than with their seedy habits. The level-headed storytelling and remarkable acting make *Stranger* into a striking ballet of lust, madness, and death.

DANCING IN THE DARK ☆☆½
1986, Canada, PG-13
Martha Henry, Neil Munro, Rosemary Dunsmore, Richard Monette. Directed by Leon Marr. 93 min.

Leon Marr's diary of an extremely mad housewife is too humane to succeed as a black comedy and too ironic to play as earnest drama; it works best as a modern fable of feminist awakening. The versatile Martha Henry gives a chillingly correct performance as a woman who serves her husband and home in a state of submission and deference bordering on catatonia. When her spouse strays, she takes some most unladylike action to keep him in line. The director's attempts to make his heroine an Everywoman fail, as does much of the over-novelistic narration, but the story's specifics give it bleak wit and startling character.

DANGER LIGHTS ☆½
1930, USA
Louis Wolheim, Robert Armstrong, Jean Arthur, Hugh Herbert, Frank Sheridan, Alan Roscoe. Directed by George B. Seitz. 87 min.

This film does have a certain historical interest in that it was the first (and only) film made and shown in an early wide-screen process called "Natural Vision." Natural Vision never caught on because the cost of the equipment needed to project it was a financial risk that Depression-era theater owners were unwilling to take. But wide-screen films can't be shown on video—they have to be cut down in size in order to fit the square video screen. Historical interest aside, this is merely a standard, dull melodrama about two friends, both railroad workers (but gentlemen nonetheless), who share an affection for the same woman. So what's the point? Don't ask us—we don't release them, we just report them.

DANGEROUS ☆☆½
1935, USA
Bette Davis, Franchot Tone, Margaret Lindsay, Alison Skipworth, John Eldredge, Dick Foran. Directed by Alfred E. Green. 78 min.

Many claim that Bette Davis won her first Oscar for *Dangerous* because she lost out for *Of Human Bondage* the year before. That's probably true, because *Dangerous* isn't any better or worse than any other movie she made at Warner Bros. during this period. It's a trashy chronicle about a washed-up alcoholic actress who is revivified by an architect. She gets back on the wagon and the stage, but loses her man in the process. Fans of the star's showy histrionics (in their early form) will enjoy the film; others should stick to *All About Eve* for a better Bette and a less melodramatic look at theater life.

DANGEROUS COMPANY ☆
1982, USA (TV)
Beau Bridges, Carlos Brown, Karen Carlson, Jan Sterling. Directed by Lamont Johnson. 100 min.

The true story of ex-con Ray Johnson, who lived through twenty-seven years of crime, imprisonment, and, in the end, rehabilitation, is recreated in this limp presentation. Beau Bridges barely manages to hold up Christopher Keane's weak script.

DANGEROUS HOLIDAY ☆½
1937, USA
Ra Hould, Hedda Hopper, Guinn Williams, Jack La Rue, Jed Prouty, Grady Sutton, Franklin Pangborn. Directed by Nicholas Barrows. 58 min.

In this justifiably forgotten feature, a young violin prodigy tires of being constantly pressured to practice his music and runs away from home so that he can romp and play like other boys. His parents, assuming he's been kidnapped, call out the G-men. The only possible interest for nostalgians is in the casting of a pre-gossip Hedda Hopper as the female lead and movie character perennials Grady Sutton and Franklin Pangborn as supports.

DANGEROUSLY CLOSE ☆☆½
1986, USA, R
John Stockwell, Carey Lowell, Bradford Bancroft, Madison Mason, J. Eddie Peck. Directed by Albert Pyun. 95 min.

In this fresh (for exploitation films) mix of John Hughes-ish rich-kid/poor-kid hierarchies and your basic vengeance plot, the richies at a Northern California high school set up a vigilante group to scare the most uppity of the poor kids; inevitably, someone dies. Director Albert Pyun wraps the whole package in snappy editing and fashionably gauzy cinematography, but he also includes a streak of realism, looking at murder as the kind of escalating game today's nihilistic kids could conceivably get into. Among the best of the teen-*noir* characters is Madison Mason as a new-wave rich bitch who is edgy and blank, but who also has smarts and backbone.

DANGEROUS MOVES ☆☆½
1984, Switzerland
Michel Piccoli, Leslie Caron, Liv Ullmann, Michael Aumont, Alexander Arbatt. Directed by Richard Dembo. 96 min.

This is a mildly diverting Swiss import about two Russian chess grand masters competing in a world championship match in Geneva. Liebskind (Michel Piccoli), the elder, is an elegant and serenely devious Russian Jew trying to defend his title before his ailing heart gives out; the challenger, Fromm (Alexander Arbatt), is a dashing Lithuanian defector—self-righteous, paranoid, a candidate for the John McEnroe Good Sportsmanship award. Writer/director Richard Dembo tries to immerse us in the high theatricality of grand-master chess, but the picture ends up being about the manipulation of the two competitors by the Soviet bureaucracy. The message, though politically honorable, has the odd effect of sapping the players of their eccentricities—and of their interest as characters. Academy Award winner for Best Foreign Film.

A DANGEROUS SUMMER ☆½
1984, Australia
James Mason, Tom Skerritt, Wendy Hughes, Ian Gilmour. Directed by Quentin Masters. 100 min.

One of James Mason's last films casts him as an insurance investigator for Lloyds of London sent to check out a casino fire at an Australian resort. Was it arson or accident? Never mind that—the more important question is, why is a cast this good wasting its time in a movie this dull? Fortunately, Mason went on to make *The Shooting Party*, so this isn't his swan song.

DANGEROUS WHEN WET ☆☆½
1953, USA
Esther Williams, Fernando Lamas, Charlotte Greenwood, Jack Carson, William Demarest. Directed by Charles Walters. 95 min.

Here's another excuse to go a few laps with Esther Williams, who was glamorous when wet and pretty dull out of the pool. In this, one of her better vehicles, Esther trains to swim the English Channel, but there's still enough time left over for some spiffy song-and-dance numbers like "I Got Out of Bed on the Right Side." Charlotte Greenwood kicks her legs; Fernando Lamas murders the English language in that marvelous way of his; and Esther treads water like a pro. If only she'd done a distaff musical version of John Cheever's "The Swimmer," perhaps film critics would have been better able to appreciate her amphibian charms.

DANIEL ☆☆
1983, USA, R
Timothy Hutton, Amanda Plummer, Joseph Leon, Mandy Patinkin, Lindsay Crouse, Edward Asner, Tovah Feldshuh. Directed by Sidney Lumet. 129 min.

A splintered and unconvincing adaptation of E. L. Doctorow's audacious fictionalization of the Rosenberg case. Like the book, the movie cuts between the events leading up to the execution of the "Isaacsons" and the fate of their grown children—Susan (Amanda Plummer), a Radcliffe radical who's beginning to go mad, and Daniel (Timothy Hutton), a guilt-paralyzed grad student. But director Sidney Lumet never finds the complex shape and shifting tone needed to clarify the volatile material.

DANIEL AND THE DEVIL

See *The Devil and Daniel Webster*

DANIEL BOONE ☆½
1936, USA
George O'Brien, Heather Angel, John Carradine, Ralph Forbes, Dickie Jones. Directed by David Howard. 75 min.

In legend, Daniel Boone was a peace-loving pioneer who settled land in Virginia. In this cheap programmer, Daniel Boone is the leader of white mobs who brutally attack Kentucky Indians. John Ford may be able to transcend this sort of racist formula, but David Howard clearly cannot.

DANNY BOY ☆½
1941, Great Britain
David Ferrar, Wilfrid Lawson, Ann Todd, Grant Tyler, John Warwick. Directed by Oswald Mitchell. 67 min.

Where *do* they dig these things up? Only Anglophiles of an extremely nostalgic bent will have any interest in watching this tearjerker about a Broadway star who returns to England to locate the husband and child she abandoned earlier. There is some minor comic relief, and a few songs are dubbed in for the nonsinging Ann Todd; none of it has anything to do with the title tune.

DANNY BOY ☆☆½
1984, Ireland, R
Stephan Rea, Honor Heffernan, Veronica Quilligan, Alan Devlin, Peter Caffrey. Directed by Neil Jordan. 92 min.

An Irish show-band musician sees his manager being shot and decides to hunt down the killers. Visually the film could not be improved upon; the surrealistic quality of the musician's lonely flight is quite arresting. But with all the pregnant pauses, couldn't they have conceived of more original plot twists? With a liberal supply of various pretensions and an unattractive leading man, *Danny Boy* shows stylistic promise but not much else. One gets the feeling that the director thought he was going to capture all the complexities of the Northern Ireland situation in one film; he hasn't.

DANTON ★★★
1982, Poland/France, PG
Gérard Dépardieu, Wojciech Pszoniak, Patrice Chereau, Angela Winkler, Boguslaw Linda. Directed by Andrzej Wajda. 136 min.

French film idol Gérard Dépardieu stars in this historical drama of the French Revolution and the Reign of Terror. Notable for its subtle commentary on the current social upheaval in Poland, the film has been otherwise slightly overrated. Dépardieu is less than credible in the title role, and while the film occasionally fascinates, it more often degenerates into pretentious, silly nonsense. This is an important film, but ultimately not a very good one.

DARBY O'GILL AND THE LITTLE PEOPLE ★★★
1959, USA
Albert Sharpe, Janet Munro, Sean Connery, Estelle Winwood, Jack MacGowran. Directed by Robert Stevenson. 95 min.

Walt Disney live-action fantasy in which estate caretaker Darby O'Gill is unable to persuade any of the little children that the leprechauns he tells them about are real—until he captures the leprechaun king. Sean Connery had his first screen role here; fortunately, he got better.

DARBY'S RANGERS ★★½
1958, USA
James Garner, Etchika Choureau, Jack Warden, Edward Byrnes, Torin Thatcher, Bill Wellman, Jr., Murray Hamilton, Reginald Owen. Directed by William A. Wellman. 120 min.

This true-to-life (more or less) Hollywood version of World War II recounts the career of Colonel William Darby, organizer of the American Rangers, a crack squadron trained to lead attacks in the Mediterranean theater of war. The plot is a little too dispersed, with accounts of nearly every male character's love life, but Garner ties it all together with his standard charm and sincerity. Featuring a cast of familiar faces and one not-so-familiar face, who was, nevertheless, the director's son.

THE DARING DOBERMANS ★½
1973, USA, PG
Tim Considine, David Moses, Claudio Martinez, Joan Caulfield, Charles Knox Robinson, Directed by Byron Chudnow. 90 min.

Here's more four-legged fun in the vein of *The Amazing Dobermans*. Too bad these legendary beasts continue to work on the wrong side of the law, setting a bad example with another attempted robbery. However, their canine maneuvers are probably enjoyable enough to distract the kids.

DARING GAME ★★
1968, USA
Lloyd Bridges, Nico Minardos, Michael Ansara, Joan Blackman, Shepperd Strudwick, Alex Montoya, Brock Peters. Directed by Laslo Benedek. 101 min.

In this pilot for a television series that never made it, Lloyd Bridges gets back into his "Sea Hunt" togs as the leader of the "Flying Fish," a group of aerial and underwater commandos. Their assignment here is to rescue a kidnapped professor from the Latin American dictatorship where he is being held hostage. The plot is complicated by the fact that the prof's wife is an old girlfriend of Bridges. The aerial and underwater sequences are well shot and lift this up a notch.

DARIO ARGENTO'S INFERNO

See *Inferno*

THE DARK ★★
1979, USA, R
William Devane, Cathy Lee Crosby, Richard Jaeckel, Keenan Wynn, Jacquelyn Hyde, Biff Elliot, Casey Kasem. Directed by John (Bud) Cardos. 92 min.

This L.A.-based monster movie seems to have had some additional scenes added prior to release that establish the beastie as being from outer space. It doesn't make much difference, because the whole thing is pretty confusing. While writer William Devane and TV reporter Cathy Lee Crosby run around trying to find it, the monster kills people either by zapping them with laser beams from its eyes or by tearing off their heads. The actual monster, when finally shown, is disappointing, as is the lack of plot motivation and development.

THE DARK COMMAND ★★½
1940, USA
John Wayne, Claire Trevor, Walter Pidgeon, Roy Rogers, George "Gabby" Hayes, Porter Hall, Marjorie Main, Joseph Sawyer, J. Farrell MacDonald. Directed by Raoul Walsh. 91 min.

Quantrill's Raiders are terrorizing Kansas settlements in the period after the Civil War, and the people are sick and tired of it. So they get themselves a new marshall to take care of the desperadoes. And who do you think that might be? No, not Marjorie Main! It's two-fisted Texan John Wayne, who cleans up the territory and woos Claire Trevor in his spare time. Good, robust Western adventure, which director Walsh keeps moving at his usual rapid pace.

THE DARK CRYSTAL ★★½
1982, Great Britain, PG
Jim Henson, Kathryn Mullen, Frank Oz, Dave Goelz, Brian Muehl. Directed by Jim Henson and Frank Oz. 94 min.

Directed by Jim Henson and Frank Oz, the team that created the Muppets, this lavish adventure fantasy features a dazzling array of Tolkienesque sets and a cast of charmingly eccentric puppet creatures. It's more than enough to keep kids entertained—though if you're past the age of ten, you may find the movie on the bland side. The creations of Henson and Oz are fun to look at, but they never tickle your imagination. Perhaps that's because their dialogue consists of unplayable B-movie clinkers like "You must follow the greatest sun to the home of Aughra!"

DARK EYES

See *Demon Rage*

DARK EYES OF LONDON

See *The Human Monster*

DARK JOURNEY ★★½
1937, Great Britain
Vivien Leigh, Conrad Veidt, Joan Gardner, Anthony Bushell, Ursula Jeans. Directed by Victor Saville. 82 min.

The young, beautiful Vivien Leigh did not flower into a great actress until *Gone with the Wind*, but the handful of early British films she made do show her promise. In this one, she plays a French Mata Hari in 1915 Sweden who falls in love with her German counterpart. Conrad Veidt, normally the villain in this kind of film, gets a rare chance to play a romantic lead, and his sharp, Teutonic stares make this a very offbeat vis-à-vis indeed. The screenplay is curiously sympathetic to German spies, but it is intricately plotted and handsomely produced.

THE DARK MIRROR ☆☆½
1946, USA
Olivia De Havilland, Lew Ayres, Thomas Mitchell, Richard Long. Directed by Robert Siodmak. 85 min.

🐈 In this, the least noteworthy of the many movies featuring big-name actresses as twin sisters, Olivia De Havilland is divided up as a sweet young girl and her vicious, insane twin. A murder is committed and both are present at the scene of the crime. A standard whodunit, enlivened only by the novelty of seeing double.

THE DARK NIGHT OF THE SCARECROW ☆☆½
1981, USA (TV)
Charles Durning, Robert F. Lyons, Claude Earl Jones, Lane Smith, Tonya Crowe, Larry Drake, Jocelyn Brando. Directed by Frank De Felitta. 97 min.

🐈 A moderately creepy tale of small-town vigilantism and revenge in which prejudiced local dimwits seize the opportunity to hunt down a retarded man when a little girl who befriends him is attacked. But have they really gotten rid of the man who they think is the wellspring of evil? Predictable and soft, as TV restrictions demand, but works well within its formula.

DARK OF THE NIGHT ☆☆
1985, New Zealand
Heather Bolton, David Letch, Margaret Umbers, Suzanne Lee. Directed by Gaylene Preston. 88 min.

☠ A *Christine* for the foreign middle-class, this New Zealand feature is running on fuel of a very low octane rating. Red-haired Heather Bolton winningly plays an antique-shop employee who purchases a Jaguar with more than knocks under the hood. While she drives to her parents' house, strange noises issue from the auto, hitchhikers appear and disappear without opening the door, and haunting music swells through the trees. This efficient if small ghost-story vehicle is wrecked by the memory of the ace who used to drive this track: Alfred Hitchcock. Neither comic nor horrific, *Dark* stays squarely in the middle of the road.

DARK PASSAGE ☆☆½
1947, USA
Humphrey Bogart, Lauren Bacall, Agnes Moorehead, Bruce Bennett. Directed by Delmer Daves. 106 min.

🎭 A criminal escapes from death row and undergoes plastic surgery to change his face (which we've never seen). And what's this? The result looks just like Humphrey Bogart! Holed up in Lauren Bacall's apartment while he recovers, Bogie is menaced by crafty villainess Agnes Moorehead, and it's not long before he feels the call of the criminal wild again. Delmer Daves's film isn't as much fun as it sounds; confined mostly to a single set, it's static and frequently silly, one of Bogart's lesser efforts.

DARK PLACES ☆½
1974, Great Britain, PG
Christopher Lee, Joan Collins, Herbert Lom, Jane Birkin, Robert Hardy, Jean Marsh. Directed by Don Sharp. 91 min.

☠ The resolutely dull Don Sharp, who gave the world a disproportionate share of the bad British thrillers of the past few decades (several Fu Manchu entries, a few bad Alistair MacLean adaptations, and the feeble 1979 remake of Hitchcock's *The 39 Steps*) again fails to live up to his name in this undistinguished melodrama. The administrator of a mental hospital, seeking a cache of money in a dead man's house, is possessed by the spirits of those who once lived there, and kills several other treasure seekers. Even the ordinarily resourceful cast can't do anything with this one. Written by Joseph Van Winkle, whose surname irresistibly suggests that he worked on this while asleep.

THE DARK RIDE ☆½
1982, USA, R
James Luisi, Susan Sullivan, Martin Speer, Hillary Thompson, John Karlen. Directed by Jeremy Hoenack. 83 min.

☠ A psychopathic killer terrorizes the California roads, picking up pretty young hitchhikers whom he rapes and murders. The police are unable to stop him, and he flaunts his ability to elude detection with sadistic glee. Purportedly based on the Ted Bundy case, *The Dark Ride* is, in fact, a formulaic police thriller devoid of novelty. Murky photography, rudimentary plotting, and the obligatory psychological explanation for the killer's behavior do nothing to improve matters. Dull.

THE DARK SECRET OF HARVEST HOME ☆☆½
1978, USA (TV)
Bette Davis, David Ackroyd, Rosanna Arquette, Rene Auberjonois, John Calvin, Norman Lloyd, Linda Marsh, Joanna Miles, Michael O'Keefe, Richard Venture. Directed by Leo Penn. 118 min.

☠ In this suspenseful horror, a harried couple moves to a small New England village seeking peace and quiet, and soon finds that the town has its own rules about everything from clothing to marital relations, not to mention a very unusual harvest festival. Good performances, especially from Bette Davis as the widow who rules her neighbors with an iron hand, will keep your attention. Unfortunately, the video version is missing nearly two hours of footage shown in the original telecast, when the film appeared as a miniseries. Based on Thomas Tryon's novel *Harvest Home*.

DARK STAR ☆☆☆½
1974, USA, G
Dan O'Bannon, Dre Pahich, Brian Narelle. Directed by John Carpenter. 83 min.

☠ Director John Carpenter's first film is a maniacally brilliant satire of *2001*. A spaceship has been sent on a mission to destroy unstable planets, and its crew has finally gone stir crazy. Among their many problems is the lack of toilet paper, a beach ball–like alien running around the ship, and a talking bomb that wants to go off. A very funny and incisive look at human nature, with some great slapstick moments. *Dark Star* was the launching pad for the talents of Carpenter and actor Dan O'Bannon (who later went on to write the screenplay for *Alien*.)

DARK VICTORY ☆☆☆☆
1939, USA
Bette Davis, George Brent, Geraldine Fitzgerald, Humphrey Bogart, Ronald Reagan. Directed by Edmund Goulding. 105 min.

🎭 Bette Davis is overwhelming in this exquisite tearjerker. None of the remakes touches this one in the honesty of its emotion and the depth of the passion that create the dying heroine's victory over the dark. George Brent displays unsuspected expertise as her husband, while Geraldine Fitzgerald is lovely as her best friend. Yet both must take second honors to Davis. She responds to Edmund Goulding's unsentimental direction with one of the most heartfelt jobs of her distinguished career. Davis's voice, not always the most versatile of her talents, achieves the note of the true tragedienne in the final scenes.

DARLING ☆☆☆½
1965, Great Britain
Julie Christie, Dirk Bogarde, Laurence Harvey, Roland Curran, Jose Luis de Villalonga, Basil Henson. Directed by John Schlesinger. 122 min.

🎭 Julie Christie rose to stardom and won an Academy Award as a young woman who rises through the modeling world to an empty marriage with a wealthy nobleman. Frederic Raphael's script is essentially a rehash of old Joan Crawford films laced with sex and profanity, but the cast is extraordinary. Harvey is properly repellent as a selfish lover, while Bogarde gives one of his best performances as the true love who gets dumped. Christie is an unfinished actress here, but has a tremendously intriguing personality—vital and passionate beneath a shallow, glittering surface.

D.A.R.Y.L. ☆☆☆
1985, USA, PG
Barret Oliver, Mary Beth Hurt, Michael McKean, Kathryn Walker, Colleen Camp, Josef Sommer. Directed by Simon Wincer. 100 min.

A childless couple, Michael McKean and Mary Beth Hurt, wants to give young Daryl a loving home, but there's more to this little wonder boy than meets the eye—that's why the U.S. government wants him destroyed. Josef Sommer, as the doctor who created D.A.R.Y.L., is caught in the middle. Pulling on the same heartstrings as the box-office hit *E.T.*, this top-quality family film has a little of everything in it, from Marvin Hamlisch music to Little League baseball to airplane acrobatics. If it doesn't bother you that the moviemakers are trying to cash in on everything you've ever liked before, including *Pinocchio*, this modern-day fairy tale will afford you a great escape.

DAS BOOT

See *The Boat*

DAUGHTER OF DR. JEKYLL ☆
1957, USA
John Agar, Gloria Talbott, Arthur Shields, John Dierkes. Directed by Edgar G. Ulmer. 67 min.

This is one of the less memorable horror quickies from that wonderful drive-in summer of 1957, when every third movie was a low-budget monster epic. British lass Janet Smith learns from her guardian that her real last name is not Smith but—Jekyll! Of course, the news is immediately all over town, and when the locals start waking up dead, who do you think they blame? Edgar Ulmer made dozens of low-budget films in the forties, many only now being hailed as genre classics; this is not one of them.

DAUGHTER OF HORROR ☆☆
1955, USA
Andrea Barrett, Brunoa VeSota, Angelo Rossito. Directed by John Parker.

Famous as the movie showing when the Blob makes its movie-theater appearance in *The Blob*, this bizarre exercise features unsynchronized sound and a demented voice-over by future Johnny Carson sidekick Ed McMahon. Sometimes described as an art-house experiment in *film noir* stylistics, this is low-budget exploitation whose minimal plot involves a young woman's descent into madness and murder. With Angelo Rossito, most recently seen as the dwarfed Master half of Masterblaster in *Mad Max Beyond Thunderdome*. (a.k.a.: *Dementia*)

DAUGHTERS OF DARKNESS ☆☆½
1971, USA/France, R
Delphine Seyrig, Daniele Ouimet, John Karlen, Andre Rau, Paul Esser, Georges Jamin. Directed by Harvey Kumel. 87 min.

This may be the best lesbian vampire movie ever made—which isn't saying too much. It is a lot spookier and more erotic than *The Hunger* and it ends up striking multiple blows for feminism. A young couple bumps into a vampire countess at a Belgian resort, where the husband (John Karlen) grows increasingly surly as his wife is lured away. The vampire is another icy blonde, but Delphine Seyrig brings a teasing imperiousness to the role. Based on the legend of Elisabeth Bathory.

DAVID AND BATHSHEBA ☆☆☆
1951, USA
Gregory Peck, Susan Hayward, Raymond Massey, Kieron Moore, Jayne Meadows, James Robertson Justice, Francis X. Bushman, Gwyneth (Gwen) Verdon. Directed by Henry King. 153 min.

Whereas the recent *King David* with Richard Gere is one of the most laughable of all biblical epics, this earlier version starring Gregory Peck as David is one of the least—a surprisingly sturdy, low-key retelling of how David fought the Philistines, conquered Goliath, and married Bathsheba (Susan Hayward). While Henry King's direction lacks the cartoon color and excitement of a Cecil B. De Mille pageant, it also avoids the usual phoniness. Gwen Verdon has a nice bit as a specialty dancer.

DAVID COPPERFIELD ☆☆☆½
1935, USA
Freddie Bartholomew, Frank Lawton, W. C. Fields, Elizabeth Allan, Jessie Ralph, Lionel Barrymore, Basil Rathbone, Edna May Oliver, Maureen O'Sullivan, Roland Young. Directed by George Cukor. 133 min.

Charles Dickens's tale about young David and his many eccentric friends and enemies still comes alive in this lavish MGM production—one of the best of the Dickens adaptations. Like the book, it is episodic, sentimental, and occasionally slow. But using a marvelous all-star cast, *David Copperfield* focuses on the colorful characterizations created by the author, and George Cukor's touch produces a collection of fascinating character gems that never resorts to caricature. Adapting great literature to film was clearly the forte of producer David Selznick, who worked frequently with Cukor; other Selznick projects included *Little Women, Anna Karenina, A Tale of Two Cities*, and *Gone with the Wind*.

DAVID COPPERFIELD ☆☆½
1970, Great Britain
Richard Attenborough, Robin Phillips, Edith Evans, Laurence Olivier, Michael Redgrave, Ralph Richardson. Directed by Delbert Mann. 118 min.

Studded with jewels from the British stage, this third adaptation of Charles Dickens's classic adds up to a strangely cosmetic ornament. Picking up the story from the second half of the book, we find David (Robin Phillips), a young man just back from exile, pacing up and down a deserted beach as barren and inert as his life now seems to be. The background of his predicament is given in choppy flashbacks, and this technique washes over most of the film's relentlessly droning momentum. Ralph Richardson glitters as Micawber, but Laurence Olivier and Richard Attenborough are flushed away in minute cameos. Although the period is competently evoked, there was less cinematic mire, and more of Dickens's fire, in George Cukor's 1935 version with wiry Basil Rathbone and wily W. C. Fields.

DAVID HOLZMAN'S DIARY ☆☆☆½
1967, USA
L. M. Kit Carson, Penny Wohl, Louise Levine, Michael Levine, Robert Lesser, Fern McBride. Directed by Jim McBride. 74 min.

Jim McBride, who directed the remake of *Breathless*, first came to attention with this influential fictional diary, a movie whose cinéma vérité surface is so convincing it sucks you right into the illusion that you're watching the daily life of a down-and-out young filmmaker. The movie is joky and freewheeling in the tradition of experimental sixties youth cinema, and if it sometimes gets on your nerves, it also captures the tenor of struggling-artist self-consciousness as few films have.

DAWN OF THE DEAD ☆☆☆
1979, USA, X (self-imposed)
David Emge, Ken Foree, Scott Reiniger, Gaylen Ross. Directed by George Romero. 125 min.

George Romero works a surprising degree of irony, wit, and observation into this ultraviolent sequel to *Night of the Living Dead*. Under the weight of the plague of cannibal zombies depicted in the first film, the very fabric of civilization is beginning to break down. Martial law has been established, cities are crumbling, the National Guard has degenerated into a mob of trigger-happy psychopaths, and the general population is inclining toward anarchy. Four people escape to a shopping mall and indulge in a consumer fantasy charade until they learn that you can run, but you can't hide. With splattery effects by gore-master Tom Savini. Followed by *Day of the Dead*.

DAWN OF THE MUMMY ½☆
1981, USA, X
Brenda King, Barry Sattels, George Peck, Joan Levy. Directed by Frank Agrama. 88 min.

A fashion crew—a photographer, models, and sundry hangers-on—working on location in Egypt accidentally awakens mummies whose habits mirror those of post–*Night of the Living Dead* cannibal zombies. Standard exploitation whose brief moments of extreme gore are the only lively spots on a generally dull horizon. Only for fans of violent horror with absolutely nothing else to do.

DAWN ON THE GREAT DIVIDE ☆☆
1942, USA
Buck Jones, Rex Bell, Raymond Hatton, Mona Barrie, Robert Lowrey, Silver. Directed by Howard Bretherton. 63 min.

Cowboy star Buck Jones had long passed the peak of his popularity when he made this, his last feature; just prior to its release, he was killed in the infamous fire at the Cocoanut Grove nightclub in Boston. That bit of trivia aside, this is a somewhat better-than-average but still unmemorable low-budget Western. Scout Buck Jones and his horse Silver guide a wagon train carrying railroad supplies and settlers through dangerous Western territory on their way to Oregon.

DAWN PATROL ☆☆☆
1938, USA
Errol Flynn, David Niven, Donald Crisp, Basil Rathbone, Barry Fitzgerald. Directed by Edmund Goulding. 103 min.

Eight years after the Howard Hawks original, Warner Bros. remade this World War I Royal Flying Corps saga utilizing some of the same aerial footage. This time, Errol Flynn and David Niven play buddies in the Fifty-ninth Squadron who risk almost certain death on dangerous flights for the "dawn patrol." More romantic than the earlier film, but notable for eschewing a happy ending and any extraneous love interests (the cast is all male).

DAWN RIDER ☆☆
1935, USA
John Wayne, Marion Burns, Yakima Canutt. Directed by Robert N. Bradbury. 53 min.

A cowpoke tries to avenge his father's murder. A good B Western. John Wayne *is* the Dawn Rider.

THE DAY AFTER ☆☆☆
1983, USA (TV)
Jason Robards, JoBeth Williams, Steve Guttenberg, John Lithgow. Directed by Nicholas Meyer. 120 min.

This wildly controversial, widely seen depiction of life after the nuclear holocaust is less a film than an unflinching catalogue of shocking horror and suffering. Unrelentingly bleak, the movie has a cumulative power that will either affect or numb the viewer. An excellent cast does as well as can be expected, but the real star is the spectacle of complete devastation. Do not watch this movie unless you are well steeled.

THE DAY AND THE HOUR ☆☆☆
1963, France/Italy
Simone Signoret, Stuart Whitman, Genevieve Page. Directed by René Clément. 115 min.

The turbulent times of the Nazi occupation of France are captured in an emotionally fulfilling drama helmed by superb French director René Clément and acted with delicacy by two imposing French actresses. Even that hulk Stuart Whitman shucks off his usual cloddishness. He commands our rapt attention as a soldier rescued by Signoret, whose husband had suffered at the hands of the loathsome Nazis. Forceful suspense tale about imperiled lives, and a graceful love story in the bargain.

A DAY AT THE RACES ☆☆☆
1937, USA
Groucho, Chico, and Harpo Marx, Allan Jones, Maureen O'Sullivan, Margaret Dumont. Directed by Sam Wood. 109 min.

This marks the beginning of the Marx brothers' long downhill slide at MGM Studios—though this film boasts its share of classic bits. Groucho is Dr. Hackenbush, a veterinarian engaged to treat the hypochondriacal Margaret Dumont. The final "Who Dat Man?" number, with Harpo gallivanting through a black ghetto like the Pied Piper of Shantytown, represents one of the most appalling lapses of taste in Hollywood history.

THE DAYDREAMER ☆☆☆
1966, USA
Paul O'Keefe, Jack Gilford, Ray Bolger, Margaret Hamilton; voices of Hayley Mills, Burl Ives, Tallulah Bankhead, Boris Karloff, Terry-Thomas, Victor Borge, Ed Wynn, Patty Duke, Sessue Hayakawa. Directed by Jules Bass. 101 min.

This children's feature is made palatable to adult audiences by the same gimmick used by the recent Muppet features—amusing cameos by recognizable stars. In this case, only the voices of a dozen actors are used, though for puppets designed in their likenesses. Any children who were raised on fairy tales and not television will enjoy these adventures of the thirteen-year-old Hans Christian Andersen as he imagines encounters with the characters who would later form the basis of his stories.

THE DAYDREAMER ☆☆½
1975, France
Pierre Richard, Bernard Blier, Marie Pacome, Marie Christine Barrault. Directed by Pierre Richard. 90 min.

That comic goof, Pierre Richard, demonstrates the slapstick charm that would later make him a popular favorite with American audiences in *The Tall Blond Man with One Black Shoe* and *Les Compères*. Carrying on the tradition of lovable klutzes dating back to the silent era, Richard practically demolishes a Paris ad agency as he tries to learn the ropes. Richard's comic chaos is irresistible, even in embryonic form. A hit-or-miss affair, but with enough levity to justify giving it a look.

DAY FOR NIGHT ☆☆☆½
1973, France, PG
Jacqueline Bisset, François Truffaut, Jean-Pierre Leaud, Valentina Cortese, Jean-Pierre Aumont. Directed by François Truffaut. 116 min.

Truffaut's funny and tender valentine to the people who make movies won an Oscar for Best Foreign Film. Truffaut stars as the director who keeps his film afloat despite the constant chaos created by his eccentric cast and crew. Truffaut also helped write the screenplay of this satirical look at the human side of filmmaking. Truffaut allows us fascinating revelations about the deceptive art of cinema and intimate looks at the people behind the scenes. The only drawback is the dubbing; but, for this particular work, subtitles would have distracted from the director's intricate conception.

THE DAY IT CAME TO EARTH ☆
1979, USA, PG
Wink Roberts, Roger Manning, Bob Ginnaven, Delight DeBruine, George Gobel. Directed by Harry Z. Thomason. 89 min.

The day *what* came to earth? Don't ask dumb questions—the moviemakers don't have time to bother with trivia like that. A meteor crashes into a lake in which a gangster was sent for a swim in his best pair of cement overshoes. Radiation from the meteor (or maybe it's an alien force living inside it—we're not quite sure) revives the corpse, which goes shambling off in search of revenge and a decent plastic surgeon. Unreleased for two years, which is understandable; why they released it at all, isn't.

THE DAY OF THE ANIMALS ☆☆½
1977, USA, PG
Christopher George, Lynda Day George, Leslie Nielsen, Richard Jaeckel, Ruth Roman, Michael Ansara. Directed by William Girdler. 98 min.

Not just birds, rats, frogs, or nematodes, but all the animals in a National Park turn against mankind in this chiller. Thank God the killer bees are still down in French Guiana.

THE DAY OF THE COBRA ☆☆
1980, Italy
Franco Nero, Sybil Danning, Mario Marazana, Enio Girolane, Licinia Lentini. Directed by Enzo G. Castellari. 95 min.

There are a few nice touches to Franco Nero's character of a down-at-the-heels detective who is rehired by a narcotics bureau to track down an old nemesis. Unfortunately, he can't overcome a soporific plot that refuses to become awakened even by the frequent fighting. Good locations in San Francisco and Genoa, and arguably the world's *worst* title song.

DAY OF THE DEAD ☆½
1985, USA, X (self-imposed)
Richard Liberty, Howard Sherman. Directed by George Romero. 103 min.

This is the disappointing completion to Romero's "Living Dead" trilogy, begun with *Night of the Living Dead* (1968) and *Dawn of the Dead* (1979). A group of scientists tries to find a way to control the hordes of cannibalistic cadavers that have overrun the Earth. To complicate matters, the researchers are at the mercy of their commanding and psychopathic military officers. In between the all-too-few bursts of gore, the movie is filled with scenes of bad actors shouting even worse dialogue at each other. While the climax is appropriately nauseating, *Day of the Dead* is a bloody bore.

THE DAY OF THE DOLPHIN ☆☆
1973, USA, PG
George C. Scott, Trish Van Devere, Paul Sorvino, Frtiz Weaver, John Korkes, Edward Herrmann. Directed by Mike Nichols. 104 min.

Heroic scientists, evil government agents, and talking dolphins are the ingredients of this occasionally compelling but fatally misconceived adventure film. Nichols and screenwriter Buck Henry can't decide whether to make a humanist drama, a conspiracy thriller, or a "Wild Kingdom"–style exploitation of the wonders of aquatic life, so they combine all three in a leapfrogging plot that will leave you either entertained or numb with disbelief. Younger viewers will, however, enjoy the incredible dolphin footage and comic book story without being overly bothered by the blustery performances or thematic confusion.

THE DAY OF THE JACKAL ☆☆☆½
1973, Great Britain/France
Edward Fox, Alan Badel, Tony Britton, Cyril Cusak, Michael Lonsdale, Eric Porter, Derek Jacobi. Directed by Fred Zinnemann. 141 min.

The Jackal is an assassin hired by a group of dissident generals to kill French president de Gaulle in this taut, deliberate thriller based on the bestselling novel by Frederick Forsyth. The film follows the Jackal as he makes his preparations, intercutting with the discovery by French and British police of the plot and their efforts to discover the killer. The film's length works in its favor, building up details so that the ending is able to generate considerable suspense, despite the fact that we know the outcome.

THE DAY OF THE LOCUST ☆☆☆½
1975, USA, R
Donald Sutherland, Karen Black, William Atherton, Burgess Meredith, Geraldine Page, Bo Hopkins, Billy Barty, Natalie Schafer. Directed by John Schlesinger. 143 min.

Complex, violent, disturbing adaptation of Nathaneal West's novel loosely based on his experiences as a Hollywood screenwriter in the thirties. William Atherton plays the wide-eyed Hollywood art director who falls for a starlet (Karen Black). Donald Sutherland plays a depressed man who becomes equally obsessed with the woman. The performances are excellent and the production, worked on by many of the same people who made *Midnight Cowboy*, is meticulously designed and shot. The meaning, if any, to the film's grim and bitter vision, may be difficult to understand without first reading West's book, but the striking imagery alone makes the film worth seeing.

THE DAY OF THE TRIFFIDS ☆☆☆
1963, Great Britain
Howard Keel, Nicole Maurey, Janette Scott, Kieron Moore, Mervyn Johns, Evan Roberts. Directed by Steve Sekely. 93 min.

Here's another in that time-honored genre of apocalyptic killer-vegetable movies. After a spectacular meteor shower blinds most of mankind (yes, we know that doesn't make any sense, but it's not supposed to, this is science fiction), the meteors hatch spores that grow into triffids, giant ambulatory killer plants. This is not nearly as dumb as it sounds; in fact, it's pretty good, written and performed with enough intelligence that you're willing to suspend your disbelief. Ex–musical star Howard Keel plays a sailor who, having escaped blindness, becomes mankind's sole hope. We wonder if Keel sings the opening song from *The Rocky Horror Picture Show* in his nightclub act these days—you know, the one with the line that goes, "And I really got hot/When I saw Janette Scott/Fight a triffid that shoots poison and kills."

THE DAY THE BOOKIES WEPT ☆☆
1939, USA
Joe Penner, Betty Grable, Richard Lane, Tom Kennedy, Thurston Hall, Jack Arnold. Directed by Leslie Goodwins. 53 min.

Cab driver Joe Penner comes into some money and is duped into spending it on a nag passed off as a racehorse; he sets out to turn it into a winner anyway. Better make sure and hit the Pause button if you step out to the kitchen for a beer, as this short, pedestrian comedy is liable to be over by the time you get back.

THE DAY THE EARTH CAUGHT FIRE ☆☆½
1961, Great Britain
Janet Munro, Leo McKern, Edward Judd, Peter Butterworth. Directed by Val Guest. 99 min.

Apocalyptic sci-fi with an intriguing premise: unplanned simultaneous nuclear test explosions at the North and South poles send the Earth off its axis and heading into the sun. Unfortunately, the script works so hard to make this farfetched idea plausible that it leaves the plot no believable resolution. The use of newspaper offices for settings provides verisimilitude as well as an effective plot contrivance.

THE DAY THE EARTH STOOD STILL ☆☆☆☆
1951, USA
Michael Rennie, Patricia Neal, Sam Jaffe, Hugh Marlowe. Directed by Robert Wise. 92 min.

Based on Harry Bates's story "Farewell to the Master," this is one of the most intelligent and literate science-fiction films. The urbane spaceman Klaatu and his imposing robot Gort land in Washington, D.C., to peacefully warn earthlings about their foolish use of nuclear weapons and are met with immediate and violent resistance. A landmark of the genre that was one of the first movies to deal effectively with the fear of atomic war and to feature a benign alien as its protagonist. Also one of the few pictures at its time to aim its stirring message at adult rather than kiddie audiences.

THE DAY THE LOVING STOPPED ☆☆
1981, USA (TV)
Valerie Harper, Dennis Weaver, James Canning, Dominique Dunne, Ally Sheedy. Directed by Daniel Mann. 100 min.

This is a capably acted but over-familiar domestic drama. Two extraordinary young actresses, Ally Sheedy and the late Dominique Dunne, invest this house-divided material with conviction and dignity, but we've tuned into this TV "Divorce Court" fodder once too often. Harper and Weaver play an embattled couple, and the dissolution of their marriage causes great pain for their uncomprehending youngsters.

THE DAY THEY ROBBED THE BANK OF ENGLAND ☆☆☆
1960, Great Britain
Aldo Ray, Elizabeth Sellars, Hugh Griffith, Peter O'Toole, Kieron Moore, John Le Mesurier. Directed by John Guillermin. 85 min.

This painstaking turn-of-the-century caper film is based on an event of legendary proportions that may never have happened. A group of Irish dissidents, seeking to raise money for the fight for home rule, set about to rob the Bank of England of a large cache of gold bullion stored in its vaults, by breaking in from underneath through an abandoned sewer. Like most caper films, emphasis is placed on detail over characterization, though Peter O'Toole, in his screen debut, is excellent as the guard who becomes involved in the plot.

THE DAY TIME ENDED ☆
1980, USA, PG
Jim Davis, Christopher Mitchum, Dorothy Malone, Scott Holden. Directed by John (Bud) Cardos. 79 min.

This is a very confusing movie; we sat through the whole thing and we're still not quite sure exactly what it's supposed to be about. A family moves into a modern solar-powered house. Suddenly, radiation from three supernovas that exploded a few centuries ago hits Earth. A miniature space critter appears to the family's daughter and pantomimes for something or other, followed soon after by a mean-looking spaceship. Before the family can call the bank and see if they can cancel the mortgage, however, a few dinosaurs show up for a brawl, and the whole thing ends with some *Close Encounters*–type UFOs and special effects. Made in 1978.

DAYS OF HEAVEN ☆☆☆½
1978, USA, R
Richard Gere, Brooke Adams, Linda Manz, Sam Shepard. Directed by Terence Malick. 95 min.

Nestor Almendros's Oscar-winning cinematography for *Days of Heaven* lingers in the memory of some as the most creative and exquisite camerawork of recent years. Unfortunately, it is much harder to recall the details of Terence Malick's icy narrative. The tale of a young woman torn between two men, set in the Texas panhandle on the eve of World War I, has an elegiac elegance of form, but the content is perhaps deliberately left vague. Malick places too much import on a device that worked in *Badlands*: a young girl narrates the horrible events in the story in the same flat, streetwise fashion that she gives to the descriptions of the beautiful countryside. Linda Manz reads her narration with an appropriate coarseness, but the effect is just too forced to carry such a heavy emotional load. Brooke Adams, in the pivotal role, has some rapport with Sam Shepard (who emerges as the best drawn of the characters). Richard Gere, however, never the warmest of actors, simply drifts along and becomes a part of the scenery. *Days of Heaven* is, on a certain level, a triumph of understated splendor, but Malick's reserve too often suggests mere emptiness.

DAYS OF OLD CHEYENNE ☆☆
1943, USA
Don "Red" Barry. Directed by Elmer Clifton. 56 min.

Red Barry plays a rough, tough cowboy confronting a crooked political boss. Guns, horses, and good action.

DAYS OF THRILLS AND LAUGHTER ☆☆☆½
1961, USA
Compiled by Robert Youngson. 93 min.

Dozens of these compilation films that cannibalize old silents have appeared over the years. Most of them speed up the proper showing time, or ladle on a cornball narration, or jumble the clips together haphazardly, so that our pleasure is minimized. This documentary overcomes these common failings for two reasons: the clips are magnificent, and many of them are rarely seen. Also, the film derives a giddy power from juxtaposing the breathtaking comedy scenes with the hair-raising last-minute escape sequences. You'd do better to see the silents in their entirety; but if that isn't possible, this is thrilling and funny enough to serve as an intro to the magic of silent movies.

DAYS OF WINE AND ROSES ☆☆☆½
1962, USA
Jack Lemmon, Lee Remick, Charles Bickford, Jack Klugman, Alan Hewitt, Jack Albertson. Directed by Blake Edwards. 117 min.

This is the powerfully pessimistic story of a young couple torn apart by alcoholism, which begins as the shared vice that holds their marriage together, and ends by destroying it. Lee Remick's strong performance wasn't really a surprise, but at the time Jack Lemmon's was; like the director, Blake Edwards, Lemmon was best known for his work in light comedy. Based on a "Playhouse 90" television drama by J. P. Miller, the film consistently surprises with its undisguised bitterness. Henry Mancini wrote the Oscar-winning title song.

DAYTON'S DEVILS ☆½
1968, USA
Rory Calhoun, Leslie Nielsen, Lainie Kazan, Eric Braeden (Hans Gudegast), Barry Sadler. Directed by Jack Shea. 107 min.

Those devilish guys want to pull off the daring heist of a U.S. Air Force base. They do so in an entirely predictable, unsuspenseful, and cut-and-dried manner. The only suspense derives from wondering whether Lainie Kazan's impressive chest will pop out of her clothes or not.

D.C. CAB ☆☆½
1983, USA, R
Max Gail, Adam Baldwin, Mr. T, Charlie Barnett, Gary Busey, DeWayne Jessie, Irene Cara. Directed by Joel Schumacher. 99 min.

This lively, formulaic comedy shuttles between fast gags and hectic action. Gary Busey, Mr. T, and a cast of talented unknowns are D.C. Cab, a ragtag Washington taxi company that comes under the leadership of an ambitious young cabbie (Adam Baldwin, who looks like one of the more thriving members of the Kennedy clan). The drivers themselves are a spirited bunch, but once the new boss quashes their anarchic antics, they need something else to do, and so writer/director Joel Schumacher turns them into the heroes of a stock kidnapping melodrama (*The B Team?*) in which they employ their hacking skills to save the two brat kids of an ambassador. The movie also employs some inspirational working-class commentary—e.g., Mr. T standing on the steps of the Lincoln Memorial and growling, "I like what I become these last few weeks, and I ain't never going back to what I was before." (a.k.a.: *Streets Fleet*)

D-DAY THE SIXTH OF JUNE ☆☆½
1956, USA
Robert Taylor, Richard Todd, Dana Wynter, Edmond O'Brien, John Williams. Directed by Henry Koster. 106 min.

As with most Hollywood war films, the war itself in *D-Day the Sixth of June* becomes a mere backdrop to the romantic story at hand. Too bad, because the film promises to depict graphically (as in *The Longest Day*) events leading up to the day the Allied forces invaded Normandy and turned World War II around. As it stands, the film concentrates on a love triangle involving a British commander (Richard Todd), his wife (Dana Wynter), and an American officer (Robert Taylor) and is directed by Henry Koster (*The Bishop's Wife, Come to the Stables*) for maximum schmaltz. The conclusion is predictably romantic but will make modern audiences groan. Originally shot in Eastmancolor and Cinemascope.

DEAD AND BURIED ☆½
1981, USA, R
James Farentino, Jack Albertson, Dennis Redfield, Lisa Blount, Michael Pataki, Melody Anderson. Directed by Gary A. Sherman. 92 min.

A small coastal town harbors a grim secret: For some reason its inhabitants are periodically compelled to gather into mobs and slaughter hapless passers-through while recording the entire gruesome business on film. Violent and illogical, with a twist ending that doesn't make a great deal of sense. From a story by *Alien* coauthor Dan O'Bannon.

DEAD EASY ☆½
1982, Australia, R
Scott Burgess, Rosemary Paul, Tim McKenzie, Max Phipps. Directed by Bert Deling. 90 min.

Three young people—a hooker on dope (Rosemary Paul), a nightclub manager (Scott Burgess), and a suspended cop (Max Phipps)—form an unlikely alliance in a battle with mobsters in Sydney's lurid Kings Cross area. This Aussie release, aimed at the youth market, lacks the necessary experience but at least delivers a hair-raising crosstown auto chase for a finale.

DEAD END ☆☆☆
1937, USA
Joel McCrea, Sylvia Sidney, Humphrey Bogart, Wendy Barrie, Claire Trevor, Allen Jenkins, Marjorie Main, Ward Bond, the Dead End Kids. Directed by William Wyler. 92 min.

Sam Goldwyn's big, glossy version of a Warner Bros. melodrama stars almost everyone who ever appeared in this kind of a film. Humphrey Bogart as "Baby Face Martin," Joel McCrea and Sylvia Sidney as the poor, young lovers, Wendy Barrie and Claire Trevor as prostitutes, and so on. Lillian Hellman adapted Sidney Kingsley's play, retaining the New York waterfront setting and the theme of class conflicts, but removing some of the sting along the way. It's well made in the Wyler/Goldwyn manner but not as juicy or exciting as such seedy Warner's pics as *Marked Woman*. The best part is the magnificent closing shot.

DEAD-END DRIVE-IN ☆☆
1986, Australia, R
Ned Manning, Natalie McCurry, Peter Whitford, Wilbur Wilde. Directed by Brian Trenchard-Smith. 92 min.

This lowbrow variation on the postapocalypse world of the *Mad Max* films thankfully has a few bright ideas of its own—such as reimagining the title location as a futuristic prison camp where inmates are subjected to a steady and inescapable barrage of exploitation films. Obviously, someone connected with the film had a sense of humor, and it shows in the odd, amusing touches that punctuate each scene. Nothing special on the whole, but better than most of its ilk.

DEAD KIDS

See *Strange Behavior*

DEADLINE ☆☆
1980, USA
Sharon Masters, Marvin Goldhar. Directed by Mario Azzopardi. 85 min.

Successful horror novelist Stephen Lessey finds his comfortable life disintegrating around him: his wife is distant, his agent hounds him for a new novel even as he suffers from writer's block, a movie adaptation of another book isn't going well, and his students denounce his work as violent pornography. Preachy horror film in which all the horrific material consists of set pieces that Lessey generates as he tries to start work on the new book, a handy way of not integrating them into the body of the film. Interesting idea gone awry.

THE DEADLY AFFAIR ☆☆☆
1967, Great Britain
James Mason, Simone Signoret, Maximilian Schell, Harriet Andersson, Harry Andrews, Lynn Redgrave, Roy Kinnear, David Warner. Directed by Sidney Lumet. 107 min.

This better-than-average espionage drama is based on John Le Carré's first novel, *Call for the Dead*. James Mason excels, as usual, as a civil servant who has doubts about the official explanation for the death of a British intelligence officer (suicide) and begins to delve into the case. Of course, he finds a web of complications and cover-ups. Direction by Sidney Lumet keeps the deliberately paced story from seeming too slow.

DEADLY BLESSING ☆½
1981, USA, R
Maren Jensen, Jeff East, Ernest Borgnine, Linda Hamilton, Lois Nettleton. Directed by Wes Craven. 102 min.

A young woman living near a strange religious cult finds her husband, a former member, slain under mysterious circumstances. Feeling threatened by the cult's members, she calls in her two college friends to keep her company. After that, the bodies start to pile up. *Blessing* gets off to a promising suspenseful start but degenerates into a very bizarre and confusing horror film. The "surprise" climax is totally ridiculous.

DEADLY ENCOUNTER ☆☆
1982, USA (TV)
Larry Hagman, Susan Anspach, James Gammon, Michael C. Gwynne, Jose Chavez, Jack Dunlap. Directed by William A. Graham. 100 min.

In this chopper spectacular, Larry Hagman enjoys himself immensely in change-of-pace heroics totally unlike his dastardly doings on "Dallas." He plays a helicopter-riding hero who rescues an ex-girlfriend from getting mauled by the mob. The superb stunt work is this production's ace in the hole, since the mechanics of the plot often grind the vehicle to a halt. Still, the copters whirl by photogenically; this is a passable time killer for action aficionados.

DEADLY EYES ☆☆½
1982, USA, R
Sam Groom, Sara Botsford, Scatman Crothers, Cec Linder, Lisa Langlois. Directed by Robert Clouse. 93 min.

A low-budget, high-impact screamfest, this is about some New York rats who abandon their netherworld and attempt a mainstream urban life-style by attacking people with the zeal of a landlord zeroing in for an eviction. Stumbling across some steroids in the docks, the Hamlinesque creatures pump themselves up and begin dining out on the Big Apple's populace. If you suffer from rat-aphobia, this film will leave you uncomfortable watching a Mickey Mouse cartoon. Even a baby gets it in this tightly scripted chiller, which ranks with *Willard* and *Of Unknown Origin* as the most unsettling of all mousterpieces. And watch out for that subway scene.

DEADLY FORCE ☆
1983, USA, R
Wings Hauser, Joyce Ingalls, Paul Shenar, Al Ruscio. Directed by Paul Aaron. 95 min.

This brutal action pic would make a perfect double bill with *Vice Squad*, another sleaze classic starring rodent-faced Wings Hauser. There he played the pimp villain; here he plays an antihero cop tracking down a psychopath while his domestic problems distract him and other members of the force get in his way by insisting he play by the rules. Naturally, our hero proves he knows best how to rid the city's streets of scumbags. Unfortunately for the film's credibility, Hauser elicits virtually no sympathy (he's the Jack Palance of the eighties) and his overemphatic acting would have been better suited to portraying the psychopath.

DEADLY FRIEND ☆☆
1986, USA, R
Matthew Laborteaux, Kristy Swanson, Michael Sharrett, Anne Twomey, Anne Ramsey. Directed by Wes Craven. 99 min.

The uneven horror director Wes Craven is capable of making imaginative and even shocking horror films (see *A Nightmare on Elm Street* and *The Hills Have Eyes*) and just as capable of dreck (*The Last House on the Left*, *Deadly Blessing*, and many more). This by-the-book entry falls somewhere in between; it's Craven at cruising speed—a smooth ride, but one without risks or flourishes. The theme is reanimation, but instead of a mad scientist, Craven gives us a brilliant teenager (Matthew Laborteaux) who transplants the computer-chip brain of his pet robot into the body of the pretty girl next door, who's just been beaten to death by her drunken dad. But the girl who comes back to life isn't the demure young thing she once was, something the local bad guys soon discover. Occasionally skilled and loaded with special effects, but silly and undistinguished.

THE DEADLY GAME ☆☆
1977, USA (TV)
Andy Griffith, Mitzi Hoag, James Cromwell, Claude Earl Jones, Sharon Spellman, Dan O'Herlihy, Hunter von Leer. Directed by Lane Slate. 100 min.

In this sequel to the TV movie *Winter Kill*, that perfect embodiment of rustic authority Andy Griffith investigates the Army's involvement in a chemical spill. He may have been hoping for another series, but there's nothing terribly exciting about this down-home sleuthing with the usual detective bloodhounding and easily deducible mystery.

DEADLY GAMES ☆☆½
1980, USA, R
Steven Railsback, Sam Groom, Denise Galin. Directed by Scott Mansfield. 94 min.

Small-town Vietnam war buddies—one a handsome policeman, the other a scarred, crippled owner of a movie theater—play all kinds of games, from a monster-movie board game of their own devising to a cat-and-mouse game of murder and concealment. A girl comes between them and learns which one is the killer and which the silent accomplice, but she would have done better to leave well enough alone. Moody, complicated psychological horror film that is a cut above average.

DEADLY HERO ☆☆☆
1976, USA, R
Don Murray, Diahn Williams, James Earl Jones, Lilia Skala, George S. Irving, Treat Williams. Directed by Ivan Nagy. 99 min.

This surprisingly good low-budget thriller was shot entirely on location in New York City. Street cop Don Murray saves a woman (Diahn Williams) from an attacker, but his methods are so unnecessarily harsh that she makes a complaint to his superiors; as a result, the cop begins to harass her in order to silence her. It's a neat twist, but audiences may have trouble getting a hold on the story, as the woman's character isn't developed sufficiently to command our full sympathy.

DEADLY SHAOLIN KICKS ☆½
Tan Teo-Liang, Lo Lieh, King Kung, Tsai Hung. Directed by Huang Lung.

In this historical epic with kung fu action passages, a cop chases down eight map thieves. Passable production highlighted by Tan Teo-Liang's nifty leg work. (a.k.a.: *Flash Legs*)

DEADLY SHAOLIN LONGFIST ☆☆
Mike Wong, Elton Chong, Bruce Cheung, Natassa Chan, Chan Fung, Lewis Ko. Directed by Phillip Chan.

Another revenge plot is the frame for this merely average martial-arts film. A young man learns the Shaolin longfist technique in order to avenge the death of his teacher, who was killed after a gold-trade swindle. Nicely executed action sequences are, unfortunately, badly put together, but there are welcome bits of comic relief.

DEADLY STRANGERS ☆☆
1974, Great Britain
Hayley Mills, Simon Ward. Directed by Sidney Hayers. 93 min.

If you have anything like a suspicious mind, the culprit is only too obvious in the *Deadly Strangers*. Although Hayley Mills and Simon Ward perform competently, they are too stiff for real excitement; however, the story is sufficiently interesting to keep one's halfhearted attention.

THE DEADLY STRIKE ☆½
Ho Tsun Tao, Chen Hsing, Tang Wei, Lung Fei. Directed by Huang Lung. 91 min.

This is a kung fu Western, sort of, with new police captain Ho Tsun Tao arriving in a new town with the express purpose of breaking up the gang of Chen Hsing. For manpower, he seeks recruits from the local prison. Dull martial arts without the usual gore and little in the way of spectacular fights.

DEADMAN'S CURVE ☆☆½
1978, USA (TV)
Richard Hatch, Bruce Davison, Pamela Bellwood, Susan Sullivan, Dick Clark. Directed by Richard Compton. 100 min.

This conventional but affecting biography deals with the dark side of the lives of that sunny singing duo of the sixties, Jan and Dean. The optimistic surf-and-sand ambience that inspired their music is captured well. Somehow, this makes the tragedy that follows even more unsettling, as the group's success story is cut short by a car crash that left Jan crippled and hospitalized for over three years.

DEAD MEN DON'T WEAR PLAID ☆☆½
1982, USA, R
Steve Martin, Rachel Ward, Carl Reiner. Directed by Carl Reiner. 89 min.

This parody of the thrillers of the 1940s doesn't work on its own terms, being too smug and knowing in its unaffectionate use of the clichés of the period. The device of interjecting Steve Martin as the bumbling private detective into clips from seventeen old movies backfires. Reiner has the lines designed to make the stars look silly. Martin has the lines; the others have the charisma. Reiner's direction is flat and dull throughout, but the carefully matched black-and-white cinematography and art direction are excellent, and it's hard to dislike a movie whose "supporting cast" includes Humphrey Bogart, Bette Davis, James Stewart, Ava Gardner, and Barbara Stanwyck, among many others.

DEAD MEN WALK ☆
1943, USA
George Zucco, Mary Carlisle, Dwight Frye, Fern Emmett, Robert Strange. Directed by Sam Newfield. 63 min.

Sometimes they even make movies, as this lifeless effort proves. George Zucco plays the twin Clayton doctors, Lloyd and Elwyn, one of whom dies and comes back to life. He spends his nights raiding the village for subjects for his demonic practices, aided by his hunchbacked assistant Zolarr (Dwight Frye). Sam Newfield made so many movies, usually of about this quality, that he often resorted to using pseudonyms. One shudders to think that he may have put his real name on this one because he was proud of it. (And that'll be the *only* time you'll shudder, too.)

DEAD OF NIGHT ☆☆☆½
1945, Great Britain
Michael Redgrave, Googie Withers, Mervyn Jones, Roland Culver, Sally Ann Howes, Basil Radford. Directed by Cavalcanti, Charles Crichton, Basil Dearden, Robert Hamer. 102 min.

This early terror anthology, in which four separate stories are held together with a framing plot, is generally regarded as the best anthology and indeed one of the best fright films ever made. Architect Mervyn Jones has been troubled by odd dreams; when he takes a business trip to a British estate, he meets a group of people, each of whom has figured in his dreams. They in turn relate stories of supernatural experiences they have had. The best-remembered segment stars Michael Redgrave as a ventriloquist who is taken over by his stage dummy; that basic story has been remade as a feature film several times (most recently in 1978's *Magic*), but never as well as here.

THE DEAD ZONE ☆☆½
1983, USA, R
Christopher Walken, Martin Sheen, Brooke Adams, Herbert Lom. Directed by David Cronenberg. 103 min.

This sedate horror film with an emphasis on human problems comes from a novel by Stephen King. After lingering in a coma for five years, a man (Walken) awakens to find himself able to read a person's past, present, and future by the mere touch of his hand, a gift that makes him neither healthy nor wealthy nor even wise. Directed by Canada's reigning macabre filmmaker, also responsible for *They Came from Within*, *Rabid*, *The Brood*, *Scanners* and *Videodrome*; the main attraction here is seeing David Cronenberg's and King's very different styles of horror mesh to interestingly low-key effect.

DEAL OF THE CENTURY ½☆
1983, USA, PG
Chevy Chase, Sigourney Weaver, Gregory Hines, Vince Edwards, William Marquez. Directed by William Friedkin. 98 min.

In this clunky, rambling, hopelessly heavy-handed send-up of the American arms industry, Chevy Chase plays an independent arms contractor who scuttles through Central America hawking weapons with all the sprightly good cheer of a door-to-door vacuum salesman. This dimestore irony might have been cooked up on the old "Saturday Night Live," but to spread it over a two-hour movie, replete with a convoluted caper plot and imitation–*Star Wars* dogfight, is a laborious feat indeed.

DEAR DEAD DELILAH ☆½
1972, USA
Agnes Moorehead, Michael Ansara, Will Geer, Dennis Patrick, Patricia Carmichael. Directed by John Farris. 90 min.

For the talented Agnes Moorehead, who like so many fine actresses turned to low-budget Grand Guignol in the sixties and seventies, this impoverished example of the genre was an unfortunate swan song. As a dying matriarch whose estate is being picked apart by greedy hangers-on, she takes a backseat to the ax murders, decapitations, and grotesqueries that are the genre's hallmarks.

DEAR DETECTIVE ☆☆
1979, USA (TV)
Brenda Vaccaro, Arlen Dean Snyder, Ron Silver, Michael MacRae, R. G. Armstrong, M. Emmet Walsh. Directed by Dean Hargrove. 100 min.

This pilot for a short-lived TV series was a less successful remake of the 1977 French film *Dear Inspector*. Brenda Vaccaro plays a police sergeant who dates a professor while investigating the sexually tinged murders of three city councilmen and a school board member. It's an odd mixture of lighthearted romance and crime drama that doesn't quite work, despite an interesting resolution and a winning performance by Vaccaro.

DEAR INSPECTOR ☆☆☆
1977, France
Annie Girardot, Philippe Noiret, Catherine Alric, Hubert Deschamps. Directed by Philippe De Broca. 105 min.

Philippe De Broca's romantic mystery about a policewoman whose profession interferes with her love life is leavened by delightful performances and deft pacing. Annie Girardot and Philippe Noiret make an unglamorous but convincingly well-matched couple, and despite a slightly slow start, the director cleverly interweaves the murder investigation with the romantic byplay until the two threads meet in the climax. Remade in 1979 for American television as *Dear Detective*, which was the original American release title of this film.

DEATH AT LOVE HOUSE ☆½
1976, USA (TV)
Robert Wagner, Kate Jackson, Sylvia Sidney, Mariana Hill, Joan Blondell, John Carradine, Dorothy Lamour. Directed by E. W. Swackhamer. 73 min.

In this gothic camp, a writer and his wife move into the mansion of long-dead Hollywood starlet Lorna Love, whose creepy spirit begins molesting their familial bliss. It's a pinch of *Sunset Boulevard*, a dash of *The Shining*, and buckets of boredom. Kate Jackson, post "Rookies," pre-Angels looks petulant and miffed throughout, and Robert Wagner, required to fall in love with a horny ghost, looks appropriately glum.

DEATHCHEATERS ☆☆½
1976, Australia
John Hargreaves, Grant Page, Margaret Gerard, Noel Ferrier, Drew Forsythe. Directed by Brian Trenchard Smith. 96 min.

There's not a whole lot of plot, and you can never be too sure that the actors aren't reading their few lines from cue cards, but things like that scarcely matter in this kind of rock 'em, sock 'em adventure. Costar Grant Page, the Australian Hal Needham, also coordinated the elaborate stuntwork in this story about two ex–Vietnam commandos, now working as movie stuntmen, who are hired by the government to reclaim some important papers from an Asian bad guy. Constant action of a fairly nonviolent nature along with an overall lack of seriousness make this satisfactory.

DEATH CORPS

See *Shock Waves*

DEATH CRUISE ☆☆
1974, USA (TV)
Richard Long, Polly Bergen, Edward Albert, Kate Jackson, Celeste Holm, Tom Bosley. Directed by Ralph Senensky. 78 min.

No, it's not a mystery set aboard "The Love Boat," although the familiar cast of TV faces have probably guest-starred on that squeaky-clean series at one point or another. Here they add a comfortable blandness to what should be the tense atmosphere of a seagoing chiller. In a Grim Reaper lottery, five or six winners of a luxury cruise discover they're earmarked for being permanently crossed off the ship's guest list. It's an average TV-movie mystery, as viewers guess who'll make it back to shore in a film that builds all the excitement of an on-deck shuffleboard tournament.

DEATHDREAM ☆☆☆
1972, USA, PG
John Marley, Lynn Carlin, Richard Backus, Henderson Forsythe, Anya Ormsby. Directed by Bob Clark. 90 min.

In this good zombie film, Andy Brooks, killed in Vietnam, is brought back to a horrifying semblance of life by the desperate wishes of his mother. His return divides his family and brings violence to his small hometown. Equal parts W. W. Jacob's *The Monkey's Paw* and topical exploitation from the director and screenwriter (Bob Clark and Alan Ormsby) of *Children Shouldn't Play with Dead Things*. Special effects by Tom Savini (*Dawn of the Dead*), on his first film job. (a.k.a.: *Dead of Night*)

DEATH GAME ☆
1977, USA, R
Sondra Locke, Coleen Camp, Seymour Cassel, Beth Brickell. Directed by Peter Traynor. 89 min.

This is not one of those so-bad-that-it's-funny efforts—though it *is* pretty bad—but the plot is so unaccountably weird that you may sit there with your eyes glued to the screen to see what happens next. Two girls worm their way into the house of a wealthy businessman, seduce him, and then refuse to leave. Along the way they smear ketchup and maple syrup on the furniture, drown a delivery boy in the aquarium, tie up and torture their host, and generally show a lack of good manners. You won't believe the ending. Originally made in 1974, but not released until 1977. (a.k.a.: *The Seducers*)

DEATH HUNT ☆½
1981, USA, R
Charles Bronson, Lee Marvin, Andrew Stevens, Carl Weathers, Ed Lauter, Angie Dickinson, Henry Beckman. Directed by Peter Hunt. 96 min.

It's easy to imagine the title of this film as the spontaneous attitude toward the director felt by audiences as they're leaving the theater. For over an hour and a half, Canadian mounties led by Lee Marvin chase Charles Bronson across the Arctic. It's ostensibly based on a real-life case, but we always thought movies were supposed to be *more* interesting than real life.

DEATH IN VENICE ☆☆☆☆
1971, Italy
Dirk Bogarde, Bjorn Andresen, Silvana Mangano, Marisa Berenson, Mark Burns. Directed by Luchino Visconti. 130 min.

The film features gorgeous photography of Venice and the sumptuous strains of the adagietto from Gustav Mahler's Fifth Symphony. But beneath the stylistic opulence is an over-literal adaptation of Thomas Mann's novella about a famous writer (turned into a Mahleresque composer/conductor here) who becomes infatuated with a beautiful blond boy, the essence of beauty itself. Dirk Bogarde, looking as pale as if he were wearing a death mask, is the central glory of this elaborate embellishment of the novella. Inordinately romantic and lush, the film is more a summation of Luchino Visconti's obsession than it is of Mann's thematic concerns; those who condemn the film for not being the novel have anesthetized themselves to the pleasures of Visconti's recounting of *l'amour fou* against a backdrop of sentimental decadence. An expressive, resonant work.

DEATH JOURNEY ☆½
1975, USA, R
Fred Williamson. Directed by Fred Williamson. 96 min.

One-man studio Fred Williamson once again produces and directs a vehicle for himself. This time he takes his moves from Clint Eastwood, as a private detective assigned to transport a government witness from coast to coast in forty-eight hours. For fans of Williamson only, which means that Fred will probably be the first one to own a copy of this.

DEATH KISS ☆☆
1933, USA
Bela Lugosi, David Manners, Adrienne Ames, John Wray, Edward Van Sloan. Directed by Edwin L. Marin. 74 min.

Despite the title and the presence of three of the stars of *Dracula*, this is not a vampire movie, but a mildly diverting murder mystery set in a movie studio. While filming a gangster movie, in which a character is gunned down after being given a signaling kiss, the director yells "Cut!" and we find that the actor really has been shot. From then on it's the usual stuff, more interesting for the cast than anything else. Bela Lugosi plays the studio manager and Edward Van Sloan (Van Helsing in *Dracula*) the film's director.

DEATH LIST

See *Terminal Choice*

DEATH OF A HOOKER

See *Who Killed Mary What's-'Er-Name?*

DEATH OF A SALESMAN ☆☆½
1951, USA
Fredric March, Mildred Dunnock, Kevin McCarthy, Cameron Mitchell. Directed by Laslo Benedek. 115 min.

Time has been unkind to this early adaptation of Arthur Miller's play, despite a very fine, well-modulated performance by Fredric March as the sixty-three-year-old traveling salesman whose life is beginning to disintegrate. Benedek's direction is stagy and overemphatic, and the dialogue has been rewritten in parts by Stanley Roberts, who is, to put it kindly, not Arthur Miller's equal. Because of the superb 1985 television version starring Dustin Hoffman and directed by Volker Schlondorff, this one seems all the more unnecessary.

DEATH OF A SALESMAN ☆☆☆☆
1985, USA (TV)
Dustin Hoffman, Kate Reid, John Malkovich, Stephen Lang, Charles Durning. Directed by Volker Schlondorff. 135 min.

A stunningly powerful and moving television adaptation of Arthur Miller's play (adapted from an acclaimed Broadway production with the same cast) redeems the drama's too-often-sullied reputation—here nothing about Miller's language or dramaturgy seems clumsy or evasive. Dustin Hoffman isn't what we expect as Willy Loman—he's short and spry, whiny rather than overbearing, and finally ineffably touching; his scenes with John Malkovich's brilliantly nuanced Biff are as fine a display of American acting style as we've seen in many a year. Volker Schlondorff's subtle, unemphatic direction is all one could ask, especially in the scenes where Willy slips into memory and delusion. If you doubt that *Death of a Salesman* is one of the great works of the American theater, don't miss this emphatic affirmation.

DEATH OF A SOLDIER ☆½
1986, Australia, R
James Coburn, Reb Brown, Bill Hunter, Maurie Fields, Michael Pate. Directed by Philippe Mora. 93 min.

Set during World War II, when hundreds of thousands of American soldiers were bivouacked in Australia, *Death of a Soldier* is based on the true story of a psychopathic American serviceman who murdered three women and was summarily hanged by a military court. The ingredients of an interesting tale are here: the clash of cultures, the Jekyll/Hyde murderer, the military conspiracy, the barely repressed wartime hysteria. But in the hands of Philippe Mora—best known for such ghastly pictures as *The Beast Within* and *The Howling II*—the material turns to dross. Every potential nuance is steamrollered across; lots of pretty cinematography just can't save the day.

THE DEATH OF BRUCE LEE ☆½
Ron Van Cliff, Charles Bonet. Directed by Tommy Loo Chung.

The "Black Dragon," Ron Van Cliff, and his buddy, Chuck Bonet, search for the true reason why Bruce Lee died. They don't find it. Spare exploitation of the man essentially synonymous with the genre.

DEATH ON THE NILE ☆☆½
1978, Great Britain, PG
Peter Ustinov, David Niven, Bette Davis, Angela Lansbury, Mia Farrow, George Kennedy, Maggie Smith, Jack Warden, Olivia Hussey, Simon MacCorkindale, Lois Chiles, Jon Finch. Directed by John Guillermin. 140 min.

In this follow-up to *Murder on the Orient Express*, everything is slower: the setting is a boat instead of a train, Hercule Poirot is played by Peter Ustinov instead of Albert Finney, and the director is stodgy John Guillermin (*King Kong*) instead of speedy Sidney Lumet. After some sweeping, gorgeous footage of Egyptian ruins, we're shut up in a paddle-wheeled Nile tour steamer while the bulbous Belgian grills a boatload of superstar suspects in the murder of snooty heiress Lois Chiles. Guessing the killer is pretty tough, but by the time the solution arrives you'll have been so calmed by this slowly rolling movie that you may hardly care.

DEATH RACE 2000 ☆☆
1975, USA, R
David Carradine, Sylvester Stallone, Simone Griffith, Mary Woronov. Directed by Paul Bartel. 78 min.

Here's some tongue-in-cheeck action from the director of *Eating Raoul* and the screenwriter of *Little Shop of Horrors* and *A Bucket of Blood*. It's the year 2000, and jaded America has a new national sport, a cross-country demolition derby in which the drivers get bonus points for running over pedestrians. A black-suited David Carradine is the national champ, Frankenstein; pre-*Rocky* Sylvester Stallone is his arch-rival, Machine Gun Joe Viterbo. Without being an out-and-out comedy, it's still pretty much as silly and camp as it sounds. Sequel: *Deathsport*.

DEATH RAY 2000 ☆½
1981, USA (TV)
Robert Logan, Dan O'Herlihy, Penelope Windust, Ann Turkel, Maggie Cooper, Clive Revill, Ji-Tu Cumbuka. Directed by Lee H. Katzin. 96 min.

This torpid made-for-TV adventure is heavily derived from the James Bond films and "The Man from UNCLE." Robert Logan plays the suave agent of a fictitious intelligence group who teams up with a sexy spy (Ann Turkel) to save the world from imminent disaster. A silly low-grade imitation of its betters; this became the short-lived TV series "A Man Called Sloane," with Robert Conrad in Logan's role.

DEATH RIDES THE PLAINS ☆½
1944, USA
Bob Livingston, Al "Fuzzy" St. John. Directed by Sam Newfield. 53 min.

Livingston and Fuzzy try to track down a man who draws prospective buyers to his ranch to kill and rob them. An average B Western and not such a bad story.

DEATH RIDE TO OSAKA ☆☆
1983, USA (TV)
Jennifer Jason Leigh, Ann Jillian, Thomas Byrd, Mako, Carolyn Seymour. Directed by Jonathan Kaplan. 100 min.

Though hot stuff for a TV movie, this is still only mildly salacious for the jaded tastes of videophiles. If you like your sleaze with lots of innuendo, you may be satisfied with the scattered bits of soft-core porn you'll discover. A Sweet Young Thing with no discernible talent gets her big chance to sing and dance way over in the mysterious Orient. Little does she know what those tired Japanese businessmen like to do for relaxation. It seems they crave teenage white goddesses. Yikes, girls, stick with the USO! The plot thickens as the importunate lass's all-American dolt of a boyfriend stalks Japan to get Pollyanna the hell out of Osaka. Somehow, the talented director manages to create an eerie portrait of a nightclub netherworld where bedmates are peddled along with cigarettes. Solid support from Ann Jillian as a jaded sexual chorine expected to strut her stuff in better hotel suites everywhere. (a.k.a.: *Girls of the White Orchid*)

DEATH SENTENCE ☆☆½
1974, USA (TV)
Cloris Leachman, Laurence Luckinbill, Nick Nolte, William Schallert, Yvonne Wilder. Directed by E. W. Swackhamer. 78 min.

Of all the gimmicky ideas ever to be manipulated into a TV movie, this premise is one of the most surefire. With the evidence flying fast and furious all around her, Cloris Leachman, playing a juror at a murder trial, is befuddled by an astonishing set of circumstances that may point to her husband as the killer. The contrivances are not altogether plausible, but Leachman shows her mettle as the suspicious wife, and the suspense is engendered with careful, taut economy and force.

DEATHSPORT
★★
1978, USA, R
David Carradine, Claudia Jennings, Richard Lynch, Jesse Vint, H. B. Haggerty. Directed by Henry Suso, Allen Arkush. 83 min.

Roger Corman's New World studios, always quick to cash in on an exploitable idea, took a few years to rip off their own *Death Race 2000* by mixing it with the *Star Wars* variety of futuristic antifascism. The result is only sporadically amusing and almost never exciting, mostly because this one doesn't have director Paul Bartel and screenwriter Charles B. Griffith. Set in the year 3000 A.D., it's your basic outer-space Western, with the good guys (the ones with the horses and sabers) versus the bad guys (who are known as "Statesmen" and ride motorcycles) and never much doubt about the outcome.

DEATH SQUAD
★★½
1974, USA (TV)
Robert Forster, Michelle Phillips, Claude Akins, Mark Goddard, Melvyn Douglas. Directed by Harry Falk. 78 min.

This TV movie plays hardball with an interesting premise about a pack of vigilante cops who take the law into their own hands by meting out expedient justice. A brutal, briskly directed action flick, *Squad* dishes out the urban paranoia with conviction and presents a frightening portrait of lawlessness posing as order. This appeared the same year as Clint Eastwood's similarly plotted *Magnum Force* and, for once, the TV movie is more interesting.

DEATH STALK
★½
1974, USA (TV)
Vic Morrow, Vince Edwards, Anjanette Comer, Carol Lynley, Robert Webber. Directed by Robert Day. 72 min.

No, it's not a horror film about killer celery, just a TV movie with a plot ripped off from *Deliverance*. Two men and their wives, on a rafting vacation, are attacked by escaped convicts who take off with the women and leave the men behind. A good cast makes it bearable, but you can do better than this.

DEATHSTALKER
★
1984, USA, R
Richard Hill, Barbi Benton, Richard Brooker, Lana Clarkson, Victor Bo. Directed by John Watson. 80 min.

It gets one star for inventive decapitations, but that's about all there is to say in defense of this generic sword-and-sorcery saga. A blond Adonis searches for the magic medallion and cuts down his hulky enemies, one by one. Everywhere our hero turns, he's confronted by *Playboy* Amazons (including the hilariously incompetent Barbi Benton), who lose no time unveiling their tanned, fleshy bosoms.

DEATHTRAP
★★
1982, USA, PG
Michael Caine, Christopher Reeve, Dyan Cannon, Irene Worth, Henry Jones. Directed by Sidney Lumet. 115 min.

Ira Levin's Broadway smash was an entertaining stage mystery that played off of the limitations of physical space—which is to say, they shouldn't have made a movie out of it. The convoluted plot begins with Michael Caine, a playwright on the tail end of a string of flops, deciding with wife Dyan Cannon to kill Christopher Reeve, one of his former students, so that he can steal a play Reeve has written and pass it off as his own. The performances of the actors are far too campy for the script; one scene, in which Caine pouts and calls Reeve a "big creep," is unintentionally hilarious.

DEATH VALLEY
★★★
1982, USA, R
Paul Le Mat, Catherine Hicks, Stephen McHattie, A. Wilford Brimley, Peter Billingsley. Directed by Dick Richards. 87 min.

A youngster on vacation with his divorced mother and her new boyfriend sees a vicious murder while they're driving over the backroads of the desolate Southwest. The only adult who really believes him is—you guessed it—the psychopathic killer, who wants the young witness silenced. Sleazy, creepy, and well-directed, *Death Valley* is a traveler's nightmare that would make a nice double bill with Robert Harmon's *The Hitcher*, which explores another on-the-road peril in worst-case terms.

DEATH WATCH
★★½
1979, France/Germany, PG
Romy Schneider, Harvey Keitel, Harry Dean Stanton, Max von Sydow, Therese Liotard. Directed by Bertrand Tavernier. 100 min.

Bertrand Tavernier (*The Clockmaker*, *A Sunday in the Country*) directed and cowrote (with David Rayfiel) this witty but pretentious sci-fi thriller about a TV show that records the last days of terminally ill patients. Harvey Keitel plays a cameraman assigned to one dying young woman (Romy Schneider) and Harry Dean Stanton portrays the show's producer. The cast is good but looks out of place; Max von Sydow is thrown in at the end as Schneider's husband for a touch of Ingmar Bergmanism. Attempts at satirizing the media and the public's morbid curiosity inevitably bog down in talky muddle. Filmed in Scotland.

THE DEATH WHEELERS

See *Psychomania* (1971).

DEATH WISH
★★
1974, USA, R
Charles Bronson, Vincent Gardenia, Hope Lange, Steve Keats, William Redfield, Stuart Margolin. Directed by Michael Winner. 93 min.

This was the prototype—along with *Walking Tall*—of the vigilante vengeance genre. Bronson plays a Manhattan architect whose wife and daughter are savagely raped. When the wife dies and the daughter becomes a vegetable, he decides to get even by killing every creep in town—and it's a big town. Very pedestrian direction by Winner, an Englishman. Followed by two sequels.

DEATH WISH II
★½
1982, USA, R
Charles Bronson, Jill Ireland, Robert Sherwood, Vincent Gardenia, J. D. Cannon, Anthony Franciosa. Directed by Michael Winner. 89 min.

The usual excuse for sequels being worse then their progenitors is that they were rush jobs churned out by hacks instead of the original creators. In this case, *Death Wish II* is just as bad as—in fact even worse than—the original precisely *because* the same director made it. As before (and as in the even worse follow-up, below) Bronson is on the streets bashing the butts of those miscreants that the police and courts are just too wimpy to handle themselves, even though they're obviously lowly scum who don't deserve to be sucking the same air as decent citizens like you and me. In other words, more reactionary paranoia. Former Led Zeppelin guitarist Jimmy Page provides a score that even Zep fans, most of whom blew out their eardrums years ago, despise.

DEATH WISH III
½★
1985, USA, R
Charles Bronson, Deborah Raffin, Ed Lauter, Martin Balsam, Gavin O'Herlihy. Directed by Michael Winner. 92 min.

Amazingly enough, it's even worse than *I* and *II*. The timing was certainly apt, 1985 being the year of *Rambo* and *Com-*

mando; in fact, it's surprising that the producers didn't think to throw in a few Russians for Bronson to blow away. Bronson is back in New York, where the flimsiest possible plot setup gives him an excuse to go after a gang of punks, first with guns, then with bigger guns, and finally with a missile launcher. Unforgivably for a director with as much experience as Winner, this isn't even technically competent—you'll find yourself constantly playing with the color and focus knobs to try and correct problems that the filmmakers never bothered with, further proof of the contempt they have for the audiences to whom they're selling this garbage.

THE DECLINE OF THE AMERICAN EMPIRE ☆☆☆½
1986, Canada
Dominique Michael, Dorothee Berryman, Louise Portal, Geneviève Rioux, Pierre Curzi, Rémy Girard, Yves Jacques, Daniel Briere, Gabriel Arcand. Directed by Denys Arcand. 95 min.

This French-Canadian comedy about eight friends sitting around discussing their sexual experiences is a quirky, satisfying mélange of literacy and scabrous humor. The first half cuts back and forth between the talk of the four men as they assemble dinner for the evening and the equally frank dialogue of the four women as they work out at the gym. In the second half, the two groups join each other and the party begins. The principals are Rémy (Rémy Girard), the smooth, controlled, womanizing host, who tells outrageously funny stories with a smug smile, and his wife of fifteen years (Dorothee Berryman), an agreeable, easily shocked woman who has no idea her husband has been fooling around. They're a pair of dyed-in-the-wool bourgeois, and that's why they have the most to lose. There's nothing here but the characters and the entertaining chatter and Denys Arcand's elegant, gliding camera—and it's enough. The intercutting between the men and the women sets up simultaneous comic structures, each with its own set of private jokes and personal recognitions. It's a smashingly democratic comedy, with sex as the great equalizer.

THE DECLINE OF WESTERN CIVILIZATION ☆☆☆½
1981, USA
Circle Jerks, Black Flag, Fear, X, Catholic Discipline, the Germs (these are punk rock groups). Directed by Penelope Spheeris. 100 min.

Penelope Spheeris's remarkable documentary on the Los Angeles hard-core punk scene makes the punk spectacle at once horrifying and hypnotic. Interspersing interviews with concert footage, Spheeris introduces us to bands like Black Flag, the Germs, Catholic Discipline, and Fear, and the effect is like descending into a cultural inferno. Few of these performers, except the discordantly blazing X, can play their instruments or carry a tune, but their violent gatherings aren't so much concerts as California tribal rites.

DECOY FOR TERROR
See *Playgirl Killer*

THE DEEP ☆☆
1977, USA, PG
Robert Shaw, Jacqueline Bisset, Nick Nolte, Louis Gossett, Eli Wallach. Directed by Peter Yates. 124 min.

The underwater photography is very beautiful, better-looking than anything else of its kind. That aside, producer Peter Guber and director Yates have made of Peter Benchley's best-seller a racist, sexist, and downright silly fiasco. The plot, about a young couple and a grizzled treasure hunter who explore an undersea wreck that hides still another undersea wreck, is unwieldy to begin with, and Yates renders it as jerkily as possible. The action scenes undercut their own suspense and the thrills are tacky and formulaic. Instead of the light summer chiller this should have been, it's a hollow, offensive waste of time.

DEEP END ☆☆☆
1970, West Germany/USA, R
John Moulder-Brown, Jane Asher, Diana Dors. Directed by Jerzy Skolimowski. 88 min.

In this stylishly directed, complex drama, famed writer Skolimowski makes a smooth transition to the film media. The film works in a downward spiral as an impressionable adolescent develops a wild crush on a beautiful bathhouse attendant. As his fantasies about her grow in intensity, he begins to act on his impulses by planning to eliminate his rival for her affections and to woo the older woman no matter what the cost. Moulder-Brown is astonishingly good as the obsessed youth; and the film is disturbing and imaginative, particularly in the chilling denouement.

DEEP IN MY HEART ☆☆½
1954, USA
Jose Ferrer, Helen Traubel, Merle Oberon, Doe Avedon, Walter Pidgeon, Paul Henreid, Ann Miller, Gene Kelly, Jane Powell, Howard Keel, Vic Damone. Directed by Stanley Donen. 132 min.

This MGM musical is at odds with itself. Although the film is about operetta stalwart Sigmund Romberg, the film is laced with musical-comedy guest appearances. One relishes the fact that this isn't another overstuffed bio like *The Great Caruso*, but the bright song-and-dance spots only liven the film up a bit without transforming it. The high spots include Gene Kelly dancing with his brother Fred to "I Love to Go Swimmin' with Wimmen" and Ann Miller doing a torrid dance to "It." So you can disrespectfully fast-forward through Romberg's life and get to the numbers by such stars as Jane Powell, Howard Keel, and Vic Damone.

DEEP RED: HATCHET MURDERS ☆☆☆½
1976, Italy, R
David Hemmings, Daria Nicolodi, Gabriele Lavia, Clara Callemai, Macha Menil. Directed by Dario Argento. 98 min.

In this top-notch psycho-thriller, set in a warped city of the mind in which nothing is what it seems and darkness lurks behind the eyes of the loveliest little girl, an English pianist living in Rome becomes enmeshed in a web of brutal murder and insanity after he witnesses the bloody demise of one of his neighbors. It is both convoluted and stylish. Argento has also directed *The Bird with the Crystal Plumage, Cat O'Nine Tails*, and others. (a.k.a.: *The Hatchet Murders*)

THE DEEP SIX ☆☆
1958, USA
Alan Ladd, Diane Foster, William Bendix, Keenan Wynn, James Whitmore, Efrem Zimbalist, Jr., Joey Bishop, Ross Bagdasarian, Jeanette Nolan. Directed by Rudolph Mate. 105 min.

This is a standard World War II naval adventure with one twist: our hero is a Quaker who must overcome his crewmates' snickers about his pacifism. Ladd in the lead and Bendix as his pal Frenchy Shapiro set new standards for religious tolerance as they mow down those godless Japanese left and right. Featuring Ross Bagdasarian as a sailor with a girl in every port, Joey Bishop as (what else?) the ship's clown, and James Whitmore as a dedicated guy. Wasn't World War II a great time for brotherhood?

THE DEER HUNTER ☆☆☆☆
1978, USA, R
Robert De Niro, Christopher Walken, John Cazale, John Savage, Meryl Streep, George Dzundza. Directed by Michael Cimino. 183 min.

Michael Cimino's controversial masterpiece about three Pennsylvania steelworkers who leave their small town for the horrors of Vietnam was perhaps the first mainstream film to posit that the war was bad but the soldiers who fought it were nonetheless heroes. This opened it up to scathing criticism from both liberals and conservatives, but most conceded that it was a work of astounding emotional power and skill, perhaps the first great screen depiction of the Vietnam experience. Cimino's epic work is divided into three sections. The first is a beautifully realized wedding sequence that also serves as a send-off for heroes Michael, Nick, and Steven. The second, taking place in Vietnam, is a war sequence of wrenching genius. In the last hour, the three men realize their fates as human beings and Americans on both sides of the globe. Notwithstanding the later debacle of *Heaven's Gate*, Cimino here proves himself in superb control of his actors and story, treating his painful material with balance, integrity, and intelligence (although he overemphasizes the awkward allegorical motifs). Standouts in the fine cast include the unforgettable performance of Walken, as the most fragile of the three men, and Streep, a vivid and eloquent presence in an almost wordless role. Attack it, argue with it, interpret it your own way, but you must see this extraordinary work about friendship, war, love, and loss. Winner of five Academy Awards.

DEFIANCE
☆☆½
1980, USA, PG
Jan-Michael Vincent, Theresa Saldana, Fernando Lopez, Danny Aiello, Art Carney, Lenny Montana. Directed by John Flynn. 102 min.

Filmed prior to *The Warriors*, this film about gang violence in an urban neighborhood was withheld from release for a while in the wake of the real-life violence that the other film allegedly obscured. Seaman Vincent, in between trips, takes a room in a decaying New York neighborhood and becomes involved with some of the longtime residents who refuse to move out despite harassment by a local street gang. Vincent teaches them to stand up to the gang, while trying to decide whether to leave for sea duty or remain. Better than most of its ilk, but still too violent and reactionary to make a serious statement.

THE DEFIANT ONES
☆☆☆½
1958, USA
Tony Curtis, Sidney Poitier, Theodore Bikel, Lon Chaney, Jr., Cara Williams. Directed by Stanley Kramer. 97 min.

Stanley Kramer's literal style was never put to better use than in this racial drama. Though the quasi-liberal attitudes seem a little dated now, the drama itself still packs a powerful punch. Tony Curtis and Sidney Poitier are at their best, playing escaped convicts who are chained together and are therefore forced to tolerate one another. This simplistic approach to the complex problem of racism is a bit more tolerable than it might sound, given that the film was made in the very early stages of the civil rights movement. Stanley Kramer's direction (aided enormously by Sam Leavitt's Oscar-winning camerawork) is admirably straightforward and nonsensational.

A DELICATE BALANCE
☆☆☆
1973, USA, PG
Katharine Hepburn, Paul Scofield, Lee Remick, Kate Reid, Betsy Blair, Joseph Cotten. Directed by Tony Richardson. 132 min.

Tony Richardson may be known for his cinematic virtuosity in films like *Tom Jones* and *The Loved One*, but this American Film Theater adaptation of Edward Albee's Pulitzer Prize–winning play is stagebound. As in *Who's Afraid of Virginia Woolf?*, Albee penetrates the seemingly calm surfaces of the American middle class; this time, the story deals with an aging couple (Hepburn and Scofield) who try to hold their family together during the visit of some unwanted houseguests (Cotten and Blair). Despite fine acting, the film sometimes resembles a pretentiously postmodern *On Golden Pond*. The film is noteworthy because it is one of the few movie roles for England's Paul Scofield, one of the very great actors of this era.

DELIRIUM
☆½
1979, USA, R
Debi Chaney, Turk Cekovsky, Terry Ten Broeck, Barron Winchester, Nick Panouzis. Directed by Peter Maris. 90 min.

This cookie-cutter drive-in fare is from the same company that produced *Take Time to Smell the Flowers* and *Stingray*. Two Vietnam vets, backed by rich businessmen, start a private vigilante organization to find and kill "crooks" found innocent by regular judicial processes. Panouzis plays the mute killer of young women whose transcontinental murder spree occupies most of the plot. Mindless and unremarkable.

DELIVERANCE
☆☆☆½
1972, USA, R
Burt Reynolds, Jon Voight, Ronny Cox, Ned Beatty, James Dickey. Directed by John Boorman. 109 min.

John Boorman's now-classic film is both adventure tale and morality fable. James Dickey's screenplay, based on his own novel, details how four city businessmen encounter hostile Appalachian natives while shooting the rapids on a weekend trip. Vilmos Zsigmond's photography is excellent and there are striking moments, including the sexual assault of one of the men, but the film trades in the book's ruminations on ethics and existence for machismo and excitement. An interesting, occasionally disturbing film, but definitely not the great work it has been said to be.

DELTA FORCE
☆
1986, USA, R
Lee Marvin, Chuck Norris, George Kennedy, Shelley Winters, Hanna Schygulla, Susan Strasberg, Robert Vaughn, Bo Svenson. Directed by Menahem Golan. 126 min.

Exploitation filmmaking hits a new low. Chuckie boy helms a trained commando crew who are experts at defusing hijacking situations. Not only does the film rip off a real-life event, it throws in every horrible detail surrounding it. (At least the Cannon Films research department is on its toes.) The hijacking of TWA Flight 847 is reproduced here as if it were a TV docudrama, cross-pollinated with the virulent spores of a mindless, junky action pic like *Invasion U.S.A.* Portraying the German flight attendant is international critics' darling Hanna Schygulla, once compared to Dietrich but now ripe for comparisons with Karen Black in *Airport 1975*.

DELTA FOX
☆
1977, USA
Richard Lynch, Priscilla Barnes, Stuart Whitman, John Ireland. Directed by Beverly and Ferd Sebastian. 92 min.

This is claptrap about a smuggler eluding capture across the country and about all the assorted movie clichés who pursue him along the way. If an adventure flick can't manage the plot mechanics adroitly and bores you to tears during all the foolproof action sequences, then there's no hope. Substandard.

DELUSIONS OF GRANDEUR
☆☆☆
1971, France
Yves Montand, Louis De Funes, Alice Sapritch, Karin Schubert, Alberto De Mendoza. Directed by Gerard Oury. 105 min.

The fourth of Oury's massive, richly clad French period comedies adds to the amiable costume jewelry of his previous works one genuine diamond: the Montand–De Funes pairing. Loosely based on Hugo's *Ruy Blas*, its fulcrum is the uneasy balance between the nobles' tax collector and his peasant victims. The intricate plot starts with De Funes as the collector; Montand, whose sympathies are always with the underclass, secures the position by unwittingly rescuing the king and queen from some explosives. Setting out to equalize France, Montand falls into disfavor and is sold into the slave trade. Lavishly detailed and rich in costumes and color, *Delusions* is often guilty of substituting mugging for acting, but the comic grandeur of its principals is a shining thing to watch.

DEMENTIA

See *Daughter of Horror*

DEMENTIA 13 ☆☆½
1963, USA
Luana Anders, William Campbell, Bart Patton, Mary Mitchell, Patrick Magee. Directed by Francis Ford Coppola. 81 min.

Just out of UCLA, Coppola was already experimenting with genre conventions, and this inexpensive Roger Corman–produced horror film has many imaginative touches. Luana Anders plays a woman seeking her late husband's fortune while an ax-murderer prowls the estate. The shock effects are of the William Castle variety, but Coppola shows his first signs of promise (and his last for a couple of pictures) in what was his second film (the first was the soft-porn *Tonite for Sure*). Filmed in Ireland.

DEMETRIUS AND THE GLADIATORS ☆☆½
1954, USA
Victor Mature, Susan Hayward, Michael Rennie, Debra Paget, Anne Bancroft, Jay Robinson, William Marshall, Richard Egan, Ernest Borgnine. Directed by Delmer Daves. 101 min.

In this sequel to the biblical epic *The Robe*, the Roman slave Demetrius, who in the original sat at Christ's feet as he was crucified, struggles with his newfound faith while trying to deliver the garment worn by Christ to the apostle Peter. Of course, temptations (of the female variety) and tribulations (mostly caused by that wacky emperor Caligula) abound. Director Daves was fond of showy camera technique, particularly complicated crane shots, and he had lots of chances to display it in this Cinemascope spectacle. Unfortunately, very little of that translates well when reduced down to video proportions.

DEMON ☆☆½
1977, USA, R
Tony LoBianco, Sandy Dennis, Sylvia Sidney, Sam Levene, Robert Drivas, Mike Kellin, Deborah Raffin. Directed by Larry Cohen. 87 min.

A New York City police detective investigating a rash of unusual murders (the perpetrators all admit to their crimes while explaining that "God told me to") uncovers a bizarre link between the killings and his own past. Marred by poor production values, but another amazing idea from the writer/producer/director of *It's Alive*, *The Stuff*, and others. Originally called *God Told Me To*.

THE DEMON ☆
1981, USA
Cameron Mitchell, Jennifer Holmes, Craig Gardener, Zoli Markey, Peter J. Elliott. Directed by Percival Rubens. 94 min.

The Demon meanders through two entirely different stories—without ever managing to link them through anything other than the presence of the titular demon, a structural device that is interesting but serves absolutely no purpose. With the exception of one real surprise about three-quarters of the way through, it offers not a single original shock or twist on genre conventions, and it's maddeningly inconclusive as well. Something inhuman kidnaps young Emily Parker and later stalks a schoolteacher, spying on her from the shadows and telephoning her at odd hours. So what?

DEMONIAC ☆
1980, Spain
Pierre Taylor, Olivier Mathod, Françoise Goussart. Directed by Jesus Franco. 87 min.

At God's behest, an excommunicated seminarian terrorizes the degenerates of Paris, murdering whores, temptresses, and sundry sinners. He is hunted both by local police and by an agent from Interpol, tempted by all manner of loose women, and cultivated by the publisher of a magazine that specializes in sadomasochistic melodrama, to which he has submitted an autobiographical article. Prolific Spanish exploitation director Franco has taken this unpromising material and rendered it absolutely stultifying. *Demoniac* is shamelessly padded with shots of the maniac wandering the streets, people dancing in tacky discotheques, and scenic views of Paris, while its various murders are given perfunctory treatment at best. In this type of film, this is a major failing. Dull, dull, dull.

DEMONOID ☆
1979, USA, R
Samantha Eggar, Stuart Whitman, Roy Cameron Jensen. Directed by Alfred Zacharias. 85 min.

An excavation in Mexico uncovers a metal hand that exerts a malefic influence over all those who come into contact with it. They are driven to acts of gory violence and can escape only by destroying their own hands. Generally silly and virtually indistinguishable from a host of similar efforts; likely to amuse only die-hard horror fans desperate for something to watch. Not released until 1982. (a.k.a.: *Demonoid—Messenger of Death*)

DEMONOID—MESSENGER OF DEATH

See *Demonoid*

DEMON RAGE ½☆
1978, USA, R
Lana Wood, Britt Ekland, Kabir Bendi, Don Galloway, John Carradine, Sherry Scott. Directed by James Polakof. 98 min.

A neglected wife attracts a demon lover to her modern house by the sea; his presence causes considerable dismay to her husband, friends, and teenaged daughter. *Demon Rage*'s relatively respectable cast cannot save it from the fact that it is phenomenally boring, a supernatural sex-thriller that seems wedded to the notion that all supernatural phenomena are better left to the imagination of the viewer. Since it contains nothing much—with the exception of some perfunctory colored lighting—to spark that imagination, this is a misguided assumption. Natalie Wood's sister, Lana, plays the wife and Britt Ekland a friend of the family whose husband is decapitated in the basement. (a.k.a.: *Satan's Mistress, Dark Eyes, Fury of the Succubus*)

DEMONS ☆☆
1986, Italy
Fiore Argento. Directed by Lamberto Bava. 90 min.

In between its bursts of gore, this stylish Italian horror film has some pertinent things to say about the relation of film violence to the people who are watching it. *Demons* makes its bloody points when the titular characters invade a theater showing a slasher film, and the patrons soon find the action in their seats far more horrific than what's on the screen. There are some unnecessary sadomasochistic detours en route to the catastrophic payoff, but director Lamberto Bava keeps the killings fast and furious and displays some chillingly imaginative touches to rival his father Mario (*Black Sunday*). Still, the effect of all this might have been greater if the picture were subtitled.

DEMON SEED ☆☆
1977, USA, R
Julie Christie, Fritz Weaver, Gerrit Graham, voice of Robert Vaughn. Directed by Donald Cammell. 94 min.

Julie Christie plays a woman whose marriage to a scientist (Fritz Weaver) is crumbling. He spends too much time with his many computers, which seem to be able to do most anything—and one of them decides to rape his wife. Soon after she learns she is pregnant, yet another unmemorable horror tale is under way. Christie and Weaver are good actors, but you'll be laughing instead of screaming at *Demon Seed*.

LE DERNIER COMBAT ★★★
1984, France, R
Pierre Jolivet, Jean Bouise, Fritz Wepper, Jean Reno. Directed by Luc Besson. 90 min.

Sharply etched sci-fi filmed in stark black and white *sans* dialogue, this film probes the interdependencies of human relationships after the apocalypse. In an imaginative odyssey, it affords insight into the developing friendship of a wordless wanderer and a doctor holed up in his hospital. While detailing the emotions still possible in this bleak, numbing environment, the film provides its own quiet authority along with a constant ability to delight and surprise us. Based on a J. G. Ballard novel, the film will please fans of action fantasy films like *Mad Max* and *Quest for Fire*, yet will also give the audience something to think about.

DERZU UZALA ★★★★
1975, Japan/Russia
Maxim Munzuk, Yuri Solomine. Directed by Akira Kurosawa. 140 min.

In this superior survival drama, a gold hunter helps an explorer learn to cope with the rigors of Siberia, and both men learn that they must keep their spirits as well as their bodies thriving in order to survive. Due to Kurosawa's continual struggles to find backing in his own country, this magisterial nature epic was a Soviet-Japanese coproduction. The joint venture yielded fecund results: the Spartan atmosphere of existence in these harsh wastelands has been captured with startling effectiveness. At all times, the two protagonists are related to the vast landscapes that fill the screen with a savage and barren beauty; in fact, Kurosawa's genius makes this icy environment into a supporting character. Much of the effect is, unfortunately, diminished on video. Winner of an Academy Award for Best Foreign Film.

DESERT BLOOM ★★★
1986, USA, PG
Jon Voight, JoBeth Williams, Ellen Barkin, Annabeth Gish, Allen Garfield. Directed by Eugene Corr. 106 min.

This sincere, powerful, often touching family drama is set against a striking backdrop—the first, secret A-bomb tests in the Nevada desert. It's 1950, and thirteen-year-old Rose Chismore (Gish) awaits the Big Bang while suffering through a home life that's almost as explosive. Her stepfather (Voight) is a crank and a brute, and her mother (Williams) is a loving but ineffectual dummy given to platitudes like "Promises don't butter the bread—the proof is in the pudding." Enter flamboyant, sexy Starr (Barkin), the kind of aunt every teenage girl should have; when she arrives in Vegas for a quickie divorce, some very familiar conflicts begin to percolate. First-time director Eugene Corr is unexpectedly handy at overcoming his own slow, housebound script, and he's helped by Voight's startlingly precise, vivid work as the emotionally crippled drinker, Jack. In the central rose, Gish turns in a lovely performance that gives the small-scale story what it needs.

THE DESERT FOX ★
1951, USA
James Mason, Cedric Hardwicke, Jessica Tandy, Luther Adler, Everett Sloane, Leo G. Carroll, Richard Boone, Desmond Young, Dan O'Herlihy. Directed by Henry Hathaway. 88 min.

This is nonsensical tripe about those poor, misguided German soldiers and generals who were fighting under the command of that incompetent bully, Adolf Hitler. Working from Brigadier Desmond Young's memoirs, Nunnally Johnson has scripted a film that is not only simpleminded, but a history lesson that is perilously close to being neofascist. It's surprising that it was ever made, and even more shocking that it was a box-office success. The "Fox" of the title is Field Marshal Erwin Rommel (James Mason), the man who led the Führer's North African campaign, and he is given the most sympathetic treatment imaginable. In addition to its ideological offenses, the film is artistically shoddy and unclearly structured. The sequel was called *The Desert Rats* (1953).

DESERT HEARTS ★★★
1986, USA, R
Helen Shaver, Patricia Charbonneau, Audra Lindley, Andra Akers, Gwen Welles, Dan Butler, James Stanley. Directed by Donna Deitch. 97 min.

A very interesting premise results in an often poignant love story by first-time director Donna Deitch. In 1959, a woman travels to Reno to get a divorce and finds herself attracted to a young, free-spirited lesbian. The relationship between the older, cold Columbia University professor and the sexy, earthy woman occasionally shows us something about women's feelings and sexual roles; but audiences also get long, dreary conversations about Life. The acting is solid and Charbonneau is very appealing as the artist; even Audra Lindley shows more than one could hope for, given her work on TV's "Three's Company" and "The Ropers." Helen Shaver is vulnerable and touching as the eastern academic.

THE DESERT OF THE TARTARS ★★
1976, France/Italy/Iran, PG
Vittorio Gassman, Giuliano Gemma, Helmut Griem, Philippe Noiret, Fernando Rey, Jean-Louis Trintignant, Max von Sydow. Directed by Valerio Zurlini. 140 min.

As dry as the desert in which it is set, this is another European drama made available to you through the advent of the VCR. You'll have to be extremely patient, as this failed bit of existentialism spends a lot of time going nowhere. A sort of cross between *Grand Illusion* and *The Keep*, it is set in a desert fortress surrounded by a deserted village. Stationed there are a group of hard-core professional soldiers awaiting a Tartar attack that may or may not ever occur. An excellent international cast does what it can, but this is a lifeless venture. Dubbed into English.

THE DESERT RATS ★★½
1953, USA
Richard Burton, James Mason, Robert Douglas, Torin Thatcher. Directed by Robert Wise. 88 min.

This follow-up to the *The Desert Fox* rights the wrong of the previous film by presenting a less sympathetic portrait of Field Marshal Rommel, commander of the Nazi troops in North Africa. The story now concentrates on a British captain (Burton) who resists the Axis forces in the battle of Tobruk. Burton is excellent, but Mason (as Rommel) has little to do in brief segments that tie the film together. Like its predecessor, *Rats* is a scrappy mixture of studio and outdoor action footage, but this one doesn't offend.

DESERT TRAIL ★½
1935, USA
John Wayne, Mary Kornman. Directed by Cullen Lewis. 54 min.

Wayne stars in this average horse-opera tale of mistaken identity.

DESIRE ★★★½
1936, USA
Marlene Dietrich, Gary Cooper, John Halliday, William Frawley, Akim Tamiroff, Ernest Cossart. Directed by Frank Borzage. 89 min.

After becoming a producer, Ernst Lubitsch hired directors like George Cukor, Otto Preminger, and, for this film, Frank Borzage to duplicate his celebrated "Lubitsch touch." This is by far the most successful imitation-Lubitsch—better in some ways than the real article. (Borzage even pokes fun at Lubitsch's airless, hothouse style of mise-en-scène.) Dietrich, at times resembling a department store mannequin, plays a jewel thief out to dupe Cooper, a wealthy car designer. Her character spends so much time trying to outwit his that their unlikely romance becomes almost an afterthought in the Edwin Justus Mayer—Waldemar Young—Samuel Hoffenstein screenplay (based on a German play and film). Dietrich seems to be enjoying her break from playing Von Sternberg heroines and Cooper is as goofy-sexy as ever. A witty, enjoyable treat, but a little creepy.

DÉSIRÉE ★★½
1954, USA
Jean Simmons, Marlon Brando, Merle Oberon, Michael Rennie, Cameron Mitchell, Elizabeth Sellars, Carolyn Jones. Directed by Henry Koster. 110 min..

Henry Koster's heavy, sugarcoated storytelling clashes with Marlon Brando's fire-and-ice performance in this highly fictionalized account of Napoleon's mistress. Jean Simmons stars as Désirée, Napoleon's true love and the peasant girl who becomes queen of Sweden, but it is Brando who steals the spotlight. He played Napoleon to fulfill a contractual commitment—and it shows—but he does not offer a darker, less romantic portrayal than those of Albert Dieudonne (*Napoleon*), Charles Boyer (*Conquest*), and Rod Steiger (*Waterloo*). The rest of the film is a laughable love-triangle soap, with Josephine (Oberon) lashing out at "the other woman." Video viewers will lose some of the Cinemascope splendor, but the sets and costumes are still impressive.

DESK SET ★★★½
1957, USA
Spencer Tracy, Katharine Hepburn, Joan Blondell, Gig Young, Dina Merrill. Directed by Walter Lang. 103 min.

Tracy and Hepburn are such brilliant farceurs that they make even the wispiest material seem hilarious. For their eighth teaming, Phoebe and Henry Ephron adapted William Marchant's play about an absentminded computer expert (Tracy) who is preparing to install a high-tech system in the reference section (headed by Hepburn) of a major corporation. The two eggheads hit it off, much to the consternation of Kate's sometime fiancé (Gig Young). The setup is perfect for Tracy's sidesplitting double takes and several scintillating Hepburn-Tracy exchanges (their rooftop lunch tête-à-tête is priceless). Hepburn was often at her most appealing with Tracy; just one of their knowing glances says more than a whole canon from another screen team.

DESPAIR ★★★½
1978, West Germany/France
Dirk Bogarde, Andrea Ferreol, Volker Spengler, Klaus Lowitsch. Directed by Rainer Werner Fassbinder. 119 min.

Fassbinder's brightly stylish, big-budget, English-language feature, wryly written by Tom Stoppard from the novel by Vladimir Nabokov, somehow manages to meld these large, divergent talents into a dense, layered film. Dirk Bogarde stars as Hermann Hermann, a middle-aged chocolate manufacturer who plunges to the depths of melancholia when he realizes that his cozy little life will probably never change. Perhaps it is Nabokov who comes through most strongly in this plight of a man who wants to muliply himself—literally—toward freedom, but succeeds only in fragmenting his life. Fassbinder's eclectic visual sense allows for a nice objectification of Hermann's interior life. He surrounds the alienated émigré with glass and mirrors and sends him to a strange movie about twins and a meeting with his doppelgänger.

DESPERATE CHASE

See *Blood of the Dragon*.

DESPERATE JOURNEY ★★★
1942, USA
Errol Flynn, Ronald Reagan, Raymond Massey, Nancy Coleman, Alan Hale, Arthur Kennedy, Sig Ruman. Directed by Raoul Walsh. 107 min.

Quite similar, in both plot line and propagandistic intent, to Michael Powell and Emeric Pressburger's *49th Parallel* and *One of Our Aircraft Is Missing*, this is an Americanized version of the story about the group of soldiers shot down in enemy territory trying to make their way back home. It's much more self-consciously flag-waving than the British films—a few segments seem laughable without the context of war—but, thanks to the rapid pacing of master action director Raoul Walsh, it's also much more exciting, and holds up quite well.

DESPERATE LIVES ★★★
1982, USA (TV)
Diana Scarwid, Doug McKeon, Helen Hunt, William Windom, Art Hindle. Directed by Robert Lewis. 100 min.

This problem drama—an earnest stay-away-from-drugs pic—succeeds in presenting an accurate portrait of confused adolescents. It doesn't sentimentalize them, nor does it preach about the dangers of drug abuse so sanctimoniously that it ends up as a modern-day *Reefer Madness*. The plot line follows one particular case as a caring counselor tries to reach a brother and sister who deal with their problems by escaping into drugs. Provocative.

DESPERATE LIVING ½★
1977, USA, X
Liz Renay, Mink Stole, Edith Massey, Mary Vivian Pearce, Cookie Mueller. Directed by John Waters. 90 min.

This is John Waters's worst and most pretentious film. Grotesque, snail-paced, and surprisingly humorless for Waters, the movie never recovers from the fact that Divine isn't in it. A lady wrestler and a murderess express their love by invading Mortville, a haven for criminals. There they revolt against a grossly wicked queen (played by Edith Massey, who's stymied by the seriousness of the enterprise). The meanings of this twisted metaphysical fairy tale will escape you; the camp value is nil. Except for one smashing early sequence in which Mink Stole has a semi-breakdown over the phone, the film is a disappointment. Disgusting without being liberating, cruel without being funny; this is desperate filmmaking.

DESPERATELY SEEKING SUSAN ★★★
1985, USA, PG-13
Rosanna Arquette, Aidan Quinn, Madonna, Laurie Metcalf, Steven Wright, Anne Carlisle, Anne Magnuson, John Lurie, Richard Hell, Shirley Stoler, Arto Lindsay, Richard Edson. Directed by Susan Seidelman. 103 min.

Beneath one of the most annoyingly overused plot devices of all time—woman is hit on the head, wakes up and thinks she's someone else—Susan Seidelman's breezy, feminist-hip film is a slickly packaged bundle of pleasant surprises, a comic romance that turns enough unexpected corners to keep your eyebrows raised. Roberta (Rosanna Arquette), a New Jersey housewife who follows the escapades of Susan (Madonna) through personal ads in the newspaper, starts to hang out in the East Village—and everyone gets the idea she's Susan herself. As she escapes from suburbia into a darkly colorful underworld, she learns to break away from the male projections that have been foisted upon her and enjoy the fun of reinventing herself. Madonna doesn't get far beneath her plethora of jewelry and costumes, but Arquette is endearing.

DESPERATE WOMEN ★½
1978, USA (TV)
Susan Saint James, Dan Haggerty, Ronee Blakely, Susan Myers, Ann Dusenberry, Max Gail, Randolph Powell. Directed by Earl Bellamy. 100 min.

In this desperate attempt at comedy, Western style, three feisty gals dumped kerplunk in the middle of the desert are left to feed the vultures. Instead, they join forces with an ex-gunman and plan revenge. As they track a human set of buzzards, their allegedly comic escapades to thwart the Prairie varmints who left them to die provide a few laughs. But this is not in a league with *Cat Ballou*.

DESTINATION GOBI
1953, USA ☆½
Richard Widmark, Don Taylor, Casey Adams, Murvyn Vye, Darryl Hickman, Martin Milner. Directed by Robert Wise. 89 min.

Someone out there in Hollywood thought that a movie about a bunch of World War II American sailors wandering around the Gobi desert trying to get the natives to help them battle the Japanese would make a good movie, so who are we to argue? It gets points for a certain weirdness value—sailors in the desert??—and for the familiar TV faces in the cast, including Martin Milner ("Adam-12"), Earl Holliman ("Police Woman"), Alvy Moore (Mr. Drucker on "Green Acres"), and Darryl Hickman. Want more? Well, costar Don Taylor went on to direct *Damien: Omen II* and *Escape From the Planet of the Apes*; Casey Adams's real name was Max Showalter, which he went back to using after 1963; and Ross Bagdasarian later became better known as David Seville, creator of Alvin and the Chipmunks. As for director Robert Wise, he was the editor who chopped up Orson Welles's original version of *The Magnificent Ambersons* while Welles was out of the country, and as if that weren't bad enough, went on to direct *Star Trek—the Movie*. We promise, reading this trivia is much more fun than actually watching *Destination Gobi*.

DESTINATION MOON
1950, USA ☆☆☆
John Archer, Warner Anderson, Tom Powers, Dick Wesson. Directed by Irving Pichel. 91 min.

Though not as visually enthralling or interesting as *Things to Come*, this film, too, is a milestone in the history of science-fiction films for its cerebral and fairly realistic (for its time) handling of a trip to the Moon. Everything's described and done with meticulous detail; however, only when the rocketship gets to the planetoid do things start to get interesting. The most entertaining sequence involves a superfluous cameo by Woody Woodpecker. Produced by George Pal.

DESTINATION TOKYO
1943, USA ☆☆½
Cary Grant, John Garfield, Alan Hale, John Ridgely, Robert Hutton, Tom Tully, Whit Bissell. Directed by Delmer Daves. 135 min.

Or, "What Part the Submarine Played in Winning the Pacific War." Overlong but involving World War II rouser casts noncombatant Grant as the captain of an American sub on its way from San Francisco to Tokyo as part of a mission to pave the way for an attack on a Japanese aircraft carrier. Director Daves provides a fine feel for his characters, many of whom stand out from the usual melting-pot war-film cast.

THE DESTRUCTORS
1974, Great Britain, PG ☆½
Michael Caine, Anthony Quinn, James Mason, Maureen Kerwin, Marcel Bozzuffi. Directed by Robert Parrish. 89 min.

In this pale thriller derived from *The French Connection* (as was almost every other action film in the early seventies), Anthony Quinn plays the American narcotics officer out to bring in or bring down James Mason, an international drug czar operating out of Marseilles. Though he gets top billing, Michael Caine has only a supporting role as a hired killer—but he's the best thing in the movie, so they got that right. The sound of Mason's distinctively British voice trying to employ a French accent is quite jarring.

DESTRY RIDES AGAIN
1939, USA ☆☆☆
James Stewart, Marlene Dietrich, Brian Donlevy, Charles Winninger, Mischa Auer, Una Merkel, Billy Gilbert. Directed by George Marshall. 94 min.

The bizarre teaming of Stewart and Dietrich is still the most interesting feature of this celebrated but overrated Western. The blend of genres is pleasant and the cast is perfect, but the film is no *Stagecoach*. Stewart plays the pacifist sheriff of an untamed western town and Dietrich is the dance-hall hostess who gives him a hard time. Of course, he shows his violent nature (i.e., manhood) and she gets her just deserts (for being a "bad" girl), but then, why should the story be different from any other of the day? The knockout fight between Marlene and Una Merkel, and Marlene's camp classic song "See What the Boys in the Back Room Will Have" are the highlights. Remade as *Frenchy* (1950) and *Destry* (1954).

THE DETECTIVE
1968, USA ☆☆½
Frank Sinatra, Lee Remick, Jacqueline Bisset, Jack Klugman, Ralph Meeker, Horace MacMahon, Lloyd Bochner, William Windom, Robert Duvall. Directed by Gordon Douglas. 114 min.

Sinatra's fans may enjoy him in this grim, nasty police procedural about a detective trying to unravel a homosexual slaying while coping with a nymphomaniacal wife and corruption in the force. The treatment of blacks and homosexuals is the worst kind of late-sixties pseudoliberalism—the kind that portrayed both groups with exaggerated negative stereotypes. The story, however, is compelling enough to hold one's attention.

DETECTIVE STORY
1951, USA ☆☆☆
Kirk Douglas, Eleanor Parker, Horace MacMahon, William Bendix, Lee Grant. Directed by William Wyler. 103 min.

Wyler demonstrates his expertise in translating Broadway hits into taut, satisfying screen entertainments (as he did before this with *The Little Foxes* and *The Desperate Hours*). Kirk Douglas juts his jaw with authority as the by-the-book detective who becomes hardened over the years after dealing with deceitful crooks as part of his daily routine. He becomes so brutalized that he begins treating everyone around him in the same rigid manner, unable to forgive his wife when a terrible secret from her past emerges. The film is a triumph of sharp direction, and is an actor's showcase. Look for Lee Grant in the small, flashy role of a pickpocket, a role that propelled her to mini-stardom as one of our best character actresses. Grant has become a talented film director in recent years.

DETOUR
1945, USA ☆☆☆
Tom Neal, Ann Savage, Claudia Drake, Edmund MacDonald, Tim Ryan. Directed by Edgar G. Ulmer. 68 min.

Edgar G. Ulmer (*Bluebeard*, *Ruthless*) directed this classic, gritty Poverty Row *film noir*. Tom Neal plays a hitchhiking pianist who is implicated in two murders he did not commit. The familiar story is made fascinating by "existential" dialogue, striking camera angles, Ann Savage's bizarre femme fatale, and dashes of Chopin on the soundtrack. One can immediately see where Godard and Truffaut got some of their inspiration. Low budget never looked so good.

DETROIT 9000
1973, USA, R ☆☆
Alex Rocco, Hari Rhodes, Vonetta McGee, Scatman Crothers. Directed by Arthur Marks. 106 min.

Cops 'n' robbers in the Motor City, this would fall into the black exploitation category except that it has an integrated cast. Cops Rocco and Rhodes investigate the theft of money from a fund-raising dinner for a black gubernatorial candidate. Rocco is good, and the script tries for a cynical atmosphere but spends most of its time chasing around Detroit via car, boat, and helicopter. (The number "9000," by the way, refers to the code used to indicate an officer in trouble.) (a.k.a.: *Police Call 9000*)

THE DEVIL AND DANIEL WEBSTER
1941, USA ☆☆☆☆
Walter Huston, James Craig, Edward Arnold, Anne Shirley, Simone Simon, Jane Darwell, Gene Lockhart, John Qualen. Directed by William Dieterle. 109 min.

Here's a real find that was probably overlooked because it came in the same year from the same studio (RKO) as *Citizen Kane*. Stephen Vincent Benét's variation on *Faust* is given many clever twists in this imaginative comedy-fantasy. James Craig plays a poor farmer who makes a deal with the devil ("Mr. Scratch," brilliantly played by Walter Huston), but is rescued from damnation by Daniel Webster (Arnold), a smooth-talking lawyer. Dieterle's atmospheric direction has rarely been better (thanks partly to Van Nest Polglase's art direction), the performances are hugely enjoyable, and Bernard Herrmann's score won a deserved Oscar. (a.k.a.: *Daniel and the Devil*, *All That Money Can Buy*, and *Here Is a Man*)

THE DEVIL AND MAX DEVLIN
1981, USA, PG ☆☆
Elliott Gould, Bill Cosby, Julie Budd, David Knell, Adam Rich, Susan Anspach. Directed by Steven Hilliard Stern. 96 min.

In this Walt Disney farce Bill Cosby, whose career was not exactly in high gear at the time, is the devil, sending dead soul Elliott Gould back to earth to recruit three innocent souls. Don't worry about the PG rating; the Disney folks just tossed in some mild nastiness because they finally figured out what a kiss of death the G rating was at the box office. Gains half a star for not having either Tim Conway or Don Knotts.

THE DEVIL AND MISS JONES
1941, USA ☆☆☆
Charles Coburn, Jean Arthur, Robert Cummings, Spring Byington, William Demarest. Directed by Sam Wood. 97 min.

This ersatz Frank Capra/Preston Sturges comedy stars Charles Coburn as a millionaire who pretends to be a clerk in order to investigate working conditions at the department store he owns. Mostly fluffy comedy, but pleasant and inoffensive.

THE DEVIL AT 4 O'CLOCK
1961, USA ☆☆
Spencer Tracy, Frank Sinatra, Kerwin Mathews, Jean-Pierre Aumont, Grégoire Asian, Alexander Scourby, Cathy Lewis, Barbara Luna. Directed by Mervyn LeRoy. 125 min.

This disaster epic came a decade before the onslaught of films like *The Towering Inferno*, *Earthquake*, and *Avalanche*, but it lacks the same schlocky appeal. Director Mervyn LeRoy is too earnest with Liam O'Brien's screenplay (from a novel by Max Cotto) about a priest (Tracy) and three convicts who rescue a children's leper hospital from volcanic destruction on a South Seas island. The eruption sequences are spectacular, but the drama is tedious; it needs more bad dialogue and about a dozen more has-been stars to make it work as camp, and much, much more than that to make it anything better.

THE DEVIL BAT

See *Killer Bats*

DEVIL DOG: THE HOUND OF HELL
1978, USA (TV) ☆½
Richard Crenna, Yvette Mimieux, Kim Richards, Ike Eisenmann, Victor Jory, Lou Frizzell, Ken Kercheval, R. G. Armstrong. Directed by Curtis Harrington. 102 min.

In this camp horror, a happy suburban family is terrorized by their possessed pet. (The *Hound of Hell* subtitle is meant to remind viewers that they're not going to see a documentary about everybody's favorite chocolate snack.) If the premise doesn't make you smile, neither will the movie, which lacks even a nuance of genuine terror. The title performer is somewhat more convincing than most of his costars.

DEVIL DOLL
1964, Great Britain ☆☆½
Bryant Halliday, William Sylvester, Yvonne Romaine. Directed by Lindsay Shonteff. 80 min.

A ventriloquist and his hostile dummy pique the curiosity of a newspaperman, who finds a much better story than he had anticipated. Sleazy atmosphere and quirky narrative make this an unexpectedly effective horror picture with some genuinely creepy moments. (Ultimately it can't match the ventriloquist's-dummy segment of *Dead of Night*.)

DEVIL GIRL FROM MARS
1954, Great Britain ☆½
Hazel Court, Adrienne Corri, Hugh McDermott, Patricia Laffan. Directed by David MacDonald. 76 min.

In another version of an all-time favorite male fantasy, a gorgeous female Martian arrives on Earth to gather up men for breeding purposes. Unfortunately, she lands in England and no one wants to go with her, so she has to resort to using her giant robot to goose them along. For some reason, British sci-fi makers are unable to construct robots that are anything less than totally laughable, and this movie features one of the sillier ones.

DEVIL IN THE HOUSE OF EXORCISM
1975, Italy, R ☆½
Telly Savalas, Elke Sommer, Robert Alda, Alida Valli. Directed by Mario Bava. 93 min.

A tourist in Rome wanders into a twilight zone of murder, madness, and diabolism after seeing a mural of the devil on the wall of an old church. This stylish but consummately confusing film exists in two versions, Bava's original (entitled *Lisa and the Devil*) and this version, in which the tourist is possessed by the devil, vomits bizarre objects, blasphemes, and tells the tale of her demented experiences to the priest assigned to conduct her exorcism. There is little to choose between them; either way, illogical entertainment from the director of *Black Sunday*, *Twitch of the Death Nerve*, *Blood and Black Lace*, and many lesser genre films. (a.k.a.: *The House of Exorcism*)

THE DEVILS
1971, Great Britain, R ☆☆☆½
Vanessa Redgrave, Oliver Reed, Dudley Sutton, Max Adrian, Gemma Jones, Michael Gothard. Directed by Ken Russell. 109 min.

A homosexual king, a priest immersed in pleasures of the flesh, and a convent full of writhing, blaspheming nuns who may or may not be possessed by the devil populate a hysterical film about hysteria in seventeenth-century France. Arguably Russell's best effort, equal parts violent, ecstatic, and grotesque, adapted from Aldous Huxley's historical study, "The Devils of London."

THE DEVIL'S ASSIGNMENT
1985, Hong Kong ½☆
Richard Kao, Albert Lee, Polly Chen, Lei Chun. Directed by George Lai and Kim Sze Hin. 89 min.

This has an abundance of plot, with bad guys out to get the secret papers from good guys; lots of twists, with double-crosses and a mysterious helper—it all adds up to a confusing story with only adequate kung fu. The print quality used for the video is the usual very low genre standard.

DEVIL'S BRIGADE ☆☆
1968, USA
William Holden, Cliff Robertson, Vince Edwards, Andrew Prine, Claude Akins, Richard Jaeckel, Jeremy Slate, Richard Dawson, Dana Andrews, Michael Rennie, Carrol O'Connor, Harry Carey, Don Megowan. Directed by Andrew V. McLaglen. 131 min.

This is another *Dirty Dozen* clone, though a particularly uninspired one. Whereas its model had legitimate drama—Will these misfits learn to work together?—the situation here is comparatively dull: a U.S. and a Canadian squadron are joined together for a special mission in World War II. Director McLaglen tries to differentiate between the rowdy Americans and the more reserved and specialized Canadians, but it's all just killing time until the final, disappointing mission.

THE DEVIL'S EYE ☆☆☆
1960, Sweden
Jarl Kulle, Bibi Andersson, Nils Poppe, Gertrud Fridh, Gunnar Bjornstrand. Directed by Ingmar Bergman. 90 min.

Even though it deals with all of his favorite subjects—sex, God, and the devil—this comedy is not one of Bergman's major works; though it has its visual moments, it is, on the whole, too talky and static. Irritated by the virginity of a country priest's daughter, Satan sends Don Juan to earth to seduce her, but the tables are turned and the impassioned seducer falls in love. Music by Scarlatti lends an appropriately light touch to this art-house favorite.

THE DEVIL'S PLAYGROUND ☆½
1946, USA
William Boyd, Andy Clyde, Rand Brooks, Elaine Riley, Robert Elliott. Directed by George Archainbaud. 62 min.

Don't be misled by the fascinating title or the presence of a female screenwriter (Doris Schroeder). This is purely formula Hopalong Cassidy in which Hopalong (Boyd) saves a lady (Riley) from a gang of no-goodniks. Fast and competent, but nothing new.

THE DEVIL'S RAIN ☆½
1975, USA, PG
Ernest Borgnine, Eddie Albert, Ida Lupino, William Shatner, Tom Skerritt, John Travolta. Directed by Rubert Fuest. 85 min.

The Preston family is tormented in a variety of ways by evil Satanist Corbis and his band of eyeless followers. Extremely silly, but Borgnine as the Prince of Lies (complete with Ram's head), Travolta in a minor role, and ten full minutes of devil worshipers melting in the devil's rain are compensatory factors.

THE DEVIL'S UNDEAD ☆½
1975, Great Britain, PG
Peter Cushing, Christopher Lee, Diana Dors. Directed by Peter Sasdy. 90 min.

Several members of the van Traylen trust, a charitable institution, die under what might be termed mysterious circumstances. A doctor accidentally drawn into the affair uncovers a bizarre plot with disturbing implications. Far too confusing for its own good, though with an interesting premise. (a.k.a.: *Nothing But the Night* and *The Resurrection Syndicate*)

DEVIL'S WEDDING NIGHT ☆
1973, Spain, R
Mark Damon, Sara Bay. Directed by Paul Solvay. 85 min.

Countess Dracula's magic ring attracts many young women to her castle, where they become blood sacrifices at the hands of her degenerate accomplice. The accomplice's brother, an archaeologist, comes to investigate and doesn't think highly of what he finds. Much flesh and few thrills in this Spanish horror film starring Sara Bay (*Lady Frankenstein*) and Mark Damon (*The Fall of The House of Usher*).

DEVONSVILLE TERROR ☆☆☆
1983, USA
Paul Wilson, Robert Walker, Jr., Donald Pleasence, Suzanna Love. Directed by Ulli Lommel. 97 min.

The estimable plot of this surprisingly good witchcraft tale deals with a curse uttered by three witches executed in 1683. Years later, three women arrive in Devonsville, where mysterious things start happening. Building suspense and eliciting goose bumps, this Chiller Theater item proceeds on the premise that these three visitors may be the tools of the dead souls of the witches, or the dead witches reincarnated. Not just a horror job, the film also touches on issues of feminism. Way above average; even Pleasence's hamminess doesn't relegate this to the camp scrap heap.

DIABOLIQUE ☆☆☆☆
1954, France
Simone Signoret, Vera Clouzot, Charles Vanel, Paul Meurisse. Directed by Henri-Georges Clouzot. 114 min.

A much-imitated French suspense classic, it already owed something to such Hollywood thrillers as *Suspicion* and *Gaslight*. Clouzot directed this spine-tingler about a wife (Vera Clouzot) and mistress (Signoret) who murder their mutual mate, a tyrannical, sadistic headmaster at a rural boarding school. Later they discover that the corpse is missing. Clouzot has said, "I only sought to amuse myself and the child that sleeps in all our hearts—the child who hides her head under the bedclothes and begs, 'Daddy, Daddy, frighten me.'" He succeeded, with a carefully constructed tale based on the novel by Pierre Boileau and Thomas Narcejac (their *D'Entre les Morts* became Hitchcock's *Vertigo*), and a twist ending that raises the film to yet loftier realms. Successfully remade in 1976 as the TV movie *Reflections of Murder*. (a.k.a.: *Les Diaboliques* and *The Fiends*)

LES DIABOLIQUES

See *Diabolique*

DIAL M FOR MURDER ☆☆☆½
1954, USA
Ray Milland, Grace Kelly, Robert Cummings, John Williams, Anthony Dawson. Directed by Alfred Hitchcock. 105 min.

This is Alfred Hitchcock's most successful adaptation from the stage, a conventional but highly entertaining thriller about a cad (Ray Milland) who plans the "perfect murder" of his wife (Grace Kelly). Robert Cummings is the persistent (and rather obnoxious) boyfriend who sees through his plot, and John Williams is the veddy British police inspector. Hitchcock filmed *Dial M* in 3-D; unfortunately, the video version doesn't utilize the technology.

DIAMONDS ARE FOREVER ☆☆½
1971, Great Britain, PG
Sean Connery, Jill St. John, Charles Gray, Lana Wood, Jimmy Dean, Bruce Cabot, Lois Maxwell. Directed by Guy Hamilton. 119 min.

At forty-one, Sean Connery proved he could still cut it as 007, but weariness was showing and this would be Connery's last James Bond outing for twelve years. The plot mechanics were also getting wearisome at this point, though not nearly as perfunctory as in the recent Roger Moore epics (*For Your Eyes Only*, *A View to a Kill*). *Diamonds* tosses together a diamond heist caper with yet another madman-blowing-up-the-world plot. The real fun is supplied by the supporting cast, who shine in individual vignettes: Jimmy Dean as a billionaire; Bruce Glover and Putter Smith as good-humored hit men; and Donna Garrat and Trina Parks as black-belt cuties named Bambi and Thumper.

DIARY OF A HITCHHIKER

See *Diary of a Teenage Hitchhiker*

DIARY OF A MAD HOUSEWIFE ☆☆½
1970, USA, R
Carrie Snodgress, Frank Langella, Richard Benjamin, Peter Boyle, Alice Cooper. Directed by Frank Perry. 95 min.

From the late-sixties–early-seventies "So, middle class life isn't all that it's cracked up to be" school of sociological filmmaking, this movie is based on Sue Kaufman's best-selling novel about a bored, unfulfilled housewife who retreats from her status-conscious husband into a love affair with a physically satisfying but no less selfish writer. Snodgress is good as the housewife, Benjamin whiny as her husband, and Langella attractive as the "other man." None of it really goes anywhere.

THE DIARY OF ANNE FRANK ☆☆☆
1959, USA
Millie Perkins, Joseph Schildkraut, Shelley Winters, Richard Beymer, Lou Jacobi, Ed Wynn. Directed by George Stevens. 170 min.

This is a melodramatic but moving film version of the hit Broadway play about a Jewish family hiding from the Nazis in an Amsterdam attic for two years. Director Stevens is perhaps too true to the story's stage origins, but it's an actor's film anyway. Winters received a Best Supporting Actress Oscar, though the entire cast is quite fine, with the exception of Perkins, who looks right for the part but is never really convincing.

DIARY OF A TEENAGE HITCHHIKER ☆½
1979, USA (TV)
Charlene Tilton, Dick Van Patten, Katherine Helmond, James Carroll Jordan, Katy Kurtzman, Christopher Knight. Directed by Ted Post. 100 min.

Charlene Tilton is *bad*, but this is only a TV movie, so she's not nearly bad enough. And she learns her lesson: Don't hitchhike! There's psychos out there! (a.k.a.: *Diary of a Hitchhiker*)

DIARY OF A YOUNG COMIC ☆½
1979, USA (TV)
Richard Lewis, Stacy Keach, Dom De Luise, Bill Macy, George Jessel, Gypsy Boots. Directed by Gary Weis. 67 min.

Real-life comedian Richard Lewis stars as Billy Gondola, a young New Yorker who wants to make it as a stand-up comic in Hollywood. This short, mediocre telefilm makes a wry statement or two and might elicit an occasional chuckle, but most of the material is dull and hackneyed. The better-known stars listed above only make cameos.

DICK TRACY ☆☆½
1945, USA
Morgan Conway, Anne Jeffreys, Mike Mazurki, Jane Greer. Directed by William Berke. 62 min.

The lantern-jawed detective who loved tangling with colorful crooks like Flattop and Pruneface reached the height of his screen fame in this fast-paced, economical actioner. An entire B-movie series followed this one and delighted a generation of schoolboys at Saturday matinees. The comic-strip shenanigans suffer from budgetary restrictions, but the movie transcends its shoestring limitations with a low-key, no-nonsense approach to playing cops and robbers.

DICK TRACY MEETS GRUESOME ☆☆½
1947, USA
Ralph Byrd, Boris Karloff, Anne Gwynne, Edward Ashley, June Clayworth. Directed by John Rawlins. 65 min.

Ralph Byrd replaced Morgan Conway as Dick Tracy in this outing, but the real news is that Boris Karloff plays Gruesome, a baddie who kills his victims by stuffing them into a furnace. It's a tribute to Karloff that he could make routine films like this one scarier than they have any right to be.

DICK TRACY RETURNS ☆☆
1938, USA
Ralph Byrd, Lynn Roberts, Charles Middleton, Lee Ford, Michael Kent. Directed by William Witney and John English. 100 min.

In the thirties and forties, the Saturday matinee crowd got to anticipate the dauntless detective's return every week; it's a treat for nostalgia buffs to have Dick back again and available wherever a video store can be found. In this serialized adventure, Tracy battles the usual verminous villains in a film possessed of a dippy, modest sort of charm. For today's younger audiences used to the technical splendors of *Raiders of the Lost Ark* and other films that set out to kill you with cleverness and special effects, the film's limited resources may seem deficient, like an artifact from the prehistory of moviemaking, but the slapdash fantasies of yesteryear made up in resourcefulness and pacing for what they lacked in budget and technique. (This is part of a series available on video.)

DICK TRACY'S DILEMMA ☆☆
1947, USA
Ralph Byrd, Lyle Latell, Kay Christopher, Jimmy Conlin, Ian Keith. Directed by John Rawlins. 60 min.

Dick Tracy thrusts out that famous oversized jaw and sticks out his neck as he grapples with more underworld chicanery. This adventure packs the usual fast-paced wallop as Dickie is pitted against the Claw, who wants to get his claws on a fur robbery racket (which is actually a cover-up for an insurance scam). Action fans are in for a treat as Dick uses his sleuthing skills against the Legendary Lobster. And guess how the metal-handed mobster meets his demise? The climax is, to say the least, electrifying.

DICK TRACY VS. CUEBALL ☆☆
1946, USA
Morgan Conway, Anne Jeffreys, Lyle Latell, Rita Corday, Dick Wessel. Directed by Gordon Douglas. 62 min.

Gordon Douglas's impressive canon (*Them*, *Young at Heart*) includes this Dick Tracy vehicle. When the series moved over from Republic to RKO, it got better production design but not better scripts. In this one, Dick is one step behind a killer of jewel thieves. Wessel as Cueball (the killer) is truly grotesque and his screen exit is memorable, but Conway is a colorless Tracy, and Jeffreys overacts as usual as Tess Truehart. Stick with Chester Gould's comic strip.

DIE! DIE! MY DARLING! ☆☆½
1965, Great Britain
Tallulah Bankhead, Stefanie Powers, Peter Vaughan, Donald Sutherland. Directed by Silvio Narizzano. 97 min.

The legendary Tallulah Bankhead, in her last movie, plays a deranged woman whose son has died. When the girl he was going to marry (Stefanie Powers) comes to visit at her mansion, the old woman demands that she get religion and live out the rest of her life as a virgin until she's reunited with the son of eternity. For some reason the girl refuses, so she's held prisoner and spends the rest of the picture trying to escape. The results are not terribly suspenseful, but Tallulah chews up the scenery, and in addition to Powers, there is another future star in Donald Sutherland, who plays a goon.

DIE LAUGHING ☆
1980, USA, PG
Robby Benson, Linda Grovenor, Charles Durning, Elsa Lanchester, Bud Cort. Directed by Jeff Werner. 108 min.

You won't. You won't even get a bit queasy. Robby Benson, who stars as a bozo on the run (never mind why) from fascist hit men, Communists, the police, and numerous other irate groups, cowrote, coproduced, and wrote a few songs for this lame farce. That's four errors—someone get this guy off the field!

DIE SCREAMING, MARIANNE
1970, USA, R
Susan George, Barry Evans, Chris Sandford, Leo Glen. Directed by Pete Walker. 99 min.

In case you couldn't tell from the title, this is a horror movie. This one has Susan George, fresh from getting abused by the master (Sam Peckinpah, in *Straw Dogs*), being abused by amateurs who evidently wish to kill her before she reaches the age of majority. Unremarkable.

A DIFFERENT STORY
1978, USA, R
Perry King, Meg Foster, Valerie Curtin, Peter Donat. Directed by Paul Aaron. 107 min.

Boy meets girl, boy marries girl, boy and girl have baby, quarrel, make up, and so on. What's so different, you ask? Well, the boy (Perry King) is gay! And so is the girl (Meg Foster)! He flounces around fluffing sofa cushions while she, uh, acts really tough, you know, like a *man*. This must rank as one of the most charmless, least enlightened looks at homosexuality in screen history, from the "fem" and "butch" characterizations to the attitude that they can take the cure and convert. Foster and King try hard, but both look appropriately shamefaced throughout.

DIGBY, THE BIGGEST DOG IN THE WORLD
1974, Great Britain, G
Jim Dale, Spike Milligan, Angela Douglas, John Bluthal, Norman Rossington, Milo O'Shea, Richard Beaumont. Directed by Joseph McGrath. 88 min.

The title tells it all: British funnymen Dale and Milligan play second fiddle to a sheepdog that drinks from the wrong bowl and grows to the size of a dinosaur. Will poor Digby be consigned to life as a sideshow attraction? Will animal psychologist Dale ever get his best friend back? Is there in all of England a fire hydrant big enough to withstand Digby's power? We're not big on canine comedies; dogs belong in dramatic fare like *The Doberman Gang* or *Old Yeller*. Besides, the animal featured here just isn't charismatic enough to carry the show.

DILLINGER
1973, USA
Warren Oates, Ben Johnson, Michelle Phillips, Cloris Leachman, Harry Dean Stanton, Richard Dreyfuss, John Ryan. Directed by John Milius. 96 min.

Leave it to John Milius (*Red Dawn*) to make one of the most violent gangster pictures of the 1970s. Action fans won't be disappointed with this heavily fictionalized view of the depression or of the notorious bank robber and killer John Dillinger. Famous thirties faces like Pretty Boy Floyd, Baby Face Nelson, and "The Lady in Red" (a wasted Cloris Leachman) are brought to life with a minimum of embarrassment by the cast, but they are overshadowed by the deluge of blood and bullets. Philipps, of The Mamas & The Papas, makes her debut. The story was also filmed in 1945.

DIMPLES
1936, USA
Shirley Temple, Frank Morgan, Helen Westley, Robert Kent, Delma Byron, Stepin Fetchit, John Carradine, the Hall Johnson Choir. Directed by William A. Seiter. 78 min.

By 1936, Shirley Temple was the queen of American movies; she'd also been doing it long enough that she had the whole cute routine down pat. As a result, this is pretty uninspired. Shirley and daddy Frank Morgan try to remain together in 1850s New York, despite Morgan's thieving impulses. The more cynical among you may be amused at a few scenes, such as the one in which Dimples joins a minstrel show and gets to play Little Eva in *Uncle Tom's Cabin*.

DINER
1982, USA, R
Mickey Rourke, Kevin Bacon, Daniel Stern, Steve Guttenberg, Timothy Daly, Ellen Barkin, Paul Reiser. Directed by Barry Levinson. 110 min.

Writer-director Barry Levinson paints an original, very witty portrait of impending adult life in Baltimore of the late 1950s. A group of friends gather frequently at an all-night diner and discuss the goings-on in their lives, providing us with a running commentary of the actual glimpses of their individual lives that we see between these bull sessions. Though the movie is more a slice of life than a carefully plotted story, it's a wonderfully baked, deliciously spiced, carefully cut slice. And if that's not enough, it features a super cast of young stars whose careers were catapulted by the film's critical success.

DINGAKA
1965, South Africa
Stanley Baker, Juliet Prowse, Ken Gampu, Alfred Jabulani. Directed by Jamie Uys. 98 min.

The maker of the inexplicably popular *The Gods Must Be Crazy* has been cranking out films in South Africa for almost thirty-five years; this is one of the few others available in this hemisphere, and it only supports the conclusion that Jamie Uys's films are permeated with condescension at best (or racism at worst) toward blacks. Like *Gods*, this story depicts the clash between black African and white European culture, though here it is played for drama. Also like *Gods*, it takes for granted that (1) the two races are best off staying apart from each other and (2) Negroes belong in the jungle, the better to practice heathen rituals to their hearts' content. The drama is based on the murder of a native girl and her father's attempt to seek justice through the white man's law, and while it pretends to be a serious examination of the differences between the two societies, it boils down to a defense of the "separate but equal" dogma; black beliefs and practices are generally played for laughs.

DINNER AT EIGHT
1933, USA
Marie Dressler, John Barrymore, Lionel Barrymore, Jean Harlow, Wallace Beery, Billie Burke, Roland Young. Directed by George Cukor. 113 min.

This film was one of MGM's biggest money-makers in the thirties, due to an unprecedented all-star cast. Invitations to a dinner party set a network of stories going, all of which are resolved by the time guests sit down to eat at that magical hour. This comedy-drama has the flavor of a soap, touching on everything from sickness to love affairs to financial distress. Cukor manages admirably to keep such a star-studded, plot-filled production smooth and expressive.

DINNER AT THE RITZ
1937, Great Britain
Annabella, Paul Lukas, David Niven, Francis L. Sullivan. Directed by Harold D. Schuster. 80 min.

Annabella tries too hard to be charming, but Paul Lukas is an appealing villain in this better-than-usual suspense story. The love story between David Niven and Annabella seems inconsequential next to Francis L. Sullivan's fruitily campy malevolence. Harold D. Schuster moves the complex story along, although to no great effect.

DINO
★★★
1957, USA
Sal Mineo, Brian Keith, Susan Kohner, Frank Faylen, Joe DeSantis. Directed by Thomas Carr. 93 min.

Sal Mineo expands on his *Rebel without a Cause* character in this small film based on an award-winning TV drama by Reginald Rose. A youth who has been abused all his life, Dino treats the world around him as he feels it has treated him, until an understanding parole officer brings out his humanity. This was Mineo's best film role, and Brian Keith is also very good as the juvenile caseworker who helps him.

DIPLOMATIC COURIER
★★½
1952, USA
Tyrone Power, Patricia Neal, Stephen McNally, Hildegarde Kneff, Karl Malden, Lee Marvin. Directed by Henry Hathaway. 98 min.

Tyrone Power was past his matinee-idol days by this time, and he doesn't really bring anything to this standard cold-war espionage story that any other competent actor couldn't. As a State Department courier, he is sent to Austria to pick up documents from a fellow agent. When the agent is killed by Soviets, Power sets out to retrieve the papers and avenge his friend's death. Patricia Neal has a good part as a wacko who isn't quite what she appears to be. What makes the whole thing watchable is the always solid direction of Henry Hathaway, one of those admirably and unlimitedly productive Hollywood studio directors that you could call a hack and mean it as a compliment.

EL DIPUTADO
★★★
1979, Spain, R
Jose Sacristan, Maria Luisa San Jose, Jose L. Alonso, Angel Pardo. Directed by Eloy de la Yglesia. 111 min.

Quite a controversial film when it was released in Spain, this is liable to confuse American audiences not intimately familiar with the political events of the last decade of Spanish history, and will perhaps turn off those with an antipathy toward explicit homosexuality. Like the British film *Another Country* and the German *Colonel Redl*, this uses homosexuality as a metaphor for political and social decay, though without condemning it. There may be more of a market for this story, which follows the career of a Spanish congressman torn by his sexual and political inclinations, among gay audiences than among those more interested in its underlying themes. As a political polemic, this tends to ramble, and long, talky sequences do not translate well into a foreign language. Worth checking out. (a.k.a.: *The Congressman*)

THE DIRT BIKE KID
★½
1986, USA, PG
Peter Billingsley, Stuart Pankin, Anne Bloom, Patrick Collins, Sage Parker. Directed by Hoite C. Caston. 90 min.

A dull, bumbling action comedy, it is aimed primarily at juvenile motorbike buffs such as the title character (played by Peter Billingsley of *A Christmas Story*), a young teen whose slightly magical moped helps him battle a nasty banker who wants to tear down the local hot-dog stand. No suspense whatsoever is generated in the tedious plot or the ho-hum bike footage.

THE DIRTY DOZEN
★★★½
1967, Great Britain
Lee Marvin, Ernest Borgnine, Charles Bronson, Jim Brown, John Cassavetes, Richard Jaeckel, George Kennedy, Trini Lopez, Donald Sutherland, Telly Savalas, Robert Webber, Robert Ryan, Clint Walker, Ralph Meeker. Directed by Robert Aldrich. 149 min.

This is pretty much the ultimate macho war movie, if you bear in mind that "macho" has a slight connotation of fantasy to it; though we all know that war is really hell, movies like this make it look more like an extended night out with the boys. During the latter days of World War II, Major Marvin takes twelve soldiers, all facing death sentences for various crimes, and offers them a governmental pardon if they will undertake a potentially suicidal mission behind enemy lines. Two-thirds of the movie deals with their training and Marvin's efforts to make loyal, obedient soldiers out of a pack of recalcitrant misfits while fighting pressure from Army brass to cancel the mission. The interplay of the actors in the large but uniformly excellent cast makes the final third of the film, in which the mission is actually undertaken, almost anticlimactic. Aldrich has always done well with this sort of manly, gung-ho action fare, and this is one of his best.

THE DIRTY DOZEN: THE NEXT MISSION
★★
1985, USA (TV)
Lee Marvin, Ernest Borgnine, Richard Jaeckel, Ken Wahl, Larry Wilcox. Directed by Andrew McLaglen. 104 min.

The original *Dirty Dozen* was dirty indeed: a brutal, misogynistic action exercise involving a cutthroat band of convicts who are sprung by the military to perform a mission with a built-in death risk. Somehow, some of the dozen from that violent but powerful action flick have survived that ordeal, and now must survive being in this second-rate TV movie. This sanitized version does not offer the rip-roaring thrills of its predecessor. The impact is lessened by the softened language and the toned-down violence as Major Lee Marvin returns with a suicide mission against the Nazis, along with former Dirty Dozeners Borgnine and Jaeckel.

DIRTY HARRY
★★½
1971, USA
Clint Eastwood, Harry Guardino, Reni Santoni, Andy Robinson, John Vernon. Directed by Don Siegel. 102 min.

Don Siegel's brass-knuckle style of filmmaking and Clint Eastwood's macho/mysterious persona blend perfectly in this magnum-powered shoot-'em-up. A maniacal killer is spreading a bloody reign of terror over helpless San Francisco and only one man can stop him—Dirty Harry (Eastwood), described by director Siegel as "a tough cop and a racist sonofabitch." The only Dirty Harry film that really shows the darker side of the tough cop, and the source for Eastwood's own *Tightrope*, a more self-conscious study of his lawman myth. Today this film looks dated and cheap, and that adds to the sewer-level thrills.

DIRTY MARY, CRAZY LARRY
★★
1974, USA, PG
Peter Fonda, Susan George, Adam Roarke, Vic Morrow, Roddy McDowall. Directed by John Hough. 93 min.

Fast cars, fast women, redneck cops and *Easy Rider*'s Peter Fonda as the very heroic antihero—who could ask for anything more in a mid-seventies road-action pic (other than, perhaps, a sensible story, an exciting climax and a more credible plot impetus than Fonda's wish to join the ranks of the great NASCAR racing champs)? Viewers who've seen and survived all of Burt Reynolds's fast-car flicks will know what they're getting into here, and find a pleasingly low-key, funny film of its kind, with Susan George playing a rambunctiously bawdy sexpot as only she can. Good, unfussy direction by Hough (*The Legend of Hell House*).

DIRTY TRICKS
★
1980, Canada, PG
Elliott Gould, Kate Jackson, Arthur Hill, Rich Little. Directed by Alvin Rakoff. 94 min.

In this "satire" on the world of academia, Elliott Gould plays a Harvard history professor (wait, it gets worse) who, between dealing with his less idealistic and scrupulous colleagues, one of whom has written a book on the sex lives of the founding fathers (pretty funny stuff, eh?), gets mixed up in a government plot to cover up some documents implicating George Washington in a political scandal. The only funny thing in the entire movie is

Gould's beard, which makes him look like Larry Talbot on a moonlit night.

THE DISAPPEARANCE ☆☆
1977, Canada
Donald Sutherland, Francine Racette, David Hemmings, Virginia McKenna, Christopher Plummer, John Hurt, David Warner. Directed by Stuart Cooper. 88 min.

Pity the poor Canadian filmmakers: they have an abundance of Canadian-born stars who seem to feel a responsibility to make features in their home country, and the national government has a generous program to develop a film industry, but in two decades of trying they've yet to turn out more than a couple of memorable features. Maybe if they had to turn a profit and weren't receiving so much help from the government. . . . Anyway, this is a mood piece about a gun-for-hire (Donald Sutherland) who accepts an assignment to Britain, all the while preoccupied by his failing marriage and the subsequent disappearance of his wife. It is really a shame to see such a good cast as this try their best to bring life to such drag material.

THE DISAPPEARANCE OF AIMEE ☆☆☆½
1976, USA (TV)
Faye Dunaway, Bette Davis, James Sloyan, James Woods, John Lehne, Lelia Goldoni, Severn Darden. Directed by Anthony Harvey. 110 min.

This is an absorbing glimpse backward at a fascinating historical occurrence. In 1926, Aimee Semple McPherson, the Bible-thumping saleslady of the Lord, suddenly disappeared for a short time, causing endless speculation, reams of publicity, and a circus of a court hearing. Along with Agatha Christie's unscheduled departure that same year, Aimee's disappearance was the most notorious now-you-see-her-now-you-don't case of the time. Since the famed evangelist enjoyed a full sex life away from the sanctity of the tents, her whereabouts were not necessarily at a religious retreat. The full richness of the roaring twenties is recreated evocatively, and the details of the vanishing act aren't neatly explained away for us. Probably Faye Dunaway's finest work for television, and Bette Davis is stingingly brilliant as her mother.

DISCONNECTED ☆½
1985, USA
Frances Raines, Mark Walker, Carl Koch, Ben Page, Carmine Capobianco. Directed by Gorman Bechard. 81 min.

This low-budget horror movie, made in Waterbury, Connecticut, has some occasional flashes of style, though not enough to provide it with any real distinction. A sales clerk at a video store and her twin sister become involved with a teenager who may or may not be the slasher killer that the police are looking for. There are enough digs at the conventions of slasher films here to indicate that the filmmakers were aware of the clichés of the genre; unfortunately, whatever their intentions may have been, they never break away from them.

THE DISCREET CHARM OF THE BOURGEOISIE ☆☆☆☆
1972, France/Spain/Italy, PG
Fernando Rey, Stephane Audran, Jean-Pierre Cassel, Delphine Seyrig, Michel Piccoli. Directed by Luis Buñuel. 105 min.

Director Buñuel takes aim at all of his favorite targets—politics, the church, the military, and mankind in general—in a much more subdued and genial manner than usual; the result won him the Oscar for Best Foreign Film. It's all held together by the device of a group of friends, South American diplomats gathered in Paris, trying to meet and have dinner but being continually frustrated by events real, surreal, and imaginary. The Monty Python troupe derived much of the style of their television show, in which events seem to randomly flow from one to another, from Buñuel, an inspiration that is most obvious here. Great fun, though those not familiar with Buñuel must remember that half the time the joke is intended to be on the viewer. The video version, from Media Home Entertainment's Cinematheque Collection, has been resubtitled for easier reading.

DISHONORED LADY ☆½
1947, USA
Hedy Lamarr, Dennis O'Keefe, John Loder, William Lundigan, Morris Carnovsky, Natalie Schafer. Directed by Robert Stevenson. 82 min.

This highly charged melodrama will be sure to remind viewers of a knockoff of Hitchcock, but it lacks the flair of the master. A career woman changes her identity for no good reason, falls in love with a scientist, finds herself charged with murder, and has her past catch up with her. Hedy Lamarr would have to be a much better actress to give these proceedings much conviction; Stevenson could have taken a little more control over the meandering pace.

DIVA ☆☆☆☆
1982, France
Wilhelmena Wiggins Fernandez, Frederic Andrei, Richard Bohringer, Thuy An Luu, Jacques Fabbri. Directed by Jean-Jacques Beineix. 123 min.

New Wave meets high fashion meets full-color *film noir* in Jean-Jacques Beineix's stylish, atmospheric debut film. An eighteen-year-old Parisian postman falls under the spell of an elusive black American diva, illegally tapes one of her performances, and becomes embroiled in a series of dangerous intrigues. The involved story is only secondary, however. The film enchants through its strange and beautiful images, mesmerizing score (by Vladimir Cosma), and mysterious, offbeat characters. A motorcycle chase through the Paris Métro is among the film's most exquisite sequences.

DIVINE MADNESS ☆
1980, USA, R
Bette Midler. Directed by Michael Ritchie. 93 min.

Depending on your point of view, this film version of Bette Midler's stage show is either too much of a good thing or unendurable.

THE DIVINE NYMPH ☆
1979, Italy
Laura Antonelli, Terence Stamp, Marcello Mastroianni, Michele Placido. Directed by Giuseppe Patroni Griffi. 90 min.

After her role in *Wifemistress* made her the hottest thing to hit the art-house circuit since Sonia Braga, Laura Antonelli's old movies began creeping out of the closets to which they had been so long and justifiably confined. In this one, made in 1976, Laura takes her clothes off a lot, proving once again that nudity and eroticism are not the same thing. The turgid plot is set in Italy circa 1920 and has her carrying on affairs with two wealthy men, ruining both of them in the process.

DIVORCE, AMERICAN STYLE ☆☆½
1967, USA
Dick Van Dyke, Debbie Reynolds, Jean Simmons, Jason Robards, Van Johnson, Joe Flynn, Shelley Berman, Lee Grant, Tom Bosley, Dick Gautier. Directed by Bud Yorkin. 109 min.

Before their vast success with television series like *All in the Family* and *Maude*, Bud Yorkin and Norman Lear made television series–style movies like this supposedly adult satire on marriage and divorce. Director Yorkin and writer Lear have concocted several sitcom-ish set pieces but, aside from some frank dialogue and sexual innuendo, they resemble leftovers from "Love, American Style," a TV show no doubt inspired by this film. The cast makes *Divorce* mildly diverting, but even they are strictly in the TV-personality groove.

DIVORCE HIS—DIVORCE HERS ☆½
1973, USA (TV)
Elizabeth Taylor, Richard Burton, Carrie Nye, Barry Foster, Gabriele Ferzetti. Directed by Waris Hussein. 148 min.

Two-time celebrity splitters Elizabeth Taylor and Richard Burton were certainly well equipped to handle a marital-anguish double feature; it's a pity they chose this dull, sappy, sudsy TV melodrama to lay their strife on the TV table. *Divorce His—Divorce Hers* is, as its title suggests, two separate but related films, each telling the story of the same breakup from a different perspective. Unfortunately, both halves abandon emotional realism or specificity in favor of unending screams across the room, fistfights, and hysterics. Carrie Nye makes the two stars look good by comparison, but this overlong, pointless exercise is still an embarrassment for all concerned.

THE DIVORCE OF LADY X ☆☆½
1938, Great Britain
Merle Oberon, Laurence Olivier, Binnie Barnes, Ralph Richardson, Morton Selten. Directed by Tim Whelan. 90 min.

With Laurence Olivier as the romantic lead, Robert Sherwood as co-screenwriter, and Technicolor photography, this comedy should have been better than just pleasant, lightweight fluff. Merle Oberon plays a mystery woman with a shady past who attracts the interest of a young lawyer (Olivier). The mistaken-identity plot is draggier than it ought to be, but the cast puts over the familiar situations effectively.

DIXIE: CHANGING HABITS ☆☆½
1983, USA (TV)
Suzanne Pleshette, Cloris Leachman, Kenneth McMillan, John Considine, Geraldine Fitzgerald, Judith Ivey. Directed by George Englund. 104 min.

This telefilm about the friendship between a madam sentenced to ninety days in a convent and the gritty mother superior in charge of changing her ways isn't as cheesy as its premise makes it sound, thanks to the lightly comic work by Cloris Leachman and Suzanne Pleshette. Still, it's neither as offensive nor as funny as it could have been. Judith Ivey, one of the more talented young actresses in America, plays a small role.

DIXIE DYNAMITE ☆½
1976, USA, R
Warren Oates, Christopher George, Jane Anne Johnstone, Wes Bishop. Directed by Lee Frost. 89 min.

Action south of the Smith and Wesson line. Warren Oates and Christopher George star as Georgia moonshiners who get caught and escape to Latin America. Now that's what we call the Deep South.

D.O.A. ☆☆½
1949, USA
Edmond O'Brien, Pamela Britton, Luther Adler, Beverly Campbell (nee Garland), Lyn Baggett, William Ching. Directed by Rudolph Mate. 83 min.

The story of a man who is poisoned but has a few days before his death to track down his killers is a great idea but only a fair movie. The opening finds Edmond O'Brien as a tax man on a San Francisco business trip who arrives at a police station to report a murder—his own! After that stunner, the film dissipates slightly as flashbacks tell how he tried to find out why he was poisoned. Some suspense is worked up, but much of the action is cloudy and the denouement is anticlimactic. An expressionistic *noir* style would have been more appropriate than the seedy, on-location look here, and the supporting cast is barely adequate, but the premise holds the film together for most of its length. One minor but annoying mistake was to have the soundtrack tweet every time O'Brien passes a pretty woman. Remade in 1970 as *Color Me Dead*.

DOC SAVAGE ... THE MAN OF BRONZE ☆
1975, USA, G
Ron Ely, Paul Gleason, William Lucking, Michael Miller, Eldon Quick. Directed by Michael Anderson. 100 min.

This attempt to rehabilitate the thirties comic-strip superhero as an icon for contemporary kids falls dismally flat. The awful jungle adventure veers between straightfaced sub–Indiana Jones exploits and deliberate camp, neither of which is in the least appealing. Ron Ely, a latter-day screen Tarzan, is certainly bronze as the hero, but his matched set of California tan and teeth is no substitute for the screen charisma he desperately lacks. The film features a particularly unpleasant score by Frank DeVol and a brief appearance by Pamela Hensley as a jungle-ette with special feelings for Doc.

THE DOCTOR AND THE DEVILS ☆☆
1985, USA, R
Timothy Dalton, Jonathan Pryce, Twiggy, Julian Sands, Stephen Rea, Beryl Reid. Directed by Freddie Francis. 92 min.

This is a sort of Hammer horror film with a much fancier set of credentials than usual. It's been adapted by Ronald Harwood (*The Dresser*) from an unproduced play by Dylan Thomas. In terms of physical production, the film's re-creation of nineteenth-century England is extraordinary, but ace horror director Freddie Francis may have spent too much time working on *The Elephant Man* (as cinematographer) because he keeps trying to pump up this film with portentous meaning and social commentary. The film ends up closer to *Sweeney Todd* than to *Dracula Has Risen from the Grave*, and it only succeeds as an all-out horror assault in one classic scene in which a tipsy old lady (superbly played by Beryl Reid) proves exceedingly difficult to kill.

DOCTOR AT LARGE ☆☆½
1957, Great Britain
Dirk Bogarde, James Robertson Justice, Muriel Pavlow, Donald Sinden, Shirley Eaton, Cyril Chamberlain, Derek Farr, George Coulouris, Lionel Jeffries. Directed by Ralph Thomas. 104 min.

This third entry in the series begun with *Doctor in the House* shows a slight slip down in quality but will still be more than sufficient to please fans of these films, and Anglophiles in general. After having survived his first appointment in *Doctor at Sea*, Simon is back at the hospital at which he trained, trying to gain the position of house surgeon. The main obstacle is chief consultant James Robertson Justice, who remembers only too well Simon's days as an intern. Humor is episodic and amiable, not unlike a British *M*A*S*H* but without the social commentary.

DOCTOR AT SEA ☆☆☆
1955, Great Britain
Dirk Bogarde, Brigitte Bardot, Brenda de Banzie, James Robertson Justice, Maurice Denham, Geoffrey Keen, Joan Sims. Directed by Ralph Thomas. 93 min.

This is the first sequel to *Doctor in the House*. Fresh out of medical school, Simon (Dirk Bogarde) signs on as ship's doctor on an all-male boat under the direction of captain James Robertson Justice, and both play essentially the same characters as in the previous film. Brigitte Bardot shines in an early role as one of several women that the ship is forced to take on board. Not quite as funny as the first, but still recommended for those with a taste for English humor.

DR. BLACK, MR. HYDE ☆½
1976, USA, R
Bernie Casey, Rosalind Cash, Marie O'Henry, Ji-Tu Cambuka, Milt Kogan, Stu Gilliam. Directed by William Crain. 87 min.

First came *Blacula*, then came *Blackenstein*, and finally: *Dr. Black, Mr. Hyde* (originally called *Dr. Black, Mr. White*—to make its social stand absolutely clear from the outset). Dr. Pride, a doctor who works in the slums of Watts but cannot quite control his yearning for the accoutrements of high honky living, devises a serum that turns him into a murderous, degenerate albino. Racist horror featuring special effects by Stan Winston (*The Entity*, *The Hunger*), who couldn't quite come to grips with the problem of making a black actor look convincingly white.

DOCTOR BUTCHER, M.D. (MEDICAL DEVIATE) ☆
1979, Italy, R
Ian McCulloch, Alexandra Cole, Peter O'Neal. Directed by Francesco Martino. 81 min.

"He is a depraved, sadistic rapist; a bloodthirsty homicidal killer . . . and he makes house calls!" "Doctor Butcher *loves* New York . . . there are so many victims!" And so on. What really goes on is this: a series of grisly murders in New York leads a doctor and an anthropologist to an isolated area occupied by native cannibals, crumbling zombies, and the demented doctor. Gross Italian exploitation that doesn't live up to its title, slightly reedited for American release. (a.k.a.: *Queen of the Cannibals*)

DOCTOR DETROIT ½☆
1983, USA, R
Dan Aykroyd, Howard Hesseman, Donna Dixon, Lydia Lei, T. K. Carter. Directed by Michael Pressman. 89 min.

A disaster conceived by Bruce Jay Friedman along the lines of *The Nutty Professor*, this unbearably leaden farce is about a fussy academic (Dan Aykroyd, in a desperate performance) who's drawn into a world of pimps and whores, and who creates a bizarre alter ego—the master pimp, Doctor Detroit—to get himself out of tight spots. The character is a zany, all right—with his steel hand and yellow fright wig, he's like Truman Capote impersonating Dr. Strangelove. But we never see any connection between Detroit and the absentminded professor who dredges him up: it's just a turn, and a mighty sloppy and tedious one.

DOCTOR DOLITTLE ☆
1967, USA
Rex Harrison, Samantha Eggar, Anthony Newley, Richard Attenborough, William Dix, Geoffrey Holder, Peter Bull. Directed by Richard Fleischer. 152 min.

One of the most expensive flops ever to come out of Hollywood, this failed children's epic eventually cost Twentieth-Century Fox an estimated $18 million—and that's in 1967 dollars. The Hugh Lofting stories on which the screenplay was based, about an eccentric British country doctor who discovers that he can talk to animals, are whimsical and charming and not at all a bad basis for a movie. But director Richard Fleischer should have taken a cue from his father, Max, and made an animated feature. The distinguished cast does what it can with the absurdly silly screenplay, but you just *know* that after this movie they all went home and framed that old Hollywood adage, the one about never working with children or animals. The ridiculous special effects include the Pushmi-Pullyu, a two-headed dancing llama (the appearance of which coincides with Sir Richard Attenborough singing "I've Never Seen Anything Like It," although you're not sure if he means the beast or the movie) and the eight-ton, forty-foot-long Great Pink Sea Snail, which by itself cost the studio $65,000. And be forewarned that Anthony Newley plays a character named Matthew Mugg, who does—incessantly.

DR. EHRLICH'S MAGIC BULLET ☆☆☆½
1940, USA
Edward G. Robinson, Ruth Gordon, Otto Kruger, Donald Crisp, Maria Ouspenskaya, Donald Meek, Albert Basserman, Louis Calhern. Directed by William Dieterle. 103 min.

The story of Dr. Paul Ehrlich provided Warner Bros. with material for another of their liberal "social conscience" biography-melodramas. Actually, it's a distinguished film and, in many ways, superior to the Pasteur and Zola bios. Robinson gives one of his best, most restrained performances as Ehrlich, the discoverer of 606 (the first cure for syphilis). The John Huston–Heinz Herald–Norman Burnside screenplay follows Ehrlich from his early struggles in a Berlin hospital to his discovery of the controversial serum and eschews many of the usual dramatic excesses inherent in the genre. Even Ruth Gordon (as the doctor's wife) does a relatively restrained job. An absorbing, neglected antique.

DR. HECKYL AND MR. HYPE ☆☆☆
1980, USA, R
Oliver Reed, Sunny Johnson, Maia Danzuger, Mel Welles, Virgil Frye, Jackie Coogan, Corinne Calvert, Dick Miller. Directed by Charles B. Griffith. 99 min.

This parody of the Dr. Jekyll–Mr. Hyde story has an ugly podiatrist drinking a bottle of patent medicine and turning into dashing Oliver Reed. (One of the best moments in the film is when he first looks into the mirror and exclaims, "Good God, I'm beautiful!") This was written and directed by Roger Corman veteran Charles Griffith, who wrote the scripts for (among countless others) the original *Little Shop of Horrors* and *A Bucket of Blood*, and this is in the same wacko mold. The cast features Corman veterans Dick Miller and Mel Welles (Mr. Mushnick from *Little Shop*), along with Jackie Coogan as Sergeant Fleacollar, the desk sergeant at the local dungeon.

DOCTOR IN DISTRESS ☆☆½
1963, Great Britain
Dirk Bogarde, James Robertson Justice, Samantha Eggar, Barbara Murry, Donald Houston, Dennis Price, Leo McKern, Frank Finlay. Directed by Ralph Thomas. 102 min.

The last of the *Doctor* series to feature Dirk Bogarde, although two more were made with the continuing character of irascible head of surgery James Robertson Justice. This time around, Justice falls in love with a lady physiotherapist and depends on Bogarde to help him through the trials and tribulations, even though Bogarde is going through his own with Samantha Eggar, a model and actress. Just the thing you're looking for if the *Carry Ons* are too lowbrow for you but you don't quite get Monty Python.

DOCTOR IN THE HOUSE ☆☆☆
1954, Great Britain
Dirk Bogarde, Kenneth More, Donald Sinden, Donald Houston, Key Kendall, James Robertson Justice, Joan Sims, Shirley Eaton. Directed by Ralph Thomas. 92 min.

This film is the first—and easily the best—in a long series of *Doctor* movies that have been perennially popular in Britain (not unlike the *Carry On* series). In it we are introduced to four young medical students whom we follow through the five years of their studies. It's similar to the *Stripes*/*Police Academy*–type of institutional satire, with the students pulling all kinds of pranks and shenanigans but, in the end, developing the greatest respect for the institution itself—in other words, ultimately humorous not anarchistic. James Robertson Justice is properly burly and gruff as the school's lecturer in surgery. Editor Gerald Thomas, the director's brother, later went on to direct all of the *Carry On* movies. Sequels currently available on videotape include *Doctor at Large*, *Doctor at Sea*, and *Doctor in Distress*.

DR. JEKYLL AND MR. HYDE ☆☆☆☆
1931, USA
Fredric March, Miriam Hopkins, Rose Hobart, Edgar Norton. Directed by Rouben Mamoulian. 90 min.

This is the best version of the oft-filmed Robert Louis Stevenson story about the peaceful doctor whose evil half periodically emerges. Fredric March won the Academy Award for best actor, but the film is made by the intricate Victorian London settings and the stylish direction of Mamoulian. For his transformation scene, March wore different layers of makeup, each sensi-

DR. JEKYLL AND MR. HYDE ★★★
1941, USA
Spencer Tracy, Ingrid Bergman, Lana Turner, Donald Crisp, Ian Hunter, Barton MacLane, C. Aubrey Smith. Directed by Victor Fleming. 127 min.

This film is one of the more effective of MGM's overproduced horror movies, perhaps because the background of Victorian repression in Robert Louis Stevenson's classic novel so perfectly fit the studio's decorous style. Spencer Tracy is surprisingly good as the tormented Dr. Jekyll and his ravenous alterego, Mr. Hyde—whom he plays without the benefit of transmogrifying makeup. Ingrid Bergman is sexy as Jekyll's fiancée.

DR. JEKYLL AND SISTER HYDE ★★
1971, Great Britain
Ralph Bates, Martine Beswick, Gerald Sim, Lewis Fiander. Directed by Roy Ward Baker. 87 min.

Debonair Dr. Jekyll tests his elixir of life on an insect, and *voilà!*—It works—with one minor catch: the bug's sex has been changed from male to female. Imagine what happens when he tests it on a man, and you have the novel premise of this variation on the split-personality classic, with Martine Beswick as a voluptuous female psychotic. Nice idea, but the filmmakers' unwillingness (or inability) to take advantage of the material's comic potential keeps it from success. Still, an intriguing if simple piece of gimmickry.

DR. JEKYLL'S DUNGEON OF DEATH ★
1980, USA, R
James Mathers, John Kearney. Directed by James Woods. 90 min.

The grandson of Dr. Jekyll (whom we don't recall as having had any children) sets up shop in the United States. Aside from developing the usual aggression-releasing serum, which he doesn't seem to require himself, Dr. J. gets his kicks out of lobotomizing and then torturing his family. About a third of this no-budget junk consists of karate footage, for no particularly good reason. The James Woods who directed is *not* the actor of the same name, and James Mathers is apparently no relation to Jerry "The Beaver" Mathers, which is too bad: the movie would then at least have had something interesting about it.

DR. KILDARE'S STRANGE CASE ★★½
1940, USA
Lew Ayres, Lionel Barrymore, Laraine Day, Sheppard Strudwick, Nat Pendleton, Emma Dunn. Directed by Harold S. Bucquet. 76 min.

Strange is right . . . and reactionary. When Kildare (Lew Ayres) isn't advising an elderly Jewish patient against the evils of mahjongg, he's giving insulin shock therapy to the mentally disturbed. The *noir*-ish climax in which Kildare treats the nut case is almost on a par with scenes from *The Exorcist* (for thrills, shocks, and unintended laughs). Fans of the series will gobble this up; others should first become acquainted with a more conventional entry—say, *Young Dr. Kildare*.

DR. NO ★★★
1962, USA
Sean Connery, Ursula Andress, Jack Lord, Joseph Wiseman, Bernard Lee. Directed by Terence Young. 111 min.

The first of the James Bond films is a good, solid beginning to the series. Sean Connery makes his debut as 007, the world's coolest superspy, battling the nefarious Dr. No in the photogenic West Indies, and Andress is the first of a long line of Bond women, Honey Ryder. Producers Albert Broccoli and Harry Saltzman didn't really find their lighthearted, gadget- and action-packed groove until *From Russia with Love* and *Goldfinger*, but *Dr. No* is still fast-paced fun.

DOCTOR OF DOOM ★
1962, Mexico
Lorene Velazquez, Armando Silvestre, Elizabeth Campbell, Roberto Canedo. Directed by Rene Cardona. 77 min.

Anticipating the popularity of wrestling stars in this country by over two decades, the Mexicans gave a boost to their horror film industry in the sixties by teaming their monsters with wrestlers—and female ones, to boot. South-of-the-border superstars Gloria Venus and the Golden Rubi have to do battle with the titular bad guy and his two laboratory creations, Gomar the human ape and Vendetta, an artificially created female wrestler! As must fun as it sounds, thanks to bad acting, worse dubbing, even *worse* dialogue, and more bad twists than the entire Chubby Checker catalogue. Gomar returned in *Night of the Bloody Apes*, while Gloria Venus and the Golden Rubi were back in *The Wrestling Women vs. the Aztec Mummy*.

DR. PHIBES RISES AGAIN ★★★
1972, Great Britain, PG
Vincent Price, Robert Quarry, Valli Kemp, Hugh Griffith, Gerald Sim, Beryl Reid, Peter Cushing, Terry-Thomas, Fiona Lewis. Directed by Robert Fuest. 88 min.

Given that, in the original *The Abominable Dr. Phibes*, Vincent Price killed off the surgeons who botched his late wife's operation with devices based on the plagues of ancient Egypt, it seems appropriate that he ventured to Egypt in this amusing sequel to try to find a fabled elixir that will restore her to life. Trouble is, he has a rival who is looking for the same potion, so Phibes once again resorts to bumping off the competition one by one in a series of clever, inventive ways. Price is wonderfully hammy, and this vehicle appropriately exploits him.

DOCTOR STRANGE ★★½
1978, USA (TV)
Peter Hooten, Clyde Kusatsu, Jessica Walter, Eddie Benton, Philip Sterling, John Mills. Directed by Philip DeGuere. 94 min.

This telefilm adaptation of the popular Marvel Comics superhero saga is more entertaining than many other recent comic book–to–film transitions. Writer-director DeGuere succeeds where others have failed by keeping the spirit light and the pace fast. Peter Hooten is only adequate as the psychiatrist invested with mystic powers that enable him to enter the fourth dimension, but Jessica Walter is ripely amusing as his archfoe.

DR. STRANGELOVE OR: HOW I LEARNED TO STOP WORRYING AND LOVE THE BOMB ★★★★
1963, Great Britain
Peter Sellers, George C. Scott, Sterling Hayden, Slim Pickens, Keenan Wynn, Peter Bull, James Earl Jones. Directed by Stanley Kubrick. 93 min.

Peter Sellers stars as the U.S. president, a British captain, and the inventor of the bomb in Stanley Kubrick's highly acclaimed black comedy about a mad general who orders a nuclear attack on the Soviet Union. Sellers gives one of his most memorable performances in this terrifying, funny, and influential *tour de force*. The satirist Terry Southern wrote the film's offbeat screenplay along with Peter George and Kubrick himself. Even now, more than 20 years later, Kubrick's film makes a devastating timely statement about the perils of the nuclear age.

DOCTORS WEAR SCARLET

See *The Bloodsuckers*

DOCTOR SYN
1937, Great Britain ☆½
George Arliss, Margaret Lockwood, John Loder, Roy Emerton. Directed by Roy William Neill. 81 min.

One of several film versions of a popular British adventure novel about a village priest who moonlights as a notorious pirate, this suffers from the miscasting of veteran ham George Arliss in the title role. They rewrote the story to try and make it more palatable to Arliss's fans, but it still doesn't work, though to be fair none of the other movies (a Disney version and one with Peter Cushing retitled *Night Creatures*) was very interesting, either. It was Arliss's last picture.

DR. TERROR'S HOUSE OF HORRORS
1965, Great Britain ☆☆½
Peter Cushing, Christopher Lee, Roy Castle, Donald Sutherland, Max Adrian, Neil McCallum, Jeremy Kemp, Michael Gough. Directed by Freddie Francis. 98 min.

Freddie Francis is a better cameraman than director, but this uneven horror mélange has a few good shudders. The premise, a solid one, involves five train passengers who are told by a sinister stranger that they will each die a horrible death. The separate stories vary in originality and suspense—one of them is yet another variation of "The Hands of Orlac"—but a cast of horror-film pros (Peter Cushing, Christopher Lee, Michael Gough, etc.) drives it through the slow spots. *Note:* This was the first of the Amicus multistory packages, which would later include *Torture Garden* and *Tales from the Crypt*.

DOCTOR ZHIVAGO
1965, Great Britain ☆☆½
Omar Sharif, Julie Christie, Tom Courtenay, Rod Steiger, Rita Tushingham, Alec Guinness, Ralph Richardson. Directed by David Lean. 197 min. (two cassettes).

As spectaculars go, *Dr. Zhivago* is decent entertainment, but on any serious level, the film is overblown and devoid of directorial insight. A triumph for art director John Box and composer Maurice Jarre, whose "Lara's Theme" is plugged in ad nauseam throughout. The acting is variable but never completely without interest, with the unfortunate and devastating exception of Omar Sharif in the title role. One of David Lean's least personal epics.

DODES 'KA-DEN
1970, Japan ☆☆
Yoshitaka Zushi, Junzaburo Ban, Kiyoko Tange, Kin Sugai, Toshiyuki Tonomura, Shinsuke Minami. Directed by Akira Kurosawa. 140 min.

Akira Kurosawa's first color film is rough, tedious going even for his most ardent admirers, a long but shallow and episodic tale of a group of impoverished shantytown dwellers in contemporary Japan. Two drunk husbands trade wives, a couple lives out a tortured marriage because of the wife's long-past affair, a timid girl is oppressed by her family, and a semiretarded young man imagines himself to be a trolley car going on the day's rounds (the title is an evocation of the car's motor sounds). Handsomely stylized but uninvolving, the film has no emotional center, and ends as little more than a collection of anecdotes and fables, the last thing we expect from the master of epic filmmaking.

DODGE CITY
1939, USA ☆☆☆
Errol Flynn, Olivia De Havilland, Ann Sheridan, Bruce Cabot, Frank McHugh, Alan Hale, John Litel, Victor Jory, Ward Bond, Monte Blue. Directed by Michael Curtiz. 100 min.

This is an A production all the way! A great cast, a Max Steiner score, color, and a good taming-a-tough-town story. Errol Flynn plays a foreign mercenary who becomes sheriff and runs up against saloon owner Bruce Cabot, who may be involved in a nefarious cattle-trading scheme. Michael Curtiz (*Casablanca*) is a more than capable director: the action never lets up. Ann Sheridan is just perfect in her part as a saloon girl. A robust, old-fashioned crowd-pleaser.

DODSWORTH
1936, USA ☆☆☆☆
Walter Huston, Ruth Chatterton, Mary Astor, Paul Lukas, David Niven, Maria Ouspenskaya. Directed by William Wyler. 90 min.

A remarkably moving and often depressing film, *Dodsworth* comes close to anticipating the mature melodrama of *Viaggio in Italia*, Roberto Rossellini's classic of travel despair and marital alienation. A retired businessman takes a boat trip to Europe and watches as his wife engages in a series of dispiriting affairs with younger men. Walter Huston, who played the role of Sinclair Lewis's antihero on Broadway, moves through the part with intelligence and feeling. Rudolph Mate's camerawork is polished and deep, creating a space that reveals the character's shallowness and *faux* elegance. The ending, though contrived, is pure Hollywood-happy.

DOG DAY AFTERNOON
1975, USA, R ☆☆☆☆
Al Pacino, John Cazale, Charles Durning, Carol Kane, Chris Sarandon, Sully Boyar. Directed by Sidney Lumet. 130 min.

The film is based on a true incident in which a would-be robber held up a Brooklyn bank to get money for a sex-change operation for his homosexual lover, only to wind up trapped inside the bank with the employees as hostages and hordes of police, FBI men, reporters, and onlookers outside. Alternately (often simultaneously) hilarious and tragic, this is worth repeated viewings in order to enjoy the wealth of characterization and details that can easily be buried by the strength of Al Pacino's performance and the rapid pace. Two of Sidney Lumet's gifts, for using New York locations to good advantage and for developing complex, ambiguous characters, are strongly evinced here. Frank Pierson's screenplay won an Academy Award.

A DOG OF FLANDERS
1959, USA ☆☆☆
David Ladd, Donald Crisp, Theodore Bikel, Max Croiset, Monique Ahrens, Patrasche. Directed by James B. Clark. 97 min.

This is an outstanding children's feature that adults should enjoy for its low-key mood and beautiful photography. Young Dutch lad David Ladd wants to become an artist, but the impoverished life that he and his grandfather (Donald Crisp) lead precludes the necessary training. When Gramps dies, Ladd and his faithful dog struggle to get by on their own. The dog, Patrasche, is the same one that played the title role in Walt Disney's *Old Yeller*.

DOGPOUND SHUFFLE
1975, Canada ☆☆☆½
Ron Moody, David Soul, Pamela McMyler, Ray Stricklyn, Raymond Sutton. Directed by Jeffrey Bloom. 95 min.

In this modest, surprisingly affecting drama, a former tap dancer, now a bum in Vancouver, must raise thirty dollars to redeem his beloved dog from the pound. Most of the film details the comic misadventures that befall him as, eschewing charity, he revives his old act, first in a local dive and then at a posh party, with lots of small complications that are very large problems for someone in his position. The film almost miraculously avoids the mawkishness that inherently threatens such a story at almost every turn. A steady-eyes, winsome gem, as befits a film starring actors named Moody and Soul.

THE DOGS OF WAR
1981, Great Britain, R ☆☆☆
Christopher Walken, Tom Berenger, Colin Blakely, JoBeth Williams, Hugh Millais, Paul Freeman. Directed by John Irvin. 101 min.

John Irvin's action film about mercenaries is probably better than anyone had a right to expect, considering its source: a laundry list of guns and ammo in the form of a novel by Frederick Forsyth. Christopher Walken plays a mask-faced gat-for-hire on a reconnaissance mission to check out the African dictator whose government he plans to topple. The first half of the film lays out an effective multi level sketch of colonial corruption, and seems to be adding up to something really exciting. But during the coup itself, the narrative loses coherence and the movie becomes another forgettable and excessively violent shoot-'em-up. Walken, however, is smooth and steady throughout.

LA DOLCE VITA ☆☆☆☆
1960, Italy/France
Marcello Mastroianni, Anita Ekberg, Anouk Aimee, Alain Cuny, Yvonne Furneaux, Magnoli Noel, Nadia Gray, Lex Barker. Directed by Federico Fellini. 174 min.

Federico Fellini's dark, vertiginous portrait of Rome as a glamorous inferno marked the birth of the phantasmagoric style that characterized his celebrated middle period—*8 ½*, *Juliet of the Spirits*, *Satyricon*. Marcello Mastroianni is the journalist who's both seduced and appalled by the apocalyptic decadence around him, and Anita Ekberg is the superstar who takes him on a midnight joyride. The episodic screenplay was written by Fellini, with Tullio Pinelli, Brunello Rondi, and well-known author Ennio Flaiano. Although much of the dialogue is in a slangy Roman dialect that is lost in translation, the video version from Republic Pictures is preferable to the dubbed prints that show up on TV. However, the widescreen compositions are not translatable to the small screen. Note the score by the brilliant Nino Rota.

$ (DOLLARS) ☆½
1972, USA, R
Goldie Hawn, Warren Beatty, Gert Frobe, Robert Webber, Scott Brady. Directed by Richard Brooks. 119 min.

Goldie Hawn and Warren Beatty make a cute if cloying couple in this humdrum, unfunny caper film about a bank security man and a hooker who team up to pull off a $1.5 million robbery. Brooks's writing and direction here are totally off the mark; as in his later *Wrong Is Right* and *Fever Pitch*, he's so overemphatic that you may see an element of parody he didn't intend. If you stick around through the interminable development, you'll be rewarded with a final chase that's more chaotic than climactic.

DOLL FACE ☆☆½
1945, USA
Vivian Blaine, Carmen Miranda, Perry Como, Dennis O'Keefe, Martha Stewart, Michael Dunne. Directed by Lewis Seiler. 80 min.

This modest musical is about a burlesque queen who auditions for a Broadway show. There's no Technicolor, and whatever was risqué about Gypsy Rose Lee's play (on which this is based) is scrubbed squeaky-clean in Leonard Praskins's script. But at least Carmen Miranda is around to supply her own special brand of fruity flavor. Vivian Blaine could have taken a few hints from Carmen and put more of the *Guys and Dolls* sass into the stripper role. Still, it's light, fast, and fun. Perry Como sings the big number: "Dig You Later." (a.k.a.: *Come Back to Me*)

THE DOLLMAKER ☆☆☆½
1984, USA (TV)
Jane Fonda, Levon Helm, Geraldine Page, Amanda Plummer, Susan Kingsley, Ann Hearn, Dan Hedaya, Christine Ebersole, Studs Terkel. Directed by Daniel Petrie. 140 min.

Jane Fonda won an Emmy for her TV-movie debut in this poignant, powerful adaptation of Harriette Arnow's novel about an illiterate mother from the Kentucky hills who must learn a new way of life when she moves to Detroit during World War II. Her performance is remarkably fine, lacking many of the irritating mannerisms that have come to characterize her recent motion picture work, and if the drama is predictable in the way of so many uplifting TV movies, it's done with exceptional taste and skill. Hume Cronyn cowrote the screenplay with Susan Cooper.

A DOLL'S HOUSE ☆☆☆
1973, Great Britain
Jane Fonda, Edward Fox, Trevor Howard, Delphine Seyrig, David Warner. Directed by Joseph Losey. 103 min.

Jane Fonda gives a vibrant performance that resonates through this otherwise staid and cautious adaptation of the classic Henrik Ibsen play. She plays the young, flighty banker's wife who undergoes a crisis and discovers both her potential strength and her husband's oppressive ways. Unfortunately, slack direction and weak support from David Warner, Edward Fox, and Trevor Howard render the male characters one-dimensional and make Ibsen's melodrama seem simpleminded; there is no tension in the sexual battle and there is no doubt as to the eventual victor. Nicely photographed in beautiful Roros, Norway. This movie had a limited theatrical run and was premiered, in most places, on television. Interestingly, this was one of two versions of *Doll's House* made in 1973; the other version had Claire Bloom in the pivotal role of Nora.

DOMINIQUE ☆
1978, Great Britain
Jean Simmons, Cliff Robertson, Jenny Agutter, Simon Ward, Judy Geeson. Directed by Michael Anderson. 100 min.

In this imponderable mystery, Jean Simmons is either (a) floating about because she's a ghost, (b) wandering about in suspended animation because of her Etruscan bracelet, or (c) not really dead at all, but hatching a scheme to torment the husband who drove her to madness. Confused? You still will be by the time this tedium winds down to its unremarkable climax. Devoid of any style or flair, the film is notable for taking one of our most talented actresses, Jean Simmons, and limiting her to a few, scattered, soft-focus ramblings. A piffle of a ghost tale that builds no suspense, despite using every scare device from every supernatural movie ever made.

THE DOMINO PRINCIPLE ☆☆½
1977, USA, R
Gene Hackman, Candice Bergen, Richard Widmark, Mickey Rooney, Edward Albert, Eli Wallach. Directed by Stanley Kramer. 97 min.

Written by Adam Kennedy from his best-selling novel, this Lew Grade production stars Gene Hackman and Candice Bergen as a couple fighting a faceless assassination network. All the dramatic conflicts in this paranoia-laced thriller collapse like so many dominoes. In the twilight of his career, Stanley Kramer tried to pump life into genre pictures as if a whole generation of Robert Altmans and Martin Scorseses had never happened. But *Oklahoma Crude* and *The Domino Principle* are not viable alternatives to the new American cinema; they're flat star vehicles that give their casts nothing meaty to enact. It's not an appalling failure, just peremptory.

DOÑA FLOR AND HER TWO HUSBANDS ☆☆☆
1977, Brazil, R
Sonia Braga, Jose Wilker, Mauro Mendonca. Directed by Bruno Barreto. 110 min.

In this pleasant Brazilian comedy, Sonia Braga plays a woman married to a sexy high roller who dies at thirty-three, leaving her to wed the boring, respectable town pharmacist. But then her first husband reappears—naked and visible only to her. The husbands never come to life as characters, but Braga's effortless sensuality is ravishing. Remade as the American *Kiss Me Goodbye*.

THE DON IS DEAD
1973, USA, R ☆☆
Anthony Quinn, Frederic Forrest, Robert Forster, Al Lettieri, Angel Tompkins, Charles Cioffi. Directed by Richard Fleischer. 96 min.

This straightforward, clumsy rip-off of *The Godfather* is helped slightly by the work of a decent cast and Richard Fleischer's competent hackwork. The plot has the death of a Mafia overlord sparking a territorial war, but the battling family herein is thoroughly incompetent—the Corleones would have squashed these small-time hoods without blinking. The version on video has been cut by about twenty minutes, eliminating some of the lead-footed pacing of the original.

DONNER PASS—THE ROAD TO SURVIVAL
1978, USA (TV) ☆☆
Robert Fuller, Andrew Prine, Michael Callan, Diane McBain, John Anderson, John Doucette, Cynthia Eilbacher. Directed by James L. Conway. 100 min.

This is a grim account of a strange chapter in the settling of the West, in which a party of westward-ho pioneers was forced to eat those who didn't survive the hardship in order to stay alive. If the film had taken a less sanitized approach to the issue of all-American cannibalism this might have been unbearable to watch. As it is, it's fairly tame—yet gripping, because of the intrinsic power of the material itself.

DONOVAN'S REEF
1963, USA ☆☆☆½
John Wayne, Lee Marvin, Jack Warden, Elizabeth Allen, Cesar Romero, Dorothy Lamour, Jacqueline Malouf, Dick Foran, Mike Mazurki. Directed by John Ford. 112 min.

John Ford gives free rein to his comic impulses, and viewers will delight in the boozy battles and annual birthday brawl as John Wayne and Lee Marvin tear up a South Seas island. There is a slightly serious side, too, to this tale of three Navy veterans who have settled in polynesia: when one of the old sailor's daughters comes down from Boston, the Duke passes off her half-Polynesian siblings as his own children. The ensuing comic mix-ups are balanced by a nice story of racial understanding. Lots of fun, with a warmhearted, patriotic streak. Many Ford fans regard this as his last great film.

DON'S PARTY
1976, Australia, R ☆☆☆½
Ray Barrett, Claire Binney, John Hargreaves, Pat Bishop, Graeme Blundell, Jeannie Drynan. Directed by Bruce Beresford. 90 min.

David Williamson's play built around the old theatrical conceit—the use of a party as a metaphor for some aspect of the human condition—is adapted into a bawdy, exceptionally well-acted film. The occasion is the Australian national election in 1969, when the Conservatives were ousted for the first time in decades. The revelers are liberal-socialist university types, with a token conservative couple to round things out, and watching the election results on television soon gives way to arguing, adultery, and alcohol. The goings-on are indigenously Australian, but the characters are universal types (although the fine cast keeps them from becoming stereotypes). Director Bruce Beresford filmed this on a single set, the house where the party takes place, and does a nice job of breaking up its stage origins without adding extraneous material.

DON'T ANSWER THE PHONE
1980, USA, R ☆
James Westmoreland, Flo Gerrish, Ben Frank, Nicholas Worth, Stan Haze, Gary Allen. Directed by Robert Hammer. 94 min.

A fleshy, physical-culture-obsessed maniac with a religious fixation dabbles in the world of pornography before settling down to a career as a rapist/murderer. "Don't answer the phone—he knows you're alone!" warned the ads, though the killer spends less time terrorizing women on the telephone—with the conspicuous exception of a call-in psychiatrist—than he does sweating in his home weight room. Sleazy and distasteful.

DON'T BE AFRAID OF THE DARK
1973, USA (TV) ☆☆½
Kim Darby, Jim Hutton, Barbara Anderson, William Demarest. Directed by John Newland. 74 min.

In this effective made-for-TV thriller, newlyweds inherit a house occupied by small, grotesque creatures. The suspense mounts as the young husband refuses to believe in the menace. Good special effects and camerawork.

DON'T CRY, IT'S ONLY THUNDER
1982, USA (TV), PG ☆☆½
Dennis Christopher, Susan Saint James, Roger Aaron Brown, Lisa Lu, Thu Thuy. Directed by Peter Werner. 108 min.

This is an earnest, fact-based tale of a determined doctor (Susan Saint James) and a G.I. Joe (Dennis Christopher) who wears his heart on his sleeve. The two team up to make an orphanage in Vietnam a workable proposition. As they overcome the odds, you'll be moved by their interaction with the hapless children. Although the film suffers from incipient TV-movie-itis with all plot points neatly tied up and the battleground horrors only dramatized up to a certain discreet point, the film is still compelling. A competent war weepie.

DON'T DRINK THE WATER
1969, USA, G ☆☆½
Jackie Gleason, Estelle Parsons, Joan Delaney, Ted Bessell, Richard Libertini, Michael Constantine, Avery Schreiber, Howard Morris. Directed by Howard Morris. 98 min.

Jackie Gleason and Estelle Parsons play Americans on vacation in Europe in this adaptation of a play by Woody Allen. Typical of his writing of the sixties, this is pretty much a nonstop barrage of one-liners in the Allen formula, all loosely hung on a plot that has a Jewish caterer and family running into assorted problems behind the iron curtain. Sporadically funny, although Allen's lines are so identifiable with his own style of delivery that they sound peculiar coming from others. Richard Libertini has a nice bit as a priest gone a bit daffy after years of political asylum in an embassy.

DON'T FENCE ME IN
1945, USA ☆☆
Roy Rogers, George "Gabby" Hayes, Dale Evans. Directed by John English. 71 min.

This amusing, well-crafted Western features singing, dancing, shooting, and more. Evans plays a magazine photographer who comes to Roy Rogers's ranch for a story on Wildcat Kelly, a notorious bad guy from way back. Cole Porter wrote the title song.

DON'T GO IN THE HOUSE
1980, USA, R ½☆
Dan Grimaldi, Robert Osth, Ruth Dardick, Charles Bonet. Directed by Joseph Ellison. 82 min.

Physically and emotionally scarred by his insanely religious mother (who burned his arms over an open flame when he misbehaved as a child), a young man lures women into his house, soaks them with gasoline, and then burns them alive in a specially constructed room. With the exception of a dream sequence on a beach (in which blackened corpses rise from a rift in the sand and drag the killer to some unspecified, ghastly fate), this is a mechanical series of dreary horrors; nasty and uninteresting.

DON'T LOOK IN THE BASEMENT ☆
1973, USA
William McGee, Annie MacAdams, Rosie Holotik, Jessie Lee Fulton. Directed by S. F. Brownrigg. 95 min.

Don't watch this movie. The standard the-maniacs-have-taken-over-the-asylum plot is almost totally without redeeming interest for anyone, including those who like to laugh at bad movies—this doesn't even try hard enough to be able to fail amusingly. With any given Edward D. Wood, Jr., movie you can at least guffaw at the inept sincerity; this is just inept.

DON'T LOOK NOW ☆☆☆½
1973, Great Britain, R
Julie Christie, Donald Sutherland, Hilary Mason, Clelia Matania. Directed by Nicholas Roeg. 110 min.

Nicholas Roeg transforms wintry Venice into a mysterious labyrinth of illusions in this sophisticated, haunting thriller. Trying to forget the death of their young daughter, John and Laura Baxter find themselves faced with a maze of terrifying premonitions that form a bizarre connection between their past and future, and offer the possibility of dreaming their daughter back to life. The ending is genuinely startling, and the undercurrent of tension between man's will and his imagination is made quite compelling by Roeg's direction and Anthony Richmond's elegant, icy cinematography. Based on a short story by Daphne Du Maurier.

DON'T OPEN THE WINDOW ☆☆½
1974, Italy, R
Arthur Kennedy, Ray Lovelock, Christine Galbo. Directed by Jorge Grau.

Produced in Italy and shot in London as *The Living Dead at Manchester Morgue*, this is a *Night of the Living Dead*-derived cannibal zombie picture (a form at which Italian horror filmmakers excel—see also *Zombie, Dr. Butcher, M.D. (Medical Deviate), Day of the Zombies, The Gates of Hell, Seven Doors of Death*, and many, many others). It posits an experimental device designed to kill insects with ultrasonic waves that instead resurrects the dead. Once restored to life, the dead kill, maim, and splatter the living all over the screen. Very bloody gore festival that should please fans to no end.

DON'T RAISE THE BRIDGE, LOWER THE RIVER ☆☆
1968, Great Britain
Jerry Lewis, Terry-Thomas, Patricia Routledge, Jacqueline Pearce, Bernard Cribbins. Directed by Jerry Paris. 99 min.

Two Jerrys don't make merry, not even when you take them over to merry old England. Under the direction of TV hack Jerry Paris, Jerry Lewis provides an argument for the superiority of his perennial spastic character by abandoning it in favor of a straighter role as a would-be entrepreneur involved in an assortment of complicated and nefarious schemes. Terry-Thomas and Bernard Cribbins prove that they are not the same person, and provide some much-needed comic relief. This is a mediocre Jerry Lewis movie, compared to some that are genuinely inventive and funny, like *The Nutty Professor*.

DOOMED TO DIE ☆½
1940, USA
Boris Karloff, Grant Withers, Marjorie Reynolds, Melvin Lang. Directed by William Nigh. 67 min.

The last of five mysteries made by impoverished Monogram studios, featuring Boris Karloff as the Oriental detective Mr. Wong, it looks as if everyone involved here was out to get the thing over with, collect his or her paycheck and go home. The murder victim is a shipping tycoon, and the solution is provided when Wong reveals several clues unavailable to the audience, always a disservice in a mystery.

THE DOOMSDAY FLIGHT ☆☆
1966, USA
Jack Lord, Edmond O'Brien, Hatherine Crawford, John Saxon, Van Johnson, Michael Sarrazin, Edward Asner, Greg Morris. Directed by William Graham. 100 min.

With all of the unreleased classics around, one has to wonder why MCA Home Video decided to put this one on the market. The Rod Serling screenplay is taut, and the cast is recognizable; however, this television movie is very undistinguished. A psychopath (Edmond O'Brien) threatens to blow up a passenger jet, and an FBI man (Jack Lord) tries to locate the bomb. Well received in its time, the movie now seems hackneyed and strident. For Jack Lord fans only.

DOPE ADDICT

See *Reefer Madness*

DOPED YOUTH

See *Reefer Madness*

EL DORADO ☆☆☆½
1967, USA
John Wayne, Robert Mitchum, Christopher George, Arthur Hunnicutt, Michelle Carey, Charlene Holt, James Caan, Paul Fix. Directed by Howard Hawks. 126 min.

Howard Hawks tells a good, old-fashioned tale about violence and male bonding out on the frontier. John Wayne plays a gunman who comes to the aid of a drunken sheriff (Robert Mitchum). Cast in the mold of Hawks's "buddy films," this rollicking Western by the old master features good performances all around.

DORIAN GRAY ☆☆
1970, Italy/Liechtenstein/West Germany, R
Helmut Berger, Richard Todd, Herbert Lom, Marie Liljedahl, Margaret Lee, Maria Rohm, Isa Miranda. Directed by Massimo Dallamano. 93 min.

The original Hollywood rendition of Oscar Wilde's *The Picture of Dorian Gray* was not great, but it is impressive next to this updated remake. Here, Helmut Berger woodenly plays Dorian, the young man who sells his soul in order to be eternally youthful; only his portrait becomes older. Herbert Lom more skillfully plays an epicene Satan, originally incarnated by George Sanders. The production is slick and flashy only to cover up the lousy script, not helped by atrocious English dubbing. (a.k.a.: *The Secret of Dorian Gray*)

THE DORM THAT DRIPPED BLOOD ☆
1982, USA, R
Laurie Lapinski, Stephen Sachs, David Snow, Pamela Holland, Daphne Zuniga. Directed by Jeffery Obrow and Stephen Carpenter. 85 min.

After the end of the semester, some students stay behind to help clean out a dorm slated for renovation. But wait, there's a mad killer on the loose! He wipes them out mercilessly, one by one, until . . . Scary stuff, eh, boys and girls? Okay, so it's *not* so scary. But Count Floyd promises you that next week we'll have a *really* scary movie, a good one, like maybe *The Blood-Sucking Monkeys From West Miflin, Pennsylvania*.

DOUBLE BUNK ☆☆
1961, Great Britain
Ian Carmichael, Janette Scott, Sidney James, Liz Fraser, Dennis Price, Graham Stark. Directed by C. M. Pennington-Richards. 92 min.

Two newlyweds, unable to find housing, buy a houseboat. Of course, it's falling apart, but they manage to pull it together in time to win a race by film's end. Minor British comedy-farce that is dominated less by Ian Carmichael's whimsy than by veteran *Carry On*-er Sidney James's incessant mugging; if there were ever a British version of the Three Stooges, James would surely be one of them.

THE DOUBLE, DOUBLE CROSS ½☆
Hong Kong
James Wang Yu, Chia Ling, Chang Li.

Typical Jimmy Wang Yu movie set in contemporary Hong Kong. This time he uses a knife.

DOUBLE DRAGON IN LAST DUEL ½☆
1985, Hong Kong
Kang Ho, Mae Li, Jum Soon Park, Bong Choi. Directed by Key Nam Nam. 90 min.

You'll need a map and a compass to find your way through this twisted, confusing tale of intrigue and revenge. A hint: the two guys in black pajamas are the good guys, but, no, they don't know each other. Crisp kung fu, but not enough of it. A score stolen from *The Empire Strikes Back*.

A DOUBLE LIFE ☆☆☆
1947, USA
Ronald Colman, Signe Hasso, Shelley Winters, Edmond O'Brien. Directed by George Cukor. 103 min.

The writing-directing team of Ruth Gordon, Garson Kanin, and George Cukor usually came up with frothy, sophisticated comedies like *Adam's Rib*, *The Marrying Kind*, and *Pat and Mike*, but in their first collaboration, they produced this dark, grim, *noir*-ish melodrama about an actor who becomes so obsessed with his stage role of Othello that he begins to live the part in real life. Oscar-winner Ronald Colman is too elegant to play the insane thespian and surprisingly bad (as is the rest of the cast) in the onstage *Othello* sequences. Still, the story is a good one and Cukor's usual polished direction (complemented by Milton Krasner's photography) makes this a visual treat.

THE DOUBLE MCGUFFIN ☆☆
1979, USA, PG
Ernest Borgnine, George Kennedy, Elke Sommer, Ed (Too Tall) Jones, Vincent Spano, Dion Pride. Directed by Joe Camp. 101 min.

Don't be fooled by the PG rating: this is the kind of thing that theaters show at Saturday matinees in the hope that mothers who want to go shopping will drop off their kids and supply them with sufficient funds to buy out half the concession stand. It's a mystery with pubescent sleuths, quite in the mold of most Disney output of the last thirty years, with Elke Sommer offering a bit of skin early on to avoid the dreaded G rating. The voice of Orson Welles takes over the soundtrack at one point to explain, for the benefit of those viewers who may not have made an in-depth study of Hitchcock (which is to say, the entire audience) just what a "McGuffin" is. (No, it's not a new sandwich at McDonald's.) From the creator of *Benji*.

DOUBLE NEGATIVE ☆½
1980, Canada
Michael Sarrazin, Susan Clark, Anthony Perkins, Howard Duff, Kate Reid, Al Waxman. Directed by George Bloomfield. 96 min.

Here is yet another tepid Canadian mystery-thriller that mistakes obfuscation for style. Michael Sarrazin plays a journalist confined to a mental institution after the murder of his wife; Susan Clark is his lover who springs him and helps him find the killer while hoping he doesn't freak out again; and Anthony Perkins is the dead wife's lover. Sarrazin is badly miscast—you never believe that this is someone who could go over the edge at any minute. Perkins steals the show with all of his usual psycho tricks, while Clark has little to do. Two negatives don't make a positive.

DOUBLE TROUBLE ☆☆
1967, USA
Elvis Presley, Annette Day, John Williams, Yvonne Romain, Chips Rafferty. Directed by Norman Taurog. 90 min.

This is *not* the film in which Elvis played dual roles (that was *Kissin' Cousins*). He's besieged by two females and two jewel thieves—apparently the rock star is unwittingly carrying some diamonds in his suitcase. The ensuing chases, skirmishes, and romantic interludes come across like *Goldfinger* with musical numbers. Presley sings "Long-Legged Girl," "Could I Fall in Love?" "I love Only One Girl," and even "Old MacDonald Had a Farm."

DOWN AND DIRTY ☆☆☆
1978, Italy, R
Nino Manfredi. Directed by Ettore Scola. 115 min.

In direct contrast to the Chaplinesque character he usually plays, Nino Manfredi goes for all-out grotesque as the one-eyed patriarch of a Rome slum family, out to defend his personal fortune from the twenty-odd relatives with whom he shares a grimy one-room shanty. It's a comedy, and quite funny if you don't mind the continual degradation. Well played by a large cast of nonprofessional actors.

DOWN AND OUT IN BEVERLY HILLS ☆½
1986, USA, R
Bette Midler, Nick Nolte, Richard Dreyfuss. Directed by Paul Mazursky. 103 min.

This movie is mediocre in every respect, which makes it awful in an especially insidious way. Nick Nolte plays Jerry, a bum who lives off the haute-cuisine garbage of Beverly Hills. After his dog, Kerouac, runs off with a shapely, food-dispensing jogger, Jerry is so despondent that he fills his pockets with stones and throws himself into the swimming pool of coat-hanger magnate Richard Dreyfuss and wife Bette Midler; they rescue him and take him in as a guest, and the rest of the movie implausibly details his beneficial effects on this neurotic, wealth-stultified family. The film's attempts at humor are unoriginal when not offensive, and its emotional paralysis is epitomized by the feebly inadequate responses of Dreyfuss to the triple betrayal he suffers at the hands of Nolte, who has sex with his wife, mistress (the maid), and, finally, daughter. Midler and Dreyfuss surprisingly gained career turn-arounds in this less-than-average film.

DOWN ARGENTINE WAY ☆½
1940, USA
Betty Grable, Don Ameche, Carmen Miranda, Charlotte Greenwood, J. Carrol Naish, Leonid Kinskey, the Nicholas Brothers. Directed by Irving Cummings. 94 min.

Even the dancing of Betty Grable, Charlotte Greenwood, and the Nicholas Brothers can't save this turkey. Grable, who stepped in for an ailing Alice Faye and became a star, plays an American heiress who falls for a South American horse trainer (Don Ameche with an accent). Terrible as Ameche is, he's never as annoying as Leonid Kinskey who plays Betty's travel guide. Carmen Miranda (in her debut) is around for three songs, including "South American Way" and "Mama Yo Quiero," but that's it! The plot is numbing, the numbers poorly filmed, and the color muddy.

DOWN BY LAW ☆☆☆½
1986, USA, R
Tom Waits, John Lurie, Roberto Benigni, Ellen Barkin, Nicoletta Braschi, Billie Neal, Rockets Redglare, Vernel Bagneris. Directed by Jim Jarmusch. 106 min.

This is a despairing, austerely beautiful comedy by the director of the cult smash *Stranger than Paradise*. *Down by Law* is a straight-faced send-up of prison-break films, shot in stunningly gloomy black and white by Robby Mueller. The somber narrative unites a small-time pimp, a down-and-out DJ, and a very confused Italian card shark in a New Orleans jail, then follows them as they trudge through the bayou looking for the road to freedom. Jim Jarmusch's movie's are bleak existential jokes, and they're unlike the work of any other American director; the overwhelming sense of anomie will leave you either laughing or completely cold. John Lurie and Tom Waits are effective as two of the jailbirds, although both are terminally dour (you're never seen fewer smiles in a comedy)—it's up to expressive Italian comic Roberto Benigni, whose robustly fractured English is sidesplitting, to give the film a heart and soul with a grave and witty performance.

DOWN DAKOTA WAY ☆☆
1949, USA
Roy Rogers, Dale Evans, Pat Brady, Monte Montana, Trigger. Directed by William Witney. 67 min.

The plot—something about outlaws and an outbreak of hoof-and-mouth disease in a cattle herd—is a bit convoluted. But good direction, above-average production values, and a rugged performance by Roy Rogers make for a passable Western.

DOWNHILL RACER ☆☆☆½
1969, USA
Robert Redford, Gene Hackman, Camilla Sparv. Directed By Michael Ritchie. 101 min.

Plot takes a backseat to breathtaking location scenery and dazzling camerawork in this tale of an arrogant ski bum trying to win a spot on the United States Olympic team. Robert Redford effectively underplays as the aloof antihero who is rapidly racing downhill in terms of human compassion. Michael Ritchie's directorial debut is well worth watching for its unforgettable imagery.

DOWN MEXICO WAY ☆☆
1941, USA
Gene Autry, Smiley Burnette, Fay McKenzie, Harold Huber, Sidney Blackmer. Directed by Joseph Stanley. 77 min.

There is slick, silly fun from Gene Autry and sidekick Smiley Burnette in this B Western, in which our hero pursues nefarious bandits south of the border. Lots and lots of songs, with a *motorcycle* chase, of all things, as the climax. The title song was a pop standard for many years.

DOWN TEXAS WAY ☆
1942, USA
Buck Jones, Tim McCoy, Raymond Hatton, Luana Walters. Directed by Howard Bretherton. 55 min.

This standard entry in Monogram's "Rough Riders" series of B-minus Westerns has U.S. marshals Buck, Tim, and Sandy looking for a small-town businessman's killer. Much horseplay, some gunplay, no screenplay, but fun for genre or nostalgia buffs.

DRACULA ☆☆☆
1931, USA
Bela Lugosi, David Manners, Dwight Frye, Helen Chandler. Directed by Tod Browning. 75 min.

If not the definitive version of Bram Stoker's *Dracula*, this film is certainly the one whose images have passed most completely into popular vampire iconography: black-and-white photography with an expressionist edge, Lugosi's classic performance, and dialogue like: "I never drink . . . wine." Based on an awkward stage play, the film retains a stiff, mannered feel, but it's still the yardstick by which other vampire films are measured. Directed by the prolific Tod Browning, whose work includes the truly horrific *Freaks*. *Dracula*'s popularity helped launch Universal Studios on the classic horror chain that includes *Frankenstein*, *The Black Cat*, and *The Wolf Man*.

DRACULA ☆☆☆
1973, USA (TV)
Jack Palance, Simon Ward, Nigel Davenport, Pamela Brown, Fiona Lewis, Penelope Horner, Murray Brown. Directed by Dan Curtis. 100 min.

This above-average rendition of the Bram Stoker novel was made for television with considerable panache by Dan Curtis (*Dark Shadows*, *The Night Stalker*). The location filming in Yugoslavia and England helps, as does the excellent supporting cast, but the best part is Jack Palance as the Count, in a performance that is as evil as one might expect but also surprisingly elegant.

DRACULA (1974)

See *Andy Warhol's Dracula*

DRACULA ☆☆
1979, USA
Frank Langella, Laurence Olivier, Donald Pleasence, Kate Nelligan, Trevor Eve. Directed by John Badham. 109 min.

This is a lush gothic retelling of Bram Stoker's novel with an all-star cast. Full of bats, wolves, cobwebs, storms, lunatics, and repressed Victorian women, it lacks the metaphorical robustness of Hammer vampire films like *Horror of Dracula*, and its large budget buys little of any value beyond elaborate window dressing. Frank Langella's sexy, tongue-in-cheek Broadway performance is flat and unmemorable on screen and Laurence Olivier gives another of his hammy latter-day jobs. From the director of *Saturday Night Fever*, *Blue Thunder*, *Wargames*, and others.

DRACULA AND SON ☆
1976, France, PG
Christopher Lee, Bernard Menez, Marie-Hélène Briellat, Anna Gael. Directed by Edouard Molinaro. 88 min.

Reputedly a pretty funny movie in the French original, this vampire comedy was cut and reedited by the American distributors, who also rewrote the dialogue. The result is awfully dumb, with the younger Dracula speaking in a bad imitation of Don Adams. The story has the Draculas being kicked out of Transylvania by the new Communist government, who considers vampires bad for the party image. From the director of *La Cage aux Folles*.

DRACULA'S CASTLE

See *The Blood of Dracula's Castle*

DRACULA'S DOG ☆☆
1978, USA, R
Michael Pataki, Reggie Nalder, Jose Ferrer, Libbie Chase. Directed by Albert Band. 90 min.

Well, they'd already made *Dracula's Daughter*, *Son of Dracula*, *Brides of Dracula*, and *House of Dracula*, and what good is a house and family without man's . . . er, vampire's best friend? The title canine, Zoltan, after being brought back to life in the usual manner, does the same for the family slave (Reggie Nalder, who plays pretty much the same role in Tobe Hooper's adaptation of Stephen King's *Salem's Lot*) after which they head off to Los Angeles to find the last living descendant of the Dracula family. Of course, there's a Van Helsing type in pursuit, this time played by Jose Ferrer.

A fair number of unintentional laughs, though not so many as the ridiculous title might indicate.

DRACULA'S LAST RITES
1980, USA, R
Patricia Lee Hammond, Gerald Fielding, Victor Jorge, Michael Lally, Mimi Weddell. Directed by Domonic Paris. 88 min.

They had one or two good ideas for this "modern" horror film, but the director, screenwriter, and performers all lacked the talent to make anything out of it. This vampire named Alucard (get it?) is the town mortician and is in cahoots with the sheriff and doctor to get not-quite-dead accident victims who won't put up much of a fuss when he drains what warm blood they have left. It's all played straight, but you can get a few cheap yocks by watching for production flaws, like intruding microphones and visible tops of sets.

DRACULA VS. FRANKENSTEIN
1971, USA
J. Carol Naish, Lon Chaney, Jr., Zandor Vorkov, Regina Carrol, Russ Tamblyn, Angelo Rossitto, Jim Davis, John Bloom, Forrest J. Ackerman. Directed by Al Adamson. 90 min.

One of those so-bad-you've-got-to-see-it atrocities, this is the worst film ever from director Al Adamson, which is really saying something. One can only hope that J. Carrol Naish and Lon Chaney were too old to realize what they were doing here: it would be awful to think that they went to their graves soon afterward with this on their consciences. The wheelchair-ridden Naish plays Dr. Frankenstein, who is still carrying on his usual experiments in a lab underneath an amusement park. Chaney is his assistant, who has no dialogue and little to do except kill teenyboppers and bring back their heads to the doc. Dracula is played by some bozo who (wisely) uses the pseudonym Zandor Vorkov; as if he didn't just *look* funny enough, every time he speaks his words are filtered through an echo chamber. The most unbelievable thing of all is that they weren't kidding. The scene where Drac deals with the pastyfaced monster created by Doc F. anticipates *Monty Python and the Holy Grail* by a good five years.

DRAGNET
1954, USA
Jack Webb, Ben Alexander, Richard Boone, Virginia Greeg, Stacy Harris. Directed by Jack Webb. 93 min.

Jack Webb as Sergeant Joe Friday wants "just the facts, ma'am." That's also what the audience gets in this tedious movie version of the popular radio and TV series: all facts, no action. Following a brutal slaying, we see every detail of the police investigation of it, a commendable but boring way to visualize a manhunt for the screen. Webb's direction is almost as stiff as his performance.

DRAGON CLAWS
Hong Kong
Huang Cheng-Li, Dragon Lee, Kitty Chui, James Lau, Philip Chan. Directed by Godfrey Ho. 90 min.

Kam Fu (Huang Cheng-Li) Is after the Shaolin Temple's four secret kung fu books, and Wong Lung (Dragon Lee) must stop him. This better-than-average costume drama boasts nice sets and costumes as well as good martial arts and choreography. We are also treated to some training scenes as Wong Lung studies Wu Fat kung fu from a Shaolin priest. Although the translation leaves something to be desired, and some fight scenes are unnecessarily speeded up, Huang Cheng-Li and Dragon Lee are worthy opponents and absolutely fabulous martial artists.

DRAGON DEVIL DIE

See *Blooded Treasury Fight*

DRAGON FORCE OPERATION
1985, Hong Kong
Long Tien Cheung, Nancy Yen, Chan Tien Tai. Directed by Tyrone Hsu. min.

Violence escalates to a flashpoint after a lowly but cocky coolie kills his boss's German shepherd. The comparison of Chinese men to dogs, long a colonialist insult, is here unearthed like an old bone and chewed to dust. A version of "Blowin' in the Wind" is used as the theme song.

THE DRAGON KID
Hong Kong
Yiu Tien-Lung, Tzudo Yien-Yung, Chu Ching, Tu Kuo Ying, Huang Yung Kwang, Meng Yuan, Shang-Kuan Liang, Wang Fei. Directed by Shen Jiang.

A man and woman from a Peking Opera troupe are persuaded by the townspeople to try to recover a jade statue from the local gangsters. The star, Yiu Tien-Lung, bears a striking resemblance to the famous Bruce Lee. His fighting style is also similar.

DRAGON, LIZARD, BOXER
Ramon Zamora, Tan Tao-Liang, Meng Fei, Edna Diaz, Philip Coo. Directed by Lo Ke.

The kung fu action is interrupted too often by an absurd plot about two brothers escaping Saigon and getting mixed up with island treasure and gold thieves. Meng Fei and Tan Tao-Liang try hard, but this one is beyond help.

DRAGON PRINCESS
1981, Japan
Sonny Chiba, Etsuko Shiomi, Yasuaki Kurtata, Jiro Yabuki, Riu Kenji, Kiyoichi Sato. Directed by Hiroshi Kouira. 81 min.

So-so kung fu action is somewhat redeemed by a veneer of feminist concerns. When a master is seriously injured and unable to win a prestigious karate instructor position, his daughter steps in and saves the day. Average film, poorly photographed.

DRAGON SEED
1944, USA
Katharine Hepburn, Walter Huston, Aline MacMahon, Turhan Bey, Akim Tamiroff, Hurd Hatfield, Frances Rafferty, Agnes Moorehead, Henry Travers. Directed by Jack Conway, Harold S. Bacquet. 144 min.

MGM did so well adapting Pearl Buck's *Good Earth* that they probably thought they could repeat the magic with Buck's epic *Dragon Seed*; they almost did. The chronicle of a Chinese peasant village under attack by the Japanese in 1937 contains some effective and suspenseful moments, but is most enjoyable as camp. Imagine Katharine Hepburn, Akim Tamiroff, and Agnes Moorehead as Orientals and you have a pretty good idea what the film is like. Best scenes (non-campy): the Japanese hunt down and attack a young girl in the woods, and Hepburn poisons the Japanese general's duck banquet. Lengthy, but too colorful (for both better and worse) to be boring.

DRAGON'S GREATEST REVENGE

See *Bruce Le's Greatest Revenge*

DRAGONSLAYER
1981, USA, PG
Peter MacNicol, Ralph Richardson, Caitlin Clarke, Albert Salmi. Directed by Matthew Robbins. 108 min.

In this majestic and unjustly neglected fantasy film a young apprentice sorcerer goes on a quest to vanquish an evil dragon that is terrorizing the countryside. On his voyage, he comes across a corrupt king who gives the realm's young virgins to the beast in return for protection. A beautifully made film, it paints a vivid picture of the Dark Ages. Although the pace lags a bit, the concluding battle between an eccentric wizard (Ralph Richardson) and the dragon is a stunner. The film received Oscar nominations for its fabulous special effects (done by Industrial Light and Magic) and for the rich score by Alex North. Coproduced by Disney Pictures.

DRAW! ☆☆½
1984, USA (TV)
Kirk Douglas, James Coburn, Alexandra Bastedo, Graham Jarvis, Derek McGrath, Jason Michas, Len Birman. Directed by Steven Hilliard Stern. 98 min.

A made-for-cable Western, this puts two veteran stars of Western action flicks back in the saddle with surprisingly felicitous results. It's a semicomic riff on the durable plot line of the trusty sheriff who must bring an old-time desperado back to justice. While there's nothing new under this particular Western sun, Kirk Douglas and James Coburn exhibit seamless teamwork in an entertaining sagebrush saga from which genre fans will draw a lot of pleasure.

DREAMCHILD ☆☆☆½
1985, Great Britain, PG
Coral Browne, Ian Holm, Peter Gallagher, Caris Corfman, Nicola Cowper, Jane Asher. Directed by Gavin Millar. 100 min.

This biographical fantasy is about Alice Liddell (the little girl Lewis Carroll wrote his *Alice* books for) and Alice Hargreaves (the starchy Victorian lady she became). The story follows the elderly Alice (Coral Browne) to New York in 1932, where she is to receive an honorary degree on Carroll's centenary. A touch of Alice's old playfulness emerges as she perceives that she can make money by exploiting America's hunger for hoopla. But as the film flashes back to her idyllic childhood, she realizes she must come to terms with her buried recollections of Carroll's unrequited love for her. Browne is very moving as Mrs. Hargreaves, and Ian Holm (in a splendid performance) manages to make the repressed, romantic Carroll sad and touching without ever seeming pathetic; he's as much the dreamchild as Alice. Written by Dennis Potter (*Pennies from Heaven*).

DREAMER ☆½
1979, USA, PG
Tim Matheson, Susan Blakely, Jack Warden, Richard B. Shull, Chris Schenkel. Directed by Noel Nosseck. 90 min.

What could be more gripping, more dramatic, more cinematic than a film about . . . bowling? The idea sounds like a parody, a struggle for fame in the sports mode à la Rocky, replete with Bill Conti theme song, but set in a bowling alley. Unfortunately, they're not kidding. The idea is about as hopeful as a seven-ten split, but rather than pick up the spare, this proceeds directly into the gutter. Well, maybe it's not that bad, but it is pointless, even given the dull nature of the subject.

DREAM FOR CHRISTMAS ☆☆☆
1973, USA (TV)
Hari Rhodes, Beah Richards, Lynn Hamilton, George Spell, Marlin Adams, Robert Doqui, Ta-Ronce Allen. Directed by Ralph Senensky. 100 min.

A Starry-eyed ode to optimism, this was written by Earl Hamner, the man who penned "The Waltons." A black preacher moves his family from the stability of Arkansas to a poor congregation in L.A., where domestic upheaval and readjustment problems await them. Although you can guess where the film's heading at all times, it's blessed with a gifted cast that maximizes the emotional impact and makes this a perfect addition to traditional family film viewing for the holidays.

DREAMING FIST WITH SLENDER HANDS ☆☆½
1980, Hong Kong
Lung Fei, Hu Chin. Directed by Karl Liao. 80 Min.

Beyond the bizarre title lies a refreshing comedy about a pair of Laurel and Hardy–ish bumblers who wander the Chinese countryside trying to find Uncle Te-Ah. Although they are looking for advanced kung fu training, they are accomplished enough to hire on to protect a village and to tangle with all comers. Eventually they fall in with different masters and learn exotic techniques through excruciating, wacky exercises.

DREAM LOVER ☆☆½
1986, USA, R
Kristy McNichol, Ben Masters, Paul Shenar, Justin Deas, John McMartin, Gayle Hunnicut. Directed by Alan J. Pakula. 104 min.

Kristy McNichol assays a difficult role with taste and skill; unfortunately, she plays it without much support from the script and director. As a troubled, sensitive woman, McNichol seems right on target. She plays a flautist who comes to the big city but finds out that her dreams of success are no match for her anxieties about the Big Apple. The story about her attempt to rid herself of nightmares doesn't begin to answer its own questions about science and the mind, and the movie doesn't quite work as a thriller, either—one gets the feeling that Alan J. Pakula has trod this ground too often in better movies, like *Klute* and *Sophie's Choice*.

DREAM OF PASSION ☆☆
1978, Greece, R
Melina Mercouri, Ellen Burstyn, Andreas Voutsinas, Despo Diamantidou, Dimitris Papamicanel. Directed by Jules Dassin. 110 min.

Writer/director Jules Dassin has devised a bizarre way of making Euripides's *Medea* "relevant." In this insufferably pretentious film, he's cast his wife, Melina Mercouri, as an international actress who, upon returning to her native Greece to play Medea on the stage, meets a real-life Medea (Ellen Burstyn), an American woman imprisoned for killing her three children. Unfortunately for us, their identities merge. This is supposed to affect Mercouri's performance of Medea, but her theatrical rantings remain uniformly noisy throughout, so it's hard to tell. Dassin's attempts to make the self-absorbed breast-beating of a glamorous international actress rate alongside the passion of Medea are pretty hilarious, but stuck in the middle of this kitsch is one sublime performance: Burstyn's hypnotic, terrifying portrait of the murderess.

DREAMSCAPE ☆☆½
1984, USA, PG-13
Dennis Quaid, Max Von Sydow, Christopher Plummer, Eddie Albert, Kate Capshaw. Directed by Joseph Ruben. 99 min.

Small-scale sci-fi fun. A telepath becomes involved in a scientific experiment that involves projecting people into other people's dreams for therapeutic reasons. Along the way, he becomes enmeshed in a sinister plot to assassinate the president of the United States using a psychopathic dream infiltrator. With some scary, if extremely literal, dreams, and nice performances.

DRESSED TO FIGHT ☆☆½
Tien Peng, Ling Yun, Lung Chun-Erh. Directed by O Yang Chyuang.

Fabulous sets and an intriguing—if somewhat confusing—story highlight this quest yarn about a young man looking for the enigmatic figure who is behind some very strange occurrences. The search leads to Cloud City, where our hero must battle a fanatical cult that refuses to let him leave. Sounds like a party we once attended. . . .

DRESSED TO KILL ★★
1946, USA
Basil Rathbone, Nigel Bruce, Patricia Morrison, Edmond Breon, Frederick Worlock. Directed by Roy William Neill. 72 min.

Not to be confused with the Brian De Palma movie of the same name, this is just another in the 1940s Sherlock Holmes series. Holmes and Watson chase down bank robbers in this outing, which is based, like the others, on a Sir Arthur Conan Doyle story; but it is basically a routine adventure distinguished by the presence of Basil Rathbone and Nigel Bruce. (a.k.a.: *Sherlock Holmes and the Secret Code*)

DRESSED TO KILL ★★★½
1980, USA, R
Michael Caine, Angie Dickinson, Nancy Allen, Keith Gordon. Directed by Brian De Palma. 105 min.

A sort of fantasy remake of *Psycho*, this is one of Brian De Palma's best movies, as scary and funnily self-conscious as the director's *Carrie*. A transsexual killer, armed with a straight razor, terrorizes a sexually repressed housewife (Angie Dickinson), a tough-talking hooker (Nancy Allen), and the housewife's computer-whiz teenager son (Keith Gordon). *Dressed to Kill* takes place in a world of repression, a world of prurience and pent-up desire. Here sex, violence, even a casual conversation all have the same pornographic allure. A sizzler.

THE DRESSER ★★★½
1983, Great Britain, PG
Albert Finney, Tom Courtenay, Edward Fox, Zena Walker, Eileen Atkins. Directed by Peter Yates. 118 min

As "Sir," an actor/manager touring the British provinces during World War II with his rickety Shakespearean company, Albert Finney projects a ravaged grandeur. Finney and director Peter Yates have transformed Ronald Harwood's cut-and-dried 1980 play about the relationship between Sir and his dresser (played here by Tom Courtenay) so that the focus is now on the aging, bellowing actor—and that's exactly where it belongs. The result is a tribute to grand acting as the epitome of human alchemy. Superb performances from both leads.

DRILLER KILLER ★★
1979, USA
Carolyn Marz, Jimmy Laine, Baybi Dey, Bob De Frank, Peter Yellen, Harry Schultz, Tony Coca Cola and the Roosters. Directed by Abel Ferrara. 90 min.

A disturbed painter living in nightmare SoHo gets a power drill with a portable battery pack and takes his frustrations to the streets, where he drills to death bums, crazy people, his slimy homosexual art dealer, and several others. Bleak, low-budget psychological horror film with an authentic downtown New York ambience, lots of blood, and an obsession with eyes. From the director of the stylish, if sleazy, *MS.45* and *Fear City*.

THE DRIVE-IN MASSACRE ½★
1976, USA, R
Jake Barnes, Adam Lawrence. Directed by Stuart Segall. 78 min.

Patrons of a drive-in whose employees are all sleazy and/or mentally abnormal are slaughtered by a maniac; the police are baffled. Cheap gore effects, a meandering story line, and a rip-off ending—in which a voice purporting to be that of the theater manager warns you that the killer was never caught and is thought to be loose in the very theater in which you are viewing this film—conspire to make this a dull and tacky experience. Needless to say, viewing this at home will considerably reduce the impact of that thrilling twist ending.

THE DRIVER ★★★
1978, USA, PG
Ryan O'Neal, Bruce Dern, Isabelle Adjani. Directed by Walter Hill. 90 min.

Walter Hill is at his best when he is handling characters whose destiny matches his own directorial intention. The desperate flight of the gang in *The Warriors* precisely echoes Hill's own speedy, straightforward style, and in *48 HRS.*, Eddie Murphy explodes the released convict's energy just like the movie's story of the cop out of control. In *The Driver*, dispassionate Ryan O'Neal plays a coldly efficient getaway driver in a lean, even stripped-down, movie on wheels. The characters may be ciphers, the plot minimal, but what matters here is the movement—even the cop, played by a wired-down Bruce Dern, has to get up to the driver's speed if he wants to catch him.

THE DRIVER'S SEAT ★½
1974, Italy, R
Elizabeth Taylor, Ian Bannen, Mona Washbourne, Andy Warhol. Directed by Giuseppe Patroni Griffi. 105 min.

Never put into general theatrical release, *The Driver's Seat* is a bizarre tale of a woman who roams through Rome seeking candidates to murder her. Men assume it is sex she is after and she states: "It is not sex I want, it is death." From a novel by Muriel Spark, *The Driver's Seat* is very weird indeed; its only redeeming feature is Elizabeth Taylor's highly unusual performance.

THE DROWNING POOL ★★
1976, USA, PG
Paul Newman, Joanne Woodward, Anthony Franciosa, Murray Hamilton, Gail Strickland, Melanie Griffith, Richard Jaeckel, Coral Browne. Directed by Stuart Rosenberg. 108 min.

Nine years after the moderate success of *Harper*, Paul Newman returned to the role of Ross MacDonald's world-weary detective (called Lew Archer in the novels) for this disappointing follow-up. The star is as charming as ever, but the unexceptional plot is rendered both dull and unbelievable by pedestrian direction and writing. Joanne Woodward's scenes with Newman—there are all too few—are wonderfully played, and Coral Browne has a nice, brief turn as an acidulous southern matriarch.

THE DRUM (1938):

See *Drums*

DRUM ½★
1976, USA
Ken Norton, Warren Oates, Isela Vega, Pam Grier, Yaphet Kotto. Directed by Steve Carver. 110 min.

Bad-movie lovers will want to snare this one. It's a sequel to the hilariously inept *Mandingo*, and guess what? This is even worse. Lurid trash about a superstud slave who's dynamite in the boxing ring and packs a wallop in bed, too. It's the kind of movie in which white women drool over the strapping bucks and white men are portrayed as drunken, racist oafs plagued by impotency problems. Naturally, the slaves rise up to kill de Massa, but maybe they should have revolted against the filmmakers. Exploitative rubbish, but those cotton fields are filled with cheap laughs and tawdry thrills.

DRUMBEAT ★★½
1954, USA
Alan Ladd, Audrey Dalton, Marisa Pavan, Robert Keith, Rudolfo Acosta, Charles Bronson, Elisha Cook, Jr., Frank de Kova. Directed by Delmer Daves. 107 min.

Director Delmer Daves spent a large part of his youth living with various Indians in the Southwest, so his Westerns always had more of a true feel for the Indians than did most others of the time. In this one, which Daves also wrote and produced, Alan Ladd plays a frontiersman sent by President Grant to prevent an uprising by the Modoc Indians. Difficulties arise both from the leader of the Modocs (Charles Bronson, using his stage name for the first time—he was billed in films before this as "Charles Buchinsky") and from local whites; the whites would just as soon the Army go into the Indian fort and massacre them all, even though Grant wants a nonmilitary solution. This is not a great Western (although Daves made several, including *3:10 to Yuma* and *Broken Arrow*) but a surprisingly good one. The transition from the film's original Cinemascope presentation will hurt a video viewing.

DRUMS ☆☆☆
1938, Great Britain
Sabu, Raymond Massey, Valerie Hobson, Joseph Livesey, David Tree, Desmond Tester. Directed by Zoltan Korda. 101 min.

This rousing, lavish production is set in India, and concerns a young would-be prince (Sabu) and his vicious, anti-British uncle. The uncle kills the father then goes after the life of the young man himself. In the late 1930s, no one in Hollywood was producing these exotic adventures as well as London's Alexander Korda, and here brother Zoltan directs skillfully. The quality of the Technicolor, a rarity in 1938, has degenerated, but the film is still a consistent visual pleasure. Originally released as *The Drum*.

DRUMS ALONG THE MOHAWK ☆☆☆½
1939, USA
Henry Fonda, Claudette Colbert, Edna May Oliver, John Carradine, Arthur Shields, Roger Imhof, Ward Bond. Directed by John Ford. 103 min.

This exciting adventure tale was John Ford's first color feature. Lamar Trotti and Sonya Levien's screenplay takes an especially hostile view toward the Indians in the story of a farm couple settling in the West around the time of the Revolutionary War; yet, like his *Stagecoach*, Ford's invigorating direction overcomes the unenlightened ideology. Henry Fonda is good as the Mohawk Valley farmer combating the odds. Claudette Colbert looks less comfortable in the wide open spaces as his put-upon colonial wife, but does manage to hold her own. The usual ripe support comes from Edna May Oliver, and Ford regulars John Carradine and Arthur Shields. Another bad history lesson becomes great entertainment.

DRUNKEN ARTS AND CRIPPLED FIST ☆☆½
The Yuen Family, Simon Yuen, Yuen Chien, Lo Lieh, Li Yi-Min, Hsia Kuan-Li. Directed by Yuen Chien Yu.

This is one of the best of the drunken-style, comic kung fu movies that followed in the wake of Jackie Chan's classic *Drunken Master*. Here a young man (Li Yi-Min) from a family harassed by bandits is sent to a kung fu teacher. Some very impressive fighting punctuates the usual training-camp hijinks as competitive martial artists continually test each other's skills.

DRUNKEN SWORDSMAN ☆☆
Hong Kong
Yo Hua, Shih Rong, Lung Fei, Yen Han-Se, Lo Lieh, Chen Chiang-Lung, Chen Yun-Ching. Directed by Chang Jen-Tsei.

A foolish, would-be hero poses as the famous Drunken Swordsman until he meets up with the real Drunken Swordsman (Yo Hua). A few laughs, a plot that's not run-of-the-mill revenge motif, and some good sword fighting make this above average.

DUBARRY WAS A LADY ☆☆½
1943, USA
Lucille Ball, Red Skelton, Gene Kelly, Virginia O'Brien, Donald Meek, Zero Mostel, Louise Beavers, George Givot. Directed by Roy Del Ruth. 101 min.

The bright musical sequences redeem the hash made out of Cole Porter's sunny Broadway show starring Ethel Merman and Bert Lahr. Lucy and Red are not exactly Ethel and Bert, but the real damage done here is the tampering with the original property, cleaning up the sauciness at every turn. Although the plot remains the same (a nightclub hatcheck boy quaffs a Mickey Finn and dreams that he's Louis XV, and that the chanteuse he fancies is Dubarry), almost all of the effervescent Porter score was scrapped for less memorable material. The cast commands attention, however, and the film's highlights include Gene Kelly's dazzling dance to "Do I Love You?" (a Porter standard) and the snappy finale to "Friendship." Spirited, but not first-rate.

THE DUCHESS AND THE DIRTWATER FOX ☆☆
1976, USA, PG
George Segal, Goldie Hawn, Conrad Janis, Thayer David, Sid Gould. Directed by Mel Frank. 105 min.

Here's another programmed comedy from producer-director-screenwriter Mel Frank, one of Hollywood's prime arguments against the *auteur* theory. His standard method is to build a backdrop for his featured performers, then stand back and let them go through their business. If he's working with someone strong enough to carry a picture, as in most of his films with Bob Hope, he achieves modest results. But the likes of George Segal and Goldie Hawn need some direction and focus. Cast as a frontier gambler and a dance-hall girl, Segal and Hawn do little but mug and pratfall through the cardboard Western story. *Duchess* is only for fans of Hawn, as tolerant a bunch as ever frequented a movie theater.

DUCK SOUP ☆☆☆☆
1933, USA
Groucho, Harpo, Chico and Zeppo Marx, Margaret Dumont, Louis Calhern, Raquel Torres, Edgar Kennedy. Directed by Leo McCarey. 72 min.

Duck Soup is the Marx Brothers' supreme paean to the absurd. The Marx Brothers were always vulnerable to their supporting talent; when they had great writers, like S. J. Perelman, they were great, and when they had weak material they could be flat and overbearing. Here, for the first time, they worked with a first-rate comedy director, and Leo McCarey continually knocks things askew and keeps the ball rolling. Less a series of skits than their other films, *Duck Soup* is like an ever-speeding row of dominoes leading to a complete, anarchic collapse. Its pointed satire, here directed at war and despotism, is right on the mark. And the mirror sequence is a comedy classic—brilliant, innocent, funny. The Paramount films, of which this is the last, are wilder and more raw than the later, tamer MGM works.

DUEL ☆☆☆
1971, USA (TV)
Dennis Weaver. Directed by Steven Spielberg. 75 min. (released theatrically in 1983 at 88 min.)

For a short while in the early seventies, some made-for-TV movies offered a real B-movie alternative to regular broadcast fare. This oddball existentialist drama, pitting a lone driver against a mysterious, death-dealing tractor-trailer rig, may be the best of the lot. Dennis Weaver stars as the salesman on his last road trip, and young Steven Spielberg attracted a lot of attention for his flashy, highly edited style of direction.

DUEL IN THE SUN ☆☆☆☆
1946, USA
Jennifer Jones, Gregory Peck, Joseph Cotten, Lionel Barrymore, Lillian Gish, Herbert Marshall. Directed by King Vidor. 138 min.

David O. Selznick's attempt to create an epic Western to match his success with *Gone with the Wind* resulted in one of Hollywood's most highly wrought, explosively acted films. Selznick cast his future wife, Jennifer Jones, in the pivotal role of Pearl, the half-Mexican girl struggling to find a position in the wealthy McCanless family and caught between the good son and the bad seed. The real story of the film is Pearl's attempt to choose between her erotic desires and her desire to be good. Jones plays Pearl as a young, panting wanton always only half in control of herself. Although the film has come to be regarded as a camp classic, it seizes authentic classic status by matching the florid acting with a rich visual style and an exquisitely framed landscape. The film's success is partially dependent on the use of advisers who had also worked in silent films. In addition to King Vidor's precise direction, Joseph von Sternberg was hired to give Jennifer Jones her keyed-up look, and Lillian Gish, Herbert Marshall, and Lionel Barrymore all give stellar, intelligently gestured performances.

THE DUELLISTS ☆☆☆½
1977, Great Britain, PG
Keith Carradine, Harvey Keitel, Albert Finney, Edward Fox, Cristina Raines. Directed by Ridley Scott. 95 min.

This sumptuous adaptation of a Joseph Conrad story was the first film by British director Ridley Scott (*Alien*, *Blade Runner*). Along with cinematographer Frank Tidy and writer Gerald Vaughan-Hughes, Scott put together the most entrancing swashbuckler of the seventies, a grand-obsession story set in Napoleonic France and starring Harvey Keitel as a compulsive, honor-mad dueler who chases aristocratic Keith Carradine across Europe, challenging him, dueling him, and challenging him again. Tense, visually astonishing, and vastly entertaining.

DUEL OF CHAMPIONS ☆½
1961, Italy
Alan Ladd, Franca Bettoja, Franco Fabrizi, Robert Keith. Directed by Ferdinando Baldi. 105 min.

By this point in his failing career, Alan Ladd had galloped way out of the Western range of his greatest triumph, *Shane*, and into the less hallowed ground of a gladiator epic. It's sad to watch the once-handsome movie star gracing a colossal coliseum spectacle that was more properly Steve Reeves's territory. Still, a movie star has to eat, and the aging Ladd heaves his chest and does his level best to convey heroic force as the leader of a Roman contingent of good guys.

DUEL OF THE IRON FIST ☆
1971, Hong Kong
Ti Lung, David Chaing, Yo Hui, Wang Pong, Ku Feng, Wang Chung, Cheng Lei, Chuen Yuan, Yang Chih Ching, Cheng Kang Yeh, Hsia Hui. Directed by Chang Chech.

If you've seen enough cheap, independently produced kung fu films, this Shaw Brothers studio production will look like heaven: there's beautiful set design, good production values, and attractive Ti Lung as the hero. Melodramatic David Chiang plays Rover, an assassin with a scratchy throat who comes to Ti Ling's aid; together they chop through a battalion of baddies before paying the ultimate price. A swinging-arm–style slasher movie.

DUEL OF THE SEVEN TIGERS ☆☆
1982, Hong Kong
Yang Pan Pan, Philip Ko, Lam Man Wei, Hsia Huang-Li, Chin Long, Chiu Chi Ling, Casanova Wong.

A disgruntled Shaolin monk goes to Japan and develops a style of fighting that becomes known as karate. He sends his best pupil to China, where he insults the locals, beats the best fighter, and closes all the kung fu schools. It's up to Chin Long to capture China's honor. This has excellent martial arts, including a textbook temple fight between a Monkey stylist and a Crane fighter. The film's highlight is a Peking Opera scene where pretty Hsia Kuang-Li (*The Leg Fighters*) balances plates while managing to take on all comers.

DUMB BOXER ½☆
Lee Chin Wen, Kan Kai, Lin Su Hwie. Directed by Lin Yang.

In a standard "revenge against the Japanese" story, a boy is thrown in jail, and his parents are killed. When he is released, he finds his sister and then kills his enemies. Absolutely nothing distinguishes it from scores of other fight flicks.

DUMBO ☆☆☆
1941, USA
Animated: Edward Brophy, Sterling Holloway, Cliff Edwards, Herman Bing. Directed by Ben Sharpsteen. 64 min.

This is one of the better full-length Disney cartoons, in the carefree style of the 1930s shorts. Baby elephant Dumbo is ostracized by all the other little elephants because of his enormous ears; he shows them by learning to fly with his ears. The film loses half a star for those two incredibly racist minstrel-show crows.

DUNE ☆½
1984, USA, PG-13
Kyle MacLachlan, Brad Dourif, Jose Ferrer, Kenneth McMillan, Sean Young, Sian Phillips, Linda Hunt, Max von Sydow, Sting. Directed by David Lynch. 145 min.

Forty-five million dollars, an international all-star cast, a source novel that's practically a sci-fi bible, and sets and special effects unparalleled in scope—all this went into the movie *Dune*, and who cares? Director David Lynch (*Eraserhead*) is to be applauded for grafting his very personal vision onto a big-budget studio opus, but when that vision consists mainly of slime-oozing pustules and undulating waves of genitalia-shaped earth, artistic individualism becomes a little hard on the eyes. The story, for the benefit of nonbuffs, is the worst kind of solemn, pseudomystical pomp about a galactic war for a life-controlling spice. Although voice-over dialogue was reportedly added to make the story comprehensible, you'll still need a glossary to understand the mythical babble. The actors are without exception wasted, the climax is fumbled badly, and, on videocassette, Lynch's work loses whatever grotesque grandeur it may have had on the screen.

THE DUNWICH HORROR ☆☆½
1970, USA
Sandra Dee, Dean Stockwell, Ed Begley, Sam Jaffe, Talia Coppola (Shire). Directed by Daniel Haller. 90 min.

After the well of Edgar Allan Poe titles was exhausted by AIP in the sixties it seemed smart to move on to the works of H. P. Lovecraft, whose more lurid style seemed better suited to movie adaptation. But, by this time, AIP was just grinding out junk, and the result is nowhere near as stylish or parodic as earlier efforts such as *The Pit and the Pendulum* or *The Masque of Red Death*. Coed Sandra Dee becomes involved with Moody Dean Stockwell, a student fascinated by devil worship. He turns out to be the son of the Devil himself, with a more monstrous brother locked up in the closet at home. Some nice, moody touches, especially when the brother escapes, but overall it's too laid back for its own good.

DYING ROOM ONLY ☆☆☆
1973, USA (TV)
Cloris Leachman, Ross Martin, Ned Beatty, Louis Latham, Dana Elcar. Directed by Phillip Leacock. 74 min.

In this expert suspense drama with spine-tingling atmosphere, nothing is what it seems and no one can be trusted. A couple en route to L.A. makes a definite error in judgment when they stop at a run-down diner; suddenly, the husband vanishes into the desert air without a trace. This cleverly plotted potboiler builds a mood of tension that's maintained up to the satisfying surprise ending. Taut script by sci-fi and suspense veteran Richard Matheson.

DYNAMITE CHICKEN ☆½
1971, USA, X
Richard Pryor, John Lennon, Joan Baez, Yoko Ono, Malcolm X, Andy Warhol. Directed by Ernie Pintoff. 76 min.

This is a dated pastiche of gags without giggles and skits without substance all jumbled together incoherently. It's a defused spoof without much bang, all about modern man and his social and sexual hang-ups circa 1970, back when shows like *Hair* and *Oh! Calcutta* seemed fresh and daring. Today most of the sketches merely sputter, and the film seems more chicken than dynamite.

DYNAMO ☆☆
1978, Hong Kong
Bruce Li (Ho Tsung-Tao), Ku Feng, Chaing Tao, Mary Kan. 88 min.

This modern-day story concerns Bruce Li as a kung fu movie star in Hong Kong, competing in a tournament that he must lose in order to save his girlfriend. It is an interesting inversion of the usual code by which a fighter judges himself, and as such an attempt at an objective look at the genre.

E

THE EAGLE FIST ★★½
Hong Kong
Chi Kuan-Chun, Cheng Kay Ying. Directed by Cheng Kay Ying.

This is one of the best of the technique and training movies. Graceful Chi Kuan-Chun carries the action with his precise form and effortless style—his acrobatic flair gives his mastery of eagle kung fu real panache.

THE EAGLE HAS LANDED ★★½
1977, Great Britain, PG
Michael Caine, Donald Sutherland, Robert Duvall, Jenny Agutter, Donald Pleasence, Anthony Quayle, Jean Marsh, Treat Williams, Larry Hagman. Directed by John Sturges. 123 min.

This solidly entertaining World War II "what if" yarn is about a German plot to kidnap Winston Churchill and hold him as a bargaining chip in Berlin. Screenwriter Tom Mankiewicz can't quite get past the essential silliness of the plot, but he does a good job trying, and the cast is less constrained by uniforms and accents than is usual in all-star war films. Based on a novel by Jack Higgins.

EAGLES ATTACK AT DAWN ★★
1970, Israel
Yehoram Gaon, Rick Jason, Peter Braun, Yoseph Shiloah, Arik Lavi, Yehuda Barkan. Directed by Menahem Golan. 90 min.

Like the British after World War II, the Israelis seem to love to glorify their own war exploits by making movies about them. In this one, a commando squad raids an Arab base to free some Israeli prisoners. Dull and predictable.

THE EARRINGS OF MADAME DE... ★★★★
1953, France/Italy
Charles Boyer, Danielle Darrieux, Vittorio De Sica. Directed by Max Ophuls. 105 min.

German director Max Ophuls was one of the greatest of all filmmakers. *The Earrings of Madame de...* marks the peak of his illustrious French period that also yielded *La Ronde, Le Plaisir,* and *Lola Montes*. The screenplay by Ophuls and Marcel Achard portrays a fairly conventional love triangle involving a general, his bored wife, and a dashing baron. What Ophuls does with the material makes it fascinating viewing. Aided by fluent and sophisticated cinematography by Christian Matras, Ophuls creates a series of rich compositions that comment on the follies of the bourgeoisie and the power struggles within personal relationships. Ophuls turns what many would call trash into something almost infinitely resonant.

EARTH ★★★★
1930, USSR
Semyon Svashenko, Stepan Shkurat, Mikola Nademsky, Yelena Maximova, Pyotr Masokha. Directed by Alexander Dovzhenko. 63 min.

Earth is a unique and breathtaking work that is more akin to lyric poetry than narrative cinema. There is a slip of a plot about peasants who want to buy a tractor and reactionary landholders who strike out at the village chairman, but don't be deterred by the mundane story. The film is a miraculous series of images of death and rebirth; Dovzhenko's obvious love of everything on which he turned his camera resulted in severe criticism of the work, including charges of pantheism. Certainly *Earth* is unlike anything else in 1930s cinema, and for viewers who are put off by Eisenstein's hauteur and Vertov's socialism, this is the perfect entrée into Soviet cinema.

EARTH VS. THE FLYING SAUCERS ☆
1956, USA
Hugh Marlowe, Joan Taylor, Donald Curtis, Morris Ankrum, John Zaremba, Tom Browne Henry, Grandon Rhodes. Directed by Fred F. Sears. 82 min.

This movie is cheaply made outer-space paranoia from the Eisenhower era that plays as pure camp today. A stolid squad of military men realize that there's trouble in the air when their defense satellites start falling out of the sky. The culprits are humanoids in flying saucers. The solution: a death ray, of course, along with the kind of hasty "scientific" explanation that provided a good laugh even in 1956.

THE EARTHLING ★★½
1980, USA/Australia, PG
William Holden, Ricky Schroder, Jack Thompson, Olivia Hamnett. Directed by Peter Colinson. 97 min.

Who's cuter—young Ricky Schroder or a koala bear? Here's your chance to compare both, as orphan Schroder is adopted by dying curmudgeon Holden and taught to be one with the Australian outback. There are times when the visual fawning over the (admittedly gorgeous) Australian bush country is so overdone that one longs for Mad Max to buzz by and rip things up, but stick with it and, in the end, you'll find it touching.

EARTHQUAKE ☆½
1974, USA, PG
Charlton Heston, Ava Gardner, Lorne Greene, Marjoe Gortner, Barry Sullivan, George Kennedy, Victoria Principal, Richard Roundtree, Genevieve Bujold, Walter Matthau. Directed by Mark Robson. 123 min.

At the peak of the "disaster" film cycle in the 1970s came this disaster about various people affected by an L.A. earthquake. At the time, audiences were treated to a new device called Sensurround, which caused sound waves to be shot through their seats during the quake sequences. On video (and in the safety of your own home), there's nothing left but a parade of stars looking embarrassed by all the silly dialogue they mouth. One of them, Walter Matthau, wisely used an alias (his real name) in the credits. Director Mark Robson (*Champion, Von Ryan's Express*) and co-screenwriter Mario Puzo (*The Godfather*) should have followed suit. Let us not forget, however, that Robson is the man who gave us *Valley of the Dolls*.

EASTER PARADE ★★★★
1948, USA
Judy Garland, Fred Astaire, Peter Lawford, Ann Miller, Clinton Sundberg. Directed by Charles Walters. 103 min.

Fred Astaire and Judy Garland create musical fireworks in this neatly constructed backstage yarn about a dancer who molds a singer into his vaudeville partner. Irving Berlin's classic score includes "Stepping Out With My Baby," "A Couple of Swells," "Shakin' the Blues Away" and, of course, the title tune. There may be more stylish and clever MGM musicals, but this is a chance to see and hear some of the screen's greatest musical talents work together, and the results are spectacular.

EAST OF EDEN
1955, USA ★★★★
James Dean, Raymond Massey, Burl Ives, Julie Harris. Directed by Elia Kazan. 115 min.

A sensitive and troubled youth rebels against the domination of his father in director Kazan's still powerful adaptation of John Steinbeck's novel, which transports the biblical story of Cain and Abel to California on the eve of World War I. Thanks to playwright John Osborne's biting script and the sterling direction, *Eden* is anything but dated, and its pacifist sentiments and gut-wrenching emotionalism caused it to become a critical and popular hit. Most memorably, the film gave James Dean his breakthrough role as the teenager who constantly bucks the authoritarian figures around him. The actor's dashing looks and the magnetic honesty of his performance made him into a generation's idol. Filmed in Cinemascope.

EAST OF EDEN
1980, USA (TV) ★★½
Timothy Bottoms, Jane Seymour, Bruce Boxleitner, Soon-Teck Oh, Karen Allen, Hart Bochner, Sam Bottoms, Warren Oates, Howard Duff, Anne Baxter, Lloyd Bridges, M. Emmet Walsh. Directed by Harvey Hart. 240 min.

Although this made-for-TV miniseries adaptation of John Steinbeck's epic novel is much more faithful to the original text than was the 1955 movie, it's inferior in almost every other way since it sorely lacks the epic scope of Elia Kazan's filmmaking and the charisma and mastery of James Dean and Jo Van Fleet. Here the saga of brothers at war over a duplicitous woman becomes standard miniseries fodder, although Jane Seymour is outstanding and appropriately coldblooded as Kate Ames (the role that won Van Fleet an Oscar). Note: the video version has been cut by approximately 150 minutes from the original telecast length.

EASY COME, EASY GO
1967, USA ★½
Elvis Presley, Dodie Marshall, Pat Priest, Pat Harrington, Elsa Lanchester, Frank McHugh. Directed by John Rich. 97 min.

Presley's Paramount musicals were never as trashy-fun as his MGM efforts, and this one is particularly bad. He plays a navy man who hunts for a treasure chest off the California coast but winds up with less than he expected. You will feel likewise after just a few minutes of this feeble effort. For the record, this was Presley's twenty-third film, and he sings "Sing, You Children" and "Yoga Is As Yoga Does."

EASY MONEY
1983, USA, R ★★
Rodney Dangerfield, Joe Pesci, Geraldine Fitzgerald, Jennifer Jason Leigh. Directed by James Signorelli. 95 min.

Rodney Dangerfield gets no respect as a contented slob forced to mend his ways so that his wife can inherit $10 million from the estate of her snobbish mother. Bland borscht-belt comedy with a few sparkling moments—like the "Regular Guy" fashion show—buried in a swamp of tired one-liners about sex and drugs. Clean up the language and it could be a television sitcom.

EASY RIDER
1969, USA, R ★★★½
Peter Fonda, Dennis Hopper, Jack Nicholson, Karen Black, Luke Askew, Robert Walker. Directed by Dennis Hopper. 94 min.

Fonda and Hopper cycle through America, the imminent collapse of the '60s counterculture hot on their trail. Hippies on choppers carrying dope! The film became a landmark, mostly owing to the ultracool, contemptuous characterizations by the two leads, balanced by the romantically harsh portrait of America. This is a jumpy, nervous film that finally criticizes its alienated subjects by revealing their greed and lack of values. Watch Jack Nicholson steal the show as he sinks his teeth into his first good, wild loner role.

EASY VIRTUE
1927, Great Britain ★★
Isabel Jeans, Franklyn Dyall, Eric Bransby Williams, Ian Hunter. Directed by Alfred Hitchcock. 75 min.

Adapted from a Noel Coward play (a melodrama, not a farce), this early, silent Hitchcock is unusual in its subject matter and for its special visual effects. Most importantly, it has, until now, been hard to find even for the director's most dedicated fans. Beginning in a divorce court, the story examines the seamy past of a well-bred woman whose former indiscretions now threaten her marriage into an upper-crust family. The electronic music track is a recent addition.

EAT MY DUST!
1976, USA, PG ★★½
Ron Howard, Christopher Norris, Dave Madden. Directed by Charles Griffith. 89 min.

Over half of the running time of this drive-in classic is taken up by a mammoth car chase. It's unpretentious, straight-ahead fun, in which plot is secondary to mayhem and the odd jokey detail, as might be expected in a movie made by Roger Corman alumnus Charles Griffith (*Little Shop of Horrors*, *A Bucket of Blood*).

EATEN ALIVE
1976, USA, R ★½
Neville Brand, Mel Ferrer, Carolyn Jones, Marilyn Burns, Stuart Whitman. Directed by Tobe Hooper. 96 min.

The second film by Tobe Hooper (*The Texas Chainsaw Massacre*) jangles the nerves with cacophonous electronic sound effects and unremitting violence. But the movie is nearly plotless and so badly written that we never believe in any of the characters, much less tremble for them. Various unsuspecting victims (including Mel Ferrer, pop-eyed William Finley, who had the title role in *Phantom of the Paradise*, and *Chainsaw*'s Marilyn Burns) stumble into a ramshackle swampland rooming house, where they are bloodily dispatched by histrionic psycho Neville Brand. We'll admit to applauding the scene in which an obnoxious, yappy little dog named Snuffy becomes an hors d'oeuvre for the killer's pet crocodile. The C&W songs that Hooper wrote for the soundtrack are sometimes funny (pick hits: "The Man I Found in My True Love's Arms Was Her Brother" and "Them Drugstore Cowboys Ain't Worth One Hair on a Real Cowboy's Chest").

EATING RAOUL
1982, USA, R ★★★
Paul Bartel, Mary Woronov, Robert Beltran, Buck Henry. Directed by Paul Bartel. 83 min.

After directing a series of sub-B pictures (*Death Race 2000*, *Private Parts*, and *Naughty Nurses* among them), Paul Bartel hit the big time with this good-natured, warped independent comedy about an uptight L.A. couple, Paul and Mary Bland, who pose as whip-wielding sexual fantasists in a money-making scheme worthy of Lucy Ricardo. The title gives away more than one might wish, but the plot of the film isn't as germane to its humor as the needling observations it serves up about the kinky and the prudish, and their respective fetishes. Look for Buck Henry as a lecherous bank man.

EBIRAH, HORROR OF THE DEEP

See *Godzilla vs. the Sea Monster*

EBOLI

See *Christ Stopped at Eboli*

EBONY, IVORY AND JADE
1979, USA, PG ☆
Bert Convy, Debbie Allen, Martha Smith, Claude Akins, Nina Foch. Directed by John Llewellyn Moxey. 78 min.

The promo for this black exploitation entry about three female athletes attending an international competition says, "They can lick any man ever made." This is one of those tired-blood exploitation flicks in which even the fisticuffs lack conviction. If you don't find it depressing to watch the talented Nina Foch play second banana to a young and unpromising cast, then you're bound to be crushed by Bert Convy's unctuous smile, which reduces all dramatic conflicts to the level of a confession on "Celebrity Tattletales."

ECHO PARK
1986, Austria/USA, R ☆☆☆
Susan Dey, Tom Hulce, Michael Bowen, Christopher Walker. Directed by Robert Dornhelm. 92 min.

Marilyn Monroe and Charlie Chaplin lived there once . . . and it hasn't changed much, that lovable Echo Park. This slow-burning, colorful film features Susan Dey, who wants to be an actress but delivers strip-o-grams instead; Tom Hulce (fresh from *Amadeus*), who pens poetry between pizza deliveries; and Michael Bowen, who builds his body for wacky entrepreneurial reasons of his own. Hopeful town, that Los Angeles! All in all, despite the slightly nonlinear crook to Michael Ventura's modest script, this *Park* is worth visiting for an hour and a half.

ECHOES
1983, USA ☆☆½
Richard Alfieri, Nathalie Nell, Mercedes McCambridge, Ruth Roman, Gale Sondergaard. Directed by Arthur Allan Seidelman. 89 min.

A nifty premise for a suspenseful outing (a student suffers from a nightmare in which his twin, who apparently died at birth, sets out to obliterate him) is never allowed to reach its potential. In the world of low-budget filmmaking, some of the cleverest ideas suffer the slings and arrows of uninspired casting and unfocused scripting. Still, this film's mysterious echoes insinuate themselves into our minds and give us a jolt or two.

ECSTACY
1933, Czechoslovakia ☆☆½
Eddy Kiesler (Hedy Lamarr), Andre Nox, Pierre Nay, Jaromir Rogoz. Directed by Gustav Machaty. 88 min.

Why would anyone want to sit through this rickety old Czech melodrama about a bored wife, her impotent husband and her handsome lover? Because young Hedy Lamarr (then Eddy Kiesler) makes a mesmerizing screen appearance. The twenty-year-old Viennese beauty runs nude through the woods, swims likewise in a lake, and has an orgasm (shown in facial close-up). The rest of the film, a combination of *Lady Chatterly's Lover* and Hedy's personal life at the time, documented in her book *Ecstacy and Me*, is completely forgettable. Some of the postproduction footnotes are more interesting than the film itself: Hedy's then-husband Fritz Mandl tried unsuccessfully to purchase all existing prints; the film was banned in several countries, including Germany and the United States; and underground prints of the film have been made that extend the famous sequences by repeating them over and over again. This film is a historic curiosity.

EDDIE AND THE CRUISERS
1983, USA, PG ☆☆☆
Michael Pare, Tom Berenger, Ellen Barkin, Matthew Lawrence, Joe Pantoliano. Directed by Martin Davison. 92 min.

This *Citizen Kane*-style mystery is structured around the brief life and fame of a mythical rock singer and his band. Strong performances by Michael Pare and Tom Berenger (as singer Eddie and his cowriter), a strong soundtrack by John Cafferty and the Beaver Brown Band, and a flashback format in which the dreamy neon scenes from the past threaten at every moment to overwhelm the dreary contemporary footage help to make the film an above-average diversion.

EDDIE MACON'S RUN
1983, USA, PG ☆☆½
John Schneider, Kirk Douglas, Lee Purcell, Leah Ayres, Tom Noonan. Directed by Jeff Kanew. 95 min.

"Dukes of Hazzard" star John Schneider made his screen debut in a film not unlike his series, and he is not nearly as bad as one might expect. This time Schneider is on the wrong side of the law as a (falsely accused) prison escapee. Douglas, in his sixty-fourth film, gnashes his teeth nicely as the cop who pursues Schneider through Texas. A surprisingly acceptable car-chase picture.

EDGE OF FURY
1981, Hong Kong, R ☆☆
Bruce Li, Tommy Lee, Andrew Sage, Michael Danna. Directed by George Ho. 90 min.

This is martial arts stuff with an American businessman framed for drug charges in Bangkok. Fortunately, he had the forethought to hire Bruce Li as his chauffeur. (Hey, Bruce Lee impersonators have to have some kind of daytime jobs to support themselves, and if driving someone else's car was good enough for the real life Lee in *The Green Hornet*, why should Li kick?) Much else *is* kicked, to everyone's presumed satisfaction.

EDITH AND MARCEL
1983, France ☆½
Evelyne Bouix, Marcel Cerdan, Jr., Charles Aznavour, Jacques Villeret. Directed by Claude Lelouch. 180 min.

Unless you count yourself among the devotees of *la petite Piaf*, this true-life love story is, unfortunately, a gargantuan bore, an epic-length retelling of the love affair between Edith Piaf and boxer Marcel Cerdan, which ended tragically with Cerdan's death in a 1949 plane crash and Piaf's emotional dissolution soon thereafter. Evelyne Bouix is a creditable Piaf, but Claude Lelouch overloads the film with imbecilic casting gimmicks: Bouix plays a dual role; Cerdan, Jr., woodenly plays his father; Charles Aznavour plays himself; and after a few minutes of this you'll want to play another movie.

EDUCATING RITA
1983, Great Britain ☆☆☆½
Michael Caine, Julie Walters, Michael Williams, Maureen Lipman. Directed by Lewis Gilbert. 110 min.

Michael Caine portrays a boozy, cynical professor and Julie Walters plays his ignorant pupil, Rita, who yearns to be educated and urbane. Excellent performances by both of these actors help make this updated version of *Pygmalion* charming and entertaining. But the story has a decidedly anti-intellectual bent, and its message is, in the end, gratingly simplistic. Walters is a revelatory joy.

EERIE MIDNIGHT HORROR SHOW
1977, Italy, R ☆½
Stella Carnachia, Chris Auram, Lucretia Love. Directed by Mario Gariazzo. 80 min.

Originally released as *The Tormented*, the film's title was changed by the distributors when they sold it to cable television, presumably in order to cash in on the success of *The Rocky Horror Picture Show*, even though the two have nothing in common. This movie is more a rip-off of *The Exorcist*, with a woman taken over by a spirit that had been held captive in a statue in an Italian church. Equal parts dull soft-core sex and dull bloodless horror.

THE EGG AND I ★★★
1947, USA
Claudette Colbert, Fred MacMurray, Marjorie Main, Percy Kilbride, Richard Long. Directed by Chester Erskine. 104 min.

Here's yet another city-folk-move-to-the-country movie, but it's better than most of them. Based on the apparently autobiographical novel by Betty MacDonald, the film's city mice are played by Fred MacMurray and Claudette Colbert, who are about ten years too old for their parts but who go through the highly predictable chicken farming gags with ease. This was their sixth teaming and, although it lacks the sharpness and spontaneity of their 1930s work, they actually manage to conceal the fact that they were probably bored silly with each other. Among the country mice are Ma and Pa Kettle, as played by Marjorie Main and Percy Kilbride (their first teaming), who make the film. As a sort of slapstick corrective to *The Grapes of Wrath*, it's a pretty funny stew.

THE EGYPTIAN ★★½
1954, USA
Jean Simmons, Edmond Purdom, Victor Mature, Gene Tierney, Michael Wilding, Bella Darvi, Peter Ustinov, John Carradine, Henry Daniell. Directed by Michael Curtiz. 140 min.

Michael Curtiz was always more at home with *film noir* (*Mildred Pierce*, *The Unsuspected*) than with big, superbudget spectacles. Mika Waltari's best-seller is the source of the tale about an Egyptian doctor (Edmond Purdom) who clashes with the Pharaoh. Bits from Michael Wilding, Peter Ustinov, and Judith Evelyn as the Queen Mother are colorful, but the film is no different from *Land of the Pharaohs* or *The Ten Commandments*, only less enjoyable. Originally in Cinemascope.

THE EIGER SANCTION ★★½
1975, USA, R
Clint Eastwood, George Kennedy, Jack Cassidy, Vonetta McGee, Thayer David. Directed by Clint Eastwood. 128 min.

With a Trevanian novel as its source and Clint Eastwood in the lead, viewers will undoubtedly expect more suspense than this movie delivers. Eastwood seems genuinely embarrassed by the poor dialogue, and he directs himself to be even more wooden than his usual screen persona. The movie is awfully long, and the climbing sequences, shot on location in Switzerland, are unconvincing despite an extensive buildup. George Kennedy and Jack Cassidy deliver performances that tip over into broad comedy.

8½ ★★★★
1963, Italy
Marcello Mastroianni, Anouk Aimee, Claudia Cardinale, Sandra Milo. Directed by Federico Fellini. 135 min.

Italian director Fellini's semiautobiographical, landmark masterpiece about a famous film director who has reached an impasse in both his art and his love life. Although it's confusing, the film is always stimulating as it frantically juxtaposes fantasy with reality in an imaginative effort to psychoanalytically and comically depict the director's search for inspiration. The acting, led by Mastroianni, is top-notch all around, and the editing and photography are astonishing, making the work a study in the art of film. (Try to see this marvel on a big movie screen, too.)

8 MILLION WAYS TO DIE ★★½
1986, USA, R
Jeff Bridges, Rosanna Arquette, Alexandra Paul, Andy Garcia, Randy Brooks. Directed by Hal Ashby. 115 min.

Lawrence Block's novel becomes a violent, foul-mouthed, grubby thriller, another variation on the overused *film noir* pairing of cop and call girl. The cop—in this case, an alcoholic narc booted from the L.A. sheriff's force—is Matthew Scudder (played by Jeff Bridges, whose performance is a sharp study in ragged dissipation). When a skittish prostitute suddenly appears in his life only to be murdered, he joins forces with a mean-mouthed whore (Arquette) to hunt down the killer. Director Ashby doesn't try for slickery, but he packs so much energy into the final, frenetic action scenes that their drab look doesn't really offend. The attempts at serious drama, most notably the hackneyed A.A. meetings, are laughably strained and intrusive, but when the film stays on course, it's a fulfilling sleaze-wallow. The film also features a sizzlingly funny, inventive performance by Andy Garcia as a jabbering arriviste drug runner with a ponytail, a taste for surrealist architecture, and a sno-cone machine.

EL AMOR BRUJO ★★½
1986, Spain, PG
Antonio Gades, Cristina Hoyos, Laura Del Sol, Juan Antonio Jiminez, La Polaca. Directed by Carlos Saura. 100 min.

With their fruitful collaborations on *Blood Wedding* and *Carmen*, director Carlos Saura and dancer-choreographer Antonio Gades demonstrated a unique ability to translate the energy of dance narratives into cinema. While not as successful as their two earlier works, *El Amor Brujo* (Love, the Magician) is nonetheless a strikingly stylized and often beautifully danced drama. The story, such as it is, interweaves ritual and fantasy as newlyweds in an arranged wedding are torn apart by the groom's murder and reunited when his ghost returns.

ELECTRIC DREAMS ★★½
1984, Great Britain, PG
Lenny Von Dohlen, Virginia Madsen, Maxwell Caulfield, Voice of Bud Cort. Directed by Steve Barron. 96 min.

Music video director Steve Barron moves to the big screen in this surprisingly entertaining tale about an extremely unusual love triangle between a man, a woman, and a home computer. The ideas never stop coming, and the camera never stops moving as the mischievous machine creates love songs for the beautiful Virginia Madsen and makes life miserable for the nerdy Lennie von Dohlen. But there's not enough substance to go with the flashy visuals as the computer tries to decipher human emotions. The soundtrack was created by Giorgio Moroder.

THE ELECTRIC HORSEMAN ★★
1979, USA, PG
Jane Fonda, Robert Redford, Valerie Perrine, Willie Nelson, John Saxon. Directed by Sydney Pollack. 120 min.

This utterly ersatz message movie lives in a world that looks as if it's meant to be ours, but isn't quite anybody's. For instance, when was the last time you saw a Barbara Walters-like network reporter (Jane Fonda, natch) covering a corporate convention? Or a Bruce Jenner-like athlete (Robert Redford, as a rodeo star who's just too famous to be true) touring the boonies to plug breakfast food? Or a race horse (swiped by a wised-up Redford from the firm that exploits them both) that could outrun a pack of police cars? Sydney Pollack's film does have its deft moments, and Willie Nelson makes pleasant company in his small debut role, but before this film even gets started, there won't be a suspended disbelief in the house. Under the circumstances, not even Redford and Fonda can work up any chemistry.

ELENI ★½
1985, USA, PG
Kate Nelligan, John Malkovich, Linda Hunt, Oliver Cotton, Ronald Pickup, Rosalie Crutchley. Directed by Peter Yates. 117 min.

This film trivializes a tragic era in European history by skimming the surface of events and assuming the viewer's sympathy and outrage rather than doing anything to actively elicit them. It is based on the excellent book by Nicholas Gage, a *New York Times* investigative reporter whose mother was executed by a Communist guerilla firing squad during the occupation of post-World War II

Greece. The film juxtaposes the life of Eleni, a peasant woman who was killed for no better reason than as an example to other Greeks, with the efforts of the adult Gage to find the Communist leader who ordered the execution. As Gage, Malkovich is so lost within his character's obsessiveness that there is nothing for us to grab onto. But the real hole in the film is Kate Nelligan, badly miscast as Eleni, an error compounded by director Yates's absurd heroization of her. The only good performace, ironically, is given by Oliver Cotton as the leader who ordered the executions.

ELEPHANT BOY ☆☆☆
1937, Great Britain
Sabu, W. E. Holloway, Walter Hudd, Alan Jeayes, Wilfred Hyde White. Directed by Robert Flaherty and Zoltan Korda. 91 min.

Sabu made his film debut in this adaptation of Rudyard Kipling's story "Toomai of the Elephants." When his father is killed in a tiger hunt, the elephant that Toomai and his grandfather rode and cared for is taken and given to another hunter who mistreats it, leading Toomai to steal back the beloved pachyderm and take it into the jungle. The visually striking (and still impressive) exterior scenes were filmed by Robert Flaherty (*Nanook of the North*).

THE ELEPHANT MAN ☆☆☆½
1980, USA, PG
Anthony Hopkins, John Hurt, Anne Bancroft, John Gielgud, Wendy Hiller, Freddy Jones. Directed by David Lynch. 125 min.

David Lynch's stylish, powerful film depicts the haunting true story of John Merrick, a horribly deformed man who rises from an abused freak-show attraction to become a respected member of British society. Lynch, who directed the cult classic *Eraserhead*, conveys a highly individualized, disturbing vision of the human condition, and John Hurt provides a moving performance as Merrick. The film, set in Victorian London, is elegantly photographed in black and white.

THE ELEPHANT MAN ☆☆½
1982, USA (TV)
Philip Anglim, Kevin Conway, Penny Fuller, Glenn Close, David Rounds, Richard Clarke. Directed by Jack Hofsiss. 102 min.

The story of John Merrick, the grotesquely deformed Englishman whose mistreatment briefly became a cause célèbre in nineteenth-century London, was first retold in a play by Bernard Pomerance that won a 1978 Tony Award. This telefilm is an adaptation of that work, retaining original cast members Anglim, who suggests Merrick's deformity without makeup, and Conway, as his compassionate doctor. The performances are good and the cumulative effect is inevitably moving, but David Lynch's 1980 film of the same name told the story with more grace, skill, and impact.

11 HARROWHOUSE ☆☆½
1974, Great Britain, PG
Charles Grodin, Candice Bergen, John Gielgud, Trevor Howard, James Mason, Helen Cherry. Directed by Aram Avakian. 95 min.

How much you enjoy this caper film about a huge cache of diamonds vacuumed out of a London safe depends on your feelings for—or against—star Charles Grodin, who plays the docile, self-deprecating thief and who also wrote the film's dry narration. His soft-spoken, urban-contemporary cadences seem a bit out of place here, but he's funny enough to energize a plot that too often drags. Bergen isn't as much of a zombie here as she was in many of her other early films, and Gielgud, as the imperturbably haughty theft victim, is, as always, beyond compare. (a.k.a.: *Anything for Love*)

ELIMINATORS ☆½
1986, USA, PG
Andrew Prine, Denise Crosby, Patrick Reynolds, Conan Lee, Roy Dotrice. Directed by Peter Mahoogian. 96 min.

Mad scientists! Mercenaries! Rifle-toting diesel dykes! Force fields! Cute robots! Time travel! Neanderthal men! Native ceremonies! Mandroids! Ninjas! Weird machines! A ghastly plan to bring the world to its *knees*! All this and not much more in a low-budget science-fiction action/adventure with lots of elements that don't really amount to much. And hey—it's self-referential as well: one character wonders aloud whether he's in some kind of comic book or something. Or something.

ELLIS ISLAND ☆☆
1984, USA (TV)
Faye Dunaway, Richard Burton, Claire Bloom, Ann Jillian, Judi Bowker, Kate Burton, Lila Kaye, Stubby Kaye, Ben Vereen, Melba Moore, Alice Krige, Emma Samms, Milo O'Shea, Cherie Lunghi. Directed by Jerry London. 327 min.

This is an example of the miniseries at its most resolutely formulaic—a multifamily, multigenerational saga of immigrants to Our Great Nation and the pitfalls, fortunes, triumphs, and heartbreaks that awaited them when they arrived on our shores from Europe at the dawn of the twentieth century. *Ellis Island* lacks the lurid plot lines that would make it entertaining trash, but it's not written or directed with enough imagination to make it work on any higher level. What few pleasures there are in the bloated running time can be found in the performances of Faye Dunaway, Claire Bloom, and Richard Burton (one of his last) and daughter Kate.

ELMER ☆☆☆
1977, USA
Philip Swanson, Elmer Swanson. Directed by Christopher Cain. 82 min.

A variation of the old "boy and his dog" standby makes for an entertaining family film in this early effort from the director of *The Stone Boy* and *That Was Then, This Is Now*. In this film, the boy is blind and the dog is an old hound going through second childhood (puphood?) Stranded in the wilderness, they help each other out as best they can. Quite good for children, and adults will enjoy it as well.

ELMER GANTRY ☆☆☆☆
1960, USA
Burt Lancaster, Jean Simmons, Dean Jagger, Arthur Kennedy, Shirley Jones, Patti Page, John McIntire. Directed by Richard Brooks. 146 min.

Sinclair Lewis's sensational novel is brought to the screen with old-fashioned fire and brimstone by Richard Brooks—his best movie by leagues. Burt Lancaster gives one of his most charismatic performances as the hypocritical Southern preacher, and Jean Simmons is remarkable as the honest evangelist he unwittingly drags down, their relationship culminating in a grand, Ibsenesque conflagration. Andre Previn contributes an effective score.

ELVIRA MADIGAN ☆☆☆☆
1967, Sweden
Pia Degermark, Thommy Berggren, Lennart Malmen, Nina Widerberg. Directed by Bo Widerberg. 95 min.

A beautiful use of color points up the delicacy and control of this exquisite love story set against a backdrop of nineteenth-century Sweden. The plot is sublimely simple—an army officer takes off with a circus tightrope dancer only to find that their idyllic lifestyle is running counter to an unsympathetic outside world. Yet *Elvira Madigan* is not an indictment of the harsh realities that they encounter, but a joyous ode to the couple's tenderness. A near flawless bit of cinema written, directed, and edited by Bo Widerberg. The wonderful Mozart score adds to the pleasure.

EMANUELLE AROUND THE WORLD ☆
1980, Italy
Laura Gemser. Directed by Joe D'Amato. 92 min.

Laura Gemser, the Emanuelle with one "m," gets heavy-lidded with a number of very bad German thespians. Rated zzzzzz.

EMANUELLE IN AMERICA ☆½
1977, Italy
Laura Gemser, Gabriele Tinti, Roger Browne. Directed by Joe D'Amato. 87 min.

The Gemser Emanuelle is less a Sylvia Kristel–style searcher for sexual fulfillment than an investigator of sexual crimes. Here, she invades a harem, overcomes a stud farm, and uncovers a seduction plot involving LSD and porno films. Heavily edited, but still hard soft-core, the film's only appeal is the alluring, Eurasian beauty of Gemser.

EMANUELLE IN BANGKOK ½☆
1977, Italy, R
Laura Gemser, Gabriele Tinti, Ivan Rssimov, Kioke Mahoco. Directed by Joe D'Amato. 94 min.

A definite loser in the fake Emanuelle series, this travel feature *does* show lots of scenery of Thailand and Casablanca, and even features a famous Thai body massage. But the sexual liaisons are chopped up and far less revealing than, say, *Emanuelle, The Queen*, and there is absolutely no plot. The best scene is a battle between a mongoose and a cobra.

EMANUELLE IN EGYPT ☆
1977, Italy, R
Laura Gemser, Annie Belle, Al Cliver, Gabriele Tinti, Susan Scott, Theodore Chaliapin. Directed by Brunello Rondi. 86 min.

This movie is a Michelin guide to Egypt, as it might be edited by Bob Guccione: ". . . and here are the splendors of the temple of Ramses II, a perfect place to get naked." Laura Gemser plays a fashion model who becomes entangled with a matriarch, her two daughters, and a holy man. Tinti gives one of his patented angry lover performances, and Belle, star of her own movies, shows up with a short haircut. There are very mild nude scenes, with an interesting, Italian antipornographic slant. After all, how erotic can simulated sex be when it's staged on a desert, surrounded by the bloodied bodies of dead men?

EMANUELLE IN THE COUNTRY ☆
1978, Italy
Laura Gemser, Tony Raggetti, Aldo Ralli, Aldo Sambrell, Lorna Green, Gabriele Tinti. Directed by Alan W. Cools. 90 min.

A young woman doctor takes up practice in a small northern Italian town, hides her fiancé in her apartment, helps a young man win the mayor's daughter, and takes a lot of showers. Not really an *Emmanuelle* movie, it's actually a standard italian comedy that stars Laura Gemser, the second Emmanuelle (or the one-"m" Emanuelle, if you prefer).

EMANUELLE, THE QUEEN ☆½
1979, Italy
Laura Gemser, Gordon Michell, Gabriele Tinti. Directed by Ilias Milonakins. 90 min.

Laura Gemser is a cool, seductive Emanuelle, but her films have a nasty undertone of sexual violence. This Greek-sponsored outing is indistinguishable from her Italian movies—weakly plotted, jammed with sex that is choppily cut to avoid the hard-core hint. (a.k.a.: *Emanuelle Queen Bitch* and *Emanuelle Queen of Sados*)

EMBRYO ☆
1976, USA, PG
Rock Hudson, Diane Ladd, Barbara Carrera, Roddy McDowall, Dr. Joyce Brothers. Directed by Ralph Nelson. 108 min.

Rock hits rock bottom as a doctor with a bunch of fetuses in his lab. He grows one of them into a woman very rapidly, and things go smoothly with the beautiful creature until he has sex with her. Talented Diane Ladd plays Hudson's jealous housekeeper. *Embryo* remains embryonic—it never develops into anything worthwhile.

THE EMERALD FOREST ☆☆☆
1985, USA, R
Powers Boothe, Charley Boorman, Meg Foster, William Rodriquez, Yara Vaneau, Dira Paes. Directed by John Boorman. 115 min.

This visually rich and emotionally empty film offers four quests: a father searches for ten years for the son who was kidnapped by a shadowy Brazilian Indian tribe; the son goes after his tribe's sacred stones; the tribe searches for their kidnapped women in the strange world outside of the jungle; and the son searches for his father to help free the women from a brothel. Tribal life is rendered in a pristine, eroticized, *National Geographic* style—the women of the tribe, especially the stunning Dira Paes, look more like models from Rio than subsistence-level Indians—and the issues of dwindling tribal populations that are raised by the film are never really addressed.

THE EMIGRANTS ☆☆☆☆
1971, Sweden, PG
Liv Ullmann, Eddie Axberg, Allan Edwall, Svenolof Bern, Max Von Sydow. Directed by Jan Troell. 148 min.

Jan Troell's film about Swedish families coming to nineteenth-century America is both a somber story of frontier courage and a tribute to the new land these pioneers helped civilize. Along with Ingmar Bergman, the director is one of the few Swedish filmmakers who have succeeded in creating a film American audiences could embrace. Perhaps it travels so well because the story line about our forbears' courage speaks to anyone who migrated to America, and to the majority of us who had relatives move here from other nations generations ago. In effect, this magnificently photographed film is everyone's story. As acted superlatively by Ullmann and Von Sydow, this is a heartbreaking saga about how losses are often a part of emigration, and how enormous sacrifices are needed to make the smallest gain against poverty or the elements. The hardships these characters endure are staggering, and their pain in Scandinavia and struggles in America are recorded with great poignancy. The film is a stirring salute to the spirit of the poem engraved on the Statue of Liberty, but it is neither a rabble-rousing nor a sentimental one; it's filmed in an expansive style that suits the epic scope of the subject matter. An excellent sequel, *The New Land*, followed.

EMILY ☆☆
1976, Great Britain, R
Koo Stark, Sarah Brackett, Victor Spinetti, Jane Hayden, Constantin de Goguel, Ina Shriver. Directed by Henry Herbert. 87 min.

Former consort to the court Koo Stark plays Emily, a young girl finishing up finishing school, with a light, breezy, come-on sensuality that makes this soft-core film fun to watch, despite its narrative inanities. Emily comes of age over and over again in this period piece of England in the late 1920s, as the plot moves from one excuse to another for people to disrobe. If you can ignore the musical score by poetaster Rod McKuen, then a fun time is guaranteed for all.

EMMANUELLE ☆
1974, France
Sylvia Kristel, Alain Cuny, Daniel Sarky. Directed by Just Jaeckin. 105 min.

Not explicit enough to be called pornography, but too worthless to be treated as anything else, *Emmanuelle* was a huge international success and spawned several sequels. It's the story of a young wife whose inattentive husband, a French diplomat, leaves her alone in Bangkok to discover the joy of sex. Notable only for its status as the first X-rated non-"art" film to be released by a major distributor, *Emmanuelle* may be a historical footnote, but it's still dull, silly junk.

EMMANUELLE BLACK AND WHITE ½☆
1978, Italy
Antonio Gizmondo, Maria Luisa Longo, Rita Manna, Percy Hogan. Directed by Mario Pinzauti. 95 min.

Forget the title—this movie has nothing to do with the *Emmanuelle* series—it's actually a rip-off of the *Mandingo*-style southern plantation yarns, featuring lots of sexual violence and depictions of black slaves enduring endless abuse at the hands of their white masters. The movie has enough liberalism to render it a little more harmless than most, and it's so badly dubbed, with some of the world's worst dialogue, that it can be silly and fun. A slightly overweight cast indulges in slightly explicit sex scenes.

EMMANUELLE 4 ☆
1984, France
Sylvia Kristel, Mia Nygren, Patrick Bauchau, Deborah Power, Sophie Berger, Sonia Martin. Directed by Francis Giacobetti (earlier credited to Francis Leroi and Iris Letans). 95 min.

Exploitation producers everywhere, take a lesson: when the starlet of your soft-core film series reaches that problematic age when letting it all hang out might *hurt* the box office, don't despair. Simply borrow a page from *Emmanuelle 4*, in which the thirty-five-year-old heroine (Sylvia Kristel, who created the role in 1975) is dispatched to Brazil for a body lift, and emerges from surgery a gorgeous virgin played by a new actress (twenty-year-old Mia Nygren). Other than that neat trick, this is the same old middle-class businessman's peep show with a little sex, a lot of nudity, and too much talk. *Note:* European prints were originally shown in 3-D.

EMMANUELLE II, THE JOYS OF A WOMAN ☆½
1976, France, X
Sylvia Kristel, Umberto Orsini, Catherine Rivet. Directed by Francis Giacobetti. 92 min.

Emmanuelle's chief joy here is listening to other people's smutty stories; director Francis Giacobetti's is montage. There are some lovely dalliance sequences, all of them soft-core, awash in the fuzzy focus, rich color, and soupy Michel Legrand music that seemed to be in vogue.

THE EMPEROR JONES ☆☆½
1933, USA
Paul Robeson, Dudley Digges, Frank Wilson. Directed by Dudley Murphy. 72 min.

Paul Robeson's most important screen acting role was in Dudley Murphy's flamboyant film of Eugene O'Neill's play. Remembered chiefly as a specimen of the expressionistic theatrical styles of the 1920s, the movie employs extravagantly artificial sets to tell O'Neill's story of an ex-Pullman porter (Robeson) who has become the king of a West Indian island. The film is stiff and difficult to watch now, but Robeson and Dudley Digges—as Jones's cynical white adviser—are very fine indeed.

EMPEROR OF THE NORTH

See *Emperor of the North Pole*

EMEPEROR OF THE NORTH POLE ☆☆☆½
1973, USA, R
Lee Marvin, Ernest Borgnine, Keith Carradine, Charles Tyner, Elisha Cook, Jr. Directed by Robert Aldrich. 119 min.

Late Robert Aldrich films are often repellently violent (*The Longest Yard*, *The Choirboys*), yet this gutsy, macho adventure yarn builds up to a bloody showdown that is not only dramatically satisfying but also emotionally liberating. It's one of the few Aldrich movies where the father is triumphant. In 1933 Oregon, evil is represented by Ernest Borgnine's savage train conductor; good is represented by Lee Marvin's hobo who is determined to ride the train cars at any cost while teaching a novice (Keith Carradine) the ropes. The sappy buddy-buddy scenes between Marvin and Carradine are the least successful part of Christopher Knof's screenplay (mainly because Carradine performs so badly), but the Marvin-Borgnine interactions are remarkable, particularly in the final savage confrontation. (a.k.a.: *Emperor of the North*)

EMPIRE OF THE ANTS ☆
1977, USA, PG
Joan Collins, Robert Lansing, John David Carson, Albert Salmi, Jacqueline Scott, Pamela Shoop. Directed by Bert I. Gordon. 89 min.

Veteran schlockmeister Bert I. Gordon adapted this laughable creepy-crawly horror film from an H. G. Wells story, but its spirit is pure American International–style 1950s junk. Joan Collins plays a corrupt Floida realtor trying to peddle swampy island property to a boatload of unsuspecting clucks. But it's evidently not nice to fool Mother Nature or potential investors and, soon enough, ten-foot insects stake a very hostile claim to the same turf. This was Collins's thirty-third film, and one of the few she says she'd like to forget; if you've seen some of the ones she doesn't mind remembering, you know this is fair warning. The movie features an especially woeful performance by John David Carson, son of Johnny.

THE EMPIRE STRIKES BACK ☆☆☆
1980, USA, PG
Mark Hamill, Harrison Ford, Carrie Fisher, Billy Dee Williams, Alec Guinness, Frank Oz. Directed by Irving Kershner. 124 min.

George Lucas's surefire *Star Wars* sequel boasts the most accomplished display of special effects—and the most dazzlingly beautiful science-fiction imagery—the movies have ever mounted. Director Irvin Kershner conjures up a glittering sense of menace, and there are uniformly better performances from Mark Hamill, Carrie Fisher, and the gang. What some viewers find disappointing is the film's ominous intellectual pretensions. Lucas strives to push his comic book daydream toward the Homeric, and the film lacks the throwaway, toy shop trashiness that made *Star Wars* so much fun.

ENCHANTED ISLAND ☆☆½
1958, USA
Dana Andrews, Jane Powell, Ted de Corsia, Don Dubbins. Directed by Allan Dwan. 94 min.

This low-budget adaptation of Herman Melville's novel *Typee* is the story of a sailor who deserts a whaling ship and finds love on a South Seas island. Allen Dwan was perhaps the quintessential B movie director: a natural, unpretentious storyteller, capable of real invention on both grand and intimate scales. There's even some unexpected black humor in an extended sequence in which Andrews believes he is going to be the island natives' next meal. (Andrews always had a knack for finding Hollywood's weirder projects). Add Jane Powell as a dark-haired Polynesian and you have a campy treat.

THE END ☆☆☆
1978, USA, R
Burt Reynolds, Dom DeLuise, Sally Field, Joanne Woodward, Kristy McNichol, David Steinberg, Norman Fell, Carl Reiner, Pat O'Brien, Myrna Loy, Robby Benson, Strother Martin, Jock Mahoney. Directed by Burt Reynolds. 100 min.

Like almost every Burt Reynolds comedy, this one (about a slightly shady salesman who discovers that he's dying of a rare blood disease and decides to kill himself rather than die a slow death) is more an excuse to string together a lot of comic bits and cameo appearances than a film with a unified plot. Reynolds himself mugs too much, a tendency that his beard seems to encourage, but there are funny turns from most of the rest of the cast, including Pat O'Brien and Myrna Loy as his parents, Robby Benson (believe it or not) as a priest, and, especially, Dom DeLuise, who, as a schizophrenic strangler, pretty much takes over the movie every time he's onscreen.

END OF DESIRE ☆☆
1962, France
Maria Schell, Christian Marquand, Pascale Petit, Ivan Desny. Directed by Alexandre Astruc. 86 min.

The film is a rather stolid, bloodless look at peccadilloes among the aristocracy. Based on a de Maupassant story, which leads one to expect something airy with a twist, the film slogs away without that *je ne sais quoi* that gives his stories their timeless charm. Doggedly mediocre, the film is too much soap opera and not enough irony. It is redeemed only by Schell's shining performance as the neglected wife of a bounder.

END OF THE ROAD ☆☆
1970, USA, X
Stacy Keach, Harris Yulin, James Earl Jones, Dorothy Tristan, James Coco. Directed by Aram Avakian. 110 min.

This seldom-seen adaptation (by Terry Southern) of the novel by John Barth received an X rating for its self-conscious grotesquerie rather than for explicit sex; in particular, the final scene, which portrays a graphically botched illegal abortion, may be hard for many to view. The film is the usual late sixties concoction of antiestablishment symbols and light show, with a story about a pair of teachers at Johns Hopkins University to fall back on when the director has nothing better to do. Cinematography by Gordon Willis.

END OF THE WORLD ☆½
1977, USA, PG
Christopher Lee, Sue Lyon, Kirk Scott, Lew Ayres, MacDonald Carey, Dean Jagger. Directed by John Hayes. 87 min.

This tepid sci-fi with religious overtones starts out promisingly enough, with Christopher Lee playing a priest who is taken over by an alien out to destroy the earth. (Seems we earthlings are polluting the universe.) Unfortunately, it never goes anywhere. Blame can presumably be placed on the head of director John Hayes, who also edited, both at a somnolent pace.

ENDANGERED SPECIES ☆☆☆½
1982, USA, R
Robert Urich, JoBeth Williams, Hoyt Axton, Paul Dooley, Peter Coyote. Directed by Alan Rudolph. 97 min.

Barely released into the theaters by MGM, this is one of the best of the post-1970s conspiracy thrillers. New York City cop Robert Urich goes to the midwest and discovers a paramilitary organization doing germ warfare experiments on cattle. Gripping, cerebral, and very exciting in its depiction of the little man against a hidden network of super patriots who are sponsored by forces in the government, this movie never got the attention it deserved. It is filled with great offbeat characterizations by Urich, Williams, and Dooley. Don't miss this neglected suspense classic.

ENDGAME ☆☆
1983, USA, R
Al Cliver, Moira Chen, George Eastman, Jack Davis, Al Yamanouchi, Mario Pedone. Directed by Steven Benson. 96 min.

It's 2025 A.D., the Bomb has fallen, and the national pastime is watching "Endgame," in which professional killers hunt each other down for glory and money, all on TV. A group of pacifistic mutants hires the star of "Endgame" to lead them out of the city and into a new land where they will begin a new society and reform the human race. This Italian-made adventure throws in scraps from *The Most Dangerous Game, The Tenth Victim, Escape from New York, Road Warrior, Terminator,* spaghetti Westerns, ninja movies, *The Seven Samurai,* professional wrestling, and God knows what else. Unfortunately, no one bothered to stir this soup, and the result is predictable and dull, without a bit of humor.

ENDLESS LOVE ☆½
1981, USA, R
Brooke Shields, Martin Hewitt, Shirley Knight, Don Murray, Richard Kiley, Beatrice Straight. Directed by Franco Zeffirelli. 115 min.

In the hands of that great swooner Franco Zeffirelli, Scott Spencer's extraordinary novel about a teenage boy consumed by obsessive love becomes one of the more disgraceful adaptations in movie history. Martin Hewitt stars as the idealistic teenager who stakes is life and soul on the ecstatic purity of his love for the young daugher (Brooke Shields) of a bohemian couple. Although the book made the boy's madness seem accessible and even attractive, the movie is like a weepy pop song about misunderstood teens.

ENDLESS NIGHT ☆☆½
1971, Great Britain
Hayley Mills, Hywel Bennett, Britt Ekland, George Sanders, Per Oscarsson, Lois Maxwell. Directed by Sidney Gilliat. 95 min.

This is spooky stuff about a rich American girl who marries her chauffeur and buys a dream mansion. Of course, the house turns out to be less a dream than a nightmare. Based on an Agatha Christie novel, this is thin and not very engagingly acted (despite the good cast), but it does have its share of suitably scary sequences, aided by a Bernard Herrmann score.

THE ENDLESS SUMMER ☆☆☆
1966, USA
Directed by Bruce Brown. 95 min.

Bruce Brown's ode to the joys of surfing—he wrote, produced, directed, shot, edited, and narrated—is as pure and charming an artifact of the mid-1960s as filmgoers are likely to find. Brown went around the world searching for the perfect wave, and set against his amazing footage are silly jokes, straight-faced observations of native rituals, and consumer guide assessments of each beach's bikini quotient. It may not be a great film or even a very good one, but if we had packed a time capsule in 1966, this would be nestled alongside our Batman comics and our Supremes 45s.

THE ENEMY BELOW ☆☆☆
1957, USA
Robert Mitchum, Curt Jurgens, Al (David) Hedison, Theodore Bikel, Kurt Kreuger, Frank Albertson, Doug McClure. Directed by Dick Powell. 98 min.

Good special effects and the American debut of Curt Jurgens are the highlights of this World War II submarine epic. Jurgens and Robert Mitchum are cast as adversaries, captains of a German sub and an American minesweeper playing cat-and-mouse games with each other. Actor-turned-director Dick Powell filmed two endings for this film and used the more upbeat one, stressing the camaraderie of all soldiers despite the uniforms they wear.

ENEMY MINE ☆☆½
1985, USA, PG
Dennis Quaid, Lou Gossett, Jr., Brion James, Lance Kerwin. Directed by Wolfgang Petersen. 110 min.

This movie at first resembles a pastiche but ultimately proves itself to be somewhat better, as a warring earthman and alien band together after being marooned on a hostile world. As the gruff space fighter (Quaid) and the fearsome-looking Drac

(Gossett) overcome their mutual hatred, director Petersen uses his actors and immense sets to create a stylish and humane movie. Although the central relationship occupies only a portion of the picture, it is humorous and moving, thanks to Gossett's good performance as the lizard-creature. The latter section, where the earth attempts to rescue the Drac's child from evil space miners, has difficulty holding up. The film is uneven, but it's a step up from the regular effects-oriented fare.

THE ENFORCER ☆☆
1976, USA, R
Clint Eastwood, Harry Guardino, Bradford Dillman, Tyne Daly. Directed by James Fargo. 96 min.

This third installment in the "Dirty Harry" series marks the point at which Clint Eastwood began to walk through them, presumably saving his energy for the more ambitious projects that his financial cut from this no doubt paid for. This time around, Harry Callahan is on the trail of some nasty terrorists, burdened by his bleeding heart bureaucrat superiors and an unwanted female partner (Tyne Daly). There is an occasional nice touch, but this is formula all the way.

ENIGMA ☆☆½
1982, Great Britain/France, PG
Martin Sheen, Brigitte Fossey, Sam Neill, Derek Jacobi, Michel Lonsdale, Frank Finlay. Directed by Jeannot Szwarc. 100 min.

It seems that these Cold War dramas about international agencies and nefarious governmental chicanery will never pass out of fashion. Somehow, as long as Robert Ludlum or John Le Carre keep churning out best sellers, there will be an audience for all these spies who come in from the cold. *Enigma* is neither the best nor the worst of these complicated intrigues; the KGB sends out its ace assassins to eliminate some Soviet dissidents with a low tolerance level for the Kremlin. Like other double-dealing spy thrillers, *Enigma* is better on your VCR than it was on the big screen. Perhaps it's because you can replay the most confusing parts at will and figure out what the heck's going on.

ENOLA GAY: THE MEN, THE MISSION, THE ATOMIC BOMB ☆☆½
1980, USA (TV)
Billy Crystal, Kim Darby, Patrick Duffy, Gary Frank, Gregory Harrison, Ed Nelson. Directed by David Lowell Rich. 150 min.

This sturdy dramatization is based on the memoirs of Paul Tibbets, the man who headed the mission that dropped the first atomic bomb. As a history lesson, the film is competent, but it's less valuable as a character study of these dutiful men; details of their emotional turmoil are handled superficially. Given the awesome task they were assigned to carry out, more depth was in order for expressing the plight of these order-followers, including any self-doubts they felt about what they had to do. A strong cast impersonates these shadowy historical figures with aplomb, but the drama unfolds in typically timid TV-movie fashion, and the opportunity to probe this history-changing mission and its devastating results is largely missed.

ENSIGN PULVER ☆☆
1964, USA
Robert Walker, Burl Ives, Millie Perkins, Walter Matthau, Larry Hagman, James Farentino, James Coco. Directed by Joshua Logan. 104 min.

This is a disappointing sequel to *Mister Roberts*, especially given the fact that it was also written and directed by Joshua Logan. The title character was played by Jack Lemmon in the earlier film, and he won an Oscar for it. He's replaced here by the much less talented Robert Walker. The other bit of bad casting was in replacing James Cagney with Burl Ives. The film is flat and meaningless, without the human virtues that redeemed the original.

ENTER LAUGHING ☆☆½
1967, USA
Jose Ferrer, Shelley Winters, Elaine May, Jack Gilford, Reni Santoni, Janet Margolin, David Opatoshu, Michael J. Pollard, Don Rickles, Rob Reiner. Directed by Carl Reiner. 112 min.

A rich, diverse comic cast manages to make the most of this how-I-broke-into-showbiz comedy, based on director Carl Reiner's own experiences but actually adapted from a stage play by Joseph Stein. The theatricality of the piece comes through here, and it's never quite as funny as you want it to be, due to a surprisingly dour performance by Reni Santoni in the leading role of the stage-struck young man. Fortunately, Winters, Ferrer, Gilford, and May are around to steal the show.

ENTER THE DRAGON ☆☆☆½
1973, R
Bruce Lee, John Saxon, Jim Kelly. Directed by Robert Clouse. 97 min.

The kung fu genre became popular and Bruce Lee achieved legendary status in this first martial arts picture distributed by a major studio. Lee plays an adventurer who infiltrates the island of a mad scientist bent on taking over the world, and soon finds himself battling the villain's minions. This is an enjoyable comic book film filled with spectacular karate fights, all of which display Lee at his balletic and shrieking best; it is a tongue-in-cheek movie that never stops moving, and one that is superior to the schlocky imitators that followed it.

ENTER THE GAME OF DEATH ☆☆
1980, Hong Kong
Bruce Le (Huang Kin-Lung), Yang Sze, Chaing Tao, Chang Li. Directed by Joseph Velasco. 90 min.

Important, secret documents that pertain to the security of China are stolen by the Japanese, and Bruce Le is sent to retrieve them. The multitalented Mr. Le also directed his own martial arts sequences in this film.

ENTER THE NINJA ☆½
1981, USA, R
Franco Nero, Susan George, Sho Kasugi, Christopher George. Directed by Menahem Golan. 101 min.

Franco Nero plods through his role as a ninja assassin. There are really only two ways to play a martial arts hero—à la the simpleminded, sincere Chuck Norris style or the sly trickster persona of Bruce Lee—but Nero mistakenly tries for a brooding sincerity that slows down an already dull film. Although there are some good Mike Stone/Sho Kasugi battles, Golan's inept direction muddles the standardized, glossy Cannon Production. Both *Return of the Ninja* and *Ninja III: The Domination* are better outings in the series.

THE ENTERTAINER ☆☆☆½
1960, Great Britain
Laurence Olivier, Brenda DeBanzie, Albert Finney, Alan Bates, Joan Plowright, Roger Livesey. Directed by Tony Richardson. 97 min.

This film is important both as a document of a pioneering trend in English theater and motion pictures, and as a record of a famous stage performance. When John Osborne's *The Entertainer* was first produced on the English stage (along with other plays such as Osborne's *Look Back in Anger* and Shelagh Delaney's *A Taste of Honey*), the event was regarded as a breath of fresh but controversial air, blasting the genteel tradition of quality English theater. The kitchen-sink school of realism, full of gritty dialogue, natualistic settings, and bleak story lines, reflected a nation's social unrest filtered through a feeling of angst. This film is a prime example of the cinema of the angry young man; a metaphor for the decline of England. Playing a loser who treats everyone in his life as an audience he's grown tired of, Laurence Olivier, in one of his greatest performances, gives a disturbing edge to the character of Archie Rice, a has-been music hall comedian. The film's achievement is to force us to examine our own failures by confronting the self-delusions of this desperate soul.

ENTERTAINING MR. SLOANE ★★★
1969, Great Britain
Beryl Reid, Peter McEnery, Harry Andrews, Alan Webb. Directed by Douglas Hickox. 94 min.

Time has taken some of the sting out of Joe Orton's play, which outraged audiences in 1964. But the film version, which provides a different ending, offers a quartet of wonderful performances and more than enough to relish for those with a taste for the perverse. Mr. Sloane, a young drifter of dubious past, is taken in as a boarder in a house populated by Kath, a middle-aged widow who has only recently discovered the joy of lust, her brother Ed, a sadistic, repressed homosexual, and their old buzzard of a father. The ending isn't as outrageous as could be hoped for (or might be expected), but there is a great deal of clever malice along the way.

THE ENTITY ★½
1983, USA, R
Barbara Hershey, Ron Silver, Jacqueline Brookes. Directed by Sidney J. Furie. 119 min.

A woman is sexually assaulted by a vicious incubus and seeks help from friends, psychiatrists, and psychic researchers, all to no avail in this graphic horror film that is more often embarrassing than terrifying. It is an attempt at intelligent genre filmmaking that doesn't really succeed, despite good production values and the efforts of a professional cast.

ENTRE NOUS ★★★
1983, France
Miou Miou, Isabelle Huppert, Guy Marchand, Jean-Pierre Bacri, Patrick Bauchau. Directed by Diane Kurys. 110 min.

This film is a sensitive, somewhat overpraised tale of two long-suffering women who find more love and companionship in their friendship than they did in their very traditional marriages. Following their fortunes from the end of World War II through the fifties, the film succeeds in detailing the painful process of their liberation, and it wisely avoids painting their husbands as black-hearted villains. Something in the director's attitude toward these women is a bit smug, though; we're meant to respond to these feminist icons (based on the director's own mother and the mother's best friend), but the actresses seem to be playing symbols, not women. Some viewers may perceive the women not as victims freeing themselves from dead marriages so much as self-centered dilettantes who want to see life through their rose-colored friendship. (a.k.a.: *Coup de Foudre*)

EQUINOX ★★
1971, USA, PG
Edward Connell, Barbara Hewitt, Robin Christopher, Fritz Leiber, Frank Boers, Jr. Directed by Jack Woods. 80 min.

A group of students searching for their missing professor comes across an ancient book that conjures up all manner of demons from another dimension. This was originally made as a 16-mm short feature by a group of horror movie fans; the stop-motion monsters they created impressed a producer enough to add some extra footage and release it in a full-length version. All things considered, the film is impressive but not very good. Frank Boers, Jr. later changed his last name to Bonner and played Herb on TV's "WKRP in Cincinnati."

EQUUS ★★
1977, Great Britain, R
Richard Burton, Peter Firth, Colin Blakely, Eileen Atkins, Jenny Agutter, Joan Plowright. Directed by Sidney Lumet. 138 min.

This film is a major disappointment. Adapting Peter Shaffer's much-lauded play, director Sidney Lumet replaces theatrical symbolism with cinematic "realism," but he can't shake the essentially allegorical, sparse, and, above all, stage-oriented nature of the story. The result is a textbook case on how *not* to adapt a play for the screen. Burton, as the troubled psychiatrist who tries to find out why a young man blinded six horses, gives a performance transferred intact from Broadway; it's an honorable but competely failed piece of work—overemphatic, strident, and tendentious. Peter Firth is somewhat better, though still unsteady, as the patient. Much of the blame here goes to Shaffer, who hadn't yet learned the differences between a play and a screenplay, and to Lumet, who was unable to find a consistent or compelling style out of his usual milieu.

ERASERHEAD ★★★
1977, USA
Jack Nance, Laurel Near, Charlotte Stewart, Judith Anna Roberts. Directed by David Lynch. 90 min.

David Lynch's midnight classic *Eraserhead* blends paranoia, claustrophobia, and the ultra macabre into a truly unique story about a young man whose life changes dramatically when his girlfriend gives birth to a grotesque, premature baby. That's not a plot summary but merely one event in a surreal, ghoulish web of actions that defy placement in a linear narrative. In black and white, with a soundtrack nearly drowned out by the roars of Lynch's industrial hell on earth, *Eraserhead* is, for many, almost unbearable to sit through. Everyone is deformed, attacked, mutilated, and miserable, and you may feel the same way after letting Lynch inflict his oozy, pulsating visual obsessions upon you. Regardless of its unfollowable story and stomach-churning qualities, though, *Eraserhead* isn't a cult "so-weird-it's-good" movie, but the striking and original debut of an important director. Steel yourself and see it, but prepare to squint at a video image that will render much of the dark action almost indecipherable.

ERENDIRA ★★★
1983, Mexico/France/West Germany
Irene Papas, Claudia Ohana, Michael Lonsdale, Oliver Wehe, Rufus. Directed by Ruy Guerra. 103 min.

Gabriel Garcia Marquez adapted his fanciful comic fable about a domineering matriarch (Irene Papas) who sets up her granddaughter (Claudia Ohana) as an itinerant prostitute, and his voice comes through in the extravagant images and the baroque accumulation of grotesque detail. Ohana plays Erendira as an impressive beauty who retreats into the solitude of her somnambulism. She's all but eclipsed by Papas, whose Grand Guignol performance as the grandmother is a mesmerizing mixture of lunacy and imperturbability.

THE ERRAND BOY ★★★
1961, USA
Jerry Lewis, Brian Donlevy, Howard McNear, Sig Ruman, Fritz Feld, Iris Adrian, Kathleen Freeman, Joe Besser, Mike Mazurki. Directed by Jerry Lewis. 93 min.

Jerry's supposed to be an unknowing studio snitch sent out to uncover the moviemaking money wasters, but the plot quickly goes by the boards as the Idiot runs into irresistible gag opportunities. There are some funny parodies of Hollywood; however, this madhouse Lewis set piece is less an excursion through the world of filmmaking than it is a paranoid look at a nervous world where everything is fake and things fall apart. The scene that features a New York intellectual explaining the genius, humanity, and acting ability of the goofy errand boy (read: Jerry) has to be seen to be believed.

ESCAPE ★
1982, Italy, R
Anthony Steffen, Ajita Wilson, Cynthia Lodett. Directed by Edward Muller. 100 min.

Lusty female prisoners try to keep their flimsy prison khakis from falling off long enough to escape from a South American jungle penal colony. If you can believe that there actually would be a jungle penal colony for women in South America, then you might even fall for some of the rest of this balderdash. Rather more brutal than the usual women's prison stuff, if you can imagine that, with rapes, beatings, tortures, and eye scratchings by the dozen. There is also hilariously bad dubbing, especially in the ad-libbed crowd scenes, which sound like they're all done by three people using different funny voices. (a.k.a.: *Escape From Hell*)

THE ESCAPE ARTIST ☆☆½
1982, USA, PG
Raul Julia, Griffin O'Neal, Teri Garr, Joan Hackett, Desi Arnaz, Sr., Gabriel Dell, M. Emmet Walsh, Jackie Coogan. Directed by Caleb Deschanel. 96 min.

Caleb Deschanel, cinematographer of *The Black Stallion* and *The Right Stuff*, made his directorial debut with this gentle, atmospheric fable about a teenage boy (Griffin O'Neal, son of Ryan) who runs away from home to become a magician. The story makes no sense whatsoever, but the random ideas that float in and out of the narrative are genuinely original. Had the plot been conceived with the same thought and care that went into Dean Tavoularis's production design, it might have been great. As it stands, *The Escape Artist* is only a curiosity, albeit an intermittently enchanting one. Produced by Francis Coppola's company, Zoetrope.

ESCAPE FROM ALCATRAZ ☆☆☆
1979, USA, PG
Clint Eastwood, Patrick McGoohan, Roberts Blossom, Larry Hankin. Directed by Don Siegel. 112 min.

In this highly impressive feature from the team of Eastwood and Siegel, the actor gives a superbly controlled performance as an inmate of the prison from which California governor McGoohan claims there's no escape. Based on an actual story, the film's point of view is too ambiguous to be considered politically rightist, a criticism often leveled against Eastwood and Siegel. If anything, *Alcatraz* seems to support a liberal argument against unfair prison conditions. It would be to deny the smooth efficiency of the filmmaking, however, to read anything into this fine entertainment; it's low-key, stark, and gripping.

ESCAPE FROM THE BRONX ☆½
1985, Italy, PG
Mark Gregory, Henry Silva, Valeria D'Obici, Timothy Brent, Paolo Malco. Directed by Enzo G. Castellari. 82 min.

This is a ridiculous film with a title inaccurately cribbed from *Escape from New York*—the characters here aren't trying to escape; they want to stay. It seems the corrupt government is trying to demolish what's left of the Bronx in order to put up a huge, futuristic condo. No, it's not supposed to be a joke, although the dubbing of Bronx accents over the voices of Italian actors is on a par with the dubbing on Godzilla films. Henry Silva provides the only touch of professionalism as the chief bad guy.

ESCAPE FROM FORT BRAVO ☆☆☆
1953, USA
William Holden, Eleanor Parker, John Forsythe, William Demarest, William Campbell, Polly Bergen, Carl Benton Reid. Directed by John Sturges. 98 min.

Television and the VCR will never be adequate substitutes for motion picture projection of some films because many cameramen in the forties were working in a medium that doesn't translate to a video screen. If you show a film shot in a wide-screen process on a squarish video screen, you lose up to half the picture. This is particularly distressing in films like this, a better-than-average Civil War Western set in a Union fort from which a group of confederate prisoners make an escape. Cinematographer Robert Surtees, one of the best, shot the film for a wide-screen format and made good use of the Arizona locales, all of which will be lost if you watch this on TV. It's still a spiffy story, mind you, with a great Indian raid at the end, but there's so much more to movies like this than just plot.

ESCAPE FROM HELL

See *Escape*

ESCAPE FROM NEW YORK ☆½
1981, USA, R
Kurt Russell, Lee Van Cleef, Ernest Borgnine, Donald Pleasence, Isaac Hayes, Adrienne Barbeau. Directed by John Carpenter. 99 min.

John Carpenter's futuristic thriller takes off from an enticing premise. The year is 1997, and the entire island of Manhattan has been converted into a maximum security prison. When Air Force One crash-lands inside the city's fifty-foot walls and the President of the United States (Donald Pleasence) is kidnapped, the prison's newest, most dangerous criminal, war hero Snake Plisken (Kurt Russell), is sent to retrieve him. The visual possibilities of a trashed, post-apocalyptic Manhattan would appear to be endless, but Carpenter simply strews some rubble around, shrouds everything in a fog, and turns the city into an anonymous junk heap. The result is so thinly imagined (and woodenly acted) that it plays like a hundred other bargain basement action films.

ESCAPE FROM THE PLANET OF THE APES ☆☆☆
1971, USA, G
Roddy McDowall, Kim Hunter, Bradford Dillman, Sal Mineo, Ricardo Montalban, Natalie Trundy. Directed by Don Taylor. 97 min.

The third of the *Apes* films is the best of the sequels, with heroic simians Roddy MacDowall and Kim Hunter escaping their blown-up planet to travel back to the 1970s and allow viewers to learn of the creation of the ape planet. Taken as a whole, the series will confound anyone who tries to figure out the chronological order of the action—it's best not to think about it too much while you sit back and enjoy this cleverly conceived tale of the weird events that started it all. *Escape* and its sequel, *Conquest of the Planet of the Apes*, constitute a virtually separate story within the series, and you won't fully understand this film without seeing the one that follows.

ESCAPE TO ATHENA ☆☆
1979, Great Britain, PG
Roger Moore, Tella Savalas, David Niven, Claudia Cardinale, Richard Roundtree, Stefanie Powers, Sonny Bono, Elliott Gould. Directed by George P. Cosmatos. 125 min.

A typical low-grade Lew Grade presentation, this is yet another failed entry in the long series of *Dirty Dozen* imitators, the *Kelly's Heroes* subgroup. An internationally disparate group of prisoners in a Greek prison camp during World War II plot to escape and take some Greek art treasures with them. The inspired casting includes Roger Moore as the Nazi commandant and Sonny Bono as an Italian guerilla fighter. We never could figure out why Sonny didn't get the lead in *Rambo* after the fierce portrayal he turns in here. Produced by David Niven, Jr., which explains why Niven, Sr. is in the cast. I wonder what everyone else's excuses were?

ESCAPE TO BURMA ☆½
1955, USA
Barbara Stanwyck, Robert Ryan, David Farrar, Murvyn Vye, Lisa Montell, Reginald Denny. Directed by Allan Dwan. 86 min.

Robert Ryan, wanted for a murder that he didn't commit, hides out on the teak plantation owned by Barbara Stanwyck, with whom he soon falls in love. His hiding place is discovered, however, leading to the obligatory chase through the Burmese jungle. This was one of the last of almost 400 films directed by Allan

Dwan; let's be charitable and assume that by this time he was a bit weary. Still, no movie that gives you Barbara Stanwyck in jungle khakis is totally without merit.

ESCAPE TO THE SUN ½☆
1972, Great Britain/Israel
Laurence Harvey, Josephine Chaplin, John Ireland, Jack Hawkins, Lila Kedrova. Directed by Menahem Golan. 105 min.

Golan-Globus Productions have long specialized in nonsensical adventure tales featuring gimmicky plots and all-star casts who always seem to have been spliced in from other bad movies. In this one, directed by Golan himself, a group of plucky Soviet Jews tries to wave bye-bye to Russia, but their plans are cut short by some nasty Kremlinites who seem to have learned their tactics by watching American propaganda films about the Nazis.

ESCAPE TO WITCH MOUNTAIN ☆☆☆
1975, USA, G
Eddie Albert, Ray Milland, Donald Pleasence, Kim Richards, Ike Eisenmann, Reta Shaw, Walter Barnes, Denver Pyle. Directed by John Hough. 97 min.

Of the dozens of live-action comedy adventures churned out by Buena Vista studios (a division of Disney) in the 1960s and 1970s, this is one of the few genuinely enjoyable ones. Kim Richards and Ike Eisenmann play a brother and sister with inexplicable psychic powers; it seems that they're actually extraterrestrials, stranded on Earth as babies. When bad guy Ray Milland pegs them as witches, they must use their special abilities to stay out of his clutches and find their way home. Adults may tire of the film quickly, but it's more literate and energetic than most Disney films of the time, and all the performances are ingratiating. Followed by a sequel, *Return from Witch Mountain*.

ESCAPADE IN JAPAN ☆☆½
1957, USA
Cameron Mitchell, Teresa Wright, Jon Provost, Philip Ober. Directed by Arthur Lubin. 93 min.

This mild adventure film has built-in kid appeal. Boasting exceptionally eye-catching locales, this escapade involves a Japanese tyke who joins forces with an American youngster who's just survived a plane crash. The helpful Asian lad joins his new American pal on a long journey to locate the boy's parents. What gives the film some dramatic juice is the care with which this unexpected friendship is developed and the lack of self-consciousness in the two talented youngsters' acting styles.

E.T. THE EXTRA-TERRESTRIAL ☆☆☆☆
1982, USA, PG
Dee Wallace, Henry Thomas, Peter Coyote, Robert MacNaughton, Drew Barrymore, K. C. Martel, Sean Frye. Directed by Steven Spielberg. 116 min.

The most financially successful film of all time weds state-of-the-art special effects to a simple, poignant and enduring story about a lonely ten-year-old who finds a friend in the form of a stranded, wise space creature aching to return to his home planet. You will remember the magnificent, wizened creation of Carlo Rambaldi, the delicate and perceptive work of Spielberg and cinematographer Allan Daviau, and the genuinely moving finale. But seeing it a second time, you'll discover forgotten pleasures, such as the story's masterful construction and Henry Thomas's solemn, understated performance. For all of its hilarious vignettes and charming child's-eye views, this is really a story about the end of childhood, told with an underlying and necessary melancholy that is the mark of a clear-eyed, mature director. Spielberg has since overworked the film's themes and emotions in so many other movies that you may never want to see another suburban home, wide-eyed kid, or cute alien again. However, despite the rip-offs, derivations, and commercialization that followed, *E.T.* remains the director's one unqualified triumph. Not on video at press time, but release in early 1988 is a possibility.

ETERNAL WOMAN

See *The Love of Three Queens*

ETERNALLY YOURS ☆☆
1939, USA
Loretta Young, David Niven, Broderick Crawford, Hugh Herbert, Billie Burke, C. Aubrey Smith, Raymond Walburn, Zasu Pitts, Eve Arden, Herman the Rabbit. Directed by Tay Garnett. 95 min.

Light comedy turns to dreary drama in this tale about a woman who marries a magician and then objects to his profession. Loretta Young is gooier than ever, David Niven is stiffer than ever, and the dream supporting cast is wasted in a dull, dated debate about power relations in marriage. Middling production values don't help the sluggish narrative.

EUNUCH OF THE WESTERN PALACE ☆½
1982, Hong Kong
Tsung Hwa, Meng Fei, Wang Tao, Lo Lieh. Directed by Wu Ma. 80 min.

Except for the simple-minded documentary introduction, there's little about eunuchs in this run-of-the-mill period kung fu film. Some nice swordplay and above-average production values flesh out the story of a gang-of-four's attempt to keep a secret letter out of the wrong hands.

EUREKA ☆☆½
1982, USA/Great Britain, R
Gene Hackman, Theresa Russell, Rutger Hauer, Jane Lapotaire, Mickey Rourke, Joe Pesci, Ed Lauter, Helena Kallianiotes. Directed by Nicolas Roeg. 130 min.

Overlong, overambitious, and wildly overblown, Nicolas Roeg's epic, oddball melodrama is almost compulsively watchable nonetheless—it's a failure that's more compelling than many other directors' successes. Gene Hackman plays Jack McCann, a fevered explorer who discovers a mother lode of gold in the Yukon. Twenty years later, during World War II, he's become the world's richest man, living in his own Caribbean island paradise—but now he's faced with a wayward daughter, a fortune-hunting son-in-law, and a coven of Florida gangsters who want a piece of his land. The patchwork plot veers merrily between conventional narrative, allegory, and surrealism, including flash-cut scenes of vertiginous sex, voodoo rites, nods to *Citizen Kane*, portentous soliloquies, and one of the most deliriously funny murder trials ever put on film. If that's not enough, there's Irish Mickey Rourke as an Italian lawyer, Italian Joe Pesci as a Jewish mobster, and Dutchman Rutger Hauer as a French playboy. Unbelievably, *Eureka* is based on a true story; even as fiction, it's impossible to explain but surprisingly easy to enjoy.

THE EUROPEANS ☆☆½
1979, USA/Great Britain, PG
Lee Remick, Robin Ellis, Wesley Addy, Tim Choate, Lisa Eichhorn, Tim Woodward. Directed by James Ivory. 90 min.

This film is a starchy, mostly humorless adaptation of Henry James's brilliantly ironic novel about a clash of values between a family of staid New Englanders and their charming and shallow European cousins, who have arrived on an ostensibly innocent visit. Although Ruth Prawer Jhabvala's screenplay preserves much of James's marvelous dialogue, the tensions, double meanings, ulterior motives, and unspoken conflicts that glimmer just below the surface are either lost altogether or made too explicit, and James Ivory's direction mummifies the film completely. What pleasures there are in *The Europeans* come from the excellence of some of the performers, in particular Lee Remick, and from the considerable Jamesian subtlety that survived the transfer from book to film. The team of Ivory, Jhabvala, and producer Ismail Merchant fared better with James's *The Bostonians* than they did here; almost everything about this film is musty.

EVIL KNIEVEL ☆☆
1972, USA, PG
George Hamilton, Sue Lyon, Bert Freed, Rod Cameron, Dub Taylor. Directed by Marvin Chomsky. 90 min.

This biography of the famed motorcycle stunt driver, who captured the American imagination in the 1960s and 1970s with his increasingly elaborate stunts and egotistical self-promotion, is short on action and long on characterization. Although it begins with a good, gritty feel for this character, the movie becomes whitewashed and moralistic, with George Hamilton as Knievel preaching at length against drugs and violence. The movie is saved by the performances of the supporting cast, Knievel's hangers-on and backers, as played by veteran character actors Freed, Cameron, and Taylor.

EVERGREEN ☆☆½
1934, Great Britain
Jessie Matthews, Sonnie Hale, Betty Balfour, Ivor MacLaren. Directed by Victor Saville. 92 min.

A Rogers and Hart score that includes "Dancing on the Ceiling," Jessie Matthews's dancing, and a not uninteresting plot somehow never add up to much fun. The story of a woman posing as her famous mother in order to win a part in a show moves too slowly and sentimentally to provide adequate bridging between numbers. The numbers themselves aren't too exciting, either, aside from a bizarre Busby Berkeley-style ensemble set to a militaristic theme. This is Matthews's most famous film; she's a likable but limited performer.

EVERY GIRL SHOULD BE MARRIED ☆½
1948, USA
Cary Grant, Franchot Tone, Diana Lynn, Betsy Drake, Alan Mowbray, Eddie Albert, Richard Gaines. Directed by Don Hartman. 84 min.

The first attempt to make overbearing Betsy Drake a star was in this queasy, unfunny comedy. Feminists will be tearing their hair out from the word go as Drake plays a department store worker who schemes (neurotically) to snare a bachelor pediatrician (Cary Grant). Her freakish notion of how to play light comedy leaves Grant looking alternately bored and embarrassed, and the rest of the talented cast look equally bemused. Produced (cheaply), directed, and cowritten by Don Hartman, the movie offers not a single laugh. At one point Grant says, "This is the most blatant display of foolishness I have ever had the misfortune to witness." Amen. Incidentally, the real-life Grant and Drake were married after the making of the film. They were also reteamed for years later in *Room for One More*.

EVERY HOME SHOULD HAVE ONE

See *Think Dirty*

EVERY MAN FOR HIMSELF ☆☆☆
1980, France/Switzerland
Isabelle Huppert, Jacques Dutronc, Nathalie Baye, Roland Amstutz, Anna Baldaccini. Directed by Jean-Luc Godard. 89 min.

Since his return to narrative filmmaking with *Every Man for Himself*, Jean-Luc Goddard appears to be romanticizing his own cinematic past while becoming increasingly apolitical. Yet, as a comment on human relationships, *Every Man for Himself* is a witty, poignant, and pictorially beautiful film. The intersecting tales of a TV director (Jacques Dutronc), his girlfriend (Nathalie Baye), and a young prostitute (Isabelle Huppert) culminate in seemingly unrelated scenes. Godard called this his "second first film" and, although it is less daring than most of his others, it is still an insightful, provocative work. (a.k.a.: *Sauve Qui Peut [La Vie]* and *Slow Motro1*)

EVERY MAN FOR HIMSELF ☆☆☆☆
AND GOD AGAINST ALL
1975, West Germany
Bruno S., Brigitte Mira, Walter Ladengast, Willy Semelrogge. Directed by Werner Herzog. 110 min.

This is a film of extraordinary emotional power from one of the modern cinema's most audacious directors. Basing his work on the true story of Kaspar Hauser, a German born around 1800 but kept in a dark cellar away from any human contact until adulthood, Herzog has fashioned a compassionate, beautifully understated film about what it means to love, to communicate, to think, and ultimately to be a human being. The provincial society he creates is marvelously detailed, but the center of the film is the stunning performance of Bruno S., an actual treated schizophrenic, who brings a stunning note of uncertainty and daring to an amazing role. (Herzog, we should remember, is also the director who made another film with his entire cast under hypnosis.) The director's challenging, individualistic work demands and rewards patient viewing—this one is worth seeking out and seeing twice. (a.k.a.: *The Legend of Kaspar Hauser*, *The Mystery of Kaspar Hauser*, and *Kaspar Hauser*)

EVERY TIME WE SAY GOODBYE ☆☆☆
1986, USA, PG-13
Tom Hanks, Cristina Marsillach, Benedict Taytlor, Anat Atzmon, Gila Almagor. Directed by Moshe Mizrahi. 97 min.

In an age when glibness and gimmickry sell tickets, it's no wonder that this utterly straightforward and conventional romantic melodrama was a box-office failure. Set in Israel during World War II, it's the story of an American officer (Tom Hanks) commissioned in the RAF and his courtship of a Spanish Jew (Cristina Marsillach) whose ancestors emigrated to the Holy Land long ago. He's the son of a Protestant minister, and her family is virulently protective of its heritage, so the inevitable crux of the film's drama is the clash between the two cultures. The tone is tasteful, muted, and subdued, contrasting well with the tumultuous atmosphere of the setting. Marsillach is attractive, and Hanks modifies his standard comedy persona into an extraordinarily engaging creation; he's a featherweight Paul Newman.

EVERY WHICH WAY BUT LOOSE ☆☆☆
1978, USA, PG
Clint Eastwood, Sondra Locke, Geoffrey Lewis, Beverly D'Angelo, Ruth Gordon. Directed by James Fargo. 114 min.

Caught somewhere between *Beach Blanket Bingo* and a Burt Reynolds trucker's special, this movie is a mess. But it's a mess whose premise is so unpretentious—Clint Eastwood as the butt of his own jokes—that it's hard not to like it. Clint plays a truck driver who is also a top-flight bare-knuckle boxer. He falls for a streetwise country and western singer (Sondra Locke) whom he pursues across the Southwest, with his brother Orville (Geoffrey Lewis, who is a perfect sad-faced foil) and a pet orangutan (Clyde) in tow. *Every Which Way* is about as loose as a movie can get without falling apart.

EVERYTHING HAPPENS AT NIGHT ☆☆½
1939, USA
Sonja Henie, Ray Milland, Robert Cummings, Maurice Moscovitch, Fritz Feld. Directed by Irving Cummings. 76 min.

One of Sonja Henie's better vehicles casts her as the daughter of a Nobel prizewinning scientist, supposedly dead but actually hiding out in Switzerland. Milland and Cummings play two rival reporters out to find the scientist and win his daughter's hand while they're at it. You probably won't be surprised to find that she straps on her ice skates and takes several spins, a few motivated by a winter sports carnival taking place in the village, and a few motivated by nothing aside from the fact that this *is* a Sonja Henie vehicle.

EVERYTHING YOU ALWAYS WANTED TO KNOW ABOUT SEX BUT WERE AFRAID TO ASK ☆☆☆
1972, USA, R
Woody Allen, John Carradine, Lou Jacobi, Louise Lasser, Anthony Quayle, Lynn Redgrave, Tony Randall, Burt Reynolds, Gene Wilder, Meredith MacRae, Geoffrey Holder, Regis Philbin. Directed by Woody Allen. 87 min.

Woody Allen's crash course in sex education is an uneven, but often very funny expedition through the comic territory of fantasy and phobia. Scenarios include Gene Wilder's problematic encounters with a standoffish sheep, a giant breast that ravages the countryside, a subtitled demonstration of exhibitionism Italian-style, and Allen's own impersonation of a cowardly sperm afraid to take the plunge. The final skit is the best.

THE EVICTORS ☆☆
1979, USA, PG
Michael Parks, Jessica Harper, Vic Morrow, Sue Anne Langdon, Jimmy Clem. Directed by Charles B. Pierce. 92 min.

If you've seen *Amityville Horror*, then you have no reason or need to see this, unless you've got a government grant to study relationships between big-budget schlock horror films and their innumerable ripoffs. Happy young couple Parks and Harper buy an old house with an, um, unsavory reputation. Their first hint should have been slimy real estate agent Vic Morrow.

THE EVIL ☆½
1978, USA, R
Richard Crenna, Joanna Pettet, Andrew Prine, Cassie Yates, Lynne Moody, Victor Buono, George O'Hanlon, Jr., Mary Louise Weller, Robert Vihavo. Directed by Gus Trikonis. 89 min.

A doctor, a psychologist, and a professor—all people with too much education and too little common sense in the face of things like supernatural manifestations—decide to turn a deserted mansion into a drug rehabilitation center. They unleash some horrible forces and are soon very sorry they didn't rent a storefront in a run-down neighborhood like other social reformers. Bad special effects undercut the already silly proceedings in this film directed by former dancer Gus Trikonis (*West Side Story*), who also brought us *Dance of the Dwarves*.

THE EVIL DEAD ☆☆½
1983, USA, R
Bruce Campbell, Ellen Sandweiss, Betsy Baker, Hal Delrich, Sarah York. Directed by Sam Raimi. 85 min.

Five young people rent a rotting cabin in the mountains and entertain themselves by reading from a book of incantations. They raise a group of horrific demons who scream, howl, and possess the teenagers to disgusting effect. Conventional genre story, given an intense rending by first-time director Sam Raimi. Audacious camerawork, stylized compositions, and wildly disorienting use of interior space combine with gory special effects to make this a rollercoaster horror movie of rare proportions.

THE EVIL MIND ☆½
1934, Great Britain/USA
Claude Rains, Fay Wray, Jane Baxter, Ben Field, Mary Clare. Directed by Maurice Elvey. 73 min.

This is a very thin tale about a down-on-his-luck mind reader (Claude Rains) who suddenly finds himself in possession of real clairvoyant powers, but only when he's with a certain mysterious woman (Jane Baxter). The soothsayer uses his newfound powers to predict horse races, impending disasters, and some very silly chance events. A love story is somehow woven into the unimaginative plot line, presumably to give Fay Wray a reason to appear. (a.k.a.: *The Clairvoyant*)

THE EVIL THAT MEN DO ☆☆
1984, USA, R
Charles Bronson, Jose Ferrer, Teresa Saldana, Rene Enriquez, Joseph Maher, Antoinette Bower. Directed by J. Lee Thompson. 90 min.

In this farfetched but satisfying thriller Charles Bronson plays a retired professional killer called back into service to knock off the Doctor—a British torture specialist who's been freelancing his services to Latin American countries. Craggy and fit, his eyes glinting with the self-satisfaction of someone who's seen it all, Bronson can hardly be called a man of action anymore: at sixty-two, he's become the serene elder statesman of revenge flicks. But the direction, by veteran hack J. Lee Thompson, works up some lurid heat, especially in the climactic meeting between the Doctor and his victims, a scene almost biblical in its fury.

EVIL UNDER THE SUN ☆☆½
1982, Great Britain, PG
Peter Ustinov, Colin Blakely, Jane Birkin, Maggie Smith, Roddy McDowall, Sylvia Miles, James Mason, Diana Rigg. Directed by Guy Hamilton. 117 min.

This star-studded Agatha Christie romp is superior to *The Mirror Crack'd*, largely because the scenery's prettier. And what else is there to care about in a movie that's practically all piffle? In broad, cartoonish strokes, screenwriter Anthony Shaffer paints in a few traits, a few relationships, and a motive for murder. Peter Ustinov plays Christie's fussy Belgian detective, Hercule Poirot, and he's wonderful—a sort of idiot savant who comes alive only in the magical presence of murder. The other members of the largely British cast manage to get away with outrageously hammy performances. On the whole, the film is a familiar soothing pastime, as briefly engrossing as a crossword puzzle.

EVILSPEAK ☆
1982, USA, R
Clint Howard, R. G. Armstrong, Joseph Cortese, Claude Earl Jones, Haywood Nelson, Charles Tyner. Directed by Eric Weston. 89 min.

Fat outcast orphan Cooper Smith is miserable at the cliqueish military academy he attends until he contacts the malevolent spirit of excommunicated monk Esteban through his personal computer; then all hell breaks loose. One novel idea buried in a swamp of genre clichés cannot make this worth viewing; it's low-level diversion for serious fans only.

EXCALIBUR ☆☆☆
1981, Great Britain, R
Nicol Williamson, Helen Mirren, Nigel Terry, Nicholas Clay, Cherie Lunghi. Directed by John Boorman. 140 min.

John (*Deliverance*) Boorman directed this moody, visually magnificent retelling of the Arthurian legends, shot in Ireland with an austerity and leisure that will surprise anyone expecting a *Conan*-esque swords-and-sorcery epic. All of the familiar characters—Merlin, Arthur, Morgana, Gawain, Lancelot—interact, but their stories are watered-down children's versions. The acting is terrible (with the notable exceptions of Williamson as Merlin and Mirren a a wonderfully malevolent Morgana), but the stories will probably keep many enthralled.

THE EXECUTIONER ☆½
1970, USA, PG
George Peppard, Joan Collins, Judy Geeson, Nigel Patrick, Keith Mitchell. Directed by Sam Wanamaker. 111 min.

Joan Collins's sadly brief appearance in this film is as the wife of Keith Mitchell, a spy whom American-born British agent George Peppard despises for: 1) bungling his last mission; 2) being married to Joan Collins; 3) being a double agent. This sadly un-brief movie follows Peppard's shakedown and debriefing of Mitchell's unsavory past with flashbacks, flash-forwards, and flashlights. For a movie with so many flashes, there are surprisingly few sparks. Collins is dynamite, but the twisted chronology and slow-burning exposition cause this film to fizzle out.

THE EXECUTIONER'S SONG ☆☆☆
1982, USA (TV)
Tommy Lee Jones, Rosanna Arquette, Christine Lahti, Eli Wallach, Jordan Clarke, Steven Keats, Jenny Wright, Pat Corley, Norris Church. Directed by Lawrence Schiller. 157 min.

This film is a gripping television adaptation of Norman Mailer's account of the life and death by execution of murderer Gary Gilmore. Mailer himself compressed his thousand-page tome into a teleplay, and the result, while sometimes spotty, is mostly coherent and compelling, thanks to Tommy Lee Jones's Emmy-winning portrayal of Gilmore and Rosanna Arquette's unusually restrained work as girlfriend Nicole Baker. Note: The video version is approximately forty minutes shorter than the original telecast length but includes graphic footage not seen on television.

EXECUTIVE ACTION ☆☆
1973, USA, PG
Burt Lancaster, Robert Ryan, Will Geer, Gilbert Green, John Anderson. Directed by David Miller. 91 min.

A conspiracy theorist's wet dream semi-disguised as fiction, Executive Action attempts, with painful sincerity, to suggest that Lee Harvey Oswald was a pawn of right-wing American industrial tycoons who wanted John F. Kennedy killed for political reasons. The film's mixture of fact, fiction, and speculation is all given the varnish of truth. Although surprisingly suspenseful, it's also the most irresponsible kind of docudrama—one that intelligently raises legitimate questions about a real event and then offers outlandish, fictionalized answers as logical conclusions. Notable for Robert Ryan's last screen appearance, and a depressingly off-target screenplay by Dalton Trumbo.

EXECUTIVE SUITE ☆☆☆
1954, USA
Fredric March, William Holden, June Allyson, Barbara Stanwyck, Walter Pidgeon, Shelley Winters, Paul Douglas, Louis Calhern, Dean Jagger, Nina Foch. Directed by Robert Wise. 104 min.

Ernest Lehman's intelligent adaptation of Cameron Hawley's novel is not the most incisive commentary on big business machinations, but it suffices as gripping melodrama. When the president of the company has a heart attack and dies (the first and best scene in the film, expertly photographed by George Folsey), the various board members vie for control in a manner not unlike birds of prey. Surprisingly, there are no strong, juicy female roles (even Barbara Stanwyck is stuck playing a masochist). Robert Wise directs with more skill and less excess than usual. "Dynasty" fans take note: This is where a lot of the Carrington/Colby grit originated.

THE EX-LADY ☆☆
1933, USA
Bette Davis, Gene Raymond, Frank McHugh, Monroe Owsley, Claire Dodd. Directed by Robert Florey. 65 min.

This is not one of Bette Davis's best. In this pre-Hays Code feature, she plays a commercial artist who refuses to marry her lover. When he finally gets his way, trouble ensues in the persons of a pair of would-be seducers. Miss Davis's eccentric costumes are the high point of the whole affair.

THE EX-MRS. BRADFORD ☆☆☆
1936, USA
William Powell, Jean Arthur, James Gleason, Eric Blore, Robert Armstrong, Ralph Morgan. Directed by Stephen Roberts. 80 min.

This comedy-mystery was pretty obviously made as an attempt to cash in on the success of The Thin Man, but no one ever said that a rip-off couldn't be fun in its own right. Somewhat more useful a citizen than Nick Charles, William Powell's character here is a physician who trades barbs and quips with, and is drawn into a murder case by, his ex-wife (Jean Arthur, who spars verbally quite as well as Myrna Loy). We presume we won't be giving anything away by telling you that the couple is reunited during the course of the movie—divorce was a no-no in Hollywood, except in the more didactic varieties of melodrama. The mystery itself is well-handled, too, with the expected last-minute wrap-up.

EXODUS ☆☆☆
1960, USA, PG
Paul Newman, Eva Marie Saint, Ralph Richardson, Peter Lawford, Lee J. Cobb, Sal Mineo, John Derek. Directed by Otto Preminger. 212 min.

Otto Preminger's epic-length version of the Leon Uris novel about the Israeli struggle for independence and the Exodus incident, when a group of 400 immigrant Jews took a ship to Palestine despite the opposition of the British Governor of Cyprus, is competent. There are several good performances—by Paul Newman, Ralph Richardson, and Sal Mineo—and some rather mediocre ones—notably by Eva Marie Saint—plus some well-handled set pieces, especially a thrilling prison break. But Dalton Trumbo's script, his first under his own name after his blacklisting, is gushy and ponderous, and the film's length is wearying: After three hours of it at a Hollywood premiere-preview, Mort Sahl reportedly stood, turned to Preminger, and said, "Otto, let my people go." Ernest Gold's score is among his best. Originally in wide-screen Super-Panavision.

THE EXORCIST ☆☆☆☆
1973, USA, R
Ellen Burstyn, Linda Blair, Jason Miller, Max Von Sydow. Directed by William Friedkin. 121 min.

This film is one of the most talked-about and controversial horror movies of all time, ushering in a morbid cycle of occult pictures and a new age of cinematic gore. Director William Friedkin uses countless eye-popping shock effects to tell the blood-curdling story of poor twelve-year-old Regan's horrifying possession by the devil. The more overt of these visceral stunts include 360-degree head spins and geysers of vomit, but it's the more subliminal chills that really get to you—the drone of bees, or the split-second glimpse of the demon itself. Friedkin updates the creepy techniques of old horror films to extremes never dreamed of, and he's also got some very good performances around his effects—including Ellen Burstyn as the girl's shrieking but driven mother, Jason Miller as a doubtful priest, and Linda Blair as the sweetly innocent Regan. Although basically an example of souped-up Gothic storytelling, The Exorcist is more intelligent and scary than the countless imitative pictures that followed it. There is also trendsetting makeup by Dick Smith, and Mercedes McCambridge dubbing in the devil's guttural repartee.

EXORCIST II: THE HERETIC ☆☆½
1977, USA, R
Linda Blair, Richard Burton, Louise Fletcher, Max Von Sydow, Kitty Winn, Paul Henreid, James Earl Jones, Ned Beatty. Directed by John Boorman. 118 min.

Imagine Richard Burton as a priest being pelted with rocks by angry African natives while, somewhere in New York, Linda Blair as a satanically possessed high school student is being tripped during a tap dance number. Picture James Earl Jones as a tribal leader dressed in a toad suit spitting up marbles in Burton's face. Fathom Blair's house being torn down in an impromptu locust swarm. Yes, these are just a few of the cinematic gems written by

William Goodhart and directed by John Boorman (*Deliverance, The Emerald Forest*) in this continuation of *The Exorcist* saga. This may not be the most inane sequel in motion picture history, but it does furnish two hours of solid laughter, which is more than can be said of any four contemporary sitcoms seen back to back. *Note*: The film was reedited after a much-hooted initial release, but this version is the original.

EXPERIENCE PREFERRED... BUT NOT ESSENTIAL ☆☆☆
1983, Great Britain, PG
Elizabeth Edmonds, Sue Wallace, Geraldine Griffith, Karen Meagher, Ron Bain. Directed by Peter Duffell. 80 min.

This gentle, very mild British comedy about a teenage girl who spends a formative summer waitressing at a run-down seaside hotel has a touch of the slightly insane whimsy of Bill Forsyth's films. Before young Annie becomes a woman, she encounters an in-the-closet coworker, a demurely nude sleepwalker, and a thirty-four-year-old runaway, all in a day's work. It's more of a playlet than a full-length film, but Peter Duffell's direction creates a tone of generosity and sorrow, and the final scenes have an unexpected emotional resonance. One of several low-budget films supervised by producer David Puttnam (*Chariots of Fire, The Killing Fields*) under the umbrella title "First Love."

EXPERIMENT IN TERROR ☆☆
1962, USA
Glenn Ford, Lee Remick, Stefanie Powers, Ross Martin, Roy Poole, Ned Glass. Directed by Blake Edwards. 123 min.

Blake Edwards's darkest two hours, a mad-killer-on-the-loose thriller about a homicidal asthmatic (Ross Martin) whose pain-racked breathing is the scariest thing in the movie. Lee Remick plays the bank teller who helps FBI agent Glenn Ford trap Martin after he kidnaps Remick's sister (Stefanie Powers). The atmosphere is full of menacing sexual innuendo that never ignites.

EXPLORERS ☆☆½
1985, USA, PG
Ethan Hawk, River Phoenix, Jason Presson, Dick Miller. Directed by Joe Dante. 109 min.

A group of children takes off into space. The movie starts out like an episode of "The Twilight Zone," but it becomes something more akin to "Monty Python's Flying Circus." The beginning dutifully attempts to re-create the crowd-pleasing techniques of Steven Spielberg as the kids experiment with their ramshackle equipment, but once director Dante's stylized loony humor kicks in, *Explorers*'s tone becomes increasingly strange. By the time the film's aliens appear, what at first seemed like a grand adventure has become a one-joke idea. Kids are sure to love the film, and it has dandy visual effects by George Lucas's Industrial Light and Magic facility.

EXPOSED ☆½
1983, USA, R
Nastassia Kinski, Rudolf Nureyev, Harvey Keitel, Ian McShane, Bibi Andersson. Directed by James Toback. 100 min.

This is a ludicrous international thriller from writer-director James Toback. Toback's films (such as 1978's *Fingers*, a camp classic) are hyperbolic fantasies about characters pulled out of their safe, academic environments and into the maelstrom of lust, money, and murder. In this one, Nastassia Kinski plays a spunky small-town college student who takes off for New York, becomes a famous fashion model, and falls in love with an enigmatic counterterrorist (Rudolf Nureyev, speaking like a cross between Count Dracula ad a remedial reading student). Toback has some fun turning New York City into a sidewalk circus, but when he isn't staging one of his brutal-yet-comic fight scenes, his characters stand around and debate the film's issues. They sound like undergraduate textbooks. A prime candidate for the so-bad-it's-good school, but worth missing nonetheless.

EXPRESS TO TERROR ☆½
1979, USA
Stella Stevens, Steve Lawrence, Telly Savalas, Don Stroud, George Hamilton. Directed by Dan Curtis. 120 min.

It's always comforting to see certain actors in certain lowbrow movies—you just know that Telly Savalas and Stella Stevens aren't going to rise above their material, so you can sit back and enjoy the diversion of a mediocre action pic. A man aboard a trans-American train has to check the upper berths because someone is trying to kill him. Steve Lawrence neither sings nor acts, and he's not lonely on the latter score in this slow-moving express.

THE EXTERMINATOR ½☆
1980, USA, R
Robert Ginty, Christopher George, Samantha Eggar, Steve James. Directed by James Glickenhaus. 101 min.

A Vietnam vet decides to rid New York City of its criminals—with a blowtorch, machine gun, meat grinder, and whatever handy household items he can find. An extremely sick film that tries to evoke public outrage over thievery on the streets but is really just an excuse to unleash Stan Winston's gory, gooey makeup effects. *Death Wish* and *Ms. 45* have trod the same ground with a lot more style and much less torture. By-the-book exploitation that brings a slice of 42nd Street sleaze to your VCR.

EXTERMINATOR 2 ½☆
1984, USA, R
Robert Ginty, Mario Van Peebles, Deborah Geffner, Frankie Faison, Scott Randolph. Directed by Mark Buntzman. 89 min.

This film is a sequel to the grimy 1980 thriller about a Vietnam vet who goes on the revenge trail in New York City. One wishes that a movie-loving exterminator who has had his fill of these exploitative rip-offs of post-Vietnam paranoia would come along and wipe these Viet-vengeance flicks out. Imagine the plot possibilities as a sinewy hero in camouflage fatigues stalks the Hollywood screening circuit and wreaks his revenge.

EXTREMITIES ☆☆½
1986, USA, R
Farrah Fawcett, James Russo, Diana Scarwid, Alfre Woodard. Directed by Robert M. Young. 90 min.

William Mastrosimone's tense, gripping melodrama, adapted from his stage hit, comes off poorly as an effort at serious writing but very well as a piece of theater. The story is built around attempted rape and attempted revenge, with Farrah Fawcett as a young woman assaulted in her home by a vicious would-be rapist who had attacked her a week earlier. In an astoundingly credible physical battle, she manages to outwit and overpower him, and suddenly, attacker becomes captive and victim becomes jailer. Unfortunately, the drama drags in two roommates (poorly played by Scarwid and Woodard) to serve as mouthpieces for a protracted and unconvincing ethical debate that will discomfort some, enrage many, and satisfy very few. Fawcett, who succeeded Susan Sarandon and Karen Allen in the role on stage, gives a solid, believable performance in her toughest role yet, and James Russo is superb as her assailant. Many remarked that only a man would have written a play about rape in which the bad guy gets all the best lines; *Extremities* is worth seeing if only for the arguments it will start.

EYE FOR AN EYE ☆
1981, USA, R
Chuck Norris, Christopher Lee, Richard Roundtree, Matt Clark, Mako, Maggie Cooper. Directed by Steve Carver. 106 min.

This is a Chuck Norris opus in which the martial-arts master single-handedly breaks up a San Francisco narcotics ring. Norris has all the screen personality of a marshmallow, except when kicking his enemies. Wisely, the producers have bolstered his low-voltage acting talents with some energetic performers, including Christopher Lee, Mako, and Richard Roundtree. Maybe this should have been called *A Leg for a Leg*, but as long as Chuck's charismatic thighs and star-quality feet are in motion, Norris fans will be enthralled. We'd like to see Chuck square off against the Rockettes cast as communists who've seized control of the Christmas Show in *Invasion of Radio City Music Hall*.

EYE OF THE NEEDLE ☆☆☆
1981, Great Britain, R
Donald Sutherland, Kate Nelligan, Ian Bannen, Christopher Cazenove, Philip Martin Brown. Directed by Richard Marquand. 112 min.

This grandiose thriller takes place in the sort of romanticized old-movie world where small emotions and inconsequential actions don't exist. Donald Sutherland plays a fiendish Nazi spy who is shipwrecked on a Scottish island during a vital mission. There, he falls in love with radiant Kate Nelligan, and the fate of Europe is soon entangled in the sticky strands of a Harlequin romance. There isn't a believable moment in the entire movie, but director Richard Marquand gives it the compulsive pull of good pulp fiction. The film is based on the Ken Follett best-seller.

EYEBALL ½☆
1978, Italy, R
John Richardson, Martine Brochard, Ines Pellegrin, Silvia Solar. Directed by Umberto Lenzi. 91 min.

This is *not* the sicko movie with the mad doctor who goes around removing people's eyes and then tossing the blinded victims into his dungeon. (Not that we recommend you go see that one, either, but that was *Mansion of the Doomed*.) This is a boring Italian murder mystery that tries to pass itself off as a horror movie for American distribution. The dubbing is awful, the photography is amateurish, and the special effects are thoroughly unbelievable. In short, the film has no saving graces.

THE EYES OF LAURA MARS ☆☆½
1978, USA, R
Faye Dunaway, Tommy Lee Jones, Brad Dourif, Raul Julia. Directed by Irvin Kershner. 104 min.

Faye Dunaway is Laura Mars, a New York fashion photographer whose premonitions about murders turn out to be accurate. It seems her eyes lock with the killer's as a murder is taking place. Parts of the film are scary enough; others are simply gratuitously violent. Although the photography makes *The Eyes of Laura Mars* more stylish than most thrillers, the script isn't quite up to par. Barbra Streisand sings the theme song—this was the first movie produced alone by her then-boyfriend, Jon Peters.

THE EYES, THE MOUTH ☆☆☆
1983, Italy/France, R
Lou Castel, Angelina Molina, Emmanuelle, Riva, Michel Piccoli. Directed by Marco Bellocchio. 110 min.

A young actor, on a visit home after the suicide of his brother, struggles to maintain his own identity in the face of his feelings of responsibility toward his senile mother. He also becomes involved with his brother's fiancée, as the past begins to absorb more and more of his attention. Director Bellocchio is preoccupied with the theme of retaining personal identity in the face of the pressures of middle-class life. This film has a more positive outlook than much of his work.

EYES OF A STRANGER ☆☆½
1981, USA, R
Lauren Tewes, Jennifer Jason Leigh, John DiSanti, Gwen Lewis, Peter Dupre. Directed by Ken Widerhorn. 85 min.

Eyes of a Stranger is what happens when slightly talented people get together to make a fast buck. It's an exceptionally well-made but extremely nasty "slasher" movie about a woman (Lauren Tewes) who thinks her neighbor is the rapist who attacked her younger sister (Jennifer Jason Leigh). There are shades of *Rear Window* and some beautifully shot sequences but, overall, it's the same old misogynistic thriller material that was so popular at the time. *Note*: Some of the more excessive gore was excised before release.

EYES OF TEXAS ☆☆
1948, USA
Roy Rogers, Lynne Robert, Andy Devine. Directed by William Whitney. 71 min.

Roy Rogers and Trigger in color! U.S. Marshall must get to the bottom of some sordid foul play. One of the more exciting Rogers Westerns.

EYEWITNESS ☆☆½
1981, USA, R
William Hurt, Sigourney Weaver, Christopher Plummer, James Woods, Irene Worth. Directed by Peter Yates. 108 min.

The makers of *Breaking Away* (writer Steve Tesich and director Peter Yates) concocted this muddled, unconvincing thriller. Echoing pre-World War II Hollywood melodramas, the film has something to do with getting Russian Jews out from behind the Iron Curtain. Christopher Plummer has the pivotal role of a diplomat with some business on the side. Sigourney Weaver as a TV news reporter and William Hurt as a love-struck janitor are the couple caught up in the intrigue. The plot is so disjointed and confusing, however, that you won't remember how they all connect. A waste of a fine cast. (a.k.a.: *The Janitor*)

F

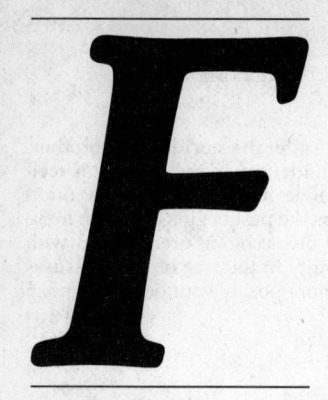

THE FABULOUS DORSEYS ☆☆
1947, USA
Tommy Dorsey, Jimmy Dorsey, Janet Blair, Paul Whiteman, William Laundigan, Art Tatum, Charlie Barnet, Ziggy Elman, Ray Banduc. Directed by Alfred E. Green. 91 min.

Fabulous they may have been, but this film of their life sure isn't. In between "Green Eyes" and "Marie," the bandleader brothers squabble and scuffle over their music and a woman (Janet Blair). Fortunately or unfortunately (depending on whether you value music or acting), the boys play themselves. At least the screenplay is less sentimental and reverential than most in the Hollywood-bio genre.

FABULOUS JOE ☆½
1947, USA
Marie Wilson, Walter Abel, Margot Grahame, Donald Meek. Directed by Bernard Carr, Harve Foster. 60 min.

A mild farce about a family man with a loquacious pooch. Animals who don't let their masters get a word in edgewise are nothing new—Francis the Talking Mule and Mr. Ed, among many others, have their partisans. Aficionados of the anthropomorphic may garner a few chuckles from this inane comedy about the bigmouthed doggie devoted to his henpecked master. Hardly fabulous, but a decent family film.

THE FACE

See *The Magician*

A FACE IN THE CROWD ☆☆☆☆
1957, USA
Andy Griffith, Patricia Neal, Lee Remick, Walter Matthau, Anthony Franciosa. Directed by Elia Kazan. 126 min.

This lacerating satire of the television industry remains one of Elia Kazan's most powerful films. Andy Griffith gives a brilliant, underrated performance as Lonesome Rhodes, a substandard Will Rogers type who is discovered and catapulted to stardom by the niece of a radio station owner (Patricia Neal). Kazan and scenarist Budd Schulberg take shots at everything from the "local-boy-makes-good" phenomenon to false advertising to Marilyn Monroe. The last half hour drags slightly, and the tone is unrelentingly bitter, but the film is always sharp, stinging, funny, and amazingly prophetic.

THE FACE OF FU MANCHU ☆☆½
1965, Great Britain
Christopher Lee, Nigel Green, James Robertson Justice, Karin Dor. Directed by Don Sharp. 90 min.

Taking note of Hammer Studios' success with reviving the horror series of the thirties and forties, some independent producers decided to take Hammer star Christopher Lee and revive another minor thirties series, based on Sax Rohmer's Fu Manchu stories. The series didn't do very well, and this is about the best of them. Lee makes a good Fu, although he doesn't look very Oriental, and he doesn't get much time onscreen. Here he's plotting to dominate the world through the threat of destruction by poison gas. Fortunately, Nayland Smith (Nigel Green) is on hand to put a halt to such nefarious doings. Should have been a lot more fun, but not bad if you can ignore the fact that Dublin, where this was filmed, does not look a whole lot like China, where the film is supposed to be set.

A FACE OF WAR ☆☆☆
1968, USA
Directed by Eugene S. Jones. 72 min.

Amazingly enough, this documentary filmed in Vietnam at the height of the war manages to avoid taking sides, sticking instead to its point that war is a tedious, dirty business. The filmmakers hooked up with a single U.S. Marine Corps regiment and stayed with them for over three months, following the day-to-day duties and experiences of the soldiers, mostly young draftees. That it does not take sides, avoiding political overtones at all costs, may be seen by some as a liability or even (given the nature of the Vietnam conflict in particular) as silent acquiesence in the "necessity" of war. Nevertheless, this is an interesting and compelling document.

THE FACE THAT LAUNCHED A THOUSAND SHIPS

See *The Love of Three Queens*

FACE TO FACE ☆☆☆½
1952, USA
"The Secret Sharer": James Mason, Gene Lockhart, Michael Pate, Albert Sharpe. "The Bride Comes to Yellow Sky": Robert Preston, Marjorie Steele, Minor Watson, James Agee. Directed by John Brahm ("The Secret Sharer") and Bretaigne Windust ("The Bride Comes to Yellow Sky"). 89 min.

These two literary adaptations are equally well done. In "The Secret Sharer," based on Joseph Conrad's story, James Mason plays a sea captain commanding his first ship. He is anxious to establish his authority, but shrinks from doing so when it requires him to mete out harsh punishment to a fugitive stowaway. In "The Bride Comes to Yellow Sky," an amusing death-of-the-Western from Stephen Crane, the last outlaw in the town of Yellow Sky sets out to gun down the sheriff, but is defeated by the latter's new civility. A very enjoyable and worthwhile program.

FACE TO FACE ☆☆☆☆
1976, Sweden, R
Liv Ullmann, Erland Josephson, Gunnar Bjornstrand, Aino Taube-Henrikson, Kari Sylwan, Sif Ruud. Directed by Ingmar Bergman. 136 min.

On the same day Dino De Laurentiis released the abominable *Lipstick*, the enterprising entrepreneur offered Ingmar Bergman's brilliant *Face to Face* to American audiences. Originally filmed as a four-part series for Swedish television, but repackaged into a single feature (as with Bergman's *Scenes from a Marriage*), *Face to Face* is a shattering examination of one woman's nervous breakdown. Bergman reworks many of his career-long themes and concerns, and the film can be seen as a distaff version of his celebrated *Wild Strawberries*. His script offers Liv Ullmann the most challenging role of her career, and she gives a bravura performance as an analyst plunging into the depths of her own madness. Ullmann is particularly devastating in a monologue sequence following her character's attempted suicide. Released just before Bergman's famous bout with Swedish tax authorities and his own nervous breakdown, *Face to Face* is often downbeat but ultimately life-affirming.

FADE TO BLACK ☆☆
1980, USA, R
Dennis Christopher, Linda Kerridge, Tim Thomerson, Morgan Paul, Marya Small. Directed by Vernon Zimmerman. 100 min.

A young man (Dennis Christopher) obsessed with the movies—and Marilyn Monroe in particular—murders his foes in ways reminiscent of his movie heroes (Dracula, The Mummy, Cody Jarrett, etc.). Showy horror film premise is given mechanical, predictable treatment; it never develops into anything more than a slasher movie for old-movie buffs. Christopher does what he can with the cinephilic psycho role and provides the film's few genuinely creepy moments.

FAHRENHEIT 451 ☆☆☆
1966, Great Britain
Oskar Werner, Julie Christie, Cyril Cusak, Anton Diffring, Jeremy Spenser. Directed by François Truffaut. 113 min.

François Truffaut's first English-language film is a dry affair, though to what extent that is intentional is open to question. Based on the novel by Ray Bradbury, the film is set in a future time in which all books have been banned and special squads of "firemen" are paid by the State to burn any reading material they can confiscate. One of these firemen, who considers himself simply an average citizen doing his job, becomes involved with a young woman who raises doubts in his mind about the justification of a totalitarian state. Truffaut's conception of the future here, like Bradbury's, is pointedly bleak and vacuous, resulting in a film that has more intellectual than emotional rewards.

FAIL SAFE ☆☆☆½
1964, USA
Henry Fonda, Walter Matthau, Fritz Weaver, Dan O'Herlihy, Larry Hagman. Directed by Sidney Lumet. 111 min.

Sidney Lumet's ever-timely, politically provocative Cold War parable is almost all talk and no action, but this does not make it any less suspenseful. When an accident triggers an unintended mission to bomb Moscow and the bomber cannot be recalled, the President of the United States (Henry Fonda) must figure out a way to avert an all-out doomsday war. With various characters representing different opinions about the nightmare at hand, the film becomes a powerful debate with built-in hypotheticals and a terrifying race-against-the-clock momentum.

FAIRYTALES ☆½
1979, USA, R
Irwin Corey, Nai Bonet, Martha Reeves, Don Sparks, Sy Richardson, Brenda Fogarty. Directed by Harry Tampa. 83 min.

A prurient musical with sets so cheap you can see them wobble and dirty jokes so old you can smell the decay. That being said, this is amusing in an irresistibly bad way. It's as if the Brothers Grimm had become oversexed and designed these sleazy storybook tales for bachelor parties everywhere. If you believe that burlesque is dead, then you'll want to view its corpse here in *Fairytales* as scantily clad cuties play fairy-tale heroines in scantily developed sketches revolving around an impotent Prince Charming. With bawdy tunes, belly dances, and the world's first sadomasochistic musical production number.

FAKE-OUT ☆½
1982, USA
Pia Zadora, Desi Arnaz, Jr., Telly Savalas, Larry Storch, Buddy Lester. Directed by Matt Cimber. 89 min.

Less a movie to showcase the plush charms of Pia Zadora than an extended commercial for her hubby's real estate holdings in Vegas, where this film was shot. Zadora portrays a hostile witness torn between spilling the beans on the Syndicate and cooling her heels in prison. The height of this gangland lunacy is reached when she teaches an aerobics class in prison (thus paving the way for Jane Fonda to do an all-exercise remake of *Caged*). We hope this doesn't start a trend toward "hot properties" in which other moguls star their girlfriends in their favorite hotels, casinos, and condos.

THE FALCON AND THE SNOWMAN ☆☆☆½
1985, USA, R
Timothy Hutton, Sean Penn, David Suchet, Pat Hingle, Lori Singer, Dorian Harewood, Boris Leskin. Directed by John Schlesinger. 132 min.

This challenging, frightening, and often bleakly funny American parable is based on the ill-fated escapades of Christopher Boyce and Daulton Lee, two young Californians who casually sold CIA secrets to the Soviet government. Director John Schlesinger doesn't try to make heroes out of the two, but he does provide compelling insights into the forces and circumstances that brought about their treachery. Steven Zaillian's script packs every scene with rich, quirky detail, and the acting is remarkable. Timothy Hutton, as the politically naive "Falcon," does his most sensitive work since *Ordinary People*, and, as his friend, the hustling, dope-dealing courier "Snowman," Penn gives one of the most calculated, complex, and intelligent performances by a young actor in years. His scenes with David Suchet, who plays the cool but eager Russian contact, are biting, witty, and truthful, the high points of a fine, disturbing film.

THE FALCON IN MEXICO ☆☆
1944, USA
Tom Conway, Mona Maris, Martha MacVicar, Nestor Paiva. Directed by William Berke. 70 min.

In this average entry in the Falcon series, our dapper hero is enlisted by a young girl to recover a portrait of herself. What intrigues him—he doesn't take on just *any* case, you know—is that the artist who painted it was supposed to have died fifteen years previously. Some Mexican location shooting gives this a better veneer than the usual B product.

THE FALCON'S ADVENTURE ☆☆
1946, USA
Tom Conway, Madge Meredith, Edward S. Brophy, Robert Warwick, Jason Robards. Directed by William Berke. 61 min.

This was the last of RKO's eleven Falcon mysteries, and the studio certainly seemed to have run out of titles by this point. Tom Conway waxes up his pencil-thin mustache and postpones his vacation once again in order to help a Brazilian beauty pursued by thieves—it seems she has her father's secret formula for manufacturing synthetic diamonds. Thanks to the Falcon's involvement, the formula is retrieved and we can today buy synthetic diamonds advertised on endless 3 A.M. television commercials.

THE FALCON TAKES OVER ☆☆☆
1942, USA
George Sanders, Lynn Bari, James Gleason, Anne Revere, Hans Conried. Directed by Irving Reis. 63 min.

This is a B film with an impeccable literary pedigree, since it's a loose adaptation of Raymond Chandler's *Farewell My Lovely* (with the Falcon stepping into Philip Marlowe's gumshoes). All the Falcon's sleuthing experiences from other entries in the series stand him in good stead here. The detective action is rousing, with the Falcon protecting a man who's ransoming a stolen necklace and also tangling with a man fleeing prison in order to pursue his wandering girlfriend. Tantalizing detective fare.

FALLEN ANGEL ☆☆☆
1945, USA
Dana Andrews, Alice Faye, Linda Darnell, Charles Bickford, Anne Revere, John Carradine. Directed by Otto Preminger. 97 min.

Otto Preminger followed up his successful *Laura* with this melodrama about a cad (Dana Andrews) who plans to throw over his wife (Alice Faye) for another woman (Linda Darnell). The plot thickens when Darnell is murdered and Andrews becomes the chief suspect. Harry Kleiner's screenplay based on Marty Holland's novel is tightly knit and the culprit is a genuine surprise, though not as daring a character choice as might be hoped for from the roundup of suspects. It's never as sharp as *Laura*, but Preminger and cinematographer Joseph LaShelle create memorable images of the noirish side of small-town life.

FALLEN ANGEL ☆☆☆
1981, USA (TV)
Dana Hill, Melinda Dillon, Richard Masur, Ronny Cox, David Hayward, Virginia Kiser. Directed by Robert Michael Lewis. 102 min.

Child pornography is the subject of this unusually hard-hitting, intelligent TV drama about a young runaway (Dana Hill) and the sinister photographer (Richard Masur) who finds his subjects by coaching a local girls' softball team. The impact of the story is only slightly diminished by the schematic nature of Lew Hunter's teleplay and the restraint necessary to meet the requirements of network standards-and-practices boards. Nothing is held back, however, in the superb performances of Hill and Masur; their work probably earned *Fallen Angel* its Emmy nomination for Outstanding Drama Special.

FALLEN IDOL ☆☆☆☆
1948, Great Britain
Ralph Richardson, Michèle Morgan, Bobby Henrey, Sonia Dresdel, Jack Hawkins. Directed by Carol Reed. 94 min.

Carol Reed has masterfully fashioned this suspenseful and romantic fairy tale from an excellent short story by Graham Greene. The script, also by Greene, details the anguish suffered by a statesman's son (Bobby Henrey) when he thinks that he has seen his idol, the family butler (Ralph Richardson), kill his shrewish wife. This is one of those rare films that center around a child's point of view without seeming naive or condescending. Despite Henrey's jarring German accent and Michèle Morgan's excessive sullenness (playing the butler's mistress), the performances are impeccable. Also notable are the lighting and camerawork, which complement each other elegantly, culminating in an exhilarating and noirish sequence in which the boy, the butler, and the mistress gleefully play hide-and-seek throughout the house while they believe that the wife is on a trip. The film's conclusion threatens to become grim and depressing (as in the original story), but Reed provides a twist that will probably satisfy everyone. Passionate and perceptive work from the director at his peak.

THE FALLEN SPARROW ☆☆☆
1943, USA
John Garfield, Maureen O'Hara, Walter Slezak, Patricia Morrison, John Banner. Directed by Richard Wallace. 94 min.

A stylish, suspenseful thriller that prefigures many a postwar film noir and features another powerhouse of a performance from John Garfield. A Spanish Civil War veteran returns to America after two years of torture in a fascist prison, but his ordeal begins anew as he's pursued by agents desperate to discover the secret that he wouldn't divulge during his captivity. Some people mistake this for an Alfred Hitchcock film; while it lacks the Master's dark humor, it does dish out the thrills with surprising regularity and force.

FALLING IN LOVE ☆☆½
1984, USA, PG-13
Meryl Streep, Robert De Niro, Jane Kaczmarek, Harvey Keitel, David Clennon, Dianne Wiest. Directed by Ulu Grosbard. 107 min.

It's often been said that the greatest actors can hold an audience's attention just by reading from the phone book. In *Falling in Love*, Robert De Niro and Meryl Streep come amazingly close to doing just that, and succeeding. Their unabashedly weepy vehicle is an updated *Brief Encounter* about two married suburbanites who meet and fall in love on their daily commute. The notion that infidelity can create a movie-sized emotional crisis in the eighties is endearing, but the screenplay is predictable, schematic, and often inarticulate—it's about as generic a romantic drama as you could imagine. De Niro and Streep are nonetheless awesome, creating characters far more human and complex than the script warrants. See it as a textbook case of great acting in a void.

FALLING IN LOVE AGAIN ☆☆
1980, USA, PG
Elliott Gould, Susannah York, Stuart Paul, Kaye Ballard, Michelle Pfeiffer. Directed by Steven Paul. 103 min.

Steven Paul's first time at the director's bat is a pointless exercise in nostalgia. Paul also produced and cowrote this story of a New York businessman who reminisces about the good old days (1940s Bronx) and learns what is really important in life. Susannah York is miscast as Elliott Gould's wife (she also had a hand in the screenplay), but their scenes are so brief that it hardly matters. The bulk of the film is about jitterbugging teens with growing pains and noisy mothers. A second-rate *Summer of '42* and a fourth-rate *Wild Strawberries*.

THE FALL OF THE HOUSE OF USHER ☆☆☆½
1960, USA
Vincent Price, Mark Damon, Myrna Fahey, Harry Ellerbe. Directed by Roger Corman. 79 min.

The first in a long line of Roger Corman–Vincent Price adaptations of Edgar Allan Poe stories, this is one of the best; it was also American-International Pictures's first big success, and pulled them out of the drive-in double-bill policy of filmmaking they adhered to in the fifties. A young man comes to the Usher family estate to claim his fiancée and learns from cadaverous Roderick Usher (Price) of the family's history of madness and Usher's intent that the line end with him. This is a very effective film, a close second to the following year's *The Pit and the Pendulum*. (a.k.a.: *House of Usher*)

THE FALL OF THE HOUSE OF USHER ☆½
1982, USA (TV)
Martin Landau, Robert Hays, Charlene Tilton, Ray Walston. Directed by James L. Conway. 101 min.

Yet another attempt to make a feature film from one of Edgar Allan Poe's masterful, inherently literate short stories. Reduced to a television movie, it becomes undistinguished haunted-house stuff in the hands of the screenwriter. Originally made in 1978, but not shown until 1982, which should tell you something.

THE FALL OF THE ROMAN EMPIRE ☆☆☆½
1964, USA
Alec Guinness, Sophia Loren, Stephen Boyd, James Mason, Christopher Plummer, Anthony Quayle, John Ireland, Mel Ferrer, Omar Sharif, Eric Porter. Directed by Anthony Mann. 185 min.

This is a rare example of an intelligently done epic film that benefits from superior contributions in all areas of production. Besides the outstanding cast, all of whom have substantial roles rather than the usual star "cameos," the film has a good claim to verisimilitude (Will Durant, coauthor of the standard reference work *The Story of Civilization*, served as consultant), a director who was at his best with wide-screen Westerns (useful experience for historical epics, as Mann proved a few years earlier with *El Cid*), a capable second-unit director (former stuntman Yakima Canutt) to keep the action scenes moving, and a musical score by Dimitri Tiomkin, one of Hollywood's best. Politically astute and played for maximum drama, this stands far above the usual TV miniseries treatment of historical topics.

FALSTAFF

See *Chimes at Midnight*

FAME
1980, USA, R   ☆☆☆
Irene Cara, Debbie Allen, Lee Curreri, Barry Miller, Paul McCrane, Gene Anthony Ray, Maureen Teefy, Anne Meara, Albert Hague. Directed by Alan Parker. 134 min.

Alan Parker's joyful, exuberant portrait of eight talented students and their four-year odyssey through New York's High School of Performing Arts comes alive with great music (by Michael Gore), energetic choreography (by Louis Falco), and a large cast of bright newcomers. The drawback here is Parker's insistence on having each kid get an angst-ridden, grandstanding scene of his own, until the film is awash in melodrama. But the first half hour, covering auditions, is a masterpiece of funky, frenetic editing. *Fame* as a whole is much grittier and smarter than the relentlessly cheerful TV series it spawned.

FAME IS THE SPUR
1947, Great Britain   ☆☆☆
Michael Redgrave, Rosamund John, Bernard Miles, Hugh Burden, Jean Shepheard, David Tomlinson. Directed by John and Roy Boulting. 116 min.

A very British drama that may confound those with no knowledge of British politics, particularly the long-standing antipathy between the Labour Party and the Tories (the major liberal and conservative elements, respectively), though it could serve as an education to those who are interested. A North Country slum boy, following the example of his grandfather, resolves to go into politics to help his oppressed fellowman. As he rises to the position of cabinet minister, his ideals fall by the wayside, and he becomes more concerned with position and power. The film is rather dry, especially considering that the Boulting Brothers became noted for comedies in the forties and fifties, but realistically made. Supposedly based on the career of Ramsay MacDonald.

THE FAMILY
1970, Italy/France   ☆☆½
Charles Bronson, Telly Savalas, Jill Ireland, Michael Constantine, George Savalas, Umberto Osini. Directed by Sergio Sollima. 100 min.

Lina Wertmüller cowrote this violent, stylish thriller filmed in New Orleans and the Virgin Islands. Bronson is his usual cool self as a hired gun who comes up against the mob when he seeks revenge on the crime boss who framed him and stole his girlfriend. Director Sollima tries to get past the clichés in the script by steamrolling over them; he doesn't succeed, but at least the film doesn't stand still long enough for you to be aware of them.

FAMILY ENFORCER
1977, USA, R   ☆☆
Joe Pesci, Joseph Cortese, Keith Davis, Ann Johns. Directed by Ralph DeVito. 89 min.

Check your hat and all questions of logic at the door. A promising mob apprentice is in a terrific hurry to move to the head of the class but doesn't realize that a crash course in crime is going to be a dangerous proposition. The gunfire flashes; the blood flows; the predictable "crime-doesn't-pay" story line resolves itself as expected.

FAMILY LIFE
1971, Great Britain   ☆☆☆½
Sandy Ratcliff, Bill Dean, Grace Cave. Directed by Ken Loach. 105 min.

Originally made for British television, this pseudodocumentary about a teenage girl's descent into schizophrenia was expanded for theatrical release, but without any obvious padding. The girl's parents are middle-class Brits who worked to make a good life for themselves and their family and are determined to keep it; when one daughter breaks away from them, they tighten their grip on the other, younger one. As the girl withdraws increasingly from the world around her, her parents unintentionally aggravate her situation by restricting her freedom. The ending is harrowing and bleak, made all the more so by the film's refusal to deal in stereotypes—the parents are seen not as ogres but as well intentioned and misguided. All of the main performances are excellent. (a.k.a: *Wednesday's Child*)

FAMILY PLOT
1976, USA, PG   ☆☆☆
Karen Black, Bruce Dern, Barbara Harris, William Devane, Cathleen Nesbitt, Katherine Helmond. Directed by Alfred Hitchcock. 120 min.

Alfred Hitchcock's final film is a clunky but amusing bauble about a phony psychic (the engagingly scattered Barbara Harris) who, along with boyfriend Bruce Dern, stumbles into a big-time kidnapping caper. Hitchcock soft-pedals the suspense to concentrate on humor (much of which is rather forced), but he's got one nice pursuit scene in a graveyard, as well as Karen Black and William Devane as a juicy pair of villains. Watch for Hitch behind an office door.

A FAMILY UPSIDE DOWN
1978, USA (TV)   ☆☆½
Fred Astaire, Helen Hayes, Efrem Zimbalist, Jr., Patty Duke Astin, Pat Crowley, Brad Rearden, Gary Swanson. Directed by David Lowell Rich. 104 min.

Fred Astaire and Helen Hayes are the main attractions in this otherwise run-of-the-mill telefilm about an aged couple whose lives are thrown into turmoil when one suffers a heart attack, forcing them to become dependent on their grown children. Predictably, issues are glossed over in favor of calculating sentiment and simplified solutions, but the cast, led by Astaire's Emmy-winning turn, is highly effective.

THE FAN
1981, USA, R   ☆☆
Lauren Bacall, Michael Biehn, Maureen Stapleton, James Garner, Hector Elizondo. Directed by Edward Bianchi. 95 min.

Broadway musical star Sally Ross (Lauren Bacall) is too busy trying to win back her ex-husband (James Garner) to notice the letters she's been getting from a demented admirer (Michael Biehn). Based on a truly exciting little novel by Bob Randall, *The Fan* has lost all of the book's humor and added much sour violence. The Broadway-style numbers are one of the few things to enjoy in the film. Bacall, in a rare contemporary screen role, is competent. Maureen Stapleton comes off best, however, as Sally's secretary, taking a small role and making the most of it.

FANDANGO
1985, USA, PG   ☆☆☆
Kevin Costner, Judd Nelson, Sam Robards, Chuck Bush, Brian Cesak, Marvin J. McIntyre. Directed by Kevin Reynolds. 91 min.

A meandering, funny, and finally quite touching passage-to-manhood story. In 1971 five guys, the Groovers, leave their college graduation to embark on an alcohol-hazed journey down to the Texas-Mexico border to fulfill a pledge they made as freshmen. The dream of friendship forever is clouded by the specter that awaits them all—Vietnam. Writing and directing for the first time, Kevin Reynolds has a tendency to make his story's structure and symbolism overexplicit, but he succeeds in sustaining a delicate flickering of merriment and sorrow throughout. His handling of the relationships and performances is exemplary, and Kevin Costner (*Silverado*, *American Flyers*) is a particularly appealing and graceful presence as the leader of the pack. Produced by Steven Spielberg's company, Amblin Entertainment.

FANNY ☆☆☆
1932, France
Raimu, Pierre Fresnay, Orane Demazis. Directed by Marc Allegret. 128 min.

In the second part of Marcel Pagnol's lovely trilogy about the tempestuous love affair of Marius (Pierre Fresnay) and Fanny (Orane Demazis), Marius is off at sea and Fanny, pregnant by Marius, finds a husband with the aid of Marius's father, César (Raimu). Marc Allegret directed. Preceded by *Marius*; followed by *César*.

FANNY ☆☆☆
1961, USA
Leslie Caron, Maurice Chevalier, Charles Boyer, Horst Buchholz, Salvatore Baccaloni, Georgette Anys. Directed by Joshua Logan. 133 min.

This poignant film drama would be all the more so if it weren't up against such an impressive pedigree: the three Pagnol films (*Marius*, *Fanny*, *César*) and the 1954 Joshua Logan–S. N. Behrman stage musical. It still works as the bittersweet tale of a young Marseilles girl whose belated reunion with the sailor who fathered her baby causes despair for everyone. Logan cast *Gigi* stars Caron and Chevalier, but wisely dropped the songs from his musical play (Harold Rome's score can still be heard in the background). Logan gets charm from Boyer and Chevalier, plaintiveness from Caron and Buchholz, and a collective lump in the throat from the audience. Lovely color photography by Jack Cardiff.

FANNY AND ALEXANDER ☆☆☆☆
1983, Sweden
Pernilla Allwin, Bertil Guve, Ewa Fröling, Allan Edwall, Gunn Wallgren, Jan Malmsjö, Jarl Kulle, Erland Josephson, Harriet Andersson. Directed by Ingmar Bergman. 197 min.

Fanny and Alexander is, in many ways, the consummate film of Ingmar Bergman's career, a resounding affirmation that a film can create a complex world and solve all of its problems with delicacy and sympathy. With a narrative spun on the grand scale of a huge, colorful tapestry, Bergman has created the personal history of the Ekdahls, a Swedish theatrical family whose life together in a provincial town at the turn of the century possesses a combination of eroticism, humor, warmth, and imagination that, in Bergman's telling, glows like a vision of domestic grace. The film concentrates on the family's two youngest members, Fanny and Alexander, a brother and sister whose charmed childhood in the family theater is abruptly ended when their father dies and their beautiful mother (played by celebrated Swedish actress Ewa Fröling) remarries, exiling them to the home of the town's severe, tormented bishop. The family rallies against their fate, however, and here Erland Josephson gives one of his most delightful performances as a Jewish magician (and beau of the family matriarch) whose spellbinding illusions reunite the Ekdahl clan and give the film some of its most stunning cinematic effects. Without a doubt Bergman's most life-affirming film, *Fanny and Alexander* is a celebration of the world of theatrical art and artifice as well as an exploration of the world of cinematic self-expression that Bergman has constructed throughout his career. 1984 Academy Award for Best Foreign Film.

FANTASIES ☆
1976, USA
Bo Derek. Directed by John Derek. 81 min.

Lurid peep show effort to unveil the splendiferous charms of Bo Derek in her teendom, long before Blake Edwards discovered she was a 10. John Derek photographs this incipient love goddess with all the finesse of a chicken hawk about to pounce. Bo's imperturbable face registers little emotion as she is pursued by panting men at an island resort. Awful.

FANTASTIC ANIMATION FESTIVAL ☆☆☆
1977, USA, PG
Animated. Various directors. 91 min.

A collection of animations from all over the world. It includes Will Vinton and Bob Gardiner's Oscar-winning *Closed Mondays*; Ian Eames's *French Windows*, with music by Pink Floyd; Steven Lisberger's *Cosmic Cartoon*; Jeffrey Hale and Derek Lamb's *The Last Cartoon Man*, Cat Stevens's *Moonshadow* (with music by guess who); Randy Cartwright's *Room and Board*; Marv Newland's *Bambi Meets Godzilla*; Jordan Belson's *Light*; Max Fleisher's *Superman vs. The Mechanical Monsters*; and Robert Swarthe's *Kick Me*.

THE FANTASTIC BALLOON VOYAGE ☆☆
1976, Mexico, PG
Hugo Stiglitz, Jeff Cooper, Carman Vicarte, Carlos East, Zamorita. Directed by Rene Cardona, Jr. 100 min.

This acceptable children's adventure tale is based on Jules Verne's *Five Weeks in a Balloon*. Like *Around the World in 80 Days*, it's a series of tame international adventures, this time led by a nineteenth-century explorer who sets out to cross Africa by balloon. If you want something for the whole family, a better choice is the Hollywood adaptation of the same story, *Five Weeks in a Balloon*.

FANTASTIC PLANET ☆☆☆½
1973, France/Czechoslovakia
Animated. Directed by René Laloux. 72 min.

René Laloux's exhilarating animation concerns a distant planet populated by two races of people: the giant blue intelligentsia known as the Draags and the tiny, primitive, human-esque Oms, who are threatened with extinction. Surreal and captivating.

FANTASTIC VOYAGE ☆☆☆
1966, USA
Stephen Boyd, Raquel Welch, Donald Pleasence, Arthur Kennedy, Edmond O'Brien, James Brolin. Directed by Richard Fleischer. 100 min.

The most expensively produced sci-fi epic of the pre-2001 era, this imaginative microcosmic fantasy turns the inside of the human body into an op art wonderland as it tells the story of a miniaturized-submarine team traveling through a man's bloodstream in an attempt to heal a clot in his brain. This may be the only science-fiction film whose climax is generated by a butterfingered nurse; if you can accept the premise, it's good corny fun.

FANTASY ISLAND ☆☆
1977, USA (TV)
Ricardo Montalban, Hervé Villechaize, Bill Bixby, Sandra Dee, Peter Lawford, Carol Lynley, Hugh O'Brian, Eleanor Parker, Victoria Principal, Dick Sargent. Directed by Richard Lang. 102 min.

The premise of this series pilot seemed more entertaining before it was rehashed 500 times over the following six years. People with a chip on their shoulder and cash in their wallet can board a plane to a tropical paradise and live out their fantasies for one weekend—but, of course, things never turn out quite as imagined. Presiding over it all are the white-suited Mr. Roarke (Ricardo Montalban) and his thigh-high sidekick Tattoo (Hervé Villechaize). As might be expected, the three stories anthologized here are somewhat more interesting than the ones that followed—but that's not saying much. A second pilot, *Return to Fantasy Island*, followed.

THE FAR COUNTRY ☆☆☆
1955, USA
James Stewart, Walter Brennan, Ruth Roman, Corinne Calvet, John McIntyre, Jay C. Flippen, Henry Morgan. Directed by Anthony Mann. 97 min.

This rousing cattle-drive drama was the fifth collaboration between star James Stewart and director Anthony Mann, whose work together yielded a collection of excellent no-frills Westerns including *Winchester '73*, *Bend of the River*, and *The Naked Spur*. This one is more of a "Northern," with Stewart and Walter Brennan herding their beef through mining camps on their way to Alaska; the cattle aren't the only ones getting pushed around, and eventually the two have to fight rustlers, swindlers, and gold diggers. Solid, well-acted fun.

FAREWELL, MY LOVELY ☆☆☆
1975, Great Britain, R
Robert Mitchum, Charlotte Rampling, John Ireland, Sylvia Miles. Directed by Dick Richards. 95 min.

Director Dick Richards tries to weave all the complex threads of Raymond Chandler's taut, hard-boiled classic into this salute to *film noir*. Richards can't quite pull it off, but he does manage an intelligent, stylish evocation of Philip Marlowe's seedy Los Angeles milieu. Richards picked Robert Mitchum—already a *film noir* icon—to play Marlowe. Mitchum makes a good Marlowe, but Bogart and Dick Powell were both more effective as the tough, lonely, incorruptible private eye. Charlotte Rampling is sexy and dangerous as the female lead.

A FAREWELL TO ARMS ☆☆½
1932, USA
Helen Hayes, Gary Cooper, Adolphe Menjou, Mary Phillips. Directed by Frank Borzage. 78 min.

The most celebrated version of Hemingway's novel contains Helen Hayes's sappy but earnest performance as a nurse who gives herself to an ambulance driver (Cooper) attached to the Italian Army during World War I. Frank Borzage invests much of the film with a strange, brooding quality, and Charles Lang's Oscar-winning camerawork is fluid and graceful. Unfortunately, the story is creaky, slow-moving, and far more romantic than Hemingway would have wanted.

THE FAR FRONTIER ☆☆
1949, USA
Roy Rogers, Gail Davis, Andy Devine, Frances Ford, Clayton Moore, Trigger. Directed by William Witney. 53 min.

A sturdy, well-paced Western. Roy uncovers an insidious smuggling scheme, sings about the far frontier, and punches out Clayton Moore, the man who would later become The Lone Ranger. The original Republic release was sixty-seven minutes long, in Trucolor. Although the box claimed that the tape was "produced from the original movie negative," the NTA Home Entertainment video version we saw was made from a television print, fourteen minutes shorter, and in black and white, as well as having periodic blackouts where the commerical interruptions would have been.

THE FARMER'S DAUGHTER ☆☆☆½
1947, USA
Loretta Young, Joseph Cotten, Charles Bickford, Ethel Barrymore, Rose Hobart, James Arness, Keith Andes, Harry Davenport. Directed by H. C. Potter. 97 min.

This top-notch political comedy should please even contemporary feminists. Loretta Young (stepping in for Ingrid Bergman) plays a wide-eyed but strong-willed Swedish woman who leaves her Minnesota farm, takes a job as a maid for a city congressman, then ends up running for Congress herself. Young (who won an Oscar) successfully portrays Katie Holstrom as both endearingly naive and irritatingly stiff-collared, and she is given impressive support by the Selznick stock company: Joseph Cotten as the employer-turned-boyfriend, Ethel Barrymore as his politically influential mother, and Charles Bickford as Katie's campaign manager. While the production lacks visual flair, that is compensated for by the engrossing content. Note: this *Farmer's Daughter* should not be confused with the 1940 film by the same title or any of the versions of *The Farmer Takes a Wife* or *The Farmer's Wife*.

THE FAR PAVILIONS ☆☆
1984, USA (TV)
Ben Cross, Amy Irving, John Gielgud, Omar Sharif, Rossano Brazzi. Directed by Peter Duffell. 108 min.

The Far Pavilions promises glamour, intrigue, and romance set against the splendors of inscrutable India. Visually, it delivers the goods, with impeccable costuming, gorgeous cinematography, and an elegant-looking, largely British cast. Unfortunately, the sight of blue-eyed Amy Irving as a bronzed Indian princess is wildly incongruous—she makes Shirley MacLaine in *Around the World in 80 Days* look like Indira Gandhi. The film's Indian flavor is about as authentic as Nehru jackets worn by rock stars of the sixties. Still, India photographs beautifully and escapists may take this Taj Mahal Harlequin romance to their hearts. The videocassette version is a massive but perhaps beneficial truncation of the original 360-minute miniseries.

FAST BREAK ☆☆
1979, USA, PG
Gabriel Kaplan, Harold Sylvester, Mike Warren, Bernard King, Reb Brown. Directed by Jack Smight. 197 min.

Tight, cautious Gabe Kaplan (TV's Kotter) stars in a college basketball comedy so determined to be harmless that you hardly notice it's there. Most of the very mild charm derives from the casting of several real athletes in the ball-playing roles; Bernard King, the Knicks's star forward, is especially engaging, and former UCLA guard Michael Warren (from TV's "Hill Street Blues") has his moments. Jack Smight (*Midway*) directed, badly.

FASTER PUSSYCAT, KILL KILL! ☆½
1966, USA
Susan Bernard, Tura Satana, Lori Williams, Stuart Lancaster, Paul Trinka. Directed by Russ Meyer. 84 min.

Three thrill-hungry, amply endowed maidens kick a man to death with some well-placed karate kicks, then kidnap his girlfriend and drag her off to a desert retreat for a sordid round of rape, sadomasochistic acts, and other unsalubrious pursuits. It's a sexploitation celebration of violence that's distasteful but full of raunchy energy.

THE FASTEST GUN ALIVE ☆☆☆
1956, USA
Glenn Ford, Jeanne Crain, Broderick Crawford, Russ Tamblyn, Allyn Joslyn, Leif Erickson, John Dehner, Noah Beery, Rhys Williams, Chubby Johnson. Directed by Russell Rouse. 89 min.

Hollywood adapts the "If-you-can't-beat-'em,-steal-from-'em" ploy: after 3-D, Cinemascope, Smell-O-Vision, and other such gimmicks failed to draw audiences away from those little boxes in their living rooms, and after *Marty*, a Hollywood adaptation of a TV drama, walked off with all the Oscars in 1955, TV-to-movie adaptations became the big thing. This one is fairly good because the original script by Frank Gilroy was adapted by himself and the director, and it was strong enough to make the transition. Peaceable shopkeeper Glenn Ford tries to hide a reputation for being the fastest quick-draw artist in the Old West because he knows that it's only a matter of time until someone quicker shows up. It still shows some TV-drama flaws, like the trick ending, but it's a good role for Ford and well played all around.

FAST FORWARD ☆½
1984, USA, PG
John Scott Clough, Don Franklin, Tamara Mark. Directed by Sidney Poitier. 100 min.

An essentially boring "Hey-kids-let's-put-on-a-show" story tricked up with break dancing, punk fashions, and interracial relationships, set in a fantasy New York where street gangs fight their turf wars on the dance floor without a modicum of bloodshed.

Eight Midwestern adolescents leave home to compete in a talent competition; complications arise arbitrarily and, once they have helped propel the narrative along its merry way, are swept away with an inane line of dialogue. Much dull disco singing and unhip dancing.

FAST TALKING ☆☆
1985, Australia
Rod Zuanic, Tony Allaylis, Chris Truswell, Gail Sweeny, Steve Bisley. Directed by Ken Cameron. 93 min.

Juvenile delinquents may not be the same all around the world, but films about them are. Despite its stunningly arid Sydney setting, this import about a high-school petty thief (Rod Zuanic) is as earnest and well intentioned as an American TV movie. Its mild exoticism alone makes it slightly appealing, and the Eurogliders contribute some good songs, but this is as formulaic as they come.

FAST TIMES AT RIDGEMONT HIGH ☆☆☆
1982, USA, R
Sean Penn, Phoebe Cates, Jennifer Jason Leigh, Ray Walston, Brian Backer, Judge Reinhold, Robert Romanus. Directed by Amy Heckerling. 92 min.

Based on Cameron Crowe's book about his one-year return to high school masquerading as a student, *Fast Times* is a healthy cut above most teen sex fare. It benefits from a witty, sympathetic, rarely crude perspective on the agonies of adolescence, and from the good performances of its ensemble cast. Sean Penn, in his debut, is a standout as Spicoli, the drug-fried surfer who has pizza delivered to his history class on the one day he shows up. Amy Heckerling, one of the few women directors working in Hollywood films, treats her female characters with a humanity unusual in this genre, and a pleasant pop soundtrack keeps the movie's simple fun burbling along.

FAST WALKING ☆
1983, USA, R
James Woods, Kay Lenz, M. Emmet Walsh, Robert Hooks. Directed by James B. Harris. 115 min.

In this paean to violence, a white prison warden becomes the pawn in a power struggle between rednecks out to bump off a charismatic black leader in jail and the leader's acolytes who are planning a prison break. Those expecting a serious indictment of the penal system will be somewhat disappointed.

FATAL ATTRACTION

See *Head On*

FATAL NEEDLES VS. FATAL FISTS ☆☆
Hong Kong
Don Wong Dao, Chaing Yi, Lo Lieh, Hwa Ling, Tommy Lee, Lee Jian Min, Hsu Song, Cheung Ping, Ge Shao Bao. Directed by Lee Tso Nan.

Nice sets, good production values, and a better-than-average story line highlight this kung-fu police yarn. Police Captain Chao (Lo Lieh) and Vice-Captain Meng Hu (Don Wong Dao) are known as the "Bandit Catchers." During a fight, Meng accidentally stabs Chao to death. Meng, feeling responsible, leaves town in a drunken state. When he awakens, he finds himself in a brothel without any money.

FATHER FIGURE ☆☆☆
1980, USA (TV)
Hal Linden, Timothy Hutton, Jeremy Licht, Martha Scott, Cassie Yates. Directed by Jerry London. 95 min.

Absorbing domestic tale of a widower who tries desperately to rebuild his relationship with two sons he hasn't seen in five years. A literate screenplay and impressive acting from Hal Linden and Timothy Hutton really bring out the anguish this torn-apart family must endure in order to come together. Deeply touching, and it never sacrifices its dramatic integrity for easy formulas and pat answers.

FATHER GOOSE ☆☆☆
1964, USA
Cary Grant, Leslie Caron, Trevor Howard, Jack Good. Directed by Ralph Nelson. 115 min.

Cary Grant plays against his usual suave image as a slovenly beach bum pressed into service as a watcher for Japanese planes on a deserted South Seas island during World War II. Reasonably happy with his solitary existence, he is annoyed to have it invaded by a French schoolteacher and her seven charges, all marooned during an escape flight. Quite funny at times, especially when the prim and proper Leslie Caron takes to the bottle as a cure for snakebite.

FATHER'S LITTLE DIVIDEND ☆☆☆
1951, USA
Spencer Tracy, Elizabeth Taylor, Joan Bennett, Don Taylor, Billie Burke, Moroni Olsen, Russ Tamblyn. Directed by Vincente Minnelli. 81 min.

MGM poured more talent into this sequel to *Father of the Bride* than many of their bigger features, and the results are charming. Spencer Tracy again plays befuddled papa to Elizabeth Taylor, who is not only married but is about to have a baby. Tracy's beautifully spontaneous work is adeptly complemented by Joan Bennett as his patient but slightly screwy wife and Billie Burke and Moroni Olsen as rich, obnoxious in-laws. Tracy's attempt to babysit the uncooperative tyke provides the comic and unexpected dramatic highlight of the film.

THE F.B.I. STORY ☆☆½
1959, USA
James Stewart, Vera Miles, Murray Hamilton, Larry Pennell, Nick Adams, Parley Baer, Joyce Taylor. Directed by Mervyn LeRoy. 149 min.

Based on a best-selling documentary about the history and workings of the Federal Bureau of Investigation, the filmmakers here decided to show that the feds are just folks, too—and who better to do so than Jimmy Stewart? In three decades with the bureau, Stewart (given the homey name of "Chip") helps battle the Ku Klux Klan, Ma Barker, Nazis, and more mundane, down-home miscreants. Oh, yeah, and a few commies, too. The cynical may view this as Hollywood's attempt to kiss and make up after the blacklisting days; whether or not that's true, this is still a sanitized filmland version of American history. Not that it's not entertaining, mind you, but don't believe everything you see.

FEAR ☆☆½
1955, Italy/West Germany
Ingrid Bergman, Mathias Wiemann, Renate Mannhart, Kurt Krueger, Elise Aulinger. Directed by Roberto Rossellini. 91 min.

The structured story line of betrayal and blackmail, drawn from a Stefan Zweig novel, constricts Roberto Rossellini's neorealist style, leaving the director with only the image of passion, lacking all conviction. The film would fail completely were it not for the presence of Ingrid Bergman, who inflames the screen but unfortunately distances her fellow actors. An adulterous wife blackmailed by her lover's former girlfriend, she salvages the film with grace and beauty, and convincingly depicts the woman's descent into self-destructive madness upon her discovery that her husband is behind the blackmail plot. Had Rossellini the strength to extract similar performances from the cast and crew, *Fear*'s tight melodrama would shine as a gripping display of cinema, instead of ultimately disappointing.

THE FEAR CHAMBER

See *Chamber of Fear*

FEAR CITY ☆☆
1984, USA, R
Tom Berenger, Billy Dee Williams, Jack Scalia, Melanie Griffith, Rossano Brazzi, Rae Dawn Chong, Joe Santos, Michael V. Gazzo, Jan Murray, Ola Ray. Directed by Abel Ferrara. 96 min.

Unusually stylish low-budget exploitation from the director of the cult hits *Driller Killer* and *Ms. 45*, as well as several episodes of TV's "Miami Vice." Fear City is, of course, the Big Apple, and you'd be afraid, too, if you were a lesbian stripper on drugs being pursued by a slasher with a G-string fetish. Abel Ferrara litters the screen with corpses, sex, and blood, so be warned: *Fear City* is *not* an example of genuine artistry overcoming a tawdry plot, but is simply a sleazy film made with just enough flair to give it a little punch.

FEAR IN THE NIGHT ☆☆½
1972, Great Britain
Judy Geeson, Ralph Bates, Peter Cushing, Joan Collins. Directed by Jimmy Sangster. 85 min.

Fear in the Night, one of Hammer Films' better entries, has an unusually well-maintained sense of loneliness and persecution in this tale of a young woman's fear that her husband's new job at a boys' school will bring out a recurrence of some terrible past events. Judy Geeson is admirably neurotic, while Peter Cushing gives a fully realized portrait of a kinky suspect.

THE FEARLESS HYENA ☆☆
1979, Hong Kong
Jacky Chan, Yen Si Kuan, Li Kuen. Directed by Jacky Chan.

Incredible, multitalented Jacky Chan directed, choreographed, and starred in this kung-fu opus about a young man defending his family honor against a warring clan. Magnificent fight scenes supplement the usual plot.

THE FEARLESS VAMPIRE KILLERS, OR, PARDON ME, BUT YOUR TEETH ARE IN MY NECK ☆½
1967, Great Britain
Jack MacGowran, Roman Polanski, Sharon Tate, Alfie Bass, Ferdy Mayne. Directed by Roman Polanski. 110 min.

Although there are some technically impressive aspects to this horror parody, including the photography and the location shooting, this is, in general, a film so inane that it's hard to believe Roman Polanski made it. It's difficult to judge his contribution: the American print was trimmed by twenty minutes, redubbed, reedited, and given a moronic cartoon title sequence, all over his objections. Still, the evidence left here doesn't indicate how it could have been much better. Jack MacGowran and Polanski play a vampire hunter and his assistant, both as drooling boobs: other sources of humor are a Jewish vampire (not bothered by crucifixes) and a gay vampire. The only saving grace is the appearance of Sharon Tate, who wasn't much of an actress but at least had some screen presence.

FEARLESS YOUNG BOXER

See *Avenging Boxer*

FEAR NO EVIL ☆☆
1981, USA, R
Stefan Arngrim, Elizabeth Hoffman, Kathleen Rowe McAllen, Frank Birney, Daniel Eden. Directed by Frank Laloggie. 96 min.

A seedy high-school outcast proves to be the Antichrist in disguise, and when he exercises his fiendish powers, the results are grim indeed. Rotting corpses rise from the ground, spectators and participants in a passion play bleed spontaneously, a macho bully grows breasts and commits suicide; it remains for a trio of angels in human guise to put things right. Quirky low-budget oddity with a new-wave score.

FEELIN' UP ½☆
1976, USA, R
Malcolm Groome, Kathleen Seward, Rhonda Hansome, Tony Collado. Directed by David Secter. 83 min.

The box this movie comes in is a good example of the misleading advertising too frequently used to sell old movies retreaded for the video market. The actual movie bears almost no relation to the description given on the package, which would have us believe that it's about a sixteen-year-old boy who "quits school . . . [and] ventures to New York," where he finds a "new, wild and sex-filled life." In fact it's about a twenty-six-year-old yuppie who quits one job and goes traveling before he gets another one, having a couple of tepid quasi-sexual encounters along the way; but, as with pulp paperback books, there's far less sex—and what there is is far less exotic—than the package copy would have the gullible buyer believe. Even in its own right, the movie itself is awful.

FELLINI SATYRICON ☆☆☆
1969, Italy/France
Martin Potter, Hiram Keller, Max Born, Salvo Randone, Mario Romagnoli, Magali Noel, Capucine, Alain Cuny. Directed by Federico Fellini. 136 min.

The Rome of Petronius Arbiter (who died A.D. 66) becomes Federico Fellini's playground in this extravagant, shamelessly self-indulgent fantasy. Few films meander so endlessly; few seem so deliriously unable to tell a story (though one can dimly perceive a picaresque tale of a young boy's search for manhood). For all the splendors of the set design, this film is unimaginably ugly in spirit. Instead of Petronius's salute to sensuality, Fellini gives us the last rites for Roman decadence. The famous director loves to boast of how he pored over thousands of photos of bizarre faces before casting his films, but couldn't his prepreproduction have consisted of some work on the script? This gilded freak show is the Fellinian approximation of a Disneyland Theme Park, only we sail through Depravityland while hideous attractions condemning sexuality pop out with boring regularity. An unsalubrious blend of Pier Paolo Pasolini and Cecil B. De Mille.

FEMALE TROUBLE ☆☆☆
1974, USA, X
Divine, David Lochary, Mink Stole, Edith Massey, Mary Vivian Pierce, Cookie Mueller. Directed by John Waters. 95 min.

John Waters's best film, made for $25,000, is a tasteless, raunchy, outrageously campy "melodrama" about Dawn Davenport (Divine), a sixteen-year-old girl who assaults her own mom with a Christmas tree when she doesn't get the cha-cha heels she covets, and from there embarks on a life of degradation worthy of Mildred Pierce—including rape, mutilation, motherhood, disfigurement, kidnapping, and murder. Divine's performance is simply unmatchable—it's safe to say that nobody but a 325-pound transvestite could have played Dawn with such verve and dedication. Only his/her rape scene is a little hard to take—until you look closely and realize that Divine is playing both parts. Behind all the shock value lurks a clever filmmaker and knowing parodist, and much of the dialogue is pricelessly funny. Waters's films are not for everyone—many would argue that they're not for *anyone*—but those willing to experience his unique fusion of sleaze and art would be well-advised to start with this film rather than the repellent *Pink Flamingos*.

FER-DE-LANCE ☆
1974, USA (TV)
David Janssen, Hope Lange, Ivan Dixon, Jason Evers. Directed by Russ Mayberry. 120 min.

Snakes stalk the crew members of a submarine in this long and dreary made-for-TV movie thriller. It takes an eternity for the snakes to attack and, when they do, it isn't much to get excited about. This is not the worst, but one of the most boring animals-gone-amok movies. (a.k.a. in Great Britain as *Death Dive*)

FERRIS BUELLER'S DAY OFF ☆½
1986, USA, PG-13
Matthew Broderick, Mia Sara, Alan Ruck, Jeffrey Jones, Jennifer Grey, Cindy Pickett, Charlie Sheen. Directed by John Hughes. 103 min.

Hollywood corrupts, and Hollywood power corrupts absolutely. Take the case of John Hughes, who won respect for a series of comedies starring Molly Ringwald that dared to depict teens as human beings. With *Ferris Bueller's Day Off*, he made exactly the kind of dumb teen flick to which his earlier films seemed the antidote—and had his biggest hit yet. Bueller (Matthew Broderick) is a rich, arrogant Chicago brat inexplicably beloved by all; the film is about his day of hooky and high jinks around the North Shore with his vacant girlfriend (Mia Sara) and nerdy pal (Alan Ruck) in tow, and the insanely vindictive high-school principal (Jeffrey Jones) in pursuit. Between overblown gags the self-obsessed little twerp gazes into the camera and delivers homilies about enjoying life that will send you screaming. Broderick's usual charm seems to be on vacation, and Sara acts like she's phoning in her role from the Twilight Zone—only the talented Jennifer Grey and Charlie Sheen emerge unsullied. Hughes's work is as slick as ever, but the cynical, materialist message comes off as a regurgitated *Risky Business*.

FERRY TO HONG KONG ☆☆
1958, Great Britain
Curt Jurgens, Orson Welles, Sylvia Syms, Jeremy Spenser, Noel Purcell. Directed by Lewis Gilbert. 113 min.

There's not really much to this overlong melodrama about a driver, booted out of several countries, who takes refuge on a ferryboat running between Macao and Hong Kong. Diffident at first, he springs to action to save the ship when it is attacked by Chinese pirates. Fans of Orson Welles may want to look at some of it, though—he gives an outrageously hammy, murkily inconsistent performance the likes of which was not seen again until Marlon Brando made *The Missouri Breaks* in 1976. As the ferryboat skipper who detests his passengers, Welles employs an obviously fake (and consistently changing) accent, and gives every appearance of having total contempt for the director.

FEUD OF THE WEST ☆☆
1936, USA
Hoot Gibson, Joan Barclay, Buzz Barton, Reed Howes, Robert Kortman. Directed by Harry Fraser. 62 min.

Western adventure. (Had you not figured that out from the title or the presence in the cast of people named "Hoot" and "Buzz," characters such as "Whitey," "Wild Horse Henderson," "Six-Bits," and "Bart Hunter" would soon have tipped you off.) A bit above par, with some elements of mystery as Hoot Gibson gets involved with murders connected to a range feud.

FEVER PITCH ½☆
1985, USA, R
Ryan O'Neal, Giancarlo Giannini, Catherine Hicks, Chad Everett. Directed by Richard Brooks. 94 min.

Arguably one of the most inept films to have been released by a major studio (MGM/UA) in several years, *Fever Pitch* means to take a long, hard look at the world of gambling as seen through the eyes of an investigative sportswriter who's secretly hooked on Lady Luck. The script must have been moldering in a drawer since 1950, and should have stayed there—there's something wrong with a film that plays like an antigambling public service announcement and then allows its indebted hero to pay off his chits by going on a $96,000 lucky streak. Thomas Dolby's score is merely the worst element in a film that deserves some other worsts: Worst Movie about Gambling Ever, Worst Movie about Journalism Ever, Silliest Vomiting Scene Ever, and, against stiff competition, Absolutely Worst Performance by Ryan O'Neal. Ever. If you see it, you'll have something to tell your grandchildren when they ask you what your biggest regret is.

fFOLKES ☆☆½
1980, Great Britain, PG
Roger Moore, James Mason, Anthony Perkins, Michael Parks, David Hedison, Jack Watson, Jeremy Clyde. Directed by Andrew V. McLaglen. 99 min.

Roger Moore plays both with and against his James Bond/Simon Templar image to good effect in this amiable, if minor, adventure. He plays the title character, an eccentric, woman-hating, ocean-bound mercenary hired by the British government to rescue an oil ship being held ransom by terrorists. Director Andrew McLaglen is best known for several of John Wayne's last films, brawling good-ol'-boy affairs that used Wayne's heroic image as a form of mild self-parody. He goes for the same thing here, down to surrounding his hero with the expected sidekicks, but Moore's image isn't solid enough to support this kind of self-effacement. Jeremy Clyde used to be half of Chad and Jeremy, for those keeping track.

FIDDLER ON THE ROOF ☆☆☆½
1971, USA, G
Topol, Norma Crane, Leonard Frey, Molly Picon, Michael Glaser. Directed by Norman Jewison. 180 min.

An unknown in this country when he was picked for the lead (a surprise to nearly everyone, who just assumed that Zero Mostel, the stage Tevye, would play him on screen as well), Israeli actor Topol brings extraordinary grace and physicality to the role of Tevye in Norman Jewison's stirring film version of the great Broadway musical about life in the tiny Russian-Jewish village of Anatevka. Although occasionally sappy and cute, it remains one of the few epic musicals that lives up to its grand scale. The songs, including such standards as "If I Were a Rich Man," "Sunrise, Sunset," "Do You Love Me?," and "Tradition," are milked for all they're worth.

THE FIENDISH PLOT OF DR. FU MANCHU ☆☆½
1980, USA, PG
Peter Sellers, Sid Caesar, Helen Mirren, David Tomlinson. Directed by Piers Haggard. 100 min.

This excruciatingly witless pulp-thriller send-up, based on Sax Rohmer's characters, ought to be buried a great and respectful distance from star Peter Sellers. Playing both the evil Oriental genius Fu Manchu (who's now 168 years old) and his archenemy Nayland Smith, Sellers offers just enough of his gifts to make an admirer nostalgic. It's not enough, however, to distract us from the lack of narrative drive and the low level of comic invention. When desperation sets in, director Piers Haggard and writers Jim Moloney and Rudy Dochtermann rely on racial slurs, aimed primarily at Orientals and delivered by Sid Caesar.

THE FIEND WHO WALKED THE WEST ☆½
1958, USA
Hugh O'Brian, Robert Evans, Dolores Michaels, Linda Cristal, Stephen McNally, Ron Ely, Edward Andrews. Directed by Gordon Douglas. 101 min.

Advertised as a "horror Western," this is really just a remake of *Kiss of Death*, with that film's psychotic gangster killer being replaced by a Western counterpart. As the vicious killer, Robert Evans (who later took over Paramount Pictures) beats up his girlfriend, scares another one into having a miscarriage, shoots an old lady with a bow and arrow, and breaks a woman's neck. Can you say "misogyny," boys and girls? Directed in typical hack style by Gordon Douglas.

FIEND WITHOUT A FACE ★★½
1958, Great Britain
Marshall Thompson, Terence Kilburn, Michael Balfour, Kim Parker. Directed by Arthur Crabtree. 77 min.

Surprisingly nasty science-fiction/horror, in which invisible vampirelike killers terrorize an air force base and its environs, butchering locals and making the military installation unpopular. An American officer gets to the bottom of matters. The main attractions are the great tentacled brains (finally visible because of weird radiation) creeping along on their spinal cords like inchworms.

FIESTA ★★½
1941, USA
Ann Ayars, George Negrete, George Givot, Armida, The Guadalajara Trio, José Arias and His Mexican Tipica Orchestra. Directed by LeRoy Prinz. 44 min.

Producer Hal Roach managed to pack a love-triangle story and five production numbers into this very brief Latin-flavored musical comedy. Ann Ayars plays a woman who travels to her father's Mexican hacienda in order to sort out her romantic problems. Along the way, there are songs and dances in breathtaking Technicolor. Directed, choreographed, and coproduced by LeRoy Prinz. Not to be confused with the similar but duller Esther Williams *Fiesta* (1947).

THE FIFTH FLOOR ★
1980, USA, R
Bo Hopkins, Dianne Hull, Patti D'Arbanville, Sharon Farrell, Mel Ferrer, Robert Englund. Directed by Howard Avedis. 87 min.

This lurid horror film has a pretty disco singer locked up in a nuthouse for temporary insanity (all those drugs, you know) who finds that the psycho ward isn't the best place to pick up new fans. Those looking for enlightenment about the state of our mental institutions may be somewhat disappointed. Sleaze-hunters will, however, enjoy the presence of Robert Englund (Freddy Krueger in the *Nightmare on Elm Street* films) as a mild-mannered schizophrenic in a doctor's coat.

THE FIFTH MUSKETEER ★½
1979, Austria/Great Britain, PG
Beau Bridges, Sylvia Kristel, Ursula Andress, Cornel Wilde, Ian McShane, Lloyd Bridges, Alan Hale, Jr., José Ferrer, Rex Harrison, Olivia De Havilland. Directed by Ken Annakin. 103 min.

Despite the title, which seems to have been provided at the last minute in order to cash in on the success of Richard Lester's *The Three Musketeers* and *The Four Musketeers*, this is really a version of Alexandre Dumas's *The Man in the Iron Mask*. While director Ken Annakin tries for the same half-parodic, half-swashbuckling tone as in Lester's films, he has neither the visual nor the comic flair to pull it off. The result is a tedious, overblown version of a story that is stale to begin with. The sole spark of life comes from the casting of Lloyd Bridges, Cornel Wilde, José Ferrer, and Alan Hale, Jr., as the Musketeers. Beau Bridges is merely silly, and Sylvia Kristel (of *Emmanuelle*) proves that had she kept her clothes on in the first place, she'd never have gotten into films at all.

55 DAYS IN PEKING ★★
1963, USA/Spain
Charlton Heston, David Niven, Ava Gardner, Flora Robson, Paul Lukas, John Ireland, Harry Andrews, Robert Helpmann, Leo Genn. Directed by Nicholas Ray and Andrew Marton. 154 min.

Despite directorial credit to Nicholas Ray (who started the film), the stodginess of this overlong epic is more akin to the style of Ray's "second-unit director" Andrew Marton (who finished it). Charlton Heston plays an American soldier who participates in the Boxer Rebellion of 1900 in China and gets involved with the widow of a Russian diplomat. The chief problem lies in the Philip Yordan/Bernard Gordon screenplay, which is not only poorly written and confusingly structured but also sympathizes with the colonialists, a point of view that by 1963 was morally questionable. Ray manages some impressive shots in Super Technirama 70 (which will be lost on video), but it is evident that he is more at home with tightly knit melodramas (*In a Lonely Place*, *Rebel without a Cause*) than with large-scale historical spectacles.

52 PICK-UP ★★½
1986, USA, R
Roy Scheider, Ann-Margret, Vanity, John Glover, Robert Trebor, Lonny Chapman, Kelly Preston, Doug McClure, Clarence Williams III. Directed by John Frankenheimer. 114 min.

In this adaptation of an Elmore Leonard thriller, director John Frankenheimer tries for the cryptic cool of a post-"Miami Vice" neo-*film noir*, but his old-school humanism is somewhat at odds with the new moral ambiguities. Roy Scheider plays a businessman who has to confront his feelings for his wife (Ann-Margret) when he's forced to reveal the affair for which he's being blackmailed. The plot is functional but impersonal, and Frankenheimer's attempts to pump it up with an in-depth look at marital woe are little more than window dressing. The main reason to see the picture is John Glover's highly entertaining performance as a gleeful, homicidal extortionist.

THE FIGHTER ★★
1983, USA (TV)
Gregory Harrison, Glynnis O'Connor, Pat Hingle, Steve Inwood, Justin Lord. Directed by David Lowell Rich. 96 min.

This muscular boxing drama gives handsome Gregory Harrison a chance to spar emotionally with some rather tired material. In the thirties John Garfield would have played the contender, and this film brings little more to the game than an old Warner Bros. fight flick. The point of these Ring Cycles is to give male movie stars a chance to flex their pectorals and run around in silk trunks. By those criteria, hubba-hubba Harrison really rings the bell. As a believable actor in a no-holds-barred melodrama, he ends up on the ropes due to a woozy script. For sheer beefcake appeal, tune in to Harrison's *For Ladies Only*. Here he's agreeable, but he can't redeem the punch-drunk teleplay.

FIGHT FOR YOUR LIFE ★
1978, USA, R
William Sanderson, Robert Judd, Yvonne Ross, Lela Small, Catherine Peppers, Reginald Bythewood, Daniel Faraldo, Peter Yoshida, Bonni Martin. Directed by Robert A. Endelson. 89 min.

A low-budget reworking of *The Desperate Hours*. Three slavering convicts—led by a psychopathic Southerner named Kain—invade the peaceful home of the middle-class Turner family, whose patriarch—a preacher—abhors all forms of violence. The Turners are subjected to racial humiliations, physical brutality, and psychological torture until they can take no more and fight back; and when they do, they fight dirty. The violent, mean, and exploitative attitude of *Fight for Your Life* is nowhere better demonstrated than in the video cover art, which depicts a screaming blond girl menaced by a switchblade (an image that does not appear in the film), presumably on the theory that terrorized nubile white girls sell more tapes than equally terrorized black families. Starring William Sanderson of *Blade Runner*.

FIGHTING BACK ★★½
1980, USA (TV)
Robert Urich, Bonnie Bedelia, Richard Herd, Howard Cosell. Directed by Robert Lieberman. 104 min.

Another inspirational biopic, this time about football great Rocky Bleier. Robert Urich as the glorified football legend and Bonnie Bedelia as his supportive wife transform the usual dross of rah-rah sports figure tributes into a touching drama of rebirth and determination. Bleier, crippled badly in Vietnam, returns to the pro-ball arena to forge a new career as both a topflight player and a leader his teammates can look up to.

FIGHTING CARAVANS ½☆
1931, USA
Gary Cooper, Lili Damita. Directed by Otto Brower and David Burton. 91 min.

Indians attack caravans. Bother only if you *really* like Gary Cooper.

THE FIGHTING DRAGON ☆
1980, Hong Kong
Bruce Liang, Soji Kurata, Yang Sze. Directed by Peng Chien.

A combination revenge and break-up-the-bad-gang film that is saved only by Soji Kurata's convincing performance. Unfortunately, there's far too little fighting; Bruce Liang, playing a cop, has only two small fight scenes, and he has little chance to show off a kicking technique rivaling that of Tan Tao Liang or John Liu.

THE FIGHTING KENTUCKIAN ☆☆☆
1949, USA
John Wayne, Vera Hruba Ralston, Oliver Hardy, Philip Dorn, Marie Windsor, Grant Withers. Directed by George Waggner. 100 min.

This John Wayne–produced Republic vehicle is far above his usual B Westerns. Part of the credit has to go to Oliver Hardy in a rare character role; his comic foil is expert and memorable. Credit also goes to George Waggner, who, in addition to directing, wrote the script around an actual historic oddity: in the early nineteenth century, land in Alabama had been granted to French veterans of Napoleon's army. Here they struggle to hold their homesteads in spite of duplicitous local politicians and hostile neighbors. Fortunately for them, the Duke falls in love with a young French lass. Lots of brawling and equal amounts of romance.

FIGHTING MAD ☆½
1977, US/Philippines
James Inglehart, Leon Isaac Kennedy, Carmen Argenziano, Jayne Kennedy. Directed by Cirio H. Santiago. 83 min.

A notable example of dishonest packaging. This junk is marketed as a steamy Jayne Kennedy action flick, but it's actually the boring story of her husband's search for vengeance against two war-buddy hoods. Kennedy has an embarrassing stab at a nightclub act, but mostly she tries to maintain her dignity in a small, thankless part. Tepid dishwater from the Robert E. Waters/Cirio H. Santiago sleaze team. (a.k.a.: *Vampire Hookers*)

THE FIGHTING SEABEES ☆☆½
1944, USA
John Wayne, Susan Hayward, Dennis O'Keefe, William Frawley, Leonid Kinskey, Grant Withers. Directed by Edward Ludwig. 100 min.

Typical John Wayne war film features the star as a navy man who persuades Congress to furnish his men with arms. In the meantime, he participates in a love triangle with a war correspondent (Susan Hayward) and a naval officer (Dennis O'Keefe). There's less gung-ho action than in most war films (thanks to Republic's typically meager budget), but the climax set around a supply depot dutifully brings out the big guns. This is the film in which the Duke gets shanghaied into a jitterbug.

FILLMORE ☆☆½
1972, USA
Jefferson Airplane, Hot Tuna, the New Riders of the Purple Sage, Quicksilver Messenger Service, the Grateful Dead, Santana. Directed by Richard T. Heffron. 105 min.

So-so rock movie shows products of the San Francisco phenomenon in concert: the Grateful Dead, Jefferson Airplane (yes, youngsters, that's what they used to be called), Quicksilver Messenger Service, the New Riders of the Purple Sage, and other groups. The focus is on the closing of the Fillmore West, a great sixties concert house, and the elegiac atmosphere of the film is a better reason to see it than the only-fair performances.

FINAL ASSIGNMENT ☆
1980, Canada
Geneviève Bujold, Michael York, Burgess Meredith, Colleen Dewhurst. Directed by Paul Almond. 101 min.

This unintentionally silly suspense film wastes a good cast, all of whom at least look properly embarrassed. Geneviève Bujold plays a Canadian reporter in Moscow (which looks suspiciously like Montreal) who discovers evidence of Russian experiments with steroids involving young children. She gets help compiling evidence from Michael York, a Soviet bureaucrat, and Colleen Dewhurst, a scientist involved in the experiments whose daughter needs to be smuggled out of the country to get a brain operation in the United States. And then, there's Burgess Meredith. Enough said?

FINAL CONFLICT

See *Omen III—The Final Conflict*

THE FINAL COUNTDOWN ☆☆
1980, USA, PG
Kirk Douglas, Martin Sheen, Katharine Ross, Ron O'Neal, Charles Durning, Victor Mohica. Directed by Don Taylor. 104 min.

The dopey plot, which has an enormous modern aircraft carrier, the USS *Nimitz*, thrown backward in time to the day before the attack on Pearl Harbor, couldn't possibly interest anyone over draft age. But it's not the plot that counts. The movie's true subject is America's military might. Director Don Taylor (*Damien, Omen II*) isn't much on storytelling or characterization—how could he be, with rock-jawed warriors like Kirk Douglas and Martin Sheen mouthing dialogue that seems to have traveled backward in time along with the vessel? But Taylor has a knack for presenting the sheer spectacle of weaponry. Listening to the booms and roars of the Dolby soundtrack, or watching the sharply edited footage of missiles being launched and giant helicopters lifting off, one eventually catches on: this movie's auteur is not the director, it's the U.S. Navy. Still, the film doesn't actually deliver the spectacular battle between F-111's and Japanese Zeroes that the promotion and the first ninety-nine minutes promise us; only two or three lousy planes are shot down.

FINAL EXAM ☆
1981, USA, R
Cecile Bagdadi, Joel Rice. Directed by Jimmy Huston. 90 min.

From the long line of horror movies named, in the tradition of *Halloween* and *Friday the 13th*, after noteworthy days of the year (e.g., *Mother's Day, Prom Night*, and a few million others). Which is to say, another slasher movie. This one is thoroughly undistinguished, and if you just want to see a slasher movie, you only need grab this one if no others are available. *Final Exam* doesn't even have any gore, the absence of which would be a positive attribute in any other movie.

FINAL JUSTICE ☆☆
1985, USA, R
Joe Don Baker, Vanantino Venantini, Rossano Brazzi, Bill McKinney. Directed by Greydon Clark. 90 min.

This predictable but slickly produced action film from the estimable director of *Satan's Cheerleaders* plays like *Dirty Harry Goes to Italy*, with the film borrowing liberally from the Clint Eastwood formula films. Joe Don Baker plays a macho sheriff who enjoys taking the law into his own hands. That's why he ends up bounced off the Dallas police force and sent to patrol the Mexican border. But Joe Don soon gets to strut his independent stuff when he's assigned to deliver a murderer abroad and turn him over to Italian authorities. A main course of vigilantism with a side dish of spaghetti.

THE FINAL OPTION ☆
1982, Great Britain, R
Judy Davis, Richard Widmark, Lewis Collins, Robert Webber, Edward Woodward, Ingrid Pitt. Directed by Ian Sharp. 122 min.

Ridiculous right-wing antiterrorist junk, in which the international peace movement is portrayed as a pastime for spoiled, sex-obsessed rich kids who wouldn't mind blowing up the world to stop nuclear proliferation. That being the case, Her Majesty's special forces employed herein need feel no qualms about wiping them right out, which they do. Dull, unconvincing attempt at rabble-rousing; the filmmakers should give the rabble a little credit next time.

THE FINAL PROGRAMME

See *The Last Days of Man on Earth*

THE FINAL TERROR ½☆
1981, USA, R
Adrian Zmed, John Friedrich, Daryl Hannah, Rachel Ward, Mark Metcalf. Directed by Andrew Davis. 82 min.

For you, viewers, the terror is just beginning. This wretched horror film came out of the rerelease woodwork in the mid-eighties to capitalize on the career prominence of several of its stars. They would probably have preferred that this gibberish stayed unexhumed. To be watched only by those who can't get enough of teenagers being eliminated in graphic detail.

FINDERS, KEEPERS ☆☆☆½
1984, USA, R
Michael O'Keefe, Beverly D'Angelo, Louis Gossett, Jr., David Wayne, Pamela Stephenson, Ed Lauter, Brian Dennehy. Directed by Richard Lester. 96 min.

This genial, whacked-out farce comes reasonably close to re-creating the topsy-turvy, money-mad universe of screwball comedies of the forties. As an update of the works of Preston Sturges, this film clocks more laughs than more widely heralded modern comedies like *Arthur* or *S.O.B.* What's so delicious about this fractious farce is that there are so many off-the-wall characters; and when the film's pacing slackens or stumbles over a too-complicated plot twist, the zany protagonists are there to take over and brighten the material. Among those tickling our ribs are the ex-manager of an all-girl roller derby team, a foul-mouthed actress, a professional thief, and the world's oldest living train conductor, all of whom cross paths with a coffin that contains a fortune in stolen loot instead of housing the remains of a Vietnam-war hero. How these lovable, ridiculous pieces of humanity fit themselves into this film's comic jigsaw puzzle will leave you breathless with surprise.

A FINE MESS ☆
1986, USA, PG
Ted Danson, Howie Mandel, Richard Mulligan, Stuart Margolin, Maria Conchita Alonso, Jennifer Edwards, Paul Sorvino. Directed by Blake Edwards. 100 min.

Blake Edwards hits absolute bottom—the title says it all. Ted Danson and Howie Mandel play a pair of buddies who make a killing on a fixed horserace and are then pursued by a mob boss's two inept thugs (Richard Mulligan and Stuart Margolin). The title is meant to evoke Laurel and Hardy (indeed, the project was originally intended as a remake of *The Music Box*), but our heroes seem more like Dean Martin and Jerry Lewis. Danson is the wrong actor to portray a strutting cocksman—there's a fatal lack of irony in his macho poses—and Mandel, playing the allegedly adorable spastic screw-up, is irritatingly antic. And Edwards strips the movie down to slapstick routines so "classic" they're DOA.

FINGERS ☆☆
1977, USA, R
Harvey Keitel, Tisa Farrow, Jim Brown, Michael V. Gazzo, Marian Seldes, Carole Francis. Directed by James Toback. 91 min.

The first film directed by James Toback (who wrote *The Gambler*) is extravagantly, entertainingly bad, so flagrant you almost want to see it again. It's as if Toback had read Dostoyevski and Mailer and seen all of Welles and Scorsese, and yet had experienced nothing. Harvey Keitel's concert pianist spends half his time strong-arming delinquent claims for his loan-shark father (Michael V. Gazzo) and the other half practicing for a Carnegie Hall audition he's been pushed into by his pianist-gone-mad mother (Marian Seldes). Keitel is a quintessentially Mailer-esque artist, "encouraging the psychopath in himself" and finally releasing his angst in a *Taxi Driver*-style murder. Toback has even written an iconic role for his own black idol, Jim Brown.

FINIAN'S RAINBOW ☆☆☆
1968, USA
Fred Astaire, Petula Clark, Tommy Steele, Don Francks, Keenan Wynn, Barbara Hancock. Directed by Francis Ford Coppola. 140 min.

Francis Ford Coppola was not yet fully in command of the medium when he transferred the Broadway musical *Finian's Rainbow* to the screen. The belated adaptation of the 1947 show is too reverential to its stage origins to really take off as a great movie musical. Those origins, however, are captivating enough to make viewing worthwhile. The story involves an Irish father and daughter looking for gold near Fort Knox, Kentucky. On their journey, the young lassie (Petula Clark) meets a handsome guitarist (Don Francks) while the old man (Fred Astaire) runs into a mischievous leprechaun (Tommy Steele). The "social conscience" subplot about a racist senator looks dated, but the score, which includes "How Are Things in Glocca Morra?" and "Look to the Rainbow," is timeless and beautifully performed, especially in the more intimate numbers and in Astaire's extended dance routines. Though lacking the personal stamp of later Coppola musicals (*One from the Heart*, *The Cotton Club*), *Finian* does work as a pleasing preservation of a classic stage show. Originally filmed in Panavision 70.

FINNEGAN BEGIN AGAIN ☆☆☆½
1985, USA (TV)
Mary Tyler Moore, Robert Preston, Sam Waterston, Sylvia Sidney, Giancarlo Esposito. Directed by Joan Micklin Silver. 105 min.

This is one of the best made-for-cable films, one that doesn't try to overextend itself and instead utilizes characters that work well on a small screen. Mary Tyler Moore, who despairs of ever finding something meaningful in her life, is a middle-aged schoolteacher involved in an affair with a married mortician; Robert Preston is a sixty-five-year-old surly newspaperman saddled with a sick older wife and a demotion to the lonely hearts column. Of course, they eventually meet and fall in love, but that this development doesn't seem forced is due to director Joan Micklin Silver (*Between the Lines*, *Chilly Scenes of Winter*), who has a charming, offhand way with such things.

FIRE! ☆☆½
1977, USA (TV)
Ernest Borgnine, Vera Miles, Patty Duke Astin, Alex Cord, Donna Mills, Lloyd Nolan, Neville Brand, Ty Hardin, Gene Evans. Directed by Earl Bellamy. 98 min.

During the 1970s Irwin Allen churned out nearly a dozen successful disaster films, one of which was *The Towering Inferno*. Apparently once was not enough, and for this TV effort he moved the fire out of the city and into the forest, with a whole community menaced by the rapidly spreading blaze. While not as exciting as his big-screen sensations, the fire footage is impressive, and in this video version, cut by forty-six minutes from its original broadcast length, the soap-opera histrionics of the cast are kept to a merciful minimum.

FIRE AND ICE ☆☆
1983, USA
Animated: Susan Tyrrell, Maggie Roswell, William Ostrander, Stephen Mendel. Directed by Ralph Bakshi. 81 min.

Animated cartoon for adventure buffs. Fans of the fantastic artwork of Frank Frazetta will be pleased to see his influence at work here, even though the animation was rotoscoped from live footage. Certainly this is more strikingly designed than the usual Saturday morning cartoon fare. The rather overdeveloped plot concerns an overdeveloped set of protagonists, sort of animated clones of Arnold Schwarzenegger and the late Jayne Mansfield. These two fight the good fight as they're swept up in a power conflict between rival factions.

FIRECRACKER ☆½
1981, Philippines
Jillian Kesner, Darby Hinton, Raymond King. Directed by Cirio Santiago. 83 min.

Here's a scene that could only exist in a kung-fu movie directed by the indomitable Cirio Santiago (*Vampire Hookers*): a karate instructor played by Jillian Kesner fights off two would-be rapists while wearing only her panties! She's searching for her sister, who disappeared while reporting on a martial arts contest. And if she doesn't find her, she'll probably beat someone up while completely naked.

FIRE DOWN BELOW ☆☆½
1957, Great Britain
Jack Lemmon, Robert Mitchum, Rita Hayworth, Herbert Lom, Bonar Colleano, Bernard Lee, Anthony Newley. Directed by Robert Parrish. 116 min.

This moderately engaging sea adventure isn't up to the talents of its stars or its scenarist, Irwin Shaw. Robert Mitchum and Jack Lemmon are small-scale smugglers whose friendship runs aground over Lemmon's love for woman-with-a-past Rita Hayworth. When Lemmon's life is imperiled in an accident, the rambling story takes a grim turn. Both men are good, but Hayworth, late in her career, was miscast as the seductress and looks ill at ease throughout.

FIRE FESTIVAL

See *Himatsuri*

FIREFOX ☆½
1982, USA, PG
Clint Eastwood, Freddie Jones, David Huffman, Warren Clarke, Ronald Lacey, Stefan Schnabel. Directed by Clint Eastwood. 124 min.

Clint Eastwood plays a crack American fighter pilot ordered to penetrate the innermost levels of Russian security and steal the country's latest war gadget—a gleaming supersonic missile transport that renders all other weapons obsolete. Eastwood directed the film, but the Cold War–paranoia theme hasn't brought out his flair for action-packed mythmaking. We've seen these espionage bits before, in countless old spy movies, and the climactic high-tech dogfight sequence is about as riveting as a curling match.

FIREMEN'S BALL ☆☆☆
1968, Czechoslovakia
Josef Kolb, Vaclav Stockel, Marie Jazkova, Josef Svet. Directed by Miloš Forman. 73 min.

A small-town gathering in honor of a local fire chief turns to chaos in Miloš Forman's cute, rather rambling comic parable of life in contemporary Czechoslovakia. The loose plotting and hapless characters suggest an Eastern European *Nashville*, but Forman's style is so meandering that the film never quite takes hold. Nevertheless, it gave him international attention and later brought him to this country and success with *One Flew over the Cuckoo's Nest*, *Amadeus*, and others.

FIRE OVER ENGLAND ☆☆½
1937, Great Britain
Flora Robson, Raymond Massey, Laurence Olivier, Vivien Leigh, Leslie Banks, James Mason. Directed by William K. Howard. 92 min.

Flora Robson's Queen Elizabeth steals the show from both young Laurence Olivier and Vivien Leigh in this tale of Britain's struggle against the Spanish Armada. Robson is almost matched by Raymond Massey playing the villainous Philip of Spain, but this is Robson's film, one of the few to give her a starring role. Olivier and Leigh, both married to others at the time, were already showing the romantic fireworks that would lead them to their famous marriage three years later. This was the first of three films they did together (the other two being *21 Days* and *That Hamilton Woman*). Unfortunately, while Olivier gets a chance to sing and wield a sword and Leigh looks beautiful, neither have roles that even begin to tap into their tremendous capabilities. The action scenes are competent but obviously limited by budget restrictions. The sort of film Hollywood generally did better.

FIREPOWER ☆☆
1979, Great Britain, R
Sophia Loren, James Coburn, O. J. Simpson, Eli Wallach, Anthony Franciosa, George Grizzard, Vincent Gardenia, Andrew Duncan, Billy Barty, Victor Mature. Directed by Michael Winner. 104 min.

This is another one of those international pseudo-epic intrigue films, in which they toss in all the right ingredients (big-name cast, European scenery, commercial director) but forget to stir the damn thing. Widow Sophia Loren persuades the U.S. government to help her find the reclusive Greek industrialist who had her husband bumped off. It all gets quite complicated after that. Not interesting, mind you, just complicated. O. J. Simpson's acting here is better than in *The Towering Inferno*, which isn't saying much.

FIRESTARTER ☆☆
1984, USA, R
Drew Barrymore, David Keith, Martin Sheen, George C. Scott, Art Carney, Louise Fletcher. Directed by Mark L. Lester. 115 min.

Based on a novel by Stephen King, this is a naively paranoid tale about a little girl with psychokinetic powers and the various villains—including representatives of the government-supported "shop" (read: CIA)—who want to exploit her. Weak special effects, and an all-star cast that lacks the conviction to make it all work, but slick.

FIREWALKER ☆☆
1986, USA, PG
Chuck Norris, Lou Gossett, Melody Anderson, Will Sampson, Sonny Landham, John Rhys-Davies. Directed by J. Lee Thompson. 110 min.

A light-spirited but heavy-handed comedy-adventure starring Chuck Norris, arguably the least expressive actor of the decade. As a soldier of fortune hunting for an Aztec treasure with Lou Gossett, he does better than usual just by playing his own image for laughs and keeping the karate to a blessed minimum. If you've already seen all of the better cliff-hanging adventures that this rips off (from *Indiana Jones and the Temple of Doom* on upward) and you're in an undemanding mood, this may pass the time; the comparative mildness of the violence makes this more suitable for kids than most films like it.

FIRE WITH FIRE
1986, USA, PG-13 ☆☆
Craig Sheffer, Virginia Madsen, Jon Polito, Kate Reid, David Harris. Directed by Duncan Gibbins. 103 min.

This mixture of *Endless Love* and *Cool Hand Luke* for the MTV generation details the passions that arise when a virginal Catholic schoolgirl develops an obsessive attraction to a detainee at a juvenile prison camp. Although the leads are likable and the sexual sparks fly between them, their eventual flight from the law isn't convincing for a minute. Still, the hopelessly romantic should get a charge out of these doomed lovers-on-the-run.

FIRST BLOOD
1982, USA, R ☆☆☆
Sylvester Stallone, Richard Crenna, Brian Dennehy, David Caruso. Directed by Ted Kotcheff. 97 min.

Sylvester Stallone's first hit outside the *Rocky* series was this intense, stunningly photographed B movie (by Andrew Laszlo, who did the similar *Southern Comfort*) about a burnt-out Vietnam vet who's tagged a vagrant by a small-town police force and goes on a violent rampage—busting heads, laying booby traps, dispatching his victims with brilliantly ironic timing. The movie loses some steam when the National Guard is called in, but the violence is crisply staged and the thrills are anchored by Stallone's mute anguish; he may be better at expressing physical pain than any actor alive. Followed by the much worse but monumentally successful *Rambo*.

FIRST BLOOD, PART TWO

See *Rambo: First Blood, Part Two*

FIRSTBORN
1984, USA, PG ☆☆
Peter Weller, Christopher Collet, Teri Garr, Corey Haim. Directed by Michael Apted. 93 min.

Part after-school special, part dark fairy tale, and one silly movie. Everything's sunny in Jake's house until Mom brings home a shifty but charming driver named Sam. Jake isn't pulled into the pseudo-father's act and becomes even more suspicious of Sam when he discovers cocaine in his mother's bedroom. Unfortunately, it's too late for Jake to act; his mother has been turned into a cokehead, and everyone in the house is under the spell of evil Sam. This film goes from the sublime to the ridiculous, mixing concrete family melodrama with overt allegorical symbolism. Despite the fact that *Firstborn* is about as subtle as an explosive, the acting is so good that it might have one rooting during the final confrontation between Jake and Sam. One instance of a movie that probably would have avoided the gratuitous violence and drug abuse if it had been produced for television.

THE FIRST DEADLY SIN
1980, USA, R ☆☆
Frank Sinatra, Faye Dunaway, David Dukes, George Coe, Brenda Vaccaro, Jeffrey De Munn, Anthony Zerbe, James Whitmore. Directed by Brian Hutton. 112 min.

What possessed Old Blue Eyes to return to the screen at the age of sixty-five in the role of an aging cop pursuing a demented killer? Perhaps he hankered to play a straight dramatic lead, and he does so without fanfare, but what a dull, downbeat, predictable vehicle he chose. As his quarry, David Dukes makes a jolting, creepy killer, but Faye Dunaway has one of the most unrewarding roles in recent history: as Sinatra's wife, she spends most of the film in a hospital bed, tubes up her nose, eyelids fluttering weakly, cooing last words at the understandably befuddled Frankie. On video, some of the night scenes are so muddy as to be unwatchable. Based on a good novel by Lawrence Sanders.

FIRST FAMILY
1980, USA, R ☆½
Bob Newhart, Gilda Radner, Madeline Kahn, Richard Benjamin, Harvey Korman, Rip Torn. Directed by Buck Henry. 104 min.

There are few sadder spectacles than that of an essentially nice man trying desperately to give offense and failing utterly—as writer/director Buck Henry does here. His political farce flails about wildly but connects with no targets worth hitting. Mostly it pokes fun at emergent African nations (because their citizens talk funny), at presidential daughters (Gilda Radner is forever horny), and at generalized bureaucratic imcompetence (Harvey Korman acting klutzy and self-serving).

THE FIRST LEGION
1951, USA ☆☆½
Charles Boyer, William Demarest, Lyle Bettger, Barbara Rush, Leo G. Carroll, Walter Hampden, Wesley Addy, H. B. Warner. Directed by Douglas Sirk. 86 min.

Douglas Sirk's glossy religious drama, based on a popular play of the 1930s, is a highly watchable if finally trite treatment of the old miracles-can-really-happen theme. When an aged priest at a Jesuit seminary suddenly regains the use of his legs, a young Father (Charles Boyer) is skeptical of the claims of divine intervention. The good story is completely undermined by the ending, but since Sirk's direction gives the same soap-opera patina to every scene, you may not mind.

FIRST LOVE
1970, Great Britain/France/Switzerland, R ☆☆½
Dominique Sanda, John Moulder-Brown, Maximilian Schell, Valentina Cortese. Directed by Maximilian Schell. 90 min.

Loosely based on the 1860 Ivan Turgenev novella, *First Love* is a romantic recollection of a sixteen-year-old boy's infatuation with a callous flirt. Set against a backdrop of the fading Russian middle class, Maximilian Schell's first foray into the directorial fires proves to be an inoffensive and forgettable tale of wide-eyed innocence and the cruel destruction of that innocence. Dominique Sanda shines as the lovely heartbreaker, and Sven Nykvist's cinematography is customarily superb.

FIRST LOVE
1977, USA, R ☆☆½
William Katt, Susan Dey, John Heard, Beverly D'Angelo, Robert Loggia. Directed by John Darling. 92 min.

John Darling has turned Harold Brodkey's story "A Sentimental Education" into a craftsmanlike—but self-righteous—film. Its hero, a hardworking college student, has an unhappy affair with a troubled rich girl and sends her packing. Though we're meant to applaud his adherence to an idea of perfect, Dante-esque love, we wind up thinking it cruel and stubborn—why is he so unwilling to learn from his experience? Susan Dey is assured and convincing, and her low, cool voice seems just right for the dream-girl role, while William Katt, a golden boy often compared with Robert Redford, is more reminiscent of a young Sterling Hayden as a tough guy whom passion has made vulnerable.

FIRST MEN IN THE MOON
1964, Great Britain ☆☆☆
Edward Judd, Lionel Jeffries, Martha Hyer, Eric Chitty. Directed by Nathan Juran. 102 min.

In this British sci-fi lark based on a novel by H. G. Wells, a U.N. team makes what they think is the first landing on the moon only to find a British flag there with a scroll dated 1899. They track down one of the names on the scroll to an old age home, where the last surviving member of the expedition gives them the story. Lionel Jeffries, one of the most engaging of British character actors, steals the show as usual as the eccentric leader of the first lunar flight in Victorian times. Neat special effects by Ray Harryhausen help make this an enjoyable package. Peter Finch plays a bit part as a process server.

FIRST MONDAY IN OCTOBER ☆☆
1981, USA, R
Walter Matthau, Jill Clayburgh, Barnard Hughes, James Stephens, Ian Sterling, Joshua Bryant. Directed by Ronald Neame. 98 min.

This comedy about the first woman nominated to the Supreme Court is a sub–Neil Simon farce, a stew of political clichés spiced with insufferably "snappy" one-liners. Jill Clayburgh is Ruth Loomis, the archconservative from Orange County, and Walter Matthau is David Snow, the bellowing William O. Douglas type who tries to set her straight.

THE FIRST NUDIE MUSICAL ☆☆☆
1976, USA, R
Stephen Nathan, Cindy Williams, Bruce Kimmel, Diana Canova, Leslie Ackerman. Directed by Bruce Kimmel. 100 min.

Bruce Kimmel wrote the screenplay, music, and lyrics, and codirected and starred in this comedy about a porno director who tries for the big time by directing the first nudie musical. What makes this work is the essential innocence of the characters and story, even during the staging of such production numbers as "Dancing Dildoes." No, Cindy Williams doesn't take off her clothes, and shame on you for asking.

THE FIRST TEXAN ☆☆
1956, USA
Joel McCrea, Felicia Farr, Jeff Morrow, Wallace Ford, Abraham Sofaer, Jody McCrea, Chubby Johnson. Directed by Byron Hasken. 81 min.

Joel McCrea, who also starred in Westerns called *The Oklahoman* and *The Virginian*, here moves a little south to portray Sam Houston, who led the revolt of the Texans against Mexican rule in the 1800s and became the first president of the Republic of Texas. Director Byron Haskin had previously worked as a newspaper cartoonist, director of photography and special-effects man, so his outdoors and battle scenes are adept and visually polished. Jody McCrea is Joel's son.

THE FIRST TIME ☆☆☆
1983, USA
Tim Choate, Wallace Shawn, Marshall Efron, Wendie Jo Sperber, Krista Errickson. Cathryn Damon, Wendy Fulton. Directed by Charlie Loventhal. 90 min.

Pretentious film professors, aspiring directors, and women's colleges get the satirical skewer in a small-scale effort of real charm and frequent inventiveness, about a seventeen-year-old would-be Steven Spielberg and his virgin efforts on screen and off. Young director Charlie Loventhal, under the tutelage of Brian De Palma, has assembled a delightfully quirky cast, including Wallace Shawn as an egotistical auteur, Marshall Efron as an overly solicitous college adviser, and Larry "Bud" Melman of "David Letterman" fame in a tiny, startling cameo. Rough around the edges and made on a shoestring budget, *The First Time* isn't perfect, but it emanates energy, goodwill, and zesty humor. Shame, however, on its video distributor (Thorn EMI) for doing a sloppy film-to-tape transfer, packaging it as a stupid sex comedy, and cutting six minutes from the theatrical released version. It's a disservice to the film and the audience.

THE FIRST TURN-ON ☆½
1984, USA, R
Georgia Harrell, Michael Sanville, Googy Gross, John Flood, Al Pia, Betty Pia, Gilda Gumbo, Susan Kaufman. 85 min.

Troma, the maker of this and such other available-on-video gems as *Feelin' Up*, *Stuck on You*, and *When Nature Calls*, aims to be nothing more (or less) than the eighties version of what Roger Corman and American-International Pictures were to the fifties—producers of cheap, quick, dumb drive-in movies that make lots of money by catering to drive-in audiences. So to say that this movie is juvenile and silly is not to call it a failure. As in any Troma film, the story, which has four boys at summer camp trapped in a cave and passing the time by telling stories about how they lost their virginity, is a loose excuse for a lot of gags of varying quality. It's very cheap and full of undressed young women, though in its own odd way it's actually antisexist. If nothing else, Troma can be credited with genuinely trying to please its audiences.

FIRST YANK INTO TOKYO ☆½
1945, USA
Tom Neal, Barbara Hale, Marc Cramer, Richard Loo, Keye Luke, Benson Fong, Leonard Strong. Directed by Gordon Douglas. 82 min.

Without the World War II anti-Japanese hysteria, and with plastic surgery as common today as appendectomies, this shocker from America's wartime film industry seems terribly dated, insulting, and silly. However, the vehement support for the fledgling atomic bomb is now rather chilling; the movie hit the theaters just after the bombings in Japan resulted in V-J Day. Tom Neal stars as an army pilot who undergoes facial surgery, sneaks into Japan, and rescues an engineer with some A-bomb secrets. Richard Loo stands out with one of his villainous-Oriental performances, and Keye Luke (the Charlie Chan series, "Kung-Fu") plays a Korean operative.

FISH HAWK ☆☆
1979, Canada, PG
Will Sampson, Charlie Fields, Geoffrey Bowes, Mary Pirie. Directed by Donald Shebib. 97 min.

The excellent Native American actor Will Sampson (*One Flew over the Cuckoo's Nest*) is sadly underutilized in this acceptable family fare about a drunken Indian who mends his ways. Abused by the white men who displaced his people (and who brought the smallpox that killed most of his tribe), even though he is an educated man, Fish Hawk ignores their taunts and retreats into the bottle. He comes to a sense of self-worth when he befriends a farm family and their young son. Well-intentioned, but rather awfully done.

THE FISH THAT SAVED PITTSBURGH ☆
1979, USA, PG
Julius Erving, James Bond III, Stockard Channing, Jonathan Winters, Margaret Avery, Jack Kehoe, Meadowlark Lemon, Flip Wilson, Kareem Abdul-Jabbar. Directed by Gilbert Moses. 102 min.

Though few movies can lay claim to pairing the histrionic talents of an actress like Stockard Channing with the athletic grace of a Julius Erving, almost any film can rightfully claim to be better than this legendary bomb. Channing plays a daffy astrologer who works her magic on an ailing basketball team. Once she figures out that the team's sign is Pisces, it's only a hop, and a jump shot to the championship. The film is depressingly cheap-looking and extraordinarily unfunny, but there are some great wide-lapel, polyester outfits and lots of trashy disco tunes. Ah, the seventies.

F.I.S.T. ☆☆½
1978, USA, PG
Sylvester Stallone, Rod Steiger, Peter Boyle, Melinda Dillon, Tony Lo Bianco. Directed by Norman Jewison. 145 min.

Norman Jewison's broad-backed, heavily clichéd epic treatment of the rise and fall of Johnny Kovak, a corrupt labor leader based on Jimmy Hoffa. The scenes of labor violence, set in late-thirties industrial Cleveland, are visually dynamic and exciting, but the rest of the movie is tiresome and confusing. In order to beat management, Kovak makes an alliance with the mob, selling out his union. Decades go by and he's still doing business with the Mafia; we're supposed to think that although Kovak acts in a corrupt way, he's not corrupt inside—whatever that means. As Kovak, Sylvester

Stallone is pulled this way and that by the compromising, sentimental screenplay (which he cowrote with Joe Eszterhas), and he never finds the character. The sleepy eyes and thickening voice seem all wrong for a supposedly shrewd, iron-willed labor leader. Melinda Dillon and Tony Lo Bianco are both wasted.

A FISTFUL OF CHOPSTICKS

See *They Call Me Bruce?*

A FISTFUL OF DOLLARS ☆☆☆
1964, Italy
Clint Eastwood, Gian Maria Volonte, Marianne Koch. Directed by Sergio Leone. 96 min.

Clint Eastwood's iconic Man with No Name drifts into a corrupt town and plays both ends against the middle to his own advantage. A violent, nihilistic fantasy on classic Western themes, based in part on Akira Kurosawa's *Yojimbo*; it is the first Italian Western to achieve international success, and also Eastwood's stepping-stone to stardom. Stylized and stylish, it features one of the four quirky soundtracks composed for Sergio Leone by Ennio Moricone. Followed by *For a Few Dollars More; The Good, The Bad and The Ugly;* and *Once upon a Time in the West.*

FIST OF FURY II ☆
1976
Bruce Li (Ho Tsung-Tao), Ku Feng, Tong Yim Chen, Ngai Ping O. Directed by To Lo Po.

It's the Japanese vs. the Chinese in Shanghai during the 1920s, with Bruce Li imitating Bruce Lee. Here's a conundrum worthy of Lao Tzu: is it a greater exploitative rip-off if a Bruce Lee imitator stars in an imitation of a Bruce Lee movie? Tune in this average copycat film for the answer.

FIST OF VENGEANCE ☆
Hong Kong
Kung Bun, Shoji Kurata, Lu Pi Chen, Tsao Chien, Lu Ping, Chen Hui Lou, Youg Lung, Pai I Feng, Tang Hsin, Has Su, with the special participation of Chiang Chih Yang and Yu Sung Chao. Directed by Chen Hung Man.

Kiro-san (Shoji Kurata), a Japanese fighter, arrives to escort a shipment of red sand, which is used in the forging of high-grade steel. This is an early "Chop Socky," before Hong Kong became a little more sophisticated in making martial-arts movies.

FISTS OF FEAR, TOUCH OF DEATH ½☆
1980, Hong Kong
Bruce Lee (clips from old movies), Ron Van Clief, Aaron Banks, Bill Louis, Teruyuki Higa, John Flood. Directed by Matthew Mallinson. 90 min.

One of the worst Bruce Lee exploitation films of all time! The premise of the movie is to find a successor to Lee through a series of elimination bouts held in Madison Square Garden. Actually, this is a facade behind which lurks Aaron Banks and his Martial Arts Expo. Banks is given the chance to tell the viewer what a great friend he was to Bruce, and to speculate on his demise. The only noteworthy sequence is the one in which Bill Louis rescues a woman from muggers.

FISTS OF FURY ☆☆☆
1972, Hong Kong, R
Bruce Lee, James Tien, Maria Yi, Han Ying Chieh, Tony Liu, Nora Miao, Li Hua Sxe. Directed by Lo Wei. 103 min.

The first Bruce Lee martial-arts movie. A young man (Lee) leaves his family in Hong Kong to work in Bangkok at an ice factory, where he discovers that his boss is operating a drug-running scheme. The bad guys try to buy him off, seduce him with women, and kill him—but Bruce is having none of that. The final fight between Lee and the Big Boss (Han Ying Chieh) is considered a classic. An average story with cheesy production values, but when Lee starts fighting, watch out!

THE FISTS, THE KICKS AND THE EVIL ☆☆
Hong Kong
Ku Feng, Yang Sze, Bruce Liang, Philip Kao Fei.

Our hero (Bruce Liang) searches for the killers of his teachers. Standard story line but beautiful fights.

A FIST TOO FAST

See *The Legendary Strike*

FITZCARRALDO ☆☆☆½
1982, West Germany, PG
Klaus Kinski, Claudia Cardinale, Jose Lewgoy, Grande Othelo. Directed by Werner Herzog. 150 min.

Visionary director Werner Herzog's offbeat, sprawling epic about a mad Irishman's quest to build the South American jungle's first opera house is one of his best if least-controlled films. As the obsessed protagonist Fitzgerald, Klaus Kinski gives what is by now a patented mad-genius performance, but his rolling eye and flyaway hair are well-suited here. The film is filled with sudden and surprising moments of great, strange beauty; and the climax, which involves a ship being pulled over a mountain, is one of the most spectacularly filmed scenes in Herzog's career.

FIVE DAYS ONE SUMMER ☆½
1982, Austria/USA, PG
Sean Connery, Betsy Brantley, Lambert Wilson, Jennifer Hilary, Isabel Dean, Gerald Buhr, Anna Massey. Directed by Fred Zinnemann. 108 min.

This is a romantic melodrama, set against the backdrop of the French Alps. The year is 1930, and Sean Connery is a married Scottish doctor who takes a girl half his age (Betsy Brantley) on a mountain-climbing holiday. Even with the charismatic Connery, the film is about as much fun as falling off Mt. Everest. One brings reservoirs of good feeling to the film because of Zinnemann's illustrious career, but his celebrated magic with actors is nowhere in evidence. You'll be rewarded instead with a plodding love triangle *aux Alpes*, a tale told unimaginatively except for one eerie sequence involving a man who'd been buried alive and perfectly preserved in the ice for decades. This icy, unconvincing film is so dated in technique that it also seems to have been preserved in a crevasse, and the sub–D. H. Lawrence subtext never quite thaws the film out.

FIVE EASY PIECES ☆☆☆☆
1970, USA
Jack Nicholson, Karen Black, Lois Smith, Susan Anspach, Fannie Flagg, Sally (Ann) Struthers, Helena Kallianotes. Directed by Bob Rafelson. 98 min.

Five Easy Pieces could easily have been just another antiestablishment "road picture." Bob Rafelson, however, turned the story of an oil-rigger who travels home to his dying father into a perceptive, picaresque adventure. After the seminal *Easy Rider*, Jack Nicholson consolidated his star status with this volatile, charismatic portrait of a working-class man from a highly cultured background. It's Nicholson's show, but the supporting cast is equally colorful: Karen Black as his pregnant girlfriend, Susan Anspach as a piano student with whom he becomes smitten, and Helena Kallianotes as a tough-talking hitchhiker. Rafelson has never duplicated the brilliance of his work here, which also includes highly innovative editing (by Christopher Holmes and Gerald Sheppard) and edgy, intense camera movements (by Lazslo Kovacs). A modern American "must see."

FIVE FINGERS ★★★½
1952, USA
James Mason, Danielle Darrieux, Richard Loo, Michael Rennie. Directed by Joseph L. Mankiewicz. 108 min.

This is as elegant a spy entertainment as you're likely to encounter. Joe Mankiewicz, the cinema's master of verbal virtuosity, brings his urbanity and malicious wit to bear on this classic double-cross tale set during World War II. Playing a fastidious valet to a British diplomat, James Mason exhibits supremely well-concealed self-interest as a devious espionage agent who knows how to sidestep detection with real agility. Wryly amusing and suspenseful, with Mason at his best in an unusual role.

FIVE WEEKS IN A BALLOON ★★½
1962, USA
Red Buttons, Fabian, Barbara Eden, Cedric Hardwicke, Peter Lorre, Richard Haydn, Barbara Luna, Billy Gilbert, Herbert Marshall, Reginald Owen, Henry Danielle, Mike Mazurki, Raymond Bailey. Directed by Irwin Allen. 101 min.

Schlockmeister Irwin Allen set out to duplicate the success of *Around the World in 80 Days* in this adaptation of a Jules Verne story that tries to be both parody and adventure. A group of British adventurers, led by Sir Cedric Hardwicke and accompanied by American reporter Red Buttons, sets out on a mission to cross Africa by balloon to claim previously untaken land before slave traders arrive. Most of the humor is provided by the cast of veteran character actors, especially Billy Gilbert as a sneezing sultan, but overall it's only adequate. After this, Allen abandoned the movies for ten years to create such seminal sixties TV shows as "Voyage to the Bottom of the Sea" and "Lost in Space."

FIXED BAYONETS ★★½
1951, USA
Richard Basehart, Gene Evans, Michael O'Shea, Richard Hylton, Craig Hill, Henry Kulky. Directed by Samuel Fuller. 92 min.

An early, and typical, film from that "authentic American primitive" (in the words of critic Andrew Sarris), writer/director Samuel Fuller. This is an old war plot undated to the then-current Korean "conflict": a platoon of soldiers is left behind to cover the rest of the regiment as they retreat. Of course, the platoon includes one representative of every ethnic group inhabiting the world today, and we get to explore a few psyches in depth. But this is a Sam Fuller picture, and there's no room for bull. Humor is minimal, in fact nonexistent, and tension is high—you don't know until the end who, if anyone, will survive. Richard Basehart, as a corporal who can't bring himself to kill, starts off weakly but gets better as the film progresses.

THE FLAME AND THE ARROW ★★★
1950, USA
Burt Lancaster, Virginia Mayo, Robert Douglas, Aline MacMahon, Frank Allenby, Nick Cravat. Directed by Jacques Tourneur. 89 min.

One of the ridiculous but enjoyable adventures that, for a while, made ex–circus acrobat Burt Lancaster the Errol Flynn of the fifties. Set in medieval Italy, Lancaster plays a Robin Hood type, helping the local peasants against the cruelties of the local despot. Director Jacques Tourneur, best known for the remarkably subtle horror thrillers he made for producer Val Lewton in the forties, shows a flair for action here as well, milking the scenes with Lancaster going through his tumbling paces for all they're worth. Nick Cravat, who plays Lancaster's mute sidekick, was also his circus partner in their pre-movie days, so the two work well together. With the usual rousing Max Steiner score, this makes for quite an entertaining package.

FLAME OF THE BARBARY COAST ★★½
1945, USA
John Wayne, Ann Dvorak, Joseph Schildkraut, William Frawley, Virginia Grey, Butterfly McQueen. Directed by Joseph Kane. 91 min.

Republic Pictures's Poverty Row depiction of the San Francisco earthquake is not unlike an erupting anthill. This low-budget rehash frames the famous 1906 earthquake around a love triangle involving a rancher (John Wayne), a singer (Ann Dvorak) and a gambler (Joseph Schildkraut). Dvorak (in one of her few leading-lady roles) is a better actress than Jeanette MacDonald, but don't expect another *San Francisco* or you will be disappointed.

FLAME OF THE ISLANDS ★★
1955, USA
Yvonne De Carlo, Zachary Scott, Howard Duff, Kurt Kasznar, Barbara O'Neil, James Arness. Directed by Edward Ludwig. 90 min.

The islands are the Bahamas, and the flame is sultry Yvonne De Carlo, a hard-luck chanteuse who's part owner of a gambling den–nightclub in this hard-nosed B romantic drama. She has four men vying for her affections, insidious underworld types moving in on her turf, and a proverbial "past"—predictable stuff, but enjoyable of its kind, with De Carlo singing "Bahama Mama" along the way.

THE FLAMINGO KID ★★★
1984, USA, PG-13
Matt Dillon, Richard Crenna, Hector Elizondo, Jessica Walter, Fisher Stevens, Molly McCarthy. Directed by Garry Marshall. 100 min.

Teen heartthrob Matt Dillon gives the best performance of his career in director Garry Marshall's funny, intelligent drama about growing up. Dillon plays Jeffrey Willis, a good kid from Brooklyn who—to the dismay of his plumber father, who dreams of sending him to college—becomes attracted to the crude philosophies of a fast-talking, nouveau-riche card hustler he meets at the El Flamingo, the crass Long Island country club where he spends the summer as a cabana boy. Marshall, the man behind "Happy Days" and "Laverne and Shirley," has created a deftly crafted, upbeat satire that amuses but is never trivial. Set in 1963, the film boasts an exceptional soundtrack featuring such classic period artists as The Silhouettes and Sam Cooke.

FLAMING STAR ★★½
1960, USA
Elvis Presley, Steve Forrest, Barbara Eden, Dolores Del Rio, John McIntire, Richard Jaeckel, L. Q. Jones. Directed by Don Siegel. 92 min.

Aside fom the title song, which is heard only over the opening credits, Elvis Presley sings only one song in this, his first overtly "dramatic" film. He plays a half-breed Indian who is accepted neither by his mother's tribe nor by the white settlers nearby. A good screenplay by Nunnally Johnson and Claire Huffaker, and passable direction by Siegel, compensate for Elvis's stoical approach.

FLASH AND THE FIRECAT ★½
1975, USA, PG
Roger Davis, Tricia Sembera, Dub Taylor, Richard Kiel, Joan Shawlee. Directed by Fred and Beverly Sebastian. 84 min.

This flashily empty action picture upholds the gangster tradition of *Bonnie and Clyde* with none of the insight, technique, or acting brilliance of that celebrated film. Instead, we have two misunderstood kids hightailing it around in search of the perfect heist. Whizzing along in their dune buggies, the cast kicks up quite a sandstorm of movie clichés but not enough to blind us to the film's almost complete lack of merit.

FLASHDANCE ★★★
1983, USA, R
Jennifer Beals, Michael Nouri, Lilia Skala, Sunny Johnson, Kyle T. Heffner, Belinda Bauer. Directed by Adrian Lyne. 96 min.

Upbeat and inspirational, this vehicle for newcomer Jennifer Beals relies more on its exuberant music and electrifying choreography than on plot. In short, it's like a series of good music videos woven together by romance and a simple success story. Bringing torn sweatshirts and a personal new-wave flair to the screen, coyly alluring Beals portrays a welder-by-day/club-dancer-by-night who dreams of becoming a ballerina. Michael Nouri, her boss on the construction site, loves and encourages the eighteen-year-old. The *Flashdance* theme song deservedly won an Oscar.

FLASH GORDON ★★★
1980, USA, PG
Sam J. Jones, Max von Sydow, Melody Anderson. Directed by Michael Hodges. 121 min.

Underrated and overlooked. Dino Di Laurentiis's big-budget version of the 1936 serial *Perils from the Planet Mongo* plays the Flash Gordon saga as pure camp. But if the story is a throwaway, the visuals are a psychedelic treat. Ex–Fellini production designer Danilo Donati conjures up a dazzling fairy-tale universe somewhere between *2001* and *The Wizard of Oz*, and the Frederick's-of-Neptune costumes and hilariously trashy rock score (by Queen) only add to the gaudy, Day-Glo splendor of it all. A blond slab of beefcake named Sam J. Jones is Flash, and Max von Sydow does an enjoyable turn as Ming the Merciless.

FLASH LEGS

See *Deadly Shaolin Kicks*

A FLASH OF GREEN ★★★
1984, USA, PG
Ed Harris, Blair Brown, Richard Jordan, George Coe, Jean De Baer, Joan Goodfellow. Directed by Victor Nuñez. 121 min.

This grim tale of compromised morality, bleakly executed by independent director Victor Nuñez (*Gal Young 'Un*), captures a torpid, tawdry Florida ambience better than the much-vaunted *Body Heat*. Bored small-town reporter Jimmy Wing (Ed Harris) takes on an investigative job and finds himself enmeshed in a plot to blackmail the ecology-minded opponents of a land-development scheme. A sincere portrait of diminished self-respect and scrabbling for survival; unfortunately, the cast plays everything so close to the vest that the viewer often remains in the dark as to character motivations. The John D. MacDonald novel upon which the film is based has been seriously underrated and is one of the few of his works that transcends its genre origins.

FLASHPOINT ★★
1984, USA, R
Kris Kristofferson, Treat Williams, Rip Torn, Kevin Conway, Kurtwood Smith, Tess Harper. Directed by William Tannen. 93 min.

Kris Kristofferson and Treat Williams are border patrol buddies who stumble onto an old political conspiracy. Produced by HBO, the film does suffer from a TV-movie lethargy. *Flashpoint* had a limp theatrical run; however, it was a mild hit when released on video—probably due to the presence of Kristofferson and Williams.

FLAT TOP ★★½
1952, USA
Sterling Hayden, Richard Carlson, Bill Phipps, John Bromfield, William Schallert. Directed by Lesley Selander. 83 min.

The title refers to a U.S. Air Force carrier ship, the location of yet another film about callow young men becoming tough, able fighters. Sterling Hayden plays the ship's C.O., the demanding sort because he knows it's best for his men, but the movie is much more fun if you imagine he's playing a younger version of Colonel Ripper, his character in *Dr. Strangelove*. Lots of newsreel footage supplies verisimilitude, and it is passable as far as it goes, but when you consider that the director served as an assistant to, among others, Fritz Lang and W. S. Van Dyke II, you might have hoped that he'd been paying more attention to what his superiors were doing when *he* was training.

FLESH AND BLOOD ★½
1985, USA, R
Rutger Hauer, Jennifer Jason Leigh, Tom Burlinson, Jack Thompson, Susan Tyrrell. Directed by Paul Verhoeven. 126 min.

The first English-language film by Dutch director Paul Verhoeven (*The Fourth Man*) is a turgid, gory, overlong medieval epic whose inept script and sluggish story line contain much more blood than flesh. Most of the latter belongs to Rutger Hauer, as a renegade swordsman seeking to overthrow the local lord, and Jennifer Jason Leigh, as the lusty lass who secretly longs to be pillaged, plundered, overthrown, and abused. By the time you see Susan Tyrrell swaggering about in animal skins and bellowing randy shouts of encouragement, you'll know not to take it too seriously; by the time bubonic plague sets in, you'll know you've been watching long enough.

THE FLESH EATERS ★
1964, USA
Martin Kosleck, Rita Morley, Ray Tudor. Directed by Jack Curtis. 82 min.

Cheap, sleazy, zero-budget horror films aren't, as some believe, an invention of the 1980s—here's an ugly little antique made a generation ago, reportedly by independent hacks whose most notable previous work was in the soft-core porn biz. The unoriginal plot pits a pair of air-crash survivors on a desert island against a mad scientist (Martin Kosleck) experimenting with the creation of the tiny title characters. Not to be believed.

FLESH FEAST ½★
1970, USA
Veronica Lake, Phil Philbin, Chris Martell, Heather Hughes, Martha Mischon. Directed by B. F. Grinter. 72 min.

Veronica Lake should have restored her peekaboo hairdo for this film and then hid behind it in shame. This maggoty thriller could serve as a companion piece to the timeless *They Saved Hitler's Brain*; it deals with a crazed scientist who takes time off from her experimentation on aging to do some terribly nasty things to Der Führer himself, who's apparently been alive all these years after all. It's so bad you may end up rooting for Hitler.

FLESH GORDON ★
1974, USA, X
Jason Williams, Suzann Fields, Joseph Hudgins, William Hunt. Directed by Howard Ziehm and Michael Benveniste. 78 min.

A film that strains for the campy humor found in the thirties serials but falls utterly flat, *Flesh* lacks even the promised soft-core sexiness. Does include some good special effects.

FLETCH ★★½
1985, USA, PG
Chevy Chase, Dana Wheeler-Nicholson, Tim Matheson, Kareem-Abdul Jabbar. Directed by Michael Ritchie. 98 min.

This comedy-mystery about a wisecracking reporter trying to break a story that's much bigger than he realizes gives Chevy Chase an opportunity to smirk his way through a variety of disguises, some funny, some not. There's fast-moving action (in a plot full of holes), but your enjoyment of *Fletch* will rise or fall on how well you stomach Chase's consistently smug, smartass acting style. He gets better zingers than usual from Andrew Bergman's script, but still gives a fundamentally lazy performance in an entertaining, wholly forgettable film.

FLIGHT FROM GLORY ★★☆
1937, USA
Chester Morris, Whitney Bourne, Onslow Stevens, Van Heflin, Richard Lane. Directed by Lew Landers. 66 min.

This exciting, tautly directed adventure presented an interesting obverse to such Howard Hawks airplane dramas as *Dawn Patrol* and *Only Angels Have Wings*. Rather than the standard Hawksian male camaraderie, Landers presents a group of fliers who are torn apart by their insecurities and the dangerous conditions under which they work. Onslow Stevens, who runs a flight service on a hazardous route over the Andes, specializes in finding pilots who have been discredited elsewhere, giving them employment, and keeping them in debt to him so that they can't leave. He hires Van Heflin, a cowardly flier who brings with him his beautiful wife (Whitney Bourne); as the only woman in an all-male operation, she causes predictable turmoil. Had the Hayes Code people really been doing their duty, they wouldn't have let the ending pass as is.

FLIGHT OF THE EAGLE ★★½
1982, Sweden
Max von Sydow, Goran Stangertz, Lotta Larsson, Sverre Anker Ousdal, Clement Havari. Directed by Jan Troell. 141 min.

A true-life adventure story of a balloon flight to the North Pole, based on the 1897 notebooks of explorer S. A. Andree (von Sydow). Although handsome and stately, it is too slow-moving and methodical to be of much interest to anyone besides exploration buffs. Von Sydow's quiet dignity in the central role is a great help.

FLIGHT OF THE NAVIGATOR ★★★½
1986, USA, PG
Joey Cramer, Cliff De Young, Howard Hesseman, Veronica Cartwright, Sarah Jessica Parker, Matt Adler, voice of "Paul Mall." Directed by Randal Kleiser. 89 min.

Since the dawning of the Age of Spielberg, no Hollywood formula has been more overworked than the twelve-year-old-boy-meets-cute-alien genre. What a pleasure, then, to discover an addition to the canon that stakes out its own turf and comes up with its own very winning combination of fantasy, humor, adventure, and drama. It's 1978, and young David (played with spunk by Joey Cramer) has been sent into the woods by his mom and dad to fetch his younger brother. He trips, falls in a ditch, and knocks himself out. Rubbing his head, he wakes up and returns home—only to find that home is gone and that even though he's still twelve, it's now eight years later. The first half of the film doesn't stint on the fright and disorientation the young hero feels when he reunites with his shocked family, and as we and he slowly discover the extraterrestrial case for his absence, the film never loses its heart. The second half of the film is a delightfully funny joyride in a talking spaceship (the very familiar voice is credited to "Paul Mall," a pseudonym for Paul Reubens, better known and loved as Pee-Wee Herman). Fast-moving, full of surprises, and a treat for kids and their parents.

THE FLIGHT OF THE PHOENIX ★★★½
1965, USA
James Stewart, Richard Attenborough, Peter Finch, Hardy Kruger, Ernest Borgnine, Ian Bannen, Dan Duryea, George Kennedy, Barrie Chase. Directed by Robert Aldrich. 149 min.

There's something about Jimmy Stewart and planes. He eloped in one in *You Gotta Stay Happy* (1949), took a nosedive in both *No Highway in the Sky* (1951) and *The Glenn Miller Story* (1955), was recalled to air-force duty in *Strategic Air Command* (1955), and crossed the Atlantic as Charles Lindbergh in *The Spirit of St. Louis* (1957). In this tense, exciting adventure yarn, Stewart plays a veteran pilot who mans a rickety craft over the North African desert. After his twin-engine plane is forced down in a sandstorm, he and his passengers must either survive their days and nights in the desert, waiting for a rescue party, or build from the wreckage a single-engine plane that will take them home. Despite the familiar tale and clichéd characters, Aldrich creates one of the best films of this type and gets solid, granular work from the cast. It is typical of a macho sixties film, however, for its only female role is that of a dancing vision (as played by Barrie Chase).

FLIGHT TO MARS ★★☆
1951, USA
Marguerite Chapman, Cameron Mitchell, Arthur Franz, Virginia Huston, John Litel, Morris Ankrum. Directed by Lesley Selander. 71 min.

This was the first all-color space movie, which is hardly enough of a distinction to make you rush right out and get a copy. It's better than the usual Monogram Studios production, but not by a whole lot. The crew of the first flight to Mars discovers an underground civilization. Needless to say, foreign civilizations in films of the fifties, especially underground ones, are bad news, so our crew has its work cut out for them. Lesley Selander was one of the very few Hollywood directors to have worked his way up from assistant director, a position he filled on such quality films as *The Thin Man*, *A Night at the Opera*, and *Fury*. Given the unexceptional quality of this sci-fier, the rarity of such upward mobility in the studio system may not have been so surprising.

THE FLIM-FLAM MAN ★★★
1967, USA
George C. Scott, Sue Lyon, Michael Sarrazin, Harry Morgan, Jack Albertson, Alice Ghostley, Albert Salmi, Slim Pickens, Strother Martin. Directed by Irvin Kershner. 104 min.

Taking off on W. C. Fields's maxim that "You can't cheat an honest man," this amiable Southern comedy follows veteran con artist George C. Scott as he teaches his trade to young drifter Michael Sarrazin. The rationale that you can only steal money from those who have already shown themselves to be greedy and dishonest may make for dubious morality, but it also provides a lot of funny moments as the pair connive their way across the rural south. The second-unit director, who was responsible for the memorable chase scene in which an entire town is practically flattened, was veteran stuntman Yakima Canutt.

FLOOD! ★½
1976, USA (TV)
Robert Culp, Martin Milner, Carol Lynley, Barbara Hershey, Richard Basehart, Cameron Mitchell, Teresa Wright, Roddy McDowall. Directed by Earl Bellamy. 98 min.

This second-rate Irwin Allen disaster film lacks his usual spectacular effects and massive vistas of destruction. Instead, we're given a small-screen version of an all-star cast playing residents of a lakeside fishing community faced with dangerously high water. If they save themselves by opening the dam, they'll lose their fish and thus their livelihood. The town's greedier minds prevail, but the film is all wet long before the flood arrives. Inane, even for this genre.

FLOWER DRUM SONG ★★★
1961, USA
Nancy Kwan, James Shigeta, Jack Soo, Miyoshi Umeki, Juanita Hall, Benson Fong. Directed by Henry Koster. 133 min.

Who can forget Kenneth Tynan's dismissal of this show as "The World of Woozy Song"? Well, movie-musical lovers may be able to overlook that remark, since this film version's colorful charms outweigh its failings, chief among which is the protracted running time. The plot involves several unresolved romances, including that of a picture bride from China and the smooth-talking nightclub owner who, after sending for her, has shifted his amorous interest to a nitery performer. A good-natured musical with terrific choreography and lovely melodies that keep the film from overstaying its welcome, even though someone seems to have fallen asleep in the editing room.

THE FLY ☆☆☆
1958, USA
Vincent Price, Al (David) Hedison, Herbert Marshall, Patricia Owens. Directed by Kurt Neumann. 94 min.

While trying to perfect a device that will transport matter through space in the wink of an eye, Andre DeLambre scrambles his atoms with those of a housefly, leaving him in a fine mess. From the view through the giant fly's eye to the fly with DeLambre's head trapped in a spiderweb bleating "Help me! Help me!" it is an arch and self-conscious horror picture. With Vincent Price as the no-nonsense DeLambre brother (though his performance still borders on hysteria) and a screenplay by James (*Shogun*) Clavell.

THE FLY ☆☆☆½
1986, USA, R
Jeff Goldblum, Geena Davis, John Getz, Joy Bouchel, Les Carlson. Directed by David Cronenberg. 95 min.

This film is not so much a remake of the sci-fi original as an intelligent rethinking of the story, about a misguided scientist whose genes are melded to a fly's during a teleportation accident. As the unfortunate inventor, Jeff Goldblum is so likable that he gives the film tragic dimensions while undergoing an inexorable transformation into a half-human insect. The extreme gore that accompanies the metamorphosis seems integral to the story, and director David Cronenberg handles the macabre material with his usual outrageous sense of humor and a newly minted attitude of sympathy. Superior to the 1957 film, except for its attenuated ending.

FLYING DEUCES ☆☆☆
1939, USA
Stan Laurel, Oliver Hardy, James Finlayson. Directed by Edward A. Sutherland. 69 min.

After failing in a suicide attempt, two bumblers throw their lives away by joining the French Foreign Legion. Laurel and Hardy's greatest gift was in making the horrifying and violent into a graceful melody, and the best moments of this film occur when the boys are fighting their situation—in the laundry, in jail, or in a runaway plane. Watch for Stan's Harpolike playing on his bedsprings while Ollie sings "Shine on Harvest Moon." Directed by Eddie Sutherland, who worked for Charlie Chaplin, directed Douglas Fairbanks and W. C. Fields, and was married to Louise Brooks.

FLYING DOWN TO RIO ☆☆½
1933, USA
Dolores Del Rio, Gene Raymond, Fred Astaire, Ginger Rogers, Paul Roulien. Directed by Thornton Freeland. 89 min.

A classic by default. Although the lavish south-of-the-border musical headlines Dolores Del Rio, Gene Raymond, and Paul Roulien in a tedious romantic triangle, dance aficionados remember the film as the debut coupling of fourth- and fifth-billed players—Fred Astaire and Ginger Rogers. Unfortunately, the team dances together for only a couple of minutes and, while Vincent Youmans's score is catchy and pleasant, it is, except for Fred and Ginger's contributions, poorly performed. Some of the film is so amateurish, in fact, that it can best be seen as camp. *Top Hat* fans, beware.

FLYING LEATHERNECKS ☆☆☆
1951, USA
John Wayne, Robert Ryan. Directed by Nicholas Ray. 103 min.

Wayne, a tough marine commander, must work out tension in the heat of battle with Robert Ryan and his squadron of flying leathernecks. Director Nicholas Ray strings together many macho clichés to create an occasionally interesting war movie. The combat scenes, which include real war footage, are the most compelling. Wayne's performance is up to par.

FLYING TIGERS ☆☆½
1942, USA
John Wayne, John Carroll, Anna Lee, Paul Kelly, Mae Clarke. Directed by David Miller. 98 min.

Yet another wartime feature glorifying the efforts of Our Fighting Men, this film has a little panache in the flying sequences that compensates for the cheapness of the production. The "Flying Tigers" are American flyers stationed in China who take up the fight against the Yellow Menace prior to the bombing of Pearl Harbor. Featuring a foreword written by Generalissimo Chiang Kai-shek!

FM ☆½
1978, USA, PG
Michael Brandon, Eileen Brennan, Alex Karras, Cleavon Little, Martin Mull, Cassie Yates. Directed by John A. Alonzo. 110 min.

The perfunctory plot of this soundtrack album masquerading as a movie concerns a group of radio station deejays who rebel against their conservative corporate bosses and play the kind of music they know their radical fans want to hear: Jimmy Buffett, Bob Welch, Steve Miller, and Linda Ronstadt. *This* is revolutionary? No, but there's a lot of it, and although the cast of comedians is for the most part wasted, Ronstadt and Buffett do turn in decent concert appearances.

THE FOG ☆☆½
1980, USA, R
Adrienne Barbeau, Jamie Lee Curtis, Hal Holbrook, Janet Leigh. Directed by John Carpenter. 91 min.

This creepy and atmospheric horror yarn has ghosts of a drowned leper colony seeking vengeance against the small New England town that benefited from their murders a hundred years ago. Low-budget horror director John Carpenter, who was handed a bigger budget for this film after the success of *Halloween*, acquits himself honorably with this brooding and suspenseful gothic thriller. Graced with the usual pounding synthesizer score by Carpenter and Alan Howarth.

FOLIES BERGÈRE ☆☆☆
1935, USA
Maurice Chevalier, Merle Oberon, Ann Sothern, Eric Blore, Ferdinand Munier. Directed by Roy Del Ruth. 84 min.

When a property is hot, it's hot. In 1935, Darryl F. Zanuck bought the French musical *L'homme des Folies Bergère*, remade it that year as *Folies Bergère*, then again in 1941 as *That Night in Rio*, and yet again in 1951 as *On the Riviera*. Today everyone agrees that the first remake is the best. It's a light, saucy concoction about a French millionaire (Maurice Chevalier, although Zanuck wanted Charles Boyer) who discovers a lookalike counterpart in a Folies Bergère singer and uses the situation to smooth out his business and romantic problems. Chevalier has a great time in what would become his last American leading-man role, and he gets delicious support from Merle Oberon as the millionaire's wife and Sothern as the singer's girlfriend. The musical highlight is a Busby Berkeleyish item with chorus girls in oversized straw hats. Also known as *The Man from the Folies Bergère*.

FOLIES BOURGEOISES

See *The Twist*

FOLLOW ME, BOYS! ☆☆½
1966, USA
Fred MacMurray, Vera Miles, Lillian Gish, Charlie Ruggles, Kurt Russell, Steve Franken, Tim McIntire. Directed by Norman Tokar. 131 min.

This typical Walt Disney comedy-drama stars Fred MacMurray as a dedicated Boy Scout leader in a small town in the 1930s. This is more effective than most, if you don't mind the obviousness of the heart-tugging effects. Lillian Gish is, as always, charming as a slightly batty old woman who decides to give away a large portion of land to the Boy Scouts, only to be tried for incompetency by a greedy nephew. Overlong, but otherwise good family entertainment.

FOLLOW THAT CAMEL ☆☆
1967, Great Britain
Phil Silvers, Jim Dale, Peter Butterworth, Charles Hawtrey, Joan Sims, Kenneth Williams. Directed by Gerald Thomas. 95 min.

The *Carry On* gang carries on again, this time in the French Foreign Legion. Phil Silvers injects some much-needed new comic blood into the series as a Bilko-esque sergeant who tries to bilk everyone within his reach. Familiar shenanigans, but expertly handled by a cast of comic pros.

FOLLOW THE FLEET ☆☆☆
1936, USA
Fred Astaire, Ginger Rogers, Randolph Scott, Harriet Hilliard (Nelson), Astrid Allwyn, Betty Grable, Lucille Ball. Directed by Mark Sandrich. 110 min.

Long withheld from distribution by Irving Berlin, who composed its score, this is not one of the great Fred Astaire–Ginger Rogers dance fests, but it has its sparkling moments, especially an enchanting *pas de deux* entitled "Let's Face the Music and Dance."

THE FOOD OF THE GODS ☆☆
1976, USA, PG
Ida Lupino, Marjoe Gortner, Pamela Franklin, Ralph Meeker, John McLiam. Directed by Bert I. Gordon. 88 min.

Rats, wasps, and other small animals grow to outrageous proportions and terrorize the countryside after devouring a mysterious goo. Ida Lupino and Marjoe Gortner appropriately overplay this camp item (based on a story by H. G. Wells) and some of the effects are truly gruesome, but one keeps waiting for the giant mammary from *Everything You Always Wanted to Know About Sex . . .* to make its appearance and drown all the other bad actors. Not up to the standards of *Them* and *Tarantula*.

FOOL FOR LOVE ☆☆½
1985, USA, R
Sam Shepard, Kim Basinger, Harry Dean Stanton, Randy Quaid. Directed by Robert Altman. 105 min.

Sam Shepard's *Fool for Love* is a theatrical desert set in a real one. Not one of his best plays, it is as inviting and kinetic as a cactus; the stage version, however, gained power from its very claustrophobia. Robert Altman's adaptation—"an exploded play," Shepard called it—of this story of two ex-lovers in a Western motel room loses even this modicum of fire. Shepard as the bucked cowboy is weirdly unmenacing, though Kim Basinger as his lover (or is it sister?) steams. Harry Dean Stanton waltzes from ghost to guest, becoming both the owner of the motel and the surreal spark for many flashbacks. Manic crosscuts and a lunatic jukebox-roping scene can't save this earnest, near-admirable work.

FOOLIN' AROUND ☆☆½
1980, USA, PG
Gary Busey, Annette O'Toole, Cloris Leachman, Tony Randall, Eddie Albert, John Calvin. Directed by Richard T. Heffron. 111 min.

Gary Busey plays Harold Lloyd, more or less, in this dopey but amiable comedy about a college freshman from the Midwest who becomes smitten with the local beauty. Trouble is, she's both rich and engaged. As you can probably tell, this is another variation on the Slobs vs. the Snobs, with Busey and Eddie Albert, the Earthy Patriarch type, against Young Snob Fiancé John Calvin and Bourgeois Snob Mother Cloris Leachman, with supercilious butler Tony Randall on the sidelines to look down on it all. A pleasant enough way to waste two hours, if you're sure you have nothing better to do.

FOOLISH WIVES ☆☆☆☆
1921, USA
Erich Von Stroheim, Mae Busch, Maud George, Cesare Gravina. Directed by Erich Von Stroheim. 85 min.

This is one of the major silent films and a milestone in the checkered career of the noted director. As an actor, Erich Von Stroheim was known as "the man you love to hate," but his principal claim to genius was as a director obsessed with realistic production design. Since he created his films without a high regard for budget overruns, he quickly became known as "the *director* you love to hate" by most Hollywood studios. *Foolish Wives* is a stunning example of Von Stroheim's predilection for background detail, yet the story line is not swallowed up by the impeccable costuming and massive sets. Billed as "the million-dollar movie," *Wives* unveils a lurid world of purchasable sex. An ersatz count (played by Von Stroheim) seduces monied married women and then graciously relieves them of the burden of great wealth by blackmailing them. The original running time was much longer, but Von Stroheim's films always suffered at the hands of studio cutters—the lost footage of *Foolish Wives* is one of Hollywood's great tragedies.

FOOLS ½☆
1970, USA
Jason Robards, Katharine Ross, Roy C. Jenson, Scott Hylands. Directed by Tom Gries. 97 min.

This film is a garish conceit of a love story that's supposed to break our hearts. Since it's impossible to care about the thwarted romance of an outspoken horror-film star and a neurotic lawyer's wife, *Fools* cleverly makes us squirm in our seats. This real stinker wrecked Katharine Ross's bid for feature-film stardom and revealed that Jason Robards is not palatable as a leading man. Unbearable.

FOOTLIGHT PARADE ☆☆☆½
1933, USA
James Cagney, Joan Blondell, Ruby Keeler, Dick Powell, Guy Kibee. Directed by Lloyd Bacon. 104 min.

Three spectacular Busby Berkeley production numbers climax this Depression-era Warner Bros. musical: "Honeymoon Hotel" is risqué fun in a honeymoon suite; "By a Waterfall" submerges Berkeley's kaleidoscopic routines in water; and "Shanghai Lil" pairs the offbeat hoofing talents of James Cagney and Ruby Keeler. Otherwise, the film is all Jimmy's. He plays a feisty young theatrical director who invents musical prologues for motion picture audiences who are tired of live stage shows. Cagney's energy, a good supporting cast and a fast pace help the film along to its dynamite finale.

FOOTLOOSE ☆☆
1984, USA, PG
Kevin Bacon, Christopher Penn, Lori Singer, John Lithgow, Diane Wiest. Directed by Herbert Ross. 106 min.

Small-town kids just want to dance, but a town ordinance—wholeheartedly supported by the local Bible-thumping preacher—holds that such carrying-on paves the highway to hell. Led by a transfer student whose notion of civil rights was fostered in Chicago, the oppressed youngsters manage to have their prom and stay within the bounds of the law, too. Upbeat message in a slick, attractive package; a hit title song performed by Kenny Loggins.

FOR A FEW DOLLARS MORE ☆☆☆
1965, Italy
Clint Eastwood, Lee Van Cleef, Gian Maria Volonte, Klaus Kinski. Directed by Sergio Leone. 130 min.

This film is the second (see also *A Fistful of Dollars*, *The Good, the Bad and the Ugly*, and *Once Upon a Time in the West*) of director Sergio Leone's revisionist explorations of classic Western themes through a glass, violently. Two bounty hunters, a displaced Southern aristocrat (Van Cleef) and Eastwood's Man with No Name, join forces to round up the psychotic El Indio and his gang of cut-throat misfits. Another offbeat soundtrack by Ennio Morricone (who did all four of Leone's Westerns) and Klaus Kinski as a malevolent hunchback.

FORBIDDEN PLANET ☆☆☆☆
1956, USA
Leslie Nielsen, Walter Pidgeon, Anne Francis, Earl Holliman. Directed by Fred McLeod Wilcox. 98 min.

Imaginatively done, better than virtually all of the other science-fiction films of its time, *Forbidden Planet* is an eerie and awe-inspiring look at humans and aliens at odds with the machinery they have created. Shakespeare's *The Tempest* moves to outer space when a group of intergalactic explorers is marooned on the forboding planet of Altair VI and meets up with a slightly mad scientist and his beautiful daughter. While the technical jargon and pretty effects seem juvenile at first glance, the story's Freudian complexities start to unravel when the crew members find themselves at the mercy of an "Id" monster, the externalized thoughts of the distraught researcher. This landmark film of its genre was also famous for introducing Robby the Robot, who spoke 187 languages and distilled his own bourbon. The excellent visuals were created by Walt Disney Studios.

FORBIDDEN TRAIL ☆½
1936, USA
Buck Jones, Barbara Weeks. Directed by Lambert Hillyer. 65 min.

An average Buck Jones oater with a strained comic overtone. Jones may not be a comedian, but he does perform well as a cowboy, and the movie contains a good portion of riding and shooting.

FORBIDDEN WORLD ☆☆
1982, USA, R
Jesse Vint. Directed by Allan Holzman. 82 min.

A space adventurer discovers that the inhabitants of an experimental research station have produced a horrifying monster that is decimating their ranks. Although promoted as a "new-wave" science-fiction movie—by virtue, one supposes, of the fact that several characters wear sunglasses in space—it is in fact a conventional *Alien*-derived exercise in which confined space + vicious killer on the loose = bloody fun for all. The creature meets a particularly vile fate by way of a cancerous liver that it imprudently devours.

FORBIDDEN ZONE ☆☆☆
1980, USA
Hervé Villechaize, Susan Tyrrell, Marie-Pascale Elfman, Viva. Directed by Richard Elfman. 76 min.

This self-consciously strange, silly film was created expressly for the midnight-movie crowd, who never exactly took it to heart. The creators of the rock group Oingo Boingo have fashioned a mythical kingdom, run by Hervé Villechaize and Susan Tyrrell and populated by all sorts of loonies. Shot in black and white on deliberately cheap, tacky sets (designed by star Marie-Pascale Elfman), this is equal parts *Cabinet of Dr. Caligari*, *Rocky Horror Picture Show*, *Desperate Living*, *Eraserhead*, Monty Pythonish video graphics, and Betty Boop; in fact, the whole thing resembles nothing so much as a live-action Max Fleischer cartoon. With lots of great songs, including some old thirties novelty tunes that the performers lip-synch.

FORCED ENTRY ½☆
1984, USA
Tanya Roberts, Ron Max, Nancy Allen, Robin Leslie. Directed by Jim Sotos. 83 min.

Brutal, lurid, and recommended only for fans of the Marquis de Sade. It was shot in 1975 and then reedited (from the looks of this abomination, the usable footage should have reduced the film's running time to about forty seconds). A vicious rapist-killer meets his match when he tries to force himself on Tanya Roberts. A tribute to the sweaty-palms set and all those dirty old men who used to frequent porn houses in their trench coats. (a.k.a.: *The Last Victim*)

FORCED VENGEANCE ☆½
1982, USA, R
Chuck Norris, Mary Louise Weller, Camilla Griggs, Michael Cavenaugh. Directed by James Fargo. 90 min.

Chuck Norris has made better movies than this, though he's made more that are equally as forgettable and indistinguishable. This time he's the head of security at a Hong Kong gambling casino out to avenge the death of his girlfriend. Written, directed, and fought by rote.

FORCE: FIVE ☆½
1981, USA, R
Joe Lewis, Pam Huntington, Mater Bong Soo Han, Richard Norton. Directed by Robert Clouse. 95 min.

More Kung Phooey from Robert Clouse, who had better luck with this action formula in *Enter the Dragon*. A motley crew of five people join forces and martial-arts specialties to rescue a young girl from enslavement in a religious cult. It's like a bad musical with good choreography—the fight sequences are super, but the actual story is one long stage wait in between fights.

FORCE OF EVIL ☆☆☆
1948, USA
John Garfield, Beatrice Pearson, Thomas Gomez, Roy Roberts, Marie Windsor. Directed by Abraham Polonsky. 78 min.

Abraham Polonsky was blacklisted shortly after writing and directing this allegorical crime drama about a syndicate lawyer (John Garfield) who yearns to go straight. Heavily inspired by Clifford Odets, the film suffers from the melodramatic overkill of its celebrated "poetic" dialogue and its descent-into-hell finale. But it also has the kind of crusading ardor that's all but disappeared from the American screen.

A FORCE OF ONE ☆
1979, USA, PG
Chuck Norris, Jennifer O'Neill, Clu Gulager, Ron O'Neal. Directed by Paul Aaron. 96 min.

Karate-chopper Chuck Norris, world champ or not, is a tight, dull screen presence, and when he does unfold his lethal limbs (which isn't often) the all-too-functional fighting style is as cool and limited as he is. At least Bruce Lee brought balletic showmanship to his exploits. The film is competently directed (by *A Different Story*'s Paul Aaron), but the drug-smuggling-cum-revenge-fantasy plot is strictly from TV. Jennifer O'Neill sports an unbecoming concentration-camp haircut.

FORCE 10 FROM NAVARONE ☆☆½
1978, USA, PG
Robert Shaw, Harrison Ford, Edward Fox, Barbara Bach. Directed by Guy Hamilton. 118 min.

A cloddish but enjoyable throwback, this is the sort of World War II movie (a sequel to *The Guns of Navarone*) in which a hard-bitten American sergeant (Harrison Ford) can still exclaim "This place is crawling with Krauts!" and "If those panzers get across that bridge they'll go through this country like a dose of salts!" The bridge in question is in Yugoslavia: Robert Shaw and Edward Fox have been assigned to blow it up. On the way to the inevitable big explosion (a special-effects washout) the limeys encounter the likes of beautiful double-agent Barbara Bach ("Day are shpies! Keel dem!") and hulking Yugoslav leader Richard Kiel ("Com frens! Vee eat! Vee drink! And den vee keel some Chermans!"). From the novel by Alistair MacLean.

FOREIGN BODY ☆☆½
1986, Great Britain, PG-13
Victor Banerjee, Warren Mitchell, Geraldine McEwan, Denis Quilley, Amanda Donohoe, Anna Massey, Trevor Howard. Directed by Ronald Neame. 100 min.

A minor but amusing film recalls the English social comedies of Roy Boulting—in the 1960s it would have been made with Peter Sellers doing his Nehru impression. Here we have popeyed Victor Banerjee in danger of becoming a self-parody as an Indian émigré who tries to better his lot in England after a lifetime of menial tasks. He lucks into a position as doctor for the smart set and comic complications ensue. Agreeable, but not inspired.

FOREIGN CORRESPONDENT ☆☆☆☆
1940, USA
Joel McCrea, Laraine Day, Herbert Marshall, George Sanders, Albert Basserman, Robert Benchley. Directed by Alfred Hitchcock. 119 min.

Among the most entertaining of Alfred Hitchcock's Hollywood projects, *Foreign Correspondent* succeeds as war propaganda at the same time that it addresses more profound questions about the nature of identity, evil, and the tension between appearance and reality. Joel McCrea plays an American crime reporter who is sent to investigate rising hostilities in Europe. When he witnesses the assassination of a Dutch diplomat, he becomes enmeshed in dangerous international intrigue. Although the narrative flags at a couple of junctures, most of the film thrills and fascinates. Hitchcock spent about $1.5 million making this movie, his greatest budget up to that time. Several extraordinary scenes—the assassination amid a sea of umbrellas, the encounter at a windmill that spins backward, and, of course, the climax in the airplane—suggest the money was well spent.

FOREPLAY ☆
1975, USA, R
Zero Mostel, Estelle Parsons, Pat Paulsen, Jerry Orbach, George S. Irving, Andrew Duncan. Directed by Robert J. McCarty, Bruce Malmuth, and John G. Avildsen. 100 min.

This mess can be at least partially explained: it was originally intended as four short episodes about sex by four directors (thus the title, which would have been a pun). However, one of the segments was considered too explicit to be released. As a result, several years later this was reedited (badly) into a single story line and released in this form. What is left has Zero Mostel sadly wasted as the ex-President of the United States explaining his downfall. This leads to segments with Pat Paulsen fooling around with a blow-up doll, a frustrated writer, and finally Mostel being blackmailed into having sex with his wife on national television. Wasn't one of the big selling points of videocassettes that complete, unedited versions of movies would become available? On the other hand, on the evidence of what's left here, the original probably wasn't any better.

THE FOREST ½☆
1983, USA
Dean Russell, Michael Brody, Elaine Warner. Directed by Don Jones. 90 min.

A party of campers breaks up when cannibals have half of them for dinner. Don't bother.

FOREVER EMMANUELLE ½☆
1982, Italy/France, R
Annie Belle, Emmanuelle Arsan, Al Cliver, Orso Maria Guerrini. Directed by Anonymous. 89 min.

This teasing, talky rip-off of the Sylvia Kristel Emmanuelles has very mild, heavily edited sex scenes and loads of conversations about sex. Even the Philippine locations make a perfunctory and unsatisfying appearance.

FOREVER YOUNG ☆☆☆
1983, Great Britain
James Aubrey, Nicholas Gecks, Karen Archer, Jason Carter, Julian Firth, Liam Holt. Directed by David Drury. 85 min.

There's shattered dreams, growing up, growing older, envy, and rock and roll. It could be a steaming teen pic, but it's not. Instead, the title song floats gently in our ears, the camera drifts over "real people" faces, and the past and the future invade the present. Father Michael is young and newfangled enough to sponsor fifties church dances where he serves as the lead vocalist for the band. But when Michael's best friend turns up, black-and-white memories of old times—when they would sing and girls would smile—begin to stir. Also stirring is a single mother whose son adores Father Michael, and the lad is disturbed by the friend's sudden arrival.... If it sounds like a lot of plot for a short film, it is, but first-time director David Drury gives his characters room to breathe and to think in this intimate, entrancing slice of life. Part of the British "First Love" series.

FOR HEAVEN'S SAKE ☆☆½
1950, USA
Clifton Webb, Joan Bennett, Robert Cummings, Edmund Gwenn, Joan Blondell, Gigi Perreau, Harry Von Zell, Tommy Rettig, Charles Lane. Directed by George Seaton. 92 min.

They're no angels, they're Clifton Webb and Edmund Gwenn, respectively tart and cuddly as a pair of celestial beings in charge of matching unborn children with their parents. (We bet you didn't know that fetuses, in the 1950s, looked just like kid stars Tommy Rettig and Gigi Perreau.) Perreau and Rettig have their eyes on nice folks who need just a little otherworldly help before they can clear the way to conceiving them. Good fun for Webb's fans, and populated with a host of bright character actors.

FOR LADIES ONLY ☆
1981, USA (TV)
Gregory Harrison, Marc Singer, Viveca Lindfors, Louise Lasser, Lee Grant, Patty Davis. Directed by Mel M. Damski. 100 min.

This embarrassing television melodrama concerns a young male stripper (Gregory Harrison) who is ruthlessly pursued by women with only one thing on their minds. Though played straight, it does have some laughs—especially when Harrison sings his own songs. The video version has some spicy scenes not included for network TV; however, they're about as hot as your Aunt Esther's chili. Look for Patty (Reagan) Davis, and credible actresses Louise Lasser, Viveca Lindfors, and Lee Grant trying to hide.

FOR LOVE OF IVY
☆☆½
1968, USA
Sidney Poitier, Abbey Lincoln, Beau Bridges, Carroll O'Connor, Nan Martin. Directed by Daniel Mann. 100 min.

What begins as a satire on an upper-middle-class white family quickly becomes a cautious, boring love story about the family's maid and a trucker who secretly runs a gambling casino. Given the period in which it was made, *Ivy* was a step forward in representing a romance between two black people. Unfortunately, it is a dull and passionless affair, with Sidney Poitier (who wrote the original story) giving his standard "perfect black male" performance.

FOR ME AND MY GAL
☆☆☆½
1942, USA
Judy Garland, Gene Kelly, George Murphy, Marta Eggerth, Ben Blue, Richard Quine, Horace (Stephen) McNally. Directed by Busby Berkeley. 104 min.

Although acknowledged as a corny musical recommended for some nifty songs and dances, *For Me and My Gal* has been unjustly neglected in another area. Director Busby Berkeley (in his best post–Warner Bros. work) magnificently evokes the seedy world of World War I vaudeville with dressing room scenes that are unbearably claustrophobic. Berkeley also gets a powerful performance from Gene Kelly (in his film debut) as a draft-dodging hoofer. Much of the rest of the film is geared to Judy Garland (his dance partner), who brings out the story's melodramatic kitsch, but the filmmaking is always of the highest quality. Best numbers include "Ballin' the Jack" and the famous title song.

THE FORMULA
☆½
1980, USA, R
George C. Scott, Marlon Brando, Marthe Keller, John Gielgud, G. D. Spradlin, Beatrice Straight, Richard Lynch. Directed by John G. Avildsen. 118 min.

Writer-producer Steve Shagan (who adapted his own best-seller) and director John Avildsen (*Rocky*) have based this torpid conspiracy thriller on a startling historical msytery: the Nazi formula for synthetic fuel disappeared at the end of World War II and has yet to resurface. George C. Scott, spouting hard-boiled dialogue, plays a Los Angeles homicide detective who stumbles across the answer; the trail leads him to a megalomaniacal oil magnate played by Marlon Brando. Doing a gloating caricature of a capitalist, Brando creates a cardboard villain. Opaque and interminable, *The Formula* is a bore. And since (as in most films of its ilk) it presents the oily conspirators as omnipresent and invincible, this supposed rabble-rouser succeeds only in confirming the passivity of a jaded public. At least the Scott-Brando scenes have some edge, but they are few and far between.

FOR PETE'S SAKE
☆☆½
1974, USA, PG
Barbra Streisand, Michael Sarrazin, Estelle Parsons, William Redfield, Molly Picon. Directed by Peter Yates. 90 min.

Streisand is the whole show in this broad slapstick farce about a Brooklyn housewife who inadvertently becomes involved in crime and prostitution while trying to help her struggling husband. Director Peter Yates has placed *Bringing up Baby* in *French Connection* country and come up with a sloppy, wildly uneven, but occasionally funny outing. Peter Bogdanovich's thirties *hommage*—*What's Up, Doc?*—was lighter and more consistent, but Streisand again manages to pull the loose parts together.

FORT APACHE
☆☆☆
1948, USA
John Wayne, Henry Fonda, Shirley Temple, John Agar, Ward Bond, Pedro Armendariz, Victor McLaglen. Directed by John Ford. 127 min.

This thinly disguised account of the Little Big Horn massacre is one of John Ford's better Westerns, the first installment of his "cavalry trilogy." Henry Fonda is surprisingly effective as the Custer figure, the martinet who runs a frontier fort, and John Wayne is in top form as the sergeant who pronounces a version of Ford's "when-the-truth-and-the-legend-are-at-odds,-print-the-legend" benediction. But the subplots—low comedy from Victor McLaglen, romance between Shirley Temple (as Fonda's daughter) and John Agar (Shirley Temple's real-life husband)—are below par, not as fully integrated into the director's overall plan as in *She Wore a Yellow Ribbon* and later Westerns.

FORT APACHE, THE BRONX
☆☆½
1981, USA, R
Paul Newman, Edward Asner, Rachel Ticotin, Pam Grier, Danny Aiello, Ken Wahl. Directed by Daniel Petrie. 125 min.

The film's depiction of the crumbling South Bronx, which is viewed from a cop's down-and-dirty perspective, must be among the most lavish visualizations of urban rot ever attempted. To the extent that the movie never rises to a higher vantage, it leaves itself open to the charges of distortion leveled against it by protest groups. However, it isn't the point of view so much as director Daniel Petrie's seeming squeamishness about sticking with it that accounts for the film's flaws. The plot (deftly pieced together by screenwriter Heywood Gould from the actual experiences of two New York cops) is too intricately interwoven, too patterned for a film that means to make an issue of the senselessness of things. And Paul Newman's enjoyable performance as our old friend, The Last Honest Cop, seems oddly anachronistic in this nihilistic context.

FOR THE LOVE OF BENJI
☆☆
1977, USA, G
Patsy Garrett, Cynthia Smith, Allen Fiuzat, Ed Nelson, Peter Bowles. Directed by Joe Camp. 85 min.

The money-making mutt returns for another dewy-eyed romp—this time in Greece—under the direction of Joe Camp. Benji is cute enough, but Lassie had a wider range of facial expressions, not to mention better writers. How much dogged conviction could even the most talented pooch bring to this tripe? While the Grecian locales are a plus, they can't alleviate the tiresome familiarity of Benji chasing his own tail.

FORTRESS
☆
1985, Australia (TV)
Rachel Ward, Sean Garlick, Rebecca Rigg, Robin Mason, Marc Gray, Beth Buchanan, Asher Keddie, Bradley Meehan. Directed by Arch Nicholson. 105 min.

Except for the obligatory obscenities and macabre violence, this made–for–HBO drama is just another dim-witted TV movie, more exploitative and less intelligent than most of its network cousins. The setting is Australia, where Rachel Ward plays a schoolteacher who, along with nine cherubic tykes, is abducted by gunmen and spirited away to the outback. What happens then won't surprise anyone who's read or seen *Lord of the Flies*—we all know that the cutest children have the most barbaric impulses. Ward is a good actress under any circumstances, but this is more like Linda Blair material.

THE FORTUNE
☆☆
1975, USA, PG
Warren Beatty, Stockard Channing, Jack Nicholson, Florence Stanley, Richard B. Shull. Directed by Mike Nichols. 95 min.

Beatty, Nicholson, and Nichols, a phenomenally talented trio, here joined forces and bent over backward to make the one kind of film for which none of them had any facility—a period lowbrow farce. The results are predictably witless and uninspired, with the stars trapped in a harebrained plot about two con men pursuing a wealthy heiress (Channing, in the film's only on-target performance). Beatty tries ferociously hard to look casual and relaxed, Nicholson scowls miserably, and the director seems to have fallen out of love with the project about halfway through shooting. The audience is left with a debacle that, if not quite on the order of the same year's *Lucky Lady* and *At Long Last Love*, is still well worth missing.

THE FORTUNE COOKIE ★★★½
1966, USA
Jack Lemmon, Walter Matthau, Ron Rich, Cliff Osmond, Lurene Tuttle, Noam Pitlik, Ned Glass, Sig Ruman, William Christopher. Directed by Billy Wilder. 125 min.

Billy Wilder's bitter comedy about football, insurance, fraud, lawyers, civil rights, and whatever else he can get his hands on is very uneven; the only consistently first-rate performance is from Walter Matthau (who won an Oscar here for Best Supporting Actor) as a divinely inspired shyster attorney helping his brother-in-law (Jack Lemmon, playing the straight man) to bilk a football team after a minor incident. Cliff Osmond, as a private investigator assigned to expose Lemmon's fakery, is quite good; his assistant is played by Noam Pitlik, who later directed most of the episodes of television's "Barney Miller." Filmed in black and white, possibly to remind you of Wilder's other film about the insurance business, *Double Indemnity*.

FORTY CARATS ★★
1973, USA, PG
Liv Ullmann, Edward Albert, Gene Kelly, Binnie Barnes, Deborah Raffin, Nancy Walker. Directed by Milton Katselas. 108 min.

This limp romantic comedy was based on a slightly more potent Broadway hit. The sitcom story follows a divorcée who is having an affair with a younger man while her daughter is involved with an older man. Besides the slim material, the miscasting of Liv Ullmann is the film's biggest problem. She looks much too young to be the mother of Deborah Raffin; Gene Kelly looks too old to be her ex-husband and Edward Albert seems just right for her as the "younger" man. Ullmann was the hottest thing going when she won this role, and the attempt to make her a "commercial" star didn't fare too well.

48 HRS ★★★
1982, USA, R
Nick Nolte, Eddie Murphy, Annette O'Toole, James Remar. Directed by Walter Hill. 96 min.

A fast-talking convict (Eddie Murphy) gets two days of freedom to help a cop (Nick Nolte) track down a killer in this high-speed, foulmouthed action comedy that launched Eddie Murphy's movie career. Director Walter Hill specializes in explosive "man's world" movies, and this one is arguably his most successful (putting aside the fact that all women are portrayed as either bimbos or lesbians, and that poor Annette O'Toole literally phones in her part). The numerous gunfights and fistfights are presented with bloody, kinetic intensity, and Murphy's comic-conspiratorial rapport with the camera is astonishing. It's easy to see why Nolte chose to sit back and underplay his way through this one—with Murphy around, there was no point in even trying.

FORTY GUNS ★★½
1957, USA
Barbara Stanwyck, Barry Sullivan, Dean Jagger, John Ericson, Gene Barry, Robert Dix, Eve Brent. Directed by Samuel Fuller. 76 min.

Barbara Stanwyck is an outlaw leader pursued by the law in the Tombstone Territory of old Arizona. Director Sam Fuller's violent themes and mobile camerawork get a workout in this frontier shoot-'em-up. Yet even scenes of Babs in black leather whipping her all-male cowboy gang into submission can't overcome the shoddy B-level theatrics, and Barry Sullivan supplies nothing as the marshal. Uselessly shot in Cinemascope.

THE 49TH PARALLEL ★★★
1941, Great Britain
Leslie Howard, Raymond Massey, Laurence Olivier, Anton Walbrook, Glynis Johns, Finlay Currie. Directed by Michael Powell. 123 min.

This was the first collaboration between Michael Powell and Emeric Pressburger, who went on as a team to codirect, write, and produce some of the finest British films of the forties and fifties. Made during the height of anti-Nazi fervor, it's a taut, suspenseful film about a group of survivors from a sunken German U-boat trying to make their way across Canada to reach the United States. Laurence Olivier and Raymond Massey's parts are little more than cameos, but the rest of the cast is more than up to the task of carrying the film. Also known as *The Invaders*.

42ND STREET ★★★★
1933, USA
Warner Baxter, Bebe Daniels, George Brent, Una Merkel, Ruby Keeler, Guy Kibbee, Ned Sparks, Dick Powell, Ginger Rogers. Directed by Lloyd Bacon. 90 min.

This is perhaps the quintessential let's-put-on-a-show musical, with Warner Baxter as the ailing director who gives his all for the love of show biz. It features the usual backstage clichés (half of which were invented for this movie), as well as magnificent Busby Berkeley dance numbers that include "Shuffle off to Buffalo" and the legendary title tune. Today Bebe Daniels's highfalutin star is a camp classic, and the fresh yet crude naïveté of the other performers lends the film its greatest appeal.

FOR YOUR EYES ONLY ★★
1981, Great Britain, PG
Roger Moore, Carole Bouquet, Chaim Topol, Lynn-Holly Johnson, Julian Glover, Jill Bennett, Cassandra Harris. Directed by John Glen. 127 min.

This James Bond thriller descends beyond the baroque into a sort of saggy decadence—and its star, Roger Moore, sags with it. Moore's 007 is no longer an arch charmer but a limp, harried old biddy who seems severed from every drive and passion, and he's surrounded by the most blandly down-to-earth decor the Bond series has yet seen. As Bond's girl, Carole Bouquet looks rather unhappy about the whole thing; she and Moore act as if they'd never dream of actually touching each other.

FOR YOUR LOVE ONLY ★★
1976, Germany
Nastassja Kinski, Christian Quadflieg, Judy Winter, Klaus Schwarzkopf. Directed by Wolfgang Petersen. 97 min.

This film is only for those who love mush-mouthed Nastassja Kinski, who, although an international celebrity, has rarely demonstrated one iota of acting ability or personality. At least she demonstrates a sort of youthful ebullience here, instead of the zombie acting style she adopts when working on bigger-budgeted films. In this threadbare soaper, "Nasty's" forbidden alliance with her teacher leads to a crash course in blackmail and murder. Someone else is eager to teach her a few things after school, so La Kinski has to eliminate this new oversexed, would-be blackmailer. Released in 1982.

FOUL PLAY ★★★
1978, USA, PG
Goldie Hawn, Chevy Chase, Burgess Meredith, Rachel Roberts, Dudley Moore, Marilyn Sokol. Directed by Colin Higgins. 116 min.

Goldie Hawn gives a warm, knowing performance as a shy San Francisco librarian who stumbles on a harebrained murder scheme, but she's used mostly as a screamer, to be jumped at from dark corners. This push-button scare tactic is used so crudely that we always see it coming. Chevy Chase—as the cop who comes to Goldie's rescue—is always drawing his lips up over his teeth in the romantic scenes, like a horse begging for sugar, but the way he understates his lines makes even the thinnest jokes seem funny.

THE FOUNTAINHEAD ★★★
1949, USA
Gary Cooper, Patricia Neal, Raymond Massey, Kent Smith, Henry Hull, Ray Collins, Paul Stanton, Robert Douglas, Jerome Cowan. Directed by King Vidor. 114 min.

Late in his career, King Vidor was turning out florid, wildly melodramatic films like *A Duel in the Sun*, *Beyond the Forest*, and *Ruby Gentry*. The most satisfying of these was his adaptation of Ayn Rand's best-seller *The Fountainhead*. Stylized with deliberately artificial sets and chiaroscuro lighting, Vidor (and screenwriter Rand) tell the story of Howard Roark, a rugged individualist who combats various obstacles to achieve the materializaton of his unpopular architectural designs. While the sexual symbolism is obvious, Patricia Neal's performance as a neurotic playgirl is laughable, and some may see this as nothing more than camp. But the philosophical subtext, Vidor's perverse visuals, and Raymond Massey's surprisingly moving performance as a William Randolph Hearst-type newspaper publisher makes this film, like its hero, out of the ordinary.

THE FOUR DEUCES ★★½
1975, USA, R
Jack Palance, Carol Lynley, Warren Berlinger, Adam Roarke, E. J. Peaker. Directed by William Bushnell. 87 min.

This rousing old-fashioned comedy-drama has solid narrative strengths and lots of bloodletting. Accomplished scenery-chewer Jack Palance is usually a bit much in a lead role, but his overbaked ham acting serves this featherweight story line quite well. The Four Deuces refers to the gambling house Palance devotes himself to when he's not romancing his sweetie or defending his property from crazy mobsters with machine guns.

FOUR FACES WEST ★★½
1948, USA
Joel McCrea, Frances Dee, Charles Bickford, William Conrad, Dan White, Joseph Calleia. Directed by Alfred E. Green. 96 min.

Based on a story (vaguely derived from *Les Misérables*) that appeared in the *Saturday Evening Post*, this Western doesn't rely heavily on shoot-outs, chases on horseback, barroom brawls, and the other stock components of the B western. Joel McCrea is the cowboy who robbed a bank to help save his father's ranch and is now trying to evade dogged sheriff William Conrad. Well performed by all. McCrea and Frances Dee were costars in real life as well: their marriage has lasted for over fifty years.

THE FOUR FEATHERS ★★★½
1939, Great Britain
Ralph Richardson, June Duprez, C. Aubrey Smith, Clive Baxter, Jack Allen. Directed by Zoltan Korda. 115 min.

Zoltan Korda's highly satisfying action film about bravery and cowardice and the British Empire is a stiff-upper-lip adventure that's nearly in a class with great ones like *Gunga Din*. Ralph Richardson is an officer in Africa who is unjustly branded a coward and struggles to redeem himself. C. Aubrey Smith does a classic bit playing war games on a dinner table.

FOUR FEATHERS ★★½
1977, USA (TV)
Beau Bridges, Robert Powell, Simon Ward, Richard Johnson, Jane Seymour, Harry Andrews. Directed by Don Sharp. 110 min.

The fifth go-round for the renowned adventure tale. An Englishman must summon up his courage and show he's not a coward by helping out his army comrades during an insurrection in the Sudan. The durable yarn is probably strong enough to withstand even a mediocre production, but this is a fairly stirring retelling, with a sharp, predominantly British cast and meticulous production values. Good, old-fashioned action tale.

FOUR FOR TEXAS ★★
1963, USA
Frank Sinatra, Dean Martin, Anita Ekberg, Ursula Andress, Charles Bronson, Victor Buono, Richard Jaeckel, Jack Elam, Fritz Feld, Percy Helton, Jonathan Hale. Directed by Robert Aldrich. 124 min.

A silly Western pitting Frank Sinatra and Dean Martin against each other as feuding mercenaries who must join forces to fight off banker Victor Buono and gunman Charles Bronson. It has lots of in-jokes and kidding around, along with cameo appearances by the Three Stooges and Arthur Godfrey. It would have been better if it went for all-out camp, but director Robert Aldrich occasionally insists on breaking up the tomfoolery and trying to make a movie, which only spoils things.

FOUR FRIENDS ★★
1981, USA, R
Craig Wasson, Jodi Thelen, Reed Birney, James Leo Herlihy, Lois Smith. Directed by Arthur Penn. 115 min.

Steve Tesich (*Breaking Away*) wrote the screenplay, based partly on his own experiences, for this allegorical story of a young immigrant coming of age in the 1960s. The four friends of the title (which is misleading, as only two of them are really major characters) are the immigrant, two high-school buddies, and the flaky girl they all love. As the girl, Georgia (every time she's around, "Georgia on My Mind" pops up on the soundtrack), Jodi Thelen is so brainlessly obnoxious that it's hard to believe that she can command so much loyalty, although Craig Wasson plays the immigrant youth as such a dullard that maybe it makes sense. The script is so full of flag-waving sentiments that it's a wonder that Arthur Penn, who was heavily involved with liberal politics in the sixties, took on this project at all; it may be that tension that causes so much of the film to ring false.

THE FOUR HORSEMEN OF THE APOCALYPSE ★★
1961, USA
Glenn Ford, Ingrid Thulin, Charles Boyer, Paul Henreid, Lee J. Cobb, Paul Lukas, Karl Boehm, Yvette Mimieux. Directed by Vincente Minnelli. 153 min.

This isn't Vincente Minnelli's worst film (that was either *Goodbye Charlie* or *A Matter of Time*), but it comes very close. Metrocolor and Cinemascope only emphasize the anachronisms in this turgid, glossy remake of the Rudolph Valentino silent classic. Now the story takes place one war later (World War II), with Glenn Ford playing the heir of an Argentine cattle baron who gets involved in the French Resistance. No one plays self-righteousness better than Glenn Ford, but he is as far removed from Valentino's exotic sexiness as one can get. Ingrid Thulin, one of the best actors in the Ingmar Bergman stable, plays the society woman with whom Ford becomes involved. Unfortunately, Thulin's English was so hard to understand that she had to be post-synched by Angela Lansbury, and the effect makes her performance distancing, to say the least. A case of a movie made at the wrong time by the wrong people.

THE 400 BLOWS ★★★★
1959, France
Jean-Pierre Léaud, Patrick Auffray, Claire Maurier, Albert Rémy, Guy Decomble, Georges Fiamant. Directed by François Truffaut. 97 min.

François Truffaut's first feature film was considered a seminal work of the French New Wave upon its release; it has since come to be considered a classic portrait of early adolescence. Truffaut based this captivating study of a troubled young truant in juvenile hall on his own childhood, and he used Jean-Pierre Léaud to portray alter-ego Antoine Doinel in four more films (*Love at Twenty*, *Stolen Kisses*, *Bed and Board*, and *Love on the Run*) over the next twenty years. But Léaud was never again as effective or touching as in this sensitive, simply told film. The last shot, ending in a freeze frame, is one of the most famous and most imitated in modern cinema.

THE FOUR MUSKETEERS
1974, Panama, PG ★★★½
Oliver Reed, Raquel Welch, Richard Chamberlain, Michael York, Frank Finlay, Christopher Lee, Jean-Pierre Cassel, Geraldine Chaplin, Simon Ward, Faye Dunaway, Charlton Heston. Directed by Richard Lester. 103 min.

Richard Lester's continuation of his very engaging *Three Musketeers* was shot at the same time and is nearly as pleasing. The performances, led by Raquel Welch's ditsy Constance and Faye Dunaway's saber-toothed seductress, are uniformly masterful, tongue-in-cheek but never condescending. And Lester's direction, though not as out-and-out funny as in the first film, is actually richer in characterization, detail, and emotion. The two films are best seen as a double feature; viewed together, they become a seamless, quite special entertainment.

THE FOUR SEASONS
1981, USA, PG ★★½
Alan Alda, Carol Burnett, Jack Weston, Len Cariou, Rita Moreno, Sandy Dennis, Bess Armstrong. Directed by Alan Alda. 107 min.

An examination of the ups and downs of a friendship among three middle-aged, middle-class couples, *The Four Seasons* is a bland, mechanical, and, above all, "instructive" reflection of the lives of its (presumably) middle-aged, middle-class audience. The movie's slick evenhandedness undercuts the meaning of the friendships, and the themes don't have any weight; they're just hoops for the characters to jump through. Written by Alan Alda.

THE FOURTH MAN
1984, Netherlands ★★★
Renee Soutendijk, Jeroen Krabbe, Thom Hoffman. Directed by Paul Verhoeven. 104 min.

A seedy, bisexual novelist is drawn into an affair with a beautiful young woman who seems to be the subject of the hallucinatory dreams that plague his sleep. This steamy brew of hysterically erotic imagery is spiced up with violence and baroque religion; it is difficult to determine just how ironic Paul Verhoeven is being about the fatality of sexual attraction. Is the glossy young widow really the black widow?

FOXES
1980, USA, R ★★★
Jodie Foster, Cherie Currie, Sally Kellerman, Randy Quaid. Directed by Adrian Lyne. 106 min.

The first half hour of this "troubled teenagers" film is all style and no substance as director Adrian Lyne tests the neon look he later employed in *Flashdance*. Once the filmmaker has gotten this optical flair out of his system, he lets *Foxes* get down to the business of providing an insightful and emotional look at a group of young women trying to cope with life in Los Angeles's fast lane. By the end of their journeys of self-discovery, the picture has been able to glean some real understanding of a plastic world filled with drugs, violence, and meaningless sex. Produced by David (*Chariots of Fire*) Putnam.

THE FOXES OF HARROW
1947, USA ★★½
Rex Harrison, Maureen O'Hara, Richard Haydn, Victor McLaglen, Vanessa Brown, Hugo Haas, Dennis Hoey, Roy Roberts. Directed by John M. Stahl. 115 min.

Set in the New Orleans of the 1820s, this historical melodrama is a polished but uncompelling production. Rex Harrison plays an adventurer of illegitimate birth whose ambition is to break into New Orleans society by accumulating wealth on the riverboats, marrying into an aristocratic family, and building an estate like the one his mother had lived on in Ireland. He achieves his goals, but loses the love of his wife (Maureen O'Hara) along the way. The few dramatic highlights seem to be plotted like points on a graph.

FOXTRAP
1986, USA/Italy, R ★
Fred Williamson, Chris Connelly, Arlene Golonka, Donna Owen, Beatrice Palme, Cleo Sebastian, Lela Rochon. Directed by Fred Williamson. 88 min.

Unsung auteur Fred Williamson is at it again, directing his ninth mindless, slam-bang action film starring his very favorite actor. Here he plays a bodyguard hired to find his boss's daughter, reported to have vanished in Europe. Low on action and common sense, the film is nonetheless an often hilarious vanity vehicle for Williamson, who styles himself as the heir to James Bond's mantle. A sequel is promised, but we won't hold our breath.

FOXTROT
1976, Mexico/Switzerland, R ★½
Peter O'Toole, Charlotte Rampling, Max von Sydow, Jorge Luke. Directed by Arturo Ripstein. 91 min.

Peter O'Toole is wasted once again in this empty, pretentious drama, though some of the blame is his own: when he does get a chance to act here, he pulls out moves that seem totally inappropriate to his character. He plays an Eastern European aristocrat who flees with his wife to a desert island to escape World War II. Once there, the couple become involved in a class war with their servants. The film was presumably inspired by Renoir's *Rules of the Game*. (a.k.a.: *The Other Side of Paradise*)

FRAMED
1975, USA, R ★½
Joe Don Baker, Conny Van Dyke, Gabriel Dell, John Marley, Brock Peters, H. B. Haggerty. Directed by Phil Karlson. 106 min.

The director, star, and writer (Mort Briskin) of the execrable *Walking Tall* join forces again for another revenge action film that while not as morally repugnant as the earlier film, still goes overboard in stacking its cards on the side of the hero. Sent to jail on a phony charge by some crooked cops, Joe Don Baker serves out his term and then seeks his revenge. The denouement may not be bloody enough for its intended audience; this is neither particularly offensive nor exciting.

FRANCES
1982, USA, R ★★½
Jessica Lange, Sam Shepard, Jeffrey De Munn, Kim Stanley, Jordan Charney. Directed by Graeme Clifford. 139 min.

On the verge of a promising film career in the thirties, Frances Farmer began her slow descent from the Hollywood heights to the depths of alcoholism, mental illness, and incarceration in an asylum at the whim of her insane mother. While *Frances* exposes the heartless conformity imposed by show business on those who want to get ahead, it tries to pigeonhole a devastating true-life horror story with preconceived points the filmmakers want to make. This film didn't need a fictionalized savior in the person of Sam Shepard, nor did it need to follow the prescribed course of all conventional Hollywood biopics—Farmer's story is so shocking and heart-rending that it would have been more powerful if it had been written and directed less hysterically. Only in Jessica Lange's dazzling performance, as a tormented woman whose greatest sin was an inability to put up false fronts even to save her career, does the film rise out of the mundane and move us as it should.

FRANCIS
1950, USA ★★½
Donald O'Connor, Patricia Medina, ZaSu Pitts, Ray Collins, John McIntire, Eduard Franz, Frank Faylen. Directed by Arthur Lubin. 91 min.

Yes, that's Francis, as in the Talking Mule. This is the first of seven Francis films, and the best of the lot, though hardly distinguishable from the six others. Donald O'Connor plays the GI who discovers the chattering critter, who will of course talk to no one except him (unless a five-star general orders him to). The unbelievable premise is worked out in a manner that doesn't require too much suspension of disbelief, which is to say that you can laugh at this without feeling too dumb. Chill Wills supplies the voice of Francis. Director Arthur Lubin later went on to create a television series called "Mr. Ed," about a talking horse. Creativity like that leaves mere mortals in awe.

FRANCIS OF ASSISI ☆½
1961, USA
Bradford Dillman, Dolores Hart, Stuart Whitman, Pedro Armendariz, Cecil Kellaway, Eduard Franz, Finlay Currie. Directed by Michael Curtiz. 105 min.

This lackluster Hollywood religious epic should have been much better than it is, given the high production budget and the track record of Michael Curtiz, whose penultimate film it was. As Francis, the Catholic saint who founded the Franciscan order and could reputedly communicate with animals, Bradford Dillman lacks the necessary charisma to convince an audience that he could persuade others to abandon their worldly possessions and follow him. The scene in which he receives his vocation from a heavenly voice is only slightly less ridiculous than the one in *Monty Python and the Holy Grail*. Acceptable for Sunday-school classes, maybe, but no one over the age of twelve will be able to tolerate it. It does get an extra half star, though, for being better than the next version of the life of Francis, *Brother Sun, Sister Moon*.

FRANKENSTEIN ☆☆☆½
1931, USA
Colin Clive, Boris Karloff, Mae Clarke, John Boles. Directed by James Whale. 71 min.

In the 1930s and 1940s, Universal Studios was famous for its horror films, and *Frankenstein* was one of the first and greatest. Colin Clive's, and Boris Karloff's performances as the mad scientist and the monster, respectively, have become indelible pop-culture archetypes, and the film is rich with scenes which are now horror-film benchmarks—the corpse robbery, the midnight funeral, and, most memorably, the creation of the monster. Working in a visual style drenched in shadows and gothic turrets, James Whale sustains fear and foreboding even in the nonhorror scenes. His version, notwithstanding countless remakes, is the *definitive Frankenstein*. Now available from MCA Home Video in a full-length version with long-missing footage restored.

FRANKENSTEIN ☆☆
1973, USA (TV)
Robert Foxworth, Susan Strasberg, Bo Svenson, John Karlen, Heidi Vaughn. Directed by Glenn Jordan. 130 min.

TV has become the final resting place of a movieland monster who refuses to stay dead and buried. In addition to the old Universal classic films, TV has given us a made-for-cable reproduction of a Broadway play and a superlative film called *Frankenstein: The True Story*, which followed the essentials of Mary Shelley's book with rewarding results. This version is rather like the British Hammer films, only without as much violence. In other words, there are beautiful sets and costumes, a lot of fatuous mumbo jumbo about the ethics of scientific experimentation, some good acting, and, unfortunately, a dearth of chills. Like Frankenstein's monster, this story is indestructible in any version, even a lackluster one like this. A handsome retelling but not a monster hit. The video version has been limited slightly from the original.

FRANKENSTEIN CREATED WOMAN ☆☆½
1967, Great Britain
Peter Cushing, Susan Denberg, Robert Morris, Thorley Walters, Michael Ripper. Directed by Terence Fisher. 92 min.

Having run out of ways to make ugly monsters with the previous entry in the series, *The Evil of Frankenstein* (in which, as you recall, the monster seemed to have a face covered in pie dough), the executives at Hammer decided to try an opposite tack. This time, Dr. F. takes the body of a scarred and crippled girl who drowned herself, transplants the soul of her boyfriend, who was executed for a murder he didn't commit, and somehow winds up with Susan Denberg, ex-*Playboy* centerfold. An interesting variation, and surprisingly sexy for the time.

FRANKENSTEIN ISLAND ☆
1983, USA
John Carradine, Cameron Mitchell, Andrew Duggan, Robert Clarke, Steve Brodie, Tain Bodkin, Laurel Johnson. Directed by Jerry Warren. 90 min.

The title refers to the presence of yet another descendant of Doctor Frankenstein on the island where this cheapoid is set, but we think it's more suitable as a description of the movie itself—a shambling monstrosity concocted out of parts scrounged from a dozen other movies, all sloppily sewn together. There are mad scientists, hypnotized zombies, jungle girls (all of whom, despite the reference to "seminude Amazons" on the cassette jacket, remain demurely clad in two-piece leopard skins), a werewolf, some people who grow fangs for no particular reason, and a monster that shows up at the last minute and does absolutely nothing but stumble around and growl while the rest of the cast participates in the longest, dullest fight ever seen. The "stars" of this mess really have only bit parts—John Carradine appears two or three times as a ghost in scenes highly reminiscent of Bela Lugosi's in *Glen or Glenda*. No gore, no sex, no violence, no fun.

FRANKENSTEIN MEETS THE SPACE MONSTER ½☆
1965, USA
James Karen, Robert Reilly, Nancy Marshall, Lou Cutell, Marilyn Hanold. Directed by Robert Gaffney. 75 min.

This awful, bargain-basement sci-fi film is set in Puerto Rico, where evil Princess Marcuzan (Marilyn Hanold) and her dwarf sidekick Nadir (Lou Cutell) are nabbing island women to repopulate their planet. "Frankenstein" turns out to be nothing more than a stranded American android disfigured by a crash who determines to save Puerto Rico from its own illegal alien problem. Horror fans will find it especially deplorable.

FRANKENSTEIN MEETS THE WOLFMAN ☆☆☆
1943, USA
Lon Chaney, Jr., Patric Knowles, Ilona Massey, Bela Lugosi, Maria Ouspenskaya, Lionel Atwill, Dennis Hoey, Dwight Frye. Directed by Roy William Neill. 72 min.

One of the better entries in the Universal cycle of thirties and forties monster movies. Brought back to life by grave robbers who desecrated his tomb, Larry Talbot (Lon Chaney, Jr.) finds that he still has this problem with his disposition every full moon and goes to Baroness Elsa Frankenstein for help. Of course, in looking over the ruins of the castle, they find that big green guy with the stiff walk. All the usuals are on hand, including Lionel Atwill as the burgomeister who doesn't like those lights up at the castle, Dwight Frye as the most rabid of the lynchers, and Dennis Hoey playing more or less the same part he had in all the Sherlock Holmes films. Ironically, Bela Lugosi, who plays the monster here (and rather stiffly), turned down the part in the 1931 *Frankenstein* because it offered no dialogue.

FRANKENSTEIN—1970 ☆½
1958, USA
Boris Karloff, Tom Duggan, Jana Lund, Donald Barry. Directed by Howard W. Koch. 83 min.

This dull monster movie never even provides a monster for the audience to gasp at. (How many dull horror movies have you stayed awake through just to see what the monster looked like at the end? Not here.) Boris Karloff, as a third-generation Dr. Frankenstein, wants to build a new body so he can transplant his own brain into it—seems the Nazis messed up the one he has. To get a nuclear reactor for his lab, he agrees to let a television crew film in his castle. The monster dies before it can even get its bandages off.

FRANKENSTEIN 3-D

See *Andy Warhol's Frankenstein*

FRANTIC ☆☆☆
1958, France
Jeanne Moreau, Maurice Ronet, Georges Poujouly, Yori Bertin. Directed by Louis Malle. 90 min.

A devilishly clever "perfect murder" outing. Director Louis Malle smoothly extracts extreme tension from this involved situation, investing the proceedings with a welcome veneer of cynicism. A man and his impatient mistress attempt a shortcut to divorce by removing her spouse with an almost foolproof plan, only to stand by helplessly as the plot goes awry due to unforeseen circumstances. The film is classily photographed in black and white, jazzily scored, and exquisitely acted. Tart suspense with a bitter-lemon twist of an ending.

FRATERNITY VACATION ☆☆
1985, USA, R
Stephen Geoffreys, Cameron Dye, Sheree J. Wilson, Leigh McCloskey. Directed by James Frawley. 89 min.

At last! A beach movie that keeps such exploitative elements as sex, nudity, and gross gags down to a minimum in favor of a female lead who isn't treated like a piece of meat and an odd assortment of likable characters. Chief among them is nerdy Wendell Tvedt, who accompanies his lusty frat brothers to Palm Springs in search of nubile young women. What the gawky kid ultimately discovers is that his innocent awkwardness places him far above his sex-crazed competitors in the estimation of the beautiful girl they're all after. Like *Revenge of the Nerds*, this film has a humane sweetness that seems to decry the genre smut that has come before it. A real surprise with a lot of enjoyable laughs.

THE FREAK MAKER ☆½
1973, Great Britain
Donald Pleasence, Brad Harris, Michael Dunn, Julie Ege, Jill Haworth. Directed by Jack Cardiff. 92 min.

This tarted-up, dismal revamp of the classic horror film *Freaks* comes complete with a mad scientist and all the trappings. It never draws us into the twisted perspective of society's perpetually peripheral citizens; instead, it uses the "freaks" only for shock value. Watching *Freaks*, we felt pity when the sideshow folks were mistreated, and then we felt revulsion at the pervasive grotesquerie. (Of course, any horror film of questionable taste must have Donald Pleasence in the cast; here he shows signs of becoming the latter-day John Carradine.) Playing the Master Mutator, Pleasence leads a dual life as a respected humanitarian and a nutty professor fond of hybridizing people and things into creatures like the Lizard Woman. Your skin may crawl, but this creepy movie won't scare you.

FREAKS ☆☆☆☆
1932, USA
Wallace Ford, Olga Baclanova, Leila Hyams, Roscoe Ates, Harry Earles, Daisy and Violet Hilton. Directed by Tod Browning. 64 min.

Tod Browning's oddly sympathetic horror classic was out of release for many years before repertory-house revivals in the seventies brought it cult status. (While the film was being made at MGM, the Hollywood stars were less than thrilled to be breaking bread with this film's cast at the MGM commissary, and it does take a bit of getting used to them—the director used deformed nonactors, so be warned.) Based on a Todd Robins short story called "Spurs," the film zeroes in on the sealed-off universe of a cut-rate carnival, where a midget becomes the husband of an Amazon who conspires with a strongman to kill the midget for his money. What makes the film masterful is the constant reversal of our expectations. Initially, the freaks are viewed in a heroic light while the "normals" are seen as vile outsiders. But there's strength in numbers, and when the freaks actively pursue revenge on their persecutors, it's a horrifying spectacle. The once-shocking climax is a bit of a letdown, but this deeply unsettling production remains one of the great horror films.

FREAKY FRIDAY ☆☆
1976, USA, G
Jodie Foster, Barbara Harris, John Astin, Patsy Kelly. Directed by Gary Nelson. 95 min.

Jodie Foster is a teenager who switches bodies with her suburban mother (Barbara Harris) for one day in a predictable, pessimistic, and humorless Walt Disney comedy directed by Gary Nelson.

FREEBIE AND THE BEAN ☆☆
1975, USA, R
Alan Arkin, James Caan, Alex Rocco, Valerie Harper, Loretta Swit, Jack Kruschen. Directed by Richard Rush. 113 min.

After trashing the film for its racist jokes and violent, corruptly likable cops, reviewers felt compelled to note that the audience at the screening they attended laughed heartily throughout. James Caan plays a cop nicknamed "Freebie" because of his predilection for coercing on-the-job gratuities from local merchants, and Arkin is his partner "Bean," so named because he's a Chicano. They drive around a lot, insult each other, drive around some more, kill some bad guys, drive cars off bridges and into third-floor apartments, and so forth. Lots of people loved it. What can we say?

FREE SPIRIT

See *The Belstone Fox*

THE FRENCH CONNECTION ☆☆☆☆
1971, USA, R
Gene Hackman, Fernando Rey, Roy Scheider, Tony LoBianco, Marcel Bozzuffi. Directed by William Friedkin. 104 min.

William Friedkin's superbly executed cop thriller brought the genre into the modern era with tough, foulmouthed narc Jimmy "Popeye" Doyle in pursuit of an international heroin ring and its multimillion-dollar cache of dope. Ernest Tidyman's taut, furiously paced script structures the entire movie as a series of chases, the most memorable being a car-versus-train race through Brooklyn that must be one of the most nerve-racking vehicle duels on film. The novelty of cops who look and sound like real people has diminished since *The French Connection* was released, due partly to the host of imitations and rip-offs it spawned, but it still packs a whallop as dynamic action entertainment, masterfully handled on all levels. Eddie Egan and Sonny Grosso, the former cops whose real-life exploits inspired the film, appear as Simonson and Klein. Academy Awards for Best Picture, Director, Actor (Hackman), Screenplay Adaptation, and Film Editing.

FRENCH CONNECTION II ☆☆☆
1975, USA, R
Gene Hackman, Fernando Rey, Bernard Fresson, Jean-Pierre Castaldi, Cathleen Nesbitt. Directed by John Frankenheimer. 119 min.

"Popeye" Doyle goes to France in pursuit of the nefarious heroin magnate Charnier in this solidly entertaining follow-up to the hugely popular 1971 hit. Gene Hackman and Fernando Rey reprise their roles to fine effect, each adding fresh nuances of characterization and insight to what could have been stock roles. John Frankenheimer's direction, however, is not up to Friedkin's, and the chase scenes, desperately trying to top the original's by adding everything from a trolley to a yacht, fall noticeably short. The film's middle section, in which cop Doyle is kidnapped, forcibly addicted to heroin, and then left to withdraw or die, is outstanding and allows Hackman to do some of his most impressive work. Overall, a good sequel to a great movie.

FRENCH LESSON ☆☆
1986, Great Britain, PG
Jane Snowden, Alexandre Sterling, Diana Blackburn, Oystein Wiik, Jacqueline Doyen, Raoul Delfosse. Directed by Brian Gilbert. 90 min.

This dull, nostalgic romance concerns a teenage British girl whose trip to Paris for language instruction proves equally educative in the ways of love. The 1961 setting seems right, but Jane Snowden's teasing performance makes her character too calculating for full sympathy. Produced by David Puttnam and very much in the vein of his "First Love" series of tiny, discreet romantic films.

THE FRENCH LIEUTENANT'S WOMAN ☆☆☆½
1981, Great Britain, R
Meryl Streep, Jeremy Irons, Patience Collier, Lynsey Baxter, Hilton McRae. Directed by Karel Riesz. 123 min.

By interweaving John Fowles's modern Victorian drama with the story of a cast and crew making a film out of the Fowles novel, Karel Reisz attempts to reflect and comment on the novel's conventions in an inventively layered story that examines the lives of the people who are dramatizing it. It's not as effective as the book, which united nineteenth- and twentieth-century ideas in a single, vibrant narrative of a tragic romance between a proper young man and a mysteriously fallen woman. Here some of the contemporary sequences are banal, but in the period story, which constitutes the greater part of the film, Meryl Streep and Jeremy Irons (in his first major screen role) sizzle with emotion, intelligence, and sensuality. Screenplay by Harold Pinter.

THE FRENCH LINE ☆☆
1953, USA
Jane Russell, Gilbert Roland, Arthur Hunnicut, Mary McCarty. Directed by Lloyd Bacon. 102 min.

Jane's breasts in 3-D were the original selling points of this paper-thin musical about an oil heiress who falls for a singer en route to Paris. Now there's very little to recommend aside from the star's sense of humor, Jack Cole's vulgar staging (the number in the bathtub should not be missed), and a splashy use of Technicolor. Directed by the same man who gave us 42nd Street.

FRENCH POSTCARDS ☆☆☆
1979, USA, PG
Miles Chapin, Valerie Quennessen, Blanche Baker, Debra Winger. Directed by Willard Huyck. 92 min.

This is a frothy and charming road movie from the writing team that brought you Indiana Jones and the Temple of Doom. Postcard's virtually plotless action is concocted around the travails of a group of exchange students studying in Paris for the year. The film is not so much a travelogue as an examination of youthful relationships, all of which, thanks to the capable young cast, are warm and believable. Occasionally it seems like a strained farce, but the film is far more like champagne bubbles. Jean-Jacques Beineix, who later went on to make Diva, served as the second-unit director here.

THE FRENCH WOMAN ☆½
1977, USA, R
Françoise Fabian, Robert Webber, Klaus Kinski, Dayle Haddon. Directed by Just Jaeckin. 110 min.

This better-than-average soft-core opus from the director of Emmanuelle concerns a Parisian madame whose girls get involved in some politically touchy situations. The film is made with some style and imagination, but its heavy-handed ending doesn't add up, given all the sex that leads up to it. Contains a particularly good, and dubbed, cast. (a.k.a.: Madame Claude)

FRENZY ☆☆☆☆
1972, Great Britain, R
Jon Finch, Anna Massey, Barry Foster, Barbara Leigh-Hunt, Jean Marsh, Alex McCowen, Vivien Merchant, Billie Whitelaw. Directed by Alfred Hitchcock. 116 min.

A vicious strangler (Barry Foster) terrorizes London, and a hot-headed bartender (Jon Finch) finds himself trapped in a nightmarish web of circumstantial evidence that very nearly leads him to the gallows. Perhaps the last great Alfred Hitchcock film, Frenzy is set in a universe in which everyone is guilty of something and it is only by chance that the protagonist isn't the necktie killer. More violent and less sardonically witty than most of the director's earlier work, but very effective.

FRIDAY THE 13TH ☆½
1980, USA, R
Betsy Palmer, Adrienne King, Harry Crosby, Kevin Bacon. Directed by Sean S. Cunningham. 95 min.

This milestone in body-count filmmaking was much reviled by critics and adored (to the tune of a reported $70 million) by audiences worldwide. Camp Crystal Lake is closed after the brutal murder of a group of teenage counselors. Years later, "Camp Blood" is reopened and a new batch of nubiles arrive. One by one they die, courtesy of the special-effects talents of Tom (Dawn of the Dead) Savini. The film, directed by the producer of Last House on the Left, features a muffled, sobbing score by Henry Manfredini that has become a series trademark. Five sequels to date, and no end in sight to the career of deformed killer Jason.

FRIDAY THE 13TH, PART V— A NEW BEGINNING ½☆
1985, USA, R
Corey Feldman. Directed by Danny Steinmann. 96 min.

Gore galore can't perk up this lackluster fourth sequel to a movie phenomenon, and the special effects aren't up to series par. Young Tommy Jarvis, traumatized by having killed Jason with a machete, is released from an asylum into a halfway house for disturbed adolescents. His peers soon find themselves being systematically slaughtered, apparently by the resurrected Jason.

FRIDAY THE 13TH, PART IV— THE FINAL CHAPTER ☆
1984, USA, R
Crispin Glover, Kimberly Beck, Corey Feldman, Joan Freeman. Directed by Joseph Zito. 90 min.

This dishonestly titled entry picks up where Part III left off, raising its repulsive and, by now, rote splatter quotient. The apparently dead Jason is taken to a local hospital, where he revives and slaughters his way to freedom. Nearby, two isolated cabins house a group of lusty teens and a family looking for some peace and quiet. The body count begins to rise once again in this very mechanical entry in an already mechanical series. Jason is killed by a small boy with a monster-movie fixation, paving the way for a fourth sequel. Very gross special effects by Tom Savini, who bowed out of Parts II and III reportedly because he thought they were stupid, but returned to consign Jason to his final resting place. He did not succeed, as audiences flocked back for the gore of Part V in this inexplicably popular and seemingly endless series.

FRIDAY THE 13TH, PART VI—JASON LIVES ½☆
1986, USA, R
Thom Mathews, Jennifer Cooke, Renee Jones, Kerry Noonan, Darcy DeMoss, Tom Fridley. Directed by Tom McLoughlin. 85 min.

The titles get longer, the scares become more numbingly familiar, the corpse count mounts, and the box-office inexplicably rolls on for what may be the most mindlessly mechanical exploitation series ever to hack and slash its way out of a major studio. (Paramount gets the blame.) Some stabs at ghoulish humor and an implicit acknowledgment of its own stupidity characterize this entry, but it's basically interchangeable with the other five.

FRIDAY THE 13TH, PART 3 ☆
1982, USA, R
Dana Kimmell, Richard Brooker, Catherine Parks, Paul Kratka. Directed by Steve Miner. 96 min.

This film is a dreary installment in the series in which a group of young people rent a house *near* Camp Crystal Lake and learn that the crazed killer Jason is willing to broaden his horizons. Shown theatrically in 3-D, this second sequel looked a little tired in its relentless rehashing of the who's-going-to-get-it-and-how formula, but it still packed theaters across America. It looks at the end as though Jason is dead, but he isn't.

FRIDAY THE 13TH, PART 2 ☆
1981, USA, R
Amy Steel, John Furey, Adrienne King, Kirsten Baker. Directed by Steve Miner. 87 min.

This *Friday the 13th* sequel is predictable, but it delivers the goods. Five years later, a new owner reopens Camp Crystal Lake, unmindful of its bloody past. A brand-new group of counselors is imported and slaughtered accordingly, this time with the help of Carl *(The Wolfen)* Fullerton, whose effects work underwent considerable editing to preserve the film's "R" rating (imperiled by public outcry over explicit violence in cinema prompted in part by *Friday the 13th*). Director Steve Miner returned for Part 3.

THE FRIENDLY PERSUASION ☆☆☆☆
1956, USA
Gary Cooper, Dorothy McGuire, Marjorie Main, Anthony Perkins, Richard Eyer, Samantha. Directed by William Wyler. 137 min.

William Wyler's often maligned Hollywood craftsmanship was in top form in this touching drama. Adapted from a best-selling novel by Jessamyn West, the story is a series of episodes in the lives of a Quaker family—the title is a pun on their preferred name of the Society of Friends. Gary Cooper is perfectly cast as the father of an Indiana family in the 1860s, forced to come to grips with the Civil War. Anthony Perkins, in his first screen role, is outstanding as the son who, despite Quaker pacifism, goes off to war. Well acted by all and sensitively made, with plenty of gentle humor, this is the type of film that they mean when they talk about how "they don't make them like they used to."

FRIGHT ☆☆
1971, Great Britain
Susan George, Honor Blackman, Ian Bannen, John Gregson, George Cole. Directed by Peter Collinson. 87 min.

This British psycho-killer film will induce the titular emotion only in those who haven't seen a horror movie in the past fifteen years; it has its effective moments but, compared to most recent films, it's very tame. Susan George agrees to baby-sit a young boy in a creepy old house. That very night, however, the boy's father breaks out of the psycho ward, and . . . but we don't want to give it all away, just in case you *have* been living in a cave since *Halloween*.

FRIGHT NIGHT ☆☆
1985, USA, R
Chris Sarandon, William Ragsdale, Amanda Bearse, Stephen Geoffreys, Roddy McDowall. Directed by Tom Holland. 105 min.

When the audience laughs during the scary scenes and cringes during the parts that are meant to be funny, there is definitely something wrong; horror and comedy intermixed have rarely made each other look so bad. A teenager (William Ragsdale) discovers a vampire (Chris Sarandon) living next door and sticks his neck out to save the world from the bloodsucker. Unable to do it alone, he enlists the help of a phony TV "vampire killer" (Roddy McDowall), and together they resort to the usual stuff—crucifixes, stakes, and sunlight. With more holes in the plot than all of the victims have in their necks, this hit-and-run teen flick is merely a vehicle for makeup artists to strut their grotesquely gory stuff.

THE FRISCO KID ☆☆
1979, USA, PG
Gene Wilder, Harrison Ford, Ramon Bieri, Val Bisoglio, George Ralph Di Cenzo, Leo Fuchs, Penny Peyser. Directed by Robert Aldrich. 122 min.

Gene Wilder stars as a nineteenth-century Polish rabbi adrift in the Wild West. But it's Harrison Ford—as the gunslinger who befriends Wilder—who redeems portions of this heavy-handed mix of Western spoof and ethnic humor with his unsinkable aplomb. The lack of plot development turns the film into a series of short action sequences that are neither original nor funny. Be prepared for an overdose of *oy veys* and *oy gevalts*.

FRISSONS

See *They Came from Within*

FRITZ THE CAT ☆☆☆
1972, USA, X
Directed by Ralph Bakshi. 78 min.

One of the few Ralph Bakshi animated features to have some genuine audacity and wit. R. Crumb's classic comic-book cat becomes a friendly, collegiate, irrepressibly horny creature who gets pulled into a series of erotic misadventures, including an imaginatively drawn ghetto sequence. Followed by the far inferior sequel, *The Nine Lives of Fritz the Cat*.

FROGMEN ☆☆½
1951, USA
Richard Widmark, Dana Andrews, Gary Merrill, Jeffrey Hunter, Warren Stevens, Robert Wagner, Harvey Lembeck, James Gregory, Parley Baer, Jack Warden. Directed by Lloyd Bacon. 96 min.

This solid thriller concerns the activities of the U.S. Navy's Underwater Demolition Teams (UDTs), which worked during World War II at clearing away underwater obstacles that could prevent landings on enemy beaches. It's one of those films where a skeletal plot serves as an excuse to show the audience how an experienced and dedicated group of craftsmen perform their jobs. In one particularly tense episode, a UDT sneaks up on a Japanese submarine base to plant explosives, and the effect is heightened by the absence of any sound except for the gurgling of air bubbles. Director Lloyd Bacon, who trained with Mack Sennett, has a knack for action and split-second cutting that he puts to good use here.

FROGS ☆☆½
1972, USA, PG
Ray Milland, Sam Elliott, Joan Van Ark, Adam Roarke, Judy Pace. Directed by George McGowan. 87 min.

Flannery O'Connor meets *Willard*. This being an American-International movie, *Willard* of course wins. A Southern family, formerly aristocratic but now just rich, gathers for the annual kiss-up-to-the-patriarch-so-he-won't-cut-us-out-of-his-will weekend. Because the family fortune was made in a terribly unecological industry, the local swamp fauna (and, in one case, flora) get together to do this not-so-happy clan in. The title is slightly misleading; the amphibians mentioned get the most discussion on the soundtrack, but equal screen time is given to various lizards, snakes, crabs, spiders, turtles, and what-have-you. Not as silly as it sounds, but reasonably fun.

FROM BEYOND ☆☆½
1986, USA, R
Jeffrey Combs, Barbara Crampton, Ted Sorel, Ken Foree, Carolyn Purdy-Gordon. Directed by Stuart Gordon. 85 min.

Though it lacks the giddy gore and exuberantly grotesque spirit of *Re-Animator*, *From Beyond* does have that film's director, stars, and H. P. Lovecraft source material. The result is a comedown that's still several cuts above most current horror films. Jeffrey Combs, so good as *Re-Animator*'s mad doctor, here plays Crawford Tillinghast, a scientist who suffers a mental collapse when his mentor experiments with a machine that stimulates the brain's pineal gland. (What happens to the pineal gland when it's stimulated? Believe us, you don't want to find out.) With the help of a straitlaced but secretly libidinous court psychiatrist (Barbara Crampton), Tillinghast returns to the lab to battle snaggletoothed flying eels, tumorous zombies, and his own worst impulses. *From Beyond* is structured conventionally, but Combs and Crampton are resourceful actors who strike an almost perfect balance between humor and horror, and Stuart Gordon's inventiveness isn't limited to eyeball-suckings and brain-chompings—he's a horror director to watch.

FROM BEYOND THE GRAVE ☆☆½
1973, Great Britain, PG
Ian Bannen, Ian Carmichael, Peter Cushing, Diana Dors, Margaret Leighton, Donald Pleasence, Nyree Dawn Porter, David Warner, Lesley Anne Down, Angela Pleasence. Directed by Kevin Connor. 98 min.

This efficient horror anthology from England's Amicus Films isn't really anything special—just entertaining, well acted, and a welcome substitution of spooky plotting for grotesque gore. Peter Cushing plays a dotty but practical exorcist called in to remove a pesky invisible gremlin from a man's shoulder; Donald Pleasence and daughter Angela are also impressive in a creepy little fable about voodoo. The unusually high quality of the cast and Kevin Connor's brisk direction make this worthwhile for fans of horror done the slightly old-fashioned (and, we think, more honest) way.

FROM CHINA WITH DEATH

See *Wits to Wits*

FROM HELL TO VICTORY ☆☆
1979, France/Italy/Spain
George Peppard, George Hamilton, Horst Buchholz, Capucine, Sam Wanamaker, Jean-Pierre Cassel. Directed by Hank Milestone (Umberto Lenzi). 100 min.

A group of friends of varying nationalities—American, German, French, British—agree in pre–World War II Paris to meet on that same spot a year hence. Of course the war intervenes, and we get to see re-creations of most of the major battles in the European theater of action, all neatly set apart from each other by titles. The plot is little more than a frame for a series of war episodes, and there's nothing you haven't seen dozens of times before. The cast does its best and the production level is high, but the direction and script are rote.

FROM HERE TO ETERNITY ☆☆☆½
1953, USA
Burt Lancaster, Montgomery Clift, Deborah Kerr, Frank Sinatra, Donna Reed, Philip Ober, Ernest Borgnine. Directed by Fred Zinnemann. 118 min.

This still-powerful adaptation of James Jones's 1951 novel won Oscars for Best Picture, Direction (Fred Zinnemann), Screenplay (Daniel Taradash), Supporting Actor (Frank Sinatra), and Supporting Actress (Donna Reed). Zinnemann originally planned Jones's vision of soldiers on the eve of Pearl Harbor to be epic in length, but producer Harry Cohn demanded that the footage come in at under two hours. The result is a compromise, but this "economical" treatment is far preferable to the 1979 miniseries and subsequent TV series also based on the book. Montgomery Clift outdistances everyone in the acting department as a persecuted young private, but curiosity still surrounds the offbeat casting of Deborah Kerr as an American blonde who shares extramarital kisses with a sergeant (Burt Lancaster) while lolling on the beach in a black two-piece suit (the part was originally meant for Joan Crawford), Sinatra as a (non-singing) private in the first of his many "comeback" performances, and Reed, television's perfect mother, as a prostitute. A Hollywood classic that really holds up.

FROM MAO TO MOZART ☆☆☆☆
1980, USA
Isaac Stern, David Golub, Tan Shuzhen. Directed by Murray Lerner. 88 min.

This superb documentary concerns a cultural-exchange tour by violin virtuoso Issac Stern, who visited the People's Republic of China in 1979. The most enthralling passages show Stern's work with talented Chinese students, who tended to play with their heads rather than their hearts. The film is a revealing record of Stern's musical genius and a stirring examination of the creative process and the joys of musicianship, brilliantly produced by Walter Scheuer. Academy Award winner for Best Documentary.

FROM NOON TIL THREE ☆☆☆
1976, USA, PG
Charles Bronson, Jill Ireland, Douglas V. Fowley, Stan Haze, Bert Williams. Directed by Frank D. Gilroy. 98 min.

Novelist/director Frank D. Gilroy, to his credit, insists on making his own movies. They're seldom financial successes, and the execution seldom lives up to the conception, but they're almost always a refreshing change of pace. In this one, Charles Bronson plays against character (quite well, too) as an amateur Western bandit who, thanks to a premature account of his life written by a widow with whom he had an affair (Bronson's real-life wife, Jill Ireland), attains legendary status. It takes the script a while to get going, and even when it does, it often seems unsure of itself. Nice try, though, and likable despite its faults.

FROM RUSSIA WITH LOVE ☆☆☆½
1963, Great Britain
Sean Connery, Daniela Bianchi, Lotte Lenya, Pedro Armendariz, Robert Shaw, Bernard Lee, Lois Maxwell. Directed by Terence Young. 118 min.

James Bond takes on evil SPECTRE agents Rose Klebb (Lotte Lenya) and Red Grant (Robert Shaw) in one of the most exciting and suspenseful films of the series. The climax is a stylized fight-to-the-death on a night-train sleeper bathed in ultraviolet light. Sean Connery is 007—the only 007.

FROM THE LIFE OF THE MARIONETTES ☆☆☆
1980, West Germany, R
Robert Atzorn, Christine Buchegger, Martin Benrath, Rita Russek. Directed by Ingmar Bergman. 104 min.

Shot in Germany, Ingmar Bergman's icy dissection of a sex murder picks up all the cinematic vocabulary of alienation that's familiar from the New German Cinema (and from Michelangelo Antonioni before that). The movie begins with a luridly colored prologue in which a bright young businessman (Robert Atzorn) strangles a prostitute and sodomizes her corpse. The movie then fades to gray, gray black-and-white, as Bergman moves back and forth in time, searching for an explanation in a series of dour, talky tableaux. There are several fine supporting performances, but Robert Atzorn, in the lead, yields so little to the camera that we never feel for him.

FROM THE MIXED-UP FILES OF MRS. BASIL E. FRANKWEILER

See *The Hideaways*

FROM THE TERRACE   ☆☆½
1960, USA
Paul Newman, Joanne Woodward, Myrna Loy, Ina Balin, Leon Ames, Barbara Eden, George Grizzard, Patrick O'Neal, Raymond Bailey, Ted De Corsia. Directed by Mark Robson. 144 min.

This adaptation of a popular John O'Hara potboiler was an undisguised attempt to create a major success in the vein of *Peyton Place* and, while it doesn't begin to approach that standard, it is an enjoyable trashy melodrama nonetheless. Paul Newman plays the lower-class kid who rises to financial success on Wall Street, meanwhile torn between his socially acceptable marriage and true love with a small-town girl. Myrna Loy steals the show as Newman's alcoholic mother, though the rest of the performances are as good as or better than what this kind of thing deserves. You won't believe a minute of it, especially the ending, but it's a good time-killer.

THE FRONT   ☆☆½
1976, USA
Woody Allen, Zero Mostel, Herschel Bernardi, Michael Murphy, Andrea Marcovicci. Directed by Martin Ritt. 95 min.

Woody Allen looks uncomfortable making a rare appearance in a film he neither directed nor wrote. He plays a restaurant cashier who achieves fame fronting for blacklisted television writers during the fifties. Director Martin Ritt and screenwriter Walter Bernstein, once blacklisted themselves, successfully re-create the grim McCarthy era but fail to focus on their subject matter. Aside from Zero Mostel's larger-than-life performance as a blacklisted comic, the film is curiously and frustratingly unmoving. Being one of the very few films about the blacklisting, however, *The Front* should probably be seen. It is unfortunate that it does not make a more powerful statement.

THE FRONT PAGE   ☆☆☆½
1931, USA
Adolphe Menjou, Pat O'Brien, Mary Brian, Edward Everett Horton, Walter Catlett, Mae Clarke. Directed by Lewis Milestone. 103 min.

Try to catch your breath during this rapid-fire comedy, adapted from the Broadway smash. It's the tale of the tumultuous relationship of an avid editor and his star reporter, both of whom belong to that strange brotherhood, the Press. The newshounds to whom a scoop means more than life itself are mercilessly ribbed in this film which paradoxically seems madly in love with what it's satirizing. As good as this is, it lacks the glow of the Cary Grant–Roz Russell remake, *His Girl Friday*, in which the reporter's character was changed to a woman and the film was charged with sexual tension. But this is superior to Billy Wilder's remake with Walter Matthau and Jack Lemmon.

FULL CIRCLE

See *The Haunting of Julia*

THE FULLER BRUSH MAN   ☆☆☆
1948, USA
Red Skelton, Janet Blair, Don McGuire, Hillary Brooke. Directed by S. Sylvan Simon. 93 min.

The zany Red Skelton is at his best stumbling, tripping, and falling into one predicament after another in this slapstick comedy. After losing his job as a street cleaner, he tries to impress his girl (Janet Blair) by proving he can succeed as a salesman for the Fuller Brush Company. This task turns into a circus of murder, mystery, and mayhem. As the evidence points increasingly toward him, he tries to clear his name, win back his girl, and discover the murderer.

FULL MOON IN PARIS   ☆☆
1984, France, R
Pascale Ogier, Fabrice Luchini, Tcheky Karyo, Christian Vadim. Directed by Eric Rohmer. 102 min.

The fourth and in every way least interesting film in Eric Rohmer's "Comedies and Proverbs" series concerns, as do the others, the comic misfortunes that occur when a young woman tries to engineer her own romantic life. This time, the protagonist is Louise (Pascale Ogier), a gratingly naive waif who, pleading the need for "space," takes a small apartment in Paris away from her lover. She soon realizes that having two houses is as problematic as having two men, and she approaches both topics with such undue sobriety that you soon realize she can only be . . . yes, a French yuppie. From the evidence here, French yuppies are as boring as the Yankee variety, and they don't even have good nightclubs. Viewers in search of a good Eric Rohmer film should seek out any of the preceding films in the series: *The Aviator's Wife*, *Le Beau Mariage*, or *Pauline at the Beach*.

FUNERAL IN BERLIN   ☆☆½
1966, Great Britain
Michael Caine, Paul Hubschmid, Oscar Homolka, Eva Renzi, Guy Doleman. Directed by Guy Hamilton. 102 min.

This standard but entertaining spy thriller is the second and best of three attempts to create another James Bond out of Len Deighton's Harry Palmer. As he did in *The Ipcress File*, Michael Caine plays the intelligence expert, soft-spoken Cockney spy Harry Palmer, this time on assignment in East Berlin, where a Communist spy is about to defect. There isn't much new here, but fans of the genre will enjoy it; producer Harry Saltzman, director Guy Hamilton and production designer Ken Adam all worked on the Bond series, and they know how to deliver the goods. Followed by *Billion Dollar Brain*.

THE FUNHOUSE   ☆☆☆½
1981, USA, R
Elizabeth Berridge, Shawn Carson, Jeanne Austin, Jack McDermott, Cooper Huckabee. Directed by Tobe Hooper. 96 min.

Surprisingly, this umpteenth entry in the horny-teens-vs.-hairy-psychos horror cycle isn't half bad. Directed by Tobe Hooper (*The Texas Chainsaw Massacre*), it's full of the usual acne-ridden teenage dialogue (Larry Block is responsible) and the usual bland acting—but only by the kids. The assorted ghouls haunting the eerie carnival that becomes the scene of several crimes are wonderfully played by such pungent hams as Kevin Conway, William Finley, and, God bless 'er, Sylvia Miles. And what's really wonderful about *Funhouse* is its awareness of what a horror movie is all about: underneath the chases and chills, this is a demented exploration of what draws us to horror, of the fascination of fear. It doesn't take us long to realize that the funhouse, with its gruesome creatures leaping from every shadow, is a metaphor for the horror movie itself. The creepiest since *Alien*, *Funhouse*'s monster is a wonderful creation designed by Rick Baker.

FUN IN ACAPULCO   ☆☆
1963, USA
Elvis Presley, Ursula Andress, Elsa Cardenas, Larry Domasin, Paul Lukas. Directed by Richard Thorpe. 97 min.

The singing of Elvis Presley and the sight of Ursula Andress and Mexico make this Presley tunefest slightly above average.

He plays a trapeze artist who must choose between Andress and a bullfighter (Elsa Cardenas). All is sorted out to tunes like "Bossa Nova Baby" and "The Bullfighter Was a Lady." Tolerable formula stuff.

FUNNY FACE ☆☆☆½
1957, USA
Audrey Hepburn, Fred Astaire, Kay Thompson, Michael Auclair, Robert Fleming. Directed by Stanley Donen. 103 min.

An outstanding score by George and Ira Gershwin graces this excellent musical. Far from director Stanley Donen's best work, the film is nonetheless visually striking, marked by careful editing and imaginative uses of color. Fred Astaire plays a fashion photographer who falls in love with the "funny face" of a brainy bookstore clerk, Audrey Hepburn. The story, which has a decidedly anti-intellectual flavor, never soars; but it does provide an amusing backdrop for several memorable musical numbers. Astaire is as graceful and dapper as ever, and "Let's Kiss and Make Up" is perhaps the film's most interesting dance routine.

FUNNY GIRL ☆☆☆
1968, USA
Barbra Streisand, Omar Sharif, Kay Medford, Anne Francis, Walter Pidgeon, Lee Allen. Directed by William Wyler. 147 min.

Barbra Streisand's powerhouse film debut is still the main attraction in William Wyler's meandering biography of comedienne Fanny Brice. Streisand sings such endearing hits as "People," "Don't Rain on My Parade," and "My Man," and although she never really becomes Fanny Brice, her own forceful personality is in itself fascinating to watch. The first half of the film, detailing the rise of the star, is lively and amusing, but the second half, detailing the star's domestic strife, is laborious and overlong. Omar Sharif is appropriately debonair as Nicky Arnstein, Fanny's handsome gambler-husband, and Walter Pidgeon is appropriately paternal as Flo Ziegfeld. But it's Streisand's show, and she is electrifying in what may be the finest two-and-a-half hours on screen. Sequel: *Funny Lady*.

FUNNY LADY ☆☆½
1975, USA, PG
Barbra Streisand, James Caan, Omar Sharif, Roddy McDowall, Ben Vereen, Carole Wells. Directed by Herbert Ross. 137 min.

Barbra Streisand bulldozes her way through this sequel to the show and film that made her a star. It's a continuation of *Funny Girl*, the Fanny Brice story, charting Brice's years in radio and film and her troubled marriage to entrepreneur Billy Rose (James Caan). The numbers are lavish (by seventies musical standards), and Streisand sings evergreens like "More Than You Know," "Am I Blue?," and "It's Only a Paper Moon" in her inimitable manner. Still, her galvanic, strident personality gets in the way of any sympathy we might have for her character. Once again, Streisand is in need of a director who can really direct her. The film becomes little but a showcase for her excesses.

A FUNNY THING HAPPENED ON THE WAY TO THE FORUM ☆☆☆½
1966, USA
Zero Mostel, Phil Silvers, Jack Gilford, Michael Crawford, Annette André, Buster Keaton. Directed by Richard Lester. 99 min.

Vaudeville meets ancient Rome in this lively adaptation of Stephen Sondheim, Larry Gelbart, and Bert Shevelove's Broadway musical. Not more than three Sondheim songs survived in the transfer to the big screen, but it hardly matters. Director Richard Lester (*A Hard Day's Night*, *The Three Musketeers*) keeps things fast and funny through his customarily rapid jump-cutting style. The fractured story line deals with a Roman slave's attempt to help his master's son elope and earn freedom for himself. The Melvin Frank/Michael Pertwee screenplay jumbles borscht-belt humor, British sat-ire, and a big Broadway sound to ridiculous and hilarious effect. Low point: Buster Keaton bumping into trees. High point: Jack Gilford's drag version of "Lovely."

FUN WITH DICK AND JANE ☆☆☆
1977, USA, PG
Jane Fonda, George Segal, Ed McMahon, Dick Gautier, Fred Willard. Directed by Ted Kotcheff. 95 min.

Jane Fonda, reminding us that she is one of America's funniest, sexiest comediennes, and George Segal play a conventional upper-middle-class couple who find themselves in desperate financial straits when Segal loses his job as an aerospace engineer. They turn to crime, first because their backs are against the wall and later because they find it a wicked sexual turn-on.

THE FURIOUS ½☆
Hong Kong
Cen Wei-Min, Lo Lieh, Ku Feng, Huang Ka Tat. Directed by Joseph Velasco.

A band of halfhearted martial artists is formed to break up a ring of international drug smugglers. An old-hat plot, less-then-adequate action choreography, and production values painful to the eye, heart, and mind all combine to produce fury in anyone unfortunate enough to sit through this. A dog, even within the worst of the genre.

THE FURTHER ADVENTURES OF THE WILDERNESS FAMILY

See *The Wilderness Family: Part 2*

FURY ☆☆☆☆
1936, USA
Spencer Tracy, Sylvia Sidney, Walter Abel, Edward Ellis, Walter Brennan, George Walcott, Frank Albertson. Directed by Fritz Lang. 94 min.

German-born Fritz Lang directed this dark, relentlessly terrifying landmark film. *Fury* tells the tale of a good, average American man (Spencer Tracy) who is lynched for a crime he didn't commit. As in his other work, Lang explores the corruption of the human spirit by mobs and systems. In Lang's world, we see men stripped of their individuality, dehumanized. As they seek revenge on the society that has destroyed their faith in humanity, Langian protagonists inevitably become as evil as their oppressors. *Fury* is particularly noteworthy for its innovative treatment of a film-within-a-film, namely footage of the lynching that serves as court evidence and represents a sort of cinematic truth. Hollywood norms required—contrary to the director's vision—that the audience's sympathies lie with a *white* lynching victim, which wasn't, of course, the way it usually happened in life. The improbable ending wasn't Lang's idea, either.

THE FURY ☆☆☆
1978, USA, R
Kirk Douglas, Amy Irving, Andrew Stevens, John Cassavetes. Directed by Brian De Palma. 118 min.

Director Brian De Palma moves from a single telekinetic teenager (*Carrie*) to a pack of telekinetic teens in this silly but enjoyable Alfred Hitchcock pastiche that mixes spies, car chases, and exploding bodies. Secret agent Kirk Douglas, whose telepathic son is kidnapped by his ruthless boss, enlists the aid of a youth with similar powers to track him down. This high-class, goofy drive-in fun is shockingly outrageous, a rip-off with style. It contains the grossest of his "shock-out" endings, with John Cassavetes literally blowing his top, a scene that is repeated several times for our enjoyment. Even John Williams's powerful score owes something to

Hitchcock's favorite composer, Bernard Herrman. (Not related to the great Fritz Lang film of the same name.)

FURY OF KING BOXER
Hong Kong ☆
Jimmy Wang Yu, Kuo Shu Chiang, Tsum Mee, Wong Yung, Tin Yen. Directed by Tse Hing.

This muddled story takes place in the period after the Boxer Rebellion. Perhaps its confusion derives from the producers' understandable eagerness to think the rebellious boxers were pugilists of an earlier era.

FURY OF SHAOLIN FIST
1977, Hong Kong ☆
Chen Jung Li, Shik Chuan, Chen-I, Chiang Pin, Chiao Chiao, Meng Li, Wang Lai, Miao Tien, Liang Feng, Sung Ling, Li Chiang. Directed by Li Chih Sho, Liu Yeh. 66 min.

This movie has absolutely nothing to do with Shaolin or the Styles. One villain has a whip, and the others swing their arms a lot. Worth buying only if it's cheaper than a blank tape.

FURY OF THE SHAOLIN MASTER
Hong Kong ½☆
Yo Hua, Tsai Tsuan Han, Chen Hsing, Pan Ying Tzu, Wen Chiang Lung, Yin Pao Lien, Kao Fei, Yo Yang, Wo Chin. Directed by Lin Tuti.

This Chinese rip-off of the Itto Ogami and "The Babycart Series" chronicles a policeman's attempt to track down the man who slaughtered his family. Accompanying the hero is an endearing four-year-old child. Unfortunately, the movie doesn't really develop the relationship between the two. One consolation: Yo Hua, the policeman, is a crisp, precise swordsman (very reminiscent of the Japanese Chambara film technique).

FUTURE-KILL
1985, USA, R ☆
Edwin Neal, Marilyn Burns. Directed by Ronald W. Moore. 83 min.

For those who care, the redoubtable stars of *Texas Chainsaw Massacre* are reunited in this thriller. Set in the hazy future (and no doubt equally inspired by *Streets of Fire* and *The Road Warrior*), the film deals with the clash of wills between—get this—a fraternity house and a bunch of deranged antinuke didacts. The film is implausible and bizarre, but not intriguing. It would have been better if they had crossed *Revenge of the Nerds* with *Silkwood* and passed it off as the shape of things to come.

FUTUREWORLD
1976, USA ☆☆
Peter Fonda, Blythe Danner, Arthur Hill, Yul Brynner, Stuart Margolin. Directed by Richard T. Heffron. 107 min.

In this sequel to *Westworld*, leftover robots from the first film reproduce and plot to take over the world. Michael Crichton's original film built terror from a mildly satirical premise—people paying money to live out their childhood playtime fantasies. This has none of that, degenerating quickly into standard sci-fi stuff.

FUTZ
1969, USA ☆☆½
Seth Allen, John Bakos, Mari-Claire Charba. Directed by Tom O'Horgan. 92 min.

Tom O'Horgan, who gained notoriety as the director of *Hair* on Broadway, adapted this from his presentation of Rochelle Owen's play. The plot, which *Futz* purposely obscures for a while, has to do with a farmer in an Appalachian community who is in love with his pig. The film is an allegory about freedom of choice designed to alternately attract and repel audiences. Not for all tastes, and probably too obscure even for many inclined to sample it. A sixties relic, for better or worse.

FUZZ
1972, USA, PG ☆☆½
Burt Reynolds, Yul Brynner, Jack Weston, Tom Skerritt, Raquel Welch, Peter Bonerz, Charlie Martin Smith. Directed by Richard A. Colla. 92 min.

With a cast like this based on one of the "87th Precinct" novels by Ed McBain (who wrote the screenplay using his real name, Evan Hunter), *Fuzz* should have been much better. For years McBain has been doing with these books what "Hill Street Blues" has been so acclaimed for in the eighties: drawing a portrait of the day-to-day minutiae of police procedure, along with glimpses into the lives of his cops. Given the cumulative effect of the books, the movie will probably appeal most to those unfamiliar with McBain, who can judge it solely as a less human *M*A*S*H* (an obvious influence, particularly in the squad-room scenes). Funny for the most part, but finally too lighthearted to succeed.

F/X
1986, USA, R ☆☆☆
Bryan Brown, Brian Dennehy, Diana Venora, Cliff DeYoung, Mason Adams, Jerry Orbach, Joe Grifasi. Directed by Robert Mandel. 107 min.

The title of this entertaining, unpretentious thriller is filmese for "special effects," and they play a central role in the taut narrative. The hero is a film-gore expert (Bryan Brown) who specializes in creating bulletholes, blood splatter, and dismemberments for horror films. When the Justice Department hires him to fake the assassination of a mobster–turned–federal witness, he finds himself the scapegoat in a murder conspiracy and must use his technical genius to save his life. The fast-moving plot has too many loose ends to move as smoothly as it should, but the offbeat casting of Australian actor Brown as the special-effects whiz works well, and some very clever moments give a charge to the slightly contrived climax. More amusing than suspenseful overall, but good fun on that level.

FYRE
1978, USA ☆
Lynn Theel, Allen Goorwitz, Frank Sivero, Tom Baker, Cal Haynes, Bruce Kirby. Directed by Richard Grand. 82 min.

A seventeen-year-old girl is raped, and the next day her mother, father, and brother go on a picnic, get beat up, and drive off a cliff! Time to leave the old hometown. Eight years later, she's a prostitute, in love with a violent con, looking to do anything to get out of her trap. Like their desperate heroine, the filmmakers descend to the depths of low-level titillation to succeed; as the film progresses, we move from disco dancing (gee), to cocaine snorting (wow), to underage, underfed girls in their panties kissing each other (yikes!).

G

GABLE AND LOMBARD
1976, USA, R
James Brolin, Jill Clayburgh, Allen Garfield, Red Buttons, Melanie Mayron, Morgan Brittany. Directed by Sidney J. Furie. 131 min.

☆

Someday someone will undoubtedly produce a film consisting of clips from movies with bad Clark Gable impersonations. He will include Mike Connors in *Harlow* (1965), Edward Winter in *Moviola: The Scarlett O'Hara War* (1980), and Boyd Holister in *Grace Kelly* (1983), but most of the footage will consist of James Brolin in this film. While Brolin dodders around in tuxedos wrinkling his forehead and muttering, Jill Clayburgh, playing Carole Lombard but looking like Little Orphan Annie, screeches and hits him for two hours. Worse than being the kind of bad film you can laugh at, *Gable and Lombard* is consistently dull. Note: Morgan Brittany repeated her Vivien Leigh in *Moviola: The Scarlett O'Hara War*.

GABRIELA
1983, Brazil, R
Sonia Braga, Marcello Mastroianni, Antonio Cantafora. Directed by Bruno Barreto. 102 min.

☆☆

The voluptuous Sonia Braga stars in this backwater romance about an impoverished peasant nymph who gets hot and heavy with a local tavern owner (Marcello Mastroianni). The oppressive social tensions director Bruno Barreto builds into the movie are never fully explored, but Braga heats up the screen as the insatiable woman who can't seem to keep her clothes on, if that's your idea of a good time.

GALAXINA
1980, USA, R
Stephen Macht, Dorothy Stratten, James David Hinton, Avery Schreiber, Ronald Knight. Directed by William Sachs. 95 min.

☆½

The only attraction of this halfhearted, low-budget spoof of the sci-fi genre is Dorothy Stratten, the slain *Playboy* Playmate whose life and death was the subject of *Star 80*. Those inclined to view her as a tragically wasted talent might do better to view *They All Laughed* than this muck, in which her abysmal acting takes a backseat to the lazy script and Avery Schreiber's incessant mugging. All things considered, it's unfunny and ghoulish.

GALAXY OF TERROR
1981, USA, R
Edward Albert, Zalman King, Erin Moran, Sid Haig, Ray Walston, Grace Zabriskie, Bernard Behrens. Directed by B. D. Clark. 80 min.

☆½

A group of astronauts on a mission to assist a marooned ship find themselves trapped in an alien structure—a sophisticated psychological torture chamber designed to confront each victim with his/her worst fear in its nastiest possible form—around whose very bend awaits some disgusting object/creature/experience. This film is seriously indebted to *Alien*, with some cosmic pretensions in the form of Ray Walston as the master gameplayer who presides over the entire grim experience. Gross derivative fun. (a.k.a.: *Mindwarp: An Infinity of Terror* and *Planet of Horrors*)

THE GALLANT HOURS
1960, USA
James Cagney, Dennis Weaver, Ward Costello, Richard Jaeckel, Les Tremayne, Raymond Bailey, William Schallert. Directed by Robert Montgomery. 115 min.

☆☆½

As is often the case, compelling real-life events make for a dull movie. This is a pseudodocumentary about a short period in the career of Admiral William Halsey during the early stages of World War II, a decisive period for the Pacific battles of the entire war. There are no battle scenes: the story instead follows the war of strategy played out between Halsey and his Japanese counterpart, Admiral Yamamoto. It's intelligently written by Frank D. Gilroy and Beirne Lay, Jr., but too talky and slow for most war fans. James Cagney's characterization is excellent, however, and he is set off well by Dennis Weaver, who provides a needed touch of humor as his assistant.

GALLIPOLI
1981, Australia, PG
Mark Lee, Mel Gibson, Bill Kerr, Robert Grubb, David Argue, Tim McKenzie. Directed by Peter Weir. 110 min.

☆☆☆☆

Peter Weir (*The Last Wave*, *The Year of Living Dangerously*) directed this powerful, acclaimed epic starring Mel Gibson and Mark Lee as two young Australian soldiers who participate in the disastrous Turkish campaign of 1915, which climaxed with the massacre of Australia's troops at Gallipoli. *Gallipoli* makes a searing antiwar statement; Weir directs seamlessly and elicits fine performances from the entire cast.

GAMBIT
1966, USA
Shirley MacLaine, Michael Caine, Herbert Lom, Roger C. Carmel, Arnold Moss, John Abbott. Directed by Ronald Neame. 107 min.

☆☆☆

Michael Caine and Shirley MacLaine are well paired in this lighthearted caper film. As a cockney thief and his Eurasian accomplice, they conspire to rob smug Arab potentate Herbert Lom of a priceless statue. Unlike most films of its type, this manages to sustain an even tone throughout without lapsing into nasty counterpoint or just becoming dull.

THE GAMBLER
1974, USA, R
James Caan, Paul Sorvino, Lauren Hutton, Morris Carnovsky, Jacqueline Brookes, Burt Young. Directed by Karel Reisz. 109 min.

☆☆☆½

James Caan gives one of his finest performances in Karel Reisz's muted, brutal, beautifully textured study of a compulsive gambler whose efforts to pay off his debts have a cataclysmic effect on those around him. Though slow and, at times, murky, *The Gambler* benefits from a strong, well-conceived script by James Toback and beautiful acting from the large supporting cast, especially Paul Sorvino and Burt Young as two cold-blooded loan shark collectors and Lauren Hutton as Caan's sympathetic friend. Victor Kemper did the fine, dark cinematography, and Roger Spottiswoode, who later directed *Under Fire*, supervised the editing.

THE GAME IS OVER
1966, France
Jane Fonda, Peter McEnery, Michel Piccoli, Tina Marquand, Jacques Mondon, Simone Valere. Directed by Roger Vadim. 85 min.

☆☆

One of Jane Fonda's earliest starring roles was in this glossy drama directed by then-spouse Roger Vadim. The story updates the Émile Zola novel *La Curée* about a young woman (Jane Fonda) who falls in love with the son of her elderly, wealthy husband. A picturesque film, and Fonda's performance is decent but nothing special. (a.k.a.: *The Kill*)

GAME OF DEATH ★★½
1979, Hong Kong
Bruce Lee, Dean Jagger, Kareem Abdul-Jabbar, Hugh O'Brian, Chuck Norris, Danny Inosanto, Gig Young, Colleen Camp, Mel Novak. Directed by Robert Clouse. 100 min.

Perhaps the most famous Bruce Lee exploitation film, *Game of Death* outstripped even *Enter the Dragon* in popularity. The story concerns a martial-arts actor who runs into trouble with a group of mobsters trying to control his career. Lee died during the making of the film, and producer Raymond Chow used a stand-in to complete it. The result is a mediocre genre film with one redeeming quality—the last ten minutes of pure Bruce Lee action, in which he engages in a bizarre, climactic battle with Kareem Abdul-Jabbar.

GAME OF DEATH II ★★
1981, Hong Kong
Bruce Lee (Hah), Tang Lung (Kim Tai-Chung), Huang Chen-Li, Casanova Wong, Miranda Austia. Directed by Ng See-Yuen.

Outtakes of Bruce Lee's performance in *Enter the Dragon* were stitched into a plot about Bruce's brother seeking his killer. Believe it or not, this is considered one of the best of the Bruce Lee exploitation films, and the display of martial arts is wonderful (though the fight scenes are speeded up a bit). At any rate, it's better than *Bruce Lee: His Last Days, His Last Nights*.

THE GAMMA PEOPLE ★
1956, Great Britain
Paul Douglas, Eva Bartok, Leslie Phillips, Walter Rilla, Philip Leaver, Martin Miller. Directed by John Gilling. 78 min.

This predictable, tepid horror film concerns two reporters in Europe who accidentally discover a mad scientist's plan to turn children into robotic geniuses by bombarding them with gamma rays. Despite some funny moments with the children, this clumsy plot is handled with a conspicuous lack of care.

GANDHI ★★★½
1982, Great Britain/India, PG
Ben Kingsley, Candice Bergen, Edward Fox, John Gielgud, Trevor Howard, John Mills, Martin Sheen, Ian Charleson. Directed by Richard Attenborough. 188 min.

A stirring, reverential epic about India's spiritual and political leader Mohandas Gandhi. In some ways, the film's portrayal of the pacifist movement in India and Gandhi's espousal of passive resistance is rather elementary, but the film wisely focuses on the charismatic figure of the man himself. In its attention to detail, its sweeping panoramas, its ability to combine large-scale action scenes with those contemplating philosophical returns, the film recalls the tradition of quality filmmaking best exemplified by David Lean, another impeccable craftsman who creates masterful epics. A thinking man's epic and a colorful history lesson, this film was rewarded with a mantelful of Oscars, including Best Picture, Best Actor, Best Screenplay, and Best Director.

GANGS OF SONORA ★½
1941, USA
Robert Livingston, Bob Steele, Rufe Davis. Directed by John English. 56 min.

The Three Mesquiteers aid Wyoming in the fight for entrance into the Union. The subplot of the tough-as-hickory newspaperwoman may prove more interesting than the sagebrush gang fight.

THE GANGSTER ★★★
1947, USA
Barry Sullivan, Belita, Joan Lorring, Akim Tamiroff, Henry Morgan, John Ireland, Sheldon Leonard, Elisha Cook, Jr., Leif Erickson, Shelley Winters. Directed by Gordon Wiles. 82 min.

Two years before James Cagney played a psychotic gangster in Raoul Walsh's *White Heat*, Monogram Studios brought out this interesting psychological study of a slum-reared gang leader who also turns out to be his own worst enemy. Unlike the later film, though, there is little action in this one, so it didn't fare well at the box office, but it's still worth checking out for fans of the genre. Barry Sullivan is quite good as the friendless hood, and Shelley Winters has a small part.

THE GANG THAT COULDN'T SHOOT STRAIGHT ★★
1971, USA, PG
Jerry Orbach, Leigh Taylor-Young, Jo Van Fleet, Lionel Stander, Robert De Niro, Hervé Villechaize, Joe Santos, Paul Benedict, Burt Young. Directed by James Goldstone. 96 min.

Jimmy Breslin's comic novel about an inept gang of South Brooklyn Italians was able to get away with a lot of ethnic stereotypes primarily because Breslin understands the types he writes about. This film version, on the other hand, tends to bring those clichés right to the forefront and lean on them rather than use them for flavoring, and the result varies between dull and downright offensive. It does have a few funny scenes, though, and is, at least, well-cast.

GARBO TALKS ★★★½
1984, USA, PG-13
Anne Bancroft, Ron Silver, Catherine Hicks, Howard DaSilva, Betty Comden. Directed by Sidney Lumet. 105 min.

Sidney Lumet directed this hip New York comedy about a dutiful son desperately trying to fulfill his cancer-stricken mother's last wish—to meet the reclusive 1930s screen star. This is one of the first "yuppie" satires, with many fine points to make about the trendy but empty executive life-style; it's also a movie with many beautifully human moments, including Anne Bancroft's delirious monologue to her idol. *Garbo* talked, and unfortunately no one went to see her at the movies, but the film has started to get the attention it deserved on videotape.

GARDE A VUE ★★★½
1981, France
Michael Serrault, Lino Ventura, Guy Marchand, Romy Schneider. Directed by Claude Miller. 87 min.

This complex, never-a-dull-moment melodrama about a murder investigation is just perplexing enough to keep audiences on the edge of their seats throughout. Two staunch investigators badger a model citizen suspected of slaying two little girls. The film details the relationship between the two dogged policemen, as well as their relationship with the alleged criminal, in a manner that counterpoints the ongoing investigation of the crime. A superb *policier* with the full-throttle treatment the French seem to do best, it has a dazzling supporting performance by the late Romy Schneider as the accused man's embittered wife.

THE GARDENER

See *Seeds of Evil*

THE GARDEN OF ALLAH ★★★½
1936, USA
Marlene Dietrich, Charles Boyer, Basil Rathbone, C. Aubrey Smith, Tilly Losch, John Carradine, Joseph Schildkraut, Lucille Watson. Directed by Richard Boleslawski. 80 min.

This irresistibly velvety kitsch was one of the earliest features to utilize the three-strip Technicolor process, and the results are dazzling. Cameramen W. Howard Greene and Hal Rossen create orange Sahara sunsets that are more stunning than the real thing in this story of a Trappist monk who is lured out of his vow of celibacy and into marriage by an exotic temptress. Director Richard Boleslawski's last completed film would be nothing but a series of spectacular shots if it weren't for Charles Boyer's beautiful, understated performance as the conscience-torn monk. This was Boyer's first American film, and he practically learned his English phonetically; however, when his big, dark eyes start welling up, it's sheer poetry.

GARDEN OF THE DEAD
1972, USA ☆
Phil Kennealy, Duncan McCloud, Lee Frost, Eric Stern. Directed by John Hayes. 90 min.

An undistinguished and grossly derivative living-dead film featuring standard zombie makeup by Joe Blasco, who also created the disgusting parasites of David Cronenberg's *They Came from Within*. On an isolated prison farm, a group of convicts amuse themselves by inhaling the fumes of the formaldehyde they are supposed to be decanting as part of their rehabilitation through honest labor.

THE GARDEN OF THE FINZI-CONTINIS
1970, Italy/West Germany, R ☆☆☆
Dominique Sanda, Lino Capolicchio, Helmut Berger, Fabio Testi. Directed by Vittorio De Sica. 95 min.

This laudable, but not altogether successful, film concerns a wealthy Jewish family living in Ferraro, Italy, at the height of World War II. As scripted, *Garden* is searing drama, powerfully juxtaposing the family's blasé attitude within their garden walls with the fate that awaits them outside. But as filmed, the story is marred by a preponderance of sixties-style mise-en-scène, soft-focus photography, and intrusive zooms. Worse still, its mood of impending doom is never left to the viewer to discover, but is imposed on him through sappy music and ominous shots of clouds on the horizon. De Sica's best film in twenty years, it is nonetheless a pale reminder of his earlier greatness.

GAS
1981, Canada, PG ☆½
Sterling Hayden, Susan Anspach, Peter Aykroyd, Donald Sutherland. Directed by Les Rose. 94 min.

An unscrupulous oil baron (Sterling Hayden) creates an artificial gas shortage in a small Midwestern town, and the inhabitants respond by fighting their way, tooth and claw, to the gas pumps. This film features Donald Sutherland as an airborne DJ, Susan Anspach as a befuddled news reporter, and Peter Aykroyd (Dan's brother) as the world's klutziest black belt. It was supposed to be topical when it came out in the days of OPEC oil shortages. It wasn't funny in that context, and it's even duller now.

GASLIGHT
1944, USA ☆☆☆½
Ingrid Bergman, Charles Boyer, Joseph Cotten, Angela Lansbury, Dame May Whitty. Directed by George Cukor. 114 min.

Ingrid Bergman's Academy Award–winning performance is one of the most heartbreaking to watch in the long line of "wives-in-distress" roles for 1940s heroines. This gloomy glimpse of Victorian villainy stars Charles Boyer as a suavely malicious husband who tries to drive his loving wife (Bergman) over the edge. George Cukor's claustrophobic mise-en-scène is actually enhanced by MGM's typically overstuffed set design. Only Joseph Cotten's bland detective hero is out of place in this atmospheric, European-style melodrama.

GAS PUMP GIRLS
1979, USA, R ☆
Kirsten Baker, Sandy Johnson, Leslie King, Huntz Hall. Directed by Joel Bender. 90 min.

Three perky girls help out an ill uncle by turning his business from a gas station to a dull disco. Of course the women are well endowed, and naturally they find several excuses to bare their bosoms. Ho-hum. Veteran character actors Joe E. Ross and Mike Mazurski appear as hoods.

GAS-S-S-S!; OR, IT MAY BECOME NECESSARY TO DESTROY THE WORLD IN ORDER TO SAVE IT
1969, USA ☆☆☆
Robert Corff, Elaine Giftos, Bud Cort, Talia Coppola (Shire), Ben Vereen, Cindy Williams, Alex Wilson, Lou Oricopio, Country Joe and the Fish, George Armitage. Directed by Roger Corman. 79 min.

A *very* strange film, even for Roger Corman, and if that doesn't make you want to rush right out and get it, you may as well stop reading right here. One of those maleficent gases that the government is always making in underground laboratories escapes, killing everyone on Earth over the age of twenty-five. Some of the survivors get together, smile on their brothers, try and love one another right now (well, it *was* 1969), and head for a pueblo commune in New Mexico. Along the way they meet up with a road bandit named Billy the Kid, a rock star named F. M. Radio, and a pocket of before-their-time yuppies led by Marshall McLuhan. At the end, a lightning storm brings all the dead adults back to life (a nice touch for you zombie fans) and things look bad for our heroes until the day is saved by John Kennedy, Martin Luther King, Che Guevara, and Edgar Allan Poe. (a.k.a.: *Gas-s-s-s*)

GATE OF HELL
1954, Japan ☆☆☆½
Machiko Kyo, Kanzuo Hasegawa, Isao Yamagata. Directed by Teinosuke Kinugasa. 89 min.

This strikingly photographed color film was one of the first to acquaint Western audiences with Japanese filmmaking. In twelfth-century Japan, a woman resists the sexual ardor of an invading warlord. The art direction and costumes are magnificent, and the film won both a special Academy Award for Best Foreign Film and the Golden Palm at the Cannes Film Festival.

THE GATES OF HELL
1981, Italy ☆
Christopher George, Lynda Day George. Directed by Lucio Fulci. 88 min.

A New England priest commits suicide in a graveyard; his action lays open the gates of hell, through which issue crumbling hordes of cannibal zombies. Tipped off by a psychic, a New York City police detective investigates the strange goings-on, and the blood and guts flow freely. This very gory, derivative Italian horror movie is not for nongenre fans, but it delivers some shocks.

THE GATHERING
1977, USA (TV) ☆☆☆
Edward Asner, Maureen Stapleton, Lawrence Pressman, Stephanie Zimbalist, Bruce Davison, John Randolph. Directed by Randal Kleiser. 92 min.

This weepy TV drama transcends the limitations of its "Daddy's-going-to die" story line. A successful businessman calls his family together for a Christmas reunion to reveal the news of his impending death and to try to instill a sense of family before it's too late. Edward Asner is superb as the hard-driving entrepreneur who put his career before his family, and he's matched every step of the way by Maureen Stapleton as his neglected wife. A worthwhile gathering of solid talent both in front of and behind the camera, particularly James Poe, who did the solid screenplay. Followed by a sequel.

GATOR ☆☆
1976, USA, PG
Burt Reynolds, Jack Weston, Lauren Hutton, Jerry Reed, Alice Ghostley. Directed by Burt Reynolds. 116 min.

Burt Reynolds's sequel to *White Lightning* (1973) springs moonshiner Gator McCluskey from jail once again to pursue some criminals who *really* deserve to be behind bars. It's nothing special, but the star's directorial debut is perfectly serviceable, as is the redneck-baiting action and by-the-book plot. It's much easier on the nerves than the brain-atrophying *Cannonball Run* films that followed, and good fun of its kind. Poor Lauren Hutton, however, seems completely adrift.

GATOR BAIT ☆½
1976, USA
Claudia Jennings, Sam Gilman, Doug Dirkson, Clyde Ventura, Bill Thurman. Directed by Fred and Beverly Sebastian. 93 min.

If you can get your kicks watching grown men salivate over a voluptuous swamp siren named Desirée (and if you behave in general like teenage boys who have just seen their first *Playboy* centerfold), then this sleazy exploitation pic about Desirée's murderous designs on her admirers may keep you alert. Others may be swamped by the gratuitous violence and tinges of sadism lurking around the edges of this sexcapade. Claudia Jennings is indeed eye-filling as the boggy babe, but you need a hard-core drive-in mentality to enjoy it.

THE GAUNTLET ☆☆☆
1977, USA, R
Clint Eastwood, Sondra Locke, Pat Hingle, William Prince, Bill McKinney, Michael Cavanaugh, Carole Cook, Mara Corday. Directed by Clint Eastwood. 108 min.

Not just another Clint Eastwood renegade-cop movie, this one was directed by Eastwood himself and it's a lot of fun. Eastwood's dim, drunken Ben Shockley, who must escort a witness (Sondra Locke) that everyone wants killed back to trial, is his most touching, vulnerable characterization in years. For once, you feel there's something behind the scrunched-up eyes and bullet-biting grimace. Eastwood's direction occasionally has a charming eccentric touch.

THE GAY DECEIVERS ☆
1969, USA, R
Kevin Coughlin, Larry Casey, Brooke Bundy, Jo Ann Harris, Michael Greer, Sebastian Brook, Jack Starrett, Richard Webb, Elosie Hardt, Jeanne Baird, Marishka, Mike Kopscha, Robert Reese, Christopher Riordan. Directed by Bruce Kessler. 97 min.

This dated farce doesn't offer a drop of genuine humor but instead floods the screen with offensive stereotypes and obnoxious gags. A couple of regular guys pretend to be gay in order to avoid the draft. They move into a homosexual apartment building (?) and much unhilarity results as they try to sneak girls in under the eyes of their effeminate landlord and their tough recruiting officer. Michael Greer attempts to subvert his outré role as the landlord by injecting a *lot* of camp silliness; however, he comes off much the worse for it.

THE GAY DIVORCÉE ☆☆☆½
1934, USA
Fred Astaire, Ginger Rogers, Alice Brady, Edward Everett Horton, Eric Blore, Eric Rhodes. Directed by Mark Sandrich. 107 min.

In this musical comedy of errors about a divorce case, Fred Astaire and Ginger Rogers fulfill the promise of *Flying down to Rio* as they trip the light fantastic by the English seaside. The novelty numbers like "Let's K-nock K-nees" are painless enough for fans to sit through while waiting for Fred and Ginger to glide sensuously through "Night and Day." The highlight of the movie is the kiss while they're dancing "The Continental," the tune that won the first Academy Award for best song. Edward Everett Horton and Eric Blore are there to complicate the foolish plot; the dreamy art deco sets are there to complement the improbable fairy-tale pursuits of the leads; and Fred and Ginger are there to demonstrate romantic perfection on the dance floor.

THE GENERAL ☆☆☆☆
1927, USA
Buster Keaton, Glenn Cavender, Jim Farley, Marian Mack. Directed by Buster Keaton. 81 min.

Buster Keaton's greatest comedy (along with *Sherlock, Jr.*) could be described as a balletic duet between Keaton and a runaway locomotive. Buster plays a would-be Confederate who tries to win his train back from a platoon of Union soldiers. The logistics alone make the film an astounding spectacle. Most of the film was shot aboard and atop a speeding train, with Buster taking more risks per scene than a trapeze artist. Unfortunately, it is impossible to recommend a video version of this film. Badly scratched and horribly washed-out prints strip this masterpiece of its meticulous attention to detail; indeed, oftentimes Buster's facial takes are impossible to read. Further, this movie demands the kind of careful viewing and absolute absorption that are endemic to watching a projected film, and this state of awareness is difficult to achieve in front of a television. Hopefully, Keaton's work will soon be accorded the kind of video transfer provided by the CBS Playhouse Chaplin series.

GENERAL DELLA ROVERE ☆☆☆½
1960, Italy
Vittorio De Sica, Hannes Messemer, Sandra Milo, Giovanna Ralli. Directed by Roberto Rossellini. 129 min.

This fine Roberto Rossellini film is blessed with his carefully measured direction and thoughtful pacing. Vittorio De Sica shines as a con artist forced to portray a big-shot Resistance leader. You'll be both amused and surprised as the actor can't shake off his role and discovers that his life has been altered and his identity radically changed. A haunting film whose climax will be hard for viewers to forget.

GENERATION ☆☆☆½
1954, Poland
Tadeusz Lomnicki, Urszula Modrzynska, Tadeusz Janczar, Zbigniew Cybulski. Directed by Andrzej Wajda. 90 min.

This study of a teenage boy who joins the Resistance during the Nazi occupation of Poland was made during a government crackdown on filmmaking there, and is somewhat more schematic and didactic than Andrzej Wajda's other early work. Still, it's told with admirable conviction and emotional honesty, and serves as an absorbing example of how Wajda was able to create a work of art around a prescribed political "message." Look for a very young Roman Polanski (who studied with Wajda) in a small role. (a.k.a.: *Pokolanie*)

GENERATION ☆
1969, USA
David Janssen, Kim Darby, Carl Reiner, Peter Duel, Andrew Prine. Directed by George Schaefer. 104 min.

With Henry Fonda in the lead, this was a big success on Broadway—a sort of tired businessman's special in which everyone could sympathize with the Papa Bear hero and get smashed during intermission in order to get through the rest of the play. (Certainly, drinking at home while watching this could only enhance your enjoyment.) Onscreen, this is a labored domestic comedy about a young with-it couple who decide to deliver their expected child themselves, thus irritating wifey's traditionalist father. Stoic David Janssen lacks Fonda's charisma, which makes this even more tedious.

GENEVIEVE
1953, Great Britain ☆☆☆☆
Dinah Sheridan, John Gregson, Kay Kendall, Kenneth More, Joyce Grenfell, Geoffrey Keen. Directed by Henry Cornelius. 86 min.

Car-race comedies are pretty tricky business. They can be detoured by witless gags and subplots (*The Great Race, Cannonball Run*) or they can be right on track, as with this 1954 British gem. Here the race between two couples returning from the Brighton car rally is made captivating by several unexpected twists and turns in the William Rose screenplay, four charming performances (Kay Kendall stands out as the least enthusiastic participant), and the sheer joie de vivre of the production. A trifle, but an engaging, offbeat one. Note: the famed harmonica player Larry Adler composed the theme music and appears in the film.

GENTLE GIANT
1967, USA ☆☆
Dennis Weaver, Vera Miles, Clint Howard, Ralph Meeker, Huntz Hall. Directed by James Nielson. 93 min.

It's the gentle family film that led to the long-running TV series "Gentle Ben," about a boy and the grizzly bear he befriends. If you're fond of animal stories and have always enjoyed Smokey the Bear commercials, this will be right up your alley. Somehow, it's easier to cuddle up to a dog or horse (or even a dolphin) than it is to embrace this oversized teddy bear. Mildly appealing.

GENTLEMAN JIM
1942, USA ☆☆½
Errol Flynn, Alexis Smith, Jack Carson, Alan Hale, Minor Watson. Directed by Raoul Walsh. 104 min.

This snazzy boxing flick, purportedly a biography of boxer Gentleman Jim Corbett, is really an excuse to allow Errol Flynn to strut his stuff. Although the truth about Corbett (not to mention the boxing world) is short-changed, this is a reasonably diverting film, since Flynn was probably the most ingratiating action hero since the days of Douglas Fairbanks. Today we're stuck with Sylvester Stallone; at least Flynn was charming, and he certainly could do more than punch out supervillains and spout platitudes.

GENTLEMAN'S AGREEMENT
1947, USA ☆☆☆
Gregory Peck, Dorothy McGuire, John Garfield, Celeste Holm, Anne Revere, June Havoc, Albert Dekker, Jane Wyatt, Dean Stockwell, Sam Jaffe. Directed by Elia Kazan. 118 min.

Elia Kazan's heavily laureled social drama gets high marks for its effort and intentions, but its expose of anti-Semitism in America was slightly contrived to begin with and hasn't aged well. Gregory Peck brings dignified restraint to his role as magazine reporter Phil Green, who goes undercover to write "I Was a Jew for Six Weeks." As Green becomes Greenberg, he finds prejudice can hit uncomfortably close to home. A large, talented cast doesn't harangue or lecture even when the screenplay does, but the idea of exploring anti-Semitism by having someone "normal" impersonate a Jew seems particularly specious. Nonetheless, a groundbreaker in its time that won Oscars for Best Picture, Director, and Supporting Actress (Celeste Holm).

GENTLEMEN PREFER BLONDES
1953, USA ☆☆½
Jane Russell, Marilyn Monroe, Charles Coburn, Tommy Noonan, Norma Varden, Elliott Reid. Directed by Howard Hawks. 91 min.

Marilyn Monroe sings "Diamonds Are a Girl's Best Friend" and gets caught in a ship porthole, but that's about it for this cheeky, colorful, but surprisingly straightforward film. Marilyn and Jane Russell play showgirls set loose in Paris in a hunt for fame, fortune, and romance. Thanks to Howard Hawks and Monroe, the film has acquired a cult following over the years, but both director and star have had better material with which to work. It's mild and painless fluff, but that's all. Anita Loos's novel of the twenties had real bite to it, both indulging and satirizing a beautiful girl's ability to sell herself dearly and manipulate men easily; the film lacks the book's scathing humor.

GENTLE SAVAGE
1978, USA, R ☆☆
William Smith, Gene Evans, Barbara Luna, Joe Flynn. Directed by Sean MacGregor. 85 min.

This revisionist Western contains a credible, if predictable, premise: a white man, guilty of raping his stepdaughter but hoping to frame an Indian for the crime, whips up the latent hostility in the townspeople against the Indian community, which is thus forced to group together to defend itself.

THE GEORGE RAFT STORY
1961, USA ☆☆½
Ray Danton, Jayne Mansfield, Julie London, Frank Gorshin, Barrie Chase, Barbara Nichols, Margo Moore, Neville Brand, Robert Strauss, Herschel Bernardi. Directed by Joseph M. Newman. 105 min.

What the real George Raft, who was still alive when this was made, thought of this biopic, and how much of it is true, he never said—but who goes to the movies for verisimilitude anyway? In this entertainingly schlocky biography, we follow Raft from his beginnings as a dancer through his entry into movies, his associations with the real underworld, and his waning popularity, culminating with his comeback in *Some Like It Hot*. As one of the women in Raft's life, Jayne Mansfield gets thrown into a swimming pool and otherwise does lots of what she did best—stand around and get stared at. Ray Danton went on to direct such classics as *Crypt of the Living Dead* and *The Deathmaster*.

GEORGE STEVENS: A FILM MAKER'S JOURNEY
1985, USA ☆☆☆
Documentary. Directed by George Stevens, Jr. 113 min.

George Stevens has been a seriously underrated director, and this film, directed by Stevens's son, certainly sets the score straight on that point. Unfortunately, it does little to explicate exactly what it was that gave Stevens such a deft comic touch and a prescient feeling for character relationships. The clips from Stevens's films—including *Alice Adams; Gunga Din; Shane; Giant; The More, The Merrier*; and many others—are marvelously chosen and presented. The interviews with, among others, Pandro Berman, Katharine Hepburn, Douglas Fairbanks, Jr., and Josephine Mankiewicz, are generally dull, eulogistic comments that uniformly praise the director as a careful craftsman and a very nice man. Certainly the most startling part of the film is the previously unseen color footage Stevens shot while serving in Europe during World War II. The war, with its fresh-faced teenaged soldiers, is brought home with a poignant immediacy. An important film for anyone seriously interested in the golden age of Hollywood.

GERVAISE
1956, France ☆☆☆
Maria Schell, François Périer, Suzy Delair, Mathilde Casadesus. Directed by René Clément. 120 min.

Director René Clément began his career as a maker of documentaries, and that approach still shows here. Émile Zola's melodrama about alcoholism and the poor is pared down here to concentrate on the life of Gervaise, a woman who struggles to fight her way out of poverty and make a better life for her children, but who finally succumbs to the influence of her drunken husband. The era of nineteenth-century France is well evoked. As a whole it may be too depressing for some audiences; it is recommended only for those who don't require a happy ending. Dubbed into English.

THE GETAWAY ☆☆
1972, USA, PG
Steve McQueen, Ali MacGraw, Ben Johnson, Sally Struthers, Al Lettieri, Slim Pickens, Richard Bright, Bo Hopkins. Directed by Sam Peckinpah. 122 min.

This dull, overlong chase film about a just-released con and his wife (Steve McQueen and Ali MacGraw) who pull off a bank robbery and promptly go on the lam was Sam Peckinpah's one out-and-out attempt at a non-auteurist commercial success. Had he treated the story with any of the viscerality he brought to *The Wild Bunch* or *Straw Dogs*, he might have been able to turn Walter Hill's shoddy script into something watchable, or at least coherent. Instead, the director stages a few undeniably exciting set pieces that are afloat in a sea of confusing, stagnant drama. McQueen, always underappreciated as an action hero, is fine here, but MacGraw is miscast and embarrassingly bad. Based on the grisly novel by Jim Thompson.

GET CRAZY! ☆☆
1983, USA, R
Daniel Stern, Malcolm McDowell, Allen Goorwitz, Gail Edwards, Miles Chapin, Ed Begley, Jr., Lou Reed, Howard Kaylan, Lee Ving, John Densmore, Bobby Sherman, Fabian Forte, Franklin Ajaye, Mary Woronov, Paul Bartel, Jackie Joseph, Dick Miller. Directed by Allan Arkush. 92 min.

Trying to cook up a vivacious youth comedy in the spirit of his *Rock 'n' Roll High School*, director Allan Arkush had what sounds like a promising idea: a peek into the backstage goings-on at a famed Manhattan rock palace loosely based on the Fillmore East. Unfortunately, the movie is so relentlessly zany it plays like a feature-length episode of "The Monkees." Daniel Stern brings his usual boyish charm to the lead role; Malcolm McDowell is disastrously miscast as a Mick Jagger–style superstar.

GET OUT YOUR HANDKERCHIEFS ☆☆☆
1978, France
Gérard Depardieu, Patrick Dewaere, Carol Laure, Riton. Directed by Bertrand Blier. 100 min.

In Bertrand Blier's subversively funny sex farce, Gérard Depardieu plays a young husband whose wife (Carol Laure) has fallen into an alarming depression; Patrick Dewaere is the Mozart-fixated stranger he enlists to help snap her out of it. The movie appears to share the men's baffled view of her illness, and yet it also makes them the butt of every joke. *Get Out Your Handkerchiefs* turns male attitudes into a farce for all time, a pure, absurdist sexual myth.

GETTING EVEN ☆
1986, USA, R
Edward Albert, Audrey Landers, Joe Don Baker, Rod Pilloud, Billy Streater. Directed by Dwight Little. 90 min.

Formerly called *Hostage Dallas*, this vapid thriller is lethargic and thrill-less. The tangled mess of a plot starts off with a U.S. government–ordered theft of a poisonous gas developed by the Russians. From there, the deadly chemical is appropriated by a shifty tycoon who, out to make a quick buck, ransoms the gas for $50 million. Minimal excitement is unleashed at the finale as the good guys grab the chemicals before Dallas can be gassed out of existence.

GETTING IT ON ☆
1983, USA, R
Martin Yost, Heather Kennedy, Jeff Edmond, Kathy Brickmeier, Mark Alan Ferri, Charles King Bibby. Directed by William Olsen. 96 min.

This adolescent sex comedy uses a perverse premise to justify some mild nudity. A couple of sniveling high-school boys decide to get thrills and bucks by using hidden cameras to make secret videotapes of naked high school girls. "C'mon, Sally, dump the towel," one of the boys urges as he watches a girl getting ready for a shower. She doesn't. It's that sort of drivel.

THE GETTING OF WISDOM ☆☆½
1980, Australia, PG
Susannah Fowles, Barry Humphries, John Waters, Sheila Helpman. Directed by Bruce Beresford. 100 mins.

Although Australian director Bruce Beresford's film conforms to the boarding-school-chronicle genre in most respects, there's a crucial discrepancy: while most such tales purport to be about the building of character, *The Getting of Wisdom* seems to chart the degeneration of one. Laura Rambotham (Susannah Fowles) starts out with a fiery imagination, a strong native intelligence, and a fierce sense of independence. Her mother, a postmistress in the Australian outback, packs her off to a snooty school in Melbourne, and her matriculation seems to involve the child mostly in deceit and treachery. Beresford presents the process with such cheeriness and acrobatic photography that it's hard to know how he wants us to take it. Has Laura learned something that we aren't privy to? Yes, indeed, to judge from the autobiographical novel the film is based on; the "wisdom" she gets is the growing awareness of herself as an artist—as a novelist, in fact. But the film, made for home consumption, fails to stress Laura's writing, and without it the movie seems arbitrary and scattershot.

GETTING STRAIGHT ☆☆½
1970, USA, R
Elliott Gould, Candice Bergen, Robert F. Lyons, Jeff Corey, Cecil Kellaway, Jeannie Berlin, Gregory Sierra, Harrison Ford. Directed by Richard Rush. 126 min.

Of the multitude of youth-oriented films of the early seventies, this is one of the better ones, if only because it tries to present characters who are in the middle of the era's extremes. Elliott Gould, who seems to have been in every other movie released in 1970, plays a Vietnam veteran who is working on his master's degree in education. Older than the mass of campus radicals, he agrees with their complaints but dislikes their methods, preferring to get on with his studies and teaching so he can get out of school. Unfortunately, the film has dated badly and now works only in its comic sequences, the best of which has Gould arguing with a member of his exam committee who is convinced that *The Great Gatsby*'s Nick and Gatsby were homosexuals. Harrison Ford has a small part in a party scene.

GETTING WASTED ☆
1980, USA, PG
Brian Kerwin, Stephen Furst, Cooper Huckabee, Wendy Ratstatter. Directed by Paul Frizler. 98 min.

This entirely trite, almost quaintly inoffensive military school nonstory only remotely resembles the promotional description on the video box, which suggests hippies, drugs, free love, and a school takeover. It is actually nothing but a series of very hackneyed adolescent episodes tied together with hit songs from the sixties. The whole thing is done by formula, and every "creative" decision was made by following the path of least intellectual resistance. One shudders to think that time and money are getting wasted on this cinematic sub-kitsch.

GHIDRAH THE THREE-HEADED MONSTER ☆☆½
1965, Japan
Yosuke Natsuki, Yuriko Hoshi, Hiroshi Koizumi. Directed by Inoshire Honda. 85 min.

Hang around Toho studios long enough and, no matter how bad a monster you started out as, they'll make you a good monster sooner or later. In this rubber-suit epic, Godzilla, Mothra, and Rodan join forces to kick the butt of Ghidrah, a three-headed dragon hatched out of a meteor. Of course, they knock over a few buildings in the process. . . . Director Inoshire Honda did pretty much every other Japanese giant-monster movie of the past twenty years; this is a bit better than the rest, but not much. The comparatively high rating is for camp value only.

THE GHOST AND MRS. MUIR ☆☆☆
1947, USA
Gene Tierney, Rex Harrison, George Sanders, Edna Best, Robert Coote, Natalie Wood, Vanessa Brown. Directed by Joseph L. Mankiewicz. 104 min.

Joseph L. Mankiewicz tried and failed to produce a mystical, pro-feminist fantasy, but the result is not without its charms. Gene Tierney plays a writer, a spunky turn-of-the-century widow who wants to live an independent life with her daughter (young Natalie Wood) in a British coastal hamlet. While residing in her new home, she is visited by the handsome, restless ghost of a sea captain (Rex Harrison) who falls in love with her while trying to break up her romance with a foppish book publisher (George Sanders). While Tierney is adequate in her role and Sanders is a little too seedy for comfort, Harrison is a joy as the all-too-human spirit. The ending of Philip Dunne's screenplay is predictable in the Hollywood way, but what comes before is slightly offbeat in treatment if rather conventional in theme. Later made into a television series.

GHOSTBUSTERS ☆☆☆
1984, USA, PG
Bill Murray, Dan Aykroyd, Harold Ramis, Sigourney Weaver, Rick Moranis. Directed by Ivan Reitman. 107 min.

This major theatrical hit serves as an apocalyptic comedy showcase for its three stars. The wispy plot involves discredited Columbia University parapsychologists who enter into the spirit of free enterprise by setting up shop as freelance ghostbusters and find their services in surprising demand by New Yorkers plagued by everything from poltergeists to bloodthirsty demon dogs. Bill Murray steals the show with his chaffing blandishments, and Dan Aykroyd slides by as the unregenerate hipster, but Harold Ramis's performance is strained.

THE GHOST GOES WEST ☆☆☆½
1936, Great Britain
Robert Donat, Eugene Pallette, Jean Arthur, Everly Gregg, Elsa Lanchester, Arthur Seaton. Directed by René Clair. 85 min.

Humorist Robert Sherwood wrote the screenplay for this amusing comedy, director René Clair's first film after leaving France to escape from the Nazis. Like *Ruggles of Red Gap*, this pokes fun at Americans who go to Europe to acquire culture, usually by trying to buy it. In this case, Eugene Pallette buys a Scottish castle and has it transported, stone by stone, to Florida. Along with the castle comes its penniless heir and the high-spirited ghost of one of his forebears (both played by Robert Donat). Donat, Pallette, and Jean Arthur make a splendidly comic trio (or should that be quartet?) in this charming satire that hardly shows its age.

GHOSTKEEPER ½☆
1980, USA
Riva Spier, Murray Ord, Sheri McFadden, Georgie Collins. Directed by James Makichuk. 87 min.

This appallingly poor horror film concerns a group of snowmobiling tourists stranded in the frozen North Woods. What lurks in the old house where they find shelter, other than the mysterious proprietress? Will any of them escape with their lives? Most importantly, will anything remotely resembling a ghost, or even a scare, show up before the closing credits?

THE GHOSTLY FACE ☆
Hong Kong
L. F. Sang Guran, Chen Hui, Chen Pao. Directed by S. K. Yang.

A mysterious masked man steals a valuable sword and kills a respected leader. His daughter vows to avenge his death. As an added attraction for *National Geographic* fans, this film contains scenes of Bali tribal ceremonies.

THE GHOST OF FLIGHT 401 ☆☆
1978, USA (TV)
Ernest Borgnine, Gary Lockwood, Kim Basinger, Howard Hesseman, Russell Johnson, Eugene Roche. Directed by Steven Hilliard Stern. 101 min.

The idea for this telefilm was ripped from the pages of your favorite supermarket tabloid—after a plane goes down in the Florida Everglades, the spectral figure of the pilot returns to haunt other flights in the area. (Gee, imagine it as a weekly series . . .) The film is mildly amusing, not very scary, and populated with actors probably destined to haunt TV movies like this for the rest of their careers. (a.k.a.: *The Crash of Flight 401*)

GHOST PATROL ☆
1936, USA
Tim McCoy, Claudia Dell, Walter Miller, Wheeler Oakman, Slim Whitaker. Directed by Sam Newfield. 58 min.

Government agents are sent into cowboy territory to investigate a series of mysterious plane crashes, which turn out to be caused by mobsters with a ray gun who rob the planes of government bonds. Don't ask us why this is available on videocassette; at under an hour's running time, they could at least have had the generosity to make it part of a double feature.

GHOST SHIP ☆½
1952, Great Britain
Dermot Walsh, Hazel Court, Hugh Burden, John Robinson, Joss Ambler, Joan Carol, Josh Ackland, John King Kelly. Directed by Vernon Sewell. 69 min.

In this very dull British horror film, with no scares or suspense to speak of, a Canadian couple in England buys a steamboat to use as a vacation ship. Unfortunately, they didn't pay enough attention when they were warned that the ship was haunted, and the resident ghost doesn't take kindly to their presence. The best that can be said for this is that it is competently made and brief.

GHOSTS ON THE LOOSE ☆
1943, USA
The East Side Kids, Bela Lugosi, Ava Gardner. Directed by William Beaudine. 62 min.

No, the East Side Kids are on the loose, with an uninventive script and poor Bela Lugosi, slumming once more in a Poverty Row production. Sadly, it's not a real Bowery Boys movie but an East Side Kids adventure from the period 1940–43; those films had even worse scripts than anything the Dead End Kids or the Bowery Boys ever perpetrated. Adding insult to injury, the plot entangles the Kids in a scheme to expose a nest of Nazis, and there's nary a ghost in sight.

GHOST STORY ☆☆☆
1981, USA, R
Craig Wasson, Alice Krige, Fred Astaire, John Houseman, Melvyn Douglas, Douglas Fairbanks, Jr. Directed by John Irvin. 110 min.

Peter Straub's chilling horror novel is partially thawed out in this liberty-taking cinematic adaptation. An inadvertent murder committed by a group of old men in the past comes back to haunt them in the form of a vengeful but nonetheless beautiful spirit. British director John Irvin substitutes outright scares for endless buildups to the various characters' demises, but also lends the picture a creepy atmosphere of decay. Filmed in a nightmarish New England town, abetted by Albert Whitlock's matte work. Dick Smith's ghoulish makeup effects provide the real shocks in this brooding gothic melodrama.

THE GHOUL
1975, Great Britain, R
Peter Cushing, John Hurt, Gwen Watford, Alexandra Bastedo, Veronica Carlson, Steward Bevan. Directed by Freddie Francis. 88 min.

A father and his cannibal son—kept carefully confined in a locked attic room—spell disaster for a fun-loving group of young people who happen onto their isolated estate. This restrained twenties period piece won't please gore fans, though it delivers some minor bloodletting at the end. Directed by cinematographer Freddie Francis (*The Innocents, Dune*), whose sense of composition has always been far superior to his sense of narrative, as *The Skull, Dracula Has Risen from the Grave*, and many others attest.

GHOULIES
1985, USA, PG-13
Peter Liapis, Lisa Pelikan, Jack Nance, Bobbie Bresee, Mariska Hargitay. Directed by Luca Bercovicci. 81 min.

An amateur sorcerer conjures up malicious imps to do his bidding; they prefer to listen to his vicious, long-dead father, a serious practitioner of the black arts determined to live again. Is this a crass attempt to cash in on the success of *Gremlins?* Sure. It's just another derivative thriller, but with the occasional engaging touch. With what amounts to a guest appearance by Jack Nance, the star of David Lynch's *Eraserhead*.

GIANT
1956, USA
Elizabeth Taylor, Rock Hudson, James Dean, Mercedes McCambridge, Jane Withers, Chill Wills, Carroll Baker, Dennis Hopper. Directed by George Stevens. 201 min.

Although George Stevens's early work (*Alice Adams, Swingtime*) has graceful innocence, it's his later blockbusters, such as *Shane, The Greatest Story Ever Told*, and *Giant*, for which he will be best remembered. Stevens won his second Best Director Oscar for this adaptation (screenplay by Fred Guiol and Ivan Moffat) of Edna Ferber's novel. At three hours and twenty minutes, the film is expectedly episodic, but it's a surprisingly streamlined chronicle of the life and times of a Texas land baron (Rock Hudson), his humanitarian wife (Elizabeth Taylor), and his ranchhand-turned-rival (James Dean). Hudson (who received the only Academy Award nomination of his career) and Taylor are surprisingly good in parts that require them to age twenty-five years, but it is Dean (in his last performance) who steals the show as the sullen cowboy who rises in society after striking an oil well. Some of the sequences are sketchily drawn and the killing off of the manipulative Mercedes McCambridge character early on was a mistake, but overall it's one of the few epics that consistently satisfies. Note: lost footage was recently restored in reissues of the film, but the extant video version is, alas, not that edition.

THE GIANT SPIDER INVASION
1975, USA
Steve Brodie, Barbara Hale, Leslie Parrish, Alan Hale, Robert Easton, Bill Williams. Directed by Bill Rebane. 82 min.

A black hole in space permits spiders of all shapes and sizes—fat ones, skinny ones, great big juicy ones—to cross from another dimension and terrorize a small Wisconsin town. Spectacularly bad special effects (look at those literal Volkswagen bugs) enliven this low-budget big-bug movie, but it takes the right frame of mind to enjoy it.

G.I. BLUES
1960, USA
Elvis Presley, Juliet Prowse, James Douglas, Robert Ivers, Leticia Roman. Directed by Norman Taurog. 104 min.

When Elvis Presley returned from army training in West Germany, Paramount immediately cast him as . . . a G.I. in service in West Germany! (It must have been coincidental.) Surprisingly, the film is slightly better than the Presley standard (which isn't saying much). Norman Taurog helmed this reworking of *Sailor Beware* (filmed three times before) with Presley as a wolf betting his army pals that he can get a date with nightclub dancer Juliet Prowse (a step up from Mary Ann Mobley). Musical numbers include "Blue Suede Shoes," "Wooden Heart," and "Shoppin' Around."

GIDEON'S TRUMPET
1980, USA (TV)
Henry Fonda, José Ferrer, John Houseman, Fay Wray, Sam Jaffe, Dean Jagger, Dolph Sweet, David Clennon. Directed by Robert Collins. 104 min.

This intriguing television film is based on the case of Clarence Earl Gideon, an uneducated driver who accomplished the amazing feat of petitioning the Supreme Court for a retrial after he was convicted of burglary. What makes his story amazing is the fact that he gained access to the Supreme Court without the aid of a lawyer—the right to be represented by legal counsel regardless of ability to pay was, in fact, the issue he fought for and eventually won. The script was based on the book by Anthony Lewis, who has a bit part as a reporter. Henry Fonda is very moving as Gideon. This powerful film reminds us that citizens with little formal education can personally effect landmark civil liberties rulings, thereby protecting us all!

GIDGET
1959, USA
Sandra Dee, James Darren, Cliff Robertson, Arthur O'Connell, Joby Craig, Yvonne Craig. Directed by Paul Wendkos. 95 min.

It's the ultimate Beauty and the Beach teen pic that paved the waves for a half-dozen sequels and hundreds of poor imitations. Surfer Sandra Dee is caught in a love quadrangle between a young, handsome surfer, a mature, handsome beach bum, and her surfboard. Later Gidget went Hawaiian, became a TV series, and got married in her own TV movie, but this is the ultimate Gidget pic.

GIDGET GOES HAWAIIAN
1961, USA
Deborah Walley, James Darren, Michael Callan, Carl Reiner, Peggy Cass, Eddie Foy, Jr. Directed by Paul Wendkos. 101 min.

The world's first Valley Girl gets uprooted and transplanted to Hawaii, with boyfriend James Darren in hot pursuit. The *Gidget* films were about as accurate a portrait of the youth of their time as the *Friday the 13th* installments are of ours; unfortunately, there's no maniac in a hockey mask to come by and hack up these teenyboppers when they become too insufferable. A fact: no actress ever played Gidget twice!

GIDGET GOES TO ROME
1963, USA
Cindy Carol, James Darren, Jessie Royce Landis, Cesare Danova, Jeff Donnell. Directed by Paul Wendkos. 101 min.

Gidget leaves her surfboard behind (her fans overdosed on California sunsets and pounding waves) for European locales. She experiences all of the expected romantic complications while the audience is kept awake by the ever-changing picture-postcard shots of the Eternal City. It's like trying to watch a romantic comedy from inside a Viewmaster. However, if you're a fan of Gidget in her many guises, you'll like it.

LA GIFLE
1974, France
Lino Ventura, Annie Girardot, Isabelle Adjani, Francis Perrin, Jacques Spiesser. Directed by Claude Pinoteau. 98 min.

This is the kind of domestic comedy-drama that might appeal to those who upgrade everything half a star if it's in a foreign language. Isabelle Adjani, in an early role, plays a teenager living with her divorced father, a teacher who doesn't understand her. There are some funny scenes, but nothing particularly memorable; more sharply drawn characters would have helped.

THE GIFT ☆☆
1982, France/Italy, R
Pierre Mondy, Clio Goldsmith, Claudia Cardinale, Jacques François. Directed by Michel Lang. 105 min.

In this frothy French sex comedy, Pierre Mondy, a jowly middle-ager with a goofy grin that resembles Harry Reasoner's, plays a retiring banker whose coworkers give him a farewell present—a high-class hooker (Clio Goldsmith) who pretends she's fallen for him. Mondy brings a note of humble humanity to the early scenes, but once he and his new "mistress" arrive in Venice, the movie devolves into a tiresome caper comedy.

GIFT FOR HEIDI ☆☆
1958, USA
Douglas Fowley, Sandy Descher, Van Dyke Parks. Directed by George Templeton. 71 min.

The treacly tyke returns to do good deeds, spread emotional fulfillment, and change lives for the better in this sweet, unexceptional kiddie fare. The story's been done to death, and this retelling is only slightly more animated than several cartoon versions of this material, but it's a surefire sentimental heart-tugger. Good for smaller kids.

THE GIG ☆☆☆
1985, USA
Wayne Rogers, Cleavon Little, Andrew Duncan, Jerry Matz, Daniel Nalbach, Warren Vache, Joe Silver, Jay Thomas. Directed by Frank D. Gilroy. 85 min.

This wry, touching seriocomedy deals with an amateur jazz combo of middle-aged men who suddenly get their first professional engagement—two weeks at a Catskills resort—and find themselves reexamining their friendships, ambitions, and dreams during their stay. Writer-director Frank Gilroy has an almost infallible ear for the way these men kvetch, bicker, and conciliate, and his homely, semidocumentary style of shooting serves the story well. Good performances from the entire cast, and a priceless one from Joe Silver as the owner-manager of the seedy Paradise Manor who forces the Dixieland sextet to play nothing but rhumbas, waltzes, and "Hava Nagila."

GIGI ☆☆☆½
1958, USA
Leslie Caron, Louis Jourdan, Maurice Chevalier, Hermione Gingold, Jacques Bergerac, Eva Gabor. Directed by Vincente Minnelli. 116 min.

Vincente Minnelli's prettified adaptation of the Colette novel about a turn-of-the-century Parisian coquette was one of his most acclaimed musicals, garnering nine Academy Awards. Visual elegance of a high order and a sophisticated tone combine to make this a treat; while it lacks the high-kicking exuberance of earlier MGM musicals, it overflows with infectious spirits. Leslie Caron blossomed in the title role, an alluring beauty being pursued by man-about-town Louis Jourdan and watched over by professional bon vivant Maurice Chevalier. Chevalier and Hermione Gingold are charming in their duet "I Remember It Well," and the title tune and Chevalier's "Thank Heaven for Little Girls" also stand out.

GILDA ☆☆☆½
1946, USA
Rita Hayworth, Glenn Ford, George Macready, Steven Geray. Directed by Charles Vidor. 110 min.

Portraying a darker side of life than most Hollywood films had yet dared, this early *film noir* conveys the story of a passionate love-hate triangle between mysterious South American casino owner George Macready, his young American right-hand man, and Macready's glamorous new wife. With keen lighting, suggestive photography, and sensual interaction between characters, the mood of Charles Vidor's picture can best be described as a paradoxically intense malaise. Its conclusion may seem contrived, but only because it tries to free the audience from this intensity. Rita Hayworth's evocative portrayal in this film added new dimension to her career as an actress.

GILDA LIVE ☆☆☆
1980, USA, R
Gilda Radner, Paul Shaffer, Don Novello, Rouge. Directed by Mike Nichols. 96 min.

In 1979, Gilda Radner took her comedic creations from "Saturday Night Live" to Broadway, and this filmed stage show (seamlessly assembled from four different performances) captures much of the energy and smartly conceived humor of her TV appearances. All of Radner's "SNL" characters show up, including the eternally crude newswoman Roseanne Roseannadanna, deaf but opinionated Emily Litella, and teenage nerd-ette Lisa Loopner, whose rendition of "The Way We Were" is the show's high point. Radner's fans will love it; those unfamiliar with her characters may be left cold.

GIMME SHELTER ☆☆☆½
1970, USA
Rolling Stones, Jefferson Airplane, Melvin Belli. Directed by David Maysles, Albert Maysles, and Charlotte Zwerin. 91 min.

This stunning "rockumentary" deals with the Rolling Stones's tragic Altamont concert in December of 1969, where one of the Hell's Angels security guards knifed a spectator to death. The Stones, the Jefferson Airplane, and Ike and Tina Turner performed, but something went awry—in the concert's conception, planning, and organization—and Altamont signaled the end of innocence for the Woodstock generation. The film's tone is dark rather than celebratory, and the bad vibes are palpable. The Maysles were major figures in the early years of cinéma-verité documentary filming.

GINGER ☆
1971, USA
Cheri Caffaro, Cindy Barnett, Kerr Kerr, William Granneli. Directed by Don Schain. 89 min.

This is a stunning film—by the time it's over (if you make it all the way through to the end), you'll be as stunned as if you'd been using a cattle prod for a Q-tip. A confused young socialite finds her niche in life by helping a private detective wipe out a gang of white slavers in New Jersey. The video version is thirteen minutes shorter than the theatrical release, and all this time appears to have been trimmed from the ending: our heroine is knocked out by one of the bad guys, things look bad, and all of a sudden she's at the airport discussing the case with her employer! As Ginger, Cheri Caffaro's only talent seems to be that she's willing to take her clothes off, undeterred by the fact that she's about as sexy as Mr. Greenjeans. With its stupid dialogue, appalling racism, and static direction, it was followed by two sequels (*Girls Are for Loving* and *The Abductors*) that are even worse! A visual lobotomy.

GINGER AND FRED ☆☆☆☆
1986, Italy/France/West Germany
Giulietta Masina, Marcello Mastroianni, Franco Fabrizi, Frederick Von Ledenburg, Martin Blau, Toto Mignone, Augusto Poderosi. Directed by Federico Fellini. 126 min.

Two ex-lovers and small-time performers, reunited on a television extravaganza, uncover a few moments of warmth and nostalgia in a world of grotesque freaks and raucous mayhem. Marcello Mastroianni and Giulietta Masina are wonderful as a two-bit dance team who once had a brief moment in the sun as imitators of Fred Astaire and Ginger Rogers. Meeting each other after so many years, they find themselves changed and distanced, but Federico Fellini reveals their deep sympathy, sadness over aging, and generous wisdom. Fellini is far less generous to the medium of television; he seems to revel in its overblown cheapness and its voracious appetite for absolutely anything—there is a parade of bizarre acts, including a midget dance troupe, a salacious transvestite, a cow with eighteen teats, and cheesy impersonators of Proust, Kafka, and Ronald Reagan. The combination of human comedy and artificial spectacle is unsettling and very, very pointed. The road to hell, according to Maestro Fellini, is paved with television sets.

GINGER IN THE MORNING ☆☆½
1973, USA (TV)
Sissy Spacek, Monte Markham, Mark Miller, Susan Oliver, Slim Pickens. Directed by Gordon Wiles. 89 min.

Before her big break in *Carrie*, Sissy Spacek could be spotted guest-starring in various TV series and emoting in a few TV movies. This is one of her fresher outings as an apprentice actress. It's a latter-day flower child romance about a buttoned-down businessman who finds romance when he picks up the hitchhiking Sissy. She's impressed by his solid strength and caring; he's drawn to her lovable, free-spirited approach to life. It's a dated concept, but the cast is personable and the film is semicaptivating, even though the idea of romance on the open road is now a dangerous proposition.

THE GIRL CAN'T HELP IT ☆☆½
1956, USA
Jayne Mansfield, Tom Ewell, Edmond O'Brien, Julie London. Directed by Frank Tashlin. 99 min.

As *Will Success Spoil Rock Hunter?* and this film prove, Jayne Mansfield was not just the poor man's Marilyn Monroe. While she lacks MM's softer edges and incandescence, Mansfield was the essential 1950s sex goddess, an undulating salute to the male mammary fixation. Her gleeful self-parody hinted at an underlying pathos, and her shrewd handling of her publicity suggests a keen intelligence not always utilized in her screen work. In this cartoonish look at the vagaries of pop music success, Jayne's animated figure is put to good use as she portrays a gangster's tootsie who'd rather bake pies than cut records. Naturally she squeals her way to stardom, accompanied by such rock-and-roll greats as Little Richard and Fats Domino. Brassy fun.

GIRL CRAZY ☆☆☆
1943, USA
Mickey Rooney, Judy Garland, Gil Stratton, Robert E. Strickland, Rags Ragland, June Allyson, Nancy Walker, Guy Kibee, Tommy Dorsey and his Orchestra. Directed by Norman Taurog. 99 min.

Mickey Rooney is *Girl Crazy*, so his father ships him out West where the quiet and fresh air will calm his overactive hormones. The Mick runs into Judy Garland and a great Gershwin score, and he ends up sublimating his sex drive into energetic singing and dancing. The score includes both "Embraceable You" and "I Got Rhythm" (staged by Busby Berkeley, who was booted as director). Having June Allyson, the cute little simp, sing "Treat Me Rough" is nothing short of kinky—and delightful. This is the eighth pairing of Mick and Judy—here they stage a *rodeo* to raise money to save the college. . . .

GIRLFRIENDS ☆☆☆
1978, USA, PG
Melanie Mayron, Eli Wallach, Bob Balaban, Anita Skinner, Viveca Lindfors. Directed by Claudia Weill. 86 min.

With this offbeat, often charming film, ex-documentarian Claudia Weill (*The Other Side of the Sky: A China Memoir*) presents her first fiction feature, shot on a shoestring budget in New York. Although it has a pleasingly authentic surface, the story is quite conventional. Two twenty-fivish ex-college chums struggle to preserve their friendship after their lives diverge; Susan (Melanie Mayron) pursues a career in photography, while Anne (Anita Skinner) opts for safe-but-stifling wifehood and motherhood.

THE GIRL FROM PETROVKA ☆
1974, USA, PG
Goldie Hawn, Hal Holbrook, Anthony Hopkins, Gregoire Aslan, Anton Dolin. Directed by Robert Ellis Miller. 103 min.

Goldie Hawn plays a Russian free spirit who draws little hearts on her cheeks with makeup—that is, when she's not wearing her heart on her sleeve as she pines for an American newsman with a love that can never be. Ah, the pathos . . . the allegorical representation of U.S.–Soviet relations . . . the self-conscious cuteness of the star, who gives the kind of all-out love-me performance that might shame even Liza Minnelli. Hal Holbrook is forced to sit by and look admiringly at Goldie, who sports some of the ugliest duds in screen history, a contemptuous American notion of what a poor, drab Russkie might mistake for fashion. All in all, as offensive as it is schmaltzy, which is to say, VERY.

GIRL HAPPY ☆☆½
1965, USA
Elvis Presley, Shelley Fabares, Mary Ann Mobley, Nita Talbot, Gary Crosby, Jackie Coogan. Directed by Boris Sagal. 96 min.

There's something playfully reassuring about the Elvis Presley universe: no one gets hurt or killed, people dance on the beach, and Mary Ann Mobley is allowed to sing in a nightclub in this totally artificial world. Elvis plays a bandleader hired to chaperon a club owner's nubile daughter on her Fort Lauderdale vacation. Of course, he falls in love with the girl, but not before he sings hits like "Wolf Call," "Do Not Disturb," "Puppet on a String," and "Startin' Tonight." Not *Viva Las Vegas*, but not a disgrace either.

A GIRL IN EVERY PORT ☆☆½
1952, USA
Groucho Marx, Marie Wilson, William Bendix, Don Defore, Gene Lockhart, Dee Hartford. Directed by Chester Erskine. 86 min.

Not to be confused with Howard Hawks's silent classic by the same name, this low-budget comedy is based on a story called "They Sell Sailors Elephants." Actually, it's about two sailors (Groucho Marx and William Bendix) who purchase a useless racehorse and try to swap it for a true thoroughbred. The Irwin Allen–Irving Cummings, Jr., production is as cheap as they come and the Chester Erskine screenplay doesn't exactly overflow with gags, but the cast, including classic "dumb blonde" Marie Wilson (television's "My Friend Irma"), is a great comedy ensemble.

THE GIRL MOST LIKELY ☆☆☆
1958, USA
Jane Powell, Cliff Robertson, Kaye Ballard, Keith Andes, Tommy Noonan, Una Merkel, Kelly Brown. Directed by Mitchell Leisen. 98 min.

RKO's last film (it was released after they had folded) was this lively musical remake of *Tom, Dick and Harry*. Jane Powell is more appealing than Ginger Rogers (who starred in the original) and perfectly cast as the small-town girl who must choose between three suitors. Energetic musical numbers (choreographed by Gower Champion) accompany Powell's dalliance with each man, but the best musical moment is her bittersweet rendition of "I Don't Know What I Want." Other refreshing Hugh Martin–Ralph Blane songs and hilarious support from Kaye Ballard as the best friend are additional assets. A remake that, for once, is at least as good as the original.

GIRLS ARE FOR LOVING ☆☆
1973, USA, R
Cheri Caffaro, Timothy Brown, Jocelyn Peters. Directed by Don Schain. 90 min.

This film is the apotheosis of the character of sexy superspy Ginger and the apes and the swan song of the series that began with *Ginger* and included *The Abductors*. If not for the performance of Cheri Caffaro, this movie would be just another sexual exploitation flick, but Caffaro infuses her role with an antiphallic venom that places *Girls Are for Loving* in the stream of feminist films of Chantal Ackerman and Lizzie Borden. Her movies, with their recurring depictions of castration, are the only direct semiotic attacks on the signifier of male domination, and, coupled with Caffaro's frank pride in her degraded body (the blemishes and sags), Ginger tends to erase the whole idea of a sexually titillating, voyeuristic positioning. Caffaro's intentionally inept musical numbers, with their awkward staging and jerky camera movements, dismantle theories of pleasure in the cinema—she mouths "I'm everything you need" and "Real, Real Woman" while confronting the viewer with an assault on the eyes and ears. Plus some great Virgin Islands location shooting.

GIRLS! GIRLS! GIRLS! ☆☆
1962, USA
Elvis Presley, Laurel Goodwin, Stella Stevens, Jeremy Slate, Guy Lee. Directed by Norman Taurog. 106 min.

This film is not to be confused with *Girl Happy* or *The Trouble with Girls*. In this outing, Elvis Presley plays a fishing-boat captain by day, nightclub singer by night who gets mixed up with a wealthy woman who disguises herself as a working woman. Sound confusing? It's not. Stella Stevens (singing for herself) portrays a fellow club singer. Songs include "Return to Sender," "Never Let Me Go," and "The Nearness of You."

GIRLS JUST WANT TO HAVE FUN ☆☆½
1985, USA, PG
Sarah Jessica Parker, Lee Montgomery, Morgan Woodward, Ed Lauter, Helen Hunt. Directed by Alan Metter. 87 min.

Real teenagers should appreciate the scattershot energy and caustic wit of stars Sarah Jessica Parker and Helen Hunt. These kids stuff *Girls Just Want to Have Fun* with enough snap and sass to gloss over a hackneyed story of a girl who wants to dance on TV. A definite cut above the usual juvenilia.

GIRLS OF THE WHITE ORCHID

See *Death Ride to Osaka*

GIRLS SCHOOL SCREAMERS ☆
1986, USA, R
Mollie O'Mara, Sharon Christopher, Mari Butler, Beth O'Malley, Vera Gallagher. Directed by John Finegan. 82 min.

Do you ever get the feeling that someone is grinding out bad horror films just to fill the shelves of video stores, since all the good movies are already rented before you get there? Be forewarned, this is another unappetizing slasher-rama, courtesy of Troma. Seven young students, accompanied by a decrepit nun, visit a haunted house where they're supposed to take inventory of the art treasures. Suffice to say that all the screaming is done onscreen; you've seen it all before.

GIVE 'EM HELL HARRY! ☆☆☆
1975, USA
James Whitmore. Directed by Steve Binder. 102 min.

The most obvious problem of this tape-to-film transfer of James Whitmore's stage performance as Harry S Truman is that it remains a theatrical one-man show. Despite this and the rather uneven production quality of the transfer, it's a near-triumph capturing James Whitmore's tour de force as the feisty, likable thirty-third President of the United States. Only late in his career did Whitmore emerge as something more than a secondhand Spencer Tracy, and he makes Truman come alive without makeup or mannerisms.

GIVE ME A SAILOR ☆☆
1938, USA
Martha Raye, Bob Hope, Betty Grable, Jack Whiting, J. C. Nugent, Clarence Kolb. Directed by Elliott Nugent. 71 min.

This vehicle for Martha Raye will appeal mostly to her fans, with Bob Hope lending what support he can to a weak farce. He and Jack Whiting are brothers, both naval officers. Both are in love with Betty Grable, who favors Whiting, so Hope plots to get him together with homely sister Raye (which would suit her just fine). They get nowhere until Raye accidentally wins a "beautiful legs" contest and begins to attract attention. Strained and unbelievable.

GIVE MY REGARDS TO BROAD STREET ☆½
1984, Great Britain, PG
Paul McCartney, Bryan Brown, Ringo Starr, Barbara Bach, Linda McCartney. Directed by Peter Webb. 109 min.

Paul McCartney plays a naïve musician who has lost the master tracks for his new record but just can't understand why all of the grown-ups are so upset. Unfortunately, naïveté here looks like stupidity, and the retreading of classic Beatles songs looks like cupidity on the part of McCartney. Endlessly narcissistic, it just goes to show that, in some cases, if someone else doesn't rip off your talent, you'll eventually end up degrading yourself. A tired, old-man's version of what the music video audience wants out of film, and a cynical misreading of a nonexistent audience's expectations.

GIZMO ☆☆☆
1980, USA, G
Directed by Howard Smith. 79 min.

This good-humored documentary, compiled from archive footage by Howard Smith (*Marjoe*), concerns unsung inventors and their Rube Goldberg–like creations. The film veers toward cruelty in its treatment of some of the wide-eyed hicks and cheerful exhibitionists on view, and Smith has burdened his film with superfluous narration, slapsticky sound effects, and—worst of all—gooey folk-rock ditties that accompany each montage. Like any compilation film, *Gizmo* is uneven, but it's funny at least half the time—about twice as much as your average Hollywood comedy.

THE GLADIATORS ☆☆½
1969, Sweden
Directed by Peter Watkins. 102 min.

Peter Watkins, who made the mock documentary *The War Game* (about the aftermath of a nuclear war) for the BBC, which then refused to air it, went on to get Swedish backing for this feature. Set in the future, the film portrays a global society where the world powers meet periodically to stage small-scale mock wars, broadcast worldwide on television. Too dry for the usual science-fiction crowd (who will recognize the premise as the plot of an old "Star Trek" episode), this goes on to occupy far more time than Watkins has ideas to fill.

THE GLASS HOUSE ☆☆☆½
1972, USA (TV)
Vic Morrow, Alan Alda, Billy Dee Williams, Clu Gulager, Scott Hylands, Tony Mancini. Directed by Tom Gries. 73 min.

Truman Capote's *In Cold Blood* furnished the movie screen with one of the most brutal films of the sixties; his *The Glass House* did likewise for the small screen in the seventies. This Emmy Award–winning TV movie is as gritty and nearly as violent as any R-rated prison feature of the day. It focuses on the adjustments made by a newly installed prison guard (Clu Gulager) and a recent inmate (Alan

Alda). Filmed in Utah State Prison with many real-life prisoners, the movie is sizzling and realistic. (a.k.a.: *Truman Capote's The Glass House*)

GLEN AND RANDA ★★½
1971, USA, X
Steven Curry, Shelly Plimpton, Woodrow Chambliss, Gary Goodrow. Directed by Jim McBride. 94 min.

This seldom-seen feature was the first commercial release from sixties experimentalist Jim McBride (*David Holzman's Diary*), who more recently directed the remake of Jean-Luc Godard's *Breathless*. Set in a time twenty years after the nuclear apocalypse, the film follows the wanderings of two post-bomb youngsters seeking a mystical city. The "X" rating is for frontal nudity, a strict no-no at the time, so don't get the impression that this is a sex feature. Cheaply made, and edited over McBride's objections, this has its moments of great beauty, although the general viewer may be merely confounded by the lack of activity.

THE GLENN MILLER STORY ★★★
1954, USA
James Stewart, June Allyson, Henry Morgan, Charles Drake, Frances Langford, Marion Ross, Louis Armstrong, Gene Krupa. Directed by Anthony Mann. 116 min.

Although best known for working with Jimmy Stewart in intense little Westerns (*Bend in the River, The Naked Spur*), Anthony Mann also guided Stewart through this sudsy but enjoyable biography of bandleader Glenn Miller. The bespectacled Stewart actually resembles Miller, and he gives a fine, sensitive performance (with trombone solos dubbed by Murray MacEachem) as the man who moved a generation with his arrangements of "Tuxedo Junction," "Stairway to the Stars," "Chattanooga Choo Choo," and "Pennsylvania 6-5000." June Allyson gives one of her more likable performances as Miller's wife and handles the difficult final scene (the news of Miller's untimely death during World War II) with restraint. An additional musical highlight is the Louis Armstrong–Gene Krupa duet "Basin Street Blues." Note: this was the last film to be shot in three-strip Technicolor.

GLEN OR GLENDA? ★
1953, USA
Bela Lugosi, Daniel Davis (Edward D. Wood, Jr.), Lyle Talbot, Timothy Farrell. Directed by Edward D. Wood, Jr. 67 min.

One star is all that this film can get under any kind of objective critical standards. However, as a camp classic, this is a four-star movie if there ever was one. An astonishingly incoherent mishmash of fiction, stock footage of city scenes, and psychobabble narration, *Glen or Glenda?* could be interpreted as reflecting the confusion of its protagonist, a closet transvestite. More realistically, though, it reflects the combined sincerity and total lack of talent of director Edward D. Wood, Jr., the legendary Worst Director of All Time. Wood, a transvestite who bragged that he wore a bra and panties under his uniform when he was a Marine, stars (under the pseudonym "Daniel Davis") as a character presumably based on himself. There are innumerable, pointless scenes with Bela Lugosi sitting in a wizard's den delivering incoherent lines about fate, ontology, and God knows what else. In the touching finale, Davis/Wood's fiancée agrees to share her wardrobe with him. Must be seen to be believed. (a.k.a.: *I Led Two Lives; I Changed My Sex; He or She*)

THE GLITTER DOME ★★
1984, USA (TV)
James Garner, Margot Kidder, John Lithgow, Colleen Dewhurst, John Marley. Directed by Stuart Margolin. 100 min.

Joseph Wambaugh's bleak police novel about child pornography has been listlessly adapted into a film that shows all of the story's melodramatic weaknesses. Colleen Dewhurst is funny in a couple of brief scenes, and John Lithgow, whose cop character is forced to experience the most convulsive mechanics of the plot, makes a heroic effort, but James Garner and Margot Kidder are mystifyingly mismatched leads. Stuart Margolin (Angel on "The Rockford Files"), in addition to directing, produced, wrote the music, and played a small role. Contains violence and nudity.

GLORIA ★★★
1980, USA, PG
Gena Rowlands, John Adames, Buck Henry, Julie Carmen. Directed by John Cassavetes. 123 min.

This smoky, violent little genre piece could only have been done by John Cassavetes's wife, Gena Rowlands, who plays a tough former gun moll shielding a wise-mouthed seven-year-old from the mob; it's a broad, powerful, funny performance that sweeps the picture along. Without it, there wouldn't be much to enjoy except some effectively seamy *film-noir* atmosphere and a succession of clumsily staged action scenes. While Oscar-nominated Rowlands holds the center marvelously, the movie feels underpopulated around the edges, and it's occasionally a bit monotonous.

GLORIFYING THE AMERICAN GIRL ★★½
1929, USA
Mary Eaton, Edward Crandall, Eddie Cantor, Helen Morgan, Rudy Vallee. Directed by Millard Webb. 80 min.

In some well-known MGM musicals, the Ziegfeld style of decadent opulence is successfully imitated. In this early sound effort, Ziegfeld himself produced the pageantry (his only film), but it falls far short of his own standard. Part of the problem is that instead of a "Follies" or revue of songs and sketches, he has provided a tiresome plot—about a showgirl who forsakes marriage for a career—that makes the film feel twice as long as it is. The other problem is that the film suffers from many technical difficulties (it was shot at Paramount's ill-equipped Astoria Studios), especially regarding sound. Still, the goods are delivered in the last reel, which is not only lavish (one number was originally shot in Technicolor, though prints no longer exist) but captures the raw, young talents of Helen Morgan, Eddie Cantor, and Rudy Vallee on film. And if you don't blink, you can catch, as part of the "first night" audience, Mayor and Mrs. James Walker, Noah Beery, Texas Guinan, Irving Berlin, Johnny Weissmuller, Ring Lardner, Adolph Zukor, Charles Dillingham, and Mr. and Mrs. Ziegfeld.

THE GLOVE ★★
1978, USA
John Saxon, Rosey Grier, Joanna Cassidy, Joan Blondell, Jack Carter, Aldo Ray. Directed by Ross Hagen. 91 min.

This improbable adventure mixes ultra-violence with comic cameos by Hollywood veterans. The shelves of video stores are stocked with slam-bang action pictures, and this one barely gets passing grades. The plot concerns a bounty hunter who's thinking of changing careers but first has to learn that he can't handle a vengeance-minded ex-con with kid gloves. The gimmick here is that when the reprobate villain gets his hands on his victims, he's wearing super-strong steel gloves. What next? A thriller with Michael Jackson strangling people with his sequined mitt?

THE GNOME-MOBILE ★★
1967, USA
Walter Brennan, Tom Lowell, Ed Wynn, Richard Deacon, Cami Sebring. Directed by Robert Stevenson. 84 min.

This Walt Disney film stars Walter Brennan in a double role as a man and as one of two gnomes searching for a lost colony—presumably of other gnomes. As Brennan and his grandchildren set out to relocate the gnomes, they encounter Sean McClory, an evil sideshow owner, who kidnaps the gnomes for his own troupe. Unfortunately, the spectacular rescue scene is followed by an anticlimactic ending involving a romance between Tom Lowell and Cami Sebring. Ellis Kadison wrote the screenplay, an adaptation of a novel by Upton Sinclair.

THE GO-BETWEEN ☆☆☆½
1971, Great Britain
Julie Christie, Alan Bates, Margaret Leighton, Michael Redgrave, Michael Gough, Edward Fox, Dominic Guard. Directed by Joseph Losey. 116 min.

When paired as screenwriter and director, British playwright Harold Pinter and American expatriate Joseph Losey always brought out the best in each other. Here, working from a novel by L. P. Hartley, they have created an insightful, charming, and revealing film, their best work together. (They also worked on *The Servant* and *Accident*.) Michael Redgrave plays an elderly bachelor remembering a summer in his youth spent at the country estate of an aristocratic family. Sexually naive, he is employed as the "go-between" to carry messages and arrange assignations between the family's daughter, with whom he thinks himself in love, and a young farmer. All of the major performances are excellent, especially that of Margaret Leighton as the girl's mother. Moody and often slow, but worth the time and attention.

GOBOTS: BATTLE OF THE ROCK LORDS ☆☆
1986, USA, G
Animated. Margot Kidder, Roddy McDowall, Michael Nouri, Telly Savalas. Directed by Ray Patterson. 75 min.

(1) The GoBots are robots that can transform themselves into cars, airplanes, trucks, etc. (2) The Guardians (who are good GoBots) and the Renegades (who are bad GoBots) are locked in a deadly feud. If you needed to read that explanation, this film would probably not interest you, although your kids might enjoy it. If you already knew what a GoBot is and what it does, then you may like this elemental animated feature about the robot heroes waging a war against the Rock People.

THE GODDESS ☆☆½
1958, USA
Kim Stanley, Lloyd Bridges, Steven Hill, Betty Lou Holland, Joan Copeland, Bert Freed, Burt Brinckerhoff, Gerald Hiken, Elizabeth Wilson, Patty Duke, Joyce Van Patten, Joanne Linville. Directed by John Cromwell. 105 min.

This glossy but idiotic melodrama concerns the rise and fall (but never success) of a neurotic, self-destructive actress in Hollywood. Kim Stanley made a spectacular screen debut as the disturbed young woman, giving a performance full of the kind of nuance and subtlety wholly lacking in the rest of the film. Paddy Chayefsky's script aims for an acute psychological portrayal, but some of its Freud-primer "insights" are shameful, as are the prattling, endless monologues that once passed for theatrical realism. Chayefsky reportedly modeled his actress after Marilyn Monroe (there are echoes of Frances Farmer as well) but made her so overwhelmingly selfish that she's unredeemed by any noble qualities at all. See it only for Stanley's performance; she played leading roles in only two films, and her extraordinary talent is evident throughout.

THE GODFATHER ☆☆☆☆
1972, USA, R
Marlon Brando, Al Pacino, James Caan, Richard Castellano, Robert Duvall, Diane Keaton, Talia Shire, Sterling Hayden, Richard Conte. Directed by Francis Ford Coppola. 175 min.

Francis Ford Coppola's gangster film about the Mafia has achieved such classic status that many have forgotten the controversies surrounding its original release: the negative representation of Italian-Americans and the sympathetic portrayal of gangsters and killers (problems also found, incidentally, in Mario Puzo's best-selling novel, on which the film is based). These difficulties are in many ways reconciled by the sheer brilliance of the filmmaking; so far, this is one of the high points of Coppola's checkered career. He paints a vast, dark canvas of characters and events, concentrating on the concern of Don Corleone (Marlon Brando) about the son who will succeed him as Godfather. The action begins in the mid-1940s and spans several years (then several more in the sequel *The Godfather, Part II*, maintaining a remarkable authenticity). The ensemble of Method actors is superb, with Brando's Oscar-winning Don almost outshined by Al Pacino's likable-soldier-turned-ruthless-gangster. A remarkable film. See also *The Godfather 1909–1959—The Complete Epic.*

THE GODFATHER 1909–1959— THE COMPLETE EPIC ☆☆☆☆
1977, USA, R
Al Pacino, Marlon Brando, Diane Keaton, Robert Duvall, James Caan, Robert De Niro, Talia Shire, Lee Strasberg, John Cazale. Directed by Francis Ford Coppola. 450 min. (3 cassettes)

Here it is! The entire *Godfather* clan on cassette. Don Corleone, Michael, Sonny, Kay, Fredo, Tom, and the star-making performances of Al Pacino, Robert De Niro, Diane Keaton, Robert Duvall, and Talia Shire. This seven-hour-plus edition was first presented in a very similar format on network television; while deleting a few of the more violent moments, Francis Ford Coppola restored previously unseen footage from both *The Godfather* and *The Godfather, Part II* and reedited the narrative into chronological order. Although its impact on video may be slightly diminished, this is probably the best way to view Coppola's brilliant gangster saga. (a.k.a.: *The Godfather Epic*; *The Godfather Saga*)

THE GODFATHER, PART II ☆☆☆☆
1974, USA, R
Al Pacino, Robert Duvall, Diane Keaton, Robert De Niro, John Cazale, Talia Shire, Lee Strasberg, Troy Donahue, Harry Dean Stanton, Michael V. Gazzo. Directed by Francis Ford Coppola. 200 min.

The Godfather, Part II has a problem: while it considerably enriches the original *Godfather*, it also needs to be seen with it to be fully appreciated as an epic depicting the rise and fall of one Mafioso family. In *Part II*, the new Godfather (Al Pacino) is faced with crooked business partners, disloyal brothers, and a wife (Diane Keaton) who disapproves of his activities. Meanwhile, the film recalls, in extended flashback sequences, how the young immigrant Don Corleone (Robert De Niro) built the now-collapsing empire. Much of the production (which won seven Oscars, including Best Picture)—acting, direction, period design—is as good as, if not better than, the original. A must-see film, all the more after a screening of the first. See also: *The Godfather 1909–1959—The Complete Epic.*

THE GODSEND ☆☆
1979, Great Britain, R
Cyd Hayman, Malcolm Stoddard, Angela Pleasence, Angela Barr. Directed by Gabrielle Beaumont. 90 min.

Another killer-kid movie in the tradition of *The Omen*, *The Exorcist*, and *It's Alive!*, but without the gore or shocks—or, for that matter, most of the interest. A strange young woman shows up at the doorstep of a rural British couple, has a baby, and then disappears. As the child grows up, it begins to bump off the couple's real children. The whole thing is rather vague and unexplained, more psychological (dealing with the effects of their children's deaths on the couple) than terrifying. Angela Pleasence, who plays the stranger, is the daughter of Donald.

GOD'S LITTLE ACRE ☆☆½
1958, USA
Robert Ryan, Aldo Ray, Tina Louise, Buddy Hackett, Vic Morrow, Rex Ingram, Michael Landon. Directed by Anthony Mann. 112 min.

Once upon a time, Erskine Caldwell's novels of Georgia farm life, *Tobacco Road* and *God's Little Acre*, were considered "adult only" reading and roundly condemned by Legions of Decency everywhere. We mention this bit of historical trivia because you would otherwise never think twice about the "raciness" of this fairly faithful adaptation. Robert Ryan is excellent as the farm owner who is possessed by the mad notion that there is gold buried on his land and devotes all of his energies (and those of his two sons) to finding it. The counterplot involves Ryan's son-in-law, Aldo Ray, who is taken by the equally simplistic notion that he can revive the town's dying economy if he can reopen the closed cotton mill. This is all done with more humor than might be apparent, although the underpinnings are allegorically moralistic.

THE GODS MUST BE CRAZY ☆½
1980, South Africa, PG
Marius Weyers, Sandra Prinsloo, N!xau, Jamie Uys. Directed by Jamie Uys. 109 min.

The leader of a Bushman tribe stumbles upon a Coke bottle, sees it as a gift from the gods, and takes it back to his clan—only to discover that the mysterious glass object brings more trouble than good. He makes a pilgrimage to throw the bottle off the edge of the world, and the journey leads to increasingly madcap encounters with representatives of Western civilization. Veteran director Jamie Uys is adept at broad slapstick and scored an international success with this film, but *Gods* evinces a patronizing attitude toward its black characters, turning them all into noble savages or buffoonish bandits.

GOD TOLD ME TO

See *Demon*

GODZILLA 1985 ☆
1985, Japan, PG
Raymond Burr, Keiju Kobayashi, Ken Tanaka, Yasuko Sawaguchi, Shin Takuma, Eitaro Ozara, Teketoshi Naito, Nobuo Kaneko, Takeshi Katoh. Directed by Kohji Hashimoto and R.J. Kizer. 91 min.

"All New!" screamed the ads, and they were basically telling the truth; this is not some old monster movie tricked up with newly shot footage. It is, however, a complete throwback to the early Godzilla movies, rubber monster extravaganzas that thrilled a generation of moviegoers who had not been weaned on the state-of-the-art special effects that characterize contemporary horror/exploitation films. Once again, the King of the Monsters breathes flames, causes deadly tidal waves, flattens cities with his tremendous feet, and terrorizes hordes of Japanese citizens. The action is framed with gratuitous stateside footage featuring Raymond Burr (included to save American viewers from having to watch a film totally filled with foreigners). Scientists are baffled, military men outraged, and philosophers humbled by the thought of the awesome natural powers Godzilla embodies; the result is solemn and silly almost beyond belief.

GODZILLA, THE KING OF THE MONSTERS ☆☆☆
1956, Japan
Raymond Burr, Takashi Shimura, Momoko Kochi, Akira Takarada. Directed by Terry Morse (American version), Inoshiro Honda (original Japanese version). 80 min.

The first and best of the Japanese giant monster films has been the fearsome dinosaur Godzilla rising out of the ocean and destroying most of Tokyo. Although it's no *King Kong*, the movie is well done and often overdramatic, with some awesome scenes of destruction. Scenes involving Raymond Burr were added for the American release. The Japanese-language version had a strong antinuclear message that was toned down for the film's importation.

GODZILLA VS. MONSTER ZERO

See *Monster Zero*

GODZILLA VS. MOTHRA ☆☆½
1964, Japan
Akira Takarada, Yuriko Hiroshi Koisumi, Yu Fujiki. Directed by Inoshiro Honda. 90 min.

One of the early Godzilla sequels, this is also one of the better ones, with some semblance of a plot and halfway decent special effects. Godzilla, still a bad guy at this point in his career, bumps off Mothra early on, but not before Mothra has left behind two eggs. And Tokyo hardly gets demolished at all! (a.k.a.: *Godzilla vs. the Thing*)

GODZILLA VS. THE SEA MONSTER ☆½
1966, Japan, PG
Akira Tadarada, Toru Wantabe. Directed by Jun Fukada. 80 min.

This movie is not to be confused with *Godzilla vs. Megalon*, *Godzilla vs. the Cosmic Monster*, *Godzilla vs. the Thing*, *Godzilla vs. Mechagodzilla*, or *Godzilla vs. Cleveland*. This is one of the ones in which the big G. is a good guy, saving humanity from various bad-guy monsters of similar size, just so that it's a fair fight. (*Godzilla vs. the Wolfman*, for instance, wouldn't be very interesting, except possibly as a sequel to *Bambi Meets Godzilla*.) His foe is Ebirah, a crustacean out to avenge the increased popularity of sushi bars or some such thing. The film features Mothra, those two-inch twins the Alilenas, and the usual mind-boggling special effects, so you really get your money's worth here. (a.k.a.: *Ebirah, Horror of the Deep*)

GODZILLA VS. THE THING

See *Godzilla vs. Mothra*

GOING APE! ☆½
1981, USA, PG
Tony Danza, Jessica Walter, Stacey Nelkin, Danny De Vito, Art Metrano. Directed by Jeremy Joe Kronsberg. 88 min.

The screenwriter of *Every Which Way But Loose* makes his directorial debut with a more ambitious project: instead of one wacky, scene-stealing orangutan, this movie has three. (Or four, if you want to count Tony Danza. Or five, if you want to count Danny De Vito.) Danza inherits the three apes from his uncle, a circus owner who leaves him $5 million on the condition that they be treated well for several years. Not as proudly, stupidly dumb as *Every Which Way*, but still pretty dumb.

GOING BERSERK ☆
1983, USA, R
John Candy, Joe Flaherty, Eugene Levy, Alley Mills, Pat Hingle, Richard Libertini, Paul Dooley. Directed by David Steinberg. 85 min.

How could you go wrong with a movie built around three of the best talents from "SCTV," the funniest and most bizarrely creative television show since the original "Saturday Night Live"? By reducing the trio to mere players and turning over the direction and writing to David Steinberg, that's how. The loose plot, which often gives way to random skits, has John Candy as a chauffeur and aspiring drummer engaged to be married to the daughter of a congressman. He is kidnapped by a religious sect that is under government investigation, and they hypnotize him into trying to kill the congressman. Candy does his best with a pile of crude, puerile jokes, at least half of which involve talking about his penis. Joe Flaherty and Eugene Levy are totally wasted, the former especially having nothing else to do but play second banana to Candy. Even Richard Libertini falls flat as the cult leader. A lamentable waste of talent.

GOING IN STYLE ☆☆☆½
1979, USA, PG
George Burns, Art Carney, Lee Strasberg, Charles Hallahan, Pamela Payton-Wright. Directed by Martin Brest. 97 min.

🤓 In outline, this film by Martin Brest (*Beverly Hills Cop*) sounds as though it has a case of the formula cutes: a comic caper yarn about three aged roomies (George Burns, Art Carney, and Lee Strasberg) who join forces to knock over a bank. But unlike so many cuddly-oldster movies, this one is *about* something: old people are useless because we make them feel useless. All three of the performers are brilliant, and so is their twenty-eight-year-old writer-director. A single word, a double take, a line that would read like nothing on the printed page—all are transmuted into the provocations to laughter or tears. There is no mechanical prodding. Brest has created a comedy of character that embraces us all.

GOING MY WAY ☆☆☆½
1944, USA
Bing Crosby, Barry Fitzgerald, Risë Stevens, Frank McHugh, Gene Lockhart, William Frawley. Directed by Leo McCarey. 126 min.

🎭 *Going My Way* and its sequel, *The Bells of St. Mary's*, never seemed to fit into the Leo McCarey canon (*Duck Soup, The Awful Truth*), yet he won writing and directing Oscars for the first, and may well be better remembered for the pair than for all the rest of his films. Despite a lack of subversive humor and technical invention, *Going My Way* is one of the best sentimental holiday movies ever made, thanks to McCarey's heart-tugging skills and the likable byplay of its stars. Bing Crosby plays singing priest Father Chuck O'Malley, who is sent to take over the work done by Old World pastor Barry Fitzgerald. Their charming confrontations are interrupted by a pleasant batch of tunes including "Swinging on a Star" and "Too-ra-loo-ra-loo-ra." Subplots involving Fitzgerald's grandmother and opera diva Risë Stevens are elaborate digressions, but they don't hurt the film. Sidenote: Fitzgerald was nominated by the Academy of Motion Picture Arts and Sciences for both Best Actor and Best Supporting Actor Awards, thus putting him in competition with himself. (He won the latter award, Crosby himself claiming the former.)

GOING PLACES ☆☆½
1974, France, R (edited)
Gérard Depardieu, Patrick Dewaere, Miou-Miou, Jeanne Moreau. Directed by Bertrand Blier. 117 min.

🌍 In this lacerating "buddy" film, calculated almost too carefully to shock and outrage, the two heroes are stupid, brutal, hateful thugs on a spree of casual crime and cruelty. Bertrand Blier means his work to be a scathing social indictment and, against all odds, it succeeds more often than not, thanks to the strong work of his cast. (Jeanne Moreau, in particular, is gravely moving in a remarkable and brief appearance.) But the semiexplicit sex and relentless violence may numb you long before the end. The version on videocassette is dubbed, adequately.

GOING STEADY ☆
1979, Israel/West Germany, R
Yiftach Katzur, Jonathan Segal, Zachi Noy, Yvonne Michaelis. Directed by Boaz Davidson. 90 min.

🌍 This is a sequel (one of many) to a very popular Israeli film called *Lemon Popsicle*. If you haven't seen that one, don't worry: it's merely another in the endless series of oversexed-teenager flicks that have been with us every summer for the past fifteen years or so. The plot is as intricate and densely wrought with sociological implications as ever in this genre: a trio of guys growing up in the fifties (you can tell by the songs played on the soundtrack) spend eight days a week trying to find, um, intimate female companionship. Directed, with no apparent style or interest, by the sensitive creator of *Hospital Massacre* and *The Last American Virgin*.

GOIN' SOUTH ☆☆
1978, USA, PG
Jack Nicholson, Mary Steenburgen, Christopher Lloyd, John Belushi, Veronica Cartwright, Richard Bradford, Jeff Morris, Danny De Vito. Directed by Jack Nicholson. 101 min.

🤓 Jack Nicholson directed and starred in this rambling, intermittently amusing yarn about a headstrong young spinster (Mary Steenburgen) who marries a condemned horse thief (Nicholson) because she needs someone to work her gold mine. Most of the jokes are sophomoric, but the sight of Nicholson mugging and leering into the camera for two hours has its own slobby charm. John Belushi gives a funny performance in the tradition of the Frito Bandito school of Mexican villainy.

GO, JOHNNY, GO! ☆☆½
1958, USA
Jimmy Clanton, Alan Freed, Chuck Berry, Eddie Cochran, Richie Valens, The Cadillacs, The Flamingos, Jackie Wilson. Directed by Paul Landres. 75 min.

🎵 This obvious story concerns a young orphan boy who rises to rock-and-roll stardom with the help of D.J. Alan Freed. The plot is negligible, but the movie is a must-see for fans of fifties rock and roll for performances by the stars in the credits. This was the only film appearance of Richie Valens, who died in the same plane accident that killed Buddy Holly.

GOLD DIGGERS OF 1933 ☆☆☆½
1933, USA
Dick Powell, Ruby Keeler, Joan Blondell, Warren William, Ginger Rogers, Aline MacMahon, Guy Kibbee. Directed by Mervyn LeRoy. 96 min.

🎵 Exhilarating, vulgar, cynical—this flamboyant musical choreographed by Busby Berkeley was all that and more: a delirious concoction about sex, money, and puttin' on a show. Hear Ginger Rogers sing "We're in the Money" in pig Latin! See sixty, count 'em, sixty chorines light up in the dark and play violins as they do the "Shadow Waltz." Watch a lascivious midget leer at necking couples in the "Pettin' in the Park" number! You get all that musical magic in one movie, plus a nonstop barrage of wisecracks from veteran comics and a juicy plot about Red Hot Mamas getting the most out of life from some easily led Sugar Daddies. Irresistible.

THE GOLDEN AGE OF COMEDY ☆☆☆½
1957, USA
Laurel and Hardy, Carole Lombard, Ben Turpin, Will Rogers, Harry Langdon. Directed by Robert Youngson. 78 min.

🤓 A sterling collection of classic scenes from silent-film comedies. Like that other exceptional compilation film, *Days of Thrills and Laughter*, this superb group of film clips avoids the pitfalls of cuteness, haphazard selection, and overly intrusive narration. It's a sort of primer in early film comedy and your teachers are, among others, Will Rogers, Ben Turpin, and Laurel and Hardy. A cavalcade of rollicking comedy that climaxes in some legendary pie-fighting scenes.

GOLDEN BOY ☆☆½
1939, USA
Barbara Stanwyck, Adolphe Menjou, William Holden, Lee J. Cobb, Joseph Calleia. Directed by Rouben Mamoulian. 98 min.

🎭 Clifford Odets's famed stage success is the basis for this classic but disappointing screen drama that introduced William Holden as a boy faced with a choice between two incompatible careers—violinist or prizefighter. Although better came later in his career, Holden shows talent playing the torn youth and Lee J. Cobb hams it up appropriately as his immigrant father. Barbara Stanwyck also scores in her scenes as a tough society girl but loses ground in the mushier moments as Holden's love interest. The story itself may also have appeal, but it is filmed unimaginatively, which is surprising considering director Rouben Mamoulian's other screen credits (*Love Me Tonight, Dr. Jekyll and Mr. Hyde, Summer Holiday*), and it strips the original play of its social and political significance.

THE GOLDEN CHILD ☆
1986, USA, PG-13
Eddie Murphy, Charles Dance, Charlotte Lewis, Victor, J. L. Reate, Randall (Tex) Cobb. Directed by Michael Ritchie. 93 min.

It wants to be at once a mystical adventure, an urban thriller, and an Eddie Murphy bash; the result is such a muddle that it borders on the unwatchable. Murphy plays a finder of lost children who gets mixed up in a plot to rescue the Golden Child, a sacred being who's been kidnapped by a group of devil worshippers. The director, Michael Ritchie, seems to be crying "H-E-L-P!" There are scenes so drippy it's hard to believe he filmed them with a straight face, and his awareness of the material's worthlessness makes the film seem almost embarrassed for itself. As for Murphy, there's an ugly air of superiority to his work here: everyone around him has been made to look pitifully stupid. *The Golden Child* is a comedy for people who'll respond automatically to whatever is put in front of them—it turns its audience into a laugh track. (Yes, we *know* it was a big box-office hit—alas!)

GOLDENGIRL ☆☆
1979, USA, PG
Susan Anton, James Coburn, Curt Jurgens, Robert Culp, Leslie Caron. Directed by Joseph Sargent. 104 min.

This adequate sports suspense film deals with a statuesque athlete whose training for the Olympic track team involves weird drugs and manipulation by creepy proto-Nazis, including her dad. Nothing terribly exciting or original here except for Susan Anton, who, though no actress, is oddly right in the role of someone slightly superhuman. Curt Jurgens provides a healthy dose of scenery-chewing as the requisite mad scientist.

THE GOLDEN LADY ☆
1979, Great Britain, R
Christina World, Suzanne Danielle, June Chadwick, Stephan Chase. Directed by José Larraz. 96 min.

No, it's not *The Return of Ginger*, but it's almost as bad—certainly in the same league as *Angel of H.E.A.T*. A gorgeous female superspy and her three partners become involved with a battle among various international interests for an oil-rich territory in the Mideast. If you must watch one of these things, this gets the nod over *Ginger* or *Angel* because the star, a Danish actress of indiscernible thespic ability, looks better without her clothes on than does Ginger, and takes them off more often than Marilyn Chambers. Which, we might warn you, isn't much. Better to catch up on your sleep than watch this.

GOLDEN RENDEZVOUS ☆½
1977, Great Britain
Richard Harris, Ann Turkel, David Janssen, Burgess Meredith, John Vernon, Dorothy Malone, John Carradine. Directed by Ashley Lazarus. 103 min.

You may recognize the title as being that of an Alistair MacLean thriller, from which this film was in fact adapted. You may also recall that, out of the dozen or so MacLean books adapted to the screen, only three (*Guns of Navarone*, *Ice Station Zebra*, and *Where Eagles Dare*) were any good. You may do a little statistical analysis and come to the conclusion that this one, about a gambling boat being held captive by terrorists, is probably not worth your time, a conclusion with which we heartily agree.

THE GOLDEN SEAL ☆½
1983, USA, PG
Steve Railsback, Michael Beck, Penelope Milford, Torquil Campbell. Directed by Frank Zuniga. 94 min.

This children's adventure story concerns a young boy who finds the mythical golden seal of the Aleutian Islands and tries to stop it from being killed by bounty hunters. Unfortunately, the drawn-out travelogue sequences of nature, accompanied by sentimental scores, overwhelm the film. Its director, Frank Zuniga (*Wilderness Family* saga), spent a lengthy apprenticeship at Disney Studios, which is all too noticeable. The characters and their interactions are mere derivatives of past nature programs and family shows. But children and animal lovers will probably enjoy this film.

GOLDEN STALLION ☆☆
1949, USA
Roy Rogers, Dale Evans. Directed by William Witney. 67 min.

Roy Rogers takes a murder rap for Trigger, who falls in love and becomes the leader of the pack of wild horses. In this wildly improbable Western, the color photography, the horses, and the songs add up to a highly enjoyable romp. Silent-film comedian Chester Conklin makes an appearance as an old duffer.

THE GOLDEN VOYAGE OF SINBAD ☆½
1974, Great Britain, G
John Philip Law, Caroline Munro, Tom Baker, Douglas Wilmer. Directed by Gordon Hesler. 105 min.

This dullish, hokey children's entertainment has Sinbad in quest of a magic statuette and doing battle with evil sorcerer Koura for its control. Kids weaned on post–*Star Wars* special effects may be bored by Ray Harryhausen's old-fashioned visual work, although his array of well-designed monsters does provide a few impressive scares. John Philip Law (*Barbarella*) is as wooden as they come playing Sinbad, but that's almost what the script calls for. Filmed in "Dynarama."

GOLDFINGER ☆☆½
1964, Great Britain
Sean Connery, Honor Blackman, Gert Frobe, Shirley Eaton, Harold Sakata, Bernard Lee, Lois Maxwell, Bert Kwouk. Directed by Guy Hamilton. 112 min.

The third James Bond film was the first directed by Guy Hamilton, who took over from Terence Young. It was also the point at which the series began to slide into a formula. It has its memorable characters, especially Oddjob and the outrageously monikered Pussy Galore, and the assault on Fort Knox is visually stunning, but overall it's more calculated than inspired.

GOLD OF THE AMAZON WOMEN ☆½
1979, USA (TV)
Bo Svenson, Anita Ekberg, Donald Pleasence, Richard Romanus, Maggie Jean Smith. Directed by Mark Lester. 100 min.

Talk about camp—if Maria Montez were alive today, this is the kind of flick she'd want to sign up for. Two fortune hunters stumble upon a tribe of Amazon ladies and make such an impression on the girls that they chase the lucky guys all the way back to the Big Apple. Pulchritudinous Anita Ekberg literally leads the cast of chesty emoters, who could conceivably be considered Jungle Feminists. Occasionally enjoyable in its all-encompassing silliness, with lots of inane dialogue.

THE GOLD RAIDERS ☆½
1951, USA
The Three Stooges (Moe Howard, Shemp Howard, Larry Fine), George O'Brien, Sheilah Ryan, Monte Blue, Lyle Talbot, Fuzzy Knight. Directed by Edward Bernds. 56 min.

You're interested in this film because it features the Three Stooges. You decide against it because (1) the Stooges are only here as support to washed-up cowboy star George O'Brien, who plays the Old West's first insurance salesman (a concept that sounds a lot funnier than it is); (2) it has Shemp instead of Curley; (3) the Stooges were at their best in their shorts, never in the few feature-length films they made; and (4) director Edward Bernds, who directed many of the Stooges's shorts as well as a goodly number of Blondie, Bowery Boys, and other series comedies, was able to do this sort of thing in his sleep and from all appearances did so here. If you must watch it, bear in mind how unfair it was that Larry never got the attention he deserved.

THE GOLD RUSH ☆☆☆☆
1925, USA
Charlie Chaplin, Mack Swain, Georgia Hale, Tom Murray, Betsy Morrissey, Henry Bergman, Malcolm Waite. Directed by Charles Chaplin. 72 min.

This perennial crowd-pleaser invariably appears on critics' lists of the ten best films of all times, and deservedly so. The setting is perfect: the urbane, dandyish Tramp was never so out of place as he is waddling around the Frozen North in his tight little jacket without an overcoat. The gruff gold-mad prospectors, too, are perfect foils, and the Tramp is the unlikeliest hero for this success-in-the-wilderness yarn. *The Gold Rush* is a wicked satire on the whole Jack London manly-adventure school—watch Charlie battle storms, face starvation, and deck the barroom tough while never losing his quintessential, delicate aplomb. The movie's marvelous look is the result of extensive location shooting in the Sierras. The New Year's Eve dinner remains as poignant and affecting as ever; Chaplin's dance of the rolls provides a perfect leavening of this sad scene. Be very careful in purchasing a videotape of this film. Inferior quality versions abound, especially in the bargain bins. In 1942, Chaplin himself cut the film slightly and added a soundtrack that includes his own narration.

THE GOLDWYN FOLLIES ☆☆½
1938, USA
Adolph Menjou, Vera Zorina, The Ritz Brothers, Andrea Leeds, Edgar Bergen, Charlie McCarthy, Phil Baker, Kenny Baker. Directed by George Marshall. 115 min.

All-color, all-singing, all-dancing, but not all that interesting a musical. George Gershwin died during the postproduction of this large-scale, Ziegfeldish musical, and his featured songs make a better legacy than the rather dull, overlong film that contains them. Highlights include "Love Is Here to Stay," "I Love to Rhyme," "I Was Doing All Right," and the Water Nymph ballet, starring Vera Zorina and choreographed by George Balanchine. Low points are the plot, as always, and the silly attempts to blend in some high culture (classical ballet, operatic arias) along with the show-biz good times.

GOLIATH AND THE BARBARIANS ☆½
1959, Italy
Steve Reeves, Chelo Alonso, Bruce Cabot, Giulia Rubini. Directed by Carlo Campogalliani. 85 min.

The scene is Italy and the year is 568 A.D. Times are savage and life is cheap, though not as cheap as the budget of this Italian muscle epic. Steve Reeves, the Arnold Schwarzenegger of his generation but without the screen personality or humor, saves Rome from the hordes of barbarian rape-and-pillagers led by Bruce Cabot. Filmed in "Totalscope," a wide-screen process that won't translate to your television screen, which means that you'll get to see fewer mountains.

GOMAR, THE HUMAN GORILLA

See *Night of the Bloody Apes*

GONE ARE THE DAYS

See *Purlie Victorious*

GONE IN 60 SECONDS ☆☆
1974, USA, PG
H. B. Halicki, Marion Busia, Jerry Daugirda, James McIntyre, Ronald Halicki. Directed by H. B. Halicki. 105 min.

Ninety-three cars, over half of them police cars, get demolished in the central car chase sequence of this movie. That was probably a record until *The Blues Brothers*, for whatever that's worth. The big chase lasts forty-five minutes onscreen, but that still leaves us with an hour of impenetrable plot about a luxury-car theft ring. Director/star H. B. Halicki also wrote and produced this. In publishing, these things are put out by what are known as "vanity presses."

GONE WITH THE WIND ☆☆☆☆
1939, USA
Vivien Leigh, Clark Gable, Olivia De Havilland, Thomas Mitchell, Hattie McDaniel, Butterfly McQueen, George Reeves, Victor Jory, Jane Darwell, Cliff Edwards, Tom Tyler, Yakima Canutt, Ward Bond. Directed by Victor Fleming. 217 min.

This film is above criticism. It was an event at the time of its release and it remains a perennial favorite whose sharply defined characters continue to elicit adulation and whose plot lines continue to inspire the writers of countless TV miniseries. An army of craftsmen, spearheaded by designer William Cameron Menzies and dominated by David O. Selznick (plus four different directors on the project), all driven to make this the epic to end all epics, succeeded in perfectly realizing Margaret Mitchell's Civil War romance and reached the apogee of Hollywood filmmaking technique. Just as *Gone with the Wind* limns the passing of a way of life, the film version is also a kind of swan song to the Hollywood dream factory. It's not that it's the greatest movie ever made, but that it's Hollywood's greatest production, with that legendary search for the actress to play Scarlett O'Hara, a fitting symbol of a crazy commitment to narrative moviemaking. For once, the budget and commitment show on the screen—with many great moments like the camera pullback at the train station where Scarlett walks among the wounded, or the scene where she and Mammy fashion a dress out of Miss Ellen's portieres. Atlanta burns, Scarlett yearns for Ashley, and Rhett finally doesn't give a damn; and Hollywood has never topped this dazzling love story.

GOODBYE, COLUMBUS ☆☆☆½
1969, USA, R
Richard Benjamin, Ali MacGraw, Jack Klugman, Nan Martin, Michael Myers, Lori Shelle. Directed by Larry Peerce. 104 min.

Philip Roth's piercing novella about a young Jewish man's coming of age is only intermittently successful, but often hilarious and observant, as a film. Richard Benjamin plays the lower-middle-class youth who courts a spoiled, wealthy girl, much to the chagrin of both families. The humor and pathos of Roth's writing come through in some sharply observed sequences, but too frequently director Larry Peerce favors caricatures over characters. Benjamin does much better than Ali MacGraw, who is attractive but inept playing the country club girl of his dreams.

GOODBYE EMMANUELLE ☆
1978, France
Sylvia Kristel, Umberto Orsini, Alexandra Stewart. Directed by François Leterrier. 95 min.

In this slow-moving soft-core film, the languid Sylvia Kristel lords it over a few guys and gals but falls hard for a filmmaker. The seriousness of the film, more genteel than the Italian rip-offs with Laura Gemser, prevents any lighthearted enjoyment. Worse, there's nothing of substance in the film to justify its sobriety.

GOODBYE, FAREWELL AND AMEN

See *M*A*S*H: Goodbye, Farewell and Amen*

THE GOODBYE GIRL ☆☆☆
1977, USA, PG
Richard Dreyfuss, Marsha Mason, Quinn Cummings, Paul Benedict, Barbara Rhodes, Theresa Merritt, Michael Shawn, Nicol Williamson. Directed by Herbert Ross. 110 min.

Another odd couple battles its way to romance in Neil Simon's movie. As Simon-watchers might expect, the film is calculated, predictable, shameless in its heart-tugging, and often scarcely credible. But as a young actor, Richard Dreyfuss unleashes his dizzying, apparently boundless energy and yet manages to be a believable romantic lead (he won an Academy Award for his performance). Marsha Mason, a warm, likable performer, is unfortunately stuck with an unlikable role as the whining hoofer who's been loved and left by a succession of handsome actors.

GOODBYE MR. CHIPS ☆☆☆
1939, Great Britain
Robert Donat, Greer Garson, Paul Henried, Lyn Harding, Austin Trevor, Terry Kilburn, John Mills. Directed by Sam Wood. 114 min.

The classic movie of James Hilton's novel has dated somewhat, but Robert Donat is still superb and the definitive "Mr. Chips," the hard-nosed but well-liked British schoolmaster who becomes one of his school's eternal fixtures. Unfortunately, the rest of the film reeks of MGM "prestige": the polished sets (even in a mountaintop scene), the drippy, romantic music, and the ubiquitous "prestige picture lady" Greer Garson (her debut, playing Chips's young wife). The R. C. Sherriff/Claudine West/Eric Mashwitz screenplay is calculated in its heart-tugging. Donat, in an Oscar-winning performance, is the reason to catch this erstwhile favorite.

GOODBYE NEW YORK ☆½
1985, Israel, R
Julie Hagerty, Amos Kollek, David Topaz, Aviva Ger. Directed by Amos Kollek. 90 min.

Amos Kollek's Israeli comedy is as kosher as Manischewitz—and as unpalatably syrupy, with the characterless bouquet of an off-year Woody Allen. Kollek gives a tendentious twist to his breathless-but-brainy protagonist, a New York yuppie (played by Julie Hagerty): she's a Gentile jammed with dehumanizing, Jewish American Princess traits. Having walked out on her husband in a Valium haze, she hops on a plane and wakes up, sans luggage and money, in Tel Aviv. There she's befriended by all things Judaic and lands on a kibbutz, but she finds the summer-camp routine hard to take.

GOODBYE, NORMA JEAN ☆
1976, USA, R
Misty Rowe, Terrence Locke, Patch Mackenzie, Preston Hanson. Directed by Larry Buchanan. 95 min.

This film is a low-class biography of Marilyn Monroe's early years, when she was a struggling young actress sexually manipulated by a series of men, none of whom made good on his promise to make her a star. The resolutely uninvolving screenplay keeps Marilyn (then Norma Jean Baker) a cipher, although Misty Rowe does a credible imitation and has a few sensitive moments. To be exploitative and boring is a fatal combination for any film but especially for a movie bio like this, whose attempts at sleaze are as phony as its stabs at truth.

THE GOODBYE PEOPLE ☆
1984, USA, PG
Martin Balsam, Judd Hirsch, Pamela Reed, Ron Silver, Gene Saks. Directed by Herb Gardner. 105 min.

If you thought you said good-bye to clichéd "little people" characters in the early sixties, you were wrong. These are garden-variety Herb Gardner people who could have been lifted from early drafts of *A Thousand Clowns* or *Thieves*; in other words, life's losers who are winners at heart. The only problem is that Gardner's conception of lovable people and yours may not be the same. Hanging out on a Coney Island boardwalk are a hot-dog vendor with grandiose dreams, his daughter who lives in a perpetual identity crisis, and a professional display maker. They cross paths and change each other's lives for the better—or so we're led to believe. Relentlessly coy and unoriginal, as dramatically run-down as Coney Island itself.

THE GOOD EARTH ☆☆☆☆
1937, USA
Paul Muni, Luise Rainer, Walter Connolly, Tilly Losch, Charley Grapewin, Jessie Ralph, Soo Yong, Keye Luke, Roland Lui. Directed by Sidney Franklin, George Hill. 138 min.

The odds were against it. MGM, the prestige family-picture factory, slanted the eyelids of the renowned Yiddish theater actor Paul Muni (*Scarface*) and Viennese discovery Luise Rainer (*The Great Ziegfeld*'s Anna Held) in Pearl S. Buck's chronicle of a Chinese peasant family's rise to wealth and power. Surprisingly, the film was not only a respectable adaptation (by Talbot Jennings, Tess Slesinger, and Claudine West) but a great Hollywood epic in its own right (and the last production of maverick producer Irving Thalberg, who died during the filming). Muni and Rainer are triumphant (she won her second consecutive Oscar, beating out Greta Garbo in *Camille*) and the other, mostly non-Oriental cast members fit into their roles comfortably. Special notice should also go to Karl Freund's cinematography which gives the images an eloquent look without being offensively glossy, and to Slavko Vorkapich's montages of Arnold Gillespie's special effects, which include a riot, a storm, and a locust swarm. Note: original prints were in Sepia Tone.

GOOD GUYS WEAR BLACK ☆☆
1979, USA, PG
Chuck Norris, Anne Archer, Lloyd Haynes, James Franciscus, Dana Andrews, Jim Backus. Directed by Ted Post. 96 min.

This is one of Chuck Norris's first films as a good guy, after being the bad guy against Bruce Lee; you can tell the difference because he's still alive at the end. The plot, which handily keeps the action scenes from getting too repetitious, is sort of an amalgamation of *Rambo* and *Missing in Action*, but without a Vietnam locale. Norris, an ex–army commando whose specialty was rescuing P.O.W.'s from behind enemy lines, has his peaceful postwar life interrupted when someone begins to kill off the other members of his unit. It all ties in with a government conspiracy to cover up some wartime wrongdoings. Norris had yet to develop more than the most rudimentary acting skills at this point, so he wisely keeps quiet and lets his feet do the talking. Fans will be happy.

GOOD LUCK, MISS WYCKOFF

See *The Shaming*

GOOD NEIGHBOR SAM ☆☆☆
1964, USA
Jack Lemmon, Romy Schneider, Dorothy Provine, Michael Conners, Edward Andrews, Louis Nye, Edward G. Robinson. Directed by David Swift. 130 min.

The only thing unusual about this domestic comedy is that it runs about thirty minutes longer than most of its type. Otherwise, it's a breezy farce about a San Francisco adman who gets into complications and misunderstandings when he agrees to pose as his sexy Viennese neighbor's husband for her to collect a large inheritance. Lemmon is a master at this sort of surreal suburban farce, and there are several sharp jabs at modern advertising strewn about the James Fritzell–Everett Greenbaum screenplay. Some cutting at the beginning and end of the film might have helped, but the slow spots here aren't ruinous.

GOOD NEWS
★★★½
1947, USA
June Allyson, Peter Lawford, Joan McCracken, Mel Torme, Patricia Marshall. Directed by Charles Walters. 95 min.

A musical that looks better and better as the years go by, this old-fashioned collegiate show with a plot right out of the 1930s is spruced up with memorable DeSylva-Brown-Anderson standards, dynamic choreography, and all the splashy production values MGM could muster. Peter Lawford, a football hero but an academic washout, gets tutored by June Allyson so he can bring up his grades in time to play the Big Game. College was never like this, but this sugar-coated, toe-tapping fantasy is very good news for lovers of what is now a lost breed of musical-comedy entertainment. With "Pass That Peace Pipe" and the lift-you-out-of-your-seat "Varsity Drag" numbers as standouts, brilliantly staged by the underrated choreographer Robert Alton.

GOOD SAM
★★★
1948, USA
Gary Cooper, Ann Sheridan, Ray Collins, Edmund Lowe, Joan Lorring, Clinton Sundberg, Louise Beavers, Ruth Roman, William Frawley. Directed by Leo McCarey. 114 min.

Leo McCarey lightly mocks Frank Capra's syrupy brand of humanism in this amusing but overlong postwar comedy. Gary Cooper plays an out-of-control Good Samaritan who goes to such lengths as cosigning bank loans for mere acquaintances and taking in boarders. Ann Sheridan plays the bighearted man's frustrated wife. Most of the gags revolve around Sheridan's displeasure with Cooper's altruism. Her "hysterical laughter" scene is especially memorable. Unfortunately, McCarey lets the film run too long, padding it with such scenes as an uncomfortable Cooper mingling with a bunch of bobby-soxers. A good idea gone slightly awry.

THE GOOD, THE BAD AND THE UGLY
★★★★
1967, Italy/Spain
Clint Eastwood, Lee Van Cleef, Eli Wallach. Directed by Sergio Leone. 180 min.

The third of Italian director Sergio Leone's loosely connected "dollars" trilogy (see also *A Fistful of Dollars* and *For a Few Dollars More*) and his penultimate brutal reworking of classic Western themes and plots (see also *Once upon a Time in the West*). It is a picaresque look at the American Civil War through the eyes of three opportunistic criminals in search of a cache of gold; egged on by Ennio Morricone's wailing score, they lie, cheat, steal, kill, and offer cynical observations amid the carnage about the hopelessly corrupt nature of the world. The film offers a jaundiced confirmation of the myth that the West was created by the action of forceful individuals. The film is violent (one contemporary reviewer suggested that the words "burn," "gouge," and "mangle" might be profitably substituted in the title), funny, and panoramic. Squeezed onto the video screen, it loses the edges of Leone's extraordinary compositions (and viewers may miss key parts of action and character delineations that occur offscreen).

THE GOONIES
★★½
1985, USA, PG
Sean Astin, Josh Brolin, Jeff B. Cohen, Ke Huy Quan, Corey Feldman, John Matuszak. Directed by Richard Donner. 97 min.

A group of misfit ten-year-olds go on a subterranean search for pirate gold in a disappointingly plastic product of the Steven Spielberg assembly line (he conceived and produced it), written by protégé Chris Columbus (*Gremlins*). It's the Goonies' last big adventure, since they'll all have to split up the next day when their homes are razed in favor of a golf course—that is, unless they can get the loot. The theme of childhood's transient magic, which Spielberg put forth so gently in *E.T. The Extraterrestrial*, is here subordinated to an endless process of noisy action gags and screaming kids in dark, ugly locations. The child actors are uneven, although lead Sean Astin has the same sensitive, wise face as Henry Thomas in *E.T.*; he gives the often silly antics an emotional force. When the gang discovers an ancient pirate ship in an underground cavern, you'll get a taste of the dress rehearsal for Spielberg's long-awaited *Peter Pan* that this could have been. Instead, it becomes *Indiana Jones and the Temple of Doom* with midgets.

THE GOOSE BOXER
★★★
1979, Hong Kong
Charles Heung, Kao Fei, Li Hai Sheng, Tian Qing, Dai Hsiao Yan. Directed by Dai Shifu.

In this genuinely funny and charmingly offbeat film, the hero mistakenly uses a sex manual to learn kung fu and then tries to use the techniques "Pushing a Cart Uphill" and "Rowing Upstream" on his flabbergasted opponent. Charles Heung, as the hapless, goose-roaster hero, is a wonderful comic and a charmingly inept warrior. An exceptional music score, combined with crystal-clear choreography and very good fighting, lifts this far, far above the average.

GORATH
★½
1964, Japan
Ryo Ikebe, Akihiko Hirata, Jun Tazaki, Takashi Shimura. Directed by Inoshiro Honda. 83 min.

Fans of Japanese monster epics will probably be disappointed by this insufficiently camp entry in the long line of Inoshiro Honda films. Gorath is the name given to a giant stellar body on a collision path with Earth. The Japanese version has a giant walrus that is unleashed when scientists divert the impending collision, but for some reason it was deleted from the American release. The dubbing is also not as bad as usual, which also diminishes the laughs. What's left is a mediocre sci-fi film, long on rational explanation but short on cheap thrills. Set in the "future" year of 1980.

GORGO
★★★
1961, Great Britain
Bill Travers, William Sylvester, Vincent Winter, Bruce Seton. Directed by Eugene Lourie. 78 min.

This well-done English elaboration on the *Godzilla* theme has a giant prehistoric beastie on a rampage through London while searching for its captured baby. Monster fans should be pleased by some spectacular building-stomping. Shows that a story of this type can be pulled off with a reasonable amount of intelligence and technical sophistication.

THE GORGON
★★★
1964, Great Britain
Peter Cushing, Christopher Lee, Barbara Shelly, Richard Pasco, Michael Rippe. Directed by Terence Fisher. 83 min.

This is one of the better Hammer horrors, with loads of the usual Victorian English atmosphere and a monster that, in best monster fashion, you don't get to see until the very end. This time it's Christopher Lee's turn to play the good guy, an investigator sent to a rural village to figure out why the locals have been turning to stone. As he should have guessed right away, it's the reincarnation of Medusa, who displays her snaky charms only when the moon is full. Barbara Shelly is the girl possessed by the demon, and Peter Cushing plays the doctor harboring her for research purposes.

THE GORILLA
★★
1939, USA
James, Harry, and Al Ritz, Anita Louise, Patsy Kelly, Lionel Atwill, Bela Lugosi, Joseph Calleia. Directed by Allan Dwan. 65 min.

The Ritz Brothers play private detectives in this well-paced but unexceptional comic whodunit, the third remake of the play by Ralph Spence. A haunted house, a gorilla on the loose, typical Ritz antics, and not enough Lugosi.

GORKY PARK ☆☆
1983, USA, R
William Hurt, Lee Marvin, Brian Dennehy, Ian Bannen, Joanna Pacula, Alexei Sayle, Alexander Knox. Directed by Michael Apted. 130 min.

Martin Cruz Smith's best-selling mystery about a triple murder in Moscow was a set of Chinese boxes—a moral dilemma wrapped inside a murder set inside a society of evasions and half-truths. But the film version never clarifies the central relationship between William Hurt's Arkady Renko, a Soviet civil-police-force detective investigating the murders, and Irena (Joanna Pacula), a mysterious Siberian beauty who may be involved. There's no tension and not much payoff; it's just a hollow thriller set against dark, claustrophobic landscapes.

GOSPEL ☆☆☆½
1982, USA
The Hawkins Family, The Clarke Sisters, The Mighty Clouds of Joy, James Cleveland, Shirley Caesar. Directed by David Levick and Frederick Ritzenberg. 92 min.

This floor-stomping concert film is the perfect companion piece to *Say Amen, Somebody*. It doesn't try to explore the roots of gospel music; it shows how much power the music has even in its most contemporary show-biz forms. Churning performances are provided by the Hawkins Family, the Clarke Sisters, and the Mighty Clouds of Joy. Beautifully edited by Glenn Farr.

GOTCHA! ☆
1985, USA, PG-13
Anthony Edwards, Linda Fiorentino, Nick Corri, Alex Rocco. Directed by Jeff Kanew. 96 min.

This clichéd and offensive entry in the teen-fantasy market features a freshman virgin (Anthony Edwards) who can't get a date but is a whiz at one of those campus spy games in which teams score points by shooting "enemies" with paint pellets when they least suspect it. Unable to score with any of the resident blond bimbos who are portrayed here as jiggling teases, our hero takes off for Europe on vacation, where he is seduced by a beautiful spy who involves him in smuggling microfilm out of East Germany. In the closing shot, he gets even with one of the aforementioned bimbos by shooting her in the posterior with a paint pellet, an action we are supposed to cheer. From the director of *Revenge of the Nerds*, a masterpiece of sensitivity compared to this misogynistic tripe.

GO TELL THE SPARTANS ☆☆☆
1978, USA, R
Burt Lancaster, Craig Wasson, Jonathan Goldsmith, Marc Singer, Joe Unger, Dennis Howard, David Clennon, Evan Kim. Directed by Ted Post. 114 min.

In this effective parable of the Vietnam War, the strength is mostly in the writing. Set in the early days of American involvement, when the nature of the war was first becoming clear, the story follows a platoon of G.I.'s making a hopeless last stand against thousands of Vietcong (the title draws a parallel with the Battle of Thermopylae). The movie tells us about the Vietnam horror rather than evoking it, but it also grants the men who fought a measure of heroism.

GO WEST ☆☆☆
1940, USA
Marx Brothers, John Carroll, Diana Lewis, Robert Barrat. Directed by Edward Buzzell. 82 min.

The Marx Brothers went thataway into the wide open spaces, and the West was never the same again. There's a hilarious opening in a train station and a wild train ride finale; in between, however, is a tiresomely straight plot about a land deed and two feuding families. The brothers keep things moving and their presence is always welcome, but this is far from their best outing.

GRACE QUIGLEY ☆
1985, USA, PG
Katharine Hepburn, Nick Nolte, Chip Zien, Kit Le Fever, Elizabeth Wilson. Directed by Anthony Harvey. 87 min.

In her forty-fifth film, Katharine Hepburn plays a spunky old lady who enlists the services of a hit man (Nick Nolte) to knock off some of her aged friends, the ones who are just too sick, tired, or annoyed to keep on living. Even for a black comedy, it's a rather sour premise, but it's executed so poorly that you'll be offended more by its ineptitude than by its bad taste. The star has certainly earned the right to pick her own projects, but why she put this one at the top of her list and tried for years to get it made is anybody's guess. A longer version, titled *The Ultimate Solution of Grace Quigley*, was prepared for release by the director but is unavailable on video.

THE GRADUATE ☆☆☆☆
1967, USA
Dustin Hoffman, Anne Bancroft, Katharine Ross, William Daniels, Murray Hamilton. Directed by Mike Nichols. 105 min.

To say that *The Graduate* is one of the funniest, wisest generation-gap films ever made is to shortchange it considerably, although its lasting popularity among teenagers and college students testifies to one of the many durable aspects of its appeal. Mike Nichols's film hits all of its targets with methods ranging from high farce to melancholy comedy, abetted by an irreverent, acidic screenplay from Buck Henry and Calder Willingham. The Graduate is Benjamin Braddock, coming home from college only to be barraged with careerism from his parents, seduced by the infamous Mrs. Robinson, and finally ensnared by her daughter Elaine. But a character who could easily have become an enigmatic, hollow center is made unforgettably vivid by Dustin Hoffman, who, in his first big role, invests Ben with just the right blend of calmness and hysteria. His first encounter with Mrs. Robinson (a deliciously blasé Bancroft) is a pinnacle of comic terror. There are too many other classic scenes to enumerate them all here, but pay close attention to the last shot and its fillip of bittersweet, unexpected ambiguity. The wonderful song score by Paul Simon and Art Garfunkel, which includes "The Sounds of Silence," "Mrs. Robinson," and "Scarborough Fair," is one of those things that, like the film, will never go out of style. Academy Award: Best Director.

GRADUATION DAY ☆½
1981, USA
Christopher George, Patch MacKenzie, E. Danny Murphy, E. J. Peaker, Michael Pataki. Directed by Herb Freed. 96 min.

This shameless grotesquerie is another version of *Friday the 13th*, in which apple-cheeked adolescents are offed by a loony. You're supposed to care whether the killer is one of the teachers, or a spaced-out student, or simply a visiting nut case with a grudge against the acne set. You won't. Low marks for writing, failing grades for direction, and the entire cast should be sent to the principal for their acting.

GRAMBLING'S WHITE TIGER ☆½
1981, USA (TV)
Bruce Jenner, Harry Belafonte, LeVar Burton, Deborah Pratt, Dennis Haysbert. Directed by Georg Stanford Brown. 100 min.

This earnest brotherhood-of-man sports flick concerns a California quarterback who became the only white player on the all-black Grambling College team. Based on the book *My Little Brother's Coming Tomorrow*, the film follows pat TV movie formulas and resolves racial conflicts as quickly as it sets them up. The biggest fumble of all was casting Bruce Jenner, a hopelessly clunky dramatic actor, who delivers his lines with all the intensity he brought to his Tropicana Orange Juice commercials.

GRAND HOTEL ☆☆☆
1932, USA
Greta Garbo, John Barrymore, Joan Crawford, Wallace Beery, Lionel Barrymore, Lewis Stone, Jean Hersholt. Directed by Edmund Goulding. 115 min.

Prime kitsch about a plush Berlin hotel full of fascinating people, this is the movie that spawned all the fine-kettle-of-fish films, from *Stagecoach* to *The Towering Inferno*. What makes it an enduring pleasure is its extraordinary stars. Surprisingly, the best performance comes from the least distinguished performer of the bunch: Joan Crawford. Her wide-eyed young secretary who witnesses a murder is some of the best work she's ever done. By contrast, all the others overact shamefully, including Greta Garbo (miscast) as a world-weary ballerina, John Barrymore as her crooked nobleman lover, Wallace Beery as a sleazy businessman, and Lionel Barrymore as a dying old man. Campy but enjoyable melodrama.

GRAND ILLUSION ☆☆☆☆
1937, France
Jean Gabin, Pierre Fresnay, Erich von Stroheim, Marcel Dalio, Julien Carette, Dita Parlo, Gaston Modot. Directed by Jean Renoir. 111 min.

One of cinema's greatest masterpieces and Jean Renoir's first international success, this profoundly moving antiwar film tells the story of a group of French aviators who are imprisoned in a German castle during World War I. Erich von Stroheim and Pierre Fresnay star as two aristocratic officers—remnants of a passing order—who are divided by nationality but united by class and outlook. Renoir helped write the screenplay, which is based on one of his own short stories, and his pacifist sentiments are made all the more stirring by his refusal to show any battle footage and by his downplaying of the melodramatic aspects of the tale. The majestic cinematography by Claude Renoir (Jean's nephew) and Christian Matras powerfully complements the inspired direction; and von Stroheim, Fresnay, Jean Gabin, and Dita Parlo all give masterful, creative performances. Amusing footnote: von Stroheim had been living in the United States for so long that he had to relearn his native German for this role. (a.k.a.: *La Grande Illusion*)

GRANDMASTER OF SHAOLIN KUNG FU ☆½
1982, Hong Kong
Philip Cheung, King Kong, Burt Chan, Pearl Lin, Gordon Lee, Toshiro Kusugi, Ming Tong. Directed by Godfrey Ho. 88 min.

This occasionally interesting costume drama concerns the legend of Dharma's secret kung-fu book and Chun's (Philip Cheung) struggle to get it to avenge his parents' deaths. No, that's not *the* King Kong listed in the credits. Competently directed martial arts.

GRAND PRIX ☆☆
1966, USA
James Garner, Eva Marie Saint, Yves Montand, Toshiro Mifune, Brian Bedford, Françoise Hardy, Donal O'Brien, Jessica Walter, Adolfo Celi. Directed by John Frankenheimer. 179 min.

What made this an exciting viewing experience in a theater—the spectacle of sensational auto-racing sequences shot in Cinerama—will be reduced to the level of a video game on a TV screen. That leaves the "human drama" about the off-track lives and loves of an international assemblage of drivers on the Grand Prix circuit, which is fairly dull stuff—certainly not enough to sustain your interest for three hours.

GRAND THEFT AUTO ☆☆½
1977, USA, PG
Ron Howard, Nancy Morgan, Marion Ross, Don Steele. Directed by Ron Howard. 89 min.

This follow-up to *Eat My Dust* is another demolition derby from the Roger Corman factory. The main human beings on screen are a pair of newlyweds, but that's not important—lots of cars get sped around and crunched up. Ron Howard, on vacation from "Happy Days" and prior to *Splash*, cowrote the script with his father, Rance; the editor was Joe Dante (*Gremlins*) and the second unit director was Allan Arkush (*Rock and Roll High School*).

GRANDVIEW U.S.A. ☆½
1984, USA, R
Jamie Lee Curtis, C. Thomas Howell, Patrick Swayze, Troy Donohue, Jennifer Jason Leigh, William Windom. Directed by Randal Kleiser. 97 min.

This bittersweet slice-of-life follows the romantic adventures of three "little people" who live normal lives in a small Midwestern town. The city itself doesn't have the palpable presence it should have, but the lumpy, schematized plot is acted with some success by a talented cast headed by Patrick Swayze and Jamie Lee Curtis, who are thrown into a whirlwind of adultery, romance, and financial chicanery. Unfortunately, the attentions of director Randal Kleiser seem most drawn by the teen member of the cast, C. Thomas Howell, who receives the sort of glamor-puss treatment that used to be reserved for ingenues.

THE GRAPES OF WRATH ☆☆☆☆
1940, USA
Henry Fonda, Jane Darwell, John Carradine, Charley Grapewin, Dorris Bowden, Russell Simpson, John Qualen. Directed by John Ford. 129 min.

John Ford's Depression-era masterpiece, based faithfully on John Steinbeck's social commentary classic, chronicles the plight of a family of Oklahoma farmers who are forced from their home and decide to head for California in search of better times. As myths become lies and their quest becomes a series of disappointments, the family must struggle to stay alive and united. Jane Darwell won an Oscar for her compelling performance as the spirited mother of the Joad clan, and Henry Fonda is powerful as her idealistic, ex-convict son. The essential relationship between the people and the land, a central Steinbeck theme, is captured and emphasized by the evocative, expansive, and often brutally realistic cinematography of Gregg Toland, who brings to the landscape a depth of field that complements Steinbeck's depth of meaning. The entire film resounds with imagery, but the final tableau, in particular, echoes with a truly stirring, unforgettable ambiguity.

THE GRASS IS GREENER ☆☆☆
1960, Great Britain
Cary Grant, Deborah Kerr, Robert Mitchum, Jean Simmons, Moray Watson. Directed by Stanley Donen. 104 min.

Who cares if a movie is all window dressing when the dressing is Cary Grant, Deborah Kerr, Robert Mitchum, and Jean Simmons? This smooth prattle about bedroom politics, taken from the play by Hugh and Margaret Williams, resembles second-rate Noel Coward (Coward even wrote one bad song for the film), but it's carried off with panache by the four principals. Kerr plays the wife of an English earl (Grant) who is swept off her feet by Mitchum, playing a rich American tourist. Simmons practically steals the show from all three as the gossipy friend of the estranged couple who sets her sights on Grant. Stanley Donen directed smoothly but without adding anything to the play. The loss of the wide screen on video is not too regrettable here.

THE GRATEFUL DEAD ☆☆
1977, USA
The Grateful Dead. Directed by Jerry Garcia. 131 min.

🎵 Jerry Garcia and his hairy horde relive those fabulous sixties in this ersatz-psychedelic concert film, which Deadheads will adore (they're as prominent in the movie as the group itself) and others will probably find on the dull side. Director Garcia should probably be commended for covering all the basic requirements of the concert-film genre, but he should have used an editor to pare down the running time. Guest shots of Jefferson Airplane, Janis Joplin, and Quicksilver Messenger Service provide relief from the group.

GRAVE OF THE VAMPIRE ☆☆☆
1973, USA, R
William Smith, Michael Pataki, Kitty Vallacher. Directed by John Hayes. 91 min.

In this grim, effective, low-budget horror film the pale gray baby of a girl raped by a vampire grows into a man determined to avenge himself on his undead father. The psychopathological undertones are very creepy indeed.

GRAVEYARD TRAMPS

See *Invasion of the Bee Girls*

GRAY LADY DOWN ☆
1978, USA, PG
Charlton Heston, David Carradine, Stacy Keach, Ned Beatty, Stephen McHattie, Ronny Cox. Directed by David Greene. 111 min.

This film is everything a disaster movie shouldn't be but usually is—drab, sluggish, overlong, underacted, and utterly unsuspenseful. It concerns a sunken submarine and the efforts of those within and without to retrieve it. Nothing about the underwater footage is as tense as, say, *The Poseidon Adventure*, and Charlton Heston may be the only actor who could make the enterprise seem even more boring than it is.

GREASE ☆☆½
1978, USA, PG
John Travolta, Olivia Newton-John, Stockard Channing, Jeff Conaway, Didi Conn, Jamie Donnelly, Dinah Manoff, Barry Pearl, Kelly Ward. Directed by Randal Kleiser. 110 min.

🎵 This noisy, undistinguished pastiche of fifties musicals is worth seeing for John Travolta. Funny-looking as well as beautiful, Travolta is a romantic hero with an ingratiating streak of self-parody. Unfortunately, his energy is released only intermittently here and, among the supporting players, only Stockard Channing gives her performance any heat. Olivia Newton-John, toothy and unspeakably bland, makes you wish that a juvenile delinquent would come along and stomp on her.

GREASED LIGHTNING ☆☆½
1977, USA, PG
Richard Pryor, Beau Bridges, Pam Grier, Cleavon Little, Vincent Gardenia, Richie Havens, Julian Bond, Earl Hindman, Minnie Gentry. Directed by Michael Schultz. 96 min.

Director Michael Schultz's loose-limbed approach seems suited to Richard Pryor, who stars as the first black stock-car driver, Wendell Scott. Schultz retains much of the agreeably bantering style of his previous films (*Car Wash, Cooley High*) and again shows a remarkable knack for depicting the complexities of relationships with a few swift, subtle strokes. Pryor's fine performance is matched by Cleavon Little's, as Pryor's oldest friend, and by Beau Bridges's as Pryor's poor white mechanic.

GREASER'S PALACE ☆☆½
1972, USA
Albert Henderson, Michael Sullivan, Luana Anders, Toni Basil, Stan Gottlieb, Hervé Villechaize, Allan Arbus. Directed by Robert Downey. 91 min.

Robert Downey, who emerged from the ranks of the American independent avant-garde with the underground classic *Putney Swope* in 1970, faded away in the seventies and was last seen directing the abominable *Mad* magazine movie *Up the Academy*. In this weird but ultimately pointless allegory, he's at about a halfway point. A zoot-suited new Messiah lands in the Old West and sets about resurrecting the dead and doing other miraculous things. Like his other features, this has its moments, but it's a hit-and-miss proposition.

GREASE 2 ☆☆
1982, USA, PG
Maxwell Caulfield, Michele Pfeiffer, Adrian Zmed, Lorna Luft, Eve Arden, Sid Caesar, Leif Green, Tab Hunter, Connie Stevens. Directed by Patricia Birch. 114 min.

🎵 *Grease* was, at best, a pleasant, energetic update of an Elvis Presley movie. The same cannot be said of this misbegotten sequel, which harnesses a similar plot, the same choreographer (now also director), a few supporting players, and one song from the original. Patricia Birch may be one of the few female directors working in Hollywood and the plot does involve a female high-school student's insatiable desire for a leather-clad cyclist, but, feminist issues aside, this is an amateurish derivation of a derivation, with forgettable songs and a colorless cast.

GREAT ALLIGATOR ☆
1980, Italy
Barbara Bach, Mel Ferrer, Richard Johnson. Directed by Sergio Martino. 80 min.

This film is a half-baked combination of *Alligator* and *Piranha*—we never knew that John Sayles had such a following overseas. Unfortunately, it's entirely lacking in either the wit or the panache that lifted those films above genre status. The owner of a tropical resort refuses to close down, even though an ancient native god has been reincarnated as an alligator and is feeding on both locals and guests alike. Too bad it didn't get the cast and crew while it was at it.

THE GREAT AMERICAN BROADCAST ☆☆½
1941, USA
Alice Faye, Jack Oakie, John Payne, Cesar Romero, Mary Beth Hughes, The Ink Spots, The Nicholas Brothers, The Wiere Brothers. Directed by Archie Mayo. 92 min.

🎵 The *Tin Pan Alley* trio (Alice Faye, Jack Oakie, and John Payne) were reunited (sans Betty Grable, who went on to bigger and better things) in this spurious but lively history-of-radio musical. None of the new Mack Gordon–Harry Warren songs went on to the Hit Parade, but "I've Got a Bone to Pick with You" and "Albany Bound" are more than serviceable. Highlights include specialty numbers by the Nicholas and Wiere brothers and cameos by Eddie Cantor, Jack Benny, Kate Smith, Rudy Vallee, and Walter Winchell.

THE GREAT BANK HOAX ☆☆½
1977, USA
Richard Basehart, Burgess Meredith, Paul Sand, Ned Beatty, Michael Murphy. Directed by Joseph Jacoby. 89 min.

The cutesy title suggests a cornball caper film, but the film delivers a bit more punch than expected. As a takeoff on the Watergate scandal, the film is funny in a broad way, with ample opportunities for the cast's farceurs to provide lots of drollery. It lacks the acerbic charm of such other Watergate satires as *Nasty Habits*, but the film is energized by its comic actors. (a.k.a.: *The Great Georgia Bank Hoax*)

THE GREAT CARUSO ★★½
1951, USA
Mario Lanza, Ann Blyth, Dorothy Kirsten, Jarmila Novotna, Marina Koshets, Carl Benton Reid. Directed by Richard Thorpe. 109 min.

Most screen biographies of performers are so full of melodramatic clichés that this famous rendering of the life of Enrico Caruso is, by contrast, refreshingly subdued. Unfortunately, under the capable but uninventive direction of Richard Thorpe, it's too subdued, often lapsing into ennui. Swaggering, vociferous Mario Lanza became a major star after playing the Italian opera singer who died at an early age, and it's his singing (with sopranos Dorothy Kirsten and Jarmila Novotna) of passages from *Pagliacci, Martha, Aïda, Rigoletto, Tosca,* and *La Boheme* that makes the film enjoyable and his performance excusable. There's no excuse, however, for Ann Blyth, playing Caruso's patrician wife. She gets to sing, too (a contract stipulation, no doubt), anticipating her performance in that other great film biography, *The Helen Morgan Story*. We recommend that you fast-forward between opera passages.

THE GREAT DAN PATCH ★★½
1949, USA
Dennis O'Keefe, Gail Russell, Ruth Warrick, Charlotte Greenwood. Directed by Joseph M. Newman. 94 min.

This breezy racetrack yarn features two of Hollywood's most appealing B film stars, Dennis O'Keefe and Gail Russell. This horse picture is a bit slow in the stretch, but the cast gives it the whip as they breezily play the roles of owners of the Great Dan Patch, champion trotter. Various vignettes about exciting races and the family's horse-training tribulations are handled with aplomb. Slow moving but recommended for racetrack fans.

THE GREAT DICTATOR ★★★½
1940, USA
Charlie Chaplin, Jack Oakie, Reginald Gardiner, Henry Daniell, Billy Gilbert, Paulette Goddard. Directed by Charles Chaplin. 127 min.

Criticized upon release for depicting the Führer as a harmless nincompoop, Charlie Chaplin's famous sound comedy (his first) stands up today as a timeless satire of totalitarianism. Chaplin plays both Adolf Hitler (called Hynkel here) and the unassuming look-alike barber who comes to take his place. There are memorably funny scenes (the meeting between Hynkel and Jack Oakie's Mussolini figure) as well as moments that attain an almost unearthly beauty (Chaplin's pas de deux with a luminous globe). Chaplin's final harangue about world peace lays a preachy and sentimental egg so big it practically ruins the ending, but what comes before remains fresh and sweet in the memory.

THE GREAT ESCAPE FROM WOMEN'S PRISON ★½
1980, USA
Cheung Pu San, Won Mei Feung, Ko Chueng. Directed by Ding Chung.

This offbeat kung-fister about the Japanese occupation of Manchuria has few fights and loads of degradation. Offensive and graphic scenes of the Korean patriot women being tortured are somewhat offset by the plucky prisoners' humorous tales of killing men. The film is marred by poor sound quality in the dubbed English and a bad job of putting the wide-screen film on the small screen.

THE GREATEST ★★
1977, USA/Great Britain, PG
Muhammad Ali, Ernest Borgnine, John Marley, Lloyd Haynes, Robert Duvall, James Earl Jones, Dina Merrill, Paul Winfield. Directed by Tom Gries. 101 min.

Muhammad Ali is a knockout starring in his own life story, but the movie is a rather shabby attempt to depict the loudmouthed champ as both a plucky underdog and a pillar of Islam. Ali's manager, Muslim leader Herbert Muhammad, had more of a hand in making this film than either the screenwriter, Ring Lardner, Jr., or the feckless director, the late Tom Gries. Much here is sanctimonious (and scarcely believable) Muslim apology, and as biography it's little more than an outline. There are plenty of sloppy directorial errors, too, and the ending implies, oddly enough, that winning, for Ali as for Rocky, merely means going the distance.

THE GREATEST MAN IN THE WORLD ★★½
1980, USA, G
Brad Davis, Carol Kane, William Prince, Reed Birney, John McMartin, Howard da Silva. Directed by Ralph Rosenblum. 51 min.

Jack Smurch (Brad Davis) is an obnoxious, boozing ignoramus who seeks fame as the first aviator to circle the globe. James Thurber's 1931 tale, questioning the phenomenon of media-made celebrity, was filmed for public television's fine "American Short Story" series.

THE GREATEST SHOW ON EARTH ★★★
1952, USA
Betty Hutton, Cornel Wilde, Charlton Heston, James Stewart, Dorothy Lamour, Gloria Grahame, Henry Wilcoxon, Lyle Bettger, Lawrence Tierney, Emmett Kelly. Directed by Cecil B. De Mille. 151 min.

De Mille's penultimate film is hardly the greatest film on earth (or even his own greatest), but it is entertaining in a hokey sort of way. Amid a barrage of grotesque songs, parades, and specialty acts, a story actually emerges. It's a love triangle between the circus owner (Charlton Heston), a high flyer (Betty Hutton), and a new trapeze attraction (Cornel Wilde). More interesting developments occur between a sadistic elephant trainer (Lyle Bettger) and his assistant (Gloria Grahame, in a part originally meant for Lucille Ball, who was pregnant). Jimmy Stewart steals the acting honors playing a clown with a secret (he's never seen without makeup) and those who stay with the whole movie will also get a glimpse of a few guest celebs, including Bob Hope and Bing Crosby. Enjoyable today primarily for its trashiness, *Show* was, astonishingly, awarded the Best Picture Oscar of 1952.

THE GREATEST STORY EVER TOLD ★
1965, USA
Max von Sydow, Charlton Heston, Carroll Baker, Sal Mineo, Claude Rains, Shelley Winters, John Wayne, Ed Wynn. Directed by George Stevens. 141 min.

The longest movie ever made—or at least it seems that way. The films that George Stevens (*Swingtime, Alice Adams*) made in his later career were deliberate and stately works such as *Giant* and *Shane*. By the time he made this one, he was no longer making movies; he was creating events, and you're expected to respond with automatic respect. If you've ever started to doze during a Sunday sermon that threatened to go on until Judgment Day, you'll have some idea of what you're in for. As if the picture-book prettiness and reverential atmosphere weren't bad enough, the director populates the film with movie stars playing famous folks from the Bible. Most jarring of these intrusions is Roman centurion John Wayne, intoning in his unmistakable voice, "This truly was the son of God." A misfortune for all concerned, but the hardy cynic will have plenty to howl over. The film is available in various running times, but sl-l-l-l-low at any length. In fairness to Stevens, it must be noted that he was less than completely satisfied with the film.

GREAT EXPECTATIONS ★★★★
1946, Great Britain
John Mills, Valerie Hobson, Bernard Miles, Francis L. Sullivan, Finlay Currie, Martita Hunt, Anthony Wager, Jean Simmons, Alec Guinness. Directed by David Lean. 118 min.

Few films of Charles Dickens's work have the rich visual style or emotional resonance of this enduring masterpiece by David Lean. Although it inevitably eliminates many of the details and minor characters that filled the novel, this *Great Expectations* hews close to the original narrative and evinces an intelligence and classicism extremely rare in literary adaptations. John Mills is fine as Pip, the impoverished young man who finds both joy and disillusionment at the hands of a wealthy family. But it's the supporting cast that haunts the memory: Martita Hunt as the scary, pathetic Miss Havisham, Jean Simmons as the young, spoiled Estella, and Finlay Currie as Magwitch, the terrifying convict on the moors. The artistry and skill that Lean puts into every scene, coupled with Guy Green's painterly black-and-white cinematography, should impress all but the fiercest Dickens purists.

THE GREAT GABBO ☆☆½
1929, USA
Erich von Stroheim, Betty Compson, Donald Douglas, Margie Kane. Directed by James Cruze. 89 min.

In this incongruous mixture of horror movie and backstage musical, the Great von Stroheim plays the Great Gabbo, a ventriloquist whose affection for a showgirl (Betty Compson) is only slightly more obsessive than his kinship with his dummy. The premise is surefire, and there are some genuinely creepy moments in the scenes where Gabbo talks with his squeaky-voiced dummy across the breakfast table. It is to the film's disadvantage, however, that James Cruze (Compson's offscreen husband), rather than von Stroheim, directed; it's a primitive-looking, slow-moving early talkie with production numbers thrown in that are almost as creepy as the horror scenes. Not up to *Dead of Night*, *Devil Doll* (1964), or even *Magic*.

THE GREAT GATSBY ☆
1974, USA, PG
Robert Redford, Mia Farrow, Karen Black, Bruce Dern, Sam Waterston, Scott Wilson. Directed by Jack Clayton. 144 min.

F. Scott Fitzgerald's works compete with Ernest Hemingway's as the hardest to portray accurately on screen, and 1974's *The Great Gatsby* definitely puts Fitzgerald out in front. Jack Clayton is able to make a pretty shallow film out of an ugly, sad book by glossing over all Gatsby's negative traits—leaving the character almost nonexistent, a fact underscored by Robert Redford's timid performance. Further, the social fabric of the era and of the central characters is virtually demolished in favor of a crude and vapid sentimentality. The good—Bruce Dern; the mediocre—Karen Black; and the bad—Lois Chiles all intermingle with practically nothing to tell them apart. Mia Farrow must be rated the worst of the film's acting horrors; her Daisy seems not only anorexic but only half awake. Yet all the blame does not go to Farrow, who is an excellent actress in better situations. Jack Clayton was able to translate the enigmatic *Turn of the Screw* into the extraordinary *The Innocents*, so his complete failure here must be seen as a forgivable misunderstanding of the work.

GREAT GENERAL ☆
1977, Hong Kong
Meng Fei. 67 min.

In the beginning of the Chia Ching period of the Ming Dynasty, Japanese pirates invade the coastline. This movie has beautiful costumes, but that's all.

THE GREAT GUNDOWN ☆☆
1977, USA, PG
Robert Padilla, Malila St. Duval, Richard Rust, Steven Oliver, David Eastman. Directed by Paul Hunt. 95 min.

Although director/cowriter Paul Hunt worked as a production assistant to Orson Welles, he doesn't seem to have picked up any knowledge except how to bring in a feature on a low budget. This Western shows much more the influence of Sam Peckinpah, with a little Sergio Leone thrown in, as good and bad guys bite the dust in record numbers. The story concerns outlaw Robert Padilla, in trouble with both sides of the law, but it's just a frame on which to hang innumerable shoot-outs. Competent for what it is, though, and Peckinpah fans may want to check it out.

GREAT GUNS ☆½
1941, USA
Stan Laurel, Oliver Hardy, Sheila Ryan, Dick Nelson, Edmund MacDonald. Directed by Monty Banks. 73 min.

Stan Laurel and Oliver Hardy join the Texas cavalry to be with their beloved employer, whom they serve as gardener and chauffeur. Although there are some good gags, this is a far cry from the duo's glory days and is recommended only to those fans who've seen everything else. Alan Ladd has a bit part.

THE GREAT LOCOMOTIVE CHASE ☆☆½
1956, USA
Fess Parker, Jeffrey Hunter, Jeff York, John Lupton, Don Megowan, Claude Jarman, Jr., Harry Carey, Jr., Slim Pickens. Directed by Francis Lyon. 87 min.

This colorful Walt Disney flick is based on an actual Civil War incident that also inspired Buster Keaton's *The General*. Fess Parker, who was also making Davy Crockett pictures for Disney at the time, stars as a Union spy sent to hijack a Confederate supply train. Certainly unobjectionable for the children, but what child of the eighties will want to watch this?

THE GREAT MCGONAGALL ☆½
1975, Great Britain
Spike Milligan, Peter Sellers, Julia Foster, Clifton Jones, Victor Spinetti. Directed by Joseph McGrath. 95 min.

Only hard-core devotees of television's "The Goon Show" are going to be able to wend their way through this impenetrable, very British comedy. Peter Sellers appears only briefly, although the fact that he plays Queen Victoria will make this a must-see for his fans. It's almost all Spike Milligan, who plays an illiterate and unemployed weaver who dreams of becoming England's poet laureate. Milligan is a very strange fellow, both in his writing and in his offscreen life (he was once arrested in a British art gallery for signing his name to some of the works of art on display), and given that predilection and the thicker-than-molasses Scots accent he uses here, this is rough going. Milligan cowrote the screenplay with director Joseph McGrath, who also directed such admirable British comedies as *Thirty Is a Dangerous Age, Cynthia*, and *The Magic Christian*, but after this he seems to have drifted back into British television.

THE GREAT MOUSE DETECTIVE ☆☆☆
1986, USA, G
Animated: Vincent Price, Barrie Ingham, Val Bettin, Susanne Pollatschek, Candy Candido, Alan Young. Directed by John Musker, Ron Clements, Dave Michener, Burny Mattinson. 72 min.

The Disney Studios' adaptation of a popular children's book is inventive, amusing, and even charming, but nothing in it really dazzles or enchants. The story has Basil of Baker Street, a rodent gloss on Sherlock Holmes, out to rescue a toymaker kidnapped by archenemy Professor Ratigan (beautifully dubbed by Vincent Price). The animators slavishly attempt to emulate classic Disney and the film has been made with obvious craftsmanship, but the characters are angular and lack detail. Still, the movie is pleasant and will probably seem like an ice cream sundae to kids raised on the shoddy, faceless hackery of *My Little Pony*, the GoBots, Smurfs, et al.

THE GREAT MUPPET CAPER ☆☆☆
1981, Great Britain, G
Jim Henson's Muppets, Diana Rigg, Charles Grodin, Robert Morley, John Cleese, Peter Ustinov, Jack Warden. Directed by Jim Henson. 95 min.

As a secretary who becomes a top fashion model, single-handedly apprehends a ring of jewel thieves, and finds true happiness with a skinny amphibian (Kermit the Frog), Miss Piggy achieves a magnetic presence; not since Joan Crawford has an actress so zealously and meticulously cultivated her screen image. *The Great Muppet Caper* is, first and foremost, a vehicle for its porky star, though it's also a touching tongue-in-cheek tribute to moviemaking itself.

THE GREAT NORTHFIELD, MINN. RAID ☆☆☆
1972, USA, PG
Cliff Robertson, Robert Duvall, Luke Askew, R. G. Armstrong, Dana Elcar, Elisha Cook, Jr., Royal Dano. Directed by Philip Kaufman. 91 min.

The first major film from director Philip Kaufman (*Invasion of the Body Snatchers, The Right Stuff, The Wanderers*), this is another of the "revisionist" Westerns that were popular at the time. Kaufman wrote the screenplay based on research he did into the lives of outlaws Jesse James and the Younger Brothers while a history major at the University of Chicago. The film follows the gang as they travel from Missouri to Minnesota to rob what advertises itself as the biggest bank in the West. As James, Robert Duvall turns in a quirky, unusual performance.

THE GREAT RACE ☆☆
1965, USA
Jack Lemmon, Tony Curtis, Natalie Wood, Peter Falk, Ross Martin, Vivian Vance, George Macready, Dorothy Provine. Directed by Blake Edwards. 163 min.

This big, uneven, and unconscionably long *hommage* to the slapstick clowns is a fairly witless offering. The plot (screenplay by Arthur Ross) is surefire (it concerns the shenanigans of the contestants in a turn-of-the-century New York–to–Paris car race), yet in Edwards's butterfingered hands there are fewer laughs than in *Cannonball Run* (which covered similar terra firma). It's not all his fault; Tony Curtis and Natalie Wood bring all the inept pseudo-charm they displayed in *Sex and the Single Girl* to their roles here, and Jack Lemmon should be spanked for his hammy, mustached arch-villain.

THE GREAT ST. TRINIAN'S TRAIN ROBBERY ☆½
1966, Great Britain
Frankie Howerd, Reg Varney, Desmond Walter Ellis, Cyril Chamberlain, Dora Bryan. Directed by Frank Launder, Sidney Gilliat. 94 min.

The last sequel to the *The Belles of St. Trinian's*, the series of British comedies based on Ronald Searle's popular comic about a girls' school populated entirely by monstrous, conniving little brats, is the weakest of the bunch. This one is similar to but nowhere near as good as the British classic *The Ladykillers*: a group of thieves robs a train of $7 million dollars and stash the loot in an abandoned mansion. When they return to retrieve it, however, the building has been taken over by St. Trinian's, and they must contend with the school's charges and equally rotten staff in order to dig it up. A good slapstick train race at the end helps to liven things up.

THE GREAT SANTINI ☆☆☆
1979, USA, PG
Robert Duvall, Blythe Danner, Michael O'Keefe, Lisa Jane Persky. Directed by Lewis John Carlino. 115 min.

A touching, impeccably acted drama about a marine colonel (Robert Duvall) whose gung-ho militaristic ethics extend to the way he treats his wife and kids. The tenuous relationship between him and his increasingly rebellious son (Michael O'Keefe) forms the core of an emotional exploration of a man who can't—or won't—accommodate his personality to fit his family. Duvall gives one of his finest performances; he and O'Keefe won well-deserved Oscar nominations for their work. Ideal for home-video viewing, where the film's small-scale charms aren't swallowed up by the big screen. Based on Pat Conroy's novel. (a.k.a.: *The Ace*)

THE GREAT SCOUT AND CATHOUSE THURSDAY ☆☆
1976, USA, PG
Lee Marvin, Oliver Reed, Robert Culp, Elizabeth Ashley, Kay Lenz, Strother Martin, Sylvia Miles, Howard Platt. Directed by Don Taylor. 102 min.

Were this Western comedy in as bad taste as it seems to think it is, it might have been fairly funny. As it is, though, the continual smirking references to sex, V.D., and prostitution never stray past the PG level and quickly become tiresome. Lee Marvin, in a role somehow meant to remind viewers of his Oscar-winning performance in *Cat Ballou*, steals a truckload of jailbound prostitutes in 1908 Colorado to use in a scheme to get money owed him by a former partner, now a rich man. Oliver Reed has played some strange roles in his time, but this one, as a Harvard-educated half-breed Indian who schemes to get even with the white man by infecting the wives with V.D., has to be the strangest.

THE GREAT SKYCOPTER RESCUE ☆
1982, USA
Aldo Ray, William Marshall, Terry Michos, Terri Taylor, Alex Manner, Russell Johnson, Richard C. Adams. Directed by Lawrence D. Foldes. 96 min.

If bad acting, missing plots, and no direction bother you, miss this stinker. On the other hand, if you think that ultralight planes and copters are really cool and disc jockeys are neat people.... Two guys team up to build experimental aircraft and fight bad guys who are trying to take over a town. Yes, that's the Professor from "Gilligan's Island" (Russell Johnson) playing the scientist.

THE GREAT SMOKEY ROADBLOCK ☆☆
1976, USA
Henry Fonda, John Byner, Dub Taylor, Susan Sarandon, Melanie Mayron. Directed by John Leone. 84 min.

This harmless comedy concerns a grandpa trucker who's fallen on hard times. Before the powers-that-be can take back his beloved rig, this Motor Age Cowboy flaunts rules and regulations to attempt one final cross-country assignment. It's *Smokey and the Bandit* whittled down, replete with "land sakes" down-home humor. This would practically be a family film if only the old galoot weren't hauling a cargo of homeless harlots! Meager creativity, but the wheels of adventure keep rolling along smoothly for the non-discriminating.

THE GREAT TEXAS DYNAMITE CHASE ☆☆½
1976, USA, R
Claudia Jennings, Jocelyn Jones, Johnny Crawford, Chris Pennock. Directed by Michael Pressman. 90 min.

This fun exploitation film concerns a pair of hard-lovin', dynamite-totin' women who turn the tables on society, seducing men and robbing banks. Claudia Jennings and Jocelyn Jones have a good, offhanded chemistry that breezes the movie along as the girls meet at a robbery, join up on the road, and become underground celebrities. The action is rousing and sexy.

THE GREAT TRAIN ROBBERY ☆☆½
1979, Great Britain, PG
Sean Connery, Donald Sutherland, Lesley-Anne Down, Alan Webb, Malcolm Terris, Robert Lang. Directed by Michael Crichton. 111 min.

Victorian England has never looked better—plush, burnished, and bronzed—than in this rather tiring caper film, the story of a sophisticated thief (Sean Connery) and his ingenious robbery of a cache of gold bound for the Crimea. It was written and directed by Michael Crichton (from his best-seller), but it really belongs to the people who created its elegant atmosphere, especially its great cinematographer, the late Geoffrey Unsworth (*Cabaret*). You've probably seen everything in this movie before, and it has the pacing of a military parade; the first hour concerns the drawn-out capture of three keys, one after another. We suggest a good, strong cup of coffee while watching. Donald Sutherland gives a jumpy, pop-eyed performance as a lock expert and beautiful Lesley-Anne Down brings a strange mixture of voluptuous eroticism and mindless precision to her role as Connery's willing moll. (a.k.a.: *The First Great Train Robbery*)

THE GREAT WALDO PEPPER ☆☆½
1975, USA, PG
Robert Redford, Bo Svenson, Bo Brundin, Susan Sarandon, Edward Herrmann, Geoffrey Lewis, Margot Kidder. Directed by George Roy Hill. 107 min.

The gallant, silk-scarved pilots who made their reputation as daredevils in the 1920s are the subject of George Roy Hill's visually spectacular, gently emotional salute to the glory days of aviation. Pepper (Robert Redford), a great flyer who just missed combat in World War I, now barnstorms in an aerial circus, hoping to challenge a great German ace (Bo Brundin) to a showdown in the skies. William Goldman's quirky script falls completely apart by its conclusion, but until then Hill succeeds in creating a pleasingly atmospheric tale. Good, unaffected work from the actors, especially Redford and Susan Sarandon.

A GREAT WALL ☆☆
1986, USA
Peter Wang, Sharon Iwai, Kelvin Han Yee, Li Qinqin, Hu Xiaoguang. Directed by Peter Wang. 102 min.

A pleasant, minuscule comedy about a Chinese computer expert (director and cowriter Peter Wang) who journeys with his wife and son to visit relations in Beijing after thirty years in the United States. Switching from quiet details of Chinese life to the sitcom-style cultural assimilation of the Americanized family, Wang makes it seem as if we'd stumbled into an episode of "Father Knows Best." The cast is very ingratiating (though too many of the characters are simply cute), but in the end the movie leaves the heart of its subject frustratingly unexamined. Notable as the first American feature to shoot extensively in Communist China.

THE GREAT WHITE HOPE ☆☆☆½
1970, USA, PG
James Earl Jones, Jane Alexander, Lou Gilbert, Joel Fluellen, Chester Morris, R. G. Armstrong, Hal Holbrook, Moses Gunn, Lloyd Gough, Scatman Crothers. Directed by Martin Ritt. 102 min.

James Earl Jones and Jane Alexander (in her screen debut) recreated their stage roles as heavyweight boxing champion Jack Johnson and his white mistress. The true story (Johnson's name here is changed to "Jack Jefferson"), set in 1910, follows the fighter from his position at the top of the world—the first black boxing champion, flaunting his success in every way he can—through his downfall. The two stars are excellent (each was nominated for an Academy Award), and the rest of the film is up to the standard they set. Director Martin Ritt has compiled a world that is so consistent in its set hierarchy of standards that a boat-rocker like Johnson is doomed from the start. The movie slows down a bit during the section in which the couple flee the country to escape a prison sentence, but it is otherwise well paced and exciting.

THE GREEKS HAD A WORD FOR THEM

See *Three Broadway Girls*

THE GREEK TYCOON ☆
1978, USA, R
Jacqueline Bisset, Anthony Quinn, Raf Vallone, Edward Albert, James Franciscus, Charles Durning. Directed by J. Lee Thompson. 106 min.

This movie was made for people whose primary source of news is the *National Enquirer*. He's a shipping magnate from Greece, she's the glamorous widow of an assassinated American president, and any relation to persons living or dead is purely intentional, not to mention smarmy, speculative, and resolutely uninvolving. What tries to be a jet-set romance set in the international playgrounds of the rich ends up as a sedative. Anthony Quinn and Jacqueline Bisset seem to have been cast because they fit the costumes, and sulk through the film as if they were being forced to stay after school.

THE GREEN BERETS ☆☆
1968, USA
John Wayne, David Janssen, Jim Hutton, Aldo Ray, Raymond St. Jacques, Jack Soo, Bruce Cabot, Patrick Wayne. Directed by John Wayne, Ray Kellogg, Mervyn LeRoy (uncredited). 135 min.

John Wayne's political views concerning the Vietnam War are not kept secret in this film. This was Hollywood's first attempt to deal with the American involvement in the war between North and South Vietnam, but the treatment is consistently simpleminded and reactionary. Even if one buys Wayne's romantic vision, disappointment is inevitable because the film is so poorly made. In a variation on his World War II movie roles, Wayne plays a colonel of the U.S. Special Forces who resists attacks on his camp by the Vietcong (equated with the Indians from Western movies. Wayne's camp is even tagged "Dodge City"!). Emotionally manipulative subplots include one soldier's ill-fated friendship with a Vietnamese orphan and a liberal American reporter's slow understanding of why U.S. involvement is vital. The film ends with a legendary technical blunder in which the sun sets in the east! Even *Rambo* fans will feel cheated.

GREEN DOLPHIN STREET ☆☆½
1947, USA
Lana Turner, Van Heflin, Donna Reed, Richard Hart, Frank Morgan, Edmund Gwenn, Dame May Whitty, Reginald Owen, Gladys Cooper, Linda Christian. Directed by Victor Saville. 141 min.

Two sisters fall in love with the same man, and near-tragedy ensues when he marries the wrong girl (Lana Turner); it seems that a slip of the pen made him write "Marianne" instead of "Marguerite" in a letter of intent to their father. If you're not already groaning, you may enjoy this richly decorated, lavishly produced, but completely harebrained soap opera. The story, set in 1840, jumps clumsily from Turner's shaky marriage in the New Zealand wilderness to the truly depressing life of lonely sibling Donna Reed back home on the British isle of St. Pierre. The leads are uniformly bland, but the great character actors in smaller roles will hold your attention, and a spectacular earthquake is worth the long wait—if only it had been shot in Technicolor. Based on a novel by Elizabeth Goudge that won the first "MGM Writing Contest."

GREEN EYES ☆☆☆
1976, USA (TV)
Paul Winfield, Jonathan Lippe, Victoria Racimo, Rita Tushingham, Claudia Bryar, Royce Wallace. Directed by John Erman. 100 min.

Excellent heart-tugging drama about an ex-G.I. who, fed up with his post-Vietnam malaise, returns to Vietnam to try to locate the son he left behind with the boy's prostitute mother. Paul Winfield gives a flawless performance as the troubled man trying to catch up with his past, and the script elicits our tears without soap-opera machinations.

GREEN ICE ☆
1981, Great Britain, PG
Ryan O'Neal, Anne Archer, Omar Sharif, John Larroquette. Directed by Ernest Day. 115 min.

If you can believe Ryan O'Neal as an electronics engineer, you might even believe some of the rest of this inane caper film, which has him leading a robbery of emeralds being held on the top floor of a Colombian skyscraper. For those of you big on locations, only part of the movie was filmed in Colombia. Rolling Stone Bill Wyman provides the music.

THE GREEN JADE STATUETTE ☆☆
1981, Hong Kong
Chi Kuan-Chun, Meng Fei, Wo Kum, Wang Kuan-Hsing, Kam Ming, Lung Fei, Mau Chou. Directed by Lee Tso Nam.

Chi Kuan-Chu and adorable Meng Fei, two of the finest actors working in martial-arts movies, enliven this yarn about a stolen statuette. Mix in some nice sets, a few plot turns, and a mood-setting soundtrack, and you have an above-average kung-fu film.

GREEN KILLER ☆
1985, Hong Kong
Pak Ying, Yun Tat Wah, Ngai Chui Wah. Directed by Lo Kay. 80 min.

A cop tries to find his buddy's killers in this excruciatingly bad police procedural. The confused story, told in flashback, has something to do with immigrant criminals in Hong Kong turning toy guns into real rods. The production values are very poor, and the fight sequences ordinary. Contains nudity.

GREEN PASTURES ☆☆☆
1936, USA
Rex Ingram, Oscar Polk, Eddie "Rochester" Anderson, Frank Wilson, Abraham Gleaves, the Hall Johnson Choir. Directed by Marc Connelly, William Keighley. 93 min.

Warner Brothers's typically lavish adaptation of this Pulitzer Prize–winning play isn't as racist as it may sound, although it does have more than its share of condescension. It's a retelling of the Old Testament as imagined by a young black child living in the Old South, who pictures the stories in terms of the people and places around him. Rex Ingram makes for an outstanding screen presence as "de Lawd," and if you just bear in mind the era in which this was made, you'll be able to relax and enjoy.

THE GREEN ROOM ☆☆½
1978, France
François Truffaut, Nathalie Baye, Jean Daste, Jean-Pierre Moulin, Jane Lobre, Patrick Maleon. Directed by François Truffaut. 94 min.

Because the Henry James novellas on which François Truffaut's film is based, "The Altar of the Dead" and "The Beast in the Jungle," are so probing and cogent, and because the movie is properly atmospheric, you may feel doubly cheated by its ultimate failure to enlighten. Truffaut himself plays the obsessed hero, a provincial journalist whose dedication to the memory of his dead wife expands to include people he has scarcely met and to shut out attachment to living things, particularly a gentle young woman (Nathalie Baye). James's stories are about missed opportunities, but Truffaut is so wan and secretive an actor that one never senses the humanity that's meant to be going to waste. The whole enterprise feels half-baked: an attempt by Truffaut to mesh his own fevered perceptions with the stately and sober meditations of James.

GREGORY'S GIRL ☆☆☆½
1981, Scotland
Gordon John Sinclair, Dee Hepburn, Alex Norton, Clare Grogan. Directed by Bill Forsyth. 99 min.

In this disarmingly sweet tale of teenage romance from director Bill Forsyth (*Local Hero*), the hero, Gregory (Gordon John Sinclair), is a gentle fellow with a touch of the nerd in him. Smitten by a beautiful classmate (Dee Hepburn), he sets about wooing her in the only way he knows how—innocently, haphazardly, occasionally with surprising charm. The movie is really nothing more than an extended anecdote, but Forsyth captures the bumbling comic poetry of adolescence.

GREMLINS ☆☆☆
1984, USA, PG
Zach Galligan, Phoebe Cates, Hoyt Axton, Polly Holliday, Dick Miller, Judge Reinhold. Directed by Joe Dante. 105 min.

This blockbuster comic horror film bears the producer-plotter influence of Steven Spielberg. Good-natured Bill receives an unusual present from his spacey father: a furry little animal called a mogwai that sings and is just as cute as can be. But its offspring (produced parthenogenetically—just add water) are vicious scaly monsters who wreak havoc in Bill's hometown. Although mean-spirited, the film is not half as mean as it could be, except when the Phoebe Cates character explains why she hates Christmas. Nonetheless, the little creatures (designed by Chris Walas) are a wonder, and the movie's look, a cartoonish grotesque reminiscent of Joe Dante's work in *Twilight Zone—The Movie*, is often just as funny as the action itself. The film's PG rating outraged many moviegoers, who objected to its violence, and the clamor over *Gremlins* and *Indiana Jones* led to the creation of the PG-13 rating in the summer of 1984.

GRENDEL GRENDEL GRENDEL ☆☆☆
1982, Australia
Animated: Peter Ustinov, Keith Michell, Arthur Dignam, Julie McKenna. Directed by Alexander Stitt. 88 min.

Based on John Gardner's novel *Grendel*, a retelling of the legend of Beowulf from the point of view of the monster, this clever animated feature is more accessible for general audiences than the book, substituting a measure of humor for some of Gardner's heavier philosophizing. On the other hand, this isn't merely watered-down and turned into a children's cartoon; it's that rare creature, an animated film that kids *and* their parents can enjoy. Designer/director/screenwriter Alexander Stitt presents Grendel as a rather peaceful mama's boy of a monster, likable even if he does occasionally dine on a local villager. By contrast, Beowulf is a pompous little twerp who is already assured of his position in history.

THE GREY FOX ☆☆☆½
1982, Canada
Richard Farnsworth, Jackie Burroughs, Wayne Robson, Ken Pogue, Timothy Webber. Directed by Philip Borsos. 92 min.

Francis Ford Coppola's Zoetrope Studios presented this small Canadian gem about Bill Miner, a stagecoach robber who was released into the twentieth century after thirty-three years in San Quentin. In his first leading role after appearing in over 300 films as a stuntman, extra, and bit player, Richard Farnsworth gives a subtle, elegant performance as the ruddy-faced gentleman robber. Borsos's direction is understated and sure, and the photography is often stunningly beautiful.

GREYSTOKE—THE LEGEND OF TARZAN, LORD OF THE APES ☆☆☆☆
1984, Great Britain, PG
Christopher Lambert, Ralph Richardson, Andie MacDowell, Ian Holm. Directed by Hugh Hudson. 129 min.

Finally, the cinema has decided to take author Edgar Rice Burroughs's loinclothed hero seriously, and no better director than Hugh Hudson (*Chariots of Fire*) could have mounted this lavish and expensive production. He has effectively turned pulp fiction into celluloid art in telling the story of an English lord raised in the jungle by apes and then found and brought to the civilized, but less rational world. As this "wild child" tries to adjust to the aristocracy, Hudson turns the movie into a sophisticated comedy of manners, but one that still retains its earlier savage atmosphere. A number of dignified performances grace the elegant surroundings, among them French actor Christopher Lambert as the noble savage and Ralph Richardson in his last appearance as the doddering but loving head of the Greystoke estate. Rick Baker's ape guises are some of the best animal costumes yet seen on the screen, adding to an excellent realization of a story that has now become legend. Written by Robert Towne, under the pseudonym of P. H. Vazak.

GRIFFIN AND PHOENIX: A LOVE STORY ☆½
1976, USA (TV)
Peter Falk, Jill Clayburgh, John Lehne, Randy Faustino, Sally Kirkland. Directed by Daryl Duke. 100 min.

Okay, so Peter Falk is this guy who finds out he's gonna die of cancer, so he splits from his family. Meanwhile there's this girl who's really young and pretty and active and she finds out that she's gonna bite it, too, which is so ironic because she's so young and pretty and active, and then they meet, and it's *really* ironic, because both of them have names that are like these old Greek monsters that kept dying and getting reborn and dying again, so they get together and pretend they're kids and steal cars, and it's really just so, so sad that you'll be crying all over the couch, unless you're too busy vomiting on it.

THE GRIM REAPER ½☆
1981, Italy, R
Tisa Farrow, Saverio Vallone, Vanessa Sterger, George Eastman, Zora Kerova, Mark Bodin, Bob Larsen. Directed by Joe D'Amato. 81 min.

While touring the Greek islands by boat, a group of youthful tourists lay over in a picturesque village whose population is conspicuous by its absence. The reason: a disfigured, insane ghoul is loose among them, compelled by his madness to kill and maim. This predictable horror film, liberally laced with blood and gore, fails to rise above the level of the extremely dull. Director Joe D'Amato was previously responsible for the series of Italian *Emmanuelle* rip-offs with Laura Gemser.

GRIP OF THE STRANGLER

See *The Haunted Strangler*

THE GRISSOM GANG ☆☆☆
1971, USA, R
Kim Darby, Scott Wilson, Tony Musante, Irene Dailey, Robert Lansing, Connie Stevens, Joey Faye, Ralph Waite. Directed by Robert Aldrich. 127 min.

Robert Aldrich's film was treated badly upon its initial release, but time has been kind to it. The random violence doesn't seem as shocking now as it once did, and as a whole the film is thus more acceptable. Set in 1931 Kansas, it concerns the kidnapping of a young heiress by a vile group, one of whom she comes to love. Aldrich's films have always had a fascination with the ugly and perverse, and this one occasionally seems to revel in it (though not in the sense of, say, a John Waters film), but it is nevertheless compelling.

GRIZZLY ☆
1976, USA, PG
Christopher George, Richard Jaeckel, Andrew Prine, Joan McCall. Directed by William Girdler. 90 min.

The baddest bear of them all goes wild in a national park. The trailer says he has "the largest jaws on land." Read that as poor special effects, no plot, and a monster that doesn't show his face for the first twenty minutes.

THE GROOVE TUBE ☆☆☆
1974, USA, R
Chevy Chase, Richard Belzer, Ken Shapiro, Buzzy Linhart, Jennifer Wells. Directed by Ken Shapiro. 75 min.

This sometimes tedious but mostly funny lampoon of television in the form of bits of imitation programming was put together by Ken Shapiro, who honed this by taking his video performances to colleges across the country in the late sixties and early seventies. Some of the bits are sophomoric (a kiddie-show clown who reads from *Fanny Hill*), but there are enough surreally weird sequences to make repeated viewing worthwhile. Shapiro went on to the more conventional "Modern Problems."

THE GROUP ☆☆
1966, USA
Candice Bergen, Joan Hackett, Elizabeth Hartman, Shirley Knight, Joanna Pettet, Jessica Walter, James Broderick, Larry Hagman, Hal Holbrook, Carrie Nye, Kathleen Widdoes, Richard Mulligan. Directed by Sidney Lumet. 150 min.

With *The Group*, Sidney Lumet tried and failed to fill George Cukor's shoes as a "woman's director." Lumet may be unsurpassed at creating tough, realistic police dramas, but he was apparently unable to turn Mary McCarthy's best-selling novel about eight Vassar College girls and their postgraduate adventures into either a slick forties-type "woman's picture" or an insightful drama about women's issues. The various plot lines stay relatively close to the book (except that the one lesbian character's story is watered down), but the re-creation of New York in the thirties and forties is glaringly inaccurate. Under the circumstances, even the more talented cast members (Shirley Knight, Jessica Walter, James Broderick, and Hal Holbrook) look amateurish and ill at ease.

GRUESOME TWOSOME ☆
1967, USA
Elizabeth Davis, Chris Martel, Rodney Bedell. Directed by Herschell Gordon Lewis.

Mrs. Pringle and her idiot son prey upon the college girls who room in their old dark house: he murders them and she turns their hair into valuable wigs. A badly made black comedy from the legendary father of splatter films; far less amusing than, say, *Color Me Blood Red* or *2000 Maniacs*.

GUADALCANAL DIARY ☆☆☆
1943, USA
Preston Foster, Lloyd Nolan, William Bendix, Richard Conte, Anthony Quinn, Richard Jaeckel, Roy Roberts, Lionel Stander, Miles Mander. Directed by Lewis Seiler. 90 min.

This film is an up-to-the-minute account of the war in the Pacific, with the usual disparate cast of characters all drawn together as brothers in battle. A good flick of its kind, the plot follows a Marine Corps division from their assignment to the Pacific theater through arduous battle with the Japanese on to victory and withdrawal as replacements arrive. William Bendix steals the show as usual as "Taxi" Potts, a Brooklyner whose civilian occupation was—well, see if you can guess.

THE GUARDIAN ☆½
1984, USA (TV)
Martin Sheen, Louis Gossett, Jr., Arthur Hill, Tandy Cronyn. Directed by David Greene. 102 min.

This bland, preachy movie deals with urban safety and apartment security. Lou Gossett is a creepy, threatening security specialist hired to protect a New York apartment building, and Martin Sheen lounges through his part as a liberal tenant who becomes shocked at Lou's strong-arm methods. The surprise ending is mildly surprising. HBO movies are, if anything, generally duller than network television productions; this one proves the rule.

GUESS WHO'S COMING TO DINNER? ☆☆☆
1967, USA
Katharine Hepburn, Spencer Tracy, Sidney Poitier, Katharine Houghton, Cecil Kellaway, Beah Richards. Directed by Stanley Kramer. 108 min.

This film is to be enjoyed primarily as the final starring vehicle for Spencer Tracy and Katharine Hepburn, though it does not represent their best work. At the time of its release, the liberal good intentions of the director were amply rewarded, but the film seems dated now. Since interracial romance is no longer such a hot potato, the film seems like a rather cozy 1940s romance, especially since all the characters are from the upper financial and professional crusts—Poitier plays a World Health Organization doctor who falls in love with Katharine Houghton while both are vacationing in Hawaii. But if you're in the mood for a fairy tale about love conquering racial stereotyping, then this is for you. Unbelievably, this won Academy Awards for Best Screenplay and for Best Actress, surely two of the graver miscarriages of Oscar justice.

GUEST IN THE HOUSE ☆☆☆½
1944, USA
Anne Baxter, Ralph Bellamy, Aline MacMahon, Ruth Warrick, Jerome Cowan, Marie McDonald, Percy Kilbride, Margaret Hamilton. Directed by John Brahm. 121 min.

This forgotten beauty combines family melodrama with horror film elements. John Brahm's meticulous, expressionistic compositions (complemented by sinuous camerawork by Lee Garmes) turn a middle-class American home inside out in this story of a manipulative young woman who takes over the household in which she is a guest. Anne Baxter is always at her best playing wicked women—she's better and more attractive here than in her more prestigious early films (*Swamp Water*, *The Magnificent Ambersons*). Baxter also gets juicy support from Aline MacMahon, Marie McDonald, Percy Kilbride, and Margaret Hamilton (as a snoopy maid). A happy surprise, highly recommended.

GULAG ☆½
1985, Great Britain (TV)
David Keith, Malcolm McDowell, David Suchet, Warren Clarke, Nancy Paul, Brian Pettifer. Directed by Roger Young. 120 min.

Red-baiting aside, this is a derivative, ugly made-for-cable movie. Produced when the eighties' cold war was in one of its icier moments, *Gulag* describes how an American athlete is framed by the KGB and tossed into one of the prisons in the Soviet gulag system. There, he attempts to escape with two friends. The escape isn't worth two minutes of *The Great Escape*, and the earlier "we have ways of making you talk" interrogation scenes are right out of bad anti-Nazi movies of the forties. The cable-TV brand of titillation comes in the form of flashback sequences of the man's wife—taking a shower! Liberals will have trouble with the political statement; everyone will have trouble with the phony drama.

GULLIVER'S TRAVELS ☆☆½
1977, Great Britain/Belgium
Richard Harris, Catherine Schell, Norman Shelly, Meredith Edwards; voices of Michael Bates, Graham Stark, Julian Glover, Roger Snowden. Directed by Peter Hunt. 80 min.

Once again, the filmmakers have taken Jonathan Swift's very adult and savage political satire and turned it into children's fare by distilling it down to its fantastical elements. As such, it's fine for the kids, a combination of live action and animation, with Richard Harris suitably cast as Gulliver. Next time they decide to remake this, though, we'd like to offer a modest proposal . . .

THE GUMBALL RALLY ☆
1976, USA, PG
Michael Sarrazin, Normann Burton, Gary Busey, Susan Flannery, Steven Keats, J. Pat O'Malley, Raul Julia. Directed by Chuck Bail. 107 min.

This road-race retread has a gang of would-be "wacky" characters participating in an auto derby from New York to California. Idiotic car-crash high jinks alternate with unerotic sex scenes. There are a couple of homages to the great Wile E. Coyote–Roadrunner cartoons. If only *The Gumball Rally* could match them in either humor or sophistication.

GUMSHOE ☆☆½
1972, Great Britain, G
Albert Finney, Billie Whitelaw, Frank Finlay, Janice Rule, Carolyn Seymour, Fulton Mackay. Directed by Stephen Frears. 85 min.

Though its plot is wobbly and its quality fluctuates wildly from one scene to the next, *Gumshoe* gets by on the oddball charm of its premise and the delightful versatility of its leading man. Albert Finney plays a number-caller at a Liverpool bingo hall who decides to cheer himself up by advertising his services as a private detective. What follows is an appropriately convoluted mystery alternately played straight and spoofed. Some of Finney's deadpan dialogue is priceless, and kids old enough to follow the story line should love it.

GUNBUS

See *Sky Bandits*

GUNFIGHT AT THE O.K. CORRAL ☆☆½
1957, USA
Burt Lancaster, Kirk Douglas, Rhonda Fleming, Jo Van Fleet, John Ireland, Earl Holliman, Dennis Hopper, Ted De Corsia, DeForest Kelley, Martin Milner, Lee Van Cleef, Jack Elam. Directed by John Sturges. 122 min.

In this OK Western, Burt Lancaster (as Wyatt Earp) and Kirk Douglas (as Doc Holliday) team up to take on the Clanton Gang in a despairing, sunset-of-the-Old-West movie that finally loses its themes in the machinations of the lengthy narrative—including a final, almost elegiac shoot-out that anticipates Sam Peckinpah. Lancaster and Douglas give appealing performances, but the screenplay, by Leon Uris, never gives them enough latitude to explore the moral dimensions of Western heroism. John Sturges (*The Magnificent Seven*) directed in a rugged but overambitious fashion.

THE GUNFIGHTER ☆☆☆
1950, USA
Gregory Peck, Helen Wescott, Millard Mitchell, Jean Parker, Karl Malden, Ellen Corby, Richard Jaeckel. Directed by Henry King. 84 min.

Twentieth Century–Fox, with its clean, polished photography and sets, was hardly the most appropriate studio to produce this tough B western; yet it is surprisingly (and enjoyably) grubby. Gregory Peck stars as Jimmie Ringo, a notorious ex-gunman who is unable to live down his past while he courts his estranged wife and son. The story (by William Bowers and Andre de Toth) builds to a suspenseful climax while the screenplay (by Bowers and William Sellers) is laced with light and much-welcome humor. Helen Wescott is a bland female lead, but the rest of the cast is just right. This was Academy Award–winning cinematographer Arthur C. Miller's penultimate film.

GUNGA DIN ☆☆☆☆
1939, USA
Cary Grant, Victor McLaglen, Douglas Fairbanks, Jr., Sam Jaffe, Eduardo Ciannelli, Joan Fontaine. Directed by George Stevens. 117 min.

It doesn't matter that director George Stevens's elaboration of Rudyard Kipling's poem centers more around the friendship of three sergeants in British colonial India than around the title character who saves the day—it's still one of the most endearing and entertaining adventure films ever made. Magnificently staged and vividly shot battle scenes between the British Lancers and the

Indian Thugs add color to an already strong story line and top-notch cast. The final tableau is a bit overdramatic, but by that point in the epic you won't care.

GUNG HO!
☆☆
1943, USA
Randolph Scott, Grace MacDonald, Alan Curtis, Noah Beery, Jr., J. Carrol Naish, Robert Mitchum, Milburn Stone. Directed by Ray Enright. 88 min.

The title says it all. Cowboy hero Randolph Scott steps into uniform to play the leader of a specially picked group of marine recruits sent to make a raid on Japanese-held Makin Island. The usual war chauvinism and heroics abound. By the way, this was one of eighteen film appearances made by Robert Mitchum in 1943.

GUNG HO
☆☆
1986, USA, PG-13
Michael Keaton, Gedde Watanabe, George Wendt, Mimi Rogers, Soh Yamamura, Rodney Kageyama, Clint Howard. Directed by Ron Howard. 120 min.

The art of Japanese management is the target of this artlessly hostile comedy about the clash of cultures that erupts when a group of Tokyo auto executives tries to revitalize a failing Tennessee auto plant, only to discover that its amiably slothful workers are unwilling to meet them halfway. Mediating between East and West is a fast-talking, belligerent hustler; Michael Keaton plays the role so crudely and charmlessly that the nominal hero comes off as an Ugly American even on home turf. The makings of a good satire about the blue-collar work force are all in place, but the union boys are so loutish that you'll probably be rooting for Japan. Gedde Watanabe and Soh Yamamura have some very good moments, and *Gung Ho* moves briskly even with a running time of two hours. Later a TV series with Watanabe reprising his role and Scott Bakula taking over Keaton's.

A GUN IN THE HOUSE
☆½
1981, USA (TV)
Sally Struthers, David Ackroyd, Dick Anthony Williams, Joel Bailey, Jeffrey Tambor, Millie Perkins. Directed by Ivan Nagy. 100 min.

A housewife who shot an assailant is dragged over the coals by an ambitious prosecuting attorney. Could this really happen in America? Of course....

THE GUNS AT BATASI
☆☆☆
1964, Great Britain
Richard Attenborough, Jack Hawkins, Flora Robson, John Leyton, Mia Farrow, Graham Stark. Directed by John Guillermin. 102 min.

Hard-core Anglophiles will be the best audience for this examination of the characters and motivations of British soldiers stationed in Africa during the politically uneasy days of the early 1960s, caught between the colonial government and the country's revolutionary forces. Director John Guillermin, an ex-RAF officer, keeps the proceedings morally ambiguous to emphasize the do-as-you're-taught quality of the British military, best exemplified by Richard Attenborough as a by-the-book sergeant. Mia Farrow's debut.

THE GUNS OF AUGUST
☆☆☆½
1964, USA
Narrated by Fritz Weaver. Directed by Nathan Kroll and Miriam Arsham. 99 min.

An excellent compilation of documentary footage on World War I, this is also an interesting technical exercise: producer Nathan Kroll set out to make a film of Barbara Tuchman's Pulitzer Prize–winning book about the beginnings of "the Great War" by using what existing film footage there was of the era. One has to approach it with an inclination to learn something about the subject. The entire project is commendably objective, a lesson in history that shows that warfare was no less foul a human endeavor when it lacked the mechanization that came into prominence during World War II and later.

GUNS OF FURY
☆☆
1945, USA
Duncan Renaldo, Roger Pryor, Martin Garruluga, Cecilia Callejo. Directed by John McCarthy. 64 min.

This is an overloaded title for a rather tame film. Its prior title, *The Cisco Kid Returns*, hits the mark more accurately. (Duncan Renaldo was the fourth Cisco Kid, and this was the first of his three films in the role.) Renaldo scored so well that he repeated the role in the "Cisco Kid" TV series. The plot concerns the Kid's rescue of a youngster from a villainous varmint, and he later has to prove he didn't kidnap the kid himself. Routine gun-toter.

THE GUNS OF NAVARONE
☆☆☆☆
1961, USA
Gregory Peck, David Niven, Anthony Quinn, Anthony Quayle, Irene Papas, James Darren, James Robertson Justice, Stanley Baker, Richard Harris. Directed by J. Lee Thompson. 159 min.

One of the best World War II adventures ever to come out of Hollywood, this is an evening's worth of solid entertainment that never bogs down in overplotting. A handpicked group of Allied officers and guerrilla fighters is sent on a seemingly suicidal mission to destroy an enormous, heavily guarded German fortress in the Aegean Sea. Based on the Alistair MacLean novel, this created a formula that Hollywood is still trying to repeat, seldom with any success. The excellent cast works together well, the action and special effects are believable and impressive, and there's nary a trace of self-parody in the entire thing.

GUS
☆☆½
1976, USA, PG
Edward Asner, Don Knotts, Gary Grimes, Tim Conway, Liberty Williams, Dick Van Patten, Bob Crane, Johnny Unitas, Dick Butkus, Harold Gould, Tom Bosley. Directed by Vincent McEveety. 96 min.

In this standard Walt Disney comedy, a cast of TV regulars plays second banana to an animal, in this case a field goal–kicking mule who moves a last-place pro football team into the NFL championship. Edward Asner utilizes his typical dour attitude as the team's owner, Don Knotts acts nervous, Tim Conway bumbles around, and Dick Butkus does a well-informed impression of a dumb jock. You won't believe it for a minute, but the kids will probably fall for it. From a story by cartoonist Ted Key ("Hazel").

GUYANA—CULT OF THE DAMNED
☆
1980, Mexico/Spain/Panama, R
Stuart Whitman, Gene Barry, John Ireland, Joseph Cotten, Bradford Dillman, Jennifer Ashley, Yvonne DeCarlo. Directed by Rene Cardona, Jr. 90 min.

We can all use a touch of sleaze now and again, but this ghoulish Mexican quickie, directed by *Survive*'s Rene Cardona, Jr., doesn't deliver. The film keeps trying to turn into *Ilsa, She-Wolf of the SS* (there are a couple of garish torture scenes), but it never quite gets there; and who wants tact (of all things!) in an exploitation picture? Stuart Whitman makes a tedious ass of himself, ranting groggily as the Reverend Jim Johnson, who lures his glassy-eyed followers to a Kool-Aid party at a jungle settlement called "Johnsontown." Sensitive souls hardly need to be warned off this movie, but even diehard trash fanciers may find its use of actual news footage of the mass suicide a bit revolting—in the wrong way. Best line: "Yes, it was a big night for death."

GUYANA TRAGEDY: THE STORY OF JIM JONES
★★★½
1980, USA (TV)
Powers Boothe, James Earl Jones, Irene Cara, Veronica Cartwright, Colleen Dewhurst, Brad Dourif, Rosalind Cash, LeVar Burton. Directed by William A. Graham. 206 min.

This is the best of several films made in the wake of the 1978 mass suicides in Guyana. The TV movie sticks close to the facts and has the guts to tell a relentlessly downbeat story with a madman as its protagonist. Powers Boothe won an Emmy for his astounding portrayal of Jim Jones as an evil visionary. He and a superb cast hold your attention all the way. It's a fine, tough film that takes its label of tragedy seriously and resists exploitative depiction even in its final, sickening scenes.

GUYS AND DOLLS
★★★
1955, USA
Marlon Brando, Jean Simmons, Frank Sinatra, Vivian Blaine, Stubby Kaye, Sheldon Leonard, Veda Ann Borg. Directed by Joseph L. Mankiewicz. 150 min.

This is one of the most delightful Broadway musicals ever written, but its flavor and zest are somewhat diminished in this awkward but pleasant adaptation. Somehow, the set stylization seems wrong for this movie version, and the direction is too matter-of-fact to make Damon Runyon's characters engage us fully. But Frank Loesser's tuneful songs are among Broadway's finest, and they keep the film bouncing over some rough spots. The male leads are at cross-purposes with the material. Frank Sinatra wanted Marlon Brando's part and Brando wanted to be in another movie. But Vivian Blaine is superb re-creating her stage triumph as adenoidal Adelaide, and Jean Simmons turns the rather bland role of musical heroine Sarah Brown into one of the most charming leads in movie musicals. Fortunately, the moments of enchantment outweigh the dull patches.

THE GUY WITH SECRET KUNG FU
★★
Hong Kong
Meng Fei, Yuen Nan Hsi, Chen Sha Lih, Yang Fei Sai, Wang Chi, Chang Feng, Tan Siu Lin, Chung Tien. Directed by Joe Law.

This is a better-than-average kung-fu flick, thanks largely to the performance of Meng Fei. Hung Wen-Teng (Meng Fei), Hung Sze-Kuan's son, and Hu A-Piao (Yuen Nan Hsi), Hu Wei-Chiun's son, were fond of helping the weak and fighting against the Chings. In this story they team up to defeat the evil "Dragon Gang," a sorcerer, and his nearly invulnerable "demon."

GYMKATA
★★
1985, USA, PG-13
Kurt Thomas, Tetchie Agbayani. Directed by Robert Clouse. 92 min.

Gymnast Kurt Thomas makes his debut in this martial-arts saga directed by Robert Clouse (*Enter the Dragon*), undisputed American king of the kung-fu flick. Clouse adopts that almost mythical detachment from character that permeates Asian action pictures: the actors assume ritualistic roles in the service of the hero, who undergoes endless tests of his fitness and ability. The director's elliptical handling of the plot and his rigid adherence to action-as-ceremony give *Gymkata* an unusual feel, but the story itself is too dull and silly for direction to make much of a difference.

GYPSY
★★½
1962, USA
Rosalind Russell, Karl Malden, Natalie Wood, Ann Jillian, Faith Dane, Betty Bruce, Roxanne Arlen. Directed by Mervyn LeRoy. 149 min.

Broadway blitzkrieg Ethel Merman lost out to Rosalind Russell in playing her most famous creation, Mama Rose, in the film adaptation of Arthur Laurents's *Gypsy*. Producer-director Mervyn LeRoy opted for Russell because her own brand of mannish energy seemed even more appropriate in the role of Gypsy Rose Lee's monstrous stage mother. LeRoy's other decisions were less judicious: the settings waver uncomfortably between highly stylized theatricalism and gritty film "realism"; a few of the more Broadwayesque Jules Styne–Stephen Sondheim songs ("Mr. Goldstone, I Love You") could have been eliminated, while "Together, Wherever We Go" surely should have been retained; Karl Malden is a washout as Mama Rose's manager-boyfriend; and Natalie Wood, though convincing as a gawky youth, fails in her scenes of "transformation" into a voluptuous and witty burlesque star. The best number remains "You Gotta Have a Gimmick," a quick lesson on the art of stripping, performed by a trio of experts (Faith Dane, Betty Bruce, and Roxanne Arlen). Russell is partially dubbed by Lisa Kirk.

H

HAIL MARY ☆☆½
1985, France/Switzerland, R
Myriem Roussel, Philippe Lacoste, Thierry Rode, Manon Andersen, Malachi Jara Kohan. Directed by Jean-Luc Godard. 78 min.

Jean-Luc Godard's revisionist (to put it mildly) view of the Virgin Birth drew picket lines and fierce denunciations from the Catholic Church during its theatrical release. Its concept must have seemed considerably more controversial on paper than on screen, where it plays like a fragmented Sunday-morning parable with some nonerotic nudity thrown in. Godard's Mary (the beautiful, somber-faced Myriem Roussel) is an unwed gas-station attendant and basketball player; Joseph is her platonic boyfriend, understandably befuddled when she announces her pregnancy; Gabriel is not an angel but a cabbie. Though it begins with Godard's signature cinematic tics, the mood of the film becomes softer and richer as it continues, and the result, though not brilliant, is anything but blasphemous. Also on the Vestron cassette is *The Book of Mary*, Anne Marie Mieville's touching twenty-eight-minute short about a girl's reaction to her parents' separation. Aurore Clement, Bruno Cremer, and Rebecca Hampton star.

HAIR ☆☆☆☆
1979, USA, R
Treat Williams, John Savage, Beverly D'Angelo, Annie Golden, Dorsey Wright, Don Dacus, Cheryl Barnes, Nicholas Ray, Charlotte Rae. Directed by Miloš Forman. 121 min.

John Savage is the young Midwestern innocent who comes to New York City during the sixties to join the army, only to be initiated into the hippie counterculture by long-haired Treat Williams and his exuberant compatriots. Debutante Beverly D'Angelo takes up with the group too, captivated by their contagious spirit. With effective changes made in the script, Miloš Forman's movie version of this intoxicating musical improves upon the original stage play. Through spectacularly unconventional numbers, colorful Central Park scenes, and inspired acting, the fast-paced film represents a past age and tells a timeless, albeit farfetched, story. Twyla Tharp's choreography is dynamite, but the most memorable aspect of the movie is Williams's heroic, charismatic, truly magnetic performance. Songs include "Age of Aquarius," "Let the Sunshine In," and "Good Morning Starshine."

HALF MOON STREET ☆☆
1986, USA, R
Sigourney Weaver, Michael Caine, Patrick Kavanagh, Faith Kent, Ram John Holder, Keith Buckley, Annie Hanson. Directed by Bob Swaim. 90 min.

A misguided adaptation of Paul Theroux's perceptive, icily witty novella *Doctor Slaughter*, this film concerns an emancipated young woman who works in a geopolitical research institute in London by day and a tony escort service by night. As she begins to fall—ever so slightly—for one of her clients, an elderly member of the House of Lords, she becomes a pawn in a political game she knows nothing about. Despite game tries by the two miscast stars (Sigourney Weaver is too old for her role and Michael Caine far too young for his), the dozens of slight alterations and Hollywoodizations that are routine in other film adaptations nearly ruin this one: to tamper with the tone or substance of Theroux's consummately crafted writing is to ruin it.

HALF SHOT AT SUNRISE ☆☆
1930, USA
Bert Wheeler, Robert Woolsey, John Rutherford, George MacFarlane, Roberta Robinson, Dorothy Lee, Edna May Oliver. Directed by Paul Sloane. 75 min.

The comedy team of Bert Wheeler and Robert Woolsey were smashes in the Follies, socko on the vaudeville circuit, and boffo with movie crowds in the thirties; now they are forgotten by audiences everywhere. Their comedy is always simple, bright stuff, and here they play two doughboys posing as officers while chasing girls in Gay Paree. The film will give you a good feel for early comedy, music, and dance films, but don't expect the Marx Brothers—we clocked it, and there was less than a chuckle per quarter hour.

HALLOWEEN ☆☆☆
1978, USA, R
Jamie Lee Curtis, Donald Pleasence, Nancy Loomis, P. J. Soles, Charles Cyphers, Kyle Richards, Tony Farlow. Directed by John Carpenter. 90 min.

Michael Myers, whose violent insanity may well be the result of demonic possession, escapes from the mental home where he has been incarcerated after murdering his older sister and returns home to kill some more. He stalks and slaughters several baby-sitters before the survivor learns once and for all that there is indeed a bogeyman. Consummate craftsmanship makes a conventional genre story into something special; the film goes easy on the bloodletting, but the subjective camera is relentless and highly effective. *Halloween* was one of the most profitable independent features ever made, and launched the damsel-in-distress career of Jamie Lee Curtis.

HALLOWEEN III—SEASON OF THE WITCH ☆
1983, USA, R
Tom Atkins, Stacey Nelkin, Dan O'Herlihy. Directed by Tommy Lee Wallace. 96 min.

This very disappointing second sequel to John Carpenter's skillful *Halloween* abandons the character of Michael Myers in favor of a fanciful tale about a malevolent toymaker whose Halloween masks conceal a deadly secret. The screenplay is weak and illogical, the direction uninspired, and the special effects silly. (Not to be confused with *Season of the Witch*, an alternate release title of George Romero's *Jack's Wife*.)

HALLOWEEN II ☆
1981, USA, R
Jamie Lee Curtis, Donald Pleasence, Charles Cyphers, Lance Guest. Directed by Rick Rosenthal. 92 min.

Michael Myers resumes his bloody doings, picking up only moments after the events that conclude *Halloween*, but much gore can't make up for the fact that Rick Rosenthal isn't the technician that John Carpenter is, and that *Halloween II* is less a sequel than an inferior imitation. Rosenthal publicly blamed Carpenter for tampering with the film (claiming that he was responsible for a number of ultraviolent inserts), but whatever the truth of the charges, it quickly faded from view like the endless *Prom Nights*, *Maniacs*, *Graduation Days*, and *Final Exams* it so resembles. Followed by *Halloween III—Season of the Witch*.

HAMBURGER...THE MOTION PICTURE ☆☆
1986, USA, R
Leigh McCloskey, Dick Butkus. Directed by Mike Marvin. 87 min.

Leigh McCloskey plays a stud so delicious that all girls ogle him with relish in this agreeably banal fast-food farce. A large inheritance is his if he can get a college degree, but he can't handle all the courses. Starved for change, he enrolls in Busterburger Hamburger College and the film becomes a veritable Whopper of spicy sight gags. If the thought of fat people exploding from an overdose of laxatives doesn't strike you as funny, don't put *Hamburger* on your menu. Often funny screenplay by Donald Ross.

HAMLET ☆☆☆☆
1948, Great Britain
Laurence Olivier, Eileen Herlie, Jean Simmons, Basil Sydney, Peter Cushing, Stanley Holloway, and Anthony Quayle. Directed by Laurence Olivier. 153 min.

Sir Laurence Olivier produced, directed, and starred in this magnificent, intelligent, comprehensible, screen interpretation of the Bard's famed tragedy. Fluid camerawork, atmospheric settings, and brilliant performances make it the most satisfying and engrossing film version of any of Shakespeare's plays, including Olivier's own adaptations of *Henry V* and *Richard III*. Some parts from the original play are omitted or altered, but only to better suit the medium. Olivier won a Best Actor Oscar for his insightful portrayal of the resolute Prince of Denmark, and the film was the first non-American production ever to win the Academy Award for Best Picture.

HAMMERSMITH IS OUT ☆☆½
1972, Great Britain, R
Elizabeth Taylor, Richard Burton, Peter Ustinov, Beau Bridges, Leon Ames, Leon Askin, John Schuck, George Raft. Directed by Peter Ustinov. 108 min.

This labored, grotesquely comic update of the Faust myth gave Elizabeth Taylor and Richard Burton their tenth opportunity to star together, and despite reasonably good performances from both, it's ultimately disappointing. Burton plays asylum inmate Hammersmith, who gains his freedom by promising local dolt Billy Breedlove (Beau Bridges) eternal power. Taylor plays slatternly waitress Jimmie Jean Jackson, the apple of Billy's eye. Peter Ustinov's direction is fine, but the film's look is relentlessly ugly in the "mod" way of 1972.

HAMMETT ☆☆½
1983, USA, R
Frederic Forrest, Marilu Henner, Peter Boyle, Elisha Cook, Jr., Sylvia Sidney, Samuel Fuller, R. G. Armstrong, Roy Kinnear, Royal Dano. Directed by Wim Wenders. 93 min.

The laborious two-year struggle to get *Hammett* released after disastrous preview screenings is not reflected in the film itself. *Hammett* is no disgrace, merely a somewhat pointless exercise in style by director Wim Wenders. Conceived as an homage to Dashiell Hammett, the film follows the author himself on a fictitious search for a missing Chinese girl in 1920s San Francisco. The period decor is exemplary, and Wenders's mise en scène reflects a very high-level skill. Further, Frederic Forrest, while not ideally cast—could this man have written *The Maltese Falcon?*—gives a persuasive, sympathetic account of an underwritten role. Marilu Henner is likewise attractive—a mixture of Gail Patrick and Myrna Loy—as his sometimes girlfriend. Wenders has cast old-timers like Elisha Cook, Jr., shrewdly, and the film is not dull. It just doesn't do more than jell into a coherent whole; there is no sense of building tension or burgeoning love, and even the humor seems to be seen behind a screen. As *Hammett* drifts to its conclusion, one is left dissatisfied without ever being bored.

THE HAND ☆☆☆½
1981, USA, R
Michael Caine, Andrea Marcovicci, Annie McEnroe, Bruce McGill. Directed by Oliver Stone. 104 min.

This impressive but somewhat silly psychological thriller is a noteworthy successor to *The Beast with Five Fingers* and *The Hands of Orlac*. A cartoonist has his hand severed in an automobile accident, and he finds that he can't adjust to the loss. Soon, his marriage and life begin to disintegrate with the reappearance of the bloody hand, which has a nasty habit of murdering people that the cartoonist doesn't like. But does the crawling appendage really exist, or is it just in the character's mind? A very good performance by Michael Caine and effectively claustrophobic direction from Oliver Stone make this into an involving shocker, marred by a stupid conclusion. The "hand" effects were done by Carlo Rambaldi, who later went on to create *E.T.*

HANGAR 18 ☆
1980, USA, PG
Darren McGavin, Robert Vaughn, Gary Collins, James Hampton, Joseph Campanella, William Schallert, Cliff Osmond. Directed by James L. Conway. 93 min.

This dull, witless movie about a White House conspiracy to suppress information concerning a UFO has no flair whatsoever for production values: it uses little plastic models for the spaceships and, it would seem, little plastic people for the actors (including such cellophane talents as Gary Collins and Darren McGavin). "Based on reported fact," *Hangar 18* offers the startling revelation that man is descended from a race of superintelligent beings who, millions of years ago, visited earth and mated with the apes. The movie itself is the imbecilic offspring of *Close Encounters* and *Capricorn One*. Of no redeeming value, but not tasteless or amusing enough to qualify as kitsch.

HANG 'EM HIGH ☆☆½
1968, USA
Clint Eastwood, Inger Stevens, Ed Begley, Pat Hingle, Arlene Golonka, James MacArthur, Ben Johnson, Bruce Dern, Alan Hale, Jr., Dennis Hopper. Directed by Ted Post. 114 min.

The American film industry just doesn't have the off-the-wall supporting characters and deadpan cynicism of the real made-in-Italy spaghetti Westerns. On the other hand, Clint Eastwood *is* Clint Eastwood, and this film is worth a look. Here he plays a tough hombre who's tracking down the nine men who didn't quite hang him. With pedestrian direction by Ted Post and music by Ennio Morricone, Eastwood delivers lines when he could be throwing lead. As Tuco said in *The Good, the Bad and the Ugly*, "If you have to shoot, shoot. Don't talk."

HANKY PANKY ☆½
1982, USA, PG
Gene Wilder, Gilda Radner, Kathleen Quinlan, Richard Widmark, Robert Prosky, Josef Sommer. Directed by Sidney Poitier. 110 min.

This heavy-handed chase comedy leans too hard on Gene Wilder's charm as an architect wrongly sought for a crime and miscasts Gilda Radner as a romantic interest. A promising beginning and some potentially clever situations give way to substandard comic shenanigans, and it's a shame to see gifted-comic-cutup Radner ill-used yet again.

HANNAH AND HER SISTERS ☆☆☆☆
1986, USA, PG-13
Woody Allen, Michael Caine, Mia Farrow, Barbara Hershey, Dianne Wiest, Carrie Fisher, Max von Sydow, Daniel Stern, Maureen O'Sullivan, Lloyd Nolan, Tony Roberts, Sam Waterston, Julie Kavner, Joanna Gleason. Directed by Woody Allen. 106 min.

In this exquisite, beautifully orchestrated Manhattan ensemble comedy, Woody Allen's comic and serious impulses have finally coalesced into a single embracing vision. For the first time, he views the other characters with the same love and understanding he's always lavished on his own obsessions. The film is about sisters Hannah, Lee, and Holly (Mia Farrow, Barbara Hershey, and Dianne

Wiest), and their husbands, lovers, children, parents, friends. Hannah's husband (Michael Caine) has become fatally infatuated with beautiful, unformed Lee, while Holly, a frazzled wreck, is desperately trying to find direction in life. On the fringes of the movie wanders Woody himself as Hannah's ex-husband, a hypochondriac whose brush with death sends him on a crazed quest to discover the value of life. It's a discovery Allen already seems to have made as a writer and director; every scene is funny, true-to-life, and enriching in a way his films have seldom been, or tried to be, before. It's also acted with beautiful self-effacement by a large cast composed of some familiar faces and some that should be. Yale President Benno Schmidt, Jr., plays a doctor advising Woody his sperm count is too low to conceive a child. It's Woody's only failure in this wondrous masterpiece! Winner of three Academy Awards: Best Original Screenplay, Best Supporting Actor (Caine), and Best Supporting Actress (Wiest).

HANNA K. ☆½
1983, USA/France, R
Jill Clayburgh, Jean Yanne, Gabriel Byrne, David Clennon, Mohammed Bakri, Oded Kotler. Directed by Costa-Gavras. 108 min.

This misconceived political melodrama has a flagrantly bad performance by Jill Clayburgh in the perhaps unplayable central role. Clayburgh is a Jewish lawyer from America now living in Israel, assigned to defend a Palestinian trying to reclaim his homeland. This causes problems with the other men in her life, namely her Israeli lover (and courtroom rival) and her Catholic husband. The poor script has ideological tentpoles where there should be characters, and Costa-Gavras, usually right at home with political material (Z, Missing), does uncertain work here.

HANOVER STREET ☆
1979, Great Britain, PG
Harrison Ford, Lesley-Anne Down, Christopher Plummer, Alec McCowen, Richard Masur, Michael Sacks, Max Wall. Directed by Peter Hyams. 109 min.

Peter Hyams's numbingly awful wallow in old-guard Hollywood bathos is the biggest unintentional laugh-getter since Ross Hunter's *Lost Horizon*. It's a straight-faced attempt at reviving the World War II star-crossed romance (American flight lieutenant falls for married British nurse), but it's so full of ludicrous errors that it seems a hilarious send-up of the films it sets out to lionize. Hyams gussies up his production with a sumptuous forties ambience, but he proves as lame a stylist as he is a writer. As the love-torn nurse, Lesley-Anne Down is classy enough to transcend her tacky surroundings. But Harrison Ford is charmless and sullen as the romantic fly-boy, and Christopher Plummer debases himself once again as Down's boorish husband.

HANS CHRISTIAN ANDERSEN ☆☆
1952, USA
Danny Kaye, Farley Granger, Jeanmaire, Joey Walsh, Philip Tonge. Directed by Charles Vidor. 112 min.

Danny Kaye does his usual eager-beaver bit in this sweet, mild, rather dorky biography of the traveling storyteller who falls in love with a beautiful ballerina. The highly hummable score was written by Frank Loesser, though even kids may find the story a bit on the gooey side. Nonetheless, the presentation strives for a storybook quality with charm and magic found in its humor, song, and dance. A high point to watch for is Kaye singing "The Ugly Duckling" to Peter Votrian, a perky schoolboy.

THE HAPPIEST MILLIONAIRE ☆☆½
1967, USA
Fred MacMurray, Tommy Steele, Greer Garson, Geraldine Page, Gladys Cooper, Leslie Ann Warren, John Davidson. Directed by Norman Tokar. 144 min.

Several different running times are available, so you may be seeing a different version on TV, on video, and at a revival house. This is a high-spirited, fairly enjoyable musical romp, one that's blessedly written directly for the screen. One wishes that this film were more infectious and less predictable, but this zany tale about the goings-on in the mansion of a free-spirited Philadelphia millionaire has its moments. Of course, if the songs were more memorable and the dances more exciting, this might have been first-rate instead of just a mild diversion. The top-notch cast brings exuberance to the film, but the material needed more kick than the Disney studio was willing to provide. (Note: the TV version is 118 minutes long.)

HAPPILY EVER AFTER ☆☆
1986, Brazil
Regina Duarte, Paulo Castelli, Pataricio Bisso, Flavio Galvao, Felipe Martins. Directed by Bruno Barreto. 92 min.

This murky modern fairy tale of sexual adventure comes from the director of the much more enjoyable *Dona Flor and Her Two Husbands*. A bourgeois, bored housewife has a chance run-in with an opportunistic bisexual drug-dealing hustler; before she knows it, she's off for a weekend of cocaine and carnality, with the hustler's maternal drag-queen friend in tow. Bruno Barreto makes the story and the characters more endearing than one might think possible, but his plotting is witless and the ending renders the film almost pointless.

HAPPY BIRTHDAY TO ME ☆☆
1981, Canada, R
Melissa Sue Anderson, Glenn Ford, Lawrence Dane, Sharon Acker, Tracey Bregman, Lisa Langlois. Directed by J. Lee Thompson. 120 min.

The poster for this horror movie promises "six of the most bizarre murders you will ever see," and two of them—especially one involving a succulent shish-kebab dinner—truly are high-class homicides. Unfortunately, the film lacks the satirical invention to turn its characters—an elite clique of students at a fancy prep school—into a bunch of sniveling snobs. Instead, they're the same damned Archie Comics adolescents who've been bumped off in every fright flick since *Jaws 2*.

THE HAPPY HOOKER ☆
1975, USA, R
Lynn Redgrave, Jean Pierre Aumont, Nicholas Powell, Tom Poston, Lovelady Powell. Directed by Nicholas Sgarro. 96 min.

Why Cannon, a good sleaze outfit if ever there was one, decided to make such a prissy, antiseptic version of Xaviera Hollander's exploitative autobiography will forever remain a mystery. But they did, and it's a dull, dressed-up version of some pretty naked material. Best scene—Lynn Redgrave's striptease for Tom Poston (playing a businessman roué).

THE HAPPY HOOKER GOES TO HOLLYWOOD ☆
1980, USA, R
Martine Beswicke, Adam West, Phil Silvers, Richard Deacon, Edie Adams, Chris Lemmon. Directed by Alan Roberts. 85 min.

Martine Beswicke (who vamped James Bond in *Thunderball*), following in the distinguished footsteps of Lynn Redgrave and Joey Heatherton, plays Xaviera Hollander. No sex to speak of, and no particularly interesting things to say about Hollywood; in fact, the highlight of this drive-in special is watching Adam West (Batman) in drag. You can imagine what the *dull* parts are like.

THE HAPPY HOOKER GOES TO WASHINGTON ☆
1977, USA
Joey Heatherton, George Hamilton, Ray Walston, Jack Carter, Larry Storch, Billy Barty. Directed by William A. Levy. 86 min.

Don't they ever get tired of this plot? The grumpy wet blankets who are trying to spoil our heroes' innocent fun turn out to be venal perverts, and our heroes just have to expose them.

This time, a Senate committee is out to get our heroine, Xaviera (Joey Heatherton), but she uses call girls to expose their warped sexual fantasies. A great low-rent supporting cast is wasted, and, no, there are no real sex scenes.

HAPPY MOTHER'S DAY, LOVE, GEORGE

See *Run, Stranger, Run*

HAPPY NEW YEAR ☆☆☆½
1979, Hungary
Istvan Bujtor, Erika Bodnar, Andras Balint, Judit Meszieri. Directed by Rezso Szoreny. 84 min.

This comparatively light but uncommonly convincing story concerns three chemists (two men and one woman) who have worked diligently together for months and decide to go out on New Year's Eve for a little relaxation. They are joined by a stranger, one man's wife, and two other women friends and, as the night wears on and the pace of the evening becomes more Dionysian, a sort of collegiate truth-game they're playing gets out of hand and repressed feelings and desires come disruptively to the surface. Within the single day of the classical convention, this bright film manages some very telling observations about life without the lugubriousness that often hovers an inch behind them. This is a deft, original, and memorable film. (Hungarian title: *Buek*)

HARBOR CITY

See *Port of Call*

HARDBODIES ☆
1984, USA, R
Grant Cramer, Teal Roberts, Gary Wood, Cindy Silver. Directed by Mark Griffiths. 88 min.

This film tells the story of three middle-aged men searching for "hardbodies" on the California beaches. The leers-and-tears drama not only insists that these pathetic dolts are being ridiculed by their young-harlot girlfriends, but also invites the viewer to voyeuristically enjoy the few dozen bared breasts. In other words, just like the dirty old men in the film, we can dispassionately use these young bodies while being consoled that they aren't worth the trouble of involvement. Such double-dealing is hardly a "bigger and better deal." Followed by a sequel, *Hardbodies 2*, in 1986.

HARDBODIES 2 ½☆
1986, USA, R
Brad Zutaut, Brenda Bakke, Fabiana Udenio, James Karen, Alba Francesca, Roberta Collins. Directed by Mark Griffiths. 88 min.

This barely related sequel to a minor sexploitation hit manages to be much, much worse than its predecessor (and that's really saying something). Director Mark Griffiths and starlet Roberta Collins are the only holdovers from the original in this new story line about a Hollywood movie crew arriving in the Greek isles to shoot a film. They soon discover more local color than they had bargained for. The same old tired titillation routines and the less-than-professional quality of the filmmaking put this near the bottom of an already undistinguished genre.

HARD CHOICES ☆☆☆
1984, USA
Margaret Klenck, Gary McCleery, John Seitz, John Sayles, John Snyder, Liane Curtis, J. T. Walsh, Spalding Gray. Directed by Rick King. 90 min.

For its first half, Rick King's handsomely shot low-budget feature is an earnest drama about a dedicated social worker (Margaret Klenck) trying to protect the rights of a frightened juvenile offender (Gary McCleery) in a brutal adult prison. Then the film takes an astonishing turn into both the sublime and the ridiculous as she busts him out of jail and they head down to the Florida Keys for an idyll of illicit and very steamy passion. King manages to hold your attention simply by confounding your expectations, and the film, made on a low (half-million-dollar) budget, is most engrossing when least plausible. Soap-opera veteran Klenck and newcomer McCleery give powerhouse performances that deserve to be discovered, and John Sayles and performance artist Spalding Gray provide entertaining cameos. Based on the article "The Lawyer Vanishes," which appeared in *Rolling Stone* magazine in 1983.

HARDCORE ☆☆
1979, USA
George C. Scott, Peter Boyle, Season Hubley. Directed by Paul Schrader. 108 min.

Paul Schrader, compelled by obsessive devotion and lack of imagination, continues to remake John Ford's classic *The Searchers*. The pathological search for the sexually corrupted young woman may have clicked for Martin Scorsese in *Taxi Driver*, but under Schrader's heavy-handed direction, it seems simpleminded and flat. George C. Scott is unconvincing as the prude rube from Grand Rapids adrift in the Los Angeles sewer, but Peter Boyle makes a nice corrupt private detective.

HARD COUNTRY ☆☆½
1981, USA, PG
Jan-Michael Vincent, Kim Basinger, Michael Parks, Tanya Tucker, Gailard Sartain. Directed by David Greene. 104 min.

This film is a palatable but undistinguished attempt to cash in on *Urban Cowboy*. The attractive lead players are a plus, as are the country-and-western trimmings that punch up the project's conventionality. Jan-Michael Vincent plays a ne'er-do-well with a surfeit of charm: he's more interested in fooling around than in settling down. Sultry Kim Basinger gives him a run for his money in this colorful but undistinguished drama.

A HARD DAY'S NIGHT ☆☆☆½
1964, Great Britain
John Lennon, Paul McCartney, George Harrison, Ringo Starr, Wilfrid Brambell, Victor Spinetti, Anna Quayle. Directed by Richard Lester. 85 min.

Richard Lester's stylishly mod romp features the Fab Four in their first and greatest movie. This funny and exhilarating film captures the lads from Liverpool in their early and endearing innocence. We see a day in the life of the group as the Beatles, all in their early twenties, try to come to terms with their spectacular success. Wilfrid Brambell is charming and unforgettably funny as Paul's crochety grandfather. The Beatles sing about a dozen tunes, all of them passionately performed and imaginatively photographed. And even those who don't dig all that "yeah, yeah, yeahing" will be uplifted by the film's wit, intelligence, and good-natured irreverence.

HARD DRIVER

See *The Last American Hero*

THE HARDER THEY COME ☆☆☆½
1973, Jamaica, R
Jimmy Cliff, Carl Bradshaw, Janet Bartley, Ras Daniel Hartman, Basil Keane, Bobby Charlton. Directed by Perry Henzell. 109 min.

The original reggae classic still rocks as Jimmy Cliff leads his one-man rebellion against the exploitation of the Jamaican music mafia. The first native Jamaican feature, the movie has an absorbing sense of place and a fierce anticolonial bent, and places the hero's fight in the larger political context of freedom from oppression. Cliff is the genuine article, a great charismatic presence. The movie is in Jamaican-English patois and subtitled, and the pulsating soundtrack features reggae superstars Toots and the Maytals and Cliff singing such hits as "Pressure Drop," "Many Rivers to Cross," and the great "You Can Get It If You Really Want."

THE HARDER THEY FALL ★★★
1956, USA
Humphrey Bogart, Rod Steiger, Jan Sterling, Mike Lane, Max Baer, Edward Andrews, Harold J. Stone. Directed by Mark Robson. 109 min.

Humphrey Bogart's last film was this boxing movie from the man who gave us *Champion*. This is a darker but more reflective film (based on a novel by Budd Schulberg) about the managers and promoters who exploit their fighters and create ringside hype. Bogart wearily but masterfully plays a cynical reporter who breaks from the numbers game in order to expose the corruption therein. Rod Steiger hams as usual as a shrewd but shifty promoter, and Max Baer is much too old to play a fighter, but Bogart and the rest of the company fit perfectly into the milieu. Not the best film of its type, but perhaps more honest than the rest.

HARDHAT AND LEGS ★★½
1980, USA (TV)
Kevin Dobson, Sharon Gless, Ray Sierra, Charlie Aiken. Directed by Lee Philips. 80 min.

The awful title and not-much-better premise make a surprisingly enjoyable TV movie, thanks to the performances of the two leads and a predictably snappy script by, of all people, Ruth Gordon and Garson Kanin. Kevin Dobson plays a construction worker who meets and falls in love with an attractive female psychiatrist (Sharon Gless). Problems arise in the form of his habitual gambling.

HARDLY WORKING ★★
1981, USA, PG
Jerry Lewis, Susan Oliver, Harold J. Stone, Deanna Lund, Buddy Lester. Directed by Jerry Lewis. 90 min.

This film hardly works. Jerry Lewis goes straight for the heart as a clown who tries for the nine-to-five. This isn't classic Lewis; however, his series of foul-ups at various jobs has scattered chuckles. What is hard to take is Lewis's pandering—of course most of the other characters love him, but do we really need all of those shots of his girlfriend mooning at him while he makes an ass of himself? The film is also stuffed with product plugs—Jerry must have raised money for the film by promising to include shots of everything from Dunkin' Donuts to Goodyear Tires; the movie actually has a commercial for Budweiser featuring the Clydesdales.

HARD TIMES ★★★
1975, USA, PG
Charles Bronson, James Coburn, Jill Ireland, Strother Martin, Maggie Blye, Michael McGuire, Robert Tessier. Directed by Walter Hill. 97 min.

For this Depression-era action film about a wanderer who earns his living by winning barefisted, illegally staged boxing bouts, Charles Bronson had the good fortune to team up with the only director whose sensibilities may be tougher than his own—Walter Hill (*The Warriors, 48 HRS*). The result was this better-than-average star vehicle, with impressively seedy atmosphere and taut drama to balance the bloody fight sequences. In his first film as director (he also cowrote the script), Hill handles Bronson with a canniness that others have since missed, simply by giving the Great Stone Face almost no dialogue. Now, if someone would only do the same for Chuck Norris . . .

HARD TO HOLD ★½
1984, USA, PG
Rick Springfield, Janet Eilber, Patti Hansen, Albert Salmi. Directed by Larry Peerce. 93 min.

Rick Springfield—Australian pop singer turned American soap-opera star turned American pop singer—makes his bid for big-screen stardom with a very bland story about a pop singer who's in love with a woman who thinks his life-style is more than a little ridiculous. Springfield is attractive enough but defeated by a dreary screenplay and genuinely horrible dialogue. Not much fun.

HARD TRAVELING ★★
1986, USA, PG
J. E. Freeman, Ellen Geer, Barry Corbin, James Gammon, Jim Haynie. Directed by Dan Bessie. 99 min.

This somber mood piece set at the tail end of the Depression is overearnest and underdramatic. The source material is the semiautobiographical novel *Bread and a Stone*, by Alvah Bessie, once a jailed member of the Hollywood Ten, and the screenplay has been written and directed by his son Dan; though clearly a labor of love, it could have used more art. The story centers around a poor drifter who finds happiness with a farm woman and then goes on trial for an accidental murder committed during a well-intentioned robbery. It's a populist quasi-tragedy with the unfortunate simplicity of a moral fable.

THE HARD WAY ★★½
1942, USA
Ida Lupino, Dennis Morgan, Joan Leslie, Jack Carson, Gladys George. Directed by Vincent Sherman. 109 min.

This chronicle of a woman (Ida Lupino) who pushes her sister (Joan Leslie) to Broadway stardom is well made but needs to be trashier to be effective. Lupino scores as the determined older sibling and her machinations are enjoyable to watch, but coming eight years before *All about Eve*, the film's preachy morality destroys the fun well before the inevitable conclusion. While Lupino naturally steals the show, Jack Carson nearly matches her with a beautifully subdued performance as a third-rate vaudevillian who falls for Leslie. Dennis Morgan is also better than usual playing Carson's handsome partner. Only Joan Leslie strikes a bland note as the supposedly innocent but talented young lady causing all the fuss. Entertaining, but not the film it could have been.

A HARD WAY TO DIE ★★
1979, Hong Kong
Billy Chong, Carl R. Scott, Louis Neglia, Hau Chin-Sing, Joseph Jennings, Ma Shung-Tak, Liang Siao-Sung, Kim Bill. Directed by Hwa I-Hung.

Billy Chong fans will be delighted to see him in top form. His charismatic acting and powerfully controlled fighting are talent and skill enough for three people. As a bonus, he's capably aided by Carl R. Scott—they're fighting an Arizona gang while searching for Chong's grandfather.

HAROLD AND MAUDE ★½
1972, USA, PG
Ruth Gordon, Bud Cort, Vivian Pickles, Cyril Cusack. Directed by Hal Ashby. 90 min.

Hal Ashby's cult classic is a cutesy black comedy about the romance between a teenage rich boy (Bud Cort) who stages jokey fake suicides and an eighty-year-old woman (Ruth Gordon) who spouts moronic homilies about wildflowers and the life force. Despite patches of amusingly bloody slapstick, it remains an insufferable piece of sixties free-spirit sentimentality. The film is a popular double feature at revival houses with the equally saccharine *King of Hearts*. Good song score by Cat Stevens.

HARPER ★★★
1966, USA
Paul Newman, Lauren Bacall, Julie Harris, Arthur Hill, Janet Leigh, Pamela Tiffin, Robert Wagner, Robert Webber, Shelley Winters, Harold Gould, Strother Martin. Directed by Jack Smight. 121 min.

William Goldman's exciting, witty screenplay adaptation of Ross MacDonald's novel *The Moving Target* gave Paul Newman his first opportunity to play sardonic California private eye Lew Archer (here renamed Harper). The complex plot has him hunting down the missing husband of unloving Lauren Bacall; along the way, he must sort through the collection of oddballs who knew the husband. The dialogue is crisp, Newman is as amiable as ever, and the ripe performances of the large supporting cast will tide you over the stretches when director Jack Smight seems to be asleep at the wheel. Newman returned to the role in 1975 for the much less successful *Drowning Pool*.

HARPER VALLEY P.T.A. ☆½
1978, USA, PG
Barbara Eden, Ronny Cox, Nannette Fabray, Susan Swift, Louis Nye, Pat Paulsen, John Fiedler. Directed by Richard Bennett. 93 min.

In the grand tradition of *Convoy*, *Ode to Billy Joe*, *The Night the Lights Went Out in Georgia*, *Girls Just Want to Have Fun*, ad nauseam, here is another movie based on a hit song. Barbara Eden is the freethinkin' mom who socks it to the assorted hypocrites of the local school board by exposing their various vices in public. The film was later made into a television series, from which this can be distinguished only by its lack of a laugh track.

HARRAD SUMMER

See *Student Union*

HARRY AND SON ☆☆
1984, USA, PG
Paul Newman, Robby Benson, Ellen Barkin, Joanne Woodward, Ossie Davis, Judith Ivey. Directed by Paul Newman. 118 min.

Paul Newman directed and starred in this story of a Miami construction worker and his aspiring-novelist son. The TV-movie style story and screenplay by Ronald L. Buch pairs the fellas off with Joanne Woodward as a friendly neighbor (for Newman) and Ellen Barkin as a pregnant woman (for Robby Benson), but most of the attention is on Harry and son, whose confrontation scenes are tedious and unconvincing. A waste of Newman, Woodward, and Judith Ivey in a supporting role.

HARRY AND TONTO ☆☆
1974, USA, R
Art Carney, Ellen Burstyn, Larry Hagman, Chief Dan George, Geraldine Fitzgerald, Josh Mostel, Barbara Rhoades, Cliff DeYoung. Directed by Paul Mazursky. 115 min.

Paul Mazursky's Ugly Americanized version of Bergman's *Wild Strawberries* features Art Carney as Harry, an aging widower who, after facing eviction, decides to travel across the country with Tonto, his pet cat, planning to meet his daughter and two sons en route. Carney, who won an Oscar as the old man in search of himself, is too young for a role that is already an abstract and distanced view of what elderly men are like. Others in the cast—Ellen Burstyn as his daughter, Geraldine Fitzgerald as an old love, and Barbara Rhoades as a prostitute—contribute nice bits, but they are lost in a meandering narrative. Mazursky would later return to the self-exploratory theme in *Tempest* (1982), with slightly improved results. In the meantime, he has turned the real issue, the plight of the homeless elderly, into a cutesy "road" movie.

HARRY AND WALTER GO TO NEW YORK ☆½
1976, USA, PG
James Caan, Elliott Gould, Michael Caine, Diane Keaton, Charles Durning, Lesley Anne Warren, Val Avery, Jack Gilford, Carol Kane, Michael Conrad, Burt Young, Bert Remsen. Directed by Mark Rydell. 120 min.

Unfortunately, it's not Harry and Walter but the audience who get mugged in this alleged comedy. As a pair of hopeless vaudevillians, James Caan and Elliott Gould are sent to prison after a carnival incident and meet supercrook Michael Caine, who starts them on the road to a wonderful new career as safecrackers. The best that can be said for this is that it does a good job of evoking the New York of the 1890s. But pairing Caan and Gould was a terrible casting decision, and the script and direction provide endless hysterics in place of slapstick.

HARRY IN YOUR POCKET ☆☆½
1973, USA, PG
James Coburn, Michael Sarrazin, Trish Van Devere, Walter Pidgeon, Michael C. Gwynne. Directed by Bruce Geller. 103 min.

This moderately entertaining comedy aims for the feel of *The Flim-Flam Man*, with James Coburn and Walter Pidgeon as two veteran pickpockets who take youngsters Michael Sarrazin and Trish Van Devere under their tutelage. *Harry in Your Pocket* is a well-made film, shot in various authentic Northwestern urban locations, but Coburn in the lead role is vaguely problematic. He's best cast as either a villain or a charming stinker; the scenes in which he exhibits a touching protectiveness toward his older partner here throw his character off-kilter.

HARRY'S WAR ☆☆
1981, USA
Edward Herrmann, Geraldine Page, Karen Grassle, David Ogden Stiers, Salome Jens. Directed by Keith Merrill. 98 min.

A mailman gets riled up when his aunt is charged a small fortune in back taxes. The ways in which he gets even will appeal to anyone who resents the very idea of the IRS's existence. But the potentially funny situations are defused by rather slovenly writing and heavy-handed direction.

HARRY TRACY ☆☆
1982, Canada, PG
Bruce Dern, Helen Shaver, Michael C. Gwynne, Gordon Lightfoot. Directed by William A. Graham. 111 min.

Buce Dern is wasted yet again in this amiable but dull Western made in Canada (in case you couldn't tell from the supporting cast). Like a more humorous version of *The Grey Fox*, Dern plays an outlaw who has become an anachronism, though he's been at his chosen profession too long to give it up. Gordon Lightfoot, who looks rather heavy on his feet here, proves that as an actor he makes a pretty good singer.

HATARI! ☆☆½
1962, USA
John Wayne, Elsa Martinelli, Red Buttons, Hardy Kruger, Gerard Blain, Bruce Cabot. Directed by Howard Hawks. 159 min.

The rough and tumble world of masculine high jinks is always a part of the Howard Hawks world, but in *Hatari!* there's nothing else to the film—no mission, not even a conflict within the group. The film, which tracks the adventures of a group of animal trappers in Africa, is enlivened by some great action sequences as they chase giraffes, wildebeests, and rhinos by jeep. However, at something over two-and-a-half hours, it will wear out its welcome by the end. The romantic squabbles involving the two women are forced and silly, and not much of the humor works. John Wayne scores as usual with his rough-hewn portrayal of the group leader. The rest of the cast is a mixed bag; Hawks was reportedly not pleased by their work. Henry Mancini had a hit with the theme song, "Baby Elephant Walk."

THE HATCHET MURDERS

See *Deep Red: Hatchet Murders*

THE HATFIELDS AND THE MCCOYS ★★
1975, USA (TV)
Jack Palance, Steve Forrest, Richard Hatch, Karen Lamn, James Keach, Robert Carradine, Gerrit Graham, Joan Caulfield. Directed by Clyde Ware. 74 min.

The Western did not die in the mid-seventies—it was resurrected in TV-movieland. There's a lot of shooting and sneering in this ho-hum version of America's most famous family feud (for even more ho-hum hokum, see Sam Goldwyn's version, *Roseanna McCoy*, 1949), but it's never any better than a single episode of "Gunsmoke." Former beauty Joan Caulfield plays Sarah McCoy, and Jack Palance plays (and, to his credit, plays down) Hatfield, but neither of them makes the production any more exciting.

HAUNTED HONEYMOON ★★
1986, USA, PG
Gene Wilder, Gilda Radner, Dom DeLuise, Jonathan Pryce, Paul L. Smith, Peter Vaughan. Directed by Gene Wilder. 88 min.

Is Gilda Radner ever going to appear in a good movie? The odds are slim if she keeps serving as leading lady to husband Gene Wilder, a fine comic actor but a lousy *auteur*. He wrote and directed this very tepid horror spoof about a thirties radio star who returns to his ancestral mansion with his new bride and starts to lose his marbles when things go bump in the night. Dom DeLuise, decked out in elaborate drag, provides a few laughs, but as you'd expect, there's too much Gene and too little Gilda, and Wilder shows no appreciation of her comic potential or his own.

THE HAUNTED STRANGLER ★★½
1958, Great Britain
Boris Karloff, Anthony Dawson, Elizabeth Allan, Derek Birch. Directed by Robert Day. 81 min.

This film is an often gripping thriller with glimpses of the old Jekyll-and-Hyde story line. Boris Karloff is a writer who can't refrain from investigating a twenty-year-old murder case, and his fascination with it soon brings him more than a byline: somehow, against his will, Boris is reenacting the strangler's crimes. The baffled police can't figure out who's committing the heinous murders. Pretty scary fright-night special as the killer's spirit infiltrates Boris's body and he starts bumping the locals off like clockwork.

THE HAUNTING ★★★½
1963, USA
Julie Harris, Richard Johnson, Claire Bloom, Russ Tamblyn, Lois Maxwell, Fay Compton. Directed by Robert Wise. 112 min.

This elegant ghost story is based on Shirley Jackson's *The Haunting of Hill House*. Contemporary audiences jaded by too much gore and special effects in their horror films may get fidgety, but those who can appreciate quality filmmaking will relish the difference between this and, for instance, *The House Where Evil Dwells*. An expert in paranormal studies accompanied by two psychically gifted women and one cynic investigate "disturbances" in a house where a murder occurred years before. Sensing their presence, the house comes alive and tries to repeat history. The director's achievement is in making the menace of this mysterious mansion palpable while revealing that the neuroses of the living make them susceptible to the house's evil.

THE HAUNTING OF JULIA ★★½
1976, Canada/Great Britain, R
Mia Farrow, Keir Dullea, Tom Conti, Jill Bennett, Robin Gammell, Cathleen Nesbit. Directed by Richard Loncraine. 96 min.

This offbeat, understated horror film comes from the director of *Brimstone and Treacle*. A pale, ethereal Mia Farrow stars as a woman who becomes unhinged after the tragic death of her young daughter (in the first, extremely harrowing scene of the film). Is her daughter's spirit haunting the house, or is it a manifestation of her own guilt? Though ultimately predictable, this quiet chiller will please those who like their horror with a delicate touch. The film was based on the novel *Julia* by Peter Straub. (a.k.a.: *Full Circle*)

THE HAUNTING OF M ★
1981, Scotland
Nini Pitt. Directed by Anna Thomas. 90 min.

This hopelessly muddled supernatural thriller is a mélange of Henry James, Bram Stoker, and "Columbo." An independent, opium-puffing actress (Nini Pitt) suspects that her vain little sister is under the spell of an evil incubus and sets out to discover the Shameful Family Secret that makes the ghost walk. Unfortunately, producer/writer/director Anna Thomas takes such feverish delight in the oldest scare-movie clichés that she never deems it necessary to do anything with them.

HAVING IT ALL ★½
1982, USA (TV)
Dyan Cannon, Barry Newman, Hart Bochner, Melanie Chartoff, Sylvia Sidney. Directed by Edward Zwick. 100 min.

A far-from-snappy rip-off of Alec Guinness's *Captain's Paradise*, which was also badly revamped as the French film *My Other Husband*. A standard plot about a bigamist who shuttles between New York and Los Angeles, with a wife in each city. Neither the complications nor the characters' responses to them are particularly engaging. Even with an attractive cast, *Having It All* has little to offer.

HAWAII ★★★
1966, USA
Julie Andrews, Max von Sydow, Richard Harris, Torin Thatcher, Gene Hackman, Jocelyn Lagarde. Directed by George Roy Hill. 171 min.

This impressive if somewhat impassive epic is based on another mammoth James Michener tome (the film tackles only a portion of the overlong book). This ambitious undertaking creates a vivid tapestry of the period during which the Hawaiian Islands were invaded, so to speak, by zealous missionaries who changed the lives of the locals, not necessarily for the better. The film conveys to us how the unspoilt Hawaiian paradise was tainted by the outsiders on a large scale; it really is one of the last of the old-fashioned Hollywood epics, since that format has found a new home as the TV miniseries. As with all traditional epics, there's a stab at romance with missionary wife Julie Andrews tempted by the longing glances of captain Richard Harris. Better on the TV screen; the scope is diminished, but you can take time out now and then for a breather.

HAWK THE SLAYER ★★
1980, Great Britain
Jack Palance, John Terry, Bernard Bresslaw, Ray Charleson, Peter O'Farrell, Harry Andrews, Roy Kinnear, Ferdy Mayne. Directed by Terry Marcel. 93 min.

In this sword-and-sorcery fantasy two brothers—one dedicated to the powers of light, the other to those of darkness—battle for possession of a magic sword. Jack Palance is the insane, disfigured Voltan who utterly overshadows pretty boy John Terry as his nice brother in this *faux*-medieval drama with special effects galore. Although made too early to profit from the box-office boom in sorcery flicks, *Hawk the Slayer* is actually pretty entertaining for those viewers inclined to this sort of material.

HAWMPS! ★★½
1976, USA, G
James Hampton, Christopher Connelly, Slim Pickens, Denver Pyle, Jack Elam, Frank Inn. Directed by Joe Camp. 126 min.

The makers of *Benji* came up with an enjoyable family film, as opposed to a children's film: adults can enjoy this slapstickery, if such is their taste, on the same level as the kids. The story is based on an actual attempt made in the 1850s to use camels in the U.S. infantry. Camels being the ornery critters that they are, you can imagine the complications that ensued. *Hawmps*'s major drawback is that it's far too long, and the material wears thin easily. But it's well played by a supporting cast of Western veterans, especially Jack Elam as the bad guy. Animal trainer Frank Inn and Higgins, the star of *Benji*, make cameo appearances during the saloon fight.

HAXAN

See *Witchcraft through the Ages*

HEAD ☆
1968, USA
The Monkees (Peter Tork, Davey Jones, Micky Dolenz, Mike Nesmith), Annette Funicello, Timothy Carey, Logan Ramsey, Vito Scotti, Victor Mature. Directed by Bob Rafelson. 86 min.

This example of pseudo-psychedelia, starring the most famous pseudo-rock group of the 1960s, is utterly unbearable to watch unless you're a nostalgite or one of the new generation of Monkees fans. After the demise of their TV show, the gang took to the big screen for this silly subteen imagining of the drug culture in which everything from Vietnam to Victor Mature gets twitted. But for God's sake—do you really want to see the Monkees condescend to the rest of pop culture? The intentionally incoherent screenplay is by Bob Rafelson and Jack Nicholson.

HEAD OFFICE ☆☆
1986, USA, PG
Judge Reinhold, Lori-Nan Engler, Richard Masur, Eddie Albert, Jane Seymour, Rick Moranis, Danny De Vito, Michael O'Donoghue, Don Novello, Don King, Wallace Shawn. Directed by Ken Finkleman. 90 min.

A young business-school grad (Judge Reinhold) goes to work for a huge conglomerate and discovers that, despite its TV slogan, it's not really "the company that cares about people." (Apparently he never took a course in public relations.) His revenge is exacted in the way of so many similar mechanical comedies, in which retribution depends on the hero being only slightly less stupid than his nemeses. Director Ken Finkleman (*Airplane 2*) manges some blackly humorous early scenes, in which backstabbing, coronaries, and suicides are all viewed as part of a normal first day on the job. But the promise of wit soon disintegrates into silly, familiar situations and a ratio of ten cartoonish gags to one bright moment. Reinhold (the addled young detective in *Beverly Hills Cop*) is so mild-mannered he almost disappears, but Rick Moranis has a couple of terrific scenes as a rabid adman.

HEAD ON ☆☆
1980, Canada
Sally Kellerman, Stephen Lack, John Huston, Lawrence Dane, John Peter Linton, Mina E. Mina. Directed by Michael Grant. 98 min.

This uncomfortable mixture of comedy and psychological drama may interest some, but it generally fails to sustain any consistent tone. A child psychologist (Sally Kellerman) and a professor of psychology (Stephen Lack) meet in an automobile accident and become involved in a bizarre sexual relationship in which each takes turns fulfilling the other's fantasies by playing out children's nursery rhymes. The two leads are good, but John Huston is generally wasted and the screenplay often seems to be going for obscurity for its own sake.

HEAD OVER HEELS

See *Chilly Scenes of Winter*

THE HEARSE ½☆
1980, USA
Trish Van Devere, Joseph Cotten, David Gautreaux, Donald Hotton, Med Florey. Directed by George Bowers. 100 min.

Joseph Cotten appears in one of the greatest films of all time (*Citizen Kane*). He also appears in one of the worst (*The Hearse*). Well, everybody has to eat.

HEARTACHES ☆☆½
1981, Canada
Margot Kidder, Annie Potts, Robert Carradine, Winston Rekert. Directed by Donald Shebib. 90 min.

Margot Kidder and baby-voiced Annie Potts are an odd couple of Canadian women who take a Toronto apartment together and try to help each other with their problems. Kidder is a wanderer who can't pass up any man who attracts her; Potts is hiding from her husband and contemplating aborting the child she is carrying, whose father was her husband's best friend. Although the plot is very predictable, the two stars are worth watching. From the director of that Canadian classic *Goin' down the Road*.

HEART BEAT ☆☆½
1980, USA, R
Nick Nolte, Sissy Spacek, John Heard, Ray Sharky, Anne Dusenberry, Margaret Fairchild, Tony Bill, Kent Williams, Stephen Davies. Directed by John Byrum. 109 min.

Writer-director John Byrum attempts to evoke waves of fifties nostalgia while dishing up soap-operatic tribulations loosely based on Carolyn Cassady's memoirs of her life with husband Neal and their buddy Jack Kerouac. It isn't a boring movie—if anything, there is more color and more background than Byrum can handle. The first third of the story jerks its way through the Eisenhower era, lurching from vignette to vignette, but, as photographed by Laszlo Kovacs, it's a captivating Edward Hopper landscape of cafeterias and flophouses. Once the movie settles down to portraying a suburban ménage à trois, however, the period details begin to seem oppressive and overdone, the dialogue (previously kept to a minimum) wildly overwritten. The actors look perfect, but Byrum often encourages their worst qualities. Nick Nolte (as Cassady) turns into a koala bear on speed, and John Heard (as Kerouac) throws deafening tantrums. Only Sissy Spacek, well within her range as the mewling Carolyn, emerges unscathed.

HEARTBEEPS ☆
1981, USA, PG
Andy Kaufman, Bernadette Peters, Randy Quaid, Kenneth McMillan. Directed by Allan Arkush. 79 min.

Sentimentality and sweetness can be welcome in a film to a point—but not when it's as sugary as molasses. That's the case here as a group of ever-so-cute robots search for happiness in what's supposed to be the world of 1995, but seems like Universal's back lot. On their jolly way, these overbearing automatons exchange lots of pathos and stupid social commentary. Rarely has such good makeup and mechanical gadgetry graced such a bad movie.

HEARTBREAKERS ☆☆☆
1984, USA, R
Peter Coyote, Nick Mancuso, Carole Laure, Max Gail, Carol Wayne, Kathryn Harrold. Directed by Bobby Roth. 98 min.

A "buddy" film taken to a psychologically discomforting extreme. The plot concerns the long-standing palhood of businessman Eli (Nick Mancuso) and artist Blue (Peter Coyote). Each is about thirty-five, pretty well off, good-looking, and aware of which socially correct Los Angeles spots to frequent; each is also helplessly in adolescent sexual competition with the other. Around women they become unwittingly abusive high-school brats, afraid of commitment and more than willing to leave hurt feelings and battered egos in their wake. Bobby Roth's elliptical, foreign-feeling style isn't for everyone, and will seem slightly secondhand if you've seen the films of Bertrand Blier (especially *Get out Your Handkerchiefs*). But those in tune with *Heartbreakers* will find thoughtful performances from Mancuso, Coyote, and Carol Wayne; a slick Tangerine Dream score; and Michael Ballhaus's crystalline cinematography in the service of an unusual look at a troubled friendship.

THE HEARTBREAK KID ★★★½
1972, USA, PG
Charles Grodin, Cybill Shepherd, Jeannie Berlin, Eddie Albert. Directed by Elaine May. 104 min.

Neil Simon's original screen comedy remains one of his funniest. Charles Grodin became a star as a man who becomes disenchanted with his new bride on their Miami honeymoon and dumps her for a young girl. The first half is serious, but overall the film rates high as a whole. Jeannie Berlin, daughter of director Elaine May, is perfect as the unsuspecting bride whose annoying habits lead to trouble. She, along with Eddie Albert as Cybill Shepherd's daddy, won Oscar nominations.

HEARTBREAK RIDGE ★½
1986, USA, R
Clint Eastwood, Marsha Mason, Mario Van Peebles, Eileen Heckart, Bo Svenson, Ramon Franco, Boyd Gaines, Moses Gunn, Everett McGill. Directed by Clint Eastwood. 128 min.

Clint Eastwood's old-fashioned basic-training saga has the great scowler as a marine veteran fighting to keep militaristic values alive in a Marine Corps gone soft. Clint has some sadistic fun in the early basic-training scenes (he introduces himself to his recruits by smashing their cassette player against a far wall) and, as always, his screen personality is scabrously entertaining; for fans, Eastwood pictures have become purifying comic rituals—he practically has a pact with the audience. Yet it's hard to keep from wishing he weren't such a clod behind the camera. Eastwood gets a halfway convincing rivalry going with Mario Van Peebles (who plays a jivey, self-mocking black recruit), but the rest of the movie is so wooden it could give you splinters. Climax: the invasion of Grenada, which comes off as exactly the sort of exhibitionistic ode to American superiority—the stacked-deck war game—that it was.

HEARTBURN ★★½
1986, USA, R
Meryl Streep, Jack Nicholson, Jeff Daniels, Maureen Stapleton, Richard Masur, Stockard Channing, Steven Hill, Catherine O'Hara, Miloš Forman, Natalie Stern, Karen Akers, Joanna Gleason, John Wood. Directed by Mike Nichols. 108 min.

In adapting her occasionally autobiographical, hilariously vengeful tell-all novel of a very pregnant wife who discovers that her husband is philandering, Nora Ephron took out most of the identity-guessing games and the corrosive wit. The result is a much more conventional comedy-drama about the domestic strife of two journalists who never should have married in the first place. Until its last third, the film coasts successfully on the star power of Meryl Streep, giving an unusually light, consistently funny performance, and of Jack Nicholson, cynical, wry, and charming as her unfaithful spouse. But then Mike Nichols's direction loses its comic zest, the story begins to repeat itself, and the appalling waste of the wonderful supporting cast (so underused that they might as well be extras) becomes ever more annoying. Streep and Nicholson (who replaced Mandy Patinkin two weeks into the shooting) make a terrific team, but *Heartburn* runs out of gas. Watch for John Wood in an amusing parody of Alastair Cooke.

THE HEART IS A LONELY HUNTER ★★½
1968, USA
Alan Arkin, Sondra Locke, Laurinda Barrett, Stacy Keach, Cicely Tyson. Directed by Robert Ellis Miller. 122 min.

This film is an uneven, tentative adaptation of Carson McCullers's novel about the friendship between a deaf-mute (Alan Arkin) and a teenage girl (Sandra Locke) in a tense Southern town. Arkin, though overly mannered, gives a challenging, strongly conceived performance that won him an Oscar nomination, and the rest of the cast is good if unremarkable. But Robert Ellis Miller's direction (from a script by Thomas C. Ryan) unwittingly exposes all of the novel's weaknesses of structure and plotting, and diminishes its emotional impact—onscreen it's a weepy melodrama with only traces of McCullers's peculiar artistry. James Wong Howe did the very pretty pastel-hued cinematography.

HEARTLAND ★★★
1979, USA
Rip Torn, Conchata Ferrell, Barry Primus, Lilia Skala, Megan Folsom. Directed by Richard Pearce. 95 min.

Set in the Wyoming of 1910, this beautifully photographed independent feature tells the story of a Denver widow (Conchata Ferrell) who takes a job as a housekeeper for a gruff Scottish rancher (Rip Torn) and ends up joining him in a marriage of convenience. As the characters prepare to face the brutal, isolating winter, they quietly attain heroic proportions.

HEART LIKE A WHEEL ★★★½
1983, USA, PG
Bonnie Bedelia, Beau Bridges, Anthony Edwards, Leo Rossi. Directed by Jonathan Kaplan. 113 min.

This exciting and unexpectedly realistic film follows the progress of Shirley Muldowney, a New Jersey housewife who tries to become a champion in the male-dominated sport of hot-rod racing. The film isn't so much concerned with its hot rods as with the troubled personal life of its heroine. In addition to winning more medals than her macho trackmates, *Heart Like a Wheel* perceptively looks at Muldowney's troubled love life, which includes a messy divorce and an affair with an arrogant "funny" car driver. Bonnie Bedelia gives an affecting performance as Muldowney, whose grit and ambition make her, and the film, come into a first-place finish. It's a movie that's inspirational without being corny, and one that was mostly neglected until the critics discovered it.

HEART OF THE GOLDEN WEST ★★
1942, USA
Roy Rogers, Smiley Burnette, George "Gabby" Hayes. Directed by Joseph Kane. 65 min.

Roy Rogers offers a steamboat service to foil a crooked trucker who has raised the rates for moving cattle. Rogers and the good guys have it out with the trucker and the bad guys, and sing cowboy tunes too! An above-average, well-budgeted B Western.

HEART OF THE RIO GRANDE ½★
1942, USA
Gene Autry, Smiley Burnette, Fay McKenzie. Directed by William Morgan. 68 min.

A spoiled girl is sent to a dude ranch where she finds sunshine, vigor, and prairie spirit. Action and drama both fail in this sloppy B Western. Only for deeply devoted Gene Autry fans.

HEART OF THE STAG ★★
1983, New Zealand, R
Bruno Lawrence, Terence Cooper, Mary Regan, Anne Flannery. Directed by Michael Firth. 94 min.

Austere melodrama about a domineering sheep rancher who forces himself on his daughter and the tensions created by an aggressive, pleasant driver who begins working on the farm. Director/writer Michael Firth evinces a good feel for the beauty and isolation in the New Zealand landscapes, but the story never engages the interest its explosive subject requires.

HEARTS AND MINDS
1974, USA, R ☆☆☆☆
Directed by Peter Davis. 112 min.

This extraordinary, scathing documentary about American involvement in Vietnam was one of the first films to suggest that we shouldn't have been there, a proposition that almost kept it unreleased. When it finally did appear, it won a Best Documentary Oscar and helped to establish a new tone for serious Vietnam films. Peter Davis, who also made the memorable CBS documentary "The Selling of the Pentagon," makes no bones about his contempt for American military and political leaders, but he doesn't say so; rather, he juxtaposes stark footage of bombed-out Vietnamese villagers with the rah-rah speeches and interviews of the army brass at home, and simply lets them hang themselves with their own words. It's polemical, unashamedly angry filmmaking that after more than a decade remains remarkably effective—startlingly so, in that it was finished only a year after the last American soldiers were evacuated.

HEAT
1972, USA, R (originally X) ☆☆½
Joe Dallesandro, Sylvia Miles, Andrea Feldman, Pat Ast. Directed by Paul Morrissey. 100 min.

Paul Morrissey's ghoulish, campy update of *Sunset Boulevard* is a grotesque, amateurish freak parade, but it's also smart, compelling, and in a strange way closer to the truth about Hollywood whores, gigolos, and fringe-dwellers than Billy Wilder's film ever could have been. The unexpectedly solid (for an Andy Warhol film) story has somnolent stud Joey Davis (Joe Dallesandro) servicing a well-off older woman (Sylvia Miles), a never-was star now reduced to game-show guest shots. Miles makes her character a pathetic, funny, and touching distillation of celebrity lost, and gives the film some of its most memorably acid moments. Though billed as an Andy Warhol production, *Heat*, like *Trash* and *Flesh*, was actually directed by protégé Morrissey and evinces his own unique style. The presence of denizens of Warhol's film "factory" is often hard to stomach, and one performance, that of Andrea Feldman as Miles's insane daughter, is a rather horrifying piece of exploitation—the disturbed actress committed suicide soon after production ended. Score by John Cale.

HEAT AND DUST
1983, Great Britain, R ☆☆☆
Julie Christie, Greta Scacchi, Sashi Kapoor, Christopher Cazenove, Nickolas Grace, Madhur Jaffrey. Directed by James Ivory. 130 min.

In this intriguing tale a British woman (Julie Christie) journeys to India and into her family's history. Investigating the life of her great-aunt, she discovers her own existence is taking a similarly rebellious turn and falls under the spell of a strange and mysterious land and its people. This slow, sumptuous, and detailed production is best in the extended flashbacks, which feature a striking debut from the young actress Greta Scacchi as Christie's ancestral counterpart. It's one of the stronger entries from the long-standing independent filmmaking team of director James Ivory, producer Ismail Merchant, and screenwriter Ruth Prawer Jhablava.

HEAT OF DESIRE
1983, France ☆☆
Clio Goldsmith, Patrick Dewaere, Jeanne Moreau, Guy Marchand. Directed by Luc Beraud. 90 min.

The late Patrick Dewaere stars in this drama of a university professor seduced by a siren in Barcelona. You don't have to be a film scholar to recognize that this is a rip-off of *The Blue Angel*, but the trashy, melodramatic elements are given a pseudo-literary style, and Dewaere as the teacher and Clio Goldsmith as the seductress exude a sufficient amount of erotic charm.

HEATWAVE
1983, Australia, R ☆☆☆
Richard Moir, Judy Davis, Chris Haywood, Bill Hunter, Anna Jemison. Directed by Phillip Noyce. 92 min.

This confusing but stylish political drama was directed by skilled Australian Phillip Noyce. Corruption in the real-estate business is the backdrop for a fiery relationship between a young architect (Richard Moir) determined to see his new project to completion and a radical (Judy Davis) who wants it stopped at any cost. The fine cast gets maximum mileage out of the story's complex development, but too many plot threads tangle for the ambiguous conclusion to be as effective as the setup. Fine cinematography from Vincent Monton and an atmospheric score by Cameron Allan are both strong contributions.

HEAVEN CAN WAIT
1978, USA, PG ☆☆☆
Warren Beatty, Julie Christie, James Mason, Charles Grodin, Dyan Cannon, Buck Henry, Jack Warden. Directed by Warren Beatty and Buck Henry. 100 min.

This updated, all-star remake of the great 1941 fantasy film *Here Comes Mr. Jordan* is not quite as good as the original, but it still makes perfect family entertainment, and it admittedly has more modern-day appeal. In the earlier version Robert Montgomery plays a prizefighter, but in this one Warren Beatty plays a Los Angeles Rams quarterback who is mistakenly summoned to heaven before his time and returns to earth in a millionaire's body. Life the second time around is complicated by his longing to play football again, his romance with Julie Christie, and the murderous plotting of his inherited wife (Dyan Cannon) and secretary (Charles Grodin). Codirector Buck Henry joins the fun as the overambitious messenger from heaven who screws up, and James Mason serves as his boss, the amenable Mr. Jordan.

HEAVEN HELP US
1985, USA, R ☆☆☆
Andrew McCarthy, Donald Sutherland, Kevin Dillon, John Heard, Mary Stuart Masterson, Malcolm Danare. Directed by Michael Dinner. 103 min.

The original title of this clear-eyed reminiscence of growing up Catholic in 1960s Brooklyn was *Catholic Boys*; Tri-Star should have let it stand. *Heaven Help Us* isn't the *Porky's* clone its ad campaign suggested, though it occasionally descends into prankish pratfalls. First-time screenwriter Charles Purpura has fashioned an accurate, sometimes incisive period piece that's also a touching coming-of-age film. The story concerns a new kid in town and his experiences with sadistic Brothers, school bullies, and first romance. The outstanding young cast members all turn in strong work, with top honors going to Andrew McCarthy's sensitive handling of the lead and Malcolm Danare's portrayal of the smartest, nerdiest boy at St. Basil's. It's a charming minor movie that's finally more anti–Catholic school than anti-Catholic.

HEAVENLY BODIES
1985, Canada, R ☆☆
Cynthia Dale, Richard Rebiere, Walter George Alton. Directed by Lawrence Dane. 89 min.

A young woman opens her own aerobics studio and then fights to hold onto it when the operation is threatened by a rival dancer. Not nearly as bad as it could be, *Heavenly Bodies* suffers from a *Perfect*-ish miscalculation of just how much aerobics one movie can absorb; yet it does have a sense of humor about itself, and its blue-collar heroines are steamily appealing. Catchy music by The Dazz Band, The Tubes, and Bonnie Pointer; script cowritten by Toronto *Star* film critic Ron Base.

THE HEAVENLY KID
1985, USA, PG-13 ☆½
Lewis Smith, Jane Kaczmarek, Richard Mulligan, Mark Metcalf, Jason Gedrick. Directed by Cary Medoway. 89 min.

A teenager killed in an auto accident years before returns as an angel to help a fellow adolescent. This movie seems to be a last-gasp teen comedy, desperately blending the usual awkward kid (who wants, more than anything else, to get lucky) with that old Hollywood warhorse device—the guardian angel. A tired cliché mix that lacks even the requisite vulgarity.

HEAVENS ABOVE! ☆☆☆
1963, Great Britain
Peter Sellers, Cecil Parker, Isabel Jeans, Eric Sykes, Bernard Miles, Ian Carmichael, Roy Kinnear, Malcolm Muggeridge. Directed by John and Roy Boulting. 118 min.

Peter Sellers gives one of his usual hysterical performances to reasonably comic effect as a working-class parson placed in an upper-class village. He tries to help his parishioners, but inadvertently makes things worse. This lesser Boulting Brothers comedy is still funny but aims at too many targets to really demolish any.

HEAVEN'S GATE ☆½
1980, USA, R
Kris Kristofferson, Christopher Walken, Isabelle Huppert, John Hurt, Jeff Bridges, Joseph Cotten, Sam Waterston, Brad Dourif. Directed by Michael Cimino. 219 min. (original version)

Not the worst film ever made, just the most money-losing (between $30 and $50 million, depending on who's talking), the most briefly released (one week, one theater), and perhaps the dullest. Director Michael Cimino was fresh from the multiple-Oscar success of *The Deer Hunter* when he embarked on this notoriously hyperinflated extravaganza and almost single-handedly killed United Artists in the process. More people know the story of the production than of the film itself, possibly because its plot, stripped of excess and embroidery, would fit neatly into a Crackerjacks box. Ostensibly, it has something to do with Wyoming's Johnson County "wars" of the 1880s, in which cattlemen banded together in a mercenary posse against immigrants horning in on their land and beef. Cimino probably would have been slammed for rampant historical inaccuracy if critics hadn't instead chosen to attack the pomposity and emptyheadedness that fill every frame. In four hours, only Vilmos Zsigmond's cinematography emerges as an artistic or technical success. Note: Only the long version of *Heaven's Gate* is available on videocassette. A later version, trimmed by seventy-one minutes, was released in a brief national run.

HEAVY TRAFFIC ☆
1973, USA, X
Joseph Kaufman, Beverly Hope Atkinson, Frank De Kova, Terri Haven. Directed by Ralph Bakshi. 76 min.

Ralph Bakshi's animated feature about a cartoonist's journey into the grubby New York underground isn't as funny as his *Fritz the Cat* but is just as offensive. Everything from *The Godfather* to the physically deformed are shot down without a modicum of subtlety. Not for most tastes.

HEIDI ☆☆☆
1937, USA
Shirley Temple, Jean Hersholt, Marcia Mae Jones, Mary Nash. Directed by Allan Dwan. 88 min.

Shirley Temple's last commercial blockbuster, *Heidi* is one of her best films. Although Temple gets involved in some typical melodramatic plot twists, Allan Dwan keeps an element of caustic wit bubbling just below the surface. He is aided by Miss Temple—a mediocre actress perhaps, but an astonishingly unlachrymose one. The toughness and cleverness she evinces may be less an intentional characterization than elements of her personality, but they enrich the film. Jean Hersholt also infuses his stock performance with a knowing wink, which makes the pathos of his big scenes all the stronger. Lush production values and a satisfying conclusion make *Heidi* a pleasant viewing experience—far more entertaining and confidently accomplished than the pundits would have.

HEIDI ☆☆☆
1968, USA (TV)
Maximilian Schell, Jean Simmons, Walter Slezak, Michael Redgrave, Jennifer Edwards. Directed by Delbert Mann. 110 min.

This film is the oft-told tale of a poor but brave moppet who's forced to venture beyond her simple Swiss Alps cottage and ends up changing the lives of those she meets with her warmth and innate goodness. The sentiment is not piled on too thick, and it's impossible not to be moved by the scene in which Heidi is separated from her granddad. Sweet without being saccharine, though we still prefer Shirley Temple's 1937 version.

HEIDI'S SONG ☆☆
1982, USA, G
Animated. Directed by Robert Taylor. 94 min.

That little Miss Do-gooder is back again, yodeling sweet sounds up and down the Alps in a tuneful, conventional cartoon. The production fairly oozes dirndls and sweetness and light, but that's to be expected of Heidi. The Hanna-Barbera animation style is proficient without being imaginative, but it does lend a little variety to the overworked story line. The real moments of distinction reside in the tunes of the accomplished Burton Lane, whose melodies are distinctive and lilting.

THE HEIRESS ☆☆☆½
1949, USA
Olivia de Havilland, Montgomery Clift, Ralph Richardson, Miriam Hopkins, Vanessa Brown. Directed by William Wyler. 115 min.

A solid, finely wrought adaptation of the play based on the Henry James novella *Washington Square*. William Wyler's directorial meticulousness is well suited to this studied tale of the plain Jane who learns cruelty at the hands of her masters and pridefully relinquishes a shot at happiness with a fortune hunter who claims to be a changed man. As the repressed wallflower, de Havilland gives a flawless, technically brilliant performance, but she does not fully engage our hearts.

HE KNOWS YOU'RE ALONE ☆½
1980, USA, R
Don Scardino, Caitlin O'Heaney, Elizabeth Kemp, Tom Rolfing, Lewis Arlt. Directed by Armand Mastroianni. 92 min.

This horror film provides standard slice-and-dice action as a psychopathic killer (driven around the bend by the fiancée who left him at the altar) stalks brides-to-be. One plucky young thing escapes his clutches, but his death offers no assurance of her safety: there is another jilted groom in the wings, just waiting to take his place. Dull and mechanical, though the heroine is less infuriatingly passive than is the genre norm.

HELDORADO ☆
1946, USA
Roy Rogers, George "Gabby" Hayes, Dale Evans, Paul Harvey, the Sons of the Pioneers, Trigger. Directed by William Witney. 70 min.

This film is barely a Western at all—Roy Rogers goes to Las Vegas during Heldorado festival week and becomes a cowpoke gumshoe in pursuit of racketeers. Good thing he's got his two sidekicks Gabby and Trigger in tow. Only for diehard fans of Roy and Dale.

HELLCATS OF THE NAVY ☆☆☆
1957, USA
Ronald Reagan, Nancy Davis, Arthur Franz, Robert Arthur, William Leslie, William Phillips. Directed by Nathan Juran. 81 min.

The penultimate feature of Ronald Reagan's career before he entered politics is fascinating on two counts: it is his only pairing with his second wife (and First Lady) Nancy Davis, and it casts him in a not entirely likable role. Reagan plays a World War II navy commander in charge of detecting Japanese mines for other submarines. When his character closes the hatch of his submarine on a fellow frogman (and romantic rival) during a mission, his second-in-command begins to question his decision-making abilities. The rumblings of a sub–*Caine Mutiny* plot, the bizarre, awkward love scenes between the Reagans, and the revisionist Reagan character make this a much more interesting film than one would expect. Note: this film was Nancy's last role after several unsuccessful years as a starlet.

THE HELLFIGHTERS ☆☆½
1968, USA
John Wayne, Katharine Ross, Vera Miles, Bruce Cabot, Jim Hutton. Directed by Andrew V. McLaglen. 121 min.

John Wayne fans won't be disappointed watching the Duke in modern surroundings as a fighter of oil-well fires, zipping around the world while trying to make amends with his estranged wife. This film is more enjoyable than it has any right to be, given the thinness of the plot and dramatic situations, but it is saved by some satisfying action sequences and sturdy performances from a cast that knows enough not to try to compete with exploding oil wells.

HELLFIRE ☆☆
1948, USA
William Elliot, Marie Windsor. Directed by R. G. Springsteen. 90 min.

William Elliot plays an ex-gambler who tries to convince a woman bandit (Marie Windsor) to give herself up so he can use the reward money to build a church. A lively, well-acted, well-written tale of guns and redemption.

HELLHOLE ½☆
1985, USA, R
Judy Landers, Ray Sharkey, Mary Woronov, Marjoe Gortner, Richard Cox, Edy Williams, Terry Moore. Directed by Pierre de Moro. 95 min.

The asylum in which amnesiac Judy Landers is trapped and tormented can legitimately be called a hellhole, but so can any room in which you get stuck watching this abysmal movie. An undercover medical-board agent tries to help the victimized Landers escape the switchblade of psychopath Ray Sharkey and the needle of mad scientist Mary Woronov; meanwhile sex, nudity, and sadomasochism have no redemptive potential with this banal script, artless acting, and raunchy humor.

HELL NIGHT ☆
1981, USA, R
Linda Blair, Vincent Van Patten, Peter Barton, Jenny Neumann, Suki Goodwin, James Sturtevant, Kevin Brophy. Directed by Tom deSimone. 101 min.

College freshmen are subjected to an annual ritual involving a night spent on an isolated, walled-in estate with a gruesome history. The twist—of course—is that the dreadful stories are true: the estate is inhabited by deformed mutants and this is the year they decide to show the young people just how they really feel about trespassers. One more post-*Halloween* stalk-and-slash picture, starring the ever-tacky Linda Blair and directed by exploitation veteran deSimone, who also has to his credit the sluts-in-the-slammer epic, *The Concrete Jungle*.

HELLO, DOLLY! ☆☆½
1969, USA
Barbra Streisand, Walter Matthau, Michael Crawford, Tommy Tune, Louis Armstrong, Marianne McAndrew. Directed by Gene Kelly. 148 min.

Gene Kelly directed this screen version of the famed musical play based on Thornton Wilder's *The Matchmaker*, but it lacks the vitality of the earlier films he directed with Stanley Donen (*On the Town, Singin' in the Rain*). The weighty Twentieth Century–Fox production runs too long to sustain interest as Barbra Streisand plays the meddling matchmaker who, after years of providing service to others, sets her sights on an eligible and wealthy bachelor (Walter Matthau) for herself. Matthau squirms as the cantankerous Horace Vandergelder, and Streisand is too young to play Dolly Levi, a role formerly filled out on stage by such divas as Carol Channing, Pearl Bailey, and Ginger Rogers, but the two provide humor and energy that is sorely missed everywhere else in the production. Jerry Herman's score is just serviceable, and Michael Kidd's choreography is surprisingly mechanical and uninspired. The best numbers, however, do take off: "Before the Parade Passes By," which ends on an exhilarating crane shot, and the title song in which Streisand shares a few magical moments with Louis Armstrong. A big lumbering failure, but not without its compensations.

HELL'S ANGELS FOREVER ☆☆
1983, USA, R
The Hell's Angels, Willie Nelson, Jerry Garcia, Johnny Paycheck, Bo Diddley. Directed by Richard Case. 93 min.

Unless you have an undying passion to see the Hell's Angels, this soporific tribute is better left on the shelf. The burly, raucous bikers couldn't be seen in a more favorable light than in this semidocumentary of their travels. Unfortunately, except for their own circumspect utterances, one never really learns about the gang. Also, don't be misled by the names of Willie Nelson, Johnny Paycheck, Jerry Garcia, Bo Diddley, etc. They either appear briefly or sing over the grainy bike-riding footage.

HELL'S ANGELS ON WHEELS ☆☆
1967, USA
Jack Nicholson, Adam Rourke, Sabrina Scharf, Sonny Barger. Directed by Richard Rush. 95 min.

Jack Nicholson did a lot of this kind of thing before he started to get parts in movies with budgets over five figures. He plays a gas-station attendant nicknamed Poet who joins up with the Hell's Angels but makes the mistake of getting too interested in leader Adam Rourke's girlfriend. The film was photographed by Laszlo Kovacs. For Nicholson fans and sixties archivists only.

HELL'S ANGELS 69 ☆☆
1969, USA
Tom Stern, Jeremy Slate, Conny Van Dyke, G. D. Spradlin, Sonny Barger. Directed by Lee Madden. 97 min.

Two rich kids trick the Hell's Angels into supplying a diversion while they rob Caesar's Palace. Less than happy about this when they find out, the Angels set out for revenge. Featuring real-life Angels Sonny Barger, Terry the Tramp, and others as themselves, from a time when they were considered basically good guys with somewhat rowdy temperaments.

HELL'S HINGES ☆☆☆½
1916, USA
William S. Hart, Clara Kingsley, Jack Standing, Alfred Hollingsworth. Dirreted by William S. Hart. 65 min.

Film scholars won't want to miss this imaginative forerunner of many early sound Westerns, about a spineless preacher assigned to Hell's Hinges, one of the least-tamed towns in the West. The story is an antique, but William S. Hart's command of the fast-moving narrative and action-filled crowd scenes remains impressive, and *Hell's Hinges* is a welcome addition to the still scant collection of early films available on video. Video Yesteryear has released a good print with a full musical score.

HELL'S HOUSE ☆½
1932, USA
Junior Durkin, Pat O'Brien, Bette Davis, Charley Grapewin, Junior Coughlan. Directed by Howard Higgin. 72 min.

A boy's state reformatory is the setting of this low-grade melodrama, ancient-feeling in style and execution. Perhaps director Howard Higgin was still uncomfortable with the advent of sound; his dialogue is leaden beyond belief. Amid the clumsy amateurism, Pat O'Brien stands out as the toughest of the inmates; look for an early appearance by Bette Davis. Some shorter prints are in circulation, and they only make the piecemeal plot more confusing.

THE HELLSTROM CHRONICLE ☆☆☆
1971, USA, G
Lawrence Pressman. Directed by Walon Green. 90 min.

We've come a long way in educational documentaries about insects, but this pioneer feature still contains some of the best footage of these creatures this side of "Nova." David Seltzer's often ludicrous narration (as spoken by Lawrence Pressman as "Dr. Nils Hellstrom") makes a gloomy plea for ecology while reveling in sensational insect wars. The point of view is fuzzy, to say the least, but rarely have ants, bees, locusts, and butterflies provided such exciting screen material.

HELL TO ETERNITY ☆☆½
1960, USA
Jeffrey Hunter, David Janssen, Vic Damone, Patricia Owens, Sessue Hayakawa. Directed by Phil Karlson. 132 min.

Battle excitement abounds in this journeyman war film based on real-life events. The striking action sequences pump life into the predictable handling of the story of war hero Guy Gabaldon, who was reared by Japanese foster parents and who distinguished himself fighting for Uncle Sam in World War II. Jeffrey Hunter excels as the brave fighter who also has to battle prejudicial attitudes toward the people who raised him.

HELTER SKELTER ☆☆☆
1976, USA (TV)
George DiCenzo, Steve Railsback, Nancy Wolfe, Marilyn Burns. Directed by Tom Gries. 200 min.

This riveting made-for-TV adaptation of Curt Gentry and Vincent Bugliosi's book documents the Manson "family" murders of Sharon Tate and Rosemary LaBianca. Steve Railsback, chilling as the deranged Charles Manson, is well supported by the essentially unknown cast. Some of the material has been watered down for television, and the four-hour storytelling is often episodic, but it is an important film and the only one on its subject.

THE HENDERSON MONSTER ☆☆
1980, USA (TV)
Jason Miller, Christine Lahti, Stephen Collins, David Spielberg, Nehemiah Persoff. Directed by Waris Hussein. 105 min.

In this queasy combination of ponderous science fiction and exciting love story, Jason Miller plays a megalomaniacal scientist who experiments with genes without considering human safety. Christine Lahti steals the film as a concerned research scientist whose conscience is troubled by her boss's work. Thrills are few and far between.

HENRY IV ☆☆☆☆
1985, Italy, PG-13
Marcello Mastroianni, Claudia Cardinale, Leopoldo Trieste, Paolo Bonacelli, Luciano Bartoli, Latou Chardons. Directed by Marco Bellochio. 95 min.

A bravura performance by Marcello Mastroianni gives just the right depth and shading to the Luigi Pirandello play about a madman who thinks that he is Henry IV, living in the year 1064, eternally atoning to the Pope for his excommunication. Of course, it's a bit more complicated than this—Mastroianni plays the madman as both Lear and the Fool; a deluded man who may or may not be truly crazy, both victim of and commentator on his situation. The movie is wonderfully accessible. Its complexities never weight down the humorous drive of the film, and Claudia Cardinale and Mastroianni evoke a genuinely moving portrait of two middle-aged romantics who have seen their lives stolen from them. Nicely photographed by Giuseppi Lanci; complemented by a good, jazzy score by Astor Piazzolla.

HERBIE GOES BANANAS ☆½
1980, USA, G
Cloris Leachman, Charles Martin Smith, John Vernon, Harvey Korman, Fritz Feld, Stephan W. Burns. Directed by Vincent McEveety. 100 min.

Herbie the Volkswagen goes south of the border, but he never makes it to the race. *Bananas*, the fourth adventure of Herbie the Love Bug, is one of the weakest of the series. Cloris Leachman, Harvey Korman, and Fritz Feld give out a few chuckles, but the story wanders well off the map. No real child will buy Joaquin Garay III's sugary portrait of the moppet Paco. Director Robert Stevenson had a much better feel for the little car, and his two films, *The Love Bug* and *Herbie Rides Again*, are far better.

HERBIE GOES TO MONTE CARLO ☆☆
1977, USA, G
Dean Jones, Don Knotts, Julie Sommars, Jacques Martin. Directed by Vincent McEveety. 105 min.

Lovable Bug Herbie, the Volkswagen with the most, is reunited with his owner, Disney stalwart Dean Jones, for a race from Paris to Monte Carlo. Kids should enjoy the road trip, and they'll laugh at Don Knotts as a bumbling mechanic sidekick. Some very nice location shooting in France, a plot about diamond thieves, and a love story between Herbie and a Lancia named Giselle.

HERBIE RIDES AGAIN ☆☆½
1974, USA, G
Helen Hayes, Ken Berry, Stefanie Powers, John McIntire, Keenan Wynn, Huntz Hall, Fritz Feld. Directed by Robert Stevenson. 88 min.

This warmhearted kid fare comes from the Disney Studios. Mean old man Alonzo Hawk (Keenan Wynn) is out to evict a sweet old lady (Helen Hayes) from her charming San Francisco firehouse. Problem is, he sends his goofy nephew, Ken Berry, who falls in love with the old lady's miniskirted friend, played by Stefanie Powers. Of course, Herbie the Volkswagen steals the show from the veteran cast. Stick around for the really cute wedding.

HERCULES ☆☆
1959, Italy
Steve Reeves, Sylva Koscina, Fabrizio Mioni, Ivo Garrani. Directed by Pietro Farncisci. 107 min.

A pectoral masterpiece! Shapely Steve Reeves, with the help of Joe Levine's publicity muscle, turned this grunt-and-groan superhero flick into a runaway box-office hit. Hundreds of chesty gladiators followed in Reeves's sandals with similar epics about weight-lifting warriors. Today, the action crowd prefers kung fu to spear tossing, but maybe some savvy mogul will put Chuck Norris in a toga and cast him opposite Arnold Schwarzenegger in the Romulus and Remus story.

HERCULES ☆
1983, Italy, PG
Lou Ferrigno, Brad Harris, Sybil Danning, William Berger, Rosanna Podesta. Directed by Lewis Coates (Luigi Cozzi). 99 min.

This film deserves a place of distinction on the all-time honor roll of Hollywood stinkers. The sets are cardboard; the dialogue blather; the special effects could be duplicated in a home planetarium; the monsters look as if they'd been slapped together from the guts of 100 transistor radios; and the muscle-bound Lou Ferrigno, with his small, sloping shoulders and nonexistent neck, looks like a turtle in repose and like Jerry Lewis when he desperately tries to run. Did we mention that it's boring, too?

HERE COMES MR. JORDAN ☆☆☆½
1941, USA
Robert Montgomery, Claude Rains, James Gleason, Edward Everett Horton, Evelyn Keyes, Rita Johnson, John Emery. Directed by Alexander Hall. 93 min.

The highly enjoyable film that Warren Beatty remade as *Heaven Can Wait* (1978) blends comedy, drama, and fantasy to pleasing effect. Robert Montgomery plays a prizefighter who finds himself prematurely summoned to heaven by an overzealous celestial messenger (Edward Everett Horton). With the help of an angel, Mr. Jordan (Claude Rains), the boxer acquires a new body for himself, that of a scheming millionaire, in order to return to earth. While the story does not hold up all the way, getting bogged down in its own intricacies, the cast brings it off. James Gleason is a particular delight playing Montgomery's perplexed manager.

HERE IS A MAN

See *The Devil and Daniel Webster*

THE HERO ☆☆
1971, Great Britain/Israel, PG
Richard Harris, Romy Schneider, Kim Burfield, Maurice Kaufman, Yossi Yadin, Shraga Friedman. Directed by Richard Harris. 97 min.

Richard Harris made his directorial debut with this low-key, uneven study of the friendship between a ten-year-old Israeli boy (Kim Burfield) and an aging soccer star. Harris plays his role decently, but as a director he's gimmicky and overwrought, and he leads the film toward a predictable win-one-last-game-for-the-kid climax that seems to drag on for hours. (a.k.a.: *Bloomfield*)

THE HERO ☆
Hong Kong
Jimmy Wang Yu, Chiao Chiao. Directed by Wang Hung Chang.

Jimmy Wang Yu's nefarious nemeses kill his mother and his girlfriend, moving him to exact bloody and brutal revenge on all of them. By the end of this tired martial-arts entry, the screen is so littered with corpses that the film just grinds to a halt—there's nobody left to kill. And thankfully, no possibility of a sequel.

HERO AT LARGE ☆☆½
1980, USA, PG
John Ritter, Anne Archer, Bert Convy, Kevin McCarthy, Harry Bellaver, Anita Dangler. Directed by Martin Davidson. 98 min.

An unemployed actor (John Ritter) is hired to run around New York in tights and cape promoting the new movie *Captain Avenger*. When he foils a grocery store holdup, heroism is his—but will he perpetuate the myth or doff the disguise? This mild, unassuming comedy plays more effectively on video than it did in the theaters; watching it at home may allay the nagging suspicion that both the screenplay and the star are better suited to television. Ritter and love interest Anne Archer are both fine in an amiable, sitcomish way, and there are some funny moments, although none that you can't see coming well beforehand.

HEROES ☆
1977, USA, PG
Henry Winkler, Sally Field, Harrison Ford, Val Avery, Olivia Cole, Hector Elias, Dennis Burkley. Directed by Jeremy Paul Kagan. 119 min.

Absolutely unbearable. Henry Winkler was at the height of his TV stardom as the Fonz on "Happy Days" when he jumped to the big screen and landed in this cloying crud about a kooky, wacky guy who meets a crazy, nutty gal and embarks on a cross-country escapade with her. The reason he's so endearingly unusual is that he's a Vietnam vet suffering from post-trauma stress syndrome, though director Jeremy Paul Kagan and writer James Carabatsos seem to equate this with a terminal case of the cutes. Sally Field and Winkler (whose movie career this came close to demolishing) are as charming as aging Mouseketeers, and when Kagan brings in Vietnam as a shrugged-off excuse, he treats a serious subject with a callous stupidity that typifies the film.

HEROES IN THE LATE MING DYNASTY ½☆
1985, Hong Kong
Carter Huang, Han Ying-Chieh.

A confused and dull film that lacks even outstanding fighting. An evil emperor is out to kill the loyalist families.

HEROES OF SHAOLIN ☆☆½
1977, Hong Kong
Chen Hsin, Ding Hwa Chong, Lo Lieh, Lung Chun Erh, Huang Cheng Li, Chan Ming Lieh, Ge Shao Bao, Yuan Kwei, Yuan Biu, Pai Lin, Chen Mei Na. Directed by William Chang. 90 min.

Tu Ta Shen (Chen Hsing) agrees to care for a great fighter's son and to help the rebels against Na Pa Ting (Huang Cheng Li) and the Manchu invasion. Above-average martial arts, choreography, and a twist ending.

A HERO'S TEARS ☆☆
Hong Kong
Ling Yun, Bok Shao-Fong, Lung Chun-Erh, Chung Hwa, Yung Chung. Directed by Li Tao.

An unusually somber kung-fu movie helped along by capable direction, *A Hero's Tears* tells the story of "Three Days Light," a famous hired killer who endures a dangerous search for the medicines that will cure his sister's blindness.

HERO TATTOO WITH 9 DRAGONS ☆☆
1981, Hong Kong
Chen Kuan-Tai, Chia Ling, Chih Chung Tien, Ku Tseng, Chen Sung Yung, Tsai Hung, Ma Chi, Cheng Kang Yeh, Li-Ho, Hung Liu, Chu Pen Ho. Directed by Pao Huseh Li. 84 min.

Ser Tah-Lung (Chen Kuan-Tai) teams up with an innkeeper, his wife (Chia Ling), and a monk in order to defeat the evil Kau and his band of murderers. This above-average film has fine acting, good photography, and sharp, clean martial-arts choreography.

HESTER STREET ☆☆☆☆
1975, USA, PG
Carol Kane, Steven Keats, Dorrie Kavanaugh, Mel Howard. Directed by Joan Micklin Silver. 92 min.

Joan Micklin Silver's lovely, intelligent portrait of the plight of immigrant Jews settling on New York City's Lower East Side tells the story of a quickly Americanized tailor (Steven Keats) whose new values are shaken when he's joined by his wife and the trappings of the old country that she can't give up. Carol Kane plays Gitl as a woman desperately trying to please her husband and at the same time rebelling against him; her acting here is so on-target that she virtually disappears into the character. Shot in black and white on a low budget, *Hester Street*, which looks like a dusty tintype come to life, marked a fine debut for director Silver. In English and in Yiddish (with subtitles).

HE WALKED BY NIGHT ★★½
1948, USA
Richard Basehart, Scott Brady, Roy Roberts, Whit Bissell, Jim Cardwell. Directed by Alfred L. Werker. 79 min.

In this solid police procedural Los Angeles's finest are assigned to track down a devious psychotic killer on the loose. Richard Basehart is very impressive as the deranged but crafty villain, and director Alfred Werker does solid B-level work, eliminating the frills and leaving plenty of room for gunplay and a fairly exciting climax taking place *under* the streets of the city. Beware cut versions.

HEY, GOOD LOOKIN'! ★½
1982, USA, R
Animated. Directed by Ralph Bakshi. 86 min.

After the novelty of the animation wears off (in about five minutes), this becomes little more than an obnoxious nostalgia flick about life on the streets of Brooklyn in the 1950s, in which the only point in continuing to watch is to listen to the tunes. Ralph Bakshi's animation is better than it was in his previous few features (*Wizards, Lord of the Rings*) because he relies less on Rotoscoping, the process of tracing over film of live actors. But it's still far from the level of his *Fritz the Cat*.

HEY, I'M ALIVE! ★★
1975, USA (TV)
Edward Asner, Sally Struthers, Milton Selzer, Hagan Beggs. Directed by Lawrence Schiller. 90 min.

Based on a true story, this made-for-TV drama documents the forty-nine days two people survived after a plane crash in the Great North wilderness. Edward Asner is good as always, but Sally Struthers is screechy and annoying. Adequate, but holds no one's attention.

THE HIDEAWAYS ★★★
1973, USA
Ingrid Bergman, Sally Prager, Johnny Doran, Madeline Kahn. Directed by Fielder Cook. 105 min.

In this enchanting tale of children's dreams and abilities, Claudia Kincaid (Sally Prager) is an imaginative twelve-year-old who runs away with her younger brother Jamie (Johnny Doran) to prove (to herself and her parents) that nothing is impossible. Their innocence and Claudia's cleverness enable them to hide out in the Metropolitan Museum of Art for a week. Claudia becomes entranced with a Renaissance statue and, in an attempt to find its creator, tracks down the donor (played masterfully by Ingrid Bergman). The ensemble acting by Bergman, Prager, and Doran is both fresh and charming. Also known as *From the Mixed-Up Files of Mrs. Basil E. Frankweiler*; based on D. J. Konigsburg's excellent children's book of the same name.

HIDE IN PLAIN SIGHT ★★½
1980, USA, PG
James Caan, Jill Eikenberry, Robert Viharo, Joe Grifasi, Barbara Rae, Danny Aiello, Kenneth McMillan, Thomas Hill. Directed by James Caan. 92 min.

James Caan's directorial debut, about a beleaguered blue-collar worker (Caan) battling the government to get his children back (his wife's second husband is a sequestered Mafia stool pigeon), has nothing original to say about official callousness and red tape. Caan is playing a sort of Saint Prole, glumly superior to everyone around him, and his romance with a shy schoolteacher (Jill Eikenberry) is *On the Waterfront*–style schmaltz. Still, this is a precise and promising first effort: Caan's depiction of working-class Buffalo is rich and saddening, and he has a nice touch with small, revealing details.

THE HIDEOUS SUN DEMON ★
1959, USA
Robert Clarke, Patricia Manning, Nan Peterson, Patrick Whyte. Directed by Robert Clarke. 74 min.

Hideous, to say the least. A scientist fond of tampering with Mother Nature turns hideous when the sun's rays hit him after a little accident he's had with radiation. What was he doing exposing himself to near-lethal radiation? Why weren't those fifties scientists more careful? Naturally, everyone in the film runs away screaming when they see he's turned into a scaly monster, but you may run away screaming with laughter.

THE HIDING PLACE ★★
1975, USA, PG
Julie Harris, Eileen Heckart, Arthur O'Connell, Jeanette Clift. Directed by James F. Collier. 145 min.

A terribly long, pious, well-intentioned and tedious tale of Christian endurance during World War II, this is a true story (based on the book of the same title) of what happened to a Dutch family that hid Jews from the Nazis. The truly unusual acting is direct and persuasive, but the travelogue shooting and staggeringly simpleminded theology just about ruin it. Produced with an ample budget by an adjunct of the Billy Graham Evangelistic Association.

HIGH ANXIETY ★★
1977, USA, PG
Mel Brooks, Madeline Kahn, Cloris Leachman, Harvey Korman, Ron Carey, Howard Morris, Dick Van Patten, Charlie Callas. Directed by Mel Brooks. 94 min.

Watching Mel Brooks's harmless, uninspired homage to Alfred Hitchcock, it's hard to imagine that he's the same daring satirist who made the modern classic *The Producers* and the ultimate movie spoof *Young Frankenstein*. In this low-grade, childish farce, Brooks's notion of homage is to restage famous sequences from *Psycho*, *Vertigo*, and *The Birds* and then tack on screwy endings. There are some funny moments, but most of the high spirits result from Brooks's getting the audience to congratulate itself for being hip enough to catch his references.

HIGH CRIME ★
1973, Italy/Spain, PG
Franco Nero, James Whitmore, Delia Boccardo, Fernando Rey, Duilio Del Prete. Directed by Enzo G. Castellari (a.k.a. Enzo Girolami). 103 min.

This failed experiment in cultural confusion is like a trip through the halls of the United Nations: characters from various countries speak in an assortment of dialects, often shifting from a Brooklyn to a northern Italian accent and then back again. Similarly, the plot line thrusts a straightforward American crime story—a cop's fight against the Mob—into a confused, obscure tale of vendettas and familial obligations. The man who plays Harry S Truman (James Whitmore) is not a convincing Old World Commissioner. In all this chaos, the film does manage some unmerited moments of sadistic cruelty.

THE HIGHEST HONOUR ★★
1982, Australia/Japan, R
John Howard, Atsuo Nakamura, Stuart Wilson, Steve Bisley. Directed by Peter Maxwell. 99 min.

Released in this country shortly after the success of *Merry Christmas Mr. Lawrence*, this story, set in a Japanese prison camp in Singapore during World War II, follows the relationship of an Australian and a Japanese officer both condemned to death. Almost forty-five minutes were trimmed from the original Australian release, and what remains is seriously lacking in plausible character exposition, relying instead on standard war clichés. (a.k.a: *Southern Cross*)

HIGH ICE ☆½
1980, USA (TV)
David Janssen, Tony Musante, Madge Sinclair, Dorian Harewood, Warren Stevens, Gretchen Corbett, Allison Argo. Directed by Eugene S. Jones. 97 min.

Four mountain climbers find themselves stranded on a cliff, and the film follows the endeavors of a forest ranger and a colonel trying to extricate them. A lot of tedious discussion about how best to bring about the rescue cuts down on the suspense level. Leave it on the ledge.

HIGHLANDER ☆☆½
1986, Great Britain, R
Christopher Lambert, Sean Connery, Clancy Brown, Roxanne Hart. Directed by Russell Mulcahy. 110 min.

Video director Russell Mulcahy comes a long way from his Duran Duran shorts and *Razorback*'s murderous warthogs with this gigantic fantasy concerning a centuries-old blood duel between immortals. While the director's predilection for fancy shots and special effects makes *Highlander* resemble an epic rock video, his imagery has poetry for the first time. Alternating between sixteenth-century Scotland and present-day Manhattan, Mulcahy injects everything with a gloriously glossy vision. Christopher Lambert struggles to overcome his impenetrable French accent as the heroic Scotsman, Clancy Brown is a delightful S-and-M villain, and Connery is winning as the token mentor who helps Lambert master his powers. These people are constantly getting into swordfights, spouting Zen wisdom, or absorbing lightning bolts. While not much of this makes sense, it's still a delightful mess of a movie in which everything is constantly coming out of left field. *Highlander* might be the most completely wacked-out film to emerge from the MTV morass of the eighties.

HIGH NOON ☆☆☆½
1952, USA
Gary Cooper, Thomas Mitchell, Lloyd Bridges, Katy Jurado, Grace Kelly, Otto Kruger, Lon Chaney, Jr., Henry Morgan, Lee Van Cleef, Sheb Wooley, Jack Elam. Directed by Fred Zinnemann. 85 min.

Fred Zinnemann's well-made Western has been overpraised, probably because of its showy moralism and ideal Aristotelian structure (the running time of the movie exactly matches that of the action on screen). Gary Cooper, who won his second Oscar for this performance, is splendid as the only man in town with the guts and honor to stand up to a pack of desperadoes. Grace Kelly got her first big break playing Cooper's wife, and Katy Jurado is memorable as the sheriff's ex-girlfriend. The conventional but solid filmmaking style is perfectly suited to the material and builds nicely to the inevitable but suspenseful conclusion. It's all pulled together further by Dmitri Tiomkin's Oscar-winning theme song.

HIGH NOON, PART II: THE RETURN OF WILL KANE ☆½
1980, USA (TV)
Lee Majors, David Carradine, J. A. Preston, Michael Pataki, Katherine Cannon, Pernell Roberts, M. Emmet Walsh, Frank Campanella. Directed by Jerry Jameson. 100 min.

This mediocre Western drama wouldn't look as bad as it does if it hadn't aimed to be a sequel to one of the outstanding Western films. Will Kane and wife return years later to face new troubles. Recommended only to those who don't know the original. Written by novelist Elmore Leonard, an unknown at the time who presumably needed the money.

HIGH PLAINS DRIFTER ☆☆☆
1973, USA, R
Clint Eastwood, Verna Bloom, Marianna Hill, Mitchell Ryan, Jack Ging, Stefan Gierasch, Ted Hartley, Robert Donner, John Hillerman. Directed by Clint Eastwood. 105 min.

An enigmatic drifter wanders into the corrupt Western town of Lagos and, after receiving a less-than-warm welcome from the townspeople, undertakes to clean it up. Strongly influenced by the stylized Sergio Leone Westerns (*A Fistful of Dollars* and others) that made Clint Eastwood an international star, *High Plains Drifter* carries his Man with No Name just one step further away from the common run of humanity, positioning him as a vengeful angel of death whose retribution is swift, sure, and cosmically just. Stark, violent, and very Italian, though shot in the United States.

HIGHPOINT ☆½
1980, Canada, R
Christopher Plummer, Richard Harris. Directed by Peter Carter. 91 min.

Call it *Lowpoint* instead. It's an alleged black comedy about a C.I.A. plot to rub out a king who doesn't fit in with their projected world view. They hire a hit man, but the king gets wise and disappears. Like many other disgruntled consumers, the C.I.A. wants its money back, but the hired killer doesn't offer his services with any guarantee and wants to keep the loot. As far as this anemic comedy caper is concerned, we can only say *Caveat emptor*.

HIGH RISK ☆☆☆
1981, USA, R
James Coburn, Lindsay Wagner, James Brolin, Anthony Quinn, Cleavon Little, Bruce Davison, Ernest Borgnine, Chick Vennera. Directed by Stewart Raffill. 74 min.

Cheech and Chong aren't the only ones cashing in on drug humor. This clever action comedy features James Brolin, Cleavon Little, Bruce Davison, and Chick Vennera as four Americans who travel to Bolivia (on Adios Airlines) to steal $5 million from a dope ring led by James Coburn. This plucky, jokey film resolutely refuses to do the expected. Take a chance on this one.

HIGH ROAD TO CHINA ☆
1983, USA, PG
Tom Selleck, Bess Armstrong, Wilford Brimley, Jack Weston, Robert Morley. Directed by Brian G. Hutton. 105 min.

This film is a lame recycling of *Raiders of the Lost Ark*, with Bess Armstrong as a rich flapper in twenties Istanbul and Tom Selleck as the boozing flying ace who agrees to find her long-lost father. From its blatantly fake air battles to its musty title (shades of Marco Polo and other junior-high-history faves), the picture is one endless, big-budget yawn.

HIGH SCHOOL CONFIDENTIAL! ☆☆☆
1958, USA
Russ Tamblyn, Mamie Van Doren, John Drew Barrymore, Jan Sterling, Jackie Coogan. Directed by Jack Arnold. 85 min.

What with John Drew Barrymore bursting forth with jive poetry and Mamie Van Doren bursting out of her blouses, the film is a feast for the eye and ear—and the mind, too. Catch this cool plot line: Russ Tamblyn (looking at least thirty-five) is a narcotics agent, and the good guys decide he's gotta go undercover as a high-school student to break up a dope ring. To make his masquerade more credible, Tamblyn is given a guardian, an "aunt" in the voluptuous form of Mamie Van Doren (who has some strange ideas of what aunts do for nephews). Can he expose the sleazy dope peddlers, or will the high-school hopheads and their protectors discover his ruse? Will he be able to keep his paws off mature schoolmarm Jan Sterling? Will he blow his cover by smooching with a teenager who realizes he kisses like a middle-aged man? You will be overwhelmed by these and other questions in this exploitative rock-'n'-rollin' treat.

HIGH SIERRA ☆☆☆½
1941, USA
Humphrey Bogart, Ida Lupino, Alan Curtis, Arthur Kennedy, Joan Leslie, Henry Hull, Henry Travers. Directed by Raoul Walsh. 99 min.

Humphrey Bogart is mesmerizing in this classic crime melodrama about a just-paroled gangster who must pull off one last job for the powerful Mob boss who had him sprung. As he plans the heist, he gets one last taste of unspoiled innocence in a brief rendezvous with a crippled farm girl before returning to life on the edge. John Huston and W. R. Burnett's script was perhaps the first to treat the gangster as a romantic antihero without bringing an overstated moral condemnation upon him. Although many of its scenes seem clichéd now, *High Sierra* was the movie that invented those clichés. Ida Lupino is a challenging presence as a seen-it-all moll, and Raoul Walsh's thematically rich, hard-hitting direction skillfully paces the movie toward its inevitable climax in the great mountains of Northern California. It stands up well.

HIGH SOCIETY
1956, USA ☆☆½
Grace Kelly, Bing Crosby, Frank Sinatra, Celeste Holm, John Lund, Louis Armstrong. Directed by Charles Walters. 107 min.

MGM refurbished their 1940 hit *The Philadelphia Story* by adding Technicolor, Vistavision, and Cole Porter songs, but they barely captured the charm of the original. Grace Kelly (in Katharine Hepburn's role) now plays the icy heiress whose marriage plans are interrupted by the appearance of her ex-husband (Bing Crosby in Cary Grant's role) and a nosy reporter (Frank Sinatra in Jimmy Stewart's role). The stars are likable and put over the John Patrick reworking of Philip Barry's play, but no one is up to his or her predecessor's standard. The best moments are primarily musical: Crosby and Sinatra's "Well Did You Evah?", Sinatra and Celeste Holm's "Who Wants to Be a Millionaire?", and every bit of Louis Armstrong. Decent in its own right, but like quality champagne that has gone flat.

THE HILLS HAVE EYES
1977, USA, R ☆☆☆
Susan Lanier, Robert Houston, Michael Berryman, Dee Wallace, James Whitworth. Directed by Wes Craven. 89 min.

A family en route to California takes a detour into the desert, where they find themselves besieged by a clan of murderous mutants. Class warfare is waged on a very personal scale as the white-bread Carters ("They were a normal American family . . . they didn't want to kill, but they didn't want to die!") defend themselves from an aggressive underclass that wants the family's food, their possessions, and their flesh. Great art direction by Robert A. Burns (*The Texas Chainsaw Massacre*); director Wes Craven has also been responsible for *Last House on the Left, Summer of Fear, Swamp Thing, A Nightmare on Elm Street,* and other genre efforts. Superior.

THE HILLS HAVE EYES II
1984, USA, R ☆
Michael Berryman, John Bloom, Janus Blythe. Directed by Wes Craven. 88 min.

"So you think you're lucky to be alive?" jeered the promotion for this sequel to the ferocious *The Hills Have Eyes*. Sadly, that tone has no counterpart in the film. Bobby Carter, survivor of his family's massacre in the desert by vicious mutants some years earlier, is now married to Ruby (now Rachel), the mutant family's one normal member; together they run a garage where Bobby tries to develop a new motor fuel. When Rachel and a gang of motorcyclists go into the desert to test it, they get lost, and of course, the remnants of the mutant family are lying in wait . . . The result is dull, dull, dull, and padded with flashbacks to the first film; by the time the family dog gets *his* flashback, one can only shake one's head in mute amazement.

HIMATSURI
1985, Japan ☆☆½
Kinya Kitaoji, Kiwako Taichi, Ryota Nakamoto, Norihei Miki, Rikiya Yasuoka. Directed by Mitsuo Yanagimachi. 120 min.

The themes of this striking, elliptical drama—the mystical aspect of nature, the fight against modernization—and its dense symbolism may have resonated more strongly in Japan. The setting is a tiny fishing village threatened with demolition and replacement by a modern park. Tatsuo, one of the members of the lumber crew, grows increasingly distraught at the job, although his own relationship with the natural world is erratic. Tough going, but thoughtful and visually impressive.

THE HINDENBURG
1975, USA, PG ☆
George C. Scott, Anne Bancroft, William Atherton, Roy Thinnes, Gig Young, Burgess Meredith, Charles Durning, Richard Dysart. Directed by Robert Wise. 125 min.

When the best catastrophe that disaster-purveyors can think of is an exploding dirigible, and names like Gig Young and Roy Thinnes fill out the requisite "all-star" cast, you know there's trouble. Fortunately, *The Hindenburg* will probably put you to sleep before you realize how awful it is. Nefarious Nazis, a German countess, ad execs, and card sharks are all aboard this Love Boat of the skies. Who will live? Who will die? Don't even bother fast-forwarding to the blowup for the effects—the best finale the producers could provide (on a then-astronomical $15 million budget) was 1937 newsreel footage of the actual crash, intercut with shots of the star either escaping or exploding. After this, only *Meteor* was needed to kill the genre.

HIROSHIMA, MON AMOUR
1959, France/Japan ☆☆☆☆
Emmanuelle Riva, Eiji Okada, Stella Dassas, Bernard Fresson. Directed by Alain Resnais. 88 min.

One of the seminal works of the French New Wave, Alain Resnais's story of an affair between a Japanese architect (Eiji Okada) and a French actress (Emmanuelle Riva) working on an antiwar film in Hiroshima is a Proustian whirl of memory and emotion. The movie's antibomb message has never been more relevant, and its dark, desultory mood is memorable. Marguerite Duras contributed the tense, spare screenplay; it is interesting that this very *auteurist* film bears such a similarity to her fiction. Georges Delerue wrote the marvelous score.

HIS DOUBLE LIFE
1933, USA ☆☆☆
Roland Young, Lillian Gish, Montague Love, Lumsden Hare, Lucy Beaumont, Charles Richmond. Directed by Arthur Hopkins. 67 min.

This delightful adaptation of a popular British stage farce is marred only by the lackadaisical adaptation done by director Arthur Hopkins, whose first film this was. Roland Young, best remembered as the star of the *Topper* films, plays an artist who is erroneously reported dead when an accident befalls his valet. This gives him a chance to attend his own funeral (where he is booted out for crying too loudly) and start his life over. Ultimately, he's hauled into court and tried for plagiarizing himself! Frothy fun.

HIS GIRL FRIDAY
1940, USA ☆☆☆☆
Cary Grant, Rosalind Russell, Ralph Bellamy, John Qualen, Helen Mack. Directed by Howard Hawks. 92 min.

A delightful reworking of Ben Hecht and Charles MacArthur's classic newspaper comedy, *The Front Page*. Howard Hawks accelerated the pace of the already lightning fast material and substituted a woman, deliciously played by Rosalind Russell, for the ordinarily male role of reporter Hildy Johnson. The results are superior to and more creative than both the 1931 version starring Adolphe Menjou and Pat O'Brien and the 1974 attempt starring Walter Matthau and Jack Lemmon. This time, a romantic element emerges between Hildy and ex-husband Walter Burns (Cary Grant), who manipulates her to ditch her dull fiancé (Ralph Bellamy) and return to his paper as his star reporter. The wisecracks in the Charles Lederer screenplay are fired like torpedoes, generally hitting their mark, and the actors are choreographed with the camera for maximum slapstick effect. The dark undertone of the piece, involving a fight for a scoop on an escaped criminal, is magnificently juxtaposed against the overall comic fury. A brilliant example of "seamless" Hollywood filmmaking and one of the last and greatest screwball comedies of that era.

HIS KIND OF WOMAN ☆☆☆
1951, USA
Robert Mitchum, Jane Russell, Raymond Burr, Charles McGraw, Marjorie Reynolds. Directed by John Farrow. 120 min.

This is your kind of movie if you like tongue-in-cheek adventure. Pity poor Robert Mitchum, who gets involved in a scheme to steal his identity. Someone's going to kill him so that mob czar Raymond Burr can take his place, but Mitchum isn't compliant enough to relinquish his life to the rotund Raymond. Terrific performances, and Jane Russell gets one of her few decent roles. (Rumor has it that the film's original title was *Bust-Top*.)

HISTORY IS MADE AT NIGHT ☆☆☆
1937, USA
Jean Arthur, Charles Boyer, Colin Clive, Leo Carrillo. Directed by Frank Borzage. 97 min.

A superb moody love triangle directed by ace romanticist Frank Borzage, whose films like *Moonrise* and *Man's Castle* have an iridescent romantic glow that other directors of love stories have seldom matched. Colin Clive's a cad whose shaky marriage to Jean Arthur reaches the breaking point when continental lover Charles Boyer enters the picture. An original, deeply felt film with persuasive star power generated by the leads.

HISTORY OF THE WORLD, PART I ☆
1981, USA, R
Mel Brooks, Dom DeLuise, Madeline Kahn, Harvey Korman, Cloris Leachman, Ron Carey, Gregory Hines, Pamela Stephenson, Shecky Greene, Jack Carter, Jan Murray, Sid Caesar, Orson Welles (Narrator). Directed by Mel Brooks. 93 min.

Mel Brooks's sloppy, smirky historical parody fills the screen with the reek of desperation. It's like an amalgam of the godawful parts of *Blazing Saddles*, with Brooks doing his usual borschtbelt comic shtick as Moses, Louis XVI, and Torquemada. Everything about the film—from the witless jokes to the crummy photography—is cheap and reductive, and stupid literalism is the modus operandi.

THE HIT ☆☆½
1984, Great Britain
John Hurt, Terence Stamp, Tim Roth, Laura Del Sol, Fernando Rey, Bill Hunter. Directed by Stephen Frears. 98 min.

A sort of deadpan road comedy overhung by a brooding menace, *The Hit* had the tag line "Even bad guys have bad days," and the movie recounts the misadventures of an icy hit man attempting to bring a stool pigeon to the slaughter. Terence Stamp plays the intended victim, a Pollyanna who doesn't seem to mind his fate, but John Hurt dominates the film as the withdrawn killer. Not for the easily bored. There's little action and lots of plot improbabilities, but there are loads of arid Spanish landscapes and good support from Tim Roth and Laura Del Sol. The terrific title instrumental by Eric Clapton is more memorable than Paco De Lucia's score.

THE HITCHER ☆☆☆½
1986, USA, R
C. Thomas Howell, Rutger Hauer, Jennifer Jason Leigh, Jeffrey DeMunn, John Jackson. Directed by Robert Harmon. 97 min.

A sleepy teen driving through the empty Southwest picks up a hitchhiker who, we learn very quickly, is a brutal, unredeemed personification of Death. The taunting, vicious game of cat-and-mouse that follows makes for one of the most riveting, psychologically canny thrillers in years, a superbly crafted exercise in highway terror that borrows a page or two from Steven Spielberg's *Duel* but has a lean, menacing energy all its own. First-time director Robert Harmon and writer Eric Red don't waste a word or image and never resort to cheap scares, and John Seale's cinematography and Mark Isham's music place the horror on a bleakly beautiful canvas. This film is not for everyone (especially the squeamish), but it is superb of its kind, and Hauer's incarnation of the villain is beyond reproach. Watch it alone.

HIT LADY ☆☆
1974, USA (TV)
Yvette Mimieux, Joseph Campanella, Clu Gulager, Dack Rambo, Keenan Wynn. Directed by Tracy Keenan Wynn. 78 min.

Versatile Yvette Mimieux wrote and starred in this poker-faced drama about a woman who loves . . . and kills. Strangely enough, this works. One question: was it Miss Mimieux's idea to constantly appear in a bikini?

HITLER ☆☆½
1962, USA
Richard Basehart, Cordula Trantow, Maria Emo, Martin Kosleck. Directed by Stuart Heisler. 107 min.

This film is an upsetting but rather malnourished examination of the Hitler mythos. Instead of a steady stream of blatant melodramatics, it somberly concentrates on a character study of Adolf Hitler. This approach has its own rewards, particularly in Richard Basehart's playing of the mad ruler. The problem is that there's nothing of sufficient interest in the writing or direction to sustain this character study as a cinematic experience. It plays like one of Hal Holbrook's one-man shows, sidetracked into a full-blown movie.

HITLER'S CHILDREN ☆☆☆
1943, USA
Tim Holt, Bonita Granville, Kent Smith, Otto Kruger, H. B. Warner. Directed by Irving Reis and Edward Dymtryk. 83 min.

A '40s exploitation film that's chock full of pumped-up melodrama and enough goose-stepping energy for a dozen wartime propaganda flicks. It purports to show how demeaning life under the swastika was for the young and impressionable. It seems that junior membership in the Master Race takes an awful toll, especially for those Aryan adolescents who won't shout "Heil, Hitler!" on command. The hardship for those nonconforming teens is dwelt on in loving detail, certainly more than is necessary for propaganda purposes. Tame by today's standards, but still enjoyably tawdry.

HITLER: THE LAST TEN DAYS ☆☆
1973, Great Britain/Italy, PG
Alec Guinness, Simon Ward, Doris Kuntsmann, Adolfo Celi, Diane Cilento, John Bennett. Directed by Ennio de Concini. 106 min.

Alec Guinness is a master of disguise—in *Kind Hearts and Coronets*, he played eight different roles! So who better to play Adolf Hitler in a drama about Der Führer's last days in the bunker with Eva Braun, Joseph Goebbels, and all the rest? The problem is not that Guinness is physically or dramatically unconvincing, but that any representation of Hitler inherently borders on exploitation or unintended camp. Hitler is simply too iconographically powerful to be tossed off by an actor who might as well be playing Willie Loman or Lear. Even G. W. Pabst's *Last Act* (1955), which covers nearly identical ground, is uncomfortable to watch. Strain as filmmakers do to understand the "human" side of Hitler's evil, the efforts are invariably laughable. This particular venture has the look of a slapped-together European coproduction, and even if it were better, we would still feel offended.

HOBSON'S CHOICE ☆☆☆☆
1954, Great Britain
Charles Laughton, John Mills, Brenda de Banzie, Daphne Anderson, Prunella Scales, Richard Wattis, Derek Blomfield, Helen Hayes, Julien Mitchell. Directed by David Lean. 107 min.

This film is one of the peaks of English comedy. Charles Laughton plays his most enthralling comic role as the boisterous drunk of the title, a lazy shoemaker who treats his eldest daughter (Brenda de Banzie) like a slave—until she elopes with his best workman (John Mills) and threatens to drive him out of business.

THE HOLCROFT COVENANT ☆
1985, Great Britain, R
Michael Caine, Anthony Andrews, Victoria Tennant, Lilli Palmer, Mario Adorf, Michael Lonsdale, Bernard Hepton. Directed by John Frankenheimer. 112 min.

Neither a big-name cast nor a team of three scriptwriters nor even a good suspense director could make this adaptation of a Robert Ludlum potboiler seem anything other than murky, muddled, and dull. Michael Caine plays an American who discovers that his father's billions are being used to establish a Fourth Reich in Germany; was ever neo-Nazi intrigue this dull or ineptly plotted? Some of the dialogue-heavy scenes between Caine and the film's pseudo-mystery woman (the incompetent Victoria Tennant) are so ludicrous that they come off as pure camp.

HOLD THAT GHOST ☆☆☆½
1941, USA
Bud Abbott, Lou Costello, Richard Carlson, Joan Davis, Evelyn Ankers, Marc Lawrence, Shemp Howard. Directed by Arthur Lubin. 86 min.

This thigh-slapping Abbott and Costello comedy ranks as their funniest film, one that still delivers ample laughs today. In this haunted house comedy, the boys get mixed up with a dying racketeer who spills the beans about his hidden fortune. Somehow this leads Bud Abbott and Lou Costello, along with a few other innocents, to a mystery mansion where sidesplitting supernatural antics ensue. Some of the routines are priceless, particularly a low-comedy dance between Costello and Joan Davis (in the classic role of Camille Brewster, a professional screamer for radio shows). Carefully sifted blend of thrills and belly laughs; these hilarious goings-on still offers chuckles for everyone.

HOLD THE DREAM ☆☆
1986, USA (TV)
Deborah Kerr, Jenny Seagrove, Stephen Collins, James Brolin, Claire Bloom, Paul Daneman, Fiona Fullerton, Nigel Havers, Liam Neeson, Suzanna Hamilton, Pauline Yates. Directed by Don Sharp. 195 min.

No, hold onto the more substantial predecessor, *A Woman Of Substance*; unfortunately this sequel, though beautifully appointed, barely cuts the mustard dramatically. Barbara Taylor Bradford should never have handled this adaptation of her novel herself, because the wobbliness of its structure damages the enterprise from start to finish. Some scenes are repetitions in terms of representing the characters' emotions, while others leave us unsatisfied because events are talked about rather than shown—and the bits and pieces we do get are the wrong ones. The original miniseries was an involving rags-to-riches melodrama, the equivalent of a good bestseller and certainly one of the most entertaining miniseries ever to hit TV. Here Emma Hart's granddaughter tries to uphold Grandma's dreams while suffering through *les affaires du coeur* and backstabbing business deals. The boardroom intrigue simply doesn't generate the excitement of the original tale of a vengeful lass and her upward triumphs against the rich folk who used her ill. Lacking that scope, this mildly enjoyable soap is further hampered by poor acting from the male leads.

HOLIDAY INN ☆☆☆☆
1942, USA
Bing Crosby, Fred Astaire, Marjorie Reynolds, Virginia Dale, Walter Abel. Directed by Mark Sandrich. 101 min.

TV stations usually play this tuneful musical on New Year's Eve, but you can rent it whenever you want on cassette. (The lavish color remake *White Christmas* is splashier but not nearly as dazzling; and, of course, Danny Kaye is no substitute for Fred Astaire.) A laid-back nightclub performer (Bing Crosby) tires of the dizzy show-biz whirl and retires to his own inn, which he will only open on holidays. This provides an opportunity for a cornucopia of Irving Berlin songs for all occasions, including the Oscar-winning "White Christmas." When Marjorie Reynolds, a struggling song-and-dance girl, arrives to dance away the holidays at the inn, Bing's former partner (Astaire) shows up and tries to woo her away with promises of a big-time career in Hollywood. This magical black-and-white musical is Astaire's best between the time he left Ginger and his crowning glory at MGM, *The Band Wagon* (1953). Photographed in that pearly Paramount style, with plenty of romantic possibilities, the film's chief claim to glory is Astaire tripping the light fantastic in any number of graceful routines by himself or with Marjorie Reynolds, who should have gone on to major stardom after this film.

HOLLYWOOD BOULEVARD ☆☆☆
1976, USA, R
Candice Rialson, Mary Woronov, Rita George, Jeffrey Kramer, Dick Miller, Paul Bartel, Jonathan Kaplan, Charles B. Griffith, Joe McBride, Commander Cody and His Lost Planet Airmen. Directed by Joe Dante and Allan Arkush. 83 min.

An in-joke from beginning to end. Allan Arkush (*Rock 'n' Roll High School*) and Joe Dante (*Gremlins*) began their careers putting together trailers from terrible Filipino movies that Roger Corman's New World Pictures bought up for U.S. release. They decided that they could do better themselves and made Corman an offer he couldn't refuse—a movie shot in ten days that would cost only $60,000. The result is this spoof, assembled mostly from leftover footage from various New World releases and glued together with a plot about murders at a small studio that pretty much resembles operations at New World. A must for Corman fans, this is at its best when it is technically the worst—it would be a continuity department's nightmare if the flaws weren't deliberate. The cast includes such B icons as Mary Woronov and director Paul Bartel (*Eating Raoul*), scriptwriter Charles B. Griffith, and the immortal Dick Miller.

HOLLYWOOD HOTEL ☆☆½
1937, USA
Dick Powell, Lola Lane, Rosemary Lane, Frances Langford, Ted Healy, Glenda Farrell, Benny Goodman and His Orchestra. Directed by Busby Berkeley. 109 min.

Busby Berkeley's last film for Warner Brothers is a trifle next to his earlier triumphs (*42nd Street*, *Footlight Parade*, *Dames*). The numbers, including the opener "Hooray for Hollywood," are inventive but much less spectacular than his previous routines. Also, Berkeley was never as adept as a "book" director, and the plot tends to lag. In all fairness, the Jerry Walk/Maurice Leo/Richard Macaulay screenplay about a saxophonist (Dick Powell) who gets caught between a movie star (Lola Lane) and her understudy (Rosemary Lane) during a premiere doesn't mine the situation for all it's worth. Cameos from others besides the ill-at-ease Louella Parsons would have been welcome. At least the Johnny Mercer–Richard A. Whiting score includes "I'm Like a Fish out of Water" and the routine in the drive-in (close to Berkeley's best).

HOLLYWOOD HOT TUBS ☆
1984, USA, R
Donna McDaniel, Michael Andrew, Paul Gunning, Edy Williams, Katt Shea. Directed by Chuck Vincent. 102 min.

In its better moments, this soft-core sexploitation film aspires to mediocrity. The title pretty much says it all: a troublesome

California teenager, in order to stay out of jail, takes a job with his uncle's plumbing business and gets involved with hot tubs and the nubile maidens who, at least according to movies like this, inhabit every one of them.

HOLLYWOOD OUTTAKES AND RARE FOOTAGE ☆☆
1983, USA

The lurid, *National Enquirer*–esque ads for this compilation film lead you to expect a cavalcade of dirty celebrity underwear (or an amusing array of bloopers), but the movie is something less: a shapeless pseudodocumentary that offers precious little in the way of campy fun. There are a few worthwhile clips. James Dean, shortly before his death, warns the youth of America about the perils of driving fast on the highway; Joan Crawford sweetly tucks her kids into bed and then makes a plea for the Jimmy Fund. But to see these choice tidbits, you've got to sit through a lengthy publicity sequence with Judy Garland and Mickey Rooney, an uneventful clip from the 1939 Oscars, twenty meandering minutes from the Hollywood premiere of *A Star Is Born*, and Humphrey Bogart's last costume fitting. The overall effect is depressing—in short, a slapdash history lesson of interest only to film buffs.

HOLLYWOOD VICE SQUAD ☆½
1986, USA, R
Ronny Cox, Frank Gorshin, Leon Isaac Kennedy, Carrie Fisher, Ben Frank, Trish Van Devere, Joey Travolta. Directed by Penelope Spheeris. 95 min.

Apparently, the director of the very interesting youth-in-revolt films *Suburbia* and *The Boys Next Door* has to pay the rent just like the rest of us, and probably did so with this plodding rip-off of "Hill Street Blues" and "Miama Vice." Unfortunately, it has neither the substance of the former nor the style of the latter—the cops on view here are a boring bunch. Weirdest performance in the very weird cast is that of Frank (Riddler) Gorshin as a pimp.

HOLOCAUST ☆☆☆☆
1984, USA (TV)
Fritz Weaver, Rosemary Harris, Meryl Streep, James Woods, Tovah Feldshuh, Joseph Bottoms, Blanche Baker. Directed by Marvin Chomsky. 450 min. (three cassettes)

A shattering docudrama about the mass extermination of the Jews under the Nazi regime, this film attains maximum impact by following the fortunes of one particular family—a cultured professor, his wife, and their children; wisely, the expert script unfolds its horrors only after we've come to know and respect this family. Thus, the calamities that befall them—including the divided loyalties of former acquaintances, the sudden disappearance of friends, the separation from loved ones, the cattle-car transports to oblivion, and the ultimate agony of the concentration camps—hit us with devastating impact. This was a major television undertaking; and if this fictionalized treatment lacks the forcefulness of such documentaries as *Shoah*, it's still to be commended for its excellence of execution and for reminding us of an unparalleled evil that we must never forget. Skillfully conceived and written by Gerald Green and expertly produced by Herbert Brodkin, this TV series had a worldwide impact. When shown on German TV, not long after its American debut, it received enormous ratings and resulted in greatly increased study of the Holocaust by German students.

HOLOCAUST SURVIVORS ☆☆½
1982, USA (TV)
Kirk Douglas, Pam Dawber, Eric Douglas, Robert Clary. Directed by Jack Smight. 104 min.

A timely but fruitless attempt to combine romance and politics. A father and daughter, visiting the 1981 World Conference of Holocaust Survivors, engage in love affairs that tangentially comment upon the Holocaust. The background is unusual for a love tale and the scenery is fetching, but the daughter's romance offers little worth remembering. The mature affair of Kirk Douglas with his long-lost love from World War II offers more resonance and adds emotional weight to this well-intentioned twin story line. A commendable and diligently acted film, it's unfortunately not the sweeping emotional experience intended. (a.k.a.: *Remembrance of Love*)

HOLOCAUST 2000 ☆½
1978, Italy/Great Britain
Kirk Douglas, Simon Ward, Agostina Belli, Anthony Quayle, Virginia McKenna, Alexander Knox. Directed by Alberto De Martino. 96 min.

This film comes from the era when Kirk Douglas apparently decided to become a science-fiction star, to judge from turkeys like this, *The Final Countdown*, and *Saturn 3*. In this *Omen* rip-off, he plays an industrialist who hires his son as an engineer at his nuclear-power plant. He soon comes to realize that his son, cleverly named "Angel," is really the Antichrist and plans to use the plant to destroy the world. It is sort of a pinhead's guide to the Book of Revelations. Originally shown theatrically as *The Chosen*.

THE HOLY INNOCENTS ☆☆☆½
1984, Spain, PG
Francisco Rabal, Alfredo Landa, Terele Pavez, Belen Ballesteros, Juan Sachez, Susan Sanchez, Juan Diego. Directed by Mario Camus. 108 min.

This solemn, meditative pastoral saga, about a family of tenant farmers in Northern Spain who live under the oppression of their aristocratic landlords, uses a series of gentle vignettes and understated scenes to accumulate astonishing emotional power. The most compelling of the dramas focuses on Paco (Alfredo Landa), the aging papa and favorite of one of the callous young masters, and on Azarias (Francisco Rabal), Paco's slow-witted brother-in-law, whose eccentricities the impoverished clan must conceal in order to protect their own welfare. Though the pace is deliberate and the structure initially confusing (most of the film takes place in flashback), Mario Camus's direction is beautifully textured, delicately weaving his story throughout the vast countryside and quietly exposing the unspeakable cruelty of the class system under Francisco Franco's rule. This is an exceptionally distinguished, rich work for demanding viewers. (Rabal and Landa shared a Best Actor Prize at the 1984 Cannes Film Festival.)

HOLY TERROR

See *Alice, Sweet Alice*

HOMBRE ☆☆☆½
1967, USA
Paul Newman, Fredric March, Richard Boone, Diane Cilento, Cameron Mitchell, Barbara Rush. Directed by Martin Ritt. 110 min.

Paul Newman is excellent as a white man raised by Apaches who finds it hard to adjust to the narrow-minded world of eastern Arizona in the 1880s. Tautly directed by Martin Ritt, *Hombre* follows him through a series of prejudicial encounters until he gets to prove his worth as leader of a disparate group of stagecoach travelers trying to survive against a band of robbers headed by Richard Boone. If the setting and situation are reminiscent of John Ford's *Stagecoach*, it is intentional; unfortunately, the characters' spoken truisms, which often come across as platitudes, aren't. Leisurely paced, *Hombre* is, by and large, a powerful study of differing human natures forced to accommodate themselves to a life-threatening situation.

THE HOME AND THE WORLD ☆☆☆☆
1984, India
Victor Banerjee, Swatilekha Chatterjee, Soumitra Chatterjee. Directed by Satyajit Ray. 130 min.

Satyajit Ray's splendid period melodrama intertwines a calamitous romantic triangle with violent political turmoil. The hero, an enlightened maharaja named Nikhil (Victor Banerjee), encourages his wife, Bimila (Swatilekha Chatterjee), to reject the restrictions of purdah and open herself up to Western culture. The first man he introduces her to is his old friend Sandip (Soumitra Chatterjee), a charismatic radical who makes Nikhil seem fussy and inert. However, Bimila lacks the experience to know that this renegade intellectual is an egotist and a flatterer, and that he's using her as an ideological and sexual conquest. Filmed mostly in lush interiors, the movie is full of loving portraiture and lingering images; Ray's genius is for storytelling that engages us not just in his characters' isolated dramas but also in their ongoing coexistence.

HOMEBODIES ☆☆☆
1974, USA, PG
Peter Brocco, Frances Fuller, William Hansen, Ruth McDevitt. Directed by Larry Yust. 96 min.

This sadly neglected tongue-in-cheek horror film deals with six elderly tenants who will not stop at murder to circumvent unfair eviction. The low-budget suspense works well because the grisly events occur surreptitiously, and because director and cowriter Larry Yust is not afraid to toy with audience sympathy. This brand of black humor is not for everyone, but it is expertly done.

THE HOMECOMING ☆☆☆
1971, USA (TV)
Patricia Neal, Richard Thomas, Edgar Bergen, Ellen Corby, Cleavon Little, Dorothy Stickney, William Windom. Directed by Fielder Cook. 100 min.

Earl Hamner revised his script for *Spencer's Mountain* to create this Christmas favorite that eventually served as the basis for the long-running series "The Waltons." Whether you liked the series or not, this film is worth a look for its beautiful craftsmanship, lovely acting, and poignant plot, all of which place it well above the average telefilm. It's Christmas Eve 1933 on Walton's Mountain, and as the night wears on Pa still hasn't arrived home safely; the story grows more touching as the family clings together in the face of a possible disaster. Patricia Neal won an Emmy nomination for her fine work, and you may recognize many series regulars in the supporting cast.

HOME IN OKLAHOMA ☆☆
1946, USA
Roy Rogers, George "Gabby" Hayes, Dale Evans, Carol Hughes. Directed by William Whitney. 72 min.

Roy Rogers plays a newsman hunting down the killers of a cattle rancher with sidekicks Gabby and Evans. The film is a well-directed, exciting oater. Trigger makes a cameo!

HOME MOVIES ☆☆
1979, USA
Kirk Douglas, Nancy Allen, Keith Gordon, Gerrit Graham, Vincent Gardenia. Directed by Brian De Palma. 90 min.

The ultimate student film, this is the end result of a course taught by Brian De Palma at Sarah Lawrence College, in which students learned how to make a movie by actually making a movie. Kirk Douglas plays a cult leader who exhorts his followers not to be "extras in their own life." He singles out one particular nebbish (Keith Gordon, who went on to become possessed by a car in *Christine*) and counsels him to go after his flaky brother's girlfriend. It's all professionally done, but uninspired; six screenwriters are credited, and the fragmented nature of the film suggests that each contributed a few separate bits that were later sutured together. Gerrit Graham steals the show, as usual, as Gordon's brother.

HOME OF THE BRAVE ☆☆☆½
1949, USA
James Edwards, Douglas Dick, Steve Brodie, Jeff Corey, Lloyd Bridges, Frank Lovejoy. Directed by Mark Robson. 88 min.

If Richard Brooks's "The Brick Foxhole" (about wartime homophobia) could become *Crossfire*, a film about wartime anti-Semitism, then Arthur Laurents's *Home of the Brave* (a Broadway play about wartime anti-Semitism) could become *Home of the Brave*, one of the first Hollywood films to deal with wartime racism. After all, prejudice is prejudice no matter who the victim is (which is the point of most of these "social conscience" films of the late forties). This one hasn't dated as badly as the others (*Gentleman's Agreement*, *Pinky*), thanks primarily to Carl Foreman's blistering adaptation and James Edwards's moving performance as the black G.I. who suffers a mental breakdown after being persecuted by his own outfit during a mission. (Edwards's own promising career would soon be destroyed by the Hollywood Blacklist.) Mark Robson's direction is somewhat too theatrical for a war film, but he keeps the action taut and skillfully integrates the flashback sequences.

HOME TO STAY ☆☆½
1978, USA (TV)
Henry Fonda, Michael McGuire, Frances Hyland, David Stambaugh, Kirsten Vigard. Directed by Delbert Mann. 74 min.

This highly sentimental but often effective TV drama concerns a teenage girl who fears that her lively grandfather (Henry Fonda) is about to be placed in a nursing home and embarks on a runaway trek with him across Illinois (the story was filmed in Canada). Much soppier than it needed to be, but Fonda's performance hits every note perfectly, and he makes it worth watching.

HOMETOWN USA ☆☆½
1979, USA, R
Gary Springer, David Wilson, Brian Kerwin, Pat Delaney, Julie Parsons. Directed by Max Baer. 93 min.

The true hometown of this 1950s hot-rod picture is the turf scrawled by *American Graffiti*; their plots are like matching tattoos. A virginal geek (Gary Springer), who happens to look like Elvis Presley, is driven through some cute vignettes to ultimate maturity by his slick buddies (David Wilson and Brian Kerwin), who also happen to look like Elvis Presley. With music by Richie Valens, Jimmy Clanton, and Little Richard, and set decoration by drive-in waitresses on roller skates, this unoriginal period soft-ploitation film nonetheless tries hard to poke fun at Anytown, and it sometimes hits the target.

HOMEWORK ☆
1982, USA, R
Joan Collins, Wings Hauser, Betty Thomas, Michael Morgan, Shell Kepler. Directed by James Beshears.

Two popular early-eighties trends converge: oversexed teenage boys being seduced by older women, and Joan Collins. What makes this a particularly bad example of the former (not one of your great subgenres to begin with) is that the filmmakers seemed to feel that because they had Collins for box-office draw they didn't need any wit, drama, or other redeeming qualities. The plot, for what it's worth, casts her as a biology teacher at the local high school who seduces one of her students. She has one nude scene, but a double was used, so it lacks even celebrity skin value.

HONEYBOY ☆
1982, USA (TV)
Erik Estrada, Morgan Fairchild, James McEachin, Robert Costanzo, Yvonne Wilder. Directed by John Berry. 100 min.

Erik Estrada and Morgan Fairchild chew scenery, emote, project, steam up, chill out, and do everything short of climbing in the ring together in an attempt to dominate this movie. Unfortunately, this isn't as good as a Leon Isaac Kennedy film; if you want to see a bad film about someone punching his way out of poverty, see *Penitentiary* or *Body and Soul*.

HONEYCHILE ★★½
1951, USA
Judy Canova, Eddie Foy, Jr., Alan Hale, Jr., Walter Catlett. Directed by R. G. Springsteen. 90 min.

Judy Canova possessed a true belter's voice in addition to a sunny comedy style. This hokey vehicle concerns Judy's attention-getting forays into the music-publishing business. Primarily for fans as she slams home the down-home comedy and shatters glass with her voice.

THE HONEYMOON KILLERS ★★★
1969, USA, R
Shirley Stoler, Tony Lo Bianco, Dotha Duckworth. Directed by Leonard Kastle. 115 min.

This grisly, low-budget thriller was based on the case of two multiple murderers who were executed at Sing Sing in 1951. Tony Lo Bianco and Shirley Stoler are an unusual but effective match as the killers who pose as a nurse and her brother to murder lonely, wealthy women after stripping them of their savings. This was one of the late François Truffaut's favorite American films.

HONEYSUCKLE ROSE ★★
1980, USA, PG
Willie Nelson, Dyan Cannon, Amy Irving, Slim Pickens, Joey Floyd, Charles Levin, Priscilla Pointer, Mickey Rooney, Jr., Diana Scarwid. Directed by Jerry Schatzberg. 119 min.

Country-and-western great Willie Nelson makes a wooden leading man in this wretched life-on-the-road "remake" of the 1939 Ingrid Bergman vehicle *Intermezzo*. As country singer Buck Bonham, Nelson cheats on spouse Dyan Cannon with beautiful guitar-instructor Amy Irving. There are lots of Nelson songs, but the story was hokum even in 1939, and Jerry Schatzberg (*The Seduction of Joe Tynan*) isn't director enough to rise above it. Genuine feeling is what country music is all about, but there's precious little of it here.

HONKY TONK FREEWAY ★★
1981, USA, PG
Beau Bridges, Hume Cronyn, Beverly D'Angelo, William Devane, George Dzundza, Teri Garr, Joe Grifasi, Howard Hesseman, Paul Jabara, Geraldine Page, Jessica Tandy, Deborah Rush. Directed by John Schlesinger. 107 min.

This episodic, witless collage about a group of oddballs converging on a small town in Florida strives for the same kind of panoramic view of American culture that *Nashville* put across so effectively. But it's too disconnected and sour about its characters and landscape to be funny, let alone meaningful. British director John Schlesinger seems to feel nothing but contempt for the crudely drawn "little people" who populate the story, and his work is terribly heavy-handed in a comic context. A few of the performers do very well, notably Joe Grifasi as a garbageman–turned–bank robber and Beverly D'Angelo as a waitress with unchallengeable loyalty to the International House of Pancakes, but they succeed by working against the script rather than with it.

HONKEYTONK MAN ★½
1982, USA, PG
Clint Eastwood, Kyle Eastwood, John McIntire, Verna Bloom, Tim Thomerson. Directed by Clint Eastwood. 122 min.

This film is one of the sorrier indulgences in Clint Eastwood's career as a director-star. His Red Stovall is a hard-drinking country-and-western singer who's dying of tuberculosis—and that may be more than even Eastwood's biggest fans can stomach. Quaint and predictable, the movie is basically a down-home road comedy, with our hero boozing it up, escaping chance brushes with the law, and guiding his adoring fourteen-year-old nephew (played by his son, Kyle) through various rites of passage. Viewers who thrive on camp may enjoy the sight of Eastwood singing country-and-western songs: clenching his teeth, spitting out lyrics with the same steely snarl he once used to strike terror in the hearts of punks, he comes on like a cross between Johnny Cash and Boris Karloff.

HONOR AMONG THIEVES ★★★
1968, France/Italy, R
Charles Bronson, Alain Delon, Brigitte Fosey. Directed by Jean Herman. 93 min.

In this tricky, suspenseful, claustrophobic thriller, a mercenary hired as part of a heist scam and a doctor who's absconded with some funds find themselves bound together in a race against the clock when they get locked together in a bank vault over one weekend. The blue-collar criminal is casing the joint, while the white-collar crook is trying to put back money he pilfered. Both men fear detection when officials open the vault on Monday, but the plot thickens when the duo discovers that thieves less honorable than they may have set them up to be discovered in the vault. Suspense builds up intricately as the weekend flies by and the threat of discovery becomes more certain. (a.k.a.: *Farewell, Friend*)

HONOR THY FATHER ★★★
1973, USA (TV)
Joseph Bologna, Brenda Vaccaro, Raf Vallone, Richard Castellano. Directed by Paul Wendkos. 99 min.

Often unjustly dismissed as a rip-off of *The Godfather*, this television film is a factual account of the family life of a Mafia branch. Consciously smaller in scope and without the mythologizing of the Francis Ford Coppola film, this is a compelling look at otherwise average citizens who happen to derive their living from organized crime. The ethical neutrality of the approach may be difficult to justify, since it may seem to some like tacit approval of these criminals; but within its limitations, the film is well handled. From the book by Gay Talese, who spent months researching and living with the Bonnano family, whose names have not been changed.

THE HOOKED GENERATION ½★
1969, USA, R
Jeremy Slate, Steve Alaimo, John Davis Chandler, Willie Pastrano, Cece Stone. Directed by William Grefe. 92 min.

Brutal, relentless, raping and murdering as casually as they shoot drugs, and bearing names like Acid and Dum Dum—are *these* the children of the sixties? That's what this unconsciously reactionary film seems to be snorting as it blithely chronicles the picaresque mayhem wreaked by three amoral zombies crashing through the Western wilds in a quest devoted exclusively to buying and selling dope. The filtered psychedelic scenes alone make this film so dated it seems to be cast in stone. Only Jeremy Slate as the gang leader and John Davis Chandler as his heroin-hooked lackey approach professional levels; the rest of the cast and crew find that an elusive goal.

HOOPER ★★★
1978, USA, PG
Burt Reynolds, Jan-Michael Vincent, Sally Field, Brian Keith, John Marley, James Best, Adam West, Alfie West, Robert Klein. Directed by Hal Needham. 99 min.

Exhilarating, funny, and surprisingly intelligent, this film is Burt Reynolds's best stunt yet. Reynolds has made a movie about the Hollywood hypocrisy he's been sneering at all along, and there hasn't been such an affectionate, believable depiction of moviemaking since François Truffaut's *Day for Night*. Reynolds plays a top stuntman facing twin perils—middle age and Hollywood's hunger for dangerous stunts—and the movie treats both in tough-minded Howard Hawks fashion. Most of it is just throwaway entertainment, but *Hooper* is also—astonishingly—the absurdist comedy about death that Reynolds tried for, and bungled, in *The End*.

HOPPITY GOES TO TOWN ★★★
1941, USA
Animated: Kenny Gardner, Gwen Williams, Jack Mercer, Ted Pierce, Mike Meyer, Stan Freed, Pauline Loth. Directed by Dave Fleischer. 77 min.

As children, watching it on TV, we were enthralled by Max and Dave Fleischer's animated feature about big-city insects searching for a safer home, much preferring it to any of the Disney pictures. We remember droll, engagingly feisty characters (the eponymous hero, a grasshopper, wears a felt hat jammed on his head, like a reporter in a thirties comedy); heart-stoppingly goopy songs (by Frank Loesser and Hoagy Carmichael!); and dazzling animation, notably some perspective views from the tops of skyscrapers. Perhaps what's most appealing, especially to kids, is the idea of a complete, miniature society coexisting with the larger one. (a.k.a.: *Mr. Bug Goes to Town*)

HOPSCOTCH ★★
1980, USA, PG
Walter Matthau, Glenda Jackson, Ned Beatty, Sam Waterston, Herbert Lom, Douglas Dirkson. Directed by Ronald Neame. 104 min.

Walter Matthau plays another rumpled and resourceful middle-ager—a crack secret agent on the lam from his former cronies—in this mediocre comedy. Kicked downstairs, Matthau begins writing a scandalous exposé of the Agency and spends the rest of the movie hopscotching from country to country and disguise to disguise. Of course, the movie means to be loved for its zaniness; Matthau's Miles Kendig is every company man who ever got a raw deal from his boss, and his adversaries, notably Ned Beatty and Douglas Dirkson, are ''Hogan's Heroes''–style buffoons. *Hopscotch* reunited Matthau with his *House Calls* costar Glenda Jackson; they come off here like the Wallace Beery and Marie Dressler of the eighties.

HORROR EXPRESS ★★★
1972, Spain
Peter Cushing, Christopher Lee, Telly Savalas, Silvia Tortosa. Directed by Eugenio Martin. 88 min.

A clever and genuinely scary shocker. The bloody fun on this chilly train ride begins when someone foolishly opens up a crate containing the remains of "The Missing Link" and is taken over by the monster. Momentum and bodies build as the creature's consciousness jumps from body to body, leaving the befuddled Peter Cushing and Christopher Lee to figure out what is going on. Watch for Telly Savalas as an unlucky Cossack. (a.k.a.: *Panic on the Trans-Siberian Express*)

HORROR HOSPITAL ★★★
1973, Britain, R
Michael Gough, Robin Askwith, Dennis Price, Vanessa Shaw, Skip Martin. Directed by Antony Balch. 91 min.

From the opening (in which Dennis Price casts a connoisseur's eye over Robin Askwith's crotch) to the climax (in which the disfigured ghoul who runs the sinister country clinic runs into the quicksand), this is a gleeful mixture of motifs from William Burroughs and memories of Anglo horrors of the 1950s. Antony Balch's only full-length feature concerns a mad Pavlovian doctor whose body is a hulk of third-degree-burn tissue, boring holes in young persons' brains in an attempt to master their minds totally. Sophisticates of undergrowth horror have never been better cared for. Ingeniously blending the macabre with the satirical, *Horror Hospital* may be as bizarre as anything you've ever seen.

THE HORROR OF DRACULA ★★★
1958, Great Britain
Christopher Lee, Peter Cushing, Michael Gough, Melissa Stribling. Directed by Terence Fisher. 82 min.

The sensual, athletic vampire count taints many Victorian women, who succumb all too readily to his deadly embrace. Scientist/scholar van Helsing forces him into the purifying rays of the morning sun after a protracted pursuit, but it is clear that this is only the beginning of a continuing struggle. This film is a lush, gothic reworking of Universal's 1931 *Dracula* by England's Hammer Films, which tackled all the classics in films like *The Curse of Frankenstein, The Mummy, Curse of the Werewolf, The Phantom of the Opera, The Two Faces of Dr. Jekyll*, and many sequels. Purely from an entertainment point of view, this is the best version of the Bram Stoker story, with a superb Christopher Lee as the most animalistic and active Dracula yet seen on screen. This was also the first Dracula to explore the sexual side of the vampire, albeit rather tamely by contemporary standards. Fast pacing and an effective music score lead to an exciting climax.

THE HORROR OF PARTY BEACH ½★
1964, USA
John Scott, Alice Lyon, Allen Laurel, Marilyn Clark, Eulabelle Moore. Directed by Del Tenney. 82 min.

Part musical, part horror film, part survey of 1960s collegiate dating habits, part beach-blanket movie, part cautionary tale about industrial pollution, and altogether awful in the most wonderful way possible. Industrial waste dumped into the ocean causes some bits of brine, bones, and sunken sludge to transmute into fishy monsters that rise from the ocean depths to suck blood. Nonstop hilarity reigns as the thirsty fishies invade a girls' pajama party (apparently to stop those repressed coeds from singing more folk songs), frighten a stereotyped black maid into revealing all of her latest voodoo prevention devices, and leave an entire community in need of mass transfusions. If seeing overage college kids do the Zombie Stomp doesn't double you over with laughter, then watching the dumb monsters attack a mannequin will. There are a few scary moments, particularly from the actress playing Tina, whose close-ups make the monsters look pretty by comparison. This ranks as one of the twelve most enjoyable bad films, along with *The Conqueror, Maniac* (1934), *Plan Nine from Outer Space, Reefer Madness, Valley of the Dolls, Robot Monster, Attack of the Fifty Foot Woman, Cobra Woman, Glen or Glenda, Scream For Help*, and *Savage Streets*. (You're welcome to add your own enjoyable bad films here.)

HORROR ON SNAPE ISLAND

See *Tower of Evil*

HORROR PLANET ★½
1981, Great Britain, R
Judy Geeson, Jennifer Ashley, Stephanie Beacham, Robin Clark. Directed by Norman J. Warren. 93 min.

Here is still another science-fiction horror movie deeply indebted to *Alien*. Raped by a slimy monster beneath the surface of a barren planet, a member of an archaeological team starts to slaughter her colleagues to support her unnatural pregnancy. A sleazy, gory, and ultimately not particularly exciting film originally called *Inseminoid*.

HORROR RISES FROM THE TOMB ½★
1972, Spain
Paul Naschy. Directed by Carlos Aured. 90 min.

It's almost inconceivable that anyone could enjoy this bottom-of-the-barrel horror film from Spain. The rising horror of the title is a knight beheaded for witchcraft in the fifteenth century. Five hundred years later, he awakens to haunt his lookalike descendant and make a nuisance of himself. Unbearable.

THE HORSE IN THE GRAY FLANNEL SUIT ★★
1968, USA, G
Dean Jones, Diane Baker, Lloyd Bochner, Fred Clark, Ellen Janov, Morey Amsterdam, Kurt Russell, Lurene Tuttle. Directed by Norman Tokar. 114 min.

This heavy-handed, ugly-looking, overlong comedy was made by Disney at a time when the studio's product was coming to resemble bloated versions of television sitcoms, with no appeal to children or adults. This one owes a debt to "Bewitched," as studio stalwart Dean Jones plays a harried ad executive who comes up with the idea of using a horse to sell aspirin (it so happens that his daughter likes to ride). Unfunny complications ensue. The Madison Avenue satire falls flat, and the modestly talented cast is wasted.

A HORSE NAMED COMANCHE

See *Tonka*

THE HORSE'S MOUTH   ☆☆☆½
1958, Great Britain
Alec Guinness, Kay Walsh, Mike Morgan, Michael Gough, Ernest Thesiger. Directed by Ronald Neame. 97 min.

Joyce Cary's novel becomes a very funny film, directed competently if not imaginatively by Ronald Neame. Alec Guinness, who wrote the script, delivered one of his most beguiling performances as Gully Jimson, an eccentric artist, mystic, and scoundrel who lives wherever he can find an intriguing surface on which to paint. The character's impulse to paint on any bare wall leads to several amusing vignettes. Guinness, in particular, makes it all well worth watching.

HORSE SOLDIERS   ☆☆☆½
1959, USA, PG
John Wayne, William Holden. Directed by John Ford. 120 min.

John Wayne and William Holden star in John Ford's underrated extravaganza about blood, romance, and glory in the Civil War. Ford, perhaps the greatest storyteller in American cinema, relates an engrossing tale of a Colonel (Wayne) and a Major (Holden) who are ordered by General Ulysses S. Grant to sever a crucial enemy rail link deep in Confederate territory. Ford provides humor, drama, and the masterly cinematography for which he is acclaimed. Ford, Wayne, and Holden all seem at home in this picturesque Civil War "Western" and together overcome an occasionally flawed screenplay.

HORTON FOOTE'S 1918

See *1918*

THE HOSPITAL   ☆☆☆½
1971, USA, PG
George C. Scott, Diana Rigg, Barnard Hughes, Nancy Marchand, Frances Sternhagen, Robert Walden. Directed by Arthur Hiller. 102 min.

The cast is excellent in Paddy Chayefsky's witty, observant, and harshly ironic look at an incredibly mismanaged hospital. George C. Scott plays a doctor who is forced to investigate the mysterious deaths of several staff workers; he also falls for a woman who is trying to get her father released from the hospital. The mystery plot is played down for several amusing vignettes, including one devastating sequence in which Frances Sternhagen as an emergency ward nurse bullies patients for their Blue Cross and Blue Shield forms. Arthur Hiller's crude caricatures work well in this milieu, but it is Chayefsky's screenplay that provides the real bite. Strong, funny stuff.

HOT DOG . . . THE MOVIE   ☆
1984, USA, R
David Naughton, Patrick Houser, Tracy N. Smith, Shannon Tweed, Frank Koppola. Directed by Peter Markle. 96 min.

This winter-fun exploitation comedy combines instant replays of downhill skiing with lots of anal jokes and oral sex. The ski footage provokes the most immediate oohs and aahs (director Peter Markle knew just how much deep blue sky you need in the background to make a stunt skier seem to be soaring), but the story is just another dumb youth-anarchy bash (*Animal Lodge*?).

HOTEL   ☆☆½
1967, USA
Rod Taylor, Catherine Spaak, Karl Malden, Melvyn Douglas, Merle Oberon, Richard Conte, Michael Rennie, Kevin McCarthy, Carmen MacRae. Directed by Richard Quine. 124 min.

Arthur Hailey's best-seller comes to the screen with its multistranded plot intact and a nearly all-star cast playing out the melodramatics with gusto. Rod Taylor is a young hotel manager faced with the problem of convincing his racist, antiunion boss (Melvyn Douglas) to modernize and thus ensure survival. For more lurid plot lines, we refer you to the various guest suits. Glossy, tacky, trashy, and often quite entertaining; it became a TV series in 1983 with James Brolin in Taylor's role.

THE HOTEL NEW HAMPSHIRE   ☆½
1984, USA, R
Jodie Foster, Beau Bridges, Rob Lowe, Nastassia Kinski, Wilford Brimley, Amanda Plummer, Wallace Shawn, Dorsey Wright, Matthew Modine. Directed by Tony Richardson. 110 min.

Adapting John Irving's phantasmagorical novel, director Tony Richardson packs in almost all the author's lunatic subplots and catches the giddy yet downbeat sentimentality, the slapstick *weltschmerz*. But under such close inspection, the book gives off an odd aura of neurasthenia—perhaps because Irving provides more life-and-death episodes than we can digest in one sitting. Among the performers who get right into the knockabout spirit are Jodie Foster, Rob Lowe, Beau Bridges, and Wallace Shawn.

HOT LEAD AND COLD FEET   ☆½
1978, USA, G
Jim Dale, Karen Valentine, Don Knotts, Jack Elam, John Williams, Darren McGavin. Directed by Robert Butler. 90 min.

The ads for this comedy Western from the Disney Studios showed Don Knotts sunk to his nostrils in quicksand. He was standing on his horse, no doubt. Even children will have to be in a very undemanding mood to enjoy this lackluster "family film."

HOT MOVES   ☆
1984, USA, R
Michael Zorek, Adam Blair, Jeff Fishman, Johnny Timko, Jill Schoelen, Debi Richter. Directed by Jim Sotos. 85 min.

A clinic for the acne set on the various sizes and shapes of female breasts. It could be mild drivel if only it didn't toe the idiotic, sexist line of "it's okay for normal boys, but only *bad* girls do it." In this movie the bad girls are a sex-starved older woman, screechy prostitutes, a gaggle of bosomy beach blankets, and a male transvestite. It earns its single star as a consolation prize for having no stars in its cast.

THE HOT ROCK   ☆☆☆
1972, USA
Robert Redford, George Segal, Ron Leibman, Paul Sand, Zero Mostel, Moses Gunn, Charlotte Rae, William Redfield. Directed by Peter Yates. 105 min.

Wry and knowing, *The Hot Rock* succeeds by not wasting a bit of its precious resources: the cast is uniformly convincing and clever, Yates's direction is snappy, and Donald Westlake's excellent source novel provides a clearly thought out, yet comically convoluted yarn. George Segal and Robert Redford may not be Paul Newman and Robert Redford, but they hit it off as contrasting crooks, and Segal is able to provide the foil that Redford so desperately requires. The story involves the theft of a diamond and the subsequent troubles that arise when the gem is abandoned in a police station. Needless to say, it all works out in the end, but along the way there are more odd, surprising touches than seasoned viewers could hope for in a thriller.

HOTROD
☆½
1979, USA (TV)
Gregg Henry, Pernell Roberts, Robin Mattson, Grant Goodeve, Robert Culp, Ed Begley, Jr. Directed by George Armitage. 97 min.

This formulaic racing movie was made for television. The good guy is a young hotshot with the talent to make up for his lack of backing. The bad guy is his rich-boy opponent, whose father (Robert Culp) is one of the sponsors of the race. The flag is down—one of them wins and you lose. (a.k.a.: *Rebel of the Road*)

H.O.T.S.
☆
1979, USA, R
Susan Kiger, Lisa London, K. C. Winkler. Directed by Gerald Sindell. 95 min.

Another *Animal House* rip-off—this time it's a group of sorority sisters who expose themselves around campus and let their pet seal create havoc. Mindlessness, nudity, and seal jokes abound.

HOT STUFF
☆½
1979, USA, PG
Dom DeLuise, Jerry Reed, Suzanne Pleshette, Luis Avalos, Ossie Davis. Directed by Dom DeLuise. 103 min.

In his first film as both actor and director, Dom DeLuise has taken a stale and unfunny cops-as-clowns premise and invested it with too many tired jokes and too few rapturous comic inventions. As Miami undercover cops who set up a "police sting" fencing operation, DeLuise and likable cohorts Suzanne Pleshette, Jerry Reed, and Luis Avalos mug, bumble, and trade caustic barbs. Only the amiable collection of crooks and kooks—introduced in quick comic strokes—gives the film a modicum of mirth. Glutted with crashing cars, knockabout chases, and buffoonish free-for-alls, *Hot Stuff* never rises above its formula trappings—it wallows in them.

HOT TIMES
½☆
1974, USA, R
Henry Cory, Gail Lorber, Amy Farber, Bob Lesser, Steve Curry. Directed by Jim McBride. 82 min.

This ugly, unpleasant sexploitation film concerns an oversexed teenager who journeys from Queens to Times Square in search of sex. The intended comedy is obscured by the overwhelmingly seedy, pornography-level production values and the barely disguised hostility toward men and women alike. Thoroughly depressing.

THE HOUND OF THE BASKERVILLES
☆☆☆
1959, Great Britain
Peter Cushing, Andre Morell, Christopher Lee, Marla Landi, David Okley, Miles Malleson, Francis De Wolff, Ewen Solon. Directed by Terence Fisher. 88 min.

No, this isn't the famous Basil Rathbone version. Instead, Peter Cushing (as Sherlock Holmes) and Christopher Lee (as Baskerville—the *romantic lead*) head up a lurid Hammer Film Studios production of the classic Conan Doyle yarn that looks more like a horror movie than a Holmes thriller. Still, Cushing is a crisp, benign master sleuth, and Andre Morell makes a surprisingly sturdy Dr. Watson. Lots of atmosphere and gore, and the usual British character traits.

HOUSE
☆½
1986, USA, R
William Katt, George Wendt, Richard Moll, Kay Lenz, Mary Stavin, Michael Ensign, Erik Silver, Mark Silver. Directed by Steve Miner. 93 min.

A horror writer (William Katt)—estranged from his actress wife and haunted by the mysterious disappearance of their little boy—inherits from his aunt the very house where the child vanished. Unable to write, he must confront the literal demons of his Vietnam experience before the pieces of his life can fall back into place. A weird comedy/horror film whose tone fluctuates wildly from scene to scene. Produced by Sean S. Cunningham (producer of Wes Craven's *Last House on the Left*, director of *Friday the 13th*) and directed by Steven Miner, who helmed the second and third installments in the triskaidekaphobe's nightmare saga. Weak and only intermittently interesting. Followed by a sequel in 1987.

THE HOUSE ACROSS THE BAY
☆☆☆
1940, USA
George Raft, Joan Bennett, Lloyd Nolan, Gladys George, Walter Pidgeon. Directed by Archie Mayo. 86 min.

In this gripping revenge drama the standard plot mechanics grind themselves out as expected, but the cast performs with enough panache to transform the material. While her rather hard-nosed criminal husband (George Raft) is doing time, Joan Bennett takes the opportunity to fall hard for Walter Pidgeon. Unfortunately for Bennett, Raft's years behind bars have not left him a forgiving soul, and he decides to get even. Suspenseful and absorbing, and Bennett and Pidgeon make a watchable, dreamy team of onscreen lovers.

THE HOUSE BY THE CEMETERY
½☆
1981, Italy, R
Katherine MacColl, Giovanni de Nari, Paolo Malco, Giovanni Frezza. Directed by Lucio Fulci. 86 min.

A family moves into the shunned Freudstein mansion and is troubled by a variety of supernatural manifestations. A child ghost, blood everywhere, and a maggotty scientist hiding out in the basement provide ample opportunity for the undiscerning fan of gross-out horror films to be entertained. From the incredibly prolific Italian director of *The Gates of Hell*, *Seven Doors to Death*, and other many equally disgusting films.

HOUSE CALLS
☆☆½
1978, USA, PG
Walter Matthau, Glenda Jackson, Art Carney, Richard Benjamin, Candice Azzara, Dick O'Neill, Thayer David. Directed by Howard Zieff. 98 min.

Director Howard Zieff (*Slither*, *Hearts of the West*) no longer looks so promising in this conventional comic romance. Glenda Jackson plays a pinch-faced divorcée who demands fidelity from her men; the film lauds her old-fashioned spunk. Walter Matthau is serenely confident as the playboy doctor tamed by Jackson. Accepting him as a sex object is surprisingly easy, but the snappy dialogue sometimes makes this movie seem more like a Punch-and-Judy show than a romantic comedy.

HOUSE OF DOOM

See *The Black Coat*

THE HOUSE OF EXORCISM

See *Devil in the House of Exorcism*

HOUSE OF FRANKENSTEIN ☆☆½
1944, USA
Boris Karloff, J. Carroll Naish, Lon Chaney, Jr., Elena Verdugo, George Zucco, John Carradine, Glenn Strange. Directed by Erle C. Kenton. 71 min.

The monster series showed signs of wear at this point, but Universal Studios persisted. Even when in need of major script surgery, the three Big Monsters—Frankenstein, Dracula, and the Wolf Man—still had plenty of life in them. Mad Scientist Boris Karloff and his hunchbacked sidekick take a pleasure trip through Transylvania and encounter Dracula. As if that weren't hair-raising enough, the Wolf Man turns up to beat his hairy chest and cause a ruckus; bringing up the rear is Frankenstein, lumbering along in need of a battery recharge. This is sort of the *Grand Hotel* of horror films. The triumvirate of fiendish foes isn't exactly terrifying, but having them around is like having Halloween at your fingertips all year round.

THE HOUSE OF LONG SHADOWS ☆
1982, USA
Vincent Price, John Carradine, Peter Cushing, Christopher Lee, Desi Arnaz, Jr. Directed by Pete Walker. 85 min.

A brash young writer, painfully overacted by Desi Arnaz, Jr., bets his publisher that he can write a gothic horror story in twenty-four hours and repairs to the isolated Baldpate manor to do so. He is distracted by the eccentric Grisbane family, who have a terrible secret to hide. Too many twists spoil the plot, and the all-star horror cast can't save it. Dumb and stilted, despite the classic moment when Price hisses "Don't interrupt me while I'm soliloquizing" to an unmannered supporting player.

THE HOUSE OF SEVEN CORPSES ☆☆½
1973, USA
John Ireland, Faith Domergue, John Carradine, Carol Wells. Directed by Paul Harrison. 90 min.

This cheap but moderately well-conceived film deals with the making of a horror flick. A film crew makes the mistake (in some cases the fatal mistake) of going on location to a haunted house. They yearn for authenticity and atmosphere, but this particular spook house is a bit more haunted than anyone suspected. Soon the house claims a few more victims—but *is* it the evil house, or a ghost, or just a member of the film crew? Not very imaginative, the film tends to coast on the surefire story line without bringing much inventiveness to bear. Still, it's worth a look for fans of the genre.

HOUSE OF USHER

See *The Fall of the House of Usher*

HOUSE OF WAX ☆☆☆
1953, USA
Vincent Price, Frank Lovejoy, Phyllis Kirk, Carolyn Jones, Charles (Buchinski) Bronson. Directed by Andre de Toth. 88 min.

Jeepers, creepers, wait until you see Vincent Price trying to recruit human dummies for his new wax museum. Originally presented in 3-D, this horror flick was a sensation back then; today some of its 3-D effects seem extraneous to the central action, but the swirling black-cloak shenanigans of Price hold up extremely well. Having been disfigured and cheated by his ex-partner, and with his sanity destroyed by having seen his beloved waxworks go up in flames, he tries to recoup his losses and start over. Naturally, kidnapping reluctant humans, killing them, and pouring hot wax all over them is the first idea that comes to mind. No one gets as much mileage out of hamminess as Price, and his makeup job (his face seems to be dripping calamine lotion) will have you jumping out of your seat. There are lots of shots of people being pursued under the gaslights, and Phyllis Kirk gives Fay Wray a run for her money in the scream department. Not first-rate, but the jolts are still effective.

HOUSE OF WHIPCORD ☆☆
1974, Great Britain, R
Barbara Markham, Patrick Barr, Ray Brooks, Anne Michelle, Penny Irving. Directed by Peter Walker. 102 min.

Known for his string of sex films, Peter Walker directs a British *Caged Heat* with a twist. A proper, elderly couple run a private prison for women of "loose morals," where the female victims are subject to the usual whips, rats, and hangings. While the film runs the typical capture-and-rescue gamut, its uptight, puritanical British setting adds an interesting taboo quality to its otherwise standard titillation.

THE HOUSE ON GARIBALDI STREET ☆☆☆
1979, USA (TV)
Topol, Martin Balsam, Leo McKern, Janet Suzman, Nick Mancuso. Directed by Peter Collinson. 100 min.

This top-flight political melodrama concerns the means by which the Israelis nabbed Nazi war criminal Adolph Eichmann in Argentina, where he was living under an assumed name, and brought him to trial. An exceptionally good cast brings the historical events to life, and the semidocumentary flavor proves an absorbing way to tell this tale of justice triumphant.

THE HOUSE ON HAUNTED HILL ☆☆☆
1958, USA
Vincent Price, Carol Ohmart, Richard Long, Alan Marshal, Elisha Cook, Jr. Directed by William Castle. 75 min.

In the late fifties and early sixties, a television phenomenon called Fright Night or Chiller Theater became an important part of the viewing habits of college kids and teenagers. On Saturday nights after midnight, young people could gather around the set and watch their favorite horror host unreel a spook show just like this one. It's the perfect Chiller Theater movie (and still a lot of fun to sit around and watch)—it's gimmicky, set in a haunted house, features a respectable quota of thrills without distracting you from pigging out on pizza, and is just scary enough to get your girl/boy friend to jump into your lap on occasion. It's an enjoyable potboiler about an immensely rich man who offers invited guests $50,000 if they can survive for one night in a spook house—but Vincent Price doesn't really intend to shell out that cash in every single case. Ranking with *The Tingler* as the best of the William Castle horror flicks, *House on Haunted Hill* should be watched with all the lights out and with as much junk food as you can carry to the TV room.

HOUSE ON SORORITY ROW ☆☆½
1983, USA, R
Eileen Davidson, Kathryn McNeil, Lois Kelso Hunt. Directed by Mark Rosman. 90 min.

Seven graduating sorority sisters are murdered, one by one, after they accidentally kill their aging housemother. This film is better than the usual psycho-killer stuff, thanks to some good acting and a director who appears to have been interested in what he was doing.

THE HOUSE THAT DRIPPED BLOOD ☆☆☆½
1971, Great Britain, PG
Denholm Elliott, Peter Cushing, Christopher Lee, Ingrid Pitt, Jon Pertwee. Directed by Peter Duffell. 101 min.

This is the best of the Amicus horror anthologies, with five stories that vary in tone to provide an overall satisfying package. The stories are held together by the victims' common residence in the house of the title. A mystery writer comes face to face with the killer in one of his stories; a wax museum holds the usual surprises; an adorable little girl experiments with a voodoo doll in Daddy's image; and a horror-film star gets a bit too involved in his work. Screenplay by Robert Bloch (*Psycho*), with plenty of in-jokes and arch bits (but almost no gore, the promise of the title notwithstanding).

THE HOUSE THAT VANISHED

See *Scream and Die*

THE HOUSE WHERE EVIL DWELLS ☆
1982, USA, R
Edward Albert, Susan George, Doug McClure, Amy Barrett, Mako Hattori. Directed by Kevin Connor. 88 min.

This brutal, bankrupt horror film benefits slightly from an unusual locale. A family ignores warnings about moving into an old house in Japan. Failing to even seek out a Nipponese ghostbuster, the foolhardy family moves right in. There are a few ectoplasmic chills, but the derivativeness of the script is not dispelled by the sense of déjà vu that haunts this film. It takes more than moving a haunted house flick to the Land of the Rising Sun to turn it into something original. This is *The Amityville Horror* wrapped in a kimono.

HOWARD THE DUCK ☆
1986, USA, PG
Lea Thompson, Jeffrey Jones, Ed Gale, Chip Zien, Tim Robbins. Directed by Willard Huyck. 111 min.

It began in the 1970s as a Marvel Comic whose cigar-chomping, wise-quacking protagonist became a cult hero. It ended, we hope forever, with this egg laid by George Lucas's production company, reportedly costing in the neighborhood of $34 million. That averages to $17 million per laugh, and about $1.95 per bad pun. The plot, for the record, concerns the arrival of the title character on Planet Earth, specifically Cleveland, and his quasi-romance with a punk singer (Lea Thompson) who apparently has a web fetish. In the second hour the low comedy gives way to endless, spectacularly boring special effects created by Lucas's Industrial Light and Magic Company; too bad they didn't lavish more care on Howard, who looks like a plastic window display.

HOW FUNNY CAN SEX BE? ☆½
1976, Italy, R
Giancarlo Giannini, Laura Antonelli, Alberto Lionello. Directed by Dino Risi. 97 min.

It must be a lot funnier than this collection of redundant vignettes starring Giancarlo Giannini and the luscious Laura Antonelli. Eight sketches united by a common theme of incipient sexual excitement, dragged down by a naughty vulgarity but never uplifted by anything truly obscenely hilarious.

HOW I WON THE WAR ☆☆
1967, Great Britain
Michael Crawford, John Lennon, Roy Kinnear, Jack MacGowran, Lee Montague. Directed by Richard Lester. 109 min.

Made by Richard Lester in the early years of what became a long decline, this conventional antiwar film makes its rather worn points by that most tiresome method, the absurdist parable. In this send-up of the "valiant British Army" movies of the World War II era, an officer watches his men get picked off one by one; unfortunately, when they die they don't leave the film, they simply get painted a solid color and drift around as distracting "ghosts" for the rest of the picture. Terribly dated, and a bit of a pain.

THE HOWLING ☆☆½
1981, USA, R
Dee Wallace, Patrick Macnee, Dennis Dugan, Christopher Stone, Belinda Balaski, Kevin McCarthy, John Carradine, Slim Pickens. Directed by Joe Dante. 91 min.

A California TV reporter (Dee Wallace of *E.T.*) stumbles over a few mutilated corpses and discovers that werewolves are alive and well in director Joe Dante's and screenwriter John Sayles's satiric, yet terrifying modern horror tale. A nice mix of werewolves as both sexual renegades and hardheaded businessmen. The startling special effects were created by Rob Bottin. Sayles is funny in a cameo role.

HOWLING 2 . . . YOUR SISTER IS A WEREWOLF ½☆
1984, USA/France/Italy, R
Christopher Lee, Annie McEnroe, Reb Brown, Sybil Danning. Directed by Philippe Mora. 91 min.

This shoddy, all-but-incomprehensible werewolf flick is a nominal sequel to *The Howling*, but it lacks that film's cast, creative team, and wit and the plot has only the most tenuous connection to the original. In place of John Sayles's script, there's hackwork whose best line of dialogue is contained in the title, and murky "Transylvania" scenes that don't look like a back lot so much as a backyard. The ubiquitous Sybil Danning is featured as a 10,000-year-old lycanthrope with excessive body hair, and a weary-looking Christopher Lee intones solemnly about the full moon.

HOW THE WEST WAS WON ☆☆☆
1963, USA
George Peppard, Debbie Reynolds, Carroll Baker, James Stewart, Henry Fonda, John Wayne, Gregory Peck. Directed by John Ford, George Marshall, and Henry Hathaway. 155 min.

This solid, inspirational Western deals with the pioneer spirit and how it tamed the West. The mammoth undertaking required three directors and an all-star cast, and was especially designed for the cinema screen; consequently, its impact is diluted on the tiny tube. Still, the film exhibits a real epic sprawl and a sense of the spectacular as the pioneers buck the ravages of nature and the temper tantrums of Indians. Hollywood craftsmanship at its most enjoyable.

HOW TO BEAT THE HIGH COST OF LIVING ☆☆
1980, USA, PG
Jane Curtin, Susan St. James, Jessica Lange, Fred Willard, Garrett Morris, Eddie Albert, Dabney Coleman, Richard Benjamin, Art Metrano, Ronnie Schell, Sybil Danning. Directed by Robert Scheerer. 102 min.

By normal standards, this farce about three financially strapped housewives who make ends meet by turning to genteel robbery is merely mediocre; considering the abilities of its cast, it's a criminal waste of talent. Jane Curtin (who later reteamed with Susan St. James for TV's "Kate and Allie") comes off best, honing her prim, sharp-tongued "Saturday Night Live" persona into a satisfying characterization. She and Dabney Coleman (as a softhearted cop) share the movie's one genuinely funny scene. But St. James can't surmount the idiocies of the script, and Jessica Lange looks none too happy muddling through her vacuous role.

HOW TO BREAK UP A HAPPY DIVORCE ☆½
1976, USA (TV)
Barbara Eden, Hal Linden, Marcia Rodd, Peter Bonerz, Harold Gould. Directed by Jerry Paris. 72 min.

A woman tries to make her ex-husband jealous in order to win him back in a film that wasn't worth seeing even when you could watch it for free on NBC. It smells like a failed pilot, is riddled with TV semistars, and now has a new life as video debris. If this sort of thing appeals to you, just stay home and turn on any network. You'll be grateful for the commercials.

HOW TO MARRY A MILLIONAIRE   ☆☆½
1953, USA
Lauren Bacall, Marilyn Monroe, Betty Grable, William Powell, Cameron Mitchell, David Wayne, Fred Clark, Rory Calhoun. Directed by Jean Negulesco. 96 min.

Marilyn Monroe bumps into walls when not wearing her eyeglasses and Lauren Bacall and William Powell trade a few quips, but otherwise this is a much-overrated comedy. It moves sluggishly from the full orchestra rendition of the "Street Scene" opening to its predictable "love over money" conclusion. The premise—how three women (Monroe, Bacall, and Betty Grable) set out to revel in the glamorous life and marry millionaires—has great possibilities that are never fulfilled. A wide screen and color print might have made the film easier on the eye, but it couldn't make it any funnier.

HOW TO STUFF A WILD BIKINI   ☆☆
1965, USA
Annette Funicello, Dwayne Hickman, Frankie Avalon, Harvey Lembeck, Buster Keaton, Mickey Rooney. Directed by William Asher. 90 min.

The Beach Party series, American International Pictures's attempt to cash in on the burgeoning teen market, began running down fairly quickly and by 1965 was in a tottering yet hysterical state. The film is a mix of several confusing plots: Frankie Avalon in Tahiti gets Bwana (Buster Keaton) the witch doctor to watch Dee Dee (Annette Funicello). Peachy (Mickey Rooney) is a press agent out to exploit Cassandra—who was sent by Bwana to distract Ricky from Dee Dee. Confused? Well, this perfect party movie will straighten you out. Interestingly sparing in its use of Avalon, and clever in covering the pregnant Funicello.

HUCKLEBERRY FINN   ☆☆☆½
1939, USA
Mickey Rooney, Walter Connolly, William Frawley, Rex Ingram, Lynne Carver, Clara Blandick. Directed by Richard Thorpe. 90 min.

Richard Thorpe may have been ousted from *The Wizard of Oz* set for lack of imagination, but he's in good form here with this earthy, well-acted adaptation of Mark Twain's classic novel. Done on a low budget, the film is less self-conscious than some of the other MGM literary adaptations (*A Tale of Two Cities, David Copperfield*) and the casting is perfect: Mickey Rooney as Huck, Rex Ingram as Jim, and William ("Fred Mertz") Frawley as "The Duke." This is not a great film but is perhaps the best of all the movie versions, which included those made in 1931, 1960, 1974, and 1975. Note: MGM also planned to make a musical Huck Finn in the mid-fifties starring William Warfield as Jim, but it never materialized. (a.k.a.: *The Adventures of Huckleberry Finn*)

HUCKLEBERRY FINN   ☆☆
1975, USA (TV)
Ron Howard, Sarah Selby, William L. Erwin, Frederic Downs, Rance Howard, Jack Elam, Shug Fisher, Antonio Fargas, Donny Most, Merle Haggard. Directed by Robert Totten. 74 min.

Mark Twain's funny, powerful saga of racism and friendship on the Mississippi has been diluted into a saccharine made-for-TV movie. The ABC network cast Ron Howard ("Richie Cunningham") as Huck and Donny Most ("Ralph Malph") as Tom Sawyer, evidently seeking to capitalize at the time on the popularity of their TV series, "Happy Days." The pacing is often slow, and the film never comes close to evoking the flavor of Twain's Mississippi adventure. The production almost completely lacks the savage bite, wry humor, and moving warmth of the original novel. A narrator made up to look like the author periodically interrupts the film with tedious snippets that try far too hard to be wise and charming. Frequent, brief blackouts that no one bothered to cut let us know where the commercials would have been.

HUD   ☆☆☆½
1963, USA
Paul Newman, Melvyn Douglas, Patricia Neal, Brandon de Wilde. Directed by Martin Ritt. 112 min.

Hud explodes as a conflict between principles and profits, Old West and New, father and son. Stern and moral Homer Bannon (Melvyn Douglas) doesn't see life on the ranch the same way that his arrogant, amoral son Hud (Paul Newman) does. Newman's charismatic presence fills out the part of a son who would rather sell diseased cattle than have the herd rightfully destroyed. His father's will eventually rules, and the resulting annihilation of the herd graphically depicts the demise of an antiquated life-style; with the death of the longhorns, so goes Homer Bannon's Old West. Fine performances in this tragedy of character keeps this adaptation of Larry McMurtry's novel tense without indulging in melodrama. Although Newman didn't win the Oscar the whole cast deserved, Patricia Neal and Melvyn Douglas did. Martin Ritt's direction is masterful.

HUEY LONG   ☆☆½
1985, USA
Directed by Ken Burns. 88 min.

Was Huey Long a martyred radical or an eccentric egotist caught up in the political machinery of his day? Ken Burns's documentary attempts to answer that question with biographical data, newsreel footage, and interviews with those who knew him (his son, his sister, Tom Wicker, Robert Penn Warren, and several Louisiana citizens). For those whose only knowlege of Long is that he provided Warren with the model for the political demagogue in *All the King's Men*, this should prove enlightening and worthwhile. For others, however, many questions remain about the man who has been credited with inspiring much of Roosevelt's New Deal, and the film never comes to a clear point of view of its own. A well-packaged profile, but one that refuses to confront the most perplexing aspects of its subject.

THE HUMAN DUPLICATORS   ☆½
1964, USA
George Nader, Barbara Nichols, George Macready, Dolores Faith, Richard Kiel, Hugh Beaumont, Richard Arlen. Directed by Hugo Grimaldi. 80 min.

This cheesy science-fiction film came a little late for its Red-scare theme of Martians coming to earth and replacing humans with exact android copies. It features a quirky cast, including perennial B-player George Nader, Richard Kiel (he was "Jaws" in a couple of James Bond films), and the Beaver's dad Hugh Beaumont; all of them, unfortunately, seem to have been replaced by androids on the first day of shooting. The tacky production values make this good for a few laughs but not much else.

HUMAN EXPERIMENTS   ☆☆
1980, USA, R
Jackie Coogan, Aldo Ray, Ellen Travolta, Linda Haynes, Geoffrey Lewis. Directed by J. Gregory Goodell. 82 min.

A pretty itinerant singer is erroneously convicted of murder and sentenced to life imprisonment at the Gates Correctional Institution. There she finds herself immersed in the usual sluts-in-the-slammer clichés—butch inmates, strip searches, sadistic guards, and gratuitous nudity—with an added dimension: head psychiatrist Hans Kline plays a warped psychopath who indulges his penchant for ridiculous experiments in behavioral modification at the expense of pretty inmates. Though *Human Experiments* (in spite of its spectacularly lurid title) lacks the maniacal energy of *Caged Heat* or *Hellhole*—two sterling examples of the women-in-prison form—it is fairly entertaining within its obvious limitations. (a.k.a.: *Beyond the Gate*)

THE HUMAN MONSTER   ☆☆½
1939, Great Britain
Bela Lugosi, Hugh Williams, Greta Gynt, Edmond Ryan, Wilfred Walter. Directed by Walter Summers. 76 min.

Bela Lugosi fans will enjoy this murder melodrama. He gets to play a much better part than usual, and he actually looks as though he's trying most of the time. Based on an Edgar Wallace thriller (all of which had more lurid titles than their content justified), the movie casts Lugosi as a doctor running a home for the blind who has an insurance scam going—if any of his charges die, he collects on the insurance. So naturally he helps them along, with the aid of his brutish assistant. This was made in Ireland, which was not obliged to follow the Hays Office Production Code, and is thus more violent than American horror movies of the time.

HUMANOIDS FROM THE DEEP ☆☆½
1980, USA
Doug McClure, Ann Turkel, Vic Morrow, Cindy Weintraub. Directed by Barbara Peeters. 80 min.

This horror howler has oversexed aquatic creatures inseminating the women of a small coastal town. The Comic-book fun is a lot better than *The Horror of Party Beach*, with a befuddled Doug McClure trying to figure out how to knock off the pesky but deadly critters. The film is notable for Rob Bottin's interesting makeup effects and a concluding scene that's a direct steal from *Alien*. Even if you don't enjoy somebody dressed in a fish costume jumping on top of a naked woman, the cast plays it in the right spirit.

HUMONGOUS ☆
1981, Canada, R
Janet Julian, David Wallace, Janit Baldwin, John Wildman. Directed by Paul Lynch. 93 min.

This film is the standard "stranded on an island" chiller. Instead of a conventional maniac stalking the surf, we have a half-man half-beast (known to his friends as Humongous, apparently). He decides to rid the world of a few more teens after these Clearasil-heads make the mistake of dropping by his island unannounced. The worst aspect of this terrible monster flick is the number of night scenes that transferred so poorly to videotape. Watching this, you'll think your eyes need a quick trip to Pearle Vision Center.

THE HUNCHBACK OF NOTRE DAME ☆☆☆☆
1939, USA
Charles Laughton, Maureen O'Hara, Edmund O'Brien, Cedric Hardwicke, Thomas Mitchell, George Zucco. Directed by William Dieterle. 115 min.

During the heyday of the German silent film, Director William Dieterle was an ex-actor (he played the lead in Leni's *Waxworks*) and he brought with him a gothic thoroughness to many a Hollywood film. His masterpiece, *Hunchback*, has seldom been bettered as an evocation of medieval life, while Charles Laughton's portrayal of the grotesque Quasimodo makes even that of Lon Chaney look feeble, bringing great pathos to the stunted creature's predicament. The film centers on the interrelation between opposites, beauty and ugliness, religion and superstition, prejudice and tolerance. The atmosphere of ignorance, terror, and cruelty becomes, on occasion, one of almost supernatural horror.

THE HUNGER ☆☆
1983, USA, R
Catherine Deneuve, David Bowie, Susan Sarandon. Directed by Tony Scott. 100 min.

A world-weary malaise hangs over and eventually overwhelms this slight, sedate horror of manners. A chic, ageless vampire and her companion—suddenly and fatally ill after 300 years of undead life—stalk New York's neon lights, crossing the path of a young gerontologist with unexpected results. The first feature by director Tony Scott, brother of Ridley Scott (*Blade Runner*), it is glossy, stunningly photographed, and erotic. Lots of look fleshes out a not-too-substantial narrative.

HUNTER ☆½
1971, USA (TV)
John Vernon, Steve Ihnat, Sabrina Scharf, Fritz Weaver, John Schuck, Barbara Rhoades, Davy Jones. Directed by Leonard J. Horn. 73 min.

This made-for-TV movie, from the producer of the series "Mission: Impossible," was the pilot for a series that never made it, and is unrelated to the later series of the same title. In fact, this pilot sat on the shelf for two years before the network would air it, which should tell you something. A scheme to brainwash government agents and use them for terrorist activities comes to light when one of the agents is injured in a racing accident. The government sends the agent's double to take his place and break up the operation. How seriously can you take a spy movie in which the lead is played by *Animal House*'s Dean Wormer?

THE HUNTER ☆☆½
1980, USA, PG
Steve McQueen, Eli Wallach, Kathryn Harrold, LeVar Burton, Ben Johnson, Tracey Walter. Directed by Buzz Kulik. 97 min.

Steve McQueen's last feature before his untimely death was almost universally panned by critics upon its initial release. (They all seemed to be expecting another *Bullitt*). It's actually an entertaining if innocuous action film with a lot more character than gunplay. McQueen plays real-life bounty hunter Ralph "Papa" Thornton, an anachronism who still lives in Chicago and makes a living by tracking down escaped criminals and bail jumpers. There are amusing in-jokes (McQueen, a prize-winning racer in real life, plays Thornton as the world's worst driver) and some odd tender moments between him and his pregnant girlfriend (Kathryn Harrold). It's all too loose and uncohesive—characters are introduced and then inexplicably drop out of sight—but it suggests that, had he lived longer, McQueen could have done interesting things with his aging-bad-boy screen presence.

HURRICANE ☆½
1974, USA (TV)
Larry Hagman, Jessica Walter, Barry Sullivan, Will Geer, Martin Milner, Michael Learned, Frank Sutton. Directed by Jerry Jameson. 78 min.

It's disaster time as the rain pours over a script that's all wet to begin with and a group of clichéd characters comes to grips with love and death. Luckily, the wind howls loudly enough to drown out some of the dialogue. Just another cliffhanger in which Mother Nature threatens to wipe out some lackluster performers; would that she had been more successful.

THE HURRICANE EXPRESS ☆☆
1932, USA
John Wayne, Tully Marshall, Conway Tearle, Shirley Grey, J. Farrell McDonald. Directed by Armand Schaefer and J. P. McGowan. 80 min.

This abridgment of the original twelve-episode poverty-row serial features the boyish John Wayne in his most agreeably awkward stage. He springs into pursuit of the Wrecker, the unknown villain responsible for his father's death in the sabotage of the Hurricane Express train. Like Fantomas, the Wrecker is a master of disguise and can impersonate each of the other characters, nearly all of whom become suspect at one point or another. Every chapter of the serial left the hero for dead, only to have its successor reveal his escape; the format encouraged repetitiousness and padding, which this streamlined version helps to reduce. (Director J. P. McGowan was earlier responsible for some of the best of the "Hazards of Helen" railroad series.)

HURRY UP, OR I'LL BE THIRTY ☆½
1971, USA, R
John Lefkowitz, Linda De Coff, Ronald Anton, Maureen Byrnes, Danny De Vito. Directed by Joseph Jacoby. 88 min.

George Trapani is running a money-losing business, fighting with his family, carrying a spare tire, and looking for love in all the wrong places as his birthday ominously approaches. You may sympathize, but do you really want to see a movie about him? Joseph Jacoby's independent comedy, produced on a shoestring, has some nice touches—including an early performance by Danny De Vito—but most of it is glum and amateurish.

HUSSY ☆½
1979, Great Britain, R
Helen Mirren, John Shea, Paul Angelis, Murray Salem, Jenny Runacre. Directed by Matthew Chapman. 95 min.

In this dreary melodrama Helen Mirren (who was so brilliant in *Cal* and poignant in *White Nights*) never attempts to rise above the level of her performance in *Caligula*. She has one steamy sex scene and displays her body a little, but refuses to shed any light on her character, a passive prostitute. John Shea plays the American who wants to take her away from it all, even if it means becoming involved in a crime with her psychotic ex-boyfriend. Worst of all, half the movie was seemingly shot in London's cheesiest nightclubs, and viewers are forced to endure several horrid acts.

HUSTLE ☆☆
1975, USA, R
Burt Reynolds, Catherine Deneuve, Ben Johnson, Paul Winfield, Eileen Brennan, Eddie Albert, Ernest Borgnine, Catherine Bach, Jack Carter. Directed by Robert Aldrich. 120 min.

Burt Reynolds receives more credit than any other actor for attempting roles outside of his usual métier, that slick good-ol'-boy persona, but the movies generally sink under the weight of all of his acting baggage. It's really a pity when he drags down a fine, crisp director like Robert Aldrich; here he's helped, in a curious way, by Steve Shagan's leaden script: the movie is stuffed full of morose gabbing about the immorality of the world. The story, about a cop who fails to talk his girlfriend out of her job as a call girl while he fails to solve the case of a dead young runaway, ends up where it began—almost. Lacks the charm and astringent grip of Aldrich/Reynolds's *The Longest Yard*.

THE HUSTLER ☆☆☆½
1961, USA
Paul Newman, Piper Laurie, George C. Scott, Jackie Gleason, Murray Hamilton, Myron McCormick. Directed by Robert Rossen. 135 min.

In this blistering, provocative poolroom drama, Paul Newman gained stardom by playing Fast Eddie Felsen, a two-bit pool player who travels to Chicago to challenge Minnesota Fats, the all-time champ. Robert Rossen and Sidney Carroll's screenplay, based on the novel by Walter Tevis, exposes the corruption of the business without taking sides, and director Rossen, in his penultimate film, achieves some of his bleakest, most despairing imagery with the help of Gene Shuftan's brilliant, Academy Award–winning widescreen photography. On video, some of the action is located off the screen (Rossen originally staged it at the far ends to comment on the alienation of the characters), but enough is captured to reveal the essence of the drama. Superb but depressing film. Followed in 1986 by Martin Scorsese's sequel *The Color Of Money*, for which Newman won an Academy Award reprising his role here.

HUSTLING ☆☆☆
1975, USA (TV)
Lee Remick, Jill Clayburgh, Monte Markham, Alex Rocco, Melanie Mayron. Directed by Joseph Sargent. 120 min.

One of the better made-for-TV movies about prostitution, Lee Remick plays a Gail Sheehy–type news magazine reporter who follows a prostitute (Jill Clayburgh) through a typical week. The film is well acted, especially by Clayburgh, and intelligently scripted by Fay Kanin. Contains many tough, uncompromising scenes and a sharp New York City ambience.

HYSTERICAL ☆☆½
1983, USA, PG
Bill, Mark, and Brett Hudson, Julie Newman, Bud Cort, Robert Donner, Murray Hamilton, Clint Walker, Keenan Wynn, Richard Kiel, John Laroquette. Directed by Chris Bearde. 86 min.

This zany comedy has to pull out all of the stops in order to succeed. It certainly tries hard enough, but it lacks the wit and talent to take it over the top. When the Hudson Brothers had their own TV show in the seventies, they were billed as a cross between the Marx Brothers and the Beatles; unfortunately, they were more like a cross between the Ritz Brothers and the Monkees—lots of cornball jokes and dull pop songs. At least this movie spares viewers the songs. As recompense, though, kooky sight gags are added to the cornball jokes. Bill Hudson plays a trashy novelist who tries to write a serious book in a haunted lighthouse; all he can come up with is "All work and no play makes Casper a friendly ghost." Mark and Brett Hudson play intrepid explorers who try to solve the mystery after having consumed lots of LSD. Amusing enough nonetheless.

I

I AM A FUGITIVE FROM A CHAIN GANG ☆☆☆½
1932, USA
Paul Muni, Glenda Farrell, Helen Vinson, Preston Foster, Allen Jenkins. Directed by Mervyn LeRoy. 85 min.

In the 1930s, Warner Brothers was known for producing "social protest" films like *Black Fury* and *They Won't Forget*. One of the best of these topical entertainments was this chain-gang exposé starring Paul Muni as a returning veteran who gets sent to a vicious convict camp for a crime he didn't commit. Based on the autobiographical story by Robert E. Burns, *I Am a Fugitive from a Chain Gang* is one of the bleakest yet most powerful films to emerge from Hollywood during the Depression (so powerful, in fact, that the Georgia chain-gang system was reformed soon after its release). The famous final shot is truly unforgettable.

I AM CURIOUS (BLUE) ☆☆
1968, Sweden, X
Lena Nyman, Borje Ahlstedt, Vilgot Sjoman. Directed by Vilgot Sjoman. 103 min.

I Am Curious (Blue) is a disappointing follow-up to *I Am Curious (Yellow)* that covers exactly the same territory, and the cast and director seem bored with the shenanigans. There is a lot of deadly discussion in this movie; most of it concerns Sweden's political life in the 1960s. The central plot again focuses on a young actress who is having an affair with her director and, yes, the director again plays the director. And there's even less sex to boot.

I AM CURIOUS (YELLOW) ☆☆☆
1967, Sweden, X
Lena Nyman, Vilgot Sjoman, Peter Lindgren, Borje Ahlstedt, Chris Wahlstrom, Magnus Nilsson, Marie Goranson. Directed by Vilgot Sjoman. 110 min.

After this film was seized by U.S. Customs as obscene material, most audiences (especially the critics) were disappointed that it didn't live up to its sensational reputation. Without the brouhaha, and without elevated expectations, the film does succeed on its own terms; it's simply about a confused young woman attempting to find her way through politics—sexual and otherwise. Lena Nyman is quite good as the pudgy, impassioned heroine searching for justice and satisfaction, and the film-within-a-film conceit is now less common and therefore less irritating than it once was. It's worth a look for historical perspective on sex in the cinema: although the film was not submitted for a rating, it was released as an X—nowadays, it's strictly an R item.

ICE CASTLES ☆☆½
1978, USA, PG
Lynn-Holly Johnson, Robby Benson, Colleen Dewhurst, Tom Skerritt, Jennifer Warren, David Huffman. Directed by Donald Wrye. 113 min.

This better-than-average ice opera concerns a skater from Iowa whose dreams of Olympic gold are dashed after a crippling accident. Like the old movies it emulates, *Ice Castles* is full of colorful star turns bolstering the unaffected lead performance of newcomer Lynn-Holly Johnson, soft, lyrical camerawork by Bill Butler, and syrupy but puissant theme music by Marvin Hamlisch. Consistently calculated for emotional response but well done by the standards of contemporary melodrama.

THE ICE PIRATES ☆
1984, USA, PG
Robert Urich, Mary Crosby, Michael D. Roberts, Anjelica Huston, John Matuszak, John Carradine. Directed by Stewart Raffill. 96 min.

Finally, someone had the bright idea to do a *Star Wars* rip-off with tongue in cheek. Too bad it wasn't someone with a bit of talent for parody, or anything else, because this is a dull and obvious yawn. Outer-space pirates zoom around seeking the universe's most precious commodity—water—and in so doing meet up with a kidnapped princess and an evil empire. The supporting cast isn't bad, especially Anjelica Huston, but the two stars should go back to television where they belong.

ICE STATION ZEBRA ☆☆☆
1968, USA
Rock Hudson, Ernest Borgnine, Patrick McGoohan, Jim Brown, Tony Bill, Lloyd Nolan, Gerald S. O'Loughlin, Buddy Hart. Directed by John Sturges. 152 min.

Aside from *The Guns of Navarone*, this is about the only successful adaptation of an Alistair MacLean novel. A spy satellite containing valuable film footage crash lands in the Arctic, and the United States and the Soviet Union engage in a race via submarine to retrieve it. From then on, it's tense action and double-crosses galore. In the best action-movie tradition, the actors restrict their efforts to trying not to bump into the furniture. Filmed in "Super Panavision," this was shown theatrically in Cinerama, so expect plenty of camera pans as they try to cram it all onto your video screen.

ICEMAN ☆☆☆½
1984, USA
Timothy Hutton, John Lone, Lindsay Crouse, Danny Glover. Directed by Fred Schepisi. 99 min.

This vastly underrated and very believable film concerns a group of scientists resurrecting a Neanderthal man who has been frozen in Arctic ice for thousands of years. After putting the caveman in a vivarium, the researchers decide on his fate while one of their number tries to communicate with the "iceman" as a human being. The movie takes a plot that has been done idiotically in the past and makes it work—thanks to the respectful handling of the subject matter. John Lone is thoroughly convincing as the noble savage, while Timothy Hutton gives an understated performance as the scientist who will do anything to save him. Filmed at actual glaciers in Canada, with Bruce Smeaton's haunting score giving much atmosphere to the already freezing surroundings.

I CHANGED MY SEX

See *Glen or Glenda?*

I CONFESS ☆☆☆
1953, USA
Montgomery Clift, Anne Baxter, Karl Malden, Brian Aherne, Dolly Haas, O. E. Hasse. Directed by Alfred Hitchcock. 95 min.

This unusual Alfred Hitchcock thriller stars Montgomery Clift as a Catholic priest faced with an impossible moral dilemma. During confession, a rectory servant tells him that he has committed a murder. When Clift is mistakenly arrested for the murder, he must obey the canonical code, even in a court of law, and not reveal what he has learned in confession. The premise is an intriguing variation on the usual tale of an innocent man trapped and destroyed by circumstantial evidence. But the pacing is heavy-handed, and the melodrama lacks Hitchcock's usual humor. Clift is inappropriately subdued and fails completely to project any sense of turmoil or anguish. But Hitchcock never did anything that was completely without interest, and this film is still worth a couple of hours of your time. Strikingly photographed, on location, in Quebec.

I COVER THE WATERFRONT ☆☆½
1933, USA
Claudette Colbert, Ben Lyon, Ernest Torrance, Hobart Cavanaugh, Maurice Black, Harry Bereseford, Purnell Pratt. Directed by James Cruze. 72 min.

The story, involving the torrid romance between a corrupt seaman's free-spirited daughter and a waterfront reporter, is wobbly, but good production values and excellent performances by Claudette Colbert and Ernest Torrance (in his last role) may make it worth a look. You'll find the character interplay more interesting than the somewhat dated adventure-on-the-seas action, and you may be surprised at the sexual candor (for the time) with which the unmarrieds' affair is depicted. Based on a novel by Max Miller.

IDIOT'S DELIGHT ☆☆
1939, USA
Clark Gable, Norma Shearer, Edward Arnold, Joseph Schildkraut, Burgess Meredith, Laura Hope Crews. Directed by Clarence Brown. 105 min.

Clark Gable is a two-bit vaudevillian and Norma Shearer a former conquest of his (in Omaha) now masquerading as a Russian countess, in the roles Alfred Lunt and Lynn Fontanne created on stage. Maybe it was an updating of *Heartbreak House* that Robert E. Sherwood had in mind when he assembled all these disparate types at an Alpine resort on the eve of an apocalypse (World War II was a cinch to predict). Whatever the motives behind his play, its author still tacked on an upbeat ending for Hollywood. There's a political warning here somewhere, but in practical terms the menace is Shearer. This part actually *calls* for posturing, and she drains out much of the junky delight we might otherwise have extracted from this.

I DISMEMBER MAMA ☆
1982, USA, R
Zooey Hall, Geri Reischl, Joanne Moore Jordan, Greg Mullavey. Directed by Paul Leder. 88 min.

A must-see for lovers of great titles attached to horrendous horror films! Mother love takes the rap again as our demented hero, Albert (Zooey Hall), lashes out at women all because he wants to kill his overprotective Mommy again and again. Wait until you see poor Albert gambol about with an eleven-year-old, marry her in a mock Victorian ceremony, and then sweatily fight off his carnal impulses. Featuring a leading man resembling an anorectic Warren Beatty cast as Dracula, a love theme entitled "Poor Albert," an almost total absence of gore or any scares, sound recording of a quality not heard since the first talkies, and a cast that seems to be rehearsing its first dramatic scene for an adult-education class, *I Dismember Mama* is a film you may want to chop into little pieces.

THE IDOLMAKER ☆☆½
1980, USA, PG
Ray Sharkey, Tovah Feldshuh, Peter Gallagher, Paul Land, Joe Pantoliano, Maureen McCormick. Directed by Taylor Hackford. 117 min.

This variation on a fifties oft-used plot (*Expresso Bongo, The Girl Can't Help It, A Face in the Crowd*) about a promoter who catapults a no-talent into stardom plays down the satire for psychodrama. Ray Sharkey plays a struggling songwriter who ends up making stars out of *two* talentless young men (Paul Land, Peter Gallagher) while romancing a publicity agent (Tovah Feldshuh). The Edward Di Lorenzo screenplay makes some deft observations about the rock-star phenomenon, but it dwells on the simpleminded notion that the business invariably corrupts by bringing out the worst in even the sweetest people. Fortunately, the well-picked cast makes the story line seem fresh, and the period re-creation is above average.

I DREAM TOO MUCH ☆☆½
1935, USA
Lily Pons, Henry Fonda, Eric Blore, Osgood Perkins, Esther Dale, Lucille Ball, Scotty Beckett. Directed by John Cromwell. 95 min.

Yet another of Hollywood's attempts to make a movie star out of an opera singer. This time it's petite Lily Pons, here playing the wife of a struggling composer (Henry Fonda). Pons gets to do numbers like the "Bell Song" from *Lakmé*, but fails to project the same kind of charm evident in her contemporaries (Grace Moore, Jeanette MacDonald). This is an enjoyable musical, despite the Depression-era look. A few more popular selections in the Jerome Kern score might have helped.

IF ... ☆☆☆☆
1969, Great Britain, R
Malcolm McDowell, Richard Warwick, David Wood, Christine Noonan, Robert Swann, Peter Jeffrey, Mona Washbourne. Directed by Lindsay Anderson. 111 min.

Lindsay Anderson achieves brilliant stylization verging on surrealism in this powerful, shocking tale of life in a repressive upper-class boys' school in England. Malcolm McDowell heads a well-used cast, but it's not essentially an actor's movie. The brutality with which the young men's lives are destroyed is stunningly meshed into a cohesive, cogent whole, which functions equally well as allegory and straightforward drama. Far better than either of Anderson's subsequent institutional attacks, *O Lucky Man* and *Brittania Hospital*.

IF YOU COULD SEE WHAT I HEAR ☆
1982, Canada, PG
Marc Singer, R. H. Thompson, Sarah Torgov, Shari Belafonte Harper, Douglas Campbell, Helen Burns. Directed by Eric Till. 103 min.

The latest entry in the Canadian-schlock-inspirational-romance genre is, believe it or not, a slapstick comedy about blindness. The hero, Tom Sullivan, is a blind college student who spends most of his time lurching around like Frankenstein's monster, crashing into everything in—or not in—sight. It's up to a golden-haired, doe-eyed Catholic girl to save him by revealing the meaning of true love. How sweet it isn't!

IF YOU DON'T STOP IT, YOU'LL GO BLIND ☆☆
1974, USA, R
George Spencer, Pat Wright, Jane Kellem, Garth Pillsbury, Russ Marin. Directed by Bob Levy. 80 min.

If you don't know from the title alone, we're not going to tell you. This film consists of nothing more than a few dozen ancient dirty jokes, all acted out by an ensemble of faceless characters. It's pretty cheesy and not at all titillating, but it's nice to know that it's there on the video rack waiting for you during those times when you just need a good dirty joke to cheer you up.

IF YOU KNEW SUSIE ☆☆
1948, USA
Eddie Cantor, Joan Davis, Allyn Joslyn, Charles Dingle. Directed by Gordon Douglas. 90 min.

Late Eddie Cantor vehicles had an air of desperation; witness this slim farce about an ex-vaudevillian who inherits a fortune in back pay from the U.S. government. Joan Davis as the wife almost outmugs old "Banjo Eyes" (a not inconsiderable feat). Hit songs include "My Brooklyn Love Song" and "What Do I Want with Money?" No comedy classic.

I HATE BLONDES ★★½
1981, Italy
Enrico Montesano, Jean Rochefort, Corinne Cleary, Ivan Desny. Directed by Giorgio Capitani. 89 min.

Enrico Montesano, "the Italian Woody Allen," plays an Italian schlemiel who ghostwrites for an incredibly successful mystery writer (Jean Rochefort). (The title of their latest tough-guy book provides the title of the movie.) This freewheeling farce about their mishaps with publishers and the underworld is reasonably funny, if less than fresh. Recommended for those who find movies funnier when they have subtitles.

I HEARD THE OWL CALL MY NAME ★★★½
1973, USA (TV)
Tom Courtenay, Dean Jagger, Paul Stanley, Marianne Jones, George Clutesi. Directed by Daryl Duke. 74 min.

One of the most critically praised TV movies of its day, this powerful drama deals with faith in God and in oneself. A young American priest is transferred to a remote village in British Columbia, where he finds his training is inadequate for coping with the demands of the post. The hardships endured by the Indians in his charge make him question his calling. Beautifully adapted from Margaret Craven's book, the film deals with a spiritual subject without being phonily pious or resorting to heavenly choirs on the soundtrack.

IKIRU ★★★★
1952, Japan
Takashi Shimura, Nabuo Kaneko, Kyoko Seki, Miki Odagiri. Directed by Akira Kurosawa. 140 min.

This muted masterpiece is cited by many critics as being the most moving portrait of the vicissitudes of aging yet captured on celluloid. While dying of cancer, a small-time civil servant wonders why his life has had so little meaning. Deciding not to go gentle into that good night, he works feverishly to have a playground built, as if that single act will somehow justify his existence. The film is an overpowering, albeit depressing, work of art. Akira Kurosawa, who has proven again and again that he is the master of epic filmmaking (*Throne of Blood, Ran*), reveals here his talent for quiet, contemporary melodrama.

I KNOW WHY THE CAGED BIRD SINGS ★★★½
1979, USA, G (TV)
Diahann Carroll, Ruby Dee, Esther Rolle, Roger E. Mosley. Directed by Fielder Cook. 96 min.

This exceptionally good biographical drama is based on Maya Angelou's poetical reminiscences of her Depression-era childhood. Set in the South, this TV movie conveys the sensation of growing up black during the poverty-wracked 1930s, as the young Maya Angelou and her brother are shunted back and forth between their paternal grandmother in Arkansas and their mother in St. Louis, two strong-willed women who clash over how best to raise the children. Sensitive, delicately acted.

I LED TWO LIVES

See *Glen or Glenda?*

ILL MET BY MOONLIGHT ★★
1956, Great Britain
Dirk Bogarde, Marius Goring, David Oxley, Cyril Cusack, Laurence Payne, Michael Gough, Wolfe Morris. Directed by Michael Powell and Emeric Pressburger. 104 min.

Not that you'd ever guess from the title, which seems to indicate a bad date, but this is another British World War II film recounting a mission in which the Brits invaded enemy territory and made the Germans look stupid. (Well, at least they make them look stupid in the movie.) This time around, the occupied territory is Crete, and the mission is to kidnap a ranking German general and smuggle him out, thus wounding German morale and bolstering that of the local resistance. Silly but acceptable war fare. (a.k.a.: *Night Ambush*)

THE ILLUSTRATED MAN ★★★
1969, USA, G
Rod Steiger, Claire Bloom, Robert Drivas, Don Dubbins, Jason Evers, Tom Weldon. Directed by Jack Smight. 103 min.

This film is really four different sketches bound together on a single canvas—which happens to be Rod Steiger's body. In this classic adaptation of a Ray Bradbury story, Robert Drivas meets Steiger, who rips off his shirt and lets his body talk. Drifting into regions of allegory and biblical hermeneutics, two of the three tattoo stories present Steiger and Claire Bloom as Adam and Eve figures; the third drops Steiger onto a planet exhibiting a perpetual downpour. Although perhaps blurred by too many directorial touch-ups, it is well acted, colorful, and balanced.

I LOVE MY . . . WIFE ★½
1970, USA
Elliott Gould, Angel Tompkins, Brenda Vaccaro, Dabney Coleman. Directed by Mel Stuart. 95 min.

Elliott Gould has sexual hang-ups. Do you care? A grossly unfunny, off-color comedy that throws in a lot of "daring" sex talk and a barrage of innuendo without much wit or sophistication. If you love your wife—indeed, if you love yourself—don't rent this.

I LOVE YOU ★★½
1981, Brazil, R
Sonia Braga, Paulo Cesar Pereio. Directed by Arnaldo Jabor. 104 min.

A mysterious, glamorous woman waltzes into the life of a brokenhearted bra manufacturer and, pretending to be a prostitute, engages him in a very sexy whirlwind romance. By the time her real identity is out, it's too late—they're in love. This breezy, dumb erotic comedy has Sonia Braga, the reigning sex queen of South American cinema, at the helm. (a.k.a.: *Eu Te Amo*)

I LOVE YOU, ALICE B. TOKLAS ★★★
1968, USA
Peter Sellers, Jo Van Fleet, Leigh Taylor-Young, Joyce Van Patten, David Arkin, Herb Edelman, Salem Ludwig, Louis Gottlieb, Grady Sutton. Directed by Hy Averback. 92 min.

Peter Sellers is wonderful as a furtive, square Los Angeles lawyer who eats some brownies laced with pot and mutates into a long-haired weirdo. Marvelously written by Larry Tucker and Paul Mazursky, this is a pre–*Bob and Carol and Ted and Alice* social comedy and a splendid evocation of the sixties. The director, alas, was Hy Averback, and the film suffers from his pedestrian pacing.

I LOVE YOU ALL

See *Je Vous Aime*

I LOVE YOU, I LOVE YOU NOT

See *Together?*

ILSA, SHE-WOLF OF THE SS ½★
1980, USA, X
Dyanne Thorn, Jo Jo Deville, Sandi Richman, Uschi Digard, Wolfgang Roehm. Directed by Don Edmonds. 95 min.

Lamentable, this is one of the hottest "cult" rental items at local video stores everywhere. (It's best not to let the mind linger over what that says about the taste of video renters.) *Ilsa* is exploitation filmmaking guaranteed to offend everyone (except sadists and sexual perverts fond of Nazi regalia). According to its prologue, the film is loosely based on actual cases of medical atrocities committed by scientists in concentration camps. Certainly this film is an atrocity that ranks with the rankest. Ilsa, a hard-to-satisfy Fräulein Doctor who vents her sexual frustration on her unfortunate "patients"—guinea pigs being tested for their tolerance to pain—meets her match in an American P.O.W. whose ability to quench Ilsa's lust leads to her downfall. (But not until we've witnessed a steady stream of vile torture scenes that are paraded here like dance numbers in a musical.)

I'M ALL RIGHT, JACK ☆☆☆½
1960, Great Britain
Ian Carmichael, Peter Sellers, Terry-Thomas, Richard Attenborough, Dennis Price, Margaret Rutherford. Directed by John and Roy Boulting. 104 min.

This very funny farce has a wonderful British cast directed by the Boulting brothers, who excelled at this sort of thing. Ian Carmichael is a naive young man who takes a job with his uncle's firm and manages to get on the bad side of both management and the union. Peter Sellers won the British Academy Award for his role as a union leader.

I MARRIED A MONSTER FROM OUTER SPACE ☆☆☆
1958, USA
Tom Tryon, Gloria Talbott, Ken Lynch, John Eldredge, Maxie Rosenbloom. Directed by Gene Fowler, Jr. 78 min.

Despite the lurid title, this is an unusually well-made film from the fifties subgenre of paranoid science fiction (*Invasion of the Body Snatchers*, for example). Just prior to his marriage to Gloria Talbott, Tom Tryon is taken over by an alien being, one of a group who have come to this planet to propagate their race. Director Gene Fowler, Jr., was a film editor for Fritz Lang, and the lessons he learned from Lang show to good effect here.

I MARRIED A WITCH ☆☆½
1942, USA
Veronica Lake, Fredric March, Cecil Kellaway, Robert Benchley, Susan Hayward, Elisabeth Patterson. Directed by René Clair. 76 min.

Certain European auteurs such as Fritz Lang, Ernst Lubitsch, Douglas Sirk, and Max Ophuls created masterpieces while working within the Hollywood studio system. René Clair, on the other hand, went from highly inventive French comedies like *Le Million* and *A Nous la Liberté* to middle-gear American fluff like *The Flame of New Orleans* and this film (originally started by Preston Sturges). Veronica Lake plays a sexy witch who ends up marrying a descendant of the man who had her burned in a seventeenth-century Salem trial. Lake looks cute and March is suitably baffled and blustery, but the comedy is thin and the fantasy elements, though technically satisfying, are not fully explored. Incidentally, this film, not the 1945 film titled *Bewitched*, was the inspiration for the popular TV series "Bewitched."

I MARRIED A WOMAN ☆½
1958, USA
George Gobel, Diana Dors, Adolphe Menjou, Jessie Royce Landis. Directed by Hal Kanter. 84 min.

This pea-brained sitcom was designed to cash in on George Gobel's TV persona. Gobel plays a harried adman who can't be blamed for his reluctance to go to work since he's got Diana Dors waiting for him at home. Not many laughs, unless you're a Gobel devotee.

I'M DANCING AS FAST AS I CAN ☆☆☆
1982, USA, R
Jill Clayburgh, Nicol Williamson, Dianne Wiest, Joe Pesci, Geraldine Page, Richard Masur, John Lithgow, James Sutorius. Directed by Jack Hofsiss. 106 min.

Despite several structural and dramatic flaws, this film rivets the viewer's attention. Jill Clayburgh plays Barbara Gordon, the real-life documentary filmmaker whose dependency on Valium lands her in a mental institution. Although David Rabe's screenplay (based on Gordon's book) convincingly builds up to the addiction, the withdrawal scenes alternate between the harrowing (Gordon abused by her live-in boyfriend) to the laughable (Gordon foaming and convulsing at the beach). The final scenes during her stay in the hospital are a little too pat. The film actually feels like three stylistically different and artistically unequal films, but the cast manages to hold the pieces more or less together: Jill Clayburgh gives her best performance since *An Unmarried Woman*; Nicol Williamson is frightening as her sadistic lover; Dianne Wiest is refreshing as her psychiatrist; and Geraldine Page steals the show as a gutsy cancer patient about whom Barbara is making her documentary. Deficiencies aside, this is a worthwhile and at times fascinating glimpse into a terrifying world.

THE IMAGEMAKER ☆½
1986, USA, R
Michael Nouri, Anne Twomey, Jerry Orbach, Jessica Harper, Farley Granger, Richard Bauer. Directed by Hal Weiner. 93 min.

This low-budget comic drama was produced at the same time as *Power*, and shares that film's unimaginative use of media manipulation as a subject. Michael Nouri (*Flashdance*) plays a deranged public-relations whiz whose elaborate scheme to raise money for a film he wants to make involves sexual blackmail and a faked on-air suicide. The film's ambivalence toward its hero briefly diverts one's attention from the utterly preposterous story. Despite the dramatic extremeties, no fresh points are made.

IMITATION OF LIFE ☆☆☆☆
1959, USA
Lana Turner, John Gavin, Juanita Moore, Susan Kohner, Robert Alda, Sandra Dee, Dan O'Herlihy, Troy Donahue, Mahalia Jackson. Directed by Douglas Sirk. 124 min.

One of the screen's all-time great melodramas, the last in the series of Ross Hunter/Douglas Sirk films made for Universal (*Magnificent Obsession*, *All That Heaven Allows*, *Written on the Wind*) and the last Sirk directed before prematurely retiring. Sirk's brilliantly precise and ironic mise-en-scène once again places his sudsy material (*Imitation* is based on the Fannie Hurst novel and the 1934 John Stahl movie) From the seductive title sequence of cascading jewelry, to the heartwrenching funeral finale, Sirk masterfully integrates music, color, and camerawork (by Russell Metty) to tell the tale of two single mothers and the trouble they encounter in raising their daughters. Modern audiences will doubly appreciate the sensitive treatment of the racial and working-woman themes. In such a film the performances need not be particularly outstanding, but Susan Kohner should be noted for playing the black daughter passing for white. Don't let the genre fool you; this is a great film.

THE IMMORTAL BACHELOR ☆☆
1977, Italy
Monica Vitti, Giancarlo Giannini, Vittorio Gassman, Claudia Cardinale, Renato Pozzetto. Directed by Marcello Fondato. 95 min.

Monica Vitti, who has become a very charming comedienne, plays a devoted wife who just loves being slapped around by hubby Giancarlo Giannini, a handsome, macho devil who likes it when she yells at him. During one of their knock-down, drag-out (but terribly sensual) battles, Giannini disappears down a sewer and Vitti is accused of murdering him. But would she kill such a hunk? No, thinks juror Claudia Cardinale, who wishes her husband, Vittorio Gassman, would try knocking her around a bit. This boring, predictable, slovenly film by Marcello Fondato would be bad even if its attitudes weren't so absurdly sexist and pathological.

IMPERIAL VENUS ☆☆
1962, Italy/France, PG
Gina Lollobrigida, Stephen Boyd, Gabriele Ferzetti, Raymond Pellegrin. Directed by Jean Delannoy. 120 min.

Jean Delannoy's second-rate historical spectacle is one of the dullest of the many films delving into the private lives of the Bonaparte clan. Here, the subject is Napoleon's seminymphomaniacal sister Paolina (as incarnated by sixties sexpot Gina Lollobrigida) and her disastrous dalliances, all set against tedious march-of-time pageantry. The original version may have been better; this English-language edition, shot simultaneously but not released in the United States until 1971, is much shorter than the European cut.

IMPULSE ☆☆
1984, USA, R
Meg Tilly, Hume Cronyn, John Karlen, Bill Paxton, Amy Stryker. Directed by Graham Baker. 91 min.

The inhabitants of a small town begin to behave in bizarre and violent ways, and nobody is looking for the problem's source. This old premise is nicely packaged, but there's no real spark to the production and the film lacks the imagination to carry its ideas out—most people give in to very ordinary impulses.

INCENSE FOR THE DAMNED

See *The Bloodsuckers*.

IN COLD BLOOD ☆☆☆
1967, USA
Robert Blake, Scott Wilson, John Forsythe, Paul Stewart, Jeff Corey. Directed by Richard Brooks. 134 min.

The famous Truman Capote nonfiction novel came to the screen in a long, chilling black-and-white semidocumentary of undeniable power and unrelieved unpleasantness. While one can't quibble with the artful look of the film or the consummate acting, one has to question the author and director's motives in exploiting both a "good" story and our own obsession with real-life tales of senseless murders. Just how serious a study of the criminal mind this is is open to question, but it is nevertheless a compelling crime story. But did the victims, the Clutters, have to be depicted so unfeelingly as personality-less sitting ducks?

THE INCREDIBLE HULK ☆☆½
1977, USA (TV)
Bill Bixby, Lou Ferrigno, Susan Sullivan, Jack Colvin, Susan Batson, Charles Siebert. Directed by Kenneth Johnson. 94 min.

This film is a dead-on retelling of the Marvel Comics yarn about a meek scientist who, through a laboratory accident, occasionally becomes an enraged green monster. At its insouciant best, it's trying for a cross between "The Fugitive" and *Doctor Jekyll and Mr. Hyde*, and it does manage to capture comic mogul Stan Lee's wise-guy attitudes toward businessmen, bookworms, women, cops . . . you name it. Pilot for the television series; the video version has been shortened.

THE INCREDIBLE JOURNEY ☆☆½
1963, USA
Emile Genest, John Drainie, Tommy Tweed, Sandra Scott, Syme Jago. Directed by Fletcher Markle. 86 min.

If you've never heard of any of the cast members in this Disney opus, don't worry—they're only supporting players to a trio of animals. After their owner gives them away to a friend, two dogs and a cat travel across two hundred miles of Canadian wilderness to rejoin their original family. Heartwarming family fare, short enough that it doesn't wind up causing heartburn.

INCREDIBLE MASTER BEGGARS ☆☆½
1985, Hong Kong
Bruce Leung, Ku Feng, Han Kuo Tsai, Li Tang Ming, Li Hai Sheng, Lui I Fan, Pan Yao Kun. Directed by Tu Lu Po.

Bruce Leung, an astounding acrobat with a fast, powerful technique, is showcased in this story of a beggar who learns the Tan Toi style and uses it to avenge the murder of his girlfriend. Recommended.

THE INCREDIBLE ROCKY MOUNTAIN RACE ☆☆
1977, USA (TV)
Christopher Connelly, Forrest Tucker, Larry Storch, Whit Bissell, Bill Zuckert. Directed by James L. Conway. 100 min.

This comic trifle dips very lightly into historical fact—it details a race between a young Mark Twain (spouting aphorisms even at this point in his career) and his archrival Mike Fink. It is neither incredible nor particularly credible, just forgettable. The race is the high point of this pleasant slice of regional roughhousing.

THE INCREDIBLE SARAH ☆☆
1976, Great Britain, PG
Glenda Jackson, Daniel Massey, Yvonne Mitchell, Douglas Wilmer, David Langton, Simon Williams. Directed by Richard Fleischer. 105 min.

This highly sanitized biography of the legendary Sarah Bernhardt is primarily a vehicle for the incredible Glenda Jackson to display her considerable talents. She's a great actress, but here the film around her is so flimsy and her own work so hammy and histrionic that she becomes, of all things, boring. Those who seek to understand the great reputations of either Bernhardt or Jackson will come away unenlightened.

INCREDIBLE SHAOLIN THUNDERKICK ☆½
1985, Hong Kong
Benny Tsui, Eagle Han, Mandy Choi, Phlip Yuen, Vincent Lee, Sandy Kwon, Bobby Nam, Simon Yuen, Harold Siu. Directed by Godfrey Ho. 90 min.

Here an absolutely irrelevant title is tacked on to a decent martial-arts fest. It's the usual revenge story beefed up by good fighting (choreographed by Eagle Han) and acting. Sharp direction by Godfrey Ho.

THE INCREDIBLE SHRINKING MAN ☆☆☆½
1957, USA
Grant Williams, Randy Stuart, Paul Langton, William Schallert, April Kent. Directed by Jack Arnold. 81 min.

This is one of the enduring science-fiction classics. Even Lily Tomlin's comic sex-change update can't vitiate the impact of the original film, which manages to disturb and move us even after repeated viewings. Jack Arnold, who also had fright-night luck with *Creature from the Black Lagoon*, has wrought the rare film that presents the kind of serious science fiction found more often in books than on celluloid. Accidentally exposed to radiation, the film's protagonist discovers to his horror that he's rapidly shrinking day by day; the process is inexorable. In addition to its contemplative subtext, the film delivers an abundance of nail-biting moments, particularly when the man is attacked by a house cat and then falls into the basement, where his survival attempts are both pitiable and frightening. Don't miss this.

THE INCREDIBLE SHRINKING WOMAN ☆☆☆
1981, USA, R
Lily Tomlin, Charles Grodin, Ned Beatty, Henry Gibson, Elizabeth Wilson, Mike Douglas. Directed by Joel Schumacher. 88 min.

Trapped in a TV-commercial-nightmare version of suburbia known as Tasty Meadows, Lily Tomlin absorbs a mixture of noxious household chemicals and promptly begins to shrink. The visual lampoon of suburban tackiness is superbly detailed, but the film's satiric content is meager; when it switches gears into slapstick farce, one is more than ready for the change. It's in the second half that we make the acquaintance of a gorilla named Sidney (actually special-effects whiz Rick Baker in his state-of-the-art gorilla suit), who gives off superstar vibes. Charles Grodin's teensy "takes" are more perfectly calibrated than ever. First-timer Joel Schumacher directs with no little energy but little enough wit.

THE INCREDIBLE TORTURE SHOW

See *Bloodsucking Freaks*

INCUBUS ☆
1982, Canada, R
John Cassavetes, John Ireland, Helen Hughes, Kerrie Keane, Erin Flannery. Directed by John Hough. 90 min.

This nasty horror film is not redeemed by the occasional touches of humor or the presence of John Cassavetes, who, we will presume, was raising money for one of his own projects. He plays a doctor who moves to a small town with his teenage daughter. Instead of peace and quiet, though, he finds a demon on a rape-and-murder spree. Director John Hough came to this from Disney films; he certainly hit the opposite extreme here.

INDEPENDENCE DAY ☆☆
1983, USA, R
Kathleen Quinlan, David Keith, Frances Sternhagen, Cliff De Young, Dianne Wiest, Josef Sommer, Bert Remsen, Richard Farnsworth. Directed by Robert Mandel. 110 min.

Kathleen Quinlan is a sensitive, artistic, beret-clad girl who's desperate (but unready) to make a break with her family in Smalltown, U.S.A. David Keith is the neighborhood boy she falls in love with. It's all unbelievably gloppy, but at least there's a great supporting performance by Dianne Wiest as a battered wife.

THE INDESTRUCTIBLE MAN ☆☆½
1956, USA
Lon Chaney, Jr., Marian Carr, Casey Adams, Ross Elliott, Stuart Randall, Robert Shayne. Directed by Jack Pollexfen. 70 min.

Lon Chaney, Jr., the Indestructible Ham, plays a bank robber who is electrocuted and brought back to life (not unlike his role in *Man-Made Monster*, though he was a good guy there). He hides out with his ex-girlfriend, a stripper, and sets out to kill the rest of his gang that turned him in. Enjoyable trashy fifties melodrama with a few authentically scary moments.

INDIANA JONES AND THE TEMPLE OF DOOM ☆☆½
1984, USA, PG
Harrison Ford, Kate Capshaw, Ke Huy Quan, Roshan Seth, Amrish Puri, David Yip, Dan Aykroyd. Directed by Steven Spielberg. 118 min.

If you haven't already seen this, be forewarned: this sequel to *Raiders of the Lost Ark* eliminates the hip, moviewise manipulation of the first film in favor of a nonstop parade of gruesome, repulsive shocks. These include a torture scene in which a high priest pulls the heart out of his victim and then lowers the still-living body into molten lava, a Himalayan feast with entrées such as baby snakes, eyeball soup, and monkey brains (served in the original container) and a journey through a dank tunnel filled with oversized scorpions, centipedes, and other bugs. (The worst torture of all, though, is Kate Capshaw, who screams shrilly from beginning to end: she is to Fay Wray what a chainsaw is to a scalpel.) Steven Spielberg's technique is undeniably the most bravura display you're likely to see for some time, but he too often uses it to produce loud, noisy roller-coaster shocks without pause or relief. The movie is acceptable for male thirteen-year-olds, younger children should perhaps be kept away from it (though its effect is diminished on television), and parents are recommended to pass it up to retain their pleasant memories of the original.

INDISCREET ☆☆☆
1958, Great Britain
Ingrid Bergman, Cary Grant, Phyllis Calvert, Cecil Parker, David Kossoff. Directed by Stanley Donen. 100 min.

In this cream puff, Cary Grant and Ingrid Bergman team up for the second time (the first was Alfred Hitchcock's *Notorious*) in a paper-thin comedy about an actress who falls for a diplomat in London. After he lies about his marital status, she plots her "revenge" (the highlight of the film). Stanley Donen's direction generally settles for a simple translation of Norman Krasna's play *Kind Sir*, but he does get to quote Rouben Mamoulian's split-screen bed scene from *Love Me Tonight*, and, as in Donen's musicals (*Seven Brides For Seven Brothers, Funny Face*), the production values are always first-rate. Grant, incidentally, is one of those few actors able to get away with playing cads, and Bergman makes masochism equally pleasurable to watch. Quite a pair, these two.

INDISCRETION OF AN AMERICAN WIFE ☆☆☆
1954, USA/Italy
Jennifer Jones, Montgomery Clift, Richard Beymer, Gino Cervi. Directed by Vittorio De Sica. 63 min.

An entire movie about a couple parting in a train station might not seem like a great idea, but director Vittorio De Sica has invested the nonnarrative with great sensitivity and style. Jennifer Jones, playing a woman torn between her husband and her lover (Montgomery Clift), gives one of the best performances of her career. Clift is also moving, but he's foolishly cast as an Italian and pushed too far into his "sensitive male" persona. It was also Selznick's idea to film the Cesar Zavattini/Truman Capote screenplay in a huge, cavernous Italian railway station, and cameraman G. R. Aldo does some beautiful work with the single set. The original eighty-seven-minute version titled *Terminal Station* was not released until 1983 and is not (as yet) available on video.

I NEVER PROMISED YOU A ROSE GARDEN ☆☆½
1977, USA, R
Bibi Andersson, Kathleen Quinlan, Ben Piazza, Lorraine Gary. Directed by Anthony Page. 96 min.

Kathleen Quinlan's performance as the teenage schizophrenic heroine of Joanne Greenberg's bestseller is so extraordinary that it's really a shame it's not showcased in a better film. Anthony Page's movie falls into the trap of turning the outbursts of patients in a mental hospital into actor's shticks and lingering on them for their freaked-out entertainment value. It's sad to see actresses like Signe Hasso and Diane Varsi tearing themselves apart for the camera (although Susan Tyrrell is actually rather good). And Anthony Page and his screenwriters, Gavin Lambert and Lewis John Carlino, have foolishly made Quinlan's violent fantasies explicit—hence ridiculous.

INFERNO ☆☆½
1978, Italy, R
Leigh McCloskey, Irene Miracle, Sacha Pitoeff, Daria Nicolodi, Eleanora Giorgi. Directed by Dario Argento. 107 min.

Once again Dario Argento expends all of his energy on eye-catching visuals with little attention paid to characterization or rudimentary logic. Still, although this isn't equal to his genuinely frightening *Suspiria*, *Inferno* will give fright-night fans a pretty hellish time. A young man returns from Europe to investigate his sister's brutal death; his questions open up a can of worms and greatly disturb some demon worshipers known as the "three mothers."

THE INFORMER ★★★½
1935, USA
Victor McLaglen, Heather Angle, Preston Foster, Joseph Sawyer. Directed by John Ford. 91 min.

John Ford's overpraised (for all the wrong reasons) story of guilt and Catholic redemption seems thematically obvious now, but it is still strikingly played and photographed, resembling nothing so much as a German expressionist version of a Warner Brothers's gangster melodrama. As Gypo Nolan, the down-at-his-heels lug who turns in a former IRA partner to the police and wrestles with his conscience in nighttime Dublin, Victor McLaglen is a brute force of nature, and it's hard to resist the oft-told story that Ford tricked him into giving as good a performance as he did by wearing him down and then telling him that they were only rehearsing.

INFRA-MAN ★½
1976, Hong Kong, PG
Terry Liu, Wang Hsieh, Lin Wei Wei. Directed by Hua-Shan. 89 min.

A scientist is turned into a super-robot to fight the monstrous hordes of Princess Dragamon, who is bent on taking over the world. This extremely silly kiddie fare has some interesting effects and sets. Inadvertently hilarious moments occur when Infra-Man and blimplike, outrageously costumed creatures have kung-fu fights.

INHERIT THE WIND ★★★½
1960, USA
Spencer Tracy, Fredric March, Gene Kelly, Florence Eldridge, Dick York, Donna Anderson, Claude Akins, Harry Morgan. Directed by Stanley Kramer. 127 min.

The Stanley Kramer canon is a frustrating one: while his themes are noble, his style is invariably pedestrian. His movies often seem more like college theses on social problems than films. *Inherit the Wind*'s stage roots (play by Jerome Lawrence and Robert E. Lee) only intensify this dilemma: Ernest Laszlo's camera does a few artful tilts and pans, but never disguises Kramer's proscenium arch. This is the one where Spencer Tracy goes head-to-head with Fredric March in a thinly disguised variation on the famous 1925 Monkey Trial, in which a schoolteacher named Scopes was prosecuted for teaching the theory of evolution. Tracy (as Henry Drummond—that is, Clarence Darrow) wins not only in the liberal righteousness of the piece but also in the acting sweepstakes. March plays the Bible-thumping prosecuting attorney, the William Jennings Bryan character. Unfortunately, aside from Tracy and Florence Eldridge (March's real-life wife), no one in the cast is able to transcend the simplistic characters they've been handed. Gene Kelly fans should note that this is one of his few nonmusical roles; he plays a cynical reporter covering the trial.

THE INHERITANCE ★★½
1976, Italy
Anthony Quinn, Fabio Testi, Dominique Sanda, Luigi Proietti, Adriana Asti, Paolo Bonalelli. Directed by Mauro Bolognini. 121 min.

Dominique Sanda won the best-actress award at Cannes for her portrayal of a thoroughly evil and coldhearted woman on the make. But while Sanda is seductive and the film visually graceful, the story is utterly predictable. Sanda sleeps her way to the top, wedding the son (Luigi Proietti) of a wealthy baking family and then bedding the clan's misanthropic patriarch (Anthony Quinn) as well. It's the umpteenth examination of the greedy aspirations of the Italian middle class of the 1880s, and the movie's atmosphere of total corruption feels more like Harold Robbins than like anything from the nineteenth century.

INHERITOR OF KUNG FU

See *Two Graves of Kung Fu*

THE INHERITORS ★★
1984, West Germany
Nikolas Vogel, Roger Schauer. Directed by Walter Bannert. 89 min.

A troubled teenager is drawn into the Nazi youth movement in the country of its origin, in a film that starts intelligently but becomes downright ludicrous once the boy is totally possessed by his fascist friends. Director Walter Bannert is full of good intentions here, and unfortunately lets a tendency toward exploitation and extremism get in the way of telling the story correctly. Even though *The Inheritors* has strong scenes and performances, it's an ultimately laughable look at a very serious problem. Subtitled, with an appropriately melodramatic Gustav Mahler soundtrack.

THE INITIATION OF SARAH ★★½
1978, USA (TV)
Kay Lenz, Shelley Winters, Kathryn Crosby, Morgan Brittany, Morgan Fairchild, Tony Bill, Tisa Farrow, Robert Hays. Directed by Robert Day. 104 min.

Trashy but highly entertaining TV gothic about sorority rivalry. When two sisters arrive at college, the beautiful one (Morgan Brittany) instantly sheds her sibling and pledges to the powerful-gorgeous-malign-bitch house, while Sis (played sweetly by Kay Lenz) gets dumped in with the rejects and handed a roommate named Mouse and a housemother who's into the black arts. Sure enough, the pretty women start dropping like flies. It's as silly as it sounds, but energetic nonetheless, with knowingly hammy performances from Shelley Winters and Morgan Fairchild. Tom Holland, who cowrote the story, went on to script *Psycho II* and *Fright Night*.

THE IN-LAWS ★★★
1979, USA, PG
Peter Falk, Alan Arkin, Richard Libertini, Nancy Dussault, Penney Peyser, Arlene Golonka, Michael Lembeck, Ed Begley, Jr. Directed by Arthur Hiller. 103 min.

In the movies, anything is possible. As witness this sub–Neil Simon farce about two loudmouthed, middle-aged bunglers, which turns out to be surprisingly deft and entertaining. Alan Arkin, as a cowardly New York dentist, and Peter Falk, as an international plotter who drags the two of them into a harebrained intrigue, have roles so perfectly suited to their gifts that they can wear them casually, like rumpled old suits. The performances have a calming ease, and so does Arthur Hiller's direction, which generates neither excitement nor hysteria. Scenarist Andrew Bergman's eagerness to throw in any gag he can think of—whether it fits or not—keeps us on our toes, and most of the jokes are quite clever.

IN LOVE WITH AN OLDER WOMAN ★★½
1982, USA (TV)
John Ritter, Karen Carlson, Jamie Rose, Jeff Altman. Directed by Jack Bender. 100 min.

This better-than-average TV comedy-drama features John Ritter as a junior partner in a stuffy San Francisco law firm who becomes involved with a carefree, fortyish woman. Things proceed in true romantic fashion until her past begins to creep in and disrupt things. From the novel *Six Months with an Older Woman* by David Kaufelt.

IN NAME ONLY ★★★
1939, USA
Carole Lombard, Cary Grant, Kay Francis. Directed by John Cromwell. 102 min.

Cary Grant and Carole Lombard make such a sexy pair that it's unfortunate that their one major team-up should be in this soap-opera triangle and not a witty screwball comedy. Actually, Kay Francis walks off with this one as Grant's cold, vindictive wife. Francis is mesmerizing. She commands Grant's rich aged parents by acting the sweet wife while simultaneously tormenting her husband. It's the only role with much depth, but the two stars deliver smooth performances. Grant is marginally better in the serious scenes, but Lombard, even in the worst parts, shines with a luminosity outside the range of her costars.

THE INN OF THE SIXTH HAPPINESS ☆☆☆
1958, USA
Ingrid Bergman, Curt Jurgens, Robert Donat, Athene Seyler, Ronald Squire. Directed by Mark Robson. 158 min.

An overlong but affecting tribute to one woman's courageous mission in pre–World War II China. In her later career, Ingrid Bergman never looked as incandescent as she does here, playing Gladys Smith, the Englishwoman who mother-henned a group of children to safety while enemy troops closed in from all sides. Among the film's pleasures are a moving final screen performance from Robert Donat as a sympathetic mandarin and the lush photography. Bergman's performance as the dedicated missionary was a role she would later parody and win a Best Supporting Actress Oscar for in *Murder on the Orient Express*.

THE INNOCENT ☆☆☆½
1976, Italy/France
Giancarlo Giannini, Laura Antonelli, Jennifer O'Neil, Rian Morelli, Massino Girotti. Directed by Luchino Visconti. 115 min.

In its first half Luchino Visconti's posthumous final film, loosely based on the 1892 Gabriele D'Annunzio novel, is a sensuous, ironic comedy. Then the transitions begin to lurch, the scenes begin to drag, and the tone veers toward a melodramatic tinniness that is antithetical to Visconti's usual operatic grandeur. Giancarlo Giannini, suffering mightily, plays a preening, adulterous dandy who's secure in his belief that, as a freethinking rationalist, he's above petty emotions like jealousy. The movie is about Giannini's comeuppance: his humiliating loss of control when his beautiful wife, Laura Antonelli, takes a lover of her own and has a child by him. What you'll remember is the way Visconti's camera glides about amid the exquisite furnishings of several palazzi—and among the pink-skinned, smooth-faced gentlefolk who are the movie's human furniture.

IN OLD AMARILLO ☆½
1954, USA
Roy Rogers, Estelita Rodriguez, Pinky Lee. Directed by William Witney. 67 min.

This film is not up to par with Roy Rogers's usual, but it has an interesting story idea about drought and ecology. Industrialists want to drive out the cattlemen and Rogers turns a ne'er-do-well youth into a good guy.

IN OLD CALIFORNIA ☆☆½
1942, USA
John Wayne, Binnie Barnes, Albert Dekker, Edgar Kennedy. Directed by William McGann. 88 min.

John Wayne carries this complicated B Western, playing a druggist from the East who has to battle both Gold Rush gunmen and a typhoid epidemic. The film has a nicely realized, Old West setting. Wayne's masculine competency is well matched by Edgar Kennedy's comic relief.

IN OLD NEW MEXICO ☆½
1945, USA
Duncan Renaldo, Martin Garralaga, Gwen Kenyon. Directed by Phil Rosen. 62 min.

Duncan Renaldo debuts as the Cisco Kid. The Kid works to clear a señorita who is charged with murder. An O.K. Cisco flick, if you like this sort of thing.

IN OLD OKLAHOMA

See *War of the Wildcats*

IN PRAISE OF OLDER WOMEN ☆½
1978, Canada, R
Tom Berenger, Karen Black, Susan Strasberg, Helen Shaver. Directed by George Kaczender. 108 min.

In this soft-core pornography a Hungarian writer reminisces over the past twenty years of his life and his many affairs with women older than himself. Weak erotica masquerading as romance will appeal to neither audience, although the cast is above average for this sort of film.

IN SEARCH OF HISTORIC JESUS ☆
1980, USA, G
John Rubinstein, John Anderson, Nehemiah Persoff, Brad Crandall, Andrew Bloch, Morgan Brittany, Walter Brooke, Annette Charles. Directed by Henning G. Schellerup. 91 min.

This Sunn Classics opus seeks to demonstrate that the Bible provides an accurate historical account of events, but it plays so fast and loose with the Gospels that it's bound to offend anyone who's really interested in them. The movie alternates between interviews with "scientists" (at least one of whom is a familiar TV character actor—uncredited, of course) and long, inept, inaccurate enactments of Bible stories. Not only does the movie fabricate dialogue and events, it does so at the expense of the unsurpassably beautiful stories in the Bible itself. About the worst movie ostensibly based on the Bible ever made.

IN SEARCH OF NOAH'S ARK ☆
1976, USA, PG
Directed by James L. Conway, Steven Gray. 95 min.

Sunn Classics, the producers who brought you such gems of unrevealed knowledge as *Chariots of the Gods* and *In Search of Historic Jesus*, brings you another rubbishy pseudodocumentary about Noah's Ark. Just for visual interest: they reconstructed it and restage the loading of the animals.

IN SEARCH OF THE CASTAWAYS ☆☆½
1962, Great Britain
Hayley Mills, Maurice Chevalier, George Sanders, Wilfrid Hyde-White, Wilfrid Brambell. Directed by Robert Stevenson. 100 min.

This Walt Disney fantasy adventure is based on a Jules Verne story. A French scientist comes across a message in a bottle revealing the location of a sea captain who disappeared mysteriously several years before. He sets off on his trail with the captain's two children and an aristocratic shipowner. Assorted breathtaking adventures follow, all played with tongues firmly in the veteran British cheeks of the cast. There is an especially funny bit by Wilfrid Brambell (Paul's grandfather in *A Hard Day's Night*) as one of the captain's crew. Entertaining and fun, if occasionally a bit obtuse.

INSEMINOID

See *Horror Planet*

INSERTS ☆☆
1975, Great Britain, X
Richard Dreyfuss, Veronica Cartwright, Jessica Harper, Bob Hoskins, Stephen Davies. Directed by John Byrum. 117 min.

Inserts was one of the last X-rated movies to come out of a major studio (United Artists), and certainly one of the strangest. Set in a decaying Hollywood mansion at the beginning of the sound era, it's the story of a washed-up director (Richard Dreyfuss) known as the Boy Wonder, now reduced to shooting pornographic two-reelers with a stoned starlet (Veronica Cartwright) and the dumbest of dumb studs (Stephen Davies). The "inserts," genital close-ups meant to be edited into the finished product, are seen in just enough detail to warrant an X without becoming hard core. The actors, particularly Dreyfuss, invest their roles with a conviction so fierce it's almost admirable, but director John Byrum's one-set, real-time screenplay is dreadfully pretentious, a blend of witless repeated epigrams, melodramatic twists, and such endless sexual conversation that you may begin to feel as seedy as the characters. Still, some decent Old Hollywood atmosphere, nasty in-jokes, and the literal and figurative ballsiness of the acting almost make it worthwhile.

INSIDE MOVES ☆☆½
1980, USA, PG
John Savage, David Morse, Diana Scarwid, Amy Wright, Tony Burton, Bill Henderson, Steve Kahan, Jack O'Leary, Bert Remsen. Directed by Richard Donner. 113 min.

This movie means well—all over the place. It begins with a suicide attempt by a twitchy misfit (John Savage) who survives to spend the rest of the film as a cripple, rediscovering his own worth and the joys of living. Most of the action takes place in Max's Bar, a Bay Area dive where the lovable handicapped congregate. The pivot of the plot is a gimpy basketball hopeful (David Morse) who uses Savage's money to finance an operation, becomes a big-league hoop star, and then turns his back on his old friends—even moving in on Savage's girl (Diana Scarwid). But fear not; in high-class humanist mush like this, instant self-realization and reform are de rigueur. Laszlo Kovacs's evocative, golden lighting is gorgeous, and Morse and Scarwid are perfectly cast low-key performers. Savage, however, while funny and likable for a time, wears out his welcome pretty quickly—feverishly high-strung, he's the new Sandy Dennis.

INSIDE OUT ☆☆
1975, Great Britain/West Germany, PG
Telly Savalas, Robert Culp, James Mason, Aldo Ray, Guenter Meisner, Adrian Hoven, Wolfgang Lukschy, Charles Korvin, Lorna Dallas. Directed by Peter Duffel. 97 min.

This cute but contrived caper film is notable for its surprising lack of violence and its deadly lack of surprises. Telly Savalas steals this show about a pack of adventurers who spring a Nazi war criminal from prison to help them find some buried German gold.

INSIDE THE THIRD REICH ☆☆½
1982, USA (TV)
Rutger Hauer, Derek Jacobi, Blythe Danner, John Gielgud, Elke Sommer, Ian Holm, Trevor Howard, Robert Vaughn, Maria Schell, Stephen Collins, Randy Quaid, Viveca Lindfors, Renee Soutendijk, Mort Sahl. Directed by Marvin J. Chomsky. 300 min.

This TV miniseries adaptation of Albert Speer's book about his work under Adolf Hitler is disappointingly shallow, but illuminated by a large and talented cast. Rutger Hauer's sober, intelligent portrayal of Speer will hold your attention even when Derek Jacobi's cold-eyed Hitler threatens to veer into caricature. There are fine moments and performances throughout, but the dressy, glossy, and functional treatment endemic to so much of network television seems inappropriate here.

THE INSPECTOR GENERAL ☆☆☆
1949, USA
Danny Kaye, Walter Slezak, Barbara Bates, Elsa Lanchester, Gene Lockhart, Alan Hale, Benny Baker, Walter Catlett. Directed by Henry Koster. 101 min.

Danny Kaye has another field day in this elaborate, colorful film version of Nikolai Gogol's classic play. He plays a traveling medicine-show man who is mistakenly identified as a government official while passing through a small town. Henry Koster's direction is more stylish than usual, particularly in the song numbers, and the supporting cast members are up to their assignments. The real energy, however, is provided by Kaye. His brand of buffoonery may be a matter of taste, but it's perfectly suited to the material here, providing several sidesplitting moments. (Title in Great Britain: *Happy Times*)

INTERIORS ☆☆☆½
1978, USA, PG
Kristin Griffith, Mary Beth Hurt, Richard Jordan, Diane Keaton, E. G. Marshall, Geraldine Page, Maureen Stapleton, Sam Waterston. Directed by Woody Allen. 99 min.

Woody Allen gets serious, and we mean SERIOUS. This absolutely straight-faced examination of the emotional and psychological trials of a wealthy WASP family threw off audiences that remembered Allen's brilliant parody of the same kind of clan in *Annie Hall*. But *Interiors* means to be taken at face value and, despite its shortcomings, it deserves that much. The lingering close-ups, the angst-filled speechmaking, the ominous silences, and the meticulous color scheme all pay homage to the director Allen most admires, Ingmar Bergman. Many scenes seem like inadvertent parody or second-rate imitation of Bergman's work, but enough of the film succeeds to give it a dramatic life of its own. Blistering performances by Geraldine Page as a middle-aged woman who suffers a breakdown when she discovers her husband's infidelity, by Diane Keaton as her most neurotic, bitter daughter, and by Maureen Stapleton as the immensely likable "other woman" will rivet your attention and get you through most of the textbook symbolism and the occasional turgid moment. But the film seems made more for Allen than anyone else, and you may rightly ask why he bent over backward to dramatize the same situations that he treats so brilliantly and incisively in comedy. It adds up to a very impressive misstep.

INTERMEZZO ☆☆☆
1939, USA
Leslie Howard, Ingrid Bergman, Edna Best, Ann Todd, John Halliday. Directed by Gregory Ratoff. 73 min.

In an economic venture of the late 1930s, Hollywood imported a number of recent European hits (*Algiers*, *A Woman's Face*, *Gaslight*) and remade them scene-for-scene. The most famous of these projects was David O. Selznick's version of the Swedish film *Intermezzo*. Selznick's coup, of course, was casting Ingrid Bergman in the role she originated in 1936, and it is her sparkling American film debut that lights up this well-made but conventional soap opera. Bergman plays a music teacher who comes between her mentor, a world-famous violinist (Leslie Howard), and his long-suffering wife (Edna Best). It's the usual love triangle with the usual cop-out ending, but Gregg Toland's silky camerawork, liberal doses of Edvard Grieg on the soundtrack, and the exquisite young Bergman make this a pleasure to see and hear. (Title in Great Britain: *Escape to Happiness*)

INTERNATIONAL VELVET ☆☆☆
1978, Great Britain, PG
Tatum O'Neal, Christopher Plummer, Anthony Hopkins, Nanette Newman, Dinsdale Landen. Directed by Bryan Forbes. 125 min.

In this sequel to *National Velvet*, Velvet Brown is a grown woman, childless and divorced, who gives support to an orphan girl (Tatum O'Neal) who wants to ride on the Olympic equestrian team. It's a fine family film, one that will engage new audiences as well as satisfy those who fondly remember the original with Elizabeth Taylor. And unlike most family films, it's not so cloying or saccharine that adults will have to force themselves to watch it.

THE INTERNS ☆☆½
1962, USA
Michael Callan, Cliff Robertson, James MacArthur, Nick Adams, Suzy Parker, Haya Harareet, Stefanie Powers, Telly Savalas. Directed by David Swift. 120 min.

This flashy, entertaining male-dominated soap puts an attractive cast through some pretty sleazy paces. Will these starry-eyed idealists be able to withstand the pressure of their first brush with the hassles of big-city hospital life? Our favorite scene involves hyperactive Michael Callan freaking out on uppers, but you'll also be held in thrall by the more subdued nonacting of Suzy Parker and the improbably named Haya Harareet. For those who need a prescription for trashy fun.

IN THE DEVIL'S GARDEN

See *Assault*

IN THE GOOD OLD SUMMERTIME ☆☆½
1949, USA
Judy Garland, Van Johnson, S. Z. Sakall, Buster Keaton, Spring Byington. Directed by Robert Z. Leonard. 102 min.

This film was nostalgic even in 1949. If you loved the old days, you'll love this movie. Judy Garland stars as a clever girl who works in a music store (an opportunity to display her talent as comedienne as well as songstress) while waiting to meet her secret pen pal. Van Johnson plays her verbal sparring partner at work. A subplot concerning the owner of the shop, his secretary, and a supposed Stradivarius keeps us occupied until we realize that Judy's "Dear Friend" is none other than Johnson. Even if you are familiar with the story from any of its previous settings (all of them based on Miklos Laszlo's play *The Shop around the Corner*), see it for the songs "I Don't Care," "Play That Barber Shop Chord," and "Wait Until The Sun Shines, Nellie" that give this version its zing. Careful viewers will spot baby Liza in the last sequence.

IN THE HEAT OF THE NIGHT ☆☆☆
1967, USA
Sidney Poitier, Rod Steiger, Warren Oates, Quentin Dean, Lee Grant. Directed by Norman Jewison. 109 min.

Sidney Poitier first portrayed policeman Virgil Tibbs in this often-effective whodunit. In Stirling Silliphant's screenplay, based on the novel by John Ball, Tibbs is a visitor in a Southern town who is asked by the police chief (Rod Steiger) to investigate the murder of a wealthy factory owner. Along the way, Tibbs encounters resistance and outright prejudice from the townspeople. The Steiger-Poitier confrontations have spark, but the rest of the murder mystery is uninvolving and the racial issue is, by contemporary standards, simplistically handled. Norman Jewison would return to this genre with *A Soldier's Story* in 1984, achieving similar results. *In the Heat of the Night* won five Academy Awards, including Best Picture and Best Actor (Steiger); it was followed by two sequels starring Poitier, *They Call Me MISTER Tibbs!* and *The Organization*.

IN THE SHADOW OF KILIMANJARO ☆
1986, USA/Great Britain/Kenya, R
John Rhys-Davies, Timothy Bottoms, Irene Miracle, Michele Carey, Calvin Jung. Directed by Raju Patel. 97 min.

This strictly-from-hunger horror flick concerns some ravenous baboons who don't take a famine lying down and decide to add humans to their diet. Clichés abound as various factions oppose or recommend evacuation, but all this debate is just a smokescreen for the film's main event of baboons feasting on flesh. Grisly and grotesque, but no real chills.

INTO THE NIGHT ☆
1985, USA, R
Jeff Goldblum, Michelle Pfeiffer, David Bowie, Irene Papas. Directed by John Landis. 115 min.

Director John Landis has made a home movie with all of his Hollywood friends who weren't doing anything else at the time. Watch for cameos by such famous filmmakers as Paul Mazursky, Roger Vadim, and David Cronenberg amid a greatly puzzling search for missing gems. Jeff Goldblum does a great job of looking quizzically at the repulsive violence going on around him; it's the first time that an actor could qualify for the best featured facial performance. The usually capable Landis has constructed a very slick and totally vacuous film that makes no sense. Let this movie disappear into the night.

INTOLERANCE ☆☆☆☆
1916, USA
Lillian Gish, Robert Harron, Mae Marsh, Constance Talmadge, Bessie Love, Seena Owen. Directed by D. W. Griffith. 123 min.

This film is considered by many to be the greatest ever made; certainly it ranks among the most daring and innovative. In four contiguous parts silent film maestro D. W. Griffith conducts a cinematic symphony interweaving three different tales of man's inhumanity to man through the ages, blended with a modern tale about an innocent boy wrongfully accused of a crime. The director masterfully crosscuts between the various strands of the narrative, and as the central contemporary story reaches a crescendo, the cutting becomes faster-paced; the film builds to its climax as if the individual sequences were going to collide and break the film apart—it's still very exciting, even sixty years after Griffith's experiments in technique are old hat. It features fantastic sets that put Cecil B. De Mille to shame, and it's paced with enough energy to dwarf most of the film epics that followed in its wake.

THE INTRUDER WITHIN ☆☆
1981, USA
Chad Everett, Joseph Bottoms, Jennifer Warren, Rockne Tarkington. Directed by Peter Carter. 86 min.

The real scares are few and far between in this earthbound *Alien* story. Chunky Chad Everett is the tool pusher on an oil rig that sucks up a few nasty eggs from the frosty bottom, and Joseph Bottoms is the geologist who may be a company rat or a mad scientist. The story is confusing—is this a monster or a virus that drives people crazy? Television movie squeamishness prevents the gore that would tell the whole story.

THE INVADERS

See *49th Parallel*

INVADERS FROM MARS ☆☆½
1953, USA
Jimmy Hunt, Helena Carter, Leif Erickson. Directed by William Cameron Menzies. 78 min.

Invaders from Mars predates *Invasion of the Body Snatchers* by three years and, while not as cleverly directed or acted, deserves some credit as inspiration for the later film. This Cold War parable about a little boy who must save the day when Martians turn his parents and friends into zombielike slaves echoes the 1949 film *The Window* in its story of a child who cannot convince anyone of the vital knowledge he possesses. It was made in the same year as *The 5,000 Fingers of Dr. T*, one of the very few other science-fiction films with a child as epicenter in a heroic sense of the word. William Cameron Menzies, designer of *Things to Come*, did not direct the narrative scenes with much panache, but the very artlessness of the before/after home life works in the picture's favor, making the flatness of life-style appear to be more a matter of degree than an obvious change.

INVADERS FROM MARS ☆☆
1986, USA, PG
Hunter Carson, Karen Black, Louise Fletcher, Laraine Newman, Timothy Bottoms, James Karen. Directed by Tobe Hooper. 100 min.

Director Tobe Hooper's remake of the science-fiction classic goes terribly wrong when he tries to mix childlike nightmares with inept black comedy. The film starts out promisingly enough when young David Gardner witnesses a Martian craft land near his house. Dad goes out to investigate and —uh oh! Soon nearly everybody's a red planet zombie as the kid desperately tries to find someone who will believe his fantastic story. But idiotic comedy takes over when the U.S. armed forces storm the organic space ship and encounter a horde of creatures whose fearsome illusions are dispelled when they move about like drunken toads. It's a real shame when one considers the effort that went into this expensive production, but there is one great moment when an officer says "Don't worry, son—marines aren't afraid to kill Martians!"

INVASION OF THE BEE GIRLS ☆☆
1973, USA, R
Victoria Vetri, William Smith, Anitra Ford, Cliff Osmond, Ben Hammer. Directed by Virgil Vogel. 85 min.

It has its moments, but it definitely does not live up to the promise of that title. The plot concerns the growing phenomenon of certain beautiful women who end up literally loving their dates to death. As science fiction, this film is pedestrian. As camp, it's fun but second-rate (although watching some of those sleazeballs drool over these queen bees before they expire is worth the price of the rental). The film buzzes along as expected, but a few parts are good enough to make this a sporadic honey of a parody.

INVASION OF THE BODY SNATCHERS ☆☆☆
1956, USA
Kevin McCarthy, Dana Wynter, Larry Gates, King Donovan, Carolyn Jones, Jean Willes, Ralph Dumke, Virginia Christine, Tom Fadden. Directed by Don Siegel. 80 min.

Don Siegel's thrilling B movie concerns a small town besieged by seed pods that grow into replicas of the townfolk and then supplant them. It hardly seems relevant now whether Siegel intended the pods to symbolize the Commies or the forces of McCarthyism (both sides have been amply argued). Despite its monster-mash title, the true terror at the heart of the film grows not from political paranoia, but from the obsession with social conformity that marked the fifties.

INVASION OF THE BODY SNATCHERS ☆☆☆½
1978, USA, PG
Donald Sutherland, Brooke Adams, Leonard Nimoy, Veronica Cartwright, Jeff Goldblum, Art Hindle, Lelia Goldoni, Kevin McCarthy. Directed by Philip Kaufman. 115 min.

This richly enjoyable modern horror story is even more fun than the 1956 Don Siegel classic on which it's based. Once again, vegetable pods arrive from deep space to replace humans with emotionless replicas. But this time the characters are so intense, attractive, and idiosyncratic that it's poignantly clear what they have to lose. With a terrific turn by Leonard Nimoy as a smooth-as-silk pop psychologist.

INVASION USA ☆☆
1985, USA, R
Chuck Norris, Richard Lynch, Melissa Prophet, Alexander Zale, Alex Colon. Directed by Joseph Zito. 100 min.

Listen up, you knee-jerking liberals! You've been gettin' soft in your consumerism, leavin' the door wide open for blood-drinking Commie invaders! Luckily, Chuck Norris and his trusty twin machine guns are on our side, stopping the scum in their attempts to blow up white middle-class churchgoers and schoolbuses. What's better here is that Norris shoots, karate-chops, and blows up the bastards with more style than in his previous flicks (this one almost seems like a real movie). Pacifists need not watch this paean to superpatriotism, but those who are up for over an hour of great explosions and enough bodies to open a cemetery in Cuba will lap this one up. On the Rambo scale, this here picture rates an eight.

INVESTIGATION ☆☆
1979, France, R
Victor Lanoux, Jean Carmet, Valerie Mairesse, Michel Robin, Jacques Richard, Gerard Jugnot. Directed by Étienne Perier. 117 min.

This slow, methodical *policier* offers some small rewards for the patient. In a small town whose livelihood rests on the fortunes of one factory, the owner's wife disappears and is later found dead. Evidence points to her husband (Victor Lanoux), who'll close the factory if he's arrested. It's up to the tired but determined investigator (Jean Carmet) to uncover the truth before the townspeople close ranks around a possible killer. The film is overlong and has few surprises, but it does provide an unusual glimpse of the work of an investigating judge (there's no American equivalent), and Lanoux and Carmet make a good cat and mouse.

THE INVINCIBLE ½☆
Hong Kong
Wei Tzu-Yun, Angela Mao Ying, Chia Ling, Lo Lich, Wang Kuan-Hsing, Shih Szu. Directed by Chen Hung Mir.

This gory, boring martial-arts cheapie has more in common with Italian maniac-on-the-prowl flicks than with the genre to which it pretends to belong. The fight scenes are faked and extended by laughably obvious photography and editing. Also known as *Swift Shaolin Boxer*; not to be confused with an equally execrable kung-fu film called *The Invincible*, with Jimmy Wang Yu.

INVINCIBLE KUNG FU TRIO ☆☆
Hong Kong
Meng Fei, John Liu, Angela Mao-Ying, King Kung. Directed by Joe Law.

Another Meng Fei (*Prodigal Boxer I & II*) costumer, as he plays the famous historical figure Fong Shih-Yu. Aided by friends Hung Hsi Kuan and Lu Ah Tsai, he fights Wu Tang and the Chings. Everything about this film is top drawer—good photography, colorful sets, and dynamic martial arts.

THE INVINCIBLE SIX ☆☆
1968, USA/Iran
Elke Sommer, Stuart Whitman, Curt Jurgens, James Mitchum, Ian Ogilvy. Directed by Jean Negulesco. 96 min.

This film is yet another version of *The Seven Samurai*, this time with a contemporary setting in which a ragtag group of adventurers come to the aid of peasants in a Middle Eastern village. Competently made by veteran director Jean Negulesco, whose last film this was, but that's really about all you can say for it.

INVITATION AU VOYAGE ☆☆½
1983, France, R
Laurent Malet, Aurore Clement, Mario Adorf, Nina Scott, Raymond Bussieres. Directed by Peter Del Monte. 93 min.

After the death of his twin sister/lover, a young man (Laurent Malet) carries on his romantic obsession by putting her corpse in an instrument case, throwing it on the car roof, and taking off on a jaunt across France. Half morbid horror film and half New Wave romance, *Invitation au Voyage* has the cryptic, gloomy, elegantly abstract tone of *Diva*, and fans of that film will most likely appreciate the straightfaced insanity of this one. But the story itself is too anecdotal, and the tone too studied, for the film to be a success. Incidentally, Malet himself is an identical twin whose brother Pierre starred in *The Basileus Quartet*.

INVITATION TO A GUNFIGHTER ☆☆
1964, USA
Yul Brynner, Janice Rule, George Segal, Pat Hingle, Brad Dexter, Alfred Ryder. Directed by Richard Wilson. 91 min.

If cultured killing has a name, it is Jules Gaspard D'Estaing. Yul Brynner, playing that sexy, silent gunfighter, arrives in a post–Civil War Western town at the request of Mr. Brewster, the local land baron, who resides in that Psycho mansion built behind the Bates Motel. Unfortunately, the offbeat plot becomes a contortionist's dream: the killer first accepts the temporary assignment because of his love for Ruth (Janice Rule) and later rejects the commission because of Ruth's love for D'Estaing's intended victim. With a love triangle, a mercenary against the townsfolk, and the good outcast against the power boss, things become so muddled you can never tell on which side of the line of fire you stand. Despite capable performances from Brynner and George Segal, everyone becomes a victim of this confused ramble. This is one invitation you should refuse.

INVITATION TO HELL ☆☆
1984, USA (TV)
Robert Urich, Joanna Cassidy, Susan Lucci, Joe Regalbuto, Kevin McCarthy, Patricia McCormack, Soleil Moon Frye. Directed by Wes Craven. 98 min.

This weak, meek horror film was directed by Wes Craven, who shows none of the ability to generate real chills that he demonstrated in *A Nightmare on Elm Street*. These scares are strictly small-screen, with Robert Urich as a scientist who moves his family to a new suburban community and falls under the spell of Susan Lucci as an agent of Hell with an offer of membership in a very enticing country club. The writing is hackneyed and careless, and Lucci wouldn't pass as a Stepford Wife, let alone a hell-spawned siren.

INVITATION TO THE DANCE ☆☆☆
1956, USA
Gene Kelly, Tamara Toumanova, Igor Youskevitch, Carol Haney, Claire Sombert, Diana Adams, Belita, David Kasday, Daphne Dale. Directed by Gene Kelly. 93 min.

Gene Kelly must have been in a particularly lofty mood when he conceived this ambitious project—a series of three separate tales told entirely through dance. A lot of it is strained and pretentious, but the final "Sinbad the Sailor" number (with music from Nikolai Rimsky-Korsakov's *Scheherezade*) is quite effective, featuring Kelly amid the cartoon creations of Hanna-Barbera. A noteworthy attempt at "popular art," the film bombed at the box office.

IN WHICH WE SERVE ☆☆☆½
1942, Great Britain
Noel Coward, John Mills, Bernard Miles, Celia Johnson, Joyce Cary, Kay Walsh, Michael Wilding, Richard Attenborough. Directed by Noel Coward and David Lean. 115 min.

This film is a sterling example of British stiff-upper-lip militarism. Though this was the directorial debut of David Lean (previously an editor), it's really Noel Coward's show entirely—he codirected it, wrote the screenplay, composed the music, and produced and starred in it. The story concerns the life of a British destroyer and the men on board, who must fight against worsening odds when their ship is bombed by the Germans. Coward's fine writing, excellent ensemble work from the large cast, and energetic photography by Ronald Neame (who went on to direct *The Poseidon Adventure*) make it more than worthwhile, although its brand of wartime sentiment has necessarily waned in emotional impact with the passage of time.

I OUGHT TO BE IN PICTURES ☆½
1982, USA, PG
Walter Matthau, Dinah Manoff, Ann-Margret, Lance Guest, Lewis Smith. Directed by Herbert Ross. 108 min.

One of the worst in the assembly-line series of film adaptations of Neil Simon plays. Spunky, grating Dinah Manoff moves in with her crumpled, burnt-out screenwriter dad (Walter Matthau), whom she has not seen in sixteen years. Ann-Margret, as Matthau's studio hairdresser and girlfriend, mediates for two hours in their badly lit Los Angeles hovel as they wisecrack their way to a reunion. Ann-Margret comes off like an emcee introducing two comics at a bad weekend in the Catskills. Matthau actually makes something of his role, but Simon hasn't even provided his usual quota of almost funny lines. Formulaic, and not even a good formula at that.

I REMEMBER MAMA ☆☆☆
1948, USA
Irene Dunne, Barbara Bel Geddes, Oscar Homolka, Philip Dorn, Cedric Hardwicke, Edgar Bergen, Rudy Vallee, Ellen Corby. Directed by George Stevens. 137 min.

Not recommended for the cynical, this perennial holiday favorite is an experience in unabashed, uplifting sentiment. Set in San Francisco in the early part of the twentieth century, the film is a series of reminiscences about the life of an immigrant family and the mother who held them all together. Irene Dunne had her most fondly remembered role here as the Norwegian mother; Ellen Corby is also very good as Aunt Trina. It's a bit too long—director George Stevens tends to milk every emotional moment (and there are lots of them)—but those who are inclined to wallow won't mind.

IREZUMI ☆½
1984, Japan
Masay Utsunomiya, Tomisaburo Wakayama. Directed by Yoichi Takabayashi. 88 min.

Despite the intentions, this overheated tale of sexual obsession delivers only steamy soft-core porn. A tattoo master's methods require an unorthodox approach—the women he tattoos experience such intense pain, his apprentice must engage them in intercourse during the process. The film's mystical sexuality doesn't travel well to these shores, and it's not recommended for feminists.

IRMA LA DOUCE ☆☆☆½
1963, USA
Shirley MacLaine, Jack Lemmon, Lou Jacobi, Herschel Bernardi, Bruce Yarnell. Directed by Billy Wilder. 146 min.

Billy Wilder has once again turned light, frothy material into something complex and completely entertaining. Wilder and co-writer I. A. L. Diamond eliminated the songs from Alexander Breffort's stage musical and replaced them with a thoughtful exploration of gender roles. A *Guardsman*-type plot soon develops that complicates matters but leads to one of Wilder's great twist endings. Jack Lemmon as the bumbling cop who winds up a pimp and Shirley MacLaine as the hooker "with a heart of gold" infuse their patented roles with more warmth than usual, and the film's ugly use of color actually works in its favor. As for the explicit material, what was once considered vulgar now looks fresh, candid, and sophisticated.

THE IRON DUKE ☆½
1934, Great Britain
George Arliss, Gladys Cooper, A. E. Matthews, Ellaline Terriss, Allan Aynesworth, Felix Aylmer, Lesley Wareing, Edmund Williard. Directed by Victor Saville. 88 min.

As usual, history and the laws of decent moviemaking are rewritten to accommodate George Arliss. In this biography of the Duke of Wellington, which exists only as a vehicle for Arliss, some events are changed, invented, or tidied up to give him more fodder. It was acceptable in its time for his fans, particularly in Great Britain, where Wellington is a national hero, but modern audiences are going to be hard pressed to find much entertainment in this slow-moving, bogus production.

IRON EAGLE ☆☆
1986, USA, PG-13
Louis Gossett, Jr., Jason Gedrick, David Suchet, Tim Thomerson, Larry G. Scott, Caroline Lagerfelt, Jerry Levine. Directed by Sidney J. Furie. 116 min.

An army kid enlists the aid of a tough air-force-reserve colonel to rescue his father from behind enemy lines, in a gung-ho action film that's completely machine-tooled but not without a couple of pleasures. Chief among them is Louis Gossett, Jr., in a virtual reprise of his role in *An Officer and a Gentleman*, as the experienced pilot who must turn the cocky young flyer into a man. His authoritative presence, though familiar and corny, lends the movie some weight. Unfortunately, he's saddled with teen star Jason Gedrick, who looks like he's more interested in joining the Brat Pack than the Air Force Academy. Some of the jingoistic in-flight action scenes are rousing, but the screenplay feels overworked and the producers have shoehorned in a mediocre soundtrack in a trite, obvious way—it seems the young ace can only detonate targets and incinerate Arabs to a rock beat.

IRON FIST OF KWANGTUNG

See *Cantonen Iron Kung Fu*

IRON NECK LI ☆☆
Hong Kong
Chi Kuan Chun, Hang Han, Hang Jui, Ku Man Ching, Ng Hsiao Chan, Ching Chen, Choi Mung, So Jin Ping, Chen Hoi, Kong Yang, Lung Se, Se Ho Tao, Tsai Hung. Directed by Chang Jen Chieh.

This lightweight story of three heroes traveling the countryside and righting wrongs is a middleweight in martial arts. There's a lot of variety, but none of the fight sequences are exemplary.

IRRECONCILABLE DIFFERENCES ☆☆☆
1984, USA, PG
Ryan O'Neal, Shelley Long, Drew Barrymore, Sharon Stone, Sam Wanamaker. Directed by Charles Shyer. 112 min.

The premise, which has a little girl seeking a divorce from her warring parents, is too cutesy to stomach; thankfully, it's just the pretext for a surprisingly mature seriocomic study of a Hollywood marriage on the rocks. Told mostly in flashbacks, it follows screenwriters Albert and Lucy from their first encounter through their hits and flops on- and offscreen, a subject which Shyer and his wife Nancy Myers, who cowrote *Differences*, presumably know well. There's a good performance from Ryan O'Neal and a dynamite one from Shelley Long, and you'll also find some clever, acid observations of Tinseltown life—watch Albert direct a musical version of *Gone with the Wind* starring his tone-deaf girlfriend. A treacly ending doesn't serve the film well, though, and Drew Barrymore is insufferably coy.

ISABEL'S CHOICE ☆☆
1981, USA (TV)
Jean Stapleton, Peter Coyote, Richard Kiley, Betsy Palmer, Mildred Dunnock. Directed by Guy Green. 100 min.

This film is a workmanlike, occasionally touching star vehicle for Jean Stapleton. It poses the question: what should the woman-behind-the-man do when the businessman she taught how to succeed is told he must take an early retirement? In a TV movie, do you think this corporate secretary is going to stay in the company and worry about her own career or not? Tune in for the obvious answers.

I SENT A LETTER TO MY LOVE ☆☆
1981, France, PG
Simone Signoret, Jean Rochefort, Delphine Seyrig. Directed by Moshe Mizrahi. 96 min.

Yet another austere art-house bore from director Moshe Mizrahi. Simone Signoret is Louise, a self-sacrificing mother hen who lives in a modest Brittany cottage with her brother, Gilles (Jean Rochefort), an invalid since childhood. Terrified that her brother may die, Louise advertises in the newspaper for a gentleman companion and receives but a single reply—from Gilles. The movie is a plodding paean to dignified martyrdom, with Signoret cast as the same sort of matriarchal hag she played in *Madame Rosa*.

THE ISLAND ☆
1980, USA, R
Michael Caine, David Warner, Angela Punch McGregor, Frank Middlemass, Don Henderson, Dudley Sutton, Zakes Mokee. Directed by Michael Ritchie. 114 min.

British journalist Michael Caine is assigned on short notice to write about the Bermuda Triangle disappearances. Along with his son, whom he had promised to take on vacation, he crashes on a remote island and becomes the prisoner of a tribe of violent, inbred pirates. This gives director Michael Ritchie an excuse to trot out a number of torture devices that escalate in repulsiveness as the movie rolls along; watching this dim-witted, exploitative junk is torture of another kind. Everything down to the climactic massacre is predictable and dull, and the film would never have been made but for its basis in an equally trashy but more popular novel by Peter Benchley (*Jaws*).

THE ISLAND AT THE TOP OF THE WORLD ☆☆½
1974, USA
David Hartman, Donald Sinden, Jacques Marin, David Gwillim. Directed by Robert Stevenson. 95 min.

In 1907 Arctic explorers discover a valley near the North Pole that is heated by a volcano and inhabited by Vikings who might be the descendants of Erik the Red. It's a Walt Disney production, but don't let that worry you; while this is good family entertainment, it's not icky-sweet stuff with swarms of children traveling the globe. The special effects are the film's highlights.

ISLAND CLAWS ½☆
1980, USA, PG
Robert Lansing, Barry Nelson, Steve Hanks, Nita Talbot. Directed by Herman Cardenas. 91 min.

This film is an hysterically funny bomb! A cheapie retrograde horror flick, it's not even as believable as *Attack of the Crab Monsters* (1957). You see, there's all this experimentation transpiring in this island paradise, but no one suspects it's dangerous until some of the populace start disappearing. Wait until you see the "monster" as it clacks its way to clawdom onscreen. Tojo Studios, responsible for the lowest budget science-fiction creations, would have sent this giant lobster back to the drawing board—and they would put *anything* on screen. A seafood spectacular—only a lobster does the dining.

ISLAND OF DR. MOREAU ☆
1977, USA, PG
Burt Lancaster, Michael York, Nigel Davenport, Barbara Carrera, Richard Basehart, Nick Cravat, The Great John "L." Directed by Don Taylor. 98 min.

Shipwrecked Andrew Braddock washes up on an island inhabited by a mad scientist who transforms the local wildlife into half-human creatures—Hyenaman, Boarman, Dogman, etc. Everybody's at the party except the Wolf Man. Aside from the colorful natives, this adaptation of an H. G. Wells story lacks vitality and conviction, and it is doomed by excessive sobriety. But with Barbara Carrera playing Maria, the Catwoman, the story does add new meaning to the term bestiality. This island is definitely not a Club Med vacation spot.

ISLANDS IN THE STREAM
1977, USA, PG ★★
George C. Scott, David Hemmings, Gilbert Roland, Susan Tyrrell, Richard Evans, Claire Bloom, Julius Harris, Hart Bochner, Brad Savage. Directed by Franklin J. Schaffner. 105 min.

Franklin Schaffner's adaptation of Ernest Hemingway's posthumously published novel is determinedly old-fashioned, full of pseudopoetic elegies to the sea, sappy, stifled-sob sentiment, tragic man-of-action posturing, and awkward contrasts between Claire Bloom's Wife Who Won't Go Away and Susan Tyrrell's Golden-Hearted Whore. In short, it's almost an unintentional parody. George C. Scott delivers a carefully crafted performance as Thomas Hudson, a sculptor in self-imposed exile on a Caribbean island, but Denne Bart Petitclerc's bland screenplay gives him little to work with, and Franklin J. Schaffner has had the bad taste to play up the novel's autobiographical aspects. The movie's technique is as anachronistic as its tone, and for all its grandiose visions of waves and shoals and the like, it looks cheap: one of the best sequences, a marlin-fishing expedition, is ruined by grainy photography and primitive process shots. There are tearjerking moments, but they add little resonance to a hollow film.

ISLE OF THE DEAD
1945, USA ★★★
Boris Karloff, Ellen Drew, Marc Cramer, Alan Napier, Jason Robards, Skelton Knaggs. Directed by Mark Robson. 72 min.

This is one of the superb series of low-key, atmospheric horror films made by producer Val Lewton for RKO in the 1940s. Like *The Cat People, I Walked With a Zombie, Bedlam,* and others, this creates a feeling of lurking dread through unseen implications rather than vivid exposition. The story concerns a disparate group of travelers shipwrecked on a quarantined Greek island. As more and more of the characters die of the plague, the film begins to touch on that most haunting of all fears, that of being buried alive. Boris Karloff has a more subdued role than usual as a Greek general trying to keep his troops safe from the disease.

I SPIT ON YOUR GRAVE
1973, USA, R ★
Camille Keaton. Directed by Meir Zarchi. 98 min.

This still-notorious film now seems tame in the gore and nudity departments, but its violence against women is still outrageous. Disguised as a distaff revenge flick, it concerns a female writer who is raped on the grass, sodomized on the rocks, and beaten to a pulp in her summer home. (She's even ridiculed as a writer.) To its credit, the film starts slowly and cleverly escalates the violence that holds our attention in the absence of any real suspense. But the film's real purpose is to invite male viewers to be cheerleaders at a brutal gang rape. Not for children or feminists of any age.

I STAND CONDEMNED
1935, Great Britain ★½
Harry Baur, Laurence Olivier, Penelope Dudley-Ward, Robert Cochrane, Morton Selten, Athene Seyler, Walter Hudd. Directed by Anthony Asquith. 76 min.

This is a British remake of a French film about a Russian soldier (the very young Laurence Olivier) who falls in love with a nurse against the objections of her mean father. When the young man is wrongly subjected to a treason trial, only the hateful old man's testimony can save him. Will he or won't he? Very little of interest is generated in this tedious melodrama; some of the actors, notably Harry Baur, seem not to be speaking the lines that you're hearing, and even Olivier looks glum. (a.k.a.: *Moscow Nights*)

IT CAME FROM BENEATH THE SEA
1955, USA ★★½
Kenneth Tobey, Faith Domergue, Donald Curtis, Ian Keith, Harry Lauter. Directed by Robert Gordon. 80 min.

In this nifty sci-fi creature feature, San Francisco gets it. Sea serpents in the fifties ignored the example of the timid Loch Ness monster and surfaced to cause as much destruction as possible. An H-bomb explosion bothers one of them on the ocean floor, so, with the help of Ray Harryhausen's special-effects team, this squidlike beast visits Frisco. The giant octopus oozes up to the city by the bay and starts grabbing everyone it can lay a tentacle on (but somehow misses Tony Bennett). Good fun.

IT CAME FROM HOLLYWOOD
1982, USA, PG ★½
Dan Aykroyd, John Candy, Cheech and Chong, Gilda Radner. Directed by Malcolm Leo, Andrew Solt. 80 min.

On paper, it sounds like a treat: a schlock anthology with snippets from nearly 100 bad movies. But *It Came from Hollywood* appears to have been made by people with even less talent and sensitivity than the lesser lights whose sorry work they exploit. Ridiculously short, the movie is padded with stupifyingly dumb comic sketches by hosts Dan Aykroyd and Cheech and Chong, and most of the "golden turkeys" on display here are presented in such teensy fragments that it's like having a pesky sibling continually switch channels on you with a remote control.

IT CAME FROM OUTER SPACE
1953, USA ★★
Richard Carlson, Barbara Rush, Charles Drake, Russell Johnson, Joseph Sawyer. Directed by Jack Arnold. 90 min.

This is an unusually high-budgeted and elaborately presented (wide-screen, stereo sound, 3D) science-fiction film from the pre-*2001* days, when science fiction was the province of assembly-line cheapies. Unfortunately, all the expense only pads out a mediocre movie with neutral aliens crashlanding on Earth, where scientist Richard Carlson tries to keep the locals from lynching them until they can repair their ship. From the director of *Creature from the Black Lagoon*, and based on a story by Ray Bradbury.

IT CAME UPON A MIDNIGHT CLEAR
1984, USA (TV) ★
Mickey Rooney, George Gaynes, Barrie Youngbellow, Annie Potts, Sary Bager, Scott Sremes. Directed by Peter H. Hunt. 104 min.

The sticky seasonal sentimentality of this film is guaranteed to have you reaching for a bottle of Emetrol to keep your Christmas dinner down. Gramps is going to kick the bucket, but he gets permission from a gruff but cute angel to spend one last Yuletide with his perky grandkid, who will really miss the old galoot. Considering that it is especially sad to lose a loved one over the holidays, this film seems opportunistic, calculatedly appealing to emotions in a way that, if one takes it to heart, is dispiriting and depressing.

IT COULD HAPPEN TO YOU
1939, USA ★★★
Stuart Erwin, Gloria Stuart, Raymond Walburn, Douglas Fowley, Clarence Kolb. Directed by Alfred Werker. 64 min.

This wacky, cheap comedy has some very strange overtones. A Milquetoast copywriter finally comes up with the big sales pitch and begins living it up. In a *noir*ish twist, he finds himself accused of murder, sitting on death row, with only his wife to defend him. Bassett-eyed Stuart Erwin has a rare starring role, and he makes the most of it, though mouthy blonde Gloria Stuart grabs quite a bit of the attention. Erwin later went on to star in the television series "The Trouble with Father." Another obscure Hollywood comedy rescued from oblivion by Kartes Video (see also *All over Town, Slightly Honorable*).

IT HAPPENED AT LAKEWOOD MANOR

See *Ants*

IT HAPPENED ONE NIGHT ☆☆☆☆
1934, USA
Clark Gable, Claudette Colbert, Walter Connolly, Roscoe Karns, Alan Hale. Directed by Frank Capra. 105 min.

This vintage Frank Capra comedy is one of the two movies ever to win the five major Academy Awards—for Best Picture, Director, Screenplay, Actor, and Actress. (The other was *One Flew over the Cuckoo's Nest*.) A cagey, hot-tempered reporter stumbles onto the big story he needs when he helps a pampered, runaway heiress in her attempt to marry against her father's wishes. The exhilarating chemistry between Clark Gable and Claudette Colbert is always magic, and their trek from Florida to New York affords us some great comic moments, such as the classic hitchhiking sequence. Incidentally, the undershirt industry has never been the same since this movie came out, because Gable didn't wear one in it.

IT HAPPENED ONE SUMMER

See *State Fair* (1945)

I, THE JURY ☆
1982, USA, R
Armand Assante, Barbara Carrera, Alan King, Laurene Landon, Geoffrey Lewis, Paul Sorvino, Judson Scott. Directed by Richard T. Heffron. 111 min.

This updated remake of Mickey Spillane's so-so potboiler has hard-nosed sleuth Mike Hammer hunting down an old pal's killer, providing metronomic installments of nudity and violence along the way. The plot still works well enough, but Larry Cohen's screenplay is humorless, bare-bones material, and Armand Assante isn't nearly as charismatic or credible as Stacy Keach was in the subsequent TV series "Mickey Spillane's Mike Hammer."

IT LIVES AGAIN ☆☆
1978, USA, R
Frederic Forrest, Kathleen Lloyd, John P. Ryan, John Marley, Andrew Duggan, Eddie Constantine. Directed by Larry Cohen. 91 min.

The premise of *It's Alive*—a killer baby—was just ridiculous enough to catch you off guard and make for a genuinely scary, if very perverse thriller. Never one to resist beating a good idea into the ground, however, producer/writer/director Larry Cohen (*The Stuff*, *Q*) came up with this sequel featuring *three* killer babies and hordes of yet-unborn ones. It's not easy to make babies, who have an attack range of about three feet, very terrifying, even with some typically disgusting Rick Baker makeup, and Cohen's not up to the job. The ending delivers some reasonable chills, though.

IT RAINED ALL NIGHT THE DAY I LEFT ☆☆
1978, USA, R
Louis Gossett, Jr., Sally Kellerman, Tony Curtis. Directed by Nicolas Gessner. 100 min.

The locale is a remote, arid region of Africa where the vengeful Sally Kellerman hoards the only water supply (because she holds the natives responsible for the death of her husband). Traveling salesmen Tony Curtis and Louis Gossett, Jr., become entangled with her by the time violence breaks out, and luckily for them the merchandise they've been selling is military hardware.

IT'S ALIVE ☆½
1974, USA, PG
John Ryan, Sharon Farrell, Guy Stockwell, Andrew Duggan, Michael Ansara. Directed by Larry Cohen. 95 min.

A baby who kills the delivery room staff and moves on to greener pastures is definitely not meant to be taken seriously, and *It's Alive* has several insanely straightfaced plot absurdities. As long as she meant it to be a parody, Sharon Farrell can be credited with an effective, bug-eyed portrayal of superbabe's mother. The conclusion, set in a sewer, is fairly unpleasant without being truly scary.

IT'S A MAD, MAD, MAD, MAD WORLD ☆½
1963, USA
Spencer Tracy, Jimmy Durante, Milton Berle, Sid Caesar, Ethel Merman, Buddy Hackett, Mickey Rooney, Dick Shawn, Phil Silvers, Terry-Thomas, Jonathan Winters, Eddie "Rochester" Anderson, Buster Keaton, Jerry Lewis, Jack Benny. Directed by Stanley Kramer. 192 min.

It's a bad, bad, bad, bad movie! Producer/director Stanley Kramer thought that if he grouped together all the living (though some looked pretty dead) comics of the day, he would end up with a funny movie. He was wrong. The plot involves several individuals' attempts to find some hidden booty buried by an eccentric billionaire (Jimmy Durante). Spencer Tracy, the only real actor in the cast, actually makes something out of his role as the police chief who gets caught up in the case. That's a testament to Tracy, but shame on Stanley Kramer for putting the ailing actor through strenuous stunts, and further shame on the supposedly liberal director for having gags like Eddie "Rochester" Anderson falling into the lap of the Lincoln Memorial. For a change, one misses nothing from not seeing this in its original Cinerama format.

IT'S A WONDERFUL LIFE ☆☆☆½
1946, USA
James Stewart, Donna Reed, Lionel Barrymore, Gloria Grahame, Henry Travers, Beulah Bondi, Thomas Mitchell, H. B. Warner. Directed by Frank Capra. 129 min.

A prime example of audiences seeing only what they want to see, this much-beloved film is considered by many to be Frank Capra's most heartwarming work, even though it is filled with a strong sense of melancholy and even outright depression. The story follows the life of a frustrated small-town businessman (James Stewart) who is rescued from suicide by an angel and shown what life would have been like in his town had he never lived. Perhaps more appropriate at Veterans' Day than at Christmas, when *It's a Wonderful Life* is customarily shown, the film reflects the changed perspectives of director/screenwriter Capra and star Stewart, both of whom had just returned from service in World War II; no longer are they able to generate the fully blown mystique of joy pervasive. The film's happy ending is certainly eagerly anticipated but carries so much less resonance and emotion than the earlier, moodier scenes as to appear almost halfhearted. The script has a strong dollop of sentimentality which, designed as it was by a master of sentimentality, of course works. But, the most honest characterization in the film comes from Gloria Grahame, who registers most strongly for being the least-sentimentalized part of the narrative.

IT'S CALLED MURDER, BABY ☆
1982, USA, R
John Leslie, Cameron Mitchell, Lisa Trego. Directed by Sam Weston. 94 min.

For those who don't believe that a little editing can make a big difference, we present Case Study #1: when this film was a mere seven minutes longer, it was called *Dixy Ray—Hollywood Star*, and won nearly a dozen major awards. Of course, the seven minutes were of hard-core pornography, and the awards were from the Adult Film Association of America, whose members were apparently impressed at seeing a film with a plot. Without the seven minutes, it's a very feeble semiparody of a hardboiled detective story about an actress being blackmailed. (The longer version, in which the actors do what they do best, is also available.)

IT SHOULD HAPPEN TO YOU ☆☆☆
1954, USA
Judy Holliday, Jack Lemmon, Peter Lawford, Michael O'Shea, Vaughn Taylor. Directed by George Cukor. 86 min.

This film is an engaging comedy from the team that created *Born Yesterday* (star Judy Holliday, director George Cukor, screenwriter Garson Kanin). Holliday plays a daffy, ambitious young woman who decides to put an end to her obscurity by renting a huge Columbus Circle billboard with her name, Gladys Glover, emblazoned on it. The trick works and she is soon pursued by a super-smooth soap heir (Peter Lawford), much to the chagrin of her boyfriend, a wide-eyed 16mm filmmaker played by Jack Lemmon in his screen debut. Even those who do not care for the very specialized talents of Holliday will be consistently amused.

IT'S IN THE BAG ☆☆☆
1945, USA, PG
Fred Allen, Jack Benny, William Bendix, Binnie Barnes, Robert Benchley, Jerry Colonna, John Carradine, Sidney Toler, Don Ameche, Rudy Vallee. Directed by Richard Wallace. 87 min.

Fred Allen discovers that he has inherited $12 million from his late granduncle; the only catch is that the money was hidden in a chair that seems to have disappeared, setting off a race among various parties to get it first. The plot is merely a loose excuse to cram in a lot of star bits, most of which are quite funny. Fans of old radio will especially want to see the enactment of the long-standing Fred Allen–Jack Benny radio feud. Mel Brooks remade the basic story as *The Twelve Chairs* in 1970.

IT'S MY TURN ☆☆☆½
1980, USA, R
Jill Clayburgh, Michael Douglas, Charles Grodin, Beverly Garland, Steven Hill, Teresa Baxter, Joan Copeland, Daniel Steven. Directed by Claudia Weill. 91 min.

This romantic comedy by Claudia Weill (*Girl Friends*) is a slight, lumpy, pleasant film about a nice, liberated Jewish girl who has no problems at all—until she finds out what she's been missing. Kate Gunzinger (Jill Clayburgh) is a Chicago mathematics professor whose relationship with lover Charles Grodin is warm and enjoyable—maybe to a fault, since these two don't really seem to communicate very much. When Kate travels to New York to be interviewed for a job and to attend her widowed father's second wedding, she drifts into an affair with Ben (Michael Douglas), her new stepbrother and a former baseball player; the tenderness and sympathy she feels—connectedness, she calls it—make her wish her life weren't quite so neat. Weill and screenwriter Eleanor Bergstein know, however, that you don't rediscover the joys of old-fashioned commitment and change your life in one weekend. What's most admirable is their scrupulous refusal to attempt to sway our judgment, to manipulate us into unthinking agreement.

IVANHOE ☆☆☆½
1952, Great Britain
Robert Taylor, Elizabeth Taylor, Joan Fontaine, George Sanders, Emlyn Williams, Robert Douglas, Finlay Currie, Felix Aylmer, Basil Sydney. Directed by Richard Thorpe. 107 min.

King Richard the Lionhearted is still imprisoned in Austria in this rousing swashbuckler, and the great knight Ivanhoe does more than anyone to make life difficult at home for the king's evil brother, John—even more than Robin Hood himself, who makes a dashing guest appearance. This is MGM's finest adaptation of Sir Walter Scott. Elizabeth Taylor is both young and dazzling as his love interest.

IVANHOE ☆☆☆
1982, USA (TV)
James Mason, Anthony Andrews, Sam Neill, Michael Hordern, Olivia Hussey, Julian Glover, John Rhys-Davies. Directed by Douglas Camfield. 148 min.

This fifth version of the Walter Scott classic about Saxon derring-do is overlong but opulent, lushly produced, and gracefully acted by a large and talented cast. Anthony Andrews, though slighter than one might wish for the title role, has the charisma to make his larger-than-life hero credible, and Olivia Hussey is appropriately demure as Rebecca—only Lysette Anthony hits a slightly wrong note as Rowena. The production values cannot be faulted, which is reason enough to give this *Ivanhoe* a look.

IVANNA

See *Scream of the Demon Lover*

IVAN THE TERRIBLE ☆☆☆☆
1945, Russia
Nikolai Cherkassov, Ludmila Tselikovskaya, Serafina Birman, Piotr Kadochnikor, Alex Abrikosor, Vsevolod Pudovkin, Mikhail Zharor. Directed by Sergei Eisenstein. 96 min.

Castles with dark, twisty corridors, characters who grimace and shift their eyes like overgrown puppets, brooding, mystical music by Sergei Prokofiev—the first half of Sergei Eisenstein's two-part black-and-white film turns the life of the famous Russian czar into a gothic Shakespearean nightmare, a story so slow and deliberate that the action might be taking place underwater. Yet if one gives this oddball epic a chance it is a tantalizing experience. Eisenstein's images have a larger-than-life grandeur, and Nickolai Cherkassov turns Ivan into a spendid icon of ambition and despair.

IVAN THE TERRIBLE, PART II ☆☆☆☆
1946, Russia
Nikolai Cherkassov, Serafina Birman, Piotr Kadochnikov, A. Ngebrov. Directed by Sergei Eisenstein. 90 min.

The second half of Sergei Eisenstein's eccentric masterpiece is, like *The Godfather, Part II*, a slower, darker, more contemplative extension of its predecessor. Ivan is recalled to the throne by the people of Moscow only to see his closest comrades desert him. More overtly Shakespearean than Part I (there's even a play-within-a-play scene reminiscent of *Hamlet*), the movie features several unforgettable sequences, including the opening "human chess game" and an entire reel shot in dazzling (if primitive) early color.

I WALKED WITH A ZOMBIE ☆☆☆☆
1943, USA
Frances Dee, Tom Conway, James Ellison, Edith Barrett. Directed by Jacques Tourneur. 69 min.

A nurse is hired by the owner of a sugar-cane plantation to care for his catatonic wife, who may be a zombie or merely the victim of the pressures of living so far from civilization. The lurid title is misleading, for *I Walked with a Zombie* is another restrained horror film produced for RKO by Val Lewton, also the guiding force behind the original *Cat People*, *The Seventh Victim*, and others. Atmospheric black-and-white photography, striking imagery and a plot that draws its inspiration from no less a literary source than *Jane Eyre*.

I WANT HER DEAD

See "W"

I WANT TO LIVE! ☆☆☆½
1958, USA
Susan Hayward, Simon Oakland, Virginia Vincent, Theodore Bikel. Directed by Robert Wise. 120 min.

The style of serious, earnest humanist filmmaking exemplified by directors Robert Wise and Stanley Kramer has recently fallen out of favor, and not without some reason—their films often valued didacticism over drama and opinionating over art. At their best, however, the films were powerful as both melodrama and indictment: such is the case with this still-gripping account of Barbara

Graham, imprisoned and eventually sent to the gas chamber for a murder she didn't commit. Wise puts the legal system and the use of capital punishment on trial, and convicts them; the final scenes are as powerful as anything done on the subject since. Holding it all together as Graham is Susan Hayward, in a superb, moving performance that won her a well-deserved Academy Award.

I WILL FIGHT NO MORE FOREVER ☆☆☆
1975, USA (TV)
James Whitmore, Ned Romero, Sam Elliott, Nick Ramos, Emilio Delgado. Directed by Richard T. Heffron. 100 min.

This film tells the gripping true-life tale of the attempted migration of the Nez Percé Indian tribe. Under their leader, Chief Joseph, the Indians tried to leave their reservation and move to Canada, but they were hampered by the U.S. government, which sent out the cavalry to force them back to government-sponsored lands. Interesting as a history lesson about a little-known occurrence and engrossing as a drama about a people who have suffered at the hands of Uncle Sam for hundreds of years.

I WILL, I WILL . . . FOR NOW ☆☆
1976, USA, R
Elliott Gould, Diane Keaton, Paul Sorvino, Victoria Principal, Robert Alda, Candy Clark, Warren Berlinger. Directed by Norman Panama. 107 min.

Diane Keaton and Elliott Gould, as an unhappily divorced couple, decide to give marriage another try under the auspices of the "New Permissiveness." The trouble is that by the time this movie was made, the "New Permissiveness" wasn't so new anymore, so this resembles nothing so much as a TV sitcom, with "The Naughty F Word" thrown in to ensure an R rating. What little the movie has going for it derives from the presence of Keaton and Gould, both below par.

IZZY AND MOE ☆☆½
1985, USA (TV)
Jackie Gleason, Art Carney, Cynthia Harris, Zohra Lampert, Dick Latessa. Directed by Jackie Cooper. 96 min.

This comic telefilm about two ex-vaudevillians who become Prohibition agents is modestly entertaining and skillfully made, but it amounts to a huge missed opportunity considering that it reunited Jackie Gleason and Art Carney for their first non-"Honeymooners" venture in thirty years. Both are great fun to watch, but Carney takes top acting honors for his hilarious portrayal of the reluctant fed. It could be worse, but it should be better.

J

JABBERWOCKY ☆☆☆
1977, Great Britain, R
Michael Palin, Max Wall, Deborah Fallender, John Le Mesurier, Terry Jones, Neil Innes, David Prowse. Directed by Terry Gilliam. 100 min.

Like *Monty Python and the Holy Grail*, which Terry Gilliam codirected, this comedy views medieval England as a milieu of incredible filth, poverty, and casual violence, and struck many viewers as ugly and unpleasant. And those were the ones who *liked* it. The humor is not generally black or brutally satirical, as it is in the later Python films; rather it is merely low, like a British version of Mel Brooks. But if you're not bothered by all of the above, or can at least tolerate it, *Jabberwocky* is often quite funny, improving on repeated viewings. Fellow Pythonite Michael Palin stars as a cooper's apprentice who journeys to the seat of the kingdom to seek his fortune and gets involved quite unintentionally in a quest for the monstrous title beast. Palin is, as always, very funny, as is British comic Max Wall as King Bruno the Questionable. Another troupe member, Terry Jones, has a precredits cameo as the monster's first victim.

JACK THE RIPPER ☆½
1976, West Germany/Switzerland, R
Klaus Kinski, Josephine Chaplin, Herbert Fox, Lina Romay. Directed by Jesse Franco. 82 min.

Klaus Kinski has been making films for almost forty years, almost all of them bad except those made with Werner Herzog. And Spanish horror director Jesse (a.k.a Jesus) Franco has almost never made anything even competent. This needlessly gory story of the infamous London murderer wastes Kinski yet again; it wasn't released in this country until after the popularity of the Herzog *Nosferatu*. Female lead Josephine Chaplin is another daughter of Charles.

JACKSON COUNTY JAIL ☆☆
1976, USA, R
Yvette Mimieux, Tommy Lee Jones, Robert Carradine, Frederic Cook, Mary Woronov, Howard Hesseman, Betty Thomas. Directed by Michael Miller. 89 min.

Downbeat action drama, produced by Roger Corman, about a woman whose cross-country drive turns into a nightmare when she's robbed, raped, jailed, and finally forced to take it on the lam with a fellow inmate. Yvette Mimieux and Tommy Lee Jones are both very effective, and the sordid story line is handled with more taste than one might expect from New World. But the film leaves too much unresolved in an overreaching, heavy handed conclusion. Screenwriter Donald Stewart later won an Academy Award for *Missing*.

JACOB TWO-TWO MEETS THE HOODED FANG ☆☆☆½
1977, Canada, G
Stephen Rosenberg, Alex Karras, Guy L'Ecuyer, Joy Coghill, Earl Pennington. Directed by Theodore J. Flicker. 80 min.

This is a delightful children's fantasy that just might appeal more to adults who are willing to overlook its technical deficiencies than to children weaned on *Star Wars/Raiders* superspectacles. Jacob Two-Two, a schoolboy so named because he has to say everything twice (adults never listen to him the first time), has a dream that he has been sent to a children's prison camp as punishment for having insulted adults. The camp is ruled by the Hooded Fang, an ex-wrestler who hates kids. Director Flicker (*The President's Analyst*), who wrote the screenplay from a novel by Mordecai Richler, originally filmed this in 1976; the version that was finally released was heavily edited by the producer.

JACQUELINE BOUVIER KENNEDY ☆☆
1981, USA (TV)
Jaclyn Smith, James Franciscus, Rod Taylor, Stephen Elliott, Claudette Nevins, Donald Moffat. Directed by Stephen Gethers. 150 min.

A reverential ode to the former First Lady from her childhood up until the assassination of her husband. Not as bad as Cheryl Ladd as Princess Grace, nor Jaclyn Smith as Florence Nightingale, nor Lynda Carter as Rita Hayworth, but why must so many tiny, plasticized TV talents trot out their mechanical voices and vapid personalities as they persist in playing legendary stars and charismatic historical personages? What next? Heather Locklear as Cosima Wagner? Tanya Roberts as Maria Callas? Loni Anderson as Gertrude Stein? Pia Zadora as Joan of Arc!

THE JADE CLAW ☆☆
1979, Hong Kong
Billy Chong, Simon Yuen, Chu Tit Wo, David Woo, Ma Shung Tak, Chaing Tao. Directed by Hwa I-Hung.

The Yuen family contributes some of their patented choreographic magic and, with Billy Chong, lifts this revenge fantasy into the realm of the worthwhile. Good Eagle-style kung fu.

JAGGED EDGE ☆☆½
1985, USA, R
Glenn Close, Jeff Bridges, Peter Coyote, Leigh Taylor-Young, Robert Loggia. Directed by Richard Marquand. 108 min.

A San Francisco newspaper heiress is found slain and her publisher husband is accused, but the district attorney is out for a conviction and Jeff Bridges hires one of the D.A.'s former assistants to defend him. This is an enjoyable but strictly secondrate lady-in-distress thriller that's like a modern-day *Suspicion* (1941). *Jagged Edge* wants to be an elaborate Hitchcockian portrait of moral ambiguity, but it's closer to "Perry Mason"; the director provides sleek machine surfaces but doesn't deliver the psychological complexity he promises; and the courtroom scenes turn into a huge surprise party full of unexpected witnesses. It's the equivalent of a fast read, but a more dynamic leading lady might have made this *Edge* a bit sharper.

JAILHOUSE ROCK ☆☆
1957, USA
Elvis Presley, Judy Tyler, Mickey Shaughnessy, Vaughn Taylor, Jennifer Holden, Dean Jones, Anne Neyland. Directed by Richard Thorpe. 96 min.

The title sequence is probably the most exhilarating musical number in an Elvis Presley film. Beyond that, it's the usual Presley fare, this time about a young convict, jailed for manslaughter, who learns to play the guitar and rises to stardom. As the convict, Presley exhibits a forceful Method acting style that would never be tapped again, and Judy Taylor is excellent as his girlfriend. Too bad their material is so routine.

JAKE SPEED
1986, USA, PG ☆
Wayne Crawford, Dennis Christopher, Karen Kopins, John Hurt, Leon Ames, Donna Pescow, Barry Primus, Monte Markham. Directed by Andrew Lane. 104 min.

A pinch of *Raiders of the Lost Ark*, a dash of *Romancing the Stone*, and a gallon of rip-off, this plodding tongue-in-cheek action thriller has a neat premise: a hero of paperback pulp novels comes to life and gets involved in a real Grade Z adventure. There's also a ripely witty, very uncharacteristic performance by John Hurt as a comic villain. The rest is misery, dragged down by the presence of wooden Wayne Crawford in the lead (he's also the producer—talk about a coincidence!).

JAMAICA INN
1939, Great Britain ☆☆
Charles Laughton, Maureen O'Hara, Robert Newton, Leslie Banks, Emlyn Williams. Directed by Alfred Hitchcock. 107 min.

Hitchcock or no Hitchcock, this is a bad movie . . . though not quite as bad as some have claimed. The Daphne du Maurier story, adapted by Sidney Gilliat, Joan Harrison, and J. B. Priestley, features Maureen O'Hara as an innocent who discovers that her uncle (Robert Newton) is involved with a pirate posing as an aristocrat (Charles Laughton). Hitchcockian moments shine through (Laughton's introduction and stunning exit), but many of the action scenes and the general filmmaking is shockingly amateurish (for Hitchcock or anyone). Could the master have left for America midway through production and allowed producer-star Laughton to take over? It's a possibility not worth exploring. This one gives the auteur theory a bad name. Remade for television in 1985.

JAMES DEAN
1976, USA (TV) ☆☆
Stephen McHattie, Michael Brandon, Dane Clark, Meg Foster, Candy Clark, Jayne Meadows. Directed by Robert Butler. 97 min.

James Dean's short life was so quickly transformed into the stuff of pop-culture myths—just take a look, for instance, at the ways in which his spectral presence informs *September 30, 1955*, and *Come Back to the Five and Dime, Jimmy Dean, Jimmy Dean*—that a straightforward film biography would be welcome. Unfortunately, this isn't it—it's a reminiscence of Dean from the memoirs of William Bast, who lived with Dean when both were acting students. Stephen McHattie is an interesting choice for the title role; he seems to get Dean's essence down, even if some of the specifics are wrong. The drama itself, though, is uninformative.

JANE AUSTEN IN MANHATTAN
1980, USA/Great Britain, PG ☆☆
Anne Baxter, Robert Powell, Sean Young, Kurt Johnson, Katrina Hodiak, Tim Choate, Nancy New, Chuck McCaughan, John Guerrasio, Michael Wager. Directed by James Ivory. 108 min.

An oddity and a disappointment from the usually reliable filmmaking team of director James Ivory and screenwriter Ruth Prawer Jhabvala (*A Room with A View*, *The Bostonians*). This is one of their rare films set in the present, and their portrayal of the theatrical demimonde of contemporary New York is uncertain. Anne Baxter (in her last film role) plays an acting teacher and would-be producer; Robert Powell is her rival, an avant-garde director. When a previously unknown manuscript by Jane Austen surfaces, the two want to stage it in distinctly different ways, and the war heats up. An interesting premise given some elegant moments by Ivory, but it's awkward and unconvincing on the whole.

JANE DOE
1983, USA (TV) ☆☆☆
Karen Valentine, William Devane, Eva Marie Saint, David Huffman, Stephen Miller, Jackson Davies. Directed by Ivan Nagy. 100 min.

This expert suspense film benefits greatly from Karen Valentine's appealing TV presence. Leaving her ingenue cuteness behind, she plays a woman found buried alive. Although she's found in time, when she recovers she has no memory of past events. Unfortunately, her memory returns in spurts and her would-be killer (a real surprise) is not too keen on having his identity revealed. As a damsel-in-distress thriller, this capably acted drama keeps you both guessing and rooting for its heroine throughout. Taut drama enhanced by a clever teleplay.

JANIS
1974, USA, PG ☆☆½
Directed by Howard Alk, Seaton Findlay. 96 min.

Joplin, of course. This documentary traces the life and times of the gravel-voiced queen of the rock-and-roll blues from her pre–Big Brother and the Holding Company days. Not a great piece of filmmaking, although Joplin is such a galvanizing presence (onstage and off) that it hardly matters. By concentrating on concert footage, though, the film doesn't really delve much into the more lurid and dramatic aspects of her offstage life.

THE JANITOR

See *Eyewitness*

THE JAPANESE CONNECTION
1978, Hong Kong ½☆
Cheung Lik, Hsia Wen, Kong Ho Yon, Yukio Fomeno, Raymond. Directed by Kong Hung.

This trifling karate film lacks fighting, acting, and a real story. The bare-bones plot: a woodcarver is persuaded to help two men rob a crook for money and jewels. Yukio Fomeno and Raymond were the karate champions of Japan and the Philippines, respectively.

JASON AND THE ARGONAUTS
1963, Great Britain ☆☆☆½
Todd Armstrong, Gary Raymond, Honor Blackman, Nigel Green. Directed by Don Chaffey. 104 min.

A marvelous fantasy that has Jason and his intrepid crew (with Hercules along for a ride) on a quest for the Golden Fleece. Before possessing the fabled item, they must fight the Hydra and a number of other fearsome creatures. This intelligent and visually spectacular retelling of several Greek legends was filmed on location in the Mediterranean. The stop-motion special effects are superbly done by Ray Harryhausen, whose work is at the top of its form here. Chief among them is the concluding classic sword duel between Jason and several skeletons, a sequence which inspired a generation of new special-effects technicians.

JAWS
1975, USA, R ☆☆☆☆
Roy Scheider, Robert Shaw, Richard Dreyfuss, Lorraine Gary, Murray Hamilton, Peter Benchley. Directed by Steven Spielberg. 125 min.

This Grade A horror film engendered an unprecedented amount of surfside paranoia. Peter Benchley's screenplay, based on his own novel (which was in turn patterned vaguely after *Moby Dick*), is turned into nail-biting suspense by Steven Spielberg. The story of a Long Island police chief's battle with officials and townspeople over the handling of a couple of shark attacks becomes a nerve-racking suspense adventure as the policeman (Roy Scheider), an oceanographer (Richard Dreyfuss), and an experienced hunter (Robert Shaw) set out to kill the Great White. Spielberg is better at manning his mechanical shark (as in the brilliant opening sequence) than directing his actors, but he does get gritty, solid work from all three leading men. Everything about the film is far superior to either of *Jaws*'s sophomoric sequels, and the film holds up well next to Spielberg's more recent successes.

JAWS OF DEATH ☆½
1976, USA, PG
Richard Jaeckel, Harold Sakata, Luke Nalperin, John Davis Chandler. Directed by William Grefe. 91 min.

Sort of an aquatic version of *Willard*, in which crusty Everglades denizen Richard Jaeckel and his funny friends get even with those who would use the sharks for their own ends. Recommended only if you feel a need for the opposing point of view to that presented in the famous *Jaws* films. (a.k.a.: *Mako: The Jaws of Death*)

JAWS OF THE DRAGON ☆½
1976, Hong Kong
James Nam, James Taylor. 90 min.

Bad guys in red high-heeled boots, nudity, car chases, a rape, guns, and nasty killings—sounds great, doesn't it? Maybe in some other movie; here it's all unremittingly dreary.

JAWS 3-D ☆
1983, USA, PG
Dennis Quaid, Bess Armstrong, Simon MacCorkindale, Louis Gossett, Jr., Lea Thompson, John Putch. Directed by Joe Alves. 97 min.

A thirty-five-foot great white shark invades the equivalent of Florida's Seaworld and inconveniences a few tourists; the result is as thudding and prosaic as the *Airport* pictures. We wait for the sea park to open; we watch Lou Gossett, Jr., as its designer, impersonate an oak tree; we ogle Bess Armstrong as she rides around on the backs of porpoises in a wet suit. Finally, after ninety minutes, the shark arrives and director Joe Alves delivers the "thrills": random, generic glimpses of a shark fin sliding through the water, with an occasional gnawed-off limb shoved into our faces via the surprisingly shoddy 3-D process (which doesn't work when you're watching this on your TV).

JAWS 2 ☆☆
1978, USA, PG
Roy Scheider, Lorraine Gary, Murray Hamilton, Joseph Mascolo, Jeffrey Kramer, Collin Wilcox, Ann Dusenberry, Mark Grunner, Barry Coe. Directed by Jeannot Szwarc. 117 min.

The thrills are still there, but the humor and theatrical flair that made *Jaws* so much fun are gone. In an obvious grab for the teenage audience, the writers send a lot of kids out on the water in sailboats; their bickering and jiving makes the movie trivial and homey, like a wilderness adventure picture. Left all alone to fight the shark, Roy Scheider gives a warm, large-scale performance, but this time the shark really is just an eating machine (although it's hard to see how even a machine could digest so many meals in so short a time).

THE JAYNE MANSFIELD STORY ☆☆
1980, USA (TV)
Loni Anderson, Arnold Schwarzenegger. Directed by Dick Lowry. 97 min.

This made-for-television movie takes a fan-magazine approach to biography. Loni Anderson portrays the voluptuous young starlet. She's buxom enough for the role, but she's really not a very good actress. Loni is, however, a major thespian talent compared to her muscle-bound costar, Arnold Schwarzenegger. How much you'll enjoy this movie depends in large part on how much pleasure you get from ogling these two exemplary bodies.

THE JAZZ SINGER ☆☆☆
1927, USA
Al Jolson, May McAvoy, Warner Oland, Eugenie Besserer, Otto Lederer, Bobbie Gordon, Richard Tucker, Nat Carr, William Demarest. Directed by Alan Crosland. 88 min.

Although not really the first sound film, Alan Crosland's musical was the first talkie to have any commercial impact. It stars Al Jolson as a nice Jewish boy who loves his mother and finds it hard to choose between singing in the synagogue (like his father) or on Broadway. Soppily sentimental and frequently boring, it was still a trailblazer, the first of the "You're-going-out-there-a-youngster-but-you've-got-to-come-back-a-star" movies. And Jolson, all energy, is terrific. "You ain't heard nothing yet."

THE JAZZ SINGER ☆½
1980, USA, PG
Neil Diamond, Laurence Olivier, Lucie Arnaz, Catlin Adams, Franklyn Ajaye, Paul Nicholas, Sully Boyar, Mike Kellin. Directed by Richard Fleischer. 115 min.

Beneath his billowing, game-show-host hair, warbler Neil Diamond glowers and pouts and simmers, playing the son of an Orthodox cantor (Lord Larry Olivier) who abandons the faith to seek fame, wealth, and good vibes on the Los Angeles music scene. Incidents of grandiloquent lunacy abound, but director Richard Fleischer hasn't enough ginger in him to capitalize on them. It's all played numbly straight. Lord Olivier squanders his gifts more shamelessly than ever before, pulling out all the icky-gooey stops. Probably Neil Diamond would have done the same with his gifts if he'd had any, but . . .

JE VOUS AIME (I LOVE YOU ALL) ☆☆
1981, France
Catherine Deneuve, Jean-Louis Trintignant, Serge Gainsbourg, Gerard Depardieu, Alain Souchon, Christian Marquand. Directed by Claude Berri. 105 min.

In response to François Truffaut's *The Man Who Loved Women*, French director Claude Berri serves up Catherine Deneuve as a professional woman, now approaching middle age, who reflects back upon all the men she's loved but never kept hold of. The tempting cast and a little bit of titillation notwithstanding, the story is far too flaccid to arouse anyone.

JEKYLL AND HYDE . . . TOGETHER AGAIN ☆☆½
1982, USA, R
Mark Blankfield, Bess Armstrong, Krista Errickson, Tim Thomerson. Directed by Jerry Belson. 87 min.

By all rights, this should have been unwatchable—an updated version of the Jekyll/Hyde story with a doctor who becomes a party animal when he snorts a new wonder drug (yes, there are cocaine jokes by the score). And it really is quite dumb. Still, it gets a good number of laughs from the maniacal performance by Mark Blankfield of the execrable "Saturday Night Live" rip-off "Fridays": he expends so much energy grunting, leering, and loping along, like some bizarre combination of Robin Williams and Dwight Frye, that he can get away with the stalest jokes simply through excess. Steve Martin lookalike comic Tim Thomerson also lends some humor; both he and Blankfield deserve a better script.

JENNIFER ☆
1978, USA, PG
Lisa Pelikan, Bert Convy, Nina Foch, Amy Johnston, John Gavin, Jeff Corey, Louise Hoven, Ray Underwood. Directed by Brice Mack. 90 min.

We like the scene in which a spoiled-rich-kid rapist has his head bitten off by a giant snake—with the noggin in its mouth the serpent looks like the main course at a Brobdingnagian dinner party. Apart from this, it's a Grade Z rip-off of *Carrie*, with attractive Lisa Pelikan—she was the young Julia in the film of that name—as a hillbilly scholarship student at a posh girls' school who is persecuted by her upper-crust classmates. With the snakes at her command, she takes her revenge.

JENNY ☆☆
1970, USA
Marlo Thomas, Alan Alda, Elizabeth Wilson, Vincent Gardenia, Marian Hailey. Directed by George Bloomfield. 89 min.

TV favorites Marlo Thomas and Alan Alda star in this bittersweet romantic yarn about an unmarried pregnant woman who falls in love with a draft-dodging young filmmaker. Director George Bloomfield, also from television, obviously wanted to make an American *A Man and a Woman*. He uses flashy camera and editing techniques and a filmmaking background in the story. However, he can't disguise the preachy moralizing and the sentimental performances. Strictly the type of material usually made for television.

JEREMIAH JOHNSON ☆☆☆
1972, USA, PG
Robert Redford, Will Geer, Stefan Gierasch, Allyn Ann McLerie. Directed by Sydney Pollack. 107 min.

Sydney Pollack's leisurely, reverent saga tells the story of society dropout/mountain man Jeremiah Johnson, who began life as a trapper in the Rocky Mountains in 1825. Robert Redford gives his usual understated, almost reluctant performance, but for once it fits his character perfectly, and Pollack's direction gently interweaves scenes of adventure and suspense with moments of reflection and introspection. The screenplay (coauthored by John Milius) tends to be pompous and grandiloquent about the philosophical issues it raises, while not answering enough of the small, practical questions any viewer will have about Johnson's way of life. But the often-vivid canvas of man in and against the wilderness will draw audiences in, especially—but by no means exclusively—children.

THE JERICHO MILE ☆☆☆
1979, USA (TV)
Peter Strauss, Richard Lawson, Roger E. Mosley, Brian Dennehy, Billy Green Bush, Ed Lauter, William Prince, Miguel Pinero. Directed by Michael Mann. 100 min.

Peter Strauss won an Emmy for his passionate work in this engrossing drama about a lifer at Folsom Prison who strives to become a world-class runner and fights to be allowed to compete in the Olympic trials. The prison atmosphere is exceptionally convincing for a TV movie, and director Michael Mann (creator of "Miami Vice") provides a handsome, hard-edged texture and a taut script. Emmys also went to the teleplay by Mann and Patrick Nolan, and to the editing.

THE JERK ☆☆
1979, USA, R
Steve Martin, Bernadette Peters, Catlin Adams, Mabel King, Richard Ward, Dick Anthony Williams, Bill Macy, M. Emmet Walsh, Dick O'Neill. Directed by Carl Reiner. 104 min.

Steve Martin's first star vehicle is a lurching, ugly-looking film that still manages to be quite hilarious in places—thanks to his hyperactive brand of nerdiness. Martin plays a tow-headed, thirty-year-old waif who leaves his black parents to make his way in the world. This warped Horatio Alger burlesque might be even funnier if director Carl Reiner didn't show such a penchant for crude racial and sexual stereotypes.

JESSE JAMES ☆☆☆
1939, USA
Tyrone Power, Henry Fonda, Nancy Kelly, Randolph Scott, Henry Hull, Slim Summerville, Brian Donlevy, John Carradine, Donald Meek, Jane Darwell. Directed by Henry King. 105 min.

The history of outlaw Jesse James is severely sanitized in this visually impressive Technicolor Western. In this version of their story, the James Brothers begin to rob trains in vengeance for the murder of their mother by a railroad agent. When Jesse gives himself up later on in order to receive a lighter sentence, he is doublecrossed and escapes, "forced" once again into a life of crime. Although this is a dubious piece of historical revisionism, it is exciting entertainment nevertheless. The following year brought a sequel, *The Return of Frank James*.

JESSE JAMES AT BAY ☆½
1941, USA
Roy Rogers, George "Gabby" Hayes, Sally Payne, Pierre Watkin, Ivan Miller, Hal Taliaferro, Gale Storm. Directed by Joseph Kane. 56 min.

Roy Rogers plays two roles: a Missouri Robin Hood named Jesse James (unlike any other Jesse in the movies) and a real bad guy. Seasoned viewers will have little trouble figuring out who wins in the end. There's all kinds of other stuff thrown in: a couple of female reporters right out of a thirties B movie, an evil railroad baron, and lovable Gabby Hayes, gumming his way through the witty palaver.

JESSE JAMES MEETS FRANKENSTEIN'S DAUGHTER ☆
1966, USA
John Lupton, Nestor Paiva, Narda Onyx, Estelita, Jim Davis, Cal Bolder. Directed by William Beaudine. 85 min.

Hack director William Beaudine's last film is a worthy companion piece to his abominable *Billy the Kid vs. Dracula*—call him the pioneer of the cheapo horror Western. Here, Narda Onyx plays a descendant of Frankenstein who has designs on Jesse James's sidekick—she decides to replace his brain with a spare she has lying around. Where's Baron Von Frankenstein when we need him most, to give moribund movies like this one some life?

JESUS CHRIST, SUPERSTAR ☆☆½
1973, USA, G
Ted Neeley, Carl Anderson, Yvonne Elliman, Josh Mostel. Directed by Norman Jewison. 107 min.

Like Robert Altman, director Norman Jewison seems most interested these days in adapting stage works to the screen. But whereas Altman makes a point of limiting his mise-en-scène to the physical boundaries of the stage production, Jewison, in such films as this, *A Soldier's Story*, *Agnes of God*, and *Fiddler on the Roof*, insists on opening it up. In a conventional production such as *Fiddler* he has obtained outstanding results, but with something more abstract, such as *Jesus Christ, Superstar*, the results are at best unnecessary and at worst annoying and obtrusive. The stage production, itself adapted from the popular "rock opera" by Andrew Lloyd Webber and Tim Rice, depended to a great degree on physicality, and Jewison is not able to provide a cinematically equivalent form of viscerality by adding tanks and jet fighters to his authentic desert locations. As for content, anyone who is converted to Christianity by this rendering of the last days of Christ will remain so only until they happen to wander in front of a screening of *Mohammed, Messenger of God*. Or even *Fiddler on the Roof*.

JESUS OF NAZARETH ☆☆☆☆
1977, USA (TV)
Robert Powell, Anne Bancroft, Ernest Borgnine, James Farentino, Stacy Keach, Ian McShane, Laurence Olivier. Directed by Franco Zeffirelli. 371 min. (three cassettes).

With Franco Zeffirelli (*Romeo and Juliet, Taming of the Shrew*) directing this compelling and original biblical spectacle, we are spared the pitfalls of the genre. We're not forced to sit through a passing parade of great moments from the Bible (*King of Kings*), nor are we expected to swallow massive doses of false piety (as in the visually impressive but soporific *The Greatest Story Ever Told*). Leading a superb cast, Robert Powell impresses as Jesus by adding a human dimension to playing this divine personage. Although the film met with considerable criticism from various religious groups, this intensely felt chronicle of the life and teachings of Christ succeeds as a religious document without sacrificing the intimate drama of the participants, who never are portrayed as if they just stepped off a gilt-edged holy card.

JET OVER THE ATLANTIC ☆☆½
1960, USA
Virginia Mayo, Guy Madison, George Raft, Ilona Massey. Directed by Byron Haskin. 95 min.

Some old, mediocre films are released on video because they feature a salable name performer, some because they have exploitable themes or titles, some because they're so bad that they're fun. Why they saw fit to make this available is anyone's guess; there are no big stars, and you've seen the story—an airplane in flight from New York to Europe is discovered to have a bomb on board—many times before. It's all professionally done and mildly engrossing, but unless you're a terminal George Raft fan, why bother?

JEWEL OF THE NILE ☆☆
1985, USA, PG
Michael Douglas, Kathleen Turner, Danny De Vito, Avner Eisenberg, Spiros Focas. Directed by Lewis Teague. 105 min.

Six months after the repartee-gilded surprise hit *Romancing the Stone*'s happy ending, Michael Douglas and Kathleen Turner have begun to tarnish. So when Arab potentate Spiros Focas hires romance novelist Turner to chronicle his building of a kingdom, she jumps at his hook, eventually dragging Douglas and comic relief Danny De Vito along to pop her out of trouble. The problem is, the tarnish never fades. Turner acts contractually bound, Douglas is as stiff as gunmetal, and the dialogue (so Cowardesque in Diane Thomas's glitzy script for *Stone*) is less stylish than a state highway. There are fireworks, but none of them are verbal: visually exciting, *Jewel* features well-crafted acrobatics by Avner Eisenberg and the Flying Karamazov Brothers. Unfortunately, it pales next to its predecessor, which makes it pale indeed.

JEZEBEL ☆☆☆½
1938, USA
Bette Davis, Henry Fonda, George Brent, Fay Bainter, Donald Crisp, Margaret Lindsay. Directed by William Wyler. 104 min.

Bette Davis did not get to play Scarlett O'Hara in *Gone With the Wind*, but she did win her second Oscar by portraying yet a different sort of convention-flouting Southern vixen in this elaborate and beautifully made antebellum melodrama. Her character's flirtatious, conniving ways with the menfolk of New Orleans (including George Brent and young Henry Fonda) are called to a halt by the yellow fever epidemic of 1853. Davis is in her element, giving a surprisingly restrained performance, and is royally showcased by a superbly mounted production. Special attention should go to Ernest Haller's cinematography in this often-neglected costume epic.

THE JIGSAW MAN ½☆
1984, Great Britain, PG
Michael Caine, Laurence Olivier, Susan George, Robert Powell. Directed by Terence Young. 96 min.

Michael Caine and Laurence Olivier star in this muddled, boring, unintentionally funny spy thriller about a British agent who, while working for the KGB, defects back to his home country only to be pursued by spies on both sides. *Sleuth* fans will be disheartened to find that Caine and Olivier share no more than two scenes together. Add incompetent Susan George as Caine's daughter, sluggish pacing, and a fudged action climax and you have a major disaster that is all the more disappointing because the source novel (by Dorothy Bennett) is not uninteresting. Candidate for worst moment: a flashback love scene between seventy-seven-year-old Olivier and thirty-four-year-old George (playing her own mother).

JIMMY THE KID ☆½
1982, USA
Gary Coleman, Dee Wallace, Ruth Gordon. Directed by Gary Nelson. 85 min.

For Gary Coleman fans only. If you are one, nothing we can say about his studied cuteness, his mechanical wisecracking, or his artificial charm will change your mind. Seeing this is like watching a windup toy designed to make smartass remarks. The derivative plot concerns bungling kidnappers who pinch the offspring of some show-biz folks but discover the little brat is not all that eager to give up the excitement of his predicament. It's a brotherly love comedy as kid and kidnappers learn important lessons in humanity from each other. Shallow and coy, but smoothly professional in its sitcom way.

JINXED! ☆☆
1982, USA, R
Bette Midler, Rip Torn, Ken Wahl, Jack Elam, Val Avery, Benson Fong. Directed by Don Siegel. 103 min.

While this quirky comedy was being made, there was much publicity about the feuding between star Bette Midler, director Don Siegel (*Dirty Harry*), and costar Ken Wahl. The turmoil obviously had its effect; *Jinxed!* is a highly unfocused film. Midler plays a singer stuck in Reno, plotting to get rid of her creepy gambler-boyfriend Rip Torn. "I'm gonna say something to you I've never said to a man before," Midler tells partner-in-crime Wahl. "Help me murder Harold." Indeed, Midler's wit may be the one saving grace of the movie.

J-MEN FOREVER ☆☆☆
1979, USA
Phil Proctor, Peter Bergman. Directed by Phil Proctor, Peter Bergman, Richard Patterson. 80 min.

This is a film in the style of Woody Allen's *What's Up, Tiger Lily?* Firesign Theater's Phil Proctor and Peter Bergman have made a comedy by dubbing new dialogue onto previously existing footage. Here, though, they have used a number of different films, mostly adventure serials of the thirties and forties, occasionally inserting themselves (in matching black-and-white footage) to patch up the narrative. Their new "plot" pits various superheroes—Captain America, Rocket Man, Shazam, here collectively known as the J-Men—against the evil Caped Madman, who wants to bring this country to its knees by polluting the radio waves with rock and roll. Of course, it's loaded with drug jokes and rock music (by The Tubes and Billy Preston).

JO JO DANCER, YOUR LIFE IS CALLING ☆☆
1986, USA, R
Richard Pryor, Debbie Allen, Art Evans, Fay Hauser, Barbara Williams, Carmen McRae, Paula Kelly, Diahann Abbott. Directed by Richard Pryor. 97 min.

In this autobiographical saga, which Richard Pryor produced, directed, cowrote, and starred in, the comic has become a victim of the personality—that of the cowardly con artist/clown—he forged in more than a dozen mediocre movies. As legendary comic Jo Jo Dancer lies swathed in bandages in the burn ward, his "alter ego" rises from his body and proceeds to skip through the turning points of his life. In his concert films, Pryor is a confessional, taboo-shattering satirist who brims with tales of his insensitive behavior, but now he's here to tell us that the big bad world is to blame for his mishaps, his cocaine addiction, his accident. He's a victim, a mere pawn. Of what? Of a childhood spent in his grandmother's brothel; of fat, racist nightclub owners; of wives who get bored when he's on the road and take to wild partying; of drugs and sleaze and fate. The movie is fatally lacking in texture, atmosphere, and drama.

All that holds it together is the soggy sanctimony of the new, born-again Pryor, who comes off as a timid, blubberingly sincere man without a trace of anger or exuberance.

JOAN OF ARC ☆☆
1948, USA
Ingrid Bergman, José Ferrer, George Couloris, Francis L. Sullivan, Gene Lockhart, Ward Bond, John Ireland, Hurd Hatfield, George Zucco. Directed by Victor Fleming. 145 min.

Ingrid Bergman's first falling-out with the critics was with this slow-moving, unconsciously long rendition of Maxwell Anderson's *Joan of Lorraine*. Ten years earlier, Bergman would have been ideal as the Maid of Orleans; here she's physically and temperamentally too mature to play the peasant girl who fights for France during the Hundred Years War. The Technicolor production is lavish, and José Ferrer's film debut as the Dauphin provides energy, but director Victor Fleming (*The Wizard of Oz*, *Gone with the Wind*) too often lets the characters talk incessantly without moving the camera. Bergman would again try to play Joan in Rossellini's *Joan at the Stake*, but to no better effect. For those seeking a good Joan of Arc movie, try *The Passion of Joan of Arc*, *Joan, the Woman*, or even *Saint Joan*.

JOE ☆☆☆
1970, USA, R
Peter Boyle, Dennis Patrick, Susan Sarandon, K. Callan. Directed by John G. Avildsen. 107 min.

The title character of this small film is a blue-collar hard-hat bigot (terms which were, at the time of the film's release, all but synonymous). Much less lovable or forgivable than the television character, Joe is most proud of his collection of World War II weaponry, which he dreams of being able to use on the "hippies, faggots, and niggers" that he sees as the enemy. In the best parts of the film, he develops an odd relationship with an upper-middle-class advertising executive who, in a fit of rage, murdered the junkie-lover of his wayward daughter. Although *Joe* finally degenerates into a forced, inflammatory climax, the bulk of the film is provocative and subtly frightening, with a performance by Peter Boyle that he has yet to equal, and strong, certain direction from John G. Avildsen (*Rocky*), who photographed this minor low-budget classic in various New York street locations.

JOE KIDD ☆☆☆
1972, USA, PG
Clint Eastwood, Robert Duvall, John Saxon, Don Stroud, Stella Garcia, James Wainwright, Gregory Walcott. Directed by John Sturges. 87 min.

Like Clint Eastwood's more recent *Pale Rider*, this is basically an old-fashioned Western adventure that benefits from expert handling, including the script by novelist Elmore Leonard and the beautiful location photography by Bruce Surtees. Once again, steely-eyed Eastwood is a vaguely sketched gunfighter, this time on the side of Spanish-American landholders trying to protect their claim against evil land baron Robert Duvall. Good action sequences, little blood or gore.

JOE PALOOKA ☆☆☆
1934, USA
Jimmy Durante, Lupe Velez, Stuart Erwin, Marjorie Rambeau, Robert Armstrong, William Cagney, Thelma Todd. Directed by Benjamin Stoloff. 80 min.

Jimmy Durante, the biggest nightclub comedian of his time, foundered a bit in his transition to the screen and stuck his legendary schnozz into a few stinkers before he came up with this winner. The role of a fast-talking, lamebrained fight manager was a natural, and the comic-strip story of a punch-drunk fighter in love with booze, dames, and the wrong end of a boxing glove only improves with age. Though Durante is in fine form and even sings "Inka Dinka Doo," look to the supporting players for the really crazy comedy. Marjorie Rambeau is the standout, playing the mother of bum-turned-champ Joe Palooka. Stuart Erwin is funny as the fighter, but Lupe Velez, the Mexican spitfire, is even better as a girl with dollar signs in her eyes and Palooka in her mitts. Al McSwatt is played by William Cagney, Jimmy's brother. The film's original title was *Palooka*.

JOHN CARPENTER'S THE THING

See *The Thing*

JOHNNY BELINDA ☆☆☆½
1948, USA
Jane Wyman, Lew Ayres, Charles Bickford, Agnes Moorehead, Stephen McNally, Jan Sterling, Rosalind Ivan, Monte Blue, Alan Napier. Directed by Jean Negulesco. 101 min.

Jane Wyman won a well-deserved Oscar here for her portrayal of a deaf-mute in a Nova Scotia fishing village. She is brought out of her shell by the arrival of a young doctor, who teaches her sign language and provides her with something she has seldom had, the ability to communicate with those around her. The story takes a melodramatic turn with a rape, a murder, and a final trial scene, but the film avoids sensationalism, concentrating on character rather than lurid situation.

JOHNNY BELINDA ☆☆½
1982, USA (TV)
Rosanna Arquette, Richard Thomas, Dennis Quaid, Candy Clark, Roberts Blossom. Directed by Anthony Harvey. 100 min.

Although this version updates the popular tearjerker without any damage, it's simply not as effective at milking tears as the two previous versions. The story line concerns a deaf-mute girl who's regarded as little more than an animal by her family until a kindly doctor educates her and introduces kindness into her loveless existence. It's surefire melodrama, yet the perpetually overvalued Rosanna Arquette lacks the luminous qualities that both Jane Wyman and Mia Farrow brought to the role; she doesn't transform this durable star vehicle into anything memorable.

JOHNNY DANGEROUSLY ☆☆½
1984, USA, PG-13
Michael Keaton, Joe Piscopo, Marilu Henner, Griffin Dunne, Peter Boyle. Directed by Amy Heckerling. 90 min.

This silly send-up of classic gangster films has an unusually good cast. Sight gags and one-liners alternate with elaborate but often unsuccessful set pieces and weird conceptual humor as a Lower East Side waif makes good in organized crime while his younger brother (whom he, needless to say, put through law school) wages a war on the underworld that would put the combined efforts of Eliot Ness and J. Edgar Hoover to shame. Often predictable, but harmless and sporadically funny.

JOHNNY GOT HIS GUN ☆☆½
1971, USA
Timothy Bottoms, Jason Robards, Marsha Hunt, Diane Varsi, Donald Sutherland, Tony Geary, David Soul. Directed by Dalton Trumbo. 111 min.

The stories behind this movie are, ironically, much more interesting than the movie itself. Writer-director Dalton Trumbo was one of the Hollywood Ten, serving ten months in prison for refusing to testify before the House Un-American Activities Committee about alleged Communist sympathies. This film—about a soldier who loses his arms, legs, and face on the last day of World War I and is confined to a hospital bed by doctors who consider him a vegetable even though his mind still functions perfectly—was based on his own novel, written in 1939 in anticipation of World War II. Most of the actors and technical staff worked for deferred payment.

The film was originally to have been directed by Luis Buñuel, who reportedly helped Trumbo with the script. Unfortunately, the film has nothing more to say than that war is bad, mostly to the young who are sent to it by the old, and aside from strong opening and ending sequences, it doesn't even say that particularly well. Memorable moment: Donald Sutherland, as Jesus Christ in a nightmare sequence, tells the hapless hero to leave him be—"You're a very unlucky boy, and it may rub off."

JOHNNY GUITAR
☆☆☆½
1954, USA
Joan Crawford, Sterling Hayden, Mercedes McCambridge, Scott Brady, Ben Cooper. Directed by Nicholas Ray. 110 min.

Nicholas Ray, the man behind *Rebel without a Cause*, directed this unusual cult classic. *Johnny Guitar* goes far beyond the conventions of the Western, addressing questions of sexual politics more characteristic of fifties melodrama. Ray rejects traditional narrative structures, tending to shun action in favor of atmosphere and emotion. The film features two women feuding over a man and a railroad, an inversion of the norms of this typically male-dominated genre. Joan Crawford's strong, masculine portrayal of Vienna surprised many when the film first appeared. The result of Ray's iconoclasm is a dark, compelling, psychological Western.

JOHNNY NOBODY
☆☆☆
1961, Great Britain
Nigel Patrick, Yvonne Mitchell, Aldo Ray, William Bendix, Cyril Cusack. Directed by Nigel Patrick. 88 min.

In many ways, this a more taut and satisfying thriller than Alfred Hitchcock's *I Confess*. An Irish priest extends his duties beyond the confessional by trying to piece together the clues in a murder case. *Johnny Nobody* will keep you glued to your seat as the snooping cleric investigates the death of an alcoholic writer, a case the authorities would like to close quickly.

JOHNNY TIGER
☆½
1966, USA
Robert Taylor, Chad Everett, Geraldine Brooks, Brenda Scott. Directed by Paul Wendkos. 102 min.

This is a drab concoction about a half-breed teacher who is trying to find a place in the white man's world without being untrue to any of his progenitors. The studios must have owed Robert Taylor a film on his contract, or vice versa; they certainly didn't have much luck building Everett into a movie star.

JOHNNY TREMAIN
☆½
1957, USA
Hal Stalmaster, Luana Patten, Jeff York, Sebastian Cabot, Dick Beymer, Walter Sande, Rusty Lane. Directed by Robert Stevenson. 80 min.

Although the times—the American Revolution—were exciting, this film is not. It's the story of a young silversmith's political awakening as he conspires with the Massachusetts Founding Fathers to oust the Redcoats. This feeble replay of history follows the schoolbook text written by Esther Forbes at a word-by-word pace; we didn't like the book and we hated the movie.

JOKES MY FOLKS NEVER TOLD ME
½☆
1978, USA, R
Dixie Edgar, Daniel Fee, Sandy Johnson, Hal Lindon, Raven De La Croix. Directed by Gerry Woolery. 82 min.

The worst thing about this movie is that it's nothing but stale jokes: they're about as funny as famine. Maybe Attila the Hun told European villagers these jokes in lieu of maiming, torturing, and sacking their village.

JONATHAN LIVINGSTON SEAGULL
☆
1973, USA, G
Voices of James Franciscus, Juliet Mills, Hal Holbrook, Philip Ahn, David Ladd, Dorothy McGuire, Richard Crenna. Directed by Hal Bartlett. 101 min.

An exasperatingly mawkish screen translation of Richard Bach's early-seventies, ten-million-copy best-seller about a Zen-obsessed bird whose flights eventually take him to a higher plane of existence. Whatever charms the story had, its archly cute dialogue was not among them; here a number of otherwise reputable actors mouth lines that are, pardon the pun, for the birds. Worse yet, J.L.S.'s midflight transitions are accompanied by (ugh!) Neil Diamond songs. The endless bird footage resembles the ugly slides that some theaters show before their main feature. Read the book: not only is it slightly more entertaining, but it takes less time to get through.

JOSEPH ANDREWS
☆☆½
1977, Great Britain, R
Peter Firth, Ann-Margret, Michael Hordern, Beryl Reid, Jim Dale, Peter Bull, John Gielgud, Peggy Ashcroft, Hugh Griffith, Natalie Ogle. Directed by Tony Richardson. 103 min.

With his superb 1963 adaptation of Henry Fielding's novel *Tom Jones*, Tony Richardson would seem to have established himself as the ideal director to film Fielding's dense, bawdy, picaresque works. However, as a return to the same territory, *Joseph Andrews* is a disappointment. Fielding's story of a young man's quest to find his true identity in a maze of concealed parentages remains a joy, and Richardson has captured its lewd aspects as well as the vivid eighteenth-century English countryside; as well, there are fine performances from Peter Firth as Joseph and Ann-Margret as Lady Booby. What's missing is the sense that Fielding's classic novel was much more than an extended dirty joke—the detail, the dialogue, the irony, and the keen sense of class structure that made it a great novel have been scooped out.

JOSHUA THEN & NOW
☆☆½
1985, Canada, R
James Woods, Gabrielle Lazure, Alan Arkin, Michael Sarrazin, Linda Sorensen, Alan Scarfe, Ken Campbell, Kate Trotter, Alexander Knox. Directed by Ted Kotcheff. 129 min.

This comedy from writer Mordecai Richler and director Ted Kotcheff, who made *The Apprenticeship of Duddy Kravitz*, has enough faults to drive you crazy, yet its dogged integrity makes it admirable, too. The story's like a literary *Once upon a Time in America*: Joshua Shapiro (James Woods) is a successful Canadian Jewish writer dogged by a domestic scandal; he spends most of the film recalling his past, from his childhood in the Montreal Jewish underworld, through his writer's apprenticeship in London, his marriage to a wealthy senator's daughter, and his rise to celebrity as a talk-show habitué in Canada. Woods is best with the tawdry side of his character; he grows flatter when Joshua escapes the gutter. And he isn't helped out much by Richler's script, which fails to bridge Joshua's light and dark sides. But director Kotcheff fills out the material with his cautious realism, and the film is certainly engrossing.

LE JOUR SE LEVE
☆☆☆½
1939, France
Jean Gabin, Jules Berry, Arletty and Jacqueline Laurent. Directed by Marcel Carne. 95 min.

Marcel Carne directed this acclaimed melodrama in a dark, atmospheric style. Writer Jacques Prevert crafted the film's intricate story of a man (Jean Gabin) under siege by the police for a murder circumstances forced him to commit. The narrative, told in flashback, moves slowly but compellingly. The photography is stylized, graceful, and tense. Maurice Jaubert's score effectively conveys the claustrophobic inexorability of the tale. (a.k.a.: *Daybreak*)

JOURNEY BACK TO OZ ☆☆
1974, USA
Animated: Liza Minelli, Milton Berle, Margaret Hamilton, Ethel Merman, Paul Lynde, Mickey Rooney, Risë Stevens. Directed by Hal Sutherland. 90 min.

Pretty decent animated-film sequel to *The Wizard of Oz*. Since our memories of those characters are so precious, the idea of a return trip is appealing, but the film boasts the usual primary color animation, the usual tepid musical score, the usual disappointments. Nothing distinctive, but pleasant enough, and the familiar voices of the cast are strong enough to lighten the heavy sweetness. (Even as a disembodied voice, though, Liza Minnelli is no substitute for Judy Garland.)

JOURNEY INTO FEAR ☆☆☆½
1942, USA
Joseph Cotten, Orson Welles, Dolores Del Rio, Agnes Moorehead, Ruth Warrick. Directed by Norman Foster and Orson Welles. 71 min.

Though officially directed by Norman Foster, *Journey into Fear* is very much an Orson Welles film. The script, based on Eric Ambler's novel, is by Welles and Joseph Cotten; Welles stars in it and directed parts of it; and the story and characters bear distinct resemblances to some of his later films (*The Lady from Shanghai, The Trail*). The film is a thriller with Cotten as a naive American engineer dragged off by Nazis to prevent him from arming Turkish ships. He then stumbles into increasingly dangerous situations. The labyrinthine plot is dominated by Welles as Colonel Haki, a menacing Turkish police chief. Studio editing created the confusion in some of the earlier scenes, but the last reel is cinematic tension on a par with the best of Alfred Hitchcock.

JOURNEY OF NATTY GANN ☆☆☆½
1985, USA, PG
Meredith Salenger, John Cusak, Ray Wise, Lainie Kazan, Barry Miller, Verna Bloom, Scatman Crothers. Directed by Jeremy Kagan. 101 min.

As far as family entertainment goes, this is a breath of fresh air. During the Depression, a feisty kid hits the road to seek out her father, separated from her by unfortunate circumstances. In order to survive the cross-country ordeal, she adopts the life-style of a hobo and, in the course of her travels, this appealing tomboy grows up before our eyes. Her adventures are made more bearable by the strange companionship of a wolf who befriends and protects her. Breathtaking photography and endearing performances make this spunky girl's odyssey into maturity a gripping experience and a must-see for animal lovers.

JOURNEY TO THE CENTER OF THE EARTH ☆☆☆½
1959, USA
James Mason, Pat Boone, Arlene Dahl, Diane Baker, Thayer David, Alan Napier. Directed by Henry Levin. 132 min.

This wildly enjoyable adventure film, along with Disney's *Twenty Thousand Leagues under the Sea* and *Mysterious Island* (1961), proves that, with the proper budget, Jules Verne is a movie natural whose books make terrific family entertainment. Heading a perilous, one-of-a-kind expedition, James Mason leads his intrepid crew into the bowels of the earth, where they encounter prehistoric dimetrodons and bubbling forces of nature just itching to do the whole bunch of them in. Along for the ride in this downward spiral into excitement are Gertrude, a scene-stealing duck, and Pat Boone, more animated than he's ever been before or since.

JOURNEY TO THE CENTER OF THE EARTH (1978)

See *Where Time Began*

JOY HOUSE ☆☆☆
1964, France/USA
Alain Delon, Lola Albright, Jane Fonda, Sorell Brooke. Directed by René Clement. 98 min.

A preposterous but inventive and enjoyable tongue-in-cheek thriller, one of those convoluted melodramas in which not even the cast and crew seem to be fully aware of where the plot is taking them. As with *The Big Sleep* (1946), the confusion doesn't prevent the film from being a zesty entertainment. Director René Clement thrives in the hothouse environment he's created for this film. The ironic tale concerns a handsome ne'er-do-well (Alain Delon) on the lam after carrying on with the moll of an unforgiving gangster. By accident, he providentially stumbles into the clutches of Lola Albright and her ingenuous cousin, Jane Fonda, both of whom have their own mysterious reasons for providing him with sanctuary. The cast is irresistible, and the sex appeal of the players radiates from the screen. Why Albright's sensuality didn't lead her to major stardom after this film is another mystery.

THE JOY OF SEX ☆☆½
1984, USA, R
Cameron Dye, Michelle Meyrink, Colleen Camp, Christopher Lloyd. Directed by Martha Coolidge. 93 min.

This gaggle of sex and scatology from the otherwise talented director of *Valley Girl* manages to gain a tiny bit of comic momentum. A teenager mistakenly believes that she's dying and does everything possible to lose her virginity, only to have her attempts at intercourse end in humorous disaster. The actors do their best with the stupid material, with Christopher Lloyd giving a hilarious performance as a berserk gym teacher. National Lampoon had their name removed from this picture.

JOYRIDE ☆☆½
1977, USA, R
Desi Arnaz, Jr., Robert Carradine, Melanie Griffith, Anne Lockhart. Directed by Joseph Ruben. 92 min.

Half teen, half lean and stylish, *Joyride* is a joyride compared to other exploitation jalopies. Uncharacteristically, it begins when the sexy stars *leave* the beach; bored with la-la Los Angeles, they crave the furrowed icescape of Alaska. Sadly, the barren frontier forces them to turn to robbery, violence, casual sex, and foul language. (It *is* a teen film, after all.) But the stars, particularly Desi Arnaz, Jr., sometimes betray more loss than gloss. Until the final, inexplicable ten minutes, the film is surprisingly bleak. It would have been nice, and more in keeping with this film's troubled tone, to see these mindless teens crash-land.

JOYSTICKS ☆
1983, USA, R
Joe Don Baker, Leif Green, Jim Greenleaf, Scott McGinnis. Directed by Greydon Clark. 87 min.

After you've seen enough of these teenagers-against-the-world comedies, you begin to search desperately for *anything* of interest. Here, it's Jeff Greenleaf's maniacal performance as the requisite gross-master, the flatulent Dorfus. John Voldstad (one of the Darryls from TV's "Newhart") appears as a bumbling heavy. The rest is *nada*.

JUAREZ ☆☆☆
1939, USA
Paul Muni, Bette Davis, Brian Aherne, Gilbert Roland. Directed by William Dieterle. 132 min.

William Dieterle had already directed 1938's Best Picture, *The Life of Émile Zola*, when Warner Bros. gave him the job of handling Paul Muni in another prestige film, *Juarez*. Unfortunately, Dieterle does not get a handle on the complex, sometimes deceitful actions of Mexico's hero. (Muni's penchant for sentimentality reduces his characterization to that of a simple soul who has greatness thrust upon him.) This is in contrast to the fascinating nuances that Bette Davis and Brian Aherne bring to the Emperor Maximilian and Carlotta. They emerge as the most passionate and intelligent figures in the drama, and Juarez himself becomes intrusive on what is clearly the more developed story. Davis underplays the subtle stages of Carlotta's incipient madness to great effect, until, in the film's highlight, her mind gives way in a lyrical, deeply moving outburst. Tony Gaudios's photography is extraordinary in its use of tiny spaces within broad vistas—enclosing the royal pair in a web spun by a buffoon.

JUBILEE ☆½
1978, Great Britain
Jenny Runacre, Jordan, Little Nell, Toyah Wilcox, Richard O'Brien, Adam Ant, Orlando. Directed by Derek Jarman. 103 min.

This feature film inspired by the punk movement of the late 1970s was named after the same British national celebration that provoked the Sex Pistols's punk anthem "God Save the Queen." That three-minute song, however, has more energy than all 103 minutes of this interminable, impenetrable, pseudo-existentialist yawn. The "plot"—a Warholesque look at the escapades of a girl gang of punks (punkettes?) in a disintegrated London of the near future—is framed by a story bringing Queen Elizabeth I into the future to observe the goings-on. The cast features several stars of *The Rocky Horror Picture Show* and future pop star Adam Ant, but they're only minor supporting characters. The music, by Brian Eno, Siouxie and the Banshees, and others, is seldom used and hardly audible.

JUDEX ☆☆☆½
1963, France
Channing Pollock, Francine Berge, Michel Vitold, Edith Scob, Theo Sarapo, Sylva Koscina, Jacques Jouhanneau. Directed by Georges Franju. 95 min.

Director Georges Franju's successful homage to the French film serials of the early, silent days is appealing for its authentic simplicity, adventurousness, and melodrama. Franju re-creates this early charm by not attempting to improve upon the genre's conventions. Instead, he retells the classic tale of the criminal who falls in love, rights his wrongs, and becomes a virtuous person. While film buffs will enjoy the freshness Franju brings to an early cinemantic genre, ordinary audiences will discover genuine entertainment in its crazy plotting.

JUDGE HORTON AND THE SCOTTSBORO BOYS ☆☆☆☆
1976, USA (TV)
Arthur Hill, Vera Miles, Lewis J. Stadlen, Ken Kercheval, Ellen Barber. Directed by Fielder Cook. 100 min.

This exemplary film, bristling with energy, is executed with the courage of its convictions in full force. A top-flight cast gives this unfortunately true story bite and immediacy. In 1931, nine black men were arrested and convicted for raping two promiscuous white women. Because of the pervasive prejudice of the times, the men never were given a fair trial at the hands of several all-male, all-white juries. The focus of this tale of racial inequality is on the judge, who bravely reversed the jury's popular decision and saved several of the accused from hanging at the risk of his own career and safety. The story is cogently adapted from the book *The Scottsboro Boys* and superbly directed by Fielder Cook. Some of the language in the courtroom trial has been toned down to meet network standards of the mid-seventies.

JUDGE PRIEST ☆☆☆½
1934, USA
Will Rogers, Henry B. Walthall, Tom Brown, Anita Louise, Stepin Fetchit, Hattie McDaniel. Directed by John Ford. 80 min.

John Ford's vision of the American folk and Will Rogers's folksy acting sweetly realize the story of the domestic and social trials of a lazybones, mint julep–drinking judge in the postreconstructionist South. *Priest* is based on the stories of Irwin S. Cobb, and Dudley Nichols wrote the screenplay. As Ford said, however, no one could write for Rogers, and it is his asides that make the slow-moving film sparkle. Today the film seems to reveal the explicit oppression of the black Southerner through the racist stereotypes expertly enacted by Stepin Fetchit and Hattie McDaniel. Unfortunately, most tape versions of this film are extremely muddy and dark, and the sound quality is poor.

JUDGEMENT AT NUREMBERG ☆☆☆½
1961, USA
Spencer Tracy, Burt Lancaster, Richard Widmark, Marlene Dietrich, Maximilian Schell, Judy Garland, Montgomery Clift, William Shatner, Edward Binns, Kenneth MacKenna, Werner Klemperer. Directed by Stanley Kramer. 190 min.

Stanley Kramer's wrenching though schematic drama about a German judge (Burt Lancaster) on trial at Nuremberg for war crimes began as a segment of TV's "Playhouse 90" in the 1950s. This greatly expanded version is very compelling on video, where its intimate characterizations and pungent performances can be appreciated in detail. Abby Mann's Oscar-winning screenplay has moments of unnecessary bombast, as if denouncing Nazi atrocities were somehow controversial; for the most part, however, it sticks with one complex, specific, and moving story line. Spencer Tracy underplays the presiding American jurist very effectively, and Judy Garland, Marlene Dietrich, and Montgomery Clift each have scene-stealing turns as witnesses, but top honors and a Best Actor Oscar went to Maximilian Schell for his impassioned portrayal of the defendant's lawyer.

JUGGERNAUT ☆☆
1974, Great Britain, PG
Richard Harris, Omar Sharif, David Hemmings, Anthony Hopkins, Shirley Knight, Ian Holm. Directed by Richard Lester. 109 min.

So-so thriller about a bomb threat on a luxury liner made in the wake of the enormous success of the seaborne disaster film *The Poseidon Adventure*. Director Richard Lester keeps the action and drama moving as best he can, but the plot is subdued and dull, and the climax, involving which of two wires must be cut to save the ship, is so hackneyed that it's fatiguing to watch. Fans no longer in the grip of disastermania will find *Juggernaut* a standard-issue drama that takes far too long to reach its formulaic end.

JULES AND JIM ☆☆☆☆
1962, France
Oskar Werner, Henri Serre, Jeanne Moreau, Marie Dubois, Vanna Urbino. Directed by François Truffaut. 110 min.

This delicate, reflective study of the long friendship of two men and the woman they both love may be the most fully realized of François Truffaut's early works, and is certainly among the most durable. *Jules and Jim* spans twenty years, ending in 1930, and working in period seemed to relax the director after the tightly strung, stylized *Shoot the Piano Player*; the camerawork is unfussy and the scenes are gently played and paced with leisure. With its long, languid scenes and lack of action, this was for a time regarded as the quintessential "art" film, but there's nothing pretentious or rarefied about this engaging dramatic romance. Jeanne Moreau is incandescent as the mercurial Catherine, and Oskar Werner and Henri Serre are excellent as the men in her life.

JULIA ☆☆☆
1977, USA, PG
Jane Fonda, Vanessa Redgrave, Maximilian Schell, Jason Robards, Hal Holbrook, Rosemary Murphy, John Glover, Lisa Pelikan, Meryl Streep, Susan Jones. Directed by Fred Zinnemann. 116 min.

Lillian Hellman's tantalizing memoir of her friendship with an underground leftist activist identified only as Julia is given a full-scale period piece treatment by Fred Zinnemann, and the result is an impeccably mounted, beautifully acted, and finally rather static drama. A gallery of famous literary intellects—Dashiell Hammett, Dorothy Parker, Alan Campbell—populates the tale, but like Hellman's story, the film is less compelling as history and/or politics than as the story of an odd and troubled friendship. Even in that capacity, Alvin Sargent's screenplay constantly promises more than it delivers—the plot ultimately evaporates rather than concludes. But see it for Jane Fonda's wiry intensity as the young Hellman—it's the best of her many "driven-woman" performances—and for Vanessa Redgrave's dazzling, impassioned portrayal of Julia. Academy Awards went to Redgrave, Jason Robards, and Sargent's script.

JUMPIN' JACK FLASH ☆☆½
1986, USA, R
Whoopi Goldberg, Stephen Collins, John Wood, Carol Kane, Annie Potts, Peter Michael Goetz, Roscoe Lee Browne, Jon Lovitz, Phil Hartman, Jim Belushi, Tracey Ullmann. Directed by Penny Marshall. 98 min.

Whoopi Goldberg's breezy, completely assured comic performance makes this creaky spy caper easy to watch even when the plot falls apart—very few screen comics have her bravado and instant audience rapport. Here she plays a computer operator who starts receiving mysterious messages on her terminal from a British spy code-named Jumpin' Jack Flash, who desperately needs her help. Her efforts to save him get her into hot water with spies, counterspies, and triple agents. The story is poorly worked out and first-time director Penny Marshall has no sense of pacing (though she does good work in individual scenes). It's up to Whoopi to carry the ball with a series of comic set pieces, and she almost consistently pulls it off.

THE JUNGLE BOOK ☆☆☆
1942, USA
Sabu, Joseph Calleia, John Qualen, Frank Puglia, Rosemary DeCamp. Directed by Zoltan Korda. 109 min.

This delightful family film boasts producer Alexander Korda's typically scrupulous production values and a captivating performance by Sabu as the wild child raised by wolves. Definitely the best version of Kipling's classic, the film is pure jungle escapism, a bit silly at times but entertaining.

JUNGLE HEAT ☆½
1984, USA, PG
Peter Fonda, Deborah Raffin, John Amos, Carlos Palomino. Directed by Gus Trikonis. 93 min.

This film consists of some standard fifties adventure plots insufficiently beefed up for eighties audiences. Anthropologist Deborah Raffin hires broken-down Vietnam vet Peter Fonda to fly her into the jungles of South America to hunt for pygmies; instead, she finds monsters and love, not necessarily in that order of importance, though the viewer will be equally indifferent toward both.

JUNIOR BONNER ☆☆☆½
1972, USA, PG
Steve McQueen, Robert Preston, Ida Lupino, Ben Johnson, Joe Don Baker. Directed by Sam Peckinpah. 100 min.

The Old West never really died—it exists today under the guise of regional rodeo shows. Sam Peckinpah, best known for his bloodbath action-adventure films, has fashioned an affectionate coda to that still-vital Western scene, whose principals drive beat-up Chryslers, their horses pulled in trailers attached to the rear bumper. Of particular interest is the film's titular character (ruefully played by Steve McQueen) who, at the age of forty, is saddled with the tag of "almost-over-the-hill" rodeo star. To prove his worth he must break a mean-spirited bull that embarrassed him during his last meet. Romantic at its core, *Junior Bonner* never sacrifices character for situation, offering several touching portraits of men desperately trying to keep alive a waning tradition. Robert Preston and Ida Lupino lend a touch of class as McQueen's estranged parents.

THE JUNKMAN ☆
1982, USA, PG
H. B. Halicki, Christopher Stone, Susan Shaw, Lang Jeffries, Lynda Day George, The Belmonts. Directed by H. B. Halicki. 96 min.

Since the 1970s, automobile crashes have become *de rigueur* in action or comedy chases, and here is the apotheosis of this trend. Compleat filmmaker H. B. Halicki produced and directed, wrote the screenplay, did the production design, and appears in the film, but the result is a dubious personal distinction. The real honors belong to the stuntmen who race and wreck the cars or to the assembly line that could keep them coming.

JUST BETWEEN FRIENDS ☆☆☆
1986, USA, PG-13
Mary Tyler Moore, Christine Lahti, Sam Waterston, Ted Danson, Salome Jens, Susan Rinell, Timothy Gibbs, Jane Greer, Mark Blum. Directed by Allan Burns. 120 min.

This affecting, wonderfully acted seriocomedy about the friendship between two women shoulders the burden of more melodramatic plot twists than it can bear—writer/director Allan Burns stirs in death, infidelity, and single parenthood without managing the careful shifts in tone that made *Terms of Endearment* (to which this owes much) a success. What emerges still has enough humor, pathos, and humanity to provide consistent pleasure. Mary Tyler Moore is fine as the sheltered wife and mother whose new best friend turns out to be her husband's lover, but it's Christine Lahti's sharp, moving, rousingly funny portrayal of the "other woman" that you'll long remember. Burns was cocreator of Moore's long-running TV series, and if parts of *Just between Friends* sound like a sitcom, at least it's a very good one.

JUST ONE OF THE GUYS ☆
1985, USA, PG
Joyce Hyser, Clayton Rohner, Billy Jacoby, Toni Hudson. Directed by Lisa Gottlieb. 100 min.

A serious-minded if simpering teen queen dons shirt and trousers and enrolls in a high school across town to get the scoop on life among the guys and win a journalism contest, in Lisa Gottlieb's cheesecake feminist film. Her notion of male impersonation, alas, consists of punky swagger and a bark like Barbra Streisand's; the cross-dressed Joyce Hyser makes Michael Jackson look like Clint Eastwood. With its leering horny-boy humor, its oddball assortment of high-school Morks and dorks, and its endlessly upturned lunchroom tables, the film doesn't aim higher than *Porky's Meets the Pulitzers*.

JUST TELL ME WHAT YOU WANT ☆☆☆½
1980, USA, R
Alan King, Ali MacGraw, Myrna Loy, Keenan Wynn, Tony Roberts, Dina Merrill, Peter Weller. Directed by Sidney Lumet. 112 min.

Who would have thought that the often-dubious talents of Sidney Lumet, Alan King, and Ali MacGraw could come up with a rich, supple, thoroughly rewarding comedy-drama? Adapting her own novel, Jay Presson Allen fashioned an incisive exploration of the lives of New York's upper crust *sans* the usual melodramatic excesses. Stand-up comedian Alan King gives a remarkably subtle performance as a wealthy businessman who plots to keep his favorite mistress (Ali MacGraw) from deserting him for a younger but financially less stable man (Peter Weller). Playing the kept woman who yearns to be free, MacGraw finally shows signs of genuine acting talent. She's just as good letting King have it in Bergdorf Goodman's as she is revealing her intimate side to Keenan Wynn (as King's business rival) over a drink. Dina Merrill also registers strongly as King's neurotic wife. Oswald Morris's photography captures the polished look of forties office-to-bedroom comedies (they've even cast Myrna Loy as King's devoted secretary), but director Lumet goes a step further, getting beneath those elegant surfaces and revealing a tantalizing picture. Vastly underrated at the time of its release, this one deserves another look.

JUST THE WAY YOU ARE ☆
1984, USA, PG
Kristy McNichol, Michael Ontkean, Kaki Hunter, Andre Dussollier, Catherine Salviat, Robert Carradine, Alexandra Paul, Lance Guest, Timothy Daly. Directed by Edouard Molinaro. 95 min.

What's worse than a soggy, cliché-ridden romantic comedy? A soggy, cliché-ridden romantic comedy with a handicapped heroine. Kristy McNichol plays a young flutist with one leg permanently disabled by a childhood bout of encephalitis. During a solo tour of Europe, she has a plaster cast substituted for her leg brace and then takes off for a wild week of experimentation at a ski resort, where she can pretend to be just another victim of the slopes. Director Edouard Molinaro trots out the sort of hoary bits that were old when the pyramids were young—viz., McNichol and friends riding in a hot-air balloon and clamoring at one another about how wonderful it is to live life to the fullest. Costarring the unredeemable Michael Ontkean.

JUST YOU AND ME, KID ☆
1979, USA, PG
George Burns, Brooke Shields, Lorraine Gary, Nicholas Coster, Burl Ives, Ray Bolger, Carl Ballantine, Keye Luke. Directed by Leonard Stern. 95 min.

Sickly sweet. George Burns plays an aging vaudevillian sheltering runaway teenage hooker Brooke Shields (in a forced, awkward performance). He spouts so many wretched homilies that one begins to hope he'll get a Mickey in his epsom salts. He and the other senior citizens in the cast try to keep the geriatric cuddliness to a minimum, but director Leonard Stern and writer Oliver Hailey sabotage their efforts with a mawkish, very condescending story line.

K

KADDISH ★★★½
1984, USA
Yossi Klein, Zoltan Klein, and Family. Directed by Steve Brand. 92 min.

Yossi Klein, the main figure in this moving documentary, is the son of a Holocaust survivor who, in 1944, buried himself in a bunker for six months to escape the Nazis. The film is a record of the tormented son's legacy—the philosophical and emotional peregrinations of a young man who thinks he can't live up to his past yet can't face it down, either. Yossi himself is an edgy, mercurial presence, and director Steve Brand films him over a period of five years, during which his hair keeps changing length, beards sprout and then vanish, and his feelings about his father and the Holocaust fluctuate between paranoia and a desire for transcendence. Yossi is as much existentialist as Jew, continually trying on new masks and adopting new purposes, and the movie conveys his pain so efficiently that it's impossible not to find some phase of his struggle with which to identify.

KAGEMUSHA ★★★½
1980, Japan
Tatsuya Nakadai, Tsutomo Yamazaki, Kenichi Hagiwana, Shuji Otaki. Directed by Akira Kurosawa. 160 min.

Akira Kurosawa's epic film must be counted among the most visually beautiful war movies ever made; emotionally, it is at once stirring and forbidding. The marvelous actor Tatsuya Nakadai plays both an embattled sixteenth-century warlord, Shingen Tanaka, and the grubby thief, known only as Kagemusha ("the shadow warrior"), who impersonates the lord for three years after his death to ensure the morale of his troops and the respect of his enemies. In adopting Shingen's gestures and postures, the thief acquires some of the lord's indomitable spirit. The video version of this lengthy, complex film comes on two cassettes, and you might find it best to watch it in two viewings: Kurosawa's film is one of ideas more than actions (although there are some savage, lavishly mounted battle scenes), and it needs to be digested slowly.

KAMIKAZE '89 ★★
1983, West Germany
Rainer Werner Fassbinder, Franco Nero, Petra Jokisch, Nicole Heesters. Directed by Wolf Gremm. 106 min.

In a grim, utopian future Germany, Inspector Jansen investigates a bomb threat and uncovers a conspiracy directed against the vast Media Combine. This is a cheap, vaguely surreal mystery, interesting primarily for the presence of German director Rainer Werner Fassbinder in the leading role.

KANAL ★★★★
1956, Poland
Tadeusz Janczar, Teresa Isewska, Misczyslaw Glinski. Directed by Andrzej Wajda. 94 min.

As the Nazis conquer Warsaw in 1944, a band of heroic Polish resisters takes to the city's sewers in a futile effort to escape. Wajda's film, which takes place mostly within these dark, diseased underground passages, is still one of the most harrowing and painful dramas ever made about World War II. His direction, from the first astonishing pan of an endless line of Poles filing through their ruined city, is a triumph of substance and style. *Kanal* is rough going even for the strong-stomached, but very much worth seeing. (a.k.a.: *They Loved Life*)

THE KANSAS CITY MASSACRE ★★½
1975, USA (TV)
Dale Robertson, Bo Hopkins, Robert Walden, Mills Watson, Scott Brady, Matt Clark, John Karlen. Directed by Dan Curtis. 96 min.

This is a sequel to the 1974 TV film *Melvin Purvis, G-Man*. It continues the true-life adventures of Purvis (again played by Dale Robertson) in the 1930s as he combatted Pretty Boy Floyd, Baby Face Nelson, and John Dillinger. Director Dan Curtis has a good feel for period dialogue and detail, and he builds to the shoot-'em-up finale of the title with fast-paced filming. Unfortunately, television standards soften the story a bit; this is one subject that would have been better served by big-screen freedom.

KANSAS TERRORS ★½
1939, USA
Robert Livingston, Raymond Hatton, Duncan Renaldo. Directed by George Sherman. 57 min.

Robert Livingston returns to the Three Mesquiteers series, replacing John Wayne, and he ably resumes his rule in righting wrongs. The fierce action is set on a strange south-of-the-border island. Livingston plays much of the film in a Lone Ranger mask.

KAOS ★★★
1985, Italy, R
Margarita Lozano, Claudio Bigagli, Franco Franchi, Cicio Ingoassia, Biagio Barone, Omero Antonutti, Enrica Maria Modugno, Directed by Paolo and Vittorio Taviani. 188 min.

Directors Paolo and Vittorio Taviani want to touch viewers on a level that transcends words, logic, and expectation. But in stripping away the trappings of naturalism, as well as the emotional undercurrents of empathy, they make it harder to reach epiphanies in their films than to be swept up by the accumulated force of a character's passion. *Kaos* is an anthology of four Pirandello short stories set in turn-of-the-century Sicily, plus a prologue and an epilogue. The stories share the mythos of peasant folklore as well as the fabulously desolate Sicilian landscape. But after the first (and best) story, "The Other Son," about a peasant madwoman who recalls the terrible event that drove her into herself, the sequences come surprisingly close to being metaphysical brain teasers on the order of a highbrow "Twilight Zone"; that the Tavianis are adapting Pirandello—and not Ray Bradbury—begins to seem a mixed blessing.

THE KARATE KID ★★★½
1984, USA, PG
Ralph Macchio, Noriyuki (Pat) Morita, Elizabeth Shue, William Zabka. Directed by John G. Avildsen. 126 min.

Director John G. Avildsen reworks his *Rocky* themes for teenagers in this movie about an underdog getting the best of his oppressors; and he proves that cosmetic surgery can indeed make a trite idea into an appealing one. A big-city show-off (Ralph Macchio) moves to California and gains the instant hatred of a group of karate-trained punks. Through his friendship with an aged martial arts master (Noriyuki Morita), the youth gains maturity and fighting skills, not to mention the chance to retaliate against his foes. Avildsen takes a long time unraveling his plot, with lots of "Kung Fu"–like scenes of Macchio learning the martial arts from his mentor. This is a sweet and likable film, with Morita's standout performance earning him an Oscar nomination. The rock group Survivor ("Eye of the

Tiger") provides the pulsating theme song. Followed by a sequel in 1986.

THE KARATE KID PART TWO ☆☆
1986, USA, PG
Ralph Macchio, Noriyuki "Pat" Morita, Yuji Okumoto, Danny Kamekona, Tamlyn Tomita. Directed by John G. Avildsen. 113 min.

Mentor Miyagi (Noriyuki Morita) takes Daniel-san (Ralph Macchio) to his home in Okinawa to reaffirm family ties and settle a blood feud, but the setting might as well be Southern California again in this dull retread, which is short on character development and long on meaningless carnage. Original screenwriter Robert Mark Kamen and director John G. Avildsen show how tired their *Rocky*-like theme has become by laying back and letting their clichéd plot flow along with the assurance of a guaranteed formula. But whenever Morita is on the screen as the inscrutable martial arts master, the picture takes on emotional resonance. He's a golden beacon in this watchable but totally inconsequential movie that could have done without the karate and the kid altogether.

KASPAR HAUSER

See *Every Man for Himself and God Against All*

THE KEEP ☆½
1984, USA, R
Scott Glenn, Alberta Watson, Robert Prosky. Directed by Michael Mann. 96 min.

Despite the warnings of superstitious locals, Nazi soldiers occupy the Keep, a strange fortress nestled high in the Romanian mountains, where they are systematically destroyed by some evil force. Big-budget horror movie with wide-reaching philosophical implications that generates no impact at all.

THE KEEPER ☆
1976, Canada, R
Christopher Lee, Tell Schreiber, Sally Gray, Ian Tracey. Directed by Tom Drake. 88 min.

An intended successor to the amalgamation of self-parody and cheap shock effects that marked the grade-Z British horror series starring the ubiquitous Christopher Lee, who here plots to collect the fortunes of the insanely rich inmates of his asylum by killing off other prospective heirs. Only for the insatiable horror buff.

KELLY'S HEROES ☆☆☆½
1970, USA/Yugoslavia, PG
Clint Eastwood, Telly Savalas, Don Rickles, Donald Sutherland, Carroll O'Connor, Gavin MacLeod, Stuart Margolin, Harry Dean Stanton. Directed by Brian G. Hutton. 148 min.

A ridiculous but very enjoyable World War II caper flick, *Kelly's Heroes* is obviously inspired by *The Dirty Dozen* and could almost qualify as a parody of it. During the cleanup period at the end of the European part of the war, a disparate group of infantry soldiers discovers the existence of a German cache containing $16 million in gold bullion and decides to steal it. Eastwood is his usual laid-back self, and therefore gets lost among the likable hamming of the rest of the cast, particularly Sutherland as an anachronistic World War II hippie.

THE KENNEL MURDER CASE ☆☆☆½
1933, USA
William Powell, Mary Astor, Eugene Pallette, Ralph Morgan, Helen Vinson, Jack LaRue. Directed by Michael Curtiz. 73 min.

Probably the best of the fifteen movies featuring novelist S. S. Van Dine's elegant New York detective Philo Vance; it is also the last one in which William Powell starred as Vance. It's pretty much a standard drawing-room mystery, down to the "One of the people in this room is . . . the killer!" finale, but it's so well done as to be a paradigm of the type. Curtiz's direction is excellent, possibly because he had a separate dialogue director to help him out.

KENT STATE ☆☆½
1981, USA (TV)
Talia Balsam, Ellen Barkin, Jane Fleiss, John Getz, Keith Gordon, David Marshall Grant, Roxanne Hart, Michael Higgins, Jeff McCracken. Directed by James Goldstone. 120 min.

James Goldstone won an Emmy for his sensitive direction of this unusually thoughtful, sober telefilm about the events that led up to the killing of four Kent State University students by National Guardsmen during an antiwar demonstration on the campus in May 1970. *Kent State* is marked by a welcome attention to atmosphere and detail as well as solid performances by the young, talented cast, who bring the churning, divisive conflict to life. MCA Home Video loses half a star for cutting thirty minutes of the original telecast length; this is one of the few TV movies that deserves to be seen in its entirety.

THE KENTUCKY FRIED MOVIE ☆☆☆
1977, USA, R
Donald Sutherland, George Lazenby, Henry Gibson, Bill Bixby, Tony Pow, Richard A. Baker, plus 110 bits and cameos. Directed by John Landis. 90 min.

This is a rarity—a blackout-style spoof of movies and TV that's genuinely funny. The handiwork of the Los Angeles theater troupe that went on to make *Airplane!*, this hit-or-miss compendium of media gags works by lampooning the form of various movies and TV shows as well as the content. The acting is terrific, too, because all the characters, fished by the hundreds from the L.A. talent pool, are natural-born caricatures: luscious porn queens, hulking musclemen, blandly handsome news commentators, and karate champs able to leap tall buildings in a single bound.

KEROUAC: THE MOVIE ☆☆
1985, USA
Jack Coulter, David Andrews, Jonah Pearson, John Rousseau, Patrick Turner, Michael Warner, Seth Goldstein, Leon Benedict. Directed by John Antonelli. 78 min.

A brief, unsteady quasi-documentary that mixes dramatized scenes from Jack Kerouac's life and work with documentary interview footage. The multiple layers of visual fabrication represent a disservice to a writer so obsessed with sincerity. And too often the dramatizations are clumsy, betraying the rhythms of the voice-over narration from Kerouac's texts. This device is less illuminating, not to mention less entertaining, than the interviews with beat types that fill out the film. *Kerouac's* highlights are its two clips of the real Kerouac: the young, fast-talking bard and the older alcoholic bloat. Its great flaw is its failure to explain how the one turned into the other. The film also includes interviews with Kerouac's colleagues and friends John Clellon Holmes, William Burroughs, Seymour Krim, Michael McClure, Joyce Johnson, Allen Ginsberg, Carolyn Cassady, and Gilbert Millstein.

KEY EXCHANGE ☆½
1985, USA, R
Ben Masters, Brooke Adams, Daniel Stern, Danny Aiello, Tony Roberts. Directed by Barnet Kellman. 95 min.

Yuppie group therapy disguised as a dull, trite romantic comedy. Writer Philip (Ben Masters) can't bring himself to commit to his long-time girlfriend (Brooke Adams). When she wants to exchange keys to their ever-so-chic apartments, Philip begins spouting whiny psycho-babble about "space" and "relationships" and then goes out to ride his bike. For most of the film's length, you'll have to watch the charming Adams adrift without a real role, and put up with Ben Masters's insufferable sulking, smirking, and smugness—the only person he seems to be in love with is himself. Kevin Scott and Paul Kurta adapted their bubble-headed screenplay from an off-Broadway hit by Kevin Wade.

KEY LARGO ☆☆☆½
1948, USA
Humphrey Bogart, Lauren Bacall, Edward G. Robinson, Lionel Barrymore, Claire Trevor, Marc Lawrence, Monte Blue. Directed by John Huston. 101 min.

John Huston's atmospheric melodrama set on a stormy island off the Florida coast stars Humphrey Bogart as an ex-Army major who becomes involved in a small hotel owned by the father and widow of a wartime comrade. Edward G. Robinson costars as a gangster marooned on the island and Claire Trevor, as his alcoholic moll, steals the film in the performance that won her an Academy Award. A potent mix of gangster cruelties and a postwar search for values, the movie becomes a tense chess game between Robinson's bull-like power and Bogie's slowly awakening integrity. Karl Freund's camera captures the story's claustrophobic tension in the oppressive Florida summer.

THE KID ☆☆☆☆
1921, USA
Charlie Chaplin, Jackie Coogan, Edna Purviance, Chuck Reisner, Lita Grey (Chaplin). Directed by Charles Chaplin. 60 min.

In Chaplin's first feature, the Tramp finds an abandoned baby and raises him to be a copartner in street living. A very funny look at tender parenting and rough-and-tumble survival, the movie has the pair engaging in dreaming, con games, and police-dodging. Jackie Coogan is the perfect tonic for anyone sick of the precocious smarminess of modern slick kids like Ricky Schroder (*The Champ*) or TV's Gary Coleman; Coogan is winsome and genuine, never affected or corny. (Did he really grow up to be Uncle Fester on "The Addams Family"?) CBS/Playhouse has packaged the film with a Chaplin short, *The Idle Class*.

KIDCO ☆☆
1984, USA, PG
Scott Schwartz, Maggie Blye, Clifton James, Charles Hallahan. Directed by Ronald Maxwell. 104 min.

Taking a sitcom approach to slight material about a little tyke who becomes an ace capitalist, this tale about kids making their Junior Chamber of Commerce pipe dreams come true has moments of unforced charm, but a more creative approach instead of a traditional one might have brought some sense of wonder to the story line. It's a decent family film, ideal when you want something palatable for all ages, even though it will not have anyone jumping up and down on the sofa in excitement. Maybe it will encourage kids to go out and make their own perfectly ordinary family films in retaliation.

THE KID FROM BROOKLYN ☆☆½
1946, USA
Danny Kaye, Vera-Ellen, Virginia Mayo, Walter Abel, Eve Arden, Steve Cochran, Lionel Stander. Directed by Norman Z. McLeod. 113 min.

A remake of Harold Lloyd's *The Milky Way* should be the perfect showcase for Danny Kaye's schlemiel persona, but this film is never as good as the original. Danny plays a milkman who unwittingly becomes a prizefighter, and it is his manic if specialized brand of bumbling that keeps the padded, overlong production afloat. Kaye's send-up of Martha Graham in Sylvia Fine and Max Liebman's "Pavlova" is the highlight, and Eve Arden is around for her quota of wisecracks, but Kaye gets no help from either Virginia Mayo as his perennially plastic inamorata or Vera-Ellen as his hyperactive singing and dancing sister. Unless you are a Kaye fanatic, stick with the Lloyd film.

THE KID FROM LEFT FIELD ☆☆½
1979, USA (TV)
Gary Coleman, Robert Guillaume, Tab Hunter, Tricia O'Neil, Gary Collins, Ed McMahon. Directed by Adell Aldrich. 100 min.

A warmhearted, sentimental bit of wishful thinking from the world of sports. A homespun 1953 film has been refashioned into a Gary Coleman vehicle and, in all fairness, the diminutive star is not too grating on the nerves as the young catalyst in a World Series victory. The story involves an ex-baseball star who passes on a winning strategy to the losing San Diego Padres through his son (Coleman), who is the team's bat boy. The movie is cute, but not cloying.

KIDNAPPED ☆☆
1960, Great Britain
Peter Finch, James MacArthur, Bernard Lee, Niall MacGinnis, John Laurie, Finlay Currie, Peter O'Toole. Directed by Robert Stevenson. 97 min.

The folks at Walt Disney Studios must have thought it was pretty funny to have this version of the Robert Louis Stevenson adventure adapted and directed by another Robert Stevenson (no relation). Aside from that in-joke, though, this is a very dull movie. Children will have trouble following the plot (eighteenth-century Scottish youth is cheated out of his inheritance by his uncle and kidnapped to be sold in the New World as an indentured servant) because of the studio's misguided (albeit admirable) efforts to render authentic Scots accents and provide historical background.

THE KIDNAPPERS ☆☆☆½
1954, Great Britain
Duncan Macrae, Jean Anderson, Adrienne Corri, Theodore Bikel, Jon Whitely. Directed by Philip Leacock. 93 min.

Charming film, set in turn-of-the-century Nova Scotia, about two boys who steal an abandoned baby because their stern grandfather won't let them have a pet. Director Philip Leacock had worked since 1935 making documentaries, so one of the strengths of this film is his feel for the rural locations; another is the performances of the two young actors who play the boys. Delightful family fare. (a.k.a.: *The Little Kidnappers*)

THE KIDS ARE ALRIGHT ☆☆☆½
1979, USA, PG
The Who (Peter Townshend, Roger Daltrey, John Entwistle, Keith Moon). Directed by Jeff Stein. 108 min.

Your opinion of the above rating is, of course, based on your predilection for The Who, the subject of this compilation documentary. Every public figure of note should have a biographer as meticulous and loving as Jeff Stein, who put together two decades worth of film clips, television interviews, and assorted other public appearances by one of the few bands with a valid claim to speak for "my generation." Fans will also enjoy the songs culled from a live performance staged especially for this film. Non-fans should still enjoy this history of an engaging and occasionally thoughtful bunch of loonies, especially the late drummer Keith Moon, who describes himself to one interviewer as a "rust repairer and full-time survivor."

KID MILLIONS ☆☆☆
1934, USA
Eddie Cantor, Ethel Merman, Ann Sothern, George Murphy, Warren Hymer, Jesse Block, Eve Sully. Directed by Roy Del Ruth. 90 min.

This big-budget Eddie Cantor musical has aged well. Cantor plays his usual nebbish role, and here he inherits millions and takes a trip to Egypt—of course, there are plenty of ancient gags about harems, mummies and torture chambers. The highlight of the film is the Technicolor finale set in an ice cream parlor in Brooklyn, where the musical standard is set by Ethel Merman's rousing (what else?) song-belting. Cantor does his blackface number: here it's Irving Berlin's *Mandy*.

THE KID WITH THE BROKEN HALO ☆☆
1982, USA (TV)
Gary Coleman, Robert Guillaume, June Allyson, Mason Adams, Ray Walston, John Pleshette. Directed by Leslie Martinson. 100 min.

Gary Coleman's just a kid again here doing what he does best—acting as a buttinski, meddling in the lives of others, and transforming them for the better. He portrays a fledgling angel who won't get his wings until he does some good deeds for three families in need of an angelic boost. Coleman, as an angel, is a concept that may leave cynics yearning for hell, but if you're a fan, tune in for a liberal sampling of Gary's patented charm.

THE KID WITH THE 200 I.Q. ☆☆
1983, USA (TV)
Gary Coleman, Robert Guillaume, Harriet Nelson, Dean Butler, Mel Stewart. Directed by Leslie Martinson. 96 min.

What? You're looking *here* for a review of a Gary Coleman TV movie? What more do you need to know? That he plays a thirteen-year-old genius who goes to college? That he's just as cute as a button? The question isn't so much whether you want to watch this, as whether you can stand anymore pint-sized mugging.

THE KILL

See *The Game Is Over*

KILL AND KILL AGAIN ☆
1980, Hong Kong
James Ryan, Anneline Kriel, Michael Mayer, Marloe Scott-Wilson, Bill Flynn, Ken Gampu, Stan Schmidt, Norman Robinson, John Ramsbottom. Directed by Ivan Hall. 100 min.

Steve Hunt (James Ryan) gathers a number of martial artists to rescue Horatio Kane (John Ramsbottom), inventor of a mind-control drug made from potatoes (that wouldn't be vodka, would it?), from the demented billionaire Marduk (Michael Mayer). This sequel to the popular *Kill or Be Killed* has a much less energetic plot, although it retains original director Ivan Hall, star Ryan and karateographer Norman Robinson. All in all, it's a disappointment.

KILLBOTS

See *Chopping Mall*

KILL CASTRO ½☆
1978, USA, R
Stuart Whitman, Caren Kaye, Robert Vaughn, Woody Strode, Albert Salmi, Michael Gazzo, Sybil Danning, Raymond St. Jacques. Directed by Peter Barton. 90 min.

Stuart Whitman plays a sea captain coerced by CIA agent Robert Vaughn into joining a plot to assassinate Fidel; the Mafia will also lend assistance, since the Agency is providing it entrée for drug trafficking into Cuba. Whatever promise this idea holds for you, forget it; even Castro could find no relief in the results. (a.k.a.: *Cuba Crossing*)

KILLER BATS ☆
1941, USA
Bela Lugosi, Suzanne Kaaren, Dave O'Brien, Guy Usher, Yolande Mallott. Directed by Jean Yarborough. 67 min.

A truly awful piece of horror filler from a tiny studio that somehow snagged Bela Lugosi for what looks like very fast work. Bela plays a mad scientist in the employ of a ruthless cosmetics firm. When he decides to take revenge on all who have wronged him, he does it by creating a scented shaving lotion that attracts the title creatures to whomever wears it. The bats are laughable; the rest is just dull. (a.k.a.: *The Devil Bat*)

THE KILLER ELITE ☆☆
1975, USA, PG
James Caan, Robert Duvall, Arthur Hill, Gig Young, Mako, Bo Hopkins, Burt Young. Directed by Sam Peckinpah. 123 min.

Strange, hyperbolic conspiracy thriller from Sam Peckinpah, blending the CIA, the FBI, an international assassination plot, and the mid-1970s kung fu craze into one breathless, muddled story about two hired killers tracking each other down. Caan and Duvall both give solid performances, but *The Killer Elite* isn't an actor's movie—it's Peckinpah's bleak, bitter contribution to the political-paranoia genre of the Watergate era. Although it's impossible to follow and parts of it make no sense at all, the film has the director's touch all over it, and Peckinpah's fans will approve. United Artists reportedly demanded cuts in the film to ensure a PG rating; there's just as much violence here as in the director's other films, but less of it is bloody.

KILLER FISH ☆
1978, Italy/Brazil, PG
Lee Majors, Karen Black, James Franciscus, Margaux Hemingway, Marisa Berenson, Gary Collins. Directed by Anthony Dawson (Antonio Margheriti). 101 min.

The nasty nibblers get to dine out on an all-star cast in this cheap horror quickie about a group of gem smugglers stranded on a boat and snapping at each other, unaware of what else is snapping in their neighborhood—a school of piranhas. The gems are at the bottom of the sea, and when the divers go after them, we learn that what goes down doesn't necessarily come up. There are some good moments, but by the gory climax, you may feel as if you've eaten bad clams.

KILLER FORCE ☆☆
1975, USA, R
Telly Savalas, Peter Fonda, Hugh O'Brian, Christopher Lee, O. J. Simpson, Maud Adams. Directed by Val Guest. 100 min.

One of several movies that Telly Savalas starred in around the time of his "Kojak" popularity, this is a competently made action picture that has a few too many plot threads in the way of the fisticuffs and shootouts. Set in South Africa, it features Savalas as the head of security at a diamond mine who, with his wisecracking assistant (Peter Fonda), is on the tracks of a gang of thieves. Hugh O'Brian and O. J. Simpson play against type as gang members, though both are outdone by a particularly nasty Christopher Lee.

A KILLER IN EVERY CORNER ☆
1974, Great Britain, PG (unofficial)
Joanna Pettet, Patrick Magee, Max Wall, Eric Flynn, Don Henderson, Petra Markham, Peter Settelen. Directed by Malcolm Taylor. 80 min.

The mad doctor invites three unsuspecting psychology students to his laboratory/house for some criminal experiments in the workings of the mind. Though the film is not exactly Bergman, if you read the house as a metaphor for the mind, then maybe you'll plug into this film's higher aspirations. But even a serious philosophical reading couldn't rescue this from its predictable plot and noncommittal acting. And without a foundation of camp humor, a visit to this killer-infested abode isn't even fun. (The PG rating was assigned by the distributor—the M.P.A.A. did not rate this film.)

KILLER OF SNAKE, FOX OF SHAOLIN ☆☆
Hong Kong
Carter Huang, Cheung Li, Cheung Pi San, Au Wai Ying, Au Yet Fan. Directed by San Pao.

For a change, here's a martial arts movie in which the plot takes precedence over the fighting. A young man (Carter Huang) aids Miss Wang Koo and her father, little suspecting that they possess magical powers. There are good costumes and sets.

KILLER ON BOARD ☆½
1977, USA (TV)
Claude Akins, Patty Duke Astin, Frank Converse, William Daniels, George Hamilton, Murray Hamilton, Susan Howard, Jane Seymour, Beatrice Straight. Directed by Philip Leacock. 98 min.

This tedious TV film might be subtitled "Death of the Love Boat Guest Stars," but don't look for the title murderer in the cast list; it's not a disgruntled passenger but a deadly virus that's cutting down the cruise list, while stalwart Beatrice Straight tries to keep things under control. We won't reveal which of the guest stars make it safely into port—we're just grateful that it didn't become a series, with different forms of pestilence guesting every week.

THE KILLERS ☆☆
1964, USA
Lee Marvin, John Cassavetes, Angie Dickinson, Ronald Reagan, Clu Gulager, Normal Fell, Claude Akins. Directed by Don Siegel. 95 min.

Don Siegel's fast-moving but dull version of the Hemingway short story was originally made for TV, but when the networks saw how violent it was, it was immediately shunted off to theaters. Lee Marvin stars as a businessman-assassin and John Cassavetes and Angie Dickinson are lovers in this story of a mechanic hunted for having double-crossed a crime kingpin. Ronald Reagan, in his last big-screen appearance, plays an emotionless mob hit man.

KILLING 'EM SOFTLY ☆
1985, Canada
George Segal, Irene Cara, Clark Johnson, Nicholas Campbell, Joyce Gordon. Directed by Max Fischer. 81 min.

It's been a long time since the screen has seen a pair of lovers with more irritating mannerisms and less personal chemistry than George Segal and Irene Cara, who transform this film from a merely awful action-comedy with songs to a thoroughly unbearable one. Without a strong director to rein him in, Segal is pure ham, and Cara simply looks lost in this tale of a band manager and a young woman on the run from a murder charge.

THE KILLING FIELDS ☆☆☆☆
1984, Great Britain, R
Sam Waterston, Dr. Haing S. Ngor, John Malkovich, Craig T. Nelson, Athol Fugard. Directed by Roland Joffé. 141 min.

A first-time director, a first-time writer and a nonprofessional actor combine to create an unlikely triumph—a film of astonishingly emotional power that opens a painful American wound in depicting the U.S. abandonment of Phnom Penh during its fall. Taking as its story the friendship between *New York Times* reporter Sydney Schanberg and his loyal Cambodian photographer Dith Pran, *The Killing Fields* covers several years, including a period after the war when Schanberg had returned to the comforts of home while Pran went through a living hell in the labor camps and devastated countryside, which give the film its title. The politics are sketched in too hastily for the film to be as effective a polemic as it wishes, but when director Joffé stays with the two men, the emotion generated is heartfelt and intelligent. As Schanberg, Sam Waterston gives a performance that bravely resists an overly sympathetic reading. The Cambodian Ngor is the real star, however, and makes Pran's odyssey unforgettable. His wrenching work deservedly won an Academy Award, as did Jim Clark's editing and Chris Menges's documentary-style cinematography—strong contributions to a film whose few shortcomings of structure and dramatization pale beside its virtues.

THE KILLING KIND ☆☆☆
1973, USA
John Savage, Ann Sothern, Ruth Roman, Cindy Williams. Directed by Curtis Harrington. 95 min.

An obscure film from Curtis Harrington, who's better known for his more subtle shockers, such as *Games* and *What's the Matter with Helen?* This is a more brutal, less cinematographically ornate exercise in suspense. Perhaps a member of the Norman Bates fan club, Savage's character, a tormented mama's boy, unleashes his pent-up emotion and aggression by performing his own variation on Swiftian birth control. There is a superb performance by Sothern, always an original and usually an underappreciated presence, as his overprotective mommy.

THE KILLING OF RANDY WEBSTER ☆☆½
1981, USA (TV)
Hal Holbrook, Dixie Carter, Jennifer Jason Leigh, James Whitmore. Directed by Sam Wanamaker. 104 min.

Another true-life tale of cover-up—the perfect material for a TV movie. A rebellious teen steals a van, is pursued by the police, and is then gunned down. Later, the cops try to absolve themselves of responsibility as the boy's parents doggedly pursue the matter until the facts are revealed. One's responsiveness to this is apt to be complicated by the fact that the unfortunate boy did commit the crime of theft, initially. If he were just a young innocent, the film would seem too slanted; this way there's just enough uncomfortable reality to make this carry the ring of truth.

THE KILLING OF SISTER GEORGE ☆☆☆
1968, USA, X
Beryl Reid, Susannah York, Coral Browne, Ronald Fraser, Patricia Medina, Hugh Paddick, Cyril Delevanti. Directed by Robert Aldrich. 138 min.

An effective, if overheated, melodrama about a lesbian love affair, adapted by Robert Aldrich from a rather too-well-made play by Frank Marcus. At work, Beryl Reid is the Mary Worth–like heroine of a British soap opera; at home, she's a violent (but oddly sympathetic) alcoholic who lords it over her childlike mod girlfriend, played by Susannah York. Coral Browne is the hissing, dragon-lady radio producer who plots to remove Reid from the air (by killing off her Sister George character) and steal York from her.

THE KILLING STONE ☆½
1978, USA (TV)
Gil Gerard, J. D. Cannon, Nehemiah Persoff, Jim Davis, Corinne Michaels. Directed by Michael Landon. 100 min.

A tiresome series pilot written and directed by Michael ("Little House on the Prairie," "Highway to Heaven") Landon, who hoped for but did not get another series. Somehow, the family man with pretensions to sainthood is ill-equipped to handle the post-Watergate paranoia on display here. Unjustly incarcerated for a decade, a crusading writer leaves prison and picks up where he left off in a search for the killer of a U.S. senator's son. The film stars a stone-faced Gil Gerard straining credibility as the imperturbable reporter.

KILLJOY ☆☆☆
1981, USA (TV)
Kim Basinger, Stephen Macht, Robert Culp, Nancy Marchand, Ann Dusenberry, John Rubinstein. Directed by John Llewelyn Moxey. 100 min.

Intriguing mystery about the investigation of a beautiful girl's death and the suspects who try to cover their tracks. Fans of films like Otto Preminger's *Laura* will enjoy all of the fancy backtracking as the detective tries to figure out who bumped off the comely daughter of a swinging surgeon, who himself would have seemed a much more likely candidate for murder. The film has some satisfying sleuthing, and is not that easy to deduce.

KILL OR BE KILLED ☆½
1980, USA, PG
James Ryan, Charlotte Michelle, Norman Combes, Stan Schmidt, Norman Robinson, Danie DuPlessis. Directed by Ivan Hall. 90 min.

Karate master Steve Hunt (James Ryan) is lured to a martial arts tournament in the desert, not knowing that he will have to kill in order to survive. There is lots of action in this American-made karate film, and an above-average plot involving an enemy coach who's a former Nazi commando. Followed by *Kill and Kill Again*.

KILL SQUAD ☆☆
1981, Hong Kong
Jean Claude, Jeff Risk, Jerry Johnson, Bill Cambra, Gary Fung, Francisco Ramirez. Directed by Patrick G. Donahue. 85 min.

A Vietnam veteran calls his buddies together to avenge the death of his wife, and his permanent paralysis. A sort of kung fu *Death Wish* that is badly dubbed but has decent action.

KILLZONE ☆
1985, USA, R
Fritz Matthews, Ted Prior, David James Campbell. Directed by David A. Prior. 89 min.

That great cliché of the 1970s, a deranged Vietnam veteran, is resuscitated and caught up in a postwar military training exercise in the United States. His mind snaps and he thinks he's back in the jungles of Nam, where survival depends on the ability to kill and kill again. Where this premise leads is pretty obvious, and soon the entire USA is in danger of becoming eponymous killzone. Standard low-budget action/adventure.

KIND HEARTS AND CORONETS ☆☆☆½
1949, Great Britain
Dennis Price, Valerie Hobson, Alec Guinness, Joan Greenwood, Audrey Fildes. Directed by Robert Hamer. 105 min.

This is one of the best of the Ealing Studios comedies. Dennis Price has star billing as an amoral young man who discovers that he is eighth in line of succession to the fortune of the Duke of Chalfont, and sets out to kill the other seven. The movie really belongs to Guinness, however, who plays all seven victims and the Duke himself. The best part about his performance(s) is that he doesn't resort to broad burlesque (even as Aunt Agatha, the family suffragette), but underplays each role, letting us savor the joke of his multi-casting rather than forcibly reminding us of it by poking himself through every character. A delight from beginning to end.

A KIND OF LOVING ☆☆☆½
1962, Great Britain
Alan Bates, June Ritchie, Thora Hird, Bert Palmer, Gwen Nelson. Directed by John Schlesinger. 112 min.

An intelligent, sensitive study of the domestic strife of a young British couple forced to marry when the girl becomes pregnant; eventually, both realize that their union is loveless, but can they turn it into something more? This is the first film directed by John Schlesinger (who went on to make *Midnight Cowboy* and *Sunday Bloody Sunday*), and it provides Alan Bates with his first really good screen role; the direction and acting are exquisite, treading a careful line between the dramatic and the documentary, and the screenplay by Willis Hall and Keith Waterhouse is unusually perceptive.

THE KING AND I ☆☆☆☆
1956, USA
Yul Brynner, Deborah Kerr, Rita Moreno, Martin Benson, Terry Saunders, Rex Thompson, Alan Mowbray. Directed by Walter Lang. 133 min.

One of the best of the Broadway-to-Hollywood conversions, Rogers and Hammerstein's musical celebration of East meeting West stars Yul Brynner in his Oscar-winning performance as the marvelously formidable King of Siam, and Deborah Kerr as the spirited, charmingly civilized British teacher. The romantic clash of their temperaments is inevitable, and culminates in one of the screen's most beautiful musical invitations, "Shall We Dance?" Gorgeous uses of color, costumes, pageantry, and dance do not detract from the story's drama, but rather enhance it. Other magical moments include "Getting to Know You," "Hello Young Lovers," and the "Small House of Uncle Tom" ballet.

THE KING BOXER ½☆
1980, Hong Kong
Lee Lin, Lin, Liu Lan Ying, Chuan Tieng Pao Chao, Johnny Nai Nam, Soji Kuratea, Meng Fei. Directed by Kung Min.

For Meng Fei (*Invincible Kung Fu Trio*, *Prodigal Boxer I & II*) completists only. This was Meng Fei's first role, and that may be reason enough to watch, but the movie is pretty hard on audiences. Filmed in Thailand, the dull story concerns a Thai boxer out to avenge the death of Mr. Chiao (Meng Fei).

KING CREOLE ☆☆½
1958, USA
Elvis Presley, Carolyn Jones, Walter Matthau, Dolores Hart, Dean Jagger, Vic Morrow, Raymond Bailey. Directed by Michael Curtiz. 116 min.

One of the better of the early Elvis dramas, though more for Michael Curtiz's direction than for anything in the script or performances. The King plays a youth in New Orleans who is saved from a life of crime when he discovers he has talents as a singer. Trouble is, the local mobster wants him to sing at *his* club. With thirteen songs, the best of which were written by Leiber and Stoller. The script was adapted from the Harold Robbins novel *A Stone for Danny Fisher*.

KING DAVID ½☆
1985, USA, R
Richard Gere, Edward Woodward, Denis Quilley, Alice Krige. Directed by Bruce Beresford. 113 min.

Richard Gere as a break-dancing King David might tickle the more perverse viewer, but this tacky, monumentally misbegotten project is too dull to be consistently campy. Edward Woodward is subtle in his delineation of King Saul, but Gere is awful. His depiction, posture, and attitude are those of a Bowery Boy comedian.

KINGDOM OF THE SPIDERS ☆☆
1977, USA, PG
William Shatner, Tiffany Bolling, Woody Strode, Natasha Ryan, Altovise Davis. Directed by John (Bud) Cardos. 94 min.

In this adequate bug shocker, an Arizona doctor (William Shatner) and entomologist (Tiffany Bolling) battle an arachnid invasion that makes the *Empire of the Ants* look positively piddling by comparison. The very familiar theme of nature's attack on man being just deserts (the tarantulas turn to human meals after pesticide spraying poisons their food) is given no fresh twists here, but some of the "action" scenes, which reportedly used 5,000 real tarantulas, are effectively grisly. Shatner, still squaring his jaw and pontificating into the camera like Captain Kirk, stays right in tune with the film's B-level spirit.

THE KINGFISHER CAPER ☆☆
1975, South Africa, PG
David McCallum, Hayley Mills, Jon Cypher, Volente Vertotti. Directed by Dirk De Villiers. 90 min.

A must-see if you're interested in seeing how diamonds are mined nowadays. Otherwise, you can take or leave this muddled drama about a miner in love with the sister of the man who is dallying with his wife. Along with apartheid, this film is a good reason to hold a grudge against South Africa.

A KING IN NEW YORK ☆☆☆☆
1957, Great Britain
Charlie Chaplin, Dawn Adams, Oliver Johnston, Maxine Audley, Harry Green, Sidney James, Jerry Desmonde, Michael Chaplin. Directed by Charles Chaplin. 105 min.

Chaplin's last film in which he starred (followed only by the disappointing *A Countess from Hong Kong*) takes cruel swipes at a crazy, avaricious America. He plays a broke monarch who travels to the States after a revolution and winds up plugging rancid booze on TV. The political satire is rather strident in its attack on McCarthyist red scares; however, there is plenty of hilariously trenchant social satire as the king visits an ultraliberal school, a movie house, and a rock and roll club. Chaplin, who had been driven out of the U.S. by government harassment, can be forgiven a certain amount of spleen; indeed, it is remarkable that he was able to find anything humorous in the situation. This was Chaplin's first British production and his cast is extremely deft in their portrayal of Americans (and Europeans); the locations, however, are very unconvincing.

KING KONG ☆☆☆☆
1933, USA
Fay Wray, Bruce Cabot, Robert Armstrong, Victor Wong. Directed by Merian C. Cooper and Ernest B. Schoedsack. 100 min.

The first and best version of the monkey meets girl story has showman Carl Denham, the beautiful actress Ann Redman, and crew journeying to mysterious Skull Island in search of prehistoric creatures rumored to be living there. The explorers find the beasts, and a giant ape named Kong who falls in love with Ann. When she goes back to New York City, so does the now-incapacitated ape. Havoc soon results as Kong breaks loose, all leading to the classic conclusion atop the Empire State Building. This is a romantic and brooding monster film that made Kong into the most popular leading man of his day. Pioneering in its use of stop-motion animal and matte effects, all of which still stand up, this film resurrected the faltering RKO studios and became an enormous hit. The video version has many famous scenes that were cut for early TV, among them Kong's stripping off Wray's clothing and stepping on unlucky island villagers. It was remade as an awful 1976 film with Rick Baker jumping about in an ape suit. Accept no substitutes for this screen gem.

KING KONG ☆½
1976, USA, PG
Charles Grodin, Jessica Lange, Jeff Bridges, Rene Auberjonois. Directed by John Guillermin. 134 min.

Dino De Laurentiis's $22 million remake of probably the greatest boy's-book fantasy ever put on film (by Ernest Schoedsack and Merian Cooper) is a procession of stiff set pieces devoid of flow, tension and cumulative power. Screenwriter Lorenzo J. Semple has made the dreadful mistake of killing the romantic adventure with 1970s cynicism, put-ons, and sour little jokes; Jessica Lange turns Fay Wray's reluctant beauty into a flipped-out prom cutie; and director John Guillermin (*Towering Inferno*) misses every opportunity for excitement. The special effects are wasted on blurry color, awkward process shots, and a mechanical forty-foot-tall monster that, when it appears (most of the time we're watching a guy in a monkey suit), isn't nearly as interesting as the eighteen-inch animated model of 1933. Followed by a sequel in 1986.

KING KONG LIVES ☆
1986, USA, PG-13
Brian Kerwin, Linda Hamilton, John Ashton, Peter Michael Goetz, Frank Maraden, Peter Elliot, George Yiasomi. Directed by John Guillermin. 105 min.

Never content to let sleeping apes lie, producer-impresario Dino De Laurentiis resurrected the big lug for this somnolent sequel to his 1976 remake of the original. In case you were naive enough to believe that Kong *died* when he toppled off the World Trade Center, this film informs you that no, he was just in a coma. After a heart transplant, Kong finds romance with Lady Kong and, by the end of the film, there's even a Baby Kong. Unrelentingly dumb and clumsy; the only scary moment is when you realize that there may be a sequel on the way.

THE KING OF COMEDY ☆☆☆½
1983, USA
Robert DeNiro, Jerry Lewis, Diahnne Abbott, Sandra Bernhard, Fred DeCordova. Directed by Martin Scorsese. 101 min.

"Better to be king for a night than schmuck for a lifetime," says Rupert Pupkin, the "hero" of Martin Scorsese's disquieting black comedy about an aspiring (and awful) comic who kidnaps a famous talk show host. As a study of the American obsession with celebrity, the movie is devastatingly accurate, sometimes to a fault. Robert DeNiro portrays his repulsive character, a man who keeps a life-size cardboard cutout of Liza Minelli in his basement, with such consummate showbiz phoniness that you're almost forced to turn away. Jerry Lewis, as the Johnny Carson figure, has undertaken a clever, change-of-pace role. *King of Comedy* is too contemptuous of its characters—all of whom are indeed schmucks for a lifetime—but very few movies aim at the targets of fame and fandom, and this one hits the bulls-eye. Good screenplay by former *Newsweek* film critic Paul Zimmerman.

KING OF THE COWBOYS ☆☆
1943, USA
Roy Rogers, Smiley Burnette. Directed by Joseph Kane. 67 min.

Most B Westerns are detective movies in cowboy drag, and this neat Roy Rogers thriller even has a reference to Hitchcock's *The 39 Steps*—the secret code is given from a mystic's stage act. This is one of Roy's best, with music from the Sons of the Pioneers.

KING OF THE GRIZZLIES ☆½
1970, USA, G
John Yesno, Chris Wiggins, Hugh Webster, Jack Van Evera. Directed by Ron Kelly. 93 min.

The human cast takes a back seat to the bears of the title in this weak, overlong Disney entry. There's an ostensible story line about an Indian's relationship to a cub as it grows to maturity, but the film is really an excuse for the exciting animal footage, which itself grows tedious from overexposure. The film is slow going, for both kids and adults.

KING OF THE GYPSIES ☆
1978, USA, R
Eric Roberts, Sterling Hayden, Shelley Winters, Susan Sarandon, Judd Hirsch, Brooke Shields, Annette O'Toole, Annie Potts. Directed by Frank Pierson. 112 min.

In his eagerness to turn out an ersatz *Godfather* saga, writer-director Frank Pierson has botched a great film subject—the cultural and criminal netherworld of American Gypsy tribes. The story of Gypsy prince Dave Stepanowicz (played by Eric Roberts in his smoldering screen debut), who drops out of tribal life but is inexorably drawn back in, bears a superficial resemblance to Michael Corleone's in *The Godfather*. But Roberts's struggles with the tangled blood ties of the Gypsy world just go on and on, and the uniformly boorish acting (by Judd Hirsch, Sterling Hayden, and others) makes them seem sordid rather than tragically heroic.

KING OF HEARTS ☆☆½
1966, France/Italy
Alan Bates, Genevieve Bujold, Adolfo Celi, Pierre Brasseur. Directed by Philippe De Broca. 102 min.

This antiwar fable was an enormous hit with college audiences in the late 1960s and early 1970s, playing for years in some cities, but now it looks dated and somewhat simpleminded. As a hero guaranteed to appeal to the average freshman English major, Alan Bates is a poetry-reading, pigeon-tending Scottish soldier during World War I who is sent to defuse a bomb in a small French town. What he doesn't know is that the residents of the town have fled, leaving only the lunatics from the local asylum to run things. The terribly obvious point, that even madmen are saner than those who choose to engage in warfare, is driven home when troops from two opposing sides meet and kill each other down to the last man. Children might enjoy this, there being nothing more objectionable than a few scenes inside a lunatic simulation of a bordello, but its appeal to adults is limited to those with nostalgia for their student days. (a.k.a.: *Le Roi de Coeur*)

THE KING OF JAZZ ☆☆☆½
1930, USA
Paul Whiteman and his Orchestra, John Boles, Bing Crosby and the Rhythm Boys, Laura la Plante, Glenn Tryon, Walter Brennan. Directed by John Murray Anderson. 101 min.

Before Rouben Mamoulian, Busby Berkeley, Fred Astaire, and the entire Arthur Freed unit, there was *King of Jazz*, one of the most daring and original musicals ever made. Released during the vogue for plotless, all-star revues, this two-strip Technicolor extravaganza boasts a series of brilliant set pieces directed by John Murray Anderson. Highlights include Paul Whiteman and his Orchestra performing "Rhapsody in Blue" and Bing Crosby and the Rhythm Boys singing "A Bench in the Park." The "Melting Pot of Jazz" finale is truly breathtaking and, although the comedy sketches (by Harry Ruskin and Hal Mohr) aren't up to the musical portions, it hardly matters. This is a spectacular, forgotten musical great.

KING OF KINGS ☆☆☆½
1927, USA
H. B. Warner, Joseph Schildkraut, James Neill, Joseph Striker, Robert Edeson, Sidney D'Albrook, David Imboden, Charles Belcher, Clayton Packard, Robert Ellsworth, Charles Requa, John T. Price, Jacqueline Logan, Rudolph Schildkraut. Directed by Cecil B. deMille. 155 min.

During the height of the Roaring '20s, Cecil B. deMille released his silent, epic-length celluloid Gospel story as seen through the eyes of Mary Magdalene. With a skillful combination of symbol and spectacle, the extravagant director created cinema's finest example of decadent spirituality. Within the visual splendor are moments of religious simplicity, and powerful moments such as the introduction of Jesus as he gives sight to a blind man. H. B. Warner's restrained personification of Christ radiates dignity and purpose in a difficult performance that no reasonable person will find offensive. What *is* questionable is deMille's tendency toward overzealous renderings of both the small and the large events, an inflation that one quickly recognizes as the director's signature. Yet it is precisely his grandiosity and visual assault that place this film above the less realized *Ben Hur* and *The Ten Commandments*. DeMille's brilliant casting of Joseph Schildkraut and his son Rudolph as Caiaphas and Judas indicates the perversity and artistic vision needed to create a Christ story that overlaps the visual indulgence with spiritual quest. Silent.

KING OF KUNG FU
See *Enter the Game of Death*

KING OF THE MOUNTAIN ☆½
1981, USA, PG
Harry Hamlin, Joseph Bottoms, Dennis Hopper, Deborah Van Valkenburgh, Dan Haggerty. Directed by Noel Nosseck. 90 min.

This film consists of an hour and a half of cars racing around Hollywood's hilly Mulholland Drive at night, and it is only slightly less dull than it sounds. There are lots of existentialist machismo, a few songs from Deborah Van Valkenburgh, and, just for a change of pace, Dennis Hopper as an aging hippie.

KING, QUEEN AND KNAVE ☆☆½
1972, Great Britain/West Germany
David Niven, John Moulder-Brown, Gina Lollobrigida, Mario Adorf. Directed by Jerzy Skolomowski. 92 min.

Nabokov's witty, darkly comic novel about a department store magnate whose nephew may be replacing him in the bedroom as well as the boardroom comes to the screen with its brittle edge blunted by Jerzy Skolimowski's faulty direction; he has a terrible time trying to milk comedy scenes for maximum effect. Although he's drawn a wickedly funny performance out of Gina Lollobrigida as the rich witch who seduces her unsophisticated nephew into plotting his uncle's demise, he allows Moulder-Brown and Adorf to overact outrageously. Still, the source material is so rich that a number of laughs hit the mark. Not the sophisticated delight it should have been, but pretty good camp.

KING RAT ☆☆☆½
1965, USA
George Segal, Tom Courtenay, James Fox, Patrick O'Neal, Denholm Elliott, John Mills, Leonard Rossiter, Gerald Sim. Directed by Bryan Forbes. 134 min.

Grim, excellent story set in a Japanese P.O.W. camp during World War II. George Segal has seldom been as good as he is here, playing a U.S. corporal who gets by quite nicely by conning the other prisoners and dealing in their goods. As in other films with a similar setting (*Bridge on the River Kwai, Merry Christmas Mr. Lawrence*), there is a good deal of attention paid to the ways in which the British prisoners maintain their class structure, although here they tend to band together in opposition to Segal's character. Screenplay by Bryan Forbes, based on a novel by James Clavell, who drew from his own experiences as a P.O.W.

KING'S ROW ☆☆☆½
1941, USA
Robert Cummings, Ann Sheridan, Ronald Reagan, Claude Rains, Charles Coburn, Judith Anderson, Maria Ouspenskaya. Directed by Sam Wood. 127 min.

Bedtime for Bonzo may be Ronald Reagan's most famous movie, but *King's Row* is undoubtedly his best. It's a superior soap opera about small-town lives and loves in turmoil during wartime, with good performances not only from the stars but also from the "B" players in the large cast. Adapting a novel by Henry Bellamann that was at the time considered fairly lurid, Casey Robinson managed to preserve most of its touchier aspects, including a hint of incestuous feelings between two of the characters. Reagan (not one of them) plays a wounded GI whose legs are amputated, and he wakes up from surgery to utter the one immortal line of his film career (and later, the title of his autobiography): "Where's the rest of me?"

KING SOLOMON'S MINES ☆☆☆
1950, USA
Deborah Kerr, Stewart Granger, Richard Carlson, Hugo Haas, Lowell Gilmore, Kimursi, Siriaque, Baziga. Directed by Compton Bennett and Andrew Marton. 102 min.

The *Out of Africa* of its day, this romance/travelogue/adventure was one of the first movies to be filmed entirely in Africa. Deborah Kerr plays a prim British woman who enlists the aid of an adventurer (Stewart Granger in a role usually played by Errol Flynn) to find her husband in the legendary mines of King Solomon. Before the two are overcome by jungle fever and in each other's arms, they must contend with animals, natives, and her watchful brother (Richard Carlson). Neither Compton Bennett nor Andrew Marton were able to disguise the hoary, predictable melodrama, but Oscar-winning cinematographer Robert Surtees achieves so many great landscape shots that leftover footage was used in MGM's *Watusi* (1959). Remade in 1985.

KING SOLOMON'S MINES ☆
1985, USA, PG-13
Richard Chamberlain, Sharon Stone, Ken Gampu, Herbert Lom, John Rhys-Davies. Directed by J. Lee Thompson. 100 min.

Ostensibly, this is a remake of the durable H. Rider Haggard book, *Alan Quatermain*, already filmed on several occasions (though never as badly as it is here). What emerges is a ragged, witless attempt to ape *Raiders of the Lost Ark* rather than to present a straightforward version of this tale of a perilous hunt for diamonds in Africa. Sharon Stone is a one-woman screechathon; Richard Chamberlain, who's so persuasive as a hero on TV miniseries, lives up to the author's name in this flop—haggard with a capital H. The movie was partially filmed in Zimbabwe and was followed by a sequel, *Allan Quatermaine and the Lost City of Gold*.

KIPPS ☆☆☆
1941, Great Britain
Michael Redgrave, Diana Wynyard, Arthur Riscoe, Phyllis Calvert, Hermione Baddeley. Directed by Carol Reed. 95 min.

An illiterate shop clerk in Victorian England inherits a fortune and various vultures come out to turn him into a "gentleman" and swindle him. Based on the satirical novel by H. G. Wells, this adaptation is a bit lacking in focus but comes across as fine entertainment for Anglophiles who don't mind a bit of moralizing.

KISMET ☆☆☆
1944, USA
Ronald Colman, Marlene Dietrich, James Craig, Edward Arnold, Joy Ann Page. Directed by William Dieterle. 100 min.

A lavishly entertaining escapist fable woven of Technicolor cinematics, Oriental scenery, and musical numbers. Ronald Colman is a beggar who poses as a prince and falls for Marlene Dietrich, the gold-painted, sultry dancing girl. James Craig is a caliph who poses as a gardener's son and falls for Colman's beautiful peasant daughter. Entitled *Oriental Dream* when shown on television, the film was adapted in 1955 as a Broadway musical.

KISS ME GOODBYE ☆½
1982, USA, PG
Sally Field, James Caan, Jeff Bridges, Paul Dooley, Claire Trevor, Mildred Natwick, William Prince, Dorothy Fielding. Directed by Robert Mulligan. 101 min.

A 1930s-style ghost comedy with a me decade sensibility, this film is really about "finding yourself." James Caan is the ghost of a rakish, Bob Fosse–like choreographer who comes back to haunt his chic New York wife (played by Sally Field, with girlish hysterics). He sits by her bed making obnoxious remarks while she tries to make love to her straitlaced Egyptologist fiancé (Jeff Bridges, in a gangly and charming performance reminiscent of Jimmy Stewart). But Caan can't join in the fun—the movie's too prudish for that. Charlie Peters's formulaic, forcibly bubbly script is a junior bigh school student's idea of sophisticated screwball comedy, and it's at odds with the soggy direction by Robert Mulligan—who probably thought he was directing a problem drama. A remake of the Brazilian film *Doña Flor and Her Two Husbands*.

KISS ME KATE ☆☆☆
1953, USA
Kathryn Grayson, Howard Keel, Ann Miller, Tommy Rall, Keenan Wynn, James Whitmore. Directed by George Sidney. 109 min.

A top MGM extravaganza, but one expects more from a filmization of one of the theater's finest musical comedies. The best way to curb one's disappointment is to keep envisioning Judy Garland, or Jane Powell, or Patricia Morrison, or even Carmen Miranda, in the role Kathryn Grayson so inadequately fills. Aside from her, the clever backstage plot about a Lunt and Fontanne of musical comedy starring in a musical version of *The Taming of the Shrew* holds up exceedingly well. That strapping baritone, Howard Keel, rips with gusto into his best screen role, equally at home as Petruchio or as Bill Graham, the show's beleaguered producer. In several numbers, that one-woman whirlwind Ann Miller taps the roof off. Best of all, the film contains one of the indisputably great dance numbers in the history of Hollywood musicals, "From This Moment On" (a Cole Porter number not from the original show), sizzlingly interpreted by six terrific dancers, including Bob Fosse and Carol Haney.

KISS ME, KILL ME ☆½
1976, USA (TV)
Stella Stevens, Michael Anderson, Jr., Dabney Coleman, Claude Akins, Bruce Boxleitner, Pat O'Brien, Robert Vaughn. Directed by Michael O'Herlihy. 78 min.

An exercise in tedium in which a female member of the D.A.'s investigative team places herself in jeopardy in order to trap a mad killer. There are too many mad killers lurking in TV movies as it is; this one adds nothing new to the questionable pastime of watching helpless women tracked by psychotics.

KISS MEETS THE PHANTOM OF THE PARK ☆
1978, USA (TV)
KISS (Paul Stanley, Gene Simmons, Ace Frehley, Peter Criss), Anthony Zerbe, Carmine Caridi. Directed by Gordon Hessler. 96 min.

Those of you who weren't at that awkward age in the mid-1970s may not remember the rock group Kiss—four mild heavy-metal types with a great deal of makeup, a great lack of talent, and a major if short-lived adolescent cult following. This movie is for anyone out there who still has all their albums—and for absolutely nobody else. The imbecilic plot has the guys trying to foil a maniac who's producing Kiss replicas; director Gordon Hessler eventually went on to Sho Kosugi movies; we're not kidding when we call that a big step up.

KISS OF THE SPIDER WOMAN ☆☆☆☆
1985, USA/Brazil
William Hurt, Raul Julia, Sonia Braga, Jose Lewgoy, Nuno Leal Maia, Antonio Petrim, Denise Dumont, Milton Goncalves. Directed by Hector Babenco. 119 min.

A homosexual window dresser arrested on a morals charge shares a cell with a political prisoner in an unnamed Latin American country. Their initial distrust and suspicion give way to a growing dependence; in this harrowing world of lost souls, a complex story of love, friendship, and loyalty unfolds. Director Hector Babenco creates a claustrophobic two-man show, relying almost completely on his actors to carry the drama. William Hurt nearly jumps off the screen with a performance that is wildly theatrical and pushed to the edge of control. He is matched by Raul Julia, who executes with a glowering intensity never shown in his previous work. Manuel Puig's source novel used the device of having Molina (Hurt), the window dresser, narrate remembered film plots as a way of whiling away time. This allowed the novel to open up and gave the two men, so opposed to each other, a common language and bedrock grounds for understanding each other. In the film, Molina tells one film story, and it serves a different function, highlighting the differences between the two men and forcing them back into the sordid real world, where they work their differences out in very elemental human terms. The net effect is an intensely moving drama about ravaged humanity in the modern police state.

KITTY AND THE BAGMAN ☆☆
1982, Australia, R
John Stanton, Liddy Clark, Val Lehman, Gerard McGuire, Collette Mann, Reg Evans. Directed by Donald Crombie. 95 min.

This meandering Australian film about a couple of rival vice queens in the Roaring '20s ends up drowning in its overdressed sets and period costumes, which are meant to evoke the American gangster classics of the 1930s. Director Donald Crombie has some visual flair, but his leisurely, dawdling approach is deadly to a plot full of improbabilities and oversized characters like Kitty (Liddy Clark), a naive English bride who becomes a rough-and-ready madam.

KITTY FOYLE ☆☆½
1940, USA
Ginger Rogers, Dennis Morgan, James Craig, Edward Ciannelli, Gladys Cooper, Ernest Cossart. Directed by Sam Wood. 108 min.

After writing the trenchant novel *Johnny Got His Gun*, Dalton Trumbo was assigned by RKO to adapt Christopher Morley's equally hard-hitting *Kitty Foyle, The Natural History of a Woman*. Somewhere along the way, however, the treatment was glossed and lacquered to death. Kitty's divorce and class conflict have been retained, but the emphasis has been shifted to the two men in her life, turning the film into a conventional love triangle. This wouldn't be so ruinous if it weren't for the completely forgettable performances by Dennis Morgan (as the Philadelphia Galahad) and James Craig (as the struggling young doctor). If you cannot guess which one Kitty ends up with, you haven't seen enough Hollywood movies. Ginger Rogers darkened her hair to play Kitty and won an Oscar for it, but we would rather see her blonder and dancing with Fred Astaire.

KITTY: RETURN TO AUSCHWITZ ☆☆☆☆
1979, Great Britain (TV)
Directed by Peter Morley. 88 min.

A gripping documentary that haunts us because it compresses the horrors of the Holocaust into a single case. We somehow understand the devastation of Nazi genocide more clearly by following the plight of one woman who's persuaded herself to return to the scene of German crimes against her. The film is an emotionally lacerating experience as Kitty journeys with her son to try to explain to him and to us how she managed to survive, and what that survival cost her. The film is one of the best documentaries on this subject now available on video.

KLUTE ☆☆☆½
1971, USA, R
Jane Fonda, Donald Sutherland, Roy Scheider, Jean Stapleton. Directed by Alan J. Pakula. 114 min.

Jane Fonda won an Academy Award for her smashing performance as a sophisticated New York call girl in Alan J. Pakula's emotionally gripping thriller. Donald Sutherland costars as a small-town detective who falls in love with her while stalking a sadistic customer who is trying to kill her. The film is a searing portrait of a woman whose physical attractiveness and financial success can't compensate for her rock-bottom self-esteem. The long conversations between Jane and her psychiatrist may seem a trifle long-winded, but the film ultimately gives the viewer the feeling of knowing everything about the victimized prostitute.

THE KNACK, AND HOW TO GET IT ☆☆☆
1965, Great Britain
Rita Tushingham, Ray Brooks, Michael Crawford. Directed by Richard Lester. 84 min.

Richard Lester imbues this film version of a middling stage farce with the same anarchic, gag-a-minute style he used to such great effect with the Beatles and Peter Sellers. The story is simple—one friend teaches another how to score with the opposite sex—but the visual jokes are nonstop and the portrait of London's Carnaby Street is an Anglophile's delight.

KNICKERBOCKER HOLIDAY ☆☆½
1944, USA
Nelson Eddy, Constance Dowling, Charles Coburn, Ernest Cossart, Richard Hale, Shelley Winters, Glenn Strange. Directed by Harry Joe Brown. 85 min.

Nelson Eddy is hardly the most engaging presence and Charles Coburn is no Walter Huston (who played his part on Broadway), but this adaptation of Kurt Weill and Maxwell Anderson's flop musical retains some of the best songs (including the haunting "September Song") and political meat of the original. Eddy plays an underground newsman who locks horns with Peter Stuyvesant and falls in love with the daughter of a Dutch politician. Quaintly charming but lacks the elegance of the Jeannette MacDonald–Nelson Eddy pairing.

KNIFE IN THE WATER ☆☆☆½
1962, Poland
Leon Niemczyk, Jolanta Umecka, Zygmunt Malanowicz. Directed by Roman Polanski. 94 min.

A lean, elliptical film that encapsulates, for those who don't like foreign films, all the slow-moving, obscure, and inconclusive traits of the international art cinema. The stripped-down story begs for an invasion of allegorical meaning, and there is something of Poland's larger, generational conflict between the war-scarred, Stalin-era survivor and the new, directionless youth; the young man may be attractive and aggressive, but the older man is tougher, crueller and more adept. As much as anything, this is a young director's film, and Roman Polanski is fascinated by the slow movements across the horizontal axis of the screen.

KNIGHTRIDERS ☆½
1981, USA, R
Gary Lahti, Ed Harris, Amy Ingersoll, Tom Savini, Christine Forrest, Patricia Tallman, Warner Shook, Brother Blue. Directed by George A. Romero. 145 min.

Give this film a point for weirdness, but that's about all there is to say in defense of George Romero's interminable, impersonally directed Camelot-on-motorcycles saga. It's about a traveling band of cyclists staging tournaments for local yokels in the California countryside, with doomed visionary King Arthur (Ed Harris) doing his damnedest to keep his knights from surrendering to the blandishments of television and glossy fan magazines. Romero tries for a medieval-pastoral feel, replete with airs and jousting, but the knights are colorless, the damsels offensive stereotypes, and in his motion picture debut as Merlin, Brother Blue is . . . well, at least it kept him off the streets.

KNIGHTS OF THE CITY ☆½
1986, USA, R
Leon Isaac Kennedy, Nicholas Campbell, The Fat Boys, Smokey Robinson. Directed by Dominic Orlando. 87 min.

The Royals, a tough multiethnic Miami street gang, try to get off the mean streets by getting into the wild world of rock and roll. Internal conflicts, social pressures, and a vicious rival gang make things difficult. With choreographed fights, stereotypical characters, predictable plotting, and the flash in the pan Fat Boys, heavyweight rappers whose members include "The Human Beat Box."

KNOCK ON ANY DOOR ☆☆☆
1949, USA
Humphrey Bogart, John Derek, George Macready, Allene Roberts, Susan Perry, Mickey Knox, Barry Kelley. Directed by Nicholas Ray. 98 min.

Humphrey Bogart and director Nicholas Ray team up for a tight melodrama on juvenile delinquency in a film shot for Bogart's independent production company. Bogie plays the Perry Mason role, attempting to prove the innocence of a young hood accused of murder. With unrelenting action and realistic locations, this courtroom investigation into the causes and lives of wild youth hits hard and fast, and the end's shocking revelation keeps the film honest.

KNUTE ROCKNE—ALL AMERICAN ☆☆½
1940, USA
Pat O'Brien, Ronald Reagan, Gale Page, Donald Crisp, Albert Basserman, John Sheffield. Directed by Lloyd Bacon. 84 min.

It was Ronald Reagan's idea to film this tribute to the famous Notre Dame football coach, yet Warner Bros. was hesitant to cast Reagan as player George Gipp. Totally lacking the exposé elements of Robert Rossen's sports meoldramas (*Body and Soul*, *The Hustler*) and the humorous details of recent movies (*The Longest Yard*, *North Dallas Forty*), this film seems tepid and sanctimonious by comparison. It is, however, competently made, and sports fans will like O'Brien's gruff portrayal of Rockne. *Note*: The current video print available is fourteen minutes shorter than the original and is missing Reagan's celebrated line "win it for the Gipper."

KOTCH ☆☆☆
1971, USA, PG
Walter Matthau, Deborah Winters, Felicia Farr, Charles Aidman. Directed by Jack Lemmon. 114 min.

Walter Matthau does an admirable job of restraining himself from giving in to ninety-five percent of the potential cuteness available in this script about a seventy-two-year-old widower doing his best to resist being put in an old folks' home by his daughter-in-law, who finds him to be too much of a bother. Rather than be committed, Kotch takes off on his own, eventually setting up house with a pregnant teenager who needs a place to stay while she has her child. Jack Lemmon's directorial debut is mostly unobtrusive, designed to give his star every chance to shine. This aids Matthau's performance, but hurts the rest of the film by failing to provide enough background or contrast.

KOYAANISQATSI ☆☆☆
1983, USA
Directed by Godfrey Reggio. 87 min.

The title of this wordless, non-narrative study of American technology's intrusion on the natural world is Hopi for "life out of balance," and director Godfrey Reggio actually manages to build a compelling motif by juxtaposing the landscape with man's persistent violation of it. Koyaanisqatsi also means "a way of life that calls for another way of living," and herein lies the problem—Reggio's prescription for a better world seems based on the principle that everything "ugly" must go. This condescending ethos is fine when applied to oil trucks or rotting slums; but when he implies that poor, old, or unattractive people should also keep off the grass, and preferably the planet, it becomes a little hard to take. Though they're often maddening and wrongheaded, the images are vivid and sometimes truly haunting. Equal credit must go to Ron Fricke's virtuoso cinematography, and to a stunning score by Philip Glass, which is likely to outlive the film itself.

KRAMER VS. KRAMER ☆☆☆☆
1979, USA, PG
Dustin Hoffman, Meryl Streep, Justin Henry, Jane Alexander, JoBeth Williams, Howard Duff, George Coe. Directed by Robert Benton. 105 min.

An intelligent, moving account of a New York advertising executive and his young son struggling to make it alone after mom (Meryl Streep) leaves home. Veteran Dustin Hoffman outdoes himself in this box-office smash, and newcomer Justin Henry is both endearing and believable as the child caught in the middle of a heartrending custody battle. The characters and the case are multi-dimensional, absorbing, provocative—anything but flat, pat, or cut-and-dried. Emotional types should be warned to have a hanky handy. Oscars were awarded for Best Picture, Actor (Hoffman), Supporting Actress (Streep), and Director and Screenplay Adaptation (both Robert Benton).

KRONOS ☆☆
1957, USA
Jeff Morrow, Barbara Lawrence, John Emery, George O'Hanlon, Morris Ankrum. Directed by Kurt Neumann. 78 min.

Better-than-average 1950s science fiction. Outer-space creatures seek to conquer Earth by sending down a giant robot to absorb all of the planet's energy. It lands in Mexico and advances toward California, trampling everything in its path and growing as it picks up more energy. The special effects are not much by today's standards, but they were top of the line in their day, and still remain not all that bad.

KRULL ☆☆☆
1983, Great Britain, PG
Ken Marshall, Freddie Jones, Lysette Anthony, Bernard Bresslaw. Directed by Peter Yates. 117 min.

British film director Peter Yates draws on his theatrical background to create this stagy fantasy film. Much of the action takes place on grand sets as a young king (Marshall, of TV's "Marco Polo") must fight the minions of the evil beast to regain the hand of his princess and save his world. *Krull* is at its best during its stylized stagebound sequences, all of which are enhanced by James Horner's marvelous score. The film's otherwise cut-and-paste quest is enhanced by Yates's inherent sense of grandeur, and the vivid and emotional performances by the predominantly English cast. It's an entertaining if hackneyed picture that has some magic in it.

KRUSH GROOVE ☆☆
1985, USA, R
Blair Underwood, Run-DMC, Sheila E., Fat Boys, Kurtis Blow. Directed by Michael Schultz. 97 min.

Although break-dancing movies began hitting the screens earlier, this was the first film to showcase the more assertive, interesting art of rapping. The styles and the sounds are now, but the plot appears to have been lifted from an old Alan Freed quickie. Director Michael Schultz uses the story (about the ups and downs of an independent record company) as an excuse to string together performance scenes, including Run-DMC's funny, awesomely arrogant "King of Rock" and Sheila E.'s transfixing "A Love Bizarre"; the songs are so lively they almost make you forget the vapid plot, which keeps coming back with deadening regularity.

KUNG FU ☆☆½
1972, USA (TV)
David Carradine, Barry Sullivan, Keye Luke, Richard Loo. Directed by Jerry Thorpe. 90 min.

This pilot for the well-received series tells the story of a half-Chinese, half-American shaolin monk who flees to the American West after killing a nobleman. The narrative structure of dreamy flashbacks of temple life played against the harsh racism of the frontier works very nicely, and the movie succeeds with David Carradine's spacey, mellowed performance.

KUNG FU ARTS: MONKEY, HORSE, AND TIGER ☆
1984, Hong Kong
Carter Huang, Lo Lieh, Ching Ts Ning, Sida The French Monkey Star, Ge Kung Tsong, Cheng Ming-Yang, Yu Hon, Huang Huei-Lang, Liu Wen Ding, Pen Huei-Gin. Directed by Lee Geo-Shou and Lee Shi-Giei.

Lo Lieh and Carter Huang fight it out for control of the clan. Don't let this one make a monkey out of you; there's nothing in the way of interesting fighting styles.

KUNG FU COMMANDOS ☆☆
1982, Hong Kong
John Liu, Shang Kuan Lung, Chen Lung, Hso Chung-Hsu, Ting Hwa-Choong, Cheng Ching. Directed by Chang Hsin-Yi. 90 min.

Sher Ting Kan (John Liu) takes five unskilled mercenaries on a mission to rescue a rebel held in a fortress. This is essentially a showcase for the prodigious talents of Liu—watch as he delivers fourteen rapid-fire kicks without putting his foot down!

KUNG FU CRUSHER

See *The Bone Crushing Kid*

KUNG FU OF THE EIGHT DRUNKARDS ☆☆
1980
Meng Fei, Lo Lieh. Directed by Wu Ma.

This is a reworking of the better *Snakes in Eagles Shadow*, with Meng Fei in the Jacky Chan role. See it for the martial arts choreography only.

KUNG FU-RY ☆
1972, Hong Kong
Lee Sheung, Pai Ying. Directed by Fung James. 90 min.

Modern-day Hong Kong is the setting for this story of an assassin who finally gets his just desserts.

L

LABYRINTH
1986, USA, PG
Jennifer Connelly, David Bowie, Jim Henson's Muppets. Directed by Jim Henson. 101 min.

☆☆

Jim Henson generally stitches his muppets together with more care than his movies—which is why his human characters seem so stuffy and cotton-mouthed. A few turns away from his more ingenuous *The Muppet Movie*, *Labyrinth* is unhelpfully helmed by humans who utter leaden phrases such as, "Nobody said life was fair," and wander across a plot so arbitrary even children might scream. David Bowie, the goblin-king, kidnaps Jennifer Connelly's baby brother and dares her to rescue him via an enormous labyrinth leading to his goblin castle in the mountains. The preceding is, of course, merely an excuse for a picaresque adventure that is often amusing and stunningly crafted. Unfortunately, Bowie moans his musical numbers and Connelly is almost numbing to watch. Worse, Henson has mistaken this movie for a muppet and stuffed it with wads of padding. There are some great special effects (by George Lucas's Industrial Light and Magic studio), but this cute toy just plods through the labyrinth.

LADY CAROLINE LAMB
1972, Great Britain/Italy, PG
Sarah Miles, Jon Finch, Richard Chamberlain, Ralph Richardson, Laurence Olivier, John Mills, Margaret Leighton, Pamela Brown. Directed by Robert Bolt. 122 min.

☆☆

Elegant period recreations are packed with overripe life in this highly melodramatic, fey depiction of the illicit romance between Lady Caroline Lamb and George Gordon, Lord Byron. Director Robert Bolt, who had worked as a writer for David Lean, gets caught in the push-pull between the high-mindedness and the heavy breathing, and the film may draw an archly amused reaction. Richard Chamberlain, marvelously miscast, is no namby-pamby verse slinger—he's a two-fisted poet who tosses off punches just like he dashes off epics. Sarah Miles has even more fun—she gets to shock everyone by appearing at a costume party as a blackamoor slave, stabs herself, and even incites Italian peasants to murder. The tragic end of the characters may be a little hard to take, but if you've made it that far, you'll probably enjoy it.

LADY CHATTERLEY'S LOVER
1981, Great Britain/France, R
Sylvia Kristel, Nicholas Clay, Shane Briant, Ann Mitchell, Elizabeth Spriggs. Directed by Just Jaekin. 107 min.

☆☆

Cannon Films has somehow managed to be faithful to D. H. Lawrence and boring at the same time. Sylvia Kristel—as the wife of a crippled mine owner—has an affair with the estate's gamekeeper. Attempts at melodrama and suspense fail, and director Just Jaekin (*Emmanuelle*, *The Perils of Gwendoline in the Land of Yik-Yak*) tosses in soft-porn love scenes that are about as sexy as a sewing basket. Some nice cinematography and adequate performances can't lift this film above the banal.

THE LADY CONSTABLE
Hong Kong
Angela Mao Ying, Wang Kuan-Hsing, Chia Ling. Directed by Chang Hsin-Yi.

☆☆

The famous female police constable Tien Ying-Hung (Angela Mao Ying), the famous swordsman Teng Lin (Chia Ling), and Prince Chen Wang's bodyguard, Hung Yi (Wang Kuan-Hsing), are all after the gang that stole Prince Cheng's "Night-shining Pearl." Apart from some unnecessary special effects (which always seem to diminish the impact of the unaided kung fu), the martial arts choreography is very good. Chia Ling is as engaging and impish as ever, and makes a good contrast to Angela Mao Ying's staunch Lady Constable. Both are believable, and their kung fu is very strong. Wang Kuan-Hsing looks just as good and nicely rounds out the team.

LADY FOR A NIGHT
1941, USA
Joan Blondell, John Wayne, Philip Merivale, Blanche Yurka, Edith Barrett. Directed by Leigh Jason. 88 min.

☆☆

Unmemorable story set in the Old South, with Joan Blondell as a gambling boat operator who tries to marry her way up in society, but in the process becomes involved in a murder. The potentially interesting casting of Blondell and John Wayne never really delivers.

LADY FRANKENSTEIN
1971, Italy, R
Sarah Bey, Joseph Cotten, Mickey Hargitay, Paul Muller. Directed by Mel Welles. 84 min.

☆

A simultaneously lurid and coy exploitation film that trades on sleazy innuendo without delivering the goods. Beautiful Tania Frankenstein transplants the brain of her wimpy longtime suitor into the lust-inspiring body of a retarded servant. The resulting creature is supposed to hunt down and kill her father's last, disastrous experiment, but it has other ideas.

LADY FROM LOUISIANA
1941, USA
John Wayne, Ona Muson. Directed by Bernard Vorhaus. 82 min.

☆

This is a feeble movie about love and vice that nevertheless has a good cast.

THE LADY FROM SHANGHAI
1948, USA
Orson Welles, Rita Hayworth, Everett Sloane, Glenn Anders. Directed by Orson Welles. 87 min.

☆☆☆½

Orson Welles's foray into *film noir* is stylish, feverish, and more than a little bit muddled. Welles plays an Irish sailor who falls for the wife of a millionaire lawyer. Soon an intricate murder plot is under way. The film, like most of Welles's post-*Citizen Kane* works, is a compromise of artistic vision and studio decree (Columbia edited this one mercilessly), but Welles triumphs by creating striking set pieces, the most famous being the meeting in the aquarium, the nightmare in the funhouse, and the shootout in the hall of mirrors. Welles also, against producer Harry Cohn's wishes, cropped and bleached Hayworth's hair and turned her character into *film noir*'s most fatal femme. (Welles and Hayworth, incidentally, were already ending their stormy four-year marriage by the time the film was released.) One may quibble about Welles's brogue, but otherwise, *Lady* showcases Hayworth at her sexiest, and Everett Sloane contributes a memorable portrait as the crippled, manipulative husband. One of the more interesting films in one of Hollywood's most fascinating genres.

LADY HAMILTON

See *That Hamilton Woman*

LADYHAWKE
1985, USA, PG ★★★
John Wood, Michelle Pfeiffer, Rutger Hauer, Matthew Broderick, Leo McKern. Directed by Richard Donner. 121 min.

Richard Donner's colorful, dashing medieval fantasy stars Rutger Hauer and Michelle Pfeiffer as cursed lovers—he's a wolf by night, she's a hawk by day—and Matthew Broderick as the pickpocket who helps them live happily ever after. Donner's strong suits are pageantry and kinetics; he wins over audiences at the simplest levels of drama, humor, and spectacle, but he's unable to imbue the events with folkloric passion or poetry. Although it's easy to be carried along by the movie's visual sweep and pop romanticism (Vittorio Storaro's iridescent cinematography and Wolf Kroeger's imaginative production design make for an impossibly gorgeous escapist backdrop), *Ladyhawke* has the lasting emotional effect of a nice warm bath.

LADY IN A CAGE
1964, USA ★★½
Olivia de Havilland, James Caan, Jeff Corey, Ann Sothern, Rafael Campos, Scatman Crothers. Directed by Walter Grauman. 93 min.

A thriller more fascinating for its pretensions than for its thrills. Olivia de Havilland has a field day as a wealthy widow who is trapped in a private elevator while thieves and thugs invade her home. Producer-screenwriter Luther Davis has given Olivia pseudo-poetic dialogue and a Freudian-angled subplot involving her son, while director Walter Grauman has thrown in a few shock effects (some of the violence was cut at the time of release, and the film was banned in England). It's a curious, ugly cross between Grand Guignol and a contemporary psychological thriller.

THE LADY IN RED
1979, USA, R ★½
Pamela Sue Martin, Robert Conrad, Louise Fletcher, Dick Miller. Directed by Lewis Teague. 93 min.

Yet another New World gangster flick with lots of blood, nudity, and enough exploitative elements to make any sleaze fan's day, this film is based on the factual (so we're told) exploits of John Dillinger's gun moll, who was present at his shooting in her infamous red dress. The cast, which includes some very good actors, seems as though it can't wait to get off the set. The film was written by John Sayles, who teamed up with director Lewis Teague for the enjoyable horror spoof *Alligator*, their next and much better low-budget outing. (a.k.a.: *Guns, Sin, and Bathtub Gin*)

LADY JANE
1985, Great Britain, PG-13 ★★★
Helena Bonham Carter, Cary Elwes, Michael Hordern, Jane Lapotaire, John Wood, Sara Kestleman. Directed by Trevor Nunn. 144 min.

A sterling costume drama in which gorgeous costumes and impeccable set design threaten to overwhelm the historical goings-on, this film is a respectable retelling of the tragic nine-day reign of Lady Jane Grey and her husband, who innocently endeavored to change the face of history with high ideals, only to be sacrificed to stronger powers. Like all good "Masterpiece Theater"–style dramas, the film can't be faulted in terms of production values, literate writing, or characterizations. But this potentially devastating portrait of how personal ambition upsets the balance of power goes astray in opting for a lush Romeo-and-Juliet approach to the story. Somehow, serious history starts to go by the wayside, as Jane's love affair is compromised with the sort of romanticism obviously aimed at a teen audience (the kind of pastel-pretty attitude that's better suited to *Endless Love* or *The Blue Lagoon*). Flawed, but a compelling history lesson nevertheless.

THE LADYKILLERS
1955, Great Britain ★★★½
Alec Guinness, Peter Sellers, Katie Johnson, Cecil Parker, Frankie Howerd. Directed by Alexander Mackendrick. 94 min.

Alec Guinness heads a gang of nasty but rather feckless bank robbers who move in on little old lady Katie Johnson, never suspecting that she will innocently destroy them in the end. Graced by fine performances and a hint of "Goon Show" zaniness, this quirky post-Ealing farce is one of the funniest, most original British comedies of the 1950s.

LADY OF BURLESQUE
1943, USA ★★★
Barbara Stanwyck, Michael O'Shea, J. Edward Bromberg, Iris Adrian, Marion Martin, Pinky Lee. Directed by William Wellman. 90 min.

Based on Gypsy Rose Lee's breezy mystery novel, *The G String Murders*, this modest comedy-mystery allows Barbara Stanwyck to cut loose with one of her most enjoyable performances. Whether bumping and grinding to the tune of "Take It on the G String" or playing amateur sleuth in order to solve a murder, she's a wisecracking, earthy delight. So are all the supporting strippers who face a final curtain when a crazed strangler skulks around backstage at the Burlesque Theater. This is a crisp mystery that doesn't take itself too seriously, and has lots of funny, bitchy dialogue in the cramped quarters of the dressing room as the ecdysiasts pull each others' hair out while hoping the maniac will kill off their rivals.

LADY OF THE HOUSE
1978, USA (TV) ★★½
Dyan Cannon, Zohra Lampert, Armand Assante, Colleen Camp, Susan Tyrrell. Directed by Ralph Nelson and Vincent Sherman. 100 min.

An above-average TV vehicle for feisty, gutsy Dyan Cannon as Sally Stanford, the Northern California madam who took a step up (or a step down) from satisfying clients' libidos to taking care of her constituent's needs as mayor of Sausalito. Apparently, life in the San Francisco suburbs is not as placid as it looks to the eyes of tourists. Sally claims she picked up the tricks of her trade only after she was falsely accused of running a bordello by her former husband, a high-priced shyster who celebrated their divorce by framing her on prostitution charges. A nicely done melodrama about success being the best revenge (or is it really about strange bedfellows making politics?).

THE LADY ON THE BUS
1978, Brazil, R ★★
Sonia Braga, Nuno Leal Maia, Jorge Doria, Paulo Cesar Percio, Ivan Setta. Directed by Neville d'Almeida. 104 min.

There is a popular strain of opinion that feels that Sonia Braga's talent in films consists entirely of throwing her clothes off at any available moment. To which we respond, well, if someone has to do it, it might as well be Sonia. In this follow-up to *Dona Flor and Her Two Husbands*, Sonia is having trouble with her first husband, with whom she is frigid. While he gnashes his teeth in frustration, she goes to outside sources for help—namely, any other male who passes by. This seldom rises above the level of soft-core porn, though it's done with a measure of lightness and charm that makes it palatable.

LADY SCARFACE
1941, USA ★★½
Judith Anderson, Dennis O'Keefe, Arthur Shields, Eric Blore, Frances Neal. Directed by Frank Woodruff. 65 min.

That provocative title and the tantalizing promise of eagle-eyed villainess Judith Anderson are enough to set an old movie buff's mouth watering. But Dame Judith is sadly underused as a distaff Capone and the film is neither a grisly gangsterama nor a camped-up exercise in mobster role reversal. Rather, it's an agreeable programmer about a wisecracking cop and a dedicated lady reporter cracking a crime ring with their ace detective work. The chief virtue of this energetic crookbusters yarn lies in the snazzy performance of Dennis O'Keefe, the most insouciant of all B movie-star heroes.

LADY SINGS THE BLUES ☆☆☆
1972, USA, R
Diana Ross, Richard Pryor, Billy Dee Williams, James Callahan, Paul Hampton, Virginia Capers, Ned Glass, Isabel Sanford. Directed by Sidney J. Furie. 144 min. (2 cassettes)

Motown Records coproduced this grim, assaultive biography of Billie Holiday. They hoped to spotlight the talents of their reigning star Diana Ross, and in the goal of creating a showcase, the film is completely successful. Ross's acting is startlingly natural, easy and emotionally spontaneous, and her singing, though it may dissatisfy Holiday purists, is a canny blend of imitation, homage, and revision. If the movie had been able to match her gripping performance instead of coast on it, *Lady Sings the Blues* might have been great. Instead, director Sidney J. Furie and the screenwriters turn Holiday's unhappy romantic life and battle with drug addiction into the fodder of another melodramatic showbiz biography, exploiting much, illuminating little, and inevitably cheapening the life it studies by turning it into the stuff of myth. Still, it packs an undeniable emotional punch, in the vein of the later, very similar film *The Rose*.

A LADY TAKES A CHANCE ☆☆☆
1943, USA
Jean Arthur, John Wayne, Charles Winninger, Phil Silvers, Mary Field, Grady Sutton, Hans Conreid. Directed by William Seiter. 85 min.

In this enjoyable comedy-romance in a Western setting, Jean Arthur, as a New York working girl, takes a vacation excursion to the West and falls in love with rodeo cowboy John Wayne. Like all good cowboys, of course, the Duke would rather be with his horse than tied down with a gal, so she gets herself stranded and has to endure the rodeo life until her bus returns. There is a terrific barroom scene, without which no minor John Wayne movie would be complete.

THE LADY VANISHES ☆☆☆½
1938, Great Britain
Margaret Lockwood, Paul Lukas, Michael Redgrave, Dame May Whitty. Directed by Alfred Hitchcock. 96 min.

A sweet old lady disappears on a train, and a young woman and her male companion become convinced that a conspiracy is afoot. This is *the* spy thriller from Hitchcock's British period, a lighthearted, action-packed romp from start to finish. Hitchcock blends adventure with satire as he hurls the film's central protagonist, Margaret Lockwood, into a world of magic, music, deception, uncertainty, and romance.

THE LADY VANISHES ☆
1979, Great Britain, PG
Cybill Shepherd, Elliott Gould, Angela Lansbury, Herbert Lom, Arthur Lowe. Directed by Anthony Page. 99 min.

This is one of the few remakes of an Alfred Hitchcock film, by a director apparently determined to do as many things wrong as Hitchcock did right. The story, one of Hitchcock's lighter ones, is still intermittently winning; it concerns a young lady who becomes enveloped in an elaborate plot when she rather whimsically decides to investigate the sudden disappearance of an old woman during a train trip. This heavy-handed retelling is not helped at all by the awful performances of Cybill Shepherd (this was her between-fame period) and charmless stumblebum Elliott Gould.

THE LAND THAT TIME FORGOT ☆☆½
1975, Great Britain, PG
Doug McClure, John McEnery, Susan Penhaligon, Declan Mulholland. Directed by Kevin O'Connor. 91 min.

Saturday morning kid stuff, from a story by Edgar Rice Burroughs, along the lines of those old movie serials but without the self-consciousness of Steven Spielberg's ventures into the same area. Trouble is, it's also lacking in most of the thrills as well. A German U-boat picks up some survivors from an Allied ship during World War I, and the whole group stumbles onto an Antarctic island populated by dinosaurs and other critters presumed extinct.

LASERBLAST ☆½
1978, USA, PG
Kim Milford, Cheryl Smith, Roddy McDowall, Keenan Wynn. Directed by Michael Raye. 90 min.

Star Wars meets *Beach Blanket Bingo*. Dumb jock Kim Milford finds an alien ray gun in the desert, then uses it to wipe out the high schoolers who have been bothering him, and other stars who have come by to collect their paychecks for an obvious day's work on this low-budget picture. *Laserblast* is a dud.

LASSITER ☆☆
1984, USA, R
Tom Selleck, Lauren Hutton, Bob Hoskins, Ed Luther, Jane Seymour. Directed by Roger Young. 100 min.

Tom Selleck plays a lovable jewel thief in this World War II adventure set in London. Poor Selleck has had three flops in a row in his tangential screen career; this film, *High Road to China*, and *Runaway* are not the means with which to become the new Clark Gable. Here, Selleck and his creative team can't decide whether his persona should be Cary Grant or Harrison Ford. As a result, all the little-boy charm and palatable machismo that constitute his small-screen identity dissipate on the big screen. Sometimes, he seems more like Robert Wagner badly crossed with Lee Horsley, but matinee idols are few and far between and it would be premature to dismiss Selleck as a film star.

THE LAST AMERICAN HERO ☆☆☆½
1973, USA
Jeff Bridges, Valerie Perrine, Geraldine Fitzgerald, Gary Busey, Ed Lauter, Art Lund. Directed by Lamont Johnson. 100 min.

A gritty racetrack drama brimming over with lots of backwoods local color. With persuasive charm, Jeff Bridges plays a part-time moonshiner who nurses ambitions of winning a race-car championship against the big boys. Lamont Johnson effortlessly captures the dusty Southern ambiance of race tracks populated by down-home speed enthusiasts and drivers' groupies. The film is a commendable slice of naturalism. (a.k.a.: *Hard Driver*)

THE LAST AMERICAN VIRGIN ☆
1983, USA, R
Lawrence Monoson, Diane Franklin, Steve Antin, Louisa Moritz. Directed by Boaz Davidson. 90 min.

A leering, stupid teenage comedy in the *Porky's* vein, but much more inept. The "original" plot—young lad frets about his inability to "do it" for the first time, all the while having all sorts of ribald adventures with his friends—doesn't have even the pretense of sensitivity that these types of films usually have in order to claim "redeeming social value" (the equivalent of the "educational" status sought by old-time porno movies). On top of everything else, it's boring, too. It's become a perennial on so-called adult cable stations.

THE LAST CHALLENGE OF THE DRAGON ½☆
1980, Hong Kong
Shih Kien, Yang Sze, Ou Yang So Fei, Kuan Shan, Steve Chan, Anna Jones, Chen Li Li. Directed by Steve Chan. 90 min.

The nefarious Mr. Wong, dope pusher and all-around lousy guy, is out to corrupt the children of a kung fu master. Yawn.

THE LAST COMMAND ★★★
1955, USA
Sterling Hayden, Anna Maria Alberghetti, Richard Carlson, Arthur Hunnicutt, Ernest Borgnine, J. Carrol Naish, Otto Kruger, Slim Pickens. Directed by Frank Lloyd. 110 min.

A better-than-average Republic Western about the events leading up to and concluding with the battle of the Alamo. Because he lacked the star value and therefore the iconographic stature of John Wayne, Sterling Hayden makes a better Jim Bowie than did Wayne in *The Alamo*, which came out only a few years later. The movie is a bit too long, but the production values and the battle sequences are far better than the usual Republic low-budget films.

LAST CRY FOR HELP ★★½
1979, USA (TV)
Linda Purl, Tony LoBianco, Shirley Jones, Murray Hamilton, Grant Goodeve. Directed by Hal Sitowitz. 100 min.

A harbinger of the recent spate of movies made for television (*Silence of the Heart, Surviving*) dramatizing an alarming trend—teenage suicide. In this disturbing drama, a high school student can't cope with the fear that she won't measure up to her parents' dreams for her. The detailing of her downward descent into depression and suicidal tendencies is carefully wrought and breathtakingly acted by Linda Purl, who's not always shown to such good advantage in her TV films.

THE LAST DAYS OF MAN ON EARTH ★★½
1974, Great Britain, R
Jon Finch, Hugh Griffith, Patrick Magee, Graham Crowden. Directed by Robert Fuest. 76 min.

Author Michael Moorcock's foppish mad scientist, Jerry Cornelius, makes the jump to the movies in this wacked-out, broadly satirical effort. It's hard to tell just what is going on as Jerry battles his psychopathic brother and a group of equally crazy researchers for a formula that will change mankind's genetic structure, but the film's vignettish structure offers many laughs. It's better in parts than as a whole, and it has a great one-joke ending along the lines of *A Boy and His Dog*. Directed by Robert Fuest with the same outrageous style as his *Dr. Phibes* movies. (Runs eighty-nine minutes in the original version entitled *The Final Programme*.)

LAST DAYS OF POMPEII ★★★
1935, USA
Preston Foster, Basil Rathbone, Dorothy Wilson, David Holt, Alan Hale. Directed by Ernest Schoedsack. 96 min.

A disgruntled blacksmith forges ambitions of becoming a celebrated gladiator in this extremely interesting non-DeMille epic with thrilling action sequences and a fire-spewing climax that remains a model of fine special effects work. It's decidedly exciting, even if the story creaks in spots.

THE LAST DETAIL ★★★½
1973, USA, R
Jack Nicholson, Randy Quaid, Otis Young, Michael Moriarty, Carol Kane. Directed by Hal Ashby. 105 min.

When two career navy officers (Jack Nicholson and Otis Young) are given the unpleasant task of escorting a petty thief (Randy Quaid) to an unjust eight-year term in a New Hampshire brig, they decide to give their naive prisoner a taste of the high life en route. Nicholson shines as the cocky Buddusky in one of Hal Ashby's most heartfelt comedies. Nicholson and Quaid both won Oscar nominations, as did Robert Towne's intelligent, ironic script, adapted from a novel by Darryl Ponicsan.

THE LAST DRAGON ★★½
1985, USA, PG-13
Taimak, Vanity, Chris Murney, Julius J. Carry III. Directed by Michael Schultz. 108 min.

A free-for-all in cultural borrowing between black and white cultures, Motown primo Berry Gordy's urban fairy tale is a colorful little jive caper in which members of each represented ethnic group crib from one another. Former Prince choir girl Vanity plays a disco-less VJ, and she sparkles whenever she sings, flirts, or cusses out her hairdresser; but eloquent she's not. Throw in an Armenian villain, a series of foiled kidnappings, some Asians eager to rap, and a soul food restaurant that sells pizza, and you've got a culture clash louder than the sound system at Vanity's club. Michael Schultz, who has made some of the worst films of the past ten years (*Sgt. Pepper's Lonely Hearts Club Band, Scavenger Hunt*) has, surprisingly enough, turned out a fun piece of junk this time around. (a.k.a.: *Berry Gordy's The Last Dragon*)

LAST EMBRACE ★★½
1979, USA, R
Roy Scheider, Janet Margolin, John Glover, Sam Levene, Charles Napier, Christopher Walken. Directed by Jonathan Demme. 103 min.

Jonathan Demme's homage to Hitchcock has a government agent (Roy Scheider) pursuing a killer while running from his corrupt bosses and recovering from a nervous breakdown. It's technically proficient and occasionally clever, but oddly unengaging—one senses that Demme is out of his element with such a calculating, impersonal thriller (he's best known for *Stop Making Sense* and *Melvin and Howard*). The screen is abuzz with nods to Hitchcock's films, including a smart variation on a scene from *Foreign Correspondent* and a very obvious bow to *Psycho*. Filmmakers have certainly perpetrated worse Hitchcock ripoffs than this one, which at least is both blatant and stylish in its derivation, but why not see the originals instead?

LAST FIST OF FURY

See *Bruce Li in New Guinea*

THE LAST FLIGHT OF NOAH'S ARK ★★
1980, USA, G
Elliott Gould, Genevieve Bujold, Ricky Schroder, Vincent Gardenia, Dana Elcar. Directed by Charles Jarrot. 97 min.

Silly Disney adventure for less discriminating children and fans of Ricky Schroder, an idolization that should not be encouraged. He gets to cry his cute little eyes out numerous times over the potential fate of a plane (and later ship) full of animals that missionary Genevieve Bujold has conned shady pilot Elliott Gould into transporting to a South Pacific island. Thank God Schroder and Gould weren't on the *real* Noah's Ark, and that we didn't all turn out to be their descendants.

THE LAST HORROR FILM ½★
1984, USA, R
Joe Spinell, Mary Spinell, Caroline Munroe. Directed by David Winters. 87 min.

A disgusting taxi driver/gore hound decides to make his own horror movie, starring pinup girl Jana Bates (played by pinup girl Caroline Munroe), whom he stalks at Cannes. This is gross exploitation with the star of *Maniac*; opportunistic and mechanical.

THE LAST HOUSE ON THE LEFT ★★
1972, USA, R
David Hess, Lucy Grantham, Sandra Cassel, Marc Sheffler, Fred Lincoln. Directed by Wes Craven. 85 min.

"Can a movie go *too far*?" asked one flawlessly calculated ad for this film. "To avoid fainting, keep repeating 'It's only a movie . . . only a movie . . . only a movie.'" A group of sociopaths rape and murder two teenage girls, then unwittingly take refuge in the suburban home of one girl's parents. Bloody revenge is exacted. Brutal and raw; from the director of *The Hills Have Eyes* and *A Nightmare on Elm Street*, and produced by Sean S. Cunningham, who went on to make his mark as the director of *Friday the 13th*.

THE LAST LAUGH ☆☆☆☆
1924, Germany
Emil Jannings, Max Hiller, Maly Delschaft, Hans Unterkirchen. Directed by F. W. Murnau. 73 min.

The proud but aging doorman of a luxury hotel is demoted to washroom attendant and stripped of his life's pride and joy, his ornate uniform. This is particularly interesting as an early exercise in subjective camerawork; there is almost no dialogue, and feelings are expressed both through camera angle and the expressionistic acting of Emil Jannings. The obviously tacked-on ending was added at the producers' insistance; faced with this necessity, F. W. Murnau made it as ridiculous as possible.

THE LAST MARRIED COUPLE IN AMERICA ☆☆
1980, USA, R
Natalie Wood, George Segal, Richard Benjamin, Arlene Golonka, Valerie Harper, Marilyn Sokol, Dom DeLuise, Alan Arbus. Directed by Gilbert Cates. 102 min.

This highly disappointing comedy is not without its pleasures. Natalie Wood and George Segal play an L.A. couple who witness several close friends go through divorces. Eventually, Segal has an extramarital affair that leads to their own breakup, a fling with the single life, and an inevitable reunion. This supposedly "modern" comedy espouses old-fashioned values as solid as granite, only thinly disguised under its satire of "trendy" relationships and raunchy dialogue. The movie wants to have its cake and eat it, too, but the moralizing is hollow and the satire unoriginal. The cast, however, considerably brightens the proceedings: Wood, in one of her last performances before her untimely death, is a much better comedienne than she was earlier in her career, Segal complements her nicely, and Valerie Harper delivers a ripe, zesty cameo as a divorcée who encourages Segal's infidelity. *Interesting footnote*: Segal and Wood have a slapstick fight scene that is astonishingly similar to the one between Alan King and Ali MacGraw in *Just Tell Me What You Want*, a film released on the same day!

THE LAST METRO ☆☆☆½
1980, France, PG
Catherine Deneuve, Gerard Depardieu, Jean Poiret, Heinz Bennent. Directed by François Truffaut. 133 min.

François Truffaut's mastery of conventional storytelling reached its apogee here. Most of the acolytes of the French New Wave dismissed this movie as a sellout to the enemy, i.e., the traditional "well-made" film. But if this production isn't innovative, it is an exemplary piece of narrative filmmaking with fully fleshed-out characters. During World War II, a woman (Catherine Deneuve) bravely carries on the tradition of her Jewish husband's theater group as a sort of dramatic resistance activity after the Germans invade Paris. Deneuve's mate directs the troupe's clandestine activities while hidden in the depths of the theater. The film was an Oscar nominee for Best Foreign Film; available only in a dubbed version, at least for now.

THE LAST MILE ☆☆½
1932, USA
Howard Phillips, Preston Foster, George E. Stone, Noel Madison, Paul Fix, Al Hill. Directed by Sam Bischoff. 69 min.

This sanitized version of a noted play about convicts on death row doesn't have the punch it once did, though it's still a good melodrama. Socially concerned audiences of the 1980s may be surprised to see that this film doesn't take a stand on, or even examine, the issue of the death penalty. Instead, it looks at the effects of such a sentence on the men who receive it. The movie provides a "happier" ending than the play by dividing its central character into two men—one an unrecalcitrant killer who stages a prison rebellion, the other an innocent young man wrongly condemned. Remade less successfully in 1958 with Mickey Rooney.

LAST NIGHT AT THE ALAMO ☆½
1983, USA
Sonny David, Lou Perry, Steve Matilla, Tina Hubbard. Directed by Eagle Pennell. 80 min.

Independent director Eagle Pennell masticates this slice of Texas life. Pennell betrays the usual Indian attitude of affection for the subject by making his crew of barroom misfits as stupid and inarticulate as possible, and he directs the film with the condescending detachment of a snide provincial aristocrat lording over the peasant dances. *Alamo*, centered on the last night of a local Houston bar, is really a sweaty, one-act, one-set play shot with static, heavily significant camera angles—a sort of black-and-white television movie of a fake Sam Shepard play acted by the theater class of a low-rent prep school.

THE LAST OF THE MOHICANS ☆☆☆
1936, USA
Randolph Scott, Binnie Barnes, Heather Angel, Henry Wilcoxen, Bruce Cabot. Directed by George B. Seitz. 91 min.

Elaborate adaptation of the James Fenimore Cooper classic set in the woods of colonial America during the French and Indian War. There is lots of action as a small band of hero types guide two women through the wilds, trying to keep them from the clutches of Magua and his savage tribe. Bruce Cabot makes a formidable evil Indian, and the ending is one you won't easily forget.

LAST OF THE MOHICANS ☆☆
1977, USA (TV)
Steve Forrest, Ned Romero, Andrew Prine, Robert Tessier, Don Shanks. Directed by James L. Conway. 100 min.

The oft-filmed James Fenimore Cooper classic comes to the small screen with an emphasis on rip-roaring action. It's settlers vs. the Indians in a "Classics Illustrated"–style version of the frontier saga covering the exploits of Hawkeye and Natty Bumpo during the French and Indian War. A colorful but predictable schoolboy adventure.

LAST OF THE RED HOT LOVERS ☆☆½
1972, USA, PG
Alan Arkin, Sally Kellerman, Paula Prentiss, Renee Taylor. Directed by Gene Saks. 98 min.

In this fairly amusing farce from the Neil Simon machine, Alan Arkin plays a fish restaurant owner, married twenty-two years, who yearns to have an affair. He attempts this with three different screwed-up ladies in his mother's apartment. Arkin is funny, as are the three women (especially Renee Taylor), though this is far from Simon at his best.

THE LAST OF SHEILA ☆
1974, USA, R
James Coburn, James Mason, Joan Hackett, Ian McShane, Raquel Welch, Dyan Cannon. Directed by Herbert Ross. 120 min.

Stephen Sondheim, Broadway's brilliant composer, and Anthony Perkins cowrote this unpleasant mystery. The enterprise, dealing with James Coburn's efforts to bring his wife's hit-and-run killer to justice, is written and played as a party game—without emotion or depth. The large cast includes James Mason and

Ian McShane, who both play with knowing winks that offset their nasty roles. The others, most especially Dyan Cannon and Raquel Welch, are fully as one-dimensional as their roles.

LAST PLANE OUT ½☆
1983, USA
Jan-Michael Vincent, Lloyd Batista, Julie Carmen. Directed by David Nelson. 98 min.

Jan-Michael Vincent is the reporter caught in the wrong place at the wrong time in this very wrong film. Suspiciously similar to *Under Fire*, *Last Plane Out* crashes under the weight of bad acting, bad plot, bad everything. Vincent may have a tough time getting out of Somoza's Nicaragua, but this film had a more difficult time getting into the neighborhood theater: it never made it.

THE LAST REMAKE OF BEAU GESTE ☆☆½
1977, USA, PG
Marty Feldman, Ann-Margret, Michael York, Peter Ustinov, James Earl Jones, Trevor Howard, Henry Gibson, Terry-Thomas, Avery Schreiber. Directed by Marty Feldman. 83 min.

Marty Feldman's comic variation on *Beau Geste* also sends up *Four Feathers*, *Gunga Din*, and every Foreign Legion drama ever to come out of England, but the raucous, anything-for-a-laugh style is straight from Mel Brooks. More jokes miss than hit here, but the weak gagmaking is almost overcome by wonderful ham acting. The plot has aged lord of the manor Trevor Howard seeking to adopt a son and heir; to acquire dashing Michael York, he must also take "identical" twin Marty. The broad humor is a matter of (mostly bad) taste, but even purists should smile when Gary Cooper turns up in recut footage from William Wellman's 1939 version. (The original, from 1926, starred Ronald Colman; Doug McClure starred in the 1966 remake.)

LAST RESORT ½☆
1986, USA, R
Charles Grodin, Robin Pearson Rose, John Ashton, Ellen Blake, Megan Mullaly, Christopher Ames, Jon Lovitz, Gerrit Graham, Brenda Bakke, Phil Hartman. Directed by Zane Buzby. 84 min.

Agony. The note of desperation sounded in the title of this inane comedy turns out to be more than accurate; most bad comedies are made by untalented people trying to be funny, but this one seems to have been made by untalented people too lazy to make the effort. The resort is a twelfth-rate variation on the recent spate of disastrous-vacation movies, with Charles Grodin as the hapless head of an oversexed clan on the loose at a tropical hotel. Tasteless, witless, virtually plotless, and thoroughly hopeless; we'd rather have sun poisoning than go on this trip.

LAST RIDE OF THE DALTON GANG ☆½
1979, USA (TV)
Cliff Potts, Randy Quaid, Larry Wilcox, Jack Palance, Sharon Farrell, Harris Yulin, Bo Hopkins. Directed by Dan Curtis. 150 min.

Director Dan Curtis (best known for his supernatural fright flicks like *The Night Stalker*) comes a cropper with this bungled Wild West opus. Gunfights galore punctuate this compendium of Western clichés about the Dalton gang. The framing device that opens and closes the film in the Hollywood heyday of the 1930s is an empty, none-too-clever device that doesn't obscure the paucity of fresh material here.

LAST RITES

See *Dracula's Last Rites*

THE LAST STARFIGHTER ☆☆½
1984, USA, PG
Lance Guest, Robert Preston, Dan O'Herlihy, Catherine Mary Stewart. Directed by Nick Castle. 100 min.

An amiable and sometimes clever movie in which aliens from another galaxy come to collect Alex, a particularly proficient videogame player, hoping to persuade him to become a starfighter in a desperate intergalactic war. It beats life in the Starlight, Starbright trailer camp, so Alex goes for it.

LAST SUMMER ☆☆☆½
1969, USA
Richard Thomas, Barbara Hershey, Cathy Burns, Bruce Davison. Directed by Frank Perry. 97 min.

Frank Perry directed and Eleanor Perry wrote the screenplay for this study of four teenagers testing their upper-middle-class morality during their summer vacation. Thomas and Davison play buddies who befriend two girls, one alluring and flighty, the other repressed. The conclusion to their game playing is devastating and the buildup is edgy and intense. Though the symbolism tends to be heavy-handed, this is undoubtedly Frank Perry's best work to date.

LAST TANGO IN PARIS ☆☆☆☆
1972, Italy/France, R
Marlon Brando, Maria Schneider, Darling Legitmus, Jean-Pierre Leaud, Catherine Sola, Mauro Marchetti. Directed by Bernardo Bertolucci. 130 min.

This film was widely hailed at its release for revolutionizing the cinematic depiction of sex. Before *Last Tango in Paris*, films dealing with sex were *de facto* required to make a choice between emphasizing lust and emphasizing genuine feeling—on the one side were all varieties of pornography, from the mildest teen turn-ons to the most X-rated skin flicks; on the other were romances covering the whole spectrum of sentimentality, marriage movies, "sensitive" but inexplicit elaborations of the social forms physical love was permitted to take. With *Last Tango*, these two hitherto mutually exclusive threads were joined, in a story that shows the complex interdependency of love and lust in the imaginative space between two people whose emotional involvement is anything besides static. Marlon Brando, in a remarkable performance—in both French and English—that was to some extent ad-libbed, plays an aging American aimlessly looking for a new apartment the day after his wife's suicide; he encounters Maria Schneider in an empty flat both are inspecting, and they abruptly and passionately make love. They then form a "no names, no pasts" compact with each other, and continue to meet in their anonymous hideaway, initially for sex only. Gradually, she begins to develop genuine love for Brando, but because of the unusual circumstances, cannot conceive how their affair can be given a more permanent status. She ends up marrying somebody else, and only then—and only after getting very drunk—can Brando declare his love for her and propose marriage. But it's too late. This is a film of innumerable elusive moods superbly evoked by Bernardo Bertolucci's camera and the principals' performances; with a lush Gato Barbieri score.

LAST TRAIN FROM GUN HILL ☆☆☆
1959, USA
Kirk Douglas, Carolyn Jones, Anthony Quinn, Earl Holliman, Brad Dexter. Directed by John Sturges. 94 min.

Top-notch Western about a long-suffering marshal who's bound and determined to catch that last train with a murder suspect understandably reluctant to take the journey with him. You get not only a shoot-'em-up "good guys vs. bad guys" flick, but also a character study and a nail-biting suspense film. John Sturges (who also directed *The Magnificent Seven* and *Bad Day at Black Rock*) is a master at these wide-screen adult Westerns that don't sacrifice character for mindless action.

THE LAST TYCOON ★★★
1976, USA, PG
Robert DeNiro, Tony Curtis, Robert Mitchum, Jeanne Moreau, Jack Nicholson, Donald Pleasence, Ingrid Boulting, Ray Milland, Dana Andrews, Theresa Russell, Peter Strauss, John Carradine, Jeff Corey, Angelica Huston. Directed by Elia Kazan. 122 min.

Perhaps because the F. Scott Fitzgerald novel on which this is based was never finished, Elia Kazan's film version (from a script by Harold Pinter) has a vaguely empty, soulless feel; but then again, given the subject matter, it may have been intended that way. Robert DeNiro is cast against type as Monroe Stahr, boy wonder film producer in 1930s Hollywood. (Fitzgerald's model was Irving Thalberg.) Most of the stellar cast appear in small roles.

THE LAST UNICORN ★★★
1982, USA, G
Animated. Directed by Arthur Rankin, Jr., and Jules Bass. 88 min.

In this animated tale of a lonely unicorn who searches for her lost kinfolk, the usual G-rated sweetness is tempered by a beautifully sustained sense of magic and mystery. The movie also has some scary and sexually suggestive imagery, as well as a host of enchanting voices, including Alan Arkin's as a nebbishy magician, Angela Lansbury's as a witch, and Robert Klein's as a wisecracking butterfly.

THE LAST WALTZ ★★★★
1978, USA, PG
The Band, Bob Dylan, Neil Young, Joni Mitchell, Van Morrison, Eric Clapton, Neil Diamond, The Staples, Muddy Waters, Emmylou Harris, Ringo Starr. Directed by Martin Scorsese. 117 min.

This documentary of The Band's farewell concert, featuring some of rock's premier talents, is among the most stylish and exciting of its kind. Martin Scorsese's masterful direction avoids most of the clichés and self-seriousness that often plague rock films. Bob Dylan and the late Muddy Waters contribute two of the film's most outstanding performances. Eric Clapton's guitar work is polished but far from his best. The finale, with The Band onstage with all those rock and roll legends, is momentous.

THE LAST WAVE ★★★
1977, Australia, PG
Richard Chamberlain, David Gulpilil, Olivia Hamnett. Directed by Peter Weir. 106 min.

Australian director Peter Weir delves into the occult in his first major film, an eerie mood piece about a lawyer (Richard Chamberlain) defending aborigines charged with ritualistic murders. While creating an ominous, almost oppressive atmosphere, Weir explores the relationships and attitudes between two cultures that, at times, are galaxies apart. His handling of the opening, a brief, stunning set piece in which a schoolhouse is battered by a rock storm, demonstrates a very sure touch, and the murky, mystical finale is quite powerful.

THE LAST WINTER ★★
1984, USA/Israel, PG
Kathleen Quinlan, Yona Elian, Zipora Peled, Michael Schnider. Directed by Riki Shelach Missimoff. 92 min.

A sometimes stale bagel with a large smear of improbability on it. Two women both believe they've identified their missing husbands in some news footage, one of whom is an Israeli and the other an American. And one of them is, of course, destined for some bad news; but we won't give away any of the startlingly original plot.

THE LAS VEGAS STORY ★★½
1952, USA
Jane Russell, Victor Mature, Vincent Price, Hoagy Carmichael, Jay C. Flippen, Brad Dexter. Directed by Robert Stevenson. 87 min.

Jane Russell and Victor Mature were fleshy icons of dazed Hollywood sex, and the past-their-prime pairing of them in this crime story is juicy and satisfying. Vincent Price plays Russell's weakling husband who gets framed for a murder, and Mature is Russell's ex-lover who also happens to be a local cop. The film really succeeds on the basis of its tough, seedy atmosphere. Though the plot is a bit too neat and optimistic for real *film noir*, this movie should satisfy the genre fans. Hoagy Carmichael, as a lowlife pianist, plays "The Monkey Song," and Russell warbles "My Resistance Is Low" and "I Get Along Without You Very Well."

THE LATE SHOW ★★★★
1976, USA, PG
Art Carney, Lily Tomlin, Bill Macy, Eugene Roche, Joanna Cassidy, Howard Duff. Directed by Robert Benton. 94 min.

An affectionate, melancholy salute to the bygone era of hardboiled private eyes and hardboiled private eye films. Art Carney plays Ira Wells, a kind, aging detective who's too old and weary to continue dealing in intrepid pursuit and casual gunplay. When L.A. oddball Margo (Lily Tomlin) hires him out of semiretirement, a charming and wistful pair of sleuths is born. Neither Carney nor Tomlin has done better work since, and writer-director Robert Benton, working in an unfamiliar genre, strikes a perfect balance between straightforward appreciation, send-up, and ironic comment on the tough, romantic whodunits from which *The Late Show* derives. Fans of 1940s Hollywood will especially enjoy it, but there's something for everyone in this funny, touching and wholly original film.

LATINO ★½
1985, USA
Annette Cardona, Robert Beltran, Tony Plana, Julio Medina, Gavin McFadden. Directed by Haskell Wexler. 105 min.

This well-intentioned but clumsy propaganda about the Nicaraguan civil war was written and directed by ace cinematographer Haskell Wexler, who brings great subtlety to his images but none whatsoever to his narrative. The political slant is contra-*contra*, which should delight Democrats and rile Republicans, but whatever your political bent, you'll be more bored than stirred. The threadbare story concerns a military advisor (Robert Beltran) sent to Honduras to help the contra forces and who predictably begins to have second thoughts when he sees what's going on. The film was shot handsomely in Nicaragua by Tom Sigel.

THE LAUGHING POLICEMAN ★★★
1974, USA, R
Walter Matthau, Bruce Dern, Lou Gossett, Albert Paulsen, Anthony Zerbe, Cathy Lee Crosby. Directed by Stuart Rosenberg. 111 min.

The novels of Swedish husband-and-wife team Maj Sjowall and Per Wahloo were breakthroughs in police procedural writing, exploring the personal life and social conscience of their thoughtful, melancholy detective, Martin Beck. Walter Matthau is a poor piece of casting for the rumpled hero; instead of melancholy, he projects grouchiness, and thoughtfulness on *his* face looks like dyspepsia. Bruce Dern's role was created out of whole cloth, but it's pretty thin work—he's an ugly, unappealing character. Still, there's enough of the complex plot to make the film work as a very good whodunit.

LAURA ★★★★
1944, USA
Dana Andrews, Gene Tierney, Clifton Webb, Vincent Price, Judith Anderson. Directed by Otto Preminger. 88 min.

Sterling performances, moody ambiance, and caustically brittle dialogue highlight this elegantly urbane *film noir* about a methodical detective investigating the murder of femme fatale Laura Hunt, only to have her turn up alive. A tough detective out of his element with a gang of Park Avenue swells, a terrifically intriguing mystery, and Gene Tierney's cold/hot characterization of Laura add up to perfect entertainment. Otto Preminger's harsh view of the glittering society and his morbid fascination with the sexual allure of an allegedly dead woman pull this film up to the status of a classic of the forties.

LAURA ☆
1979, France, R
Maud Adams, Dawn Dunlap, James Mitchell. Directed by David Hamilton. 95 min.

This is among the most powerful, fastest-acting sleeping aids available without a doctor's prescription. David Hamilton, the well-known photographer of gauzy, pubescent female forms, wrote the original story and directed this silly yarn about a pedophiliac sculptor who wants to use his ex-lover's daughter as his new model. When he loses his sight, he's afraid he'll have to abandon the project. The resourceful young woman thinks up a crazy way for him to carry on—care to guess how he does it? It's not worth watching this movie to find out—he goes by *touch*! (a.k.a.: *Laura: Shadows of Summer*)

THE LAVENDER HILL MOB ☆☆☆☆
1951, Great Britain
Alec Guinness, Stanley Holloway, Sidney James, Alfie Bass, Marjorie Fielding. Directed by Charles Crichton. 82 min.

Charles Crichton's delightfully droll comedy stars Alec Guinness, in one of his most amusing and remarkable performances, as a bespectacled bank clerk who plans a massive gold heist with the help of a windy cohort (Stanley Holloway). T. E. B. Clarke won an Oscar for his witty, well-paced screenplay. Audrey Hepburn makes a cameo. A joy throughout.

THE LAWLESS FRONTIER ☆½
1935, USA
John Wayne, Sheila Terry, George "Gabby" Hayes, Yakima Canutt, Earl Dwire. Directed by Robert N. Bradbury. 52 min.

A tad cornball. It involves a half-breed who terrorizes desert ranchers, rustles cattle, and chases women, and the sheriff is less than helpful—looks like it's time for the Duke. Gabby Hayes provides the usual great support, here as the girl's crusty, dusty, desert-rat dad.

LAWLESS RANGE ☆☆
1935, USA
John Wayne, Sheila Manners, Earl Dwire, Yakima Canutt. Directed by Robert N. Bradbury. 54 min.

Standard sagebrush yarn, well-directed, filmed, and acted. John Wayne steals the show, and even sings a few prairie songs.

LAWRENCE OF ARABIA ☆☆☆☆
1962, USA
Peter O'Toole, Alec Guinness, Anthony Quinn, Jack Hawkins, Jose Ferrer, Anthony Quayle, Claude Rains, Arthur Kennedy, Omar Sharif. Directed by David Lean. 222 min.

David Lean's sumptuous epic adventure about T. E. Lawrence, the British cartographer who became a hero when he led the Arab revolt against Damascus, is a bit too long and a bit self-consciously mammoth, but brilliant acting and Lean's sure hand make it one of the most enduringly popular screen spectaculars. Peter O'Toole's charismatic portrayal of Lawrence shot him to stardom; the character's homosexual side, though not skirted, is left in the background except for one memorable scene. What remains most vivid is a series of beautifully shot and edited action set pieces, and the dynamic *tour de force* work of Alec Guinness, Claude Rains and Jose Ferrer in supporting roles. *Lawrence of Arabia* won a Best Picture Academy Award, and also picked up trophies for direction, cinematography, editing, art direction, sound, and Maurice Jarre's much-parodied score. Unfortunately, the wide-screen splendor of Freddie Young's camerawork is all but lost in the video rendering, where you're seeing about thirty percent of the original Super Panavision 70 image. Much of the mastery of David Lean's films is inherent in his use of the entire frame; it's hard to think of a film that suffers in home viewing more than this one. But it's a masterpiece nonetheless.

LAY OUT ½☆
Hong Kong
Chen Kuan-Tai, Chen Sha Lih, Hu Chin, Shih Jong Tien, Tien Yee, Chaing Tao, Cheng Kang Yeh. Directed by Pao Li.

What does this movie have going for it? A tired and confusing revenge plot, martial arts that are as convincing as professional wrestling, and a horribly unintelligible soundtrack—in short, nothing.

LEAVE 'EM LAUGHING ☆☆☆
1981, USA (TV)
Mickey Rooney, Anne Jackson, Allen Goorwitz, Elisha Cook, Jr., William Windom, Red Buttons. Directed by Jackie Cooper. 100 min.

Inspirational TV drama about a professional clown who wears his heart on his sleeve. While struggling with a bout of terminal cancer, instead of giving in to self-pity, he worries about the welfare of others. Mickey Rooney plays a real-life clown, Jack Thum, who struggled to provide a home for dozens of unwanted kids. Moving without being maudlin, this tale of self-sacrifice is lifted out of the mundane disease-of-the-week syndrome by Rooney's superb work as the clown who does more than make people laugh. It's a role tailor-made for Rooney, and he comes through brilliantly.

THE LEGACY ☆☆
1979, USA, R
Katharine Ross, Sam Elliott, John Standing, Roger Daltrey, Ian Hogg, Margaret Tyzack. Directed by Richard Marquand. 100 min.

The right elements for a horror treat are all in place: a lavish country manor in England, a group of guests assembled for no apparent reason, and a series of violent deaths that will eventually leave just one person to inherit a mantle of evil. Unfortunately, elements are all they are—*The Legacy* is long on clichés and short on sense, and anyone who's seen one haunted mansion movie will be able to stay at least three steps ahead of the predictable plot. (a.k.a.: *The Legacy of Maggie Walsh*)

LEGACY OF BLOOD

See *Blood Legacy*

LEGAL EAGLES ☆☆☆
1986, USA, PG
Robert Redford, Debra Winger, Daryl Hannah, Terence Stamp, Steven Hill, Brian Dennehy, John McMartin, Jennie Dundas, Roscoe Lee Browne. Directed by Ivan Reitman. 116 min.

Ivan Reitman's jaunty comedy-mystery, set in the high-powered world of Manhattan's art galleries, law firms, and auction houses, tries to re-create the kind of witty rivalry and bright banter associated with the best Hepburn-Tracy films. It doesn't come close—Reitman (*Ghostbusters*) and his writers (the team that scripted *Top Gun*) don't have the style or comic imagination to pull it off. What they *do* have are Robert Redford and Debra Winger, and that's enough. He plays an assistant D.A. prone to insomnia and tap dancing; she's a defense attorney given to midnight food binges and outlandish explanations to the jury. When they're thrown together on an art fraud case involving slightly crazed sexpot Daryl Hannah, sparks begin to fly. Too often, that's literally true—the film is overstuffed with explosions, fires, and searing special effects. Reitman didn't need to rely on these visual tricks; all the heat this movie needs is provided by the two stars, as relaxed, comic, and charming as they've ever been. With the flick of an eyebrow or the twitch of a half-smile, they give something extra to every line and infuse the film with a wonderfully edgy sense of adult romance.

LEGEND ☆☆
1986, USA, PG
Tom Cruise, Mia Sara, Tim Curry, David Bennet, Alice Playten, Billy Barty. Directed by Ridley Scott. 88 min.

As long as it lingers in the arena of evil, where Tim Curry (playing a satanic colossus known as the Lord of Darkness) proclaims his badness in mesmerizing high style, Ridley Scott's extravagantly silly, barely coherent dungeons-and-goblins fantasy has an over-the-top, pop-Wagnerian zip. Tom Cruise, romping around in a Jackson Browne haircut and ragamuffin duds, plays Jack o'the Green, a noble young sprite out to rescue Princess Lili (the gorgeous Mia Sara) and save the world from a wintry curse. The script is full of god-awful blather about good and evil and the forces of light and darkness, and though Scott creates some atmospheric shots, he seems to have lifted most of his images from old storybooks. With its billowy images of fairies, elves, and unicorns, *Legend* should have hypnotized us with its wondrous strangeness; instead, it plays like the ultimate shampoo commercial.

THE LEGENDARY STRIKE ☆☆
Hong Kong
Chu Kwon, Angela Mao Ying, Carter Huang, Li Ting Ying, Chang Ing, King Kung, Casanova Wong. Directed by Kwang Feng.

During the time of Emperor Kang Hsi's rule, Lord Yung (Carter Huang) hired a Japanese to transport "Dharuma's Relic," a large pearl. Tan, a fighter, and Miss Chin Lan (Angela Mao Ying) team up in order to steal the pearl and to defeat the Chings. The martial artistry is inspiring and the choreography is well thought out. The story is interesting, if confusing.

THE LEGEND OF BILLIE JEAN ☆
1985, USA, PG-13
Helen Slater, Peter Coyote, Christian Slater, Keith Gordon, Barry Tubb, Yeardley Smith. Directed by Matthew Robbins. 94 min.

A ludicrously muddled attempt at populist mythmaking. A teenage girl becomes a folk hero when she takes her little brother on the run after the kid accidentally shoots a mean guy. Although Billie Jean is ready to turn herself in (what exactly did she do wrong, anyway?), she wants the $608 for her brother's vandalized bike because "fair is fair." "FAIR IS FAIR!" chant the town teens, who start wearing "I love Billie Jean" T-shirts and calling upon her to rescue children and the mistreated all through Texas. The cynical, empty-headed attempts to manipulate the audience into cheering her on would be offensive if they weren't so inept. However, when B.J. sees *Joan of Arc* on TV and decides to cut her blond hair, the better to be a martyred icon, you may want to give the movie a good, hard slap.

THE LEGEND OF HELL HOUSE ☆☆☆
1973, Great Britain, PG
Roddy McDowall, Gayle Hunnicutt, Clive Revill, Pamela Franklin. Directed by John Hough. 95 min.

The film's visual pyrotechnics are a bit overdone—as though the director were trying to camouflage the familiarity of the plot. However, overlooking the sense of *déjà vu*, this is an above-average thriller about four psychic researchers who agree to spend a week in a haunted house because they believe they are professionals with the ability to take the situation firmly in hand. The ghosts under their scrutiny have other prankish ideas in mind and begin trying out a few experiments of their own on the harried scientists. This is a good goose-bumper that bears favorable comparison to *The Haunting*.

THE LEGEND OF KASPAR HAUSER
See *Every Man for Himself and God Against All*

THE LEGEND OF SLEEPY HOLLOW ☆☆½
1980, USA (TV)
Jeff Goldblum, Dick Butkus, Meg Foster, Paul Sand, John Sylvester White, Laura Campbell. Directed by Henning Schelluerup. 98 min.

Jeff Goldblum *looks* like an Ichabod Crane, and he is a fine actor. That's reason enough to see this film, originally produced by NBC as part of their "Classics Illustrated" series. This is a reasonable adaptation of the Washington Irving yarn, though it emphasizes humor at the expense of chills.

LEGEND OF THE BROKEN SWORD
See *Dressed to Fight*

THE LEGEND OF THE LONE RANGER ☆
1981, USA, PG
Klinton Spilsbury, Michael Horse, Christopher Lloyd, Matt Clark, Juanin Clay, Jason Robards, John Bennett Perry, John Hart. Directed by William A. Fraker. 98 min.

Trotting out every scrap of Lone Ranger mythology, director William A. Fraker has rehashed a clichéd vision of the Old West that ends up exhibiting all the aesthetic depth of a shampoo commercial. *Legend* is a depressing genre homage-cum-update that evinces no respect for or understanding of the much better films that are its source. Shameful!

LEG FIGHTERS ☆☆½
1980, Hong Kong
Tan Tao-Liang, Hsia Kuan-Li, Chin Lung, Peng Kang, Sun Yung-Chi, Wang Hsieh, Tsai Hung, Wang Yiu, Cheng Pao. Directed by Li Tso-Nan.

In one of the greatest leg fighting movies since *Top Hat*, Hsia Kuang-Li (*Duel of the Seven Tigers*) and Chin Lung play stubborn students who must learn leg fighting from Tan Tao Liang in order to defeat a heinous villain. Astaire and Rogers they ain't, but did you ever see Fred and Ginger flying through the air and kicking Reng Kang's butt? Highly recommended.

LEGS ☆☆½
1983, USA (TV)
Gwen Verdon, John Heard, David Marshall Grant, Sheree North, Maureen Teefy, Shanna Reed. Directed by Jerrold Freedman. 100 min.

This is a high-stepping drama with spiffy dancing and a plum supporting role for great Broadway dancer Gwen Verdon as choreographer to the Rockettes. Parts of the drama are as resolutely bland as the Christmas Show at Radio City Music Hall, but this exposé of the showbiz heartbreaks of dime-a-dozen dancers striving for the few openings in the Rockettes line does pack more dramatic kick than tales of those kvetchy teenage twerps on "Fame." If only Hollywood had used Verdon at the height of her powers instead of throwing these character parts her way now.

LENNY ☆☆☆½
1974, USA, R
Dustin Hoffman, Valerie Perrine, Jan Miner, Gary Morton. Directed by Bob Fosse. 112 min.

Dustin Hoffman's brilliantly edgy, hopped-up portrayal of Lenny Bruce—the beat generation's prophet-jester-sadist—greatly aids

Bob Fosse's dark look at Lenny and the alternate demons of drug addiction and obscenity charges that he had to face. There are lengthy scenes of Bruce's greatest monologues along with pseudo-vérité interviews with other characters. Fosse, however, presents everything with the same off-putting combination of lurid gawking and cool detachment, so that this depiction of a troubled, complex life, though showy and intermittently poweful, is not invariably illuminating. Hoffman does, however, find something in Bruce, as does Valerie Perrine in her role as his gorgeous, strung-out wife Honey. The film was nominated for six Academy Awards, including Best Picture, Actor, and Actress.

THE LENNY BRUCE PERFORMANCE FILM ☆☆
1967, USA
Lenny Bruce. No director credited. 61 min.

The only filmed record of Lenny Bruce, live, uncensored and in front of an audience, was made in San Francisco late in 1965. Technically, it's a horror—grainy, shakily shot and at times barely audible. Unfortunately, Bruce himself isn't good enough here to make this worth seeing for anyone except the curious; this was very late in Bruce's career, and most of the hour consists of him reading from and commenting on the transcripts of his obscenity trials. The film is more sad than funny overall, but there are moments of the caustic brilliance that made his reputation.

THE LEOPARD MAN ☆☆☆
1943, USA, PG
Dennis O'Keefe, Jean Brooks, Margo, Isabel Jewell, James Bell. Directed by Jacques Tourneur. 59 min.

Jacques Tourneur's last film for producer Val Lewton is based on a Cornell Woolrich thriller about a series of murders in a New Mexico town, blamed on a runaway circus leopard. The mosaic narrative, with the focus shifting from one character to another and back again, was a favorite Lewton device and allowed his directors ample opportunity to build suspense and liberally toss in red herrings. Although this isn't as consistently eerie as *I Walked with a Zombie* or *The Cat People*, the film is still a worthwhile entry in the horror field, and one scene, in which a young girl is slaughtered outside the door to her home, is tremendously effective.

LEPKE ☆½
1975, USA, R
Tony Curtis, Anjanette Comer, Michael Callan, Vic Tayback, Milton Berle. Directed by Menahem Golan. 110 min.

One of the dullest of the many ripoffs inspired by the success of *The Godfather*. Tony Curtis plays Louis Lepke Buchalter, head of the 1930s crime syndicate known as Murder Inc., and although the film makes a few halfhearted attempts to re-create him as the Jewish Don Corleone, the script doesn't have the style, atmosphere, or imagination to support even this one idea. The violent set pieces are staged blandly, and token appearances by an impressive rogues' gallery—Lucky Luciano, Dutch Schultz, Legs Diamond—can't enliven the cheap, banal proceedings.

LES GIRLS ☆☆½
1957, USA
Gene Kelly, Taina Elg, Kay Kendall, Mitzi Gaynor. Directed by George Cukor. 114 min.

This sophisticated script (one that manages to tweak the pretensions of the Japanese film *Rashomon* in a lighthearted manner) deals with the nature of truth as perceived by several interested parties rehashing the past. The problem is that it's too clever for this musical's ultimate well-being, since the screenplay doesn't lend itself to musicalization; the numbers all seem to come out of left field. Still, the physical production has a lustrous sheen that's bewitching. Kay Kendall is smashing as one of three full-time dance partners and part-time girlfriends to Gene Kelly's song-and-dance wolf. His amorous pursuits become the focus of a libel suit when one of the gals (Kendall) publishes her self-serving memoirs. Not top drawer, but the Jack Cole choreography is vigorous, and even second-rate Cole Porter is better than most composers.

LET IT BE ☆☆☆
1970, Great Britain, G
The Beatles (John Lennon, Paul McCartney, George Harrison, Ringo Starr), Yoko Ono, Billy Preston. Directed by Michael Lindsay-Hogg. 80 min.

This documentary following the Beatles at work in the recording studio is fascinating mostly because of what came afterward: The album they were recording, "Let it Be," turned out to be their last group work, and they broke up shortly before the film's release. Given that knowledge, viewers had a tendency to read too much into the minor disagreements and squabbles that marked the creative process. Aside from a few songs performed for a street crowd from the roof of their recording studio, there are really no live performances in this film. But for fans of the group, stage director Michael Lindsay-Hogg has captured a fascinating look at the tensions and harmonies that permeated their work and their public personae.

LET'S DO IT AGAIN ☆☆½
1975, USA, PG
Sidney Poitier, Bill Cosby, Calvin Lockhart, John Amos, Denise Nicholas, Ossie Davis, Jimmie Walker. Directed by Sidney Poitier. 110 min.

This semi-sequel to *Uptown Saturday Night* is an infectiously cheerful low-comedy caper, a sort of all-black *Sting* that also owes a lot to Abbott and Costello and, for that matter, Fred Flintstone and Barney Rubble. The plot has lodge brothers Sidney Poitier and Bill Cosby scamming some no-good gangsters by backing a spindly prizefighter (Jimmie Walker, then hugely popular thanks to TV's "Good Times"). Director-star Poitier seems a little uncomfortable with comedy, and, for the most part, takes a backseat to the antics of Cosby, Walker and Ossie Davis. Nothing special overall, but very pleasant on its own terms.

LET'S SCARE JESSICA TO DEATH ☆☆½
1971, USA, PG
Zohra Lampert, Barton Heyman, Kevin O'Connor, Gretchen Corbett, Alan Manson, Mariclare Costello. Directed by John Hancock. 89 min.

A young woman (Zohra Lampert) recovering from a nervous breakdown seeks peace in a rustic Connecticut country house and gets just the opposite, in an offbeat, creepy thriller that's a love generation variation on the classic vampire tale. The film has enough bizarre atmosphere and detail to make up for its amateurish moments, and Lampert is an intriguing, mercurial presence even when the script pigeonholes her into playing the standard hysterical victim. John Hancock went on to direct *Bang the Drum Slowly*.

LET'S SPEND THE NIGHT TOGETHER ☆½
1983, USA, PG
The Rolling Stones. Directed by Hal Ashby. 94 min.

Let's not, Mick; you're getting a bit old for this sort of thing. This concert film from the Rolling Stones's appropriately named "Still Life" tour is predominantly a string of close-ups of Mick Jagger gesticulating broadly for the people in the cheap seats in the sports arenas in which the band played, while guitarists Keith Richard and Ron Wood act like ten-year-olds and rhythm section Charlie Watts and Bill Wyman try not to look their age. With all the expected songs, only one of which ("You Can't Always Get What You Want") benefits from live performance. This is for die-hards only.

THE LETTER ☆☆☆½
1940, USA
Bette Davis, James Stephenson, Herbert Marshall, Frieda Inescourt, Gale Sondergaard. Directed by William Wyler. 95 min.

Bette Davis, playing a murderess trying to retrieve an incriminating letter, had one of her best roles in William Wyler's skillful rendering of Somerset Maugham's work. This overheated melodrama has seen service before as a vehicle for Jeanne Eagels and would later showcase Brenda Marshall and, then, Lee Remick in a TV movie, but no one has surpassed Davis as the adulterous plantation wife who has trysts in the moonlight with a rotter whose Eurasian wife doesn't forgive Bette for bumping off her wandering husband. Pauline Kael called this performance the greatest study of a woman's sexual hypocrisy in film history, but Davis, incredibly, was passed over for an Oscar in favor of Ginger Rogers in *Kitty Foyle*. The lush cinematography creates a mysterious black and white shadow world that is exploited to the hilt by Wyler's savvy direction. There's also that immortal line of dialogue, "With all my heart, I still love the man I killed."

A LETTER OF INTRODUCTION ☆☆½
1938, USA
Adolphe Menjou, Andrea Leeds, Edgar Bergen, George Murphy, Rita Johnson, Eve Arden, Ann Sheridan. Directed by John M. Stahl. 100 min.

Andrea Leeds stars as a struggling actress who wants to make it big without the help of her arrogant, movie star father (Adolphe Menjou). John Stahl provides effective direction for this well-written, finely cast melodrama that is interesting throughout. Edgar Bergen, with Charlie McCarthy and Mortimer Snerd, contributes some funny moments.

LETTER TO BREZHNEV ☆☆☆
1985, Great Britain, R
Alexandra Pigg, Margi Clarke, Peter Firth, Alfred Molina, Tracy Lea. Directed by Chris Bernard. 94 min.

This ruefully funny love story is set in rainy, impoverished Liverpool, where two factory girls hit the local bars one night looking for a good time and one of them finds true love—in the form of a cherubic Russian sailor (Peter Firth) who's on very brief shore leave. Will cultural differences, family objections, and political bureaucracy be able to keep them apart? Don't bet on it; you may be surprised at director Chris Bernard's portrayal of England as a world behind an iron curtain of its own. It's very gloomy and a bit repetitive, and the Liverpudlian accents are sometimes harder to decipher than the Russian ones, but the touching tale is full of small, unexpected rewards.

A LETTER TO THREE WIVES ☆☆☆
1949, USA
Ann Sothern, Linda Darnell, Jeanne Crain, Paul Douglas, Kirk Douglas, Thelma Ritter, Jeffrey Lynn. Directed by Joseph L. Mankiewicz. 102 min.

Joseph Mankiewicz avoids the unpleasant and hollow cynicism that pervades much of his work in this story of three women, each of whom receives a letter from a mutual friend saying that she has run off with one of their husbands—leaving them to ponder which one. The worst segment, dealing with Jeanne Crain and Jeffrey Lynn, is so listlessly written and directed that one wonders how Mankiewicz could ever have envisioned the film as even longer—*A Letter to Four Wives*. Ann Sothern's section, dealing with crass commercialism and a deeper discord than the other tales, is potentially the finest story and Sothern achieves a real sophistication on top of Mankiewicz's arch pretense. Unfortunately, the script goes only so far before backtracking into farce for a weak conclusion. The third and most popular story has Paul Douglas and Linda Darnell offering expertly timed performances as the most comical of the three couples. The director is blessed with the ability to step back and let people like Thelma Ritter do their stuff with a minimum of interference. Mankiewicz won Academy Awards for Best Director and Best Screenplay.

LIANNA ☆☆
1983, USA, R
Jon DeVries, Linda Griffiths, Jane Hallaren, Jo Henderson, Jesse Solomon, Jessica Wight MacDonald, Maggie Renzi. Directed by John Sayles. 110 min.

John Sayles settled on a fashionable subject in his second film, a drab, rather precious story about a housewife (Linda Griffiths) who falls into a lesbian affair with her night school professor, moves out on her oppressive husband, and tries to piece together a brave new life. Sayles's usual sparkling dialogue is always in evidence, but it never hides the shallowness of the movie, which amounts to a thin, doctrinaire coming-out-of-the-closet story.

LIAR'S MOON ☆☆
1981, USA, PG
Matt Dillon, Cindy Fisher, Christopher Connelly, Hoyt Axton, Susan Tyrrell, Broderick Crawford. Directed by David Fisher. 105 min.

An otiose love story short on logic. It's been released with different endings, but, with or without a happy fade-out, the film bombed and did nothing for Matt Dillon's career. As usual, he scratches his armpits, mumbles his dialogue and manages to look adorably long-suffering in a way that teenybopper girls are apt to faint over. He's poor but decent; she's rich but love-starved. Quicker than you can say "Romeo and Juliet" in a down-home accent, Matt and his honey are fleeing those adults and establishment types who don't understand them. This film is only for impressionable teens who thought *Pretty in Pink* made sense, too.

THE LIBERATION OF L. B. JONES ☆½
1970, USA
Lee J. Cobb, Anthony Zerbe, Roscoe Lee Browne, Lola Falana, Lee Majors, Barbara Hershey. Directed by William Wyler. 102 min.

Overheated Southern Gothic, à la *Hurry Sundown* and *The Chase*. In these films, a good percentage of the decaying Southern populace are satyrs and nymphomaniacs, as sexually indulgent as they are racially prejudiced. All Southern hell breaks loose when a black man discovers that his wife is dallying with a white policeman. This is a simplistic drama so preachy about racial attitudes that one feels as if one were trapped in a high school civics class. The great director William Wyler's swan song has some energy, but his detached style seems at odds with the purple passions on display.

LT. ROBINSON CRUSOE, U.S.N. ☆☆
1966, USA
Dick Van Dyke, Nancy Kwan, Akim Tamiroff, Arthur Malet, Tyler McVey. Directed by Byron Paul. 110 min.

It's conceivable that children might love the beginning of this movie, when a navy pilot parachutes into the sea, lands on an island, meets a similarly shipwrecked chimp, and builds a South Seas suburbia, complete with a golf course. However, the kids will get bored and mom may get offended at the second half, when Crusoe meets up with an island girl (Nancy Kwan), leads a silly island women's revolt, and flees from Kwan after he's inadvertently proposed to her. Dick Van Dyke tries hard, and he looks every bit the simple, industrious American, but he has so little to work with that the film simply sputters out.

THE LIFE AND ASSASSINATION OF THE KINGFISH ☆☆½
1977, USA (TV)
Ed Asner, Nicholas Pryor, Diane Kagan, Fred Cook, Gary Allen. Directed by Robert Collins. 100 min.

The creators of this political horror story could have taken a more constructive path by more closely following the classic 1949 version of the rise and fall of Huey Long. A lot of the bite of that film, *All the King's Men*, is missing here as clichéd writing and lackluster direction vitiate the impact of a powerhouse cautionary tale. That the film succeeds at all is due solely to Ed Asner's bravura performance as the cracker-barrel politician whose fall from grace illustrated the truthfulness of Lord Acton's maxim that "absolute power corrupts absolutely." Also, this true tale is such a compelling one in itself that the viewer is pulled into the saga of the Louisiana governor and U.S. senator who pleaded for the rights of the common man even as he played fast and loose with the law.

THE LIFE AND DEATH OF COLONEL BLIMP ☆☆☆½
1943, Great Britain
Roger Livesey, Anton Walbrook, Deborah Kerr, Ursula Jeans, Albert Lieven, Felix Aylmer, Roland Culver, James McKechnie. Directed by Michael Powell and Emeric Pressburger. 163 min.

The character of Colonel Blimp, the creation of the English cartoonist David Low, was a caricature of Britain's officer class on the threshhold of World War II—too old and portly, too bound by an outmoded code of honor, to withstand Nazi ruthlessness. Brought to life in Michael Powell and Emeric Pressburger's handsome color production at the turning point of the war, however, Blimp became the romanticized figure of all the best of British qualities—old-fashioned, perhaps, but liberally fair-minded, good-humored, and persevering. The story follows its hero (Roger Livesey, because Laurence Olivier was unavailable) throughout the century, maintaining his friendship, despite their national differences, with his German counterpart (Anton Walbrook). In a bright whim of casting, Deborah Kerr plays the three different redheads in Blimp's life. The film is a richly detailed, splendidly absorbing emblem of the nation, and of its once-proud national cinema, at its finest hour.

THE LIFE AND TIMES OF JUDGE ROY BEAN ☆☆☆
1972, USA, PG
Paul Newman, Victoria Principal, Anthony Perkins, Ned Beatty, Jim Burk, Tab Hunter, John Huston, Stacy Keach, Roddy McDowall, Jacqueline Bisset, Ava Gardner, Anthony Zerbe, Richard Farnsworth. Directed by John Huston. 120 min.

John Huston's revisionist fantasy of the Old West is genial and amusing, even when it's overly episodic and a bit too loose with historical facts. Paul Newman cleans up the character of the title, the West's infamous "hanging judge," who here becomes a nice guy with a couple of grudges. There's a sequence in which Newman and Victoria Principal, as his Mexican wife, dance with a lovable bear to the strains of Andy Williams singing a song called "Marmalade, Molasses and Honey," and it is to Huston's credit that the scene does not make you want to throw up. The film was written by John Milius.

LIFEBOAT ☆☆☆
1944, USA
Tallulah Bankhead, Walter Slezak, Canada Lee, Henry Hull, Mary Anderson, Heather Angel, William Bendix. Directed by Alfred Hitchcock. 96 min.

Hitchcock's experiment with a single set throws a motley gang of survivors from a torpedoed liner into a small lifeboat. The film gives a metaphor for the unification of the Allies: The lifeboat rescues, then turns against, a Nazi picked up from a sunken submarine. The script, by John Steinbeck and Jo Swerling, contains a lot of class stratification and wartime pontificating, and Hitchcock is content to sit back, let them talk, and cut in some great reaction shots. Tallulah Bankhead lords over the other passengers like a Hollywood queen at a local diner, and her performance, when it's in gear, transcends the rest of the film. This movie, reviled by many, is genuinely entertaining and never loses its steady momentum.

LIFEFORCE ☆☆½
1985, USA, R
Steve Railsback, Matilda May, Peter Firth, Frank Finlay. Directed by Tobe Hooper. 105 min.

This is a state-of-the-art effects film with its heart planted in the science fiction B movies of the 1950s. A space shuttle mission discovers a gigantic alien craft inside of Halley's Comet. Upon exploring the ship, the astronauts find three human-looking aliens on board, beings who reveal themselves to be soul-sucking vampires when brought back to Earth. It's a high-energy combination of *Dawn of the Dead* and *Star Wars* that never takes itself seriously. With its breakneck pace and astounding visuals, *Lifeforce* is a crazy, entertaining movie.

LIFEGUARD ☆☆½
1976, USA, PG
Sam Elliott, Anne Archer, Kathleen Quinlan, Stephen Young, Parker Stevenson, Sharon Weber. Directed by Daniel Petrie. 96 min.

The many interesting moments of this offbeat drama add up to a watchable but inconclusive film. Sam Elliott gives a fine performance as an overaged beach boy who wonders if endless summer is what he really wants when a more stable job beckons; Anne Archer plays his girlfriend from high-school days, wondering if the magic is still there. The film is low-key and often perceptive. Paramount Home Video has made the idiotic decision to package this as "A Joan Collins Video Selection," and she introduces the film *à la* Alastair Cooke.

THE LIFE OF EMILE ZOLA ☆☆☆½
1937, USA
Paul Muni, Joseph Schildkraut, Gale Sondergaard, Gloria Holden, Donald Crisp, Louis Calhern, Harry Davenport, Erin O'Brien Moore. Directed by William Dieterle. 116 min.

Zola-the-novelist is downplayed in favor of Zola-the-activist in this lavishly mounted Warner Bros. biography. Norman Reilly Raine's Oscar-winning screenplay from a story by Heinz Herald and Geza Herczeg concentrates on Zola's crusade to help the falsely accused Jewish soldier Alfred Dreyfuss (Best Supporting Actor Joseph Schildkraut), who spent years on Devil's Island before being released. Though liberal in Warner's best social conscience manner, it is curious that the word "Jew" is never uttered. Despite that lapse, this is still a fine, moving Hollywood biography, with Paul Muni giving one of his last satisfying performances before becoming the ham he would remain thereafter.

LIFE WITH FATHER ☆☆☆
1947, USA
William Powell, Irene Dunne, Edmund Gwenn, ZaSu Pitts, Elizabeth Taylor, Martin Milner, Jimmy Lydon, Emma Dunn. Directed by Michael Curtiz. 118 min.

One of the theater's perennial favorites is turned into a respectable if slightly stuffy film. The plot, such as it is, finds William Powell playing a stern, turn-of-the-century patriarch finally getting the baptism he missed all those years ago. Donald Ogden Stewart's faithful adaptation of the Howard Lindsay-Russel Crouse play remains too theatrical in tone to take off as solid screen comedy, and Michael Curtiz directs too unobtrusively, displaying none of the finesse exhibited by Vincente Minnelli in *Meet Me in St. Louis* and Otto Preminger in *Centennial Summer*. The result is like a glorified Andy Hardy movie; as such, it's entertaining but no classic. Irene Dunne and the young Elizabeth Taylor shine brightly in the cast. Unimaginative use of Technicolor.

THE LIFT ☆☆½
1983, Holland, R
Huub Stapel, Willeke Van Ammelrooij, Josine Van Dalsum, Hans Veerman. Directed by Dick Maas. 90 min.

A killer elevator—just when you thought you'd seen it all. It's not a bad idea, and has some nice Hitchcockian touches, but there's nothing here to make this film particularly memorable. Dutch director Dick Maas never generates any real tension with this material; you expect the killings to come on schedule, as cued by the *Jaws*–like music, and sure enough . . .

THE LIGHT AT THE EDGE OF THE WORLD ☆½
1971, USA/Spain/Lichtenstein
Yul Brynner, Kirk Douglas, Samantha Eggar, Fernando Rey. Directed by Kevin Billington. 119 min.

A drab adventure tale spiced up with some romance and based on a Jules Verne tale, this low-wattage story tells of a lighthouse keeper who accidentally casts his beacon on a shipwreck swarming with scavengers. Naturally, pirates don't stay in business by letting witnesses live, so the buccaneers decide to punch his lights out. In between brawls, Yul Brynner and Kirk Douglas (the good guy) find time to pursue the token love interest (Samantha Eggar).

THE LIGHT IN THE FOREST ☆☆½
1958, USA
Fess Parker, Wendell Corey, Joanne Dru, James MacArthur, Jessica Tandy, John McIntyre, Carol Lynley, Rafael Campos, Directed by Herschel Daugherty. 93 min.

Decades have passed since its initial publication, but Conrad Richter's touching novel of a young white boy raised by Indians in the early days of America is still read in grade schools everywhere. This film adaptation from Walt Disney isn't as durable and gives way to candy-coated silliness, but the basic merit of the story is preserved. James MacArthur plays the young man who reluctantly returns to the white world when a treaty orders the return of all hostages, but he longs for the Indian world of his youth. The film is oversimplified but touching, and kids will like it.

LIGHTS OF OLD SANTA FE ☆½
1944, USA
Roy Rogers, George "Gabby" Hayes, Dale Evans. Directed by Frank McDonald. 78 min.

This Roy Rogers film has the cowboys joining up with Gabby Hayes's ramshackle rodeo tour. Roy does a little nifty riding aboard Trigger.

THE LIGHTSHIP ☆☆½
1986, USA, PG-13
Robert Duvall, Klaus Maria Brandauer, Tom Bower, Robert Costanzo, Badja Djola, William Forsythe, Arliss Howard. Directed by Jerzy Skolimowski. 90 min.

This grim, claustrophobic shipboard melodrama is made compelling by the work of its two stars. Oddly, the more flamboyant Klaus Maria Brandauer has the less showy role; he plays the captain of a retired ship moored off the mid-Atlantic Coast, trying to overcome his past and raise his young son. Suddenly, the ship is boarded by a band of fugitives led by a psychotic menace (Robert Duvall), a hurricane nears, and tension mounts. Silly and overblown, but it has its moments.

LILI ☆☆☆
1953, USA
Leslie Caron, Mel Ferrer, Kurt Kaznar, Jean-Pierre Aumont, Zsa Zsa Gabor. Directed by Charles Walters. 81 min.

This intimate small-scale MGM musical is pleasant but slightly too sweet. Leslie Caron, hot off *An American in Paris*, plays a young French waif (what else) who joins a carnival and falls for a handsome magician. That's the plot. Charles Walters (*Good News*, *Easter Parade*) nicely integrates the slight Paul Gallico tale with song and dance. Unfortunately, the theme song, "Hi Lili, Hi Lo," is a pain (Bronislau Kaper inexplicably won an Oscar for it) and the climactic dance is marred by Mel Ferrer's inability to partner Caron. Still, this one is better than some of Metro's musical heavyweights and is expertly acted by the ensemble. Children will especially enjoy Lili's dance with the puppets.

LILIES OF THE FIELD ☆☆☆½
1963, USA
Sidney Poitier, Lilia Scala, Lisa Mann, Isa Crino, Stanley Adams. Directed by Ralph Nelson. 93 min.

A delightful comedy-drama about accepting responsibility for others. Although most interracial brotherly love movies tend to cloy, this one is hard to resist. An itinerant handyman (Sidney Poitier) keeps to himself and never hangs around long enough to reach out to others. Then, out in the desert, he encounters a determined Mother Superior who views him as the answer to her prayers and the instrument through which her chapel will be built. The budding relationship between the optimistic nun and the resolute loner is handled with clarity and warmth, and you'll enjoy watching the nun con the handyman into doing God's work. The hand-clapping "Amen" sequence is a rousing high point and Poitier deservedly won the first Academy Award ever given a black man for Best Actor.

LILITH ☆☆☆½
1964, USA
Warren Beatty, Jean Seberg, Kim Hunter, Peter Fonda, Gene Hackman, Jessica Walter, Anne Meacham. Directed by Robert Rossen. 114 min.

An extraordinary, provocative film about a destructive love affair between an alluring schizophrenic and a troubled male attendant at a progressive mental institution. Exquisitely photographed in black and white by Eugene Shuftan, *Lilith* visually captures an eerie twilight world where states of madness blend seamlessly with perceived reality, a world in which a sensitive therapist (Warren Beatty) is led into viewing life through the eyes of his schizophrenic lover (Jean Seberg). Years ahead of its time, this disturbing movie is among the best American films dealing with mental illness and is the only American film to properly capture Seberg's incandescent beauty and talent.

LILY IN LOVE ☆☆☆
1985, USA
Maggie Smith, Christopher Plummer, Elke Sommer, Adolph Green, Szabo Sandor. Directed by Karoly Makk. 103 min.

Ferenc Molnar's *The Guardsman* provided a rare screen vehicle for Alfred Lunt and Lynn Fontanne, and this uncredited remake proves that the story is durably romantic and elegant. Graceful farceurs Christopher Plummer and Maggie Smith play a vain actor and his wife, a playwright who tells him he's no longer the man she has in mind for the romantic lead of her new script. When he disguises himself as a would-be Don Juan to get the role, his performance works too well. Visually drab, but the stars bring to their roles a sophistication rarely seen these days.

LIMELIGHT ☆☆☆☆
1952, USA
Charles Chaplin, Claire Bloom, Sydney Chaplin, Buster Keaton, Andre Eglevsky, Melissa Hayden. Directed by Charles Chaplin. 138 min.

Sentimentality was always an important part of Chaplin's artistic repertoire, and *Limelight* is Chaplin's deepest, most self-indulgent exploration of the theme of the suffering individual. This is by no means a complaint—the film is frank in its concerns and equally forthright about its desire to elicit tears and sympathy; to cavil about this movie's sentimentality is akin to complaining that it is difficult to understand the words during an opera. Chaplin plays a broken-down music hall entertainer who cannot make people laugh but does find someone to cheer up. He rescues a struggling ballerina from suicide and manages to convince her that life is worth living, even as he is reduced to begging in the streets. In a sense, this movie is a return to the Tramp character's vulnerability, and, especially, to the final moments of *City Lights*; however, now Charlie has grown too old for the girl he has saved, and he must watch her drift away from him. Chaplin's performance as Calvero is, of course, stunning, but be prepared to be swept away by Claire Bloom's sad sweetness. The famous, all-too-brief sequence that finally unites the two greatest comic talents of our century, Chaplin and Keaton, is very, very funny. It is also heartbreakingly poignant to see how much the two men have aged. Because of political pressure, the film had only a partial release in 1952, and Chaplin's score (which contains the hit "Smile") won the 1972 Academy Award when it was finally released.

LINCOLN CONSPIRACY ☆½
1977, USA, G
Bradford Dillman, Robert Middleton, John Anderson, John Dehner, Whit Bissell. Directed by James L. Conway. 90 min.

Did you know that when John Wilkes Booth assassinated Lincoln he was in cahoots with several anti-Reconstruction members of the Senate? Did you know that Booth really escaped to Canada and that someone else was buried in his grave? Did you know that Sunn Classics made millions in the 1970s with such pseudo-documentary drivel as this, *In Search of Noah's Ark*, *In Search of Historic Jesus*, and *Chariots of the Gods*? The film does gain half a star for having a few good actors in the cast who, troopers all, actually try to get through this tripe.

LINK ☆☆½
1986, USA, R
Terence Stamp, Elizabeth Shue, Steven Pinner, Richard Garnett, David O'Hara, Kevin Lloyd, Joe Belcher. Directed by Richard Franklin. 103 min.

Ape intelligence is the focus of this moderately entertaining suspense film by the director of *Psycho II*. Terence Stamp plays a weird professor studying primate behavior in his secluded cottage. All is well until a new assistant with new ideas shows up and Link, the old ape who functions as a sort of houseboy, decides to demand a little respect. An abundance of good camera effects and interesting touches compensate for the silly moments and overall thinness of the plot.

THE LION IN WINTER ☆☆☆½
1968, Great Britain
Peter O'Toole, Katharine Hepburn, Jane Merrow, John Castle, Timothy Dalton, Anthony Hopkins. Directed by Anthony Harvey. 135 min.

James Goldman's hit play, a sort of twelfth-century *Who's Afraid of Virginia Woolf?*, is translated to the screen by director Anthony Harvey with more regard for dialogue than for cinema. Peter O'Toole reprises the role he played four years earlier in *Becket*, that of Henry II, now some years older. Concerned about who to name as his successor to the crown, he spends a day haranguing it out with his three acknowledged male heirs, his exiled wife, his mistress, and her brother, the king of France. Katharine Hepburn, as the queen, won a Best Actress Oscar, but it's O'Toole who enlivens the film with his customary panache.

LIPSTICK ☆
1976, USA, R
Margaux Hemingway, Chris Sarandon, Perry King, Anne Bancroft, Mariel Hemingway. Directed by Lamont Johnson. 89 min.

This is trashy, sensational garbage in which talentless Margaux Hemingway plays a top fashion model who is pursued and then raped by a disturbed avant-garde musician (Chris Sarandon). After she goes after her kid sister (played by real-life kid sister Mariel), she guns him down in the parking lot, striking a blow for women's equality everywhere. It's hard to say which is worse: viewing the grueling rape scene repeatedly (thanks to trial sequence flashbacks) or being subjected to Dino De Laurentiis's *Death Wish* ideology, which caps this offensiveness. It's understandable that most of these dubiously talented folks would have made this exploitation picture, but why is Anne Bancroft involved? At one point, the rapist smears lipstick on the mirrors; you'll want to do the same to your TV screen while watching this junk.

LIQUID SKY ☆☆☆
1983, USA, R
Anne Carlisle, Paula Sheppard. Directed by Slava Tsukerman. 114 min.

This is a cool and self-conscious science-fiction oddity. Aliens who feed on the chemical byproduct of human orgasms and heroin highs, land, fortunately enough, on the roof of a Manhattan loft populated variously by rapists, drug addicts, trendsetters of various sexes and persuasions, and their voyeuristic entourages. It's informed by a brittle sense of humor and a weird veneer that barely conceals more weirdness. Russian émigré Slava Tsukerman portrays New York and its avant-garde subculture with an originality you may never see again—his eye for city life is at once jaundiced and full of gentle wonderment.

LISA AND THE DEVIL

See *Devil in the House of Exorcism*

LISBON ☆☆
1956, USA
Ray Milland, Maureen O'Hara, Claude Rains, Yvonne Furneaux, Francis Lederer. Directed by Ray Milland. 98 min.

This is a slow-moving adventure of international intrigue set in the Portuguese capital, produced and directed by star Ray Milland. He plays an American dilettante dabbling in smuggling who comes under the employ of evil Claude Rains. The story is predictable and, since Republic Pictures used Trucolor, the images are brilliantly and thoroughly artificial-looking.

LISTEN TO YOUR HEART ☆☆
1983, USA (TV)
Kate Jackson, Tim Matheson, Cassie Yates, George Coe, Will Nye, Tony Plana. Directed by Don Taylor. 100 min.

Listen to your common sense and skip this will-o'-the-wisp romance about two coworkers who fall in love in the Windy City. Scanty plot development and the debatable charms of Kate Jackson won't result in a scintillating romantic comedy for some viewers, but if you're in the mood for a light, nondemanding tête-à-tête between two attractive players, then ignore us and watch this. Any movie with sassy second banana Cassie Yates is worth catching.

THE LIST OF ADRIAN MESSENGER ☆☆½
1963, USA
George C. Scott, Dana Wynter, Clive Brook, Herbert Marshall, Kirk Douglas, Jacques Roux. Directed by John Huston. 98 min.

A witty adventure story about a retired British Intelligence officer (George C. Scott) tracking down a killer who is a master of disguise. The suspense mechanism never quite works, and the cameo stars—Tony Curtis, Robert Mitchum, Burt Lancaster, and Frank Sinatra—are so heavily disguised that they don't engage any interest. Clive Brook, quintessential Brit and silent screen star, came out of retirement for the movie, and he's always worth seeing. Although John Huston could handle spoof, as he proved with *Beat the Devil*, the timing here is just a hair off.

LISZTOMANIA ☆
1975, Great Britain, R
Roger Daltrey, Sara Kestleman, Paul Nicholas, Fiona Lewis. Directed by Ken Russell. 110 min.

This is a complete embarrassment from the ever-excessive hand of Ken Russell. Masquerading as a would-be biography of the Hungarian composer Franz Liszt, *Lisztomania* reimagines him as the first pop idol, complete with wild clothes and screaming groupies. Although Roger Daltrey of The Who is an apt casting choice, the concept would have trouble filling a five-minute revue sketch, and, stretched to feature length, it becomes intolerable. Worse yet, Russell ladles on fantasies of the most misogynistic sort, with profusions of gigantic concrete phalli, sluttish courtesans and Rick Wakeman's truly dreadful music. Russell's directorial style can be defended in almost any of his other films—here, there's just no excuse.

LITTLE BIG MAN ☆☆☆
1970, USA, PG
Dustin Hoffman, Faye Dunaway, Martin Balsam, Richard Mulligan, Chief Dan George, Jeff Corey. Directed by Arthur Penn. 147 min.

A sprawling, picaresque tragicomic Western about Jack Crabb, half-white, half-Indian, the only white survivor of the battle of Little Big Horn. In this adaptation of the National Book Award-winning novel by Thomas Berger, director Arthur Penn manages to capture Berger's ambivalences and bawdiness, but can't really do justice to the pro-Indian tone, although the remarkable performance of Chief Dan George helps. Dustin Hoffman gives a rich and searching performance as Crabb, who ages from adolescence to over 120 in the frame story. Richard Mulligan is also good as George Armstrong Custer, played here as an overblown loony.

LITTLE CAESAR ☆☆☆½
1930, USA
Edward G. Robinson, Douglas Fairbanks, Jr., Glenda Farrell, William Collier, Jr. Directed by Mervyn LeRoy. 77 min.

One of the first and most-imitated sound-era gangster films, *Little Caesar* and its morality tale of a mobster's rise and fall echo William Wellman's *Public Enemy* and Howard Hawks's *Scarface*, both of which have aged better. Burdened by drab, often static direction and somewhat perfunctory plotting, the film is notable only for Edward G. Robinson. His lively, inventive work as the power-mad thug Rico gives the character and film a psychological and sexual charge that keeps the tone of *Little Caesar* surprisingly modern over fifty years later.

LITTLE DARLINGS ☆
1980, USA, R
Kristy McNichol, Tatum O'Neal, Armand Assante, Matt Dillon, Maggie Blye. Directed by Ronald Maxwell. 95 min.

Troubled rich girl Tatum O'Neal and troubled poor girl Kristy McNichol compete to see who can lose her virginity first— along the way, they learn about life. The movie bullies you with its summer-camp frolicking, its bright, bright color, and all those nymphets in bikinis giving moral lessons to their elders. McNichol gives it a certain luster, though; her performance seems to be taking place in the half-formed feelings behind her face, which makes her a perfect embodiment of that unformed condition known as adolescence. What begins as a commentary on the exaggerated importance we still place on virginity ends in "wait till you're ready" platitudes that convey the opposite message. It's an offensive film with smug attitudes about sexuality so that all you're left with is semi-soft-core porn for the acne set. If you've ever dreamed of being shanghaied to a pajama party attended by horny teenage girls, then this is the movie for you.

THE LITTLE DRUMMER GIRL ☆☆
1984, USA, R
Diane Keaton, Klaus Kinski, Yorgo Voyagis. Directed by George Roy Hill. 130 min.

Though the relentless ambiguity of John LeCarre's world of weary spies is not impossible to render on film, it is difficult, and this adaptation is not a successful one. A miscast Diane Keaton in the role of a young actress seduced by the real-life theater of international espionage is a serious debit, and Klaus Kinski turns in a stylized caricature of a performance that might fit into some other film but is entirely out of place in this one. A classic example of interesting material crushed into a sorry state of dull lifelessness.

THE LITTLE FOXES ☆☆☆☆
1941, USA
Bette Davis, Herbert Marshall, Teresa Wright, Richard Carlson, Charles Dingle, Carl Benton Reid, Dan Duryea, Patricia Collinge, Jessie Grayson. Directed by William Wyler. 116 min.

Lillian Hellman's play about a family of greedy, calculating Southern aristocrats remains surprisingly fresh decades later, and William Wyler's adaptation of it plays better than the juiciest of prime-time soap operas. The dialogue is witty and acid (Dorothy Parker and Alan Campbell worked with Hellman on the screenplay), and Bette Davis's performance as Regina, the shrewdest, cruelest member of the clan, may be the best of her career; watching her here, you will realize why she is considered one of the great American screen actresses. She's ably supported by Teresa Wright and Patricia Collinge as, respectively, her good-hearted daughter and alcoholic sister-in-law, and by Herbert Marshall, who hits every emotion perfectly as her ailing husband. The film is still exemplary as an adaptation of a theatrical work, and great fun as well. Followed by a "prequel," *Another Part of the Forest* (1948).

THE LITTLE GIRL WHO LIVES DOWN THE LANE ☆☆
1976, USA/Canada/France, PG
Jodie Foster, Martin Sheen, Alexis Smith, Mort Shuman, Scott Jacoby. Directed by Nicolas Gessner. 94 min.

Strange little drawing-room horror film about a thirteen-year-old girl (Jodie Foster) living alone in her late father's house and killing the strangers who want to interfere. She's the good guy; the bad guys are an officious Mrs. Gulch type (Alexis Smith) and her child-molester son (Martin Sheen), who have their own ideas about how to bring up the girl. Jodie Foster is never uninteresting, even in the unlikeliest of roles, but this slow-moving Gothic isn't up to the talents of its cast, and the scares, with a couple of notable exceptions, are quite halfhearted. Laird Koenig, adapting his own novel, wrote the screenplay.

LITTLE HOUSE ON THE PRAIRIE ☆☆½
1974, USA (TV)
Michael Landon, Karen Grassle, Melissa Gilbert, Melissa Sue Anderson, Victor French. Directed by Michael Landon. 100 min.

This is a heartwarming film, and it became a long-running series, so fans will find this a welcome entry on their video shelves. Laura Ingalls Wilder based her popular series of children's books on the real-life experiences of her family, who journeyed from Wisconsin to the Kansas prairies after the Civil War. It's a touching slice of Americana for the show's fans, but a tolerance for saccharine and for Landon's telegraphed acting is required from cynics.

LITTLE LADIES OF THE NIGHT ☆☆
1977, USA (TV)
David Soul, Lou Gossett, Linda Purl, Clifton James, Carolyn Jones, Lana Wood, Kathleen Quinlan. Directed by Marvin Chomsky. 100 min.

An unconvincing exposé about the grimy nether world of teenage prostitution. Eschewing exploitation, the film focuses on a teenager who doesn't find understanding at home, but finds worse cruelty awaiting her when she runs away from home and falls into the hands of treacherous pimps. Unfortunately, the earnest acting can't make up for the typical sanitized TV-movie examination of street life. True, the intention is to reveal the plight of troubled teens rather than to milk interest in sleazy subject matters, but the urban horrors have to be palpable for this to work; they're not.

LITTLE LORD FAUNTLEROY ☆☆☆
1936, USA
Freddie Bartholomew, Dolores Costello, Guy Kibbee, Jessie Ralph, Mickey Rooney, C. Aubrey Smith. Directed by John Cromwell. 98 min.

A Brooklyn urchin softens hearts en route from rags to riches as he becomes heir to a British title. Independent of MGM, producer David O. Selznick converted Frances Hodgson Burnett's classic novel into a classic film. Freddie Bartholomew, who played David Copperfield for Selznick in 1935, is in the leading role again, but a stellar cast does justice to a gamut of colorful character sketches.

LITTLE LORD FAUNTLEROY ☆☆½
1980, USA (TV)
Alec Guinness, Ricky Schroder, Colin Blakely, Eric Porter, Rachel Kempson. Directed by Jack Gold. 100 min.

Superb production values and Alec Guinness's starchy elegance are the highlights of this version of the popular Frances Hodgson Burnett novel about the poverty-stricken tyke from America who inherits a magnificent estate in England. But if we had to choose between the unctuous manner of Freddie Bartholomew in the original film and the unbearable smarminess of Ricky Schroder in this remake, we'd hold out for Freddie. With a different child star in the lead role, this film might have been a superior production instead of just a passably good one.

LITTLE MAD GUY ☆☆☆
Simon Yun, Ng Ming Tsai, Fan Mui Sang, Tiger Yang. Directed by Singloy Wang.

This movie is a change of pace: a kung fu comedy. In this yarn, an overweight kung fu master attempts to capture a notorious bandit for the reward money. It's a funny, likable mixture of slapstick and martial arts, with excellent action footage.

LITTLE MEN ☆☆☆
1940, USA
Kay Francis, Jack Oakie, George Bancroft, Jimmy Lydon, Ann Gillis. Directed by Norman McLeod. 84 min.

One of Kay Francis's better vehicles from the later years of her film career. Based on the sequel to Louisa May Alcott's *Little Women* (given the big-budget classic treatment by MGM in 1933), this film, although it can't boast as stellar a cast or as big a budget as *Women*, has its own merits, not the least of which is Francis's no-nonsense portrayal of the grown-up Jo March, now running an orphanage for boys. The updating hasn't done much harm, and the sweet-tempered essence of Alcott's book shines through.

THE LITTLE MINISTER ☆☆☆
1934, USA
Katharine Hepburn, John Beal, Donald Crisp, Andy Clyde, Beryl Mercer. Directed by Richard Wallace. 110 min.

Lovely period piece made during the first flush of Hepburn's stardom at RKO. Based on the James M. Barrie tale about a Scottish minister who becomes smitten with a local lass, the film is refreshingly sentimental without ever becoming saccharine.

LITTLE MISS MARKER ☆☆☆
1934, USA
Shirley Temple, Adolphe Menjou, Dorothy Dell, Charles Bickford, Lynne Overman, Sam Hardy, Edward Earle. Directed by Alexander Hall. 78 min.

Shirley Temple fans will be thrilled to see the little moppet surrounded by one of her strongest stories. In this adaptation of a Damon Runyon work, Miss Marker is a little girl left as security for a debt owed to a bookie. When her father dies, she is suddenly the "property" of a whole gang of tough cookies and track rats. Producer B. P. Schulberg did a great job of packaging talent—the supporting players here, especially Adolphe Menjou and Charles Bickford, are golden, and Alexander Hall's direction is sure-handed and always focuses on Temple. Our favorite part: a glorious production number that is a low-life version of The Knights of the Round Table, with the boys and the Depression Darling singing "Sidewalks of New York."

LITTLE MISS MARKER ☆☆
1980, USA, PG
Walter Matthau, Julie Andrews, Tony Curtis, Bob Newhart, Lee Grant, Sara Stimson, Brian Dennehy. Directed by Walter Bernstein. 112 min.

Gifted screenwriter Walter Bernstein (*Semi-Tough*, *The Front*) chose for his directorial debut yet another version of Damon Runyon's square, sloshy classic about a bookie and an orphan. Whereas Adolphe Menjou and Shirley Temple were simpatico in the 1934 version, Walter Matthau and Sara Stimson are not. Add Julie Andrews as an icy heiress who somehow takes to Matthau, Tony Curtis as an epicene gangster, some extremely slow delivery, some disturbing innuendo about Stimson sharing Matthau's bed, and you end up with pretty sorrowful family entertainment. *Note*: Don't let the video distributors fool you; they have been marketing this film with cover art à la *The Sting*.

A LITTLE NIGHT MUSIC ☆☆½
1978, Austria/West Germany, PG
Elizabeth Taylor, Diana Rigg, Len Cariou, Lesley-Anne Down, Hermione Gingold, Christopher Guard. Directed by Harold Prince. 110 min.

A little less music might have helped this screen adaptation of Stephen Sondheim's musical (based on Ingmar Bergman's *Smiles of a Summer Night*). Hugh Wheeler's merry-go-round plot deals with the romantic follies of several Viennese upper crusts. Director Harold Prince is obviously paying homage to those sophisticated, "integrated" musicals of the 1950s (e.g., *Gigi*) by smoothly incorporating the songs into the narrative. His efforts are defeated by his own weak staging of the numbers, and by the poor musical performances of the cast. When Liz Taylor sings "Send in the Clowns," a very great song, you'll want to send in a vocal coach. Because its sources are a good musical and a superb film, this actually works overall, despite the many flaws.

THE LITTLE PRINCE ☆½
1974, USA, G
Steven Warner, Richard Kiley, Bob Fosse, Gene Wilder, Joss Ackland, Clive Revill, Donna McKechnie. Directed by Stanley Donen. 88 min.

Antoine de Saint-Exupery's classic children's parable gets the Stanley Donen-Lerner and Lowe treatment, becoming a cloying, wholly forgettable musical. The author's delicately constructed web of fantasy becomes thunderously overexplicit as soon as it's put on screen, and attempts to represent the story's more tangled allegory are laughable. Young, golden-locked Steven Warner is an amazingly accurate personification of the book's odd little illustrations, but he seems wan and sleepy throughout. Bob Fosse is an irresistible Snake; Gene Wilder is a *very* resistible Fox, who's made to mouth some of the movie's most saccharine platitudes. Parents with fond recollections of the melancholy tale may think their children will enjoy it on film. They won't.

THE LITTLE PRINCESS ☆☆½
1939, USA
Shirley Temple, Richard Greene, Anita Louise, Cesar Romero. Directed by Walter Lang. 95 min.

Shirley Temple's first color feature splashes her into this story of a little Victorian girl's search for her battle-victim father. No longer a tiny moppet, Shirley does an admirable job of acting, and has one of her best dance sequences, with lanky Arthur Treacher. The story is based on a well-known tearjerker, *Sara Crewe* by Frances Hodgson Burnett, and puts Shirley through some horrible degradations at the hands of cruel adults and heartless kids—consequently, some smaller children may find parts of the film upsetting. Look for Cesar Romero as the kindly Indian servant Ram Dass.

THE LITTLE RED SCHOOLHOUSE ☆☆
1936, USA
Frank Coghlan, Jr., Dickie Moore, Ann Doran, Lloyd Hughes, Corky. Directed by Charles Lamont. 64 min.

Because it relies heavily on the juvenile appeal of its now-obscure star, today's audience may have a little trouble getting involved in this movie. Junior Coghlan shot to fame as a four-year-old in silent films, and his freckle-faced boyishness kept him working through the 1920s and into the 1930s. By the time of this film, however, he was outgrowing these parts, and this morality fable about a boy who leaves home and school and becomes involved with big-city crooks would be hard to swallow with a seven-year-old Jackie Coogan in the lead. The movie is helmed by Universal veteran Charles Lamont—director of Abbott and Costello and a darling of certain French auteurists.

A LITTLE ROMANCE ☆☆½
1979, USA, PG
Laurence Olivier, Diane Lane, Thelonious Bernard, Arthur Hill, Sally Kellerman, David Dukes, Broderick Crawford. Directed by George Roy Hill. 108 min.

It's hard to be unkind to this frail little farce about a charming *bon vivant* who helps two youngsters elope. Unfortunately, the film is so wispy, it wilts away before it even gets started. Diane Lane plays the bored daughter of an American movie actress (Sally Kellerman) who falls for a French boy (Thelonious Bernard) while staying in Paris. Lane (in her debut) is more appealing here than in her later performances, but the real charm comes from the great Laurence Olivier as the boulevardier. Broderick Crawford plays himself in a cameo.

A LITTLE SEX ☆½
1982, USA, R
Tim Matheson, Kate Capshaw, Edward Herrmann, John Glover, Wallace Shawn, Joan Copeland. Directed by Bruce Paltrow. 94 min.

Poor Michael. He's good looking, successful, has a beautiful girlfriend . . . but the guy just can't restrain himself from having sex with every woman he meets. If this premise doesn't move you to instant sympathy, then the hero's predicament in *A Little Sex* probably won't keep you in thrall. The drab, humorless writing and yuppie cutout characters won't win any converts either, although the very pretty New York locations might. Tim Matheson and Kate Capshaw are attractive performers who don't try hard enough to overcome their material, but a few moments of sweetly offbeat interplay do emerge from this otherwise lead-footed comedy.

THE LITTLE SHOP OF HORRORS ☆☆☆½
1960, USA
Jonathan Haze, Jackie Joseph, Jack Nicholson, Mel Welles, Dick Miller, Myrtle Vail. Directed by Roger Corman. 70 min.

Roger Corman shot this black comedy in only a few days, but it's still one of his best pictures. A gigantic talking plant brings fame and fortune to its bookish owner, as long as the owner commits murder to feed it. Jack Nicholson has a frightfully funny cameo as a masochistic dentist's patient. Charles Griffith's clever screenplay was later adapted to the stage as a hit musical with the same title, which in turn was filmed in 1986.

LITTLE SHOP OF HORRORS ☆☆☆½
1986, USA, PG-13
Rick Moranis, Ellen Greene, Vincent Gardenia, Steve Martin, Jim Belushi, John Candy, Christopher Guest, Bill Murray, Tichina Arnold, Tisha Campbell, Michelle Weeks. voice of Levi Stubbs. Directed by Frank Oz. 88 min.

Former Muppeteer Frank Oz might strike many as an odd choice to direct a movie musical, but his snappy, sassy, and spirited adaptation of the Off-Broadway hit (which in turn was adapted from Roger Corman's 1960 cheapie) is a delightful surprise, one of the only screen musicals in recent years to keep you laughing and leave you humming. The picturesque rundown setting is, of course, Skid Row, where nebbish Seymour Krelborn (Rick Moranis) falls in love with ditsy blond bimbo-waif Audrey (the incomparable Ellen Greene) and names a feral-looking plant Audrey II in homage. The bizarre plant revitalizes business, but it's out for blood—human blood. The spoofy dialogue and tuneful songs (by Howard Ashman and Alan Menken) are just this side of camp, and from the first number, Oz's graceful style as a musical director is abundantly clear. With Steve Martin and Bill Murray in sidesplitting cameos as a sadistic dentist–cum–Elvis impersonator and his masochistic patient ("I need a root canal . . . a long, slow root canal," Murray sighs), spectacular sets by Roy Walker, and a doo-wopping girl group chorus named Crystal, Chiffon, and Ronette to comment on the action.

LITTLE TREASURE ☆
1985, USA, R
Margot Kidder, Ted Danson, Burt Lancaster. Directed by Alan Sharp. 97 min.

The mystery isn't why Tri-Star, a subsidiary of the Coca-Cola Company chose to shelve this numbing comedy-drama, but why it was made at all—it doesn't have a single appealing, let alone marketable, aspect. Margot Kidder plays a stripper who journeys to Mexico for a brief reunion with her father (Burt Lancaster); after his death, she hooks up with a traveling projectionist (Ted Danson) to search for the money her dad supposedly buried in a ghost town decades ago. Writer-director Alan Sharp tries to point up the pathetic desperation of their small, hopeless lives with painful exchanges like: "I'm close to the edge." "Oh yeah? We're *all* close to the edge." This being a Tri-Star film, when its characters walk that edge, they usually find a nice cold can of Coca-Cola there; it would be a reprehensible example of art-as-advertisement if more than twelve people had seen the film.

LITTLE WOMEN ☆☆☆☆
1933, USA
Katharine Hepburn, Joan Bennett, Frances Dee, Paul Lukas, Douglass Montgomery, Spring Byington, Edna May Oliver. Directed by George Cukor. 115 min.

This is one of the many literary classics that were turned into cinematic greats by producer David O. Selznick. Fine performances (particularly by young Hepburn as the noble Jo March), teamed effectively with George Cukor's straightforward style of directing, bring to life Louisa May Alcott's inspirational chronicle of family life during the Civil War.

LIVE AND LET DIE ☆☆½
1973, Great Britain, R
Roger Moore, Jane Seymour, Yaphet Kotto. Directed by Guy Hamilton. 121 min.

The previous non-Sean Connery Bond film, *On Her Majesty's Secret Service*, had been atypically serious and a failure. The introduction of the new James Bond, Roger Moore, meant a new tone for the series. *Live and Let Die* is the first one to be more comedic than suspenseful. Moore's lightweight condescending attitude infects the film with a sense of boredom early in the story, although the actor delivers his *bon mots* competently. This one has more locations than action, but the sidetrack into a Southern sheriff character proved popular.

LIVES OF A BENGAL LANCER ☆☆☆½
1935, USA
Gary Cooper, Franchot Tone, Richard Cromwell, Sir Guy Standing, C. Aubrey Smith, Monte Blue, Kathleen Burke. Directed by Henry Hathaway. 110 min.

This adventure on the grand scale set in a British badlands military school embellishes the melodramatic account of distrust between a father and son with lots of local flavor and exotic locations. Gary Cooper and Franchot Tone set out to rescue a colonel's son after he's kidnapped by a local tribal leader named Mohammed Khan. Tone's light comic style prevents the melodrama from overwhelming the film, and the fast action, particularly in the explosive battle scene, disguises any narrative improbability. There's an ingenious mixture of comedy, adventure, drama, and travelogue that swells the proportions of this film and certifies it as classic cinema. If you thought *Raiders of the Lost Ark* did it all, check out these lives.

LIVING FREE ☆☆
1972, Great Britain, G
Susan Hampshire, Nigel Davenport, Geoffrey Keen, Peter Lukoya. Directed by Jack Couffer. 91 min.

This sequel to *Born Free* lacks the emotional power and graceful storytelling of the first film, but if you loved the story of Elsa, you may want to see the slightly soggy follow-up that recounts the efforts of Joy and George Adamson (now played by Susan Hampshire and Nigel Davenport) to raise Elsa's three cubs. Children will be bored by the overemphasis on tedious adult plot lines, but the African scenery is still beautiful and the lions themselves are charismatic performers.

LOCAL HERO ☆☆☆☆
1983, Great Britain
Peter Riegert, Burt Lancaster, Fulton MacKay, Denis Lawson, Norman Chancer, Peter Capaldi, Jenny Seagrove. Directed by Bill Forsyth. 111 min.

Bill Forsyth, Scotland's foremost filmmaker, wrote and directed this delightful, offbeat comedy about a Texas oil executive sent to a coastal village in Scotland to purchase the drilling rights for his company. Forsyth fills this alternately joyous and melancholy fantasy with Capraesque images, surrealistic touches, and echoes of *Brigadoon*. The film—perhaps the finest work from this highly original and talented young director—casts a warm and magical spell. The only drawback is that when the reels stop spinning, we're forced to leave Forsyth's enchanted celluloid universe.

THE LOCH NESS HORROR ½☆
1982, USA, PG
Barry Buchanan, Miki McKenzie, Sandy Kenyon, Eric Scott. Directed by Larry Buchanan. 93 min.

The horror element in this film is as questionable as the existence of the beast itself. The illusive monster just happens to surface when some local poachers attempt to capture it and then wreaks a justifiable havoc on those who crossed its troubled waters. With movies like this, it's no wonder the real thing prefers to lead a solitary life.

THE LODGER ☆☆☆
1926, Great Britain
Ivor Novello, Marie Ault, Arthur Chesney, Malcolm Keen. Directed by Alfred Hitchcock. 91 min.

Hitchcock had his first major success with this highly enjoyable mystery-thriller. Fresh from working at UFA (Erich Pommer's German production company), Hitchcock returned to his native England to direct and cowrite this by-now-familiar tale of a mysterious boarder who is suspected of being Jack the Ripper. It's a plot Hitch would elaborate on later and better in *The 39 Steps*, *Suspicion*, and *Frenzy*. Stylistically, there are stilted moments, but already the master was beginning to experiment (note the transparent ceiling sequence) and seems to have picked up some hot tips from his German Expressionist forebears (Murnau, Pabst, Lang); a good start by one of cinema's greatest storytellers. (a.k.a.: *The Phantom Fiend* and *The Case of Jonathan Drew*)

LOGAN'S RUN ☆☆☆
1976, USA, PG
Michael York, Richard Jordan, Jenny Agutter, Peter Ustinov, Farrah Fawcett-Majors. Directed by Michael Anderson. 120 min.

An ambitious and fairly successful look at a post-nuclear future where, in order to control the population, no one is allowed to live past thirty. To enforce this rule, "sandmen" terminate those who try to escape their fate. One of these police officers is recruited to find a reputed sanctuary for the "runners," and discovers the world outside of his dome. A good pace and some spectacular action sequences keep things moving along. Notable for its excellent, glittery set design (most of the interiors were shot at a shopping mall), this is one of the money-making sci-fi pictures that paved the way for *Star Wars*.

LOLITA ☆☆☆☆
1962, Great Britain
James Mason, Shelley Winters, Peter Sellers, Sue Lyon. Directed by Stanley Kubrick. 152 min.

Stanley Kubrick managed to transfer most of the story of *Lolita* to the screen, but his version sacrifices most of the wit of Nabokov's savage, cartoonish original in favor of a sweeter, more human tone. James Mason is extraordinary as Humbert Humbert, the pedophile with a yen for the provocative nymphet Lolita. The actor suggests a type of ruined greatness which is in direct opposition to the nonentity that Humbert really is, but it must be stressed that his performance is full of passion and a painful self-mockery that is unflinching and brutally funny. Shelley Winters, as Lolita's mother, has been restrained and directed by Kubrick into what is probably her best performance—the only one that exploits and blends her somewhat dull serious-actress persona with the blowsy-broad aspect of her talent. The role is closest to the novel's original conception and Winters benefits from some astounding jokes. She even surpasses Nabokov's original in her depiction of horror in the awakening of Humbert's true passion. Sue Lyon is less spectacular in scope but deeper and more sympathetic. This Lolita is tempting without being repulsively condescending, and her fate, Kubrick's biggest switch from the novel, is deserved in this context. If anything seems out of place in Kubrick's sad, whispery world, it is Peter Sellers as Lolita's seductive joker. Sellers plays the book's insanity for all he's worth; it isn't his fault that he is diminished by the others' emotive performances.

THE LONELIEST RUNNER ☆☆½
1976, USA (TV)
Lance Kerwin, Brian Keith, DeAnn Mears, Melissa Sue Anderson, Michael Landon. Directed by Michael Landon. 90 min.

A TV movie unusual in that its subject is chronic teenage bedwetting. Lance Kerwin sensitively plays a youth who is taunted and punished by his parents, especially his wicked mother, for dampening his sheets at night. Based on writer/producer/director and costar Michael Landon's own childhood experiences, it's a combination of *Mommie Dearest* and *Chariots of Fire* as the young boy grows up to be an Olympic gold medal runner (played by Landon). It is incredible that even Landon, who must have had a lot of clout at NBC in 1976, could get this "poor me" childhood revenge fantasy on the air. It is even more incredible that, in 1984, he could finance a barely released theatrical remake called *Sam's Son*, with himself again writing, directing, and playing himself as a grown-up. How many more trips back to his obviously painful past must audiences endure?

LONELY ARE THE BRAVE ☆☆☆
1962, USA
Kirk Douglas, Walter Matthau, Gena Rowlands, Michael Kane, Carroll O'Connor, William Schallert, George Kennedy. Directed by David Miller. 107 min.

Another "Death of the Western" Western, but this time done with more attention to character than is usual. Kirk

Douglas plays an old hell-raising cowboy who returns to his homestead in New Mexico and finds himself at immediate odds with the demands of modern life. This is one of Douglas's best roles ever, and he plays it in a deceptive way that almost masks death with humor. Even so, Walter Matthau steals the show, as usual, as the sheriff who hunts him down after he engineers a jailbreak.

THE LONELY GUY ☆☆½
1984, USA, R
Steve Martin, Charles Grodin, Judith Ivey, Steve Lawrence, Robyn Douglass, Merv Griffin, Dr. Joyce Brothers. Directed by Arthur Hiller. 90 min.

A prime example of too many cooks spoiling the broth. Bruce Jay Friedman's hilarious collection of essays—a neurotic Jewish guide to life for the unwilling single male—is herein adapted by Neil Simon, turned into a screenplay by Stan Daniels and Ed Weinberger (of "The Mary Tyler Moore Show") for a film starring Steve Martin and Charles Grodin and directed by Arthur Hiller; all of the above tear this in different ways, and the film lurches wildly between some marvelously surreal and touching moments and the most awful, leaden sitcom plot complications. At its best, this is not just another dumb Steve Martin comedy but—well, a *smart* Steve Martin comedy, with a Chaplinesque quality that makes you laugh at scenes that you could as easily cry at. Forget the plot, see this to enjoy the first half, with veteran "L.G." Charles Grodin showing Martin the tricks of survival for a single guy in the big city, but turn it off halfway through to spare yourself an awful performance by Judith Ivey and a long, labored parody of the ending of *The Graduate*.

LONELY HEARTS ☆☆☆
1981, Australia, R
Wendy Hughes, Norman Kaye, Jon Finlayson, Julia Blake, Jonathan Hardy. Directed by Paul Cox. 95 min.

This offbeat romantic comedy from Australia chronicles a love affair between two vulnerable misfits, a piano tuner and an office worker, who meet through a computer dating service. The award-winning performances of Wendy Hughes and Norman Kaye breathe life into a film occasionally marred by Paul Cox's heavy-handed direction. Cox wrote the film's unusual, often amusing screenplay.

THE LONELY LADY ½☆
1983, USA, R
Pia Zadora, Lloyd Bochner, Bibi Besch, Joseph Cali, Jared Martin. Directed by Peter Sasdy. 92 min.

Don't be misled by critics who said this was merely a dull Bad Movie; this is a terrific BAD MOVIE, deserving of inclusion in that privileged pantheon of trash headed by *Valley of the Dolls* and *The Carpetbaggers*. If you can't get enough cheap thrills picking up a tabloid in your local supermarket, then let Pia Zadora's character sleep her way into your heart. Here, the starlet is really a budding authoress who, en route to creating a prizewinning and highly symbolic and meaningful screenplay about the human condition, marries an impotent screenwriter who pilfers her ideas, and leaves her unsatisfied nymphet's body ripe for seduction by a randy stud, who impregnates her and then ditches her. It's inevitable that she become a cocaine-addicted slut and suffer a breakdown that is a complete surprise to her harried mother (who insists there's never been any of that mental stuff on her side of the family).

THE LONE RANGER ☆☆½
1956, USA
Clayton Moore, Jay Silverheels, Lyle Bettger, Douglas Kennedy, Charles Watts. Directed by Stuart Heisler. 86 min.

This was the big-screen version of the small-screen hit. In the 1950s, it was the ultimate salute to a TV show if it managed to rate a wide-screen theatrical feature. As Westerns go, this is a lackadaisical oater; it's possible to get just as much bang out of TV reruns. Still, Tonto is here to speak pidgin English, and Silver is here to whinny majestically, and the Ranger's here to uphold the Western code of honor. This true American folk hero and his adventures are appealing and exciting enough to interest any kemosabe.

LONE WOLF MCQUADE ☆½
1983, USA, PG
Chuck Norris, David Carradine, Barbara Carrera, Leon Isaac Kennedy, Robert Carver. 105 min.

Chuck Norris is the good guy, David Carradine is the bad guy, and there are some other characters who fill in the time until the climactic big fight. Come on, you can't really *hate* a Chuck Norris movie; they're too dumb to take seriously, and they deliver just what they promise in the most economical fashion.

LONG AGO TOMORROW

See *The Raging Moon*

THE LONG DARK HALL ☆☆½
1951, Great Britain
Rex Harrison, Lilli Palmer, Tania Heald, Henrietta Barry, Anthony Dawson, Denis O'Dea. Directed by Anthony Bushell. 86 min.

An innocent married man is accused of and tried for the murder of a showgirl. The audience is tipped off early on as to the identity of the real killer, so the suspense here is in watching the web of circumstantial evidence being drawn shut around the accused. However, you never really believe that an eventual happy ending is ever jeopardized. Rex Harrison is interesting in a different sort of role for him.

LONG DAY'S JOURNEY INTO NIGHT ☆☆☆☆
1962, USA
Katharine Hepburn, Sir Ralph Richardson, Dean Stockwell, Jason Robards, Jr. Directed by Sidney Lumet. 136 min.

Sidney Lumet's grim film of what is perhaps the greatest American play is graced by the luminous performances of a flawless ensemble. (They were awarded a joint acting prize at the Cannes Film Festival.) Some have quibbled over the staginess of the presentation here, but the close-ups and restricted camerawork enhance the feeling of claustrophobia. Never has a film so clearly grasped the pain of a family's disintegration; the human failures and the recriminations build to such an impact that audiences are wiped out by the end of this demanding film. It's Hepburn's greatest dramatic performance, despite all her later Oscars. Even those who claim she's miscast here do not deny the extraordinary power she brings to the role of the genteel mother who's become a drug addict. There is sterling support from Ralph Richardson as the second-rate stage ham, Jason Robards as the alcoholic wastrel, and Dean Stockwell as the playwright's surrogate. This is a great film of Eugene O'Neill's finest play.

THE LONG DAYS OF SUMMER ☆☆
1980, USA (TV)
Dean Jones, Joan Hackett, Ronnie Scribner, Louanne, Donald Moffat, Andrew Duggan, David Baron. Directed by Dan Curtis. 78 min.

A sequel of sorts to the 1978 TV film *When Every Day Was the Fourth of July*, this is a formulaic period piece about a Jewish family suffering under the prejudices of a WASPy Northeastern town during the 1930s. Producer-director Dan Curtis has the right details and atmosphere for this semiautobiographical reminiscence, but the drama never catches fire. There is a good performance by Dean Jones, the only cast member from the first film, as the father.

THE LONGEST DAY ☆☆½
1962, USA
John Wayne, Robert Mitchum, Henry Fonda, Robert Ryan, Rod Steiger, Robert Wagner, Paul Anka, Fabian, Mel Ferrer, Tommy Sands, Eddie Albert, Jeffrey Hunter, Peter Lawford, Richard Burton, Sean Connery, Roddy McDowall. Directed by Andrew Marton, Ken Annakin, Bernhard Wicki, Darryl F. Zanuck (uncredited). 169 min.

The longest movie. Darryl F. Zanuck's interminable epic about the D day invasion by the Allied forces is a good film if you enjoy watching an all-star cast grenade each other in Cinemascope. The first half, depicting the French, German, British, and American preparations, is chock full of unconvincing representations of famed military leaders (Roosevelt, Eisenhower, Rommel, et al). The second half gets down to business and does not disappoint. Unfortunately, home viewers will miss the impact of the battle scenes on video. Still, Richard Burton and Robert Mitchum stand out in the cargo of stars, and Zanuck's intentions seem honorable enough. Directorial credit goes to Andrew Marton, Ken Annakin, and Bernhard Wicki, but Zanuck reportedly directed more than half of the film. Screenplay by Cornelius Ryan, based on his own book.

THE LONGEST YARD ☆☆☆
1974, USA, R
Burt Reynolds, Eddie Albert, Michael Conrad, Ed Lauter, Bernadette Peters. Directed by Robert Aldrich. 125 min.

Burt Reynolds fans will enjoy this prison yarn that finds Reynolds as a pro football star sent to prison on a trumped-up charge. Once there, he gets caught in the machinations of the typically corrupt warden (Eddie Albert, who oozes villainy) and plays in a climactic guards-vs.-prisoners football game. It's all pretty silly, with some jarring moments of violence, but overall this is a crowd pleaser.

THE LONG GOOD FRIDAY ☆☆☆½
1980, Great Britain, R
Bob Hoskins, Helen Mirren, Dave King, Eddie Constantine, George Coulouris. Directed by John Mackenzie. 114 min.

The performance of Bob Hoskins, who looks like Phil Collins after an overdose of Dr. Jekyll's Wonder Tonic, as a reigning London mobster, is reason enough to see this powerful British gangster film. On the eve of a major deal with the Mafia to finance a casino he wants to build, Hoskins finds his holdings and underlings being inexplicably blown up, and sets out to find out why. His Harold Shand is that rarity of movie bad guys, one that can evoke understanding and even sympathy without becoming a likeable or desirable character. The supporting cast is excellent as well, especially Helen Mirren as Shand's mistress, a woman who maintains her position through brains and beauty.

THE LONG HOT SUMMER ☆☆☆½
1958, USA
Paul Newman, Joanne Woodward, Orson Welles, Anthony Franciosa, Lee Remick, Angela Lansbury. Directed by Martin Ritt. 117 min.

A fiery screen adaptation of two William Faulkner stories, plus his novel *The Hamlet*, all blended together into an actors' field day. There's no replacement for star power, as exemplified by Welles's performance as a Southern landowner who hires a drifter (Paul Newman) with a bad reputation, a man he hopes will marry his intellectual daughter (Joanne Woodward) and someday share in his fortune. Naturally, Welles's weak-willed wastrel of a son isn't keen on sharing his legacy with an alleged barn-burning wanderer. This is a zesty melodrama, superior to the 1985 TV remake that starred Don Johnson and Judith Ivey in Newman and Woodward's roles.

LONG JOHN SILVER ☆☆½
1954, Australia
Robert Newton, Kit Taylor, Connie Gilchrist, Eric Reiman, Syd Chambers, John Brunskill, Harry Hambleton, Rod Taylor. Directed by Byron Haskin. 106 min.

More rousing pirate adventures, with Robert Newton once again chewing up the scenery in this sequel to the 1950 *Treasure Island*. The usual action and roguery abounds, with Master Jim Hawkins again sharing the ride with the one-legged cook, here promoted to captain, but Newton is the whole show and he knows it. With a young Rod Taylor, here billed as "Rodney."

LONG JOURNEY BACK ☆☆½
1978, USA (TV)
Mike Connors, Cloris Leachman, Stephanie Zimbalist, Katy Kurtzman, Howard McGillin, Nicolas Coster. Directed by Mel Damski. 100 min.

This is a moist-eyed but effectively "inspirational" TV drama about a teenage girl who must fight to rebuild her body and spirit after a horrible bus accident nearly kills her. Good performances from veterans Mike Connors and Cloris Leachman as her parents and from Stephanie Zimbalist as the spirited teen who won't let herself give in to misery make this highly watchable, though no less predictable.

THE LONG RIDERS ☆☆☆
1980, USA, R
David Carradine, Keith Carradine, Robert Carradine, James Keach, Stacy Keach, Dennis Quaid, Randy Quaid, Christopher Guest, Nicholas Guest, Kevin Brophy, Harry Carey, Jr., Pamela Reed, James Remar. Directed by Walter Hill. 98 min.

Walter Hill's somber Western has stunning cinematography by Ric Waite, passages of beautifully choreographed gunplay and an appropriately elegiac mood, plus one great casting/concept coup: actors who are real-life siblings play the legendary outlaw brothers. The Keaches are Jesse and Frank James, the Carradines are the Younger gang, and so on. Unfortunately, there's not enough going on in the way of a plot to make it a great movie: the screen is too cluttered with historical cameos and self-consciously mythic moments. Hill is the modern master of the tough-guy movie, and he gets the 1880s ambience right without romanticizing his heroes, but the staging is static and finally dull. The Keaches come off best in the large cast—not surprisingly, since they cowrote the screenplay with Bill Bryden and Steven Philip Smith.

THE LONG VOYAGE HOME ☆☆☆☆
1940, USA
John Wayne, Thomas Mitchell, Ian Hunter, Barry Fitzgerald, John Qualen, Wilfred Lawson, Mildred Natwick, Ward Bond, Joseph Sawyer. Directed by John Ford. 103 min.

This is an episodic film following the lives of a group of seamen on a tramp steamer carrying a load of explosives across the Atlantic Ocean. Regular John Ford scenarist Dudley Nichols adapted this from four one-act plays by Eugene O'Neill, but the overall concerns are typical of Ford—the feel of male camaraderie and the sense of community. The cast plays as an ensemble, and is uniformly excellent, as is the striking photography of Gregg Toland.

A LONG WAY HOME ☆☆☆
1981, USA (TV)
Timothy Hutton, Brenda Vaccaro, George Dzundza, Paul Regina, Rosanna Arquette, John Lehne. Directed by Robert Markowitz. 100 min.

A stunning and unpretentious performance by Tim Hutton (before he found his Oscar and an overabundance of self-awareness as an actor) sets off this heart-tugging tale of a teen searching for his brother and sister, who'd been placed in different foster homes earlier. Hutton is extremely moving as he tries to reunite a family his parents callously lost interest in; and Brenda Vaccaro matches his intensity as a caring outsider who tries to make the bureaucratic system work for him.

LOOK BACK IN ANGER ☆☆☆
1958, USA
Richard Burton, Claire Bloom, Edith Evans, Mary Ure, Donald Pleasance. Directed by Tony Richardson. 99 min.

Imagine a point in the history of British theater when it was possible to shock audiences by having a realistic scene layed out in front of an ironing board, and you will have *Look Back in Anger* in context. John Osborne's celebrated play is well-filmed by Tony Richardson with Richard Burton as Jimmy Porter, temperamental market stall holder and first of the British angry young men.

LOOKER ☆☆½
1981, USA, PG
Albert Finney, James Coburn, Susan Dey, Leigh Taylor-Young. Directed by Michael Crichton. 94 min.

Director Michael Crichton's high-tech thrillers started to get just a little ridiculous with this nonsensical, but nonetheless dazzling combination of mind-controlling computers, laser guns, and murdered models. Albert Finney plays a plastic surgeon who is drawn into this craziness, and finds a plot to zap television audiences with hypnotic advertisements. Everything looks great and is a lot of fun to watch, but it's an experience akin to playing a videogame. One of the progenitors of Crichton's later, overly stylized pictures (*Runaway*, for example).

LOOKING FOR MR. GOODBAR ☆☆☆
1977, USA, R
Diane Keaton, Tuesday Weld, William Atherton, Richard Kiley, Richard Gere, Tom Berenger. Directed by Richard Brooks. 135 min.

A harrowing morality play about singles bars and the perils of promiscuity. Adapting Judith Rossner's novel, director Richard Brooks has played up the split personality of protagonist Terry Dunn, a schoolteacher by day who cruises New York's low-life watering holes in search of semi-anonymous sex. That she ends up meeting Mr. Wrong will come as no surprise—*Goodbar* telegraphs the punishment it has in store for its heroine early on. What makes the rather vicious tale work is the conviction with which Brooks delineates his story's ugly milieu. There's also fine acting from Diane Keaton (at the time, it was overshadowed by her near-simultaneous appearance in *Annie Hall*), and from Tuesday Weld, Oscar-nominated as her unstable sister. *Goodbar* also marks Richard Gere's first major screen appearance, and one of his better performances.

THE LOOKING GLASS WAR ☆½
1970, Great Britain
Christopher Jones, Pia Degermark, Ralph Richardson, Anthony Hopkins, Paul Rogers. Directed by Frank Pierson. 108 min.

A John LeCarre novel is turned into a tepid spy thriller you'll want to leave out in the cold. Christopher Jones risks attractive life and limb to take some pictures of a rocket hidden behind the Iron Curtain. There's the usual predictable double-dealing, and a stiff-upper-lip British cast of supporting players float in the vacuum created by Jones and leading lady Pia Degermark, who pose with great self-assurance and act with little conviction.

LOOKIN' TO GET OUT ☆½
1982, USA, R
Jon Voight, Ann-Margret, Burt Young, Bert Remsen, Jude Farese, Allen Keller. Directed by Hal Ashby. 105 min.

After peaking with 1978's *Coming Home*, director Hal Ashby hit a long downhill stretch that he has yet to pull out of. Star Jon Voight cowrote this abysmal story about two New York bozos who head to Las Vegas to make a killing. The only interesting thing about the entire film is its depiction of Vegas as a universe unto itself, with its own laws and codes of behavior. Voight seems to have borrowed all of his mannerisms and his accent from costar Burt Young. This is the worst movie about gambling until *Fever Pitch* came along.

LOOSE SHOES ☆½
1980, USA
Bill Murray, Howard Hesseman, David Landsburg, Ed Lauter, Susan Tyrrell. Directed by Ira Miller. 74 min.

And the filmmakers trip all over them. This is one of those smart-alecky send-ups of movies—not as good as *Kentucky Fried Movie* and not as bad as *National Lampoon Goes to the Movies*. A grab bag of preview parodies, with some funny standouts like "Skateboarders from Hell." Watch "SCTV" or "Not Necessarily the News" instead, if you want some genuinely funny ribbing of Hollywood's lesser achievements. (a.k.a.: *Coming Attractions*)

LORD JIM ☆☆½
1965, USA
Peter O'Toole, Eli Wallach, James Mason, Curt Jurgens, Paul Lukas, Jack Hawkins. Directed by Richard Brooks. 154 min.

As a Saturday matinee adventure tale in the forties, this would have been reasonably good, but it's supposed to be an adaptation of Joseph Conrad's famous novel. Once again, Richard Brooks (*The Brothers Karamazov* and *Something of Value*) captures great moments from the plot and sweeps the story along energetically, but all psychological dimensions and deeper meanings are either obscured or jettisoned. In fact, when Peter O'Toole actually tries to act, he seems out of place in this tale of a young seafarer who can never quite pull his life together after he is branded as a coward. Not bad, but it's not Conrad's book by a long shot.

LORD OF THE RINGS ☆½
1978, USA, PG
Animated: Christopher Guard, William Squire, John Hurt, Michael Sholes, Dominic Guard. Directed by Ralph Bakshi. 133 min.

Strictly for fans of the J. R. R. Tolkien trilogy upon which this is based, although even they will be disappointed—this covers about half of the three books and ends abruptly; the sequel, which was to have comprised the remainder of the story, never materialized. Nonfans, or those who haven't read the books, will have no idea what is going on amid the mass of bizarre characters in this impenetrable fantasy about a quest for a ring that provides enormous but corrupting power. Ralph Bakshi's Rotoscoping process of animation provides some interesting effects, though it more often looks as if he has merely traced over stills of actual actors, which is essentially what the process involves.

THE LORDS OF DISCIPLINE ☆☆½
1983, USA, R
David Keith, Robert Prosky, Mark Breland, G. D. Spradlin, Rick Rossovich, Michael Biehn, Barbara Babcock, Mitchell Lichtenstein, Judge Reinhold, Bill Paxton. Directed by Franc Roddam. 103 min.

Racism in a Southern military academy is the subject of this familiar melodrama, made compelling by a roster of fine young actors. Mark Breland plays the academy's first black cadet, who becomes the target of harassment and intimidation by a group known as "The Ten," who want to scare him out of the school. Military schools and their attendant codes of behavior have been somewhat overworked in recent years; if you liked *Taps* or TV's *Dress Gray*, this may be for you.

THE LORDS OF FLATBUSH ☆☆
1974, USA, PG
Perry King, Henry Winkler, Sylvester Stallone, Paul Mace, Susan Blakely, Maria Smith, Paul Jabara. Directed by Stephen F. Verona and Martin Davidson. 85 min.

This is passable but dull 1950s nostalgia made on the heels of *American Graffiti*. The Lords are four Brooklyn high school seniors who like to hang out, skip school, make out, fool around, hang out, skip school . . . The sitcom writing and slack direction keep the film's motor idling, but the three principals, seen here before they became stars, provide some nice character touches. For a much wiser look at the same era, see *The Wanderers*.

LOSIN' IT ☆☆
1982, USA, R
Tom Cruise, Jack Earle Haley, Shelley Long, John Stockwell, John P. Navin, Jr. Directed by Curtis Hanson. 104 min.

The fortuitous casting of Tom Cruise and Shelley Long just before their big breakthroughs (his in *Risky Business*, hers in TV's "Cheers") can't really save but does enliven this run-of-the-mill sex comedy about four teens on the loose in Tijuana. Both actors give sensitive performances, and Long in particular makes a valiant attempt, largely successful, to keep her role from turning into cliché. But the all-too-familiar antics of desperately shed virginity and farcically stuffed underpants define the film and its intended audience.

LOST AND FOUND ☆½
1979, USA, PG
Glenda Jackson, George Segal, Maureen Stapleton, Hollis McLaren, John Cunningham, Paul Sorvino. Directed by Melvin Frank. 112 min.

If you find this, lose it. Even if you like *A Touch of Class*, you'll be disappointed by this reteaming of the schticky George Segal and the brittle Glenda Jackson in a romantic comedy about a mismatch. The film's rife with pratfalls and burned-out one-liners. A cute widow and a college professor meet at a ski resort and make the mistake of marrying. Graded "D."

THE LOST HONOR OF KATHERINA BLUM ☆☆☆
1975, West Germany, R
Angela Winkler, Mario Adorf, Dieter Laser, Heinz Bennent. Directed by Volker Schlondorff and Margarethe von Trotta. 97 min.

A young woman's life is destroyed by the emotional brutality of the police and the scandal press after she unknowingly spends the night with a fugitive, in a compelling if not entirely successful adaptation of Heinrich Boll's labyrinthine novel. Boll's storytelling created a deceptively random patchwork of characters and events, building to a devastating finale in which every plot line converged. The film can't achieve that shattering cumulative effect, but it does offer a finely nuanced central performance by Angela Winkler, and inspired, surprisingly seamless team direction that works to moving effect. *Note*: The videocassette version is nine minutes shorter than the original release; the film was skillfully remade for American television in 1984 as *The Lost Honor of Kathryn Beck*.

THE LOST HONOR OF KATHRYN BECK

See *Act of Passion*

LOST IN AMERICA ☆☆☆½
1984, USA, R
Albert Brooks, Julie Hagerty, Maggie Roswell, Garry Marshall. Directed by Albert Brooks. 91 min.

In this meandering, episodic comedy showcasing director-actor Albert Brooks's smarmy persona, a hot young advertising executive and his wife liquidate their assets, buy a monster Winnebago, and set out to explore the America that they missed out on seeing during their single-minded pursuit of financial success. It seemed like a good idea at the time. This is a deadpan comedy of contemporary American manners; acerbic, understated, and ideally suited to small-screen viewing.

LOST IN THE STARS ☆
1974, USA, G
Brock Peters, Melba Moore, Raymond St. Jacques, Clifton Davis, Paul Rogers, Paulene Myers, Paula Kelly, Alan Weeks. Directed by Daniel Mann. 114 min.

This Kurt Weill-Maxwell Anderson musical was a fragile construction to begin with—a Broadway operetta with the unlikely subject of South African racial violence. Anderson's book is awkward, but considering the excellence of Weill's score and the timeliness of the material, this film adaptation is a huge disappointment. Stylized, threadbare, overacted, and undersung, it brings out the worst aspects of the stage version while hiding all of its virtues. The awful choreography, leaden pace, and ineptitude of the sung sections all suggest the work of filmmakers who know absolutely nothing about musical theater. The film was originally presented as part of the American Film Theater series, which abruptly and understandably terminated after this was released.

THE LOST KUNG FU SECRET ☆½
Hong Kong
David Chaing, Tsai Hung, Hon Fong, Hu Gun, Chiang Choug. Directed by Joe Law.

During the Ching Dynasty, a corrupt warlord attempts to use Christianity to control the people and take over the country. David Chaing plays a patriot attempting to unmask the warlord's underling (Tsai Hung). This is a better-than-average production with location shooting, attractive costumes, and plenty of fighting. Chaing, especially, is in top form, though his acting skills have not quite kept pace with his martial arts development.

THE LOST MOMENT ☆☆☆
1947, USA
Robert Cummings, Susan Hayward, Agnes Moorehead, Joan Lorring, Eduardo Ciannelli. Directed by Martin Gabel. 89 min.

A solid, intriguing drama based on Henry James's novella *The Aspern Papers* and put together by some of the impressive talents of Orson Welles's radio troupe, the Mercury Players—Martin Gabel (this was his only directorial effort), screenwriter Leonardo Bercovici, and actress Agnes Moorehead (with an extraordinary makeup job here as a 105-year-old woman). Publisher Robert Cummings, seeking some love letters written by a long-dead poet to Miss Moorehead, travels to her mansion in Venice and becomes involved with Susan Hayward, her psychotic niece. The film is not a total success, and it is occasionally murky, but, on the whole, it's well done.

THE LOST SQUADRON ☆☆☆
1932, USA
Richard Dix, Mary Astor, Erich Von Stroheim, Joel McCrea, Robert Armstrong. Directed by George Archainbaud. 72 min.

A spellbinding action film that is only a bit stiff in the joints after all these years. With a top-notch cast, *Squadron* unfolds a strange tale about two down-and-out flyers forced to repeat their real-life death-defying stunts in front of a movie camera. The hitch is that the director of their film is a stickler for authenticity and more dangerous than their World War I enemies. Considering the high casualty rate for stuntpeople in recent years, the film's contentions about the dangers of making make-believe believable seem particularly relevant.

THE LOST WEEKEND ☆☆☆☆
1945, USA
Ray Milland, Jane Wyman, Philip Terry, Howard Da Silva, Doris Dowling, Frank Faylen, Mary Young. Directed by Billy Wilder. 101 min.

Although its subject matter has since been exhausted in dozens of features and TV films, Billy Wilder's lacerating study of three days in the life of an alcoholic writer who goes on a lonely, desperate bender was the first such treatment, and a milestone in Hollywood's willingness to depict social problems. Although Paramount produced and released it with reluctance, the film was rewarded with Oscars for Best Picture, Best Director, Best Screenplay (Wilder and Charles Brackett) and Best Actor. Ray Milland broke with his romantic-lead image to star here as the haunted, angry drunk, and it's the best work he ever did. Wilder's tough-minded direction is still compelling, and some of the episodes are no less vivid than they were at the time. The happyish ending, a departure from Charles Jackson's source novel, isn't in line with the rest of the film, but was probably a necessary concession to studio dictates.

LOVE AND ANARCHY ☆☆☆½
1973, Italy
Giancarlo Giannini, Mariangela Melato, Lina Polito, Pina Cel, Eros Bagni. Directed by Lina Wertmuller. 108 min.

One of Lina Wertmuller's most completely realized projects, a disturbing contemplation of fascism and the resultant moral squalor and decadence under Il Duce, is certainly the film that launched her in the United States. Sexy and dynamic Giancarlo Giannini plays a politically driven assassin who wants to rid the world of Mussolini. In the midst of striving to change the Italian political machine, he becomes smitten with a prostitute in the brothel where he's hiding out. The sparks between Giancarlo and the fiery Mariangela Melato set this deeply felt film aflame with passion. Unlike Wertmuller's other films, this one is not awash in political rhetoric; the tumultuous affair of the leads stays in view as a counterpoint to the political situation. Points are made, but not at the expense of the human drama, making this an exceptional look at an unsavory epoch.

LOVE AND BULLETS ☆½
1979, Great Britain
Charles Bronson, Rod Steiger, Jill Ireland, Strother Martin, Bradford Dillman, Henry Silva. Directed by Stuart Rosenberg. 103 min.

Charles Bronson pursues gangster girl Jill Ireland against an Alpine background, but it's the same old urban USA crime plot with ubiquitous bad guys out to stop him cold. Meanwhile, he must struggle with his romantic impulses for Jill. For die-hard Bronsonites and Swiss travelogue fans only.

LOVE AND DEATH ☆☆☆½
1975, USA, PG
Woody Allen, Diane Keaton, Olga Georges-Picot, Harold Gould, James Tolkan, Henry Czarniak. Directed by Woody Allen. 89 min.

This witty lampoon of the great Russian novels and foreign films stars Woody Allen—who also wrote and directed—as Boris Grushenko, a skinny coward in the Russian army during the Napoleonic Wars. Boris expounds with girlfriend Sonja (Diane Keaton) on the great questions of Life, Love, and Death. Allen's comic instincts carry this movie and keep the lesser scenes from taking too much away from the truly hilarious moments.

LOVE AT FIRST BITE ☆☆☆
1979, USA, PG
George Hamilton, Susan Saint James, Richard Benjamin, Dick Shawn, Arte Johnson, Sherman Hemsley, Isabel Sanford. Directed by Stan Dragoti. 96 min.

George Hamilton's first intentional foray into outlandish comedy was this sometimes heavy-handed but often funny spoof of Dracula movies. In Robert Kaufman's script, the Count is escaping from behind the Iron Curtain and settles in modern Manhattan, where he meets up with a flippant fashion model. Hamilton displays some unexpected comic timing, but everyone else mugs outrageously: Arte Johnson as Dwight Frye, Dick Shawn as a cop, Richard Benjamin as a neurotic psychiatrist, and even talented Susan Saint James (in her brief sexpot phase) as the model (Director Stan Dragoti should have used his then-wife Cheryl Tiegs). There are sporadic laughs, but the pacing is slow and uneven. The intended highlight is a disco number with Hamilton and Saint James dancing to "I Love the Nightlife," but the camerawork misses all the humor.

THE LOVE BUG ☆☆☆
1969, USA, G
Dean Jones, Michele Lee, David Tomlinson, Buddy Hackett, Joe Flynn, Benson Fong, Joe E. Ross. Directed by Robert Stevenson. 108 min.

The box office smash of 1969, *The Love Bug* was a major revitalization for Disney Studios and began the four-movie series that includes *Herbie Rides Again*, *Herbie Goes to Monte Carlo*, and *Herbie Goes Bananas*. A second-rate race driver gets a magical, mischievous Volkswagen that helps him win all of his big races. Buddy Hackett gives comic relief as the spaced-out mechanic, but even funnier are Benson Fong as an enigmatic helper, Joe Flynn as a baddie, and Joe E. Ross as a lost detective. The film was produced by the great Disney mainstay, Bill Walsh, who also contributed to the screenplay. Robert Stevenson, director of films ranging from *Back Street* to *Mary Poppins*, lends a very sure hand and a good, light touch.

LOVE BUTCHER ☆☆
1983, USA, R
Eric Stern. Directed by Mikel Angel, Don Jones. 80 min.

A schizophrenic cripple named Caleb does gardening work for a variety of bored, sluttish California bitches who regret their mistreatment of him when his brother/alter ego Lester comes to even up the score. This is exploitation of a high order, featuring horrible set design, moderately gruesome murders (committed on the theme of gardening tools), ridiculous psychology, and some excruciating acting. However, it can be entertaining, particularly when Lester adopts a series of outlandish disguises in order to gain access to the homes of his victims-to-be.

LOVE CHILD ☆☆½
1982, USA, R
Amy Madigan, Beau Bridges, Mackenzie Phillips, Albert Salmi. Directed by Larry Peerce. 96 min.

Although this prison drama received only minimal theatrical distribution, it's well worth seeing as a showcase for the talented young actress Amy Madigan (*Alamo Bay*, *Twice in a Lifetime*). She gives a superlative, subtly shaded performance as Terry Jean Moore, an inmate in a women's prison who's impregnated by a guard and then fights for the right to keep her baby. Based on fact and powerfully told, although Larry Peerce's direction is occasionally overemphatic.

LOVE FROM A STRANGER ☆☆½
1947, USA
Sylvia Sidney, John Hodiak, John Howard, Isobel Elsom. Directed by Richard Whorf. 80 min.

This film is an Americanized remake of a 1937 British film starring Ann Harding and Basil Rathbone. In this thriller squarely in the *Suspicion-Gaslight* tradition, Sylvia Sidney doing fine work as the distraught heroine who slowly comes to suspect that her new husband may be a murderer and that she may be the next victim. Though it lacks the originality or style that would make it memorable, it's a good time-passer, the sort of brisk, no-frills suspense film that Hollywood used to turn out in its sleep.

LOVE HAPPY ☆☆
1949, USA
Groucho, Chico, and Harpo Marx, Eric Blore, Ilona Massey, Vera-Ellen, Marilyn Monroe. Directed by David Miller. 85 min.

Even the most devoted Marx Brothers fan will be distraught at the sight of their last film effort. In this feeble farce, Harpo takes the spotlight (such as it is) while Groucho appears briefly at the beginning and end, and Chico is completely pushed into the background. The Ben Hecht-Frank Tashlin-Mac Benoff screenplay gives the brothers almost nothing to work with in a convoluted plot about a theater company that gets mixed up with jewel thieves. Incidental pleasures come from a walk-on by young Marilyn Monroe, a dance by Vera-Ellen, and the appearance of Ilona Massey (who does not sing), but the boys look too old and tired to be chasing people around rooftops and leering at pretty girls. Cheap production values don't help either.

LOVE IN THE AFTERNOON ☆☆½
1957, USA
Audrey Hepburn, Gary Cooper, Maurice Chevalier, John McGiver. Directed by Billy Wilder. 130 min.

Billy Wilder's witty, wistful evocation of romance in Paris isn't one of his masterpieces, but it's still several notches above the work of most other directors. Audrey Hepburn plays the daughter of a private eye who specializes in divorce cases; reading in her father's files about a Lothario whose track record with women seems unmatched, she decides to track him down and finds herself falling in love. Many critics feel this was Wilder's homage to another great émigré comedy director, Ernst Lubitsch, and the sweet depiction of budding romance and melancholy undertone of innocent youth meeting weary experience (exemplified by the choice to cast the much-older Gary Cooper as Hepburn's love) do seem to evoke Lubitsch's films more than Wilder's body of work.

A LOVE IN GERMANY ☆☆☆½
1984, France/West Germany, R
Hanna Schygulla, Pyotr Lysak, Elisabeth Trissenaar, Marie-Christine Barrault, Armin Mueller-Stahl, Daniel Olbrychski. Directed by Andrzej Wajda. 119 min.

Powerful drama, boasting a riveting performance by Hanna Schygulla. During World War II, in the small village of Brombach, a German housewife (Schygulla) carries on a passionate affair with a Polish P.O.W. (Pyotr Lysak) while her husband is away fighting. Andrzej Wajda's study of Fascist oppression can be read as yet another parable of modern-day Poland. The story builds to a shattering climax. See it, primarily, for the astonishing emotional presence of Schygulla, whose performance finds meaning and resonance throughout.

LOVE IN THE CITY ☆☆½
1953, Italy
Ugo Tognazzi, Maresa Gallo, Caterina Rigoglioso, Silvio Lillo, Angela Pierro. Directed by Carlo Lizzani, Michelangelo Antonioni, Dino Risi, Federico Fellini, Cesare Zavattini, Umberto Maselli, Alberto Lattuada. 110 min.

This film consists of six serio-comic episodes dealing with love and sex in the city of Rome, all done in a pseudo-neorealist style. The serious segments involve a prostitute, interviews with attempted suicides, and a servant girl who abandons her illegitimate child. The humorous ones concern a dance hall, a marriage agency, and the reactions of Italian girlwatchers. The Federico Fellini and Michelangelo Antonioni segments give some indication of their later styles, though they contain little of major interest. Some versions of this do not have the first segment (about the prostitute) and run only ninety minutes. (a.k.a.: *Amore in Citta*)

LOVE IS A MANY-SPLENDORED THING ☆☆½
1955, USA
William Holden, Jennifer Jones, Torin Thatcher, Isobel Elsom, Murray Matheson. Directed by Henry King. 102 min.

Romance aplenty in Hong Kong, with a five-handkerchief ending. In this corner is William Holden, American press correspondent whose wife refuses to give him a divorce. In this corner is Jennifer Jones, Eurasian doctor and widow, torn between love and a desire to return to her homeland. Oscars were awarded for Best Song and Best Costume Design.

LOVE LAUGHS AT ANDY HARDY ☆☆☆½
1946, USA
Mickey Rooney, Lewis Stone, Sara Haden, Fay Holden, Bonita Granville, Lina Romay, Dick Simmons, Clinton Sundberg. Directed by Willis Goldbeck. 93 min.

Postwar angst drips over the Hardys's white picket fence and oozes onto their beautifully manicured lawn in what was to be the last film (until a 1950s reunion) in the series. Mickey Rooney, after two years in the service, plays Andy Hardy returning home from World War II only to find that his bride-to-be is marrying another. This is pretty grim stuff for the apple pie and jalopy world of Carvel, and director Willis Goldbeck stresses the bleakness by casting former evil-child incarnate Bonita Granville as the deceptive fiancée (her character incestuously marries her guardian and has the nerve to make Andy the best man), and by setting most of the action at night, creating *noir*-ish textures. There are a few attempts to recapture the rambunctiousness of Andy's prewar days (e.g., a tacked-on happy ending), but there are also a number of unusually touching scenes (including an exquisite cameo by Dorothy Ford as an extremely tall girl), and nothing can veil the terrifying world-weariness of Rooney's eyes (he was twenty-six at the time and already into his second troubled marriage). The message is clear: Andy Hardy has grown up and lost his innocence. This is a devastating, black end to a bleach-white movie serial.

THE LOVELESS ☆
1982, USA, R
Willem Dafoe, Marin Kanter, Robert Gordon. Directed by Kathryn Bigelow, Monty Montgomery. 83 min.

Working on a small budget, Kathryn Bigelow and Monty Montgomery codirected a bike movie celebrating the 1950s through the eyes of the 1980s. Where earlier bike films like *The Wild One* were forced to concentrate on plot, this deliberately slips its story into the background in order to linger over all the latent erotic material of the period that other films only hinted at in their posters. Unfortunately, *The Loveless* seems enraptured by surface details of the period—advertising displays, pop art icons, etc. There's no drama here, only texture, in this tedious tale of a loner antihero who wrangles with the local bigots and sleeps with the wrong girl. It's pretentiously cool and fraught with hidden meaning known only to the filmmakers.

LOVE LETTERS ☆☆½
1983, USA, R
Jamie Lee Curtis, James Keach, Amy Madigan, Bud Cort, Matt Clark, Bonnie Bartlett. Directed by Amy Jones. 98 min.

The unusual, melancholy screen presence of Jamie Lee Curtis is the best reason to see this independently produced tearjerker about a young disc jockey who discovers love letters written to her late mother by an unknown suitor, and begins to reexamine her own romantic life as a result. The whole film is keyed to Curtis's reactions, but, great reactor that she is, it's not enough to carry the whole show. Nevertheless, it's the kind of interestingly low-key mood piece that wouldn't come out of a major Hollywood studio. It's attentively cast right down to the smallest roles; Amy Madigan is especially good as Curtis's worldly neighbor.

LOVELINES ½☆
1984, USA, R
Michael Winslow, Greg Bradford, Mary Beth Evans. Directed by Rod Amateau. 93 min.

Cheap youth exploitation movies like this are financed on the assumption that teenage audiences will be attracted to the promise of sex and frivolity like flies to molasses. Well, teenagers, beware: The comedy is clumsy, and no sex is delivered when the all-girl band meets the local telephone company.

LOVE ME TENDER ☆☆½
1956, USA
Elvis Presley, Richard Egan, Debra Paget, Robert Middleton, Neville Brand, Mildred Dunnock, Bruce Bennet, L. Q. Jones. Directed by Robert D. Webb. 94 min.

Elvis's film debut shows that he hasn't developed the extraordinary thespic skills that marked such later classics as *Fun in Acapulco* and *Viva Las Vegas!* He plays the youngest son of a Texas clan during the Civil War. When his oldest brother (Richard Egan) is reported killed, he marries his fiancée (Debra Paget), which doesn't sit too well with the brother when he returns. Aside from the title tune, Elvis also sings the classics "Poor Boy," "Let Me," and the immortal "We're Gonna Move."

THE LOVE OF THREE QUEENS ☆½
1954, Italy/France
Hedy LaMarr, Gerard Ouy, Massimo Serato, Robert Beatty, Cathy O'Donnell. Directed by Marc Allegret, Edgar Ulmer. 90 min.

What does an aging actress with little talent but a lot of beauty do when her studio contract runs out? If she's Hedy LaMarr (in 1953), she runs off to Montegelato, Italy, to make a three-hour epic in which she gets to play Helen of Troy, Empress Josephine, and Genevieve de Brabant. What was to be the crowning achievement of the Viennese-born movie star's career was whittled down to half its length on release and failed miserably wherever it played (it has never been shown theatrically in the United States). As it stands, it's still too long. The device that gets Hedy into costume (she looks best as Josephine, worst as Genevieve) is having her portray a woman who must decide what to wear to a masked ball. She then imagines herself as each of the above sirens of history. Promise shown by codirector Edgar Ulmer and composer Nino Rota goes unfulfilled. (a.k.a.: *Eternal Woman* and *The Face That Launched a Thousand Ships*)

LOVE ON THE RUN ☆☆½
1979, France, PG
Jean-Pierre Léaud, Marie-France Pisier, Dorothee, Claude Jade, Julien Bertheau, Daniel Mesguich. Directed by François Truffaut. 93 min.

This is the last and one of the least interesting of Truffaut's chronicles of the life and times of alter ego Antoine Doinel (Jean-Pierre Léaud), who first appeared in *The 400 Blows* (1959), and went on to a brief appearance in the international anthology *Love at Twenty* (1963) as well as starring roles in *Stolen Kisses* (1968) and *Bed and Board* (1970). This chapter is illustrated with clips from parts one through four, but it's the wrong place for anyone unfamiliar with the series to begin, and it's a commonplace romantic drama on its own. Doinel, now thirty-three, doesn't seem to have gotten any wiser in the intervening years, and his naïveté wears thin here. Léaud is so closely identified with the role that it's hard to fault his performance, and the supporting cast is excellent; this is in no way a trashing of the superb *400 Blows*, but it isn't anything like a fulfillment of it, either.

LOVERS AND LIARS ☆
1979, Italy, R
Goldie Hawn, Giancarlo Giannini, Laura Betti. Directed by Mario Monicelli. 96 min.

In this droopy-eared, flea-bitten dog of a formulaic, dubbed sex comedy, the usual misunderstandings and infidelities are paraded before us with an ersatz international flavor. Giancarlo Giannini looks more somnolent than ever, and Goldie Hawn explodes with a veritable Vesuvius of mannerisms. It's a leering star vehicle that affords little amusement. (a.k.a.: *Travels with Anita*)

LOVERS AND OTHER STRANGERS ☆☆☆
1970, USA
Gig Young, Bea Arthur, Bonnie Bedelia, Anne Jackson, Harry Guardino, Michael Brandon, Richard Castellano, Cloris Leachman. Directed by Cy Howard. 106 min.

Sort of *The Father of the Bride* of the seventies, only more like the Family of the Bride, this is a congenial grouping of vignettes about the impact that a couple's decision to marry has on their two families, with all the different factions choosing sides. There is rippling hilarity throughout, but only a modicum of belly laughs. Unlike earlier wedding comedies, this isn't a fluffy farce; we can really identify with these family squabbles.

LOVE SCENES ☆
1983, USA, R
Tiffany Bolling, Franc Luz, Julie Newmar, Jack Carter, Daniel Pilon, John Warner Williams, Britt Ekland, Dee Dee Bradley. Directed by Bud Townsend. 90 min.

Not satisfied with merely showing soft-core junk, the Playboy Cable TV Channel decided to go for vertical integration and start producing it as well. It's here on videocassette just in case you're not fortunate enough to have cable. This is a story highly reminiscent of *S.O.B.*, but without the humor: A fading actress is persuaded by her husband and agent to do an erotic film. Sexual situations abound until the final happy reunion of husband and wife, the fatuous element of "redeeming social significance" that used to be invoked to justify this kind of trash. Directed rather dully by Henry Jaglom's ex-father-in-law, Bud Townsend.

LOVESICK ☆☆½
1983, USA, PG
Dudley Moore, Elizabeth McGovern, Alec Guinness, John Huston. Directed by Marshall Brickman. 94 min.

Dudley Moore and Elizabeth McGovern make an oddly mismatched romantic pair in this languorous comedy about a psychiatrist who falls in love with one of his patients. Unfortunately, the film is funnier when it sticks to Moore and his oddball clientele (played amusingly by a host of familiar New York faces) than when the dizzy McGovern wanders in for what descends into a gooey romance. There are some well-observed moments of city life that call to mind director Marshall Brickman's start as a Woody Allen collaborator, and deft turns by Alec Guinness and John Huston. But *Lovesick* is ultimately interesting only around its edges.

LOVES OF A BLONDE ☆☆☆☆
1964, Czechoslovakia
Hana Brejchova, Vladimir Pucholt, Antonin Blazejovsky, Josef Sebanek. Directed by Milos Forman. 88 min.

This is a gently human coming-of-age comedy with an undertone of melancholy that's beautifully sustained. A love-starved young worker in an all-girl factory falls for an offbeat musician at a dance one night, follows him to Prague, and has a head-on collision with romantic disillusionment in the form of his parents. This is probably the best of Milos Forman's Czechoslovakian work, demonstrating his uncanny ability to draw you into the most alien of scenes or situations, and extracting telling details from the most unlikely moments.

LOVE SONGS ☆½
1986, Canada/France
Catherine Deneuve, Richard Ancocina, Christopher Lambert, Jacques Perrin, Nick Mancuso, Dayle Haddon, Charlotte Gainsbourg. Directed by Elie Chouraqui. 107 min.

A mediocre May-July romance that's burdened with eight excruciating, treacly pop songs—we know that contemporary French rock is bad, but this is ridiculous! Michel Legrand's mawkish, overinsistent ditties keep bursting onto the soundtrack whenever writer-director Elie Chouraqui runs out of plot (which, for the record, has a married woman entering an affair with an up-and-coming singer ten years her junior). Catherine Deneuve's beauty remains undiminished, but she's not a good enough actress to overcome the absence of a strong director, and the appeal of dull, luggish Christopher Lambert remains elusive.

LOVE'S SAVAGE FURY ☆
1979, USA (TV)
Jennifer O'Neill, Perry King, Raymond Burr, Robert Reed, Connie Stevens, Ed Lauter. Directed by Joseph Hardy. 100 min.

Oh, come on, now. Turn the television set off and watch dust collect on the tube if you can't do any better than this small-screen rip-off of *Gone with The Wind*. This is only for the less discriminating pulp romance market and terminal "Brady Bunch" groupies.

LOVE STORY ☆☆½
1970, USA, PG
Ali MacGraw, Ryan O'Neal, John Marley, Ray Milland, Katherine Balfour. Directed by Arthur Hiller. 100 min.

The title says it all—this romantic drama, as definitive as it is generic, will leave you either weeping or rolling in the aisles, depending on whether your temperament tends toward the moonstruck or the cynical. The most popular screen tearjerker ever, *Love Story* depicts the romance between rich, handsome, brilliant Harvard student Oliver Barrett IV (Ryan O'Neal) and poor, beautiful, brilliant Radcliffe student Jenny Cavalleri (Ali MacGraw). But the film's real trump card is played in its first line, when Ollie sighs, "What can you say about a twenty-five-year-old girl who died?" The film can be attacked on infinite levels—for its banality, its blatant manipulation, its mannequin–like acting, and its saccharine beautification of everything from immense wealth to terminal (unspecified) illness. But none of this explains why audiences adore it and went back again and again. Making a crowd-pleasing blockbuster means never having to say you're sorry, even if you're screenwriter Erich Segal, who committed perhaps the most lasting artistic sin of all—with this movie, he created the genre of novelization. If none of this has seriously dissuaded you, you're going to love it. Followed by *Oliver's Story*.

LOVE STREAMS ☆☆☆☆
1984, USA, PG-13
John Cassavetes, Gena Rowlands, Diahnne Abbott, Seymour Cassel, Margaret Abbott, Jakob Shaw. Directed by John Cassavetes. 122 min.

Good theater often leads the audience to understand its characters through the incessant abrasion of talk; attitudes, poses, falsehoods are gradually worn away, and something marvelously human comes into being. Films, on the other hand, show their characters' humanity through quick revelations—the sidelong glance, an overseen, fleeting facial expression. John Cassavetes may be the film director most concerned with using both methods of exposition. He is unafraid to let his characters talk, and he's always watching them closely, carefully. Here his direct approach to cinema is perfectly mirrored by the script's (adapted from Ted Allan's play) unpitying look at its people, and further deepened by the cathartic integrity of the actors. Cassavetes's own performance, as a dissipated writer used to feeding off other people, is a wonder—so honest, so clear, that it is painful to watch. He is even more generous to his wife and costar, Gena Rowlands, and her portrayal of the writer's neurotic sister rejected by her husband and daughter plumbs the depths of pathos and self-abnegation; both will haunt the viewer long after the movie ends. The movie is long—the video version regrettably has been trimmed from 141 minutes—and draining, but it is a tour de force of personality imprinted on the screen.

LOVING COUPLES ☆☆☆
1980, USA, PG
Shirley MacLaine, James Coburn, Susan Sarandon, Stephen Collins, Sally Kellerman. Directed by Jack Smight. 98 min.

This is an enjoyable, much-underrated comedy about modern relationships in which Shirley MacLaine and James Coburn play married doctors who, tired of each other, each seek out younger romantic partners. Subsequently, both couples wind up vacationing at the same Malibu resort where jealousy erupts. The stars, particularly the women, are charming and accurately fill out the chic quadrille. Add Sally Kellerman delightfully playing a nymphomaniac and the film becomes a sophisticated, adult farce, far superior to that other 1980 MacLaine sex comedy, *A Change of Seasons*. Screenplay by Martin Donovan.

LOVING YOU ☆☆
1957, USA
Elvis Presley, Lizabeth Scott, Wendell Corey, Dolores Hart, James Gleason. Directed by Hal Kanter. 101 min.

A sort of musicalized *Face in the Crowd*, only the face is Elvis Presley's. Lizabeth Scott plays a manipulative agent who turns a guy from the sticks into a rock-and-roll star. He thinks she's his girl, but she only has eyes for her estranged bandleader husband (Wendell Corey). Elvis's fans needn't worry: he ends up with cute Dolores Hart. Songs include "Teddy Bear" and "Hot Dog."

LOW BLOW ½☆
1986, USA, R
Leo Fong, Akosua Busia, Cameron Mitchell, Troy Donahue. Directed by Frank Harris. 85 min.

Even a slam-bang action picture needs more plotting and characterizations than this dull action film about a millionaire who pays some commando types to break into a religious cult and rescue his daughter. It's brutal without being a bit exciting. Originally called *Savage Sunday*.

LUCAS ☆☆½
1986, USA, PG-13
Corey Haim, Kerrie Green, Charlie Sheen, Courtney Thorne-Smith, Winona Ryder, Guy Boyd. Directed by David Seltzer. 90 min.

David Seltzer's sweet, minor paean to the agonies and foibles of early adolescence avoids many of the pitfalls of other teen films simply by treating its subjects as human beings; like a Disney nature movie, it shows that our happy ecosystem has room for nerds and jocks, prom queens and wallflowers, all functioning in harmony. Unfortunately, the gently optimistic tale of a goggle-eyed lad's longing for an older "woman" he can't have begins to cloy when young Lucas stops making passes and starts trying to catch them on the football field. The story eventually degenerates into *Rocky* redux, and Corey Haim isn't as expressive an embodiment of Lucas as one would like. But there are good moments all the way through, and a fine, subtle performance by Charlie Sheen as a sympathetic jock.

LUCKY JIM ☆☆½
1957, Great Britain
Ian Carmichael, Terry-Thomas, Hugh Griffith, Sharon Acker, Jean Anderson. Directed by John Boulting. 95 min.

Strangely, this Boulting brothers farcical adaptation has aged into exhaustion, while the Kingsley Amis novel upon which it is based has risen to the status of a small classic. Choppily edited and inconsistently shot, it squeezes the pathos and stylishness of Amis down into a softly amusing pulp. Ian Carmichael is a minor professor in a minor rural college, beset by the beastliness of being British. With a hankering for Sharon Acker (a Canadian), Carmichael involves himself with ceremonies, processionals, politics, fights, drunks, voyeurism, and car crashing. Spurred by their earlier farce successes, *Private's Progress* and *Brothers-in-Law*, the Boultings have mounted the same slapstick horse; it might have run faster under more subtle, less heavy-handed jockeying.

LUCKY TEXAN
1934, USA ☆½
John Wayne, Barbara Sheldon, George "Gabby" Hayes, Yakima Canutt. Directed by Robert N. Bradbury. 56 min.

Some good John Wayne-Gabby Hayes comic repartee gives a lift to this routine, man-accused-of-friend's-murder yarn. Watch the way veteran director Robert N. Bradbury handles the railroad/car/horse chase scene.

LUNCH WAGON
1980, USA, R ☆½
Pamela Jean Bryant, Rosanne Katon, Candy Moore, Rick Podell, Rose Marie, Chuck McCann. Directed by Ernest Pintoff. 88 min.

This is a raucous jiggle comedy about a bevy of buxom cuties who run a lunch wagon near the work site of some chauvinistic construction workers. It's a combination of soft-core sexuality, off-color jokes, and even has a caper movie subplot about a cache of diamonds. As far as laughs are concerned, rate this one out to lunch. (a.k.a.: *Lunch Wagon Girls*; *Come 'n' Get It*)

LUST FOR A VAMPIRE
1970, Great Britain ☆☆☆
Michael Johnson, Suzanna Leigh, Ralph Bates, Barbara Jefford. Directed by Jimmy Sangster. 95 min.

A lusty, full-blooded vampire tale based on Sheridan Le Fanu's "Carmilla," this material has seen service in films as disparate as the silent film *Vampyr* and Roger Vadim's *Blood and Roses*. Sensual and strikingly atmospheric, the film covers the burgeoning romance of a surprisingly sophisticated schoolgirl who has a crush on a novelist visiting the old castle that houses the girls' school she attends. He's interested in the other world; little does he know that that is exactly where this supernatural miss comes from. There is a modicum of real scares, but lots of frissons as the vampiress yearns to mingle her hot blood with the handsome writer's.

LUST IN THE DUST
1985, USA, R ☆☆
Divine, Tab Hunter, Lainie Kazan, Nedra Volz, Geoffrey Lewis. Directed by Paul Bartel. 85 min.

A rangy, likeable companion piece to *Blazing Saddles*. Unfortunately, this parody mines only the most obvious Western flick clichés as a desperado, a Clint Eastwood clone, an itinerant honky-tonk singer, and an oversexed cantina proprietress all vie to be the first to find a fortune in gold. The director tries to take that *Polyester* pair, Divine and Tab Hunter, out of Baltimore and plop them down in the Wild Wild West for comic effect. Paul Bartel (*Eating Raoul*) displays a fatal niceness of attitude that proves he's not the man to play John Waters (*Polyester*) or Paul Morrissey (*Trash*). Although he loves the low humor of camp put-ons, he lacks the cruelty that's sometimes an essential ingredient of camp. *Lust*, like Bartel's *Not for Publication*, lacks even the rudimentary sharpness and vitriol of a "Carol Burnett Show" take-off of old movies. That being said, there are some good vulgar laughs from Divine looking like the Rocky Mountains in drag and from Nedra Volz as a long-in-the-tooth saloon girl.

THE LUSTY MEN
1952, USA ☆☆☆
Susan Hayward, Robert Mitchum, Arthur Kennedy, Arthur Hunnicutt, Frank Faylen, Burt Mustin. Directed by Nicholas Ray. 112 min.

Ex-rodeo star Robert Mitchum returns to the ranch of his youth and inspires cowhand Arthur Kennedy to enter the rodeo circuit. Soon, Kennedy becomes a success and fame begins to change him. This drama benefits from sturdy performances from the principals and Nick Ray's strong, sure direction.

LUTHER
1974, Great Britain, G ☆☆½
Stacy Keach, Patrick Magee, Hugh Griffith, Alan Badel, Leonard Rossiter, Maurice Denham. Directed by Guy Green. 112 min.

This is an American Film Theater adaptation of the three-act drama by John Osborne about the life of Martin Luther, the sixteenth-century founder of Protestantism. In the title role, Stacy Keach is pretty much the whole show, and he handles it magnificently. Unfortunately, the film that's going on around him isn't up to that level, and drags on for too long.

LUV
1967, USA ☆☆
Jack Lemmon, Peter Falk, Elaine May, Nina Wayne, Eddie Mayehoff. Directed by Clive Donner. 96 min.

The relaxation of moral codes in the late 1960s allowed Hollywood to deal explicitly with topics like impotence and wife-swapping. Unfortunately, the eagerness to represent such "taboo" areas on screen resulted in a glut of disappointing and exploitative films like this smutty adaptation of Murray Schisgal's Broadway play. The plot is still amusing—an unhappily married man (Peter Falk) schemes to introduce his wife (Elaine May) to his suicidal best friend (Jack Lemmon) in order to obtain a divorce and marry his mistress. But the cast (particularly May and Lemmon), mugs outrageously, and *Luv*'s look is muddy and unattractive. A few years and a few Neil Simon scripts later, Hollywood would be expert in doing this sort of thing.

M

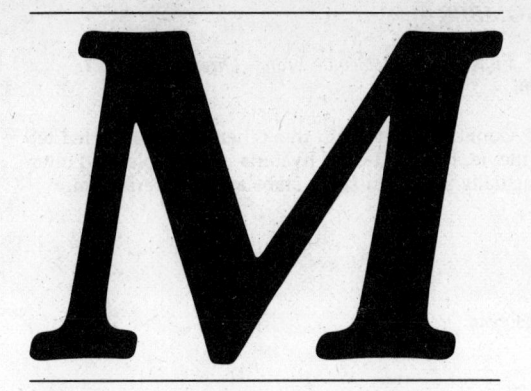

M ☆☆☆☆
1931, Germany
Peter Lorre, Ellen Widmann, Gustav Grundgens, Inge Landgut. Directed by Fritz Lang. 99 min.

A child-murderer is brought to questionable justice in this harrowing drama, one of the greatest films to grow out of the German Expressionistic movement. *M* is the mark chalked on the dark overcoat of the Dusseldorf murderer (Peter Lorre) as both the police and the underworld attempt to track him down; in the film's final quarter, Lorre's brilliantly acted scenes of entrapment and confession are among the first on film to sympathetically probe the criminal mind. Fritz Lang's use of subjective sound was virtually unprecedented at the time and enhances the film's superbly grim atmosphere. Avoid the dull 1951 American remake—Lang's *M* is the one to see.

MACARONI ☆☆½
1985, USA/Italy, PG
Jack Lemmon, Marcello Mastroianni. Directed by Ettore Scola. 102 min.

Pairing Jack Lemmon and Marcello Mastroianni, respectively the American and Italian embodiments of everyman-as-schmuck, was an inspired idea, but it didn't work in this fizzled vehicle. Lemmon plays an American businessman who returns to Naples for the first time since World War II and runs into an old buddy (Mastroianni) whose sister was Lemmon's wartime sweetheart. For forty years, Mastroianni has been writing his sister love letters and signing Lemmon's name, painting him as a heroic journalist with a full, exciting, satisfying life. Trying for nostalgia, director Ettore Scola (*We All Loved Each Other So Much, Down and Dirty*) ends up with a tone of forced whimsy, and the two stars don't get to do much beyond recapping their old, reliable shticks.

MacARTHUR ☆☆
1977, USA, PG
Gregory Peck, Ed Flanders, Dan O'Herlihy, Marj Dusay, Sandy Kenyon, Nicolas Coster. Directed by Joseph Sargent. 128 min.

This is an obvious but failed attempt to do for General Douglas MacArthur what the film *Patton* did for that other flamboyant World War II general: portray both the attractive and the objectionable sides of a man who was a brilliant strategist but also a hopeless egomaniac. The problem is that neither the production nor the director (whose primary experience has been in television) could grasp the kind of scope that such an undertaking would require, and in trying to project a larger-than-life character have only come up with a big frog in a small lily pond. Peck does what he can with the title role, but the support to flesh it out and provide a context just isn't there.

MACBETH ☆☆☆½
1948, USA
Orson Welles, Jeanette Nolan, Dan O'Herlihy, Roddy McDowall, Edgar Barrier, Alan Napier, Peggy Webber. Directed by Orson Welles. 90 min.

Shooting on a shoestring budget and using flimsy sets left over from old Westerns, Orson Welles turned the Bard's tragedy into a highly stylized nightmare that seems to be taking place in a gothic ghost town. The effect is strange, patchy, and oddly haunting. Unfortunately, the version released on videocassette is not Welles's complete one, but that which the studio trimmed (from 106 to ninety minutes) and redubbed (they didn't like the Scottish accents). This is particularly annoying given that Welles's full version was restored a few years back. It's still a must-see for Welles fans.

MACBETH ☆☆☆½
1971, Great Britain
Jon Finch, Francesca Annis, Martin Shaw, Nicholas Selby, John Stride, Stephan Chase, Paul Shelley, Terence Bayler. Directed by Roman Polanski. 140 min.

Roman Polanski and Kenneth Tynan create a sensational and hypnotic version of Shakespeare by emphasizing the play's bloody, orgiastic elements and suppressing its pageantry of state. The movie is remarkably faithful to the Bard, and it is the clearest filmed exposition of *Macbeth*. At the time of its release, it was considered very daring (due mostly to one nude scene), but the film lacks the free-ranging genius of Kurosawa's *Throne of Blood* and the expressionistic bombast of Welles's interpretation. The cast is expert, the direction both crisp and unsettling, and the set design (by Wilfrid Shingleton) is a perfectly realized nightmare. The film versions of this play offer the best opportunity to compare three very different, very good translations of Shakespeare.

MACKENNA'S GOLD ☆☆
1969, USA
Gregory Peck, Omar Sharif, Camilla Sparv, Telly Savalas, Julie Newmar, Keenan Wynn, Raymond Massey, Burgess Meredith. Directed by J. Lee Thompson. 128 min.

This is a full-scale, full-throttle attempt at a Western epic. Some of the sprawl is appealing, and the film is visually magnificent, but it never overcomes the unevenness of the script, nor can it surmount the ragged editing (because the film was heavily cut before its initial release). This failed epic concerns a cutthroat search for a lost canyon that's supposed to house a cache of gold. Everyone in this stellar cast is ready to stab everyone else in order to get there first. The action never ceases as the stars are hell-bent-for-leather to satisfy their greed; if only there were more real suspense and less emphasis on unconvincing plot twists.

THE MACKINTOSH MAN ☆½
1973, Great Britain, R
Paul Newman, Dominique Sanda, James Mason, Harry Andrews. Directed by John Huston. 98min.

John Huston perhaps found that Paul Newman was as unsuited to his understated style as Hitchcock discovered in 1966's *Torn Curtain*. Newman sleepwalks through the mazelike plot without contributing much humor or grace. Dominique Sanda is attractive, but she's made to resemble Valli in *The Third Man* (right up to the ending stolen from that masterpiece). Huston is on secure ground only with the British supporting cast, several of whom—like James Mason and Harry Andrews—offer expertly timed, light performances.

MACON COUNTY LINE ☆☆
1974, USA, R
Alan Vint, Jesse Vint, Max Baer, Cheryl Walters, Geoffrey Lewis, Joan Blackman, James Gammon, Leif Garrett, Doodles Weaver. Directed by Richard Compton. 89 min.

Anti-Southern paranoia fuels this energetic, lurid drama about two Chicago brothers (Alan and Jesse Vints) who venture into redneck territory circa 1955 and find themselves mistaken for a pair of killers and subjected to Confederate vengeance. Max Baer (Jethro on "The Beverly Hillbillies") wrote the screenplay with Richard Compton and has a juicily crude role as the meanest good-ol'-boy sheriff you'd ever want to meet, and although much of the film is obvious and predictable, at least it has the courage of its own trashy convictions. A sluggish but better-cast sequel, *Return to Macon County*, followed in 1975.

MADAME BOVARY ☆☆☆
1949, USA
Jennifer Jones, Van Heflin, Louis Jourdan, James Mason, Christopher Kent (Alf Kjellin), Gene Lockhart, Gladys Cooper, George Zucco. Directed by Vincente Minnelli. 115 min.

It was inevitable that MGM would remake *Madame Bovary* and that Vincente Minnelli would be chosen to direct, but this fourth go-round is surprisingly intelligent as well as lavish. The thematic and stylistic concerns of Gustave Flaubert's novel are generally dispensed with by the screenwriter (Robert Ardry) in favor of the plot about a nineteenth-century wife who meets a tragic end after an act of indiscretion. It's all very stylish, but Minnelli's Ophulsesque effects work best in the ball sequence. The film is superior to the 1934 Jean Renoir version only in that Jennifer Jones is more convincingly cast as Emma Bovary than was aging, heavyset Valentine Tessier. Also made in 1932 and 1937.

MADAME ROSA ☆½
1977, France
Simone Signoret, Claude Dauphin, Samy Ben Youb, Costa-Gavras. Directed by Moshe Mizrahi. 105 min.

This is an example of the sort of humane, well-intentioned and mediocre art house film that audiences love because it makes feelings they already have seem noble. As Madame Rosa, the frayed, wheezing old ex-prostitute who now ekes out a living in Paris's Belleville district caring for the children of whores, Simone Signoret delivers her usual self-pitying, beauty-martyred-by-age performance that nevertheless won her France's Cesar Award for Best Actress.

MADAME SIN ☆☆
1972, Great Britain
Bette Davis, Robert Wagner, Denholm Elliott, Gordon Jackson. Directed by David Greene. 100 min.

This pilot for a proposed television series never really makes up its mind whether it's a campy, humorous piece or a serious crime story. The well-photographed, glamorous Bette Davis plays in her former grand style, and she is occasionally splendid. Her entrance is particularly good, although it is stolen from *The Lady from Shanghai*. Robert Wagner, however, is painfully sincere and a drag on what little momentum David Greene achieves. The conclusion has a nasty irony that is pleasing.

MADAME X ☆☆½
1966, USA
Lana Turner, John Forsythe, Ricardo Montalban, Burgess Meredith, Keir Dullea, Constance Bennett. Directed by David Lowell Rich. 99 min.

Having been filmed several times before (and once since), this version of *Madame X* is the best known. It's a corny old soap opera given a high-gloss treatment that should please fans of the tearjerker/camp variety. As the woman who is forced away from her family by circumstance (and a nasty mother-in-law), only to encounter them years later in a new identity, Lana Turner, though never a great actress, turns in a solid performance; and Constance Bennett, in her last screen appearance, is quite good. Producer Ross Hunter, known for extravagant productions, has gone all out with this one; it's trash of the very highest order.

MADAM KITTY

See *Salon Kitty*

THE MAD BOMBER ☆
1973, USA
Chuck Connors, Vince Edwards, Neville Brand. Directed by Bert I. Gordon. 104 min.

Chuck Connors is perfect in this otherwise halfhearted terrorist movie. His dead-eyed hysteria is plausible, and intermittently, he actually sneaks in some stabs at characterization.

MAD DOG

See *Mad Dog Morgan*

MAD DOG MORGAN ☆☆☆
1976, Australia
Dennis Hopper, Jack Thompson, David Gulpilil, Frank Thring. Directed by Philippe Mora. 102 min.

This is a visually stunning albeit violent tale of legendary Australian outlaw Daniel Morgan. Relying heavily upon our identification with revenge, *Morgan* effectively deals with unsympathetic characters who populate an equally unsympathetic environment. As the title character, Dennis Hopper shines, conveying a feeling of paranoia through consistent development of his character rather than the usual psycho mannerisms. Evocative, penetrating, and powerful—a rare glimpse into the anatomy of aberrant behavior. (a.k.a.: *Mad Dog*)

MADE FOR EACH OTHER ☆☆☆
1939, USA
Carole Lombard, James Stewart, Charles Coburn, Lucile Watson. Directed by John Cromwell. 90 min.

This touching family melodrama about a young couple struggling with marriage and parenting is perfectly leavened by the comic talents of Carole Lombard and James Stewart. The story is slightly constructed but engaging and affecting, and the near death of the couple's child is handled with emotion and suspense. The screenplay is by Jo Swerling, who also wrote for Hitchcock, Borzage, and Capra.

MADIGAN ☆☆☆½
1968, USA
Richard Widmark, Henry Fonda, Inger Stevens, Harry Guardino, James Whitmore, Susan Clark, Michael Dunn, Don Stroud. Directed by Don Siegel. 101 min.

An excellent, tautly suspenseful police procedural about a New York City detective's three-day hunt for an escaped murderer. There is good use of city locations and no-frills direction by Don Siegel (*Dirty Harry*) that never lets the pace flag; all of the performances, from Henry Fonda's as the police commissioner to Michael Dunn's as a local bookie, go beyond the call of duty in a genre film. Richard Widmark later reprised the title role for a short-lived television series.

MAD MAD KUNG FU ☆½
Hong Kong
Simon Yuen, Chin Long, Cheng Kang Yeh, Kao Fei, Chaing Tao. Directed by Chien Yuet.

The story of a noodle vendor (Chin Long) who comes to the aid of a beggar who is being harassed by the town bullies, and gets trapped into becoming a hero. It's just wonderful the way these actors can wrap their bodies around one another in endless combinations—the last fight, between Chin Long and Kao Fei, is a perfect example of this. What imagination!

MAD MAX
1980, Australia, R ☆☆½
Mel Gibson, Joanne Samuel, Hugh Keays-Byrne. Directed by George Miller. 90 min.

A stylish and violent exercise in mayhem that, despite a bargain-basement budget, packs a solid entertainment punch into its short running time. In a deteriorating future, an ultraviolent urban police force protects the civilized population from psychopathic biker gangs. Max is the pride of the force until his family is destroyed by motorcyclists; he abandons faith in the legal process and takes the law into his own hands, with bloody results. *Mad Max* launched the career of Mel Gibson, who followed it with the much pricier *Road Warrior* and *Mad Max Beyond Thunderdome*.

MAD MAX BEYOND THUNDERDOME
1985, Australia, PG-13 ☆☆☆
Mel Gibson, Tina Turner, Bruce Spence, Angry Anderson. Directed by George Miller and George Ogilvie. 108 min.

The latest installment in the adventures of this nihilistic hero adds sweep to the post-apocalyptic story, but loses some of the savagely violent action that made the series so popular. The gruff Max tries to save a band of feral children from falling into the corrupt clutches of Auntie Entity. Gibson as Max is effectively overshadowed by pop singer Tina Turner, making her film debut as the malevolent ruler of a seedy city. The global destruction and descent into savagery that were partially shown in *Mad Max* and *The Road Warrior* are fully realized in this visually clever and opulent film, but it's a somewhat empty-feeling epic that relies more on set design than innovative action.

MAD MAX 2

See *The Road Warrior*

MAD MONSTER PARTY?
1967, USA ☆☆
Animated: Boris Karloff, Phyllis Diller, Ethel Ennis, Gale Garnett. Directed by Jules Bass. 94 min.

This silly, sweet-natured fun has the great monsters of cinema—Frankenstein, Dracula, the Wolfman, the Mummy, Phyllis Diller—gathering at the castle for a big, rocking bash. It's agreeable, quintessentially 1960s camp fare, and the stop-motion look of the animation (Jules Bass, of Rankin-Bass Productions, supervised) gives all of the ghoulies the same familiar, wobbly, mildly arthritic-looking gait that you usually see only on the company's TV Christmas specials.

MAEDCHEN IN UNIFORM
1931, Germany, PG ☆☆☆
Dorothea Wieck, Herta Thiele, Emilia Unda, Hedy Schlichter. Directed by Leontine Sagan. 87 min.

In its time, this was controversial enough to provoke a lawsuit when exhibitors attempted to show it in America (several years later, it was distributed here). The lesbian theme is tastefully handled in this poignant drama set in a girls' boarding school, where a shy student (Herta Thiele) and a teacher enter a relationship. The film is powerful and well-acted, although its cinematic technique is sometimes rudimentary. Remade in Germany in 1958.

THE MAFU CAGE

See *My Sister, My Love*

MAGIC
1978, USA, R ☆☆
Anthony Hopkins, Ann-Margret, Burgess Meredith, Ed Lauter, E. J. Andre, Jerry Houser. Directed by Richard Attenborough. 106 min.

William Goldman wrote this mechanical thriller about a professional ventriloquist (Anthony Hopkins) whose murderous alter ego, as represented by his dummy Fats, begins to take over his personality. *Magic* owes a great debt to the Michael Redgrave segment of the British classic *Dead of Night*, which was a lot smarter and scarier. Though the film is easy to watch and intermittently entertaining, Richard Attenborough's clumsy direction doesn't allow any of the plot twists to come as surprises. The casting of Hopkins as the fast-talking New York protagonist and Ann-Margret as a blowsy hotel manager is so totally in error that you have to suspect that the studio executives at Fox were out to lunch the day the decisions were made.

MAGICAL MYSTERY TOUR
1967, Great Britain (TV) ☆☆½
The Beatles (George Harrison, John Lennon, Paul McCartney, Ringo Starr), Victor Spinetti, Mandy Weet, Derek Royle, George Claydon, Ivor Cutler. Directed by The Beatles. 60 min.

As well as anyone can tell, this is all pretty much Paul's fault, and it's only better than *Give My Regards to Broad Street* because it has better songs and a better cast (i.e., all four Beatles). They do seem to be making up this BBC television special as they go along; the plot makes no sense at all unless you have the record album and the accompanying booklet. Even for all of its indulgence, the whole mess is occasionally endearing, like the first music videos were before they got slick and expensive. Songs include "Magical Mystery Tour," "The Fool on the Hill," "Flying," "Blue Jay Way," "Your Mother Should Know," and "I Am the Walrus."

THE MAGIC CHRISTIAN
1970, Great Britain ☆☆½
Peter Sellers, Ringo Starr, Isabel Jeans, Wilfred Hyde-White, Richard Attenborough, Leonard Frey, Laurence Harvey, Christopher Lee, Spike Milligan, Raquel Welch, John Cleese, Graham Chapman, Roman Polanski, Yul Brynner, John Le Mesurier, Dennis Price. Directed by Joseph McGrath. 92 min.

Like the often-filmed *Brewster's Millions*, this is basically a farce about all the great things you could do if you were filthy rich. Peter Sellers plays the world's richest man, Sir Guy Grand, who spends his time amiably proving that you can do anything with money and that people will do anything for it. It really has no plot to speak of, just a spiraling series of gags and practical jokes that climaxes with proper Brits wading into a pool, specially constructed by Grand, containing equal parts animal blood, urine, manure, and pound notes. In between, he adopts Ringo Starr (who has nothing to do but does it most engagingly), stages a mock cruise of a new luxury liner powered by topless female galley slaves, stages quail hunts with antiaircraft artillery, bribes a policeman (ex-Goon Spike Milligan) to eat a traffic ticket, and so forth. Monty Python fans would do well to check it out, as would all fans of English humor, although the ending fails because it has nowhere in particular to go. Sellers cowrote the screenplay with director Joseph McGrath and Terry Southern, and the score contains some good songs by former Beatles protégés Badfinger.

THE MAGIC FLUTE
1974, Sweden, G ☆☆☆☆
Josef Kostliger, Irma Urrila, Birgit Nordin. Directed by Ingmar Bergman. 135 min.

We're so used to Ingmar Bergman's more gloomy views of the human condition that we may forget he's the same director who gave us such comedies as *Smiles of a Summer Night*. Although this is a fairly conventional rendering of the opera without a lot of cinematic daring, it's nonetheless a whimsically stylized and beautifully photographed version that translates the material without any damage. Unafraid to call attention to the artifice of the piece, Bergman draws us into an enchanted world of dashing princes rescuing princesses while the forces of good and evil swirl about in the background. This *Flute* is indeed magic as conceived by Bergman and should be a model for other screen operas. George Bernard Shaw said that this opera's music was the only music fit for the mouth of God, and it's hard to argue with that after listening to the film's soundtrack. It's blissful, enchanting, and as easy to sit through as *Amadeus*.

THE MAGICIAN ☆☆☆½
1958, Sweden
Max von Sydow, Ingrid Thulin, Gunnar Bjornstrand, Bibi Andersson, Naima Wifstrand, Lars Ekborg. Directed by Ingmar Bergman. 102 min.

Ingmar Bergman channels his moody introspection into this horror tale about a nineteenth-century magician and his troupe who plot revenge on the authorities who try to expose him as a charlatan. This is not as great as Bergman's other "middle-period" films (*Smiles of a Summer Night*, *Wild Strawberries*), but once again, his accomplished cast and crew create dazzling set pieces within a formally and intellectually challenging framework. (a.k.a.: *The Face*)

THE MAGICIAN OF LUBLIN ☆½
1979, USA, R
Alan Arkin, Louise Fletcher, Valerie Perrine, Shelley Winters, Lou Jacobi, Warren Berlinger. Directed by Menahem Golan. 105 min.

Cannon president Menahem Golan meets Nobel laureate Isaac Bashevis Singer, and despite an all-star cast and a tony production, Singer loses. Singer's dark, adult fable is set in turn-of-the-century Warsaw, where a shrewd, libidinous magician (Alan Arkin) wins temporary notoriety by claiming the ability to fly. Golan's heavy-handed direction causes Singer's subtlety to sink like a stone, and except for Arkin's wry turn, the cast is stiff and unappealing.

THE MAGIC OF LASSIE ☆
1978, USA, G
Lassie, James Stewart, Mickey Rooney, Stephanie Zimbalist, Pernell Roberts, Alice Faye. Directed by Don Chaffey. 99 min.

Children, poor things, are talked down to. That's all right, they're used to it. Maybe that's why they like Lassie so much; she doesn't talk at all. What is really unforgivable is when they're *sung* down to by people who can't sing (such as James Stewart, Mickey Rooney, and Alice Faye) or shouldn't sing (such as Debby Boone). Couple this constant croaking with an orchestral score that swells yet never arrives, and you have a film that's short on magic and hard on Lassie. Vindictive grape lover Pernell Roberts lifts Stewart's grandson's fluffy collie after a botched business transaction and shunts her to Colorado. Lassie escapes and Stewart tries to find her; at every turn in their trying search for each other there are tearjerking near-fatalities and glitches, and the journey to the requisite happy ending is larded with ersatz pathos.

MAGIC TOWN ☆☆☆
1947, USA
James Stewart, Jane Wyman, Kent Smith, Regis Toomey, Donald Meek, Ned Sparks. Directed by William A. Wellman. 103 min.

If this folksy little comedy-drama resembles a Frank Capra film, it is probably because Capra's independent film company (Liberty Films) helped produce it and because Robert Riskin (Capra's most frequent writer) wrote the screenplay. In some ways, it's even better (or at least less overbearing) than some 1940s Capra. James Stewart plays a pollster who wants to strike pay dirt by exploiting a small town to represent Anytown, USA, in a human interest story. When the local newspaper editor (Jane Wyman) exposes his scheme, the town becomes the eye of a tabloid hurricane. William Wellman's somber approach to the tale leaves some of the humorous aspects unexplored, but there are several quietly charming moments along the way. Stewart and Wyman are a likable pair.

THE MAGNIFICENT AMBERSONS ☆☆☆☆
1942, USA
Joseph Cotten, Anne Baxter, Tim Holt, Agnes Moorehead, Dolores Costello, Ray Collins. Directed by Orson Welles. 88 min.

Some camps like this even better than *Citizen Kane*. Orson Welles's follow-up to *Kane* was supposedly tampered with by RKO (when weren't his films being tampered with?), but this adaptation of Booth Tarkington's novel remains one of the most compelling cinematic depictions of American small-town life. Welles does not appear in the film (he starred in a 1939 radio version), but he does supply the witty, ironic narration to the story of a spoiled, arrogant heir (Tim Holt) who destroys everyone within his orbit. Welles also interweaves engaging but pointed commentary about the economic and social changes brought about by the Industrial Revolution. Despite the general unevenness of the acting (Holt and Anne Baxter are stilted, although Agnes Moorehead gives a tour de force as the neurotic spinster aunt), the film is superb in almost every other department (Stanley Cortez's deep-focus cinematography expands on Gregg Toland's work in *Kane*). The film is not as earth-shaking as *Citizen Kane*, but it's almost as powerful in its own quiet, forceful way.

THE MAGNIFICENT FIST ☆
1978, Hong Kong
Carter Huang, John Wai, Kam Ki Jue, Mok Yuen Char, Hui I Lin, Chue Jin. Directed by Kam Aug.

This is a drab Carter Huang action picture in which he attempts to protect his "well-shaped, 200-year-old" ginseng plant against a horde of covetous Japanese. For tea nuts only.

MAGNIFICENT MATADOR ☆☆☆
1955, USA
Anthony Quinn, Maureen O'Hara. Directed by Budd Boetticher. 94 min.

A matador is faced with initiating his son into the bullring in this intensely felt evocation of the demands of the last great blood sport. Budd Boetticher, the writer and director, began his Hollywood career as a technical adviser on the bullfighting scenes for *Blood and Sand*, and lavishes a loving effort both on his subject and the Mexican countryside.

MAGNIFICENT OBSESSION ☆☆☆½
1954, USA
Jane Wyman, Rock Hudson, Barbara Rush, Agnes Moorehead, Otto Kruger. Directed by Douglas Sirk. 107 min.

Based on the Lloyd C. Douglas novel, this *Obsession* is far superior to the 1935 version starring Irene Dunne and Robert Taylor. It's an expertly made melodrama about a reckless playboy (Rock Hudson) who devotes his life to helping the young widow (Jane Wyman) he accidentally injures. Douglas Sirk's meticulous mise-en-scène perfectly complements a plot that often becomes a surreal collage of events, and the mystical elements of the story add a richness that raises the film from mere entertainment to something truly thought provoking.

THE MAGNIFICENT SEVEN ☆☆☆½
1960, USA
Yul Brynner, Steve McQueen, Eli Wallach, Horst Buchholz, James Coburn, Charles Bronson, Robert Vaughn. Directed by John Sturges. 126 min.

Hollywood's colorful, enjoyable remake of *The Seven Samurai* is highlighted by an amazing assortment of nascent superstars. Among the paid gunslingers who team up against bandits in a small Mexican town are Charles Bronson, a mostly silent James Coburn, Steve McQueen (doing great moves with a sawed-off shotgun), and Yul Brynner, who comes through with a kingly performance as the gang leader he later parodied in *Westworld*. John Sturges effectively demythologizes the Western by concentrating equally on character and action: Each of the seven gunfighters has a personal reason, aside from the small amount of money they are being paid, for participating in the defense of the village. Neither of the sequels is up to par.

MAGNUM FORCE ★★½
1973, USA, R
Clint Eastwood, Hal Holbrook, Felton Perry, Mitchell Ryan, David Soul, Tim Matheson, Robert Urich. Directed by Ted Post. 122 min.

There's an interesting thematic twist to this first sequel in the *Dirty Harry* series; here, vigilante cop Callahan must track down a band of renegade officers in a case that will test the same system he sorely opposes. As always, Clint Eastwood's cooly calculated performance suggests that there's more going on in his character than he'll allow the script to show, but, this time around, he has a fairly intricate story written by John Milius (*Red Dawn*) and Michael Cimino (*The Deer Hunter*) to back him up. Healthy doses of violence appear with reassuring regularity to remind you that, despite its small pretensions, this is still a Dirty Harry flick with a vengeance.

MAHLER ★★
1974, Great Britain
Robert Powell, Georgina Hale, Lee Montague, Antonia Ellis. Directed by Ken Russell. 110 min.

Ken Russell's pseudo-biography of the Austrian composer is memorable for the director's by now familiar excesses. It uses dream sequences, grotesque fantasies, and flashbacks to disguise an ultimately conventional music bio about misunderstood genius. You won't learn much about the man or the musician, but you will see Cosima Wagner interpreted as a whip-cracking Nazi sex goddess, singing lyrics to Wagner's "Valkyrie" so tasteless they must be heard to be believed. In the midst of this idiocy, Robert Powell manages to give an appealing and insightful performance as Mahler.

MAHOGANY ★½
1975, USA, PG
Diana Ross, Billy Dee Williams, Anthony Perkins, Jean-Pierre Aumont, Nina Foch, Beah Richards. Directed by Berry Gordy, Tony Richardson. 109 min.

Riding on the crest of her Oscar nomination for *Lady Sings the Blues*, Diana Ross sunk in this follow-up rags-to-riches yarn, this time concerning a small-time fashion designer who becomes an international model. Ross and the rest of the talented cast are wasted in stereotyped roles and forced to mouth inane dialogue. Anthony Perkins's patented *Psycho* bit provides the most fascinatingly bad performance, but the others are merely routinely awful. The largest mistake, obviously, was in conceiving a Diana Ross movie without songs, although the hit "Do You Know Where You're Going To?" comes from this film. It's a tedious trash wallow, even for Ross fans.

MAID'S NIGHT OUT ★½
1938, USA
Joan Fontaine, Allan Lane, Hedda Hopper, George Irving, William Brisbane. Directed by Ben Holmes. 64 min.

This is a simpering farce of mistaken identity among the upper crust. He's really an aristocrat with a penchant for studying fish. And she's really not the maid at all, but a blueblood lass whose family is in a financial reversal. With witless retreads of thirties comedies like this, it's no wonder the screwball comedy was dealt a death blow. It's only for old film buffs apt to appreciate the resuscitative efforts of the supporting cast.

THE MAIN EVENT ★★
1979, USA, PG
Barbra Streisand, Ryan O'Neal, Paul Sand, Whitman Mayo, Patti D'Arbanville. Directed by Howard Zieff. 110 min.

Made in the mold of the Hepburn-Tracy comedies, *The Main Event* fails to provide much old-fashioned fun. Barbra Streisand and Ryan O'Neal, who proved a winning team in *What's Up, Doc?*, are reunited. Barbra's a bankrupt perfume manufacturer and her only asset is broken-down boxer O'Neal. It's hate at first sight and, of course, later—love. It all resembles a sitcom, but sitcoms don't often have a larger-than-life star like Streisand—she is often funnier than the material. Patti D'Arbanville scores briefly as O'Neal's chronically coughing girlfriend.

MAJOR BARBARA ★★★
1941, Great Britain
Wendy Hiller, Rex Harrison, Robert Morley, Robert Newton, Sybil Thorndike, Deborah Kerr. Directed by Gabriel Pascal. 115 min.

This film version of George Bernard Shaw's wild satire about the daughter of an armaments millionaire who joins the Salvation Army and then quits when it accepts a donation from her father, is stiff and theatrical, but that scarcely matters—not when Rex Harrison and Wendy Hiller are staging Shaw's glittering verbal battles. The rest of the cast is nearly as marvelous.

MAJOR DUNDEE ★
1965, USA
Charlton Heston, Richard Harris, James Coburn, Jim Hutton, Warren Oates. Directed by Sam Peckinpah. 124 min.

Mitch Miller's Sing Along Gang performs the title song during the opening credits, and indeed this choppily edited early Sam Peckinpah film often seems to have no more continuity than a medley of old favorites. Charlton Heston plays a cavalry officer pursuing a vicious Apache into Mexico to rescue the three white children he's kidnapped (a blatant echo of *Rio Grande*, 1950). But the story is narrated off-screen from the diary of one of the troopers, which has a distancing effect, as have the numerous, largely irrelevant subplots. Heston, Richard Harris, and James Coburn deliver the expected grizzled performances, and the Mexican location filming is gorgeous, but the thing's been done a thousand times before. Senta Berger supplies the obligatory speck of romance. Compare this with 1969's *Wild Bunch* to see how much Peckinpah improved in four years.

MAKE ME AN OFFER ★★½
1980, USA (TV)
Susan Blakely, Patrick O'Neal, John Rubinstein, Bruce Bauer, Edie Adams, Kathleen Lloyd, Carole Cook, Stella Stevens. Directed by Jerry Paris. 97 min.

The cutthroat world of Beverly Hills real estate is the setting of this made-for-TV satire with a mild feminist slant. Susan Blakely plays a loyal wife who works to put her husband through law school, and gets dumped when he graduates. Untrained, she takes a job with a realtor and soon learns that making more money than your ex is the best revenge—or is it? Most of the good opportunities for satire are lost in a sitcom-style succession of quick, simplistic scenes, but Blakely is ingratiating in the leading role.

MAKE MINE MINK ★★★
1960, Great Britain
Terry-Thomas, Athene Seyler, Billie Whitelaw, Hattie Jacques, Elspeth Duxbury, Irene Handl, Jack Hedley, Ron Moody. Directed by Robert Asher. 118 min.

The older actors, particularly Athene Seyler, use every trick to enliven this thin but charming tale of a quartet of senior citizens who turn to a life of innocent if profitable crime. Leisurely paced, the film does boast some hysterical situations and the pros in the cast keep it consistently amusing.

MAKING LOVE ★★
1982, USA, R
Michael Ontkean, Kate Jackson, Harry Hamlin, Wendy Hiller, Arthur Hill, Nancy Olson. Directed by Arthur Hiller. 113 min.

This is a gloves-on treatment of homosexuality, in which a married doctor (Michael Ontkean) finds himself unable to suppress the feelings he has for men, and drifts away from his wife (Kate Jackson) into the bed of an out-of-the-closet novelist (Harry Hamlin). Although it's refreshing to see any big-studio film that doesn't portray gays as suicidal (*The Boys in the Band*) or homicidal (*Cruising*), *Making Love* is too much the opposite—almost suffocatingly tasteful and cautious. All the performances are good, and the obligatory love scene between Ontkean and Hamlin is handled with something between tact and cowardice. The movie is entirely inoffensive, if that is any criterion by which to make or watch a film.

MAKING THE GRADE ☆☆
1984, USA, R
Judd Nelson, Jonna Lee, Gordon Jump, Walter Okewicz, Dana Olsen. Directed by Dorian Walker. 105 min.

This is a fairly brainless rerun of the slobs-vs.-snobs routine, with a Jersey kid hired by a rich kid to attend his last year of prep school for him: Of course, there are all the predictable clashes between street culture and the squeaky-clean preppies, with a score of alligator jokes. The direction is at best competent, the editing is bad, and it features the phoniest break-dancing scene of all of 1984, a year when almost every movie had a break-dancing scene. But you can't really dislike it: Judd Nelson has star charisma, though it's poorly used here, and there are several winning supporting players who do well with clichéd roles. Best of all is Dana Olsen as Palmer Woodrow III, the rich kid with no shame at all about claiming his God-given rights to wealth, arrogance, and self-indulgence—"I'm rich," he tells his best (and only) friend. "I don't *have* to be nice."

MALCOLM ☆☆
1986, Australia, PG-13
Colin Friels, John Hargreaves, Lindy Davies, Chris Haywood, Charles Tingwell, Beverly Philips. Directed by Nadia Tass. 90 min.

Colin Friels gives a charming performance as a mildly retarded thirty-year-old man who has an astounding knack for mechanical gadgetry, but *Malcolm* is even slower than its title character and not as inventive. The centerpiece of this offbeat comedy is a hilariously improbable bank heist pulled off courtesy of the hero, but before and after, it just wanders along. *Note: Malcolm* was a minor milestone in a way that has nothing to do with content—it was the first theatrical film to be produced by a video company (in this case, Vestron).

MALIBU BEACH ☆½
1978, USA, R
Kim Lankford, James Daughton, Susan Player Jarreau. Directed by Robert J. Rosenthal. 93 min.

Perfectly titled and perfectly mindless, *Malibu Beach* should offend no one who is prepared to enter a theater with those two words on the marquee. A blonde lifeguard (Kim Lankford) and her friend are importuned by a tanned muscle man and two geeks. Pot is smoked. The geeks get the women and the muscle man goes off with a schoolteacher to give her a few lessons. Pot is smoked. The movie comes to an end. Volleyball, anyone?

THE MALTA STORY ☆☆½
1953, Great Britain
Alec Guinness, Jack Hawkins, Anthony Steel, Muriel Pavlow, Flora Robson, Renee Asherton. Directed by Brian Desmond Hurst. 103 min.

Filmed on location in Malta, this retrospective war film honors the historic role of the RAF fliers against the Axis invasion (and, by extension, the valiant resistance of the Maltese population). Sober performances mitigate the conventionality of the material, with Alex Guinness as the contemplative hero.

THE MALTESE FALCON ☆☆☆☆
1941, USA
Humphrey Bogart, Mary Astor, Jerome Cowan, Gladys George, Sydney Greenstreet, Peter Lorre, Elisha Cook, Jr., Lee Patrick, Barton MacLane, Ward Bond, Walter Huston. Directed by John Huston. 100 min.

Humphrey Bogart stars as Dashiell Hammett's cool, cynical private eye, Sam Spade, in this classic tale of deception, greed, and a priceless, jewel-encrusted statuette. At the story's outset, Spade's partner, Miles Archer (Jerome Cowan), is murdered and, as Spade puts it, "When a man's partner is killed, he's supposed to do something about it." The film marked John Huston's directorial debut, one of the most impressive in the annals of American cinema. Huston also wrote the screenplay, which remains faithful to the tone, plot, and themes of Hammett's novel. Huston established a sinister mood in *The Maltese Falcon* that made it a pivotal, early example of *film noir*. Bogart's Spade is, appropriately, less vulnerable than his portrayal of Raymond Chandler's incorruptible sleuth, Philip Marlowe, in Howard Hawks's 1946 *The Big Sleep*. Sydney Greenstreet, in his first screen role, and the rest of this excellent cast, provide Bogart with admirable support. Look for the director's father, Walter Huston, as Captain Jacobi.

MAME ☆☆
1974, USA, PG
Lucille Ball, Beatrice Arthur, Robert Preston, Jane Connell, Bruce Davison. Directed by Gene Saks. 133 min.

Mame has its flaws but in parts it's a grandly old-fashioned movie no musical fanatic can miss. Lucille Ball, sixty-two at the time of filming, took much abuse for being hazily photographed and for her less-than-Streisand singing. Still, she has style and charm and is a funny Auntie Mame. Beatrice Arthur is spectacular, re-creating her Tony-winning role as Mame's best friend, and Robert Preston lends solid support. Gene Saks, who directed *Mame* on Broadway, is more than a bit heavy-handed with the film. Jerry Herman's all-hit score is a delight, as are Theodora Van Runkle's gorgeous costumes. The story, having gone from novel to stage to screen to stage and now screen again, holds up. *Mame* is fine as innocuous family entertainment. The PG rating is for several words that now turn up occasionally on network TV.

A MAN ALONE ☆☆½
1955, USA
Ray Milland, Mary Murphy, Ward Bond, Raymond Burr, Arthur Space, Lee Van Cleef, Alan Hale, Douglas Spencer, Thomas B. Henry. Directed by Ray Milland. 95 min.

With this offbeat Western, actor Ray Milland proves that he can handle the director's reins as well as act. He plays a fugitive who holes up with a young woman and her father in a cabin that's been quarantined for yellow fever infection. The claustrophobic dynamics are nicely balanced by the outside threat of a lynch mob that's aching to get a noose around Milland's neck; both stories are well developed, and the conclusion manages a surprise. The supporting cast acquits themselves nicely, and seasoned viewers will welcome Ward Bond, Lee Van Cleef, and especially Raymond Burr as a nefarious banker. Although the heightened tensions will occasionally spill over into ripe melodrama, this is an under-recognized little treat. Filmed in Republic's oddly-hued Trucolor process.

A MAN AND A WOMAN ☆☆☆
1966, France
Anouk Aimée, Jean-Louis Trintignant, Valerie LaGrange, Pierre Barouk. Directed by Claude Lelouch. 102 min.

The quintessential make-out movie of the 1960s has lost some of its sparkle over the years, but Anouk Aimée and Jean-Louis Trintignant still make a formidable romantic duo and the infectious Francis Lai score helps the film soar above the soapsuds. A racing car driver whose wife has died finds emotional fulfillment with a young widow in a love story that was so irresistible that Claude

Lelouch himself plagiarized it in *Another Man, Another Chance*. An Academy Award winner for Best Foreign Film; followed in 1986 by a sequel, *A Man and a Woman: 20 Years Later*.

A MAN AND A WOMAN: 20 YEARS LATER ☆☆
1986, France, PG
Anouk Aimée, Jean-Louis Trintignant, Richard Berry, Evelyne Bouix, Marie-Sophie Pochat, Patrick Poivre D'Arvor. Directed by Claude Lelouch. 120 min.

Claude Lelouch's late-in-coming sequel to his 1966 international hit is well-intentioned but rather inane; having come up with the concept of reuniting his lovers, he forgot to throw in a coherent or believable plot. Jean-Louis, the race-car driver, is now a race organizer, while Anne, the script girl, has become a successful film producer. This gives Lelouch a chance to throw in film-within-a-film footage, intermingle it with "reality," throw in flashbacks from *A Man and a Woman*, and generally dawdle over the interplay between Life and Art which, as presented here, is somewhat less fascinating than he intends. Jean-Louis Trintignant and Anouk Aimée still set off the occasional spark, and the Francis Lai score remains humable, but the simplicity of the first film is replaced by a crush of empty technique and glib observation.

A MAN, A WOMAN AND A BANK ☆☆☆
1979, Canada, PG
Donald Sutherland, Brooke Adams, Paul Mazursky, Allen Magicovsky. Directed by Noel Black. 100 min.

This is a funny, entertaining romp that received only limited theatrical distribution in this country. Donald Sutherland and Paul Mazursky (in his first major acting role) play a pair of computer hackers who plug into the computer systems of a bank under construction so that, when the bank is completed, they can make their own "withdrawals" at will. Brooke Adams is charming as Sutherland's love interest, who doesn't know what's going on until late in the game. (a.k.a.: *A Very Big Withdrawal*)

A MAN CALLED ADAM ☆☆
1966, USA
Sammy Davis, Jr., Louis Armstrong, Ossie Davis, Cicely Tyson, Frank Sinatra, Jr., Peter Lawford, Mel Torme, Lola Falana, Jeanette Du Bois. Directed by Leo Penn. 96 min.

Nobody knows the trouble Sammy has seen. As an ultracool cat, the Candy Man has to contend with a lot of uptight whites who resent his bluesy horn, his way with the ladies, and his hip patter. There's something a tad nauseating about having to swallow synthetic Sammy as the troubled hero while greats like Louis Armstrong, Cicely Tyson, and Ossie Davis are forced to play fawning, defeated sycophants. Worse, the entire structure of racism boils down to a conspiracy of mean people who like picking on this sensitive artist. Cruel movie buffs may appreciate Sammy Davis, Jr.'s outrageous overacting; his crying scene is sure to provoke laughs. On the up side, Nat Adderly did fine work dubbing the horn playing, and Benny Carter's score is generally first-rate.

A MAN CALLED HORSE ☆☆½
1970, USA, R
Richard Harris, Judith Anderson, Jean Gascon, Manu Tupou, Corinna Tsopei, Dub Taylor, William Jordan. Directed by Elliot Silverstein. 114 min.

An English aristocrat wanders off into Sioux country in order to discover himself, and winds up the captive of his involuntary hosts. But, being the tough and smart white man that he is, he naturally withstands all of the torture and, in due course, scalps and fights his way to the top of the tribe. If this kind of racist paternalism doesn't put you off and you can wade through Richard Harris's comically heavy philosophical mumblings, the movie does offer an interesting look at native American culture, and the story is relatively well told. The only satisfying sequence for fans of real Westerns is the exciting, well-mounted battle between the Sioux and the Shoshone. Followed by *Return of A Man Called Horse* and *Triumphs of A Man Called Horse*.

A MAN CALLED TIGER ☆
1972, Hong Kong, X
Jimmy Wang Yu, Maria Yi, James Tien, Han Yin-Chien, Okada Kawai. Directed by Lo Wei. 79 min.

Jimmy is in Japan trying to solve his father's murder. James helps him, and Han is the bad guy. The movie is murder, but all Jimmy Wang Yu movies are audience killers.

MANDINGO ½☆
1975, USA, R
James Mason, Susan George, Perry King, Richard Ward, Brenda Sykes, Ken Norton, Lillian Hayman, Paul Benedict, Ji-Tu Cumbuka, Ben Masters. Directed by Richard Fleischer. 126 min.

It takes a lot to offend us, and since *Mandingo* is one of the few films that succeeds, we can't dismiss it without a few words of gape-jawed amazement. Here, from a major studio (Paramount), is a film so puerile, racist, and sexist in intent and artless in execution that it defies description and belief. Highlights include: James Mason's mean plantation patriarch trying to cure his rheumatism by digging his sore toes into a slave child's stomach; Susan George sidling up to the "big black buck" of the title (Ken Norton) to whisper, "Pleasure me, Mandingo"; her brother becoming jealous (seems he slept with his sister when they were thirteen and still misses it) and taking a lash to a slave mistress of his own; and a climactic birth scene in which everyone, including the mother, is wondering what color the new arrival will be. We bet you didn't know the Civil War began because the races kept hopping into bed together. All we know is that somebody must have slept with somebody else to get this movie made; there's just no other explanation. Followed by a sequel, *Drum*.

MANEATER

See *Shark!*

A MAN FOR ALL SEASONS ☆☆☆☆
1966, Great Britain
Paul Scofield, Robert Shaw, Wendy Hiller, Orson Welles, Susannah York, Vanessa Redgrave, John Hurt. Directed by Fred Zinnemann. 120 min.

Six Academy Awards, including Best Picture, Best Director, and Best Actor (Paul Scofield), went to this powerful film version of Robert Bolt's play about the explosive ideological battle between Sir Thomas More (Scofield) and King Henry VIII (Robert Shaw). The issues and debates are all delineated too neatly and clearly, but Fred Zinnemann's sumptuous production generates great emotion out of what could have turned into a long-winded history lesson or a costume-heavy soap. The great cast, somewhat too mindful of the seriousness and nobility of their subject, does distinguished but low-key work. Scofield, though, is masterly—articulate, graceful, and passionate—as the conscientious objector to Henry's misdeeds, and he holds you in thrall even when the screenplay degenerates into speechifying. Scofield, one of our greatest actors, has, alas, made very few films since this now-classic biography.

MAN FRIDAY ☆☆½
1975, Great Britain, PG
Peter O'Toole, Richard Roundtree. Directed by Jack Gold. 109 min.

British colonialism and racism are satirized by taking the story of Robinson Crusoe and retelling it from the point of view of Crusoe's "hired servant," Friday. It's an intriguing idea, but one that is never developed beyond the noble-savage, uptight-white-man stereotypes. Peter O'Toole is very good, but he's ultimately limited by the fact that the role is essentially more caricature than character. Richard Roundtree, on the other hand, seems unable to play his role as anything but a stereotype. The movie was filmed in Puerto Vallarta, Mexico.

THE MAN FROM ATLANTIS ☆☆
1977, USA (TV)
Patrick Duffy, Belinda Montgomery, Art Lund, Dean Santoro, Victor Buono. Directed by Lee H. Katzin. 100 min.

Get in the swim with some splashy sci-fi as Patrick Duffy flips his fins in the briny deep before he rode the range to stardom in "Dallas." Sporting an impressive physique and somewhat less exceptional acting skills, Duffy plays the last remaining survivor of the famed suboceanic city, and he raises his webbed hand in the defense of the American Way and non-chlorinated swimming pools. A bit drippy, but fun.

MAN FROM MUSIC MOUNTAIN ☆½
1943, USA
Roy Rogers, Bob Nolan and The Sons of the Pioneers, Ruth Terry. Directed by Joseph Kane. 71 min.

Cattlemen versus the sheep ranchers in one of Roy's better outings. He plays a singing star who sides with the sheep, and Ruth Terry, soon to be replaced by Dale Evans, gives a nice light touch to the love interest.

THE MAN FROM SNOWY RIVER ☆☆½
1982, Australia, PG
Kirk Douglas, Tom Burlinson, Sigrid Thornton, Terence Donovan, Tommy Dysart, Bruce Kerr. Directed by George Miller. 105 min.

At the time of its American release, this Australian feature was already that country's highest-grossing movie ever, surpassing *Star Wars* by a wide margin. This undoubtedly has to do with the story's status as something of an Aussie folk classic, derived from a popular poem written around the turn of the century, about a boy who comes of age while helping to save a herd of wild bush horses from an American rancher. The story is less resonant for American audiences, who may not quite fathom why the director is taking such epic measures in dealing with such a simple story. (The director, we must note, is *not* the George Miller of *Mad Max* fame.) Kirk Douglas plays two roles, the rancher (read: "despoiler of the land") and his brother, a sort of outback-dwelling benevolent version of Long John Silver.

THE MAN FROM THE FOLIES BERGERE

See *Folies Bergere* (1935).

THE MANGO TREE ☆☆½
1977, Australia
Geraldine Fitzgerald, Robert Helpmann, Christopher Pate, Gerard Kennedy, Gloria Dawn. Directed by Kevin Dobson. 92 min.

This is a slow-moving, atmospheric movie about coming of age in Australia during the World War I years. Geraldine Fitzgerald dominates the film with a straightforward, dramatic performance as a feisty, independent grandmother. It's a very "Masterpiece Theater"–style production done with impeccable taste but no directorial flair.

MANHATTAN ☆☆☆☆
1979, USA, R
Woody Allen, Diane Keaton, Michael Murphy, Mariel Hemingway, Anne Byrne, Meryl Streep. Directed by Woody Allen. 96 min.

This wonderful, bittersweet saga of love in the city stars Woody Allen as a comedy writer torn between an affectionate schoolgirl, Mariel Hemingway, and a neurotic intellectual, Diane Keaton. The film is a joy throughout, funny, touching, poignant. The romance is real and wrenching; the characters ring true. The chemistry between Allen and Keaton has never been better. Hemingway, in her best performance by far, is perfect as Allen's innocent and appealing young love interest. Meryl Streep, as Allen's ex who has discovered lesbianism, is superlative as usual. Gordon Willis's elegant black-and-white cinematography superbly conveys the film's picturesque, romantic tone. (The video version preserves the entire wide-screen image and looks beautiful.) Whether you see it alone or with a sweetheart, this romantic masterpiece will do your soul good.

THE MANHATTAN PROJECT ☆☆
1986, USA, PG-13
John Lithgow, Christopher Collet, Cynthia Nixon, Jill Eikenberry, John Mahoney, Paul Austin. Directed by Marshall Brickman. 120 min.

Unlike the imaginative comedy-thriller *WarGames*, this film can't suck us into its improbable adventures involving Armageddon; we never suspend our disbelief. A teenage boy, long on technical genius but short on tolerance for grown-ups, decides to build his own atomic bomb as a science project in order to protest secret government testing and pollution of the environment. Unfortunately for the film, this teen savior's motives come across as those of a petulant schoolboy eager to put one over on the Establishment, rather than those of a concerned citizen fighting against the misuse of power. Filled with lots of zingy one-liners and capably acted across the board, the film remains a flaky, uninvolving enterprise that fails to cross a thinking man's thriller with juvenile fun. Retitled *The Manhattan Project: The Deadly Game* on video.

MANHUNTER ☆☆☆
1986, USA, R
William L. Petersen, Kim Greist, Joan Allen, Brian Cox, Dennis Farina, Stephen Lang, Tom Noonan. Directed by Michael Mann. 118 min.

This frightening, exceptionally intense crime thriller was written and directed by Michael Mann, the creator of "Miami Vice," and he obviously relished the lack of small-screen constraints. His signature touches—the pulsing soundtrack, the sharp visuals, the overdressed cops—are all in place, but the story they serve is fierce and gripping, unlike all TV and most other movies. William L. Petersen plays an ex-investigator who used to specialize in tracking serial killers by becoming, in a way, their mental doubles—imagining what they see, how they kill, what they dream, and who they'll target next. Still recovering from a case that brought him to the edge of psychosis, he reluctantly returns to duty, in pursuit of a maniac who massacres whole families by the full moon. Mann is superb at unlayering the mental processes of his too-dedicated hero, and he's helped by Petersen's quiet, masterful performance. Scary, and, at its best, enthralling.

MANIAC ☆
1934, USA
Bill Woods, Horace Carpenter, Ted Edwards, Phyllis Diller, Thea Ramsey, Jennie Dark, Marvel Andre. Directed by Dwain Esper. 57 min.

Fans of the outrageous must see this collection of peccadilloes from cinema's inglorious past. When Hollywood's Production Code went into effect in the early thirties, tight clamps were placed on the subject matter films could examine. Fortunately for sensation-starved fans, cheesy sub-industry producers began making movies that revealed such juicy tidbits as drug addiction, animal abuse, torture, medical operations, miscegenation, mutilations, and nudity. *Maniac* is remarkable mostly for the sheer variety of its distasteful acts. The plot, complete with psuedo-scientific jibberish about criminal insanity, concerns a washed-up actor who marries a doctor and assumes the doctor's identity and profession. Cat lovers will definitely want to give this a miss.

MANIAC ½☆
1980, USA, X (self-imposed)
Joe Spinell, Caroline Munro, Gail Lawrence (Abigail Clayton), Kelly Piper, Rita Montone, Tom Savini. Directed by William Lustig. 87 min.

A mother-fixated psychopath terrorizes New York, murdering women and bringing their scalps home to his dingy apartment in Queens. This is an excuse for a movie, structured around a series of spectacularly gross special effects designed by Tom (*Dawn of the Dead*) Savini, who makes a cameo appearance as a man who gets his head blown off with a shotgun inside a car. Disgusting, sleazy, and mechanical.

THE MAN IN GREY ☆☆☆
1943, Great Britain
Margaret Lockwood, James Mason, Phyllis Calvert, Stewart Granger, Martita Hunt. Directed by Leslie Arliss. 116 min.

Phyllis Calvert, repelled by the cruel mistreatment of her husband (James Mason) and the machinations of the woman she supposes to be her friend (Margaret Lockwood), takes refuge in the arms of Stewart Granger. This decorous feature, set in the early 1800s, was an immense success among British audiences during World War II and brought stardom to all four principals. Its succulent melodrama offered the escapism of romantic intrigue among the spoiled aristocracy of another era, yet it also mirrored the barely suppressed violence of the war years.

THE MAN IN THE IRON MASK ☆☆☆
1939, USA
Louis Hayward, Joan Bennett, Warren William, Joseph Schildkraut, Alan Hale, Walter Kingsford, Marion Martin. Directed by James Whale. 119 min.

Based on the Alexander Dumas tale of regal intrigue and musketeer heroics during the reign of Louis XIV, this extravaganza lends itself to good old-fashioned family viewing. Louis Hayward plays both the French king and the king's twin brother, a noble young swashbuckler who is forced to hide his identity behind an iron mask.

THE MAN IN THE IRON MASK ☆☆☆½
1977, USA (TV)
Richard Chamberlain, Patrick McGoohan, Louis Jourdan, Jenny Agutter, Ian Holm, Ralph Richardson, Vivien Merchant. Directed by Mike Newell. 100 min.

This tricky swashbuckling entertainment provided Richard Chamberlain with one of his most believable roles since he became the king of the TV costume pictures. Sometimes, Richard seems a bit too studied in these historical hero roles, as though he thought he was still playing Hamlet in repertory. But he's superb here playing King Louis XIV's twin brother who was believed dead. While rebarbative villains conspire against him, Chamberlain joins a plot to replace his brother. This is a superlative adventure tale replete with dazzling swordplay and sparkling production values.

THE MAN IN THE SANTA CLAUS SUIT ☆☆
1978, USA (TV)
Fred Astaire, Gary Burghoff, John Byner, Nanette Fabray, Harold Gould, Bert Convy. Directed by Corey Allen. 100 min.

A forced tour de force for Fred Astaire, who's a nimble farceur but not up to the demands of delineating the multiple roles he plays here. He's not as comically brilliant as Peter Sellers; however, he does possess that fabled Astaire charm, which sweeps all carping criticism before it. Eminently showable during the yuletide season, this film is a slight confection about several people whose lives are magically transformed when they rent a Santa Claus suit with very special properties.

THE MAN IN THE WHITE SUIT ☆☆☆☆
1952, Great Britain
Alec Guinness, Joan Greenwood, Cecil Parker, Michael Gough, Ernest Thesiger, Edie Martin. Directed by Alexander Mackendrick. 84 min.

A thoroughly beguiling parable on the machinations of capitalism in which Alec Guinness plays a frustrated chemist who discovers a wonder yarn with everlasting properties. His magical, dirt-repellent, indestructible suit is regarded with horror by both the cloth manufacturers and the trade unions, who unite to suppress the threat to their livelihoods. "Why can't you scientists leave things alone?" says Edie Martin, one of Ealing's perennial old ladies. This is a super comedy with a hard edge.

THE MANIONS OF AMERICA ☆☆½
1981, USA (TV)
Kathleen Beller, Pierce Brosnan, Steve Forrest, Simon MacCorkindale, Barbara Parkins, Kate Mulgrew, Anthony Quayle. Directed by Charles S. Dubin and Joseph Sargent. 270 min.

If Scarlett O'Hara were picking potatoes instead of cotton, she might have ended up in this lavish TV epic. Insurrections, patriotic folderol, family scandals, and tragic affairs all bubble together in a tasty but rather sludgy Irish stew. Dramatically, things get as thick as Barry Fitzgerald's accent as the Manions prove, with their various double dealings, that they're as American as the next guy. Luckily, there are no leprechauns assisting the clan in their fight for upward mobility in the New Land. Written by veteran soap opera creator Agnes Nixon, the film is a glorified Harlequin Romance with sturdy production values and lots of shamrocky sentimentality. Originally a six-hour miniseries.

THE MANITOU ☆
1978, USA, R
Susan Strasberg, Tony Curtis, Michael Ansara, Stella Stevens, Ann Sothern, Burgess Meredith. Directed by William Girdler. 104 min.

What would you do if a bump on the back of your neck suddenly turned out to be a tumorlike cocoon rapidly metamorphosing into the growing fetus of a three-hundred-year-old Indian? Like Susan Strasberg, you might scream a lot, seek the help of the more experienced performers in the cast to abort the unwanted "baby," and pray that you'll never have to act in a bomb like this again. As in so many recent horror films, a good if grotesque premise is mishandled into lifelessness by filmmakers who can only imitate their betters, not learn from them.

MAN OF FLOWERS ☆☆☆
1984, Australia
Norman Kaye, Alyson Best, Chris Haywood. Directed by Paul Cox. 91 min.

Surrounded by a tasteful decor of wealth and art, a gentle eccentric man worships the sensuality of flowers, studies drawing and flower arrangement, but tragically is unable to appreciate beauty except from afar. Some fine performances and an interweaving of dreamlike sequences depicting childhood memories, together with some beautiful photography, make for a wise yet witty film. An unusual combination of nutty, almost macabre humor and moments of great pathos, which is no small accomplishment.

MAN OF LA MANCHA ☆½
1972, USA, PG
Peter O'Toole, Sophia Loren, James Coco, Harry Andrews, John Castle. Directed by Arthur Hiller. 130 min.

On stage, whatever one thought of its pretensions, this musical built an undeniable power out of crisscrossing the life of Cervantes with the picaresque adventures of his legendary creation, Don Quixote. Plodding and hopelessly literal-minded, the film version doesn't tilt at windmills; it sinks in the mud. An impossible nightmare of failed conceits, this film is redeemed only by Peter

O'Toole's eccentric knight-errant and by Sophia Loren's astonishingly good performance as the earthy Dulcinea. If the filmmakers had scrapped the lugubrious score, these two stars might have saved the film.

THE MAN THEY COULD NOT HANG ☆☆
1939, USA
Boris Karloff, Lorna Grey, Robert Wilcox, Roger Pryor, Don Beddoe. Directed by Nick Grinde. 61 min.

In this typical Boris Karloff mad-doctor movie from the 1930s, he's a sympathetic character for the first half of the movie—a scientist working on a method of suspending life in patients so that difficult operations can be facilitated. But the police interrupt him during one such experiment, refuse to let him revive the patient, and try him for murder. After he is executed, his assistant brings him back to life and he sets out for revenge on the judge and jury who convicted him.

MANTIS FIST FIGHTER

See *Thundering Mantis*.

MANTIS VS. FALCON CLAWS ☆½
Hong Kong
Alain Ko, Gary Cho, Sonny Man, Bob Ng, Mike Cheun, Vincent Lee. Directed by Mitch Wong. 90 min.

Yet another story of an average man forced to take arms against a sea of misfortune. In this one, Wang, a silk merchant, must learn kung fu in order to retrieve his stolen goods from the evil Falcon Ma. It's not much on sets or costumes, but it does have some nice choreography. Unfortunately, the fight scenes have been speeded up photographically.

THE MAN WHO COULD WORK MIRACLES ☆☆☆
1936, Great Britain
Roland Young, Ralph Richardson, Edward Chapman, Ernest Thesiger, Joan Gardner, George Zucco, George Sanders. Directed by Lothar Mendes. 82 min.

Typical H. G. Wells story: A department store milquetoast (Roland Young) is magically endowed by the gods with powers to do anything. In using his gifts against his oppressors, he causes near apocalypse. Young is one of the few character actors who could carry a feature all alone, and the special effects of this fantasy are still impressive (though slightly less so than those in *Things to Come*). The problem is that the tone is often too serious for its own good, and Lothar Mendes's direction is ponderous in that 1930s British way.

THE MAN WHO FELL TO EARTH ☆☆☆½
1976, Great Britain, R
David Bowie, Candy Clark, Buck Henry, Rip Torn. Directed by Nicolas Roeg. 140 min.

Nicolas Roeg's beautiful, complex pop-art film has become a science-fiction cult classic. David Bowie plays a frail and exotic extraterrestrial who splashes down into a Southwestern lake and, in a noble attempt to find water for his people, is overcome by modern technology, American capitalism, and earthly love. Roeg has constructed a highly offbeat, intellectual film, but there is so much going on that the story is occasionally hard to take. Despite its unwieldiness, the film succeeds through sheer originality and directorial flair. Bowie's performance is haunting and unique. Don't expect a "family movie," however; there's enough nudity for the British to have given it an X rating. Based on a novel by Walter Tevis, author of *The Hustler*.

THE MAN WHO HAD POWER OVER WOMEN ☆½
1970, Great Britain, R
Rod Taylor, Carol White, James Booth, Penelope Horner, Charles Korvin, Alexandra Stewart, Clive Francis. Directed by John Krish. 89 min.

In this dull, overstated sex comedy set in swinging 1970s London, Rod Taylor, looking droopy and glum, plays a middle-aged talent agency executive who leaves his young wife for a series of minor sexual escapades. Clive Francis gives a wonderfully unpleasant portrayal of an egomaniacal rock star, but the rest of the film is familiar foolishness that makes the bad mistake of reaching for significance.

THE MAN WHO HAUNTED HIMSELF ☆☆
1970, Great Britain, PG
Roger Moore, Hildegard Neil, Alistair Mackenzie, Hugh Mackenzie, Thorley Walters, Freddie Jones, Gerald Sim. Directed by Basil Dearden. 94 min.

Wearing a wimpy mustache, Roger Moore plays a conservative businessman who, in a rare fit of reckless driving, gets into an accident that almost kills him. When he recovers, he begins to discern signs of a double of himself raising a ruckus with his life by acting in a most un-conservative manner. It's an interesting premise, unsatisfyingly handled: The second Moore should have been given more screen time, and the ending is weak.

THE MAN WHO KNEW TOO MUCH ☆☆☆
1934, Great Britain
Peter Lorre, Edna Best, Leslie Banks. Directed by Alfred Hitchcock. 84 min.

An American family on vacation finds itself entangled with spies and hurled into chaos in Hitchcock's first version of this classic suspense tale. Although some laud the gritty simplicity of this early film, the director's 1956 remake is smoother and more visually sophisticated. Hitchcock once commented that "the first version was the work of a talented amateur and the second was made by a professional." The film nonetheless boasts a fine cast, and Peter Lorre's performance as the elegant villain is especially good.

THE MAN WHO KNEW TOO MUCH ☆☆☆½
1956, USA
James Stewart, Doris Day, Daniel Gelin, Brenda De Banzie, Bernard Miles, Christopher Olsen. Directed by Alfred Hitchcock. 119 min.

Lost are Peter Lorre's villain and the husband and wife team-sleuthing, but Hitchcock's VistaVision and Technicolor remake is vastly superior to his own 1934 British original. The glossy Paramount production aside, this version—which is also about a vacationing couple's attempt to recover their kidnapped child—contains some of Hitchcock's most diverting and suspenseful set pieces, including a murder attempt in Albert Hall and a false lead in a taxidermy shop. Hitchcock's audacious plot digressions (from the John Michael Hayes–Angus McPhail screenplay), scene blackouts, and comedy relief (particularly in the closing bit) have rarely been equaled in his films. James Stewart and Doris Day work beautifully together as the slightly crass American couple who are reluctantly drawn into a world of political espionage in their attempt to find their son (a chilling scene—their best—finds Stewart sedating an hysterical Day after she is told of the kidnapping). Day's repetitious rendition of "Que Sera Sera," though necessary to the plot, is the one camp element of this otherwise sizzling suspense film.

THE MAN WHO LOVED CAT DANCING ☆½
1973, USA, PG
Burt Reynolds, Sarah Miles, Lee J. Cobb, Jack Warden, George Hamilton, Bo Hopkins. Directed by Richard C. Sarafian. 114 min.

This is a movie as long, boring, and pointless as its title. Burt Reynolds plays a cowboy who protects a woman (Sarah

Miles) fleeing both her husband and a gang of train robbers. Feminists will have trouble with a woman portrayed to enjoy being abused. Others will have trouble with the plodding story and shameful waste of character actors like Jack Warden and Lee J. Cobb. It's a major bore.

THE MAN WHO LOVED WOMEN ☆☆
1977, France
Charles Denner, Brigitte Fossey, Nelly Borgeaud, Leslie Caron, Nathalie Baye. Directed by François Truffaut. 119 min.

François Truffaut's oddly enervated story of a compulsive Casanova who skulks through a series of affairs as though he were living out a prison sentence. Charles Denner is the hero, a Don Juan so dour he's almost reptilian. And Truffaut, though clearly intending the story as a sort of autobiography, obviously didn't have his heart in it: The film is terse, facile, charmless, and not really as good as Blake Edwards's 1983 Americanization of it.

THE MAN WHO LOVED WOMEN ☆☆☆
1983, USA, R
Burt Reynolds, Julie Andrews, Kim Basinger, Cynthia Sykes, Barry Corbin. Directed by Blake Edwards. 118 min.

In his remake of a lesser François Truffaut film, Blake Edwards has cast Burt Reynolds in the role of a compulsive Don Juan, a promiscuous sculptor both sated and starved by love. But Edwards is one writer-director who doesn't indulge the smirky Reynolds persona; rather, he enlarges it. Reynolds's David Fowler is a man brought low by his woman chasing, a man so aggressively spunky in pursuit that he's laughable, so depressed in flight he's poignant. The movie isn't a knockdown comedy, though it has some hilarious bits; instead, Edwards shuffles flashbacks, subplots, and digressions into a series of anecdotal revelations that chart David's breakdown, recovery, and demise. The scenes with David and his adoring shrink (Julie Andrews) get a bit pedantic (who wants all this Freud in a farce?), but it's also a pleasure to see Edwards confounding his audience's expectations instead of pandering to them.

THE MAN WHO SHOT LIBERTY VALANCE ☆☆☆½
1962, USA
James Stewart, John Wayne, Vera Miles, Lee Marvin, Edmond O'Brien, Andy Devine, John Carradine, Jeanette Nolan, John Qualen, Woody Strode, Denver Pyle, Strother Martin, Lee Van Cleef. Directed by John Ford. 122 min.

James Stewart is a lawyer who becomes famous for shooting Liberty Valance, a notorious galoot played with a wonderfully wicked flair by Lee Marvin. John Wayne is the cowboy who takes personal umbrage at Stewart's nonviolent Eastern ways, and Vera Miles is the lady for whose attentions they vie. This study of Western nobility is classic John Ford material, though the picture is too long and appears to have been shot on decaying, cheap sets.

THE MAN WHO WASN'T THERE ☆
1983, USA, R
Steve Guttenberg, Jeffrey Tambor, Art Hindle, Morgan Hart, Lisa Langlois. Directed by Bruce Malmuth. 111 min.

A weak story and a comedy script with no jokes. The worst aspect of this straining farce, however, is the utterly charmless Steve Guttenberg, who generates no interest for his smarmy State Department employee enmeshed in a chase for some formula that renders people invisible. This is a film that couldn't make a profitable theatrical release and, therefore, was dumped on the cable and video market. It earns one star for the good-looking Washington locations. Originally in 3-D.

THE MAN WHO WOULD BE KING ☆☆☆☆
1975, USA, PG
Sean Connery, Michael Caine, Christopher Plummer, Shakira Caine, Saeed Jaffrey. Directed by John Huston. 129 min.

Sean Connery and Michael Caine are fine in this invigorating adaptation of a Rudyard Kipling tale about two British soldiers and con men who try to cheat the holy men of Kafiristan out of their sacred riches by persuading them that Connery is their long-awaited god. This is one of director John Huston's most broadly painted and realized films, with the ironic, almost bitter ending that marks (although some would say mars) many of his best films.

THE MAN WITH BOGART'S FACE ☆½
1980, USA, PG
Robert Sacchi, Franco Nero, Michelle Phillips, Olivia Hussey, Sybil Danning, Misty Rowe, Victor Buono, Herbert Lom, Jay Robinson, George Raft, Yvonne De Carlo, Mike Mazurki, Victor Sen Young, Buck Kartalian. Directed by Robert Day. 106 min.

The one movie that Robert Sacchi could ever have made, at least in a starring role: The professional Humphrey Bogart impersonator plays a man who has his face altered by plastic surgery to look like Bogart, changes his name to "Sam Marlowe," and sets himself up as a private investigator. From thereon in, it's a low-grade parody of *The Maltese Falcon*, with a lot of respectable character actors doing little but killing time. Sacchi undeniably looks like Bogart, but there's already plenty of real Bogart on video, so why settle for an imitation?

THE MAN WITH ONE RED SHOE ☆½
1985, USA, PG
Tom Hanks, Lori Singer, Dabney Coleman, Jim Belushi. Directed by Stan Dragoti. 92 min.

Another aborted attempt at remaking a French farce (this time *The Tall Blond Man with One Black Shoe*) into a slapstick American comedy. The talented Tom Hanks is wasted in this singularly unfunny tale about a musician who is unwittingly used as a pawn by rival CIA men. This is a movie that's constantly hitting you on the head with big, destructive jokes, resulting in headaches rather than laughter.

THE MAN WITH THE GOLDEN ARM ☆☆☆
1955, USA
Frank Sinatra, Eleanor Parker, Kim Novak, Darren McGavin, Arnold Stang, Robert Strauss. Directed by Otto Preminger. 119 min.

Considering his acting career as a whole, Frank Sinatra does a surprisingly marvelous job here, mixing the perfect blend of vulnerability and savvy as a professional card dealer who takes the long slide into heroin addiction. The film was a shocker in its time, and Otto Preminger soaks it in his trademark juicy lasciviousness and murky mise en scène. Though the story is all melodramatic contrivance, both Eleanor Parker and Kim Novak provide authentic support. Nelson Algren, who wrote the original novel, raised legendary hell with Preminger and it's easy to see what his beef was: Very little remains of Algren's social conscience and leftist politics—the dealer becomes a junkie here not because of postwar maladjustment and urban helplessness, but out of thrill-seeking, hedonistic indulgence. Elmer Bernstein's jazz score is one of his best.

THE MAN WITH THE GOLDEN GUN ☆½
1974, USA, PG
Roger Moore, Christopher Lee, Britt Ekland, Maud Adams, Herve Villechaize, Bernard Lee, Lois Maxwell, Desmond Llewellyn. Directed by Guy Hamilton. 125 min.

A leading candidate for the booby prize as the worst James Bond film of all time, this movie is Roger Moore's second outing in the role. It features Britt Ekland and Maud Adams as guest bunnies, and for a villain offers Christopher Lee with a plastic third nipple pasted to his chest. If we had Bond's license to kill, we'd start here.

THE MAN WITH TWO BRAINS ★★★
1983, USA, R
Steve Martin, Kathleen Turner, David Warner, Paul Benedict, James Cromwell, George Furth. Directed by Carl Reiner. 90 min.

Until *All of Me*, this was the only Steve Martin movie as wild and crazy as its manic hero. Martin plays Dr. Michael Hfuhruhurr, a famous brain surgeon caught between two loves: his taunting, bitch-goddess wife who's only after his money, and a disembodied female brain that sits in the laboratory of a brooding mad scientist. Martin and director Carl Reiner take this story to the outer limits of campy chaos. The film features the immortal line, "Into the mud, scum queen!," a wonderfully steamy performance by Kathleen Turner, and a guest appearance by Merv Griffin that almost makes up for the rest of his career.

MAN, WOMAN AND CHILD ★½
1983, USA, PG
Martin Sheen, Blythe Danner, Craig T. Nelson, David Hemmings, Billy Jacoby. Directed by Dick Richards. 101 min.

This is another sudsy tale from a book by Erich Segal, who gave the world *Love Story*, *Oliver's Story*, and a few others we've thankfully forgotten. Martin Sheen plays a happily married UCLA professor who discovers that his one moment of extramarital passion, a decade ago in France, produced a son who is being sent to his care now that the mother has died. Understandably, this produces a bit of tension between Sheen and his wife and children, but it's nothing you couldn't see done more interestingly on daytime television.

THE MANXMAN ★★½
1929, Great Britain
Carl Brisson, Malcolm Keen, Anny Ondra. Directed by Alfred Hitchcock. 85 min.

Hitchcock's last silent film is so rare that it will naturally command interest—despite its director's disavowals—particularly since it incorporates themes of personal loyalty and moral equivocacy. A lawyer (Malcolm Keen) rejects marriage in the pursuit of his career, then discovers that his lover (Anny Ondra), now the wife of his lifelong friend (Carl Brisson), is pregnant with his own child. What's more, as a newly appointed judge, the man of law must rule on the case of the woman after she attempts to resolve the dilemma by suicide. (Electronic music has been added to this tape.)

MARATHON ★★
1980, USA (TV)
Bob Newhart, Anita Gillette, Leigh Taylor-Young, Herb Edelman, Dick Gautier, John Hillerman. Directed by Jackie Cooper. 100 min.

A man with a casual approach to jogging, and a serious regard for his marriage, suddenly goes head over heels for a lithesome lady jogger. In order to scratch his seven-year itch, this very married man becomes a marathon racer and exhibits signs of leaving his marriage back at the starting point as he races off in pursuit of his vanishing youth. This is a fairly feeble comedy that sprints by merrily on occasion due to Newhart's ace timing and the welcome presence of his personable female costars.

MARATHON MAN ★★★½
1976, USA, R
Dustin Hoffman, Laurence Olivier, Roy Scheider, William Devane, Marthe Keller, Fritz Weaver. Directed by John Schlesinger. 126 min.

The star (Dustin Hoffman) and director (John Schlesinger) of *Midnight Cowboy* team again to create another riveting portrait of New York City. This time, Hoffman plays the innocent, a student and marathon runner pursued by a Nazi war criminal (Laurence Olivier) who believes that the young man has knowledge of some valuable diamonds. William Goldman's screenplay, based on his novel, becomes confusing at times but eventually straightens itself out, and Schlesinger's *noir*ish tonality sustains the sudden jumps in location and action. Several set pieces are memorable: the innocent argument in midtown traffic that triggers all the events to come; Hoffman tortured with a drill in Olivier's dentist's chair; Hoffman chased on city highways in nothing but his pajama bottoms; and Olivier (who gives one of his best latter-day performances) recognized in the diamond district by a concentration camp survivor (Lotta Andor-Palfi). The conclusion is slightly disappointing, but otherwise this is a superb thriller.

MARCH OF THE WOODEN SOLDIERS

See *Babes in Toyland*

MARGARET ATWOOD'S SURFACING

See *Surfacing*

MARIA'S LOVERS ★★
1984, USA, R
Nastassja Kinski, John Savage, Robert Mitchum, Keith Carradine, Bud Cort, Vincent Spano. Directed by Andrei Konchalovsky. 103 min.

Young Ivan Bibic (John Savage) comes home from his World War II internment in a Japanese POW camp haunted and obsessed with rekindling his childhood romance with the angelic Maria. He succeeds in making miserable everyone with whom he comes into contact, including his gruff father (Robert Mitchum), sensitive coworker (Bud Cort) and, of course, Maria (Nastassja Kinski). Despite the unusual cast and near painterly cinematography, it's a riotous pastiche of disconnected elements that never coalesce.

MARIE ★★★
1985, USA, PG
Sissy Spacek, Jeff Daniels, Keith Szarabajka, Morgan Freeman, Fred Thompson. Directed by Roger Donaldson. 111 min.

This is a consistently involving true story. Tennessee parole board chairman Marie Ragghianti took on Governor Ray Blanton when she discovered his cronies were selling pardons; so the character has to be both tough and naive, a difficult combination that's nevertheless well within the range of Sissy Spacek. Her predicament never changes: She's always a sensitive woman surrounded by goons who are ganging up on her, and her final victory—though inevitable—is well-handled. Spacek is wonderful

MARIUS ★★★
1931, France
Raimu, Pierre Fresnay, Orane Demazis, Alida Demazis, Charpin. Directed by Alexander Korda. 125 min.

The first part of playwright Marcel Pagnol's touching trilogy about the romance of Marius and Fanny introduces us to the characters and pits Marius's love for Fanny against his love for the sea. Director Alexander Korda shows a flair for capturing the pace and atmosphere of Marseilles life, even though all he has done has been essentially to film the stage play, with its entire cast, that had been running for three years in Paris. The other segments of the Trilogy, *Cesar* and *Fanny*, are also available on videocassette.

MARJOE ★★★
1972, USA, PG
Marjoe Gortner. Directed by Sarah Kernochan and Howard Smith. 88 min.

This is an intriguing documentary about the child who went from being a prodigy preacher to being a fast-talking adult evangelist capable of mesmerizing audiences with his charismatic delivery. The film won an Oscar for best documentary, but it seems very selective as to the facts presented concerning the title figure. It's fascinating material, but there was one unfortunate consequence of the film's release—Marjoe was so moved by its reception that he decided to become an actor and try to find salvation through stardom. Anyone who's ever seen him act can consider that they've done penance for their sins.

MARLENE ★★★½
1983, West Germany
Directed by Maximilian Schell. 96 min.

What becomes a legend most? If the legend is Marlene Dietrich, nothing could be more image-enhancing than this wonderfully fragmented portrait of the screen goddess by her *Judgment at Nuremberg* costar Maximilian Schell. Dietrich, past eighty when this was shot, chose to stay off camera; she's combative, contentious, unsentimental and determined to protect her privacy. Schell, however, is just as determined to discover the woman behind the icon. A generous and well-selected array of film clips is punctuated by their talks, disagreements, and battles, allowing the film to become both the story of its own making and a dazzling depiction of Dietrich then and now. Funny, moving, and altogether unique. Winner of an Academy Award nomination for Best Documentary.

MARNIE ★★★
1964, USA
Tippi Hedren, Sean Connery, Diane Baker, Martin Gabel, Louise Latham, Alan Napier, Bruce Dern, Henry Beckman. Directed by Alfred Hitchcock. 120 min.

This marks the beginning of Alfred Hitchcock's slow decline: The case-study scenario is fascinating, but you can feel the sweat behind the camera movements. Tippi Hedren is a frigid kleptomaniac, and Sean Connery is the dashing lover-employer desperate to get to the bottom of her little problem. With a growing reputation among many Hitchcock buffs, the movie features Bruce Dern's movie debut, "innovative" use of color (the screen turns bright scarlet whenever Hedren begins to lose her grip), and the director's most ludicrous Freudian resolution since *Spellbound*. You can spot Hitchcock making his usual cameo appearance coming out of a hotel room.

MARRIAGE IS ALIVE AND WELL ★★
1980, USA (TV)
Joe Namath, Jack Albertson, Melinda Dillon, Judd Hirsch, Susan Sullivan, Nicholas Pryor. Directed by Russ Mayberry. 100 min.

These loosely connected stories about marital ups and downs resemble an overextended episode of an altar-bound "Love American Style." Joe Namath's a photographer specializing in weddings and his observations cement these tales together. It's painless and unexceptional.

MARRIAGE OF A YOUNG STOCKBROKER ★★½
1971, USA, R
Richard Benjamin, Joanna Shimkus, Elizabeth Ashley, Adam West, Patricia Barry. Directed by Lawrence Turman. 95 min.

This is a strange, flawed seriocomedy about the deterioration of a marriage due to the pressures of modern times. It's a bizzare cross between *La Notte* and *The Awful Truth*; some of the scenes are intriguing, but the whole just doesn't jell. However, it's worth seeing for the stylish performances, even though the uncertainty of tone eventually does the film in.

THE MARRIAGE OF MARIA BRAUN ★★★★
1979, West Germany, R
Hanna Schygulla, Klaus Lowitsch, Ivan Desny, Gottfried John, Gisela Uhlen, Gunter Lamprecht, Hark Bohm. Directed by Rainer Werner Fassbinder. 120 min.

R. W. Fassbinder's biting seriocomic study of a young wife's ascension to economic and personal power in postwar Germany may have been his finest achievement—it's more accessible than his earlier films, and not burdened by the baroque flourishes of his later ones. Hanna Schygulla's sexy, seething portrayal of Maria Braun won her international attention, and Fassbinder depicts her character as just one element in his complex tableau of a country gripped by both ambition and disillusionment. Angry and original down to its shocker of an ending, and graced with crystalline cinematography by Michael Ballhaus, it's the perfect film to introduce Fassbinder to newcomers and a fine one for the director's fans to revisit.

MARRY ME, MARRY ME ★★★
1969, France
Elizabeth Weiner, Regine, Claude Berri, Luisa Colpeyn. Directed by Claude Berri. 87 min.

This is an effervescent romantic comedy with the naughty sparkle French filmmakers seem to instill instinctively. An encyclopedia salesman from Paris falls madly in love with a Belgian girl who's pregnant. This film is madcap comic melee that includes its share of touching moments.

MARTIAL MONKS OF SHAOLIN TEMPLE ★½
1983, Hong Kong
Dragon Lee, Wong Chen Li, Petty Suh, Jose Wong. Directed by Godfrey Ho. 90 min.

Director Godfrey Ho really understands his genre—his kung fu films are about eighty percent fighting with only the leanest plots and characterizations. Here, he and martial arts director Philip Yuen serve up a banquet of esoteric fighting styles as a bad guy tries to take over a monastery.

THE MARTIAN CHRONICLES ★★½
1980, USA (TV)
Rock Hudson, Gayle Hunnicutt, Roddy McDowall, Darren McGavin, Maria Schell, Bernadette Peters, Fritz Weaver, Bernie Casey. Directed by Michael Anderson. 300 min. (three cassettes)

A generally worthwhile enterprise, this lavish miniseries works on a grand scale to capture the flavor of Ray Bradbury's sci-fi classic. Rock Hudson heads the cast as the space explorer who journeys to discover what happened to the members of two previous space crews now missing in the cosmos. While the adventure angle of this lost-in-space extravaganza builds excitement, the comedy portions just don't mesh well with the suspense segments. We're left with a potpourri of intriguing elements that don't quite jell as a single entry.

MARTIN ★★★½
1978, USA, R
John Amplas, Lincoln Maazel, Christine Forrest, Tom Savini, George A. Romero. Directed by George A. Romero. 95 min.

Martin—a young man who may or may not be a vampire in the supernatural sense of the term—engages in blood-drinking practices while living with the old-country relative who considers him a family curse and is determined to save his tormented soul. *Martin* is a sophisticated meditation on the iconography of vampirism that lacks the accessibility of George Romero's other films. Set in a crumbling corner of Pittsburgh, it features a hauntingly awkward performance by John Amplas as the vampire, Romero himself as a jocular modern priest who explains that exorcism isn't like what you see in the movies, and makeup artist Tom Savini (who supplied the movie's effects) as a lower-class creep. Complex and well crafted, it is perhaps Romero's best film to date.

MARTY ★★★½
1955, USA
Ernest Borgnine, Betsy Blair, Joe De Santis, Esther Minciotti. Directed by Delbert Mann. 90 min.

Four Academy Awards (Best Picture, Actor, Director, and Screenplay) went to this low-budget film version of Paddy Chayefsky's famous inner-city melodrama about Marty, the lonely Bronx butcher who finds love at the Stardust Dance Hall with an equally withdrawn teacher. Chayefsky's realistically biting dialogue and characters made this into a hit with lonely hearts all over the world (it also captured the Palme D'Or at the Cannes Film Festival). Adapted from a live television play starring Rod Steiger, it contains one of the most memorable opening lines in the American cinema, "What do you wanna do, Marty?"

MARVELOUS STUNTS OF KUNG FU ☆
Hong Kong
Ling Yun, Wang Kuan-Hsing, Hsia Ling-Ling, Ling Fei, Chang Kuan-Lung. Directed by Chin Sheng-En.

Not so marvelous. A cocky young man (Wang Kuan-Hsing) arrives in town, incurs the wrath of the local bullies, and must learn kung fu from a fortune teller before seeking revenge. Second-rate martial arts action interrupts an oh-so-familiar plot.

MARY AND JOSEPH: A STORY OF FAITH ☆
1979, USA (TV)
Jeff East, Blanche Baker, Colleen Dewhurst, Stephen McHattie, Lloyd Bochner, Paul Hecht. Directed by Eric Till. 100 min.

This is as puerile an examination of biblical history as such other TV classics as "Solomon and Sheba" and "Last Days of Pompeii." With the most rudimentary acting prowess, Blanche Baker and Jeff East reverentially delineate the characters of Mary and Joseph, the parents of Christ. Nazareth was never like this; the level of believability is such that the two leads seem to be experiencing nothing more than a temporary room shortage at the local Marriott.

MARY OF SCOTLAND ☆☆
1936, USA
Katharine Hepburn, Fredric March, Florence Eldridge, Douglas Walton, John Carradine, Robert Barrat, Moroni Olsen, Alan Mowbray, Donald Crisp. Directed by John Ford. 123 min.

One of the films that almost killed the career of the young Katharine Hepburn; watching it, you'll be surprised that it didn't. She plays the role of Mary Stuart, the rightful claimant to the throne of England over Henry VIII's illegitimate daughter Elizabeth Tudor, with a perpetually quivering lower lip that suggests that she is going to burst into tears if they don't hand over the throne right this minute. Aside from the handsome production, particularly the expressionistic trial scene, this is notable to film historians primarily as one of the very few John Ford films with female protagonists; that said, Florence Eldridge's Elizabeth is much more interesting than Hepburn's Mary.

MARY POPPINS ☆☆☆☆
1964, USA
Julie Andrews, Dick Van Dyke, David Tomlinson, Glynis Johns, Ed Wynn, Arthur Treacher, Karen Dotrice, Matthew Garber. Directed by Robert Stevenson. 140 min.

A supercalifragilisticexpialidocious musical treat boasting the most enjoyable combination of live action and animation ever on film. A capstone of Walt Disney's career and the winner of thirteen Academy Award nominations, this sweet fantasy follows the occupational adventures of a nanny who can fly, transport her charges into a chalk drawing on a sidewalk and, above all, magically transform the troubled households that she drops into and out of. The cheery score (Academy Award for best song: "Chim Chim Cheree"), the spirited choreography, the personable actors, and the flawless production design make this one of Hollywood's better original musicals. Julie Andrews won an Academy Award for Best Actress. That award is certainly open to debate, but she is winsome and winning and manages to coax Dick Van Dyke's best screen work out of him.

Highlights: the dance of the chimney sweeps on the rooftops and the "Jolly Holiday" animated picnic sequence.

MARY WHITE ☆☆☆½
1977, USA (TV)
Ed Flanders, Kathleen Beller, Fionnula Flannagan, Tim Matheson, Donald Moffat. Directed by Jud Taylor. 100 min.

This is an exquisitely acted biographical film drawn from the poignant contemplations of newspaper editor William Allen White on the occasion of his teenaged daughter's tragic death in 1921. Not many TV films take the chance of concentrating on detailed characterizations and mood, instead of pat formulas and dramatic shorthand that move the story along on a shallow level; but everything about this exemplary film is unusual. It's a quality production in which we can empathize with this father's pride in his free-spirited daughter and his shattering sense of loss when she is accidentally killed.

MASADA ☆☆½
1984, USA (TV)
Peter O'Toole, Peter Strauss, Barbara Carrera, David Warner, Anthony Quayle. Directed by Boris Sagal. 120 min.

This superbly acted, meticulously researched historical melodrama recounts with admirable detail the first-century siege of Masada, a mountain fortress of the Jews. Peter O'Toole spearheads the superlative cast with his portrayal of the Roman general Cornelius Flavius Silva, and David Warner, playing O'Toole's devious rival, won an Emmy for Best Supporting Actor. The late Boris Sagal, in his best directorial work ever, creates a first-rate epic with a suspenseful twist to the plot. There is, however, a tremendous drawback—the videocassette presents less than a quarter of the eight hours Masada ran when it was a TV miniseries. Most of the story's dynamism and scope is predictably lost in the cut.

M*A*S*H ☆☆☆☆
1970, USA, R
Donald Sutherland, Elliott Gould, Tom Skerritt, Robert Duvall, Sally Kellerman, Jo Ann Pflug, Rene Auberjonois, Roger Bowen, Gary Burghoff, John Schuck, G. Wood, Fred Williamson, Bud Cort, Danny Goldman. Directed by Robert Altman. 116 min.

If you loved the increasingly drippy sitcom descendant, which wore its heart on its sleeve in a way that Robert Altman would never dream of, you won't be prepared for the brutality of the original if you've never seen it. The movie M*A*S*H is quite another thing from "Little House on the Korean Prairie," it is an often heartlessly funny film about people living in a heartless situation. Donald Sutherland's Hawkeye would chew up and spit out Alan Alda's in the same mouthful as the other "Regular Army clowns." The movie was the first of Altman's multi-character extravaganzas, and its blend of 1960s irreverence and 1970s cynicism instantly established him as the director most in tune with the zeitgeist of his era.

M*A*S*H: GOODBYE, FAREWELL AND AMEN ☆½
1983, USA (TV)
Alan Alda, Mike Farrell, Loretta Swit, Harry Morgan, Jamie Farr, William Christopher, David Ogden Stiers. Directed by Alan Alda. 120 min.

This is the last episode of the enormously popular sitcom "M*A*S*H," which finally ended after having gone on for eight years longer than the actual Korean War. This compiles all the faults of the show in its dying days: all of the best cast members were gone, giving way to standard TV caricatures; the writing was sappy and overtly sentimental; and, worst of all, Alan Alda had taken over behind the scenes as well as on camera. The result is pretentious, smarmy, and bathetic, the kind of thing that gives liberalism a bad name. Alda is so smug, both as a performer and as director, that you want to kick the screen every time he comes on, which is often.

MASK ★★★½
1985, USA, PG-13
Cher, Eric Stoltz, Sam Elliott, Richard Dysart, Harry Carey, Jr. Directed by Peter Bogdanovich. 120 min.

The true story of Rocky Dennis, a teenage boy afflicted with a form of giantitis, which caused his head and skull to swell into a grotesque, misshapen appearance. The film doesn't so much dwell on the disease (he had it since boyhood) but on his reactions to life with those around him, especially his roustabout mother (Cher) and her biker boyfriends. *Mask* generally avoids pathos except in a few irresistibly tear-jerking scenes. And although Rocky is shown as an essentially strong young man who has already learned to deal with a lot of problems, there are just enough peeks beneath the veneer to establish a real human being instead of a saint. Quibbles arise mostly from a slight problem with tone—a few more downbeat aspects would have helped round it out—and background. (For instance, how do Rocky and his mom manage to live in more than reasonable comfort with no visible sign of income?) The film, however, is superbly performed by Cher and Eric Stoltz, and very good for the family despite the MPAA rating, which is entirely due to a few mild profanities.

MASSACRE AT CENTRAL HIGH ★★½
1976, USA, R
Derrel Maury, Andrew Stevens, Kimberly Beck, Robert Carradine. Directed by Renee Daalder. 85 min.

When a bright, shy new kid enrolls at the local high school, he becomes the instant target of bullies and creeps. That's hardly new material for teen exploitation; what *is* new is writer-director Renee Daalder's method of giving our hero just retribution—he decides to kill everyone. Yes, everyone. This surf-set *Apocalypse Now* alternates between amateurism and jolting displays of style, with the requisite sex and violence enthusiastically thrown in. Repulsive it may be, but it deserves credit for going that extra mile in the high school genre, and it will keep your attention from beginning to end. Double-feature this with *Carrie* for a *real* revenge of the nerds.

MASSACRE IN ROME ★★★
1973, Italy, PG
Richard Burton, Marcello Mastroianni, Leo McKern, John Steiner, Delia Boccardo. Directed by George Pan Cosmatos. 103 min.

Based on actual historical events, this film details a reprisal taken by the German command during its occupation of Rome in World War II when they had threatened to kill ten Italians for any German soldier killed by the resistance. After a resistance attack results in thirty-three dead Germans, the head of German security (a good performance by Richard Burton) sets in motion the execution of 330 Italians. His chief antagonist is a low-level Vatican priest (Marcello Mastroianni), who cannot rouse his superiors to do anything about the upcoming massacre. It's a compelling story, well made and well played.

MASS APPEAL ★★
1984, USA, PG
Jack Lemmon, Zeljko Ivanek, Charles Durning, Louise Latham, Talia Balsam. Directed by Glenn Jordan. 99 min.

This is the film version of one of those May-December problem plays in which a young idealist rekindles the faith of an aging cynic. The cynic is Father Tim Farley, playwright Bill C. Davis's poke at the worldly compromises of the post-Vatican II Catholic Church; as played by Jack Lemmon, he's an irrepressible gagmeister who considers the collection plate his weekly Nielsen rating. The idealist is Dolson (Zeljko Ivanek, who has all the charisma of a scowling border guard), a firebrand seminarian who scorns the little white lies Farley's life is sprinkled with. Director Glenn Jordan does the usual "opening up" job on Davis's one-set, two-character drama, but the play still seems cramped, and the issues it raises are treated with timid sentimentality. Lemmon gives an effusive performance.

MASSIVE RETALIATION ★½
1985, USA
Jason Gedrick, Tom Bower, Karlene Crockett, Peter Donat, Marilyn Hasset. Directed by Thomas Cohen. 90 min.

This is a regressive drama about Neanderthal mind-sets during the pre-nuclear Apocalypse. Three couples whose mettle was previously untested fight fiercely for their territory as some frightened townspeople decide to hole up with them in their remote country home. (If the Big Bomb burst, how much safer would this rural sanctuary be, anyway?) There are meretricious thrills; it was done much better on "The Twilight Zone" in the 1960s, in an episode about the neighbors trying to squeeze into the only available family bomb shelter on the block. There are no frissons here, and no food for thought.

MASTER KILLER ★★★
1978, Hong Kong
Liu Chia-Hui, Huang Yu (Young Wang Yu), Lo Lieh, Liu Chia-Yung, Hsu Shao-Chiang, Yu Yong. Directed by Liu Chia-Liang. 113 min.

Up until the release of this movie, most kung fu films forced the viewers to accept the hero's expertise in the martial arts. This film changed all that. Liu Yu Te (Liu Chia-Hui), later called San-Te, goes to the Shaolin temple to learn kung fu so that he may avenge his family's murder by the Manchus. At the end of the film, San-Te opens a thirty-sixth chamber in Shaolin to teach young men kung fu in order to resist the Manchus. Nearly one hour of the movie's 113 minutes is devoted to San-Te's training. Thank you, Liu Chia-Liang.

MASTER OF TIGER CRANE ★★
1983, Hong Kong
Huang Cheng-Li, Benny Tsui, Stan Yuen, Chis Bo, Perry Lang, Kathy Lee. Directed by Sammy Lee. 90 min.

Steven's (Benny Tsui) brother, Allan, is kidnapped and his teacher killed by Silver Fox (Huang Cheng-Li) and his sister. The only clue to the crimes is a necklace left accidentally by Silver Fox. Steven must try to find the owner of the necklace and rescue his brother. The film contains wonderful martial arts, if a less-than-gripping story.

THE MASTER RACE ★★★
1944, USA
George Coulouris, Nancy Gates, Lloyd Bridges, Osa Massen, Stanley Ridges. Directed by Herbert J. Biberman. 96 min.

This is another naughty Nazi spectacular. Awash in swastikas, the film is full of menacing villains with that "vee haff vays" look in their eyes. The plot is founded on the precept that you can't keep a good master race down; even when Hitler's world crumbles, one of his henchmen is a never-say-die kind of guy who decides to carry on in the Führer's goose-steps by plotting more vicious deeds. It's a compelling propaganda film with persuasive performances (particularly by the bad guys, who were all pretty much stuck playing Nazi swine throughout their careers).

MATILDA ★
1978, USA, G
Elliott Gould, Robert Mitchum, Harry Guardino, Clive Revill, Roy Clark, Lionel Stander. Directed by Daniel Mann. 105 min.

A down-on-his-luck theatrical agent (Elliott Gould) gets a shot at the pot of gold by managing heavyweight contender Matilda—a boxing kangaroo. This is the kind of film they used to call "family entertainment," but if you let your kids grow up watching idiotic drivel like this, what kind of movies will they enjoy as adults? The fine cast must have been paid a fortune to play second fiddles to an uncredited animal—no doubt they were relieved that *Matilda* went down for the count at the box office.

A MATTER OF LIFE AND DEATH ☆☆½
1946, Great Britain
David Niven, Kim Hunter, Robert Coote, Richard Attenborough, Kathleen Byron, Raymond Massey. Directed by Michael Powell and Emeric Pressburger. 104 min.

This overdone British allegory tries to be so many things at once that it eventually falls apart under its own weight; still, it can be enjoyed in bits, especially the performance of David Niven and the scenes in Heaven. Niven plays an RAF pilot, shot down on his way back from a mission, who, thinking he's about to die, gives his last words to a WAC (Kim Hunter) on the radio. He miraculously survives and falls in love with the nurse; however, Heaven sends an emissary to tell him that his time on Earth is really up. He refuses to go, and is given a trial in Heaven. (a.k.a.: *Stairway to Heaven*)

A MATTER OF TIME ☆½
1976, Italy-USA, PG
Liza Minnelli, Ingrid Bergman, Charles Boyer, Spiros Andros, Tina Aumont, Fernando Rey, Isabella Rossellini. Directed by Vincente Minnelli. 99 min.

Vincente Minnelli disowned the release cut of this period piece, even though it starred his daughter Liza. One day, someone will resurrect a complete version of the film, but for now we are left with a shambles, partially redeemed by the bitterwsweet scenes played by Ingrid Bergman and Charles Boyer. The plot, or what's left of it, follows the rise of a hotel maid (Minnelli) to movie stardom. Bergman plays the eccentric countess who helps her, and Boyer is the elderly woman's estranged husband. Mr. Minnelli's penchant for jumbling fantasy, music, and melodrama does not work here. *A Matter of Time* never takes off in any of these genres, nor does it jell as a compound genre homage. A chief problem, aside from the studio butchery, is the presence of Liza Minnelli, who gives a nauseatingly spunky performance. Given the dreary results, it is not surprising that Vincente Minnelli did not direct a film after this one.

MAUSOLEUM ☆½
1983, USA, R
Marjoe Gortner, Bobbie Bresee, Norman Burton, La Wanda Page. Directed by Michael Dugan. 96 min.

Possessed by a demon as a result of a family curse, a beautiful blonde (Bobbie Bresee) makes a most killing femme fatale. Former evangelist Marjoe Gortner is cast as her husband, but this time the exorcist is going to have to be a friendly psychiatrist (Norman Burton) and not a man of the cloth. Bresee's breasts and some unusual camerawork are the most salient redemptions for this classically conceived sex chiller, but because of a spate of legal squabbles surrounding the film, it is hard to know who deserves credit for the latter assets.

MAX DUGAN RETURNS ☆☆
1983, USA, PG
Marsha Mason, Jason Robards, Donald Sutherland, Matthew Broderick. Directed by Herbert Ross. 98 min.

More pap from Neil Simon, with Marsha Mason as a widowed schoolteacher whose long-lost father, Max Dugan (Jason Robards), arrives after a twenty-eight-year absence with a suitcase full of stolen money and a proposed deal: she gets the money ($687,000) if Max can get to know his grandson (Matthew Broderick). The movie is a debased fairy tale that says it's all right to be a little dishonest in your work as long as you bring a little sunshine into other people's lives. Could this be Simon's attempt at an apologia for his own career?

MAXIE ☆½
1985, USA, PG
Glenn Close, Mandy Patinkin, Ruth Gordon, Valerie Curtin, Barnard Hughes. Directed by Paul Aaron. 90 min.

The only fun to be derived from this lame comedy is guessing who should have played Glenn Close's dual role. She's competent but full in her standard characterization of a down-to-earth working wife. However, as the unflappable 1920s flapper, complete with bleached curls and "bee's knees" accent, she conclusively proves that her proficiency as an actress can't help her in a part requiring star personality. As a result, this film about a San Francisco couple (with a cute dog, a cute marriage, and cute domestic problems) whose lives are magically transformed when the spirit of a long-dead starlet inhabits the wife's body and tries to reactivate her career, is constantly put to shame by the ghost of good romantic comedies past. Tedious, and Close's performance ranks as the miscasting of the decade.

MAXIMUM OVERDRIVE ☆
1986, USA, R
Emilio Estevez, Pat Hingle, Laura Harrington, Yeardley Smith, John Short, J. C. Smith. Directed by Stephen King. 97 min.

Maximum overkill. This is the kind of idea that was better handled as a trim thirty-minute episode of the old "Twilight Zone" series. Here the material about machinery and appliances running amok is padded out and delivered in a style best described as overemphatic. At a truck stop, a cross-section of American idiots is terrorized by all of the various electrical items, big and little, that are supposed to serve men, not serve them up. As for Stephen King, whose directorial bow this was, he has promised never to do it again. If he breaks his word, may the reels of this film rise up and attack. Cloddishly directed and gratingly performed, this may be the first good-ol'-boys horror flick; we hope it won't set a trend.

MAYERLING ☆☆☆½
1936, France
Charles Boyer, Danielle Darrieux, Suzy Prim, Jean Dax, Debucourt. Directed by Anatole Litvak. 90 min.

One of the all-time great screen romances, based, at least in part, on fact, this film concerns Archduke Rudolph of Austria, heir to the throne, who defies convention and his father by falling in love with the Baroness Marie Vetsera, a match judged unsuitable for the future emperor. The film's title refers to the estate where the lovers ended their lives in a suicide pact in 1889. Charles Boyer is excellent; he wisely refused to allow the film to be dubbed into English on the ground that only his voice should accompany his performance.

MAYTIME ☆☆☆½
1937, USA
Jeanette MacDonald, Nelson Eddy, John Barrymore, Herman Bing, Tom Brown, Lynn Carver, Sig Ruman, Billy Gilbert. Directed by Robert Z. Leonard. 132 min.

This intoxicatingly schmaltzy film is the most irresistible of the Jeanette MacDonald–Nelson Eddy screen operettas. We may never know the glories of the Technicolor version started by Edmund Goulding in 1936 and scrapped after the untimely death of producer Irving Thalberg, yet this black-and-white adaptation could hardly be improved upon. In Noel Langley's extremely loose adaptation of the 1917 show, Jeanette plays a prima donna who marries her mentor (John Barrymore) out of both pity and gratitude, even though she loves an adoring street singer (Eddy). Her actions lead to a moving if melodramatic finale, after which ghostly reflections of the "singing sweethearts" croon down a pathway of flowered trees (this and other scenes were originally filmed in Sepia Tone). MacDonald is at her loveliest as the gushing young singer (and surprisingly convincing as an old woman in a framing story) and Eddy is more relaxed than usual, especially in a clever street song number. Still, it is Barrymore, in one of his last decent roles, who steals the show with his special brand of sadomasochistic intensity. Regrettably, only one Sigmund Romberg song survives from the stage (the rest of the score is an uneven potpourri) but, otherwise, the production gleams with the best talent MGM's money could buy.

MAZES AND MONSTERS

See *Rona Jaffe's Mazes and Monsters*

McCABE AND MRS. MILLER ☆☆☆☆
1971, USA, R
Warren Beatty, Julie Christie, Rene Auberjonois, Shelley Duvall, Michael Murphy, Keith Carradine. Directed by Robert Altman. 121 min.

An evocative Western that re-creates a period when one form of civilization, the brothel, was taming the clapboard towns out on the edge of the wilderness. Warren Beatty is mesmerizing as a fast-talking pipe dreamer who teams up with Julie Christie, Oscar-nominated as a hardened whore who tries not to let her romantic inclinations for Beatty interfere with her business sense. Never have Robert Altman's predilections for overlapping dialogue and misty cinematography been so suited to his theme of people being judged, not by what they accomplish, but by how big their dreams are.

McQ ☆☆
1974, USA, PG
John Wayne, Eddie Albert, Diana Muldaur, Colleen Dewhurst, Clu Gulager, Al Lettieri. Directed by John Sturges. 114 min.

John Wayne, who turned down the lead role in *Dirty Harry*, attempts to rectify that mistake by showing his fans that he can be just as much of a brute in blue as was Clint Eastwood. Of course Eastwood, a good quarter of a century younger, didn't have to worry about the loss of credibility incurred by having to wear a bad toupee and corset while chasing thugs around city streets. But what the hell, you either love John Wayne movies or ignore them. For those in the former category, in this one he plays a Seattle cop (apparently a city with no mandatory retirement law) who can't understand why his lily-livered superiors object to such interrogatory tactics as throwing suspects off of buildings. There are also hippies, drug smugglers, and other scum that you don't have to feel sorry for when McQ beats the crap out of them.

McVICAR ☆☆½
1980, Great Britain, R
Roger Daltrey, Adam Faith, Cheryl Campbell, Steven Berkoff, Brian Hall, Jeremy Blake. Directed by Tom Clegg. 111 min.

In his first starring nonmusical role, Roger Daltrey of The Who acquits himself quite adequately as an actor. In this true story of thief John McVicar and his attempts to escape from a high-security British prison, he combines a sense of pugnacity with a cold intelligence to good effect. The screenplay was cowritten by director Tom Clegg and the real McVicar, based upon his best-selling autobiography. It's a smaller-scale, less glorified version of *Papillon*; with a soundtrack of Daltrey songs, just in case.

THE MEAN SEASON ☆☆½
1985, USA, R
Kurt Russell, Mariel Hemingway, Richard Masur, Richard Jordan. Directed by Phillip Borsos. 106 min.

This intriguing but uneven suspense drama revolves around a touchy ethical question—what happens when a reporter gets too close to his source? A lot, as it turns out, if the reporter is covering the crimes of a serial murderer and his source—seeking publicity, attention, and a good mouthpiece—is the killer himself. *The Mean Season* is sharp and taut when it stays in the milieu of crime reportage, but director Phillip Borsos cheapens it considerably with low-level fake scares and hokey news headlines whirling onto the screen. Kurt Russell does very fine, restrained work as the duped journalist, but Mariel Hemingway is hopeless as his whiny girlfriend.

MEAN STREETS ☆☆☆☆
1973, USA, R
Harvey Keitel, Robert DeNiro, Amy Robinson, Cesare Danova, Richard Romanus. Directed by Martin Scorsese. 110 min.

This is an electrifying portrait of a troubled young man's fall from grace in a local Mafia family, set to the beat of the Rolling Stones and the Ronettes, and enriched by a palpable evocation of New York City. Early in his career, Martin Scorsese seemed more interested in the guilt-obsessed, compulsively Catholic Harvey Keitel character with his uptight philosophical angst; but, even here, Robert DeNiro steals the show with his mannered, crazy-boy histrionics. The movie is a jazzed junkyard of burned-out characterizations, an *I Vitelloni* of Little Italy. Best scene: a magical rooftop confrontation between DeNiro and Keitel after DeNiro's Johnny Boy has been shooting at the Empire State Building.

MEATBALLS ☆☆
1979, Canada, PG
Bill Murray, Harvey Atkin, Kate Lynch, Kristine DeBell, Russ Banham, Chris Makepeace. Directed by Ivan Reitman. 92 min.

Bill Murray is the whole show in this amiable but witless summer camp comedy. Murray, in his first feature after his success on "Saturday Night Live," is likably raunchy as an activities director who is more interested in the female counselors than in the crew of misfits to which he is assigned. The rest of the film shifts from crude slapstick to sentimental drama about one particular outcast (Chris Makepeace). Even Murray can't survive scenes with the latter. The sequel, *Meatballs Part II*, was even worse.

MEATBALLS PART II ☆½
1984, USA, PG
Archie Hahn, John Mengatti, Richard Mulligan, John Larroquette, Paul Reubens, Tammy Taylor. Directed by Ken Weiderhorn. 96 min.

The original *Meatballs* had exactly one thing going for it: Bill Murray. *Meatballs Part II* does not have Bill Murray. A little simple arithmetic tells us that one minus one equals zero. Credit watchers may have spotted the presence of John Larroquette (of TV's "Night Court") and Paul Reubens (better known in his Pee Wee Herman persona). Neither has much of anything to do here except stand around and try not to get in the way of the usual geeks at summer camp. Where is *Friday The 13th*'s Jason when you *need* him? Followed by *Meatballs III*.

THE MECHANIC ☆☆
1972, USA, PG
Charles Bronson, Jan-Michael Vincent, Keenan Wynn, Jill Ireland. Directed by Michael Winner. 100 min.

Mechanical. A professional killer (Charles Bronson) trains a newcomer while making a deal with the Mafia. This is a slickly made B action melodrama that contains a few tense moments and Bronson's usual low-key performance, but is basically formula fare. It's better, however, than many of Bronson's more recent films.

MEDIUM COOL ☆☆☆½
1969, USA, X
Robert Forster, Verna Bloom, Robert Blankenship, Peter Bonerz, Marianna Hill. Directed by Haskell Wexler. 110 min.

Ace cinematographer Haskell Wexler wrote, directed, and shot this corrosive portrait of a TV cameraman (Robert Forster) who distances himself from the political tumult of the times. The movie adopts a critical perspective toward the relationship between politics and the media as it touches on such epochal events as the 1968 Democratic convention and the assassinations of Robert Kennedy and Martin Luther King. Unfortunately, the personal story takes a back seat to the explosive documentary footage. The "X" rating is for a brief sex scene that wouldn't guarantee this an "R" if released today. It's an important film for today's voters so frequently manipulated by TV news.

THE MEDUSA TOUCH ☆☆
1978, Great Britain, R
Richard Burton, Lee Remick, Lino Ventura, Derek Jacobi. Directed by Jack Gold. 110 min.

Richard Burton has the ability to predict and cause deaths, leading his distraught psychiatrist Lee Remick to try and kill him. A slow and stupid exposition builds to a smashing climax at Westminster Abbey. It's a good suspense film, but with a silly performance by Burton.

MEET JOHN DOE ☆☆☆½
1941, USA
Gary Cooper, Barbara Stanwyck, Edward Arnold, Walter Brennan, Spring Byington, James Gleason, Gene Lockhart, Rod La Roque, Regis Toomey. Directed by Frank Capra. 129 min.

In Frank Capra's darkest film, Gary Cooper plays a hobo plucked from the streets to participate in a stunt to sell newspapers. He gradually falls for the hokum he's peddling, and "John Doe Societies" spread across the land, urging folks to be nice to one another. But when Cooper realizes the goodwill he's preaching is intended as a cover for vested fascist interests, he turns on his backers. Capra's populism is a little shopworn here, but Cooper's aw-shucks John Doe has a devilish side Jimmy Stewart could never bring to these roles, and the final scene at the Empire State Building's summit is a corny gem. It doesn't end the way it should have, but then you can only ask for so much from the movies.

MEET ME IN ST. LOUIS ☆☆☆☆
1944, USA
Judy Garland, Margaret O'Brien, Lucille Bremer, Mary Astor, Tom Drake, Marjorie Main, June Lockhart, Harry Davenport, Leon Ames. Directed by Vincente Minnelli. 113 min.

Judy Garland shines as the girl in love with "The Boy Next Door" in Vincente Minnelli's masterpiece about a middle-class family in St. Louis, circa 1903. The ever-so-slight plot has a threatened move to New York throwing the whole family in an uproar, and the viewer is quickly drawn to these staid, stay-at-home types who don't want to leave their hometown just as the World's Fair is coming. The film is a unique blend of heartfelt nostalgia, glorious color and set design, and exhilarating musical numbers. It contains at least two classic sequences: First, the visually rich, spooky evocation of a children's-eye-view of Halloween—a bit of film history that has been cribbed by movies from *E.T.* to *Halloween*. And, Margaret O'Brien's strangely melodramatic tantrum in the snow, followed by Judy Garland's attempt to comfort her with "Have Yourself a Merry Little Christmas." It's still a perfect family entertainment, with a strong Christmas appeal.

MEGAFORCE ☆
1982, USA, PG
Barry Bostwick, Persis Khambatta, Michael Beck, Edward Mulhare, Henry Silva. Directed by Hal Needham. 99 min.

This movie is like a cop show transported to the future—a bad cop show. Megaforce is the mean, lean law enforcement machine that we can all expect in our futures. The film is abysmally directed, routinely photographed, and indifferently acted.

MELANIE ☆☆½
1982, Canada, PG
Glynnis O'Connor, Paul Sorvino, Burton Cummings, Don Johnson, Trudy Young. Directed by Rex Bromfield. 109 min.

Melanie is a good mother, but she's illiterate. So her husband, played by a clean-shaven (i.e., pre-"Miami Vice") Don Johnson, takes their son away to Los Angeles. When she follows them, she meets a songwriter (Burton Cummings) who encourages her to learn to read and write and to fall in love with him. She is assisted in achieving those goals by a lawyer (Paul Sorvino) who handles her divorce and her custody hearing. This movie could be much better if it weren't so episodic—characters appear only to almost immediately disappear, and the focus shifts so often that the net result is a thematic blur. The camerawork and the credit sequences have the look of a film class project, but at least the acting is professional. *Melanie* is a diverting little film, but not much more than that.

MELODY RANCH ☆☆½
1941, USA
Gene Autry, Jimmy Durante, Ann Miller, George "Gabby" Hayes. Directed by Joseph Santley. 80 min.

Gene Autry is invited back to Torpedo, Arizona as an honorary sheriff and soon leaps into action against the bad men. There are good tunes, good direction, a good story, and good performances by Autry, Jimmy Durante, and Ann Miller; it's a funny film.

MELODY TRAIL ☆½
1935, USA
Gene Autry, Smiley Burnette, Buck. Directed by Joseph Kane. 61 min.

Gene Autry and some blond cowgirls sing, chase cattle rustlers, and engage in other Western antics. You have to wait awhile for the action, but it's good when it finally comes. Autry's all right, but Buck is even better.

MELVIN AND HOWARD ☆☆☆☆
1980, USA, R
Paul LeMat, Mary Steenburgen, Jason Robards, Pamela Reed, Elizabeth Cheshire. Directed by Jonathan Demme. 96 min.

The story of Melvin Dummar, the milkman who may or may not have been named by Howard Hughes as a $156-million beneficiary, is the loose basis for a generous American fable that's filled with delightfully funny touches and real respect for its characters. The film is primarily concerned with Melvin and his comical odyssey of jobs, wives, and financial disarray, although Jason Robards makes Hughes a wonderfully loony, wraithlike presence at the beginning and the end. It's one of the only films about "little people" that neither condescends to nor deifies them, thanks as much to Bo Goldman's bright, episodic screenplay as to Jonathan Demme's thoughtful direction. Mary Steenburgen won an Oscar playing Dummar's wife Lynda.

THE MEMBER OF THE WEDDING ☆☆☆
1952, USA
Ethel Waters, Julie Harris, Brandon de Wilde, Arthur Franz, Nancy Gates, James Edwards. Directed by Fred Zinnemann. 91 min.

Carson McCullers's characterizations often take wing, and in this film a trio of breathtaking performances from Ethel Waters, Brandon de Wilde, and a young Julie Harris really soar. Harris plays the petulant, put-upon Frankie, an imaginative girl growing into adolescence. The loneliness and fear of a teenager have rarely been captured so well. Harris gets to react to situations ranging from sex to race to the death of her only friend. Fred Zinnemann's direction owes a lot to the film's stage origins, but what the movie lacks in visual imagination it makes up for in the ensemble playing of the Broadway cast.

MEN . . . ☆☆☆
1985, West Germany
Heiner Lauterbach, Uwe Ochsenknecht, Ulrike Kriener, Janna Marangosoff, Dietmar Bar. Directed by Doris Dorrie. 99 min.

They may be willful, silly, childish, and impossible to understand, but director Doris Dorrie likes the title character of her playful comedy in spite of their shortcomings, and so will you. *Men . . .* begins as a comedy of infidelity and obsession; on his wedding anniversary, thirty-fiveish ad executive Julius Armbrust discovers that his wife is having an affair with Stefan, a shaggy relic of 1960s rebeldom. Julius tracks his cuckolder in secret, and when Stefan advertises for a roommate, guess who takes a false identity and moves in? Dorrie doesn't do what you might expect with the farcical premise—she has Julius and Stefan become, if not friends, then at least brothers under the skin. Her ideas run out before the film does, but her portrait of two guys looking for a second childhood in middle age can flicker between amusement, irony, and generosity with a skill and ease that marks her as a talent to watch.

MENAGE ☆☆☆☆
1986, France
Gerard Depardieu, Michel Blanc, Miou-Miou, Bruno Cremer, Jean-Pierre Marielle, Michel Creton, Caroline Sihol. Directed by Bertrand Blier. 84 min.

This is a dizzying sexual farce that's always one step ahead of the audience—in fact, it moves so fast that the director seems to be racing to keep up with it. (You feel as the characters do—cut adrift and soaring.) Viewing conventional sexuality as a straitjacket, the film hurls us into the heady freedom and eventual anarchy that result when men and women stop behaving according to centuries of social-sexual conditioning. A burly burglar (Gerard Depardieu) who flouts the law and flaunts his sexual preference for men, transforms the lives of an impoverished couple like a Pied Piper of sexuality. As he introduces them to the joys of housebreaking, he cagily seduces the mousy, resistant husband with the full cooperation of his wife. Once their new arrangement divorces the trio from normality, the role reversals and shifts in sexual domination multiply until they have to create their own brave new world. This is a wildly imaginative and wickedly funny film; even when it turns bitter, we're still on a high.

THE MEN FROM UTAH ☆
1934, USA
John Wayne, Polly Ann Young, George "Gabby" Hayes, Yakima Canutt, George Cleveland. Directed by Robert N. Bradbury. 57 min.

Another B western, with John Wayne as undercover frontier cop (see *Randy Rides Alone*), this film's a circular ride on the open range—the same scenery over and over. It seems that the production company shot themselves a rodeo and insisted on repeating that footage in all their films. In this film, the same cow is lassoed so many times it should be suffering from an incurable case of whiplash. The camp dialogue adds some tiny welcome relief.

MEN IN WAR ☆☆☆
1957, USA
Robert Ryan, Aldo Ray, Vic Morrow, Robert Keith, James Edwards, Scott Marlowe. Directed by Anthony Mann. 104 min.

Korean War films usually seem to be small-scale, gritty films about individuals in isolation, especially when contrasted with the heroic tone of World War II films. *Men in War*, about the attempt of a lieutenant to rejoin his battalion, considers the war only in terms of the characters' nervousness, fatigue, and conflict with each other. The movie consists of a long march through hostile territory precisely measured by tired footsteps and individual deaths. The film is remarkably tense, and the soldiers' deaths are genuinely affecting. Robert Ryan stands out as the insomniac lieutenant barely in command, and Aldo Ray delivers one of his patented rock-hard performances.

THE MEN'S CLUB ☆
1986, USA, R
David Dukes, Richard Jordan, Harvey Keitel, Frank Langella, Roy Scheider, Craig Wasson, Treat Williams, Stockard Channing, Gina Gallegos, Gwen Welles, Cindy Pickett, Jennifer Jason Leigh, Ann Wedgeworth, Ann Dusenberry. Directed by Peter Medak. 100 min.

This is a trite confessional drama that's waterlogged with the monologues of the seven thoroughly unlikable middle-aged men who get together to trade quips, barbs, and teary half-truths. Despite a great cast, the film makes no use of any of its performers under Peter Medak's bland, unfocused direction, and Leonard Michaels's terrible, arch script combines every cliché of bad theater with some new ones all his own—the film plays like a heterosexual version of *The Boys in the Band*.

MEPHISTO ☆☆☆½
1981, West Germany/Hungary, R
Klaus Maria Brandauer, Krystyna Janda, Ildiko Bansagi, Karin Boyd. Directed by Istvan Szabo. 135 min.

As Hendrik Hofgen, a seething, ambitious actor who barters himself to the Nazis in exchange for their applause and adoration, Klaus Maria Brandauer gives a joyously hammy performance—moaning, screaming, throwing his arms about, and gazing rapturously into mirrors. Telling the story of Hofgen's rise to glory, director Istvan Szabo is content to condemn his protagonist because, like Germany itself, he's an empty vessel who takes on the character of whatever he's filled with. That may be a glib metaphor for what an actor is, but this Oscar winner for Best Foreign Film generally manages to transcend it.

MERRY CHRISTMAS, MR. LAWRENCE ☆☆☆½
1983, Great Britain/Japan, R
Tom Conti, Ryuichi Sakamoto, David Bowie, Takeshi. Directed by Nagisa Oshima. 122 min.

Nagisa Oshima's ambitious drama, in English and Japanese, is set in a POW camp during World War II, and studies the brutal relationship between an arrogant, samurai-inspired Japanese commander and the cultured, high-spirited British prisoner (Tom Conti) he abuses. What results is a powerful, ambiguous meditation on eroticism and violence, and on the inevitable clash that results from the proximity of opposing cultures. All of the actors are excellent, especially David Bowie as the cool, courageous New Zealander who becomes the spiritual inspiration of the film. The fabulous score is by Japanese pop star Ryuichi Sakamoto, who also plays the commander.

MESA OF LOST WOMEN ☆
1953, USA
Jackie Coogan, Richard Travis, Mary Hill. Directed by Ron Ormond, Herbert Tevos. 70 min.

This reaches the pleateau of junk early on, and stays there. Special consideration must be given to the plot line, about a crazed scientific genius intent on launching a new race of creatures combining the most stunning properties of beautiful women with deadly spiders. Several unfortunates fall into this web of master race activities, but you won't be frightened; you'll be too busy laughing at the dialogue.

THE MESSAGE

See *Mohammad: Messenger of God*

METALSTORM: ☆
THE DESTRUCTION OF JARED SYM
1983, USA, PG
Jeffrey Byron, Mike Preston, Tim Thomerson, Richard Moll, Kelly Preston, Larry Pennell. Directed by Charles Band. 84 min.

Would that they'd destroyed this movie instead. Set "on a distant world in another age" (clever, huh?), *Metalstorm* follows the efforts of peacekeeping ranger "Finder" Jack Dogen to track down the evil Jared Sym before he can take over the desert planet Lemuria and use it as a stepping-stone to taking over the universe, or some such thing. This is a thoroughly hokey sci-fi fantasy whose theatrical run was distinguished only by 3-D effects—and we all know how annoying 3-D movies are on television.

METEOR
1979, USA, PG ☆☆
Sean Connery, Natalie Wood, Karl Malden, Brian Keith, Henry Fonda, Martin Landau, Trevor Howard, Richard Dysart. Directed by Ronald Neame. 103 min.

A comet hurtles toward earth as an all-star cast tries to stop it, in this big-budget disaster film whose chilly box-office reception put the genre in a temporary coma. *Meteor* is no worse than most films of its kind, although there's an awful lot of talk and little action as Russians Brian Keith and Natalie Wood and Americans Henry Fonda and Sean Connery fight to stave off the inevitable. They huff and they puff, but the catastrophic dramatics that are Ronald Neame's specialty (he also directed *The Poseidon Aventure*) don't get into gear until that great ball of fire bakes the Big Apple. It's a long wait, but some spectacle fans will find it worthwhile.

METEOR MONSTER
1958, USA ☆
Anne Gwynne, Gloria Castillo, Stuart Wade, Gilbert Perkins. Directed by Jacques Marquette. 65 min.

This is a graze Z horror film about a gorillalike town dummy transformed into a murderous maniac by a fireball from outer space. He roves the countryside on a rampage while his protective mama (Anne Gwynne) tries to shield him from the increasingly suspicious authorities. Some unintentionally funny moments and mild camp value may make this worth a look for the morbidly curious. Originally the bottom end of a double bill with the howler *The Brain from Planet Arous*, this was once called *Teenage Monster*.

METROPOLIS
1926, Germany ☆☆☆☆
Brigitte Helm, Alfred Abel, Gustav Froelich, Fritz Rasp. Directed by Fritz Lang. 87 min. (restored, with a new soundtrack, in 1984)

Oppressed workers rebel against the futuristic city they helped to create in director Fritz Lang's spectacular vision of the twenty-first century. Besides being a strong political statement, this is *the* premier example of German expressionism—a mad amalgam of weird camera angles and striking set designs that creates a film as vivid and creepily haunted as a dream. Musician Giorgio Moroder (*Flashdance*) practically (and brilliantly) reconstructed the movie with the help of a computer-generated color and a pop soundtrack, also adding in previously "lost" footage that helped to clarify the story. *Note*: There are also video versions of *Metropolis* without the added footage that are available with a variety of older soundtracks; however, some of these are copies of horribly transferred prints—beware of low-priced versions.

MIAMI VICE
1984, USA (TV) ☆☆½
Don Johnson, Philip Michael Thomas, John Diehl, Saundra Santiago, Michael Talbott, Gregory Sierra, Miguel Piñero. Directed by Thomas Carter. 99 min.

Shootouts, car chases, blackmail, murder—it's all here, along with the designer clothes, designer architecture, and designer music that made this the glossiest cop show on TV. If the names Crockett and Tubbs don't ring any bells for you, you may wonder what all the fuss was about; if you didn't catch on until after the first season, here's a chance to sample the pilot, which actually had a juicy plot to accompany its slick soundtrack. Best reason to see it: the early New York sequences. Biggest disappointment: the absence of Edward James Olmos, whose hypnotically stone-faced Castillo didn't show up until several episodes later. The video version differs very slightly from that shown on TV.

MIAMI VICE II: THE PRODIGAL SON
1985, USA (TV) ☆☆
Don Johnson, Philip Michael Thomas, Edward James Olmos, Pam Grier, Penn Jillette. Directed by Paul Michael Glaser. 98 min.

Crockett and Tubbs head north in this feature-length second-season opener of the popular series, but this shot-in-New York episode marked the beginning of a long letdown; there's not enough Miami or vice, just wall-to-wall music (including Glenn Frey's "You Belong to the City"), overwrought stylistic maneuverings, a not-very-clever plot, and Don Johnson and Philip Michael Thomas staring soulfully at each other and themselves. You can take the boys out of Miami . . . but you'll end up with just another humdrum cop show.

MICKI AND MAUDE
1984, USA, PG-13 ☆☆½
Dudley Moore, Ann Reinking, Amy Irving, Richard Mulligan, Lu Leonard, Wallace Shawn. Directed by Blake Edwards. 115 min.

A bigamist's two wives become pregnant at (almost) the same time in this sex farce whose charming performances only partially conceal its arrogantly antifeminist perspective. Dudley Moore is fine as the TV producer whose lawyer wife is too busy to have a baby, and Amy Irving proves a deft comedienne as Wife #2, a cellist. The message here is that bigamy is OK if he loves them both, a premise that turns rancid long before the story has run its course.

MICROWAVE MASSACRE
1979, USA ½☆
Jackie Vernon, Loren Schein, Al Troupe, Claire Ginsberg, John Harmon. Directed by Wayne Berwick. 75 min.

There is something genuinely horrifying in this movie: the performance of comic Jackie Vernon. After five minutes of his singsong delivery, you'll be hiding under the covers. If you last through the entire film, you may find yourself acting just like him, shuffling around the house in sloppy clothes, mumbling to yourself in a daze. Gore fans will not be satisfied, as this tale of a construction worker who develops a strange "taste" for women shows nothing more graphic than a store mannequin being sawed to pieces.

MIDNIGHT COWBOY
1969, USA, X (later R) ☆☆☆☆
Dustin Hoffman, Jon Voight, Sylvia Miles, John McGiver, Brenda Vaccaro, Barnard Hughes, Bob Balaban, Viva, Taylor Mead, Paul Morrissey. Directed by John Schlesinger. 119 min.

A naive Texas boy shamed by his past and bored with his life comes to New York to become a stud for hire; what he finds instead is the degradation of street life and hustling in contemporary (circa 1969) Manhattan. A Hollywood groundbreaker in its time, the movie's lurid forays into the New York inferno have dated, but the characters—Dustin Hoffman's Ratso Rizzo and Jon Voight's raw, guileless Joe Buck—remain memorable. This and *Butch Cassidy and the Sundance Kid*, released around the same time, were the progenitors of the endless cycle of 1970s "buddy" movies, none of which had half the feeling shown here. Hoffman and Voight were both nominated for Oscars (they lost to John Wayne's self-parody in *True Grit*); the film won in the categories of Best Picture, Director, and Screenplay. The "X" rating was later changed to an "R."

MIDNIGHT EXPRESS
1978, USA, R ☆☆☆½
Brad Davis, John Hurt, Irene Miracle, Mike Kellin. Directed by Alan Parker. 121 min.

A harrowing account of American college student Billy Hayes's arrest, incarceration, and subsequent escape from a Turkish prison for hashish smuggling, *Midnight Express* is one of the most skillful exploitation films ever made (and one of a small handful to be nominated for a Best Picture Oscar). But exploitation it remains, especially in its relentlessly voyeuristic (and racist) depiction of the horrors of Turkish jails, and in the considerable liberties it takes with the events on which it is based. Alan Parker's direction is consistently intense, as are the tour de force performances of Brad Davis and John Hurt; notable as well is Giorgio Moroder's pulsating synth score, a classic of its kind. Enjoy it as terrific suspense, but take the grandstanding commentary it pretends to provide with a grain of salt. Oliver Store's screenplay won an Academy Award.

MIDNIGHT MADNESS ☆
1980, USA, PG
David Naughton, Debra Clinger, Eddie Deezen, Brad Wilkin, Stephen Furst, Michael J. Fox. Directed by David Wechter and Michael Nankin. 110 min.

Puerile, loose-jointed comedy for the low-SAT college set in which a group of smarmy collegiates participates in an all-night scavenger hunt; and not all of them play fair. Lots of silly slapstick, amorphous performances, and pitifully unfunny one-liners abound in this vulgar and out-of-control film. Look for Michael J. Fox as the sympathetic little brother.

A MIDSUMMER NIGHT'S DREAM ☆☆☆
1935, USA
James Cagney, Dick Powell, Olivia de Havilland, Mickey Rooney, Ian Hunter, Joe E. Brown, Hugh Herbert, Ross Alexander. Directed by Max Reinhardt and William Dieterle. 117 min.

This fantasy farce broke ground in Hollywood, demonstrating that Shakespeare could indeed work on the silver screen. The unreal elements of the tale lend themselves conveniently to the power of film, and the poetry is preserved by both the script and the fluidity of Oscar winner Hal Mohr's camera. Shakespeareans will be generally pleased by the production's respect for the original, and by the added effect of an enchanting Mendelssohn score; but inconsistencies in the acting will inevitably bother some. Mickey Rooney's Puck is debatable, but at least James Cagney's Bottom is a surefire favorite.

A MIDSUMMER NIGHT'S SEX COMEDY ☆☆☆
1982, USA, PG
Woody Allen, Mia Farrow, Jose Ferrer, Mary Steenburgen, Tony Roberts, Julie Hagerty. Directed by Woody Allen. 88 min.

This attractive but strangely trivial Woody Allen romp depicts a winsome game of romantic musical chairs set at a summer house party around the turn of the century. The beautiful countryside is captured by Gordon Willis's fine cinematography and perfectly complemented by Santo Loquasto's sumptuous costuming. Allen completists won't want to miss it, and others might find it a pleasant diversion. On the whole, the film ranks among the more forgettable creations of this great American filmmaker. The film, following the hostile and unpopular *Stardust Memories* and preceding the superbly crafted *Zelig*, seems to have been a transitional work of a groping director, and, with its references to Shakespeare and Bergman's *Smiles of a Summer Night*, seems the farthest from Allen's strikingly original core works.

MIKE'S MURDER ☆½
1984, USA, R
Debra Winger, Paul Winfield, Darrell Larson, Mark Keyloun. Directed by James Bridges. 109 min.

This barely released drama unfolds on the sleazy high-tech byways of Los Angeles, telling the story of a woman who delves into the drug and crime culture revolving around the disappearance of her old lover. Conceived as a vehicle to reunite Debra Winger and James Bridges (who worked together on *Urban Cowboy*), it's almost a complete failure, eschewing a coherent story and interesting situations in favor of long scenes of moody, pointless exposition and atmosphere. Winger can't do a thing with her hapless, unmotivated character, but Darrell Larson makes a strong impression as a psychotic hood. Reynaldo Villalobos's cinematography does wonders with the slick, gaudy L.A. locations.

MIKEY AND NICKY ☆☆☆½
1976, USA
Peter Falk, John Cassavetes, Ned Beatty, Rose Arrick, William Hickey, Joyce Van Patten, M. Emmet Walsh. Directed by Elaine May. 119 min.

Elaine May's film, long unreleased, is about two hoods, Peter Falk and John Cassavetes, who grew up together. Belying May's comedic background, this is a dark melodrama about two friends who find out they're not friends after all. It has the structure of a classic *film noir*: All the action takes place on a single night, as Nicky, with Mikey at his side, is tracked through mean streets by a bumbling hit man (Ned Beatty). Its scenes build from moments of pain and intensity to eruptive climaxes and then linger on, like smoke from a spent shell. The movie takes as many chances as a tightrope walker—May's method calls for high-powered improvisation, and she gets it from an agile cast. Cassavetes is the grand *seigneur* of this type of acting, and he meets his match in Falk, who parries with his own imperturbable calm.

MILDRED PIERCE ☆☆☆☆
1945, USA
Joan Crawford, Ann Blyth, Jack Carson, Zachary Scott, Eve Arden. Directed by Michael Curtiz. 109 min.

Taking off from a James Cain novel, director Michael Curtiz creates one of the most masochistic women's tearjerkers ever made, and fuses it to a coolly murderous *film noir* story line. Joan Crawford successfully bakes her way out of the kitchen to become the head of a restaurant chain. When not being abused by men, she's busy paying for the increasingly criminal misdeeds of her evil daughter. Never has a working woman been punished with more vigor for abandoning the marital bed than in this high-rolling guilt trip. With an Oscar-winning turn by Crawford as super-martyred Mildred, and a commendably snotty performance by Ann Blyth as her venomous demon-child, Veda.

MILITANT EAGLE ☆☆
Hong Kong
Lin Yun, Wei Tzu-Yun, Yen Nan-Hsi, Pai Ying, Lu Ping, Hsued Han, Yang Hsiu Chian, Chang Ching Ha, Choe Yue. Directed by Kim Chin.

At the end of a period of war and unrest, an Imperial Decree was issued temporarily suspending all taxes in an effort to ease the country into an era of peace and prosperity. In one area, however, the corrupt town bosses choose to ignore the decree and continue to tax and harass the people. Chao Chu Lang (Lin Yun), brother-in-law to the town boss, comes to the aid of the people. This beautifully costumed and well-choreographed film should not be missed by martial arts fans.

THE MILKY WAY ☆☆☆½
1936, USA
Harold Lloyd, Adolphe Menjou, Verree Teasdale, Helen Mack, William Gargan, George Barbier, Dorothy Wilson, Lionel Stander, Charles Lane, Marjorie Gateson. Directed by Leo McCarey. 83 min.

Leo McCarey's nonstop visual comedy meshes perfectly with that of Harold Lloyd; neither was ever more supremely funny than in this knockout of a screwball comedy. Harold is the milquetoast who, through a blend of persuasion and duplicity involving the middleweight boxing champ (William Gargan), is transformed into the "fighting milkman" of the ring, hilariously intoxicated by his own publicity. The supporting cast withholds no comic punches, either; especially good are Adolphe Menjou (the promoter), Lionel Stander (his dumbbell sidekick), Verree Teasdale (his hard-boiled fiancée), Helen Mack (the milkman's little sister), and Marjorie Gateson as the stuffy social hostess who picks up on all the hero's defensive maneuvers in no time.

MILLHOUSE: A WHITE COMEDY ☆☆☆½
1971, USA
Richard M. Nixon. Directed by Emile de Antonio. 92 min.

For those with a poor memory who think that former President Richard Milhous Nixon was a popular guy until the Watergate scandal, this lacerating, sarconic, astonishing documentary will provide some needed perspective. Emile de Antonio has compiled clips of Nixon's public career and interviews with various journalists and political commentators, all showing that Nixon had always been a conniving political opportunist. Valuable historically, the film presents in its entirety Nixon's famous TV Checkers speech that Nixon buffs, and his many enemies, will relish and may want to own. The American television networks were too scared to run this powerful condemnation of the then-incumbent president.

THE MILPITAS MONSTER ½☆
1976, USA
Douglas Hagdohl, Scot Henderson, Scot Parker, Daniel Birkhead. Directed by Robert L. Burrill. 81 min.

This is yet another horror movie that never got a theatrical release, although at least this time you can credit distributor VCI with honesty: They make no bones about the fact that this is garbage. It's even actually about garbage, with a monster created somehow or other in a huge garbage dump south of San Francisco. In true monster fashion, it attacks the local sock hop. The distributors are trying to pass this off as one of those so-bad-it's-funny films under the umbrella title "Le Bad Cinema," and they're half right: it *is* bad. Sole sources of interest for trivia buffs are the narration by veteran commercial voice Paul Frees (Bullwinkle, the Pillsbury Doughboy) and sound effects by Ben Burtt, who went on to win an Oscar for *Star Wars*.

MIN AND BILL ☆☆☆
1930, USA
Wallace Beery, Marie Dressler, Dorothy Jordan, Marjorie Rambeau. Directed by George Hill. 70 min.

Dated and creaky, but the power of Wallace Beery and Marie Dressler's teamwork survives. Their gin-soaked voices, craggy faces, and gruff delivery convey both tenderness and power; they've weathered the years better than a lot of the pretty people of their era at MGM. Beery and Dressler portray grizzled waterfront denizens kicked around by life. Still, they take a stand when the authorities try to remove Marie's daughter to a better environment. It's heart-tugging, and the ineffable Dressler won a Best Actress Oscar for her work here.

MINDWARP: AN INFINITY OF HORRORS

See *Galaxy of Terror*

A MINOR MIRACLE ☆☆
1983, USA, G
John Huston, Pele, Peter Fox. Directed by Raoul Lomas. 100 min.

The miracle is that anyone's still making decent, unpretentious family films like this one anymore. It's a winning little entertainment about another endangered species—a Roman Catholic home for orphaned boys, run by a roving old lion, John Huston. The crusty Huston's presence in a warmhearted part like this is the most miraculous stroke of all; not exactly his cup of Ovaltine, to be sure, but a relief from his usual casting as an imperious madman or senile pervert.

THE MIRACLE OF THE BELLS ☆
1948, USA
Fred MacMurray, Alida Valli, Frank Sinatra, Lee J. Cobb, Charles Meredith. Directed by Irving Pichel. 120 min.

Going My Way meets *Sunset Boulevard*. Alida Valli, as a Hollywood starlet, does the stake scene from *Joan of Arc* and then dies from exhaustion. Frank Sinatra (as a priest) sings, and the starlet rises from the dead just in time for the premiere of her picture. Believe it or not, it's all played straight.

MIRACLE ON 34TH STREET ☆☆☆½
1947, USA
Maureen O'Hara, John Payne, Edmund Gwenn, Gene Lockhart, Natalie Wood, William Frawley, Thelma Ritter, Percy Helton. Directed by George Seaton. 95 min.

This delightful holiday classic is a fantasy that has Kris Kringle going to work as Macy's Santa and trying to convince a little girl (a very young Natalie Wood) that the fat man does indeed exist. Edmund Gwenn is wonderful—the eternal image of St. Nick—and received an Academy Award for his performance. The highlight is the courtroom scene, in which, while debating Gwenn's sanity, the very existence of Santa Claus is put on trial.

THE MIRACLE WORKER ☆☆☆☆
1962, USA
Anne Bancroft, Patty Duke, Victor Jory, Inga Swenson, Andrew Prine, Kathleen Comegys. Directed by Arthur Penn. 107 min.

Anne Bancroft and Patty Duke both deliver powerhouse, Oscar-winning performances playing the teacher Annie Sullivan and her blind-deaf pupil Helen Keller. Their tour-de-force acting carries this film deep into the viewer's memory, and certain scenes—most notably, the moment when Helen realizes the relationship between the cold, wet substance cascading over her hands and the word "water"—will never be forgotten. Director Arthur Penn has had such a meandering, inconsistent career that one looks perhaps too hard for flaws in individual films. *The Miracle Worker* stands up under scrutiny. The movie was not particularly successful when first released, but it has become a sentimental classic through repeated television screenings.

THE MIRACLE WORKER ☆☆☆½
1979, USA (TV)
Patty Duke Astin, Melissa Gilbert, Diana Muldaur, Charles Siebert. Directed by Paul Aaron. 100 min.

Based on William Gibson's classic play about the life of Helen Keller, this television remake falls slightly short of the original version. Patty Duke Astin played Helen Keller in the original and shines once again as the remarkable teacher, Annie Sullivan. Set in 1887, the film depicts both the struggle and triumph that Annie and her student—the young deaf, mute, and blind Helen Keller—experience.

MISCHIEF ☆½
1985, USA, R
Doug McKeon, Catherine Mary Stewart, Kelly Preston, Chris Nash, Graham Jarvis. Directed by Mel Damski. 97 min.

Horny teenagers in 1956 Ohio struggle ceaselessly to get lucky. If you have a hunch that you've seen this before, you're right. Here, we have the nerd, the school slut he's hopelessly lusting after, the nice girl next door, the new kid in town (who has an "attitude"), about a zillion James Dean quotes, and a few dozen songs on the soundtrack, most of which did not come out until *after* 1956. From the director of *Yellowbeard*.

THE MISERS
1970, USA, R ☆
William Smith, Bernie Hamilton, Adam Roarke, Daniel Kem, Houston Savage, Gene Cornelius, Paul Koslo, John Garwood, Ana Korita, Lillian Margarejo, Paralumen Paul Nuckles. Directed by Jack Starrett. 95 min.

A sloppy, cheap knock-off of Robert Aldrich's *The Dirty Dozen*. Why motorcycle bums would be employed by the U.S. government to free a CIA agent held captive by the North Vietnamese is left unexplained. But that's only one of the many illogical scenarios that take place in this motorcycle-war picture. Technical aspects such as camerawork and acting are minimally accomplished; however, there is enough bloody violence to please even *Rambo* fans.

THE MISFITS
1961, USA ☆☆☆½
Clark Gable, Marilyn Monroe, Montgomery Clift, Thelma Ritter, Eli Wallach. Directed by John Huston. 124 min.

Its cast of legendary Hollywood greats, directed by the prolific John Huston, is the main reason to watch this affected study of loneliness and renewed hope. The last film for Clark Gable and Marilyn Monroe, it portrays the subtle ways in which a divorcée and three modern-day cowboys change each other's lives when they meet in Reno, Nevada. Focusing on interactions, particularly between Gable and Monroe, the film manages to be emotionally engaging, though not narratively satisfying. Arthur Miller, Monroe's husband at the time of the filming, wrote the strained screenplay, creating Monroe's role specifically for her. Gable's part seems tailor-made for him as well; and although both of these leads give very fine performances, Montgomery Clift does more with a smaller, less-defined part. The last third of the film, in which the misfits set out to round up wild horses, contains vigorous action sequences and is the film's high point. There is strong support from Alex North's cogent score.

MISFITS OF SCIENCE
1985, USA (TV) ☆½
Dean Paul Martin, Kevin Peter Hall, Mark Thomas Miller, Courteney Cox, Jennifer Holmes, Mickey Jones, Eric Christmas, Edward Winter, Larry Linville, Kenneth Mars. Directed by James D. Parriott. 96 min.

The feature-length pilot for a flop series from 1985 is an unsuccessful attempt to wed second-rate science-fiction adventure to a joky, self-conscious style of humor. Four misfits, each endowed with superhuman but relatively useless abilities, band together with a young scientist and his very tall assistant to fight wrongdoing everywhere. Tiresome silliness that's better suited to Saturday morning than prime time.

MISHIMA
1985, USA, R ☆☆
Ken Ogata, Mashayuki Shionoya, Junkichi Orimoto, Go Riju. Directed by Paul Schrader. 115 min.

Japanese novelist Yukio Mishima was a showman, a searcher, and a bit of a nut case. No movie could possibly capture his full emotional extravagance, and *Mishima*, despite some vivid moments, is an exasperatingly misconceived attempt. The movie features three overlapping sections in contrasting styles: a framing device presenting Mishima's last day, on which he launched a coup attempt and then committed hara-kiri; biographical fragments from Mishima's youth; and lavish excerpts from three novels, shot in a lurid, hothouse style. Paul Schrader has reduced Mishima's life to a parade of abstractions, canonizing him as a glowering demigod of art and death—and so we get a gloss over the ideas without an inkling of the personality in which they were rooted. (It should be noted, though, that Schrader was forbidden by Mishima's widow to deal with much of the writer's personal life, including his flamboyant homosexuality.) As Mishima, the splendid actor Ken Ogata barely gets a chance to act.

MISS ANNIE ROONEY
1942, USA ☆☆½
Shirley Temple, William Gargan, Guy Kibbee, Peggy Ryan, Gloria Holden, June Lockhart. Directed by Edwin L. Marin. 84 min.

The adorable child star Shirley Temple went through an awkward adolescence but still held onto her stardom in pleasant vehicles like this one. The perpetually pouty cutie plays a poverty-stricken girl who has a crush on a poor little rich boy. Will true love bridge the difference in their backgrounds? In this painless period entertainment, it does. Note: Temple received her first screen kiss here.

MISS JULIE
1950, Sweden ☆☆☆½
Anita Bjork, Ulf Palme, Andes Henrikson, Marta Dorf, Lissa Alandh. Alf Sjoberg. 92 min.

From Strindberg's play about a woman's self-destruction, Swedish director Alf Sjoberg has fashioned an extraordinary cinematic exercise. Sjoberg avoids flashbacks by having past and present coexist onscreen, using camera movement instead of fades and cuts. Anita Bjork's portrayal of Julie is one of the great screen performances, and she is given able support by Ulf Palme as the brutish Jean.

MISS MARY
1986, Argentina, R ☆☆½
Julie Christie, Sofia Viruboff, Donald McIntire, Barbara Bunge, Nacha Guevara, Eduardo Pavlovsky. Directed by Maria Luisa Bemberg. 102 min.

Julie Christie gives a fine performance in the title role of this period drama about an English governess who arrived in Argentina just before World War II to supervise the upbringing of the children of an aristocratic family. She comes in conflict with the strict family patriarch, not realizing that at the same time his oldest son is becoming infatuated with her. Handsomely mounted by the director of the somewhat more compelling *Camila*, the story is gracefully told but lackadaisical and finally pointless.

MISS SADIE THOMPSON
1953, USA ☆☆½
Rita Hayworth, Jose Ferrer, Aldo Ray, Charles Bronson. Directed by Curtis Bernhardt. 91 min.

Flamboyant star vehicle for the luscious Rita Hayworth, who was entering the downward slide from love goddess to character actress. Even with her age starting to show, she has presence to burn and her brio enables this musicalization of Somerset Maugham's "Rain" to catch fire. At her best in the musical numbers, she had also matured as a dramatic actress by this time, and makes Sadie's flirtations—first with the sailors, and later with religion—both seem credible. Not as powerful as the versions with Jeanne Eagels or Joan Crawford, but it is provocative, and, for Hayworth fans, a cause for rejoicing.

THE MISSILES OF OCTOBER
1974, USA (TV) ☆☆☆
William Devane, Martin Sheen, Howard da Silva, Ralph Bellamy. Directed by Anthony Page. 155 min.

Originally an "ABC Theatre" presentation, this well-handled depiction of President Kennedy's trials during the Cuban missile crisis was one of television's first docudramas. The blend of suspense and history lesson, though less powerful than it could be, stands up nicely. William Devane's superb portrayal (he was one of the first actors to play JFK) brought him a great deal of attention, and Martin Sheen provides fine support as brother Robert. Overall, *Missiles* eschews controversy in favor of reverence, but still provides the kind of taut debate drama that's ideally suited to the small screen.

MISSING ☆☆☆☆
1982, USA, PG
Jack Lemmon, Sissy Spacek, John Shea, Melanie Mayron, Charles Cioffi. Directed by Costa-Gavras. 122 min.

In Costa-Gavras's pointed telling of the true story about a young American journalist who disappears from his home in Chile where he worked for a "liberal" newspaper, the menacing reality of the post-Allende repression becomes increasingly more clear, as the journalist's wife and father run up against endless walls of patronizing bureaucracy in their futile search for him. Like his distraught characters, Costa-Gavras has a neat way of slowly changing the consciousness of his audiences as he lets the disturbing facts slip along this journey of discovery. Even though the real villains here are the politicians who are constantly giving the couple the runaround, this high-tension political thriller is hardly anti-American. Rather, *Missing* is a chilling depiction of the abuse of power and of life under a military dictatorship. Nominated for several Oscars, including Best Picture, Actor, Actress, and Director, it won for Best Screenplay.

MISSING IN ACTION ☆
1984, USA, R
Chuck Norris, M. Emmet Walsh, James Hong, Lenore Kasdorf. Directed by Joseph Zito. 101 min.

Chuck Norris karate chops, strangles, and machine guns what seems to be the entire Vietnamese army in his quest to find a group of American MIAs. This is a distinctly awful piece of Cannon exploitation with a warped mentality that relegates the Vietnamese to the kind of evil Asian stereotypes last seen in World War II movies, and elevates Chuck to a self-righteous demigod. Despite some well-handled stunts, what *Action* lacks is excitement. The same kind of story was done with more class, if no more brains, in *Rambo: First Blood Part 2*.

MISSING IN ACTION 2: THE BEGINNING ½☆
1984, USA, R
Chuck Norris, Soon-Teck Oh, Steven Williams, Bennett Ohta, Joe Michael Terry. Directed by Lance Hool. 96 min.

Chuck Norris returns as the one-man demolition team out to get back at the Vietnamese for having the impertinence to ruin America's perfect military win-loss record. Set ten years before the first *Missing in Action*, this one features a solid hour of the sadistic prison-camp overlord Colonel Yen's torturing Norris and his buddies with rats, mock executions, and gladiatorial contests. Naturally, an hour of torture calls for an hour of retribution, and the film delivers. Lining up every cruelty on the Vietnamese side and all heroism on the American side, the MIA movies recast Vietnam as a World War II B movie with long-suffering GIs grimacing at inhuman Japs. The anger that's being expressed may be heartfelt, but instead of making audiences think, the film just makes them want to smash heads, which Norris does in an especially revolting way: The scene in which he exacts his revenge on Colonel Yen is sickening. So is the movie!

THE MISSION ☆☆½
1986, Great Britain, PG
Robert De Niro, Jeremy Irons, Ray McAnally, Liam Neeson, Aidan Quinn, Ronald Pickup, Charles Low, Cherie Lunghi, Daniel Berrigan. Directed by Roland Joffe. 128 min.

In this guilty-liberal historical epic set in the South American rain forests in the mid-eighteenth century, Jeremy Irons plays a Jesuit missionary who Christianizes the Guaraní Indians; Robert De Niro (in a catatonic performance) is a ruthless slave trader who undergoes a crisis of conscience and becomes a priest himself. When the region is transferred from Spain to Portugal and it's learned that the Portuguese officials want to enslave the Guaraní, the two enter a life-and-death struggle to save the Indians. This is a snazzily photographed but woefully impersonal movie; together director Roland Joffe, screenwriter Robert Bolt, and producer David Puttnam reduce the tradition of British-humanist filmmaking to a series of abstract poses. Joffe, after his brilliant debut with *The Killing Fields*, treats the Guaraní so patronizingly that he seems almost nostalgic for the days of colonialism; moral injustice is just one more colorful splotch on his palette. Winner of the Palme D'Or at the 1986 Cannes Film Festival, and an Academy Award for Chris Menges's cinematography.

THE MISSIONARY ☆☆½
1982, Great Britain, R
Michael Palin, Maggie Smith, Trevor Howard, Denholm Elliott, Michael Hordern, Graham Crowden, Neil Innes, Phoebe Nicholls. Directed by Richard Loncraine. 93 min.

This is not—we repeat, *not*—a Monty Python movie. Yes, it was written by and stars Pythonite Michael Palin, but that's only one-sixth of the troupe. And while this is quite a funny and amusing film in its own way, people expecting Pythonesque humor will be disappointed. The movie is set in 1906, and Palin plays a missionary recalled from Africa by the Bishop of London to do some work at home. His mission: "Go out amongst the prostitutes, find what it is they do and stop them from doing it." This he does, with the aid of Lady Ames (Maggie Smith), who sets him up with funds from her rich husband (Trevor Howard). It's full of nice bits, all in properly dry British style, and if they don't finally add up to much of a whole, it's well-enough made that you won't mind.

THE MISSOURI BREAKS ☆☆
1976, USA, PG
Marlon Brando, Jack Nicholson, Harry Dean Stanton, Randy Quaid, Frederic Forrest. Directed by Arthur Penn. 126 min.

A classic example of too many cooks spoiling the broth. In this case, the broth is an anti-Western written by Thomas McGuane (*Rancho Deluxe*), one of the more outstanding American novelists of the past twenty years; directed by Arthur Penn (*Bonnie and Clyde*, *Little Big Man*), a man with no little talent for examining American myths; and starring Marlon Brando and Jack Nicholson, both at the peak of their careers, fresh from *Last Tango in Paris* and *One Flew Over the Cuckoo's Nest*, respectively. And it's a mess, mostly due to Brando, who seems to be doing everything he can to amuse himself regardless of whatever is supposed to be going on in the film. By itself, his performance is actually pretty funny in an insane way, and the contributions of Penn, McGuane, and, especially, Nicholson all have aspects to recommend them. But as a whole, forget it. In fact, it might just be fun to have this videotape just so you can go over it and see what it might have been.

MISTER ROBERTS ☆☆☆
1955, USA
Henry Fonda, Jack Lemmon, James Cagney, William Powell, Betsy Palmer, Ward Bond, Harry Carey, Jr. Directed by John Ford and Mervyn LeRoy. 123 min.

Auteurists will have a field day determining the relative contributions of the two directors; others will be pleasantly amused and possibly moved by this Warner Bros. adaptation of Thomas Heggen and Joshua Logan's stage play. There are still too many theatrical kinks not ironed out—the group scenes look as though they are ready to take off into musical numbers—but the leading players make it work. Henry Fonda plays the lieutenant who, in order to get a transfer, goes head to head with James Cagney, the mulish captain of a World War II cargo ship. Cagney does splendid comic variations on Humphrey Bogart's Captain Queeg; William Powell (in his last film) graces the screen with his gentle wit as the ship's doctor; and Oscar winner Jack Lemmon plants the seeds of his career playing the rambunctious Ensign Pulver. The film really belongs, however, to Fonda as the quietly authoritative "Mister Roberts." It was followed by a sequel in 1964, *Ensign Pulver*, directed by Joshua Logan.

THE MISTRESS ☆☆½
1953, Japan
Hideko Takamine, Hiroshi Akutagawa, Eijiro Tono, Jukichi Uno, Choko Iida. Directed by Shiro Toyoda. 106 min.

In this slow, delicate study of sexual longing and shame, one of the earlier Japanese films to appear on American movie screens, Hideko Takamine portrays a young woman whose chances for marriage are ruined by a rape-seduction. She agrees to be taken as a mistress by an unscrupulous man whose promise to marry her is a false one. Its tragic overtones are predictable, but the story moves with unusual grace and dignity. (a.k.a.: *Wild Geese*)

MISTRESS OF THE WORLD ☆☆
1960, Sweden
Martha Hyer, Sabu, Carlos Thompson, Gino Cervi, Micheline Presle, Lino Ventura. Directed by William Dieterle. 98 min.

A Swedish physicist and his Cambodian assistant, who have developed a "formula that could destroy the world," are kidnapped by agents of an unspecified enemy, supervised by the cruel Madame Le Tour, the would-be Mistress of the World. An international team of spies is formed to trace them. The trail leads through the nightclubs and waterfronts of Europe, and ends up in Cambodia, where there is a lot of good location shooting. There are the usual genre ingredients, not excluding the professor's lovely daughter who falls in love with the chief sleuth. Not great, but it's still surprisingly watchable, perhaps because of the pre-007 naïveté of it, or because of the beautifully furnished interiors.

MISUNDERSTOOD ☆½
1984, USA, PG
Gene Hackman, Henry Thomas, Rip Torn, Huckleberry Fox, Susan Anspach. Directed by Jerry Schatzberg. 91 min.

This unrelieved tearjerker might have died onscreen were it not for the presence of Gene Hackman. He plays an American tycoon in Tunisia, a man so emotionally out of touch that, after his wife dies, he can barely break the news to his children; indeed, this tycoon loathes his own repressed nature so much that he slights the son who most resembles him and dotes on the son who most resembles the mother. This post-*Kramer vs. Kramer* father-and-sons sob story pushes its conflicts to shameless, heart-tugging extremes, but Hackman manages to come out with his dignity intact. From the moment you see him standing at his wife's graveside, his erect posture knocked aslant by loss, he gives the character a credibility the story itself never earns.

MIXED BLOOD ☆½
1985, France
Marilia Pera, Richard Ulacia, Geraldine Smith, Rodney Harvey, Angel David, Pedro Sanchaz, Linda Kerridge, Ulrich Berr. Directed by Paul Morrissey. 97 min.

Andy Warhol's protégé Paul Morrissey gained a cult following in the early 1970s for his sleazy, campy dissections of urban lowlife (*Heat, Trash, Flesh*). Here, he returns to the drug-scarred, bloodstained New York slum known as Alphabet City for a less-than-scintillating black comedy. The threadbare plot concerns the efforts of a deranged gangleader-cum-den mother (Marilia Pera) to protect her brood of underage criminals from a bloody drug war. Morrissey's trademark touches—explosions of violence, deadpan humor, scenes that drag on forever, and sublimely incompetent acting—are all in place, as are the murky dialogue and muddy camerawork endemic to low-budget filmmaking. Except for Pera's extravagantly trashy star turn (though burdened by a severe language barrier), the result is labored throughout, and often incomprehensible.

MOBY DICK ☆☆☆
1956, USA
Gregory Peck, Richard Basehart, Orson Welles, Harry Andrews, Joseph Robertson Justice. Directed by John Huston. 115 min.

A whaling voyage becomes one man's obsessive crusade against the monstrous white whale that maimed him. Adapted by director John Huston and Ray Bradbury from Herman Melville's classic novel, the film conveys a visual, textured intensity that complements the personal intensity of Captain Ahab. Action scenes are effective; an elaborate nautical set recaptures the period's aura; but Gregory Peck is lackluster in the role of Ahab (he and Huston apparently argued over the best approach to the role, and Huston was eventually satisfied, but Peck was never completely comfortable with the performance). Orson Welles is the dominant actor.

MODERN GIRLS ☆
1986, USA, PG-13
Daphne Zuniga, Virginia Madsen, Cynthia Gibb, Clayton Rohner, Chris Nash, Steve Shellen, Rich Overton, Pamela Springsteen. Directed by Jerry Kramer. 82 min.

"Sleazy broads" is more like it; haven't the three ladies in this low, low, low comedy heard that the sexual revolution is over? Kelly, Margo, and Cece are the titular heroines who cast off their dull daytime jobs to prowl Los Angeles's clubs, do a lot of drugs, nearly get picked up, practically get raped, and many other tedious almost-activities. Notwithstanding the fact that the film stars three otherwise attractive performers and that the script was written by a woman, this is about as feminist as "The Flintstones" and a lot less funny.

MODERN PROBLEMS ☆½
1981, USA, PG
Chevy Chase, Patti D'Arbanville, Mary Kay Place, Nell Carter, Brian Doyle-Murray, Dabney Coleman. Directed by Ken Shapiro. 92 min.

This lame Chevy Chase vehicle is typical of many of the comedies starring "Saturday Night Live" alumni—the writing feels rushed and secondhand, relying heavily on visual gags and special effects to compensate for a one-joke premise, and the star is left to shuffle around and smirk. The single gag here has Chase as an air-traffic controller who gains telekinetic powers after a brush with radioactivity. He proceeds to perpetrate all manner of trickery on those around him, when it's really Chase's arrogant character who you'd like to see get it in the face. Featuring Nell Carter keeping one Hollywood stereotype alive and well by playing a black maid who runs around screaming about voodoo.

MODERN ROMANCE ☆☆☆
1981, USA, R
Albert Brooks, Kathryn Harrold, Tyann Means, Bruno Kirby, James L. Brooks. Directed by Albert Brooks. 102 min.

Fans of Albert Brooks's recent success *Lost in America* would do well to check out this, his second full-length feature as writer-director-star. Like Woody Allen, he makes movies about contemporary American neuroses as displayed by his own, more abrasive persona. Though not as sweet or accessible, this is Brooks's *Annie Hall*: His character, an L.A. film editor, breaks up with his girlfriend and spends the rest of the movie changing his mind, finding excuses to call her on the phone, strengthening his determination to start anew, and generally acting like a complete jerk. Brooks's comic situations build very slowly, so much so that many viewers tend to nod off before the payoff; the jokes are, however, carefully structured, which makes a repeated viewing of this rewarding.

MODERN TIMES ☆☆☆☆
1936, USA
Charlie Chaplin, Paulette Goddard, Henry Bergman, Chester Conklin, Stanley Sanford, Hank Mann, Louis Natheaux, Allan Garcia. Directed by Charles Chaplin. 85 min.

Pointed satire was always in Chaplin's arsenal of comic weapons, and in *Modern Times* he uses it as a destructive scalpel for a brilliant dissection of contemporary culture. The film begins in a factory where Charlie works on an assembly line, and the pace and pressure cause him to have a nervous breakdown. Unemployed, he gets arrested after ironically becoming involved in a strike; then, after his release from prison, he falls for a girl on her way to jail—now he wants to get back in. Their two lives become intertwined and they work in a restaurant before being forced on the run. The movie is a slippery slope of insecurity for the Tramp and his gamine girlfriend, and every stop is less a resting place than one more step closer to the final dispossession of life on the road. Chaplin and Paulette Goddard make a great team: Her comic talents and energetic demeanor make her Chaplin's strongest leading lady since the days of Mabel Normand and Edna Purviance. The movie looks great, too. Chaplin spent $1.5 million and constructed two huge sets—the factory actually worked. Released in 1936, the movie was, like *City Lights*, nearly a silent film, and marked Chaplin as a unique artist in the film industry. It was also his last use of the Tramp character.

MOGAMBO ☆☆☆½
1953, USA
Clark Gable, Ava Gardner, Grace Kelly, Donald Sinden. Directed by John Ford. 115 min.

John Ford's exciting jungle romance features a glorious cast masterfully filmed on location in Africa. A remake of *Red Dust*, which appeared in 1932 with Clark Gable and Jean Harlow, *Mogambo* is a sexy, humorous tale of adventure and sexual politics in the wilderness. Gable exudes suave, masculine cool as Victor Marswell, the tough, capable guide for the anthropologist Donald Nordley (Donald Sinden). Gable's costars, Ava Gardner as the woman who wants Victor, and Grace Kelly as the anthropologist's wife, both contribute exceptional performances.

MOHAMMAD: MESSENGER OF GOD ☆
1977, Saudi Arabia/Libya, PG
Anthony Quinn, Michael Ansara, Irene Papas, Johnny Sekka, Martin Benson, Andre Morell, Neville Jason, Michael Forest. Directed by Moustapha Akkad. 179 min.

Would that this three-hour non-epic about the founder of the Islam religion were as interesting as the story behind its making; first-time producer-director Moustapha Akkad wanted to make the Muslim version of *The Ten Commandments* or *The Robe* and spent seven years putting it together. Along the way, he had to persuade various Arab leaders to finance it, all the while assuring them that it would be reverent and not break the religious rule that neither Mohammad's personage nor voice (or, for that matter, his shadow) be depicted. He finally obtained financing from that well-known Libyan entertainment mogul Colonel Qadaffi, and turned out this extremely dull sand saga in which the part of the prophet is played by the camera; the closest you ever get to a glimpse of the great man is a few views of his camel stick. When it was finally released in Washington, a band of Black Muslims stormed the local B'nai B'rith and took 100 hostages, demanding that the film not be shown. Their reaction would have been more understandable had they actually been inside a theater showing it, demanding to be let out. (a.k.a.: *The Message*)

THE MOLLY MAGUIRES ☆☆☆
1970, USA
Sean Connery, Richard Harris, Samantha Eggar, Frank Finlay, Anthony Zerbe, Bethel Leslie. Directed by Martin Ritt. 124 min.

A gritty, interesting historical film from doggedly iconoclastic director Martin Ritt, for only those viewers willing to immerse themselves in a complicated and slow-moving story. The drama is set in the Pennsylvania of 1876, where a group of coal miners unwilling to tolerate employer abuses any longer rebelled. Sean Connery is the leader of the miners, and Richard Harris is the spy hired by the bosses to insinuate himself among the workers. Beautifully textured and detailed, though a little too long for its own good. Cinematography by James Wong Howe.

MOMMIE DEAREST ☆☆½
1981, USA, PG
Faye Dunaway, Diana Scarwid, Steve Forrest, Howard da Silva. Directed by Frank Perry. 129 min.

This camp classic portrays the tormented relationship between bitchy star Joan Crawford and her daughter Christina—which includes everything from insanity to fist fights. Adapted from Christina's best-selling book, *Mommie* provides an interesting look at Hollywood's inside life, though all of it might not seem terribly believable. There is, however, a monumental performance from Faye Dunaway, who utters the picture's most memorable line: "No more wire hangers—EVER!" Paramount successfully marketed *Mommie* as a midnight movie with the headline, "The biggest mother of them all."

MONA LISA ☆☆☆
1986, Great Britain, R
Bob Hoskins, Cathy Tyson, Michael Caine, Clarke Peters, Kate Hardie, Robbie Coltraine. Directed by Neil Jordan. 100 min.

Mona Lisa decries the exploitation of prostitutes and damns the aristocratic scum who abuse them, but there's a tragic and glamorous eroticism to be found under the grit of this poignant morality fable. A feisty ex-con (Bob Hoskins) learns his lessons the hard way when he descends into England's menacing world of sex for sale to drive a beautiful black hooker named Simone to her tricks. The conniving streetwalker waves her sensual spells about the squat antihero until he is enraptured enough to help her find a missing hooker friend. George's haunting encounters with a soulless legion of pubescent whores are effectively counterbalanced by the film's comedy of manners, especially when Simone tries to give her hopelessly lower-class charge some social graces. Director Neil Jordan handles these wild mood swings with class, building suspensefully to the bizarre and violent conclusion. The performers do the complex material justice, especially Michael Caine, who has one of his best roles as a satanic pimp.

THE MONEY PIT ☆½
1986, USA, PG
Tom Hanks, Shelley Long, Joe Mantegna, Philip Bosco, Alexander Godunov, Maureen Stapleton, Josh Mostel, Yakov Smirnoff. Directed by Richard Benjamin. 91 min.

Tom Hanks and Shelley Long are yuppie lovers who buy a stately suburban-country mansion that turns out to be a renovation nightmare. The stairway collapses, and Hanks falls onto the floor; a bathroom faucet spurts disgusting brown goo, and Hanks falls onto the floor; the wall sockets catch fire, the roof leaks buckets, and the bathtub crashes through the ceiling and onto the floor. The problem with movies like this is that the endless spiral of disaster becomes as frustrating for the audience as it is for the characters. Director Richard Benjamin has the normally funky Hanks playing a kind of junior version of himself; Hanks gets to do a lot of vintage-Benjamin pleading, whining, and repressed yelling. It all would have worked better as a four-minute Pink Panther cartoon.

MONIKA ☆☆☆½
1952, Sweden
Harriet Andersson, Lars Ekborg, John Harryson, Georg Skarstedt, Dagmar Ebbesen. Directed by Ingmar Bergman. 96 min.

Anyone who criticizes Ingmar Bergman for dealing with elitist subject matter should witness this scalding melodrama from his early period. Harriet Andersson and Lars Ekborg play a struggling young couple in south Stockholm who must deal with an unwanted pregnancy. The screenplay by Bergman and Per Anders Fogelstrom never glosses over the hardships faced by the couple, and Bergman is equally uncompromising in his direction. From the opening satire of Hollywood B movies to the devastating closing shot, *Monika* is a searing reminder of Bergman's storytelling economy and skill. (a.k.a.: *Summer with Monika*)

MONKEY BUSINESS ☆☆☆☆
1931, USA
Groucho, Harpo, Chico, and Zeppo Marx, Thelma Todd. Directed by Norman Z. McLeod. 78 min.

A rollicking, frenetically paced film in the Marxian mold, *Monkey Business* features the brothers as stowaways on a ship and then as bodyguards for gangsters. Each decides to impersonate Maurice Chevalier to get off the boat. As with most Marx Brothers films, the story feels improvised, thrown together. But so what: At this time the brothers were still fairly new to Hollywood, and the film crackles with their unbounded energy and sense of a limitless, new canvas of comedy.

MON ONCLE ☆☆☆½
1958, France
Jacques Tati, Jean-Pierre Zola, Alain Becourt, Adrienne Servantie. Directed by Jacques Tati. 110 min.

Jacques Tati's savage satire of mechanized living details the lives of a middle-class couple with a fetish for gadgets. Their white-walled house is stocked with the latest easy-living gimmicks, and Tati has riotous fun taking his bumbling hero, Mr. Hulot, on a grand tour of the place. The movie has its longueurs, though; it wasn't until a decade later, with *Playtime*, that Tati unveiled the full force of his satiric vision.

MON ONCLE D'AMERIQUE ☆☆☆☆
1980, France
Gérard Depardieu, Nicole Garcia, Roger Pierre, Marie DuBois, Nelly Bourgeaud, Henri Laborit. Directed by Alain Resnais. 123 min.

The role of dominance in human behavior may seem a tad dry as a subject for a movie. In the hands of director Alain Resnais (*Hiroshima Mon Amour*), this premise allows for a wry poke at scientific theorizing and a delightfully engaging story about three people trying to be happy in an abrasive world. The film is constructed on two levels: Henri Laborit lectures on his behavioral theory, and we get to see three characters act out their lives in ways that first seem to confirm the good doctor's thesis. Then, as in life, things begin to get interestingly confused, and the story begins to confound and contradict Laborit's psychological pigeonholing. Combine this with Dusan Makavejev's *W.R.—Mysteries of the Organism* for a great science-and-life double feature.

MONSIEUR VERDOUX ☆☆☆½
1947, USA
Charlie Chaplin, Martha Raye, Mady Correll, Allison Roddan, Robert Lewis, William Frawley, Fritz Leiber. Directed by Charles Chaplin. 122 min.

Based on an idea by Orson Welles, this splendid black comedy casts Charlie Chaplin not as the Tramp but as a refined, elegant murderer of rich women. "Verdoux feels that murder is a logical extension of business," Chaplin has explained, and with dark but never morbid humor the film depicts its sympathetic, detached killer performing his sanguinary deeds to support himself and his crippled wife after his legitimate business fails. Chaplin fans who are familiar only with the little tramp may be bored with some of the excessively talky scenes, especially when Chaplin starts to philosophize. It was however, his own personal favorite.

MONSIGNOR ☆
1982, USA, R
Christopher Reeve, Genevieve Bujold, Fernando Rey, Jason Miller, Joe Cortese, Adolfo Celi, Leonardo Cimino. Directed by Frank Perry. 122 min.

An American army chaplain (Christopher Reeve) works his way into the power structure of the Vatican, committing enough sins along the way to put him on the other side of the confessional until the Second Coming. Someone should have locked Reeve in a dark room and made him atone for appearing in this monstrosity, perhaps the worst of his many attempts to prove that under the big red "S" lay a Serious Actor. The plot machinations and stiff "international" cast couldn't hack it on the shoddiest TV miniseries. The funniest scene has Genevieve Bujold as a randy nun who gets Father Chris all hot under the clerical collar.

MONSTER A GO-GO ½☆
1965, USA
Phil Morton, June Travis, George Perry, Henry Hite, Lois Brooke. Directed by Bill Rebane. 70 min.

Yet another instance where the story behind the making of the film is far more interesting than the film itself: Gorehound Herschell Gordon Lewis (*Blood Feast, 2000 Maniacs, Color Me Blood Red*) had just completed a feature called *Moonshine Mountain*, intended (as were all of his films) for the drive-in/grind house market. He wanted the receipts from both halves of the double bill, so he bought an unfinished film called *Terror at Half Bay* that producer-director Bill Rebane had run out of money for, added a few more feet of film and a narrator to give it continuity, and released it as *Monster a Go-Go*. What minimal plot there is concerns a hunt for an astronaut, played by Henry Hite, "the world's tallest man," who emerges from a space capsule doused with radiation. This monster has almost no go-go at all—Hite appears for a grand total of less than a minute. Definitely *not* a "so-bad-it's-funny" film, this is simply unwatchable. The only good thing is the music by a surf band called The Other Three; the title song contains the lyric, "You may come from beyond the moon/But to me you're just a goon."

THE MONSTER CLUB ☆☆
1980, Great Britain
Vincent Price, John Carradine, Stuart Whitman, Donald Pleasance, Britt Ekland, Richard Johnson, Simon Ward, UB 40, Patrick Magee. Directed by Roy Ward Baker. 97 min.

A writer of horror stories is invited by a vampire—who assures him that all the monsters *love* his writing—to a raucous discotheque frequented by ghouls, werewolves, zombies, and sundry creatures. There he hears tales of a lonely, whistling monster, a family of persecuted vampires and a town of ghouls, in between noisy musical diversions and dissertations on the family tree of monsters. This is a well-produced but extremely uneven anthology horror film with some nice moments.

MONSTER ZERO ☆☆
1966, Japan
Nick Adams, Akira Tadarada. Directed by Inoshiro Honda. 90 min.

Planet X makes a deal with Earth to borrow Godzilla and Rodan (it's OK, we weren't using them at the time, anyway) in order to battle Ghidrah, but then turns around and sics all three monsters on us! Have you ever heard of anything so dastardly? Of course, the evil aliens have to hypnotize Godzilla and Rodan to do all kinds of things they wouldn't otherwise do, like stomp around Tokyo and knock over lots of buildings. Just for those who have trouble keeping these things straight, Godzilla is the radioactive green dinosaur, Rodan is the flying pterodactyl, and Ghidrah is the three-headed fire-breathing dragon from outer space. (a.k.a.: *Godzilla vs. Monster Zero*)

MONTENEGRO ☆☆½
1981, Sweden/Great Britain, R
Susan Anspach, Svetozar Cvetkovic, Erland Josephson, Patricia Gelin. Directed by Dusan Makavejev. 98 min.

The most accessible film by Dusan Makavejev (*WR: Mysteries of the Organism, The Coca-Cola Kid*) looks like one of those hip liberation comedies from a decade ago, but it's also got a streak of euphoric humor. Susan Anspach is Makavejev's mad housewife, a wigged-out madonna who leaves her rich businessman husband and follows a pack of garlicky Slavic immigrants to their sleazy, festive nightclub, where she spends three days "finding herself." The story is rather banal, but it's occasionally funny and sexy.

MONTE WALSH ☆☆½
1970, USA, R
Lee Marvin, Jack Palance, Jeanne Moreau, Mitch Ryan, Jim Davis, Bear Hudkins, Ray Guth, Allyn Ann McLerie. Directed by William A. Fraker. 108 min.

Another Death of the West film about cowboys and encroaching civilization, *Monte Walsh* is handled with such meditative pacing and melancholic deliberation that it continually threatens to put the viewer to sleep. Interest is maintained by the presence of Lee Marvin and Jack Palance, two bad-guys icons from classic films who manage to come across as aging ranch hands ready to give up the range. As the frontier shrinks and ranching suffers, economic troubles force the two men to reconsider their lives and try to settle down. Death interferes, though, and Walsh (Marvin) is forced into a last showdown. First-time director William Fraker (*Legend of the Lone Ranger*) manages to conjure up a grimy, naturalistic view of the dog-eared West that is effective but points up his debt to Sam Peckinpah and the superior *The Wild Bunch*.

MONTY PYTHON AND THE HOLY GRAIL ☆☆☆
1974, Great Britain, R
Graham Chapman, John Cleese, Terry Gilliam, Eric Idle, Michael Palin. Directed by Terry Gilliam and Terry Jones. 90 min.

The Monty Python troupe, extending their irreverent half-hour comedy show to feature length, more or less, retains the bare bones of the legend of King Arthur and his knights' search for the Holy Grail. Unexpected and outrageous turns come in the form of a killer rabbit, the decapitation of a "you are there"-type of reporter, a castle of lusty young maidens, a fey depiction of Robin Hood and his merry men, and much, much more. Uneven, like the TV series and all the other Python films, but with so many solid laughs that the duds don't matter.

MONTY PYTHON LIVE AT THE HOLLYWOOD BOWL ☆☆☆½
1982, Great Britain, R
Graham Chapman, John Cleese, Terry Gilliam, Eric Idle, Terry Jones, Michael Palin, Carol Cleveland, Neil Innes. Directed by Terry Hughes and Monty Python. 77 min.

Filmed in 1980, this elegantly shot, well-sustained series of vintage sketches finds the Monty Python troupe closer than ever to its Cambridge Footlights origins. Python fans will recognize such timeless routines as the lumberjack song, "Crunchy Frog," and Eric Idle's "Nudge, nudge—say no more!" from the opening lines; for the uninitiated, this is a succinct and delightful introduction to the comedy of a discombobulated culture.

MONTY PYTHON'S LIFE OF BRIAN ☆☆☆☆
1979, Great Britain, R
Graham Chapman, John Cleese, Terry Gilliam, Eric Idle, Terry Jones, Michael Palin, Carol Cleveland, Neil Innes, Spike Milligan. Directed by Terry Jones. 93 min.

Monty Python's gonzo gospel was condemned as "blasphemous," even though its barbs are directed not at Jesus but at the mortals He walked among. Graham Chapman plays "Brian called Brian," an ordinary schmo who spends most of his life on the run, either from Roman centurions or from followers who are certain he's the Messiah. It's the Pythons' best feature because they managed to work all of their concerns into a single cohesive plot, without losing the spontaneity of their earlier work. Memorable bits include Michael Palin's lisping Pontius Pilate, a stoning attended entirely by women dressed as men (all played by men in the first place), endless political haranguing from the People's Front of Judea (or is it the Judean People's Front?), and the closing song, "Always look on the Bright Side of Life." Producer George Harrison has a bit part. (a.k.a.: *Life of Brian*)

MONTY PYTHON'S THE MEANING OF LIFE ☆☆☆½
1983, Great Britain, R
Graham Chapman, John Cleese, Terry Gilliam, Terry Jones, Eric Idle, Michael Palin, Carol Cleveland: Directed by Terry Jones. 101 min.

This series of sketches from the Python troupe is funny, grotesque, savage, and, true to its title, quite philosophical. By placing their cheeky Swiftian musings front and center, the Pythons have abandoned some of the anything-goes irreverence—the comedy of absolutely no redeeming social value—that made their earlier work so memorable. The lack of a cohesive plot, however, does provide them some of the freedom to segue seemingly at random from bit to bit, one of the joys of the television series. This is not a good introduction to the troupe for the unfamiliar, as there are several sequences here whose primary purpose seems to be to offend as many as possible; these include an *Oliver!*-style production number about the evil of birth control entitled "Every Sperm is Sacred," a graphic organ donation sequence (seems the donor thought the donation would take place *after* he had died), and the infamous scene in which the world's fattest man eats one mouthful too many at an elegant restaurant, and then explodes.

THE MOON IN THE GUTTER ☆☆
1983, France R
Nastassja Kinski, Gerard Depardieu, Victoria Abril, Bertice Reading. Directed by Jean-Jacques Beineix. 125 min.

This is an utterly artificial evocation of a pulp world gone wild. A longshoreman institutes his own investigation into the rape and subsequent suicide of his younger sister; it plunges him into a surreal world of erotic danger in which nothing and no one can be taken at face value. Based on the novel by American writer David Goodis (whose work formed the basis for *Shoot the Piano Player* and other films), this is a disappointment from the director of *Diva*.

THE MOON IS BLUE ☆☆
1953, USA
Maggie McNamara, William Holden, David Niven, Tom Tully, Dawn Addams. Directed by Otto Preminger. 95 min.

Oh, the fuss they made over this "blue" comedy when it was first released! This unexceptional Broadway hit was made into a film by Otto Preminger, who had to release the film without a production code seal. Despite its tepid comedy, *Moon* was deemed unreleaseable because the cast used words like "virgin." None of the controversy hurt the film at the box office. As a piece of cinematic history, the film deserves its place in a time capsule. As a study of sexual mores, it is indispensable for historians of the 1950s. As a movie, though, it's just a standard sex farce about a girl who'd rather fight than join the ranks of the "tarnished."

MOONLIGHTING ☆☆☆½
1982, Great Britain, PG
Jeremy Irons, Eugene Lipinski, Jiri Stanislaw, Eugeniusz Hackiewicz. Directed by Jerzy Skolimowski. 97 min.

In this galvanizing political allegory, Jeremy Irons portrays a bilingual Polish construction foreman sent to work in Great Britain as a cost-saving measure. As a stranger in a strange land, with his native country on the brink of revolution, he finds himself unsure of his friends, his allegiances, and his beliefs. Irons delivers a brilliant performance as a man playing solitaire with his psyche. Although the film functions somewhat elliptically as drama, it's devastatingly effective as a study of Poland's national identity in turmoil. Under great pressure to keep the film timely, Jerzy Skolimowski wrote, cast, shot, and edited the film in less than three months.

MOONLIGHTING ☆☆☆½
1985, USA (TV)
Cybill Shepherd, Bruce Willis, Alyce Beasley, Jim McKrell, Dennis Lipscomb, John Medici, Dennis Stewart. Directed by Robert Butler. 98 min.

We like the series, and we like this pilot episode, which introduced millions to the gumshoe with the big mouth and the model with the slow burn. Aficionados who came late to "Moonlighting" will learn how Maddie lost her fortune, how she first met Dave, and even such useful trivia as the original name of the Blue Moon Detective Agency. Series creator Glenn Gordon Caron's teleplay has none of the brushes with surrealism that characterized later episodes, but there's plenty of sharp wordplay, romantic chemistry, and a lively and unusually clever plot; and Bruce Willis and Cybill Shepherd each give a new dimension to the definition of small-screen sex appeal. If you've never seen them, there's no better place to start.

MOONLIGHT SWORD AND JADE LION ★★
Hong Kong
Angela Mao Ying, Don Wang Dao, So Chan Ping, Lung Kwan Yee, Man Kwong Lung, Kwong Ming, Tong Lik, Ng Ka Yan, Cheung Fong Ha, Show Lo Fai, Yuen Sum, Man Cheung San. Directed by New Kwong Lam.

Chiu Shiao Yen (Angela Mao Ying) is sent to find her teacher's brother because he knows who killed her parents. The confusing plot is further aggravated by the cut-rate production. Angela Mao Ying's usual vivaciousness is lacking and Don Wang Dao is hardly seen at all.

MOON OF THE WOLF ★★½
1972, USA (TV)
David Janssen, Bradford Dillman, John Beradino, Geoffrey Lewis, Royal Dano, Barbara Rush. Directed by Daniel Petrie. 73 min.

What with werewolf flicks enjoying new popularity (*Teen Wolf, Silver Bullet*), fans of this subgenre will want to reconsider this TV chiller about a modern monster wolfing down his victims in the Louisiana bogs and environs. The swamps provide appropriately mist-shrouded atmosphere, but plot logic is also lost somewhere in the blue bayou; this problem prevents this promising thriller from being anything more than a passable fright flick.

MOONRAKER ★★★
1979, Great Britain, PG
Roger Moore, Lois Chiles, Michael Lonsdale, Richard Kiel, Corinne Clery, Bernard Lee, Desmond Llewelyn, Lois Maxwell. Directed by Lewis Gilbert. 126 min.

For the eleventh entry in the James Bond series, producer Albert Broccoli dropped the spy-versus-spy intrigue of the Sean Connery era completely, in favor of a cartoonish, effects-laden, light-spirited style better suited to Roger Moore, and almost as entertaining. This installment isn't quite as clever or well crafted as *The Spy Who Loved Me*, but the gimmick, which has 007 traveling into outer space to foil a world-conquest plot, is irresistible. Lois Chiles is cold and drab as the requisite Bond bedmate, but there's a very funny subplot involving the return of Richard Kiel's steel-toothed villain Jaws (who gets his very own girlfriend), and a bang-up finale.

MOONSHINE COUNTY EXPRESS ★★
1977, USA, PG
John Saxon, Susan Howard, William Conrad, Maureen McCormack, Claudia Jennings, Dub Taylor. Directed by Gus Trikonis. 95 min.

Three breathtaking sisters (Susan Howard, Maureen McCormack, and Claudia Jennings) are heiresses to a fortune in cornsqueezin's after the demise of their paw. Before they can get their goods to market, though, they've got to break the moonshine monopoly of their father's suspected killer (William Conrad). The kick of this swill is agreeable enough if you've got the hankering.

THE MOON SPINNERS ★★★
1964, Great Britain/USA, G
Hayley Mills, Peter McEnery, Joan Greenwood, Pola Negri, Eli Wallach. Directed by James Neilson. 118 min.

This is a spritely adventure that showcases the moonstruck charms of Hayley Mills, Disney's golden girl. Hayley and her aunt (the delicious Joan Greenwood) vacation on the isle of Crete, where they are welcomed with less than open arms. Soon they're enmeshed in a life-and-death mystery involving smuggling, stolen jewels, and a few thieves who don't want strangers poking their noses into their gem trafficking. The film has some pleasant romancing, a few mild chills, and a memorable cameo from silent film legend Pola Negri.

MORGAN! ★★★
1966, Great Britain
David Warner, Robert Stephens, Vanessa Redgrave. Directed by Karel Reisz. 97 min.

Odd black comedy that was highly popular in art houses and on college campuses in the late 1960s. David Warner, in his first starring role, plays the title character, a not-all-there artist whose wife divorces him after she can no longer tolerate his weirdness. Undeterred by her remarriage to a paragon of normality, Morgan sets out to win her back through the unlikeliest of strategies. Although retaining the knee-jerk sympathy always given to the disenfranchised of the world in the movies, *Morgan* has lost much of its charm in the years since the film's release; removed from the context of the Love Generation, when alienation by itself seemed commendable, this nut evokes more pity than identification.

THE MORNING AFTER ★★½
1986, USA, R
Jane Fonda, Jeff Bridges, Raul Julia, Diane Salinger, Richard Foronjy, Geoffrey Scott, Kathleen Wilhoite, James Haake, Don Hood. Directed by Sidney Lumet. 103 min.

Playing an alcoholic actress who wakes up next to a man with a knife stuck in his chest, Jane Fonda shows more life—more enjoyment of acting—than she has in years. Wearing a pile of big blond hair, she has a hardbitten elegance here, and she's funny and nasty and sexy—she lets herself revel in the trashy fun of being a broad. This thriller isn't much, but Fonda acts with the sudden, instinctive shifts of tone, brittle intelligence, and tough humor that have characterized her best work. As the ex-cop who helps her out, Jeff Bridges gives a performance different from anything he's done: his shambling, drawling placidity balances Fonda's coiled tension. It's too bad, though, that the two of them really don't get a chance to connect. Individually, the performances are fine, but the script's limitations and Sidney Lumet's clumsy direction keep the picture from amounting to much.

MORNING GLORY ★★½
1933, USA
Katharine Hepburn, Douglas Fairbanks, Jr., Adolphe Menjou, C. Aubrey Smith. Directed by Lowell Sherman. 74 min.

Katharine Hepburn is here in all her tremulous early glory. Whether she deserved the 1933 Academy Award for Best Actress remains open to question. Kate fearlessly captures the stridency and arrogance of Eva Lovelace, the fledgling actress who lives and breathes the "theatah." Determined not to fade into obscurity, Kate puts affairs of the heart on the back burner and becomes an overnight sensation in this slightly creaky but sturdy warhorse. Remade as *Stage Struck* in 1958.

MORTUARY ½★
1981, USA, R
Lynda Day George, Christopher George, Mary McDonough, David Wallace, Bill Paxton. Directed by Howard Avedis. 90 min.

A film half-embalmed with ideas stolen from better horror movies. A teenage girl (the usual stupid brave soul who's oversexed and fond of wandering out alone at night when she's in fear of her life) doesn't believe her daddy's death was an accident. Who's that stalking her in the black opera cape? Why doesn't her seance-loving mommy believe she's in danger? You'll figure out answers to these questions early on, and you will not be entertained by some graphic how-to embalming lessons. A sick, boring movie except for a tremendously silly ending involving a wedding ceremony with some very dead guests.

MOSCOW DOES NOT BELIEVE IN TEARS ☆☆½
1980, U.S.S.R.,
Vera Alentova, Irina Muravyova, Raisa Ryazonova, Natalia Vavilova. Directed by Vladimir Menshov. 150 min.

This pleasant but rather wan story of three provincial girls who come to Moscow to find a man is a Soviet variation of a standard Hollywood formula. In the first half, set in 1958, we meet the heroines and watch them undertake small, girlish adventures. But during the second half, when sensitive, intelligent Katerina lands herself a quirkily macho prole, the movie becomes both a Soviet *Unmarried Woman* and a mild piece of propaganda, a demonstration that Russians can have their consumerist society and their classless society at the same time. This somehow won the Oscar for Best Foreign Language Film, over such competition as Truffaut's *The Last Metro* and Kurosawa's *Kagemusha*. Go figure.

MOSCOW NIGHTS

See *I Stand Condemned*

MOSCOW ON THE HUDSON ☆☆½
1983, USA, PG
Robin Williams, Maria Conchita Alonso, Cleavant Derricks, Alejandro Rey, Elya Baskin, Yakov Smirnoff. Directed by Paul Mazursky. 115 min.

As Vladimir Ivanoff, a Russian saxophone player who defects to the United States during a stop at Bloomingdale's, Robin Williams gives his first emotional screen performance. Up through the poignant and hilarious defection scene, this comedy by Paul Mazursky is a perfect showcase for Williams's balancing act of a performance. But when Vladimir tries to make a life for himself in his new country, all director Paul Mazursky can do is fill the screen with lovable ethnics and bamboozle us with a lot of cheery homilies about "freedom." The ending, in which a group composed of every ethnic type under the sun begins to recite the Declaration of Independence, would embarrass a seventh grade civics class.

THE MOSQUITO COAST ☆☆½
1986, USA, PG
Harrison Ford, River Phoenix, Helen Mirren, Jadrien Steele, Andre Gregory, Conrad Roberts, Martha Plimpton, Dick O'Neill, Hilary Gordon, Rebecca Gorden, Butterfly McQueen. Directed by Peter Weir. 118 min.

A disappointing adaptation of Paul Theroux's nightmarish adventure novel about crackpot inventor Allie Fox, who rails against American consumerism and waste, relocates his hapless family to Central America to start anew in the jungle and, when his new empire crumbles, begins to slide from eccentricity into madness. The power of the novel is in its disillusionment; told from the perspective of Allie's teenaged son, it chronicles a *Swiss Family Robinson*-style escapade gone terrifyingly wrong, and becomes the story of a boy's belief in his father's wisdom curdling into cynicism. But Paul Schrader's script stacks the deck by making Allie's wife and kids sullen and wary, and Allie a charmless tyrant from the beginning, and Peter Weir's usual talent for depicting cultural dislocation deserts him in the jungle scenes. The film has some notable assets, chiefly Harrison Ford's masterful, on-target performance, his best work yet, as the brutally domineering Allie, but the narrative is too lopsided and the characters (except for Allie) too underdeveloped to compel attention.

THE MOST DANGEROUS GAME ☆☆☆
1932, USA
Joel McCrea, Fay Wray, Leslie Banks, Robert Armstrong, Steve Clemento, Noble Johnson. Directed by Ernest B. Schoedsack and Irving Pichel. 61 min.

The men who brought you *King Kong* first presented its female star here, in one of the oldest and most imitated pulp horror films, about a deranged Russian count who lives on a lonely island, and entertains himself by hunting whatever human prey happens to be stranded there. Joel McCrea and Fay Wray play the unfortunate innocents who find themselves ensnared; the fun begins when the diabolical Zaroff agrees to let them go—that is, if they can survive the night. You've seen variations in everything from the credited remake, *A Game of Death*, to *Cat's Eye*, but the original still makes for fast-paced, hokey fun. Based on the famous short story of Richard Connell.

MOTEL HELL ☆☆
1980, USA, R
Rory Calhoun, Paul Linke, Nancy Parsons, Nina Axelrod, Wolfman Jack, Elaine Joyce. Directed by Kevin Connor. 102 min.

Moderately amusing black comedy with lots of uninventive stretches. Rory Calhoun and his tubby sister are spicing up their smoked sausages with a secret ingredient that Sweeney Todd and the entire Texas Chainsaw Massacre clan would have endorsed heartily. Rory sinks his teeth into this character role, but the combination of all that hamminess with all that sausage still doesn't add up to a very meaty horror parody.

MOTHER AND DAUGHTER— ☆☆½
THE LOVING WAR
1980, USA (TV)
Tuesday Weld, Frances Sternhagen, Kathleen Beller, Jeanne Lang, Edward Winter, Directed by Burt Brinckerhoff. 98 min.

This tasteful, efficient melodrama concerns three generations of mothers and daughters who seem to take an inordinately long time to learn from their mistakes. This is really Tuesday Weld's show, and the resourceful actress bites off a little more than she can chew with her portrayal of a woman from her teenaged pregnancy to the birth of her grandchild. The drama is too intimate and small-scale to sustain the abrupt shifts in time, but the stars make it interesting viewing.

MOTHER LODE ☆½
1982, USA, PG
Charlton Heston, John Marley, Nick Mancuso, Kim Basinger. Directed by Charlton Heston. 101 min.

This contemporary search for gold pans out as nothing but fool's gold: it looks the same, but it just doesn't have any real value. Perhaps because of his directorial involvement, Charlton Heston really has his heart in this one, but the secondary players appear flaky, and the whole film has an inauthentic ring. With a more coherent team effort, they might have struck it rich, but nobody's going to fight the claim they've staked here.

MOTHER'S DAY ☆☆
1980, USA, X (self-imposed)
Tiana Pierce, Deborah Luce, Rose Ross, Holden McGuire, Billy Ray McQuade. Directed by Charles Kaufman. 98 min.

Three camping girlfriends are kidnapped by a pair of bestial brothers who indulge their fantasies of rape and murder in a cluttered shack in the woods under the watchful supervision of their cackling mother. The girls, terrorized, have no alternative but to fight back any way they can. This is a standard violent revenge horror film with an overlay of social commentary that never gets in the way of the sordid goings-on. Some striking imagery and an undercurrent of genuinely demented humor elevate *Mother's Day* above many other films of this kind, but it is not for the squeamish.

MOTHRA ☆☆
1962, Japan
Lee Kresel, Franky Sakai, Hiroshi Koizumi, Kyoko Kagawa. Directed by Inoshiro Honda. 100 min.

Mothra may be one of the best examples of the genre of Japanese giant monster movies. In the tradition of *Rodan*, this particular creature is an enormous flying moth that raises havoc throughout the world as it searches for a pair of foot-high women. The usual gamut of exploding miniature buildings and fleeing mobs follows. *Mothra* came out before movies of this type got really silly, and it's graced with better than usual special effects. It is appealing juvenilia from the same people who brought you a large fire-breathing lizard named Godzilla.

THE MOUNTAIN MEN
1980, USA, R
Charlton Heston, Brian Keith, Victoria Racimo, Stephen Macht, John Glover, Seymour Cassel. Directed by Richard Lang. 102 min.

☆

Charlton Heston rolls off another mountain but fails to provide any commandments. He's a bloodthirsty Jeremiah Johnson who's taken on the responsibility of protecting a runaway Indian squaw from the predictable attacks launched by her former Indian lover. Dressed as a bear, Heston and his irritating sidekick Brian Keith swear their way from one boring bloody encounter to the next, while a bombastic musical score attempts to keep you from falling asleep. It's quite a challenge. You may want to keep your eyes open for the scenery and Victoria Racimo's infrequent appearances.

MOUNTAINTOP MOTEL MASSACRE
1986, USA, R
Bill Thurman, Anna Chappell, Will Mitchel, Virginia Loridans. Directed by Jim McCullough. 96 min.

½☆

Another low point for the horror genre in which a psychotic senior citizen (who must have gone to a motel management school run by *Psycho's* Mrs. Bates) treats her guests to a most inhospitable stay as she sneaks up to their rooms and bumps them off! The motel doesn't even feature cable television or vibrating beds, both of which are more entertaining than this grisly, predictable film.

THE MOUSE THAT ROARED
1959, Great Britain
Peter Sellers, Jean Seberg, Leo McKern, David Kossoff, Monty Landis. Directed by Jack Arnold. 83 min.

☆☆☆½

The world's smallest nation, a Central European duchy called Grand Fenwick, declares war on the United States—it's planning to lose without bloodshed and then beef up its failing economy with American foreign aid. Unfortunately, through no fault of its own, Grand Fenwick wins. This breezy political farce remains delightful, as does Peter Sellers's triple performance: He made a much better Grand Duchess of Fenwick than did Margaret Rutherford in the sequel, *Mouse on the Moon*.

MOVERS AND SHAKERS
1985, USA, PG
Walter Matthau, Charles Grodin, Vincent Gardenia, Tyne Daly, Bill Macy, Gilda Radner, Steve Martin, Penny Marshall, Nita Talbot, Luana Anders. Directed by William Asher. 79 min.

☆☆

In this Hollywood satire cowritten and produced by star Charles Grodin and director William Asher (of the mid-'60s *Beach Party* films), Walter Matthau is a studio head determined to honor the memory of his mogul boss by making a meaningful movie out of the title of a sex manual, *Love in Sex*; Grodin plays the naive screenwriter called in to script the opus. The film's assault on the movie industry quickly deflates into a corny muddle, and it loses hold of its own meager story as it rambles on. The nub of the joke is that *Love in Sex* is never going to be more than a "concept"—and *Movers and Shakers*, hitched to the empty folly of a nonexistent movie, can't travel very far.

MOVIE HOUSE MASSACRE
1984, USA
Mary Woronov, Jonathan Blakely, Lynne Darcy, Cynthia Hartline, Lisa Lindsley, Pam McCormack, Dee-Dee Hoffman. Directed by Alice Raley. 75 min.

½☆

Ironically, considering the subject matter, this lame horror parody never played at a real movie house (it was first released on video), which is just as well; had it ever played in a theater, there might have been a real movie house massacre as the angry patrons streamed into the lobby demanding their money back. Three employees of a chain of movie theaters try to clean up a haunted movie house so that they can reopen it, but they (and the cheerleader friends of one of them) are swiftly dispatched by the spook. Mary Woronov, who must have the same agent as Klaus Kinski, is only featured in a small supporting part, and she's the only remotely professional player here. Incompetent from beginning to end—and not funny, either.

MOVIE MOVIE
1978, USA, PG
George C. Scott, Trish Van Devere, Eli Wallach, Red Buttons, Barbara Harris, Barry Bostwick, Harry Hamlin, Art Carney, Ann Reinking, Kathleen Beller, George Burns. Directed by Stanley Donen. 107 min.

☆☆☆½

Forget those "rent-two-for-the-price-of-one" video specials; this is what they used to call a swell night at the movies, 1930s style. In Stanley Donen's affectionate, delightfully funny pastiche of Hollywood's golden age, you get not one but two movies. *Dynamite Hands* is a punch-drunk boxing drama, a sort of tarnished *Golden Boy* with Harry Hamlin fisticuffing his way to glory in glorious black and white; that gives way to the bottom of the bill, *Baxter's Beauties of 1933*, a lavish Technicolor musical that sweetly skewers Busby Berkeley, the Big Broadcast, and the Broadway Melody films. Each parody goes on a bit too long, but lovers of old movies shouldn't pass up this cross-eyed glance backward.

MOVING VIOLATIONS
1985, USA, PG
John Murray, Jennifer Tilly, James Keach, Brian Backer, Sally Kellerman, Wendie Jo Sperber, Fred Willard. Directed by Neal Israel. 90 min.

☆

Nepotism writes the ticket here: Bill sibling John Murray, Meg sibling Jennifer Tilly, and Stacy sibling James Keach are featured in this twaddle-laden comedy about bad drivers in traffic school conspired against by a cop and a judge. The film's less amusing than being stuck in a traffic jam in July with a wired-up insurance salesman; its skeletal plot is hung with a number of unrelated skits whose bones can barely stand on their own (including Clara "Where's the beef?" Peller neighing her one line). And John Murray is the exact opposite of his brother, a thoroughly unendearing smart ass; you want to throttle him after about five minutes, a feeling that doesn't fade by film's end.

MR. AND MRS. SMITH
1941, USA
Carole Lombard, Robert Montgomery, Gene Raymond, Jack Carson, Lucile Watson, Philip Merivale, William Tracy. Directed by Alfred Hitchcock. 95 min.

☆☆☆

Constantly renewed interest in the Hitchcock canon ensures that there will always be fans puzzling over this screwball comedy. Some claim they see themes and obsessions from the master's suspense films, but, in actuality, the film owes more to the cinema of Mitchell Leisen and Gregory La Cava than to Hitchcock's other work, and only infrequently does Hitchcock make his sinister presence known. In Norman Krasna's sophisticated but not consistently funny screenplay, Carole Lombard and Robert Montgomery discover that their marriage license has been invalid all these years and that they are technically single. The premise keeps the first half of the film going, but the second half runs out of steam. However, it is always well acted by the leads—Lombard is at her sexiest here—and it's beautifully photographed by Harry Stradling.

MR. BLANDINGS BUILDS HIS DREAM HOUSE ★★★½
1948, USA
Cary Grant, Myrna Loy, Melvyn Douglas, Reginald Denny, Sharyn Moffett, Jason Robards, Lurene Tuttle: Directed by H. C. Potter. 93 min.

This spiffy comedy about the postwar American dream gone awry hasn't aged a bit; just multiply all of the figures by about 300% to account for inflation. Unable to take another day of having to share his morning shaving water with his wife and numerous other discomforts of apartment living, New Yorker Jim Blandings decides to buy a house in the suburbs. He makes the mistake of purchasing a run-down shack. No problem, he says, we'll tear it down and build our own from scratch. Then the problems *really* begin. Cary Grant and Myrna Loy, each just on the comfortable side of middle age, are perfect (and perfectly matched) as the married couple who discover that a God-given right to a house of one's own is no help in dealing with architects, contractors, and recalcitrant nature. Remade in 1986 as *The Money Pit.*

MR. BUG GOES TO TOWN

See *Hoppity Goes to Town*

MR. HULOT'S HOLIDAY ★★★★
1953, France
Jacques Tati, Nathalie Pascaud, Michelle Rolla, Valentine Camax. Directed by Jacques Tati. 86 min.

This is one of the cinema's comedy classics featuring Jacques Tati's remarkable creation, Mr. Hulot, the ultimate innocent abroad who calmly wanders through life, acting as an unwitting catalyst for the chaos that usually erupts around him. Hulot, in his first outing, owes a bit to Chaplin, a tad to Langdon, but he is a Gallic unique—Tati is the French answer to the great Neapolitan comic, Toto, and both of these men are the last true slapstick clowns.

MR. KLEIN ★★★
1977, France
Alain Delon, Jeanne Moreau, Michel Lonsdale, Juliet Berto. Directed by Joseph Losey. 122 min.

This moving, moody drama deals with guilt, complicity, and redemption during World War II. Alain Delon plays Klein, a Catholic art dealer who exploits Jews in need of cash by buying their paintings at artificially low prices. As it happens, the authorities mistake him for a Jewish namesake who they're seeking for arrest; the story becomes more complex as Klein finds himself insatiably curious about his counterpart. A valuable addition to the growing body of film work about the Holocaust, although its murkiness prevents it from achieving as much power as it might.

MR. LOVE ★★
1986, Great Britain, PG-13
Barry Jackson, Maurice Denham, Margaret Tyzack, Linda Marlowe, Christina Collier. Directed by Roy Battersby. 92 min.

This thoughtful but awfully morose comedy concerns a British village gardener and the throngs of grieving women who mourn at his funeral (we're not giving anything away; that's the first scene). Did his meek and mild exterior conceal the soul of a Lothario, or did he just make a lot of friends? This gentle character study works some ironic variations on the theme of François Truffaut's (and Blake Edwards's remake of) *The Man Who Loved Women*, but it's so self-effacing that it fades from memory even while you watch.

MR. LUCKY ★★★
1943, USA
Cary Grant, Laraine Day, Charles Bickford, Gladys Cooper, Alan Carney, Paul Stewart. Directed by H. C. Potter. 98 min.

In this breezy, forgettable romantic drama, Cary Grant plays a World War II racketeer who charms and hustles a Park Avenue socialite (Laraine Day), turning her war-effort charity into the "New York underworld relief fund." Her attempts to reform do make their mark and, combining love and patriotism, they take on the mob together. Although the story line may prove dated, the RKO set design has never looked more polished, and Grant is as classy as ever.

MR. MAJESTYK ★★
1974, USA, PG
Charles Bronson, Al Lettieri, Linda Cristal, Alejandro Rey, Lee Purcell. Directed by Richard Fleischer. 109 min.

Charles Bronson once again takes on the forces of Evildom single-handedly. Evildom loses. This time, he's a melon farmer in Colorado who insists on hiring lovable Mexican migrant workers instead of workers okayed by the mob. Aside from the unsubstantiated insistence that unions are run by the Mafia, there's little here that is either offensive or particularly exciting. (Vegetarians may, however, be horrified at one scene in which thousands of innocent melons are machine-gunned as an act of recrimination.) The film was directed in one of his more competent periods by veteran hack Richard Fleischer from a script by crime novelist Elmore Leonard.

MR. MOM ★★
1983, USA, PG
Michael Keaton, Teri Garr, Martin Mull, Ann Jillian, Jeffrey Tambor, Christopher Lloyd, Graham Jarvis. Directed by Stan Dragoti. 108 min.

This is a tacky, big-screen sitcom about an automotive engineer (Michael Keaton) who gets fired and becomes a house husband while his wife (Teri Garr) scales the ladder of success as an ad executive, making him feel like that much more of a schlub. The filmmakers have barely bothered to dust off the role-reversal clichés (the movie even features that time-honored bit in which a washing machine goes berserk). As usual, screenwriter John Hughes relies almost entirely on his grab bag of *National Lampoon* anti–middle-class smarminess for knee-jerk jokes. That this is at all amusing is due to the ability of the cast to make such tired material bearable, though it's a disappointment seeing Keaton given almost no chance to cut loose.

MR. MOTO'S LAST WARNING ★★½
1939, USA
Peter Lorre, Ricardo Cortez, Virginia Field, John Carradine, George Sanders. Directed by Norman Foster. 70 min.

In the Mr. Moto novels by John P. Marquand, the character of the polite Japanese spy is deucedly ambiguous—he's a lot more intelligent than the blustery Americans who condescend to involve him in their affairs, but (because of the incipient racism of the time) he's also untrustworthy, opportunistic, and loyal only to his country's right-wing plans. Fox was smart to cast Peter Lorre; his menacing, snide delivery gives the figure a real bite in these otherwise bland adventure films. This late entry in the series has Moto attempting to save the French fleet and is set against the backdrop of the Suez Canal. George Sanders is tasty as a snotty villain.

MR. PEABODY AND THE MERMAID ★½
1948, USA
William Powell, Ann Blyth, Irene Hervey, Andrea King, Clinton Sunberg. Directed by Irving Pichel. 89 min.

Before *Splash* came this feeble mermaid comedy-fantasy. A lot of talent but not much energy went into this story about an older married man (William Powell) who thinks he is having an innocent fling with a mermaid (Ann Blyth). Powell subtly personifies a man in a mid-life crisis, but Blyth's wide-eyed, near-mute performance as the amphibious girl grows excessively coy and lacks the knowing humor of Glynis Johns (who played a similar role in *Miranda* the year before). Slow, and not funny, but at least Russell Metty's soft-focus camerawork lends it an appropriately dreamlike quality.

MR. ROBINSON CRUSOE
1932, USA ★★★
Douglas Fairbanks, William Farnum, Maria Alba, Earle Brown. Directed by Edward Sutherland. 71 min.

This silly adventure parody is a good deal of fun, especially for fans of the senior Fairbanks's athletic style. In a sort of hybrid of de Maupassant's "The Bet" and Defoe's *Robinson Crusoe*, he plays a well-to-do sort who bets that he can live alone on a tropical island for a year, making do with only his hands and wits. Less than halfway through, he's already built himself what could pass in New York these days for prime condo space! An unconvincingly made-up but still lovely "Girl Friday" (Maria Alba) and a good score by Alfred Newman add their own sparks. It's amazing how fit and trim Fairbanks looks in this, his next-to-last film, made four years before his untimely death n 1936 at 49.

MRS. BROWN, YOU'VE GOT A LOVELY DAUGHTER
1968, Great Britain, G ★★
Peter Noone, Keith Hopwood, Derek Leckenby, Karl Green, Stanley Holloway, Lance Percival, Sheila White, Sarah Caldwell. Directed by Saul Swimmer. 95 min.

Mrs. Brown is a dog, the pet greyhound of a rowdy and rambling group of English rock and rollers who are better known as Herman's Hermits. This madcap flick erratically follows the exploits of the band, their dog, and the real Brown family, complete with lovely daughter Judy. The film breezes along like a pop song, with a brief refrain of light regrets and a coda of love as Herman loses a girl. It would take help to turn this tapping tale into *A Hard Day's Night*, but with a host of happy tunes it's good for a quick spin on the old VCR.

MR. SMITH GOES TO WASHINGTON
1939, USA ★★★★
James Stewart, Jean Arthur, Claude Rains, Edward Arnold, Guy Kibbee. Directed by Frank Capra. 129 min.

This superb, engrossing Frank Capra classic succeeds as human drama, political satire, and screwball comedy. James Stewart plays a naive young boy scout leader who becomes a senator, only to find his idealistic illusions shattered by the corrupt realities of Washington. The Senator courageously fights the system, as Stewart contributes one of the most memorable performances of his career. Jean Arthur is also effective as his jaded political secretary who gradually comes to believe in Stewart and the ideals he represents. The masterful screenplay by Sidney Buchman won an Academy Award.

MRS. R.'S DAUGHTER
1979, USA (TV) ★½
Cloris Leachman, Season Hubley, Donald Moffat, Ron Rifkin, Stephen Elliott. Directed by Dan Curtis. 100 min.

A worthless film that seems more concerned with providing an acting showcase for Cloris Leachman than it does with handling the touchy subject matter with any delicacy. When her daughter is raped, Mrs. R. rails out against the injustice of the criminal justice system as a tired rehash of the "where are the victim's rights" syndrome is trotted out. The overall impact is as impersonal as Mrs. R.'s name in the film's title.

MRS. SOFFEL
1984, USA, PG ★★★½
Diane Keaton, Mel Gibson, Matthew Modine, Edward Herrmann, Trini Alverado: Directed by Gillian Armstrong. 110 min.

A beautifully acted romantic drama filled with emotional explosions and a sensual fervor. Working from a true story, director Gillian Armstrong (*My Brilliant Career*) ushers us into the ice-cold clamminess of 1901 industrial Pittsburgh, where Kate Soffel (Diane Keaton), the repressed Victorian wife of a prison warden, becomes infatuated with convicted murderer Ed Biddle (Mel Gibson) and ends up helping him and his brother (Matthew Modine) to escape. As Biddle woos Mrs. Soffel with sentimental doggerel and an animal magnetism that just won't quit, she becomes a rejuvenated woman. Armstrong is a tough-minded director who doesn't hide the heartache beneath the pair's ebullience.

MR. WONG, DETECTIVE
1938, USA ★½
Boris Karloff, Grant Withers, Maxine Jennings, Evelyn Brent, Lucien Prival. Directed by William Nigh. 69 min.

The first of five Mr. Wong mysteries, a series instigated by Monogram Studios to try to duplicate the success of those other Oriental sleuths Mr. Moto and Charlie Chan. Unfortunately, Englishman Boris Karloff was much less believable as a Chinese detective than the German Peter Lorre was as a Japanese Mr. Moto. Here, he tracks down a gang of spies who are killing people with glass bombs containing poison gas.

MS. 45
1980, USA, R ★★★½
Zoe Tamerlis, Steve Singer, Jack Thibeau. Directed by Abel Ferrara. 84 min.

This underground sleeper has a beautiful, mute young woman getting raped twice in the same day. After killing her second attacker, she uses his gun to murder all of the men she encounters on her nightly vigilante rounds. This is a far superior film to *Death Wish*, with Zoe Tamerlis (who bears a striking resemblance to Nastassja Kinski) giving a beguiling performance as the unbalanced protagonist who is anything but a heroine. It's a sleek and violent picture, shot in seedy New York City locations. Listen for the marvelous jazz score by Joseph Delia.

THE MUMMY
1932, USA ★★★
Boris Karloff, Zita Johann, David Manners, Edward van Sloan, Bramwell Fletcher, Noble Johnson. Directed by Karl Freund. 72 min.

Less a "horror" film than an eerie mood piece, this is slow going at times but definitely worth the attention. Boris Karloff appears in full wrappings in only one scene, at the beginning, but it's a memorable one: Alone with an archaeologist in his desecrated tomb, he slowly comes back to life after a 3,700-year nap and frightens the young man literally out of his wits. He plays the remainder of the film in more realistic, but still unusual, makeup, trying to persuade young Zita Johann that she is the reincarnation of his beloved. Director Karl Freund, whose first feature this was (he also directed *Mad Love* and several features before winding up his career as a cameraman on the "I Love Lucy" show) was a cinematographer in Germany during the height of expressionism, and also worked on *Metropolis* and *The Last Laugh*.

THE MUNSTERS' REVENGE
1981, USA (TV) ★½
Fred Gwynne, Al Lewis, Yvonne De Carlo, Jo McDonnell, K. C. Martel, Sid Caesar, Howard Morris. Directed by Don Weis. 100 min.

Once upon a time in TV Land there was a fairly funny monster spoof called "The Addams Family," in which Carolyn Jones and John Astin captured the sophisticated flair of the ghoulish Charles Addams cartoons. Copycatting their success but missing the point, another network created "The Munsters," a much broader, sillier sitcom that nonetheless has its partisans. This TV movie is one of those reunion pics, reuniting the stars fifteen years after the show went off the air, and compounding the mistake by wasting Sid Caesar and Howard Morris in supporting roles. For those who missed the Munster clan, this lame movie has them coping with a crazed scientist who's come up with robot lookalikes of Herman, Lily, and Grandpa. No amount of monster makeup can hide the actors' aging, and fans may look in vain for series regulars Butch

Patrick and Pat Priest, neither of whom attended this family get-together.

THE MUPPET MOVIE ☆☆☆½
1979, USA, G
Jim Henson's Muppets, Frank Oz, Jerry Nelson, Richard Hunt, Dave Goelz, Charles Durning, Austin Pendleton, Scott Walker. Directed by James Frawley. 98 min.

In their much-heralded move from the tube to the big screen, the Muppets pack along their special brand of charm and wit for an entertaining, music-filled journey to Hollywood and stardom. It's Kermit's big dream to get that major studio contract, instead of performing in a Doc Hopper television commercial for fried frogs legs, or, worse yet, ending up in the frying pan himself. When Orson Welles (one of the film's fifteen cameos) finally signs the "standard furry animal" contract, it's a bittersweet cinematic reference in this generally self-aware film: Kermit gets the contract from the man who could never secure one himself. The casual references to other films—from *High Noon* to *Attack of the Fifty-Foot Woman*—and the movie's own sincere self-mockery—"I just turned to page eighty-seven of the script and"—keep the mood light and entertaining. The unobtrusive special effects, which allow full body movement, visually reflect this big-screen freedom. Steve Martin as an arrogant waiter, Dom De Luise as a drifting Hollywood agent, and Mel Brooks as the mad scientist determined to give the frog an "electronic cerebrectomy" spice up the film's wacky humor. Although the middle bogs down somewhat (too many cameos), the Muppets' bubbling enthusiasm is highly contagious.

THE MUPPETS TAKE MANHATTAN ☆☆☆½
1984, USA, G
Jim Henson's Muppets, Louis Zorich, Juliana Donald, Lonny Price, Art Carney, James Coco, Dabney Coleman, Gregory Hines, Linda Lavin, Elliott Gould, Liza Minnelli, Brooke Shields, John Landis, Edward I. Koch. Directed by Frank Oz. 93 min.

Easily the zippiest and most inventive of the three Muppet movies. Our cloth companions are still stuck in the middle of a tiresome story (in this one, they're would-be stars trying to make it on Broadway—generic enough for you?), but Muppeteers Jim Henson and Frank Oz have loosened up a bit, throwing in some lavish cinematic set pieces, a terrific new-style Muppet character named Rizzo the Rat, and a wedding for Kermit and Miss Piggy that's both rowdier and more romantic than anyone might have expected. As usual, there are lots of guest stars to keep adults amused after the novelty of the Muppets wears off, but they're not really necessary: Kermit and Co. hold their own quite well, thank you.

MURDER ☆☆☆½
1930, Great Britain
Herbert Marshall, Nora Baring, Phyllis Konstam, Edward Chapman, Esme Percy. Directed by Alfred Hitchcock. 108 min.

A juror goes outside the system in an effort to prove an actress is innocent of a murder she has been convicted of committing. In this finely crafted early Hitchcock talkie, the director uses a theatrical backdrop to delve into the problems of artifice and reality. Hitchcock's treatment of this satirical whodunit yarn incorporates hints of surrealism and German expressionism. The performances are all quite good in this elegant and entertaining work.

MURDER BY DEATH ☆
1976, USA, PG
Alec Guinness, Peter Falk, Peter Sellers, Maggie Smith, David Niven, Eileen Brennan, Truman Capote. Directed by Robert Moore. 95 min.

Neil Simon had a good idea in combining all of the top fictional detectives at a party and having them solve a murder. Alas, if only he had evinced a shred of knowledge about any one of them in this too-cute-for-words misfire. David Niven and Maggie Smith fare best: Their Nick and Nora Charles caricatures are based on the best-known movie detective team, and Simon copies their delivery slavishly. Eileen Brennan is also quite fresh in her rendition of Sam Spade's Gal Friday. The rest of the cast sinks like stones.

MURDER BY DECREE ☆☆☆
1979, Canada/Great Britain, PG
James Mason, Christopher Plummer, Donald Sutherland, Geneviève Bujold, Susan Clark, David Hemmings, Frank Finlay, John Gielgud, Anthony Quayle. Directed by Bob Clark. 121 min.

Sherlock Holmes continues to provide fodder for filmmakers who aren't the least bit interested in the Conan Doyle stories; this film fashions an adventure for the master sleuth out of whole cloth and gives him an appropriately large-scale nemesis: Jack the Ripper. The story's brutality is too explicit and contemporary to make this fully credible as a Holmes adventure, but an all-star cast makes it very diverting, with top honors going to Christopher Plummer and James Mason's rich, full-bodied portrayals of Sherlock Holmes and Dr. Watson.

MURDER BY PHONE ☆☆
1980, Canada, R
Richard Chamberlain, John Houseman, Sara Botsford, Robin Gammell, Gary Reineke, Barry Morse. Directed by Michael Anderson. 79 min.

The killer does it by telephone in this Canadian shocker, but Ma Bell doesn't want word to get out. Richard Chamberlain stars as a former student activist, now environmentalist, whose experience with establishment cover-ups leads him to play detective when he gets a line on the murders.

MURDERER'S ROW ☆☆
1967, USA
Dean Martin, Ann-Margret, Karl Malden, Camilla Sparv, James Gregory, Beverly Adams. Directed by Henry Levin. 108 min.

Ann-Margret bugaloos, frugs, stomps, and even jitterbugs in her best disco dance performance prior to *C.C. and Company*. Unfortunately, Dean Martin is supposed to be the star, and he keeps stealing time for a dumb yarn about Karl Malden attempting to melt down Washington. But Ann-Margret steals back every scene she's in—with her kittenish cooing and her tongue-on-lips sensuality, she makes Dino look like a dirty old man flushed out of a boarding school locker room. This is not the best of the Matt Helm superspy series.

MURDER IN TEXAS ☆☆
1981, USA (TV)
Katherine Ross, Sam Elliot, Farrah Fawcett, Andy Griffith, Craig T. Nelson, G. W. Bailey. Directed by Billy Hale. 100 min.

Yet another television murder movie that's "based on a true story." A plastic surgeon kills his wife so he can hook up with another woman. Or did he? A father's desperate search for justice. A video company's desperate attempt to trim down an overblown 200-minute courtroom drama. An audience's desperately fruitless search for entertainment.

MURDER MOTEL ☆½
1974, Great Britain
Robyn Millan, Derek Francis, Ralph Bates, Edward Judd, Allan McClelland. Directed by Malcolm Taylor. 80 min.

Some places you check into, but don't check out. Other places you just drive on by. Well, don't bother to check this one out. It's a standard murder-for-hire film, with unconvincing acting and an inane story line. Despite the appearance of actor Ralph Bates, this murderous roadside reststop will never live up to the reputation of the Bates Motel.

MURDER, MY SWEET ☆☆☆☆
1944, USA
Dick Powell, Claire Trevor, Mike Mazurki. Directed by Edward Dmytryk. 95 min.

Raymond Chandler felt that Dick Powell was the best of the screen's Philip Marlowes, and from this film, it's easy to understand why. Powell is a perfect hard-case detective using every method to gain results, and he goes over his lines like a mean fat kid chewing on a stolen Maryjane. Edward Dmytryk is a consistently underrated director, and he turns in a marvelously dark, convoluted tale of a private eye's two cases converging on him like a vise. This is a must-see *noir* classic. The novel on which the film is based, *Farewell, My Lovely*, was turned into an eponymously titled 1977 movie starring the legendary Robert Mitchum.

MURDER ON FLIGHT 502 ☆☆
1975, USA
Hugh O'Brian, Robert Stack, Polly Bergen, Fernando Lamas, Walter Pidgeon. Directed by George McCowan. 98 min.

A plane on a transoceanic flight becomes the setting for a high-flying mystery, as a letter reveals that a murderer is on the passenger list. Big surprise, huh? This is the standard tailspinning with more TV-movie sputtering than any real driving suspense. Will the stewardess get bumped off? Will it turn out it's only a plot to stop the in-flight movie? No, it's just another mediocre movie about a crazed assassin.

MURDER ON THE ORIENT EXPRESS ☆☆☆½
1974, Great Britain, PG
Albert Finney, Lauren Bacall, Martin Balsam, Ingrid Bergman, Jacqueline Bisset, Jean-Pierre Cassel, Sean Connery, John Gielgud, Wendy Hiller, Anthony Perkins, Vanessa Redgrave, Rachel Roberts, Richard Widmark, Michael York, Denis Quilley. Directed by Sidney Lumet. 127 min.

A grandly old-fashioned mystery is brought to life by Sidney Lumet's lavish direction, Paul Dehn's tight script, and an all-star cast that, for once, really is made up entirely of stars. Agatha Christie's Hercule Poirot novel, written in 1934, was one of her best—she put her Belgian detective on a luxury train, trying to solve a murder with too many suspects. On screen, her occasionally mechanical plotting works like a dream, every cog and wheel in perfect order. It's unquestionably the best screen adaptation of her work, and the almost unrecognizable Albert Finney makes a dazzlingly funny and on-target Poirot. *Murder* may seem tedious to viewers unused to Christie's leisurely way with a mystery, but those who know her work will be enraptured with the film's high style. Ingrid Bergman won an Academy Award for Best Supporting Actress.

MURDERS IN THE RUE MORGUE ☆☆☆
1971, USA, PG
Jason Robards, Herbert Lom, Chrstine Kaufmann, Adolfo Celi, Lilli Palmer, Maria Perschy, Michael Dunn. Directed by Gordon Hessler. 87 min.

Not to be confused with the 1933 Lugosi-Fox menagerie, this third adaptation of Poe's classic detective story is by far the most lively of the *Morgues*. The victims, grizzled with bizarre claw marks, all turn out to be business bedfellows of sinister theater manager Jason Robards; his wife (Christine Kaufmann) often wakes up screaming. Many scenes are shot as ghostly hallucinations, and the climax strikes a chord reminiscent of *Phantom of the Opera*. Lavishly costumed and filmed as if through a haunted camera, the movie's tight plot piles on momentum until a jarringly pedestrian ending.

MURPH THE SURF ☆☆
1975, USA, PG
Robert Conrad, Don Stroud, Donna Mills, Robyn Mills, Luther Adler, Paul Stewart, Burt Young. Directed by Marvin Chomsky. 105 min.

Real-life crooks Jack Murphy and Allan Kuhn were unsavory beach bums who gleaned a lot of publicity from a string of burglaries in the Miami area. In this fictionalized treatment, they smoothly pull off the heist of the Star of India diamond. With an extensive background in cheap movies, Don Stroud brings a nice sleaze to the role of the nasty titular creature, and Robert Conrad is okay as the more sympathetic partner. The direction by Marvin Chomsky is sure-handed if pedestrian, and the big speedboat chase scene along Miami's inland waterway is surprisingly good. (a.k.a.: *Live a Little, Steal a Lot*).

MURPHY'S LAW ☆
1986, USA, R
Charles Bronson, Kathleen Wilhoite, Carrie Snodgress, Robert F. Lyons, Richard Romanus, Angel Tompkins. Directed by J. Lee Thompson. 97 min.

Someone must have thought that having Charles Bronson on the run from a homicidal woman *and* the police was enough of an idea for a movie—obviously they didn't bother to work in any dialogue, plot, or characterizations. The movie is nothing more than a series of brief, violent confrontations directed in a dull, ham-handed fashion. Kathleen Wilhoite tries her best to put some energy into her role as a punk who somehow got handcuffed to Chuck; she fails.

MURPHY'S ROMANCE ☆☆½
1985, USA, PG
Sally Field, James Garner, Brian Kerwin, Corey Haim, Dennis Burkley. Directed by Martin Ritt. 100 min.

Concept: Sally Field and James Garner in a small midwestern town. No doubt, the studio thought that would make a commercial film. However, they did need something for Sally and Jim to do. So they gave the Concept a title, *Murphy's Romance*, to let the consumer know that Jim will fall in love with Sally. Unfortunately, they forgot to have any of this take place in the movie. So what we have instead is lots of Sally being a spunky, independent, cute-as-a-button woman, occasionally Garner being his laconic self, and a plotless subplot with Sally's ex-husband hanging around trying to weasel his way back into her Levi's. It's a cute, pointless, and forgettable film.

MURPHY'S WAR ☆☆½
1971, Great Britain
Peter O'Toole, Sian Phillips, Philippe Noiret, Horst Janson, John Hallam. Directed by Peter Yates. 108 min.

Peter O'Toole's dramatically intense performance as a fighting Irishman who is the sole survivor of a German U-boat attack is the main reason to see this complicated, adult action film, from the director (Peter Yates) of *Bullitt* and the writer (Stirling Silliphant) of *In The Heat of the Night*. Murphy's superhuman struggle to win a personal war against the killers of his men is generally compelling, and action fans should be satisfied.

THE MUSIC MAN ☆☆☆½
1962, USA
Robert Preston, Shirley Jones, Buddy Hackett, Hermione Gingold, Paul Ford, Pert Kelton, Ron Howard. Directed by Morton Da Costa. 151 min.

This is an exuberant, thoroughly entertaining screen adaptation of Meredith Willson's smash Broadway musical about a smooth-talking con artist who sells a small town the idea of a marching band, installs himself as leader—and then has to make good on his promise. Unlike so many screen musicals that fall apart because of poor casting, this one has the star who originated the title role, and Robert Preston's oversized brass and bluff works perfectly with Shirley Jones's demure charm as Marian the librarian. Though a little long, it should please kids and adults with its celebratory spirit and now-classic score (including "76 Trombones," "Trouble," and "Till There Was You").

MUTANT ☆☆
1983, USA, R
Wings Hauser, Bo Hopkins, Jennifer Warren, Jody Medford. Directed by John "Bud" Cardos. 98 min.

In this zombie horror film, improperly stored toxic wastes turn a townful of solid citizens into vicious yellow-blooded zombies with a lust to kill; vacationing brothers find themselves in the middle of a fine mess. *Mutant* is enlivened by an electric performance by Wings Hauser, who is also displayed advantageously in *Vice Squad*. It might make a nice double bill with Graham Baker's *Impulse*, which has a similar theme.

THE MUTATIONS
See *The Freak Maker*

THE MUTILATOR ☆
1984, USA, R or unrated
Jack Chatham, Ben Moore, Frances Raines, Bill Hitchcock. Directed by Buddy Cooper. 86 min. (both versions)

A college student and his friends take a trip to the beach, where they plan to close up his demented father's condo for the season. They are systematically slaughtered and hung on hooks in a closet in the garage; who could the killer be? This is a formula body-count film with an ending so obvious that there must be a twist. But there isn't. It's available in both R-rated and unedited versions on videocassette.

MUTINY ON THE BOUNTY ☆☆☆☆
1935, USA
Clark Gable, Charles Laughton, Franchot Tone. Directed by Frank Lloyd. 135 min.

Based on historical fact and Nordhoff and Hall's best-selling novel, this Academy Award winner is one of the great adventure films of all time—better than the 1962 remake and 1984's *The Bounty*. Though the cinematography is superb, even by today's standards, the movie hinges more on the complex character of a formidable Captain Bligh, which Charles Laughton handles here with uncanny skill and realism. Clark Gable leads the crew of mutineers and the cast of supporting actors in one of his most penetrating performances.

MUTINY ON THE BOUNTY ☆☆½
1962, USA
Marlon Brando, Trevor Howard, Richard Harris, Hugh Griffith, Richard Haydn, Tim Seely, Gordon Jackson. Directed by Lewis Milestone. 179 min.

This is the longest and in many ways the strangest of the three big-screen versions of the battle between Captain Bligh and Fletcher Christian, based, like the first film, on the Nordhoff-Hall adventure tale (the third, *The Bounty*, used other sources). Veteran director Lewis Milestone was well-equipped to helm this lavish, large-scale production, and the story of men on an eighteenth-century ocean voyage slowly turning against their tyrannical martinet of a leader is a great one. Where this version goes wrong is in the acting: Trevor Howard makes a fine Bligh, but Marlon Brando's Fletcher Christian is a disaster that sabotages the film; as many have said, it takes a great actor to give a performance this bad. Much of the Panavision 70 splendor will be lost on video.

MY AMERICAN COUSIN ☆☆☆
1985, Canada, PG
Margaret Langrick, John Wildman, Richard Donat, Jane Mortifee, T. J. Scott, Camille Henderson. Directed by Sandy Wilson. 95 min.

This amiable, nostalgic coming-of-age romance swept the Genie Awards (the Canadian equivalent of the Oscars), and it's easy to see why—its title notwithstanding, *My American Cousin* is one of the few Canadian films to provide any sense of a national identity. The plot is set in 1959 (which seems on the verge of becoming an emblematic end-of-youth year), and involves the flirtation between twelve-year-old Sandy and her brash older cousin, who arrives from L.A. with a ducktail haircut, a sleek Cadillac, and a lesson for Sandy in the shortfalls of valuing surface over substance. Margaret Langrick and John Wildman are engaging screen newcomers, and Sandy Wilson's screenplay offers some deft touches within a very quickly recognizable formula.

MY BEAUTIFUL LAUNDRETTE ☆☆☆½
1985, Great Britain, R
Daniel Day Lewis, Gordon Warnecke, Saeed Jaffrey, Roshan Seth, Shirley Ann Field, Rita Wolf, Derrick Branche. Directed by Stephen Frears. 93 min.

A sociopolitical-ethno-sexual comedy set in modern London, where native British poor boys and canny, ambitious Pakistani immigrants jostle for a piece of the economic pie, *My Beautiful Laundrette* is a cluttered, funny, startlingly well-observed delight. The multi-stranded plot follows young Omar (Gordon Warnecke) in his attempts to make a run-down laundromat given to him by his uncle both prosperous and chic. Enlisting the aid of his friend and lover Johnny (Daniel Day Lewis), he makes the enterprise a success but learns some unexpected lessons about cultural identity in a changing world. *Laundrette* was directed by an Englishman and written by a Pakistani, Hanif Kureishi, which may help to explain its remarkably balanced, clear-eyed perspective—this is a film that knows all races, classes, ages, and sexual orientations well enough to laugh about them. Every scene is pointed, bright, and insightful enough to sit through twice.

MY BEST FRIEND'S GIRL ☆☆½
1983, France
Isabelle Huppert, Coluche, Thierry Lhermitte, Farid Chopel. Directed by Bertrand Blier. 99 min.

Director Bertrand Blier (*Get Out Your Handkercheifs*) trots out his familiar triad of two inseparable buddies who end up sharing the same woman. Pascal is a handsome ski bum who picks up a sexy dish named Viviane only to watch her seduce his schlubby best friend. The playful insolence of the setup is unmistakably Blier, but what's missing are the sweetness and animal desperation that made the director's previous heroes so memorable. Isabelle Huppert scampers through the film in a variety of Frederick's of Hollywood numbers, and still manages to give a sly, modulated performance.

MY BLOODY VALENTINE ☆½
1981, Canada, R
Paul Kelman, Lori Hallier, Neil Affleck, Keith Knight, Alf Humphreys. Directed by George Mihalka. 91 min.

Despite its lurid title and a promising pickax murder to get things rolling, this horror film is just a mediocre variation on the old killer-at-the-big-dance theme. This time, the party takes place in an abandoned coal mine, allowing for a number of gloomy shafts and tunnels as locales for stalking the victims. The dull, overage cast cries out to be led by Jamie Lee Curtis, but she was busy with her own *Prom Night*. Or was it *Terror Train*?

MY BODYGUARD ☆☆☆
1980, USA, PG
Chris Makepeace, Adam Baldwin, Matt Dillon, Ruth Gordon, Martin Mull, Paul Quandt, Joan Cusack, John Houseman. Directed by Tony Bill. 97 min.

Tony Bill used a cast of talented, then-unknown kids and nice Chicago locations to film this bright, uplifting tale of an underdog's victory in the *Karate Kid*/*Breaking Away* mold. Chris Makepeace plays a smart, slight kid who finds himself the target of a vicious bully (Matt Dillon) in his new school. He enlists the protection of the misunderstood class monster (Adam Baldwin), a strong, silent type with a tragic past, but he eventually learns that he'll have to fight his own battles. The pacifist message gets awfully muddled by the end, and adults Ruth Gordon and Martin Mull are unnecessary distractions, but if you were ever the class shrimp, you'll root hard during the climactic showdown. Look for Jennifer Beals (*Flashdance*) in a tiny debut role.

MY BRILLIANT CAREER ☆☆☆½
1979, Australia, G
Judy Davis, Sam Neill, Wendy Hughes, Robert Grubb, Max Cullen. Directed by Gillian Armstrong. 101 min.

This film is a consistently engaging mixture of romantic comedy and feminist uplift. The central romance, between an enraptured and frustrated country girl (the radiant Judy Davis) and a laconic gentleman farmer (Sam Neill) who seems ideal for her, is undercut by the heroine's simmering desire to write. The career vs. marriage conflict seems trumped up here because the alternatives to marriage in rural Australia at the turn of this century were very bleak. But this is still a brisk, enjoyable movie, with some wonderful supporting performances.

MY CHAUFFEUR ☆½
1986, USA, R
Deborah Foreman, Sam Jones, Sean McClory, E. G. Marshall, Howard Hesseman, Penn & Teller. Directed by David Beaird. 96 min.

David Beaird's very routine lowbrow comedy was, oddly, well received by critics, some of whom went so far as to call it feminist. To its credit, it does flash peddle men as well as women—an Equal Opportunity Exploiter. Deborah Foreman plays a spunky driver who shakes things up at a misogynistic limo firm, and Sam Jones is the wealthy stuffed shirt who finds her attractive—and also strangely familiar. (Exactly why the latter is true is resolved in a rather grotesque subplot.) Jones (of *Flash Gordon*) has a couple of nice scenes, but Foreman has been bizarrely misdirected to emote like the mutant offspring of Cyndi Lauper and Gidget.

MY DARLING CLEMENTINE ☆☆☆½
1946, USA
Henry Fonda, Linda Darnell, Victor Mature, Walter Brennan, Cathy Downs, Tim Holt, Ward Bond, Alan Mowbray, John Ireland, Jane Darwell. Directed by John Ford. 97 min.

Perhaps not a classic on the level of John Ford's own *She Wore a Yellow Ribbon* or *The Searchers*, *My Darling Clementine* nonetheless makes the work of most other Western directors look like hackery; Ford was almost alone in his ability to make the myths of the Old West take on the stature of both legend and high drama. This is the Gunfight at the O.K. Corral Story, with Henry Fonda as Wyatt Earp and Victor Mature as Doc Holliday. Although Mature isn't everything one might want in the role, the other performances and Ford's mastery more than compensate. The story was later filmed by John Sturges as *Gunfight at the O.K. Corral*, with Burt Lancaster and Kirk Douglas.

MY DEAR SECRETARY ☆☆☆
1948, USA
Kirk Douglas, Laraine Day, Keenan Wynn, Helen Walker, Rudy Vallee, Florence Bates, Irene Ryan. Directed by Charles Martin. 94 min.

The working woman who really wants to settle down with a husband was a frequent subject for movies during Hollywood's heyday and was more than fair game for humorous treatment. Laraine Day proves herself a capable if workmanlike comedienne, playing a prim secretary who marries her wayward novelist boss. Kirk Douglas is a little out of his element as a writer—he seems always on the verge of pulling a gun; and while playing comedy it seems like he's waiting for his next *film noir* assignment. However, this bright face carries everything along in its endless stream of crazy plot twists, and the attentive support by Keenan Wynn and Rudy Vallee constantly reassures the viewer that they are in excellent hands. By the time the movie ends, you may not recall who wrote what book or who thought whose wife was fooling around with whom, but trust us, you won't care.

MY DINNER WITH ANDRE ☆☆☆½
1981, USA
Wallace Shawn, Andre Gregory. Directed by Louis Malle. 10 min.

Louis Malle's fascinating and thoroughly successful cinematic experiment features an enrapturing two-hour dinner conversation between two divergent personalities, Andre Gregory, the theater director, and Wallace Shawn, the actor and playwright. The two basically play themselves, and the film's final "screenplay" was culled from dozens of hours of dialogue that they wrote and improvised. Louis Malle works subtly and persuasively within the narrow bounds he sets for himself. The camerawork is lively and imaginative but never obtrusive or self-conscious. The resulting achievement is vivid, provocative, funny, and spellbinding—a dazzling spiritual odyssey that never leaves the dinner table.

MY FAIR LADY ☆☆☆☆
1964, USA
Rex Harrison, Audrey Hepburn, Stanley Holloway, Wildred Hyde-White, Gladys Cooper, Jeremy Brett, Theodore Bikel. Directed by George Cukor. 170 min.

Lerner and Loewe's delightful musical, based on George Bernard Shaw's *Pygmalion*, is gloriously transferred to the screen by director George Cukor and his splendid leads. Earnest acting lends the film more substance than most musicals have. The role of Professor Henry Higgins, who energetically endeavors to transform crude cockney girl Eliza Doolittle (Audrey Hepburn) into a lady, was a tailor-made for Rex Harrison on both stage and screen. Songs in this octuple Oscar winner include "I Could Have Danced All Night," "Get Me to the Church on Time," and "The Rain in Spain"; however, it's Marni Nixon's voice coming out of Audrey Hepburn's mouth.

MY FAVORITE BRUNETTE ☆☆☆
1947, USA
Bob Hope, Dorothy Lamour, Peter Lorre, Lon Chaney, Jr., John Hoyt. Directed by Elliott Nugent. 87 min.

This is a breezy wisecracking comedy in which Bob Hope plays a long-suffering photographer who can't resist coming to Dorothy Lamour's rescue, even though he ends up on the mob's most-wanted list. Hope and Lamour bounce beautifully off each other and the gags fly fast and furious from the sidesplitting supporting cast, especially Peter Lorre as a bad guy who keeps throwing tantrums and knives at Hope.

MY FAVORITE WIFE ☆☆½
1940, USA
Cary Grant, Irene Dunne, Randolph Scott, Gail Patrick, Ann Shoemaker, Scotty Beckett, Donald MacBride. Directed by Garson Kanin. 88 min.

Considering its reputation and all the talent involved, this film should be much better. This is one of many comic variations on Alfred Lord Tennyson's *Enoch Arden* (others include *Too Many Husbands* and *Our Wife*), the one about a wife who is surprised by the reappearance of her first husband after marrying another. Sam and Bella Spewack's script, from a story by the Spewacks and Leo McCarey, adds an extra twist by changing the genders of the above characters. Unfortunately, there is very little to laugh about once the premise is established. The film even tries to remake highlights from McCarey's superior *The Awful Truth* (1937), also starring Cary Grant and Irene Dunne, and Dunne pushes too hard as Ellen Arden, the "favorite wife." At least RKO didn't spare anything on the look of the film (Van Nest Polglase's art direction as photographed by Rudolph Mate).

MY FAVORITE YEAR ☆☆☆☆
1982, USA, PG
Peter O'Toole, Mark Linn-Baker, Jessica Harper, Joseph Bologna, Bill Macy, Lainie Kazan, Lou Jacobi, Selma Diamond, Cameron Mitchell. Directed by Richard Benjamin. 92 min.

This is a fizzy, irresistible farce set in the mad backstage world of 1950s television comedy. The year is 1954, and Alan Swann (Peter O'Toole), a swashbuckling Hollywood star in the Errol Flynn mold, has agreed to be the guest star on a successful live TV show called Comedy Cavalcade (modeled after Sid Caesar's *Your Show of Shows*). To ensurb his sobriety, the producers entrust him to the care of a hero-worshipping young comedy writer (Mark Linn-Baker). Directing for the first time, Richard Benjamin shows a flair with actors, and O'Toole gives a great performance: Waltzing through the picture dispensing chivalry and noblesse oblige, he turns debauchery into a kind of grandeur.

MY LITTLE CHICKADEE ☆☆☆
1940, USA
Mae West, W. C. Fields, Joseph Calleia, Dick Foran, Ruth Donnelly, Margaret Hamilton, Donald Meek, Fuzzy Knight, George Moran. Directed by Edward Cline. 83 min.

This is a disappointing film when you consider its potential. The screen characters fashioned by Mae West and W. C. Fields are exaggerated burlesques of the American woman and man, and had they brought them together with flair, the results would almost certainly have been memorable. Instead, their "collaboration" on the screenplay seems to consist of half of a Fields movie welded to half of a West movie, with little real interaction between the two. The plot is reminiscent of *Destry Rides Again*, with the pair meeting up in a lawless Western town. It has some funny moments, of course—enough for fans of either star, in fact—but overall, don't expect too much.

MY LITTLE PONY: THE MOVIE ☆
1986, USA, G.
Animated: Madeline Kahn, Tony Randall, Danny DeVito, Rhea Perlman, Cloris Leachman, Jon Bauman, Alice Playten. Directed by Michael Joens. 87 min.

My Little Pony wants to be *your* little pony—and you can arrange this at your local toy emporium, where the huggable horsies with the combable manes can be had for a song. Not coincidentally, the very same song serves as lead-in to Saturday morning commercials for the product and as theme for the movie—an animated amalgam of music, adventure, and advertising. The plot is as simple as the minds who dreamed up this latest Toys-R-movie stars exercise in parent abuse: A wicked witch and her daughter, inhabitants of the "Volcano Of Doom," are out to eradicate the frolicsome ponies with cute little designs on their haunches. To this end, they create a marauding purple goo called the Smooze that can only be combatted by the "utter flutter" of the faraway Flutter Ponies. The songs and crises are borrowed from sources as diverse as *My Fair Lady* and *The Spider*, but Disney, of course, is the guy whose creative pocket is most often picked.

MY MAN GODFREY ☆☆☆☆
1936, USA
William Powell, Carole Lombard, Alice Brady, Gail Patrick, Eugene Pallette, Mischa Auer. Directed by Gregory La Cava. 94 min.

In perhaps the finest and funniest screwball comedy ever made, two daughters in a family of socialites are assigned to find a "forgotten man" during a scavenger hunt, and the bum they bring home is adopted into their scatterbrained clan. Part of the pleasure comes in watching the dapper, unflappable William Powell play the high-society dropout who becomes a bemused butler in the Bullock household, and Carole Lombard, the most natural and breezy of comediennes, is equally fine. *Godfrey*'s comedy, as directed by Gregory La Cava, is still fresh and frenetic, and the whole film is a charming reminder of an era when people went to the movies to forget their troubles and see the idle rich at play.

MY NEW PARTNER ☆☆☆½
1984, France, R
Philippe Noiret, Thierry Lhermitte, Regine, Grace De Capitani. Directed by Claude Zidi. 107 min.

Claude Zidi is the French equivalent of someone like Stan Dragoti, a director of popular comedies that do consistently well at the box office and poorly with critics. So when this comedy won the public's heart over such competition as *A Sunday in the Country* and *Full Moon Paris*, the critics were properly appalled. But this is very funny stuff, and it's good to see humor applauded. The story is probably familiar: A veteran cop has his regular cycle of collecting graft from the pimps and pickpockets of his district interrupted by the presence of a new partner, an idealistic young police academy graduate. But Philippe Noiret is so outrageous as the cop on the take that you're won over by the sheer magnitude and single-mindedness of his scheming. The ending is too sentimental, and this problem could easily have been avoided; still, there probably had to be some measure of lip service paid to the "crime doesn't pay" message the public demands.

MY OTHER HUSBAND ☆½
1986, France, PG
Miou-Miou, Roger Hanin, Eddie Mitchell, Dominique Lavanant. Directed by Georges Lautner. 110 min.

Miou-Miou plays a woman who divides her time between Paris, where she lives with her husband, and Trouville, where she has two children and a lover she met during her 10-year separation. This post-feminist heartwarmer toys with farcical elements but keeps reaching for something "higher"; the result is wobbly and unfocused. Director Georges Lautner veers away from the jealousies and passions of his characters, and his resolution is as impromptu as it is contrived. Meanwhile, Miou-Miou, a fine actress, is robbed of her distinctive sensuality.

MY PAL TRIGGER ☆☆
1946, USA
Roy Rogers, Dale Evans, George "Gabby" Hayes. Directed by Frank McDonald. 79 min.

With a larger budget, more impressive sets, and a stronger story line, Republic hoped to lift this Roy Rogers movie to the top of the bill. This vehicle tells the story of the birth of the legendary Trigger and thus, for fans of the series, is a must to see.

MYRA BRECKINRIDGE ☆
1970, USA, X
Raquel Welch, Mae West, John Huston, Rex Reed, Farrah Fawcett, Roger C. Carmel, George Furth, Calvin Lockhart, Jim Backus, John Carradine, Andy Devine, Grady Sutton, Tom Selleck. Directed by Michael Sarne. 94 min.

A homosexual movie nut (critic Rex Reed) gets a sex-change operation and, in the person of Raquel Welch, goes to Hollywood to devastate mankind, Hollywood, and America, not necessarily in that order, or in *any* kind of order at all. The director and producer rejected Gore Vidal's screenplay adaptation of his novel—whether they used any screenplay at all is questionable, because *Myra Breckinridge* is an incoherent, aimless, terminally "hip" hodgepodge of gaudy visuals interspersed with old movie clips. This was one of the first (and only) major Hollywood productions to receive an X rating, though now it would have to be spiced up in order to be assured of an R. Aside from the various thirties and forties idols shown in clips, there is the questionable spectacle of such prewar supporting players as Andy Devine, Grady Sutton and John Carradine in "cameo" appearances, as well as future television sex stars Farrah Fawcett and Tom Selleck in parts they'd probably rather forget. Sole saving grace: Mae West, who *does* show her age, but who was at least allowed to write her own lines. The movie lacks even camp value, mostly because that's just what it tries so hard to achieve.

MY SCIENCE PROJECT
☆½
1985, USA, PG
John Stockwell, Fisher Stevens, Dennis Hopper, Richard Masur. Directed by Jonathan R. Betuel. 95 min.

Movie teenagers seem to have a knack for endangering civilization with their ill-advised uses of advanced technology, and films with this type of plot usually have great special effects and no comprehensible script. Here's yet another that can sit beside *Weird Science* and its mediocre ilk. This time, a bunch of car-obsessed kids find an alien time-warp generator and turn their school into a living museum of prehistory and future shock. Director Jonathan Betuel and his inept cast all seem to think that what they're doing is particularly clever, but it's all resoundingly funny and unimaginative, and somewhat nasty toward the end. The dazzling visuals by the Disney technicians make this absurd stuff almost watchable.

MY SISTER, MY LOVE
☆☆½
1978, USA, R
Lee Grant, Carol Kane, Will Geer, James Olson. Directed by Karen Arthur. 99 min.

This is a very strange, independently produced psychological horror film about two obsessively close sisters who keep their anthropologist father's memory alive by dwelling in a house full of monkeys and tropical foliage. Older sis Lee Grant is comparatively normal, but young Carol Kane has major problems with her simian housemates—she likes to maim, torture, and kill them in her spare time. Appropriately overheated performances and the genuine oddity of its premise may hold your attention, although not much finally comes of it. (a.k.a.: *The Mafu Cage*).

THE MYSTERIANS
☆☆☆
1959, Japan
Kenji Sahara, Yumi Shirakawa, Momoko Kochi, Akihiko Hirata. Directed by Inishiro Honda. 85 min.

This is the first Japanese sci-fi film to get a full-scale American release—and it's still one of the silliest (and liveliest) entries in the low-budget apocalypse-now genre. It features giant robots destroying most of Japan (of course—what would an Inishiro Honda movie be *without* Tokyo getting trashed?) and aliens lusting after earth women. And all this at a time when American movies like *Sayonara* were dealing with minor matters like miscegenation. Great fun.

MYSTERIOUS FOOTWORKS OF KUNG FU
☆½
Hong Kong
Chaing Tao, Chen Hui-Min, Charles Huang, Betty Ting. Directed by Chen Wah.

Charles Huang (*The Goose Boxer*) fans may be disappointed by the lackadaisical early fight scenes in this story of a simpleminded man who attempts to break up a drug ring run by Shrimp and Crab. Chen Hui-Min, who can kick faster than most people can punch, has a small supporting role.

MYSTERIOUS ISLAND
☆☆½
1961, Great Britain
Michael Craig, Joan Greenwood, Michael Callan, Gary Merrill, Herbert Lom, Beth Rogan, Percy Herbert, Dan Jackson, Nigel Green. Directed by Cy Enfield. 101 min.

Although not reaching the depths of *20,000 Leagues Under the Sea*, this Jules Verne adaptation does have some meaty action in the form of oversized roosters, bees, and a bad case of crabs. Escapees from a Confederate prison camp commandeer an observation balloon that ends up on a something-less-than-fantasy island. Two women wash up on the beach to complete the Swiss Family Robinson in this overgrown stockyard. Finally, our underwater hero, Captain Nemo, shows up to explain that this island is his laboratory to solve world hunger and that the island is about to blow up. Surprise! As the volcano explodes, the refugee community escapes, but the valiant captain stays behind to see his livestock become the world's largest Kentucky Fried Chicken. Good Ray Harryhausen effects keep the visuals interesting, including the memorable beeswax entombment sequence.

MYSTERIOUS ISLAND OF BEAUTIFUL WOMEN
☆½
1979, USA (TV)
Steven Keats, Jamie Lyn Bauer, Kathryn Davis, Rosalind Chao, Deborah Shelton. Directed by Joseph Pevney. 96 min.

Just as the title sounds more like an *idea* for a title than the real thing, this brainless TV concoction plays more like a concept for a comic book than a film. A crew of oil riggers crashes on a tropical paradise, but its population of scantily clad ladies (with names like Bambi and Flower) doesn't exactly bring out the welcome wagon. There are a few laughs from the film's occasional acknowledgment of its own stupidity, but why bother?

THE MYSTERIOUS TWO
☆
1982, USA (TV)
John Forsythe, James Stephens, Priscilla Pointer, Robert Pine, Noah Beery. Directed by Gary Sherman. 100 min.

This is a pilot originally called "Follow Me if You Dare." Watch this stultifying mess if you dare. It took the network that showed this bomb several years to foist this on an unsuspecting public. A couple of space aliens visit Earth to recruit hardy souls for a glamorous new life-style in the Great Beyond. If you decided not to join the Naval Reserves or the Peace Corps, maybe you'd be interested in catching the extraterrestrials' recruiting pitch.

THE MYSTERY OF ALEXINA
☆☆½
1986, France
Vuillemin, Valerie Stroh, Veronique Silver, Bernard Freyd, Pierre Vial, Marianne Basler. Directed by Rene Feret. 86 min.

This is a quietly engrossing piece of sexual esoterica—the true story of a young hermaphrodite in nineteenth-century France who was classified as a female at birth and, when male sexual characteristics began to appear, was reviled and despised. Rene Feret's film is never prurient, and by its end it becomes a rather touching love story. As Alexina, Vuillemin gives an extremely subtle and convincing performance befitting the bizarre but well-handled tale.

THE MYSTERY OF KASPAR HAUSER

See *Every Man for Himself and God Against All*

THE MYSTERY OF PICASSO
☆☆☆½
1957, France
Pablo Picasso. Directed by Henri-Georges Clouzot. 85 min.

The creation of a painting may be the most elusive and difficult to depict of all the visual arts; we can watch a canvas fill, but we can't see the composition and structure that's already in the artist's mind. Director Henri-Georges Clouzot doesn't overcome this problem, but he comes closer to portraying the creation of a painting—the forethought, the caprice, the experiments, the imagination, the frustration—than we would have thought possible. The artist, of course, is Pablo Picasso, and the art appears line by line, shape by shape, on a blank screen, using a kind of transparent glass that allows us to see only the art, not the artist. Uneven and at times exasperating—Picasso destroyed all of the canvases before or upon completion—but an extraordinary portrait of an artistic imagination at work. Shot in 1956, the film was entangled in legal problems with the estates of Clouzot and Picasso and was virtually unreleased for thirty years.

THE MYSTERY OF THE MARIE CELESTE

See *Phantom Ship*.

MY SWEET CHARLIE   ★★★½
1970, USA (TV)
Patty Duke, Al Freeman, Jr., Ford Rainey, William Hardy, Nobel Willingham. Directed by Lamont Johnson. 97 min.

Although this two-character drama flopped on Broadway, it succeeds beautifully on TV. With a minimum of preachiness, it probes the budding relationship of two people who suddenly find themselves social outcasts. They've been conditioned to despise each other: he's a black activist lawyer on the run and she's a poor-white-trash girl expecting a baby. Thrown together by fate, forced to hide in the same small house, the two loners break through the racial prejudices that had separated them. Patty Duke deservedly won an Emmy; both she and Al Freeman, Jr. give exemplary performances in a production that helped legitimize made-for-TV movies.

MY TUTOR   ★★
1983, USA, R
Matt Lattanzi, Caren Kaye, Kevin McCarthy, Arlene Golonka. Directed by George Bowers. 97 min.

Mediocre passage-to-manhood comedy, which benefits slightly by substituting silly sentiments for leering jokes. Bobby's flunked his French college boards, so his rich dad hires luscious Terry the tutor to coach him for the summer. Needless to say, they end up speaking the international language. Give Caren Kaye credit for refusing to play another dumb blonde in a role that clearly asks for one, but her relatively sensitive work can't pull the film out of its adherence to the meretricious attitude, so familiar by now, that beautiful women were put on earth solely to teach lusty teens the way of love.

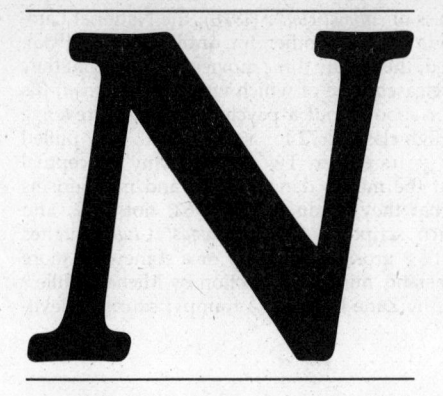

N

NADIA
☆½
1984, USA/France/Yugoslavia (TV)
Talia Balsam, Carrie Snodgress, Conchata Ferrell, Joe Bennett, Jonathan Banks, Johann Carlo. Directed by Alan Cooke. 100 min.

Reverent, thoroughly dull biography of Nadia Comaneci, the Rumanian athletic sensation who mesmerized a worldwide audience by scoring the first perfect tens ever in Olympic gymnastics competition in 1976. This rather late-in-coming attempt to rekindle those memories is a failure as human drama, and the restaged competition footage doesn't hold a candle to the real thing. Johann Carlo plays the teenage Nadia; Sonja Kereskenski doubles in the gymnastics scenes.

THE NAKED AND THE DEAD
☆☆☆
1958, USA
Aldo Ray, Cliff Robertson, Raymond Massey, William Campbell, Richard Jaeckel, Joey Bishop, L. Q. Jones, James Best, Robert Gist, Lili St. Cyr. Directed by Raoul Walsh. 131 min.

The best thing about Raoul Walsh's adaptation of Norman Mailer's account of Marines in World War II is Aldo Ray's crusty performance as the platoon's sergeant. He captures something of the book's hard-boiled earthiness; everyone else in the film has gone through the sanitization process into a typical Hollywood ethnic unit. The worst of them is Joey Bishop, playing a comic Jew who carries much of the movie's interest; Cliff Robertson is better as a lordly officer who finds out that he's only human. Walsh directs with his customary muscular efficiency, and he gets mileage out of the tension and boredom inherent in being on the front line in the hellish Pacific theater. Overall, it's far better than the average war film, if not a great insight into one of the better books on the war.

THE NAKED CAGE
☆☆
1986, USA, R
Shari Shattuck, Angel Tompkins, Lucinda Crosby, Carole Ita White. Directed by Paul Nicholas. 97 min.

Women-behind-bars pictures have to be very bad indeed not to deliver some basic exploitation entertainment value; *The Naked Cage* comes through with flying colors. Sensitive Michelle is imprisoned unjustly, and despite her best efforts to adjust to jailhouse life she is victimized by Rita, a full-fledged psychotic whose false testimony landed her in jail in the first place. The warden is a corrupted lesbian, the guards are demented sadistic rapists, and the other prisoners are a bad lot of whores, thieves, liars, and drug addicts in tight, short uniforms. Sex, violence, and action galore make this sleazy fun for fans of the form.

THE NAKED FACE
☆☆
1984, USA, R
Roger Moore, Rod Steiger, Elliott Gould, Art Carney, Anne Archer. Directed by Bryan Forbes. 98 min.

A low-voltage suspense thriller about a psychiatrist (Roger Moore) being investigated for a murder he didn't commit, at the same time that the real killer is hunting him down. An involved subplot about the doctor's testimony in an old cop-killing case—the cops hate him for winning the killer an insanity plea—doesn't really work here as well as it did in Sidney Sheldon's compact, effective novel. Moore is a yawn, but the end does generate a couple of chills.

THE NAKED NIGHT

See *Sawdust and Tinsel*

THE NAKED PREY
☆☆☆
1966, USA
Cornel Wilde, Gert Van Den Bergh, Ken Gampu. Directed by Cornel Wilde. 94 min.

Cornel Wilde flexes his directorial muscles in this taut, brutal exercise in unrelenting suspense. Echoing the plot of *The Most Dangerous Game*, this adventure tale proceeds at breakneck speed as Wilde eludes death at the hands of African savages. The tribesmen give him a head start at escape, only to close in for the kill later. There is breathless action; and not for the squeamish as Wilde out-savages the natives.

THE NAME OF THE ROSE
☆☆
1986, France/Italy/West Germany, R
Sean Connery, F. Murray Abraham, Christian Slater, Elya Baskin, Feodor Chaliapin Jr., William Hickey, Michael Lonsdale, Ron Perlman. Directed by Jean-Jacques Annaud. 128 min.

A prestige production with a rigorously somber look and a solemn tone throughout. Seeing this film is a bit like being forced to attend Sunday school; it's not a movie but a duty, because it's based on the renowned bestseller by Umberto Eco (a book that everyone seems to have read and that nobody will admit they had a hell of a time getting through). The plot concerns a murder investigation in a forbidding medieval monastery, where disagreements over banned books and acts of heresy provide the motivation behind some unsolved crimes. The film's physical reproduction of fourteenth-century life can't be faulted, but stripped of Eco's philosophical ponderings, the plot is finally somewhat clumsy. It's well-made but lifeless, and often so dark that it's hard to see.

NAPOLEON
☆☆☆☆
1927, France
Albert Dieudonne, Antonin Artaud, Pierre Batcheff, Vladimir Roudenko. Directed by Abel Gance. 240 min.

One of the great long-lost classics of the silent screen, the original six-hour *Napoleon* was shown only twenty-four times in Europe before being cut up and reedited in endless permutations by international distributors. (The version that played in New York in 1929 was only seventy minutes long!) Director Abel Gance himself spent most of his life trying to have it seen, adding sound and tinted sequences over the years. In the late 1970s, film historian Kevin Brownlow spent years going through piles of footage and reassembling the film into the best possible approximation of its original form; it was finally shown under the sponsorship of Francis Coppola. Some of Gance's most awesome sequences, particularly the final three-screen triptych (the first instance of the wide-screen process that Hollywood didn't pick up until the 1950s), are diminished or lost again in transferring the film to video, but the sheer fervor and imagination of the filmmaker in depicting the early life of the French leader still come through magnificently.

NAPOLEON
☆☆½
1955, France
Daniel Gelin, Raymond Pellegrin, Sacha Guitry, Michele Morgan, Orson Welles, Daniele Darrieux, Lana Marconi, Erich Von Stroheim, Maria Schell, Jean Gabin. Directed by Sacha Guitry. 115 min.

This little-known historical epic offers some lavish sets and colorful star turns, but little else. Writer-director-star Sacha

Guitry has assembled a great international cast to play scenes from the life of Emperor Napoleon. Unfortunately, neither Daniel Gelin's young Bonaparte nor Raymond Pellegrin's older Napoleon stir up very much passion, and the sweep of the production is a mere whisk next to Abel Gance's recently restored 1927 *Napoleon*. The fun is in watching the players make mincemeat of history: Guitry as the storyteller Talleyrand, Michele Morgan as a sexy Josephine, Orson Welles as a sly Hudson-Lowe and, best of all, Erich Von Stroheim as an intense Beethoven. The original running time was 190 minutes.

NASHVILLE ☆☆☆☆
1975, USA, R
Barbara Baxley, Ned Beatty, Karen Black, Ronee Blakley, Keith Carradine, Geraldine Chaplin, Shelley Duvall, Allen Garfield, Henry Gibson, Scott Glenn, Barbara Harris, Michael Murphy, Cristina Raines, Lily Tomlin. Directed by Robert Altman. 159 min.

This brilliantly detailed, epic collage of the lives of twenty-four unforgettable characters during five hectic days in Nashville—the city where showbiz and politics merge—is one of the greatest American films of the 1970s. Altman has created a triumphantly idiosyncratic portrait of American strength, weakness, folly, and grace in a film that slides between tragedy and comedy with a remarkably lifelike fluidity. Constantly overlapping dialogue gives many of the scenes a narrative richness and naturalism that verges on the poetic. The huge cast (many of whom wrote the songs they sing in the film, superb country-music spoofs) does splendid work as an emsemble, and still allows performances of particular incisiveness—Lily Tomlin's and Ronee Blakeley's foremost among them—to shine through. Politics, pop culture, and personal relationships blend to create a cinematic rarity—a highly individual but all-encompassing vision of America. Stay with *Nashville*—its apparent early rambling conceals a carefully calculated structure not fully evident until the last scene.

NATE AND HAYES ☆☆
1983, USA/New Zealand, PG
Tommy Lee Jones, Michael O'Keefe, Max Phipps, Jenny Seagrove, Grant Tilly. Directed by Ferdinand Fairfax. 100 min.

Adventure on the high seas, with Tommy Lee Jones as an eighteenth-century "blackbirder" (slaver) and Michael O'Keefe as the man whose finacée he helps rescue. The screenplay, by David Odell and John Hughes (*Sixteen Candles, The Breakfast Club*), wobbles very unsteadily between straightforward swashbuckling fare and comic book parody, with a surprising measure of violence thrown in. It's not very successful in the end, but interestingly told and well-acted by Jones.

NATIONAL LAMPOON'S ANIMAL HOUSE ☆☆☆
1978, USA, R
John Belushi, Tim Matheson, John Vernon, Verna Bloom, Thomas Hulce, Cesare Danova, Donald Sutherland, Karen Allen, Mary Louise Weller. Directed by John Landis. 109 min.

A cast of real pros makes this famed frat house comedy many grades higher than the rest: John Belushi incites a cafeteria food fight; Tim Matheson beds the dean's wife (Verna Bloom) during a wild toga party; Thomas Hulce gets "high" with his professor (Donald Sutherland); and John Vernon, as the dean, conducts Nazi-like drill sessions. The Harold Ramis-Douglas Kenny-Chris Miller screenplay is less raucous than National Lampoon's magazine humor and goes for some cheap laughs, but it is funny. John Landis (*The Blues Brothers, An American Werewolf in London*) directs in an appropriately crude yet breezy manner.

NATIONAL LAMPOON'S CLASS REUNION ☆½
1982, USA, R
Gerrit Graham, Fred McCarren, Miriam Flynn, Stephen Furst, Shelley Smith, Michael Lerner, Zane Busby, Chuck Berry. Directed by Michael Miller. 86 min.

After the success of *Animal House* (1978), the National Lampoon team didn't have another hit until *Vacation* (1983). During the fallow period, they made three movies so awful that they were barely or never released, one of which was *Class Reunion*. It's a lame, tasteless horror spoof about a psycho who seeks revenge on the Lizzie Borden High class of '72 for a cruel prank they pulled on graduation eve ten years earlier. Two of the many conceptual problems here are that the music, dances, fads, and mannerisms of the class suggest that they graduated in 1962, not 1972, and that the blackout-sketch script by John (*Breakfast Club*) Hughes can't decide whether it's a gross-out comedy or a somewhat more mature satire. There is static, mirthless direction by Michael Miller, but a nice performance by Zane Busby as a trampy, sarcastic devil-woman.

NATIONAL LAMPOON'S EUROPEAN VACATION ☆☆
1985, USA, PG-13
Chevy Chase, Beverly D'Angelo, Jason Lively, Dana Hill, Eric Idle, Victor Lanoux. Directed by Amy Heckerling. 98 min.

The ever-so-smarmy Griswolds win a trip to the Continent on the game show "Pig in a Poke" in this generally disappointing follow-up of the much funnier *National Lampoon's Vacation*. These ugly Americans were more appealing at home than they are abroad, and director Amy Heckerling doesn't evince the comic timing or style of the first film's director, Harold Ramis. The script (by *Vacation* writer John Hughes and Robert Klane) manages to work a few fresh variations on the original, but it's inconsistent, badly structured, and too lazy to go for anything but the cheap laugh. Chevy Chase and Beverly D'Angelo, though clearly bored reprising their roles, do credible work, but the film arches with the absence of the other comic actors—Anthony Michael Hall, Imogene Coca, John Candy—who populated the first, and lacks the crafty humor they were given.

NATIONAL LAMPOON'S VACATION ☆☆☆
1983, USA, R
Chevy Chase, Beverly D'Angelo, Anthony Michael Hall, Dana Barron, Randy Quaid, Imogene Coca, Christie Brinkley, John Candy. Directed by Harold Ramis. 100 min.

A family vacation turns into a comic nightmare in this barbed, often very funny satire of American materialism at its tackiest. Chevy Chase plays ultra square Clark Griswold, who packs his wife and kids into the car and heads west for a week of fun at Walley World. But somewhere between a stop-off at the home of their dirt-farmer relations and a visit to the world's second largest ball of twine, all goes awry. As with the best of the *Lampoon* satires, gross gags share space with edgy, well-observed situational humor, and anyone who's ever suffered through a never-ending trip with the family will recognize more than they might expect. Credit goes to Harold Ramis's fast-paced direction, John Hughes's pungent script, and good performances by the whole cast, including Anthony Michael Hall's very appealing presence as one of the kids, and Chase's dead-on dad.

NATIONAL VELVET ☆☆☆
1944, USA
Mickey Rooney, Elizabeth Taylor, Anne Revere, Donald Crisp, Angela Lansbury, Jackie Jenkins, Reginald Owen, Terry Kilburn. Directed by Clarence Brown. 125 min.

The durable Enid Bagnold story of a girl and her horse was done to perfection in the MGM crowd-pleaser starring Elizabeth Taylor and Mickey Rooney in what are, perhaps, their best performances as juveniles. The story is very simple and awfully mawkish, but no less moving for being so calculated. Children should love the whole thing, although adults may sit by and be entertained by the familiar, wonderful supporting cast. Followed thirty-five years later by a sequel, *International Velvet*.

NATIVE SON ★★½
1986, USA, PG
Victor Love, Carroll Baker, Akosua Busia, Matt Dillon, Art Evans, John Karlen, Elizabeth McGovern, John McMartin, Geraldine Page, Oprah Winfrey, David Rasche. Directed by Jerrold Freedman. 112 min.

Richard Wright's powerful novel about a confused, poor black teenager who murders a white girl has proved a difficult one to translate to film; in 1951 it was filmed poorly in Argentina with Wright himself in the leading role of Bigger Thomas, and this American Playhouse production, with newcomer Victor Love as Bigger, isn't much more successful. Richard Wesley's screenplay is first didactic and then unbelievable, and Love's remote performance fails to evoke sympathy or even interest. The supporting cast ranges from good (Matt Dillon) to terrible (Oprah Winfrey, in a cameo that suggests her work in *The Color Purple* was a fluke), and the production is handsome but unengaging.

THE NATURAL ★★½
1984, USA, PG
Robert Redford, Glenn Close, Barbara Hershey, Joe Don Baker, Robert Duvall, Kim Basinger, Wilford Brimley, Richard Farnsworth. Directed by Barry Levinson. 134 min.

Robert Redford, returning to the screen after four years, is naturally a pleasure to watch as Roy Hobbs, a fictive baseball player whose dream to be the best is sidetracked by intriguing twists of plot and a cruel twist of fate. Mounted as a mythical rendition of Bernard Malamud's first novel, the film ultimately forfeits realism in exchange for an uplifting, Disney–like movie experience. It would be considerably more powerful and memorable if it ended the way the book does; but in terms of pure entertainment, the story is failsafe and the cast is top-notch.

NATURAL ENEMIES ★½
1979, USA, PG
Hal Holbrook, Louise Fletcher, Peter Armstrong, Elizabeth Berridge, Steve Austin, Viveca Lindfors, José Ferer. Directed by Jeff Kanew. 100 min.

This grim, sordid drama concerns a publisher who's seized one day with the desire to murder his wife and children, just because. "All men think of killing their families," he informs us in appropriately sober narration. "Some do it. Some do not." How illuminating. Morbid and unpleasant, this is a shallow treatment of the most serious of subjects and fails to make us understand the first thing about what drives men to murder, despite the endless talk about that very topic.

NEA (A YOUNG EMMANUELLE) ★★★
1976, France/West Germany
Sani Frey, Ann Zacharias, Francoise Brion, Micheline Presle, Heinz Bennent, Ingrid Caven. Directed by Nelly Kaplan. 105 min.

This is a film that has less in common with other *Emmanuelle* products than it does with director Nelly Kaplan's more overtly feminist movies like *La Fiancee du Pirate*. A young woman writes an explosive erotic novel after doing a bit of first- and second-hand research. Although the film offers the usual titillations associated with Emmanuelle Arsan's writings, it is remarkably clear-eyed in detailing the young girl's feeling of being decidedly underwhelmed by male sexuality.

'NEATH THE ARIZONA SKIES ★½
1935, USA
John Wayne, Sheila Terry, Jay Wilsey (Buffalo Bill, Jr.). Directed by Harry Fraser. 56 min.

John Wayne must save a kidnapped Indian girl and do in all sorts of bad men. This is a cheaply made film with lots of shooting, cattle, and an undeniable energy about it.

NEIGHBORS ★★½
1981, USA, PG
John Belushi, Dan Aykroyd, Cathy Moriarty, Kathryn Walker, Tim Kazurinsky. Directed by John G. Avildsen. 91 min.

A promising project that went wrong somewhere. Blame probably belongs to director John Avildsen and screenwriter Larry Gelbart for misadapting the excellent Thomas Berger novel of the same title. Belushi and especially Dan Aykroyd are excellently cast. Belushi, cast against type, plays a fiftyish suburbanite whose life is disrupted by an exceedingly weird and unpredictable pair of new neighbors, pugnacious Aykroyd and alluring Cathy Moriarty. The book's subversive point of view is replaced by one going strictly for laughs, with a radically softened ending. What's left isn't bad, but only in spurts. Bill Conti's musical score is one of the worst and most intrusive in recent years. Belushi's last film will disappoint those looking for more in the *Animal House* vein, but will reward those who suspected that he had potential for more than just buffoonish comedy.

NETWORK ★★★½
1976, USA, R
Peter Finch, William Holden, Faye Dunaway, Robert Duvall, Wesley Addy, Ned Beatty, William Prince, Beatrice Straight, Marlene Warfield. Directed by Sidney Lumet. 120 min.

Paddy Chayefsky's lacerating satire of the television industry begs to be taken as a scathing indictment of the manipulative scum that foists tube trash on the mindless masses; as a black comedy it's often funny and nasty enough to score its points with humor. Peter Finch, in his last role, plays a network anchorman fired after years of service. He breaks down on the air, and his deranged rantings send the Nielsens skyward and the megalomaniacal, string-pulling programmer (Faye Dunaway) into ecstasy; she dubs him the Mad Prophet of the Airwaves, and a star is born. Finch and Dunaway's robust, over-the-top performances won them Oscars, and Beatrice Straight was also honored for her brief, histrionic turn as an unappreciated wife. Nominated here as well were Ned Beatty as one of the corporate powers-that-be, and William Holden, who gives the best performance in the thankless role of Chayefsky's mouthpiece. There are many great moments and hysterical set pieces.

NEVADA SMITH ★★½
1966, USA
Steve McQueen, Karl Malden, Brian Keith, Arthur Kennedy, Suzanne Pleshette, Raf Vallone, Janet Margolin, Howard da Silva, Martin Landau. Directed by Henry Hathaway. 132 min.

After the success of his Hollywood-trash melodrama *The Carpetbaggers*, Joseph E. Levine decided to spin off one of that film's characters into a very loosely related prequel; this highly watchable Western saga was the result. Steve McQueen, alternately charismatic and wooden, plays a young man whose parents are brutally slain at the outset; vowing vengeance, he sets out to find and kill the three murderers (Karl Malden, Arthur Kennedy and Martin Landau). Although riddled with cowboy clichés and padded to a ridiculous length, the story beneath the flab is a good one. Remade for television in 1975.

NEVER A DULL MOMENT ★★½
1968, USA
Dick Van Dyke, Edward G. Robinson, Dorothy Provine, Henry Silva, Joanna Moore, Tony Bill, Slim Pickens, Jack Elam, Ned Glass, Mickey Shaughnessy. Directed by Jerry Paris. 99 min.

If you look very hard, you can find one or two dull moments here. Or three or four or. . . . This mediocre Disney comedy has art-loving gangster Edward G. Robinson mistaking TV actor Dick Van Dyke for a hit man, with the predictable farcical consequences. Both Van Dyke and director Jerry Paris should never have left television neither was able to break away from the habits they learned in that medium. Like many Disney comedies, the best thing about this is the large cast of recognizable supporting actors.

NEVER CRY WOLF ★★★½
1983, USA, PG
Charles Martin Smith, Brian Dennehy, Zachary Ittimangnag, Samson Jorah. Directed by Carroll Ballard. 105 min.

Another marvelous animal adventure film by the director of *The Black Stallion* in which Charles Martin Smith portrays a scientist chosen to study the Alaskan wolves to determine if they are responsible for the disappearing caribou herds. What follows is simply not a 1950s–style Disney nature film (although Disney studios did produce this), but a thoughtful, inspiring voyage of self-discovery as a man realizes his role within nature as the most dangerous animal on earth.

THE NEVERENDING STORY ★★
1984, Great Britain/West Germany, PG
Noah Hathaway, Barrett Oliver, Moses Gunn. Directed by Wolfgang Petersen. 92 min.

If children's movies were divided along the lines of what children really want to see and what their parents would like them to want to see, this film could define the latter category. A bright, sensitive youngster acquires a mysterious book only to realize as he reads it that he is part of the story, and that the salvation of its mythical land of Fantasia is his responsibility. There are some throwaway Borgesian notions about fictions-within-fictions, but this is basically a lackluster children's diversion with too much message.

NEVER ON SUNDAY ★★★½
1959, Greece
Melina Mercouri, Jules Dassin, Georges Foundas, Titos Vandis, Despo Diamantidou. Directed by Jules Dassin. 97 min.

Melina Mercouri plays a spirited prostitute, and Jules Dassin (her real-life husband) is the intellectual who comes to Greece and tries to give her some culture. Dassin also directed this good-natured sex comedy which achieved major international success when it first appeared. Credit for that probably goes to Mercouri's rowdy, sexy award-winning performance and the catchy theme song rather than to the story itself, which will be familiar to anyone who's seen *Pygmalion* or its numerous offshoots.

NEVER SAY NEVER AGAIN ★★★
1983, USA, PG
Sean Connery, Klaus Maria Brandauer, Max von Sydow, Barbara Carrera, Kim Basinger, Bernie Casey, Alec McCowen, Edward Fox. Directed by Irvin Kershner. 130 min.

Sean Connery's return to the role of James Bond after twelve years was in this loose remake of *Thunderball*. It centers on SPECTRE's heist of a couple of nuclear warheads, and it's pretty tired stuff, with pedestrian action sequences and a predictable underwater finish. But Barbara Carrera and *Mephisto's* Klaus Maria Brandauer make a stunning pair of villains, and Connery, who plays 007 as older, wiser, and wearier, gives *Never Say Never Again* something no other Bond film has ever had: emotional resonance. For devotees of the series, this one is a must.

THE NEW CENTURIONS ★★½
1972, USA, R
George C. Scott, Stacy Keach, Jane Alexander, Rosalind Cash, Erik Estrada. Directed by Richard Fleischer. 103 min.

Based on Joseph Wambaugh's novel, which was culled from his own experiences as an L.A. cop, this film is to the men in blue what John Wayne's *The Green Berets* was to the marines; a recruitment film for general consumption. This reflects the Nixon-era swing of public opinion to the opposite extreme from the "Off the pigs!" cries of the late 1960s. The title refers to an equation of today's police with the Roman centurions, the last stronghold of that civilization against the barbarians who eventually overtook it. Fortunately, director Richard Fleischer is incapable of creating a film with any real depth, so while it never sinks to the camp depths of *Green Berets*, it stays at the level of glib, unconvincing entertainment.

THE NEW FRONTIER ★½
1935, USA
John Wayne, Muriel Evans, Warner Richmond. Directed by Carl Pierson. 54 min.

There is two-fisted action as the Duke serves as trail boss for a wagon train of pilgrims in his second film for Republic. The story and prodution values are just above the rather crude level found in Monogram films.

NEWMAN'S LAW ★½
1974, USA, PG
George Peppard, Roger Robinson, Eugene Roche, Gordon Pinsent, Louis Zorich, Abe Vigoda. Directed by Richard Heffron. 98 min.

This is a rote, resolutely formulaic action film that casts George Peppard as an honest loner cop who's wrongly suspended from the force. Needless to say, that doesn't stop him from advancing the cause of law and order by going after an international drug ring. But for the moderate violence, it would be easy to confuse this with a TV movie or any one of the dozens of cop shows that flourished in the early 1970s; it's certainly no more original than most of them were.

NEWSFRONT ★★★
1978, Australia
Bill Hunter, Gerard Kennedy, Angela Punch McGregor, Wendy Hughes, Chris Hayward, John Ewart, Bryan Brown. Directed by Phillip Noyce. 110 min.

This sweet and lively Australian film chronicles the lives of two brothers who work for rival Australian newsreel companies in the late forties and early fifties. Director Phillip Noyce mixes great hunks of irresistible newsreel footage with his fictional material, artfully blurring the line between the documentary and the fictional. Lovely compositions and textures abound, and Noyce has managed to forge believable characters out of familiar types: Bill Hunter as the gruff, idealistic Len; Gerard Kennedy, thoroughly sympathetic as his hustling brother Frank; and Wendy Hughes, appropriately wistful as Amy, the colleague both the brothers love.

NEW YORK, NEW YORK ★★★½
1977, USA, PG
Robert DeNiro, Liza Minnelli, Mary Kay Place, Barry Primus, Lionel Stander. Directed by Martin Scorsese. 163 min. (Original release, 153 min.)

Martin Scorsese takes the conventions of 1940s musicals, melodramas, and romantic comedies and ingeniously turns them inside out to create a new kind of musical—one that embodies the exhilarating magic of old Hollywood while exploring the validity of the romantic lessons that audiences so eagerly assimilated. Scorsese's first cut was reportedly close to four hours; this version, which includes footage restored after the original release, is somewhat less than three, and inevitably somewhat jumpy in tone and style. It still offers beautiful performances by Robert DeNiro and Liza Minnelli as a bandleader and his wife at war, swinging music from the big-band era, flashes of directorial genius and the now-standard title song. All in all, it's an insightful adult entertainment, and possibly the director's most unfairly underappreciated work.

NEXT STOP, GREENWICH VILLAGE ☆☆☆½
1976, USA, R
Lenny Baker, Shelley Winters, Ellen Greene, Lois Smith, Christopher Walken, Dori Brenner, Antonio Fargas, Lou Jacobi, Mike Kellin, Jeff Goldblum. Directed by Paul Mazursky. 111 min.

This is a splendid autobiographical comedy by Paul Mazursky that's set in the 1950s. Mazursky's surrogate hero is Larry Lapinsky, a hyperkinetic Jewish hipster who dreams of becoming an actor and moves from his safe Brooklyn home to a ratty apartment in the Village—a world of beatniks and rent parties that Mazursky portrays with satire and affection. Shelley Winters gives a definitive performance as Larry's clinging mother, and the late Lenny Baker is superb in the lead role. Taunting and jiving like Lenny Bruce, he lends this nostalgic film a veracious edge.

NEXT VICTIM ☆½
1974, Great Britain
Carroll Baker, T. P. McKenna, Maurice Kaufman, Ronald Lacey, Ian Gelder, Brenda Cavendish, Max Maxon. Directed by James Ormerod. 80 min.

Alone in her apartment building for a holiday weekend, a woman confined to a wheelchair discovers that she's intended as the next victim of a runaway killer in this hybrid of *Whatever Happened to Baby Jane?* and *Are You in the House Alone?* Immobility and isolation are the elements of great horror, but low production values muddled the essential tension in what otherwise might have been a simple, effective story. Still, low-budget horror films are not particularly renowned for their cinematic flair, and if you can overlook the cheaper shots, the central premise may grab you.

NICHOLAS AND ALEXANDRA ☆☆½
1971, Great Britain, PG
Michael Jayston, Janet Suzman, Roderic Noble, Fiona Fullerton, Ania Marson, Lynne Frederick, Harry Andrews, Tom Baker, Michael Bryant, Maurice Denham, Jack Hawkins, Ian Holm, Curt Jurgens, John McEnery, Eric Porter, Michael Redgrave, Alan Webb, Irene Worth, Laurence Olivier. Directed by Franklin J. Schaffner. 185 min.

Franklin Schaffner's retelling of the troubled lives of the last Russian Czar and Czarina is overstuffed with visual splendor, spectacularly decorative crowd scenes, historical portent, and all-star appearances, but someone forgot to stir in the drama. Although Janet Suzman makes a compelling Alexandra, Michael Jayston is a very bland Nicholas, and James Goldman's script tends to stoop to obvious manipulation and very silly name-dropping ("Who is this Stalin fellow anyway?"). The wide-screen mastery will be lost on video, and the story feels lopped off, too, but the overwhelming display of pageantry and a number of small, sharp star turns make it passable epic entertainment; the art direction and costume design won Oscars. The film is based on a popular historical study by Robert K. Massie, who also wrote *Peter the Great*.

NICHOLAS NICKLEBY ☆☆☆☆
1947, Great Britain
Derek Bond, Cedric Hardwicke, Sally Ann Howes. Alfred Drayton, Vida Hope, Stanley Holloway, Vera Pearce, Cyril Fletcher, Fay Compton. Directed by Alberto Cavalcanti. 105 min.

Quite possibly one of the finest screen adaptations of a Dickens novel, along with David Lean's stately (and very different) *Great Expectations*. The book, one of the author's most enormous and gangly, is neatly compressed: Nicholas (Derek Bond) fends off the malefactions of his scheming uncle (Cedric Hardwicke) to restore prosperity and happiness to his family. Alberto Cavalcanti captures all the ebullience of Dickens's three-dimensional characters while keeping a brisk, sparkling clip to the pacing.

NIGHT AMBUSH
See *Ill Met by Moonlight*

NIGHT AND DAY ☆☆
1946, USA
Cary Grant, Alexis Smith, Monty Woolley, Mary Martin, Ginny Simms, Jane Wyman, Eve Arden, Dorothy Malone. Directed by Michael Curtiz. 132 min.

Cary Grant has only given two bad performances in his career. One was in *Arsenic and Old Lace* as the frenetic Mortimer Brewster. The other was in this flaccid, sugarcoated biography of Cole Porter, playing the composer himself. Grant looks stiff and uncomfortable and is not the least bit helped by having to play love scenes opposite bland, dreary Alexis Smith. Monty Woolley and Jane Wyman generate some excitement in their scenes but the drama of the man (Porter's life from pre-World War I Yale to post-World War II Broadway) remains artificial and uninvolving. This would not be a major problem if only the musical sequences were noteworthy. Unfortunately, most of Porter's tunes are either heard in fragments or thrown away in big, badly staged production numbers. Redeemable features include Grant and Ginny Simms dueting "You're the Top," Mary Martin singing "My Heart Belongs to Daddy," and Estelle Sloan tap dancing to "Just One of Those Things." Otherwise, it's a sadly inadequate tribute to a great artist.

A NIGHT AT THE OPERA ☆☆☆☆
1935, USA
Groucho, Chico, and Harpo Marx, Allan Jones, Kitty Carlisle, Margaret Dumont, Sig Ruman. Directed by Sam Wood. 96 min.

The Marx Brothers's madness always bordered on the surreal and this, arguably their best film, is a devastating satire on the pomp and pretension surrounding grand opera. While crossing the ocean with an Italian opera company, the brothers contrive to help two young singers (Allan Jones, Kitty Carlisle) get a break. In the first of their films for MGM, Groucho, Chico, and Harpo lost "straight" brother Zeppo and gained a few extra musical numbers, but the changes do not get in the way of the film. The stuffed stateroom scene, the backstage chase, and the Groucho-Chico contract dispute are all classic moments in this, their most popular vehicle.

THE NIGHTCOMERS ☆½
1972, Great Britain
Marlon Brando, Stephanie Beacham, Thora Hird, Harry Andrews, Verna Harvey. Directed by Michael Winner. 96 min.

An interesting concept that remains just that throughout this failed chiller. A painful sense of missed opportunities is prevalent here, especially since Marlon Brando is in such good form as the embodiment of evil. This prequel to Henry James's Gothic novella *The Turn of the Screw* purports to tell us what evils befell the children at the hands of their governess, Miss Jessel (Stephanie Beacham) and her lover, Peter Quint (Brando). But instead of frightening us, the film merely revels in its sadism, with no insight into the characters and no accumulation of suspense. It's almost worth seeing, however, for Brando.

NIGHT CRIES ☆☆
1978, USA (TV)
Susan Saint James, Michael Parks, Jamie Smith Jackson, William Conrad, Cathleen Nesbitt. Directed by Richard Lang. 100 min.

Admittedly, there are a few tingles here, but once again television takes subject matter requiring sensitivity and trashes it in order to fit a suspense formula. A mother has recurring nightmares that push her to the realization that her dead baby may actually be alive somewhere and in desperate need of her. The film is rather heartless in milking scares—certainly it isn't recommended to anyone who's recently suffered the loss of a child.

NIGHT CROSSING ★★
1981, Great Britain, PG
John Hurt, Jane Alexander, Doug McKeon, Keith McKeon, Beau Bridges, Glynnis O'Connor, Ian Bannen. Directed by Delbert Mann. 106 min.

Walt Disney Studios was in a brief, unhealthy adolescence when this was made, and it shows. Caught in the transition between family fare and the purely adult features which were to follow, they came up with a very uneasy compromise: a Cold War adventure for the kids. John Hurt and Jane Alexander play the heads of an East German clan that's planning to defect by flying a hot-air balloon over the Berlin Wall. This gives the filmmakers a chance to combine the stark brutality of vicious border guards with merry scenes of chipper tots preparing for the big adventure. At its worst, it plays like "Heidi Joins the Resistance," but decent acting and direction compensate for the bursts of thematic schizophrenia.

NIGHT GALLERY ★★
1969, USA (TV)
Joan Crawford, Ossie Davis, Richard Kiley, Roddy McDowall, Barry Sullivan, Tom Bosley, Rod Serling (host). Directed by Boris Sagal (Part 1), Steven Spielberg (Part 2), Barry Shear (Part 3). 95 min.

This pilot for Rod Serling's supernatural anthology series (1970–73) is of interest only for its central segment, one of Steven Spielberg's earliest directorial assignments. Otherwise, it's a fairly tepid rehash of the kind of story that was one of the dullest aspects of the old "Twilight Zone," with each part depicting a guilty person who's creatively punished for past misdeeds. The Spielberg episode, with Joan Crawford hamming it up as a blind millionairess willing to do anything to see, unsurprisingly evinces more style and energy than the other two (one about a scheming nephew, the other about a Nazi on the run), both of which are strictly fast-forward material. That Serling wrote all three makes their generally hackneyed quality especially disappointing.

NIGHT GAMES ★½
1980, USA, R
Cindy Pickett, Joanna Cassidy, Barry Primus, Paul Jenkins, Gene Davis. Directed by Roger Vadim. 100 min.

This is prolonged semi-erotic foreplay from Roger Vadim at his most slavering. Cindy Pickett, later of numerous TV series, stars as a Beverly Hills housewife traumatized by a rape in her past and now given to haunting nightmares and screaming fits. The sex therapy she gets is probably not recommended by the American Psychiatric Association, and the R rating limits the on-screen action to heavy breathing, heavy kissing, and heavy implication. Pickett at least looks beautiful; the film, in which glorious downtown Manila doubles for L.A., does not.

NIGHTHAWKS ★★★
1981, USA, R
Sylvester Stallone, Billy Dee Williams, Lindsay Wagner, Persis Khambatta, Nigel Davenport, Rutger Hauer. Directed by Bruce Malmuth. 99 min.

This energetic, well-staged cop thriller was one of Sylvester Stallone's more successful attempts to break out of the *Rocky* mold. Here, he plays an embryonic variation on Rambo as a New York detective with fifty-two Vietnam kills under his belt, now pursuing a diabolical international terrorist who's on a sadistic rampage through New York. Sly downplays the heroics, giving a performance of comparative restraint, but the film belongs to Rutger Hauer, whose cleverly icy portrayal of the sleek villain is memorably monstrous. ("You're going to a better place," he tells his victims before slicing them up.) It's worth seeing for director Bruce Malmuth's deft action work, including a dazzler set on the Roosevelt Island tramway with *Star Trek*'s bald bombshell Persis Khambatta as Hauer's accomplice. But if you don't guess the "twist" ending beforehand, you're just not paying attention.

A NIGHT IN HEAVEN ★
1983, USA, R
Christopher Atkins, Lesley Ann Warren, Robert Hogan, Carrie Snodgress, Deborah Rush, Denny Terrio. Directed by John G. Avildsen. 92 min.

A college professor, ignored by her husband, falls for a very young male stripper who happens to be one of her students, in a slimy and indescribably stupid exploitation film. Lesley Ann Warren, a talented actress, deserves much better than this, but Christopher Atkins, who's making a career out of playing male bimbos, is right in his element. Something of the film's quality is connoted by the fact that Denny Terrio, the grinning host of TV's "Dance Fever," gives one of the better performances.

NIGHTMARE ★
1981, USA, R
C. J. Cooke, Mik Cribben, Kathleen Ferguson. Directed by Romano Scavolini. 97 min.

A murderous psychopath is released from a mental institution, his madness supposedly controlled by medication. It isn't, and after a brief foray into the fleshpots of New York's Times Square, he embarks on a murderous rampage. Does this plot sound familiar? *Nightmare* offers the usual low-budget brew of bloody mayhem, cardboard cutout characters (the better to cut them down with dispatch), and dreamy flashbacks whose ostensible purpose is to establish a motive for the manic's madness; in fact, they are just an opportunity for gratuitous titillation involving the killer's fat father and a dominatrix. *Nightmare*'s great claim to fame is that its original theatrical advertisements promised special effects by splatter king Tom Savini, only to recant when Savini—who had no involvement with the film—threatened to sue.

NIGHTMARE CITY

See CITY OF THE WALKING DEAD

NIGHTMARE IN WAX ★½
1969, USA
Cameron Mitchell, Anne Helm, Scott Brady. Directed by Bud Townsend. 91 min.

The Phantom of the Opera meets *House of Wax*: A former movie studio makeup artist now runs a Hollywood wax museum, having been given the boot (as well as some major scars) by his former employer. Seems they both lusted after the same actress, and now our hero plots revenge. Hmmm, wonder where he gets those amazingly realistic-looking wax statues of all the famous stars from his old studio? You, the viewer, will of course have no difficulty spotting that the wax statues are cleverly simulated by real people, who do occasionally have trouble keeping still while on camera. In fact, seeing how long you can stand still and pretend to be a statue might be a better way of spending your time than watching this rehash.

A NIGHTMARE ON ELM STREET ★★★½
1984, USA, R
Heather Langenkamp, John Saxon, Ronee Blakley, Amanda Wyss, Nick Corri, Robert Englund. Directed by Wes Craven. 94 min.

Wes Craven, the splatter-film maven who made *Last House on the Left* and *The Hills Have Eyes*, has come up with a crafty horror yarn about four high school friends who share the same nightmare—a nightmare that comes true unless you're lucky enough to wake up in time. The cackling psycho who runs through this dream is a comically creepy fellow (with his burned-up face topped by a battered snap-brim hat; he looks like Mr. Green Jeans' psychotic cousin), and the movie boasts a good deal of generally startling imagery. Heather Langenkamp shows more talent than the usual shrieking teen star, and Robert Englund actually manages to give a performance underneath his deep-fried makeup. Followed by a sequel, *A Nightmare on Elm Street Part 2: Freddy's Revenge.*

A NIGHTMARE ON ELM STREET PART 2: FREDDY'S REVENGE ☆☆½
1985, USA, R
Mark Patton, Robert Englund, Kim Myers, Robert Rusler, Clu Gulager, Hope Lange, Marshall Bell, Melinda O. Fee, Thom McFadden, Hart Sprager. Directed by Jack Sholder. 85 min.

The Walsh family gets a great deal on the Thompson house on Elm Street, only vaguely aware that something dreadful happened there five years earlier, but soon they—particularly teenage Jesse—become aware that the past is still disturbingly present. The house is unbearably hot, pets and appliances behave in strange and destructive ways, and Jesse's sleep is deranged by the figure of a deformed maniac whose razor-tipped hands soon reach out into the waking world to kill and maim. Though this sequel to *A Nightmare on Elm Street*, directed by Jack Sholder (*Alone in the Dark*), lacks the complexity of the first film and sometimes reduces its potentially unnerving material to the level of cliché, it is still more interesting than much of what passes for horror filmmaking. A double bill of the two should guarantee some very sweet dreams. Followed by a sequel, *A Nightmare on Elm Street Part 3: Dream Warriors.*

NIGHTMARES ☆½
1983, USA, PG
Christina Raines, Emilio Estevez, Richard Masur, Veronica Cartwright. Directed by Joseph Sargent. 99 min.

This is a timid horror anthology with no framing story and four segments concerning a classic piece of folklore (do *you* always check the back seat before you get in?), a sinister video game, a possessed car, and a monster rat. Made for television but released theatrically; professionally put together but bland.

NIGHT, MOTHER ☆☆½
1986, USA, PG-13
Sissy Spacek, Anne Bancroft, Ed Berke, Carol Robbins, Jennifer Roosendahl. Directed by Tom Moore. 96 min.

Marsha Norman's Pulitzer Prizewinning play about an unhappy woman who tells her mother of her intention to commit suicide comes to the screen, and perhaps fittingly self-destructs. Making his first film, director Tom Moore, who handled the original staging, doesn't understand that what might work in the theater as an expression of alienation and isolation can have the opposite effect on screen. If you can swallow your objections to the speciousness of the story line, you can enjoy a showcase for two powerful actresses at the top of their form. But once you question this play's contrived reason for being—that this beaten soul (Sissy Spacek) would choose to play out her suicide in front of her never-say-die mother (Anne Bancroft), then the film begins to unravel and one starts to wonder whether Norman isn't more interested in juicy dramatics than she is in saying anything profound about suicide.

NIGHT OF THE CREEPS ☆☆☆
1986, USA, R
Jason Lively, Jill Whitlow, Tom Atkins, Steve Marshall. Directed by Fred Dekker. 88 min.

A creepy, suspenseful scare-a-thon that plays by the genre rules, managing an absurdist sense of humor without cutting in on the chills. When a cryogenically frozen body is moved as part of a fraternity initiation, the "creeps" are let loose. This is not a reference to the frat brothers but to creatures that burst through the brain leaving the victim-host a zombie. The creeps had been left by some nasty extraterrestrials years before, and they seize this second opportunity to zombify the world with frightening results for viewers.

NIGHT PARTNERS
1983, USA (TV)
Yvette Mimieux, Diana Canova, Arlen Dean Snyder, M. Emmet Walsh, Patrcia McCormack, Patti Davis, Larry Linville. Directed by Noel Nosseck. 97 min.

Just what you wanted to spend money on—a mediocre pilot for a series that never happened. *Night Partners* owes a debt to the success of the series "Cagney and Lacey" in its pairing of two lady crime fighters (Yvette Mimieux and Diana Canova), but these women are merely amateurs who join forces with the Bakersfield police in a special civilian crime prevention program. The film was inspired by a true story, which again proves that fascinating fact can make boring fiction. Ronald Reagan's daughter Patti appears as a rape victim.

THE NIGHT THE LIGHTS WENT OUT IN GEORGIA ☆☆
1981, USA, PG
Kristy McNichol, Mark Hamill, Dennis Quaid, Sunny Johnson, Don Stroud, Arlen Dean Snyder. Directed by Ronald F. Maxwell. 120 min.

Dennis Quaid plays a country singer who is at least as interested in boozing and carousing as he is in singing, much to the dismay of his manager and sister, Kristy McNichol, who wants to get them off the honky-tonk circuit. As usual, the plot has almost nothing to do with the song from which the film took its title.

NIGHT MOVES ☆☆½
1975, USA, R
Gene Hackman, Jennifer Warren, Susan Clark, Edward Binns, Melanie Griffith, James Woods. Directed by Arthur Penn. 95 min.

Arthur Penn has a conventional streak (*Target*) and this *hommage au noir* has more than its share of familiar expositional devices and character sketches. Fortunately, Penn is also a skillful filmmaker and this Alan Sharp mystery about a private eye's search for a runaway (Melanie Griffith, Tippi Hedren's real-life daughter) builds to a suspenseful payoff. The infusion of the detective's urban *angst* would seem pretentious in the hands of someone other than Gene Hackman. Uneven technically (shoddy camerawork, excellent editing) but acceptable for mystery buffs.

NIGHT OF THE BLOODY APES ☆
1968, Mexico
Directed by Rene Cardona. 85 min.

In the late 1950s and early 1960s, Mexico churned out a slew of horror films inspired by the Universal classics of the 1930s. They have a cult following of their own, partly for the fact that they managed to look like they were about thirty years older than they were, but mostly for the ineptitude of the English dubbing and acting that made Bela Lugosi and John Carradine look like Richardson and Gielgud. This isn't one of those. Instead, it's a gory if equally amateurish monster epic with the standard mad scientist transplanting the heart of a gorilla into the body of his dead son. Naturally, this revives the son and turns him into a half-gorilla whacko, a phenomenon not regularly documented in the *New England Journal of Medicine.* (a.k.a. *Gomar, the Human Gorilla*)

NIGHT OF THE CLAW

See *ISLAND CLAWS*

NIGHT OF THE COBRA WOMAN ☆
1971, USA, R
Joy Bang, Marlene Clark, Roger Garrett, Vic Diaz. Directed by Andrew Meyer. 85 min.

A woman in the Philippines develops a sort of one-woman snake-worshiping cult that involves stripping down to her bra and panties with a succession of bad actors. The ubiquitous Filipino actor Vic Diaz (*Vampire Hookers, Fighting Mad*) plays his usual disgusting part.

NIGHT OF THE COMET ☆☆½
1984, USA, PG-13
Catherine Mary Stewart, Mary Woronov, Robert Beltran, Kelli Maroney. Directed by Thom Eberhardt. 100 min.

This is a clever comedy of post-apocalypse manners. Halley's Comet passes over the earth, reducing most of its population to piles of dust. Of the survivors, the majority become shambling, degenerate zombies mad for human blood. Two cute sisters Valley girl-speak their way through decimated Los Angeles, kept company by a hunk who may just be the last man on earth. With its pop-oriented visual style, offbeat humor, and a requisite appearance by Mary Woronov, *Comet* seems to have been constructed for a cult audience.

NIGHT OF THE DEMON ☆☆☆½
1957, Great Britain, PG
Dana Andrews, Peggy Cummins, Niall MacGinnis, Maurice Denham. Directed by Jacques Tourneur. 83 min.

An ancient parchment inscribed with runic symbols has the power to summon primeval evils, demonic ghouls from places outside of time and space. Prosaic situations turn into nightmares as a scientist travels the path from skepticism to uncertainty in terror. Based on the classic M. R. James short story "Casting the Runes," and directed in an atmospheric understated style that wrings out every ounce of suspense, this film was underrated at the time of its release, but has since been hailed as a horror classic by aficionados. It's a spine-tingler that delivers tension all the way up to and including its terrifying climax of demonic pursuit.

NIGHT OF THE GHOULS ☆
1959, USA
Kenne Duncan, Duke Moore, Tor Johnson, Valda Hansen, John Carpenter, Paul Marco, Criswell. Directed by Edward D. Wood, Jr. 69 min.

This follow-up to *Plan 9 from Outer Space*, most everyone's all-time favorite bad movie, was unseen until the success of Edward T. Wood's other features on the camp circuit led to its video release. Wood fans will be disappointed; it has neither Bela Lugosi nor Timothy Farrell and his fabulous neckties, previous Wood staples, and it's not so-bad-it's-funny; it's just dull. The creaky plot, which involves no ghouls, concerns a fake swami (cleverly named Dr. Acula) who unsuspectingly resurrects some of the citizenry of the local graveyard. No, that's not the same John Carpenter in the cast. For prime Wood, look for *Glen or Glenda* or *The Sinister Urge*. (a.k.a.: *Revenge of The Dead*)

THE NIGHT OF THE GRIZZLY ☆½
1966, USA
Clint Walker, Martha Hyer, Keenan Wynn, Nancy Kulp, Kevin Brodie. Directed by Joseph Pevney. 102 min.

When you show pleasant people solving ordinary, if extreme, problems, you have yourself a fairly routine, uninspired Western. In this film, the land baron has a sense of humor and the marauding bear is like Grizzly Adams with a hangover. But if you're interested in a story about a down-and-out ex-lawman rancher who hunts down a grizzly bear to get bounty money to save the ranch, this film may satisfy.

NIGHT OF THE HOWLING BEAST ☆
1975, Spain
Paul Naschy, Grace Mills, Silvia Solar, Gil Vidal. Directed by Armando de Ossorio. 87 min.

Paul Naschy is the king of hokey Spanish horror; if he's ever made a good movie, it's been hidden somewhere so as not to spoil his reputation. In this sequel to *Frankenstein's Bloody Terror* (which was actually a werewolf movie onto which the American distributor stuck the Frankenstein name for no apparent reason), Wolfman Paul howls at the Tibetan moon while on an expedition there. Competently filmed in spots, which might only prove the law of averages.

THE NIGHT OF THE IGUANA ☆☆☆½
1964, USA
Deborah Kerr, Richard Burton, Ava Gardner, Grayson Hall, Sue Lyon, Cyril Delevanti. Directed by John Huston. 125 min.

Searing adaptation of the Tennessee Williams Broadway hit. In a remote corner of Mexico, which seems to have been abandoned by God, a busload of tourists reluctantly mingle with some down-on-their-luck misfits stranded at a decrepit hotel run by resident earth mother Ava Gardner (in perhaps her best screen performance). Time seems to be running out for these lost souls, especially Richard Burton as a defrocked priest-turned-tour guide, and Deborah Kerr as a sensitive soul searching for fulfillment in the company of the world's oldest living poet. The film has steamy atmosphere, glorious Williams dialogue, and explosive performances.

NIGHT OF THE JUGGLER ☆☆
1980, USA, R
James Brolin, Cliff Gorman, Richard Castellano, Linda G. Miller, Barton Heyman, Abby Bluestone, Dan Hedaya, Mandy Patinkin. Directed by Robert Butler. 101 min.

A New York cop searches for his kidnapped daughter, in a dim-witted but furiously paced thriller that serves as little more than a long excuse for a mind-deadening tally of car chases and collisions. James Brolin, looking thick and surly beneath a heavy beard, plays the stalwart, unstoppable hero with aplomb; like most of the cast, he seems capable of better work than this. The kidnapper (Cliff Gorman) is a bundle of drooling, mother-fixated clichés, and his motives are implausible even within their somewhat ludicrous context. At least it moves quickly.

NIGHT OF THE LIVING DEAD ☆☆☆☆
1968, USA
Duane Jones, Judith O'Dea, Russell Streiner, Karl Hardman. Directed by George A. Romero. 96 min.

The dead rise from their graves, compelled by some unknown force to kill and devour the living. A small group of individuals, trapped in an isolated farmhouse, tries to ward off the relentless zombies whose ranks swell by the hour. The movie that *Variety* claimed ". . . sets a new low in box-office opportunism (and) casts doubt on all concerned, including exhibs who decide to play it." Ninety minutes of unrelenting horror shot in Pittsburgh in gritty black and white; a nightmare still as potent as the year it was made.

THE NIGHT OF THE SHOOTING STARS ☆☆☆☆
1982, Italy, R
Omero Antonutti, Margarita Lozano, Claudio Bigagli. Directed by Paolo and Vittorio Taviani. 106 min.

The Taviani Brothers have given us a new and entrancing vision of the greatest battle yet fought—World War II as a particularly savage fairy tale. The movie follows a young woman's childhood memories of the war's concluding days, when her entire community was forced to make a treacherous journey from Nazi troops in Tuscany to meet liberating American soldiers in the south of Italy. The film is an affecting mix of touching sentimentality and graphic battle violence, one that depicts mankind's monstrous mistreatment of itself, but at the same time celebrates ideals of love, courage, and freedom. Often terrifying, yet always beautiful, this is one of the most lyrical and powerful war films ever made. It was a prizewinner at Cannes.

NIGHT OF THE ZOMBIES
1983, Italy, R
Directed by Vincent Dawn. 102 min.

A government-funded project to alleviate hunger in the Third World turns out—after many disgusting goings-on—to hinge on turning the poor into cannibal zombies so they'll eat each other. This novel premise, unveiled near the end, is the best part of a standard Italian *Dawn of the Dead*-derived gross-out that features bloody special effects galore. It's not a particularly entertaining variation on the basic clichés, but it's enlivened by a few gory set pieces.

NIGHT PATROL
1985, USA, R
Linda Blair, Pat Paulsen, Jaye P. Morgan, Jack Riley, Billy Barty, Murray Langston, Pat Morita. Directed by Jackie Kong. 84 min.

With the above cast and lots of gross-out humor, this outrageously low-down farce threatens to make *Police Academy* look respectable. But there are actually a few slivers of wit floating around in the sludge. Director Jackie Kong keeps the sex jokes and awful puns whizzing by at *Airplane!* velocity, and the film's eagerness to step over the line of decency gives it a certain shameless flamboyance. There are amusing grade-C turns by Linda Blair, Pat Paulsen, and by Billy Barty as a midget police captain with a digestive problem. Definitely not for the sensitive.

THE NIGHT PORTER
1974, Italy/USA, R
Dirk Bogarde, Charlotte Rampling. Directed by Liliana Cavani. 117 min.

This look at the romantic side of S&M created quite a controversy when it was scheduled for release in the USA after having been tried for obscenity in Italy, and after breaking box-office records around Europe. The controversy died rather quickly as soon as the film got here and people got a chance to see it. Long, tedious, and anything but erotic, this equation of political fascism with emotional fascism could spark interest only in a viewer who is extremely open-minded and who has resided within a cave since 1956. Dirk Bogarde plays the title character, an ex-Nazi concentration camp guard now working at a hotel in Vienna. Along comes a camp survivor, a woman whom he had raped and abused in sadomasochistic activities. Of course, they immediately resume their "relationship," much to the distress of his pals, other surviving Nazis who fear that they will be exposed. The film is well-photographed in appropriately somber, brooding tones, but otherwise it's a drag.

THE NIGHT RIDERS
1939, USA
John Wayne, Ray Corrigan. Directed by George Sherman. 57 min.

John Wayne and story are up to par. The Three Mesquiteers fight a corrupt land grab.

NIGHT SHIFT
1982, USA, R
Henry Winkler, Michael Keaton, Shelley Long, Gina Hecht, Pat Corley, Bobby DiCicco, Nita Talbot. Directed by Ron Howard. 105 min.

Terrific performances and Ron Howard's very sure comic touch energize what could have been an abominably tasteless comedy about two morgue managers who become pimps (well, "love brokers," if you want to use their term) for a corps of goodhearted hookers whose previous agent was slain. Henry Winkler is meek and pasty enough to bring off the milquetoast role, and he takes a back seat to Michael Keaton, who sizzles in his first major role as Henry's fast-talking, deranged partner, a self-proclaimed "idea man" whose brainstorms are on the order of "Feed tunafish the mayonnaise *first*! Save a step!" As Keaton revels in his new profession—"You could never do this in Russia," he reminds us—love blossoms between Winkler and Shelley Long, who plays the kind of prostitute every man would love to reform. The film begins to fall apart near the end, but Howard and his writers (Lowell Ganz and Babaloo Mandel, who reteamed for *Splash*) give it a bright and surprisingly romantic spirit.

THE NIGHT STALKER
1972, USA (TV)
Darren McGavin, Carol Lynley, Simon Oakland, Ralph Meeker, Claude Akins, Larry Linville, Elisha Cook. Directed by John Llewellyn Moxey. 74 min.

Down-and-out newspaperman Carl Kolchak uncovers the story of a lifetime: The homicidal maniac who has been terrorizing Las Vegas is a bona fide vampire. But his efforts to make this information public knowledge (both for the good of the public and his own career) are thwarted at every turn—by his editor, by the police, and by the medical examiner's office. Kolchak takes matters into his own hands, but his efforts go unappreciated and he is soon on the road again. Ingenious and well-crafted vampire variation that was made for American television but released theatrically in Europe; it was directed by the very erratic John Llewellyn Moxey, who distinguished himself with *Horror Hotel* before settling for a series of routine thrillers. The film generated a TV series, "Kolchak: The Night Stalker," and a sequel, *The Night Strangler*.

THE NIGHT THEY RAIDED MINSKY'S
1968, USA
Jason Robards, Britt Ekland, Norman Wisdom, Forrest Tucker, Harry Andrews, Joseph Wiseman, Denholm Elliott, Elliott Gould, Jack Burns, Bert Lahr. Directed by William Friedkin. 100 min.

With detailed art direction that perfectly re-creates the atmosphere of old New York's Lower East Side, this fast-paced comedy captures all the excitement and cheap thrills of a night at a burlesque theater. Although the Amish girl-turned-stripper story line runs G-string thin—it doesn't bear close examination—the truly awful singing of those rowdy songs and a host of very talented character actors—all with their own perspective—keeps things rolling merrily along. Rudy Vallee does a voice-over introduction, and Bert Lahr, in his last film appearance, plays an affectionate aging comic seen, unfortunately, only at the beginning and the end. But it's Britt Ekland's sensual striptease—who'd have thought an Amish girl would have moves like these?—that deservedly brings down the house.

NIGHT TIME IN NEVADA
1947, USA
Roy Rogers, Adele Mara, Andy Devine. Directed by William Witney. 67 min.

Roy Rogers goes after the man who stole his cattle, and Andy Devine entertains well as the bungling, helpful police officer. The movie is only average, but Roy sings "The Big Rock Candy Mountain."

NIGHT TRAIN TO MEMPHIS
1946, USA
Roy Acuff, Adele Mara, Irving Bacon. Directed by Lesley Selander. 66 min.

Country musician Roy Acuff plays the hero who comes between the hillbillies and the railroad in this corny movie. There is an offensive use of black players Nicodemus Stewart and Nina Mae McKinney for some dubious comedy.

THE NIGHT VISITOR
1970, USA, PG ★★★
Max von Sydow, Trevor Howard, Liv Ullman, Per Oscarsson, Rupert Davies, Andrew Kier. Directed by Laslo Benedek. 106 min.

An excellent cast, including a trio of Ingmar Bergman regulars, is the main reason to see this good if minor thriller. Max von Sydow, a peaceable Swedish farmer, is falsely accused of a vicious murder and committed to an insane asylum by his sister (Liv Ullman) and her husband (Per Oscarsson). The experience really does drive him insane, and he concocts an ingenious plan to wreak revenge while supplying himself with a perfect alibi. It's rather slow going, and the ending is a letdown, but it's interesting watching nonetheless.

NIGHT WARNING
1982, USA ★★½
Susan Tyrrell, Jimmy McNichol, Julia Duffy, Bo Svenson. Directed by William Asher. 90 min.

A febrile horror movie whose message is that young love conquers all, including multiple murders, illegitimate parentage, and sexual prejudices. Laced with a pernicious undertone of cruelty and sadism, this incredible concoction makes the fatal mistake of cluing us in to the killer's identity from the outset. The familiar scare tactics carry more stylistic conviction than in most slasher pictures, although the ramshackle plotting must also survive the onslaught of Susan Tyrrell's full-throttle performance. As Cheryl, an overly possessive aunt fond of fondling her nephew and discussing her problems with the preserved head of her lover (which she keeps in the basement!), Tyrrell really keeps this implausible farrago of stimuli consistently entertaining. Perpetually in motion, her mannerisms rival those of Geraldine Page, and one can only hope she will one day star in a remake of *Whatever Happened to Baby Jane?* with Shelley Winters.

NIGHTWING
1979, USA, PG ★
Nick Mancuso, David Warner, Kathryn Harrold, Stephen Macht, Strother Martin. Directed by Arthur Hiller. 110 min.

Before he created E.T., special effects ace Carlo Rambaldi designed the bats for this tepid little shrieker about a Southwestern Indian reservation menaced by the little monsters. The problem is that Rambaldi's bats are about as scary as the Smurfs—they're nothing you couldn't handle with a broomstick and a little diligence. The native American locale means that you're going to hear a lot of blather about evil shamans, sacred ground, and the Turbulent Wrath of the Spirits. Italian Nick Mancuso plays the Indian who went to Yale and briefly strayed, but has not forgotten the old ways. He spouts enough prairie folklore to send an entire troop of Boy Scouts screaming for the exits, and you leaping for the "off" button.

NINE DEATHS OF THE NINJA
1985, USA, R ½★
Sho Kosugi, Brent Huff, Emilia Lesniak, Blackie Dammett, Regina Richardson. Directed by Emmet Alston. 94 min.

In the kung fu genre generated by Bruce Lee, this is the fourth bout for Sho Kosugi, whose determination to outlive Lee extends even to posterity: Among the cast are his sons Kane and Shane, who sound as if they were inspired by Hollywood movie greats. Kosugi, who is not above camping up his ninja sagas, leads a squad of rescuers kicking and screaming after an American tour bus that is hijacked in the Philippines by an odd variety of political misfits.

9½ WEEKS
1986, USA, R ★
Mickey Rourke, Kim Basinger, Margaret Whitton, David Margulies, Christine Baranski, Karen Young. Directed by Adrian Lyne. 115 min.

A fiasco of jaw-dropping proportions. In Adrian Lyne's glazed, torpid movie about a sadomasochistic affair, Mickey Rourke is a rich commodities broker who picks up the sultry yet vague Kim Basinger and leads her, circle by circle, into the exquisite hell of psychological domination. In the world according to director Lyne (*Flashdance*), sex is just another image, and life is an empty, soft-core daydream. He portrays bent sex as a replacement for consumerism—as the thing bored folks do when there's nothing left to buy. There's no force to the obsession, because Basinger's heroine/victim is such a cipher she barely has a soul to lose. And Rourke just smirks his way through the movie; he's passed beyond narcissism into a kind of death-defying smugness. *Note*: The version on video includes scenes not shown in the American theatrically released version; they don't help at all. Based on the novel by the pseudonymous Elizabeth McNeill.

NINE TO FIVE
1980, USA, PG ★★½
Jane Fonda, Lily Tomlin, Dolly Parton, Dabney Coleman, Sterling Hayden, Elisabeth Fraser, Henry Jones. Directed by Colin Higgins. 110 min.

Three overworked and underpaid secretaries plot to take over the office from their ogre of a boss. This box-office hit was hailed by feminists as a plea for improved working conditions, but it owes more to *I Love Lucy* than to *Born in Flames*. In the last half of the film, for example, most of the polemics are sidetracked by frantic, unfunny slapstick. Still, it's agreeable if lightweight escapism notable for Lily Tomlin playing the wisecracking senior office worker who is unfairly passed over for a promotion, and for Dolly Parton (in her screen debut) as a sweet but tough woman who doesn't go in for after-hours "funny business." Jane Fonda as the newcomer learning the ropes is both miscast and awful. The highlight is a fantasy sequence in which the three women daydream of killing the boss, each in her own special way.

1918
1984, USA, PG ★½
Matthew Broderick, Hallie Foote, William Converse-Roberts, Rochelle Oliver, Michael Higgins. Directed by Ken Harrison. 91 min.

This Texas-set family saga should be called *When Bad Things Happen to Dull People*. It's tidy enough to fit on a sampler: Every citizen we meet in the fictional town of Harrison assumes his or her proper square in screenwriter Horton Foote's homespun tapestry. Not only is *1918* stagy and "theatrical" in the worst way, but it's dull, resoundingly undramatic, and written so poorly that you'll hardly believe Foote's previous work included *Tender Mercies* and *To Kill a Mockingbird*. Foote simply presents the characters and then has misfortunes befall them. When the film ends, you may feel as if you've just seen Part 5 of a miniseries you'd hoped to avoid. The sets and costumes look like sets and costumes, and although Hallie Foote (the writer's daughter) gives a good, in-period performance as a beleaguered wife, the usually reliable Matthew Broderick is startlingly awful. Followed by a related film, *On Valentine's Day*. (a.k.a.: *Horton Foote's 1918*)

1984
1984, Great Britain, R ★★½
John Hurt, Suzanna Hamilton, Richard Burton, Cyril Cusack, Gregor Fisher, James Walker, Andrew Wilde. Directed by Michael Radford. 122 min.

Someone had to do the obvious and make a film of the book in the year of the book and, although it was a race against time and copyright, Michael Radford managed it. (A previous version was directed by Michael Anderson in 1955.) The film is a scrupulously fair version of Orwell's novel, from its 1940s design to its chilling story of a future society in which actions, thoughts, and emotions are controlled. The washed-out, eyesore look of the film is, if hideous, at least appropriate, and Richard Burton, in his last screen role, gives a strong performance as the interrogator who finally brings Winston Smith (John Hurt) to love Big Brother. *1984* is overlong, and made with such unvarying good taste and somber restraint that it finally becomes rather dull, but the obvious care Radford has taken mitigates many of its flaws. With a score by Eurythmics, truncated shortly before release, and a final dedication to Burton.

1941 ☆☆☆
1979, USA, PG
John Belushi, Christopher Lee, Toshiro Mifune, Ned Beatty, Robert Stack, Dan Aykroyd, Treat Williams, Nancy Allen, Tim Matheson, Warren Oates, Dianne Kay. Directed by Steven Spielberg. 118 min.

This freewheeling story of post-Pearl Harbor war panic in California is a slapstick account of the American entry into World War II, beginning with an off-course Japanese submarine surfacing between the limbs of a nude bather in California, and ending with chunks of L.A. real estate sliding away. With its astonishing fantasy of flights and crashes, an illuminated ferris wheel that rolls into the ocean, and a few sensational sets, this mammoth entertainment is due for reappraisal since it was savaged by the critics when first released.

92 IN THE SHADE ☆☆
1975, USA, R
Peter Fonda, Warren Oates, Margot Kidder, Burgess Meredith, Harry Dean Stanton, William Hickey, Louise Latham, Sylvia Miles, Elizabeth Ashley. Directed by Thomas McGuane. 91 min.

Thomas McGuane's gloomy, cynical novel about a rivalry between two small-time fishing guides in the Florida Keys doesn't come across well in this screen adaptation, which he wrote and directed. Peter Fonda plays a young boatman who starts a war he can't win with the deranged Warren Oates, but neither character is as interesting as those on the story's fringes, and the plot goes nowhere. McGuane's salty script is shot through with despair and an unspoken but clear disgust with the establishment. The sporadic speechmaking about democracy and nonintervention suggests that the frail story was meant as a metaphor for weightier matters, but it eventually crumbles under the weight of its pretensions.

99 AND 44/100% DEAD ☆½
1974, USA, PG
Richard Harris, Edmond O'Brien, Bradford Dillman, Ann Turkel, Constance Ford, Chuck Connors. Directed by John Frankenheimer. 98 min.

Richard Harris underplays as usual as a hired gun caught up in a gang war between rival mobsters Edmond O'Brien and Bradford Dillman. The "Batman"-style pop-art opening credits promise a campy spoof along the lines of *Modesty Blaise*, but it wavers uncertainly between that and straight action. John Frankenheimer does all right with most of the shoot-'em-up sequences, but he seems at a loss for how to handle the rest of this unfocused film.

NINJA EXTERMINATORS ☆
Hong Kong
Han Koon-Wan Lun, Hun Chung Sin, Au Su Leung, Richy Lam. Directed by Tai Cher.

Ho-hum action and a routine plot about a police inspector (he's attempting to clear a man of trumped-up murder and rape charges) all but bury this film—until an exciting finale injects life into the proceedings.

NINJA III: THE DOMINATION ☆☆
1984, USA, R
Sho Kosugi, Lucinda Dickey, Jordan Bennet, David Chung. Directed by Sam Firstenberg. 95 min.

A fierce action picture wrapped in a dull story of a young woman's possession—a sort of Bruce Lee meets *The Exorcist*. The girl inhabited by the spirit of a deadly black ninja is woodenly portrayed by the nonetheless appealing Lucinda Dickey, the young star of *Breakin' 1* and *2*. Dickey's amateurish fighting and stodgy acting are offset by the graceful, humorous Sho Kosugi, and the movie's first fifteen minutes are absolute dynamite. The film suffers from a standardized Golan-Globus prepackaged feel and features several stupid aerobics sequences.

NINOTCHKA ☆☆☆½
1939, USA
Greta Garbo, Melvyn Douglas, Ina Claire, Sig Ruman, Felix Bressart. Directed by Ernst Lubitsch. 110 min.

"Garbo Laughs!" ballyhooed the ads for this sparkling romantic comedy about a stodgy Russian emissary (Greta Garbo in her first American comedy role) who meets a charming American capitalist (Melvyn Douglas) while on assignment in Paris. The satire leveled at the Soviets is predictable and director Ernst Lubitsch never had a good sense of pace, but individual scenes showcase the Garbo talent at its best. There have been retreads and remakes of *Ninotchka* (including the Cole Porter musical *Silk Stockings*), but none of them have Greta Garbo's mesmerizing performance.

THE NINTH CONFIGURATION ☆☆☆
1980, USA
Stacy Keach, Jason Miller, Scott Wilson, Ed Flanders, Neville Brand, Moses Gunn. Directed by William Peter Blatty. 118 min.

Unfairly underrated when first released as *Twinkle, Twinkle, Killer Kane*, this intriguing film has improved with age. If you liked *The Manchurian Candidate* or *Winter Kill*, you'll want to give it a chance to work its quirky spell on you. Delving into the myths surrounding the Pentagon's imperturbability, the film examines the unorthodox psychiatric treatment received by top-ranking military officers in a secret research program. Based on William Peter Blatty's surreal novel, the movie is a suspenseful, thoughtful drama probing the nature of sanity and madness. There are superb actors in an occasionally confusing but highly original film. (a.k.a.: *Twinkle, Twinkle, Killer Kane*)

NOBODY'S FOOL ☆½
1986, USA, PG-13
Rosanna Arquette, Eric Roberts, Jim Youngs, Mare Winningham, Louise Fletcher, Gwen Welles, Stephen Tobolowsky, Ann Hearn, Belita Moreno, Charlie Barnett. Directed by Evelyn Purcell. 107 min.

In this foolish small-town comedy screenwrite, Beth Henley (a Pulitzer Prize-winner for *Crimes of the Heart*) fails to distance herself from this loose, sloppy material based on her own youthful pining for an acting career. A slightly whacked-out country bumpkin whose self-esteem was shattered by the town stud slowly builds a positive image of herself by trying out for amateur theatrics. When a visiting Shakespearean troupe sets up shop in her community, she falls for acting and for a darkly handsome technician who manufactures magic for her on and off the stage. This is congealed fantasy masquerading as a screenplay, and Henley's condescending attitude toward the locals is offensive and familiar. Although Eric Roberts is effectively subdued as the brooding Prince Charming, Rosanna Arquette makes a rather tattered and pushy Cinderella.

NOBODY'S PERFECT ☆☆
1968, USA
Doug McClure, Nancy Kwan, James Whitman, David Hartman, Gary Vinson. Directed by Alan Rafkin. 103 min.

The spirit of the sixties lurks beneath even the innocuous decks of oceanic comedies like *McHale's Navy*, *The Wackiest Ship in the Army*, and this film. Here, the strict and microcosmic shipboard ranking is genially gutted by a low-level grunt (Doug McClure) who is smart and sympathetic but against the fine grain of the manual. It seems that some Eastern establishment figure from Annapolis (Gary Vinson) always erects roadblocks to fun. In the end, the grunt finds vindication proving that rules were made to be bent. More consistent than most ship-operas, *Nobody's Perfect* features watertight performances but a merely service-level script. The antics, like strewing the skipper's cabin with cockroaches, sometimes seem less manic than anemic; a middling movie, but it floats.

NOCTURNA ☆
1979, USA
Yvonne De Carlo, John Carradine, Nai Bonet, Tony Hamilton, Brother Theodore. Directed by Henry Tampa. 85 min.

Dracula's granddaughter is short on cash, so she turns the family castle into the swinging Hotel Transylvania. This is a vanity production for esteemed belly dancer Nai Bonet, who gyrates her way through an unending supply of gauzy, artfully slit costumes. The disco sounds of 1970s divas Vicki Sue Robinson and Gloria Gaynor are piped in while seminude starlets writhe in pleasure and Yvonne De Carlo glowers distractedly.

NO DEPOSIT NO RETURN ☆
1976, USA, G
David Niven, Darren McGavin, Don Knotts, Herschel Bernardi, Barbara Feldon, Kim Richards, Brad Savage. Directed by Norman Tokar. 112 min.

Even the most distinguished of screen actors will always have at least a couple of dogs in his career; this is one of David Niven's. He plays, somewhat tiredly, the grandfather of two irrepressible tykes put in his charge by their carefree mother. A pair of comically bumbling kidnappers soon gives the youngsters more of an adventure than they'd ever hoped for. This being a Disney adventure, everything works out happily and there's nothing in it to scare kids—nor to interest them.

NOMADS ☆☆
1986, USA, R
Pierce Brosnan, Lesley-Anne Down, Ann-Maria Montecelli, Adam Ant, Hector Mercado, Josie Cotton, Mary Woronov, Frank Doubleday, Frances Bay, Tim Wallace. Directed by John McTiernan. 95 min.

A doctor has a disturbing emergency room experience with a bloody, apparently demented derelict and soon finds herself forced to relive the terrifying last days of the doomed man. He turns out to have been a world-famous French anthropologist, fatally intrigued by a band of urban wanderers who are actually malevolent spirits in the forms of punks, junkies, and whores. This well-made, sometimes genuinely creepy film is sadly undermined by a weak ending, but it features great performances from all involved, including a supporting cast of rock singers and cult personalities.

NO MERCY ☆☆
1986, USA, R
Richard Gere, Kim Basinger, Jeroen Krabbe, George Dzundza, Gary Basaraba, William Atherton, Terry Kinney, Bruce McGill, Ray Sharkey. Directed by Richard Pearce. 107 min.

This handsome but predictable (and implausible) cop thriller set in sultry New Orleans, where a Chicago cop (Richard Gere) out to avenge his partner's murder finds himself involved with a beautiful woman (Kim Basinger) who's the bought-and-paid-for property of the crime lord of a red-light district (seen in the same context in *Angel Heart*) called Algiers. Gere gives another one of his scowling poster-boy performances, and Basinger, who seems to have been hosed down before every shot, is properly decorative but almost mute; individually they're sexy, but the chemistry between them is nonexistent, and for much of the film's unfortunate first half they run through the bayou chained together, looking coiffed and grumpy. What works in Jim Carabatsos's script is the cartoonish he-man dialogue and the portrayal of the menacing, virtually indestructible villain (the Dutch actor Jeroen Krabbe, sporting a ninja ponytail and a lead coat), but there's not an original moment in his slack plotting and stock characterizations. Stylishly directed by Richard Pearce, whose previous work (*Heartland* and *Country*) doesn't prepare you for the brutality and lurid neon look of this film.

NONE BUT THE LONELY HEART ☆☆☆
1944, USA
Cary Grant, Ethel Barrymore, Barry Fitzgerald, June Duprez, Jane Wyatt, George Coulouris, Dan Duryea, Roman Bohnen. Directed by Clifford Odets. 110 min.

Cary Grant never won an Oscar; he was nominated, however, for this showy, all-out dramatic role as an East End drifter who tries to help his dying mother by working for a gangster. Playwright Clifford Odets (*Golden Boy*, *The Country Girl*) wrote the screenplay and made his directorial debut here, but the artistic strain shows: There are too many talky passages in difficult-to-understand cockney. Jane Wyatt is too American as Grant's love interest, but Ethel Barrymore (who won a Best Supporting Actress Oscar) is perfect as his terminally ill mother.

NO NUKES ☆☆
1980, USA, PG
Concert/documentary. Performances by Jackson Browne, Crosby, Stills and Nash, The Doobie Brothers, John Hall, Bonnie Raitt, Gil Scott-Heron, Carly Simon, Bruce Springsteen, James Taylor, Jesse Colin Young, others. Directed by Julian Schlossberg, Danny Goldberg, and Anthony Potenza. 103 min.

The benefit concerts staged in 1979 by Musicians United for Safe Energy (MUSE) marshaled an impressive array of talent for a worthy cause—but how much shoddiness can a worthy cause excuse? Shamefully rotten sets (by Crosby, Stills and Nash, among others) alternate with dull ones (by John Hall and a few more), and all have been execrably photographed and edited; even Bruce Springsteen can't save the show, though he does his damnedest with roof-raising versions of "Thunder Road" and "Quarter to Three." It's occasionally stirring, but mostly secondhand in feeling.

NO RETREAT, NO SURRENDER ½☆
1986, USA, PG
Kurt McKinney, Jean Claude Van Damme, J. W. Fails, Kathie Sileno. Directed by Corey Yuen. 90 min.

They just don't come any worse than this—amateur actors, terrible post-dubbing, laughably poor martial arts stuntwork, a non-English-speaking supporting cast, a would-be Russian villain with a French accent, and an extended homage to Bruce Lee by an actor playing (we kid you not) his ghost. The scattershot plot concerns a young fighter who idolizes Lee, who luckily becomes undead just in time to train him for a match with monster-Commie Ivan. Even the title is a ripoff—from a Bruce Springsteen lyric.

THE NORMAN CONQUESTS ☆☆☆
1977, Great Britain
Richard Briers, Penelope Keith, Tom Conti, David Troughton, Penelope Wilton. Directed by Herbert Wise. Three tapes, 100 min. each.

British television adapted this trilogy from a series of plays by Alan Ayckbourn, a popular comic playwright sometimes referred to as the English Neil Simon. As with all of Ayckbourn's idiosyncratic work, *The Norman Conquests* was far more successful in the U.K. then in the U.S., where it had a short run on the Broadway stage. Each segment of the trilogy explores relationships among the same cast on the same weekend at the same home. Although each play stands alone, the three interconnect such that the events in each occur simultaneously with the others. When a character leaves the living room in one segment, he may be entering a bedroom in another. The device works niftily and testifies to Ayckbourn's indisputable abilities as a craftsman. As an artist, however, the playwright often falls short. The humor is quintessentially English—droll and understated. Ayckbourn imbues the characters with a calculated inertia, revealing the sadness and emotional chaos lurking beneath the comic veneer. But the pacing becomes increasingly leaden, despite largely good performances from this particular cast. Ayckbourn's characterizations tend to be more shallow than clever and his comic touch falters nearly as often as it succeeds.

NORMA RAE ☆☆☆½
1979, USA, PG
Sally Field, Ron Liebman, Beau Bridges, Pat Hingle, Barbara Baxley, Gail Strickland. Directed by Martin Ritt. 114 min.

Sally Field won both the Academy Award and the Cannes film festival prize for her vivid portrayal of a Southern textile worker whose unremarkable life is changed by the arrival of a union organizer (Ron Liebman) from New York. Martin Ritt's triumphant mounting of this depiction of a brave, unforgettable woman is among his best work; he's right at home with this kind of populist-inspirational material. Field, even for nonfans, is especially impressive—you can see her struggling (successfully) to make Norma Rae a real woman, warts and all, and deglamorize herself in the process. Norma Rae isn't terribly complex, but on its own level it's thoroughly successful. The lovely theme song, "It Goes Like It Goes," won an Oscar.

THE NORSEMAN ½☆
1978, USA, PG
Lee Majors, Cornel Wilde, Mel Ferrer, Jack Elam, Chris Connelly, Kathleen Freeman, Charles B. Pierce, Jr. Directed by Charles B. Pierce, Sr. 90 min.

This is one of the worst Viking movies ever made, and if you think about what stinkers most Viking movies are, you'll realize what powerful company that puts this in. Tenth-century Prince Thorvald (good Viking name, eh?) sets sail for America to rescue his father, who has been captured there by savage eye-gouging Indians. Lee Majors, whose production company funded this farce, looks like he's out for a weekend at the health club, while Cornel Wilde at least has the sense to stay out of his way. Charles B. Pierce, Jr. has the distinction of being the only member of the cast to look even vaguely like a real Viking.

EL NORTE ☆☆☆½
1983, USA
Zaide Silvia Gutierrez, David Villalpando, Ernesto Gomez Cruz, Alicia del Lago, Eraclio Zepeda, Stella Quan. Directed by Gregory Nava. 139 min.

This powerful, lyrical film tells the tale of the harrowing exodus of two persecuted Indians, a brother and sister, from Guatemala to "El Norte," the United States. Director Gregory Nava has filled this exquisitely photographed work with a series of startling, lingering close-ups of objects that together form a haunting thematic thread traversing the narrative. In its style and imagery, Nava's film recalls the tone of Gabriel Garcia Marquez. James Glennon is responsible for the beautiful cinematography that graces this disturbing, provocative film. Nava and his wife, Anna Thomas, won an Oscar nomination for their screenplay.

NORTH BY NORTHWEST ☆☆☆½
1959, USA
Cary Grant, Eva Marie Saint, James Mason, Jessie Royce Landis, Leo G. Carroll, Philip Ober. Directed by Alfred Hitchcock. 136 min.

A series of imaginative set pieces—a crop-dusting attack, a disrupted auction, a chase on a cross-country locomotive, a scramble on the faces of Mt. Rushmore—all highlight one of Hitchcock's most romantic, stylish, and suspenseful thrillers. Cary Grant plays an unsuspecting American businessman who becomes embroiled in a sinister espionage plot; Eva Marie Saint costars as a beautiful double (or triple) agent with whom he falls in love. Saint is not the most alluring of Hitchcock heroines, but Grant and James Mason are matchless as hero and villain, respectively. It's Hitchcock at his most playful.

NORTH DALLAS FORTY ☆☆☆
1979, USA, R
Nick Nolte, Mac Davis, Dayle Haddon, Bo Svenson, Dabney Coleman, John Matuszak, Charles Durning, G. D. Spradlin. Directed by Ted Kotcheff. 120 min.

This sardonic, foulmouthed comedy-drama about life on and off the gridiron for an aging wide receiver (Nick Nolte) shares a lot with Semi-Tough in its jaundiced, wise view of the psychology of professional sports, but this film cuts a little closer to the bone. Nolte, thick and bruised, wryly underplays the athlete who's living on painkillers and post-game parties, and wondering about life after Super Bowl Sunday. Mac Davis is also good as his wisecracking best friend, the quarterback. The perspective (which comes from Peter Gent's book) doesn't idolize the athletes, and they're more human here than in many more conventional sports dramas.

NORTH OF THE GREAT DIVIDE ☆☆
1950, USA
Roy Rogers, Penny Edwards, Roy Barcroft, Trigger, The Riders of the Purple Sage. Directed by William Witney. 67 min.

This is routine but enjoyable fare from Roy Rogers, with one interesting twist here—the cowboy's on the side of the Indians, defending them from gunslinging evil palefaces. Penny Edwards substitutes effectively in the Dale Evans role, and solid direction from William Witney keeps you from noticing that by this point, the Republic series had pretty much run out of gas.

NORTHERN PURSUIT ☆☆☆
1943, USA
Errol Flynn, Julie Bishop, Helmut Dantine, John Ridgely, Gene Lockhart, Tom Tully, Monte Blue, Bernard Nedell. Directed by Raoul Walsh. 93 min.

Errol Flynn lends his masculine dash to this story of Nazis in the frozen North. He plays a mountie who tracks down a spy and, by affecting fascist leanings, infiltrates his ring. Julie Bishop is just fine in her undemanding role of the faithful woman who tags along so that the Nazis will have someone to capture; Helmut Dantine is suitably evil as the villain. Flynn's stalwart acting finds companionable direction in the machine-tooled efficiency of Raoul Walsh, and this should please fans of forties action films. There are plenty of fights and gun battles to keep things rolling, and the snowy location shooting is crisp and good-looking.

NOSFERATU ☆☆☆☆
1922, Germany
Max Schreck, Gustav von Wangenheim, Greta Schroeder, Alexander Granach. Directed by F. W. Murnau. 72 min. in original American release; see review.

F. W. Murnau's classic silent vampire film about a stick-thin, spiderlike apparition who arrives in Bremen in a rat-infested death ship, carrying his own coffin under one arm and spreading plague. Murnau's use of fast motion and expressionistic lighting may seem campy at first, but the creaky, silent-film ambience actually embodies, more than any other vampire film, the Victorian sexual nightmares immortalized by Bram Stoker's novel. Max Schreck's vampire is one of the most visually memorable characterizations in horror history. Note: Nosferatu exists in many different versions on video, some with music and some without; the prints used range in running time from fifty-four to eighty-seven minutes; we recommend viewing the longest version you can find. (a.k.a. Nosferatu the Vampire, not to be confused with Carl Dreyer's Vampire)

NOSFERATU THE VAMPYRE ☆☆☆½
1978, West Germany
Klaus Kinski, Isabelle Adjani, Bruno Ganz, Ronald Torpor. Directed by Werner Herzog. 106 min.

Werner Herzog's Nosferatu recreates F. W. Murnau's silent film in color and sound. Made up in whiteface with front-

and-center fangs, Klaus Kinski plays another in his and Herzog's gallery of dangerous eccentrics (he also portrayed Aguirre and Fitzcarraldo), this time the most isolated social outcast of all the vampires. The settings are constantly atmospheric, and the images are often nothing less than astonishing—like the raft of coffins swept down a torrential river or the 10,000 specially bred rats that plagued the set. Although it lacks the force of the original silent version with a remarkable Max Schreck, this dreamy re-creation offers subtle pleasures and is often spellbinding due to a superb cast, especially Isabelle Adjani as the pure heroine and Ronald Torpor as Nosferatu's insane groupie.

NO SMALL AFFAIR ☆☆½
1984, USA, R
Jon Cryer, Demi Moore, George Wendt, Peter Frechette, Elizabeth Daily, Anne Wedgeworth, Jennifer Tilly. Directed by Jerry Schatzberg. 103 min.

Typical adolescent fantasy about a sixteen-year-old camera nut who falls for a twenty-two-year-old rock singer and won't stop bugging her until he's helped her to win fame and fortune—but director Jerry Schatzberg treats his characters with unusual respect and gets modestly pleasing results. As the love-struck hero, Jon Cryer adds a surprisingly sour tang to the usual bubbly-dreamer clichés. As his object of his desire, Demi Moore is convincing in the role of an ambitious small-timer whose middling career is starting to turn her bitter. Interesting, if only because it's so much more brittle than most teen films.

NOT FOR PUBLICATION ☆☆
1984, USA/Great Britain, R
Nancy Allen, David Naughton, Laurence Luckinbill, Alice Ghostley, Richard Paul, Barry Dennen. Directed by Paul Bartel. 87 min.

This Paul Bartel comedy casts Nancy Allen as a reporter for a National Enquirer–type weekly and David Naughton as her sidekick-photographer. The very old-fashioned plot has the charming couple crusading to clean up a politically dirty town and restore their paper to its former greatness. The exposition is so excessive and the twists so tedious that you may want to write it off as a total failure, but amid the muck and mire are a few moments of stingingly funny satire. Good performances from the two leads make it bearable.

NOTHING IN COMMON ☆☆½
1986, USA, PG
Tom Hanks, Jackie Gleason, Eva Marie Saint, Hector Elizondo, Barry Corbin, Sela Ward, Bess Armstrong. Directed by Garry Marshall. 118 min.

The ways in which adults interact (or refuse to) with their aging parents is a potentially great theme, and although Garry Marshall's comedy-drama makes a valiant attempt to explore it, it just doesn't work—the humor is bright and convincing, but the drama is soggy. Tom Hanks plays a fast-talking, obnoxious young ad executive who, when a woman asks if he's involved with anyone, replies, "Does self-involved count?" But when his parents split up and one becomes ill, feelings of filial duty, resentment, and love come to the surface for the first time in years. The ad agency scenes, in which he tries to win the account and the daughter of an airline president, are sitcom-clever, and Hanks gives a wonderful, versatile performance in an only semi-sympathetic role. But all of the other characters are just sketched in, and Jackie Gleason and Eva Marie Saint, as the parents, have nothing but the most familiar clichés to work with. It's an honorable failure, though, and worth a look if the subject interests you. Later a television series.

NOTHING PERSONAL ☆☆
1980, Canada/USA, PG
Donald Sutherland, Suzanne Somers, Lawrence Dane, Dabney Coleman, Roscoe Lee Browne, Saul Rubinek, Catherine O'Hara, Kate Lynch, Eugene Levy, Joe Flaherty, Joe Rosato. Directed by George Bloomfield. 96 min.

The cast of this tired populist farce is so loaded with pleasant faces, few used to good advantage, that they almost manage to hide the lack of a screenplay. But only almost. Donald Sutherland, as a professor of constitutional law, and Suzanne Somers, in her film debut as a top Washington attorney (isn't typecasting a terrible thing?) team up to keep the government from killing baby seals. The measure of the film's success comes when you find yourself rooting for the guys with the clubs. Somers is marginally better here than on television, but only because she gets to say *real* dirty things instead of pubescent ones.

NOTHING SACRED ☆☆☆
1937, USA
Carole Lombard, Fredric March, Charles Winninger, Sig Ruman. Directed by William Wellman. 75 min.

Carole Lombard, one of the screen's greatest comediennes, sparkles as a young woman used by a newspaper for a circulation stunt. Screenwriter Ben Hecht, himself a veteran journalist and author of The Front Page, takes a razor both to mendacious journalists and to the morbid public with his lacerating story about a girl's supposed dying of radiation poisoning.

NO TIME FOR SERGEANTS ☆☆½
1958, USA
Andy Griffith, Myron McCormick, Nick Adams, Murray Hamilton, Howard Smith, Don Knotts. Directed by Mervyn LeRoy. 111 min.

From the wacky military comedies of the 1950s that caused cold war senators to reevaluate America's preparedness to fight the commies, this one mixes "The Andy Griffith Show" and "Gomer Pyle" as Andy himself plays the backwoodsman who disrupts the Air Force with his simple but honest approach to life. Director Mervyn LeRoy's third attempt at the story—with several actors taking roles from previous versions—makes the comedy smooth and facile, if slightly familiar. Myron McCormick does an excellent slow burn as the sergeant who wants to put Griffith far, far away. The film's a must for Griffith Show fans because it includes a hilarious cameo from none other than Don Knotts.

NOT MY KID ☆☆☆
1985, USA (TV)
George Segal, Stockard Channing, Viveka Davis, Crista Denton. Directed by Michael Tuchner. 100 min.

A harrowing TV drama about teenage drug addicts that explores the crisis of a suburban family when mom and dad discover their fifteen-year-old daughter (Viveka Davis) is an alcoholic methadone addict who's becoming increasingly violent. The extreme horror of the situation is made unusually credible by fine acting and direction, but the group therapy and recovery scenes take a turn toward predictability.

NOTORIOUS ☆☆☆☆
1946, USA
Ingrid Bergman, Cary Grant, Claude Rains, Leopoldine Konstantin, Louis Calhern. Directed by Alfred Hitchcock. 101 min.

Hitchcock is at his most gripping in this taut, exquisitely filmed and finely acted romantic spy thriller. Ingrid Bergman plays a woman with a past whom the United States enlists to spy on Nazi activities in Brazil after the war. Cary Grant is an equally hardened American agent whose cynicism keeps him from expressing his love for Bergman. This film contains some of the most memorable moments in the Hitchcock catalog—the prolonged passionate embrace; the revelation in the wine cellar; the climactic, painfully suspenseful descent down the staircase; and many, many others. Grant's performance is among the greatest of his career; Bergman is exquisite. Claude Rains is suave and sinister, the exemplary Hitchcockian villain. Together, they make this tale of romance and deception utterly compelling.

NOT QUITE PARADISE
☆½
1986, USA, R
Sam Robards, Joanna Pacula, Ewan Stewart, Selina Cadell. Directed by Lewis Gilbert. 157 min.

If this film is "not quite" paradise, then paradise itself must be a major disappointment. Hurled like puppets by an arbitrary scriptwriter onto kibbutz Kfar Ezra, a dozen caricatures amble around searching for the worst moments to deliver banal punch lines. There are two British boys who, being British, think of nothing but Swedish sex; there is the New York Jewish family who apparently believes every good cliché needs some people to enact it. Joanna Pacula and Sam Robards are puzzlingly heartless as *Paradise*'s Adam and Eve, the directing and editing were done with sledgehammers and hatchets, and the script is about as hilarious as the Suez Canal.

NOUS ETIONS UN SEUL HOMME

See *We Were One Man*

NOW AND FOREVER
☆
1983, Australia, R
Cheryl Ladd, Robert Coleby, Carmen Duncan, Christine Amor. Directed by Adrian Carr. 92 min.

Angels die hard—when they can't get work in overstuffed miniseries, silly comedies, or "Night of 100 Stars" specials, they go to Australia in the hopes that someone will remember their mid-1970s glory days. This time, Cheryl Ladd opts for the suffering wife role as a young woman whose husband is wrongly imprisoned for rape. What can she do but sit at home, change her costume, cry a little, change her costume, cry some more, think about changing her costume again . . . and, of course, promise to love him now and forever. The gauzy, tame sex scenes makes this less suitable for voyeurs than for Danielle Steele fans who like to daydream about how much fun it would be to live in an exotic land, have a sad past, and be able to cheer up just by looking in the closet.

NO WAY TO TREAT A LADY
☆☆½
1968, USA
Rod Steiger, Lee Remick, George Segal, Eileen Heckart, Murray Hamilton. Directed by Jack Smight. 108 min.

This darkly comic crime drama would be nothing without the virtuoso performance of Rod Steiger as a literal lady-killer with a mother fixation who is chased by a harried police detective (George Segal). Steiger's disguises in the murder scenes (as a priest, handyman, cop, old woman, etc.) give the film color and the hammy actor a chance to really show his stuff. Unfortunately, the romance between Segal and Lee Remick (as a museum tour guide) is pedestrian, and the Jewish-comedy schtick with Eileen Heckart as Segal's overbearing mother looks like the worst outtakes from *Butterflies Are Free* (you wish Steiger would bump *her* off). The resolution is also predictable and poorly staged, with Steiger in a shamefully long, operatic death scene. It's best to see this for the good if undisciplined star at work.

NOWHERE TO RUN
☆☆☆
1978, USA (TV)
David Janssen, Stefanie Powers, Allen Garfield, Neva Patterson, Linda Evans. Directed by Richard Lang. 100 min.

As if running all over the place in "The Fugitive" wasn't enough, David Janssen took on this TV film about trying to escape from the clutches of his mercenary wife and her tenacious private detective. The characterizations are well-drawn and you'll be rooting for Janssen as he tries to finagle his way out of a tight spot in order to be free of his former wife's money lust. A top-notch TV cast will make you glad you stayed put to watch this wily husband's schemes unfold.

NOW, VOYAGER
☆☆☆
1942, USA
Bette Davis, Claude Rains, Paul Henreid, Gladys Cooper, Janis Wilson. Directed by Irving Rapper. 118 min.

Bette Davis is superb as a neurotically repressed Boston heiress who is transformed by psychiatrist Claude Rains from an obsessively aloof spinster to a vibrant young woman. Paul Henreid plays the impossible object of her affections in this ultra-glossy melodrama. Davis's acting field day is enhanced by Max Steiner's Oscar-winning score, Henreid's stylish cigarette-lighting technique, and the immortal last line, "Don't let's ask for the moon, we have the stars!" Unfortunately, too many dippy scenes with child actress Janis Wilson severely cloy in the latter half of the film. Davis fans, however, will not be disappointed.

NUDO DI DONNA
☆☆½
1984, Italy/France
Nino Manfredi, Eleonora Giorgi, Jean-Pierre Cassel, George Wilson, Carlo Bagno. Directed by Nino Manfredi. 112 min.

Nino Manfredi directed, cowrote, and starred in this subtitled Italian comedy that recalls—but falls far short of—Germi's 1960s bedroom farces. Manfredi's movie begins at a leisurely pace and soon becomes genuinely boring. The film has a fair amount of dialogue and none of it very interesting. Some of the lighting and cinematography do, however, have a certain stylized appeal. The film marks the debut of Eleonora Giorgi—a beautiful, soft-featured blonde with liquid blue eyes—who does well within the material's limitations. The film has little nudity but several well-done erotic sequences. (a.k.a.: *Portrait of a Woman Nude*)

LA NUIT DE VARENNES
☆☆☆½
1982, Italy/France, R
Marcello Mastroianni, Jean-Louis Barrault, Hanna Schygulla, Harvey Keitel, Jean-Claude Brialy. Directed by Ettore Scola. 133 min.

Ettore Scola set this sumptuous drama of the French Revolution on a stagecoach, with a fascinating cast of characters—including Marcello Mastroianni as Casanova, Hanna Schygulla as a lady-in-waiting, and Harvey Keitel as Tom Paine—traveling together and discussing the climate of their times. Gradually, they realize that they are in the direct wake of the flight of Louis XVI and Marie Antoinette from Paris, and that the most earthshaking political event of their century has begun. The dialogue is generally witty, and the lavish sets and costumes are added attractions.

NUMBER SEVENTEEN
☆☆½
1932, Great Britain
Leon M. Lion, Anne Grey, John Stuart, Donald Calthrop, Barry Jones, Garry Marsh. Directed by Alfred Hitchcock. 63 min.

One of Hitchcock's most bewildering films, with atypically vague characterizations and a muddy plot about jewel thieves, this film is based on a play, but, as short as it is, the talky exposition becomes quite tedious. Still, this early feature has no lack of technical marvels: moody gothic shots, a dizzying cinematic *pas de deux* with an old staircase (that collapses to leave our heroes stumbling in midair), and a breathtaking train chase at the climax.

NURSE
☆☆
1980, USA (TV)
Michael Learned, Robert Reed, Tom Aldredge, Hattie Winston, Antonio Fargas, Jon Matthews. Directed by David Lowell Rich. 104 min.

Acceptable if uninspired TV adaptation of Peggy Anderson's best-seller about a newly widowed woman who goes back to grueling employment as head nurse in an overcrowded metropolitan hospital. Michael Learned, of "The Waltons," is restrained and intelligent in the title role, but Sue Grafton's teleplay is standard "Medical Center"-style fare, and sudsier than it should be. *Nurse* later became a one-hour series that appeared briefly during the 1981–82 season.

NURSE EDITH CAVELL ☆☆
1939, USA/Great Britain
Anna Neagle, Edna May Oliver, George Sanders, May Robson, ZaSu Pitts, H. B. Warner, Robert Coote. Directed by Herbert Wilcox. 97 min.

A rigid, stiff-upper-lip retelling of the heroics of a World War I nurse who was put to death by a German firing squad for helping refugees sneak across the border to freedom. The veteran cast plays it nobly and calmly, so much so that you begin to miss the melodramatics that might have made it less reverent and more entertaining. Herbert Wilcox's staging is slow and uncinematic, and the film's high-mindedness makes it unbearably dull. ZaSu Pitts, Edna May Oliver, and May Robson come off the best as three wealthy women who finance the underground effort.

NUTCRACKER ☆½
1986, USA, G
Hugh Bigney, Vanessa Sharp, Patricia Barker, Wade Walthall, The Pacific Northwest Ballet. Directed by Carroll Ballard. 89 min.

Can this be the same Carroll Ballard who directed *The Black Stallion* and *Never Cry Wolf*? This film of the 1983 Pacific Northwest Ballet production designed by Maurice Sendak is a terrible disappointment: meandering, semicoherent, and visually tepid beyond belief. The enchanting Tchaikovsky score aside, the ballet itself is little more than a series of set pieces revolving around little Clara and her nutcracker prince. But Ballard hasn't begun to solve the problems of translating a stage work to the screen. Maurice Sendak's hyperbolic backgrounds look colorless and threadbare here, like a series of enlarged storyboards, and the dancers, none of whom take to the camera, are photographed from lackluster angles that make the film look neither "open" nor "closed," just meaninglessly cramped.

THE NUTTY PROFESSOR ☆☆☆☆
1963, USA
Jerry Lewis, Stella Stevens, Del Moore. Directed by Jerry Lewis. 107 min.

Jerry Lewis concocts a brilliant comic essay on personality and success. As professor Julius Kelp, he is a bumbling, jittery bug hopelessly in love with one of his students. With the aid of modern chemistry, he transforms himself into Buddy Love, a slick, reptilian crooner who must be bitter Jerry's memory of Dean Martin. The film is a satire on *Dr. Jekyll and Mr. Hyde* and on contemporary social attitudes toward attractiveness: In the world of this movie only the monsters succeed, and Kelp's descent into Buddy Love is the genuinely frightening desire for ruthless manipulative power. Jerry Lewis captures this fragmentation of personality in a marvelously jumbled style of filmmaking replete with a screaming color scheme. Stella Stevens performs well as the alternately sexy and prim coed, but Jerry's acting buries everyone in its brash, steamrolling vigor.

O

THE OBLONG BOX ★★½
1969, Great Britain
Vincent Price, Christopher Lee, Alastair Wiliamson, Hilary Dwyer, Peter Arne, Michael Balfour, Rupert Davies. Directed by Gordon Hessler. 91 min.

The Oblong Box was the thirteenth Edgar Allan Poe entry by American International Pictures, and its story of witchcraft and redemption shows signs of wear and tear. In nineteenth-century England, an aristocrat keeps his crazy, disfigured brother imprisoned in their family manor house. The brother escapes and embarks on a bloody trail of revenge. An average chiller compared to classic Poe movies made by Roger Corman (*The Fall of the House of Usher, The Tales of Terror*).

OBSESSION ★★½
1976, USA, R
Cliff Robertson, Genevieve Bujold, John Lithgow. Directed by Brian De Palma. 110 min.

Obsession is perhaps Brian De Palma's purest excursion into Hitchcock homage. The story, heavily indebted to themes from *Vertigo*, concerns a New Orleans businessman fascinated by a young Italian girl who bears an uncanny resemblance to his late wife, the victim of a mysterious kidnapping. De Palma eventually loses control of the peculiarly icy ambience that is in intriguing counterpoint to the nominal obsession of the tale. The lush cinematography and Bernard Herrmann's overworked score (his last one) are also effective at first, but the entire enterprise becomes ridiculous in its final sequences; the laughable misuse of Hitchcock's encircling camera pan in *Vertigo* is an inadequate substitute for believable characterization and motivation. Cliff Robertson plays the magnate with the proper seething detachment, but Genevieve Bujold fails to create a believable bridge between her two roles. John Lithgow, however, is excellent as Robertson's smooth business partner. His own particular obsession is eventually revealed in more depth than are those of the central pair. Written by Paul Schrader.

OCEAN'S ELEVEN ★★½
1960, USA
Frank Sinatra, Dean Martin, Sammy Davis, Jr., Peter Lawford, Angie Dickinson, Richard Conte, Cesar Romero, Patrice Wymore, Joey Bishop. Directed by Lewis Milestone. 127 min.

It's almost inconceivable how Frank Sinatra and his "rat pack" pals persuaded the gifted, politically liberal director Lewis Milestone (*All Quiet on the Western Front*) to helm one of their self-indulgent romps. Still, this farce about eleven former war buddies who plot to heist five Las Vegas casinos is entertaining in a laid-back sort of way. It's the kind of film where songs are thrown in but never crystallize into full-fledged musical numbers, stars like Red Skelton, George Raft, and Shirley MacLaine show up in cameos but don't do very much, and all the women are window-treated as dressing. Some real performances are delivered by Richard Conte and Cesar Romero; everyone else gets by on charm. Cute titles by Saul Bass.

THE OCTAGON ★★½
1980, USA, R
Chuck Norris, Karen Carlson, Lee Van Cleef, Art Hindle, Carol Bagdasarian, Jack Carter. Directed by Eric Karson. 103 min.

Chuck Norris meets the Ninja. As usual, Chuck is a retired martial arts master who really doesn't want to beat people up anymore, but this time, he's persuaded by a rich girl who wants him to bump off some terrorists. Seems the head terrorist is Chuck's old nemesis from the kung fu academy, and they have a score to settle. If you're a fan, this is one of the better Norris films because it has some of his best action scenes, as choreographed by Chuck and Aaron Norris. Music by former Blood, Sweat and Tears member Dick Halligan.

OCTAMAN ★
1971, USA
Kerwin Matthews, Pier Angeli, Jeff Morrow, Norman Fields. Directed by Harry Essex. 90 min.

Octaman is half-man, half-octopus, and not half as much fun as *The Creature from the Black Lagoon*. Despite the delectably monstrous creation concocted for the title role, the film plumbs the depths of mediocrity as the octo-creature surfaces during an expedition to Mexico.

OCTAVIA ★
1982, USA, R
Susan Curtis, Neil Kinsella, Jake Foley, G. B. File, Tom Wayne. Directed by David Beaird. 93 min.

A thoroughly inane melodrama disguised as a modern-day fairy tale, and such a guilelessly stupid one that it almost bears watching. Octavia (Susan Curtis) is a young blind woman imprisoned in a big house with her mean father, who throws her into traffic when she gets out of line just to remind her who's boss. Simpering and insanely chipper, she lolls around the mansion in filmy white dresses until she discovers an escaped convict (Neil Kinsella) hiding out in the garden. Together they flee to the wilderness on a white stallion, each hoping to find a better life. It's hard to feel no sympathy at all for a blind, abused girl, but Curtis must have attended Charmlessness School, and her endless prattle about witches, trolls, and fairies makes you want to throttle the little ninny. And by the way, how does she know that Pluto "looks like a golf ball"?

OCTOBER

See *Ten Days That Shook the World*

OCTOPUSSY ★★★
1983, USA, PR
Roger Moore, Louis Jourdan, Maud Adams, Vijay Amritraj, Steven Berkoff. Directed by John Glen. 122 min.

Roger Moore's sixth outing as 007 isn't as good as the masterful comic strip *The Spy Who Loved Me*, but it's perfectly satisfying nonetheless, an increasing rarity with James Bond films. Ostensibly, the plot concerns the superagent's attempts to halt the launching of a nuclear missile by a subversive German general, but the international intrigue isn't as memorable as the snazzy clown-chase opening, the carnival climax, or the island of beautiful women where Bond is briefly, joyously imprisoned. Maud Adams, who appeared eight years earlier in *The Man with the Golden Gun*, here portrays the title temptress, becoming the first Bond-ette to show up twice.

THE ODD ANGRY SHOT ★★½
1979, Australia
Graham Kennedy, John Hargreaves, John Jarratt, Bryan Brown, Graeme Blundell. Directed by Tom Jeffrey. 90 min.

As it did in this country, involvement in the Vietnam war caused a great deal of moral consternation and confusion in Australia, which sent a number of mostly volunteer troops there. This film examines some of those problems through the eyes of a group of Aussie Special Air Service troops, an elite branch stationed in Vietnam. Though not draftees, most are volunteers and not professional soldiers. Alternately comic and tragic, the film looks at war as a situation that a group of men are thrown into and forced to accept, often in ways typical to the Australian national character.

THE ODD COUPLE ☆☆☆
1968, USA
Jack Lemmon, Walter Matthau, John Fiedler, Herbert Edelman, David Sheiner, Larry Haines. Directed by Gene Saks. 105 min.

Neil Simon's wistful, very funny evocation of the lonely life in Manhattan is one of his best plays, and infinitely preferable to his later, more serious mode; this film adaptation is a little shrill but otherwise very entertaining. Jack Lemmon plays fussbudget Felix Unger, dumped by his wife and forced into cohabitation with slob sportswriter Oscar Madison (Walter Matthau). Odd they are, but also a wonderful, hangdog pair. The film was the basis for the highly successful, quite different TV series, which in turn spawned a less successful all-black version entitled "The New Odd Couple"; Simon later put the play back on Broadway with women instead of men as the protagonists.

THE ODD JOB ☆☆½
1980, Great Britain
Graham Chapman, David Jason, Diana Quick, Simon Williams, Bill Paterson. Directed by Peter Medak. 86 min.

Monty Python addicts and fans of the Ealing Brothers' British comedies of the 1950s will be the best viewers for this black farce about an upper-middle-class twit (Graham Chapman) who hires a hit man to murder him. He then changes his mind and spends the rest of the movie trying to get away from the killer (in underworld argot, an "odd job man") and break the contract, which specifies that anything Chapman says after the initial deal is to be disregarded. Along the way he encounters all sorts of British stereotypes, including *Comfort and Joy*'s Bill Paterson as a bobby. Director Peter Medak (*The Ruling Class*) is competent but uninspired. The film is a disappointment, but not without its virtues for fans of British comedy.

THE ODESSA FILE ☆☆½
1974, Great Britain, PG
Jon Voight, Maximilian Schell, Mary Tamm, Martin Brandt, Maria Schell, Sybil Danning, Derek Jacobi. Directed by Ronald Neame. 128 min.

In 1963 Hamburg, a determined journalist (Jon Voight) hunts down a secret network of ex-SS officers planning to overthrow Israel. This predictable, often plodding entry in the Nazis-in-hiding genre doesn't measure up to efforts like *The Boys from Brazil* and *Marathon Man*, but even if the outcome is obvious, Voight's low-key work and Maximilian Schell's chilling portrayal of his nemesis are reason enough to follow along. Based on a somewhat more effective novel by Frederick Forsyth.

ODE TO BILLY JOE ☆
1976, USA, PG
Robby Benson, Glynnis O'Connor, Joan Hotchkis, Sandy McPeak, James Best, Terence Goodman. Directed by Max Baer. 105 min.

The Bobbie Gentry song of the title was so memorable on the radio in 1967 because it was such an eerie evocation of mood, a three-minute piece of Southern Gothic in which we significantly never learn just why "Billy Joe McAllister jumped off the Tallahatchie bridge." In the screenplay by Herman Raucher (*Summer of '42*), we find out why, and a good song is ruined. Robby Benson and Glynnis O'Connor do their puppy-love bit yet again, this time in 1953 Mississippi, and although this is a cut above most of its ilk, it will be palatable only to those who haven't yet had their fill of films about the sensitivity of youth.

OFF BEAT ☆☆
1986, USA, PG
Judge Reinhold, Meg Tilly, Cleavant Derricks, Jacques D'Amboise, Joe Mantegna, Anthony Zerbe, Harvey Keitel. Directed by Michael Dinner. 91 min.

A second-rate, shambling comedy about a meek librarian (Judge Reinhold) roped into impersonating a policeman at a cops' variety show. He soon finds out how hard it is to shed the disguise when a pretty policewoman (Meg Tilly) falls for him. There are a number of nice, gently funny scenes before the film becomes bogged down in the action climax so many comedy directors seem to think they can't do without, and Tilly is sweetly effective. Reinhold, however, relies so heavily on his droning voice and bland, wiseass smile that you may fall asleep in the middle of one of his lines.

AN OFFICER AND A GENTLEMAN ☆☆☆½
1982, USA, R
Richard Gere, Debra Winger, Louis Gossett, Jr., David Keith, Lisa Blount, Lisa Eilbacher, Rogert Loggia. Directed by Taylor Hackford. 125 min.

Richard Gere gives his most substantive performance ever as an unruly Marine enlistee who, under the persistent training of hard-nosed Louis Gossett, becomes an officer, and under the persistent love of feisty local girl Debra Winger, becomes a gentleman. His most compelling lesson of pride and self-worth, however, comes from the misfortune of his best friend, played earnestly by standout David Keith. Though gender stereotypes prove somewhat overbearing, this movie manages a unique mesh of realism and fairy tale, comedy and tragedy; and boasts of one of the sexiest love scenes permitted under an R rating. Oscars went to Gossett and the film's theme song, "Up Where We Belong."

OFF THE WALL ☆½
1983, USA, R
Paul Sorvino, Rosanna Arquette, Patrick Cassidy, Monte Markham, Mickey Gilley, Gary Goodrow, Lewis Arquette. Directed by Rick Friedberg. 85 min.

Two Northern boys hitchhiking in the South get thrown into a Southern prison on a trumped-up charge in this weak comedy rather obviously inspired by *Stir Crazy*. The cast tries to deal with flimsy jokes by overplaying, a tactic that doesn't work. Fans of Rosanna Arquette should be warned that she makes only a brief appearance.

OF HUMAN BONDAGE ☆☆½
1934, USA
Leslie Howard, Bette Davis, Frances Dee, Reginald Owen. Directed by John Cromwell. 83 min.

Of Human Bondage is best remembered as Bette Davis's breakthrough picture. Davis does indeed play the waitress Mildred with uncommon vividness, and her sexuality is almost palpable; no other version makes the male character's obsession for her so real or so clearly outlined. However, she is too often out of control; director John Cromwell never integrates her into the rest of the film—good for Davis but bad for Leslie Howard. He gives a more complete but slightly dull performance as a clubfooted doctor. Frances Dee fares best with the casual viewer, for she plays her role with lovely understatement.

OF HUMAN BONDAGE ☆☆
1964, Great Britain
Kim Novak, Laurence Harvey, Siobhan McKenna, Robert Morley, Roger Livesey, Nanette Newman. Directed by Ken Hughes. 98 min.

This was the third go-round (following versions in 1934 and 1946) for Somerset Maugham's weepie about an exquisitely sensitive doctor whose love for a tin-hearted waitress nearly brings him to ruin. The story is good, if not good enough to justify three films, and the characters provide rich acting opportunities for the right performers. Laurence Harvey and Kim Novak are, alas, the wrong performers; he's too hard-edged to portray a tortured aesthete, and she lacks the range and intuition the role of Mildred requires.

OF UNKNOWN ORIGIN ☆
1983, USA
Peter Weller, Jennifer Dale, Lawrence Dane, Shannon Tweed. Directed by George Cosmatos. 88 min.

This is a strange thriller in which a young businessman becomes obsessed with the notion that his brownstone is home to a giant rat, which, in fact, it is. Not the supernatural story it first appears to be, but hardly realistically plausible either; it's just misguided and silly.

OH, ALFIE ☆☆
1975, Great Britain, R
Alan Price, Jill Townsend, Paul Copley, Joan Collins, Rula Lenska, Robin Parkinson. Directed by Ken Hughes. 102 min.

This sequel to 1966's *Alfie* has a claim to authenticity since it's based on the sequel to the novel from which the earlier film was adapted. But it's quite a step down in quality, with Alfie's sexual meanderings played up for titillation value and a moral that seems tacked on at the end as an excuse for what's gone on before. Alan Price, the British songwriter/performer, makes his film debut as an actor here, and although he has a definite roguish charm, director Ken Hughes relies too heavily on it. The movie features Rula Lenska, for the edification of those Americans who still think she was invented by a shampoo company.

OH, CALCUTTA! ☆½
1972, USA, X
Bill Macy, Raina Barrett, Mark Dempsey, Samantha Harper, Mitchell McGuire, Margo Sappington, Nancy Tribush, George Welbes. Directed by Jacques Levy. 105 min.

Of historical or nostalgic value only; it's amazing to recall while watching this that there was a time when *Oh, Calcutta!* and *Hair* were often used as phrases synonymous with "the moral rot and decadence of our times." But where *Hair* was adapted into an excellent film, this is nothing more than a videotaped performance of the original Broadway show, shot in September 1970 and released to theaters, with an added pastoral scene, two years later. And the content doesn't save the presentation; these ten sketches satirizing sex and sensuality are painfully dated and only intermittently funny in a sitcom way. John Lennon, Jules Feiffer, Robert Benton, Dan Greenburg, David Newman, and Sam Shepard, among others, contributed sketches, although the credits don't mention who wrote what. The long-running play was conceived by Kenneth Tynan.

OH DAD, POOR DAD, MAMA'S HUNG YOU ½☆
IN THE CLOSET AND I'M FEELING SO SAD
1967, USA
Rosalind Russell, Robert Morse, Jonathan Winters, Barbara Harris, Hugh Griffith. Directed by Richard Quine. 86 min.

Oh viewer, poor viewer, they've hung Arthur Kopit's play in the closet and you'll be feeling so sad if you rent this. Whatever merit Kopit's savage attack on momism had in the theater is lost in this overblown production that tries desperately to be "with it" in a 1960s manner. Rather than the modest black-and-white production it should have had, the film is burdened with a grimly freewheeling directorial style that owes too much to *Tom Jones*. Black comedies (*The Loved One, How I Won the War, Candy*) were in vogue in the 1960s, but few of them worked because subtlety was abandoned in favor of elbowing the audience in the ribs until their rib cages were crushed. In this abject failure, Jonathan Winters keeps appearing in a bubble at the top of the screen to rattle off unfunny one-liners that comment on the action as if the audience is too stupid to understand that this is an outrageous put-on. Shamefully, the film wastes a superb cast, including the indefatigable Roz Russell, who must have relished playing a character who's conceived as Auntie Mame crossed with the Countess in Durrenmatt's *The Visit*.

OH GOD! ☆☆
1977, USA, PG
George Burns, John Denver, Teri Garr, Paul Sorvino. Directed by Carl Reiner. 110 min.

Just for safety's sake, one should probably be wary of giving God a bad review, and thankfully, here it's not strictly necessary. George Burns is a nice, grandfatherly version of the Almighty (as Burns himself remarked, they're fairly close in age), but one wishes his God had chosen a funnier vehicle for his return to earth or a more interesting person to bless than grocery clerk John Denver. The worldly travails experienced by Denver and clan exert all the interest of an ingrown toenail, but Burns, even spouting the most ridiculous aphorisms, proves a reassuring presence. He wrings as much charm out of the role as possible—the rest of the film is less than a religious experience. Followed by two sequels, *Oh God Book II* and *Oh God! You Devil*.

OH GOD BOOK II ☆½
1980, USA, PG
George Burns, Louanne, Suzanne Pleshette, David Birney. Directed by Gilbert Cates. 94 min.

Oh, God, no more! George Burns's easygoing, low-key charm carried the first entry in this surprisingly popular series; even he can't save the follow-up. If John Denver seemed a bit treacly to you in the original, wait until you meet Louanne, the wide-eyed, robotic small person (she *must* be a real child, but we can't quite believe it) who plays the tot chosen by the Almighty comic to spread the word of love and peace. Watching this kid deliver homilies seems more like a plague visitation than a blessed event. Followed by *Oh God! You Devil*.

OH GOD! YOU DEVIL ☆☆
1984, USA, PG
George Burns, Ted Wass, Ron Silver, Roxanne Hart, Eugene Roche, Robert Desiderio. Directed by Paul Bogart. 96 min.

Having played God the Granddad twice before, George Burns now has a grand old time as the Devil. In his Beelzebub guise, he's a show-biz agent named Harry Tophet who takes as his protégé an unsuccessful songwriter (Ted Wass) willing to sell his soul to make it as a rock star. Cranking out the tired wisecracks with that rusty voicebox of his (and gobbling his cigar like a pacifier between lines), the ninetyish Burns is certainly one of film comedy's natural wonders. But, then, as Samuel Johnson once observed of a dog walking on its hind legs, what's remarkable is not that the trick is done well but that it is done at all.

OH HEAVENLY DOG! ☆
1980, USA, PG
Chevy Chase, Jane Seymour, Benji, Omar Sharif, Donnelly Rhodes, Alan Sues, Robert Morley. Directed by Joe Camp. 103 min.

The title gets it half-right, and we don't mean it's heavenly. Benji buffs may get a kick out of the pup's performance (directed by the animal's longtime collaborator, Joe Camp), but even kids will be put off by the inane plot, which has private eye Chevy Chase murdered and then reincarnated in canine form in order to solve his own slaying. Here, even a little of Chase's patented smugness is too much, and the producer who decided to cast Jane Seymour as a romantic lead opposite an animal should be locked in a kennel.

O'HARA'S WIFE ★★½
1982, USA, PG
Edward Asner, Mariette Hartley, Jodie Foster, Perry Lang, Tom Bosley, Ray Walston, Allen Williams, Richard Schaal, Nehemiah Persoff. Directed by Williams S. Bartman. 87 min.

An amiable, romantic gloss on *Topper*, this comedy-drama has Edward Asner as a grieving widower whose late wife (Mariette Hartley) returns in spectral form to give his sagging spirits a lift. You've seen it before, but it's a pleasant enough time-passer, with a nice, bewildered performance from Asner and good support from Jodie Foster.

OKLAHOMA! ★★★
1955, USA
Gordon MacRae, Shirley Jones, Charlotte Greenwood, Gloria Grahame, Gene Nelson, Rod Steiger, James Whitmore, Eddie Albert, Barbara Lawrence. Directed by Fred Zinnemann. 145 min.

The belated screen adaptation of *Oklahoma!*, one of Broadway's most beloved musicals, inaugurated an era of large-scale, carbon-copy transcriptions of popular shows (*The Music Man*, *The Sound of Music*). Still, this early example is less stagey and heavy-going than the rest. The original idea was to make it a "Method" musical with Paul Newman as Curley, Joanne Woodward as Laurey, and Barbara Cook as Ado Annie. They all tested, but it just didn't work out, so safe, pallid Gordon MacRae and Shirley Jones were cast instead (well, at least they could sing) and the part of Ado Annie was given to the delightful Gloria Grahame. Like the show, the plot had nothing more to depict than Laurey's choice of her escort to the big dance. The score, which includes "People Will Say We're in Love," "Oh, What a Beautiful Morning," and "Surrey with the Fringe on Top," is arguably the richest, best work Rodgers and Hammerstein ever did (and it was their first collaboration). Agnes DeMille's avant-garde choreography in the dream sequence is jarring, but the other dances are a splendid recreation of her Broadway work. *Note:* originally filmed in Todd-AO (a wide-screen process).

OKLAHOMA ANNIE ★½
1952, USA
Judy Canova, John Russell, Grant Withers, Roy Barcroft, Emmett Lynn. Directed by R.G. Springsteen. 89 min.

Silly cornball comedy with big-voiced Judy Canova as a country shopkeeper who yearns to snag the handsome new sheriff and become a deputy herself. The antics are as broad as those on "Hee Haw" and awfully dumb, and the script recycles gags so old they're covered with cobwebs, but Canova's fans or nostalgia buffs may enjoy it anyway.

THE OKLAHOMA KID ★★★
1939, USA
James Cagney, Humphrey Bogart, Donald Crisp, Rosemary Lane, Harvey Stephens, Ward Bond. Directed by Lloyd Bacon. 85 min.

Spirited saga that James Cagney galvanizes with his presence. Set in the Cherokee Strip when settlers were scrambling for land, this snappy Western features Jimmy as a vengeance-minded sagebrusher out to settle a score with landowner Humphrey Bogart (who seems mighty uncomfortable acting on the lone prairie). The film moves at a fast clip, with some well-timed comic interludes adding up to good entertainment.

THE OLD BARN DANCE ★½
1938, USA
Gene Autry, Smiley Burnette, Helen Valkis, Walter Shrum and His Colorado Hillbillies, The Maple City Four. Directed by Joseph Kane. 60 min.

Cowboy crooner Gene Autry does what's expected of him in this routine feature. He and his pals earn their living by selling horses to ranchers until a tractor company puts them out of business. They then move on to a job as musical performers on a radio show, but it's not all rags to riches. Of interest to nostalgians and country music historians.

OLD BOYFRIENDS ★½
1979, USA, R
Talia Shire, Richard Jordan, Keith Carradine, John Belushi, John Houseman, Buck Henry, P.J. Soles. Directed by Joan Tewkesbury. 103 min.

After a psychiatrist suffers a mild nervous breakdown, she decides to cheer herself up by contacting all her old flames. (Think about this: Would hunting up all of your ex-loves pull *you* out of the doldrums?) This vehicle for Talia Shire has "vanity production" stamped all over it; as the star yaks away about relationships and space and deep feelings, you'll wish someone would have her committed. Instead, she goes on a merry rampage through her past that culminates in a humiliation of her old high school crush (John Belushi) and a seduction of the younger brother of her one (and dead) true love. With psychiatrists like this, who needs patients? Some good performers are wasted.

THE OLD CORRAL ½★
1937, USA
Gene Autry, Smiley Burnette. Directed by Joseph Kane. 52 min.

Gene Autry plays a singing sheriff in this dull prairie yarn. There's lots of music and all of it pretty awful.

OLD ENOUGH ★★½
1984, USA, PG
Sarah Boyd, Rainbow Harvest, Neill Barry, Danny Aiello, Susan Kingsley, Roxanne Hart, Fran Brill, Alyssa Milano, Gerry Bamman. Directed by Marisa Silver. 91 min.

A tough, charming independent feature about the unlikely friendship of two Manhattan girls—one a spry, innocent WASP; the other a beautiful working-class Italian Catholic who's just crossed over the line into sexual awareness. What starts out as a comic contrast between the two classes turns into a touching and surprisingly savvy look at what it means to grow up. The film was directed by the twenty-four-year-old Marisa Silver, whose mother is director Joan Micklin Silver (*Chilly Scenes of Winter*); apparently a gift for sly social observation runs in the family.

THE OLD GUN ★★★
1976, France
Philippe Noiret, Romy Schneider. Directed by Robert Enrico. 141 min.

A brutal but engrossing French revenge tale about a partisan physician whose wife and child are slain by Nazis during the final German retreat from France at the tail end of World War II. A virtuoso performance by Philippe Noiret as the family man turned exterminator and an intricate screenplay laced with flashbacks of the doctor's life *chez famille* add interesting twists to the overworked revenge plot. Despite the poor English dubbing, this import's potency remains undiminished.

OLD YELLER ★★★
1957, USA
Dorothy McGuire, Fess Parker, Tommy Kirk, Kevin Corcoran, Chuck Connors, Spike. Directed by Robert Stevenson. 83 min.

As Bill Murray asked in *Stripes*, "Who didn't cry when Old Yeller died?" One of the more durable Disney non-animated features, this perennial heart-tugger is about a big, lovable mongrel who shows up out of nowhere and is adopted by a Texas frontier family. Along the way, he helps protect them from such less-friendly wilderness critters as a bear, a wolf, and a pack of rampaging boars. The ending is even more heartrending than the death of Bambi's mother.

OLIVER! ★★★
1968, Great Britain, G
Mark Lester, Ron Moody, Oliver Reed, Harry Secombe, Shani Wallis, Jack Wild, Hugh Griffith. Directed by Carol Reed. 153 min.

♪ Carol Reed's clamorous, cheerful adaptation of the musical based on *Oliver Twist* opts to discard Dickens's narrative mastery in favor of a large-scale, family-oriented, resolutely upbeat production style. Although no great service to the author, it stood on its own well enough to win six Academy Awards, including Best Picture, Director, and Song Score. Lionel Bart's cloying music is a disappointment, but the handsome, elaborate production design is very impressive, and Mark Lester's Oliver, Ron Moody's Fagin, and Jack Wild's Artful Dodger are good enough to enthrall youngsters and make the film's excessive length bearable for adults. Unfortunately, much of the Panavision splendor of Oswald Morris's cinematography will be lost on the small screen.

OLIVER'S STORY ★
1978, USA, PG
Ryan O'Neal, Candice Bergen, Nicola Pagett, Edward Binns, Benson Fong, Charles Haid, Kenneth McMillan, Ray Milland. Directed by John Korty. 90 min.

It took eight years for Hollywood to produce a sequel to the phenomenally popular *Love Story*, and the result of the long wait seems a rather nasty joke: In casting a romantic interest to preppy Oliver Barrett (Ryan O'Neal), the producers obviously couldn't use Ali MacGraw—she died in the original. Who better to replace her than the only other actress of the 1970s who matched MacGraw's stupefying inexpressiveness—Candice Bergen. This was her last really bad performance, and it's a stinker—she plays an heiress to the Bonwit Teller fortune, although you may confuse her with one of that store's window dummies. O'Neal (also at his worst here, or close) falls for her—but will he be able to shake the memory of dear, dead Ali? Whether or not you enjoyed the original, save yourself the disappointment of this continuation; even Francis Lai's insistent love theme will get on your nerves.

OLIVER TWIST ★★
1933, USA
Dickie Moore, Irving Pichel, William Boyd, Doris Lloyd, Barbara Kent, Sonny Ray, Clyde Cook. Directed by William Cowen. 70 min.

Careful—this isn't the one you want! Either get the 1968 musical version (retitled *Oliver!*) or the '48 straight version with Alec Guinness; both of those are outstanding productions of the Dickens classic. This production of the Dickens classic is cheaply and poorly done, with child star Dickie Moore an appalling Oliver. The rest of the cast isn't much better, each looking as though this were just another studio assignment. It still has some interest for the story alone, although it has been severely eviscerated to keep the running time down to seventy minutes.

O LUCKY MAN! ★★½
1973, USA, R
Malcolm McDowell, Rachel Roberts, Mona Washbourne, Lindsay Anderson, Ralph Richardson. Directed by Lindsay Anderson. 174 min.

A modern-day comic parable about greed, crime, and punishment, punctuated by the sardonic but sometimes clumsy songs of Alan Price. Lindsay Anderson, Malcolm McDowell, and writer David Sherwin collaborated on this study of a young coffee salesman's rise and fall, the second film in the Mick Travis trilogy that began with *If . . .* and concluded with *Brittania Hospital*. Critically acclaimed upon its release, *O Lucky Man!* has not aged well, suffering from a mammoth running time and an overly precious script. It's not nearly as pungent as *If . . .*, and functions more successfully as a cult artifact than as anything else.

LOS OLVIDADOS ★★★★
1950, Mexico
Alfonso Mejia, Miguel Inclan, Estela Inda, Roberto Cobo. Directed by Luis Buñuel. 88 min.

Luis Buñuel's first truly commercial success is this astounding drama about "delinquent" children living in Mexico City and how they corrupt one poor youth. Capturing a world of bleakness—beggars, cripples, abandoned buildings, and slums—Buñuel conveys the razor's-edge existence of these lost children with chilling and stunningly poetic intensity. The surreal touches, including an ultra-Freudian dream sequence, and the sleek photography are seemingly out of place, yet may be seen as biting commentary on the dubious relationship between documentary and fiction film. This is an ironic, incisive and, finally, powerful film. (a.k.a.: *The Young and the Damned*)

THE OMEGA MAN ★★
1971, USA, PG
Charlton Heston, Rosalind Cash, Anthony Zerbe, Paul Koslo, Eric Laneuville. Directed by Boris Sagal. 98 min.

In a Los Angeles where dusk is longer than the day (both beautifully photographed by Russell Metty), Charlton Heston cruises barren streets and, by night, staves off surfer–like zombies in priestly robes who want to occupy his luxury penthouse. In this solid adaptation of Richard Matheson's novel *I Am a Legend* set in a post-plague 1976, Heston plays a scientist who develops a serum and searches for unrobed people; Rosalind Cash is delicious as one of his finds. Unfortunately, the midsection with Cash either sags or soars, depending on whether you hate digression or admire human interaction and wit. The intelligent Heston delivers many awkward soliloquies and the film ends with a crucifixion, which is exactly what the ending deserves.

THE OMEN ★★★
1976, USA, R
Gregory Peck, Lee Remick, David Warner, Billie Whitelaw, Leo McKern, Harvey Stephens, Patrick Troughton. Directed by Richard Donner. 111 min.

The Antichrist, a changeling child born of a jackal and foisted upon the U.S. ambassador to Britain and his unsuspecting wife, wreaks elaborate havoc on all those who inhibit his plans to bring about Armageddon in this century. This is a groundbreaking big-budget horror movie whose respectable cast, expensive special effects, and exceptional production values ultimately compensate for its silliness and lack of conviction. Pay particular attention to the Gregorian chants-on-acid soundtrack that was used in both sequels—*Damien—Omen II* and *Omen II—The Final Conflict*—in a desperate attempt to inject some life into them.

OMEN III—THE FINAL CONFLICT ★
1981, USA, R
Sam Neill, Rossano Brazzi, Lisa Harrow, Don Golden, Mason Adams. Directed by Graham Baker. 108 min.

The very weak second and last sequel to *The Omen*. Grown to adulthood, demonic Damien (now played by Sam Neill) rules the Thorne industrial empire and aspires to a position in the diplomatic corps—the better to stir up trouble in the world—pausing only to direct tortured monologues to a life-size figure of the crucified Jesus and abuse women who make the mistake of becoming sexually involved with him. A group of monks try to kill him and instead die in dreadful ways, but the apocalypse is nonetheless averted, as no astute viewer needs to be told. (a.k.a.: *The Final Conflict*)

OMEN II

See *Damien—Omen II*

ON A CLEAR DAY YOU CAN SEE FOREVER ★★★
1970, USA, G
Barbra Streisand, Yves Montand, Jack Nicholson, Larry Blyden, Bob Newhart, Simon Oakland, Pamela Brown. Directed by Vincente Minnelli. 129 min.

Paramount reasoned that teaming the premier musical comedy star of the year (Barbra Streisand) with the premier musical comedy director of yesteryear (Vincente Minnelli) would result in artistic and box-office magic. Unhappy with the results, however, the studio tampered endlessly with the footage, releasing it so long after it was made that Streisand's clothes and hairdos were already out of style. Today, it is possible to appreciate the film less as a musical (the Alan Jay Lerner-Burton Lane songs are well sung but given almost no staging, and very few remain from the 1967 Broadway production) than as a wistful coda to Minnelli's Hollywood career. It is primarily Minnelli's bittersweet touches, and not Streisand's funny but loud performance as a telepathic young woman under the care of a psychologist, that give the film warmth and feeling. Jack Nicholson fans should know that the actor's performance was just one of the casualties of the studio edit (among other things, his duet with Streisand was cut).

ON ANY SUNDAY ☆☆☆
1971, USA, G
Bruce Brown, Steve McQueen, Mert Lawwill, Malcolm Smith. Directed by Bruce Brown. 89 min.

Bruce Brown, who wrote, directed, and produced the classic surfing documentary *The Endless Summer*, attempts to do the same thing here for the sport of motorcycle racing, with good results. Steve McQueen, an amateur racer of some repute, was enlisted here to add star value to the film, but the real star is the photography of the high-speed racing. Brown examines various types of motorcycle races, including motocross racing, ice racing, and English racing (in which the riders are disqualified if their feet ever touch the ground). The film is exciting and entertaining, even for those who are not racing fans.

ONCE BITTEN ☆
1985, USA, PG-13
Lauren Hutton, Jim Carrey, Cleavon Little, Karen Kopins, Skip Lackey, Thomas Ballatore. Directed by Howard Storm. 97 min.

What do you call a horror-comedy that's neither scary nor funny? Several titles come to mind, but *Once Bitten* will do. Lauren Hutton is alluring but utterly wasted as a thirsty vampire in quest of that teen-pic standby, the young male virgin. Jim Carrey plays the young man who must bed his girlfriend or become one of the undead. Lame frat-house sex jokes alternate with Hutton slavering over young male flesh and Cleavon Little generally disgracing himself as her limp-wristed sidekick.

ONCE IN PARIS ☆☆
1978, USA
Wayne Rogers, Gayle Hunnicutt, Jack Lenoir, Philippe March. Directed by Frank Gilroy. 100 min.

Frank Gilroy's independently made romantic comedy (he also wrote and produced) is, like many of his films, moderately charming as it unfolds and forgettable as soon as the credits roll. Wayne Rogers, one of the more affable members of TV's original "M*A*S*H" ensemble, plays an American writer sent to the City of Lights to doctor a script. If only someone had injected life into Gilroy's own work, which has his hero falling hard for a beautiful Englishwoman (Gayle Hunnicutt). The extramarital complications that follow have moments of poignancy, but the script and direction are much too mild for any real humor or drama to emerge.

ONCE UPON A SCOUNDREL ☆☆☆
1973, USA
Zero Mostel, Katy Jurado, Tito Vandis, Priscilla Garcia. Directed by George Schaefer. 90 min.

Director George Schaefer has put together a surprisingly innocent and enjoyable fable in this feature that was unseen in this country until years after it was made. Zero Mostel plays a ruthless rich man in a small Mexican town who tries to coerce a girl into marrying him by having her fiancé imprisoned on trumped-up charges. The people of the town, in order to change his ways, drug him and, upon his waking, pretend that they can neither see nor hear him, convincing him that he is a ghost condemned to wander the earth doing good deeds before he can rest. Quite funny in parts, this is one of those rare films that the whole family can enjoy without the older members feeling slightly benumbed. The movie is beautifully photographed by veteran Mexican cameraman Gabriel Figueroa.

ONCE UPON A TIME IN AMERICA ☆☆☆☆
1984, USA, R
Robert DeNiro, James Woods, Tuesday Weld, Elizabeth McGovern, Treat Williams, James Hayden. Directed by Sergio Leone. 227 min.

This brilliant gangster saga spanning forty-five years in the lives of two small-time hoods in New York was called a Jewish *Godfather* by some critics, but it owes no debt to Coppola's work. The astonishingly rich, mythic, and introspective tone that Sergio Leone gives the film is uniquely his own. As the story glides back and forth between 1923, 1933, and 1968, many of the scenes take on a hallucinatory, fantastic quality—the entire climax may, in fact, be a drug-induced delusion. Although violent and brutal, especially in its treatment of women, *America* sustains its complex story beautifully. Robert DeNiro, in the central role, has never been better. At nearly four hours, this challenging and rewarding movie seems not a minute too long. *Note: Once Upon a Time in America* is also available in its U.S. theatrical version, which is 93 minutes shorter. This studio recut destroyed so much of the film's mastery that Leone disowned it, and it is emphatically not recommended.

ONCE UPON A TIME IN THE WEST ☆☆☆½
1969, USA/Italy
Henry Fonda, Charles Bronson, Claudia Cardinale, Jason Robards, Keenan Wynn, Jack Elam. Directed by Sergio Leone. 165 min.

Italian director Sergio Leone's epic reworking of traditional Western motifs, about the coming of the cross-country railroads and the final taming of the frontier. Charles Bronson as a nameless protagonist (more a zombie than Clint Eastwood ever was in *A Fistful of Dollars*, *For a Few Dollars More* or *The Good, The Bad and the Ugly*) out for revenge, Henry Fonda as a sadistic villain, the garrulous Jason Robards as a roguish outlaw, and Claudia Cardinale as a woman tough enough to stand up to all of them. More introspective than the "dollars" trilogy, it features a stunningly stylized opening in a minimalist train station; a sequence shot in Monument ("John Ford Country") Valley; a wealth of explicit references to other Westerns; and the last of Ennio Morricone's strange soundtracks.

THE ONE AND ONLY ☆
1978, USA, PG
Henry Winkler, Kim Darby, Gene Saks, William Daniels, Harold Gould, Herve Villechaize, Polly Holliday, Ed Begley, Jr., Brandon Cruz. Directed by Carl Reiner. 98 min.

Oh, Henry! If the abysmal *Heroes* nailed the coffin of Henry Winkler's film career shut, this follow-up threw dirt on the lid and danced on the grave. Never have a star's TV charms so thoroughly abandoned him on the big screen as here, where Winkler plays a dandyish Gorgeous George–type of wrestler who's meant to be an endearing kook (as in *Heroes*) but comes across as an egomaniacal dork. Kim Darby, who, like Henry, is a good decade too old for her role, is the love interest. Endless gay jokes, midget jokes, and rectal function jokes abound, and you haven't seen what unattractive is until you've checked out the less-than-muscular star poured into a blonde wig, fur undies, and pink leotards. It's mortifying embarrassment for all concerned, although the star did begin to redeem himself by staying off the screen for four years after this came out.

THE ONE AND ONLY GENUINE ORIGINAL FAMILY BAND
☆½
1968, USA
Buddy Ebsen, Janet Blair, Lesley Ann Warren, John Davidson, Walter Brennan, Kurt Russell, Goldie Hawn, Richard Deacon, Wally Cox. Directed by Michael O'Herlihy. 117 min.

By the late 1960s, the Disney Studios could do almost nothing right. In this lamentable *Mary Poppins* imitation, a musical family rises to prominence during the 1888 presidential campaign between Grover Cleveland and Benjamin Harrison. Based on the autobiography of Laura Bower Van Nuys, it's not the stuff from which great musicals are made. Lesley Ann Warren and John Davidson (the lovebirds in *The Happiest Millionaire*) are reunited here, but the real news is that the film features both Kurt Russell and Goldie Hawn (her debut), who would go on to costar in *Swingshift* fifteen years later.

ONE ARMED VS. NINE KILLERS
☆
Hong Kong
Jimmy Wang Yu, Lo Lieh, Chung Hwa.

Jimmy Wang who? Jimmy Wang *Yu*. He was the hero of *The Hero*, and now he's back in a kung fu flick whose title should provide all the explanation you need as to why the odds are against him. He's missing one of those limbs they always say is "registered as a deadly weapon," and a cadre of bad guys would like to remove the remaining one. Guess who wins? Yu, yes; you, no.

ONE BODY TOO MANY
☆☆
1944, USA
Jack Haley, Jean Parker, Bela Lugosi, Bernard Nedell, Lyle Talbot. Directed by Frank McDonald. 74 min.

The superfluous body of the title of this lighthearted mystery would seem to be Bela Lugosi, once again cast in a forgettable red-herring role as a butler who didn't do it. Jack Haley is likable enough as an insurance salesman who arrives at an old dark house too late to do his potential customer any good. Mistaken for a private eye, he must solve the murder and protect his vulnerable client from things that go bump in the night.

ONE CRAZY SUMMER
☆½
1986, USA, PG
John Cusack, Demi Moore, Bobcat Goldthwait, Joel Murray, Curtis Armstrong, John Matuszak. Directed by Savage Steve Holland. 95 min.

This determined-to-be-wild-and-crazy youth comedy has a certain cruel comic flair, but it's very minor. John Cusack is a seventeen-year-old aspiring artist who hopes to gain admission to the Rhode Island School of Design by illustrating a love story. And when he accompanies a friend on a summer trip to Nantucket in search of material, he falls for a singer (Demi Moore) he meets along the way. Writer-director Savage Steve Holland, whose first film was *Better Off Dead*, has a gift for conceptual cartoon gags and goofy details, but when he tries to haul in teen movie mechanics, he's lost. In the end, the movie turns into just another wish-fulfillment melodrama.

ONE DARK NIGHT
☆☆
1983, USA, R
Meg Tilly, Adam West, Robin Evans, Melissa Newman, Elizabeth Daily, Leslie Speights. Directed by Tom McLoughlin. 89 min.

This standard horror item about a group of teens spending one night in a mausoleum has a few nice things going for it, including the screen debut of Meg Tilly, an appearance by Adam West (TV's "Batman"), and some rotting-corpse special effects that belie its modest budget. It's too bad that writer-director Tom McLoughlin has put them in the service of a humdrum, familiar plot. Some of the moments are more funny than scary, although to the film's credit, much of the humor seems intentional.

ONE DEADLY OWNER
☆
1974, Great Britain
Donna Mills, Jeremy Brett, Robert Morris, Laurence Payne. Directed by Ian Fordyce. 80 min.

In this Rolls-Royce *Christine*, a young model finally gets her dream car only to discover it's possessed by the spirit of a murder victim. It's all too much and the poor girl is literally driven to the brink of madness when the dead previous owner gives her the lowdown. Although more amusing than John Carpenter's botched Plymouth Fury story, this used car is still a clunker, dragging its chassis in low gear through a winding plot.

ONE DOWN, TWO TO GO
☆½
1983, USA, R
Fred Williamson, Jim Brown, Jim Kelly, Richard Roundtree. Directed by Fred Williamson. 84 min.

This is a film that karate experts should have kicked into better shape; as it stands, they'll have to foot the blame for the results. Assorted martial arts maestros fight petty unfairness in the world of championship karate matches. Can they stop the rigging of these competition bouts? Just one more action flick down, and there's probably another 1,000 like it to go.

ONE-EYED JACKS
☆☆☆☆
1961, USA
Marlon Brando, Karl Malden, Pina Pellicer, Katy Jurado, Ben Johnson, Slim Pickens, Larry Duran, Sam Gilman, Timothy Carey, Miriam Colon, Elisha Cook, Jr., Rudolph Acosta. Directed by Marlon Brando. 137 min.

Stanley Kubrick was originally set to direct this, but Marlon Brando took over for his only outing behind the camera. The result was a criminally underrated psychological Western—a forerunner to the great revisionist Westerns of the 1960s and early 1970s. Brando plays an outlaw who devotes his life to getting revenge against Karl Malden, the old crony who betrayed him and has since become a sheriff. Brando's directorial style is, like his acting, at once larger than life and powerfully detailed, and the film's slow, meditative surface gives way to an epic theme: the intrusion of the modern corporate mentality into the purity of the West. The splendid photography is by Charles Lang.

ONE FLEW OVER THE CUCKOO'S NEST
☆☆☆☆
1975, USA, R
Jack Nicholson, Louise Fletcher, Will Sampson, William Redfield, Brad Dourif, Scatman Crothers, Danny DeVito, Michael Berryman, Peter Brocco. Directed by Milos Forman. 133 min.

Ken Kesey's 1962 best-seller was adapted into the only movie since *It Happened One Night* (1934) to win the five major Academy Awards—Best Picture, Director, Screenplay, Actor, and Actress. Jack Nicholson delivers an ingenious, truly unforgettable performance as rebellious MacMurphy, the mental hospital patient who undermines the tyranny of stoic Nurse Ratched (Louise Fletcher) and breathes new life into his otherwise spiritless fellow patients. Interaction between the actors is so refreshingly, tangibly real, so inspired, that we are compelled not merely to sympathize with the insane, but also to identify with them; not only to cry for them, but also to laugh with them. Impeccably directed by Milos Forman, the film dissolves preconceived boundaries between normality and abnormality, establishing itself as one of those rare movies that can both broadly entertain and subtly change us.

ONE FRIGHTENED NIGHT ☆☆☆
1935, USA
Charley Grapewin, Mary Carlisle, Arthur Hohl, Wallace Ford, Hedda Hopper, Regis Toomey. Directed by Christy Cabanne. 67 min.

Half "it was a dark and stormy night" murder mystery and half-parody, this antique is a lot better than it has any right to be, and a good bit of fun. A rich old geezer is spending the night in his eerie old house with his family, all just waiting for him to die so they can inherit his money. When the presumed heiress is killed, it all gets going. The movie features Hedda Hopper in her pre-columnist starlet days.

ONE FROM THE HEART ☆☆
1982, USA, R
Teri Garr, Frederic Forrest, Raul Julia, Nastassja Kinski, Lainie Kazan, Harry Dean Stanton, Luana Anders. Directed by Francis Ford Coppola. 101 min.

Francis Coppola ushers us through a theatrical wonderland of prettily painted sets and elaborate cinematography, all of it edited in the magically smooth style made possible by video technology. This legendary folly sank Zoetrope studios. It is by no means unwatchable, but the story—about a discontented couple (Teri Garr and Frederic Forrest) who venture into Las Vegas on the Fourth of July and find glamorous new fantasy lovers—has all the verve and electricity of a checkers game. Coppola's one successful innovation is his use of Tom Waits's music, which plays perpetually in the background like an operatic score. This is an enormously disappointing trifle from one of our genuinely talented film directors.

ONE MAGIC CHRISTMAS ☆☆½
1985, USA, PG
Mary Steenburgen, Harry Dean Stanton, Gary Basaraba, Arthur Hill, Elizabeth Harnois. Directed by Philip Borsos. 89 min.

This attempt by the Disney studios to create a new Christmas classic has so much going for it that it's a real disappointment when, about halfway through, it stumbles and never recovers. It begins by dealing with a very real and pressing question: What do you do when you're facing bad financial times and the kids are expecting the usual Christmas visit from Santa Claus? Mary Steenburgen, working double shifts at the local supermarket to support the family since her husband's layoff, is soured on the idea of Christmas. So an angel is sent to cheer her up, in the best *It's a Wonderful Life* manner, by showing her how things could be worse. Unfortunately, the worst things we see happen (and it is not immediately clear that they will be set right at film's end) are terrifying to the point of sadism toward the audience, *especially* young children, and the resolution is absolutely forced and unbelievable. Casting Harry Dean Stanton as the angel was a brilliant stroke, although the way he is used in some of the scenes may give parents cause to warn their children about talking to strange men on the street.

ONE MAN JURY ☆☆
1978, USA, R
Jack Palance, Chris Mitchum, Pamela Shoop, Angel Tompkins. Directed by Charles Martin. 104 min.

This film is not dull. In fact, it makes *Death Wish* look as if it were designed as a recruitment advertisement for the beauties of urban living. Dissatisfied with the shortsightedness of the law and the loopholes through which criminals can evade the system, a law-and-order freak goes looking for felons. It's an ugly-looking film that suits the ugliness of the theme. It's also brutal and fast-paced; if you like this violent subgenre, you could do worse.

ONE MILLION YEARS B.C. ☆☆
1966, Great Britain
Raquel Welch, John Richardson, Percy Herbert, Jean Waldon, Robert Brown. Directed by Don Chaffey. 100 min.

In this updated version of Hal Roach's 1940 kitschy *One Million B.C.* (D.W. Griffith allegedly contributed to the directing of the original), young Turk Tumak becomes disgruntled (literally) with his father, the leader of the rock people. Setting out on his own, Tumak escapes the wrath of both a giant lizard and a brontosaurus, finally reaching the ocean shore and the arms of Raquel Welch. Although Ms. Welch's performance doesn't quite match up to the hard seductiveness of her whip-cracking galley master in *The Magic Christian*, her appearance in man's first bikini, along with the steady grunts and groans on the soundtrack, raises this film to a suitably steamy level. The young couple spend their days visiting each other's respective tribes, until the rock people spoil the party by attacking the shell people. A volcano interrupts the bloodshed, hot lava pouring over members of both tribes. The film ends with one of those "We can make this meaningful, if we make it relevant to contemporary society" images: A black mushroom cloud rises over the newly constituted shell/rock tribe.

ONE NIGHT STAND ☆☆☆
1984, Australia
Tyler Coppin, Cassandra Delaney, Jay Hackett, Saskia Post, Midnight Oil. Directed by John Duigan. 95 min.

This is a comedy-drama-antinuclear-propaganda-rock concert-romance that's much less pretentious and more engaging than its schizophrenically hybrid nature would lead you to believe. Set casually on the eve of world destruction, the plot has four young adults, three Australians and a U.S. sailor gone AWOL, taking refuge in the Sydney Opera House, where they get drunk, flirt, fight, play strip poker, and finally steel themselves for the apocalypse that awaits them beyond the walls. The rock group Midnight Oil makes a brief appearance to perform "Short Memory," a song that's as blatantly partisan as the film itself, which makes no bones about its contempt for both American and Soviet defense policies. It's worth a look, especially if you already agree with its political slant.

ONE OF OUR AIRCRAFT IS MISSING ☆☆☆½
1941, Great Britain
Godfrey Tearle, Eric Portman, Hugh Williams, Bernard Miles, Hugh Burden, Googie Withers, Peter Ustinov. Directed by Michael Powell and Emeric Pressburger. 100 min.

Like their earlier feature, *49th Parallel*, this Michael Powell-Emeric Pressburger feature concerns a group of six soldiers making their way across enemy territory after their vehicle has been struck down by the enemy. In this case, however, the soldiers are Brits instead of Nazis, so rather than show the murderous methods employed for survival by the latter, the script plays up the strength and bravery of the British fliers trying to get back to England through Holland. The film is well acted and quite suspenseful.

ONE ON ONE ☆½
1977, USA, PG
Robby Benson, Annette O'Toole, G.D. Spradlin, Gail Strickland, Melanie Griffith. Directed by Lamont Johnson. 98 min.

This meek, mawkish drama about a slightly dull-witted high school basketball star who's in danger of losing an athletic scholarship was written by its star, Robby Benson, and his father, Jerry Segal. Unless you think of Benson as multitalented, stay away. *One on One* scores some points against the business of sports, but none that weren't made more forcefully in *All the Right Moves*. And why Benson's mumbling, bumbling, graceless presence brought him brief teen fandom in the 1970s is still a mystery; his mere appearance can numb a viewer more quickly than almost anyone we've seen since Fred MacMurray in "My Three Sons."

ONE RAINY AFTERNOON ☆½
1936, USA
Francis Lederer, Ida Lupino, Hugh Herbert, Roland Young, Erik Rhodes, Donald Meek, Mischa Auer, Countess Liev de Maigret. Directed by Rowland V. Lee. 75 min.

One rainy afternoon is the amount of time we suggest you spend with this forgettable 1930s comedy, and then only if it's a particularly *dull* rainy afternoon. Something must have been lost in the translation of this adaptation of a popular French comedy. A young man sits down next to a woman in a movie theater and, mistaking her for his girlfriend, kisses her. She has a conniption, he is arrested, the contretemps gets in all the newspapers, and the girl and he end up falling in love. Preston Sturges is credited with cowriting the lyrics for the two songs: Too bad they didn't let him write the dialogue as well.

ONE SHOE MAKES IT MURDER ☆☆
1982, USA (TV)
Robert Mitchum, Mel Ferrer, Angie Dickinson, John Harkins, Jose Perez. Directed by William Hale.

This is a fairly polished detective yarn that benefits from Robert Mitchum's tough-guy persona and Angie Dickinson's jaded glamour. Hard-boiled Mitchum plays a washed-up private eye who becomes entangled in a hard-to-fathom case involving a gambling bigshot's unfaithful wife. The film was culled from the novel *So Little Cause for Caroline*, but the book's rougher edges have been ironed out to make a smooth, unexceptional TV thriller. A little more pizzazz was in order.

ONE SINGS, THE OTHER DOESN'T ☆½
1977, France
Valerie Mairesse, Therese Liotard. Directed by Agnes Varda. 105 min.

Agnes Varda's feminist comedy-drama explores the friendship of two women at a turning point of gender consciousness-raising. Suzanne, the older woman, has two illegitimate children as a legacy of the flower-child era, and Pauline, the younger woman, is a blithely unworried child of the 1970s, the first semi-adult of the postlib generation. Varda is unabashedly didactic, but she's also a wise enough filmmaker to give the central relationship wit and warmth; it's easy to overlook the fact that both women are really more ideological props than believable characters. Intelligent and light-spirited nonetheless, it's a mainstream feminist work, and as such a comparative rarity.

ONE STEP TO HELL ☆½
1967, USA
Ty Hardin, Pier Angeli, George Sanders, Rossano Brazzi, Helga Line. Directed by Sandy Howard. 90 min.

This is a cornball costume drama with an international cast acting with all the enthusiasm of actors trapped in a public service announcement. Of course, it would be hard to muster much interest in still another trackdown scenario about a lawman trying to rid the African bush of murderous varmints. If that sounds like a Western transposed to Africa, it's not surprising: that's exactly what it is.

1,001 RABBIT TALES

See *Bugs Bunny's 3rd Movie: 1,001 Rabbit Tales*

ONE TOUCH OF VENUS ☆☆½
1948, USA
Ava Gardner, Robert Walker, Dick Haymes, Eve Arden, Tom Conway, Olga San Juan. Directed by William Seiter. 81 min.

Mary Pickford was a better actress than producer. In overseeing this adaptation of the S.J. Perelman-Ogden Nash-Kurt Weill Broadway musical about a statue of Venus that comes to life, the former silent screen idol nixed director Gregory La Cava in favor of reliable but bland William Seiter and, to play Venus, Ginger Rogers and Deanna Durbin in favor of Ava Gardner (beautiful, but she can't act, sing, or dance). She also threw out twelve of the sixteen Nash-Weill songs and all of the fascinating Agnes DeMille ballet sequences. To anyone who saw the 1944 show (starring Mary Martin in her first adult role), the film must have seemed a horror. Yet today, without a contemporary touchstone to compare it with, it's fairly pleasant, thanks to a lively supporting cast and the few melodies (including the haunting "Speak Low") that remain.

ONE TRICK PONY ☆☆½
1980, USA, R
Paul Simon, Blair Brown, Rip Torn, Joan Hackett, Alan Goorwitz, Mare Winningham, Lou Reed, Harry Shearer, Tiny Tim, the Lovin' Spoonful, the B-52's, Sam and Dave. Directed by Robert M. Young. 98 min.

Paul Simon also wrote and scored this film, in which he plays a singer who made it with one big hit a decade ago and has now been reduced to opening shows for New Wave bands. Conflicts arise from his wife, who wants him to settle down, and his record company, pushing for material that's more Top 40. Once you get used to Simon playing a character that's different from himself—when a pop singer makes a movie, we just naturally assume that he's going to play himself—you can settle in and enjoy a lot of good songs and in-jokes about the music community. (The best is in the casting of Lou Reed as a Richard Perryish producer.) The drama succeeds by not aspiring too high or going for "big" scenes; it may be minor, but better a minor success than an ambitious failure.

ONE, TWO, THREE ☆☆☆
1961, USA
James Cagney, Arlene Francis, Pamela Tiffin, Horst Bucholz, Lilo Pulver, Hans Lothar, Howard St. John. Directed by Billy Wilder. 108 min.

This is a Cold War comedy in which the director keeps the gags flying so fast that you won't have time to catch your breath—if a one-liner falls flat, another whizzes by a few seconds later to make you laugh. James Cagney's a Coca-Cola bigwig who's perturbed when his boss's daffy daughter marries a Communist. It's certainly not as polished as Billy Wilder's other anticommunist free-for-all script, *Ninotchka*, but in its good-naturedly vulgar way, it's hilarious, with Cagney delivering the jokes with his inimitable rapid-fire dexterity. (This was his last role until his celebrated cameo in *Ragtime* twenty years later.)

ONE WILD MOMENT ☆☆½
1980, France
Jean-Pierre Marielle, Victor Lanoux, Agnes Soral, Christine Dejoux. Directed by Claude Berri. 88 min.

This prototypical French sex comedy has a premise just spicy enough to make it interesting: On the Riviera, a middle-aged man begins an affair with his best friend's teenage daughter. Director Claude Berri manages to make the most of the comic possibilities—he even has the befuddled father enlist the aid of the guilt-stricken culprit in a search for the man who defiled his daughter. Berri also wants the pleasure of exploring the affair's emotional ramifications for all concerned—but do you really want to see halfhearted sensitivity in a musical-beds farce? Whatever the answer, you'll probably enjoy the antics here a bit more than in the subsequent Americanization, *Blame It on Rio*.

ON GOLDEN POND ☆☆½
1981, USA, PG
Henry Fonda, Katharine Hepburn, Jane Fonda, Dabney Coleman, Doug McKeon. Directed by Mark Rydell. 109 min.

Film echoed life in this popular box-office hit about a crotchety father (Henry Fonda, in his last role) who reaches a final truce with his once-antagonistic daughter (Jane Fonda). The union of the real-life father-daughter pair may have seemed like a casting coup, but although Henry is sturdy and workmanlike, Jane is surprisingly (and ironically) unconvincing. Katharine Hepburn, as the old man's resilient Yankee wife, supplies the real fun in Ernest Thompson's adaptation of his own Broadway play. Both she and Henry Fonda (also paired for the first time) won Oscars for their work (his first, her fourth). In their scenes together, they turn this mawkish, old-fashioned family melodrama into something golden indeed.

ON HER MAJESTY'S SECRET SERVICE ☆½
1969, Great Britain
George Lazenby, Diana Rigg, Telly Savalas, Ilse Steppat, Gabriele Ferzetti. Directed by Peter Hunt. 140 min.

In the agonizing four-year period between *You Only Live Twice* and *Diamonds Are Forever*, George Lazenby stepped into Sean Connery's blazers to play 007 on this occasion. (Remarkably, Lazenby, whose immortality ended with this film, looks like a cross between Connery and his eventual replacement, Roger Moore.) The novelty, however, of having a different man play James Bond (a fact that the film readily acknowledges) soon becomes tiresome because Lazenby completely lacks Connery's sense of humor and style. The film's villain (Telly Savalas as a Russian) is also less interesting than usual and, although she tries hard, Diana Rigg is wasted in the role of the society playgirl that Bond ends up marrying. *Service* also offers the first dull action sequences in a James Bond flick, foreshadowing things to come in more recent entries, and the plot is both convoluted and interminable. It's no wonder so many can't remember this one is a James Bond film.

THE ONION FIELD ☆☆☆½
1979, USA, R
John Savage, James Woods, Ted Danson, Franklyn Seales, Ronny Cox, David Huffman, Christopher Lloyd. Directed by Harold Becker. 126 min.

Deeply dissatisfied with the previous screen adaptations of his works (*The New Centurions*, *The Choirboys*), crime writer Joseph Wambaugh closely supervised this factual drama about the kidnapping of two cops, the murder of one of them, and the toll of the nightmarish experience on the partner who lived. The result is a sterling tale of justice miscarried, abetted by four terrific performances. Ted Danson, as the slain cop, and Franklyn Seales, as the weaker of the criminals, give admirably understated performances, allowing you to rivet your attention to John Savage, as the officer who, as the trials drag on for years, begins to crumble, and James Woods, a terrifying incarnation of the calculating killer. It's not always as clearly or neatly told as it might have been, but the story's oddities come from its close adherence to the facts, and Wambaugh's refusal to sacrifice truth for drama is hard to fault.

THE ONLY GAME IN TOWN ☆
1970, USA
Elizabeth Taylor, Warren Beatty, Charles Braswell, Hank Henry, Olga Valery. Directed by George Stevens. 113 min.

George Stevens's twenty-fifth, last, and arguably worst film is best avoided, even (or perhaps especially) if you admire his other work or the two stars. It's a draggy two-character drama based on a flop play by Frank Gilroy and set in an ugly studio-built Las Vegas. Elizabeth Taylor plays an overaged, overweight, overwrought chorine hoping to find love in the arms of gambling addict Warren Beatty. Beatty, thirty-two when this was shot, stepped in when fifty-five-year-old Frank Sinatra bowed out; the characters are so unbelievable and the dialogue so maudlin that it doesn't matter. It's shudder-inducing embarrassment.

THE ONLY WAY ☆☆☆½
1970, USA/Denmark/Panama
Martin Potter, Jane Seymour, Ove Sprogoe. Directed by Bent Christensen. 98 min.

This powerful low-budget film is based on a true incident in Danish history in which, following that country's occupation by the Nazis, more than 7,000 Jews were evacuated to Sweden in a few nights. A good deal of the film is given to establishing the cultural assimilation of the Jews in Denmark, who were accepted to the point where they were not regarded (either by themselves or non-Jews) as other than average pre-invasion citizens. It's an inspiring addition to the record of humanitarian forces that were mobilized during the Holocaust.

ONLY WHEN I LAUGH ☆☆
1981, USA, R
Marsha Mason, James Coco, Kristy McNichol, Joan Hackett, David Dukes. Directed by Glenn Jordan. 120 min.

Neil Simon reworked his play *The Gingerbread Lady* into this maudlin comedy-drama about showbiz stereotypes, the subject he knows best. Marsha Mason plays an alcoholic actress who returns from a dry-out clinic to reestablish ties with her emotionally wounded teenage daughter; her weepy, histrionic work won an Oscar nomination, as did James Coco and Joan Hackett for supporting performances that do little to illuminate the best-friend stock roles of Unhappy Gay Actor and Woman Afraid of Getting Old. Ignored was the subtle, intelligent work of Kristy McNichol, who makes you root for the daughter to ditch these pathetic, self-indulgent adults and depart for greener pastures or better movies. It's the playwright's time-proven blend of witty babble and huggy uplift, and on those terms, it should please his fans.

ONLY WITH MARRIED MEN ☆☆
1974, USA (TV)
David Birney, Michele Lee, John Astin, Judy Carne, Dom DeLuise, Gavin MacLeod. Directed by Jerry Paris. 78 min.

Not even Claudette Colbert and Cary Grant in their prime could have redeemed this fluff, which wrestles with the New Morality and gets slammed to the mat. Michele Lee headlines this coquettish comedy as a bachelorette who eases the singles scene by confining herself to married men, who presumably aren't looking to get married and are therefore "safe." Farcical complications abound as a bachelor fakes a marriage and tries to capture the marriage-shy maiden's heart. It's harmless fun, but the sexual implications would be disturbing if the film were intended as anything more than a comic striptease.

ON THE BEACH ☆☆☆½
1959, USA
Gregory Peck, Ava Gardner, Fred Astaire, Anthony Perkins, Donna Anderson. Directed by Stanley Kramer. 134 min.

A grim, still-powerful black-and-white drama about nuclear war and how the citizens of Melbourne prepare for the inevitable. The John Paxton-James Lee Barrett screenplay (based on the novel by Nevil Shute) focuses on a submarine captain (Gregory Peck), an embittered woman (Ava Gardner), an atomic scientist (Fred Astaire), and two hysterical newlyweds (Anthony Perkins and Donna Anderson). Stanley Kramer's direction is more affecting than usual, perhaps because of the doom-laden theme, and the final shots say more than any more graphic depiction could. Stanley Kubrick's *Dr. Strangelove* did hit closer to home, and *Fail Safe* was, strictly speaking, a better drama, but this was one of the first atomic menace movies and it remains a chilling picture, even bleaker and more uncompromising than the TV movie *The Day After*.

ON THE EDGE ☆☆
1986, USA, PG-13
Bruce Dern, John Marley, Bill Bailey, Jim Haynie. Directed by Rob Nilsson. 86 min.

This is a rather wet-eyed inspirational sports drama that should appeal primarily to those who view jogging as a religious activity. The acolyte here is Bruce Dern, training for the oldest footrace on the West Coast and psyching himself up with exercise, mental preparation, and talk, talk, talk—enough bubble-headed blather about going over the edge, hitting the wall, and personal triumph to make your head hurt more than his feet.

ON THE NICKEL
1980, USA ★★
Donald Moffat, Ralph Waite, Hal Williams, Penelope Allen, Jack Kehoe. Directed by Ralph Waite. 96 min.

Ralph Waite of "The Waltons" produced, wrote, directed, and costars in this well-intentioned but failed attempt to paint a portrait of life on skid row (in the film's street slang, the "nickel"). He plays a bum whose best friend (Donald Moffat), an alcoholic who has managed to remain on the wagon, tries to help him without being pulled back into the street himself. What could have been an American adult variant on Luis Buñuel's *Los Olvidados* instead becomes overly sentimental, offering no explanation for why these men are this way except that they are responsible for themselves.

ON THE RIGHT TRACK
1981, USA, PG ★★
Gary Coleman, Maureen Stapleton, Michael Lembeck, Norman Fell, Lisa Eilbacher. Directed by Lee Philips. 98 min.

This is a glorified TV movie (even though it was released in theaters) with the pint-size wonder, Gary Coleman, a little Mr. Buttinski, combining the determined cuteness of Shirley Temple with the sophisticated wisecracking style of a Flip Wilson. Because of his ability to play the ponies successfully, Gary becomes a popular little fellow. But he's also a lovable, homeless orphan who lives out of a train station locker (in fact, he's small enough to crawl inside and live there, but he doesn't, perhaps fearing that a critic would lock him in). Naturally, a happy home is in store for plucky Gary in this agreeable, lightweight comedy.

ON THE TOWN
1949, USA ★★★
Gene Kelly, Frank Sinatra, Jules Munshin, Ann Miller, Betty Garrett, Vera-Ellen. Directed by Gene Kelly and Stanley Donen. 98 min.

This musical follows the amorous adventures of three sailors—Gene Kelly, Frank Sinatra, and Jules Munshin—during an action-packed twenty-four-hour leave in New York City. The three sing and dance their way through the colorful sights of Manhattan, and the girls they meet along the way—Ann Miller, Betty Garrett, and Vera-Ellen—prove to be the best tour guides a sailor could hope for. Though still fast-paced and energetic, *On the Town* has lost much of its appeal over the years. What was once considered revolutionary—the location shooting, the special effects, the story-within-the-story ballet sequence, etc.—now looks dated or just plain ordinary. Also, although the "new" Hollywood songs are serviceable, the elimination of Broadway's original score was a sad mistake. All in all, it's the dance numbers that hold up best.

ON THE WATERFRONT
1954, USA ★★★★
Marlon Brando, Eva Marie Saint, Rod Steiger, Karl Malden, Lee J. Cobb, Martin Balsam, Fred Gwynne. Directed by Elia Kazan. 108 min.

Marlon Brando won his first Oscar for a breathtaking, emotionally charged performance in Elia Kazan's profound study of a confused young dockworker caught up in union struggles on the New York waterfront. In her screen debut, Miss Saint confidently carries her own weight as the young woman who loves and inspires Brando, and Rod Steiger proves himself a talent in the role of Brando's corrupt brother. Boris Kaufman's cinematography gives the film visual intensity, and Leonard Bernstein supplies the final touches for this model drama with his commanding score. Winner of eight Academy Awards, including Best Picture.

ON VALENTINE'S DAY
1986, USA, PG ★★★
William Converse-Roberts, Hallie Foote, Michael Higgins, Steven Hill, Rochelle Oliver, Richard Jenkins, Carol Goodheart, Matthew Broderick. Directed by Ken Harrison. 106 min.

Horton Foote has written nine plays in his cycle about small-town Texas life called *An Orphan's Home*, and this is the second play from the cycle to be made into a film. Ken Harrison again teams with Foote, and this time out their grasp of the material is sure-handed and affecting. The film is set before the time of *1918* and provides insights into the characters that were missing in that movie. Most of the action concerns the early married life of Elizabeth and Horace Robedaux, marvelously played by Foote's daughter Hallie and William Converse-Roberts. There is little more to the film than the quiet speech of gentle people talking to each other; though Foote is a good writer with an ear for dialogue, it is disappointing that the characters never get the chance to change through circumstances. The period is beautifully evoked, and the film's satisfactions, though small, are many.

OPERATION AMSTERDAM
1958, Great Britain ★★½
Peter Finch, Eva Bartok, Tony Britton, Alexander Knox, Malcolm Keen, Tim Turner. Directed by Michael McCarthy. 104 min.

Once again, the British properly pat themselves on the back for having done such a smashing job in World War II by making a movie to celebrate one of the many daring missions pulled off by their crack troops. Problem is that, having spent much of that decade grinding out films like this, the most exciting mission left unfilmed by 1958 involved smuggling industrial diamonds out of Holland circa 1940 (just to make sure the Nazis wouldn't get them). To add some thrills, and to kill some spare time, the Brits also blow up an oil dump before bidding a fond farewell to the land of tulips and dikes. However, it's well enough made and played.

OPERATION C.I.A.
1965, USA ★★½
Burt Reynolds, Kieu Chinh, Danielle Aubrey, John Hoyt, Cyril Collack. Directed by Christian Nyby. 90 min.

This is a sharp action tale with more than passing interest due to the story's location. Burt Reynolds fans will enjoy seeing a young, sleek Burt embroiled in spyjinks in Vietnam as he attempts to abort an assassination attempt in Saigon. The background details about political subversiveness and the creation of a nightmarish world where citizens are perpetually at the mercy of their government give this film a lot of narrative thrust.

OPERATION FRED
Great Britain ★★½
Danny La Rue, Lance Percival, Alfred Marks. Directed by Bob Kellett. 90 min.

English audiences have a definite taste for high drag and unless you have a high tolerance for mistaken-identity plots and cross-dressing humor, you'd better steer clear. This elaborately plotted, but rather drably photographed star vehicle for that ingenious female impersonator Danny La Rue doesn't feature the wild burlesquing of a Benny Hill or Milton Berle. Rather, La Rue can pass quite adequately for a woman; and the comedy proceeds from the situations his gender-bending leads him into. It's breezy fun if you like English whimsy like the *Carry On* series, but it has none of the serious underpinnings of *Tootsie* or the big laughs of *La Cage aux Folles*. Still, it's a feast for lovers of double entendres and the art of ribbing our sexual conditioning.

OPERATION PETTICOAT
1959, USA ★★½
Cary Grant, Tony Curtis, Joan O'Brien, Dina Merrill, Gene Evans, Arthur O'Connell, Virginia Gregg, Gavin MacLeod, Marion Ross. Directed by Blake Edwards. 124 min.

In *Some Like It Hot*, Tony Curtis does a devastating impression of Cary Grant. Logic followed that in Curtis's next film, he would costar with Grant. They play commanders of a dilapidated submarine carrying nurses, Filipino families, and a goat through

World War II Philippines. There's something unsettling about extracting jokes out of the war setting (as Edwards did again, and even more tastelessly, in *What Did You Do in the War, Daddy?*), and most of the sight gags have to do with the gobs squeezing past the buxom nurses in the sub's narrow passageways. The saving grace is Grant. He can make even slight and slightly offensive material seem fresh and funny. Otherwise, this is *Das Boot* as envisioned by Jerry Lewis.

OPERATION THUNDERBOLT ☆☆☆
1977, Israel
Yehoram Gaon, Assaf Dayan, Ori Levy, Arik Lavi, Klaus Kinski, Sybil Danning. Directed by Menahem Golan. 120 min.

This is one of three films that came out at roughly the same time concerning the Israeli commando raid on the airport at Entebbe, Uganda, in 1976, where terrorists were holding Jewish passengers captive. (The other two, *Raid on Entebbe* and *Victory at Entebbe*, were made for television.) This is the best of the three because it lacks an overload of "special guest stars" and because it was made with the cooperation of the Israeli government, giving it a verisimilitude lacking in the other versions. Surprisingly, though, it is *not* merely a piece of patriotic self-congratulation, but a solid, believable action film. Klaus Kinski stands out in the mostly nonprofessional cast as a German terrorist.

ORCA ☆
1977, USA, PG
Richard Harris, Charlotte Rampling, Will Sampson, Bo Derek, Keenan Wynn, Robert Carradine. Directed by Michael Anderson. 92 min.

Audiences have Dino De Laurentiis to thank for this cheapjack *Jaws* rip-off, which has a killer whale seeking vengeance on the sailor (Richard Harris) who inadvertently maimed his pregnant mate. Charlotte Rampling stands by to offer sober explanations of Orca's behavior, and Bo Derek has a pre-*10* appearance as—what else?—the resident sexpot. It's all ludicrous and uninvolving, Harris is all ham, and you could create more impressive special effects in your bathtub. There's even an awful theme song, "My Love, We Are One," presumably crooned by the title character to his amour.

ORDEAL BY INNOCENCE ☆½
1984, Great Britain, PG
Donald Sutherland, Faye Dunaway, Christopher Plummer, Ian McShane, Diana Quick, Phoebe Nicholls, Sarah Miles. Directed by Desmond Davis. 87 min.

The right ingredients—an all-star cast, an Agatha Christie plot, a generally slick production—are all in place, but this whodunit set in 1958 lacks the style, wit, and suspense of *Murder on the Orient Express* or even *Death on the Nile*. Without a Miss Marple or Hercule Poirot to anchor her plots, Christie was usually a bit lost, and their absence here makes the talky, tangled plot seem barely worth unraveling. Donald Sutherland fills in as an extremely uninspired sleuth, and Faye Dunaway, prominent billing notwithstanding, appears only briefly, as the victim.

THE ORDEAL OF DR. MUDD ☆☆☆½
1980, USA (TV)
Dennis Weaver, Susan Sullivan, Richard Dysart, Michael McGuire, Nigel Davenport, Arthur Hill. Directed by Paul Wendkos. 143 min.

This is a perfectly realized TV film about a little-known historical fact. Having unwittingly aided the wounded John Wilkes Booth after he assassinated Lincoln, Dr. Samuel Mudd was charged with abetting Booth and sentenced for his alleged complicity to the penal colony at Shark Island. This is a harrowing treatment of a man swept up in an historical tide he's unable to swim against; and Dennis Weaver is astonishingly right in every detail as the unfortunate Dr. Mudd. This is one of the few TV remakes that bears favorable comparison with the theatrical original, in this case John Ford's memorable *The Prisoner of Shark Island*.

ORDINARY PEOPLE ☆☆☆☆
1980, USA, R
Donald Sutherland, Mary Tyler Moore, Timothy Hutton, Judd Hirsch, Elizabeth McGovern, M. Emmet Walsh. Directed by Robert Redford. 123 min.

Robert Redford's directorial debut is a truly penetrating and compassionate drama about the hidden desperation of an upper-middle-class suburban family forced to come to terms with a repressed family tragedy. Donald Sutherland, Mary Tyler Moore, and son Timothy Hutton create an extraordinary portrayal of ordinary people who are emotionally crippled by their denial of the past. Judd Hirsch turns in a sincere performance as the psychiatrist who gets involved by way of treating Conrad (Hutton) after his release from a hospital. Academy Awards went to the film, Redford, Hutton, and Alvin Sargent, who adapted Judith Guest's novel for the screen.

THE ORGANIZATION ☆☆
1971, USA, PG
Sidney Poitier, Barbara McNair, Gerald S. O'Loughlin, Sheree North, Fred Beir, Allen Garfield, Raul Julia. Directed by Don Medford. 105 min.

Sidney Poitier's third outing as detective Virgil Tibbs lacks the punch of *In the Heat of the Night*; it's just a competent, workmanlike police procedural set in San Francisco. The politically tinged plot has Tibbs opposing the police force to assist a group of anti-drug activists who will use any method to foil a ring of heroin smugglers, but there's nothing terribly interesting about the tale or the telling. Barbara McNair makes a blink-and-you-miss-it appearance as Tibbs's wife, and Dan Travanti ("Hill Street Blues") and Max Gail ("Barney Miller") also have small roles.

ORPHANS OF THE STORM ☆☆☆
1921, USA
Lillian Gish, Dorothy Gish, Joseph Schildkraut, Frank Puglia, Catherine Emmett. Directed by D.W. Griffith. 125 min.

This is one of D.W. Griffith's finest, a brilliantly staged epic of the French Revolution with a slightly tiresome romantic melodrama threaded through it. Lillian and Dorothy Gish, playing sisters, escape the clutches of a debauched nobleman, are separated, and spend most of the movie trying to get back together. Griffith recreates a detailed vision of eighteenth-century Paris, and his scenes of mob violence are thrilling, even if the plot is somewhat less than plausible.

ORPHAN TRAIN ☆☆☆
1979, USA (TV)
Jill Eikenberry, Kevin Dobson, Linda Manz. Directed by William Graham. 156 min.

This is a superior TV film without any filler—just a strong narrative vigorously directed. And although it deals with children, it does not sentimentalize the material. Based on an historical novel, this uplifting film captures a true sense of the mid-1800s as a persevering social worker leads a group of impoverished orphans to new lives out on the American frontier. It's a vivid history lesson and an enthralling TV film filled with drama and a spirit of adventure.

ORPHEUS ☆☆☆☆
1949, France
Jean Marais, Francois Perier, Maria Casares, Marie Dea. Directed by Jean Cocteau. 86 min.

This is one of screen magician Jean Cocteau's luminous explorations of the creative process and romantic love. Building his own highly stylized version of the Orpheus legend, Cocteau spins a mysterious, shimmering tale about a modern poet's descent into hell in search of his beloved. It's a journey to the underworld that is made dangerous by the guiding spirit of the Princess of Death, by whom Orpheus becomes entranced. This is a landmark film—

mesmerizing, with arresting imagery (Death takes joyrides on a motorcycle), and an iconoclastic use of cinematic conventions and properties.

THE OSCAR ☆
1966, USA
Stephen Boyd, Elke Sommer, Tony Bennett, Jill St. John, Joseph Cotten, Milton Berle, Eleanor Parker, Edie Adams, Ernest Borgnine, Ed Begley, Walter Brennan, Broderick Crawford, Peter Lawford, Jack Soo. Directed by Russell Rouse. 119 min.

"He has no genitalia, and he's holding a sword," Dustin Hoffman once remarked upon winning the golden statuette that's at the heart of this camp classic—Hollywood's delirious paean to its own incessant greed and vulgarity. It's appropriate that this unintentionally hilarious melodrama about a rat actor (Stephen Boyd) in quest of the Academy Award should be every bit as castrated as the idol it worships. You won't find any genuine Tinseltown grit here, just the coy, shallow scum that's flogged to life by a gloriously tacky 1960s cast (see above). This film has no redeeming features—it exerts a fascination comparable to the first time you find out that a chicken can live and walk without a head.

THE OSTERMAN WEEKEND ☆☆½
1983, USA, R
Rutger Hauer, John Hurt, Burt Lancaster, Meg Foster, Dennis Hopper, Craig T. Nelson. Directed by Sam Peckinpah. 105 min.

Four friends get together for an annual weekend in the country with their wives. But this time something is different: Their host has allowed a deranged CIA agent to wire his house with video and audio equipment because he has been convinced that his four friends are all involved in an anti-U.S. conspiracy. There are bizarre performances, weird double and triple crosses, and the usual slow-motion violence in the last film by director Sam Peckinpah, also responsible for *Straw Dogs, The Wild Bunch, Bring Me the Head of Alfredo Garcia,* and others. From the novel by Robert Ludlum.

OTELLO ☆☆☆
1986, USA, PG
Placido Domingo, Katia Ricciarelli, Justino Diaz, Petra Malakova, Urbano Barberini, Massimo Foschi. Directed by Franco Zeffirelli. 124 min.

Franco Zeffirelli's lush, picturesque adaptation of what some critics call Verdi's greatest opera should please and delight cineastes; opera buffs may have more to quarrel with—the libretto has been cut, and some of the supporting roles are poorly sung. However, Placido Domingo gives a spectacular singing and acting interpretation of the jealous Moor, Justino Diaz is properly malevolent as Iago, and Zeffirelli's robust, splendidly active staging cannot be faulted. All in all, it's a worthy companion to the director's *La Traviata,* and a confirmation of Domingo's stature as the preeminent opera actor of our time.

THE OTHER SIDE OF MIDNIGHT ☆½
1977, USA, R
Marie-France Pisier, John Beck, Susan Sarandon, Raf Vallone. Directed by Charles Jarrot. 165 min.

Sidney Sheldon's glittery, garbagy novel comes to the screen in an engorged rendering that doesn't even meet its cheesy goal. The plot concerns a young, vengeful French actress and the two men in her life, a dashing flyer and a Greek tycoon. By the time the closing credits weigh in three hours later, you'll feel as if you've experienced the characters more fully than a mere nightmare would allow. A wire-hanger abortion scene is thrown in for good gratuitous measure. Even if you're a sleaze hunter, there are better bargains to be found.

THE OTHER SIDE OF PARADISE
See *Foxtrot*

THE OTHER SIDE OF THE MOUNTAIN ☆☆
1975, USA, PG
Marilyn Hassett, Beau Bridges, Belinda Montgomery, Nan Martin, William Bryant, Dabney Coleman. Directed by Larry Peerce. 101 min.

In the 1950s, downhill skier Jill Kinmont was an Olympic sure shot until a tragic accident during a trial competition left her paralyzed below the shoulders. This film biography details the accident, and her efforts to adjust to life as a paraplegic; it's not bad, just dull and unable to surmount the clichés of its uplift-and-inspiration genre. Marilyn Hassett is attractive as Kinmont, and Beau Bridges does well as the man in her life, but the downbeat ending should deter all but the most devoted from the sequel.

THE OTHER SIDE OF THE MOUNTAIN PART II ☆½
1978, USA, PG
Marilyn Hassett, Timothy Bottoms, Nan Martin, Belinda Montgomery, Gretchen Corbett, William Bryant, James Bottoms, Charles Frank. Directed by Larry Peerce. 97 min.

Real life has the ring of bad fiction in this dreary sequel to the drama about skier Jill Kinmont's efforts to overcome her paralysis and built a new life for herself. Larry Peerce's followup milks every tear it can, using so many clips from the first film that this one almost seems superfluous, unless you were on the edge of your seat at the end of the original, wondering if Kinmont would ever find happiness. She did, but you won't if you sit through this.

OUR DAILY BREAD ☆☆☆☆
1934, USA
Karen Morley, Tom Keene. Directed by King Vidor. 80 min.

This is an austere, naturalistic portrait of Depression America that demonstrates the regenerative power of the native soil over the broken spirit of the urban poor. An archetypal couple starts a communal farm, and the group learns that cooperation and understanding are necessary for success. Although its concern for social significance reflects the goals of 1930s art more than 1980s thematic taste, King Vidor's breathtaking visual realization is as powerful as ever. The scene of cutting an irrigation ditch, which Vidor directed to the beat of a metronome, is justifiably famous and often excerpted to teach the dynamics of movement and editing.

OUR FAMILY BUSINESS ☆☆½
1981, USA (TV)
Sam Wanamaker, Vera Miles, Ted Danson, Ray Milland, Deborah Carney, James Luisi, Ayn Ruyman, Chip Mayer. Directed by Robert Collins. 74 min.

This slickly photographed look at a Mafia clan was a bit ahead of its time. Although it didn't make it from pilot status, a similar 1985–86 pilot called "Our Family Honor" did. The attempt to squeeze a *Godfather*esque epic into the confines of a TV film is commendable but hardly viable. Although the film's examination of loyalties and chicanery within the various mob factions is often exciting and sufficiently different from standard TV fare, it fails to explore the mobster myths with any complexity. It simply lacks the savagery and dark underpinnings that made the Coppola *Godfather* films so extraordinary.

OUR RELATIONS ☆☆☆
1936, USA
Stan Laurel, Oliver Hardy, Betty Healy, Daphne Pollard, James Finlayson, Alan Hale. Directed by Harry Lachman. 72 min.

Whereas some of Laurel and Hardy's MGM features are cramped with musical numbers and subplots (*The Bohemian*

Girl, Swiss Miss), this comedy nugget gives the boys plenty of elbow room. Laurel and Hardy play both nagged husbands and look-alike sailors on leave. As one could imagine, there are more than a few hilarious misunderstandings, and the gags include one priceless sequence in a phone booth. It's an absolute must for fans but recommended to all. *Note:* Stan produced for the first time with this film.

OUR TOWN ☆☆☆
1940, USA
Frank Craven, William Holden, Martha Scott, Fay Bainter, Beulah Bondi, Thomas Mitchell. Directed by Sam Wood. 90 min.

Thorton Wilder's Pulitzer Prize-winning play looks on screen like little more than an expertly made Andy Hardy movie. With the play's ending disastrously altered and strikingly sparse set design filled in, the results are often conventional (much like other small-town movies made around World War II) and its life-affirming message severely diminished. It's a nostalgic look at the many denizens of a turn-of-the-century New Hampshire hamlet, including two young lovers (William Holden and Martha Scott) and their respective families. The talented cast and solid production values make this pleasing fare but the film is far from classic status.

OUR TOWN ☆☆½
1975, USA (TV)
Hal Holbrook, Sada Thompson, Robby Benson, Glynnis O'Connor, Barbara Bel Geddes, Ned Beatty, Ronny Cox. Directed by George Schaeffer. 90 min.

This celebrated TV transcription of Thornton Wilder's Pulitzer Prize-winning play is more faithful but less gripping than the 1940 Hollywood film. Director George Shaeffer decided to follow Wilder's stage directions by rote, stripping away most of the props and sets and, although the cast opens nonexistent doors with great skill, the effect (on film) is jarringly theatrical. This production should be praised, however, for retaining the uncompromising but life-affirming conclusion that was missing in Hollywood's adaptation. Otherwise, the cast does its best with this reverent but unexciting version of the great play: Hal Holbrook is perfect as the gruff, omniscient "stage manager," Barbara Bel Geddes is charming as Robby Benson's mother, and even Benson and Glynnis O'Connor (costars in *Ode to Billy Joe*, *Jeremy*, and *Walk Proud*) are sweet and unaffected as the gawky small-town lovers.

OUT CALIFORNIA WAY ☆
1946, USA
Monte Hale, Adrian Booth, John Dehner, The Riders of the Purple Sage. Directed by Lesley Selander. 67 min.

This is a dopey comedy about the making of B Westerns in Hollywood. There are no shoot-'em-ups, no action, no fun, and no personality in Monte Hale, who's a poor man's Roy Rogers (the real one makes a cameo appearance) in this short-lived Republic series.

THE OUTCAST ☆☆½
1954, USA
John Derek, Joan Evans, Jim Davis, Catherine McLeod, Slim Pickens, Harry Carey, Jr., Bob Steele. Directed by William Witney. 90 min.

John Derek acquits himself quite well in this standard but action-packed Western made in the days before he went on to become a photographer and developer of sexy female stars. He plays a rancher's son seeking to regain his late father's property after his uncle has seized it on the basis of a forged will. Ex-serial director William Witney keeps things moving at a serviceable clip.

OUTLAND ☆☆☆
1981, USA, R
Sean Connery, Peter Boyle, Frances Sternhagen, James Sikking. Directed by Peter Hyams. 109 min.

Peter Hyams's high-tech science-fiction film has rightfully been called "*High Noon* in outer space." In the righteous tradition of Gregory Peck, Sean Connery plays a marshal at a planetary mining colony who runs afoul of the drug-smuggling head of operations. Despite the immense size of the place and the seedy characters, everything begins to seem like a Western when a group of assassins is sent to dispatch Connery, and the "townsfolk" are too frightened to help the "sheriff." Hyams lacks the tight dramatic pacing of Fred Zinnemann, but his cluttered visual sense and romanticized violence make for an interesting genre hybrid.

THE OUTLAW ☆☆½
1943, USA
Jane Russell, Jack Beutel, Walter Huston, Thomas Mitchell, Joe Sawyer, Mimi Aguglia. Directed by Howard Hughes, (Howard Hawks). 123 min.

The saga of Billy the Kid has been filmed in widescreen (*Billy the Kid*, 1930), in Technicolor (*Billy the Kid*, 1940), with neurosis (*The Left-Handed Gun*, 1958), opposite Dracula (*Billy the Kid Meets Dracula*, 1966), and splattered with blood (*Pat Garrett and Billy the Kid*, 1974), but Howard Hughes tops them all with this raunchy rendering. Hughes not only broke a few Production Code rules with his depiction of sexual themes but also gave Billy his only (thus far) happy ending. The decadent entrepreneur enlisted some superior Hollywood talent to put together this item, campy even in 1943—director Howard Hawks (uncredited), screenwriter Jules Furthman, cinematographer Gregg Toland, composer Victor Young, and character actors Thomas Mitchell (as Pat Garrett) and Walter Huston (as Doc Holliday)—but the real highlight is Hughes's revolutionary "bosom art" gimmick. Hughes not only "discovered" the buxom Jane Russell (here playing Rio, a Latin temptress) but designed her bras for the film, or so legend has it. Originally filmed in 1941, *The Outlaw* was held up by censorship problems until its limited 1943 release. A much-shortened 1947 release finally emerged, but this video print is one of the longer, steamier versions available.

OUTLAW BLUES ☆☆
1977, USA, PG
Peter Fonda, Susan Saint James, John Crawford, Michael Lerner, James Callahan. Directed by Richard T. Heffron. 101 min.

This amiable country-and-western comedy pokes fun at media star-making, with Peter Fonda as an ex-con who's got a knack for strumming a guitar, and Susan Saint James as the showbiz maven who falls for her new protégé. The car chases are substandard and the plot, about a nasty superstar who tries to steal Fonda's title tune, would be more at home in an Elvis Presley movie. Still, some nice moments rise above the formula, and the stars are perfectly pleasant.

THE OUTLAW JOSEY WALES ☆☆
1976, USA, PG
Clint Eastwood, Chief Dan George, Sondra Locke, Bill McKinney, John Vernon, Paula Trueman. Directed by Clint Eastwood. 135 min.

Clint Eastwood's fifth directorial effort was his last Western until *Pale Rider* (1985) and it's an unfortunately clumsy, very standard revenge saga. Clint plays a peaceable farmer who seeks bloody retribution after his family is slain . . . and we mean bloody. Wales becomes a frontier forerunner of Dirty Harry, piling up corpses at a rate beyond belief (and, one would think, beyond the confines of the PG rating as well). Eastwood can be a very effective director, but this slackly paced, muddled effort doesn't show it; with its straightforward lift of *Death Wish*'s plot, it may satisfy action buffs more than Western fans.

OUT OF AFRICA ☆☆☆½
1985, USA, PG
Meryl Streep, Robert Redford, Klaus Maria Brandauer, Michael Kitchen, Mallick Bowens, Michael Gough, Rachel Kempson, Suzanna Hamilton. Directed by Sydney Pollack. 158 min.

Sydney Pollack's romantic drama about an early chapter in the life of writer Isak Dinesen derives from five different literary sources, including fiction, reminiscence, and biography. Not surprisingly, it's shaky as a history lesson, but what's impressive is how well it's sustained as both an epic entertainment and an intimate, unusual love story shot on location in Africa. The film's starting point is the independently-minded Dinesen's arrival in East Africa to start a farm; once there, she begins to question her marriage of convenience to a caddish baron (Klaus Maria Brandauer) and falls in love with a Thoreauish man of the wilderness, Denys Finch-Hatton (Robert Redford). Redford's performance, needlessly cryptic and high-minded, is all wrong, but Meryl Streep is magnificent, finding every nuance of her cool, stubborn character, and Brandauer makes a largely unsympathetic man likable. Kurt Luedtke's screenplay is full of anecdotes, vignettes, and details, all wisely chosen, and David Watkin's cinematography and John Barry's score provide all the travelogue grandeur the film requires. There are lovely costumes designed by Milena Canonero. Winner of seven Academy Awards, including Best Picture, Director, Screenplay Adaptation, Cinematography, and Original Score.

OUT OF BOUNDS ☆☆½
1986, USA, R
Anthony Michael Hall, Jenny Wright, Jeff Kober, Meatloaf. Directed by Richard Tuggle. 93 min.

A naive boy from Cedar Rapids pays a visit to his older brother in Los Angeles, looking forward to a summer of fun and adventure in the big city. Unfortunately, he finds less fun and much more adventure than he had in mind when his red tote bag gets mixed up with another on the Los Angeles Airport carousel with an identical bag—identical, that is, except for the heroin it contains and the murderous psychopaths who want it. In his first dramatic role, Anthony Michael Hall (Sixteen Candles, The Breakfast Club, Weird Science) runs, hides, pretends to be a cool L.A. punk, kidnaps motorcyclists, rendezvouses with sociopaths, falls in love, and generally takes a tour of the Los Angeles underworld as seen through the eyes of a fairly hip set designer. Director Richard Tuggle (Tightrope) keeps things moving right along and the results are pretty entertaining. Jeff Kober is a standout as the heroin dealer from hell.

OUT OF SEASON ☆☆
1975, Great Britain
Vanessa Redgrave, Cliff Robertson, Susan George. Directed by Alan Bridges. 90 min.

Like much of director Alan Bridges's less impressive work (The TV Brief Encounter Pary), this will appeal most to terminal Anglophiles and those to whom "Masterpiece Theater" is the highlight of the week. Twenty years after an affair with the owner of a seaside hotel, a man returns for a visit. The owner now has a daughter, fully grown, who could be the man's daughter; both mother and child set their sights on him. It's all quite misty and vague, so if you like to read between the lines you'll love it. (a.k.a.: Winter Rates)

OUT OF THE BLUE ☆☆☆
1947, USA
Virginia Mayo, George Brent, Turhan Bey, Ann Dvorak, Carole Landis. Directed by Leigh Jason. 84 min.

In this effervescent, undeservedly obscure romantic trifle, upright George Brent suffers no end of complications when he discovers a beautiful stranger knocked out flat in his apartment. This is a lighthearted concoction with Ann Dvorak delightfully wacky as a comedienne. It's hard to believe she's so adept since she spent so many years playing hard-boiled neurotics at Warner Bros.

OUT OF THE BLUE ☆☆
1980, USA, R
Linda Manz, Sharon Farrell, Dennis Hopper, Raymond Burr, Don Gordon. Directed by Dennis Hopper. 94 min.

Dennis Hopper seems to have conceived his fervid study of a tough, Johnny Rotten-worshiping tomboy (Linda Manz) as the American tragedy to end all American tragedies. Alas, his ambition far outstrips his talent. Instead of giving us a small, disturbing portrait of a child on the edge, he turns his characters into cracked metaphors for evil and tosses in an apocalyptic finish that's meant to explode the ulcer festering at the heart of the American family. It's all very facile, though Hopper contributes a startling performance as Manz's passionate wreck of a father.

OUT OF THE PAST ☆☆☆½
1947, USA
Robert Mitchum, Jane Greer, Kirk Douglas, Rhonda Fleming, Richard Webb. Directed by Jacques Tourneur. 95 min.

A detective falls for a duplicitous woman with disastrous results in this grimly cynical film noir, one of the best of the genre. Director Jacques Tourneur builds his characters superbly while keeping the action dark, shadowy and impressively suspenseful, and one couldn't ask for a better, sexier performance than that of Robert Mitchum, or of Jane Greer, who plays the sweet-faced, utterly evil femme fatale. Their acting helps make Out of the Past that rare film noir that allows you to believe that lust can indeed motivate any action. The film was remade and modernized in 1984 as Against All Odds, with Greer playing the mother of the character she created.

THE OUT-OF-TOWNERS ☆½
1970, USA, G
Jack Lemmon, Sandy Dennis, Sandy Baron, Anne Meara. Directed by Arthur Hiller. 98 min.

Doesn't Neil Simon ever throw anything away? This, his first original screenplay, was meant to be one of the segments in his play Plaza Suite, but was wisely dropped. Why Simon felt compelled to pick it up and put it on the screen is a mystery; this noisy, imbecilic farce about a couple's disastrous trip to New York isn't any funnier on screen than it would have been as a playlet. Although they lose their luggage (of course) early on, Jack Lemmon and Sandy Dennis did remember to pack a steamer trunk full of their overly familiar tics, whines, shrugs, twitches, and brays; they're such an unpleasant pair that you actually begin to enjoy seeing them pelted with urban misfortune. Now, if only the screenplay would follow their lead and go back where it came from.

OUTRAGEOUS! ☆☆½
1977, Canada, R
Craig Russell, Hollis McLaren, Richard Easley, Helen Shaver. Directed by Richard Benner. 96 min.

Fans of La Cage aux Folles will take to this misfit comedy about a female impersonator yearning for acceptance from friends and associates. Noted impersonator Craig Russell plays an outcast, a gay male who is looked down upon by many of his fellow gays for performing at drag bars. He joins forces with Liza, a schizophrenic young woman who thinks she is being pursued by an imaginary creature named "The Bonecrusher." That these two persevere and succeed without giving in to the pressures of the world makes for an upbeat, enjoyable viewing experience. Russell is especially memorable when he does his routines, which include impersonations of Mae West, Barbra Streisand, Tallulah Bankhead, Bette Davis, and others.

OUTRAGEOUS FORTUNE ☆☆☆½
1987, USA, R
Shelley Long, Bette Midler, George Carlin, Peter Coyote, John Schuck, Anthony Heald, Robert Prosky. Directed by Arthur Hiller. 92 min.

This hilariously bawdy screwball comedy was written by a young, witty feminist screenwriter (Leslie Dixon) who indeed gets almost everything right. This auspicious writing debut is greatly aided by the wacky antics and generally wonderful acting of the whole cast. Bette Midler, the riotous vulgarian of Hollywood's mid-1980s, is matched step by rude step by the ineffably prim Shelley Long. They are delicious, both together and separately. Paul Newman and Robert Redford beware—this is the first major female buddy comedy, and certainly the only one to date in which the protagonist is momentarily incapacitated during a fearful chase scene because she breaks her fingernail. Don't worry that much of the adventure is implausible—it starts in New York, detours to Mexico with a spaced-out contribution from George Carlin, and winds up on a stage with Long playing Hamlet. Director Arthur Hiller, who has done his share of hackwork over the years, displays a deft and knowing hand in this unpredictable romp. Just sit back and enjoy the ribald, perceptive screenplay and two perfectly mismatched actresses.

THE OUTSIDERS ☆☆☆
1983, USA, PG
Matt Dillon, Ralph Macchio, C. Thomas Howell, Tom Cruise, Leif Garrett, Diane Lane, Rob Lowe. Directed by Francis Ford Coppola. 90 min.

This stylized, melodramatic adaptation of S.E. Hinton's best-selling novel may not be director Francis Coppola's best, but it's not as disappointing as many critics were so quick to judge it to be. The plot spins slowly around young Oklahoma greasers who get caught up in a rich/poor conflict as they search for meaning and manhood. Strong performances from the all-star teenage cast carry it along. Some memorable cinematographic scenes, an adequate musical score, and a stirring end raise the work well above teen-flick status. Coppola was inspired enough to do another Hinton film, *Rumblefish*.

OUTSIDE THE LAW ☆☆
1921, USA
Lon Chaney, Priscilla Dean, Wheeler Oakman, Ralph Lewis, E.A. Warren. Directed by Tod Browning. 77 min.

This crime melodrama written, produced, and directed by Tod Browning is below the standards of his later work with Lon Chaney, but it's an interesting example of the early work of both. Set in San Francisco's Chinatown, the story pits Chaney, as a vicious criminal, against a young couple, destined for lives of crime by the circumstances in which they were raised but set on the straight and narrow by film's end. The movie is pretty hokey overall, with an adorable blond infant on hand to mug in the grand manner and win over the heroine's heart. This is a silent film, and the video was duplicated from a reconstructed print and shows signs of wear and tear; still, silent film aficionados will be grateful to Blackhawk Films for making this available.

OVER THE BROOKLYN BRIDGE ☆
1984, USA, R
Elliott Gould, Margaux Hemingway, Shelley Winters, Carol Kane, Sid Caesar, Burt Young. Directed by Menahem Golan. 108 min.

Cannon Films head Menahem Golan has never been known for his light comedic touch as a director, and this abominable romance between a Jewish restaurateur (Elliott Gould) and a "classy" gentile (Margaux Hemingway) has all the wit, warmth, and sophistication of "Chuck Norris Meets Emmanuelle." If the outrageous ethnic characterizations don't drive you away screaming, Gould's mugging, Hemingway's ineptitude, and Shelley Winters's presence surely will.

OVER THE EDGE ☆☆☆½
1979, USA, PG
Matt Dillon, Vincent Spano, Michael Kramer, Pamela Ludwig. Directed by Jonathan Kaplan. 95 min.

You can catch a few rising stars in this frenetic youth-in-revolt film, made by former New World action director Jonathan Kaplan. A planned community has been built solely for adults' needs and the town's bored and dissatisfied teenagers are pricked into acts of vandalism. A skillful and perceptive film, taken from a script by Kaplan and Tim Hunter (director of the sensitive Matt Dillon vehicle, *Tex*), *Edge* is a remarkable examination of the generation gap. Among the teen pictures that followed, none has dealt as well with sex and drugs. Dillon is excellent in his first role as a doomed delinquent.

THE OWL AND THE PUSSYCAT ☆☆☆
1970, USA, R
Barbra Streisand, George Segal, Robert Klein, Allen Garfield, Roz Kelly. Directed by Herbert Ross. 96 min.

Though stagebound and claustrophobic, Buck Henry's screen adaptation of Bill Manhoff's two-character play is delightful entertainment. George Segal plays an aspiring writer who allows a prostitute (Barbra Streisand) to spend the night in his apartment after indirectly causing her eviction. The resulting verbal exchanges about his writing and her "modeling" is loud, fierce, and extremely funny. As with so many adaptations, however, the attempts to "open up" the play with additional characters and New York location shooting are obtrusive, and the final reel gets sloppy and sentimental. But Streisand (in her first non-singing role) and Segal contribute some of their best work to date in this ribald and raunchy farce.

OXFORD BLUES ☆☆
1985, USA, PG-13
Rob Lowe, Ally Sheedy, Julian Sands, Michael Gough. Directed by Robert Boris. 93 min.

A tepid remake of *A Yank at Oxford* wherein brash boy Rob Lowe sneaks his way into Oxford to win the hand of a beautiful socialite. If this plot doesn't seem contrived enough, just wait for the ridiculous rites of passage that Lowe undergoes to become a mature Oxfordian. It's a passably entertaining, but irritatingly condescending film that depicts the English as snobby snits and the Americans as none too bright. The quality of Ally Sheedy's bubbly performance is strictly a matter of personal taste.

P

THE PACK ★★½
1977, USA, R
Joe Don Baker, Hope Alexander-Willis, Richard B. Shull, R.G. Armstrong, Ned Wertimer, Delos V. Smith, Jr., Richard O'Brien. Directed by Robert Clouse. 99 min.

If, for some reason, you're looking for a mildly scary horror movie that you can show to the whole family without worrying about excessive gore, blood, or violence, this will do. Set on an island resort, the beasties are a pack of dogs, formerly pets, who were abandoned at the end of the summer by their owners and reverted to savagery in order to survive. They have grown in numbers to the point where they begin attacking the vacationers, keeping them stranded and unable to leave the island. Director Robert Clouse, who made some of the better upscale kung fu films (including the acknowledged classic of the genre, *Enter the Dragon*), is better with fighting people than fighting dogs, but this has some satisfactory chills.

PADRE PADRONE (FATHER MASTER) ★★★★
1977, Italy
Omero Antonutti, Saverio Marioni, Marcella Michelangeli, Fabrizio Forte. Directed by Paolo and Vittorio Taviani. 114 min.

A brilliant film by the brothers who directed *The Night of the Shooting Stars*, this story of the conflict between a young, crushingly ignorant Sardinian shepherd and his brutal father is raw, passionate, and breathtakingly innovative. Instead of drawing you in with narrative movement, the film comes at you in explosive emotional bursts, conveying both the terrible isolation of the Sardinian hills and an exhilarating feel for what is shared within that isolation: fear, joy, sexuality, and shame. It's a beautifully focused drama, perhaps even more moving than their later works.

A PAIN IN THE A— ★½
1974, France/Italy, PG
Lino Ventura, Jacques Brel, Caroline Cellier, Nino Castelnovo, Jean-Pierre Darras. Directed by Edouard Molinaro. 90 min.

Director Edouard Molinaro and scenarist Francis Veber were the creative team behind *La Cage aux Folles* and its first sequel, and you'll recognize their hyperventilating, clamorous comic style in this halfhearted comedy. Don't be surprised if you recognize the plot as well, a silly sketch about a hit man and a would-be suicide who keep interfering with each other's plans; Billy Wilder remade it a few years later in the equally dull *Buddy Buddy*. Lino Ventura and Jacques Brel are an adequate team, but they don't have the charisma or grace to win their bouts with physical comedy, and their slapstick predicaments are strained and very familiar. Despite some clever scenes, this is a dud, unless you have a very special affection for French farce.

PAINT YOUR WAGON ★½
1969, USA, PG
Clint Eastwood, Lee Marvin, Jean Seberg, Harve Presnell, Ray Walston, William O'Connell. Directed by Joshua Logan. 164 min.

Clint Eastwood is not the least talented performer ever cast in a musical, but rarely has such an inept song-and-dance man been surrounded by such an equally inept cast. Josh Logan must have thought it was a cute idea to have spaghetti-Western star Eastwood and recent Oscar winner Lee Marvin (*Cat Ballou*) croak their way through this multimillion-dollar adaptation of Alan Jay Lerner and Frederick Loewe's 1951 Broadway hit about two California gold miners and the woman (Jean Seberg) they both love. Whatever is left of the beautiful score ("I Talk to the Trees," "Wandrin' Star," "They Call the Wind Maria") is trampled on by the non-singing leads, who are scarcely any better in their dialogue scenes (thanks partly to Lerner's plodding screenplay). Location filming (in Panavision and Technicolor) in Baker, Oregon is the only merit of the production—but even that's severely hurt by the transfer to video.

PAINTED DESERT ★½
1931, USA
William Boyd, Helen Twelvetrees, William Farnum, Clark Gable. Directed by Howard Higgin. 79 min.

This is an attractively photographed but ever-so-average B Western. Don't miss Clark Gable's first screen appearance as Brett!

PAISAN ★★★½
1946, Italy
Carmela Sazio, Robert van Loon, Dots M. Johnson, Alfonsino, Maria Michi, Gar Moore. Directed by Roberto Rossellini. 90 min.

Roberto Rossellini and Federico Fellini cowrote this compelling six-episode anthology of life in occupied Italy during its liberation by the Allies at the end of World War II. It's an uneven film, but a few of the vignettes are quite powerful, particularly the final episode, in which partisans and OSS soldiers are massacred in the Po Valley. It was Rossellini's first film after his neorealist breakthrough, *Open City*, made the previous year.

PALE RIDER ★★★
1985, USA, R
Clint Eastwood, Michael Moriarty, Christopher Penn, Carrie Snodgress, Sydney Penny, Richard Dysart. Directed by Clint Eastwood. 113 min.

Clint Eastwood has constructed a somewhat artificial but grandly stirring all-purpose Western that combines the ecological commentary of George Stevens with the gritty action of Sergio Leone. It's a majestically staged picture that's basically an art film in gunfighter's clothing, replete with not-so-subtle symbolism. Borrowing much of the plot of Stevens's *Shane*, Eastwood once again plays a loner with no name who rights injustices with a fast trigger finger and a cockeyed stare. The villains here are an evil mining magnate and his deadly posse who terrorize a group of defenseless gold prospectors. Once Clint arrives on his pale horse and begins to thwart the industrialist's machinations, matters become violent. This is a slow and studious movie with an inordinate number of landscape shots, but one that's well made and maintains interest. It's a peculiar mixture of pacifist sentiments and outright action with a lot of fine characterizations, especially from Eastwood with his patented gruff coolness, and the usually eccentric Michael Moriarty getting down to earth as a prospector.

THE PALEFACE ★★★
1948, USA
Bob Hope, Jane Russell, Robert Armstrong, Iris Adrian. Directed by Norman Z. McLeod. 91 min.

This Western parody may be Bob Hope's best non-*Road* movie, a good showcase for his often underrated but highly influential style of film comedy. (Woody Allen's on-screen characters in particular owe a strong debt to Hope.) The screenplay, cowritten by ex-cartoonist Frank Tashlin, casts Hope as a none-too-heroic Eastern dentist with Miss Russell as Calamity Jane, who enlists his unwilling support in bringing in a gang of desperados. There's enough story and visual interest to balance the eternal wisecracks and one-liners from Hope, the reliance on which sank most of his later movies. Academy Award for Best Song ("Buttons and Bows").

PALOOKA

See *Joe Palooka*

PALS OF THE GOLDEN WEST ☆
1952, USA
Roy Rogers, Dale Evans, Pinky Lee, Trigger. Directed by William Witney. 67 min.

This is the last of the innumerable singing Westerns that Roy Rogers churned out for Republic Pictures, and not one of his best—he and the formula were very tired. There are a couple of songs and a grimmer-than-usual script about a border patrolman pitted against Mexican smugglers. Happily, good old Trigger, "the smartest horse in the world," teams with Roy's pooch Bullet to lend aid.

PALS OF THE SADDLE ☆☆
1938, USA
John Wayne, Ray Corrigan, Max Terhune, Doreen McKay. Directed by George Sherman. 55 min.

John Wayne replaces Bob Livingstone, and The Three Mesquiteers continue as always, here cleaning up some munitions smugglers. The Three Mesquiteers was a very popular series for Republic, and the films are above the average for that genre. Look for Max Terhune as Lullaby, providing good comic relief with the added oddball twist of ventriloquism.

PANDORA'S BOX ☆☆☆☆
1928, Germany
Louise Brooks, Fritz Kortner, Franz Lederer, Gustav Diessl. Directed by G.W. Pabst. 110 min.

This silent-era masterpiece is, for now, the only opportunity for the serious buff or scholar to see a Louise Brooks film (or a G.W. Pabst film) on video, and it shouldn't be missed. The heroine of Pabst's tragic moral tale is Lulu, a carefree, callous tramp who devastates the men in her life on her way to a shocking rendezvous with Jack the Ripper. The grim narrative belongs to the nineteenth-century style of stage melodrama, but Pabst's work is joltingly ahead of its time—the panoramic, deep-focused crowd scenes, the unusual understatement of the acting, and the frank sexuality all point to the work of future filmmakers. Brooks is beautiful and expressive, and Pabst's photography of her, whether in lingering close-up or reflective long shot, is a stirring directorial tribute. Some sequences, most notably the murder trial and the final encounter on a foggy night, are unforgettable. *Note:* The Embassy Home Entertainment release is a restored full-length print with a newly recorded score.

PANIC AT LAKEWOOD MANOR

See *Ants*

PANIC IN ECHO PARK ☆☆
1977, USA (TV)
Dorian Harewood, Robin Gammell, Catlin Adams, Ramon Bieri, Movita. Directed by John Llewellyn Moxey. 78 min.

This movie is not to be confused with the vastly superior *Panic in the Streets*, another film about trying to block the spread of an epidemic. In this adequate TV movie, Dorian Harewood once again rises above his material as a dedicated doctor battling red tape from both the city government and his own hospital. Suspense builds along predictable lines as Dr. Dorian tries to find the root cause of the deadly disease threatening the city.

PANIC IN NEEDLE PARK ☆☆☆½
1971, USA, R
Al Pacino, Kitty Winn, Alan Vint, Richard Bright. Directed by Jerry Schatzberg. 110 min.

This film probes the needle subculture of New York—where love and betrayal, harrowing humor, and tragedy pivot on a pinpoint. Director Jerry Schatzberg and Al Pacino (in his first starring role) have tapped veins of both irony and pathos, but the subplot in which Pacino pulls the upscale Kitty Winn into the sordid depths injects the plot with real tragedy. Scripted by "New Journalists" Joan Didion and John Gregory Dunne, and scored with scathing street sounds, *Panic* has a startling near-documentary buzz.

PANIC ON THE 5:22 ☆½
1974, USA (TV)
Ina Balin, Bernie Casey, Linden Chiles, Andrew Duggan, Dana Elcar, Lynda Day George, Laurence Luckinbill. Directed by Harvey Hart. 78 min.

A silly action TV film about a group of passengers on a private train who must fight for their lives against three armed robbers who may be planning to kill them. A number of unintentionally funny moments and Ina Balin's ridiculous star turn as a countess derail this nonsense long before its conclusion. Predictable tripe.

PANIQUE ☆☆☆½
1946, France
Viviane Romance, Michel Simon, Paul Bernard. Directed by Julien Duvivier. 95 min.

The great Michel Simon stars in Julien Duvivier's taut adaptation of a Georges Simenon novel. Simon plays an innocent stranger, framed for murder by a pair of unscrupulous lovers and hunted by a heedless mob. The movie flirts with social commentary and deep thinking, but most of the time it's as suspenseful a thriller as you could wish for. In French, with English subtitles.

THE PAPER CHASE ☆☆☆
1973, USA, PG
Timothy Bottoms, Lindsay Wagner, John Houseman, Graham Beckel, Edward Herrmann, Craig Richard Nelson. Directed by James Bridges. 111 min.

Long a favorite among college students and uncertain pre-professionals, this engaging comedy-drama tells of a first-year law student in an intellectual wrangle with a brilliant, imperious professor (John Houseman) and a romantic one with his daughter (Lindsay Wagner). Director James Bridges, shooting at Harvard and in Canada, perfectly captures the imposing, scary architectural grandeur of an Ivy League college, and Timothy Bottoms is fine as the scholar unwittingly caught in a war of wills. The script, however, has scenes of pomposity and ineptitude, and the tone of much of the film, especially the ending, is pure 1970s disillusionment-is-so-romantic drivel. But the ecclesiastical atmosphere of a law school is splendidly conveyed, and Houseman, who won an Academy Award for this film, brilliantly distills every student's greatest fears into one unforgettable characterization. The film later became an acclaimed television series that ran, first on network, then on cable, for several years.

PAPER MOON ☆☆☆
1973, USA, PG
Ryan O'Neal, Tatum O'Neal, Madeline Kahn, John Hillerman, P.J. Johnson, Randy Quaid. Directed by Peter Bogdanovich. 101 min.

A Depression America that is alternately homey and hard-bitten is brilliantly evoked in Peter Bogdanovich's sentimental movie about an odd-couple team of con artists. Tatum O'Neal is very good as the orphan who latches onto the small-time flimflam man played by her father, Ryan. Their comic backchat is funny, though their relationship doesn't change much over the course of the movie. Madeline Kahn almost steals the show as a has-been floozie, and P.J. Johnson holds her own playing a put-upon maid. The movie is really a series of comic vignettes, and it lacks the focus of its source novel, *Addie Pray* by Joe David Brown. On the whole, however, the movie's machinery clicks along nicely. The combination of Laszlo Kovacs's sharp black-and-white photography and contemporary music like "Keep Your Sunny Side Up" and "Let's Have Another Cup of Coffee" generates an authentic feel.

PAPER TIGER ☆½
1976, Great Britain, PG
David Niven, Toshiro Mifune, Hardy Kruger, Ando, Ronald Fraser, Jeff Corey. Directed by Ken Annakin. 101 min.

Don't be fooled by the star value of the cast: This is a sub-Disney version of the kind of thing that Shirley Temple did decades earlier, with the grown-ups top billed but really only there for support. The tyke here is a Japanese golfball (dimples galore) named Ando; as the son of ambassador Toshiro Mifune, he, along with his tutor, David Niven, are kidnapped by terrorists. Of course, Ando manages to outwit the bad guys, as well as Niven and Hardy Kruger (as a German journalist). There is no subtlety in sight as the filmmakers hammer into your head how wonderful it is that a Briton, a Japanese, and a German can put aside their residual World War II hatreds and work together.

PAPILLON ☆☆☆
1973, USA, PG
Steve McQueen, Dustin Hoffman, Victor Jory, Don Gordon, Anthony Zerbe, Bill Mumy, George Coulouris, Gregory Sierra. Directed by Franklin J. Schaffner. 150 min.

Popular, engrossing but overlong film based on the memoirs of Henri Charriere, who escaped from the infamous penal colony of Devil's Island after eight attempts. Much of the film's time is spent detailing the horrors of prison life, and, without becoming overtly sadistic or horrifying, it is a numbing experience. Steve McQueen is very good in a more restrained role than usual; Dustin Hoffman is likewise good as a counterfeiter also sentenced to the prison, a variation on his Ratso Rizzo in *Midnight Cowboy*. The film should have been at least twenty minutes shorter, though. However, it has a screenplay by Lorenzo Semple, Jr., and Dalton Trumbo, who has a bit part at the beginning of the film as the prison commandant.

PARADISE ☆
1982, USA, R
Willie Aames, Phoebe Cates. Directed by Stuart Gillard. 100 min.

It's hard to believe that any actor could legitimately be called "the poor man's Christopher Atkins" or that any movie seeking to rip off a better one would choose as creative inspiration *The Blue Lagoon*. But *Paradise*, with artfully loinclothed Willie Aames pursuing temporarily loinclothed Phoebe Cates, fits the bill. After both sets of parents are killed, the two young naifs flee through the Arabian desert to a scenic oasis. Fearing for their lives, they decide to have a lot of sex. Well plotted it isn't, but in a movie of this ilk, one supposes that's beside the point.

PARADISE ALLEY ☆
1978, USA, PG
Sylvester Stallone, Lee Canalito, Armand Assante, Frank McRae, Anne Archer, Kevin Conway. Directed by Sylvester Stallone. 109 min.

After Sylvester Stallone's meteoric rise to fame with *Rocky*, he made his directorial debut with this less-than-memorable action comedy about three lower-class brothers from New York who aspire to greater things. It's odd to see Stallone play comedy—imagine an elephant trying to play the piano (or just cast your mind back to *Rhinestone*). Despite some funny moments and some surprisingly handsome filmmaking, this is ninety-percent insufferable, even for Sly's legion of fans.

PARADISE CANYON ☆☆
1935, USA
John Wayne, Yakima Canutt. Directed by Carl Pierson. 53 min.

In this better-than-average Western with good action, direction, and story, John Wayne plays a government agent investigating a counterfeiting operation near the Mexican border. Watch for the spine-tingling high-dive scene.

PARADISE, HAWAIIAN STYLE ☆☆
1966, USA
Elvis Presley, Suzanna Leigh, James Shigeta, Donna Butterworth, Irene Tsu, Marianna Hill, Linda Wong. Directed by Michael Moore. 91 min.

The variations on the Presley formula here include a nine-year-old costar (Donna Butterworth) and location shooting in Hawaii—causing this to play like a combination of *It Happened at the World's Fair* and *Blue Hawaii*. Elvis's legion of fans should be pleased. El operates a helicopter service, gets grounded by the FAA when a pack of frisky pups causes him to lose control of his chopper, and risks his license when he takes off to rescue his injured coworker. The King sings "House of Sand" and "Queenie Wahine's Papaya" with pixie Butterworth, and solos on "You Scratch My Back," "This Is My Heaven," and the title tune. Watch for the big luau production number, "Drums of the Island."

PARADISIO ☆
1956 (Released 1961), Great Britain, R
Arthur Howard, Eva Waegner. Directed by Pseudonymous. 82 min.

New World Video is marketing this ancient British "nudie" item as a so-bad-it's-funny treat, and there are a few laughs in discovering what passed for dirty during the Eisenhower era, but only a few. Arthur Howard (Leslie's brother) plays an Oxbridge professor on a European jaunt who discovers that the special sunglasses he's brought along allow him to see natives of many lands stark naked. Of course, these natives tend to be shapely young women, Howard never looks below their waists, and you should see his paroxysms of pain when a *man* (ugh!) happens to pass within his field of vision. You may want to hang on until the three-breasted woman appears, but we wouldn't recommend it. Oddly enough, the nude sections of the film appear to have been shot in 3-D; in the video version, they're just tinted red, and when Howard exhorts you to put on *your* glasses, you may feel a bit left out.

THE PARALLAX VIEW ☆☆☆
1974, USA, R
Warren Beatty, Paula Prentiss, Hume Cronyn, William Daniels. Directed by Alan J. Pakula. 102 min.

Conspiracy buffs will enjoy this Watergate-era thriller about a journalist who becomes the last surviving witness of a political assassination. His investigation leads him to a truth that's far worse than his nightmares. Alan J. Pakula has crafted a generally fine suspense film, blending everything from a fictionalized Warren Commission to a satanic CIA into a heady brew of perceptive paranoia. It's marred only by a disappointing (although logical) conclusion.

PARANOIA ☆
1969, Italy
Carroll Baker, Lou Castel, Colette Descombes, Tino Carraro. Directed by Umberto Lenzi. 91 min.

A dull, distasteful blend of *La Dolce Vita* and *The Servant*, made during Carroll Baker's sex-bomb exile in Italy, this S&M "thriller" wallows in the star's kinky enslavement to a slimy bisexual couple with designs on her fortune. Moral: An oversexed fool and her lire are soon parted.

PARASITE
1982, USA, R ☆
Robert Glaudini, Demi Moore, Lula Berovici, Vivian Blaine, Cherie Currie, James Davidson, Al Farr. Directed by Charles Band. 85 min.

In a future America, a doctor creates a mutated parasite that he thinks will be used to some good end by the government. Instead, he learns that it is to be taken over by the nefarious "merchants" who aspire to world domination and will stop at nothing to find him. This is a murky fusion of *They Came from Within* and *Alien*, set in a post-apocalypse landscape originally rendered in passable 3-D. Some gory parasite effects that burst out of one character's stomach and another's face are diverting, but generally dull.

THE PARASITE MURDERS

See *They Came from Within*

PARDON US
1931, USA ☆☆½
Stan Laurel, Oliver Hardy, James Finlayson, Wilfred Lucas, Walter Long. Directed by James Parrott. 55 min.

Stan and Ollie stand outside a store, dreaming up a recipe. Since the store sells hops and malt, they decide to whip up a batch of beer. Before you can say "prohibition," the boys are in the slammer, set for a clever send-up of hard-boiled prison pictures. This is their first starring feature, and they are in fine mettle, though the staging is stiff and director James Parrott has no flair. Ollie does a number in blackface that is offensive, but Stan's sequence with the dentist is fresh and hilarious.

THE PARENT TRAP
1961, USA ☆☆½
Hayley Mills, Maureen O'Hara, Brian Keith, Charlie Ruggles, Una Merkel, Leo G. Carroll, Joanna Barnes, Cathleen Nesbitt, Ruth McDevitt. Directed by David Swift. 129 min.

Although this Disney family comedy isn't really much better than most of its ilk, its wish-fulfillment premise may exert a real emotional pull on some kids (not to mention some former kids). The gimmick has young Hayley Mills playing identical twins who don't meet each other until one summer at camp. Discovering that their parents divorced and split them up shortly after their birth, they conspire to get mom (Maureen O'Hara), a Back Bay socialite, back together with dad (Brian Keith), a Western rancher. The idea that a little youthful ingenuity can patch up a broken marriage is perhaps not the healthiest proposition to foist upon youngsters, but you can't help rooting for Mills, and the antics are enjoyable even when they're at their most sugary. Followed by a made-for-TV sequel in 1987.

PARIS BLUES
1961, USA ☆☆☆
Paul Newman, Joanne Woodward, Sidney Poitier, Diahann Carroll, Louis Armstrong. Directed by Martin Ritt. 98 min.

There are quite a few good reasons to see this film—a great jazz score by Duke Ellington, some gorgeous Parisian scenery captured by the legendary French cameraman Christian Matras (*Grand Illusion*, *Lola Montez*), a very good cast of stars—but, ultimately, the movie is obscured by the cloud of ideas emanating from its screenplay. Martin Ritt, heir to the socially conscious filmmaking of Elia Kazan and director of fine films like *Hud* and *Norma Rae*, riffs around with the characters and their intertwined stories, but never quite zeros in on them.

PARIS HOLIDAY
1958, USA ☆☆½
Bob Hope, Fernandel, Anita Ekberg, Martha Hyer, Preston Sturges. Directed by Gerd Oswald. 100 min.

Bob Hope's vehicles don't exactly become hopeless with the passing years, but their topicality does cause them to sputter and creak like an aging boat. The amiable, ambling script casts Preston Sturges as a playwright whose new work unmasks the antagonists in a Paris currency scandal. Hope, perched to produce the play in America, ventures on board a wacky freighter to France; Anita Ekberg is there to wrest the script from him, and non-English-speaking Fernandel (he gets subtitles!) is there to wrest Ekberg from him. The rest—including a stunt-filled stint in a mental institution and a wily helicopter escape—is fairly arbitrary. The movie is well paced and as solid as one could reasonably expect; although its age lines are getting starker and its laugh lines far less deep, it is a pleasant enough vacation.

PARIS, TEXAS
1984, West Germany/France, R ☆☆☆
Harry Dean Stanton, Nastassja Kinski, Dean Stockwell, Aurore Clement, Hunter Carson. Directed by Wim Wenders. 145 min.

A meditative, slow-moving but often interesting film written by Sam Shepard (*True West*, *Fool for Love*) and directed by Wim Wenders (*Kings of the Road*, *Hammett*). It is essentially a modern family melodrama in which a drifter (Harry Dean Stanton) is returned to his son (Hunter Carson) after several years' absence. Together, they search for the child's mother (Nastassja Kinski), who now works in a Texas "lonely hearts" parlor. The performances are good (except for the miscast Kinski), the photography by Robby Muller outstanding, and the dialogue terse and funny. Unfortunately, the deliberate pacing, unexplained story elements, and unsatisfying conclusion will probably annoy more than intrigue most viewers.

THE PARK IS MINE
1985, USA (TV) ☆½
Tommy Lee Jones, Helen Shaver, Yaphet Kotto, Eric Petersen. Directed by Steven Hilliard Stern. 95 min.

Tommy Lee Jones had a bad time in Vietnam and, obviously, so did his friend who goes bonkers and kills himself (but not before planting a terrific bee in Tommy Lee's bonnet: Hold Central Park for ransom in order to dramatize the plight of the forgotten vet). After his friend dies, he catches the spirit of the enterprise, not wanting to let such a good idea go to waste. So he plants explosives and takes over Central Park just as if he were back in Nam. HBO, for which this was made, should be ashamed of exploiting the adjustment problems of Vietnam veterans in this pea-brained action picture.

PARLOR, BEDROOM, BATH
1931, USA ☆☆½
Buster Keaton, Charlotte Greenwood, Reginald Denny. Directed by Edward Sedgwick. 72 min.

MGM had a way of bulldozing talent, turning a quirky performer into just another one of their galaxy of stars. Buster Keaton may have been the most unfortunate victim of this system, and this film illustrates Buster's on-screen problems in the early 1930s. The film is a straight, stagey farce whirling around the stolid Keaton like a storm whipping a flag, and no concessions are granted to Keaton's intellectual, meticulous comic development. The best moments are early in the film, shot on location at Keaton's gorgeous mansion.

PARTING GLANCES
1986, USA ☆☆½
Richard Ganoung, John Bolger, Steve Buscemi, Adam Nathan, Kathy Kinney, Patrick Tull, Yolande Bavan. Directed by Bill Sherwood. 90 min.

Bill Sherwood's first film is a low-budget but slick and precise anatomization of Manhattan's gay yuppie demimonde, set on the Upper West Side. The not-very-interesting protagonists are young lovers Michael and Robert, about to attend a farewell party for the latter, whose job transfer threatens to disrupt their relationship. At the heart of the plot is a fairly conventional romantic story, but Sherwood leavens it with jolts of acutely observed social comedy and wry, thoughtful wit. Unfortunately, both main characters are underdeveloped and generically acted, but Steve Buscemi's vivid, challenging portrayal of a musician with AIDS heads a list of distinguished supporting performances. The film is not for everyone, but it is a minor ground breaker in its subject matter and an unusually assured writing and directorial debut.

PARTISANS OF VILNA ☆☆☆
1986, USA
Documentary narrated by Roberta Wallach. Directed by Josh Waletzky. 130 min.

This is a moving documentary that mixes archival footage and contemporary interviews to create an oral history of the courageous Jews of Vilna, Lithuania, who fought against the advancing Nazi army during World War II even as their religious community was decimated. As a documentarian, Josh Waletzky makes up for his lack of cinematic creativity by studious, quiet earnestness, and although many of the survivors' recollections are less than galvanizing, the film ultimately succeeds as a moving work of scholarship.

PARTNERS ☆½
1982, USA, R
Ryan O'Neal, John Hurt, Kenneth McMillan, Robyn Douglass, Jay Robinson, Denise Galik. Directed by James Burrows. 91 min.

Francis Veber, author of *La Cage aux Folles* and *Les Comperes*, wrote this comedy about a rabidly heterosexual detective teamed up with a gay police clerk in order to track down a killer of homosexuals in Los Angeles. Like most of Veber's work, it has just enough laughs to make you feel guilty for laughing at something so overloaded with cheap stereotypes, even with (or maybe because of) the phony liberal plea for "understanding" with which it ends. It's easy to snicker at macho Ryan O'Neal being forced to cruise gay bars, though the mechanism that evokes the humor is pretty vile. It's harder to justify the character of his partner, played by the wasted John Hurt as a simpering, overly sensitive non-male. In the end, this is probably not truly mean-spirited, but only those who view it as such are liable to find much humor in it.

PARTS: THE CLONUS HORROR

See *The Clonus Horror*

PASSAGE OF THE DRAGON

See *Twins of Kung Fu*

A PASSAGE TO INDIA ☆☆☆☆
1984, Great Britain, PG
Judy Davis, Victor Banerjee, Peggy Ashcroft, James Fox, Alec Guinness, Nigel Havers, Richard Wilson, Michael Culver, Antonia Pemberton, Art Malik. Directed by David Lean. 163 min.

One of the world's greatest directors made a triumphant return after an absence of fourteen years. In his gratifying and often visually stunning adaptation of E.M. Forster's 1924 novel, David Lean uses his concrete, literal style to conjure up the magic of an alien atmosphere. Following Adela Quested (Judy Davis) and her prospective mother-in-law, Mrs. Moore (Peggy Ashcroft), into the city of Chandrapore, we see both their astonishment at the callousness of the English overlords and the women's desire to find the "real India"—a search that culminates in their trip to the Marabar Caves, where Adela may or may not have imagined a rape attempt by their host, the warm yet anguished Dr. Aziz (Victor Banerjee). Ashcroft and Banerjee give the strongest performances in the standout cast; only Alec Guinness, playing an Indian philosopher, goes over the top into eccentricity. Nominated for eleven Academy Awards, and a winner for Ashcroft's supporting performance and Maurice Jarre's score. Lean may be the world's best editor of the wide screen, and his movies suffer greatly by being chopped down to video size.

PASSAGE TO MARSEILLES ☆☆½
1944, USA
Humphrey Bogart, Michele Morgan, Claude Rains, Philip Dorn, Sidney Greenstreet, Peter Lorre, Helmut Dantine. Directed by Michael Curtiz. 110 min.

From the folks who gave you *Casablanca:* same director (Michael Curtiz), producer (Hal Wallis) and studio (Warner Bros.); similar production crew (including composer Max Steiner) and cast (Humphrey Bogart, Claude Rains, Sidney Greenstreet, Peter Lorre, etc.); but not the same magic. The problem is that the film is more propaganda (a lengthy tribute to the French Resistance) than drama (about some Devil's Island escapees who join the French), and what drama there is is poorly handled—at one point there is a flashback within a flashback within a flashback. Bogart never seems to dominate the action the way he should, and Michele Morgan, though attractive and a good actress, is no Ingrid Bergman, and is given a bland assignment. It's recommended primarily if you're tired of watching *Casablanca* for the umpteenth time.

THE PASSENGER ☆☆☆☆
1975, Italy/France/Spain
Jack Nicholson, Maria Schneider, Jenny Runacre, Ian Hendry, Stephen Berkoff, Ambrose Bia. Directed by Michelangelo Antonioni. 119 min.

It is 1975 and the International Art Cinema is in crisis. The years of film's political urgency are over, the avant garde coherency of European masters like Godard, Antonioni, Resnais and Pasolini has, finally, completely fragmented. Against this brick wall runs, headlong, *The Passenger*. In its deadpan acting and on-again/off-again thriller narrative, it sums up the ennui and imitativeness of a dying art community. The aridity of the "artistic," though, is perfectly balanced by the film's visual stylishness—Jack Nicholson's Hollywood glamour and Maria Schneider's earth-moppet sexiness, the incredible tracking shots (including a legendary final take), the marvelously organic Antonio Gaudi architecture, the elegance of the road. The film is, finally, an elegy to a lost, loved art, declaring at once, "Look at what we could do," and "Wouldn't it be silly to try it again?" The film's story is about a TV reporter who assumes another man's identity and attempts to take over his profession as an idealistic gunrunner; the film's setting covers Chad, Munich, London, Spain, and North Africa; both the setting and the story are summatory catalogues of the poetic ideology, the alienating distance, the beauty and the closure of great filmmaking.

PASSION FLOWER HOTEL

See *Boarding School*

PASSION OF JOAN OF ARC ☆☆☆☆
1928, France
Falconetti, Eugene Sylvain, Maurice Schutz. Directed by Carl Theodor Dreyer. 77 min.

Universally admired as one of Carl Dreyer's masterworks, this silent classic is a rigorous exploration of the physical trials and spiritual agonies of Joan of Arc as she is interrogated mercilessly before being burned at the stake. Dreyer's style is deliberately austere and the constant use of close-ups makes the film doubly harrowing. Falconetti gives one of the silent screen's most devastating performances; it was so demanding that she retired from the screen after giving it—the image of her passionate face remains in the forefront of film icons.

PATERNITY ☆☆
1981, USA, PG
Burt Reynolds, Beverly D'Angelo, Lauren Hutton, Norman Fell, Elizabeth Ashley, Paul Dooley, Juanita Moore. Directed by David Steinberg. 94 min.

David Steinberg (and writer Charlie Peters) must have pieced together this foolish fluff from the front pages of the weekly tabloids. Burt Reynolds plays a childless bachelor who interviews a series of surrogate mother candidates. It's hard to get through the first interview, however, because Reynolds is at his most smug. The not uninteresting premise becomes predictable and, thanks to Burt, offensive. The movie wastes the talents of Beverly D'Angelo, Lauren Hutton, and Elizabeth Ashley.

PAT GARRETT AND BILLY THE KID ☆☆☆
1973, USA, R
Kris Kristofferson, James Coburn, Richard Jaeckel, Chill Wills, Jason Robards, Bob Dylan, Rita Coolidge, Barry Sullivan, Elisha Cook, Jr. Directed by Sam Peckinpah. 106 min.

James Coburn, aging but still elegant, pursues his one-time outlaw friend across an emotional landscape streaked with a kind of ambiguous half-light. Both Billy and Garrett are tarnished by life, or rather the love-and-death chain that links them. That this kind of romantic and repressive masculine love should be expressed in images redolent of the grave seems entirely accurate. *Pat Garrett and Billy the Kid* is a whole necrology of the West. It's brilliant in parts, so allow the rest to slide by . . . not difficult given Bob Dylan's soundtrack.

PATHS OF GLORY ☆☆☆☆
1957, USA
Kirk Douglas, Ralph Meeker, Adolphe Menjou, George Macready, Wayne Morris, Timothy Carey. Directed by Stanley Kubrick. 86 min.

Stanley Kubrick's sharp, harrowing film, based on an actual incident from World War I, deals with many of the same issues as Peter Weir's 1981 antiwar indictment, *Gallipoli*, but with far greater impact. The film chronicles the court-martial of three innocent French soldiers on charges of cowardice, an action designed to salve a pompous and cruel general's vanity. The film is vivid, disturbing, and realistic. With fearful symmetry, Kubrick depicts the relentlessness of war and the system that gives rise to the warrior mind-set. This is an enduring classic.

PATRICK ☆½
1978, Australia, PG
Susan Penhaligon, Robert Helpmann, Rod Mullinar, Bruce Barry, Julia Blake, Maria Mercedes, Helen Hemingway. Directed by Richard Franklin. 96 min.

What was reputedly a good film in its original incarnation (having won the Grand Prize at a French Fantasy Film Festival in 1978) is unpersuasive and unfrightening in this form, which has been trimmed by almost half an hour and features a rerecorded dubbed soundtrack. After killing his mother and her lover, Patrick lapses into a coma. At the hospital where he is kept alive by machines, a new nurse begins to discover that, far from being brain dead as well, Patrick is able to control the environment around him through telepathy, which he puts to use when his doctor wants to pull his plugs. Director Richard Franklin went on to *Road Games* and *Psycho II*, both of which indicate that this might be worth tracking down in its original form.

THE PATSY ☆☆½
1964, USA
Jerry Lewis, Ina Balin, Everett Sloane, Phil Harris, Keenan Wynn, Peter Lorre, John Carradine, Hans Conreid, Phil Foster, Richard Deacon, Scatman Crothers, Nancy Kulp. Directed by Jerry Lewis. 100 min.

If you have even the slightest aversion to Jerry Lewis, avoid this movie. It may well trigger your gag reflex, because this is Jerry at his most unrestrained. After a popular singer dies, his avaricious management team attempts to make a shy bellboy (Lewis) into the newest sensation. Fans, of course, will revel in the master's manic characterizations, especially in the scene where he tries to learn voice from Hans Conreid. There is a great moment when our hero, now a star, forgives everyone who wronged him. What a guy! Look for Ed Wynn, Ed Sullivan, Mel Torme, Hedda Hopper, and George Raft in cameo roles.

PATTON ☆☆☆☆
1970, USA
George C. Scott, Karl Malden, Michael Bates, Karl Michael Vogler, Edward Binns, Tim Considine. Directed by Franklin J. Schaffner. 173 min.

Subtitled "Salute to a Rebel," this film about one of World War II's most notorious hawks was a risky venture at a time when this country was torn apart over the issue of our involvement in Vietnam; that the film was a major hit testifies to its objective treatment of General George S. Patton, a man who had his own ideas about how wars should be fought regardless of what his superiors thought. George C. Scott gives an astounding performance, both hero and lunatic at the same time. Director Franklin J. Schaffner achieves the equally amazing feat of not letting Scott overwhelm the rest of the film, with brilliantly panoramic re-creations of some of the major battles of the war. Both star and director won Oscars (although Scott declined to accept his); the film also won awards for Best Picture, screenplay (Francis Ford Coppola and Edmund H. North), sound, editing, and set direction.

PAULINE AT THE BEACH ☆☆☆½
1983, France, R
Arielle Dombasle, Amanda Langlet, Pascal Greggory, Feodor Atkine, Simon de la Brosse, Rosette. Directed by Eric Rohmer. 95 min.

This is the third and most charming of Eric Rohmer's romantic film series entitled "Comedies and Proverbs." The proverb here illustrated is "a wagging tongue bites itself," and the wagging tongues are those of a sophisticated sexpot (Arielle Dombasle) on a vacation jaunt to Normandy, her young cousin Pauline (Amanda Langlet), and the anthropologist, surf bum, beach boy, and candy girl with whom they flirt and dally. The sexual roundelay hinges on the misunderstanding caused by good intentions, and watching it unravel in a series of pungent, well-observed conversations is a delight. Though small in scale, it's a sophisticated and charming miniature, with Dombasle and Langlet the standouts in a top-notch cast. Media Home Entertainment's videocassette has been re-subtitled for easier reading. (For the curious, the other films in Rohmer's series so far include *The Aviator's Wife, Le Beau Marriage, Full Moon in Paris*, and *Summer*.)

LA PAURA

See *Fear*

THE PAWNBROKER ☆☆☆½
1965, USA
Rod Steiger, Geraldine Fitzgerald, Brock Peters, Jaime Sanchez, Thelma Oliver, Marketa Kimbrell. Directed by Sidney Lumet. 115 min.

In Sidney Lumet's powerful study of a concentration camp survivor who loses touch with his own humanity, the symbols crash noisily through the thin story line. Everything in the film stands for something—the Harlem pawnshop where Sol Nazerman (Rod Steiger) works, the gay black mobster with whom he is in unholy alliance, the stockboy named Jesus who suffers for the sins of others. But *The Pawnbroker* remains a moving experience despite its schematism, thanks primarily to Steiger's superbly controlled portrayal of a man on guard against his own nightmarish memories. Lumet's depiction of Harlem doesn't wear well, and his flashbacks become showy with repetition, but when he focuses on Steiger, the effect is shattering.

PAYDAY
★★★½
1972, USA, R
Rip Torn, Elayne Heilveil, Ahna Capri, Michael C. Gwynne. Directed by Daryl Duke. 103 min.

The performance of Rip Torn in his best screen role is reason enough to see this film, an opportunity few had during its theatrical release. He plays Maury Dann, a country-and-western singer whose career has stopped just a step away from stardom. For over thirty-six hours of his life, we watch this unlikable but captivating character perform, abuse his entourage, pop pills, and all but live in his Cadillac. Torn's ability to submerge himself into a despicable character is equal to that of Robert DeNiro or Jack Nicholson, and this is one of the very few starring roles he has had that have been equal to his talents.

PEARL OF THE SOUTH PACIFIC
★
1955, USA
Virginia Mayo, Dennis Morgan, David Farrar, Murvyn Vye, Lance Fuller, Basil Ruysdael, Lisa Montell. Directed by Allan Dwan. 85 min.

This pearl's no gem. Three evil white men want to steal the natives' collection of black pearls, but the local white patriarch, looking after the best interests of his natives, wants to stop them. In the face of goodness, two of the wicked triumvirate change their minds, while the third dies from hardheadedness and a native spear. Two out of three's not bad, but this movie is. Even the local color isn't colorful, and the deadly octopus looks suspiciously like an escapee from Woolworth's novelty department.

PEE-WEE'S BIG ADVENTURE
★★★½
1985, USA, PG
Pee-Wee Herman (Paul Reubens), Elizabeth Daily, Mark Holton, Diane Salinger, Judd Omen, James Brolin, Morgan Fairchild. Directed by Tim Burton. 92 min.

The great film critic James Agee once called silent film comedian Harry Langdon "a baby dope fiend." If he ever tried this with Pee-Wee Herman, who captures something of Langdon's infantile, spasmodic eccentricity, Pee-Wee would undoubtedly retort, "I know you are, but what am I?" Pee-Wee is a beatific angel with a mean streak and a smart mouth. In his first film, he travels cross-country to recover his precious, stolen bicycle. The real adventure, though, is in watching Paul Reubens's brilliant manipulation of set design and props—to this overgrown kid, the world is a toy box to be rifled. First-time director Tim Burton has a real flair for this hopped-up lunacy; he recalls Frank Tashlin's shiny, primary-colored 1950s comedies—indeed, Burton, like Tashlin, worked for the Disney studios, and they both have something of a cartoon spirit. There is a nice, kooky score by Danny Elfman of Oingo Boingo.

PEGGY SUE GOT MARRIED
★★★★
1986, USA, PG-13
Kathleen Turner, Nicolas Cage, Barry Miller, Catherine Hicks, Joan Allen, Kevin J. O'Connor, Barbara Harris, Don Murray, Maureen O'Sullivan, Leon Ames. Directed by Francis Coppola. 104 min.

If you could relive your life, what would you change? Such questions get answered only in the movies, but we wish that all dreams come true were as beautifully realized as they are in this masterful bittersweet comedy. Kathleen Turner plays a middle-aged mother, separated from her husband and reluctantly attending her twenty-fifth high school reunion. When she arrives, the memories come flooding back and she faints. Awakening to find herself in 1962, Peggy Sue encounters her family, friends, and fiancé (Nicolas Cage) with that rare gift, twenty-twenty foresight. Jerry Leichtling and Arlene Sarner's screenplay triumphs by depicting Peggy Sue as a grown woman browsing through her own past with hopes and regrets intact, and many of the scenes are as poignant as they are funny. Turner's superb, subtle performance gives the film even more emotional resonance, and Cage has worked out a brave, risky characterization for her nerdy Don Juan of a husband. The supporting cast, led by Barry Miller, is a delight, and Francis Coppola's direction is his finest in many years. Ironically, *Peggy Sue* had a troubled production history, with Coppola replacing Penny Marshall and Turner replacing Debra Winger, but given the result, we wouldn't have it any other way.

PENDULUM
★★
1969, USA
George Peppard, Jean Seberg, Richard Kiley, Charles McGraw, Robert F. Lyons. Directed by George Schaefer. 106 min.

Detective George Peppard tracks down vicious rapist-murderer Robert L. Lyons only to see the conviction thrown out by the Supreme Court on vague constitutional grounds. When Peppard's adulterous wife is murdered, however, he finds himself accused of the crime and in a similar position of being presumed guilty until proven innocent. The big issues of the rights of the accused are essentially evaded here by the script's stacking of the deck—the bad guy is only slightly less obvious than the one in *Dirty Harry*. This also hurts the half of this film that just wants to be a murder mystery, because you guess whodunit way before the ending.

PENITENTIARY
★★½
1979, USA, R
Leon Isaac Kennedy, Thommy Pollard, Badja Djola, Hazel Spears, Gloria Delaney, Chuck Mitchell. Directed by Jamaa Fanaka. 99 min.

Though this depiction of prison life is supposed to be some kind of bedrock realism, exploitation aficionados will recognize the milieu as the male cousin to all of those great women's prison pictures—*Chained Heat, Caged Heat*, etc. It's a fantasy world of "shocking" events: crazed cons, sexual assaults, beatings, *outre* performances, and cartoon boxing. Leon Isaac Kennedy has very few lines and thus turns in his best performance, and, on the whole, this is far superior to the sequel, *Penitentiary II*, and Kennedy's remake of *Body and Soul*. The story is simple: A guy gets thrown into prison, refuses to submit to the sexual demands of his cell mate, and reveals himself to be a great boxer. Not only that, he also lives by the saintly prison code of the "self-satisfied": "What five fingers can't get done, don't get done," he tells a young con who thinks our hero is out to molest him.

PENNIES FROM HEAVEN
★★★½
1981, USA, R
Steve Martin, Bernadette Peters, Jessica Harper, Christopher Walken, Vernel Bagneris, John McMartin, Jay Garner, Tommy Rall. Directed by Herbert Ross. 107 min.

Steve Martin and Bernadette Peters are bitter, star-crossed lovers in this bold, imaginative, lavish reworking of Depression-era musicals. Dennis Potter, who adapted his own BBC series for the screenplay, and director Herbert Ross fashion an audaciously bizarre, grisly musical that eerily re-creates the duality of 1930s Hollywood glamour and the gloomy reality it concealed. This is an art film of shifting, conflicting perspectives—the grim melodrama of pathetic lives is constantly undermined by the parallel text of glossy musical numbers; no attempt is made to wed the two essentially different movies, and viewers must either grow annoyed with the conflict or discover a relationship for themselves. In a film that constantly distances the audience with its obtrusively dubbed musical numbers, Martin gives a harsh, emotionally distancing performance as a viciously self-centered businessman teetering on the edge of financial and personal collapse.

PENNY SERENADE
★★★½
1941, USA
Irene Dunne, Cary Grant, Beulah Bondi, Edgar Buchanan, Ann Doran, Eva Lee Kuney, Leonard Willey. Directed by George Stevens. 120 min.

A beautifully acted tearjerker about a small-town publisher and his wife who desperately want to adopt a baby, and finally succeed, only to face an unexpected tragedy. Cary Grant gives one of his most sensitive performances as the flustered but always caring husband and father, and Irene Dunne's work stays as far from maudlin excess as is possible within the strictures of her role. George Stevens gracefully moves from scenes of domestic comedy to overt melodrama, and the carefully etched characters keep the transitions almost believable. It's undeniably weepy and manipulative, but, in the multi-handkerchief genre, it holds up surprisingly well. Screenplay by Morrie Ryskind.

THE PEOPLE ☆☆½
1971, USA (TV)
Kim Darby, William Shatner, Diane Varsi, Laurie Walters, Dan O'Herlihy. Directed by John Korty. 74 min.

A strange sci-fi tale that will have educators in the audience thinking twice before moving to remote areas. Based on Zenna Henderson's novel, the film follows the travails of an unusually conscientious young teacher (Kim Darby). The film manages some striking Northern California location photography and occasional shudders, but this eerie portrait of taciturn parents and their oddly well-behaved children is rather muted science fiction, without much momentum built up.

THE PEOPLE NEXT DOOR ☆☆
1970, USA
Julie Harris, Stephen McHattie, Eli Wallach, Hal Holbrook, Cloris Leachman, Deborah Winters. Directed by David Greene. 93 min.

A TV problem drama that is padded and puffed up to make it to the big screen. Even when first released, this film seemed dated; now it's ready for a time capsule. Parents who have given their daughter "everything" just about collapse when it turns out all she really wants is drugs. A fine cast contends with the writer's preachiness and sledgehammer dramatizing.

THE PEOPLE VS. JEAN HARRIS ☆☆☆
1981, USA (TV)
Ellen Burstyn, Martin Balsam, Richard Dysart, Peter Coyote, Sarah Marshall. Directed by George Schaefer. 150 min.

The ramifications of the Jean Harris case are still being discussed, even after two controversial books and continuing debate about her innocence. When Harris, the headmistress of a fashionable girls' school, shot her long-time lover, "Scarsdale Diet" doctor Herman Tarnower, all America seemed to jump on the bandwagon with speculation. Is it any wonder that a television network rushed into the fray with a film more quickly than you could say "Blind Justice"? Because some of the facts of the case may still be debatable, this film still slams across a cogent tale of a woman scorned and the unladylike way in which that fury was released. This was a rushed production, but there's nothing rushed or second-rate about Ellen Burstyn's meticulous performance, which netted her an Emmy nomination.

PEPE LE MOKO ☆☆☆☆
1937, France
Jean Gabin, Mireille Balin, Line Noro, Lucas Gridoux, Gabriel Gabrio, Saturnin Fabre. Directed by Julien Duvivier. 90 min.

The crime drama was an extraordinary prototype of the American *film noir* actually issued from French director Julien Duvivier. The setting is the sordid underworld of the Casbah, in Algiers, and Jean Gabin plays an internationally famous gangster holed up there because it's the one place the police can never penetrate. He must, however, protect himself from both the French authorities and the Algerian natives in order to survive. The film has a dark, despondent tone, but it's full of lively scenes like the killing of a stoolie (to the sound of raucous piano music) and a thrilling chase through the alleys of the Casbah.

PERFECT ☆☆
1985, USA, R
John Travolta, Jamie Lee Curtis, Marilu Henner, Jann Wenner, Laraine Newman. Directed by James Bridges. 125 min.

A film that should be re-titled *Half Right*. John Travolta plays a ruthless *Rolling Stone* reporter in the process of covering two stories, one involving a crooked businessman, and the other about health clubs serving as the "new singles bars." While on the latter assignment, he falls in love with a beautiful and troubled aerobics instructor (Jamie Lee Curtis). A movie with ideas that don't come together and a mediocre script, it fails to convince with any of its heavy-handed points about journalistic responsibility. There are good performances by several members of the cast, including Travolta and Laraine Newman. *Rolling Stone* editor Jann Wenner manages to turn in an unconvincing portrayal of himself.

PERFECT STRANGERS ☆☆
1984, USA, R
Anne Carlisle, Brad Rijn, John Woehrle, Matthew Stockley, Stephen Lack, Otto Von Wernherr. Directed by Larry Cohen. 90 min.

A hit man discovers that a toddler has witnessed one of his murders in this low-budget, low-key suspense film. Writer-director Larry Cohen does swift, skilled work, and his plotting doesn't really fall apart until the end. However, the story's been told before with more style, and the sexism with which the divorced-mother heroine and her tough feminist friends are portrayed is jolting and unpleasant. (a.k.a.: *Blind Alley*)

PERFORMANCE ☆☆½
1970, Great Britain, X
Mick Jagger, James Fox, Anita Pallenberg, Michelle Breton. Directed by Donald Cammell and Nicolas Roeg. 106 min.

In any objective sense, *Performance* is not really a very good film, and those who are easily roused to moral indignation by the decadence of our time would be well-advised to stay away (as would those who are easily bored). But for the more jaded and/or indulgent, this does have a perverse, creepy fascination; even when it's being quite vile, it is more viscerally vile than almost any other film. The bare-bones plot has James Fox as a gangster hiding out from his ex-cronies in a house owned by retired rock star Mick Jagger. The two personalities begin to merge, the macho gangster experimenting with drugs and perversity and the singer discovering violence and cruelty. Jagger is not a very good actor, though he was called on only to pose here, and he sings only one song, the striking "Memo from Turner." The film is loaded with every arty trick that the two first-time directors could think of, generally to no solid effect. Don't be misled by the X rating; were this to be released nowadays, they'd probably have to spice it up a bit to be insured an R.

PERIL ☆☆
1985, France, R
Christophe Malavoy, Nicole Garcia, Michel Piccoli, Richard Bohringer, Anemone, Anais Jeanneret. Directed by Michel Deville. 100 min.

Michel Deville's erotic thriller has an admirably complex plot, but it's directed and acted without any passion, and the result is much less engaging than it should be. Christophe Malavoy plays a guitarist hired to give a wealthy couple's daughter music lessons. He begins an affair with the mother, and quickly finds himself entrapped in a byzantine plot involving a purloined microfilm, a local voyeur, an incriminating videocassette, and a melancholy paid assassin (*Diva's* Richard Bohringer, in an excellent performance). The intrigue is clever if a bit indecipherable, but Deville's detached, ironic style doesn't serve his story well.

THE PERILS OF GWENDOLINE IN THE LAND OF THE YIK-YAK ☆
1984, France, R
Tawny Kitaen, Brent Huff, Zabou. Directed by Just Jaeckin. 88 min.

Director Just Jaeckin (*Emmanuelle*) turns out another one of his idiotic soft-core opuses, with picture-perfect heroes who lose their clothes at every opportunity. Based on a risqué French comic strip (which could only be better than the film), *Gwendoline* follows the adventures of a monosyllabic he-man and a helpless damsel who find a hidden city filled with G-string-clad amazons. Even the action sequences are badly staged in the haste for someone's top to fall off. This is undoubtedly the worst of the *Raiders* rip-offs.

THE PERILS OF PAULINE ☆☆☆
1947, USA
Betty Hutton, John Lund, Billy de Wolfe, William Demarest, Constance Collier. Directed by George Marshall. 96 min.

Betty Hutton is at her lively best in this lighthearted musical biography of silent screen star Pearl White. The P.J. Wolfson-Frank Butler screenplay pokes fun at both early screen serials (White was the star of *The Perils of Pauline*) and theatrical types. Hutton's galvanic gesticulations are perfect for this role, and the Frank Loesser songs include "Papa Don't Preach to Me." The last half hour gets sappy and slightly draggy, but the rest is breezy, fast-paced fun.

PERSONA ☆☆☆☆
1966, Sweden
Liv Ullmann, Bibi Andersson, Gunnar Bjornstrand. Directed by Ingmar Bergman. 83 min.

A major modern European film that represents a key stage in Ingmar Bergman's development. The title refers to a mask, and also to the personality behind it. Liv Ullmann plays an actress who suffers a complete breakdown, losing her power of speech during a performance of *Electra*, when the person and the mask become estranged. Psychiatric nurse Bibi Andersson gradually finds herself drawn into a mesmerizing exchange of personalities. Bergman deals with questions of communication, sexuality, and identity, while also including non-narrative sequences about the nature of film itself and how the idea came to him. The result is one of his purest, most uncompromising and inexplicit films. (*Trivia note*: This was the inspiration for Woody Allen's *Interiors*.)

PERSONAL BEST ☆☆
1982, USA, R
Mariel Hemingway, Patrice Donnelly, Scott Glenn, Kenny Moore, Jim Moody, Larry Pennell. Directed by Robert Towne. 124 min.

The first film directed by screenwriter Robert Towne is a dull paean to the beauty of human striving. Towne follows a pair of runners (Mariel Hemingway and Patrice Donnelly) over a period of four years, as they fall into a lesbian affair and prepare for the 1980 Olympic pentathlon trials. The movie is a bit fuzzy about its post-feminist attitudes, but Michael Chapman's cinematography is extraordinary; with dazzling clarity, he brings the athlete's world of straining muscles and avid concentration directly to your senses.

THE PERSONALS ☆☆☆
1982, USA, PG
Bill Schoppert, Karen Landry, Paul Eiding. Directed by Peter Markle. 90 min.

A film that gives us a very believable look at being middle-aged and single. Set in a world where husbands cry and relationships don't always work out, *The Personals* depicts the efforts of a recently divorced male trying to meet women through a newspaper's personals column. Director Peter Markle doesn't feel the need to indulge in overly cerebral situations or the glamorized Hollywood antics of such pictures as *Starting Over*; instead he tries for something disarmingly honest and succeeds. Even the dialogue here seems to have been taken from somebody's cocktail party. The cast of unknowns does well, especially Bill Schoppert as the all-too-human protagonist.

PETE'S DRAGON ☆☆
1977, USA, G
Helen Reddy, Jim Dale, Mickey Rooney, Red Buttons, Shelley Winters, Sean Marshall, Jean Kean, Jim Backus, Jeff Conaway, voice of Charlie Callas. Directed by Don Chaffey. 134 min.

The Disney people were just trying too hard with this attempt to create another perennial family classic. The best thing about it is the combination of animation with live action; the problem is that they *know* that that's the best thing, and didn't care enough to work more on the other elements of the film—story, songs, characters, etc. The homely dragon is likable, though it's not on-screen for enough of the film's excessive running time. Two and one-quarter hours is a long time to expect kids to sit still. (It's also far longer than you should expect any adult to be able to tolerate the grating Helen Reddy.)

PETIT CON ☆☆☆
1984, France, R
Bernard Brieux, Guy Marchand, Caroline Cellier, Souad Amidou. Directed by Gerard Lauzier. 90 min.

The title translates roughly as "little shmuck," and the protagonist of this bright comedy is just that, a hopelessly self-involved, wonderfully melancholy teenage boy. He tells his befuddled parents he's taking drugs just to spite them, begins a pathetic affair with a wrong-side-of-the-tracks tramp, and, in his spare time, jots diary entries such as: "Am I a genius? Am I a madman? Which?" Writer-director Gerard Lauzier makes gentle mockery of adolescent angst while allowing all of his characters their humanity and letting even the young man redeem himself eventually. There are fine performances, especially from Guy Marchand as the hopelessly bourgeois father who flinches every time his creepy kid calls him a fascist.

THE PETRIFIED FOREST ☆☆☆
1936, USA
Leslie Howard, Humphrey Bogart, Bette Davis, Charley Grapewin. Directed by Archie Mayo. 83 min.

A fleeing killer holds a group of people hostage at a desert café, in a talky but still taut melodrama adapted from Robert Sherwood's play. It's unmistakably theatrical in its language and filming, and some of the story's big themes have dated. The acting, though, is uniformly excellent, and provides a fortuitous chance to see Bette Davis and Humphrey Bogart at the start of their careers, and Leslie Howard at the height of his, giving a standout performance as a disillusioned intellectual.

PHANTASM ☆☆☆
1979, USA, R
Michael Baldwin, Bill Thornbury, Reggie Bannister. Directed by Don Coscarelli. 87 min.

Two brothers investigate a spooky funeral home and find that its alien caretakers are turning fresh corpses into evil dwarfs. This is a low-budget strikingly original horror film, with a surrealistic style that owes something to George Romero. It's often very scary, with some ingenious special effects, the most notorious of which is a flying metal ball that drills its victims' brains out.

THE PHANTOM EXPRESS ☆½
1932, USA
J. Farrel MacDonald, William Collier, Jr., Sally Blane, Alex Axelson, Deirdre Martin, Hobart Bosworth. Directed by Emory Johnson. 65 min.

This is a creaky railroad melodrama about a ghostly train that keeps appearing just long enough to force other trains off the tracks. There are the requisite pair of lovers, Swedish comedy relief, and numerous dark and stormy nights: Even in 1932, this kind of stuff must have seemed awfully dated. J. Farrel MacDonald began his career in the early days of silent movies; in addition to acting, he also directed, but he is best known as one of John Ford's informal ensemble players.

THE PHANTOM FIEND

See *The Lodger*

PHANTOM KUNG FU ☆
Hong Kong
Wang Kuan-Hsing, Don Wong Dao, Chang Yi, Lee Kuen, Chin Min. Directed by Lee Tso Nan.

This is a rather confusing story of the Chings vs. the Mings, starring some of Hong Kong's great martial artists/actors. Unfortunately, *Phantom* also suffers from poor photography and choppy editing.

THE PHANTOM OF THE OPERA ☆☆☆☆
1925, USA
Lon Chaney, Mary Philbin, Gibson Gowland, Norman Kerry. Directed by Rupert Julian. 101 min.

This is the most celebrated filming of the old chestnut. Blackhawk Video has released a lavish, partially color-tinted tape of the classic melodrama set in the Paris of the 1880s, with that master of bizarre makeup, Lon Chaney, in full Grand Guignol flight. He plays a hideously disfigured former maestro living in the vaults beneath the Paris Opera House who is obsessed with a young singer and conducts a reign of terror to further her career. The Claude Rains (1943) version had real opera thrown in, but this one has more chills, and Chaney's tortured villain-hero is one of his best. The famous unveiling scene is still a shocker. This movie originally ran at 101 minutes; all of the video versions are shorter (owing to the fact that they have transferred the film to tape at a higher projection speed—unfortunate, because it cripples the film's pacing, but, so far, unavoidable).

PHANTOM SHIP ☆½
1935, Great Britain
Bela Lugosi, Shirley Grey, Arthur Margetson, Edmund Willard, George Mozart. Directed by Denison Clift. 80 min.

Bela Lugosi's presence and the title might lead you to expect scarier fare than this middling high-seas suspense film delivers. The original title, *The Mystery of the Marie Celeste*, was a more accurate description of the non-supernatural goings-on in 1872, when a ship of tough British sailors comes upon a vessel sailing near them that's completely bereft of crew members. Some very moderate chills follow, but they're ruined by a framing story and a very obvious explanation.

THE PHANTOM TOLLBOOTH ☆☆
1970, USA, G
Butch Patrick (live sequences); voices of Mel Blanc, Hans Conried, Shep Menken, Candy Candido, others (animated sequences). Directed by Chuck Jones, Abe Levitow, and David Monahan. 90 min.

Norton Juster's splendid children's book about a boy who journeys into a magical land becomes pedestrian kiddie fare under the hand of ex-Looney Tunes master Chuck Jones (this was his first feature). Some of the more complex symbols and references, charming on the page, become cloying and obvious on-screen, and the framing live-action scenes are cheap and banal. Very young children won't mind the dated pop art animation, but they'll probably be stumped by the profusion of briefly seen, mostly undifferentiated characters.

PHAR LAP ☆☆
1984, Australia, PG
Judy Morris, Tom Burlinson, Martin Vaughan, Ron Leibman, Vincent Ball, Celia de Burgh. Directed by Simon Wincer. 108 min.

A horse is a horse—of course. Except, that is, if it's the hero of this lavish Australian film about a champion racer of the 1920s and 1930s—in which it's the equestrian answer to Jesus Christ. After arriving from New Zealand, Phar Lap is purchased by a corrupt American businessman (Ron Leibman) and then hooked up with a rosy-cheeked lad (Tom Burlinson) who develops, as they say, a bond with the beast. The horse is then dragged through the mud by a scheming, greedy mankind too sunk in vice to recognize the savior in its midst. Simon Wincer is the latest Australian director to serve up cinematic simplemindedness as a virtue. His film relies on lush cinematography, period costuming, and prettified track competition to gloss over a creative void.

PHASE IV ☆☆☆
1974, USA, PG
Michael Murphy, Nigel Davenport, Lynne Frederick, Allan Gifford. Directed by Saul Bass. 86 min.

Superintelligent ants menace a group of research scientists in the desert, in a horror film that has more in common with the insect documentary *The Hellstrom Chronicles* than with *Them*. Director-designer Saul Bass isn't trying to make just another thriller here, and loads his debut film with some fantastic visual touches as the scientists try to find some way to destroy the diabolical little buggers. It's intelligently done and notable for its excellent use of the ant actors.

THE PHILADELPHIA EXPERIMENT ☆
1984, USA, PG-13
Michael Pare, Nancy Allen, Bobby DiCicco, Eric Christmas. Directed by Stewart Raffill. 102 min.

The experiment fails! A naval experiment goes awry, catapulting a warship from the Philadelphia Harbor circa 1942 into another dimension, where it creates a vortex that threatens to destroy the world forty years later.

THE PHILADELPHIA STORY ☆☆☆½
1940, USA
Cary Grant, Katharine Hepburn, James Stewart, Ruth Hussey, John Howard, Roland Young, Virginia Weidler, Henry Daniell, John Halliday. Directed by George Cukor. 112 min.

This delightfully sophisticated comedy, set in Main Line society, revolves around the impending wedding of heiress Tracy Lord (Katharine Hepburn) to commoner George Kittredge (John Howard). But Tracy's ex, C.K. Dexter Haven (Cary Grant) and Maccaulay Connor (James Stewart) step in and force her to rethink things. Donald Ogden Stewart based his screenplay on the play of the same name, which Philip Barry wrote with Hepburn in mind. The dialogue is eloquent, witty, incisive. Kate is perfect, of course, and very beautiful. Stewart won a well-deserved Best Actor Oscar for his deft performance.

A PIANO FOR MRS. CIMINO ☆☆☆
1982, USA (TV)
Bette Davis, Penny Fuller, Keenan Wynn, Alexa Kenin, George Hearn, Christopher Guest, Graham Jarvis. Directed by George Schaefer. 100 min.

Among actresses of her stature and generation, Bette Davis has been virtually alone in finding a rewarding haven for her talents in television; this is one of her best TV movies. She gives a fine, touching performance as an elderly woman declared senile and incompetent after the death of her husband; when she fights to retake control of her life, she alienates her well-meaning but unthinking children. Director George Schaefer showcases his star with great care, and the other performers wisely stand back and let Davis take center stage.

PICNIC
1955, USA ★★★
William Holden, Kim Novak, Rosalind Russell, Arthur O'Connell, Susan Strasberg. Directed by Joshua Logan. 113 min.

Joshua Logan, who also directed the stage version of William Inge's Pulitzer Prize-winning play, here opens up the one-set drama with a vengeance, although much of the intensity of the piece is obfuscated through meaningless local details and Logan's use of overly lush color. William Holden, a mite old for his role, is a drifter whose passage through a small Midwestern town greatly affects the lives of several women. Kim Novak has been castigated by some for merely playing herself in the role of the pretty, dumb homecoming queen with whom Holden becomes involved, but her performance has at least a shy dignity at odds with the overly theatrical, and she and Holden share the high point of the film—the electric moment when they dance together. Rosalind Russell's job is so at odds with her usual image that her portrayal of the desperate, man-hungry spinster either astounds or seems to be merely an effective stunt. The others range from old pros (Arthur O'Connell) to strident newcomers (Susan Strasberg), but the largest complaint with this well-crafted movie is the absence of a strong directorial vision to unify and give meaning to the separate strands of the story.

PICNIC AT HANGING ROCK
1975, Australia, PG ★★★
Rachel Roberts, Dominic Guard, Helen Morse, Jacki Weaver, Vivean Gray, Kirsty Child. Directed by Peter Weir. 115 min.

A perplexing mood mystery of Victorian Australia unfolds as three young girls and their teacher picnic at an ominous geological formation and disappear soon after. One girl, later found alive, has no recollection of what actually happened, and the film probes the puzzle of their bizarre and unfathomable adventure. Director Peter Weir's customarily elusive approach to his material works well here, but the film may still leave viewers frustrated. The symbolism is heavy going and some expositional scenes go on far too long. Ultimately, Weir (*The Year of Living Dangerously*, *Witness*) is better at creating atmosphere than telling stories. *Picnic* is offbeat and interesting but lacks real depth.

PICTURE MOMMY DEAD
1966, USA ★★½
Don Ameche, Martha Hyer, Zsa Zsa Gabor, Susan Gordon, Maxwell Redd, Wendell Corey, Signe Hasso, Anna Lee. Directed by Bert I. Gordon. 88 min.

A compact, occasionally clever chiller with the overused plot hook of a disputed inheritance. Susan Gordon, the director's daughter, plays a young girl apparently possessed by the soul of her late mother, doing battle with her father (Don Ameche) and greedy stepmother (Martha Hyer). It's predictable but often amusing, thanks to the hammy performances of the cast's veterans and some appropriately baroque moments.

THE PICTURE OF DORIAN GRAY
1945, USA ★★★
Hurd Hatfield, George Sanders, Donna Reed, Angela Lansbury, Peter Lawford. Directed by Albert Lewin. 110 min.

MGM's lavish, atmospheric version of *Dorian Gray* preserves enough of the wit, horror, and decadence of Oscar Wilde's novella to make it worthwhile. Albert Lewin (*The Moon and Sixpence*, *Pandora and the Flying Dutchman*) wrote the screenplay and directed the story of a young Victorian man who never ages but whose portrait reveals all the sins and deterioration throughout his life. Highlights of the film are Angela Lansbury's touching performance as the music hall singer who falls for Dorian's charms, George Sanders's pungent quips, and the spectacular revelation of the portrait itself (in Technicolor in some prints). They easily atone for the episodic pace and bland romantic subplot starring Donna Reed and Peter Lawford. Wilde fans will probably approve of the adaptation.

A PIECE OF THE ACTION
1977, USA, PG ★★
Sidney Poitier, Bill Cosby, James Earl Jones, Denise Nicholas, Hope Clarke. Directed by Sidney Poitier. 135 min.

A very long, occasionally bright but mostly tedious comedy in the *Uptown Saturday Night*/*Let's Do It Again* vein. Sidney Poitier again costars with Bill Cosby and directs, but this time the story, in which they play a pair of thieves blackmailed into helping out a group of ghetto kids, is sweet where it should be sharp. There are some engaging comic episodes along the way, but it's predictable from the opening scenes, and the cast used up its best gags in the earlier films.

PIECES
1983, Italy/Spain ★
Christopher George, Paul Smith, Edmund Purdom, Lynda Day George. Directed by Juan Piquer Simon. 89 min.

The most ghastly horror spectacles are mangled human sculptures: That moment in *Happy Birthday to Me*, for instance, when Melissa Sue Anderson croons the title song to a table of mangled corpses in party hats. *Pieces* had the potential to become just such a bloody tableau—a tale of a mental mutant stalking a college campus mutilating naked women for a human jigsaw puzzle. Unfortunately, even this hope is dashed as the film limps along like an incredibly long prelude to an obscure Swedish porn film that never occurs. Although the actors have American names, the dialogue appears to have been dubbed from the Venusian, and the characterization is so poor it must have been coached by a lumberjack. The script and sound editing were done with a chainsaw, and horror purists will balk at the bloated detective subplot. The idea was decent, but it has been hacked to pieces.

PILLOW TALK
1959, USA ★★★
Doris Day, Rock Hudson, Tony Randall, Thelma Ritter, Nick Adams, Allen Jenkins, Marcel Dalio, Lee Patrick. Directed by Michael Gordon. 110 min.

Now that Rock Hudson films will be viewed with a certain degree of morbid curiosity, it should be mentioned right off that in this comedy, Rock's character pretends to be gay for part of the narrative. Hudson plays a playboy songwriter who sees this as the only way of winning over his party-line nemesis, an interior decorator played by (who else?) Doris Day. In what was Hudson and Day's first of three unions, producers Ross Hunter and Martin Melcher (Day's husband) packaged the stars in posh sets, garish color, and wide-screen. It's the kind of film where people talk in sexual innuendo (or what passed for risqué in 1959) in nightclubs, offices, and deluxe highrise apartments. Everything is artificial, from the ridiculous plot contrivance of having the two characters share a party line to Day's peroxide blond hair color. Yet the film works much like a situation comedy episode, and often better because of the skilled cast and the playful if dopey use of music and Cinemascope (slightly distorted on tape). For the record, Oscar-nominated Day sings, but only light, comic numbers, and Stanley Shapiro and Maurice Richlin's Oscar-winning script competed that year against their script for *Operation Petticoat*.

PINK FLAMINGOS
1973, USA ★½
Divine, Mink Stole, David Lochary, Edith Massey, Mary Vivian Pearce, Danny Mills, Cookie Mueller. Directed by John Waters. 95 min.

Yes, it's the notorious cult film that midnight moviegoers have been gagging at for years. What can you say about a film capped off with a coda in which a 300-pound tranvestite munches on poodle droppings? John Waters's later films, *Female Trouble* and *Polyester*, were both cruel and funny, but this spiteful odyssey through lower Baltimore has all the appeal of shouting obscenities at nuns or spitting in the face of someone who just wished you "good morning." From her tacky trailer home, La Divine and her family (including a son who has threesomes with a live chicken and a girl, and an obese, dim-witted mother with an egg fetish) hold court as the filthiest people alive. But the Gross-out Gorgon is soon challenged by the Marbles, an enterprising duo that impregnates and imprisons hippie hitchhikers to sell their babies to lesbian couples. In a better film, this might pass as an indictment of the middle class, since the Marbles are disgusting for profit, whereas, for Divine and son, criminal behavior is an artistic expression. But overall, you may feel as if someone has set up a home movie camera to record the sights of a typical day in hell.

PINK FLOYD—THE WALL ☆☆½
1982, Great Britain, R
Bob Geldof, Christine Hargreaves, James Laurenson, Bob Hoskins, Eleanor David. Directed by Alan Parker. 99 min.

Roger Waters, Pink Floyd's bassist and the writer-conceptualist of the best-selling album upon which this film is based, has seldom made any effort to hide his contempt for a large part of his audience. Like the album, this film both panders to and looks down on the audience, and in order to really enjoy it you have to be either too dumb to realize you're being sneered at or arrogant enough to consider yourself "in" on the whole thing. Bob Geldof, in his pre-"St. Bob" days, is featured as a rock star on the verge of a nervous implosion, but the real protagonist here is the nightmarish imagery created by director Alan Parker and animator Gerald Scarfe. It's an ugly, bleak, and depressing film, but it is also undeniably fascinating.

THE PINK PANTHER ☆☆☆½
1964, USA
David Niven, Peter Sellers, Robert Wagner, Capucine, Claudia Cardinale, Fran Jeffries, John Le Mesurier. Directed by Blake Edwards. 115 min.

Fans of later entries in the often hilarious *Pink Panther* series may be moderately disappointed with this initial entry, as Peter Sellers's Inspector Clouseau is a supporting character instead of the lead and because the level of slapstick is less inspired than in some sequels. On the other hand, Sellers's outrageous accent and buffoonery are often hysterically funny and there are many riotous sight gags. Clouseau keeps his eye on jewel thief David Niven planning to steal the fabulous Pink Panther.

THE PINK PANTHER STRIKES AGAIN ☆☆☆½
1976, Great Britain, PG
Peter Sellers, Herbert Lom, Colin Blakely, Leonard Rossiter, Lesley-Anne Down, Bert Kwouk. Directed by Blake Edwards. 103 min.

The best of the three Pink Panther films that Peter Sellers and Blake Edwards made when they picked the character back up in the 1970s. This time around, Inspector Clouseau's chief adversary (aside from the world of sense and order) is none other than Chief Inspector Dreyfus (Herbert Lom), his old superior officer, now driven insane as a result of Clouseau's bumbling. In the best serial villain fashion, Dreyfus has taken over a castle where he plays an organ maniacally and devises a death ray capable of vaporizing buildings from thousands of miles away. You can see most of the jokes coming a mile away, which is exactly what makes most of them as funny as they are; a case of familiarity breeding contentment.

PINOCCHIO ☆☆☆☆
1940, USA
Animated: Dickie Jones, Cliff Edwards, Christian Rub, Evelyn Venable, Walter Catlett. Directed by Ben Sharpsteen and Hamilton Luske. 88 min.

Walt Disney's second animated feature, based on the story by Carlo Collodi, marked a high point for the studio. The visual details alone should be enough to keep you dazzled, but the film also masterfully blends action, music, horror, and melodrama. Dickie Jones supplies the voice of Pinocchio, the wooden puppet who comes alive through the spell of a fairy and whose nose grows to great lengths when he's caught lying. Cliff Edwards, who sings "When You Wish Upon a Star" and "Give a Little Whistle," ghosts Jiminy Cricket, Pinocchio's friend and the film's storyteller. Despite a few lapses into typical Disney sentimentality, *Pinocchio* is one of the best animated features from that or any other studio.

PIONEER WOMAN ☆☆½
1973, USA (TV)
Joanna Pettet, William Shatner, David Janssen, Lance LeGault, Helen Hunt. Directed by Buzz Kulik. 78 min.

In this generally commendable Western drama about overcoming insurmountable odds in the untamed West, a family pulls together when they strike out for farmland in Nebraska and have to meet incredible hardships, including fights with recalcitrant squatters who won't relinquish their territory. The film is slanted from the woman's point of view, which is refreshing in the Western genre, and the cast plays rural types with rugged conviction.

PIRANHA ☆☆☆
1978, USA
Bradford Dillman, Heather Menzies, Kevin McCarthy, Keenan Wynn, Dick Miller, Barbara Steele. Directed by Joe Dante. 92 min.

John Sayles (*Alligator*) wrote and Joe Dante (*Gremlins*) directed this fish-with-teeth story. Our heroes unwittingly release mutant fresh-water piranhas, originally intended for Vietnam's Mekong Delta, into a resort lake; the results turn the peaceful waters red as our overzealous nibblers make a watery picnic out of many vacationers and a camp filled with innocent children. This "little *Jaws*" bustles with humor and vitality, complete with cinematic in-jokes and sardonic wit: It is an excellent example of New World's black comedy and cinematic parody. Leave it to Roger Corman to make fishing fun again.

PIRANHA PART 2: THE SPAWNING ☆
1981, Italy/USA, R
Tricia O'Neil, Steve Marachuk, Lance Henriksen, Leslie Graves. Directed by James Cameron. 88 min.

In the original, Dr. Mengers warned us that this might happen—but oh, if only it could have been prevented. James Cameron (*Terminator*) directs an inconsistent adventure in a land where tropical tourists are subjected to a sea and air attack by flying—yes, flying—piranhas. (How's that for evolutionary development?) With only a few visually exciting moments, particularly the deceptive opening credit sequence, this film might still have succeeded had it emulated the action of the original and not strained for character development. If *Piranha* ripped off *Jaws*, *The Spawning* rips off *Jaws II*; it's that bad.

THE PIRATE ☆☆☆☆
1948, USA
July Garland, Gene Kelly, Gladys Cooper, Walter Slezak, The Nicholas Brothers. Directed by Vincente Minnelli. 102 min.

The setting is a small Caribbean island in the 1800s, where Judy Garland dreams of the passion and excitement of love with a notorious pirate. This exuberant parody, full of Cole Porter songs, is glorious and sophisticated entertainment, an immense and lavish production that is nevertheless as enchantingly weightless as a daydream. At the time of its initial release, this musicalization of a Broadway vehicle for Lunt and Fontanne was a box-office disappointment, despite the high-powered performances of Garland, who's delightful in a gutsy, change-of-pace role, and Gene Kelly, whose over-the-top takeoff on Douglas Fairbanks, Sr., is vastly amusing. This is one of the best of the MGM musicals, and its songs include "Love of My Life," "You Can Do No Wrong," and the classic "Be a Clown."

THE PIRATE MOVIE
1982, Australia, PG ☆
Christopher Atkins, Kristy McNichol, Ted Hamilton, Bill Kerr, Maggie Kirkpatrick. Directed by Ken Annakin. 99 min.

A running leap at the bandwagon of *The Pirates of Penzance*, then in the prime of its Broadway success, this falls flat on its face but still insists on coughing up saltwater in the viewer's face. After falling off a tourist boat, Kristy McNichol dreams herself into a bastardization of the Gilbert and Sullivan operetta with a song score consisting of one-half G & S (with new lyrics) and one-half bubblegunk rock and roll. The nonstop parade of dumb gags derived from other popular movies (*Jaws, Star Wars*, etc.) and such "hip" gags as a black pirate sending a white victim down the plank with a cry of, "Hang five, honky!" are in no way to be mistaken for comedy. Kristy awakens at the end, with a sense of relief equal to the viewer's upon finding that escape is just an "off" button away.

PIRATES
1986, France/Tunisia, PG-13 ☆½
Walter Matthau, Cris Campion, Damien Thomas, Olu Jacobs, Charlotte Lewis. Directed by Roman Polanski. 117 min.

Walter Matthau's boisterous performance as Captain Red can't hold this tedious high-seas adventure together, nor can his outrageous energy submerge the picture's jumbled plot. *Pirates*, Roman Polanski's first picture in seven years, is best during its first portion, when Red and his youthful companion Frog are taken aboard a hellish galleon and then subtly encourage the crew to mutiny against their snide Spanish officers. But once the ship has been taken and the foes dispatched, the movie's swashbuckling steam runs out and the plot drags on forever. Polanski's strong visual sense keeps things running, but this lush production doesn't amount to anything more than crude, mechanical entertainment.

THE PIRATES OF PENZANCE
1983, USA, G ☆☆½
Linda Ronstadt, Kevin Kline, Angela Lansbury, Red Smith, George Rose, Tony Azito. Directed by Wilford Leach. 112 min.

In the film version of Joseph Papp's New York Shakespeare Festival production, director Wilford Leach retains all the whimsical bits of business he invented for the stage show. Unfortunately, he's no filmmaker, and the movie's oppressive cuteness ends up distracting you from the lyrics and music of Gilbert and Sullivan; watching this *Pirates*, you keep expecting Smurfs to pop up from the bushes gabbling "Poor Wandering One." However, the singing is often gorgeous.

THE PIT
1981, USA, R ☆½
Sammy Snyders, Jennie Elias, Sonja Smits, Laura Hollingsworth. Directed by Lew Lehman. 96 min.

A geeky small-town boy finds a pit in the woods at the bottom of which live weird hairy troglodytes. He comes to think of them as his friends and hurls down to them a number of people who have tormented him in large ways and small; they are devoured. When he is no longer able to feed the creatures, he helps them to escape, with predictably bloody results. *The Pit* suffers from a strange schizophrenia, seeming at some points to be a conventional monster movie and at others a psychological thriller in which all the demons are the product of the mind of a lonely, sexually obsessed, outcast youngster. The two elements never quite mesh, but *The Pit* is fairly entertaining nonetheless, and many of those thrown into the pit richly deserve their gory fate.

THE PIT AND THE PENDULUM
1961, USA ☆☆☆
Vincent Price, John Kerr, Barbara Steele. Directed by Roger Corman. 80 min.

Vincent Price, thinking he is back in the Spanish Inquisition, revels in torture tactics and terrorizes visitor John Kerr, who ventures into Price's eerie castle in the hope of uncovering the mystery of his sister's death. This bone-chilling elaboration of the Edgar Allen Poe short story has great effects—despite laughable dialogue at times—and is the second of eight Roger Corman/Poe/Price projects.

PIXOTE
1981, Brazil, R ☆☆☆☆
Fernando Ramos da Silva, Jorge Juliano, Marilia Pera. Directed by Hector Babenco. 127 min.

This brutal, chilling, superb portrait of Brazil's abandoned youth focuses on the story of one ten-year-old for whom survival—by means of prostitution, drugs, or murder—is everything. Without exploitation or cheap sentimentality but with an unrelentingly dismal tone, this film is truly shocking and deeply affecting. Team this with Buñuel's classic *Los Olvidados* for the ultimate double feature on child crime.

A PLACE IN THE SUN
1951, USA ☆☆☆½
Montgomery Clift, Elizabeth Taylor, Shelley Winters, Keefe Brasselle, Raymond Burr, Ann Revere. Directed by George Stevens. 122 min.

George Stevens won an Oscar for his direction of this overpraised adaptation of Theodore Dreiser's *An American Tragedy*. Stevens's style is relentlessly authoritative, resulting in an exquisitely handsome, somber film that can be criticized for its lack of any spontaneity or warmth, for an uncomfortable feeling that this was a film created to be a masterpiece. Most of the filmmaking is too conventional for that, but Elizabeth Taylor *is* breathtakingly beautiful as the rich, gorgeous object of Montgomery Clift's desire, and the pair almost shock in the eroticism of their love scenes, heightened by Stevens's extreme close-ups. (This was the first and best of their three films together.) Shelley Winters is almost too drab by contrast, but her performance as Clift's working-class wife is the only one in the film that gives the viewer a sense of genuine poignancy.

PLACES IN THE HEART
1984, USA, PG ☆☆½
Sally Field, Danny Glover, John Malkovich, Lindsay Crouse, Ed Harris. Directed by Robert Benton. 110 min.

This golden-hued drama about a young widow trying to save her Texas farm during the Depression was the most popular of the triad of farm films released in late 1984, probably because it takes the Reagan-era position that natural, personal, and financial disasters can all be overcome with a little good, hard work. Writer-director Robert Benton's nostalgic film is beautiful looking and often well observed, and much of the acting, including a notable film debut by John Malkovich, is fine. But the gross oversentimentalization of every scene, culminating in a ludicrous finale, is maddening—like the Oscar-winning, overpraised performance of Sally Field, *Places* begs way too hard for the approval of its audience.

THE PLAGUE DOGS
1982, USA, PG ☆☆☆
Animated: John Hurt, James Bolam, Christopher Benjamin, Judy Geeson, Barbara Leigh-Hunt. Directed by Martin Rosen. 86 min.

This beautifully animated drama concerns a pair of dogs, imprisoned by vicious lab experimenters, who escape from their confines only to find themselves hunted mercilessly. The film is based on a novel by Richard Adams and directed by Martin Rosen, who also handled the author's *Watership Down*. While many of the visual elements on display here remain within the classical animation tradition, the grim story and characterizations are in almost defiant contrast to Disney cuteness. Not for young children, but lovers of animation should seek it out.

PLANET OF THE APES
1968, USA, G ★★★½
Charlton Heston, Roddy McDowall, Kim Hunter, Maurice Evans, James Whitmore, Linda Harrison. Directed by Franklin J. Schaffner. 112 min.

One of the most exciting and successful science-fiction adventures ever made takes a simple, clever premise—time-traveling astronauts land on a planet where talking, "civilized" apes have enslaved human beings—and fashions an entertainment that works on all cylinders: horror, action, social comedy, and mild political allegory. Of the principal actors, only the stalwart Charlton Heston plays a human; the others are encased in John Chambers's and Dan Striepeke's superbly mobile and convincing simian makeup, the likes of which had never been seen before. The film strives for social commentary at times, but it never slows down the breakneck pace of a consistently creative screenplay by Michael Wilson and Rod Serling, which deftly unlayers ape society as an extension of human political trends. It's great fun, especially but by no means exclusively for children. Followed by *Beneath the Planet of the Apes*.

PLANET OF HORRORS

See *Galaxy of Terror*

PLANET ON THE PROWL
1965, Italy ★
Giacomo Rossi-Stuarti (Jack Stuart), Ombretta Colli (Amber Collins), Peter Martell. Directed by Anthony M. Dawson (Antonio Margheriti). 80 min.

This is a bottom-of-the-barrel Italian sci-fi film about a renegade planet on a collision course with Earth and the team of stalwart scientists trying to get it back on track before it's too late. It's too clumsy and poorly made to be enjoyable even on its own shlocky terms. Originally released as *War Between the Planets*.

PLAN NINE FROM OUTER SPACE
1959, USA ★
Bela Lugosi, Tor Johnson, Vampira. Directed by Edward Wood, Jr. 79 min.

This is another legendary debacle in the oeuvre of Edward Wood, Jr. Second-banana vampires, effeminate aliens and paper-plate flying saucers are thrown together in this jumbled mess with no apparent reason other than cutting the budget to $1.98. The film's narrator, Criswell, pretty much sums it up: "There comes a time in every man's life when he just can't believe his eyes." Bela Lugosi died during production—he obviously saw the dailies.

PLATOON
1986, USA, R ★★★★
Charlie Sheen, Tom Berenger, Willem Dafoe, Keith David, Kevin Dillon, John C. McGinley. Directed by Oliver Stone. 111 min.

Oliver Stone's great combat film about the horrors of Vietnam is one of the finest war films ever made, on a par (on its own very different terms) with masterpieces like Jean Renoir's *Grand Illusion* and Stanley Kubrick's *Paths of Glory*. Stone, himself a Vietnam vet, also wrote the remarkable screenplay and brings his own experiences to bear with searing impact. This lacerating masterpiece makes clear, in terse writing and powerful images, some basic facts about our grunts in Vietnam that many Americans (and American filmmakers) chose to ignore in the 1960s and early 1970s, and which millions of others never knew—that the slogging, awful fighting on the ground was done largely by our poor and uneducated, who knew little of why they were there or what the war was about. A flawless cast, led by Charlie Sheen's poignant incarnation of the young infantryman whose experiences form the film's heart, gives unforgettable performances in this shattering history lesson. *Platoon* should be required viewing for anyone who has seen the reams of drivel Hollywood has produced on the same subject, from *The Green Berets* to *Rambo*. Winner of four Academy Awards, including Best Picture and Best Director.

PLAYERS
1979, USA, PG ★
Ali MacGraw, Dean-Paul Martin, Maximilian Schell, Steve Guttenberg, Pancho Gonzalez. Directed by Anthony Harvey. 120 min.

In its day, this was a bomb notable enough to solidify Ali MacGraw's reputation as a contender for Worst Actress of the 1970s, and to put the acting career of Dean Martin's son Dean-Paul on semipermanent hold. With its reputation diminished, now it's just one more turkey from the recent cinematic past. The world of professional tennis is the setting for this irritating romance between pro Martin and gigolette MacGraw. They pout and preen and paw at each other until you'll wish someone would end it all with a couple of well-placed backhands.

THE PLAYGIRL KILLER
1970, Canada ½★
William Kerwin, Jean Christopher, Neil Sedaka, Andree Champagne, Mary Lou Collins. Directed by Enrick Santamaran. 90 min.

Unrelievedly awful, no-budget Canadian horror about a deranged artist with the nasty habit of killing and freezing his models when he no longer has use for their squirming and pouting. The actresses are marginally less stiff before being frozen than after, and William Kerwin is nobody's idea of a fun psycho. Features an unfortunate singing appearance by Neil Sedaka. (a.k.a. *Decoy for Terror*)

PLAYING FOR KEEPS
1986, USA, PG-13 ★½
Daniel Jordano, Matthew Penn, Leon W. Grant, Mary B. Ward, Marisa Tomei, Jimmy Baio, Harold Gould, Kim Hauser. Directed by Bob Weinstein and Harvey Weinstein. 105 min.

Another rock and roll update of the "let's put on a show" genre, with a run-down country hotel substituting for the summer stock barn, and an ethnically balanced, not-too-talented cast replacing Mickey Rooney and Judy Garland. This film seems conceived for the video market, aimed at teens in search of a movie to listen to while they neck, eat junk food, or do homework. Basted together with an enjoyable sampling of top-forty tunes on the soundtrack, the film's skimpy plot concerns some adolescents who convert (against impossible odds, of course) a dilapidated hotel into a fantasy-fulfilling music-blasting resort for teens. A long playing album in the form of an awfully long-playing movie.

PLAY IT AGAIN, SAM
1972, USA, PG ★★★½
Woody Allen, Diane Keaton, Tony Roberts, Jerry Lacy, Susan Anspach, Jennifer Salt, Joy Bang. Directed by Herbert Ross. 87 min.

Woody Allen adapted this film's screenplay from his hit Broadway show and enlisted Herbert Ross to direct. The result is funny, sweet, and touching, if less maniacally original than some of the films Allen himself has directed. Allen stars as a lovably neurotic movie buff with a Humphrey Bogart fixation. Following Bogie's example, he finds himself in love with his best friend's wife, played irresistibly by Diane Keaton, and their romance culminates in his dream come true—replaying the parting scene from *Casablanca*. The ghost of Bogart materializes in Allen's fantasies: "Dames are simple," Bogart advises. "I've never known one that didn't understand a slap in the mouth or a slug from a .45." An early exploration by Allen of the relationship between cinema and "reality," issues he would later treat more profoundly in *Zelig* and *The Purple Rose of Cairo*.

PLAY MISTY FOR ME ★★★½
1971, USA, R
Clint Eastwood, Jessica Walter, Donna Mills, John Larch, Jack Ging. Directed by Clint Eastwood. 95 min.

Clint Eastwood's directorial debut was this searing thriller about a disc jockey who gets involved with a psychotic fan. Eastwood's use of crosscutting and camera movement to create Hitchcockian suspense is surprisingly effective, and Jessica Walter's performance as the jealous, obsessive woman is chillingly realistic. Eastwood would later return to themes of sexual paranoia in Richard Tuggle's *Tightrope* and in his own Dirty Harry epic *Sudden Impact*. He obviously owes much of his success in this first (and so far best) film, however, to old master Don Siegel (*Dirty Harry*, *The Beguiled*), who plays a small role as a bartender. The ending is a cop-out and the Eastwood-Donna Mills romance is conventional, but the film has a compulsive pulp quality that makes it hard *not* to watch.

PLAYTIME ★★★½
1967, France
Jacques Tati, Barbara Dennek, Jacqueline Lecomte, Valerie Camille. Directed by Jacques Tati. 123 min.

Jacques Tati's endearing M. Hulot continues his adventures in this bittersweet comedy. Filmed with minimum dialogue but maximum play with sound effects, *Playtime* is a beautifully made film about a Frenchman who becomes enamored of an American tourist in Paris. Their adventures are set in Orly Airport, a modern office building, and, most amusingly, a seemingly posh restaurant. The gags build slowly and many occur simultaneously, making a second viewing almost mandatory. Some viewers, however, will be irritated by the lack of narrative, but Tati's Keatonesque figure and his commentary on our modern age is both funny and poignant.

PLAZA SUITE ★★★
1971, USA, PG
Walter Matthau, Maureen Stapleton, Barbara Harris, Lee Grant, Louise Sorel. Directed by Arthur Hiller. 114 min.

Adapted from Neil Simon's Broadway hit, this film consists of three comedies all set in the same suite of New York's Plaza Hotel, and all featuring Walter Matthau (in a variety of bad hairpieces). In the first, he and Maureen Stapleton play a suburban couple on a second honeymoon that ends up with the discovery of infidelity. The second casts him as a Hollywood producer out to seduce his high school flame (Barbara Harris), who is more interested in talking about Jill St. John and Frank Sinatra. The third features Matthau and Lee Grant as parents on the wedding day of their daughter, who locks herself in the bathroom with a case of cold feet. Matthau wears rather thin, and the differentiations he tries to make between his three characters quickly become rather obvious. The actresses, though, are all outstanding. One of Simon's better plays, *Plaza Suite* suffers from an inadequate translation to film, especially in the farcical last story.

PLENTY ★★★
1985, USA, R
Meryl Streep, Charles Dance, Tracey Ullman, Sting, John Gielgud, Ian McKellen, Sam Neill, Burt Kwouk. Directed by Fred Schepisi. 120 min.

David Hare's screen adaptation of his wildly ambitious play attempts to synthesize the whole of the British political and psychological character after World War II into the story of one fascinating, enigmatic woman. As a teenager, Susan Traherne fought in the French Resistance; for the next fifteen years, she tries to recapture that heroic purity in herself and everyone she meets, and when that fails, she drifts into cruelty, irrationality and finally madness. The complex narrative is compelling scene by scene, but it never coheres into a story that allows us to understand Susan as much more than a sympathetic pain in the ass. Still, Meryl Streep's performance goes a long way toward pulling the fragmentary character together, and the supporting cast is superb, with brilliant work from John Gielgud and an extraordinary appearance by Sting as a working stiff whom Susan befriends and then betrays. Hare's writing sizzles with wit and intelligence, but those unfamiliar with his demanding work might do better to start with *Wetherby* than with *Plenty*.

THE PLOUGHMAN'S LUNCH ★★★
1984, Great Britain, R
Tim Curry, Jonathan Pryce, Rosemary Harris, Charlie Dore, Frank Finlay. Directed by Richard Eyre. 100 min.

A sophisticated and cutting inquiry into the lives of British yuppie journalists, the new wave of poseurs and "pseuds" who are clawing their way up the ladder in Thatcher's England. The protagonist, James (Jonathan Pryce, of *Brazil*) is a young fraud who edges uncomfortably around anything that recalls his working-class heritage. While researching a revisionist history of the Suez crisis, he becomes entangled in a romantic triangle with his buddy (Tim Curry) and the buddy's old school chum (Charlie Dore); the film draws parallels between public and private opportunism that, though sometimes strained, lend the story considerable resonance.

POCKETFUL OF MIRACLES ★★★
1961, USA
Glenn Ford, Bette Davis, Hope Lange, Arthur O'Connell, Peter Falk, Thomas Mitchell, Edward Everett Horton, Ann-Margret, Sheldon Leonard, Mickey Shaughnessy. Directed by Frank Capra. 136 min.

Frank Capra's last film is a bighearted tribute to the classic sentimental comedies that he made in the 1930s and 1940s. Capra had used the Damon Runyon story "Madame la Gimp" for *Lady for a Day*, and this is a glamorized remake of that movie. *Miracles* doesn't so much try to re-create the Depression era as it does to serve up an artificial, Hollywood-bred cast of crusty characterizations and glossy sets. Watch closely and you'll see appearances by supporting greats Fritz Feld, Mike Mazurki, Jack Elam, Snub Pollard, and Doodles Weaver. Bette Davis does a fine job as Apple Annie, the Broadway beggar who discovers that her daughter is coming home from a Spanish convent school expecting to be entertained by her society *grande dame* mother. Glenn Ford plays the bootlegger who reluctantly helps the old crone pass herself off as one of the upper crust; he is a little stiff and forced as a comedian. Peter Falk finds his niche as the hilarious hood Joy Boy, and he steals every scene he's in. This is a fun, affectionate comedy from one of the greats.

POLICE ★★½
1985, France
Gerard Depardieu, Sophie Marceau, Richard Anconina, Pascal Rocard, Sandrine Bonnaire. Directed by Maurice Pialat. 113 min.

A strong but oddly uninvolving *policier* from the director of the brutal, fascinating family drama *A Nos Amours*. With a bigger budget, Maurice Pialat stays in safer territory this time with a straightforward tale of a tough cop (Gerard Depardieu) using a young woman to lead him to her Tunisian boyfriend's drug stash. The cop, Mangin, is a sort of "Dirty Henry"—he irks his department by not playing by the rules, he's a loner, he gets intensely involved in his cases, and so on, in the manner of dozens of recent screen lawmen. Depardieu's solid, bearish performance keeps the film focused, but the film was reportedly rewritten during shooting and the plot meanders badly.

POLICE ACADEMY ★★
1984, USA, PG
Steve Guttenberg, G.W. Bailey, George Gaynes, Kim Cattrall, Michael Winslow, Bubba Smith, David Graf, Andrew Rubin. Directed by Hugh Wilson. 95 min.

This zany slapstick comedy is *Stripes* with the police force instead of the Army and has dull, eager-to-please Steve Guttenberg in place of the blissfully unhinged Bill Murray. The new "lady mayor" of an unnamed American city has lifted all requirements for entry into the local police academy; everyone and his brother is now free to sign up, and, naturally, everyone does. The movie is a throwaway from beginning to end, but there's enough dirty-minded audacity to provoke a few laughs. Followed by three sequels.

POLICE ACADEMY 3: BACK IN TRAINING ☆
1986, USA, PG
Steve Guttenberg, Bubba Smith, David Graf, Michael Winslow, Art Metrano, Tim Kazurinsky, Bobcat Goldthwaite, George Gaynes, Leslie Easterbrook. Directed by Jerry Paris. 82 min.

As one critic noted succinctly, *Police 3* is worse than *Police 2*, which was awful. The infamous Lassard Academy is faced with being put out of business, and so its star graudates (including the unctuous Steve Guttenberg, big Bubba Smith, and human sound effects machine Michael Winslow) are called back to retrain the new recruits. There's the usual noisy slapstick, and even the few funny bits would work better if the timing weren't off (the gags are telegraphed and ruined by superfluous reaction shots). What little does go right here is due mostly to Bobcat Goldwaite as an insane punk biker and Tim Kazurinsky as his persnickety roommate—a constipated little windup toy. Followed by a sequel, *Police Academy 4: Citizens on Patrol.*

POLICE ACADEMY 2: THEIR FIRST ASSIGNMENT ☆½
1985, USA, PG
Steve Guttenberg, Bubba Smith, David Graf, Michael Winslow, Bruce Mahler, Marion Ramsey, Colleen Camp, Howard Hesseman. Directed by Jerry Paris. 87 min.

Steve Guttenberg returns to lead the world's lowliest cops into the streets in the sequel to the 1984 blockbuster—an awful marriage of serial hyperbole and sporadic high jinks. Guttenberg drops the half-baked Bill Murray imitation of Part One and serves up his lines in his much more palatable *Diner* style. When it's not undercut with feeble lines and palsied rhythms (which is more than half the time), *First Assignment* works vaguely like "Car 54, Where Are You?" before screeching to a halt. Followed by *Police Academy 3: Back In Training.*

POLICE CALL 9000

See *Detroit 9000*

POLICEWOMAN CENTERFOLD ☆☆
1983, USA (TV)
Melody Anderson, Ed Marinaro, Donna Pescow, Corinne Carroll, Greg Monaghan, Bert Remsen, David Spielberg, Michael LeClair, David Haskell. Directed by Reza S. Badiyi. 96 min.

A willing lady cop consents to the solicitations of a girlie magazine. When her new image circulates around town, she's seen as no lady by the citizenry, and may soon be no cop if the police force has its way. This average made-for-TV picture displays several popular television stars and takes its story from actual incidents involving women whose all-too-public poses have jeopardized their lives and jobs.

POLLYANNA ☆☆☆
1920, USA
Mary Pickford, J. Wharton James, Katherine Griffith, William Courtleigh, Herbert Prior, Helen Jerome Eddy, Howard Ralston. Directed by Paul Powell. 60 min.

Mary Pickford always radiates sunshine on the screen, and she is the perfect Pollyanna. As the sweet girl who warms the heart of her shriveled old aunt and helps out the poor orphan Jimmy and the lonely bachelor Mr. Pendleton, Pickford manages the difficult task of never becoming cloying. She does this by acting with energy and conviction, and when Pollyana gets run over by a car, the character's personality is turned around with expert economy and believability. The movie has a good period feel and a nice small-town look, and it's far superior to the Disney remake. Silent, but available with an organ score from Blackhawk Films.

POLLYANNA ☆☆½
1960, USA
Hayley Mills, Jane Wyman, Richard Egan, Nancy Olson, Karl Malden, Adolphe Menjou, Donald Crisp, Agnes Moorehead, Reta Shaw. Directed by David Swift. 133 min.

Although mawkish and cloying, this film is not really as bad as you might expect. This pre-World War I story about a child who's a die-hard optimist (they call her "the glad girl"), and who infects a whole town with her cheerful spirit, cried out for the overproduced, garish, jubilant style of a Walt Disney family film and that's exactly what it got. Fortunately, into the bargain went a supporting cast filled with great character actors, and a star-making performance by Hayley Mills, whom you can't hate even when she's at her most Pollyannaish in the melodramatic climax. It's ideal for young kids, or grown-ups with a sweet tooth. Originally made in 1920, with Mary Pickford.

POLTERGEIST ☆☆☆
1982, USA, R
JoBeth Williams, Craig T. Nelson, Beatrice Straight, Dominique Dunne, Zelda Rubenstein. Directed by Tobe Hooper. 114 min.

Steven Spielberg once called this the dark side to *E.T.* A suburban family finds its tract house troubled by a host of frightening paranormal phenomena emanating from the graveyard that was plowed under in the name of urban development and now lies beneath their swimming pool. Produced and—according to persistent rumor—partially directed by Steven Spielberg, *Poltergeist* is a slick and polished ghost story in a contemporary setting, with good performances, lots of special effects, and energy. The supporting cast, in an attempt to provide comic relief, overacts shamelessly.

POLTERGEIST II—THE OTHER SIDE ☆☆
1986, USA, PG-13
Craig T. Nelson, JoBeth Williams, Will Sampson, Julian Beck, Heather O'Rourke, Zelda Rubinstein, Oliver Robins, Geraldine Fitzgerald. Directed by Brian Gibson. 91 min.

The original *Poltergeist* was a special effects hodgepodge held together by the palpable love and terror of the Freeling family. The sequel has no scare logic, and no real story; it's one slack, disconnected scene after another. Various omens remind us that something bad is about to happen; wispy ghosties fly out of Will Sampson's campfire, little Carol Anne (Heather O'Rourke) gets calls from the beyond on her toy telephone, and the blobby mystic Tangin (Zelda Rubinstein) babbles on about "a presence, . . . something terrible." What actually is frightening here is the late Julian Beck as Kane, a nineteenth-century cult leader resurrected as a cadaverous Southern gentleman, a grinningly malevolent old coot in string tie and parson's hat. Beck, who was in the last stages of cancer when the film was made, exploits the physical effects of his disease for its full measure of implied moral rot; beneath the ravagement, though, he's obscenely, maniacally alive. The rest of the cast might be acting in a vacuum.

POLYESTER ☆☆½
1981, USA, R
Divine, Tab Hunter, Mary Garlington, Edith Massey, David Samson, Ken King, Mink Stole, Stiv Bators. Directed by John Waters. 86 min.

John Waters's demented send-up of suburbia is his slickest, most "tasteful" product to date, and one of his funniest. Follow the worm-eaten adventures of Francine Fishpaw (Divine), an elephantine housewife driven to alcoholic despair by her fiendish family and then rescued by Todd Tomorrow (Tab Hunter), a dashing stud in a white Corvette. Waters's wild card, as always, is the gleeful sadism of his characters; acts of gratuitous mayhem make them come alive. The great Edith Massey plays Cuddles. Theatrical showings of this film were actually accompanied by Odorama cards; you won't miss them.

THE POM POM GIRLS ☆
1976, USA, R
Robert Carradine, Jennifer Ashley, Lisa Reeves, Michael Mullins, Bill Adler. Directed by Joseph Ruben. 90 min.

Get out your pompoms and join in the juvenile fun as vapid teenagers (played by actors well past their acne years) throw food, exchange witless insults, and leer at each other as though innuendos and dirty party games were preferable to the real thing. It's a desultory comedy at best.

A POOR LITTLE RICH GIRL ☆☆☆
1917, USA
Mary Pickford, Medeline Traverse, Charles Wellesley, Gladys Fairbanks, Frank McGlynn, Emile La Croix, Marcia Harris, Maxine Hicks. Directed by Maurice Tourneur. 64 min.

Mary Pickford here has the opportunity of working with a first-rate director, Maurice Tourneur, and she makes the most of it. As Gwendolyn, the pampered girl who is not allowed to play or socialize, Pickford could have tugged at the heartstrings; instead, she bounces from one escapade to another, enlivening the proceedings with humor and verve. Tourneur, an artist who had worked with Auguste Rodin, has a matchless eye, and this film's simple beauty and delicately sustained atmosphere are thrilling. The movie is based on Eleanor Gates's stage tearjerker. Available from Blackhawk films with a muscial score.

POOR WHITE TRASH ½☆
1957, USA
Peter Graves, Lita Milan, Timothy Carey. Directed by Harold Daniels. 70 min.

This was quite a drive-in favorite in 1961 (although the film was originally released in 1957 and flopped) because of a crass ad campaign in which cops were supposed to boot out unescorted kids from screenings. The film, about a fifteen-year-old Bayou beauty caught in a sexual tug-of-war between a Yank architect and a backwoods bully, is almost incidental to the film's reputation. Neither provocative nor involving, it does, however, still live up to the "trash" part of its title.

POP ALWAYS PAYS ☆☆½
1940, USA
Leon Errol, Dennis O'Keefe, Marjorie Gateson, Walter Catlett, Adele Pearce. Directed by by Leslie Goodwins. 65 min.

A bright, modest "B" film that is a festival of double takes from ace comic Leon Errol. He plays a beleaguered head of household who's easily manipulated into doing what his family wants. Pop foolishly makes a bet that if his prospective son-in-law can raise $10,000, then Errol will match the sum as a wedding gift. The sight gags fly fast and furious when he himself doesn't have the money to put up or shut up. Father may not know best, but he does know how to get the most laughs as he tries to steal his wife's jewelry and discovers he may have hidden the stolen bracelet in a can headed for the city dump. The film is silly but entertaining—Errol was a much underrated comic.

THE POPE OF GREENWICH VILLAGE ☆☆☆
1984, USA, R
Eric Roberts, Mickey Rourke, Daryl Hannah, Geraldine Page. Directed by Stuart Rosenberg. 122 min.

In this funny, underrated caper picture, two woebegone Italian cousins commit what looks to be an easy robbery. In the process, they accidentally kill a corrupt policeman and find themselves with both the clannish police and the Mafia out for their blood. This meandering male bonding film about life on the fringes suffers slightly from slack direction, which allows an inconsistency of tone to develop. Eric Roberts and Mickey Rourke deliver a workshop on post-1970s acting styles, with Rourke mumbling through the Actors Studio/Brando/DeNiro lineage, and Roberts chewing up the nervous psychotic, gangster/Widmark/Nicholson heritage.

POPEYE ☆☆☆½
1980, USA, PG
Robin Williams, Shelley Duvall, Ray Walston, Paul Smith, Paul Dooley, Richard Libertini. Directed by Robert Altman. 114 min.

Of the recent spate of revisionist musicals (*New York, New York, One From the Heart*), this is one of the most enjoyable. Jules Feiffer's script and Robert Altman's direction courageously attempt to duplicate the cartoon world of E.C. Segar's classic comic strip and, although they are not always successful, the sheer boldness of their endeavor gives the film a uniquely stylized look that is refreshing. Robin Williams is superb as Popeye, skillfully negotiating between the cartoon legend and a fuller characterization underneath. Shelley Duvall is perfectly cast as the gangling Olive Oyl and has some beautifully timed slapstick moments. The action beomes chaotic and less interesting toward the end with the introduction of Ray Walston as Popeye's long-lost father, but, until then, this is a charming offbeat treat.

PORKY'S ☆
1982, Canada, R
Mark Herrier, Dan Monahan, Wyatt Knight, Kim Cattrall, Roger Wilson, Scott Colomby, Kaki Hunter, Alex Karras, Susan Clark. Directed by Bob Clark. 94 min.

This is the teen-move trendsetter that made $150 million by replaying the anarchic goings-on of *Animal House* with a kind of smirky, peep show puritanism. The raunchy boys from Angel Beach High peek into the girl's shower room and then head out to a redneck bordello called Porky's—all in the vain hope of getting laid. Bob Clark directed, and his touch is about as light as a bulldozer. The movie also features the singularly uncharismatic Dan Monahan as Peewee. Followed by two sequels.

PORKY'S REVENGE ½☆
1985, USA, R
Dan Monahan, Wyatt Knight, Tony Ganios, Mark Herrier, Kaki Hunter, Scott Colomby, Nancy Parsons, Chuck Mitchell. Directed by James Komack. 94 min.

Here are more lascivious thrills with the Angel Beach High kids and their arch-nemesis, Porky Wallace, who's now running a brothel aboard a showboat and trying to extort a point-shaving deal from the basketball coach. This yawner is even messier and more rushed than the bizarre *Porky's II*. These movies are like pro wrestling: Given enough time, the bad guys eventually get to be heroes. Still, everything is as obvious—and, ahem, appealing—as the Swedish exchange student who starts each line with, "Ja, ja."

PORKY'S II: THE NEXT DAY ☆
1983, Canada, R
Mark Herrier, Dan Monahan, Wyatt Knight, Roger Wilson, Kaki Hunter, Scott Colomoby, Nancy Parsons, Edward Winter. Directed by Bob Clark. 95 min.

The raunchy boys from Angel Beach High are back; this time they're facing off against a growly backwoods preacher who wants to halt Angel Beach's biracial production of *Romeo and Juliet*. Like the first *Porky's*, this is adolescent slapstick stripped down to its bare bones, and its mirky, voyeuristic tone is dispiriting. Followed by *Porky's Revenge*.

PORTNOY'S COMPLAINT ☆☆
1972, USA, R
Richard Benjamin, Karen Black, Lee Grant, Jill Clayburgh, Jeannie Berlin, Jack Somack. Directed by Ernest Lehman. 101 min.

Once again, Hollywood proves that some books just should not be brought to the big screen. Philip Roth's novel was a brilliantly sustained monologue, in the form of a repressed Jewish man's psychotherapy sessions, that gained notoriety for its Rabelaisian sexual candor, and more precisely, for its hilariously true rendition of masturbatory practices of the American male. The film, however, hardly even tries to incorporate the humanity of Roth's writing, turning it instead into a long Jewish sex joke couched in a ridiculously unlikely romantic setting (never has a Michel LeGrand score been so inappropriate) to make it "less offensive." If you aren't familiar with the novel, or if you can manage not to compare it with the film, you can at least enjoy good performances by Richard Benjamin, and, more especially, Karen Black, although almost the entire remaining cast probably would like to forget their work here.

PORT OF CALL ☆☆
1948, Sweden
Nina-Christine Jonsson, Bengt Eklund, Berta Hall, Erik Hell, Mimi Nelson. Directed by Ingmar Bergman. 100 min.

One of Ingmar Bergman's earliest films was this quite conventional romance between a sailor (Bengt Eklund) on leave in a seaside city and the dance hall girl (Nina-Christine Jonsson) with whom he quickly becomes infatuated. Bergman proves himself adept at handling romantic complications, but this is a very long way from the mastery he would later acquire, even as early as *Smiles of a Summer Night*. (a.k.a.: *Harbor City*)

PORTRAIT OF A SHOWGIRL ☆☆
1982, USA (TV)
Lesley Ann Warren, Rita Moreno, Dianne Kay, Tony Curtis, Barry Primus. Directed by Steven H. Stern. 100 min.

Before she hit her stride in *Victor, Victoria*, Lesley Ann Warren specialized in playing good girls with bad reputations in glitzy TV films. This underdeveloped portrait purports to lay bare the life of a Las Vegas gypsy, as if show dancers were on a par with Mary Magdalene. It's fairly watchable, with sterling support from Rita Moreno, but the film is an empty exercise in Las Vegas neon, full of sound and sequins signifying nothing.

PORTRAIT OF A STRIPPER ☆½
1979, USA (TV)
Lesley Ann Warren, Edward Herrmann, Vic Tayback, Sheree North, K.C. Martel. Directed by John A. Alonzo. 100 min.

Poor Lesley Anne Warren! She has to take it off in order to put food on the table for her little tyke. And then Sonny Boy's granddad tries to use her life as an ecdysiast as an excuse to get custody of the kid. And she's not even a career stripper! It's the old melodramatic "throw-her-out-into-the-snow" routine, punched up here with a few bumps and grinds.

THE POSEIDON ADVENTURE ☆☆☆
1972, USA, PG
Gene Hackman, Ernest Borgnine, Red Buttons, Carol Lynley, Roddy McDowall, Stella Stevens, Jack Albertson, Shelley Winters, Leslie Nielsen, Pamela Sue Martin, Arthur O'Connell, Eric Shea. Directed by Ronald Neame. 117 min.

This is the first entry in the 1970s' cycle of "disaster" films, and the best by miles. When a luxury liner capsizes beneath a tidal wave, an all-star cast led by rugged priest Gene Hackman must undertake a thrillingly perilous journey to the bottom—now the top—of the ship. Although much of the initial exposition is inevitably clumsy, once the wall of water hits, it's action all the way. All of the actors give juicy, caricatured performances, but our favorite is Shelley Winters as the corpulent Jewish mama who insists against all reason that she can undertake a dangerous swim—she won an Oscar nomination. The move was produced by Irwin Allen, the real auteur of this genre, who directed some of the action sequences here, and who went on to the spectacles, *The Towering Inferno*, *The Swarm*, and the terrible sequel *Beyond the Poseidon Adventure*.

POSSESSED ☆☆
1931, USA
Clark Gable, Joan Crawford, Wallace Ford, Skeets Gallagher. Directed by Clarence Brown. 77 min.

This is a mediocre soap opera about a working girl (Joan Crawford) who leaves her poor but honest small-town life for a morally bankrupt existence as a "kept woman" (thus the title) in New York City. She quickly wins the love of a jet-setter (Clark Gable, sans mustache) but learns too late the cost of her sin. Nobody played lower-class ambition better than Crawford in the 1930s, but Gable is utterly wooden, and the story, equating urban life with moral rot, was a ridiculous antique even at the time. Of some historical interest is the film's attitude toward money, a mixture of intense longing and deep resentment that spoke more strongly to a Depression-era audience than it does today. It's not to be confused with the 1947 film of the same name, which also starred Crawford.

POSSESSION ☆☆☆
1981, France/West Germany, R
Isabelle Adjani, Sam Neill, Heinz Bennent, Margit Carstensen, Michael Hogben. Directed by Andrzej Zulawski. 97 min.

A married woman decieves both her husband and her longtime lover with yet another amour, a slimy monster whose origins are shrouded in obscurity. This is a heady mix of violence and sexual weirdness with an exceptional cast, top-notch production values, and a disgusting monster created by Carlo (*E.T.*) Rambaldi. It's heavily edited from the European-released version, which won Isabelle Adjani a Best Actress prize at the Cannes Film Festival.

THE POSTMAN ALWAYS RINGS TWICE ☆☆☆½
1946, USA
Lana Turner, John Garfield, Cecil Kellaway, Leon Ames, Hume Cronyn. Directed by Tay Garnett. 113 min.

James M. Cain's steamy novels (*Mildred Pierce*, *Double Indemnity*) were ideally suited to the slowly eroding standards of Hollywood's Production Code of the 1940s, and this *Postman* may just be the steamiest adaptation from a Cain source. MGM, home of Greer Garson, Andy Hardy, and mother love, bought up the prints of previously existing French (*Le Dernier Tournant*, 1939) and Italian (*Obsession*, 1942) versions and proceeded to cast their resident sexpot Lana Turner as the scheming woman who seduces a handyman (ex-Warner's bad boy John Garfield) into killing her boring husband (Cecil Kellaway) and collecting the insurance money. The plot is not unlike the one in *Double Indemnity* and at least half a dozen other Hollywood melodramas, but Turner and Garfield generate a lot of heat that is often missing from those other films, especially in the late-night rendezvous in the kitchen and in a pre-*From Here to Eternity* beach scene with Lana in a dazzling white bikini. As the lovers become more distant in the second half of the story, a showdown of legal wits between Leon Ames and Hume Cronyn perks things up. Tay Garnett reached a peak in his *noir* period; this is, without question, his best film. Remade in 1981.

THE POSTMAN ALWAYS RINGS TWICE ☆☆☆
1981, USA, R
Jack Nicholson, Jessica Lange, John Colicos, Christopher Lloyd. Directed by Bob Rafelson. 121 min.

Adapting James M. Cain's 1934 novel of illicit love and murder in a dusty California roadhouse, director Bob Rafelson and screenwriter David Mamet have made a more hot-blooded (and faithful) but ultimately less interesting film than the 1946 *film noir* classic. They've treated what should be an engrossingly sleazy story with a stateliness and visual respect that drains its lust and energy. What makes it work, to a considerable degree, are the two leads. Jack Nicholson gives a strong, calculated performance that's sometimes too intelligent for the character he plays; Jessica Lange is a knockout, and deservedly got her first critical recognition for her work as beautiful, bloodthirsty Cora. Unfortunately, they work better separately than together, and their steamy encounter atop a kitchen table seems more uncomfortable than passionate. The distinguished literary critic Edmund Wilson called Cain "the poet of the tabloid murder."

POTEMKIN

See *Battleship Potemkin*

POT O' GOLD ☆☆
1941, USA
James Stewart, Paulette Goddard, Horace Heidt, Charles Winninger, Mary Gordon. Directed by George Marshall. 84 min.

There's not much comic gold at the end of this rainbow. This is an undemanding musical comedy about a debutante whose staid daddy despises vulgar big band music; naturally, his eager-to-swing daughter pesters him to book Horace Heidt's band on his radio program. When not functioning as an agent, she still has time to truck her way into James Stewart's heart. This was the second big band musical for the luscious Paulette Goddard (*Second Chorus* was the first); judging from the results, she should have forced her manager to jitterbug on glass.

POWDERKEG ☆☆
1970, USA (TV)
Rod Taylor, Dennis Cole, Michael Ansara, Fernando Lamas, Lucianna Paluzzi. Directed by Douglas Heyes. 100 min.

This pilot for the series "The Bearcats" is a camped-up adventure tale that yearns for the scope of big-screen cape films like *The Professionals*. Two soldiers of fortune accept the challenge of bringing back a hijacked train, but their plans get derailed by obstacles from all sides. The overall impact is now powderkeg; it's merely dynamite sputtering with a wet fuse, that fuse being the derivative, piecemeal script. Mild excitement is all aficionados of action flicks get.

POWER ☆☆
1986, USA, R
Richard Gere, Julie Christie, Kate Capshaw, Gene Hackman, Denzel Washington, E. G. Marshall, Beatrice Straight, J.T. Walsh, Michael Learned, Fritz Weaver, Matt Salinger. Directed by Sidney Lumet. 110 min.

Perhaps hoping that modern audiences could still get all hot under the collar at the revelation that political success involves manipulation, Sidney Lumet made this study of an "image expert" as blustery as possible. What emerges is a lot of smoke and no fire. Richard Gere plays a media consultant fielding three clients in state races and apparently engineering a small South American revolution on the side. Are we aghast at the fact that this amoral snake takes on candidates regardless of their political views? Do we shudder to think that evil Arab sheiks and corrupt American businessmen are in collusion to support candidates who will help them? This mixture of the obvious and the paranoid gives the film some energy, but it's hopelessly wide-eyed and silly, and the ending, which attempts to prove that honest politicians can win just by being themselves, is an offensive piece of lip service to populism that denies everything else in the film.

P.O.W.—THE ESCAPE ☆☆
1986, USA, R
David Carradine, Charles R. Floyd, Mako, Steve James, Phil Brock. Directed by Gideon Amir. 90 min.

"Everybody goes back home," swears Colonel James Cooper, summing up in a single rallying cry the plot that is credited to no fewer than six writers (including director Gideon Amir). Like Chuck Norris's *Missing in Action*—also produced by notorious exploitation house Cannon Films—*P.O.W.—The Escape* uses Vietnam as the backdrop for some standard action-adventure in uniform. Led by the ever-tough David Carradine (*Deathrace 2000*, *Kung Fu*), a motley band of military misfits blasts its way out from behind enemy lines; the result is adequate entertainment of its kind. It's not too spectacular (that would strain the budget), nor too demanding (that would strain the minds of its intended audience), but solid.

PRAIRIE MOON ☆☆
1938, USA
Gene Autry, Smiley Burnette. Directed by Ralph Staub. 58 min.

Three tough kids from Chicago show up at Gene Autry's ranch in this amusing, superior B Western. Autry sings "Hoofbeats on the Prairie" and other good old sagebrush tunes.

PRAY FOR DEATH ½☆
1986, USA, R
Sho Kosugi, Donna Kei Benz, Michael Constantine, James Booth, Shane Kosugi, Kane Kosugi. Directed by Gordon Hessler. 90 min.

Pray for many things—pray that you'll never have to see another martial arts flick. Pray that you'll get through this one without your eardrums being split by the sounds of limbs crashing against each other, or the thudding of a hackneyed revenge plot. Pray that Sho Kosugi doesn't play the grown-up Ralph Macchio in a "Karate Kid" sequel.

PRAY TV ☆☆½
1982, USA (TV)
John Ritter, Ned Beatty, Richard Kiley, Madolyn Smith, Louise Latham, Jonathan Prince. Directed by Robert Markowitz. 98 min.

This is an above-average TV movie with a timely theme—the influence of electronic evangelists on the current religious and political scenes. Ned Beatty plays the leader of a growing national flock, and John Ritter is the new minister who comes into his employ and begins to find his mentor's spirituality lacking. The film doesn't go as far or as deep a you might wish, but it's well acted and cogent more often than not.

PREMATURE BURIAL ☆☆½
1962, USA
Ray Milland, Hazel Court, Richard Ney, Heather Angel, Alan Napier. Directed by Roger Corman. 81 min.

Ray Milland stars as a sister-loving recluse shaken to the roots with his fear of being buried alive. This movie is great for doctor-fearing patients, and spooky fun for all. The third of Roger Corman's versions of Poe (following *The House of Usher* and *The Pit and the Pendulum*), *Burial* has the creepy feeling, overblown set design, and loosely adapted screenplay that mark the series. It's richly entertaining, with Corman's customary directorial flair, but the wide-screen impact is dulled by television's small dimensions.

PREPPIES ☆
1984, USA, R
Dennis Drake, Steven Holt, Peter Brady Reardon, Nitchie Barrett, Katt Shea. Directed by Chuck Vincent. 85 min.

This was coproduced by cable TV's Playboy Channel, which should tell you everything you need to know. It's a lowbrow comedy about three losers at a prep school, made about three years after the preppie fad had faded. They're set up with a trio of "loose women" in order to keep them from passing an important exam—if they flunk out, their cousin gets their inheritance. Former hardcore director Chuck Vincent makes lots of these movies; the fact that a few of them have been quite good seems to be nothing more than the law of averages at work.

THE PRESIDENT'S MISTRESS ☆☆
1978, USA (TV)
Beau Bridges, Susan Blanchard, Karen Grassle, Larry Hagman, Joel Fabiani. Directed by John Llwellyn Moxey. 100 min.

The title is just a come-on, so don't expect too much heat. It's an unexceptional TV thriller about a man who learns his sweet sister has shared her favors with the president and secured secrets for the Soviets. Unsurprisingly, he ends up in hot water after sis gets bumped off for reasons of international expediency.

PRETTY BABY ☆☆
1978, USA, R
Keith Carradine, Susan Sarandon, Brooke Shields, Frances Faye, Antonio Fargas, Gerrit Graham, Mae Mercer, Diana Scarwid, Barbara Steele. Directed by Louis Malle. 109 min.

Louis Malle's portrait of a twelve-year-old girl who becomes a prostitute in New Orleans' notorious Storyville is not pornographic—nor is it particularly engrossing. Though perfectly cast, Brooke Shields remains a very childish twelve-year-old and we never understand why Keith Carradine, pointlessly unappealing as the photographer E.J. Bellocq, falls in love with her. It's a strangely inert movie, though it was photographed by Sven Nykvist and looks absolutely sumptuous.

PRETTY IN PINK ☆
1986, USA, PG-13
Molly Ringwald, Harry Dean Stanton, Jon Cryer, Andrew McCarthy, Annie Potts, James Spader. Directed by Howard Deutch. 96 min.

Although the credited director is Howard Deutch, whose previous works consisted of rock videos, this is a John Hughes film just as *Poltergeist* and *The Goonies* were Steven Spielberg Films. Hughes, credited as writer and executive producer, has herein concocted a teenage fairy tale that ranges from stupidly unbelievable to downright offensive. The plot is ancient—poor girl and rich boy fall in love but are kept apart by social pressures. You'd never know that Molly Ringwald, as the girl, was supposed to be "poor" if everyone didn't talk about it so much; does your idea of poverty-stricken extend to teenagers with their own cars and telephone answering machines? As a fantasy, this might be acceptable along the lines of Hughes's *Sixteen Candles*, but *Pink* begs to be taken as a realistic portrayal of teen problems. There is talent in the cast, but no outlet for it; Harry Dean Stanton is wasted in a role that finally requires nothing more than that he look paternal.

THE PRIDE AND THE PASSION ☆☆
1957, USA
Cary Grant, Frank Sinatra, Sophia Loren, Theodore Bikel. Directed by Stanley Kramer. 132 min.

A misfired cannon. Visually, it's an impressive, handsome epic, but the director has such a heavy hand that he can't get by with the kind of sexy semi-camp history that was DeMille's forte. As it is, it's hard to take the miscast leading players seriously in this turgid tale about some French fighters to haul off a cannon in nineteenth-century Spain. Cary Grant appears ludicrous in period costumes and, in their love scenes, looks as if Sophia Loren could crush him at will. The romance is flat; the action remains supine, but the cannon is photogenic and demonstrates real power and flash, something the human stars are lacking. The film is nothing to be proud of.

PRIDE AND PREJUDICE ☆☆½
1940, USA
Greer Garson, Laurence Olivier, Mary Boland, Edmund Gwenn, Maureen O'Sullivan. Directed by Robert Z. Leonard. 117 min.

This full-dress MGM period spectacle stays surprisingly close to the letter of Jane Austen's great novel, but the spirit is a little different. More broadly played and less minutely observed than it should have been, the film still sustains a wonderfully entangled comedy of manners. Greer Garson is too old and starchy to play the vibrant Elizabeth, but Laurence Olivier, as the unemotional object of her affection, is superb, magnificently chilly and clipped. The literate screenplay adaptation, by Aldous Huxley and Jane Murfin, allows you to forgive many deficiencies elsewhere.

THE PRIDE OF JESSE HALLAM ☆☆½
1981, USA (TV)
Johnny Cash, Brenda Vaccaro, Ben Marley, Eli Wallach, Guy Boyd. Directed by Gary Nelson. 105 min.

This is a well-intentioned exploration of a serious issue, TV-style—in this case, illiteracy. Johnny Cash plays a coal miner forced to confront his problem for the first time when he gets a new job in a new city; thanks to the help of sympathetic schoolteacher (Brenda Vaccaro), he begins to overcome his disability. It's predictably uplifting but nicely done, with stoic Cash and fast-talking Vaccaro playing well together.

PRIDE OF THE BOWERY ½☆
1941, USA
The East Side Kids, Donald Haines, David Gorcey. Directed by Joseph Lewis. 60 min.

The East Side Kids (who are really the Dead End Kids, who are really the Little Tough Guys, who are really the Bowery Boys) run amok once more. Mugs, an amateur boxer, joins the Civilian Conservation corps in order to get in shape cheaply. This is a drab formula comedy filmed on half a shoestring; it's strictly an excuse for military academy–type gags and is listed in *The Films of the Bowery Boys* as possibly the worst of the East Side Kids series.

PRIDE OF THE YANKEES ☆☆☆½
1942, USA
Gary Cooper, Teresa Wright, Babe Ruth, Walter Brennan, Dan Duryea, Elsa Janssen, Ludwig Stossel, Virginia Gilmore, Bill Dickey, Ernie Adams, Pierre Watkin. Directed by Sam Wood. 128 min.

Probably the best baseball film ever made—and also one of the better Hollywood bios, with Gary Cooper turning in a superb performance as Lou Gehrig, the legendary first baseman who died at the height of his career. Teresa Wright is also outstanding as Gehrig's devoted wife, and the final scene, in which real footage of Gehrig's farewell speech at Yankee Stadium is intercut with restaged scenes, is extremely moving. Daniel Mardell's edition won an Academy Award; the same story was retold in a 1977 TV movie, *A Love Affair: The Eleanor and Lou Gehrig Story*.

PRIEST OF LOVE ☆☆½
1981, Great Britian, R
Ian McKellen, Janet Suzman, Ava Gardner, Penelope Keith, Sir John Gielgud, James Faulkner, Jorge Rivero. Directed by Christopher Miles. 125 min.

This selective dramatization of the life of D.H. Lawrence is an honorable try, and avoids most of the "and then I sat down to write" clichés associated with film biographies of writers. Unfortunately, *Priest of Love* also misses Lawrence's genius by a mile, reducing him to a colorful, articulate eccentric surrounded by a coven of even more extreme characters. Though the script touches on his early relationships and battles with literary censors, the focus is on his wife Frieda, and Janet Suzman's wild, impressive but slightly hysterical work necessarily eclipses Ian McKellen's carefully restrained portrayal. The film is worth seeing for Lawrence admirers; it's at least as interesting as most of the screen adaptations of his novels.

PRIME CUT ☆☆
1972, USA, R
Lee Marvin, Gene Hackman, Angel Tompkins, Gregory Walcott, Sissy Spacek, Eddie Egan. Directed by Michael Ritchie. 86 min.

A violent gangster story, with some vague touches of satire. The front for the mob's operations here is the cattle industry: Kansas boss Gene Hackman uses his stockyards as a cover for a drug and prostitution ring. Feminists will undoubtedly be appalled at the sight of prostitutes being kept in cattle pens, although director Michael Ritchie seems to intend it as mordant commentary on woman's role in capitalist society. (His subsequent film, *Smile*, is a more incisive satire on another side of the same issue, the Great American Beauty Pageant.) One can't help but worry, though, that the intended audience for this film is probably watching it and considering installing a pen of their own. Some of the gorier murders have been obviously cut in the video version.

PRIME SUSPECT ☆☆½
1982, USA (TV)
Mike Farrell, Teri Garr, Veronica Cartwright, Lane Smith, Barry Corbin, James Sloyan, Charles Aidman. Directed by Noel Black. 100 min.

Call this the small screen's *Absence of Malice*. A busybody reporter follows the trail of a hot scoop without worrying how many innocent people get hurt. Naturally, a model citizen is suspected unfairly in the sex slayings of young girls, and this poor innocent is presumed guilty by his community-at-large. It's a loaded swipe at the power of the press, with some effective moments, but the issues are given a cursory examination, and dramatic points are scored with too much facility.

THE PRINCE AND THE PAUPER ☆☆☆½
1937, USA
Errol Flynn, Billy Mauch, Bobby Mauch, Claude Rains, Alan Hale, Henry Stephenson, Barton MacLane. Directed by William Keighley. 118 min.

Fine acting and a thorough production job do justice to Mark Twain's magnificent yarn of two young boys, one poor and one rich, who decide to trade places—it's not, of course, such a difficult switch since the two have identical faces. It's still charming family entertainment, enhanced by Erich Wolfgang Korngold's precious musical scoring. Remade in 1978 as *Crossed Swords*.

THE PRINCE OF CENTRAL PARK ☆☆☆½
1977, USA (TV)
Ruth Gordon, T.J. Hargrave, Lisa Richard, Brooke Shields, Mark Vahanian. Directed by Harvey Hart. 76 min.

In this engaging yarn based on the Evan Rhodes novel, two orphans set up housekeeping in a tree in Central Park after fleeing their foster home. Gradually, they develop a relationship with a little old lady who befriends them and gains their confidence. This TV film was so well received that several people have since tried to turn it into a Broadway musical. Ruth Gordon's pixieish spirit is put to good use here, and the children are refreshingly natural, not the standard sugary types off the TV assembly line.

PRINCE OF THE CITY ☆☆☆☆
1981, USA, R
Treat Williams, Jerry Orbach, Richard Foronjy, Paul Roebling, Don Billett, Lindsay Crouse, Kenny Marino, Bob Balaban, Carmine Caridi, Michael Beckett. Directed by Sidney Lumet. 167 min.

Director Sidney Lumet and actor Treat Williams share the credit for this enthralling police melodrama about honesty, loyalty, corruption, and victimization. Williams gives an engaging, multifaceted performance playing a character modeled after Robert Leuci, the young detective who, in the Knapp Commission hearings, blew the whistle on New York's illustrious Special Investigation Unit (the men who cracked the "French Connection," among other cases). Lumet's precise direction tells the story not as a clear-cut tale of a virtuous hero exposing venal crooks, but as a complex series of confrontations that slowly draws an ordinary cop into spying on, and turning in, his friends and partners. The movie consists mostly of long interviews and meetings, and viewers who are easily bored, or even slightly inattentive, will become lost somewhere in the movie's 167 minutes. But for the involved audience, the film has many rewards. Lumet has a great feel for New York City (*Dog Day Afternoon* and *Serpico*), and he captures it in grim, muted tones of gray and brown. The script is by Jay Presson Allen, and includes dialogue taken from original tapes of Leuci.

THE PRINCESS AND THE PIRATE ☆☆½
1944, USA
Bob Hope, Virginia Mayo, Walter Brennan, Victor McLaglen, Walter Slezak, Maude Eburne, Hugo Haas, Marc Lawrence. Directed by David Butler. 92 min.

In pirate days, princess Virginia Mayo is traveling incognito because she loves a commoner. Bob Hope is a not-yet-ready-for-small-time-performer she's thrown together with. Walter Slezak, Victor McLaglen, and Walter Brennan are after them. Bing Crosby puts in a surprise appearance as Mayo's lover, much to Hope's dismay ("That bit player from Paramount . . . That's the last picture I'll make for you, Mr. Goldwyn!"). It's wartime escapism at its most insistent, feathery, and routine, but if you're not too familiar with Hope's comedy, this may seem a most bracing throwaway.

PRINCESS DAISY ☆☆½
1983, USA (TV)
Merete Van Kamp, Lindsay Wagner, Paul Michael Glaser, Robert Urich, Claudia Cardinale, Rupert Everett, Stacy Keach, Sada Thompson. Directed by Waris Hussein. 200 min.

More best-selling "class" trash from Judith Krantz, who always adds a veneer of "Lifestyles of the Rich and Famous" to her work, thus disguising the essential seediness of the material. Princess Daisy survives rape, incest, and other assorted lesser evils in her rise to prominence, but the real drama lies in the glamorous locales, lavish sets, and continual parade of changing designer fashions worn by the female stars. As Daisy, Merete Van Kamp makes a rather wilted leading lady.

THE PRISONER OF SECOND AVENUE ☆☆½
1975, USA, PG
Jack Lemmon, Anne Bancroft, Gene Saks, Elizabeth Wilson, Florence Stanley, Sylvester Stallone. Directed by Melvin Frank. 99 min.

Neil Simon at his most clamorous. Adapting his grimly funny play about a high-strung executive driven to the edge of a breakdown by the pressures of New York life, the playwright has turned the city into a headachy conflagration of noisy garbage trucks, rude neighbors, bad smells, and thin walls. But what could have become a comic study of the Big Apple as a circle of hell is hampered by Melvin Frank's heavy-handed direction and Simon's overreliance on tired, clichéd situations and rat-a-tat dialogue. As in all of his movies, the fast pace and sharp lines keep it watchable, but everything else about *Prisoner* is shrill, overemphatic, and familiar.

THE PRISONER OF ZENDA ☆½
1979, Great Britain, PG
Peter Sellers, Lynne Frederick, Lionel Jeffries, Elke Sommer, Gregory Sierra, Jeremy Kemp, Graham Stark. Directed by Richard Quine. 108 min.

Peter Sellers was never selective enough about the parts he took, and as a result he followed up one of his best performances (*Being There*) with this, a feeble parody that emphasizes all of his worst qualities as a comic actor. It's especially unfortunate because this was his last completed film before his death. In this spoof of the Hollywood perennial about the commoner who impersonates the King of Ruritania in order to keep his evil brother from seizing the throne, Sellers plays three parts: the old king (in a brief death scene), his heir (with a lisp), and the commoner double, with a straight but unintelligible Cockney accent á la Michael Caine. (The leading lady was Sellers's last wife.)

PRISONERS OF THE LOST UNIVERSE ☆½
1983, USA (TV)
Richard Hatch, Kay Lenz, John Saxon, Dawn Abraham, Ray Charleson. Directed by Terry Marcel. 90 min.

A cheesy entry in the *Son of Star Wars* sweepstakes that's somehow entertaining on the most primitive, comic-book level. A feisty career girl and a cohort are reluctantly swept into the future, where they must deal with a menacing warrior who has the hots for the liberated lady, contend with a derivative script that must have been conceived under a dunce cap, and encounter a plethora of fanciful creatures that seem to be wearing rental tags from a discount costume warehouse. If you want to be prisoners of this for a lost hour and a half, it's painless.

PRIVATE BENJAMIN ☆☆☆
1980, USA, R
Goldie Hawn, Eileen Brennan, Armand Assante, Hal Williams, Robert Webber, Sam Wanamaker. Directed by Howard Zieff. 110 min.

In this snappily directed crowd-pleaser, Goldie Hawn stars as a pampered Jewish-American Princess who joins the Army expecting excitement and glamour and soon discovers, to her horror, that it ain't like the TV commercials. Supported by an excellent cast, Goldie is charming en route to self-esteem, deftly managing a role that combines comedy and substance.

PRIVATE BUCKAROO ☆☆½
1942, USA
The Andrews Sisters, Joe E. Louis, Donald O'Connor. Directed by Edward Cline. 68 min.

Unassuming, generally delightful B movie featuring the Andrews Sisters. A world-famous band gets to make sweet music for Uncle Sam when its members are drafted into the service. They decide that the most patriotic thing they can do is to raise the barracks roof with song in a big boot-camp variety show. This is a musical produced with a paucity of funds but an abundance of talent. It is foot-stomping entertainment, especially for fans of the big band sound.

PRIVATE CONVERSATIONS: ON THE SET OF "DEATH OF A SALESMAN" ☆☆☆
1985, USA
Directed by Christian Blackwood. 82 min.

A compelling, behind-the scenes look at the 1984 Broadway revival (and rethinking) of Arthur Miller's *Death of a Salesman*, in which Dustin Hoffman stepped into Willy Loman's shoes and gave a unique interpretation of the role. (The brilliant results are available for all to see in the cassette of the televised adaptation.) Christian Blackwood's fairly straightforward interview-and-footage study of the making of the play is a worthy companion piece to the film, and stands nicely on its own as a document of the artistic process.

PRIVATE EYES ☆☆½
1980, USA, G
Tim Conway, Don Knotts, Trisha Noble, Bernard Fox, John Fujioka, Fred Struthman, Mary Nell Santacroce. Directed by Lang Elliot. 91 min.

Fans of the team of Tim Conway and Don Knotts will want to seek out this, their finest hour. Believe it or not, they make fairly good Scotland Yard detectives, and their high-gear hijinks find affinity with the British daffiness. They're trying to save a young woman whose parents have perished in a suspicious accident. The dungeon scene is a treat.

A PRIVATE FUNCTION ☆☆☆
1985, Great Britain, R
Micahel Palin, Maggie Smith, Denholm Elliott, Bill Paterson. Directed by Malcolm Mowbray. 96 min.

A very British satire about two quintessentially British topics, the class system and food. Michael Palin plays a chiropodist in post-World War II Yorkshire with a wife (Maggie Smith) whose amibtion to rise in the local social scale is awkwardly incompatible with his position as a lowly toenail clipper. A local group of Tories is illegally raising a pig in order to celebrate the wedding of Queen Elizabeth (in a period when all food, and especially meat, was strictly rationed); the pig of course falls into the hands of Palin and Smith, who sees it as her ticket up in the world, if only she can get her timid husband to slaughter it. The film is equal parts low farce and drawing room satire, from a screenplay by "Beyond the Fringe" alumnus Alan Bennett.

PRIVATE LESSONS ☆
1981, USA, R
Howard Hesseman, Sylvia Kristel, Eric Brown, Pamela Bryant. Directed by Alan Myerson. 87 min.

An insipid little comedy about a shy teenager (Eric Brown) who gets seduced by his older housekeeper (Sylvia "Emmanuelle" Kristel). Written by humorist Dan Greenberg from his own novel, it's a collection of third-rate slapstick and drearily obvious double entendres, all of which boil down to the same coy sentiment: It sure is cute to be young, male, and horny.

THE PRIVATE LIFE OF DON JUAN ☆☆
1934, Great Britain
Douglas Fairbanks, Binnie Barnes, Merle Oberon, Joan Gardner, Benita Hume, Clifford Heatherley, Melville Cooper, Bruce Winston. Directed by Alexander Korda. 79 min.

The writers and director of *The Private Life of Henry VIII* followed up with this surprisingly humorless and dull debunking of the legends of the famous Spanish lover, not unlike what Fellini did with his *Casanova* but without the visual style. When we meet the Don, Miguel de Manara, he is aging and retired, cared for by his worshipful staff; we learn that much of his mystique is built around fantasy, the wish of so many women that such a lover merely exist. This was Douglas Fairbanks, Sr.'s last film.

THE PRIVATE LIFE OF HENRY VIII ☆☆☆
1933, Great Britain
Charles Laughton, Merle Oberon, Robert Donat, Binnie Barnes, Elsa Lanchester, Wendy Barrie. Directed by Alexander Korda. 97 min.

Don't expect a rousing British history lesson on the order of *Becket* or *A Man for All Seasons*. This movie is nonsense, but it's also bawdy and enjoyable nonsense. Charles Laughton won an Oscar and international acclaim playing the sixteenth-century king who marries on six different occasions. It's Laughton's show all right, and he makes a meal out of Henry, providing some delightfully campy moments. Also attention-getting is young Merle Oberon, playing wife number two, beheaded for not siring Henry a son, and Elsa Lanchester (Laughton's then real-life wife) playing Anne of Cleves. Robert Donat and Binnie Barnes, unfortunately, are saddled with a dull romantic subplot. The Lajo Biro-Arthur Wimperis screenplay provides some juicy asides in this entertaining, colorful showcase.

THE PRIVATE LIFE OF SHERLOCK HOLMES ☆☆☆☆
1970, USA/Great Britain, PG
Robert Stephens, Colin Blakely, Irene Handl, Christopher Lee, Stanley Holloway. Directed by Billy Wilder. 125 min.

This film is ambiguous enough to be viewed as either a Sherlock Holmes update, parody, or demythification, but ultimately none of that is important; what this film is really about is director Billy Wilder's sheer joy in making movies, and though it is seldom recognized as such, it's one of his very best. Colin Blakely is at once more comic and more forthright as Dr. Watson than Nigel Bruce, but it is Robert Stephens who shines as Holmes, undercutting the traditional view of the Baker Street detective in ever-so-subtle ways. Christopher Lee also deserves mention for a lovely performance in one of the best parts he was ever permitted after being typecast as Dracula, that of Holmes's brother, Mycroft. Thoroughly delightful.

THE PRIVATE LIVES OF ELIZABETH AND ESSEX ★★★
1939, USA
Bette Davis, Errol Flynn, Olivia de Havilland, Vincent Price, Donald Crisp, Henry Daniell, Henry Stephenson, Alan Hale, Leo G. Carroll. Directed by Michael Curtiz. 106 min.

Hollywood must be fascinated with British royalty. All three of Maxwell Anderson's Tudor plays (*Elizabeth the Queen, Mary of Scotland,* and *Anne of the Thousand Days*) have been filmed, the first two more than once. This Warner Bros. version of *Elizabeth the Queen* is one of the most famous, thanks primarily to its leads. In spite of impressive production credits (Sol Polito-W. Howard Greene photography, Eric Wolfgang Korngold music, and Orry-Kelly costumes), it is the dynamic teaming of Bette Davis and Errol Flynn that makes this memorable. The stars reportedly hated each other (and weren't too fond of director Michael Curtiz, either) but were paired anyway after their success in *The Sisters*. Here, however, Bette plays (to the hilt) the bald, aging, and crotchety Elizabeth (Perc Westmore's old-age makeup is outstanding) to Flynn's dashing but impulsive Lord Essex. Even at thirty-one, Davis does more with the role than she would in the similar *The Virgin Queen* sixteen years later.

PRIVATE PRACTICES: THE STORY OF A SEX SURROGATE ★★½
1986, USA
Narrated by Noreen Hennesey. Directed by Kirby Dick. 75 min.

This is a straightforward, nonexploitative documentary about a subject that can't help but exert a certain voyeuristic fascination: the work of a professional sexual surrogate, a therapist who treats the sexual dysfunctions of her male clients by active participatory experience. Filmmaker-interviewer Kirby Dick asks the questions you'd ask, and sensitively depicts the relationship between surrogate Maureen Sullivan and two of her patients. But the surrogate's own inner conflicts are explored only tangentially. Still, it's a creditable job on a difficult subject.

PRIVATE SCHOOL ★
1983, USA, R
Phoebe Cates, Matthew Modine, Betsy Russell, Michael Zorek, Ray Walston, Sylvia Kristel. Directed by Noel Black. 97 min.

Another reluctant-virgin teen-sex comedy, somewhat enlivened by a recognizable, attractive cast. Everything is standard—from the voyeuristic boys who climb the walls of the girls' school to the bitchy coed who gets just desserts—and nothing is fresh or funny. Phoebe Cates and Matthew Modine are the lead couple, and their love scene, right out of *From Here to Eternity*, is oh-so-sensitive.

PRIVATES ON PARADE ★★★
1984, Great Britain, R
John Cleese, Denis Quilley, Nicola Pagett, Joe Melia, Michael Elphick, Patrick Pearson. Directed by Michael Blakemore. 96 min.

A ragtag show-biz unit of the British Army is assigned to put on a "Jungle Jamboree" for the troops in Okinawa, in a warmly funny though less sharp adaptation of the stage play, filmed with deliberate artifice and stylization. The film's heroes are the mostly gay, very campy members of the theatrical troupe, and the villains are the stuffed shirts and bureaucrats (personified by John Cleese) with whom they do verbal combat. It's a jumpy story that can't quite support its wild shifts from revue to black comedy to melodrama to fantasy, but its high spirits and humanity make it genuinely affecting. Denis Quilley plays it to the hilt and admirably avoids caricature as the company's grande dame and mother hen. Written for stage and screen by Peter Nichols.

THE PRIZE FIGHTER ★★
1979, USA, G
Tim Conway, Don Knotts, David Wayne, Robin Clarke, Cisse Cameron, Mary Ellen O'Neill. Directed by Michael Preece. 99 min.

If you can mistake the jitterbug hysterics of Tim Conway and Don Knotts for comedy, you will probably love this movie about boxing in the 1930s. The period is sketched in pretty broad strokes, and there are plenty of gangsters, mugs, chiselers, and dames to keep you entertained. Conway produced and wrote this, and for what it's worth, he manages to capture the feeling of an average Disney product of the 1970s. Kids will probably be the best audience.

PRIZZI'S HONOR ★★★★
1985, USA, R
Jack Nicholson, Kathleen Turner, Anjelica Huston, William Hickey, John Randolph, Lee Richardson, Robert Loggia. Directed by John Huston. 129 min.

Celebrated director John Huston has placed a perfectly cut gem in an equally magnificent setting. The gem is Jack Nicholson's characterization of Charley Partanna, the smart-dumb enforcer for a Brooklyn mob. The setting is a cogent, crisply satirical black comedy—the kind that we laugh our way through before finally realizing that the joke's on us. With Huston directing, we can be sure that every twist, every jab, every delicious irony, is intentional. The film's brilliance is enhanced further by a very strong supporting cast. A throwback to the 1940s, stunning Kathleen Turner captivates with her multidimensional portrayal of a contract killer who comes between Charley's heart and his adopted family's honor. Huston's dark-complexioned, sharp-featured daughter Angelica provides a very amusing contrast as the serpentine outcast of the Prizzi clan. And William Hickey, playing the shriveled, shrill-voiced don of the Italian mob, delivers a scintillating parody of the legendary Don Corleone. An Oscar winner for Best Supporting Actress (Huston).

THE PRODIGAL BOXER ½★
1980, Hong Kong
Meng Fei, Lee Lam-Lam, Pa Hung, Sun Nam, Suma Wah-Lung, Tung Chui-Po, Wong Yee-Tin. Directed by Chai Yang-Min.

Fong Shi-Yu (Meng Fei), an adorable champion of the townspeople, is blamed for the death of a friend of the town bullies. They kill Fong's father and injure his mother. After rigorous training, supplied by his mother (!), he is ready to exact his own revenge. This is one of Meng Fei's first movies, and it affords an historical perspective on his development as a martial artist and actor.

THE PRODIGAL BOXER PART II ★★
1982, Hong Kong
Meng Fei, Shoju (Yasuaki) Kurata, Tan Tao-Liang, Bruce Law, Chang Yee, Cherry Lung, Jojo Uy. Directed by Au Yang Chu.

Fong Shi Yu (Meng Fei) returns and he's better than ever! He's wanted for the murder of Commander Ma's men, and Dragon Lee (Shaju Kurata) teams with Ma to obtain vengeance and reward. Overall, the fighting in this movie is excellent, but special attention must be given to Meng Fei's first fight scene using a fan (shown during the opening credits). He's progressed a great deal, as an actor and a martial artist, since *The Prodigal Boxer*.

THE PRODUCERS
☆☆☆
1968, USA
Zero Mostel, Gene Wilder, Kenneth Mars, Estelle Winwood, Renee Taylor, Christopher Hewett, Dick Shawn, Lee Meredith. Directed by Mel Brooks. 88 min.

Mel Brooks's feature debut (he wrote and directed) is wildly uneven but contains many great moments. Zero Mostel, in his best screen role, plays a bankrupt producer who, with the help of his milquetoast accountant (Gene Wilder), plots to swindle some old ladies into investing in a flop show and to then run away with their money. The early Mostel/Wilder scenes are extremely broad but contain some hilarious bits and are generally funnier than the fragmented account of how, later, the two put together their ill-fated show. The show itself, a musical titled "Springtime for Hitler," is the highlight of the film. Brooks's directorial talent would later improve, but his raucous sense of humor is in full evidence here.

THE PROFESSIONALS
☆☆☆
1966, USA
Burt Lancaster, Lee Marvin, Jack Palance, Robert Ryan, Woody Strode, Claudia Cardinale, Ralph Bellamy, Joe De Santis. Directed by Richard Brooks. 117 min.

Four mercenaries are hired to rescue a millionaire's wife from the stronghold of a Mexican bandit. After they've sprung her, though, they find out she has no intention of going back to her despicable husband. Now the men are in a bind: Do they honor their contract like professionals and return her against her will, or do they do the chivalrous thing and help her to escape to her lover? You may be able to guess, but don't let that deter you from this bracing Western. It has all the earmarks of a decadent work in that venerable genre—dynamite and machine guns, antiheroes enacted by aging performers, a taste of spaghetti-Western cynicism—but it's a good, wholesome shoot-'em-up for the entire family. There is crisp dialogue and flashy direction from Richard Brooks, and a decent score by Maurice Jarre.

PROMISE AT DAWN
☆☆½
1970, USA/France
Melina Mercouri, Didier Haudepin, Assaf Dayan, Francois Raffoul, Jules Dassin, Fernand Gravey. Directed by Jules Dassin. 101 min.

This is a promising but rather overbaked filmization of Romain Gary's memoirs of life with Mama. Mama was a larger-than-life actress who swept Junior up in her international adventures. As played by that slice of Athenian ham, Melina Mercouri, the woman is a bit too much like Auntie Mame to be convincing dramatically, but it's a handsome production and the filtered-through-memory soapsuds aren't without some passion.

PROMISES IN THE DARK
☆☆
1979, USA, PG
Marsha Mason, Ned Beatty, Susan Clark, Michael Brandon, Kathleen Beller, Donald Moffat, Bonnie Bartlett. Directed by Jerome Hellman. 115 min.

This is an unabashed tearjerker without enough drama to make it compelling. Kathleen Beller plays a high school student stricken with terminal cancer, and Marsha Mason is the widowed doctor who begins to come out of her shell while treating the girl. Beller plays the patient with one-note nobility, but the focus is really on Mason, whose good if familiar work is the best thing about the film. Even as soap opera, it's very soft, dated stuff.

PROM NIGHT
☆☆½
1980, Canada, R
Jamie Lee Curtis, Leslie Nielsen, Eddie Benton. Directed by Paul Lynch. 91 min.

A better-than-average dead teen festival with a masked maniac out to avenge the years-old murder of a little girl. Now the participants in the terrible deed are in high school, and given the title, you can probably guess what happens next. There are some moments of real suspense with scream queen Jamie Lee Curtis giving her all. Unintentional comic highlight: a severed head rolling down the disco floor.

PROPHECY
☆
1979, USA, PG
Talia Shire, Robert Foxworth, Armand Assante, Richard Dysart, Victoria Racimo. Directed by John Frankenheimer. 95 min.

This John Frankenheimer monster is a laughable horror film that would have seemed trite in 1969, much less 1979. Mercury poisoning from industrial pollution is creating mutated monsters in the woods of Maine, who take out their fire on a team of environmentalists investigating the circumstances. Frankenheimer tries very hard and does everything absolutely wrong. You'll be rooting for the monster to come along and gobble up Talia Shire just to stop her from whining.

THE PROTECTOR
☆☆
1985, USA/Hong Kong, R
Jackie Chan, Danny Aiello, Bill Wallace. Directed by James Glickenhaus. 94 min.

Considering its chopsocky star and hack director (*The Exterminator*), this international action flick is better than you'd think. Chinese lead Chan doesn't have to use his garbled English much as an evil cop who gets involved in the kidnapping of a Manhattan drug lord's daughter by a rival Hong Kong businessman. Soon enough Chan is in the Far East with his foul-mouthed buddy busting up massage parlors and mowing down the bad guys as they attempt to rescue the woman and clean up the Orient's drug traffic. The exotic locations lend extra class to the fantastic stunt work and offbeat characterizations.

PROTOCOL
☆½
1984, USA, PG
Goldie Hawn, Chris Sarandon, Richard Romanus, Andre Gregory, Gail Strickland, Cliff De Young, Ed Begley, Jr., Kenneth Mars, Kenneth McMillan. Directed by Herbert Ross. 96 min.

A Goldie Hawn movie. That tells you everything you need to know. This time, she's a Washington cocktail waitress who accidentally prevents an assassination. She winds up a public heroine and a patsy for some shady State Department types who want to marry her off to an Arab ruler in exchange for a military base. The first half is straightforward comedy, with naive Goldie running amok in diplomatic circles. The second half, though, veers uncomfortably into adventure as Goldie gets caught up in a Middle East revolution and returns home to deliver a final patriotic speech second in unctuousness only to the one in *Rambo*. The film was written by Buck Henry, a funny guy who lacks a gift for political satire (as demonstrated earlier in *Day of the Dolphin* and *The First Family*).

PROVIDENCE
☆☆☆½
1977, France/Switzerland, R
John Gielgud, Dirk Bogarde, Ellen Burstyn, David Warner, Elaine Stritch, Cyril Luckham, Denis Lawson, Kathryn Leigh-Scott. Directed by Alain Resnais. 110 min.

Alain Resnais's first English-language film is an intellectual shell game—we're inside the feverish mind of a dying author (superbly played by John Gielgud) who's creating his latest novel out of fragments of the lives of his own family members. The Freudian premise is a bit obvious and the dialogue is incredibly florid, though this is at least partly intentional—some of what we hear are imaginations of scenes from the old man's novel, and it's hard to tell where the line is drawn. Many regard this as a masterpiece; at the very least, the acting is excellent and the direction sharp, seductive, and dreamlike.

THE PROWLER
1981, USA, R ☆
Farley Granger, Christopher Goutman, Vicki Dawson, Laurence Tierney, Cindy Weintraub, John Seitz. Directed by Joseph Zito. 88 min.

A brutal psychopathic killer stalks a small town, slicing and dicing residents courtesy of splattery special effects provided by Tom Savini (*Dawn of the Dead*). This is a mechanical slasher movie from the director of *Friday the 13th—The Final Chapter*. Look, if you are so inclined, for some extremely gory effects work, but expect little else. (a.k.a.: *Rosemary's Killer*)

THE PSYCHIC
1978, Italy, R ½☆
Jennifer O'Neill, Gabriele Ferzetti, Marc Porel. Directed by Lucio Fulci. 89 min.

As a symbol of the film's artistic integrity and homogeneous feel, consider this: Jennifer O'Neill speaks in her own voice, but the others are dubbed from the Italian. Consider also this: Although it is a "thriller" about a pretty woman having psychic flashes of impending deaths, it has all the excitement of small-claims court. When she's not flash-forwarding unconvincingly, O'Neill is ineptly attempting to convince incredulous authorities to take decisive action. Like walk out on this film. Or explain why it was ever made.

PSYCHO
1960, USA ☆☆☆☆
Janet Leigh, Anthony Perkins, Vera Miles, Martin Balsam, John Gavin, Simon Oakland. Directed by Alfred Hitchcock. 109 min.

A woman is brutally murdered in the isolated Bates Motel; her lover and sister follow her trail and uncover a web of madness and murder. Perhaps the most studied, imitated, and parodied horror film of all time, *Psycho* broke the ground for a generation of horror films and set a standard few can measure up to; it is still shocking, despite its relative restraint. Followed by a sequel in 1983, and another in 1986.

PSYCHOMANIA
1971, Great Britain ☆☆½
George Sanders, Beryl Reid, Nicky Henson, Mary Larkin. Directed by Don Sharp. 95 min.

A gang of bikers follows their leader, a pretty boy dedicated at birth to Satan, literally to hell and back—they commit suicide and return from the grave as zombie psychopaths who wreak havoc before they are stopped through the efforts of their leader's pretty girlfriend, who finds that she cannot, after all, stand by her man in everything. It's a slick mixture of humor and horror that works much better than most, from the director of *Kiss of the Vampire, Curse of the Fly*, and others. (a.k.a.: *The Death Wheelers*)

PSYCHO SISTERS
1972, USA, PG ☆☆½
Susan Strasberg, Faith Domergue, Charles Knox Robinson. Directed by Reginald LeBorg. 76 min.

Almost entirely unseen until its release on videocassette, this is that rare instance where something halfway decent has been rescued from oblivion by the VCR craze. After the death of her husband, Susan Strasberg moves in with sister Faith Domergue (the 1950s star of such drive-in favorites as *It Came from Beneath the Sea* and *This Island Earth*). Unfortunately, Faith is having her own problems these days—still readjusting to life outside of the insane asylum where she'd been residing for the past few years; she also has to contend with the voice of her dead mother. Not at all what the title (this was originally released as *So Evil My Sister*) and the lurid cover art would indicate, though by no means a great film—just a pleasingly scary movie.

PSYCHO III
1986, USA, R ☆☆☆
Anthony Perkins, Diana Scarwid, Jeff Fahey, Roberta Maxwell. Directed by Anthony Perkins. 100 min.

It doesn't have the sheer brilliance of the original or the overwhelming trickiness of the first sequel, but this addition to the saga of poor mama's boy Norman Bates and his troubled motel does have Anthony Perkins behind and in front of the camera. His directorial debut proves an unexpected asset—Perkins knows his character inside and out, and he's great fun to watch in this often suspenseful but more often campy chiller. When a disturbed ex-nun and conniving drifter arrive at the newly reopened Bates Motel, Mom starts "talking" again, Norman goes off the deep end, and the body count begins. Like most sequels, it's unnecessary, but at least it's slash with class, and Perkins is ever more mesmerizing in the role.

PSYCHO II
1983, USA, R ☆☆½
Anthony Perkins, Meg Tilly, Vera Miles, Dennis Franz, Robert Loggia, Hugh Gillin. Directed by Richard Franklin. 113 min.

Released from the mental asylum where he was placed twenty-two years earlier, Norman Bates returns home to his dilapidated motel and tries to resume a normal life. But the past is inescapable, and soon his fragile grip on sanity begins to dissolve, precipitating a new wave of bloody violence. A project doomed to failure by *its* past, *Psycho II* is gimmicky and predictable, except when it sacrifices all other elements in favor of surprising plot twists. Anthony Perkins's twitchy performance is admirably intense but clichéd (even though his *original* performance as Bates is essentially the source of the cliché), and director Richard Franklin is not—as one hardly needs to say—the craftsman that Hitchcock was. Followed by *Psycho III*.

PSYCH-OUT
1968, USA ☆☆
Susan Strasberg, Dean Stockwell, Jack Nicholson, Bruce Dern, Adam Roarke, Max Julien, Henry Jaglom, The Strawberry Alarm Clock. Directed by Richard Rush. 95 min.

LSD, STP, Haight-Ashbury, blind runaways, philosophy-spouting acid-heads, love beads, hallucinations—thanks to the erstwhile American International Pictures, all the glory of the drop-out era will live on in films like this one forever. *Psych Out* isn't quite as astonishing as the previous year's *The Trip* (although it shares cast members Bruce Dern, Jack Nicholson, and Susan Strasberg) or as coherent as the following year's *Easy Rider*, but it's an essential installment for those who want to see how exploitation filmmakers tried to become subversive during the age of free love and cheap drugs. It is well directed by Richard Rush (who later made *The Stunt Man*), and produced, unbelievably, by Dick Clark.

PT 109
1963, USA ☆☆
Cliff Robertson, Ty Hardin, James Gregory, Robert Culp, Grant Williams, Lew Gallo, Errol John, Michael Pate, Robert Blake, William Douglas. Directed by Leslie H. Martinson. 140 min.

In this profile of courage, Cliff Robertson plays a smug, self-righteous and young JFK as he practices for the presidency in the South Pacific during World War II. The incidental conflicts of the small patrol boat take on dramatic excesses that ludicrously attempt to elevate them to the mythical stature of Ulysses's adventures, and the heroics of Kennedy would qualify him not for chief executive, but for sainthood. Viewed today, this film reinforces your belief in manifest destiny and the Kennedy mystique.

PUBERTY BLUES
1981, Australia, R ☆☆
Neil Schofield, Jad Capelja, Geoff Rhoe, Sandy Paul. Directed by Bruce Beresford. 87 min.

In this familiar coming-of-age hokum with an Australian accent, two Sydney girls (Nell Schofield and Jad Capelja) attempt to ingratiate themselves into the "in-crowd"—"in" meaning those with a penchant for drugs, sex, and squeezing blackheads. This is an early Bruce Beresford effort, obviously released to capitalize on the successes of the later-made *Breaker Morant* and *Tender Mercies*.

THE PUBLIC ENEMY ☆☆☆½
1931, USA
James Cagney, Jean Harlow, Edward Woods. Directed by William A. Wellman. 83 min.

A landmark film, *The Public Enemy* established James Cagney as the quintessential gangster. William A. Wellman directed this saga of a boy (Cagney) who, shaped and corrupted by the mean streets of Chicago, turns to a life of crime. The film would be little without Cagney. He plays the part with a complexity and depth that makes his character at once despicable, sympathetic, and romantic. Watch for the scene where Cagney shoves half a grapefruit in Mae Clarke's face!

PUMPING IRON ☆☆½
1977, USA, PG
Lou Ferrigno, Arnold Schwarzenegger, Mike Katz, Franco Columbu, Ed Corney, Ken Waller, Serge Nubert, Robin Robinson, Marianne Claire, Matty and Victoria Ferrigno. Directed by George Butler and Robert Fiore. 85 min.

A successful documentary alternative to the Jane Fonda workout tape, this movie brings character and charm to the fitness craze at its craziest. This is the real thing—bodybuilders at the Mr. Olympia competition. There is a lot of real-life muscle flexing, with lots of behind-the-scenes ploys and plots. Arnold Schwarzenegger's for real, too, acting tough and out-psyching the Brooklyn sheet-metal worker Lou Ferrigno. Perhaps this explains why Schwarzenegger could retire to become the Terminator, while Ferrigno had to settle for playing "The Incredible Hulk."

PUMPING IRON II: THE WOMEN ☆☆
1985, USA
Lori Bowen, Carla Dunlap, Bev Francis, Rachel McLish, Kris Alexander, Lydia Cheng, Steve Michalik, Randy Rice. Directed by George Butler. 107 min.

This is a sardonic, entertaining semidocumentary about the phenomenon of women's bodybuilding. Organized around the Caesars Palace World Cup, the movie combines staged scenes with cinéma vérité footage to tell the tale of two physiques: reigning champ Rachel McLish, a relatively traditional combination of sinew and coquetry, who hails fom Venice, California, and hefty challenger Bev Francis, an Australian power-lifter whose strapping, unmistakably masculine physique (she must down anabolic potboilers for breakfast) put her at center stage. The matchup becomes Valley Girl versus Road Warrior, as the judges debate the relative merits of mass and proportion in a sport where "femininity" has become an abstract concept.

PUPPET ON A CHAIN ☆☆
1972, Great Britain/Holland, PG
Sven-Bertil Taube, Barbara Parkins, Alexander Knox, Peter Hutchins. Directed by Geoffrey Reeve. 97 min.

Based on a lesser novel by Alistair MacLean (*The Guns of Navarone, Ice Station Zebra*), the highlight of this post-*French Connection* action film is a fast-paced speedboat race along the narrow canals of Amsterdam. (The chase sequence was directed by Don Sharp, a director for Hammer Studios in the early 1960s.) That aside, this is an average bit of espionage with an American agent tracking down the leader of a major European drug-smuggling ring. There are no major thrills, but a modicum of style and competent technical credits make this watchable.

PURLIE VICTORIOUS ☆☆½
1963, USA
Ossie Davis, Ruby Dee, Sorrell Booke, Godfrey Cambridge, Alan Alda, Beah Richards. Directed by Nicholas Webster. 97 min.

This is an adaptation of the delightful Broadway comedy (later turned into the musical "Purlie") that seems a bit diminished on the movie screen, let alone on the video picture tube. The play's buoyant energy and high spirits seem artificial here; but if one can overlook the staginess, a good time can still be had with this update of old Negro folk tales of modern times. It's a brash, clumsily filmed story of a fast-talking preacher getting the best of an unscrupulous Simon Legree landowner. (a.k.a.: *Gone Are the Days*)

THE PURPLE HEART ☆☆☆
1944, USA
Dana Andrews, Richard Conte, Farley Granger, Kevin O'Shea, Donald Barry, Sam Levene, Charles Russell, John Craven, Trudy Marshall, Tala Birell. Directed by Lewis Milestone. 99 min.

Eight Americans, members of a bomber crew captured following an air raid on Tokyo, are tried in a Japanese courtroom for the deaths of some civilians. This grippingly contrived wartime propaganda film, tautly directed by Lewis Milestone, was allegedly based on fact, but was scripted by high-minded producer Darryl Zanuck under a pseudonym. Its aim, besides the reminder about the unflinching courage of our fliers, was to delineate the gamut of personal cruelty and the psychological aberration in the Japanese character, and to this virulent end it succeeded as well as or better than any other diatribe of its era. It's a dark, fascinating historical document that retains its impact today, though of course for rather different reasons.

PURPLE HEARTS ☆
1984, USA, R
Ken Wahl, Cheryl Ladd, Stephen Lee, Annie McEnroe, Paul McCrane, David Harris. Directed by Sidney J. Furie. 116 min.

In his continuing quest (*The Boys in Company C, Iron Eagle*) to turn military adventure into the warfaring equivalent of Harlequin Romance, Sidney J. Furie hit his low point with this entry, which manages to be as laughable a war film as it is a soap opera. Perky Cheryl Ladd and mumbling Ken Wahl play a Vietnam army nurse and doctor who are stationed apart, but sneak off to see each other whenever they can get away from the open wounds and all that messy medical work. Lines that were clichés several wars ago are repeated with straight faces here, and the is-he-or-isn't-he (dead) story line gives way to a truly ludicrous conclusion. The insignia of the late Ladd Co. at the beginning of the movie might lead you to expect that this is a vanity production for Cheryl, but she's so badly used it must be an accident of fate.

PURPLE RAIN ☆☆½
1984, USA, R
Prince, Apollonia Kotero, Morris Day, Clarence Williams III, Olga Karlatos. Directed by Albert Magnoli. 111 min.

Purple Passion comes to the small screen! Rock's sexiest self-promoter, Prince, has created a rock and soul romance that is part performance art, part personal melodrama, part steamy fairy tale and 100 percent style. Apollonia Kotero debuts as the protégée of his dreams, and although some may find her fawning devotion a bit too much, it displays Prince's estimation of his own attractiveness. There are great musical numbers (the score won Prince an Academy Award), and Morris Day steals the show as the slimy, cagey foil to Prince's heavy-breathing, pouting kid-heroics.

THE PURPLE ROSE OF CAIRO ☆☆☆☆
1985, USA, PG
Mia Farrow, Jeff Daniels, Danny Aiello, Edward Herrmann, Dianne Wiest, Stephanie Farrow, Van Johnson, John Wood. Directed by Woody Allen. 82 min.

An imaginative triumph. Among Allen's films, this one is in the same aesthetic neighborhood as *A Midsummer Night's Sex Comedy* and *Zelig*—like them, it's a wistful mixture of realistic and fantastic elements that are combined according to the logic of your imagination. The story concerns a Depression-era waitress (Mia Farrow) who goes to the movies a lot to forget about her dull life and drab marriage. One night, the handsome star (Jeff Daniels) of a romantic movie she's seen several times notices her in the audience and steps out from the screen and into her life. Later, she goes back into the movie with him, to the consternation of his fellow actors. The actions and responses of the people in both worlds, once the possibility of the transmigration is accepted, are basically realistic, and it is this mixture of rigor and laxity that gives *Purple Rose* the elevating, melancholy quality of a dream we regret to awaken from. It's a delight.

THE PURPLE TAXI ☆½
1977, France/Italy/Ireland, R
Charlotte Rampling, Philippe Noiret, Agostina Belli, Peter Ustinov, Fred Astaire, Edward Albert, Jr., Mairin O'Sullivan, Jack Watson. Directed by Yves Boisset. 120 min.

Lush Ireland acts as the backdrop for a collection of rich expatriates who seek shelter and a new identity. All the characters in this European Common Market product have amazing pasts, including a troubled young man who smoked opium with a girl who subsequently died in a fire, for which he continues to blame himself. And then there's the woman who refuses to speak, possibly because she has fallen in love with a tortured and despicable co-artist. And finally there's Fred Astaire, peversely suggesting that Ireland is an elephant's graveyard, but only for those who fail to select their own demise. There are too many memories and too much angst in this Irish stew to make it tasty.

THE PURSUIT OF D.B. COOPER ☆☆☆
1981, USA, PG
Robert Duvall, Treat Williams, Kathryn Harrold, Ed Flanders, Paul Gleason, R.G. Armstrong, Nicolas Coster, Cooper Huckabee, Christopher Curry. Directed by Roger Spottiswoode. 100 min.

D.B. Cooper, in case you're young or short of memory, was the name given by the man who hijacked a 727 between Portland and Seattle in November 1971, and parachuted out of it somewhere between with $200,000 in ransom. Neither he nor the money, nor any trace of either, was ever found, despite an intensive manhunt. It's not really necessary to know any of that to enjoy this film though, because it's an entirely fictional story about who D.B. might have been. As played by Treat Williams, he's just a good old boy who wanted to win back his estranged wife and have a good time without having to worry about money. Most of the film consists of the two of them racing around the Western states trying to evade capture by William's old Green Beret sergeant, now an insurance investigator. It's minor but enjoyable, thanks to the charms of the performance; Williams and Kathryn Harrold have a few scenes that are quite erotic for a PG film.

PURSUIT TO ALGIERS ☆½
1945, USA
Basil Rathbone, Nigel Bruce, Marjorie Riordan, Rosalind Ivan, Martin Koslek. Directed by Roy William Neill. 65 min.

This one's a *musical* thriller, with an elementary song by Doctor Watson. A typical if slightly substandard Holmes mystery set primarily on a ship bound for Algiers, it features jewel thieves and mythical kingdoms.

PUTNEY SWOPE ☆☆☆
1969, USA
Stanley Gottlieb, Allen Garfield, Ramon Gordon, Arnold Johnson, Buddy Butler. Directed by Robert Downey. 84 min.

Robert Downey's crazed, quasi-underground comedy about blacks taking over a Madison Avenue ad agency isn't nearly as outrageous today as it was in 1969; indeed, its very premise no longer makes sense. But if the iconoclastic mood has lost resonance, the parodies of TV commercials—always the best part of the film—are still hilarious.

PYGMALION ☆☆☆½
1938, Great Britain
Wendy Hiller, Leslie Howard, Wilfrid Lawson, Marie Lohr, Scott Sunderland, Jean Cadell, David Tree, Violet Vanbrugh, Cathleen Nesbitt. Directed by Anthony Asquith and Leslie Howard. 96 min.

Four writers adapted George Bernard Shaw's play about a haughty professor and a cockney flower girl to the screen; their goal seems to have been to stay as close to the original text as possible, and wisely so. Leslie Howard makes a typically chilly Shavian hero, but his Henry Higgins has a saving touch of humanity, and Wendy Hiller's Eliza Doolittle is a marvel—cheeky, even a bit pugnacious, always warm and womanly. Howard himself codirected (with Anthony Asquith), and this version of the play later apotheosized as *My Fair Lady* is smooth, civilized, and enjoyable throughout.

Q

QB VII
1974, USA (TV) ★★★
Anthony Hopkins, Ben Gazzara, Juliet Mills, Leslie Caron, Edith Evans, Jack Hawkins, Lee Remick, John Gielgud, Dan O'Herlihy, Anthony Quayle. Directed by Tom Gries. 313 min.

Leon Uris's effective courtroom drama introduced the miniseries form to a mass American audience, and like many of its successors, this one is a mixture of the soapy and the serious, the oversimplified and the genuinely compelling. The case is libel: The plaintiff is a respected Jewish doctor (Anthony Hopkins) and the defendant is an American author (Ben Gazzara) who painted him as a war criminal in a thinly disguised characterization in a novel. The serpentine maneuverings of the trial, based on a real suit brought against Uris after the publication of *Exodus*, will hold you in thrall even when Edward Anhalt's teleplay lags or melodramatizes. Fine acting from all the principals, and especially incisive supporting performances by Jack Hawkins, as the judge, and Anthony Quayle, who won an Emmy as one of the lawyers.

Q—THE WINGED SERPENT
1982, USA, R ★★
Michael Moriarty, David Carradine, Candy Clark. Directed by Larry Cohen. 92 min.

Another quirky Larry Cohen (*It's Alive*, *God Told Me To*) horror movie, this time concerning a winged serpent—apparently an avatar of the Aztec god Quetzelcoatl—that swoops down from its nest in the Chrysler Building to devour unwary New Yorkers. A small-time criminal locates the monster's lair and uses his knowledge to try to pull off the one big score he has always dreamed of, and much mayhem ensues. The movie is laced with offbeat humor and a curious, muted subtext concerning the nature of deity.

QUACKSER FORTUNE HAS A COUSIN IN THE BRONX
1970, Ireland, R ★★★
Gene Wilder, Margot Kidder, Eileen Colgen, Seamus Ford. Directed by Waris Hussein. 90 min.

This is a delightful low-key comedy about a Dublin fertilizer salesman who would rather scoop up manure as a freelancer than have to deal with the conformist stuff he'd have to shovel if he joined the masses in a less unusual occupation. True love in the form of an American college girl tempts him, as progress forces him to consider another line of work. The film is offbeat and original from the word go. (a.k.a.: *Fun Loving*)

QUADROPHENIA
1979, Great Britain, R ★★½
Phil Daniels, Mark Wingett, Philip Davis, Leslie Ash, Garry Cooper, Toya Wilcox, Sting (Gordon Sumner), Trevor Laird. Directed by Frank Roddam. 120 min.

Frank Roddam's invigorating punk-rebellion film, loosely based on the 1973 album by The Who, depicts the conflicts between Mods and Rockers circa 1964. The story of an angry-but-sensitive Mod (Phil Daniels) who is led by a series of shocks and betrayals to yearn for more fulfillment than gang life can provide, *Quadrophenia* becomes a nearly universal rites-of-passage saga. What's hard to fathom is how passionate these kids were about poses and trappings that seem distant to us.

QUARTET
1981, Great Britain/France ★★
Isabelle Adjani, Alan Bates, Maggie Smith, Anthony Higgins, Armelia McQueen. Directed by James Ivory. 101 min.

The Ivory-Merchant-Jhabvala production team has made a number of noteworthy literary adaptations, including *A Room With A View* and *The Bostonians*, but *Quartet* is not one of their more sterling achievements. They've drained the spark and personality out of Jean Rhys's superb novella about a young West Indian woman staying with a rich British couple, and what remains is a richly decorated but empty film whose action is meaningless and whose characters are impenetrable. Maggie Smith is, as always, marvelous, but Rhys's very personal story is ill served by this film.

QUEEN OF THE CANNIBALS

See *Doctor Butcher, M.D. (Medical Deviate)*

THE QUEEN'S DIAMONDS

See *The Three Musketeers* (1973)

QUERELLE
1982, West Germany/France, R ★½
Brad Davis, Franco Nero, Jeanne Moreau, Gunther Kaufmann, Hanno Poschl, Laurent Malet. Directed by Rainer Werner Fassbinder. 105 min.

Rainer Werner Fassbinder's last film, an adaptaion of Jean Genet's 1947 novel *Querelle de Brest*, looks like a lurid dream, with livid sunsets, a phallus-decorated ship, and streets that simply sweat color. Visually mesmerizing, it's also, sadly, a thorough failure, tacky where it means to be stylized and drooling when it tries for eroticism. Sailor-suited Brad Davis plays the title role of a bloodthirsty seaman on leave in the seaport of Brest—he looks and acts like a lawn jockey at an S&M bar, but still manages to make sirens sing and sailors salivate all over town. It's very dispiriting, not only because the film is nothing like Genet, but because Fassbinder's inspirations here—overproduced studio melodramas and male porn—seem unworthy of such slavish and extended homage.

QUEST FOR FIRE
1981, France/Canada, R ★★½
Everett McGill, Ron Perlman, Rae Dawn Chong, Nameer El-Kadi. Directed by Jean-Jacques Annaud. 97 min.

Quest was vaunted as the most anthropologically correct early-man movie, complete with a grunted language created by Anthony Burgess and a body language devised by pop anthropologist Desmond Morris; however, the film rarely catches fire. The primitive heroes are all thoughtful, caring individuals, but they seem transplanted from a Hollywood movie—even worse, they are the blue-eyed leaders of a dark-haired race. Occasionally, the film's well-intentioned depictions of the quest for knowledge are embarrassingly obvious, such as when a more advanced woman (Rae Dawn Chong) teaches the crude Cro-Magnon man (Everett McGill) the missionary position. Some wonderful landscape photography fills out the mechanical story.

QUEST FOR LOVE ☆☆
1971, Great Britain
Joan Collins, Tom Bell, Denholm Elliott, Laurence Naismith, Lyn Ashley, Juliet Harmer, Neil McCallum. Directed by Ralph Thomas. 90 min.

An intriguing premise is terribly wasted in this pedestrian science-fiction melodrama, released on video to cash in on Joan Collins's inexplicable popularity. A physicist is blown into a parallel universe where he is a philandering playwright. He struggles to convince his wife that he is a new man; however, when he manages to redeem himself, she dies. He returns to the real world, where he now must find the woman and save her life.

A QUESTION OF GUILT ☆☆½
1978, USA (TV)
Tuesday Weld, Ron Leibman, Peter Masterson, Alex Rocco, Viveca Lindfors, Lana Wood, M. Emmet Walsh. Directed by Robert Butler. 96 min.

This disappointingly tepid but occasionally compelling police melodrama owes its plot to a controversial murder case in New York, in which a woman's personal life became a point of prosecution when she was accused of killing her young daughter. Here, Tuesday Weld gives a good if oddly dispassionate performance, but she's stuck in a script that always lets you stay two steps ahead of it.

A QUESTION OF HONOR ☆☆½
1982, USA (TV)
Ben Gazzara, Paul Sorvino, Robert Vaughn, Tony Roberts, Danny Aiello, Steve Inwood, Anthony Zerbe. Directed by Jud Taylor. 134 min.

This gritty, hard-hitting drama of police corruption is very much in the vein of Sidney Lumet's considerably better *Prince of the City*. Robert Vaughn plays a government investigator determined to root out corruption in the force, and Ben Gazzara is the good but confused cop who becomes his quarry. While a compelling film, it is not particularly fresh or insightful, although writer Budd Schulberg provides some pointed dialogue. Note: the video version, released by VCL, is slightly shorter than the version originally telecast.

A QUESTION OF LOVE ☆☆☆
1978, USA (TV)
Gena Rowlands, Jane Alexander, Ned Beatty, Bonnie Bedelia, Clu Gulager, James Sutorius. Directed by Jerry Thorpe. 100 min.

A real-life custody battle that generated great controversy gets a sensitive television treatment bolstered by fine performances. Gena Rowlands plays a lesbian parent faced with losing her two sons because of her sexual preference. Jane Alexander plays her lover, and Clu Gulager is the ex-husband who brings her to court. The climactic trial, intelligently written, raises complex questions without haranguing or exploiting, and, as always, Rowlands and Alexander are very good.

A QUESTION OF SILENCE ☆☆½
1983, Holland
Cox Habbema, Edda Barends, Nelly Frijda, Henriette Tol, Eddy Brugman. Directed by Marleen Gorris. 92 min.

A housewife, for no good reason, tries to shoplift a piece of clothing from a retail store. When she is apprehended by the manager, two other women, who know neither her nor each other, also start to pocket merchandise. The three of them then beat the manager to death, kicking and pummeling him in a blind, dispassionate manner. That is how this feminist film opens. The balance of it deals with the trial of the three women, who refuse to offer a motive for their actions. The film gains points for being well made and for unearthing an occasional keen psychological observation, but in the end it is a conundrum. It isn't so stupid as to postulate that this one unknown man deserved to die for the sins visited upon the trio by the respective men in their lives, but it's hard *not* to feel that that's really all it has to say.

QUICKSILVER ☆☆
1986, USA, PG
Kevin Bacon, Jami Gertz, Paul Rodriguez, Gerald S. O'Laughlin, Rudy Ramos, Larry Fishburne, Andrew Smith, Whitney Kershaw. Directed by Tom Donnelly. 106 min.

In this combination of *Footloose* and *Trading Places*, Kevin Bacon scowls incessantly as a young stockbroker who, after losing his parents' life savings on a bad day at the market, chucks his successful career and becomes a bicycle messenger. Of course, the world of messengers is blown up to a melodramatic extreme—these guys are so busy dealing with dope-dealing bad guys and staging macho races that you wonder when they get any work done. A never-ending soundtrack of potential hit singles and the absence of excessive sex or violence make this palatable for young teens, who will be more willing than adults to overlook the individualist hooey that permeates the script.

QUIET COOL ☆☆
1986, USA, R
James Remar, Adam Coleman Howard, Daphne Ashbrook, Jared Martin, Nick Cassavetes, Fran Ryan. Directed by Clay Borris. 80 min.

This adequate, no-frills action film concerns a tough New York cop (James Remar) busting a ring of marijuana mobsters in a small town in northern California. Remar, the memorable villain of *48 HRS* and *The Cotton Club*, isn't as forceful a screen presence when he's on the right side of the law, but the film looks good and moves briskly, and Jacques Haitkin's cinematography is better than most work in the genre.

THE QUIET EARTH ☆☆½
1985, New Zealand, R
Bruno Lawrence, Alison Routledge, Peter Smith. Directed by Geoffrey Murphy. 91 min.

A strangely subdued end-of-the-world fantasy that manages to tread some fresh ground. Bruno Lawrence plays the apparent sole survivor of an "accident" that's simply erased all human life from earth. For a while, overtaken with delirium at having the world to himself, he has a fine time unfettering his wildest impulses, becoming the merry lord of the apocalypse. But when he encounters two other survivors and learns that their own doom may be imminent, the conflicts and the drama turn conventional. The special effects are kept extremely modest in favor of a story that's limited but also quite original.

THE QUIET MAN ☆☆☆☆
1952, USA
John Wayne, Maureen O'Hara, Barry Fitzgerald, Ward Bond, Victor McLaglen, Mildred Natwick, Arthur Shields. Directed by John Ford. 129 min.

John Ford's beguiling romance stars John Wayne as an American boxer who returns home to his native Ireland and falls in love with a fiery, red-haired Irish lass (Maureen O'Hara). Next to *Stagecoach*, Ford's 1939 classic, *The Quiet Man* is the finest film John Wayne ever appeared in. As always, the Ford-Wayne collaboration elicits some of the greatest work either one of them has ever done. The story held intense personal interest for Ford, whose father had emigrated from Ireland a century earlier. Ford depicts an Ireland that is as idyllic as it is unrealistic, looking to the country of his forbears with passionate reverence. The result is charming, uplifting, and extremely funny. The film garnered seven Oscar nominations. Ford won his fourth award as Best Director, and Winton C. Hoch won his third for his exquisite panoramic cinematography.

QUINTET ☆
1979, USA, R
Paul Newman, Vittorio Gassman, Fernando Rey, Bibi Anderson, Brigitte Fossey, Nina Van Pallandt, David Langton, Tom Hill. Directed by Robert Altman. 100 min.

Robert Altman's apocalpytic fantasy, set in a future ice age, is a low for him, as well as for most of the cast members, and was roundly and rightly dismissed on its original release. Instead of a plot, there's an extended, facile metaphor about life as an endgame; in this case, it's called Quintet, the "pawns" are real people, and when you're out, you're out. This causes the pelt-clad cast to suffer through such embarrassments as Nina Van Pallandt sitting on-screen with an arrow through her head for what seems like hours until someone resolves it by saying, "Death is always arbitrary." It is notable only in that the stagy, theatrical production foreshadows the style, if not the quality, of the play adaptations (*Streamers; Fool for Love; Come Back to the Five and Dime, Jimmy Dean, Jimmy Dean*) that would restore Altman's badly tarnished reputation after this bomb.

QUO VADIS ☆☆½
1951, USA
Robert Taylor, Deborah Kerr, Peter Ustinov, Leo Genn, Patricia Laffan, Finlay Currie. Directed by Mervyn LeRoy. 171 min.

They threw the Christians to the lions, but they should have thrown them the script. However, if you like all-star spectaculars and enjoy the mindlessly mammoth, this entertainingly nonsensical big-budget Roman candle from MGM is for you. Rome conveniently forms a burning backdrop for Robert Taylor's burning passion for Deborah Kerr. It's a mixed romance—he's a Roman and she's a Christian, thus potential lion bait. For the price of a rental, you also get Nero fiddling around, magnificent sets, and Sophia Loren as an extra!

R

RABBIT TEST ☆
1978, USA, PG
Billy Crystal, Joan Prather, Alex Rocco, Doris Roberts, George Gobel, Imogene Coca, Jimmie Walker, Alice Ghostley, Paul Lynde, Rosey Grier. Directed by Joan Rivers. 84 min.

If you've ever wondered why Joan Rivers's talk show monologues contain so much self-hatred, this skeleton in her closet, in which Billy Crystal plays the world's first pregnant man, may be the answer. It's an odious, offensive, resolutely unfunny mess that's little more than a badly photographed assemblage of weakly connected incidents and painful one-liners, with the blame resting squarely on director-cowriter Rivers. Her much-maligned husband Edgar (Rosenberg) produced, and her daughter Melissa, ten at the time, is listed as associate producer. We think this must be a joke—surely a ten-year-old could do better than this. Despite a bushel of all-star cameos ranging from Paul Lynde to Rosey Grier (all right, maybe not *all* stars), it's a truly pathetic waste of film.

RABID ☆☆½
1976, Canada, R
Marilyn Chambers, Frank Moore, Joe Silver. Directed by David Cronenberg. 90 min.

This is a weird, violent horror cheapie, in which an experimental skin graft turns pretty Rosie into a vampire plague carrier. Director David Cronenberg (*They Came from Within, The Brood, Scanners, Videodrome,* and *The Dead Zone*), Canada's reigning horror genre filmmaker, is at his most conventional here, but his film is still bloody and generally perverse. It's also notable for being Marilyn Chambers's first adult venture outside the world of hard-core porn.

RACE FOR YOUR LIFE, CHARLIE BROWN ☆☆
1977, USA, G
Animated. Directed by Bill Melendez. 75 min.

The title suggests some intriguingly dark possibilities; perhaps this entry will have the Peanuts gang pursued by *Friday the 13th*'s Jason. Nope. It's just a meek, unmenacing big-screen version of the TV specials that has the whole group of regulars, including Snoopy and Woodstock, troop off to summer camp, get involved in a big canoeing race, and grow up a bit in the process. There are moments of wistful charm, but something about Charles Schulz's characterizations gets lost when it moves off the page, and the vaguely deformed look of the kids (huge bald heads, squat legs, bucket ears) has the unfortunate effect of making the camp look like a hospice.

RACE WITH THE DEVIL ☆½
1975, USA, PG
Peter Fonda, Warren Oates, Loretta Swit, Lara Parker, R.G. Armstrong, Clay Turner. Directed by Jack Starrett. 88 min.

As further proof that there are some things that money just can't buy, this major studio (Twentieth Century-Fox) attempt to make the kind of action-horror film that small studios and the independents do with such cheesy panache falls flat on its face. The plot is prime Wes Craven stuff, with some vacationing suburbanites taking their motor home to rural Texas, where they encounter a band of backwoods Satanists engaged in human sacrifices; like Craven, director Jack Starrett seems to be drawing parallels between middle-class Americans and their sub-societal counterparts. It doesn't try very hard, or very successfully, and most of this is hackneyed chase and shoot-out stuff. Only Warren Oates manages to rise above the material.

RACHEL AND THE STRANGER ☆☆☆½
1948, USA
Loretta Young, Robert Mitchum, William Holden, Tom Tully, Sara Haden. Directed by Norman Foster. 93 min.

A real treat, an adult Western in which a taciturn farmer takes a bondswoman in marriage out on the frontier. When a handsome visitor stops by and regards her as a beautiful woman, not just a glorified servant, her husband's eyes are finally opened and an interesting triangle is formed. Will Rachel hit the trail with the attractive stranger, or wait for her husband's passion to ignite? Full-bodied performances make this Western yarn top-notch.

RACHEL, RACHEL ☆☆½
1968, USA, R
Joanne Woodward, James Olson, Kate Harrington, Estelle Parsons, Geraldine Fitzgerald. Directed by Paul Newman. 101 min.

Paul Newman made his directorial debut with this earnest but overrated drama about a spinster. Joanne Woodward is excellent as the woman who thinks she'll be alone forever until a childhood friend reenters her life. The proceedings are pretty slow, however, as the script does not match the acting.

RACING WITH THE MOON ☆☆☆
1984, USA, PG
Sean Penn, Elizabeth McGovern, Nicolas Cage, John Karlen, Rutanya Alda, Carol Kane. Directed by Richard Benjamin. 108 min.

Sean Penn plays a small-town California wise guy in this touching drama about coming of age during World War II. The movie centers on Penn's prickly, tentative romance with a young woman, disarmingly rendered by Elizabeth McGovern. Richard Benjamin's direction expertly paces the film's key comic scenes, including a marvelously inept roller-skating performance by Penn. The references to the war and other scenes of high melodrama are so deliberately handled that they may seem forced; however, the expert ensemble playing of the actors carries the film.

RAD ☆
1986, USA, PG
Bill Allen, Lori Loughlin, Talia Shire, Ray Walston, Jack Weston, Alfie Wise. Directed by Hal Needham. 91 min.

Hal Needham has enough trouble making watchable films when he has the services of big-name cats and powerful automobiles (witness *Cannonball Run, Stroker Ace,* and *Smokey and the Bandit*); here, his witless direction takes on a low-rent cast riding undersized bicycles. Unless you are harboring the delusion that BMX racing is long overdue as a thrilling Olympic event, you will be bored silly at this story of a young local who wants to compete in a glamorous national race. The highlight of the film is John Schwartzman's credit sequence of trick bicycle riding; the low point is another embarrassment for the talented Ray Walston.

RADIOACTIVE DREAMS ☆
1986, USA, R
John Stockwell, Michael Dudikoff, Lisa Blount, Michele Little, Don Murray, George Kennedy. Directed by Albert F. Pyun. 95 min.

This not-very-funny fallout comedy rips off a half-dozen commercial hits with extremely limited results. Safely tucked away from the radiation of the postapocalyptic years, two goof-offs raised only on 1940s detective fiction emerge from their hiding place and have to cope with a new world of desolation, made worse by factions that are after the pair's possession—the last remaining nuclear weapon in captivity. A mismash that mixes detective spoofs with nuclear knucklehead comedy and typical action-genre stuff.

RADIO DAYS ☆☆☆☆
1987, USA, PG
Mia Farrow, Seth Green, Julia Kavner, Michael Tucker, Dianne Wiest, Wallace Shawn, Diane Keaton. Directed by Woody Allen. 88 min.

In this stunning, funny movie, Woody Allen merges two sides of his own early life: the magical, illusory world of commercial radio shows and the earthy, real life of radio's audience. Essentially, this is a poignant concept—that we as audiences find escape from our own situations by investing emotions in someone else's fakery. Allen is aware of the melancholic aspects of the relationship between people and their mass-produced dreams, but he has the ironist's eye for every bit of silliness and ridiculousness. Ultimately, his message is the standard Allen benevolent balm: everyone, even the glamorous radio stars, are people, and all people share the same dreams and frustrations. The scenes of Allen's childhood rival Fellini's *Amarcord* in their vulgar hilarity. His evocation of the period, filmed in Astoria Studios, is gorgeous.

RAFFERTY AND THE GOLD DUST TWINS ☆☆½
1975, USA, R
Alan Arkin, Sally Kellerman, Mackenzie Phillips, Alex Rocco, Charlie Martin Smith, Harry Dean Stanton, Louis Prima. Directed by Dick Richards. 91 min.

In this fitfully amusing adventures of an odd trio traveling through some of the seamier regions of the American southwest, Sally Kellerman and Mackenzie Phillips are a couple of hitchhikers who persuade driving instructor Alan Arkin to give them a ride by sticking a gun in his face; they, of course, resolve their differences while on the road. Arkin and Kellerman coast through on their characterizations, but enough slack is taken up by teenage Phillips, Charlie Martin Smith, and especially the ever-reliable Harry Dean Stanton to make this of some interest, if not particulaly commendable. Shown on TV as *Rafferty and the Highway Hustlers*.

RAFFERTY AND THE HIGHWAY HUSTLERS

See *Rafferty and the Gold Dust Twins*

RAGE ☆☆☆
1980, USA (TV)
David Soul, James Whitmore, Yaphet Kotto, Caroline McWilliams, Sharon Farrell, Vic Tayback, Craig T. Nelson. Directed by by William A. Graham. 100 min.

A thought-provoking topical drama that endeavors to view the crime of rape from the perspective of the rapist, this film guides viewers through a program designed to rehabilitate sex offenders and fills us in on their case histories. The controversial subject matter may not draw a sympathetic response from all audience members, but the film is not an apology for criminal behavior—rather, it is an attempt to understand what drives men to acts of violence. Unexpectedly, David Soul is quite effective at unleashing the rage inside himself as a man whose intense anger at women stems from a childhood of being sexually abused. The film boasts an expressive script and well-modulated ensemble playing.

RAGE OF ANGELS ☆☆½
1983, USA (TV)
Jaclyn Smith, Ken Howard, Deborah May, Armand Assante, Ronald Hunter, Kevin Conway, George Coe. Directed by Buzz Kulik. 195 min.

This is a high-gloss, low-brainpower miniseries adaptation of Sidney Sheldon's pop page-turner about a brilliant, beautiful young attorney and her affairs with a ruthless mob lawyer and a senatorial candidate. It's satisfactory trash with a brisk plot that wastes no time with unnecessary frills like realism or characterization; Jaclyn Smith's one-dimensional performance proves ideally suited to the genre. The version on video is complete. Followed by a sequel.

THE RAGE OF PARIS ☆☆☆
1938, USA
Douglas Fairbanks, Jr., Danielle Darrieux, Helen Broderick, Mischa Auer, Louis Hayward, Harry Davenport. Directed by Henry Koster. 77 min.

A trifling but bewitching confection that was supposed to launch the tantalizing Danielle Darrieux as an American movie star. It's our loss that she did not find filming here a satisfying experience and fled back to France, because she's quite charming in this Cinderella story about a would-be model who's persuaded to masquerade as a soignée rich girl in order to snag a rich husband. The cast is made up of able farceurs like Mischa Auer and Helen Broderick; and Douglas Fairbanks and Darrieux strike romantic sparks together. It is an iridescent comedy that, in its inconsequential way, still captivates.

RAGGEDY MAN ☆☆☆½
1981, USA, PG
Sissy Spacek, Eric Roberts, Sam Shepard, William Sanderson, Tracey Walter, Henry Thomas, Carey Hollis, Jr. Directed by Jack Fisk. 94 min.

This is the first film directed by Sissy Spacek's husband, art director Jack Fisk, which really capitalizes on her appealing vulnerability as an actress. In this period piece set in a small Texas town during World War II, she plays a stuck-at-home divorcée who becomes prey to a couple of small-town psychotics. This film is so insightful as a character study of emotional casualties on the home front that its violent excesses in the final half hour seem unnecessary. Overlooking the overloaded climax in which Spacek is terrorized by the two thugs, this is superior filmmaking and a very promising directorial debut.

RAGING BULL ☆☆☆☆½
1980, USA, R
Robert DeNiro, Cathy Moriarty, Joe Pesci, Frank Vincent, Nicholas Colasanto. Directed by Martin Scorsese. 129 min.

The rise and fall of middleweight boxing champion Jake LaMotta becomes one of the finest films about boxing ever made. Director Martin Scorsese incisively explores the violent and destructive nature of the man both in and out of the ring, detailing his two failed marriages, his brief reign as prizefighter, his falling in with gangsters, and his years in decline as a third-rate nightclub comic. Robert DeNiro's Oscar-winning performance is more riveting than any of his other psychopathic roles (*Mean Streets*, *Taxi Driver*), and he is given solid support by Cathy Moriarty as his second wife and Joe Pesci as his nice-guy brother. Minor flaws in period detail and editing are eclipsed by otherwise superb production design and brilliant black-and-white cinematography (by Michael Chapman). Unlike *Rocky* and its sequels, *Raging Bull* is unafraid to show the ugly side of the boxing profession and the people in it.

RAGING MASTERS OF TIGER AND CRANE

See *Master of Tiger Crane*

THE RAGING MOON ☆☆☆
1971, Great Britain
Malcolm McDowell, Nanette Newman, Georgia Brown, Bernard Lee, Gerald Sim, Michael Flanders, Margery Mason. Directed by Bryan Forbes. 110 min.

We can all be grateful that, for every ten deservedly unseen sex and horror exploitation unknowns dredged up for the video cassette market, there is the occasional seldom-seen feature like this that gets a second chance. Adapted and directed by Bryan Forbes, one of the best but least recognized British directors of the 1960s, this is an uplifting romance on a downbeat theme. A callow young man loses both of his legs in a soccer injury and is confined to a home for cripples, where he meets a girl who has been there for six years. Malcolm McDowell exhibits much of the somewhat suspect boyish charm he employed in different ways in *If . . .* and *A Clockwork Orange*, and is well matched by Nanette Newman (Forbes's wife). It's not a great film, but one that discerning viewers will be pleased to discover. (a.k.a.: *Long Ago Tomorrow*)

RAGTIME ☆☆☆½
1981, USA, PG
Howard E. Rollins, James Cagney, James Olson, Brad Dourif, Elizabeth McGovern, Mary Steenburgen, Mandy Patinkin, Pat O'Brien, Kenneth McMillan. Directed by Milos Forman. 155 min.

Author E.L. Doctorow's multifaceted portrait of turn-of-the-century American life is exquisitely detailed in director Milos Forman's (*Amadeus*) cinematic adaptation of the book. The film delicately weaves its fictive subplot of a black man trying to find justice with such historic events as the assassination of Sanford White, and, like any picture attempting to cover such a broad scope of events, this one has a cramped feeling to it. But credit Forman for doing very well with a nearly impossible task; *Ragtime* has a finely tuned sense of nostalgia and a remarkable cast of actors, among them James Cagney returning to the movies as a crusty police commissioner. It's a sometimes slow and bumpy ride through early America, but one that's often dazzling and absorbing. Nominated for several Academy Awards, including Best Supporting Actor (Rollins) and Best Supporting Actress (McGovern).

RAIDERS OF BUDDHIST KUNG FU ☆☆
Liu Chia-Hui, Mike Wong, John Kelly, Sarah Sit, Alan Kwok, Brian Park, Edward Youn, Paul Yuen. Directed by Godfrey Ho. 85 min.

Guest appearances by kung fu masters and a climactic battle of a beach punctuate this routine entry about a conspiracy to take over some sacred territory. It's one of the few films of this type, however, to feature a brother-sister kung fu team.

RAIDERS OF THE LOST ARK ☆☆☆☆
1981, USA, PG
Harrison Ford, Karen Allen, Wolf Kahler, Paul Freeman, Ronald Lacey, John Rhys-Davies, Denholm Elliott. Directed by Steven Spielberg. 115 min.

Harrison Ford is Indiana Jones, the ruggedly charismatic archaeologist who races the Nazis through Africa in search of the Ark of the Covenant, making hair's-breadth escapes at every turn. Producers George Lucas and Steven Spielberg demonstrate their amazingly accurate instincts for popular entertainment by combining the dynamic, razzle-dazzle spirit of 1930s adventure serials with deliciously dry humor and ingenious special effects. A bumbling but feisty Karen Allen accompanies our indefatigable hero, making more trouble than love; and a bespectacled Ronald Lacey serves as the quintessential villain in this thrill-after-thriller. Followed by a sequel, *Indiana Jones And The Temple of Doom*.

RAID ON ENTEBBE ☆☆
1977, USA (TV)
Peter Finch, Martin Balsam, Horst Bucholz, John Saxon, Yaphet Kotto, Charles Bronson, Sylvia Sidney, Jack Warden, Tige Andrews, James Woods, Harvey Lembeck. Directed by Irvin Kershner. 113 min.

This by-the-book unfolding of the Israelis' rescue of the planeload of hostages held at Uganda's Entebbe Airport is politically correct—Israelis/good, terrorists/bad, Idi Amin/real bad— and crisply executed. The huge cast collected a passel of Emmy nominations, including Peter Finch for his last role, and an Emmy was won by cinematographer Bill Butler. The video version is cut from an original 150 minutes.

THE RAILWAY CHILDREN ☆☆☆
1970, Great Britain
Dinah Sheridan, Bernard Cribbins, William Mervyn, Iain Cuthbertson, Jenny Agutter, Sally Thomsett. Directed by Lionel Jeffries. 108 min.

It's not a Disney film, but it would have made a fine one—a group of adorable moppets in Edwardian England whose father is unjustly jailed must go live in a small railroad village on the moors. The film is picturesque, pleasantly acted (a very young Jenny Agutter plays the oldest of the children), and only rarely saccharine, although it finally slides into triviality as the family's poverty is glossed over in favor of a few silly subplots.

RAIN ☆☆☆
1932, USA
Joan Crawford, Walter Huston, William Gargan, Walter Catlett, Guy Kibbee. Directed by Lewis Milestone. 92 min.

The first sound version of Somerset Maugham's *Sadie Thompson*—the hardened prostitute stranded on the island of Pago Pago with an outfit of Marines and a fanatical missionary. It is the first of Joan Crawford's meaty dramatic roles, and she seized the opportunity splendidly. An immense critical and box-office failure in 1932, the film is more impressive today and Crawford, though she often disparaged this performance, is very persuasive as the tropical trollop who's mesmerized by the hypocritical Reverend Davidson. Although the supporting cast comprises a rather hammy background for Crawford's tour de force, the film's message about the cruel self-righteousness of many so-called Christians comes across forcefully and with great stylistic conviction.

RAINBOW BRITE AND THE STAR STEALER ½☆
1985, USA, G
Animated: Bettina, Patrick Fraley, Peter Cullen, Robbie Lee, Andrew Stojka, David Mendenhall, Les Tremayne, Monna Marshall. Directed by Bernard Degries and Kimio Yabuki. 85 min.

Hallmark Productions manufactured this feature-length animated ad for the insipidly cutesy "Rainbow Brite collection" it markets to unwary tykes. In the movie, the cartoon characters must save the world, but the deadly production spells nothing but doom for anyone exposed to it. Too dreadful a punishment for wicked children.

THE RAIN PEOPLE ☆☆☆½
1969, USA, R
Shirley Knight, James Caan, Robert Duvall, Andrew Duncan. Directed by Francis Ford Coppola. 102 min.

This is an interesting, somewhat upsetting early film from Francis Ford Coppola about a housewife who, discovering that she is pregnant for the first time, takes off in the family station wagon for parts unknown. Along the way, she meets up with an ex-football player who has been rendered mentally deficient by a game injury, and a motorcycle cop seething with personal guilt and rage. The themes are the acceptance and rejection of responsibility, certainly a pressing social issue of the time (though, believe it or not, there seems to be no Vietnam allegory here). Shirley Knight is a bit too neurotic as the housewife, but James Caan turns in an especially compelling performance as the dim-witted jock. Coppola filmed this on "found locations": He set out with a small crew over eighteen states, the same as those covered in the script, and filmed on whatever he found in those areas, integrating into the story anything that struck his interest.

RAINTREE COUNTY ★★★
1957, USA
Elizabeth Taylor, Montgomery Clift, Eva Marie Saint, Lee Marvin, Nigel Patrick, Rod Taylor, Agnes Moorehead. Directed by Edward Dmytryk. 168 min.

A gargantuan love story based on one of the most popular best-sellers of the 1940s, *Raintree County* was not rapturously received by the critics, but maybe they were reacting to how obviously the film sold itself as another *Gone with the Wind*. It wasn't, but it *was* a huge money-maker, and it's easy to see why. If you've ever enjoyed an overblown network miniseries and love big stars and consummate, decorative re-creations of historical periods, you'll be glad that this tale of a man's search for the meaning of life never gets in the way of the passionate love scenes. In this Civil War version of *The Razor's Edge*, Montgomery Clift searches for the elusive raintree of happiness while coping with the horror of war and the pain of marriage to a half-mad Southern belle (Liz Taylor, who goes off the deep end just in time for Monty to end up with saintly Eva Marie). It is lavish and colorful enough to sweep away most criticism, including any complaints about its length. The troubled production shut down halfway through filming when Clift was involved in a near-fatal car accident that left him disfigured; as a result, his appearance differs from scene to scene. *Note:* The version on video does not include twenty minutes of footage cut after the film's initial engagements.

RAISE THE TITANIC! ★½
1980, USA/Great Britain, PG
Jason Robards, Richard Jordan, David Selby, Anne Archer, Alec Guinness. Directed by Jerry Jameson. 112 min.

If you thought the *sinking* of the Titanic was a disaster, wait until you see this numbingly stupid adventure about a group of Russians and Americans racing to raise it. The convoluted plot, adapted from Clive Cussler's best-seller, has both nations in quest of precious minerals in the ship at the bottom of the sea, but for a film that cost $35 million, there's precious little in the way of special effects to merit the sum, and absolutely nothing in the way of interesting drama or compelling characters to make it worth seeing. The best disaster films aren't exactly intimate human stories, but at least they have spectacular, panoramic action to make up for it; films like this and *Meteor* are merely enormous without being impressive in the least, and their mammoth budgets effectively killed one of the most enjoyably cheesy genres of the 1970s.

A RAISIN IN THE SUN ★★★½
1961, USA
Sidney Poitier, Claudia McNeil, Ruby Dee, Diana Sands, Ivan Dixon, John Fiedler, Louis Gossett. Directed by Daniel Petrie. 128 min.

Lorraine Hansberry's eloquent stage drama about a black family facing upheaval when they look for a way out of the Chicago ghetto and into a "closed" neighborhood has lost none of its power and poignance over the years, and this film version is a fine if not very cinematic adaptation. Moving performances by Sidney Poitier as the angry young man looking for financial security and Claudia McNeil as the benevolent matriach will hold your attention, and Daniel Petrie's unfussy, restrained direction is just what this articulate play demands.

RALLY

See *Safari 3000*.

RAMBO: FIRST BLOOD PART TWO ★★
1985, USA
Sylvester Stallone, Richard Crenna, Charles Napier. Directed by George P. Cosmatos. 98 min.

This is a rousing sequel to *First Blood*, with Sylvester Stallone as a near-superhuman Vietnam vet returning to that country to rescue American MIAs. It's nonstop action from beginning to end, with Stallone battling insurmountable odds to get to safety, and the best of the lowly pack of revisionist, Reagan-era Vietnam films that includes *Uncommon Valor* and *Missing in Action*.

RAMPARTS OF CLAY ★★★★
1970, France/Algeria, PG
Leila Schenna and the people of Tehouda, Algeria. Directed by Jean-Louis Bertucelli. 87 min.

With local actors and on-site locations, Jean-Louis Bertucelli's neorealist approach imaginatively captures a woman's struggle to overcome the restraints her fellow villagers ritualistically impose on her. Sparse and beautiful, the film overlays various levels of oppression; Leila Schenna is subservient within the village, while the villagers themselves are dependent upon a corporate salt-mining operation for their livelihood. By extension, one reads a metaphor for the French occupation of Algeria. This layering of attitudes, in combination with the simplicity of the directorial style, creates a unique, powerful, and moving experience, and a committed film. There is virtually no dialogue.

RAN ★★★★
1985, Japan/France, R
Tatsuya Nakadai, Akira Terao, Jinpachi Nezu, Daisuke Ryu, Mieko Harada, Peter (Shinnosuke Ikehata). Directed by Akira Kurosawa. 160 min.

The title means "chaos," but Akira Kurosawa may never have made as controlled a film as this austere, savage masterpiece, his twenty-seventh and valedictory effort. Drawing on *King Lear*, *Macbeth*, and his own *Throne of Blood*, the director has fashioned a sixteenth-century epic about an aged feudal lord (Tatsuya Nakadai) who cedes his power to the greediest of his three sons, provoking a bloody battle for the kingdom and becoming an outcast in the process. Kurosawa planned *Ran* for ten years, composing every shot long before filming; not surprisingly, many of the scenes are a little distant and stiff, more reflective than dramatic. But the tale unfolds with a scope and precision that perhaps no other contemporary director could have achieved. As the story moves gracefully from one plot to the next, you'll see brilliant acting by Mieko Harada as a vicious Lady Macbeth-like noblewoman, stunning drama in Nakadai's ravaged face as he wanders the "blasted heath," and depictions of warfare ranking with the most beautiful and spectacular ever filmed. Takao Saito's cinematography captures every subtlety in the country horizons, and Toru Takemitsu's score is an artistic triumph in itself. Though its power will be greatly diminished on video, *Ran* is still a resonant, often astounding achievement. It won an Academy Award for Best Costume Design.

RANCHO NOTORIOUS ★★★
1952, USA
Marlene Dietrich, Arthur Kennedy, Mel Ferrer, Gloria Henry, William Frawley, Jack Elam. Directed by Fritz Lang. 89 min.

Fritz Lang brings *film noir* concerns to a Western story with results that are not always successful but are often fascinating. Arthur Kennedy, searching for the murderer of his fiancée, follows a clue to a lonely ranch run as a hideout for fugitives by saloon singer Marlene Dietrich. In the style of revenge melodramas of the 1970s (*Death Wish*, *Walking Tall*, even *Straw Dogs*), Lang's characters fall victim to the corruption of civilization as they become the same as those they seek revenge on. The stylized outdoor sets are an unexpected plus, but that damn "Ballad of Chuck-O-Luck" has got to go.

RANDY RIDES ALONE ★★
1934, USA
John Wayne, Alberta Vaughan, George "Gabby" Hayes, Earl Dwire, Yakima Canutt. Directed by Harry Frazer. 60 min.

A pre-*Stagecoach* John Wayne plays an undercover lawman determined to derail an express office robbery gang. Although the film doesn't quite live up to its exciting opening, an all-around good cast gives an all-around good performance.

RAPE OF LOVE ☆☆½
1979, France, R
Nathalie Nell, Alain Foures, Michele Simonnet, Pierre Arditi. Directed by Yannick Bellon. 117 min.

This is a sincere attempt to present an accurate portrait of both the iniquities of the legal system toward, and the unfairness of bourgeois stereotypes regarding, the crime of rape. Stripped of sensationalism, the film doesn't preach too much; rather, it lets the characters speak for themselves. What's unique about the film is its insight into the reactions of the families of the rapists and how the crime affects them. Compared with sensationalized American films like *Lipstick*, this is a well-balanced and sensitive, albeit talky, treatment of the violation of a woman.

RAPPIN' ☆☆
1985, USA, PG
Mario Van Peebles, Tasia Valenza, Charles Flohe, Leo O'Brien, Eriq La Salle, Richie Abanes, Ruth Jaroslow. Directed by Joel Silberg. 92 min.

Who would have guessed that rappin' would hang around as an authentic low-class art form while break dancing dribbled off into the never-never land of white suburbia? This movie is hardly the definitive piece, and it lacks the great raps of *Krush Groove*, but it has a nice street-level gutsiness and naïveté. A young ex-con comes home and fights against local politicos, local hoods, and the big bad guy, a landlord. Mario Van Peebles (Melvin's son) plays Rappin' Hood, the hero, and his boyish charm and humorous good looks are the best thing about the movie. The raps are by Force M.D.'s, Ice T, T-force, and Tuff, Inc., and the cheap look is courtesy of Cannon Films.

THE RARE BREED ☆☆½
1966, USA
James Stewart, Maureen O'Hara, Brian Keith, Juliet Mills, Don Galloway, David Brian, Jack Elam, Ben Johnson, Harry Carey, Jr. Directed by Andrew V. McLaglen. 97 min.

A hornless white-faced Hereford bull named Vindicator carries the seeds for a new West, and it is Sam Burnett's responsibility to see that the prize stud, along with his previous owner, Martha Price, arrive safely at the Bowen cattle ranch. When Vindicator gets lost on the Bowen ranch and subsequently dies, Martha loses her faith in a genetically controlled future and Sam loses his hold on Martha. If a bull named Vindicator may seem a bit much, this Western at least amuses, with good performances from the entire herd.

RASHOMON ☆☆☆☆
1951, Japan
Scinobu Hascimoto, Toshiro Mifune, Akira Kurosawa, Machiko Kyo, Masayuki Mori, Takashi Shimura. Directed by Akira Kurosawa. 90 min.

Akira Kurosawa's (and Japan's) international movie breakthrough views the murder of a lord and the rape of his wife from the point of view of four protagonists, all antithetical to each other. Almost anyone would admit that its theme of "the unknowability of truth" is trite, and that the loopholes in its plot line stretch plausibility to the limit. However, few films are as visually stunning or as meticulously detailed. In the end, *Rashomon* is a study not of truth but of ego, which stands between men and truth.

RATBOY ☆
1986, USA, PG-13
Robert Townsend, Sondra Locke, Christopher Hewett, Larry Hankin, Sydney Lassick, Gerrit Graham, S. L. Baird. Directed by Sondra Locke. 105 min.

The French critics loved this; please remember that they also adore Jerry Lewis. Not nearly as accomplished as M. Jerry, Mlle. Locke makes her directorial debut with the finesse and "sudden impact" of . . . well, of one of her performances. Whimsical but strident, this fable concerns the discovery of a strange creature, part boy, part rodent, who gets caught in a commercial rattrap. This easily disparagable enterprise yearns to be a bittersweet fairy tale about how an innocent being is exploited by various hucksters out to make a buck by hyping his freakiness into celebrity status. While this notion is intriguing, the treatment is heavy-handed and maladroit.

THE RATINGS GAME ☆☆½
1984, USA (TV)
Danny DeVito, Rhea Perlman, Gerrit Graham, Ronnie Graham. Directed by Danny DeVito. 89 min.

This is a fairly sunny made-for-cable outing about a self-made man who learns how to manipulate a TV ratings service so he can turn all of the shows he produces into hits. Danny DeVito is a master at milking laughs from vulgarity, and he's in fine fettle as the devious would-be tycoon. However, the combination of DeVito and Rhea Perlman may prove too heady for lovers of subtlety.

THE RATS ARE COMING! THE WEREWOLVES ARE HERE!
1972, USA/Great Britain, PG
Berwick Kaler, Hope Starsung, Jackie Korvellis. Directed by Andy Milligan. 97 min.

A family of werewolves suffers from excessive inbreeding that has made one brother a drooling idiot, a sister a twisted rat fancier, and the patriarch an enervated cripple. This is a cheap, stupid and badly made horror film written and directed by Staten Island-based Andy Milligan, also responsible for *The Body Beneath*, *Guru the Mad Monk*, and other dull exploitations.

RATTLE OF A SIMPLE MAN ☆☆☆½
1964, Great Britain
Harry H. Corbett, Diane Cilento, Thora Hird, Charles Dyer, Michael Nedwin. Directed by Muriel Box. 96 min.

A sharply observed romantic comedy about two sleepy people who wake up to love after a chance encounter. She's a stripper who also entertains gentlemen callers at home; he's a tongue-tied mama's boy from Manchester out for his big night in the wicked city. Egged on by his boisterous buddies, he goes home with the free-spirited dame and, as his defense mechanisms melt away and her false bravado drops aside, the two hesitant strangers realize that they were made for each other. Based on a London stage hit, this charming character study deserves to reach a wider audience.

THE RAVEN ☆☆
1935, USA
Boris Karloff, Bela Lugosi, Irene Ware, Lester Matthews, Samuel S. Hinds. Directed by Louis Friedlander. 60 min.

The second of four films inspired by the classic Poe poem, and the first of two to feature Boris Karloff, this version teams him with Bela Lugosi in a bout of classic horror, laced with allusions to other Poe melodramas. A mad plastic surgeon (Lugosi) forces the grotesquely disfigured Karloff to perform dastardly deeds in payment for corrective surgery. The "Pit and the Pendulum" scene provides a fine example of American horror from the 1930s, but if you seek a more interesting version of "The Raven," check out Roger Corman's comic classic from 1963.

THE RAVEN ☆☆☆
1963, USA
Vincent Price, Peter Lorre, Boris Karloff, Hazel Court, Olive Sturgess, Jack Nicholson, Connie Wallace, William Baskin, Aaron Saxon. Directed by Roger Corman. 85 min.

Roger Corman's satire of the Edgar Allan Poe treatments he himself invented starts with a lugubrious Vincent Price mooning over the whereabouts of his paramour. "Where is my lost Lenore?" he implores as a raven flaps about the room. At which point the organ swells and, from within the raven, Peter Lorre's irritated voice replies, "How the hell should I know?" Need we say more? A very young Jack Nicholson costars.

RAW DEAL ☆☆½
1986, USA, R
Arnold Schwarzenegger, Kathryn Harrold, Sam Wanamaker, Paul Shenar, Darren McGavin. Directed by John Irvin. 97 min.

Arnold Schwarzenegger destroys the Chicago mob without messing up his hair or three-piece suit in a thriller that may not have much clarity, but contains a lot in the way of well-staged destruction and style. As in Chuck Norris's *Code of Silence*, the Windy City and its gangsters pump life into an often stilted macho man. Arnold plays an ex-intelligence agent who infiltrates the city's Mafia in order to wipe it out for his vengeful boss, and a chance for reemployment. This the incredibly indestructible Austrian hulk does in an awesome finale that rivals anything in the mass-destruction genre. The usually sedate British director John Irvin (*Turtle Diary*) might seem out of place amid the bloodshed, but he gives the monosyllabic star a sleek environment in which to blow away a barrage of wonderfully slimy characters, and a bit of (gasp) intelligence to do it with. This might be just another vehicle for Schwarzenegger, but it drives like a Cadillac.

RAW FORCE ☆
1981, Hong Kong
Cameron Mitchell, Jillian Kesner, Rey King, Jeff Benny. 90 min.

Martial artists get shipwrecked on an island of cannibalistic monks who need a continuous supply of live girls to eat. Yum, yum.

RAZORBACK ☆☆
1984, Australia, R
Gregory Harrison, Arkie Whiteley, Bill Kerr, Chris Haywood, David Argue, Judy Morris. Directed by Russell Mulcahy. 95 min.

A giant, vicious, baby-murdering boar rampages across the Outback in one of the more watchable, though failed, man-versus-monster films to appear recently. Director Russell Mulcahy had previously done pioneering work in rock videos; as might be expected, his first feature is more pleasing to look at than to listen to or think about. The presence of "name" star Gregory Harrison is jarringly asynchronous with the film's arid, Down Under rhythms, but his effectively low-key work offsets many of the misgivings we may feel about the silly premise—a pig is simply not a horror archetype.

THE RAZOR'S EDGE ☆☆☆
1946, USA
Tyrone Power, Gene Tierney, Clifton Webb, Anne Baxter, Herbert Marshall, John Payne. Directed by Edmund Goulding. 146 min.

Some regard this film as a solemn bore; others feel Twentieth Century Fox's glossy approximation of Somerset Maugham's rambling novel is some sort of classic. Although it doesn't exhibit a complex understanding of the main character's spiritual quest, it works smashingly well as an austere, metaphysical tale that follows our hero from the mist-shrouded heights of the Himalayas to the lower depths of Parisian boites. Never has there been a greater filmic argument for the effectiveness of star-powered acting or for the pleasures that shimmery black-and-white cinematography can afford. Tyrone Power and Gene Tierney are incredibly poignant; as the defeated Sophie, Anne Baxter won a best supporting actress Oscar for this performance. The film is best appreciated when viewed after the elephantine remake with Bill Murray (a vanity production that plays lke a "Saturday Night Live" outing with the ghost of Maugham as host).

THE RAZOR'S EDGE ☆½
1984, USA, PG-13
Bill Murray, Theresa Russell, Catherine Hicks, Denholm Elliott, James Keach, Peter Vaughn, Brian Doyle-Murray. Directed by John Byrum. 130 min.

There were traces of a good idea in this project, a remake of the Somerset Maugham novel first filmed with Tyrone Power as a vehicle for Bill Murray's dramatic debut. The part of Larry Darrell, who becomes disillusioned with his empty, middle-class Chicago existence after seeing the horrors of World War I and sets off around the world in search of something worth learning, seems tailor-made for a side of Murray that had previously only been hinted at in his comedic roles. Unfortunately, the movie also stresses his comedic persona, and the result is often astoundingly inappropriate. Add to that a rebalancing of the story to emphasize all of the most melodramatic parts, an awful performance by Theresa Russell as a "fallen woman," and a sanctimonious 1960s attitude and you've got a movie applying the razor's edge to its own wrists. It gains an extra half star because it seems to be sincere and has nice scenery.

REACHING FOR THE MOON ☆☆☆
1931, USA
Douglas Fairbanks, Bebe Daniels, Edward Everett Horton, Bing Crosby, Jack Mulhall, Helen Jerome Eddy. Directed by Edmund Goulding. 62 min.

This is a finger-snapping comedy-musical. With one of Douglas Fairbanks, Sr.'s few talkie appearances and tunes by Irving Berlin, what more could you ask for? Well, check out the rest of the cast and you'll see why this dated but bubbly comedy is guaranteed to put a smile on your face. Years before *Arthur*, this comedy was dealing with the comical effects inebriation has on a wealthy playboy. It's a vintage champagne comedy; lots of fizz in it, and it hasn't gone flat over the years.

THE REAL BRUCE LEE ½☆
1979, Hong Kong
Bruce Lee, Dragon Lee. Directed by Jim Markovic. 100 min.

Included in this film are some clips of Bruce Lee from his non-martial arts movies. Korean martial artist Dragon Lee tries to carry on in the "Bruce Lee" tradition. He can't.

REAL GENIUS ☆☆☆½
1985, USA, PG
Val Kilmer, Gabe Jarret, Michelle Meyrink, William Atherton. Directed by Martha Coolidge. 104 min.

Director Martha Coolidge (*Valley Girl*) answers many a filmgoer's prayer by making a substantial and genuinely funny youth comedy that's as smart as its characters. Instead of a bunch of hormonally crazed teenagers, *Real Genius* concerns itself with a group of brilliant college students who are desperately at work on a laser system for their nasty professor who, unbeknownst to them, wants to use their talents to create the ultimate weapon. The inspired method they use to foil his plans is a tribute to the movie's intelligence. The very appealing class of young Einsteins is headed by Val Kilmer, who wittily plays a cerebral young scientist in the wisecracking style of Bill Murray. The writing team responsible for the genre's noisier efforts (*Police Academy* among them) shows that they may have grown up in a picture that almost lives up to its title.

REAL LIFE ☆☆½
1979, USA, PG
Charles Grodin, Frances Lee McCain, Albert Brooks, J.A. Preston, Matthew Tobin. Directed by Albert Brooks. 99 min.

Previously known for his uniquely funny films for the early years of *Saturday Night Live*, Albert Brooks brings his original brand of humor to the big screen in a hilarious spoof of television's cinéma vérité portraits of "typical American families." In this surprisingly experimental and professional first feature, Brooks cast himself as a documentary filmmaker who will stop at nothing to capture "real life" on film. Charles Grodin and Frances Lee McCain are excellent as the hapless couple whose life he invades. Brooks's whining, manic-depressive style of comedy is an acquired taste but once acquired, it will leave you rolling in the aisles with laughter.

RE-ANIMATOR ☆☆☆☆
1985, USA, X (self-imposed)
Jeffrey Combs, Bruce Abbott, Barbara Crampton, David Gale, Robert Sampson, Gerry Black, Carolyn Purdy-Gordon, Peter Kent, Barbara Picters. Directed by Stuart Gordon. 86 min.

Herbert West, a medical student whose audacity greatly outweighs his common sense, devises a serum that can reanimate the dead. The state in which they return to consciousness is generally horrifying, but West persists, convinced that if only his specimens were *fresher* the results would be better. From this very basic horror movie notion (specifically based on H.P. Lovecraft's short story "Herbert West—Reanimator"), screenwriter Dennis Paoli and director Stuart Gordon have fashioned a knockout horror movie whose sense of grand guignol farce in no way undermines the effectiveness of its ghastly imagery. There is a bloodbath featuring perhaps the best visual pun in horror movie history (to say more would spoil the fun of discovering it in context) and some surprisingly good performances, especially from Jeffrey Combs as the fanatical West and Bruce Abbott as his reluctant partner.

REAR WINDOW ☆☆☆☆
1954, USA, PG
James Stewart, Grace Kelly, Thelma Ritter, Raymond Burr, Wendell Corey, Judith Evelyn. Directed by Alfred Hitchcock. 112 min.

In one of Hitchcock's greatest films, and perhaps the one that tops them all for the sheer purity of its entertainment, James Stewart plays an action photographer immobilized in his apartment by a broken leg. He idles away his days by spying, through a telephoto lens, on his neighbors across the courtyard. Naturally, he sees what he shouldn't—or does he? Not only does Hitchcock give his most fascinating and disturbing definition of what it means to watch a "silent film" of other people's lives, but he integrates the themes and emotions of the film into a plot that will keep you riveted. Stewart epitomizes the Hitchcockian hero in one of his best performances, and no one could ask for a more luminous incarnation of 1950s womanhood than Grace Kelly. Accolades must go as well to John Michael Hayes's script (adapted from a Cornell Woolrich short story), and to the color cinematography of Robert Burks. More than thirty years later, *Rear Window* is still an enriching, revivifying film experience.

REBECCA ☆☆☆☆
1940, USA
Joan Fontaine, Laurence Olivier, Judith Anderson, George Sanders. Directed by Alfred Hitchcock. 130 min.

Hitchcock's first American film tells the dark tale of a pretty young woman who marries a wealthy widower haunted by the memory of his dead wife, Rebecca. The couple lives in Manderly, a mansion that makes Citizen Kane's Xanadu seem upbeat by comparison, with a terrifyingly icy servant, Mrs. Danvers (Judith Anderson). Hitchcock successfully conveys the brooding, gothic mood of the best-selling Daphne Du Maurier novel on which the film is based. This masterfully photographed classic won Oscars for Best Picture and cinematography; Joan Fontaine and Olivier each earned a nomination.

REBECCA OF SUNNYBROOK FARM ☆☆½
1917, USA
Mary Pickford, Eugene O'Brien, Marjorie Daw, Josephine Crowell, Helen Jerome Eddy, Charles Ogle. Directed by Marshall Neilan. 77 min.

All of the sweetness and light that is associated with the book *Rebecca of Sunnybook Farm* also applies to Mary Pickford, the great silent star. It was inevitable that Pickford play the role of the treacly heroine who is sent to live with her aunts when her mother can no longer afford to raise her children herself. The story moves all over the place, covering many episodes from Kate Douglas Wiggins's novel. There's the very happy ending, of course, but prior to that there is a storm, a boarding school, and the death of one of the aunts. Pickford elevates Rebecca with acting that is remarkable for its natural charm and evanescence. Though it is not quite up to *The Poor Little Rich Girl* of the same year, it is quintessential sentimental silent drama.

REBECCA OF SUNNYBROOK FARM ☆☆☆½
1938, USA
Shirley Temple, Randolph Scott, Jack Haley, Bill "Bojangles" Robinson, Gloria Stuart. Directed by by Allan Dwan. 74 min.

Everyone's favorite curly-topped kid is an aspiring and inspiring radio starlet in this fun but typical Shirley Temple movie. It takes its title from a popular children's book, but the two stories are unrelated. Shirley's dance with Bojangles Robinson adds sugar, and romance between Gloria Stuart and Randolph Scott adds a very mild spice.

REBEL ☆☆
1986, Australia, R
Matt Dillon, Debbie Byrne, Bryan Brown, Bill Hunter, Ray Barrett, Julie Nihill, John O'May, Kim Deacon. Directed by Michael Jenkins. 89 min.

This bizarre, ill-conceived romantic drama concerns an American G.I. (Matt Dillon) who deserts Down Under and hooks up with a very small-time nightclub performer (Debbie Byrne) who may be able to help him get out without being caught. Inappropriately splashy and theatrical nightclub numbers are interspersed with the oddly jumpy plot; the result is an occasionally ambitious but almost comically uneven effort. Byrne and Bryan Brown do nice work; Dillon is unconvincing.

REBEL OF SHAOLIN

See *Shaolin Traitor*

REBEL OF THE ROAD

See *Hotrod*

REBEL WITHOUT A CAUSE ☆☆☆☆
1955, USA
James Dean, Natalie Wood, Sal Mineo, Jim Backus, Dennis Hopper, Nick Adams, Ann Doran. Directed by Nicholas Ray. 111 min.

The acting careers of James Dean, Natalie Wood, and Sal Mineo were all cut short by unfortunate deaths, but not before they had made a lasting impression together on film as three troubled teenagers at odds with their middle-class world. It starts out slowly, but once viewers have climbed safely aboard, director Nicholas Ray's exploration of adolescent alienation picks up, managing to be both turbulent and sensitive. Dean's character is truly absorbing, complemented well by the others. The shadowy, disorienting cinematography effectively intensifies the mood of the film, but Ray's compositions are lopped at the edges of the small screen.

RECKLESS ☆½
1984, USA, R
Aidan Quinn, Daryl Hannah, Adam Baldwin, Kenneth McMillan, Cliff De Young, Lois Smith, Dan Hedeya. Directed by James Foley. 93 min.

This flashy, empty-headed high school romance looks as if it was made for MTV, and is about as well acted as an average rock video. Aidan Quinn plays a rebel given to sullen fits in which he pretends to drive his motorcycle over a cliff. Daryl Hannah is a popular girl unhappy with her crowd and looking for a "real" man. Finally, they have perfect, glossy sex in a pool and a boiler room. Ah, high school. Both principals look as if they've been attending for about eleven years, but that's almost a convention of the teen-dream genre. This one is strictly for adolescent wishful thinkers.

RECKLESS DISREGARD ☆☆½
1985, USA (TV)
Leslie Nielsen, Tess Harper, Frank Adamson, Ronny Cox, Kate Lynch, Henry Ramer, Sean McCann. Directed by Harvey Hart. 94 min.

This is an interesting, provocative made-for-cable drama in the journalist-bashing genre. Leslie Nielsen plays a crusading TV reporter on a show called "Hourglass" (no resemblance to "60 Minutes" intended, we swear) whose report on a clinic that issues unnecessary medical prescriptions destroys the reputation of an innocent doctor (no resemblance to a lawsuit filed against Dan Rather—really). A good cast makes it work, and there's plenty of food for thought even if Charlie Haas's teleplay stacks the deck more than it should.

THE RED BALLOON ☆☆☆☆
1956, France
Pascal Lamorisse. Directed by Albert Lamorisse. 34 min.

This classic French children's fable about a sensitive grade-schooler who's befriended by a magical red balloon, much to the bemusement (and jealousy) of his fellow kids, is a lyrical, surprisingly moody fantasy that was once part of every child's movie-going experience, and should be again.

RED DAWN ☆½
1984, USA, PG-13
Patrick Swayze, C. Thomas Howell, Lea Thompson, Powers Boothe, Charlie Sheen, Harry Dean Stanton. Directed by John Milius. 114 min.

In John Milius's hands, a politically audacious premise—the first full-scale Soviet invasion of the United States—becomes a dull, plodding adventure fantasy about eight down-jacketed high-schoolers who take on the combined forces of Cuba, Nicaragua, and the Russian army. The movie is nothing more than an overscaled grade B combat flick with our righteous young renegades hiding out in the Rocky Mountain wilderness, picking off some Russians, trekking through endless fields of wheat, blowing up a few more Russians, and so on. Milius obviously thinks he's saying something important about honor, might, and our loss of military will, but his story is so farfetched, his characters so bland and one-dimensional, that even right-wingers in the audience may have to psych themselves up to cheer. Worst of all, on a very mean subtextual level this movie seems to be about a gang of isolationist white supremacists conducting raids on black and Hispanic towns.

RED FLAG: THE ULTIMATE GAME ☆☆☆
1981, USA (TV)
William Devane, Barry Bostwick, Joan Van Ark, George Coe, Debra Feuer, Fred McCarren, Linden Chiles. Directed by Don Taylor. 100 min.

A sharp teleplay and persuasive performances add up to an adventure tale with bite. A lot of macho myths about courage under fire and the nature of warfare are given an acute analysis in this rugged action yarn about two feuding fighter pilots involved in war games. Old hostilities don't fade away as their mutual antagonism resurfaces with deadly results during the fighter-pilot training missions that they're in charge of.

THE RED HOUSE ☆☆☆
1947, USA
Edward G. Robinson, Lon McCallister, Judith Anderson, Rory Calhoun, Julie London, Allene Roberts. Directed by Delmer Daves. 100 min.

An embittered cripple tries to curb his ward's natural curiosity about a dank dwelling; soon she and her boyfriend embark on an investigation of the red house that nearly costs them their lives. The film won an Academy Award for best original story, but today the plot line has been done to death in dozens of TV movies. Eerie occurrences abound on the land surrounding the red house and viewers will have a pretty good time figuring out the mystery. Lots of psychological overtones replace the usual floating ghosts and clawed hands coming out of the wall that customarily frequent these stormy-night chillers; this is a more thoughtful haunted house movie in which a crime from the past haunts the lives of the characters in the present. There are enough red herrings and shudders to keep the melodrama bubbling throughout.

THE RED-LIGHT STING ☆½
1984, USA (TV)
Farrah Fawcett, Beau Bridges, Harold Gould. Directed by Rod Holcomb. 100 min.

Viewers expecting entertainment are apt to get stung by this inane undertaking. Cops take charge of a brothel in order to move in on some big, bad crooks. Farrah Fawcett still acts with her hairstyle here, and the others are stymied by the flimsy script.

RED NIGHTMARE

See *The Commies Are Coming, The Commies Are Coming*

RED RIVER ☆☆☆☆
1948, USA
John Wayne, Montgomery Clift, Joanne Dru, Walter Brennan, Coleen Gray, John Ireland, Noah Beery, Jr., Harry Carey, Sr., Harry Carey, Jr., Paul Fix, Mickey Kuhn, Chief Yowiachie, Ivan Perry, Ray Hyke. Directed by Howard Hawks. 126 min.

This splendid Western features the remarkable trio of John Wayne, Montgomery Clift, and Walter Brennan. Clift, who became a star after this movie, plays a smart young cowhand who rebels against Wayne's slit-eyed, hardened cattle baron (his foster father) in the midst of an epochal roundup. The movie is remembered for its panoramic shots of cattle on the move, but its real revelation is the complex performance that director Howard Hawks coaxes out of Wayne. The sweeping, rich narrative manages to include a great number of what might seem genre clichés in a lesser work, but Hawks implements them in a way that makes us understand their value as emotional and symbolic underpinnings of almost all Westerns. It's a must-see, even—and perhaps especially—if you've never counted the Western among your favorite film experiences.

THE RED SHOES ☆☆☆½
1948, Great Britain
Moira Shearer, Anton Walbrook, Robert Helpmann. Directed by Michael Powell and Emeric Pressburger. 132 min.

The stunning Technicolor photography by Jack Cardiff and Moira Shearer's exquisite dancing are the best-remembered elements of *The Red Shoes*, but a recent appraisal reveals a more complex and rich narrative than originally supposed. The tale of the young ballet star's troubled relationship with all but her driving force, the dance, is given depth by Anton Walbrook as the seemingly heartless ballet master. Walbrook achieves much of the witty sadness that infuses his performance in the later Max Ophuls films. Shearer, although not a consummate actress, does project an unusually strong combination of natural charm and determination. Further, her dancing is not only technically superb but she is also able to remain in character while doing the ballet pieces. Michael Powell had flirted with undercurrents of despair and misery in some of his earlier genteel comedies, but *The Red Shoes* emerges as one of the best examples of a film that has more depth than its many fans either know or acknowledge.

REDS
1981, USA, PG ☆☆☆☆
Warren Beatty, Diane Keaton, Edward Herrmann, Jerzy Kosinski, Jack Nicholson, Paul Sorvino, Maureen Stapleton, Gene Hackman. Directed by Warren Beatty. 196 min.

This is a large-scale (over three hours) epic based on the life and times of Communist journalist John Reed. The plot covers his journey from Greenwich Village to Petrograd, his romance with columnist Louise Bryant, his takeover of the fractured Communist party and his imprisonment in a Russian jail. The film emphasizes the sweep and romance, over the far more interesting political intrigue. Beatty, likable as Reed (he won the Best Director Oscar) and Diane Keaton, superb as Bryant, are equaled by the supporting cast, which includes Jack Nicholson (nominated for the Best Supporting Actor Oscar as Eugene O'Neill), Jerzy Kosinski, Maureen Stapleton (won the Best Supporting Actress Oscar as Emma Goldman) and Gene Hackman. The film's best moments, however, are a series of interviews with real-life acquaintances of Reed. Some of the familiar faces include Henry Miller, Adela Rogers St. Johns, Will Durant, and George Jessel. Their colorful commentary reminds us how inadequate most screen biographies are in re-creating famous chapters from history.

RED SONJA
1985, USA, PG-13 ☆½
Arnold Schwarzenegger, Brigitte Nielsen, Sandahl Bergman, Paul Smith, Ronald Lacey. Directed by Richard Fleischer. 89 min.

Even the sword 'n' sorcery crowd, a notoriously undiscriminating lot, will be bored with this film about a female version of Conan the Barbarian. The character was created by Conan's Robert E. Howard, but the blame here lies with screenwriter George MacDonald Fraser, who should stick to writing pulp fiction—he fails to pick up on either the camp humor or the action potential of the material. Nor does director Richard Fleischer, who managed to make *Conan the Destroyer* an enjoyable romp, help matters with his unflagging literalness. On the other hand, it could have been worse—Brigitte Nielsen could have insisted that her future husband, Sylvester Stallone, play the Schwarzenegger part.

REEFER MADNESS
1936, USA, PG ☆☆
Dave O'Brien, Dorothy Short, Warren McCollum, Lillian Miles, Carleton Young, Thelma White. Directed by Louis Gasnier. 67 min.

This is the famous, antique antimarijuana tract that dramatizes the dangers of the devil weed by showing stoned kids turning into perverts, zombies and murderers. Amusing at times, but the combination of misinformation and exploitation in a film about drugs is dispiriting, no matter how campy the intent or execution. Even in 1936, the opium den scenes must have seemed farfetched; our favorite is the manic stint at the piano by one of the dazed teens. (a.k.a.: *Tell Your Children, The Burning Question, Doped Youth,* and *Dope Addict*)

REFLECTIONS IN A GOLDEN EYE
1967, USA ☆☆½
Marlon Brando, Elizabeth Taylor, Brian Keith, Julie Harris, Robert Forster, Zorro David. Directed by John Huston. 109 min.

An interesting failure from John Huston. Adapting Carson McCullers's novel of the repressed emotions of a homosexual colonel, his wife, and a young private at a Southern army post, the director, for the first hour, manages to create an extraordinary atmosphere of seething, hidden passion about to explode—by the time you realize that absolutely nothing is going to emerge from this ominous portent, the film's almost over. The plot swirls around a gallery of Georgia gothics, drained of the humanity they had on the page and left merely grotesque. Best among them are Elizabeth Taylor, bitchy, funny, and vital as the colonel's frustrated wife, and Brian Keith, as the weak-willed hypocrite with whom she has an affair. In the pivotal role of the half-mad colonel, however, Marlon Brando is irredeemably awful; emoting robotically and mumbling through a misconceived accent, he seems not to have seen his lines before the cameras rolled. (The part was originally to have gone to Montgomery Clift, who might have been brilliant.) On balance, *Reflections* is less interesting for what it says than for how it says it, and it is, in spite of its flaws, well worth a look for film buffs. *Note*: The videocassette version is in full Technicolor, not the de-saturated semi-Sepia tint that was originally used.

REFORM SCHOOL GIRLS
1986, USA, R ☆☆½
Linda Carol, Wendy O. Williams, Sybil Danning, Pat Ast. Directed by Tom DeSimone. 94 min.

Since every women's prison picture is a tongue-in-cheek creation by its very nature, any attempt at parodying this infamous genre has to end up being another repetition of the formula, with exaggerated emphasis on the old familiar cliches for comic effect. Which is exactly what *Reform School Girls* is, fusing the plots of two of the best babes-behind-bars movies, *Caged* and *Caged Heat*, and spiking the mixture with several inspired additions. Principal among these is the ingenious triple-threat casting of Andy Warhol star Pat Ast, exploitation perennial Sybil Danning, and punk star Wendy O. Williams as three of the evil ladies governing the school's activities. The school itself is populated by a bevy of well-aged minors who model various looks in lingerie while reciting dialogue that would make John Waters proud. Director Tom DeSimone already trod this ground with *The Concrete Jungle*, so even when the proceedings aren't funny, they qualify as top-notch exploitation fare.

REHEARSAL FOR MURDER
1982, USA (TV) ☆☆☆
Robert Preston, Lynn Redgrave, Patrick Macnee, Lawrence Pressman, William Russ, Madolyn Smith, Jeff Goldblum, William Daniels. Directed by David Greene. 104 min.

"Columbo" creators Richard Levinson and William Link coauthored this clever, elegant whodunit, set in a Broadway theater where a playwright (Robert Preston) stages a reading of his newest work, aiming to identify and trap the killer of his leading lady (Lynn Redgrave). An intricate flashback-and-fantasy structure will keep you guessing about the characters and incidents down to the last minute. Though not quite as sharp as the team's earlier *Murder by Natural Causes*, this entry is still a savory mystery of a kind too rarely seen, evoking genuine suspense. Winner of a Mystery Writers of America Award.

THE REINCARNATION OF PETER PROUD
1975, USA, R ☆☆½
Michael Sarrazin, Jennifer O'Neill, Margot Kidder, Corneila Sharpe, Paul Hecht. Directed by J. Lee Thompson. 104 min.

Max Erlich's best-seller becomes a promising screen thriller that loses some steam in the final quarter. Michael Sarrazin is the man who realizes he has lived before and just happens to hook up with the daughter of his former wife. The suspense mounts continuously and Margot Kidder gives a challenging performance.

REMEMBER MY NAME
1978, USA ☆☆½
Geraldine Chaplin, Anthony Perkins, Moses Gunn, Berry Berenson, Jeff Goldblum, Alfre Woodard. Directed by Alan Rudolph. 95 min.

Alan Rudolph was Robert Altman's protégé before he began directing, and in this odd, elliptical drama about a "wronged" woman who gets out of jail and reinvades the life of her ex-husband, Altman's influence shows. Full of ominous pauses and incomprehensible behavior, *Remember My Name* is despicably pretentious at times. What makes it involving, however, are the weirdly intense performances of Geraldine Chaplin and Anthony Perkins and the lush, evocative blues score performed by Alberta Hunter. Rudolph has a good eye for detail but little narrative sense, and thus the fringes and subplots of his movie are often more interesting than the shallow and derivative story at its center.

REMO WILLIAMS: THE ADVENTURE BEGINS... ☆½
1985, USA, PG-13
Fred Ward, Joel Grey, Wilford Brimley, J.A. Preston, George Coe, Charles Cioffi, Kate Mulgrew. Directed by Guy Hamilton. 121 min.

Logy, dispiriting macho-man fantasy. Remo Williams (Fred Ward) is a New York cop who's plucked from the rank and file by a top-secret government organization and given a new identity. Our hero comes under the tutelage of a Korean Zen-discipline master (Joel Grey) who spends an hour teaching him to dodge bullets from five feet away. And how does the Zen secret agent use his new knowledge? Why, he goes out and blows the villain to smithereens. Ward is a lusty, freewheeling actor, but he and Grey (as a sub-*Karate Kid* guru) have zero rapport. Based on the popular series of *Destroyer* novels, *Remo Williams* cried out to be a zippy, fanciful yarn, but Guy Hamilton, who made *Goldfinger*, directed it in the slack, grungy cop-movie-style of a dozen low-grade Frank Sinatra thrillers.

THE RENDEZVOUS OF WARRIORS ☆
Hong Kong
Betty Ting Pei, Paul Chiang, Pai Ying. Directed by Jimmy Shaw Fung.

This modern-day story concerns a double-cross. Betty Ting Pei pays her boyfriend to kill her "business associates." In the end they all end up as dead as the plot.

RENEGADE MONK ☆☆
Liu Chung Liang (John Liu), Hwang Hsing Shaw, Ko Shou Liang, Kar Yang, Liu Ming. Directed by Chang Shin I.

An exciting manhunt for a killer monk is peppered with super fight scenes. Unfortunately, a dreary subplot about a princess and a peasant slows up the action, and the production is cluttered with special effects. It's a disappointing kung fu opus.

REPO MAN ☆☆☆½
1984, USA, R
Emilio Estevez, Harry Dean Stanton, Tracey Walter, Vonetta McGee. Directed by Alex Cox. 92 min.

Emilio Estevez, all bulging eyes and clenched fists, makes a hysterically tense protégé for the laid-back repo king (Harry Dean Stanton). This is car-culture craziness with a razor-sharp edge. Surreally seedy Edge City rocks with thrill-crazy punks, nihilistic automobile repossessers, lobotomized scientists, secret government, agents, and a stolen 1960 Chevrolet Malibu worth $20,000. It's a picture about the real weirdness underneath the surface weirdness, that does for Los Angeles and its "white suburban punks" what *Liquid Sky* did for Soho artists.

REPULSION ☆☆☆½
1965, Great Britain
Catherine Deneuve, Ian Hendry, John Fraser, Patrick Wymark. Directed by Roman Polanski. 105 min.

Roman Polanski's direction is at its best in this macabre, erotic story of a woman torn between her craving for and loathing of men. Her psychopathic tendencies are revealed detail by detail in a suspense-filled horror tale of alarmingly skilled perversity. Catherine Deneuve is hauntingly beautiful and perfectly cast in the challenging role of the unhinged young woman, and Gerard Brach's screenplay has been worked out with a care and intelligence unusual in this genre. Some of the special effects are genuinely startling.

RETURN FROM WITCH MOUNTAIN ☆☆½
1978, USA, G
Bette Davis, Christopher Lee, Kim Richards, Ike Eisenman. Directed by John Hough. 93 min.

Returning from an extraterrestrial vacation, Kim Richards and Ike Eisenman reprise their alien personae of Disney's stellar-grossing *Escape to Witch Mountain*. Here they are pitted against Christopher Lee and an admirably feisty Bette Davis (it was Ray Milland in the first one) who want to twist the sacred siblings' powers to their evil ends: namely, the takeover and exploitation of Earth. The climax comes where it should—in a faceoff near the end—and the road there is Disney-smooth, but *Return* lacks the naive freshness and preadolescent appeal of the original.

THE RETURN OF A MAN CALLED HORSE ☆☆☆½
1976, USA, PG
Richard Harris, Gale Sondergaard, Geoffrey Lewis, Bill Lucking, Jorge Luke. Directed by Irvin Kershner. 129 min.

In this flawlessly directed sequel to *A Man Called Horse*, Richard Harris plays an advocate of Indian rights who refuses to remain in his comfortable life-style and tries instead to improve the lot of his blood brothers, the Yellow Sioux, who've suffered the exploitation of the white man for years. The penetration of the Indian mystique is so much more powerful than we're used to from Hollywood's customary treatment of Indians that the film practically overwhelms the audience—it has the ring of truth. Followed by a sequel, *Triumphs of a Man Called Horse*.

RETURN OF BRUCE ☆
Hong Kong
Bruce Le (Huang Kin-Lung), Meng Fei, Lo Lieh, Chaing Tao, Chang Li, Elizabeth Oropesa, Gina Velasco, James Nam. Directed by Joseph Velasco.

After killing a gangster in a fight, Bruce escapes to Manila to search for his parents. While there, he is involved with white slavery. This is below average, but what Bruce-imitator movie isn't?

THE RETURN OF FRANK CANNON ☆½
1980, USA (TV)
William Conrad, Allison Argo, Arthur Hill, Burr DeBenning, Joanna Pettet, Diana Muldaur. Directed by Corey Allen. 96 min.

Those who miss the exploits of the portly detective will no doubt be glad he's back. Others may be hard put not to snore through this attempt at reviving the "Cannon" series. This time, the Orson Welles of sleuths abandons retirement to solve the riddle of an old buddy's apparent suicide. Better Cannon should have played cards with Barnaby Jones in the Old Detectives Home than have come back in this uninspired mystery.

RETURN OF FRANK JAMES ☆☆☆½
1940, USA
Henry Fonda, Gene Tierney, Jackie Cooper, Henry Hull, John Carradine, J. Edward Bromberg, Donald Meek, Lloyd Corrigan. Directed by Fritz Lang. 92 min.

Fritz Lang's tense, terse direction makes this a superior sequel to 1939's *Jesse James*. Beginning with the ending of that film, in which the Ford Brothers gun down Jesse despite his attempts to lead a straight life, this follows older brother Frank as he leaves his farm to track down the killers and even the score. Given Lang's past penchant for the theme of revenge, it would have been interesting to see what he could have done with this were he not hampered by the Hays Code restrictions that an outlaw could not be portrayed in too sympathetic a light. It's a good job nevertheless.

THE RETURN OF MARTIN GUERRE ★★★½
1982, France
Gerard Depardieu, Bernard Pierre Donnadieu, Nathalie Baye, Roger Planchon, Maurice Jacquemont, Isabelle Sadoyan. Directed by Daniel Vigne. 111 min.

Gerard Depardieu stars in this intelligent adaptation of the famous, true story of a weak sixteenth-century peasant who returns home strong, lively, and lusty after years away at war. His reappearance and metamorphosis are celebrated until, despite the entreaties of his adoring wife, he is called to trial for impersonation. Depardieu is completely convincing as the French villager, and the film is exceptionally attractive, with historically accurate evocations of the dress and life-style of the period. Director Daniel Vigne uses this still-fascinating story as a vehicle for a poignant statement on marriage and relationships. Available on videocassette in both dubbed and subtitled versions.

RETURN OF THE BADMEN ★½
1948, USA
Randolph Scott, Robert Ryan, Anne Jeffreys, George "Gabby" Hayes, Jacqueline White. Directed by Ray Enright. 89 min.

This Western version of *Destroy All Monsters* assembles all the great bad guys from the frontier for a dramatic encounter with the virtuous and retired lawman Vance (Randoph Scott). The action centers on the confrontation between Vance and an incredibly sadistic Sundance Kid. All in all, it's like taking on all those goons from your high school class, only this time you've got the upper hand.

RETURN OF THE DRAGON ★★½
1973, Hong Kong, R
Bruce Lee, Nora Miao, Chuck Norris. Directed by Bruce Lee. 90 min.

Bruce Lee preens, struts, and directs himself in the story of a Hong Kong bumpkin who comes to Rome to help protect a family restaurant. The melodramatic story may be silly, the sets cheesy, the 1970s fashions tacky, the music a rip-off of a Morricone score, but everything is saved by the kinetic perfection of Bruce Lee, martial artiste. Lee is blindingly fast and his kung fu is believable, precisely exaggerated, and vicious. Unfortunately, his fight sequences, particularly his dazzling nunchaka work, are cropped by the squeeze down to television size, and video viewers will miss seeing where blows land. The Coliseum showdown with Chuck Norris is a classic, especially the moment where Lee reaches in and grabs a handful of Norris's blond chest pelt. The print used for the videotape is very grainy and the dubbing job is only fair.

RETURN OF THE FLY ★★
1959, USA
Vincent Price, Brett Halsey, David Frankham. Directed by Edward L. Bernds. 80 min.

This is the sequel to *The Fly*. If you recall the ending of the original, you will no doubt think it highly unlikely that the fellow with the fly's head would be doing any returning, and you're right; in the best monster-movie tradition, it's his son mucking around with the same matter-transporter stuff that got his father in trouble. The movie is predictable but has several good scenes. Director Edward L. Bernds made a lot of Bowery Boys and Three Stooges films.

RETURN OF THE JEDI ★★★
1983, USA
Mark Hamill, Harrison Ford, Carrie Fisher, Billy Dee Williams, Anthony Daniels, Peter Mayhew, Sebastian Shaw, Ian McDiarmid, Frank Oz, and various Ewoks. Directed by Richard Marquand. 132 min.

After the empire struck back, you demanded more, and got it. More effects, more monsters, more action—more of the original elements that make the *Star Wars* trilogy so popular. Chapter Three picks up with Hans Solo imprisoned on Carbonite, and his friends involved in a desperate rescue attempt. From the Jabba hut to the moons of Endor, Richard Marquand's self-effacing direction allows the actors and the aliens to shine in their simple but satisfying way. All the mysteries created in the first two films—what's between Hans and Leia or what's betwen Leia and Luke, and just what is the relationship between Luke and this Darth Vader?—find their obvious answers as the crosscutting three-way battle climax grinds the entire saga to a rightful and blessed end.

RETURN OF THE KUNG FU DRAGON ★★½
1978
Tsai Hon, Ling Feng, Cheng Lik, Tung Li Chuan Yun, Tien Yei. Directed by Yu Chik-Lim.

Mythological and philosophical elements upgrade this kung fu vehicle. It's obvious, however, that the film was made by Confucians because the baddie is (unconvincingly) a Taoist monk. Sound Kung-Fusing? Never mind. Just sit back and enjoy the fancy footwork.

RETURN OF THE LIVING DEAD ★★
1985, USA, R
Clu Gulager, James Karen, Don Calfa, Thom Matthews, Beverly Randolph, John Philbin, Jewel Shepard, Miguel Nunez. Directed by Dan O'Bannon. 91 min.

You've heard of the undead? These are the fun dead. A lab manager messes with canisters containing the corpses from *Night of the Living Dead* and the stiffs come to life and start looking for parties to crash. They find one at a nearby graveyard, where they munch on the brains of some mohawked punks as music by the Cramps, the Damned, and the Flesheaters plays on the soundtrack. Scientists join the punks, then medics and cops join punks and scientists, and all end up as meals for the zombies. Not to be confused with George Romero's living dead films, this outing is more send-up than remake, and, as such, is only moderately amusing.

THE RETURN OF THE PINK PANTHER ★★★
1975, Great Britain, G
Peter Sellers, Herbert Lom, Christopher Plummer, Catherine Schell, Bert Kwouk, Victor Spinetti, Carol Cleveland. Directed by Blake Edards. 113 min.

After ten years away from the character, Peter Sellers and director Blake Edwards brought back inspector Clouseau when both were at low points in their careers. As usual, the purposely trite mystery plot exists only as a background for Sellers to make shambles out of all around him, in the most pretentious possible way. Running gags include the Inspector's assistant, Kato, whose job it is to keep him on his toes by attacking him at unannounced moments, and Herbert Lom's perpetual sputtering and chagrin as the Inspector's superior officer. It's amusing, if not the best of the series; a warm-up for *The Pink Panther Strikes Back* (1976).

RETURN OF THE RED TIGER ★
Hong Kong
Bruce Le (Huan Kin-Lung), James Nam, Anita Wong, Danny Moor, Peter Ng, Jack Chung, Lisa Lam, Jack Tam. Directed by James Nam. 105 min.

In this exceptionally poor martial arts movie, Bruce Le is a pathetic mute idiot in love with a girl, who gets involved with two rival gangs scheming to steal some microfilm.

RETURN OF THE SECAUCUS SEVEN ★★★½
1980, USA
Mark Arnott, Gordon Clapp, Maggie Cousineau, Adam Lefevre, Bruce MacDonald, Jean Passanante, Maggie Renzi. Directed by John Sayles. 100 min.

John Sayles wrote and directed this exhilarating, funny drama (made for $60,000) centering on seven former 1960s activists who gather at a New Hampshire farmhouse and try to come to terms with their friendships, careers, and the end of hippie idealism. The film, Sayles's directorial debut, spawned a series of slicker remakes that peaked with *The Big Chill* and quickly fell off to lesser rehashes like *St. Elmo's Fire* and *Windy City*. Sayles's imaginative direction and intelligent script, and the rough but spirited performances by the largely unknown actors make this one of the finest examples of American independent filmmaking.

THE RETURN OF THE SOLDIER ☆☆☆½
1982, Great Britain, PG
Alan Bates, Glenda Jackson, Julie Christie, Ann-Margret, Ian Holm, Frank Finlay. Directed by Alan Bridges. 101 min.

Shell-shocked in World War I, a British army captain suffers from a peculiar form of amnesia that blots out all of his post-adolescent life. Having suddenly forgotten all passion for his beautiful, shrewish wife, he wants only to rekindle his teenage affair with a farm girl, now a drab, married woman. Alan Bridges's faithful adaptation of Rebecca West's novel is almost too restrained for its own good but still remarkably perceptive about the class consciousness and emotional repression that formed the fabric of Edwardian society. Alan Bates gives a dignified performance, but it's the three ladies who shine, playing superbly against type. Julie Christie portrays the snobby, venomous wife to perfection, Ann-Margret is astonishingly natural as her plain, timid cousin, and Glenda Jackson does what may be her most restrained work as the soldier's reluctant long-lost love. Bridges's style tends slightly toward the gaseous in a few scenes, but they don't seriously mar this otherwise excellent work.

THE RETURN OF THE TALL BLOND MAN WITH ONE BLACK SHOE ☆☆☆
1974, France, PG
Pierre Richard, Jean Rochefort, Mireille Darc, Yves Robert, Jean Carmet, Paul le Person. Directed by by Yves Robert. 89 min.

This sequel to (you guessed it) *The Tall Blond Man with One Black Shoe* is a notch below the original but still more than satisfactory for fans of Pierre Richard's shambling charm. The same spies who made life hell for innocent violinist Francois in the earlier film are back, once again using him as a pawn to wipe each other out. As in most any Pierre Richard film, most of the humor comes from his character's inability to deal with everyday situations, coupled with his singularly unwarranted self-confidence. Written by Francis Veber (*La Cage aux Folles, La Chevre*).

RETURN OF THE TIGER ☆☆
1976
Ho Sung-Tao (Bruce Li), Paul Smith, Angela Mao Ying, Chang I, Lung Fei, Hsieh Hsing. Directed by Jimmy Shaw.

Bruce Li ("Bruce Lee's successor") goes undercover in Taiwan, assisted by a female cop. There are decent fight scenes, but it's really just another cash-in on Bruce Lee's name without the real chun-tzu. (a.k.a.: *Silent Killer from Eternity*)

RETURN OF THE VAMPIRE ☆☆½
1943, USA
Bela Lugosi, Frieda Inescort, Nina Foch, Roland Varno, Miles Mander. Directed by Lew Landers, Kurt Neumann. 69 min.

Universal Studios, the reigning horror producers of the 1930s and 1940s, never exploited the Dracula character the way they did their other monsters, although they held the copyright. This put quite a crimp in the career of Bela Lugosi, who was so strongly identified with the Count but in fact only played him three times in the movies—in the original *Dracula*, the 1946 parody *Abbott and Costello Meet Frankenstein*, and here (although for contractual reasons the character is named "Armand Tesla"). Revived when a Nazi bomb disinters him, Lugosi goes through his paces in the foggy streets of London accompanied by a werewolf assistant. Surprisingly well-done for a low-budget thriller, especially considering that director Lew Landers made eight other movies that year!

RETURN TO EARTH ☆☆☆
1976, USA (TV)
Cliff Robertson, Ralph Bellamy, Shirley Knight, Charles Cioffi. Directed by Jud Taylor, 78 min.

This is a compelling biographical film based on the true story of Buzz Aldrin, who had a difficult time putting both his feet back on the ground after his heady, heroic adventures in outer space. The film examines Aldrin's breakdown after he fails to readjust to civilian life after the high of having made his famous moon walk of 1969. It's a sincere drama, owing mostly to Cliff Robertson's ability to convey Aldrin's self-doubts with such conviction.

RETURN TO MACON COUNTY ☆½
1975, USA, PG
Nick Nolte, Don Johnson, Robin Mattson, Robert Viharo, Eugene Daniels, Matt Greene, Devon Ericson. Directed by Richard Compton. 89 min.

If you saw *Macon County Line*, then you know that a sequel wasn't really possible—this is more of a variation on the same theme (two buddies venture down South and are wrongly accused of something or other), but with an all-new cast. Nick Nolte and Don Johnson, before their success, make a good pair, but there's nothing remotely suspenseful or exciting about the meandering plot. It's much more reminiscent of a Burt Reynolds car-chase comedy than of the *Walking Tall*-style of hard, cold meanness that made the first film a surprising success. The change from an R to a PG rating just about tells the whole story.

RETURN TO OZ ☆☆½
1985, USA, PG
Fairuza Balk, Nicol Williamson, Jean Marsh, Piper Laurie, Matt Clark. Directed by Walter Murch. 110 min.

This lackluster Disney follow-up to MGM's classic *The Wizard of Oz* has Dorothy returning to the magical land of Oz, which she discovers has been turned to stone by the evil Gnome King. After gathering an odd assortment of friends, including a robot and a talking pumpkin head, Dorothy tries to restore the city to life. Even though it's beautifully made and acted, the film lacks the proper energy and pace to make itself really interesting. It's a disappointment, considering all the time and love that have gone into this mammoth project. Former sound man Walter Murch has done a wonderful job of depicting author L. Frank Baum's mystical world, but he never really brings it to life. There are some remarkable special effects, including the realistic puppetry and animation techniques.

REUBEN, REUBEN ☆☆☆
1983, USA, R
Tom Conti, Kelly McGillis, Roberts Blossom, Cynthia Harris, E. Katharine Kerr, Kara Wilson. Directed by Robert Miller. 101 min.

Tom Conti earned an Oscar nomination for his wry, charming performance as Gowan McGland, a minor Scottish poet boozing and seducing his way through the women's club circuit in New England. More a caustic social satire than the comedy it was marketed as, *Reuben* has a deadpan, offhand coldness inherited from Peter De Vries's source novel. McGland is a tough character to get audiences to like, and he is really attractive only in relation to the desolate suburban culture leeches from whom he derives his income, if not most of his identity. The engaging Kelly McGillis does serve as an attractive ideal for the dissolute poet, and Roberts Blossom, playing the character derived from Herman Shulman's play *Spofford*, is genuinely likable in his small role.

REVENGE ★★★
1971, USA (TV)
Shelley Winters, Stuart Whitman, Bradford Dillman, Carol Rossen, Roger Perry. Directed by Jud Taylor. 78 min.

Shelley Winters cuts loose in an obvious but sure-fire gimmick of a script. Not willing to let her daughter's rape go unpunished and not daunted by little matters like taking the law into her own chubby hands, Winters traps the man she suspects inside a cage in her basement and metes out her own punishment. Can you imagine many things scarier than being locked up in the basement by Shelley Winters? But did she lock up the right man? The film is vastly entertaining due to a taut script and to that divine ham, Shelley.

REVENGE OF THE CHEERLEADERS ½★
1976, USA, R
Jerii Woods, Rainbeaux (Cheryl) Smith, Helen Lang, Carl Ballantine. Directed by Richard Lerner. 88 min.

Cheerleaders save the school, if not the movie, by giving their mischievous all to foil a dastardly plot. Carl Ballantine is hammily effective as the wacked-out principal. The story is a drag, there's no sex (really), and all of the jokes (loosely defined) are weak double entendres.

REVENGE OF THE DEAD

See *Night of the Ghouls*

REVENGE OF THE DRAGON ★★
Hong Kong
Alexander Lou, Liu Hau Yi, Lou Chun, Tien Lung, Yang Hsiung, Chien Hsun, Wang Hau, Tsing Kuo Chung. Directed by Robert Tai.

Kids and kung fu! What could be better, or more wholesome? A group of children survive a massacre and learn kung fu in order to exact a violent revenge. Fortunately, all of the children in this movie are phenomenal kung fu performers.

REVENGE OF THE NERDS ★★★
1984, USA, R
Robert Carradine, Julie Montgomery, Anthony Edwards, Curtis Armstrong, Ted McGinley, Bernie Casey, Michelle Meyrink. Directed by Jeff Kanew. 90 min.

After forming their own fraternity, a kind of Animal House for dorks, the freshman nerds at Adams College unite to fight off the local jocks and jockettes. There are the inevitable scenes with guys who wear plastic pen holders and abominably ugly glasses making fools of themselves, yet the makers of this enormously friendly—and witty—teen sex comedy actually get you to care about their social-misfit heroes. From the "hip" Beatles poster that adorns the fraternity to Robert Carradine's painfully unspontaneous guffaw, the movie milks for all it's worth the nerds' desperate desire to fit into the mainstream.

REVENGE OF THE NINJA ★★★
1983, USA, R
Sho Kosugi, Keith Vitali, Virgil Frye, Arthur Roberts. Directed by Sam Firstenberg. 88 min.

This is great martial arts fun that's an *Indiana Jones*–like machine of thrills and action. A former master ninja moves to America after his family is wiped out, then finds himself embroiled in a heroin-smuggling operation led by a rival, an extremely nasty ninja. Lots of fights ensue, all of which are well staged by Kosugi. The final fifteen-minute confrontation between the ninja is a stunner.

THE REVENGE OF THE PINK PANTHER ★★½
1978, Great Britain, PG
Peter Sellers, Herbert Lom, Robert Webber, Dyan Cannon, Burt Kwouk. Directed by Blake Edwards. 99 min.

The fifth Blake Edwards-Peter Sellers Pink Panther film is, aside from the first (in which Sellers was only a supporting character) the most tedious. You know exactly what Clouseau is going to do (and say) well in advance, a built-in fault that Edwards tries to overcome by making the gags bigger and better. Unfortunately, all this does is to take one medium-size laugh and spread it out over a longer period of time than it can bear. Plot, as usual, is almost meaningless in the face of Sellers's continual fumblings, overblown contrivances, and mispronunciations.

REVENGE OF THE STEPFORD WIVES ★★
1980, USA (TV)
Sharon Gless, Julie Kavner, Audra Lindley, Don Johnson, Arthur Hill, Mason Adams, Ellen Weston. Directed by Robert Fuest. 104 min.

This TV-movie follow-up is an unnecessary extension of a film that was not exactly a masterpiece to begin with. Those soulless housewives finally rebel against the chauvinist mentality that's turned their suburban paradise into a Disneyland of sexist fantasies. The primary appeal of this none-too-sexy picture is catching TV stars Sharon Gless and Don Johnson in their journeyman days; Gless is, as always, a sexy and striking presence, but Johnson demonstrates that only a rare and serendipitous series of events could have propelled him to stardom. Followed by another made-for-TV sequel, *The Stepford Children*, in 1987.

THE REVENGE OF THE TEENAGE VIXENS FROM OUTER SPACE ★
1986, USA
Lisa Schwedop, Howard Scott, Amy Crumpacker, Sterling Ramberg, Julian Schembri. Directed by Jeff Farrell. 84 min.

Yes, the terrible title of this independent film is meant as a spoof of cheap 1950's sci-fi, as is the film itself, but it's hard to parody a genre that itself provides such a full measure of humor. Female aliens arrive on our planet hungry for some down-to-earth sex, but interpersonal contact with them proves to have some nasty side effects. Cheap and slipshod.

REVOLT OF THE ZOMBIES ★★
1936, USA
Dorothy Stone, Dean Jagger, Roy D'Arcy, Robert Noland, George Cleveland. Directed by Douglas Biggs. 62 min.

An early horror film set in, of all places, Cambodia, where an expeditionary team is dispatched to squelch a revolting tribe of zombies. A corny, awful romantic plot is tough to sit through, but the zombies themselves are amusing, careening in all directions and not terribly scary.

REVOLUTION ★★
1985, USA/Great Britain, PG
Al Pacino, Donald Sutherland, Nastassja Kinski, Annie Lennox. Directed by Hugh Hudson. 123 min.

This retelling of the American Revolution, directed by Englishman Hugh Hudson, is visually spectacular but bloated and boring. As a colonist who doesn't want to get involved, an incredibly miscast Al Pacino rolls his eyes and wanders through the anarchistic colonies with his son, finding himself at every battle important in the founding of the United States. The alternately elegant and grimy settings all feel right and the jerky camera movements give the film a needed sense of immediacy, but what's being done and said on the screen is idiotic. Hudson envisions the colonists as a gruff but noble people, while the British are portrayed as the kind of hideously sneering villains who deserve violent death. Unfortunately, *Revolution* has only a few moments when the bad guys get their comeuppances, and the beautiful scenery can't compensate for the overwhelmingly narrative mediocrity.

RHINESTONE ☆
1984, USA, PG
Sylvester Stallone, Dolly Parton, Richard Farnsworth, Ron Leibman, Tim Thomerson, Steven Apostle Pec. Directed by Bob Clark. 111 min.

Detractors of the *Rocky* series probably wish this film had ended Sylvester Stallone's film career. (It almost ended Dolly Parton's.) In a reversal of *Easter Parade*, Parton plays a country singer who makes a bet with her lecherous manager (Ron Leibman) that she can turn the first hick she sees into a country star. The hick turns out to be New York cabbie Stallone. Unlike the stars of *Easter Parade*, however, Parton is like a blowup doll with spurs and Stallone's singing evokes painful memories of Clint Eastwood's and Lee Marvin's in *Paint Your Wagon*. Directed by Bob Clark (*Porky's*), the film is laughable—but not funny.

RICH AND FAMOUS ☆☆
1981, USA, R
Candice Bergen, Jacqueline Bisset, Hart Bochner, David Selby, Matt Lattanzi. Directed by George Cukor. 117 min.

George Cukor's last film (he was eighty-two) is something less than a triumphant valedictory; careers don't always end cleanly, and with this film, our foremost women's director was reduced to directing two parodies of actresses. It's a thin, crass update of *Old Acquaintance* about a lifelong rivalry between two women, a cheerfully crude author of trashy best-sellers (Candice Bergen) and a grumpy, unfulfilled serious novelist (Jacqueline Bisset). Some of Cukor's touch is evident; he may be the only director ever to coax a completely unselfconscious, funny performance out of Candice Bergen, who's smart enough to play her character as the cartoon it is. But Bisset, mouthing pretentious lines about what it means to be a writer, is unbearable. This would be satisfying bitchery if someone hadn't given it a post-feminist veneer; the scene in which Bisset goes all mushy as she begins to lust for the succulent young flesh of hustler Matt Lattanzi is an appallingly debased moment, a last, snarled concession to studio dictates from the normally decorous Cukor.

RICHARD PRYOR HERE AND NOW ☆☆☆
1983, USA, R
Richard Pryor. Directed by Richard Pryor. 83 min.

This is another uproarious chapter in what has become the funniest continuing fictional autobiography in American art and entertainment. Richard Pryor's concert film, made months after his near-fatal accident, finds him in a more relaxed mood than we've seen before. The comedian faces up to new stumbling blocks (sobriety and success), and he uses his candor to penetrate sexual and racial "forbidden zones." It's too bad that he only halfheartedly tries to pierce the obfuscating curtains of show biz and celebrity.

RICHARD PRYOR LIVE ON THE SUNSET STRIP ☆☆☆½
1982, USA, R
Richard Pryor. Directed by Joe Layton. 82 min.

Not as funny as *Richard Pryor Live in Concert*, this still has more laughs per minute than almost anything else you're liable to find in your local video store. It's full of Pryor's scathing barbs on sex, racism, and especially himself—this was his return to the screen after nearly burning himself to death freebasing cocaine (which incident provides one of the film's funniest single moments at the end). The only drawback to this is that Pryor spends too much time with a few set pieces that he has obviously worked out carefully. As bits of acting, they're good enough, but they disrupt the tempo, like some aging star's shot for a best supporting Oscar in the middle of an action film. As usual, none of the jokes are reprintable here.

RICHARD III ☆☆☆☆
1956, Great Britain
Laurence Olivier, John Gielgud, Ralph Richardson, Claire Bloom, Alex Clunes, Cedric Hardwicke, Stanley Baker, Pamela Brown, Michael Gough. Directed by Laurence Olivier. 158 min.

This is a stagy, conventional interpretation of middling-good Shakespeare. Why is it a great film? Well, the player's the thing, and Laurence Olivier lights up the screen—limping, plotting, rudely stamping, spitting out lines scarce half made-up, and brimming with conviction. For the illiterati, this is about the scheming, evil, murderous duke who sets out to make himself king. How he achieves it and how he loses it are fascinating, but the real genius—of both Shakespeare and Olivier—is that this consummate villain remains a compelling and irresistible character.

RICHES AND ROMANCE

See *The Amazing Adventure*

THE RIDDLE OF THE SANDS ☆☆
1978, Great Britain
Michael York, Jenny Agutter, Simon MacCorkindale, Alan Badel. Directed by Tony Maylam. 98 min.

Adapting a turn-of-the-century adventure by Erskine Childers, considered to be the first modern spy novel, director Tony Maylam has fashioned a dull, distressingly drab suspense film. Michael York plays a bored foreign service officer whose vacation on a yacht turns into international intrigue as he uncovers a German plot to invade England. He and Jenny Agutter (reteaming after *Logan's Run*) are an attractive pair, and the plot is clever, but viewers used to the brisker pace of more contemporary thrillers may find it tedious.

RIDERS OF DESTINY ☆½
1933, USA
John Wayne, Cecelia Parker, George "Gabby" Hayes, Al "Fuzzy" St. John. Directed by R.N. Bradbury. 66 min.

John Wayne plays a government agent sent to work out a water controversy. Weak story, OK horses.

RIDERS OF THE ROCKIES ☆½
1938, USA
Tex Ritter, Yakima Canutt. Directed by R.N. Bradbury. 59 min.

Singing cowpoke Tex Ritter goes after bad guys on the frontier; good Tex, but standard oats opera.

RIDE THE HIGH COUNTRY ☆☆☆☆
1962, USA
Randolph Scott, Joel McCrea, Mariette Hartley, Ronald Starr, Edgar Buchanan, R. G. Armstrong, Warren Oates, John Anderson, L. Q. Jones. Directed by Sam Peckinpah. 94 min.

Sam Peckinpah's elegiac attitude toward the Western was most fully developed in *The Wild Bunch*, in which an aging gang confronts the beginning of the twentieth century. The seeds of this idea, though, are found in this film, with beautiful photography and inspired performances. Joel McCrea and Randolph Scott bring incalculable history to their roles as aging gunfighters who are on their last job guarding the shipment of gold, and in truth, this was Scott's last film. Peckinpah's story of the passing of time was also the story of the passing of a great film genre, and this is the last great old-fashioned Western. Made in wide screen, it loses a bit of grandeur on tape.

RIDING ON AIR
1937, USA ☆
Joe E. Brown, Guy Kibbee, Florence Rice, Vinton Haworth, Anthony Nace, Harlan Briggs. Directed by Edward Sedgwick. 58 min.

In his adventures here, taken from a series of *Saturday Evening Post* stories, Joe E. Brown plays a small-town newspaperman who gets mixed up with smugglers, a remote-control airplane, and a stock swindler, all on the way to true love. Brown mugs, fumbles, and yowls throughout, and it may be a bit much for nonfans to take.

RIDIN' ON A RAINBOW
1941, USA ☆
Gene Autry, Smiley Burnette, Mary Lett, Carol Adams. Directed by Lew Landers. 76 min.

This movie involves Gene Autry, a bank robbery, and a showboat. It sounds good, but none of it fits together very well. A better script, faster pacing, and some more cattle would have helped.

RIFIFI
1954, France ☆☆☆½
Jean Servais, Carl Mohner, Magali Noel, Jules Dassin, Robert Manuel. Directed by Jules Dassin. 115 min.

A taut, suspenseful progenitor of dozens of robbery caper films since, from *The Killing* to *The Brink's Job*, *Rififi* is still one of the masterpieces of the genre. The planning of a jewel heist is at the center of this drama but, as we all know, there is no honor among thieves, and Jules Dassin's portrayal of the ways in which the petty suspicions and innate distrustfulness of the robbers slowly doom their enterprise makes for compelling viewing.

RIGHT OF WAY
1983, USA (TV) ☆☆
Bette Davis, James Stewart, Melinda Dillon, Priscilla Morrill. Directed by George Schaefer. 106 min.

It's hard to believe that Bette Davis and James Stewart never acted together before *Right of Way*, and it is very disappointing to see them finally united in the service of such an unsuccessful vehicle. Here, they play an old couple who decide to end their lives together when the wife finds out she is dying. In comes their daughter (Melinda Dillon), a social worker who tries to change their minds. It turns into a tedious polemic that leaves its two stars depicted as cutesy oldsters. The film is lamentable for the talent it wastes.

THE RIGHT STUFF
1983, USA, PG ☆☆☆½
Charles Frank, Scott Glenn, Ed Harris, Dennis Quaid, Sam Shepard, Veronica Cartwright, Pamela Reed, Jeff Goldblum. Directed by Philip Kaufman. 193 min.

This is a faithful adaptation of Tom Wolfe's best-selling account of the life and times of the Mercury project astronauts. It is concerned equally with the "hard science" that propelled planes beyond the sound barrier and eventually landed a man on the moon, and with the "technological astrology" that enthralled the American public. There is great ensemble acting, fabulous photography, and a relatively sophisticated approach to the blend of media manipulation and genuine hard work and heroism that conspired to make the Mercury 7 the idols of a generation.

RING OF BRIGHT WATER
1969, Great Britain ☆☆½
Bill Travers, Virginia McKenna, Peter Jeffrey, Jameson Clark. Directed by Jack Couffer. 107 min.

Children young enough to enjoy animal adventures will adore this tale of a man and his pet otter without questioning many of the plot oddities. The production and cinematography are generally superior, and the ending is a real tearjerker, almost too much so for anyone impressionable enough to have watched this far. Based on Gavin Maxwell's book, it was made by some of the same team responsible for *Born Free*.

RIO BRAVO
1959, USA ☆☆☆☆
John Wayne, Dean Martin, Angie Dickinson, Walter Brennan, Ricky Nelson, Ward Bond, Claude Akins. Directed by Howard Hawks. 141 min.

The postwar years marked a time of reexamination for many of Hollywood's most traditional film genres, and *Rio Bravo* was Howard Hawks's most untraditional Western. Shot almost entirely in interiors and eschewing any examination of the myths of the Western frontier, the film studies a small group of men under extreme pressure. John Wayne stars as an aging sheriff attempting to hold a prisoner while under siege from the prisoner's family. Aiding him is his crippled sidekick, played on the edge of comic ridiculousness by Walter Brennan, and his alcoholic ex-deputy, played under control by Dean Martin. In essence, *Rio Bravo* is more a film of the 1950s than it is a Western film. Its themes of characters struggling with their limitations and its notions of social interdependency are concerns that are evident in the contemporary films of Douglas Sirk and Nicholas Ray. The movie draws on many sources, including Jules Furthman's screenplay for the silent film classic *Underworld* and, indeed, the film has a smell of the trapped, urban milieu of the gangster film. The character Feathers, played by Angie Dickinson, is a badly used moll lifted right from the gangster film, and the only real Western figure is John Wayne, a self-conscious icon complete with his belt buckle from *Red River*.

RIO CONCHOS
1964, USA ☆☆
Richard Boone, Stuart Whitman, Tony Franciosa, Wende Wagner, Jim Brown, Vito Scotti, Edmond O'Brien. Directed by Gordon Douglas. 105 min.

This is the kind of Western that Hollywood was making at the time that Sergio Leone was beginning to take apart the genre in Italy with *A Fistful of Dollars*, to which this is an interesting comparison for fans of the Western. Four tough guys in the post-Civil War West, each differently motivated, set out to stop an ex-Confederate officer who is supplying guns to the Apaches as a way of wreaking vengeance on the North. Director Gordon Douglas is big on action, but in the Hollywood tradition: The comparison with Leone is interesting only in order to see how Leone took similar material and reworked it. In short, it's mediocre.

RIO GRANDE
1950, USA ☆☆☆☆
John Wayne, Maureen O'Hara, Ben Johnson, Claude Jarman, Jr., Harry Carey, Jr., Chill Wills, J. Carrol Naish, Victor McLaglen, Sons of the Pioneers. Directed by John Ford. 105 min.

While the cavalry fights the Apaches, family member fights family member in this John Ford classic. When her son drops out of West Point to join his father in the fighting on the Texas frontier, Mrs. Yorke (Maureen O'Hara) arrives at her husband's post determined to take her son back to the military academy. As an actress whose strength equals John Wayne's, O'Hara convincingly portrays a wife who fails to understand her husband's unswerving commitment to military duty; her incomprehension is understandable considering that her husband destroyed her family's Southern home fifteen years earlier during the Civil War. Only her husband's courageous acts, including a daring raid across the Rio Grande and into Mexico to rescue a group of children, place the Colonel's attitude in perspective. The emphasis on familial relationships elevates this film above the boundaries of a simple cowboy picture and places it in the realm of the philosophical, a study of the problematic issues of power and compassion in the family. This is the last of the famous cavalry trilogy begun with *Fort Apache* and continued by *She Wore a Yellow Ribbon*.

RIO LOBO ★★½
1970, USA, G
John Wayne, Jorge Rivero, Jennifer O'Neill, Jack Elam, Mike Henry, Sherry Lansing, Jim Davis, George Plimpton. Directed by Howard Hawks. 114 min.

Careful—don't confuse this with *Rio Bravo* or *El Dorado*, two other Howard Hawks-John Wayne Westerns. This was Hawks's last film, and although it looks like something he could have done in his sleep, members of the Hawks-as-*auteur* cult will tell you that it is a major accomplishment, an opinion they'd hold to even if it turned out that the director was somnambulating when he made it. The story has to do with the Duke as an ex-Civil War colonel out to find the traitors whose actions resulted in the death of one of his younger officers. It's reasonably entertaining, as well as beautifully filmed in the manner of all Hawks Westerns. Jennifer O'Neill proves that she should never been have allowed in front of the kind of camera that takes thirty-two exposures per second, and journalist George Plimpton gets to bark the line, "I got your warrant right here, Sheriff," before being blown away by the Big Guy.

RIOT IN CELL BLOCK 11 ★★★
1954, USA
Neville Brand, Emile Meyer, Frank Faylen, Leo Gordon, Robert Osterloh, Paul Frees. Directed by Don Siegel. 80 min.

This is a compact, effective prison drama about a group of inmates rioting for changes who come up against a system they just can't beat. Director Don Siegel (who also made *Dirty Harry* and the original *Invasion of the Body Snatchers*) doesn't let a scene or a reaction run one second longer than it should, and his furious, tense pace keeps the somewhat familar action exciting. Good ensemble work from the "inmates" and a strong pro-reform slant make it compelling. Producer Walter Wanger reportedly based *Riot* on his own feelings after being jailed for shooting Jennings Lang (at the time, the agent of Wanger's wife Joan Bennett).

THE RIPPER ★
1985, USA
Tom Schreier, Mona Van Pernis, Wade Tower, Tom Savini. Directed by Christopher Lewis. 103 min.

The name of special effects artist Tom Savini, who did all the gore effects for *Dawn of the Dead*, *Friday the 13th*, and numerous others, is prominently featured here, but fans should be warned that he's only here as an actor, and then only for the finale. This made-for-video horror tale is standard slasher stuff, with women killed and disemboweled at regular intervals by a mysterious killer in a small Midwestern city. The target audience for this junk will probably not mind the poor video quality; dull, padded plot; and silly supernatural denouement, but viewers with any sensitivity should stay away.

RISKY BUSINESS ★★
1983, USA, R
Tom Cruise, Rebecca De Mornay, Joe Pantoliano, Richard Masur, Curtis Armstrong, Bronson Pinchot. Directed by Paul Brickman. 99 min.

Young capitalists-in-training in Chicago learn that life can be just a pornographic dream when one of their number, charged with watching over his parents' house in their absence, turns it into a nonstop erotic cabaret with the help of some nubile prostitutes. The movie is slick and ingratiating, with an eerie soundtrack by Tangerine Dream.

RITA HAYWORTH: THE LOVE GODDESS ★½
1983, USA (TV)
Lynda Carter, Michael Lerner, John Considine, Jane Halloren, Alejandro Rey, Aharon Ipale. Directed by James Goldstone. 104 min.

This is a standard rags-to-riches-to-misery TV biographical film that doesn't begin to capture the allure, charisma, and talent that made Rita Hayworth one of Hollywood's most memorable sex symbols. E. Arthur Kean's teleplay starts in 1934, then skids to a halt in 1952, before many of the most dramatic events of its subject's life had occurred. Otherwise, it offers no particular insight, and Lynda Carter isn't nearly the actress or the icon that Hayworth was—her performance is more an impersonation than an interpretation.

THE RITZ ★★★
1976, Great Britain, R
Jack Weston, Jerry Stiller, Rita Moreno, Kaye Ballard, F. Murray Abraham, Paul B. Price, Treat Williams, Bessie Love. Directed by Richard Lester. 91 min.

Richard Lester (*A Hard Day's Night*, *The Three Musketeers*) directed this overblown, uneven, but often funny farce about a man who hides out in a gay bathhouse in order to escape the mobsters sent by his father-in-law. In the posh Manhattan club, he meets an amorous ex-Army buddy, a bad Puerto Rican singer, and the brother-in-law sent to kill him. The jokes in Terrence McNally's screenplay, based on his own play, are hit-and-miss, many crude and obvious, but the cast is ingratiating and the setting original. It is intermittently enjoyable.

RIVALS OF THE DRAGON ½
Hong Kong
Jeffrey Chan, Yuen Tak, Chan Wah Lung, Joseph Yeung, Ken Thomson, Pardon Au, Dickson Wong, Stephen Chiu, Thomas Hope, William Cobalt, Samuel Kent, Lily Taylor. Directed by Yeung Kwan and Florence Yu. 86 min.

Master Chen, a kung fu teacher in California, gets involved with the local gang. The movie tries for laughs but misses.

THE RIVER ★★½
1984, USA, PG-13
Mel Gibson, Sissy Spacek, Shane Bailey, Becky Jo Lynch, Scott Glenn, Don Hood, Billy Green Bush, James Tolkan, Bob W. Douglas. Directed by Mark Rydell. 122 min.

The last of 1984's great rural life trilogy (*Country*, *Places in the Heart*), *The River* washes over the very familiar terrain of a family's desperate struggle to hold onto their land by battling developers, bankers, and high waters. Sissy Spacek dominates the film as the mythic American earth mother, but she cannot give this old mule the kick it needs to get going. Although attentive camerawork gives a detailed account of life down on the farm, it also transforms that hard life into a series of beautiful pictures, which undermines the film's social reality. Mel Gibson's overly reserved acting complicates matters by creating an emotional vacuum. Yet this film does have its brilliant moments, as when the frustrated farmer seeks employment as a scab in a faraway factory. Perhaps as time separates the three farm films, *The River* will be able to stand on its own; right now, it's in third place.

RIVER RAT ★★
1984, USA, PG
Tommy Lee Jones, Martha Plimpton, Brian Dennehy, Shawn Smith, Nancy Lea Owen, Norman Bennett, Tony Frank, Angie Bolling. Directed by Tom Rickman. 93 min.

Coal Miner's Daughter director Tom Rickman returns to the South to combine a Twain riverboat adventure with Cajun mysticism in this small film about a father and his daughter establishing a relationship. Coming home from a thirteen-year jail sentence, Billy meets his daughter for the first time. As the two discover a common bond in their appreciation of the Mississippi, the past reemerges in the figure of a prison psychologist who wants a share of Billy's loot. The combination of a family drama and adventure story makes for enjoyable viewing, but the film suffers from a series of unlikely acts—timely lightning bolts and convenient runaway boats—attributed to supernatural forces. Although the final revelation arrives abruptly, the film, for the most part, glides smoothly along like a pleasant Deep South afternoon spent on the river.

ROAD AGENT ☆
1952, USA
Tim Holt, Noreen Nash, Mauritz Hugo, Dorothy Patrick. Directed by Lesley Selander. 60 min.

In a B-minus Western, hero Tim Holt defends good, honest ranchmen against a dastardly baron who's charging them exorbitant tolls to move their cattle. Without the songs and romance on the range that made the Roy Rogers and Gene Autry series durable fun, there's nothing going for this tiresome, formulaic entry, made as the bottom half of a double bill.

ROAD GAMES ☆☆☆
1981, Australia, PG
Stacy Keach, Jamie Lee Curtis, Marion Edward, Grant Page. Directed by Richard Franklin. 101 min.

While moving a load of pork across the Australian outback, a truck driver who has picked up a hitchhiker begins to notice that one of his fellow motorists has done a number of strange things. He confides his suspicions to his passenger and together they decide to do a little investigating, but she vanishes at their next stopover. In this stylist nightmare road movie with a mean streak, director Richard Franklin brings a fine touch to this exercise in Hitchcockian suspense with a wrong-man twist.

ROADHOUSE 66 ☆½
1984, USA, R
Judge Reinhold, Willem Dafoe, Kate Vernon, Karen Lee. Directed by John Mark Robinson. 94 min.

In this artificial road movie, Judge Reinhold is cast as a preppy who undergoes his rites of passage under the guidance of a burnt-out rocker (Willem Dafoe) and the abuse of a gang of rednecks. Despite all of *Roadhouse*'s blaring vintage music and superfluous car chases, the movie runs out of gas very quickly and by the end of Reinhold's high-octane journey, his character and the film still remain unlikable.

ROAD TO BALI ☆☆½
1952, USA
Bob Hope, Bing Crosby, Dorothy Lamour, Murvyn Vye, Peter Coe, Ralph Moody. Directed by Hal Walker. 91 min.

If you've never seen a Hope-Crosby road movie, this might be a good place to start. The boys are in fine form, trading quips and tunes; it's in color; and there are walk-ons by Humphrey Bogart, Jane Russell, and Martin and Lewis: Think of it as a big, long music video from a strange, ancient culture. It's all mindless fun and very mild sexiness, as our stars become South Seas divers and try to save Princess Dorothy Lamour's treasure. Songs include "Chicago Style," "Moonflowers," and "To See You"—none are awful, but none are memorable.

ROAD TO SALINA ☆☆½
1970, France/Italy, R
Robert Walker, Jr., Rita Hayworth, Mimsey Farmer, Ed Begley, Directed by Georges Lautner. 95 min.

It should be awful—a French-Italian coproduction using post-dubbed American stars and European locations to double for Mexico—but it's not; in fact, it lingers in the memory longer than it deserves to. Robert Walker Jr., the very image of his father, plays an opportunistic drifter who happens by a roadside gas station on the sun-scorched road. Its deluded owner (Rita Hayworth, terrific throughout) thinks he's her long-lost son and treats him like royalty. Her daughter (Mimsy Farmer) knows the guy's a fake, but allows his free ride to continue in exchange for some quasi-incestuous sex. The passages of torrid lovemaking, flashbacks within flashbacks, dazed hippie dialogue, and an overdose of late 1960s disaffection will leave you either mind-tripped, bummed out, or turned off; those who like their drama deliriously convoluted shouldn't miss it.

ROAD WARRIOR ☆☆½
1981, Australia, R
Mel Gibson, Bruce Spence. Directed by George Miller. 95 min.

This slick, violent and endlessly kinetic follow-up to Mad Max is less a sequel than a reworking of the same themes and images with a far more substantial budget, a flashy exercise in the iconography of automobiles and leather men against a barren outback landscape. Max, a former policeman burnt out by personal tragedy and years of wandering around post-apocalypse Australia, helps a ragged group of civilized survivors to escape from a spectacularly vicious gang of cycle savages with ferocious haircuts and fetishistic clothes. (a.k.a.: *Mad Max 2.*) Followed by *Mad Max Beyond Thunderdome.*

ROARING FIRE ☆½
Japan
Henry Sanada, Sue Shiomi, Sonny Chiba, Miki Yamasita, Emily Yokoyama. 95 min.

Henry Sanada plays a cowboy in Texas (!) who had been kidnapped as a baby, and finds out about his true heritage only when his "father" dies. He then travels to Japan searching for his brother and sister, and finds much more than he bargained for—murder, intrigue, enemies, and countless opportunities for unarmed showdowns.

THE ROARING TWENTIES ☆☆☆
1939, USA
James Cagney, Priscilla Lane, Humphrey Bogart, Jeffrey Lynn. Directed by Raoul Walsh. 104 min.

This highly popular gangster classic from Warner Bros. features James Cagney and Humphrey Bogart together for the third and final time. Cagney, Bogart, and Jeffrey Lynn play World War I comrades who become embroiled in the bootlegging racket when they return to Prohibition America. Raoul Walsh's intelligent direction, a taut, well-plotted screenplay, and the joyous spectacle of watching Cagney and Bogart on-screen together, combine to make this still worthwhile nearly half a century after its release.

THE ROBE ☆☆
1953, USA
Richard Burton, Jean Simmons, Victor Mature, Michael Rennie, Richard Boone, Jay Robinson. Directed by Henry Koster. 135 min.

Yes, the Cinemascopic 3-D spectacle is now reduced to the small screen without 3-D and with the Cinemascope scarcely mattering. Everything looks squeezed together, as if the Roman Empire had been pressed in by Barbarians on either side. Richard Burton (nominated for an Oscar—for his diction, apparently) is the pagan whose involvement in the crucifixion of Christ transforms his life. He becomes both the keeper of Jesus' robe and the keeper of the Christian faith, which does not sit too well with the Roman power brokers. Everyone seems awed by the Theme, and Jean Simmons is once again wasted as the decorative love interest. But, if you like pomp and pageantry, by all means put on *The Robe*.

ROBERT ET ROBERT ☆☆☆
1979, France
Charles Denner, Jacques Villeret, Jean-Claude Brialy, Regine, Germaine Montero, Macha Meril. Directed by Claude Lelouch. 105 min.

Claude Lelouch will be forever known as the man who made the lush, romantic *A Man and a Woman*. For those who feel he is slick and facile, *Robert et Robert*—a Gallic buddy film—will be a down-to-earth, humane treat; for those who hope for another sentimental hankyfest, this may be a slight disappointment. Here two bachelors look for love and sex and settle for friendship before achieving final success. On-target satire of dating services.

ROBIN AND MARIAN ☆☆☆½
1976, Great Britain, PG
Sean Connery, Audrey Hepburn, Robert Shaw, Richard Harris, Nicol Williamson, Denholm Elliott, Ian Holm. Directed by Richard Lester. 106 min.

This is a charming oddity—an elegiac ode to dashing Robin Hood and pristine Maid Marian that picks up the romance twenty years later, when derring-do has turned to cynicism and fitness has given way to flab. The script by James Goldman (*The Lion in Winter*) never makes as much of the premise as it could, but stars Sean Connery and Audrey Hepburn, both idols slightly past their heyday, are ideal casting choices and give the drama a bittersweet edge. Those who like their legends unadulterated will quickly take offense, but others will find a touching, funny, and well-sustained drama, performed and directed with splendor and restraint.

ROBIN HOOD (1938)

See *The Adventures of Robin Hood*

R.O.B.O.T.

See *Chopping Mall*

ROBOT MONSTER ½☆
1953, USA
Selena Royle, George Nader, Claudia Barrett. Directed by Phil Tucker. 63 min.

This is a camp masterpiece. You will recognize the hybrid creature, Ro-Man, because from the neck down he's a gorilla, and from the neck up he's a diver. Poor Ro-Man has come to destroy the planet Earth, and somehow one typical American family has escaped his wrath. Whether or not this nuclear family will survive forms the plot of this woeful sci-fi flick that will astound you with its insights into the mysteries of the universe at the same time it pulverizes you with laughter due to the cheesiness of its none-too-special effects.

THE ROBOT VS. THE AZTEC MUMMY

See *Aztec Mummy Double Feature*

ROCKETSHIP X-M ☆☆
1950, USA
Lloyd Bridges, Osa Massen, John Emery, Noah Beery, Jr., Hugh O'Brian, Morris Ankrum. Directed by Kurt Neumann. 77 min.

One of the first of the 1950s science-fiction films, this is occasionally ludicrous in retrospect, but then who knew in 1950 what the future was going to bring? Five scientists on the first manned flight to the moon miss their destination and land on Mars instead, where they find the remnants of a civilization destroyed by nuclear war.

ROCK 'N' ROLL HIGH SCHOOL ☆☆½
1979, USA, PG
P.J. Soles, Vincent Van Patten, The Ramones, Mary Woronov, Paul Bartel, Clint Howard. Directed by Allan Arkush. 94 min.

Here's a freewheeling mishmash of drive-in flicks, 1950s rock and roll movies, and the sleazy side of MTV. P.J. Soles plays a high school student and the biggest fan of the Ramones, a macabre-looking punk rock band. While she anxiously waits for their upcoming concert, the school principal does some after-hours research on the detrimental effects of hard rock music on laboratory mice. There's also a school takeover, a literarlly explosive finale, and many more assorted subplots. The satire is uneven, but the spirits are always high in this happy surprise from executive producer Roger Corman. *Note*: Mary Woronov and Paul Bartel (of *Eating Raoul* fame) do not share their scenes.

ROCK, ROCK, ROCK! ☆☆½
1956, USA
Tuesday Weld, Jacqueline Kerr, Ivy Schulman, Alan Freed, The Moonglows, Teddy Randazzo, Chuck Berry, Johnny Burnette Trio, LaVern Baker, The Flamingos, Frankie Lymon and the Teenagers. Directed by Will Price. 85 min.

Fans of 1950s rock and roll should go out of their way to pick up this cheesy artifact of the times: The plot and production are laughable, but some of the artists who perform herein made no other film appearances. In her film debut, thirteen-year-old Tuesday Weld (who fortunately went on to better things) must raise money to buy herself a strapless gown for the big dance after Daddy takes away her charge privileges. Her singing was dubbed by Connie Francis, but the real musical highlight is Frankie Lymon and the Teenagers singing "I'm Not a Juvenile Delinquent," later immortalized in *Pink Flamingos*. Filmed on location in the Bronx.

ROCKTOBER BLOOD ☆
1984, USA, R
Tray Loren, Donna Scoggins, Cana Cockrell, Renee Hubbard, Ben Sebastian. Directed by Beverly Sebastian. 88 min.

A heavy-metal rock star executed for a murder spree returns to life to haunt the woman who testified against him in this low-budget, barely competent horror thriller, written by the husband-and-wife team of Ferd and Beverly Sebastian. More than the usual dose of bloody violence and a headache-inducing rock score differentiate but do not distinguish this entry from dozens of cheap scare films made on similarly impoverished budgets and imaginations.

ROCKY ☆☆☆½
1976, USA, PG
Sylvester Stallone, Talia Shire, Burgess Meredith, Burt Young, Carl Weathers. Directed by John G. Avildsen. 119 min.

One of the film trivia questions of the 1990s may be: What was the only film for which Sylvester Stallone won a Best Screenplay Oscar nomination? At least so far, it's *Rocky*, the sweet boxing fable about a down-and-out Philly slugger who gets one miraculous shot at the champ. If you've never seen it, separate yourself from the deification of the title character that occurred in the sequels. You'll find a well-told tale with an outlook at once inspirational and ironic, beautiful performances (not the least of which is Stallone's), and strong, gritty direction by John G. Avildsen that helped make this Best Picture Oscar winner the sleeper hit of the 1970s. Despite the often execrable work that Stallone has done more recently, *Rocky* still stands as an uplifting winner, with full credit belonging to its creator-star.

ROCKY IV ☆½
1985, USA, PG
Sylvester Stallone, Dolph Lundgren, Carl Weathers, Talia Shire, Burt Young. Directed by Sylvester Stallone. 90 min.

Stallone's inexhaustible ego is the real heavyweight in this dully propagandistic continuation of the Rocky mythos, wherein the Italian Stallion journeys to Russia to beat the crap out of Ivan Drago (Dolph Lundgren), a Soviet super-fighter who's knocked Apollo Creed out of the competition for good. In addition to the match, Rocky also gets to deliver a ridiculously facile pacifistic speech to hundreds of cheering Russians, one that even Mikhail Gorbachev stands up for! Since the whole movie's edited like an MTV video, it flies by painlessly. But it's saddening to realize that this reactionary trash was actually the highest-grossing entry of any of the *Rocky* films, and one of the huge box-office hits of 1985.

ROCKY MOUNTAIN RANGERS ☆☆
1940, USA
Robert Livingston, Raymond Hatton, Duncan Renaldo, Rosella Towne. Directed by George Sherman. 55 min.

The Three Mesquiteers, Republic's most popular good-guy team, return for an above-average B Western outing. Robert Livingston, replacing John Wayne in the series, doubles as the villain (the "Laredo Kid") in a predictable but satisfyingly taut entry.

ROCKY III ☆½
1982, USA, PG
Sylvester Stallone, Talia Shire, Carl Weathers, Burgess Meredith, Mr. T. Directed by Sylvester Stallone. 95 min.

This punch-drunk installment in the series is best remembered for introducing Mr. T to millions of moviegoers, a dubious accomplishment but the only one the film can call its own. The only twist here is that Apollo Creed is now in Rocky's camp as the Philly legend gears up for a face-off with the menacing T. Sylvester Stallone again wrote and directed, and it's depressing to watch the other characters play ever more peripheral roles in a story increasingly concerned with Sly's, uh, Rocky's attempt to cope with the pitfalls of fame, wealth, and success. *Rocky III* was a huge money-maker, actually outstripping both of the films that preceded it, but it continues Stallone's needless violation of the first film's exuberant underdog spirit. And it isn't over yet.

ROCKY II ☆☆
1979, USA, PG
Sylvester Stallone, Talia Shire, Burt Young, Carl Weathers, Burgess Meredith. Directed by Sylvester Stallone. 119 min.

Sylvester Stallone took over directorial chores from John Avildsen for this follow-up to his 1976 smash, with the predictable result being the first appearance of a halo above the title character's head. About the best one can say for *Rocky II* is that it's a crowd-pleaser, less a sequel than a slick second round to a boxing saga that apparently will never end. (You don't have to be a genius to figure out early that the film ends with a rematch between Rocky and nemesis Apollo Creed.) The film is best in the early scenes, which pick up right where *Rocky* left off and bring back most of the vigor of the first film's climax. But the odd, charming details and human scope of *Rocky* are wholly absent here, and Stallone gives his fellow actors offensively short shrift. In light of what followed, one wishes he had left well enough alone.

RODAN ☆☆½
1957, Japan
Kenji Sawara, Yumi Shirakawa, Akihiko Hirato. Directed by Inoshiro Honda. 70 min.

Director Inoshiro Honda's answer to his previously successful *Godzilla* has an equally gigantic pterodactyl waking up from its slumber inside a volcano and wreaking havoc across Japan. There are some great atmospheric moments at the beginning, but the film quickly becomes a pedestrian horror outing as it moves along. It contains better special effects than most of its ilk.

LE ROI DE COEUR

See *King of Hearts*

ROLLERBALL ☆☆☆
1975, USA, R
James Caan, John Houseman, Maud Adams, John Beck, Moses Gunn, Pamela Hensley, Ralph Richardson. Directed by Norman Jewison. 123 min.

In the near future, an athlete (James Caan) who excels in the brutal, bloody international sport of rollerball causes trouble for the powers that be when he becomes too famous; his efforts to beat the system form the plot of this shakily conceived but entertaining exercise in sci-fi suspense. Although there are scripted mumblings about computers, multinational corporations and dehumanization, the core of *Rollerball* is the game itself, a combination of roller derby, hockey, and open warfare that's thrillingly filmed. Most of the cast takes it all too seriously, but Ralph Richardson has a brief, sparkling role as a kindly old computer genius assigned to tend the master memory bank, Zero.

ROLLER BOOGIE ☆☆
1979, USA, PG
Linda Blair, Jim Bray, Beverly Garland, Roger Perry, Jimmy Van Patten, Kimberly Beck. Directed by Mark L. Lester. 103 min.

It would be cruel to say that this roller-disco film is really about weightlifting, but one involuntarily groans as the plump Linda Blair is thrust skyward by her anemic, puny skating partner. Linda plays a spoiled rich flute prodigy who dallies away the summer with a crowd of working-class skating buffs. Will the skating rink be paved over by a shopping mall? Will Linda stay with her new boyfriend or go off to Juilliard? Will the memory of roller disco live long enough to make this video comprehensible? Who cares? Watch this one for Linda's trash-queen makeup and sidesplittingly tight costumes.

ROLLERCOASTER ☆½
1977, USA, PG
George Segal, Richard Widmark, Timothy Bottoms, Henry Fonda, Harry Guardino. Directed by James Goldstone. 119 min.

The script of this very meek suspense film is by the usually estimable team of Richard Levinson and William Link, the creators of TV's "Columbo" and "Murder She Wrote." This time, their plotting skill didn't carry over to the big screen. The plot has a mad-genius extortionist (Timothy Bottoms) threatening to create havoc in a major amusement park unless he's paid handsomely. This is less a disaster film than a suspense procedural, with good guy George Segal trying to track down the loony before all hell breaks loose. Action fans will have to wait until the last half hour to be placated. Originally shot in "Sensurround."

ROLLING THUNDER ☆☆
1977, USA, R
William Devane, Tommy Lee Jones, Linda Haynes, Lisa Richards, Dabney Coleman, Cassie Yates. Directed by John Flynn. 99 min.

For a while, this looks as if it is going to be an honest examination of the tribulations faced by homecoming Vietnam veterans: William Devane, as a U.S. major who was tortured for eight years in a Viet Cong POW camp, returns home a wooden, emotionless shell, caring little that his wife and son have become attached to his best friend. But then psycho killers murder his family, and it's time for the usual Vietnam vet killing-machine stuff. As written by Paul Schrader, this is in some ways similar to his *Taxi Driver*, but with all of the worst parts magnified.

ROLLOVER ☆☆
1981, USA, R
Jane Fonda, Kris Kristofferson, Hume Cronyn, Josef Sommer, Bob Gunton, Macon McCalman, Ron Frazier. Directed by Alan J. Pakula. 118 min.

A sincere but failed attempt to present the world of high finance in the sinuous, money-is-erotic style of "Dynasty" or a Jackie Collins novel while shoe-horning in a fairly complex political plot. The title refers to a common practice of keeping market investments stable from year to year, and the film tries to explore the possibility that a conspiracy to withdraw all foreign money from American banks could get off the ground and destroy the international monetary system. Who's behind it? Arabs, of course; they're always the bad guys when something devious yet completly inexplicable is going on. It's up to Jane Fonda and Kris Kristofferson, both made up so thickly that they look like putty additions to Mount Rushmore, to stop the madness, but their labyrinthine maneuverings are too reliant on conversations to be compelling as fast-moving suspense.

ROMANCE AND RICHES

See *The Amazing Adventure*

ROMANCE OF A HORSE THIEF ☆☆
1971, USA/Yugoslavia, PG
Yul Brynner, Eli Wallach, Jane Birkin, Oliver Tobias, Lainie Kazan. Directed by Abraham Polonsky. 101 min.

A horse opera with Polish horses and no singing, this lavish but mediocre epic is very sluggish getting to the finish line. Events pile up at every turn: Cossack Yul Brynner commandeers horses from his quaint peasant village for Tsar Nicholas; quaint peasants revolt, thus casting off their simple charms; Brynner's protégé Oliver Tobias frees his treason-tried revolutionary girlfriend and flees across the border. Eventually the film grinds to a halt, but not before muddling its murky Marxism by keeping its honey-dipped camera trained on the most hackneyed locations for the most unbelievable lengths of time. It's quite a comedown for director Abraham Polonsky (*Tell Them Willie Boy Is Here*).

ROMANCING THE STONE ☆☆☆
1984, USA, PG
Michael Douglas, Kathleen Turner, Danny DeVito, Zack Norman, Alfonso Aram, Manuel Ojeda. Directed by Robert Zemeckis. 105 min.

Kathleen Turner injects roustabout charm into this story of a Manhattan-based romance novelist who travels to Colombia to save her sister and ends up going on a hair-raising treasure hunt. The zippy *Raiders of the Lost Ark* scenario is breathlessly paced, but what anchors it is the fun of seeing a mousy writer of fantasy caught up in her own swashbuckling saga. Unfortunately, Michael Douglas is the daredevil adventurer and he fails to convince as a charmer or hero.

ROMAN HOLIDAY ☆☆☆½
1953, USA
Gregory Peck, Audrey Hepburn, Eddie Albert. Directed by William Wyler. 119 min.

A gloriously filmed (on location) celebration of love in the Eternal City. Gregory Peck is an expatriate newspaperman whose big scoop is Princess Audrey Hepburn's mysterious disappearance while on diplomatic duty in Rome. To keep her under wraps, he takes her on a whirlwind tour of the city, and somewhere in between ice cream on the Spanish Steps and dancing on the Tiber, he realizes that he has met the princess of his dreams. William Wyler beautifully blends comedy and drama, and Hepburn gives a luminous, glamorous performance in a wonderfully old-fashioned high-style tradition. She and Peck are an almost achingly romantic pair.

THE ROMAN SPRING OF MRS. STONE ☆☆½
1961, USA
Vivien Leigh, Warren Beatty, Coral Browne, Jill St. John, Lotte Lenya, Jeremy Spenser, Stella Bonheur. Directed by Jose Quintero. 103 min.

This very downbeat tearjerker is based on a novel by Tennessee Williams, a cogent but cruel work that proved a perfect opportunity to reunite the playwright with his *Streetcar* star Vivien Leigh. Returning to the screen after six years, Leigh looks beautiful but fragile and a little bit haggard—a very apt choice to play Karen Stone, a middle-aged widow who travels to Rome for a peaceful rest and finds herself attracted to, and humiliated by, a handsome, mercenary gigolo (played by a very young Warren Beatty). Beatty is callow and ill at ease with the delicate Leigh; their work is bettered by Lotte Lenya's juicy turn as a vicious procuress. Although there are some sharply observed moments, it eventually descends to a vaguely misogynistic, very depressing wallow.

ROMANTIC COMEDY ☆☆½
1983, USA, PG
Dudley Moore, Mary Steenburgen, Frances Sternhagen, Janet Eilber, Ron Leibman. Directed by Arthur Hiller. 103 min.

This is an adaptation of a play by Bernard Slade, a Neil Simon manqué whose works are very popular with community and dinner theater groups. Dudley Moore and Mary Steenburgen are Broadway collaborators who, over the years, find their platonic relationship developing into—aw, we won't give it away for you. After this and such recent efforts as *Six Weeks*, *10*, and *Unfaithfully Yours*, if Dudley gets any more cuddly he'll have to join the Care Bears. He and Steenburgen make a charming, attractive couple, the movie has some chuckles and some sniffles, and you won't remember any of it tomorrow morning.

THE ROMANTIC ENGLISHWOMAN ☆☆½
1975, France/Great Britain, R
Glenda Jackson, Michael Caine, Helmut Berger, Beatrice Romand, Kate Nelligan, Michel Lonsdale, Nathalie Delon. Directed by Joseph Losey. 115 min.

This is a clever, well-acted but self-consciously cryptic tale of a bored husband and wife and the drug-smuggling gigolo who comes into their lives. The screenplay was written by Tom Stoppard, and his love of wordplay, mirror images, plots within plots, and self-referential jokes meshes well with Joseph Losey's directional style. But the characters seem less flesh and blood than careful constructions for the writer's whims. It's engrossing in sections, but emphatically less than the sum of its parts.

ROMEO AND JULIET ☆☆☆½
1968, Great Britain/Italy
Leonard Whiting, Olivia Hussey, Milo O'Shea, Michael York, John McEnery. Directed by Franco Zeffirelli. 152 min.

Franco Zeffirelli's adaptation of Shakespeare's play is so openly romantic, and so skillfully "contemporary" while remaining faithful to its fifteenth-century Verona locations, that you can almost (but not quite) forgive the director for cutting major passages of dialogue as if they were so much deadwood. At least the remaining words belong to Shakespeare, and Leonard Whiting and Olivia Hussey make a touchingly ardent pair of lovers. (Their balcony scene remains one of the most beautiful evocations of Shakespeare's language on screen.) If at times the staging and acting seem closer to *West Side Story* than they should be, there's much to be said for a film that doesn't just assume Shakespeare is timeless, but proves it.

ROME, OPEN CITY ☆☆☆☆
1945, Italy, PG
Anna Magnani, Aldo Fabrizi, Marcello Pagliero, Maria Michi. Directed by Roberto Rossellini. 101 min.

Roberto Rossellini's classic set the tone and style for the Italian neorealist movement (it was shot on the streets of Rome at the same time as the city was being liberated from the Germans). It's actually closer to the pre-World War II Italian "white telephone melodramas" than many of the neorealist films to come (*Paisan*, *The Bicycle Thief*), but it did pave the way for the others. Anna Magnani, as usual, is unforgettable. She plays the pregnant wife of an underground resister, and her performance atones for some of the supporting players—who are pressed into such cardboard roles as a knife-sucking lesbian Nazi. Federico Fellini cowrote the screenplay.

RONA JAFFE'S MAZES AND MONSTERS • ★★½
1982, Canada (TV)
Tom Hanks, Wendy Crewson, David Wallace, Chris Makepeace, Lloyd Bochner, Peter Donat, Anne Francis, Vera Miles, Susan Strasberg. Directed by Steven Hilliard Stern. 97 min.

A role-playing fantasy game not unlike Dungeons and Dragons becomes a dangerous obsession for a troubled college student in an intriguing, suspenseful TV drama based on Rona Jaffe's novel. The plot machinations become familiar when the young man disappears and his friends embark on a search using clues from the labyrinthine game, but Tom Lazarus's script is an often compelling exploration of the game and its players, and Tom Hanks is appropriately intense as the unwitting victim. (a.k.a.: *Mazes and Monsters*)

ROOM AT THE TOP ★★★½
1958, Great Britain
Laurence Harvey, Simone Signoret, Heather Sears, Donald Wolfit, Ambrosine Philpotts, Donald Houston, Raymond Huntley. Directed by Jack Clayton. 117 min.

Generally credited with being the first of the British "kitchen sink" dramas, this tough, sensual adaptation of John Brine's novel casts Laurence Harvey as the opportunist who sacrifices his love for sexy Simone Signoret in order to make his way to the top in a Northern England town by marrying the daughter of the local factory boss. Signoret won a richly deserved Oscar for her performance, as did screenwriter Neil Paterson.

THE ROOMMATE ★★½
1986, USA (TV)
Lance Guest, Barry Miller. Directed by Nell Cox. 90 min.

This is a schematic but amiable seriocomedy, based on John Updike's short story "The Christian Roommate." It's 1952, and Orson (Lance Guest), a straitlaced, repressed college freshman, finds himself burdened with maniacal roommate Henry (Barry Miller), a leftist pacifist vegetarian whose eccentricity exhausts Orson's efforts to accommodate. If you're thinking of *The Odd Couple*, you're on the right track, but don't expect many laughs in this poignant, beautifully mounted but overly sober variation. It was originally shown on PBS's "American Playhouse."

ROOM SERVICE ★★★
1938, USA
Groucho, Chico, and Harpo Marx, Lucille Ball, Ann Miller, Frank Albertson, Donald MacBride. Directed by William A. Seiter. 76 min.

The Marx Brothers match wits with the managers of a hotel while they work to put on a play. Harpo sprays fake measles onto a young playwright, a turkey escapes in the hotel room, Chico smuggles in a moose head . . . In general, the RKO releases are not as funny as the early Paramount films, and this is not classic Marx Brothers—Harpo doesn't even have a harp solo—but it's still very funny. Although the movie doesn't have music, it does have an uncharacteristically solid plot.

A ROOM WITH A VIEW ★★★½
1986, Great Britain
Helena Bonham Carter, Julian Sands, Daniel Day Lewis, Denholm Elliott, Maggie Smith, Simon Callow, Judi Dench, Rosemary Leach, Rupert Graves, Fabia Drake. Directed by James Ivory. 115 min.

From E.M. Forster's 1908 novel about the sexual and social awakening of young Lucy Honeychurch, James Ivory has fashioned a splendid adaptation, as elegant as all of his films, but more lively and energetic than any of them. The sumptuous period recreations are by now familiar; the unexpected pleasures come in the pungent wit and brisk pace—we're not used to classics retold with such a light touch. As Ivory's camera glides seductively through the city of Florence and then the country parishes of England, the film celebrates the barely corseted romantic longing of its protagonists, reveling in the wit of each camera angle and line of dialogue. (The screenplay is by Ivory's longtime collaborator Ruth Prawer Jhabvala.) The tiny, inexpressive Helena Bonham Carter is a distressing choice for Forster's mercurial heroine, conveying the proper immaturity but little spark. Fortunately, she's backed up by the intelligent, perfectly italicized performances of veteran character actors Maggie Smith and Denholm Elliott and promising newcomers Julian Sands and Daniel Day Lewis. Even Forster purists should find little cause for quarrel. Academy Awards went to Jhabvala's screenplay, the art director, and the costume design.

ROOSTER COGBURN ★★
1975, USA, PG
John Wayne, Katharine Hepburn, Anthony Zerbe, Strother Martin, Richard Jordan, John McIntire. Directed by Stuart Millar. 107 min.

This is a sequel to *True Grit* with large measures of *The African Queen* offered as a starring vehicle for the never-before-teamed Katharine Hepburn and John Wayne. Wayne is amusing, as he always was after he learned to parody himself, but Hepburn is the weak link as yet another fierce old spinster.

ROPE ★★★½
1948, USA, PG
James Stewart, Farley Granger, John Dall, Cedric Hardwicke, Joan Chandler, Constance Collier. Directed by Alfred Hitchcock. 80 min.

Grand Guignol in a New York skyscraper. Two former college friends kill off a third, stuff the body in a trunk and use it as a cocktail table to entertain the college professor (James Stewart) whose theories inspired the killing. Thrill killing is not, of course, what their teacher had in mind and, during the course of this grisly gathering, he unravels the senseless crime. Filmed in a dizzying series of ten-minute takes to appear as one continuous shot, Hitchcock's first color film is a highly stylized, slightly talky experiment that holds up much better today than one would have surmised from the negative critical reports of the late forties.

THE ROSE ★★½
1979, USA, R
Bette Midler, Alan Bates, Frederic Forrest, Harry Dean Stanton, David Keith, Barry Primus. Directed by Mark Rydell. 134 min.

This very loose fictionalized retelling of the life of Janis Joplin embraces every rise-and-fall-of-a-star cliché in screen history. When we first meet the Rose (Bette Midler) battling with her manipulative manager (Alan Bates), she's already on the skids, and it's all downhill from there. The film is elevated from the trash heap by Midler's natural, sizzlingly emotional portrayal of the wrecked superstar, a tour de force performance in a role that desperately calls for one. Her singing, including soaring versions of the bluesy "When a Man Loves a Woman" and "Stay with Me," as well as the title ballad, is "acted" as well, in a style that's a marked departure from her own. Despite its cheap, oversimplified qualities, the drug-and-booze-soaked odyssey on display is a harrowing one. Midler and Frederic Forrest (as one of the Rose's amiable flings) were both Oscar nominees.

ROSELAND ★★
1977, USA, PG
Teresa Wright, Lou Jacobi, Don de Natale, Louise Kirkland, Geraldine Chaplin, Helen Gallagher, Joan Copeland, Christopher Walken, Conrad Janis, Lilia Skala, David Thomas, Edward Kogan, Madeline Lee, Stan Rubin. Directed by James Ivory. 103 min.

Three vignettes about sorrowful people dancing their little lives away in the famous old ballroom on New York's West 52nd Street. Christopher Walken (in an expert performance) is a thirtyish gigolo dividing his time between Joan Copeland and Geraldine Chaplin; Teresa Wright dreams of her dead husband while Lou Jacobi dutifully attends her; and Lilia Skala and David Thomas are two oldsters who refuse to admit age and sit down. As directed by James Ivory, the movie feels like a "sensitive" TV drama from 1955, and despite a number of extremely good performances, it's resolutely condescending and mawkish.

ROSE MARIE ☆☆☆
1936, USA
Jeanette MacDonald, Nelson Eddy, James Stewart, Reginald Owen, Allan Jones, George Regas, Gilda Gray, David Niven(s). Directed by W.S. Van Dyke II. 110 min.

Jeanette MacDonald and Nelson Eddy's single most famous film is not really their best. It lacks the elegance of *Maytime*, the reflexive humor of *Sweethearts*, the outlandish camp of *New Moon*, and the great scores of all three films. True, this is the one where they sing "The Indian Love Call" ("When I'm Calling Youooo . . ."), but the rest has gotten a little musty over the years. Jeanette plays a Canadian opera singer (MGM wanted Grace Moore) who treks across the Rockies to aid her fugitive brother (young Jimmy Stewart). Nelson plays the Northwest mounted policeman who always gets his man (or woman, as the case may be). The singing sweethearts have some lively banter (supplied by Francis Goodrich, Albert Hackett, and Alice Duer Miller) and sing the Rudolph Friml score beautifully, if only infrequently together. It is the supporting cast that steals this one: Lean and mean Stewart, Gilda Gray as a honkytonk singer (her duet with Jeanette is a pip), Allan Jones as "Romeo" to Jeanette's "Juliet" in an opera sequence, and David Nivens (later Niven) as one of her backstage suitors. It is still a vastly better film than either the 1927 silent with Joan Crawford or the 1954 widescreen and color remake with Ann Blyth.

ROSEMARY'S BABY ☆☆☆☆
1968, USA, R
Mia Farrow, John Cassavetes, Ruth Gordon, Maurice Evans, Sidney Blackmer, Ralph Bellamy, Patsy Kelly, Charles Grodin, Elisha Cook, Jr. Directed by Roman Polanski. 134 min.

One of the most haunting thrillers ever made, *Rosemary's Baby* is based on Ira Levin's best-seller about a young married couple who move into an old building in New York. Strange neighbors are only the beginning of their problems, and when the wife becomes pregnant (not to mention how she becomes pregnant) things really get creeepy. In lesser hands, this could have turned out badly, but Roman Polanski has done a remarkable job, eliciting fine performances from Mia Farrow and Ruth Gordon (who won an Oscar for her performance). From start to finish, *Rosemary's Baby* is truly chilling.

ROSEMARY'S KILLER

See *The Prowler*

ROSIE: THE ROSEMARY CLOONEY STORY ☆☆
1982, USA (TV)
Sondra Locke, Tony Orlando, Penelope Milford, John Karlen, Robert Ridgely, Cheryl Anderson, Joey Travolta, Katherine Helmond, Kevin McCarthy. Directed by Jackie Cooper. 95 min.

This unenlightening TV biography tells the story of singer Rosemary Clooney, whose huge success masked a bitterly unhappy personal life and eventually gave way to barbiturate addiction and a nervous breakdown (she later recovered from both). Sondra Locke isn't a good physical match for Clooney, nor is she up to the acting requirements of the role, and Tony Orlando is ridiculous as husband José Ferrer. The flashback format keeps the film's drama very conventional; somewhat better are the musical numbers, original Clooney recordings lip-synched by Locke.

ROUGE BAISER ☆☆½
1986, France
Charlotte Valandrey, Lambert Wilson, Marthe Keller, Gunter Lamprecht, Laurent Terzieff. Directed by Vera Belmont. 110 min.

A stylish, nostalgic romance about a headstrong fifteen-year-old girl's first love, with a couple of twists—the setting is 1952 France, and the young heroine (Charlotte Valandrey) is, of all things, an ardent Communist (one of many who felt they owed allegiance to Stalin for saving them from the Nazis). When she's bonked on the head during a protest rally, she ends up in the flat of a handsome but hopelessly bourgeois capitalist photographer (Lambert Wilson). Director-writer Vera Belmont gives their affair a funny and bittersweet ideological gloss, and the cast is pleasant and attractive even if the story is finally conventional.

ROUGH CUT ☆½
1980, USA, PG
Burt Reynolds, Lesley-Anne Down, David Niven, Timothy West, Patrick Magee, Isobel Dean. Directed by Don Siegel. 113 min.

Apparently not having learned his lesson in *At Long Last Love*, Burt once again tries to pass himself off as the Cary Grant of the 1980s, with results similar to (and only slightly better than) those of Tom Selleck in *Lassiter*. As a jewel thief in London, he is lured into attempting to steal $30 million of uncut diamonds (hence the title) by Scotland Yard inspector David Niven, who is about to retire and wants this final arrest as a final feather in his cap. Don Siegel, one of our best action directors, has no faculty at all for the sort of sophisticated comedy that this aspires to be.

ROUGHNECKS ☆☆
1980, USA (TV)
Steve Forrest, Sam Melville, Ana Alicia, Cathy Lee Crosby, Vera Miles, Harry Morgan, Stephen McHattie. Directed by Bernard McEveety. 200 min.

A long, sporadically entertaining tale about oil wildcatters who are rough-and-tumble tough guys in the field but who melt into romantic softies under the influence of women (in shorter supply than oil, apparently). It's a crude oil adventure, but there are some fair action segments for the undiscriminating.

'ROUND MIDNIGHT ☆☆☆½
1986, USA, R
Dexter Gordon, Francois Cluzet, Gabrielle, Sandra Reaves-Philips, Lonette McKee, Christine Pascal, Herbie Hancock, Martin Scorsese. Directed by Bertrand Tavernier. 130 min.

Bertrand Tavernier's contemplative drama works its magic in a roundabout way, letting the memorable jazz renditions by a superb ensemble of musicians comment on the story line. A black musician (played by jazz great Dexter Gordon), wounded by lack of acceptance in the U.S., moves to France. There, he finds a home in Parisian jazz circles where he develops a relationship with a jazz enthusiast who weans him off alcohol and lovingly watches over him until he begins playing at his peak again. In almost documentary fashion, the powerful musical sequences enable us to appreciate this burned-out man's desire to keep performing, and to comprehend what that smoky, smoldering music means to the French acolyte out to save his idol from self-destruction. This is a unique, soulful, and expressive tribute to the art of jazz. Academy Award winner for Best Original Score (Herbie Hancock).

ROUND-UP TIME IN TEXAS ☆
1937, USA
Gene Autry, Smiley Burnette, Maxine Doyle, Champion. Directed by Joseph Kane. 54 min.

You won't see much of the Lone Star State in this loony musical-cowboy-adventure film, which drops genial Gene Autry onto the South African veld in search of diamonds . . . if the voodoo doesn't get him first. Even for a very old B film, *Round-Up* is prehistoric in style and content. This version is trimmed by nine minutes from its theatrical release version.

ROUSTABOUT ☆☆½
1964, USA
Elvis Presley, Barbara Stanwyck, Joan Freeman, Leif Erickson, Sue Anne Langdon, Pat Buttram. Directed by John Rich. 101 min.

Elvis Presley and Barbara Stanwyck, two actors with an affinity for black leather, team up in this carnival musical melodrama. Elvis plays a biker who is hired by Barbara to sing for her carny customers. That's until he gets a better offer at a rival show. The plot is straight from *Billy Rose's Jumbo*, but instead of Rodgers and Hart, you get Leiber and Stoller. Elvis sings "It's a Wonderful World," "It's Carnival Time," and "Carney Town." Joan Freeman is the love interest, but Elvis has more chemistry with Barbara.

ROYAL WEDDING ☆☆☆
1951, USA
Fred Astaire, Jane Powell, Peter Lawford, Sarah Churchill, Keenan Wynn, Albert Sharpe, Viola Roache, James Finlayson. Directed by Stanely Donen. 93 min.

In response to the 1946 marriage of Princess Elizabeth to Philip Mountbatten, Duke of Edinburgh, MGM built around some location wedding footage one of their slickest Technicolor musical treats. Fred Astaire and Jane Powell play a brother-and-sister dance team touring London during the coronation who split up when she marries a lord (Peter Lawford). (Alan Jay Lerner's screenplay culls the plot from Astaire's own life: His sister Adele left their act during a 1928 London tour to marry Lord Charles Cavendish.) Jane Powell, replacing a pregnant June Allyson and an ill Judy Garland, is cute and sassy as the flirtatious young lady, but she only just gets by on the dance floor. Sarah Churchill (Winston's daughter) doesn't give Astaire much more to dance with as his obligatory vis-à-vis. Ultimately, Fred is best alone: With a coat rack in a gymnasium or up and down the walls of his hotel suite, Astaire (and choreographer Nick Castle) create breathtakingly dexterous routines. Astaire dancing on the ceiling is one of the greatest routines in the history of film musicals. Otherwise, Stanley Donen (in his first solo directing job) keeps the formula moving briskly, the Lerner-Burton Lane score yields a few hits ("Too Late Now," "You're All the World To Me"), and Albert Sharpe has a cute bit as Churchill's American-hating father.

R.S.V.P. ☆½
1984, USA, R
Harry Reems, Veronica Hart. Directed by Lem Amero. 87 min.

This low-budget, R-rated sex comedy always disappoints on all counts. The dialogue, of course, is awful, the humor is nonexistent, and the story, a vague vehicle for all the sex, is boring and inane. But the worst part is that the promised payoff—a zany, wild orgy—is pretty tame and very brief. This representative of the genre—whose premise involves a Hollywood party for a novelist—boasts a cast of actors known for their X-rated roles.

RUBY GENTRY ☆☆½
1952, USA
Jennifer Jones, Charlton Heston, Karl Malden, Josephine Hutchinson. Directed by King Vidor. 82 min.

This film is not as florid as other late King Vidor work (*Duel in the Sun, The Fountainhead, Beyond the Forest*) and not as much fun, either. Much as she did in *Duel*, Jennifer Jones plays a backwoods woman who upsets her benefactor's household and seeks revenge on those who betrayed her. The ingredients for a great, trashy melodrama are all there, but Jones is more subdued than usual, Charlton Heston lacks the charisma of Gregory Peck and Gary Cooper, Sylvia Richards's screenplay misses the necessary hyperbole, and the feeble budget shows (color would have helped). It's disappointing but adequately steamy, with Karl Malden giving a dress rehearsal for *Baby Doll*.

RUDE BOY ☆☆½
1979, Great Britain, R
Ray Gange, The Clash, Caroline Coon. Directed by Jack Hazen, David Mingay. 133 min.

This is a semi-improvised portrait of post-punk Britain that follows an anarchic slob's attempt to discover an identity for himself by becoming a roadie for punk band The Clash, "The Only Band That Matters." Termed "disgusting" by the easily offended British press, the movie features some alarming scenes of the police in action, but owes its cult status almost entirely to the concert footage of The Clash, a truly exciting live band. Fans of the band may wish to keep the fast forward control at hand for the times when they are not on camera.

RULES OF THE GAME ☆☆☆☆
1939, France
Nora Gregor, Jean Renoir, Marcel Dalio, Pauline Dubost, Mila Parely. Directed by Jean Renoir. 110 min.

It is difficult to understand the backlash created by *Rules of the Game* in 1939, but then great works of art are often at the center of controversy. After its Paris opening, the audience rioted, the distributors excised over thirty minutes, and the Nazis banned it. Nearly two decades later, after Jean Renoir had reconstructed his "lost" masterpiece with the help of two archivists, critics started to add it to their "ten best ever" lists. Although planned as a modern version of Alfred de Musset's *Les Caprices de Mariane*, with subtextual commentary about the disintegration of a culturally rich but ignorant society (France was about to fall to the Nazis), the film is too complex and many-leveled to be pigeonholed. Indeed, even some of the narrative is difficult to understand on a literal level. The central story that does emerge concerns a wealthy landowner, his wife (Nora Gregor, though Renoir originally wanted Simone Simon), and her aviator-lover. At a weekend party, they join their guests and servants in a wicked comedy of manners accompanied by the music of Mozart, Chopin, and Johann Strauss. Soon, their comedy turns to tragedy. Christian Matras's brilliantly mobile camera is only one of the many elements that make this a masterpiece.

THE RULING CLASS ☆☆☆
1972, Great Britain, R
Peter O'Toole, Alastair Sim, Arthur Lowe, Harry Andrews, Coral Browne, Michael Bryant, Graham Crowden, Kay Walsh. Directed by Peter Medak. 154 min.

There are so many wonderful bits in this peculiar, unmistakably British film that you're almost willing to overlook the parts that drag on and on, even though they could easily have been edited. After the perverse accidental death of the thirteenth Earl of Gurney, his son assumes the peerage. Trouble is, young Jack is a paranoid schizophrenic who thinks that he is, in his words, "J.C., the god of love." Needless to say, this causes no end of consternation to his family, who do their best either to have him cured or marry him off and produce an heir so that they can have him tossed back in the bin. The film is equal parts heavy-handed British satire and music hall farce, with all of the stodgy characters breaking into thoroughly incongruous songs at any time. As the new earl, Peter O'Toole turns in an amazing performance that is by itself more than enough reason to see this; he received an Academy Award nomination for his efforts.

RUMBLEFISH ☆☆☆½
1983, USA, R
Matt Dillon, Mickey Rourke, Diane Lane, Dennis Hopper, Vincent Spano, Christopher Penn, Nicolas Cage, Tom Waits. Directed by Francis Ford Coppola. 94 min.

This is an underrated myth about the process of mythmaking—dreamy and self-referential. Francis Ford Coppola explodes over the mark with his second S.E. Hinton novel adaptation, stylizing the visuals and stripping down the epigrammatic dialogue at the expense of clarity. Alienated teenagers rumble and philosophize in a Nietzschean wasteland whose black-and-white splendor is disrupted twice with fleeting flashes of color. As the story revolves around the strained relationship of two brothers, one struggling to escape the other's shadow, the film does manage to intensify to a compelling climax. Like *The Outsiders*, this mood piece features an impressive teenage cast and a great performance by Tom Waits as a fry cook. Score by Stewart Copeland of The Police.

A RUMOR OF WAR ☆☆☆½
1980, USA (TV)
Brad Davis, Keith Carradine, Michael O'Keefe, Brian Dennehy, Perry Lang. Directed by Richard T. Heffron. 200 min.

Hailed as the first TV film to deal with the Vietnam experience, this adaptation of the best-seller by Philip Caputo is a gripping study of the torments of Vietnam and the way conventional notions of patriotism failed our fighting men in this war, which was unlike any other. With powerhouse delivery, the film traces the evolution of a sincere college kid into a gung-ho Marine and finally into a burned-out fighting machine who's charged with murders committed back in Nam. Uneasy echoes of the My Lai massacre resound throughout the film, but this is no rip-off of a headline horror story; it's a devastating tragedy about failed expectations and a no-win war.

RUNAWAY ☆☆½
1984, USA, PG-13
Tom Selleck, Gene Simmons, Cynthia Rhodes, Kirstie Alley. Directed by Michael Crichton. 99 min.

In the near future, household robots are as common as toasters, and when they malfunction, homeowners simply call the special police "runaway" squad. But when an evil genius begins programming them to kill, disaster looms. This is a slick film, with a silly sense of humor and some mild suspense. Look for the little metal spiders loaded with acid venom, and for former Kiss member Gene Simmons as the eye-rolling maniac. It's a perfect B film; and for a mad-robot home-video double feature, pair it with Crichton's own *Westworld* or, even better, *The Terminator*.

THE RUNAWAY BARGE ☆½
1975, USA (TV)
Bo Hopkins, Tim Matheson, James Best, Nick Nolte, Jim Davis, Christina Hart. Directed by Boris Segal. 78 min.

This is not a runaway hit, just another mediocre time-killer about real men making a name for themselves by eking out a living on a riverboat, and right in modern times, too. Numerous close scrapes and death-defying adventures kept the stuntmen's union busy, and the personable cast makes the shenanigans palatable.

RUNAWAY TRAIN ☆☆
1985, USA, R
Jon Voight, Eric Roberts, Rebecca De Mornay, Kyle T. Heffner, John P. Ryan, T.K. Carter, Kenneth McMillan. Directed by Andrei Konchalovsky. 112 min.

This is a gut-slamming, brutal action film with an overlay of existential platitudes straight from a freshman philosophy class. Jon Voight plays Manny, the meanest prisoner in the toughest maximum-security prison in the coldest region of Alaska; Eric Roberts plays a constantly chattering convicted rapist who reveres him. The two engineer an escape by swimming through a sewer and trudging through an icy wasteland, but they make the mistake of leaping aboard a train bound for nowhere at ninety miles an hour. Director Andrei Konchalovsky gets some impressively bleak footage of the locomotive hurtling past glaciers and ice-covered mountains, but the dialogue, pseudo-Nietzschian prattle about man battling himself and nature, is embarrassing. Voight's performance wavers between mere hamminess and frightening ferocity, but Roberts is robustly, intensely awful in ways that we rarely see in contemporary American films. The film carries the credit "based on a screenplay by Akira Kurosawa," though as rewritten by Djordje Milicevic, Paul Zindel, and Edward Bunker, it's unrecognizable as Kurosawa's work.

RUNNING BRAVE ☆☆½
1983, Canada, PG
Robby Benson, Pat Hingle, Claudia Cron, Denis LaCroix, Jeff McCracken. Directed by D.S. Everett (Don Shebib). 105 min.

In the grand Hollywood tradition of ludicrous racial impersonations by white actors, Robby Benson plays a half-Sioux track star. (Guess he didn't learn his lesson after his performance as a Chicano in *Walk Proud*.) Based on the true story of Billy Mills, who won an amazing upset victory in the 10,000-meter run at the 1964 Tokyo Olympics, the film and its star are sincere and determined. Inspired, no, but this is a Buena Vista presentation, so the first order of business is to make it palatable for the whole family.

RUNNING OUT OF LUCK ☆
1985, Great Britain
Mick Jagger, Jerry Hall, Rae Dawn Chong, Dennis Hopper. Directed by Julien Temple. 90 min.

It had to happen. First video clips were made of hit songs from movies. Then, movies began to include videolike interludes to generate record sales which in turn could help make the film a hit. The final, logical step had to be a movie made to do nothing but promote songs, and here it is: a collection of seven videos for Mick Jagger's 1985 album "She's the Boss," joined in a film that boasts a flimsy plot line, moronic dialogue, and pitiful performances. The film is set in Brazil where Mick (playing himself) gets mugged after walking off the set of a video, and ends up in the desert where he works on a plantation, makes friends with a hooker (Rae Dawn Chong), and meets lots of people who have never heard of him—a rock star's nightmare. The videos lurking in this mess are only average, and poor Mick seems like an aging camp version of himself; only Chong comes off looking good. Next time, Mick will, we hope, restrain his artistic impulses (he cowrote and produced), and leave filmmaking to filmmakers.

RUNNING SCARED ☆☆½
1986, USA, R
Billy Crystal, Gregory Hines, Joe Pantoliano, Steven Bauer, Darlanne Fluegel. Directed by Peter Hyams. 106 min.

Director Peter Hyams gives his versatile stars a lot to do in this entertaining but formulaic crime action-comedy, more realistic but much less exciting than the similar *48 HRS*. There's a slightly forced, cutesy feeling to the antics of two Chicago cops who try to stay alive in the face of gunrunners and drug smugglers who are blocking their way to a sunny retirement in Key West. Gregory Hines and Billy Crystal work well together and toss off the one-liners with ease, but Hyams pigeonholes them into a tired car-chase big-finale format that ought to be retired once and for all.

RUN SILENT, RUN DEEP ☆☆☆
1958, USA
Clark Gable, Burt Lancaster, Jack Warden, Brad Dexter, Don Rickles, Nick Cravat, Mary LaRoche, Eddie Foy III. Directed by Robert Wise. 93 min.

This is one of the best World War II submarine pictures ever made. Combining elements of *Moby Dick* and *The Caine Mutiny*, this psychological action film has Clark Gable playing a submarine captain who's single-mindedly pursuing the Japanese destroyer that sank his previous sub, and Burt Lancaster as his executive officer who takes over command when Gable's monomania begins to seem dangerously unbalanced. But events soon lead them to see eye to eye, and some gripping nautical battles ensue. It's a grim, no-frills war picture, with only a brief scene with Mary LaRoche as commander Gable's wife to punctuate the masculine atmosphere.

RUN, STRANGER, RUN
☆☆
1973, USA
Ron Howard, Cloris Leachman, Bobby Darin, Tessa Neal, Simon Oakland, Thayer David, Patricia Neal. Directed by Darren McGavin. 90 min.

A young man (Ron Howard) comes to a small, isolated town to discover the truth about his parentage; his inquiries precipitate a spate of brutal murders that leaves bodies scattered across the landscape like autumn leaves. This is a body-count horror film just slightly ahead of its time, directed by gruff character actor Darren McGavin. Some fun for fans of the form. (a.k.a.: *Happy Mother's Day, Love, George*)

RUSSIAN ROULETTE
☆☆
1975, USA, PG
George Segal, Cristina Raines, Bo Brundin, Denholm Elliott, Gordon Jackson, Peter Donat. Directed by Lou Lombardo. 93 min.

This is a passable suspense drama set in 1970 and starring a fairly restrained George Segal as a Canadian Mountie trying to foil an assassination plot against then-Soviet Premier Alexei Kosygin (who appears in newsreel footage) on his visit to Vancouver. The complex intrigue involves, of course, the KGB and the CIA—where would low-budget spy-vs.-spy films be without them? There's nothing new here, but the Canada location is at least a mild departure from the formula.

THE RUSSIANS ARE COMING, THE RUSSIANS ARE COMING
☆☆☆
1966, USA
Carl Reiner, Eva Marie Saint, Alan Arkin, Brian Keith, Jonathan Winters, Theodore Bikel, Paul Ford, Tessie O'Shea. Directed by Norman Jewison. 124 min.

An overlong but often delightful comedy about Cold War paranoia, based on Nathaniel Benchley's novel *The Off-Islanders*. The plot has a Russian submarine running aground just off a Nantucket-like isle whose residents distrust mainlanders, let alone Commies. When some of the hapless crew members venture ashore for help, the town fights back against the Russian "invasion" with all its might. Norman Jewison lacks a comic director's sense of composition and timing, and the pace drags a little, but there are a number of ripely funny performers, led by Alan Arkin's Oscar-nominated work as the innocent Soviet sailor who finds himself in hot water. Also nominated for Best Picture, Best Screenplay, and Best Editing.

RUSTLERS' RHAPSODY
☆☆
1985, USA, PG
Tom Berenger, G.W. Bailey, Marilu Henner, Andy Griffith, Fernando Rey, Patrick Wayne. Directed by Hugh Wilson. 88 min.

Hugh Wilson, the director of *Police Academy*, misses the mark with this parody of singing cowboy westerns. As Rex O'Herlihan, a pastiche of Gene Autry, Hopalong Cassidy, and Roy Rogers dressed up in Cleavon Little's wardrobe from *Blazing Saddles*, Tom Berenger comes across as merely bland. The supporting characters aren't strong (except for a funny bit by, of all people, John Wayne's son Patrick), and there are few solid laughs—Wilson's forte is gleefully juvenile humor, but except for an annoying amount of homosexual jokes, this is more affectionate than offensive.

RUTHLESS PEOPLE
☆☆☆½
1986, USA, R
Danny DeVito, Bette Midler, Judge Reinhold, Helen Slater, Anita Morris, Bill Pullman, William G. Schilling. Directed by Jim Abrahams, David Zucker, and Jerry Zucker. 93 min.

A crude, caustic and scorchingly funny adult farce that puts the slapstick talents of the *Airplane!* team in the service of a complex, almost perfectly orchestrated plot. A venomous miniskirt merchant (Danny DeVito) plots to kill his shrewish wife (Bette Midler); when she's kidnapped by a sweet, inept young couple, he refuses to ransom her. That's merely the springboard for a series of fantastically convoluted subplots involving blackmail, a sexy videotape, a neighborhood serial killer, and "the world's stupidest man." DeVito gives his most assured comic performance to date, and Midler steals every scene she's in with her over-the-top hysterics as the "pasty-faced troll" who wants sweet revenge on her hateful husband. Even the normally bland Judge Reinhold and Helen Slater are exceptionally good as the guileless kidnappers. The comedy is often broader and noisier than it needs to be, and there are moments when it sags; at its best, though, it's as funny as any American film in years. Special praise goes to Dale Launer's debut screenplay, which, apart from a minor debt to O. Henry's "The Ransom of Red Chief," is that rarity, a genuine original.

RYAN'S DAUGHTER
☆☆☆
1970, Great Britain
Robert Mitchum, Trevor Howard, Sarah Miles, Christopher Jones, John Mills, Leo McKern, Barry Foster. Directed by David Lean. 192 min.

David Lean is a filmmaker so skilled at making lengthy, visually grandiose epics for the wide screen (*Lawrence of Arabia, Dr. Zhivago, Bridge on the River Kwai*) that he almost persuades us that trying to make an epic out of this fairly small story was the right and proper thing to do. It wasn't, though. Set in Ireland during the country's British occupation in World War I, the story concerns Sarah Miles as the spoiled wife of impotent schoolteacher Robert Mitchum and mistress of British soldier Christopher Jones. Mitchum is badly miscast, although he makes more of his role than one could really have hoped. John Mills won an Academy Award as Best Supporting Actor for his role (also against type) as a hunchbacked village idiot. Freddie Young also picked up an Oscar for the beautiful camerawork, but—and this could be a fatal problem for home viewing—much of the 70mm wide-screen presentation will be lost on a small screen.

S

SABOTAGE ★★★½
1936, Great Britain
Oscar Homolka, Sylvia Sidney, John Loder, Desmond Tester, Joyce Barbour. Directed by Alfred Hitchcock. 76 min.

One of Hitchcock's most poignant early films is based on Joseph Conrad's novel *The Secret Agent* (Hitchcock also filmed a movie called *The Secret Agent* in 1936, but that one was based on Somerset Maugham's *Ashenden*). The story involves a movie theater manager's wife (Sylvia Sidney) who suspects her husband (Oscar Homolka) of sabotage. Hitchcock uses an austere Expressionistic style to tell the offbeat tale, and the construction of the bomb-on-the-bus and knife-on-the-table scenes displays his celebrated montage technique at its nerve-racking best. Although his vision is bleak, this skillfully crafted thriller is curiously moving. (a.k.a.: *A Woman Alone*)

SABOTEUR ★★★½
1942, USA
Priscilla Lane, Robert Cummings, Norman Lloyd, Otto Kruger, Vaughan Glaser, Murray Alper, Dorothy Peterson, Alma Kruger. Directed by Alfred Hitchcock. 106 min.

Arson in an airplane factory, an unjustly accused worker, and the innocent man's dogged cross-country chase after the actual saboteurs are the plot elements in this top-notch Alfred Hitchcock suspense thriller. Made during World War II, it is not without its patriotic speeches, but its breadth of vision keeps them in perspective with several lurid minor characters—circus freaks, a saboteur's demented little son, a thuggish butler. Some nice footage of New York City, and all, of course, superbly and distinctively shot and edited.

SACCO AND VANZETTI ★★★
1971, Italy/France
Gian Maria Volonte, Riccardo Cucciolla, Cyril Cusack, Milo O'Shea, Rosanna Fratello. Directed by Giuliano Montaldo. 121 min.

This historical drama about the trial and subsequent execution of the two immigrants in 1927 Massachusetts takes the view that they were innocent, an issue still hotly debated in some circles. Arrested for theft, a crime to which they confessed, the two were accused of planning the robbery in order to raise money for anarchist causes. The film makes a good argument for its position, although it does dwell a bit too much on some unnecessarily emotional scenes to score viewer points. Music by Ennio Morricone and Joan Baez.

THE SACKETTS ★★
1979, USA (TV)
Jeff Osterhage, Tom Selleck, Sam Elliott, Glenn Ford, Ben Johnson, Gilbert Roland, Ruth Roman, Jack Elam, Mercedes McCambridge. Directed by Robert Totten. 200 min.

Splendiferous scenery and a bevy of television hunks don't really wake up this poorly paced television movie. Based on works by Louis L'Amour, the film does have a feeling of authenticity about the West, but its story of the battle between two powerful clans lacks the primal fire of great Westerns like *My Darlin' Clementine*. Here the conflict seems melodramatic, the stuff of soap opera, and the adventures of the three brothers lack dramatic focus.

SACRED GROUND ★★
1983, USA, PG
Tim McIntire, Jack Elam, Mindi Miller, Serene Hedin, Eloy Phil Casados, L. Q. Jones. Directed by Charles B. Pierce. 100 min.

The "sacred ground" of the title is an Indian burial ground that is settled by a frontier family. The best thing about this movie is that it eschews a simpleminded sensationalist approach to detailing the clash of cultures. Instead, it balances the resolution of the problem with the daunting task of making a life in an untamed country.

THE SACRIFICE ★★★
1986, Sweden
Erland Josephson, Susan Fleetwood, Valerie Mairesse, Allan Edwall, Gudrun Gisladottir, Sven Wollter. Directed by Andrei Tarkovsky. 145 min.

Andrei Tarkovsky's epic drama about a self-loathing intellectual (Erland Josephson) obsessed with what he's sure is the impending collapse of Western culture is an anomaly—the sort of symbolic, personal art film associated with the international cinema of the 1960s. The movie is infuriating and intriguing, obscure and obvious: Tarkovsky's themes (sin, guilt, death, rebirth) are the sort that invite ponderousness, and his deliberate technique (long, long tracking shots) loads everything with significance. The effect is akin to watching an even more insular and stripped-down version of one of Ingmar Bergman's chamber dramas. But just as you're ready to give up on the film, it takes on an understated power, and Josephson's fine performance allows us to see the end of the world as a symptom of human spiritual crisis. The extraordinary cinematography is by Bergman mainstay Sven Nykvist.

THE SAD SACK ★★★
1957, USA
Jerry Lewis, David Wayne, Phyllis Kirk, Peter Lorre. Directed by George Marshall. 98 min.

Jerry is at war with the army again, but this time without Dean Martin playing the foil for his endearing ineptitude. As a whiz kid with two left feet, Lewis gets tripped up with psychiatrists, spies, and Arabs, pulling it off solo in this fast-paced, funny comedy. While Lewis fans indulge, even Martin fans are bound to chuckle.

SAFARI 3000 ★½
1982, USA, PG
Stockard Channing, David Carradine, Christopher Lee. Directed by Harry Hurwitz. 91 min.

This film gives us auto racing on location across Zimbabwe and South Africa, with David Carradine, as an old Hollywood stunt driver, competing against Christopher Lee, as heir to the murderous Borgias, and Stockard Channing, as Carradine's tagalong. It's great terrain, but the action never revs up too much. (a.k.a.: *Rally* and *Two in the Bush*)

SAFETY LAST ★★★½
1923, USA
Harold Lloyd, Mildred Davis, Bill Strothers, Noah Young. Directed by Fred Newmeyer, Sam Taylor. 71 min.

Although Harold Lloyd is generally ranked with Chaplin, Keaton, and Langdon as one of the great silent comedians, and he was consistently the most popular comedy star of the 1920s, his style is less individual than theirs. He was more of a social comedian, a sort of vulnerable Douglas Fairbanks, and his movies are usually stories of the boy next door making his way in the world. This is not by way of denigrating Lloyd; certainly his best films, *The Freshman* and *Speedy*, are among the best ever made. *Safety Last*, though not so inventive, includes the most famous Lloyd sequence. After failing to make a success of himself in the big city, our hero undertakes to climb a skyscraper for a one-thousand-dollar prize. He plans to let a friend take over after the first couple of floors, but when things go awry, he ends up climbing alone and almost falls off the building's huge clock face. Lloyd was a master of thrills, and the clock-hanging sequence was done on a set specially constructed on the roof of a downtown building. Even today, the unmistakably authentic danger is spine-tingling.

SAGEBRUSH TRAIL ☆½
1934, USA
John Wayne, Lane Chandler, Nancy Shubert, Yakima Canutt. Directed by Armand Schaefer. 53 min.

This early John Wayne, done at the time he was punching the clock in countless B Westerns, has him sharing the bill with Lane Chandler in this Monogram Studios tale of an escaped con who makes good.

SAHARA ☆☆☆
1943, USA
Humphrey Bogart, Bruce Bennett, Lloyd Bridges, Rex Ingram. Directed by Zoltan Korda. 97 min.

Bogart leads a tank crew across the Sahara. He's the commander of the usual Hollywood grab-bag outfit, and Rex Ingram stands out as the unruffled Sudanese soldier marching his Italian prisoner across the sands. The desert photography was very nicely realized by Rudolph Mate, and the story carries enough tension to get over the improbabilities and the patriotic soliloquies.

SAHARA ☆
1983, USA, R
Brooke Shields, Lambert Wilson, Horst Buchholz, John Rhys-Davies, Ronald Lacey, John Mills, Steve Forrest, Cliff Potts. Directed by Andrew V. McLaglen. 104 min.

This has a lot of incidental similarities to Bo Derek's *Bolero*; released at the same time (and by the same people, Cannon Films), with the star's kin calling the shots (Teri Shields is credited as Executive Producer here), this is also about a willful young woman in the 1920s who sets off to Arabia in order to find what has previously been denied her. The difference is that, whereas Bo was looking for the Big O, Brooke wants to race her daddy's car in an international rally. "But young ladies don't drive race cars," she is told. No problem—Brooke just slaps on a mustache and everybody's happy. At least *Bolero* was a so-bad-it's-funny movie; as directed by action veteran Andrew V. McLaglen, *Sahara* has a minimal competence that its script can't live up to, raising this to the level of the merely bad.

THE SAILOR WHO FELL FROM GRACE WITH THE SEA ☆☆
1976, Great Britain, R
Kris Kristofferson, Sarah Miles, Jonathan Kahn, Earl Rhodes. Directed by Lewis John Carlino. 105 min.

In adapting Yukio Mishima's circumspect novel of honor and betrayal at a Yokohama seaport, writer-director Lewis John Carlino has transplanted the tale to Devon, England, and come up with a film that is moody, evocative, erotic, and finally nonsensical. Imagine a version of *Anna Karenina* filmed along Miami Beach, and you may begin to get a sense of the cultural dislocation that occurs here. Mishima's complex, tormented tale of a sexually malnourished widow, the sailor who beds her, and the pubescent son who resents the older man is uniquely Eastern in philosophy and spirit, and deliberately bizzare within that context. Carlino treats it with a straight face but doesn't seem quite to understand it; what emerges is all portent and allegory, with little substance or meaning. There are good performances and torrid love scenes from the two principals, but poor acting from Jonathan Kahn and Earl Rhodes as pompous, cant-spouting brats.

ST. BENNY THE DIP ☆☆☆
1951, USA
Dick Haymes, Nina Foch, Roland Young, Lionel Stander, Freddie Bartholomew. Directed by Edgar G. Ulmer. 80 min.

This low-budget melodrama was masterfully directed by Edgar G. Ulmer, the poverty-row Orson Welles. Ulmer, a new darling of the auteur criticism set, was renowned for bringing his personal touch to films with almost nonexistent budgets. Among his more noteworthy projects were *Detour*, *Carnegie Hall*, and this charming opus about low-life con artists who pose as clergymen and then find the costume is getting under their skin. The director's considerable skill turns this fragile conceit about confident tricksters going straight into something singularly charming and daffy.

ST. ELMO'S FIRE ☆☆
1985, USA, R
Rob Lowe, Emilio Estevez, Ally Sheedy, Andrew McCarthy, Mare Winningham, Judd Nelson, Demi Moore. Directed by Joel Schumacher. 110 min.

A close-knit group of college friends try to adjust to life after school. The film desperately tries to be a young adult's *Big Chill*, but is hobbled by lots of meaningless psycho-babble and exaggerated comic vignettes. A cast comprised of some of the best young talent then in Hollywood is thoroughly wasted by the artificial script and meandering direction, with only Mare Winningham surviving the mess, as a social worker with a crush on the aimless Rob Lowe. It's a shame that such fine actors couldn't have done something better than this.

THE SAINT IN LONDON ☆☆½
1939, Great Britain
George Sanders, Sally Gray, David Burns, Gordon McLeod. Directed by John Paddy Carstairs. 77 min.

No actor was better suited to *Saint*-hood than dapper, dry George Sanders, and this entry in the series, the first to be shot in England, was one of the most enjoyable. The plot has Simon Templar going up against an international counterfeiting ring. The only drawback is the resolutely bumbling portrayal of the crooks, which quickly wears thin. Based on Leslie Charteris's novel *The Million Pound Day*.

THE SAINT IN NEW YORK ☆☆
1938, USA
Louis Hayward, Kay Sutton, Sig Rumann, Jonathan Hale, Jack Carson. Directed by Ben Holmes. 72 min.

Well before Roger Moore's popular incarnation of Leslie Charteris's suave detective on television in the 1960s, the Saint turned up in a number of films; this was the first, with Louis Hayward a little too dopey and juvenile to play the hero effectively. A good supporting cast and unusually fast pace make up for some of the technical and dramatic deficiencies, but RKO made a smart move in replacing Hayward with George Sanders in subsequent Saint films. (Hayward did return for the last entry, *The Saint's Girl Friday*, in 1953.)

ST. IVES ☆☆
1976 USA, PG
Charles Bronson, John Houseman, Jacqueline Bisset, Harry Guardino, Harris Yulin, Dana Elcar, Maximilian Schell. Directed by J. Lee Thompson. 94 min.

Neither the best nor the worst of the Charles Bronson oeuvre, this workmanlike mystery casts him as a crime novelist who becomes embroiled in a real conspiracy when he crosses tracks with a rich old criminal (John Houseman) who wants him to foil a blackmail scheme. With Houseman doing a Sydney Greenstreet impression as the baddie, Jacqueline Bisset as a sumptuous femme fatale, and a brief, bizarre appearance by Maximilian Schell, this should have been better—more *noir*-ish, more mysterious, more moody. As it stands, it's a passable but unexceptional crime drama, too predictable to merit attention.

SAINT JACK
1979, USA, R ☆☆☆½
Ben Gazzara, Denholm Elliot, James Villiers. Directed by Peter Bogdanovich. 115 min.

Ben Gazzara delivers a wonderful performance as an unregenerate pimp in Singapore. Although the film wallows in the seamy world of whorehouses and cynical expatriates, it delivers an acute portrait of a man deciding not to take the final plunge in abandoning his self-respect. It's a fascinating glimpse of petty corruption and small-time exploitation set within the larger context of America's Vietnamization of Asia—eventually the bankrupt antihero refuses to run the U.S.-sponsored brothel for servicemen. The movie gives a good realization of the Paul Theroux novel, and may be Peter Bogdanovich's most controlled and unassuming film.

THE SAINT STRIKES BACK
1939, USA ☆☆½
George Sanders, Wendy Barrie, Jonathan Hale, Jerome Cowan, Neil Hamilton. Directed by John Farrow. 67 min.

The first of four *Saint* films featuring George Sanders as Simon Templar, a role as tailor-made for him as Sherlock Holmes was for Basil Rathbone. Here he journeys to San Francisco to help solve the murder of an innocent man and persuade the man's daughter not to turn to crime herself for vengeance. Well made for a B picture.

THE SAINT TAKES OVER
1940, USA ☆☆
George Sanders, Wendy Barrie, Jonathan Hale, Paul Guilfoyle, Morgan Conway. Directed by Jack Hively. 68 min.

George Sanders made his third appearance as amateur detective Simon Templar in this solid series entry, which has the Saint combatting a gang of horse-race riggers who aren't above murder. Sanders is as pleasing as ever here, but it's very much a B film, from the brief running time to the fly-by-night look of the production.

SAKHAROV
1984, USA (TV) ☆☆☆½
Jason Robards, Glenda Jackson. Directed by Jack Gold. 117 min.

This dramatization of the life of the courageous Soviet dissident was widely hailed when first released by HBO, and it helped focus world attention on the plight of the Russian physicist. The message is on target and gains power as it moves along. David W. Rintels's screenplay makes an engrossing story. Jason Robards's effective, low-key performance is aided by Glenda Jackson, who is compelling and believable as the dissident's second wife.

SALEM'S LOT—THE MOVIE
1979, USA (TV) ☆☆½
David Soul, James Mason, Lance Kerwin, Bonnie Bedelia, Lew Ayres. Directed by Tobe Hooper. 126 min.

Stephen King's clever vampire chiller is the only one of his novels to be adapted for television; the videocassette version is heavily edited from the four-hour miniseries, and includes some previously unused footage. Not surprisingly, the story seems jumpy and fragmented in this form, and it's not as scary as the big-screen King films that are unconstrained by network standards. There's still some effective neck biting, taut direction by Tobe Hooper, and a delicious performance by James Mason as the hero's dignified, toothy nemesis.

SALOME WHERE SHE DANCED
1945, USA ☆
Yvonne De Carlo, Rod Cameron, Walter Slezak, Albert Dekker, Marjorie Rambeau, J. Edward Bromberg, David Bruce. Directed by Charles Lamont. 90 min.

One of the all-time howlers of the 1940s, this film somehow caught the appreciative eye of film critic James Agee. It's a sophomoric tale about a dancing girl who bumps and grinds her way to superspydom. Try to picture Mata Hari doing the dance of the seven veils and you'll get some idea of what you're in for. Laughs galore for those who approach the film in the right caustic spirit.

SALON KITTY
1977, Italy/West Germany/France, X ☆½
Helmut Berger, Ingrid Thulin, Therese Ann Savoy, Bekim Fehmiu, John Steiner. Directed by Giovanni Tinto Brass. 110 min.

A sort of low-budget *The Damned*, with all your favorite Nazi depravities on display. It doesn't have much style, but they didn't skimp on the kinkiness. Madame Kitty (Ingrid Thulin) runs a brothel catering to Germans with bizarre tastes; but she also spies on the SS officers in attendance for commandant Helmut Berger. With Berger and Thulin around, the echoes of Visconti's film are unavoidable, but this is no more than a campy send-up with lots of exploitative material. It's a perfect companion piece to the lurid *The Night Porter*, but that's not necessarily a recommendation—remember, Brass was also responsible for much of *Caligula*.

SALT OF THE EARTH
1954, USA ☆☆½
Rosaura Revueltas, Juan Chacon, Will Geer, David Wolfe, Mervin Williams. Directed by Herbert J. Biberman. 94 min.

This film was presented by the International Union of Mine, Mill & Smelter Workers, its star was a real-life union leader, and its producer was in trouble with Congress. Welcome to the 1950s, when men were Mexican, women were men, and work was as rare as a hurricane named Juan. *Salt* details, with very little spice, a strike in aptly named Zinc Town, New Mexico; the "bosses" are evil incarnate. Despite Rosaura Revueltas's bright acting and some impressive journeyman directing and cinematography, the film doesn't pay off fully; still, it's a valuable cinematic record of a political attitude virtually never seen in American films at that time.

SALVADOR
1986, USA, R ☆☆☆
James Woods, Jim Belushi, Michael Murphy, John Savage, Elpedia Carrillo, Tony Plana, Cynthia Gibb. Directed by Oliver Stone. 122 min.

Reporter Richard Boyle cowrote the screenplay for this nightmarish venture into El Salvador, based on his own experiences in the early 1980s, and he's turned himself into a near-mythic Great American Journalist—on the front line of every battle, on the periphery of every historic moment, at the ready to tell dictators of both right and left where to shove their propaganda. If you can ignore the slightly egomaniacal tone of the enterprise, you'll find an angry, churning drama of life during wartime, intensely political in nature but canny enough not to get too partisan. At its best, it has the immediacy of *The Killing Fields*; at its frequent worst, it's Abbott and Costello south of the border, with the porcine Jim Belushi subbing for Lou as a disk jockey friend of Boyle's along for the ride. James Woods makes Boyle the kind of crude, bigmouthed know-it-all who's disliked all the more because he *does* know it all, and his tough, honorable characterization holds *Salvador* together when all else fails, which is often.

THE SALZBURG CONNECTION ☆½
1972, USA, PG
Barry Newman, Anna Karina, Klaus Maria Brandauer, Udo Kier, Karen Jenson, Whit Bissell. Directed by Lee H. Katzin. 92 min.

Helen MacInnes's exciting best-seller has been turned into a dreary, lifeless film, badly padded out with minimal location footage shot in Austria. Barry Newman is as listless and unmotivated as ever as an American lawyer investigating a hoax and uncovering some secret Nazi documents. The film gains half a star for the presence of Klaus Maria Brandauer (*Mephisto*) and Udo Kier (Andy Warhol's *Dracula* and *Frankenstein*) in early roles.

SAMAR ☆
1962, USA
George Montgomery, Gilbert Roland, Ziva Rodann, Joan O'Brien, Nico Minardos. Directed by George Montgomery. 89 min.

In this dull vehicle, actor-writer-director George Montgomery plays the head of a nineteenth-century penal colony in the Philippines. He leads the prisoners on an escape from the awful agonies of prison into the awful agonies of the jungle. Exploitation tends to have a short shelf life, and this one is no better than most recent cheap action films, just more dated.

SAME TIME, NEXT YEAR ☆☆½
1978, USA, PG
Ellen Burstyn, Alan Alda, Ivan Bonar, Bernie Kuby, Cosmo Sardo, David Northcutt, William Cantrell. Directed by Robert Mulligan. 119 min.

Pleasantly old-fashioned, rather literal adaptation of Bernard Slade's hit play about an adulterous couple who meet for one weekend a year over twenty-six years. The passing of time is represented by new hats and different hairstyles for Ellen Burstyn, and some truly tacky montages that reduce everything from hula hoops to the My Lai massacre into tiny video images. Despite the relentlessly schematic style and motormouth dialogue, the notion of "illicit fidelity" becomes charming, due more to Burstyn's dignified, funny, and touching performances than to Alan Alda's one-note morosity. Absolutely unoriginal, but quite satisfying in its familiar way. Johnny Mathis and Jane Olivor sing the requisite Marvin Hamlisch theme song, "The Last Time I Felt Like This." Major scenes filmed at the Heritage House in Mendocino, on the northern coast of California.

SAMSON AND DELILAH ☆☆☆
1949, USA
Victor Mature, Hedy Lamarr, George Sanders, Angela Lansbury, Henry Wilcoxon, Russ Tamblyn, Moroni Olsen, Fritz Leiber, Mike Mazurki, George Reeves. Directed by Cecil B. De Mille. 128 min.

Groucho Marx once remarked that what was wrong with *Samson and Delilah* was that Victor Mature had larger breasts than Hedy Lamarr. Actually, bigness is what's *right* with the film, because for Cecil B. De Mille, bigger was always better. This biblical epic may not be filled with great actors, but there are lots of them, as well as lots of extras, mammoth sets, intricate costumes, and whatever else money could buy. The story is right out of the Old Testament—almost: Samson still slays a thousand with the jawbone of an ass and pulls down the pillars of the temple, but he also spends considerably more time dallying with Delilah. Bonus attraction: unlike most epics of the time, this was *not* filmed in a wide-screen process, so you won't lose half of the image on your television screen.

SAMSON VS. THE VAMPIRE WOMEN ☆
1961, Mexico
Santo, Lorena Velazquez, Jaime Fernandez, Maria Duval, Ofelia Montesco. Directed by Alfonso Corona Blake. 89 min.

Santo, the Hulk Hogan of his time and place, becomes Samson thanks to the miracle of bad dubbing in this Mexican wonder (as in, "I *wonder* what was going through their minds when they made this?" or "I *wonder* why I'm watching this?"). As a masked and caped crimefighter, Samson battles female vampires and their burly male slaves. Lorena Velazquez, head Vampire Woman, was later promoted to Wrestling Woman and her own movies (*Doctor of Doom, Wrestling Women vs. the Aztec Mummy*).

SAM'S SONG

See *The Swap*

SAN ANTONIO ☆☆½
1945, USA
Errol Flynn, Alexis Smith, S. Z. "Cuddles" Sakall, Victor Francen, Florence Bates. Directed by David Butler. 110 min.

In a standard but satisfying elaboration on a Western cliché, a lone good guy tames a tough town and wins the love of an even tougher saloon singer. Errol Flynn seems a little out of place on the frontier, but Alexis Smith is just right, and the gallery of character actors from Warner Bros.' stable is consistently amusing to watch. Raoul Walsh did uncredited work as the codirector. Technicolor.

SANDERS OF THE RIVER ☆☆☆
1935, Great Britain
Paul Robeson, Nina Mae McKinney, Leslie Banks. Directed by Zoltan Korda. 98 min.

It's ostensibly about the British presence in Africa, but its *raison d'être* is the imposing presence of expatriate Paul Robeson, who found few opportunities for dramatic or musical stardom in all-white 1930s Hollywood. Filmed on location in Africa, *Sanders* concerns a river patrol officer and some stiff-upper-lip imperialists. Worth watching for Robeson's majestic acting; he also gets to sing a folk song here.

THE SAND PEBBLES ☆☆☆
1966, USA
Steve McQueen, Candice Bergen, Richard Crenna, Mako, Simon Oakland, Richard Attenborough, Larry Gates. Directed by Robert Wise. 179 min.

Rousing adventure tale that effectively showcases McQueen's low-key heroic style. The epic story sprawls all over land and sea in China during the 1920s, as McQueen tangles with his commanders after becoming aware of the political situation there. When not battling his superiors or engaging in military confrontations, Steve has time to pursue missionary Candice Bergen for romance. The action sequences have appealing sweep, even if the director lets the pace flag too often. It's a big-budget spectacular in which human emotions do manage to surface occasionally.

THE SANDPIPER ☆☆
1965, USA
Elizabeth Taylor, Richard Burton, Eva Marie Saint, Charles Bronson, Robert Webber, Torin Thatcher. Directed by Vincente Minnelli. 115 min.

The most memorable thing about this bloated soap opera is Johnny Mandel's theme song, "The Shadow of Your Smile." Aside from that, the biggest thrill here is watching Elizabeth Taylor attired in a series of increasingly lower-cut sweaters, culminating in as close to a nude scene as 1965 would allow. She plays a nonconformist artist who has an affair with the minister who is her son's headmaster (Richard Burton). It's all very lushly filmed on location at Big Sur in California, and if you weren't paying attention you might think that there was something going on here. Charles Bronson is featured as a beatnik sculptor.

THE SANDS OF IWO JIMA ★★★
1949, USA
John Wayne, John Agar, Adele Mara, Forrest Tucker, Wally Cassell, James Brown, Arthur Franz, Julie Bishop, Richard Jaeckel, Martin Milner. Directed by Allan Dwan. 110 min.

John Wayne received the second of three Academy Award nominations for his role here as a tough Marine Corps training sergeant during World War II. He's up against John Agar as an officer's son who has no desire to be a soldier but whom Wayne must whip into shape anyway. You can pretty much guess what happens two scenes ahead of time, but this is well done nevertheless, especially in the battle scenes, which include actual war footage. The Wayne character dies before the end of the film; but an essentially similar character was resurrected for flag-waving purposes in *The Green Berets*.

SAN FERNANDO VALLEY ★½
1944, USA
Roy Rogers, Dale Evans, Jean Porter, Ed Gargan, Trigger, the Sons of the Pioneers. Directed by John English. 74 min.

This rambling, slightly overlong Western-musical for Republic Pictures has Roy wooing ranch mistress Dale, and incidentally hunting down some ne'er-do-well guntoters. Cute songs, light fare, and a nice appearance by Ed Gargan make this fun for fans of the king of fast food and fast films.

SAN FRANCISCO ★★★
1936, USA
Clark Gable, Jeanette MacDonald, Spencer Tracy, Jack Holt, Jessie Ralph, Ted Healy, Shirley Ross, Margaret Irving, Harold Huber, Al Shean, Roger Imhof, William Ricciardi, Charles Judels. Directed by W. S. Van Dyke. 115 min.

You couldn't quite call it the original *Earthquake*, but this nifty slice of Americana does boast an enjoyable disaster-movie climax, complete with jittery cameras and falling balsa-wood pillars. Clark Gable, Spencer Tracy, and a surprisingly sexy Jeanette MacDonald are locals caught up in a melodramatic love story. Anita Loos wrote the script, D. W. Griffith handled the crowd scenes, and W. S. Van Dyke directed.

SANJURO ★★★
1962, Japan
Toshiro Mifune, Tatsuya Nakadai, Reiko Dan, Yozo Kayama. Directed by Akira Kurosawa. 96 min.

Later in Akira Kurosawa's career, no actors would serve his artistry more fully than Toshiro Mifune and Tatsuya Nakadai; here they're together in a rousing action tale—a sequel to *Yojimbo*—set in mid-nineteenth-century Japan. Mifune plays a brilliant, bold swordsman leading a band of inexperienced youths in revolt against corrupt town leaders. Funny, fast, and fierce, though lacking the technical or thematic richness of many of Kurosawa's other films.

SANTA AND THE THREE BEARS ★½
1970, USA, G
Animated: Hal Smith, Jean Van Der Pyl, Annette Ferra, Bobby Riha. Directed by Tony Benedict. 63 min.

Discriminating parents should certainly be able to find better holiday fare for the younger children than this cartoon feature. The three bears of the title aren't the ones that Goldilocks ran into, but a mother bear and her two cubs living in Yellowstone National Park. The cubs refuse to hibernate until the saintly old forest ranger dresses up as Santa Claus for them. With some innocuous songs but absolutely no moral lesson.

SANTA CLAUS—THE MOVIE ★★½
1985, USA, PG
David Huddleston, John Lithgow, Dudley Moore. Directed by Jeannot Szwarc. 110 min.

In spite of its obvious prepackaging, this big-budget fantasy from the writers and producers of *Superman* is modest fun. The filmmakers have turned Santa Claus (David Huddleston) into a jolly fat superhero. To give him a nemesis, they've created the world's ultimate capitalist in the person of industrialist John Lithgow, who, with his constantly enraged face and huffing renditions of dialogue, looks like the bull from Picasso's *Guernica*. These two marvelously overdrawn characters clash when the industrialist uses one of Santa's dejected elves (played by a cherubic Dudley Moore) to manufacture magical candy canes. A surprisingly enjoyable and often involving piece of commercialism for director Jeannot Szwarc, who envisions Manhattan as a land of advertising tie-ins and Santa's shop as an energetic toy sale at Macy's. Huddleston is so good as St. Nick that you might want to sit on his lap.

SANTA FE STAMPEDE ★½
1938, USA
John Wayne, Ray Corrigan, Max Terhune, William Farnum. Directed by George Sherman. 56 min.

Another entry in Republic's popular Three Mesquiteers series has the Duke leading his gang of good guys into battle against a corrupt justice of the peace. This dull B Western was one of the many Wayne sleepwalked through for Republic and Monogram, and one of the last before his big breakthrough in *Stagecoach* (1939).

SANTA FE TRAIL ★★★
1940, USA
Errol Flynn, Olivia de Havilland, Raymond Massey, Ronald Reagan. Directed by Michael Curtiz. 110 min.

Six army officers are ordered to destroy John Brown and his men. Michael Curtiz directed this well-made historical drama. The film's point of view often seems confused, but excellent performances by Raymond Massey as John Brown and Errol Flynn as Jeb Stuart keep the story credible. Ronald Reagan plays Flynn's West Point comrade George Custer, and he's not all that bad.

SANTEE ★★
1973, USA, PG
Glenn Ford, Michael Burns, Dana Wynter, John Larch, Jay Silverheels, Harry Townes, Robert Wilke, Robert Donner. Directed by Gary Nelson. 93 min.

Glenn Ford can't seem to muster enough energy in his role of a bounty hunter to perk up this saddle-weary Western. After his own son is killed, he adopts the son of an outlaw he has tracked down. For diehard sagebrush addicts only. Why not try a John Ford Western instead?

SAPPHIRE ★★★
1959, Great Britain
Nigel Patrick, Yvonne Mitchell, Michael Craig, Paul Massie, Bernard Miles. Directed by Basil Dearden. 92 min.

When a beautiful black student is murdered, police discover that she was passing for white, and their investigation becomes the center of controversy. The same team responsible for *Victim* (1961) created this sharp police drama that also revolves around a then-daring topic, miscegenation. With its clever use of flashbacks filling in the details of the case piece by piece, *Sapphire* holds up today as a gripping tale of a girl who led a double life. Yvonne Mitchell gives a standout performance.

SAPS AT SEA
1940, USA ★★★½
Stan Laurel, Oliver Hardy, James Finlayson, Richard Cramer, Ben Turpin, Harry Bernard. Directed by Gordon Douglas. 57 min.

Saps at Sea was one of the last Hal Roach comedies that the screen's greatest comic duo made before being drawn into a disastrous contract with Twentieth Century-Fox. It has all the hallmarks of the pair's great work: leisurely pacing, an atmosphere of nonchalance, a clever story premise; and, as a bonus, Harry Langdon—a great silent comedian in his own right—worked on the script. After Ollie has a nervous breakdown in his factory job, he decides to relax by boating; unfortunately, Stan is along to help. Stanley's attempts at aid are nothing short of sadism, but Ollie dished it out as well. James Finlayson, master of the slow burn, provides capable support.

THE SATAN BUG
1965, USA ★★½
George Maharis, Richard Basehart, Anne Francis, Dana Andrews, Ed Asner. Directed by John Sturges. 114 min.

Shogun author James Clavell wrote the adaptation of this moderately suspenseful drama about a powerful plague-creating virus that falls into the hands of a would-be terrorist, and the story (from a novel by Alastair MacLean) churns along quickly enough to let you tolerate the cardboard characterizations and paper-thin premise. On the side of the law is a federal investigator (George Maharis); his nemesis is a renegade millionaire (Richard Basehart) who manages to infiltrate the government's top-secret labs and steal the bug. It all adds up to low-grade but infectious entertainment.

SATAN'S CHEERLEADERS
1977, USA ½★
Kerry Sherman, John Ireland, Yvonne DeCarlo, Jacqueline Cole, Jack Kruschen, John Carradine. Directed by Greydon Clark. 92 min.

The devil has gone too far this time: going after Linda Blair in *The Exorcist* was one thing, but possessing nubile all-American teenagers is unforgivable. The girls are perturbed when they catch the janitor peeking into their locker room, but they're unaware that the randy old gent is in league with Beelzebub. After being delivered into the hands of the local sheriff and his wife, the girls must contend not only with demonic possession, but also with the horror of acting opposite the horrendous thesping of John Ireland and Yvonne DeCarlo, surefire candidates for admission if there's really a hell for ham actors. Gimme a B! Gimme an A! Gimme a D! What does it spell? *Satan's Cheerleaders*!

SATAN'S SCHOOL FOR GIRLS
1973, USA (TV) ★½
Pamela Franklin, Kate Jackson, Jo Van Fleet, Roy Thinnes, Lloyd Bochner, Cheryl Jean Stoppelmoor (Ladd). Directed by David Lowell Rich. 74 min.

Poor Pamela Franklin has a helluva time trying to prove her sister didn't commit suicide at a posh girls' school. Talk about alternative education! Judging from this film, the students are being trained in the Black Arts (and also in how to reach new heights of inept acting). A TV movie, and a derivative, inferior one except for Franklin, who is, as usual, too good for her material.

SATAN'S SKIN
See *The Blood on Satan's Claw*

SATURDAY NIGHT FEVER
1977, USA, PG and R (2 versions) ★★★½
John Travolta, Karen Lynn Gorney, Donna Pescow, Barry Miller, Julie Bovasso. Directed by John Badham. 108 min. (PG); 119 min. (R).

John Travolta shot to stardom playing Tony Manero in this music- and dance-filled drama about a working-class Brooklyn kid who lets loose each weekend at a local disco. It's the granddaddy of just about every pop-music movie released since, and a must for any student of 1970s pop culture in all its tacky greatness. Whether by luck or skill, Travolta gave a performance accurate and incisive enough to earn him an Oscar nomination, and his dancing is still electrifying. Director John Badham is quite sharp in his depiction of teenagers who can only let themselves live it up by dancing or destruction, and the Bee Gees score is the last word in disco. (Watch for the ominous appearance of a *Rocky* poster on Tony's wall—it was Sylvester Stallone who directed the execrable 1983 sequel, *Staying Alive*.) Note: On videocassette, *Saturday Night Fever* is available in its original R-rated form and in the PG version that was released later to capitalize on a huge teenage audience, most of whom had seen it already anyway. The shorter version is missing one significant scene, and a lot of the grit that makes the movie more than just pop trash. The R version is recommended.

SATURDAY THE 14TH
1981, USA, PG ★
Richard Benjamin, Paula Prentiss, Severn Darden, Jeffrey Tambor, Kari Michaelsen, Kevin Brando. Directed by Howard R. Cohen. 79 min.

A sludgy, ineptly written and directed send-up of you-know-what and all of the films it spawned. Slasher films are certainly ripe for parody, and a haunted house may be as good a framework as any, but Howard Cohen could stand to take a few lessons from the lowest horror hack in shot composition and storytelling. As the couple who moves into the cobwebby mansion, Richard Benjamin and Paula Prentiss don't manage to wring a single laugh out of the deadly script.

SATURN 3
1980, Great Britain, R ★★½
Kirk Douglas, Harvey Keitel, Farrah Fawcett. Directed by Stanley Donen. 88 min.

Slick sci-fi fun with an interesting variation on the monster-meets-girl theme. Psychotic astronaut Harvey Keitel brings down his pet robot to an Edenlike planetary research center that houses lovers Kirk Douglas and Farrah Fawcett. It isn't long before a large and deadly "snake" is running around this paradise lusting after the sexy spacewoman. A film that's graced with excellent set design by John Barry, and a remarkable robot. A change of pace for one of the directors who brought you *Singin' in the Rain*.

SATYRICON
See *Fellini Satyricon*

SAUL AND DAVID
1965, Italy/Spain ★★½
Norman Wooland, Gianni Garko, Luz Marques, Elisa Cegani, Pilar Clemens. Directed by Marcello Baldi. 118 min.

Those with a taste for Italian historical epics may want to track this one down in the religion section of their local video store. It is a straightforward rendering of the biblical rivalry between King Saul, who is slowly losing his faculties, and his young protégé, David. Some of the sequences are too talky, but it is generally exciting and fortunately lacks gratuitous sex and violence.

SAUVE QUI PEUT (LA VIE)
See *Every Man for Himself*

SAVAGE ☆½
1973, USA (TV)
Martin Landau, Barbara Bain, Will Geer, Barry Sullivan, Susan Howard, Dabney Coleman, Pat Harrington. Directed by Steven Spielberg. 77 min.

Steven Spielberg's little-known farewell to the small screen is a disappointment even if your expectations are low. It's pedestrian hackwork with a dull storyline about a pair of ace journalists (played by the stupefying Martin Landau and Barbara Bain) on the trail of a Supreme Court nominee with a shady past. The teleplay is cowritten by Richard Levinson and William Link, two of TV's finest writers, and it reeks of a pilot for a nonexistent series.

SAVAGE ATTRACTION ☆☆
1983, Australia/West Germany, R
Kerry Mack, Ralph Schicha, Judy Nunn, Clare Binney, Lydia Greibohm. Directed by Frank Shields. 93 min.

A bored Australian carnival worker finds herself in a very bad marriage with a quiet German man who begins talking about *his* country where there are lots of people who share his dream. Before long, she's sitting around Munich watching Leni Riefenstahl movies while her husband disappears on mysterious long trips. Based on the true story of Christine Maresch, the movie does have the ring of authenticity—what writer would dare put a fictional heroine through an abortion, beatings, a suicide attempt, an attempted abduction, and shootings by crossbow and rifle? This slow-paced melodrama is marketed, with the usual delicacy and logic, as a racy film about a teenaged sexpot.

THE SAVAGE BEES ☆☆
1976, USA (TV)
Ben Johnson, Michael Parks, Paul Hecht, Horst Buchholz, Gretchen Corbett. Directed by Bruce Geller. 99 min.

Those lovable pests are at it again, this time invading Louisiana via a banana boat to spread a plague that may end up destroying the city's Mardi Gras celebration. It's up to sheriff Ben Johnson to haul out the bug spray, while entomologist Gretchen Corbett provides solemn explanations of their stinging behavior, that is, until they . . . If you haven't seen *The Bees*, *The Killer Bees*, or *The Swarm*, you may as well jump in here; if you enjoy it, catch the sequel, *Terror Out of The Sky*. Edited by (we kid you not) George Hively.

SAVAGE ISLAND ☆
1985, USA/Italy/Spain, R
Linda Blair, Ajita Wilson, Christina Lai, Anthony Steffen. Directed by Nicholas Beardsley, Edward Muller. 79 min.

Producers from three countries labored to make one piece of junk. As Woody Allen did with *What's Up, Tiger Lily?*, American Nicholas Beardsley here took a foreign genre junker (women in jungle prison), chopped out a third of it, and added a new frame story (with Linda Blair, both of whose fans should note that she's here for only a few minutes). Featuring a woman with a surprising reaction to snakes, many busty women falling out of their clothes, and some of the worst dubbing ever in a film without giant Japanese monsters.

THE SAVAGE IS LOOSE ☆
1974, USA, R
George C. Scott, Trish Van Devere, John David Carson, Lee H. Montgomery. Directed by George C. Scott. 114 min.

It's really a shame that this wasn't a good, or even remotely competent film, because it might have accomplished something. Star George C. Scott produced and directed, then also distributed the film to theaters himself, hoping to buck the system of Hollywood middlemen who gobble up the lion's share of a film's profits and then fudge it in the paperwork at the expense of both filmmakers and exhibitors. Unfortunately, the film is a complete mess, two hours of pseudo-Darwinian babble mixed with generous doses of Freud. Scott and wife Trish Van Devere (his wife in real life as well) are stranded on a tropical island with their infant son. As the boy (played by Johnny Carson's son) grows up, he develops certain, uh, animal attractions toward the only human female on the island—Mom. Featuring some of the most ludicrous dialogue you've ever heard, along with equally bad acting.

SAVAGES ☆☆
1974, USA (TV)
Andy Griffith, Sam Bottoms, Noah Berry. Directed by Lee H. Katzin. 72 min.

Mildly suspenseful man-against-man film has a jaded, selfish attorney (Griffith) chasing a young man through the desert in an attempt to cover up an accidental killing. Made by TV's big producers, Aaron Spelling and Leonard Goldberg (*Love Boat, Dynasty*).

SAVAGE SAM ☆
1963, USA
Brian Keith, Tommy Kirk, Kevin Corcoran, Dewey Martin, Jeff York, Marta Kristen. Directed by Norman Tokar. 103 min.

This is Disney product at its nadir—a falsely sugary, overlong, and even offensive tale of a Texas posse trying to retrieve a pair of kidnapped kids from an Apache tribe. Tommy Kirk and Kevin Corcoran were two of the least appealing products of the Disney youth factory, and the tone of the film, which alternates sluggish action with low comedy, is distracting. The subject matter is less likely to upset kids than to bore them.

SAVAGE STREETS ☆☆
1984, USA, R
Linda Blair, Robert Dryer, Sal Landi, Johnny Venocur, Scott Mayer, John Vernon. Directed by Danny Steinmann. 93 min.

Pavement-pounding, tire-screeching vigilante flick whose sleazy plotting, muscular direction, salacious dialogue, and overwhelming aura of smuttiness make this an exploitation classic. Poor Linda Blair has been in trouble before but the urban blight here outdoes the locusts who plagued her in *Exorcist II*. Her angelic, deaf-mute sister is gang-raped by foaming-at-the-mouth punksters who, ever on the prowl for mischief, next pitch Linda's best girlfriend off a bridge on the eve of her wedding. Is it any wonder Linda strikes back? With her Frederick's of Hollywood leather togs and Annie Oakley marksmanship, Linda's Rambo-ette makes Movieland's savage streets safe for sex-and-violence-fanciers everywhere.

SAVANNAH SMILES ☆☆☆
1982, USA, PG
Mark Miller, Donovan Scott, Chris Robinson, Michael Parks, Bridgette Anderson, Peter Graves. Directed by Pierre De Moro. 105 min.

An embraceable family film about two bumbling kidnappers who stumble upon a rich little runaway and plan to collect a reward. Instead they become grumpy temporary foster parents and demonstrate more love for this little kid than her upscale but neglectful parents ever did. A modest but engaging comedy with a delightful performance by Bridgette Anderson as the determined little Goldilocks who wants to hang onto her two newfound parents.

SAVE THE TIGER ☆☆☆½
1973, USA, R
Jack Lemmon, Jack Gilford, Laurie Heineman, Norman Burton, Patricia Smith. Directed by John G. Avildsen. 100 min.

This early 1970s update on *Death of a Salesman* and *The Man in the Grey Flannel Suit* casts Jack Lemmon as a small-time garment manufacturer in crisis. While preoccupied with wartime memories, he considers burning down his factory in order to collect on his insurance. This bitter, depressing look at one man's mid-life crisis has an uncompromising flavor that is both repellent and powerful, and Lemmon's Oscar-winning performance hits all the right notes. The sour, unpleasant characters and perspective will appeal mainly to those who see water pitchers as half empty rather than half full, but the film is impressively done, and still packs a powerful punch. Jack Gilford is excellent as Lemmon's business partner.

SAVING GRACE ☆
1986, USA, PG
Tom Conti, Giancarlo Giannini, Fernando Rey, Erland Josephson, Patricia Mauceri, Donald Hewlett, Edward James Olmos. Directed by Robert M. Young. 112 min.

Papal pabulum that isn't helped a bit by its engaging star or international supporting cast. Tom Conti plays fictional pontiff Leo XIV, who tires of the Vatican and decides to become a Pope of the populace. He drifts into a destitute Italian village and starts to help its peasant residents, doing good deeds and keeping his real identity a secret. Unbelievably tedious and sentimental, the film is also about ninety minutes too long for its Sunday-morning-TV parable of a plot. Publicity credited the screenplay to "Joaquin Montana," although it was reportedly written by director Robert Young, Conti, Richard Kramer, and David S. Ward (*The Sting*).

SAWDUST AND TINSEL ☆☆☆½
1953, Sweden
Harriet Andersson, Ake Groenberg, Hasse Ekman, Anders Ek, Annika Tretow, Kiki. Directed by Ingmar Bergman. 82 min.

This haunting early Bergman film follows the sordid lives of a troupe of down-and-out circus performers from the turn of the century. Love and betrayal again form the plot for the legendary director's exploration of helplessness, humility, and humanity. And what better location for it all than under the big top? While many of his psycho-stylistics are still in the experimental stage here, Bergman successfully evokes a backdrop of depression against which our own beliefs and prejudices can be visualized and tested. This mental drama is most apparent in the scene where a circus clown must carry his feeble wife from the stream where she bathed nude through a gauntlet of erotomaniacal soldiers. An important film for Bergman fans. (a.k.a.: *The Naked Night*)

SAY AMEN, SOMEBODY ☆☆☆½
1982, USA, PG
Directed by George T. Nierenberg. 100 min.

This highly entertaining documentary concerns gospel singers. The heart and soul of the movie is "Mother" Willie Mae Ford Smith, a St. Louis singer who was sixty-eight when she cut her first record and who now wears the beatific expression of a young girl in a church choir. Producer/director George T. Nierenberg doesn't quite find a way to convey the drama of gospel's history, but when he focuses on the singing of Smith and her disciples, the movie has power to spare. Featuring Thomas A. Dorsey, Sallie Martin, the Barrett Sisters, and the O'Neal Brothers.

SAY GOODBYE, MAGGIE COLE ☆☆
1972, USA (TV)
Susan Hayward, Darren McGavin, Michael Constantine, Nichelle Nichols, Dane Clark, Beverly Garland, Jeanette Nolan. Directed by Jud Taylor. 75 min.

Susan Hayward gave her final performance in the title role of this sudsy telefilm about a recently widowed doctor who returns to practice at a clinic in the mean streets of Chicago. The maudlin story is no different from that of an average medical-drama-series episode, but Hayward was expert at making hackneyed material work, and she almost pulls it off here.

SAY HELLO TO YESTERDAY ☆☆
1971, Great Britain
Jean Simmons, Leonard Whiting, Evelyn Laye, John Lee. Directed by Alvin Rakoff. 91 min.

Murky May-December romance that plays like an archetypal soap opera. However, the brilliant Jean Simmons had so few starring vehicles in her career (she always seemed to be Richard Burton's or Kirk Douglas's leading lady, but rarely had a film built around her) that fans may want to bask in her latter-day radiance as she succumbs to her passion for a boy young enough to be her son. The material's trite, but Simmons transforms the lachrymose events.

SAYONARA ☆☆☆½
1957, USA
Marlon Brando, Red Buttons, Miyoshi Umeki, Miko Taka, James Garner, Martha Scott. Directed by Joshua Logan. 147 min.

In a beautifully acted love tale, an American pilot becomes smitten with a Japanese entertainer during the Korean War. Paul Osborn adapted the splashy James Michener tome; the interracial love stories strain after tragedy but instead settle into familiar soap opera patterns. In addition to Marlon Brando's ill-fated affair, there's a tearjerking subplot involving Red Buttons and Miyoshi Umeki, whose romance is destroyed by prejudice and Army interference. Both Buttons and Umeki were awarded supporting actor Oscars. A bit sappy by today's standards, it still exerts a pull on our emotions.

SAY YES ☆
1986, USA, PG-13
Lissa Layng, Art Hindle, Logan Ramsey, Jonathan Winters, Maryedith Burrel, Jensen Collie. Dircted by Yust Camera. 88 min.

A feeble comedy about a man who's got to get married in a big hurry in order to rake in a 250-million-dollar inheritance, this is even worse than the remake of *Brewster's Millions*, which had a similar greed-based plot line. Hollywood used to crank out these breezy comedies by the dozens, but this one smacks of frenetic desperation. Reportedly, Winters's scenes were added to save a hopelessly flawed product. Poor Jonathan deserves better than this.

SCALPS ½☆
1983, USA, R
Kirk Alyn, Carroll Borland, Jo Ann Robinson, Richard Hench, Forrest J. Ackerman. Directed by Fred Olen Ray. 82 min.

Six archeology students go out to the desert to dig for Indian artifacts, until one is possessed by the evil spirit of renegade warrior Black Claw. He slaughters his friends in various ineptly bloody ways and undergoes a gross physical transformation into a vicious Indian. The film's lack of technical sophistication extends to its inclusion of an early montage of the mutilated victims that effectively dispels any rudimentary suspense as to their fates that might have existed. A boring low-budget horror movie.

SCANDALOUS ☆½
1984, USA, PG
Robert Hays, John Gielgud, Pamela Stephenson, Jim Dale, M. Emmet Walsh, Bow Wow Wow. Directed by Rob Cohen. 94 min.

Exploitation masters Larry and Rob Cohen have never had trouble wringing a few laughs out of the proceedings in their other films (*It's Alive, The Stuff*). But when they sat down to write an out-and-out comedy, they forgot that they had to compensate for the lack of a monster with more jokes. The result, this failed attempt at a 1940s-style mystery comedy, is flat and empty. Robert Hays, as an American newscaster, becomes caught up in various shady schemes masterminded by veteran con artist John Gielgud and his niece Pamela Stephenson. Sir John is used as he was in *Arthur*, so that his outrageous actions (e.g., dressing up in leather regalia to attend a punk concert) would contrast with his stately British accent and posture. That's about as clever as this gets.

SCANNERS ☆☆
1981, Canada, R
Jennifer O'Neill, Stephen Lack, Patrick McGoohan, Charles Shamata. Directed by David Cronenberg. 102 min.

This is a favorite of David Cronenberg cultists, and the one that began to win him wide critical notice; nonfans, however, may have a little trouble discerning what all the shouting's about. The "scanners" are a race of genetic mutants with telepathic abilities, eagerly sought for both pro- and antigovernment work. Cronenberg sets his sights on too many targets, and therefore never really hits any of them. What remains with you afterward is an unsettled feeling and the memory of some excruciating special effects, mostly of people blowing up from within, shown in great detail—veins popping out, etc. For the strong of stomach only.

SCARAMOUCHE ☆☆½
1952, USA
Stewart Granger, Eleanor Parker, Janet Leigh, Henry Wilcoxon, Nina Foch, Mel Ferrer. Directed by George Sidney. 118 min.

The Rafael Sabatini novel about a young adventurer seeking the nobleman who murdered his friend gets the full MGM costume treatment here, with the French Revolutionary atmosphere missing but the sets, spectacle, and derring-do in full throttle. It's hokey material even for the time, and nobody in the cast seems to know whether to go for laughs or play it straight. The action is often incomprehensible, but at least it moves along quickly. Originally made in 1923, with Ramon Novarro in Granger's role.

SCARECROW ☆☆☆
1973, USA, R
Gene Hackman, Al Pacino, Dorothy Tristan, Eileen Brennan, Ann Wedgeworth. Directed by Jerry Schatzberg. 112 min.

One of the better 1970s "buddy" films, a subgenre that goes back at least as far as *Of Mice and Men* but that really came into its own in the wake of *Midnight Cowboy* and *Butch Cassidy and the Sundance Kid*. In this version, recent San Quentin parolee Gene Hackman, hitchhiking to Pittsburgh, where he plans to use his savings to open a car wash, meets up with Al Pacino, a sailor on his way to see the five-year-old child whose mother he abandoned before its birth. Hackman is the closed-off one, Pacino the clownish extrovert; of course, each brings out the inner depths of the other. Generally too heavy-handed (in one scene Hackman, who wears innumerable layers of clothing, saves Pacino from a beating in a bar by doing a mock striptease, removing his clothing and his psychic armor in a bit of symbolism right out of Freshman Lit.), but saved by the performances, especially Hackman's and those of the supporting actresses. Winner of the Golden Palm at Cannes.

SCARED TO DEATH ☆½
1980, USA, R
John Stinson, Diana Davidson, Jonathan David Moses, Toni Jannotta. Directed by William Malone. 95 min.

The police, suspecting a conventional murderer, are mystified, and who can blame them? It's actually genetic engineering gone awry that's produced this sci-fi horror, now lurking in the sewers of L.A. and using its expansive tongue to suck the life out of its victims. Writer-director William Malone designed the monster himself, obviously after seeing the one in *Alien*.

SCARFACE ☆☆☆½
1932, USA, PG
Paul Muni, Ann Dvorak, Karen Morley, Osgood Perkins, Boris Karloff, George Raft. Directed by Howard Hawks. 99 min.

Paul Muni radiates sheer nastiness as the gangster Tony Camonte in this Howard Hawks masterpiece. Subtitled *The Shame of the Nation* to satisfy the censors, this harsh, gripping saga shares little of the romanticism that characterizes the other films of this genre. Camonte, loosely based on Al Capone, is a mean and ugly gangster with a scar across his face that suggests an inner twistedness, a deeper disfigurement. Camonte begins as a gunman and then ruthlessly seizes control from the mob boss, Johnny Lovo (Osgood Perkins). Ben Hecht crafted the film's exciting, bloody, psychologically dense screenplay. Hawks's direction is, of course, outstanding and far exceeds that of the Brian De Palma rip-off.

SCARFACE ☆☆½
1983, USA, R
Al Pacino, Michelle Pfeiffer, Steven Bauer, Mary Elizabeth Mastrantonio, Robert Loggia. Directed by Brian De Palma. 169 min.

As a remake of Howard Hawks's taut, sleek gangster classic, Brian De Palma's foray into the genre is a dud; judged on its own, it's pretty mediocre—a foulmouthed, blood-soaked excursion into Cuban racketeering in Miami. The protagonist is criminal refugee Tony Montana (Al Pacino), a low-life hood who floats to the top of Florida's cocaine industry by carefully choosing whom to befriend and whom to expend. All the while, he nurtures an obsession for his beautiful sister (Mary Elizabeth Mastrantonio) and a coke habit that would make an elephant's trunk disappear. Oliver Stone's screenplay has some terrific lines (none quotable here) and Pacino's mesmerizing, underappreciated performance keeps the film going during the long stretches in which De Palma's direction becomes turgid or lazy. This *Scarface* has excess everywhere that the original had subtlety; see it only if your tolerance for gore and De Palma are high.

THE SCARLET AND THE BLACK ☆☆☆
1983, USA (TV)
Gregory Peck, Christopher Plummer, John Gielgud, Raf Vallone, Barbara Bouchet. Directed by Jerry London. 155 min.

Based on the book *The Scarlet Pimpernel of the Vatican*, this expert thriller is a catch-me-if-you-can suspense drama that features Gregory Peck in his TV movie debut. He toplines the cast as a heroic Vatican official who ignores the precepts of neutrality by becoming instrumental in aiding prisoners of war during the dark days of Germany's occupation of Rome. The excitement derives from the fact that a wily Nazi (Christopher Plummer) suspects the subterfuge and is determined to put an end to Peck's good-samaritanism, and to Peck, too. Fast-paced, uncommonly stylish wartime thriller.

THE SCARLET LETTER ☆☆
1934, USA
Colleen Moore, Hardie Albright, Henry B. Walthall, Alan Hale, William Farnum. Directed by Robert G. Vignola. 70 min.

Unfortunately, this is the only version of Nathaniel Hawthorne's classic currently available on videotape: the 1926 silent version with Lillian Gish and the 1975 West German version directed by Wim Wenders are both far superior. The basic undeniably bleak story of Hester Prynne, a Puritan woman who is stigmatized when she bears an illegitimate child and refuses to name the father, a righteous minister, has been lightened with some inappropriate comic relief. It's a pity, too, because the leads are well cast, particularly Colleen Moore as Hester.

THE SCARLET PIMPERNEL ☆☆☆½
1934, Great Britain
Leslie Howard, Merle Oberon, Raymond Massey, Joan Gardner, Nigel Bruce, Anthony Bushnell. Directed by Harold Young. 95 min.

This feast-for-the-eyes adaptation of Baroness Orczy's novel is served up on the silver screen by producer Alexander Korda. Leslie Howard, dynamically doubling as a British socialite and a friend to those in need during the French Revolution, is the main course, though not a ham. Elaborate sets and costumes spice things up, maybe even too much.

THE SCARLET PIMPERNEL ☆☆☆
1982, USA (TV)
Anthony Andrews, Ian McKellen, Jane Seymour, James Villiers, Eleanor David, Malcolm Jamieson. Directed by Clive Donner. 150 min.

TV-movie producers have a predilection for remaking classic film versions of famous novels; often, they're more faithful to the source material, but they rarely match the vigorous filmmaking qualities of the original productions. This *Pimpernel* is a lushly mounted, impeccably acted swashbuckler, but Anthony Andrews is no Leslie Howard and the larger-than-life role of the Pimpernel requires a more florid movie-star presence. Andrews, a good actor, is better at suggesting the Pimpernel's foppish alter ego than he is at socking across that revolutionary activist's heroic stature. Fans of derring-do and aficionados of costume dramas will find much to admire in the lavish production, based on two Baroness Orczy books, *The Scarlet Pimpernel* and *El Dorado*.

SCARLET STREET ☆☆☆½
1945, USA
Edward G. Robinson, Joan Bennett, Dan Duryea. Directed by Fritz Lang. 103 min.

Edward G. Robinson is a henpecked cashier dragged into the gutter by a scheming roundheel and her pimping boyfriend. Joan Bennett and Dan Duryea play the two low-rent chiselers who chip away at Robinson's self-esteem like demented Rodins carving a naked old man out of a lump of liver. Lang's dark vision, nurtured in the German expressionist cinema, found the perfect outlet in the postwar cynicism of American *film noir*. Lang delivers an austere, obsessive remake of Jean Renoir's *La Chienne*.

SCARRED ☆
1985, USA
Jennifer Mayo, Jackie Berryman, David Dean, Randolph Pitts, Shandra Beri, Neva Miner. Directed by Rose-Marie Turko. 85 min.

In a run-of-the-mill documentary-style story, an unmarried mother is forced by her circumstances into, yes, a life of prostitution. The moral dimensions of her fate are presented with TV crudity, and the graphic depiction of the squalor of her milieu rivals that of Andy Warhol's *Bad*. A pitying fellow hooker and a good-hearted pimp supply the obligatory warmth and smarmy understanding this troubled young woman is so touchingly in need of. Sentimentally antisentimental, with no credible statement about prostitution, and certainly nothing resembling acting, to redeem it.

SCARS OF DRACULA ☆☆½
1971, Great Britain, R
Christopher Lee, Dennis Waterman, Jenny Hanley, Wendy Hamilton. Directed by Roy Ward Baker. 96 min.

The last of the good Hammer Studios Dracula movies is also the last period Dracula. After this, they made the mistake of bringing the count into modern times (*Dracula A.D. 1972*). This film is in the mold of *Dracula Has Risen from the Grave* and *Taste the Blood of Dracula*, if not as cleverly titled, with ridiculous amounts of blood, lusty wenches, and more religious imagery than St. Patrick's Cathedral. Christopher Lee's characterization of Dracula by this time had moved to the direct opposite of Bela Lugosi's, a snarling, bloodthirsty animal as opposed to the suave seducer.

SCAVENGER HUNT ½☆
1979, USA, PG
Richard Benjamin, James Coco, Scatman Crothers, Cloris Leachman, Cleavon Little, Roddy McDowall, Robert Morley, Richard Mulligan, Tony Randall, Dirk Benedict, Willie Aames, Richard Masur, Avery Schreiber, Vincent Price, Meat Loaf, Ruth Gordon, Liz Torres, Pat McCormick, Arnold Schwarzenegger. Directed by Michael Schultz. 116 min.

Comedies that are so overloaded with stars and guest stars that they never get around to being really funny are not hard to find—in fact, Michael Schultz made two of them (*Car Wash* and *Sergeant Pepper's Lonely Heart's Club Band*) prior to this. *Scavenger Hunt* has the distinction, however, of having a large cast that is entirely unlikable and obnoxious; not only that, but the movie is so long that they all get sufficient time on screen to torment you. The premise is that rich old geezer Vincent Price dies and leaves his entire 200-million-dollar estate to whichever of his relatives wins a scavenger hunt. The various factions form into teams, bicker incessantly, and fall down a lot. The "nice" team, who you realize all along are going to win, are bland and unengaging—you root for them (if at all) only because you hate everyone else so much. We laughed exactly once.

SCENES FROM A MARRIAGE ☆☆☆
1973, Sweden (TV)
Liv Ullmann, Erland Josephson, Jan Malmsjo, Bibi Andersson, Gunnel Lindblom. Directed by Ingmar Bergman. 168 min.

Bergman's microscopic study of an unhappy couple's shattering breakup and its aftermath is nowhere near the masterpiece that critics called it in the 1970s, and how could it be? American audiences see only half of the film, which was originally made as a five-hour television miniseries in Sweden. Bergman supervised the cuts for the U.S. release, but few works of genius (which this may have been) could survive the loss of fifty percent of their footage and then woeful dubbing without seeming jumpy, arbitrary, even boring. What remains is a tribute to Bergman's extraordinary talents as a writer and director—a moving drama that scaled the highs and lows of a troubled relationship with remarkable precision. Erland Josephson's good performance and Liv Ullmann's great one both suffer from the cutting and dubbing—the film's many brilliant aspects are sabotaged in one way or another throughout. Read Bergman's full-length screenplay, published in the United States in book form, for an idea of what you're missing. Bergman's *Face to Face* and *Fanny and Alexander* underwent similar TV-to-film adaptations, but somehow survived with more integrity.

SCHIZO ☆½
1977, Great Britain, R
Lynne Frederick, John Leyton, Stephanie Beacham, John Fraser. Directed by Pete Walker. 92 min.

Not widely released in this country, this British chiller is most notable for being one of the few starring features of Lynne Frederick, Peter Sellers's wife at the time of his death. Apparently taking a cue from her husband's many multiple performances, she plays a young woman who may or may not be a schizophrenic killer, never having gotten over the childhood trauma of seeing her mother killed by a maniac. A few mildly gory murders and a twist ending aren't enough.

SCHLOCK (THE BANANA MONSTER) ☆☆½
1971, USA
Saul Kahan, Joseph Piantadosi, Eliza Garrett, John Landis. Directed by John Landis. 80 min.

A sloppy, irreverent parody, this was John Landis's first— and most agreeable—movie. After such inspired silliness, his projects became infected with elephantiasis (see *The Blues Brothers*). A gorillalike monster, a sort of distant relative of King Kong, goes on a rampage and tears at the very fabric of small-town life with hysterically funny results. Watch this for the scene in which a blind girl mistakes the furry fiend for a seeing-eye pooch. You'll never again sit through the blind-hermit scene in *Bride of Frankenstein* without cracking up.

SCHOOL SPIRIT ☆½
1985, USA, R
Tom Nolan, Elizabeth Foxx, John Finnegan, Larry Linville, Daniele Arnaud, Marta Kober, Tom Hudson. Directed by Alan Holleb. 90 min.

A morbid little story about a college kid who runs head-on into a truck and returns to campus as a ghost to consummate his relationship with a curvaceous coed. Given its premise, its low-budget values, and its witless script, this movie isn't as bad as it could be—it's innocent and dopey, and the characters seem almost human. Still, there are more amusing ways to pass time—like almost any TV sitcom.

SCORE ☆½
1973, USA/Yugoslavia
Claire Wilbur, Calvin Culver, Lynn Lowry, Gerald Grant, Carl Parker. Directed by Radley Metzger. 90 min.

Radley Metzger, the European equivalent of Russ Meyer, made a shaky transition to the more explicit 1970s with this comedy about a swinging couple out to seduce the naive newlyweds next door. The twist is that the wife wants the wife and the husband the husband. This may be of some significance to aficionados of softcore porn for being the first (and one of the very few) films to give equal treatment to straight and gay sex, all with the usual Metzger voluptuousness, though as a comedy it's negligible.

SCREAM AND DIE ½☆
1974, Great Britain, R
Andrea Allan, Karl Lanchbury, Maggie Walker. Directed by Joseph Larraz. 98 min.

A clumsy, lurid horror film from England, this is about a knife-wielding maniac who stalks buxom young ladies (he apparently learned his trade from all the other knife-wielding maniacs in equally sleazy films), and the gorgeous model who witnesses one of his killings, but doesn't suspect just how close the murderer is to her heart. Originally released as *The House That Vanished*.

SCREAM AND SCREAM AGAIN ☆☆½
1970, Great Britain
Vincent Price, Christopher Lee, Peter Cushing, Christopher Matthews, Judi Bloom. Directed by Gordon Hessler. 94 min.

Director Gordon Hessler shows some stylish traits throughout this atypical AIP horror film, though the end result never lives up to its promise. The main plot has mad doctor Vincent Price trying to create a superhuman race from leftover bits of victims he has killed. There's also a parallel subplot set in an Eastern European police state, the significance of which doesn't become clear until the film's end. It was considered quite gruesome at the time, though it shouldn't bother anyone nowadays. Christopher Lee and Peter Cushing are relegated to supporting roles, lest anyone think that this was to be a summit meeting of horror stars.

SCREAM BABY SCREAM ☆☆½
1970, USA, R
Ross Harris, Eugenie Wingate, Chris Martell, Suzanne Stuart, Larry Swanson. Directed by Joseph Adler. 91 min.

Four hippie art students take painting class, hang out and/or perform in cool psychedelic clubs, take acid trips, and wear groovy clothes. Their idyll ends when Charles Butler, renowned painter of macabre portraits and scenes, enters their lives. With the help of an insane doctor over whom he wields unholy influence, Butler is determined to make over the real world into something resembling his nightmare canvases, and so he does. Low-budget horror with lots of entertaining elements, including a pretty girl turned into a Picassoesque grotesque in three dimensions.

SCREAM FOR HELP ½☆
1985, Great Britain/USA, R
Rachael Kelly, David Brooks, Marie Masters, Rocco Sisto, Lolita Lorre, Corey Parker. Directed by Michael Winner. 90 min.

A thoroughly, almost deliriously incompetent thriller directed by ham-fisted hack Michael Winner, *Scream for Help* is an irresistible loser with a couple of real belly laughs. Teenager Christie just *knows* her nasty stepdad Paul is planning to kill her rich dodo of a mother—the basement switchbox is rewired to deadly effect, the brakes on the family car fail, and she even catches him *in flagrante* with another woman. But will she be able to prove it before it's too late? Not in this movie, where everyone in the town is suffering from severe stupidity, caused by overexposure to plot contrivances. Features hefty helpings of sleazy violence, a central performance by zaftig teen Rachael Kelly that's squarely in the tradition of Linda Blair, a script full of howlers by Tom Holland (*Psycho II*), and the worst musical score of the 1980s. Don't miss it.

SCREAM OF THE DEMON LOVER ½☆
1971, Spain/Italy, R
Agostina Belli, Jeffrey Chase, Jennifer Hartley, Antonio G. Escribano. Directed by Jose Luis Merino. 76 min.

Sleazy, poorly produced, execrably dubbed foreign horror film about a nineteenth-century baron murdering local girls to use them as raw material in his experiments with carbon regeneration, and the beautiful assistant who must stop him before she becomes the next victim. Pure trash that, like so many cheap horror films, is retitled and repackaged to look like an American production. (a.k.a.: *Ivanna*)

SCREAMS OF A WINTER NIGHT ☆
1979, USA, PG
Matt Borel, Gil Glascow, Patrick Byers, Mary Agen Cox, Robin Bradley. Directed by James L. Wilson. 91 min.

The Bergman pun of the title is about as clever as this horror anthology gets. Ten college kids go camping at a remote lake area that's rumored to be haunted and spend a night sitting around the campfire telling scary stories (well, they're *supposed* to be scary). Filmed in 16 mm, this is very low-budget and very tame.

SCREEN TEST ½☆
1986, USA, R
Michael Allen Bloom, Robert Bundy, Paul Leuken, David Simpatico, Mari Laskarin. Directed by Sam Auster. 84 min.

A low-budget, retrograde sex comedy about four horny men who pretend to produce a low-budget, retrograde porn video in order to "meet" beautiful women. "Wait!" says one. "We need some sort of outline—a script—or else it'll come out like shit!" Duly noted. Features a porn marquee reading "Amphibioids from the Deep Rape Your Favorite Network Soap Stars," a very tedious Siskel-and-Ebert parody, and a rude speculation about the upper anatomy of "Dukes of Hazzard" star Catherine Bach.

SCROOGE ☆☆½
1970, Great Britain, G
Albert Finney, Alec Guinness, Edith Evans, Kenneth More, Michael Medwin, Laurence Naismith, David Collings, Richard Beaumont. Directed by Ronald Neame. 115 min.

Young children will enjoy this splashy, visually rich musicalization of the Charles Dickens classic *A Christmas Carol*, with Albert Finney in heavy makeup doing a gloriously hammy turn as the greatest reformed humbug of them all. Adults are advised to do household chores during Leslie Bricusse's gooey songs, and pay attention only to the lovely performances by everyone from Edith Evans (as the wraithlike Ghost of Christmas Past) to young Richard Beaumont, thankfully unmaudlin as Tiny Tim. *Scrooge* is perfectly serviceable, but for a more definite adaptation, hunt down either the 1951 Alastair Sim standard or, better still, the superb 1984 telefilm starring George C. Scott, both of which are also available on cassette.

THE SEA AROUND US ☆☆☆
1953, USA, PG
Narrator: Don Forbes. Directed by Irwin Allen. 61 min.

Unbelievably, before Irwin Allen swarmed into towering infernos of disaster films, he cowrote and produced this hour-long documentary adaptation of Rachel L. Carson's best-seller about the sea. There are whales instead of wails, and eels instead of squeals—all shot seamlessly and edited swimmingly. Music by Paul Sawtell and photo effects by Linwood Dunn tide it over. Short, but worth the trip from port.

SEA DEVILS ☆☆☆
1953, Great Britain
Yvonne De Carlo, Rock Hudson, Maxwell Reed, Denis O'Dea. Directed by Raoul Walsh. 90 min.

Rock Hudson is a Guernsey Island fisherman-turned-smuggler and Yvonne De Carlo a British spy posing as a French countess in this excellent cloak-and-dagger costume yarn set during the time of Napoleon I. Hudson mistakenly thinks she's a French spy, but when the French pierce her disguise and imprison her, he about-faces and chivalrously goes to her rescue. Hair-raising adventure combined with high-society intrigue make this a winning diversion. In Technicolor.

THE SEA HAWK ☆☆½
1940, USA
Errol Flynn, Flora Robson, Claude Rains, Brenda Marshall, Donald Crisp, Alan Hale, Henry Daniell, Una O'Connor, James Stephenson, Gilbert Roland, William Landigan, Julien Mitchell, Montague Love, J. M. Kerrigan, Fritz Leiber. Directed by Michael Curtiz. 127 min.

A highly regarded but only average swashbuckler, this is taken, with liberties, from Rafael Sabatini's tale of feuding Elizabethan families and recast as a pirate/Robin Hood vehicle for Errol Flynn. Directed with a great deal of zip by Michael Curtiz, and handsomely photographed by Sol Potito. Too bad Flynn looks like he's getting tired of all the derring-do, Claude Rains is almost unrecognizable in one of his least distinguished villain roles, and Brenda Marshall provides merely soggy love interest. Only Flora Robson holds court as a boisterous Queen Elizabeth. Well made, but certainly not another *Adventures of Robin Hood*.

SEANCE ON A WET AFTERNOON ☆☆☆
1964, Great Britain
Kim Stanley, Richard Attenborough, Patrick Magee, Nanette Newman, Maria Kazan. Directed by Bryan Forbes. 115 min.

A muted (maybe *too* muted) but engrossing psychological thriller. Tired of the public's and the media's refusal to take her gifts seriously, a medium persuades her mild-mannered, subservient husband to initiate a kidnapping scheme that will propel her to prominence when she reveals the missing child's whereabouts. Tension mounts as the expedient plot backfires and the demented mind reader loses her grip on reality. A disturbing film that cooks along on a low burner. Kim Stanley's performance is overpowering and details the process of a mental breakdown with uncanny skill.

SEARCH AND DESTROY ☆☆
1981, USA, PG
Perry King, Don Stroud, George Kennedy, Tisa Farrow, Park Jong Soo. Directed by William Fruet. 93 min.

Sure, it's cheap, but it's also nice and gritty. It is ham-fisted, but also two-fisted. The film gives a nice slice of working-class Vietnam vets' lives, but is still only a slow, routine actioner. In other words, it's average. A Vietnamese ex-ARVN soldier chases the remnants of the squad that abandoned him in battle—a nice twist on the usual veteran-as-loner-against-indifferent-society routine.

THE SEARCHERS ☆☆☆☆
1956, USA
John Wayne, Jeffrey Hunter, Vera Miles, Ward Bond, Natalie Wood, Lana Wood, John Qualen, Henry Brandon. Directed by John Ford. 119 min.

No director made better Westerns than John Ford, and many would argue that *The Searchers* is the best he ever made. Although he was actually adapting a serialized novel by Alan LeMay, Ford seems to have rethought the entire story in cinematic terms, and the result is a film that comments and expands upon the Western genre as a whole. If you know it only by reputation, you may be surprised at its bleak, almost frightening psychological acuity and the unexpected savagery of its heroes as well as its villains. John Wayne plays Ethan Edwards, a stoic frontiersman who returns to his brother's homestead after the Civil War, only to witness the massacre of his family and the kidnapping of his young niece by hostile Comanches. With his adoptive nephew (Jeffrey Hunter), Edwards embarks on a search for the girl that turns into an obsessive quest spanning many fruitless years. Ford's thematic concerns were never more skillfully woven into a story than they are here, and Wayne never topped his work as Edwards, a subtle and skilled portrayal that reveals both the dark and heroic sides of the archetypal Western loner. The beauty of Winton C. Hoch's rich, twilight-hued cinematography is diminished on video, but that shouldn't deter you from seeing this brooding masterpiece, a film whose style and themes echo through the work of many of today's best-known filmmakers.

THE SEA SHALL NOT HAVE THEM ☆☆☆
1954, Great Britain
Michael Redgrave, Dirk Bogarde, Bonar Colleano, Anthony Steel, Nigel Patrick, Nigel Green, Rachel Kempson. Directed by Lewis Gilbert. 92 min.

High waters and high drama in this sincere and biting story of a British aircraft downed in the icy waters of the North Sea keep this English "male bonding" movie afloat. The four downed flyers spend a couple of anxious days bobbing helplessly in a dinghy while the British navy conducts its search. Sharp intercutting between the survivors and their rescuers propels the film full steam ahead toward the dramatic conclusion, which takes place off the German-occupied shores of Belgium. With excellent performances, Michael Redgrave and Dirk Bogard *become* heroes.

SEA WIFE ☆
1957, Great Britain
Joan Collins, Richard Burton, Basil Sydney, Ronald Squire, Cy Grant. Directed by Bob McNaught. 82 min.

This dreadful adventure of the ocean has one attraction, so riotous in concept that it lends the film genuine camp status: Joan Collins plays a nun. That said, it should be added that one performance, no matter how inadvertently funny, is no reason to suffer through this ridiculous tale. Most of it takes place in flashback, with Collins and three men (now, *that's* more like it) stuck in a dinghy after their ship has been torpedoed. Richard Burton plays the RAF officer who falls in love with her. Thoroughly silly, and even Burton can't really scrape together a good performance here.

THE SEA WOLVES ☆☆½
1980, USA/Great Britain, PG
Gregory Peck, Roger Moore, David Niven, Trevor Howard, Patrick Macnee. Directed by Andrew V. McLaglen. 120 min.

Rip-snorting action tale about some over-the-hill British Army specialists who have to get their mitts on a German radio transmitter. There's no doubt that these senior saviors are going to come through with flying colors, so viewers can settle back and enjoy how all the action formulas work themselves out. It's a better-than-average World War II adventure, a sort of tongue-in-cheek *Guns of Navarone*. All-American Gregory Peck has as much trouble with his English accent as he did with his German one in *The Boys from Brazil*, but he has the authority to make us believe in his heroic presence. The other stars are accomplished, if a bit too suave for their assignments.

SECOND CHORUS
1940, USA ☆
Fred Astaire, Burgess Meredith, Paulette Goddard, Artie Shaw and orchestra, Charles Butterworth. Directed by H. C. Potter. 83 min.

🎵 Those who feel this is Fred Astaire's worst musical will get no argument here (though *Finian's Rainbow* should at least make the final balloting). Whoever got the idea of involving Fred in these big-band monkeyshines without supplying decent choreographic opportunities ought to be beaten with a stack of Artie Shaw records. Added liabilities are the undistinguished score and the garbled plot line about two collegiate musicians trying to strike a happy chord with the same girl. Paulette Goddard, who's usually so cheery and effusive, is a lummox on and off the dance floor and succeeds in being Astaire's second worst partner of all time—the signal honor of first worst going to Joan "Elephant Walk" Fontaine in *Damsel in Distress*).

SECRET ADMIRER
1985, USA, R ☆☆½
C. Thomas Howell, Kelly Preston, Lori Loughin, Fred Ward. Directed by David Greenwalt. 90 min.

This is a teenage *Cyrano de Bergerac*, with a handsome youth (C. Thomas Howell) receiving a love letter from a mysterious admirer. Soon enough, the paper gets into the hands of a number of parents and kids, resulting in a lot of comic havoc. A fresh and very funny youth picture that's thankfully spare on sex and gross gags, and one that also takes a surprisingly honest look at teenage relationships.

SECRET AGENT
1936, Great Britain ☆☆☆☆
John Gielgud, Madeleine Carroll, Robert Young, Peter Lorre. Directed by Alfred Hitchcock. 93 min.

This satirical spy thriller is among the most complex and unusual of Hitchcock's British films. John Gielgud and Madeleine Carroll pose as a married couple to carry out a secret mission, and, through well-intentioned naiveté, become involved with deception and murder. Peter Lorre is a Mexican hired killer. The director achieves a tense balance between sardonic wit and taut suspense. Lorre plays his part with maniacal humor and stands out in this fine cast.

SECRET HONOR
1984, USA, R ☆☆☆½
Philip Baker Hall. Directed by Robert Altman. 90 min.

Robert Altman directed the film version of Donald Freed and Arnold M. Stone's Richard Nixon play—a ninety-minute monologue in which our deposed president performs a drunken rite of self-justification, outlining a conspiracy theory so labyrinthine it outdoes anything your local streetcorner orator ever dreamed of. Freed and Stone caricature the spluttering obscenities and inchoate thoughts, the erratic speech patterns of the private Nixon America discovered in the Watergate transcripts. And Philip Baker Hall gives an admirably crazed performance, building his paranoid fits into a lathered crescendo. The result is one of the most biased, deranged, and entertaining political movies ever made.

THE SECRET LIFE OF AN AMERICAN WIFE
1968, USA ☆½
Walter Matthau, Anne Jackson, Patrick O'Neal, Edy Williams, Richard Bull. Directed by George Axelrod. 92 min.

George Axelrod has written brilliant comic screenplays, such as *Breakfast at Tiffany's* and *Lord Love a Duck* (which he also directed), but this black comedy talks itself to death. A frustrated housewife poses as a prostitute and offers her services to one of her husband's clients. The cast tries hard but the bright spots are infrequent, and whatever attracted Axelrod to this subject matter isn't apparent from the indifferent comedy results on view.

THE SECRET LIFE OF WALTER MITTY
1947, USA ☆☆½
Danny Kaye, Virginia Mayo, Boris Karloff, Fay Bainter, Ann Rutherford, Thurston Hall, Reginald Denny, Fritz Feld. Directed by Norman Z. McLeod. 108 min.

James Thurber's short story is used as a jumping-off point for a series of Danny Kaye routines, all tied together by an unnecessary plot about real-life spies. As the daydreaming Milquetoast who escapes his dull job and nagging mother into various fantasies, Kaye goes through bits as a sea captain, a surgeon, a riverboat gambler, etc. It has its moments, but it's not prime Kaye. Boris Karloff does have a very funny scene in which he pretends to be a psychiatrist and tries to convince Kaye that he's insane.

THE SECRET OF NIMH
1982, USA, G ☆☆☆
Animated: Elizabeth Hartman, Derek Jacobi, Dom DeLuise, John Carradine, Peter Strauss. Directed by Don Bluth. 82 min.

The artists at the then-new Aurora animation studios have resurrected the full-length "classical" cartoon (*à la* Disney) with skill and charm. Director Don Bluth and company heap on the visual details (the golden glow of a candle, rippling reflections in splashing water, and so on), and their story of a pack of superintelligent rats who live in their own high-tech, underground city whizzes right along. It's just good enough to make you wish it were better—less derivative and philosophically richer. Still, it's easily among the best recent animated features.

SECRET PLACES
1985, Australia ☆☆½
Marie-Theres Relin, Tara MacGowran, Cassie Stuart, Claudine Auger, Jennie Agutter. Directed by Zelda Barron. 98 min.

A well-meaning but overly genteel coming-of-age film about the friendship of two adolescents in World War II England. A troubled German refugee has difficulty adapting to her new life in a British girls' school, where the students hold a great deal of resentment toward the Germans. Plot strands involving other students and the girls' home lives are never woven together properly, and the project is directed with too much reverence. Still, the insight into adolescent growing pains makes up for the film's Masterpiece Theatre-ish overtones.

THE SECRET POLICEMAN'S OTHER BALL
1982, Great Britain, R ☆☆☆½
John Cleese, Peter Cook, Michael Palin, Graham Chapman, Eleanor Bron, Rowan Atkinson, Pamela Stephenson, Sting, Peter Townshend, John Williams, Phil Collins, Jeff Beck, Eric Clapton. Directed by Julien Temple and Roger Graef. 91 min.

Poorly filmed and edited, this is a compilation of often hilarious skits and musical performances from two concerts given in London to benefit Amnesty International, a worthy organization benefiting victims of political persecution. The lack of credits will be frustrating to American audiences, as will much of the dialect, especially that in a very funny monologue by an unidentified British comic who looks like Curly of the Three Stooges. There are also numerous famous but uncredited faces in the finale, an all-star sing-along of "I Shall Be Released." Of the comedy bits, the best feature John Cleese and Pamela Stephenson as a couple tormenting each other at a bus stop, and Peter Cook and Rowan Atkinson as cultists gathered on a mountaintop to await the end of the world. Of the musical sections, Townshend performs "Won't Get Fooled Again" with classical guitarist John Williams, Sting and Phil Collins turn in good solo renditions of their songs, and Jeff Beck and Eric Clapton sing a duet in blistering fashion.

SECRETS
1978, USA, R ☆
Jacqueline Bisset, Per Oscarsson, Robert Powell, Shirley Knight Hopkins. Directed by Philip Saville. 92 min.

A 1971 film released in 1978 to cash in on Jacqueline Bisset's popularity has a longish nude scene of the stunning Bisset. Nothing else. Jumbled, amateurishly made, the movie is the story of a family in which all of the members have had surreptitious sex.

SECRETS
1982, Great Britain, R ☆☆½
Helen Lindsay, John Horsley, Anna Campbell-Jones, Daisy Cockburn. Directed by Gavin Millar. 75 min.

A gentle, well-directed import, set in 1963, about a thirteen-year-old girl's discovery of the adult world of sex and betrayal. Anna Campbell-Jones plays young Louise, who discovers some contraceptives in a secret box belonging to her late father. Their existence causes confusion and debate among her school chums—what are they, anyway?—and more serious woe for her mother. Nicely handled, though very minor and markedly inconsistent in its tone.

SECRETS OF WOMEN
1952, Sweden ☆☆½
Anita Bjork, Karl Arne Holmsten, Jarl Kulle. Directed by Ingmar Bergman. 108 min.

Three young wives briefly separated from their husbands trade bittersweet reminiscences in an early, minor comedy-drama by Ingmar Bergman. The themes of fidelity, betrayal, and solitude that would mark his greatest films are present here in embryonic form, but *Secrets of Women* remains conventional and uninvolving, due partly to its flashback format, and partly to the fact that its central story of a pregnant woman and her weak-willed lover is the least interesting one. The film is well acted by all, although poor dubbing detracts from the performances.

THE SECRET WAR OF HARRY FRIGG
1968, USA ☆☆
Paul Newman, Sylva Koscina, Tom Bosley, Andrew Duggan, James Gregory, John Williams, Charles D. Gray, Vito Scotti, Norman Fell, Buck Henry. Directed by Jack Smight. 110 min.

An uninspired but passable World War II comedy, quite a flourishing genre in the 1960s. When five Allied generals are captured by the Germans, goof-off private Harry Frigg is disguised as a general and sent into the camp to find out why they haven't taken advantage of ample opportunities to escape. Paul Newman coasts by on his charm, though he spends too much of the movie's first half mugging mindlessly.

THE SEDUCTION
1982, USA, R ☆
Morgan Fairchild, Michael Sarrazin, Andrew Stevens, Vince Edwards. Directed by David Schmoeller. 104 min.

In this nonthriller, Morgan Fairchild makes two serious mistakes. First, she crosses paths with a deranged photographer who wants to ravish her in the flesh after a shutterbug courtship of picture-snapping. Second, she makes the more damaging mistake of allowing the film's director to photograph her with her hair dripping wet; without her celebrated bouffant hairdo, her minimal screen presence evaporates completely. Morgan Fairchild uncoiffed is the most terrifying sight awaiting you here in this substandard damsel-in-distress horror film.

THE SEDUCTION OF JOE TYNAN
1979, USA, R ☆☆
Alan Alda, Barbara Harris, Meryl Streep, Rip Torn, Melvyn Douglas, Charles Kimbrough, Blanche Baker, Adam Ross, Carrie Nye, Chris Arnold. Directed by Jerry Schatzberg. 107 min.

Alan Alda seems to delight in putting little cracks in his nice-guy image. Unfortunately, this melodrama (which he wrote and starred in) about the professional and domestic crises of a revered, Edward Kennedy–type senator is cheaply staged and thoroughly muddled. Alda obviously thinks he's saying something important about American political life, but all he's really done is graft a tired situation-drama about a man who has an affair and doesn't spend enough time with his family onto a blandly "topical" hash of political clichés. The result is all the more grating for Alda's self-importance. Meryl Streep gives a good performance as the Southern labor lawyer who "seduces" Joe Tynan.

THE SEDUCTION OF MIMI
1974, Italy, R ☆☆☆
Giancarlo Giannini, Mariangela Melato, Agostina Belli, Elena Fiore. Directed by Lina Wertmüller. 89 min.

Lina Wertmüller's story of a man who goes to absurd lengths to defend his sexual honor but is too frightened to do anything about his political honor stars Giancarlo Giannini as the distracted hero playing musical beds and Mariangela Melato as his mistress, a sort of Marxist Aphrodite. The film is notable for a grotesque scene in which Giannini beds down with an obese woman, and the wide-angle lens reveals her derriere in all its flabby splendor. Later filmed in a reconceived version with Richard Pryor entitled *Which Way Is Up?*

SEEDS OF EVIL
1974, USA ½☆
Joe Dallesandro, Katharine Houghton, Rita Gam. Directed by Jim Kay. 97 min.

A ludicrous, seedy-looking horror flick, which will never be recommended by Better Homes and Gardens, let alone by Better Critics and Reviewers. A gardener with a green thumb for cultivating evil has the knack of transforming oversexed women into oversized shrubs after he has his way with them. Only Katharine Houghton manages to resist this greenhouse effect. A film of monumental ineptitude, acted with consummate torpor by Joe Dallesandro, who conveys sexual menace with all the intensity of a clipped hedge, and with false graciousness by Houghton, who wins the 1974 Lady Bountiful Award (usually given to Trish Van Devere) for acting like a debutante in the receiving line of a coming-out party. Shot in Puerto Rico. (a.k.a: *The Gardener*)

SEEMS LIKE OLD TIMES
1980, USA, PG ☆☆
Goldie Hawn, Chevy Chase, Charles Grodin, Robert Guillaume, Harold Gould, George Grizzard, Yvonne Wilder, T. K. Carter, Judd Omen, Marc Alaimo. Directed by Jay Sandrich. 102 min.

The smoothest, most enjoyable movie ever fashioned from an original Neil Simon script. It follows the well-defined laws of bedroom farce, a genre that Goldie Hawn, Chevy Chase, and Charles Grodin—as wife, ex-husband, and new husband, respectively—navigate with some skill. Unfortunately, Simon also employs a tasteless, racist subtext: much of the comedy—when Chase isn't hiding under a bed or falling down, or when Hawn isn't acting flummoxed or Grodin priggish—derives from racial stereotyping. Director Jay Sandrich (a TV sitcom veteran) isn't the sharpest comedic hand we've seen, but the writing is so overstuffed with gags that, had most of them paid off, the film might have curdled into overheated muck.

SEE NO EVIL
1971, Great Britain ☆☆☆
Mia Farrow, Dorothy Allison, Robin Bailey, Diane Grayson. Directed by Richard Fleischer. 89 min.

In a way, this Richard Fleischer thriller was ahead of its time, because it foreshadows later forays into mayhem like *Halloween* and *Friday the 13th*. Attacked at the time of its release for excessive violence, this is a reasonably controlled exercise in terror, falling somewhere between a damsel-in-distress thriller and the contemporary slasher film. Farrow plays a blind girl whose relatives are wiped out by a vengeful killer, who keeps a watchful eye on her for most of this scary film's length. A real nail-biter.

SEIZE THE DAY ☆☆☆
1987, USA (TV)
Robin Williams, Joseph Wiseman, Jerry Stiller, John Fiedler, Tony Roberts, William Hickey, Eileen Heckart, Jo Van Fleet, Glenne Headly, Richard B. Shull, Fran Brill. Directed by Fielder Cook. 93 min.

Robin Williams gives an affecting dramatic performance as a middle-aged loser trying to get back on his feet in this sour, ruefully funny adaptation of Saul Bellow's novel. Williams plays Tommy Wilhelm (born Wilhelm Adler), fired from his job as a kiddie-furniture salesman, squeezed by his estranged wife for support payments, pressured by his girlfriend to get a divorce, and routinely humiliated at the hands of his benignly sadistic father (Joseph Wiseman), an elderly doctor who despises his son's mediocrity. Williams, though good, falters in some of his big moments and the film as a whole isn't dramatized as much as it might have been, but Wiseman's brilliant work will rivet your attention.

THE SELL OUT ☆☆
1976, Great Britain, PG
Richard Widmark, Oliver Reed, Gayle Hunnicutt, Sam Wanamaker, Peter Frye. Directed by Peter Collinson. 88 min.

A couple of good action sequences, including a car chase finale, aren't enough to make this espionage drama more than mildly interesting. Retired CIA agent Richard Widmark, now living in Israel, decides to help out Oliver Reed, his former associate, currently the object of a manhunt by both the Russians and the Americans. Along the way, the Israelis, who don't cotton to having their home turf used as a battleground, join in the fun and games. The characters give lots of speeches about how awful all of this killing is, usually right before or after the filmmakers have shown us some, just so we can see for ourselves.

SEMI-TOUGH ☆☆½
1977, USA, R
Burt Reynolds, Kris Kristofferson, Jill Clayburgh, Robert Preston, Bert Convy, Roger E. Mosley, Lotte Lenya, Richard Masur, Carl Weathers, Brian Dennehy, Mary Jo Catlett. Directed by Michael Ritchie. 107 min.

If only Michael Ritchie's adaptation of Dan Jenkins's bestseller were about football, or team relations—or something that might justify its setting in the midst of a Miami gridiron squad on its way to the Superbowl. Instead, *Semi-Tough* is a slick, contemptuous redneck-chic movie that devotes most of its time to a farcical attack on New Age consciousness-raising movements. The film views psychic seekers—and intellectuals and businessmen and devout Christians—as ninnies and offers only a sort of juvenile nihilism as an alternative. Burt Reynolds's performance here is good enough to make you wish it were housed in a worthier film. Kris Kristofferson and Jill Clayburgh, though, are miscast and unconvincing.

THE SENATOR WAS INDISCREET ☆☆☆
1947, USA
William Powell, Ella Raines, Peter Lind Hayes, Arleen Whelan, Hans Conried. Directed by George S. Kaufman. 81 min.

A charming lamebrain farce about political machinery jammed up with human imperfections. Expert farceur William Powell shines as a ditzy senator who watches the complications pile up when a juicy political diary slips out of his hands. It has the rapid-fire pacing and snappy dialogue that all the classic Kaufman-Hart comedies had in abundance; perhaps George S. Kaufman's direction had something to do with that. Crackling hilarity.

THE SENDER ☆☆½
1982, Great Britain, R
Kathryn Harrold, Zeljko Ivanek, Shirley Knight, Paul Freeman. Directed by Roger Christian. 92 min.

A young man, simultaneously coddled and tormented by his insanely religious mother, finds himself in a mental hospital after a suicide attempt. One psychiatrist devotes herself to tying to uncover the source of his troubles, only to learn that he has a remarkable mental power: he can "send" his terrifying nightmares into other people's minds, an experience that is very unpleasant indeed. Unusually well-made psychological horror film enlivened by a series of grotesque dream sequences that are as bloody as they are bizarre.

THE SENIORS ☆
1978, USA, R
Dennis Quaid, Jeffrey Byron, Gary Imhoff, Edward Andrews, Alan Reed, Priscilla Barnes. Directed by Rod Amateau. 87 min.

Four lovable college seniors hustle a foundation grant to study the sex lives of college girls and end up opening a sex institute where businessmen make a donation to participate in the research. Right. In other words, four sleazes become cynical pimps, and viewers are invited to laugh along. Look for Priscilla Barnes (TV's "Three's Company") in a nonspeaking role as a "nympho who likes to cook and clean."

A SENSE OF LOSS ☆☆☆
1972, USA/Switzerland
Directed by Marcel Ophuls. 135 min.

Following the enormous success of his brilliant documentary *The Sorrow and the Pity*, Marcel Ophuls turned to the conflict in Northern Ireland; the result was this compelling though not definitive study. To capture the turbulence and confusion, Ophuls used a profusion of voices, emcompassing street kids, revolutionaries, and the politically enfranchised. Thankfully, he doesn't bully the viewer toward a particular stance or solution, but chooses instead to try to define the scope and complexity of the issues involved. The cumulative effect is moving, but be warned: the accents make some of the soundtrack unintelligible.

THE SENSUOUS NURSE ☆
1978, Italy, R
Ursula Andress, Jack Palance, Mario Pisu, Duilio Del Prete, Stefano Sabelli. Directed by Nello Rossati. 79 min.

In case you don't have a so-called adult cable station in your area and always wondered what it would be like, here's your chance to find out: this bomb is a staple in those markets. A lecherous old count refuses to die, even though his sexual escapades have landed him in the hospital with a heart attack. To hasten him along, his greedy heirs hire a blond bombshell to "nurse" him into the grave. It's really rather sad to see Ursula Andress at her age still having to take off her clothes to get movie parts, although on the other hand she gives no evidence here of having any other credentials to offer.

THE SENTINEL ☆☆
1977, USA, R
Chris Sarandon, Cristina Raines, Martin Balsam, John Carradine, Jose Ferrer, Ava Gardner, Arthur Kennedy, Burgess Meredith, Sylvia Miles, Deborah Raffin, Eli Wallach, Christopher Walken, Jerry Orbach, Beverly D'Angelo, Tom Berenger, William Hickey, Jeff Goldblum. Directed by Michael Winner. 91 min.

This is one of the lesser examples of the school of religious horror films (*Rosemary's Baby*, *The Omen*, *The Exorcist*). A model rents an apartment in a Brooklyn Heights building and begins to notice that her neighbors are, well, sort of *weird*. Turns out they're either demons or priests, all out to secure the entranceway to hell, which just happens to be located in the building. Director Michael Winner has no touch for subtlety, as he demonstrated in all three of the *Death Wish* films—the devil, for instance, is played by Burgess Meredith as a raging queen, and when the script calls for the minions of hell to arise, Winner uses real sideshow freaks and human monsters. The effect is creepy, but you feel abused. The large cast is used to no great advantage, least of all to distract attention from Cristina Raines, who is quite bad.

A SEPARATE PEACE ☆½
1972, USA, PG
John Heyl, Parker Stevenson, Peter Brush, Victor Bevine, Scott Bradbury. Directed by Larry Peerce. 105 min.

John Knowles's unctuous, self-satisfied novel about preppies enduring their last year of school before being shipped off to fight World War II is given an appropriate visual treatment, full of shimmering snow-covered fields and sparkling sunlight to contrast with the rottenness of the "real" world. The leaders of the graduating class are Finny, an athletic daredevil, and Gene, his bookish best friend who betrays him. Sample of deep dialogue: "If war can drive somebody crazy, then it's real, all right." Movies like this could make you start to think nicer things about *Rambo*.

SEPARATE TABLES ☆☆☆½
1958, USA
David Niven, Deborah Kerr, Burt Lancaster, Rita Hayworth, Wendy Hiller, Cathleen Nesbit, Gladys Cooper. Directed by Delbert Mann. 99 min.

In the hands of a sterling cast, Terence Rattigan's pair of one-act plays becomes a memorably touching film drama. The setting is a cozy seaside hotel in England where an unhappy couple and some unhappy singles play out their private romance dramas and hushed tragedies. David Niven won an Academy Award for his superbly etched portrait of an ex-colonel who inflates his past heroics to impress a timid spinster (Deborah Kerr); Burt Lancaster and Rita Hayworth are also fine as a divorced couple attempting a reunion. An Oscar also went to Wendy Hiller as the resort's proprietress whose affair with Lancaster is crushed by the appearance of his ex-wife. Later remade for television with Alan Bates and Julie Christie.

SEPARATE VACATIONS

See *Separate Ways*

SEPARATE WAYS ☆½
1981, USA, R
Karen Black, Tony LoBianco, Sharon Farrell, Robert Fuller, Arlene Golonka, David Naughton, William Windom. Directed by Howard Avedis. 92 min.

Soap suds in suburbia, about a couple who discover that something is amiss with their marriage when they both have affairs. The message that you have to fall apart to come together is tame, tired, and overworked—the movie plays like a self-help manual for the terminally dull, and the ending is simply hopeless. Karen Black and Tony LoBianco have both done much stronger work.

SERENADE ☆☆½
1956, USA
Mario Lanza, Joan Fontaine, Sarita Montiel, Vincent Price, Joseph Calleia. Directed by Anthony Mann. 121 min.

Musicals were clearly not Anthony Mann's forte, but this musical soap opera has more bite than his previous *Glenn Miller Story*. James M. Cain's seamy novel about a vineyard worker who rises to prominence as a singer was adapted to fit the talents of ex-MGM glutton Mario Lanza. With the allusions to the singer's homosexuality removed, what is left is a fairly juicy catfight between a chi-chi society woman (Joan Fontaine) and the Mexican spitfire (Sarita Montiel) who really loves him. Lanza looks a little lost in Douglas Sirk country, but he is right at home singing "Serenade," "My Destiny," "Ave Maria," and many others.

THE SERGEANT ☆½
1968, USA/France, R
Rod Steiger, John Philip Law, Ludmila Mikael, Frank Latimore, Elliott Sullivan. Directed by John Flynn. 107 min.

A desperate, oafish attempt to present a modern depiction of homosexuality—modern, that is, in the somewhat reactionary Hollywood climate of the late 1960s—by showing how the passion of its poor pathetic victims will ultimately destroy them. It's more offensive than even the most limp-wristed comic treatments of gays, if only because it takes itself so seriously. Rod Steiger plays a hard-as-nails war hero who is consumed by a possession-obsession for a handsome young recruit. The subject of homosexuality in the military can be compelling, even when handled as obliquely as it is in *Reflections in a Golden Eye*, but this film botches it badly, and Steiger's flagrant overplaying (he acts repression by pursing his lips and bulging his eyes) is exhausting to watch.

SERGEANT MATLOVICH VS. ☆☆☆
THE U.S. AIR FORCE
1978, USA (TV)
Brad Dourif, Marc Singer, Frank Converse, William Daniels, Stephen Elliott, Rue McClanahan. Directed by Paul Leaf. 100 min.

An earnest, worthwhile TV movie depicts a celebrated case of sexual discrimination, a no-win situation for an air force veteran who challenged the legality of Uncle Sam's bias against homosexuality. Brad Dourif is, for once, remarkably restrained and effective as a reluctant hero coming to grips with his sexuality and finding the courage to confront the homophobic attitudes of the military establishment.

SERGEANT PEPPER'S ☆
LONELY HEARTS CLUB BAND
1978, USA, PG
Peter Frampton, Barry, Robin and Maurice Gibb, Alice Cooper, Billy Preston, Steve Martin, George Burns, Donald Pleasence, Earth, Wind and Fire. Directed by Michael Schultz. 111 min.

The entrepreneurs behind *Saturday Night Fever* pulled together this virtual desecration of classic Beatles tunes by inflating them into a stupid, obvious, cartoonish story line, and putting them in the mouths of such 1970s pop icons as Peter Frampton and the Bee Gees. Watching the disco brothers Gibb and arena rocker Frampton cough out the great music on their tissue-thin voices will remind you that 1978 was not a banner year for pop tunes (the year's other big musical was the film *Grease*). What there is of the script, not surprisingly, stinks. You'd be better off with *A Hard Day's Night*, *Help!* or any old Beatles album.

SERGEANT YORK ☆☆☆½
1941, USA
Gary Cooper, Walter Brennan, Joan Leslie, George Tobias, Stanley Ridges, Margaret Wycherly, Ward Bond. Directed by Howard Hawks. 134 min.

Top-notch propaganda and first-rate drama, this cleverly crafted screenplay helped Gary Cooper sell the American war effort. Gary won his first Oscar as Alvin York, the crack marksman who suffered pangs of conscience when he was drafted. It's a thoughtful story of grace under pressure as York tries to reconcile his pacifist leanings with the exigencies of survival on the battlefield. How he manages to square his Bible-influenced philosophy with his desire to defend his country adds up to a somewhat simplified but gratifying exercise in hero worship. One of Warner Bros.' prouder achievements in biographical drama

SERIAL
1980, USA, R ☆☆
Martin Mull, Tuesday Weld, Jennifer McAlister, Sam Chew, Jr., Sally Kellerman, Anthony Battaglia, Nita Talbot, Bill Macy, Pamela Bellwood, Barbara Rhoades, Christopher Lee, Tom Smothers, Peter Bonerz. Directed by Bill Persky. 91 min.

Cyra McFadden's observant satire of life in ultra-mellow Marin County, California, has been turned into a raunchy sitcom by director Bill Persky. Persky has retained the characters' names, faddish pursuits, and psycho-babbly dialogue, but he's replaced McFadden's fair-mindedness with a condescension that turns the people into goonish cartoons. Tuesday Weld has a presence that even a bad script can't spoil, but Martin Mull (overdoing Barth Gimble) and Tom Smothers (as a spacey minister) have rarely looked worse.

THE SERPENT'S EGG
1977, USA/West Germany, R ☆☆
Liv Ullmann, David Carradine, Gert Frobe, Heinz Bennent, Gynn Turman, James Whitmore. Directed by Ingmar Bergman. 119 min.

Even the greatest of directors can make a misstep, and this drab, derivative mess by Ingmar Bergman proves it. Working outside of Sweden for the first time, Bergman had the misfortune to meet up with producer Dino De Laurentiis, who was to the 1970s what Golan and Globus are to the 1980s. The result was his highest-budgeted film, and one of his least successful. The milieu is 1923 Berlin, where Liv Ullmann plays a seedy whore who works part-time in a seedier cabaret, and David Carradine is an American circus performer who begins to lose his mind in the decadent, unfamiliar atmosphere. The English-language screenplay (by Bergman) is so poorly constructed and awkwardly played that the cumulative effect is one of watching a second-rate Bergman imitator or skilled parodist.

SERPICO
1973, USA, R ☆☆☆½
Al Pacino, John Randolph, Jack Kehoe, Biff McGuire, Barbara Eda-Young. Directed by Sidney Lumet. 130 min.

Sidney Lumet, working in the realistic crime drama milieu that is his forte, adapts Peter Maas's novel about the New York City maverick cop Frank Serpico. Lumet gets a raw, gutsy performance from Al Pacino as the officer who refuses to take graft, and his depiction of Serpico's dangerous raids is explosively violent. In some ways, *Serpico* feels like a warm-up for Lumet's similar, superior *Prince of the City* (1981). It's Pacino you come away remembering.

THE SERVANT
1963, Great Britain ☆☆☆½
Dirk Bogarde, Sarah Miles, James Fox, Wendy Craig. Directed by Joseph Losey. 115 min.

Director Joseph Losey's dark and decadent adaptation of Harold Pinter's first screenplay is a sardonic household study of the fickleness of power and the daily moral hypocrisies of the British upper class. An aristocratic playboy (James Fox) has his staid life turned inside out by a sinister butler (Dirk Bogarde), who starts out as the man's servant but ends up as his lover and master. Full of disturbing implications and exceptional acting, this is one of Losey's most tantalizing and complex films.

SESAME STREET PRESENTS: FOLLOW THAT BIRD
1985, USA, G ☆☆½
Jim Henson's "Sesame Street" muppets, Caroll Spinney, Jim Henson, Frank Oz, Sandra Bernhard, John Candy, Chevy Chase, Joe Flaherty, Waylon Jennings, Dave Thomas, Paul Bartel. Directed by Ken Kwapis. 88 min.

This child's movie will also amuse adults. It's a *Canary, Come Home*–style adventure about that gawky eight-footer, Big Bird, who must travel back to Sesame Street after the Feathered Friends Society places him for adoption with the Dodo family—a snooty crew whose members goose-step to the approved pecking order of Jane Fonda workouts, DeSoto ownership, and a rigid nine-to-five worm hunt. As Bird heads for home, his Sesame Street pals fan out to search for him, and he runs into such human luminaries as Paul Bartel, Sandra Bernhard, and Waylon Jennings. The filmmakers buttress the story by trashing the targets we love to hate: conformity, greed, and bad food.

SESSIONS
1983, USA (TV) ☆½
Veronica Hamel, Jeffrey DeMunn, Jill Eikenberry, David Marshall Grant, George Coe. Directed by Richard Pearce. 100 min.

A woman's film, this is about a call girl who works the swanky side of the Big Apple, but comes to view her superficial lifestyle with increasing disdain. Inordinately glossed over, the film is full of surface revelations; a blue-ribbon hooker must somehow see the light and realize there is more to life than shopping at Bloomingdale's every day. Ex-model and "Hill Street Blues" regular Veronica Hamel brings a seductive sleekness to her portrayal of a professional toy for men, but we're not really interested in how her time on an analyst's couch enables her to spend less time in bed with her clients. Recommended only for those who want their trash binges to be redeemed by the illusion of deeper meanings; this is like putting Sidney Sheldon on the same shelf with Freud.

SESSION WITH THE COMMITTEE

See *The Committee*

THE SET-UP
1949, USA ☆☆☆½
Robert Ryan, Audrey Totter, George Tobias, Alan Baxter, Wallace Ford. Directed by Robert Wise. 72 min.

This is one of the grittier boxing movies, from a time when pugilistic dramas were in vogue and dealt with serious emotional quandries and not whether Sylvester Stallone's punch could knock out the Communist menace. A fighter goes several rounds with his conscience when the powers-that-be want him to turn crooked. Robert Ryan is one cool customer as the hard-boiled has-been who struggles to resist corruption and uphold the purity of his profession. Overwrought in spots, but a clean knockout with lots of fancy dramatic footwork from Ryan.

SEVEN
1979, USA, R ☆½
William Smith, Guich Koock, Barbara Leigh, Art Metrano, Martin Kove. Directed by Andy Sidaris. 106 min.

Formulaic action film that never strays from the hard-violence-and-soft-sex road that fans of this genre seem to find so consistently satisfying. William Smith plays a mercenary hired by the government to break a crime ring—needless to say, he's not the type to use polite negotiation. There are some stabs at humor, but this isn't the kind of film you watch for its wit.

SEVEN BEAUTIES
1975, Italy, R ☆☆☆☆
Giancarlo Giannini, Fernando Rey, Shirley Stoler, Elena Fiore, Enzo Vitale. Directed by Lina Wertmüller. 115 min.

This is a remarkable, searing film about the degradations men will endure in war. Giancarlo Giannini plays a macho Italian faced with the horrors of life in a concentration camp and forced to consider whether mere survival is enough or not. This is Lina Wertmüller at her flashiest and most outrageous, and if the film is sometimes repulsive, it's also vivacious and remarkably stylized. Consensus rates this as Wertmüller's crowning achievement; the Oscar nomination she won for *Seven Beauties* was the first ever accorded to a woman director.

SEVEN BLOWS OF THE DRAGON ☆☆☆
1972
David Chaing, Ti Lung, Wang Chung, Lily Ho, Tetsuro Tamba, Ku Feng. Directed by Chang Cheh.

Complex historical saga about "The Honorable 108," who were rebels against the oppressive Sung dynasty. Beautiful period sets and costumes and striking martial arts sequences atone for excesses of blood and nudity. (a.k.a.: *The Water Margin*)

SEVEN BRIDES FOR SEVEN BROTHERS ☆☆☆½
1954, USA
Howard Keel, Jane Powell, Jeff Richards, Russ Tamblyn, Tommy Rall. Directed by Stanley Donen. 103 min.

A young woman accepts a marriage proposal from a handsome stranger and then finds herself keeping house for him and his six rambunctious brothers in this unabashedly pat but light and lively musical. All dated and hokey elements are forgivable because of the exuberant, athletic dance numbers choreographed by Michael Kidd. It's worth watching just for the barn-raising scene. And don't worry about confusing the seven brothers—they all wear different colored bright shirts.

SEVEN DAYS IN MAY ☆☆☆
1964, USA
Burt Lancaster, Kirk Douglas, Fredric March, Ava Gardner, Edmond O'Brien, Martin Balsam, George Macready, Whit Bissell, John Houseman, Malcolm Atterbury. Directed by John Frankenheimer. 120 min.

Rod Serling wrote the screenplay for this exciting, still-topical drama about a group of right-wing extremists led by a maniacal general (Burt Lancaster) plotting to overthrow the president (Fredric March). It seems they object to his recently signed nuclear treaty with Russia, and think he's soft on communism. The it-can't-happen-here scenario is made surprisingly credible, and excellent performances in even the smallest roles will hold your attention even when the script sinks into sermonizing. This film, incidentally, marked John Houseman's screen debut at the age of sixty-two.

SEVEN DOORS TO DEATH ☆
1944, USA
Chick Chandler, June Clyde, George Meeker, Michael Raffetto, Gregory Gay, Rebel Randall. Directed by Elmer Clifton. 60 min.

In this dull poverty-row mystery, a young architect has to solve a double murder in which he is wrongly suspected. The seven doors are all shop entrances that lead into the courtyard where the dastardly deed was committed. What this picture needs is a Monte Hall: "Okay, behind door number one, strangulation; door number two, poison; number three, defenestration . . . Which one should our contestants go for, audience?"

SEVEN GRANDMASTERS ☆☆
Li Yi Min, Lung Fei. Directed by K Joseph Kuo.

Low-budget martial arts feature about "The Champion of the Righteous Fist" defending his title against seven top fighters. Good fight scenes are lost in mediocre production.

THE SEVEN MAGNIFICENT GLADIATORS ☆☆
1983, Italy, PG
Lou Ferrigno, Sybil Danning, Brad Harris, Dan Vadis, Carla Ferrigno. Directed by Bruno Mattei. 90 min.

An evil demigod wreaks havoc on a small town. The only thing that can stop him is a magical sword. But who is worthy of wielding this weighty weapon? Only the mighty Lou, barbarian and speaker of dubbed, pretentious dialogue. A silly latter-day gladiator pic from Italy has some good old-fashioned muscleman fun.

SEVEN MILES FROM ALCATRAZ ☆☆
1942, USA
James Craig, Bonita Granville, Frank Jenks, Cliff Edwards, George Cleveland, Erford Gage, John Banner. Directed by Edward Dmytryk. 62 min.

Champ Larkin and his buddy Jimbo, serving life sentences on Alcatraz Island, escape one foggy night but get no farther than a lighthouse, which they discover has been taken over by Nazi spies. Of course, the war effort comes before their own personal freedom, and they stick around to do battle with the evil Krauts, one of whom is John Banner, who played Sergeant Schultz on "Hogan's Heroes" (typecasting starts early in Hollywood). It is standard stuff, with the best bit a fight on the lighthouse's winding staircase. When was the last time you met someone named "Erford"—or, for that matter, "Champ" or "Jimbo"?

THE SEVEN PER CENT SOLUTION ☆☆☆½
1976, Great Britain, PG
Alan Arkin, Nicol Williamson, Laurence Olivier, Vanessa Redgrave, Robert Duvall, Joel Grey, Samantha Eggar, Jeremy Kemp. Directed by Herbert Ross. 113 min.

A delightful, consistently intelligent mystery-adventure, swirling fact, fiction, speculation, and fantasy into a captivating alliance between two great psychological detectives, Sherlock Holmes and Sigmund Freud. The "solution" in the title refers to cocaine, an interest in which brings the two together, and to the conundrum they must unravel, an entanglement involving a mysterious woman (Vanessa Redgrave) and the sinister Professor Moriarty (Laurence Olivier) that takes the unlikely team across Europe. Writer Nicholas Meyer is the master of this sort of what-if plot (he also united H. G. Wells and Jack the Ripper in *Time after Time*), and his story, ably directed by Herbert Ross, is full of sharp wit and invention. There isn't a bad performance in the cast, but you'll especially enjoy Olivier, who adds another memorable name to his list of latter-day villains, and Robert Duvall, very fine as the very British Dr. Watson. Sparkling, smart, entertaining fare.

THE SEVEN SAMURAI ☆☆☆☆
1954, Japan
Toshiro Mifune, Takashi Shimura, Yoshio Inaba, Isko Kimura. Directed by Akira Kurosawa. 204 min.

One of Akira Kurosawa's action masterpieces, this is *the* definitive samurai film. Toshiro Mifune heads an excellent cast as an eager young apprentice to six veteran samurai who agree to help a community of farmers fight off a band of attacking bandits. An excellent epic, it depicts the feudal strife of sixteenth-century Japan. The movie's elegant symbolism and energetic performances make it into a spellbinding adventure, filled with moments of furious violence and subtle beauty. Kurosawa was inspired by the Westerns of John Ford in this effort, and *Samurai* may be one of the grandest films of the genre to be produced. Dust swirls around before every fight, and all of the participants have a mythic aura about them. Later remade in America as *The Magnificent Seven* (1960) and set in outer space for *Battle Beyond the Stars* (1980). The video version includes over an hour of footage cut shortly after the film's original release. Subtitled.

1776 ☆☆☆
1972, USA, G
William Daniels, Howard Da Silva, Ken Howard, Blythe Danner, John Cullum, Ray Middleton, Virginia Vestoff. Directed by Peter H. Hunt. 141 min.

This is one musical with a book solid enough to stand without music. It's a big, long screen adaptation of the Broadway musical about the events leading up to the signing of the Declaration of Independence. Screenwriter Peter Stone, opening up his own play, details the politics behind the signing, including the debate that led to the elimination of the antislavery plank. The cast members fit perfectly into their powdered wigs and larger-than-life roles. Howard Da Silva steals the show as Ben Franklin, but also memorable are William Daniels as John Adams, Ken Howard as Thomas Jefferson, and Blythe Danner as Martha Jefferson. The music and lyrics by Sherman Edwards are less memorable, but the staging, by Onna White, is handsome. Don't be put off by the setting or subject matter. Despite some lapses into excessive wholesomeness, the film generally avoids the jingoism one might expect, and it is often lively.

THE SEVENTH SEAL ☆☆☆☆
1956, Sweden
Max von Sydow, Gunnar Bjornstrand, Nils Poppe, Bibi Andersson, Bengt Ekerot. Directed by Ingmar Bergman. 96 min.

Ingmar Bergman's most acclaimed early film is this fascinating, multilayered effusion of medieval religious imagery. Bergman conflates several stories in this period piece, the most celebrated of which features Max von Sydow as a despondent knight searching for a sign of God's existence. Although couched in what Bergman sees as medieval hopes and fears, the film is remarkable for the way it touches modern sensibilities, both philosophic and erotic. Unforgettable moments include the knight's chess game with death on the beach; a strolling player's humiliation in a medieval pub; and an accused witch's torture in the woods. These individual sequences are outstanding. *The Seventh Seal* achieves a haunting quality and remains one of Bergman's most elegantly stylized films.

THE SEVENTH VEIL ☆☆☆
1945, Great Britain
James Mason, Ann Todd, Herbert Lom, Hugh McDermott, Albert Lieven, Yvonne Owen. Directed by Compton Bennett. 94 min.

After years of being treated coldly by her bachelor guardian (James Mason), orphan girl Ann Todd sets off on her own but has trouble dealing with men. The title refers to the psychological barrier behind which people hide their innermost thoughts and feelings, often from themselves; psychiatrist Herbert Lom tries to get beyond that veil in order to discover the root of the girl's troubles. The emotional drama is engrossing, if oversimplified. What distinguishes this British melodrama are the fine performances, especially Mason's.

THE SEVENTH VICTIM ☆☆☆
1943, USA
Kim Hunter, Tom Conway, Jean Brooks, Evelyn Brent, Hugh Beaumont. Directed by Mark Robson. 71 min.

Subtlety and horror rarely go hand in hand, but in the 1940s they often did, thanks to producer Val Lewton. In this, one of the least known of his series of supernatural thrillers (*The Cat People, The Body Snatcher*, et al.), Kim Hunter gets her first starring role as a young girl who discovers that her sister's disappearance is linked to a group of devil worshippers in Greenwich Village. Menace lurks everywhere in this obvious forerunner of *Rosemary's Baby*; there are fear-ridden journeys through *noir*-ish back alleys, dead men riding the subway, and even a room furnished only with a chair and a noose.

72 DESPERATE REBELS ☆½
Hong Kong
Pai Ying, Shao Gn, Wei Hai-Bing, Shieh Han, Ma Tien, Tsai Hung, Chen Shing, Wei Ts-Yon, Lung Fei. Directed by Lin Bin.

At the beginning of the Ming Dynasty, a very powerful man refuses to accept the new emperor and surrounds himself with seventy-two bodyguards. The surrealistic lighting, wonderfully imaginative sets, and beautiful costumes make this a pictorially lush film. The kung fu, however, is early 1970s, when the use of too much magic was in vogue.

THE SEVEN-UPS ☆☆
1973, USA, PG
Roy Scheider, Victor Arnold, Jerry Leon, Tony LoBianco. Directed by Philip D'Antoni. 103 min.

The producer of *Bullit* and *The French Connection* tries to do it again with another fast-moving story of unorthodox cops against a big-city background. Only problem is, this time he hired himself to direct it. There's a ten-minute car chase that rivals anything in the other two productions. But nothing in the rest of the movie, which mixes four undercover NYPD cops and a gangland kidnapping scheme, is particularly memorable. The grimy New York visuals and Don Ellis's jazz-rock score help mask the other deficiencies. Even more so than in *The French Connection*, the viewer is expected to condone and applaud the street cops' tactics of breaking the law in the name of the law.

THE SEVEN YEAR ITCH ☆☆☆☆
1955, USA
Marilyn Monroe, Tom Ewell, Evelyn Keyes, Sonny Tufts, Victor Moore, Oscar Homolka, Carolyn Jones, Doro Merande. Directed by Billy Wilder. 105 min.

When a New York publisher (Tom Ewell) sends his wife away to the country one long, hot summer, he finds himself succumbing to the treacherous temptations—liquor, cigarettes and Marilyn, the sweet, innocent, alluring blonde upstairs. Billy Wilder hangs his farce on a thin premise, but his zany comic touch and Monroe's irresistible performance keep the film upbeat and entertaining. Ewell is especially deft in the marvelous fantasy sequences, which are, for the most part, parodies of 1950s films and advertising campaigns. When Monroe begs to spend the night at Ewell's apartment because she doesn't have air conditioning, she becomes the archetypal male fantasy.

SEX ☆☆
1920, USA
Louise Glaum, Peggy Pearce, Irving Cummings, William Conklin, Myrtle Stedman. Directed by Fred Niblo. 65 min.

This lackluster silent melodrama has not picked up charm with age. A vamp breaks up a marriage and laughs at the poor, abandoned wife. Then she gets married, only to have her happiness destroyed by a home-wrecker. A real lesson to be learned, kids. Available with a musical soundtrack.

THE SEX MACHINE ☆☆
1975, Italy, R
Luigi Proietti, Agostina Belli, Eleanora Giorgi, Christian DeSica. Directed by Pasquale Festa Campanile. 80 min.

In the energy-starved future, an eccentric professor discovers that electrical power can be generated when people . . . er . . . shall we say—rub together. An Italian comedy of no manners, with a funny little satirical twist: government and religion band together to ban romantic love because it gets in the way of pure, energy-producing sex. The dubbing may make the film seem more crude than it was in Italian, and the video version has been cut from a 101-minute original.

LE SEX SHOP ☆☆☆
1974, France
Jean-Pierre Marielle, Claude Berri, Juliet Berto, Nathalie Delon, Jacques Martin. Directed by Claude Berri. 95 min.

This amiable spoof of the preoccupation with sex that followed in the wake of the sexual revolution of the 1960s was tagged with an X rating simply for its candor in dealing with its subject matter, not for any prurient material. In order to keep his business solvent, the owner of a bookstore begins to stock a line of "marital aids." As they become a greater and greater percentage of his business, he becomes fascinated by them and finds them starting to take over his life as well.

SEXTETTE ½☆
1978, USA, PG
Mae West, Timothy Dalton, Dom DeLuise, Tony Curtis, Ringo Starr, George Hamilton, Alice Cooper, Keith Moon, Rona Barrett, Walter Pidgeon. Directed by Ken Hughes. 91 min.

A dull, witless musical comedy? A disastrous end to the career of eighty-five-year-old Mae West? An embarrassment for everyone involved? Yes, *Sextette* is all this, and a suspense film to boot. The suspense revolves around the dreaded moment when the overweight, arthritic octogenarian will be revealed in close-up. Fortunately, this moment never comes. Director Ken Hughes wisely keeps Mae behind a mask of makeup and shoots her in nothing closer than medium shot through gauzy filters. Any closer, and this film would certainly qualify as a horror classic as the once-talented comedienne sidles up to beefy males one-fourth her age and delivers her famous innuendos. In this film based on her own plays is a movie star whose spicy memoirs get into the wrong hands just before her wedding to British royalty (Timothy Dalton). It is hard to select a low point—Mae and Tim singing "Love Will Keep Us Together," Mae discoing to a number by Alice Cooper, or a fashion sequence with Mae modeling gold-sequined gowns. No one, with the possible exception of George Raft, emerges unscathed by this abomination that tries to pass as camp.

SHACK OUT ON 101 ☆☆☆½
1955, USA
Terry Moore, Frank Lovejoy, Keenan Wynn, Lee Marvin, Jess Barker, Whit Bissell, Donald Murphy. Directed by Edward Dein. 80 min.

After seeing this film, you may feel like you've awakened from a three-day bender in a waterfront dive—sure you'll want a shower, but first, one more shot of that cheap whiskey. This is lowdown *film noir*, teetering on the edge of exploitation. Lee Marvin gives an *outré* performance as a sex-crazed fry cook named Slob; is he really only a pervert, or is he—worse—a Commie? Terry Moore is the waitress who knows what a truck driver's hands should feel like. She gets everyone's percolator bubbling. The rest of the cast acts with jittery looseness that emphasizes the characters' over-the-edge neurosis—Whit Bissell plays a pathological 'fraidy-cat who wants to become more manly; Keenan Wynn is great as the owner of the diner who forces Marvin to lift weights with him. An intense, claustrophobic nightmare for anyone who's ever loved run-down diners on lonely highways.

SHAFT ☆☆☆
1971, USA, R
Richard Roundtree, Moses Gunn, Gwen Mitchell, Christopher St. John. Directed by Gordon Parks. 100 min.

With liberal doses of sex and violence, this groundbreaking portrayal of an ultracool black private eye paved the way for dozens of black exploitation films, most of which didn't match its skill or style. Though no action masterpiece, *Shaft* is a furiously exciting comic-book adventure whose hero wipes out truckloads of criminals and beds whichever lassies he pleases during lulls. That this superstud was black wouldn't excite the interest today that it did fifteen years ago, but Parks's smooth, no-nonsense direction and Isaac Hayes's driving funk score are still likely to quicken a lot of pulses.

THE SHAGGY D.A. ☆☆
1976, USA, PG
Dean Jones, Tim Conway, Suzanne Pleshette, Keenan Wynn, Joanne Worley, Dick Van Patten, Vic Tayback. Directed by Robert Stevenson. 91 min.

Disney's belated follow-up to its 1959 hit *The Shaggy Dog* should satisfy fans of the original without winning any new admirers. Once again, a guileless good guy—here an aspiring district attorney—turns into a sheepdog every time a certain magical incantation is uttered. Director Robert Stevenson was the undisputed king of Walt's "family" comedies (this was his nineteenth for the studio), and he manages to keep things moving at a reasonable clip. However, if you're not already chortling at the prospect of a talking dog, stay away.

THE SHAGGY DOG ☆☆
1959, USA, PG
Fred MacMurray, Tommy Kirk, Jean Hagen, Annette Funicello, Tim Considine, Cecil Kellaway. Directed by Charles Barton. 104 min.

This badly dated farce about a talking canine was the Disney studio's first foray into the kind of dopey live-action comedy that was to become its primary output for the next fifteen years. The threadbare plot has a teenage boy finding an ancient ring whose inscription can turn him into a double of the neighbors' dog. The animal antics fight for time with a typically boneheaded Commie spy plot, and the cast overplays desperately. A sequel, *The Shaggy D.A.*, appeared in 1976.

SHALAKO ☆½
1968, Great Britain
Sean Connery, Brigitte Bardot, Stephen Boyd, Jack Hawkins, Honor Blackman, Woody Strode. Directed by Edward Dmytryk. 113 min.

This shaky Western plays itself out rather pointlessly. It's about European big-game hunters in New Mexico and how they experience more interference from the local injuns than they ever did from cannibals in Africa. It is interesting only for the all-star cast—particularly Brigitte Bardot—which completely fails to make a dent in the mainstream commercial surroundings. Filmed in Spain, which arguably looks something like New Mexico. Offbeat, but the script is porous and the direction convictionless.

SHALL WE DANCE ☆☆☆
1937, USA
Fred Astaire, Ginger Rogers, Edward Everett Horton, Eric Blore, Ann Shoemaker. Directed by Mark Sandrich. 116 min.

The plot is weaker and the film is longer than most Astaire-Rogers collaborations, but the special chemistry between Fred and Ginger is ineradicable. A dancing duo pretending to be married sets the scene and the stage for such memorable Gershwin numbers as "They Can't Take That Away from Me" and "Let's Call the Whole Thing Off."

THE SHAMING ☆
1979, USA, R
Anne Heywood, Donald Pleasence, Carolyn Jones, Robert Vaughn, Dorothy Malone, Ronee Blakley. Directed by Marvin J. Chomsky. 105 min.

This adaptation of William Inge's only novel has TV veteran Marvin Chomsky as director, and a modestly talented cast; that considered, it's no less appalling a piece of exploitation than it would have been in the hands of lesser men. Former starlet Anne Heywood was a little too old (forty-seven) and too British to play the virginal Kansas schoolteacher whose sexual awakening comes at the hands of a black janitor who rapes her, a rather grotesque alteration from the book. Everyone in the cast seems to be trying, but why? The version on video, although fairly racy for an R rating, is not the steamier cut that received European distribution. (a.k.a.: *Good Luck, Miss Wyckoff* [its original release title] and *The Sin*)

SHAMPOO ☆☆☆½
1975, USA, R
Warren Beatty, Julie Christie, Goldie Hawn, Jack Warden, Lee Grant, Tony Bill, Carrie Fisher. Directed by Hal Ashby. 109 min.

The episodic style and sexual shenanigans of this bedroom comedy add up to a surprisingly pungent, pointed look at manners and morality circa 1968 (the film takes place on the eve of Richard Nixon's election). Warren Beatty plays a womanizing hairdresser who finds that his customers are demanding more in the way of house calls than even he can provide. Beatty's charming Lothario races from one Beverly Hills mansion to the next, blowdryer at the ready, and, while *Shampoo* uses his character to incarnate every aspect of 1960s political consciousness that failed, it's the women who will stay in your mind: Goldie Hawn's bubble-headed actress, Julie Christie's bitter, self-protective mistress, Carrie Fisher's randy teenager, and Lee Grant's Oscar-winning turn as a shrewd but desperate wife. The excellent screenplay is by Beatty and Robert Towne.

SHAMUS ☆☆½
1973, USA, PG
Burt Reynolds, Dyan Cannon, John Ryan, Joe Santos, Kevin Conway, Kay Frye. Directed by Buzz Kulik. 98 min.

Burt Reynolds is in good form in this mildly parodic (though seldom jokey) private eye mystery. As an all-purpose Brooklyn tough guy turned gumshoe, he is hired to dig into a case involving a stolen cache of diamonds and smuggled munitions. The plot is soon lost, however, in a never-ending series of beatings that begin to take on the character of jokes, given Reynolds's ability to emerge from dozens of them virtually unhurt. Good location shooting gives the film atmosphere to substitute for plausibility.

SHANGHAI EXPRESS ☆☆☆☆
1932, USA
Marlene Dietrich, Clive Brook, Warner Oland, Anna May Wong. Directed by Josef von Sternberg. 84 min.

A Josef von Sternberg film is a paean to the resiliency and dignity of beauty, and Marlene Dietrich was his best expression of the luminous pearl in the gutter. Here, she meets an ex-lover on a train full of misfits fleeing the civil war. A wicked Jules Furthman script keeps the characters at each others' throats while Marlene struggles against her own degradation and attempts to save her former paramour's life. Clive Brook, the extraordinary, graceful British actor, plays the lover. Von Sternberg's single-source lighting and dreamy dissolves give the appearance of an opulently furnished hallucination, and his works remain Hollywood's most surreal, lyrical melodramas.

SHANGHAI SURPRISE ½☆
1986, USA, PG-13
Sean Penn, Madonna, Paul Freeman, Richard Griffiths, Philip Sayer, Clyde Kusatsu. Directed by Jim Goddard. 93 min.

This star vehicle is a Chinese junk. Playing a madcap adventurer (like Harrison Ford? like Errol Flynn? no, like Leo Gorcey) is Sean Penn, who acts as if he were appearing in a children's production put on in someone's basement. Worse yet is the ludicrously miscast Madonna as a saintly missionary (we can't wait for her musical remake of *The Song of Bernadette*). The out-of-their-element couple stumbles over old movie conventions, eyeing each other romantically while exchanging leaden badinage in a mildewed tale of drugs, romance, and adventure in the Orient.

SHAOLIN DEATH SQUAD ☆☆
1977
Polly Shian Kuan, Tin Peng, Carter Huang, Cheung Yeh, Chin Kang, Yih Yuan. Directed by Joseph Kuo.

The Light and Dark Killers assist a prime minister to become king. The usual kung fooey, but nicely produced action-adventure.

THE SHAOLIN DRUNKEN MONK ☆☆
1985, Hong Kong
Lau Ka-fai, Chin Yuen-san, Wong Yat-tso. Directed by Au Yeung Chun.

A skinhead avenger goes after his father's killers in this kung fu epic. Lau Ka-fai has a nice, clean fighting style—his brother Lau Ka-liang is the fight choreographer—but for a drunken-style fighter, he doesn't have much sense of fun. There is some comedy, however, in the flashback of Lau's childhood; the drunken master is a real wine barrel of laughs.

THE SHAOLIN DRUNK MONKEY ☆½
1985, Hong Kong
Elton Chong, Eagle Han, Mike Wong, Bruce Cheung, Sue Lee, Kent Chan, Robert Kwon, Christ Kong, Sunny Young. Directed by Godfrey Ho. 85 min.

Silver Eagle (Eagle Han) kills the master of the Shaolin Temple and his gang takes over the town. Mo (Elton Chong), Chu (Sue Lee), and Uncle Bo team up for revenge. The title eludes us—no drunken forms were used and we saw only two monkey techniques. Fine martial arts, but rather uninspired choreography.

SHAOLIN FIST FIGHTER ☆☆
Hong Kong
Elton Chong, Mike Wong, Beau Wan, Lewis Ko, Lung Yuen, Kelly Lun. Directed by Godfrey Ho. 90 min.

Ko Lin learns Shaolin kung fu from an old chef in order to avenge the death of his wife, murdered by the bandit Hung Lao. Godfrey Ho, Tomas Tang, and the Filmark Kung Fu Association almost always produce superior kung fu movies, as this one definitely demonstrates. The only major flaw is the obvious use of photographically accelerated fight scenes.

SHAOLIN INVINCIBLE STICKS ☆☆☆
Don Wong Tao, Hsia Kuang-Li, Chang Yi (Yee), King Kong, Lo Ei Lon. Directed by Lee Tso-Nam.

Outstanding martial arts action highlights the tale of a Stick Clan heir pitted against an evil warrior. Kung fu stick fighting at its best.

SHAOLIN KUNG FU MYSTAGOGUE ☆☆
1975
Carter Huang, Hsu Feng, Chang Yee, Chang Shao-Peng, Chin Kang. Directed by Chang Peng-I.

Too much plot and too little action in this Carter Huang movie. Carter Huang plays a kung fu pupil learning the "Eighteenth Form," while Hsu Feng is a female warrior helping a Ming prince. Thoroughly routine Kung Fu epic.

SHAOLIN: THE BLOOD MISSION ☆☆
1984, Hong Kong
Sun Kok Ming, Poou Chevng, Huang Tang Ming (Huang Cheng-Li), Lo Wah Sing, Wong Yin Fong. Directed by Leung Wing Chan. 86 min.

Ching general Yuen Fong is ordered to obtain the Loyal Heart Record, a list of the names of all the rebels. His search leads him to the Shaolin Temple. Believing the monks are hiding Ching rebels, he has the temple burned to the ground. Absolutely breathtaking kung fu! Huang Cheng-Li is perfectly cast as the evil General Yuen.

SHAOLIN TRAITOR ☆☆
1982, Hong Kong
Carter Huang, Hsang Chia Ta, Lung Chun Erh, Chang Yee. 99 min.

In this period kung fu melodrama, Carter Huang plays a Shaolin novice during the end of the Ming Dynasty. The fighter is framed for the murder of some monks and students while the real killer is a traitor working for the emperor. The action footage, of course, highlights the convoluted plot.

SHARK! ☆☆
1969, USA/Mexico, PG
Burt Reynolds, Barry Sullivan, Arthur Kennedy, Silvia Pinal, Enrique Lucero, Charles Berriochoa. Directed by Samuel Fuller. 93 min.

The lure is an undersea treasure trove in gold bullion, but it is guarded by man-eaters and the conflicting desires of each of the three adventurers come to retrieve it. Luis Buñuel's frequent star Silvia Pinal is the harpy playing against Burt Reynolds and Barry Sullivan. Even crusty old Sam Fuller disclaimed the final release, but there are moments here salty enough for his finest devotees.

SHARK RIVER ☆½
1953, USA
Steve Cochran, Carole Mathews, Warren Stevens, Robert Cunningham, Spencer Fox. Directed by John Rawlins. 79 min.

This B feature set in the Florida Everglades is more effective as a travelogue than as anything else. Two brothers set off through the swamps to escape the law and get one of them to Cuba to evade a murder charge. Along the way they encounter hostile Indians and female interest in the form of a young widow who works in the swamp as a trapper. The flora and fauna of the Everglades are considerably more interesting than the performers or the plot, although there is a decided shortage of sharks.

SHARK'S TREASURE ☆½
1975, USA, PG
Cornel Wilde, Yaphet Kotto, John Neilson, Cliff Osmond, David Canary. Directed by Cornel Wilde. 95 min.

This seafaring feature, written, produced, and directed by its star, Cornel Wilde, sat on the shelf for several years until *Jaws* became a big hit, at which time it was decided to play up the minimal shark footage and retitle it *Shark's Treasure* (the original title was simply *The Treasure*). Captain Cornel puts his ship into hock so that he can raise some money to go on a treasure hunt. He finds his treasure, but also runs afoul of some escaped convicts. Should have stayed on the shelf.

SHARKY'S MACHINE ☆☆
1981, USA, R
Burt Reynolds, Rachel Ward, Vittorio Gassman, Brian Keith, Bernie Casey, Henry Silva, Carl Holliman, Richard Libertini, John Fiedler, Darryl Hickman. Directed by Burt Reynolds. 119 min.

Tom Sharky is that old chestnut—a tough, fearless cop who, beneath it all, has Feelings—and whenever he starts gazing dewy-eyed at kids, or at gorgeous Rachel Ward (as a mysterious call girl), the movie comes to a dead halt. Not that the rest of *Sharky's Machine* is much better. Reynolds, who directed, is trying for a flashy style here, but this story of a demoted narc who assembles a "machine" of hangdog veterans to flush out an underworld chieftain is all noise and thudding cliché! As Sharky's partners, Brian Keith and Bernie Casey make the most of their sketchy roles.

SHARMA AND BEYOND ☆☆½
1985, Great Britain
Suzanne Burden, Robert Urquhart, Michael Maloney, Anthonia Pemberton. Directed by Brian Gilbert. 82 min.

A pleasant lightweight romance, this is from producer David Puttnam's "First Love" series. First-time director Brian Gilbert also wrote the quirky tale of an aspiring science-fiction writer who unwittingly falls in love with his idol's daughter. The humor is initially wistful in a way that seems appropriate to the rainy London locales and the timidities of the characters, but when Gilbert ventures into the beautiful British countryside, the mood becomes rich and merry. Although it's too low-key to hold your full attention, it is well acted and unusually gentle in spirit.

SHATTERED ☆☆½
1972, Great Britain, R
Peter Finch, Shelley Winters, Colin Blakely. Directed by Alistair Reid. 95 min.

A bravura performance by the estimable Peter Finch is the reason to see this British melodrama, released as *Something to Hide*. As an alcoholic town councilman on the Isle of Wight, harassed by a hateful boss (Colin Blakely) and a grotesque wife (Shelley Winters, typecast), Finch is reduced to a depressed isolation before lashing out with mad, inexorable violence. (a.k.a.: *Something to Hide*)

THE SHE BEAST ☆☆
1965, Italy/Yugoslavia
Barbara Steele, John Karlsen, Ian Ogilvy, Mel Welles, Richard Watson. Directed by Michael Reeves. 74 min.

This is one of only three features directed by Michael Reeves, a promising young director (twenty-one when he made this) who killed himself after the release of *The Conquerer Worm*. It's not a great film, but there are signs of an emerging talent at work. Barbara Steele, the doyenne of British horror films, plays a young bride on her honeymoon in eastern Europe who becomes possessed by the spirit of an executed witch. Mel Welles, the flower-shop owner in *Little Shop of Horrors*, plays the innkeeper.

SHEENA—QUEEN OF THE JUNGLE ½☆
1984, USA, PG
Tanya Roberts, Ted Wass, Donovan Scott, Elizabeth of Toro, France Zobda, Trevor Thomas. Directed by John Guillermin. 100 min.

The fate of the primitive Zambuli nation—imperiled by government greed and hypocrisy—rests in the hands of Sheena, the child of American doctors killed in an accident while exploring a sacred mountain. Deals lightly with political conspiracy, assassination, wildlife conservation, and the plight of traditional cultures in the modern world while dwelling on the charming idiosyncrasies of Sheena's English and the fit of her animal-skin bikini. Even dumber than one would imagine.

SHEER MADNESS ☆☆☆½
1985, Germany/France
Hanna Schygulla, Angela Winkler, Peter Striebeck, Franz Bushrieser, Agnes Fink. Directed by Margarethe von Trotta. 110 min.

Some of the finest talent in Germany collaborated on this complex yet subtle film about two women who form a friendship that threatens both their marriages. Writer/director Margarethe von Trotta (*Marianne and Julianne*) is more concerned with character study than storytelling, and the slow pace may frustrate some viewers. But the film does build to a provocative climax and a shattering yet perplexing conclusion. The cast is brilliant, particularly Hanna Schygulla as the strong-willed Olga, Angela Winkler as the neurotic Ruth, and Peter Striebeck as Ruth's caring but cloddish husband. One unexpected highlight is Schygulla's rendition (in English) of Carole King's "Will You Love Me Tomorrow?" Masterfully photographed by Michael Ballhaus in both color and, in several disturbing dream sequences, black and white. An extraordinarily delicate movie, tantalizing in its nuances.

SHE-FREAK ☆½
1966, USA
Claire Brenna. Directed by Byron Mabe. 86 min.

The producer of most of Hershell Gordon Lewis's early films wrote the screenplay for this sleazy remake of *Freaks*. A conniving waitress marries the owner of a freak show, and then has an affair behind his back. When he finds out, he kills the other, and she takes over the show. Lurid, amateurish, and dull.

SHEILA LEVINE IS DEAD AND LIVING IN NEW YORK ☆☆
1975, USA, PG
Jeannie Berlin, Roy Scheider, Rebecca Dianna Smith, Janet Brandt. Directed by Sidney J. Furie. 112 min.

The neurotic, self-obsessed heroine of Gail Parent's serio-comic novel is brought to very uneasy life by shrill actress Jeannie Berlin and shriller director Sidney J. Furie. On the page, the loony driven musings of the title character, a Jewish-American Princess who comes to New York to find a sense of personal worth and a marriageable doctor, were witty and articulate enough to redeem their stereotypical nature. Berlin's wildly self-indulgent performance makes the screen's Sheila little more than a compendium of nasty clichés, and Furie gives her mannerisms free rein. Still, there are a few moments of satisfyingly masochistic humor, and very solid work from Roy Scheider as the doctor who steadfastly resists her interest.

SHE'LL BE WEARING PINK PAJAMAS ☆☆
1985, Great Britain
Anthony Higgins, Julie Walters, Jane Evers, Janet Henfrey, Paula Jacobs. Directed by John Goldschmidt. 90 min.

A clumsy feminist comedy-drama about a group of women testing their mettle one weekend in an outdoor survival course. Naturally, they all let down their hair as they pit themselves against nature and against their own natures. Imagine *Meatballs* redone as a serious movie and your sitting through all the little campers having moments of self-realization, and you'll have some idea of what you're in for.

SHENANDOAH ☆☆☆
1965, USA
James Stewart, Doug McClure, Glenn Corbett, Patrick Wayne, Rosemary Forsyth, Philip Alford, Katharine Ross, George Kennedy, Denver Pyle. Directed by Andrew V. McLaglen. 105 min.

Jimmy Stewart plays a Virginia farmer who doesn't want to lose his sons to the Civil War in this compelling, well-acted melodrama (later adapted into a Broadway musical). It's an uncharacteristic role for the star, and he does solid work under McLaglen's direction. The combination of battle footage and quiet scenes examining the changes within the clan keeps the pace brisk; older children as well as adults should enjoy it, although youngsters might find the seemingly random violence upsetting.

THE SHERIFF OF FRACTURED JAW ☆☆½
1958, Great Britain
Kenneth More, Jayne Mansfield, Robert Morley, Ronald Squire, David Horne. Directed by Raoul Walsh. 103 min.

This often amusing Raoul Walsh comedy, about a London dandy (Kenneth More) who inherits a gun shop in the old west and travels to America to claim his inheritance, was one of the director's last films, and he gets more mileage out of the one-joke fish-out-of-water premise than you might expect. The fortuitous casting of Jayne Mansfield as a tough-mama saloon mistress also helps matters; she even gets to sing a couple of songs. If the idea of an American director shooting a comic Western in Spain with British actors doesn't dislocate you too much, give it a try.

SHERIFF OF WICHITA ☆½
1949, USA
Allan "Rocky" Lane, Black Jack, Eddy Waller, Roy Barcroft, Lyn Wilde, Clayton Moore, Eugene Roth, Truvor Bardette. Directed by R. G. Springsteen. 60 min.

For an hour-long programmer, this Republic Western proffers a plot more complex than most—it's a longstanding mystery surrounding a stolen Army payroll, anonymous missives, and a jailbreak by the lieutenant who's falsely convicted. Rocky Lane relies on routine detective protocol by getting everybody into one room to crack the caper. Some okay stunts, and, yes, that's Clayton Moore before his "Lone Ranger" days. Black Jack is the horse, not a croupier.

SHERLOCK HOLMES AND THE SECRET CODE

See *Dressed to Kill* (1946)

SHERLOCK HOLMES AND THE ☆☆½
SECRET WEAPON
1942, USA
Basil Rathbone, Nigel Bruce, Lionel Atwill, Dennis Hoey. Directed by Roy William Neill. 68 min.

By this point in the Universal series of Holmes films (this was number four out of fourteen), the Mister Spock of the detective genre has been removed from the Victorian era of author Conan Doyle's stories and transplanted into contemporary Britain, generally to do battle with the dark forces of Nazism. Here the Gestapo has employed Holmes's arch-rival, Professor Moriarty, to obtain a secret bombsight. Ostensibly adapted from Arthur Conan Doyle's short story "The Dancing Men," this may annoy purists but will be more than adequate for nostalgia buffs and fans of the series. Basil Rathbone and Nigel Bruce were born to play Holmes and Watson, and Lionel Atwill is the best of the three actors used at various points in the series to play Moriarty.

SHERLOCK HOLMES AND THE ☆☆
VOICE OF TERROR
1942, USA
Basil Rathbone, Nigel Bruce, Evelyn Ankers, Reginald Denny, Henry Daniell, Thomas Gomez, Montagu Love. Directed by John Rawlins. 65 min.

The first of the Basil Rathbone–Nigel Bruce Sherlock Holmes films in which the great detective and his sidekick were transposed from their Victorian milieu into the modern world in order to fight Nazi spies and deliver stirring speeches about the glory of the British Empire. In this one, they track down a mysterious Nazi radio broadcaster who is predicting acts of sabotage. The mystery is not bad, and Rathbone and Bruce play the characters straight, but it's quite jarring to see them in this setting.

SHERMAN'S MARCH ☆☆☆
1986, USA
Ross McElwee. Directed by Ross McElwee. 155 min.

Ross McElwee's endearing but somewhat overpraised film is a laid-back dissertation on the search for true love in contemporary times. Setting out to film a documentary on General Sherman's march to the sea, which devastated the South during the Civil War, the filmmaker encounters personal devastation when his girlfriend unexpectedly dumps him. Instead, as he films bit and pieces of his work-in-progress, his heartbreak-in-progress gets the better of him. Rather than trace Sherman's trail of destruction, McElwee unsuccessfully combs the South for Ms. Right. This is a bittersweet, rueful docucomedy that lacks a firm, controlling hand. Some shaping and reorganization was in order; still, it's a sweet though overlong odyssey of romantic yearning.

SHE'S DRESSED TO KILL ☆½
1979, USA (TV)
Eleanor Parker, John Rubinstein, Jessica Walter, Connie Sellecca. Directed by Gus Trikonis. 102 min.

A fashion designer's comeback extravaganza is spoiled when someone starts bumping off her models one by one. A substandard bitchy showbiz mystery, but the stars at least try to camp it up. Later, the producers exchanged one rip-off title for another, *Someone Is Killing the World's Greatest Models*. Under any name, it's irredeemably stupid.

SHE'S GOTTA HAVE IT ☆☆☆
1986, USA, R
Tracy Camila Johns, Tommy Redmond Hicks, John Canada Terrell, Spike Lee, Raye Dowell, Bill Lee, Joie Lee. Directed by Spike Lee. 84 min.

When was the last time you saw an urban romantic comedy with an all-black cast? When was the first time? If the answer to both questions is never, there's no better place to start than with Spike Lee's hip, jumpy first feature. It's a stylishly sexy exploration of a year in the life of Nola Darling (Tracy Camila Johns) and the men who can't live without her—stuffy, narcissistic Grier, sweet but possessive Jamie, and scrawny, irresistibly funny pest Mars (Spike Lee, in a hilarious performance). It's as uneven as many first films, filled with self-conscious technique, some of which works and some of which doesn't. But Lee, as writer, director, and performer, is a major new talent, and his film, made in just twelve days for $175,000, is smarter and more entertaining than much of what comes out of Hollywood.

SHE'S IN THE ARMY NOW ☆☆
1981, USA (TV)
Jamie Lee Curtis, Kathleen Quinlan, Susan Blanchard, Melanie Griffith, Janet MacLachlan, Dale Robinette, Julie Carmen. Directed by Hy Averback. 97 min.

After the success of Goldie Hawn's *Private Benjamin* but before the failure of the TV series it spawned came this very similar female service comedy, a pilot for a series that never took off. This one follows five women enlistees as they skirmish in the trenches and struggle with romances, all on their way to becoming good soldiers. Earl W. Wallace (*Witness*) wrote the shallow script, which covers no new ground but does allow the talents of Jamie Lee Curtis and Kathleen Quinlan to shine.

SHE WAITS ☆☆
1971, USA (TV)
Patty Duke, David McCallum, Lew Ayres, Beulah Bondi, Dorothy McGuire. Directed by Delbert Mann. 74 min.

A modern-day spook story that tries to elicit goose bumps. The film itself, unfortunately, is haunted by a creeping sense of *déjà vu*. Only a few surface tricks are used in this attempt to make a haunting film; if the creators of *She Waits* have seen Hitchcock's *Rebecca*, they haven't learned much from it. Patty Duke stars as a neurotic wife who is being controlled by the ghost of her hubby's first wife. A nice Halloweenish try, but the scares are too benign.

SHE WORE A YELLOW RIBBON ☆☆☆☆
1949, USA
John Wayne, Victor McLaglen, Ben Johnson, John Agar, Harry Carey, Jr., Joanne Dru, George O'Brien, Mildred Natwick, Chief Big Tree. Directed by John Ford. 103 min.

In his second installment in the cavalry trilogy—*Fort Apache* and *Rio Grande* completed the field—John Ford once again explores his favorite themes of civilization on the fringe of the wilderness and citizens under attack from the Indians. John Wayne gives a commanding yet restrained performance as the retiring cavalry Captain Nathan Brittles, a man shrouded in nostalgia and distanced from his contemporaries. In an attempt to prevent a war with the local tribe, the captain sympathizes with the aging chief's complaint that the young are beyond his command. Academy Award–winning Winton Hoch augments this nostalgic atmosphere with colors that glow like a campfire. When, after averting the war, Brittles retires, he sets off, in classic Western fashion, to disappear in the glowing, setting sun. No one invented and reinvented the Western like Ford: the cavalry arrives just in time to offer Brittles a new post, thus saving Wayne from obscurity and convention. Includes the quintessential Ford/Wayne line, "Don't apologize. It's a sign of weakness."

SHINBONE ALLEY ☆☆½
1971, USA
Animated: Eddie Bracken, Carol Channing, John Carradine. Directed by John D. Wilson and David Detiege. 86 min.

Clever animated film that has been toned down to appeal to kids. Archy the cockroach and Mehitabel the cat strut their stuff, but not exactly in the same sophisticated manner as they did in the Don Marquis stories that inspired this film. Still, the bubbly tunes are pleasant and the project has an offbeat, unexpected air that is refreshing.

SHINE ON, HARVEST MOON ☆☆½
1944, USA
Ann Sheridan, Jack Carson, Dennis Morgan, Irene Manning, S. Z. Sakall. Directed by David Butler. 112 min.

A corny, trivialized bio-pic of performers Nora Bayes and Jack Norworth, it is nonetheless apt to put viewers in a sunny frame of mind. The classic songs pour out one after the other, and Jack Carson and Dennis Morgan have their vaudevillian patter down to a science. Ann Sheridan was a Warner Bros. treasure, but they foolishly never came up with top-notch vehicles to showcase her gifts. In every assignment, she was the game trooper, and here she outshines second-rate material. (When opportunities like *The Man Who Came to Dinner* and *I Was a Male War Bride* presented themselves, she was dazzling.) The finale is in color.

THE SHINING ☆☆☆
1980, USA, R
Jack Nicholson, Shelly Duvall, Danny Lloyd, Scatman Crothers, Barry Nelson, Joe Turkel. Directed by Stanley Kubrick. 146 min.

Stanley Kubrick's adaptation of a popular Stephen King horror novel will delight Kubrick's fans, outrage King's, and probably puzzle everyone else. As usual, Kubrick seems to have taken a particular literary work solely for the purpose of undermining its original intentions. The horrifying moments of the film are inventions of Kubrick's, while the frightening elements of King's story have been rendered all but irrelevant. The story is set in the mammoth environment of the Overlook Hotel, closed for the winter and being watched by a troubled family: Jack Torrence, an alcoholic novelist afflicted with writer's block; his cringing wife, Wendy; and their withdrawn, clairvoyant son, Danny. The seemingly endless tracking shots, which constitute a good deal of the movie's running time, put off many viewers but serve effectively to create a feeling of claustrophobia in a wide-open environment. There are also many disquieting comic moments in Jack Nicholson's portrayal of the average American dad as psycho killer.

A SHINING SEASON ☆☆☆
1979, USA (TV)
Timothy Bottoms, Allyn Ann McLerie, Rip Torn, Connie Forslund. Directed by Stuart Margolin. 100 min.

Above-average disease-of-the-week TV flick. This inspirational tale involves a dying track star who devotes his waning energies to coaching a girls' track team to victory. Like *Brian's Song*, this is one of those rare tearjerkers that somehow aren't offensively manipulative, and the actors give very good performances.

SHIP OF FOOLS ☆☆☆
1965, USA
Vivien Leigh, Oskar Werner, Simone Signoret, Jose Ferrer, Lee Marvin, Jose Greco, George Segal, Elizabeth Ashley, Michael Dunn, Lilia Skala. Directed by Stanley Kramer. 149 min.

This is a Stanley Kramer message movie with a capital M. Souls are spiritually and physically adrift at sea on an ocean liner during the time just before World War II. Praiseworthy performances by the four leads, including Simone Signoret as a drug-addicted countess finding respite with a world-weary doctor (Oskar Werner), Lee Marvin as an alcoholic baseball has-been, and Vivien Leigh as the regal Mrs. Treadwell, another in her gallery of Southern Gothic grotesques. Also featuring two of the worst performances ever committed to celluloid: George Segal and Elizabeth Ashley as a battling but boring pair of free spirits who nearly sink the ship.

SHIVERS

See *They Came from Within*

SHOAH ☆☆☆☆
1985, France
Documentary. Directed by Claude Lanzmann. 480 min.

Shoah is the Hebrew word for Holocaust. This shattering, unforgettable masterpiece is not only one of the longest films ever made—about nine and one half hours—but one of the greatest documentaries in the history of world cinema. Its length, thanks to director Claude Lanzmann's genius, simply adds to its searing power. *Shoah* is a multilayered triumph, showing us both the darkest and the brightest sides of the human spirit. It is, on one level, a devastating documentary record and essay about The Final Solution—Hitler's unthinkable but successful effort to murder six million Jews in Europe during World War II.

One of the many cinematic inspirations that guided Lanzmann during the more than ten years that he selflessly devoted to this remarkable essay was his early decision not to use any archival or historical footage, normally and understandably utilized in most documentaries or films dealing with the Holocaust or other aspects of Hitler's Nazi empire. All of the astonishing footage seen in *Shoah* is new material, filmed in the seventies and early eighties, largely based on interviews with those rare survivors of the concentration camps. Some of the most devastating sequences are those in which Lanzmann interviews German officers, technicians, or Polish civilians who ran the trains taking the hapless victims to their deaths in the gas chambers. One German officer, responsible for the "efficient" operation of an extermination camp in Poland, calmly notes that he addressed the question as an engineer, simply carrying out his orders and trying to keep a factory assembly line moving with maximum speed and greatest cost savings.

SHOCK TREATMENT ☆½
1981, USA, PG
Jessica Harper, Cliff De Young, Richard O'Brien, Patricia Quinn, Charles Grey, Ruby Wax, Nell Campbell, Barry Humphries. Directed by Jim Sharman. 94 min.

This sort-of sequel to *The Rocky Horror Picture Show*—same director and writer, many of the same supporting cast (though as different characters), the same leading characters (though played by different actors)—has none of what its predecessor had going for it. Only arch-nerds Brad and Janet are left from *RHPS*, and they're played here by Cliff De Young and Jessica Harper (who is no Susan Sarandon). Their troubles arise from a popular TV game show in their hometown and the megalomaniacal sponsor (also played by De Young) who makes Janet into a local celebrity and has Brad tossed into the nuthouse under the control of Dr. Cosmo McKinley and his staff (as played by the staff loonies of *RHPS*). The songs, which were catchy 1950s rock-cum-Elton John pastiches in *RHPS*, are here droning syntho-pop schlock that will not inspire you to sing along.

SHOCK WAVES ☆☆½
1977, USA
Brooke Adams, Peter Cushing, John Carradine, Luke Halpin. Directed by Ken Wiederhorn. 86 min.

A group of vacationers on board a small touring boat find themselves shipwrecked on an uncharted tropical island after a nighttime encounter with an abandoned ship. The island's sole inhabitant, an elderly German, is less than hospitable and suggests that they leave as soon as possible—advice they would gladly follow if they were able. The hitch: the denizens of the surrounding waters. The pale, flaxen-haired Nazi supermen with black goggles—genetically engineered to man Third Reich submarines and forgotten since the end of the war—rise from the ocean to kill everyone in their paths, and very nearly succeed. "Once they were *almost* human," leered the ads for *Shock Waves*, which features a young Brooke Adams in a yellow bikini, Hammer studios horror veteran Peter Cushing with an elegant scar, and John Carradine in black bathing trunks. The result is surprisingly entertaining, and the amphibious Aryans are very creepy indeed. (a.k.a.: *Death Corps*)

SHOGUN ☆☆½
1980, USA, PG (theatrical version), unrated (complete version) (TV)
Richard Chamberlain, Yoko Shimada, Toshiro Mifune. Directed by Jerry London. 550 min. (complete version); 119 min. (theatrical version)

This is the American miniseries at its most gargantuan—a mammoth, often tedious version of James Clavell's jumbo novel about a British trader shipwrecked in seventeenth-century Japan who learns the ways of both geisha love and feudal war. Richard Chamberlain earned his stripes as King of the Miniseries with his creditable performance here, but the drama as a whole is very slow going and not worth the trip. Paramount Home Video has made this available in two versions: the nine-hour-plus, multicassette version contains the uncut drama, but there's also a two-hour condensation that was released overseas as a theatrical film. If you must see it, you may as well see it all.

SHOGUN ASSASSIN ☆☆½
1980, Japan/USA
Tomisaburo Wakayama, Masahiro Tomikawa, Kayo Matsuo, Minoru Ohki, Shoji Kobayashi, Shin Kishida. Directed by Kenji Misumi. 82 min.

Itto Ogami (Tomisaburo Wakayama), once the shogun's official decapitator and now a victim of his paranoia, must travel the country with his son, Daigoro, seeking work as a paid assassin. Certain changes have been made in the U.S. (dubbed) release, most notably in Daigoro's narration. These changes, rather than detracting from the original, enhance the American viewer's understanding of the complex society of feudal Japan. A wonderfully photographed movie, if you don't mind the sight of a little blood (after all, Itto Ogami *was* the official decapitator).

SHOGUN NINJA ☆
Hong Kong
Sonny Chiba, Henry Sanada, Sue Shiomi, Yuki Ninagawa, Tetsuro Tamba, Yoko Nogiwa, Makoto Sato. Directed by Noribumi Suzuki. 115 min.

First there was the television miniseries *Shogun*; then there was the ninja craze. Now, stealing from both, here's *Shogun Ninja*! A laughable tale of sixteenth-century Japan, in which two ninja clans battle over an old feud, a cache of gold, and who has the nicest pajamas.

THE SHOOTING ☆☆½
1967, USA, G
Millie Perkins, Jack Nicholson, Will Hutchins, Warren Oates. Directed by Monte Hellman. 82 min.

This arty film was shot simultaneously with another intriguing low-budget Western, *Ride in the Whirlwind*. Deceptively simple in story line, it seems to be a standard revenge tale, but this involved film is more concerned with delving into the relationships of the principals. An off-the-wall actioner in which a lot of Western clichés were tossed into the air, only to fall back down to the Western prairie in some unexpected configurations.

THE SHOOTING PARTY ☆☆
1984, Great Britain
James Mason, Edward Fox, Dorothy Tutin, Cheryl Campbell, John Gielgud, Gordon Jackson, Aharon Ipale. Directed by Alan Bridges. 97 min.

In his last film role, James Mason plays an aging aristocrat sadly presiding over the decline of the British leisure class on the eve of World War I. It's a great, melancholy performance in a musty, embalmed film. Director Alan Bridges has the ultracivilized "Masterpiece Theatre" tone down cold; unfortunately, Isabel Colegate's source novel, which uses a hunting weekend as a metaphor for the end of noble conduct during the Great War, is no masterpiece, nor even very good. There's something faintly snotty about chiding the English upper crust, in a novel written in 1980, for its inability to anticipate the events of 1914–1918, and this suffocatingly mannered film can't shake that essential arrogance. You can still savor Mason, though, and his one encounter with John Gielgud almost makes it worth seeing. *Note:* Much of the dialogue on the Thorn/EMI cassette we viewed was muffled.

SHOOTING STARS ☆☆
1983, USA (TV)
Billy Dee Williams, Parker Stevenson, Robert Webber, Edie Adams, Efrem Zimbalist, Jr., Denny Miller. Directed by Richard Lang. 100 min.

A gimmicky pilot for a failed series that no viewers will go into mourning over. Two actors are bumped from a series in which they portray private eyes. Like most out-of-work hams, they need a sideline for some quick cash, so they became—you guessed it—real-life private eyes. The mind reels at the possibilities of this premise. If they'd been in a TV movie about the Brinks job, would they have become stickup artists? If they'd played brain surgeons, would they end up working at Cedars Sinai? A mindless shoot-'em-up, chase-'em-down detective story.

THE SHOOTIST ☆☆☆
1976, USA, PG
John Wayne, Lauren Bacall, Ron Howard, Bill McKinney, James Stewart, Richard Boone, Hugh O'Brian, Harry Morgan, John Carradine, Scatman Crothers. Directed by Don Siegel. 99 min.

John Wayne's last film before his death is an appropriate swan song. He plays an aging gunfighter in 1901 Carson City, a town caught between centuries. Learning that he is dying of cancer, Wayne sets out to tidy up some loose ends and ensure that he will not die in his bed. Director Don Siegel fashions an effective valedictory for the Western, restraining the temptations to mythologize either the genre or its star and avoiding both parody and cynicism. The last of the straightforward Westerns until *Pale Rider*.

SHOOT IT: BLACK, SHOOT IT: BLUE ☆½
1982, USA, R
Michael Moriarty, Eric Laneuville, Paul Sorvino, Earl Hindman, Linda Scruggs, Bruce Kornbluth. Directed by Dennis McGuire. 93 min.

A potentially interesting story about police power and racism, the film flounders without ever clearly defining its target. Michael Moriarty plays a dim-witted cop who kills a black thief he has apprehended. Charged by the thief's widow with wrongful death, he feels sure that a jury will accept his version of the story. But the whole incident was filmed by a young photographer who wants to make a documentary about Moriarty's wife. The potential for suspense is mostly wasted, and the ending is a cop-out.

SHOOT THE MOON ☆☆☆
1982, USA, R
Diane Keaton, Albert Finney, Dana Hill, Karen Allen, Peter Weller. Directed by Alan Parker. 123 min.

An emotionally powerful but uneven drama about the ravaging effects of a marital breakup on a Southern California family. Alan Parker may be one of the least genre-bound directors currently working—his previous credits include *Bugsy Malone, Midnight Express, Fame,* and *Pink Floyd, the Wall*—and author Bo Goldman's highly personal screenplay takes no sides and creates no clear-cut winners or losers. Parker does best with Goldman's minute observations of daily life, creating an unusually credible relationship between mother Faith (Diane Keaton) and her four kids. Too often, however, Parker throws in jarring bits of business that seem totally out of place. This is particularly unfortunate in such an otherwise restrained and understated work.

SHOOT THE PIANO PLAYER ☆☆☆☆
1960, France
Charles Aznavour, Marie Dubois, Nicole Berger, Michele Mercier, Albert Remy, Jacques Aslanian, Richard Kanavan. Directed by François Truffaut. 92 min.

France's enduring love affair with hard-boiled American writers has resulted in many good movies—among others, *Coup de Torchon* (Bertrand Tavernier, from a Jim Thompson novel), *The Bride Wore Black* (Truffaut, from Cornell Woolrich), *And Hope to Die* (René Clément, from David Goodis)—but this is by far the best film. Based on Goodis's so-so novel *Down There,* Truffaut's film fashions a brilliant chart of a slow slide into the abyss of lost identity and the fugitive life. Charles Aznavour is alternately funny and desperate as a café keyboard pounder who is trying to forget his past as a concert pianist and who finds his future running out on him. A complex, intricate work done by a highly charged young director (this was Truffaut's second film). A pioneering work on the wide screen; for years, film students have been forced to see this film on chopped-off 16 mm prints. Unfortunately, the film was not put into its proper panoramic format for video and is available from discount distributors in several versions—beware scratchy, dark, and cut tapes.

SHOOT THE SUN DOWN ☆
1981, USA, PG
Christopher Walken, Margot Kidder, Geoffrey Lewis, Bo Brundin, A. Martinez, Sacheen Littlefeather. Directed by David Leeds. 93 min.

A hip cast portraying offbeat characters will invariably make for an intriguing twist on the old Western theme, right? Wrong. As they search for gold, and toss off character affectations of a sea captain, a feminist servant, and a scalp-hunter, you'll be searching for a book, a pillow, and milk and cookies.

THE SHOP ON MAIN STREET ☆☆☆☆
1965, Czechoslovakia
Josef Kroner, Ida Kaminska. Directed by Jan Kadar and Elmar Klos. 128 min.

Winner of an Academy Award for Best Foreign Film, this haunting tragicomedy is set during the early days of the Nazi occupation of Czechoslovakia. Josef Kroner plays a carpenter appointed as the "Aryan controller" of a Jewish shop run by the elderly Ida Kaminska. He becomes fond of the tenacious woman only to discover that she is about to be deported. His attempt to save her gives the film its emotional punch, and the beautifully modulated performances of the two leads turn *Main Street* into a real tearjerker that works despite some excessive sentimentality.

SHORT CIRCUIT ☆☆½
1986, USA, PG
Ally Sheedy, Steve Guttenberg, Fisher Stevens, G. W. Bailey. Directed by John Badham. 99 min.

Number Five is alive! Struck by lightning, an adorable state-of-the-art robot/soldier escapes to become a pop-culture-spouting peacenik. Cute Ally Sheedy, who first thinks he's an alien ("Oh my God, I knew they'd pick me!"), and naive programmer (read: nerd) Steve Guttenberg set out to save him from the nasty folks over in the Defense Department. The movie is too much of a good thing—every gag from *E.T.*, *Gremlins*, *Close Encounters*, and *WarGames*, plus car chases and a Pakistani (Fisher Stevens) spouting malapropisms. Some are quite clever—Number Five does John Wayne, John Travolta, etc.—but it grows very predictable. Great for kids, though.

SHORT EYES ☆☆☆½
1977, USA, R
Bruce Davison, Jose Perez, Nathan George, Don Blakely, Shawn Elliot, Tito Goya, Joe Carberry, Kenny Steward, Bob Maroff, Keith Davis, Miguel Pinero, Curtis Mayfield, Willie Hernandez, Bob O'Connell, Tony De Benedetto, Mark Margolis. Directed by Robert M. Young. 104 min.

From the very beginning, we know this is no mincing, humanitarian prison movie. In *Short Eyes*, the mostly black and Hispanic prisoners are tough and cocky, proud of their crimes and fiercely unrepentant; they're not only coping with prison life, they've mastered it. Into this bizarre civilization steps Clark Davis, masterfully portrayed by Bruce Davison. He's a "short eyes," a child molester, guilty of the one crime the other prisoners can't forgive—a milksop whom the prisoners hate not only because his twisted sexuality mirrors their own, but because his self-loathing tests their own tenuous self-respect, which is the one thing that stands between them and the abyss. Despite some staginess, this is probably the most convincing prison movie ever filmed; it's no surprise that it makes your skin crawl. Adapted by Miguel Pinero from his Obie and Drama Critics Circle Award–winning play, it boasts extraordinary performances by Pinero, Tito Goya, Kenny Steward, and Joe Carberry. (a.k.a.: *Slammer*)

THE SHOUT ☆☆☆
1979, Great Britain, R
Alan Bates, Susannah York, John Hurt. Directed by Jerzy L. Skolimowski. 87 min.

An ambitious, uneven surreal melodrama. Alan Bates is a mysterious stranger who wanders into the lives of a village couple and begins an unnerving struggle with the husband for power and for his wife. Jerzy Skolimowski conducts a raid on the vocabulary of the international art film and stuffs the movie with shock cuts, elliptically ominous dialogue, and weirdly composed frames. The narrative frame of the film, set at a lunatic asylum's cricket match, fails to provide a real anchor—it's as strange as the internal story—and doesn't work as another manifestation of the film's concern with power and impotence. The sexy intruder theme, from William Holden in *Picnic* to Zygmunt Malanowicz in Polanski's *Knife in the Water*, began to take on a portentous, socially disruptive function, and here seems stretched to the comically ridiculous, especially compared to the genuine strangeness of Terence Stamp in Pasolini's *Teorama*. Based on a short story by Robert Graves.

SHOUT AT THE DEVIL ☆☆½
1976, Great Britain, PG
Lee Marvin, Roger Moore, Barbara Parkins, Ian Holm, Rene Kolldehoff. Directed by Peter Hunt. 128 min.

In this typical but fairly energetic action-adventure film, the slam-bang stunt sequences have much more personality than the actors (or doubles) running through them. The setting is Zanzibar, Africa, on the eve of World War I in 1913, with a rowdy Irish tradesman (Lee Marvin) and a suave, naive Englishman (Roger Moore) joining forces to combat mercenary Germans as war breaks out. The few scenes in which nothing is exploding tend to lag badly. *Note:* The version on video corresponds to that of the American theatrical release; a 147-minute version was released in Europe.

SHOWBOAT ☆☆☆½
1936, USA
Irene Dunne, Allan Jones, Helen Morgan, Paul Robeson, Donald Cook, Charles Winninger, Helen Westley. Directed by James Whale. 110 min.

James Whale's direction of Jerome Kern and Oscar Hammerstein II's classic about performers on a Mississippi riverboat is cruder but livelier than the glossy MGM remake. Although Whale (*The Bride of Frankenstein*) allows condescending blackface numbers (remember, it was 1936) and botches the ending, he also underlines the pathos of the tragic miscegenation theme and achieves some startling expressionistic effects. Best of all, the cast is one of the finest ensembles in any musical, and the score is one of Kern's most memorable: Helen Morgan sings "Can't Help Lovin' That Man," Irene Dunne and Allan Jones perform the duet "Make Believe," and the wondrous Paul Robeson delivers "Ol' Man River." Not consistently great but enough magic to make it one of the more eloquent screen musicals.

SHOW BUSINESS ☆☆½
1944, USA, PG
Joan Davis, Eddie Cantor, George Murphy, Nancy Kelly, Constance Moore. Directed by Edward L. Marin. 92 min.

We would like to say, "There's no musical like 'Show Business,'" but that hyperbolic statement would be untrue. This is merely a standard backstager about Joan Davis, Eddie Cantor, and others doing their darnedest to break into show business. Unlike his performances in his early talkies, Banjo Eyes is relatively subdued here and easier to take. It's one of Davis's few headlines vehicles, and one wishes the material had more zing. Like Martha Raye, she was one of our great slapstick clowns and also knew her way around a song and dance. It's a congenial outing as long as you don't expect too much. Best number is "It Had to Be You."

SHOWDOWN AT BOOT HILL ☆☆☆
1958, USA
Charles Bronson, Robert Hutton, John Carradine, Carol Mathews, Fintan Meyler, Paul Maxey, Thomas B. Henry. Directed by Gene Fowler, Jr. 71 min.

This is a good if minor entry in the 1950s "adult" Western category. A young Charles Bronson plays a bounty hunter who guns down a wanted killer and then has to fight it out in a different way with the townspeople, who resent his interference and refuse to allow him the bounty money. John Carradine is good in a rare sympathetic role as the town barber and undertaker, the only person on Bronson's side. Tightly directed by former film editor Gene Fowler. Filmed in "Regalscope," which means less than nothing on a video screen.

A SHRIEK IN THE NIGHT ☆☆☆
1933, USA
Ginger Rogers, Lyle Talbot, Arthur Hoyt, Purnell Pratt, Harvey Clark. Directed by Albert Ray. 66 min.

A sort of follow-up to *The Thirteenth Guest* (also with Ginger Rogers and Lyle Talbot), this one concerns two rival reporters hot on the trail of a murderer who's eluded police capture. In typical B-movie fashion, the news hounds trade quips while trying to outdo each other as detectives. For a low-budget programmer, this is sleekly professional, with a dandy story line whose mystery elements are juggled with aplomb by the cast. A good example of the lean, efficient entertainment routinely provided by Hollywood in its heyday.

SID AND NANCY ☆☆☆☆
1986, Great Britain, R
Gary Oldman, Chloe Webb, Drew Schofield, David Hayman, Debby Bishop, Tony London. Directed by Alex Cox. 111 min.

Alex Cox's biography of the late punk star/junkie Sid Vicious and Nancy Spungen, the groupie girlfriend he murdered, is a triumph on all counts—a brilliant depiction of the squalid late-1970s punk scene, a bruisingly realistic antidrug horror show, and an unusual, even funny love story. To his great credit, Cox doesn't romanticize his ill-fated characters—there's nothing picturesque about their lives—but he doesn't trash them either. The seemingly straightforward story is layered with unexpected shades of drama, pathos, and stinging wit. Gary Oldman, a classically trained English actor, and the new-to-films American actress Chloe Webb couldn't be better as Sid and Nancy, and there's excellent support from Drew Schofield as Sid's eventual antagonist Johnny Rotten. Cox's direction, in only his second film, is astonishingly mature, attuned to every detail of their bizarre lives. The last third of the film, showing the couple's drugged stupor in the Chelsea Hotel, is revelatory. Beautiful photography and an excellently re-created score of Sex Pistols songs round out the achievement, a brief sojourn to hell that's worth the trip.

SIDEWALKS OF LONDON ☆☆☆
1938, Great Britain
Charles Laughton, Vivien Leigh, Rex Harrison, Larry Adler, Tyrone Guthrie. Directed by Tim Whelan. 84 min.

Charles Laughton laudably portrays a street entertainer who takes poor girl Vivien Leigh into his act, training her so well that he loses her to stardom. Rex Harrison has a small but noticeable role as the wealthy songwriter who sponsors Leigh's climb and turns the romance element into a triangle. The acting and street atmosphere carry this charmer along, though perhaps at an overly deliberate pace. (a.k.a.: *St. Martin's Lane*)

SIDEWINDER ONE ☆
1977, USA, PG
Marjoe Gortner, Michael Parks, Susan Howard, Alex Cord, Charlotte Rae. Directed by Earl Bellamy. 96 min.

If you're really, really into watching motocross racing, you may be willing to overlook the intrusive attempts at adding a plot to the otherwise adequate stunt footage. Marjoe Gortner and Michael Parks play stunt riders who are members of a troupe that is inherited by snobbish Susan Howard. The film's only suspense—will Michael or Marjoe fall in love with Susan?—is settled early, and how long can you watch motorcycle races before dozing off?

SIDNEY SHELDON'S BLOODLINE

See *Bloodline*

THE SIGN OF ZORRO ☆☆½
1960, USA
Guy Williams, Henry Calvin, Gene Sheldon, Britt Lomond, Lisa Gaye. Directed by Norman Foster and Lewis R. Foster. 91 min.

That sword-wielding savior leaves his mark on action fans in this fast-paced swashbuckler. Unfortunately, this is not so much a movie as a pasteup job of several episodes from Disney's "Zorro" series. That show was a favorite with youngsters and it did have lots of pizzazz, which is still apparent in this assemblage of footage. It may be merely a case of "great moments" from the old adventure show, but there's enough flair onscreen, and enough comic moments by Sergeant Garcia (Henry Calvin), to make this a watchable family flick.

SILENCE OF THE NORTH ☆☆
1981, Canada, PG
Ellen Burstyn, Tom Skerritt, Gordon Pinsent, Jennifer McKinney. Directed by Allan Winton King. 94 min.

Although this film had virtually no theatrical release, it's not without merit. If only it didn't suffer from such a lack of distinctive directing. Ellen Burstyn plays her patented long-suffering survivor, an independent woman struggling against such insurmountable odds as blizzards, hungry animals, starvation, and cabin fever. The brutal experience of life in the frozen wastelands is dutifully captured, particularly the toll this icy land takes on Burstyn's family, but it never seems harrowing. Somehow it remains within the careful limitations of a BBC-style drama. Despite the circumspect aspects of the production, Burstyn manages some exhilarating moments in her arduous assignment.

THE SILENCERS ☆☆½
1966, USA
Dean Martin, Stella Stevens, Dahlia Lavi, Victor Buono, Robert Webber, James Gregory, Arthur O'Connell, Cyd Charisse, Nancy Kovack. Directed by Phil Karlson. 102 min.

Matt Helm is a tacky, greasy superspy—sort of what James Bond would look like to a Carmelite nun—and the series of adventure films that Dean Martin made are coy and atrocious, what the Rat Pack types thought audiences really wanted (see also old Blue Eyes's *Tony Rome*). If all that is kept in mind, these movies (the worst two are *Murderer's Row* and *The Ambushers*) can be quite enjoyable; it's fun to see people who think you are stupid making asses of themselves. This is the first and the best of the series (though a few aficionados prefer the last, *The Wrecking Crew*). Victor Buono plays an evil genius trying to destroy a U.S. atomic testing site. But all eyes are on the women, from Cyd Charisse's opening dance, to Dahlia Lavi's deadly viper, to Stella Stevens's lovable klutz who only wants to help. A television staple.

SILENT CONFLICT ☆½
1948, USA
William "Hopalong Cassidy" Boyd, Andy Clyde, Rand Brooke, Virginia Belmont, Earle Hodgins. Directed by George Archainbaud. 61 min.

One of the last of the sixty-five or so Hopalong Cassidy Westerns that William Boyd made before turning around and selling them all to television in the late 1940s. As usual, this one features no cussin', no smokin', and almost no discernible romance or violence. Lots of horses, though, as Hopalong tracks down an evil hypnotist who has coerced one of his ranch hands into turning over the payroll. And they wonder why the Western almost died. For nostalgians and historians only.

SILENT KILLER FROM ETERNITY

See *Return of the Tiger*

SILENT MOVIE ☆☆☆
1976, USA, PG
Mel Brooks, Marty Feldman, Madeline Kahn, Burt Reynolds, Paul Newman, James Caan, Anne Bancroft, Liza Minnelli. Directed by Mel Brooks. 88 min.

Mel Brooks's send-up of the pretalkie era is audacious in one respect: it really *is* silent—except for one word whose uttering makes for one of the funnier jokes in the film. Otherwise, this falls short of the superb genre parodies the director mounted in *Blazing Saddles* and *Young Frankenstein*, although it's occasionally quite skilled and funny. The plot has filmmaker Mel Funn trying to get financing for his new picture from Engulf and Devour Studios. Best among the five superstars who have extended appearances is Anne Bancroft, who does a deft takeoff on her own glamorous image using the simple gimmick of crossed eyes.

SILENT NIGHT, BLOODY NIGHT ☆☆½
1973, USA, PG
Patrick O'Neal, Mary Woronov, John Carradine, Candy Darling, Astrid Heeren. Directed by Theodore Gershuny. 83 min.

One nasty Christmas Eve, a quiet town is disrupted by a series of odd occurrences. Jeffrey Butler, the owner and soon-to-be seller of the shunned Butler mansion, arrives claiming that he was to meet his lawyer at the house and is otherwise unable to get in. Cleverly plotted horror movie with some amusing twists.

SILENT NIGHT, DEADLY NIGHT ½☆
1984, USA, R
Robert Brian Wilson, Gilmer McCormick, Lilyan Chauvan. Directed by Charles E. Sellier, Jr. 93 min.

Traumatized by the murder of his parents by a man in a Santa Claus suit and his subsequent upbringing in a Dickensian Catholic orphanage, young Billy grows up with pathological problems about Christmas. At the age of nineteen, circumstances drive him off the deep end, and he dons a deadly St. Nick suit. Dull and formulaic horror picture, distinguished by the uproar that surrounded its theatrical release during the Christmas holidays.

SILENT NIGHT EVIL NIGHT

See *Black Christmas*

THE SILENT PARTNER ☆☆☆½
1979, Canada, R
Elliott Gould, Christopher Plummer, Susannah York, Celine Lomez, John Candy, Michael Kirby. Directed by Daryl Duke. 103 min.

This genuinely suspenseful thriller is a real treat, marred only slightly by a needlessly violent scene that the film as a whole could have done without, although it does establish what a psycho the bad guy is. Bank teller Elliott Gould manages to hide fifty thousand dollars in his lunchbox during a holdup, letting the police believe that the missing money was part of what the robber got away with. The real thief (Christopher Plummer), however, knows otherwise, and launches an elaborate scheme to get it back. Gould is surprisingly good in a rare straight role, and Plummer is frightening as the psychotic robber; both are well served by the intelligent, unpredictable script.

SILENT RAGE ☆☆
1982, USA, R
Chuck Norris, Ron Silver, William Finley, Toni Kalem. Directed by Michael Miller. 105 min.

A psychopathic killer, wounded by the police, is used by doctors as the guinea pig in an experiment in tissue regeneration. The result: an indestructible psychopathic killer who must be stopped by martial artist Chuck Norris. A minor departure from his usual adventures; still predictable, but entertaining enough.

SILENT RUNNING ☆☆½
1971, USA, G
Bruce Dern, Cliff Potts. Directed by Douglass Trumbull. 90 min.

In a change of pace from his usual bad guy–psychotic role, Bruce Dern gets to play a good guy–psychotic, a botanist on a space station containing all of the earth's remaining plant life. When the bureaucrats on Earth decide that the environment will never be able to support flora again, Dern kills his crewmates rather than jettison the cargo and takes off for parts unknown. Douglass Trumbull worked on the special effects in *2001: A Space Odyssey*, and the effects in this, his directorial debut, certainly seem to interest him more than the thin premise. Cowritten by Michael Cimino, with music by Joan Baez and Peter (P. D. Q. Bach) Schickele.

SILENT SCREAM ☆☆☆
1980, USA, R
Rebecca Balding, Barbara Steele, Cameron Mitchell, Yvonne De Carlo, Avery Schreiber. Directed by Denny Harris. 87 min.

Horror movie fans have learned to set their expectations a bit lower in this age of gore and gross-outs; therefore, as a stylistic exercise, the modest *Silent Scream* has the makings of a minor classic. With consummate control, the director glides his camera through this psychologically haunted house, through hidden passageways and cobweb-covered beams, as if he were probing the insides of a twisted mind. The script and its denouement (the usual "distant cousin of Norman Bates on a tear" plot line) lack originality, but your screams won't all be silent ones as some college students become the victims of a household that can no longer control the madness it has hidden away with faded photos, old records, and dead dreams.

SILK STOCKINGS ☆☆½
1957, USA
Fred Astaire, Cyd Charisse, Peter Lorre, Janis Paige, George Tobias, Joseph Buloff, Jules Manshin, Barrie Chase, Belita. Directed by Rouben Mamoulian. 117 min.

Entertaining, in spite of its many flaws. A musical version of the 1939 Greta Garbo–Ernst Lubitsch classic *Ninotchka* was not a bad idea, and this adaptation of Cole Porter's 1955 Broadway success features the superb dancing of Fred Astaire and Cyd Charisse in several inventive, well-integrated musical sequences. Unfortunately, substituting Charisse for Garbo in the role of the icy Soviet commissar who's warmed up during a mission in Paris is a little like trying to pass off Kool Whip as the real thing; and casting Astaire as a manipulative producer of bad movie musicals is an insult to his classiness (this was, incidentally, his last leading role). What's more, Rouben Mamoulian's use of Cinemascope awkwardly cuts off the performers in the frame—and that was before video scanners got to it. At least Janis Paige is around for a nifty spoof of Esther Williams. The creamy Cole Porter score includes "All of You," "Satin and Silk," and "Paris Loves Lovers."

SILKWOOD ☆☆☆
1983, USA, R
Meryl Streep, Kurt Russell, Cher, Craig T. Nelson, Diana Scarwid, Fred Ward, Ron Silver, Charles Hallahan, Josef Sommer, Sudie Bond, Henderson Forsythe, E. Katherine Kerr, Bruce McGill. Directed by Mike Nichols. 131 min.

In this dramatization of Karen Silkwood's one-woman battle against the Kerr-McGee nuclear fuel plant that employed her, director Mike Nichols and screenwriters Nora Ephron and Alice Arlen soft-pedal the melodrama to create a genuine modern horror story, a crawling two and a quarter hours in which the chemical, industrial, and political phobias of our age coalesce into a single all-consuming demon. Meryl Streep plays Karen Silkwood as the flirty busybody who puts her nosiness to work for the union not because she's a crusader but because she doesn't like being kept in the dark.

SILVERADO ☆☆☆½
1985, USA, PG-13
Kevin Kline, Scott Glenn, Jeff Goldblum, Rosanna Arquette, Danny Glover, Kevin Costner, Brian Dennehy, John Cleese, Linda Hunt. Directed by Lawrence Kasdan. 132 min.

To breathe life back into the Western, writer/director Lawrence Kasdan rooted through his memory for archetypal genre moments and left nothing out: we get gunplay, galloping horses, and wagon trains; a classic story about four straight-shooting outsiders who unite in a common cause; a romantic subplot about a farm girl and a drifter; and a villain who's a real low-down coyote. The result is an exceptionally pleasing entertainment and a modern rarity: not an anti-Western, a semi-Western, or a meta-Western, but a classically structured tale of pure-hearted heroes, black-hatted nemeses, and spirited frontier justice. Kasdan embraces some clichés and pokes fun at others; if you're generous enough to be able to include John Cleese, Jeff Goldblum, and Rosanna Arquette in your vision of the Wild West, you should enjoy it tremendously.

SILVER BEARS ☆☆☆
1978, USA, PG
Michael Caine, Cybill Shepherd, Louis Jourdan, Stephane Audran, Tom Smothers, David Warner, Martin Balsam, Jay Leno, Tony Mascia, Charles Gray, Joss Ackland, Jeremy Clyde. Directed by Ivan Passer. 113 min.

A thoroughly enjoyable, utterly inconsequential high-finance caper picture, this is directed by the expatriate Czech Ivan Passer (*Intimate Lighting*). Michael Caine, doing some impenetrable dirty work for an American Mafia boss, is seduced by Cybill Shepherd—who is really wonderful here—befriended by Louis Jourdan, and betrayed by, among others, Stephane Audran, David Warner, and (yes!) Tom Smothers—and Caine still ends up with all the marbles (bags of silver, actually). The gorgeous Swiss and Northern Italian scenery and Passer's leisurely pacing make it quite a lovely, relaxing two hours. From the novel by Paul Erdman.

SILVER BULLET
☆☆½
1985, USA, R
Gary Busey, Corey Haim, Megan Follows, Everett McGill, Robin Groves, Leon Russom. Directed by Daniel Attias. 95 min.

An amiable werewolf yarn, it foregoes the usual updated kinkiness of, say, *The Howling* or *An American Werewolf in London* in favor of good old-fashioned heroes out to get the monster. Though sketchily plotted, with no real focus to the story, *Bullet* nicely captures Stephen King's patented, blue-collar, small-town ethos—a squabbling family with a disabled son and an alcoholic uncle finds itself at the center of its town's trouble. A good, hammy performance by Gary Busey and a credible job by the two children—Corey Haim and Megan Follows—help to offset some weak dialogue and unconvincing support. The werewolf, of the ordinary expanding-bones-and-pulsing-flesh sort, was created by Carlo Rambaldi (*E.T.*). (a.k.a.: *Stephen King's Silver Bullet*)

THE SILVER CHALICE
☆½
1954, USA
Virginia Mayo, Pier Angeli, Jack Palance, Paul Newman, Walter Hampden, Joseph Wiseman, E. G. Marshall, Lorne Greene, Natalie Wood. Directed by Victor Saville. 142 min.

Only the very tolerant or very devoted will enjoy this second-rate religious spectacle about the young Greek sculptor who created the chalice from which Christ drank at the Last Supper, and the subsequent battle between the Romans and the Christians to gain possession of the coveted cup. This was based on a popular historical novel, and marked Paul Newman's film debut; like many of the other cast members, he tries hard but looks acutely uncomfortable mouthing the screenplay's pseudoclassical dialogue while lounging around in a toga. Jack Palance, however, is great fun to watch as the nefarious Nero.

SILVER DREAM RACER
☆½
1980, Great Britain, PG
David Essex, Beau Bridges, Cristina Raines, Clarke Peters, Harry Corbett. Directed by David Wickes. 111 min.

You'd have to be a very big fan of British pop star David Essex to sit through this dull, derivative sports fantasy about a grease monkey who trades in his coveralls for a motorcycle helmet and trains for a race that could bring him fame and glory. But will he be allowed to ride the sleek Silver Dream Racer . . . or will it fall into the hands of his rich, cocky competitor (Beau Bridges)? The best thing about the film—and that's not saying much—is the music, written and performed by the star.

SILVER HERMIT FROM SHAOLIN TEMPLE
☆☆
1985, Hong Kong
Roc Tien, Men Fei, Tien Ho, Chung Hwa, Doris Chen. Directed by Roc Tien. 86 min.

Handsome Roc Tien directs and stars in this period kung fu film that manages to capture a nice fairytale atmosphere. The Divine Steed, a heroic fighter, is suspected of killing his rivals in a contest for the hand of the princess of the Green Jade Village. Stay with the confusing story through the series of double-crosses—it's worth it.

SILVER SPURS
☆½
1943, USA
Roy Rogers, Smiley Burnette, John Carradine, Trigger, Sons of the Pioneers. Directed by Joseph Kane. 68 min.

One of the first films Roy Rogers made for Republic when he wasn't yet a big name, and the formula that would carry the series through dozens of installments wasn't quite perfected. The plot is both too silly and too complicated for much fun here, but Roy's smiling, singing presence carries this very slight entertainment along. Trimmed for video release.

THE SILVER STREAK
☆☆
1934, USA
Sally Blane, Charles Starrett, Hardie Albright, William Farnum, Irving Pichel, Edgar Kennedy. Directed by Tommy Atkins. 85 min.

No, this isn't the one with Gene Wilder and Richard Pryor, though it has more than a few similarities; like the later comedy, it's about the maiden run of the title train, a new high-speed express, from Chicago to Boulder Dam. Pretty melodramatic stuff, with the president of the railroad company shipping an iron lung out west for his son, a romance between the designer/driver of the train and the owner's daughter, and a fugitive German murderer aboard the train. Fails to generate the necessary suspense.

SILVER STREAK
☆☆½
1976, USA, PG
Richard Pryor, Gene Wilder, Jill Clayburgh, Patrick McGoohan, Ned Beatty, Richard Kiel, Scatman Crothers, Fred Willard. Directed by Arthur Hiller. 113 min.

This genial comedy-adventure, set on a supertrain from Los Angeles to Chicago, is only moderately engaging. Considering the talents of its cast, it's also surprisingly low on laughs. The story, with *Wrong Man*–ish intrigue, slick villains, and vanishing corpses, means to be a 1930s-style sophisticated romp, but director Arthur Hiller's slack execution suggests that some genres are better consigned to past films or present masters. The three stars are all quite funny, especially Richard Pryor and Gene Wilder, who reteamed later for the somewhat better *Stir Crazy*. But any movie that hires Richard Pryor and then keeps him off the screen for the first hour clearly has its funnybone in the wrong place.

SIMON
☆☆½
1980, USA, PG
Alan Arkin, Austin Pendleton, Judy Graubart, William Finley, Jayant, Wallace Shawn, Max Wright, Fred Gwynne, Madeline Kahn, Adolph Green. Directed by Marshall Brickman. 97 min.

Flipped-out scientists brainwash a neurotic psychology professor (Alan Arkin) into the belief that he's an extraterrestrial with a mission to save the world—but the only things he can think to save it from are hot-air hand-driers and ketchup in little plastic envelopes. This first solo comedy by Marshall Brickman, Woody Allen's frequent collaborator, has gloss and style and a baker's dozen laugh-out-loud sequences. It might even work, if it stuck with its initial premise. But when the focus shifts from Simon's effect on the world to the effects of fame on Simon, we lose track of what the movie is supposed to be about. Max Wright is a wonderful, feverish mouse of an actor playing a "media consultant."

SIMON, KING OF THE WITCHES
☆½
1971, USA, R
Andrew Prine, Brenda Scott, George Paulsin, Norman Burton, Ultra Violet. Directed by Bruce Kessler. 91 min.

Actually, Simon isn't quite king of the witches (or warlocks, as we always thought male witches were called), he's more of a novice, setting up shop in a Los Angeles storm sewer, the better to practice his sacrifices and spells without interruption. Confused, poorly plotted thriller that will appeal only to the undemanding.

A SIMPLE STORY ☆☆☆
1978, France
Romy Schneider, Bruno Cremer, Claude Brasseur, Arlette Bonnard, Sophie Daumier, Eva Darlan, Francine Berge, Roger Pigaut, Madeline Robinson. Directed by Claude Sautet. 107 min.

Claude Sautet (*Vincent, François, Paul, and the Others*) directed and cowrote (with Jean-Loup Dabadie) this lovely, perceptive character study set in a middle-class Parisian milieu. The depth and thickness in Sautet's images reflect his interest in the nuances and shifts of feeling in small events and limited people; and he creates richer visual and emotional textures than we would ever expect. Romy Schneider plays an industrial designer torn between two men: Bruno Cremer, gracious but inflexible, and Claude Brasseur, loutish but generous. Her character is a rather passive, loyal woman whose fine-tuned responses keep us alert to every mood. Sautet's only serious mistake is a plot that singles Schneider out as an ideal—as woman incarnate. But while Sautet's ideas may not be fresh, his vision certainly is. He gives us tangible proof of the wonder of the commonplace.

THE SIN

See *The Shaming*

SINAI COMMANDOS ☆☆½
1968, Israel
Robert Fuller, John Hudson, Ester Ullman, Avram Mor, Eli Sinai, Avram Hefner. Directed by Raphael Nussbaum. 98 min.

Actual documentary footage from the Arab-Israeli Six-Day War of 1967 helps pad out this war drama. A small Israeli unit has the task of disabling an Arab communications outpost prior to a full-scale attack on the region. Effective location shooting of the rugged desert terrain lends plausibility to this otherwise standard caper.

SINBAD AND THE EYE OF THE TIGER ☆☆
1977, USA, PG
Patrick Wayne, Taryn Power, Margaret Whiting, Jane Seymour, Patrick Troughton. Directed by Sam Wanamaker. 112 min.

Here's the third and terminal entry in the hokey mid-1970s series of kiddie adventures that began with *The Golden Voyage of Sinbad* and *The Seventh Voyage of Sinbad*. This one has him trying to free a prince from the spell of evil sorceress Zenobia. Patrick Wayne (son of John) was the third actor to play Sinbad in the series; his acting, and that of Taryn Power (daughter of Tyrone), is clumsy even for the comic-book format. Ray Harryhausen's special effects, a combination of live action and live-looking animation known as Dynarama, have since been replaced by the more technology-oriented visuals of the *Star Wars* era, but the fast-moving plot should satisfy young children without overly frightening them.

SINBAD THE SAILOR ☆☆½
1947, USA
Douglas Fairbanks, Jr., Maureen O'Hara, Walter Slezak, Anthony Quinn, George Tobias, Jane Greer, Mike Mazurki, Sheldon Leonard, Alan Napier. Directed by Richard Wallace. 116 min.

RKO produced this expensive swashbuckler as a vehicle for the younger Fairbanks's reentry into pictures upon his return from war duty, and as a return to the type of adventure film that had been so popular ten years earlier. It is big, splashy, and amusing, with a great acrobatic performance from its star, but on the whole it's a waste. There's much more talk than action, though the plot is murky and almost impossible to follow. The eighth voyage of Sinbad takes him to Arabia and an island of fabulous riches, where he mixes with a beautiful princess and a traitor on board his ship. In throbbing Technicolor. You could easily turn off the sound and not miss anything of worth, except Sheldon Leonard's one scene as an auctioneer.

SINCERELY, CHARLOTTE ☆☆½
1986, France
Isabelle Huppert, Niels Arestrup, Christine Pascal, Nicolas Wostrikoff, Jean-Michel Ribes. Directed by Caroline Huppert. 92 min.

This mystery-romance about a woman on the run from a murder rap who uses her still hopelessly infatuated ex-lover to protect her is familiar but still good fun, thanks to Isabelle Huppert's comically overwrought performance in a role created for her by her sister. As Charlotte, she tempts, teases, pouts, and lies so badly that no one but a man dumbstruck with love could believe her. Fortunately for her, that man is Mathieu (Niels Arestrup), who happily ditches his fiancée and her small son to embark on a mini-getaway spree with her. Nothing new is done with the plot, but Huppert makes it a pleasant one to revisit.

THE SINGER NOT THE SONG ☆☆
1960, Great Britain
John Mills, Dirk Bogarde, Mylene Demongeot, Laurence Naismith, John Bentley. Directed by Roy (Ward) Baker. 132 min.

Two good lead performances are all that redeem this overexplicit religious debate about a Catholic priest (John Mills) who takes over a parish in Mexico, only to find that a renegade bandit leader (Dirk Bogarde) is trying to intimidate him through a systematic series of murders. The adversaries get into a game of psychological warfare that takes increasingly unbelievable turns; occasionally, things come to a halt while the script ponders the role of free will and individual action in the Church. Dull and shapeless—the plot plays like an episode of "Davey and Goliath" gone berserk.

SINGIN' IN THE RAIN ☆☆☆☆
1952, USA
Gene Kelly, Donald O'Connor, Debbie Reynolds, Jean Hagen, Cyd Charisse. Directed by Stanley Donen and Gene Kelly. 103 min.

One of the greatest musicals ever born in Hollywood! Set during the glittery period of transition from silent films to talkies, this charming, wonderfully funny romance incorporates some of the most delightfully innovative song-and-dance numbers to be seen on the screen. The most memorable are Gene Kelly's splashy title number, Donald O'Connor's hilariously acrobatic "Make 'Em Laugh," and their amusing duet of "Moses Supposes." Debbie Reynolds plays the pretty show-biz newcomer who is threatened by the talkies because of her horrendous, high-pitched Bronx inflection. You definitely get your money's worth of entertainment from this multidimensional extravaganza. Songs by Adolph Green, Betty Comden, and Nacio Herb Brown.

SINGLE BARS, SINGLE WOMEN ☆☆½
1984, USA (TV)
Shelley Hack, Tony Danza, Paul Michael Glaser, Christine Lahti, Mare Winningham, Keith Gordon, Frances Lee McCain. Directed by Harry Winer. 101 min.

Considering that it's based on a country-and-western tune performed by Dolly Parton, this TV movie is more engaging than it has a right to be. It's like "The Love Boat" with class—a series of seriocomic vignettes set in a pickup bar/dance club, and although the situations are cliché, the dialogue has unusual zest and the performances are excellent. Outstanding as always is Christine Lahti, as a thirty-five-year-old teacher venturing into the bar for the first time, and meeting an easygoing lug nicely played by, of all people, Tony Danza. As the camera glides around the bar, picking up and then momentarily leaving each couple (or single), you'll be drawn in and perhaps unexpectedly touched.

SINGLE ROOM FURNISHED
1968, USA ☆
Jayne Mansfield, Dorothy Keller, Fabian Dean, Billy M. Greene, Martin Horsey. Directed by Matteo Ottaviano (Matt Cimber). 93 min.

This was supposed to do for Jayne what *Bus Stop* did for Marilyn and what *Carnal Knowledge* did for Ann-Margret. However, Jayne's director, Matt Cimber, was a hack. (Cimber's exploitation of sex symbols didn't end with Jayne; he later directed *Butterfly* with the unsinkable Pia Zadora.) This smudge of a movie doesn't really showcase Jayne's talents, which were more properly comedic, but she gives it the old college try. She plays a perpetually pregnant dame who's forever abandoned by men. But this fecund loser gets her revenge by becoming a prostitute and emasculating her customers with taunts (not the sort of thing to guarantee return business). Wait until you see her drive a horny sailor to suicide with shouts of "Monkey! Monkey!" If the film shows signs of raggedness, it's because Jayne was en route to finish it when she was killed in a car accident. A sad swan song.

SING YOUR WORRIES AWAY
1942, USA ☆☆
Jack Haley, Bert Lahr, Buddy Ebsen, Patsy Kelly, Sam Levene, Margaret Dumont. Directed by Edward Sutherland. 71 min.

This film might just do that, for old-movie buffs. If, however, you aren't impressed with the cast of solid-gold character actors, then the film's essential vaudevillian pleasures will be lost on you. It's an amiable, knock-about musical about some mob types making inroads into the inner circle of show biz. Second-rate material, but the first-rate musical pros slam it across with verve.

SINISTER JOURNEY
1948, USA ☆½
William Boyd, Andy Clyde, Rand Brooks, Elaine Riley, John Kellogg. Directed by George Archainbaud. 59 min.

This Hopalong Cassidy adventure is even duller than average. The usual young lovers here are torn apart by his inability to get along with her father, a feisty old railroad executive; Hopalong intervenes to set things straight when the lad is falsely accused of murder.

SINNER'S BLOOD
1983, USA ½☆
Naci Sheldon, Stephen Jacques, Cristy Beal, Parker Herriott. Directed by Neil Douglas.

This plotless bit of nothing is an example of what can happen when you make motion picture technology available to anyone at all. Two girls arrive in a small town where they are to live with their drooling uncle, shrewish aunt, peeping-tom cousin, and his whacked-out sister. Other characters, including the minister's son, his homosexual friend, and all four members of the local biker gang, pop up. A few things happen, with almost no logical connection, and then the movie stops. It doesn't end, mind you—it just stops. Maybe it's the first chapter of a rural American answer to *Berlin Alexanderplatz*.

SIN OF ADAM AND EVE
1972, Mexico, R ☆½
Candy Wilson, George Rivers (Jorge Rivero). Directed by Michael Zachary (Miguel Zacarias). 72 min.

A one-of-a-kind film. This is a straightfaced Mexican production that relates the expulsion of our forebears from the Garden and fills a gap in the Genesis tale: how will the two find one another again, pick up the pieces, and go about generating our species? (Adam's Mexican, Eve a gringo, we think; a possible clue?)

THE SIN OF HAROLD DIDDLEBOCK
1947, USA ☆☆☆
Harold Lloyd, Jimmy Conlin, Franklin Pangborn, Edgar Kennedy, Rudy Vallee. Directed by Preston Sturges. 90 min.

A middle-aged man loses his job, takes his first drink, and ends up the owner of a circus. Although the plot may be a standard Hollywood farce, the combined talents of Preston Sturges and Harold Lloyd, both at the end of brilliant comedy careers, create a standout movie. The film begins with original footage from Lloyd's *The Freshman*; then, after showing him winning the big college game and taking a job offer from an enthusiastic alumnus, the film moves on in time. Harold stagnates in the same bookkeeper job for twenty-two years. We see his abandonment of youthful diligence and his adoption of gambling, riotous living, and dependence on a weasly con man played by chinless Jimmy Conlin. The movie is strained and hyperactive, but that's the point—old man's comedy, like adult success, is achieved only over the edge of self-restraint. The film was tampered with by producer Howard Hughes; the longer running time has more of Sturges's original footage. (a.k.a.: *Mad Wednesday*, 79 min. version)

SIOUX CITY SUE
1946, USA ☆½
Gene Autry, Lynne Roberts, Sterling Holloway, Richard Lane, Ralph Sanford, the Cass County Boys. Directed by Frank McDonald. 69 min.

This was Gene Autry's first feature after returning from four years in the army, but you'd never know he'd been gone—no big welcome-back production here. Cowboy Gene is lured away from his ranch by a female talent agent who promises to make him into a Western singing star, though all she really wants to do is record his voice for a cartoon about a donkey. As usual, more singing than anything else, with six tunes and innumerable reprises.

SIROCCO
1951, USA, PG ☆☆
Humphrey Bogart, Marta Toren, Lee J. Cobb, Gerald Mohr, Zero Mostel, Vincent Renno. Directed by Curtis Bernhardt. 97 min.

This Humphrey Bogart–Marta Toren vehicle travels down a winding road. It's set in Damascus when the 1925 war between Syrians and their French occupiers frequently went underground—into graves and subterfuge. Bogart is Bogart as a near-Olympic gunrunner with a torch for the terrifying Toren, concubine of the French intelligence kingpin (Lee J. Cobb). Wooed and then wowed, Toren sees Bogart as a highway to Cairo; unfortunately, Cobb detects the flame and the screen explodes. Although the look of the film (photography by Burnett Guffey) is formula one, and the indestructible Bogart is at the helm, *Sirocco* is guilty of bad tuning and a confused sense of direction.

SISTER KENNY
1946, USA ☆☆☆½
Rosalind Russell, Alexander Knox, Dean Jagger, Philip Merivale, Beulah Bondi. Directed by Dudley Nichols. 116 min.

Rosalind Russell had to lobby for years to make this film, but her patience and the long wait were worthwhile. It's a superb bio-pic detailing the courageous crusading of a dedicated nurse who was instrumental in improving methods in the treatment of polio. Since Sister Kenny and her struggle are not well known, the story takes on an added interest. Obviously a labor of love for Russell, the film won one of her four best actress nominations for her role here; she really subdues her mannerisms and tries to inhabit this fascinating woman's life.

SISTERS
1973, USA, R ☆☆☆
Margot Kidder, Jennifer Salt, William Finley, Charles Durning. Directed by Brian de Palma. 93 min.

Siamese twins Dominique and Danielle are implicated in a brutal murder seen only by an inquisitive neighbor, whose investigations lead her into a nightmare of perversion, death, and insanity. De Palma's breakthrough film is riddled with Hitchcockian homages but still full of its own perverse energy. The highlight is an amazing nightmare flashback about the past of the twins. From the director of *Carrie, Dressed to Kill, Body Double,* and many others, all characterized by his obsession with Hitchcock and with many forms of cinematic sexual violence.

SITTING DUCKS ☆☆
1980, USA, R
Michael Emil, Zack Norman, Patrice Townsend, Irene Forrest, Richard Romanus, Henry Jaglom. Directed by Henry Jaglom. 90 min.

Henry Jaglom is known as the difficult, independent director of films like *A Safe Place* and *Tracks,* but in this film, he's going for nothing more difficult than a caper comedy, and a very mild one at that. A pair of bumblers (Zack Norman and Michael Emil) steal $750,000 from the New York Mafia and then hightail it to Miami, laughing and loving, as the saying goes, all the way. The two, while likable enough, are hardly a great comedy team, but when they pick up a hitchhiker, Patrice Townsend, the incessant bickering gives way to a sexual roundelay that's made all the more amusing by Townsend's gradually unfolding performance.

THE SIX DIRECTIONS OF BOXING ☆☆½
1979, Hong Kong
David Chaing, Simon Yuen, Yo Hua. Directed by Tyrone Hsu. 90 min.

The commissioner (Yo Hua) orders Captain Ai Chaing-feng (David Chaing) to capture Chen Hui-Chih, brother of warlord Chen Ming-Chin, and to discover their gun-smuggling plans. Lots of money was poured into this production, and it shows in the quality of the cast, costumes, sets, and choreography.

SIX KUNG FU HEROES ☆☆
Hong Kong
Han Ying Chieh, Pai Wei, Chaing Yi-Peng, Chang Ten-Wen, Li Lu-Ling. Directed by Lin Ping.

Six crippled kung fu students are each given an imperial decree starting an anti-Ching rebellion, and are instructed to deliver them to the loyal commander-in-chief. To Lo, boss of the Ching secret agents, learns of the imperial decree and tells his men to get it. This well-directed and well-filmed movie has much to its credit: good sets and costumes, comic touches, believable actors, good martial arts, and fine choreography.

SIX PACK ☆☆
1982, USA, PG
Kenny Rogers, Diane Lane, Barry Corbin, Erin Gray, Terry Kiser, Bob Hannah. Directed by Daniel Petrie. 110 min.

Kenny "I'm a gamblin' kinda guy" Rogers makes his motion-picture debut in this sentimental story of a race driver traveling around the southern stock-car circuit with six young ragamuffins in tow. There's nothing offensive here, but there's no real distinction either; it's identical to almost any evening's TV offerings.

SIX SHOOTIN' SHERIFF ☆
1938, USA
Ken Maynard, Marjorie Reynolds, Lafe McKee, Walter Long, Bob Terry. Directed by Harry Fraser. 59 min.

Ken Maynard is framed for a bank robbery, and comes back to find the men who sent him up. Being an all-American cowboy, he of course does so in the approved legal manner. Standard B Western, in which the most interesting pastimes for the viewer are (a) wondering what they fed Maynard in prison that made him put on so much weight, and (b) wondering whether his character's name, Trigger, and the aforementioned spare tire were the inspiration for the name of Roy Rogers's whinnying costar.

SIXTEEN CANDLES ☆☆½
1984, USA, PG
Molly Ringwald, Anthony Michael Hall, Michael Shoeffling, Paul Dooley. Directed by John Hughes. 93 min.

Molly Ringwald lends her patented pout to this refreshingly bright, insightfully funny movie about the traumas of teenhood. First, her family is so preoccupied with her sister's wedding that they forget Molly's landmark birthday; then, the boy she likes proves preoccupied with another girl; but, worst of all, she falls victim to the indefatigable, humiliating attentions of class geek Anthony Michael Hall, who ultimately steals the show with his devilish charm. Though tripped up by some typical teen-flick gimmicks, the script has enough substance to make even adults laugh.

SIXTEEN DAYS OF GLORY ☆☆½
1985, USA, G
Directed by Bud Greenspan. 145 min.

A rah-rah documentary tribute to the 1984 Olympic Games in Los Angeles that concentrates on the American medal sweep and makes it way too easy to forget the absence of Soviet and East German competitors. Good photography captures the winning efforts of Mary Lou Retton in gymnastics, Rowdy Gaines in swimming, Edwin Moses in the hurdles, and Joan Benoit in the first-ever Olympic women's marathon. The less noble U.S. achievements—Mary Decker's trip-up on the track and her subsequent tantrum, Carl Lewis's refusal to try for a long-jump record—go unrecorded, and 145 minutes of cheering begin to sound very hollow. Still, the sheer scope, detail, and professionalism of Greenspan's work should satisfy sports buffs and impress casual rooters.

SIX WEEKS ☆
1982, USA, PG
Dudley Moore, Mary Tyler Moore, Katherine Healey, Shannon Wilcox, Joe Regalbuto. Directed by Tony Bill. 107 min.

For audiences who identified with the protagonists in *Love Story,* here's some more unbearable schmaltz. Now that they're older, they can pull out the hankies for this tale of a dying thirteen-year-old girl who tries to get her widowed mother together with her choice of an adoptive father so that she can be part of a real family again before she dies. (Guess how long she has to live?) We're tempted to write this off with puns on the order of "Moore and Moore make less," but it isn't really their fault (although why Brit Dudley, who makes no attempt to cover up his accent, plays a politician running for Congress in California is anyone's guess; and he does deserve special blame for composing and performing the atrocious score). No, aside from the saccharine script and direction, the major irritant here is Katherine Healey as the dying lass. Wise beyond her years and precocious to the point of causing physical pain, she may have you rooting for her to die already and get it over with.

SIZZLE ☆☆
1981, USA (TV)
Loni Anderson, John Forsythe, Michael Goodwin, Richard Lynch, Leslie Uggams. Directed by Don Medford. 100 min.

This prohibition tale will leave viewers thirsty for fine acting and dramatic depth. Loni Anderson, an amply endowed actress with some comic flair, comes across as too intelligent to portray successfully a decorative dumb bunny from the sticks; nor does she have that blissful ignorance that Jayne Mansfield brought to her cartoonish performances. So the performance is neither good enough nor bad enough to make the film work. But Loni's not the only liability here; none of the actors fit the period style. All the flapper fringe and spats seem superimposed on a modern and rather plastic sensibility. More like "Fizzle."

SKIN GAME ★★★
1971, USA, PG
James Garner, Louis Gossett, Jr., Ed Asner, Susan Clark, Brenda Sykes, Andrew Duggan, Henry Jones, Royal Dano. directed by Paul Bogart. 102 min.

In this bright, episodic Old West comedy, James Garner plays—what else?—a con man who keeps selling his sidekick (Lou Gossett) as a slave, helping him escape, and moving on to repeat the scam in another town. Slavery is an awfully tenuous premise on which to build a farce, and Gossett's nobility quotient is kept a little too high for comfort, but he and Garner both turn in winning performances. Writer Peter Stone had his name removed from the credits when his script was rewritten; credited author Pierre Marton is a pseudonym. Later remade for TV as "Sidekicks," with Larry Hagman in Garner's role.

SKULLDUGGERY ★½
1970, USA
Burt Reynolds, Susan Clark, Wilfred Hyde-White, Roger C. Carmel, Edward Fox. Directed by Gordon Douglas. 105 min.

This adventure film has a few vague allegorical ideas that aren't developed too far, which is probably just as well, given the general listlessness of the cast and director. Burt Reynolds and Roger Carmel are mercenaries who tag along on a jungle expedition and discover a tribe of half-men, half-apes. Our heroes, however, consider them predominantly human—Carmel so much so that he impregnates one of the females. In order to have the slaves declared human and therefore have them freed, Reynolds brings the nature of the offspring to a court trial. At best, this is preaching to the converted; most of the time, however, the film doesn't even seem to care much about its own message. Another flop from hot-and-cold hack director Gordon Douglas.

SKY BANDITS ★
1986, Great Britain, PG
Scott McGinniss, Jeff Osterhage, Miles Anderson, Ronald Lacey, Valerie Steffen, Ingrid Held, Keith Buckley, Terrence Harvey. Directed by Zoran Perisic. 93 min.

Eighteen million dollars went into the budget of this abominably awful airborne adventure about two bank robbers who, after they're arrested and tossed into World War I, become aerial aces. Poorly acted and scripted with a laughable tin ear, the film means to wow you with its sky-high stuntwork, but the special effects are distinctly unimpressive, surprisingly so considering the budget. Originally titled *Gunbus*.

SKYLINE ★★★
1984, Spain
Antonio Resines, Beatriz-Porro, Jaime Nos, Roy Hoffman, Patricia Cisarano. Directed by Fernando Colomo. 83 min.

New York, as seen through the eyes of a cultural and political outsider, is the subject of this surprisingly charming film. Gustavo, a successful Spanish free-lance photographer, spends a summer vacation in New York hoping to make contacts that will land him a job, preferably with *Life* or *Newsweek*. His difficulties include the ever-present language barrier, how to meet girls, and why his photos won't sell when the same kind of things by other photographers are perfectly acceptable. Very low-key, with a forced ironic ending; the Spanish folk music may strike many non-Latin viewers as unintentionally funny.

SLAMMER

See *Short Eyes*

THE SLAP

See *La Gifle*

SLAPSHOT ★★★
1977, USA, R
Paul Newman, Strother Martin, Michael Ontkean, Jennifer Warren, Lindsay Crouse, Jerry Houser, Andrew Duncan, Jeff Carlson, Steve Carlson, David Hanson, Yvon Barrette, Alan Nicholls, Brad Sullivan, Stephen Mendillo, Swoosie Kurtz, M. Emmet Walsh. Directed by George Roy Hill. 123 min.

Paul Newman holds together George Roy Hill's confused, foulmouthed comedy about a down-and-out hockey team that resorts to violence to sell tickets. The film falls into the trap of glorifying the violence it pretends to deplore, and Nancy Dowd's script takes a rather naive delight in its own naughtiness. The women (Jennifer Warren as hockey coach Newman's estranged wife and Lindsay Crouse as the well-educated, hard-drinking hockey wife) are intriguing, and the roughhousing is often hilarious. Newman's performance is his best in years, and the striptease Michael Ontkean ("The Rookies") does on the ice is funny and sexy.

SLAPSTICK OF ANOTHER KIND ★
1984, USA, PG
Jerry Lewis, Madeline Kahn, Marty Feldman, John Abbott, Jim Backus, Samuel Fuller, Merv Griffin, Pat Morita. Directed by Steven Paul. 85 min.

Junk of a forgettable kind. Kurt Vonnegut undergoes the worst censorship that an artist can suffer: his ideas are embraced and translated by tiny, tiny minds. What emerges from producer-director-writer Steven Paul's vanity production is sledgehammer satire performed by a zombified cast. Two alien children are placed in the womb of a wealthy and powerful earth woman, and they are expected to grow up and save the world. However, small-minded groundlings want nothing more than to repress these odd-looking saviors. Two small blessings: the film was actually made in 1982 but the world was spared two years of its release while it sat on a shelf; and the final cut was shortened from an original running time of ninety-four minutes.

THE SLASHER . . . IS THE SEX MANIAC! ½★
1976, Italy, R
Farley Granger, Sylva Koscina. Directed by Robert Montero. 83 min.

Society adulteresses are systematically murdered by a maniac with a big knife, who leaves at the scenes of all his crimes photographic evidence of the victims' indiscretions. Inspector Capuana, himself married to a wealthy woman, conducts an investigation that goes nowhere (though he does conclude that he is looking for a sex maniac) until the killer threatens his own wife, precipitating an inevitable confrontation. A deadly dull Italian murder mystery, its greatest distinction is having been reedited into a pornographic feature called *Penetration*, reportedly a deadly dull Italian murder mystery with hard-core inserts (of potential victims being indiscreet) featuring Harry Reems and Marc Stevens.

SLAUGHTERHOUSE-FIVE ★★★★
1972, USA, R
Michael Sacks, Valerine Perrine, Ron Leibman, Eugene Roche, Sharon Gans. Directed by George Roy Hill. 104 min.

As he later did with John Irving's *The World According to Garp*, director George Roy Hill adapts the Kurt Vonnegut novel to the screen with a wonderful concision, creating a work that is faithful to its source and yet distinctly his own. Everyman Billy Pilgrim becomes "unstuck in time," living every moment in his life simultaneously: he moves randomly from the firebombing of Dresden during World War II to his boring contemporary life as an optician in upstate New York to his captivity in an intergalactic zoo on the planet Tralfamadore. Valerie Perrine made her film debut here as Montana Wildhack, a movie sex kitten who is provided as Pilgrim's mate on Tralfamadore. A surreal and very original film, aided by a marvelous Glenn Gould-adapted score by J. S. Bach.

SLAVE OF THE CANNIBAL GOD ☆
1978, Italy, R
Ursula Andress, Stacy Keach, Claudio Cassinelli, Franco Fantasia. Directed by Sergio Martino. 86 min.

There are two kinds of people in the world: those who wisely think this title couldn't possibly be attached to a movie that was worthwhile, and those who foolishly think that this title couldn't possibly be attached to a movie that didn't have a few cheap laughs. Well, those in the first group are right—it isn't; those in the second group are wrong—it doesn't. Rather than snicker at the campy antics of the cast, you'll be stupefied by the lugubrious goings-on involving Ursula Andress's potential sacrifice to some hungry gods. Certainly she's a tasty dish, but this trash doesn't even give *Cannibal Movie*–lovers any food for thought.

SLAVERS ☆½
1977, West Germany, R
Trevor Howard, Ron Ely, Britt Ekland, Ray Milland, Jurgen Goslar, Don Jack Rousseau, Cameron Mitchell. Directed by Jurgen Goslar. 102 min.

For some unknown reason, the world was subjected to a spate of execrable movies about slavery during the mid-1970s, with directors as diverse as Richard Fleischer and Russ Meyer and, as often as not, a bewildering variety of respectable thespians. The prime example is *Mandingo*, and this is another of the worst ones. Jurgen Goslar, who previously directed the atrocious *Albino*, returns to Africa for this merry story about Arab slave traders in the late 1800s. Ray Milland plays an Arab chieftain whose hobbies include using a swimming pool full of slaves for target practice.

THE SLAYER ☆
1982, USA, R
Sarah Kendall, Alan McRae, Carl Kraines. Directed by J. S. Cardone. 80 min.

Kay (Sarah Kendall) is a painter whose nightmares are turning her into a surrealist. Of more immediate concern is the title character, whose antics are turning Kay's loved ones into gore. And that's spoiling their vacation on Georgia's Tybee Island, off Savannah. But you'll survive.

SLAYGROUND ☆
1984, Great Britain, R
Peter Coyote, Billie Whitelaw, Philip Sayer, Bill Luhr. Directed by Terry Bedford. 89 min.

A darkly photographed, dully scripted, and drearily directed action pic, this seems to have cable TV written all over it. Lowlife Peter Coyote becomes targeted for murder after he accidentally kills a child. The tyke's daddy is understandably perturbed and hires a contract killer who naturally tracks him down (conveniently in a photogenic amusement park). Glum, humdrum downer. Moody atmosphere is no substitute for tension and drama.

SLEDGE HAMMER ½☆
1984, USA
Ted Prior, Linda McGill, John Eastman, Jeanine Scheer, Tim Aguilar. Directed by David A. Prior. 85 min.

This made-for-video horror film features lots of gore, a few undressed bodies, and all of the subtlety of the title instrument. In the usual slasher tradition, the story is almost nonexistent: an abused young boy kills his mother and her lover with a sledgehammer. Years later, some youngsters spending a weekend at the same house are being killed off one by one. Clever premise, huh?

SLEEPAWAY CAMP ☆☆
1984, USA, R
Feliissa Rose, Jonathan Tiersten, Karen Fields, Christopher Collett. Directed by Robert Hiltzak. 88 min.

Unusual murders, false scares, promiscuous teens, lecherous camp employees, implausible behavior in the face of gruesome events, and a maniac (strictly according to Freud) add up to fair entertainment of its kind. Relatively subdued violence.

SLEEPER ☆☆☆½
1973, USA, PG
Woody Allen, Diane Keaton, John Beck. Directed by Woody Allen. 86 min.

This enormously popular comedy represents the peak of Woody Allen's early, zany style. Allen is Miles Monroe—a well-intentioned schlemiel who works at the Happy Carrot Health Food Store in Greenwich Village—until he awakens from a supposedly routine operation to learn that he has been frozen for the past two hundred years and that it is now 2173. Diane Keaton, an able comedienne in her own right, provides a perfect foil for Allen's slapstick antics. Even Mia Farrow's outstanding comic performances in the later, more sophisticated Allen films never succeeded in duplicating the warm, energetic chemistry that Keaton achieved with Allen in such films as *Sleeper, Play it Again, Sam, Annie Hall*, and *Manhattan*.

SLEEPING BEAUTY ☆☆☆
1959, USA, G
Animated: Mary Costa, Bill Shirley, Eleanor Audley, Verna Felton, Barbara Jo Allen, Barbara Luddy, Bill Thompson, Taylor Holmes. Supervising director: Clyde Geronimi. 75 min.

Some critics saw this as the beginning of the end of Disney's Golden Age of animation, and while it's certainly not a classic on the level of *Pinocchio*, time has proven it to be more durable than many suspected. After a weak start, the animation becomes extraordinarily beautiful and the story enchants as a trio of chubby fairies raises a lovely princess in the woods to protect her from a wicked spell. Disney never did as well with human subjects as with animals: their Sleeping Beauty looks a bit like Kim Novak, and Prince Philip sings like Nelson Eddy. However, the fairies are delights, and the wicked witch Maleficent belongs in a Villainesses' Hall of Fame: she seems fashioned in equal measure out of Joan Collins, Joan Crawford, Margaret Hamilton, and Mercedes McCambridge as the voice of the devil in *The Exorcist*. The climax, in which she turns into a dragon to kill the prince, may be much too frightening for some young children.

SLEUTH ☆☆☆☆
1972, Great Britain, PG
Laurence Olivier, Michael Caine, Alec Cawthorne, Eve Channing. Directed by Joseph L. Mankiewicz. 138 min.

A witty and intriguing game of cat-and-mouse, played out between a shrewd mystery writer and a devious young man in the cluttered rooms of a lavish English country manor. *Sleuth*, adapted by Anthony Shaffer from his hugely successful play, relies on bitchy, biting dialogue, macabre twists, and one enormous trick to create its suspense—if you don't already know the *trompe l'oeil* upon which the film turns, we won't spoil it for you. Joseph Mankiewicz's direction allows Laurence Olivier to give a grand, hammy performance that teeters between genuine star turns and pure camp. Michael Caine is terrific, too. If you like mysteries with a lot of cleverness and more than a little self-mockery, *Sleuth* is about as good as they come.

SLIGHTLY HONORABLE ☆☆☆
1940, USA
Pat O'Brien, Edward Arnold, Broderick Crawford, Ruth Terry, Eve Arden, Evelyn Keyes. Directed by Tay Garnett. 75 min.

Edward Arnold plays an oily highway commissioner who will stop at nothing to rake in a few more dirty dollars. Unluckily, a hard-boiled young attorney is on his trail. Pat O'Brien is convincing, if a bit stiff, as the lawyer, but Ruth Terry is a gem, playing her part of a singer with real verve and brass. It's all carried off in a crisply efficient fashion by director Tay Garnett (*The Postman Always Rings Twice*), who has no trouble mixing murder and patter. Film noir buffs will want to catch this early, grimly humorous mystery.

SLIGHTLY SCARLET   ☆☆
1956, USA
John Payne, Arlene Dahl, Rhonda Fleming, Kent Taylor, Ted de Corsia. Directed by Allen Dwan. 92 min.

Connoisseurs of *Vertigo* should take a look at this and other mid-1950s B noirs (*Rouge Cop*, *Screaming Mimi*) to remind themselves that Alfred Hitchcock's film was not alone in bending the rules. Bending the rules, however, does not necessarily make a good film. In *Slightly Scarlet*, the characters are gray, the hero unsympathetic, and the sexuality overt, but the results are lurid and muddled rather than fresh and intriguing. The plot, based on a James A. Cain novel, has something to do with good and bad sisters involved with gangsters, corrupt city officials, and policeman John Payne. Technicolor and Superscope make this film, one of RKO's last, seem better than it is.

THE SLIME PEOPLE   ☆
1962, USA
Robert Hutton, Les Tremayne, Susan Hart, Robert Burton. Directed by Robert Hutton. 76 min.

Bloblike creatures run amok and try to take over the earth, so we'd all better watch out. Often an actor will want to direct himself in order to have a proper showcase for his underappreciated talents. We suppose Hutton directed himself here only to pick up two different paychecks in Low-Budget Land. No better, no worse than a lot of Toho Japanese Godzilla monstrosities, with the inevitable shortcuts in sets and special effects taking their toll on credibility. Slimy!

SLOW BURN   ☆½
1986, USA (TV)
Eric Roberts, Beverly D'Angelo, Raymond J. Barry, Ann Schedeen, Emily Longstreth, Johnny Depp, Henry Gibson, Dan Hedaya. Directed by Matthew Chapman. 92 min.

Director-writer Matthew Chapman was clearly attempting a contemporary *film noir* with this made-for-cable drama about a hard-bitten detective (Eric Roberts) trying to find a missing person in Palm Springs, but the result is feeble and imitative—even the main characters seem to have pilfered their life-styles from old, better movies. The miscast Roberts overplays wildly without achieving one credible scene, and Beverly D'Angelo looks forlorn; the endless narration, meant to evoke classic films, succeeds only in distancing the viewer from a quite clever plot.

SLOW MOTION

See *Every Man for Himself*

THE SLUGGER'S WIFE   ½☆
1985, USA, PG-13
Michael O'Keefe, Rebecca De Mornay, Martin Ritt, Randy Quaid, Cleavant Derricks, Lisa Langlois. Directed by Hal Ashby. 114 min.

More of the weightless sentimental claptrap Neil Simon has been turning out since about the time of *Chapter Two*. A rock singer (Rebecca De Mornay) is married to a baseball outfielder (Michael O'Keefe); she's simple and nice and in love, and so is he, but career pressure drives them apart, and they both make cloying, winsome speeches to each other in blatant attempts to wring a few smiles or tears. Director Hal Ashby presides with more grace than is warranted, but his shifting, varying contexts only emphasize how false the characters are.

SLUMBER PARTY '57   ☆
1977, USA, R
Noelle North, Debra Winger, Bridget Hollman, Mary Ann Appleseth, Rainbeaux (Cheryl) Smith, Janet Wood. Directed by William A. Levey. 89 min.

Odds-on favorite for the picture Debra Winger would most like to forget. Essentially a series of black-out sketches: the girls at a slumber party sit around reliving their loss of virginity. Cannon films can really make sex look sordid, and they are at their leering best watching high school girls in shorty nightgowns.

SLUMBER PARTY MASSACRE   ☆
1982, USA, R
Michele Michaels, Michael Villela, Robin Stille, Debra Deliso, Andre Honore, Gina Mari. Directed by Amy Jones. 78 min.

You may not believe this, but the script to this Roger Corman–produced psycho thriller was penned by none other than Rita Mae Brown. Don't expect any radical sexual attitudes, however; there is just the tiniest whiff of fresh feminism wafting over this graveyard tale. The girls are having an overnight party and the uninvited guests include silly boys and a crazed killer.

SMALL CHANGE   ☆☆☆½
1976, France, PG
Geory Desmouceaux, Philippe Goldman, Claudio Deluca, Frank Deluca, Richard Golfier, Laurent Devlaeminck. Directed by François Truffaut. 104 min.

François Truffaut's tribute to the imagination and invention of childhood follows the lives of several children in a provincial town. In this well-created, poetic comedy, the children are allowed to be spontaneous rather than precious. *Small Change* has a serious side as well, but most of the film, the most successful part, is light, witty, and often exhilarating. Truffaut has done more powerful work, and *400 Blows* may be more original; but even slight Truffaut makes for an amusing *divertissement*.

A SMALL CIRCLE OF FRIENDS   ☆☆
1980, USA, R
Brad Davis, Karen Allen, Jameson Parker, Gary Springer, Shelley Long, John Friedrich. Directed by Rob Cohen. 112 min.

There's something for everyone in Rob Cohen's sodden paean to the good old days of student turbulence: buckets of Harvard-Cambridge ambience 1967–71, fluctuating hairstyles to remind you that the times they were a-changin', and a very pretty best-friendship that turns into a ménage à trois between blond WASP Jameson Parker, spirited artist Karen Allen, and street-wise rebel Brad Davis. Unfortunately, Cohen treats everything from beery dorm pranks to Vietnam casualties with the same wet-eyed fondness; by the end, you're not sure whether to long for the Beatles or the Weathermen. The performances are good, except for the insufferable overplaying by Davis, but the atmosphere seems derived more from reading about the 1960s than from living through the era—odd, since Cohen attended Harvard at the same time as his characters. The brightness of many individual scenes keeps it entertaining, but it plays as pure fantasy, and its "big" emotions feel predigested and self-congratulatory.

A SMALL KILLING   ☆☆½
1981, USA (TV)
Jean Simmons, Ed Asner, Sylvia Sidney, Andrew Prine, J. Pat O'Malley. Directed by Steven Hilliard Stern. 100 min.

This shaky premise must have worked better in the source material novel, *Rag Bag Clan*. Still, Ed Asner and Jean Simmons generate an incredible amount of star chemistry together and make this detective trifle oddly compelling. A cop doing undercover work as a wino and a college teacher doing research among bag ladies pool resources to crack a drug ring that has murdered a bag lady who was doing courier work for them to earn a bit of cash. Not altogether believable, but the sterling cast covers a multitude of improbabilities.

SMASH-UP, THE STORY OF A WOMAN ☆☆
1947, USA
Susan Hayward, Lee Bowman, Marsha Hunt, Eddie Albert, Carl Esmond. Directed by Stuart Heisler. 103 min.

After years as a decorative ingenue, Susan Hayward was finally taken seriously by the critics with this flashy vehicle about an alcoholic, a sort of second cousin to *The Lost Weekend*. Her fans will enjoy her vibrant emoting; her detractors will be apt to make unkind remarks about how she telegraphs every emotion. She's still feeling her way as an actress here, but it's hard to look away when she's sinking her teeth into this meaty role that won her her first Academy Award nomination.

SMILE ☆☆☆
1975, USA, PG
Bruce Dern, Barbara Feldon, Michael Kidd, Geoffrey Lewis, Nicholas Pryor, Colleen Camp, Maria O'Brien, Joan Prather, Annette O'Toole, Melanie Griffith. Directed by Michael Ritchie. 113 min.

Teenage beauty pageants are the target of this sharply funny satire, one of Michael Ritchie's most consistently entertaining films. Bruce Dern and Barbara Feldon stand out as the sponsor and coordinator of a Young Miss America runoff in California, but the most memorable moments involve the young women—shrewd, calculating beauties who fight tooth and nail to see who's the sweetest of them all. Some priceless lines pin the ethos of the Me Decade to the wall like a wriggling insect, and even if the film is too affectionate about its subject to really sting, its more gentle mockery holds up nicely. Later a Broadway musical.

SMILES OF A SUMMER NIGHT ☆☆☆☆
1955, Sweden
Gunnar Bjornstrand, Eva Dahlbeck, Harriet Andersson, Ulla Jacobson, Margit Carlquist. Directed by Ingmar Bergman. 108 min.

Bergman's exquisite pastoral comedy is similar in tone to Renoir's *Rules of the Game*; it's about four couples who bicker and change partners before finding the road to true love. The ensemble acting is perfection, and the film's charm and warmth gives way to an ending of surprising impact. There's magic in the air, but the film doesn't hide from the pain and sorrow of love in a tissue of fantasy—it's an exalting work that never trivializes emotions. Served to inspire both Woody Allen's *A Midsummer Night's Sex Comedy* and Steven Sondheim's *A Little Night Music*.

SMITHEREENS ☆☆☆
1982, USA, R
Susan Berman, Brad Rinn, Richard Hell. Directed by Susan Seidelman. 90 min.

Offbeat, often perceptive low-budgeter. Wren, a New Jersey girl determined to go places in New York's New Wave scene, goes places, meets people, and makes plans, none of which come to much. Discursive exploration of terminal coolness in the Lower East Side clubland milieu, and is surprisingly sharp and on the mark. After the success of this shoestring budget feature (one of the first American independent films ever selected for Cannes), Susan Seidelman went on to direct *Desperately Seeking Susan*.

SMOKEY AND THE BANDIT ☆☆½
1977, USA, PG
Burt Reynolds, Sally Field, Jerry Reed, Jackie Gleason, Mike Henry, Paul Williams, Pat McCormick. Directed by Hal Needham. 97 min.

A long time ago in a galaxy far, far away, *Star Wars* broke every box-office record in history; that year, this low-road chase comedy was the second most popular film. Burt Reynolds had already refined his good-ol'-boy persona in *White Lightning* and *Gator* but hadn't yet become the smug talk-show standby of his later films; as the superskilled speed driver Bandit, he's actually fun to watch here, amiable and easy going. "Smokey" is, of course, Sheriff Buford T. Justice (Jackie Gleason), the blustery redneck who's hot on his trail but never quite catches up. The film has as much complexity and style as a Road Runner cartoon, and that's quite enough; if you've never seen one of these, give it a spin. Followed by two sequels.

SMOKEY AND THE BANDIT—PART III ☆
1983, USA, PG
Jackie Gleason, Jerry Reed, Paul Williams, Pat McCormick, Mike Henry, Colleen Camp, Burt Reynolds. Directed by Dick Lowry. 88 min.

A tired retread that's as bald as Burt sans toupee. Reynolds appears very briefly here, and Jerry Reed seems lonesome. The "story" has sheriff Buford T. Justice (Jackie Gleason) chasing Reed and a giant replica of Jaws across country. Paul Williams isn't the worst thing about the movie, but he sure tries. Saddest of all, the Great One was once a very funny comedian.

SMOKEY AND THE BANDIT II ☆
1980, USA, PG
Burt Reynolds, Sally Field, Jackie Gleason, Jerry Reed, Dom DeLuise, Paul Williams, Pat McCormick, Mike Henry, Brenda Lee, Mel Tillis. Directed by Hal Needham. 101 min.

Yet another sequel lacking in the charm and wit that made its predecessor a big hit. And if you recall the original *Smokey and the Bandit*, you'll realize how much trouble this one is in. This time, Burt Reynolds and sidekick Jerry Reed are hired to transport an elephant to the Republican national convention, giving rise to all sorts of elephant jokes. (When was the last time you heard a good elephant joke?) One of Reynolds's worst: he pulls out all of his least ingratiating ploys as an actor, including belching and giggling incessantly. Even the outtakes at the end look contrived—"Hey, guys, we have to have some funny outtakes for the end of the movie, can you try to screw up your lines a little more?"

SMOOTH TALK ☆☆☆½
1985, USA, PG-13
Laura Dern, Treat Williams, Mary Kay Place, Elizabeth Berridge, Levon Helm, Sarah Inglis, Margaret Welch. Directed by Joyce Chopra. 92 min.

In adapting "Where Are You Going, Where Have You Been?," Joyce Carol Oates's frightening short story of a teenage girl's unknowing flirtation with a possibly dangerous older man, screenwriter Tom Cole hasn't expanded it but built around it—the original tale is now just the last third of the film. Its gem-hard menace doesn't quite mesh with the more thoughtful, reflective first hour, but everything else in this portrait of a fifteen-year-old girl's sexual awakening is exactly right. Director Joyce Chopra and Cole have taken the locations and contexts of dozens of teen-bimbo films—trips to the mall, fights with mom, backseat necking—and refashioned them into acutely observed, poignant social drama that never condescends to the pain and uncertainty of its adolescent heroine. Laura Dern's dazzling work in the lead dominates the film, but Treat Williams does a sizzling, scary turn as Dern's sneering, soft-spoken pursuer. On the surface, it can be read as a cautionary tale, but its intelligence and complexity overrule simple labels.

SNAKE FIST FIGHTER ☆
1981, Hong Kong
Jacky Chan, Simon Yuen, Shi Tian, Tian Feng. Directed by Chin Hsin.

Probably the first Jacky Chan exploitation film! Chan's first martial arts movie was released in 1971 as *Master with Crack Fingers* and as *Little Tiger from Canton*. In 1981, this film was released, containing additional footage of Simon Yuen and Shi Tian. Note how Jacky's hair changes length throughout the film. Here he plays a waiter who defends a girl and incurs the wrath of the town bullies. Historically important to aficionados, but certainly not one of Chan's best.

THE SNAKE PEOPLE ☆
1968, USA/Mexico
Boris Karloff, Julissa, Charles East. Directed by Enrique Vergara and Jack Hill. 90 min.

What's a great star like Boris Karloff doing in tripe like this? The inane plot slithers about unsuspensefully in this south-of-the-border bomb about a police investigation of a creepy isle. Reptiles, voodoo, and LSD form a strange triad of evil on this mysterious island, where the natives are plagued by . . . strange transformations, let's call them. Strictly snake eyes. (a.k.a.: *Isle of the Snake People*)

SNAKES IN EAGLE SHADOW ☆☆☆
1978, Hong Kong
Jacky Chan, Simon Yuen, Shi Tien, Huang Jang-Li, Chiu Chi-Ling. Directed by Yuan Ho-Ping.

In his first kung fu comedy, Jacky Chan's impish antics and breathtaking martial arts skills marked him as a major star. He plays a sad-sack kitchen boy in a kung fu school who learns fighting skills from the cook. Of course he goes on to avenge the master's death, and, yes, you have seen this story before, but *Snakes* is still a fresh, lively, action film.

SNOOPY, COME HOME ☆☆☆
1972, USA
Animated: Chad Webber, David Crey, Stephen Shea, Bill Melendez. Directed by Bill Melendez. 70 min.

Not exactly inspired animation, but "Peanuts" fans will be in heaven. If the artwork isn't much more sophisticated than the simple style of the comic strip, it doesn't matter. Schultz aficionados will want to experience the gentle philosophizing, and youngsters will enjoy the antics of the fanciful beagle who embarks on an odyssey to find that rare spot where there aren't any "No Dogs Allowed" signs. This was not a TV special, but a film designed for theatrical release. Cute, cuddly, and humorous.

SNOWBALL EXPRESS ☆☆½
1972, USA, PG
Dean Jones, Nancy Olson, Harry Morgan, Keenan Wynn, Johnny Whittaker, David White, Dick Van Patten, George Lindsey. Directed by Norman Tokar. 99 min.

Manhattan insurance accountant Dean Jones gets to fulfill his long-cherished dream of leaving the rat race of the big city when he learns that he has inherited a ski lodge from a distant uncle. But when he and his family arrive, the place is a dilapidated wreck. Various comic situations ensue as they whip the place into shape for the upcoming season. Need we say that this is a Disney comedy? It's a cut above their typical 1970s product, and the cast should appeal to television fans.

SNOWBEAST ☆
1977, USA (TV)
Bo Svenson, Yvette Mimieux, Robert Logan, Clint Walker, Silvia Sidney. Directed by Herb Wallerstein. 100 min.

Frigid thriller about a treacherous monster terrorizing some ski-resort types who thought their biggest worry was a potential case of chapped lips and the inflated price of hot chocolate at the local chalet. It's the kind of snowbound horror film that should be thrown on the fire in place of another log. Pity the poor Yeti monster who has to maul such a stereotyped pack of victims.

SNOW CREATURE ☆
1954, USA
Paul Langton, Leslie Denison, Teru Shimada, Robert Kino, Robert Hinton, Jack Daly. Directed by W. Lee Wilder. 80 min.

Billy Wilder's brother directed this ridiculous abominable snowman yarn. (Or should that be, this abominable ridiculous snowman yarn?) The story is a low-rent version of *King Kong*, with an American botanist in Tibet capturing the A.S. after it makes a play for his wife; after having trouble getting it through immigration, they take it back to Hollywood, where it of course escapes. Instead of making its last stand on the tallest building in town, though, the silly-looking monster winds up in the sewers, which is where the entire film belongs. Good for a few cheap laughs.

SNOW, THE MOVIE ½☆
1982, Australia
David Argue, Lance Curtis. Directed by Robert Gibson. 73 min.

Even the Renaissance produced some clunkers. So, too, the recent awakening of the Australian cinema. There are no laughs in this sad little comedy that lumbers along after two buffoons who win a car and hightail it to a ski resort, where they add their presences to a talentless assortment presided over by a resident sex therapist.

SNOW TREASURE ☆☆
1968, USA
James Franciscus, Ilona Rodgers, Paul Anstad, Raoul Oyen, Randi Borch. Directed by Irving Jacoby. 95 min.

A group of Norwegian tykes during World War II help the Resistance smuggle a cache of gold out of the country under the eyes of the Nazis. It's not as saccharine as it sounds, though still too cute for the general action fan, and with far too much background music and skiing footage. Top-billed James Franciscus has only a small part, as a Nazi traitor.

SNOW WHITE AND THE THREE STOOGES ☆½
1961, USA
Patricia Medina, Carol Heiss, Buddy Baer, Guy Rolfe, the Three Stooges. Directed by Walter Lang. 107 min.

Let's just say this isn't the Stooges at their anarchic best. Their manic energy is flattened out here to clear the ice for Olympic skating queen Carol Heiss. Holy Sonia Henie! Heiss's figure eights are smoother than her dialogue delivery; and the attempts to shoehorn the aging Stooges into the fairy-tale plot are clumsy. Guaranteed to put the entire family to sleep.

S.O.B. ☆☆½
1981, USA, R
Julie Andrews, William Holden, Richard Mulligan, Robert Vaughn, Robert Preston, Larry Hagman, Shelley Winters, Marisa Berenson, Loretta Swit. Directed by Blake Edwards. 121 min.

All the venomous bile Blake Edwards ever had for Hollywood is spewed forth in this only halfway funny satire. Richard Mulligan stands in for Edwards, playing a high-strung director who is forced to turn his actress-wife's latest musical turkey into an exploitation film. Along the way there are digs at publicists, agents, studio chiefs, Hollywood parties, and much, much more. As in most of Edwards's films only some of the gags are on target (the slapstick party scene is especially forced), but this is one of the few uncompromisingly savage views of Tinseltown and there's a melancholy resonance here not found in most of Edwards's work. *Note*: the story is supposedly a quasi-autobiographical account of

Edwards's experiences while making wife Andrews's multimillion-dollar turkey *Darling Lili* (1969). Andrews did not bare her breasts in that film, but she does in the film-within-a-film in *S.O.B.*

SO FINE
1981, USA, R ☆½
Ryan O'Neal, Richard Kiel, Mariangela Melato, Jack Warden. Directed by Andrew Bergman. 89 min.

This crass, clamorous garment-district comedy plays like an outdated vaudeville sketch with some dirty jokes thrown in as a sop to the very bored masses. Ryan O'Neal plays an English lit. professor who revitalizes his dad's ailing business by inventing designer jeans with see-through vinyl windows in place of back pockets. A tedious loan-shark story line leads to a dull "madcap" finale in which a production of Verdi's *Otello* is trashed; Mariangela Melato plays an Italian sexpot whose bad jokes are even less funny in subtitles.

THE SOFT SKIN
1964, France ☆☆½
Jean Desailly, Françoise Dorléac, Nelly Benedetti, Daniel Ceccaldi, Jean Lanier. Directed by François Truffaut. 115 min.

One of the less interesting early works from director François Truffaut, it nonetheless has enough merit to make it worth a look. Moving away from his hallmark themes of nostalgia, memory, and adolescence, Truffaut turned to adultery as a subject, and the result was this clean and uncluttered but rather bland look at the dissolution of a marriage. Desailly plays a magazine editor who suddenly rejects his wife in favor of a beautiful young stewardess and underestimates the fierce will of his mate. Truffaut handles the situations well, but the leading players are too dull to be convincing.

SOLARBABIES
1986, USA, PG-13 ½☆
Richard Jordan, Charles Durning, Jami Gertz, Jason Patric, Lukas Haas. Directed by Alan Johnson. 94 min.

Once upon a time there was a movie called *Star Wars*, and it was good. Then there was a rip-off of *Star Wars*, and another rip-off and another. Then, in 1986, there was a rip-off of a rip-off of a rip-off of a rip-off of *Star Wars* and every other science fiction–fantasy film made since Georges Melies's *A Trip to the Moon*. The plot concerns an ethnically balanced claque of roller-skating orphans who try to bring water to their parched planet. As the skating kiddies roll by, so do the plots of *Dune*, *The Road Warrior*, and *Rollerball* and many others. A dried-out, misconceived groaner of a fairy tale.

THE SOLDIER
1982, USA ½☆
Ken Wahl, Klaus Kinski, Alberta Watson, William Prince, Jeremiah Sullivan. Directed by James Glickenhaus. 96 min.

This repellent actioner is about a CIA operative on a collision course with the KGB, which is planning to blow up a big chunk of the world's oil supply. The film plays on our paranoia about terrorists, communism, and Middle Eastern treachery and serves up this tasteless dish on a platter of spy movie clichés and bloody scare tactics better suited to a slasher movie. Ken Wahl, unable to deliver any line of dialogue running longer than three words, is aggressively charmless. Casting agents should catch this performance and remember him when any parts for a Cro-Magnon man are floating around.

SOLDIER BLUE
1970, USA ☆½
Candice Bergen, Peter Strauss, Donald Pleasence, John Anderson, Dana Elcar. Directed by Ralph Nelson. 112 min.

A violent revisionist Western, it tries, in one fell swoop, to make up for Hollywood's long-standing anti-Indian attitudes. Despite the liberal pieties, the film is saddled with one impossible conceit (unsuccessfully equating the genocide of the Red Man with the killing in Vietnam). The film's noble attempt to create an epic poem of injustice can't survive insufficiencies in the story structure. A romance is thrown in, and that also jeopardizes the seriousness of the message. Worst of all, the devastating climax, showing the massacre of an entire village, is gratuitously brutal. It doesn't slam the message across, it buries it in the blood and cavalry dust. The film won't appeal to traditional Western lovers, and it's bound to disappoint those seeking a coherent statement about American attitudes toward the Indians.

SOLDIER IN THE RAIN
1963, USA ☆☆
Steve McQueen, Jackie Gleason, Tuesday Weld, Tony Bill, Tom Poston, Ed Nelson, John Hubbard. Directed by Ralph Nelson. 87 min.

Army-barracks comedies were probably Hollywood's indirect way of dealing with the United States' intensified military maneuvers in Southeast Asia during the 1960s. There are no explicit references to Vietnam in the film, but the focus on army life in a comic vein must have provided a tonic for audiences of the day. Today *Soldier in the Rain* offers little, but at least it is less offensive than *What Did You Do in the War, Daddy?* (1966) and *The Wicked Dreams of Paula Schultz* (1968). It's a bittersweet hodgepodge about two Army sergeants and their wild escapades (most having to do with getting out of the Army). Jackie Gleason and Steve McQueen can be excellent dramatic actors, and they give the film whatever charm it possesses. Scenarists Blake Edwards and Maurice Richlin give them almost no plot and some very weak vignettes with which to work. Tuesday Weld also does her best, but her character (a dumb blonde to end all dumb blondes) is just plain irritating. Henry Mancini's musical score is overused, and even the normally welcome Tom Poston has a misfired running gag. From director Ralph Nelson, who has done better with *Requiem for a Heavyweight*, *Charly*, and *Soldier Blue*.

SOLDIER OF ORANGE
1979, The Netherlands ☆☆☆
Rutger Hauer, Jeroen Krabbe, Peter Faber, Derek De Lint, Edward Fox, Susan Penhaligon. Directed by Paul Verhoeven. 144 min.

This slow-moving, powerful World War II drama concerns the German occupation of Holland, the cataclysmic effect it had on the lives of the Dutch, and the Resistance movement that quickly began to take shape. Rutger Hauer and Jeroen Krabbe (*No Mercy*, *The Living Daylights*) do excellent work under Paul Verhoeven's thoughtful if somewhat staid direction; the baroque excesses of his later *The 4th Man* suggest that he is less than ideally suited to straightforward drama. Note: The video version of *Soldier of Orange*, released by Media Home Entertainment's Cinematheque Collection, is trimmed by twenty minutes from the theatrical release cut.

A SOLDIER'S STORY
1984, USA, PG ☆☆☆
Howard E. Rollins, Jr., Adolph Caesar, Dennis Lipscomb, Larry Riley, Robert Townsend, Denzel Washington, William Allen Young, Patti LaBelle, Wings Hauser. Directed by Norman Jewison. 101 min.

As a whodunit, Charles Fuller's play about the murder of a black sergeant on a Louisiana Army base in 1944 is hardly a model of suspense, but it succeeds as a sophisticated inquest into the nature of black self-loathing. Howard E. Rollins gives a sly, stoic performance as Captain Davenport, a kind of proto-yuppie black lawyer dispatched from Washington to investigate the murder of Sergeant Waters, an authoritarian go-getter whose gnarled psyche comes to eclipse the identity of his killer as a subject of interest. It's the contrast between Davenport and Waters—their different ways of coping with white condescension—that maintains the movie's excitement.

SOLE SURVIVOR ☆½
1969, USA (TV)
Vince Edwards, Richard Basehart, William Shatner, Lou Antonio, Larry Casey. Directed by Paul Stanley. 100 min.

This cryptic drama is about a man found wandering the Libyan desert. Apparently, he is the sole survivor of a plane crash; and the film unravels the skein of this mysterious incident, including speculation about the role he may have played in these strange circumstances. Just another lost-in-the-desert adventure with the plotting about as steady as a dune in a sandstorm.

SOLO ☆☆
1977, Australia/New Zealand, PG
Martyn Sanderson, Lisa Peer, Jock Spence, Vincent Gil, Perry Armstrong, Frances Edmund, Davina Whitehouse, Maxwell Fernie, Gillian Hope, Veronica Laurence, Val Murphy. Directed by Tony Williams. 97 min.

An unsuccessful love duet between a lone woman (Lisa Peer), hitchhiking through the isolated wilderness of New Zealand, and a solo pilot (Vincent Gil) working among the forest rangers in that part of the country. The backgrounds are gorgeous, but the story is stronger in individual scenes than as a sustained whole.

SOLOMON AND SHEBA ☆½
1959, USA
Yul Brynner, Gina Lollobrigida, George Sanders, Marisa Pavan, Harry Andrews, Finlay Currie, John Crawford. Directed by King Vidor. 139 min.

This exceedingly slow-moving biblical epic features a cast of thousands, all of whom manage to give bad performances. In relating the tempestuous love tale of the wise king who wasn't too bright where the queen of Sheba was concerned, the celebrated director saves all his energy for the battle scenes, especially the literally dazzling climax in which the Israelites hold their shields up to the desert sun and blind the Egyptians. Yul Brynner is uncharacteristically subdued, with a full head of hair, as he avoids the sultry glare of Gina Lollobrigida; she in turn acts unbearably kittenish, mouthing her lines as if she'd learned them at Berlitz. There are plenty of biblical howlers to keep you awake, though, especially the stoning of poor little Sheba, in which the lavishly made-up Lollo is used as a target by Israel's finest pitching arms and subsequently revives with only one photogenic smudge on her spectacular Technicolor face.

SOME CALL IT LOVING ☆½
1973, USA, R
Zalman King, Carol White, Tisa Farrow, Richard Pryor, Veronica Anderson, Pat Priest. Directed by James B. Harris. 103 min.

The title is only the beginning of the ambiguities in this muddled fairy-tale fantasy. A jazz musician buys "The Sleeping Beauty," a girl on display at a carnival sideshow, and takes her home to the castle where he lives with a bisexual woman and her lesbian lover. Richard Pryor is on hand for a small role as a drugged-out musician friend, along with Pat Priest of "The Munsters." Just because you don't get it, don't think that there's anything here to get.

SOME KIND OF HERO ☆½
1982, USA, R
Richard Pryor, Margot Kidder, Ray Sharkey, Ronny Cox, Lynne Moody, Olivia Cole, Paul Benjamin, David Adams, Martin Azarow, Shelly Batt, Susan Berlin. Directed by Michael Pressman. 97 min.

As Eddie Keller, an American soldier who returns from six years in a Vietcong prison camp only to be confronted by every imaginable trauma, Richard Pryor has one of his meatiest roles to date. Yet it's also one of his most conventional, and the novelty of having to reach his audience on a sentimental level does odd things to America's premier demon-possessed comic; most of all, it makes him strangely unconvincing. Director Michael Pressman dilutes every dramatic scene with a comic shtick and every comic scene with a tearjerk, and the result begins to look like a run-of-the-mill TV series.

SOME LIKE IT HOT ☆☆☆☆
1959, USA
Marilyn Monroe, Tony Curtis, Jack Lemmon, George Raft, Pat O'Brien, Joe E. Brown. Directed by Billy Wilder. 119 min.

One of the funniest American films ever! Jack Lemmon and Tony Curtis star as Chicago musicians on the lam from gangsters in this wildest of all Wilder comedies. The pair don women's clothes, join an all-girl band, and befriend a luscious, ukulele-playing vocalist, Marilyn Monroe. This jazz-age romp costars George Raft, as mobster Spats Columbo, and Joe E. Brown, as an eccentric millionaire who falls for the lumpy Ms. Lemmon. This was the fifteenth film for Wilder, who directed such renowned works as *Double Indemnity*, *Sunset Boulevard*, and *The Lost Weekend*, and his second with Monroe, following the highly successful comedy *The Seven Year Itch*. *Some Like It Hot* did not win the Oscars it deserved (Lemmon was nominated for Best Actor), but it was a hugely popular hit when it was released in 1959. Monroe is intensely appealing as Sugar, the singer with a fatal weakness for male saxophonists. Curtis is at his best. And the film's final line is a classic!

SOMEONE I TOUCHED ☆½
1975, USA (TV)
Cloris Leachman, James Olson, Glynnis O'Connor, Allyn Ann McLerie, Andy Robinson. Directed by Lou Antonio. 78 min.

What can you say about a movie on venereal disease that has a theme song? Touching upon the affairs of an architect, his expectant wife, and a teenage cutie pie, the film is more concerned with these characters pinning the blame on each other than it is with any social or moral questions. Viewers expecting a turn-on because of the subject matter will be extremely disappointed. Someone should stop the spread of dumb TV message movies.

SOMEONE'S KILLING THE WORLD'S GREATEST MODELS

See *She's Dressed to Kill*

SOMETHING FOR EVERYONE ☆☆☆
1970, USA
Angela Lansbury, Michael York, Anthony Corlan, Heidelinde Weis, Jane Carr, Eva-Maria Meineke. Directed by Harold Prince. 112 min.

In this enjoyably nasty but minor comedy of amorality, good manners and social politesse matter more than decency or honesty. A shrewd, sexy young man worms his way into the household of a down-on-her-luck countess and then uses the various family members and staff for his own financial and social betterment. Based on Harry Kessring's "The Cook," the film is needlessly drawn out by director Harold Prince's poor pacing, but it's quite amusing as it details the loathsome Lothario's bedding who he wants to get what he wants. The cast sparkles, and it's refreshing to see Lansbury in a glamorous, larger-than-life starring role.

SOMETHING OF VALUE ☆☆☆
1957, USA
Rock Hudson, Sidney Poitier, Dana Wynter, Wendy Hiller, Frederick O'Neal. Directed by Richard Brooks. 113 min.

Expert filmization of Robert Ruark's best-seller, a probing account of two friends who find themselves on opposite sides of an African civil war. While it's hard for the film to compress the voluminous material of the novel, it succeeds in fleshing out the chief characters. Playing childhood friends, Hudson and Poitier movingly enact their roles as a member of the landed gentry and a Kenyan native who possess opposing viewpoints of the Mau Mau insurrec-

SOMETHING SHORT OF PARADISE ☆½
1979, USA, PG
David Steinberg, Susan Sarandon, Jean-Pierre Aumont, Marilyn Sokol, Joe Grifasi, Robert Hitt. Directed by David Helpern, Jr. 91 min.

To put it mildly. This romance between a theater manager and a journalist has all of the self-abusing neuroses of *Annie Hall* without any of Allen's wit or creativity. Your reaction to it will depend almost entirely on the amount of affection you hold for comedian David Steinberg, whose loud, unpleasant work here would be more at home in a stand-up routine. Susan Sarandon, all fluttery stammering mannerisms, is scarcely better. Gets an extra half-star only for the terrific credit sequence.

SOMETHING TO HIDE

See *Shattered*

SOMETHING TO SING ABOUT ☆☆☆
1937, USA
James Cagney, Evelyn Daw, William Frawley, Mona Barrie, Gene Lockhart. Directed by Victor Schertzinger. 93 min.

This is pretty breezy fun for a second-string musical. Throughout his film career, tough guy Cagney had to battle against typecasting and was always delighted when he could unbutton his spats and slip on a pair of tap shoes. One wishes the songs were better and that there were more of them, and that the leading lady didn't have nonentity stamped all over her, but it *is* one of the rare opportunities to see Jimmy in a musical. Flanked by some peppy supporting performances, Cagney delights as a song-and-dance man hemmed in by the constraints of stardom. Indeed, the Hollywood star syndrome and the Big Studio system are ribbed mercilessly. The acid satire (modeled somewhat loosely after Cagney's own contretemps with Warner Bros.) keeps the film on its toes when the central romance begins to act as a soporific. Not all it could have been, but much of it is something to sing about.

SOMETHING WICKED THIS WAY COMES ☆☆½
1983, USA, PG
Jason Robards, Jonathan Pryce, Pam Grier, Diane Ladd, Royal Dano, Shawn Carson, Vidal Peterson, Mary Grace Canfield, James Stacy. Directed by Jack Clayton. 94 min.

This eerie, otherworldly tale didn't deserve the lack of attention it received in its theatrical release, and it's worth looking up for a late night show at home. It begins well, with ominous images of a train carrying a demonic carnival past a Norman Rockwell small town. But then this adaptation of Ray Bradbury's novel about a pair of children tempted into the carnival's wickedness turns both rickety and gimmicky, with special effects superimposed in an attempt to spice up the movie. Jason Robards stars as the kids' father, but Jonathan Pryce steals the show as the menacing carny master.

SOMETHING WILD ☆½
1986, USA, R
Jeff Daniels, Melanie Griffith, Ray Liotta, Margaret Colin, Jack Gilpin, Su Tissue, John Sayles, John Waters. Directed by Jonathan Demme. 113 min.

A clumsy, mechanical comedy-thriller overloaded with quirky details and schizophrenic plot turns. Jeff Daniels and Melanie Griffith play two of our newest screen clichés—he's a straitlaced Wall Street yuppie with an adventurous soul, and she's a kooky downtown type (you can tell by the bracelets, wig, and miniskirt) who wants to loosen him up. What begins as a chance meeting turns into a comic odyssey through New England, then pauses for a pastoral interlude at a high-school reunion, and finally lurches toward the finish line as an action drama. Perhaps to compensate for the lack of characterization and coherence in E. Max Frye's script, director Jonathan Demme (*Melvin and Howard, Stop Making Sense*) fills the frame with cameos, in-jokes, or inappropriate background knickknacks; you know a film is bad, and that its performers are bland, when you find yourself staring at the props.

SOMEWHERE IN TIME ☆☆☆
1980, USA, PG
Christopher Reeve, Jane Seymour, Christopher Plummer, Teresa Wright, Bill Erwin, George Voskovec, Susan French, John Alvin, Eddra Gale, Sean Hayden, Richard Matheson. Directed by Jeannot Szwarc. 103 min.

Hunky Christopher Reeve (a.k.a.: the Man of Steel) and swan-necked Jane Seymour, as romantic-fantasy lovers, are a pair of dreams come true for swoon-and-sigh-starved audiences. Reeve is a troubled modern playwright who wills himself back in time to 1912 to pursue Seymour, a turn-of-the-century actress whose photograph has captured his heart. Written by fantasy specialist Richard Matheson (*I Am Legend*) and directed by Jeannot Szwarc (*Jaws II*), the movie is a pastiche of bits from *The Ghost and Mrs. Muir, Portrait of Jennie, Laura*, and several "Twilight Zone" episodes. Yet it's acted and directed so wholeheartedly, and is so enraptured by its own schmaltziness, that any viewer with even an ounce of vulnerability is likely to be a goner. A nice, Saturday-night cry.

SONG OF FREEDOM ☆☆½
1936, Great Britain
Paul Robeson, Elizabeth Welch, George Mozart, Esme Percy, Joan Fred Emney, Arthur Williams, Ronald Simpson, Jenny Dean, Bernard Ansell, Robert Adams, Cornelia Smith, Sydney Benson, Will Hammer. Directed by J. Elder Wills. 80 min.

This is what passed for an enlightened depiction of black heritage in 1936. The mighty Paul Robeson plays a London dockworker who discovers that he is a descendant of a sixteenth-century African queen. He then becomes a famous opera singer in order to make money and return to his homeland to help his people throw off the yoke of oppression and ignorance. A 1930s *Roots* that soft-pedals its themes in favor of showcasing Robeson; recommended primarily as a rare chance to see his towering, charismatic screen presence.

SONG OF NEVADA ☆☆
1941, USA
Roy Rogers, Dale Evans, Mary Lee, Lloyd Corrigan, Thurston Hall, Bob Nolan and the Sons of the Pioneers. Directed by Joseph Kane. 75 min.

Poor Dale. She's in the arms of a dangerous city slicker while Roy is camping out with the Sons of the Pioneers. Her rich daddy finally gets Roy away from his buddies long enough for the singing sagebrusher to stop the sale of the family ranch. Look for the comic talents of Lloyd Corrigan and Mary Lee as a couple of snake-oil salespeople, and give a listen to Dale's warbling of "It's Love, Love, Love." The contemporary setting doesn't add much Western flavor.

SONG OF NORWAY ☆
1970, USA, G
Toraly Maurstad, Florence Henderson, Christina Schollin, Frank Porretta, Robert Morley, Edward G. Robinson, Oscar Homolka. Directed by Andrew L. Stone. 141 min.

Milton Lazarus's 1940s stage musical becomes a lengthy, tedious bio-pic of Edvard Grieg. It follows the composer from his early struggle for recognition in Norway to his collaboration with Henrik Ibsen on *Peer Gynt*. Along the way, there's Florence Henderson playing his Danish wife, who sings his songs while traipsing across the countryside. Also immortalized are Franz Liszt and Hans Christian Andersen. This one is so bad, it will leave you begging for Julie Andrews in *The Sound of Music*.

SONG OF TEXAS
1943, USA ☆☆
Roy Rogers, Sheila Ryan, Barton MacLane, Harry Shannon, Arline Judge, Bob Nolan and the Sons of the Pioneers. Directed by Joseph Kane. 69 min.

Standard Roy Rogers Western is a bit overloaded with songs (ten of them), but they don't detract much from the plot, a variation on the old "Lady for a Day" story. Rodeo star Roy and his buddy Harry Shannon take over a ranch with some other pals, but have to pretend that the whole operation belongs to Shannon in order not to disillusion his daughter, visiting from back east. Little gunplay or stunt riding; the big finale is a chuckwagon race!

THE SONG REMAINS THE SAME
1976, Great Britain, PG ☆
Led Zeppelin (John Bonham, John Paul Jones, Jimmy Page, Robert Plant), Peter Grant. Directed by Peter Clifton and Joe Massot. 136 min.

This concert film made during a Led Zeppelin concert at Madison Square Garden in 1973 is strictly for fans, and only the less discriminating of those. The concert footage is fleshed out with indecipherable fantasy sequences, one per band member, and some interesting scenes of the band's manager handling the whole road show from backstage. But that still leaves two hours of the band onstage, in which they perform thirteen songs—that's an average length of about nine minutes apiece—that are pretty much indistinguishable from each other. Photographed and edited in a pretentious, pseudopsychedelic way.

A SONG TO REMEMBER
1945, USA ☆☆
Cornel Wilde, Paul Muni, Merle Oberon, George Couloris, Nina Foch. Directed by Charles Vidor. 113 min.

This film will be forever remembered as the movie that brought the classics to our nation's jukeboxes as Chopin's Polonaise became "Till the End of Time." If you always imagined that Chopin bore a striking resemblance to Cornel Wilde, and if you always thought that George Sand must have looked sexy in pants and had to appear every bit as feminine-looking in them as Merle Oberon does, then this preposterous but undeniable entertaining bio-mush is for you. One thing you definitely won't want to remember is Paul Muni's fussy, high school theatrics in his portrayal of Chopin's teacher.

SONGWRITER
1984, USA, R ☆☆½
Willie Nelson, Kris Kristofferson, Melinda Dillon, Rip Torn, Lesley Ann Warren, Richard C. Serafin. Directed by Alan Rudolph. 94 min.

Director Rudolph's follow-up to his breakthrough hit *Choose Me* is a less personal and stylized project, though not without its charms. Willie Nelson and Kris Kristofferson play archetypes of modern Nashville, the latter a veteran performer who refuses to settle down and give up his carousing ways, the former his ex-partner who long ago gave up performing to become a "mogul." After he gets hustled out of his own production company, Nelson sets out to get even and get back. The story isn't much, but good performances from a large cast (especially Lesley Ann Warren as an aspiring singer and Rip Torn as a clownish promoter) and lots of irrelevant but amusing bits of business make this mildly enjoyable, if you can put up with a dozen bland country tunes that Kris and Willie might well have written in their sleep.

SON OF BLOB
See *Beware! The Blob*

SON OF FLUBBER
1963, USA ☆☆½
Fred MacMurray, Nancy Olson, Keenan Wynn, Tommy Kirk, Ed Wynn, Charlie Ruggles, Edward Arnold, Alan Carney, Jack Albertson. Directed by Robert Stevenson. 102 min.

In this sequel to the popular Walt Disney comedy *The Absent-Minded Professor*, Fred MacMurray repeats his role as Professor Brainard, eccentric genius and inventor. Along with "Flubber," a substance that can defy the laws of gravity, he concocts a "Flubber-gas" and a dry rain that can cause indoor storms. Silly stuff, but still among the best of the many Disney wacky-inventor films that it spawned. The large cast of familiar faces is the most appealing aspect for adults, while children can get by on jokes that they don't yet realize are older than their grandparents.

SON OF GODZILLA
1968, Japan ☆☆
Tadao Takashima, Akira Kubo, Bibari Maeda. Directed by Jun Fukuda. 86 min.

Pretty much a comedy this time around. (Yes, of course *all* Godzilla movies are pretty funny, but this time they were trying to be). It's not exactly clear if Godzilla is *mere* or *pere*, but there's this egg that hatches into . . . Minya, a sort of bulldog-faced junior monster that stumbles a bit and burps nonradioactive smoke rings. Lest this sound too cute for you jaded horror fans, however, there are the occasional giant mantises and spiders out to bully this new kid in the neighborhood.

SON OF KONG
1933, USA ☆☆½
Robert Armstrong, Helen Mack, Victor Wong. Directed by Ernest B. Shoedsack. 70 min.

This minor but entertaining sequel to *King Kong* has guilt-ridden showman Carl Denham (Robert Armstrong) returning to Skull Island and finding the giant ape's albino son. Although it's mostly played for laughs, the film still works on a juvenile level. The animated effects by Willis O'Brien couldn't be better. The last good movie to be made with the word *Kong* in the title.

THE SON OF MONTE CRISTO
1940, USA ☆☆½
Louis Hayward, Joan Bennett, George Sanders, Florence Bates, Lionel Royce, Montagu Love, Ian MacWolfe, Clayton Moore. Directed by Rowland V. Lee. 101 min.

Louis Hayward is a bit below par as a swashbuckling hero, though this sequel to the often-filmed *Count of Monte Cristo* has its moments of rousing adventure. As in the original, the son of Edward Dante is drawn into the court intrigues of the mythical European country now under a dictatorial ruler (here George Sanders), who is forcing a marriage to the rightful heir (Joan Bennett) in order to safeguard his rule. Sanders's despicable villainy makes up for many of the less heartfelt aspects of this chestnut.

SON OF THE SHEIK
1926, USA ☆☆☆
Rudolph Valentino, Vilma Banky, Agnes Ayres, Karl Dane, Bull Montana. Directed by George Fitzmaurice. 72 min.

Some may quibble with Valentino's eye-popping excesses, but it's still possible to comprehend what impact his dark, smoldering sexuality had on audiences of the 1920s. In this steamy desert romance, passion spills out under the blazing sun while Rudy gallops over the dunes and sets his leading lady's heart aflutter. It's his final film and he does double duty here playing both a desert ruler and the son of the sheik. Not a great movie, but quite enjoyable.

THE SONS OF KATIE ELDER
1965, USA ☆☆½
John Wayne, Dean Martin, Martha Hyer, Earl Holliman, Michael Anderson, Jr., Paul Fix, George Kennedy. Directed by Henry Hathaway. 112 min.

Entertaining Western romp, even if the stars appear a little saddle-sore and the director falls asleep at the reins once too often. One of those all-brawling, all-shouting slugfests with bits of obvious humor and lots of buddy-buddy affection tossed in. Four men show up at their mother's funeral and solemnly vow to do right by their family name in the dead woman's honor. However, a bevy of bad guys shows up and flings a few choice epithets at them, which leads to the expected round of sagebrush confrontations. Brash and invigorating, but everything you'd expect and nothing more.

SONS OF THE DESERT ☆☆☆½
1933, USA
Stan Laurel, Oliver Hardy, Charley Chase, Mae Busch, Dorothy Christy. Directed by William A. Seiter. 69 min.

A rambunctious comedy featuring Laurel and Hardy at their laugh-getting zaniest. Some critics feel that this is their best full-length film, and if it isn't that, it's definitely close. The boys sneak off for a gala trip to a convention without telling their wives their true whereabouts, offering instead an incredible story about Stan's rare tropical disease. Dressed in their lodge brother outfits and determined to raise hell, the boys are constantly thwarted in their attempts to throw off the shackles of matrimony. The hilarity builds as the danger of their better halves getting wise to them becomes more and more likely. Sidesplittingly funny.

SOPHIA LOREN: HER OWN STORY ☆
1980, USA (TV)
Sophia Loren, John Gavin, Rip Torn, Armand Assante, Theresa Saldana, Edmund Purdom. Directed by Mel Stuart. 150 min.

Oh, really, Sophia! Isn't it enough to glamorize your life by turning both adversity and triumph into bland self-advertisement—do you have to act in it, too? Sophia gives an unconvincing performance as herself. For those who prefer to pick up a *Star* magazine rather than be confronted with the reality of a famous person's life, this is perfect viewing. As such, it's as good as anything you've ever read in *Photoplay*. As for Sophia, she might as well have let Kate Jackson or Lynda Carter play her; they would have been perfect for this artificial teleplay.

SOPHIE'S CHOICE ☆☆½
1982, USA, R
Meryl Streep, Kevin Kline, Rita Karin, Peter MacNicol, Stephen D. Newman, Josh Mostel. Directed by Alan J. Pakula. 157 min.

Pakula's two-and-a-half-hour adaptation of the William Styron best-seller is doggedly faithful to the book; indeed, it ends up drowning in Styron's apparent message that survivor's guilt is, or ought to be, the human condition. Portraying a sensual Polish Catholic who has survived Auschwitz, Streep gives a funny, engaging performance for about half the movie (she won an Oscar for the role), but then, as the film begins to trot out its roster of Great Themes, her acting turns glum and unconvincing. By the time we discover what Sophie's "choice" was, we no longer care. This is Pakula's most unabashedly melodramatic and least satisfying work.

SO PROUDLY WE HAIL! ☆☆½
1943, USA
Claudette Colbert, Veronica Lake, Paulette Goddard, Sonny Tufts, George Reeves, Barbara Britton, Walter Abel. Directed by Mark Sandrich. 125 min.

It's hard to believe that Veronica Lake, Sonny Tufts, and Paulette Goddard were once taken seriously in this immensely popular salute to the nurses in the Pacific. Goddard even snagged an Oscar nomination. So did Allen Scott, who wrote the screenplay about eight nurses in the American Red Cross, their romances, and their fight to save lives in Bataan and Corregidor. Scott and director Mark Sandrich used to work on Fred Astaire–Ginger Rogers pictures at RKO and that's the kind of world to which Colbert if not the rest of the cast, seems suited; she gets her hair mussed admirably, but she never goes through the kind of traumas that made her postwar *Three Came Home* so compelling. Most of the film is flag-waving and studio-bound battle grit; it's "entertaining" in a way that should not necessarily be taken as a recommendation.

SORCERESS ½☆
1982, USA, R
Leigh Harris, Lynette Harris. Directed by Brian Stuart. 83 min.

Follow the adventures of Mira and Mara (Leigh and Lynette Harris), a pair of cuddly twins each equipped with magical powers and blank expressions. Brian Stuart directed this particularly scrappy entry in the sword-and-sorcery genre.

THE SORROW AND THE PITY ☆☆☆☆
1970, France/Switzerland
Directed by Marcel Ophuls. 260 min.

Marcel Ophuls's massive, powerful documentary about the resistance to and collaboration with Nazi occupation that went on in one French town during World War II stands as the most intelligent, intimate, and moving study yet of the moral coercion, confusion, and self-justification that went on during the war. Ophuls's point of view is at once microscopic and encompassing; he focuses tightly on Clermont-Ferrand, and within it on the residents who fought back, those who didn't, and those who couldn't, but also includes excellently chosen newsreel footage, interviews with French and British political and military leaders, photo collections, and propaganda films. What emerges is not only amazingly free of manipulation and political or emotional bullying, but, against all odds, an almost definitive film on a very complex, troublesome theme. Try if at all possible to see the subtitled version of the film, as the dubbing, though skilled, covers the real voices and their often telling qualities. Incidentally, no choice need be made between this and the film to which it's recently been compared, *Shoah*; the physical, political, and moral ground they cover is very different, and each complements and enriches the other.

SORRY, WRONG NUMBER ☆☆½
1948, USA
Barbara Stanwyck, Burt Lancaster, Ann Richards, Wendell Corey, Ed Begley. Directed by Anatole Litvak. 89 min.

High-strung suspense about a wealthy woman who accidentally hears her own murder being plotted on the telephone. This woman-in-distress melodrama fits snugly into a cycle including *Suspicion*, *Gaslight*, and *Secret Beyond the Door* and builds up suspense. Still, the expansion of Lucille Fletcher's crisp half-hour radio play into a full-length feature greatly lessens the impact, and Burt Lancaster is miserably cast as the wimpy husband. Basically, it's a one-woman show for Barbara Stanwyck, who shrieks and gasps admirably.

S.O.S. TITANIC ☆☆½
1979, USA (TV)
David Janssen, Cloris Leachman, Susan St. James, David Warner, Helen Mirren, Ian Holm, Harry Andrews. Directed by William Hale. 105 min.

The umpteenth retelling of the *Titanic* disaster is done this time in a handsome made-for-television version with a myriad of capable guest stars filling out the passengers and crew. Well above the norm for TV. If not a match for the exacting British classic *A Night to Remember*, it's at least in the league of Hollywood's *Titanic* (1953).

SOTTO . . . SOTTO ☆☆½
1984, Italy, R
Enrico Montesano, Veronica Lario, Luisa De Santis, Massimo Wertmüller, Mario Scarpetta, Isa Danieli. Directed by Lina Wertmüler. 105 min.

Don't be deceived by the title, which means "Softly . . . softly"; this is one of Lina Wertmüller's noisiest and most raucous comedies, not up to the mastery of her work in the mid-1970s, but way ahead of the debacles that followed. Once again, the theme is the battle of the sexes, and the warriors are a man and wife. He's sure that she's having an affair with another man, and sure enough, she announces she's in love with someone else—another woman. The same plot that's received somber treatment in a couple of recent American TV movies makes for broad comedy here, which almost makes up in energy what it lacks in subtlety.

SOUL MAN ☆½
1986, USA, PG-13
C. Thomas Howell, Arye Gross, Rae Dawn Chong, James Earl Jones, Melora Hardin, Leslie Nielsen, James B. Sikking, Max Wright, Jonathan (Fudge) Leonard. Directed by Steve Miner. 101 min.

The idea of a white kid who pretends to be black to win a minority scholarship to Harvard Law School is outrageous, to be sure, and also rich in possibilities. But the premise—a racial variation on *Tootsie*—is like comic dynamite that the moviemakers have dunked in water. The problem with the sub–Brat Packer C. Thomas Howell isn't just that he's as white as Wonder Bread; it's that there's no actor's juice in him. His impersonation should have been the movie's comic sparkplug, but instead the film gutlessly plunks him into low-key racist situations so he can discover that yes, there's a thing called prejudice in the world. It's when he begins courting fellow law student Rae Dawn Chong that the reason for the film's antiseptic blandness becomes clear: *Soul Man* has been made by people who pat themselves on the back for recognizing that color is only skin deep, but who wouldn't dare to show a white boy kissing a black girl unless the boy was in blackface.

SOUNDER ☆☆☆☆
1972, USA, G
Cicely Tyson, Paul Winfield, Kevin Hooks, Taj Mahal. Directed by Martin Ritt. 105 min.

Made at a time when films about blacks ranged from *Shaft* to *Blacula*, *Sounder* was such a breath of fresh air that people fell over themselves trying to praise it. The kudos were not undeserved: it is an excellent film dealing with a family struggling to remain intact against pressure from the outside world. Set in the rural South of the 1930s, *Sounder* is an outstanding family film, one that adults can watch without feeling that they have to look down. It presents rural life and prejudice with verisimilitude but without excess, conveying its emotions and platitudes gently but effectively. Superbly directed by the often underrated Martin Ritt.

THE SOUND OF MUSIC ☆☆½
1965, USA
Julie Andrews, Christopher Plummer, Eleanor Parker, Richard Haydn, Peggy Wood, Heather Menzies, Charmian Carr, Nicolas Hammond. Directed by Robert Wise. 174 min.

Still despised by the intelligentsia as the worst kind of wholesome treacle, *The Sound of Music* is actually a much better-made film than most people will give it credit for being. The problem is that the careful, overlong Twentieth Century-Fox production is almost all sugar and no spice. Based on a 1959 Rodgers and Hammerstein Broadway show starring Mary Martin, this 1965 film adaptation became one of the biggest moneymakers of all time and helped to spawn a series of clones (*Doctor Doolittle*, *Song of Norway*). The only possible explanation for the film's astronomical success is that the true story of Maria Von Trapp, a nun who forsook her vows to become a governess to a brood of children in 1930s Salzburg, offered refreshing innocence to jaded 1960s audiences. The film can still provide that kind of pleasure despite excesses of goo in the score (which includes "Climb Every Mountain," "My Favorite Things," and "Do-Re-Mi"), the Ernest Lehman screenplay, and almost every performance save Christopher Plummer's (he just looks embarrassed). The opening title song (photographed in the Alps) is still the best sequence.

SOUP FOR ONE ☆☆
1982, USA, R
Saul Rubinek, Marcia Strassman, Gerrit Graham, Andrea Martin, Richard Libertini. Directed by Jonathan Kaufer. 87 min.

Silly but endearing yarn about a not-so-swinging single and his setbacks while seeking *l'amour, toujours l'amour*. This kind of light comedy terrain has been traversed too often, and the barbs aimed at the dating scene are far from inspired. Still, it's a pleasant little riff of a movie that spins a few laughs out of the horrors of the mating ritual, and it's populated by a pleasing line-up of clever comic actors. If only Andrea Martin had had a better part and the comic observations were fresher, this cheerful grab-bag comedy might have been more than passable.

SOUTHERN COMFORT ☆☆☆
1981, USA, R
Keith Carradine, Powers Boothe, Fred Ward, Franklyn Seales, T. K. Carter, Peter Coyote, Lewis Smith. Directed by Walter Hill. 106 min.

In an uneven but often very exciting suspense film, a group of National Guardsmen goes into the Louisiana bayou on a paramilitary exercise; there the men find themselves the prey of murderous Cajuns. Director Walter Hill is well suited for this kind of bloody, stylized, all-male action (he also directed *The Warriors* and *The Long Riders*), and although he pushes too hard for a Vietnam allegory, his work here is appropriately tough and grim. Great backwoods location footage and strong acting make the film's narrative sloppiness all the more disappointing, but it's still one of the better *Deliverance* clones around.

THE SOUTHERNER ☆☆☆½
1945, USA
Zachary Scott, Betty Field, J. Carrol Naish, Beulah Bondi. Directed by Jean Renoir. 92 min.

Perhaps Jean Renoir's greatest American film (though still behind the French classics), this is a superb drama of Southern sharecroppers struggling against overwhelming odds to make their farmland self-supporting. Zachary Scott and Betty Field nicely play the farm couple fighting both nature and troublesome neighbors. Renoir's surreal, idiosyncratic touches make this simple tale far more intriguing (and far less sentimental) than both *The Grapes of Wrath* and the more recent spate of "farm" movies (*The River*, *Places in the Heart*). Good, understated, often profound work.

SOUTH OF THE BORDER ☆½
1939, USA
Gene Autry, Smiley Burnette, June Storey, Lupita Tovar, Mary Lee, Duncan Renaldo, the Checkerboard Band. Directed by George Sherman. 71 min.

Gene Autry and Smiley Burnette, as a pair of U.S. agents, visit Mexico and implement our foreign policy by sticking their noses into the latest revolution. Written around a song that was popular at the time, which we of course get to hear several times throughout the course of the flick (just in case you thought that was a trick they dreamed up with *Ode to Billy Joe*). Featuring the future Cisco Kid.

SOUTH PACIFIC ☆☆
1958, USA
Mitzi Gaynor, Rossano Brazzi, John Kerr, Ray Walston, Juanita Hall, France Nuyen. Directed by Joshua Logan. 171 min.

A Pulitzer Prize–winning musical comes to the screen in a depressingly overblown production. The leading roles are indifferently cast, and the film is awash in garish lighting effects that flood the screen to no good effect. The original musical (admittedly, it now seems dated in its recent stage revivals) was a mature achievement in its day, as it blended vignettes from James Michener's *Tales of the South Pacific* into a cohesive whole. The impact of the two intertwined stories, both interracial romances, is diluted by peremptory handling. We don't care whether all-American Nellie Forbush will accept the fact that her plantation beau has children by a native woman; and the Yankee–jungle princess romance between wooden John Kerr and inept France Nuyen is strictly formulaic stuff. Still, that magnificent score will get you through the film, and you can dream of what the movie might have been like if Doris Day or Susan Hayward (both contenders for the role) had been cast instead of pert but inadequate Mitzi Gaynor.

SOYLENT GREEN ☆½
1973, USA, PG
Charlton Heston, Leigh Taylor-Young, Chuck Connors, Joseph Cotten, Edward G. Robinson, Paula Kelly. Directed by Richard Fleischer. 97 min.

The year is 2022 and overpopulation is so bad that people are being scooped up in the streets and made into food resembling wheat thins. Charlton Heston comes to the rescue to stop the killings. Other acting heavyweights include Leigh Taylor-Young and Chuck Connors. It's all perfectly ridiculous, though it does offer Edward G. Robinson in his last screen role.

SPACECAMP ☆☆½
1986, USA, PG
Kate Capshaw, Lea Thompson, Kelly Preston, Larry B. Scott, Leaf Phoenix, Tate Donovan, Tom Skerritt. Directed by Harry Winer. 108 min.

In the wake of the explosion of the space shuttle *Challenger*, audiences weren't in the mood for this amiable adventure about a group of teenage astronaut trainees at NASA who are accidentally launched into orbit during a test aboard the shuttle. Yes, there are some similarities to reality that resonate uncomfortably, especially during the early part of the film, but once the young crew is shot into space and must fight to return to earth safely, the exciting, well-handled action takes over. *Spacecamp* is really an old-fashioned battle-troop movie recast with space cadets, all of whom must overcome their individual weaknesses and prove their mettle under a tough commander (Kate Capshaw, in the Lou Gossett role). If only the filmmakers hadn't felt it necessary to toss in a talking robot named Jinx and an obnoxious little kid who spouts lines from *Star Wars*.

SPACED OUT ☆
1981, Great Britain, R
Tony Maiden, Ava Caldell, Barry Stokes, Glory Annen, Michael Rowlatt. Directed by Norman J. Warren. 85 min.

A spaceship of Amazons transports four earthlings into intergalactic ecstasy in this crass British breast-and-bum, two-quid extravaganza. Originally titled *Outer Touch*, the American version has added some incredibly crude narration from the ship's computer. A fairly attractive cast (especially Ava Caldell, as the ship's engineer) indulges in loads of gymnastics.

SPACEHUNTER: ADVENTURES IN THE FORBIDDEN ZONE ☆
1983, Canada, PG
Peter Strauss, Molly Ringwald, Ernie Hudson, Andrea Marcovicci, Michael Ironside, Beeson Carroll, Hrant Alianak, Deborah Pratt, Aleisa Shirley. Directed by Lamont Johnson. 90 min.

The sets for this ritzy new 3-D feature appear to be modeled on *The Road Warrior*'s futuristic junk-heap universe, and the film itself is like an intergalactic toy chest—everywhere there are hooks and pulleys, rope bridges, and jungle-gym contraptions over which the hero (Peter Strauss) can scamper as he tries to save three nubile Earthwomen from the evil dictator Overdog (Michael Ironside). There's only one small problem: without glasses, the 3-D process is not effective on video.

SPACE RAIDERS ☆☆
1983, USA, PG
Vincent Edwards, Patsy Pease, David Mendenhall, Luca Bercovici, Thom Christopher. Directed by Howard R. Cohen. 82 min.

Another in the endless line of *Star Wars* clones, this one has the distinct flavor of a bunch of kids dressing up and trying to make their own *Star Wars* movie; it's not good, but it does have the appeal of fulfilling its own modest rip-off goals. It zips along painlessly with some of the feeling of a space-borne swashbuckler. With a little boy stowaway on board, interplanetary adventurers battle corporate villains as the laser guns blast away in the background, foreground, and everywhere else. Derivative, noisy, but cheesy fun nonetheless.

SPACESHIP ☆☆
1981, USA, PG
Cindy Williams, Leslie Nielsen, Gerrit Graham, Patrick Macnee. Directed by Bruce Kimmel. 80 min.

The writer/director of *The First Nudie Musical* returns with this low-budget amalgamation of *Alien* and *Airplane!*; it's pretty dumb, but it's goofy enough to draw occasional chuckles. The crew of this *Spaceship* includes out-of-it pilot Leslie Nielsen, horny scuzzball Gerrit Graham, unreasonably mad scientist Patrick Macnee, and Cindy Williams as the ship's morale officer, who tries to keep the crew's spirits high with a talent show. The monster sings a Sinatra-esque ditty called "I Want to Eat Your Face." It's short enough so that you can catch it after *Masterpiece Theatre* and still get to bed on time. (a.k.a.: *The Creature Wasn't Nice*)

SPARKLE ☆☆½
1976, USA, PG
Philip (Michael) Thomas, Irene Cara, Lonette McKee, Dwan Smith, Dorian Harewood, Mary Alice. Directed by Sam O'Steen. 98 min.

A ripely melodramatic subject—the rise and fall of a 1960s "girl group" à la the Supremes—is handled only adequately in Joel Schumacher's script, but the cast of pros will hold your attention. Philip Thomas, long before "Miami Vice," looks stiff and uneasy, but Irene Cara, Lonette McKee, and Dwan Smith are very dynamic as the singing sisters. Curtis Mayfield contributed the excellent song score, sung by Aretha Franklin.

SPARROWS ☆☆☆½
1926, USA
Mary Pickford, Gustav von Seyfferitz, Mary Louise Miller, Spec O'Donnell. Directed by William Beaudine. 84 min.

A silent feature, this has stood the test of time. Most of Mary Pickford's features have been kept out of circulation for years. Unlike some of her other vehicles, this one isn't supercharged sweetness and light. Playing a plucky youngster, Pickford energizes a suspenseful, emotionally shattering melodrama about a band of mistreated young orphans who've suffered at the hands of a cruel ward. The ending escape through the treacherous swamps as Mary and the waifs elude capture and almost fall into the gaping jaws of alligators is an horrific, stunning climax to a heart-tugging classic.

SPARTACUS ☆☆☆½
1960, USA
Kirk Douglas, Jean Simmons, Laurence Olivier, Tony Curtis, Charles Laughton, Peter Ustinov, John Gavin, Woody Strode, Nina Foch. Directed by Stanley Kubrick. 196 min.

A triumph. A literate Hollywood spectacle directed with unerring good taste (and without his later pretentious style) by Stanley Kubrick. Kirk Douglas's swagger has never been better suited to a role as he bravely graduates from Gladiator School and directly into spearheading a revolt against the Roman oppressors. Eschewing all those semibiblical, pseudoliterary dialogue problems that we come to associate with epics from Tinseltown, this film boasts a sturdy, stirring screenplay. The film neither loses sight of the intimate dramas unfolding, nor fails to make the most of every opportunity for sword-clanking action and pageantry. The standouts in the superb cast are Jean Simmons as the woman who bears Spartacus a son who will not follow his father's sandal-steps into the Arena, and Laurence Olivier as a bisexual Roman senator who prefers indoor sport with his slaves to the pleasure of watching mortal combat among the gladiators.

SPASMS ☆
1983, Canada, R
Peter Fonda, Oliver Reed, Al Waxman, Marilyn Lightstone. Directed by William Fruet. 87 min.

Hissssterically awful thriller about a giant snake on the loose. Oliver Reed, as a hunter with a telepathic connection to the big hunk of rubber, has a great time twitching his face. Some nice atmospheric touches but basically it's just a boring bloodbath.

A SPECIAL DAY ☆☆☆½
1977, Italy/Canada
Sophia Loren, Marcello Mastroianni, John Vernon, Francoise Berd, Nicole Magny, Patrizia Basso. Directed by Ettore Scola. 110 min.

In their eighth film together, Marcello Mastroianni and Sophia Loren play a homosexual radio announcer and an oppressed housewife drawn together by the ways in which they suffer under Italy's fascist regime. Their uneasy, inarticulate relationship is meant to serve as a global metaphor; the film takes place on the day of Hitler's famous "house call" on Mussolini, and the dialogue is occasionally too studied and deliberate. But Ettore Scola's sensitivity as a director of actors has never been more evident—he draws a beautiful performance from Loren and a very touching, credible one from Mastroianni (who was nominated for an Academy Award). It's small in scale and more theatrical than it needs to be, but quite effective nonetheless.

SPECIAL DELIVERY ☆½
1976, USA, PG
Bo Svenson, Cybill Shepherd, Tom Atkins, Sorrell Booke, Gerrit Graham, Michael C. Gwynne, Jeff Goldblum, John Quade, Vic Tayback. Directed by Paul Wendkos. 98 min.

Isn't "special delivery" supposed to get where it's going quickly and accurately? Then it's a poor title for this comedy-caper, because it meanders all over the place without seeming to have any idea of where it wants to go. Bo Svenson and three Vietnam vet buddies, unable to find jobs, rob a bank in desperation. During the escape, Svenson hides his share of the haul in a mailbox, overseen by artist Cybill Shepherd and dope peddler Michael Gwynne. From there, the movie brings in Mafia drug connections, romance, and hippies. TV fare boosted up with some profanity; it could have used some laughs as well.

SPECIAL EFFECTS ☆☆
1984, USA, R
Zoe Tamerlis, Brad Rijn, Eric Bogosian, Kevin O'Connor. Directed by Larry Cohen. 100 min.

Low-budget suspense about a satanic movie director (Eric Bogosian) who murders a starlet, films it, frames her hayseed husband for the crime, and then puts him in a *Star 80*–type movie playing himself opposite a perfect double of his late wife, with the cop investigating the crime as technical adviser. Convoluted enough for you? That's not all in this blend of a mystery and a sardonic look at show biz that's more heavy-handed than deft, and, considering its twists and turns, not nearly as interesting or clever as it should be. Like many of Larry Cohen's films, it's more than quirky enough to be appreciated, but unlike many, it's not quite good enough to like.

THE SPECIALIST ☆½
1975, USA, R
Adam West, John Anderson, Ahna Capri, Alvy Moore, Christiane Schmidtmer, Marlene Schmidt. Directed by Hikmet Avedis. 93 min.

Not to be confused with *The Specialists*, made for television the same year, this feature is the work of the husband/wife team of Hikmet Avedis (director) and Marlene Schmidt (producer, screenwriter, actress). Ahna Capri is a buxom gun-for-hire in a partly parodic, partly pimping actioner.

SPEEDTRAP ☆☆
1977, USA
Joe Don Baker, Tyne Daly, Richard Jaekel, Robert Loggia, Morgan Woodward. Directed by Earl Bellamy. 98 min.

A tire-screeching, rubber-peeling odyssey into crime solving. A private eye is hot on the trail of a car-purloining racket. The real trap is the script, which drags out action-movie clichés from as far back as the 1930s. It's routine racetrack stuff, on a par with your average TV action series. "Cagney and Lacey" fans will want to catch up with Tyne Daly before all her Emmies and mannerisms caught up with her.

SPEEDWAY ☆☆½
1968, USA
Elvis Presley, Nancy Sinatra, Bill Bixby, Gale Gordon, Carl Ballantine, William Schallert. Directed by Norman Taurog. 94 min.

By the late 1960s, MGM was churning out Presley musicals like hamburger meat, but *Speedway* does have the distinction of an unusual leading lady. A plastic sixties icon from her capped teeth to her vinyl boots, Nancy Sinatra is great camp fun. She plays an IRS agent assigned to curb the spending habits of racing-car driver Elvis. In tandem, they perform the big finale on psychedelic-colored cars. (You haven't lived until you've seen Nancy do "Your Groovy Self.") Frank's daughter is unquestionably the pioneer who paved the way for such talents as Joey Heatherton, Heather Locklear, and Elvis's former bride, Priscilla.

SPELL ☆
1977, USA (TV)
Lee Grant, James Olson, Susan Myers, Lelia Goldoni, Helen Hunt. Directed by Lee Philips. 78 min.

You won't be spellbound by this telekinetic twaddle about a *Carrie* clone who gets heavenly revenge on all the nasty cretins who've been making her life a living hell. A prime example of how TV movies cannibalize popular movie hits, and of how being starved for ideas and stealing them ultimately proves insufficient when you don't know what to do with them anyway.

SPELLBOUND ☆☆☆½
1945, USA
Ingrid Bergman, Gregory Peck, Leo G. Carroll, Norman Lloyd, Rhonda Fleming, Michael Chekhov. Directed by Alfred Hitchcock. 111 min.

A beautiful but repressed psychoanalyst (Ingrid Bergman) probes the subconscious of an amnesiac (Gregory Peck) in an effort to prove the man is innocent of the murder he is convinced he has committed. Many of Hitchcock's less self-consciously Freudian films make far more profound statements about the human psyche. The director stresses the isolation of the characters from their environments by photographing them against deliberately artificial backdrops. The device distracts rather than illuminates. But even lesser Hitchcock is enormously entertaining and Bergman is always fun to watch. Salvador Dali designed the film's most notable footage, his famous surrealistic dream sequence, and some prints are available with a startling color sequence at the climax. Miklos Rosza won an Oscar for his haunting musical score.

SPETTERS ☆☆
1980, Netherlands, R
Renee Soutendijk, Rutger Hauer, Hans van Tongeren, Toon Agterberg, Maarten Spanjer. Directed by Paul Verhoeven. 108 min.

This wildly melodramatic study of three motorbiking pals manages to work gang rape, homosexual blackmail, paraplegia, and suicide into an otherwise familiar framework of discontented youth. It's just as excessive and offensive, though not nearly so interesting, as Paul Verhoeven's later *The Fourth Man*, and despite Rutger Hauer's prominent billing, his role is only peripheral. The sexual antics are more explicit and male-oriented than an R rating usually permits. Dubbed. *Note*: The videocassette edition of *Spetters* is seven minutes shorter than the unrated version that appeared briefly in U.S. theaters (what's missing is still more sex). While some of Verhoeven's themes were a little clearer in the original, this mediocre film doesn't suffer all that much from a shortened running time.

SPHINX ☆
1981, USA, PG
Frank Langella, Lesley-Ann Down, John Gielgud, Maurice Ronet, Martin Benson, John Rhys-Davies. Directed by Franklin J. Schaffner. 117 min.

Director Franklin Schaffner's past efforts have included such monumentally "big" movies as *Patton*, *Papillon*, and *Nicholas and Alexandra*, and this time he's gone for extravagance to rival that of Cecil B. DeMille. This turkey is set in Egypt; the King Tut legends and architectural wonders create an exotic backdrop for a modern-day mystery. Based on Robin Cook's best-seller, the movie features Lesley-Ann Down as a young Egyptologist and Frank Langella as a UNESCO director trying to solve a murder. Naturally, they fall in love. The film is almost as unintentionally funny as *The Awakening*, but too drawn out and slow moving for really big laughs. For those stumped by the riddle of why Langella's film career didn't take off, *Sphinx* supplies the answer.

SPIDER-MAN ☆☆
1977, USA (TV)
Nicholas Hammond, David White, Michael Pataki, Hilly Hicks, Lisa Eilbacher. Directed by E. W. Swackhamer. 94 min.

Comic-book adventure about the acrobatic arachnid, a hero who achieved more prominence on TV than he ever did in the comics. The script attempts, as unsuccessfully as most TV-movie scripts, to turn various gaucheries into artless, innocent charm. It's a tangled web of a story about a college kid who gets bitten by a radioactive spider, which leaves him with certain spidery properties and a really nifty blue and red outfit that resembles a modern dance costume. Only those under the age of eight should come into this particular parlor to watch.

SPIES ☆☆☆
1928, Germany
Rudolph Klein-Rogge, Willi Fritsch, Gerda Maurus, Lupu Pick. Directed by Fritz Lang. 90 min.

Rudolph Klein-Rogge, the Rotwang of Lang's *Metropolis*, plays a Dr. Mabuse–like banker (Dr. Strangelove was modeled on this sort of frighteningly canny madman) whose vast network of spies enables him to aspire to mastery of the world. Willi Fritsch is the agent on his track whom the criminal mastermind sends Gerda Maurus to seduce. Don't count for a minute on finding the goings-on the least bit credible; but Lang charges pulp material with an eerie magnetism, largely through his visually arresting camera style and rich decor, so characteristic of the director's great German silents. This is the American release version of the film, cut by nearly half (its full length approaches three hours), so it offers only a partial view of this influential classic.

SPIES LIKE US ☆☆
1985, USA
Chevy Chase, Dan Aykroyd, Steve Forrest, Donna Dixon, Bruce Davison, Bernie Casey, William Prince. Directed by John Landis. 105 min.

Remember all those *Road* movies with Bob Hope and Bing Crosby? Well, so did director John Landis and the writers of this, and they decided to make a new one. Like the *Road* features, this is an inconsistent undertaking, and your enjoyment of it depends on your liking for Chase and Aykroyd (the latter generally wasted in another white-bread role, though not as badly as usual). The two play bottom-echelon spies sent to Pakistan as decoys to distract attention from a pair of real spies. There are a few solid laughs, but mostly just amiable silliness. As in his *Into the Night*, Landis has peopled this with cameos from about a dozen other directors, including Costa-Gavras, Terry Gilliam, Sam Raimi, Joel Cohen, Larry Cohen, and Frank Oz. The writers included Aykroyd, SCTV's Dave Thomas, and Lowell Ganz and Babaloo Mandel (*Splash*). With a *Ghostbusters* sound-alike theme song by Paul McCartney.

SPINAL TAP

See *This is Spinal Tap*

THE SPIRAL STAIRCASE ☆☆☆
1946, USA
Dorothy McGuire, George Brent, Ethel Barrymore, Rhonda Fleming, Elsa Lanchester. Directed by Robert Siodmak. 83 min.

New England, 1906, is the setting for this thriller about a series of murders of handicapped girls. Dorothy McGuire plays the young woman, mute since childhood, who may be next. Ethel Barrymore is the invalid widow and George Brent the family doctor. Quite suspenseful and often Hitchcockian, with an excellent performance from McGuire as the silent young girl.

THE SPIRAL STAIRCASE ☆☆
1975, Great Britain
Jacqueline Bisset, Christopher Plummer, John Philip Law, Sam Wanamaker, Mildred Dunnock, Gayle Hunnicutt, Elaine Stritch. Directed by Peter Collinson. 89 min.

A mediocre remake of Robert Siodmak's clever suspenser about a mute servant who knows there's a killer in her employer's bizarre mansion. Despite a fine cast and production values that easily surpass the original, the story itself hasn't worn well, and Jacqueline Bisset never ignites in what should be a showy role. Occasionally atmospheric, but nothing special.

THE SPIRIT OF ST. LOUIS ☆☆☆
1957, USA
James Stewart, Patricia Smith, Murray Hamilton, Marc Connelly. Directed by Billy Wilder. 138 min.

This earnest but protracted bio-pic captures the magisterial splendors of early aviation; we get a sense of what Charles Lindbergh felt blazing those trails with his head in the clouds. It is an attempt at a heroic epic and, owing to James Stewart's quiet authority, the film partially succeeds. The film's leisurely pace stems from trying to cover too much ground in depth, and if the film is uncharacteristically wholesome in tone, it's not marred by any of the director's occasional facile cynicism, either.

SPIRITS OF BRUCE LEE ☆
Hong Kong
Michael Chan, Sun Chia Ling, Poon Lok, Wong Tip Lam, Guh Men Tong, Chan Fei Lung. Directed by Shang Lang.

Inane dialogue and a boring story kill this film within the first ten minutes. Chan (Michael Chan) travels to Thailand looking for his brother, who went there to buy jade. He learns that his brother was robbed and killed by a gang of Thai boxers.

SPITFIRE ☆☆½
1934, USA
Katharine Hepburn, Robert Young, Ralph Bellamy, Martha Sleeper, Louis Mason. Directed by John Cromwell. 86 min.

This unusual film finds Hepburn overacting all over the place as a wild young woman growing up in an Ozark mountain community. Her character's eager intelligence unstimulated elsewhere, she buries herself in religion, and circumstances cause her to be hailed by the community as a faith healer, then vilified as a witch. Hepburn tries so hard to play the pathetic backwoods girl that she damn near succeeds. But it's nonetheless an awkward vehicle for her talents and undoubtedly one of the films that made her box-office poison three years later. Hepburn's iron will and tight contract also got her $10,000 in overtime for the single day the film went over schedule.

SPLASH ☆☆☆
1984, USA, PG
Tom Hanks, Daryl Hannah, Eugene Levy, John Candy, Dody Goodman, Shecky Greene, Richard B. Shull, Bobby Di Cicco, Howard Morris, Tony di Benedetto. Directed by Ron Howard. 111 min.

This magical comedy about a young Manhattan produce-company head who falls in love with a beautiful mermaid is both a boisterously funny farce and a romantic fairy tale that adults can believe in. Ron Howard's unruffled direction sets off his quirky cast: Tom Hanks as the straight but whimsical hero, John Candy (in his most explosive screen performance) as Hanks's hilariously randy older brother, and Daryl Hannah as Madison the mermaid, whose wide-eyed innocence and passion turn a slightly wormy Big Apple into the Magic Kingdom.

SPLATTER UNIVERSITY ½☆
1985, USA, R
Francine Forbes, Dick Biel, Cathy Lacommaire, Ric Randig. Directed by Richard W. Haris. 79 min.

Slice and dice at a Catholic university, courtesy of an escaped mental patient. Bloody, to be sure, but dreary and utterly formulaic.

SPLENDOR IN THE GRASS ☆☆☆½
1961, USA
Natalie Wood, Warren Beatty, Pat Hingle, Zohra Lampert, Audrey Christie. Directed by Elia Kazan. 124 min.

Featuring Beatty in his first screen performance, and Wood in her most compelling, this landmark coming-of-age film both poignantly and sensitively addresses the questions of sexual morality. When two high-school sweethearts, living in the roaring twenties, run up against the repressive small-town values of their community, their love is destroyed. With sizzling implications, a mythical feel, and a melodramatic style, Elia Kazan's beautifully filmed romance conveys a tearjerking sense of the confusion, pain, even devastation, caused by the discovery, the demands, and the denial of love. The ending is powerfully unsettling. William Inge's Oscar-winning screenplay was used again in 1981 for a much inferior TV remake.

SPLIT IMAGE ☆☆½
1982, USA, R
Michael O'Keefe, Karen Allen, James Woods, Elizabeth Ashley, Brian Dennehy, Peter Fonda, Michael Sacks. Directed by Ted Kotcheff. 111 min.

This Hollywood-ized cult exposé lacks the uncluttered power of the similar *A Ticket to Heaven*. Serving up juicy dollops of melodrama, the film plays up the horror-movie aspects of the situation. Interestingly, the indoctrination process is made understandable by explaining that the WASP-y boy's fascination with religion starts as a romantic interest in one of the cult members. This perverse love story gives the film a solid anchor—which it sorely needs. James Woods plays his part with unrelieved oiliness. Subtlety goes by the wayside, but in depicting the conflict between the brainwashed boy and his ineffectual, desperate parents, the film achieves a measure of power.

THE SPOILERS ☆☆☆
1942, USA
Marlene Dietrich, John Wayne, Randolph Scott, Margaret Lindsay, Richard Barthelmess, Harry Carey. Directed by Ray Enright. 87 min.

The durable Rex Beach tale gets its best sound movie treatment here (it was also filmed in 1914, 1923, 1930, and 1955), probably because of the freedom given to the seasoned players really to let loose. It could be considered a "Northern" since it takes place in Alaska, but it's got traditional Western stamped all over it. Randolph Scott and John Wayne punch each other from one end of the Yukon to the other, while Marlene Dietrich languishes as a bad girl in the background (why are they taking long-suffering Margaret Lindsay seriously when Dietrich's around?). The famous climactic fisticuffs scene doesn't disappoint and must have put several stuntmen out of commission for a while. A gutsy brawler—routine, but flavorsome.

SPOILERS OF THE PLAINS ☆☆
1951, USA
Roy Rogers, Penny Edwards, Trigger, Bullet, the Riders of the Purple Sage. Directed by William Witney. 66 min.

A good, solid semi-Western from Roy and Republic, with the twist that the villains aren't rustlers or swindlers, but foreign spies. You can almost see the cold war on the horizon in this late series entry. Dale Evans is absent, and Roy's silly songs don't interfere with the slam-bang climax.

SPOOKS RUN WILD ☆☆
1941, USA
The East Side Kids, Bela Lugosi, Dennis Moore. Directed by Phil Rosen. 64 min.

The East Side Kids strike again (just think of them as the aging Dead End Kids before they became the even more decrepit Bowery Boys). Trundled off to summer camp, the kids quake in their boots as the "Monster Killer" stalks New England campgrounds (years before *Friday the 13th* made a cottage industry out of the same idea). After their pal Pee Wee is shot, the Kids hightail it to an old dark house, in an unassuming programmer rife with haunted house hijinks. Okay blend of goosebumps and guffaws.

SPRAGGUE "MURDER FOR TWO" ☆
1984, USA (TV)
Michael Nouri, Glynis Johns, James Cromwell, Mark Herrier, Patrick O'Neal, Andrea Marcovicci, Itank Garrett, Callan White. Directed by Larry Elikann. 77 min.

Ten minutes of this pilot for a failed TV series would convince any viewer that *Spraggue* didn't deserve to be on every week. A not-so-tough Boston professor and his kooky aunt try to solve a murder case. The doctor is the bad guy.

SPRING BREAK ½☆
1983, USA, R
David Knell, Perry Lang, Paul Land, Steve Bassett, Jayne Modean, Corinne Alphen, Richard B. Shull. Directed by Sean S. Cunningham. 100 min.

Coed cheesecake in Fort Lauderdale, from the sensitive director who gave us *Friday the 13th*. Two wildmen take two average guys around to the bars and beach; they find beer, wet T-shirts, and, since the movie is a Columbia release, lots of cans of Coca-Cola. Features 1982 Penthouse Pet of the Year Corinne Alphen.

SPRING FEVER   ½☆
1983, Canada, PG
Susan Anton, Carling Bassett, Frank Converse, Jessica Walter, Lisa Brady. Directed by Joseph L. Scanlan. 93 min.

About as exciting as Canadian cuisine, a young lady whose mother is a showgirl plays in a tennis tournament. That's *all* that happens. This movie's idea of humor: a middle-aged man has a tennis ball served into his groin by our teenaged heroine. For class, there's location shooting in Florida and Vegas. Sex is supplied by a flabby troupe of male go-go dancers. And Susan Anton is the best performer, every bit as charismatic as she is talented.

SPRING SYMPHONY   ☆☆☆
1986, West Germany, PG-13
Nastassja Kinski, Herbert Gronemeyer, Rolf Hoppe, Edda Sieppel, Andre Heller. Directed by Peter Schamoni. 105 min.

This is a melodious drama about Clara Wieck, the pianist, and her passionate love for Robert Schumann, the composer. Sensibly, the film keeps the glorious music cascading over the predictable plot; still, there is more depth here than in earlier bio-pics about composers such as *Song of Love* and *A Song to Remember*. It must also be admitted that Nastassja Kinski's work here is superior to Katharine Hepburn's posturing in *Song of Love* in the same role. Nastassja isn't that affected but her voice is characterless, as is she learned English by satellite from another planet.

SPRINGTIME IN THE ROCKIES   ☆☆½
1942, USA
Betty Grable, John Payne, Carmen Miranda, Cesar Romero, Edward Everett Horton. Directed by Irving J. Cummings. 91 min.

This amiable musical lacks the exuberance and sophistication we associate with Hollywood's Golden Age and MGM's output (this came from Fox). The plot is the umpteenth look behind the scenes on Broadway, where a couple is sweetness and light on stage and cat-and-dog off. The always effervescent Carmen Miranda does a memorable "Chattanooga Choo Choo," and genre fans should appreciate the plentiful musical numbers.

SPRINGTIME IN THE SIERRAS   ☆☆
1947, USA
Roy Rogers, Jane Frazee, Andy Devine, Stephanie Bachelor, the Sons of the Pioneers. Directed by William Witney. 75 min.

Solid grade-B vehicle for Roy made during the late 1940s period when wife Dale Evans briefly hung up her spurs. This one has Roy showing a gang of wild-game killers who's boss with a fistful of good-natured tunes. The original version has been trimmed by about ten minutes, as have most of Rogers's films, for video release.

THE SPY WHO LOVED ME   ☆☆☆½
1977, Great Britain
Roger Moore, Barbara Bach, Bernard Lee, Lois Maxwell, Curt Jurgens, Richard Kiel, Caroline Munro. Directed by Lewis Gilbert. 125 min.

Eccentricity, exaggeration, plastic characters, and ludicrous dialogue are all part of the fun in this tenth James Bond adventure. The finicky and epicurean British spy teams up with a luscious Russian agent to stop the insane Curt Jurgens, who plans to destroy the world with his nuclear arsenal. "Jaws," the gimmick character of the film, a human monster with steel teeth, is Bond's nemesis. The excellent photography and production render the big action scenes absolutely breathtaking. Bond fans will, of course, be gratified by the exciting ski chases and impressive underwater sequences. A commercial smash.

SQUEEZE PLAY!   ½☆
1980, USA, R
Jim Harris, Jenni Hetrick, Al Corley. Directed by Samuel Weil. 92 min.

If the words "A Troma Film" don't scare you off, they should—Troma's the perpetrator of a series of dumb-beyond-description comedies that include *Waitress!* and *Stuck on You*, the kind of movies that make you think murderous thoughts about their makers. This entry has more of a plot than the others, but its story of a battle of the sexes on a softball field is resolutely inane and climaxes with the longest, dullest game ever played on screen. Sexist and sordid, with many of the jokes absolutely identical to those in other films by the company.

SQUIRM   ☆☆½
1976, USA, R
John Scardino, Patricia Pearcy, R. A. Dow, Carl Dagenhart. Directed by Jeff Lieberman. 93 min.

Rampaging sand worms attack a small Georgia town. Really. Actually, it's not nearly as bad as it sounds, with good, occasionally sickening special effects and a fairly realistic ending. (The producers claim at the beginning of the film that their story is based on a true incident.) Low-budget but surprisingly effective.

SQUIZZY TAYLOR   ☆☆½
1982, Australia
David Atkins, Jacki Weaver, Alan Cassell, Michael Long, Kim Lewis. Directed by Kevin Dobson. 89 min.

An oddity, but an enjoyable one, this is a mobster tale from Down Under, a fast-paced period piece that dishes out the old-fashioned gangster movie stereotypes but serves them up with an Aussie accent. Squizzy Taylor was a real-life gangster in 1920s Australia, and his exploits form the basis of this fun-loving adventure saga.

SS GIRLS   ½☆
1985, Italy, X
Gabriele Carrara, Marina Daunia. 82 min.

Pier Paolo Pasolini's movie *Salo*, a brutal depiction of violence and sexual abuse in the waning years of World War II, still raises charges of obscenity in the United States, but it is a serious, artful film. Its real crime has been the spawning of cheap, greasy rip-offs like *SS Girls*. Packaged in a box with no credits, the film looks like a guilty secret; however, it's really only a gang of tired bodies dragged off a back lot at Cinecittà for some sordid exploitation.

STAGECOACH   ☆☆☆☆
1939, USA
John Wayne, Claire Trevor, Thomas Mitchell, Andy Devine, George Bancroft, Donald Meek, Louise Platt, John Carradine, Berton Churchill, Tim Holt. Directed by John Ford. 96 min.

Stagecoach is one of those cinematic milestones that offer several perspectives on film art. John Ford returned to the Western after a thirteen-year absence, and with virtuoso technique and by introducing literary themes, he infused into the genre a radical seriousness and an openness to new ideas. Ford maintained that the film, based on a story by Ernest Haycox, actually had its roots in Guy de Maupassant's "Boule de Suif," the story of a prostitute traveling through war-ravaged France in a carriage full of bourgeois. *Stagecoach*, indeed, is less a story of the perilous trip than it is a chart of the tensions raised inside the coach between an outlaw, a prostitute, a pregnant woman, a Southern gentleman turned gambler, a bank president/embezzler, a meek whiskey salesman, and an alcoholic doctor who quickly drains the salesman's sample case. In the crucible of crisis, everyone's best and worst characteristics emerge, and by a brilliant use of reaction shots—glances edited to glances—Ford asserts the director's point of view; he's always subtly communicating the story's most salient points. John Wayne has a star-making role in the film. When he strides on camera, he's stepping out of the part of the gangly, bright cowboy he played in countless B Westerns, and into the deeper, controlled icon Ford is creating. Wayne, too, becomes an auteur of new, more interesting Westerns. All of the performances are impeccable, and each viewing is sure to turn up a new favorite. The groundbreaking score used music from many American folk songs, lending an authenticity to the movie and winning an Academy Award. An assured, mature masterpiece from one of America's most rugged, indigenous filmmakers.

STAGE DOOR ☆☆☆½
1937, USA
Katharine Hepburn, Ginger Rogers, Adolphe Menjou, Lucille Ball. Directed by Gregory La Cava. 83 min.

Big-star vehicle adapted from the Edna Ferber–George S. Kaufman Broadway play. Katharine Hepburn shines as Terry Randall, a young actress struggling with overnight success. The film gives an excellent rendering of the chatty, dormlike atmosphere associated with aspiring actresses of the late 1930s. The film gets an added bonus from the stark contrast between Ginger Rogers's assertive, worldly character and Hepburn's starry-eyed newcomer.

STAGE DOOR CANTEEN ☆☆
1943, USA
Cheryl Walker, William Terry, Katherine Cornell, Alfred Lunt, Lynn Fontanne, Katharine Hepburn, Merle Oberon, Helen Hayes, George Raft, Ray Bolger, Judith Anderson, Gertrude Lawrence. Directed by Frank Borzage. 132 min.

Frank Borzage patched together this big, boring wartime musical, which offers an enormous amount of talent but very little entertainment value. The complex and intriguing plot involves a canteen hostess (Cheryl Walker) who breaks a rule and dates a serviceman (William Terry). Along the way, we are treated to a striptease by Gypsy Rose Lee, a tap dance by Ray Bolger, band numbers from Xavier Cugat, and walk-ons by people like Alfred Lunt and Lynn Fontanne, Katharine Hepburn, Judith Anderson, Tallulah Bankhead, Helen Hayes, George Jessel, Harpo Marx, Paul Muni, George Raft, and Johnny Weismuller. The highlights are Peggy Lee and Benny Goodman's "Why Don't You Do Right?," Ethel Waters and Count Basie's "Quicksand," and Katherine Cornell (in her only screen appearance) doing a version of the "balcony" scene from *Romeo and Juliet* that is both sublime and ridiculous. Otherwise, it's not much of a movie. Color might have helped but they were on a budget, you know.

STAGE FRIGHT ☆☆☆½
1950, USA
Jane Wyman, Marlene Dietrich, Michael Wilding, Richard Todd, Alastair Sim, Sybil Thorndike. Directed by Alfred Hitchcock. 110 min.

Hitchcock's comic thriller, set in the world of London theater, stars Jane Wyman as a young drama student whose friend (Richard Todd) is accused of murdering the husband of musical-comedy star Marlene Dietrich. Far from Hitchcock's most profound work, the film nonetheless makes for amusing and involving entertainment. *Stage Fright*'s thematic richness lies chiefly in the story's theatrical milieu. Hitchcock uses the stage as a backdrop for a subtle exploration of artifice and reality, where you rarely know who is *really* acting. On this level, the final creation resembles a Sartrean existential farce.

STAGE STRUCK ☆☆½
1958, USA
Henry Fonda, Susan Strasberg, Joan Greenwood, Christopher Plummer, Herbert Marshall. Directed by Sidney Lumet. 95 min.

This film is in almost every way superior to *Morning Glory*, of which it is a remake. The one exception is Susan Strasberg, who lacks the magnetic stridency and luminous presence Katharine Hepburn possessed in the role of Eva Lovelace; it was easier to believe that Hepburn had the self-serving determination necessary to launching a theatrical career. Maybe Hepburn was, to a large extent, playing herself, but we bought all the trite show-biz clichés as part of the package. Where *Stage Struck* surpasses the earlier film is in capturing the treacherous backstage milieu. All the supporting characters are well rounded as they swim around in this unsettling environment. Lots of waspish theatrical types and tart dialogue make this a crisp show-biz tale—if one can overlook Strasberg's lack of charisma.

STAIRCASE ☆½
1969, USA/France, R
Richard Burton, Rex Harrison, Cathleen Nesbitt, Beatrix Lehman. Directed by Stanley Donen. 101 min.

This adaptation of Charles Dyer's arch play attempts to "humanize" homosexuals by showing how miserable, lonely, and self-deluding they are under the mask of gaiety; apparently this is as enlightened as things got in 1969. Harrison and Burton play a longtime couple who run a barber shop, happy to trade bitchy remarks and subtle cruelties until one of them, incredibly, gets in trouble with the law for public transvestism. Both men must also contend with the ancient, bedridden, senile mothers, perhaps meant to foreshadow their own physical declines. The script is much crueler to its characters than they are to each other, and the two stars give mincing, shamefully self-conscious performances. Music by Dudley Moore.

STAIRWAY TO HEAVEN

See *A Matter of Life and Death*

STALAG 17 ☆☆☆½
1953, USA
William Holden, Don Taylor, Otto Preminger, Peter Graves, Robert Strauss. Directed by Billy Wilder. 120 min.

William Holden (in his Oscar-winning performance) is a prisoner of war out to exploit his camp comrades. His being suspected as a German spy turns comedy to drama, but our captive capitalist, needless to say, emerges triumphant. Billy Wilder is a master at carefully setting up a situation—this time, Holden's tracking down of the real German spy in his POW camp—then letting loose with a powerful and bitterly funny twist ending. This is probably the film that influenced such later turkeys as *The Private Wars of Harry Frigg*, *The Wicked Dreams of Paula Schultz*, and the TV series "Hogan's Heroes," but that's not its fault.

STALK THE WILD CHILD ☆☆
1976, USA (TV)
David Janssen, Trish Van Devere, Benjamin Bottoms, Joseph Bottoms, Jamie Smith Jackson. Directed by William Hale. 78 min.

Can a child who's been reared by a pack of wild dogs be retrained to adapt to civilization? That is the question asked by this American revamp of Truffaut's *The Wild Child*, a far more sensitive examination of the same subject matter. This oversimplified TV movie vulgarizes the delicacy of the French film in order to appeal to the lowest common denominator of viewers craving mere excitement. It was unusual enough to spin off into an unsuccessful series called "Lucan," but the film itself has many rough edges that need the civilizing influences of a good script.

STAND BY ME ☆☆☆☆
1986, USA, R
Wil Wheaton, River Phoenix, Jerry O'Connor, Corey Feldman, Richard Dreyfuss, Kiefer Sutherland, John Cusack. Directed by Rob Reiner. 98 min.

A moving, funny, fully realized work, this film confirms Rob Reiner's stature as one of the most talented directors to emerge in recent years. The story is simple, on its surface little more than an anecdote of youthful adventure: in 1959, four twelve-year-old boys go on a search for a dead body that they know is hidden somewhere in the nearby woods. But without ever overreaching, Reiner develops many of the "big" themes—loss of innocence, passage to manhood, abandoned friendships—that have eluded so many other directors. The tale is framed as the memory of the most intelligent and sensitive of the boys, now grown up, and even the most cheerful moments are tinged with a deeply felt, almost melancholy emotional charge that's almost impossible to achieve in film. The dramatic scenes become a bit moist at times—Reiner has made the kids a little too self-aware—but his work with the young actors, who give almost flawless performances in demanding roles, is done with a sure hand. Based on a novella by Stephen King.

STAND-IN ☆☆☆
1937, USA
Joan Blondell, Humphrey Bogart, Alan Mowbray, Jack Carson, Leslie Howard. Directed by Tay Garnett. 90 min.

In this bouncy, behind-the-scenes comedy, directed and written with a knowing, smart-alecky air, a straitlaced bank official has the difficult task of bailing Colossal Pictures out of financial hot water. That's a colossal task since the studio personnel aren't too keen on tightening their belts. In between balancing the books, Milquetoast Leslie Howard tangles with movie-star stand-in Joan Blondell, and she teaches him how to live a life away from his ledgers. It's a delightfully dizzy farce populated by likable screwballs. Modestly executed; but robust hilarity results.

STANLEY ☆½
1972, USA
Chris Robinson, Alex Rocco, Susan Carroll, Mark Harris. Directed by William Grefe. 106 min.

Chris Robinson, of television's "General Hospital," plays a troubled Vietnam vet with a grudge against the world. He takes it out with the aid of his friends, the snakes. Obviously derived from *Willard* and *Ben*, though several steps below even those in quality. Unless, of course, you're more afraid of snakes than of rats.

THE STAR CHAMBER ☆☆
1983, USA, R
Michael Douglas, Hal Holbrook, Yaphet Kotto, Sharon Gless, James B. Sikking, Joe Regalbuto, Don Calfa, John DiSanti, DeWayne Jessie, Jack Kehoe, Larry Hankin, Dick Anthony Williams. Directed by Peter Hyams. 149 min.

In this ludicrous but very stylish thriller, Michael Douglas plays a judge who becomes involved with the Star Chamber, a secret society of judges that dispenses hit men to kill off the scummy criminals who have escaped proper punishment by slipping through outrageous legal loopholes. The movie means to be a sort of thinking man's *Dirty Harry*, and for a while it's carried along by the sterling craftsmanship of director Peter Hyams. But Hyams makes a glaring miscalculation by turning the Star Chamber into bad guys and suddenly asking us to become good liberals again. The movie pummels us with vigilante politics and then tells us we were wrong to get hot and bothered; in the end, it lacks the courage of its own manipulation.

STARCRASH ☆☆
1979, USA/Italy, PG
Marjoe Gortner, Caroline Munro, Christopher Plummer, David Hasselhoff, Joe Spinell. Directed by Lewis Coates (Luigi Cozzi). 92 min.

What hath *Star Wars* wrought? Galactic adventurers are recruited by the Emperor of the Universe to do battle with the evil Zarth Arn (yes, that's Zarth, not Darth). It's very cheap, even for a New World production, and what may seem like campiness to some is more probably shoddy dialogue and bad acting. Still, Caroline Munro looks great in her leather leotards.

STARDUST MEMORIES ☆☆☆
1980, USA, PG
Woody Allen, Jessica Harper, Marie-Christine Barrault, Charlotte Rampling, Laraine Newman. Directed by Woody Allen. 91 min.

Lifting his story almost point for point from Fellini's $8½$, Woody Allen made this bitter study of a big-time director beset by creative blocks, dogged by grotesque fans, angered by studios who want to pigeonhole him into doing only "funny" films, and tormented by the love of three beautiful women. Critics vilified *Stardust Memories* as a slap in the face from Allen to his audience when it was first released, and Allen's claim that it's not autobiographical seems a little disingenuous—you'd know this character was Woody even if he were played by Mr. T. That aside, Allen was right in that the film wasn't judged on its merits. Unfortunately, on its merits, it still is far from his best work—beautifully filmed and occasionally incisive. In black and white.

STAR 80 ☆½
1983, USA, R
Mariel Hemingway, Eric Roberts, Cliff Robertson, Carroll Baker, Roger Rees, David Clennon, Josh Mostel, Sidney Miller. Directed by Bob Fosse. 102 min.

Bob Fosse turns the tragic success story of Dorothy Stratten—the *Playboy* playmate who was murdered by her jealous husband/promoter—into a "hard-hitting" show-biz exposé that packs only a sucker punch. Eric Roberts gives a slimy, fascinating performance as Paul Snider, but Fosse only touches on the sexual spell that this Vancouver hustler cast over the virginal Stratten (played by an ingratiating but miscast Mariel Hemingway); in the end, we're left with the same old Hollywood saga of a wife soaring to the top while the husband who discovered her slides downhill.

STARHOPS ☆☆½
1978, USA, R
Dorothy Buhrman, Sterling Frazier, Jillian Kesner, Peter Paul Iapis, Dick Miller. Directed by Barbara Peeters. 82 min.

Cheaply made comedy of the drive-in double-feature variety is at least amiable and lacking in gross exploitation. Two carhops take over a failing drive-in restaurant from its owner and set about building up the business. They succeed with the help of a gourmet chef and some attractive roller-skaters in skimpy uniforms. Like the restaurant, this film was helmed by women—director Barbara Peeters (*Humanoids from the Deep*) and screenwriter Stephanie Rothman. This originally got a PG rating, so the filmmakers went back and dubbed in a few four-letter words to ensure an R.

A STAR IS BORN ☆☆☆½
1937, USA
Janet Gaynor, Fredric March, Adolphe Menjou, Andy Devine, Lionel Stander. Directed by William A. Wellman. 111 min.

This revealing melodrama about the system that makes and breaks stars has fascinated audiences in a number of different versions, as early as 1932 and as recently as 1976. It's the story of Esther Blodgett, a young actress whose career begins to accelerate as that of her husband, superstar Norman Maine, nosedives into alcoholism and ruin. Like many Hollywood films about Hollywood, this one ends up justifying the system it pretends to indict, but it's nonetheless an effective tearjerker, well performed by Gaynor and March and pioneering in its use of color cinematography.

A STAR IS BORN ☆☆☆☆
1954, USA
Judy Garland, James Mason, Charles Bickford, Jack Carson, Tommy Noonan, Amanda Blake. Directed by George Cukor. 181 min.

♪ One of a small handful of great movie musicals, *A Star Is Born* features Judy Garland at the peak of her career, as a rising Hollywood star whose celebrity quickly surpasses that of her older husband, Norman Maine (James Mason). A wonderful showcase for her acting and singing talents, it's also the definitive version of the story, easily eclipsing the 1937 and 1976 attempts as well as the 1932 progenitor *What Price Hollywood?* Garland's performance justifies the legendary reputation it later won—had she done nothing else, many would revere her just for this. George Cukor's direction is sensitive and impeccably controlled, and the Harold Arlen–Ira Gershwin songs, including "Born in a Trunk" and "The Man That Got Away," are delights. The video version includes nearly thirty minutes of footage, just recently restored, which were cut shortly after the film's release. Where a few minutes of the original were permanently lost to the ravages of the studio vault, the cassette retains the soundtrack and shows production stills of the missing scenes. It's a commendable job, and one that clarifies the film's justifiable reputation as a masterpiece. "Born in a Trunk" is simply one of the very greatest scenes in the history of film musicals.

A STAR IS BORN ☆½
1976, USA, R
Barbra Streisand, Kris Kristofferson, Gary Busey, Oliver Clark, Marta Heflin, Vanetta Fields, Clydie King. Directed by Frank Pierson. 140 min.

Every so often, Hollywood purges itself by remaking this masochistic show-biz tearjerker about the cost of fame, with an up-and-coming woman falling in love with a rapidly disintegrating man. The first three (counting the 1932 *What Price Hollywood?*) ranged from good to great. This one is a debacle. Both main characters have been changed from actors to singers, the better to accommodate producer-star Barbra Streisand. What emerges is an egomaniacal mess, a protracted excuse for her to make a semiconcert film interspersed with high-school amateur dramatics. The music, including the Oscar-winning "Evergreen," far outclasses the acting, but after two and a half hours, you won't care. Even Streisand's most devoted followers will be hard pressed to find any art or talent in the bullying histrionics with which she dominates the proceedings. The fine writers Joan Didion and John Gregory Dunne are credited with the patchy script, but a small army of hired pens reportedly contributed to other drafts, all for naught.

STARMAN ☆☆½
1984, USA, PG
Karen Allen, Jeff Bridges, Charles Martin Smith, Richard Jaeckel. Directed by John Carpenter. 115 min.

"There's a starman waiting in the sky/He'd like to come and meet us, but he thinks he'd blow our minds." Sentimental love story about a young widow and the benevolent alien who assumes the form of her late husband. Interference is provided by mean government scientists, who would rather dissect the visitor than let him rendezvous with his mothership and go home. This is the picture Columbia chose to develop instead of *E.T.*

STAR PACKER ☆☆
1934, USA
John Wayne, Verna Hillie, George "Gabby" Hayes, Yakima Canutt. Directed by Robert N. Bradbury. 52 min.

John Wayne packs his star on the inside of his shirt as he goes undercover in this well-paced, fight-'n'-chase Western. Robert N. Bradbury wrote and directed a ton of B Westerns, and he's a serviceable actioner—his son was cowboy star Bob Steele.

STARS ON PARADE ☆½
1944, USA
Larry Parks, Lynn Merrick, Ray Walker, Jeff Donnell, Nat "King" Cole. Directed by Lew Landers. 63 min.

♪ The stars must have been off parading somewhere else when this was made, because none of them managed to show up onscreen here. Two youngsters from Los Angeles decide to put on a talent show in order to get the interest of a Hollywood producer. The standout among the various performing acts is a young Nat "King" Cole, seen here as a jazz pianist before he attained fame as a romantic vocalist.

STARTING OVER ☆☆☆
1979, USA, R
Burt Reynolds, Jill Clayburgh, Candice Bergen, Paul Sorvino, Austin Pendleton. Directed by Alan J. Pakula. 106 min.

This entertaining seriocomedy about adjusting to the aftermath of divorce is superficially meaningful—along the lines of *Terms of Endearment* (also written by James Brooks)—but it mercifully lacks that film's unconvincing turn to tragedy. Burt Reynolds, trying to shuck off his good ol' boy image, plays a divorced man whose newly minted feelings for schoolmarm Jill Clayburgh are complicated by his deep-rooted feelings for his former wife, Candice Bergen. She's a dingbat who dreams of a successful songwriting career as the means to cap off her emancipation. The loose ends of these private lives aren't tied together satisfactorily in the final reel, but the film is a decent romantic comedy. Both Clayburgh and Bergen were considered winsome and funny enough each to receive Oscar nominations.

STAR TREK IV: THE VOYAGE HOME ☆☆
1986, USA, PG
William Shatner, Leonard Nimoy, DeForest Kelley, James Doohan, George Takei, Walter Koenig, Nichelle Nichols, Catherine Hicks, Mark Lenard, Jane Wyatt, John Schuck, Brock Peters, Robin Curtis, Majel Barrett, Robert Ellenstein, Grace Lee Whitney. Directed by Leonard Nimoy. 118 min.

This entry in the ever-popular series has a bright premise treated with mild humor but a depressing lack of style or imagination. In the twenty-third century, Earth's existence is threatened by an alien probe whose signals can be answered only by the song of the extinct humpback whale. The solution? Kirk, Spock, McCoy et al. do the Time Warp in a Klingon rustbucket (remember, the *Enterprise* was destroyed), coming back to 1986 San Francisco in order to bring two of the whales into their future. Unfortunately, stripping the cast of its high-tech sci-fi trappings reveals all of its considerable deficiencies, and under Leonard Nimoy's direction most of the time-travel jokes fall flat and the spirit of adventure lags; Don Peterman's unusually poor cinematography doesn't help. Still, this installment has plenty to satisfy Trekkies, including appearances by Mark Lenard and Jane Wyatt as Spock's parents, Majel Barrett and Grace Lee Whitney as Nurse Chapel and Yeoman Rand, and the promise of a new, improved *Enterprise* for future sequels.

STAR TREK—THE MOTION PICTURE ☆½
1979, USA, G
William Shatner, Leonard Nimoy, DeForest Kelley, James Doohan, George Takei, Nichelle Nichols, Walter Koenig, Stephen Collins, Persis Khambatta. Directed by Robert Wise. 145 min.

It took eleven years, but the low-rated sci-fi series whose five-year mission was cruelly cut short in 1968 finally made it to the big screen. Seeing this, you'll wonder why. Much of *Star Trek*'s inflated running time (it's even longer on video) is given over to director Robert Wise's endless, salivating pans across the elaborately dull sets of the new, improved *Enterprise*; when he actually focuses on the characters, it's usually for a painfully drawn-out reunion between any two of the rusty-jointed, deep-frozen crew members. The cast, once so wonderfully hammy, is forced to act as if their mere presence gives the film mythic weight, but the plot, about a mysterious missing spacecraft, is cheaper and more dim-witted than the silliest series episode.

STAR TREK III: THE SEARCH FOR SPOCK ☆☆
1984, USA, PG
William Shatner, Leonard Nimoy, DeForest Kelley, James Doohan, Walter Koenig, George Takei, Nichelle Nichols, Robin Curtis, Merritt Butrick. Directed by Leonard Nimoy. 105 min.

☢ In this latest of the *Star Trek* films, a melancholy *Enterprise* crew heads home after depositing Mr. Spock's cadaver on the newly reborn Genesis planet. But Genesis is degenerating, and Spock's body needs to be taken home to Vulcan. The aging cast goes through its characteristic paces and winks, and the audience of Trekkies presumably goes home happy. Leonard Nimoy directed this one—and he proves a singularly unexciting filmmaker.

STAR TREK II: THE WRATH OF KHAN ☆☆☆
1982, USA, PG
William Shatner, Leonard Nimoy, DeForest Kelley, George Takei, James Doohan, Nichelle Nichols, Walter Koenig, Ricardo Montalban, Kirstie Alley. Directed by Nicholas Meyer. 113 min.

☢ Everything that the 1979 original botched, this zippy, imaginative sequel gets right. With Nicholas Meyer (*Time After Time, The Seven Per Cent Solution*) at the helm, the seemingly rejuvenated, energized *Enterprise*-ers plunge into a dynamite story line taken from the old series episode "Space Seed." Returning as Kirk's nemesis after a fifteen-year (our time) banishment, Ricardo Montalban plays the deadly Khan, who in his quest for revenge becomes the most formidable villain Captain (now Admiral) Kirk has ever faced. Meyer never lets the pace flag, injects some welcome wit, and draws good performances from William Shatner and Montalban, which may be the most surprising special effect in the film. The ending will have you racing out to rent *Star Trek III*.

START THE REVOLUTION WITHOUT ME ☆☆½
1970, USA, PG
Gene Wilder, Donald Sutherland, Hugh Griffith, Jack MacGowran, Billie Whitelaw, Victor Spinetti, Ewa Aulin, Orson Welles. Directed by Bud Yorkin. 90 min.

😎 Yet another parody of the old Corsican Brothers story: two twins accidentally separated at birth, one raised in the French aristocracy, the other as a peasant, who are united by the French Revolution. This time, however, there are *two* sets of twins, each played by Gene Wilder and Donald Sutherland, and most of what's good about this farce is watching them ham it up as the aristocratic brothers. Before too long, though, in the manner of most costume comedies, this disintegrates into tedious chases and overplotting.

STAR WARS ☆☆☆½
1977, USA, PG
Mark Hamill, Carrie Fisher, Harrison Ford, Peter Cushing, James Earl Jones, David Prowse, Anthony Daniels. Directed by George Lucas. 121 min.

☢ George Lucas proves himself a comic-book artist without peer in this homage to the cheesy space-ship-and-ray-gun serials of the 1930s. Never has so much fancy technology been thrown away with such manic frivolity. The plot about warring intergalactic factions resembles old Hollywood Westerns and Buck Rogers–type serials, but it's actually a retread of Akira Kurosawa's *Hidden Fortress* (1958). Admittedly, the story is simple and the characters are shallow, but the special effects are exceptionally well done and Lucas deserves praise for creating the gushing spirit of an old-fashioned adventure movie.

STATE FAIR ☆☆☆
1945, USA
Jeanne Crain, Dana Andrews, Dick Haymes, Vivian Blaine, Donald Meek, Charles Winninger, Fay Bainter, Frank McHugh. Directed by Walter Lang. 100 min.

♪ This musical about an Iowa farm family's adventures at the State Fair is a simple, ingratiating slice of rustic Americana. Rodgers and Hammerstein contributed the songs (their only score written directly for the screen), including "That's for Me," "It's a Grand Night for Singing," and "It Might as Well Be Spring." There are lively performances by Jeanne Crain, Dana Andrews, Dick Haymes, Vivian Blaine, and, as a judge who gets progressively drunker, Donald Meek. Sharply directed by Walter Lang, the film is visually less evocative than the similar *Meet Me in St. Louis, Centennial Summer*, and *Summer Holiday*, but it integrates its numbers just as engagingly. This was a remake of a (better) 1933 film and was remade into a (worse) 1962 musical film.

STATE OF SIEGE ☆☆☆
1973, France
Yves Montand, Renato Salvatori, Jacques Weber, O. E. Hasse, Jean-Luc Bideau, Evangeline Peterson. Directed by Costa-Gavras. 120 min.

🌐 In the Uruguayan equivalent to his Academy Award–winning *Z*, Costa-Gavras fits his brand of political storytelling into a virtual formula, and the film suffers from a "Haven't-I-seen-this-before?" syndrome. His attempt at portraying the insidious involvement of the United States in other countries' political arenas (the country is not named, but everybody knows) creates a diffuse atmosphere that lacks the compulsion—emotionally and morally—that fueled its precursor. Although a strangely sentimental film—considering Yves Montand's dignified performance as the captive American torturer—it still cuts deep with its often too-vivid detailing of "investigation" techniques such as electric cattle-prodding.

STATE OF THE UNION ☆☆☆
1948, USA
Katharine Hepburn, Spencer Tracy, Van Johnson, Angela Lansbury, Adolphe Menjou. Directed by Frank Capra. 124 min.

😎 This is a decent translation of an assembly line Broadway hit, but somehow one expects more from comedy expert Frank Capra. The plot involves a presidential hopeful who wants to be in the White House but doesn't like the double-dealing of the political arena itself. Maybe the confines of the Broadway plotting and the solidified teamwork of Tracy-Hepburn proved too much for Capra's freewheeling temperament. The film is enjoyable, but resembles his other work more for its populist political sentiments than for its comedy technique. It's an efficient theatrical machine with lots of repartee and political chicanery to keep things hopping. Good, but no cigar.

THE STATIONMASTER'S WIFE ☆
1977, West Germany (TV)
Elisabeth Trissenaar, Kurt Raab, Bernhard Helfrich, Udo Kier. Directed by Rainer Werner Fassbinder. 111 min.

🌐 Another of Rainer Werner Fassbinder's cryptic studies of bourgeois depravity. The hero (played by pasty-faced Kurt Raab) is a wormy village bureaucrat whose life erupts into scandal when his voluptuous wife (Elisabeth Trissenaar) begins an affair with the local butcher. The movie means to be a satirical parable of small-town social oppression, but Fassbinder's portrait of a middle-class marriage turned poisonous becomes oppressive; as in nearly all the director's work, the doors to redemption are closed from the start. Originally made for German television, the film has some of the same high-art dazzle that Fassbinder brought to his final works.

STATION WEST ☆☆☆
1948, USA
Dick Powell, Jane Greer, Agnes Moorehead, Burl Ives, Tom Powers, Steve Brodie, Raymond Burr, Regis Toomey, Guinn "Big Boy" Williams. Directed by Sidney Lanfield. 91 min.

🤠 Depending on your point of view, this is a Western drama with gumshoe trappings or a detective story in cowboy mufti. However you view it, though, it's a solid concoction drawn from the 1940s genre gene pool. Ex–Busby Berkeley cutie Dick Powell, in the tough-guy phase of his career, plays an Army intelligence officer out to discover who's responsible for a series of government gold robberies. His investigation takes him to a Western town under the domination of a crime boss named Charlie. Charlie is played by Jane Greer, and it's all uphill from there.

STAY AS YOU ARE
1978, France, R ★★½
Marcello Mastroianni, Nastassja Kinski, Francisco Rabal, Anja Pieroni. Directed by Alberto Lattuada. 95 min.

Having had a fight with his wife, Giulio, a fifty-year-old architect, has an affair with a girl young enough to be his daughter. The trouble begins when she informs him that she might actually *be* his daughter, the illegitimate product of an affair her mother had years ago. The question of incest, which is never resolved, was used to sell this film, though its ostensible concern is with the broader issues of fatherhood in general and Giulio's mid-life crisis. Tastelessly done, it should satisfy Kinski-watchers; made before *Tess*, this was released in the U.S. in this shortened version to cash in on Miss Kinski's success in the Polanski film.

STAY HUNGRY
1976, USA, R ★★★
Jeff Bridges, Sally Field, Arnold Schwarzenegger, R. G. Armstrong, Helena Kallianiotes, Scatman Crothers, Ed Begley, Jr., Joanna Cassidy, Gary Goodrow. Directed by Bob Rafelson. 103 min.

Poorly received by those few who saw it when it first came out, *Stay Hungry* has become something of a cult film, due mostly to the recent stardom of Sally Field and Arnold Schwarzenegger and the film's loose, snobs-versus-slobs style. Set in the New South, the story centers on Jeff Bridges, a rich young man trying to force himself back into the real world after the death of his parents. Persuaded by family and friends to uphold his genteel tradition, he instead becomes involved with an odd assortment of characters at a local gym. Director Bob Rafelson (*Five Easy Pieces, The Postman Always Rings Twice*) has always shown an affinity for characters on the fringe. Unfortunately, this, like his first film, *Head*, is little more than a collection of observations and weird bits that never really pull together. It is worth seeing anyway for those unsummed parts; Schwarzenegger is especially good, a fact less surprising now than it was at the time. The same is true of Field, who was then still known only for *Gidget* and *The Flying Nun*.

STAYING ALIVE
1983, USA, PG ★
John Travolta, Finola Hughes, Cynthia Rhodes. Directed by Sylvester Stallone. 96 min.

The Stallone-ization of movies may be one of the scarier trends in American films; everything he touches turns to mud, and still makes money. If he ever goes on trial for crimes against art, this painful *Saturday Night Fever* sequel will have to be Exhibit A—he wrote it, directed it, and even gave himself a cameo. It's too awful to laugh at, with Tony Manero transplanted to Manhattan, torn between lovers and seeking his big break on Broadway in a disco version of Dante's Inferno. No acting, ugly costumes, hideous and badly shot choreography, and an appallingly amateurish song score by brother Frank Stallone. Sly told the press he was chosen for the job solely on merit. Yes, merit. Let the trial begin.

STEAMBOAT BILL, JR.
1928, USA ★★★★
Buster Keaton, Ernest Torrence, Tom Lewis, Marion Byron, Tom McGuire. Directed by Charles F. Reisner. 70 min.

Buster Keaton's career was meteoric—brilliant and brief. After 1928, his best works were behind him, and this film—along with *The Cameramen*—is the last of the great ones. Buster plays a dandy who comes to help his father run the family Mississippi riverboat. His father, the last of a crusty race, is deeply disappointed by his pipsqueak son, and he becomes less pleased when Buster falls in love with the daughter of his rival. The two boats compete in a race and Buster ... well, why spoil it? This movie contains the surrealistic cyclone sequence in which Buster takes a ride on a hospital bed and has a building fall down around him. The movie was shot on location on the Sacramento River and has the look of authenticity for which Keaton was famous. Interestingly, this was, like other Keaton films, an expensive money-loser.

STEAMING
1985, Great Britain, R ★½
Vanessa Redgrave, Diana Dors, Sarah Miles, Patti Love, Brenda Bruce, Felicity Dean. Directed by Joseph Losey. 95 min.

A very undistinguished end to the career of the fine American expatriate director Joseph Losey. *Steaming* is an unimaginative adaptation of Nell Dunn's awful play, set in a London steambath about to be shuttered. The script (by the director's wife, Patricia) introduces the bathhouse's regulars—the tart Cockney Josie (Patti Love), the edgy career woman (Sarah Miles), the repressed wife (Vanessa Redgrave)—and, in the best tradition of bad drama, gives each a turn in the spotlight and a confessional speech before wending its way to a pat conclusion. Onstage, Dunn's work had the gimmick of nudity; here, the actresses and the camera seem uncomfortable with the very thought—you'll rarely see a collection of performers more ill at ease.

STEEL
1980, USA, PG ★½
Lee Majors, Jennifer O'Neill, Art Carney, George Kennedy, Harris Yulin, Roger Mosley, Albert Salmi, R. G. Armstrong. Directed by Steven Carver. 99 min.

A group of construction workers races to complete nine floors of a skyscraper in three weeks in order to keep the bank from closing down the project. It's all in memory of their boss, who was killed while trying to help out a new member of the team. Fearing that they'll never finish on time, worker Lee Majors travels around the country rounding up first-class builders. Why any of them, or the audience, should care about the silly building is less than clear.

THE STEEL CLAW
1961, USA ★½
George Montgomery, Charito Luna, Mario Barri, Paul Sorensen, Amelia de la Rama. Directed by George Montgomery. 96 min.

Attention, George Montgomery fans: he not only stars in and directed this low-budget war adventure, but also produced and cowrote it. Attention, nonfans: this old-fashioned shot-in-the-Philippines action film is tough to sit through. Good photography can't compensate for a very old-fashioned approach to macho wartime comradeship and heroics, stiff performances, and often laughable dialogue.

STEEL COWBOY
1978, USA (TV) ★
James Brolin, Rip Torn, Strother Martin, Jennifer Warren, Julie Cobb. Directed by Harvey Laidman. 100 min.

This rough-and-tumble modern-day cowboys-and-rustlers flick features beefy James Brolin (who'd be better cast as a cigar store Indian than as a charismatic cowpoke) as a beleaguered trucker who discovers that his rig may be pulled out from under him. Quicker than you can say "convoy," Brolin's out a-rustlin' cows to pay the bills so his truck won't be repossessed; and arguing with his wife, who thinks stealing is just not government-inspected grade-A behavior. Even the stolen cattle are more expressive than the cast in this big-rig hokum about morality in the New West.

STEELYARD BLUES
1973, USA, PG ★★
Donald Sutherland, Jane Fonda, Peter Boyle, Howard Hesseman, Garry Goodrow, John Savage. Directed by Alan Myerson. 93 min.

A very uneven contemporary screwball comedy, this is about a band of misfits attempting to escape the tribulations of conventional society by flying away in an abandoned airplane they are attempting to rebuild. Donald Sutherland, the gang leader, dreams of staging demolition derbies with mobile homes; Jane Fonda is familiar as a call girl; and Peter Boyle keeps busy quelling everybody's fear of flying. Already very badly dated, the film relies heavily on an early 1970s mood of alienation to justify its characters' odd actions. If you aren't put off, you may be mystified; however, there is not enough of a story to make this a good time-passer.

STELLA DALLAS ☆☆☆☆
1937, USA
Barbara Stanwyck, John Boles, Anne Shirley, Alan Hale, Barbara O'Neil, Marjorie Main. Directed by King Vidor. 106 min.

Before Douglas Sirk and Max Ophuls came to Hollywood, people like King Vidor were making grandiose weepies that managed to transcend their inherent corniness. In this vastly superior remake of Henry King's silent *Stella Dallas*, Vidor masterfully builds up to scenes of great poignancy and eliminates many of the potentially campy excesses. Barbara Stanwyck plays a woman from the wrong side of the tracks who marries a wealthy industrialist only to find herself an outcast in his society. Stanwyck ages many years to play her role and several of her scenes with her grown daughter (played by Anne Shirley)—including the birthday party and train sequences—are among the best work she's ever done. Both women give Oscar-caliber performances, although neither won that year. Also helping to milk the tear ducts are Alfred Newman's delicate score and Rudolph Mate's fluid camerawork. Only John Boles's usual stiff male lead is less than satisfying.

STEPHEN KING'S CAT'S EYE

See *Cat's Eye*

STEPHEN KING'S SILVER BULLET

See *Silver Bullet*

THE STERILE CUCKOO ☆☆☆½
1969, USA, R
Liza Minnelli, Wendell Burton, Tim McIntire. Directed by Alan J. Pakula. 108 min.

Liza Minnelli earned a well-deserved Oscar nomination in her first starring screen role as a neurotic college freshman. Pookie Adams is an outcast who cracks jokes to hide her feelings—in this case, love for a shy student (Wendell Burton). Alan J. Pakula, in his directorial debut, shows a sensitive hand for the material, which often shifts from comedy to drama. Minnelli proves, at least in this film, that she is as fine an actress as she is a singer. The theme song, "Come Saturday Morning," also won an Oscar nomination.

STEVIE ☆☆☆
1978, Great Britain
Glenda Jackson, Mona Washbourne, Alec McCowen, Trevor Howard. Directed by Robert Enders. 102 min.

The performances in this biography of the reclusive poet Stevie Smith are so moving, precise, and beautifully controlled that it's easy to forgive the stagy, sedate direction and essentially undramatic quality of the production. The film is set in Smith's quiet country home, where she writes, thinks, and tends to her aged, loving aunt. Glenda Jackson really flies with the literate script, particularly in the lovely scenes she shares with veteran actress Mona Washbourne. *Stevie* does nothing that wasn't done just as well by the fine play on which it's based, but it's a perfectly effective adaptation.

STICK ☆☆☆
1985, USA, R
Burt Reynolds, Candice Bergen, Charles Durning, George Segal, Tricia Leigh Fisher, Dar Robinson. Directed by Burt Reynolds. 109 min.

Director/star Burt Reynolds is at his best when taking a look at a city's seamy underbelly—whether it's the menacingly violent Atlanta in *Sharky's Machine*, or the drug-infested Miami in *Stick*. Reynolds plays a macho ex-con who comes to the city with dreams of starting a new life and ends up having a price placed on his head by some murderous dope dealers. At last, Burt gets to play a man who uses his brain more than his biceps. The eccentric street characters and double-crosses of Elmore Leonard's suspense novel are brought to vivid life in this sizzling adaptation.

STILETTO ☆☆
1969, USA, R
Alex Cord, Britt Ekland, Patrick O'Neal, Joseph Wiseman, Barbara McNair, John Dehner, Titos Vandis, Roy Scheider. Directed by Bernard Kowalski. 100 min.

This adaptation of a minor Harold Robbins novel has some thrills but, unlike the titular weapon, neither sharp edges nor a point. Playboy foreign-car merchant Alex Cord performs several murders to repay a local mob leader for having once saved his life. Then he wants out, but the mob considers him one of theirs now. The film has too many characters, none sufficiently developed, and in the end you don't really care about any of them; but it moves along quickly and doesn't require any serious thinking.

STILL OF THE NIGHT ☆½
1982, USA, PG
Meryl Streep, Roy Scheider, Josef Sommer, Sara Botsford, Jessica Tandy. Directed by Robert Benton. 90 min.

A psychiatrist falls in love with a mystery woman who may or may not have killed one of his patients. More than a few nods to Hitchcock punctuate this disappointing thriller for our even more voyeuristic age. But the film suffers from a poor performance by Streep, whose idea of suggesting neurosis is to fiddle with her hair. No real thrills until the end, but that doesn't make up for the flat-footed exposition leading up to it. This does for Hitchcock what *At Long Last Love* did for 1930s musicals.

STILL SMOKIN' ☆
1983, USA, R
Thomas Chong, Richard "Cheech" Marin, Carol Van Herwijen, Hans Van Veld. Directed by Thomas Chong. 91 min.

There really is no excuse for this movie. Cheech and Chong, who began as sophomoric comedians for the drug generation (that's fine, everyone needs something to laugh at) actually fared better than anyone might have expected when they began to make movies. But this one, their fifth, isn't really a movie at all, just a badly filmed live performance with a sketchy plot tossed in. You get the impression that they were chatting in Amsterdam, where they happened to be doing a concert, and said something like, "Hey, the footage we shot of last night's show wasn't bad—let's go do some location shooting today, and we can put it out as a movie and rake in some bucks!" It's not even as if someone else acquired rights to old footage and decided to rip them off—they're ripping themselves off here, and their fans, too. Get *Cheech and Chong's Next Movie* or *Nice Dreams* instead. (a.k.a.: *Cheech and Chong Still Smokin'*)

THE STING ☆☆☆☆
1973, USA, PG
Paul Newman, Robert Redford, Robert Shaw, Charles Durning, Ray Walston, Eileen Brennan. Directed by George Roy Hill. 129 min.

Four years after George Roy Hill directed Newman and Redford in *Butch Cassidy and the Sundance Kid*, the trio teamed up again and made another huge box-office hit. Oscars for best picture, director, and screenplay went to this thoroughly entertaining comedy about two slick Chicago con men of the 1930s who revenge their friend's death by putting "the sting" on big-time gangster Shaw in a wildly elaborate swindle. Scott Joplin's delightful ragtime score, arranged by Marvin Hamlisch and highlighted by

"The Entertainer," gives the film razzle, and Hill's glittery mounting supplies the dazzle.

STING OF THE DRAGON MASTERS

See *When Tae Kwon Do Strikes*

THE STING II
☆½
1983, USA, PG
Jackie Gleason, Mac Davis, Teri Garr, Karl Malden, Oliver Reed, Bert Remsen. Directed by Jeremy Paul Kagan. 102 min.

More con games and money-making schemes in old New York—minus, of course, Paul Newman and Robert Redford. This time, the year is 1940, and Jackie Gleason and Mac Davis are the lovable con artists who face off against a wealthy racketeer (Karl Malden). They are trying to fix a boxing match. Needless to say, it's just not the same game, though David Ward repeated as writer, and Teri Garr is, as usual, fresh and appealing.

STIR CRAZY
☆☆½
1980, USA, R
Richard Pryor, Gene Wilder, Georg Stanford Brown, Erland van Lidth de Jeude, JoBeth Williams, Craig T. Nelson, Barry Corbin. Directed by Sidney Poitier. 111 min.

Richard Pryor and Gene Wilder, reteaming after *Silver Streak*, play a couple of bumbling innocents who step into a robbery and are wrongly sentenced to 132 years in jail. Their misadventures in and out of the big house form the core of this boisterous, sometimes funny comedy. *Stir Crazy* was extremely popular, probably due to a couple of riotous set pieces behind bars, but it's really nothing special—the gags here aren't funnier than those in many similar comedies, they're just louder. Wilder uses every vaudeville trick in the book, and it's a bit embarrassing to see him work so hard, only to be upstaged by a twitch of Pryor's eyebrow or a toss of his head. Later a TV series.

STOLEN KISSES
☆☆☆
1968, France
Jean-Pierre Léaud, Delphine Seyrig, Claude Jade, Michel Lonsdale, Daniel Ceccaldi. Directed by François Truffaut. 96 min.

François Truffaut's Antoine Doinel grows up into a lovelorn jerk-of-all-trades in this frothy, dewy-eyed comedy. Jean-Pierre Léaud carries on the role he began as a child in *The Four Hundred Blows*, establishing many of the sensitive-stumblebum mannerisms that would soon become his trademark. This film is cute, but has nowhere near the mastery or originality of some of the director's earlier work. This was the third in the Doinel series; it was preceded by *Four Hundred Blows* and the "Antoine et Colette" segment of *Love at Twenty*, and followed by *Bed and Board* and *Love on the Run*.

THE STONE BOY
☆
1984, USA, PG
Robert Duvall, Jason Presson, Frederic Forrest, Glenn Close, Wilford Brimley, Gail Youngs, Cindy Fisher, Mayf Nutter, Susan Blackstone, Dean Cain. Directed by Chris Cain. 93 min.

In this trite heartland version of *Ordinary People*, a sensitive twelve-year-old accidentally kills his older brother during a hunting trip and then retreats into a shell of guilt. The boy's parents (Robert Duvall and Glenn Close) don't talk out his problems with him, but their eyes reproach him for his brother's death and eventually he's driven out of the house and into the arms of his lovable old grandpa (Wilford Brimley, acting mostly with his whiskers and belly). It's hard enough to make a movie about noncommunication among gabby people, but in *The Stone Boy* the characters are so taciturn that the underplaying of the actors becomes a kind of mugging.

STONE COLD DEAD
☆☆½
1980, Canada, R
Richard Crenna, Paul Williams, Linda Sorenson, Belinda J. Montgomery, Charles Shamata. Directed by George Mendeluk. 97 min.

Not a horror film as the title might indicate, this is a reasonably engrossing Canadian thriller that will keep you entertained for an evening, even if you won't remember it the next day. Crenna plays a police sergeant investigating a sniper who likes to kill prostitutes and, with the aid of a camera mounted on the rifle barrel, photograph their deaths. Along the way, Crenna also sets out after local drug dealer and pimp Julius Kurtz (played by the diminutively menacing Paul Williams).

THE STONE KILLER
☆☆½
1973, USA, R
Charles Bronson, Martin Balsam, David Sheiner, Norman Fell, Ralph Waite, Stuart Margolin, John Ritter, Frank Campanella. Directed by Michael Winner. 95 min.

The director and star of the *Death Wish* films are teamed in an earlier, slightly less gory police thriller. New York cop Charles Bronson, transferred to the LAPD after using excessive violence on a street punk, stumbles onto a plot by gangster Martin Balsam to avenge a forty-year-old shooting by using a gang comprised of Vietnam veterans. Complicated and violent, though without the vigilante excesses that marred Bronson and Winner's later losers.

STONER
☆☆
1981, Hong Kong
George Lazenby, Angela Mao Ying, Betty Ting Pei, Whang In-Sik, Joji Takagi, Hung Chin-Po. Directed by Huang Feng. 88 min.

What happens to James Bonds after they have been put out to pasture? If they are George Lazenby (*On Her Majesty's Secret Service*), they learn karate and star in second-rate kung fu movies. In this one, Lazenby plays an agent searching through Hong Kong for a drug supplier. Angela Mao Ying steals the show from Lazenby as another high-kicking agent.

STOP MAKING SENSE
☆☆☆☆
1984, USA
The Talking Heads (David Byrne, Tina Weymouth, Chris Frantz, Jerry Harrison), Alex Weir, Bernie Worrell, Steve Scales, Edna Holt, Lynn Mabry. Directed by Jonathan Demme. 99 min.

This is arguably the best concert film ever made, bar none. Filmed records of live performances tend, at best, to make you wish you'd been there for the real thing, but director Jonathan Demme and head Head David Byrne have made this in such a precise and deceptively simple manner that the adrenaline that usually accompanies physical proximity is invoked cinematically. On most bands, such care might have been wasted, but it perfectly complements the polyrhythmic energy of the Heads. The band is visually engaging throughout, without having to rely on the standard smoke bombs and laser shows. Lead singer and songwriter Byrne, who has worked with Twyla Tharp in the past, has mastered what can only be described as a controlled simulation of lack of control. The videocassette features three songs not included in the theatrical release, "Cities" and a medley of "Big Business/I Zimbra"; the entire soundtrack is recorded in pristine twenty-four-track digital sound. You *will* dance.

STOPOVER TOKYO
☆☆
1957, USA
Robert Wagner, Joan Collins, Edmond O'Brien, Ken Scott, Reiko Oyama, Larry Keating. Directed by Richard L. Breen. 100 min.

Would you believe Robert Wagner as Mr. Moto? Well, almost; based on one of John P. Marquand's innumerable Mr. Moto stories, this substitutes a clean-cut, two-fisted American secret agent (does that sound more like Wagner?) for Mr. M. Mild chills and thrills are derived from Communist agitator Edmond O'Brien trying to cause trouble in Japan by assassinating the U.S. ambassador at the dedication of a peace monument. "Dynasty" fans will want to see the final scene in which the twenty-four-year-old Joan Collins practices her archetypal bitch persona.

STORM BOY ☆☆½
1976, Australia
Greg Rowe, Peter Cummins, David Gulpilil, Judy Dick, Tony Allison, Michael Moody. Directed by Henri Safran. 88 min.

This is an exemplary children's flick that should also do well with grown-ups who could use an evening's entertainment without the usual splash and thrash. Based on a popular Australian book, the film follows the adventures of Mike, a ten-year-old boy living with his father, a reclusive widower who makes his living as a fisherman. Starved for companionship, Mike meets up with an aborigine who gives him the nickname "Storm Boy." The two rescue some birds from hunters and Mike raises them as pets. Well made, particularly in presenting the harshness of the Australian outback environment.

STORM IN A TEACUP ☆☆☆
1937, Great Britain
Vivien Leigh, Rex Harrison, Cecil Parker, Sara Allgood, Ursula Jeans, Gus McNaughton, Edgar Bruce, Robert Hale, Arthur Wontner. Directed by Victor Saville. 84 min.

An amiable British comedy that can be described as a cross between Bill Forsyth and Frank Capra. Young reporter Rex Harrison, a novice English reporter working in Scotland, takes a story about a local tyrant and an accident with a dog and blows it up out of all proportion, thus puncturing the public image and vanity of the politician, who is running for reelection. The politician sues Harrison for slander. The final trial scene is especially reminiscent of Capra's little-guy-versus-city-hall stuff.

STORY IN TEMPLE RED CITY ☆☆
Hong Kong
Chia Ling, Hsieh Lin-Lin, Tung Li, Lung Fei, I Yuan, Tan Tao-Liang.

An ordinary political intrigue plot lulls this kung fu actioner. An evil baron tries to wipe out the royal family with the help of the sheriff (Lung Fei), a group of renegade monks, and other assorted villains. Obvious pro-Royalist melodrama marred by poor "special effects" and mediocre fight sequences.

THE STORY OF ADELE H. ☆☆☆½
1975, France
Isabelle Adjani, Bruce Robinson, Sylvia Marriott, Joseph Blatchley. Directed by François Truffaut. 95 min.

Isabelle Adjani was nominated for an Academy Award for this, the feature that first brought her to international attention. In a story based on fact, she plays the daughter of novelist Victor Hugo, a woman obsessed with a British lieutenant who seduced her but no longer wants her. She follows him to Britain and Barbados, growing more and more unhinged until she is finally taken back to Paris in a state of mental collapse. François Truffaut's direction is a bit meandering, without much of his characteristic warmth; it is Adjani's performance that is the heart of this moving tale.

THE STORY OF O ☆
1976, France, R
Corinne Cléry, Udo Kier, Anthony Steel, Jean Gaven, Martine Kelly, Christiane Minazzoli, Li Seligreen, Alain Noury, Gabriel Cattand. Directed by Just Jaeckin. 112 min.

Just Jaeckin abandons the sighs and whispers of *Emmanuelle* for the cries and whips of the submission and domination crowd. A young woman is taught just why it's fun to have men use her as an object. If the theme attracts you, it can be safely assumed that little could be said to discourage you from this torpid hooey.

THE STORY OF VERNON AND IRENE CASTLE ☆☆☆½
1939, USA
Fred Astaire, Ginger Rogers, Edna May Oliver, Walter Brennan, Lew Fields, H. C. Potter. 93 min.

This is the real Fred Astaire–Ginger Rogers swan song (they reteamed for *The Barkleys of Broadway* but their hearts weren't in that unplanned reunion—only their feet). Here for the first time they played real-life characters, the influential dance team the Castles, who popularized a number of famous dance steps, including the Castle Walk. The script also focuses on Irene's considerable fashion influence, but the film is primarily a summation of Astaire and Rogers's careers, and is only incidentally a tribute to the Castles. If Astaire and Rogers's earlier films celebrated the thrill of courtship, this film is a salute to mature marital bliss, making it less effervescent than the preceding films. The stars shine dramatically and reenact the famous Castle dance triumphs with grace. A good musical with an affecting dramatic edge.

STRAIGHT TIME ☆☆☆☆
1978, USA, R
Dustin Hoffman, Theresa Russell, Gary Busey, M. Emmet Walsh, Harry Dean Stanton. Directed by Ulu Grosbard. 114 min.

Dustin Hoffman is one of those rare actors who can submerge himself in a role with such an intensity that his "star" persona ceases to exist, and he uncannily becomes the character. This bleak movie is an example of his abilities at their best; it's a downbeat, fascinating portrayal of an ex-con who can't adjust to the outside world and does everything possible to land himself back into the environment that he knows best—jail. *Straight Time* brilliantly examines the seedy atmosphere and straggly characters in his life with a near-documentary sensibility. Among the effectively rendered characters are a social worker with whom he falls in love, a drug-addicted young man, and a burned-out worker who wants a life of crime instead of his newly found normality. Even though Ulu Grosbard puts them at a distance from us, their tragic lives are still emotionally affecting.

STRAIT-JACKET ☆½
1964, USA
Joan Crawford, Diane Baker, Leif Erickson, George Kennedy, Rochelle Hudson. Directed by William Castle. 93 min.

Before the glut of prime-time serials, older actresses' only way of finding work was in crummy thrillers like *Strait-Jacket*. Joan Crawford returns home after years in an asylum for chopping off the heads of her husband and his girlfriend. Some more ax murders take place and it seems Joan is up to her old tricks—or is it Joan? The movie is unintentionally hilarious and, despite production design by Boris Leven, it is clearly el cheapo. Crawford tries as if she were in something better, but it's no use.

THE STRANGE AND DEADLY OCCURRENCE ☆½
1974, USA (TV)
Robert Stack, Vera Miles, L. Q. Jones, Herb Edelman, Dena Dietrich. Directed by John Llewellyn Moxey. 90 min.

Not since the postwar *noir* days of *Lady in the Lake* and *Dark Passage* has the subjective camera technique been so exploited as in this made-for-TV suspense movie. We never see the strange and deadly occurrence that is menacing, for no apparent reason, our happy middle-class family. Instead, we see through "its" eyes (accompanied by heavy breathing). The denouement is so ludicrously tacked on that it makes what was otherwise a passable little thriller into something very avoidable.

STRANGE BEHAVIOR ☆☆☆
1981, New Zealand, PG
Michael Murphy, Louise Fletcher, Fiona Lewis, Dan Shor. Directed by Michael Laughlin. 98 min.

A small-town sheriff's son signs up for some psychological experiments at the local college, thinking that they will be an easy way to earn some money for school. He is wrong. Soon the town is under siege by a psychopathic murderer (or murderers), and the solution is somehow linked to the enigmatic and apparently long-dead Dr. LeSange, whose research has continued without him. A very stylish horror movie whose ironic subtext never drags the film into the realm of overt self-parody. Director Michael Laughlin displays a fine understanding of genre clichés and the above-average cast negotiates *Strange Behavior*'s tricky waters with grace. *Strange Invaders*, released two years later, is a sequel more in tone and style than in overt subject matter. (a.k.a.: *Dead Kids*)

STRANGE BREW ☆☆
1983, USA, PG
Rick Moranis, Dave Thomas, Max von Sydow, Paul Dooley, Lynne Griffin. Directed by Rick Moranis, Dave Thomas. 90 min.

Bob and Doug McKenzie (Rick Moranis and Dave Thomas) foil the dastardly plans of a greedy brewery owner (Paul Dooley) and his sinister master brewer (Max von Sydow). The beginning and end of the film showcase the stars at their free-form best, but Moranis and Thomas (who wrote and directed) have scripted things too tightly, shutting off opportunities for their nutty improvisations. The result plays like a limp Abbott and Costello movie. And what do all of the references to *Macbeth* mean?

THE STRANGE CASE OF DR. JEKYLL ☆☆☆
1968, USA/Canada (TV)
Jack Palance, Billie Whitelaw, Oscar Homolka, Leo Genn, Denholm Elliott. Directed by Charles Jarrott.

A reasonably stylish TV horror movie from producer Dan Curtis, the man responsible for "The Night Stalker," "Trilogy of Terror," and other top-notch TV chillers. While not as memorable as Fredric March in the 1932 version, Jack Palance is quite convincing in the famous dual role, moviedom's most famous split personality. The atmosphere is properly spooky and there's good support from Billie Whitelaw as Hyde's favorite victim.

STRANGE INVADERS ☆☆½
1983, USA, PG
Diana Scarwid, Paul LeMat, Wallace Shawn, Fiona Lewis, Louise Fletcher, Nancy Allen. Directed by Michael Laughlin. 94 min.

This is skewed science fiction with a surreal air, from the American gothic space invaders to the obsessed government UFO researchers. Aliens invade a small American town during the 1950s and maintain it in a kind of time warp until, thirty years later, a series of strange occurrences convinces a Columbia University entomologist and a tabloid reporter that they're onto the UFO story of a lifetime. A stylistic sequel to *Strange Behavior*.

STRANGE LOVE OF MARTHA IVERS ☆☆☆
1946, USA
Kirk Douglas, Barbara Stanwyck, Lizabeth Scott, Judith Anderson, Van Heflin. Directed by Lewis Milestone. 117 min.

A complicated *film noir* with a lot of plot strands to juggle amid those high-key shadows. This is an unrelievedly grim exploration of the darkest recesses of human guilt and the fear of skeletons rattling out of closets. Everyone here has an ulterior motive; this small town is so corrupt it makes Peyton Place and King's Row look like model communities. A murder committed long ago lives on in the tangled lives of several people, including the unhappily married Barbara Stanwyck and Kirk Douglas. A brooding film in which everyone seems to know everyone else's secret, and fear of exposure is the ruling emotion. Powerful and unremittingly downbeat.

THE STRANGER ☆☆☆
1946, USA
Edward G. Robinson, Loretta Young, Orson Welles, Philip Merivale, Richard Long, Byron Keith, Billy House, Konstantin Shayne, Martha Wentworth, Isabel O'Madigan. Directed by Orson Welles. 94 min.

Though we don't agree with Orson Welles that this is his worst film, we can certainly understand why the great showman thought so: *The Stranger* is an intense but rather unimaginative character study. Welles stars as a former Nazi official hiding out as a teacher in a Connecticut prep school. His entanglement in a murder and his eventual capture are treated in conventional, suspense-movie terms, but Welles creates a darkly fascinating portrait of the criminal mind, haunted both by fear of capture and by his own guilty visions. Edward G. Robinson plays against type as the government agent pursuing Welles.

THE STRANGER AND THE GUNFIGHTER ☆☆½
1976, Italy/Hong Kong, PG
Lee Van Cleef, Lo Lieh, Patty Shepard. Directed by Anthony Dawson (Antonio Margheriti). 107 min.

East meets West as martial arts kick their way into the spaghetti Western. Seeking buried treasure, Lee and Lo go a-wenching; it seems that the treasure map is printed in sections on the backsides of the women they seduce (an image not seen again until *Lust in the Dust*). Following one lead to another, the two heroes keep the action coming and the laughs rolling—it's a good thing, too, because the frantic pace prevents you from realizing how stupid this hybrid could be.

STRANGER FROM VENUS ☆☆½
1954, Great Britain
Helmut Dantine, Patricia Neal. Directed by Burt Balaban. 76 min.

An extraterrestrial visitor tries to bring a message of peace and a warning about global warfare to earthlings who misinterpret his motives and react fearfully. The film, a British remake of the American film *The Day the Earth Stood Still* (1951), is not nearly as memorable as the earlier version. It is an oddity in that it was remade so quickly and that Patricia Neal repeats the role she played in the earlier version. Given the budgetary restrictions, though, it is an efficient sci-fi drama with a message.

STRANGER IN OUR HOUSE

See *Summer of Fear*

STRANGER IN THE HOUSE

See *Black Christmas*

A STRANGER IS WATCHING ☆☆½
1982, USA, R
Rip Torn, Kate Mulgrew, James Naughton, Barbara Baxley, Shawn Von Schreiber. Directed by Sean S. Cunningham. 92 min.

Horror hack Sean Cunningham (*House, Friday the 13th, The New Kids*) usually creates his scares by manipulation so mechanical that it quickly loses its power—an ominous noise turns out to be just the cat, followed by the real scare, and so on, ad nauseam. There's a little of that trickery in this suspense film, but most of it is fairly honest, nerve-racking work. In a wonderfully nasty performance, Rip Torn plays a maniac who kidnaps a little girl and an anchorwoman, hiding them somewhere in New York's subterranean labyrinth of train tunnels. It's a little overplotted and forced at times, but there are plenty of scary moments and an admirable attention

STRANGER ON THE 3RD FLOOR ★★★½
1940, USA
John McGuire, Margaret Tallichet, Peter Lorre. Directed by Boris Ingster. 67 min.

This extraordinarily strange and gripping movie possesses the twisted logical conclusiveness of a nightmare. John McGuire plays a slightly unappetizing newspaperman who threatens his noisy next-door neighbor, then lies awake wondering what would happen if the guy really was murdered. Peter Lorre has a creepy, limited role as the homicidal maniac who can make bad dreams come true. The film, with its air of desperation and its quirky lighting and performances, anticipates the antiheroics of *film noir* and demonstrates that a movie can work magic with little money, an otherwise mediocre director, and an undistinguished cast. It is rumored that, while waiting to work on *Citizen Kane*, Orson Welles had a hand in this.

STRANGERS IN PARADISE ½★
1986, USA
Ulli Lommel, Ken Letner, Thom Jones, Geoffrey Barker, Gloria McCord. Directed by Ulli Lommel. 81 min.

Of the scores of hacks toiling behind the cameras of exploitation films everywhere, few come up with more inept or less appetizing results than Ulli Lommel. He followed the dreadful *Boogey Man* with this odious, atonal semimusical action film. Lommel himself assays the role of a mentalist from Hitler's Germany who's cryogenically frozen and thawed out decades later to help wipe out rock and roll. From the aural evidence on display here, you'll root for him to succeed.

STRANGERS KISS ★½
1984, USA, R
Peter Coyote, Victoria Tennant, Blaine Novak, Dan Shor, Richard Romanus. Directed by Matthew Chapman. 93 min.

In this insular and film-schoolish film, a novice actor and a gangster's girl fall in love, encouraged by their tyrannical director, while acting in a low-budget thriller; real and reel lives intertwine. Director Matthew Chapman puts a glossy pastiche of *film noir* themes and imagery in the context of an intensely self-referential narrative.

STRANGER THAN PARADISE ★★★½
1984, USA
John Lurie, Eszter Balint, Richard Edson, Cecillia Stark. Directed by Jim Jarmusch. 89 min.

This remarkable deadpan comedy, made on a shoestring budget in black and white, might be described as "Samuel Beckett meets 'The Honeymooners.'" It's also a witty takeoff on the "road" movie: its three characters travel an oddball odyssey from New York to Cleveland to Florida, all of which look like the same industrial wasteland. Told in brief scenes punctuated by blackouts, the story concerns Willie, happily living a completely inert life in SoHo; his best friend, Eddie; and Eva, a cousin who suddenly arrives from Hungary but fits right into this mellow urban landscape. The scenes in Cleveland with Willie's ancient Aunt Lotte are hysterically funny and true to life, and director Jim Jarmusch perfectly orchestrates the farcical ending. *Stranger* doesn't look or sound like any Hollywood film you've ever seen, but that only enhances its unhinged, very original charm.

STRANGE SHADOWS IN AN EMPTY ROOM ★
1977, Italy/Canada, R
Stuart Whitman, John Saxon, Martin Landau, Tisa Farrow, Gayle Hunnicutt. Directed by Martin Herbert (Alberto de Martino). 99 min.

The title must be somebody's idea of a joke; the original Italian title, which translates as *Blazing Magnums*, was much more appropriate. Cop Stuart Whitman stalks the murderer of his sister in the streets of Montreal. Maybe we're supposed to accept his grief over her death as the explanation for his peculiar insistence on beating up his suspects before he interrogates them. The plot is either incomprehensible or nonexistent.

THE STRANGE WORLD OF PLANET X

See *The Cosmic Monster*

THE STRATTON STORY ★★★
1949, USA
James Stewart, June Allyson, Frank Morgan, Agnes Moorehead, Bill Williams. Directed by Sam Wood. 106 min.

This standard Hollywood drama is made special by the fine work of James Stewart. He plays Monty Stratton, a rising young baseball pitcher tragically felled—but not for long—by the amputation of one leg. Sam Wood, who also directed *The Pride of the Yankees*, has a fine feel for the baseball milieu, and the second half of the film, detailing Stratton's efforts to rebuild his life after the operation, are moving and powerfully acted by Stewart.

THE STRAWBERRY BLONDE ★★★
1941, USA
James Cagney, Olivia de Havilland, Rita Hayworth, Alan Hale, Jack Carson, George Tobias, Una O'Connor. Directed by Raoul Walsh. 97 min.

A slight but charming comedy, it is socked across solely by the attractive cast. Olivia de Havilland has to fold her hands and wait patiently for James Cagney to come to his senses; an ambitious dentist, he understandably considers Rita Hayworth an eyeful, even though we all know Olivia's better for him. The same story was made in 1932 without songs as *One Sunday Afternoon* and remade in 1948 with songs as *One Sunday Afternoon*. Neither of those versions is as tasty as this confection, with Jimmy and Rita demonstrating how far a film can coast on real star power.

STRAW DOGS ★★★
1971, Great Britain, R
Dustin Hoffman, Susan George, Peter Vaughan, David Warner. Directed by Sam Peckinpah. 115 min.

A horror story without a trace of the supernatural in it, *Straw Dogs* is not simply a violent film, but a film *about* violence. It tells the story of a passive pacifist mathematician and his wife who must change their ways when their English manor house is attacked by crazed locals. Sam Peckinpah draws fine performances out of everyone, creating a symbol-riddled moral universe in which bloodshed, masculinity, and self-esteem must go hand in hand, a questionable premise but one which he puts forth with great subtlety and conviction. An exploitative rape scene early on leaves a foul taste, but the last half hour, an unremittingly harrowing, brilliantly edited orgy of carnage, may be Peckinpah's greatest work.

THE STREETFIGHTER ★
1975, Hong Kong, R
Sonny Chiba, Milton Ishibashi, Etsuko Shiomi.

In its original release, this movie was one of the first to receive an X rating for violence. In order to soften the violence and receive an R rating for video, massive editing was required. The result is a mess. Terry Surugy (Sonny Chiba) is a man who'll do anything, for a price. He is hired to rescue Jungo (Milton Ishibashi), a murderer, from jail. In his attempt, Surugy accidentally kills Jungo's brother. Jungo vows revenge.

STREETFIGHTERS PART II
Hong Kong ½★
Sean Lee, Lyon Chan, Mah San, Randy Lee, Joe Ho, Philip Chan, Sandy Lau, Gary Tony. Directed by Stewart Cheung. 86 min.

This convoluted modern-day hodge-podge concerns ex-cons, drug trafficking, and murder. A trite story, ridiculous dubbing, and boring martial arts.

STREET OF SHAME
1956, Japan ★★★
Machiko Kyo, Michiyo Kogure, Ayako Wakao, Aiko Mimasu, Yasuko Kawakami, Eitaro Shindo. Directed by Kenji Mizoguchi. 88 min.

The last film by the great Japanese director Kenji Mizoguchi (*Life of Oharu, Ugetsu, Sansho the Bailiff*) is one of the few that's available on videocassette. Here he dramatizes the lives of prostitutes in the Yoshiwara district, about to be put out of work by a new government decree. The realism of the performances and direction and the sympathetic portrayal of embattled women were Mizoguchi's signatures; this film is emblematic of his talent for beautiful composition and graceful, naturalistic style.

STREET PEOPLE
1976, USA/Italy, R ★½
Roger Moore, Stacy Keach, Ivo Garrani, Fausto Tozzi, Ettore Manni. Directed by Maurizio Lucidi, William Garroni. 92 min.

Roger Moore was presumably trying to break his James Bond typecasting when he accepted his role here as Ulysses, a hit man in a Sicilian gang; unfortunately, the results are about equal to Wilt Chamberlain's trying to play a Munchkin. Moore is sent here by his godfather—er, uncle—to track down a million dollars' worth of heroin smuggled into the country in a crucifix. Stacy Keach, as Moore's driver and best friend, has the only good part and makes the most of it. The bulk of this consists of endless car chases. One wonders what in here required the use of six scriptwriters, including *Shaft*'s Ernest Tidyman and future schlock director Randal Kleiser.

STREET SCENE
1931, USA ★★★
Sylvia Sidney, William Collier, Jr., David Landau, Estelle Taylor, Beulah Bondi. Directed by King Vidor. 80 min.

This stark early talkie is based on Elmer Rice's Pulitzer Prize–winning play (which he adapted to the screen himself), which helped solidify King Vidor's reputation as a film pioneer and an innovative director. Vidor's imaginative camerawork captures the harsh environment of New York tenement life and gets across Rice's concern with social problems. The cast blends into this grim milieu without seeming like Hollywood stars going slumming. The story line deals with some second-generation youngsters trying to flee the stranglehold of the impoverished environs that trapped their parents.

STREETS OF FIRE
1984, USA, PG ★½
Michael Pare, Diane Lane, Rick Moranis, Willem Dafoe. Directed by Walter Hill. 93 min.

Director Walter Hill has done far better work than this neon myth in ultraviolent drag involving a teen idol, her lover/manager, an honorable gun-for-hire, and a gang of funky leather boys led by a fetishistic fashion plate with a satanic sneer. The action is set in a never-never landscape of the mind (equal parts fabulous fifties and *film noir*) whose color-washed streets are dotted with sharp haircuts, fishnet stockings, and cool cars. A rock-and-roll fable for the MTV generation; shallow schlock for anyone older.

STREETS OF GOLD
1986, USA, R ★★½
Klaus Maria Brandauer, Adrian Pasdar, Wesley Snipes, Angela Molina, Elya Baskin, Rainbow Harvest. Directed by Joe Roth. 95 min.

Director Joe Roth and star Klaus Maria Brandauer manage to inject this clichéd studio programmer with a little feeling. Brandauer plays a former Soviet boxing champ who has been denied the chance to fight because he's a Jew. He emigrates to Brooklyn and shepherds two amateur American fighters to victory over the Soviet boxing team. Every post-*Rocky* plot twist is preordained, but Brandauer plays his character's self-pity for sharp, bitter humor; he wears the rueful grin of a man who possesses a secret and isn't about to let on what it is. Roth creates a nice sense of community in the scenes of the Russians trying to stave off the loneliness of exile by basking in each other's company, and his refusal to pump up the melodrama with Reagan-era feel-good jingoism comes to seem like a form of decency.

STREETWALKIN'
1985, USA, R ★★★
Julie Newmar, Melissa Leo, Dale Midkiff, Leon Robinson, Antonio Fargas. Directed by Joan Freedman. 88 min.

A young runaway is picked up by a silky pimp as she sits weeping in the Port Authority bus terminal; soon she is walking the streets for him while trying to keep her younger brother in school and out of trouble. When her pimp savagely beats another girl, she tries to switch her allegiance, precipitating a night of bloody violence as he hunts her down with serious intent to kill. *Streetwalkin'* delivers solid sleazy action along with some surprisingly sharp characterizations, all backed up by unusually attractive photography and editing. Directed by Roger Corman protégée Joan Freedman and featuring Julie Newmar—*Batman*'s first Cat Woman—in some red-hot lingerie.

STREETWISE
1984 ★★½
Directed by Martin Bell. 92 min.

A flawed but powerful docu-melodrama, this is about Seattle runaways who eat out of dumpsters, pimp, and turn tricks to survive. The movie is enthralling when it offers privileged glimpses of the nitty-gritty. We're led from dramatic high point to dramatic high point (including a suicide that occurred while the film was being made), and the boredom and enervation of runaway life is passed over for its terror, its anguish, its laughter-through-tears. Unfortunately, in trying to arrive at a truth more dramatic than fiction, the filmmakers never satisfy our informational needs or our desire to see relationships develop over time; they end up mirroring the kids' melodramatic fantasy of the streets as a cheap, exciting cavalcade.

STRIKE FORCE
1975, USA (TV) ★½
Cliff Gorman, Donald Blakely, Richard Gere, Joe Spinell. Directed by Barry Shear. 78 min.

In this mediocre cop movie, a modern Three Musketeers (a federal agent, a state trooper, and a New York cop) join forces to stymie a drug ring. Maybe next time they can team up and nab some TV movie producers and prevent them from making any more pointless crime flicks. Look for Richard Gere in an early role, if you manage to stay awake.

STRIKE UP THE BAND
1940, USA ★★½
Mickey Rooney, Judy Garland, Paul Whiteman, June Preisser, Larry Nunn. Directed by Busby Berkeley. 120 min.

A fairish let's-put-on-a-show musical galvanized by Mickey Rooney and Judy Garland's sparkling teamwork, including one memorable heart-on-your-sleeve ballad, "Our Love Affair." June

Preisser lends her wide-eyed support to help get the show on the road, but it never really takes flight. As usual, Busby Berkeley puts all his energy into staging the numbers and fails to energize the sagging plot line about a high school band competing in a national competition. One wishes they had stopped putting Garland in the untenable position of playing a wallflower forever waiting for Rooney to come to his senses. Worth seeing only for the stars being put through their paces.

STRIPES ☆☆☆
1981, USA, R
Bill Murray, Harold Ramis, Warren Oates, P. J. Soles, Sean Young, John Candy, John Larroquette. Directed by Ivan Reitman. 105 min.

Funnier than *Ghostbusters*. Bill Murray had his best showcase yet in this anarchic military fare about an unemployed bum who joins the Army. The basic-training set pieces are among the most hilarious Army-comedy sequences in memory. Murray takes the hang-loose irreverence of *M*A*S*H* and updates it to the video-game era, and he's ably supported by John Candy and P. J. Soles. A tacked-on rescue mission at the end waters down the comic sparkle.

THE STRIPPER ☆☆
1963, USA
Joanne Woodward, Richard Beymer, Claire Trevor, Carol Lynley, Robert Webber, Louis Nye, Gypsy Rose Lee, Michael J. Pollard. Directed by Franklin J. Schaffner. 95 min.

Joanne Woodward doesn't quite triumph over miscasting as a down-and-out showgirl who turns to stripping at the behest of her conniving manager, but her performance is the only praiseworthy aspect of this contrived, cliché melodrama, based on William Inge's flop play *A Loss of Roses*. The rest of the casting of Franklin Schaffner's first film ranges from seasoned pros (such as Claire Trevor) to inept youth (Richard Beymer) to curiosities (Gypsy Rose Lee)—but none of them can overcome Meade Roberts's screenplay, still tinged with Inge at his imitation–Tennessee Williams worst.

STRIPPER ☆☆☆
1986, USA, R
Janette Boyd, Kimberley Holcomb, Sara Costa, Loree Menton, Lisa Suarez. Directed by Jerome Gary. 90 min.

A riveting semidocumentary of women who bare all on stage, here baring their *souls* on camera for us. We follow them en route to the first annual Strip Tease Convention in Las Vegas. This revealing film compels our attention as the female exhibitionists ramble on about their private lives, their ambitions, and their philosophies. The film's remarkable achievement is that it makes us want to see each of these bump-and-grind performers win the pot of gold they're all competing for. Without being unduly exploitative, the film functions as a sort of *Chorus Line* in G-strings. All of the true-life stories of these strippers are affecting, particularly Janette Boyd's description of her life as both a working mother and an aging Las Vegas showgirl. A bit too selective in avoiding the seamier side of this particular form of show biz, but superbly edited and scored.

STROKER ACE ☆½
1983, USA, PG
Burt Reynolds, Loni Anderson, Ned Beatty, Parker Stevenson, Jim Nabors, Frank O. Hill, Bubba Smith, John Byner. Directed by Hal Needham. 96 min.

Burt Reynolds plays a champion stock-car racer in this good-ol'-boy flick. He's trying to get out of a contract with a sleazy fried-chicken king (Ned Beatty, in the film's only good performance), and he's trying to get into the favors of Loni Anderson. Jim Nabors does his Gomer Pyle shtick; however, this movie isn't quite as good as that TV series.

STROMBOLI ☆☆☆☆
1950, Italy
Ingrid Bergman, Mario Vitale, Renzo Cesana, Mario Sponzo. Directed by Roberto Rossellini. 81 min.

Roberto Rossellini's first film with Ingrid Bergman has been reviled as a simplistic bore and hailed as a masterpiece. To us, it seems a bit undramatic, but its power and beauty are undeniable. Bergman plays a Lithuanian refugee who, at the end of World War II, marries an Italian peasant she does not love in order to get out of an internment camp. Unfortunately, he lives on the isolated, terribly impoverished volcanic island of Stromboli, and the movie becomes a masterfully composed meditation on the stormy relationship between the woman and the land. Bergman has never been lovelier or more affecting.

THE STRONGEST MAN IN THE WORLD ☆½
1975, USA, PG
Kurt Russell, Joe Flynn, Eve Arden, Cesar Romero, Phil Silvers, Dick Van Patten, Harold Gould. Directed by Vincent McEveety. 92 min.

A breakfast cereal gives college student Dexter (Kurt Russell) awesome physical powers in this weakly plotted, slapdash comedy from the Disney studios, a virtual continuation of the gimmicky story lines of *The Computer Wore Tennis Shoes* and *Now You See Him, Now You Don't*. Joe Flynn and Cesar Romero return as, respectively, the perennially befuddled dean and the wealthy baddie, and Russell, who looks very tired of his role, embodies Walt's concept of the all-American boy for the last time (he was twenty-four). Slow going, even for kids.

STUCKEY'S LAST STAND ☆
1980, USA, PG
Whit Reichert, Ray Anzalone, Will Shaw, Tom Murray, Richard Cosentino. Directed by Lawrence G. Goldfarb. 92 min.

A bunch of counselors at a summer camp for rich nine-year-olds horse around a lot in their spare time. No, a maniac in a hockey mask doesn't come along and wipe them all out. No, they don't make out in a lot of soft-core sex scenes. No, they don't even visit a Stuckey's restaurant, which certainly would have livened up this dud some. Written, produced, and directed by one Lawrence G. Goldfarb, who got the money from his father; let's hope that used up his allowance for the rest of his life, so that Dad won't be bankrolling any other pointless losers like this.

STUDENT BODIES ☆☆
1981, USA, R
Kristen Riter, Matthew Goldsby, Richard Brando, Joe Flood, Joe Talarowski, Mimi Weddell. Directed by Mickey Rose. 86 min.

High school students are being killed just as they're about to have sex, and it looks like one of the teachers may be the culprit. Mickey Rose, who worked with Woody Allen on *Take the Money and Run* and *Bananas*, goes all out with good jokes and bad, but his swipes at the horror genre aren't quite up to the standards of *Airplane!*, let alone Allen. Still, there are laughs in the movie, and if you are in a silly enough mood, and if there's nothing better in sight . . .

THE STUDENT TEACHERS ☆☆½
1973, USA, R
Susan Damante, Bob Harris, Brooke Mills, John Cramer, Dick Miller, Robert Phillips, Don Steele, Charles Dierkop. Directed by Jonathan Kaplan. 79 min.

Sex, drugs, rock 'n' roll, and an unconventional education are in the course at Valley High, where student teachers change the curriculum as often as they change into and out of their clothes. This film has all the flights of fantasy that only a Roger Corman project can show, including a drug gang–Western showdown. A true Corman classic with continuous convoluted action, comedy, and an obscure social statement. Jonathan Kaplan worked the turf for the even more anarchic *Rock 'n' Roll High School*.

STUDENT UNION ☆☆
1974, USA, R
Robert Reiser, Laurie Walters, Richard Doran, Victoria Thompson, Bill Dana, Tito Vandis, Marty Allen, Emmaline Henry. Directed by Steven H. Stern. 105 min.

A sequel to *The Harrad Experiment*, this is still fitfully entertaining but, like its predecessor, awfully dated. The students at a college that stresses communal living and open sexuality (not to be confused with promiscuousness) return home for summer vacation, ready to apply what they've learned to their home environments. Bland and inoffensive, despite the subject matter.

A STUDY IN TERROR ☆☆½
1965, Great Britain
John Neville, Donald Houston, John Fraser, Georgia Brown, Anthony Quayle, Barbara Windsor, Robert Morley, Cecil Parker, Frank Finlay, Kay Walsh. Directed by James Hill. 94 min.

John Neville is Sherlock Holmes and Donald Houston is Watson in James Hill's okay thriller about the famous sleuth's meeting with Jack the Ripper.

STUNTS ☆☆☆
1977, USA, PG
Robert Forster, Fiona Lewis, Joanna Cassidy, Bruce Glover, Ray Sharkey. Directed by Mark L. Lester. 90 min.

Exploitation director Mark Lester surprisingly comes a cropper with this Howard Hawksian action picture. The story, about a maniac killing members of a movie stunt team who are making a film in San Luis Obispo, California, is mediocre in itself, though there is sufficient action to keep things moving at a reasonable pace. What lifts this up is a genuine feel of community generated in the depiction of the stunt players and their relations with each other and with "outsiders." Recommended. (a.k.a.: *Who Is Killing the Stuntmen?*)

SUBMISSION ☆½
1975, Italy, R
Franco Nero, Lisa Gastoni, Raymond Pellegrin, Andrea Ferreol, Claudia Marsani. Directed by Salvatore Samperi. 107 min.

Like *The Night Porter*, this Italian feature about sexual obsession promises more than it delivers and will only bore thrill seekers. A female pharmacist, long neglected by her husband, is taken advantage of by a cretin who works at her store, and soon finds herself no longer in control of her desires. Humorless and melodramatic, with fairly tame nudity. Dubbed in English.

SUBTERFUGE ☆☆
1969, Great Britain
Gene Barry, Joan Collins, Richard Todd, Tom Adams, Michael Rennie, Marius Goring, Suzanna Leigh. Directed by Peter Graham Scott. 89 min.

Here's what Joan Collins did before she matured into a sex symbol for yuppies with an Oedipal fix. Fans who are renting this only for her presence will be pleased to note that, given the comparative unimportance of her character, she gets an inordinate amount of screen time. She plays the wife of one of three British agents suspected of dealing with the Russians on the side. The main plot concerns Gene Barry, an American CIA agent who is coerced into helping weed out the double agent.

SUBURBIA ☆☆☆
1984, USA, R
Chris Pederson, Bill Coyne, Jennifer Clay, Timothy Eric O'Brien, Andrew Pece, Don Allen. Directed by Penelope Spheeris. 99 min.

In this melodramatic youth-in-rebellion picture with a gritty, documentary look, alienated youngsters camp out in abandoned tract houses—their sweet, gentle natures belied by their vicious punk mannerisms—and eventually come into bloody conflict with unemployed auto workers. Polemical but laid back, from the director of the punk documentary *The Decline and Fall of Western Civilization*. (a.k.a.: *The Wild Side*)

SUBWAY ☆☆½
1985, France, R
Isabelle Adjani, Christopher Lambert, Richard Bohringer, Michel Galabru, Jean-Hugues Anglade, Jean Bouise, Jean Reno, Jean-Pierre Bacri, Pierre-Ange Le Pogam. Directed by Luc Besson. 108 min.

Luc Besson's visual confection is a hip, bouncy, likably ridiculous antidote to the dullness of most contemporary French filmmaking. The plot has something to do with papers stolen by a tuxedoed punk (Christopher Lambert) during a party given by the elegant Isabelle Adjani. Some goons who work for her husband have been told to retrieve the papers, so Lambert takes refuge in the labyrinthine tunnels of the Paris Métro. All this is little more than an excuse for Besson to show us the underworld and its endless possibilities for freedom and disguise. His characters are defined by style and gesture, and his kinetic images undercut the banality of visual chic.

SUDDENLY ☆☆☆
1954, USA
Frank Sinatra, Sterling Hayden, Nancy Gates, James Gleason, Kim Charney. Directed by Lewis Allen. 77 min.

At this point in his career, a real change of pace for Frankie Boy. Playing a character with ice water in his veins, instead of his usual buddy-boy sailor, Sinatra proved his *From Here to Eternity* triumph was no flash in the pan. He plays part of a trio of hired hit men who pull into town to fulfill a death contract on the U.S. president. It will keep you on the edge of your seat, but, as with *Day of the Jackal*, one doesn't sympathize with the murderous protagonists or ever seriously think they might succeed, so the film remains a cold-blooded, effective exercise in suspense technique.

SUDDEN TERROR ☆☆½
1970, Great Britain
Mark Lester, Lionel Jeffries, Susan George, Jeremy Kemp. Directed by John Hough. 95 min.

Another version of that splendid B movie *The Window*, and this outing does that sturdy potboiler no disservice. A lad who's fond of stretching the truth has credibility problems when he's in a jam and his family won't believe he isn't just spinning tales. When he witnesses the assassination of an African president, his own life is in danger. The direction is too busy and the plot gets lost in a few too many embellishments, but the cast is self-assured and capable enough to pull this suspense thriller over the rough spots.

SUGARBABY ☆☆½
1985, West Germany, R
Marianne Sagebrecht, Eisi Gulp, Toni Berger, Manuela Denz, Will Spindler, Paul Wurges Combo. Directed by Percy Adlon. 86 min.

Percy Adlon's comedy uses Day-Glo colors and a very straight face to tell the story of a plump mortician's assistant with two consuming passions—one for sweets and the other for a scrawny, guileless young train conductor whom she discovers, pursues with a vengeance, and finally manages to seduce with good food and great sex. Adlon makes the romance between the two believable, and Johanna Neer's cinematography, lit in purple, pink and bile-green, gives *Sugarbaby* the look and atmosphere of an industrial fairy tale. A cloud of Teutonic glumness prevents this flight of fancy from taking off; it's a tasty snack, but you may be hungry an hour later.

SUGAR CANE ALLEY ☆☆☆
1983, Martinique, PG
Darling Legitimus, Garry Cadenat, Douta Seck. Directed by Euzhan Palcy. 106 min.

You might expect a film about black agricultural wage slaves in 1930s Martinique to be a bleak one, but by focusing on the education of a gifted young boy named Jose (Garry Cadenat), who is saved from a life in the cane fields by his stern, elderly grandmother, director Euzhan Palcy captures both the humiliation of life under the overseer's whip and the joys that sustain a resilient, put-upon people. The result shines like the warm summer days of childhood.

SULLIVAN'S TRAVELS ☆☆☆☆
1941, USA
Joel McCrea, Veronica Lake, Robert Warwick, William Demarest, Franklin Pangborn, Porter Hall, Alan Bridge, Robert Greig, Eric Blore, Arthur Hoyt. Directed by Preston Sturges. 90 min.

Most talented directors eventually get around to making a movie about moviemaking; however, it's a rare treat when the film is as funny and unself-conscious as *Sullivan's Travels*. A Hollywood director finds his life shallow and his art unfulfilling, so he hits the road to do research for his new project, an adaptation of the hefty tome, *O Brother Where Art Thou?* After starting off in a luxurious motor coach supplied by the studio, Sullivan (Joel McCrea) escapes his yes-men and sets off on his own. The rest of the film is taken up with a succession of comic and, occasionally, painful episodes in which the neophyte hobo gets taken in by sex-starved sisters, is saved from hunger by the down-at-the-heels starlet who becomes his traveling companion, hops railroad cars, eats in soup kitchens, and sleeps in flophouses. His moment of crisis comes when he is unjustly sent up to a prison work farm; there, during an evening's entertainment that consists of a broken-down Mickey Mouse cartoon, the director discovers the shared communion of comedy and its healing balm. Chastened, he returns to Hollywood. Preston Sturges keeps everything in the plot going at a breakneck pace, breezily blowing through scenes, confident in the expert McCrea and the sultry Veronica Lake, and buoyed by his regular gang of crackerjack supporters. A perfect tonic for mild indigestion caused by consumption of too many socially conscious melodramas.

SUMMER ☆☆☆½
1986, France, R
Marie Rivière, Lisa Heredia, Vincent Gauthier, Béatrice Romand, Carita. Directed by Eric Rohmer. 98 min.

The fifth in Eric Rohmer's series of "Comedies and Proverbs" is a slow, thoughtful mood piece about a self-pitying young woman who can't decide where or with whom to spend her summer vacation. Delphine (Marie Rivière) is the type of person whose high standards doom her to solitude; she's grown allergic to the chemistry of interpersonal contact. She journeys to Cherbourg to stay with a friend's family, but once there, cranky as ever, she soon up and leaves. The mood of the film is aesthetic melancholy, with rocky beaches and overcast skies. Marie, who in another director's hands might have been too much to take, becomes a test for the limits of Rohmer's empathy, and Rivière manages to alert you to her inner network of hope and frustration. Rohmer burrows into lonely corners of our own lives, and by patiently waiting for Marie to come out of her funk, he rewards us at the end with the vision of a soul reborn.

SUMMER CAMP ☆
1979, USA, R
Michael Abrams, Jake Barnes, Bud Bogart, Louise Carmona, Verkina Flower, Brenda Fogarty, Barbara Gold, Dustin Pacino, Jr. Directed by Chuck Vincent. 85 min.

Ever have one of those horrible dreams where for some unknown reason you're forced to repeat some horrible childhood experience, like the eighth grade—at your present age? Well, here's a movie about people who are invited back to the summer camp they attended as children for a fun-filled weekend. It's all part of a plan to raise some cash for the failing camp in this stupid drive-in comedy from former hard-core sex director Chuck Vincent. Watch this and you can have a new bad dream: that you're forced to rewatch *Summer Camp* over and over again. (By the way, we presume that the cast members who call themselves "Bud Bogart" and "Dustin Pacino, Jr." are kidding; they probably knew they'd never have to worry about agents trying to look them up for further work.)

SUMMER FANTASY ☆☆
1984, USA (TV)
Julianne Phillips, Ted Shackelford, Michael Gross, Dorothy Lyman, Paul Keenan, Danielle von Zerneck, John Wesley Shipp. Directed by Noel Nosseck. 97 min.

Although nothing special, this is not quite as much of a beach-party-bimboes film as it might first seem. The slight story concerns a seventeen-year-old girl (Julianne Phillips) who becomes the first female lifeguard at her local beach; during the summer, she turns into Her Own Woman, fighting with her family and taking the plunge with a young divorced dad (but not until she's eighteen, of course). Familiar TV faces make this easy to watch, and trivia buffs will want to note the presence of Phillips, a.k.a. Mrs. Bruce Springsteen, in the leading role.

SUMMER LOVERS ½☆
1982, USA, R
Peter Gallagher, Daryl Hannah, Valerie Quennessen, Barbara Rush, Carole Cook, Hans Van Tongeren, Lydia Lenos, Vladimiros Kiriakos, Carlos Rodriguez Ramos, Henri Behar, Rika Dialina. Directed by Randal Kleiser. 98 min.

Director Randal Kleiser (*The Blue Lagoon*) tries to give the youth of America what they've always yearned for: a pornography to call their own. Set in the Greek isles, this incredibly vapid story of a teenage ménage à trois is like a teeny-bopper's vision of the peaceable kingdom. Pretty young bodies loll topless on the beach and everything is sunshine and indolence. Peter Gallagher, Daryl Hannah, and Valerie Quennessen make a cheery threesome, but cheery is all they are; in the world according to Kleiser, there's no conflict that can't be resolved within three minutes.

SUMMER MADNESS

See *Summertime*

SUMMER MAGIC ☆☆½
1963, USA
Hayley Mills, Dorothy McGuire, Burl Ives, Deborah Walley, Eddie Hodges, Una Merkle. Directed by James Neilson. 100 min.

This sporadically magical Disney film serves to highlight Hayley Mills's girlish appeal, as a struggling family pulls together to make ends meet. Widow Dorothy McGuire fusses endearingly over her brood, who all seem to have the usual puppy loves and other less than earth-shattering dilemmas with which to cope. Insubstantial, but light and tasty in a summery sort of way.

SUMMER OF FEAR ☆☆☆
1978, USA (TV)
Linda Blair, Lee Purcell, Jeremy Slate, Ralph Bellamy, Carol Lawrence, Jeff East. Directed by Wes Craven. 100 min.

Linda Blair's not possessed this time, but she does have a witch as a guest. In this surprisingly effective TV shocker, an evil sorceress poses as a distant relative and sows seeds of dissension within a family, thus enabling her to dominate and then destroy the tight-knit suburban clan. Lee Purcell is both beautiful and frightening as the duplicitous spellbinder who has a habit of breaking up happy homes. And, for once, Blair's awkwardness as an actress works in her favor and draws the audience over to her side. She's completely believable as an ordinary outgoing teen who's shunned by her mother, appalled by witnessing her father's lewd interest in their visitor, and infuriated when she learns that her alleged relative is making funeral plans for her. A lean, nerve-racking thriller. (a.k.a.: *Stranger in Our House*)

SUMMER OF MY GERMAN SOLDIER ☆☆☆
1978, USA (TV)
Kristy McNichol, Bruce Davison, Barbara Barrie, Esther Rolle, Michael Constantine. Directed by Michael Tuchner. 100 min.

This expert TV film, based on a novel by Bette Greene, sketches an unforgettable portrait of forbidden love in a southern town during World War II. The nostalgia-laced romance involves the doomed affair between a lonely Jewish schoolgirl and a Nazi prisoner of war. Although the film's a bit on the sentimental side, the central relationship never seems contrived or melodramatic and the performances transform the material into something memorable.

SUMMER OF SECRETS ☆☆
1976, Australia
Arthur Dignam, Rufus Collins, Nell Campbell, Andrew Sharp, Kate Fitzpatrick. Directed by Jim Sharman. 100 min.

This is a strange little film, though in ways quite different from its director's previous success, *The Rocky Horror Picture Show*. Though both films were based on plays staged by Jim Sharman, this one makes little attempt to hide its origins; it is overly talky and quite set-bound. Also like *RHPS*, this has a young couple stranded, here on a remote island, with a doctor trying to restore life to a dead body, but instead of humor and affectionate genre parody, this wallows in overt style and serious absurdities, all to no discernible end.

SUMMER SOLSTICE ☆☆☆
1981, USA (TV)
Henry Fonda, Myrna Loy, Stephen Collins, Lindsay Crouse. Directed by Ralph Rosenblum. 156 min.

On Golden Pond again. Henry Fonda and Myrna Loy play lovers who reminisce about the highs and lows of their fifty years of married life while their early years are shown in flashbacks performed by Stephen Collins and Lindsay Crouse. This is a two-handkerchief movie. You'll weep because the film is so good that you really care that Loy has died, really feel Fonda's pain as he holds her dead in his arms. But if you think about it, there is another reason for crying: when actors of this caliber do die, who is there to take their places?

SUMMERTIME ☆☆½
1955, USA
Katharine Hepburn, Rossano Brazzi, Isa Miranda, Darren McGavin, Mari Aldon. Directed by David Lean. 99 min.

This is an inexplicably overrated film from David Lean. In this adaptation of Arthur Laurents's play *The Time of the Cuckoo*, Lean pushes Katharine Hepburn's aging spinster number to its limits. Against the background of Venice, Hepburn plays an American tourist who falls for a native (Rossano Brazzi) and into a canal (a stunt that cost Hepburn some permanent vision impairment). The whole film is about how Hepburn eventually gets it on with the suave Italian (in a laughable climax), so, except for the pretty scenery, there's little to recommend. (a.k.a.: *Summer Madness*)

SUMMER WISHES, WINTER DREAMS ☆☆☆
1973, USA
Joanne Woodward, Martin Balsam, Sylvia Sidney, Dori Brenner. Directed by Gilbert Cates. 93 min.

This is a real Joanne Woodward vehicle, a generally compelling and trenchant film written by Stewart Stern. Soap opera fans will be enthralled by Joanne's menopausal dilemmas. Woodward and Martin Balsam take a trip to try to rediscover their former, warmer feelings for each other, meanwhile hoping to sort out their failures with their children. There are some poignant scenes, with good acting. In the *echt* Sylvia Sidney role, Sylvia Sidney has a great death scene that generates some real emotion. Despite some reservations, Woodward and Sidney are both fine and should have won the Oscars that went that year to Glenda Jackson and Tatum O'Neal.

SUMMER WITH MONIKA
See *Monika*

SUNA NO ONNA
See *Woman in the Dunes* (1964)

SUNBURN ☆
1979, USA, PG
Farrah Fawcett, Charles Grodin, Art Carney, Joan Collins, William Daniels, John Hillerman, Eleanor Parker, Keenan Wynn, Alejandro Rey. Directed by Richard C. Sarafian. 99 min.

Farrah Fawcett takes another stab at big-time feature-film success. The movie is a comedy-thriller packed with murders, suicides, blackmail attempts, and wild car chases, material that director Richard Sarafian (*Vanishing Point*) has executed with some flair in the past. What kind of professional would hire a model as an investigator on a tough case?

SUNDAY, BLOODY SUNDAY ☆☆☆½
1971, Great Britain, R
Peter Finch, Glenda Jackson, Murray Head, Peggy Ashcroft, Maurice Denham. Directed by John Schlesinger. 110 min.

This powerful, literate drama, written by then–*New Yorker* film critic Penelope Gilliatt, explores a love triangle between a bisexual artist (Murray Head), his doctor-lover (Peter Finch), and his sometimes-mistress (Glenda Jackson). At the time, it was hailed for presenting the first noncaricatured, nonbathetic depiction of a homosexual, and Finch's superbly restrained work still stands as the finest of his career; many felt that his Oscar for *Network* was a belated accolade for this film. Jackson, though perhaps somewhat more strident than warranted, remains his equal in thoughtful nuance. The intervening years have made the film more problematic, especially regarding Murray Head's opaque characterization of the mutual lover and the almost too subdued, uneventful nature of the story. However, it remains a notable poignant essay about and for intelligent adults, a commodity one shouldn't undervalue.

A SUNDAY IN THE COUNTRY ☆☆½
1984, France, G
Louis Ducreux, Sabine Azema, Michel Aumont, Geneviève Mnich, Monique Chaumette, Claude Winter, Thomas Duval, Quentin Ogier, Katia Wostrikoff, Valentine Suard, Erika Faivre, Marc Perrone, Pascale Vignal, Jacques Poitrenaud. Directed by Bertrand Tavernier. 94 min.

Set on a single day in pre-1914 France, Bertrand Tavernier's elegiac character study centers on a serene, aging painter whose son has arrived with his family for their weekly Sunday visit. Louis Ducreux, the seventy-three-year-old French theater actor who plays the old artist, has a face that is the image of elderly kindliness.

As he begins looking back on his life's work, wondering how he could have passed through the Impressionist revolution without being touched by its most vital voices, there are moments of poignancy and fascination. Unfortunately, Tavernier fills out the rest of his story with conventional turn-of-the-century types (the stuffy bourgeois, the feminist free spirit). Despite Ducreux's cuddly presence (and despite the gorgeous, painterly photography), the movie is quaint and tedious.

SUNDAYS AND CYBÈLE ☆☆½
1962, France
Hardy Kruger, Nicole Courcel, Patricia Gozzi, Daniel Ivernel. Directed by Serge Bourguignon. 110 min.

This glossy pseudo-art film was released during a period of extraordinary ferment in European cinema and was such a box-office success here that it won an Oscar for Best Foreign Film. The story of a shell-shocked deserter (Hardy Kruger) who rediscovers human contact through his platonic relationship with a little girl (Patricia Gozzi), it's full of pregnant pauses, dewy walks by the water, and so forth, but it doesn't end up doing much with its characters beyond parading them "sensitively" across the screen.

SUNDAY TOO FAR AWAY ☆☆☆
1975, Australia
Jack Thompson, Phyllis Ophel, Reg Lyle, John Charman, Gregory Apps, Sean Scully. Directed by Ken Hannam. 90 min.

One of the first Australian features to have gained international attention in the last decade, this is a simple tale that is of interest mostly for the Aussie setting: imagine a Howard Hawks Western about a cattle ranch, transport it Down Under, and you end up with this. The focus of interest is Foley (Jack Thompson, of *Breaker Morant*), an itinerant sheep worker who wants to quit for more steady employment. A strike in protest against falling wages for shearers boosts his involvement. Like Hawks, director Hannam presents a male community where tensions incurred by backbreaking work are alleviated with assorted rivalries and brawls, all of which solidify rather than undermine the necessary sense of community.

SUNDOWN ☆☆
1941, USA
Gene Tierney, Bruce Cabot, Harry Carey, Joseph Calleia, Dorothy Dandridge. Directed by Henry Hathaway. 90 min.

This is a tough-minded wartime melodrama filtered through the usual patriotic propaganda. Unfortunately, it falls between two stools—that of a gung-ho war adventure and that of an exotic desert romance—and it doesn't emerge as a success in either category. Somehow the temperature under the blazing African sun never heats up sufficiently, though Gene Tierney is as luscious as ever as an agent for the British troops. Here even the Nazi swine seem to be about to snooze, as if they'd been in this story line once too often.

SUNFLOWER ☆☆
1970, Italy
Sophia Loren, Marcello Mastroianni, Ludmilla Savelyeva. Directed by Vittorio De Sica. 101 min.

Definitely not one of master director Vittorio De Sica's better films, this is a sticky soap opera foreshadowing those scenes of Diane Keaton scouring Russia for Warren Beatty in *Reds*. Even though her soldier-boy husband was lost on the Russian front fifteen years ago, plucky Sophia Loren hasn't given up hope. Her lamented husband has a shorter memory; he's now married to a Russian girl and Sophia's got to take steppes to get him back. Loren and Marcello Mastroianni are so wonderful together that they get away with a lot, but this sunflower is in drastic need of replanting in more fertile soil.

SUNSET SERENADE ☆☆
1942, USA
Roy Rogers, George "Gabby" Hayes, Bob Nolan and the Sons of the Pioneers, Helen Parrish, Onslow Stevens, Joan Woodbury, Frank M. Thomas, Roy Bancroft, Jack Kirk. Directed by Joseph Kane. 58 min.

For those who're really curious, or just really addicted, this is among the better Roy Rogers Westerns prior to his partnering with Dale Evans. By luck, Helen Parrish's awkwardness is partly concealed in her role of the city girl victimized by prairie toughs. Roy and the Sons of tle Pioneers pass by to rescue her and still have time to croon six cowboy ballads before the hour's past. The intended laughs are the property of Gabby Hayes.

SUPERDAD ☆
1974, USA, G
Bob Crane, Kurt Russell, Barbara Rush, Joe Flynn, Kathleen Cody. Directed by Vincent McEveety. 96 min.

Nonsense that wastes the talents of an attractive cast. The asinine premise concerns a competition between a girl's overprotective dad and her boyfriend, who has to prove himself to the papa in a sort of athletic trial by fire. In other words, a familial problem is blown up to Olympic Game proportions. Luckily, there were no follow-ups involving housewives forced to settle their disputes with daughters-in-law with three rounds of mud wrestling. Tiresome and trivial.

SUPER FUZZ ☆
1981, USA/Italy, PG
Terence Hill, Ernest Borgnine, Joanne Dru, Marc Lawrence, Julie Gordon. Directed by Sergio Corbucci. 94 min.

Miami cop Terence Hill is exposed to radiation and, in best 1950s tradition, develops superpowers. (His dubbing is so atrocious that you half expect him to grow green scales, breathe fire, and topple Tokyo, too.) This stupid slapstick comedy will insult the intelligence of even the most brain-damaged couch potato. At least Ernest Borgnine has the presence of mind to look embarrassed, though it doesn't excuse his being here.

SUPERGIRL ☆
1984, USA, PG
Faye Dunaway, Helen Slater, Peter O'Toole, Mia Farrow, Brenda Vaccaro, Peter Cook, Simon Ward, Marc McClure, Hart Bochner, Maureen Teefy, David Healy. Directed by Jeannot Szwarc. 105 min.

Newcomer Helen Slater has an ungainly, coltish allure, but as Supergirl she doesn't get a chance to *do* anything besides making goo-goo eyes at her spellbound mortal love. The filmmakers have come up with material that plays less like a Superman movie (or a DC comic) than a misguided Disney send-up. David Odell's charmless screenplay boils down to a series of misfiring camp couplets, and director Jeannot Szwarc applies TV rules of dramatic construction: instead of telling a story, he's content to drag us from one tacky special effect to the next. Faye Dunaway plays the evil witch Serena; decked out in an array of butterfly sunglasses, she seems bent on becoming our contemporary queen of kitsch.

SUPERMAN ☆☆☆
1978, USA, PG
Christopher Reeve, Marlon Brando, Gene Hackman, Margot Kidder, Ned Beatty, Jackie Cooper, Glenn Ford, Phyllis Thaxter, Trevor Howard, Valerie Perrine, Terence Stamp, Susannah York, Jack O'Halloran, Jeff East, Sarah Douglas. Directed by Richard Donner. 142 min.

The Man of Steel flew from the pages of DC Comics to the big screen; audiences cheered, and you will too. This spectacular fantasy-adventure may not be as much fun as its first sequel, but it has just about everything a live-action comic strip needs: dazzling special effects, a clear-cut set of villains, a romantic subplot, and an abundance of good humor. Christopher Reeve is an ideal Superman, stiff and wooden as Clark Kent but with just enough self-mockery to let you know he's kidding, and Margot Kidder breathes more husky-voiced life into Lois Lane than thirty years of comic books ever did. The only slow going is in the film's first third, which presents Superman's origins in the kind of scrupulous piety and detail usually accorded to Bible stories; once Superman leaves Ma and Pa Kent for the bright lights and big crimes of Metropolis, he and the film both soar. With Jackie Cooper as Perry White, Gene Hackman as Lex Luthor, and a white-wigged, rather prissy Marlon Brando as Superman's real dad, Jor-El. Followed by three sequels and the *Supergirl* spin-off.

SUPERMAN III ☆☆½
1983, USA, PG
Christopher Reeve, Richard Pryor, Robert Vaughn, Annette O'Toole, Margot Kidder, Annie Ross, Pamela Stephenson, Marc McClure. Directed by Richard Lester. 134 min.

From its very title sequence, a slapstick urban rhapsody in red, white, and blue, the third Superman adventure transcends its comic-book genre. Director Richard Lester established a lilting, puckish tone, and when he sets Superman down in a tipsy technological Metropolis or follows Clark Kent back to his high school reunion in Kansas, the movie is marvelous. But one almost wishes Lester didn't have a story to tell. Our hero has to face Robert Vaughn as a slimy multinationalist and Richard Pryor as the computer wiz whom Vaughn has co-opted, and Pryor, once again, does his cowardly buffoon act. Still, while it's up there, the movie is an enchanting pop fantasy.

SUPERMAN II ☆☆☆
1980, USA, PG
Christopher Reeve, Gene Hackman, Margot Kidder, Terence Stamp, Sarah Douglas, Ned Beatty, Jackie Cooper, Jack O'Halloran, Valerie Perrine, Susannah York, Clifton James, E. G. Marshall, Marc McClure, Pepper Martin, Peter Whitman. Directed by Richard Lester. 127 min.

Directing the sequel to 1979's overblown blockbuster, director Richard Lester takes the Superman story back to its pulpy, comic-book roots, and the result is a spectacle with style—a movie that ends up drawing its ambience from the comics' very crudeness. This time, Christopher Reeve shows us Superman's delight in impersonating the nerdlike Clark Kent, and then, when Superman falls in love with Lois Lane (Margot Kidder), his pain at having to become him. The shift from comic glee to pathos is accomplished with such extraordinary assurance that a silly adventure movie takes on the dimension of myth. With Gene Hackman, in a witty turn, as Lex Luthor, and Terence Stamp, who leads up a trio of wonderfully nasty villains from Krypton.

THE SUPERNATURALS ½☆
1986, USA, R
Maxwell Caulfield, Nichelle Nichols, Talia Blasam, LeVar Burton, Bobby DiCicco, Bradford Bancroft. Directed by Armand Mastroianni. 80 min.

Some ghosts really hold a grudge—from the Civil War to the present is a long time to stay mad. Johnny Rebs slaughtered by Union soldiers haunt the campground of some contemporary soldiers out on bivouac. Isn't it convenient that the northern soldiers just happen to camp on the same spot where the "sons of Jefferson Davis" were slaughtered years before? This is *Friday the 13th* recast with recruits, or *Night of the Living Confederacy*. The film does, however, offer the best visualization of the lyrics to the song "Mame," which state "Tonight the South will rise again."

SUPERPOWER ☆☆
1980, Hong Kong
Billy Chong, Chaing Tao, Hau Chiu Sing, Liu An Li, William Liu Tan, Liu Hao-Nien. Directed by Lin Chan Wei. 89 min.

Kung fu student Hau Chiu Sing is sent home to see his dying father. He learns that, many years before, his father had been the head of the Manchu Imperial guard, and was beaten in a contest by five Chinese kung fu experts. Kang Sze Min vows to regain face and retrieve the family honor by taking revenge on Billy Chong, the son of one of the five experts. Not bad as far as these things go.

SUPPOSE THEY GAVE A WAR AND NOBODY CAME? ☆☆½
1970, USA
Tony Curtis, Brian Keith, Ernest Borgnine, Susanne Pleshette, Ivan Dixon. Directed by Hy Averback. 113 min.

In a comic vein, the film explores the touchy relationship between an Army base and the community surrounding it. Although uncertainties in tone mar the film (which switches awkwardly from comedy to drama), one is drawn into this tale of three veteran tank officers who fight their own small-scale war with some recalcitrant rednecks. A pungent comedy with occasional serious undercurrents.

THE SURE THING ☆☆☆
1985, USA, PG-13
John Cusack, Daphne Zuniga, Nicolette Sheridan, Anthony Edwards, Boyd Gaines, Viveca Lindfors. Directed by Rob Reiner. 94 min.

Rob Reiner's second directorial stint eschews the paralyzing hilarity of his remarkable debut, *This Is Spinal Tap*, for geniality and sweetness in a more familiar context, the coming-of-age film. Though the story he tells, that of two college freshmen finding true love on a rocky cross-country trip, is overly schematic, nice observations and fresh performances keep it rolling along. As Gib, the ironic, shtick-prone John Cusack seems to want to be David Letterman when he grows up, peppering his conversation with grating asides to an invisible audience. But he's affectingly puppyish once he becomes smitten with preppy Alison (nicely played by Daphne Zuniga). The film is at its best when it's at its nastiest; otherwise, you'll smile more often than you'll laugh.

SURFACING ☆½
1980, Canada, R
Kathleen Beller, Joseph Bottoms. Directed by Claude Jutra. 90 min.

Margaret Atwood's fine novel becomes a movie that fails completely as wilderness adventure, feminist awakening, and sexual suspense tale. Kathleen Beller and Joseph Bottoms are not nearly interesting enough as performers to make sense out of the muddled screenplay, which has two couples going into the North Woods of Canada in search of the heroine's missing father. Atwood's elliptical style doesn't easily translate to the screen, and it's not helped along by Claude Jutra's flaccid direction.

SURVIVAL RUN ☆½
1980, USA, R
Peter Graves, Ray Milland, Vincent Van Patten, Pedro Armindariz, Jr., Alan Conrad, Marianne Sauvage. Directed by Larry Spiegel. 90 min.

Some California surfer kids are out cruising in their van through the Arizona desert one weekend when the van breaks down. They encounter some slimy bad guys who think that the kids have discovered their nefarious plans and decide to eliminate them. Someone seems to have forgotten to tell the folk responsible for this yawner that you can make movies like this in one of two ways: you can make it scary, or you can throw in lots of sex, nudity, and/or violence and gore.

THE SURVIVORS ☆☆½
1983, USA, PG
Walter Matthau, Robin Williams, Jerry Reed, James Wainwright, Kristen Vigard, Annie McEnroe. Directed by Michael Ritchie. 102 min.

Director Michael Ritchie's usually keen eye for satire on things American fails him here even though it's let loose on what would seem to be a perfect subject: survivalists, those people who practice for Communist invasions or the end of the world by going off into the woods and living by their wits and a pocket knife. Instead of working with each other, the three leads each seem to be off doing their own thing—Walter Matthau uses his surly charm as an unemployed gas station attendant; Robin Williams relies on improvisational zaniness as a white-collar worker who freaks when he gets fired (by his boss's parrot), and joins a survivalist group; and unpredictable Jerry Reed as an unemployed hit man (even the Mob, it seems, suffers from the recession) out to protect his identity by rubbing out the other two. There are enough random, unconnected funny moments to make this amusing, but the whole thing adds up to very little.

SUSAN SLEPT HERE
1954, USA ☆☆½
Dick Powell, Debbie Reynolds, Glenda Farrell, Anne Francis, Alvy Moore. Directed by Frank Tashlin. 98 min.

In this briskly directed romantic comedy, a May-December romance develops when a Hollywood writer (Dick Powell) has to baby-sit for Debbie Reynolds during the holidays. It's one of those mildly blue 1950s comedies in which a lot is suggested but nothing much happens. Slight escapist fare with the stars trying hard (in Reynolds's case too hard) to sock the jokes across. Not the best work by director Frank Tashlin (*Rock-a-Bye, Baby*), but the film does have flashes of his zany brilliance.

SUSPICION
1941, USA ☆☆☆½
Joan Fontaine, Cary Grant, Cedric Hardwicke, Nigel Bruce, Dame May Whitty, Isabel Jeans, Heather Angel, Leo G. Carroll. Directed by Alfred Hitchcock. 99 min.

This intense psychological drama is among the most popular and, at one time, controversial of Alfred Hitchcock's American films. A quiet English girl (Joan Fontaine) falls in love with a charming good-for-nothing (Cary Grant) and begins to suspect he is a murderer. The film's climactic twist—an ending the studio chose despite the director's objections—provides an appropriate and intriguing resolution of the tale's disparate themes. This beautifully photographed work recalls the brooding, malevolent mood of Hitchcock's first American film, *Rebecca*, which he completed a year earlier. Grant's manner is at once tongue-in-cheek and sinister, and he imbues his role with deadly tension. Fontaine's exceptional performance won her an Oscar for Best Actress.

SUZANNE
1980, Canada ☆
Jennifer Dale, Winston Rekert, Gabriel Arcand, Ken Pogue, Gina Dick. Directed by Robin Spry. 114 min.

For every good Canadian film like *The Silent Partner* or . . . (give us a moment, we'll think of another one)—well, there are at least a dozen turkeys like this romantic melodrama that even regular readers of Harlequin romances would find hard to take. Set—to no good effect—against the background of French-English strife in Quebec, the film follows three decades in the life of a young girl, who grows up misunderstood by her parents to fall in love with a ne'er-do-well whose child she bears. Unbearably goopy.

SVENGALI
1983, USA (TV) ☆½
Peter O'Toole, Jodie Foster, Elizabeth Ashley, Larry Joshua, Pamela Blair, Barbara Bryne, Ronald Weyand. Directed by Anthony Harvey. 100 min.

Despite the seemingly excellent casting of its two lead roles, this TV retelling of the story of string-puller Svengali and his puppet-protégé Trilby falls disconcertingly flat; perhaps the Dereks or Meshulam Riklis and Pia Zadora would have livened it up. Instead, we have the tale updated and set in New York City, with Jodie Foster very badly used as a struggling pop singer and Peter O'Toole camping it up maniacally as the voice teacher obsessed with manipulating her career and life. The complete lack of chemistry between the two keeps the drama remote and juiceless.

SWAMP THING
1982, USA, PG ☆☆½
Louis Jourdan, Adrienne Barbeau, Ray Wise, David Hess, Nicholas Worth. Directed by Wes Craven. 91 min.

One of the few tongue-in-cheek horror movies that actually work. When a curious professor (Louis Jourdan) drinks some funky potion and accidentally catches fire, he jumps into a swamp and emerges with a case of skin algae that could keep the Porcelana company in business for years. Inside, though, he's still a sensitive creature with the soul of a poet—and Adrienne Barbeau is still willing to be his honey. There's plenty of outrageous dialogue, and director Wes Craven treats the swamp itself as a giant comic-book frame, making sure it has the proper look of deep-dish phoniness.

THE SWAP
1969, USA, R ½☆
Robert DeNiro, Jennifer Warren, Jered Mickey, Terrayne Crawford, Martin Kelley, Lisa Blount, Sybil Danning. Directed by John Shade, John C. Broderick. 87 min.

Early in his film career Robert DeNiro made a film called *Sam's Song*, in which he played a young filmmaker. Nobody saw it, and it went unnoticed until 1979 when it was rereleased in this form to capitalize on his stardom. But don't be fooled: only about twenty minutes of the DeNiro footage is used here. The bulk of this is a new feature about the DeNiro character's brother getting out of prison and tracking down his murderer. It's very badly done; the brother, Vito, is a walking compendium of Italian punk clichés without a trace of parody, and the actors who appeared in both films give noticeably poorer performances in the new footage. Not enough DeNiro here to make this worth your time, even for his fans. (a.k.a.: *Sam's Song*)

SWAP MEET
1979, USA, R ☆½
Ruth Cox, Debi Richter, Danny Goldman, Cheryl Rixon, Jonathan Gries. Directed by Brice Mack. 84 min.

Drive-in comedy loaded with the usual horny teenagers, greasy bad guys, and dumb suburbanites. Yes, there's a swap meet as well, but it's just an excuse for the never-ending stream of jokes about middle-class kids. The best that can be said for it is that, unlike most of its ilk, it's not particularly nasty toward its subjects; on the other hand, it isn't particularly funny, either.

SWEET COUNTRY
1987, Greece, R ½☆
Jane Alexander, John Cullum, Carole Laure, Franco Nero, Joanna Pettet, Randy Quaid, Irene Papas, Jean-Pierre Aumont, Pierre Vaneck. Directed by Michael Cacoyannis. 150 min.

Michael Cacoyannis's indictment of the 1973 coup in Chile and its aftermath means to sear your soul, to scald, to lacerate: It's torture, all right, but not quite in the way Cacoyannis intended. Rarely does a film of such sober intent go as hopelessly and hilariously awry as this one, in which an international cast plays the members of a haute-bourgeois family closing their eyes and minds to the coup. It's Cacoyannis's bizarre triumph to make Chile look like New Jersey and New York look like Athens, to write dialogue so garbled as to be untranscribable, to cast performers of four different nationalities as members of one family, to make Jane Alexander give her first utterly awful performance and, most memorably, to allow Randy Quaid to play a swaggering, brutal Chilean military policeman in a performance that should drive a stake through the heart of any comic actor who has ever longed to do a "serious" role. All concerned should be embarrassed.

THE SWEET CREEK COUNTY WAR
1979, USA, PG ☆½
Richard Egan, Albert Salmi, Nita Talbot, Slim Pickens, Robert J. Wilke, Joe Orton. Directed by J. Frank James. 99 min.

This may explain why the Western died. As you watch, you keep wondering why they bothered to make it. The story about a rancher trying to fight off an evil land baron is old and hoary, as are almost all the rest of the dialogue and situations; there are no "name" stars for box-office value; there is no exploitation material (sex, graphic violence). We presume that the director's name, as credited, is a pseudonym; we can hardly say that we blame him.

SWEET HOSTAGE ☆☆½
1975, USA (TV)
Linda Blair, Martin Sheen, Jeanne Cooper, Bert Remsen, Lee DeBroux. Directed by Lee Philips. 93 min.

This drama about a young kidnap victim (Linda Blair) who begins to fall in love with her cute, loony captor (Martin Sheen) could have been much worse; television restrictions probably saved it from going the exploitation route. Sheen, giving his last "troubled youth" performance, and Blair, giving her last good one, make an oddly believable couple, and just when you tire of hearing him recite Coleridge's "Kubla Khan," the inevitable climax intervenes to terminate their romance in the woods and moisten the eyes of all romantics. It's less compelling now than it was in the wake of the Patricia Hearst kidnapping/turnabout, but still worth a look. Based on Nathaniel Benchley's novel *Welcome to Xanadu*.

SWEET LIBERTY ☆☆
1986, USA, PG
Alan Alda, Lise Hilboldt, Lillian Gish, Michael Caine, Michelle Pfeiffer, Bob Hoskins, Saul Rubinek, Lois Chiles. Directed by Alan Alda. 107 min.

Alan Alda's send-up of the movie industry is full of stale potshots and halfhearted swipes at very familiar targets: the immature director, the two-faced leading lady, the hack writer, etc. But, this being an Alan Alda film, it's nice to *everything*, including its satirical targets. Alda plays a New England historian whose novel about the American Revolution is bought by Hollywood; when cast and crew invade his tiny town for a summer of filming, he learns some hard lessons about art, truth, and Tinseltown. There are deft, lively turns by luminous Michelle Pfeiffer and comical Bob Hoskins, but every time the movie picks up some nasty satirical energy, it's back to Alda—and the haranguing, smirking, lecturing, and smugness that made the last years of "M*A*S*H" so insufferable. *Sweet Liberty* is the kind of film *S.O.B.* would wipe the floor with.

THE SWEET LIFE

See *La Dolce Vita*

SWEET WILLIAM ☆☆☆
1980, Great Britain, R
Sam Waterston, Jenny Agutter, Anna Massey, Geraldine James, Tim Pigott-Smith, Daphne Oxenford, Arthur Lowe. Directed by Claude Whatham. 92 min.

This charming, low-key sex comedy is a winning find, well worth seeing. Sam Waterston, a good actor who until recently seldom got the parts he deserved, plays a rabidly romantic playwright who can control neither his philandering nor his lying—faults he gets away with through his seeming sincerity and genuine charm. Jenny Agutter, also an overlooked thespian, is his latest conquest, who refuses to accept his faults. Based on a novel by bestselling British author Beryl Bainbridge, the tone is adult and ironic, though never melodramatic. There is also a comparative lack of explicit sex and nudity.

SWEPT AWAY . . . (BY AN UNUSUAL DESTINY IN THE BLUE SEA OF AUGUST) ☆☆☆
1975, Italy, R
Mariangela Melato, Giancarlo Giannini. Directed by Lina Wertmüller. 116 min.

Lina Wertmüller fuses her two favorite themes—sex and politics—in this rich allegory about the tumultuous pairing of a beautiful Milanese bourgeoise (Mariangela Melato) and the swarthy Sicilian deckhand (Giancarlo Giannini) with whom she finds herself marooned. There's a mammoth amount of dialogue, some clever and provocative, some tiresome, and it's a close call as to whether the story's resolution is a put-on or a revolting piece of sexism.

SWIFT SHAOLIN BOXER

See *The Invincible*

THE SWIMMER ☆☆☆
1968, USA
Burt Lancaster, Janice Rule, Janet Landgard, Diana Muldaur, Kim Hunter. Directed by Frank Perry. 94 min.

This is an intelligent, explicitly literary but also compellingly cinematic adaptation of the John Cheever short story about a confused suburbanite's odyssey across town by way of his neighbors' swimming pools. Burt Lancaster, fit and trim in his fifties, gives a subtle, expert performance as the disturbed amnesiac disconnected from his own family, and though the film's fragile conceits disintegrate before the end, it offers much food for thought along the way. *Note:* The sequence with Janice Rule was directed by Sydney Pollack.

THE SWINGING CHEERLEADERS ☆½
1974, USA, R
Jo Johnston, Rainbeaux Smith, Colleen Camp, Rosanne Katon, Ron Hajek, Mae Mercer. Directed by Jack Hill. 94 min.

The title says it all in this mid-1970s drive-in staple. A journalism student infiltrates the cheerleading squad at her high school in order to write a story on female exploitation, but becomes converted in time to help foil the coach's attempt to throw the Big Game. There is the usual soft-core sex, though less of it than is usual in this kind of thing. Director Jack Hill, a Roger Corman alumnus, keeps things going smoothly, if not interestingly.

SWING SHIFT ☆☆½
1984, USA, PG
Goldie Hawn, Kurt Russell, Christine Lahti, Ed Harris, Belinda Carlisle, Roger Corman, Fred Ward, Sudie Bond, Holly Hunter, Patty Maloney. Directed by Jonathan Demme. 100 min.

Jonathan Demme's first film after the classic *Melvin and Howard* is an affectionate salute to "Rosie the Riveter," the gal who manned the factories during World War II. The movie overflows with period pleasures (swingtime songs on the soundtrack, sun-dappled locations), but the story is just a milky, homogenized wartime romance about a woman defense worker (Goldie Hawn) who has an affair with her male coworker (Kurt Russell) while her husband (Ed Harris) is away at war. Christine Lahti won a deserved Oscar nomination for her role as the tough-talking friend. Several of Hollywood's top writers worked, uncredited, on the script, and the director had his writing credit removed after a parting of ways with producer Hawn.

SWING TIME ☆☆☆☆
1936, USA
Fred Astaire, Ginger Rogers, Victor Moore, Helen Broderick, Eric Blore, Betty Furness. Directed by George Stevens. 105 min.

Fred Astaire comes to the big city so that he can earn enough money to marry his girl back home. But then he falls in love with a pretty dance instructor—Ginger Rogers, of course. Arguably the finest of the Astaire-Rogers musicals, this film might leave you feeling good for the rest of your life. The dancing is exquisite, and Jerome Kern's score is glorious; Kern won a Best Song Oscar for "The Way You Look Tonight." George Stevens's excellent direction and light comic touch sustain interest in the nonmusical sequences as well. When Astaire fears that he will lose his beloved Rogers, he sings that he is "Never Gonna Dance Again." The scene is one of the most movingly bittersweet in the history of American musicals.

SWISS FAMILY ROBINSON ★★★½
1960, USA
Dorothy McGuire, James MacArthur, Janet Munro, John Mills, Sessue Hayakawa, Tommy Kirk. Directed by Ken Annakin. 128 min.

The durable Johann Wyss tale comes to the screen again as the shipwrecked family brings civilization to an island wilderness. The story still has meaning in our day and age when so many city folks talk about chucking it all and getting back to nature. The prime survivalists of all time, the Robinsons harness energy, domesticate wild animals, and even have to fend off swarthy pirates led by nasty Sessue Hayakawa (having a high old time as the villainous buccaneer). One of Disney's best action adventures with superlative production values. Really manages to capture the castaway flavor of innocence and freedom without losing its reassuring domesticity.

SWISS MISS ★★
1938, USA
Stan Laurel, Oliver Hardy, Della Lind. Directed by John G. Blystone. 73 min.

As mousetrap salesmen in the Alps, Ollie and Stan get caught up in an actress's scheme to make her husband jealous. An excess of plot overcrowds the picture, limiting the most successful comedy team in screen history from showing their stuff. The few classic Laurel-and-Hardy sight gags end up stealing the show.

SWORD AND THE ROSE ★★½
1953, USA
Richard Todd, Glynis Johns, James Robertson Justice, Michael Gough, Jane Barrett, Peter Copley, Rosalie Crutchley, D. A. Clarke-Smith, Ernest Jay, John Vere, Phillip Lennard, Bryan Coleman, Jean Mercure. Directed by Ken Annakin. 91 min.

This Walt Disney production of Charles Major's *When Knighthood Was in Flower* was made in England by English forces, who supply the atmosphere of the Tudor period but not enough of the full-blooded swashbuckling needed to spark the action along. As Princess Mary, the sister of Henry VIII (James Robertson Justice), Glynis Johns is going to be married off to the king of France (Jean Mercure) or, worse, the evil duke of Buckingham (Michael Gough) unless the commoner she really loves (Richard Todd) can reverse all odds.

SWORD AND THE SORCERER ★★
1982, USA
Lee Horsley, Kathleen Beller, Simon MacCorkindale, Richard Lynch, George Maharis, Richard Moll. Directed by Albert Pyun. 100 min.

Entertaining garbage. It's one of those sword-clanking adventures in which the film's highlights occur every time someone's chest heaves. Naturally this pneumatic epic offers plenty of laughs to keep our minds off the inept script about an insane ruler enslaving his people with supernatural help. By the time Lee Horsley shows up to wipe out all the wicked creeps and mythical beasts, you'll be overwhelmed by the general tackiness of the sets, costumes, and performances. It's sort of a cross between a budgetless Cecil B. DeMille and one of those Saturday night wrestling matches where the players come out and exchange threats in skimpy costumes. tumes.

SWORD OF LANCELOT ★★★
1963, Great Britain
Cornel Wilde, Jean Wallace, Brian Aherne, George Baker. Directed by Cornel Wilde. 116 min.

It didn't have the biggest budget in the world, but *Sword of Lancelot* is a handsome-looking minor epic nonetheless. Certainly, this action-packed adventure conveys more of the purity of the Arthurian legends than Hollywood's overblown film of *Camelot*. The love triangle of King Arthur, Guinevere, and Lancelot is treated with proper reverence, and the star is surprisingly creative in his capacity as the film's director.

THE SWORD OF MONTE CRISTO ★★
1951, USA
George Montgomery, Paula Corday, Berry Kroeger, Steve Brodie. Directed by Maurice Geraghty. 80 min.

An ordinary adventure saga about a beauteous miss who locates the legendary sword of Monte Cristo (hence the title) and then tries to wield it against a nefarious ruler. She enlists the aid of a heroic warrior in her pursuit of justice, and also in her search for the treasure to which the sword may hold the key. Average and unoriginal, but painless.

SYBIL ★★½
1976, USA (TV)
Sally Field, Joanne Woodward, Brad Davis, Martine Bartlett, Jane Hoffman, William Prince. Directed by Daniel Petrie. 122 min.

Sally Field made her first successful bid for recognition as a serious actress with her Emmy-winning performance as Sybil Dorsett, a woman so traumatized by her childhood that she fragments into sixteen personalities. She's very good in a challenging role, and matched all the way by Joanne Woodward (who herself made a mark as a split personality with her Oscar-winning performance in *The Three Faces of Eve*) as her psychiatrist. The original film was one of the finest then made for TV; however, eighty minutes have mistakenly been cut from the videocassette release, resulting in a messy, fragmented film. This one is worth seeing on commercial TV, interruptions and all—or better yet on pay cable.

SYLVESTER ★★
1985, USA, PG
Melissa Gilbert, Richard Farnsworth, Michael Schoeffling, Constance Towers, Peter Kowanko, Yankton Hatten, Shane Servin, Angel Salazar. Directed by Tim Hunter. 103 min.

An unfortunate, misguided movie that is too incredible for anyone over the age of seven and, with a graphic rape attempt, too brutal for children under twelve. Melissa Gilbert, of TV's "Little House on the Prairie," makes a disappointing and unconvincing feature film debut as a teenager who becomes a champion showhorse rider despite a lack of training. She also manages to raise her two younger brothers and warm the heart of a crusty old man. Director Tim Hunter can't really be faulted—he moves things along gracefully—but this is a sharp drop from his very good *Tex*.

SYLVIA ★★★
1985, Great Britain, PG
Eleanor David, Tom Wilkinson, Nigel Terry, Mary Regan. Directed by Michael Firth. 98 min.

This is a reverent, moving biography of Sylvia Ashton-Warner, the educator who developed new methods of teaching from her work with New Zealand's indigenous Maori children. Eleanor David's spirited, finely nuanced performance in the title role and Ian Paul's handsome cinematography will hold your attention, and although the narrative is conventional, there are inspiring moments. Based on Ashton-Warner's books *Teacher* and *I Passed This Way*.

T

TABLE FOR FIVE ☆½
1982, USA, PG
Jon Voight, Marie-Christine Barrault, Richard Crenna, Millie Perkins. Directed by Robert Lieberman. 122 min.

One of the most ignoble entries in the oh-so-sensitive genre that flourished briefly after *Kramer vs. Kramer*, whose sole purpose was to prove that dads make better moms than moms. Here Jon Voight plays the heart-on-his-sleeve hero, a suffocatingly sincere divorced father whose wife has remarried a perfectly decent man (Richard Crenna). This being a melodrama, not only does tragedy strike, but it's precisely the kind of tragedy that allows Voight to flex every muscle of parental goodness and exercise his tear ducts in the process. Crudely manipulative but unsure about its point of view, an obnoxious combination.

TAG: THE ASSASSINATION GAME ☆☆
1982, USA, PG
Robert Carradine, Linda Hamilton, Kristine DeBell, Perry Lang, Bruce Abbott. Directed by Nick Castle. 92 min.

TAG is one of those games that were popular on college campuses a few years back, in which opposing teams armed with guns that shoot paint pellets or suction darts stalk each other. A good film could be made about the psychological effects of such games (or the causes), but *TAG* opts instead for a predictable plot about a student who starts playing the game with real bullets. It's done with a good degree of parody, at least for the first half, but sinks down to standard chase routines by the end.

TAIPAN ☆
1986, USA, R
Bryan Brown, Joan Chen, John Stanton, Tim Guinee, Bill Leadbitter, Russell Wong, Katy Behean, Kyra Sedgwick, Janine Turner. Directed by Daryl Duke. 127 min.

This adaptation of a mammoth novel by James Clavell (*Shogun, Noble House*) plays like a miniseries thrown into a Cuisinart—long, dull, full of holes, hamhanded, and without even the requisite all-star cast or commercial breaks. Bryan Brown plays a trader facing treacherous competition from the opium and silver merchants of nineteenth-century China, and the film, the first American feature to be shot in mainland China, takes every opportunity to exploit the country's travelogue grandeur. However, such is the incompetence of the filmmakers that they succeed in making everything look like a Burbank set.

TAKE DOWN ☆☆½
1979, USA, PG
Edward Herrmann, Kathleen Lloyd, Lorenzo Lamas, Maureen McCormick, Stephen Furst, Kevin Hooks. Directed by Keith Merrill. 107 min.

Another underdog sports movie, this one was most probably inspired by *The Bad News Bears*. *Take Down* contains no surprises but has some laughs and is honest enough to be affecting. A young English teacher (Edward Herrmann) is assigned the extracurricular duty of coaching the school's perennially losing wrestling team because no one else will take it. As he warms up to his task (this high school is a loser at everything, and he begins to think that he can start to change that), the team begins to gain inspiration from him. Lorenzo Lamas, as a potential young wrestler, cannot act, but he is not called upon to. The PG rating is hardly deserved: this is perfectly acceptable family fare.

TAKE IT TO THE LIMIT ☆☆
1980, USA, PG
Barry Sheene, Russ Collins, Steve Baker, Scott Autrey, Mike Hailwood, Kenny Roberts. Directed by Peter Starr. 95 min.

This documentary about motorcycle racing won't persuade you to mortgage the house and sell the kids into slavery in order to get your own chopper, though it might amuse you for an hour and a half if you're already into the sport and "Wide World of Sports" isn't covering it this week. Producer/director Peter Starr alternates race footage and interviews with longtime champions, explaining how they manage to retain their status. The best sequence for the uninvolved is an animated bit to Arlo Guthrie's "The Motorcycle Song" ("I don't want a pickle/I just wanna ride on my *motorsickle*"). Vrroom.

TAKE THE MONEY AND RUN ☆☆☆☆
1969, USA, PG
Woody Allen, Janet Margolin, Marcel Hillaire, Jacquelyn Hyde, Lonny Chapman, Jan Merlin. Directed by Woody Allen. 85 min.

The first movie that Woody Allen directed, wrote, *and* starred in uses a mock documentary style to trace the life of crime of the lovable, would-be murderer, Virgil Starkwell. Not all the gags work in this sprawling, loosely constructed Allen effort, but enough do to make it a thoroughly enjoyable, often hysterically funny, comic gem. Although not a masterpiece in a class with *Manhattan* or *The Purple Rose of Cairo*, such early films as this one from, arguably, America's premier active filmmaker emanate a warmth that is not always as present in Allen's later, finer work. Virgil's bank holdup scene is one of the funnier in the annals of film.

TAKE THIS JOB AND SHOVE IT ½☆
1981, USA, PG
Robert Hays, Art Carney, Barbara Hershey, David Keith, Martin Mull, Tim Thomerson, Eddie Albert, Penelope Milford. Directed by Gus Trikonis. 100 min.

Fact #1: There has never been a good movie based on a popular song—e.g., *Ode to Billie Joe, The Night the Lights Went Out in Georgia, Harper Valley P.T.A.* Fact #2: There has never been a good movie made by Gus Trikonis. Fact #3: There has almost never been a good movie with Martin Mull. Fact #4: This feeble comedy about a junior executive with a megaconglomerate who is sent back to his hometown to modernize a brewery disproves none of the preceding.

TAKE YOUR BEST SHOT ☆☆
1982, USA (TV)
Robert Urich, Meredith Baxter Birney, Jeffrey Tambor, Jack Bannon, Claudette Nevins, Susan Peretz, Howard McGillin. Directed by David Greene. 96 min.

We'd usually go out of our way to watch a TV-movie scripted by the ace team of Richard Levinson and William Link, but in this one, they abandoned their usual twisty mystery for a light comedy, and they ran aground. Robert Urich plays an actor whose career and marriage are both sinking; he's a likable actor, and Levinson and Link manage to work in some wry brushes at Hollywood hypocrisy, but it's never more than mild.

THE TAKING OF PELHAM ONE TWO THREE ★★½
1974, USA, R
Walter Matthau, Robert Shaw, Martin Balsam, Hector Elizondo, Doris Roberts, Tony Roberts, Earl Hindman, James Broderick, Jerry Stiller. Directed by Joseph Sargent. 104 min.

Joseph Sargent's efficient pulse-pounder about a commandeered New York City subway train is enlivened by Walter Matthau's ingratiating comic turn as a rumpled transit authority inspector. The hijackers are demanding one million dollars to be delivered in one hour, and the old ticking-clock plot device works extremely well, tying together the parallel stories of the frantic cops and the panicked people aboard the train.

A TALE OF TWO CITIES ★★★½
1935, USA
Ronald Colman, Elizabeth Allan, Edna May Oliver, Reginald Owen, Basil Rathbone, Blanche Yurka, Henry B. Walthall, Donald Woods. Directed by Jack Conway. 121 min.

Producer David Selznick had a talent for turning literary classics into film classics, as demonstrated here by his respectful filmization of the great Dickens novel. This is a rousing depiction of London and Paris life during the French Revolution, with a vivid reenactment of the storming of the Bastille. Several lives intertwine in a web of story lines, pulling on a symphony of heartstrings, and displaying a gallery of character types. Stellar performance by Ronald Colman in the difficult role of Sydney Carton, the antihero who proves himself a far, far better friend than most.

A TALE OF TWO CITIES ★★½
1958, Great Britain
Dirk Bogarde, Dorothy Tutin, Cecil Parker, Stephen Murray, Christopher Lee, Donald Pleasence, Ian Bannen, Marie Versini. Directed by Ralph Thomas. 117 min.

One might think that a film version of Charles Dickens's classic coming from the country in which it was written would tower above them all. Alas, this respectful but stolid rendition is far less exciting than the opulent 1935 Hollywood film. Dirk Bogarde struggles playing Sydney Carton, the alcoholic lawyer who makes the ultimate sacrifice for his unrequited love during the bloody days of the French Revolution. The real zing comes from Christopher Lee's savage nobleman and Marie Versini's servant girl. Otherwise, France looks like England, and the film looks like it was made for classroom use.

TALES FROM THE CRYPT ★★★
1972, Great Britain, PG
Joan Collins, Ralph Richardson, Ian Hendry, Peter Cushing, Richard Greene, Patrick Magee. Directed by Freddie Francis. 92 min.

In this above-average Amicus horror anthology, five people meet up with an old crypt-keeper (Ralph Richardson, overacting outrageously) who shows each a vision. The smart move here was to adapt stories from William Gaines's E.C. comics, those beloved mind-warpers of the fifties that almost single-handedly brought about the creation of the Comics Code. There are quick moments of gore, mostly for punch lines. The material is treated more seriously than might be expected, or perhaps even than it deserves, but it's refreshing to see a horror movie with a big-name cast and by professional filmmakers that doesn't play it tongue in cheek.

TALES OF HOFFMANN ★★★
1951, Great Britain
Moira Shearer, Robert Rounseville, Ann Ayers, Robert Helpmann, Pamela Brown, Frederick Ashton, Meinhart Maur, John Ford, Richard Golding, Philip Leaver. Directed by Michael Powell and Emeric Pressburger. 138 min.

Here's an art film to end all art films. Michael Powell and Emeric Pressburger (*Black Narcissus, The Red Shoes*) took on Jacques Offenbach's three-act opera and the results are heavy going. Still, there is much to appreciate: Moira Shearer as the beautiful ballerina who inspires Hoffmann (played by Robert Rounseville) to relate "the three tales of my folly of love"; the Olympia Doll sequence with Shearer's singing severed head (the film's trick effects are often dazzling); Ann Ayers's rendition of "All in Vain"; and some brilliant Technicolor photography by Christopher Challis. The pace is less than brisk, but there are many rewards for patient viewers.

TALES OF ORDINARY MADNESS ★★★★
1981, Italy, X (self-imposed)
Ben Gazzara, Ornella Muti, Susan Tyrrell, Tanya Lopert, Katia Berger. Directed by Marco Ferreri. 107 min.

The poet's muse is a beautiful whore with a death wish—literally—in Marco Ferreri's corpse-cool adaptation of Charles Bukowski's scathing collection of stories, *Erections, Ejaculations, Exhibitions and General Tales of Ordinary Madness*. Ben Gazzara is perfect as he intelligently and humorously renders the lowlife of a post-Beat writer who chooses to wallow in ugliness rather than buy into the synthetic beauties available in America's cultural wasteland. Ferreri has an outsider's alienated vision of the American landscape that adds a nice, ironic level to Bukowski's obsessively participatory alienated nightmare. Hollywood and its inhabitants never looked uglier, less mythic. Extremely nice low-light photography by the great Tonino Delli Colli and a well-done score by Phillipe Sarde are wedded to a disturbing jumble of background noise emanating from radios, kids, jukeboxes, and bums.

TALES OF TERROR ★★★
1962, USA
Vincent Price, Peter Lorre, Basil Rathbone, Debra Paget, Joyce Jameson. Directed by Roger Corman. 90 min.

It's a great Chiller Theater bargain—three short horror flicks for the price of one—all loosely based on the much-pillaged works of Edgar Allan Poe. "The Cask of Amontillado" packs the most punch, as Lorre tries to wall up his adulterous wife and her boyfriend; although Vincent Price's disintegration in the third story provides a scary wind-up. The other tale offers an eerie glimpse of hypnosis, featuring another Fright Night veteran, Basil Rathbone. You'll pick your own favorite, but these three slices of classical terror all have merit.

TALES THAT WITNESS MADNESS ★★½
1973, Great Britain, R
Jack Hawkins, Donald Pleasence, Joan Collins, Kim Novak, Suzy Kendall. Directed by Freddie Francis. 90 min.

A horror anthology in the style of the Amicus productions of the time (*The House That Tripped Blood, Tales from the Crypt*), with a similar cast and veteran director Freddie Francis, this just isn't up to the level of the others. As usual, the frame story is set in a madhouse, with a possibly mad doctor (Donald Pleasence) recounting case histories of his clients to skeptical Jack Hawkins. The best story, about a man who, much to his wife's dismay, falls in love with a tree trunk, sounds a lot funnier than it is, and the capper is predictable and gross rather than suspenseful. Still, this has enough atmosphere (what British horror film hasn't?) and cheap thrills to merit at least one viewing for the dedicated horror fan.

THE TALK OF THE TOWN ★★★½
1942, USA
Cary Grant, Ronald Colman, Jean Arthur, Edgar Buchanan. Directed by George Stevens. 118 min.

This delightful comedy stars Ronald Colman as a celebrated lawyer about to be appointed to the Supreme Court who, fearing publicity, decides to lie low in a remote cottage for the summer. Little does he know that his gardener (Cary Grant) is an accused anarchist on the lam from the law and that his landlady (Jean Arthur) is determined to prove Grant's innocence with as much help from the press as possible. The deft but difficult blend of sociopolitical satire with broad slapstick is brought off beautifully by the powerhouse trio of stars. Speaking of tough decisions, just watch our heroine choose between leading men. (Even director George Stevens shot two different endings before making his decision.)

THE TALL BLOND MAN WITH ONE BLACK SHOE ☆☆
1972, France, PG
Pierre Richard, Bernard Blier, Jean Rochefort, Mireille Darc, Yves Robert. Directed by Yves Robert. 90 min.

The French have a knack for sophisticated comedy (even when it's bad it at least sounds good), but often fail at paying homage to the American silent clowns, as they do in this lightweight farce. It's a mistaken-identity plot about a bumbling cellist who becomes unwittingly mixed up with secret agents. The production is flashy and the gags elaborate, but the only payoff is tedium. Dubbing, of course, seldom helps, but this film was given a particularly bad job. Followed by a sequel, *The Return of the Tall Blond Man With One Black Shoe*, and later remade for American audiences as *The Man With One Red Shoe*.

TALL IN THE SADDLE ☆☆☆
1944, USA
John Wayne, Ella Raines, Audrey Long, George "Gabby" Hayes, Elizabeth Risdon, Ward Bond, Don Douglas, Russell Wade. Directed by Edwin L. Marin. 87 min.

The Duke riding tall says it all. His sturdy performance as a cowhand-turned-detective fuels this twisting narrative that eventually includes everything we expect from a good Western. John Wayne rides onto a ranch only to discover that someone has recently murdered his prospective employer. With subtle confidence, the cowhand slowly investigates the situation, threading his way through the complexities of dealing with feuding women and angry townsfolk. Inevitably, he solves the mystery, gets the ranch, and marries one of the quarrelsome females. Wayne's performance would border on the excessive were it not placed in contrast to the brilliant comedy of sidekick Gabby Hayes. What results is a well-rounded, thoroughly entertaining film, similar in many respects to *Stagecoach*.

THE TALL MEN ☆☆☆
1955, USA
Clark Gable, Jane Russell, Argentine Burnetti, Robert Ryan, Cameron Mitchell, Juan Garcia, Harry Shannon, Emile Meyer, Mae Marsh. Directed by Raoul Walsh. 122 min.

His leisurely and often meditative style makes Raoul Walsh one of America's most underrated directors. He directs a classic, his version of social mobility in America. An older and still wiser Clark Gable and an ex-Confederate bushwhacker stumble into a saloon, intent on making a quick holdup. In a surreal narrative twist, they opt instead to assist their intended victim in his plan to bring cattle to meat-hungry Montana. Along the route of the world's longest cattle drive, Walsh treats us to serene scenery and those wide-open spaces, augmented by discussions on success in the West and a captivating performance by the aging Gable. An additional bonus: Jane Russell as the woman who "thinks big." Who can blame her?

THE TAMARIND SEED ☆☆½
1974, Great Britain, PG
Julie Andrews, Omar Sharif, Anthony Quayle, Daniel O'Herlihy, Oscar Homolka. Directed by Blake Edwards. 123 min.

More uxoriousness from Blake Edwards, in which much of the point seems to be to make Julie Andrews (Mrs. Edwards) look more beautiful and glamorous by setting her against beautiful and glamorous surroundings. She plays a widow, just coming off of a bad affair with a married man, on vacation in the Barbados, where she meets a beautiful and glamorous Russian (Omar Sharif). Ah, but is it true love, or does their romance have anything to do with the fact that she works for an important British diplomat and that he is a Soviet attaché? Basically an old-fashioned, globe-trotting romance-cum-spy-movie, this could have used a touch more humor to lighten the mood of all those moon-lit close-ups.

THE TAMING OF THE SHREW ☆☆☆
1967, USA
Elizabeth Taylor, Richard Burton, Michael York, Cyril Cusack. Directed by Franco Zeffirelli. 122 min.

Shakespeare's quintessential battle between male and female is given real-life immediacy when the antagonists are Liz Taylor and Richard Burton. Zeffirelli's direction is energetic and colorful, there's a fine musical score by Nino Rota, and the look in Liz's eyes confirms that this is one shrew who's not likely to be tamed. Unfortunately, while Burton is at his best with Shakespeare, Liz is more at home in Edward Albee (or at least John O'Hara) territory. She screeches her way through here with a complete lack of delicacy.

TAMMY AND THE BACHELOR ☆☆½
1957, USA
Debbie Reynolds, Walter Brennan, Leslie Nielsen, Mala Powers, Fay Wray, Sidney Blackmer. Directed by Joseph Pevney. 89 min.

An enjoyable corn-pone romance arises between an innocent backwoods Miss Fixit and a pilot whose plane crashes in the stix, where he is cared for by this innocent child-woman. Quicker than you can say "Gigi" with a Southern accent, the sophisticated gent falls for the unspoiled lassie. Sequels and a TV series followed; and the film's title tune was a smash hit. It's a glorified Deanna Durbin movie for Debbie Reynolds, whose determined charm suits the artificiality of the enterprise. Still, it's homey and it probably did wonders for the dream lives of underage country girls hoping that a pilot would likewise crash-land near their houseboats.

TAMMY AND THE DOCTOR ☆☆
1963, USA
Sandra Dee, Peter Fonda, Macdonald Carey, Beulah Bondi, Margaret Lindsay. Directed by Harry Keller. 88 min.

Peter Fonda may not want to admit that, long before *Easy Rider*, he made his film debut in this sappy rural romance about the homespun heroine who experiences heart trouble over a young doctor. Sandra Dee replaced Debbie Reynolds as Tammy, the Sweetheart of the Swamps. She's an improvement, but the film itself is cloying.

TANGIER ☆☆
1946, USA
Maria Montez, Preston Foster, Robert Paige, Louise Albritton, Sabu, Kent Taylor. Directed by George Waggner. 76 min.

Camp fans will rejoice as Maria Montez dances in her spike heels all over North America. She's a lesser light in black and white than she was in the storybook color of *Cobra Woman* and *Sudan*, but the indispensable Sabu is on hand to help her butcher the English language and assist her in her plans for revenge. As an action flick, it's rather shaky; as a vehicle for La Montez, it's perfectly spiffy.

TANK ☆☆
1984, USA, PG
James Garner, G. D. Spradlin, Shirley Jones, C. Thomas Howell, Jenilee Harrison. Directed by Marvin Chomsky. 113 min.

James Garner is the saving grace of this uneven blend of revenge, dramatics, and good-ol'-boy farce, and his presence is more than *Tank* deserves. He plays a career soldier who relocates with his family to a base near a small Southern town under the heel of a corrupt sheriff. When Garner runs afoul of the constabulary by preventing a deputy from beating up a prostitute, the sheriff retaliates by arresting his son on a trumped-up charge and sending him to a particularly brutal state prison. Fortunately, Garner owns his own personal Sherman tank, and sets out to get justice. The ending is designed for laughs and vindication, but it's out of keeping with the nastiness of much of the rest of the movie.

TAPS ☆☆
1981, USA, PG
Timothy Hutton, Ronny Cox, Sean Penn, George C. Scott, Tom Cruise, Brendan Ward, Evan Handler. Directed by Harold Becker. 118 min.

When the students at an elite military academy learn that the trustees have decided to sell it to a developer of condominiums, they arm themselves and barricade the doors; a bloodbath eventually results. Exactly what position this film takes toward its subject—and for that matter, just what precisely its subject matter is supposed to be—are questions that are left too wide open for *Taps* to have any lasting power. The first half stands firmly for honor, duty, and loyalty; the ending would have us think there is something wrong with that. The attitudes of the filmmakers (including director Harold Becker, an Englishman who also directed *The Onion Field* and *The Black Marble*, and scriptwriter Darryl Ponicsan, who wrote *The Last Detail*—all works concerned with similar questions of codes of honor and conduct) seem to have been somewhere in the middle, but even they don't seem to have known quite where.

TARANTULA ☆☆☆
1955, USA
John Agar, Mara Corday, Leo G. Carroll, Nestor Paiva, Ross Elliot. Directed by Jack Arnold. 80 min.

A hair-raising thriller featuring not the usual papier-mâché Big Bug, but a convincing-looking giant creepy crawler. When the glandular arachnid escapes the clutches of the scientific community, it scuttles forth over the desert in search of people to crunch. One of the better sci-fi thrillers of the 1950s, with enough gruesome, eye-opening moments to hold the attention of a contemporary audience.

TARANTULAS: THE DEADLY CARGO ☆½
1977, USA (TV)
Claude Akins, Charles Frank, Deborah Winters, Howard Hesseman, Sandy McPeak. Directed by Stewart Hagman. 100 min.

Yech! What's worse—the sight of those hairy-legged creepy crawlers or the ridiculous script that crawls along just as insidiously? A small town is terrorized by the tarantulas, but, alas, you won't be. For some reason, TV movies about killer bees are usually better than TV movies about killer spiders, tarantulas, etc. This is a film even an entymologist couldn't love.

TARGET ☆☆
1985, USA, R
Gene Hackman, Matt Dillon, Josef Sommer, Guy Boyd, Gail Strickland. Directed by Arthur Penn. 98 min.

Arthur Penn can be a delightfully sardonic director: witness such films as *Bonnie and Clyde* and *Little Big Man*. Here he takes on the espionage picture, and goes terribly wrong. The adventures of an ex-CIA father who must cope with a disbelieving son as he searches for his kidnapped wife in spy-filled Europe could have worked with a certain amount of seriousness, but the director injects so many stereotypically idiotic chases, characters, and plot contrivances into the story that the picture ultimately becomes a berserk parody of itself. Even the usually dynamic Gene Hackman suffers under the ridiculous action and dialogue.

TARGET: HARRY ☆☆
1969, USA, PG
Vic Morrow, Suzanne Pleshette, Victor Buono, Cesar Romero, Stanley Holloway, Charlotte Rampling, Michael Ansara. Directed by Henry Neill (Roger Corman). 81 min.

One of the last films directed by Roger Corman, this was originally made for television but was never shown because it was deemed "too violent." It was eventually released overseas after Corman's brother Gene tried to get it released in this country by adding some gratuitous nude scenes (not in this version). The story is pretty much that of *The Maltese Falcon*, with Vic Morrow, Suzanne Pleshette, and Victor Buono taking the roles of Humphrey Bogart, Mary Astor, and Sydney Greenstreet, respectively. A cheapy quickie, even for Corman, but still sturdy enough to command some interest. Corman himself has a cameo role. (a.k.a.: *What's in It for Harry, How to Make It*)

TARGETS ☆☆☆½
1968, USA
Tim O'Kelly, Boris Karloff, Peter Bogdanovich, Sandy Baron, Monty Landis. Directed by Peter Bogdanovich. 90 min.

The story goes that Roger Corman had a few minutes of leftover footage from a quickly shot, incoherent film he'd made in 1963 called *The Terror*, as well as two days of shooting time owed him by Boris Karloff. He offered these and a minimal budget to his then-assistant writer Peter Bogdanovich, to do with whatever he wished, as long as the result was some kind of salable, full-length film. What Bogdanovich came up with was two stories, both excellent, that merge in the film's chilling conclusion. One involves a young man who, having accumulated an arsenal of guns, one day kills his wife and mother and then climbs a tower to snipe at passing cars. The lack of a real clue to his motivations is the strongest element of this argument for gun control. The other story follows Karloff, playing himself under a different name, as a horror star who wants to retire from movies because he feels they are no longer as horrible as what is reported on every day in the newspapers. It's a wonderful performance, of a kind he was too seldom allowed to give, and as fitting a conclusion to his career (if one overlooks a few Mexican-made cheapies he did following this in the year before his death) as this film is a beginning of Bogdanovich's.

TARTU

See *The Adventures of Tartu*

TARZAN'S REVENGE ☆☆
1938, USA
Glenn Morris, Eleanor Holm, George Barbier, C. Henry Gordon, Hedda Hopper. Directed by Ross Lederman. 70 min.

This is one of the few Tarzan films made in the 1930s without Johnny Weissmuller as the ape-man, but Glenn Morris does an admirable job on the vines, supported by good production quality, interesting scenery, a touch of humor, Eleanor Holm in the drink, and an entertaining chimp. The action moves a bit slowly, following a safari group through danger to the abode of a wicked ruler who is after Miss Holm.

TARZAN, THE APE MAN ☆☆☆½
1932, USA
Johnny Weissmuller, Maureen O'Sullivan, C. Aubrey Smith, Neil Hamilton. Directed by W. S. Van Dyke. 99 min.

There have been ape-men before this and lots of jungle swingers since. To most of us, though, Johnny Weissmuller is still the only Tarzan with a firm grasp on the Jungle Vine of Fame. Our affection for the film is a mixture of our childhood memories of being enthralled by the rugged action scenes (including that famous alligator-wrestling match) plus our adult amusement at Jane's continuing inability to improve Tarzan's rudimentary English. Despite the rampant silliness, this is a pre–Production Code film which is remarkably sensual in depicting Jane and Tarzan's jungle courtship. And even though some of this footage was lifted and reused continually, nothing detracts from the joyousness of the original.

TARZAN, THE APE MAN ☆
1981, USA, R
Bo Derek, Richard Harris, John Phillip Law, Miles O'Keeffe, Steven Strong. Directed by John Derek. 112 min.

It's not as unintentionally funny as *Bolero*, but Bo and John Derek's remake of the Tarzan story still manages its share of howlers. As Jane, who returns to Africa to seek her long-lost father, Bo nearly pushes the title character out of the picture altogether. And when Tarzan does show up, he is given little to do and no dialogue to do it with. No matter, though, as the entire film is simply an excuse to photograph Bo in various stages of undress. As John Derek explained in an interview: "There is nothing in this that says Bo has to play this naked. She could play it with her clothes on. But Bo *is* naked. She is a naked person." Just try and argue with that! The estate of Edgar Rice Burroughs sued (unsuccessfully) to block the film's release, thus giving it more publicity than it deserved.

TARZAN THE FEARLESS ☆½
1933, USA
Buster Crabbe, Jacqueline Wells, E. Alyn Warren, Edward Woods, Philo McCullough. Directed by Robert Hill. 85 min.

Sold originally as the introduction to a nine-part serial, this lame tale ends abruptly, with questions left unanswered. Plenty of padding and poor dialogue weaken the story of a scientist who falls prisoner to scoundrels in the jungle. Buster Crabbe (Tarzan) rescues the old man and then saves his daughter, falling in love with her en route. Don't bother seeing the other eight parts!

A TASTE OF HONEY ☆☆☆
1961, Great Britain
Rita Tushingham, Robert Stephens, Dora Bryan, Murray Melvin, Paul Danquah. Directed by Tony Richardson. 100 min.

A "kitchen sink" drama, one of the most popular slices of English realism, makes a safe crossing to cinema waters. Shelagh Delaney's insightful play examines the coming-of-age of an unloved teenage girl who finds temporary solace with a sailor. When he abandons her for the sea, her taste of honey proves short-lived, but she endeavors to raise her illegitimate child with the help of a homosexual friend. Despite the naturalistic bent, the film plays somewhat like a grim fairy tale about an ugly duckling who never quite turns into a swan. Instead, she comes to appreciate that her inner beauty and strength are enough to sustain her. Superb performances; and the film doesn't violate the integrity of the play. Originally, Hollywood was going to film this with Audrey Hepburn and a happy ending.

A TATTERED WEB ☆☆
1971, USA (TV)
Lloyd Bridges, Frank Converse, Broderick Crawford, Murray Hamilton. Directed by Paul Wendkos. 73 min.

This TV-movie suspenser spins an appealingly complicated yarn of guilt complexes and covered tracks. Lloyd Bridges, unfortunately, isn't quite up to the demanding role of a detective involved in a murder. When he discovers that his son-in-law is cheating on his daughter, the cop confronts the mistress and accidentally kills her. As the detective embarks on a campaign of obfuscation, all the evidence seems to point more and more to his son-in-law. Conventionally handled, but the story itself is intricate enough to ensnare most viewers in this web.

TATTOO ☆☆
1981, USA, R
Bruce Dern, Maud Adams, Leonard Frey, Rikke Borge, John Getz, Peter Iachangelo. Directed by Robert Brooks. 103 min.

This lurid study of one man's obsession is too overheated and sleazy to take seriously, but it's made with such conviction that it's not without a certain perverse fascination. Bruce Dern, who made a career out of playing borderline cases, here goes over the edge with a twitchy, maniacal performance as a tattoo artist longing to use luscious Maud Adams as his ultimate canvas. It starts off as an interesting riff on *The Collector*, but soon turns into a heavy-breathing S & M spectacle when its wholeheartedly trashy values burst to the surface. Adapted from a novel by Earl Thompson.

THE TATTOO CONNECTION ☆☆
1979, Hong Kong
Jim Kelly, Chen Hsing, Tan Tao-Liang, Chaing Tao, Yang Sze, Misake Name, Bobby Ming. Directed by Lee Tso Nan. 90 min.

This is a kung fu epic with Jim Kelly (*Enter the Dragon*) as an ex-CIA man now working as an insurance investigator sent to recover a stolen diamond from the gang of the insidious Mr. Lu (Chen Hsing).

THE TATTOOED DRAGON ☆
1973, Thailand
Jimmy Wang Yu, Samuel Hui, Sylvia Chang, James Tien, Li Kun. Directed by Lo Wei. 84 min.

Filmed in Thailand, this standard Jimmy Wang Yu film concerns a martial arts school that harbors "The Dragon" (Yu) from a gang of thieves and murderers.

TAXI DRIVER ☆☆☆☆
1976, USA, R
Robert DeNiro, Cybill Shepherd, Jodie Foster, Peter Boyle, Leonard Harris, Harvey Keitel. Directed by Martin Scorsese. 114 min.

Martin Scorsese's nightmarish drama of personal shell-shock, urban paranoia, and random bloodshed is a contemporary horror story with its roots in Arthur Bremer's attempted assassination of George Wallace. Its effects, though, have been felt long since then; its impact is hypnotic, grisly, and lasting. The film's nominal hero, Travis Bickle, lives in a netherworld between the past hell of Vietnam and the more mundane horror of New York street life, driving a cab, frequenting Times Square dives, and holing up in his grimy apartment in a solitude that's ready to explode. When he meets Betsy (Cybill Shepherd), a coolly friendly campaign worker, and Iris (Jodie Foster), a twelve-year-old prostitute, their lives come together in a shocking eruption of violence that temporarily earned *Taxi Driver* an X rating. Paul Schrader's screenplay has some problems with its perspective and development, and Scorsese's generally superb direction slips into several moments of odd overemphasis. DeNiro's central performance is, however, acting of the highest order. Standing in front of his mirror, practicing his icy glare and "You talkin' to *me*?" sneer, his Travis becomes one of the most enduring and scary icons of postwar alienation on screen.

UN TAXI MAUVE

See *The Purple Taxi*

TEACHERS ☆☆
1984, USA, R
Nick Nolte, JoBeth Williams, Ralph Macchio, Judd Hirsch, Richard Mulligan. Directed by Arthur Hiller. 106 min.

An earnest social melodrama about a lawsuit against a decaying inner-city school gets puffed up with some teenage comedy and ends as an unsatisfying mix. Nick Nolte growls through his part as the burned-out, once-great teacher like a leatherneck mercenary on the wrong side of a small war. The rest of the cast is similarly afflicted with performances that boom with significance: Ralph Macchio is television tough, JoBeth Williams is stereotyped shrill, and Judd Hirsch is the Nixonian, compromised principal.

TEA IN THE HAREM ☆☆½
1986, France
Kader Boukhanef, Remi Martin, Laure Duthilleul, Sandra Bekkouche, Nicole Hiss. Directed by Mehdi Charef. 100 min.

The protagonists of Mehdi Charef's shaggy, likable film are a couple of young Parisian toughs (Kader Boukhanef and Remi Martin) who do nothing all day but wander the streets, pick people's pockets, and, when they're bored, find a girl to fool around with. Cute and monosyllabic, these delinquents are innocent animals devoted to getting through the day as entertainingly as possible. The film's freewheeling structure isn't always satisfying, but what it gives you is a fiercely authentic understanding of characters who have grown up riding the waves of life, literally doing whatever pops into their heads. Boukhanef and Martin are both instinctive actors (and terrific camera subjects), projecting a stoned indifference to everything that's in their midst.

TEENAGE MONSTER

See *Meteor Monster*

TEEN WOLF ☆☆½
1985, USA, PG
Michael J. Fox, Scott Paulin, Jay Tarses. Directed by Rod Daniel. 90 min.

When his lupine ancestry catches up with him, a downtrodden teenager learns that happiness is being a werewolf. He turns into a superbeast who's able to score at basketball and with a snobby blonde. But through his regular transformations, the teen starts to lose his self-identity and ultimately learns that it's better to "be yourself." There are some real moments when the hapless protagonist first discovers his affliction, but then the film's satirical points and outright laughs fall flat at a frightening rate. If it weren't for the fresh and charming acting of Michael J. Fox, this would be a very bland comedy. The filmmakers should have studied Walt Disney's *The Shaggy Dog*, a movie that did the same thing with a lot more humor. Followed by a sequel.

TELEFON ☆☆☆
1977, USA, PG
Charles Bronson, Lee Remick, Donald Pleasence, Tyne Daly, Patrick Magee, Sheree North. Directed by Don Siegel. 103 min.

This engrossing spy story posits a plan initiated by the KGB under Stalin in which fifty-four agents were planted in the U.S. and hypnotized into thinking they were red-blooded Americans; upon receiving a telephone call with the proper code, they would be reactivated and set off to destroy select military sites. When a renegade Russian obtains a copy of the code book and sets off to put the long-abandoned plan into operation, the KGB sends its own operative (Charles Bronson) to stop him and avoid international embarrassment. Bronson and Lee Remick, as a double agent, make an unusual but oddly workable romantic couple, but Donald Pleasence steals the show as the Stalinist fanatic who resorts to a series of silly disguises to avoid detection.

TELL ME A RIDDLE ☆☆
1980, USA, PG
Lila Kedrova, Melvyn Douglas, Brooke Adams, Dolores Dorn, Bob Elross, Joan Harris, Zalman King. Directed by Lee Grant. 90 min.

In the hands of first-time director Lee Grant, Tillie Olsen's elliptical novella about two aging Russian-Jewish immigrants becomes a gentle, small-scale drama that doesn't really know where to go. Lila Kedrova and Melvyn Douglas star as the old couple whose fifty-year marriage has come down to enfeebled bouts of kvetching. The movie is bland and patronizing, and its attempt to turn Olsen's fragmentary narrative into a gripping series of events ends up giving scenes and characters a significance they don't warrant.

THE TELL-TALE HEART ☆☆
1963, Great Britain
Laurence Payne, Adrienne Corri, Dermot Walsh, Selma Vaz Dias. Directed by Ernest Morris. 81 min.

Edgar Allan Poe's classic short story is padded out into something long enough for a feature film by framing the story as a dream being experienced by the author. There are some creepy moments but, overall, the whole project is thin and lacking in plot.

TELL THEM WILLIE BOY IS HERE ☆☆
1969, USA, PG
Robert Redford, Katharine Ross, Robert Blake, Susan Clark, Barry Sullivan, Charles McGraw, John Vernon. Directed by Abraham Polonsky. 97 min.

After a twenty-year gap, blacklisted Abraham Polonsky directed his second film—a reexamination of the traditional lawman-and-Indian Western—with a vengeance. Robert Redford plays Coop (his name a deliberate reference to Gary Cooper), a local sheriff who spends much of his time living a peaceful life. Trouble breaks out among the Indian population when Willie (Robert Blake) kills his lover's father in self-defense. The two flee into the hills pursued by a posse of locals. The reluctant Coop quickly abandons the search, but he is forced to rejoin the group when Willie's lover is found dead and several posse members are injured. With the arrival of no less a personage than President Taft imminent, many of the townspeople believe a conspiracy to assassinate him is afoot, and they want Coop to act. The film climaxes with Coop's showdown with fugitive Willie in what amounts to a lopsided and tragic gunfight. Despite the suspension of disbelief needed to accept Blake and Katharine Ross playing American Indians, *Willie Boy* is a hard-hitting, haunting allegory and a vicious condemnation of contemporary American values.

TELL YOUR CHILDREN

See *Reefer Madness*

TEMPEST ☆☆
1982, USA, PG
John Cassavetes, Gena Rowlands, Susan Sarandon, Raul Julia, Vittorio Gassman, Molly Ringwald, Paul Stewart, Sam Robards. Directed by Paul Mazursky. 140 min.

Paul Mazursky's two-and-a-half-hour mid-life-crisis movie is an empty, pretentious mishmash that still manages to be fitfully entertaining. The premise is certainly pungent enough to put anyone off: this is a modern dress adaptation of Shakespeare, with John Cassavetes as a big shot New York architect who, fed up with Playing the Game, takes over a deserted Greek isle along with his daughter (Molly Ringwald), his new girlfriend (Susan Sarandon), and a lusty low-life servant (Raul Julia). Mazursky spikes his middle-aged moonshine with a goofy vaudeville spirit, but the movie is weighed down by Big Questions.

THE TEMPTER ☆☆½
1974, Italy, R
Carla Gravina, Arthur Kennedy, Mel Ferrer, George Coulouris, Alida Valli, Umberto Orsini, Anita Strindberg, Mario Scaccio. Directed by Alberto de Martino. 96 min.

A wealthy young woman, hysterically crippled since the automobile accident that killed her mother, becomes possessed in the wake of her beloved father's engagement to another woman. She froths at the mouth, makes lewd suggestions and gestures, has hallucinatory visions of an ancestor burned as a witch, and claims that she is carrying the Antichrist, fathered by her own brother. A very entertaining exploitation film, its debt to *The Exorcist* is evident. Heavily steeped in Catholicism and determined to outdo itself at every turn, it very nearly does. Look for the orgy of the damned.

10
1979, USA, R ☆☆☆½
Dudley Moore, Julie Andrews, Bo Derek, Robert Webber, Dee Wallace, Sam Jones, Brian Dennehy, Max Showalter. Directed by Blake Edwards. 122 min.

The delightful comedy that made Dudley Moore a star and Bo Derek a sensation. Dudley plays a songwriter whose midlife crisis wrenches him from his smart, tolerant-up-to-a-point girl friend (Julie Andrews) and sends him careening south of the border in pursuit of an elusive beauty (Derek) who rates an 11 on his 1-to-10 scale of beauty. Beneath the slick sex farce is a double-edged study of the menopausal male at his worst, and a charming cautionary tale about the dangers of pursuing a voyeuristic fantasy into the real world. Moore and Andrews are startlingly fine, and Derek is astonishingly beautiful and completely shallow—luckily for her, so is the character she plays. One of Blake Edwards's best non–*Pink Panther* films.

THE TENANT
1976, USA/France, R ☆☆☆
Roman Polanski, Shelley Winters, Lila Kedrova, Jo Van Fleet, Isabelle Adjani, Melvyn Douglas. Directed by Roman Polanski. 126 min.

In this slyly humorous horror tale, Roman Polanski plays a file clerk who rents a gloomy flat from concierge Shelley Winters and landlord Melvyn Douglas. Soon he discovers that the previous resident leaped to her death and he begins to suspect that his fellow tenants are conspiring to drive him to a similar fate. Shot in heavy, saturated colors and thick with portent, *The Tenant* is slow and oppressive going in parts, but it's masterfully handled by the director. (a.k.a.: *Le Locataire*)

TEN BROTHERS OF SHAOLIN
1979, Hong Kong ☆
Chia Ling, Chang Yi, Liang Chia-Jen, Don Wong Dao.

The ten brothers are Shaolin fighters who are protecting King Chu Chen of the Ming Dynasty from the Chings. It is a period story that is rendered with some authenticity but no original flair. The fights, too, fail to build in intensity and complexity.

THE TEN COMMANDMENTS
1956, USA ☆☆☆
Charlton Heston, Yul Brynner, Anne Baxter, Edward G. Robinson, Yvonne DeCarlo, Debra Paget, John Derek, Nina Foch, Cedric Hardwicke, Martha Scott, Judith Anderson, Vincent Price, John Carradine. Directed by Cecil B. DeMille. 219 min.

Cecil B. DeMille's endless epic is cheesy and anachronistic—what with the Egyptian harem giggling around the swimming pool like California girls, and the words of God etched by lightning bolt on the stones of Mount Sinai; both Cedric Hardwicke's English-gent old Pharaoh and Yul Brynner's Siamese young Pharaoh are hilarious. But there's undeniable majesty in Charlton Heston's Moses; when he abandons his career as Egypt's playboy prince to become the world's first abolitionist, his beard becomes almost as long as his staff. DeMille's film doesn't have much to do with the Bible, but, with its celebration of freedom through law, it's a classic document of 1950s American confidence.

TEN DAYS THAT SHOOK THE WORLD
1928, Russia ☆☆☆½
Directed by Sergei M. Eisenstein. 75 min.

Commissioned to commemorate the tenth anniversary of the 1917 revolution, this account of the ten days in which the Bolsheviks overthrew the reigning powers is one of Sergei Eisenstein's least accessible but most creative efforts: cold, rigorous, at times absurdly stylized. The film features some of the key figures and events of the period (with Trotsky's role carefully excised); but the real Marxist political meat is dramatized in such dizzying, erotic scenes as the Bolshevik soldier who tears apart the czarina's overstuffed imperial boudoir and a horse who dangles over the opening of the drawbridge in Leningrad. It is hard to believe that Eisenstein was severely criticized by his peers for being a pure formalist. *Ten Days* is a perfect example of his fusion of left-wing ideas and his formal experiments. The story is based in part on John Reed's *Ten Days that Shook the World* (which was also a source for Warren Beatty's bio of Reed in *Reds*). (a.k.a.: *October*)

TENDER COUSINS

See *Tendres Cousines*

TENDER IS THE NIGHT
1962, USA ☆☆
Jennifer Jones, Jason Robards, Jr., Joan Fontaine, Tom Ewell, Jill St. John. Directed by Henry King. 146 min.

This is an enervating film translation of a Scott Fitzgerald novel set in Europe in the 1920s that would be difficult to film under the best of circumstances (a six-hour version made for cable TV in 1985 fared even worse). Jennifer Jones has the requisite fragility for the role of Nicole, but she can't quite convey the psychosis of the character. Far worse is Jason Robards as the once-dynamic Dick Diver, whose life ends up a sacrifice to defeatism, brought on by his wife's mental illness. Because of Robards's blandness in the key role, the dual story lines of Nicole's rejuvenation and Dick's downfall never strike sparks. What we're left with is a prettified "doomed romance" set against gorgeous international backgrounds. In this superficial production, Joan Fontaine's flashy performance steals the show.

TENDER MERCIES
1983, USA, PG ☆☆☆½
Robert Duvall, Tess Harper, Allan Hubbard, Betty Buckley, Ellen Barkin, Wilford Brimley. Directed by Bruce Beresford. 89 min.

Bruce Beresford's first American film is a touching, sensitive portrait of personal redemption, set on the Texas prairie. Robert Duvall earned himself an Academy Award as Mac Sledge, a down-and-out country singer given a new lease on happiness by a lovely, lonely young widow, played with conviction by newcomer Tess Harper, and her small son. People from Sledge's past complicate matters, while the rhythms and themes of country music complement a nice screenplay (also an Oscar winner) by Horton Foote. Duvall writes and sings his own music.

TENDRES COUSINES
1980, France, R ½☆
Anja Shute, Thierry Tevini, Macha Meril, Catherine Rouvel, Pierre Vernier, Jean Rougerie. Directed by David Hamilton. 90 min.

Photographer David Hamilton applies his pretentious and inane "artistic vision"—soft-focus on soft-core subjects—to the world of moving images for the third time, and comes away with a lot of mist devoid of mystery. This round involves the sexual exploits of a young boy and the various women who populate his parents' summer estate. In line with Hamilton's own indulgent sexual fantasies, which primarily center on incest, the boy seeks the affection of his reluctant cousin, and, with World War II breaking out in Europe and toppling the conventions of peacetime society, he eventually wins her. Lame and dull. (a.k.a.: *Tender Cousins*)

TEN FROM YOUR SHOW OF SHOWS ☆☆☆☆
1973, USA
Sid Caesar, Imogene Coca, Carl Reiner, Howard Morris. Directed by Max Liebman. 102 min.

Surrounded by a brilliant writing team and hilarious second bananas, Sid Caesar starred in the most highly acclaimed comedy show of the 1950s. It's not the broad humor or rowdy shenanigans of Milton Berle or Ed Wynn, but clever satire and sharp parodies. One can discern what all the shouting was about in this compilation film, but not every sketch is a knockout. Our favorite moments are an hysterical takeoff on *From Here to Eternity* and a perfectly timed bit of physical comedy involving a cuckoo clock gone haywire. The real joy here is watching the inimitable Imogene Coca, that rubber-faced comedienne who unfortunately never again found as congenial an atmosphere as she had on this comedy series.

TEN LITTLE INDIANS ☆☆½
1965, USA
Hugh O'Brian, Shirley Eaton, Fabian, Leo Genn, Stanley Holloway, Wilfrid Hyde-White, Daliah Lavi, Dennis Price. Directed by George Pollock. 92 min.

This is the second version of the Agatha Christie mystery, first (and most successfully) filmed by René Clair in 1945 as *And Then There Were None*. Ten people, each with a guilty secret, are trapped in an Alpine mansion and killed one by one. Which of them is the killer? Unlike the Clair version and the 1975 remake, this uses Christie's original ending. The film *Clue* in 1985 was more or less a parody.

TEN LITTLE INDIANS ☆☆
1975, Italy/France/Spain/West Germany, PG
Oliver Reed, Elke Sommer, Stéphane Audran, Charles Aznavour, Richard Attenborough, Gert Frobe, Herbert Lom. Directed by Peter Collinson. 98 min.

This third film version of the Agatha Christie mystery is the least successful of the three, though it will still keep you guessing if you don't already know the plot. Ten people are summoned to a remote mansion (located, for no good reason, in Iran in this version), where they are told that each is guilty of a murder for which he cannot legally be tried and therefore will meet justice here. It soon becomes apparent, as their numbers decrease, that the host/killer is one of the ten. But which one? The enjoyment is in the plot only; the cast of international stars—with the exception of Oliver Reed, who is inexplicably jolly throughout—all look as though they would rather be somewhere else. The ending is the same as in the 1945 version, which was different from Christie's.

TENNESSEE'S PARTNER ☆☆
1955, USA
John Payne, Ronald Reagan, Rhonda Fleming, Coleen Gray. Directed by Allan Dwan. 87 min.

In a pioneer-days Western, a good cowboy (Ronald Reagan) falls in with a trigger-happy gambler and saloon proprietress. Black hats, white hats, old hat, but it's given a better-than-average production and nice performances. Based on a Bret Harte story; shot in Eastmancolor.

TEN NORTH FREDERICK ☆☆½
1958, USA
Gary Cooper, Diane Varsi, Geraldine Fitzgerald, Tom Tully, Suzy Parker. Directed by Philip Dunne. 102 min.

John O'Hara's potboiler comes to the screen with the politics and romance intact, but it seems to be awash in soap suds now. Geraldine Fitzgerald plays a shrewish Lady Macbeth, who pushes reluctant Gary Cooper into the political arena, but he is more concerned with tossing his hat onto Suzy Parker's bed. The believable May-December romance compensates for the all-enveloping histrionics of most of the cast. A tasty soap opera, but nothing distinctive.

TEN RILLINGTON PLACE ☆☆☆
1971, Great Britain
Richard Attenborough, Judy Geeson, John Hurt, Andre Morrell, Gabrielle Daye. Directed by Richard Fleischer. 111 min.

This is a chilling film treatment of the notorious John Christie murder case. Richard Fleischer has proven particularly adept at presenting true-life crime studies (*The Boston Strangler*, *Compulsion*) and this is no exception. Consistently absorbing, this grim film probes the facts behind some bizarre slayings and delves into the psychology of the killer, a Milquetoast who fills up his lonely hours by killing women and children. Richard Attenborough is frightening as the demented man; this is possibly his best screen work.

TENTACLES ☆
1977, Italy, PG
John Huston, Shelley Winters, Henry Fonda, Bo Hopkins, Cesare Danova, Claude Akins. Directed by Oliver Hellman. 90 min.

Jaws with suction cups. In this dreadful waste of talents, a giant octopus (not played by Shelley Winters, unfortunately) terrorizes a seaside resort. In what you might consider an homage to Toho studios, the monster is dispatched at the end by killer whales, formerly the bad guys in such films as *Orca*. The director, whose name is actually Ovidio Assonitis, previously gave the world *Beyond the Door*, a rip-off of *The Exorcist*.

THE TENTH VICTIM ☆☆☆½
1965, Italy
Marcello Mastroianni, Ursula Andress, Elsa Martinelli, Salvo Randone, Massimo Serato. Directed by Elio Petri. 92 min.

Ursula Andress is sexily leonine as a huntress tracking down Marcello Mastroianni. Marcello is befuddled and attracted, and he's trying to kill Ursula. It's all part of a weird futuristic game conducted in a glossy, sterile world. This is an unrecognized classic Italian comedy of the 1960s and a lighthearted work from a director better known for the intense *Investigation of a Citizen Above Suspicion*—both are good reasons for seeing the movie. An even better reason is that it is good, dirty-minded fun. Watch out for Ursula's bullet-firing bra—she'll let you have it with both barrels.

TEN TO MIDNIGHT ☆
1983, USA, R
Charles Bronson, Lisa Eilbacher, Andrew Stevens, Gene Davis, Wilford Brimley, Geoffrey Lewis. Directed by J. Lee Thompson. 100 min.

Yet another Charles Bronson variant on *Death Wish*, with Chuck taking personal vengeance on a psycho killer that some judge let off on a legal technicality. The killer is a nice, cleancut young man who prefers to disrobe before dispatching his victims. When police sergeant Bronson catches him, he strengthens his case by planting some additional evidence on the killer, resulting in the case being thrown out of court. Just in case you're still not persuaded that this scum deserves to die, he begins to terrorize Bronson's daughter. Director J. Lee Thompson used to make solid action-adventure films (the best was *The Guns of Navarone*), but in the last few years has consistently ground out gory, reactionary trash like this.

TEN WHO DARED ☆
1960, USA
Brian Keith, John Beal, James Drury, R. G. Armstrong, Ben Johnson, L. Q. Jones. Directed by William Beaudine. 92 min.

A slice of American history gets Disney-ized into a simpleminded, insufferably boring mess. The story of ten Union soldiers after the Civil War who were the first to explore the Colorado River might make for a good tale in more competent hands than these, where silly, overdrawn characters and artificial drama clutter the narrative. The pioneer spirit could never have been this dull.

TERMINAL CHOICE ☆
1985, Canada, R
Joe Spano, Diane Venora, Ellen Barkin, David McCallum, Robert Joy. Directed by Sheldon Larry. 97 min.

An unusually talented cast (including many New York thespians along with Joe Spano of "Hill Street Blues") is subjected to a succession of mysterious, mechanical deaths in a medical clinic. Successively called *Trauma*, *Critical List*, and *Death List*, this spin-off of *Coma* by any other name would be just as anesthetizing.

TERMINAL ISLAND ☆½
1973, USA, R
Phyllis Elizabeth Davis, Don Marshall, Barbara Leigh, Sean Kenney, Roger Mosley, Tom Selleck, Jo Morrow. Directed by Stephanie Rothman. 88 min.

After the future abolition (finally!) of the death penalty in the U.S., incorrigible murderers are sent to an island prison camp off the California coast. Catalina it's not. Below par for Stephanie Rothman, an interesting director (see *Working Girls*); she is a former protégée of Roger Corman who became queen of the B's, specializing in throwaway sex films for the drive-in circuit.

THE TERMINAL MAN ☆☆
1974, USA, PG
George Segal, Joan Hackett, Jill Clayburgh, Richard Dysart, Michael C. Gwynne, Donald Moffat. Directed by Mike Hodges. 104 min.

Yet another modernization of the Frankenstein story, this time based on a novel by Michael Crichton (who also wrote *The Andromeda Strain*). When a computer scientist suffers from uncontrollably violent outbursts after an automobile accident, he submits himself to an experimental operation in which electrodes are implanted in his brain to neutralize the outbursts. Of course, it all goes wrong and he becomes a full-time killing machine. George Segal is well cast (against type) as the murderous scientist, and director Mike Hodges provides some interesting baroque touches, but the film as a whole is cold, off-putting, and poorly paced—the operation scene seems to go on forever.

THE TERMINATOR ☆☆☆
1984, USA, R
Arnold Schwarzenegger, Michael Biehn, Linda Hamilton. Directed by James Cameron. 105 min.

A death-dealing robot from the future tracks down a young woman and kills everything in its path. This is really the story of the Inseminator, a regular guy from the future who is sent to impregnate a young woman before a huge birth-control device, played by snotty behemoth Arnold Schwarzenegger, can kill her and prevent the birth of a rabidly anti-robot human revolutionary. Got it? The script, by director James Cameron and producer Gale Hurd, actually has some funny little things to say about our present dependence on machines, and, in one sense, the movie tells of our domesticated mechanical friends turned against us. Gut-wrenching violence, and nonstop action.

TERMS OF ENDEARMENT ☆☆☆☆
1983, USA, PG
Shirley MacLaine, Debra Winger, Jack Nicholson, Jeff Daniels, John Lithgow. Directed by James L. Brooks. 132 min.

Affecting, poignant, manipulative, slick tearjerker about a vain woman and her beloved daughter. One of the few contemporary melodramas that work, it pulls all the stops and milks the material for all the laughs and sobs it will bear. A high-powered cast and slick, tight production values made this a smash hit at the time of its theatrical release. The film succeeds by taking its characters very seriously, and using writer Larry McMurtry's method of having them whittle away at each other, never risking the audience's intense, emotional involvement. Winner of Academy Awards for Best Picture, Best Director, Best Actress (Shirley MacLaine, beating fellow nominee Debra Winger), and Best Supporting Actor (Jack Nicholson).

TERRACES ☆½
1977, USA
Lloyd Bochner, Jane Dulo, Arny Freeman, Julie Newmar, Lola Albright, Tim Thomerson. Directed by Lila Garrett. 78 min.

A pilot for a series that never made it, this is the usual soap opera stuff tied together by the common denominator of the building in which all of the principals live. There's a married doctor having a homosexual affair, a former Vegas showgirl now living as a "kept woman," an insecure young woman having an affair with her tennis coach, an attempted suicide, and everything else that makes life worth living in Los Angeles.

TERROR ☆☆
1978, Great Britain, R
John Nolan, Carolyn Courage, James Aubrey, Sarah Keller, Tricia Walsh. Directed by Norman J. Warren. 86 min.

The best part of this average horror movie is the first quarter—a film-within-a-film about an ancient witch, made in the style of the 1960s Hammer films. It turns out to be part of a film that James Nolan is making about one of his ancestors; when he shows it to his cousin, she becomes possessed by the spirit of the witch and sets about wreaking some kind of retroactive vengeance. With suitable amounts of gore, for those so inclined.

TERROR BY NIGHT ☆☆
1946, USA
Basil Rathbone, Nigel Bruce, Alan Mowbray, Dennis Hoey, Renee Godfrey, Billy Bevan, Skelton Knaggs. Directed by Roy William Neill. 60 min.

The penultimate entry in the Rathbone-Bruce Sherlock Holmes series, which came to an end later in 1946 when producer/director Roy William Neill died. Here Baker Street's best is employed to guard a famous diamond on a train en route from England to Scotland. At least by this point World War II had ended, so the viewer is spared watching Holmes fighting Nazis and delivering patriotic speeches.

TERROR IN THE AISLES ☆½
1984, USA, R
Donald Pleasence, Nancy Allen. Directed by Andrew J. Kuehn. 84 min.

A *That's Entertainment!* of horror movies, moderated by Donald Pleasence and Nancy Allen, who dispense platitudes between clips from fright films old and new. Clearly designed to be a roller-coaster ride of thrills and chills, it suffers from excessive editing, which often destroys carefully crafted shock effects, and an eclecticism that juxtaposes footage from supernatural horror pictures and conventional thrillers to no good effect. As a result of last-minute editing designed to avoid an MPAA "X" at the time of its theatrical release, the film is less violent than it might have been, considering the subject. With a clip of Alfred Hitchcock explaining his theory of suspense.

TERROR IN THE WAX MUSEUM ☆½
1973, USA, PG
Ray Milland, Broderick Crawford, Elsa Lanchester, Maurice Evans, John Carradine, Louis Hayward, Patric Knowles. Directed by Georg Fenady. 93 min.

There may be terror in the wax museum, but it doesn't make its way out into the audience. Good cast apparently absorbed all of the production budget, leaving nothing for a writer, so instead they just rehashed the usual "Ohmigod, Martha, I think those wax figures are killing people" plot. Viewers will arrive at this conclusion some time before the characters, as they will be tipped off by the inability of the actors playing the statues to stand still for long periods of time.

THE TERROR OF TINY TOWN ½☆
1938, USA
Billy Curtis, Yvonne Moray, Little Billy, Billy Platt, Johnny Bambury. Directed by Sam Newfield. 63 min.

A pint-sized prairie saga with a minuscule budget and all-midget cast, all of whom sound as if they were dubbed in by Billy Barty, this piece about a varmint rustling cattle and stirring up a range feud is only for film freaks who will sit through *anything*.

TERROR ON TAPE ☆½
1985, USA
Cameron Mitchell; and film clips featuring Nastassja Kinski, James Earl Jones, John Carradine, Marianne Faithful, and others. Directed by Robert Worms. 90 min.

This made-for-video compilation of decapitations and shrieks is strung together by a device so obtrusive and ludicrous that—like the twenty "horror" films it frames—it soon becomes funny. Cameron Mitchell is the proprietor of the Shoppe of Horrors Video Store. His name is actually Shoppe (that's about as witty as it gets). Three customers wander in on Halloween night and ask him if he has any scary movies. Boy oh boy, does he. The clips that follow are from films so buried in time that the tape smells like a graveyard. Still, there are limbs from some overlooked genre miniclassics, such as *To the Devil a Daughter*, starring a rakish Nastassja Kinski; *Return of the Alien's Deadly Spawn*, starring a crock of hungry leeches; and the child-possession pic *Nightmare*. If anything, *Terror on Tape* shows up the genre: how much it relies on innuendo, how limited is its repertoire of frights, how close the cheap films are to the rhythms of a porn movie. It's a brisk, well-edited tape, but the Shoppe of Horrors Video Store should be demolished with an ax.

TERROR ON THE 40TH FLOOR ☆½
1974, USA (TV)
John Forsythe, Joseph Campanella, Lynn Carlin, Anjanette Comer, Pippa Scott, Don Meredith. Directed by Jerry Jameson. 72 min.

The Towering Inferno is scaled down for the small screen. Seven people are trapped on the fortieth floor of a burning skyscraper; no one knows that they're there, and they can't get word out. With as many plot complications as can be packed into one and one-quarter hour's running time.

TERROR ON TOUR ☆
1980, USA
Rick Styles, Chip Greenman, Rich Pemberton, Dave Galuzzo, Larry Thomasoff. Directed by Don Edmonds. 90 min.

The Clowns, a noisy rock band whose stage show features much simulated violence, find that a maniac has taken his inspiration from their act and is killing various of their hangers-on. The police suspect that one of the musicians might be responsible, and the climax of sorts occurs during one of their shows. Though there is the germ of an interesting idea here, *Terror on Tour* is boring and badly made—dialogue is sometimes inaudible, shots are badly staged, and the lighting is so perfunctory that when the killer is finally unmasked it is almost impossible to tell who he is. Add in endless scenes of the band partying in an ugly theater and some perfunctory psychology, and the result is deadly.

TERROR OUT OF THE SKY ☆½
1978, USA (TV)
Efrem Zimbalist, Jr., Tovah Feldshuh, Dan Haggerty, Bruce French, Lonny Chapman. Directed by Lee H. Katzin. 100 min.

. . . And right into your living room. This *Terror* is a stingless sequel to the TV movie *The Savage Bees*. Although it's impossible to tell whether any of the same insects are repeating their roles, they are pretty nifty thespians. When seen buzzing around New Orleans in the last film, the killer bees were temporarily routed, but a new bunch of pollen counters are on tap here to teach those little buggers a lesson in social amenities. No doubt this will be followed by another sequel, named *To Hive and Hive Not*.

TERROR TRAIN ☆☆½
1980, Canada, R
Ben Johnson, Jamie Lee Curtis, Hart Bochner, David Copperfield, Derek Mackinnon, Sandee Currie, Timothy Webber, Anthony Sherwood. Directed by Roger Spottiswoode. 97 min.

As a screen heroine, Jamie Lee Curtis is a swashbuckling debutante, a two-fisted dream date. Decked out like a female Errol Flynn, in a dashing pirate-cum-gypsy outfit of knee boots and belted tunic, Curtis is the best reason to see this rather limp Canadian variation on the stalk-and-kill *Halloween* formula. Some frat-house jocks and their girlfriends throw a costume party on an excursion train, and a killer wanders among them, assuming the disguise of each new victim. There are funny costumes, flashing strobes, dance numbers, magic tricks (by real-life magician David Copperfield), practical jokes, and ribald romantic entanglements. In fact, the many embellishments make it rather difficult to keep your mind on the worn-out story—which, when you think about it, is probably just as well.

THE TERRY FOX STORY ☆☆½
1983, USA
Eric Fryer, Robert Duvall, Rosalind Chao, Chris Makepeace. Directed by Ralph Thomas. 96 min.

This true story of a young man who ran a "Marathon of Hope" across Canada after losing a leg to cancer was the first movie made for cable television, and it's more well intentioned than dramatically successful. Eric Fryer, himself an amputee, resists portraying Fox as a saint or a martyr, and the film's strengths derive largely from his restraint. But Robert Duvall is oddly bland as Fox's coach, and the direction and writing do nothing to distinguish the film from a host of network-TV counterparts.

TESS ☆☆☆½
1979, France/Great Britain, PG
Nastassja Kinski, Peter Firth, John Bett, Tom Chadbon, Rosemary Martin, Leigh Lawson, Sylvia Coleridge. Directed by Roman Polanski. 170 min.

An innocently stunning Nastassja Kinski stars as the haunted, victimized heroine of Thomas Hardy's novel in Roman Polanski's sweepingly cinematic adaptation set in the countryside of England. Treated like an epic, in length and texture, the film moves at a poetically deliberate pace, drawing out the pleasure of a visually captivating experience. This compelling, fatalistic account of innocence lost, wealth gained, and love confused won Academy Awards for Cinematography, Art Direction, and Costume Design.

TESTAMENT ☆☆☆½
1983, USA, PG
Jane Alexander, William Devane, Ross Harris, Roxana Zal, Lukas Haas, Philip Anglim, Lilia Skala, Leon Ames, Lurene Tuttle, Rebecca DeMornay, Kevin Costner, Mako, Mico Olmos. Directed by Lynne Littman. 90 min.

The bomb has been dropped on San Francisco, giving everyone in the neighboring suburb of Hamlin a fatal dose of radiation.

This film spares us the physical symptoms of radiation sickness; instead, it focuses on a courageous mother of three (superbly played by Jane Alexander) who must remain stoical while her world dissolves around her. Shot for PBS's "American Playhouse" but released in theaters first, *Testament* often seems too tidy for its own good (the holocaust as staged by a neatness freak), but it also stirs up apocalyptic feelings of dread and disorientation that few other movies have given us. Lynne Littman, who came out of independent filmmaking and public TV, is one of the more gifted young women directors to emerge in the 1980s.

A TEST OF LOVE ☆☆☆½
1984, Australia, PG
Angela Punch McGregor, Drew Forsythe, Tina Arhondis, Wallas Eaton, Liddy Clark, Simon Chilvers, Monica Maughan, Mark Butler. Directed by Gil Brealey. 93 min.

One has to admire the integrity of this movie. Based on the true account of a child with cerebral palsy who was mistakenly institutionalized and deprived of all opportunities for a normal life, this film achieves the rare virtue of forcing the viewer to confront prejudice, hope, anguish, and rage by looking at the world through the eyes of one of its victims. The use of Tina Arhondis, a young lady with severe cerebral palsy, for the pivotal role assures that exact limits and possibilities of the character are never out of sight; as it turns out, Arhondis (a nine-year-old girl playing a teenager) is a fine actress. The movie never descends to sentimental weeping; this is the story of an angry young woman who understands exactly what has been denied her. Even better, the movie doesn't fall into the trap of factualizing and preaching; this is a very dramatic and moving account of a teacher and pupil who come to understand each other. The source book, *Annie's Coming Out* by Anne McDonald and Rosemary Crossley, was a major success abroad. An inspirational must-see. (a.k.a.: *Annie's Coming Out*)

TEX ☆☆☆
1982, USA, PG
Matt Dillon, Jim Metzler, Ben Johnson, Meg Tilly, Bill McKinney, Frances Lee McCain, Emilio Estevez, Phil Brock, Jack Thibeau, Tom Virtue. Directed by Tim Hunter. 103 min.

Matt Dillon has the sort of surly glamour you rarely see in teenage film stars, and in this adaptation of S. E. Hinton's novel he gets a chance to act, too. Dillon's Tex is a free-spirited adolescent living with his eighteen-year-old brother (beautifully played by Jim Metzler) in a small Oklahoma town. The interplay between these two draws you into the movie, even as the story devolves into a series of melodramatic devices; but in its own hoky, conventional way, *Tex* is more effective than the more recent Hinton adaptations (*The Outsiders* and *That Was Then, This Is Now* among them.)

TEXAS ☆☆½
1941, USA
William Holden, Glenn Ford, Claire Trevor, Edgar Buchanan, George Bancroft, Don Beddoe. Directed by George Marshall. 93 min.

An "A" cast in a B-plus Western about two Confederate army rejects whose friendship is cast asunder when they wind up on opposite sides of the law, one as a ranchhand and the other as a rustler, and on opposite sides of Claire Trevor's affection. There are some predictable bits of low-comedy business, but nice work from the leads, ripe support by Edgar Buchanan, and a shoot-'em-up climax.

THE TEXAS CHAINSAW MASSACRE ☆☆½
1974, USA, R
Marilyn Burns, Allen Danziger, Paul A. Partain, Gunner Hansen. Directed by Tobe Hooper. 83 min.

One of the most revoltingly gory cheap horror films ever made—with graphic depictions of meathook impalings, pickaxes in the head, and freshly dismembered corpses—this is also, undeniably, one of the best, with young director Tobe Hooper taking exploitative violence into previously unexplored realms. Oddly enough, *Chainsaw* is roughly based on the same real-life incident that inspired *Psycho*. If Hitchcock's film is the pinnacle of sophisticated horror, this one has the dubious distinction of being at the top of the splatter heap. Be warned, though: unless you salivate at words like "splatter," stay away. Followed by an ineffective sequel.

THE TEXAS CHAINSAW MASSACRE PART TWO ☆
1986, USA, X (self-imposed)
Dennis Hopper, Caroline Williams, Bill Johnson, Jim Siedow, Bill Moseley. Directed by Tobe Hooper. 95 min.

The original was sleazy, cheap, and very frightening; *Part Two* is equally sleazy, cheap-*looking*, and not for one second scary. In place of the first film's unpredictable, nightmarish succession of horrors, we have a mechanical, in-jokey script by *Paris, Texas* coauthor L. M. Kit Carson, who makes the action especially stupid, just to let you know he's slumming. Tobe Hooper, who doesn't appear to have learned much more about directing than he knew in 1974, does careless, often slipshod work here, but blame Cannon Films for this cynical update of the exploits of Leatherface and clan, which will please only those who think that gore and horror are one and the same.

TEXAS LADY ☆☆
1955, USA
Claudette Colbert, Barry Sullivan, Ray Collins, James Bell, Horace McMahon, John Litel, Don Haggerty, Douglas Fowley. Directed by Tim Whelan. 85 min.

RKO's last films saw aging actresses go west (see Ginger Rogers in *The First Traveling Saleslady*). In this outing, Claudette Colbert, of all people, starts a newspaper service in a Texas saloon town. Claudette, always the lady, looks very much out of place in period bustles sparring with gambler Barry Sullivan. The color photography isn't especially flattering to her, either.

THANK GOD IT'S FRIDAY ☆½
1978, USA, PG
Donna Summer, Valerie Landsburg, Terri Nunn, Chick Vennera, Ray Vitte, Mark Lonow, Jeff Goldblum, Debra Winger, the Commodores. Directed by Robert Klane. 89 min.

Robert Klane, the screenwriter of *Where's Poppa?*, makes his first film as a director, and it's a badly botched job. *T.G.I.F.* follows sixteen cartoonish characters and a band (the Commodores) through the unlikely and uninteresting tribulations of a night at The Zoo, a singularly unpleasant disco in Los Angeles. The actors are all promising and many have since gone on to bigger and better things, but they've been badly used here. There's not much dancing in the movie, either, and what little there is turns out to be a bewildering pileup of squirming bodies shot from angles that suggest dangerously drugged cameramen.

THANKS A MILLION ☆☆☆½
1935, USA
Dick Powell, Ann Dvorak, Fred Allen, Patsy Kelly, Margaret Irving. Directed by Roy del Ruth. 87 min.

This is one of those pleasant surprises from an era when Hollywood could slap together a decent musical with good intentions and a few specialty numbers. The throwaway songs are by Paul Whiteman and his renowned orchestra. The breezy plot involves a singer (Dick Powell) running for governor (certainly the film was ahead of its time, considering how far George Murphy and Ronald Reagan have gone), under the sponsorship of an acerbic promoter played by the indispensable Fred Allen. Inconsequential, but a pleasure from start to finish—in the vernacular of the time: It's just swell.

THANK YOUR LUCKY STARS ☆☆☆
1943, USA
Dennis Morgan, Joan Leslie, Eddie Cantor, Humphrey Bogart, Bette Davis, Olivia de Havilland, Ann Sheridan, John Garfield. Directed by David Butler. 127 min.

This is the kind of all-star extravaganza that Hollywood turned out by the bucketful in the 1930s (when they were generally disguised as "Follies" of one kind or another) and the 1940s (when most of them were conceived to entertain the troops). This one unites Warner Brothers's biggest stars in the service of an unimaginably silly plot that can be ignored. Humphrey Bogart makes a funny, rather sheepish appearance, Errol Flynn has an absolutely grand number, and Bette Davis sings the specialty number "They're Either Too Young or Too Old" (actually, she sort of recites it, Rex Harrison-style). Concentrate on the stars; you'll wince at Eddie Cantor's too-numerous appearances, and Dennis Morgan and Joan Leslie are as sappy a pair of juveniles as Hollywood ever dumped onscreen.

THAT CHAMPIONSHIP SEASON ☆☆½
1982, USA, R
Bruce Dern, Stacy Keach, Robert Mitchum, Martin Sheen, Paul Sorvino, Arthur Franz. Directed by Jason Miller. 108 min.

Jason Miller's play about the stars of a high school basketball team who have a reunion with their coach twenty-five years later was an outstanding theater piece, and won the Pulitzer Prize and the New York Critics' Award for Best Play in 1972. But in the ten years it took Miller to get the film made, he lost touch with his characters—they seem stiff, occasionally caricatured in the film—and the opening up of the play to bring in the decay of its setting (Scranton, Pennsylvania) is merely distracting. Of the cast, Bruce Dern is best as the simpleminded mayor, and Stacy Keach is also fine as a repressed bureaucrat. The others have their moments, but are hampered by a script that telegraphs its twists far too obviously.

THAT COLD DAY IN THE PARK ☆☆
1969, Canada, R
Sandy Dennis, Michael Burns, Susanne Benton, Luana Anders, Michael Murphy, John Garfield, Jr. Directed by Robert Altman. 91 min.

About halfway through the movie, something finally happens: she meets a silent, sullen young man in the park and takes him home with her. The ending, if you make it that far, is jolting. The videocassette version, the same one released to television, is twenty-two minutes shorter than the theatrical print—whether for better or worse, who can say?

THAT DARN CAT ☆☆☆
1965, USA
Hayley Mills, Dean Jones, Dorothy Provine, Roddy McDowall, Neville Brand, Elsa Lanchester, Ed Wynn. Directed by Robert Stevenson. 116 min.

An agreeable Disney trifle about Hayley Mills and her feline friend, a snoopy Siamese who crosses the path of some comically larcenous types. Soon the FBI is pursuing the pair in addition to tracking down some kidnappers, all adding up to a merry chase. Will the bad guys bump off Hayley and rid the cat of all nine of its lives? This dizzy family fare is worth watching to find out. A bit overextended, but good fun.

THAT HAMILTON WOMAN ☆☆☆
1941, USA
Vivien Leigh, Laurence Olivier, Alan Mowbray, Sara Allgood, Gladys Cooper, Henry Wilcoxon, Heather Angel. Directed by Alexander Korda. 128 min.

As Lord Admiral Nelson and Lady Emma Hamilton, Laurence Olivier and Vivien Leigh make a sublime pair in this stylish, stiff-upper-lip romance. Not terribly satisfying if you're looking for a good cry, and far too tame, but it's cleanly acted, well-produced, and expressively photographed by Rudolph Mate. (a.k.a.: *Lady Hamilton*)

THAT'LL BE THE DAY ☆☆☆
1973, Great Britain, PG
David Essex, Ringo Starr, Rosemary Leach, James Booth, Billy Fury, Keith Moon, Rosalind Ayres. Directed by Claude Whatham. 90 min.

Sort of a British version of *American Graffiti*, the subsequent release of which prevented it from getting the attention it deserved on this side of the Atlantic. David Essex, whose later pop hit "Rock On" earned the film its brief American release, plays a British youth growing up in the late 1950s, going through the usual trials and tribulations and working at a series of dull jobs in order to fulfill every boy's dream—to buy a guitar and start a band. In the tradition of British "kitchen sink" dramas, this is more realistic than its nostalgic American counterparts, which tend to look at past generations through rose-colored glasses. Ringo Starr is excellent as Essex's friend, Mike, and Who drummer Keith Moon (the film's musical consultant) has a nice bit as well. Sequel: *Stardust*.

THAT LUCKY TOUCH ☆☆
1975, Great Britain
Roger Moore, Susannah York, Shelley Winters, Lee J. Cobb, Jean-Pierre Cassel, Raf Vallone. Directed by Christopher Miles. 93 min.

This farce about a charming chauvinist arms dealer (who else but Roger Moore?) and his unlikely alliance with a hard-shelled feminist aims for the breeziness, sophistication, and easy repartee of an old Cary Grant film. Unfortunately, the film tries so hard you can practically hear it grunting in its effort to be casual. Director Christopher Miles is handy with the performers in the cluttered cast, but less skilled at setting up and executing the tiresome sight gags.

THAT NIGHT IN RIO ☆☆½
1941, USA
Alice Faye, Don Ameche, Carmen Miranda, S. Z. Sakall, J. Carrol Naish. Directed by Irving Cummings. 90 min.

A fetching musical featuring Fox's vivid color photography, this is saddled with one of those mistaken-identity plots that never seem to work as well as they did in Shakespeare's *Comedy of Errors*. If you can overlook the plot about a Rio big shot being mistaken for someone with a less savory background, there are compensations. Alice Faye is a bit subdued but still proves she was the premiere torch singer of the forties. And Carmen Miranda will elate musical fans with her Brazilian-bombshell presence whether she's spinning on her platform shoes or creating her own form of musical Esperanto during such numbers as "Chica Chica Boom Chic." One of those South-of-the-Border Good Neighbor Policy musicals, this was filmed earlier as *Folies Bergère* and later as *On the Riviera* with Danny Kaye.

THAT OBSCURE OBJECT OF DESIRE ☆☆☆☆
1977, France/Spain, R
Fernando Rey, Carole Bouquet, Angela Molina, Julien Bertheau, Andre Weber. Directed by Luis Buñuel. 100 min.

An aging roué relentlessly pursues a virgin and finally she agrees to let him into her bed; the catch is that he is not allowed to touch her. The man sends the young woman into the bathroom to change clothes; a different woman emerges a few moments later. Luis Buñuel serves up his usual plate of wit, irony, and surrealism. The movie is impossible to categorize; it's even difficult to follow. Suffice it to say that it's a story of frustrated expectations—even Buñuel seems so frustrated with the plot that he continually shifts settings, time, and mood. Fernando Rey is marvelous as the sensualist who is alternately bored and obsessed. Buñuel's wacky view of the world in 1977—terrorists, hijackings, a mysterious killer virus, religious radicalism—looks a lot like reality today.

THAT'S DANCING! ☆☆½
1985, USA, G
Narrators: Liza Minnelli, Gene Kelly, Ray Bolger, Sammy Davis, Jr., Mikhail Barishnikov. Directed by Jack Haley, Jr. 105 min.

This coffee-table-book approach to film history contains many colorful and entertaining film clips but fails completely at giving any kind of insight into what made them great or even how they were made. Also, the refusal of director Jack Haley, Jr., to repeat footage he used in the *That's Entertainment* films creates gaps (most notably, Gene Kelly's "Singin' in the Rain") which he fills in with stuff better left in the vaults. Still, it's good to see Fred and Ginger "pick themselves up" in *Swing Time*, Jimmy Cagney "give his regards to Broadway" in *Yankee Doodle Dandy*, and Ray Bolger in newly restored footage from *The Wizard of Oz*.

THAT'S ENTERTAINMENT! ☆☆☆☆
1974, USA, G
Narrators: Elizabeth Taylor, Liza Minnelli, Frank Sinatra, James Stewart, Gene Kelly, Fred Astaire, Mickey Rooney, Debbie Reynolds. Directed by Jack Haley, Jr. 133 min.

MGM wasn't the only studio to make a lot of movie musicals, but they certainly made the best. *That's Entertainment!* is the apt title for a dazzling array of film clips of the best of MGM musicals. There's a generous helping of magical work of Judy Garland, Fred Astaire, Gene Kelly, and Eleanor Powell. The material is well chosen, and even after two hours and thirteen minutes, you'll be wanting more.

THAT'S ENTERTAINMENT, PART 2 ☆☆½
1976, USA, G
Narrators: Fred Astaire and Gene Kelly. New sequences directed by Gene Kelly. 132 min.

Here's yet another tribute to those great MGM musicals. There are still many moments of pleasure to be had, but this time the film is weighted down by poorly filmed new sequences with "hosts" Fred Astaire and Gene Kelly and a series of tediously reverential tributes (to Paris, popular songwriters, and Frank Sinatra). Just when you're about to eject your cassette, however, there's Judy Garland, Lena Horne, Cyd Charisse, (the young) Astaire and Kelly, et al.—who resuscitate this long, sagging, disorderly compilation.

THAT SINKING FEELING ☆☆☆
1979, Scotland, PG
Robert Buchanan, John Hughes, Gordon John Sinclair. Directed by Bill Forsyth. 82 min.

This first film from Scotland's Bill Forsyth (*Gregory's Girl, Local Hero, Comfort and Joy*) will please the growing number of his fans, though others might be a bit put off by it at first. Using a group of neighborhood youths and filming in some of the drearier areas of Glasgow, Forsyth has put together a shoestring comedy about leading meaningless lives that isn't at all serious, isn't really very funny much of the time, but that is still quite charming. The story follows some bored teenagers who decide to pull off a grand theft of one hundred sinks from a local warehouse. Of course, they don't really have any profitable use for one hundred sinks; nor is the warehouse worthy of the elaborate plans they make to break into it. But that's what Forsyth's world is like: what's going on is never so important or interesting as the peripheral details. An overblown, ridiculous ending set in a hospital doesn't work at all, but he's learned better since.

THAT'S LIFE ☆½
1986, USA, PG-13
Jack Lemmon, Julie Andrews, Robert Loggia, Sally Kellerman, Jennifer Edwards, Matt Lattanzi, Chris Lemmon, Emma Walton, Cynthia Sikes, Felicia Farr. Directed by Blake Edwards. 102 min.

Just because Blake Edwards is raging against aging, does he have to make the audience feel older and wearier in the process? While a family's courageous mother (Julie Andrews) stoically awaits the verdict on her biopsy, her infantile sixty-year-old husband (Jack Lemmon) suffers from career angst, near-fatal hypochondria, and impotence. In the background, a chorus of whining, selfish children dump their petty problems into Mommy's lap while the audience waits and wonders whether she's going to die. Andrews is good and Lemmon has flashes of power, but the film's balance of slapstick and sententiousness is overbearing, and the sentimentality bloats the film further. It ends up as Edwards's home-movie salute to nepotism, with his daughter, Andrews's daughter, and Lemmon's son all demonstrating why they haven't worked much in other people's films.

THAT'S THE WAY OF THE WORLD ☆☆½
1975, USA, PG
Harvey Keitel, Ed Nelson, Cynthia Bostick, Bert Parks, Earth, Wind and Fire. Directed by Sig Shore. 99 min.

Major attractions here are the score and appearances by Earth, Wind and Fire, playing themselves as a struggling young band. Unfortunately, they serve mostly as background for this thin exposé of the music business. Harvey Keitel plays a record-company executive who tries to help EWF make it big but who is instead forced to push a watered-down family band. Keitel is good, as always, but the story and characterization aren't strong enough to give this any real impact. *Note:* That's not *the* Bert Parks.

THAT TOUCH OF MINK ☆☆½
1962, USA
Doris Day, Cary Grant, Audrey Meadows, John Astin, Dick Sargent. Directed by Delbert Mann. 99 min.

Not in the Russian-sable class as far as comedies go; more like a nice hometown synthetic fur. Cary's a tycoon who takes a fancy to poor working girl Doris. Although he sweeps her off her feet, he doesn't carry her into the bedroom until the final minutes. Velvety support from the accomplished supporting cast helps, but the two leads are not the most felicitous teaming (Day's sunny all-American goodwill paired better with Rock Hudson, and Grant's urbanity seems to distance him, as if he were dressed up to appear in an Ernst Lubitsch movie and instead somehow wandered onto the set of a TV sitcom.

THAT WAS THEN . . . THIS IS NOW ☆☆
1985, USA, PG-13
Emilio Estevez, Craig Sheffer. Directed by Chris Cain. 98 min.

Another tried and trite examination of the "good boy/bad boy" theme has two former buddies going their separate ways to ruin and salvation in a dilapidated town. Emilio Estevez, who also wrote the screenplay, has plenty of heart and acting ability, but he just isn't capable of perceiving what makes his noble teens tick. When this scene-stealing heartthrob isn't on screen, costar Craig Sheffer adequately holds attention with his suave magnetism and model's looks. Director Chris Cain handles this mediocre stuff with a welcome amount of verve, even when the material simply can't support it. One of the lesser adaptations of an S. E. Hinton novel.

THEATRE OF BLOOD ☆☆☆½
1973, Great Britain, R
Vincent Price, Diana Rigg, Ian Hendry, Harry Andrews, Coral Browne, Jack Hawkins, Robert Morley, Dennis Price, Diana Dors, Milo O'Shea. Directed by Douglas Hickox. 104 min.

Not a Roger Corman chiller but a British horror comedy, this stars Vincent Price as a Shakespearean actor determined to do in eight critics whom he believes denied him a Best Actor award. Each critic is killed in a disgusting but amusing way that relates to a scene from a Shakespeare play (decapitation, swordplay, drowning, etc.). The most memorable of these sequences involves Robert Morley as a portly critic who is stuffed to death with his own pet poodles. A delightful black comedy that gives Price his most perfect role. Not for the squeamish, but recommended to everyone else.

THEATRE OF DEATH ☆☆
1966, Great Britain, PG
Christopher Lee, Lelia Goldoni, Jenny Till, Julian Glover. Directed by Samuel Gallu. 90 min.

This surprisingly dense and subtle thriller is small-scale, but well executed. The Grand Guignol Theatre de la Mort is plagued by strange occurrences while Paris is terrorized by a blood-drinking murderer. Is the new director—Philip Darvas, the mirror image of his father (who vanished under mysterious circumstances)—a vampire? (a.k.a.: *Blood Field*)

THEM! ☆☆☆
1954, USA
James Whitmore, Edmund Gwenn, Joan Weldon, James Arness, Onslow Stevens, Sean McClory, Chris Drake, Sandy Descher, Mary Ann Hokanson, Don Shelton, Fess Parker, Olin Howlin. Directed by Gordon Douglas. 93 min.

Perhaps the best giant-bug movie ever made. It's mutant ants this time: they're poisonous, disgusting, and amazingly fertile—and to kill 'em you gotta burn 'em. The film has a wonderful quasidocumentary atmosphere and a climax that's like the end of *The Third Man*, with insects instead of Orson Welles. One of those 1950s treats that can never go stale.

THERE'S A GIRL IN MY SOUP ☆☆½
1970, Great Britain, R
Peter Sellers, Goldie Hawn, Tony Britton, Nicky Henson, Diana Dors. Directed by Roy Boulting. 94 min.

A mediocre sex comedy that coasts along entirely on the presence of its two stars. Peter Sellers plays a TV gourmet trying to fight back middle age by consorting with every female who comes his way. Goldie Hawn is a kook with whom he has a fling when she breaks up with her drummer boyfriend. Goldie has several not-very-flattering nude scenes and Sellers relies too much on the smug side of his Inspector Clouseau persona, but there are still enough bright moments to make this passable entertainment.

THÉRÈSE ☆☆☆½
1986, France
Catherine Mouchet. Directed by Alain Cavalier. 90 min.

Alain Cavalier's biographical portrait of the nineteenth-century nun known as the little flower of the Carmelites (she became famous, and was eventually canonized, when her diary was published after her death) is a film of hushed, austere beauty and exceptional power, one of the few to depict the difficult and elusive subject of religious devotion. Most of the action is played against a diorama or minimalist sets in the convent, and the almost silent interaction of the nuns combined with their fervid, ecstatic, and almost sexual love of Christ distills the essence of the cloistered religious life as very few other films have done. Stunningly photographed, with a finely nuanced performance by newcomer Catherine Mouchet as Thérèse.

THERE'S NO BUSINESS LIKE SHOW BUSINESS ☆☆☆
1954, USA
Ethel Merman, Marilyn Monroe, Donald O'Connor, Dan Dailey, Mitzi Gaynor, Johnnie Ray. Directed by Walter Lang. 117 min.

A typical 1950s musical, this is fun as long as everyone is singing and dancing, but unfortunately there's this plot that keeps getting in the way. Ethel Merman and Dan Dailey are show-biz parents; son Donald O'Connor and daughter Mitzi Gaynor follow in the family business, although son Johnnie Ray opts for the priesthood instead. Marilyn Monroe is also on hand as the hussy who steals one of the Merm's sons and, even worse, one of her numbers. Apparently nobody informed Merman that she was acting for the movies and not the stage—she storms into a room to shout the simplest line. Highlights include Monroe performing "Heat Wave" and O'Connor and Gaynor recreating one of their parents' numbers. The hokey plot keeps creeping back in, but there's plenty of splash to enjoy.

THERE WAS A CROOKED MAN... ☆☆☆
1970, USA, R
Kirk Douglas, Henry Fonda, Hume Cronyn, Warren Oates, Burgess Meredith, Lee Grant, Arthur O'Connell, Alan Hale. Directed by Joseph L. Mankiewicz. 125 min.

Typical of the kind of cynical Westerns that Hollywood was making in the late 1960s, perhaps in response to the comic-book spaghetti Westerns from Europe that were so popular here, this stands above its brethren simply for the professionalism that went into it. Director Joseph L. Mankiewicz, who usually wrote his own scripts, here uses one by Robert Benton and David Newman (*Bonnie and Clyde*) about a robber (Kirk Douglas) in an Old West prison who schemes to get out and recover his loot just as steadfastly as the reform-minded warden (Henry Fonda) tries to rehabilitate him. It's rather nasty, with the likable Douglas character wiping out friends and enemies alike to suit his purposes, and Mankiewicz does not seem entirely at home with this genre—this was his first and only Western. Well played and well made, nevertheless.

THESE HANDS DESTROY

See *Phantom Kung Fu*

THESE THREE ☆☆☆
1936, USA
Merle Oberon, Miriam Hopkins, Joel McCrea, Bonita Granville, Alma Kruger, Margaret Hamilton, Walter Brennan. Directed by William Wyler. 93 min.

In this first film adaptation of Lillian Hellman's most acclaimed stage play, *The Children's Hour*, Sam Goldwyn removed the then-taboo lesbianism but still came up with a fine film. Here the story is about a vicious schoolgirl who charges that her two teachers are involved in an extramarital affair (rather than a lesbian relationship as in the original). Though softened, the material is still potent, thanks to Hellman's forceful writing (she did the adaptation), Gregg Toland's polished camerawork, and the winning performances—Merle Oberon and Miriam Hopkins as the teachers (their best work), Bonita Granville as the lying student, and Marcia Mae Jones as her unwitting accomplice. *Note*: Wyler remade the film in 1962, restoring the original title and lesbian theme, but the results were less effective.

THEY ALL LAUGHED ☆☆☆
1982, USA, PG
Audrey Hepburn, Ben Gazzara, John Ritter, Colleen Camp, Patti Hansen, Dorothy Stratten, George Morfogen. Directed by Peter Bogdanovich. 116 min.

Peter Bogdanovich's exquisite roundelay is a celebration of improbable love and the way it triumphs in the midst of that great synchronizer, New York City. It's a gentler, less forced genre number than Bogdanovich's *What's Up Doc?* and *At Long Last Love*. The movie follows a trio of detectives who work for an agency that specializes in tailing the wives of suspicious husbands; two of the gumshoes (John Ritter and Ben Gazzara) find themselves falling in love with their marks (Dorothy Stratten and Audrey Hepburn). It's a slight story, but Bogdanovich tells it with charm and exuberance, and he has a beguilingly cockeyed way of looking at the world.

THEY CALL ME BRUCE? ☆½
1982, USA, PG
Johnny Yune, Margaux Hemingway, Ralph Mauro, Pam Huntington, Ric Mancini. Directed by Elliot Hong. 88 min.

Johnny Yune, an unfunny stand-up comic whose entire routine is based on the fact that he's Korean, produced and stars in this unfunny parody of kung fu films. As a cook and low-ranking martial artist, Yune is mistaken for Bruce Lee and gets involved with drug-smuggling mobsters. If Margaux Hemingway took any acting lessons between this and her previous starring film, *Lipstick*, the results don't show.

THEY CALL ME MISTER TIBBS! ☆☆
1970, USA, PG
Sidney Poitier, Barbara McNair, Martin Landau, Anthony Zerbe, Edward Asner. Directed by Gordon Douglas. 108 min.

This is an unmemorable sequel to *In the Heat of the Night*. You may recall Poitier, flaring with steely dignity and fierce pride, growling the sequel's title line in the original film as a response to a racist remark from Southern sheriff Rod Steiger. (You may also recall that Steiger was the one who got the Oscar.) Back in San Francisco, Tibbs tracks down a murderer, interacts with his wife and children, and generally avoids any question of race whatsoever, which may be admirable—this was one of the first Hollywood movies to star a black actor in which you weren't made conscious of it every ninety-four seconds or so.

THEY CALL ME TRINITY ☆☆
1971, Italy, PG
Terence Hill, Bud Spencer, Farley Granger, Stephen Zacharias, Dan Sturkie. Directed E. B. Clucher (Enzo Barboni). 109 min.

The film that made Terence Hill (a.k.a. Mario Girotti) an international star, this spaghetti Western is played almost entirely for laughs, and doesn't hold up well at all. Hill and stepbrother Bud Spencer set themselves up as the law in a western town, supposedly to clean up corruption but actually as part of an elaborate plan to rustle cattle from a crooked rancher. Followed by a sequel, *Trinity is Still My Name*.

THEY CAME FROM WITHIN ☆☆
1975, Canada, R
Paul Hampton, Joe Silver, Lynn Lowry, Allen Magicovsky, Barbara Steele. Directed by David Cronenberg. 88 min.

The first of David Cronenberg's series of grisly, pathological horror films (which also includes *Rabid*, *Scanners*, and *Videodrome*), this features ideas that surface in all of his work, but it suffers from its low budget. A man-made parasite spreads throughout the tenants of a high-rise apartment building, bringing out all of their base desires, resulting in mass orgies and murder sprees. Like most Cronenberg films, this tends to make less and less sense as the tempo picks up, but horror fans will have little to complain about. Produced by *Ghostbusters* director Ivan Reitman, who provided "musical supervision." (a.k.a.: *Shivers*, *The Parasite Murders*, and *Frissons*).

THEY CAME TO CORDURA ☆☆½
1959, USA
Gary Cooper, Rita Hayworth, Van Heflin, Tab Hunter, Richard Conte, Dick York, Robert Keith, Edward Platt. Directed by Robert Rossen. 123 min.

Couldn't Columbia find a better vehicle for the potentially explosive pair of Gary Cooper and Rita Hayworth than this sordid and thematically offensive Western? Both stars appear too old and too tired to generate any steam in this tale of a U.S. Army officer, circa 1916, who is sent to track down five potential Medal of Honor soldiers. Hayworth plays a bitter woman who tags along with the guys. When she chooses rape in order to prevent Cooper's capture, the movie's politics become messy and uncomfortable. Equally unsettling is the depiction of the five men's "heroic" exploits (rape, murder, etc.). This is unpleasant action posing as revisionism. Originally in Cinemascope.

THEY DIED WITH THEIR BOOTS ON ☆☆☆
1941, USA
Errol Flynn, Olivia de Havilland, Gene Lockhart, Regis Toomey, Stanley Ridges, Arthur Kennedy, John Litel, Sydney Greenstreet, Hattie McDaniel, Anthony Quinn, Charles Grapewin. Directed by Raoul Walsh. 140 min.

Boots was the last costarring vehicle for Errol Flynn and Olivia de Havilland and the only one of their eight joint ventures *not* directed by Michael Curtiz. Otherwise, there are no big differences in this Raoul Walsh super-Western except that Errol exchanges his usual saber for a bayonet to play General Custer in a highly fictionalized and reactionary retelling of Custer's last stand at Little Big Horn. Olivia, at her most attractive, plays Custer's patient but spunky wife, who brings gun-running charges against the Sharps (members of the Grant administration) after her husband's death. Ronald Reagan had played the young Custer in the previous year's Flynn–de Havilland epic *Santa Fe Trail*. For a more complex, less romantic view of Custer, try Arthur Penn's *Little Big Man*, which features Richard Mulligan as an oafish, racist military man. This film is more like *Gone with the Wind* envisioned as a glorified shoot-'em-up.

THEY DRIVE BY NIGHT ☆☆☆½
1940, USA
Ann Sheridan, George Raft, Humphrey Bogart, Ida Lupino, Alan Hale, Gale Page. Directed by Raoul Walsh. 93 min.

One of those Warner Bros. melodramas of bits and pieces lifted from earlier hits, this is surprisingly juicy in its own right. The second half is practically a remake of *Bordertown*, with Ida Lupino picking up the Bette Davis mantle as a bored housewife. The first half is a no-holds-barred tale about two brothers battling corruption in the trucking business, served up in fast-paced Warner's style. There's memorably racy dialogue, with all the stars shining, especially the saucy, sensual Ann Sheridan.

THEY GOT ME COVERED ☆☆☆
1943, USA
Bob Hope, Dorothy Lamour, Lenore Aubert, Otto Preminger, Eduardo Ciannelli. Directed by David Butler. 95 min.

All the comic bases are covered in this once topical and still amusing spy yarn. Secret agents from Germany descend upon the United States, apparently for the express purpose of chasing Bob Hope. Dorothy Lamour's around for decorative purposes and later joins in the fun, helping Bob Hope thwart various Nazi schemes to undermine America's defenses.

THEY LIVE BY NIGHT ☆☆☆
1948, USA
Farley Granger, Cathy O'Donnell, Howard Da Silva, Jay C. Flippen. Directed by Nicholas Ray. 95 min.

Nicholas Ray's debut film, about two young lovers on the run, displays his poignant themes of individuals groping for a place in the world. The movie also possesses a nightmarish *film noir* sense of entrapment, as a wilting ex-con, desperate to escape the dark underworld that brought him to his fresh-faced girl, realizes that their world is slowly consuming them. Ray's clear-eyed, sharply edited film centers on the sad romance but never loses sight of the milieu's dank undertow. From the book *Thieves Like Us* by Edward Anderson; director Robert Altman retained this title for his 1974 version.

THEY MADE ME A CRIMINAL ☆☆☆
1939, USA
John Garfield, Claude Rains, Gloria Dickson, May Robson, Billy Halop, Huntz Hall, Leo Gorcey. Directed by Busby Berkeley. 92 min.

Warner Bros. strikes again with an enjoyable hodgepodge of social realism, the Dead End Kids, and John Garfield's soul-stirring romantic defeatism. Incredibly, it was directed by Busby Berkeley, better known for his Depression-era musicals; indeed, Warner Bros. seems to have made a cottage industry out of the seedier side of the thirties. No one fit the mold of the down-on-his-luck hero better than John Garfield. Here he plays a boxer who takes to the road after believing he's killed an opponent in the ring. Can love and the Dead End Kids redeem him? Garfield's chip-on-the-shoulder style has never been as watchable as it was at this time in his career. Claude Rains is pitifully miscast as an all-American prosecutor, a part he begged not to be stuck with, but to no avail.

THEY'RE PLAYING WITH FIRE ☆
1984, USA, R
Sybil Danning, Eric Brown, Andrew Prime, Paul Clemens. Directed by Howard (Hikmet) Avedis. 96 min.

Every Sybil Danning movie is a suspense film: the suspense is how long it will be before she takes off all her clothes. (It takes about eight minutes in this one.) Danning, who has posed for *Playboy*, plays a seductive English professor who more or less rapes her excited student (Eric Brown) and coerces him into helping her scare her mother-in-law into giving up her estate. The casting of Danning as a professor has so little credibility that it's almost amusing. Brown, who appeared in *Private Lessons*, has no discernible talent. For prepubescent males only.

THEY SHOOT HORSES, DON'T THEY? ☆☆☆
1969, USA
Jane Fonda, Michael Sarrazin, Susannah York, Gig Young, Red Buttons, Bruce Dern, Michael Conrad. Directed by Sydney Pollack. 121 min.

A shabby ballroom on the shore of the Pacific Ocean is the sole set in this often compelling adaptation of Horace McCoy's 1935 novel about a marathon dance contest in Los Angeles. The central character is Gloria (Jane Fonda), a would-be actress who enters the dance contest with Robert (Michael Sarrazin, in his debut), a would-be director, in hopes of winning the prize, being discovered by a talent scout, and generally finding a reason to go on living. Sydney Pollack's handling of the political and spiritual symbolism is overblown, but the actors are good enough to keep his sermonizing in check most of the time. Red Buttons is effective playing an aging sailor, and Gig Young won an Oscar for his portrayal of the cynical promoter/announcer.

THEY WENT THAT-A-WAY AND THAT-A-WAY ☆½
1978, USA, PG
Tim Conway, Chuck McCann, Reni Santoni, Dub Taylor, Richard Kiel, Lenny Montana. Directed by Edward Montagne, Stuart E. McGowan. 95 min.

Despite the PG rating, this one is aimed strictly at the kiddie market. Tim Conway and Chuck McCann do a very feeble Laurel and Hardy impression as two cops who sneak into a prison disguised as convicts in order to locate some hidden money. Conway also wrote the story, and how much you enjoy this depends entirely on your tolerance for his dopey humor.

THEY WERE EXPENDABLE ☆☆☆
1945, USA
Robert Montgomery, John Wayne, Donna Reed, Jack Holt, Ward Bond, Louis Jean Heydt, Marshall Thompson. Directed by John Ford. 135 min.

Recently discharged Navy officer Robert Montgomery plays a Navy officer who is convinced that small, speedy patrol boats could play a big part in defeating the Japanese in the Pacific. The Duke plays a more skeptical lieutenant. Captain John Ford of the Navy Reserves plays a big part in making this a fast-moving, action-packed war story. This is one of the best of the World War II war movies, and while it's not as good a film as Ford's Westerns, the touch of the master can be seen everywhere.

THEY WON'T BELIEVE ME ☆☆☆
1947, USA
Robert Young, Susan Hayward, Jane Greer, Rita Johnson, Tom Powers, Don Beddoe. Directed by Irving Pichel. 95 min.

In a stylish *film noir*, a wastrel with an eye for the ladies has trouble juggling the women in his life and ends up to his neck in murder and mayhem. There are shades of James Cain, only instead of the usual plotting to murder a husband, this is about a man trying to eliminate his wife so he can play the field. The man's scheme fails, but through one of those 1940s twists of fate, he gets arrested anyway. Full of quirky plot turns and lots of handsome, shadowy black-and-white photography.

THEY WON'T FORGET ☆☆☆½
1937, USA
Claude Rains, Edward Norris, Allyn Joslyn, Linda Perry, Ann Shoemaker, Donald Briggs, Frank Faylen, Gloria Dickson, Otto Kruger, Lana Turner. Directed by Mervyn LeRoy. 95 min.

A celebrated early *film noir* about the murder of a small-town girl (the ravishing young Lana Turner) and the layers of corruption the crime unveils. Mervyn LeRoy's direction was at its crispest during this period, the peak of the Warner's social-conscience period. The film looks superficial next to Fritz Lang's similar *M*, but is well above the average Hollywood treatment of racial injustice and political corruption. The buildup to the murder scene still has razor-sharp effectiveness. Riveting and different.

THIEF ☆☆☆½
1981, USA, R
James Caan, Willie Nelson, Jim Belushi, Robert Prosky, Tuesday Weld. Directed by Michael Mann. 122 min.

James Caan's performance is a tour de force in this explosively violent, but visually poetic film about a master safecracker who wants to retire and settle down with his new wife. Unfortunately, a foul mob boss refuses to see the criminal's talent go to waste. A punchy piece that effectively displays Michael Mann's talent for viscerally staging his bloody action (an ability he used as a producer to make TV's "Miami Vice" phenomenally successful). Caan sweats, screams, and blows holes in many a foe to create his tensest characterization since Sonny Corleone in *The Godfather*. A remarkable crime drama that keeps you on the edge.

THE THIEF OF BAGDAD ☆☆☆☆
1924, USA
Douglas Fairbanks, Julanne Johnstone, Anna May Wong, Sojin, Snitz Edwards, Charles Belcher, Brandon Hurst. Directed by Raoul Walsh. 140 min.

Douglas Fairbanks's matchless virility was never more potent than in this rousing story of a vagrant thief who woos a princess. The magical world of old Bagdad is conjured up by the opulent sets done by William Cameron Menzies, and Fairbanks skips and jumps his way across them like a drifter demigod in a delirious universe. The film's mood is enhanced by expertly rendered special effects. Color tinting was used, too, in the theatrical original; however, this movie is in the public domain and none of the various video companies that distribute the film offers a colored copy. Although Raoul Walsh's expert handling of the big-screen action almost demands seeing this in a theater, the sexy charisma of Fairbanks, Anna May Wong (the villainess), and Julanne Johnstone comes through no matter the medium. This is one of those rare movies that was remade well—the 1940 British film is every bit as good. *Note*: Make sure that the film is not cut from its long running time, and look for an orchestrally scored video (although the organ score on Blackhawk's version is nice, too).

THE THIEF OF BAGHDAD ☆☆
1978, Great Britain/France (TV)
Peter Ustinov, Roddy McDowall, Kabir Bedu, Frank Finlay, Pavla Ustinov, Terence Stamp. Directed by Clive Donner. 100 min.

Futile revamp of the splendiferous 1940 classic (not to mention the 1924 Douglas Fairbanks gem) that had a unique fairy-tale charm, marvelously eccentric performances, and a wonderful, barbaric score by Miklos Rozsa. Kids might still enjoy the antics of the genie in the bottle and the fabled Arabian Nights adventures, but this particular magic carpet is worn thin in more than a few spots. The comic hijinks of Ustinov as the caliph with a marriageable daughter (played by his real-life daughter, Pavla) are obviously meant to make up for the script's shortcomings, but Ustinov comes across here as the poor man's Billy Gilbert. Imagination was needed here, not tomfoolery.

THIEF OF HEARTS ☆☆
1984, USA
Steven Bauer, Barbara Williams, John Getz. Directed by Douglas Day Stewart. 100 min.

When Hollywood producers began spending more and more time cutting deals in restaurants, movies began to look like nouvelle cuisine dinners—very small portions of substance, artfully arranged. About a sensitive gourmet cook who steals art objects from the homes while the owners are dining out. The dialogue even resembles the boring dinner conversation of a loudmouth couple behind you. Glitzy decor, bland food. Includes steamy scenes excised from the theatrical release.

THE THIEF WHO CAME TO DINNER ☆½
1973, USA, PG
Ryan O'Neal, Jacqueline Bisset, Warren Oates, Jill Clayburgh, Charles Cioffi, Ned Beatty, Austin Pendleton, John Hillerman. Directed by Bud Yorkin. 105 min.

Walter Hill (*The Warriors, 48 HRS*) wrote the screenplay for this thuddingly dull caper film about a computer-wizard-turned-jewel-thief who must outwit an insurance investigator trying to pin a rap on him. The script would have you believe that the thief (Ryan O'Neal) left a secure job and luxurious life for a high-tech criminal existence because he needed some excitement in his life. It's doubtful that he found it in this movie. Bud Yorkin's experience in television is evident in every frame, and Jacqueline Bisset is wasted as the barely characterized love interest.

THE THING ☆☆☆
1951, USA
Margaret Sheridan, Kenneth Tobey, Robert Cornwaithe, Douglas Spencer, James Young, Dewey Martin, Robert Nicholls, William Self, Edward Franz, Sally Creighton. Directed by Christian Nyby. 89 min.

The original adaptation of John W. Campbell's short story "Who Goes There?" enjoys quite a reputation in sci-fi circles, and its characters and chitchat are plentifully entertaining. A group of Army scientists at a remote Arctic testing station is menaced by a vegetable man from outer space; but where Campbell's monster was less a character than an insidious presence, here it's played by the young James Arness, who makes a great entrance and then spends a grand total of three minutes lumbering around like a low-budget version of Frankenstein's monster. The nominal director is Christian Nyby, but the hand of producer Howard Hawks is clearly visible in the taut, spunky dialogue. (a.k.a.: *The Thing from Another World*)

THE THING ☆☆☆
1982, USA, R
Kurt Russell, Wilford Brimley, Richard Dysart, Richard Masur, Donald Moffat, David Clennon, T. K. Carter. Directed by John Carpenter. 108 min.

John Carpenter's remake of the 1951 winner is really two films that don't quite jibe. One is a bleak story about paranoia, with scientists at an isolated Antarctic base unearthing a centuries-old extraterrestrial able to assume their shapes and identities so successfully that soon the atmosphere is poisoned by mistrust. The other is a special-effects extravaganza, with Rob Bottin's elaborate, ever-changing beast that is funny as often as it is gross (and sometimes both, as when a dismembered head sprouts spidery legs and begins to skulk away). This is Carpenter's most nihilistic film, and it is hurt by overkill. Still, it looks better with time, especially for the often maligned performances of the cast, who are *supposed* to act stoical and enervated. Featuring scenes from the earlier version. (a.k.a.: *John Carpenter's The Thing*).

THINGS ARE TOUGH ALL OVER ☆☆
1982, USA, R
Cheech Marin, Tommy Chong, Shelby Fiddis, Rikki Marin, Evelyn Guerrero, Rip Taylor. Directed by Thomas K. Avildsen. 92 min.

In their fourth screen outing, Cheech and Chong play two oil-rich Arab brothers who take off across the desert. Seems they're in hot pursuit of two mellow dope fiends—also played by Cheech and Chong. This is a bit more plot than the two can handle, but the movie has its moments. One of them is when the boys are in drag, and another finds them in the clutches of a couple of French sexpots, played by the stars' wives (it takes a special kind of comedian to have his wife play a voracious porno star). The depictions of the Arabs are nothing short of racist.

THINGS TO COME ☆☆☆☆
1936, Great Britain
Ralph Richardson, Raymond Massey, Cedric Hardwicke. Directed by William Cameron Menzies. 97 min.

A classic science-fiction film based on H. G. Wells's story follows man from his self-destruction to his glorious resurgence in the future. Revolutionary for its time, the film still holds up with its innovative special effects and intelligent approach to the subject. It was written by Wells, who saw many of his prophecies come true in later years, and produced by Alexander Korda, a distinguished filmmaker who also oversaw such fantasy masterpieces as *The Thief of Baghdad* (1940) and *The Jungle Book* (1942). Look for the dashing young Sir Ralph as a barbarian leader.

THINK DIRTY ☆☆
1970, Great Britain, R
Marty Feldman, Shelly Berman, Judy Cornwell, Julie Ege, Patrick Cargill. Directed by Jim Clark. 94 min.

Marty Feldman, the British comic who began his career as a popular writer and performer on the BBC, was a little too strange to have made it as a leading man in movies. His best role was as Igor (pronounced "eye-gor") in Mel Brooks's *Young Frankenstein*, but almost every other film he made was of poor quality. In this, his first, he plays an advertising agent who is given the task of devising a new campaign to sell oatmeal by injecting sex into the TV commercials. This is used as a jumping-off point to bring in a number of parody sequences, in the form of either suggested commercials or Feldman's daydreams, and while some are funny, the whole thing is wearying, with an overreliance on tired sex jokes.

THE THIN MAN ☆☆☆½
1934, USA
William Powell, Myrna Loy, Maureen O'Sullivan, Nat Pendleton, Minna Gombell, Porter Hall, Henry Wadsworth, William Henry, Harold Huber, Cesar Romero, Edward Ellis. Directed by W. S. Van Dyke II. 80 min.

A marvelous cocktail-lounge detective movie—funny, suspenseful, and blessed with the sparkling chemistry of William Powell and Myrna Loy as Nick and Nora Charles—this was the first and one of the best of the famed detective series based on characters in Dashiell Hammett's novel. Later *Thin Man* movies found Powell and Loy honing their sparkling repartee, although they were usually given weaker material with which to work. Incidentally, the "Thin Man" in this film is the victim, but in subsequent entries the tag referred to Powell's Nick Charles character. Followed by *After the Thin Man*.

THE THIRD MAN
1949, Great Britain ☆☆☆☆
Orson Welles, Joseph Cotten, Alida Valli, Trevor Howard, Bernard Lee. Directed by Carol Reed. 104 min.

One of the most famous suspense thrillers of its time, this is a visually complex game of cat-and-mouse made memorable by the director's use of expressionistic camera angles. Everything in *The Third Man* looks out of kilter and tilted, the canted frame technique a perfect photographic complement to the disturbing story line. A second-rate writer (Joseph Cotten) wants to locate his pal Harry Lime, of whom the authorities have a low opinion. When the police inform the innocent abroad that his friend is dead, he searches for a way to unravel the confusion surrounding Lime's death. Along the way, he gets sucked into an Old World cesspool of black marketeering and betrayal. A cynical thriller that takes a jaundiced view of post–World War II Europe; special attention should be paid to the knockout score of zither music, as well as a classic encounter on a ferris wheel between Cotten and Orson Welles.

THE THIRD MAN ON THE MOUNTAIN
1959, USA ☆☆☆
Michael Rennie, James MacArthur, Janet Munro, James Donald, Herbert Lom. Directed by Ken Annakin. 107 min.

This live-action drama from Disney has an undercurrent of emotion unusual for the studio, and an appealing performance from young lead James MacArthur. He plays the son of a legendary Swiss mountain climber who died many years earlier trying to become the first man to scale the Citadel. Now young Rudi wants to make his own attempt and stop living in his father's and the mountain's shadows. Among the best of Disney's 1950s product, with a story kids will love and a cameo appearance by MacArthur's mother, Helen Hayes.

THIRST
1979, Australia ☆☆
David Hemmings, Chantal Coutouri, Henry Silva, Max Phipps. Directed by Rod Hardy. 98 min.

A cosmetics executive descended from the notorious countess Elisabeth Bathory, a medieval Transylvanian noble who bathed in virgins' blood to preserve her youth, is kidnapped by a vampire cult determined to indoctrinate her into its bloody ways. Drinking blood, explains one vampire, is the ultimate aristocratic art—or, at least, it is in this political vampire film from Australia starring David Hemmings (*Blow-Up*). There is a certain novelty to *Thirst*'s picture of an effete upper class literally draining the lifeblood of the plebian horde, but it never goes for the big shocks. Interesting, especially for vampire completists.

13 GHOSTS
1960, USA ☆☆
Charles Herbert, Jo Morrow, Martin Milner, Rosemary DeCamp, Margaret Hamilton. Directed by William Castle. 85 min.

The best part of this movie is when William Castle comes on in the beginning to explain how to use the "ghost viewers" given out at the box office (if you got too scared by the ghosts, you could look through the proper half and presto! away they went). Castle used such gimmicks for most of his lightweight spook flicks because he knew that they were too unexceptional otherwise to attract an audience. In this one, a family of four moves into a house already occupied by a dozen ghosts, who are looking to increase their number to thirteen. Mildly entertaining, though not at all scary (unless a traumatic, childhood viewing of *The Wizard of Oz* left you with a lingering fear of wicked witch Margaret Hamilton).

13 RUE MADELEINE
1946, USA ☆☆☆
James Cagney, Annabella, Richard Conte, Frank Latimore. Directed by Henry Hathaway. 95 min.

A fast-paced semidocumentary about government agents on a secret mission to nab a murderous Nazi on the loose in France. The gritty edge of realism serves this tale well, and you'll find the exploits of the O.S.S. to be gripping throughout. Inspired by the March of Time documentary series, and featuring a solid performance by James Cagney.

THE THIRTY FOOT BRIDE OF CANDY ROCK
1959, USA ☆☆
Lou Costello, Dorothy Provine, Gale Gordon, Charles Lane, Jimmy Conlin. Directed by Sidney Miller. 75 min.

Mildly amusing children's picture about pudgy Lou's adventures with a giantess whose height poses problems in their relationship. Although twenty feet shorter than her infamous contemporary the Fifty Foot Woman, this bride is much more even-tempered and less neurotic. Costello's only film sans Abbott is strictly kiddie fare, and the luscious Dorothy Provine deserved better (if not bigger) parts.

30 IS A DANGEROUS AGE, CYNTHIA
1968, Great Britain ☆☆☆
Dudley Moore, Eddie Foy, Jr., Suzy Kendall, John Bird. Directed by Joseph McGrath. 85 min.

Dudley Moore's first film effort away from partner Peter Cook. Aside from starring, he also cowrote the screenplay and wrote and performed the music, and he really pulls it off. He plays a nightclub piano player who rallies to accomplish everything he wanted to do with his life in the six weeks before his thirtieth birthday. These include writing a hit musical and getting married, goals he hasn't even begun to work on. Occasionally veers into slapstick territory, but in such a sure manner that the viewer is carried right along.

THE 39 STEPS
1935, Great Britain ☆☆☆½
Robert Donat, Madeleine Carroll. Directed by Alfred Hitchcock. 89 min.

Not to be confused with the lesser remakes, this Alfred Hitchcock classic is among the most popular and profound of the master's British films. A man is accused of murder and must flee from the authorities to prove his innocence and stop the escape of crucial government secrets from his country. The image of sexual bondage, a common motif in Hitchcock, becomes central to the film as the man, played by Robert Donat, winds up handcuffed to reluctant Madeleine Carroll. The journey becomes a metaphor for the personal psychological odyssey of two people joined by common knowledge and guilt. This deft, taut spy thriller—at turns suspenseful and comic—anticipates many of the themes that occupied the director over the next four decades.

THE 39 STEPS
1959, Great Britain ☆☆½
Kenneth More, Taina Elg, Brenda de Banzie, Barry Jones, Sidney James. Directed by Ralph Thomas. 93 min.

Trying to follow in the formidable footsteps of Alfred Hitchcock, the filmmakers of this remake don't trip all over themselves; nor do they equal the master's quota of chills and thrills. An innocent soul gets enmeshed in the usual international espionage and somehow enlists the assistance of a beautiful lady who's initially skeptical, but then comes through with flying colors to help him. It lacks Hitchcock's wit, and the leads won't erase any memories of Robert Donat and Madeleine Carroll, but it's a briskly directed version of a foolproof story line.

30 SECONDS OVER TOKYO ☆☆☆
USA, 1944
Van Johnson, Robert Walker, Spencer Tracy, Phyllis Thaxter, Scott McKay, Robert Mitchum, Don Defore. Directed by Mervyn LeRoy. 138 min.

A good war yarn is nicely mixed with a teary-eyed romance in this patriotic film about the first attack on Japan. The action centers around the flight crew of a bomber, and everything, from the mission to the wrecking of the plane, is handled with unusual restraint. The script is by the always dependable and sometimes remarkable Dalton Trumbo.

THIRTY SIXTH CHAMBER OF SHAOLIN

See *The Master Killer*

THIS ABOVE ALL ☆☆☆
1942, USA
Tyrone Power, Joan Fontaine, Thomas Mitchell, Nigel Bruce, Gladys Cooper. Directed by Anatole Litvak. 110 min.

A glossy wartime romance that's dated but eminently watchable. Twentieth Century-Fox gave love stories like this and *The Razor's Edge* a bewitching pearly sheen—the lovestruck leading characters almost seem to glow in black-and-white, as if they've been ennobled by the power of love. Based on an Eric Knight novel, the story deals with a disillusioned soldier (Tyrone Power) who is made whole again by his affair with a courageous Britisher (Joan Fontaine). The film is tinged with World War II propaganda, but the romance was gracefully handled and still tugs heartstrings today.

THIS GUN FOR HIRE ☆☆☆
1942, USA
Veronica Lake, Alan Ladd, Robert Preston, Laird Cregar. Directed by Frank Tuttle. 80 min.

Alan Ladd and Veronica Lake remain coolly attractive in this acceptable version of Graham Greene's novel. Neither can really act in the normal sense, but their lazy indifference to one another somehow emerges as sensuous fatigue on the screen. Laird Cregar is deliciously obscene as the villain of the piece.

THIS IS ELVIS ☆☆☆
1981, USA, G
Elvis Presley, David Scott, Paul Boensh III, Johnny Harra, Lawrence Koller. Directed by Malcolm Leo, Andrew Solt. 144 min.

Surprisingly engrossing docudrama of Elvis Presley's life and career, consisting partly of footage of the real Elvis (in movies, newsreels, concert and television appearances) and partly of dramatizations. Given the quality of the rest of the narrative, it's a shame that the filmmakers couldn't think of a better way to cover the gaps in Presley's story than by having fill-in actors and actresses deliver voice-overs. Still, this is an admirable and often successful attempt to show the real Presley, the one that remained at the time of his death behind the smokescreen of drugs, guns, and paranoia. The version on videocassette includes forty-four minutes of footage not seen in theaters.

THIS IS SPINAL TAP ☆☆☆☆
1984, USA, R
Michael McKean, Christopher Guest, Harry Shearer, Rob Reiner, Tony Hendra, June Chadwick, R. J. Parnell, David Kaff. Directed by Rob Reiner. 82 min.

Rob Reiner directed this hilarious documentary, or "Rockumentary" if you will, about the leather-clad, lovably repugnant, make-believe heavy-metal band "Spinal Tap," the authors of such musical masterpieces as "Big Bottom" and "Smell the Glove." It may be a spoof, but it's so on-target that, for style and dramatic flair, it beats the rock movies it satirizes. Reiner and the cast would often simply discuss the general direction they wanted a sequence to take and then improvise it in front of the camera. The result is an energetic, eminently believable, extremely funny story. The videocassette version also has a bonus: a mock MTV video.

THIS IS THE ARMY ☆☆☆
1943, USA
George Murphy, Joan Leslie, George Tobias, Alan Hale, Charles Butterworth, Dolores Costello, Una Merkel, Stanley Ridges, Rosemary De Camp, Frances Langford, Kate Smith, Ronald Reagan, Joe Louis. Directed by Michael Curtiz. 120 min.

As a Broadway revue written to raise money and red blood counts for the Army Emergency Relief Fund during World War II, this was performed entirely by soldiers—hence the title. Many of them also appear in this film version, though only in roles that Warner Bros. couldn't fill with someone from their large roster of contract players. With lots of songs by Irving Berlin, who makes an appearance at the piano (faking rather obviously) to sing "How I Hate to Get Up in the Morning." Bet you can't guess what song Kate Smith sings.

THIS MAN MUST DIE ☆☆☆½
1970, France, PG
Michel Duchaussoy, Jean Yanne, Caroline Cellier, Lorraine Rainer. Directed by Claude Chabrol. 115 min.

A lean, compelling drama of revenge, it often transcends its genre to become a study of the nature of justice, thanks to Claude Chabrol's astutely observant direction. Michel Duchaussoy plays the father of a little boy killed by a hit-and-run driver. Seeking revenge, the man discovers that the murderer is a truly despicable character who many others wish were dead as well. Chabrol unlayers the goodness and evil of his opposing characters with precision to build to a suspenseful and harrowing conclusion. Based on the novel *The Beast Must Die* (used as the title for an unrelated film) by Nicholas Blake.

THIS PROPERTY IS CONDEMNED ☆☆½
1966, USA
Natalie Wood, Robert Redford, Mary Badham, Kate Reid, Charles Bronson, Robert Blake. Directed by Sydney Pollack. 110 min.

This story line is not exactly condemned, if a bit rickety and run-down. Based on a one-act play by Tennessee Williams, the drama's Southern gothic atmosphere is the main attraction. Natalie Wood is not convincing as a wrong-side-of-the-tracks girl who goes gaga for a boarder in her mother's house and envisions him as her passport to romance. Although Wood and Robert Redford are lovely to look at and make a nice pair, they teamed to better advantage in *Inside Daisy Clover*. Here the screenplay seems worked over and padded. Not shameful, but not very good.

THE THOMAS CROWN AFFAIR ☆☆
1968, USA
Steve McQueen, Faye Dunaway, Paul Burke, Jack Weston, Yaphet Kotto. Directed by Norman Jewison. 102 min.

This is slick, in the worst sense of the word. Steve McQueen plays the Boston millionaire who, out of boredom, plans an elaborate bank heist. Faye Dunaway plays the insurance navigator who, using woman's intuition, sets out to catch the playboy crook. The dubious morality of a movie that asks us to sympathize with an already wealthy robber is compounded by the use of Dunaway as a professional working woman more interested in her miniskirt, white stockings, and bouffant hairdo than in her assignment. Director Norman Jewison and cinematographer Haskell Wexler's use of multiple-screen technique seemed really "hip" in 1968; today they look dated and pointless. For a better romance heist movie, check out *How to Steal a Million* starring Audrey Hepburn and Peter O'Toole. Now that's real class.

THOROUGHLY MODERN MILLIE ☆☆☆
1967, USA
Julie Andrews, Mary Tyler Moore, James Fox, Carol Channing, Beatrice Lillie, John Gavin, Jack Soo. Directed by George Roy Hill. 138 min.

♪ A snazzy tune fest about a 1920s flapper thwarting a white slave ring improbably headed by that deadpan dragonlady, the great Bea Lillie, this should have musical lovers shouting, "It's the Bee's Knees!" (Bea Lillie, or Lady Peel, was scandalously underutilized and wasted in films during her long, triumphant stage career. This is a rare chance to see, however briefly, the other Queen Bea!) Although it runs out of steam in the second half, this is one of Hollywood's brightest musicals of the sixties, and Julie Andrews gives what may just be her most appealing performance. Storming the big, bad city with modern dreams of emancipation, good sport Julie finds romance and adventure. Still, Carol Channing steals the film as the archetypal Jazz Baby, contributing just the right amount of fizz to keep the film from being too sticky-sweet. If Ross Hunter had resisted inserting that Jewish wedding number—he obviously did it because he'd lost out on the rights to *Fiddler on the Roof*—this would have been even better.

THOSE GLORY, GLORY DAYS ☆☆
1984, Great Britain
Julia McKenzie, Elizabeth Spriggs, Julia Goodman, Rachel Meidman, Zoe Nathanson. Directed by Philip Saville. 77 min.

The British series of low-budget directorial debuts called "First Love" yielded varying results—in this entry, the first love is soccer, and the story is as worn out and lumpy as the ball the Spurs use. Following this local team with great diligence is a group of thirteen-year-old girls who have developed a group crush on the team and the sport itself. Writer Julie Welch doesn't make much of her offbeat premise, and the attempt at period (1961) atmosphere on a shoestring fails. Nice try, but no goal.

THOSE LIPS, THOSE EYES ☆☆
1980, USA, R
Frank Langella, Thomas Hulce, Glynnis O'Connor, Jerry Stiller, George Morfogen, Kevin McCarthy. Directed by Michael Pressman. 107 min.

Made when Frank Langella seemed destined for stardom after his success in the Broadway revival of *Dracula*, this pleasant but slight coming-of-age comedy seems tailor-made to highlight his shortcomings as well as his strengths. He plays the star of a summer theater company in 1950s Cleveland, a big frog in a small pond who still dreams of getting to Broadway. The bulk of the story concerns Thomas Hulce (between *Animal House* and *Amadeus*), a young pre-med who takes a summer job with the company and becomes dazzled by Langella's outward charm and self-confidence. As a film about mediocrity, illusion and disillusion, and nostalgia, this wastes more opportunities than it fulfills.

A THOUSAND CLOWNS ☆☆☆½
1965, USA
Jason Robards, Barbara Harris, Martin Balsam, Barry Gordon, William Daniels, Gene Saks. Directed by Fred Coe. 118 min.

An abundance of good performances make up for the occasional coyness and overt sentimentality of this adaptation of a play by Herb Gardner that could easily pass for Neil Simon. Jason Robards has a field day as a societal drop-out whose prime concerns are nurturing his own eccentricities and developing them in the orphaned nephew who lives with him. The rest of the cast is equally good, including Martin Balsam (who won the Best Supporting Actor Oscar) as Robards's uptight, haunted brother, Barbara Harris as a social worker who tries to rehabilitate him, and William Daniels as a prissy bureaucrat. Even Barry Gordon, who plays the kid, does well with the especially difficult feat of playing a smart-alecky kid without coming off like a midget in knickers. (Fred Coe was, during the 1950s, perhaps the best and most admired producer of live television drama.)

THOUSANDS CHEER ☆☆☆
1943, USA
Mickey Rooney, Judy Garland, Gene Kelly, Red Skelton, Eleanor Powell, Ann Sothern, Lucille Ball, Kathryn Grayson, Mary Astor, Lionel Barrymore, Kay Kyser, Jose Iturbi, Lena Horne. Directed by George Sidney. 100 min.

♪ United Artists had *Stage Door Canteen*, Warner Bros. had *Thank Your Lucky Stars*, and MGM came through with its own all-star variety-show war effort, *Thousands Cheer*. There's a minor romantic plot to frame the numerous, glossily produced specialty numbers, including Lena Horne singing "Honeysuckle Rose," Eleanor Powell hoofing, Judy Garland belting, and most memorably, youthful Gene Kelly dancing a wonderful duet with a mop. There are slow stretches and the comedy falls flat, but musical fans will find much to cheer.

THREADS ☆☆☆☆
1984, Great Britain/Australia (TV)
Karen Meagher, Reece Dinsdale. Directed by Mick Jackson. 110 min.

A brutal, brilliant look at nuclear holocaust and its devastating effects on the British city of Sheffield, *Threads* begs comparison to American efforts such as *The Day After* and *Testament*—and it beats both, hands down. The viewer is spared nothing of the horrors wreaked first by the bomb itself and then by its atmospheric effects, from skin-searing heat to nuclear winter, and it refuses to concede a happy or even scantly hopeful ending. As propaganda and as drama, it's superbly effective, moving, and most definitely not for the faint of heart.

THE THREAT ☆☆½
1949, USA
Charles McGraw, Michael O'Shea, Virginia Grey, Julie Bishop, Frank Conroy. Directed by Felix Feist. 66 min.

This is a crisply efficient crime drama about a vicious felon who breaks out of jail to carry out a revenge plan against those who sent him up. After kidnapping the law-abiding citizens and his ex-girlfriend, the killer begins to have doubts about his ex-partners and his current sidekicks. Talk about dissension in the ranks; everyone ends up at each other's throat in this tension-filled melodrama. It's just a B movie, but a good one, with something of the impact of bigger-budget crime-athons like *Key Largo*. Available on a double-feature cassette with *The Lady Fugitive*.

THREE AGES ☆☆☆
1923, USA
Buster Keaton, Margaret Leahy, Wallace Beery, Joe Roberts, Horace Morgan, Lillian Lawrence, Lionel Belmore. Directed by Buster Keaton and Eddie Cline. 60 min.

Buster Keaton's first feature film (though he acted the lead in the 1920 *The Saphead*) is a clever parody of Griffith's *Intolerance*. Instead of examining the various forms of intolerance through the course of history, though, Keaton shows the comic foibles of love in Prehistoric times, ancient Rome, and contemporary America. The funniest business is the intense rivalry between Keaton and his burly antagonist (Wallace Beery) as they find new technologies for attacking each other and defending themselves. Most critics have found, and Keaton himself has concurred, that the movie is actually three short comedies spliced together to make a feature; if so, it is the only set of three thematically linked shorts in silent comedy, and it is a unique treat. Admittedly not as successful as the classic Keaton works, the film has hilarious moments, and the Stone Age sequence is as funny as any of the priceless shorts. This is the first film that credits Keaton's trio of great writers: Clyde Bruckman, Joseph Mitchell, and Jean Havez.

THREE AMIGOS! ☆☆☆
1986, USA, PG
Steve Martin, Chevy Chase, Martin Short, Alfonso Rau, Patrice Martinez, Jon Lovitz. Directed by John Landis. 120 min.

This agreeably silly spoof doesn't suffer from the excesses that marred John Landis's earlier, overproduced comedies (*The Blues Brothers, Into the Night*). The big question is: why bother to rib a Western subgenre—the Mexican bandito film—which few viewers even remember? Within these limited comic boundaries, two of the three amigos manage to dispense some inspired lunacy as silent-movie heroes down on their luck (namely, Martin Short and Steve Martin—Chevy Chase seems so lackadaisical that you feel you're watching a Two Stooges movie). Going south of the border down Mexico way for what they think is a personal appearance, there screen cowboys actually end up saving a village from loathsome bandits. With two blissfully funny musical numbers—if only the rest of the film had lived up to those two peaks, it would have been terrific instead of good.

THE THREE AVENGERS ☆
1979, Hong Kong
Bruce Li (Ho Tsung Tao), Chien Yuet Sun, Michael Winston, Lin Chiao. Directed by Wong Wah Kay. 91 min.

Two Chinese and an American fight to save their martial arts school and avenge their master's death, which is twice as complex a plot as usual in this genre.

THREE BROADWAY GIRLS ☆☆☆
1932, USA
Joan Blondell, Ina Claire, Madge Evans, Lowell Sherman, David Manners. Directed by Lowell Sherman. 79 min.

Don't be discouraged by the prosaic retitling: this was originally know as *The Greeks Had a Word for Them*, and it's the venerable great-grandmother of all golddigger comedies, down to and beyond *How to Marry a Millionaire*. Joan Blondell, Ina Claire, and Madge Evans make a winning trifecta of eligible fillies game to saddle some well-heeled bridegrooms.

THE THREE CABALLEROS ☆☆☆½
1945, USA
Aurora Miranda, Carmen Molina, Dora Luz, Clarence Nash, Jose Oliveira, Joaquin Garay. Directed by Walt Disney. 70 min.

Disney created this Latin American *Fantasia* as a war propaganda film exhorting cooperation among the Americans, but a shortage of color film delayed its release until 1945. It was worth the wait. The animation wizard used every trick in the book, and even reintroduced, with moderate success, the combination of animation with live action. Donald Duck takes an extended tour of the lands of our southern neighbors. If you can tolerate the cultural clichés and the duck's inherently patronizing attitude, this extravaganza will dazzle you with its flights of imagination and its rapid-fire visual puns. This one should prove to the skeptics that animation sometimes is more than kids' stuff.

THREE COINS IN THE FOUNTAIN ☆☆☆
1954, USA
Clifton Webb, Dorothy McGuire, Jean Peters, Louis Jourdan, Maggie McNamara, Rossano Brazzi. Directed by Jean Negulesco. 102 min.

A real popcorn movie for armchair travelers and diehard romantics. According to legend, if three people throw coins in the old Roman wishing well, one of them will be granted his wish. The stories are little more than cotton-candy confections (secretary snares her boss, virginal miss tames a Casanova, career girl settles for marriage) but it's hard to resist the Italian tourist attractions and the wide-screen splendor, and, whenever the story flags, the lush strains of the title tune will revive the audience. A gossamer romantic treat, unfortunately somewhat diminished on video.

THREE DAYS OF THE CONDOR ☆☆☆½
1975, USA, R
Robert Redford, Faye Dunaway, Cliff Robertson, Max von Sydow, John Houseman. Directed by Sydney Pollack. 117 min.

An innocent CIA drone becomes caught in a murderous conspiracy within the department in one of the tautest, most suspenseful examples of the mid-1970s political paranoia film. Released in the wake of Watergate, *Condor* finds energy in an unblinking belief in evil at the highest levels of government, personified here by the clever, chilling performances of Cliff Robertson and John Houseman. Robert Redford, better than usual, plays the agency's good guy, a professional bookworm whose only street smarts come from reading spy novels. Director Sydney Pollack falters during a few frosty romantic interludes; otherwise, he weaves the narrative deftly through well-chosen New York locations and expertly sustains its tension.

THE THREE FACES OF EVE ☆☆
1957, USA
Joanne Woodward, David Wayne, Lee J. Cobb, Nancy Kulp, Vince Edwards. Directed by Nunnally Johnson. 91 min.

The *Sybil* of its day, and not really as good as its reputation. In typical 1950s fashion, this superficial, fairly compelling film seems more interested in creating a dubious acting showcase for its star than in examining the psychosis of split personalities with any depth or accuracy. Lee J. Cobb tries to separate the good Joanne from the bad Joanne (there are three of her, to be exact). His job here isn't too difficult, because the differences between the personalities are so ridiculously telegraphed and overdone. As Woodward runs around in her Freudian slip, the audience sits back and enjoys her performance in all its shallow glory. This facile interpretation of psychiatric methods won her an undeserved Oscar. Also written by the illustrious Nunnally Johnson.

THREE FACES WEST ☆☆
1940, USA
John Wayne, Sigrid Gurie, Charles Coburn, Spencer Charters, Roland Varno, Russell Simpson. Directed by Bernard Vorhaus. 79 min.

John Wayne takes on the Bureau of Agriculture in this Dust Bowl Western. Facing a stark wasteland, he eventually agrees with the government's opinion and leads a group of destitute farmers past California and into Oregon. In the Great American Northwest he finds water and two Austrian refugees fleeing Hitler. The two refugee stories ultimately don't come together, but the "duel by automobile" and Charles Coburn's German accent prove interesting. Some pointed anti-Nazi propaganda, but no *Grapes of Wrath*.

3:15—MOMENT OF TRUTH ☆
1986, USA, R
Adam Baldwin, Deborah Foreman, Rene Auberjonois, Ed Lauter, Scott McGinnis, John Scott Clough. Directed by Larry Gross. 95 min.

The less-than-gripping title refers, for those of you with short memories, to the end of the school day, when the hero of this juvenile exploitation film must face his high school tormentors. Unfortunately, this lacks the rancid nastiness of a *good* high-school-is-hell piece like *Class of 1984*, and doesn't substitute much in the way of quality or credibility. A couple of good performances, but you'll be waiting for the dismissal bell to ring.

THREE IN THE ATTIC ☆☆½
1968, USA
Christopher Jones, Yvette Mimieux, Judy Pace, Maggie Thrett, Nan Martin, John Beck. Directed by Richard Wilson. 91 min.

It's a shame that this movie isn't better. First, it has a great exploitation premise: a college stud is held prisoner by three women who attempt to exhaust him sexually. Second, this is one of the "hip" movies made by American International Pictures in the 1960s, a series that included *The Trip*, *Psych-Out*, and *Wild in the Streets*. Finally, it stars the fascinating mumbler Christopher Jones, a flash-in-the-pan star who will remind viewers of someone who has watched a lot of James Dean movies. The film begins promisingly, with Jones picking up a frosty coed (Yvette Mimieux, playing a Jersey girl) by growling Kierkegaard at her. However, it quickly slides into a hackneyed troubled-relationship tale. When the film was released it became a hit, due to the *frisson* of suggested group sex and interracial dalliances.

THREE MEN AND A CRADLE ☆½
1985, France, PG-13
Roland Giraud, Michel Boujenah, André Dussolier, Philippine Leroy Beaulieu. Directed by by Coline Serreau. 100 min.

A tedious, unfunny farce that also happens to be France's all-time box-office champ. The clichés start with the film's premise: three Parisian bachelors find a baby girl on their doorstep. Predictably, they go from having no idea what to do with her to being loving parents who dote over their little bundle of joy. Writer/director Coline Serreau toys with a dumb drug-deal subplot before moving on to her real subject: the emptiness of being single and childless. For these three, bachelor life may be an endless series of one-night stands with impossibly gorgeous fashion-model types, but it's all so—how you say?—unsatisfying. As for baby Marie, she's adorable, all right, but less a character than a device for Serreau to hang her message on. Although the picture offers almost nothing in the way of laughs, sitting through it may be a kind of doe-eyed penance for guilty singles.

THE THREE MUSKETEERS ☆☆☆
1939, USA
Don Ameche, the Ritz Brothers, Binnie Barnes, Lionel Atwill, Gloria Stuart, Pauline Moore, Joseph Schildkraut, John Carradine, Miles Mander. Directed by Allan Dwan. 71 min.

Not the gallivanting Richard Lester escapade, nor the legendary Fairbanks silent, but a hilarious musical starring Don Ameche (who sings, unfortunately) and the Ritz Brothers as flunkies impersonating the famed swashbucklers. Oddly enough, the adaptation of the Alexandre Dumas novel is rather faithful, once again involving Richelieu and Milady's plot to steal the queen's emeralds. Everyone but the Brothers plays it straight, which makes the adaptation all the more funny. The songs include "My Lady," "Viola," and the Ritz specialty "Chicken Soup." Directed by Allan Dwan, and among the finest Ritz features.

THE THREE MUSKETEERS ☆☆☆½
1973, Panama, PG
Michael York, Oliver Reed, Raquel Welch, Richard Chamberlain, Charlton Heston, Faye Dunaway, Christopher Lee, Geraldine Chaplin, Jean-Pierre Cassel, Frank Finlay. Directed by Richard Lester. 107 min.

Probably the liveliest and most enjoyable version of the oft-filmed Alexandre Dumas classic about the daring guardians of King Louis XIII. Richard Lester (*A Hard Day's Night, A Funny Thing Happened on the Way to the Forum*) concentrates on the swordplay and lighter aspects of the adventure, and he is helped immeasurably by an all-star cast that plays it with tongues firmly in cheek. Michael York is perfect as their headstrong but innocent D'Artagnan; Faye Dunaway is deliciously wicked as Milady de Winter; and Charlton Heston as Cardinal Richelieu and Raquel Welch as Constance give the best performances of their careers. MGM did it more lavishly in 1948 (with Gene Kelly) and Fox did it more ridiculously in 1939 (with the Ritz Brothers), but this one tops them all. The follow-up film, *The Four Musketeers* was shot simultaneously. (a.k.a.: *The Queen's Diamonds*)

THE THREEPENNY OPERA ☆☆☆
1931, Germany
Rudolf Forster, Carola Neher, Fritz Rasp, Lotte Lenya. Directed by G. W. Pabst. 100 min.

Bertolt Brecht and Kurt Weill's classic musical play about sexual and economic hypocrisy is set in a very mythical Soho school for beggars and cooperative for prostitutes. For years, prints were unavailable of this rendition, which is far superior to later versions. Still, while G. W. Pabst's slow, Germanic style captures the caustic irony of the original, he misses much of the playful reflexiveness (Brecht reportedly disliked this film). Heavy going but worthwhile, with Lotte Lenya outstanding in the role of Pirate Jenny.

THE THREE STOOGES MEET HERCULES ☆☆
1962, USA
The Three Stooges, Vicki Trickett. Directed by Edward Bernds. 89 min.

In a time machine the Stooges and slapstick travel back to the age of Roman galley slaves, chariot races, and the Cyclops. A bizarre blend of aged Stooges and Italian peplum.

3:10 TO YUMA ☆☆☆½
1957, USA
Glenn Ford, Van Heflin, Felicia Farr, Henry Jones, Richard Jaeckel. Directed by Delmer Daves. 92 min.

One of the best of the 1950s "modern" Westerns, a class that also included *Shane* and *High Noon*, to which this bears some resemblance. A failing farmer, who has accidentally participated in the capture of a wanted outlaw, agrees to guard him in a secluded hiding spot away from his gang until he can be transported away to trial; in return, he is offered a reward that will clear up his financial difficulties. Glenn Ford, cast against character, is superb as the slick, manipulating outlaw, as is Van Heflin as the vacillating farmer. The artificial ending, however, is a letdown. Written by Elmore Leonard.

THREE THE HARD WAY ☆☆½
1974, USA, R
Jim Brown, Fred Williamson, Jim Kelly, Sheila Frazier, Jay Robinson, Howard Platt, Alex Rocco. Directed by Gordon Parks, Jr. 93 min.

A better-than-average "blaxploitation" movie that benefits from a higher budget and less bloody violence than is standard for these thrillers. A white racist gets together an army and plots to poison the drinking water of major cities with a serum that will kill only blacks. It's up to the all-star team of Jim Brown, Fred Williamson, and Jim Kelly to stop him. Nonstop action with a dearth of humor but lots of stunt work (supervised by Hal Needham), karate, and car crashes.

THRESHOLD ☆☆☆
1983, Canada, PG
Donald Sutherland, Jeff Goldblum, Allan Nichols, Sharon Acker, Mare Winningham, John Marley, Michael Lerner. Directed by Richard Pearce. 97 min.

Originally made in 1980 but unreleased for several years because distributors thought it was noncommercial, this film about two surgeons working on an artificial heart finally saw the light of day after Barney Clark's famous operation. *Threshold* is very low-key, with emphasis on the professional concerns of average, human doctors; moral issues are raised only briefly. Donald Sutherland is excellent as the cardiac surgeon who will perform the operation, as is Mare Winningham (*St. Elmo's Fire*) as the girl chosen to be the test case. The graphic scenes of open-chest surgery, although presented clinically and not intended to shock, may be unnerving to some.

THRONE OF BLOOD ☆☆☆☆
1957, Japan
Toshiro Mifune, Isuzu Yamada, Takashi Shimura, Minoru Chiaki. Directed by Akira Kurosawa. 105 min.

One of Akira Kurosawa's masterpieces, *Throne of Blood* uses the samurai warfare of feudal Japan as the setting for a retelling of *Macbeth*. The drama is powerful, but the highlights are the astonishingly vivid, graphic battle scenes, with the screeching hiss of flying arrows and formal elegance that were to become Kurosawa's trademarks. Those who have seen *Ran* will be curious at how similar this forerunner is; the ways in which it informed Kurosawa's later work are evident and intriguing. MHE's excellent video version "letterboxes" the screen, preserving the entire wide image, and adds easy-to-read subtitles.

THUMB TRIPPING ☆½
1972, USA, R
Michael Burns, Meg Foster, Mariana Hill, Burke Burns, Mike Conrad, Bruce Dern, Joyce Van Patten. Directed by Quentin Masters. 94 min.

A cheesy little nostalgia item that must have been excavated in an archeological dig at Woodstock. *Thumb Tripping* (some call it hitchhiking) is a straightforward rip-off of *Easy Rider*'s cool-youth attitudes, without anything as heavy as that film's nasty nihilism on its head. Instead, we have Michael Burns and Meg Foster as Gary and Chay, two vague hippies traveling nowhere in particular with nothing much to say. The Big Sur scenery is pretty, but this trip has been taken way too often; even in 1972 it was a bore. Nice supporting turns from Bruce Dern, doing his usual psycho routine, and Joyce Van Patten as a runaway teenager's mom.

THUNDERBALL ☆☆☆
1965, Great Britain
Sean Connery, Claudine Auger, Adolfo Celi, Luciana Paluzzi, Bernard Lee. Directed by Terence Young. 129 min.

Packed with beauties, chases, fights, and wit, *Thunderball* concerns the kidnapping of beautiful women and big bombs by the evil SPECTRE. What better combination for a man of James Bond's talents? His superslick attack on world terrorism ends with one of the most thrilling underwater action scenes ever filmed. Good and gimmicky, with Sean Connery turning in a vintage performance (his fourth) as 007.

THUNDER BAY ☆☆☆
1953, USA
James Stewart, Joanne Dru, Gilbert Roland, Dan Duryea, Marcia Henderson, Jay C. Flippen, Antonio Moreno, Robert Monet. Directed by Anthony Mann. 82 min.

Excitement explodes from the screen like an oil well blowing its top. Jimmy Stewart and Dan Duryea are a couple of hell-bent-for-leather wildcatters who have staked a desperate bid for success on an oil field in Louisiana. They come up against a hardscrabble town of Cajuns who are worried about their shrimping grounds. Director Anthony Mann, who was creating classic Westerns with Stewart at this time, handles the confrontation with skill and complexity, introducing a pair of women who are attracted to the men but fear their influence. As is usual with Mann, the personal conflicts and desire begin to take over everyone's stated goals. The movie becomes an interesting mixture of melodrama and action that never really gets sorted out satisfactorily. The unconvincing ending won't diminish viewing pleasure, though. This makes a good double-bill entry with Louis Malle's *Alamo Bay*, a later film that dealt with Gulf shrimpers' conflict with Vietnamese immigrants.

THUNDERBOLT AND LIGHTFOOT ☆☆☆
1974, USA, R
Clint Eastwood, Jeff Bridges, George Kennedy, Geoffrey Lewis, Gary Busey, Catherine Bach, Vic Tayback, Dub Taylor. Directed by Michael Cimino. 115 min.

Michael Cimino's directorial debut (he came to Clint Eastwood's attention after writing *Magnum Force* for him) is an engaging caper film, sparked primarily by the chemistry between Eastwood's usual stolid presence and Jeff Bridges as his eager new accomplice, who persuades him to restage a bank robbery that Eastwood pulled a few years back in which the loot was lost. Bridges, who was nominated for an Academy Award here, is especially good, an extremely affable screen presence. Cimino's script is also strong, if a bit too jokey at times, but his direction shows the tendency toward unnecessary extravagance that came to a head with *Heaven's Gate*.

THUNDERING MANTIS ☆☆☆
1979, Hong Kong
Liang Chia-Jen, Huang I-Lung, Chien Yueh-Sheng, Cheng Feng. Directed by Yeh Yung-Tsu.

In this cross between *Beginning of the End* and a Bruce Lee movie, a fish delivery boy becomes a giant mantis after his best friend is killed. Powerful, bizarre kung fu feature like no other. A must for fans. (a.k.a.: *Mantis Fist Fighter*)

THUNDER IN THE CITY ☆☆☆
1937, Great Britain
Edward G. Robinson, Luli Deste, Nigel Bruce, Constance Collier, Ralph Richardson, Arthur Wontner, Annie Esmond. Directed by Marion Gering. 79 min.

This is a good comic vehicle for Edward G. Robinson, who had to travel to Britain in order to get something different from the gangster parts he was becoming typed in. He plays an American go-getter promoting an African mine rich in a newly discovered mineral. His aggressive style is pitted against the British art of salesmanship, which relies more on a sort of noble old-boy network. Nigel Bruce and Ralph Richardson lend amusing support.

THURSDAY'S GAME ☆☆☆
1974, USA, PG (TV)
Gene Wilder, Bob Newhart, Ellen Burstyn, Cloris Leachman, Martha Scott, Nancy Walker, Valerie Harper, Rob Reiner, Norman Fell. Directed by Robert Moore. 99 min.

This sparkling adult comedy, shot in 1971, was originally intended for theatrical release, but ended up instead as one of the brighter TV movies of the early 1970s. Gene Wilder and Bob Newhart play two longtime poker players who sneak out on their wives once a week even after their game breaks up. A smart commentary on the war between men and women, enlivened by a dream cast and a sharply observed script by James L. Brooks ("The Mary Tyler Moore Show," *Terms of Endearment*).

THX-1138 ☆☆☆½
1971, USA, PG
Robert Duvall, Donald Pleasence, Maggie McOmie, Don Pedro Colley. Directed by George Lucas. 88 min.

A stunning, bleak visualization of the twenty-first century where humans live in a sterile underground society, ruled over by police robots. One man, THX-1138 (Robert Duvall), tries to make it to the surface. An intelligent and thought-provoking example of the science-fiction genre, it is directed by George Lucas, who later went on to make the immensely popular (albeit more juvenile) *Star Wars*.

A TICKET TO TOMAHAWK ☆☆½
1950, USA
Dan Dailey, Anne Baxter, Rory Calhoun, Walter Brennan, Will Wright, Charles Kemper, Marilyn Monroe. Directed by Richard Sale. 90 min.

Were it not for a walk-on bit by Marilyn Monroe (one of her briefest), this film would be almost completely forgotten. Monroe plays a chorine in a number toplining Dan Dailey, but she makes her presence known. Otherwise, this light, slight Western spoof reteams Dailey and Anne Baxter from *You're My Everything* (1949). There are fewer songs but more comedy as Dailey plays a singing traveling salesman who gets mixed up in a railroad war. Baxter's gun-toting marshall's daughter is about as subtle as her Eve Harrington (in *All About Eve*, also made that year), but she plays it in the right spirit. A pleasant, slick Fox production, but Monroe fans should not be duped into thinking this is one of *her* starring vehicles.

TICKLE ME ☆☆
1965, USA
Elvis Presley, Julie Adams, Jocelyn Lane, Merry Anders, Jack Mullaney, Connie Gilchrist. Directed by Norman Taurog. 90 min.

It's true, confound it! If you've seen one Elvis Presley movie, you've seen them all. This one is no different from the others except for an especially bad title. Elvis plays a rodeo performer who searches for gold around a health spa populated by bikini-clad women. Sound funy? Bring along some feathers, because you won't be tickled by the comedy here. Songs include "Night Rider," "Dirty Dirty Feeling," "Put the Blame on Me," and "Slowly but Surely."

TIDAL WAVE ☆½
1975, Japan, PG
Lorne Green, Kiliu Kobayashi, Rhonda Leigh Hopkins, Hiroshi Fujioka. Directed by Shiro Moriana and Andrew Meyer. 90 min.

Originally a two-and-a-half-hour epic called *The Submersion of Japan*, this film depicting that country's destruction by tidal waves and earthquakes was the highest grossing film ever in Japan. For American release, however, Roger Corman's New World studios cut out about an hour, added Lorne Greene as the U.S. representative to the United Nations urging the other countries of the world to take in the Japanese, and dubbed in new dialogue. What's left doesn't make a whole lot of sense, since most of the human subplots were excised, but all the special effects (lots of miniature cities that Godzilla somehow missed destroying) were left in. A time waster.

THE TIGER AND THE PUSSYCAT ☆½
1967, USA/Italy
Ann-Margret, Vittorio Gassman, Eleanor Parker, Antonella Stani. Directed by Dino Risi. 105 min.

A tepid, sex-kittenish comedy, it concerns an Italian businessman (exhibiting every overgesticulating Italian cliché in the book) who gets entangled with a hot-tomato Americana. One of Ann-Margret's most undulating performances during her pre–*Carnal Knowledge* period, when she seemed to be the natural successor to Mamie Van Doren. Now she'd probably want to burn the prints of this worthless comedy.

TIGER BAY ☆☆☆☆
1959, Great Britain
Hayley Mills, Horst Buchholz, John Mills, Yvonne Mitchell, Megs Jenkins. Directed by J. Lee Thompson. 105 min.

A dazzling thriller–*cum*–character study about a Polish sailor who kills his girlfriend during a quarrel. In the aftermath, the desperate man kidnaps a little girl who's witnessed the crime, and the film records their blossoming friendship from initial mistrust to affection. The way in which the police trackdown of the pair dovetails with the relationship of the hapless man and the little girl transforms the drama into something exceptional, aided by astonishingly fine work from Hayley Mills and Horst Buchholz. Nerve-racking *and* emotionally gripping, a rare combination in any suspense film.

TIGER'S CLAW ☆
1980, Hong Kong
Chin Long, Shih Kien. 90 min.

Chin Long plays an undisciplined, obnoxious egotist who learns that the world's greatest fighter is in jail. He decides to break him out so that they can fight to determine who's *really* the best. Who cares?

TIGHT LITTLE ISLAND ☆☆☆☆
1949, Great Britain
Basil Redford, Catherine Lacey, Bruce Seton, James Robertson Justice, Joan Greenwood, Gordon Jackson, Comptom Mackenzie. Directed by Alexander Mackendrick. 82 min.

This droll little comedy is one of the glories of British humor on film. The citizenry of a Scottish island manage to evade concern about World War II until it hits them where they live: their liquor supply runs out, and the war effort prevents them from laying in any more. Fortunately, a freighter carrying fifty thousand cases of Scotch runs aground off their shore. Now all they have to do is get around the Home Guard officers who are watching the ship. . . .Based on a novel by Compton Mackenzie, who has a small part as the ship's captain.

TIGHTROPE ☆☆☆½
1984, USA, R
Clint Eastwood, Genevieve Bujold, Dan Hedaya, Alison Eastwood. Directed by Richard Tuggle. 114 min.

In one of Clint Eastwood's best films, he offers a challenging, low-key portrayal of a kinky police detective trying to restrain some unusual sexual appetites. His character, Wes Block, plunges headlong into the psychosexual tarpit of New Orleans's flesh industry in search of the brutal killer to whom he is linked by circumstance and, perhaps, inclination. If not precisely vulnerable, Eastwood is surprisingly twitchy, and his wallowing in the neon slime makes for some kinky viewing fun. Director Richard Tuggle was also responsible for another acclaimed Eastwood oddity, *Escape from Alcatraz*.

TILLIE'S PUNCTURED ROMANCE ☆☆½
1914, USA
Marie Dressler, Charlie Chaplin, Mabel Normand, Mack Swain, Charles Bennett, Chester Conklin, Edgar Kennedy, Charley Chase, Charles Murray, Minta Durfee. Directed by Mack Sennett. 60 min.

The first feature-length American comedy is known today for the presence of Charlie Chaplin; however, he is the supporting player in this Marie Dressler vehicle. Dressler was the star of *Tillie's Nightmare* on the stage, and she made a smooth transition to the screen, even if her acting style is played to the back rows and she couldn't sing her famous number "Heaven Will Protect the Working Girl" in a silent film. Still, Dressler is a funny actress, an agile slab always on the verge of crushing her diminutive lover. Charlie, too, is good, playing the city slicker who entices Tillie away from her farm and marries her when she inherits $3 million. Mabel Normand steals every scene she's in, playing Charlie's copartner in crime. The movie is a typical Mack Sennett pastiche, little more than a string of set pieces, but many of the pieces are quite good. The best sequence is the grand society ball, where Tillie finds her husband in the arms of another woman and goes on a rampage. The finale features the Keystone Cops, a pier, and the ocean. It's crude, vulgar, and what America loved in 1914.

TILL MARRIAGE DO US PART ☆☆
1974, Italy, R
Laura Antonelli, Alberto Lionello, Michele Placido. Directed by Luigi Comencini. 97 min.

Here's one for those who like their soft-core sex with a European accent and period costuming (or removal thereof). Italian sex symbol Laura Antonelli was at her most voluptuous when she made this romp about turn-of-the-century fiancés who discover just in time that they're brother and sister. Not surprisingly, the bride-to-be quickly finds a chauffeur to help her expend her pent-up passion. And expend, and expend, and expend—the film even includes an actual roll in the hay, minus the farm animals (they'd only get in the way). Within this undistinguished genre, you could do worse.

TILL THE CLOUDS ROLL BY ☆☆☆
1946, USA
Robert Walker, Judy Garland, Frank Sinatra, Lucille Bremer, Lena Horne, Van Johnson, Angela Lansbury, Dinah Shore, Van Heflin, June Allyson, Cyd Charisse, Kathryn Grayson, Virginia O'Brien. Directed by Richard Whorf. 137 min.

MGM musical buffs will be in ecstasy. The more discriminating will note that this is yet another whitewashed composer bio with the narrative providing a ponderous wait between numbers. This time, Jerome Kern is the man of honor and his songs, including "Look for the Silver Lining," "They Didn't Believe Me," and "Ol' Man River," are lovingly overarranged. After the sixteenth or seventeenth production number, however, a feeling of *déjà vu* is inevitable. Still, there is pleasure to be had in Judy Garland's sequences (directed by Vincente Minnelli) and George Sidney's audaciously staged finale.

TILT ☆½
1979, USA (TV)
Brooke Shields, Charles Durning, John Crawford, Ken Marshall. Directed by Rudy Durand. 104 min.

He's a modern minstrel and she's a pinball wizardess. In tandem they make a caravan all over America before encountering the big poobah of Pinball Champions, Charles Durning (Durning must have been duped into thinking this was an arcade remake of *The Hustler*). This was the film that was meant to tilt prepubescent sex idol Brooke Shields into solo stardom and, although she is more appealing here than in her later, plastic performances, the film's shoddy, see-through production values do not showcase properly whatever charm she possesses.

TIM ☆☆☆
1979, Australia
Mel Gibson, Piper Laurie, Alwyn Kurts, Pat Evison, Peter Gwynne. Directed by Michael Pate. 108 min.

Mel Gibson and Piper Laurie give admirable performances in this understated movie about an older woman who falls in love with a handsome, slightly retarded laborer. The film eschews melodramatic confrontations and plot complications; the affair is taken as an understandable, natural relationship, and the movie has an old-fashioned sentimental charm. Based on a novel by the author of *The Thorn Birds*, Colleen McCullough.

TIME AFTER TIME ☆☆☆½
1979, USA, PG
Malcolm McDowell, Mary Steenburgen, David Warner. Directed by Nicholas Meyer. 112 min.

A great idea for a science-fiction film, it lives up to its potential. H. G. Wells (Malcolm McDowell) uses his time machine to pursue Jack the Ripper (David Warner) to 1979 San Francisco. There, the Victorian author falls in love with a bank teller who shows him the ropes of the twentieth century—but the Ripper is learning right along with him. Very imaginative and a lot of fun, with McDowell and Warner standing out as "timeless" adversaries. The scene where McDowell walks into a McDonald's is hilarious. Rousing score by Miklos Rozsa. McDowell met and married Mary Steenburgen while making the film.

TIME BANDITS ☆☆☆½
1981, Great Britain, PG
John Cleese, Sean Connery, Shelley Duvall, Ian Holm, Michael Palin, Ralph Richardson, Peter Vaughn, David Warner, David Rappaport. Directed by Terry Gilliam. 113 min.

A delightful journey through time and space, as six assorted dwarfs with names like Fidgit, Wally, Og, and Vermin, and a small boy make their way through the universe armed only with their wits and a map of the bits that need repairing. The special effects are as imaginative as the film itself. This daffy star-studded romp, a throwback of sorts to *The Wizard of Oz*, is as much fun for grown-ups as kids. Coming from a Monty Python troupe member, the film does have a sharp and absurd sense of humor (especially in the disturbing conclusion), but it is also refreshingly more sardonic than other Python films.

A TIME FOR MIRACLES ☆☆½
1980, USA (TV)
Kate Mulgrew, Jean-Pierre Aumont, Rossanno Brazzi, John Forsythe, Lorne Greene. Directed by Michael O'Herlihy. 98 min.

Luminous Kate Mulgrew is a good casting choice for the role of Elizabeth Bayley Seton, the spirited New York woman who founded the Sisters of Charity nearly two hundred years ago and eventually was canonized as America's first native-born saint. Though Mulgrew is excellent, the film around her is a very standard inspirational TV biopic that offers uplift where insight would have been more welcome.

TIME LOCK ☆☆
1957, Great Britain
Robert Beatty, Betty McDowall, Vincent Winter, Lee Patterson. Directed by Gerald Thomas. 73 min.

A compact, mildly suspenseful B film from England, this is about a little boy trapped in a bank vault and the efforts of a team of experts to free him before it's too late. The no-frills look and stolid playing of the no-name cast won't exactly rivet your attention, but it's a competent movie that sticks to its subject and wastes no footage in reaching its conclusion.

THE TIME MACHINE ☆☆☆
1960, USA
Rod Taylor, Yvette Mimieux, Alan Young, Sebastian Cabot, Tom Helmore, Whit Bissell, Doris Lloyd. Directed by George Pal. 103 min.

The Academy Award–winning special effects of George Pal are usually well integrated into this adaptation of the H. G. Wells classic. Rod Taylor is a dubious intellectual but a stalwart hero as the turn-of-the-century scientist whose time machine propels him far into the future. The barbaric apelike creatures and the gentle humans are played in a way to suggest *The Time Machine*'s strong influence on the subsequent *Star Trek* and *Planet of the Apes*. Very entertaining, although it doesn't do quite as much with Wells's ideas as did *Time After Time*, in which Wells himself was a character.

THE TIME MACHINE ☆☆
1978, USA (TV)
John Beck, Priscilla Barnes, Rosemary DeCamp, Jack Kruschen, Andrew Duggan. Directed by Henning Schellerup. 100 min.

A comic-strip adventure tale that makes you want to travel back to the superior 1960 version of H. G. Wells's classic. John Beck is personable as the clever scientist obsessed with visiting the future, but neither the special effects nor the physical production will do anything to advance TV versions of science fiction.

TIME RIDER ☆
1983, USA, PG
Fred Ward, Belinda Bauer, Richard Masur, Tracey Walter, Peter Coyote, L. Q. Jones, Ed Lauter. Directed by William Dear. 94 min.

A motorcycle racer in the Southwest accidentally drives into a time warp and comes out in 1877 Mexico, where he causes quite a stir. How this reasonably promising variation on *A Connecticut Yankee in King Arthur's Court*, cowritten and scored by the estimable ex-Monkee Mike Nesmith, with a cast chock full of veteran bad guys and that plate-of-shrimp guy from *Repo Man* (another Nesmith production), could have turned out to be so drearily unimaginative and uninvolving mystifies us. See it for yourself if you don't believe us, but don't say we didn't warn you.

THE TIMES OF HARVEY MILK ☆☆☆½
1984, USA
Directed by Robert Epstein. 87 min.

A galvanizing documentary about the buoyant camera-store owner who became the first openly homosexual member of

San Francisco's board of supervisors—and who, on November 27, 1978, after only eleven months in office, was assassinated at City Hall by a former colleague. Director and coeditor Robert Epstein embroils us in the controversy surrounding the trial of Dan White, the straight-arrow family man who killed Milk (and took his own life months after being paroled). And Milk himself, looking like a cross between Lenny Bruce and Andre Gregory, emerges as both a savvy, irreverent media manipulator and an inspiring grass-roots activist whose warmth and ebullience crystallized the spirit of gay liberation. Academy Award winner for Best Documentary.

TIMES SQUARE ☆
1980, USA, R
Trini Alvarado, Robin Johnson, Tim Curry, Peter Coffield, Herbert Berghof. Directed by Alan Moyle. 111 min.

An attempt to do for punk music what *Saturday Night Fever* did for disco, which is to say, create a film whose primary purpose is to produce a blockbuster soundtrack album. The soundtrack does have lots of good songs, from such as the Talking Heads and David Johansen, but the movie around them is awful. Two teenaged girls from different sides of the tracks take to the streets of New York and get on the radio by performing their song "Damn Dog" (easily the low point of the soundtrack) on a Forty-second Street theater marquee. *Rocky Horror*'s Tim Curry, as a cynical disk jockey, does little more than sit around and sneer.

TIME STANDS STILL ☆☆☆
1981, Hungary
Istvan Znamenak, Henrik Pauer, Sandor Soth, Peter Galfy, Aniko Ivan. Directed by Peter Gothar. 99 min.

Teenagers battling their parents in the early 1960s, awkward prom nights, crazy driving, "You Are My Destiny" on the soundtrack—no, it's not *American Graffiti*, but a very interesting Hungarian approximation of it. Peter Gothar's first film is deceptively straightforward in style, following a young man through his adolescent traumas, first love, and passage to adulthood. But like almost all films from Eastern Europe, the content is in the subtext—what's almost said, what isn't quite shown, what might be going on off-screen. Viewers unfamiliar with Hungarian political events in the 1950s and 1960s will find this very rough going, but it rewards attentive viewing. Beautiful cinematography by Lajos Koltai.

THE TIN DRUM ☆☆☆☆
1979, West Germany/France, R
David Bennent, Mario Adorf, Angela Winkler, Daniel Olbrychski, Katharina Tallbach, Heinz Bennent, Charles Aznavour. Directed by Volker Schlondorff. 142 min.

Gunter Grass's novel, which attempted to fuse fifty years of German history into one surreal, allegorical, fantastically entertaining family saga, might be regarded as one of this century's least filmable literary works. Although Volker Schlondorff's adaptation condenses much of the action and eliminates the last third entirely, it's better than anyone had a right to expect. Schlondorff focuses on Oskar, the youngest member of the Matzerath clan, who at the age of three wills himself to stop growing. Schlondorff uses his stunted and ultimately demented vision to depict everything from the Weimar era to the beginnings of the postwar "economic miracle" (where he stops and the book continues). Thanks to his superb rendering of Grass's ordered chaos, and to a great lead performance by twelve-year-old David Bennent, much of the novel's power and scope makes an amazingly fluid transition to film. Well worth seeing, whether or not you're familiar with the novel. Winner of the Best Foreign Film Academy Award and the Cannes Film Festival Palme d'Or.

TIN MAN ☆☆
1983, USA
Timothy Bottoms, Deana Jurgens, John Phillip Law, Troy Donohue. Directed by John G. Thomas. 95 min.

In a corny but likable drama, a deaf young man invents a machine that enables him to hear and speak. A woman who works with a clinic for the deaf puts him in touch with a computer-manufacturing firm where he is able to improve on his inventions, without realizing that they are out to exploit him. Timothy Bottoms does well as the deaf boy in a part too obviously reminiscent of *Charly*, but the supporting cast isn't much; former teen idol Troy Donohue weighs things down as the formula bad guy in a business suit.

TIN PAN ALLEY ☆☆☆½
1940, USA
Alice Fay, Betty Grable, John Payne, Jack Oakie, the Nicolas Brothers, Esther Ralston. Directed by Walter Lang. 94 min.

Alice Faye, of the throbbing voice and languid manner, helped launch Betty Grable's career as Fox's top song-and-dance girl when they appeared together in this polished entertainment. The two adorable Fox blondes shine in this assembly-line musical about pre–World War I songwriters (John Payne and Jack Oakie), although the war is merely an unwelcome interruption in a happy outpouring of bright tunes, snappy patter, and enjoyable dances. if you like Betty and Alice, this will be right up your Tin Pan Alley.

TINTORERA . . . TIGER SHARK ☆
1977, Great Britain/Mexico, R
Susan George, Fiona Lewis, Hugo Stiglitz, Andres Garcia, Jennifer Ashley, Priscilla Barnes, Laura Lyons. Directed by Rene Cardona, Jr. 91 min.

Hungry for a bite of *Jaws*' profits, the chefs behind this Mexican-made British coproduction gambled that to serve up some scrumptious sex would further arouse the appetites of their diners. But they forgot that the shark should be the principal gourmand at the feast, and the swinging ménage à trois (including the tasty Susan George), often glimpsed in the altogether, is too rarely menaced alfresco.

TITAN FIND

See *Creature*

T.N.T JACKSON ☆
1974, USA, R
Jeanne Bell, Stan Shaw, Pat Anderson, Ken Metcalf. Directed by Cirio Santiago. 70 min.

The script of this routine karate-woman film sleeps in the subbasement even of this functionally illiterate genre. Jeanne Bell kicks off in Hong Kong, unwittingly sacking with the very frigid heroin kingpin (Stan Shaw) who iced her brother. Fights and splayed knuckles! There is a battle over a stool pigeon between boss Ken Metcalf and his floozie Pat Anderson—and somehow everybody arrives at the end credits in a hearse. Everybody but Bell, unfortunately; her seventy-minute grimace is the film's most subtle and self-referential statement.

THE TOAST OF NEW YORK ☆☆☆
1937, USA
Edward Arnold, Cary Grant, Frances Farmer, Jack Oakie, Donald Meek. Directed by Rowland V. Lee. 109 min.

It's one of those spirited Hollywood Horatio Alger stories about a businessman who storms the bastions of big business. Edward Arnold is adorably gruff as the enterprising entrepreneur, and the ill-fated beauty Frances Farmer has one of her few decent showcases as a film star. Cary Grant is also around to add some suave support and to complete the traditional love triangle.

TOBACCO ROAD
★★½
1941, USA
Charley Grapewin, Gene Tierney, Marjorie Rambeau, Dana Andrews, Ward Bond, Elizabeth Patterson. Directed by John Ford. 84 min.

A sanitized treatment of the long-running Broadway hit about dirt farmers in the South, where some give in to poverty and others try to rise above their surroundings. After his success with *The Grapes of Wrath*, one would have thought John Ford more attuned to social commentary, but he and screenwriter Nunnally Johnson seem to have scrubbed most of Erskine Caldwell's novel and Jack Kirkland's play clean of any social significance and depth. Thus the saga of Jeeter Lester and his poor white trash family is oddly uncompelling, teetering awkwardly between comedy and drama. A few charming moments do shine through.

TO BE OR NOT TO BE
★★★★
1942, USA
Carole Lombard, Jack Benny, Robert Stack, Felix Bressart, Lionel Atwill, Stanley Ridges, Sig Rumann, Tom Dugan, Charles Halton, Peter Caldwell. Directed by Ernst Lubitsch. 100 min.

Ernst Lubitsch directed this classic black comedy about an acting troupe in Nazi-occupied Poland. Lubitsch's light comic touch manages to make this explosive material wonderfully satirical rather than offensive and insensitive. His dead-on comic planning is inimitable; it must be seen because he has so few heirs. Jack Benny shines, in what is probably the greatest of his film performances, as the prissy third-rate Polish actor Joseph Tura. Carole Lombard, who was killed in a plane crash two months after the film's completion, amuses and arouses as Tura's wife, Maria.

TO BE OR NOT TO BE
★★½
1983, USA, PG
Mel Brooks, Anne Bancroft, Tim Matheson, Charles Durning, Jose Ferrer, George Gayness, Christopher Lloyd. Directed by Alan Johnson. 107 min.

This is a faithful, serviceable remake of Ernst Lubitsch's black comedy classic about a valiant Polish theater troupe struggling against the Nazi occupation. It doesn't degrade the original, but it adds virtually nothing new and can't come close to duplicating the magical comic chemistry of Jack Benny, Carole Lombard, and Lubitsch. Amusing moments from Anne Bancroft, who's able to infuse low comedy with high style more gracefully than almost any other working actress. Mel Brooks proves the perfect 1980s counterpart to Benny in the role of an inept actor with a hammy and finally transcendent faith in his own talent. There's also more of a structure to the complex story than in past Brooks films (this one was directed by longtime collaborator Alan Johnson). But when a remake is this similar to and devoted to its source, why bother doing it at all?

TO CATCH A KING
★½
1984, USA (TV)
Robert Wagner, Teri Garr, Barbara Parkins, Barry Foster, Jane Laportaire. Directed by Clive Donner. 114 min.

A lamebrain's "What if?" movie (originally made for HBO), this is about a Nazi scheme to kidnap the Duke and Duchess of Windsor for ransom. A ditzy nightclub singer and a suave nightclub entrepreneur rehabilitate their political consciences and set out to foil those naughty Nazis in 1940. Another TV movie in which nobody fits the style of the period in which the film supposedly takes place.

TO CATCH A SPY

See *Catch Me A Spy*

TO CATCH A THIEF
★★★
1955, USA
Cary Grant, Grace Kelly, Jessie Royce Landis, Charles Vanel, John Williams, Brigitte Auber. Directed by Alfred Hitchcock. 97 min.

Alfred Hitchcock's sparkling and romantic suspense thriller stars Cary Grant as a retired master jewel thief whose quiet life in his Monte Carlo villa is interrupted by a new series of robberies, perfectly executed in his style. Attempting to clear himself, he sets a trap and, in the process, falls in love with the gorgeous Grace Kelly, an American millionairess who is determined to be burglarized. Fans of Hitchcock's more macabre and spine-tingling yarns may be disappointed by this relatively tame mystery. The culprit is obvious, and apart from a wild car-chase sequence, there are few of the master's renowned set pieces. Fortunately, Grant, Kelly, and the French Riviera look terrific in color and make up for any shortcomings.

TO FORGET VENICE
★★★★
1979, Italy
Erland Josephson, Mariangela Melato, Eleanora Giorgi, David Pontremoli, Hella Petri, Fred Personne. Directed by Franco Brusati. 110 min.

A beautifully controlled, splendidly acted, and very moving meditation on growing up and growing old is directed by Franco Brusati with the creative invention and surety of touch that one usually associates with the best of Ingmar Bergman or Federico Fellini. It's set in a quiet old country house presided over by elderly, loving "aunt" Marta (Hella Petri), who had served as a maternal surrogate to three charges who still need her guidance as adults. When the two women, now lovers, and the man, with his much younger male lover in tow, arrive for a weekend, the joy of their reunion is shattered by Marta's sudden death, and all four must learn to take emotional responsibility for themselves. Brusati treats all of his highly individuated characters with great generosity, and does stunning work with the reflective, gliding flashbacks that pace the film. Mariangela Melato and Petri are outstanding and the film as a whole is a sterling achievement. Dubbed.

TOGETHER?
★★
1979, Italy, R
Jacqueline Bisset, Maximilian Schell, Terence Stamp, Monica Guerritore. Directed by Armenia Balducci. 91 min.

In her first feature, Italian writer/director Armenia Balducci presents a grim view of sexual liberation set against the sun-drenched attractions of a seaside resort filled with jet-setters. Single-mother Jacqueline Bisset carries on a running quarrel with lover Maximilian Schell, while Monica Guerritore has an equally unpleasant time with Terence Stamp. First released as *I Love You, I Love You Not*.

TO HAVE AND HAVE NOT
★★★★
1944, USA
Humphrey Bogart, Lauren Bacall, Walter Brennan, Hoagy Carmichael, Dan Seymour, Walter Sande, Walter Molnar, Dolores Moran. Directed by Howard Hawks. 100 min.

Howard Hawks supposedly bet Ernest Hemingway that he could make a movie out of Hemingway's worst book; Hemingway handed over this novel and Hawks transformed it into a marvelous, dryly comic suspenser. Humphrey Bogart plays a tough boat captain who refuses to take sides in Vichy-controlled Martinique. He meets a girl in a bar (Warner Bros. *was* hoping to repeat the success of *Casablanca*), and they become caught between the government and the Resistance. Nineteen-year-old Lauren Bacall made a stunning costarring debut as the sexy drifter, Slim, and Bogart creates one of his great cynical characterizations. Hawks's masterful direction makes the most of Warner Bros.' murky, shadow-filled visual style, and the film, though done mostly in interiors, achieves an eerie beauty. Many students of Hawks find his films of the thirties and forties separated into two categories: the woman-dominated comedies like *His Girl Friday* and *Bringing Up Baby*, and the films where men work together as a unit, such as *Only Angels Have Wings* and *Red River*. This film is a sort of hybrid—here the masculine loner learns, though his association with a woman, to take a stand for a group. The movie also represents Hollywood's ability to blend film culture with the literary world: beside Hawks and Hemingway, the movie utilized the talents of William Faulkner and screenwriter Jules Furthman.

TO HELL AND BACK ☆☆½
1955, USA
Audie Murphy, Marshall Thompson, Charles Drake, Gregg Palmer, Jack Kelly. Directed by Jesse Hibbs. 106 min.

There's something almost inevitably hokey about film autobiography—perhaps it's the spectacle of performers melodramatizing their own lives (remember *Sophia Loren: Her Own Story*?) So, while *To Hell and Back* is only average as a war film, it's nice to see Audie Murphy playing himself without too much swagger or bravado. The film follows his rise during World War II from infantryman to company commander, and depicts the heroics that earned him twenty-four decorations.

TO KILL A CLOWN ☆☆
1972, USA, R
Alan Alda, Blythe Danner, Heath Lamberts, Eric Clavering. Directed by George Bloomfield. 104 min.

A veteran of the (then current) war in Vietnam, crippled and—as becomes evident—pscyhopathic, terrorizes a couple isolated in a New England beachhouse. A telling but ploddingly unrewarding relic of its period, with sadly little opportunity for the luster of Blythe Danner, who plays Alan Alda's wife in her first screen role.

TO KILL A MOCKINGBIRD ☆☆☆
1962, USA
Gregory Peck, Mary Badham, Philip Alford, John Megna, Brock Peters, Robert Duvall, Frank Overton, Collin Wilcox, William Windom. Directed by Robert Mulligan. 129 min.

Gregory Peck's stoic strength and Lincolnesque dignity were never better suited to a project, and he won an Academy Award for Best Actor for his portrayal of Atticus Finch, a liberal white attorney who risks his neck and his legal practice to defend a black man falsely accused of rape. This memorable screen translation of Harper Lee's beloved best-seller based on her childhood reminiscences was written by Horton Foote (*Trip to Bountiful*). The courtroom scenes have the usual message-movie patina, but they really take a backseat to the film's poetic depiction of southern childhood as Finch's kids try to comprehend the complicated world of grown-up prejudices. Rarely has the camera managed to capture a child's viewpoint so accurately; and the pristine black-and-white cinematography and haunting musical score made this a magical experience. Look for Robert Duvall in the tiny but pivotal role of Boo Radley.

TO LIVE AND DIE IN L.A. ☆☆☆
1985, USA, R
William L. Petersen, Willem Dafoe, John Pankow, Debra Feuer, John Turturro, Darlanne Fluegel, Dean Stockwell. Directed by William Friedkin. 116 min.

William Friedkin's (*The French Connection, Sorcerer*) violent thriller was not a great success in the theaters, and it's a welcome video discovery. There is enough action and surprise to keep a casual audience entranced, and, for careful viewers, there is a deeper exploration of themes of responsibility, uncertainty, and the irreversibility of consequences. The story concerns a young, aggressive Secret Service agent who is hot on the trail of a vicious counterfeiter. His fierce dedication leads him outside the bound of the law, and the film charts his desperate, destructive plunge toward retribution and ultimate justice. The movie's unflinching portrayal of violence may shock some viewers. Interesting score by Wang Chung.

THE TOMB ☆½
1986, USA
Cameron Mitchell, John Carradine, Sybil Danning, Susan Stokey, Richard Alan Hench. Directed by Fred Olen Ray. 84 min.

A silly but occasionally engaging horror thriller, this one's about an ancient Egyptian priestess who comes back to life and relocates to sunny southern California to practice human-sacrifice rituals. Sybil Danning's fans will be disappointed, since the queen of the B's is in and out of the film in a blink, but John Carradine and Cameron Mitchell add some camp/nostalgia value.

TOMBOY ☆
1985, USA, R
Betsy Russell, Jerry Dinome, Kristi Somers. Directed by Herb Freed. 91 min.

No worse than most of the low-rent T & A cars-and-comedy genre, this one centering around a female mechanic out to prove she's just as good as a famous male racer. What's particularly annoying about this entry, though, is the way it keeps patting itself on the back for being "feminist," even as the filmmakers give you the umpteenth thigh shot. And Betsy Russell (*Private School, Avenging Angel*) is stupefyingly untalented.

TOM BROWN'S SCHOOLDAYS ☆☆½
1940, Great Britain
Cedric Hardwicke, Freddie Bartholomew, Jimmy Lydon, Josephine Hutchinson, Billy Halop, Polly Moran, Gale Storm. Directed by Robert Stevenson. 81 min.

An almost entirely American cast can't help but be out of place in this adaptation of the children's novel about a new boy at an English public school, though the results are by no means as bad as they might have been—in fact, the film is not nearly as insufferable as the book. Possibly in the wake of the popularity of *Goodbye, Mr. Chips*, the story is written to build up the character of the schoolmaster, played by Sir Cedric Hardwicke. The 1951 British version is better.

TOM, DICK AND HARRY ☆☆☆½
1941, USA
Ginger Rogers, Alan Marshal, Burgess Meredith, George Murphy, Phil Silvers. Directed by Garson Kanin. 86 min.

Ginger Rogers's film career underwent several metamorphoses as she transformed herself from a wisecracking doxie, to Fred Astaire's dazzling vis-à-vis, to a wacky comedienne, to her eventual self-enshrinement as a dramatic actress (at which point rigor mortis set in, and Ginger became a grande dame). This film is from a happier time in her career when she delighted in being a sparkling comedienne, and this clever script is one of her few durable comedies. She's betwixt and between, deciding among three very different suitors and she fantasizes about what her married life would be like with each. A dreamy comedy that was effectively musicalized as *The Girl Most Likely*.

TOM HORN ☆☆½
1980, USA, R
Steve McQueen, Linda Evans, Richard Farnsworth, Billy Green Bush, Slim Pickens, Elisha Cook, Jr. Directed by by William Wiard. 98 min.

This average latter-day Western about the dying years of Indian tracker Tom Horn, who found his gun-barrel justice to be out of key with the suddenly peaceable frontier of 1900, is given some energy by Steve McQueen's grim, rough-hewn performance. But despite his presence and John Alonzo's richly textured cinematography, the film isn't good enough to sustain the melancholic elegiac spirit for which it strives. Considering that scenarist Larry McMurtry has written some of the best recent Western fiction, it's disappointingly slack, running out of steam about halfway through. But McQueen and Linda Evans (as a schoolmarm) both have their moments. Horn's life was also the basis for the four-hour telefilm *Mr. Horn*, with David Carradine.

TOM JONES ☆☆☆☆
1963, Great Britain
Albert Finney, Hugh Griffith, Susannah York, David Warner. Directed by Tony Richardson. 129 min.

The amorous hero of Henry Fielding's classic novel of eighteenth-century manners and mores is brought to wild and bawdy life by the zesty direction of Tony Richardson, who never seems to take what he's doing too seriously. This is one of the most pleasurable and offbeat "costume" epics ever made, perky and cute, with just a dash of self-satirization. The events of the book race along at a breakneck pace, with the half-crazed style and droll narration providing much of the enjoyment of the movie. Albert Finney is wonderful as the lusty hero of this mock pre-Victorian soap opera, dashing about the atmospheric countryside and pursuing women like an overly energetic satyr. Academy Award winner for Best Picture and Best Director.

TOMMY ☆½
1975, Great Britain, PG
Ann-Margret, Oliver Reed, Roger Daltrey, Elton John, Eric Clapton, Keith Moon, Jack Nicholson, Robert Powell, Paul Nicholas, Tina Turner. Directed by Ken Russell. 111 min.

Ken Russell's excess is wearying in this dull, popping version of the Who's rock opera. It is also a veritable *coup de cinéma*, a genuine opera (there's no spoken dialogue) with a plethora of scenes that refuse to be forgotten. If only Russell didn't take his kitschy Christ allegories so seriously. And, more important, if only the music weren't so often awful and so badly sung. There is no good acting in the entire movie, although Ann-Margret somehow managed to win a Best Actress Oscar nomination.

TOMORROW ☆☆☆
1972, USA, PG
Robert Duvall, Olga Bellin, Sudie Bond, Richard McConell, Peter Masterson, William Hawley, James Franks, Johnny Mask. Directed by Joseph Anthony. 103 min.

Robert Duvall had his first starring role in this bleak, quiet adaptation of William Faulkner's story about a backwoods farmer who comes to care for an abandoned pregnant woman he finds passed out cold on his land. The movie might have been a study for *Tender Mercies*, what with its vast silences and its atmosphere of sodden Christian melancholy, and it's easily one of the most earnest, "uncompromised" attempts to bring Faulkner to the screen. Duvall succeeds at disappearing inside the skin of his character, but you're kept so aware of what a monosyllabic dumdum he's playing that the performance never jells. Olga Bellin is affecting.

TOM SAWYER ☆☆
1973, USA (TV)
Josh Albee, Jeff Tyler, Buddy Ebsen, Jane Wyatt, Vic Morrow, Chris Wiggins. Directed by James Neilson. 78 min.

It's not the definitive version of the Mark Twain classic, but not entirely abysmal, either. If your kids haven't seen any of the numerous versions available, they might enjoy the antics of Tom, his pal Huckleberry Finn, and the villainous Injun Joe. But no film of this tale has ever truly captured the earthy humor and twangy charm of the original.

TONKA ☆☆
1958, USA
Sal Mineo, Philip Carey, Jerome Courtland, Rafael Campos. Directed by Lewis R. Foster. 97 min.

An unexceptional family film from Walt Disney, this is in the studio's familiar a-boy-and-his-animal format. Instead of Old Yeller, the pet here is a pony named Tonka whose young master is a Sioux brave-to-be (Sal Mineo). It's not anti-Indian except in its cliché portrayal of them; the real bad guys here are Custer's cavalrymen, who want not only to eradicate the Sioux population but to seize Sal's horse. Not awful, but nothing special either. (a.k.a.: *A Horse Named Comanche*)

TONY ROME ☆☆
1967, USA
Frank Sinatra, Jill St. John, Richard Conte, Simon Oakland, Sue Lyon, Gena Rowlands, Lloyd Bochner. Directed by Gordon Douglas. 110 min.

Frankie Boy turns on the cocky charm as a crimebuster Tony Rome, who's investigating a case involving a millionaire's errant daughter who is fond of frequenting the lower depths of Miami. When she ends up inebriated in a run-down hotel, Tony's sent to find out why the poor little rich girl's gone slumming. Competently acted action flick; Sinatra fits the gumshoes admirably as the hard-boiled detective.

THE TOOLBOX MURDERS ½☆
1978, USA, R
Cameron Mitchell, Pamelyn Ferdin, Wesley Eure, Nicholas Beauvy, Tim Donnelly, Kelly Nichols. Directed by Dennis Donnelly. 93 min.

Cameron Mitchell sinks to an all-time low here—and if you've seen any of his films in the past decade, you'll realize how truly low that can be. He plays the superintendent of an apartment building who sets out to purge the building of certain sinful women (including porno star Kelly Nichols, in the film's grisliest scene). Pretty gory stuff, with people being killed by drills, screwdrivers through the skull, a nail gun, a hammer—is this really your idea of a good time? With a supporting cast of familiar television faces.

TOOTSIE ☆☆☆☆
1982, USA, PG
Dustin Hoffman, Jessica Lange, Teri Garr, Dabney Coleman, Charles Durning, George Gaynes, Bill Murray, Sydney Pollack, Geena Davis. Directed by Sydney Pollack. 110 min.

Put this on the shelf next to *Some Like It Hot* as one of the hippest, most riotous cross-dressing comedies the screen has ever seen. Its inspired premise has Dustin Hoffman as Michael Dorsey, an actor so desperate for work that he disguises himself as a woman to win a role on America's most popular soap. The temporary gig is complicated considerably when Michael falls in love with his beautiful costar as the nation falls in love with him—as a her. Eight writers, most uncredited, contributed to the seamless screenplay, and each seems to have given his or her best, giving *Tootsie* opportunities to poke fun at daytime drama, nighttime New York, and full-time aspiring actors within the framework of an ingenious romantic comedy that's better seen than described. Hoffman's work is astonishingly resourceful; he creates a female character with a personality all her own while letting you see just a little of the crafty calculation of the man behind the mascara. He's given the best support in any recent comedy, headed by Jessica Lange, an Oscar winner for her work as his sweet, slightly askew colleague, Teri Garr as a marvelously addled woman of the 1980s, Bill Murray as his sly roommate, and director Sydney Pollack as a hypertensive agent. It's a comedy worth celebrating—poignant, perceptive, and paralyzingly funny!

TOPAZ ☆☆
1969, USA
Frederick Stafford, Dany Robin, John Vernon, Karin Dor, John Forsythe. Directed by Alfred Hitchcock. 125 min.

Alfred Hitchcock's political thriller set on the eve of the Cuban missile crisis is one of the director's few unqualified duds. Leon Uris's novel about Cold-War defectors, Cuban dictators, and Russian spy rings is jumbled and confusing on screen. Some set pieces, such as the French agent hero's capture of some top-secret Cuban documents and the murder of the dictator's mistress, have the old Hitchcock zing, but the rest looks like a muddled amalgam of late 1960s spy thrillers. In the cast, only John Vernon's villainous dictator stands out. A poor film, all the more disappointing when you realize it's Hitchcock.

TOP GUN ☆☆
1986, USA, PG
Tom Cruise, Kelly McGillis, Anthony Edwards, Val Kilmer, Tom Skerritt. Directed by Tony Scott. 110 min.

This smash hit from the summer of '86 may have sex, swearing, and splashy visuals, but it is basically a reworking of such 1940s war fantasies as *The Flying Tigers*, replete with their male camaraderie and overblown patriotism. Tom Cruise is cast as Maverick, a hunky all-American flyboy who has no trouble shooting down enemy planes or piloting himself into the bed of a beautiful civilian. When tragedy strikes, Maverick must get back on his sights for the concluding Cold War fight over the Indian Ocean. These cliché shenanigans are photographed and acted with such enthusiasm that their overall effect is disarmingly enjoyable. *Top Gun* may be nothing more than a moving recruiting poster, but it is fun to look at. The theme song, Berlin's "Take My Breath Away," won an Academy Award. Paramount Home Video's cassette includes a commercial—the first on a major video release—at the beginning of the film.

TOP HAT ☆☆☆☆
1935, USA
Fred Astaire, Ginger Rogers, Edward Everett Horton, Helen Broderick, Erik Rhodes, Eric Blore. Directed by Mark Sandrich. 101 min.

Fred Astaire and Ginger Rogers are at their zesty, scintillating best. Fred falls for Ginger while tap-dancing in Edward Everett Horton's hotel room, and the two shuffle off to Venice, where things get very giddy. Irving Berlin's score is one of his loveliest, boasting "Cheek to Cheek," "Isn't It a Lovely Day," and the justly famous title number. This is the most perfectly constructed of the Astaire-Rogers films and the Art Deco sets are at their most irresistible. The comedy may be slightly fresher in the very similar *Gay Divorcee* (1934), and the numbers may soar just that much more in the very different *Swingtime* (1936), but this is the one everyone remembers and comes back to.

TOPKAPI ☆☆☆
1964, USA
Melina Mercouri, Maximilian Schell, Peter Ustinov, Robert Morley, Akim Tamiroff. Directed by Jules Dassin. 120 min.

An intricate caper film, it was inspired by the same director's marvelous *Rififi*—only this time he pulls out all the stops and coats the intricate suspense sequences with a sprinkling of broad comedy. An assembly of international riffraff pool their resources to pull off an ingenious heist utilizing acrobats and split-second timing. The film's comic tone and thrilling robbery segment influenced dozens of subsequent films—e.g., *How to Steal a Million*. Melina Mercouri and Peter Ustinov try to outmug each other; somehow Ustinov's starring role netted him a Best Supporting Actor Oscar.

TOPPER ☆☆½
1937, USA
Cary Grant, Constance Bennett, Roland Young, Billie Burke, Arthur Lake, Hedda Hopper. Directed by Norman Z. McLeod. 98 min.

Glamorous George and Marian Kirby—Hal Roach's attempt to create characters to outdrink and outrevel Nick and Nora—find the party abruptly over one dawn after a martini-induced car crash. Reduced to the blithest of spirits, the pair decide to teach the fine art of living, Kirby-style, to their long-suffering pal, Cosmo Topper. Entirely dependent on the ample charms of Cary Grant, Constance Bennett, and Roland Young, the film lacks pacing and the requisite great dialogue that could lift it to the status of a screwball classic. Still, it was a popular success that spawned two sequels and an early TV series. (Roach Studios has released a computer-colorized version of this film.)

TOPPER RETURNS ☆☆☆
1941, USA
Joan Blondell, Carole Landis, Billie Burke, Patsy Kelly, Dennis O'Keefe, Eddie "Rochester" Anderson. Directed by Roy Del Ruth. 85 min.

An effervescent, "spirited" comedy about a ghost helping her girlfriend stay alive and butting into the investigation of her own untimely demise, this was the last and also the best of the *Topper* series. While it had the feel of a B movie, it delivers more exuberant fun than many so-called A productions. If you like haunted-house mystery comedies like *Hold That Ghost* and *Ghost Breakers*, this *Topper* is tops.

TOPPER TAKES A TRIP ☆☆☆
1939, USA
Constance Bennett, Roland Young, Billie Burke, Alan Mowbray, Franklin Pangborn. Directed by Norman Z. Leod. 85 min.

Those dizzy scatterbrains (Roland Young and Billie Burke) from the original *Topper* film are back and the disembodied but beautiful Constance Bennett continues to haunt Cosmo Topper, everybody's favorite henpecked hubby. This time, ghostly Constance flies around solo (Cary Grant is present only via flashback), but still manages to stir up lots of complications for these mere mortals, as she make Topper's Riviera vacation an unforgettable experience. Still sprightly fun.

TOP SECRET ☆½
1978, USA (TV)
Bill Cosby, Tracy Reed, Gloria Foster, Sheldon Leonard. Directed by Paul Leaf. 100 min.

The top secret here must be why they ever bothered to make this drivel. Bill Cosby, one of TV's most popular stars, comes a cropper in this tedious caper film about an American spy grappling with intrigue in Italy, where he's tracking down some missing plutonium. Apparently, the producers wanted to cash in on the appeal Cos won from the "I Spy" series, but the sophistication of that show is missing here.

TOP SECRET! ☆☆☆½
1984, USA, PG
Val Kilmer, Lucy Gutteridge, Jeremy Kemp, Omar Sharif. Directed by Jim Abrahams, David Zucker, and Jerry Zucker. 90 min.

The team that brought you *Airplane!* and *Kentucky Fried Movie* do it again with hilarious sendup of spy and rock-'n'-roll films. The often indiscernible plot has teen singer Nick Rivers (Val Kilmer) going to East Europe, where he gets mixed up with a plot by neo-Nazis to take over Germany. Lots of great sight gags, although they begin to wear thin after several viewings. The best moments involve an ingeniuos parody of *The Blue Lagoon*.

TORA! TORA! TORA! ☆
1970, USA/Japan, G
James Whitmore, Martin Balsam, Jason Robards, Joseph Cotten, George Macready, Toshio Masuda, Kinji Fukasuku, Soh Yamamura, Tatsuya Mihashi, E. G. Marshall, Wesley Addy, Leon Ames. Directed by Richard Fleischer. 143 min.

If Akira Kurosawa had directed this film, as originally planned, this overweight, muddled excuse for a war film might have retained some of the power and excitement suggested in the subject matter. Here, in only two hours and twenty minutes, is the painful and stagnant replay of American bumbling on the eve of Japan's entry into the war. The attack and the film don't really take off until past the halfway point. A torrent of big-name stars, along with clouds, bombs, and more bombs, do little to save this bloated disaster film. For diehard war film fans it may be tolerable, but for everyone else it's terri! terri! terrible.

TO RACE THE WIND ☆☆☆
1980, USA (TV)
Steve Guttenberg, Randy Quaid, Mark Taylor, Lisa Eilbacher, Barbara Barrie. Directed by Walter Grauman. 105 min.

Some of the same basic biographical material here also surfaced in the play and film, *Butterflies Are Free*. This TV movie deals with the exploits of Harold Krents, a blind man who became a Harvard University honor student. It's a pleasingly lighthearted approach detailing the efforts of this man to live as normal a life as possible. As such, the film is a more palatable survey of the heartaches and triumphs of the blind than a film like *If You Could See What I Hear*.

TORCHLIGHT ☆
1985, USA, R
Pamela Sue Martin, Steve Railsback, Ian McShane, Al Corley, Rudy Ramos, Rita Taggart. Directed by Tom Wright. 90 min.

Just what serious cineasts were hungering for—an anticocaine sermon by a "Dynasty" cast member. Pamela Sue Martin left the Carrington mansion to write and star in this cautionary vehicle (her husband produced) about a young woman whose spouse falls under the influence of the deadly dust, first snorting, then freebasing and finally turning into a raving maniac. Some thought this might become our decade's *Reefer Madness*, but whereas that film perpetuated myths about marijuana, this one takes some serious truths about cocaine and manages to make them seem spurious.

TORN BETWEEN TWO LOVERS ☆☆½
1979, USA (TV)
Lee Remick, Joseph Bologna, George Peppard, Giorgio Tozzi, Molly Cheek. Directed by Delbert Mann. 100 min.

Well, if you've got to make a movie out of a popular song, this one's as good a workprint as any, and is certainly superior to the movie *Ode to Billy Joe*. With surprising frankness, the film uncovers the psychological pitfalls a woman stumbles upon when she finds emotional and sexual solace with an architect while retaining her affection and respect for her husband. A bit superficial in the manner of a glossy 1940s woman's picture, but it does try to view the situation from some new angles.

TORN CURTAIN ☆☆☆
1966, USA
Paul Newman, Julie Andrews, Lila Kedrova, Tamara Toumanova, Hans-Voerg Felmy, Wolfgang Kieling, Gunter Strack, Mort Mills. Directed by Alfred Hitchcock. 126 min.

By the mid 1960s, Alfred Hitchcock started to deal more explicitly with political themes (with this and *Topaz*, 1969), but his creative energy seemed to be running out. In this flawed but fascinating film, Paul Newman plays a nuclear physicist who pretends to defect to East Berlin in order to obtain a top-secret formula from a German scientist. Julie Andrews, in a change-of-pace role, plays Newman's attractive, tag-along girlfriend and assistant. The Brian Moore screenplay gets excessively tangled and the stars have little chemistry together, but Hitchcock manages to whip up a few near-classic set pieces that echo his earlier work—including a murder in a farmhouse, a suspenseful interrogation sequence, and a chilling moment of recognition in the middle of a ballet. If only the director had been able to sustain the rest of the film with the same expertise found in these scenes.

TORTURE GARDEN ☆☆☆
1967, Great Britain
Jack Palance, Burgess Meredith, Beverly Adams, Peter Cushing, Michael Ripper. Directed by Freddie Francis. 92 min.

One of many Amicus horror anthologies, this one is up to their usual high standards. The frame story has Burgess Meredith as a carnival seer who offers four people a glimpse into their futures, each depicted as a separate story. The first involves a kitty out to avenge it owner's death; the second a hopeful starlet who discovers the secret of Hollywood glamour; the third a possessed piano. The last and best features Jack Palance and Peter Cushing as two rival Edgar Allan Poe collectors who tangle with the ghost of the writer himself. Written (with a less tongue-in-cheek approach than later entries) by Robert Bloch.

TOSCA'S KISS ☆☆☆½
1985, Italy
Directed by Daniel Schmid. 97 min.

This documentary by Swiss director Daniel Schmid is a real find—a funny, touching, resonant study of old age and memory that neither condescends to nor sentimentalizes its subjects. Schmid took his cameras to Casa Verdi, an Italian rest home for elderly opera singers, and discovered humor, truth, and dignity among the declining divas and tremulous tenors. Many of the most seemingly infirm residents are still in glorious voice, and all, whether singing along to their old records or emoting for the cameras, are wonderfully theatrical. The film's highlight, an impromptu scene from *Tosca* with two eighty-year-olds, is a vividly emotional portrait of artists whose spirits stay vibrant even as their bodies fail.

TO SIR, WITH LOVE ☆☆☆½
1967, Great Britain
Sidney Poitier, Christian Roberts, Suzy Kendall, Lulu, Judy Geeson. Directed by James Clavell. 104 min.

In a more sentimental version of *The Blackboard Jungle*, Sidney Poitier is an American engineer who, for lack of a job in his field, accepts a year's position as a teacher in a London slum school. After realizing that the traditional syllabus will not prepare his students in any useful way for the lower-class lives that they will face upon graduation, he abandons it for lessons in grooming, self-respect, cooking, and other survival techniques. The ending is a bit mawkish, but only the most cynical will be able to resist it.

TO THE DEVIL—A DAUGHTER ☆☆
1976, Great Britain/Germany, R
Christopher Lee, Richard Widmark, Nastassja Kinski. Directed by Peter Sykes. 95 min.

This lavish but dull adaptation of the novel by Dennis Wheatley is the second in Hammer Films' proposed adaptation of his Black Magic series, following *The Devil's Bride*. Devil cultists intend to use a young girl to further their diabolical plan for world domination; a writer of books on the occult intends to stop them. Not as good as its cast would suggest, but a very young Nastassja Kinski makes a startling impression.

TO THE LIGHTHOUSE ☆☆
1984, Great Britain (TV)
Rosemary Harris, Michael Gough, Suzanne Bertish, Linsey Baxter, Pippa Guard. Directed by Colin Gregg. 120 min.

Who's afraid of adapting Virginia Woolf? Apparently not the BBC. They have fashioned a thoroughly lifeless film out of Woolf's enigmatic postmodern classic. The basic problem is that the film takes the book at its most literal level, failing to find a cinematic equivalent to the writer's literary experiments and poetic antinarrative passages. With its linear story line and conventional editing, the production becomes just another melodrama about a family living on the English seaside. Fine acting, such as Rosemary Harris's (she plays the matriarchal Mrs. Ramsey), does not disguise the formula.

THE TOUCH ☆☆½
1971, Sweden/USA
Bibi Anderson, Elliott Gould, Max von Sydow, Sheila Reid, Steffan Hallerstram, Maria Nolgard, Barbro Hiortaff Ornas, Ake Lindstrom, Mimi Wahlander, Elsa Ebbesen. Directed by Ingmar Bergman. 113 min.

Ingmar Bergman goes wrong in this earnest but misconceived soap opera about a Swedish housewife (Bibi Anderson) living in America who falls into a disastrous affair with a self-hating Jewish archaeologist (Elliott Gould). Bergman has said he wanted to use Gould because he saw the American actor as a "tragic figure," but the only thing tragic about the performance is how bizarrely out of place it is; when the smirky, apple-cheeked Gould chews away on one of Bergman's tortured monologues, the director's gloomy universe almost turns to camp.

TOUCH AND GO ☆☆
1980, Australia
Wendy Hughes, Chantal Contouri, Carmen Duncan, Jeanie Drynan, Jon English. Directed by Peter Maxwell. 92 min.

Female sexpot Robin Hoods steal from the well-off to aid the not-so-well-off—in particular, some schoolchildren whose school is threatened with foreclosure. When they tire of small jobs, they begin to plan a raid on a popular offshore resort. Light farce that mostly just wastes the talent of several good actresses, particularly Wendy Hughes (*Careful He Might Hear You*).

TOUCHED ☆☆
1982, USA, R
Kathleen Beller, Robert Hays, Ned Beatty, Gilbert Lewis, Lyle Kessler. Directed by John Flynn. 93 min.

Doubtless motived by their movie predecessors David and Lisa, Kathleen Beller and Robert Hays fall for each other while incarcerated in an insane asylum, then flee, with aspirations of finding a saner life together. Obviously well intentioned, and with a capable cast, despite the paucity of substance in the story.

TOUCHED BY LOVE ☆☆
1980, USA, PG
Deborah Raffin, Diane Lane, Michael Learned, John Amos, Cristina Raines, Mary Wickes. Directed by Gus Trikonis. 95 min.

This is an inoffensive but tiresome drama about a young nursing trainee and her charge, a cerebral palsy victim who's drawn out of her shell by a growing interest in . . . Elvis Presley! It's based on a true story, but as presented here, it's just as manipulative and sentimentally forced as any disease-of-the-week TV movie. Diane Lane gives the best performance as the stricken teenager, and she's nicely complemented by Deborah Raffin as the nurse; both actresses circumvent some, though not enough, of the script's mawkishness.

A TOUCH OF CLASS ☆☆½
1973, Great Britain, PG
Glenda Jackson, George Segal, Paul Sorvino, Hildegard Neil, K Callan. Directed by Melvin Frank. 105 min.

The oddball pairing of brashly American George Segal with cool, clipped Glenda Jackson gives this old-fashioned, Neil Simon-ish romantic comedy exactly what its title promises. He's a married executive living in London, she's a separated fashion designer, and when they meet, it's lust at first sight. The terribly cute complications that ensue are sometimes hilarious, sometimes not. Firing off the endless dialogue without pausing for air, both stars are witty and attractive. That the superb dramatic actress Jackson won an Oscar for this froth represents the Academy at its most invertedly snobbish. All in all, it's old hat, but old hats can be surprisingly comfortable and touching. Director Melvin Frank, whose credits stretch back to 1942's *My Favorite Blonde*, cowrote the script with Jack Rose.

TOUCH OF EVIL ☆☆☆☆
1958, USA
Charlton Heston, Orson Welles, Janet Leigh, Joseph Calleia, Akim Tamiroff, Marlene Dietrich, Dennis Weaver, Mercedes McCambridge, Ray Collins, Zsa Zsa Gabor. Directed by Orson Welles. 108 min.

Orson Welles's brilliant, bizarre *film noir* was his first Hollywood-made film in many years; despite some studio interference, Welles admitted that the finished product was close to the film he'd envisioned. Opening with a stunning single-take camera movement that introduces the characters and sets the volatile plot in motion in one fell swoop, the movie goes on to present one of the most disturbing, cynical portrayals of police corruption and lack of human conscience that's ever been committed to celluloid. A Mexican-born investigator (Charlton Heston) returns to his homeland to investigate a murder, but his young bride is kidnapped and he's blackmailed in an effort to buy his silence and cut short his snooping. This dogged persistence pits him against a burnt-out cop (one of Welles's most indelible characterizations) whose feverish desire to cover his tracks leads to betrayal and murder before his luck runs out. A masterpiece, with incredible cameos by Mercedes McCambridge as a lesbian gang leader, Dennis Weaver as a peeping tom, and Marlene Dietrich as a Mexican fortune teller. MCA Home Video has released the recently restored, full-length version, including fifteen more minutes of footage than most prior prints.

TOUGH ENOUGH ☆
1983, USA, PG
Dennis Quaid, Carlene Watkins, Stan Shaw, Pam Grier, Warren Oates, Bruce McGill, Wilford Brimley. Directed by Richard O. Fleischer. 106 min.

This variation of *Rocky* is half riff, half rip-off; it posits that a somewhat shrimpy Dennis Quaid can enter a Toughman contest, beat the human Godzillas who oppose him, and work his way to national exposure, all the while trying to embark upon a career as a country-and-Western singer. If that's not enough, there are black jokes, blind jokes, gay jokes, and a wet T-shirt contest.

TOUGH GUYS ☆☆
Hong Kong
Chen Kuan Tai, Chia Ling, Chen Hsing. Directed by Pao Hsiue Li.

Detective Lenghshieh (Chen Kuan Tai) tracks down the killer of a concubine and discovers political conspiracy afoot. An interesting premise gets the usual treatment, sprinkled with very routine fight footage.

TOUGH GUYS ☆☆☆
1986, USA, PG
Kirk Douglas, Burt Lancaster, Charles Durning, Eli Wallach, Dana Carvey, Alexis Smith, Billy Barty, Darlanne Fluegel. Directed by Jeff Kanew. 95 min.

Two ageless stars are the centerpiece of this wild and woolly action picture. Kirk Douglas and Burt Lancaster generate such star-power chemistry together that they make this old-fashioned comedy work. They portray two seasoned crooks fresh from a thirty-year prison stretch who do not want to go gentle into that good retirement. Tasting the contemporary crime scene, they decide on one last spree to prove that they can still outclass the modern criminal element. The two old pros make the material seem better than it is and add zest to sequences that would have floundered in lesser hands.

TOURIST TRAP
☆☆
1979, USA, PG
Chuck Connors, Tanya Roberts, Keith McDermott, Jon Van Ness. Directed by David Schmoeller. 85 min.

Vacationing teenagers happen onto Slausen's Desert Oasis, a roadside tourist attraction forgotten when a highway replaced the old road. They are at first intrigued by the genial Mr. Slausen and his lifelike mannequins, but they soon learn that his smile conceals a deadly secret. This is a low-budget horror movie with psychokinetic phenomena, screaming mannequin heads, psycho siblings, and leggy girls in some very short shorts. Not terribly original, but also not without its moments.

THE TOWERING INFERNO
☆☆½
1974, USA, PG
Steve McQueen, Paul Newman, William Holden, Faye Dunaway, Fred Astaire, Susan Blakely, Jennifer Jones, Richard Chamberlain, O. J. Simpson, Robert Vaughn, Robert Wagner. Directed by John Guillermin and Irwin Allen. 165 min.

In the biggest and most spectacular of the Irwin Allen all-star disaster entertainments that flourished in the early 1970s, a newly erected skyscraper is packed with people unaware of impending flames. It's up to the heroic team of firefighter Steve McQueen and architect Paul Newman to sort out the killable celebrities from the must-saves. The action sequences (directed by Allen) are well staged and compelling, but the personal-drama vignettes in between (John Guillermin's work) are strictly TV fare. By your third hour you may be hoping for a sudden cloudburst to douse the damn thing and get it over with. That this enjoyable but thoroughly trivial movie won an Oscar nomination for Best Picture is surely one of the sorriest footnotes in Academy history.

TOWER OF DEATH
See *Game of Death II*

TOWER OF EVIL
½☆
1972, Great Britain, R
Jill Haworth, Bryant Halliday, Anna Palk, Mark Edwards, Jack Watson, Derek Fowlds. Directed by Jim O'Connolly. 85 min.

If you watch *Tower of Evil*, you'll feel as though your seat is in the Pit of Boredom. A madman kills a bunch of people on an island. Look elsewhere for something with more gore and sex; better yet, look for something scary. (a.k.a: *Horror on Snape Island* and *Beyond the Fog*)

THE TOWER OF LONDON
☆½
1962, USA
Vincent Price, Michael Pate, Joan Freeman, Robert Brown. Directed by Roger Corman. 79 min.

A moldy history lesson from American International Pictures, this is a remake of a much more creditable historical horror tale first filmed in 1939. Vincent Price sashays around in hunchback drag as Richard III, who tries to keep his slippery grasp on the English throne by eliminating the competition. The dastardly usurper even knocks off royal children in his ruthless quest. This low-budget throne-a-rama is shoddily produced, but Price's fruity elocution and hamminess enliven the proceedings. And there's a big laugh (one of many) when the dead royal youngsters come back to haunt Vincent and you can spot the strings they fly in on.

THE TOWN THAT DREADED SUNDOWN
☆☆
1977, USA, R
Ben Johnson, Andrew Prine, Dawn Wells, Charles B. Pierce. Directed by Charles B. Pierce. 90 min.

Based on a true story about a hooded killer who terrorized the town of Texarkana, Arkansas, during 1946, this is drive-in stuff, from the director of *The Legend of Boggy Creek*, who doesn't seem to have invested any of the enormous profits from that one in this. Aside from the usual stalwart performance from the reliable Ben Johnson, who must have lost a bet or been the producer's brother-in-law, this has nothing to distinguish it.

THE TOXIC AVENGER
☆½
1985, USA, R
Andree Maranda, Mitchell Cohen, Jennifer Baptist, Cindy Manion, Mark Torgl. Directed by Michael Herz and Samuel Weil. 85 min.

A hopeless nerd, janitor at the Tromaville (Toxic Waste Capital of the World! local signs proudly proclaim) Health Club, is the victim of a vicious practical joke perpetrated by the town's vile citizens. Overcome with shame, he leaps from a window and falls headfirst into a vat of toxic waste, from which he emerges a deformed, superpowered mutant. Using his newfound powers, he sets to work cleaning up corrupt, criminally infested Tromaville and avenging himself upon those responsible for his condition. Cheap, sleazy, stupid, and cliché-ridden, *The Toxic Avenger* is—for all its complete lack of narrative subtlety, filmic invention, or technical competence—actually pretty entertaining. Bloody in an inept sort of way and brazenly sentimental—so a blind girl falls for the kind-hearted monster; you want to make something of it?

THE TOY
☆½
1982, USA, PG
Richard Pryor, Jackie Gleason, Ned Beatty, Scott Schwartz, Teresa Ganzel, Wilfrid Hyde-White, Annazette Chase, Tony King. Directed by Richard Donner. 110 min.

A black man in Louisiana sells himself to a white millionaire for the purpose of satisfying the millionaire's bored, bratty child: a shabby premise for a movie set in modern times, but an audacious performer like Richard Pryor could turn this bad joke into a scathingly funny satire on money, race, and class. Don't count on it. Pryor merely mugs, ingratiates, Uncle Toms, Stepin Fetchits, dresses in drag, walks on water to avoid piranhas ("Feets, do yo' stuff!"), and coddles the snotty rich white boy. So that the producer could not be accused of making a racist film, there are plenty of pie-eyed brotherhood-of-man speeches thrown in, thus ruining the fun for the movie's one possible audience—slavery fantasists.

TRACKS
☆☆
1977, USA
Dennis Hopper, Taryn Power, Dean Stockwell, Topo Swope. Directed by Henry Jaglom. 90 min.

Don't make tracks for this counterculture artifact about the aftermath of Vietnam. For an hour and a half we're taken inside Dennis Hopper's brain (think about *that* for a while) as he accompanies his dead pal's body back home on a train. Dennis thinks deep thoughts about the meaning of our involvement in Vietnam, and involvements in general. Heavy stuff; it took Henry Jaglom until 1985 to make a good film (*Always*).

TRADING PLACES
☆☆☆
1983, USA, R
Eddie Murphy, Dan Aykroyd, Jamie Lee Curtis, Ralph Bellamy, Don Ameche, Jim Belushi. Directed by John Landis. 106 min.

John Landis keeps the wheels turning in this funny but formulaic comedy about an executive prince and a street-hustling pauper who suddenly undergo a radical switch in life-styles. When they discover that they are rival guinea pigs in a nature-versus-nurture debate by two millionaire brothers, they join forces with an entrepreneurial young hooker (Jamie Lee Curtis) and make the class system work for them. The static script is little more than a serviceable vehicle for the estimable talents of Eddie Murphy, Dan Aykroyd, and (in her first nonhorror role) Curtis, and although they don't share nearly enough scenes, they do make a winning, ripely comic threesome.

THE TRAIL BEYOND ★★½
1934, USA
John Wayne, Verna Hillie, Noah Beery, Sr., Irish Lancaster, Noah Beery, Jr., Robert Fraser, Earl Dwire. Directed by Robert N. Bradbury. 55 min.

Yet another early 1930s John Wayne low-budget Western, this one, set in a gold mine, does contain a few nuggets—fast action and Beery's performances—but nothing to rush for. Still, if you're going to see them all, this isn't the worst one you'll come across.

THE TRAIL OF THE PINK PANTHER ★★
1982, USA, PG
Peter Sellers, David Niven, Herbert Lom, Richard Mulligan, Joanna Lumley, Capucine, Robert Loggia, Harvey Korman, Bert Kwouk, Graham Stark, Leonard Rossiter. Directed by Blake Edwards. 97 min.

Released after the death of Peter Sellers, *Trail* infuriated many of his fans, who saw it as a cheap attempt by Blake Edwards to cash in with some leftover footage of Sellers he had lying around. Edwards defended the project as a way of presenting scenes of which both he and Sellers were proud, but that had to be cut from previous *Panther* films to make way for such necessities as plot. The director's intentions were probably honorable, but the result is not: by tying the leftovers together with a frame plot (Clouseau disappeared, and a French television reporter is compiling a documentary on his career), *Trail* results in too little Sellers and too much dreck. Edwards would have done better just to have assembled the best outtakes and released them as is with a bit of voice-over narration; the Clouseau character was identifiable enough that no plot would have been needed.

TRAIL RIDERS ★★
1942, USA
John "Dusty" King, David Sharpe, Max "Alibi" Terhune. Directed by Robert Tansey. 55 min.

In case you missed it, here's the ten-day production that became number 18 in Monogram's *The Range Busters* series. As the heroes, King, Sharpe, and Terhune expose some bandits posing as a citizens' vigilante committee in Gila Springs. Sharpe is a rough-and-ready stuntman.

TRAIL STREET ★½
1947, USA
Randolph Scott, Robert Ryan, Anne Jeffreys, George "Gabby" Hayes. Directed by Ray Enright. 83 min.

This serviceable pseudohistorical Western has genre staple Randolph Scott as Bat Masterson, out to clean up the lawless burg of Liberal, Kansas, with an assist from farm agent Robert Ryan. Plenty of saloons, tunes, and two-fisted action keep the energy level high, but the colorful supporting characters will grab your interest more than the stolid leads.

THE TRAIN ★★½
1965, USA/Italy/France
Burt Lancaster, Paul Scofield, Jeanne Moreau, Michael Simon, Wolfgang Preiss. Directed by John Frankenheimer. 140 min.

A fascinating chapter in World War II history is given an adequate but uneven screen treatment. In 1944, a French railway inspector aids the Resistance in preventing the Nazis from taking French art treasures back to Germany. The pace is slow, the plot digresses, and the accents (with American Burt Lancaster cast as a Frenchman and British Paul Scofield as a German) are ludicrous, but the look is grimly authentic and the historical aspect constantly intriguing. A slow, bumpy, but rewarding ride.

TRAINED TO KILL, U.S.A. ★½
1975, USA
Stephen Sandor, Rockne Tarkington, Richard X. Slattery, Michael Lane, Heidi Vaughn. Directed by Daniel J. Vance. 91 min.

There's graphically violent fun for action fans as a Vietnam vet wipes out a vile gang that's invaded his hometown. Need we say that he dispatches them, one by one, with techniques he learned fighting in the war? If this were rated, it would definitely get an R.

THE TRAIN ROBBERS ★★½
1973, USA, PG
John Wayne, Ann-Margret, Rod Taylor, Ben Johnson, Christopher George, Bobby Vinton, Ricardo Montalban. Directed by Burt Kennedy. 92 min.

The Duke recruits a band of good ol' boys to help recover a cachet of gold that (sort of) belongs to the widder Ann-Margret. They don't plan to keep the gold themselves, mind you; although there is a reward to be had, the main point is to save the honor of the lady and her young son. In short, this is a Western suitable for the family. Bobby Vinton, at a career low point just prior to gaining new recording stardom as the Polish Prince, plays one of the lesser members of the band.

TRANSATLANTIC MERRY-GO-ROUND ★★½
1934, USA
Jack Benny, Nancy Carroll, Gene Raymond, Sidney Blackmer, Mitzi Green, the Boswell Sisters, Patsy Kelly. Directed by Ben Stoloff. 92 min.

The film gives the viewer a dizzy ride—it's sort of a murder mystery–comedy–romance. It doesn't really resolve itself satisfactorily; sleuthing and musical numbers don't mesh too well. A radio troupe becomes involved in a murder case while transmitting their program on an ocean liner at sea. This oddity boasts lots of enjoyable bits and pieces, such as Jack Benny's double takes, the Boswell Sisters' harmonizing, and child star Mitzi Green's broad impressions, all served up in a glossy Paramount production.

TRANSFORMERS: THE MOVIE ★★
1986, USA, PG
Animated: Eric Idle, Judd Nelson, Leonard Nimoy, Robert Stack, Orson Welles. Directed by Nelson Shin. 86 min.

This one is strictly for kids who gorge themselves every Saturday morning on junk-food animation—adults raised on Disney, or even "The Flintstones," will be dumbstruck not only by the spareness of the artwork but by the portentous lack of humor of the story, about Autobots clashing with Decepticons over a powerful medallion. There are good contraptions and bad contraptions; and if you know the difference between an Autobot and a Decepticon but not between this and classic animation, tune in.

TRANSYLVANIA 6-5000 ½★
1985, USA, PG
Jeff Goldblum, Joseph Bologna, Ed Begley, Jr., Carol Kane, Jeffrey Jones, John Byner, Geena Davis, Michael Richards, Norman Fell. Directed by Rudy DeLuca. 90 min.

Occasionally a movie is so bad that there is nothing good that can be said about it. In this case, though, there is one positive comment to be made: Geena Davis looks great. Other than that, this pastiche of horror clichés wastes even the microscopic comic talents of John Byner; Jeff Goldblum and Ed Begley, Jr., apparently mailed in their parts so they couldn't be held responsible. Norman Fell reaches the heights of his work on "The Ropers" as a newspaper editor who sends his reporters to Transylvania to cover a sighting of Frankenstein. Ha-ha.

TRAPPED ★★½
1949, USA
Lloyd Bridges, Barbara Paxton, John Hoyt, James Todd. Directed by Richard Fleischer. 78 min.

Not to be confused with the made-for-TV movie with James Brolin, this is a gritty G-man melodrama in which the FBI tries to crack down on a fake money operation, as the good guys stake out some shifty counterfeiters. Done in a semidocumentary style, this well-coined yarn will have you cheering for the Feds.

TRASH ★★★½
1970, USA
Joe Dallesandro, Holly Woodlawn, Jane Forth, Michael Sklar, Geri Miller, Andrea Feldman. Directed by Paul Morrissey. 103 min.

This funny, touching feature is the one film to come out of the Andy Warhol Factory in which pain and compassion transcend camp. Joe Dallesandro is the monosyllabic junkie who can't get it up, and female impersonator Holly Woodlawn is his battered-but-true girlfriend who wants him to kick his habit so they can go back on welfare and become "respectable." Paul Morrissey's unblinking camera records their low-income follies with a kind of gracious detachment, but it's Woodlawn's moving performance that finally pulls the film together, turning Morrissey's deliberately tacky aesthetic into a form of deadpan tragedy.

TRAUMA

See *Terminal Choice*

LA TRAVIATA ★★★½
1983, Italy, G
Teresa Stratas, Placido Domingo, Cornell MacNeil, Alan Monk, Axelle Gail, Pina Cei, Maurizio Barbacini, Robert Sommer, Ricardo Oneto, Luciano Brizi, Tony Ammirati. Directed by Franco Zeffirelli. 112 min.

Franco Zeffirelli's sumptuously designed production of Verdi's most popular opera (based upon the Camille story of Alexandre Dumas *fils*) is an often breathtaking achievement when the opulent scenery and indulgent camerawork don't intrude upon the splendid performances of Teresa Stratas and Placido Domingo (the sparkling score is played by the exceptional Metropolitan Opera Orchestra, conducted by James Levine with his characteristic flair for Verdi). All in all, one of the most successful operas on film.

TREASURE ISLAND ★★★
1934, USA
Wallace Beery, Jackie Cooper, Lionel Barrymore, Otto Kruger, Lewis Stone, Nigel Bruce, Charles "Chic" Sale, William V. Mong, Charles McNaughton, Dorothy Peterson. Directed by Victor Fleming. 109 min.

Peg-legged, duplicitous Long John Silver is the center of narrative gravity in this most classic of swashbucklers, and Wallace Beery, one of MGM's most popular stars of the 1930s, is perfect in the role. The surly young Jackie Cooper ("Our Gang") does a credible job as Jim Hawkins, the alert, adventurous cabin boy whose Tom Sawyer-ish thirst for adventure actually generates the treasure hunt in the first place and who is responsible for most of the plot's turns. Most of the other actors are also very good, especially Lionel Barrymore as the loyal seaman Billy Bones and Chic Sale as Ben Gunn, the half-crazed castaway who has been alone on T.I. for several years. This film version is long and a bit bombastic, but the action scenes are plentiful and satisfying, and, since the film, like the book, was intended for an audience of boys, there is not even an attempt at a romance angle. Good musical score by Herbert Stothart.

TREASURE ISLAND ★★★½
1950, USA
Bobby Driscoll, Robert Newton, Basil Sydney, Walter Fitzgerald, Denis O'Dea, Ralph Truman, Finley Currie, John Laurie. Directed by Byron Haskin. 96 min.

Disney's first full-length live-action feature remains the definitive version of Robert Louis Stevenson's adventure tale. It cleans up the story a bit, supplying a new ending and toning down the wickedness of Long John Silver, but Robert Newton plays the one-legged pirate with such panache and roguish charm that it's difficult to imagine the character as anything (or anyone) else. He even manages to best the old show-business adage never to play scenes with children or animals by stealing scenes from both! High production values are abetted by Freddie Jones's excellent cinematography. Newton returned in the sequel, *Long John Silver*.

TREASURE OF BRUCE LE ★
1985, Hong Kong
Bruce Le (Huang Kin-Loug), Chen Hsing, Chang Li, Chaing Tao, Mulo Tong. Directed by Joseph Velasco.

Joseph Velasco (*Return of Bruce*) wrote and directed this tepid Bruce Le kung fu film. Here Le seeks a stolen secret kung fu manual and encounters a Shaolin traitor and a samurai on the way. Guess what happens when they meet?

TREASURE OF MATECUMBE ★½
1976, USA, G
Robert Foxworth, Joan Hackett, Peter Ustinov, Vic Morrow, Johnny Doran, Billy Attmore, Jane Wyatt. Directed by Vincent McEveety. 117 min.

Children raised on the technical wizardry of *Star Wars* and its ilk may wonder why Disney's family comedies packed their counterparts in a generation earlier; they won't feel enlightened after seeing this sluggish, simpleminded adventure, made just a year before Lucas' film but lagging decades behind in its style and substance. The plot has two boys searching for buried treasure in the Florida Keys, and might have been a compelling tale at half the length.

THE TREASURE OF PANCHO VILLA ★½
1955, USA
Rory Calhoun, Shelley Winters, Gilbert Roland, Joseph Calleia. Directed by George Sherman. 96 min.

In a weak action-adventure set in Mexico during the Revolution, Rory Calhoun and Gilbert Roland, the former a soldier of fortune and the latter a fervent supporter of Pancho Villa, get together to pull off a huge gold robbery. The ending is straight out of *The Treasure of the Sierra Madre*. This was Shelley Winters's last picture before she retired from Hollywood for four years to return to Broadway and those great New York delis.

THE TREASURE OF THE SIERRA MADRE ★★★★
1948, USA
Humphrey Bogart, Walter Huston, Tim Holt, Bruce Bennett, Barton MacLane, Bobby (Robert) Blake. Directed by John Huston. 124 min.

In 1920 Mexico, three down-and-out Americans win some money in a lottery and decide to go prospecting for gold. They find it, but also find out some unpleasant truths about themselves as they become consumed by suspicion and greed. This is perhaps the best early film of John Huston's career; his direction shows a sureness and clarity that were often absent until his more recent films (*Prizzi's Honor*, *Under the Volcano*). Humphrey Bogart, as Fred C. Dobbs, did an about-face from the gruffly heroic roles that made him famous in the 1940s to an unscrupulous type similar to those he played in supporting roles earlier. Walter Huston, as the old-timer of the group, won an Academy Award for Best Supporting Actor; and his son won two, for Best Director and Best Screenplay Adaptation (he also has a bit role, as a white-suited American, toward the beginning of the film).

A TREE GROWS IN BROOKLYN ★★½
1974, USA (TV)
Cliff Robertson, Diane Baker, James Olson, Pamelyn Ferdin, Allyn Ann McLerie, Nancy Malone. Directed by Joseph Hardy. 78 min.

This is an acceptable but unremarkable remake of the classic 1940s film of Betty Smith's best-seller. A youngster dotes on her father, who has trouble handling the responsibilities of family life. She inherits his dreamy charm and imagination and struggles to find her place in the sun while growing up in the shadows of a tenement. Sometimes poignant, but not the unforgettable experience of the original.

THE TREE OF THE WOODEN CLOGS ☆☆☆☆
1978, Italy
Luigi Ornaghi, Francesca Moriggi, Omar Brignoli, Antonio Ferrari, Teresa Brescianini, Giuseppe Brignoli, Carlo Rota. Directed by Ermanno Olmi. 186 min.

The quiet beauty of Italian peasant life is evoked as a rich tapestry, and then, thread by thread, director Ermanno Olmi picks the tapestry apart to reveal the punishing labor and unyielding rigor behind it. Focusing on the unceasing rhythms of a tiny village in Lombardy in the late nineteenth century, Olmi shows not only the life, but also how terribly wrong things can turn when one of the *paisani* violates his station: with his son in need of new wooden shoes, a farmer cuts down a tree without permission and uses the wood to carve a pair of clogs. His harsh punishment for stealing the wood comes as an epiphanic shock that recasts the entire pastoral scene into its cultural and historical context and resonates with the viewing experience. One suddenly feels guilty for enjoying the visual spectacle and suddenly understands the ease and comfort of seeing peasant life in sentimental and rustic terms. Regrettably, the experience is provisional with a video viewing. Lacking the intense color values of film, Olmi's painterly touch is diminished, and with the screen missing its sweep, the sense of being enveloped in this atmosphere is lost. What does come through is the integrity of the nonprofessional actors and Olmi's obvious regard for them.

THE TRIAL ☆☆☆½
1962, France/Italy/Germany
Anthony Perkins, Jeanne Moreau, Romy Schneider, Orson Welles. Directed by Orson Welles. 118 min.

Orson Welles's screen version of Franz Kafka's *The Trial* is a nightmarish journey into a labyrinthine world. Filmed at the Gare d'Orsay in Paris, it is full of Wellesian surprises while remaining largely faithful to the original text. Welles doesn't imitate Kafka's claustrophobic stylization so much as find a visual equivalent for it, using mesmerizing combinations of shadow and light to create a bureaucratic inferno. Anthony Perkins makes a credible Joseph K., but the complex, surreal story may frustrate those who aren't familiar with the novel.

THE TRIAL OF BILLY JACK ☆
1974, USA
Tom Laughlin, Delores Taylor, Victor Izay, Teresa Laughlin, William Wellman, Jr. Directed by Frank Laughlin. 175 min.

The freak success of the cult hit *Billly Jack* did not yield similar results in this, its ludicrous sequel. All of the Laughlins are involved in this forgettable family affair as Billy, the half-breed peacemonger, impetuously squares off against government corruption and big-business duplicity. Only Billy is pure, noble, and capable of keeping his principles inviolate. A pitiful canonization of a two-bit counterculture hero.

THE TRIANGLE FACTORY FIRE SCANDAL ☆☆☆
1979, USA (TV)
Stephanie Zimbalist, David Dukes, Tom Bosley, Tovah Feldshuh, Janet Margolin. Directed by Mel Stuart. 100 min.

A sobering account of a tragic real-life event that proved influential in effecting changes in labor laws and job safety standards. Blessedly, all the vignetted stories about the victims and survivors of this inferno factory fire are not contrived and pat; there's a freshness about the writing and a gritty realism to the acting that makes this film something special. Most docudramas are too puffed up with the importance of the Big Historic Event, but this one takes care in first making us feel for the protagonists, and it's this emotional involvement that gives the painful historic incident its full weight.

TRIBUTE ☆½
1980, USA/Canada, PG
Jack Lemmon, Robby Benson, Lee Remick, Kim Cattrall, Colleen Dewhurst, John Marley, Gale Garnett. Directed by Bob Clark. 123 min.

We can just imagine the studio conference: "Okay, we've just bought the rights to this hot Broadway show, and Jack Lemmon has signed to play the same role that he got a Tony for. This is a combination comedy and tearjerker, so we need a director with a sensitive touch to pull it off. Anybody have any suggestions?" A hand goes up in the back: "How about the guy who made *Porky's*?" Okay, never mind that Bob Clark didn't make *Porky's* until two years later—he still ruins this with a heavy-handed approach that is exactly wrong for this kind of play, pushing it over the edge into sentimental goop. As Broadway press agent Scottie Templeton, the life of the party in public who has neglected his family for years, Lemmon fails to tone down his performance for the camera.

TRICK OR TREAT ☆☆
1986, USA, R
Marc Price, Tony Fields, Lisa Orgolini, Doug Savant, Elaine Joyce, Gene Simmons, Ozzy Osbourne. Directed by Charles Martin Smith. 97 min.

This low-octane horror film manages some funny observations about its subject, teen worship of pseudosatanic heavy-metal bands. Marc Price (Skippy of TV's "Family Ties") plays an adolescent misfit devastated at the death of rock star Sammi Curr. When he gets hold of Curr's last, unreleased recording and plays it backward, Curr returns to life. Light on scares and heavy on metal, this is almost unbearable unless you have a high tolerance for this particular musical genre. Those who do will appreciate the appearances of KISS's Gene Simmons as a DJ and Osbourne as a minister.

TRICK OR TREATS ☆
1982, USA, R
David Carradine, Carrie Snodgress, Jackelyn Giroux, Steven Railsback, Paul Bartel, Peter Jason. Directed by Gary Grover. 90 min.

A baby-sitter finds herself saddled with a singularly obnoxious child on Halloween night. The boy's elaborate and nonstop pranks, however, are not the worst that the evening holds: his dangerously insane father has escaped from a lunatic asylum and is on his way home with vengeance on his mind. *Trick or Treats* is a very weak, formulaic horror film undermined by a serious structural flaw; fully three-quarters of its running time is an elaborate boy-who-cried-wolf setup for a payoff that just doesn't arrive. Featuring what amount to cameos by several respectable actors: Carrie Snodgress and David Carradine as parents who go out to a costume party and don't come back, Steven Railsback as a boyfriend who calls in from time to time, and director Paul Bartel (*Eating Raoul*) as a bum. Dull and attenuated.

TRIGGER, JR. ☆☆
1950, USA
Roy Rogers, Dale Evans, Pat Brady, Gordon Jones, Trigger. Directed by William Witney. 68 min.

Roy Rogers confronts a gang of extortionists and a killer stallion in this pleasant B Western. The excitement wanes at points, but the heated hoof-to-hoof combat scenes between Trigger, Jr., and the maniacal stallion pay off. Shot in gloriously artificial "Trucolor."

TRILOGY ☆☆☆
1969, USA (TV)
Mildred Natwick, Maureen Stapleton, Martin Balsam, Geraldine Page, Donnie Melvin, Susan Dunfee. Directed by Frank Perry. 110 min.

An exquisitely acted and produced collection of three short stories by Truman Capote, shown separately on television and then compiled, trimmed (without detriment), and released theatrically. "Miriam," the opener and weak link, is a half-creepy, half-silly chiller about a nanny (Mildred Natwick) pushed toward madness by a vicious little girl. "Among the Paths To Eden," the second segment, is a touching playlet with Maureen Stapleton and Martin Balsam as a spinster and a widower desperate for love. Best of all, however, is "A Christmas Memory," a Southern-fried reminiscence of yuletides spent with a lovably dotty aunt (Geraldine Page in an Emmy-winning performance). The trio of fine actresses makes the overly precious storytelling easy to ignore. Screenplay by Capote and Eleanor Perry.

TRILOGY OF TERROR ☆☆½
1975, USA (TV)
Karen Black, Robert Burton, John Karlen, George Gaynes, Gregory Harrison. Directed by Dan Curtis. 90 min.

This three-part made-for-TV thriller has gained a cult following thanks to its clever, scary, and extremely well-made final story. In it, Karen Black plays a woman who buys a knife-wielding warrior doll for her boyfriend only to have it come alive and chase her around her apartment. The entire segment is good enough for viewers to sit through the first two tedious stories, which cast Black as a sexually promiscuous woman and her repressed sister, and as a seemingly repressed schoolteacher who gets involved with one of her students. Black is always interesting to watch, but only in the final tale does she receive exciting material with which to work.

TRINITY IS STILL MY NAME ☆☆½
1972, Italy, PG
Terence Hill, Bud Spencer, Harry Carey, Jr., Jessica Dublin, Yanti Somer, Pupo de Luca. Directed by by E. B. Clucher. 117 min.

A sequel to *My Name Is Trinity*, the spaghetti Western-parody that was one of the biggest box-office hits ever in Italy; this one is more overtly a comedy. Here Trinity and his dopey brother Bambino (you have to wonder when Terence Hill is cast as the *smarter* half of a pair) trying to become bandits in deference to their father's dying wish. Unfortunately, they just can't help standing up for the weak and defenseless. A discontinuous stream of sight gags, many reminiscent of silent comedies.

THE TRIP ☆☆☆
1967, USA
Peter Fonda, Bruce Dern, Susan Strasberg, Dennis Hopper, Salli Sachse. Directed by Roger Corman. 85 min.

A director of television commercials in the middle of an emotional crisis takes his first tab of LSD and encounters a Bergmanesque dwarf, psychedelic lighting effects, and a host of demons of the mind. Dedicated to the proposition that a sane person might actually decide to take acid under the supervision of the ever-demented Bruce Dern, *The Trip* invites you to "Listen to the Sound of Love . . . Feel Purple . . . Taste Green . . . Touch the Scream That Crawls Up the Wall!" From a screenplay by Jack Nicholson.

THE TRIP TO BOUNTIFUL ☆☆½
1985, USA, PG
Geraldine Page, John Heard, Carlin Glynn, Richard Bradford, Rebecca De Mornay. Directed by Peter Masterson. 106 min.

Originally a 1963 television drama starring Lillian Gish, this was redone for the movies after its author, Horton Foote, who dropped out of the business after winning an Academy Award for his screenplay for *To Kill a Mockingbird*, reemerged with *1918* and *Tender Mercies*. Unfortunately, this is one of those little dramas that works well in short form on the small tube but cannot be blown up. The minimal plot concerns an old woman, reduced to living with her insecure son and bitchy daughter-in-law in Houston, who wants to return to the small town in which she was born. Geraldine Page does her patented old-lady act, and Carlin Glynn is too much of a caricature as the shiftless daughter-in-law to achieve dramatic plausibility. Rebecca De Mornay has so little to do that she might as well have been a wax model. The sole saving grace here is John Heard; in a short play that would have benefitted from expansion, the filmmakers erred grievously in not developing his part more—he is the only character whom you feel there is more that you would like to know. However, what he does with the little time given him onscreen, especially in the closing scene, is almost enough to redeem this otherwise tedious film. Page won the Academy Award for Best Actress.

TRISTANA ☆☆☆☆
1970, Spain/Italy/France
Catherine Deneuve, Fernando Rey, Franco Nero, Lola Gaos, Jesus Fernandez, Antonio Casas. Directed by Luis Buñuel. 95 min.

The last and darkest of the films in what might be called Luis Buñeul's *Viridiana* cycle, this is the unsettling story of a young girl (Catherine Deneuve) who surrenders to the sexual longings of her benefactor (Fernando Rey). Instead of liberating the two of them, her capitulation tears them apart and transforms the pristine and beautiful Deneuve into a predatory harpy. Undeniably one of Buñuel's slowest-moving yet most powerful and bitter tracts. The plot is almost identical to *Viridiana*'s, but the conclusion is even more devastating. Though possibly one of the director's most skillful films, there is no saving grace in his vision—you come away feeling disgusted.

THE TRIUMPH OF SHERLOCK HOLMES ☆☆☆☆
1935, Great Britain
Arthur Wontner, Ian Fleming, Lyn Harding, Leslie Perrins, Jane Carr. Directed by Leslie Hiscott. 75 min.

Despite the indelible identification of Basil Rathbone as the Baker Street detective, Sherlock Holmes was played onscreen by at least two dozen other actors before Rathbone first donned the deerstalker. Arthur Wontner played him in five British films, of which this is the best, an adaptation of Arthur Conan Doyle's novel *The Valley of Fear*. Though he plays the role with less panache than Rathbone, Wontner is actually closer to the conception of Holmes found in Doyle's stories.

TRIUMPH OF THE WILL ☆☆☆
1935, Germany
Directed by Leni Riefenstahl. 110 min.

Leni Riefenstahl's famous propaganda film is a record of the 1934 Nazi Party Congress in Nuremberg, an event staged by Hitler so that Riefenstahl could film it. Most of the movie is devoted to her surging visions of Aryan splendor (vistas of clouds and mountaintops, crowds of thousands marching with Busby-Berkeley precision and set to the music of Herbert Windt), and the effect is at once unsettling and hallucinatory: watching the monstrous regime turned into such an overpowering spectacle, you can almost understand how the German people went for it. The film remains a fascinating object of study but, for all the hoopla, it is a poorly and ponderously paced documentary. An abridged version, which omits some of the speeches and marches, was reportedly edited by Luis Buñuel. This video edition is the full-length feature.

TRIUMPHS OF A MAN CALLED HORSE ☆
1982, USA/Mexico, R
Richard Harris, Ana De Sade, Michael Beck, Vaughn Armstrong, Buck Taylor, Anne Seymour. Directed by John Hough. 86 min.

The original *Man Called Horse* hit a nerve with Richard Harris's powerhouse performance, a load of philosophy about self-awareness, and its kinky scenes of punishment. *Return of a Man Called Horse* was a good sequel that added an interesting plot. *Triumphs*, inevitably, illustrates the fourth law of thermodynamics, that entropy always takes over a system, that the universe is winding down to senseless disorder. If that doesn't depress you, try this story about Harris's Indian son protecting the Sioux. Harris looks abject throughout, as though he knows that he'll never be asked to play King Arthur again.

TROLL
1986, USA, PG-13
June Lockhart, Michael Moriarty, Shelley Hack, Jenny Beck, Noah Hathaway, Sonny Bono, Gary Sandy, Brad Hall, Julia Louis-Dreyfuss. Directed by John Buechler. 86 min.

The special-effects designer of the Gremlins rip-off Ghoulies somehow gets to direct his own movie, featuring all of the same badly constructed gnomes as the earlier film. This time the beasties are trying to take over an apartment building currently occupied by an assortment of oddballs and a little girl whose family has just moved in. It's up to her brother and to June Lockhart, as the witch who lives upstairs, to stop them. This is meant to be funny, though it never is (unless you find the idea of Sonny Bono playing a would-be swinger with lines that would embarrass most sitcoms funny). All of the actors are bad, even those who should know better (Michael Moriarty, for one); Jenny Beck, who plays the little girl, is especially irritating. John Buechler has an annoying habit of trying to cover up the deficiencies of his troll effects by covering them with slime and various other bodily secretions. You never once believe in them, but you wouldn't want to touch them, or this movie, either.

THE TROLLENBERG TERROR

See *The Crawling Eye*

TRON ☆☆☆
1982, USA, PG
Jeff Bridges, Bruce Boxleitner, David Warner, Cindy Morgan. Directed by Steve Lisberger. 96 min.

The only film that takes place primarily inside a computer, it is noteworthy for its spectacular introduction of the revolutionary special-effects technique of computer animation to the screen; otherwise, *Tron* is a *Star Wars* retread. Video-game whiz Jeff Bridges is zapped into a bizarre electronic world by an evil program. There Bridges teams up with his digitized counterparts to defeat the omnipotent MCP (Master Computer Program). Enjoyable comic-book entertainment.

TROUBLE IN MIND ☆☆☆½
1986, USA, R
Kris Kristofferson, Geneviève Bujold, Lori Singer, Keith Carradine, Divine, Joe Morton, George Kirby, Albert Hall, John Considine. Directed by Alan Rudolph. 111 min.

A disillusioned former policeman, just out of prison for killing a mafia kingpin; a tough but tender woman, whose diner is the hangout for all the misfits of Rain City; a sweet couple from the backwoods, torn apart as the man drifts into a psychedelic world of violence and corruption; an effete criminal overlord, the vortex of all crime and depravity—Alan Rudolph (*Choose Me, Welcome to L.A.*) whips these *film noir* elements into a cool, beautifully photographed movie. The film is neither parody nor homage; it is a weird sort of hybrid, ironic, self-conscious, and yet essentially serious about itself. Some viewers may find it a little vague and slow, but others will be seduced by its self-deprecating sensuality. It features several songs performed by Marianne Faithfull, and rain *all* the time.

TROUBLE IN THE GLEN ☆☆
1954, Great Britain
Margaret Lockwood, Orson Welles, Forrest Tucker, Victor McLaglen, John McCallum, Eddie Byrne, Grizelda Harvey. Directed by Herbert Wilcox. 91 min.

A promising idea for a comedy goes awry, owing to a preponderance of Technicolor scenery, a dearth of sentimentality, and a lack of jokes or humorous scenes. After years in South America, Orson Welles returns to his Scottish Highlands homeland to assume his inherited title. He gets in trouble with the locals, though, when he closes up a road running through his property. American ex–Air Force officer Forrest Tucker tries to mediate, and to ingratiate himself with the laird's daughter as well. Welles gives an engaging performance, and his fans will be the most likely audience for this whimsical piffle.

THE TROUBLE WITH ANGELS ☆☆½
1966, USA
Rosalind Russell, Hayley Mills, June Harding, Binnie Barnes, Mary Wickes, Gypsy Rose Lee, Camilla Sparv. Directed by Ida Lupino. 111 min.

This film belongs to the mid-1960s "nun cycle," where rebellious young girls eventually discover the true meaning of womanhood or sisterhood. These "angels" go through the routine comedy of planning and executing mischief, followed by discovery and punishment by Mother Superior (spiritually rendered by Rosalind Russell). The comedic repetition grows nagging and tiresome, but the supporting cast of misfit nuns—the band leader who wears earplugs, a wacky swimming teacher—introduce elements of vitality. Ultimately, the trouble with *The Trouble with Angels* is that it's a little too angelic and not devilish enough. Ida Lupino directed after a thirteen-year lapse from the chair.

THE TROUBLE WITH HARRY ☆☆☆½
1955, USA, PG
Edmund Gwenn, Shirley MacLaine, John Forsythe, Mildred Natwick, Mildred Dunnock, Jerry Mathers, Royal Dano, Parker Fennelly. Directed by Alfred Hitchcock. 96 min.

This rare foray into black comedy by the master of suspense contains enough trademark strokes to satisfy his fans, and the ahead-of-its-time morbidity of its humor only ripens with age. The goings-on revolve around a number of eccentrics in a New England town (beautifully photographed in color by Robert Burks); the trouble with one of them, Harry, is that he's dead. Consternation abounds when his corpse persistently refuses to stay buried. An uncertainty in tone doesn't detract too much from writer John Michael Hayes's wry jabs at Yankee Puritanism, or from MacLaine's sparkling film debut. Look for Jerry Mathers, even smaller here than he was as the Beaver, in a juvenile performance that's every bit as cute as it means to be.

TRUCK STOP WOMEN ☆☆
1974, USA, R
Claudia Jennings, Lieux Dressler, Paul Carr, John Martino, Jennifer Burton. Directed by Mark Lester. 87 min.

Low-down road raunch—violent, crammed with country music, and acted by some real American-beefy faces—this met with surprisingly critical enthusiasm at the time of its release, and it does have an energetic charm. Mobsters attempt to take over Anna's truck stop, and Anna's daughter Rose (*Playboy* playmate Claudia Jennings) crosses her own ma.

TRUE CONFESSIONS ☆☆☆½
1981, USA, R
Robert DeNiro, Robert Duvall, Charles Durning, Rose Gregorio, Ed Flanders, Burgess Meredith, Kenneth McMillan. Directed by Ulu Grosbard. 108 min.

This absorbing adaptation of John Gregory Dunne's 1940s-era mystery novel about two brothers, a rising monsignor (Robert DeNiro) and a hard-boiled detective (Robert Duvall) who became entangled in the grisly murder of a prostitute has been mounted with great care and skill. The film delves into Catholic loyalty, guilt, and the business of religion; what emerges is a beautifully acted film. Dunne and wife Joan Didion wrote the screenplay.

THE TRUE GAME OF DEATH ½☆
Hong Kong
Bruce Lee (sic), Hsao Lung, Ali Taylor, Kamson. Directed by Chen Tien Tai Steve. 90 min.

This is nothing but a shabby copy of *Game of Death*, and that's *not* the real Bruce Lee.

TRUE GRIT ☆☆☆
1969, USA
John Wayne, Glen Campbell, Kim Darby, Jeremy Slate, Robert Duvall, Dennis Hopper, Strother Martin, Jeff Corey, John Fiedler. Directed by Henry Hathaway. 128 min.

In which John Wayne parodied his screen image of the previous forty years and, to everyone's amazement, won an Academy Award over also-rans Dustin Hoffman, Jon Voight, Richard Burton, and Peter O'Toole. As Rooster Cogburn, a one-eyed, drunken U.S. marshall called on by teenager Kim Darby to track down the killer of her father, Wayne doesn't really act so much as participate in his own good-natured debunking. The classic scene has him charging at a variety of bad guys on horseback, a rifle in each hand, the reins in his teeth.

TRUE STORIES ☆☆
1986, USA, PG
David Byrne, John Goodman, Swoosie Kurtz, Spalding Gray, Annie McEnroe, Pops Staples. Directed by David Byrne. 98 min.

David Byrne, leader of the innovative band Talking Heads, made his debut behind the camera with this arch, rather snotty take on small-town sun-belt life. The normal is made strange, human foibles become enormous deviations, and daily life turns into performance art, all in a way that only a New Yorker who spends every spare moment knocking the Midwest could enjoy. In a series of anecdotes and vignettes, Byrne (our host and narrator) buddies up to the fictional residents of Virgil, Texas, including a woman who never gets out of bed, a man who advertises for a wife on local TV, and a married couple who haven't spoken in years. The stories are reportedly drawn from tabloids, and although Byrne bends over backward to show you he *likes* these corn-fed bizarros, his praise reeks of condescension—he seems to find them quaint, or amusingly inhuman. But the joke may be on Byrne—in his dark suits and buttoned-up shirts he's a stiff, almost creepy screen presence, weirder than anybody he puts on parade in this mean-spirited freak show. Gains a star for a terrific collection of songs by the band, used well throughout the film; but when the music stops, it's only sporadically funny and at times is hateful.

TRUMAN CAPOTE'S THE GLASS HOUSE

See *The Glass House*

TUCK EVERLASTING ☆½
1980, USA
Margaret Chamberlain, Paul Flessa, Fred A. Keller, Marvin Mcnow, Joey Giambra. Directed by Fred King Keller. 90 min.

This movie isn't really everlasting, it just seems that way. Adapted from Natalie Babbit's book about a young girl who encounters a family that has discovered the secret of eternal life, this low-budget feature just drags on and on. The director, Fred Keller (Jr.—that's his father in the cast), shot this around the western New York area for an astoundingly low budget, and for the most part it's technically competent, but completely uninspired. Kids won't be interested, and adults will be asleep halfway through.

TUFF TURF ☆☆☆
1985, USA, R
James Spader, Kim Richards, Paul Mones, Robert Downey. Directed by Fritz Kiersch. 112 min.

Rebel without a Cause meets MTV in this flashy, powerful, and provocative New World number about an outcast youth who gets on the bad side of some punks, and complicates matters for himself by falling in love with the gang leader's girlfriend. Director Fritz Kiersch takes a giant step beyond his previous effort *Children of the Corn* here, pounding out the story in a frenetic visual style to match the pulsating soundtrack. The young actors keep a mean tempo with the colorful imagery, particularly James Spader, who adequately steps into James Dean's shoes. Although there are some needless exploitative bits, *Tuff Turf* is a superior and immediate youth film that isn't afraid to be offbeat. Cameo appearance by the Jim Carroll Band.

TULSA ☆☆½
1949, USA
Susan Hayward, Robert Preston, Pedro Armendariz, Chill Wills, Ed Begley, Lloyd Gough, Lola Albright. Directed by Stuart Heisler. 88 min.

The only notable thing about this oil-drilling melodrama is that Susan Hayward has a lower voice than all the men in the cast. Sue plays a rancher's daughter who becomes a wealthy, ambitious wildcatter in order to avenge the death of her father. Robert Preston plays the oil engineer who favors conservationism and tames the fiery lady beneath the gushing geysers. Preston was never much as a leading man, but, until the top-out finale, Susan displays her husky pyrotechnics and a lot of red hair (this was one of her earliest Technicolor features). Chill Wills adds welcome comic relief and sings the title song.

TUMBLEWEEDS ☆☆½
1925, USA
William S. Hart, Barbara Bedford, Lucien Littlefield, J. Gordon Russell, Richard R. Neill, Jack Murphy, Lillian Leighton. Directed by King Baggot. 76 min.

William S. Hart was the Roy Rogers of his era, with the difference that he tried to insist that the films he appeared in be as historically authentic as possible. *Tumbleweeds* tells the story of a homesteading boom in the "Cherokee Strip" between Kansas and Oklahoma, where the demand for free land was so great that the government had to organize a virtual race, with the cavalry called in to hold a ragtag assortment of wagons and buggies at the starting line. Most of the film is devoted to the vicissitudes of this race, though there is an uncomplicated romantic side-plot between Hart and Barbara Bedford. Unlike most Westerns, this has very little violence—the villains are unsportsmanlike but not wicked—with only one death in the entire film. Wholesome entertainment of the Tom Mix variety.

TUNNELVISION ☆☆
1975, USA, R
Laraine Newman, Chevy Chase, Howard Hesseman, Betty Thomas, Phil Proctor, Al Franken, Tom Davis. Directed by Brad Swirnoff, Neal Israel. 76 min.

This 1975 parody of television in 1985 lives or dies on the strength of the individual comic sketches. Most keel over, but a few are stand-up satire. "Ramon and Sonja," an obscene *All in the Family*, with a screeching Laraine Newman and a laugh track that explodes over every racial epithet, is well worth the price of the rental.

TURKEY SHOOT

See *Escape 2000*

TURK 182!
★★
1985, USA, PG-13
Timothy Hutton, Robert Culp, Darren McGavin, Kim Cattrall, Robert Urich. Directed by Bob Clark. 96 min.

In a lackluster, improbable tale of teen rebellion and famemaking; Timothy Hutton plays a borough kid who goes to bat against a city administration that refuses to acknowledge his brother's injury. The film has its heart in the right, warm spot, but embarrassed performances by Hutton, Kim Cattrall, and Robert Urich, and television-broad playing by Darren McGavin and Robert Culp sabotage the effort.

THE TURNING POINT
★★★
1977, USA, PG
Anne Bancroft, Shirley MacLaine, Mikhail Baryshnikov, Tom Skerritt, Leslie Browne, Anthony Zerbe. Directed by Herbert Ross. 119 min.

Lavishly praised when it made its debut, this story of youth and aging in the ballet world trips up a bit in retrospect, but it nevertheless remains a delicious spectacle and a caustic artists' crisis drama. Anne Bancroft movingly plays a dancer at the end of her career, while Shirley MacLaine is her old friend who hung up her points for a home life long ago and whose daughter (the ballerina Leslie Browne) shows a star's luminosity. Mikhail Baryshnikov, in his screen debut, provides a sufficiently quirky love interest, and Tom Skerritt and Anthony Zerbe are finely tuned in smaller roles. The technical work is of the highest precision (especially Robert Surtees's sure camera handling), but ultimately it strikes one as being less a ballet film than a mere palette of beautifully disguised sentimentality.

TURTLE DIARY
★★★
1985, Great Britain, PG
Glenda Jackson, Ben Kingsley, Richard Johnson, Rosemary Leach, Jeroen Krabbe, Eleanor Bron. Directed by John Irvin. 97 min.

Harold Pinter wrote the screenplay for this (based on a novel by Russell Hoban), which should tip you off that this is a film just reeking of subtlety. Ben Kingsley, a reclusive bookshop clerk, and Glenda Jackson, an equally solitary writer of children's books, meet at the zoo in front of the turtles' aquarium, and decide to steal the confined creatures and release them into the sea, where they belong. Along the way, of course, they begin to peek their heads out of their own shells. It's not nearly as maudlin as it sounds, and the prime attraction is in hearing what the two stars do with Pinter's careful language and odd details.

TUXEDO WARRIOR
★½
1985, USA
John Wyman, Carol Royle, Holly Palance, James Coburn, Jr. Directed by Andrew Sinclair. 90 min.

No, it's not Cary Grant fighting the gasoline shortage in post-Apocalypse Australia. Set in Zimbabwe, a hotbed of skullduggery, we have Cliff, owner of the Omega Bar, a sort of poverty row Rick's Place straddling the fence on matters of law and order. Whether he will join forces with his ex-girlfriend or run afoul of diamond thieves is less interesting than contemplating whether Holly Palance and James Coburn, Jr., will bring further shame on their famous fathers by persisting in their acting careers.

TWELVE ANGRY MEN
★★★½
1957, USA
Henry Fonda, Lee J. Cobb, Ed Begley, E. G. Marshall, Jack Klugman, Martin Balsam, Jack Warden, John Fiedler, Robert Webber. Directed by Sidney Lumet. 95 min.

This powerful, taut drama (adapted by author Reginald Rose from his acclaimed live television drama) concerns a lone juror (Henry Fonda) who opposes the eleven other men on the jury with his belief that they must not convict a young man on trial. This was Sidney Lumet's first film, and it's characterized by the fine performances and sense of relentless conflict that mark his best work. Winner of well-deserved Oscar nominations for Best Picture, Director, and Screenplay.

THE 12 CHAIRS
★★½
1970, USA, PG
Frank Langella, Ron Moody, Dom DeLuise, Diana Coupland, Mel Brooks. Directed by Mel Brooks. 93 min.

Mel Brooks wrote and directed this flagging, uneven remake of Fred Allen's *It's in the Bag*. It's now set in 1927 Russia, where Frank Langella plays a count who pursues twelve dining room chairs, one of which contains rare jewels. Brooks also has a small part, but otherwise this cast is not up to the stock company ensemble for which he would later be famous. Here he is working with handsome but unfunny Langella and unhandsome and unfunny Dom DeLuise. The premise is still amusing, but the second half of the film relies heavily on slapstick in lieu of funny lines or situations.

TWELVE MONTHS
★★½
1980, Japan
Animated. Directed by Yasuhiro Yamaguchi. 90 min.

Serious animation fans may want to have a look at this lovely Japanese fairy tale; parents who are trying to keep their younger kids away from the likes of *Transformers* and *He-Man* and *Masters of the Universe* can do likewise. The story is a distillation of plots from Western fairy tales. A young girl, living in the house of a wicked woman and her daughter and forced by them to do all the housework, is sent to perform an impossible task in hopes of currying favor for the others from a spoiled princess. The spirits of the woods have pity on her, however, and grant her a miracle that sends everyone else out into the woods looking for their own reward. Of course, everyone gets what they deserve in the end.

TWELVE O'CLOCK HIGH
★★★
1949, USA
Gregory Peck, Dean Jagger, Gary Merrill, Hugh Marlowe, Paul Stewart, Millard Mitchell. Directed by Henry King. 132 min.

A grim, impassioned war film, this eschews gung-ho militarism and spectacular battles in favor of a detailed psychological examination of the members of an Air Force regiment that specializes in dawn attacks. Although all of the soldiers are dedicated, some bristle under the brutal, unyielding command of the appropriately named General Savage (Gregory Peck, in a great performance), whose rigidity is intended only to make better men out of them. *Twelve O'Clock High* was unusually sensitive work from veteran director Henry King, and Dean Jagger's fine, sad performance as the soldier whose memories frame the story won an Academy Award.

TWENTY MILLION MILES TO EARTH
★★★
1957, USA
William Hopper, Joan Taylor, Frank Puglia, Thomas B. Henry. Directed by Nathan Juran. 82 min.

This is top-flight science fiction about a monster from Venus who tries to do to Italy what Godzilla has been doing to Tokyo all these years. The creature grows in size and the thrills escalate before the scientists and the military can join forces to flatten the beast like a pizza. A thrilling climactic showdown at the Coliseum, with astonishing work by special-effects master Ray Harryhausen.

20,000 LEAGUES UNDER THE SEA
★★★★
1954, USA
Kirk Douglas, James Mason, Paul Lukas, Peter Lorre, Robert J. Wilke, Carleton Young, Ted de Corsia, Percy Helton. Directed by Richard Fleischer. 127 min.

Disney brought his animated magic to life in his adaptation of the Jules Verne story of a man and his sub. Because it was Disney's most ambitious live-action film, he carefully selected the best live crew in Hollywood, ironically employing rival Max Fleischer's son Richard to direct. Disney embellished his simple story with amazing visuals and outstanding dramatic tension. James Mason brilliantly waves between madness and civility in his portrayal of a despondent scientist/sea captain who pilots his supersubmarine against a backward world filled with people who fail to appreciate his accomplishments. Disney paid particular attention to detail in reconstructing the submarine according to Verne's description: it resembles a 200-foot-long undersea monster with headlights that look like eyes in dark waters. For the interior, art director John Meehan decked out the lounge with velvet chairs, rococo ornaments, and a pipe organ, and consequently won an Oscar for it. On all accounts, this Disney's a winner for the whole family.

TWICE IN A LIFETIME ☆☆½
1985, USA, R
Gene Hackman, Ellen Burstyn, Ann-Margret, Amy Madigan, Ally Sheedy, Brian Dennehy, Stephen Lang, Darrell Larson. Directed by Bud Yorkin. 117 min.

A thirty-year marriage is cast asunder by the husband's abrupt departure for another woman, in a well-acted but dreadfully overearnest family drama that owes more to a dozen TV "problem" movies than to the *Ordinary People–Kramer vs. Kramer* prestige films to whose class it aspires. The early scenes have a surprisingly gritty working-class texture, and Gene Hackman's portrayal of a man who's sick of his dull marriage and ashamed of his own boredom is strong, subtle, and wholly convincing. But the film's generosity to all of its characters is so maddeningly fair-minded that any chance for honest conflict is smothered in good feeling. Ellen Burstyn does a decent job as the bereft wife, despite a few great-lady mannerisms, and Oscar-nominated Amy Madigan is dazzlingly good as the one family member who refuses to forgive and forget.

TWILIGHT IN THE SIERRAS ☆
1950, USA
Roy Rogers, Dale Evans, Estelita Rodriguez, Trigger, Riders of the Purple Sage. Directed by William Witney. 67 min.

A low-grade vehicle for Roy Rogers, one of the dozens churned out by Republic in the 1940s and '50s, has him battling a coven of counterfeiters. This one is cornier than usual, especially with Dale and the Riders of the Purple Sage popping in to sing at the oddest times. Shot in eye-aching Trucolor.

TWILIGHT'S LAST GLEAMING ☆☆
1977, USA/West Germany, R
Burt Lancaster, Richard Widmark, Charles Durning, Melvyn Douglas, Paul Winfield, Burt Young, Joseph Cotten, Roscoe Lee Brown, Gerald S. O'Loughlin, Richard Jaeckel, William Marshall, Leif Erickson. Directed by Robert Aldrich. 146 min.

A leftist general (Burt Lancaster) and his escaped-convict sidekick (Paul Winfield) take over a missile silo and threaten to touch off World War III if the bumbling president of the United States doesn't go to the American people with the truth. Robert Aldrich's glossy thriller is a quirky, occasionally interesting cartoon. If this cartoon were sleazier, it might be a cultish B movie, but instead it's lavish, frequently incompetent, and fraught with pretensions. Still, the comedy (intentional or not) of Oval Office decision making has its moments.

TWILIGHT ZONE—THE MOVIE ☆☆½
1983, USA, PG
Dan Aykroyd, Albert Brooks, Vic Morrow, Scatman Crothers, Bill Quinn, Martin Garner, Kathleen Quinlan, Jeremy Licht, Kevin McCarthy, John Lithgow, Abbe Lane, Donna Dixon, William Schallert, Patricia Barry. Directed by John Landis—Introduction and Segment 1; Steven Spielberg—Segment 2; Joe Dante—Segment 3; George Miller—Segment 4. 102 min.

This big-budget anthology film constantly evokes the classic TV series, but only once improves upon our fond memories of it. The episodes, each one by a different filmmaker, are cannily arranged from worst to best, beginning with John Landis's clunky morality play about a bigot (Vic Morrow, who was killed while filming a stunt sequence) who receives his comeuppance, and ending with George Miller's virtuoso remake of "Nightmare at 20,000 Feet," with John Lithgow as a hysterical airline passenger who thinks he sees a gremlin on the wing of the plane. Joe Dante works up some deranged visual energy in his cartoonish nightmare "It's a Good Life," but Steven Spielberg's "Kick the Can" is the filmmaker at his most cloying. Enjoyable overall, if you're not a diehard Rod Serling loyalist.

TWINKLE TWINKLE KILLER KANE
See *The Ninth Configuration*

TWINS OF EVIL ☆
1971, Great Britain, R
Mary Collinson, Madeleine Collinson, Peter Cushing, Dennis Price. Directed by John Hough. 82 min.

Twins of Evil has to be credited with the apotheosis of thought at Hammer Studios. If their films always have a bosomy no-talent in the lead, why not make a movie about twins and double the fun? These two girls have little talent, but they do have a lot of animation—which is more than can be said for talented veterans Peter Cushing and Dennis Price. In terms of shock, *Twins of Evil* is average Hammer—sluggish pacing with one or two chases, a soupçon of sex, and, this being 1971, Hammer's monthly foray into some discreet lesbianism.

TWINS OF KUNG FU ☆☆½
Hong Kong
Han Kwok-Choi, Jacky Lui, Chu Chi Ling, Jason Pai Piao, Michelle Mei. Directed by Lam Hung, Pasan.

A son and daughter of a kung fu teacher must find out why the village water has been poisoned and the countryside filled with corpses. Kung fu feature works as comedy, suspense and drama. Excellent fight scenes put this way above the average. (a.k.a.: *Passage of the Dragon*)

THE TWIST ☆☆
1976, France
Bruce Dern, Stéphane Audran, Ann-Margret, Sydne Rome, Jean-Pierre Cassel, Curt Jurgens, Maria Schell, Charles Aznavour. Directed by Claude Chabrol. 106 min.

Claude Chabrol's manic fascination with the follies of the upper-middle class continues in this lesser work, which received little attention on its release. Bruce Dern plays an American writer married to a Frenchwoman (Stéphane Audran), each of whom suspects the other of adultery (while wishing for as much themselves) with the big names in the rest of the international cast. The director is unable to maintain an engaging tension between the sexual comedy and social melodrama. (a.k.a.: *Folies Bourgeoises*)

TWIST AND SHOUT ☆☆☆
1984, Denmark
Adam Tonsberg, Lars Simonsen, Camilla Soeberg, Ulrikke Juul Bondo, Thomas Nielsen, Bent Mejding. Directed by Bille August. 100 min.

A sensitive, intelligent coming-of-age drama set in 1963 Denmark, which looks a lot like 1963 America—teenaged girls screaming over the Fab Four, and teenaged boys slavishly imitating them with ragged garage bands, moptops, and jackets with little velvet collars. Director Bille August keeps the tone gentle and the scale small, but his look at the experiences that push adolescents into adulthood doesn't compromise. One of his two schoolboy protagonists, Bjorn (Adam Tonsberg), enters a bittersweet first love affair with an unusual number of attendant complications; the other, Erik (Lars Simonsen), must deal with his mentally ill mother and a hypocritical martinet of a father who'd rather ignore them both. Treads familiar ground, but it's exceptionally well acted and directed. It is a sequel to August's *Zappa* (1983), although no knowledge of the first film is necessary to enjoy this one.

THE TWITCH OF THE DEATH NERVE

See *Bay of Blood*

TWO ENGLISH GIRLS ★★★½
1971, France
Jean-Pierre Leaud, Kika Markham, Stacey Tendeter, Philippe Léotard, Sylvia Marriott, Marie Mansart. Directed by François Truffaut. 130 min.

François Truffaut's melancholy, exquisitely mounted period love story is very much a companion piece to his earlier *Jules and Jim*; both films were based on novels by Henri-Pierre Roche, and this one recasts the first film's pre–World War I love triangle with two headstrong British sisters, both of whom love the same Frenchman (Jean-Pierre Leaud). Though it lacks the incandescence of *Jules and Jim*, it's a beautifully controlled study of romantic longing and repressed desire, and Nestor Almendros's impressionistic cinematography makes it perhaps the most visually beautiful of all Truffaut films. Stacey Tendeter is a little strident as the more willful of the sisters, but Kika Markham and Leaud are superb, and the direction is consistently sensitive and thoughtful. *Note: Two English Girls* was originally released at 108 minutes; the video version includes 22 minutes of footage restored by Truffaut shortly before his death.

TWO FISTS VS. SEVEN SAMURAI

See *Fist of Vengeance*

TWO FOR THE ROAD ★★★★
1967, USA/Great Britain
Audrey Hepburn, Albert Finney, William Daniels, Eleanor Bron. Directed by Stanley Donen. 112 min.

A couple traverses Europe, first as lovers, then as newlyweds, then as young parents, and finally as bored, disillusioned spouses, in a touching, witty comedy-drama. The film crosscuts between the many trips, and the jigsaw-puzzle style of Frederic Raphael's screenplay makes *Two for the Road* a refreshingly clever and unsentimental study of the journey from young love into middle-aged ennui. Audrey Hepburn, by turns buoyant and bitchy, gives one of her sharpest, least affected performances, and Albert Finney is very good as her too-often callous husband.

TWO GRAVES OF KUNG FU ★
1982, Hong Kong
Liu Chia-Yung Chen Hung-Lieh, Shek Kien, Lee Wing. Directed by Lau Ka Wing. 95 min.

Liu Chia-Yung is framed for a murder, breaks out of jail, and tracks down the real killer. The martial arts choreography represents an early cinematic form, a transitional step between the karate-style fights and kung fu proper.

200 MOTELS ★★
1971, Britain, R
Frank Zappa and the Mothers of Invention, Flo and Eddie, Ringo Starr, Theodore Bikel, Janet Ferguson, Keith Moon. Directed by Frank Zappa and Tony Palmer. 98 min.

Even die-hard fans of Frank Zappa will find this hard going, although it does have its moments. Essentially plotless, it is supposed to be a series of bits about rock stars on the road in Middle America. Who drummer Keith Moon has a funny bit as a nun, and rock satirists Flo and Eddie have a few good moments, but for the most part you'll have finger firmly fastened to the fast-forward button. Neither as funny nor as amusing as any given Zappa album.

TWO IN THE BUSH

See *Safari 3000*

TWO MULES FOR SISTER SARA ★★½
1970, USA, PG
Clint Eastwood, Shirley MacLaine, Manolo Fabregas, Alberto Morin, Armando Silvestre. Directed by Don Siegel. 105 min.

This amiable Western comedy gets a lot of mileage out of its odd-couple casting. Perky Shirley MacLaine and stoic (to put it politely) Clint Eastwood play a spunky nun and the drifter (he seems to have wandered in from a Sergio Leone picture) protecting her as they travel across the mesa. Since the director is Don Siegel (*Dirty Harry*), Eastwood's granite-faced heroics come across rather more easefully than MacLaine's chipper chatter.

TWO OF A KIND ½★
1983, USA, PG
John Travolta, Olivia Newton-John, Beatrice Straight, Charles Durning, Oliver Reed. Directed by John Herzfeld. 87 min.

Remember the scene in *A Clockwork Orange* where Malcolm McDowell's eyelids were held open with little metal clips, and he was forced to watch a movie as aversion therapy, and he threw up afterward, feeling really bad for a long time? You got it—*Two of a Kind*. This comedy about angels who help two losers save Earth from destruction thoroughly merits the label "Worst of the Eighties," but there are some poor souls out there who actually seek out bad films for their entertainment value. They should be warned that there's no mirth to be found here, planned or otherwise. One critic called it the only movie that could make *Xanadu* and *Staying Alive* look good. If that doesn't discourage you, then you deserve to see it. But bring your eyelid clips.

2000 MANIACS ★★
1964, USA
Connie Mason, Thomas Wood, Jeffrey Allen, Ben Moore. Directed by Herschell Gordon Lewis. 80 min.

This is the infamous "Bloody Brigadoon" that thrilled a generation of drive-in gore junkies. Stupid Yankee tourists are lured off the main road into the sleepy little southern town of Pleasant Valley, where a jolly centennial celebration is going on. The centennial is, however, the anniversary of the slaughter of the town's population by Northern soldiers during the Civil War, and the celebration involves bloody repayment in kind. "Yeeeeeeeehaw! The South is gonna rise again!" Gross-out exploitation from pioneering splatter moviemaker Lewis, whose *Blood Feast* broke some serious ground for today's exploitation filmmakers.

2001: A SPACE ODYSSEY ★★★★
1968, USA/Great Britain
Keir Dullea, William Sylvester, Gary Lockwood, Daniel Richter, Douglas Rain, Leonard Rossiter, Margaret Tyzack. Directed by Stanley Kubrick. 160 min.

This futuristic space opera, based on "The Sentinel" by Arthur C. Clarke, follows the nine-month search in outer space for a mysterious monolith by two astronauts and a computer named HAL with a voice and mind of its own. Though ambiguous in meaning, the film has been called everything from an apocalyptic condemnation of our modern machine age to a visual approximation of an acid "trip" to a boring series of matte shots. The storytelling is slow and the techmatic concerns repetitiously stated; but in style and substance, it is light-years ahead of most of the space sagas of the 1980s (including the sequel, *2010—The Year We Make Contact*). Although much of what was originally presented in Super Panavision and Cinerama will be lost on video, this is one of those films that ought to be seen even in a diminished format.

2010—THE YEAR WE MAKE CONTACT ☆½
1984, USA, PG
Roy Scheider, Keir Dullea, John Lithgow, Bob Balaban, Helen Mirren. Directed by Peter Hyams. 116 min.

The relentlessly reductive sequel to Stanley Kubrick's *2001*, in which a joint U.S./Soviet crew is sent to Jupiter to try to learn the real fate of the Discovery mission and unlock the secrets of the black ship, packs a bland plea for world peace into a tired plot. Blame for its dullness must rest squarely on the shoulders of director Peter Hyams (*Outland*), who also produced, wrote the screenplay, and did the cinematography. *2001*'s grandiose mysteries are reduced to banality and the narrative is *still* shrouded in obscurity. Keir Dullea, the sole returnee from the 1968 film, is almost unrecognizable.

TWO TICKETS TO BROADWAY ☆☆½
1951, USA
Tony Martin, Janet Leigh, Ann Miller, Gloria deHaven, Eddie Bracken, Barbara Lawrence, Bob Crosby, Smith and Dale. Directed by James V. Kern. 106 min.

Who says that vaudeville is dead? It's alive and kicking in this Howard Hughes–produced mishmash, which features everything from Tony Martin singing the prologue from *Pagliacci* in full regalia atop a titanic forty-five disc, to Bob Crosby ribbing a dummy replica of his brother Bing, to a series of sketches involving two Jewish deli owners (Joe Smith and Charles Dale). Otherwise, the story of five Broadway hopefuls trying to break into television creeps in between the different acts, the best of which is Ann Miller's "Worry Bird" number. Television's James V. Kern directed as if this were another "I Love Lucy" episode and Busby Berkeley did the numbers without leaving his signature. Still, it's a jaunty, unpretentious musical comedy.

TWO WOMEN IN GOLD ☆
1970, Canada
Louise Turcot, Monique Mercure, Donald Pilon, Marcel Sabourin. Directed by Claude Fournier. 90 min.

This is a silly sex farce about two housewives so bored with their husbands that they'll sleep with anybody—including traveling salesmen, as payment for their wares. When one of the unsuspecting Canucks drops dead in the heat of the moment, the complications begin. Lots of sex and not much comedy in his French-Canadian quickie, which ran seventeen minutes longer in its original release.

TWO WONDEROUS TIGERS ☆☆
Hong Kong
Johnny Chang, Yang Pan Pan, Philip Ko, Tiger Young, Charlie Chan, Mung Kwun Ha, Wilson Tong. Directed by Cheung Sum.

Young master Ma wants to marry Yuen Ah-Mai and tries to kidnap her. Tiger (Johnny Chang) and his friend Robert come to her aid. Ma goes to the Yuen home and is informed that he must first defeat Ah-Mai, her older sister and their brother in kung fu. Ma is beaten and decides to post a reward of $1,000 to anyone who can defeat the Yuens. Tiger and Robert defeat the three, and Ah-Mai chooses Tiger to marry. Now Tiger must try to collect his money. Johnny Chang is as adorable as ever, and his martial arts are first-rate. The choreography and pacing are of the highest quality.

THE TWO WORLDS OF JENNIE LOGAN ☆☆☆
1979, USA (TV)
Lindsay Wagner, Marc Singer, Allen Feinstein, Henry Wilcoxon, Linda Gray. Directed by Frank DeFelitta. 100 min.

In this clever time-travel fantasy, the two worlds of this title take place in two different centuries. When Jennie tries on an antique dress from the nineteenth century, she travels back in time and experiences a doomed love affair. Television often bungles these supernatural love stories that combine suspense and romance, but this is an exception—a wistful love triangle between a beautiful woman, the husband she treasures, and a long-ago Lothario. Quite watchable; possibly Lindsay's best TV vehicle.

U

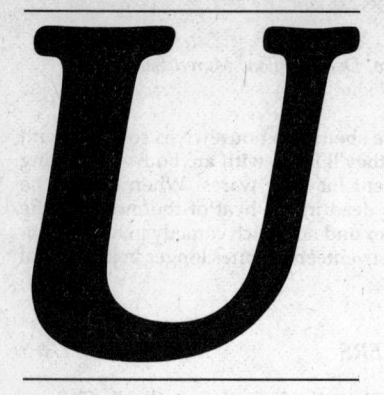

UFOria ☆☆☆
1980, USA, PG
Harry Dean Stanton, Cindy Williams, Fred Ward, Harry Carey, Jr., Beverly Hope Atkinson. Directed by John Binder. 100 min.

This winsome bit of eccentricity is like a C&W *Repo Man*—a tale of misfits, dropouts, con men, and aliens in the desert of the Southwest. Visually, it's flat and utilitarian, but some of its acting is choice—especially the scenes featuring Fred Ward as Sheldon, a drifter and good ol' boy who believes every self-dramatizing romantic-outlaw song Waylon Jennings ever wrote. He meets Arlene (Cindy Williams), a desert-town supermarket checkout girl who thinks she's destined to make contact with visiting aliens. Also in town is Sheldon's old buddy (Harry Dean Stanton), a traveling preacher. The plot hinges on extraterrestrials, but don't go expecting expensive light shows; the fun is in seeing down-home characters who are infatuated with their own fantasies.

UGETSU ☆☆☆☆
1953, Japan
Machiko Kyo, Masayuki Mori, Minuyo Tanaka, Sakae Ozawa. Directed by Kenji Mizoguchi. 96 min.

Set in war-torn sixteenth-century Japan, *Ugetsu* is generally considered to be Kenji Mizoguchi's greatest achievement. A haunting, dreamlike tale of the supernatural, the plot concerns two peasant families who leave their homes in search of fortune. An exquisite study of the illusiveness of human ambitions and relationships. Unforgettable scenes include the rape and murder of one of the peasant wives and the haunting of the woman's husband by her spirit. Mizoguchi's sensitive and progressive treatment of the female characters has given the film appeal to modern audiences. A classic, however, in any age. Full title *Ugetsu Monogatari*.

THE ULTIMATE SOLUTION OF GRACE QUIGLEY

See *Grace Quigley*

UMBERTO D ☆☆☆☆
1953, Italy
Carlo Battisti, Maria Pia Casilio, Lina Gennari. Directed by Vittorio De Sica. 89 min.

One of Vittorio De Sica's finest films, this story of a lonely old man struggling to retain his dignity in postwar Italy had perhaps more real influence than earlier, purer neorealistic films. Characterization is unusually strong, and the relationship between the man and his dog—thematic thin ice if anything is, almost impossible to handle without mawkishness—is deeply moving, thanks as much to Carlo Battisti's emotionally wrenching performance as to De Sica's astute direction.

THE UMBRELLAS OF CHERBOURG ☆☆½
1964, France
Catherine Deneuve, Nino Castelnuovo, Anne Vernon. Directed by Jacques Demy. 95 min.

The first French musical–soap opera, this concerns a young woman who is left pregnant when her boyfriend goes in the army. Though she sings the hit "I Will Wait for You," her mother makes her marry someone else while he's away. The plot is quite typical, but the fact that it is entirely sung is certainly not. The score is by Michel Legrand and also includes "Watch What Happens." Director Jacques Demy is not as creative with the visuals as he might have been, but the music is the main ticket here. Sung in the original French.

UNCOMMON VALOR ☆½
1983, USA, R
Gene Hackman, Robert Stack, Fred Ward, Patrick Swayze, Reb Brown, Randall "Tex" Cobb. Directed by Ted Kotcheff. 105 min.

A pulpy, flaccid action movie that replays the Vietnam War—and lets the Americans win. Gene Hackman is a retired Marine colonel whose son has been listed as MIA for ten years; he rounds up the son's service buddies and turns them into a crack fighting unit, and then the Sleazy Seven journey to Bangkok and shoot it out with the gooks. Director Ted Kotcheff wants to whip up a jingoistic fervor, but his soul isn't in the dirty work: the movie is flat and unconvincing, even when Kotcheff goes for the crudest Pavlovian response. Only plug-ugly Tex Cobb injects a little life with his sloppy good humor.

THE UNDEFEATED ☆☆½
1969, USA
John Wayne, Rock Hudson, Tony Aguilar, Roman Gabriel, Bruce Cabot. Directed by Andrew McLaglen. 119 min.

Thanks to John Wayne and Rock Hudson, this lethargic Civil War drama doesn't go down to total defeat. In this tale of the blue and the gray, Wayne, a former Union cavalryman, bumps into Hudson, a former champion of the Confederacy; and the erstwhile enemies team up in a new war against Juarez and his Mexican banditos (Hollywood must have decided to take a vacation from picking on the Indians). Star power transforms this elemental "best of enemies" story line into moderately gripping horse opera.

UNDER CALIFORNIA STARS ☆
1948, USA
Roy Rogers, Jane Frazee, Andy Devine, Trigger, the Sons of the Pioneers, Bullet. Directed by William Witney. 70 min.

The beginning of the worst of the many Republic Westerns with Roy Rogers now on videocassette, this one was made during a stretch when wife Dale Evans was out of the series, leaving only faithful steed Trigger to abet Roy—and in this film, he's horsenapped! Dull songs, but fans will enjoy Andy Devine's comic relief and the first appearance of Roy's dog Bullet.

UNDER CAPRICORN ☆½
1949, USA
Ingrid Bergman, Joseph Cotten, Michael Wilding, Cecil Parker, Margaret Leighton, Denis O'Dea, Jack Watling, Harcourt Williams. Directed by Alfred Hitchcock. 116 min.

This is a rarity: a Hitchcock film that's well nigh unwatchable. Photographed in a lulling Technicolor palette of yellows and browns, it's a stuffed-and-mounted period piece about an alcoholic (Ingrid Bergman) living under the thumb of her frosty husband (Joseph Cotten) in nineteenth-century Australia. Michael Wilding is the upright friend who comes to the rescue—but not before the audience has been anesthetized by the wooden dialogue and endless ballroom set pieces.

UNDER CAPRICORN ☆½
1982, Australia
Lisa Harrow, John Hallam, Peter Cousens, Julia Blake, Cathrine Lynch, Jim Holt. Directed by Rod Hardy. 110 min.

When this nineteenth-century Australian Gothic was first filmed in 1949, it was one of Alfred Hitchcock's few out-and-out failures; even the Master of Suspense couldn't get around the hamfisted expository passages and plodding plotting. Australian director Rod Hardy doesn't do much better, although the location shooting helps. A young man visiting a country mansion finds himself caught between the lord of the manor, his dipsomaniacal wife, and a malcontent housekeeper. The revelations that follow fail to startle, and you may wonder if any husband could be as stupid as the one depicted here. While we're grateful that second-rate filmmakers aren't tampering with Hitchcock's masterpieces, they might do well to let his flops alone too.

UNDER FIRE
1983, USA, R ☆☆☆
Nick Nolte, Joanna Cassidy, Gene Hackman, Ed Harris, Jean-Louis Trintignant. Directed by Roger Spottiswoode. 128 min.

In this timely better-than-average issue movie, journalists covering the war in Nicaragua become involved in the revolutionary cause; their subsequent loss of detachment raises serious ethical problems for them. Unlike *The Year of Living Dangerously*, released theatrically the same year, this film tries—if not altogether successfully—to negotiate the pitfall of becoming a steamy romance played out against a backdrop of revolution.

UNDERGROUND ACES
1980, USA, PG ☆
Dirk Benedict, Melanie Griffith, Robert Hegyes, Jerry Orbach, Frank Gorshin. Directed by Robert Butler. 93 min.

Let's put it this way: Dirk Benedict was better in "The A-Team," Robert Hegyes was funnier on "Welcome Back Kotter," and Frank Gorshin could never equal his brilliant portrayal of the Riddler in "Batman." What they do in this story about garage attendants who help a sheik get a girl won't be remembered as their career high points. If all of this isn't enough to convince . . . Melanie Griffith wears less in *Body Double*.

UNDER MEXICALI STARS
1950, USA ☆½
Rex Allen, Dorothy Patrick, Roy Bancroft, Buddy Ebsen. Directed by George Blair. 67 min.

Rex Allen was a sort of alternative Roy Rogers for a brief time in the 1950s, and his musical-Western B films for Republic are almost indistinguishable from Roy's. This one has him battling Mexican gold smugglers, and singing three songs. The plotting isn't half bad.

UNDER MILK WOOD
1971, Great Britain, PG ☆☆½
Richard Burton, Elizabeth Taylor, Peter O'Toole, Glynnis Johns, Vivien Merchant, Sian Phillips, Victor Spinetti. Directed by Andrew Sinclair. 90 min.

Despite the powerhouse cast and marvelous source material, this is a big disappointment. There are few actors more skilled than Richard Burton in reciting poetry, and his reading of Dylan Thomas's radio play about the mythical town of Llareggub gently caresses the lines with great feeling. Unfortunately, director Andrew Sinclair has accompanied Burton's narration with extremely literal visuals reminiscent of the Hammer horror films (not the least horrifying sight is Elizabeth Taylor as the perennially supine Rosie Probert), and the camera work (by Bob Huke) is a real hack job. What story there is concerns Peter O'Toole as a blind, aging sea captain searching for his lost love (Taylor in a cameo). Liz and Dick's fans should note that this is not one of their costarring features:

UNDER THE CHERRY MOON
1986, USA, PG-13 ☆
Prince, Emmannuelle Sallet, Kristin Scott Thomas, Jerome Benton, Alexandra Stewart, Steven Berkoff, Francesca Annis. Directed by Prince. 98 min.

After the surprise success of *Purple Rain*, Warner Bros. eagerly offered Prince this follow-up vehicle, a period comedy-romance set in the south of France. His Royal Badness promptly fired the director (Mary Lambert), replaced her with himself, and saw to it that he sang as little as possible. As gigolo Christopher Tracy, he pouts, preens, struts, purses his lips, and bats those mascara'd lashes more than anyone since Mae West. Jerome Benton, as his sidekick, alternately jives and shuffles as the most embarrassingly clichéd black factotum since the early talkies. And did we mention the misogyny? A laughable fiasco.

UNDER THE RAINBOW
1981, USA, PG ☆
Chevy Chase, Carrie Fisher, Eve Arden, Joseph Maher, Robert Donner, Billy Barty, Mako, Pat McCormick, Adam Arkin. Directed by Steve Rash. 97 min.

Chevy Chase's worst film—and we're not unmindful of *Modern Problems* and even *Oh Heavenly Dog*—was this tasteless, painfully unfunny midgetfest, a would-be period farce that imagines the exploits of the little people hired to play Munchkins in *The Wizard of Oz* back in 1938. Their real misdeeds, as chronicled by Aljean Harmetz in her book on the film, were a lot funnier and more scandalous than this sanitized stupidity can allow. Carrie Fisher is cute as the talent coordinator, but Chase is his usual smug self. Perhaps the reason this was made is that the star demanded a supporting cast that would look up to him, and the seventy-five or so "specialty performers" on hand here fit the bill.

UNDER THE ROOFTOPS OF PARIS
1929, France/Germany ☆☆☆
Albert Préjean, Pola Illery, Edmond Greville, Gaston Modot, Bill Bocket. Directed by René Clair. 80 min.

René Clair's first sound film is the enchanting story of a Parisian street singer whose lover takes up with his best friend. Notable for its intricate sound effects and for Lazare Meerson's evocative sets, which re-created the city of Paris on a soundstage. With English subtitles. (a.k.a.: *Under Paris Rooftops*, *Sous Les Toits de Paris*, *Under the Roofs of Paris*)

UNDER THE VOLCANO
1984, USA, R ☆☆☆½
Albert Finney, Jacqueline Bisset, Anthony Andrews, Directed by John Huston. 109 min.

John Huston directed this fiery adaptation of Malcolm Lowry's masterpiece about the final days in the life of Geoffrey Firmin—the self-destructive, alcoholic ex-British consul in Cuernavaca on the edge of World War II. Lowry's dense, jagged novel perhaps could not be fully realized on the screen. Huston used a straightforward, pitched-to-hell narrative descent that depends on Albert Finney's raging performance. Finney was nominated for the Academy Award, and gives a bravura performance, though occasionally tippling into the gutter.

UNDER WESTERN STARS
1938, USA ☆☆
Roy Rogers, Smiley Burnette, Carol Hughes. Directed by Joe Kane. 65 min.

Republic Studios made a daring move when it launched an unknown sideline player, Roy Rogers, in this relatively big-budget B Western. The gamble paid off as Roy Rogers, a handsome and authentic-looking wrangler, went on to become the most famous of the singing cowboys. Roy stands out here, and he is surrounded by a well-paced blend of action and musical numbers.

THE UNEARTHLY ☆½
1957, USA
Allison Hayes, John Carradine, Myron Healey, Sally Todd. Directed by Brooke L. Peters. 73 min.

Any movie with Allison Hayes (*Attack of the Fifty Foot Woman*) and the ubiquitous John Carradine can't be all bad, but this insipid chiller comes close. What dirty deeds does John have in mind? What happens to all those hapless souls who foolishly go into that forbidding laboratory? Strictly a late-night chiller-theater feature for insomniacs.

UNFAITHFULLY YOURS ☆☆☆½
1948, USA
Rex Harrison, Linda Darnell, Barbara Lawrence, Rudy Vallee, Lionel Stander, Kurt Krueger. Directed by Preston Sturges. 105 min.

A resounding flop in its day, *Unfaithfully Yours* has been reevaluated of late as one of Preston Sturges's best works. The film, though highly original, is really too problematical for that status. Rex Harrison is perfectly cast as a symphony conductor whose fits of jealousy compel him to imagine killing his possibly unfaithful wife in three different ways, set to three different pieces of music (by Rossini, Wagner, and Tchaikovsky). Sturges's seemingly sophisticated screenplay is built around a simplistic device of misunderstandings. Also, some of the execution is too black for any comedy (one of Harrison's murders is done with a razor in a scene as horrifying as the shower sequence in *Psycho*). Sturges tries to assuage our discomfort after these fantasies with such prolonged slapstick bits as Harrison trying (unsuccessfully) to hang himself. Also, many of the lines are just plain unfunny, and the opening buildup is interminable. It is better by default than the 1984 remake, but still an unsettling, even unpleasant comedy.

UNFAITHFULLY YOURS ☆☆½
1984, USA, PG
Dudley Moore, Nastassja Kinski, Armand Assante, Albert Brooks, Cassie Yates. Directed by Howard Zieff. 96 min.

A mildly entertaining remake of Preston Sturges's 1948 farce about an orchestra leader who suspects his wife of infidelity. When Dudley Moore's world-famous conductor unleashes a terribly clever plot to kill his wife, the comic makes the most of the slapstick routines. But Moore simply doesn't have the presence—the haughty, virulent grandeur that Rex Harrison had in the original—to lend credence to the conductor's violent passion. Nastassja Kinski, however, is a revelation; this is the first film in which she abandons her pouty hauteur for broad, bawdy European charm, and her expansive characterization manages to be as sexy as it is funny.

UNIDENTIFIED FLYING ODDBALL ☆☆½
1979, USA, G
Dennis Dugan, Jim Dale, Ron Moody, Kenneth More, Sheila White. Directed by Russ Mayberry. 93 min.

Disney's adept adaptation of Mark Twain's *A Connecticut Yankee in King Arthur's Court* derives its velocity from the same gas that sparked Twain's story: two eras crash together and become metaphors for one another. Dennis Dugan is mawkish and redeeming as the NASA wunderkind spun back in time to a dizzy sixth-century England—where he and a look-alike android dump technology on the pastures and cultivate a courtly stink. Strangely, the script is sometimes too subtle for kids, with the result that the dated special effects become a crutch instead of just decoration. Still, an enduring oddity.

UNION CITY ☆☆½
1980, USA, PG
Dennis Lipscomb, Deborah Harry, Irina Maleeva, Everett McGill, Taylor Mead, Pat Benetar. Directed by Mark Reichert. 87 min.

Fans of Blondie, the defunct New Wave band, who rent this for the ballyhooed dramatic debut of singer Debbie Harry will be disappointed; deglamorized as much as possible with a mousy brown wig and hausfrau mufti, she sinks into her surroundings rather than asserting any special talent. On the whole, though, this is an interesting, gloomy little film, beautifully shot by first-time cinematographer Ed Lachman (who trained with Wim Wenders, Sven Nyquist, and Werner Herzog). It's a grim, *noir*-ish tale about a man who becomes obsessed with trapping a vagrant who steals a drink of milk out of the bottle delivered to his door every morning. What begins as a petty complaint escalates into near madness and tragedy. Singer Pat Benetar also has a small role; music by Chris Stein.

AN UNMARRIED WOMAN ☆☆☆
1978, USA, R
Jill Clayburgh, Michael Murphy, Alan Bates, Cliff Gorman, Lisa Lucas, Penelope Russianoff. Directed by Paul Mazursky. 124 min.

A middle-aged woman whose stockbroker husband suddenly leaves her learns that there is life after divorce—especially if you live in a posh New York condo, acquire the services of a good therapist, and find a prototypical strong-but-sensitive lover who appreciates you for yourself. Paul Mazursky's uplifting drama is not the groundbreaking feminist triumph some critics called it; rather, it's a glossy, well-acted, and finally rather old-fashioned "woman's picture" with a patina of late-1970s "love thyself" consciousness-raising. On those terms, it's quite successful, and Jill Clayburgh hasn't topped the sensitive, emotionally rich work she does here, even if her final triumph seems more one of luck than spirit.

THE UNSEEN ☆½
1981, USA, R
Barbara Bach, Sidney Lassick, Stephen Furst, Lelia Goldoni, Karen Lamm, Doug Barr, Lois Young. Directed by Peter Foleg. 89 min.

Three newswomen covering a local festival find themselves forced to take lodging in a private home because all the hotels are booked solid. They soon regret having done so, for their genial host is not what he seems and something very nasty lives (but doesn't *stay*) in the cellar. It's yet another variation on a genre theme: pretty girls away from home are tormented by *something*—in this case a vicious Baby Huey of a retarded monster—horrible. Nice production values cannot redeem what is in the final accounting just one more by-the-numbers horror movie.

THE UNSINKABLE MOLLY BROWN ☆☆½
1964, USA
Debbie Reynolds, Harve Presnell, Ed Begley, Jack Kruschen, Hermione Baddeley. Directed by Charles Walters. 128 min.

This raucous musical can't be faulted for its energy level, but it pushes too hard for the homespun humor and high spirits that came naturally to the Broadway original. Somehow, Debbie Reynolds won an Academy Award nomination for Best Actress even though she seems to be portraying Ma Kettle having a musical comedy seizure. Good dancing and some pretty tunes, but Reynolds needed to be placed in physical restraints.

UNTIL SEPTEMBER ☆½
1984, USA, R
Karen Allen, Thierry Lhermitte, Christopher Cazenove, Marie-Christina Conti, Nitza Saul, Hutton Cobb. Directed by Richard Marquand. 95 min.

In this self-consciously ultraromantic trifle set in Paris, an American visitor finds love while on vacation in the City of Lights. Unfortunately, while it has the benefit of Karen Allen as the

American girl, it is also saddled with a script and direction that do not so much use and try to revivify the romantic clichés (in the manner of other such recent films as *Choose Me* and *One from the Heart*) as simply load them on. And Thierry Lhermitte, the French matinee idol who plays the love interest, comes across as a pompous, arrogant bully.

UP IN SMOKE
1978, USA, R ☆☆☆
Cheech and Chong (Richard Marin, Tommy Chong), Stacy Keach, Tom Skerritt, Strother Martin, Edie Adams, Zane Busby. Directed by Lou Adler. 117 min.

Cheech and Chong share the same anarchic qualities that brought the Marx Brothers and the Three Stooges new audiences in the 1960s and 1970s. You really have to be trying hard to hold an active dislike for them; work at it as you might, they are just too amicably dumb to hate. They weren't happy with the way their record producer, Lou Adler, directed this, their first film. They felt it was too structured, which may come as a shock to first-time viewers who find it to have a bare plot as an excuse for a lot of odd gags, many pulled from their stage shows. The drug humor, being almost entirely based on smoking dope, is not as offensive as might be expected; it's certainly no worse than the millions of drunk jokes that Hollywood has engaged in over the years. Highlight: C & C winning a punk rock contest with a song whose immortal lyric begins "My mamma talk-a to me, try to tell me how to live/ But I don't listen to her 'cause my head is like a sieve."

UP THE ACADEMY
1980, USA, R ☆½
Ron Leibman, Wendell Brown, Ralph Macchio, Tom Citera, Tom Poton, Antonio Fargas, Stacey Nelkin, Barbara Bach. Directed by Robert Downey. 87 min.

Mad magazine produced this movie, and if they had one ounce of the class-clown wit and suburban irreverence of the magazine itself, it would be irresistible to all of us who grew up devouring that rag. Instead, it's a chicken-hearted and weak-kneed attack on a very soft target—military academies—and the fun it does poke is leveled at such targets as Arabs, Jews, and homosexuals. It's not quite as bad as a lot of teen-oriented comedies, but with veteran Robert Downey (*Putney Swope, Greaser's Palace*) involved, it is plenty disappointing. Ralph Macchio as Chooch and Stacey Nelkin as delectable Candy don't embarrass themselves, but everyone else does. *Note:* Ron Leibman kept his name off the credits.

UP THE CREEK
1984, USA, R ☆☆
Tim Matheson, Stephen Furst, Jennifer Runyon, Dan Monahan, Sandy Helberg, John Hillerman, Jeff East, James B. Sikking. Directed by Robert Butler. 95 min.

Another slobs-versus-snobs teen-pic, this one more overtly derivative of *Animal House* (including using two of its stars) than most of its ilk. The four worst students at the country's worst college, Lepetomane U., are promised degrees if they can win an intercollegiate raft race. You've seen it all before, but if you like this kind of thing you won't mind seeing it again here. It's mildly ingratiating, has a few funny scenes and some good songs by Cheap Trick and Ian Hunter.

UP THE SANDBOX
1972, USA, R ☆☆☆½
Barbra Steisand, David Selby, Jane Hoffman. Directed by Irvin Kershner. 97 min.

Barbra Streisand is funny and touching as a "unfulfilled New York housewife," in one of the more underrated films of the 1970s. She spends her time fantasizing about everything from telling off her meddling mother to being with Fidel Castro. Her chauvinist husband, a college professor, is insensitive to her needs. Based on the novel by Anne Richardson Roiphe, occasionally written in the tone of a feminist tract. Should be of interest to anyone—not only Streisand fans—looking for an offbeat comedy-drama.

UPTOWN NEW YORK
1932, USA ☆☆
Jack Oakie, Shirley Grey, Leon Waycoff (Ames), George Cooper, Lee Moran, Raymond Hatton. Directed by Victor Schertzinger. 76 min.

This limp comedy-romance is notable now only as a Jack Oakie vehicle, and isn't even a particularly good example of that—though the comedian has star billing, he is essentially the comic relief here. Don't be fooled by the title, which would seem to promise a Harlem musical. It refers only to the location of the rooming house from which the heroine ponders which of her two lovers she should accept.

UPTOWN SATURDAY NIGHT
1974, USA, PG ☆☆½
Sidney Poitier, Bill Cosby, Harry Belafonte, Flip Wilson, Richard Pryor, Rosalind Cash, Roscoe Lee Browne, Lee Chamberlin, Calvin Lockhart. Directed by Sidney Poitier. 104 min.

Pleasant, often funny, low-comedy caper about two rubes (Sidney Poitier and Bill Cosby) whose search for a stolen lottery ticket takes them into a Harlem demimonde of pulpit-pounding preachers, kung fu experts, congressmen who dress up as Africans, and even a black Godfather (Harry Belafonte, doing Marlon Brando to a sizzling turn). Many of the performances in the all-black, all-star cast are such sharp, inspired riffs that it's a shame the film itself doesn't measure up. Blame must fall equally with Richard Wesley's wobbly script and Poitier's direction, generous with the actors but slackly paced and visually uninventive. Still, there's a lot of charm here, giving *Uptown* a slight edge over the companion piece that followed it, *Let's Do It Again*.

URBAN COWBOY
1980, USA, PG ☆☆☆
John Travolta, Debra Winger, Scott Glenn, Madolyn Smith, Barry Corbin, James Gammon. Directed by James Bridges. 135 min.

James Bridges's tough, spirited Texas romance between a refinery worker (John Travolta) and the fiery young woman (Debra Winger) he marries too soon can't quite decide whether it's Southern-fried *Saturday Night Fever* (a major location is Gilley's Bar) or a serious drama, but it succeeds on the strength of energetic direction and acting. This was meant as a vehicle for Travolta, and he does good, solid work, but the show is stolen by Winger—rawboned, smart, and sexy as his young lover—and by Scott Glenn as a mean, black-hatted cowboy always ready to challenge the hero. The story meanders all over the place near the end, but many of the opening scenes are well observed and detailed in the manner of the best recent screen romances, and the soundtrack is jammed with good country tunes.

URGH! A MUSIC WAR
1981, USA ☆☆☆
The Police, Wall of Voodoo, Toyah Wilcox, O.M.D., Oingo-Boingo, XTC, the Members, the Go-Go's, Klaus Nomi, Jools Holland, Steel Pulse, Devo, Echo and the Bunnymen, the Cramps, Joan Jett, Pere Ubu, Gary Numan, the Fleshtones, Gang of Four, X, Magazine, 999. Directed by Derek Burbridge. 124 min.

An assortment of New Wave bands from London, New York, and Los Angeles perform one song apiece, and if the result is something less than a great concert film, it's a veritable crash course in the punk legacy. Most of these groups play variations on the same stripped-down, bass-powered garage rock. Some of the performers (the Go-Go's, O.M.D., the Members) later went on to commercial fame with more pop-oriented material than the songs they perform here. There are riveting numbers from the Police, Oingo-Boingo, X, and Pere Ubu, as well as an unforgettable few minutes with the late

Klaus Nomi, a space-age cabaret singer whose operatic falsetto was a study in twisted passion.

USED CARS ★★★½
1980, USA, R
Kurt Russell, Jack Warden, Gerrit Graham, Frank McRae, Deborah Harmon, Joseph P. Flaherty, David L. Lander, Michael McKean, Michael Talbott, Marvey Northrup. Directed by Robert Zemeckis. 113 min.

This is a near-brilliant, neglected comedy about that great American institution, duplicitous salesmanship. Kurt Russell is a fast-talking used-car dealer caught in cutthroat competition with his local rival, the ruthless Roy Fuchs (Jack Warden). The characters go to shocking extremes to make a buck, and that's what gives this neo–Preston Sturges comedy its splendidly cynical bite. Russell offers a hilarious, motor-mouth performance as the dubious hero, and Robert Zemeckis, who later directed *Back to the Future*, sustains the furious pace with impressive control.

THE USERS ★★
1978, USA (TV)
Jaclyn Smith, Tony Curtis, Red Buttons, Alan Feinstein, Joan Fontaine, John Forsyth, George Hamilton, Darren McGavin, Carrie Nye, Michelle Phillips. Directed by Joseph Hardy. 110 min.

In a mild departure from her role on "Charlie's Angels," Jaclyn Smith plays an ex-hooker who works her way up the ladder in this mediocre adaptation of Joyce Haber's trash chronicle. An all-star cast, the kind with miles of perfect hair and row upon row of pearly teeth (yes, this is an Aaron Spelling production) backs up Smith playing very familiar movie-biz types—the down-and-out actor, the cold-blooded executive, etc. Amusing pre-"Dynasty" high-gloss fun, but too long, and crippled by network standards that kept out the sleaze at the heart of the enterprise.

UTAH ★½
1945, USA
Roy Rogers, Dale Evans, George "Gabby" Hayes, the Sons of the Pioneers. Directed by John English. 55 min.

Average B Western-musical from Republic, with Roy and Dale butting heads as a ranch foreman and an inexperienced heiress who wants to use her land to make money. Reliable laughs from Gabby Hayes, sweet songs, and only the most perfunctory bad guys in this light horse opera. *Note*: The theatrical version of *Utah* ran 78 minutes; the video release has been shortened.

UTOPIA ★
1950, France
Stan Laurel, Oliver Hardy, Suzy Delair, Max Elloy. Directed by Leo Joannon. 80 min.

Though it would be impossible to make Laurel and Hardy completely humorless, this movie comes very close. Stan was very ill at the time of the filming and it shows on his face and in his carriage; Oliver's timing seems off. The story has a good premise: the boys inherit an island that is loaded with uranium, and they are caught between the commercial possibilities and their desire to create a utopian society. Unfortunately, there's too much leaden satire, and Leo Joannon shows absolutely no directorial talent. A sad swan song from the lovable comedy duo.

UTU ★★★
1985, New Zealand, R
Anzac Wallace, Bruno Lawrence, Tim Elliott, Kelly Johnson, Wi Kuki Kaa, Tania Bristowe, Ilona Rodgers. Directed by Geoff Murphy. 104 min.

Set in 1870s New Zealand, this exotic thriller about a Maori officer who turns guerrilla when the British massacre his village keeps the audience on its toes by shifting from revenge epic to horror movie to Western to Victorian morality tale. Director Goeff Murphy lets the audience figure out the details and concentrates on suspenseful storytelling. Although he doesn't assign blame, he has an eye for the absurdities of the relationship between imperialists and natives, and for the follies perpetrated by Europeans in the wild. The cast, especially Anzac Wallace as the rebel Te Wheke and Bruno Lawrence (of *Smash Palace* and *The Quiet Earth*) as a white farmer who goes on a vengeful trek of his own, is superb.

V

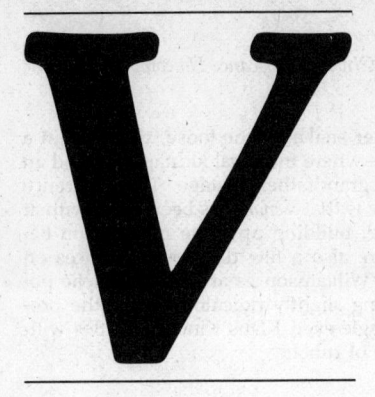

VAGABOND
1985, France ☆☆☆
Sandrine Bonnaire, Macha Meril, Stéphane Freiss, Laurence Cortadellas. Directed by Agnès Varda. 105 min.

A beautifully rendered but gritty and depressing movie that follows the final days of Mona, a lovely teenager who aimlessly wanders the countryside looking for food and smokes. Director Agnès Varda narrates the bizarre adventures with on-camera comments from "people" whose lives have been touched by the tramp, and though the performances are often enigmatic and distancing, the film has a strangely affecting and even maddening quality about it. *Vagabond* moves with Mona's weird precision, but something can be learned by keeping slow step with it.

VALLEY GIRL
1983, USA, R ☆☆½
Deborah Foreman, Nicolas Cage, Colleen Camp, Frederic Forrest. Directed by Martha Coolidge. 95 min.

This is a slice of California culture as immortalized by the Frank and Moon Unit Zappa song. Deborah Foreman stars as Julie, the ultimate L.A. teen who breaks up with her perfect Val boyfriend and, much to the embarrassment of her crowd, falls in love with a hip Hollywood punk (Nicolas Cage, in an attractive debut). Meanwhile, she has to contend with her parents, flower-child relics who run a health food store and urge her to mellow out. Martha Coolidge won praise for her direction of this cute culture clash, which includes music by Modern English, Men at Work, Eddy Grant, and the Psychedelic Furs. Nothing stupid, but nothing special.

VALLEY OF THE DOLLS
1967, USA ☆☆
Patty Duke, Barbara Parkins, Sharon Tate, Susan Hayward, Lee Grant, Paul Burke, Martin Milner. Directed by Mark Robson. 123 min.

Valley of the Dolls must surely be the greatest bad movie ever made. Artistically it ranks low, but as comic entertainment, it can't be beat. Some ill-conceived dramatic movies have occasional moments of unintentional humor; *Dolls* is so consistently hilarious that is is well worth seeing. Based on Jacqueline Susann's best-seller, the film follows three career girls and their problems with work, men, and pills (dolls). Patty Duke, who only five years earlier won an Academy Award, gives one of the worst performances in screen history as Neely O'Hara, the singing star modeled after Judy Garland. Her stay at a mental hospital is especially amusing. Barbara Parkins is Anne Welles, fresh from New England, hired on the spot by a big-time agent as his secretary ("Can she start right away, Mr. Bellamy, we're swamped!"). The late Sharon Tate has the Marilyn Monroe role, and Susan Hayward, a last-minute replacement for Judy Garland, is great as the Ethel Merman–type star. The great lines are too numerous to list.

VAMP
1986, USA, R ☆☆☆
Grace Jones, Chris Makepeace, Robert Rusler, Sandy Barron, Gedde Watanabe. Directed by Richard Wenk. 90 min.

Two cool guys decide that they can't stand living in their Animal House dorm anymore, so they agree to find a hot stripper for a big-frathouse-on-campus party in exchange for membership. Their mistake: looking for her at the wild After Dark club, where all the strippers are vicious vampire ladies with a serious lust for young blood. Unlike most vampire comedies—*Love at First Bite* and *Once Bitten*, for example—*Vamp* plays its horror elements very seriously. Fangs sprout, faces contort into gargoyle masks, blood flows fast and freely; the tone resembles that of John Landis's *An American Werewolf in London* or Joe Dante's *The Howling*—funny, but very mean indeed. In addition, *Vamp* benefits from some highly stylized, sumptuous cinematography that transforms its decaying urban setting into a neon fantasy of mean, exciting streets and picturesquely run-down hotels, clubs, and diners. Fun for horror buffs with a sense of humor.

VAMPING
1984, USA, R ☆
Patrick Duffy, Catherine Hyland, Rod Arrants, David Booze. Directed by Frederick King Keller. 110 min.

This dreary Patrick Duffy vehicle concerns a down-and-out sax player who falls in love with a young, mysterious widow whose house he has burgled. The odd, out-of-the-blue ending suggests that somewhere—about twenty-seven rewrites ago—someone had a good idea for a movie.

THE VAMPIRE BEAST CRAVES BLOOD

See *The Blood Beast Terror*

THE VAMPIRE HAPPENING
1971, West Germany ☆
Pia Degermark, Damar, Thomas Hunter, Ferdie Mayne, Ivor Murillo. Directed by Freddie Francis. 97 min.

Inane horror film has Pia Degermark (wife of the producer) as a Hollywood starlet with neck-nibblers in her bloodline, and Ferdie Mayne as the toothy Dracula substitute. Lowbrow comedy substitutes for any attempt at genuine horror; the minds behind this seem to have given up on vampires as a possibly frightening subject before they started. A lazy piece of hackwork that's a disappointment from ace cinematographer Freddie Francis, whose attempts at direction almost always fell short.

VAMPIRE HOOKERS
1978, USA, R ½
John Carradine, Kathie Dolan, Lenka Novak, Karen Stride, Trey Wilson, Bruce Fairbairn, Vic Diaz. Directed by Cirio Santiago. 82 min.

If you ever become a sailor and you're on leave in the Far East, and a friendly neighborhood prostitute takes you to a subterranean crypt that's fussily overdecorated, you're probably in trouble. Boasting a perfect score of no laughs, no chills, and no turn-ons, *Vampire Hookers* should be exposed to the first rays of the sun and left to disintegrate.

VANISHING POINT
1971, USA, PG ☆☆
Barry Newman, Cleavon Little, Charlotte Rampling, Dean Jagger, Severn Darden, Delaney & Bonnie & Friends. Directed by Richard C. Sarafian. 107 min.

This basically silly, pseudo-existential period piece will still appeal to fans of car chases, which comprise about three-quarters of the film. Ex-cop Barry Newman accepts a bet to get a car from San Francisco to Denver in fifteen hours, with considerably more granite-jawed seriousness than Burt and friends in *Cannonball Run*. Instead of Dom DeLuise, he's accompanied by Cleavon Little, a blind deejay who communicates with him over the airwaves and through some sort of ESP. Whatever initial appeal the film had is undoubtedly lessened in its reduction from a wide-screen format to television. Good rock score, though, by Delaney & Bonnie & Friends (who appear briefly), Kim Carnes, and others.

VAN NUYS BLVD. ☆☆
1979, USA, R
Bill Adler, Cynthia Wood, Dennis Bowen, Melissa Prophet. Directed by William Sachs. 93 min.

During the time when Crown International Pictures' roster teemed with teen movies, it couldn't help improving them—even if that amounted to teaching their kennel of dogs only one new trick each. On slick, quick *Van Nuys Blvd.*, beach-bum Bill Adler actually gets swamped by postadolescent feelings like, um, love; unfortunately, that doesn't happen until Adler and his meat-locker mates compile a travelogue for the unintelligent by molesting the Magic Mountain amusement park, dabbling in disco, and jetting into jail. But then comes Moon (former Playmate Cynthia Wood), pulling Adler far away from the crystalline squalor and childishness of Van Nuys Blvd. If this generally entertaining film doesn't quite follow him, at least it aspires to.

VARAN THE UNBELIEVABLE ☆½
1958, Japan
Myron Healy, Tsuruko Kobayashi, Clifford Kawada, Derick Simatsu. Directed by Jerry Baerwitz and Inoshiro Honda. 70 min.

Another gigantic beastie from the deep arises from its watery grave and vents its ire by kicking the crap out of Tokyo. Why should you find that unbelievable? It seems to happen every other week in Japan. As usual, this was sliced up and given added footage for its American release, which explains how a guy named Myron got into the Japanese cast. Varan is distinguished from other such rubber-suited building-bashers mostly by a spiky back that looks like something you'd see at a punk rock bar on Friday night.

VEGAS ☆½
1978, USA (TV)
Robert Urich, Will Sampson, Chick Vennera, Michael Lerner, Red Buttons, June Allyson, Scatman Crothers, Greg Morris, Tony Curtis. Directed by Richard Lang. 74 min.

This pilot for the TV show already has the series' tired-blood formula—a knock-off of Mannix in Glitter Gulch becomes involved in a series of phyical scrapes while he exerts no visible mental effort in solving a tedious mystery. Here he looks for another runaway girl. For Robert Urich completists (are there any?) only.

VELVET HOUSE

See *Crucible of Horror*

THE VELVET VAMPIRE ☆☆
1971, USA, R
Celeste Yarnall, Michael Blodgett, Sherry Miles. Directed by Stephanie Rothman. 82 min.

Silky smooth direction highlights this fable about a vampire who lives in the sun-baked desert. Many script improbabilities mar the sexed-up saga in which a sultry Draculette lures two L.A. swingers to her lair and tries to love them to death. Short on logic; long on stylishness. (a.k.a.: *Cemetery Girls*)

VENOM ☆☆
1982, Great Britain, R
Nicol Williamson, Klaus Kinski, Oliver Reed, Lance Halcomb. Directed by Piers Haggard. 93 min.

There's another killer snake on the loose, this time in a London town-house where maniacal kidnappers hold an asthmatic young boy and his grandfather hostage. The difference between this movie and its like is that *Venom* has been done with at least some style and suspense, building up some momentum between snake attacks. There are also a few droll performances on hand, particularly from Nicol Williamson as an ever-so-Gaelic policeman. Still, there's something slightly ridiculous about the proceedings, especially when goggle-eyed Klaus Kinski wrestles with what is obviously a long piece of rubber.

VERA CRUZ ☆☆½
1954, USA
Gary Cooper, Burt Lancaster, Denise Darcel, Cesar Romero, George Macready, Ernest Borgnine, Morris Ankrum, Charles Buchinsky (Bronson), Jack Elam. Directed by Robert Aldrich. 94 min.

This early Robert Aldrich film is a cult Western that was, arguably, an influence on the more "adult" Westerns that flourished in the 1960s. Burt Lancaster and Gary Cooper are well teamed as two soldiers of fortune on different sides who become involved in an attempt to overthrow the Mexican emperor Maximilian in the 1860s. Some slow patches throughout, but an exciting climax makes up for them.

THE VERDICT ☆☆☆½
1982, USA, R
Paul Newman, Charlotte Rampling, Jack Warden, James Mason, Milo O'Shea, Edward Binns. Directed by Sidney Lumet. 129 min.

Paul Newman delivers one of his most concentrated, brilliant performances as an alcoholic Boston attorney given one last shot at respectability by a case of medical negligence. Director Sidney Lumet's powerful, heady drama features one of the all-time great courtroom scenes and a strong supporting cast led by James Mason as the lawyer up against Newman.

VERTIGO ☆☆☆☆
1958, USA, PG
James Stewart, Kim Novak, Barbara Bel Geddes, Tom Helmore, Henry Jones. Directed by Alfred Hitchcock. 128 min.

In this Alfred Hitchcock masterpiece, James Stewart plays a retired cop suffering from vertigo and, what's worse, from a strange obsession with an elusive woman (Kim Novak) he has been hired to follow. After being unable to prevent the woman's apparent suicide, the despairing man falls into a deep depression that only recedes when he meets the woman's double, and he endeavors to transform her into his lost love. Hitchcock's compelling depiction of this character's delirious obsession results in an overwhelmingly romantic, genuinely disturbing work full of brooding passions underlined by Bernard Herrmann's influential musical score. For some, this is Hitchcock's finest, with extraordinary performances by Novak and Stewart.

VESSEL OF WRATH

See *The Beachcomber*

VICE SQUAD ☆☆
1982, USA, R
Season Hubley, Gary Swanson, Wings Hauser, Pepe Serna, Beverly Todd, Stack Pierce, Nina Blackwood. Directed by Gary A. Sherman. 97 min.

Brutal and sleazy, but effective. An L.A. cop enlists a hooker (Season Hubley) as bait to catch a psychotic pimp (Wings

Hauser) who specializes in mutilating his ladies before he murders them. Hauser turns the pimp into a truly menacing baddie, giving an eye-rolling, lip-smacking performance with the kind of calculated exaggeration the rest of the film could have used. (He also bellows out the tune "Neon Slime.") MTV veejay Nina Blackwood appears briefly as a victim, the first of many.

VICTIM ☆☆☆
1961, Great Britain
Dirk Bogarde, Sylvia Sims, Dennis Price, John Barrie, Peter McEnery. Directed by Basil Dearden. 100 min.

A noble endeavor at the time, but now merely a crisp, authoritative courtroom drama. Back in 1961, it was unheard of to make homosexuality the central focus of a film. Since the subject matter was treated sympathetically, the film was even more unusual. It's also fatally faint-hearted because the lawyer protagonist sees the light and shelves his attraction to men forever. The tricky plot deals with a scandal that breaks when a respected barrister's past threatens to wreck his reputation and compromise his ability to try a case involving a homosexual.

VICTOR/VICTORIA ☆☆½
1982, USA, PG
Julie Andrews, James Garner, Robert Preston, Lesley Ann Warren, Alex Karras. Directed by Blake Edwards. 133 min.

Blake Edwards's broad comedy gets a lavish period production in 1930s Paris and is spiced up with elaborate musical numbers; it works fairly well as a grandly old-fashioned entertainment but is never as funny or sophisticated as he'd like it to be. Based on the 1933 German film *Viktor und Viktoria*, this revision takes gender confusion as its premise to tell the tale of a woman (Julie Andrews) who masquerades as a female impersonator (that is, a man who *looks* like a woman) in order to win notoriety and fame on the cabaret circuit. Everything's fine until the she-who-would-be-he discovers true love in the person of James Garner. The same idea was brought off with infinitely more flair and humor in *Tootsie*, and as many critics pointed out, it's challenge enough for Julie Andrews to play one gender convincingly, mush less three layered ones. But the zippy support of Robert Preston, Lesley Ann Warren, and Alex Karras keeps the story a consistent diversion.

VICTORY ☆☆
1981, USA, PG
Michael Caine, Sylvester Stallone, Max von Sydow, Pele, Daniel Massey, Carol Laure. Directed by John Huston. 110 min.

John Huston's later career has been nothing if not uneven, and this misguided silliness falls into the *Phobia-Annie* area of undistinguished hit-and-run work rather than the vaunted achievement (*Prizzi's Honor, Wise Blood*) category. This World War II tale has German military leaders pulling together a soccer match between their soldiers and the American and European POWs to show them who's boss. When the Allies join forces in a plan to win the game and their freedom, the rigged, creaky plot gets into gear. Not bad overall, but slow and familiar, and the acting by semipros like Sylvester Stallone and Pele is less than stellar.

VIDEODROME ☆☆☆
1983, Canada, R
James Woods, Deborah Harry, Sonja Smits, Les Carlson. Directed by David Cronenberg. 88 min.

Pirate cable operator Max Wren (James Woods) is searching for a "new twist" in video that will satiate his sex- and violence-hungry viewers. He finds it in "Videodrome" snuff television, which, unknown to him, is designed to take over the minds of its viewers. An original and often shocking commentary on the extremes of TV shows and the people who watch them, the film is overseen under the bizarre direction of famed Canadian horror king David Cronenberg (*Scanners*). It takes several viewings to absorb the film's meanings, but it's doubtful whether many audience members will want to watch Rick Baker's extremely gory makeup effects over and over. Not recommended for those used to routine horror films or with weak stomachs.

A VIEW TO A KILL ☆☆
1985, Great Britain, PG
Roger Moore, Tanya Roberts, Christopher Walken, Grace Jones, Patrick Macnee. Directed by John Glen. 133 min.

This sixteenth entry in the eternal James Bond series is one of the weakest, with sub–*Smokey and the Bandit* stunts and unusually inane dialogue. It pits Bond against a psychotic corporate magnate who wants to corner the microchip market by blowing up Silicon Valley. There's a strong finale atop the Golden Gate Bridge, and Christopher Walken and the astonishing Grace Jones are the slickest pair of bad guys in years. But the film is too long, Roger Moore looks old, tired, and annoyed, and Tanya Roberts is howlingly awful in a role that requires little talent to begin with. Even as a cartoon, this one doesn't make it.

THE VIKINGS ☆☆
1958, USA
Kirk Douglas, Tony Curtis, Janet Leigh, Ernest Borgnine, Alexander Knox. Directed by Richard Fleischer. 114 min.

Brutal but never boring, in many ways this presaged later cheesy comic-book history epics like *Sword and the Sorcerer* and *Beastmaster* with its colorful picture of barbarian behavior and its preoccupation with violence and décolletage. So hold onto your Viking helmet as Tony Curtis and Kirk Douglas vie for the affections of highborn Janet Leigh, a competition that pales in comparison with the acting duel between Douglas and Ernest Borgnine for hammiest performance. As the Vikings invade England, the film goes from bad to Norse.

VILLAGE OF THE DAMNED ☆☆☆½
1960, Great Britain
George Sanders, Barbara Shelley, Michael Gwynne, Martin Stephens, Laurence Naismith. Directed by Wolf Rilla. 78 min.

This low-budget mood piece is a small horror classic that's spooked generations of children—and quite a few parents—since its initial appearance. In a small English village, twelve angelic youngsters born under a magic spell begin a reign of terror; with their penetrating, cold-eyed stares, they can enforce their will on anyone. Soon enough, moms and dads are dropping like flies. Wolf Rilla's direction is attentive to every scary plot possibility, and the climax is chilling in the manner of the best old "Twilight Zone" episodes. A sequel, *Children of the Damned*, followed in 1964.

VILLAGE OF THE GIANTS ☆☆
1965, USA
Tommy Kirk, Johnny Crawford, Beau Bridges, Ronny Howard, Joy Harmon, Toni Basil, Joe Turkel, the Beau Brummels, Freddy Cannon. Directed by Bert I. Gordon. 81 min.

This typically ridiculous Bert I. Gordon feature has the usual vapid plot and tacky special effects, but it also has lots of nostalgia value. Future director Ron Howard plays an eleven-year-old genius, appropriately named Genius, who invents a formula that makes things grow to huge proportions. A bunch of rock-'n'-rollin' teenagers drift into town after losing their car in an avalanche, eat food peppered with the stuff, become giants, and take over the town. Beau Bridges will never live down his role as one of the giants; as for Tommy Kirk, and Johnny ("The Rifleman") Crawford, they were already old news. But some of the Beau Brummels and Freddy Cannon tunes are good, if totally unrelated to the story; and a young Toni Basil appears as—what else?—a dancer. Remade by Gordon, in an even worse version, as *Food of the Gods*, the title of the H. G. Wells story on which he claims this was based.

THE VILLAIN STILL PURSUED HER ★★½
1940, USA
Alan Mowbray, Richard Cromwell, Anita Louise, Buster Keaton. Directed by Edward F. Cline. 67 min.

A camped-up treat, this bit of whimsy gives you an opportunity to relive the glory days of gaslight melodramas. Replete with mustache-twirling villains and goldilocked heroes, it gussies up the potboiler format with a lot of silent-movie comedy tecniques. Even in his small role, Buster Keaton is a joy and shows just how far screen humor has degenerated from his heyday in the Golden Age of Silent Comedy. A slight but agreeable comic romp.

VIOLETS ARE BLUE ★★
1986, USA, PG-13
Sissy Spacek, Kevin Kline, Bonnie Bedelia, John Kellogg, Jim Standford, Augusta Dabney. Directed by Jack Fisk. 90 min.

A wilted bouquet of romance. Modern-day conventions about character motivations are at odds with the film's yearning to be "the kind of movie they just don't make anymore." The appeal of Sissy Spacek and Kevin Kline carries the film far, but not quite far enough. They enact a happily married small-town newspaperman and his ex-girlfriend, who's now a celebrated photojournalist. After a long absence, she returns to Ocean City and falls back into her idealistic ex-flame's arms. The script is such a fragile conceit about dreams and commitments, with no meaningful dialogue to anchor it in reality and no old-fashioned love-story charm to send it soaring, that it all but blows away. The drama is minor and wispy, except for a very assured performance by Bonnie Bedelia as the contented wife, a woman who cooks balanced meals and even packs her hubby's Fruit-of-the-Looms as he prepares to leave her.

THE VIRGIN SPRING ★★★½
1960, Sweden
Max von Sydow, Brigitta Valberg, Gunnel Lindblom, Brigitta Petersen. Directed by Ingmar Bergman. 88 min.

An Academy Award for Best Foreign Film went to this grim, grinding morality play, which only Ingmar Bergman's mastery saves from being unbearably oppressive. There are images of quiet, almost rapturous beauty in this adaptation of a fourteenth-century Swedish legend about the rape and murder of a young virgin and her father's subsequent revenge. One of Bergman's favorite male leads, Max von Sydow, plays the father with a dramatic fervor rivaling his work in *The Seventh Seal* and *Shame*, and Bergman's keen theatrical intuition doesn't desert him for an instant. Believe it or not, this served as the basis for Wes Craven's horror film *The Last House on the Left*.

VIRIDIANA ★★★
1961, Spain
Silvia Pinal, Francisco Rabal, Fernando Rey, Margarita Lozano. Directed by Luis Buñuel. 90 min.

After twenty-three years in exile from his native Spain, Luis Buñuel returned to make *Viridiana* using government funds. When Franco finally saw this scathing masterpiece on corruption in the Roman Catholic Church, he banned it throughout his country. The story involves a beautiful young novice (Silvia Pinal) who, just before taking her vows, visits the estate of her uncle (Fernando Rey) and receives a stunning introduction to some of the earthier aspects of human reality. The film culminates in a devastating sequence during which a group of beggars wreaks havoc on the old man's mansion. Winner of the Grand Prix Award at Cannes in 1961, this bitter, trenchant work has remained undiminished in strength over the years.

VISION QUEST ★★½
1985, USA, R
Matthew Modine, Linda Fiorentino, Michael Schoeffling, Ronny Cox, Harold Sylvester, Charles Hallahan, J. C. Quinn, Daphne Zuniga, R. H. Thompson, Madonna. Directed by Harold Becker. 108 min.

Matthew Modine plays Louden Swain, a high-school wrestler determined to drop his weight from 190 to 168 pounds; only then will he get a crack at the finest wrestler in the city. His plunge into starvation dieting is treated with too much solemn reverence, and his romance with a tough-cookie sexpot (Linda Fiorentino) seems trumped up, but the movie remains modestly charming, with flashes of insight that put it above most other rabble-rousing fairy tales. Modine has the range and robust sensuality of a major screen star. And director Becker understands that life in high school isn't all fast times and insolent high jinks. Madonna makes a brief concert appearance to sing the theme song, "Crazy for You."

VISITING HOURS ★
1982, Canada, R
Lee Grant, Michael Ironside, William Shatner, Linda Purl, Harvey Atkin, Helen Hughes. Directed by Jean Claude Lord. 103 min.

Unfortunately, some real talent got caught in this exploitative thriller about a knife-weilding psychopath who pursues an outspoken feminist TV reporter and her nurse in a metropolitan hospital. The film is nasty not only for its repetitive knife-attack scenes but for its reactionary attitudes toward Lee Grant's character.

VISIT TO A SMALL PLANET ★★½
1960, USA
Jerry Lewis, Joan Blackman, Earl Holliman, Fred Clark, Lee Patrick, Gale Gordon, Barbara Lawson. Directed by Norman Taurog. 85 min.

Jerry Lewis faced such strong criticism in this attempt to carry Gore Vidal's stage vehicle onto the big screen that he forever abandoned the notion of acting in a structured, written comedy. Certainly, his own films didn't involve him in frustrated love stories, or have him held at bay by a normal, suburban world. Still, the flashes of Lewis's shtick now seem the freshest part of this dated satire, and Jerry's wacked-out persona is easier to understand than the provincial community of middle-class clods. Lewis plays Kreton, a mischievous alien who drops in on earth and falls for the daughter of a local television personality. Unfortunately, everyone finds out that he's from outer space, and Kreton is chased from the planet by an overzealous state militia. The film's highlight is set in a coffee house, where Jerry does a hep dance with a beatnik chick (Barbara Lawson).

VIVACIOUS LADY ★★★
1938, USA
Ginger Rogers, James Stewart, James Ellison, Beulah Bondi. Directed by George Stevens. 90 min.

In this generally laudable comedy vehicle, Ginger Rogers is pressed into service as a nonmusical performer for the first time. Miss Rogers is delightfully levelheaded as the performer who marries a teacher from a straitlaced family. James Stewart is a good match for his costar, and George Stevens's direction has excellent bits of small-town Americana that are reminiscent of his *Alice Adams*.

VIVA KNIEVEL! ★
1977, USA, PG
Evel Knievel, Gene Kelly, Lauren Hutton, Red Buttons, Leslie Nielsen, Frank Gifford, Cameron Mitchell, Marjoe Gortner. Directed by Gordon Douglas. 106 min.

Motorcycle daredevil Evel Knievel may be the least interesting public figure ever to be the subject of two movies—a biography in which he was portrayed by George Hamilton, and this unbearably stupid, egotistical homage to himself, in which Evel plays Evel, trying to outwit an evil crook who's planning to sabotage his next big stunt. Along the way, he meets Lauren Hutton, who instantly falls in love with him (*sure*, Evel) and enriches the life of old rummy mechanic Gene Kelly. There's some decent motorcycle footage, but the real stunt is watching Evel's head swell . . . and swell . . . and swell. Somehow it never explodes, but you may be rooting hard.

VIVA LAS VEGAS ★★★
1964, USA
Elvis Presley, Ann-Margret, Cesare Danova, William Demarest, Jack Carter. Directed by George Sidney. 86 min.

One of the few Elvis Presley films fit for viewing by those other than his loyal fans. Elvis plays a car-racing fan who tries to raise money to buy an engine for the car with which he hopes to win the Grand Prix. A light and lively hour and a half is bolstered by the presence of Ann-Margret, who smolders her way across the screen and makes *Viva* more than just another Elvis film.

VIVA ZAPATA! ★★★
1952, USA
Marlon Brando, Jean Peters, Anthony Quinn, Joseph Wiseman, Alan Reed, Margo, Lou Gilbert. Directed by Elia Kazan. 112 min.

New York "Method" meets Mexican folklore in this challenging, always intriguing portrait of rebel leader Emiliano Zapata. Director Elia Kazan and screenwriter John Steinbeck attempted to show the complexities and contradictions of the Mexican Revolution and they should be congratulated for not compromising their subject. Unfortunately, the compression of events and emphasis on action clouds many of the issues; the film often resembles a Western with the cowboy hats replaced by sombreros. Ultimately, the audience comes away enjoying individual moments—like the massive peasant uprising when Zapata is taken prisoner, and Zapata's wedding night during which he is taught to read—without gaining overall insight. Marlon Brando fans will enjoy watching the actor (in dark makeup and mustache) portray the fearless but simple peasant-turned-revolutionary, particularly in his scenes with Anthony Quinn (Best Supporting Actor), playing his brother Eugenio. Interesting, but not the masterpiece it wants to be.

VOLUNTEERS ★★
1985, USA, R
Tom Hanks, John Candy, Rita Wilson, Tim Thomerson, Gedde Watanabe, George Plimpton, Ernest Harada. Directed by Nicholas Meyer. 106 min.

Tom Hanks plays a filthy-rich Ivy League dandy who boards a plane to Bangkok to escape a hefty gambling debt and ends up doing a cracked tour of duty in the Peace Corps. Hanks's portrayal of the Yalie is so one-dimensional that you might assume filmmaker Nicholas Meyer was planning to take him down a notch or two; but if you did, you would be wrong. The movie often seems to be reveling in his condescension toward the natives, but it's really just a series of old gags done in a ham-fisted style that pummels the audience into submission. You'll laugh some, but you may also feel like crying uncle.

VON RYAN'S EXPRESS ★★★
1965, USA
Frank Sinatra, Trevor Howard, Brad Dexter, Edward Mulhare, James Brolin, Serge Fantoni. Directed by Mark Robson. 117 min.

This exciting World War II movie is both edifying as a character study and engrossing as a muscular action picture. Nonstop suspense awaits viewers of this thriller about prisoners of war who take over a train from the German troops and embark on a daring escape trek. What makes the suspense sequences work is that the characters are well defined intially—we root for Colonel Frank Sinatra because we've seen him transform himself from a self-centered antihero to a fearless leader who takes charge and commands respect as he engineers a plan to lead his men to safety. Exemplary action sequences.

VOYAGE OF THE DAMNED ★★
1976, USA/Spain/Great Britain, PG
Faye Dunaway, Max von Sydow, Oskar Werner, Malcolm McDowell, Orson Welles, James Mason, Lee Grant, Ben Gazzara, Katharine Ross, Luther Adler, Denholm Elliott, Jose Ferrer, Julie Harris, Wendy Hiller, Fernando Rey, Janet Suzman, Maria Schell. Directed by Stuart Rosenberg. 158 min.

An endless, melodramatic, and trivialized account of the exodus from Germany in 1939 of nine hundred Jewish citizens, who were put on an ocean liner, told they were traveling to freedom, and never given a hint that their exodus was merely a propaganda move, and an ill-fated one. It's a tragic story, but the seagoing spectacle nearly sinks under the weight of its all-star cast, each member of which is given a trite, tiny subplot that plays like a dour, grouchy segment of "The Love Boat." The wildly broad performances seem meant to compensate for the absence of any real drama, and some of the star turns are moving, but most of it comes off as an unintentionally tawdry rendition of a Holocaust tragedy, dressed in typical disaster-movie regalia.

VOYAGE TO THE BOTTOM OF THE SEA ★
1961, USA
Walter Pidgeon, Joan Fontaine, Barbara Eden, Peter Lorre, Robert Sterling, Michael Ansara, Frankie Avalon, Regis Toomey, John Litel, Howard McNear. Directed by Irwin Allen. 105 min.

Oh, the wonders that a little scientific knowledge have wrought on the underactive imagination. Here Irwin Allen, picking the bones of Jules Verne, sets the then recently discovered Van Allen Belt on fire and sends out Admiral Nelson of the USS *Seaview* as a submarine-borne firefighter. In this underwater follow-up to the more enchanting *Journey to the Center of the Earth*, the United Nations attempts to stop the good admiral from testing his theory that by shooting a Polaris missile through the polar ice cap, they could, logically, extinguish the fire in the sky. With U.N. subs in watery pursuit, the *Seaview*—so named for its all-glass front—encounters a cross-eyed giant squid and rubbery sea vegetation. When the world is safe at last, the film sinks to a waterlogged death, eulogized in song by Frankie Avalon.

VULTURES ★
1984, USA
Stuart Whitman, Meredith MacRae, Yvonne De Carlo, Aldo Ray, Jim Bailey, Greg Mullavey, Carmen Zapata. Directed by Paul Leder. 101 min.

Vultures—isn't that what they call fourth-rate filmmakers who pick the bones of dead directors to create feeble imitations of their work? This one owes a debt to the Master of Suspense, but if you get through it, you'll owe a bigger one to the makers of No-Doz. The plot concerns a series of murders among a group of human leeches waiting for a rich benefactor to die; the small-name cast is the only attraction.

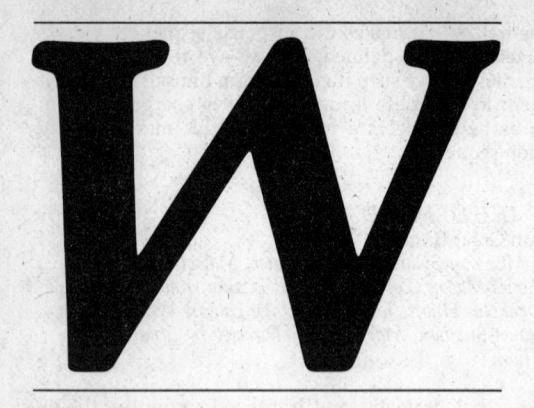

W

W ☆½
1974, USA, PG
Twiggy, Michael Witney, Dirk Benedict, John Vernon, Eugene Roche. Directed by Richard Quine. 95 min.

This plodding, unappetizing thriller, about a woman threatened by her ex-spouse, failed to launch Twiggy as a dramatic actress. While she has since proven herself a charming, elfin singer-dancer on Broadway, she's only a game amateur here. The former husband, convicted of committing her alleged murder, returns really to do the deed. His attempts to strike fear into her and her new mate are more sadistic than suspenseful.

WACKO ☆☆½
1981, USA, PG
Joe Don Baker, Stella Stevens, George Kennedy, Jeff Altman. Directed by Greydon Clark. 84 min.

Greydon Clark is one of the all-time awful directors, as he has proven time and time again in such dreck as *Joysticks* and *Satan's Cheerleaders*. But even though *Wacko* is as badly and as cheaply made as all of his other films (Clark seems to spend all of his budget on getting name casts), it's actually pretty funny. The film aims to be a parody of slasher films in the style of *Airplane!*; it comes nowhere near that high standard, but the very cheapness of the gags makes it much funnier than it has any right to be. You probably won't get most of the jokes unless you've seen every installment of *Friday the 13th*, but if you have, this will provide some laughs.

WAGES OF FEAR ☆☆☆
1953, France/Italy
Yves Montand, Charles Vanel, Peter Van Eyck, Vera Clouzot, Folco Lulli. Directed by Henri-Georges Clouzot. 138 min.

Henri-Georges Clouzot described his gripping existential thriller as "an epic whose main theme is courage." The plot concerns four losers trapped in a squalid South American shantytown; the only way they can get the money they need to escape is by trucking nitro through the jungle for the resident oil interests, who need it to cap a fire in one of their wells. In the end, the men's sole possessions are gestures of loyalty and courage that have no effect on their fates. This was the movie that inspired William Friedkin's far inferior *Sorcerer*. *Note*: The version on video is shorter than the original European release (156 minutes), but longer by far than the 104-minute American theatrical cut.

WAGNER ☆☆☆
1983, Great Britain (TV)
Richard Burton, Vanessa Redgrave, Laurence Olivier, Ralph Richardson, John Gielgud, Franco Nero, Ronald Pickup. Directed by Tony Palmer. 540 min. (complete version), 300 min. (edited version)

This miniseries, made for British television, is a slow but extraordinarily lush and handsome biography of the great composer, with Richard Burton giving his last major performance in the title role. Burton looks drawn and ill, but his work here shows him at the height of his talents; at its best, the film offers a genuine examination of one man's artistic process. It's also the only film in which Laurence Olivier, Ralph Richardson, and John Gielgud, the three giants of the English theater, share a scene; watching these venerable talents try to steal the show from each other is reason enough to see the film. Kultur Videocassettes has released the full nine-hour version of *Wagner* with the subheading "The Complete Epic," but the less committed should be satisfied with Embassy Home Entertainment's excellent five-hour version, which appeared in slightly longer form on American television.

WAGON MASTER ☆☆☆½
1950, USA
Ben Johnson, Harry Carey, Jr., Ward Bond, Joanne Dru, Charles Kemper, Alan Mowbray, Jane Darwell, Russell Simpson, Ruth Clifford, Kathleen O'Malley, James Arness. Directed by John Ford. 85 min.

A wagon train of Mormons heading for Utah faces vicious outlaws, drought and starvation, Indians, and uncrossable rivers and mountains in this handsome large-scale traditional Western from the master of the genre. For abundant romantic subplotting, there are *three* women in this wagon train; watch for James Arness, cast against his later "Gunsmoke" persona, as one of Uncle Shiloh's boys (the outlaws). Four songs by Stan Jones are performed by the Sons of the Pioneers. Perhaps not a masterpiece, but thoroughly enjoyable and one of Ford's own favorites among his Westerns.

WAITRESS! ½☆
1982, USA, R
Jim Harris, Carol Drake, Carol Bevaer, David Hunt, Renata Majer. Directed by Samuel Weil and Michael Herz. 85 min.

This indigestible movie will turn your sense of humor to stone. Troma Films specializes in amateurish "comedies" that combine scatological humor that would make a third-grader wince, jokes on the order of "Waiter, what is this fly doing in my soup?," and badly lit, awkwardly staged sex that occurs with metronomic regularity. You won't laugh, you won't smile, and, by the end, you won't believe that such dull-witted garbage gets made and distributed.

WAIT UNTIL DARK ☆☆☆
1967, USA
Audrey Hepburn, Alan Arkin, Efrem Zimbalist, Jr., Richard Crenna, Jack Warden. Directed by Terence Young. 108 min.

This smash adaptation of Frederick Knott's stage thriller works best when viewed in a movie theater where a surprise twist at the climax has audiences screaming their heads off. On the small screen, the big scares are somewhat diminished, but the film remains a polished exercise in suspense. The story's foolproof gimmick is that a blind woman is chased by three thugs in pursuit of a cache of heroin she doesn't know is in her possession. Milking every bit of Audrey Hepburn's vulnerability, the film draws you into her horrifying ordeal without surcease and plays continuous havoc with your nerves. Exceptionally well acted, particularly by Alan Arkin as the most clever and demented of the criminals.

WAKE ISLAND ☆☆☆½
1942, USA
Brian Donlevy, Robert Preston, Macdonald Carey, Albert Dekker, Barbara Britton, William Bendix, Walter Abel. Directed by John Farrow. 87 min.

Made at a time when Hollywood was concentrating on pumping up the war effort, *Wake Island* interestingly chronicles a tragic, bitter defeat of the U.S. in the South Pacific. This is the war film nearly at its finest, with dug-in leathernecks repelling wave after wave of Japanese assaults. The film manages to work in scenes of American strategy that are compelling in themselves and add scope to the battle scenes. Credit screenwriters W. R. Burnett (novelist of *Little Caesar* and *High Sierra*) and Frank Butler (*Going My Way*) for the strong story, and credit the island's 385 Marine defenders for intense, gritty heroics.

WAKE OF THE RED WITCH ☆☆☆
1948, USA
John Wayne, Gail Russell, Luther Adler, Adele Mara, Gig Young, Paul Fix. Directed by Edward Ludwig. 106 min.

A refreshing change of pace for John Wayne, who abandons his six-shooters for a scabbard in this colorful East Indies adventure. A shipping magnate and an independent-minded captain vie for a fortune in pearls. When they're not engaged in one-upmanship in their wars of commerce, they battle over the affections of dark-eyed Gail Russell, who also paired beautifully with the Duke in another atypical film, *Angel and the Badman*; their chemistry and the exotic locale transform an ordinary action picture into something special.

WALKING TALL ☆
1973, USA, R
Joe Don Baker, Elizabeth Hartman, Gene Evans, Noah Beery. Directed by Phil Karlson. 125 min.

This is a gussied-up version of a true story about Buford Pusser, a Tennessee sheriff who drove out the local mobsters with the use of a large hickory stick and a disdain for due process. Pusser's methods are as violent and as vile as those of the gangsters he opposes. (Earlier, the mob had him beaten up when he demanded back money they'd stolen from him.) The final scene, in which Pusser leaves the funeral of his wife, killed in an ambush, and runs his car into the last of the villains, is stomach-turning. Manipulative filmmaking at its worst—a good director and cast in the service of some utterly reprehensible ideals.

WALKING TALL PART 2 ☆½
1975, USA, PG
Bo Svenson, Luke Askew, Noah Beery, Angel Tompkins, Bruce Glover, Richard Jaeckel. Directed by Earl Bellamy. 109 min.

Sheriff Buford Pusser continues to bash moonshiners in his beloved hometown. Not as well made as its predecessor, and partly for that reason not as offensive, with much less yahoo-rousing violence; this time around, cars tend to get demolished more than people. (a.k.a.: *Part 2, Walking Tall*)

WALKING TALL: THE FINAL CHAPTER ☆½
1977, USA, R
Bo Svenson, Margaret Blye, Lurene Tuttle, Forrest Tucker, Morgan Woodward. Directed by Jack Starrett. 112 min.

Buford Pusser bites the dust in the last entry in the popular series of films about the brave sheriff who battled corruption on all sides even after his scrupulously honest attitude and bulldog hounding of fat cats resulted in his wife being bumped off by crime figures. Despite the lure of this originally being a true story, the thrill of watching the stoic upholder of law and order was definitely petering out at this point. One hopes this is it for big-screen sequels about Pusser, unless some writer concocts one about his deputy's being possessed by Buford's ghost.

A WALK IN THE SPRING RAIN ☆☆
1970, USA, PG
Ingrid Bergman, Anthony Quinn, Fritz Weaver, Katherine Crawford. Directed by Guy Green. 100 min.

More like a wade through a brook filled with soap suds. When Ingrid Bergman's absentminded professor husband has forgotten she's a woman with complex emotional needs, Anthony Quinn comes along to fulfill them. Older audiences may enjoy this tepid tale because of Bergman's radiance and Quinn's patented "earthy" presence, but that's about it.

A WALK IN THE SUN ☆☆☆
1945, USA
Dana Andrews, Richard Conte, George Tyne, John Ireland, Lloyd Bridges, Sterling Holloway. Directed by Lewis Milestone. 117 min.

It's nice to find a World War II movie made during the war that isn't crammed with propaganda. *A Walk in the Sun* is not quite as pacifist in tone as Milestone's earlier *All Quiet on the Western Front*, but it's just as carefully made and almost as moving. Robert Rossen's screenplay (faithful to Harry Brown's novel) deals with a troubled sergeant and his platoon's attempt to destroy a Nazi bridge in Salerno. Dana Andrews gives one of his best performances as the unstable commander, and he gets rugged support. Not a film classic, but dignified work from one of Hollywood's more independent directors.

WALTZ OF THE TOREADORS ☆☆☆
1962, Great Britain
Peter Sellers, Dany Robin, Margaret Leighton, John Fraser, Cyril Cusack, Prunella Scales, John Le Mesurier. Directed by John Guillermin. 104 min.

Peter Sellers gave one of his best performances in this adaptation of Jean Anouilh's stage farce about an aging general with a still-young eye for the ladies. He has been carrying on a platonic affair with one particular woman for seventeen years, always hampered by his nagging, invalid wife. Some of the later scenes, in which the general forces himself to the realization that his childish behavior has been an insufficient attempt to escape from the realities of his life, are wonderful in themselves, though they seem jarring juxtaposed with much of the broader humor of the rest of the film. The setting was changed from England to France, and the play evidently doesn't travel well.

THE WANDERERS ☆☆☆½
1979, USA, R
Ken Wahl, John Friedrich, Karen Allen, Toni Kalem, Linda Manz, Erland van Lidth de Jeude. Directed by Philip Kaufman. 113 min.

Philip Kaufman's erratic but extremely entertaining contribution to the gang-movie genre is set in the Bronx in 1963, just as the greaser era was giving way to the tumult of the 1960s. The expressionistic violence is too mannered, but in its scenes of teenage sexual initiation and tribal rites, *The Wanderers* is the equal of any youth movie ever made. All of the performers are excellent, but the elephantine Erland van Lidth de Jeude and the elfin Linda Manz are standouts. A strip-poker scene with Karen Allen and Ken Wahl may be the highlight; try not to miss the hilarious answer to the question, "What color is your nail polish?"

WANTED DEAD OR ALIVE ☆☆
1987, USA, R
Rutger Hauer, Gene Simmons, Robert Guillaume, Mel Harris, William Russ, Susan McDonald, Hugh Gillin. Directed by Gary Sherman. 104 min.

This routine action thriller is very loosely based on the 1958–61 television series about Old West bounty hunter Josh Randall (Steve McQueen). This film, set in the present, casts Rutger Hauer as Nick Randall, Josh's grandson; the family's left the West for Los Angeles, but they're still in the same line of work. Why the filmmakers bend over backward to refer to an almost-forgotten series is about as explicable as anything else in the silly plot, which has Nick tailing an Arab terrorist (ex-KISS member Gene Simmons) who's blown up a Los Angeles movie theater where *Rambo* was playing. Now that's taking film criticism to an extreme . . . or is it?

WAR AND PEACE
1956, USA/Italy ★★★
Audrey Hepburn, Henry Fonda, Mel Ferrer, Vittorio Gassman, Oscar Homolka, Herbert Lom, John Mills, Anita Ekberg. Directed by King Vidor. 208 min.

Despite the destructive miscasting of wooden Mel Ferrer and all-American Henry Fonda as the heroes of Tolstoy's mammoth novel, this spectacular film does capture some of the sprawl of the elaborate tome. What it lacks in intellectual content, it compensates for in solid Hollywood craftsmanship, especially in the epic battle scenes. And, in the inspired casting of Audrey Hepburn as the incandescent Natasha, the film creates an attractive focus, so that all human emotion isn't swept away by the carnage dished out by King Vidor. Within its own limited scope, that of the Hollywood epic, this is a rousing success, and Hepburn has defined the character of Natasha for several generations of filmgoers. It may not be a work of art, but it's more entertaining than the more prestigious Russian version of 1968.

WAR AND PEACE
1968, USSR ★★★★
Ludmila Savelyeva, Vyacheslav Tihonov, Hira Ivanov-Golovko, Irina Gubanova, Sergei Bondarchuk. Directed by Sergei Bondarchuk. 373 min. (four cassettes)

Sergei Bondarchuk's mammoth adaptation from Tolstoy (originally shown in two parts) is one of the most successful film versions ever of a literary masterpiece. With enormous amounts of Soviet government money at his disposal (rumors placed the budget at $100 million), Bondarchuk staged the Napoleonic battle sequences with great sweep and clarity. And a collection of fine performances, closely observed, gives a good account of the human story as well. Superior to both the American theatrical version and the "Masterpiece Theatre" serial, this *War and Peace* lasts for more than six hours, yet it's not a minute too long. The only drawback—and it's a big one—is the exceptionally poor English dubbing.

WAR BETWEEN THE PLANETS

See *Planet on the Prowl*

THE WAR GAME
1966, Great Britain ★★★★
Directed by Peter Watkins. 50 min.

This important, frightening short film about the most important social issue of our times was almost never seen by the public because its producers, who had already paid for it, were afraid of the reaction it would provoke! The BBC assigned staff director Peter Watkins to make a short "documentary" about the effects of a nuclear attack on present-day Britain. What he came up with was decreed "unsuitable for mass audiences" and kept off the broadcast waves, so Watkins quit the BBC and managed to get it shown theatrically (it eventually won the Academy Award for Best Documentary). Unlike *The Day After* or *Threads*, this does not offer fictional characters or a "plot," but presents, in newsreel-type footage, a picture of events just prior to, during, and after the dropping of the bomb. The effect is indescribably chilling, but thought-provoking as well. Unlike other antibomb films, this does not give the impression of settling the questions it raises, but instead leaves them frighteningly open.

WARGAMES
1983, USA, PG ★★★½
Matthew Broderick, Ally Sheedy, Dabney Coleman, John Wood, Barry Corbin. Directed by John Badham. 110 min.

This tech-age thriller about a teenage computer whiz who accidentally hooks into the Defense Department's Global Thermonuclear War program manages to be—simultaneously—fun, exciting, and terrifying. And you don't have to understand computers to appreciate the meaning of impending disaster or to understand the movie. Matthew Broderick shines in the lead, and young Ally Sheedy adds incidental romantic interest.

WAR HUNT
1962, USA ★★★
John Saxon, Robert Redford, Charles Aidman, Sydney Pollack, Gavin McLeod, Tommy Matsuda, Tom Skerritt. Directed by Denis Sanders. 81 min.

An interesting, austere drama about a Korean War soldier who can't restrain his bloodlust when the ceasefire is called (just in case you thought that Hollywood invented psycho vets only after Vietnam). John Saxon is surprisingly good as the sniper who continues to make nightly prowls behind enemy lines after the war is declared ended, with Robert Redford also good in his film debut as a rookie who discovers his obsession. A small-scale treat that manages to conjure up a quiet, spooky vision of warfare. The supporting cast includes director Sydney Pollack and "Love Boat" captain Gavin McLeod.

WARKILL
1967, USA ★★½
George Montgomery, Tom Drake, Conrad Parham, Eddie Infante, Henry Duvall. Directed by Ferde Grofe, Jr. 103 min.

An interesting if not entirely successful war drama, it tried to explore the issue of war from a neutral point of view—a difficult thing to do during the height of the Vietnam war. American guerilla colonel George Montgomery, trying to weed out small resistance groups of Japanese soldiers in the Philippines at the end of World War II, is accompanied by a reporter who had idolized his accomplishments without ever examining his methods. With enough action scenes to keep the average war-film fan happy.

WARLORDS OF ATLANTIS
1978, Great Britain ★★
Doug McClure, Peter Gilmore, Shane Rimmer, Lea Brodie, Cyd Charisse. Directed by Kevin Connor. 96 min.

The producer, director, and star of *Land That Time Forgot*, *At the Earth's Core*, and *The People That Time Forgot* reteam for another adventure, this time with an original screenplay instead of one based on an Edgar Rice Burroughs tale. As usual, Yank McClure and a team of adult and adolescent British explorers encounter a subsurface civilization, only this time they're under the surface of the sea. With a giant octopus, and Cyd Charisse, still looking good as Atsil, the leader of the Atlanteans.

WARLORDS OF THE 21ST CENTURY
1982, USA ★
Michael Beck, Annie McEnroe, James Wainwright. Directed by Harvey Cokliss. 91 min.

Another *Star Wars* rip-off with bargain-basement special effects, plot details lifted from dozens of sci-fi movies, and an air of desperation all its own. Taking a cue from *Mad Max*, some space-explorer types fight an energy shortage in the future.

THE WAR LOVER
1962, Great Britain ★★
Steve McQueen, Robert Wagner, Shirley Anne Field, Gary Cockrell, Michael Crawford, Al Waxman. Directed by Philip Leacock. 105 min.

This adaptation of John Hersey's compelling World War II novel comes across well visually but badly in its characterizations. As "Buzz" Rickson, ace fighter pilot obsessed with war and unable to develop normal relationships with women, Steve McQueen brings little more than a wild-eyed confusion to his part, and Robert Wagner and Shirley Anne Field, as his copilot and their common object of interest, aren't able to fill in that blank. The aerial battle scenes, however, are striking and exciting.

THE WARNING ★★½
1985, Italy
Martin Balsam, Giuliano Gemma, Ennio Antonelli. Directed by Damiano Damiani. 101 min.

In this detailed crime drama strewn with corruption and violence, the Italian underworld is out to destroy the police department through bribery and bloody "warnings." The plot becomes repetitious as crime upon crime puzzles the last two honest police officials, Martin Balsam and Giuliano Gemma. Interesting and intense investigation at times, but the production itself remains routine. This is an Italian film dubbed in English.

WARNING SIGN ★★
1985, USA, R
Sam Waterston, Kathleen Quinlan, Jeffrey De Munn, Richard Dysart. Directed by Hal Barwood. 99 min.

Director Hal Barwood has molded a high-tech thriller in the tradition of *The Andromeda Strain*, creating an atmosphere of up-to-the-minute suspense as a group of genetic researchers are trapped inside their laboratory with an invisible virus that turns them into psychopaths. Barwood pours on the action as a heroic sheriff and a burned-out scientist venture inside the institute and battle the murderous scientists while trying to cure them. This is a humanistic thriller that tries to warn its audience about the dangers of gene slicing, and often ends up silly; it's sort of an everyman's *China Syndrome*.

WAR OF THE WILDCATS ★★½
1943, USA
John Wayne, Albert Dekker, Martha Scott, George "Gabby" Hayes, Marjorie Rambeau, Dale Evans, Sidney Blackmer. Directed by Albert S. Rogell. 102 min.

This is a spruced-up retitling of *In Old Oklahoma*, a sturdy old Republic Western that'll deliver the goods to whoever chooses to wait for 'em. In the center ring, the Duke takes down Albert Dekker in the oil fields; on the sidelines there's the standard romantic interest, and Gabby Hayes for comic relief.

WAR OF THE WORLDS ★★★★
1953, Great Britain
Gene Barry, Anne Robinson, Les Tremayne, Henry Brandon. Directed by Byron Haskins. 85 min.

One of the most chilling and spectacular science-fiction films of all time, this is based on H. G. Wells's novel about a full-scale attack on the Earth by Martians. The froglike creatures prove to be impervious to bazookas, tanks, and atomic bombs as they level our planet. Byron Haskins cleverly builds up a steady level of suspense as the aliens blow up skyscrapers, topple the Eiffel Tower, and incinerate innocents, leading to a desperate and immediate climax as a noble scientist struggles to come up with a winning defense while the population of L.A. stampedes about him. Rarely will you see such spectacular destruction on the screen. Narration by Sir Cedric Hardwicke.

THE WARRIOR AND THE SORCERESS ★½
1984, USA, R
David Carradine, Luke Askew, Maria Socas, Anthony DeLongis, Harry Townes. Directed by John Broderick. 81 min.

This film is closer in spirit to Italian muscle-man films of the 1950s and 1960s than it is to latter-day fantasy films like *The Beastmaster* and *Conan, the Barbarian*. The action is well paced, and there is less of the usual blather about quests and birthrights and minions and such—if only it weren't so god-awful dull, this movie could be recommended on the basis of an utter lack of pretension. David Carradine makes a pretty puny hero and certainly does not resemble the figure on the cover art.

THE WARRIORS ★★★
1979, USA, R
Michael Beck, James Remar, Thomas G. Waites, Dorsey Wright, Deborah Van Valkenburgh. Directed by Walter Hill. 90 min.

Writer/director Walter Hill takes the existence of youth gangs as a jumping-off point for pure fantasy, an urban gothic kung-fu picture that's one of the snazzier action films of the 1970s. The story of the Coney Island Warriors, who fight their way across New York through the territories of a dozen rival gangs, has been set up to generate as many chases and fight scenes as possible. The balletic, bloodless combat episodes are startlingly tense and graceful, and Andrew Laszlo's grimly beautiful cinematography keeps the action seamless. When originally shown in New York, *The Warriors* was reportedly responsible for a couple of small in-theater riots that inspired the formation of the Guardian Angels.

WARRIORS OF THE WASTELAND ★
1983, Italy, R
Timothy Brent, Fred Williamson, Anna Kanakis, Venantino Venantini. Directed by Enzo G. Castellari. 87 min.

An undistinguished action flick, this is set in the future (which, to judge from this film, will resemble a flea-bitten set from a low-budget sci-fi movie). Two imperturbable heroes take a bunch of weaklings under their wings when blackguards threaten to dominate and destroy what's left of civilization.

THE WARRIOR WITHIN ★★
1976, Hong Kong
Bruce Lee, Chuck Norris, Moses Powell, Dan Inosanto, Fumio Demura, Chaka Zulu, Alex Sternberg, Tomojo Ebihara, Ron Taganashi, Chan Pui, Florendo Visitacion, Wai Hung, Shum Leung, Hui Cambrelen. Directed by Burt Rashby. 85 min.

The film does *not* examine the inner meaning of the martial arts. Instead, we get these great martial artists chatting and doing their stuff. This is fine and dandy, but less than satisfying. By and large, the actors are as inarticulate as athletes often are about their sports, and like athletes do little but reiterate generic clichés of enthusiasm.

WASN'T THAT A TIME! ★★★
1982, USA
The Weavers. Directed by Jim Brown. 91 min.

It's almost impossible to dislike this documentary portrait of the Weavers, even though the famous folk-singing quartet now seems strangely out of synch. Director Jim Brown adopts a tone as casual and meandering as his subjects: after gazing at some old news clippings, he'll wander over to interview some of the Weavers' spiritual children (Arlo Guthrie, Mary Travers) and then the Weavers themselves, a warm, sprightly crew who seem to bear nary a grudge against scoundrel time. The effect is that of a pleasant family reunion, and the triumphant Carnegie Hall concert that ends the film is very moving.

WATCHED ★½
1972, USA, R
Stacy Keach, Harris Yulin, Bridget Polk, Turid Aarstd, Valeri Parker. Directed by John Parsons. 93 min.

This remnant of the paranoid early 1970s tries to cover the same territory as Francis Coppola's excellent *The Conversation*, but fails to impress. Stacy Keach plays a government surveillance agent whose obsession with his job has already caused him to develop a split personality. Rather than give us a slow development of the character, writer/director John Parsons starts out with him already past the point of no return, so all we can do is watch his ongoing descent and try to guess at the factors that contributed to it. Low production values and poor camerawork don't help.

THE WATCHER IN THE WOODS ☆☆½
1980, Great Britain, PG
Bette Davis, Carroll Baker, David McCallum, Lynn-Holly Johnson, Kyle Richards, Ian Banner. Directed by John Hough. 83 min.

The only Walt Disney movie you're liable to find in the "Horror" section of your video store, this actually does make you jump. Too bad that the Gothic ghost story surrounding the shock cuts is a predictable wheeze. When a family inhabits a woodland mansion, their teenage daughter is haunted by visions— all the usual ghost-story garbage. The film is technically well made, but there isn't a moment in it of real invention. The version on videocassette may not be the same one you saw in the theaters: this was released in three different versions, one of which contained about fifteen extra minutes of special effects, not in this version.

WATCH ON THE RHINE ☆☆☆
1943, USA
Bette Davis, Paul Lukas, Geraldine Fitzgerald, Lucile Watson, George Coulouris, Donald Woods. Directed by Herman Shumlin. 114 min.

Critically acclaimed both on Broadway and on screen, this World War II relic gets points for good intentions and the zeal with which its message about democracy and the evils of Nazism is presented. It's a stirring soapbox drama about a European refugee couple who seek asylum in America only to discover that the Nazis are infiltrating our political system to track them down. Bette Davis is too sententious as the supportive wife of Paul Lukas, who deservedly won an Oscar as the brave mouthpiece for Lillian Hellman's vociferous sentiments about patriotism and the resilience of the human spirit. Somewhat dated, but still powerful.

WATCH OUT, CRIMSON BAT! ☆½
Japan
Yoko Matsuyama, Goro Ibuki, Asahi Kurizuka, Kiyoko Inoue, Nayumi Arai, Maya Maki, Mutsuhiro Toura, Jun Hamamura. Directed by Hirokazu Ichimura.

Oichi, the Crimon Bat (Yoko Matsuyama), a blind swordswoman, is asked by a dying man to deliver a scroll to Sukahara. The scroll contains the formula for a very high explosive. One in a series of stories concerning the Crimson Bat. The perfect female answer to Zatoichi.

WATER ☆
1986, Great Britain, PG-13
Michael Caine, Valerie Perrine, Brenda Vaccaro, Billy Connelly, Leonard Rossiter, Fulton Mackey. Directed by Dick Clement. 91 min.

This silly, often funny farce takes place on a tiny Caribbean island. An abandoned well spews forth a geyser of high-quality mineral water that attracts the attention of Texas oil companies, English paratroopers, French mercenaries, and Cuban guerrillas; eventually the island's doped-out English governor (Michael Caine) joins forces with the scruffy pair who make up the island's rebel movement to drive out the white oppressors. This is meant to be a heartwarming, politically correct satire of imperialism, but director Dick Clement throws in too much of everything, in the style of bad British sitcoms. Brenda Vaccaro (as a heavy-accented Latino slut) and Valerie Perrine (as a spacy environmentalist heiress) vie for the most embarrassing performance, but Vaccaro finally walks off with the honors; as her character might put it, "Jou want to throw op."

THE WATER BABIES ☆☆½
1978, Great Britain/Poland
James Mason, Billie Whitelaw, Bernard Cribbins, Joan Greenwood, David Tomlinson, Paul Luty. Directed by Lionel Jeffries. 93 min.

Best known as a familiar face in dozens of British comedies, Lionel Jeffries has also served behind the cameras as the director of several engaging children's films. This one is a combination of live action and animation, based on a Victorian-era children's novel. An apprentice chimney sweep circa 1850 has an adventure with some underwater creatures, all of whom embody various human stereotypes. He helps them escape from their captors and also learns a lesson about the Golden Rule. This has its dry spots, but in general adults should find it amusing.

WATERLOO BRIDGE ☆☆☆
1940, USA
Vivien Leigh, Robert Taylor, Lucile Watson, Virginia Field, Maria Ouspenskaya, C. Aubrey Smith. Directed by Mervyn LeRoy. 81 min.

This unabashedly hokey tearjerker is a far cry from the kind of work Mervyn LeRoy was doing at Warner Bros. (*I Am a Fugitive from a Chain Gang, They Won't Forget*). In the S. N. Behrman–Hans Rameau–George Froeschel adaptation of Robert E. Sherwood's play (first filmed in 1931 and later in 1956), LeRoy heightens the contrivances of the melodrama by allowing the score, lighting, and set design to overwhelm the action; it's one of the best examples of the overly lush type of four-hankie weepie in which MGM specialized. Robert Taylor is never a convincing Brit, but he gives what is for him an adequate performance, and Vivien Leigh, in her first post-Scarlett role, does wonders with the part of a ballerina who becomes a prostitute after her husband is believed dead. Without Leigh, the film would never have achieved the poignancy that it does.

THE WATER MARGIN

See *Seven Blows of the Dragon*

WATERMELON MAN ☆½
1970, USA, R
Godfrey Cambridge, Estelle Parsons, Howard Caine, D'Urville Martin. Directed by Melvin Van Peebles. 100 min.

An overbearing, bigoted insurance salesman (Godfrey Cambridge) wakes up one morning to discover that he has turned into a Negro. Cambridge tries hard in this one-joke movie, which wavers unsuccessfully between broad humor and social commentary, but despite his chameleonic capabilities, even he can't change this into a worthwhile effort.

WATERSHIP DOWN ☆☆☆
1978, Great Britain, PG
Animated: John Hurt, Richard Briers, Roy Kinnear, Denholm Elliott, Zero Mostel, Harry Andrews, Michael Hordern, Joss Ackland. Directed by Martin Rosen. 92 min.

For the most part, Martin Rosen's animated treatment of Richard Adams's best-seller works beautifully. It's the story of a handful of rabbits who escape their soon-to-be-bulldozed warren and set out for a new home, braving dogs, cats, humans, and a slew of warlike bunnies along the way. At first, the everyday world seems magical, but when our heroes begin to do bloody battle with their rabbit foes, the fantasy turns grimly to realism. Rosen has refused to "cartoonize" his bunnies; thus, they're harder to differentiate visually, although characterized with more individual depth. Rosen also wrote and directed the animated adaptation of Adams's *The Plague Dogs*.

WATUSI ☆☆
1959, USA
George Montgomery, Taina Elg, David Farrar, Rex Ingram, Dan Seymour, Robert Goodwin. Directed by Kurt Neumann. 85 min.

Supposedly a sequel to the popular 1950 version of the oft-filmed *King Solomon's Mines*, this is more like a retelling of the same basic story, with a great deal of footage from the earlier film reused here quite recognizably. Alan Quatermain's son returns to Africa to seek the same treasure sought by his father, and endures all of the usual jungle hardships—nasty natives, curmudgeonly crocs, etc. Recommended to those with a nostalgia for a past case of malaria, but to be taken only with quinine.

WAVELENGTH ☆☆☆
1983, USA, PG
Robert Carradine, Keenan Wynn, Cherie Currie. Directed by Mike Gray. 87 min.

In this extremely intelligent handling of a tired story line—from the man who wrote *The China Syndrome*—a young woman (Cherie Currie) receives telepathic cries for help from a trio of aliens imprisoned in a government research center. She then enlists the aid of her boyfriend and an old man to rescue them. Despite its low budget, the film has a lot of interesting visual touches as seen from the spacemen's point of view. The movie's conclusion was effectively ripped off in *Starman*.

THE WAY AHEAD ☆☆☆
1944, Great Britain
David Niven, Raymond Huntley, Billy Hartnell, Stanley Holloway, James Donald, John Laurie, Leslie Dwyer, Hugh Burden, Jimmy Hanley, Reginald Tate, Peter Ustinov, Renee Asherson, Mary Jerrold, A. E. Matthews. Directed by Carol Reed. 115 min.

Originally intended as a short army propaganda film (by scriptwriters Eric Ambler and Peter Ustinov), this World War II comedy about a group of very reluctant draftees manages to be both a decent comedy and a tribute to the British army. For a World War II feature, it is refreshingly free of both a conventional narrative and a love interest, and Carol Reed is up to Roberto Rossellini's standards in bringing semidocumentary realism to dramatic filmmaking.

WAY DOWN EAST ☆☆☆☆
1920, USA
Lillian Gish, Richard Barthelmess, Lowell Sherman, Mary Hay. Directed by D. W. Griffith. 113 min.

Every melodramatic situation is in place and flawlessly directed by D. W. Griffith. His visual genius once again redeems a hackneyed story, though Lillian Gish deserves a share of the credit for a wildly emotional performance. She plays an innocent country girl who is seduced by a wealthy landowner, only to be abandoned and disgraced. She has a baby and is driven from her community. When she flees across an ice field that suddenly breaks up, a classic piece of cinematic history is the result—watch this for a lesson in the buildup of suspense and action. Silent; available with a musical score.

WAY OF A GAUCHO ☆☆½
1952, USA
Rory Calhoun, Gene Tierney, Richard Boone, Hugh Marlowe, Everett Sloane, Enrique Chaico. Directed by Jacques Tourneur. 90 min.

Gene Tierney's star was in the descendant when she made this outdoor oater. The real star of the show is Rory Calhoun, who plays an arrogant gaucho gang leader who joins the militia to beat a murder rap. Gene plays the patrician beauty who joins up with the rebel under the pampas moon. The politics are liberal (Tierney gets pregnant before she is actually married and the military is not seen in a favorable light), yet this location-lensed (in Argentina) yarn is obviously Hollywood's capitalization on South America's own burgeoning cinema (*O Cangaceiros*, etc.)—it's a slapdash, disappointing effort.

WAY OF THE DRAGON
See *Return of the Dragon*

WAY OUT WEST ☆☆☆☆
1937, USA
Stan Laurel, Oliver Hardy, Sharon Lynne, James Finlayson, Rosina Lawrence, Stanley Fields, Vivien Oakland, the Avalon Boys, Chill Wills, Dinah (the Mule). Directed by James W. Horne. 64 min.

In this, one of the best Laurel and Hardy feature films, the duo is sent to Brushwood Gulch to deliver a gold-mine deed to the daughter of a late prospector. Of course, they bungle the deed into the wrong hands, and the movie's funniest moments occur as Stan tries to hoist Ollie to the second floor of the villain's saloon—one of the great extended gag sequences of the sound era. All of the sight gags are splendid, and the Western setting is a perfect backdrop for the pair's persnickety routines. Jimmy Finlayson provides his usual expert support as the duo's nemesis. The boys sing "In the Blue Ridge Mountains of Virginia" and perform a nice dance routine. Notable also as a film without a leading man.

THE WAY WEST ☆☆
1967, USA
Kirk Douglas, Robert Mitchum, Richard Widmark, Lola Albright, Jack Elam, Michael Witney, Stubby Kaye, Sally Field, Harry Carey, Elizabeth Fraser, William Lundigan, Patric Knowles, John Mitchum. Directed by Andrew V. McLaglen. 122 min.

This screen version of the Pulitzer Prize–winning novel by A. B. Guthrie, Jr., comes across like the book's greatest hits—a stream of vignettes with little plot or characterization. The story follows a wagon train of Missouri farmers headed out to Oregon under the leadership of disciplinarian Kirk Douglas and trail scout Robert Mitchum. The overabundance of subplots doesn't cover up the lack of a main plot, nor does the sporadic direction by Andrew McLaglen, who seems interested only in the action sequences.

THE WAY WE WERE ☆☆☆
1973, USA, PG
Barbra Streisand, Robert Redford, Bradford Dillman, Lois Chiles, Viveca Lindfors. Directed by Sydney Pollack. 118 min.

Barbra Streisand won an Oscar nomination and Robert Redford was certified superstar, and together their chemistry is incredible. The film encompasses three different decades in the stormy relationship of a politically active young woman and a writer. The lush Marvin Hamlisch score (in addition to his hit title tune) helps jerk the tears even more. Important plot development involving the "witch hunts" of the 1950s was cut out just before release and some gaps are evident, but *The Way We Were* remains a first-class romance.

WE ALL LOVED EACH OTHER SO MUCH ☆☆½
1976, Italy
Vittorio Gassman, Nino Manfredi, Stefano Satta Flores, Giovanni Ralli, Stefania Sandrelli, Aldo Fabrizi. Directed by Ettore Scola. 124 min.

This is Ettore Scola's version of the male-buddy movie so many directors in Europe were making back in the mid-1970s. The film is suffused with a sentimental leftism that grows wearying, but it also boasts splendid performances by Nino Manfredi, Vittorio Gassman, and Stefano Satta Flores, who play the three ex–war buddies. As in many Scola films, the good spirits generally override the sloppy structure, and there are some clever references to several movie classics along the way, including a cameo by Federico Fellini (who is mistaken for Roberto Rossellini).

A WEDDING ☆☆☆½
1978, USA, PG
Carol Burnett, Mia Farrow, Geraldine Chaplin, Vittorio Gassman, Lillian Gish, Dina Merrill, Lauren Hutton, Desi Arnaz, Jr., Pat McCormick, Paul Dooley, Pam Dawber, Nina Van Pallandt, Viveca Lindfors. Directed by Robert Altman. 125 min.

One of Robert Altman's most watchable films, *A Wedding* has the director's trademarks of multiple characters and some improvised dialogue, and works very well. The action takes place on the wedding day of a young man whose father has Mafia connections. The families meet, everyone revealing some sort of secret. The goings-on are often extremely funny. Altman is known for giving great freedom to his actors, and as usual obtains performances of high quality. Carol Burnett, as the mother of the bride who contemplates an affair with her new son-in-law's uncle (Pat McCormick) steals the movie, in one of her best performances.

WEDDING IN WHITE ☆☆☆
1972, Canada
Carol Kane, Donald Pleasence, Doris Petrie, Doug McGrath. Directed by William Fruet. 106 min.

This sad slice-of-life tale is set in World War II Canada. Proud and unbowed, a tight-knit family insists on a traditional wedding for their daughter, even though she's pregnant by her brother's best friend; and tongues are wagging in the community. Heart-wrenching drama about family ties.

THE WEDDING PARTY ☆☆½
1969, USA
Jill Clayburgh, Robert DeNiro, Charles Pfluger, Valda Satterfield, Raymond McNally, John Braswell, Judy Thomas. Directed by Brian De Palma, Wilford Leach, Cynthia Munroe. 90 min.

This zippy antimarriage comedy offered the screen debuts of Robert DeNiro and Jill Clayburgh (who both look a tad on the plump side) and the first directorial efforts of Brian De Palma and Wilford Leach (*The Pirates of Penzance*). The setting is a Long Island estate on the eve of a high-society wedding, to which the characters have come in order to sneer and giggle and throw stones through the windows of propriety. Stylistically, it's pure 1960s—a hybrid of 1920s visual gags, 1930s rapid-fire dialogue, and French New Wave spontaneity—and the film has such irresistible manic energy that it gets by with its questionable implication that marriage is an institution perpetuated and enforced by grasping women. The film was shot in part at Sarah Lawrence College, where De Palma and Cynthia Munroe were students at the time and Leach was on the faculty.

WEDNESDAY'S CHILD

See *Family Life*

WEEKEND OF SHADOWS ☆☆☆½
1978, Australia
John Waters, Melissa Jaffer, Wyn Roberts, Barbara West, Graham Rouse, Graeme Blundell. Directed by Tom Jeffrey. 94 min.

An excellent character study set against the background of a vigilante-like manhunt for a suspected murderer. The setting is rural Australia in the 1930s, and the local policeman, having been transferred to this out-of-the-way location after an unpleasant incident in his home city, is trying to curry favor with his superiors by tracking down a farmhand who is suspected of killing a rancher's wife. Along the way, though, the situation gets out of his control as the posse becomes more boisterous and inebriated.

WEEKEND PASS ☆½
1984, USA, R
D. W. Brown, Peter Ellenstein, Patrick Hauser, Chip McAllister, Pamela G. Kay, Hilary Shapiro, Graem McGavin, Daureen Collodel, Annette Sinclair, Grand L. Bush. Directed by Lawrence Bassoff. 92 min.

Four sailors who've just completed basic training take off for Los Angeles for some rowdy R & R. For a teenage sex comedy, the sex scenes are surprisingly tame, but that doesn't make the film any better than *Porky's II, Joysticks, Losin' It, Screwballs*, etc.

It's more like *On the Town* as envisioned by Randal Kleiser and Allen Carr.

WEIRD SCIENCE ☆☆
1985, USA, PG-13
Anthony Michael Hall, Kelly LeBrock, Ilan Mitchell-Smith, Bill Paxton. Directed by John Hughes. 91 min.

This may be the loudest and most completely incoherent American comedy since *Neighbors*, but it's also a film whose moments of inventive wit save it from total disaster. With their home computer, two nerds create a beautiful woman, a sex goddess who wreaks all sorts of havoc when she causes mutant bikers and a nuclear missile to materialize out of thin air. As the proceedings get wilder, director John Hughes lets the movie go completely out of control; this is one case where the special effects overwhelm everything else.

WELCOME TO BLOOD CITY ☆½
1977, Great Britain/Canada
Jack Palance, Keir Dullea, Samantha Eggar, Barry Morse, Hollis McLaren, Chris Wiggins. Directed by Peter Sasdy. 96 min.

A pretentious, murky clone of *Westworld*. Citizen Keir Dullea, in a role that emphasizes the first four letters of his last name, is shanghaied and tested by a secret organization recruiting killers for a fascist political group. He is mentally sent to an imaginary Western town called Blood City, ruled by sheriff Jack Palance, the most honored resident because he has the most murders to his credit. This attempt to fuse sci-fi and the Western produces a hybrid that is successful as neither.

WELCOME TO L.A. ☆½
1977, USA, R
Keith Carradine, Sally Kellerman, Geraldine Chaplin, Harvey Keitel, Lauren Hutton, Viveca Lindfors, Sissy Spacek, Denver Pyle, John Considine, Diahann Abbott. Directed by Alan Rudolph. 103 min.

The first film directed by Robert Altman protégé Alan Rudolph has some excellent performances and some pretty, Antonioni-style shooting, but it is so amateurish, so flimsy in conception, so poorly scripted, and so enervated that you're hard pressed to care about anything in it. Keith Carradine plays a songwriter whose arrival for some L.A. recording sessions provides the insubstantial center around which the film wobbles as it dourly explores the misconnections among a handful of numb, unlikable characters. Denver Pyle and Sissy Spacek are both fine, but Geraldine Chaplin is embarrassing in a rehash of her *Nashville* role, and Carradine's performance here as a blank sex object is so dull that it becomes unintentionally antierotic.

WE OF THE NEVER NEVER ☆☆☆
1983, Australia, PG
Angela Punch McGregor, Arthur Dignam, Tony Barry, Tommy Lewis, Lewis Fitz-Gerald, Donald Blitner, Sibina Willy. Directed by Igor Auzins. 132 min.

This is an Australian epic about the struggles of a white woman (Angela Punch McGregor) to make a place for herself and her husband (Arthur Dignam) in a particularly desolate region of the Australian outback. The film is based on the memoirs of Mrs. Aeneas Gunn and is so faithful to the spirit of the early 1900s that it occasionally feels old-fashioned and overly restrained. Still, McGregor delivers a fine performance as a woman who argues for her own rights in a world of men and for the rights of the aborigines in a world that is no longer theirs. Beautifully photographed by Gary Hansen.

WE'RE NO ANGELS ☆☆☆
1955, USA
Humphrey Bogart, Aldo Ray, Peter Ustinov, Joan Bennett, Basil Rathbone, Leo G. Carroll, Gloria Talbott. Directed by Michael Curtiz. 103 min.

In this droll comedy, Bogie, Aldo Ray, and Peter Ustinov play three prison escapees who descend upon a Paris shop intending to rob it; instead, they stick around to help the owner and his family through some Christmas difficulties. A few of the larger menaces, including Basil Rathbone as the greedy relative with a mortgage on the store, are taken care of with the aid of Ustinov's pet snake, which he keeps in a cigar box. This is based on a hit Broadway play, and it shows—the whole thing looks very stagebound. But the cast plays well together and manages to elevate this minor farce into an enjoyable, if not uproarious, time-killer.

THE WEREWOLF OF WASHINGTON ☆☆½
1973, USA, PG
Dean Stockwell, Katalin Kallcy, Michael Dunne, Thayer David. Directed by Milton Moses Ginsberg. 90 min.

This odd mixture of political satire and lycanthropy features Dean Stockwell as presidential press secretary Jack Whittier, who becomes a werewolf when the moon is full. "I knew the Pentagon was involved," he declares when gypsies try to warn him about wolfmen and the sign of the pentagram, and by the time he's put things into the right perspective, it's too late. High concept exploitation with its fair share of amusing moments. (a.k.a.: *Werewolf After Midnight*)

WEREWOLVES ON WHEELS ☆½
1971, USA, R
Stephen Oliver, Severn Darden, D. J. Anderson, Billy Gray, Barry McGuire. Directed by Michel Levesque. 85 min.

If only this were a little worse or a little better, it would be worth watching. As it is, this saga of bikers who run afoul of a Satanist cult is too competently made to provide cheap laughs, but too dumb and unfocused to be scary. The monsters are seen only very briefly. Featuring, as "Scarf," folk singer Barry McGuire, who had a big hit years earlier with "Eve of Destruction" and later became a gospel singer.

THE WESTERNER ☆☆☆½
1940, USA
Gary Cooper, Walter Brennan, Fred Stone, Doris Davenport, Forrest Tucker, Chill Wills, Dana Andrews. Directed by William Wyler. 100 min.

Seen today, William Wyler's classic Western is surprisingly mature and provocative—an anti-Western before its time. Like most of its contemporaries, the film is obsessed with explorations of manhood and courage, and the meaning of morality in a lawless world. But this is also a character study, and a bleakly comic one at that. Its presiding angel is Walter Brennan's Judge Roy Bean, a savage who dreams of grace, delicacy, and the love of Lilly Langtry. Brennan's performance won him an Oscar, and it's nicely balanced by Gary Cooper's star turn as the man who fatefully opposes him in a dispute over land rights.

WESTERN UNION ☆☆☆½
1941, USA
Robert Young, Randolph Scott, Dean Jagger, Virginia Gilmore, John Carradine, Slim Summerville, Chill Wills, Barton MacLane. Directed by Fritz Lang. 93 min.

Spectacularly staged and gorgeously photographed (in technicolor), this epic is about the stringing of the first telegraph cable between Omaha and Salt Lake City in 1861. Dean Jagger is Western Union's surveyor, and his life is saved by Randolph Scott, an outlaw who goes straight and works as a scout for the expedition. Trouble besets the westward-moving wagon train in the form of renegades (led by Barton MacLane) who rustle cattle and steal horses, eventually leading to a showdown between MacLane and Scott. Virginia Gilmore is the unintrusive love interest, Robert Young is an Eastern dude, and Slim Summerville is the crusty, comical camp cook. Fritz Lang tells a straight, tense, lusty story with an almost naive enthusiasm, and the film's large budget pays off in the unsurpassed Utah scenery that's present in abundance. The screenplay is by Robert Carson, based on a story by Zane Grey.

WEST OF THE DIVIDE ☆½
1934, USA
John Wayne, Virginia Brown Faire, Yakima Canutt, George "Gabby" Hayes. Directed by Robert N. Bradbury. 52 min.

The string of B Westerns that the Duke made for Monogram Pictures in the thirties are virtually all now in video; this one's half a notch better than the average. Wayne is a cowboy who tries to find his parents' killers and manages to save a girl in the process.

WEST SIDE STORY ☆☆☆☆
1961, USA
Natalie Wood, Richard Beymer, George Chakiris, Rita Moreno, Russ Tamblyn, Tucker Smith, David Winters, Tony Mordente, Simon Oakland. Directed by Robert Wise, Jerome Robbins. 151 min.

Ten Academy Awards, including Best Picture and Best Director, went to this dazzling, kinetic musical that will make you want to snap your fingers, leap over a chain-link fence, and sing in the street. Natalie Wood and Richard Beymer star as Maria and Tony, the star-crossed lovers whose future is threatened by the violence and prejudice of their families and friends; but supporting cast members George Chakiris, Russ Tamblyn, and Rita Morena provide most of the film's energy. This 1950s street-gang tribute to *Romeo and Juliet* combines innovative choreography by Jerome Robbins, music by Leonard Bernstein, and lyrics by Stephen Sondheim all so consistently marvelous that it's almost impossible to choose a favorite number. But some of the contenders are "America," "Maria," and "Tonight."

WESTWORLD ☆☆☆
1973, USA, R
Yul Brynner, Richard Benjamin, James Brolin. Directed by Michael Crichton. 88 min.

Imagine a Disneyland taken to the extreme: customers pay one thousand dollars a day to indulge in their wildest fantasies. Two friends choose the area with the Western theme where battles, horse chases, etc., are played out by robots. Soon enough, things begin to go wrong. Yul Brynner makes a believable villain in a far cry from his patented "King" role. Richard Benjamin and James Brolin are less successful, but this imaginative, well-paced thriller is still diverting fun from the masterful Michael Crichton.

WETHERBY ☆☆☆½
1985, Great Britain, R
Vanessa Redgrave, Ian Holm, Judi Dench, Susanna Hamilton, Tim McInnerney, Joely Richardson. Directed by David Hare. 102 min.

Playwright David Hare has created a difficult, adult psychological suspense drama that's perfectly suited to the medium of film, and as good as anything he's written for the stage. *Wetherby* begins in the English suburb of its title, where lonely schoolteacher Jean Travers has a casual dinner party for a few friends. Among the guests is an odd, intense young man who returns the next day, tells Jean that he wasn't the "friend of a friend" he claimed to be, and then blows his head off in front of her. The investigation of this seemingly random act of violence structures the film, which takes place in three rapidly alternating time periods. It's deliberately slow-moving and obscure about its meaning, but its cryptic, elliptical quality helps bring it to a shattering climax. The performances are superb, with Vanessa Redgrave matching the finest work she's done on film, and with her daughter, Joely Richardson, who plays her as a younger woman, a remarkable find. Hare, directing his first film, shows startling finesse, and his dialogue—ironic, spare, witty, and intelligent—crackles across the screen with an impact and insight reminiscent of Harold Pinter's best work.

WE WERE ONE MAN ★★½
1980, France
Serge Avedikian, Piotr Stanislaus, Catherine Albin. Directed by Philippe Vallois. 90 min.

In this ludicrous art film, director/producer/scenarist/editor Philippe Vallois tackles all those great Art themes—individualism, existentialism, homosexuality, and World War II. A wounded German soldier is sheltered by a mentally deficient French boy. Both are cut off from the societies in which they function, and their differences give way to bonds, culminating in an explicit love scene. Mostly confusing and pretentious, although when Vallois confines himself to delineating of character he attains some nice moments. (a.k.a.: *Nous Etions un Seul Homme*)

WHAT DO YOU SAY TO A NAKED LADY? ★★
1970, USA
Directed by Allen Funt. 90 min.

A sleazy pasteup documentary in which Allen "Candid Camera" Funt tries for a stag party ambience, as he trains his Peeping Tom cameras on unsuspecting passers-by who are caught reacting to an unclothed lovely in their midst. It's a slim premise and scanty amusement. Imagine if another clean-cut TV institution like Lawrence Welk had decided to film his champagne-music cast performing scenes from "Oh, Calcutta!" and you'll have some idea of how cheap and dispiriting this movie is. What do you say to a gimmick-conscious director-producer who's run out of ideas?

WHAT EVER HAPPENED TO AUNT ALICE? ★★★
1969, USA
Geraldine Page, Ruth Gordon, Rosemary Forsyth, Mildred Dunnock. Directed by Lee H. Katzin. 101 min.

Not a sequel to *Baby Jane*, but merely in the same vein, *What Ever Happened to Aunt Alice?* has that memorable film's director, Robert Aldrich, as its producer. Geraldine Page, at least as batty as Bette Davis, is a woman who hires lonely old ladies to be her companions. She takes their life savings, promises to invest for them, and then promptly bumps them off. Ruth Gordon is fun, as usual, as one feisty old woman who isn't so easy to get rid of. She and Page make the film seem more interesting than it really is.

WHAT EVER HAPPENED TO BABY JANE? ★★★
1962, USA
Bette Davis, Joan Crawford, Victor Buono, Anna Lee, Maidie Norman. Directed by Robert Aldrich. 132 min.

Bette Davis and Joan Crawford pull out all the stops in this wonderfully lurid, scary tale of two former screen greats going berserk. "Baby Jane" Hudson (Davis), a child star who's become a deranged old alcoholic, lives with her sister Blanche, a bigger star, who's been confined to a wheelchair since a mysterious auto accident. When Blanche decides to institutionalize Jane, her sister plots a wild revenge that includes tying her up and feeding her rats . . . well, you get the idea. Looking like an elephantine rag doll, Davis gives a great, noisy, funny, sad performance, and half the fun of this campy movie is watching the immobilized Crawford strain to outact her. Of all of the 1960s films in which aging female stars get to play evil gargoyles, *Baby Jane* is the one to see.

WHAT PRICE GLORY? ★★½
1952, USA
James Cagney, Corinne Calvet, Dan Dailey, William Demarest, Craig Hill, Robert Wagner, Marisa Pavan, James Gleason. Directed by John Ford. 110 min.

One of John Ford's lesser known works was this remake of Raoul Walsh's 1926 silent classic (from the play by Maxwell Anderson). Sound, color, songs, and a considerable dose of humor have been added to the original, but it's still the same old story about two friends fighting over a French beauty during World War I. James Cagney and Dan Dailey hog most of the footage in what amounts to a male buddy-buddy movie before that type of film was in vogue. Cagney's professionalism, however, saves it from being just another movie.

WHAT'S NEW PUSSYCAT? ★★★
1965, USA
Peter Sellers, Peter O'Toole, Romy Schneider, Capucine, Paula Prentiss, Woody Allen, Ursula Andress, Louise Lasser. Directed by Clive Donner. 106 min.

Woody Allen's first effort as a screenwriter shows the same pluses and minuses as some of the early films he directed—continual gags, some of which work and many of which don't, though they come so fast that you don't have time to stop and count. He has a supporting role as an undresser for strippers, but the brunt of the goings-on are borne by Peter O'Toole and Peter Sellers, the former as a fashion editor who has to fight women off and the latter as his sex-starved Viennese analyst. The best scene is the beginning, with Sellers and his wife having a fight that extends thoughout their entire house. The two Peters settled the question of who would get top billing by flipping a coin.

WHAT'S UP DOC? ★★★
1972, USA, G
Barbra Sreisand, Ryan O'Neal, Kenneth Mars, Michael Murphy, Madeline Kahn, John Hillerman, Randy Quaid, Mabel Albertson. Directed by Peter Bogdanovich. 94 min.

Peter Bogdanovich's homage to screwball comedies of the 1930s is a hit-or-miss affair, but it generally maintains an air of merriment. Barbra Streisand, who sings twice, plays an eccentric who disrupts the lives of a square professor (Ryan O'Neal) and his equally uptight fiancée (Madeline Kahn) while attending a convention at a posh San Francisco hotel. Bogdanovich keeps things moving, and the cast is bright and funny. Unfortunately, the director also pushes too hard to get laughs, relying too heavily on his original sources for inspiration. Screwball fans will not be disappointed, but a screening of *Bringing up Baby* is preferable to this imitation.

WHAT'S UP, TIGER LILY? ★★★
1966, USA
Tatsuya Mihashi, Miya Hana, Eiko Wakabayashi (original); Woody Allen, The Lovin' Spoonful (new footage); voice of Louise Lasser. Reedited by Woody Allen. 80 min.

A minor masterpiece. Before he'd ever peeked through a camera lens, Woody Allen took a cheesy Japanese spy thriller, removed the soundtrack, and dubbed in his own demented dialogue. The result? An often sidesplitting comedy that's the last word in laughs that come from the mismatching of sound and image. Follow the adventures of "Phil Moskowitz, lovable rogue" as he does battle with the evil Wing Fat and searches for the world's most coveted recipe for egg salad. Best line: "You'd never guess I have no pants on." Allen worked with six other writers on the new script.

WHEN A STRANGER CALLS ★★½
1979, USA, R
Carol Kane, Charles Durning, Colleen Dewhurst, Ron O'Neal. Directed by Fred Walton. 97 min.

A baby-sitter is terrorized by a persistent caller who asks with malicious glee whether she has checked the children; her increasingly frantic calls to the police finally produce the dreadful recognition that the calls originate from somewhere within the house. But wait: that's not the end. Years later, the psychotic child killer escapes from a lunatic asylum. He is pursued by a dedicated policeman and nearly undone by his uneasy relationship with an aging barfly, but eventually eludes capture and returns to the scene of his original crime to again torment the baby-sitter, now grown and with children of her own. The first third of *When a Stranger Calls* is an exceptionally well-crafted exercise in suspense; the second third a competent pursuit thriller that generates considerable sympathy for the twitchy psychopath; and the last third a funhouse ride of mechanical shocks.

WHEN'S YOUR BIRTHDAY ☆☆
1937, USA
Joe E. Brown, Marian Marsh, Edgar Kennedy, Margaret Hamilton, Maude Eburne, Granville Bates. Directed by Harry Beaumont. 77 min.

Remember Joe E. Brown? If not, best move on, because this Brown vehicle won't make much of an introduction, although old fans may feel a nostalgic twinge. He plays a boxer who plans his career with astrology—he only wins when the stars are in the proper order. A good supporting cast, including slow-burning Edgar Kennedy, keeps things from bogging down.

WHEN TAE KWON DO STRIKES ☆
1981
Angela Mao-Ying, Jhoon Rhee, Carter Huang, Whong In-Sik. Directed by Huang Feng. 95 min.

This is a no-action tale of dumb resistance fighters in dreary Japanese-occupied Korea. However, it does feature the talents of pretty Angela Mao-Ying, the first major female kung fu star.

WHEN THE LEGENDS DIE ☆☆☆
1972, USA, PG
Richard Widmark, Frederic Forrest, Luana Anders, Vito Scotti, Herbert Nelson, John War Eagle. Directed by Stuart Millar. 105 min.

This small film works much better on television than it did in theaters, where it was generally ignored on its initial release. An Indian boy, eager to experience life beyond the confines of his reservation, goes on the rodeo circuit with a hard-drinking manager. Frederic Forrest, in his debut, is good enough as the boy to overcome objections of miscasting, though it is Richard Widmark who captures the show as the cynical has-been. Some excellent rodeo photography.

WHEN THE NORTH WIND BLOWS ☆☆½
1974, USA, G
Henry Brandon, Herbert Nelson, Dan Haggerty. Directed by Stuart Raffill. 113 min.

After two rare Siberian tigers attack near the outskirts of a small Alaskan town in the early 1900s, a group of youths, accompanied by an old trapper, set out to hunt the animals down. When one boy approaches one of the tigers and is attacked, the trapper accidentally wounds the boy while attempting to save his life. Misunderstood and falsely accused, the trapper flees into the wilderness, where he befriends a family of the tigers, caring for the whelps after their mother is slain by another hunter. Pleasant family fare.

WHEN TIME RAN OUT ☆
1980, USA, PG
Paul Newman, Jacqueline Bisset, William Holden, James Franciscus, Edward Albert, Red Buttons, Ernest Borgnine, Burgess Meredith, Valentina Cortese, Alex Karras, Barbara Carrera. Directed by James Goldstone. 121 min.

Irwin Allen hauls out all his favorite clichés for this intermittently funny disaster movie about a volcano tearing apart a resort island. Paul Newman and Jacqueline Bisset are the good couple who lead the nice people to safety, while James Franciscus and Barbara Carrera pay for their greed and lust by staying behind at the doomed hotel with a whole lot of rich tourists who keep pointing at the sky and groaning. You expect the movie to climax in a volcanic explosion, but instead there's one of those interminable will-they-get-across-the-rickety-bridge sequences. The version on video is that of the original theatrical release, not the later version shown on network television.

WHEN WOMEN HAD TAILS ☆½
1970, Italy, R
Senta Berger, Giuliano Gemma, Lando Buzzanca, Frank Wolff. Directed by Pasquale Festa Campanile. 110 min.

In this slapstick sex comedy in the *Caveman/Cavegirl* vein, prehistoric man's interest in the opposite sex occurs somewhere between the discovery of fire and the invention of the wheel. The film is made with skill, if not style, and Lina Wertmuller was among the many who contributed to the screenplay. Still, even if we accept horniness as an integral part of the dawn of man, we'll take Raquel Welch in *One Million Years B.C.* over Senta Berger's object of desire here, thank you.

WHEN WORLDS COLLIDE ☆☆½
1951, USA
Richard Derr, Barbara Rush, Peter Hanson, John Hoyt, Larry Keating. Directed by Rudolph Mate. 81 min.

Pioneering special-effects work by Gordon Jennings and Harry Barndollar is the highlight of this adaptation of the Edwin Balmer/Philip Wylie sci-fi novel. The dialogue of this cast of unknowns is implausible to the point of amusement, but the tale is engaging enough in spite of the writing. An astronomer announces that in one year a star will crash into Earth and destroy it. The only hope is to escape to a planet of that star and begin civilization over again. A spaceship is constructed, launched, and successfully landed on the lifeboat planet, Zayra. None of this is accomplished without the almost insuperable snafus that you'd expect, and there is no lack of suspense, melodrama, even romance. In Tehnicolor.

WHERE EAGLES DARE ☆☆☆
1969, Great Britain, PG
Richard Burton, Clint Eastwood, Mary Ure, Michael Hordern, Patrick Wymark, Robert Beatty, Anton Diffring. Directed by Brian G. Hutton. 158 min.

This elaborate wartime action thriller has enough intrigue, complexity, and hair's-breadth escapes to satisfy the most demanding fan, although at nearly three hours you may lose interest long before the labyrinthine plot turns reach their conclusion. Richard Burton plays the head of an Allied commando force that parachutes into Bavaria to rescue a kidnapped officer from a Nazi fortress; however, nobody in Alistair Maclean's plot is quite what he seems—look for double agents, triple agents, and a lot of confusion.

WHERE'S POPPA? ☆☆☆
1970, USA, R
George Segal, Ruth Gordon, Trish Van Devere, Ron Leibman, Vincent Gardenia, Rob Reiner, Barnard Hughes, Paul Sorvino. Directed by Carl Reiner. 82 min.

This notorious black comedy still has enough kick to shock and offend. Robert Klane's screenplay, based on his own novel, tells of how an overburdened son (George Segal) desperately tries to put his lunatic mother (Ruth Gordon) in an old age home. He is assisted, poorly, by his girlfriend (Trish Van Devere) and brother (Ron Liebman). Carl Reiner's direction is obvious and coarse, but it suits the material at hand and the cast's overplaying is equally appropriate. The biggest laugh (and the biggest offense) generates from a scene involving the brother's participation in a rape. It's that kind of film, but there are a few gentle moments, a sweet ending, and a tongue-in-cheek tone to balance the hysteria.

WHERE THE BOYS ARE ☆☆½
1960, USA
Dolores Hart, George Hamilton, Yvette Mimieux, Jim Hutton, Barbara Nichols, Paula Prentiss, Connie Francis, Frank Gorshin, Chill Wills. Directed by Henry Levin. 99 min.

Spring break, Fort Lauderdale. A group of girls sort out their feelings toward boys while revelry and abandon whirl around them. Less a beach-party romp than a pre-feminist encounter session, the movie is entertaining and not terribly dated in its concerns. Most of the comedy comes courtesy of Barbara Nichols, and, especially, Jim Hutton, who achieves amazing charm with stupendous ease. This was Connie Francis's first film. Remade in 1984.

WHERE THE BOYS ARE '84   ½☆
1984, USA, R
Lisa Hartman, Russell Todd, Lorna Luft, Lynn-Holly Johnson. Directed by Hy Averback. 93 min.

Four college girls head for Fort Lauderdale for a spring break full of sun, fun, and carefree sex; things don't work out exactly the way they had planned. This is a tepid and tasteless remake of the 1960 film starring Connie Francis, spiced up with smarmy sex jokes and teasing nudity. Produced by the consummately tacky Alan Carr, also responsible for the likes of *Grease* and *Can't Stop the Music*, starring the flash-in-the-pan Village People.

WHERE THE BUFFALO ROAM   ☆☆☆
1980, USA, R
Bill Murray, Peter Boyle, Bruno Kirby, Rene Auberjonois. Directed by Art Linson. 100 min.

Anyone who thinks that Bill Murray is a one-performance actor has to see his quirky, mumbled characterization of psychotic journalist Hunter S. Thompson. The loose-jointed script follows the gonzo writer on a long strange trip, continually interrupted by his pal Lazlo (Peter Boyle), while Thompson attempts to cover everything from the Superbowl to Nixon's reelection campaign. The film hits and misses, but offers many penetrating, off-the-wall observations about a weird period of American history. The film's slapdash manner and crazy point of view make it the perfect late-night video view.

WHERE THE GREEN ANTS DREAM   ☆☆☆
1984, West Germany, R
Bruce Spence, Wandjuk Marika, Roy Marika, Ray Barrett. Directed by Werner Herzog. 100 min.

Returning to his favorite theme, the defeat of civilized western types by the power of nature, Werner Herzog transports us to the pounding heat of the south Australian drylands, where a mining company is stripping the landscape in search of uranium. Two aborigine elders try to stop the bulldozers from leveling their sacred grounds; a young geologist, caught between his bosses' demands and the aborigines' determination, succumbs to the hypnotic power of the land and its religion. As drama this is predictable stuff, and some courtroom scenes fall flat; but Herzog's lively, eccentric cast often saves him, and the film succeeds as an agglomeration of wonderful images.

WHERE THE HOT WIND BLOWS   ☆☆
1958, France/Italy
Gina Lollobrigida, Yves Montand, Pierre Brasseur, Marcello Mastroianni, Melina Mercouri. Directed by Jules Dassin. 120 min.

A fairly clumsy sex comedy about the randy residents of a small Italian village, with sex kitten Gina Lollobrigida camping it up as the town siren and Yves Montand suave and rumpled as a local *capo*. The story is utterly inane, but Jules Dassin's deft touch and the good cast give it a number of breezy moments.

WHERE THE RED FERN GROWS   ☆☆
1974, USA, G
James Whitmore, Beverly Garland, Jack Ging, Lonny Chapman, Stewart Petersen. Directed by Norman Tokar. 97 min.

Sleepy, derivative family fare about a close-knit, dirt-poor clan in the Ozarks circa 1930, with problems more than a little reminiscent of those faced by the Waltons. Nothing silly or offensive here, but certainly nothing of insight either. Of interest to those who like their children's entertainment served up with a healthy amount of hayseeds and homilies.

WHERE TIME BEGAN   ☆½
1978, Spain, G
Kenneth More, Pep Munne, Jack Taylor. Directed by Piquer Simon. 86 min.

A retelling of Jules Verne's loftily imaginative *Journey to the Center of the Earth* requires more substantial resources than are packed along on this rock-bottom expedition undertaken in Spain. The anemic prehistoric beasts are beyond their depths, and droll British comic Kenneth More's career reaches a precipitous decline with this no-cigar. Try the entertaining 1959 movie version instead if you cannot find the novel.

WHICH WAY IS UP?   ☆☆½
1977, USA, R
Richard Pryor, Lonette McKee, Margaret Avery, Dolph Sweet, Morgan Woodward. Directed by Michael Schultz. 94 min.

The Seduction of Mimi was one of Lina Wertmuller's best films; Michael Schultz's accurate but empty remake of it is his own worst. Why did Schultz want to do this movie if he didn't understand Wertmuller's original? The earlier film had a point, but this doesn't. Nowhere in *Which Way* do we find any enunciation of *Mimi*'s central irony: that it's hero is willing to defend his sexual honor, his manhood, to the point of absurdity, but is unwilling even to try to become an honorable man politically. Schultz's attempt to make a "laff riot" of Wertmuller's wry fable is like trying to make Mort Sahl perform slapstick. The result is an awkward, predictable, painfully unfunny travesty. Richard Pryor has three roles here, and he seems wasted in all of them.

WHICH WAY TO THE FRONT?   ☆☆☆½
1970, USA, G
Jerry Lewis, Jan Murray, John Wood, Steve Franklin, Dack Rambo. Directed by Jerry Lewis. 98 min.

Cynics sneered that this film would finish off the career of Jerry Lewis (it was his last completed film until *Hardly Working*, 1981), but not only had Lewis successfully come back, a reassessment of this war comedy proves that this is one auteur that got away. Lewis craftily subverts the queasy premise of Gerald Gardner and Dee Caruso's screenplay about a 4-F billionaire who bribes his servants into sailing to Italy during World War II and capturing a Nazi commander (whom he then impersonates). Themes touched upon in previous Lewis films are fully explored here: neurosis, rejection, class struggle, etc. In addition, Lewis creates a sensitive and pointed subtext about the evils of U.S. intervention in Vietnam. If all this weren't enough, Lewis's comic timing and filmmaking technique are at their zenith. Witness him impersonating the Nazi general or ordering his servants to wear the latest guerrilla attire (orange jump suits) and you'll see comedy at its best.

WHIFFS   ☆
1975, USA, PG
Elliott Gould, Eddie Albert, Harry Guardino, Godfrey Cambridge, Jennifer O'Neill. Directed by Ted Post. 101 min.

Malodorous comedy with chemical warfare as a premise—lots of laughs there, all right! Elliott Gould was once involved in testing top-secret poisonous gas (though nothing he tried could be as noxious as this film); now he uses the vapors to commit bank holdups. A stinkbomb.

WHILE THE CITY SLEEPS   ☆☆☆
1956, USA
Rhonda Fleming, Dana Andrews, George Sanders, John Drew Barrymore, Thomas Mitchell. Directed by Fritz Lang. 100 min.

A latter-day *film noir* in which Fritz Lang captures the city's underbelly as no other director could. The police are in hot pursuit of a crazed sex killer; the twist is that a newspaper offers the job of city editor to whomever gets a lead on the sex fiend's whereabouts. The idea of bestowing a job as a reward for nabbing a killer functions as a cynical reworking of the bounty-hunter motif from old Westerns. Here the director deals with the lawlessness of modern cities in a thriller that's quite critical of the news media.

WHISKY GALORE

See *Tight Little Island*

WHISPERING DEATH

See *Albino*

WHISTLE DOWN THE WIND ☆☆☆☆
1961, Great Britain
Alan Bates, Hayley Mills, Bernard Lee, Norman Bird, Elsie Wagstaffe. Directed by Bryan Forbes. 99 min.

An exemplary allegory is adapted from a novel by Mary Hayley Bell, whose daughter Hayley Mills stars. Three English kids discover a fugitive in their barn and labor under the delusion that he is Jesus Christ. Alan Bates is perfect as the desperate convict who enters into an uncertain relationship with the children, and the entire enterprise retains its air of innocence without ever succumbing to sentimentality. A gently expressive, masterful film.

WHISTLE STOP ☆☆
1946, USA
George Raft, Ava Gardner, Victor McLaglen, Tom Conway, Florence Bates, Charles Drake. Directed by Leonide Moguy. 84 min.

A failed melodrama that attempts to create a *noir* atmosphere and still have a happy ending. Ava Gardner plays a woman who returns to her small hometown of Ashbury to resume a romance with the shiftless heel (George Raft) whom she left a few years earlier. He and his doltish bartender friend (Victor McLaglen) run afoul of the town tough guy (Tom Conway), who frames them for a murder. None of the characters engenders any sympathy, and the happy ending leaves the viewer cold—they might as well have all gone to prison, for all you'll care.

THE WHITE BUFFALO ☆
1977, USA, PG
Charles Bronson, Jack Warden, Will Sampson, Kim Novak, Clint Walker, Stuart Whitman, Slim Pickens, John Carradine. Directed by J. Lee Thompson. 97 min.

Dino De Laurentiis's abominable-animal movie has a ludicrous plot, ridiculous characters (Charles Bronson as Wild Bill Hickok and Will Sampson, very awkward, as Crazy Horse), and astounding dialogue. Seen only in bits and pieces, the big albino bison Hickok and Crazy Horse are stalking looks for all the world like a fleecy, cuddly carousel animal, rocking through the snowy Black Hills while the soundtrack emits seismic rumbles. Writer Richard Sale and director J. Lee Thompson want their movie to be profound (like *Moby Dick*, of course), but, fortunately, most of the philosophical claptrap is lost amid the foggy photography, arbitrary plotting, and Cuisinart editing. A white elephant.

WHITE CHRISTMAS ☆☆☆
1954, USA
Bing Crosby, Danny Kaye, Rosemary Clooney, Vera-Ellen, Dean Jagger, Mary Wickes, John Brascia, Anne Whitfield, Sig Rumann, Grady Sutton, George Chakiris. Directed by Michael Curtiz. 120 min.

It's no classic, but Irving Berlin's hardy perennial has, as one character puts it, "plenty of schmaltz and lots of heart," enough to have pleased generations of audiences. The plot is thin: Bing Crosby and Danny Kaye (who stepped in for Donald O'Connor) play Army buddies who become a successful show-biz team after the war, eventually putting on a gala variety show to save their old general's Vermont inn from failure. Rosemary Clooney and Vera-Ellen are the sister act around to provide romantic complications. The performances range from adequate to good, but the real stars are Berlin's tunes, including "Sisters," "The Best Things Happen While You're Dancing," "Love, You Didn't Do Right By Me" (with nineteen-year-old George Chakiris as a chorus boy) and, of course, the title song. The hokey finale is a bit much; the rest is a treat.

THE WHITE DAWN ☆☆☆
1974, USA, R
Warren Oates, Timothy Bottoms, Louis Gossett, Jr., Simonie Kopapik, Joanasie Salomonie, Pilitak, Sagiaktok, Akshooyooliak. Directed by Philip Kaufman. 110 min.

This terrific early film from director Philip Kaufman (*Invasion of the Body Snatchers*, *The Right Stuff*) is about three nineteenth-century whalers who get lost in the Arctic and are rescued by Eskimos. Like *Never Cry Wolf*, the film plunges you into the heart of an imposing wilderness culture, only here a curious tug-of-war develops between the civilized men and their saviors: the Eskimos (portrayed by real natives of the Arctic) teach the whalers how to survive, but the Americans end up exploiting them.

WHITE HEAT ☆☆☆☆
1949, USA
James Cagney, Virginia Mayo, Edmond O'Brien, Margaret Wycherly. Directed by Raoul Walsh. 144 min.

Eighteen years after *Public Enemy*, *White Heat* marked James Cagney's triumphant return to the gangster fold. As Cody Jarrett, a psychotic criminal ruled only by his mother and his whim, he gave one of his nerviest, most entertaining performances. Cody runs his gang with an iron hand, but his leadership is subject to odd fits of paranoia and confusion. During a brief jail stay, he goes over the edge for good, and all hell breaks loose when he's sprung. Cagney makes Cody one of the great movie psychos, and director Raoul Walsh keeps the action hurtling at breakneck speed toward the explosive finale.

WHITE LIGHTNING ☆☆☆
1973, USA, PG
Burt Reynolds, Jennifer Billingsley, Ned Beatty, Bo Hopkins, Matt Clark, Louise Latham, R. G. Armstrong, Diane Ladd. Directed by Joseph Sargent. 101 min.

Burt Reynolds's first "good-ol'-boy" role has less silly humor than the ones that followed, with a better balance of action and tomfoolery. Moonshiner Gator McKlusky is released from prison in order to help gather evidence to convict the local sheriff, who had McKlusky's brother killed. All of the usual fisticuffs and car chases are present, but they're properly spaced so that the movie doesn't suffer from overkill. Reynolds directed the sequel, *Gator*.

WHITE LINE FEVER ☆☆☆
1975, USA, PG
Jan-Michael Vincent, Kay Lenz, Slim Pickens, L. Q. Jones, Don Porter, Sam Laws, Johnny Ray McGhee, Leigh French. Directed by Jonathan Kaplan. 89 min.

A well-respected B picture by Jonathan Kaplan. Jan-Michael Vincent is the independent trucker who refuses to carry contraband and suffers reprisals from a corrupt union in league with the Mob. It's the *Serpico* of trucking movies, and despite a surfeit of action, the film actually says something important about independent versus organized structures and is convincingly played by Vincent and Kay Lenz as the rebellious driver and his pregnant wife. Not as juicy as the old *They Drive by Night*, but more timely and pertinent.

WHITE MAMA ★★★
1980, USA (TV)
Bette Davis, Ernest Harden, Jr., Eileen Heckart. Directed by Jackie Cooper. 104 min.

Although the subject matter's a bit improbable, with Bette Davis playing a *nouveau* bag lady, the star rises above the contrivances of the script with an exceptionally good performance, one of her best TV efforts. In addition to suffering the horrors of being bounced onto the pavement, Davis has to take in a belligerent black street tough as a boarder. As the two get to know each other, the boy discovers that she cares for him, and she learns that he can fill the emotional void left by her husband's death. They comprise an unusual sort of family, which is precisely the point of this strong statement of interracial and intergenerational compatibility.

WHITE NIGHTS ★★★
1985, USA, PG-13
Mikhail Baryshnikov, Gregory Hines, Geraldine Page, Jerzy Skolimowski, Isabella Rossellini, Helen Mirren. Directed by Taylor Hackford. 135 min.

In this extremely entertaining thriller, two dancers, one a Russian defector and the other a black American expatriate, find themselves thrown together in Siberia and must overcome their differences and try to escape. The plot smacks of Cold-War paranoia and strains credibility at times, but Baryshnikov's powerful presence energizes the film remarkably—his dancing is spellbinding and unusually well shot, and his acting evinces the romantic reserve of a born star. Director Taylor Hackford elicits excellent performances from Gregory Hines and the supporting cast, and keeps the action moving in interesting, slightly off-center ways. Even if you object to the "godless Commies" tone that *White Nights* finally takes, its heavy-handed politics are completely overridden by the slickly exciting craftsmanship that has gone into it.

THE WHITE ROSE ★★
1982, West Germany
Lena Stolze, Wolf Kessler. Directed by Michael Verhoever. 108 min.

Set in Munich in the early 1940s, this gray, rather sluggish German melodrama tells the true story of five university students who distributed a series of eloquent, anti-Nazi flyers. Unfortunately, the movie's glossy, conventional style leaves us ignorant of the motives of its young characters.

THE WHITE TOWER ★★★
1950, USA
Glenn Ford, Claude Rains, Alida Valli, Oscar Homolka, Cedric Hardwicke. Directed by Ted Tetzlaff. 98 min.

An old-fashioned but quite effective melodrama about a group of climbers attempting to scale a treacherous peak of the Alps—a mountain that's defeated other intrepid risk-takers—and also solve their own problems in the process. Compare this taut, compressed drama with the kind of overblown treatment the same story would recieve as a TV movie, and you'll understand why this works so splendidly; the characters are carefully delineated, so we can share in the adventure and not just view the mindless action.

WHITE ZOMBIE ★★★
1932, USA
Bela Lugosi, Madge Bellamy, John Harron, Joseph Cawthorne. Directed by Victor Halperin. 75 min.

An eerie, unique horror movie set in Tahiti has a young couple newly arrived from New York meeting satanic-looking Bela Lugosi, the master of an army of zombies, corpses reanimated by witchcraft to work the sugar mills. The film is fluidly cinematic, filled with lengthy wordless sequences and supported by an effective musical score. Better than anything else, *White Zombie* generates its own ambience, and this aspect has been enhanced by the passing of time.

WHODUNIT ½★
1982, USA
Terry Goodman, Ron Gardner, Gary Phillips, Rick Dean, Steven Tash, Bari Suter. Directed by Bill Naud. 82 min.

A group of amateur actors about to appear in a low-budget film are stranded on a remote island; one by one, they are murdered in grisly ways, with their doom foretold by a Walkman dangling in the air. Inept horror exploitation made by people who have no business being filmmakers, with some attempts at mocking the ineptitude of the filmmaker characters that, in context, are rather pathetic.

WHO HAS SEEN THE WIND ★★½
1977, Canada
Brian Painchaud, Douglas Janor, Gordon Pinsent, Jose Ferrer, David Gardner, Patricia Hamilton, Helen Shaver. Directed by Allan King. 100 min.

This film is based on a classic Canadian children's novel, something like Tom Sawyer in Depression-era Saskatchewan. The episodic screenplay follows the growth of a young boy and his closest companions, his father, and his various pets. Along the way are incidents involving such characters as the town spinster (Patricia Hamilton) and the local drunk (Jose Ferrer, giving a much livelier performance than usual). Unfortunately, this looks more like a Cliff Notes version of the book, without any real life of its own, and is most successful as an illustrated reminder if you've read the novel.

WHO IS KILLING THE GREAT CHEFS OF EUROPE? ★★½
1978, USA, PG
George Segal, Jacqueline Bisset, Robert Morley, Jean-Pierre Cassel, Philippe Noiret. Directed by Ted Kotcheff. 112 min.

While the other actors in this farcical mystery are frantically outgesticulating one another to get laughs, Robert Morley steals the show just by tilting his chin or rounding his lips. The plot, grinding along formulaically, concerns a beautiful pastry chef (Jacqueline Bisset), her amorous ex-husband (George Segal), who is a junk-food entrepreneur, and a series of murders in which eminent chefs are done in by methods related to their famous dishes. There's no spark of wit or lunacy, but there is a great deal of pleasure in just watching Robert Morley calmly, rapturously eating the scenery.

WHO IS KILLING THE STUNTMEN?

See *Stunts*

WHO KILLED "DOC" ROBBIN ★★
1948, USA
Virginia Grey, Don Castle, George Zucco, Whitford Kane, Claire Dubrey, Grant Mitchell. Directed by Bernard Carr. 55 min.

A failed attempt by producer Hal Roach to create a new comedy series along the lines of the "Our Gang" films. This has a similar group of slightly older moppets, including two black children named "Dis" and "Dat," roaming around a haunted house trying to solve a murder of which their friend is accused. The expected slapstick situations ensue, all at a reasonably brisk pace.

WHO KILLED MARY MAGDALENE?

See *Who Killed Mary What's'ername?*

WHO KILLED MARY WHAT'S'ERNAME? ★★½
1971, USA
Red Buttons, Alice Playten, Sylvia Miles, Sam Waterston, Conrad Bain. Directed by Ernie Pintoff. 90 min.

After running up against a brick wall of official indifference, a former boxer plays detective and sets out to solve the murder of a prostitute, a crime the cops don't place high on their priority list. Red Buttons is surprisingly restrained as the amateur sleuth, and his nicely focused energy sparks the entire cast of New York actors. While the scripting delivers the standard crime-solving rigamarole, the gritty Manhattan atmosphere is captured with lots of urban angst and local color. (a.k.a.: *Who Killed Mary Magdalene?*)

WHO'LL STOP THE RAIN? ☆☆☆½
1978, USA, R
Nick Nolte, Tuesday Weld, Michael Moriarty, Anthony Zerbe, Charles Haid. Directed by Karel Reisz. 126 min.

Perhaps the harshest treatment to date of alienated Vietnam soldiers, this features Nick Nolte in a star-making performance as a cruel but charismatic heroin-smuggling vet on the lam with his buddy's addicted wife (Tuesday Weld). Karel Reisz directs a version of Robert Stone's *Dog Soldiers* that dissects the slim motivations behind an individual's desperate acts of rebellion. The film becomes a play of evil against greater evil, where viciousness and tenacity become the only good character traits.

WHOLLY MOSES ☆
1980, USA, PG
Dudley Moore, Laraine Newman, James Coco, Paul Sand, Jack Gilford, Dom DeLuise, John Houseman, Madeline Kahn, David Lander, Richard Pryor, John Ritter. Directed by Gary Weis. 109 min.

Between the surprise hit *10* and the monster success *Arthur*, this abysmal comedy came along to prove that sometimes Moore was less. Here he plays a dual role (Bad Comedy Warning Sign #1) as a desert tour guide who finds a missing book of the Bible, the Book of Herschel, whose action we then see in flashback (sign #2), with Herschel also played by Moore. The star's incessant mugging will make you long for the Star Cameos (sign #3), which in turn will make you long for the star again. Unmitigatedly awful in all departments.

WHOOPEE! ☆☆½
1930, USA
Eddie Cantor, Eleanor Hunt, Paul Gregory, John Rutherford, Spencer Charters. Directed by Thornton Freeland. 93 min.

One of the earliest screen musicals, *Whoopee!* will please genre buffs but probably bore anyone else. It came way before the Golden Age of musicals and, though certainly no classic, it numbers among its pleasures a comically jittery performance by Eddie Cantor and a couple of good Busby Berkeley production numbers. In homely black-and-white, with a soundtrack that plays like a scratchy gramophone.

WHOOPS APOCALYPSE ☆☆☆
1981, Great Britain (TV)
Barry Morse, John Barron, Richard Griffiths, John Cleese, Alexei Sayle, Ed Bishop, Bruce Montague, David Kelley, Peter Jones. Directed by John Reardon. 137 min.

A bleak comedy done by British television that takes aim at the end of the world. The movie cleverly globe-hops, briskly following the machinations of the world's power-hungry politicians—who include a deposed shah's brother, a British prime minister who thinks he's Superman, and a senile president of the United States—and everything's interspersed with a television announcer's recap. The effect is more a conventionalized Monty Python than a *Doctor Strangelove*, but it's more entertaining than most nighttime TV. Startlingly pungent, the humor often hits home, but some of the jokes are so wildly outrageous that they lack punch. After all, who would believe that the U.S. president was a daffy, washed-up ex–B-movie actor completely controlled by a fanatical, right-wing religious leader? Still, it's very interesting to see what British humorists think of the U.S. John Cleese gives another good comic turn as a mercenary terrorist and man of disguises; David Kelley is even better as the ultimate obsequious servant.

WHO'S AFRAID OF VIRGINIA WOOLF? ☆☆☆☆
1966, USA
Elizabeth Taylor, Richard Burton, George Segal, Sandy Dennis. Directed by Mike Nichols. 130 min.

Warner Bros.' Academy Award–winning screen version of Edward Albee's searing play is a major achievement, especially considering how bad a film it could have been. Elizabeth Taylor and Richard Burton, the disastrous screen pair of *Cleopatra* and *Boom!*, electrify the screen as a tormented couple who brawl their way through a night of party games and domestic hellfire that threaten to consume both of them and a visiting couple (Sandy Dennis and George Segal). Taylor and Dennis both won Oscars for their work. Mike Nichols, the theatrical director assigned his first feature, successfully translated the play to the film medium by carefully following the original text. The few attempts to "open up" the play with exteriors are distracting, and Burton's English accent is obvious, but none of these flaws get in the way of the devastating, adult drama.

WHOSE LIFE IS IT ANYWAY? ☆☆
1981, USA
Richard Dreyfuss, John Cassavetes, Christine Lahti, Bob Balaban, Janet Eilber, Kenneth McMillan, George Wyner. Directed by John Badham. 118 min.

Brian Clark's play about a talented sculptor (Richard Dreyfuss) who becomes paralyzed from the neck down and fights for the right to die is provocative only on the shallowest level. Dreyfuss delivers the cute one-liners and pat homilies with his usual smart-aleck charm, and director John Badham has done an admirable job of turning the play into a fluid piece of cinema. But since there's nothing here to suggest the pain and bitterness a quadriplegic might feel—let along a quadriplegic who begs to die—the movie has all the dramatic power of a classroom discussion.

WHO SLEW AUNTIE ROO? ☆☆
1971, USA
Shelley Winters, Mark Lester, Chloe Franks, Ralph Richardson. Directed by Curtis Harrington. 89 min.

Another horror pic to serve as an excuse for an aging Hollywood actress to chew the scenery, but not in the same league as *Whatever Happened to Baby Jane?* This film purports to tell us what happens to all those little kiddies Auntie Roo gets her pudgy hands on. A grisly retelling of "Hansel and Gretel," but despite Shelley Winters's powerhouse hamming, the chills are never delivered.

WHO'S MINDING THE MINT? ☆☆☆½
1967, USA
Jim Hutton, Dorothy Provine, Milton Berle, Joey Bishop, Bob Denver, Walter Brennan, Victor Buono, Jack Gilford, Jamie Farr, Jackie Joseph. Directed by Howard Morris. 98 min.

This typical 1960s wackiness is more successful than most, thanks to the large cast of second-banana comics assembled here by director Howard Morris, himself a perennial supporter (he's the one no one ever remembers from *Your Show of Shows*). Jim Hutton plays a would-be playboy who lives a seemingly opulent life-style by purchasing limousines and flashy clothes for a few days and then returning them. This arouses the suspicion of his boss at his place of employment, the U.S. Treasury, so when he accidentally destroys $50,000 in new bills, he realizes that telling the truth won't keep him out of jail. So he devises an alternative plan: sneak into the treasury at night and print up a batch of replacement bills. What starts out as a two-man job, however, soon becomes a gang effort, as every character from the local loonie fringe convinces Hutton that the job can't be pulled off without his or her help. Morris keeps things moving along briskly so that you don't have time to quibble over the little inconsistencies.

WHY SHOOT THE TEACHER? ☆½
1977, Canada
Bud Cort, Samantha Eggar, Chris Wiggins, Gary Reineke, John Friesen, Michael J. Reynolds. Directed by Silvio Narizzano. 96 min.

But then again, why not? Lemur-eyed Bud Cort was barely acceptable playing the dreamy heroes of *Harold and Maude* and *Brewster McCloud*, but he's impossible as Max Brown, a young teacher packed off to an impoverished rural school district in Saskatchewan at the height of the Depression. Max is meant to be a survivor, a green kid who learns to love his dour students and the harsh country landscape, but Cort never conveys the core of strength and normality that would allow us to accept this conceit. Director Silvio Narizzano (*Georgy Girl*) loses his grip on the promising realistic ambience created by the settings and supporting players when he overdoes several big scenes, and he gives Cort his head at all the wrong moments.

WICHITA ☆☆½
1955, USA
Joel McCrea, Vera Miles, Lloyd Bridges, Wallace Ford, Edgar Buchanan, Peter Graves, Mae Clarke. Directed by Jacques Tourneur. 80 min.

Director Jacques Tourneur, best known for his superb series of literate, low-key horror films (*I Walked with a Zombie, Curse of the Demon*) didn't seem to have much interest in the other assignments he undertook; this Western, while always competent, is seldom inspired. Joel McCrea plays yet another version of Wyatt Earp, the lawman who cleaned up the lawless West, while Vera Miles gets a bit more screen time than the usual Western heroine.

THE WICKED LADY ☆½
1983, Great Britain, R
Faye Dunaway, Alan Bates, John Gielgud, Denholm Elliott, Prunella Scales, Jane Purcell, Oliver Tobias. Directed by Michael Winner. 98 min.

Based on a 1945 British adventure flick of the same name, this story about a seventeenth-century woman who becomes a highwayman (highwaywoman? highwayperson?) out of boredom is played by director Michael Winner for camp value. Unfortunately, after directing so many Charles Bronson movies, he seems to have no feel for humor, and what amusement there is derives from watching such pros as Alan Bates and John Gielgud overplaying and kidding themselves. In the title role, Faye Dunaway seems to know she's being wasted, and her apparent indecision about whether to play it straight or askew drags the movie down ever more. Music by Tony Banks, keyboardist for Genesis.

THE WICKER MAN ☆☆☆
1973, Great Britain, R
Christopher Lee, Britt Ekland, Edward Woodward, Aubrey Morris, Diane Cilento. Directed by Robin Hardy. 97 min.

A priggish policeman receives an anonymous tip involving the disappearance of a child from a small rural community housed on an island off the British coast. His investigation leads him to believe that the island's population—encouraged by the eccentric Lord Summerisle—has reverted to paganism, and that the missing girl is to be sacrificed in order to insure a bountiful harvest. His Christian sensibilities are outraged, and his deductions are slightly off the mark—slightly, but dangerously. A clever puzzle created by playwright Peter Shaffer (*Sleuth*) that is perhaps too schematic for its own good, but nonetheless constitutes an unusual diversion with a potent subtext.

WIDOW'S NEST ☆☆
1977, USA/Spain
Patricia Neal, Valentina Cortese, Susan Oliver, Yvonne Mitchell, Jadwiga Baranska, Jerzy Zelnik, Lila Kedrova. Directed by Tony Navarro. 119 min.

A murky Gothic melodrama, this might better have been called *House of Dark Skeletons*. Three unmarried sisters live in a big old house in Cuba, along with one-eyed servant (and part-time witch) Patricia Neal and insane mother Lila Kedrova. A visit from their brother and his wife sparks sequences in which all three relive the past sexual traumas that led to their current loneliness. Far too long and self-conscious to have any real impact as either drama or terror.

WIFEMISTRESS ☆☆½
1977, Italy, R
Laura Antonelli, Marcello Mastroianni. Directed by Marco Vicario. 110 min.

Laura Antonelli's erotic presence invigorates this silly, sexy romp about a young wife who sets out to uncover the secret life of her husband, who has mysteriously disappeared. Although she presumes him dead, he has actually gone underground and watches from across the street as she carries on his political and sexual intrigues and is transformed from a timid housewife to a wildly adventurous woman of the world.

THE WILBY CONSPIRACY ☆☆½
1975, Great Britain, PG
Sidney Poitier, Michael Caine, Nicol Williamson, Prunella Gee, Persis Khambatta, Rutger Hauer, Joseph De Graf, Helmut Dantine. Directed by Ralph Nelson. 101 min.

Sort of a spiritual descendant of *The Defiant Ones*, this time set against the background of South Africa and its policy of apartheid. Political prisoner Sidney Poitier is released from prison but pursued by racist cop Nicol Williamson, who hopes to be led to a guerrilla leader in hiding. While on the run, Poitier hooks up with an unwilling Michael Caine, a glib engineer who generates some onscreen chemistry against Poitier's intense stoicism. There are some exciting moments, but Ralph Nelson's by-the-book direction doesn't add any flourish, and it makes no particular statement about apartheid except that it's bad.

THE WILD BUNCH ☆☆☆☆
1969, USA, R
William Holden, Ernest Borgnine, Robert Ryan, Edmond O'Brien, Warren Oates, Ben Johnson, Strother Martin, L. Q. Jones, Albert Decker, Bo Hopkins, Dub Taylor. Directed by Sam Peckinpah. 127 min.

One of the best American (and *most* American) films of the 1960s, Sam Peckinpah's epic anti-Western, or Western eulogy, was viewed in its time only in terms of its violence. For the time, it was the most bloody Hollywood film ever made, but anyone who has seen any horror film made in the last decade will be amazed at how tame it now appears. Whether the shoot-outs here are excessive and gratuitous, and whether Peckinpah has any noble intent behind them or was simply carried away with his stylized violence, are still open questions. But what remains in the film about self-destruction, masculinity, the American mythos, and the meaning of liberty is challenging and engrossing.

WILDCATS ☆½
1986, USA
Goldie Hawn, James Keach, Swoosie Kurtz, Nipsey Russell, Bruce McGill, Jan Hooks, Tab Thacker. Directed by Michael Ritchie. 104 min.

It's *Private Benjamin on the 50-Yard Line*. No, it's *Goldie Gets Protocol in a Ghetto High School*. No, it's an overly familiar comedy in which Goldie Hawn's adorable attributes are exposed in tried and true situations from her earlier hits. Goldie has to test her mettle by successfully coaching a ramshackle high school team to victory; there's not a believeable or moving minute in it. Goldie, get a new formula!

THE WILD COUNTRY
1970, USA, G ★★½
Steve Forrest, Vera Miles, Jack Elam, Ronny Howard, Frank De Kova, Morgan Woodward, Clint Howard. Directed by Robert Totten. 100 min.

In the 1960s and 1970s, when the Disney studios floundered with dozens of live-action kids' films, a favorite theme was frontier life, in which the cornball behavior of the characters seemed less anachronistic. This was one of the more palatable entries, thanks to the cast's assured work as a frontier family whose oldest boy (Ronny Howard) must grow up quickly when tragedy threatens the clan. Real-life brother Clint Howard appears as a younger sibling, and the reliably hammy Jack Elam plays a mountain man.

THE WILD DUCK
1983, Australia, PG ★★
Jeremy Irons, Liv Ullmann, Lucinda Jones, John Mellon. Directed by Henri Safran. 96 min.

This is a misguided, sentimental truncation of Henrik Ibsen's classic drama. His Norwegian characters have been transported to the outback, and his tale of a tortured family propped up by benign delusions has been rendered with the let's-just-tell-a-good-story overconfidence typical of Australian filmmakers; the resulting tone is less Ibsen-tragic than Dickens-uplifting. Liv Ullmann gives a touching, understated performance as the long-suffering wife. But Jeremy Irons, as the husband, is truly bizarre: eyes bugging, jaw muscles twitching, he sets a new standard for hammy screen neurosis.

THE WILDERNESS FAMILY: PART TWO
1978, USA, G ★★★
Robert Logan, Susan Damante Shaw, Heather Rattray, Ham Larsen. Directed by Frank Zuniga. 105 min.

Exceptionally good family fare, this is beautifully photographed in Utah and less blandly scripted than the norm. After growing disenchanted with big-city life, a construction worker gives up urban angst for the rugged unspoiled wilderness. As with *The Swiss Family Robinson*, the film's strength lies in scrutinizing how these city folk cope with Mother Nature as they leave civilization behind. It's old hat, but briskly done and suitable for all ages. (a.k.a.: *Further Adventures of the Wilderness Family*)

THE WILD GEESE
1978, Great Britain, R ★★★
Richard Burton, Hardy Kruger, Richard Harris, Stewart Granger, Roger Moore. Directed by Andrew V. McLaglen. 134 min.

This standard rugged action pic rated well enough with audiences to get a sequel in 1985, *Wild Geese II*. This is a slightly more benign version of *The Dirty Dozen*, with a pack of mercenaries doing their darnedest to retrieve a kidnapped African leader. It's undemanding fare; the actors phone in their performances and the audience can tune out mentally when the action dies down. As the leader of the pack, Richard Burton looks pained at being reduced to this tripe; it's not unlike watching John Barrymore at the end of his career.

WILD GEESE II
1985, Great Britain, R ★½
Scott Glenn, Barbara Carrera, Edward Fox, Laurence Olivier, Robert Webber. Directed by Peter Hunt. 124 min.

Neither rain nor sleet nor the death of a star nor even lack of popular interest will stay some producers from trying to cash in on a hit with a sequel—when star Richard Burton became permanently unavailable, the makers of *Wild Geese II* simply forged ahead with Scott Glenn. The idiotic plot, only vaguely related to the first film, has a team of commandos attempting to spring Rudolf Hess from Spandau for a journalist who wants a hot story. The film gets a grudging extra half-star for its cast, although if Burton *had* been in it, he'd probably have died of embarrassment. *Note*: the film *Code Name: Wildgeese*, which was made at the same time, is unrelated.

WILD HORSES
1982, New Zealand ★
Keith Aberdein, John Bach, Robyn Gibbes, Kevin J. Wilson, Bruno Lawrence, Kathy Rawlings, Tom Poata, Marshall Napier, Michael Haigh, Martyn Sanderson. Directed by Derek Morton. 88 min.

During the 1960s, it was reported that the government of New Zealand legalized the slaughter of wild horses and deer in its Tongariro National Park. It is within that context that this film locates the conflict between deer hunters (who also shoot horses) and the cowboys who merely want to round up the horses for sale. If it sounds as if a preservationsist point of view has been omitted here, so, alas, have any other points to recommend—besides "horses and real estate"—in this failed anti-Western.

WILD IN THE COUNTRY
1961, USA ★★½
Elvis Presley, Hope Lange, Tuesday Weld, Millie Perkins, John Ireland, Gary Lockwood, Christina Crawford, Jason Robards, Sr. Directed by Phillip Dunne. 112 min.

Elvis Presley doing Clifford Odets is a little like Jayne Mansfield doing John Steinbeck (*The Wayward Bus*, 1957), but Elvis at least had some acting talent. It's unfortunate, then, that Odets's adaptation of J. R. Salamanca's "The Lost Country" is just as sappy and unconvincing as all the other Jerry Wald/Twentieth Century-Fox melodramas of the day. Elvis plays a backwoods boy with untapped writing talent who has romantic problems with an older psychologist (Hope Lange), a town flirt (Tuesday Weld), and a shy girl (Millie Perkins, of *Anne Frank* fame). Although this was touted in its day as Presley's first big acting role, fans need not worry: he sings on several occasions.

WILD IN THE STREETS
1968, USA ★★½
Shelley Winters, Christopher Jones, Diane Varsi, Ed Begley, Hal Holbrook, Millie Perkins, Richard Pryor, Melvin Belli, Walter Winchell, Dick Clark. Directed by Barry Shear. 96 min.

In this youth exploitation fantasy, Christopher Jones plays Max Frost, a rock star who wields such power among "the kids" that he successfully gets the voting age lowered to fifteen and is elected president. The new head of state decrees a mandatory retirement age of thirty, and sends everyone over the age of thirty-five to concentration camps, where they are administered daily doses of LSD. Soon all of Congress is on acid. Shelley Winters plays his overbearing mom, Hal Holbrook is the liberal senator, and Richard Pryor makes his debut as Stanley X, Black Power drummer extraordinaire and author of the best-selling *Aborigine Cookbook*. Tacky and dated, with a soundtrack of plastic 1960s rock, but undeniably amusing.

THE WILD LIFE
1984, USA, R ★★
Christopher Penn, Ilan Mitchell-Smith, Eric Stoltz. Directed by Art Linson. 95 min.

A teen comedy with thumpingly serious undertones. Written by *Fast Times at Ridgemont High* screenwriter Cameron Crowe, it has a premise that's pure *American Graffiti*: kids dragging down strips in big old cars, visiting greasy spoons, partying, and making out. But Crowe's perspective has become distressingly parental. Beneath its zany humor, the movie is a souped-up version of those old high-school film strips that told you how to drive or not to smoke pot—only *The Wild Life* is more insidious because it's dressed in hipper clothes. Featuring a blond-dyed Christopher Penn, who's less charismatic than he thinks, and Eric Stoltz, whom you almost certainly won't recognize as the boy from *Mask*.

THE WILD ONE
★★★½
1954, USA
Marlon Brando, Mary Murphy, Robert Keith, Lee Marvin, Jay C. Flippen. Directed by Laslo Benedek. 79 min.

Some films become classics for reasons other than quality. *The Wild One* is such a film. The production values are cheap, the screenplay crudely developed, and the performances—with the exception of Marlon Brando's—barely competent. Brando plays an outlaw motorcyclist who is pursued by townsmen after making trouble in a small town and falling for the chief of police's daughter. Few actors have been able to match Brando's mixture of external sexuality with internal vulnerability and, in this granddaddy of all biker movies, his talents are on full display. The film is notable not only for Brando's tour de force as the troubled gang leader but also for how the John Paxton screenplay does not automatically condone the town's hysterical reaction to the gang—a liberal point of view in the Eisenhower era. In 1954, middle America panicked over the film's portrayal of corrupted youth (the film was banned in England for fourteen years). Today *The Wild One* looks tame, but Brando's work remains fresh, immediate, and exciting, one of the bravado performances of the 1950s.

THE WILD PANTHER
★
Hong Kong
Chang Shan, Wang Dao, Hon Ying, Yuen Shan, Kim Dong Hyun. Directed by Lee Tso Nan. 90 min.

Chun Min Chu, leader of the now-defunct Wild Panther unit in Vietnam, is entrusted with a map leading to a list of secret agents working in Asia. Chun's mission is to deliver the information to only one man in Seoul, Korea. Kung fu fans, beware! Although this movie does have some very realistic martial arts, the emphasis is on action and, that dreaded of all curses, guns.

THE WILD PARTY
★★½
1975, USA, R
James Coco, Raquel Welch, Perry King, Tiffany Bolling, Royal Dano, David Dukes. Directed by James Ivory. 100 min.

Hollywood of the 1920s is the setting for this frustrating but fascinating mixture of fact and fiction, camp, spectacle, and real drama. James Coco gives one of his best performances as washed-up silent-film clown Jolly Grimm, who can't make the transition to talkies but nonetheless throws a free-for-all bash to celebrate his already outmoded comeback effort. Raquel Welch, touching and effective, is his longtime mistress and Perry King is the slick, glossy matinee idol who beds her when the party turns into an orgy. Murder hangs in the air from the film's first minutes, so much so that the predictable proceedings become emotionally distant and often ring hollow. Director James Ivory is better known for his tasteful, low-key period pieces (*The Bostonians*, *A Room With A View*) but shows surprising facility with this gaudy, stylized, deliberately artificial tale. If it doesn't put you off immediately, you may be engrossed.

THE WILD RIDE
★
1960, USA
Jack Nicholson, Robert Bean, Georgianna Carter. Directed by Harvey Berman. 63 min.

This low-budget junk was made, we can only assume, before Jack Nicholson had the standing to refuse such roles. He plays a virtually sociopathic motorcyclist who steals his best friend's girlfriend and takes her off on a destructive joyride. It's awe-inspiring to contemplate the artistic distance between this and *Easy Rider*.

THE WILD RIVER
★★★★
1960, USA
Montgomery Clift, Lee Remick, Jo Van Fleet, Albert Salmi, Jay C. Flippen, James Westerfield, Barbara Loden, Frank Overton, Malcolm Atterbury, Bruce Dern, Robert Earl Jones. Directed by Elia Kazan. 115 min.

A visionary, but cleanly objective, exploration of the theme of "progress" versus "people," this has Jo Van Fleet superbly portraying an implacable octogenarian who refuses to surrender her island home to the Tennessee Valley Authority; Montgomery Clift plays the TVA representative sent to negotiate with her. During these protracted proceedings, he falls in love with the matriarch's granddaughter, played by Lee Remick. The film achieves tragic stature through Elia Kazan's deft handling of the simultaneous levels of meaning, and since it's successful on all levels, it can be viewed with equal interest for the story alone or for its artistry. Playwright Paul Osborn (who also adapted John Steinbeck's novel for Kazan's *East of Eden* [1955]) wrote the screenplay, based on *two* novels, W. B. Huie's *Mud on the Stars* and Borden Deal's *Dunbar's Cove*. A classic. The wide-screen CinemaScope format is diminished on video.

WILDROSE
★★★
1984, USA
Lisa Eichhorn, Tom Bower, Jim Cada, Cinda Jackson, Bill Schoppert. Directed by John Hanson. 95 min.

Employed at a dying Minnesota strip mine, June Lorich (Lisa Eichhorn) tries to establish an independent life, but she's hounded by her boozing ex-husband and her town's churchgoing ethics. Rick (Tom Bower), the man she loves, is a fisherman from Wisconsin who's working a lake where the fish are becoming scarce. Will they stay together? How and where will they make a living? As in his *Northern Lights*, director John Hanson is trying to combine a love story and an economic study, narrative and documentary, professional and nonprofessional actors. The film sometimes achieves a sense of reality that's both solid and heightened; Hanson, however, fares better with mood and personality than with his big themes.

THE WILD SIDE

See *Suburbia*

WILD STRAWBERRIES
★★★★
1957, Sweden
Victor Sjostrom, Ingrid Thulin, Bibi Andersson, Gunnar Bjornstrand, Naima Wifstrand. Directed by Ingmar Bergman. 93 min.

Ingmar Bergman was at the peak of his powers when he directed this richly textured film about an elderly doctor (Victor Sjostrom) who travels to his alma mater to accept an honorary degree. The man, afraid of his approaching death, journeys through a personal landscape of dreams and memories. Bergman, at age forty-two, did not simply fashion a meditation on the transience of life and the plights of the aged (which would be original and satisfying enough); he also created a subtle, profound criticism of bourgeois life and a film that ponders an entire spectrum of philosophical ideas. Sjostrom is perfect as the reserved gentleman who finally achieves insight, thanks to such fellow travelers as his daughter-in-law (Ingrid Thulin) and a teenage girl (Bibi Andersson), a reincarnation of his first love. Bergman masterfully combines the man's daily Sturm und Drang with surreal, often terrifying dream sequences—including a famous one with faceless clocks. Still an extraordinary film and arguably the best of Bergman's celebrated "middle period."

WILD STYLE
★★★
1982, USA
George Quinones, Patti Astor, Fred "Fab Five Freddy" Brathwaite, Cold Crush Bros., Fantastic Freaks, Rock Steady Crew, Electric Force. Charlie Ahearn. 82 min.

A scrappy but exuberant independent feature, this is about New York's hiphop subculture—the sassy, streetwise world of rappers, break dancers, and graffiti artists. Working on a small budget, independent director Charlie Ahearn has come up with a low-rent melodrama about a South Bronx graffiti artist ("Lee" George Quinones) who tries to realize his wildest ambitions without selling out. Ahearn is a careless storyteller, but there's a value to his slipshod approach: he refuses to sentimentalize his subject. And in the rough-

and-tumble club scenes that are the movie's highlight, the rapping and break dancing become a testament to the gritty glory of hiphop: it's poised right on the line between art and survival.

WILD TIMES ☆☆½
1980, USA (TV)
Sam Elliott, Bruce Boxleitner, Penny Peyser, Dennis Hopper, Cameron Mitchell, Pat Hingle. Directed by Richard Compton. 200 min.

A wild and wooly Western tale, this broaches some fairly fresh subject matter. These wild times are about the impresario of America's first Wild West Show and how his novel enterprise was originally launched. In some ways, this is more fun than sitting through a more pretentious treatment of the same topic (such as *Buffalo Bill and the Indians*). A good-time movie with lots of interesting character shadings and some pungent background flavor.

WILD WHEELS ½☆
1969, USA, R
Don Epperson, Robert Dix, Casey Kasem, Dovi Beams, Terry Stafford, Bruce Kimble, Evelyn Guerrero. Directed by Ken Osborne. 92 min.

A bottom-of-the-barrel 1960s motorcycle movie—hardly an elevated genre to begin with—this one, rather badly blown up to 35 mm from 16 mm, pits bad bikers against fun-lovin' dune-buggy racers on Pismo Beach. Sole points of interest, for the really desperate trivia hound, are appearances by disc jockey Casey Kasem (who was better in *The Incredible Two-Headed Transplant*, though not by much) and Evelyn Guerrero, who went on to become a Cheech and Chong sidekick in a few of their movies. Not *Easy Rider*; not even *Satan's Sadists*, for that matter.

WILLARD ☆☆½
1971, USA, PG
Bruce Davison, Ernest Borgnine, Elsa Lanchester, Sondra Locke, Michael Dante, J. Pat O'Malley. Directed by Daniel Mann. 95 min.

A disturbed young man (Bruce Davison) enlists the aid of his rodent friends to wreak revenge upon a mean boss, a meddling mother, and a nosy neighbor, in a semiclassic of the evil-animals horror subgenre. Davison plays the crazed wretch with conviction, but the real stars of the show are the deftly used rats, especially in one memorable sequence that will make you think twice the next time you eat a peanut butter sandwich. Followed by an execrable semisequel, *Ben*.

WILL: G. GORDON LIDDY ☆☆½
1982, USA (TV)
Robert Conrad, Katherine Cannon, Gary Bayer, Peter Ratray. Directed by Robert Lieberman. 100 min.

This biography of the life of Watergate mastermind G. Gordon Liddy is troublesome in that Conrad, whether deliberately or not, makes his an engrossing, almost likable character. The script concentrates less on the Watergate affair than on Liddy's time in prison, during which he asserted his "natural superiority" to win over the other prisoners and deal with the prison authorities. Based on Liddy's best-selling autobiography.

WILLIE AND PHIL ☆☆
1980, USA, R
Michael Ontkean, Ray Sharkey, Margot Kidder, Jan Miner, Tom Brennan, Julie Bovasso. Directed by Paul Mazursky. 115 min.

The memory of François Truffaut's *Jules and Jim* hangs like a pall over Paul Mazursky's movie. He means the film to be an update of that work for the American 1970s, but he's precisely the wrong director to undertake such a task. Treating the era of est and hot tubs almost without irony, Mazursky gives us characters who seem to stick together only because they've bought the same New Age slogans. Michael Ontkean and Ray Sharkey are the two pals, Margot Kidder the woman who unites and divides them. Mazursky's odd new propriety keeps him from digging very deeply into the 1970s; in other films, he would have poked fun at the encounter-session dialogue the characters here toss around—and there's even more of it in Mazursky's voice-over narration. The failure of vision evident here deteriorates to total artistic blindness in Mazursky's abominable *Down and Out in Beverly Hills* (1986).

WILLY MCBEAN AND HIS MAGIC MACHINE ☆☆
1965, Japan
Animated: Larry Mann, Billie Richards, Alfie Scopp, Paul Ligman, Bunny Cowan, Paul Sole, Pegi Loder. Directed by Arthur Rankin, Jr. 94 min.

This is unobjectionable children's animated fare made with puppets filmed in stop-action. A mad scientist builds a time machine and plans to go back in history, taking credit for all of man's important scientific discoveries. He is foiled by a young man who builds a duplicate machine and follows him through each era, from the caveman through Buffalo Bill. Some entertaining songs help move things along.

WILLY WONKA AND THE CHOCOLATE FACTORY ☆☆
1971, USA, G
Gene Wilder, Jack Albertson, Peter Ostrum, Michael Bollner, Ursula Reit. Directed by Mel Stuart. 100 min.

Five children, including a poverty-stricken youth, in a contest allowing them to tour their town's famous chocolate factory. Roald Dahl's classic children's novel *Charlie and the Chocolate Factory* always had the makings of a good children's film. But Dahl (who wrote the screenplay) and director Mel Stuart have sweetened and sentimentalized the tart original with bad songs by Leslie Bricusse and Anthony Newley and an overly cute actor playing Charlie, the one unspoiled child in the adventure. The fun now centers around Gene Wilder playing Willy Wonka, the factory owner. His deadpan delivery is the only thing adults who happen to be watching will find tolerable. The rest is like dining on a meal consisting of cake, cookies, ice cream, fudge, and chocolate milk—a child's dream, but a rather sickening one.

WILMA ☆☆
1977, USA (TV)
Cicely Tyson, Shirley Jo Finney, Jason Bernard, Joe Seneca, Denzel Washington. Directed by Bud Greenspan. 100 min.

This is another overcoming-the-obstacles bio-pic meant to shake us out of our TV-induced stupor and get us to realize that "nothing is impossible." The true-life tale sketches, in broad strokes, the life of Wilma Rudolph, a polio victim who courageously fought both her disease and people's responses to it and became an Olympic athlete, winning a Gold Medal in track. The story's an inspiring one, but there's no fire here—the actors certainly don't experience a Wilma-like triumph over the trite script and direction.

WINCHESTER '73 ☆☆☆☆
1950, USA
Jimmy Stewart, Shelley Winters, Dan Duryea, Stephen McNally, Millard Mitchell, Charles Drake, John McIntire, Will Geer, Rock Hudson. Directed by Anthony Mann. 82 min.

The films in the cycle of 1950s Westerns that Jimmy Stewart made under the direction of Anthony Mann are classics of the genre. Stewart brings a jittery vulnerability to his roles that suggests a Western hero who is closer to the tortured obsessive neurotics of postwar melodrama than to the staunch frontier-tamers who traditionally dominated these films. Four of the Mann films—*Winchester '73*, *Bend in the River*, *The Naked Spur*, and *The Man from Laramie*—can stand with the great psychological Westerns, films such as John Ford's *The Searchers*, Howard Hawks's *Red River*, and Nicholas Ray's *Johnny Guitar*; two of Mann's—this and *Bend in the River*—have been handsomely packaged and released by MCA Video. This is one of the best of the entire lot; here Stewart assumes the proportions of a full-blown paranoiac as he attempts to retrieve his stolen gun. He finds himself up against a lunatic robber, a young Indian chief, a gunrunner, an old nemesis—in short, everyone else in the movie. The powerful punches packed by the film's themes are backed by Mann's rugged style, and it all makes for a compelling, disturbing movie that will change viewers' perceptions about the limitations of the Western.

THE WIND AND THE LION ☆☆½
1975, USA, PG
Sean Connery, Candice Bergen, Brian Keith, John Huston, Geoffrey Lewis, Steve Kanaly, Vladek Sheybal, Nadim Sawalha, Roy Jenson, Simon Harrison, Polly Gottesman, Deborah Baxter, Shirley Rothman. Directed by John Milius. 119 min.

Candice Bergen plays an American lady kidnapped by an Arab chieftain (Sean Connery) in John Milius's turn-of-the-century romantic adventure. Most fun when it explores the odd diplomatic dealings of Connery's nomad and Brian Keith's Teddy Roosevelt, the movie is a bit logy and easily distracted by the desert scenery, but Connery is wonderful, a glorious portrait of Bedouin nobility. Jerry Goldsmith's rousing score received an Oscar nomination.

WINDOM'S WAY ☆☆☆
1957, Great Britain
Peter Finch, Mary Ure, Natasha Parry, Robert Flemyng, Michael Hordern, John Cairney. Directed by Ronald Neame. 108 min.

Although rather slow-moving and lacking in real drama, this well-crafted film is intelligently played and leaves the viewer with something to think about. Peter Finch plays a British doctor working on a small Far Eastern island. The natives, in a state of unrest because of poor working conditions on the local plantations, are being led toward rebellion by Communist agitation. Caught in the middle, Finch tries to reconcile labor and management, all the while working on a reconciliation of his own with his ex-wife.

WINDOWS ☆
1980, USA, R
Talia Shire, Elizabeth Ashley, Joseph Cortese, Kay Medford. Directed by Gordon Willis. 96 min.

A psychological thriller of the pull-the-wings-off-the-butterfly school, this first directorial effort by cinematographer Gordon Willis (*Manhattan*) was hooted off the screen, and may achieve camp status on video. Why is crazed lesbian Elizabeth Ashley so hot for mousy Talia Shire (who seems to wear her shapeless crocheted hat even in the shower)? And why has Ashley stuffed Talia's cat into a freezer? The answers to these and countless other questions are shrouded in mystery. Except for Willis's pretty pictures, *Windows* is a movie ugly in intention and in execution. But it's far too stupid to be worth getting angry about.

WINDS OF KITTY HAWK ☆☆☆
1978, USA (TV)
Michael Moriarty, David Huffman, Tom Bower, Eugene Roche, Scott Hylands. Directed by E. W. Swackhamer. 100 min.

A lot of interesting historical data and beautiful aerial photography are the principal merits of this handsome production about the Wright Brothers. Special emphasis is placed on the rivalries and financial difficulties that hampered these pioneers, and on the shortsightedness of various naysayers who wronged them before they had proved the validity of their ideas. What really makes the film take off is that it creates a feeling for the love of flight that inspired the Wrights to risk everything for their dream.

WINDS OF THE WASTELAND ☆☆
1936, USA
John Wayne, Phyllis Fraser, Yakima Canutt, Lane Chandler, Sam Flint, Lew Kelly, Bob Kortman. Directed by Mack V. Wright. 57 min.

In one of his better B Westerns, John Wayne's the stagecoach entrepreneur vying for that big government contract. Although far from a classic, it does show Wayne's growing abilities and confidence as an actor.

WINDWALKER ☆☆☆½
1980, USA, PG
Trevor Howard, Nick Ramos, James Remar, Serene Hedin. Directed by Kieth Merrill. 108 min.

One of the best recent films about American Indians, *Windwalker* feels authentic, from its subtitled Cheyenne and Crow dialogue to the deerhide tepees. Nature director Kieth Merrill effectively captures the frosty Utah surroundings, adding visual splendor to this fairy tale about an aged warrior who's spared from death to rescue his grandson's kin from marauding Crow braves. All of the characters have a great deal of nobility (sometimes too much of it), particularly famed British actor Trevor Howard in the title role. A beautiful picture and a refreshing change of pace from the insulting Indian stereotypes of the past.

WINDY CITY ☆☆☆
1984, USA, R
John Shea, Kate Capshaw, Josh Mostel, Jeffrey DeMunn. Directed by Armyan Bernstein. 105 min.

Another semiautobiographical film about group therapy, this one in the tradition of *The Big Chill*, and has been done with a remarkable amount of conviction and warmth. Set in Chicago, the picture details the adventures of the Rogues, childhood buddies who now have to deal with the real world as adults. Even though the movie's attempts to portray male camaraderie gets a bit pretentious at times, *Windy City* has the kind of personable characters that make it endearing.

WINGS ☆☆☆½
1927, USA
Clara Bow, Charles Rogers, Richard Arlen, Gary Cooper, Jobyna Ralston, Hedda Hopper. Directed by William A. Wellman. 139 min.

The first Best Picture in the history of the Academy Awards still stands up as a slam-bang good film. Although the original Magnoscope presentation of this silent classic has been lost, the color tinting during the aerial and battle footage (some of the best ever filmed) has been preserved. The story frame is less exciting. It's about a World War I flyer who accidentally shoots down his best friend behind enemy lines. Gary Cooper and Clara Bow were creating a lot of noise in the tabloids during this time, but they are *not* teamed here; Bow plays down her image as the woman caught between the two buddies, and Coop lasts for less than a reel. Nevertheless, a roisterous show and one of William Wellman's most freewheeling directorial jobs.

WINNING ☆☆☆
1969, USA, G
Paul Newman, Joanne Woodward, Robert Wagner, Richard Thomas, David Sheiner, Clu Gulager, Robert Quarry, Bobby Unser. Directed by James Goldstone. 123 min.

The story isn't much, but fine acting by the principals and exciting race photography make this a better-than-average melodrama. Paul Newman plays a race driver (racing is the actor's hobby in real life) who lets nothing stand in the way of his success. He marries a woman with a thirteen-year-old son (Joanne Woodward and Richard Thomas of "The Waltons"), but neglects them for his obsession, leading her to begin an affair with a rival driver. Footage of a seventeen-car crash is taken from an actual incident at the 1968 Indianapolis 500.

WIN, PLACE OR STEAL ☆☆
1975, USA, PG
Russ Tamblyn, Dean Stockwell, Alex Karras, Kristina Holland, McLean Stevenson, Alan Oppenheimer. Directed by Richard Bailey. 81 min.

It's a day at the races, 1970s style, and a pleasant enough diversion at that. A heist at the track brings some comic mayhem, highlighted by the surprise of seeing ex–Green Bay Packer Alex Karras play Oliver Hardy to Russ Tamblyn's Stan Laurel.

THE WINSLOW BOY ☆☆☆½
1948, Great Britain
Robert Donat, Margaret Leighton, Cedric Hardwicke, Marie Lohr, Neil North, Wilfried Hyde-White, Ernest Thesiger. Directed by Anthony Asquith. 117 min.

Terence Rattigan adapted his own play, which in turn was based on an actual incident in pre–World War I Britain, with excellent results. When a thirteen-year-old naval cadet is accused of stealing a small money order and is expelled from school, the boy's father takes the case through the entire British legal system, culminating in an action against the king. Well played by all, especially Cedric Hardwicke as the father and Robert Donat as the eminent barrister who agrees to take their case.

WINTER KILLS ☆☆☆½
1979, USA, R
Jeff Bridges, John Huston, Anthony Perkins, Sterling Hayden, Eli Wallach, Belinda Bauer, Elizabeth Taylor, Richard Boone, Ralph Meeker, Dorothy Malone. Directed by William Richert. 97 min.

A terrific cast enlivens this slick, straight-faced black comedy, a riff on big business, political assassination, and every conspiracy movie ever made. Jeff Bridges is a young playboy determined to track down the man who killed his brother, the president, fifteen years ago, and John Huston gives a grand, raucous performance as his dad, a lewd old tycoon who tells the kid to stop worrying and have some fun. Much more comic than Richard Condon's novel, *Winter Kills* is good paranoid fun. Watch for Elizabeth Taylor (who quit the film before its completion) in a one-word cameo.

WINTER LIGHT ☆☆☆☆
1962, Sweden
Gunnar Bjornstrand, Gunnel Lindblom, Ingrid Thulin, Max von Sydow. Directed by Ingmar Bergman. 80 min.

Winter Light is the most searing, bitter, and ironic work in the Ingmar Bergman canon. This devastating commentary on the hypocrisy of organized religion came second in a trilogy of Bergman films about self-tortured individuals and their inability to cope with life. Unlike the more meditative first (*Through a Glass Darkly*) and third (*The Silence*), *Winter Light* burns like tissue paper once it gets started. The story of a widowed pastor who wants to end his affair with one of his parishioners is both painful and fascinating to watch because Bergman has placed his sadomasochistic characters in scorchingly bright lights and sparse settings. Both Gunnar Bjornstrand and Ingrid Thulin are superb, and each has an extraordinary monologue sequence (hers directly into camera). Bergman reportedly hated making this film, but he was nonetheless at his most powerfully creative at the time.

WINTER OF OUR DREAMS ☆☆½
1981, Australia, R
Judy Davis, Bryan Brown, Cathy Downes, Baz Luhrmann, Peter Mochrie. Directed by John Duigan. 90 min.

One of the less widely seen products of the Australian film boom of the 1980s, this is a serious, uningratiating drama about two people approaching middle age after having experienced the uplifting turmoil of the 1960s. Rob (Bryan Brown) is the manager of a bookstore, unsure about his "open" marriage to a college teacher. Louise is a prostitute who is completely removed from the physical side of her profession. The link between them is Lisa, another prostitute who had an affair with Rob a decade ago and who is murdered, possibly because of her past political activism. The deliberately antierotic relationship that develops between Louise and Rob has more feeling than most of its erotic counterparts. By nature, though, the film is cold, and will only appeal to patient audiences.

WINTER RATES

See *Out of Season*

WINTERSET ☆☆
1936, USA
Burgess Meredith, Margo, Eduardo Cianelli, Edward Ellis, Paul Guilfoyle, John Carradine. Directed by Alfred Santell. 78 min.

Another classic play becomes stilted in the hands of Hollywood. Maxwell Anderson's award-winning drama inspired by the Sacco and Vanzetti case is adapted for the screen with some changes but remains too theatrical in style and tone. Burgess Meredith plays another one of his bitter hotheads, this time the son of one of the accused killers who confronts the mob about his father's conviction. Anthony Veiller's adaptation of Anderson's original remains quasi-liberal (the old man's innocence is never questioned), which is perhaps commendable, but a lot of overacting in coarse, proto-*noir* shots diffuses the story's dramatic impact.

WIN THEM ALL ☆☆½
Hong Kong
Huang Yuan-Sheng, Hu Shao, Yasuaki Kurada, Hsu Feng, Ting Feng, Tang Hsin, Kao Pao Shu. Directed by Kao Pao Shu.

Kao, chief guard of the Chi Ying Security Bureau, is killed by Iron Fingers Fan Shen (Yasuaki Kurada) after Kao stops the casino dealer from cheating the public. Kao's daughter, Tien Feng (Hsu Feng), comes to town to seek revenge. This movie is filled with good fights and, although mostly Japanese in style, does show some Chinese influences in execution of techniques and the acrobatics. This movie has one of our favorite characters: Miss Bo Po. The delightfully funny scene where she flirts with, beats, and then depants the local gang, is a pure joy. Kurada does some absolutely flawless Japanese martial arts techniques including karate, judo, jujitsu, and aikido. A fine film with a good cast and nice choreography.

WISDOM ☆
1986, USA, R
Emilio Estevez, Demi Moore, Tom Skerritt, Veronica Cartwright, William Allen Young, Richard Minchenberg. Directed by Emilio Estevez. 108 min.

This is a film you can feel good about hating: a brash, aggressively stupid populist drama written, directed by, and starring Emilio Estevez, a minimally talented actor who seems determined to become the Orson Welles of the Brat Pack. He plays John Wisdom, a young man who, facing unemployment, decides to become a Robin Hoodish robber and embarks on an interstate crime spree with his girlfriend (played by real-life girlfriend Demi Moore) in tow. Estevez on camera is more able than Estevez behind it; the emphasis in *Wisdom* is clearly on the second syllable.

WISE BLOOD ☆☆☆½
1979, USA, PG
Brad Dourif, Ned Beatty, Harry Dean Stanton, Daniel Shor, Amy Wright, Mary Nell Santacroce, John Huston. Directed by John Huston. 106 min.

John Huston's adaptation of Flannery O'Connor's first novel is quite faithful to its source, a remarkable achievement in itself given the Southern Gothic eccentricity of the book. Brad Dourif (Billy Bibbitt in *One Flew Over The Cuckoo's Nest*) is ideally cast as a lost soul who returns to his backwoods home after World War II, dons preacher's garb, and tries to establish the Church of Truth Without Christ. Preaching on streetcorners in small towns, he is taken in and used by two other preachers, one who blinded himself and the other a good-ol'-boy type. Alternately funny and bleak, not unlike Huston's *Prizzi's Honor*, *Wise Blood* is quite obviously a film made by a man who, in his mid-seventies, felt no need to make his material more palatable to a wide audience.

WISE GUYS ☆
1986, USA, R
Danny DeVito, Joe Piscopo, Harvey Keitel, Ray Sharkey, Dan Hedaya, Captain Lou Albano, Patti LuPone. Directed by Brian DePalma. 91 min.

Toward the beginning of this alleged comedy, Joe Piscopo, as a lower-echelon mob employee, is fired at half a dozen times by his employer. Unfortunately, he's wearing a bulletproof jacket and survives to make the remainder of this movie seem like an eternity in purgatory for the viewer. Imagine all of the worst excesses of Jerry Lewis, Jim Belushi, and a Johnny Carson skit all rolled into one, and you've got some idea of Piscopo's performance. The other acting is just as bad, with DeVito and Piscopo running away from Newark mobster Dan Hedaya and having all kinds of "wacky" escapades in Atlantic City. What can you say about a comedy where Captain Lou Albano gives the best performance? It's enough to make you hope that Brian DePalma finds some more Alfred Hitchcock movies to rip off.

WITCHCRAFT THROUGH THE AGES ☆☆
1922, Sweden
Maren Pedersen, Clara Pontoppidan, Elith Pio, Oscar Stribolt, Tora Teje, Johs Andersen, Benjamin Christensen, William S. Burroughs (narration). Directed by Benjamin Christensen. 90 min.

A bizarre, watchable curio from the film vaults of Sweden, this purports to show the history of the Black Arts and then relate them to the strange new practice of "neuropsychiatry." Although there are dribs and drabs of a second-rate German Expressionist style, the film's primary purpose seems to have been to titillate its viewers with odd, leering rituals and fleeting nudity. Some of the scenes are amusing indeed, but this pre-exploitation film is never really creepy and never really charming. Embassy Home Entertainment's handsome version includes English-language intertitles, a full musical score by Daniel Humair, and delightfully deadpan voiceovers by author William S. Burroughs. Watch for director Benjamin Christensen as the Devil. (a.k.a.: *Haxan* and *The Witches*)

THE WITCHES

See *Witchcraft Through the Ages*

WITCHES' BREW ☆½
1980, USA, PG
Teri Garr, Richard Benjamin, Lana Turner, Kathryn Leigh Scott, Kelly Jean Peters. Directed by Richard Shorr and Herbert L. Strock. 98 min.

Three wives, all novice witches under the tutelage of veteran Lana Turner, attempt to use their shaky powers to advance the careers of their husbands, professors at a local college. This wan comedy doesn't derive as much from the TV series "Bewitched" as it sounds, though there are moments when Richard Benjamin may remind you of a cross between Dick York and Dick Sargent. It gets better toward the end, but not so much that you'd want to sit through the whole thing. From the director of *I Was a Teen-Age Frankenstein*.

THE WITCH'S MIRROR ☆
1960, Mexico
Rosita Arenas, Armando Calvo, Isabela Vorona, Dina De Marco. Directed by Chano Urveta. 75 min.

Rosita Arenas, the Fay Wray of Mexico, is back in another no-budget thriller. After a surgeon kills his first wife, the woman's stepmother, a sorceress, seeks vengeance. She causes him to disfigure the face of his second wife, launching him onto the old mad-surgeon tactic of trying to revitalize her with skin grafts from young girls, most of whom he has to kill first (them's the breaks). Guaranteed not to give you nightmares, and pretty unlikely even to keep you awake.

WITHOUT A TRACE ☆☆
1983, USA, PG
Kate Nelligan, Judd Hirsch, David Dukes, Stockard Channing, Daniel Bryan Corkill. Directed by Stanley R. Jaffe. 120 min.

This drama about a six-year-old boy who's kidnapped on his way to school and the desperate months subsequently endured by his mother (Kate Nelligan) may affect you emotionally, but you'll more likely be annoyed that it isn't handled with more intelligence or sincerity. Nelligan's performance is excellent, but the drama is pat down to its conclusion, and no aspect of it stands up to the subsequent telefilm *Adam*. At the time of its release, producer-director Stanley Jaffe took pains to dissociate *Without a Trace* from the real-life case of Etan Patz, a New York child whose disappearance received national attention. In fact, the two stories were similar enough that the film's inadequacies seem all the more pointed.

WITH SIX YOU GET EGGROLL ☆½
1968, USA
Doris Day, Brian Keith, Pat Carroll, Barbara Hershey, George Carlin, Alice Ghostley, Vic Tayback, Jamie Farr, Mickey Deems. Directed by Howard Morris. 95 min.

If you admire *Yours, Mine and Ours*, *Mulligan's Stew*, or any of the episodes of *The Brady Bunch*, you might consider this an original and amusing comedy. Doris Day (in her last feature film role to date) plays a widow who marries a widower (Brian Keith) against the wishes of their respective children (she has three boys, he has one girl). Like most TV family sitcoms over the last two decades, the film is both coy and predictable. Add hippies and the Grass Roots and you know the film was made in 1968. Directed by Howard Morris (*Goin' Coconuts*).

WITNESS ☆☆☆½
1985, USA, R
Harrison Ford, Kelly McGillis, Alexander Godunov, Lukas Haas, Jan Rubes, Danny Glover, Patti LuPone. Directed by Peter Weir. 112 min.

An Amish child (Lukas Haas) witnesses a murder in a train station men's room while accompanying his young, recently widowed mother (Kelly McGillis) on a rare trip into the outside world. The investigation of the crime, handled by rough Philadelphia detective John Book (Harrison Ford), uncovers a network of high-level corruption that forces Book to take reluctant refuge with the Amish community; his presence acts as a lightning rod for precisely those aspects of the twentieth-century civilization that the Amish most fear and despise. From the Australian director of *Gallipoli* and *The Year of Living Dangerously*, *Witness* is another sumptuously photographed exploration of conflicting cultures and the lives that get ground up in the process. Despite its schematic premise, the film is dense, subtle, and complex, with excellent performance from Ford and McGillis. Nominated for eight Academy Awards.

WITNESS FOR THE PROSECUTION ☆☆☆☆
1957, Great Britain
Charles Laughton, Marlene Dietrich, Tyrone Power, Elsa Lanchester, John Williams. Directed by Billy Wilder. 114 min.

Billy Wilder's foray into courtroom territory is a fine exception to the usual tedium of legal dramas. As Agatha Christie's murder mystery unfolds, revealing unexpected twist after unexpected twist, the camera prowls around the courtroom, conveying a sense of shifting loyalties and mutual suspicion. Tyrone Power as the accused killer and Marlene Dietrich as his devious wife are excellent, though both are topped by the delightful virtuosity of Charles Laughton as the ailing attorney. And how could a film like this be complete without peerless John Williams, as another barrister. As usual Wilder's razor-sharp irony and supreme craftsmanship make even his trashiest material fascinating to watch. Ingenious fun.

WITS TO WITS ☆½
Hong Kong
Henry Yu Young, Sucy Mango, Shik Chien, Wang Sun, Wu Ma, Tang Chine, Bee Chiu, Yamsaikuun, Yuen Sun, Ma Chien. Directed by Wu Ma. 90 min.

Ta Tu (Sucy Mango), an unshaven country bumpkin, pickpocket, and lech, runs away from his wife, Mimi, and meets a citified con man, Pai Shuang Len (Henry Yu Young), on a train. After pulling some dirty tricks on each other, they decide to steal a large shipment of gold that is being deposited into the local bank. This modern story has better acting and direction than many other martial arts movies. A cute film, but due to the small number of fights, not much for the kung fu buff. (a.k.a.: *From China with Death*)

THE WIZ ☆☆
1978, USA, G
Diana Ross, Michael Jackson, Richard Pryor, Lena Horne, Mabel King, Nipsey Russell, Ted Ross. Directed by Sidney Lumet. 133 min.

Whatever simple pleasures *The Wizard of Oz* once provided are lost in this hyperinflated, grotesquely overproduced version of the Broadway hit, which reset the story in New York, adding different songs and an all-black cast. Diana Ross is about twenty-five years too old to play Dorothy (now a Harlem schoolteacher) as anything but a case of arrested development. Sidney Lumet has shot the film in huge, dark vistas which are off-putting to young and old alike. But the transformation of the Brooklyn Bridge into the Yellow Brick Road is a spectacular display, and Mabel King, encased in a costume of chewed rubber-dog toys, makes a great, rowdy Wicked Witch. Still, any movie that wastes Michael Jackson, Richard Pryor, and Lena Horne deserves little leeway or forgiveness.

THE WIZARD OF GORE ☆
1982, USA, R
Ray Sager, Wayne Raven, Judy Clark, Sherry Carson. Directed by Herschell Gordon Lewis. 81 min.

A mad magician decides to improve the verisimilitude of his stage act, with the rather mysterious result that what he pretends to do to his victims on stage actually happens to them after they leave the theater. Given that he pretends to saw them in half and drive spikes through their brains, that does not leave them with a good opinion of the art of prestidigitation. Yes, folks, it's another Herschell Gordon Lewis gorefest, and those of you who cherish bad (but disgusting) special effects and worse acting will be pleased to know that, in those respects, this is one of his best. Others of you who may pick this up expecting to see the Tin Man, the Cowardly Lion, and Toto will learn not to go to the video store without your glasses in the future.

THE WIZARD OF MARS ☆½
1964, USA
John Carradine, Roger Gentry, Vic McGee, Jerry Rannow. Directed by David Hewitt. 81 min.

One female and three male astronauts crash-land on Mars and wander about the terrain trying to find the "Wizard of Mars" before their oxygen supply runs out. Cheap and boring, it's loosely derived from *The Wizard of Oz*, but to no interesting effect.

THE WIZARD OF OZ ☆☆☆☆
1939, USA
Judy Garland, Ray Bolger, Bert Lahr, Jack Haley, Margaret Hamilton, Billie Burke, Frank Morgan, Charlie Grapewin, Clara Blandick. Directed by Victor Fleming. 101 min.

There's no place like home and there's no more beloved musical than this enchanting adaptation of L. Frank Baum's timeless Oz books about the adventures of Kansas girl Dorothy Gale in the land of Oz. For years, fans have been praying for the video release of this lavish Technicolor fantasy peopled with munchkins and winged monkeys playing on a yellow brick road and in an Emerald City. With her unexpected arrival on a cyclone, Dorothy strikes up friendships with a Tin Man, a Scarecrow, and a Cowardly Lion, all of whom are met by the Wicked Witch of the West as they search for their hearts' desires. Judy Garland became a full-fledged star as Dorothy (in a role originally earmarked for Shirley Temple) and her teamwork with veteran scene-stealers Bert Lahr, Ray Bolger, and Jack Haley is magical. In additon to the splendid art direction, the melodic score by Harold Arlen and E. Y. Harburg (whose "Over the Rainbow," which was almost cut from the film, won an Oscar for Best Song) is the film's biggest attraction besides the irreplaceable cast. Although critical opinion was divided when the film was first released, *Oz* has attained classic status since its arrival on television. Remade in cartoon form and continued in the Disney feature *Return to Oz*. Die-hard *Oz* fans, however, prefer to click their heels three times and wait for this film original.

WOLFEN ☆☆
1981, USA
Albert Finney, Edward James Olmos, Diane Verona, Gregory Hines, Dick O'Neill. Directed by Michael Wadleigh. 115 min.

In this occasionally stylish but dreary horror movie about a series of gory murders in New York City, director Michael Wadleigh (*Woodstock*) proposes that the bombed-out South Bronx simply be left as is, so that the supernatural wolf-creatures (known as wolfen) can roam around in it and eat the bums. We don't get to see the wolves until the very end; the result plays like a horror movie about people being attacked by Steadicams. Albert Finney is wasted as a rogue police detective, but Gregory Hines has a few nice moments as a morgue worker with a sense of humor.

THE WOLF MAN ☆☆☆½
1941, USA
Lon Chaney, Jr., Maria Ouspenskaya, Evelyn Ankers, Claude Rains, Ralph Bellamy, Patric Knowles, Bela Lugosi, Fay Helm. Directed by George Waggner. 70 min.

The first of the many grade-B werewolf movies that came out of Hollywood remains the classiest of the lot, and one of the finest horror films of the 1940s. The usual lycanthrope lore is here in abundance, and there are some amusingly hoky bits with Maria Ouspenskaya as an old gypsy soothsayer. But what's striking about this version is Lon Chaney, Jr., who, as Larry Talbot, the haunted, pathetic victim of the werewolf's bite, gave the most memorable performance of his career. Jack Pierre is responsible for the still-chilling special effects. In many ways, it's more effective than the two best-remembered Universal horror classics, *Frankenstein* and *Dracula*.

A WOMAN CALLED GOLDA ☆☆☆½
1982, USA (TV)
Ingrid Bergman, Ned Beatty, Leonard Nimoy, Judy Davis. Directed by Alan Gibson. 200 min.

This is a moving, sympathetic chronicle of former Israeli prime minister Golda Meir's life from her childhood in the U.S. through her 1977 meeting with Anwar Sadat. Ingrid Bergman's stirring final performance in the title role earned her a posthumous Emmy as Outstanding Actress, with commendable acting by Leonard Nimoy as Golda's husband and Judy Davis as the young Golda. The beautiful Bergman is made up to look astonishingly like the homely but charismatic Golda!

A WOMAN IN FLAMES ☆☆
1983, West Germany, R
Gudrun Landrebe, Mathieu Carrière, Hans Zischler, Gabriele Lafari. Directed by Robert Van Ackeren. 105 min.

🌐 Gudrun Landrebe stars in this dull, modern melodrama about a young woman who walks out on her husband to discover a life of prostitution, specializing in the sexual abuse of men. Soon after, she meets the man of her dreams (Mathieu Carrière), also a prostitute, but it is not until he suggests that they escape and open a restaurant that she realizes she can't give up her career. Robert van Ackeren is shameless enough to quote from Jean-Luc Godard's abstruse classic *My Life to Live*, but he replaces Godard's social criticism and existentialist despair with panting eroticism and character stupidity. Available only in a dubbed English version.

THE WOMAN IN GREEN ☆☆☆
1945, USA
Basil Rathbone, Nigel Bruce, Henry Daniell, Hillary Brooke, Eve Amber. Directed by Roy William Neill. 68 min.

🐈‍⬛ One of the best (and last) entries in the Rathbone-Bruce Sherlock Holmes series. Now that World War II was over, they could send Holmes back to tracking down diabolical Professor Moriarty and forget about those silly spies and patriotic speeches of the previous entries. Moriarty's racket this time involves hypnotism, murder, and blackmail. Suitably atmospheric and foggy.

THE WOMAN IN RED ☆½
1984, USA, PG
Gene Wilder, Gilda Radner, Kelly LeBrock, Charles Grodin, Joseph Bologna, Judith Ivey. Directed by Gene Wilder. 86 min.

🤓 In this mousy remake of the 1977 French farce *Pardon Mon Affaire*, Gene Wilder plays Teddy Pierce, a woozy advertising executive who falls for a beautiful model (luscious Kelly LeBrock) and launches an obsessive, mishap-ridden attempt at seduction. Wilder's genial inertness is appealing, but despite occasional tame delights, the movie winds up coddling the most sentimental sort of adultery fantasies: by the end, Wilder could be caught in bed with LeBrock by his entire familial tribe and nothing would seem at stake. Gilda Radner, Wilder's wife in real life, plays the office hag. The sappy theme song, Stevie Wonder's "I Just Called to Say (I Love You)," won an Oscar.

WOMAN IN THE DUNES ☆☆☆☆
1964, Japan
Eiji Okada, Kyoko Kishida. Directed by Hiroshi Teshigahara. 127 min.

🌐 Hiroshi Teshigahara won the Special Jury Prize at the Cannes Film Festival for this delicate, evocative visual poem—the first Japanese film ever entered in the competition at Cannes. The mythical story has a young entomologist (Eiji Okada) fall asleep while hunting for butterflies. Some villagers find him and tell him that he may spend the night in a house in a nearby sandpit. When he awakens, the ladder has been pulled up, and he is trapped there with a beautiful young woman (Kyoko Kishida) and told he must help her to fill buckets with sand every night. Nearly all the film is about the evolution of the relationship between these two isolated people. On this surreal framework, Teshigahara has woven, in visually direct black-and-white photography, a haunting meditation on eroticism, cooperation, and fate. Screenplay by Kobo Abe, based on his own novel. (a.k.a.: *Suna No Onna*)

THE WOMAN IN THE WINDOW ☆☆☆½
1944, USA
Edward G. Robinson, Joan Bennett, Dan Duryea, Robert Blake, Raymond Massey, Dorothy Peterson. Directed by Fritz Lang. 99 min.

🐈‍⬛ Despite a silly ending, Fritz Lang's complicated *film noir* is one of the darkest, most absorbing movies of the 1940s. The hero—or antihero—is homely Edward G. Robinson, and it was one of his best roles; he plays a gentle, ordinary bourgeois who suddenly finds himself on the run, sucked into a grisly murder involving Joan Bennett. Robinson's dogface becomes a mask of desperation as the district attorney (Raymond Massey) closes in on him from one side and the dead man's bodyguard (Dan Duryea) hunts him from the other. A stinging, deliciously nasty film, one of Lang's best American movies.

THE WOMAN NEXT DOOR ☆☆☆
1981, France
Gérard Depardieu, Fanny Ardant, Henri Garcin, Michelle Baumgarner, Véronique Silver, Roger Van Hool, Philippe Morier-Genoud. Directed by François Truffaut. 106 min.

🌐 This is one of the smaller and less adventurous of François Truffaut's tales of obsessive love. Gérard Depardieu plays Bernard, a happy, decent man whose new next-door neighbor (Fanny Ardant) turns out to be his lover of years before. As the two rekindle their tempestuous affair, Truffaut tries to sweep us up into the dizzying world of grand passion, but, except for a jolting garden-party scene, nothing in the movie seems spontaneous or daring. Still, Truffaut elicits beautiful performances from his two romantic leads, and though the film too often seems premeditated, it's no less engaging than much of his better work.

A WOMAN OF PARIS ☆☆☆☆
1923, USA
Edna Purviance, Adolphe Menjou, Carl Miller, Lydia Knott, Betty Morrissey, Charles French. Directed by Charles Chaplin. 81 min.

🎭 This is, quite simply, one of the most beautiful and sensitive melodramas ever made, a landmark that introduced new sophistication in character shadings. It comes from CBS's Playhouse Video, one of the finest presentations of silent films on video (see also *The Circus*, *The Gold Rush*, *The Kid*). The story is simple: after a young woman's elopement falls through, she becomes a Parisian girl-about-town and the lover of a wealthy playboy. A chance meeting leads to a reunion with her young ex-fiancé; however, tragedy lurks in the wings. The film unfolds as a series of small incidents told with a deft touch—a napkin is folded to hide its povety-worn holes, a man's collar drops from a woman's drawer, an eyebrow is raised, and a glance is averted—everything is told, yet everything is left to the viewer. Charlie Chaplin's first film for the United Artists company that he had formed with Douglas Fairbanks, Mary Plckford, and D. W. Griffith, *A Woman of Paris* was also the first film that Chaplin directed but did not star in. Chaplin conceived the film as a vehicle for his longtime costar and friend Edna Purviance, and she is supremely touching and completely natural in a demanding role. Chaplin also helped Adolphe Menjou create the suave roué that he was to play for years. Look for Charlie in a tiny role as a railroad porter.

A WOMAN OF SUBSTANCE ☆☆☆
1984, Great Britain (TV)
Deborah Kerr, Jenny Seagrove, Liam Neeson, Barry Bostwick, Diane Baker. Directed by Don Sharpe. 300 min.

🎭 Possibly the best romantic miniseries ever. Granted, it is a glorified Harlequin romance, but the dross is transformed into gold in a luminous entertainment, produced by actress Diane Baker, who's also very moving in a supporting role here. As in many lesser examples of women's fiction, *Substance* details the upward progress of a serving girl who's betrayed by men until she starts acquiring some of their unscrupulousness. She suffers at all turns, becomes pregnant, opts for a marriage of convenience, improves her business acumen, and launches an extravagant conspiracy against the upper-crust family who used her so badly. This substantial drama plays upon an audience's desire to seek revenge against all those souls from the right side of the tracks who ever made them feel like serfs.

THE WOMAN OF THE TOWN ☆☆☆
1943, USA
Claire Trevor, Albert Dekker, Barry Sullivan, Henry Hull, Marion Martin, Porter Hall, Percy Kilbride, Beryl Wallace, Glenn Strange. Directed by George Archainbaud. 87 min.

🐎 An unusual, likable Western about the early life of Bat Masterson, the journalist who made a detour from his writing career for a while to become the marshal of Dodge City. He runs the gang out of town and generally makes the streets safe for decent folk, with the help of saloon singer Dora Hand, whose occupation irks the town's other nominal do-gooders. The whole thing is reminiscent of *Destry Rides Again*, but Albert Dekker and Claire Trevor manage to avoid overt comparisons with James Stewart and Marlene Dietrich.

WOMAN OF THE YEAR ☆☆☆☆
1942, USA
Katharine Hepburn, Spencer Tracy, Reginald Owen, Fay Bainter, William Bendix. Directed by George Stevens. 122 min.

In the first and one of the greatest of the Katharine Hepburn–Spencer Tracy romances, Kate plays Tess Harding, a globe-trotting ace reporter whose wit and style charm sportswriter Sam Craig (Tracy) into marriage. Once *en ménage*, however, the romance goes on the rocks, and it's up to the down-to-earth husband to teach his beautiful overachiever the real meaning of success. There's an undeniable message here that a woman's place is behind her man, but you can't take offense at the witty, Oscar-winning script by Ring Lardner, Jr., and Michael Kanin, and you'll only marvel at the truly timeless chemistry of the screen's greatest romantic couple.

A WOMAN REBELS ☆☆☆
1936, USA
Katharine Hepburn, Herbert Marshall, Elizabeth Allan. Directed by Mark Sandrich. 88 min.

Set in nineteenth-century England, this film is still timely, addressing fundamental issues of women's rights. Katharine Hepburn comfortably plays the young woman who crusades against the male-oriented conventions of her Victorian milieu. Directed by the same man who directed the Fred Astaire–Ginger Rogers musicals, Mark Sandrich's costume drama lacks the necessary intensity and, as a result, is not as inspiring as it had the potential to be.

WOMAN TIMES SEVEN ☆☆☆
1967, USA/France/Italy
Shirley MacLaine, Michael Caine, Alan Arkin, Peter Sellers, Rossano Brazzi, Lex Barker, Robert Morley, Anita Ekberg, Philippe Noiret. Directed by Vittorio de Sica. 98 min.

Shirley MacLaine stars in seven short segments of from eight to fifteen minutes in length, each intended to delve into a different aspect of the "contemporary woman." Not surprisingly, some segments are better than others; the lesser ones seem dated and silly, particularly one with MacLaine as a flower child. But the good ones are outstanding: MacLaine and Alan Arkin as a pair of nervous lovers trying to keep a suicide pact; Peter Sellers seducing MacLaine at her husband's funeral; and MacLaine as an over-thirty housewife fantasizing about a stranger (Michael Caine, in a wonderful wordless performance) who seems to be following her friend. Vittoria de Sica filmed in Paris, and makes excellent use of the cityscape for backdrop.

A WOMAN UNDER THE INFLUENCE ☆☆½
1974, USA
Peter Falk, Gena Rowlands, Matthew Cassel, Matthew Laborteaux, Christina Grisanti, Katherine Cassavetes, Lady Rowlands, Fred Draper. Directed by John Cassavetes. 155 min.

Gena Rowlands is meant to be cracking up "under the influence" of her well-meaning, boorish husband (Peter Falk). But Rowlands's performance is so jittery and overwrought that her character seems crazy from the start, and the movie has nothing to build (or decline) toward. John Cassavetes seems to be attempting a cinéma vérité style—the scenes drag on forever and the cast is cluttered with nonprofessionals and relatives. But his framing story is finally too conventional a study of a nervous breakdown to support his more ambitious concerns. Like many of his films, though, it's compelling even when it's least successful.

WOMBLING FREE ☆½
1977, Great Britain
David Tomlinson, Frances de la Tour, Bonnie Langford, Bernard Spear, Jack Purvis, Kenny Baker. Directed by Lionel Jeffries. 96 min.

The Wombles were a group of furry creatures who starred in a popular BBC children's series in the early 1970s, singing ditties about picking up garbage and making the world a cleaner place in which to live (well, you didn't think that *all* British television was Monty Python and Masterpiece Theatre, did you?). This is their version of *The Muppet Movie*, an attempt to put their charm across on the large screen. It's unquestionably for children only, and American kids who have never seen the Wombles before may be thoroughly puzzled (and bored) by the proceedings.

THE WOMEN ☆☆☆½
1939, USA
Norma Shearer, Joan Crawford, Rosalind Russell, Mary Boland, Paulette Goddard, Phyllis Povah, Joan Fontaine, Virginia Weidler, Lucile Watson, Ruth Hussey, Marjorie Main, Hedda Hopper. Directed by George Cukor. 132 min.

Its sexual politics lurch from the emancipated to the retrograde, and Norma Shearer is almost insufferably noble until the end, but George Cukor's adaptation of Claire Booth Luce's play about a corps of back-stabbing society wives is still hugely entertaining. Cukor retained the device of a single-sex cast to show a group of women obsessed by men but not terribly fond of them: there are standout performances by Rosalind Russell as a well-heeled shrew and Joan Crawford as a gold-digging villainess who sums it up when she says, "There's a name for you ladies, but it isn't used in proper society outside of a kennel." See it, if only to enjoy a talented cast attacking the juicy roles with energy and flair. And watch for the bizarre Technicolor fashion show in the middle.

WOMEN IN CELL BLOCK 7 ☆
1974, Italy/USA, R
Anita Strinberg, Eva Czemeys, Olga Bisera, Jane Avril, Valeria Fabrizi. Directed by Rino Di Silvestro. 90 min.

Standard women-in-prison fare, a genre that refuses to go away, though we should be grateful to it for keeping Linda Blair off the streets. This one looks suspiciously like it's made up of bits and pieces of two different Italian features, mixed together with some dialogue that seldom appears to be what the characters were saying in their native language. One plot involves an innocent young girl sent to the Big House on drug charges; the other has to do with the Mafia, and ne'er the twain shall meet. Try to pretend that you're sitting in a drive-in—it'll help.

WOMEN IN LOVE ☆☆☆
1969, Great Britain, R
Alan Bates, Oliver Reed, Glenda Jackson, Jennie Linden, Eleanor Bron, Alan Webb, Vladek Sheybal, Catherine Wilmer, Michael Glough. Directed by Ken Russell. 130 min.

Ken Russell's baroque adaptation of D. H. Lawrence's novel is full of his expectedly stunning set pieces and florid sexual decoration, but it may be his most intelligent work for the big screen; you'll be surprised at how easily Lawrence's narrative style meshes with the director's own sensibilities. Glenda Jackson won an Academy Award playing the tough-minded, independent heroine, but Russell seems more interested in the male characters; the most memorable scenes are those with Oliver Reed as the chilly, superior Gerald and Alan Bates as Rupert Birkin, whose desire for a bond with Gerald forms the story's emotional core. It's difficult to follow if you haven't read the book, and only slightly easier if you have.

WOMENS PRISON MASSACRE ½☆
1986, Italy, R
Laura Gemser, Gabriele Truti, Ursula Flores. Directed by Gilbert Roussel. 87 min.

The gravest sin any exploitation film can commit is to inspire boredom—yet this cheap mixture of female nudity and bloody violence does exactly that, in spades. Four psychotic killers (all men) are brought into a women's prison where they go berserk and cause mayhem. The only vaguely entertaining part of this mess happens during the opening credits, when three of the women introduce themselves in monologue fashion ("I am a slut. Filthy slut Eileen."). The rest is a hopeless waste of time you could spend doing something productive—like watching a fun (read: funny) exploitation film like *Chained Heat* or *Reform School Girls*. Note: *Womens Prison Massacre* is also known as *Emanuelle Escape from Hell*, one of the many films in the *Emanuelle* rip-off series that star Laura Gemser.

WONDER BAR ☆☆☆
1934, USA
Kay Francis, Dick Powell, Al Jolson, Dolores Del Rio, Ricardo Cortez, Hal Le Roy, Guy Kibbee, Ruth Donnelly, Hugh Herbert. Directed by Lloyd Bacon (musical numbers directed by Busby Berkeley). 85 min.

Wonder movie! This item comes from the same studio, director, and production team that gave us *Forty-Second Street* but it's even more outrageously campy. The *Grand Hotel*–type plot has something to do with a Paris nightclub owner (Al Jolson), his star attraction (Dolores Del Rio), and a singer (Dick Powell). The musical numbers include Busby Berkeley's notoriously racist but nonetheless fascinating "Going to Heaven on a Mule," with Jolson in blackface and sets probably later used in Warner's *Green Pastures*, and the divine "Don't Say Goodnight" sequence with its dazzling use of mirrors. The usually reliable Al Dubin and Harry Warren disappoint in the music department, but otherwise the production is up to par.

WON TON TON, THE DOG WHO SAVED HOLLYWOOD ☆
1976, USA, PG
Bruce Dern, Madeline Kahn, Art Carney, Phil Silvers, Teri Garr, Ron Leibman, Augustus Von Schumacher (as Won Ton Ton). Directed by Michael Winner. 92 min.

Michael Winner (*Death Wish*) directs this leaden farce that comes alive only when silent screen star Won Ton Ton (the pooch), depressed by his fading career, hits skid row. The period recreation is every bit as convincing as Ron Leibman playing Valentino as a mincing queen. There are cameo appearances by everyone who happened to be alive in Hollywood during the filming, including: Ethel Merman, Stepin Fetchit, the Ritz Brothers, George Jessel, William Demarest, Dennis Day, Joan Blondell, Broderick Crawford, Andy Devine, and Cyd Charisse.

WOODSTOCK ☆☆☆
1970, USA, R
Joan Baez, Joe Crocker, Country Joe and the Fish, Crosby, Stills, Nash and Young, Arlo Guthrie, Richie Havens, Jimi Hendrix, Santana, Shana-na, John Sebastian, Sly and the Family Stone, Ten Years After, the Who. Directed by Michael Wadleigh. 184 min.

"Woodstock was just a lot of people walking around in the mud looking for a place to pee," sniffs one too-young-to-remember character in Ann Beattie's *Chilly Scenes of Winter*. That may be true, especially for anyone born before 1945 or after 1959, but it was still almost half a million people gathered at a farm in upstate New York waiting for the Port-o-San. As a documentary, the feeling *Woodstock* puts across wavers between "Guess you had to be there" and "Wish I'd been there," with a lot of sadness probably not intended by the filmmakers (such as nostalgia). The performances, in all of their pre-MTV primitiveness, are still fabulous, especially those by Sly and the Family Stone, the Who, Jimi Hendrix, and Joe Cocker. Michael Wadleigh's split-screen technique, which was about the only way he could even begin to approach the enormity of the event, produces mostly confusion when viewed on the television screen; but then, in this case confusion is ambient. Winner of an Academy Award for Best Documentary.

THE WORD ☆☆
1978, USA (TV)
David Janssen, James Whitmore, Florinda Bolkan, Eddie Albert, Geraldine Chaplin, Hurd Hatfield, John Huston, Ron Moody, John McEnery, Diana Muldaur, Nicol Williamson, David Ackroyd, Nehemiah Persoff, Christopher Lloyd. Directed by Richard Lang. 188 min.

The Irving Wallace novel on which this shortened version of a TV miniseries was based has an intriguing premise: what would be the repercussions to the religious establishment if a new version of the New Testament, written by a contemporary of Jesus Christ, were discovered? Too bad the premise is discarded in favor of standard detective stuff and a cop-out ending. It's an unfortunate waste of an exceptional cast on over three hours of pointless plot—but on television you expect that.

WORDS AND MUSIC ☆☆
1948, USA
Mickey Rooney, Tom Drake, Judy Garland, Vera-Ellen, Gene Kelly, June Allyson, Lena Horne, Cyd Charisse. Directed by Norman Taurog. 119 min.

Thank God the words and music belong to Rodgers and Hart, because the nonmusical portions of this film are horrendous. Surely the disjointed events depicted onscreen can't belong to them, too. Mickey Rooney as Lorenz Hart? Tom Drake as Richard Rodgers? We didn't expect them to have Leo the Lion roar out the news that Hart had crushes on the male stars of his musicals, but were all the other ludicrous distortions necessary? Luckily, no one gets to act for long stretches because the proceedings are constantly interrupted by song-and-dance spots from MGM's finest. Judy Garland and Rooney blast the roof off with "I Wish I Were in Love Again," Lena Horne purrs her way through "The Lady Is a Tramp," and Gene Kelly and Vera-Ellen do a smashing ballet to "Slaughter on Tenth Avenue." So read a truthful biography of the famous songwriting team some other time and just enjoy their music here.

WORKING GIRLS ☆☆½
1973, USA, R
Sarah Kennedy, Laurie Rose, Lynne Guthrie, Solomon Sturges, Cassandra Peterson, Mary Beth Hughes. Directed by Stephanie Rothman. 81 min.

Writer/director Stephanie Rothman brings a woman's touch to the mild exploitation she's marketing in this story of three women roommates working to achieve personal and professional fulfillment in Los Angeles. One's an artist who paints billboard ads, another's a law student–stripper, and the new face in town is willing to try *anything*. Agreeable titillation and general good spirits. The role of the boyfriend is filled by Preston Sturges's son.

THE WORLD ACCORDING TO GARP ☆☆☆
1982, USA, R
Robin Williams, Glenn Close, John Lithgow, Mary Beth Hurt, Jessica Tandy, Hume Cronyn, Swoosie Kurtz, Amanda Plummer. Directed by George Roy Hill. 136 min.

Robin Williams stars in this episodic adaptation of John Irving's best-selling novel about the comic and tragic perils of everyday life; playing the author's winsome alter ego, he is, like the film as a whole, credible but softer and less compelling than his literary counterpart. Steve (*Breaking Away*) Tesich's screenplay preserves many of the novel's grimmest incidents (including a mutilation scene that many thought would be unfilmable), but the dazzling texture of characters and details that Irving took six hundred pages to create feels rushed and arbitrary here. See it for the Oscar-nominated performances of Glenn Close, as Garp's feminist mother, and John Lithgow, as a transsexual ex-fullback, which are sustained better than any fan of the novel would have thought possible.

THE WORLD IS FULL OF MARRIED MEN ☆☆
1979, Great Britain, R
Anthony Franciosa, Carroll Baker, Sherrie Cronn, Paul Nicholas, Gareth Hunt, Georgina Hale. Directed by Robert Young. 107 min.

An enjoyably tawdry sex romp with a very faint tinge of feminism. Anthony Franciosa plays a lecherous advertising executive whose long-suffering wife (Carroll Baker) finally becomes fed up with his philandering and takes her own lover. Trash-princess Jackie Collins (*Hollywood Wives*) adapted the screenplay from her own novel, and it contains her familiar mixture of sex, violence, and bitchiness.

THE WORLD OF HENRY ORIENT ☆☆☆
1964, USA
Peter Sellers, Tippy Walker, Merrie Spaeth, Angela Lansbury, Paula Prentiss, Phyllis Thaxter, Tom Bosley. Directed by George Roy Hill. 106 min.

One would not expect a light, engaging comedy about two starstruck schoolgirls from the likes of George Roy Hill (*Butch Cassidy and the Sundance Kid, The World According to Garp*), but perhaps the crazy-quilt world of Henry Orient is not so far removed from the one inhabited by Garp. Peter Sellers plays the amorous Manhattan concert pianist Henry Orient and Tippy Walker and Merri Spaeth play the schoolgirls who trail his every move. Could Nora and Nunnally Johnson's offbeat screenplay be a wicked send-up of *The Children's Hour*? It might have been had it stayed with the two girls; instead, the point of view wanders, especially when one of the mothers (a rich bitch nicely played by Angela Lansbury) has a fling with Orient. The film is also too long, but there is enough charm along the way to make it a world worth entering.

THE WORLD'S GREATEST ATHLETE ☆☆½
1973, USA, G
Tim Conway, Jan-Michael Vincent, John Amos, Roscoe Lee Browne, Dayle Haddon, Billy DeWolfe, Nancy Walker, Howard Cosell, Frank Gifford, Jim McKay. Directed by Robert Scheerer. 92 min.

Very much in the vein of Kurt Russell's early 1970s comedies for Disney (*The Barefoot Executive, Now You See Him Now You Don't, The Computer Wore Tennis Shoes*), this one has Jan-Michael Vincent standing in as the studio's incarnation of wholesome youth. He plays a young man raised in the jungle and brought to a college campus, where he beomes an all-American phenomenon. The athletic stunts and comic subplots will delight kids, and adults looking for a Disney film could do worse.

THE WORLD'S GREATEST LOVER ☆½
1977, USA, PG
Gene Wilder, Carol Kane, Dom DeLuise, Fritz Feld, Carl Ballantine. Directed by Gene Wilder. 89 min.

Gene Wilder's noisy, helpless, unfunny comedy is his second directorial effort and further proof that he is among the few filmmakers on earth who can make themselves totally unappealing. Here he plays an aggressive, thimble-brained schnook who is drawn to 1920s Hollywood by a contest, sponsored by Dom DeLuise's movie studio, to find a rival for Rudolph Valentino. Wilder harbors odd misconceptions about humor: as a director, he equates it with noise and numbing repetition, and as an actor, he equates it with a strangled voice and popping eyes. As his wife, Carol Kane has some affecting moments; they are almost the only ones in the movie.

THE WORLD, THE FLESH AND THE DEVIL ☆☆
1959, USA
Harry Belafonte, Inger Stevens, Mel Ferrer. Directed by Ranald MacDougall. 95 min.

M. P. Shiel's time-worn sci-fi classic (first filmed as a silent in 1914) is turned into an intriguing, topical, but woefully disappointing film. In writer-director Ranald MacDougall's treatment, atomic warfare leaves Manhattan island completely desolate save for three people: a black man, a white woman, and a white man. The first third of the film, during which Harry Belafonte (and the audience) assumes he is the sole survivor, is the best part. When Inger Stevens shows up, followed by Mel Ferrer, the issue of race raises its head, but it is not adequately dealt with or clearly resolved. Another mistake was framing skyscraper compositions in Cinemascope. This film was the inspiration for such recent films as *The Omega Man, Dawn of the Dead*, and *Night of the Comet*. No relation to a 1960 Mexican film titled *World, Flesh and the Devil*.

WORLD WITHOUT END ☆☆½
1956, USA
Hugh Marlowe, Nancy Gates, Nelson Leigh, Rod Talyor, Shawn Smith. Directed by Edward Bernds. 79 min.

In better-than-average 1950s low-budget science fiction, a spaceship bound for Mars accidentally breaks the time barrier and ends up on Earth in the year 2508. By this time, of course, the surface of the planet has been wiped out by nuclear wars, so the remaining humans live underground. Having atrophied just about every part of their bodies except their brains, the Earthlings of the future decide that spacemen from the past will make good breeding stock. This was probably a career high for writer-director Edward Bernds, whose usual output consisted of Blondie, Bowery Boys, and Three Stooges programmers.

THE WORM EATERS ☆☆½
1977, USA, R
Herb Robins. Directed by Herb Robins. 80 min.

This is it—the one both of you have been waiting for, a truly awful movie that will make you groan, retch, howl, and occasionally laugh yourself sick. There's a slight chance that it was *supposed* to be funny, but we sincerely doubt it. Writer/director Herb Robins stars as a misunderstood worm breeder. He tricks people into eating special worms that turn them into "worm monsters"—the costume department wraps up their legs in brown cloth and they wriggle around on the floor. At the end of the movie, the worm people cast a fishing line into Robins's house, hook him, reel him out, and turn him into a worm monster, too; he wriggles out onto the highway and gets run over by a truck. The highlight of this, though, is watching people eat *real* worms, live, on camera, with their mouths wide open so you can see every moment of mastication. Produced by Ted Mikels, the notorious director of *The Astro-Zombies* and *Blood Orgy of the She-Devils*.

THE WRAITH ☆
1986, USA, PG-13
Charlie Sheen, Nick Cassavetes, Sherilyn Fenn, Randy Quaid, Matthew Barry, David Sherill. Directed by Mike Marvin. 90 min.

This ludicrous horror action film features the otherwise talented Charlie Sheen as the ghost of a murdered teenager who returns from the dead in a very fancy car to torment the vicious hood (Nick Cassavetes) who slew him. The hokey dialogue suggests that dead teens don't sound terribly different from living ones and can still get driver's licenses. Not a scare or surprise in sight, but there are a few funny moments courtesy of the slumming cast.

THE WRECKING CREW ☆☆
1968, USA, M
Dean Martin, Elke Sommer, Sharon Tate, Nancy Kwan, Nigel Green, Tina Louise. Directed by Phil Karlson. 104 min.

If you were ten years old in 1968 and want to enjoy some camp nostalgia of the time, go out and rent the movie version of *Batman*. If you were twenty or older, rent *The Wrecking Crew*. The fourth and last of the Matt Helm series, a parody of the James Bond films, this one is ostensibly about Helm (Dean Martin) tracking down the bad guy who hijacked a billion dollars in gold in order to ruin the international monetary system (now *that's* ambition!), but never mind that: this exists only to give Martin a chance to leer, make jokes about sex, booze, and sex, and generally look like he's still astounded that they're paying him money to do this. Sharon Tate had the best role of her too-brief career here, as an engagingly clumsy female agent. She manages to play for both laughs and sex appeal at the same time, a very difficult feat.

THE WRESTLING WOMEN VS. THE AZTEC MUMMY
1964, Mexico ☆
Lorena Velazquez, Armando Silvestre, Elizabeth Campbell, Chucho Salinas. Directed by Rene Cardona. 88 min.

Those south-of-the-border wrestling sensations Gloria Venus and the Golden Rubi, of *Doctor of Doom* fame, are back in a leading contender for the Best Movie Title of All Time. Actually, the title is misleading, because the mummy is on the same side as the wrestling women and their incompetent police boyfriend. The bad guy is an Oriental prince, with his own squad of evil female wrestlers. Written by Abel Salazar, who starred in several dozen Mexican horror movies himself before moving behind the camera. Fans will also want to see *Aztec Mummy Double Feature*.

WRITTEN ON THE WIND
1956, USA ☆☆☆½
Rock Hudson, Lauren Bacall, Robert Stack, Dorothy Malone, Robert Keith, Grant Williams, Robert J. Wilke, Edward C. Platt, Harry Shannon, John Larch. Directed by Douglas Sirk. 99 min.

Douglas Sirk is best known for his acid-etched portraits of the middle class (*Magnificent Obsession, All That Heaven Allows*), and here he tells a rich, tortured tale about the things closest to American hearts: sex, money, booze, class, and insanity. A quartet of powerhouse performances deliver the melodramatic excess needed to carry the emotional torment of an oil family gone to hell. Dorothy Malone won an Oscar for her characterization of the low-down slatternly Marylee, the daughter of the Hadley family who always seems to be haunting the oil field bars. Robert Stack is just as good as Kyle Hadley, her insecure brother, who marries the beautifully cool Lucy Moore (Lauren Bacall). At the center of these relationships is staunch Mitch Wayne, played marvelously by Hudson. Sirk surrounds them all with the glossy-looking Hadley home and a nightmarishly bleak town—a suffocating world that is caught between empty pleasures and rock-hard suffering.

W.R.—MYSTERIES OF THE ORGANISM
1971, Yugoslavia/West Germany, X ☆☆☆☆
Milena Dravic, Jagoda Kaloper, Betty Dodson. Directed by Dusan Makaveyev. 86 min.

Dusan Makaveyev seemed, at the time, with the possible exception of Jean-Luc Godard, to be the only true heir to the heroic age of Soviet montage filmmaking. In this film he is closest to Dziga Vertov, using the techniques of joining pieces of celluloid to deconstruct his topics: sexual repression, expression, and perversion. Half of the film is an examination of the theories of Wilhelm Reich, the W.R. of the title, who purported that the desire for power is the result of repressed sexuality and that sexual freedom creates positive personal energy. Although Makaveyev seems sympathetic to Reich, his outsider's look at the variety of American indulgent sexual expressions is funny, acerbic, and cynical. The other half of the film uses a narrative involving a young Yugoslavian girl's attempt to use sex as a tool of political liberation. Her destruction at the hands of an ice-blooded Russian is both a sexual crime and a daring political statement. Makaveyev's film continually leaves gaps that the viewer must fill in, and the jumbled activity of the viewing process becomes an analog to the actual disparate bits of film fighting for attention.

THE WRONG BOX
1966, USA/Great Britain ☆☆☆½
John Mills, Ralph Richardson, Michael Caine, Peter Cook, Dudley Moore, Nanette Newman, Tony Hancock, Peter Sellers. Directed by Bryan Forbes. 105 min.

A frequently riotous dark comedy, this spoofs many of the obsessions of Victorian England, including death and the repression of romantic urges. Based on the novel by Robert Louis Stevenson and Lloyd Osbourne, it is a crazy, convoluted patchwork quilt of a movie, but the sterling cast makes it work most of the way. John Mills and Ralph Richardson star as two brothers, linked by an insurance policy, determined to do away with each other (assisted by nephews Dudley Moore and Peter Cook); Michael Caine also stars as Mills's grandson, a starry-eyed young bumbler in love with a pretty young lady (Nanette Newman); and Peter Sellers is unforgettable as a degenerate doctor who offers death certificates in advance. Sluggish in spots, but generally very funny in the best British black-comedy tradition.

WRONG IS RIGHT
1982, USA, R ☆½
Sean Connery, George Grizzard, Robert Conrad, Katharine Ross, G. D. Spradlin, John Saxon, Henry Silva, Leslie Nielsen, Robert Webber, Rosalind Cash, Hardy Kruger, Dean Stockwell, Ron Moody, Cherie Michan, Tony March. Directed by Richard Brooks. 117 min.

Richard Brooks's dispiriting, satirical thriller is apparently the product of a disordered mind that wants to say something about politics and television but doesn't know exactly what. Sean Connery plays a TV newsman who stumbles across a plot to assassinate an Arab king, depose the president, and blow up New York with two atomic bombs. The movie's incoherence and lack of connection to the real world are exceeded only by its feebleness as satire; this is a film for the sort of people who can gasp and giggle when daring words like "Watergate" issue from the screen.

THE WRONG MAN
1956, USA ☆☆☆½
Henry Fonda, Vera Miles, Anthony Quayle, Harold J. Stone, Charles Cooper. Directed by Alfred Hitchcock. 105 min.

As gripping and powerful as nearly anything in the Alfred Hitchcock canon, *The Wrong Man* tells a relentlessly grim tale, unrelieved by the director's characteristic humor. Henry Fonda plays a Stork Club musician whose life is shattered when he's mistaken by witnesses and police for an armed robber. Fonda's wife (Vera Miles) is driven to madness by the seemingly futile attempts to clear her husband's name. The themes of mistaken identity and an individual being devoured by an impersonal, entrapping system are common in Hitchcock's work. This film, however, has the distinction of being based on a true story, as the director explains in a precredit sequence. Robert Burks's bleak, black-and-white cinematography and Bernard Herman's subdued, haunting score add to the movingly realistic terror Hitchcock creates.

WUTHERING HEIGHTS
1939, USA ☆☆☆½
Laurence Olivier, Merle Oberon, David Niven, Geraldine Fitzgerald, Flora Robson, Donald Crisp. Directed by William Wyler. 104 min.

Merle Oberon is a less-than-perfect Cathy, but Laurence Olivier is a splendid Heathcliff and everything else about this Sam Goldwyn adaptation of Emily Brontë's classic novel is polished and meticulous. The opening sequence is shot (by Gregg Toland, who won an Oscar) like a 1930s Universal horror movie, and the closing sequence is pure thirties romanticism. In between unreels the story of undying love between a handsome stable boy and a middle-class Englishwoman. Ben Hecht and Charles MacArthur's script neatly condenses Brontë's lengthy Victorian narrative into an economical 104-minute running time and the supporting cast is made up of some great British and pseudo-British character actors, including Flora Robson, David Niven, Geraldine Fitzgerald (in a role originally intended for Vivien Leigh), Cecil Kellaway, Hugh Williams, and Donald Crisp. Luis Buñuel's 1954 Mexican version had more cynical wit, but this one has a compulsively watchable schmaltziness. Olivier was on his way to film stardom after his wonderful performance.

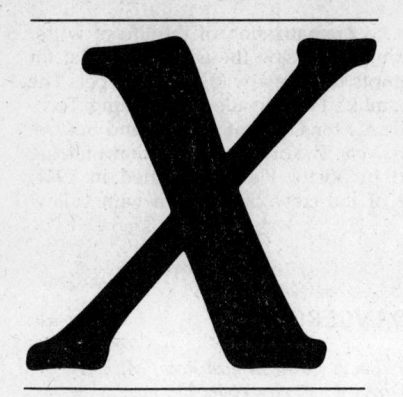

X

XANADU ☆
1980, USA, PG
Olivia Newton-John, Michael Beck, Gene Kelly, James Sloyan. Directed by Robert Greenwald. 96 min.

♪ Saccharine sludge, about a heavenly muse (Olivia Newton-John) who helps a Nice Young Guy (Michael Beck) open a roller-disco and fulfill his dreams. The pop songs and the dancing are so cheerfully inept and mindless that within minutes, you'll be longing for *Singin' in the Rain* and weeping for its star, Gene Kelly, who somehow became entrapped in this cynical spectacle. Newton-John is an attractive actress, but her taste in projects is truly perverse. After *Xanadu*, no major Hollywood movie was awful in quite the same way until her 1983 flop, *Two of a Kind*.

"X"—THE MAN WITH THE X-RAY EYES ☆☆☆
1963, USA
Ray Milland, Diana Van Der Vlis, Harold J. Stone, Don Rickles, Jonathan Haze, Dick Miller. Directed by Roger Corman. 80 min.

This memorable mad doctor movie was quite a bit better than usual AIP horror film. Ray Milland invents a serum that provides better vision; he administers too strong a dose to himself and finds that he can see through things. Unfortunately, he has no control over this: he can see through his own eyelids, and witnesses things he'd rather not see. The ending is a real shocker. *Note*: yes, it's the same Don Rickles; no, he doesn't sing.

XTRO ☆
1982, USA, R
Philip Sayer, Bernice Stegers, Simon Nash, Maryann D'Abo. Directed by Harry Davenport. 86 min.

Juicy horror film that's a perennial on the Times Square circuit, where plot and acting are secondary to gory, gooey special effects. A man is kidnapped by aliens and returned to earth three years later to begin breeding his new masters. Those of you who have seen *Alien*, of course, already know how extraterrestrials breed. For maximum effect, we recommend that you watch this with your feet in a bowl of strawberry jam.

THE XYZ MURDERS

See *Crimewave*

Y

THE YAKUZA ★★½
1974, USA, R
Robert Mitchum, Takakura Ken, Herb Edelman, Okada Eiji, Brian Keith. Directed by Sydney Pollack. 112 min.

A languorous immersion into a strange, hard-boiled, soft-focus contemporary Japan leads to a violent East/West confrontation. Japanese star Takakura Ken underplays effectively, and Robert Mitchum and Brian Keith talk tough with lots of hand-me-down dialogue courtesy of Robert Towne and Paul Schrader, the two masters of 1940s script retreading. Mitchum is the kind of performer who can make a film his own, and the movie has more in common with his slouching virility in films like *Farewell My Lovely* and *Out of the Past* than it does with the chameleon career of director Sydney Pollack. Note the haunting score by Dave Grusin. (a.k.a.: *Brotherhood of the Yakuza*)

YANKEE DOODLE DANDY ★★★½
1942, USA
James Cagney, Joan Leslie, Walter Huston, Richard Whorf, S. Z. Sakall, Jeanne Cagney, Captain Jack Young, Irene Manning, Frances Langford. Directed by Michael Curtiz. 126 min.

Warner Bros.' big and brazzy musical biography of song-and-dance man George M. Cohan transcends some unavoidable flag-waving hokeyness through the electrifying performance of James Cagney, whose stiff-backed hoofing and rapid-fire belting are still wonders to behold. Cagney's lovable, Oscar-winning portrait is more entertaining than anything Cohan himself ever committed to film, and he makes a competent but ordinary production something exhilarating to watch. The film's highlight is Cohan's chance encounter with the legendary Eddie Foy (played by Eddie, Jr.)—their exchange is priceless.

YANKS ★★★
1979, USA, R
Richard Gere, Lisa Eichhorn, Vanessa Redgrave, William Devane, Chick Vennera, Wendy Morgan, Rachel Roberts. Directed by John Schlesinger. 104 min.

Before he joined the Navy and fell for local girl Debra Winger in *An Officer and a Gentleman*, Richard Gere joined the Army and fell for local girl Lisa Eichhorn in this teary, old-fashioned World War II romance set in a small English village. John Schlesinger's direction is lush and tasteful (perhaps too tasteful). The subplot, with William Devane and Vanessa Redgrave as the more mature pair of lovers, is more interesting and better acted than the main story.

THE YEARLING ★★★½
1946, USA
Gregory Peck, Jane Wyman, Claude Jarman, Jr., Chill Wills, Henry Travers, Forrest Tucker, June Lockhart. Directed by Clarence Brown. 134 min.

If you saw *Cross Creek*, a dramatization of the life of writer Marjorie Kinnan Rawlings, you saw the source material for this story of a boy who attempts to raise a wild deer as a pet. The film is an eerie, almost dreamlike fable, made in ravishing Technicolor; it won Academy Awards for Cinematography and Set Design. An excellent family film. *Note*: The original production, starring Spencer Tracy and directed by Victor Fleming, started in 1941, but was halted when some of the crew came down with yellow fever.

THE YEAR OF LIVING DANGEROUSLY ★★½
1983, Australia/USA, PG
Mel Gibson, Sigourney Weaver, Linda Hunt, Bembol Roco, Michael Murphy, Domingo Landicho. Directed by Peter Weir. 115 min.

Peter Weir's offbeat adventure film, set in the midst of Indonesia's 1965 military coup, stars Mel Gibson as an Australian journalist who becomes romantically involved with an assistant British military attaché (Sigourney Weaver). Linda Hunt plays a Chinese-Australian dwarf who brings the lovers together and serves as the film's moral conscience. Unfortunately, Weir is more interested in creating mood than he is in detailing political intrigue, and his film leaves the viewer only superficially informed. The reportedly "hot" love scenes between Gibson and Weaver (whose British accent is embarrassingly uneven) are few and far between. Ultimately, the supporting cast, headed by the Oscar-winning Hunt and Michael Murphy, gives the film whatever grit it has.

YEAR OF THE DRAGON ★½
1985, USA, R
Mickey Rourke, John Lone, Ariane. Directed by Michael Cimino. 135 min.

An underdog cop (Mickey Rourke) tries to unravel New York's "Chinese Mafia," in an extravagant, overblown failure from Michael Cimino. To say that *Year of the Dragon* isn't nearly as bad as *Heaven's Gate* is faint praise, but that's almost more than Cimino's first film in five years deserves. Although he has an undeniable knack for staging scenes of spectacular visual grandeur and physical movement, he doesn't give *Dragon* a coherent story or credible characters to go along with it. Police chief Stanley White is Manhattan's own Rambo, going after Chinatown's criminal ruling class as if he were still in Vietnam. We're supposed to applaud his efforts and ignore the blustering, bullying, and blatant racism that he and the film almost wholeheartedly endorse. Rourke's performance is clamorous, mannered, and crassly emphatic, and model Ariane, in the potentially interesting role of an Asian-American newswoman, sleepwalks through her debut. Much of the original story seems to have been cut at random, but watch for the scenes in which our loner hero rants against the evil puppetry of the press and proudly states that his arrogant belief in his own abilities is fully justified, even if nobody else sees it. You'll wonder who's talking.

A YEAR OF THE QUIET SUN ★★½
1985, Poland
Scott Wilson, Maja Kamorowska, Hanna Skarnanka, Ewa Dalkowska, Vadim Glowna, Daniel Webb, Jerzy Nowak, Zbigniew Zapasiewicz, Tadeusz Bradecki. Directed by Krzysztof Zanussi. 106 min.

This love story about an American GI (Scott Wilson) and a Polish refugee (Maja Kamorowska) who don't speak each other's language uses the shambles of postwar Poland as a metaphor for the debris of the lovers' souls, and for the differences that finally drove a wedge between the U.S. and its allies. Krzysztof Zanussi lacks the narrative control to make the parallel structure work. With no way for the characters to impart enough basic information to each other, their lack of verbal communication becomes an irritating device. The performances of Kamorowska and Hanna Skarnanka (as her mother) are, however, exemplary.

YELLOWBEARD ☆½
1983, Great Britain, PG
Graham Chapman, Peter Boyle, Richard "Cheech" Marin, Tommy Chong, Peter Cook, Marty Feldman, Kenneth Mars, Martin Hewitt, Eric Idle, Madeline Kahn, James Mason, John Cleese, Susannah York, David Bowie, Spike Milligan, Beryl Reid, Peter Bull. Directed by Mel Damski. 101 min.

Seldom have so many funny performers been wasted in a single movie. Some of the blame must fall on Graham Chapman and Peter Cook, who cowrote the screenplay and apparently let all of their worst shared tendencies get the better of them. But the major fault is with director Mel Damski, a veteran of bad made-for-TV features. Not only does he have no idea what to do with all of these people, he seems to have been intimidated by them. So they all wander aimlessly about doing their own litte shticks, resulting in a package that contains a few funny moments but which as a whole is painful to watch. It's supposed to be a parody of pirate movies.

YENTL ☆☆½
1983, USA, PG
Barbra Streisand, Amy Irving, Mandy Patinkin, Nehemia Persoff, Steven Hill. Directed by Barbra Streisand. 134 min.

With much toil and effort, star/director Barbra Streisand turned Isaac Bashevis Singer's charming fable "Yentl, the Yeshiva Boy" into the kind of sophisticated, "integrated" musical that Hollywood gave up making around the time of *Gigi* (1958). It is obvious from her sensitive work as director (this is her debut) that the story of a pre–World War I Jewish girl who disguises herself as a boy to study the Talmud has great meaning for her. The lighting, photography and general *mise en scène* are carefully executed and neatly evoke the condescending attitudes toward women in that bygone era. Deliberate pacing aside, the surprisingly adult romantic roundelay between Streisand, Amy Irving, and Mandy Patinkin builds cleverly. It is especially unfortunate, then, that the work of Streisand as star is typically front, right, and center (when one out of three would have been more than enough) and that Streisand the songwriter didn't have enough sense to write her own songs rather than hire Michel Legrand, who contributes a series of bummers (all sung by Streisand). Better than some of her recent film efforts, and a promising debut as director, but far from an unqualified success.

YES, GIORGIO ☆½
1982, USA, PG
Luciano Pavarotti, Kathryn Harrold, Eddie Albert, Paolo Borboni, James Hong, Beulah Quo. Directed by Frnaklin J. Schaffner. 110 min.

Luciano Pavarotti makes his film debut in an embarrassing cliché-fest about an illicit love affair between an opera star and a beautiful Boston throat doctor (Kathryn Harrold). In one scene, Pavarotti—a stiff actor even by opera standards—goes up in a balloon and honors us with the John Williams–Alan and Marilyn Bergman song "If We Were in Love," while, down below, rustics in the California countryside cry "Giorgio!" and drop their milk pails and fishing rods. And so on.

YOJIMBO ☆☆☆☆
1961, Japan
Toshiro Mifune, Eijiro Tono, Isuzu Yamada. Directed by Akira Kurosawa. 110 min.

In the annals of the samurai film, this is a very close second to Akira Kurosawa's *Seven Samurai*. Toshiro Mifune is superb as a wandering samurai who enters a town beset by two warring bands. He hires himself out to both, and then proceeds to set them against each other. Kurosawa, who several years earlier made a film from a crime novel by Ed McBain, is said to have adapted this from Dashiell Hammett's *Red Harvest*; it was later remade by the Italian Sergio Leone as the spaghetti Western *A Fistful of Dollars* (just as *Seven Samurai* was remade into the American Western *The Magnificent Seven*). So whether your preferred genre is the Western, crime drama, or samurai epic, this is for you. Followed by a sequel, *Sanjuro*.

YOL ☆☆☆☆
1982, Turkey/Switzerland, PG
Tarik Akan, Halil Ergun, Necmettin Cobanoglu, Serif Sezer. Directed by Serif Goren and Yilmaz Guney. 114 min.

The 1982 Grand Prize–winner at Cannes, this searing political powerhouse is the story of five Turkish political prisoners who are granted a week's leave from jail. They return home to find a world overrun with violence and racism, where order is based on family vendettas and the violent oppression of women, especially the wives they had left behind. Yilmaz Guney conceived this film while a prisoner himself and has brought to his story an almost documentarylike intensity and passion. Viewers will remember the personal humiliations and, especially, a harrowing trip through a snowstorm. Filmed secretly after Guney's release from prison.

YOR, THE HUNTER FROM THE FUTURE ½☆
1983, Italy, PG
Reb Brown, Corinne Clery, John Steiner, Carole Andre. Directed by Anthony M. Dawson (Antonio Margheriti). 88 min.

Set in the future, but filmed in scenic present-day Yugoslavia, this unbelievably bad movie deals with the exploits of Yor, a caveman who excels at bashing in the brains of papier-mâché dinosaurs. After many idiotic adventures, our sun-bronzed hero (Reb Brown, who looks like he wandered in from Zuma beach to play the title character) discovers that he's the only genetically perfect survivor of a nuclear holocaust that took the earth back to the stone age. From there on in, Yor battles a bunch of Darth Vader clones for the remnants of civilization. Directed by everyone's favorite Italian schlockmeister, Anthony M. Dawson (*Cannibal Holocaust*).

YOTZ'IM KAVUA

See *Going Steady*

YOU LIGHT UP MY LIFE ☆
1977, Canada, PG
Didi Conn, Joe Silver, Michael Zaslow, Stephen Nathan, Melanie Mayron, Amy Letterman. Directed by Joseph Brooks. 90 min.

Joseph Brooks, who wrote, produced, directed, and scored this, formerly worked as a composer of advertising jingles, and, sure enough, this has all the depth and sincerity of a greeting card. (We should at least be thankful that he didn't cast himself as the star as well, as he did in his next feature, *If Ever I See You Again*.) Didi Conn (*Grease*) plays an aspiring pop singer who makes the mistake of consistently falling in love with the wrong men as she progresses in her career. She and gravel-voiced Joe Silver, as her father, have some moments, but the script and everything else in this is pure syrup. Docked half a star for producing the most annoying title song to become a hit single in the last twenty years.

YOU'LL FIND OUT ☆☆½
1940, USA
Kay Kyser, Peter Lorre, Boris Karloff, Bela Lugosi, Helen Parrish. Directed by David Butler, 97 min.

Any musical comedy that pairs Kay Kyser (playing himself) with the three-headed monster called Karloff-Lorre-Lugosi should be anticipated with horror even by scholars of this bathetic subgenre. Actually, *You'll Find Out* is aptly titled in its implied anticipation of pleasant surprise; hardly high-flying, it nevertheless isn't strung out, and its pace and solid musicality lift it up about two stories above Kyser's earlier *That's Right, You're Wrong*. The bandleader is hired to play Helen Parrish's twenty-first birthday in a home constructed like a wooden Egyptian tomb; Bela Lugosi arranges a seance that imperils the ingenue, and Kyser is left to unwrap the ghouls. Not dour, dull, or demanding, this film is worth finding out about.

YOU'LL NEVER GET RICH ☆☆
1941, USA
Fred Astaire, Rita Hayworth, Robert Benchley, John Hubbard, Osa Massen, Frieda Inescort. Directed by Sidney Lanfield. 88 min.

And you'll never get entertained by this lame musical comedy. It's hard to believe today, but this feeble effort put Fred Astaire back on top after a few years of being box-office poison. Fred plays a Broadway director who reluctantly joins the Army, where he gets into trouble for trying to stage a show with army brat Rita Hayworth. This was a big production for Columbia in its day, but it's a shoddy showcase next to the Astaire standard: the comedy routines in the barracks make "Hogan's Heroes" look classy; the subplot with Robert Benchley as a philandering husband is more queasy than funny; Cole Porter's score (possibly his worst) is instantly forgettable; the "Wedding Cake Walk" finale is a major embarrassment; and, most regrettably, Astaire and Hayworth dance very infrequently together. The film's one saving grace is their dance to "So Near and Yet So Far," Porter's one good song and an elegantly staged pearl. Otherwise, the "You Never" follow-up, *You Were Never Lovelier*, also with Astaire and Hayworth, is a much better film.

YOUNG AND INNOCENT ☆☆☆
1937, Great Britain
Nova Pilbeam, Derrick de Marney. Directed by Alfred Hitchcock. 80 min.

Circumstantial evidence points to a man's guilt in a murder, and the man flees the authorities and latches on to the local chief constable's beautiful daughter, who is soon persuaded to help him to prove his innocence. The story is a highly familiar one in the Alfred Hitchcock oeuvre, and is nearly identical to that of *The 39 Steps*, the superior British film released two years earlier. *Young and Innocent* develops many of the director's ideas about identity, deception, theater, and artifice that the earlier work introduced. But despite its subtle cinematography and thematic richness, the film is never very exciting or involving.

YOUNG AND WILLING ☆☆
1943, USA
William Holden, Eddie Bracken, Susan Hayward, Barbara Britton, Robert Benchley. Directed by Edward H. Griffith. 82 min.

This is a sort of backstage musical, only there isn't any music; some young and willing hopefuls try to get a show on the boards. A good chance to see some fresh-faced actors before they became big-time stars.

YOUNGBLOOD ☆☆½
1986, USA, R
Rob Lowe, Cynthia Gibb, Patrick Swayze, Ed Lauter, Jim Youngs, Fionnula Flanagan. Directed by Peter Markle. 110 min.

Peter Markle's dewy sports drama about a teenager (Rob Lowe) determined to make it in Canada's junior hockey league is a familiar but satisfying blend of genre clichés—a poor but supportive family, a good woman and wise teammate who help the hero overcome an attitude problem, and a Big Game in which all scores are settled. Markle nicely captures the cheap, grubby feeling of semipro sports, and admirably avoids the temptation of making the stakes too high, even in the crucial final match. It's an effective athletic transposition of *Flashdance*'s Winning Through Egotism credo even if pouty, pretty Lowe isn't credible as an athlete. (Except for his numerous glistening slo-mo close-ups, a double was used in the rink.) With good supporting work from Ed Lauter, as a gruff coach, and from Cynthia Gibb, as the daughter who's justifiably hoping that Lowe's face remains unscarred.

YOUNG DOCTORS IN LOVE ☆☆
1982, USA, R
Michael McKean, Sean Young, Dabney Coleman, Pamela Reed, Demi Moore. Directed by Garry Marshall. 95 min.

This fast but generally flaccid spoof attempts to do for the hospital drama what *Blazing Saddles* did for the Western. Garry Marshall, however, is no Mel Brooks, nor can his comedy maintain the frenetic pace of the Zucker-Abrahams-Zucker *Airplane!*, which clearly served as another inspiration. *Young Doctors* is closer to TV sitcoms in its religious adherence to a belief that if you have a joke every fifteen seconds, 800 will lay eggs but 100 will hit their mark. That's hardly an impressive batting average, but Michael McKean and Sean Young, stolid and stalwart, do provide some sweetly funny moments. The film is riddled with cameos by stars of TV's *General Hospital*, a nice touch only if you were a soap fan in 1982.

YOUNG FRANKENSTEIN ☆☆☆☆
1974, USA, PG
Gene Wilder, Peter Boyle, Marty Feldman, Madeline Kahn, Teri Garr, Cloris Leachman, Gene Hackman, Kenneth Mars. Directed by Mel Brooks. 108 min.

Arguably Mel Brooks's best film, and perhaps the funniest and most skillful genre parody ever made, *Young Frankenstein* is less a send-up of the original tale than it is of the lushly memorable Universal horror films of the 1930s that brought the story mass popularity. Its humor, at once broad and wry, will leave you laughing with surprise and recognition all the way. The story has the Baron's grandson (Gene Wilder) journeying to a glorious Transylvania castle to redo the famous experiment and get it right. Instead, he gets Peter Boyle, whose incarnation of the monster is hilarious, apt, and even touching. Riotous, deliciously well-calculated performances from all give the film an energy bordering on the hysterical, and Gerald Hirschfeld's superb black-and-white cinematography provides all the atmosphere anyone could ask. Best moment: Wilder and Boyle, in top hat and tails, sing "Puttin' on the Ritz."

YOUNG HERO ☆☆☆
Hong Kong
Huang Cheng-Li, Kwon Yong Moon, Wang Chiang, Wang Sha, Yuan Wu, Yuan Chu. Directed by Lo Chi Po.

Lo Chi Po's stylish *mise-en-scène* upgrades this kung fu melodrama. Po invests the traditional tale of a young man's revenge for his teacher's death with spectacular stunts and stirring visuals.

YOUNG LADY CHATTERLY ☆
1977, USA, X (unofficial)
Harlee McBride, Peter Ratray, William Beckley. Directed by Roberts Winters. 100 min.

Inane revamping of the D. H. Lawrence novel has an American heiress venturing to a British state where she proceeds to have sex with most of the locals. Nice sound effects, lousy movie.

YOUNG LOVE, FIRST LOVE ☆☆
1979, USA (TV)
Valerie Bertinelli, Timothy Hutton, Arlen Dean Snyder, Fionnula Flanagan, Dee Wallace. Directed by Steven Hilliard Stern. 101 min.

Two teenagers from different backgrounds find love in a sappy aren't-parents-terrible romance, originally titled *A Girl and a Boy: The First Time*. The script and direction are about as generic as that scrapped title implies, with the main attraction being a chance to catch Timothy Hutton before he hit it big with *Ordinary People*. He and Valerie Bertinelli are decent but unexceptional, right in line with the rest of the film.

THE YOUNG PHILADELPHIANS ☆☆☆
1959, USA
Paul Newman, Alexis Smith, Brian Keith, Billie Burke, Robert Vaughn. Directed by Vincent Sherman. 136 min.

A hopped-up soap opera that lays bare the soul of ambitious legal beagles like Paul Newman. His impatience to get to the top has something to do with his desire to wed a society girl. The film is as adept as portraying the power brokering that occurs in the legal profession as it is in dissecting the social climbing going on in elite social circles. The polished performers churn up the soap suds as passions flare, particularly Robert Vaughn as a murder defendant. His performance netted him a Best Supporting Actor Oscar nomination.

YOUNG SHERLOCK HOLMES ★★½
1985, USA/Great Britain, PG-13
Nicholas Rowe, Alan Cox, Sophie Ward, Freddie Jones, Anthony Higgens. Directed by Barry Levinson. 110 min.

Never mind that Barry Levinson (*Diner, The Natural*) is named as the director of this; it's a Steven Spielberg "presentation," and all of those look as much alike, regardless of the director, as any given MGM musical or Warner Bros. gangster melodrama of the 1930s. The idea here—Holmes and Watson meet as schoolboys in Victorian London—is iffy, but it's nicely done for the first half. Unfortunately, that promise veers off into a ridiculously obvious carbon copy of *Indiana Jones and the Temple of Doom*. And, worst of all for a Sherlock Holmes effort, there is hardly any mystery, and what there is of it is solved in a most unsatisfyingly perfunctory way. With all of the usual Industrial Light and Magic hullabaloo, and quotes from every other Spielberg film of the past five years.

THE YOUNG TIGER ★
1980, Hong Kong
Meng Fei, Maggie Li Lin Lin, Lui Chi, Fong Chu Fang. Directed by Wo Ma. 102 min.

Meng Fei plays a man who is framed for murder in this sloppy, choppy kung fu entry. Fei is arrested but the police let him escape, hoping to find the real killer by tailing him. There are few things more depressing than a poorly made martial arts movie. Almost as bad as a Jimmy Wang Yu film.

THE YOUNG WARRIORS ★
1984, USA, R
Ernest Borgnine, Richard Roundtree, James Van Patten, Lynda Day George, Dick Shawn, Anne Lockhart. Directed by Lawrence D. Foldes. 103 min.

Ernest Borgnine, Richard Roundtree, and Lynda George all have secondary roles to that of James Van Patten, who plays the leader of a frat group that organizes to gain revenge for the gang-rape of his sister but then decides to become full-time vigilantes. As usual, some dubious moralizing is thrown in to excuse the constant comic-strip violence.

YOU ONLY LIVE ONCE ★★★★
1937, USA
Sylvia Sidney, Henry Fonda, Barton MacLane, Jean Dixon, Margaret Hamilton. Directed by Fritz Lang. 86 min.

Henry Fonda plays a three-time loser who bids for happiness on the straight and narrow. Fonda gives a cold, pinched performance as the bitter yegg, and his hard-luck descent suits his character's self-pitying fatalism and overwhelming sense of guilt. Fritz Lang's flinty-eyed look at a world where the innocent little guy gets croaked by the impersonal, petty system presents a significant contrast to the Depression-era optimism of directors like Frank Capra and Busby Berkeley.

YOU ONLY LIVE TWICE ★★★
1967, Great Britain
Sean Connery, Akiko Wakabayashi, Tetsuro Tamba, Mie Hama, Lois Maxwell, Donald Pleasence. Directed by Lewis Gilbert. 116 min.

Roald Dahl adapted Ian Fleming and the results are top-gear James Bond. Super agent 007, played by Sean Connery, must wriggle out of several hairy situations (including his own apparent murder in the opening scene!) in order to stop the two superpowers from blowing up the world. This is the highlight of the Connery era of the famous series, thanks to the flashy production and quick pacing. It's too bad that Donald Pleasence, who obviously relished his role as a German baddie, does not have more to do, but Connery carries the rest of the film with his suave, disarming portrayal.

YOU'RE A BIG BOY NOW ★★★★
1967, USA
Peter Kastner, Elizabeth Hartman, Karen Black, Geraldine Page, Rip Torn, Michael Dunn, Tony Bill, Dolph Sweet, Michael O'Sullivan. Directed by Francis Ford Coppola. 96 min.

Francis Coppola presented this, his first project after his apprenticeship with Roger Corman, for his master's thesis at UCLA. But far from something dry and academic, this precursor to *The Graduate* is one of the few 1960s films about youth, sex, and growing up neurotic that hasn't badly dated—it is still fresh, amusing, original, and touching. Young schlemiel Bernard Chanticleer, in an effort to break away form his smothering parents, gets his own apartment in New York and sets out looking for love (which he keeps getting confused with sex). With a gamut of original, occasionally grotesque characters too numerous to list, a lovely debut performance by Karen Black, and an appropriately sentimental or boisterous score (as the scene merits) by John Sebastian and the Lovin' Spoonful, this is a delight from beginning to end.

YOUR PLACE . . . OR MINE ★½
1983, USA (TV)
Bonnie Franklin, Robert Klein, Tyne Daly, Peter Bonerz, Penny Fuller. Directed by Robert Day. 93 min.

This is a plodding made-for-TV romance about a recently jilted psychiatrist (winsome, whiny Bonnie Franklin) who's looking for love in all the wrong places and can't see it when it's right in front of her, in the form of divorced Robert Klein. Predictable sitcomish fare, it even recycles those tired meddlesome best friends that seem to exist primarily in TV movies. Isn't that what you bought a VCR to get away from? *Note*: The video version appears to have been slightly trimmed from the original telecast length.

YOU'VE GOT TO HAVE HEART ★★
1976, Italy, PG
Carroll Baker, Renzpo Montagnani, Ray Lovelock, Gabriella Giorgelli. Directed by Franco Martinelli. 98 min.

This is a leering—make that slobbering—Italian sex comedy about an impotent husband and the myriad efforts his family makes to excite him. If you like seeing women groped by middle-aged men and enjoy hearing extremely vulgar double entendres, you'll adore this movie. It does have a certain earthy energy, but it's extremely demeaning to the actresses, especially Carroll Baker. Although the videotape is labeled PG, the film contains R-type sex and nudity.

YOU WERE NEVER LOVELIER ★★★★
1942, USA
Fred Astaire, Rita Hayworth, Adolphe Menjou, Leslie Brooks, Adele Mara, Xavier Cugat and his Orchestra, Gus Schilling, Isobel Elsom, Barbara Brown. Directed by William A. Seiter. 97 min.

A glorious gossamer black-and-white musical, it celebrates Fred Astaire's nimble feet and Rita Hayworth's love-goddess persona. More than that, Rita was a magnificent dancer, sensual and technically self-assured, and her style meshed perfectly with Astaire's suave elegance; their breathtaking teamwork here suggests that she may have been his best partner. The serviceable plot twinkles with sparkling dialogue as Astaire, a part-time gambler, part-time hoofer becomes involved in a Cyrano de Bergerac–type plot instigated by a worried father to fan a flame in the heart of his daughter. The scheme works too well as Astaire really turns into her Lochinvar and woos Rita to a brilliant Jerome Kern score (including "I'm Old-Fashioned" and "Dearly Beloved"). Sheer delight no matter how many times you view it. The personification of 1940s musical comedy glamour.

THE YUM-YUM GIRLS ☆½
1976, USA, R
Judy Landers, Tanya Roberts, Michelle Dawn. Directed by Barry Rosen. 93 min.

This is a sporadically amusing soft-core skin flick about young models trying to make it in front of and behind the camera. Watchable only if you're into movies of this type.

Z

Z ☆☆☆☆
1968, France/Algeria
Yves Montand, Irene Papas, Jean-Louis Trintignant, Jacques Perrin, François Perrier. Directed by Costa-Gavras. 123 min.

Costa-Gavras's classic political thriller, a suspenseful exposé of the goings-on behind the right-wing takeover of Greece in 1963, was the Oscar winner for Best Foreign Language Film in 1969. Yves Montand lends warmth and dignity to the role of Gregorios Lambrakis, the parliament leader whose assassination is made to look like an accident, and Jean-Louis Trintignant is memorable as the government investigator who brings down the fascist conspirators.

ZABRISKIE POINT ☆☆½
1969, USA, R
Mark Frechette, Daria Halprin, Rod Taylor, Paul Fix. Directed by Michelangelo Antonioni. 111 min.

The marvelous Italian director Michelangelo Antonioni was not a bad choice to direct this travelogue of two rebellious youths who "find themselves" in Death Valley, but he clearly was given too much autonomy in the shooting. Like *Blow-Up*, this is about disenchantment with materialistic society, the evils of bureaucratic institutions, and the moral dilemmas of sociopolitical involvement. But departing from his subtle work in *Blow-Up*, Antonioni (who wrote the screenplay with Sam Shepard, among others) clobbers the audience with these themes and has cast stiff, amateurish actors to portray the two free spirits. Redeeming sequences include the opening college debate, the Death Valley orgy, and the explosive climax. It's a failure, however, in between.

ZAPPED! ☆½
1982, USA, R
Scott Baio, William Aames, Felice Schachter, Scatman Crothers. Directed by Robert J. Rosenthal. 96 min.

It's horny high school hijinks for the zillionth time, which is no better than the first. Scott Baio plays a science nerd who manages to acquire telekinetic powers, and before you can say "not again," the blouses and bras of nubile lassies are popping open in every corridor. It's all at the level of a subpar TV sitcom, with some dirty jokes thrown in to appease the apparently inexhaustible adolescent audience for which it was made. Willie Aames is almost totally charmless; Baio fares a bit better. They both teamed up later for the TV series "Charles in Charge."

ZARDOZ ☆☆☆
1974, Great Britain, R
Sean Connery, Charlotte Rampling, John Alderton, Sara Kestelman. Directed by John Boorman. 105 min.

A bold and original science-fiction film that's become a cult item. In the year 2293, ruthless Exterminators wipe out the defenseless Brutals at the command of a giant floating stone head named Zardoz. One of the Exterminators stows away in the statue and discovers a paradise where the inhabitants live forever. Director John (*Excalibur*) Boorman's weird visual touches are particularly striking.

ZELIG ☆☆☆☆
1983, USA, PG
Woody Allen, Mia Farrow, Garrett Brown, Stephanie Farrow, Will Holt, Sol Lomita, Mary Louise Wilson. Directed by Woody Allen. 79 min.

Woody Allen's brilliant tour de force is a documentary pastiche about the Human Chameleon, Leonard Zelig (Allen), who became an international phenomenon in the 1920s because of his uncanny tendency to assume the looks and personalities of those around him. Zelig, the ultimate conformist, finds true love with his bookish female analyst (Mia Farrow). Allen, with his talented, long-time collaborators, editor Susan E. Morse and cinematographer Gordon Willis, went to extraordinary lengths to achieve this film's unprecedented cinematic effects. Through all sorts of elaborate filmmaking magic, Zelig has been inserted into authentic period footage. We see Zelig with Jack Dempsey, Hitler, Calvin Coolidge, and many others. Just the short sequence of Zelig with Babe Ruth took five months to construct! Such intellectuals as Saul Bellow and Bruno Bettelheim look back and attempt to place him in historical context. The result is touching, whimsical, and poignant.

ZÉRO DE CONDUITE ☆☆☆½
1933, France
Jean Daste, Louis Lefèbvre, Gilbert Pruchon. Directed by Jean Vigo. 47 min.

Time and money prevented Jean Vigo from shooting his entire script about rebellion at a boys' boarding school; what emerged was nonetheless a remarkable and influential film. Told from the perspective of youngsters, *Zéro de Conduite* is full of odd, jarring touches, with the most surprising and anarchical scene being the last, when the kids bombard their teachers—many represented by stuffed mannequins—with books and pots thrown from the school roof. This sort of flirtation with unreality was handled better by Buñuel, but Vigo's knowing and sympathetic portrayal of children survives well. Nobody interested in film history should miss it. (a.k.a.: *Zero for Conduct*)

ZIEGFELD FOLLIES ☆☆☆½
1946, USA
Fred Astaire, Lucille Bremer, William Powell, Judy Garland, Gene Kelly, Lucille Ball, Fanny Brice, Lena Horne, Kathryn Grayson. Directed by Vincente Minnelli. 110 min.

While reminiscing in his celestial penthouse suite, Florenz Ziegfeld (William Powell) conjures up a revue to end all revues. Vincente Minnelli's full-scale, dazzling musical omnibus proves that MGM really *did* have more stars than the heavens: Fanny Brice wins a sweepstakes ticket in her Brooklyn flat; Fred Astaire and Lucille Bremer dance around old Chinatown; Esther Williams swims under flora and fauna; Lena Horne saunters through a South American dive; Red Skelton gets tipsy during a live television broadcast; Judy Garland, as a puffed-up celebrity, deigns to grant an interview with the press; and much, much more. Uneven results but a rich, rewarding eyeful and earful, showcasing a studio at the peak of its powers.

ZIGGY STARDUST AND THE SPIDERS FROM MARS ☆☆☆
1983, USA
David Bowie. Directed by D. A. Pennebaker. 91 min.

David Bowie's stunning performance saves this film—shot a full ten years before it was finally released—from D. A. Pennebaker's mindless direction. The soundtrack is badly mixed, the footage is murky, and the cameraman must have had seriously altered perceptions. But Bowie, immersed in the glitter-rock persona of his outrageous alter ego Ziggy Stardust, sings, mimes, and plays with manic intensity. Bowie—artist, actor and rock-'n'-roller—makes this film exciting.

ZOMBIE ☆☆
1979, Italy, unofficial X
Tisa Farrow, Ian McCulloch, Richard Johnson, Al Cliver. Directed by Lucio Fulci. 91 min.

Italian gore-maestro Lucio Fulci effectively rips off American horror master George Romero's *Living Dead* films. A group of hapless adventurers (with Mia Farrow's little sister along for the ride) land on an island inhabited by cannibalistic cadavers. Fulci lacks Romero's ability to extract social commentary from his violence, and *Zombie* is little more than an excuse to let a few makeup artists go crazy and for a number of extras to eat raw meat.

ZOMBIES OF MORA TAU ☆☆
1957, USA
Gregg Palmer, Allison Hayes, Autumn Russell, Joel Ashley, Morris Ankrum. Directed by Edward Kahn. 68 min.

Here's another feature from that wonderful drive-in year of 1957, back when zombies didn't pull out their victims' intestines on the screen but just lumbered about slowly. Who needs gore, though, when you've got Allison Hayes (*Attack of the Fifty Foot Woman*)? She joins the zombies who are guarding a sunken treasure that her husband and his partner are trying to retrieve. Fun junk.

THE ZOO GANG ☆☆
1985, USA, PG-13
Jack Earle Haley, Ramon Bieri, Ty Hardin, Eric Gurry, Jason Gedrick, Ben Vereen. Directed by John Watson and Pen Densham. 96 min.

A clunky but fairly watchable mishmash of a typical teenage gang movie and a junior chamber of commerce commercial. The Zoo Gang consists of five teenagers tired of hanging out on street corners who latch onto a run-down night eatery called The Zoo. Their new nightclub-clubhouse becomes a rousing success, until the tough Donelly Clan decides to muscle in on their turf. Not bad to rent, especially if you want to keep your kids off the street.

ZORBA THE GREEK ☆☆☆
1964, USA
Anthony Quinn, Alan Bates, Irene Papas, Lila Kedrova, George Foondras, Eleni Anousaki. Directed by Michael Cacoyannis. 145 min.

Anthony Quinn acts with such unmitigated brio that he brings to life the zesty, crusty character of Zorba. Lusty life unbounded, the ability to intensely feel simple pleasure and eloquently express wrenching pain are the Greek traits Zorba tries to instill in a silly priggish Englishman (Alan Bates) who has traveled to Crete to open up a family mine. The movie is able to extract many riches from the Nikos Kazantzakis novel, and there are fascinating parallel stories about Bates's attempts to fit in, the sad loneliness of an aging prostitute (Lila Kedrova, in an Oscar-winning performance), the hardships and labor practices involved in mining, and Zorba's own repressed, sad history. Becsuse of the author's perspective, the movie never condescends to "colorful native" depictions, and there is good earthy humor and some unflattering looks at the people. Though the Mikis Theodorakis score can become a bit tiring, the cinematography by Walter Lassally is starkly beautiful—it won an Academy Award.

ZORRO THE GAY BLADE ☆☆½
1981, USA, PG
George Hamilton, Lauren Hutton, Brenda Vaccaro, Ron Leibman, Donovan Scott, James Booth. Directed by Peter Medak. 93 min.

After George Hamilton scored as Dracula in the comedy *Love at First Bite*, he took on the task of a double comedy role, playing Don Diego, a fey son of Zorro, *and* Don's gay brother Bunny Wigglesworth. Unfortunately, this campy send-up isn't twice as funny as the earlier film; its about half as amusing and twice as labored. There are a few good chuckles for the comically deprived, and the send-up of swashbuckling old California is clever.

ZULU ☆☆½
1964, Great Britain
Stanley Baker, Jack Hawkins, Ulla Jacobsson, James Booth, Michael Caine, Nigel Green, Peter Gill, Patrick Magee. Directed by Cy Enfield. 138 min.

Zulu was shot in South Africa with a huge supporting cast, and its battle scenes were directed with verve. Played on a big screen, with its Technicolor and Techniscope intact, *Zulu* might be a rousing entertainment. On video, though, the emphasis shifts to the rather standard story of stiff-upper-lip Brit heroics. Based on the actual attack on Rorke's Drift in 1879, the movie has a weak subplot about an alcoholic missionary and his daughter. Most of the story drops away when the Zulu bodies start piling up, a development that is fine for the action, but fairly callously handled (and perhaps offensive). Richard Burton provides the narrated foreword.

ZULU DAWN ☆☆
1979, Netherlands/USA, PG
Burt Lancaster, Peter O'Toole, Simon Ward, John Mills, Denholm Elliott, Ronald Lacey, Bob Hoskins. Directed by Douglas Hickox. 117 min.

This late-in-coming, not terribly successful sequel to *Zulu* is set before the first film. A good cast brings the troubling colonialist tale of the often brutal British rule over the African Zulu tribes to life, and some excellent, large-scale battle scenes are impressive, but the drama remains remote and impersonal. The version on video restores twenty minutes of footage not seen in the film's American theatrical release.

Index

DRAMA

Abdulla's Harem. *See* Abdulla the Great
Abdulla the Great, 1
Abe Lincoln in Illinois, 1–2
Abraham Lincoln, 2
Absence of Malice, 2
Accidental, 2
Ace, The. *See* Great Santini, The
Act of Passion, 3
Adam, 3
Adam Had Four Sons, 3
Adultress, The, 4
Adventures of Nellie Bly, The, 5
Advise and Consent, 5
Affair, The, 5
Against a Crooked Sky, 6
Agatha, 7
Agency, 7
Agnes of God, 7
Airport, 8
Airport 1975, 8
Airport '79—The Concorde, 8
Airport '77, 8
Alamo Bay, 8–9
Alexander the Great, 9
Algiers, 9
Alice Doesn't Live Here Anymore, 9–10
All About Eve, 11
All God's Children, 12
All Mine to Give, 12
All the King's Men, 13
All the President's Men, 13
All the Right Moves, 13
All This and Heaven Too, 13
Aloha, Bobby and Rose, 14
Always, 14
Amadeus, 15
Amazing Howard Hughes, The, 15
Ambush Murders, The, 16
American Anthem, 16
American Dream, 16
American Flyers, 16
American Gigolo, 16–17
Amin—The Rise and Fall, 18
Among the Cinders, 18
Amos, 18
Amy, 18–19
Anatomy of a Murder, 19
And God Created Woman, 19
And Nothing But the Truth, 19
Angela, 21
Angel and the Badman, 21
Angels over Broadway, 21
Angels with Dirty Faces, 21
Animal Farm, 22
Anna Christie, 22
Anna Karenina, 22
Anne of the Thousand Days, 22–23
Annie's Coming Out. *See* Test of Love, A

Ann Vickers, 23
Another Country, 23
Another Time, Another Place, 23
Anthony Adverse, 24
Apocalypse Now, 25
Arch of Triumph, 26
Arrangement, The, 27
Assam Garden, The, 28
As Summers Die, 28
At Close Range, 29
Atlantic City, 29
Attica, 30
Autobiography of Miss Jane Pittman, The, 31
Autumn Leaves, 31
Autumn Sonata, 31

Baby Doll, 33
Baby the Rain Must Fall, 33
Back From Eternity, 34
Back Street, 34
Bad Boys, 35
Badlands, 35
Ballad in Blue, 37
Ballad of Cable Hogue, The, 37
Ballad of Gregorio Cortez, The, 37
Bang the Drum Slowly, 38
Barefoot Contessa, The, 39
Baron and the Kid, The, 39
Barry Lyndon, 39
Battered, 40
Bay Boy, The, 42
Bayou. *See* Poor White Trash
Becket, 44
Becky Sharp, 44
Beguiled, The, 45
Behind the Rising Sun, 45
Behold a Pale Horse, 45
Belizaire the Cajun, 46
Bell Jar, The, 47
Bells of St. Mary's, The, 47
Belstone Fox, The, 47
Best Little Girl in the World, The, 49
Best Years of Our Lives, The, 49
Betrayal, 50
Betsy, The, 50
Beyond Obsession, 51
Beyond the Limit, 51–52
Beyond the Valley of the Dolls, 52
Bible, The, 52
Big Mo, 53–54
Bilitis, 55
Bill, 55
Billy Budd, 55
Birdy, 57
Birth of a Nation, The, 57
Bitch, The, 57
Bittersweet Love, 57
Black Fury, 59
Black Jack, 59
Black Like Me, 59

Black Magic, 59
Black Narcissus, 60
Blame It on the Night, 61
Blonde Venus, 62
Blood and Sand (1941), 63
Bloodbrothers, 63
Blood Feud, 63
Bloodline, 64
Blood on the Sun (1945), 64
Bloomfield. *See* Hero, The
Blue and the Gray, The, 66
Blue Angel, The, 66
Blue Collar, 66–67
Blue Lagoon, The, 67
Blue Lamp, 67
Blue Max, The, 67
Blue Skies Again, 67–68
Blue Velvet, 68
Bobby Deerfield, 69
Body and Soul (1947), 69
Body and Soul (1981), 69
Bogie: The Last Hero, 70
Bolero, 70–71
Border, The, 71
Born Again, 72
Born Innocent, 72
Boss's Son, The, 72
Bostonians, The, 73
Bound for Glory, 73
Boy in Blue, The, 73–74
Boy in the Plastic Bubble, The, 74
Boys in the Band, The, 74
Boys Next Door, The, 74
Boy with the Green Hair, The, 75
Brain Wash, 76
Brave One, The, 76
Breaker Morant, 76
Breakfast Club, The, 77
Breaking Glass, 77
Break of Hearts, 77
Breakthrough, 78
Breathless, 78
Breed Apart, A, 78
Brian's Song, 78
Bridge of San Luis Rey, The, 79
Brief Encounter, 79
Brimstone and Treacle, 80
Broken Blossoms, 81
Brother Sun, Sister Moon, 81
Brubaker, 81–82
Bullfighter and the Lady, The, 83
Burn!, 84
Burning Bed, The, 84–85
Bus Is Coming, The, 85
Bus Stop, 85
Buster and Billie, 85
Butterfly, 86

Cactus, 87
Caddie, 87–88

Drama *(cont'd)*
Caine Mutiny, The, 89
Cal, 89
California Dreaming, 89
Caligula, 89
Callie and Son, 89
Call to Glory, 90
Candidate, The, 90
Cannery Row, 91
Can You Hear the Laughter?: The Story of Freddie Prinze, 92
Captain Newman M.D., 92–93
Caravaggio, 93
Cardinal, The, 93
Careful, He Might Hear You, 94
Carnal Knowledge, 94
Carnival Story, 94
Carny, 94
Carpetbaggers, The, 95
Carrington, V.C., 95
Casablanca, 96
Case of Libel, A, 96
Catherine the Great, 97
Catholics, 97
Cat on a Hot Tin Roof (1958), 98
Cat on a Hot Tin Roof (1984), 98
Caught, 98–99
Cease Fire, 99
Celebrity, 99
Certain Sacrifice, A, 99–100
César, 100
Champ, The (1931), 100
Champ, The (1979), 100–1
Champion, 101
Champions, 101
Chanel Solitaire, 101
Change of Habit, 101
Chariots of Fire, 102
Charly, 102
Chase, The, 102
Cheerleaders Wild Weekend, 103
Cheers for Miss Bishop, 104
Child Bride of Short Creek, 104
Children of a Lesser God, 104–5
Children of An Lac, The, 105
Children of Divorce, 105
Children of Sanchez, The, 105
Chimes at Midnight, 105–6
Choices, 107
Choose Me, 107
Chosen, The (1981), 107
Christmas Lilies of the Field, 108
Christmas to Remember, A, 108
Christmas Tree, The, 108
Christmas without Snow, A, 108
Christopher Strong, 109
Ciao! Manhattan, 109
Cid, El, 109
Cincinnati Kid, The, 109
Circle of Two, 110
Circus World, 110
Citadel, The, 110
Citizen Kane, 110
City in Fear, 111
City's Edge, The, 111
Clash by Night, 112
Clash of the Titans, 112
Class of '44, 112
Class of '63, 112
Claudine, 112–13
Cleopatra, 113
Clockwork Orange, A, 113–14
Cloud Dancer, 114
Clown, The, 114
Coach, 115
Coal Miner's Daughter, 115

Cocaine Cowboys, 115
Cocaine: One Man's Seduction, 116
Cockfighter, The, 116
Cockleshell Heroes, 116
Collector, The, 117
Color of Money, The, 118
Color Purple, The, 118
Come and Get It, 118
Comeback Kid, The, 118
Come Back to the Five and Dime, Jimmy Dean, Jimmy Dean, 118–19
Coming Home, 119
Competition, The, 120
Concorde, The. *See* Airport '79—The Concorde
Condemned of Altona, The, 121
Conduct Unbecoming, 121
Confessions of a Police Captain, 121–22
Conrack, 122
Conversation, The, 123
Cornbread, Earl and Me, 124
Corn Is Green, The, 124
Cotton Club, The, 125
Countdown, 125
Count of Monte Cristo, The (1934), 125
Count of Monte Cristo, the (1976), 125
Country, 125–26
Country Girl (1981), 126
Country Girl, The (1954), 126
Court Martial. *See* Carrington, V.C.
Coward of the County, 127
Cracker Factory, The, 127
Craig's Wife, 127–28
Crime and Passion, 130
Crime School, 130
Crimes of Passion, 130–31
Criminal Code, The, 131
Criminal Court, 131
Crisis at Central High, 131
Cross and the Switchblade, The, 132
Cross Creek, 132
Crossfire, 132
Crossover Dreams, 132
Crossroads, 133
Crowded Paradise, 133
Cruel Sea, The, 133
Cruising, 133
Cry for Love, A, 133
Cuba, 134
Cutter and Bone. *See* Cutter's Way
Cutter's Way, 135
Cyrano de Bergerac, 135–36

Daisy Miller, 137
Dam Busters, The, 137
Damien: The Leper Priest, 138
Dance with a Stranger, 138
Dancing in the Dark, 138
Danger Lights, 138
Dangerous, 138–39
Dangerous Company, 139
Dangerous Holiday, 139
Daniel, 139
Danny Boy, 139–40
Dark Journey, 140–41
Dark Passage, 141
Dark Victory, 141
Darling, 141–42
Daughter of Dr. Jekyll, 142
Day After, The, 143
Day of the Locust, The, 144
Days of Heaven, 145
Days of Wine and Roses, 145
Day the Loving Stopped, The, 145
Dead End, 146

Deadman's Curve, 147–48
Death Game, 149
Death of a Salesman, 149–50
Death of a Soldier, 150
Deep End, 152
Deer Hunter, The, 152–53
Defiant Ones, The, 153
Delicate Balance, A, 153
Demetrius and the Gladiators, 154
Desert Bloom, 155
Desert Hearts, 155
Desert of the Tartars, The, 155
Désirée, 156
Despair, 156
Desperate Lives, 156
Desperate Living, 156
Detective Story, 157
Devils, The, 158
Diary of a Hitchhiker. *See* Diary of a Teenage Hitchhiker
Diary of Anne Frank, The, 160
Diary of a Teenage Hitchhiker, 160
Different Story, A, 161
Dinner at Eight, 161
Dino, 162
Disappearance, The, 163
Disappearance of Aimee, The, 163
Dishonored Lady, 163
Divorce His—Divorce Hers, 164
Dr. Ehrlich's Magic Bullet, 165
Dr. Kildare's Strange Case, 166
Doctor Zhivago, 167
Dodsworth, 167
Dog Day Afternoon, 167
Dogpound Shuffle, 167
Doll's House, A, 168
Dollmaker, The, 168
Don't Cry, It's Only Thunder, 169
Don Is Dead, The, 169
Downhill Racer, 172
Dragon Seed, 173
Dreamchild, 174
Dreamer, 174
Dream for Christmas, 174
Dresser, The, 175
Drum, 175

Earthling, The, 179
East of Eden (1955), 180
East of Eden (1980), 180
Easy Rider, 180
Easy Virtue, 180
Ecstacy, 181
Egyptian, The, 182
El Cid. *See* Cid, El
Eleni, 182–83
Elephant Man, The (1980), 183
Elephant Man, The (1982), 183
Ellis Island, 183
Elmer Gantry, 183
Emperor Jones, The, 185
Emperor of the North. *See* Emperor of the North Pole
Emperor of the North Pole, 185
Endless Love, 186
End of the Road, 186
Enola Gay: The Men, The Mission, The Atomic Bomb, 187
Entertainer, The, 187–88
Equus, 188
Escape Artist, The, 189
Escape to Happiness. *See* Intermezzo
Eternally Yours, 190
Eternal Women. *See* Love of Three Queens, The

Drama *(cont'd)*
Eureka, 190
Europeans, The, 190–91
Everything Happens at Night, 191–92
Every Time We Say Goodbye, 191
Executioner's Song, The, 193
Executive Suite, 193
Ex-Lady, The, 193
Exposed, 194
Extremities, 194

Face in the Crowd, A, 196
Face That Launched a Thousand Ships, The. *See* Love of Three Queens, The
Face to Face, 196
Fail Safe, 197
Falcon and the Snowman, The, 197
Fallen Angel (1981), 198
Falling in Love, 198
Fall of the Roman Empire, The, 198
Falstaff. *See* Chimes at Midnight
Fame Is the Spur, 199
Family Life, 199
Family Upside Down, A, 199
Fanny, 200
Fantasies, 200
Fantasy Island, 200
Farewell to Arms, A, 201
Far Pavilions, The, 201
Fast Talking, 202
Fatal Attraction. *See* Head On
Father Figure, 202
Father's Love, A. *See* Bloodbrothers
Fellini Satyricon, 203
Female Trouble, 203
Ferry to Hong Kong, 204
Fever Pitch, 204
55 Days in Peking, 205
Fighter, The, 205
Fighting Back, 205–6
Fighting Seabees, The, 206
Fingers, 207
Fire over England, 208
Firstborn, 209
First Legion, The, 209
First Love (1970), 209
First Love (1977), 209
First Yank into Tokyo, 210
Fish Hawk, 210
F.I.S.T., 210–11
Five Days One Summer, 211
Five Easy Pieces, 211–12
Flame of the Barbary Coast, 212
Flame of the Islands, 212
Flat Top, 213
Fool for Love, 216
Foolish Wives, 216
Fools, 216
Force of Evil, 217
Forever Young, 218
For Ladies Only, 218
For Love of Ivy, 219
Fort Apache, The Bronx, 219
Fountainhead, The, 221
Four Deuces, The, 221
Four Friends, 221
Foxes, 222
Foxes of Harrow, The, 222
Foxtrot, 222
Frances, 222
Francis of Assisi, 223
Freaks, 224
Free Spirit. *See* Belstone Fox, The
French Lesson, 225
French Lieutenant's Woman, The, 225

French Woman, The, 225
Friendly Persuasion, The, 226
From Here to Eternity, 227
From the Terrace, 228
Front, The, 228
Fury, 229

Gable and Lombard, 231
Gallipoli, 231
Gambler, The, 231
Game Is Over, The, 231–32
Gandhi, 232
Gangster, The, 232
Garden of Allah, The, 232–33
Gathering, The, 233
Gentleman's Agreement, 235
George Raft Story, The, 235
Getting of Wisdom, The, 236
Getting Wasted, 236
Giant, 238
Gideon's Trumpet, 238
Gig, The, 239
Gilda, 239
Ginger in the Morning, 240
Give 'Em Hell Harry!, 241
Glass House, The, 241–42
Go-Between, The, 243
Goddess, The, 243
Godfather, The, 243
Godfather, The, Part II, 243
Godfather Epic, The. *See* Godfather 1909–1959, The—The Complete Epic
Godfather Saga, The. *See* Godfather 1909–1959, The—The Complete Epic
God's Little Acre, 243–44
Going My Way, 245
Golden Boy, 245
Gone with the Wind, 247
Goodbye, Columbus, 247
Goodbye Mr. Chips, 248
Goodbye, Norma Jean, 248
Good Earth, The, 248
Good Luck, Miss Wyckoff. *See* Shaming, The
Grambling's White Tiger, 250–51
Grand Hotel, 251
Grapes of Wrath, The, 251
Greased Lightning, 252
Greaser's Palace, 252
Greatest, The, 253
Greatest Show on Earth, The, 253
Greatest Story Ever Told, The, 253
Great Expectations, 253–54
Great Garbo, The, 254
Great Gatsby, The, 254
Great Santini, The, 255
Great Waldo Pepper, The, 256
Great White Hope, The, 256
Greek Tycoon, The, 256
Green Dolphin Street, 256
Green Eyes, 256
Green Pastures, 257
Grey Fox, The, 257
Greystoke—The Legend of Tarzan, Lord of the Apes, 257–58
Griffin and Phoenix: A Love Story, 258
Group, The, 258
Guardian, The, 258
Gulag, 259
Gun in the House, A, 260
Guyana—Cult of the Damned, 260
Guyana Tragedy: The Story of Jim Jones, 261

Half Moon Street, 262
Hamlet, 263

Hannah K., 264
Hanover Street, 264
Harbor City. *See* Port of Call
Hard Choices, 265
Hardcore, 265
Hard Country, 265
Hard Driver. *See* Last American Hero, The
Harder They Fall, The, 266
Hard Traveling, 266
Hard Way, The, 266
Harrad Summer. *See* Student Union
Harry and Son, 267
Hawaii, 268
Head On, 269
Heart Beat, 269
Heartbreakers, 269–70
Heart Is a Lonely Hunter, The, 270
Heartland, 270
Heart Like a Wheel, 270
Heart of the Stag, 270–71
Heat and Dust, 271
Heavenly Bodies, 271
Heiress, The, 272
Hellfire, 273
Hell's House, 274
Helter Skelter, 274
Henry IV, 274
Hero, The, 275
Hester Street, 275
Hey, I'm Alive!, 276
Hide in Plain Sight, 276
Hiding Place, The, 276
Highest Honour, The, 276
High Sierra, 277–78
Hindenburg, The, 278
History Is Made at Night, 279
Hit, The, 279
Hit Lady, 279
Hitler, 279
Hitler: The Last Ten Days, 279
Hold the Dream, 280
Holocaust, 281
Holocaust Survivors, 281
Homecoming, The, 282
Home of the Brave, 282
Home to Stay, 282
Honeyboy, 282
Honeysuckle Rose, 283
Honkeytonk Man, 283
Hooked Generation, The, 283
Horton Foote's 1918. *See* 1918
Hotel, 285
House on Garibaldi Street, The, 287
Hunchback of Notre Dame, The, 290
Hussy, 291
Hustle, 291
Hustler, The, 291
Hustling, 291

I Am a Fugitive from a Chain Gang, 292
Ice Castles, 292
Iceman, 292
Idolmaker, The, 293
If . . . , 293
If You Could See What I Hear, 293
I Heard the Owl Call My Name, 294
I Know Why the Caged Bird Sings, 294
Imagemaker, The, 295
I'm Dancing as Fast as I Can, 295
Imitation of Life, 295
Incredible Sarah, The, 296
Independence Day, 297
Indiscretion of an American Wife, 297
I Never Promised You a Rose Garden, 297
Informer, The, 298

Drama *(cont'd)*
Inherit the Wind, 298
In Love with an Older Woman, 298
In Name Only, 298–99
Inn of the Sixth Happiness, The, 299
In Praise of Older Women, 299
Inserts, 299–300
Inside Moves, 300
Inside the Third Reich, 300
Interiors, 300
Intermezzo, 300
Interns, The, 300–1
Intolerance, 301
In Which We Serve, 303
I Remember Mama, 303
Iron Dike, The, 303
Isabel's Choice, 304
Islands in the Stream, 305
I Stand Condemned, 305
It Came Upon a Midnight Clear, 305
It's a Wonderful Life, 306
Ivanhoe (1952), 307
Ivan the Terrible, 307
Ivan the Terrible, Part II, 307
I Want to Live!, 307–8
I Will Fight No More Forever, 308

Jacqueline Bouvier Kennedy, 309
Jamaica Inn, 310
James Dean, 310
Jane Austen in Manhattan, 310
Jane Doe, 310
Jayne Mansfield Story, The, 311
Jenny, 312
Jeremiah Johnson, 312
Jericho Mile, The, 312
Jesus of Nazareth, 312–13
Jezebel, 313
Joan of Arc, 314
Joe, 314
Johnny Belinda (1948), 314
Johnny Belinda (1982), 314
Johnny Got His Gun, 314–15
Johnny Tiger, 315
Johnny Tremain, 315
Jo Jo Dancer, Your Life Is Calling, 313–14
Juarez, 316–17
Jubilee, 317
Judex, 317
Judge Horton and the Scottsboro Boys, 317
Judgement at Nuremberg, 317
Judge Priest, 317
Julia, 317–18

Karate Kid, The, 320–31
Karate Kid Part Two, The, 321
Kent State, 321
Kerouac: The Movie, 321
Kill, The. *See* Game Is Over, The
Killing Fields, The, 324
Killing of Randy Webster, The, 324
Killing of Sister George, The, 324
Kind of Loving, A, 325
King David, 325
Kingfisher Caper, The, 326
King of Kings, 327
King of the Gypsies, 326–27
King's Row, 327
Kiss of the Spider Woman, 328–29
Kitty Foyle, 329
Knute Rockne—All American, 330
Kramer vs. Kramer, 330

Lady Caroline Lamb, 332
Lady Chatterley's Lover, 332
Lady for a Night, 332

Lady Hamilton. *See* That Hamilton Woman
Ladyhawke, 333
Lady Jane, 333
Lady of the House, 333
Lady Sings the Blues, 334
Last American Hero, The, 334
Last Cry for Help, 335
Last Laugh, The, 336
Last Mile, The, 336
Last Night at the Alamo, 336
Last Summer, 337
Last Tango in Paris, 337
Last Tycoon, The, 338
Last Winter, The, 338
Latino, 338
Laura (1979), 339
Leave 'em Laughing, 339
Legend of Sleepy Hollow, The, 340
Legs, 340
Lenny, 340–41
Letter, The, 341–42
Letter of Introduction, A, 342
Lianna, 342
Liar's Moon, 342
Liberation of L. B. Jones, The, 342
Life and Assassination of the Kingfish, The 342–43
Lifeboat, 343
Lifeguard, 343
Life of Emile Zola, The, 343
Lightship, The, 344
Lilies of the Field, 344
Lilith, 344
Limelight, 344–45
Lincoln Conspiracy, 345
Lion in Winter, The, 345
Lipstick, 345
Little Foxes, The, 346
Little Ladies of the Night, 346
Little Men, 347
Little Minister, The, 347
Little Red Schoolhouse, The, 348
Little Treasure, 348
Little Women, 348
Loneliest Runner, The, 349
Lonely Lady, The, 350
Long Ago Tomorrow. *See* Raging Moon, The
Long Day's Journey into Night, 350
Long Days of Summer, The, 350
Long Hot Summer, The, 351
Long Journey Back, 351
Long Way Home, A, 351
Look Back in Anger, 352
Looking for Mr. Goodbar, 352
Lookin' to Get Out, 352
Lords of Discipline, The, 352
Lords of Flatbush, The, 352–53
Lost Honor of Kathryn Beck, The. *See* Act of Passion
Lost Moment, The, 353
Lost Weekend, The, 353–54
Love Child, 354
Love Is a Many-Splendored Thing, 355
Love Laughs at Andy Hardy, 355
Loveless, The, 355
Love Letters, 355
Love of Three Queens, The, 356
Love Scenes, 356
Love's Savage Fury, 357
Love Story, 357
Love Streams, 357
Luther, 358

Macbeth (1948), 359
Macbeth (1971), 359
Madame Bovary, 360

Madame Claude. *See* French Woman, The
Madame X, 360
Made for Each Other, 360
Mafu Cage, The. *See* My Sister, My Love
Magician of Lublin, The, 362
Magnificent Ambersons, The, 362
Magnificent Matador, 362
Magnificent Obsession, 362
Mahler, 363
Mahogany, 363
Making Love, 363–64
Man and a Woman, A, 364–65
Man Called Adam, A, 365
Mandingo, 365
Man for All Seasons, A, 365
Man from Snowy River, The, 366
Mango Tree, The, 366
Man in Grey, The, 367
Man in the Iron Mask, The (1939), 367
Man in the Iron Mask, The (1977), 367
Manions of America, The, 367
Man of Flowers, 367
Man Who Could Work Miracles, The, 368
Man with the Golden Arm, The, 369
Man, Woman and Child, 370
Manxman, 370
Margaret Atwood's Surfacing. *See* Surfacing
Maria's Lovers, 370
Marie, 370
Marty, 371–72
Mary and Joseph: A Story of Faith, 372
Mary of Scotland, 372
Mary White, 372
Masada, 372
Mask, 373
Master Race, The, 373
Matter of Life and Death, A, 374
Matter of Time, A, 374
Maurice. *See* Big Mo
Mazes and Monsters. *See* Rona Jaffe's Mazes and Monsters
Mean Streets, 375
Medium Cool, 375–76
Meet John Doe, 376
Melanie, 376
Member of the Wedding, The, 376
Men's Club, The, 377
Merry Christmas, Mr. Lawrence, 377
Message, The. *See* Mohammad: Messenger of God
Midnight Cowboy, 378
Mikey and Nicky, 379
Mildred Pierce, 379
Min and Bill, 380
Miracle of the Bells, The, 380
Miracle Worker, The (1962), 380
Miracle Worker, The (1979), 380
Mishima, 381
Missiles of October, The, 381
Missing, 382
Mission, The, 382
Mr. Lucky, 390
Mr. Smith Goes to Washington, 391
Mrs. R.'s Daughter, 391
Mrs. Soffel, 391
Misunderstood, 383
Moby Dick, 383
Mohammad: Messenger of God, 384
Molly Maguires, The, 384
Mommie Dearest, 384
Mona Lisa, 384
Monsignor, 385
Moonlighting, 386
Moscow Nights. *See* I Stand Condemned
Mosquito Coast, The, 388
Mother and Daughter—The Loving War, 388

Drama (cont'd)
Murder in Texas, 392
Mutiny on the Bounty (1962), 394
My American Cousin, 394
My Bodyguard, 394–95
My Sister, My Love, 397
Mystery of Alexina, The, 397
My Sweet Charlie, 398

Nadia, 399
Name of the Rose, The, 399
Napoleon (1927), 399
Napoleon (1955), 399–400
National Velvet, 400
Native Son, 400–1
Natural, The, 401
Natural Enemies, 401
Nea (A Young Emmanuelle), 401
Newsfront, 402
Nicholas and Alexandra, 403
Nicholas Nickleby, 403
Night, Mother, 405
Night Games, 404
Night in Heaven, A, 404
Night of the Iguana, The, 406
Night Porter, The, 407
9½ Weeks, 408
1918, 408
92 in the Shade, 409
None But the Lonely Heart, 410
Norma Rae, 411
Norte, El, 411
Not My Kid, 412
Not Quite Paradise, 413
Now and Forever, 413
Now, Voyager, 413
Nurse, 413–14
Nurse Edith Cavell, 414

Octavia, 415
Ode to Billy Joe, 416
Officer and a Gentleman, An, 416
Of Human Bondage (1934), 416
Of Human Bondage (1964), 416–17
O'Hara's Wife, 418
Old Boyfriends, 418
Old Enough, 418
Oliver's Story, 419
Oliver Twist, 419
Once Upon a Time in America, 420
One Flew Over the Cuckoo's Nest, 421
One Night Stand, 422
One on One, 422
One Step to Hell, 423
One Trick Pony, 423
On Golden Pond, 423–24
Onion Field, The, 424
Only Game in Town, The 424
Only When I Laugh, 424
On the Beach, 424
On the Edge, 424
On the Nickel, 425
On the Waterfront, 425
On Valentine's Day, 425
Ordeal of Dr. Mudd, The, 426
Ordinary People, 426
Orphans of the Storm, 426
Orphan Train, 426
Oscar, The, 427
Other Side of Midnight, The, 427
Other Side of Paradise, The. *See* Foxtrot
Other Side of the Mountain, The, 427
Other Side of the Mountain Part II, The, 427
Our Daily Bread, 427
Our Family Business, 427

Our Town (1940), 428
Our Town (1975), 428
Out of Africa, 428–29
Out of Season, 429
Out of the Blue, 429
Outsiders, The, 430
Over the Edge, 430

Panic in Echo Park, 432
Panic in Needle Park, 432
Paris Blues, 434
Paris, Texas, 434
Parting Glances, 434–35
Passage to India, A, 435
Passage to Marseilles, 435
Paths of Glory, 436
Patton, 436
Pawnbroker, The, 436
Payday, 437
Penny Serenade, 437–38
People Next Door, The, 438
People vs. Jean Harris, The, 438
Perfect, 438
Performance, 438
Personal Best, 439
Petrified Forest, The, 439
Phar Lap, 440
Piano for Mrs. Cimino, A, 440
Picnic, 441
Picnic at Hanging Rock, 441
Picture of Dorian Gray, The, 441
Place in the Sun, A, 443
Places in the Heart, 443
Plague Dogs, The, 443
Platoon, 444
Players, 444
Plenty, 445
Ploughman's Lunch, The, 445
Policewoman Centerfold, 446
Poor White Trash, 447
Pope of Greenwich Village, The, 447
Port of Call, 448
Portrait of a Showgirl, 448
Portrait of a Stripper, 448
Possessed, 448
Power, 449
Pray TV, 449
Pretty Baby, 450
Pride and the Passion, The, 450
Pride of Jesse Hallam, The, 450
Pride of the Yankees, 450
Priest of Love, 450
Prince of the City, 451
Princess Daisy, 451
Private Life of Don Juan, The, 452
Private Life of Henry VIII, The, 452
Private Lives of Elizabeth and Essex, The, 453
Promises in the Dark, 454
Psych-Out, 455
Puberty Blues, 455–56
Public Enemy, The, 456
Purple Heart, The, 456
Purple Hearts, 456
Purple Taxi, The, 457

QB VII, 458
Quadrophenia, 458
Quartet, 458
Queimada! *See* Burn!
Question of Guilt, A, 459
Question of Honor, A, 459
Question of Love, A, 459
Question of Silence, A, 459
Quiet Man, The, 459
Quo Vadis, 460

Rachel, Rachel, 461
Racing with the Moon, 461
Rage, 462
Rage of Angels, 462
Raggedy Man, 462
Raging Bull, 462
Raging Moon, The, 462–63
Ragtime, 463
Rain, 463
Rain People, The, 463
Raintree County, 464
Raisin in the Sun, A, 464
Ratboy, 465
Razor's Edge, The (1946), 466
Razor's Edge, The (1984), 466
Rebel, 467
Rebel without a Cause, 467
Reckless, 467–68
Reckless Disregard, 468
Reds, 469
Red Shoes, The, 468
Reflections in a Golden Eye, 469
Remember My Name, 469–70
Remembrance of Love. *See* Holocaust Survivors
Return of the Soldier, The, 472
Return to Earth, 472
Revolution, 473–74
Richard III, 474
Right of Way, 475
Rita Hayworth: The Love Goddess, 476
River, The, 476
River Rat, 476–77
Road to Salina, 477
Robe, The, 477
Robin and Marian, 478
Rocky, 478
Rocky II, 479
Rocky III, 479
Rocky IV, 478–79
Roman Spring of Mrs. Stone, The, 480
Romantic Englishwoman, The, 480
Romeo and Juliet, 480
Rona Jaffe's Mazes and Monsters, 481
Room at the Top, 481
Rose, The, 481
Roseland, 481–82
Rosie: The Rosemary Clooney Story, 482
'Round Midnight, 482
Ruby Gentry, 483
Rude Boy, 483
Rumblefish, 483–84
Running Brave, 484
Ryan's Daughter, 485

Sailor Who Fell from Grace with the Sea, The, 487
St. Benny the Dip, 487
St. Elmo's Fire, 487
Saint Jack, 488
Sakharov, 488
Salome Where She Danced, 488
Salt of the Earth, 488
Salvador, 488–89
Samson and Delilah, 489
Sam's Song. *See* Swap, The
Sanders of the River, 489
Sandpiper, The, 489
San Francisco, 490
Saturday Night Fever, 491
Savage Attraction, 492
Savage Is Loose, The, 492
Save the Tiger, 492–93
Saving Grace, 493
Say Goodbye, Maggie Cole, 493
Say Hello to Yesterday, 493

Drama *(cont'd)*
Sayonara, 493
Scarecrow, 494
Scarlet Letter, The, 494
Scarlet Pimpernel, The, 494–95
Secret Places, 498
Secrets (1978), 499
Secrets (1982), 499
Seducers, The. *See* Death Game
Seduction of Joe Tynan, The, 499
Seize the Day, 500
Separate Peace, A, 501
Separate Tables, 501
Sergeant, The, 501
Sergeant Matlovich vs. the U.S. Air Force, 501
Sergeant Steiner. *See* Breakthrough
Sergeant York, 501
Serpico, 502
Servant, The, 502
Sessions, 502
Set-Up, The, 502
Seventh Veil, The, 504
Sex, 504
Shack Out on 101, 505
Shaming, The, 505
Shanghai Express, 506
Shattered, 507
Shenandoah, 508
Shining Season, A, 509
Ship of Fools, 509–10
Shogun, 510
Shooting Party, The, 511
Shoot It: Black, Shoot It: Blue, 511
Shoot the Moon, 511
Short Eyes, 512
Shout, The, 512
Sid and Nancy, 512–13
Sidewalks of London, 513
Sidney Sheldon's Bloodline. *See* Bloodline
Silence of the North, 513
Silkwood, 514
Silver Chalice, The, 515
Silver Dream Racer, 515
Sin, The. *See* Shaming, The
Singer Not the Song, The, 516
Single Bars, Single Women, 516
Single Room Furnished, 517
Sin of Adam and Eve, 517
Sister Kenny, 517
Six Weeks, 518
Sizzle, 518
Slammer. *See* Short Eyes
Small Circle of Friends, A, 521
Small Killing, A, 521–22
Smash-Up, the Story of a Woman, 522
Smooth Talk, 522
Soldier's Story, A, 524
Sole Survivor, 525
Solo, 525
Solomon and Sheba, 525
Some Call It Loving, 525
Some Kind of Hero, 525
Someone I Touched, 525
Something to Hide. *See* Shattered
Somewhere in Time, 526
Song of Freedom, 526
Song to Remember, A, 527
Songwriter, 527
Son of Monte Cristo, The, 527
Sophia Loren: Her Own Story, 528
Sophie's Choice, 528
So Proudly We Hail!, 528
S.O.S. Titanic, 528
Sounder, 529

Southern Cross. *See* Highest Honour, The
Southerner, The, 529
South of the Border, 529
Sparkle, 530
Sparrows, 530
Spartacus, 530–31
Spetters, 532
Spirit of St. Louis, The, 532
Spitfire, 533
Splendour in the Grass, 533
Split Image, 533
Stage Door, 535
Stage Struck, 535
Staircase, 535
Stairway to Heaven. *See* Matter of Life and Death, A
Stalag 17, 535
Stalk the Wild Child, 535
Stand By Me, 535–36
Star 80, 536
Star Is Born, A (1937), 536
Star Is Born, A (1976), 537
Stay Hungry, 539
Staying Alive, 539
Steaming, 539
Steel, 539
Steel Cowboy, 539
Stella Dallas, 540
Sterile Cuckoo, The, 540
Stevie, 540
Stone Boy, The, 541
Straight Time, 542
Stratton Story, The, 544
Straw Dogs, 544
Street Scene, 545
Streets of Gold, 545
Stripper, The, 546
Student Union, 547
Suburbia, 547
Sugar Cane Alley, 548
Summer Fantasy, 548
Summer Lovers, 548
Summer Madness. *See* Summertime
Summer of My German Soldier, 549
Summer Solstice, 549
Summertime, 549
Summer Wishes, Winter Dreams, 549
Sunday, Bloody Sunday, 549
Sunflower, 550
Surfacing, 551
Suzanne, 552
Svengali, 552
Swap, The, 552
Sweet Country, 552
Sweet Hostage, 553
Swimmer, The, 553
Sybil, 554
Sylvester, 554
Sylvia, 554

Table for Five, 555
Taipan, 555
Tale of Two Cities, A (1935), 556
Tale of Two Cities, A (1958), 556
Tamarind Seed, The, 557
Taps, 558
Taste of Honey, A, 559
Tattoo, 559
Taxi Driver, 559
Taxi Mauve, Un. *See* Purple Taxi, The
Teachers, 559–60
Tell Me a Riddle, 560
Ten Commandments, The, 561
Tender Is the Night, 561
Tender Mercies, 561
Ten North Frederick, 562

Terms of Endearment, 563
Terraces, 563
Terry Fox Story, The, 564
Tess, 564
Testament, 564–65
Test of Love, A, 565
Tex, 565
That Championship Season, 566
That Cold Day in the Park, 566
That Hamilton Woman, 566
That'll Be the Day, 566
That's Life, 567
That's the Way of the World, 567
That Was Then . . . This is Now, 567
These Three, 568
They Drive by Night, 569
They Live by Night, 569
They Made Me a Criminal, 569–70
They Shoot Horses, Don't They?, 570
Thief of Hearts, 571
This Above All, 573
This Property Is Condemned, 573
Threads, 574
Three Faces of Eve, The, 575
Three in the Attic, 575–76
Thumb Tripping, 577
Tim, 579
Time for Miracles, A, 579
Times Square, 580
Tin Man, 580
Tobacco Road, 581
To Have and Have Not, 581–82
To Kill a Mockingbird, 582
Tomorrow, 583
To Race the Wind, 585
Torchlight, 585
Torn Between Two Lovers, 585
To The Lighthouse, 585–86
Touched, 586
Touched by Love, 586
Toy, The, 587
Tracks, 587
Train, The, 588
Treasure of the Sierra Madre, The, 589
Tree Grows in Brooklyn, A, 589–90
Trial, The, 590
Trial of Billy Jack, The, 590
Triangle Factory Fire Scandal, The, 590
Trilogy, 590–91
Trip, The, 591
Trip to Bountiful, The, 591
Trouble in Mind, 592
Truman Capote's The Glass House. *See* Glass House, The
Tulsa, 593
Turning Point, The, 594
Twelve Angry Men, 594
Twelve O'Clock High, 594
Twice in a Lifetime, 595
Twist and Shout, 595–96

Under Capricorn, 598–99
Under Fire, 599
Under Milk Wood, 599
Under the Volcano, 599
Union City, 600
Unmarried Woman, An, 600
Until September, 600–1
Urban Cowboy, 601
Users, The, 602
Utu, 602

Valley of the Dolls, 603
Verdict, The, 604
Victim, 605
Violets Are Blue . . . , 606

Drama *(cont'd)*
Vision Quest, 606
Voyage of the Damned, 607

Wagner, 608
Walk in the Spring Rain, A, 609
Wanderers, The, 609
War and Peace (1956), 610
War and Peace (1968), 610
War Hunt, 610
Warkill, 610
War Lover, The, 610–11
Watch on the Rhine, 612
Waterloo Bridge, 612
Way Down East, 613
Way We Were, The, 613
Wedding in White, 614
Wednesday's Child. *See* Family Life
Welcome to L.A., 614
We of the Never Never, 614
Wetherby, 615
What Price Glory?, 616
When the Legends Die, 617
Whistle Down the Wind, 619
White Mama, 620
White Tower, The, 620
Who'll Stop the Rain?, 621
Who's Afraid of Virginia Woolf?, 621
Whose Life Is It Anyway?, 621
Why Shoot the Teacher?, 622
Widow's Nest, 622
Wild Duck, The, 623
Wild Horses, 623
Wild in the Streets, 623
Wild Party, The, 624
Wild River, The, 624
Wildrose, 624
Wild Side, The. *See* Suburbia
Will: G. Gordon Liddy, 625
Willie and Phil, 625
Wilma, 625
Windom's Way, 626
Winds of Kitty Hawk, 626
Windwalker, 626
Windy City, 626
Winning, 626–27
Winslow Boy, The, 627
Winter of Our Dreams, 627
Winter Rates. *See* Out of Season
Winterset, 627
Wisdom, 627
Wise Blood, 627–28
Without a Trace, 628
Woman Called Golda, A, 629
Woman of Paris, A, 630
Woman of Substance, A, 630
Woman Rebels, A, 631
Woman Under the Influence, A, 631
Women in Love, 631
Word, The, 632
Written on the Wind, 634
Wuthering Heights, 634

Yanks, 636
Yearling, The, 636
Year of Living Dangerously, The, 636
You Light Up My Life, 637
Youngblood, 638
Young Lady Chatterly, 638
Young Love, First Love, 638
Young Philadelphians, The, 638–39
You Only Live Once, 639

Zabriskie Point, 641
Zorba the Greek, 642

MUSICAL ♪

Absolute Beginners, 2
All That Jazz, 13
American in Paris, An, 17
Annie, 23
Apple, The, 25

Babes in Arms, 33
Band Wagon, The, 38
Barefoot in the Park, 39
Battling Hoofer. *See* Something to Sing About
Beach Blanket Bingo, 42
Beatlemania—The Movie, 43
Beat Street, 43
Bells Are Ringing, 47
Best Foot Forward, 49
Best Little Whorehouse in Texas, The, 49
Bikini Beach, 55
Blood Wedding, 65
Blue Hawaii, 67
Body Rock, 70
Breakin', 77
Breakin' II: Electric Boogaloo, 77
Breaking the Ice, 77
Brigadoon, 79
Broadway Melody of 1936, 80
Broadway Melody of 1938, 80–81
Bronze Venus, 81
Bugsy Malone, 83
Bundle of Joy, 84
Bye Bye Birdie, 86

Cabaret, 87
Cabin in the Sky, 87
Camelot, 90
Can't Stop the Music, 91
Carefree, 94
Carmen (1983), 94
Carmen (1984), 94
Carmen Jones, 94
Carousel, 94–95
Chorus Line—The Movie, A, 107
Come Back to Me. *See* Doll Face
Concert for Bangla Desh, The, 121
Connecticut Yankee in King Arthur's Court, A, 122
Copacabana (1947), 124
Copacabana (1985), 124

Daddy Long Legs, 137
Dames, 137
Damn Yankees, 138
Damsel in Distress, 138
Dangerous When Wet, 139
Danny Boy, 139
Deep in My Heart, 152
Divine Madness, 163
Doll Face, 168
Double Trouble, 171
Down Argentine Way, 171
Dubarry Was a Lady, 176
Duke Is Tops, The. *See* Bronze Venus

Easter Parade, 179
Easy Come, Easy Go, 180
Evergreen, 191

Fabulous Dorseys, The, 196
Fairytales, 197
Fame, 199
Fast Forward, 201–2
Fiddler on the Roof, 204
Fiesta, 205
Fillmore, 206
Finian's Rainbow, 207

First Nudie Musical, The, 210
Flashdance, 213
Flower Drum Song, 214–15
Flying Down to Rio, 215
Folies Bergère, 215
Follow the Fleet, 216
Footlight Parade, 216
Footloose, 216–17
Forbidden Zone, 217
For Me and My Gal, 219
42nd Street, 220
French Line, The, 225
Fun in Acapulco, 228–29
Funny Face, 229
Funny Girl, 229
Funny Lady, 229
Funny Thing Happened on the Way to the Forum, A, 229

Gay Divorcée, The, 234
Gentlemen Prefer Blondes, 235
G.I. Blues, 238
Gigi, 239
Girl Crazy, 240
Girl Happy, 240
Girl Most Likely, The, 240
Girls! Girls! Girls!, 241
Give My Regards to Broad Street, 241
Glenn Miller Story, The, 242
Glorifying the American Girl, 242
Go, Johnny, Go!, 245
Gold Diggers of 1933, 245
Goldwyn Follies, The, 247
Good News, 249
Gospel, 250
Grateful Dead, The, 251–52
Grease, 252
Grease 2, 252
Great American Broadcast, The, 252
Great Caruso, The, 253
Guys and Dolls, 261
Gypsy, 261

Hair, 262
Hans Christian Andersen, 264
Happiest Millionaire, The, 264
Happy Times. *See* Inspector General, The
Hard Day's Night, A, 265
Harder They Come, The, 265–66
Hard to Hold, 266
Head, 269
Hello, Dolly!, 273
High Society, 278
Holiday Inn, 280
Hollywood Hotel, 280

I Dream Too Much, 293
Inspector General, The, 300
In the Good Old Summertime, 301
Invitation to the Dance, 303
It Happened One Summer. *See* State Fair

Jailhouse Rock, 309
Jazz Singer, The (1927), 311
Jazz Singer, The (1980), 311
Jesus Christ, Superstar, 312

Kid Millions, 322–23
Killing 'em Softly, 324
King and I, The, 325
King Creole, 325
King of Jazz, The, 327
Kismet, 328
Kiss Me Kate, 328
Knickerbocker Holiday, 329
Krush Groove, 330

Musical *(cont'd)*
Les Girls, 341
Lili, 344
Lisztomania, 345–46
Little Miss Marker (1934), 347
Little Night Music, A, 347
Little Prince, The, 347
Little Princess, The, 347
Little Shop of Horrors (1986), 348
Lost in the Stars, 353
Love Me, Tender, 356
Loving You, 357

Magical Mystery Tour, 361
Mame, 364
Man from Music Mountain, 366
Man from the Folies Bergère. *See* Folies Bergère
Man of La Mancha, 367–68
Maytime 374–75
Meet Me In St. Louis, 376
Miss Sadie Thompson, 381
Mrs. Brown, You've Got a Lovely Daughter, 391
Music Man, The, 393
My Fair Lady, 395

New York, New York, 402–3
Night and Day, 403

Oklahoma!, 418
Oliver!, 419
On a Clear Day You Can See Forever, 419–20
One from the Heart, 422
One Touch of Venus, 423
On the Town, 425
Otello, 427

Paint Your Wagon, 431
Paradise, Hawaiian Style, 433
Pennies from Heaven, 437
Perils of Pauline, The, 439
Pink Floyd—The Wall, 442
Pirate, The, 442
Pirate Movie, The, 443
Pirates of Penzance, The, 443
Playing for Keeps, 444
Popeye, 447
Pot o'Gold, 449
Private Buckaroo, 452
Purple Rain, 456

Rappin', 465
Reaching for the Moon, 466
Road to Bali, 477
Rock, Rock, Rock!, 478
Rose Marie, 482
Roustabout, 483
Royal Wedding, 483
Running Out of Luck, 484

Scrooge, 496
Second Chorus, 498
Serenade, 501
Sergeant Pepper's Lonely Hearts Club Band, 501
Seven Brides For Seven Brothers, 503
1776, 503–4
Sextette, 505
Shall We Dance, 505
Shine On, Harvest Moon, 509
Showboat, 512
Show Business, 512
Silk Stockings, 514
Singin' in the Rain, 516
Sing Your Worries Away, 517

Something to Sing About, 526
Song of Norway, 526
Sound of Music, The, 529
South Pacific, 529–530
Speedway, 531
Springtime in the Rockies, 534
Stage Door Canteen, 535
Star Is Born, A, 536–37
Stars on Parade, 537
State Fair, 538
Story of Vernon and Irene Castle, The, 542
Strike Up the Band, 545–46
Swing Time, 553–54

Tales of Hoffmann, 556
Thank Your Lucky Stars, 566
That Night in Rio, 566
There's No Business Like Show Business, 568
This Is the Army, 573
Thoroughly Modern Millie, 574
Thousands Cheer, 574
Threepenny Opera, The, 576
Tickle Me, 578
Till the Clouds Roll By, 578–79
Tin Pan Alley, 580
Tommy, 583
Top Hat, 584
Two Tickets to Broadway, 597

Unsinkable Molly Brown, The, 600

Viva Las Vegas, 607

West Side Story, 615
White Christmas, 619
Whoopee!, 621
Wild in the Country, 623
Wild Style, 624–25
Wiz, The, 629
Wonder Bar, 632
Words and Music, 632

Xanadu, 635

Yankee Doodle Dandy, 636
Yentl, 637
You'll Find Out, 637
You'll Never Get Rich, 638
You Were Never Lovelier, 639–40

Ziegfeld Follies, 641

CHILDREN'S

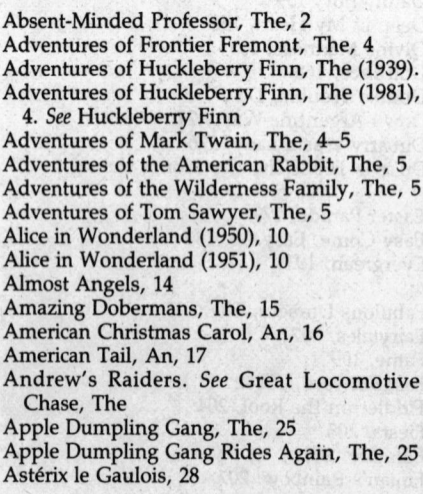

Absent-Minded Professor, The, 2
Adventures of Frontier Fremont, The, 4
Adventures of Huckleberry Finn, The (1939).
Adventures of Huckleberry Finn, The (1981), 4. *See* Huckleberry Finn
Adventures of Mark Twain, The, 4–5
Adventures of the American Rabbit, The, 5
Adventures of the Wilderness Family, The, 5
Adventures of Tom Sawyer, The, 5
Alice in Wonderland (1950), 10
Alice in Wonderland (1951), 10
Almost Angels, 14
Amazing Dobermans, The, 15
American Christmas Carol, An, 16
American Tail, An, 17
Andrew's Raiders. *See* Great Locomotive Chase, The
Apple Dumpling Gang, The, 25
Apple Dumpling Gang Rides Again, The, 25
Astérix le Gaulois, 28

Babes in Toyland, 33
Barefoot Executive, The, 39
Bears and I, The, 43
Bedknobs and Broomsticks, 44
Benji, 48
Best of Popeye, The, 49
Big Red, 54
Billion Dollar Hobo, 55
Black Beauty (1946), 58
Black Beauty (1971), 58
Black Cauldron, The, 58
Black Stallion, The, 60
Black Stallion Returns, The, 60
Bless the Beasts and Children, 62
Blue Fin, 67
Blue Fire Lady, 67
Boatniks, The, 69
Bon Voyage Charlie Brown (And Don't Come Back!), 71
Born Free, 72
Boy Named Charlie Brown, A, 74
Brighty of the Grand Canyon, 80
Bugs Bunny/Road Runner Movie, The, 83
Bugs Bunny's 3rd Movie: 1,001 Rabbit Tales, 83

Candleshoe, 90–91
Care Bears Movie, The, 93
Care Bears Movie Two: A New Generation, 93–94
Casey's Shadow, 96
Castaway Cowboy, The, 96
Cat from Outer Space, The, 97
Challenge to be Free, 100
Charlotte's Web, 102
Chitty Chitty Bang Bang, 106
C.H.O.M.P.S., 107
Christmas Carol, A (1938), 108
Christmas Carol, A (1951), 108
Cinderfella, 110
Computer Wore Tennis Shoes, The, 120–21
Condorman, 121
Courage of Black Beauty, 126
Crossed Swords. *See* Prince and the Pauper, The

Daffy Duck's Movie: Fantastic Island, 137
Darby O'Gill and the Little People, 140
David Copperfield (1935), 142
David Copperfield (1970), 142
Daydreamer, The, 143
Devil and Max Devlin, The, 158
Digby, the Biggest Dog in the World, 161
Dimples, 161
Doc Savage . . . The Man of Bronze, 164
Doctor Dolittle, 165
Dog of Flanders, A, 167
Dumbo, 177

Elmer, 183
Escapade in Japan, 190
Escape to Witch Mountain, 190

Fantastic Animation Festival, 200
Fantastic Balloon Voyage, The, 200
Fantastic Planet, 200
Follow Me, Boys!, 216
For the Love of Benji, 219
Freaky Friday, 224
From the Mixed-Up Files of Mrs. Basil E. Frankweiler. *See* Hideaways, The
Further Adventures of the Wilderness Family, *See* Wilderness Family, The: Part Two

Gentle Giant, 235
Gentle Savage, 235

Children's (cont'd)
Gift for Heidi, 239
Gnome-Mobile, The, 242–43
Gobots: Battle of the Rock Lords, 243
Golden Seal, The, 246
Golden Voyage of Sinbad, The, 246
Great Locomotive Chase, The, 254
Great Mouse Detective, The, 254
Great Muppet Caper, The 254–55
Grendel Grendel Grendel, 257
Gulliver's Travels, 259
Gus, 260

Hawmps!, 268–69
Heidi (1937), 272
Heidi (1968), 272
Heidi's Song, 272
Herbie Goes Bananas, 274
Herbie Goes to Monte Carlo, 274
Herbie Rides Again, 274
Hideaways, The, 276
Hoppity Goes to Town, 284
Horse in the Gray Flannel Suit, The, 284–85
Horse Named Comanche, A. See Tonka
Hot Lead and Cold Feet, 285
Huckleberry Finn (1939), 289
Huckleberry Finn (1975), 289

Incredible Journey, The, 296
Infra-Man, 298
In Search of the Castaways, 299
International Velvet, 300
Island at the Top of the World, The, 304

Jacob Two-Two Meets the Hooded Fang, 309
Jason and the Argonauts, 310
Jonathan Livingston Seagull, 315
Journey Back to Oz, 316
Journey of Natty Gann, 316
Journey to the Center of the Earth (1959), 316
Jungle Book, The, 318

Kidnapped, 322
King of the Grizzlies, 326

Last Flight of Noah's Ark, The, 335
Last Unicorn, The, 338
Laurel and Hardy in Toyland. See Babes in Toyland
Lt. Robinson Crusoe, U.S.N., 342
Light in the Forest, The, 344
Little House on the Prairie, 346
Little Lord Fauntleroy (1936), 346–47
Little Lord Fauntleroy (1980), 347
Living Free, 349
Lord of the Rings, 352
Love Bug, The, 354

Mad Monster Party?, 361
Magic of Lassie, The, 362
March of the Wooden Soldiers. See Babes in Toyland
Mary Poppins, 372
Matilda, 373–74
Minor Miracle, A, 380
Mr. Bug Goes to Town. See Hoppity Goes to Town
Moon Spinners, The, 387
Muppet Movie, The, 392
Muppets Take Manhattan, The, 392
My Little Pony: The Movie, 396

Night Crossing, 404
No Deposit No Return, 410
Nutcracker, 414

Old Yeller, 418
One and Only Genuine Original Family Band, The, 421
One Magic Christmas, 422
1,001 Rabbit Tales. See Bugs Bunny's 3rd Movie: 1,001 Rabbit Tales

Parent Trap, The, 434
Pete's Dragon, 439
Phantom Tollbooth, The, 440
Pinocchio, 442
Pollyanna (1920), 446
Pollyanna (1960), 446
Prince and the Pauper, The, 451

Race for Your Life, Charlie Brown, 461
Railway Children, The, 463
Rainbow Brite and the Star Stealer, 463
Rebecca of Sunnybrook Farm (1917), 467
Rebecca of Sunnybrook Farm (1938), 467
Red Balloon, The, 468
Return From Witch Mountain, 470
Return to Oz, 472
Ring of Bright Water, 475

Santa and the Three Bears, 490
Santa Claus—The Movie, 490
Savage Sam, 492
Secret of Nimh, The, 498
Sesame Street Presents: Follow That Bird, 502
Shaggy D.A., The, 505
Shaggy Dog, The, 505
Shinbone Alley, 509
Sinbad and the Eye of the Tiger, 516
Sleeping Beauty, 520
Snoopy, Come Home, 523
Son of Flubber, 527
Storm Boy, 542
Strongest Man in the World, The, 546
Summer Magic, 548
Superdad, 550
Swiss Family Robinson, The 554
Sword and the Rose, The 554

That Darn Cat, 566
Third Man on the Mountain, The, 572
Thirty Foot Bride of Candy Rock, The, 572
Three Caballeros, The, 575
Tom Brown's Schooldays, 582
Tom Sawyer, 583
Tonka, 583
Transformers: The Movie, 588
Treasure Island (1934), 589
Treasure Island (1950), 589
Treasure of Matecumbe, 589
Tuck Everlasting, 593
Twelve Months, 394
20,000 Leagues Under the Sea, 594–95

Unidentified Flying Oddball, 600

Water Babies, The, 612
Watership Down, 612
When the North Wind Blows, 617
Where the Red Fern Grows, 618
Who Has Seen the Wind, 620
Wild Country, The, 623
Wilderness Family, The: Part Two, 623
Willy McBean and His Magic Machine, 625
Willy Wonka and the Chocolate Factory, 625
Wizard of Oz, The, 629
Wombling Free, 631
Wooden Soldiers. See Babes in Toyland
World's Greatest Athlete, The, 633

HORROR/SCIENCE FICTION

Abominable Dr. Phibes, The, 2
Adventures of Buckaroo Banzai Across the Eighth Dimension, The, 4
After the Fall of New York, 6
Alchemist, The, 9
Alice, Sweet Alice, 10
Alien, 10
Alien Contamination, 10
Alien Factor, The, 10
Alien Prey, 10
Aliens, 11
Aliens from Spaceship Earth, 11
Alison's Birthday, 11
Alligator, 12
Alone in the Dark, 14
Alpha Incident, The, 14
Altered States, 14–15
American Werewolf in London, An, 17
Amityville Horror, The, 18
Amityville: The Demon, 18
Amityville 3D. See Amityville: The Demon
Amityville II: The Possession, 18
Amok. See Schizo
And Now the Screaming Starts, 19–20
Android, 20
Andy Warhol's Dracula, 20
Andy Warhol's Frankenstein, 20
Angry Red Planet, The, 22
Ants, 24
Ape, 24
Ape, The, 24
Ape Man, The, 24–25
April Fool's Day, 26
Archer, The: Fugitive from the Empire, 26
Are You in the House Alone?, 26
Arnold, 27
Astro-Zombies, The, 28
Asylum, 29
Asylum of Satan, 29
Attack of the Crab Monsters, The, 30
Attack of the 50 Foot Woman, 30
Attic, The, 30
Audrey Rose, 31
Autopsy, 31
Awakening, The 32
Awakening of Candra, The, 32
Aztec Mummy Double Feature, 32

Baby, The, 33
Babysitter, The, 33
Back to the Future, 35
Baffled, 36
Bamboo Saucer, The, 37
Barbarella, 38–39
Baron Blood, 39
Basket Case, 40
Battle Beneath the Earth, 40
Battle Beyond the Stars, 40
Battle for the Planet of the Apes, 40–41
Battlestar: Galactica, 42
Bay of Blood, 42
Beast in the Cellar, The, 43
Beast Must Die, The, 43
Beast of the Yellow Night, 43
Beast Within, The, 43
Bedlam, 44
Bees, The, 45
Before I Hang, 45
Being, The, 45–46
Ben, 47–48
Beneath the Planet of the Apes, 48
Beware! The Blob, 51
Beyond Atlantis, 51

Horror/Science Fiction *(cont'd)*
Beyond Evil, 51
Beyond the Door, 51
Beyond the Door II, 51
Beyond Tomorrow, 52
Bigfoot, 53
Big Foot, 53
Billy the Kid vs. Dracula, 56
Biohazard, 56
Birds, The, 56
Bird with the Crystal Plumage, The, 57
Black Cat, The, 58
Black Christmas, 58
Blackenstein, 58–59
Black Hole, The, 59
Black Sabbath, 60
Black Sunday (1961), 60–61
Blacula, 61
Blade Runner, 61
Blind Date, 62
Blob, The, 62
Blood and Black Lace, 62
Blood Beach, 63
Blood Beast Terror, The, 63
Blood Feast, 63
Blood Fiend. *See* Theatre of Death
Blood Legacy, 63–64
Blood of Dracula's Castle, 64
Blood of the Undead. *See* Schizo
Blood on Satan's Claw, The, 64
Blood Orgy of the She Devils, 65
Blood-Spattered Bride, The, 65
Bloodsuckers, The, 65
Bloodsucking Freaks, 65
Bloodthirsty Butchers, 65
Blood Tide, 65
Bloody Fiancée. *See* Blood-Spattered Bride
Bluebeard (1944), 66
Bluebeard (1972), 66
Blue Sunshine, 68
Boarding House, 68
Body Snatcher, The, 70
Bog, 70
Boogeyman, The, 71
Boogeyman II, The, 71
Boy and His Dog, A, 73
Boy Who Could Fly, The, 74–75
Brain, The, 75
Brain from Planet Arous, The, 75
Brainiac, The, 75
Brainstorm, The, 75
Brain That Wouldn't Die, The, 75–76
Brainwaves, 76
Brazil, 76
Bride, The, 79
Bride of Frankenstein, The, 79
Bride of the Monster, 79
Brood, The, 81
Brother from Another Planet, The, 81
Brute Man, The, 82
Buckaroo Banzai. *See* Adventures of Buckaroo Banzai Across the Eighth Dimension, The
Buck Rogers in the 25th Century, 82
Bug, 83
Burial Ground, 84
Burning, The, 84
Burnt Offerings, 85

Cabinet of Dr. Caligari, The, 87
Café Flesh, 88
Camile 2000, 90
Captain Kronos: Vampire Hunter, 92
Car, The, 93
Carrie, 95
Cars That Ate Paris, The. *See* Cars That Eat People, The
Cars That Eat People, The, 95
Castle of Evil, 96
Castle of Fu Manchu, The, 96
Cat's Eye, 98
Cathy's Curse, 98
Cat People (1942), 98
Cat People (1982), 98
Cauldron of Blood, 99
Cemetery Girls. *See* Velvet Vampire, The
Chamber of Fear, 100
Changeling, The, 101
Children, The, 104
Children of Blood. *See* Cauldron of Blood
Children of the Corn, 105
Children of the Damned, 105
Children Shouldn't Play with Dead Things, 105
Chosen, The. *See* Holocaust 2000
Christine, 108
Christmas Evil, 108
C.H.U.D., 109
City of the Walking Dead, 111
Clairvoyant, The. *See* Evil Mind, The
Class Reunion Massacre, The, 112
Clonus Horror, The, 114
Close Encounters of the Third Kind, 114
Cocoon, 116
Code Name: Trixie. *See* Crazies, The
Color Me Blood Red, 117
Communion. *See* Alice, Sweet Alice
Company of Wolves, The, 120
Conquest, 122
Conquest of the Planet of the Apes, 122
Corpse Grinders, The, 124
Corpse Vanishes, The, 124
Cosmic Monster, The, 125
Count Dracula, 125
Count Yorga, Vampire, 126
Crash of Flight 401, The. *See* Ghost of Flight 401, The
Crater Lake Monster, 128
Crawling Eye, The, 128
Crawling Hand, The, 128
Crawlspace, 128
Craze, 128
Crazies, The, 128
Creation of the Humanoids, 129
Creature, 129
Creature from Black Lake, 129
Creature from the Black Lagoon, The, 129
Creature from the Haunted Sea, The, 129
Creepers, 129
Creeping Flesh, The, 130
Creeping Terror, The, 130
Creepshow, 130
Critters, 131
Crocodile, 132
Crucible of Horror, 133
Crucible of Terror, 133
Cruise into Terror, 133
Crypt of the Living Dead, 134
Cujo, 134
Curse of Frankenstein, The, 134–35
Curse of the Cat People, The, 134
Curse of the Crying Woman, The, 134
Curse of the Demon, 134
Curse of the Living Corpse, 135
Curse of the Mummy. *See* Aztec Mummy Double Feature
Curse of the Werewolf, The, 135
Curtains, 135
Cyclops, 135

Damien—Omen II, 137
Damnation Alley, 138
Dario Argento's Inferno. *See* Inferno
Dark, The, 140
Dark Eyes. *See* Demon Rage
Dark Eyes of London. *See* Human Monster, The
Dark of the Night, 141
Dark Places, 141
Dark Ride, The, 141
Dark Secret of Harvest Home, The, 141
Dark Star, 141
D.A.R.Y.L., 142
Daughter of Horror, 142
Daughters of Darkness, 142
Dawn of the Dead, 142–43
Dawn of the Mummy, 143
Day It Came to Earth, The, 144
Day of the Animals, The, 144
Day of the Dead, 144
Day of the Triffids, The, 144
Day the Earth Caught Fire, The, 144–45
Day the Earth Stood Still, The, 145
Day Time Ended, The, 145
Dead and Buried, 146
Dead-End Drive-In, 146
Dead Kids. *See* Strange Behavior
Deadline, 146
Deadly Blessing, 146
Deadly Eyes, 147
Deadly Friend, 147
Dead Men Walk, 148
Dead of Night (1945), 148
Dead of Night (1972). *See* Deathdream
Dead Zone, The, 148
Dear Dead Delilah, 148
Death at Love House, 148–49
Death Corps. *See* Shock Waves
Death Cruise, 149
Deathdream, 149
Death Race 2000, 150
Deathsport, 151
Deathstalker, 151
Death Watch, 151
Death Wheelers, The. *See* Psychomania (1971)
Decoy for Terror. *See* Playgirl Killer
Deep Red: Hatchet Murders, 152
Deep Six, The, 152
Dementia. *See* Daughter of Horror
Dementia 13, 154
Demon (1977), 154
Demon, The (1981), 154
Demoniac, 154
Demonoid, 154
Demonoid—Messenger of Death. *See* Demonoid
Demon Rage, 154
Demons, 154
Demon Seed, 154
Destination Moon, 157
Devil Bat, The. *See* Killer Bats
Devil Dog: The Hound of Hell, 158
Devil Doll, 158
Devil Girl from Mars, 158
Devil in the House of Exorcism, 158
Devil's Rain, The, 159
Devil's Undead, The, 159
Devil's Wedding Night, 159
Devonsville Terror, 159
Diaboliques, Les. *See* Diabolique
Die! Die! My Darling!, 160
Die Screaming, Marianne, 161
Disconnected, 163
Doctor and the Devils, The, 164
Dr. Black, Mr. Hyde, 164–65
Doctor Butcher, M.D. (Medical Deviate), 165
Dr. Jekyll and Mr. Hyde (1931), 165–66
Dr. Jekyll and Mr. Hyde (1941), 166

Horror/Science Fiction *(cont'd)*
Dr. Jekyll and Sister Hyde, 166
Dr. Jekyll's Dungeon of Death, 166
Doctor of Doom, 166
Dr. Phibes Rises Again, 166
Doctor Strange, 166
Doctors Wear Scarlet. *See* The Bloodsuckers
Dr. Terror's House of Horrors, 167
Don't Answer the Phone, 169
Don't Be Afraid of the Dark, 169
Don't Go in the House, 169
Don't Look in the Basement, 170
Don't Open the Window, 170
Dorian Gray, 170
Dorm That Dripped Blood, The, 170
Dracula (1931), 172
Dracula (1973), 172
Dracula (1974). *See* Andy Warhol's Dracula
Dracula (1979), 172
Dracula's Castle. *See* The Blood of Dracula's Castle
Dracula's Dog, 172–73
Dracula's Last Rites, 173
Dracula vs. Frankenstein, 173
Dragonslayer, 173–74
Dreamscape, 174
Driller Killer, 175
Drive-In Massacre, The, 174
Dune, 177
Dunwich Horror, The, 177

Earth vs. the Flying Saucers, 179
Eaten Alive, 180
Ebirah, Horror of the Deep. *See* Godzilla vs. the Sea Monster
Eerie Midnight Horror Show, 181
Eliminators, 183
Embryo, 184
Empire of the Ants, 185
Empire Strikes Back, The, 185
Endgame, 186
End of the World, 186
Enemy Mine, 186–87
Entity, The, 188
Equinox, 188
Eraserhead, 188
Escape from New York, 189
Escape from the Bronx, 189
Escape from the Planet of the Apes, 189
E.T. The Extra-Terrestrial, 190
Evictors, The, 192
Evil, The, 192
Evil Dead, The, 192
Evil Mind, The, 192
Evilspeak, 192
Exorcist, The, 193
Exorcist II: The Heretic, 193–94
Explorers, 194
Eyeball, 195
Eyes of a Stranger, 195

Fahrenheit 451, 197
Fall of the House of Usher, The, (1960), 198
Fall of the House of Usher, The, (1982), 198
Fantastic Voyage, 200
Fear Chamber, The. *See* Chamber of Fear
Fear No Evil, 203
Fiend Who Walked the West, The, 204
Fiend without a Face, 205
Fifth Floor, The, 205
Final Conflict, *See* Omen III—The Final Conflict
Final Countdown, The, 206
Final Exam, 206
Final Terror, The, 207
Firestarter, 208

First Men in the Moon, 209–10
Flash Gordon, 213
Flesh Eaters, The, 213
Flesh Feast, 213
Flight of the Navigator, 214
Flight to Mars, 214
Fly, The (1958), 215
Fly, The (1986), 215
Fog, The, 215
Food of the Gods, The, 216
Forbidden Planet, 217
Forbidden World, 217
Forest, The, 218
Frankenstein (1931), 223
Frankenstein (1973), 223
Frankenstein—1970, 223–24
Frankenstein 3-D. *See* Andy Warhol's Frankenstein
Frankenstein Created Women, 223
Frankenstein Island, 223
Frankenstein Meets the Space Monster, 223
Frankenstein Meets the Wolfman, 223
Freak Maker, The, 224
Friday the 13th, 225
Friday the 13th, Part V—A New Beginning, 225
Friday the 13th, Part IV—The Final Chapter, 225
Friday the 13th, Part VI—Jason Lives, 225
Friday the 13th, Part 3, 226
Friday the 13th, Part 2, 226
Fright, 226
Fright Night, 226
Frissons. *See* They Came from Within
Frogs, 226–27
From Beyond, 227
From Beyond the Grave, 227
Full Circle. *See* Haunting of Julia, The
Funhouse, The, 228
Fury, The, 229–30
Fury of the Succubus. *See* Demon Rage
Future-Kill, 230
Futureworld, 230

Galaxy of Terror, 231
Gamma People, The, 232
Gardener, The. *See* Seeds of Evil
Garden of the Dead, 233
Gas-s-s-s!; Or, It May Become Necessary to Destroy the World in Order to Save It, 233
Gates of Hell, The, 233
Ghidrah the Three-Headed Monster, 236–37
Ghostkeeper, 237
Ghostly Face, The, 237
Ghost of Flight 401, The, 237
Ghost Ship, 237
Ghost Story, 237–38
Ghoul, The, 238
Ghoulies, 238
Giant Spider Invasion, 238
Girls School Screamers, 241
Gladiators, The, 241
Glen and Randa, 242
Godsend, The, 243
God Told Me To. *See* Demon
Godzilla 1985, 244
Godzilla, The King of the Monsters, 244
Godzilla vs. Monster Zero. *See* Monster Zero
Godzilla vs. Mothra, 244
Godzilla vs. the Sea Monster, 244
Godzilla vs. the Thing. *See* Godzilla vs. Mothra
Gomar, the Human Gorilla. *See* Night of the Bloody Apes
Gorath, 249
Gorgo, 249
Gorgon, The, 249
Graduation Day, 250
Grave of the Vampire, 252

Great Alligator, 252
Gremlins, 257
Grim Reaper, The, 258
Grip of the Strangler. *See* Haunted Strangler, The
Grizzly, 258
Gruesome Twosome, 258
Guest in the House, 259

Halloween, 262
Halloween III—Season of the Witch, 262
Halloween II, 262
Hand, The, 263
Hangar 18, 263
Hannah—Queen of the Vampires. *See* Crypt of the Living Dead
Happy Brithday to Me, 264
Hatchet Murders, The. *See* Deep Red: Hatchet Murders
Haunted Strangler, The, 268
Haunting, The, 268
Haunting of Julia, The, 268
Haunting of M, The, 268
Hawk the Slayer, 268
Hearse, The, 269
He Knows You're Alone, 272
Hellhole, 273
Hell Night, 273
Henderson Monster, The, 274
Hideous Sun Demon, The, 276
Highlander, 277
Hills Have Eyes, The, 278
Hills Have Eyes II, The, 278
Hitcher, The, 279
Holocaust 2000, 281
Holy Terror. *See* Alice, Sweet Alice
Horror Express, 284
Horror Hospital, 284
Horror of Dracula, The, 284
Horror of Party Beach, The, 284
Horror on Snape Island. *See* Tower of Evil
Horror Planet, 284
Horror Rises from the Tomb, 284
House, 286
House by the Cemetery, The, 286
House of Doom. *See* Black Cat, The
House of Exorcism, The. *See* Devil in the House of Exorcism, The
House of Frankenstein, 287
House of Long Shadows, The, 287
House of Seven Corpses, The, 287
House of Usher. *See* Fall of the House of Usher, The (1960)
House of Wax, 287
House on Haunted Hill, The, 287
House on Sorority Row, 287
House That Dripped Blood, The, 287–88
House That Vanished, The. *See* Scream and Die
House Where Evil Dwells, The, 288
Howling, The, 288
Howling 2 . . . Your Sister Is a Werewolf, 288
Human Duplicators, The, 289
Human Monster, The, 289–90
Humanoids from the Deep, 290
Humongous, 290
Hunger, The, 290

I Dismember Mama, 293
Illustrated Man, The, 294
Ilsa, She-Wolf of the SS, 294–95
I Married a Monster from Outer Space, 295
Impulse, 296
Incense for the Damned. *See* Bloodsuckers, The
Incredible Hulk, The, 296

Horror/Science Fiction *(cont'd)*
Incredible Shrinking Man, The, 296
Incredible Torture Show, The. *See* Bloodsucking Freaks
Incubus, 297
Indestructible Man, The, 297
Inferno, 297-98
Initiation of Sarah, The, 298
Inseminoid. *See* Horror Planet
In the Shadow of Kilimanjaro, 301
Intruder Within, The, 301
Invaders from Mars (1953), 301
Invaders from Mars (1986), 301-2
Invasion of the Body Snatchers (1956), 302
Invasion of the Body Snatchers (1978), 302
Invitation to Hell, 303
Island, The, 304
Island Claws, 304
Island of Dr. Moreau, 304
Isle of the Dead, 305
Isle of the Snake People, The. *See* Snake People, The
I Spit on Your Grave, 305
It Came from Beneath the Sea, 305
It Came from Outer Space, 305
It Happened at Lakewood Manor. *See* Ants
It Lives Again, 306
It's Alive, 306
Ivanna. *See* Scream of the Demon Lover
I Walked with a Zombie, 307

Jack the Ripper, 309
Jennifer, 311-12
Jesse James Meets Frankenstein's Daughter, 312
John Carpenter's The Thing. *See* Thing, The (1982)
Journey to the Center of the Earth (1978). *See* Where Time Began

Keep, The, 321
Keeper, The, 321
Killbots. *See* Chopping Mall
Killer Bats, 323
Killer Fish, 323
Killer in Every Corner, A, 323
Killer on Board, 324
Killing Kind, The, 324
Kingdom of the Spiders, 325-26
King Kong (1933), 326
King Kong (1976), 326
King Kong Lives, 326
Kronos (1957), 330
Kronos (1974). *See* Captain Kronos: Vampire Hunter
Krull, 330

Labyrinth, 332
Lady Frankenstein, 332
Laserblast, 334
Last Horror Film, The, 335
Last House on the Left, The, 335-36
Last House on the Left Part II. *See* Bay of Blood
Last Rites. *See* Dracula's Last Rites
Last Starfighter, The, 337
Legacy, The, 339
Legacy of Blood. *See* Blood Legacy
Legacy of Maggie Walsh. *See* Legacy, The
Legend, 340
Legendary Strike, The, 240
Legend of Hell House, The, 340
Leopard Man, The, 341
Lifeforce, 343
Lift, The, 343-44
Liquid Sky, 345

Lisa and the Devil. *See* Devil in the House of Exorcism
Little Girl Who Lives Down the Lane, The, 346
Little Shop of Horrors, The (1960), 348
Locataire, Le. *See* Tenant, The
Loch Ness Horror, The, 349
Logan's Run, 349
Love Butcher, 354
Lust for a Vampire, 358

Man from Atlantis, The 366
Maniac (1934), 366
Maniac (1980), 367
Manitou, The, 367
Man They Could Not Hang, The, 368
Man Who Fell to Earth, The, 368
Martian Chronicles, The, 371
Martin, 371
Mausoleum, 374
Maximum Overdrive, 374
Medusa Touch, The, 376
Megaforce, 376
Mesa of Lost Women, 377
Metalstorm: The Destruction of Jared Sym, 377-78
Meteor Monster, 378
Microwave Massacre, 378
Milpitas Monster, The, 380
Mindwarp: An Infinity of Horrors. *See* Galaxy of Terror
Misfits of Science, 381
Monster a Go-Go, 385
Monster Club, The, 385
Monster Zero, 385
Moon of the Wolf, 387
Mortuary, 387-88
Mother's Day, 388
Mothra, 388-89
Mountaintop Motel Massacre, 389
Movie House Massacre, 389
Mummy, The, 391
Murder Motel, 392
Mutant, 394
Mutations, The. *See* Freak Maker, The
Mutilator, The, 394
My Bloody Valentine, 394
My Science Project, 397
Mysterians, The, 397
Mysterious Two, The, 397

Neverending Story, The, 402
Night Gallery, 404
Nightmare, 404
Nightmare City. *See* City of the Walking Dead
Nightmare in Wax, 404
Nightmare on Elm Street, A, 404-5
Nightmare on Elm Street Part 2, A: Freddy's Revenge, 405
Nightmares, 405
Night of the Bloody Apes, 405
Night of the Claw. *See* Island Claws
Night of the Cobra Woman, 405-6
Night of the Creeps, 405
Night of the Demon, 406
Night of the Ghouls, 406
Night of the Howling Beast, 406
Night of the Living Dead, 406
Night of the Zombies, 407
Night Stalker, The, 407
Night Warning, 408
Nightwing, 408
1984, 408-9
Nocturna, 410
Nomads, 410
Nothing But the Night. *See* Devil's Undead, The

Oblong Box, The, 415
Octaman, 415
Of Unknown Origin, 417
Omega Man, The, 419
Omen, The, 419
Omen III—The Final Conflict, 419
Omen II. *See* Damien—Omen II
One Dark Night, 421
One Deadly Owner, 421
Outland, 428

Pack, The, 431
Panic at Lakewood Manor. *See* Ants
Panic on the Trans-Siberian Express. *See* Horror Express
Parasite, 434
Parasite Murders, The. *See* They Came from Within
Parts: The Clonus Horros. *See* Clonus Horror, The
Patrick, 436
People, The, 438
Phantasm, 439
Phantom Express, The, 439-40
Phantom of Terror, The. *See* Bird with the Crystal Plumage, The
Phantom of the Opera, The, 440
Phase IV, 400
Philadelphia Experiment, The, 440
Pieces, 441
Piranha, 442
Piranha Part 2: The Spawning, 442
Pit, The, 443
Pit and the Pendulum, The, 443
Planet of Horrors. *See* Galaxy of Terror
Planet of the Apes, 444
Planet of the Prowl, 444
Plan Nine from Outer Space, 444
Playgirl Killer, The, 444
Poltergeist, 446
Poltergeist II—The Other Side, 446
Premature Burial, 449
Prisoners of the Lost Universe, 452
Prom Night, 454
Prophecy, 454
Prowler, The, 455
Psychic, The, 455
Psycho, 455
Psychomania, 455
Psycho Sisters, 455
Psycho III, 455
Psycho II, 455

Q—The Winged Serpent, 458
Queen of the Cannibals. *See* Doctor Butcher, M.D. (Medical Deviate)
Quest for Love, 459
Quiet Earth, The, 459
Quintet, 460

Rabid, 461
Rats Are Coming, The! The Werewolves Are Here!, 465
Raven, The (1935), 465
Raven, The (1963), 465-66
Razorback, 466
Re-Animator, 467
Reincarnation of Peter Proud, The, 469
Repulsion, 470
Resurrection Syndicate, The. *See* Devil's Undead, The
Return of the Fly, 471
Return of the Jedi, 471
Return of the Kung Fu Dragon, 471
Return of the Vampire, 472
Revenge of the Dead. *See* Night of the Ghouls

Horror/Science Fiction (cont'd)
Revenge of the Stepford Wives, 273
Revolt of the Zombies, 473
Ripper, The, 476
R.O.B.O.T. See Chopping Mall
Robot Monster, 478
Rocketship X-M, 478
Rocktober Blood, 478
Rodan, 479
Rollerball, 479
Rosemary's Baby, 482
Rosemary's Killer. See Prowler, The
Runaway, 484

Sacred Ground, 486
Salem's Lot—The Movie, 488
Samson vs. the Vampire Women, 489
Satan's Mistress. See Demon Rage
Satan's Cheerleaders, 491
Satan's Skin. See Blood on Satan's Claw, The
Satan's School for Girls, 491
Saturn 3, 491
Savage Bees, The, 492
Scalps, 493
Scanners, 494
Scared to Death, 494
Scars of Dracula, 495
Schizo, 495
School Spirit, 495–96
Scream and Die, 496
Scream and Scream Again, 496
Scream Baby Scream, 496
Scream for Help, 496
Scream of the Demon Lover, 496
Screams of a Winter Night, 496
Secret of Dorian Gray. See Dorian Gray
Seeds of Evil, 499
See No Evil, 499–500
Sender, The, 500
Sentinel, The, 500–1
Seventh Victim, The, 504
She Beast, The, 507
She-Freak, 507–8
She Waits, 509
Shining, The, 509
Shivers. See They Came from Within
Schock Treatment, 510
Shock Waves, 510
Short Circuit, 511–12
Silent Night, Bloody Night, 513
Silent Night, Deadly Night, 514
Silent Night Evil Night. See Black Christmas
Silent Running, 514
Silent Scream, 514
Silver Bullet, 515
Simon, King of the Witches, 515–16
Sinner's Blood, 517
Slasher . . . Is the Sex Maniac, The, 519
Slave of the Cannibal God, 520
Slayer, The, 520
Sledge Hammer, 520
Sleepaway Camp, 520
Slime People, The, 521
Slumber Party '57, 521
Slumber Party Massacre, 521
Snake People, The, 523
Snowbeat, 523
Snow Creature, 523
Solarbabies, 524
Something Wicked This Way Comes, 526
Son of Blob. See Beware! The Blob
Son of Godzilla, 527
Son of Kong, 527
Sorceress, 528
Soylent Green, 530
Spaced Out, 530

Spacehunter: Adventures in the Forbidden Zone, 530
Space Raiders, 530
Spasms, 531
Spell, 531
Splatter University, 533
Squirm, 534
Starcrash, 536
Starman, 537
Star Trek—The Motion Picture, 537
Star Trek IV: The Voyage Home, 537
Star Trek III: The Search For Spock, 537–38
Star Trek II: The Wrath of Khan, 538
Star Wars, 538
Stephen King's Cat's Eye. See Cat's Eye
Stephen King's Silver Bullet. See Silver Bullet
Strange Behavior, 543
Strange Case of Dr. Jekyll, The, 543
Strange Invaders, 543
Stranger from Venus, 543
Stranger in Our House. See Summer of Fear
Stranger in the House. See Black Christmas
Strangers in Paradise, 544
Strange World of Planet X, The. See Cosmic Monster
Summer of Fear, 548–49
Summer of Secrets, 549
Supernaturals, The, 551
Swamp Thing, 552

Tales from The Crypt, 556
Tales of Terror, 556
Tales That Witness Madness, 556
Tarantula, 558
Tarantulas: The Deadly Cargo, 558
Teenage Monster. See Meteor Monster
Tell-Tale Heart, The, 560
Tempter, The, 560–61
Tenant, The, 561
Tentacles, 562
Tenth Victim, The, 562
Terminal Man, The, 563
Terminator, The, 563
Terror, 563
Terror in the Aisles, 563
Terror in the Wax Museum, 563–64
Terror on Tape, 564
Terror on Tour, 564
Terror Train, 564
Texas Chainsaw Massacre, The, 565
Texas Chainsaw Massacre Part Two, The, 565
Theatre of Blood, 567–68
Theatre of Death, 568
Them!, 568
They Came from Within, 569
Thing, The (1951), 571
Thing, The (1982), 571
Thing from Another World, The. See Thing, The (1951)
Things to Come, 571
Thirst, 572
13 Ghosts, 572
THX-1138, 577
Time after Time, 579
Time Bandits, 579
Time Machine, The (1960), 579
Time Machine, The (1978), 579
Time Rider, 579
Tintorera . . . Tiger Shark, 580
Titan Find. See Creature
Tomb, The, 582
Toolbox Murders, The, 583
Torture Garden, 585
To the Devil—A Daughter, 585
Tourist Trap, 587

Tower of Evil, 587
Tower of London, The, 587
Toxic Avenger, The, 587
Trick or Treat, 590
Trick or Treats, 590
Trilogy of Terror, 591
Troll, 592
Trollenberg Terror, The. See Crawling Eye, The
Tron, 592
Twenty Million Miles to Earth, 594
Twilight Zone—The Movie, 595
Twins of Kung Fu, 595
Twitch of the Death Nerve, The. See Bay of Blood
2000 Maniacs, 596
2001: A Space Odyssey, 596–97
2010—The Year We Make Contact, 597
Two Worlds of Jennie Logan, The, 597

Unearthly, The, 600
Unseen, The, 600

Vamp, 603
Vampire Beast Craves Blood, The. See Blood Beast Terror, The
Vampire Happening, The, 603
Vampire Hookers, 603
Varan the Unbelievable, 604
Velvet House. See Crucible of Horror
Velvet Vampire, The, 604
Venom, 604
Videodrome, 605
Village of the Damned, 605
Village of the Giants, 605
Vultures, 607

War between the Planets. See Planet on the Prowl
Warlords of Atlantis, 610
Warlords of the 21st Century, 610
War of the Worlds, 611
Warriors of the Wasteland, 611
Watcher in the Woods, The, 612
Wavelength, 613
Welcome to Blood City, 614
Werewolf after Midnight. See Werewolf of Washington, The
Werewolf of Washington, The, 615
Werewolves on Wheels, 615
Westworld, 615
When Worlds Collide, 617
Where Time Began, 618
White Zombie, 620
Whodunit, 620
Who Slew Auntie Roo?, 621
Wicker Man, The, 622
Willard, 625
Windows, 626
Witch's Mirror, The, 628
Wizard of Gore, The, 629
Wizard of Mars, The, 629
Wolfen, 629
Wolf Man, The, 629
World, The Flesh and the Devil, The, 633
World without End, 633
Worm Eaters, The, 633
Wraith, The, 633
Wrestling Women vs. The Aztec Mummy, The, 634

"X"—The Man with the X-Ray Eyes, 635
Xtro, 635

Yor, the Hunter from the Future, 637
You Better Watch Out. See Christmas Evil

Horror/Science Fiction *(cont'd)*
Zardoz, 641
Zombie, 642
Zombies of Mora Tau, 642

MYSTERY/SUSPENSE

Act, The, 3
Adventures of Sherlock Holmes, The, 5
Against All Odds, 7
Agent on Ice, 7
Amateur, The, 15
Anderson Tapes, The, 19
. . . And Hope to Die, 19
Andromeda Strain, The, 20
And Then There Were None, 20
Anything for Love. See 11 Harrowhouse
Apology, 25
Arabesque, 26
Asphalt Jungle, The, 28
At Gunpoint, 29

Baby Love, 33
Bad Ronald, 36
Bad Seed, The, 36
Battle Shock, 41–42
Bedroom Eyes, 44–45
Bedroom Window, The, 45
Belarus File, The, 46
Berlin Express, 48
Beyond Reasonable Doubt, 51
Big Combo, The, 53
Big Fix, The, 53
Big Heat, The, 53
Big Sleep, The (1946), 54
Big Sleep, The (1978), 54
Blackmail, 59
Black Marble, The, 59
Black Room, The, 60
Black Widow, 61
Black Windmill, The, 61
Blade, 61
Blind Alley. See Perfect Strangers
Blood Mania, 64
Blood Simple, 65
Blood Sisters. See Sisters
Blow Out, 66
Blue City, 66
Blue Knight, The, 67
Body Double, 69–70
Body Heat, 70
Boston Strangler, The, 73
Boys from Brazil, The, 74
Bullitt, 84
Bunco, 84
Butterfly Affair, The, 86

Capricorn One, 92
Case of Jonathan Drew, The. See Lodger, The
Catamount Killing, The, 97
Cat and Mouse, 97
Cat and the Canary, The (1927), 97
Cat and the Canary, The (1978), 97
Centerfold Girls, 99
Chain Reaction, 100
Chairman, The, 100
Charade, 102
Chiefs, 104
China Syndrome, The, 101
Chinatown, 106
Choice of Arms, 106
City, The, 111
Clay Pigeon, The, 113
Cloak and Dagger, 113

Cold Room, The, 117
Color Me Dead, 118
Coma, 118
Comeback, The, 118
Coogan's Bluff, 123
Cop Killer, The. See Corrupt
Cornered, 124
Corrupt, 124
Corrupt Ones, The, 124
Course du Lievre à travers les Champs. See
   . . . And Hope to Die
Critical List. See Terminal Choice
Cross Country, 132
Curse of King Tut's Tomb, The, 135
Curse of the Black Widow, 134

Dain Curse, The, 137
Dangerous Summer, A, 139
Dark Mirror, The, 141
Dark Night of the Scarecrow, The, 141
Day of the Cobra, The, 144
Day of the Jackal, The, 144
Dayton's Devils, 145
Deadly Affair, The, 146
Deadly Game, The, 147
Deadly Games, 147
Deadly Hero, 147
Deadly Strangers, 147
Dear Detective, 148
Death Kiss, 149
Death List. See Terminal Choice
Death of a Hooker. See Who Killed Mary
   What's'ername?
Death on the Nile, 150
Death Sentence, 150
Deathtrap, 151
Death Valley, 151
Destructors, The, 157
Detective, The, 157
Detour, 157
Diabolique, 159
Dial M for Murder, 159
Dingaka, 161
Dinner at the Ritz, 161
Diplomatic Courier, 162
Dixy Ray—Hollywood Star. See It's Called
   Murder, Baby
D.O.A., 164
Dominique, 168
Domino Principle, The, 168
Don't Look Now, 170
Doomed to Die, 170
Doomsday Flight, The, 170
Double Life, A, 171
Double McGuffin, The, 171
Double Negative, 171
Dragnet, 173
Dream Lover, 174
Dressed to Kill (1946), 175
Dressed to Kill (1980), 175
Driver's Seat, The, 175
Drowning Pool, The, 175
Duel, 176
Dying Room Only, 177

Echoes, 181
Eddie and the Cruisers, 181
Eddie Macon's Run, 181
Eiger Sanction, the, 182
8 Million Ways to Die, 182
11 Harrowhouse, 183
Endangered Species, 186
Endless Night, 186
Enigma, 187
Escape to Burma, 189–90
Evil under the Sun, 192

Executive Action, 193
Express to Terror, 194
Eye of the Needle, 195
Eyes of Laura Mars, The, 195
Eyewitness, 195

Face of Fu Manchu, The, 196
Fade to Black, 197
Falcon's Adventure, 197
Falcon in Mexico, The, 197
Falcon Takes Over, The, 197
Fallen Angel (1945), 197–98
Fallen Idol, 198
Fallen Sparrow, The, 198
Family Plot, 199
Fan, The, 199
Farewell, My Lovely, 201
Fear in the Night, 203
Final Assignment, 206
First Deadly Sin, The, 209
First Great Train Robbery, The. See Great Train
   Robbery, The
Five Fingers, 212
Flash of Green, A, 213
Flashpoint, 213
Fletch, 213–14
Foreign Correspondent, 218
Formula, The, 219
Fortress, 219
Frantic, 224
Frenzy, 225
Funeral in Berlin, 228
F/X, 230

Gaslight, 233
Glitter Dome, The, 242
Golden Rendezvous, 246
Gorky Park, 250
Great Train Robbery, The, 255–56
Green Ice, 256–57

Hammett, 263
Happy Mother's Day, Love, George. See Run,
   Stranger, Run
Harper, 266–67
Heatwave, 271
He Walked by Night, 276
Holcroft Covenant, The, 280
Honeymoon Killers, The, 283
Honor Thy Father, 283
Hot Rock, The, 285–86
Hound of the Baskervilles, The, 286
House Across the Bay, The, 286
How to Make It. See Target: Harry
Hurricane Express, The, 290

I Confess, 292–93
In Cold Blood, 296
In the Heat of the Night, 301
I, the Jury, 306
It's Called Murder, Baby, 306
I Want Her Dead. See W

Jagged Edge, 309
Janitor, The. See Eyewitness
Jet over the Atlantic, 313
Jigsaw Man, The, 313
Johnny Nobody, 315
Journey into Fear, 316
Joy House, 316
Juggernaut, 317

Kansas City Massacre, The, 320
Kennel Murder Case, The, 321
Key Largo, 322
Killer Elite, The, 323

Mystery/Suspense *(cont'd)*
Killjoy, 324–25
Kiss Me, Kill Me, 328
Klute, 329
Knock on Any Door, 330

Lady from Shanghai, The, 332
Lady in a Cage, 333
Lady of Burlesque, 333
Lady Vanishes, The (1938), 334
Lady Vanishes, The (1979), 334
Land That Time Forgot, The, 334
Lassiter, 334
Last Embrace, 335
Last of Sheila, The, 336–37
Last Wave, The, 338
Las Vegas Story, The, 338
Late Show, The, 338
Laughing Policeman, The, 338
Laura (1944), 338–39
Legal Eagles, 339–40
Let's Scare Jessica to Death, 341
Link, 345
Little Drummer Girl, The, 346
Lodger, The, 349
Long Dark Hall, The, 350
Looker, 352
Looking Glass War, The, 352
Love from a Stranger, 354

Mackintosh Man, The, 359
Madame Sin, 360
Madigan, 360
Magic, 361
Maltese Falcon, The, 364
Man, a Woman and a Bank, A, 365
Manhattan Project, The, 366
Manhunter, 366
Man Who Haunted Himself, The, 368
Man Who Knew Too Much, The (1934), 368
Man Who Knew Too Much, The (1956), 368
Marathon Man, 370
Marnie, 371
Mean Season, The, 375
Mike's Murder, 379
Mr. Moto's Last Warning, 390
Mr. Wong, Detective, 391
Morning After, The, 387
Murder, 392
Murder by Decree, 392
Murder by Phone, 392
Murderer's Row, 392
Murder, My Sweet, 393
Murder on Flight 502, 393
Murder on the Orient Express, 393
Murders in the Rue Morgue, 393
Mystery of the Marie Celeste, The. *See* Phantom Ship

Naked Face, The, 399
Next Victim, 403
Nightcomers, The, 403
Night Cries, 403
Night Moves, 405
Night of the Juggler, 406
Night Partners, 405
Night Visitor, The, 408
Ninth Configuration, The, 409
North by Northwest, 411
Notorious, 412
No Way to Treat a Lady, 413
Nowhere to Run, 413
Number Seventeen, 413

Obsession, 415
Odessa File, The, 416

One Body Too Many, 421
One Frightened Night, 422
One Shoe Makes It Murder, 423
Ordeal by Innocence, 426
Organization, The, 426
Osterman Weekend, The, 427
Out of the Past, 429
Outside the Law, 430

Parallax View, The, 433
Paranoia, 433
Park Is Mine, The, 434
Pendulum, 437
Perfect Strangers, 438
Phantom Fiend, The. *See* Lodger, The
Phantom Ship, 440
Picture Mommy Dead, 441
Play Misty for Me, 445
Postman Always Rings Twice, The (1946), 448
Postman Always Rings Twice, The (1981), 448–49
President's Mistress, The, 450
Prime Suspect, 451
Private Life of Sherlock Holmes, The, 452–53
Pursuit to Algiers, 457

Rear Window, 467
Rebecca, 467
Red House, The, 468
Rehearsal for Murder, 469
Return of Frank Cannon, The, 470
Revenge, 473
Rififi, 475
Road Games, 477
Rollover, 479–80
Rope, 481
Rough Cut, 482
Run, Stranger, Run, 485
Russian Roulette, 485

Sabotage, 486
Saboteur, 486
Saint in London, The, 487
Saint in New York, The, 487
St. Ives, 487–88
Saint Strikes Back, The, 488
Saint Takes Over, The, 488
Sapphire, 490
Satan Bug, The, 491
Savage, 492
Scarlet and the Black, The, 494
Scarlet Street, 495
Seance on a Wet Afternoon, 497
Secret Agent, 498
Seduction, The, 499
Seven Days in May, 503
Seven Doors to Death, 503
Seven Per Cent Solution, The, 503
Shamus, 506
Sharky's Machine, 507
She's Dressed to Kill, 508–9
Sherlock Holmes and the Secret Code. *See* Dressed to Kill (1946)
Sherlock Holmes and the Secret Weapon, 508
Sherlock Holmes and the Voice of Terror, 508
Shriek in the Night, A, 512
Silent Partner, The, 514
Silver Bears, 514–15
Silver Streak, The, 515
Sisters, 517–18
Sleuth, 520
Slightly Honorable, 520–21
Slightly Scarlet, 521
Slow Burn, 521
Someone is Killing the World's Greatest Models. *See* She's Dressed to Kill

Sorry, Wrong Number, 528
Special Effects, 531
Spellbound, 531
Sphinx, 532
Spiral Staircase, The, 532
Spraggue "Murder for Two," 533
Stage Fright, 535
Star Chamber, The, 536
Stick, 540
Stiletto, 540
Still of the Night, 540
Stone Cold Dead, 541
Stopover Tokyo, 541–42
Strait-Jacket, 542
Strange and Deadly Occurrence, The, 542
Strange Love of Martha Ivers, 543
Stranger, The, 543
Stranger is Watching, A, 543–44
Stranger on the 3rd Floor, 544
Strangers Kiss, 544
Strange Shadows in an Empty Room, 544
Strike Force, 545
Study in Terror, A, 547
Subterfuge, 547
Suddenly, 547
Sudden Terror, 547
Sunburn, 549
Suspicion, 552

Taking of Pelham One Two Three, The, 556
Target, 558
Target: Harry, 558
Targets, 558
Tattered Web, A, 559
Telefon, 560
Ten Little Indians (1965), 562
Ten Little Indians (1975), 562
Ten Rillington Place, 562
Terminal Choice, 563
Terror by Night, 563
They Call Me MISTER Tibbs!, 569
They're Playing with Fire, 570
They Won't Believe Me, 570
They Won't Forget, 570
Thief, 570
Thief Who Came to Dinner, The, 571
Thin Man, The, 571–72
Third Man, The, 572
13 Rue Madeleine, 572
39 Steps, The (1935), 572
39 Steps, The (1959), 572
This Gun for Hire, 573
Thomas Crown Affair, The, 573
Threat, The, 574
Three Days of the Condor, 575
Tiger Bay, 578
Tightrope, 578
Time Lock, 579
To Catch a King, 581
To Catch a Thief, 581
To Kill a Clown, 582
Tony Rome, 583
Topaz, 583–84
Topkapi, 584
Torn Curtain, 585
Touch of Evil, 586
Town That Dreaded Sundown, The, 587
Trauma. *See* Terminal Choice
Triumph of Sherlock Holmes, The, 591
True Confessions, 592–93
Twilight's Last Gleaming, 595
Twinkle, Twinkle, Killer Kane. *See* Ninth Configuration, The

Under Capricorn, 598

Mystery/Suspense *(cont'd)*
Vamping, 603
Vertigo, 604
Very Big Withdrawal, A. *See* A Man, a Woman and a Bank
Visiting Hours, 606

W, 608
Wait Until Dark, 608
WarGames, 610
Warning Sign, 611
Watched, 611–12
Weekend of Shadows, 614
What Ever Happened to Aunt Alice?, 616
What Ever Happened to Baby Jane?, 616
What's in It for Harry. *See* Target: Harry
When a Stranger Calls, 616–17
While the City Sleeps, 618–19
Whistle Stop, 619
White Nights, 620
Who is Killing the Great Chefs of Europe?, 620
Who Killed Mary Magdalene?. *See* Who Killed Mary What's'ername?
Who Killed Mary What's'ername?, 620–21
Witness, 628
Witness for the Prosecution, 628–29
Woman Alone, A, 486
Woman's Devotion, A. *See* Battle Shock
Woman in Green, The, 630
Woman in the Window, The, 630
Wrong Man, The, 634

Young and Innocent, 638
Young Sherlock Holmes, 639

ACTION/ADVENTURE

Abduction, The, 1
Abductors, The, 1
Accident, The, 2–3
Across 110th Street, 3
Across the Great Divide, 3
Adventure for Imperial Treasure, 4
Adventures of Captain Fabian, The, 4
Adventures of Don Juan, 4
Adventures of Robin Hood, The, 5
Adventures of Tartu, The, 5
African Queen, The, 6
Against All Odds, 7
Air Force, 7
Albino, 9
Allan Quatermain and the Lost City of Gold, 11
Allegheny Uprising, 11
Alley Cat, 11
All Quiet on the Western Front (1930), 12
All Quiet on the Western Front (1979), 12–13
All the Way, Boys, 13
Alphabet City, 14
American Commandos, 16
American Justice, 17
American Ninja, 17
Amsterdam Connection, The, 18
Amsterdam Kill, The, 18
Angel, 20–21
Angel from H.E.A.T., 21
Angels Die Hard, 21
Angels Hard as They Come, 21
Appointment in Honduras, 25
Amored Car Robbery, 26–27
Around the World under the Sea, 27
Arousers, The, 27
Ashanti—Land of No Mercy, 27

Assassination, 28
Assault, 28
Assault on Agathon, 28
Assault on Precinct 13, 28
Ator. *See* Ator, the Fighting Eagle
Ator, the Fighting Eagle, 29–30
At Sword's Point, 30
Attack Force Z, 30
At the Earth's Core, 30
Avalanche, 31
Avenging Angel, 32
Avenging Boxer, 32
Avenging Force, 32

Baby . . . Secret of the Lost Legend, 33
Back to Bataan, 34
Badge 373, 35
Bandits, Prostitutes, and Silver, 38
Bandits, The, 37–38
Band of the Hand, 38
Barabbas, 38
Barbary Coast, 39
Bataan, 40
Battle Creek Brawl. *See* Big Brawl, The
Battle Cry, 40
Battle Hell, 41
Battle of Austerlitz, 41
Battle of El Alamein, 41
Battle of Neretva, The, 41
Battle of the Bulge, 41
Battle of the Commandos, 41
Bear Island, 42–43
Beastmaster, The, 43
Because of the Cats, 44
Bedford Incident, The, 44
Below the Belt, 47
Beneath the 12-Mile Reef, 48
Ben Hur, 48
Beyond the Gate. *See* Human Experiments
Beyond the Poseidon Adventure, 52
Big Bad Mama, 52
Big Brawl, The, 52
Big Cat, The, 52–53
Big Doll House, The, 53
Big Rascal, The, 54
Big Red One, The, 54
Big Score, The, 54
Big Trees, The, 54
Big Trouble in Little China, 55
Big Wednesday, 55
Billy Jack, 55–56
Bionic Woman, The, 56
Birdman of Alcatraz, The, 56
Bird of Paradise, 56
Birds of Prey, 57
Black Arrow, The, 58
Black Belt Jones, 58
Black Godfather, The, 59
Black Hand, The, 59
Black Moon Rising, 59–60
Black Pirate, 60
Black Six, The, 60
Black Sunday (1977), 61
Blade Master, The, 61
Blazing Ninja, The, 61
Blind Fist of Bruce, 62
Blind Rage, 62
Blood and Sand (1922), 63
Blooded Treasury Fight, 63
Blood of the Dragon, 64
Blood of the Dragon Peril, 64
Blood on the Sun, 64–65
Bloody Fight, The, 65
Bloody Fist, The, 65
Bloody Mama, 66
Blue Thunder, 68

Bobby Jo and the Outlaw, 69
Bobo, 69
Bolo the Brute. *See* Bobo
Bone Crushing Kid, The, 71
Bonnie and Clyde, 71
Bonnie's Kids, 71
Borderline, 71
Born American, 72
Born Invincible, 72
Born Losers, The, 72
Bounty, The, 73
Boxcar Bertha, 73
Boys in Company C, The, 74
Brady's Escape, 75
Brain, The, 75
Brannigan, 76
Brass Target, The, 76
Brave Lion, The, 76
Bravest Fist, The, 76
Breaker, Breaker, 76
Breakheart Pass, 77
Breakout, 77–78
Break-Out from Oppression, 78
Bridge on the River Kwai, The, 79
Bridge Too Far, A, 79
Brink's Job, The, 80
Bronson Lee, Champion, 81
Brotherhood of the Yakuza. *See* Yakuza, The
Bruce, Kung Fu Girls, 82
Bruce and Shaolin Kung Fu Part I, 82
Bruce and the Dragon Fist, 82
Bruce Le's Greatest Revenge, 82
Bruce Li in New Guinea, 82
Bruce vs. Bill, 82
Bulldog Drummond Comes Back, 83
Bulldog Drummond's Bride, 83
Bullies, 84
Bury Me an Angel, 85
Bust-Top. *See* His Kind of Woman

Caboblanco, 87
Caged Heat, 88
Caged Women, 89
Call of the Wild, The (1972), 90
Call of the Wild, The (1976), 90
Cannonball, 91
Cannonball Run, The, 91
Cannonball Run 2, 91
Cantonen Iron Kung Fu, 91
Captain America, 92
Captain America II: Death Too Soon, 92
Captain Blood, 92
Captain Caution, 92
Captain Kidd, 92
Captain Scarlett, 93
Captains Courageous, 93
Cassandra Crossing, The, 96
Cast a Giant Shadow, 96
Catch Me a Spy, 97
C.C. and Company, 99
Certain Fury, 99
Chained Heat, 100
Challenge, The, 100
Challenge the Dragon, 100
Champion of Death, 101
Charge of the Light Brigade, The, 102
Charley Varrick, 102
Chase Step by Step, 102–3
China Seas, 106
Chinese Connection, The, 106
Choke Canyon, 107
Circle of Iron, 110
City on Fire, 111
Clan of the Cave Bear, The, 111–12
Class of 1984, 112
Cleopatra Jones, 113

Action/Adventure (cont'd)
Clones of Bruce Lee, The, 114
Cobra (1981), 115
Cobra (1986), 115
Cocaine Wars, 116
Code Name: Diamond Head, 116
Code Name: Wildgeese, 116–17
Code of Silence, 117
Colditz Story, The, 117
Commando, 119
Conan the Barbarian, 121
Conan the Destroyer, 121
Concrete Jungle, 121
Conqueror, The, 122
Convoy, 123
Cool Hand Luke, 123
Corsican Brothers, The (1941), 124
Cotton Comes to Harlem, 125
Crazy Mama, 128–29
Crimson Pirate, The, 131
Crossed Swords, 132
Cross of Iron, 132
Cry of the Innocent, 133–34
Cuba Crossing. See Kill Castro

Dangerously Close, 139
Daniel Boone, 139
Darby's Rangers, 140
Daring Dobermans, The, 140
Daring Game, 140
David and Bathsheba, 142
Dawn Patrol, 143
Day of the Dolphin, The, 144
Day They Robbed the Bank of England, The, 145
D-Day the Sixth of June, 146
Dead Easy, 146
Deadly Encounter, 146–47
Deadly Force, 147
Deadly Shaolin Kicks, 147
Deadly Shaolin Longfist, 147
Deadly Strike, The, 147
Deathcheaters, 149
Death Hunt, 149
Death Journey, 149
Death of Bruce Lee, The, 150
Death Ray 2000, 150
Death Ride to Osaka, 150
Death Squad, 151
Death Stalk, 151
Death Wish, 151
Death Wish II, 151
Death Wish III, 151–52
Deep, The, 152
Defiance, 153
Delirium, 153
Deliverance, 153
Delta Force, 153
Delta Fox, 153
Desert Fox, The, 155
Desert Rats, The, 155
Desperate Chase. See Blood of the Dragon
Desperate Journey, 156
Destination Gobi, 157
Destination Tokyo, 157
Detroit 9000, 157
Devil at 4 O'Clock, The, 158
Devil's Assignment, The, 158
Devil's Brigade, 159
Diamonds Are Forever, 159
Dick Tracy, 160
Dick Tracy Meets Gruesome, 160
Dick Tracy Returns, 160
Dick Tracy's Dilemma, 160
Dick Tracy vs. Cueball, 160
Dillinger, 161

Dirty Dozen, The, 162
Dirty Dozen, The: The Next Mission, 162
Dirty Harry, 162
Dirty Mary, Crazy Larry, 162
Dixie Dynamite, 164
Dr. No, 166
Doctor Syn, 167
Dogs of War, The, 167–68
$ (Dollars), 168
Donner Pass—The Road to Survival, 169
Double, Double Cross, The, 171
Double Dragon in Last Duel, The, 171
Dragon, Lizard, Boxer, 173
Dragon Claws, 173
Dragon Devil Die. See Blooded Treasury Fight
Dragon Force Operation, 173
Dragon Kid, The, 173
Dragon Princess, 173
Dragon's Greatest Revenge. See Bruce Le's Greatest Revenge
Dreaming Fist with Slender Hands, 174
Dressed to Fight, 174
Driver, The, 175
Drum, The (1938). See Drums
Drums, 176
Drunken Arts and Crippled Fist, 176
Drunken Swordsman, 176
Duellists, The, 177
Duel of Champions, 177
Duel of the Iron Fist, 177
Duel of the Seven Tigers, 177
Dumb Boxer, 177
Dynamo, 178

Eagle Fist, The, 179
Eagle Has Landed, The, 179
Eagles Attack at Dawn, 179
Earthquake, 179
Eat My Dust!, 180
Ebony, Ivory, and Jade, 181
Edge of Fury, 181
Elephant Boy, 183
Emerald Forest, The, 184
Enchanted Island, 185
Enemy Below, The, 186
Enforcer, The, 187
Enter the Dragon, 187
Enter the Game of Death, 187
Enter the Ninja, 187
Escape, 188–89
Escape from Alcatraz, 189
Escape from Hell, See Escape
Escape to Athena, 189
Escape to the Sun, 190
Eunuch of the Western Palace, 190
Evil Knievel, 191
Evil That Men Do, The, 192
Excalibur, 192
Executioner, The, 192–93
Exodus, 193
Experiment in Terror, 194
Exterminator, The, 194
Exterminator 2, 194
Eye for an Eye, 194–95

Fake-Out, 197
Family, The, 199
Family Enforcer, 199
Faster Pussycat, Kill Kill!, 201
Fast Walking, 202
Fatal Needles vs. Fatal Fists, 202
F.B.I. Story, The, 202
Fear City, 203
Fearless Hyena, The, 203
Fearless Young Boxer. See Avenging Boxer
Fer-de-Lance, 203–4

fFolkes, 204
Fifth Musketeer, The, 205
Fight For Your Life, 205
Fighting Dragon, The, 206
Fighting Mad, 206
Final Justice, 206–7
Final Option, The, 207
Fire!, 207–8
Fire and Ice, 208
Firecracker, 208
Fire Down Below, 208
Firefox, 208
Firepower, 208
Firewalker, 208
Fire with Fire, 209
First Blood, 209
First Blood Part Two. See Rambo: First Blood Part Two
Fist of Fury II, 211
Fist of Vengeance, 211
Fists of Fear, Touch of Death, 211
Fists of Fury, 211
Fists, the Kicks and the Evil, The, 211
Fixed Bayonets, 212
Flame and the Arrow, The, 212
Flash and the Firecat, 212
Flash Legs. See Deadly Shaolin Kicks
Flesh and Blood, 213
Flight from Glory, 214
Flight of the Phoenix, The, 214
Flood!, 214
Flying Leathernecks, 215
Flying Tigers, 215
Forced Entry, 217
Forced Vengeance, 217
Force: Five, 217
Force of One, A, 217–18
Force 10 From Navarone, 218
48 HRS, 220
49th Parallel, The, 220
For Your Eyes Only, 220
Four Feathers (1977), 221
Four Feathers, The (1939), 221
Four Horsemen of the Apocalypse, The, 221
Four Musketeers, The, 222
Foxtrap, 222
Framed, 222
Freebie and the Bean, 224
French Connection, The 224
French Connection II, The, 224–25
Frogmen, 226
From China with Death. See Wits to Wits
From Hell to Victory, 227
From Russia with Love, 227
Furious, The, 229
Fury of King Boxer, 230
Fury of Shaolin Fist, 230
Fury of the Shaolin Master, 230
Fyre, 230

Gallant Hours, The, 231
Gambit, 231
Game of Death, 232
Game of Death II, 232
Gator, 234
Gator Bait, 234
Gauntlet, The, 234
Gentleman Jim, 235
Getaway, The, 236
Getting Even, 236
Ghost Patrol, 237
Ghosts on the Loose, 237
Ginger, 239
Girls Are for Loving, 240–41
Girls of the White Orchid. See Death Ride to Osaka

Mystery/Suspense *(cont'd)*
Gloria, 242
Glove, The, 242
Goldengirl, 246
Golden Lady, The, 246
Goldfinger, 246
Gold of the Amazon Women, 246
Goliath and the Barbarians, 247
Gone in 60 Seconds, 247
Good Guys Wear Black, 248
Goonies, The, 249
Goose Boxer, The, 249
Gotcha!, 250
Go Tell the Spartans, 250
Grandmaster of Shaolin Kung Fu, 251
Grand Prix, 251
Grand Theft Auto, 251
Gray Lady Down, 252
Great Bank Hoax, The, 252
Great Escape from Women's Prison, The, 253
Great General, 254
Great Georgia Bank Hoax, The. *See* Great Bank Hoax, The
Great Skycopter Rescue, The, 255
Great Texas Dynamite Chase, The, 255
Green Berets, The, 256
Green Jade Statuette, The, 257
Green Killer, 257
Grissom Gang, The, 258
Guadalcanal Diary, 258
Gumball Rally, The, 259
Gunbus. *See* Sky Bandits
Gunga Din, 259–60
Gung Ho!, 260
Guns at Batasi, The, 260
Guns of Navarone, The, 260
Guns, Sin, and Bathtub Gin. *See* Lady in Red, The
Guy with Secret Kung Fu, The, 261
Gymkata, 261

Hard Times, 266
Hard Way to Die, A, 266
Hatari!, 267
Heartbreak Ridge, 270
Hellcats of the Navy, 272–73
Hellfighters, The, 273
Hell's Angels on Wheels, 273
Hell's Angels 69, 273
Hell to Eternity, 274
Hercules (1959), 274
Hercules (1983), 274–75
Hero, The, 275
Heroes in the Late Ming Dynasty, 275
Heroes of Shaolin, 275
Hero's Tears, A, 275
Hero Tattoo with 9 Dragons, 275
High Crime, 276
High Ice, 277
High Risk, 277
High Road to China, 277
His Kind of Woman, 279
Hitler's Children, 279
Hollywood Vice Squad, 281
Hometown USA, 282
Hooper, 283
Hotrod, 286
House of Whipcord, 287
Human Experiments, 289
Hunter, 290
Hunter, The, 290
Hurricane, 290

Ice Station Zebra, 292
I Cover the Waterfront, 293
Ill Met by Moonlight, 294

Incredible Master Beggars, 296
Incredible Rocky Mountain Race, The, 296
Incredible Shaolin Thunderkick, 296
Indiana Jones and the Temple of Doom, 297
Inheritor of Kung Fu. *See* Two Graves of Kung Fu
Inside Out, 300
In the Devil's Garden. *See* Assault
Into the Night, 301
Invaders, The. *See* 49th Parallel, The
Invasion USA, 302
Invincible, The, 302
Invincible Kung Fu Trio, 302
Invincible Six, The, 302
Iron Eagle, 304
Iron Fist of Kwangtung. *See* Cantonen Iron Kung Fu
Iron Neck Li, 304
It Rained All Night the Day I Left, 306
Ivanhoe (1982), 307

Jackson County Jail, 309
Jade Claw, The, 309
Jake Speed, 310
Japanese Connection, The, 310
Jaws, 310–11
Jaws of Death, 311
Jaws of the Dragon, 311
Jaws 3-D, 311
Jaws 2, 311
Jewel of the Nile, 313
Joyride, 316
Jungle Heat, 318
Junkman, The, 318

Kelly's Heroes, 321
Kill and Kill Again, 323
Kill Castro, 323
Killer Force, 323
Killer of Snake, Fox of Shaolin, 324
Killers, The, 324
Killing Stone, The, 324
Kill or Be Killed, 325
Kill Squad, 325
Killzone, 325
King Boxer, The, 325
King of Kung Fu. *See* Enter the Game of Death
King of the Mountain, 327
King Rat, 327
King Solomon's Mines (1950), 327–28
King Solomon's Mines (1985), 328
KISS Meets the Phantom of the Park, 328
Kitty and the Bagman, 329
Knightriders, 329
Knights of the City, 329–30
Kung Fu, 330–31
Kung Fu Arts: Monkey, Horse, and Tiger, 331
Kung Fu Commandos, 331
Kung Fu Crusher. *See* Bone Crushing Kid, The
Kung Fu of the Eight Drunkards, 331
Kung Fu-ry, 331

Lady Constable, The, 332
Lady in Red, The, 333
Lady Scarface, 333
Last Challenge of the Dragon, The, 334
Last Days of Pompeii, 335
Last Fist of Fury. *See* Bruce Li in New Guinea
Last of the Mohicans (1977), 336
Last of the Mohicans, The (1936), 336
Last Plane Out, 337
Last Victim, The. *See* Forced Entry
Lawrence of Arabia, 339
Lay Out, 339
Legend of Billie Jean, The, 340

Legend of the Broken Sword. *See* Dressed to Fight
Leg Fighters, 340
Lepke, 341
Light at the Edge of the World, The, 344
Lisbon, 345
List of Adrian Messenger, The, 345
Little Caesar, 346
Little Mad Guy, 347
Live a Little, Steal a Lot. *See* Murph the Surf
Live and Let Die, 348
Lives of a Bengal Lancer, 348–49
Lone Wolf McQuade, 350
Longest Day, The, 351
Longest Yard, The, 351
Long Good Friday, The, 351
Long John Silver, 351
Long Voyage Home, The, 351
Lord Jim, 352
Lost Kung Fu Secret, The, 353
Lost Squadron, The, 353
Love and Bullets, 354
Low Blow, 357

MacArthur, 359
Macon County Line, 359–60
McQ, 375
McVicar, 375
Mad Bomber, The, 360
Mad Dog. *See* Mad Dog Morgan
Mad Dog Morgan, 360
Mad Mad Kung Fu, 360
Mad Max, 361
Mad Max Beyond Thunderdome, 361
Mad Max 2. *See* Road Warrior, The
Magnificent Fist, The, 362
Magnificent Seven, The, 362
Magnum Force, 363
Mako: The Jaws of Death. *See* Jaws of Death
Malta Story, The, 364
Man Called Tiger, A, 365
Maneater. *See* Shark!
Mantis Fist Fighter. *See* Thundering Mantis
Mantis vs. Falcon Claws, 368
Man Who Would Be King, The, 369
Man with the Golden Gun, The, 369
Martial Monks of Shaolin Temple, 371
Marvelous Stunts of Kung Fu, 372
Massacre at Central High, 373
Massacre in Rome, 373
Massive Retaliation, 373
Master Killer, 373
Master of Tiger Crane, 373
Mechanic, The, 375
Men in War, 377
Meteor, 378
Miami Vice, 378
Miami Vice II: The Prodigal Son, 378
Midnight Express, 378–79
Militant Eagle, 379
Misers, The, 381
Missing in Action, 382
Missing in Action 2: The Beginning, 382
Mr. Majestyk, 390
Mistress of the World, 383
Mogambo, 384
Moonlight Sword and Jade Lion, 387
Moonraker, 387
Moonshine County Express, 387
Most Dangerous Game, The, 388
Mother Lode, 388
Mountain Men, The, 389
MS. 45, 391
Murph the Surf, 393
Murphy's Law, 393
Murphy's War, 393

Action/Adventure *(cont'd)*
Mutiny on the Bounty (1935), 394
Mysterious Footworks of Kung Fu, 397
Mysterious Island, 397
Mysterious Island of Beautiful Women, 397

Naked and the Dead, The, 399
Naked Cage, The, 399
Nate and Hayes, 400
Never Cry Wolf, 402
Never Say Never Again, 402
New Centurions, The, 402
Newman's Law, 402
Night Ambush. *See* Ill Met by Moonlight
Nighthawks, 404
Night the Lights Went Out in Georgia, The, 405
Nine Deaths of the Ninja, 408
99 and 44/100% Dead, 409
Ninja Exterminators, 409
Ninja III: The Domination, 409
No Mercy, 410
No Retreat, No Surrender, 410
Norseman, The, 411
Northern Pursuit, 411

Octagon, The, 415
Octopussy, 415
Odd Angry Shot, The, 415–16
On Any Sunday, 420
One Armed vs. Nine Killers, 421
One Down, Two to Go, 421
One Man Jury, 422
One Million Years B.C., 422
One of Our Aircraft Is Missing, 422
On Her Majesty's Secret Service, 424
Operation Amsterdam, 425
Operation C.I.A., 425
Orca, 426
Out of Bounds, 429

Panic on the 5:22, 432
Paper Tiger, 433
Papillon, 433
Paradise, 433
Paradise Alley, 433
Part 2, Walking Tall. *See* Walking Tall Part 2
Passage of the Dragon. *See* Twins of Kung Fu
Pearl of the South Pacific, 437
Penitentiary, 437
Perils of Gwendoline in the Land of the Yik-Yak, The, 438–39
Phantom Kung Fu, 440
Pirates, 443
Police Call 9000. *See* Detroit 9000
Poseidon Adventure, The, 448
Powderkeg, 449
P.O.W.—The Escape, 449
Pray for Death, 449
Prime Cut, 451
Prodigal Boxer, The, 453
Prodigal Boxer Part II, The, 453
Protector, The, 454
PT 109, 455
Puppet on a Chain, 456
Pursuit of D. B. Cooper, The, 457

Queen's Diamonds, The. *See* Three Musketeers, The (1973)
Quest for Fire, 458
Quiet Cool, 459

Race with the Devil, 461
Rad, 461
Rafferty and the Gold Dust Twins, 462
Rafferty and the Highway Hustlers. *See* Rafferty and the Gold Dust Twins

Raging Masters of Tiger and Crane. *See* Master of Tiger and Crane
Raiders of Buddhist Kung Fu, 463
Raiders of the Lost Ark, 463
Raise the Titanic!, 464
Rally. *See* Safari 3000
Rambo: First Blood Part Two, 464
Raw Deal, 466
Real Bruce Lee, The, 466
Rebel of Shaolin. *See* Shaolin Traitor
Rebel of the Road. *See* Hotrod
Red Dawn, 468
Red Flag: The Ultimate Game, 468
Red-Light Sting, The, 468
Red Sonja, 469
Remo Williams: The Adventure Begins . . . , 470
Rendezvous of Warriors, The, 470
Renegade Girls. *See* Caged Heat
Renegade Monk, 470
Return of Bruce, 470
Return of the Dragon, 471
Return of the Red Tiger, 471
Return of the Tiger, 472
Return to Macon County, 472
Revenge of the Dragon, 473
Revenge of the Ninja, 473
Riddle of the Sands, The, 474
Right Stuff, The, 475
Riot in Cell Block II, 476
Rivals of the Dragon, 476
Roadhouse 66, 477
Road Warrior, 477
Roaring Fire, 477
Roaring Twenties, The, 477
Robin Hood (1938). *See* Adventures of Robin Hood, The
Rolling Thunder, 479
Romancing the Stone, 480
Roughnecks, 482
Round-up Time in Texas, 482–83
Rumor of War, A, 484
Runaway Barge, The, 484
Runaway Train, 484
Running Scared, 484
Run Silent, Run Deep, 484–85

Safari 3000, 486
Sahara (1943), 487
Sahara (1983), 487
Salzburg Connection, The, 489
Samar, 489
Sand Pebbles, The, 489
Sands of Iwo Jima, The, 490
Savage Island, 492
Savages, 492
Savage Streets, 492
Scaramouche, 494
Scarlet Pimpernel, The, 495
Scarred, 495
Sea Devils, 497
Sea Hawk, The, 497
Search and Destroy, 497
Sea Shall Not Have Them, The, 497
Sea Wife, 497
Sea Wolves, The, 497
Sell Out, The, 500
Seven, 502
Seven Blows of the Dragon, 503
Seven Grandmasters, 503
Seven Magnificient Gladiators, The, 503
Seven Miles From Alcatraz, 503
72 Desperate Rebels, 504
Seven-Ups, The, 504
Seven Year Itch, The, 504
Shaft, 505
Shanghai Surprise, 506

Shaolin Death Squad, 506
Shaolin Drunken Monk, The, 506
Shaolin Drunk Monkey, The, 506
Shaolin Fist Fighter, 506
Shaolin Invincible Sticks, 506
Shaolin Kung Fu Mystagogue, 506
Shaolin: The Blood Mission, 506
Shaolin Traitor, 506–7
Shark!, 507
Shark River, 507
Shark's Treasure, 507
Sheena—Queen of the Jungle, 507
Shogun Assassin, 520
Shogun Ninja, 510
Shooting Stars, 511
Shout at the Devil, 512
Sidewinder One, 513
Sign of Zorro, The, 513
Silencers, The, 513
Silent Killer from Eternity. *See* Return of the Tiger
Silent Rage, 514
Silver Hermit from Shaolin Temple, 515
Sinai Commandos, 516
Sinbad the Sailor, 516
Sirocco, 517
Six Directions of Boxing, The, 518
Six Kung Fu Heroes, 518
Skullduggery, 519
Sky Bandits, 519
Slavers, 520
Slayground, 520
Smokey and the Bandit, 522
Smokey and the Bandit—Part III, 522
Smokey and the Bandit II, 522
Snake Fist Fighter, 522–23
Snake in Eagle Shadow, 523
Snow Treasure, 523
Soldier, The, 524
Something of Value, 525–26
Son of the Sheik, 527
Southern Comfort, 529
Spacecamp, 530
Specialist, The, 531
Speedtrap, 531
Spider-Man, 532
Spirits of Bruce Lee, 532–33
Spy Who Loved Me, The, 534
Squizzy Taylor, 534
SS Girls, 534
Steel Claw, The, 539
Sting of the Dragon Masters. *See* When Tae Kwon Do Strikes
Stone Killer, The, 541
Stoner, 541
Story in Temple Red City, 542
Streetfighter, The, 544
Streetfighters Part II, 545
Street People, 545
Streets of Fire, 545
Streetwalkin', 545
Stroker Ace, 546
Stunts, 547
Sundown, 550
Super Fuzz, 550
Supergirl, 550
Superman, 550–51
Superman III, 551
Superman II, 551
Superpower, 551
Survival Run, 551
Swap Meet, 552
Swift Shaolin Boxer. *See* Invincible, The
Sword and the Sorcerer, 554
Sword of Lancelot, 554
Sword of Monte Cristo, The, 554

Action/Adventure *(cont'd)*
TAG: The Assassination Game, 555
Tangier, 557
Tank, 557-58
Tartu. *See* Adventures of Tartu, The
Tarzan's Revenge, 558
Tarzan, the Ape Man (1932), 558-59
Tarzan, the Ape Man (1981), 559
Tarzan the Fearless, 559
Tattoo Connection, The, 559
Tattooed Dragon, The, 559
Ten Brothers of Shaolin, 561
Ten to Midnight, 562
Ten Who Dared, 562-63
Terminal Island, 563
Terror on the 40th Floor, 564
Terror Out of the Sky, 564
That Lucky Touch, 566
These Hands Destroy. *See* Phantom Kung Fu
They Were Expendable, 570
Thief of Baghdad, The (1924), 570
Thief of Baghdad, The (1978), 570-71
30 Seconds Over Tokyo, 573
Thirty Sixth Chamber of Shaolin. *See* Master Killer, The
Three Avengers, The, 575
3:15—Moment of Truth, 575
Three Musketeers, The (1973), 576
Three the Hard Way, 576
Threshold, 576
Thunderball, 577
Thunder Bay, 577
Thunderbolt and Lightfoot, 577
Thundering Mantis, 577
Tidal Wave, 578
Tiger's Claw, 578
Tilt, 579
T.N.T. Jackson, 580
To Catch a Spy. *See* Catch Me a Spy
To Hell and Back, 582
To Live and Die in L.A., 582
Tomboy, 582
Top Gun, 584
Top Secret, 584
Tora! Tora! Tora!, 584-85
Tough Guys (1986), 586
Tough Guys, 586
Towering Inferno, The, 587
Tower of Death. *See* Game of Death II
Tower of Terror. *See* Assault
Trained To Kill, U.S.A., 588
Trapped, 589
Treasure of Bruce Le, 589
Treasure of Pancho Villa, The, 589
Truck Stop Women, 592
True Game of Death, The, 593
Tuff Turf, 593
Tuxedo Warrior, 594
Two Fists vs. Seven Samurai. *See* Fist of Vengeance
Two Graves of Kung Fu, 596
Two in the Bush. *See* Safari 3000

Uncommon Valor, 598
Underground Aces, 599

Vanishing Point, 603-4
Vegas, 604
Vice Squad, 604-5
Victory, 605
View to a Kill, A, 605
Vikings, The, 605
Viva Knievel!, 606
Viva Zapata!, 607

Von Ryan's Express, 607
Voyage to the Bottom of the Sea, 607

Wake Island, 608-9
Wake of the Red Witch, 609
Walking Tall, 609
Walking Tall Part 2, 609
Walking Tall: The Final Chapter, 609
Walk in the Sun, A, 609
Wanted Dead or Alive, 609
Warning, The, 611
Warrior and the Sorceress, The, 611
Warriors, The, 611
Watch Out, Crimson Bat!, 612
Water Margin, The. *See* Seven Blows of the Dragon
Watusi, 612-13
Way of the Dragon. *See* Return of the Dragon
When Tae Kwon Do Strikes, 617
When Time Ran Out, 617
Where Eagles Dare, 617
Whispering Death. *See* Albino
White Buffalo, The, 619
White Dawn, The, 619
White Heat, 619
White Lightning, 619
White Line Fever, 619
Who Is Killing the Stuntmen?. *See* Stunts
Wilby Conspiracy, The, 622
Wild Geese, The, 623
Wild Geese II, 623
Wild One, The, 624
Wild Panther, The, 624
Wild Ride, The, 624
Wild Wheels, 625
Wind and the Lion, The, 626
Wings, 626
Win Them All, 627
Wits to Wits, 629
Women in Cell Block 7, 631
Womens Prison Massacre, 631-32
Wrecking Crew, The, 633-34

Yakuza, The, 636
Year of the Dragon, 636
Young Hero, 638
Young Tiger, The, 639
Young Warriors, The, 639
You Only Live Twice, 639

Zoo Gang, The, 642
Zulu, 642
Zulu Dawn, 642

COMEDY

Abbott and Costello in Hollywood, 1
Abbott and Costello Meet Captain Kidd, 1
Abbott and Costello Meet Dr. Jekyll and Mr. Hyde, 1
Abbott and Costello Meet Frankenstein, 1
About Last Night . . . , 2
Adam's Rib, 3
Admiral Was a Lady, The, 4
Adventure of Sherlock Holmes' Smarter Brother, The, 4
Affairs of Annabel, The, 6
Africa Screams, 5
After Hours, 6
After the Fox, 6
After the Thin Man, 6
Airplane!, 7-8
Airplane II: The Sequel, 8
Alfie, 9

Alfie Darling. *See* Oh, Alfie
Alice Adams, 9
Alice Goodbody, 10
Alice's Restaurant, 10
All Night Long, 12
All of Me, 12
All over Town, 12
All That Money Can Buy. *See* Devil and Daniel Webster, The
All the Marbles, 13
Almost Perfect Affair, An, 14
Almost You, 14
Amazing Adventure, The, 15
Amazing Quest. *See* Amazing Adventure, The
Amazing Quest of Ernest Bliss. *See* Amazing Adventure, The
American Dreamer, 16
American Graffiti, 17
Americathon, 17-18
And Justice for All, 19
And Now for Something Completely Different, 19
Andy Warhol's Bad, 20
Angelo My Love, 21
Angel on My Shoulder (1946), 21
Angel on My Shoulder (1980), 21
Animal Crackers, 22
Annabel Takes a Tour, 22
Annie Hall, 23
Annie Oakley, 23
Any Which Way You Can, 24
Apartment, The, 24
Apprenticeship of Duddy Kravitz, The, 25
April Fools, The, 25
Armed and Dangerous, 26
Around the World in 80 Days, 27
Arsenic and Old Lace, 27
Arthur, 27
As You Like It, 29
Atoll K. *See* Utopia
Attack of the Killer Tomatoes, 30
At the Circus, 30
At War with the Army, 30-31
Auntie Mame, 31
Author! Author!, 31
Aviator, The, 32
Awful Truth, The, 32

Bachelor and the Bobbysoxer, The, 33-34
Bachelor Bait, 34
Bachelor Knight. *See* Bachelor and the Bobbysoxer, The
Bachelor Mother, 34
Bachelor Party, 34
Back Roads, 34
Back to School, 34-35
Bad. *See* Andy Warhol's Bad
Bad Guys, 35
Bad Manners, 35
Bad Medicine, 36
Bad News Bears, The, 36
Bad News Bears Go to Japan, The, 36
Bad News Bears in Breaking Training, The, 36
Ball of Fire, 37
Baltimore Bullet, The, 37
Banana Monster, The. *See* Schlock
Bananas, 37
Bank Dick, The, 38
Barry McKenzie Holds His Own, 39-40
Basic Training, 40
Batman, 40
Battle of the Sexes, 41
Beachcomber, The, 42

Comedy *(cont'd)*
Beach Girls, The, 42
Beach House, 42
Beach Party, 42
Beat the Devil, 43
Bedazzled, 44
Bedtime for Bonzo, 45
Beer, 45
Being There, 46
Bela Lugosi Meets a Brooklyn Gorilla. *See* Boys from Brooklyn, The
Bell, Book and Candle, 46
Bellboy, The, 46
Belles of St. Trinian's, The, 47
Berry Gordy's The Last Dragon. *See* Last Dragon, The
Best Defense, 48–49
Best Friends, 49
Best Legs in the Eighth Grade, The, 49
Best of Times, The, 49
Better Late than Never, 50
Better Off Dead, 50
Between Friends, 50
Between the Lines, 50
Beverly Hills Cop, 50–51
Big Bus, The, 52
Big Chill, The, 53
Big Trouble, 54
Bill Cosby—"Himself," 55
Billy Liar, 56
Bingo Long Traveling All-Stars and Motor Kings, The, 56
Bishop's Wife, The, 57
Blackbeard's Ghost, 58
Black Bird, The, 58
Blame It on Rio, 61
Blazing Saddles, 61–62
Bliss, 62
Block-Heads, 62
Blue Money, 67
Blues Brothers, The, 67
Blume in Love, 68
Bob and Carol and Ted and Alice, 69
Bobo, The, 69
Bohemian Girl, 70
Boom in the Moon, 71
Born Yesterday, 72
Borrowed Trouble, 72
Boy, Did I Get a Wrong Number!, 73
Boys from Brooklyn, The, 74
Breakfast at Tiffany's, 76–77
Breakfast in Hollywood, 77
Breaking Away, 77
Brewster McCloud, 78
Brewster's Millions (1945), 78
Brewster's Millions (1985), 78
Brighton Beach Memoirs, 79–80
Britannia Hospital, 80
Broadway Danny Rose, 80
Broken Hearts and Noses. *See* Crimewave
Bronco Billy, 81
Buck Privates, 82
Buddy Buddy, 82–83
Buddy System, The, 83
Buffalo Bill and the Indians, or Sitting Bull's History Lesson, 83
Bullfighters, The, 84
Burning Question, The. *See* Reefer Madness
Bustin' Loose, 85
Butterflies Are Free, 86
By Design, 86

Cactus Flower, 87
Caddyshack, 88
Caesar and Cleopatra, 88

California Suite, 89
Call Out the Marines, 90
Candy Stripe Nurses, 91
Can I Do It . . . Til I Need Glasses?, 91
Can She Bake A Cherry Pie?, 91
Captain's Paradise, The, 93
Carbon Copy, 93
Carry On Behind, 95
Carry On, Cleo, 95
Carry On, Jack, 95
Carry On Nurse, 95
Carry On, Venus. *See* Carry On, Jack
Car Wash, 95–96
Casino Royal, 96
Catch-22, 97
Catholic Boys. *See* Heaven Help Us
Caveman, 99
Champagne for Caesar, 101
Change of Seasons, A, 101
Chapter Two, 101–2
Charlie Chan and the Curse of the Dragon Queen, 102
Chattanooga Choo Choo, 103
Cheap Detective, The, 103
Cheaper to Keep Her, 103
Check and Double Check, 103
Cheech and Chong's Next Movie, 103
Cheech and Chong's Nice Dreams, 103
Cheech and Chong's Still Smokin'. *See* Still Smokin'
Cheech and Chong's The Corsican Brothers, 103
Chesty Anderson U.S. Navy, 104
Chicken Chronicles, The, 104
Chilly Scenes of Winter, 105
Choirboys, The, 107
Christmas in July, 108
Christmas Story, A, 108
Chu Chu and the Philly Flash, 109
Chump at Oxford, A, 109
Circus, The, 110
City Heat, 111
City Lights, 111
Class, 112
Class of Miss MacMichael, The, 112
Class Reunion. *See* National Lampoon's Class Reunion
Clinic, The, 113
Clock, The, 113
Clockwise, 113
Club Paradise, 114–15
Cluny Brown, 115
Coast to Coast, 115
Coca-Cola Kid, The, 115
Cocaine Fiends, 115–16
Cockeyed Cavaliers, The, 116
Cocoanuts, The, 116
Cold Feet, 117
College, 117
Colonel Effingham's Raid, 117
Come Back Charleston Blue, 118
Come 'n' Get It. *See* Lunch Wagon
Comfort and Joy, 119
Comic, The, 119
Coming Attractions. *See* Loose Shoes
Commies Are Coming, the Commies Are Coming, The, 119–20
Committee, The, 120
Compromising Positions, 120
Con Artists, The, 121
Continental Divide, 123
Cooley High, 123
Corsican Brothers, The (1984). *See* Cheech and Chong's the Corsican Brothers
Corvette Summer, 125
Country Gentleman, 126

Court Jester, The, 126–27
Crackers, 127
Cracking Up, 127
Creator, 129
Creature Wasn't Nice, The. *See* Spaceship
Crimes of the Heart, 131
Crimewave, 131
"Crocodile" Dundee, 132
Curse of the Pink Panther, 135

Daniel and the Devil. *See* The Devil and Daniel Webster
David Holzman's Diary, 142
Day at the Races, A, 143
Days of Thrills and Laughter, 145
Day the Bookies Wept, The, 144
D.C. Cab, 145–46
Dead Men Don't Wear Plaid, 148
Deal of the Century, 148
Desire, 155–56
Desk Set, 156
Desperately Seeking Susan, 156
Desperate Women, 156
Devil and Daniel Webster, The, 157
Devil and Miss Jones, The, 158
Diary of a Mad Housewife, 160
Diary of a Young Comic, 160
Die Laughing, 160–61
Diner, 161
Dirt Bike Kid, The, 162
Dirty Tricks, 162–63
Divorce, American Style, 163
Divorce of Lady X, The, 164
Dixie: Changing Habits, 164
Doctor at Large, 164
Doctor at Sea, 164
Doctor Detroit, 165
Dr. Heckyl and Mr. Hype, 165
Doctor in Distress, 165
Doctor in the House, 165
Dr. Strangelove or: How I Learned to Stop Worrying and Love the Bomb, 166
Don't Drink the Water, 169
Donovan's Reef, 169
Don's Party, 169
Don't Raise the Bridge, Lower the River, 170
Dope Addict. *See* Reefer Madness
Doped Youth. *See* Reefer Madness
Double Bunk, 170–71
Down and Out in Beverly Hills, 171
Down by Law, 171–72
Dracula and Son, 172
Duck Soup, 176
Dutchess and the Dirtwater Fox, The, 176
Dynamite Chicken, 178

Easy Money, 180
Eating Raoul, 180
Echo Park, 181
Educating Rita, 181
Egg and I, The, 182
Electric Dreams, 182
Electric Horseman, The, 182
Emily, 184
End, The, 185–86
Ensign Pulver, 187
Enter Laughing, 187
Entertaining Mr. Sloane, 188
Errand Boy, The, 188
Every Girl Should Be Married, 191
Every Home Should Have One. *See* Think Dirty
Everything You Always Wanted to Know About Sex But Were Afraid to Ask, 192
Every Which Way But Loose, 191

663

Comedy (cont'd)
Ex-Mrs. Bradford, The, 193
Experience Preferred . . . But Not Essential, 194

Fabulous Joe, 196
Falling in Love Again, 198
Fandango, 199–200
Farmer's Daughter, The, 201
Fast Break, 201
Fast Times At Ridgemont High, 202
Father Goose, 202
Father's Little Dividend, 202
Fearless Vampire Killers, The, or, Pardon Me, But Your Teeth Are in My Neck, 203
Feelin' Up, 203
Female Trouble, 203
Ferris Bueller's Day Off, 204
Fiendish Plot of Dr. Fu Manchu, The, 204
Final Programme, The. See Last Days of Man on Earth, The
Finders, Keepers, 207
Fine Mess, A, 207
Finnegan Begin Again, 207
First Family, 209
First Monday in October, 210
First Time, The, 210
First Turn-On, The, 210
Fish that Saved Pittsburgh, The, 210
Fistful of Chopsticks, A. See They Call Me Bruce?
Five Weeks in a Balloon, 212
Flamingo Kid, The, 212
Flesh Gordon, 213
Flim-Flam Man, The, 214
Flying Deuces, 215
FM, 215
Follow That Camel, 216
Foolin' Around, 216
Foreign Body, 218
Foreplay, 218
For Heaven's Sake, 218
For Pete's Sake, 219
Fortune, The, 219–20
Fortune Cookie, The, 220
Forty Carats, 220
Foul Play, 220
Four Seasons, The, 222
Francis, 222–23
Fraternity Vacation, 224
French Postcards, 225
Frisco Kid, The, 226
Fritz the Cat, 226
Front Page, The, 228
Fuller Brush Man, The, 228
Fun Loving. See Quackser Fortune Has a Cousin in The Bronx
Fun with Dick and Jane, 229
Futz, 230
Fuzz, 230

Galaxina, 231
Gang That Couldn't Shoot Straight, The, 232
Garbo Talks, 232
Gas, 233
Gas Pump Girls, 233
Gay Deceivers, The, 234
General, The, 234
Generation, 234
Genevieve, 235
Get Crazy!, 236
Getting It On, 236
Getting Straight, 236
Ghost and Mrs. Muir, The, 237
Ghostbusters, 237
Ghost Goes West, The, 237

Gidget, 238
Gidget Goes Hawaiian, 238
Gidget Goes to Rome, 238
Gilda Live, 239
Girl Can't Help It, The, 240
Girlfriends, 240
Girl from Petrovka, The, 240
Girl in Every Port, A, 240
Girls Just Want to Have Fun, 241
Give Me a Sailor, 241
Glen or Glenda?, 242
Going Ape!, 244
Going Berserk, 244
Going in Style, 244–45
Goin' South, 245
Golden Age of Comedy, The, 245
Golden Child, The, 246
Gold Raiders, The, 246–47
Gold Rush, The, 247
Gone Are the Days. See Purlie Victorious
Goodbye, Farewell and Amen. See M*A*S*H: Goodbye, Farewell and Amen
Goodbye Girl, The, 248
Goodbye New York, 248
Goodbye People, The, 248
Good Neighbor Sam, 248
Good Sam, 249
Gorilla, The, 249–50
Go West, 250
Grace Quigley, 250
Graduate, The, 250
Grandview U.S.A., 251
Grass is Greener, The, 251
Graveyard Tramps. See Invasion of the Bee Girls
Great Dan Patch, The, 253
Great Dictator, The, 253
Greatest Man in the World, The, 253
Great Guns, 254
Great McGonagall, The, 254
Great Race, The, 255
Great St. Trinian's Train Robbery, The, 255
Great Scout and Cathouse Thursday, The, 255
Great Smokey Roadblock, The, 255
Great Wall, A, 256
Greeks Had a Word for Them, The. See Three Broadway Girls
Gregory's Girl, 257
Groove Tube, The, 258
Guess Who's Coming to Dinner, 258–59
Gumshoe, 259
Gung Ho, 260

Half Shot at Sunrise, 262
Hamburger . . . The Motion Picture, 262–63
Hammersmith Is Out, 263
Hanky Panky, 263
Hannah and Her Sisters, 263–64
Happy Hooker, The, 264
Happy Hooker Goes to Hollywood, The, 264
Happy Hooker Goes to Washington, The, 264–65
Hardbodies, 265
Hardbodies 2, 265
Hardhat and Legs, 266
Hardly Working, 266
Harold and Maude, 266
Harper Valley P.T.A., 267
Harry and Tonto, 267
Harry and Walter Go to New York, 267
Harry in Your Pocket, 267
Harry's War, 267
Haunted Honeymoon, 268
Having It All, 268
Head Office, 269
Head Over Heels. See Chilly Scenes of Winter

Heartaches, 269
Heartbeeps, 269
Heartbreak Kid, The, 270
Heartburn, 270
Heat, 271
Heaven Can Wait, 271
Heaven Help Us, 271
Heavenly Kid, The, 271–72
Heavens Above!, 272
Heavy Traffic, 272
He or She. See Glen or Glenda?
Here Comes Mr. Jordan, 275
Here Is a Man. See Devil and Daniel Webster, The
Hero at Large, 275
Heroes, 275
Hey, Good Lookin'!, 276
High Anxiety, 276
Highpoint, 277
High School Confidential!, 277
His Double Life, 278
His Girl Friday, 278–79
History of the World, Part I, 279
Hobson's Choice, 280
Hold That Ghost, 280
Hollywood Boulevard, 280
Hollywood Hot Tubs, 280–81
Homebodies, 282
Home Movies, 282
Homework, 282
Honeychile, 283
Honky Tonk Freeway, 283
Hopscotch, 284
Horse's Mouth, The, 285
Hospital, The, 285
Hot Dog . . . The Movie, 285
Hotel New Hampshire, The, 285
Hot Moves, 285
H.O.T.S., 286
Hot Stuff, 286
Hot Times, 286
House Calls, 286
Howard the Duck, 288
How Funny Can Sex Be?, 288
How I Won the War, 288
How to Beat the High Cost of Living, 288
How to Break Up a Happy Divorce, 288
How to Marry a Millionaire, 289
How to Stuff a Wild Bikini, 289
Hurry Up, or I'll Be Thirty, 290–91
Hysterical, 291

Ice Pirates, The, 292
I Changed My Sex. See Glen or Glenda?
Idiot's Delight, 293
If You Don't Stop It, You'll Go Blind, 293
If You Knew Susie, 293
I Led Two Lives. See Glen or Glenda?
I Love My . . . Wife, 294
I Love You, Alice B. Toklas, 294
I'm All Right, Jack, 295
I Married a Witch, 295
I Married a Woman, 295
Incredible Shrinking Woman, The, 297
Indiscreet, 297
In-Laws, The, 298
Invasion of the Bee Girls, 302
I Ought to Be in Pictures, 303
Irma La Douce, 303
Irreconcilable Differences, 304
It Came from Hollywood, 305
It Could Happen to You, 305
It Happened One Night, 306
It's a Mad, Mad, Mad, Mad World, 306
It Should Happen to You, 306–7
It's in the Bag, 307

Comedy *(cont'd)*
It's My Turn, 307
I Will, I Will . . . For Now, 308
Izzy and Moe, 308

Jabberwocky, 309
Jekyll and Hyde . . . Together Again, 311
Jerk, The, 312
Jimmy the Kid, 313
Jinxed!, 313
J-Men Forever, 313
Joe Palooka, 314
Johnny Dangerously, 314
Jokes My Folks Never Told Me, 315
Joseph Andrews, 315
Joshua Then & Now, 315
Joy of Sex, The, 316
Joysticks, 316
Jumpin' Jack Flash, 318
Just Between Friends, 318
Just One of the Guys, 318
Just Tell Me What You Want, 318–19
Just the Way You Are, 319
Just You and Me, Kid, 319

Kentucky Fried Movie, The, 321
Key Exchange, 321–22
Kid, The, 322
Kidco, 322
Kid from Brooklyn, The, 322
Kid from Left Field, The, 322
Kidnappers, The, 322
Kid with the Broken Halo, The, 323
Kid with the 200 I.Q., The, 323
Kind Hearts and Coronets, 325
King in New York, A, 326
King of Comedy, The, 326
King, Queen and Knave, 327
Kipps, 328
Kiss Me Goodbye, 328
Knack, and How to Get It, The, 329
Kotch, 330

Ladykillers, The, 333
Last American Virgin, The, 334
Last Days of Man on Earth, The, 335
Last Detail, The, 335
Last Dragon, The, 335
Last Married Couple in America, The, 336
Last of the Red Hot Lovers, 336
Last Remake of Beau Geste, The, 337
Last Resort, 337
Lavender Hill Mob, The, 339
Lenny Bruce Performance Film, The, 341
Let's Do It Again, 341
Letter to Brezhnev, 342
Letter to Three Wives, A, 342
Life and Death of Colonel Blimp, The, 343
Life of Brian. *See* Monty Python's Life of Brian
Life with Father, 343
Lily in Love, 344
Listen to Your Heart, 345
Little Darlings, 346
Little Kidnappers, The. *See* Kidnappers, The
Little Miss Marker (1980), 347
Little Romance, A, 348
Little Sex, A, 348
Local Hero, 349
Lolita, 349
Lonely Guy, The, 350
Lonely Hearts, 350
Loose Shoes, 352
Losin' It, 353
Lost and Found, 353
Lost in America, 353
Love and Death, 354

Love at First Bite, 354
Love Happy, 354–55
Love in the Afternoon, 355
Loveliness, 355–56
Lovers and Other Strangers, 356
Lovesick, 356
Loving Couples, 357
Lucas, 357
Lucky Jim, 357
Lunch Wagon, 358
Lust in the Dust, 358
Luv, 358

Macaroni, 359
Magic Christian, The, 361
Magic Town, 362
Maid's Night Out, 363
Main Event, The, 363
Major Barbara, 363
Make Me an Offer, 363
Make Mine Mink, 363
Making the Grade, 364
Malcolm, 364
Malibu Beach, 364
Man Friday, 365–66
Manhattan, 366
Man in the Santa Claus Suit, The, 367
Man in the White Suit, The, 367
Man Who Had Power over Women, The, 368
Man Who Loved Women, The, 369
Man Who Wasn't There, The, 369
Man with Bogart's Face, The, 369
Man with One Red Shoe, The, 369
Man with Two Brains, The, 370
Marathon, 370
Marriage is Alive and Well, 371
Marriage of a Young Stockbroker, 371
Marry Me, Marry Me, 371
Marx Brothers at the Circus, The. *See* At the Circus
M*A*S*H, 372
M*A*S*H: Goodbye, Farewell and Amen, 372–73
Mass Appeal, 373
Max Dugan Returns, 374
Maxie, 374
Meatballs, 375
Meatballs Part II, 375
Melvin and Howard, 376
Micki and Maude, 378
Midnight Madness, 379
Midsummer Night's Dream, A, 379
Midsummer Night's Sex Comedy, A, 379
Milky Way, The, 379–80
Miracle on 34th Street, 380
Mischief, 380
Miss Annie Rooney, 381
Missionary, The, 382
Mr. and Mrs. Smith, 389
Mr. Blandings Builds His Dream House, 390
Mr. Hulot's Holiday, 390
Mr. Love, 390
Mr. Mom, 390
Mr. Peabody and the Mermaid, 390
Mister Roberts, 382
Mr. Robinson Crusoe, 391
Mixed Blood, 383
Modern Girls, 383
Modern Problems, 383
Modern Romance, 383
Modern Times, 383–84
Money Pit, The, 384
Monkey Business, 384–85
Monsieur Verdoux, 385
Monty Python and the Holy Grail, 386

Monty Python Live at the Hollywood Bowl, 386
Monty Python's Life of Brian, 386
Monty Python's The Meaning of Life, 386
Moon Is Blue, The, 386
Moonlighting, 386–87
Morgan!, 387
Morning Glory, 387
Moscow on the Hudson, 388
Motel Hell, 388
Mouse That Roared, The, 389
Movers and Shakers, 389
Movie Movie, 389
Moving Violations, 389
Munsters' Revenge, The, 391–92
Murder by Death, 392
Murphy's Romance, 393
My Beautiful Laundrette, 394
My Best Friend's Girl, 394
My Brilliant Career, 395
My Chauffeur, 395
My Dear Secretary, 395
My Dinner with Andre, 395
My Favorite Brunette, 395
My Favorite Wife, 395
My Favorite Year, 396
My Little Chickadee, 396
My Man Godfrey, 396
Myra Breckinridge, 396–97
My Tutor, 398

Nashville, 400
National Lampoon's Animal House, 400
National Lampoon's Class Reunion, 400
National Lampoon's European Vacation, 400
National Lampoon's Vacation, 400
Neighbors, 401
Network, 401
Never a Dull Moment, 401
Next Stop, Greenwich Village, 403
Night at the Opera, A, 403
Night of the Comet, 406
Night Patrol, 407
Night Shift, 407
Night They Raided Minsky's, The, 407
1941, 409
Nine to Five, 408
Ninotchka, 409
Nobody's Fool, 409
Nobody's Perfect, 409-10
Norman Conquests, The, 410–11
North Dallas Forty, 411
No Small Affair, 412
Not for Publication, 412
Nothing in Common, 412
Nothing Personal, 412
Nothing Sacred, 412
No Time for Sergeants, 412
Nutty Professor, The, 414

Ocean's Eleven, 415
Odd Couple, The, 416
Odd Job, The, 416
Off Beat, 416
Off the Wall, 416
Oh, Alfie, 417
Oh, Calcutta!, 417
Oh Dad, Poor Dad, Mama's Hung You in the Closet and I'm Feeling So Sad, 417
Oh God!, 417
Oh God Book II, 417
Oh God! You Devil, 417
Oh Heavenly Dog!, 417
Oklahoma Annie, 418
Old Barn Dance, The, 418
O Lucky Man!, 419

Comedy *(cont'd)*
Once Bitten, 420
Once in Paris, 420
Once Upon a Scoundrel, 420
One and Only, The, 420
One Crazy Summer, 421
One Rainy Afternoon, 422–23
One, Two, Three, 423
Only with Married Men, 424
On the Right Track, 425
Operation Fred, 425
Operation Petticoat, 425–26
Our Relations, 427–28
Out California Way, 428
Outlaw Blues, 428
Out of the Blue, 429
Out-of-Towners, The, 429
Outrageous!, 429
Outrageous Fortune, 429–30
Over the Brooklyn Bridge, 430
Owl and the Pussycat, The, 430
Oxford Blues, 430

Paleface, The, 431–32
Palooka. *See* Joe Palooka
Paper Chase, The, 432
Paper Moon, 432–33
Paradiso, 433
Pardon Us, 434
Paris Holiday, 434
Parlor, Bedroom, Bath, 434
Partners, 435
Paternity, 436
Patsy, The, 436
Pee-Wee's Big Adventure, 437
Peggy Sue Got Married, 437
Personals, The, 439
Philadelphia Story, The, 440
Piece of the Action, A, 441
Pillow Talk, 441
Pink Flamingos, 441–42
Pink Panther, The, 442
Pink Panther Strikes Again, The, 442
Play It Again, Sam, 444
Plaza Suite, 445
Pocketful of Miracles, 445
Police Academy, 445–46
Police Academy 3: Back in Training, 446
Police Academy 2: Their First Assignment, 446
Polyester, 446–47
Pom Pom Girls, The, 447
Poor Little Rich Girl, A, 447
Pop Always Pays, 447
Porky's, 447
Porky's Revenge, 447
Porky's II: The Next Day, 447
Portnoy's Complaint, 448
Preppies, 449–50
Pretty in Pink, 450
Pride and Prejudice, 450
Pride of the Bowery, 450
Prince of Central Park, The, 451
Princess and the Pirate, The, 451
Prisoner of Second Avenue, The, 451
Prisoner of Zenda, The, 451–52
Private Benjamin, 452
Private Eyes, 452
Private Function, A, 452
Private Lessons, 452
Private School, 453
Privates on Parade, 453
Prize Fighter, The, 453
Prizzi's Honor, 453
Producers, The, 454
Protocol, 454
Purlie Victorious, 456

Purple Rose of Cairo, The, 456–57
Putney Swope, 457
Pygmalion, 457

Quackser Fortune Has a Cousin in The Bronx, 458
Quicksilver, 459

Rabbit Test, 461
Radioactive Dreams, 461–62
Radio Days, 462
Rage of Paris, The, 462
Raid on Entebbe, 463
Ratings Game, The, 465
Rattle of a Simple Man, 465
Real Genius, 466
Real Life, 466–67
Red Nightmare. *See* Commies Are Coming, the Commies Are Coming, The
Reefer Madness, 469
Reform School Girls, 469
Repo Man, 470
Return of the Living Dead, 471
Return of the Pink Panther, The, 471
Return of the Secaucus Seven, 471–72
Reuben, Reuben, 472
Revenge of the Cheerleaders, 473
Revenge of the Nerds, 473
Revenge of the Pink Panther, The, 473
Revenge of the Teenage Vixens From Outer Space, The, 473
Rhinestone, 474
Rich and Famous, 474
Richard Pryor Here and Now, 474
Richard Pryor Live on the Sunset Strip, 474
Riches and Romance. *See* Amazing Adventure, The
Riding on Air, 475
Risky Business, 476
Ritz, The, 476
Rock 'n' Roll High School, 478
Roller Boogie, 479
Rollercoaster, 479
Romance and Riches. *See* Amazing Adventure, The
Roman Holiday, 480
Romantic Comedy, 480
Roommate, The, 481
Room Service, 481
Room with a View, A, 481
R.S.V.P., 483
Ruling Class, The, 483
Russians Are Coming, The Russians Are Coming, The, 485
Rustlers' Rhapsody, 485
Ruthless People, 485

Sad Sack, The, 486
Safety Last, 486–87
Same Time, Next Year, 489
Saps at Sea, 491
Saturday the 14th, 491
Savannah Smiles, 492
Say Yes, 493
Scandalous, 493–94
Scarface (1932), 494
Scarface (1983), 494
Scavenger Hunt, 495
Schlock (The Banana Monster), 495
Score, 496
Screen Test, 496
Secret Admirer, 498
Secret Honor, 498
Secret Life of an American Wife, The, 498
Secret Life of Walter Mitty, The, 498
Secret War of Harry Frigg, The, 499

Seems Like Old Times, 499
Semi-Tough, 500
Senator Was Indiscreet, The, 500
Seniors, The, 500
Separate Vacations. *See* Separate Ways
Separate Ways, 501
Serial, 502
Session With The Committee, A. *See* Committee, The
Shampoo, 505–6
Sharma and Beyond, 507
She'll Be Wearing Pink Pajamas, 508
She's Gotta Have It, 509
Sheila Levine Is Dead and Living in New York, 508
She's in the Army Now, 509
Sheriff of Fractured Jaw, The, 508
Sherman's March, 508
Silent Movie, 513
Silver Streak, 515
Simon, 515
Sin of Harold Diddlebock, The, 517
Sitting Ducks, 518
Six Pack, 518
Sixteen Candles, 518
Slapshot, 519
Slapstick of Another Kind, 519
Slaughterhouse-Five, 519
Sleeper, 520
Slugger's Wife, The, 521
Smile, 522
Smithereens, 522
Snow, The Movie, 523
Snowball Express, 523
Snow White and the Three Stooges, 523
S.O.B., 523–24
So Fine, 524
Soldier in the Rain, 524
Some Like It Hot, 525
Something for Everyone, 525
Something Short of Paradise, 526
Something Wild, 526
Sons of the Desert, 528
Soul Man, 529
Soup for One, 529
Spaceship, 530
Special Delivery, 531
Spies Like Us, 532
Spinal Tap. *See* This is Spinal Tap
Splash, 533
Spooks Run Wild, 533
Spring Break, 533–34
Spring Fever, 534
Squeeze Play!, 534
Stand-In, 536
Stanley, 536
Stardust Memories, 536
Starhops, 536
Starting Over, 537
Start the Revolution without Me, 538
State of the Union, 538
Steamboat Bill, Jr., 539
Steelyard Blues, 539–40
Still Smokin', 540
Sting, The, 540–41
Sting II, The, 541
Stir Crazy, 541
Storm in a Teacup, 542
Strange Brew, 543
Stranger than Paradise, 544
Strawberry Blonde, The, 544
Stripes, 546
Stuckey's Last Stand, 546
Student Bodies, 546
Student Teachers, The, 546–47
Sullivan's Travels, 548

Comedy *(cont'd)*
Summer, 548
Summer Camp, 548
Suppose They Gave a War and Nobody Came?, 551
Sure Thing, The, 551
Survivors, The, 551–52
Susan Slept Here, 552
Sweet Liberty, 553
Sweet William, 553
Swinging Cheerleaders, The, 553
Swing Shift, 553
Swiss Miss, 554

Take Down, 555
Take the Money and Run, 555
Take This Job and Shove It, 555
Take Your Best Shot, 555
Talk of the Town, The, 556–57
Taming of the Shrew, The, 557
Tammy and the Bachelor, 557
Tammy and the Doctor, 557
Teen Wolf, 560
Tell Your Children. *See* Reefer Madness
Tempest, 560
10, 561
Ten from Your Show of Shows, 562
Thank God It's Friday, 565
Thanks a Million, 565
That Sinking Feeling, 567
That Touch of Mink, 567
There's a Girl in My Soup, 568
They All Laughed, 568
They Call Me Bruce?, 568–69
They Got Me Covered, 569
They Went That-a-Way and That-a-Way, 570
Things Are Tough All Over, 571
Think Dirty, 571
30 Is a Dangerous Age, Cynthia, 572
This is Spinal Tap, 573
Those Glory, Glory Days, 574
Those Lips, Those Eyes, 574
Thousand Clowns, A, 574
Three Ages, 574
Three Amigos!, 574–75
Three Broadway Girls, 575
Three Coins in the Fountain, 575
Three Musketeers, The (1939), 576
Three Stooges Meet Hercules, The, 576
Thunder in the City, 577
Thursday's Game, 577
Tiger and the Pussycat, The, 578
Tight Little Island, 578
Tillie's Punctured Romance, 578
Toast of New York, The, 580
To Be or Not To Be (1942), 581
To Be or Not To Be (1983), 581
Tom, Dick and Harry, 582
Tom Jones, 583
Tootsie, 583
Topper, 584
Topper Returns, 584
Topper Takes a Trip, 584
Top Secret!, 584
To Sir, With Love, 585
Touch and Go, 586
Touch of Class, A, 586
Tough Enough, 586
Trading Places, 587
Trail of the Pink Panther, The, 588
Transatlantic Merry-Go-Round, 588
Transylvania 6-5000, 588
Trash, 589
Tribute, 590
Trouble in the Glen, 592
Trouble with Angels, The, 592

Trouble with Harry, The, 592
True Stories, 593
Tunnelvision, 593
Turk 182!, 594
Turtle Diary, 594
12 Chairs, The, 594
Two for the Road, 596
200 Motels, 596
Two of a Kind, 596
Two Women in Gold, 597
Two Wonderous Tigers, 597

UFOria, 598
Ultimate Solution of Grace Quigley, The. *See* Grace Quigley
Under the Cherry Moon, 599
Under the Rainbow, 599
Unfaithfully Yours (1948), 600
Unfaithfully Yours (1984), 600
Up in Smoke, 601
Up the Academy, 601
Up the Creek, 601
Up the Sandbox, 601
Uptown New York, 601
Uptown Saturday Night, 601
Used Cars, 602
Utopia, 602

Valley Girl, 603
Van Nuys Blvd., 604
Vessel of Wrath. *See* Beachcomber, The
Victor/Victoria, 605
Villain Still Pursued Her, The, 606
Visit to a Small Planet, 606
Vivacious Lady, 606
Volunteers, 607

Wacko, 608
Waitress!, 608
Waltz of the Toreadors, 609
Water, 612
Watermelon Man, 612
Way Ahead, The, 613
Way Out West, 613
Wedding, A, 613–14
Wedding Party, The, 614
Weekend Pass, 614
Weird Science, 614
We're No Angels, 614–15
What's New Pussycat?, 616
What's Up Doc?, 616
What's Up, Tiger Lily?, 616
When's Your Birthday?, 617
When Women Had Tails, 617
Where's Poppa?, 617
Where the Boys Are, 617–18
Where the Boys Are '84, 618
Where the Buffalo Roam, 618
Where the Hot Wind Blows, 618
Which Way Is Up?, 618
Which Way to the Front?, 618
Whiffs, 618
Whisky Galore. *See* Tight Little Island
Who Killed "Doc" Robbin, 620
Wholly Moses, 621
Whoops Apocalypse, 621
Who's Minding the Mint?, 621–22
Wicked Lady, The, 622
Wildcats, 622
Wild Life, The, 623
Win, Place or Steal, 627
Winter Kills, 627
Wise Guys, 628
Witches' Brew, 628
With Six You Get Eggroll, 628
Woman in Red, The, 630

Woman of the Year, 631
Woman Times Seven, 631
Women, The, 631
Won Ton Ton, the Dog Who Saved Hollywood, 632
Working Girls, 632
World According to Garp, The, 632
World Is Full of Married Men, The, 632–33
World of Henry Orient, The, 633
World's Greatest Lover, The, 633
Wrong Box, The, 634
Wrong Is Right, 634

XYZ Murders, The. *See* Crimewave

Yellowbeard, 637
Yes, Giorgio, 637
Young and Willing, 638
Young Doctors in Love, 638
Young Frankenstein, 638
You're a Big Boy Now, 639
Your Place . . . Or Mine, 639
You've Got to Have Heart, 639
Yum-Yum Girls, The, 640

Zapped!, 641
Zelig, 641
Zorro the Gay Blade, 642

FOREIGN

Addition, 3
After the Rehearsal, 6
Aguirre, the Wrath of God, 7
Alexander Nevsky, 9
Allegro Non Troppo, 11
All Screwed Up, 13
Alsino and the Condor, 14
Amarcord, 15
American Friend, The, 16
American Soldier, The, 17
Amor Brujo, El. *See* El Amor Brujo
Amore in Citta. *See* Love in the City
And Now My Love, 19
And the Ship Sails on, 20
Angry Harvest, 22
Angst. *See* Fear
A Nos Amours, 23
A Nous la Liberté, 23–24
Antarctica, 24
Argent, L', 26
Ashes and Diamonds, 27–28
Atalante, L', 29

Bal, Le, 36
Balance, La, 36–37
Ballad of a Soldier, 37
Basileus Quartet, The, 40
Battleship Potemkin, 41
Beau Mariage, Le, 43–44
Beau-Père, 44
Belle et la Bête, La, 46
Bellissima, 47
Berlin Alexanderplatz, 48
Bête Humaine, La, 50
Betty Blue, 50
Beyond the Walls, 52
Bicycle Thief, The, 52
Birgitt Haas Must Be Killed, 57
Bizarre, Bizarre, 57–58
Black Orpheus, 60
Blood in the Streets, 63
Blood of a Poet, 64
Blow-Up, 66

Foreign *(cont'd)*
Boarding School, 68
Boat, The, 68
Boat Is Full, The, 68–69
Bob le Flambeur, 69
Bolero, 70
Book of Mary, The, 262
Boot, Das. *See* Boat, The
Boum, La, 73
Breathless, 78
Buek. *See* Happy New Year
Bye Bye Brazil, 86

Café Express, 88
Cage aux Folles, La, 88
Cage aux Folles III, La: The Wedding, 88
Cage aux Folles II, La, 88
Camila, 90
Christianne F., 107
Christ Stopped at Eboli, 109
Cicada, The. *See* Cricket, The
Cicala, La. *See* Cricket, The
Circle of Deceit, 110
Clair de Femme, 111
Clean Slate. *See* Coup de Torchon
Clockmaker, The, 113
Closely Watched Trains, 114
Clowns, The, 114
Comic Magazine, 119
Comperes, Les, 120
Confidentially Yours, 122
Conformist, The, 122
Congressman, The. *See* Diputado, El
Contempt, 122
Conversation Piece, 123
Cosi Come Sei. *See* Stay as You Are
Coup de Foudre. *See* Entre Nous
Coup de Grace, 126
Coup de Torchon, 126
Cousin, Cousine, 127
Cranes Are Flying, The, 128
Crazy Family, The, 128
Cricket, The, 130
Cries and Whispers, 130

Damned, The, 138
Dangerous Moves, 139
Danton, 140
Das Boot. *See* Boat, The
Day and the Hour, The, 143
Daybreak. *See* Jour Se Leve, Le
Daydreamer, The, 143
Day for Night, 143–44
Dear Inspector, 148
Death in Venice, 149
Decline of the American Empire, The, 152
Delusions of Grandeur, 153
Dernier Combat, Le, 155
Derzu Uzala, 155
Devil's Eye, The, 159
Diputado, El, 162
Discreet Charm of the Bourgeoisie, The, 163
Diva, 163
Divine Nymph, The, 163
Dodes 'Ka-Den, 167
Dolce Vita, La, 168
Doña Flor and Her Two Husbands, 168
Down and Dirty, 171
Dream of Passion, 174

Earrings of Madame De . . . , The, 179
Earth, 179
Eboli. *See* Christ Stopped at Eboli
8 1/2, 182
El Amor Brujo, 182
El Diputado. *See* Diputado, El

Elvira Madigan, 183
Emanuelle Around the World, 183–84
Emanuelle Escape from Hell. *See* Womens Prison Massacre
Emanuelle in America, 184
Emanuelle in Bangkok, 184
Emanuelle in Egypt, 184
Emanuelle in the Country, 184
Emanuelle Queen Bitch. *See* Emanuelle, the Queen
Emanuelle Queen of Sados. *See* Emanuelle, the Queen
Emanuelle, The Queen, 184
Emigrants, The 1984
Emmanuelle, 184
Emmanuelle Black and White, 185
Emmanuelle 4, 185
Emmanuelle II, The Joys of a Woman, 185
End of Desire, 186
Entre Nous, 188
Erendira, 188
Eu Te Amo. *See* I Love You
Every Man for Himself, 191
Every Man for Himself and God against All, 191
Eyes, The Mouth, The, 195

Face, The. *See* Magician, The
Fanny, 200
Fanny and Alexander, 200
Farewell, Friend. *See* Honor among Thieves
Fear, 202
Fire Festival. *See* Himatsuri
Fireman's Ball, 208
Fitzcarraldo, 211
Flight of the Eagle, 214
Folies Bourgeoises. *See* Twist, The
Forever Emmanuelle, 218
For Your Love Only, 220
400 Blows, The, 221
Fourth Man, The, 222
Freedom for Us. *See* A Nous la Liberte
From the Life of the Marionettes, 227–28
Full Moon in Paris, 228

Gabriela, 231
Garde a Vue, 232
Garden of the Finzi-Continis, 233
Gate of Hell, 233
General Della Rovere, 234
Generation, 234
Gervaise, 235
Get Out Your Handkerchiefs, 236
Gifle, La, 238–39
Gift, The, 239
Ginger and Fred, 239–40
Gods Must Be Crazy, The, 244
Going Places, 245
Going Steady, 245
Goodbye Emmanuelle, 247
Grande Illusion, La. *See* Grand Illusion
Grand Illusion, 251
Green Room, The, 257

Hail Mary, 262
Happily Ever After, 264
Happy New Year, 265
Haxan. *See* Witchcraft through the Ages
Heat of Desire, 271
Himatsuri, 278
Hiroshima, Mon Amour, 278
Holy Innocents, The, 281
Home and the World, The, 281–82
Honor Among Thieves, 283

I Am Curious (Blue), 292
I Am Curious (Yellow), 292

I Hate Blondes, 294
Ikiru, 294
I Love You, 294
I Love You, I Love You Not. *See* Together?
I Love You All. *See* Je Vous Aime
Immortal Bachelor, The, 295–96
Imperial Venus, 296
Inheritance, The, 298
Inheritors, The, 298
Innocent, The, 299
Investigation, 302
Invitation au Voyage, 302
Irezumi, 303
I Sent a Letter to My Love, 304

Je Vous Aime (I Love You All), 311
Jour Se Leve, Le, 315
Jules and Jim, 317
Junior Bonner, 318

Kagemusha, 320
Kamikaze '89, 320
Kanal, 320
Kaos, 320
Kaspar Hauser. *See* Every Man for Himself and God against All
King of Hearts, 327
Knife in the Water, 329

Lady on the Bus, The, 333
Last Metro, The, 336
Legend of Kaspar Hauser, *See* Every Man for Himself and God against All
Lost Honor of Katherina Blum, The, 353
Love and Anarchy, 354
Love in Germany, A, 355
Love in the City, 355
Love on the Run, 356
Lovers and Liars, 356
Loves of a Blonde, 356
Love Songs, 356–57

M, 359
Madame Kitty. *See* Salon Kitty
Madame Rosa, 360
Maedchen in Uniform, 361
Magic Flute, The, 361–62
Magician, The, 362
Man and a Woman, A: 20 Years Later, 365
Man Who Loved Women, The, 369
Marius, 370
Marriage of Maria Braun, 371
Mayerling, 374
Men . . . , 376–77
Menage, 377
Mephisto, 377
Mepris, Le. *See* Contempt
Metropolis, 378
Miss Julie, 381
Miss Mary, 381
Mr. Klein, 390
Mistress, The, 382–83
Monika, 384
Mon Oncle, 385
Mon Oncle d'Amerique, 385
Montenegro, 385
Moon in the Gutter, The, 386
Moscow Does Not Believe in Tears, 388
My New Partner, 396
My Other Husband, 396
Mystery of Kaspar Hauser, The. *See* Every Man for Himself and God against All

Naked Night, The. *See* Sawdust and Tinsel
Never on Sunday, 402
Night of the Shooting Stars, The, 406–7

Foreign *(cont'd)*
Nosferatu (1922), 411
Nosferatu the Vampyre (1978), 411–12
Nous Etions un Seul Homme. *See* We Were One Man
Nudo di Donna, 413
Nuit de Varennes, La, 413

Old Gun, The, 418
Olvidados, Los, 419
One Sings, the Other Doesn't, 423
One Wild Moment, 423
Only Way, The, 424
Operation Thunderbolt, 426
Orpheus, 426–27

Padre Padrone (Father Master), 431
Pain in the A—, A, 431
Paisan, 431
Pandora's Box, 432
Panique, 432
Passenger, The, 435
Passion Flower Hotel. *See* Boarding School
Passion of Joan of Arc, 435
Pauline at the Beach, 436
Paura, La. *See* Fear
Pepe Le Moko, 438
Peril, 438
Persona, 439
Petit Con, 439
Pixote, 443
Playtime, 445
Pokolanie. *See* Generation
Police, 445
Portrait of a Woman Nude. *See* Nudo di Donna
Possession, 448
Potemkin. *See* Battleship Potemkin
Promise at Dawn, 454
Providence, 454

Querelle, 458

Ramparts of Clay, 464
Ran, 464
Rape of Love, 465
Rashomon, 465
Return of Martin Guerre, The, 471
Return of the Tall Blond Man with One Black Shoe, The, 472
Ridin' on a Rainbow, 475
Robert et Robert, 477–78
Roi de Coeur, Le. *See* King of Hearts
Rome, Open City, 480–81
Rouge Baiser, 482
Rules of the Game, 483

Sacco and Vanzetti, 486
Sacrifice, The, 486
Salon Kitty, 488
Sang d'un Poète, Le. *See* Blood of a Poet
Sanjuro, 490
Satyricon. *See* Fellini Satyricon
Saul and David, 491
Sauve Qui Peut [la Vie]. *See* Every Man for Himself
Sawdust and Tinsel, 493
Scenes from a Marriage, 495
Secrets of Women, 499
Seduction of Mimi, The, 499
Sensuous Nurse, The, 500
Serpent's Egg, The, 502
Seven Beauties, 502–3
Seven Samurai, The, 503
Seventh Seal, The, 504
Sex Machine, The, 504
Sex Shop, Le, 504–5

Sheer Madness, 507
Shoot the Piano Player, 511
Shop on Main Street, The, 511
Simple Story, A, 516
Sincerely, Charlotte, 516
Skyline, 519
Slap, The. *See* Gifle, La
Slow Motion. *See* Every Man for Himself
Small Change, 521
Smiles of a Summer Night, 522
Soft Skin, The, 524
Soldier of Orange, 524
Sotto . . . Sotto, 528–29
Sous Les Toits de Paris. *See* Under the Rooftops of Paris
Special Day, A, 531
Spies, 532
Spring Symphony, 534
State of Siege, 538
Stationmaster's Wife, The, 538
Stay as You Are, 539
Stolen Kisses, 541
Story of Adele H., The, 542
Story of O, The, 542
Street of Shame, 545
Stromboli, 546
Submission, 547
Subway, 547
Sugarbaby, 547–48
Summer with Monika. *See* Monika
Suna No Onna. *See* Woman in the Dunes
Sunday in the Country, A, 549–50
Sundays and Cybèle, 550
Sweet Life, The. *See* Dolce Vita, La
Swept Away . . . (By an Unusual Destiny in the Blue Sea of August), 553

Tales of Ordinary Madness, 556
Tall Blond Man with One Black Shoe, The, 557
Tea in the Harem, 560
Tender Cousins. *See* Tendres Cousines
Tendres Cousines, 561–62
That Obscure Object of Desire, 566
Thérèse, 568
They Loved Life. *See* Kanal
This Man Must Die, 573
Three Men and a Cradle, 576
Throne of Blood, 576–77
Till Marriage Do Us Part, 578
Time Stands Still, 580
Tin Drum, The, 580
To Forget Venice, 581
Together?, 581
Touch, The, 586
Travels with Anita. *See* Lovers and Liars
Traviata, La, 589
Tree of Wooden Clogs, The, 590
Tristana, 591
Twist, The, 595
Two English Girls, 596

Ugetsu, 598
Umberto D, 598
Umbrellas of Cherbourg, The, 598
Under Paris Rooftops. *See* Under the Rooftops of Paris
Under the Roofs of Paris. *See* Under the Rooftops of Paris
Under the Rooftops of Paris, 599

Vagabond, 603
Virgin Spring, The, 606
Viridiana, 606

Wages of Fear, 608
We All Loved Each Other So Much, 613

We Were One Man, 616
Where the Green Ants Dream, 618
White Rose, The, 620
Wifemistress, 622
Wild Geese (1953). *See* Mistress, The
Wild Strawberries, 624
Winter Light, 627
Witchcraft through the Ages, 628
Witches, The. *See* Witchcraft through the Ages
Woman in Flames, A, 629–30
Woman in the Dunes, 630
Woman Next Door, The, 630
W.R.—Mysteries of the Organism, 634

Year of the Quiet Sun, A, 636
Yojimbo, 637
Yol, 637
Yotz'im Kavua. *See* Going Steady
Young and the Damned, The. *See* Olvidados, Los

Z, 641
Zéro de Conduite, 641
Zero for Conduct. *See* Zéro de Conduite

WESTERN

Abilene Town, 2
Alamo, The, 8
Along Came Jones, 14
Along the Navajo Trail, 14
Alvarez Kelly, 15
American Empire, 16
Americano, The, 17
Annihilators, The, 23
Apache, 24
Arizona Days, 26
Arizona Raiders, 26
Arizona Ranger, The, 26

Bad Company, 35
Bad Man's River, 35
Badman's Territory, 36
Bandolero!, 38
Barbarosa, 39
Bells of Coronado, 47
Bells of Rosarita, The, 47
Bend of the River, 48
Between God, the Devil and a Winchester, 50
Big Jake, 53
Big Show, The, 54
Billy the Kid Returns, 56
Bite the Bullet, 57
Blood on the Moon, 64
Blue Steel, 68
Boiling Point, The, 70
Boots and Saddles, 71
Border Romance, 72
Buck and the Preacher, 82
Bullwhip, 84
Butch and Sundance: The Early Days, 85
Butch Cassidy and the Sundance Kid, 85–86

Cahill, U.S. Marshall, 89
California Gold Rush, 89
Call of the Canyon, 89–90
Captain Apache, 92
Cat Ballou, 97
Cattle Annie and Little Britches, 98
Cattle Queen of Montana, 98
Cheyenne Autumn, 104
Cheyenne Rides Again, 104
Cheyenne Takes Over, 104

Western *(cont'd)*
Chino, 106
Chisum, 106
Cisco Kid Returns, The. *See* Guns of Fury
Colorado Serenade, 117
Comancheros, The, 118
Comes a Horseman, 119
Cowboy and the Senorita, The, 127
Cowboys, The, 127
Culpepper Cattle Co., The, 134

Dakota, 137
Dakota Incident, 137
Dark Command, The, 140
Dark Crystal, The, 140
Dawn on the Great Divide, 143
Dawn Rider, 143
Days of Old Cheyenne, 145
Death Rides the Plains, 150
Desert Trail, 155
Destry Rides Again, 157
Devil's Playground, 159
Dodge City, 167
Don't Fence Me In, 169
Dorado, El, 170
Down Dakota Way, 172
Down Mexico Way, 172
Down Texas Way, 172
Draw!, 174
Drumbeat, 175–76
Drums along the Mohawk, 176
Duel in the Sun, 176–77

Escape from Fort Bravo, 189
Eyes of Texas, 195

Far Country, The, 200–1
Far Frontier, The, 201
Fastest Gun Alive, The, 201
Feud of the West, 204
Fighting Caravans, 206
Fighting Kentuckian, The, 206
First Texan, The, 210
Fistful of Dollars, A, 211
Flaming Star, 212
For a Few Dollars More, 217
Forbidden Trail, 217
Fort Apache, 219
Forty Guns, 220
Four Faces West, 221
Four for Texas, 221
From Noon Til Three, 227

Gangs of Sonora, 232
Golden Stallion, 246
Good, the Bad, and the Ugly, The, 249
Great Gundown, The, 254
Great Northfield, Minn. Raid, The, 255
Gunfight at the O.K. Corral, 259
Gunfighter, The, 259
Guns of Fury, 260

Hang 'em High, 263
Harry Tracy, 267
Hatfields and the McCoys, The, 268
Heart of the Golden West, 270
Heart of the Rio Grande, 270
Heaven's Gate, 272
Heldorado, 272
Hell's Hinges, 273
High Noon, 277
High Noon, Part II: The Return of Will Kane, 277
High Plains Drifter, 277
Hombre, 281
Home in Oklahoma, 282

Horse Soldiers, 285
How the West Was Won, 288
Hud, 289

In Old Amarillo, 299
In Old California, 299
In Old New Mexico, 299
In Old Oklahoma. *See* War of the Wildcats
Invitation to a Gunfighter, 302–3

Jesse James, 312
Jesse James at Bay, 312
Joe Kidd, 314
Johnny Guitar, 315

Kansas Terrors, 320
King of the Cowboys, 326

Lady from Louisiana, 332
Lady Takes a Chance, The, 334
Last Command, The, 335
Last Ride of the Dalton Gang, 337
Last Train from Gun Hill, 337
Lawless Frontier, The, 339
Lawless Range, 339
Legend of the Lone Ranger, The, 340
Life and Times of Judge Roy Bean, The, 343
Lights of Old Santa Fe, 344
Little Big Man, 346
Lonely Are the Brave, 349–50
Lone Ranger, The, 350
Long Riders, The, 351
Lucky Texan, 358
Lusty Men, The, 358

McCabe and Mrs. Miller, 375
Mackenna's Gold, 359
Major Dundee, 363
Man Alone, A, 364
Man Called Horse, A, 365
Man Who Loved Cat Dancing, The, 368–69
Man Who Shot Liberty Valance, The, 369
Melody Ranch, 376
Melody Trail, 376
Men from Utah, The, 377
Misfits, The, 381
Missouri Breaks, The, 382
Monte Walsh, 386
My Darling Clementine, 395
My Pal Trigger, 396

'Neath the Arizona Skies, 401
Nevada Smith, 401
New Frontier, The, 402
Night of the Grizzly, The, 406
Night Riders, The, 407
Night Time in Nevada, 407
Night Train to Memphis, 407
North of the Great Divide, 411

Oklahoma Kid, The, 418
Old Corral, The, 418
Once Upon a Time in the West, 420
One-Eyed Jacks, 421
Outcast, The, 428
Outlaw, The, 428
Outlaw Josey Wales, The, 428

Painted Desert, 431
Pale Rider, 431
Pals of the Golden West, 432
Pals of the Saddle, 432
Paradise Canyon, 433
Pat Garrett and Billy the Kid, 436
Pioneer Woman, 442

Prairie Moon, 449
Professionals, The, 454

Rachel and the Stranger, 461
Rancho Notorious, 464
Randy Rides Alone, 464–65
Rare Breed, The, 465
Red River, 468
Return of a Man Called Horse, The, 470
Return of Frank James, 470
Return of the Badmen, 471
Riders of Destiny, 474
Raiders of the Rockies, 474
Ride the High Country, 474
Rio Bravo, 475
Rio Conchos, 475
Rio Grande, 475–76
Rio Lobo, 476
Road Agent, 477
Rocky Mountain Rangers, 479
Romance of a Horse Thief, 480
Rooster Cogburn, 481

Sacketts, The, 486
Sagebrush Trail, 487
San Antonio, 489
San Fernando Valley, 490
Santa Fe Stampede, 490
Santee, 490
Searchers, The, 497
Shalako, 505
Sheriff of Wichita, 508
She Wore a Yellow Ribbon, 509
Shooting, The, 510–11
Shootist, The, 511
Shoot the Sun Down, 511
Showdown at Boot Hill, 512
Silent Conflict, 513
Silverado, 514
Silver Spurs, 515
Sinister Journey, 517
Sioux City Sue, 517
Six Shootin' Sheriff, 518
Skin Game, 519
Soldier Blue, 524
Song of Nevada, 526
Song of Texas, 527
Sons of Katie Elder, The, 527–28
Spoilers, The, 533
Spoilers of the Plains, 533
Springtime in the Sierras, 534
Stagecoach, 534–35
Star Packer, 537
Station West, 538
Stranger and the Gunfighter, The, 543
Sunday Too Far Away, 550
Sunset Serenade, 550
Sweet Creek County War, The, 552–53

Tall in the Saddle, 557
Tall Men, The, 557
Tennessee's Partner, 562
Terror of Tiny Town, The, 564
Texas, 565
Texas Lady, 565
There Was a Crooked Man . . . , 568
They Call Me Trinity, 569
They Came to Cordura, 569
They Died with Their Boots On, 569
Three Faces West, 575
3:10 to Yuma, 576
Ticket to Tomahawk, A, 577
Tom Horn, 582–83
Trail Beyond, The, 588
Trail Riders, 588
Trail Street, 588

Western *(cont'd)*
Train Robbers, The, 588
Trigger, Jr., 590
Trinity is *Still* My Name, 591
Triumphs of a Man Called Horse, 591–92
True Grit, 593
Tumbleweeds, 593
Twilight in the Sierras, 595
Two Mules for Sister Sara, 596

Undefeated, The, 598
Under California Stars, 598
Under Mexicali Stars, 599
Under Western Stars, 599–600
Utah, 602

Vera Cruz, 604

Wagon Master, 608
War of the Wildcats, 611
Way of a Gaucho, 613
Way West, The, 613
Westerner, The, 615
Western Union, 615
West of the Divide, 615
Wichita, 622
Wild Bunch, The, 622
Wild Times, 625
Winchester '73, 625–26
Winds of the Wasteland, 626
Woman of the Town, The, 630–31

DOCUMENTARY
Animals Are Beautiful People, 22
Atomic Cafe, The, 29
Autopsy, 31

Beach Boys, The—An American Band, 42
Being Different, 46

Bill and Coo, 55
Bring on the Night, 80
Burden of Dreams, 84

Children of Theater Street, The, 105
Compleat Beatles, The, 120

Decline of Western Civilization, The, 152

Endless Summer, The, 186

Face of War, A, 196
From Mao to Mozart, 227

George Stevens: A Film Maker's Journey, 235
Gimme Shelter, 239
Gizmo, 241
Guns of August, The, 260

Hearts and Minds, 271
Hell's Angels Forever, 273
Hellstrom Chronicle, The, 274
Hollywood Outtakes and Rare Footage, 281
Huey Long, 289

In Search of Historic Jesus, 299
In Search of Noah's Ark, 299

Janis, 310

Kaddish, 320
Kids Are Alright, The, 322
Kitty: Return to Auschwitz, 329
Koyaanisqatsi, 330

Last Waltz, The, 338
Let It Be, 341
Let's Spend the Night Together, 341

Marjoe, 370–71
Marlene, 371
Millhouse: A White Comedy, 380
Mystery of Picasso, The, 397–98

No Nukes, 410

October. *See* Ten Days That Shook the World

Partisans of Vilna, 435
Private Conversations: On the Set of "Death of a Salesman," 452
Private Practices: The Story of a Sex Surrogate, 453
Pumping Iron, 456
Pumping Iron II: The Women, 456

Say Amen, Somebody, 493
Sea around Us, The, 496–97
Secret Policeman's Other Ball, The, 498
Sense of Loss, A, 500
Shoah, 510
Sixteen Days of Glory, 518
Song Remains the Same, The, 527
Sorrow and the Pity, The, 528
Stop Making Sense, 541
Streetwise, 545
Stripper, 546

Take It to the Limit, 555
Ten Days That Shook The World, 561
That's Dancing!, 567
That's Entertainment!, 567
That's Entertainment, Part 2, 567
This Is Elvis, 573
Times of Harvey Milk, The, 579–80
Tosca's Kiss, 585
Triumph of the Will, 591

Urgh! A Music War, 601–2

War Game, The, 610
Warrior Within, The, 611
Wasn't That a Time!, 611
What Do You Say to a Naked Lady?, 616
Woodstock, 632

Ziggy Stardust and the Spiders from Mars, 641–42